There are over seventy Rough Guide titles covering destinations from Amsterdam to Zimbabwe & Botswana

Forthcoming titles include

Bali • Costa Rica • Mallorca • Rhodes • Vietnam

Rough Guide Reference Series

Classical Music • World Music • Jazz

Rough Guide Phrasebooks

Czech • French • German • Greek • Italian • Spanish

Rough Guide Credits

Text editors:	Paul Gray, Samantha Cook, Richard Trillo
Series editor:	Mark Ellingham
Production:	Susanne Hillen, Andy Hilliard, Nicola Williamson, Link Hall
Cartography:	Melissa Flack
Marketing & Publicity:	Richard Trillo (UK), Jean-Marie Kelly, Jeffrey Kaye (US)

The authors jointly want to thank Sam Cook for getting us afloat and giving us a reassuring sense of direction; Nicola Williamson for many hours' graft beyond the call and still a surprising number of laughs; Susanne Hillen for supreme organization; Kate Berens for additional production help; Melissa Flack for dealing calmly with the maps and also Matt Welton, Sam Kirby, Mick Bohoslavec and Stratigraphics for drawing them; Andy Hilliard and Link Hall for putting in the time on the Macs so unflappably and for tolerating all those last-minute little changes, as well as Judy Pang and Alan Spicer for emergency aid; Daniel Jacobs for dropping everything in the cause of indexing; and Phil Stanton for doing a great CD just at the right moment. Most of all, we owe a huge debt to the editorial skills of Paul Gray, without whose dedication and precision the meaning would never have been quite as clear. Thanks for a very fine job Paul.

Richard: for all their help and interest in different ways, Martin Dent (Jubilee 2000), Clare Fairclough, Gael Gahagan, Terry O'Leary, Patrick Sothern (West Africa Tours), Gabrielle Marley (Truck Africa), Dan Rees (VSO), Emma Gregg and James McCormick, Chris Scott, Louis Taussig, Jean Trouillet (World Network) and Jo Winter. Most importantly, to Teresa, Alex, David and Phoebe, for putting up with it, all my love. There'll never be another summer like it. And that's a promise.

Jim: In gratitude and in love to Sallee and Arba, for their unfailing trust, support and encouragement.

Acknowledgements to readers and contributors appear on the next page.

Illustrations for "Basics", "Contexts" and the country title pages are by **Henry Iles**; incidental illustrations in "Basics" and "Contexts" by **Edward Briant**.

First published by Harrap Columbus Ltd, 1990. Reprinted 1992, 1993, 1995 by Rough Guides Ltd.
This second edition published November 1995 by Rough Guides Ltd, 1 Mercer Street, London WC2H 9QJ.

Distributed by the Penguin Group:

Penguin Books Ltd, 27 Wrights Lane, London W8 5TZ
Penguin Books USA Inc., 375 Hudson Street, New York, NY 10014, USA
Penguin Books Australia Ltd, 487 Maroondah Highway, PO Box 257, Ringwood, Victoria 3134, Australia
Penguin Books Canada Ltd, 10 Alcorn Avenue, Toronto, Ontario, Canada M4V 1E4
Penguin Books (NZ) Ltd, 182–190 Wairau Road, Auckland 10, New Zealand.

Rough Guides were formerly published in the US and Canada as Real Guides.

Typeset in Linotron Univers and Century Old Style to an original design by Andrew Oliver.

Printed by Cox & Wyman Ltd, Reading.

1312pp, includes index

British Library Cataloguing in Publication Data
A catalogue record for this book is available from the British Library.

ISBN 1-85828-101-6

West Africa

THE ROUGH GUIDE

Written and researched by

Richard Trillo and Jim Hudgens

Additional research on this edition by

Emma Gregg, Chris Scott and Jo Winter

THE ROUGH GUIDES

ACKNOWLEDGEMENTS TO READERS AND CONTRIBUTORS

All our thanks to the following readers who wrote in with comments and information, in many cases more than once.
Neville Abbott, Oluyemi Emile Akanbi, Lucia Alvarez de Toledo, Jenny Angel, Nicolas Argenti, Jack Barker, Chris Barton, Simon Batterbury, Jennifer Battiglini, RM Beatty, Tim Beddow, David Benson, David Benton, Elaine Berry, Ruud Blücker, Richard Bonnor Harris, John Bradshaw, DR Brison, Andrew Brook, Judith Brownnett, David Bumstead & Jose Diaz Urbieta, Christa Burtt, Gareth Butler, Sylvia Cabus, Chris Caine, Kate Calvert, Jan Capper, R Carman, Annie Chandler, Síle Nic Chormaic, Jan Claassen, Teresa Clarke, Phil Cole, Jeanette Coly, Florent Conings, Amanda Cooper, Philip Cooper, Tony Coren, Rebecca Corman, Graeme Counsel, David Cox, Lisa Jane Crowley, PN Dakin, Philip Davey, Catherine Davie, Heather Davis, James Demba, Alan Dempster, Ingrid Deutschmann, Tom Dohrmann, Sarah Donald, Joanna Dowell, Chris Drakeley, Richard Durkan, Ronald W van Engers, Ferdinand Fellinger, Marie Fichet & François Boillot, Jorun og Finn Kaare, Chris Frean, Herbert Frei, Trician Gilchrist, Faith Glasgow, Valerie Godsalve, Chris Goldring, Carol Gorman, Christian Graindorge, Femke Groot, Elisabeth Gruys, Keith & Mary Hallam, Henry Hallward & Georgina Hue Williams, Jackie Harris, Andrew Hart, Eddie Hefford, Andy Hibbert, Claire Hughes, Hans Huysmans, John Jackson, Steve Jackson, Andy Jones, Christopher Jones, Chris & Angela Kenny, Inez Kipfer, Joy Lawson, Hélène & Olivier Leenhardt, Sian Lewis, Dawn Lock, Jonas Ludvigsson, Greville Lushington, Roger van der Maelen, Geerdt Magiels, Lucy Maguire, Elizabeth & Deidre Mahoney, Naomi McBride, Melanie McGrath, Paula McIlwaine, Fiona McVicar & John Donnelly, W Iain Mackay, Andrew Morgan, David Mozer, Peter Newman, Sokhna Niasse, Paul Nyanzu Kwesi, Sharon Otoo, Dele Oyeleke, Andrew Pacey, Mark Painter, Alan Parker & Jacqueline Slater, Nikhil Patel, Sara Patnoy, René Pélissier, Nicola Penford, Richard Persse, Christine & Jean Pierre Pieters, Georges Platon, Wilfred J Plumbe, Sarah Pocknell, Russell Price, Pat Proden, Maurice Purslow-Tomlinson, Simon Rackston, Stuart Roberts, Lindsey Robinson, Kevin Rose, Wolfgang Roth, Koffi Kouassi Sadrac, Richard Sale, Greet van Spitoul, Marijke Swart, Jean Tanguy, Jim Taylor, Diana Temple, Daphne Topouzis, Eric Torres, Matthew Tostevin, Jane Townsend, Michal Uít, Julian Uribe, Todd Wallström, Nigel Watt, Elaine Wattam, Paul Weiberger, Emily White, Peter Whitehead, Jane Wilde, Paul Wilmshurst, Sally Wilson, Sara Withers, Tony Woods, John Wright and Jay Yasgur.

The following readers were outstandingly helpful to Richard – a thousand thanks for the huge letters and faxes, the queries answered and the chapters tried out on the ground: Gerrie Breukers (Mali), Donald Carey, Tom Dohrmann (Sierra Leone), Rosemary Faal (The Gambia), Jonathan & Siân Flower (Nouadhibou), Barry Hanson (Cameroon), Jo Hanson, Bob Harris (Ghana), Jonathan Graepne (Cape Verde), Simon Heap (Nigeria), Andy Jones (Nigeria), Margot Kokke (Nigeria & Cameroon), Marike Kloppenburg (Côte d'Ivoire), David Lawrence (Cameroon and Nigeria), Jessica Leslie (Cape Verde), Andy Lohof (Guinea), Andrew Long, Jamie and Catherine Mackenzie, James McCormick, Rexford Quaye (Accra), Lisa Washington Sow (Senegal), Robert Walker (Burkina Faso), Paul Whitfield, Trevor Wilson (Mauritania), Nikki Watson (Ghana), John Wright (Sierra Leone) and British High Commission staff in West Africa.

Jim thanks: Apou Gata Djima, Jermaine Onwubere, Dr. Boniface Obichere, Lisa Washington, Babacar So, Matthew Christensen, Kairn Kleiman, "Buster" Boahen, Vijitha Mahadevan, Duke Agunente, Tony Adedze, Anthony Mainer, Dr Teshome H. Gabriel, Julia Bromhead, Gotzon Zaratiegi, Dogbe K Mensah, Conerly Casey, Kendahl Radcliffe, Shirley Radcliffe, Bruce Bailey, Luc and Fati Denesle, Luca and Sara Guiliani, Pauline Ava, Fay Sueltz, Prince Eyango, Belinda Sunnu, Wendy Belcher, Senen Garcia and Koné Nicolas.

Continuing thanks from both authors must go to the following people who helped shape the first edition: Kabba Camara, Teresa Driver, Paul Everett, Samba M. Fye, Paul Hayward, Henry Iles, Bill Jackson, Daniel Jacobs, Monica Mackaness, Kevin Malone, Dave Muddyman, Manfred Prinz, George Senger, Chris Seward, Caroline Shaw, Hamidou Soumah, Jim Taylor, David Warne and Tony Zurbrugg.

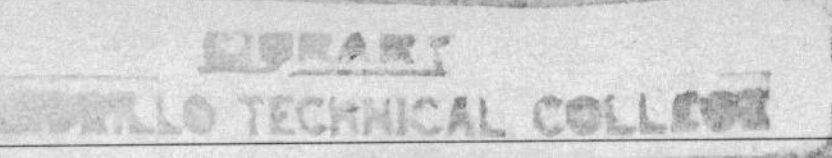

HOW THE BOOK WORKS

This book is designed to be as much use if you're visiting a single country, as for travelling widely in several. Part One, *Basics*, covers all the practical details and much of the background information useful to know *before* arrival in Africa, including full information about travelling to West Africa from the rest of the world, and useful French words and phrases. If you can't find the information you're looking for anywhere else in the book, it should be in *Basics*.

Part Two, *The Guide*, covers the countries, starting from the north with Ch 1 *Mauritania* – the only currently viable overland route from Europe – and then more or less following the coast from Ch 2 *Senegal* to Ch 17 *Cameroon*, with diversions inland for Ch 4 *Mali*, Ch 11 *Burkina Faso* and Ch 15 *Niger*. Each chapter begins with **practical information** specific to that country and a short **history**; following this is the **guide** proper, starting with the capital or largest city. If something seems to require explanation, you should find it covered in the "Practical Information" and, again, if it's not there, try *Basics*. Information about foreign embassies of each country and about flights from outside Africa will always be found in *Basics*, not the country chapter. Each country has its own **index**, somewhat more detailed than the **main index** at the end of the book.

The book's concluding section, Part Three, *Contexts*, has an annotated **reading list**, and articles introducing West African **cinema** and **music**, with recommendations for CDs to buy.

HELP US UPDATE

We've done our best to make sure that this second edition of **The Rough Guide to West Africa** is as useful, accurate and up-to-the-minute as possible, credit for which is due in large part to the fantastic response to our request in the last edition to keep us posted as you travel. Events move fast in West Africa and we can only keep it all current in future editions by hearing from readers. We are conscious of the fact that, while we have had some African contributors, the book has been largely put together on the basis of the research and opinions of white travellers, and we are therefore particularly keen to have the input of feedback from black readers.

If we've got it wrong, or you feel there are places we've overrated or under-praised, or find we've missed something good or covered something which has gone, then **please write and tell us**. Letters about obscure routes off the beaten track are as welcome as a postcard about your favourite club or hotel, and we are always trying to improve our maps. It is always a great help if information about different countries comes on different pages.

Since the first edition was published we have established more or less permanent correspondents in several countries. We would welcome hearing from anyone – either nationals or expatriates – who would like to pass on their knowledge and experience. Please write to us, marking letters **West Africa Ed 2 Update**, at:

Rough Guides, 1 Mercer Street, London WC2H 9QJ, UK or

Rough Guides, 375 Hudson St, 3rd floor, New York, NY 10014, US

Alternatively, you can send email to **mail@roughtravl.com**.

We will acknowledge all information used in the next edition and will send a free copy of this or any other Rough Guide for the best (and most legible!) letters.

LIST OF MAPS

CONTENTS

WEST AFRICA: MAIN ROUTES
To Morocco
Dakhla
WESTERN SAHARA
Zouérat
Nouadhibou
Atar
MAURITANIA
MALI
Nouakchott
Timbuktu
River Niger
Néma
St-Louis
River Senegal
Dakar
SENEGAL
Kayes
Mopti
Tambacounda
THE GAMBIA
Banjul
BURKI
FASO
Ziguinchor
Bamako
Oua
Bissau
GUINEA-BISSAU
Labé
GUINEA
Bobo-Dioulasso
Kankan
Conakry
SIERRA LEONE
CÔTE D'IVOIRE
Tamale
Freetown
Bo
GH
Nzérékoré
Bouaké
Man
Yamoussoukro
Kumasi
Monrovia
LIBERIA
Abidjan
Sassandra
Takora
N
0
500 km

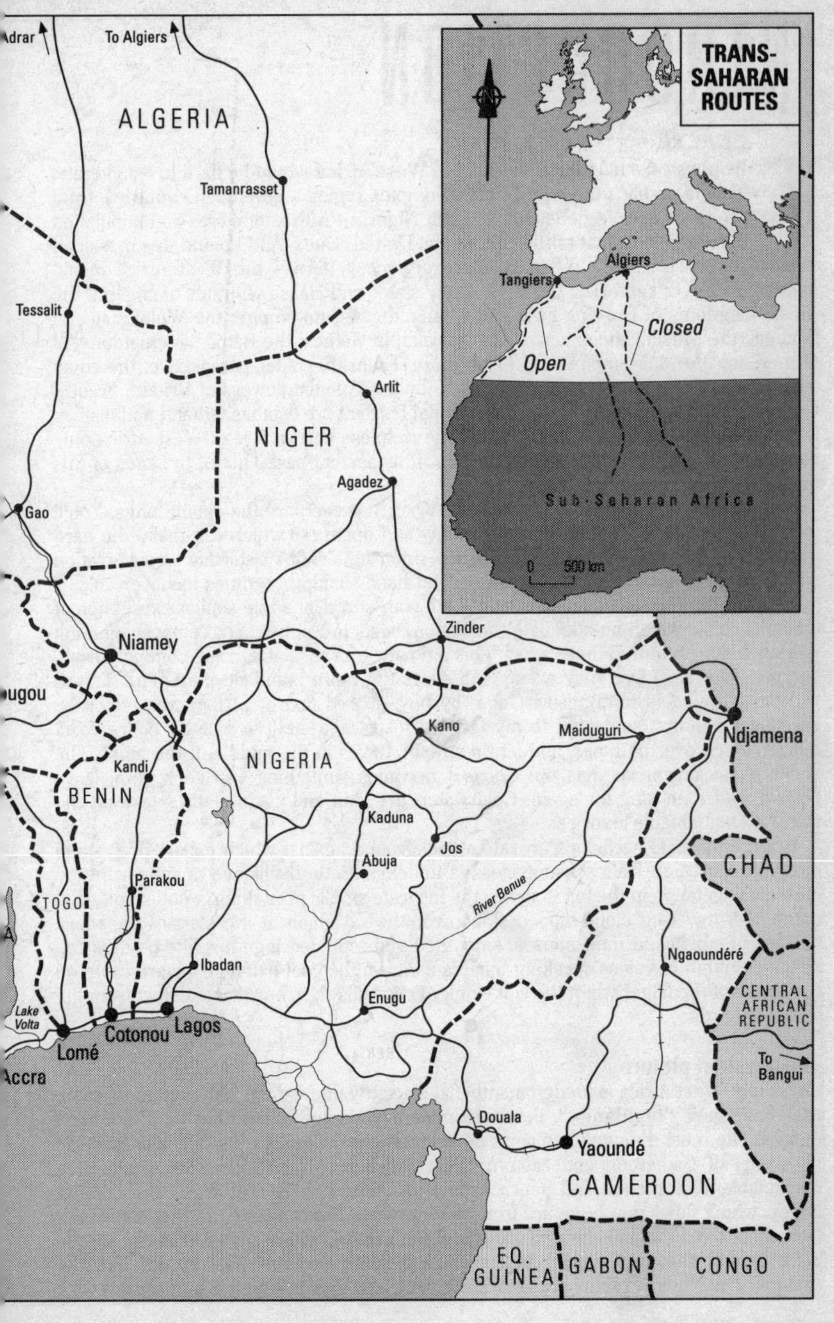

Adrar
To Algiers
ALGERIA
Tamanrasset
Tessalit
Arlit
NIGER
Agadez
Gao
Zinder
Niamey
ugou
Kano
Maiduguri
Ndjamena
NIGERIA
Kandi
BENIN
Kaduna
Jos
Abuja
CHAD
Parakou
TOGO
River Benue
Ngaoundéré
Ibadan
CENTRAL AFRICAN REPUBLIC
Enugu
Lake Volta
Lomé
Cotonou
Lagos
Accra
To Bangui
Douala
Yaoundé
CAMEROON
EQ. GUINEA
GABON
CONGO
TRANS-SAHARAN ROUTES
Algiers
Tangiers
Closed
Open
Sub-Saharan Africa
0 500 km

INTRODUCTION

The physical and cultural diversity of **West Africa** would be hard to exaggerate. This is perhaps the world's most complex region – seventeen countries, from the tiny Cape Verde Islands to giant Nigeria – with a total area and population comparable to that of the continental United States. And behind this mosaic of modern territories lies a different, more organic pattern – the West Africa of old nations built over centuries: the Yoruba city states and Hausa emirates of Nigeria; the Mossi kingdoms of Burkina Faso and Ghana; the Asante empire; the Wolof states of Senegal; the Muslim theocracy of Fouta Djalon in Guinea; the Bamiléké chiefdoms of Cameroon; the Mali empire, and many more. From this older perspective, the countries of today are imposters, fixed in place by the colonial powers of Britain, France, Germany and Portugal. Although the national borders are established and nationalism is a part of each country's social fabric, the richness and variety of West Africa only comes into focus with some understanding of its ancient past. One of the aims of this book is to bring that to the fore.

Some of the biggest pleasures of West Africa, however, are the small things. You'll encounter a degree of good humour, vitality and openness which can make the hard insularity of Western cultures seem absurd. Entering a shop or starting a conversation with a stranger without proper greetings and hand-shaking becomes inconceivable. If you stumble in the street, passers-by will tell you "sorry" or some similar expression of condolence for which no adequate translation exists in English. You're never ignored; you say hello a hundred times a day. This intimacy – a sense of barriers coming down – sharpens the most everyday events and eases the more mundane hardships. Travel, without a doubt, is rarely easy. Going by bus, shared taxi or pick-up van, you'll be crushed for hours, subjected to mysterious delays and endless halts at police roadblocks, jolted over potholes, and left in strange towns in the middle of the night. The sheer physicality never lets up. Comfort becomes something you seek, find, leave behind, and then long for again. Cold water, dry skin and clean clothes take on the status of unattainable luxuries.

But the material hardships provide a background against which experiences stand out with clarity. Africa's sensuousness is undeniable: the brilliance of red earth and emerald vegetation in the forest areas; the intricate smells of cooking, wood smoke and damp soil; towering cloud-scaped skies over the savannah at the start of the rains; villages of sun-baked mud houses, smoothed and moulded together like pottery; the singing rhythm of voices speaking tonal languages; the cool half-hour before dawn on the banks of the Niger when the soft clunk of cowbells rises on a haze of dust from the watering herds . . .

The physical picture

Physically, West Africa is predominantly flat or gently undulating. Although most countries have their **"highlands"**, these are generally rugged hills rather than mountain ranges. The most mountainous parts of the region are Guinea's Fouta Djalon and the highlands of Cameroon and eastern Nigeria (where Mount Cameroon peaks at a respectable 4000 metres and gets a little frost). The big river of West Africa is the **Niger**, which flows in a huge arc from the border of Sierra Leone, northeast through Guinea, into Mali and to the very fringes of the Sahara (where sand dunes rise on the bank behind snorting hippos) before turning south through Nigeria and into the Atlantic. The Niger is highly seasonal and river traffic depends on the annual rains.

As for the scenic environment, expectations of tropical forest are usually disappointed, at least to begin with. While the natural **vegetation** across the whole southern coastal belt is rainforest – with a gap in the Ghana-Togo area where grasslands come nearly to the coast – by far the commonest scene in the densely populated parts is of a desolate, bush-stripped landscape where dust and bare earth figure heavily. True rainforest, however, is still present in parts of Guinea, Sierra Leone, Liberia, Côte d'Ivoire, in southeast Nigeria and Cameroon. Guinea also features beautiful **savannah** lands, as does Burkina Faso. Along the **coast**, creeks and mangroves make many parts inaccessible. The best beaches are in Sierra Leone and Côte d'Ivoire, with Ghana, Senegal, The Gambia and Cameroon creditable runners-up. The currents tend to be strong, though, making many shorelines unsuitable for swimming – take care.

Where to go

If you have the time, by far the most satisfying way of visiting West Africa is **overland**, traversing the yawning expanse of the **Sahara**, arriving in the dry northern reaches of the Sahel – these days most likely in Mauritania – to the ravishing shock of an alien culture, and then adapting to a new landscape, a new climate and new ways of behaving.

Choosing **where to go** is no easy task: the region offers so much and Africa repeatedly confounds all expectations and assumptions. In the main section of the guide, the individual country introductions give an idea of what to look forward to. However, at the risk of reinforcing stereotypes, it's possible to make a few generalizations about the feel of the countries.

Of the eleven Francophone, **ex-French colonies**, the three nations most dominated by French culture and language are Cameroon, Senegal and Côte d'Ivoire; these can also be the more expensive countries to travel in, and their relatively westernized cities are inclined to be hustly. **Senegal** is an obvious choice as a base from which to launch travels: facilities are much better than in many parts of the region and the verdant **Basse Casamance** district has a remarkable network of village-based accommodation. **Côte d'Ivoire** provides a mélange of the traditional and modern, African and French. **Cameroon** – which is English-speaking in the west – blends magnificent scenery and national parks with an extraordinary richness of culture, running the whole African gamut from "Pygmy" hunting camps to Arabic-speaking trading towns and taking in the colourful kingdoms of the western highlands.

Vast, land-locked **Mali** is blessed with the great inland delta of the Niger River and, again, striking cultural contrasts – the old **Islamic cities** of Gao, Timbuktu and Djenné (on, or near the river), and the traditionally non-Muslim **Dogon country** along the rocky cliff of the Bandiagara escarpment. Other Francophone countries include the narrow strips of **Togo** and **Benin**, the latter being especially easy-going and fairly undeveloped as far as tourism is concerned; the laid-back, former revolutionary republic of **Burkina Faso**, and the remote and dramatic expanses of **Mauritania** and **Niger**. Perhaps the most impressive of the *pays francophones*, however, is the republic of **Guinea**, with only a thin overlay of European culture and an extraordinary vitality released by the end of dictatorship.

Four of the West African countries are **former British colonies**, divided from each other by the speed of the French invasion in the nineteenth century. **The Gambia** is an easy place to set out from, a winter holiday destination that's small and personable enough to feel accessible for the least adventurous visitor. The distinctive personality of **Ghana** provides flamboyant cultural experiences and its splendid, palm-lined coast, dotted with old European forts, a handful of good wildlife sanctuaries and official encouragements to the tourist industry, make it one of West Africa's most promising countries to travel in. **Sierra Leone**, while hugely likable, has always been a more demanding destination. It has some of the best beaches in the world – only minutes away from the raffish tumble of Freetown – but the civil war there rules out any recommendation to visit for the present. **Nigeria**, too, with its despised military government, is not exactly sending out messages of welcome at the moment. However, there are big travel incentives inland – in the fine uplands of the plateau and the old cities of the north, to mention just two areas. It's a hard country to come to terms with but, once you're away from the slightly psychotic manifestation of Lagos, there's no denying the ease and peace which accompany travels even here. The same cannot be said for **Liberia** – a former vassal state of the USA, nominally independent since 1847 – whose ugly civil war has all but destroyed it as a nation.

The **former Portuguese colonies** are West Africa's least-known destinations. The **Cape Verde Islands** are immediately beguiling: volcanic outcrops and desert islands in the mid-Atlantic, with a scenery and lifestyle that make them hard to leave. **Guinea-Bissau** has its own island highlights – the Bijagos – luxuriant green forests in the warm, inshore sea, as different from the Cape Verdes as it's possible to imagine.

The first recommendation in all this, is to give yourself **time**. It's tempting to try to cover as much of this fascinating region as possible. But the rewards become thinner the faster you go and, beyond a certain pace, the point of being there is lost in the pursuit of the next goal. While it may be hard to stop completely, or just to limit yourself to a small corner, that is precisely the way to get the most out of your trip – and, incidentally, also how to put the most in. In such a poor region, the idea of some kind of reciprocity is one worth keeping: everything comes back to you in the end. Patience and generosity always pay off; haste and intolerance tend to lead to disaster.

If you're travelling alone – and it's really the best way if you want to get to know West Africa rather than your travelling companion/s – it may be useful to know about the main **travellers' crossroads** in the region, where you might team up for a while or swap experiences: Nouadhibou at the edge of the desert, Bamako or Mopti in Mali, Bobo-Dioulasso in Burkina Faso, Cotonou in Benin, and Busua or Accra on the Ghanaian coast.

When to travel

Individual **climate** details are given for each country. The big consideration is not the **heat** – temperatures, in fact, only occasionally climb very much higher than you might experience in Europe – but the **humidity** and particularly the timing of the **rainy seasons**. Broadly the rains come in the "summer" months, some time between April and October. Although travel is rarely out of the question during the rains, it's obviously not an ideal time. You can be pretty sure of dry weather everywhere from mid-November to the end of January. Where the rainy seasons are very marked, the very end of the dry season is best avoided as it can be stiflingly humid. The best time to leave on an overland trip planned to last several months is September.

PART ONE

THE BASICS

GETTING TO WEST AFRICA – GENERAL INFORMATION

The most straightforward – and usually the least expensive – way to get to West Africa is by air. If you have the time, though, making your way partly overland, either with your own vehicle or using any available transport along the way, gives rewards of its own – and an unbeatable introduction to the region.

You can travel in a similar style, with most of your needs looked after, by going on an organized overland tour. These, like inclusive package holidays to West Africa, are fairly limited in choice.

There's detailed information over the following pages for travel from Britain, Ireland, North America, Australia, New Zealand, and the rest of Africa. There are also plenty of options for getting to West Africa if you're starting from France, Switzerland, Germany or the Benelux countries. We don't include those details in this book, but to get started, contact the following: in France, *Air Afrique* (☎1/44.21.33.33), *Nouvelles Frontières* (☎1/41.41.58.58) or the club *Aventures du Bout du Monde* (☎1/43.35.08.95); in Belgium, *Sabena* (☎02/723 23 23) or *Nouvelles Frontières* (☎02/513.76.36); in Switzerland, *Swissair* (☎812.12.12); in the Netherlands, *KLM* (☎20/747747); and in Germany, *Lufthansa* (☎069/255255) or an adventure travel specialist like *Därr Expeditionsservice* (☎089/28.20.32).

DISCOUNT FLIGHT TICKETS

In the main, travel agents offer tickets for scheduled flights at substantially **discounted rates** – well below the official fares agreed by *IATA*, the association to which most airlines belong. Airlines prepared to sell off their tickets through these agents have in the past been generally the less reputable ones left with the most unsold seats, but more and more major carriers are cashing in to maintain full flights. Note, however, that discounts are sometimes subject to **restrictions**: check if you have to be a student, for example, or under a certain age for them to apply.

BOOKING AND BUYING

Discount agencies are, almost without exception, respectable travel agents, even if first impressions might suggest otherwise. When **booking**, note whether the agent reserves seats directly with the airline by telephone or on a computer system, or has to go through another agent. While many agents have ticketing agreements with certain airlines and can write tickets on the premises, they may have to order some from the nominated "consolidator" of the airline concerned – usually another agent. Don't expect to see your ticket until you've paid in full.

Always get receipts and ask if your deposit is refundable, and what refund you can expect if anything goes wrong after the ticket is issued (it's wise to be insured from this point on). Also check how easy it will be to **change your reservation dates** once you've got your ticket. You can sometimes leave a round-trip ticket "open-dated" on its return portion, but in that case you'll have to make a seat reservation yourself with the airline. It's just as easy, and safer, to have a confirmed seat and change the date if necessary (and if seats are available). Note that if you book through a discount agency, you cannot deal direct with the airline on your booking until you have your ticket, though you can always quote them the details and ask them to check the reservation is held under your name. If it's not, don't panic. It will probably be held under the agent's block allocation of seats.

Airline "seasons" for West Africa vary considerably but many discounted fares are non-seasonal: they don't vary. Most student and youth fares, however, do have a seasonal structure to tie in with summer and Christmas holiday periods. **Book as far in advance as you can.** Some routes are full to capacity at peak periods, especially Christmas, and discounted seat availability is often snapped up quickly.

TICKETS AND FARES

Round-trip fares are generally of three types – short excursions (usually one month, sometimes requiring advance purchase – Apex), three-month excursions and one year (never more). A **one-way** fare (valid a year) is normally half the "yearly" fare. You may be able to fly out to one destination and back from another (an "**open jaw**"), depending on the airline and the agent's contract. In rare cases, you may also be able to purchase a ticket *back* from West Africa, before you leave – useful if you're travelling out overland. *Balkan Bulgarian Airlines* and *Egyptair* tickets can be bought like this; in the case of the latter you'll have to collect the ticket from their office in the city from which you intend to fly back. Such arrangements are often surprisingly reliable.

Once you have your ticket, check the status boxes are what you've been told: a confirmed seat on the flight will be marked "OK", a place on the waiting list "WL". If your ticket says "RQ" you're not even waitlisted, merely "requested". Note that a ticket has to be "OK" before you can actually fly.

FLIGHTS & HOLIDAYS FROM BRITAIN AND IRELAND

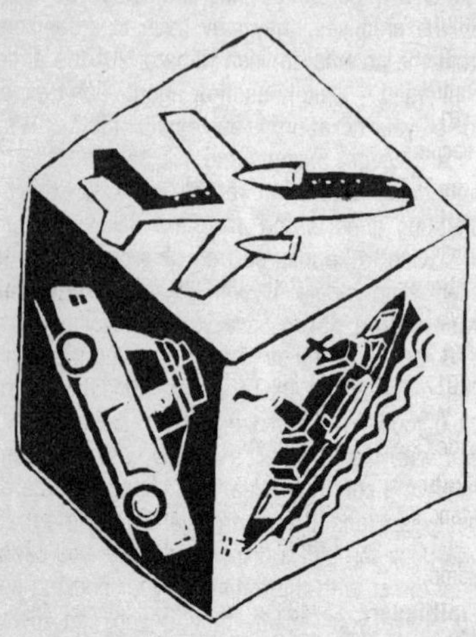

The airlines with the busiest West African schedules are the Dutch airline *KLM* and the Belgian airline *Sabena*. Both route all flights through their home airports of Amsterdam and Brussels. *British Airways* only flies to Accra and Lagos. Other useful airlines include *Air Afrique*, *Air France* and *Swissair*.

When booking in Britain, it's a good idea to check your agent is an ATOL (Air Travel Operator's Licence) holder. If not, they should be an authorized agent of an ATOL holder and thus by extension offer the same protection. An ATOL ensures that in the event of the airline going bust, your money is safe.

You can pay anything from under £400 ($600) return to nearly £700 ($1050) for a return flight from London to West Africa. Most discounted return fares fall somewhere between £400 ($600) and £500 ($750). One-ways are rarely less than £200 ($300). The cheapest fare to many destinations is often on the Russian airline, *Aeroflot*. Many *Aeroflot* schedules, however, only operate once or twice a month and most require a stopover in Moscow (basic hotel at their expense). Most of the better agents are unwilling to deal with them.

For an idea of the saving over the airlines' own fares, make a few calls to their fares departments (see p.7). Current *IATA* one-month excursion fares in the region go from around £750/$1125 to £1000/$1500. If you want to try some detective work, ask the airline for their consolidators' details. Some are only too happy, others refuse.

FLIGHTS FROM IRELAND

There are no non-stop flights from Ireland to West Africa: the best routings are via Brussels on

Sabena or, if you're flying from Belfast, via Amsterdam on *KLM* (overnight stay required). For other destinations, or more price choices, talk to a clued-up travel agent and expect to route through London or Paris – though not without incurring some delay.

CHARTER FLIGHTS

The only regular **charter flights** from Britain to West Africa are to **The Gambia** from London Gatwick and Manchester. Prices for stays of from one to four weeks range from around £200–£300 ($300–$450). You'll have to keep checking the situation with the operators – it changes from year to year (see the "Package Tours" section, p.9). Special promotions are sometimes introduced to fill seats, and these can be really excellent value.

If you're travelling to Nigeria before Christmas, check the press, especially *West Africa* magazine, for details of special charters.

HOLIDAYS FROM THE UK

The Gambia is the best-known West African package destination from Britain. Most travel agents will have a choice of brochures which include it, and it is a good place to go if you're looking for a short winter holiday, with guaranteed sun and a low-key African atmosphere that is not too over-exploited. Read the brochures carefully, ask for the full details of the hotel from the agent's manual, and look carefully through the listings in our chapter on the country. Most operators also offer summer departures (during the rainy season), which are much cheaper, and there are often good, last-minute offers available.

DISCOUNT AGENTS IN BRITAIN

Africa Travel Centre, 4 Medway Court, Leigh St, London WC1H 9QX (☎0171/387-1211; Fax 0171/383-7512). Helpful and resourceful Africa specialists offering flights, packages, overland tours, books, maps and advice.

African Travel Specialists, 98 Victoria St, Victoria House, London SW1E 5JL (☎0171/630-5434; Fax 0171/630-5470). Specialists with particularly good deals on direct flights to Accra and Lagos.

Bridge the World, 1–3 Ferdinand St, Camden Town, London NW1 (☎0171/911-0900; 24hr ☎0171/911-0830). Competitive independent travel firm.

Campus Travel, 52 Grosvenor Gardens, London SW1W 0AG (☎0171/730-8111). Nationwide student/youth specialist with over thirty branches.

Holiday Planners: London ☎0171/439-7755; Manchester ☎0161/832-3167. Excellent range of destinations, all via Brussels.

North-South Travel, Moulsham Mill Centre, Parkway, Chelmsford, Essex CM2 7PX (☎01245/492882; Fax 01245/356612). Small agency whose modest profits are devoted to developing-world charities.

Redcoat Express, Unit 3B, Gatwick Metro Centre, Balcombe Rd, Horley, Surrey RH6 9GA (☎01293/ 774141 Fax 01293/774080). West Africa specialists.

Sam Travel, 14 Broadwick St, London W1V 1FH (☎0171/434-9561; Fax 0171/494-3560). *Aeroflot* specialists.

Soliman Travel, 133 Earl's Court Rd, London SW5 (☎0171/37-6446). *Egyptair* specialists.

STA Travel, 74 Old Brompton Rd, London SW7 (☎0171/937-9962). Full range of cities and airlines for West Africa, from 20 UK offices and 120 worldwide. Special fares for students and young people.

Sunbeam Travel: London ☎0171/396-9922; Manchester ☎0161/236-3144; Glasgow ☎0141/204-1717. Good value fares to Accra and Lagos via Rome.

Trailfinders, 42–48 Earl's Court Rd, London W8 6EJ (☎0171/938-3366; Fax 0171/937-9294). Respected discount flights agency with a range of other services and several regional branches.

DISCOUNT AGENTS IN IRELAND

Thomas Cook, 118 Grafton St, Dublin (☎01/677-1721) and 11 Donegall Place, Belfast (☎01232/240 833). Reasonable range of mainstream discount fares.

USIT, O'Connell Bridge, 19/21 Aston Quay, Dublin (☎01/778117) and 31a Queen St, Belfast (☎01232/242562). Ireland's foremost student and youth specialists.

Joe Walsh Tours, 8–11 Baggot St, Dublin (☎01/678-9555). General discount agent.

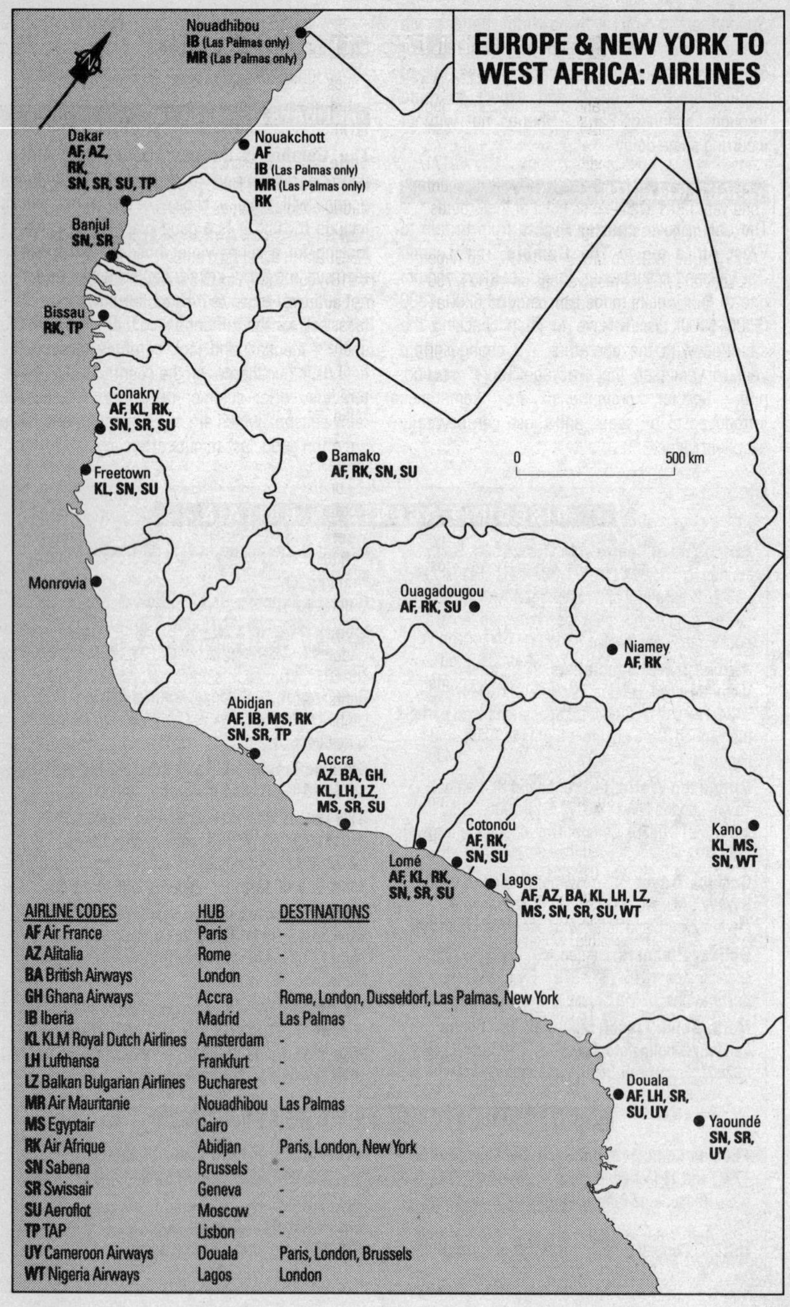

AIRLINE CODES	HUB	DESTINATIONS
AF Air France	Paris	-
AZ Alitalia	Rome	-
BA British Airways	London	-
GH Ghana Airways	Accra	Rome, London, Dusseldorf, Las Palmas, New York
IB Iberia	Madrid	Las Palmas
KL KLM Royal Dutch Airlines	Amsterdam	-
LH Lufthansa	Frankfurt	-
LZ Balkan Bulgarian Airlines	Bucharest	-
MR Air Mauritanie	Nouadhibou	Las Palmas
MS Egyptair	Cairo	-
RK Air Afrique	Abidjan	Paris, London, New York
SN Sabena	Brussels	-
SR Swissair	Geneva	-
SU Aeroflot	Moscow	-
TP TAP	Lisbon	-
UY Cameroon Airways	Douala	Paris, London, Brussels
WT Nigeria Airways	Lagos	London

AIRLINES IN THE UK

Check with the airlines for schedules and full fares. Airlines prefer to avoid being officially associated with particular agents and do not as a rule quote discounted fares. However they may refer you to their consolidator agents, for whom various addresses are given in the "Discount Agents" box.

Aeroflot (SU), 70 Piccadilly, London W1 (☎0171/355-2233; Fax 0171/355-2323). Heavily discounted one-year fares available on most of their routes through many discount agencies.

Air Afrique (RK), c/o *British Airways*, 156 Regent St, London W1 (NB: reservations on ☎0171/730-2192). Direct flight to Abidjan; many others via Paris. No UK discounts.

Air France (AF), 177 Piccadilly, London W1V 9DE (☎0181/742-6600; Fax 0181/750-4488). Flights via Paris. Discounted seats available.

Alitalia (AZ), 205 Holland Park Ave, London W11 4XB (☎0171/602-7111; Fax 0171/603-1095). Accra, Dakar and Lagos via Rome, but rarely discounted.

Balkan Bulgarian Airlines (LZ), 322 Regent St, London W1R 5AB (☎0171/637-7637; Fax 0171/637-2481). Overnight flights to Accra and Lagos via Sofia. Not a pleasant journey but reliable enough and among the cheapest.

British Airways (BA), 156 Regent St, London W1 (central reservations: ☎0181/897-4000). Good student fares available through selected agents. Some specially discounted (and unrestricted) fares.

Cameroon Airlines (UY), 44 Conduit St, London W1R 9FB (☎0171/734-7676). Non-stop flight London–Douala on Sun, arrives Douala Mon morning. Own fares.

Egyptair (MS), 31 Piccadilly, London W1V OPT (☎0171/734-2395; Fax 0171/287-1728). Flights to Abidjan, Accra, Lagos and Kano via Cairo (with an overnight at the airline's expense). Extended stopovers in Cairo are possible, which makes this an interesting alternative. Discounted fares are widely available.

Ghana Airways (GH), 12 Old Bond St, London W1R (☎0171/499-0201; Fax 0171/491-1504). Three flights a week to Accra. Economical fares direct from the airline or through agents.

Iberia (IB), 29 Glasshouse St, London W1R 5RG (☎0171/830-0011; Fax 0171/413-1262). Flights via Madrid and Las Palmas to Dakar.

KLM Royal Dutch Airlines (KL), Plesman House, 190 Gt South West Rd, Feltham, Middx, TW14 9RL (☎0181/750-9200; Fax 0181/750-9090). One of the best airlines. Flights via Amsterdam (out of Belfast, Birmingham, Bristol, Cardiff and Southampton as well as London) to a number of West African cities. Many agents offer discounted fares and one or two have longer validities and "open jaw" deals available at very competitive prices.

Lufthansa German Airlines (LH), 10 Old Bond St, London W1X 4EN (☎0345/737747). Flights to Accra and Lagos via Frankfurt. Rarely discounted.

Nigeria Airways (WT), 12 Conduit St, London W1R 0NX (☎0171/629-3717; Fax 0171/491-9644). Overnight flights direct to Kano and Lagos, but can be unreliable. Occasionally good discounted fares.

Sabena Belgian Airlines (SN), 177 Piccadilly, London W1V 9DB (☎0171/495-7272; Fax 0171/495- 0774). Top quality airline, along with *KLM*. Flights via Brussels (and ex Bristol, Dublin, Edinburgh, Glasgow, Leeds, Manchester, and Newcastle), include some less common destinations (Bamako, Niamey and Yaoundé, for example). Discounted fares available.

Swissair (SR), Swiss Centre, 10 Wardour St, London W1V 4BJ (☎0171/439-4144; Fax 0171/434-7214). Flights via Zurich and Geneva. Some discounts available.

TACV (VR). No London Office. Flights from Lisbon to Sal, Cape Verde. Through-bookings from London, using *TAP*, can be made with most discount agents in London.

TAP Air Portugal (TP), 38–44 Gillingham St, London SW1 (☎0171/828-0262; Fax 0171/931-0805). Via Lisbon to Abidjan, Bissau, Dakar and Sal. No discounts.

In the past, other mainstream package alternatives have included the Cap Skiring coast in **Senegal**, and **Sierra Leone**. At the time of writing, neither was available through a high street operator. *Caravela*, the holiday arm of the Portuguese airline *TAP*, offers holidays in **Cape Verde** and **Guinea-Bissau** and you can find a number of interesting trips through **French operators** and agents if you visit Paris.

An excellent option from Britain is the highly recommended **Ghana homestay** programme operated by *Insight Travel*, 6 Norton Rd,

PLANNING AHEAD

AIRPORTS

If you're uncertain where to fly in, this rundown of West Africa's airports might help to narrow down your choice. Another factor to consider before you buy an air ticket is whether you need a visa for that country and how easy that will be to obtain (see "Red Tape and Visas", p.19).

• **Some airports are simply best avoided**. **Lagos** (Nigeria) and **Douala** (Cameroon) do not make promising first impressions. Both are likely to be swelteringly hot and they are notoriously corrupt. Lagos, after dark, is downright unsafe and the journey to the city by taxi can be unnerving (Kano, in northern Nigeria is a less nerve-wracking international airport).

• Smaller capitals, naturally enough, have the most agreeable airports. Good candidates include **Banjul** (The Gambia), **Bissau** (Guinea-Bissau), **Sal** (Cape Verde), **Bamako** (Mali), **Ouagadougou** (Burkina Faso) and **Niamey** (Niger).

• Among medium-sized capitals, **Abidjan** (Côte d'Ivoire) is well-organized and convenient and **Accra** (Ghana), **Dakar** (Senegal) and **Conakry** (Guinea) aren't bad. **Freetown** airport is shambolic and very inconveniently located.

• **Cotonou** (Benin) is probably the best all-round choice – small and well-run, pretty much unaffected by hassles and chaos and very close to the city centre.

OVERNIGHT FLIGHTS

An additional factor is the time you will arrive. It's obviously preferable to **arrive by day**, especially in a large city – but, unfortunately, overnight flights to West Africa are in the minority. Most flights arrive in the evening, or at best the late afternoon.

These airlines operate at least some flights from Europe by night, to arrive in West Africa the next morning:

Abidjan (ex Paris)
Air Afrique and *Air France*

Accra (ex London)
Balkan Bulgarian Airlines

Bamako (ex Paris)
Air Afrique

Conakry
Aeroflot (ex London), *Air Afrique* (ex Paris)

Cotonou (ex Paris)
Air Afrique and *Air France*

Dakar (ex Paris)
Air Afrique

Douala (ex London)
Air France and *Cameroon Airlines*

Freetown (ex London)
Aeroflot

Lagos (ex London)
Air France, *Balkan Bulgarian* and *Nigeria Airways*

Niamey (ex London)
Air France

LONDON–WEST AFRICA NON-STOP

The following services operate non-stop from London to:

Abidjan *Air Afrique*, Sun

Abuja *Nigeria Airways*, Sun

Accra *British Airways*, Wed, Fri, Sun; *Ghana Airways*, Thurs, Sat

Banjul charter operators

Douala *Cameroon Airlines*, Sun

Kano *Nigeria Airways*, Mon, Wed

Lagos *British Airways*, Mon, Tues, Thurs, Sat; *Nigeria Airways*, Tues, Sat

Garstang, Preston, Lancs, PR3 1JY (☎01995/606095), in which you stay as a guest near Kumasi and participate in local life. In northern Ghana, the *Suntaa-Nuntaa* project in WA is a good way of meeting Ghanaians and participating in agro-forestry development work. Charges are modest. Contact friends of Suntaa-Nuntaa, 44 Melville Place, Leeds LS6 2LZ, UK.

WEST AFRICA BY FREIGHTER

Surprisingly perhaps, going by **cargo ship** from Europe to "the Coast" is not quite history. At the bottom end of the scale, this is an unusual and price-competitive way of travelling to West Africa. While conditions vary from adequate to luxurious depending on the ship and your choice of cabin, fares include all meals. Stays in port

BRITISH PACKAGE OPERATORS

THE GAMBIA

During the winter of 1994/95, most British operators pulled out of **The Gambia** after an over-sensitive Foreign Office travel advisory. Most were expected to resume operations in the winter of 1995/1996. The main operators to The Gambia include *Thompson, Kuoni, Going Places, Airtours* and *Hayes and Jarvis.*

The Gambia Experience, Kingfisher House, Rownhams Lane, North Baddesley, Hampshire SO52 9LP (☎01703/730888; Fax 01703/731122). Gambia specialists with a strong commitment to the country – the only British operator to continue selling holidays while the travel advisory was posted. Includes some offbeat hotels and good offers.

OTHER COUNTRIES

Caravela Tours, 38–44 Gillingham St, London SW1V 1HU (☎0171/630-9225; Fax 0171/233-9680). One- or two-week packages to Cape Verde and Guinea Bissau, including Rubane Island. Expensive.

Club Med, 106–8 Brompton Rd, London SW3 1LJ (☎0171/581-1161). All-inclusive stays at holiday villages in Senegal and Côte d'Ivoire. Fun, if you speak reasonable French, and good for families, but very insulated from anything local or West African.

will vary from a few hours to a couple of days or more. You may need to embark from a north European port. Suitable insurance cover is required, which for over-65s can be expensive.

Gdynia American Shipping Lines, 238 City Rd, London EC1V 2QL (☎0171/251-3389; Fax 0171/250-3625), are agents for *Euro-Africa Lines* which depart every ten days or so from Szczecin to Hamburg, Antwerp/Rotterdam, Las Palmas, Dakar, Banjul, Freetown, Monrovia, Abidjan, Tema, Lomé, Cotonou, Lagos, Port Harcourt, Douala and then back again (total round-trip voyage around 60–80 days). Not every port is visited on every voyage. One-way fares to Dakar/Banjul/Freetown/Monrovia start from £360 ($540) sharing a twin cabin. These are small ships, around 7000 tonnes.

The *Grimaldi Line*, 103–105 Jermyn St, London SW1Y 6ES (☎0171/930-5683; Fax 0171/839-1961), operates brand-new Italian container ships (much bigger and designed with passengers in mind, even with swimming pools) from Tilbury to Hamburg, Rotterdam, Antwerp, Le Havre, Dakar (8 days), Conakry, Freetown, Lomé, Cotonou, Lagos (13 days), Tema, Douala (17 days), then back to Tilbury. One-way fares (Europe to West Africa) start at £850 ($1275) per person sharing a three-berth outside cabin, £1066 ($1600) sharing a twin and £1400 ($2100) for a single cabin. Car tariffs start at £416 ($625) and motorbikes £240 ($360). Ships depart about every 18 days.

The German line *NSB* offers a regular West African service from Felixstowe, via Le Havre, Dakar, Conakry, Freetown, Abidjan, Tema, Lomé, Cotonou, Lagos, Libreville and Douala; then back via Abidjan, Dakar and Portugal. Fares for the 64-day round-trip, in very comfortable cabins, range from £3500 ($5250) to £5900 ($9000) depending on the cabin.

The *Strand Cruise and Travel Centre*, Charing Cross Shopping Concourse (☎0171/836-6363; Fax 0171/497-0078), has been in the business a long time and can supply full details and make bookings on all the above routes.

FLIGHTS FROM NORTH AMERICA

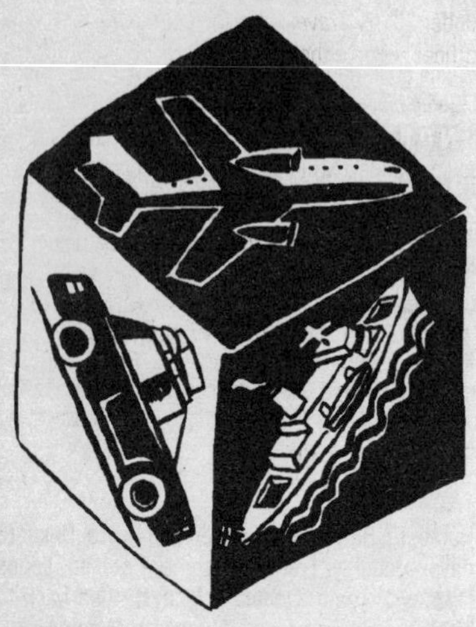

Currently the only direct flights from the USA to West Africa are *Air Afrique*'s service from New York to Dakar (continuing to Abidjan) or *Nigeria Airways'* flights to Lagos. The quickest alternatives are via Paris, Amsterdam or Brussels – where *Air France, Air Afrique, KLM* and *Sabena* connect to most Francophone capitals – or via London.

Discount fares are available by booking through one of the budget agencies (consolidators) listed on p.11. You might save money or air tickets by flying to London or Paris, stopping over for a few days and picking up a discounted flight there, but, assuming you find a cut-rate deal, you may have to be prepared to wait for a seat. You could even telephone or fax ahead from the USA or Canada. But again, you'd need to be flexible – and you could easily build up a big phone bill while trying to save money.

If you do break your journey in Europe, remember that the "two pieces" **luggage limit** that applies on trans-Atlantic flights becomes a "20kg" (44 pound) limit for the rest of the world.

FLIGHTS FROM THE EAST COAST

If you're a **student**, **youth** or **teacher**, *Council Travel* should be your first call. They offer the *Air Afrique* New York–**Abidjan** flight from around $1200 round-trip in the off-season ($1050 to **Dakar**). Compare their fares with those of *STA Travel*, who have a large international network of offices. They offer roughly $1100–1300 return to West Africa, on the basis of restricted eligibility, destination and season.

Classified advertisers in the Sunday travel section of the *New York Times* offer various discounted fares open to all, though there's generally very little direct to West Africa. Non-students will do better checking the **budget agencies**, some of whose fares are only slightly higher than those of *Council* and *STA* (sometimes as low as $1350 return to Abidjan). Good **one-way** deals are very rare.

Any of these estimates still probably make it cheaper to buy tickets in the USA compared with bolting together a trip **via London** from about $400 with an onward flight to, for example, Accra, for the equivalent of $750-plus in sterling – unless, that is, you find an exceptional deal and and don't mind spending some time in Europe.

FLIGHTS FROM THE WEST COAST

Again, it's a good idea to give *Council* and *STA Travel* a call first. Off-season, their LA–**Abidjan** fares, including *Air Afrique*'s flight from New York, plus an add-on, start as low as $1250 ($1100 to **Dakar**) and sometimes they have bargain deals open to all. Also, and especially if you're not a student, check the agents listed on p.11 (*Maharaja Travels*, for example, is very adept at finding the cheapest rates, or closer to home, *New Coast Travel*). Finally, make a search of the Sunday Travel pages of the *Los Angeles Times* or the *San Francisco Examiner/Chronicle*. Offers for low-fare travel to Africa are exceedingly rare, but you can often find really good deals on **flights to Europe**.

FLIGHTS FROM CANADA

There are **no direct flights** to West Africa from any Canadian city. You have two main options for getting there. Firstly you could fly to New York and connect with an Africa-bound flight there. Or you could fly to London or another European capital, either connecting on to West Africa, or stopping over long enough to make onward arrangements. *KLM*, via Amsterdam, has some of the best connections, with just a few hours to kill at Schiphol airport.

If you fly to London, Paris, Amsterdam or another capital in northern Europe, you're looking at anything from a rock bottom CAN$600 round-trip out-of-season fare from Toronto, or CAN$800 from Vancouver, to perhaps CAN$1000 or CAN$1200 high season. If you are a student or under 26, try *Travel Cuts*, the college agents, with offices all over the country.

USEFUL AIRLINES IN NORTH AMERICA

Air Afrique (☎1-800/456-9192) 2 flights a week from New York to Abidjan, via Dakar.

Air Canada (☎1-800/776-3000). From many Canadian cities to European cities.

Air France (US: ☎1-800/237-2747; Canada: ☎1-800/667-2747). Several flights daily to Paris from New York, plus Chicago, Houston, LA, Miami, San Francisco and Washington, all non-stop.

British Airways (US: ☎1-800/247-9297; Canada: ☎1-800/668-1059). From many North American cities to London.

Canadian Airlines (☎1-800/426-7000). From major Canadian cities to major European cities.

Ghana Airways (☎1-800/404-4262) 5 flights a week from New York to Accra, 2 via Dakar.

KLM (US: ☎1-800/374-7747; Canada: ☎1-800/361-5073). From many North American cities to Amsterdam with connections on to West Africa.

Nigeria Airways (☎212/935-2700) 2 flights a week from New York to Lagos.

Sabena (☎1-800/955-2000). Eastern US cities to Brussels, with connections on to West Africa.

South African Airways (☎1-800/722-9675) 1 flight a week from New York to Jo'burg, via Sal, Cape Verde.

TACV 535 Boylston St, 3rd floor, Boston MA 02116 (☎617/578-8940). Flights from Boston to Sal, Cape Verde, summer and Christmas only.

Virgin (☎1-800/862-8261). From many cities to London.

NORTH AMERICAN DISCOUNT AGENTS

Though all of the companies listed below offer reduced-rate tickets, some are travel "clubs" which require membership (generally around $50 and refundable if you're not satisfied). Most book flights all the way to Africa, while others are included because they have special fares to Europe – sometimes as low as $299 for LA–Paris return.

American Youth Travel Centre, 1434 2nd St, Santa Monica, CA (☎310/393-3413).

Around the World, 2241 Polk St, San Francisco, CA 94109 (☎415/673-9950).

Council Travel, Head Office: 205 E 42nd St, New York, NY 10017 (☎212/661-1450).

Discount Club of America, 61–63 Woodhaven Blvd, Rego Park, NY 11374 (☎718/335-9612).

Flytime, 45 W 34th St, Suite 305, New York, NY 10001 (☎212/760-3737).

Interworld, 3400 Coral Way, Miami, FL 33145 (☎305/443-4929).

Magical Holidays, 501 Madison Ave, New York, NY 10022 (☎1-800/223-6862).

Maharaja Travels, 393 5th Ave, New York, NY 10016 (☎1-800/223-6862).

Moment's Notice, 425 Madison Ave, New York, NY 10017 (☎212/486-0503).

New Coast Travel, 440 Lincoln Blvd, Venice, CA 90291 (☎310/452-1990).

Pan-Express Travel, 209 Mail St, San Francisco, CA 94108 (☎415/989-8282).

Spector Travel, 31 St James Ave, Boston, MA 02116 (☎1-800/879-2374).

STA Travel, Head Office: 48 E 11th St, New York, NY 10003 (☎1-800/777-0112).

Stand Buys, 311 W Superior St, Chicago, IL 60610 (membership required; ☎1-800/331-0275).

Swan Travel, 400 Madison Ave, New York, NY 10017 (☎212/421-1010).

Travel Cuts, Head Office: 187 College St, Toronto, ON M5T 1P7 (☎416/979-2406).

Travel International, Ives Building 114 Forest Ave, Suite 205, Narbeth, PA 19072 (☎1-800/221-8139).

Traveler's Advantage, 49 Music Square, Nashville, TN 37203 (membership required; ☎1-800/548-1116).

UniTravel, Box 12485, 1177 Warson Rd, St Louis, MO 63132 (☎1-800/325-2222).

Worldwide Discount Travel Club, 1674 Meridian Ave, Miami Beach, FL 33139 (☎305/534-2082).

FLIGHTS FROM AUSTRALASIA

From Australia and New Zealand, you'll have the most options if you fly first to Europe, and then connect with a flight to West Africa, though you could fly to Cairo and then on to Kano, Lagos, Accra or Abidjan on *Egyptair*, or as part of even wider travels on *Singapore Airlines* to India, then on to Addis Ababa, where *Ethiopian Airlines* will connect you to almost anywhere in West Africa.

The only **direct flights to Africa from Australia** or New Zealand currently on offer are the four flights a week that go from Sydney and Perth to southern Africa courtesy of *Qantas/Air Zimbabwe* and *South African Airways.* Two of these flights take you direct to **Johannesburg**, the other two going via **Harare**. From Johannesburg or Harare you can pick up connections to West Africa – see the next section.

AUSTRALIAN AND NEW ZEALAND AIRLINE ADDRESSES

Air New Zealand, Air New Zealand House, Queen St, Auckland (☎09/357-3000).

British Airways, 64 Castlereagh St, Sydney (☎02/258-3300) and Dilworth Building, Queen St, Auckland (☎09/367-7500).

Qantas, International Square, Jamison St, Sydney (☎02/957-0111 or 236-3636) and Qantas House, 154 Queen St, Auckland (☎09/303-2506).

Singapore Airlines, 17 Bridge St, Sydney (☎02/236-0111) and West Plaza Building, Ground Floor, corner of Customs St and Albert St, Auckland (☎09/379-3209).

AUSTRALIAN DISCOUNT AGENTS

Anywhere Travel, 345 Anzac Parade, Kingsford, Sydney (☎02/663-0411).

Brisbane Discount Travel, 360 Queen St, Brisbane (☎07/229-9211).

Discount Travel Specialists, Shop 53, Forrest Chase, Perth (☎09/221-1400).

Flight Centres, Circular Quay, Sydney (☎02/241-2422); Bourke St, Melbourne (☎03/650-2899); plus other branches nationwide except the Northern Territory.

Passport Travel, 320b Glenferrie Rd, Malvern, Melbourne (☎03/824-7183).

STA Travel, 732 Harris St, Sydney (☎02/212-1255); 256 Flinders St, Melbourne (☎03/347-4711); plus other offices in Townsville and state capitals.

Topdeck Travel, 45 Grenfell St, Adelaide (☎08/410-1110).

Tymtro Travel, Suite G12, Wallaceway Shopping Centre, Chatswood, Sydney (☎02/411-1222).

NEW ZEALAND DISCOUNT AGENTS

Budget Travel, PO Box 505, Auckland (☎09/309-4313).

Flight Centres, National Bank Towers, 205–225 Queen St, Auckland (☎09/309-6171); Shop 1M, National Mutual Arcade, 152 Hereford St, Christchurch (☎09/379-7145); 50–52 Willis St, Wellington (☎04/472-8101); plus other branches countrywide.

STA Travel, Traveller's Centre, 10 High St, Auckland (☎09/309-9995); 233 Cuba St, Wellington (☎04/385-0561); 223 High St, Christchurch (☎03/379-9098); plus other offices in Dunedin, Palmerston North and Hamilton.

FLIGHTS FROM THE REST OF AFRICA

From **South Africa**, *Air Afrique* and *South African Airways* share the Johannesburg to Abidjan route, connecting with *Air Afrique* flights across West Africa, while *Ghana Airways* flies via Harare to Accra and Lagos with onward connections and *Cameroon Airlines* flies weekly from Jo'burg to Douala via Harare and Kinshasa. *South Africa Airways* flies four times a week to Sal, Cape Verde, en route to New York. There's also a weekly *Aeroflot* link between Jo'burg and Lomé.

From **Harare**, the only direct connections are these *Ghana Airways* flights, plus flights from Harare to Douala on *Cameroon Airlines*, and to Lagos and Accra on *Balkan Bulgarian*. There are also flights from Harare to Nairobi five times a week on *Air Zimbabwe* and *Kenya Airways* – fares about £245 ($368) – with connections west from Nairobi.

From East Africa to West Africa, **Nairobi** is the natural hub for flights, though even here, where discount ticket agents thrive, special fares to West Africa, apart from the odd Apex, are unknown. There are direct flights on *Ethiopian Airlines* to Abidjan, Accra, Lagos, Lomé and Monrovia, and also – with a change of planes in Addis Ababa – to Bamako and Dakar. *Cameroon Airlines* runs flights twice a week between Douala and Naïrobi via Kinshasa and Kigali.

From **North Africa** direct flights connect **Casablanca** to Abidjan, Bamako, Conakry, Dakar, Lomé, Nouakchott and – once a month – Bissau; **Algiers** to Bamako, Dakar, Nouakchott and Ouagadougou; and **Tunis** to Dakar. Prices, even one-way, seem high, from around £200 ($300) to £350 ($525) on these routes, and you'd be lucky to find anything discounted.

OVERLAND AND ADVENTURE TRAVEL

Despite recent troubles which have effectively closed the route through Algeria to West Africa, overlanding from Europe, via Morocco and into Mauritania, is still feasible. It's the best way to get to the region if you want to become fully immersed in the identities and landscapes of West Africa: as you finally arrive on the far side of the sea of sand and rock, the first sensations of another world are ones that endure. If you don't have the time or the inclination to do the trip alone, a number of companies will take you, or meet you from a flight for an escorted overland trip through one or more countries.

If you're setting off on extensive travels, the **best time to leave** is at the end of the European summer. Especially if you plan to hitch and use public transport, you should aim to be in North Africa in September and across the Sahara in October. Throughout most of the region, this gives you at least six months before you can realistically expect to be rained upon.

TRANS-SAHARAN ROUTES

If you're planning to cross the desert you should be careful to obtain the most up-to-date information. Talk to returning travellers and read the African news magazines. Since the early 1990s there have been sporadic clashes between **Tuareg nomads** and the governments of Mali and Niger. Incidents of banditry on trans-Saharan tourists led to armed escorts for convoys and eventually to border closures.

Meanwhile, in **Algeria**, the fundamentalist GIA (Groupe Islamique Armée) has murdered

> The practical information at the beginning of each country chapter has details on overland arrival from that country's neighbours, including transport availability, road conditions and the kind of treatment you might expect from border officials. As a general rule, borders close at dusk and often on public holidays. Very few are open 24 hours.

dozens of foreigners (mostly expatriate workers) who ignored their September 1993 deadline to leave the country. As a result of the dangers of travel in Algeria, the traditional trans-Saharan routes were still effectively closed to foreigners as this book went to press, with no prospects of conditions improving sufficiently to make either of them even barely safe. A brief description is given below for information in the event of their reopening.

Mauritania has conceded to pressure from overlanders seeking an alternative route, effectively opening its northern border to southbound traffic using the **Atlantic route** that hugs the coast through southern Morocco to **Nouadhibou**, the mineral port just inside Mauritania. It's a safe enough route, though convoys lead vehicles past minefields near the Mauritanian border. Apart from a difficult section from Nouadhibou to Nouakchott along the coast (guide essential) – which can be avoided by putting your vehicle on the **ore train** heading inland – this route is relatively easy on vehicles, although scenically less impressive than the old Algerian routes.

DRIVING YOURSELF

Driving to West Africa isn't a difficult feat in itself. Many people set off with more or less unmodified road vehicles. Even a Citröen 2CV can make it if you're prepared to go slowly, take care as you drive and let it cool – and its physical lightness can be a positive advantage. But all motorized travellers (whether on two, four or six wheels) agree that the comfort and independence

THE CLOSED ROUTES AND THE TUAREG

Until the early 1990s, the main trans-Saharan routes were through **Algeria**, now a country effectively closed to foreigners because of attacks by Muslim fundamentalists. Even before the current civil war, the Algerian routes were becoming risky due to Tuareg banditry. What follows summarizes the routes as they were in the late 1980s. When overlanders start using them again, the tracks are likely to be hard to follow and what facilities that existed along the way will have fallen into disrepair.

From the Mediterranean coast, the Sahara is just a day's drive to the south – and a couple of days will see you well into the heart of it. The great majority of travellers (in their own vehicles or otherwise) used the **Hoggar**, a route with long portions of asphalt, stunning variety of scenery, and more towns to break the drive. These include historic settlements like **In Salah** and **El Goléa** and administrative outposts like **Tamanrasset**, a gathering point for desert nomads. The Hoggar mountains peak at 2908m near **Assekrem**, while around Djanet, in the east, the **Tassili** plateau reaches heights of 2154m in the remote **Tassili National Park**, the site of prehistoric **cave paintings** from an age when the Sahara was bursting with life. The last Algerian post is at **In Guezzam**, from where a 25km stretch of sandy, track-scrawled no-man's-land (sometimes a whole day's travel if you had nobody to guide you) fills the space before godforsaken **Assamakka**, the Nigérien border post. The drive from Assamakka to the start of the tarmac at **Arlit** takes around six hours.

Though less scenically compelling, the **Tanezrouft** route would be the one to choose for the most dramatic introduction to sub-Saharan Africa. It's a bigger adventure – and a more personal experience, as fewer people use it. This stretch of desert is almost completely flat and barren and distances between settlements seem staggering. Picturesque oases like **Taghit**, **Beni-Abbès** and **Timimoun** dot the route in its early stages, well to the north of the **Tropic of Cancer**. By the time you reach the end of the tarmac at **Reggane**, roughly a third of the way across, there still remains over 1300km of uninterrupted *piste* before arrival at the next town, **Gao**, in Mali, on the almost lush banks of the Niger River.

There are two main **Tuareg groups** living in the Algerian Sahara: the **Kel Ahaggar**, who occupy the Hoggar near Tamanrasset, and the **Kel Ajjer**, who live in the Tassili near Djanet. Further afield, other groups are scattered throughout the desert. Among them are the Kel Aïr and Kel Gress in Niger, and the Kel Tademaket in the Timbuktu region of Mali.

The Tuareg speak **Tamashek** (or *Tamahaq*, or numerous other spellings), a Berber dialect that's one of the few African languages with its own script. Traditionally, they controlled trans-Saharan trade, offering protection to caravans or raiding those that refused their services. Their society was highly stratified, with classes ranging from nobles to slaves, and the **Harratin**, blacks who formerly worked as indentured servants, still live in virtual chatteldom in many of the desert oases. The Algerian Tuareg have become increasingly sedentary, due in part to a government plan to settle them, and in part to the crippling effects of the drought of the mid-1980s.

of their **own vehicle** is a mixed blessing. It insulates you from the life of Africa; it's a permanent security headache, especially in towns; and it says one thing – money – to everyone you meet along the way. You can feel like a travelling circus after a few weeks of this. Taking account of fuel, maintenance and insurance, it is a fairly expensive business, too. And unless you have someone aboard who knows the vehicle inside out (and even then) any serious breakdown can be immensely tedious and costly.

The outstanding **advantages** of taking your own vehicle are that you can get off the beaten track (assuming the vehicle is sturdy enough) and visit areas that see a local vehicle only once in a toddler's lifetime. To a great extent, you can actually avoid towns and cities, or at least avoid staying overnight in them by driving out into the wilderness and camping.

One consideration can't be stressed enough – give yourself **time**. Rushing around in Africa is a bad enough idea using local transport. But to try to drive in your own vehicle with a fixed number of days and weeks is to court disaster. Allow a month, at the very least, to get from the Mediterranean to sub-Saharan Africa. It's simply not worth the work, in any case, to rush through at a breakneck pace.

If you intend to **sell your vehicle** in West Africa, your best investment would be a three-year old Peugeot 505 *familiale* station wagon – semi-automatic, petrol engine and of course left-hand drive. Most end up in service as *taxis brousse*. The best West African countries in which to sell vary depending on current import laws and economic conditions: ask as you go.

Good **books** for drivers heading to West Africa include: *The Sahara Handbook*, Simon Glen (Lascelles, 1990), *Through Africa: the Overlanders' Guide*, Bob Swain and Paula Snyder (Bradt, 1991), and the unique *Desert Biking*, Chris Scott (Travellers' Bookshop, 1993).

VEHICLE DOCUMENTS

Travelling by private vehicle drastically increases the red tape you'll have to deal with. First and foremost, you must be able to produce the vehicle's **log book**, stating ownership, country of registration and the registration, chassis and engine numbers. All these details are checked thoroughly at customs. If you're not the owner of the car you're driving, you'll need a notified document (*attestation du propriétaire* in French) stating permission to use the car. In many countries, you will be able to buy a **carte grise**, international registration certificate from the local licensing authority. This makes passage through checkpoints easier.

Your national **driver's licence** is usually acceptable, but many people get an **international driving licence**, not a bad idea, especially considering how easy to obtain and cheap they are (the British AA and other motoring organizations sell them over the counter). Their size and the official-looking stamps seem to confer extra legitimacy to border officials, and as they're translated into French and Arabic they're instantly recognizable.

A **carnet** is also taken by many motorists. These documents (again issued by associations like the AA) allow you to take your car into a country without paying import duties or a deposit. They're expensive, however, since the motoring clubs require a bank guarantee (that may be substantially more than the value of your car) before handing them out. The *carnet* is not required for a number of countries, where you make temporary importation arrangements at the border (or even at the embassy when obtaining a visa), and is specifically *not* valid in Nigeria.

Motor insurance is obligatory and varies in cost. Motorbike insurance is approximately half the cost of cars, and commercial vehicles (including minibuses with eight seats plus driver) twice as much. As soon as you cross into Mauritania, you need to buy a new policy that will cover you for all ECOWAS (Economic Community of West African States) countries. This is the **carte brun**, (brown card) insurance. It may have no genuine insurance value, but it eases checkpoint and border passage.

HITCHING AND USING PUBLIC TRANSPORT

If you're going to travel **under your own steam**, it's worth considering a cheap, one-way flight to Morocco or the Canary Isles to get started. Bearing in mind the possible cost of even a minimum number of days of travel through Europe this can be a positive saving.

Of course, you can do it the hard way. Not a few Timbuktu-bound travellers have begun the trip **hitching** to a British channel port for the crossing to France and the unpredictable haul through Spain to North Africa. Of the Mediterranean ferry ports, **Algeciras** is the cheapest and easiest embarkation point for **Morocco** with several ferries a day to Tangier

OVERLAND OPERATORS AND AGENTS IN BRITAIN

Acacia Expeditions, 5 Walm Lane, London NW2 5SJ (☎0181/451-3877). A wide variety of trans-African trips.

Africa Travel Centre, 4 Medway Court, Leigh St, London WC1H 9QX (☎0171/387-1211; Fax 0171/383-7512). The best specialist Africa agent in London, with good expertise and lots of trips to offer through many operators.

Dragoman, 18 Camp Green, Debenham, Suffolk IP14 6LA (☎01728/861133 or 0171/370-1930). Personal and creative operators with notably good trucks and competitive prices. Regular trans-African departures via Mauritania include Mali, Côte d'Ivoire and Ghana.

Encounter Overland, 267 Old Brompton Rd, London SW5 9JA (☎0171/370-6951; Fax 0171/244-9737). Specialists in long trips; several pass through Mauritania and Mali.

Exodus, 9 Weir Rd, London SW12 0LT (☎0181/675-7996; Fax 0181/673-0779). Runs several trips a year between Nairobi and London via western parts of West Africa, including Guinea.

Explore Worldwide, 1 Frederick St, Aldershot, Hampshire, GU11 1LQ (☎01252/344161; Fax 01252/343170). Highly respected small-groups operator with an excellent reputation. Trips include a 16-day "Foot Safari" in Mali from £1400 ($2100).

Guerba Expeditions, 101 Eden Vale Rd, Westbury, Wiltshire BA13 3QX (☎01373/826611; Fax 01373/858351). Acknowledged as the best African specialist operator. Trips include 7 weeks Dakar to Lomé (as part of a trans-Africa trip) for £1095 ($1650) land-only or £1750 ($2625) with flights.

Teranga Expeditions, Kingfishers, Aqueduct Lane, Alvechurch, Worcestershire R48 7BP (☎0121/447-8222; Fax 0121/445-1679). Dedicated, new overland company, aiming to offer a number of truck trips exclusively in West Africa. Prices, not including flights, range from about £100–250 ($150–375) per week.

Truck Africa, 37 Ranelagh Gardens Mansions, London SW6 3UQ (☎0171/731-6142). Personal, but professional, and enthused about by past clients. Long overland trips, London to East and Southern Africa, are the main journeys on offer.

OVERLAND OPERATORS AND AGENTS IN THE US

Adventure Center, 1311 63rd Street, Suite 200, Emoryville, CA 94608 (☎1-800/227-8747 or 510/654-1879). Wide range of tours and safaris.

African Adventure Company, 1620 S Federal Highway, Suite 900, Pompano Beach, FL 33062 (☎305/781-3933). One of the best agencies in the business, offering over 100 programmes to Africa and thousands of safari options.

Africa Travel Centre, 499 Ernston Rd, Parlin, NJ 08859 (☎1-800/631-5650 or 908/721-2929; Fax 908/721-2344). Sister company of London-based *Africa Travel Shop*.

Geo Expeditions, Box 3656, 63 S Washington St, Sonora, CA 95370 (☎209/532-0152; Fax 209/532-1979).

Global Safaris, 2601 Chapman Ave, Fullerton, CA 92631 (☎1-800/548-3140 or 714/738-7979). A wide range of safaris and good fares on many airlines.

International Bicycle Fund, 4887 Columbia Drive S, Seattle, WA 98108-1919 (☎/Fax 206/628-9314). Campaigning bicycle outfit offers tours in various parts of Africa each year, including Mali, Burkina and Benin.

Journeys, 1536 NW 23rd Ave, Portland, OR 97210 (☎503/226-7200); and at Powell's Travel Store, Pioneer Courthouse Sq, Portland (☎503/226-4849). Tailor-made trips for individuals and groups. To receive their quarterly newsletter, *The African Traveler*, send $10 annual subscription.

Safari Centre, 3201 N Sepulveda Blvd, Manhattan Beach, CA 90266 (☎1-800/223-6046 or 310/546-4411).

Spector Travel, 31 St James Ave, Boston, MA 02116 (☎1-800/879-2374). All-round Africa specialists with good West Africa knowledge.

Wilderness Travel, 801 Allston Way, Berkeley, CA 94710 (☎510/548-0420).

and to the Spanish enclave of Ceuta on the Moroccan coast. Note: there are **Rough Guides** to France, Spain and Morocco and various smaller regions along the way – invaluable travelling companions and marketable commodities as you move on!

If you camp, and have the stamina to keep hitching, there's no reason you shouldn't get to the Mauritanian side of the Sahara at remarkably little cost. The ease of hitching in Morocco compensates for the common misery of the roadside in southern Europe, though as you venture into the far southern regions of Morocco, you will simply need to be lucky: there's no public transport to the Mauritanian border and travellers without their own transport will have to find lifts with overlanders or the occasional truck. The final section of the **Western Sahara** will usually cost you to cross. Car sellers may have room for hitchers, but tourist vehicles are generally packed to the gills.

VIA THE CANARIES

One off-beat route to West Africa from the UK is **via the Canary Islands**. You can pick up exceptionally cheap last-minute **package holidays to Las Palmas**, Gran Canaria, then cancel, or possibly sell off, your seat back. Going on from Las Palmas, the shortest (and cheapest) flight to West Africa is to **Nouadhibou** in Mauritania (twice weekly on *Air Mauritanie*, around £266 – $400 – one-way). *Air Afrique* and *Iberia* fly three times a week to Dakar (some £360/$540).

But you can get **passage by boat** for a fraction of the cost of flying. The *Aramas* shipping company operates two cargo vessels that ply between Las Palmas and Nouadhibou weekly – "Caribbean Trailer" and "Cap Blanc". The officers are Spanish, the crew Ghanaian, the food good and the cabins quite adequate. The fare is less than £20 ($30) and the voyage takes about 36 hours. Apply directly to the captain.

CANADIAN OVERLAND OPERATORS AND AGENTS

The Adventure Centre, 25 Bellair St, Toronto, ON M5R 3L3 (☎416/922-7584).

Blyth & Co, 68 Scollard St, Toronto, ON M5R 1GR (☎1-800/387-1387 or 416/964-2569).

G.A.P. Adventures, 227 Sterling Rd Suite 105, Toronto, ON M6R 2B2 (☎416/535-6600 or 1-800/465-5600).

Goway Travel, 2300 Yonge St, Box 2331, Toronto, ON M4P 1E4 (☎416/322-1034); and 402 West Pender St, Vancouver V6B 1T9 (☎604/687-4004).

Trek Holidays, 8412 109th St, Edmonton, Alberta T6G 1E2 (☎403/439-9118 or 1-800/661-7265).

Westcan Treks, 8412 109th St, Edmonton T6G 1E2 (☎403/439-9118; Fax 403/439-5494).

World Expeditions, 78 George St, Ottawa, ON K1N 5W1 (☎613/230-8676).

AUSTRALIAN OVERLAND OPERATORS AND AGENTS

Access Travel, 58 Pitt St, Sydney, NSW 2000 (☎02/241-1128).

Adventure World, 73 Walker St, North Sydney, NSW 2060 (☎02/956-7766 or 008/221 931).

Africa Travel Centre, Level 12, 456 Kent St, Sydney, NSW 2000 (☎02/267-3084); Raptis Plaza, Cavill Ave, Surfers Paradise, Queensland 421 (☎075/755035). Sister company of the London-based *Africa Travel Shop*.

African Wildlife Safaris, 1st Floor, 259 Coventry St, South Melbourne, VIC 3205 (☎008/333-022 or 03/696-2899). Range of packages and safaris all over Africa. Agents in Adelaide, Brisbane, Perth and Sydney.

Journeys Worldwide, 262 Adelaide St, 2nd Floor, Brisbane 4000 (☎09/321-3930).

Sydney Adventure Centre, Suite 16, 8th Floor, Dymocks Building, 48 George St, Sydney 2000 (☎02/221-8555).

Thor Adventure Travel, 228 Rundel St, Adelaide 5000 (☎08/232-3155).

NEW ZEALAND OVERLAND OPERATORS AND AGENTS

Adventure World, 101 Great South Rd, Remuera, PO Box 74008, Auckland (☎09/524-5118).

Africa Travel Centre, 21 Remuera Rd, Newmarket, Auckland 3 (☎09/520-2000). From the same stable as the Australian company.

INCLUSIVE OVERLAND TOURS

The "overland tour" catch-all covers most of the organized holidays that don't feel like packages. Not all of them are *overland* the entire way. The fly out, tour around by truck, fly back option is increasingly popular. Note that operators sometimes run trips "in association" with each other, and the number of trips offered each year is actually quite small.

If you're interested in one of the more inexpensive (sometimes regrettably one-off) expedition companies that advertise in the travel pages of British and European papers, it's worth paying them a visit. They're often just a private trip hoping to minimize costs by taking others. Scrutinizing their literature gives a good indication of their probable preparedness and real know-how. If their prospectus looks cheap or hasty, forget it.

As a destination for specialist **American Africa operators**, West Africa is little known in comparison with East and southern Africa. Hence the all-inclusive tours that are available are mainly **adventure treks** targeting younger travellers, similar to what's on offer in Europe. You won't find *Princess Cruises* to this part of the world and even *Club Med* has only conquered a few isolated beaches.

CYCLING

If you have enough **time** (the most precious commodity), energy and stamina, it's quite feasible to consider mountain biking through Europe in the summer, down through Morocco in the autumn, loading your machine aboard a lorry for the hardest part of the Sahara crossing and then cycling where your fancy takes you through the dry season.

It is of course possible to take a sturdy touring bike, or even use a locally bought roadster. A tourer is much faster on the main roads and a fit cyclist could expect to cover 120km a day or more. But you're likely to suffer more from broken spokes and punctures at unexpected potholes and you're much less free to leave the highways. Some routes and regions for which a mountainbike is ideal are beyond the scope of other bikes.

More cycling practicalities are detailed in "Getting Around" on p.49. If you still need convincing, write to *International Bicycle Fund* (see box – "Overland Operators and Agents in the US") for details of their escorted cycle tours.

BIKES BY AIR

If time is limited, you can **fly your bike** to West Africa. To avoid paying excess baggage charges, you should write in advance to the ground operations manager of the airline, pack as many heavy items into your hand luggage as possible and arrive several hours before the flight to get to know the check-in staff. It's rare that you'll be obliged to pay.

It's much harder, as a rule, to avoid excess fees on charter flights. Let them know in advance and plead your case. The 20kg weight allowance, which your bike and luggage is likely to exceed, is a notional figure with no bearing on air safety, used to extract more profit from the passengers.

Few airlines will insist your bike be boxed or bagged. But it's best to turn the handlebars into the frame and tie them down, invert the pedals and deflate the tyres.

RED TAPE AND VISAS

All visitors to West Africa require a full ten-year passport, which should remain valid for at least six months beyond the end of the trip. Some West African countries will not allow you in with less. Allow at least one blank page per country to be visited.

If your passport has Israeli stamps, it's just as well to get a new one, though some countries will overlook Israeli stamps and several – including Côte d'Ivoire, Togo, Nigeria and Cameroon – now have diplomatic relations with Israel. If your passport gives an occupation, student, teacher or business person is best. Try to avoid declaring yourself a journalist, photographer or anything similar that might be misconstrued.

Further kinds of red tape which may entangle you on your travels include "currency declaration forms", "tourist cards", "photography permits" and international vaccination certificates.

VISA CHECKLIST

The table shows which nationalities from the main countries of Western Europe, North America, Australasia and Japan and South Africa require visas (✔) and which don't (blank). Further details are given under the "Red Tape" sections in each country's chapter.

	UK	Ireland	France	Germany	Benelux	Scandinavia*	Italy	Spain	Switzerland	Japan	Canada	USA	Australia /NZ	South Africa
Morocco					✔									✔
Niger		✔						✔	✔	✔	✔	✔	✔	✔
Mali	✔	✔		✔	✔	✔	✔	✔	✔	✔	✔	✔	✔	✔
Burkina Faso	✔	✔	✔			✔		✔	✔	✔	✔	✔	✔	✔
Mauritania	✔	✔		✔	✔	✔		✔	✔	✔	✔	✔	✔	✔
Senegal					✔	✔		✔	✔	✔	✔		✔	
The Gambia			✔		3				✔	✔		✔		✔
Cape Verde	✔	✔	✔	✔	✔	✔	✔	✔	✔	✔	✔	✔	✔	✔
Guinea-Bissau	✔	✔	✔	✔	✔	✔	✔	✔	✔	✔	✔	✔	✔	✔
Guinea	✔	✔	✔	✔	✔	✔	✔	✔	✔	✔	✔	✔	✔	✔
Sierra Leone	✔	✔	✔	✔	✔	✔	✔	✔	✔	✔	✔	✔	✔	✔
Liberia	✔	✔	✔	✔	✔	✔	✔	✔	✔	✔	✔	✔	✔	✔
Côte d'Ivoire	✔		✔	✔	✔	✔	✔	✔	✔	✔	✔		✔	
Ghana	✔	✔	✔	✔	✔	✔	✔	✔	✔	✔	✔	✔	✔	✔
Togo						1			✔	✔	✔		✔	✔
Benin	✔	✔			✔	2		✔	✔	✔	✔	✔	✔	✔
Nigeria	✔	✔	✔	✔	✔	✔	✔	✔	✔	✔	✔	✔	✔	✔
Cameroon	✔	✔	✔		✔	✔	✔	✔	✔	✔	✔	✔	✔	✔

*Scandinavia countries referred to = Denmark, Norway, Sweden and Finland

(1) visas not required except Finland; (2) Denmark and Sweden: visa not required; (3) Belgium: visa required

Currency rules, health formalities and photography are dealt with in detail further on. Other pieces of paper are mentioned in the introductory Practical Information at the beginning of relevant country chapters.

GETTING VISAS BEFORE DEPARTURE

If you're flying out to a limited number of countries on a short trip, you should get **visas** in advance. Few visas remain valid beyond three months, however, and if you'll be away for longer you'll have to procure them at the respective embassies in West Africa.

Visa regulations in West Africa are notoriously fickle and hard to pin down. While there are few rules that can't be broken in an emergency, cases do occur – too often – of people sent back hundreds of kilometres for want of a stamp. It pays to plan ahead.

Bear in mind also that a visa only constitutes "permission to apply to enter". This isn't mere pedantry. You can be turned away despite having a visa (for arriving on a one-way ticket, for example, in the case of Cameroon) and the length of **validity** of a visa may bear no relation to how long you're allowed to stay in the country when you arrive. It's almost always possible to **extend** a first stay, but in several countries it can be a serious matter if you overstay without extending.

There seems to be little sense to the who-does and who-doesn't of **visa requirements** (see table). Six countries – **Cape Verde**, **Guinea-Bissau**, **Guinea**, **Sierra Leone**, **Liberia** and **Nigeria** – require all non-West Africans to have visas.

To get a visa in your home country you'll fairly often be asked to provide evidence of a return air ticket and occasionally have to show an invitation or a covering letter stating the purpose of your trip. Tourist visas and business visas are always distinct. The latter usually require a letter from your company and often a letter from an African contact. It's always worth asking for a **multiple entry visa** (which often costs more). Should you need to go back from a neighbouring country it saves a lot of hassle.

VISA SERVICES

If you're in a hurry, need a visa for a country which doesn't have a representative in your home country, or anticipate some kind of hassle getting it, it may be worth considering a commercial **visa service**, whereby, for a set fee, you sign the application forms and mail them your passport and they do all the legwork. If you're flying straight into a country you may have little choice, since personal applications abroad by mail can take several months to process. In that specific instance, however, it is sometimes permitted to organize your visa at the airport on arrival (check that the airline won't refuse you boarding if you don't have the required visa).

A visa service can be extremely practical, if not essential, in the **USA** – where embassies are concentrated in New York and Washington DC and where each one can take six weeks (if you're lucky) or many months to process by mail. With an agency, you still need to plan ahead, but they can generally get visas in about a week; count on another two to three weeks to send the

VISA SERVICES IN THE UK

Thames Consular Services, 363 Chiswick High Rd, London W4 4HS (☎0181/995-2492). Offers a quick and personal service; for example Mali (£42) in under a week.

The Visa Service, 2 Northdown St, King's Cross, London N1 9BG (☎0171/833-2709; Fax 0171/833-1857). One of the largest visa agents. They charge £17 per visa, plus visa fees and courier fees for overseas applications.

Worldwide Visas, 9 Adelaide St, London WC2 4HZ (☎0171/379-0419; Fax 0171/497-2590). The biggest by far, with a walk-in shop and agent in Brussels for the tricky visas. £35 plus the fee for the visa itself, or £75 all-in if it's done in Brussels.

VISA SERVICES IN THE US

AAT Visa Services, 3417 Haines Way, Falls Church, VA 22041 (☎703/820-5612).

Embassy Visa Service, 1519 Connecticut Ave NW, Suite 300, Washington DC, 20036 (☎202/387-0300).

International Passports and Visas, 205 Beverly Dr, Suite 204, Beverly Hills, CA (☎310-274-2020; Fax 310/274-4581).

Travel Agenda, 119 West 57 St, Suite 1008, New York, NY 10019 (☎212/265-7887).

EMBASSIES, HIGH COMMISSIONS AND CONSULATES IN THE UK AND IRELAND

All the following offices are open Mon–Fri, unless otherwise stated.

Benin, 125–129 High St, Edgware, Middlesex HA8 7HS (☎/Fax 0181/954-8800). Open 10am–12.30pm & 2–4.30pm. Visas £25 on the spot.

Burkina Faso, 5 Cinnamon Row, Plantation Wharf, London SW11 3TW (☎0171/738-1800; Fax 0171/738-2828). Open 9am–1pm & 2–5pm. Multiple entry visa, immediate issue, £17.

Cameroon, 84 Holland Park, London W11 3SB (☎0171/727-0774).

Côte d'Ivoire, 2 Upper Belgrave St, London SW1X 8BJ (☎0171/ 235-6991; Fax 0171/259-5439). Open 9am–noon & 1–4pm. Visa costs £45.

The Gambia, 57 Kensington Court, London W8 5DG (☎0171/937-6316; Fax 0171/937-9095). Open 9.30am–5pm (closes 1pm Fri).

Ghana, 13 Belgrave Square, London SW1X 8PR (☎0171/235-4142). Open 9.30am–1pm. Return ticket routinely demanded.

Guinea-Bissau, 8 Palace Gate, London SW8 4RP (☎0171/589-5253; Fax 0171/589-9590). 3-month visas in 24hr.

Liberia, 2 Pembridge Place, London W2 4XB (☎0171/221-1036). Open Mon–Thurs 10am–3pm.

Morocco, 49 Queen's Gate Gardens, London SW7 5NE (☎0171/724-0719). Open 9.30am–1pm.

Nigeria, Nigeria House, 9 Northumberland Ave, London WC2N 5BX (☎0171/839-1244; Fax 0171/830-8746). Open 9.30am–1pm. Also at 56 Leeson Park, Dublin 6 (☎01/604 366). Return ticket or covering documentation required.

Senegal, 11 Phillimore Gardens, London W8 7QG (☎0171/937-0925; Fax 0171/937-8130). Open 9.30am–1pm & 2–4pm.

Sierra Leone, 33 Portland Place, London W1N 3AG (☎0171/636-6483 or 636-6485; Fax 0171/323-3159). Open 10am–1pm for visa application, 2.30–3.30pm for visa collection. Personal visit advisable to ensure receipt of passport.

To obtain visas for Mauritania, Cape Verde, Guinea, Mali and Niger contact the appropriate embassies in Europe (see box on p.26) or use a visa service. The French consulate in London (6a Cromwell Place, SW7; ☎0171/838-2050) may be able to help with a Togolese visa.

applications back and forth through the mail and have your passport returned. Given the expense ($15–30 per visa plus the embassy's visa fee), if you're planning on covering a lot of territory, you might just get visas for the first couple of countries to be visited and pick up the rest in Africa, checking the map on p.22 to make sure onward destinations are represented in the country you arrive in.

GETTING VISAS ALONG THE WAY

On an **overland trip**, it would seem to be simplest to pick up the visas you need along the way – were it not for the fact that some West African embassies in the region may occasionally refuse to issue visas to passport holders who could have obtained them in their own country. A further obstacle – though one that's steadily diminishing – is the lack of representation for a number of countries which have very few embassies. Plan ahead to see where you should be getting your next visa. The **visa map of West Africa** on p.22 indicates in which cities you should be able to obtain which visas. Certain nationalities will have hassles getting some of these (Britons with Nigeria, for example) so it's worth trying at the first opportunity. Even an expired visa can be a help in getting another for the same country, though reckless applications can be an expensive hobby. Take plenty of passport photos – allow three or four for each visa you expect to need.

VISA ADVICE

In the country chapters, addresses have been given in as much detail as possible in the "Listings" section at the end of each capital city. Once you've located the embassy in question – where you've any choice it's the *consulate* you need to go to – **obtaining visas** should be fairly straightforward in most cases and is often a good deal easier than sorting things out at home. Nevertheless, you ought to be prepared for an average 2–3 days' wait from application to delivery, and have a handy hotel address to use as your intended address in the country (nothing too slummy).

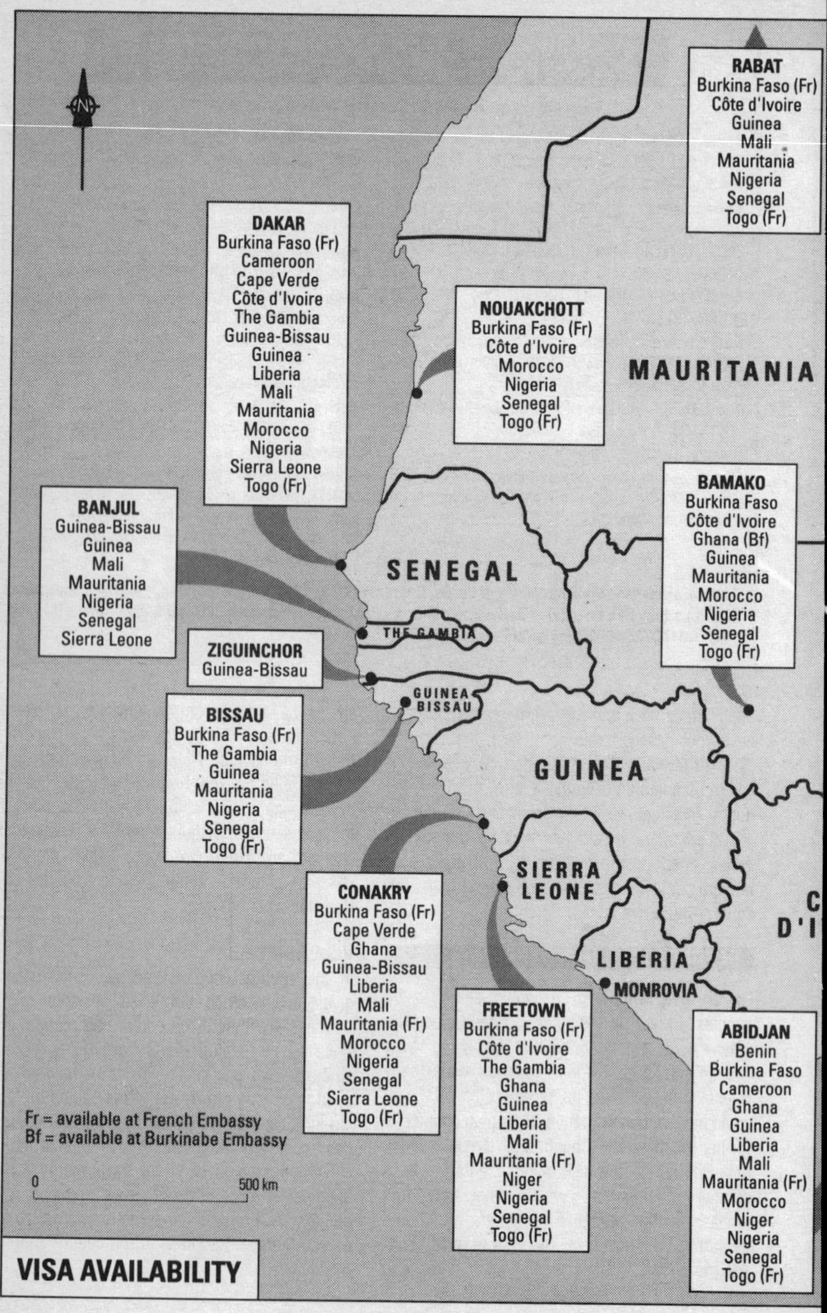
RABAT
Burkina Faso (Fr)
Côte d'Ivoire
Guinea
Mali
Mauritania
Nigeria
Senegal
Togo (Fr)
DAKAR
Burkina Faso (Fr)
Cameroon
Cape Verde
Côte d'Ivoire
The Gambia
Guinea-Bissau
Guinea
Liberia
Mali
Mauritania
Morocco
Nigeria
Sierra Leone
Togo (Fr)
NOUAKCHOTT
Burkina Faso (Fr)
Côte d'Ivoire
Morocco
Nigeria
Senegal
Togo (Fr)
MAURITANIA
BANJUL
Guinea-Bissau
Guinea
Mali
Mauritania
Nigeria
Senegal
Sierra Leone
SENEGAL
BAMAKO
Burkina Faso
Côte d'Ivoire
Ghana (Bf)
Guinea
Mauritania
Morocco
Nigeria
Senegal
Togo (Fr)
THE GAMBIA
ZIGUINCHOR
Guinea-Bissau
GUINEA BISSAU
BISSAU
Burkina Faso (Fr)
The Gambia
Guinea
Mauritania
Nigeria
Senegal
Togo (Fr)
GUINEA
SIERRA LEONE
CONAKRY
Burkina Faso (Fr)
Cape Verde
Ghana
Guinea-Bissau
Liberia
Mali
Mauritania (Fr)
Morocco
Nigeria
Senegal
Sierra Leone
Togo (Fr)
LIBERIA
MONROVIA
FREETOWN
Burkina Faso (Fr)
Côte d'Ivoire
The Gambia
Ghana
Guinea
Liberia
Mali
Mauritania (Fr)
Niger
Nigeria
Senegal
Togo (Fr)
ABIDJAN
Benin
Burkina Faso
Cameroon
Ghana
Guinea
Liberia
Mali
Mauritania (Fr)
Morocco
Niger
Nigeria
Senegal
Togo (Fr)
Fr = available at French Embassy
Bf = available at Burkinabe Embassy
0
500 km
VISA AVAILABILITY

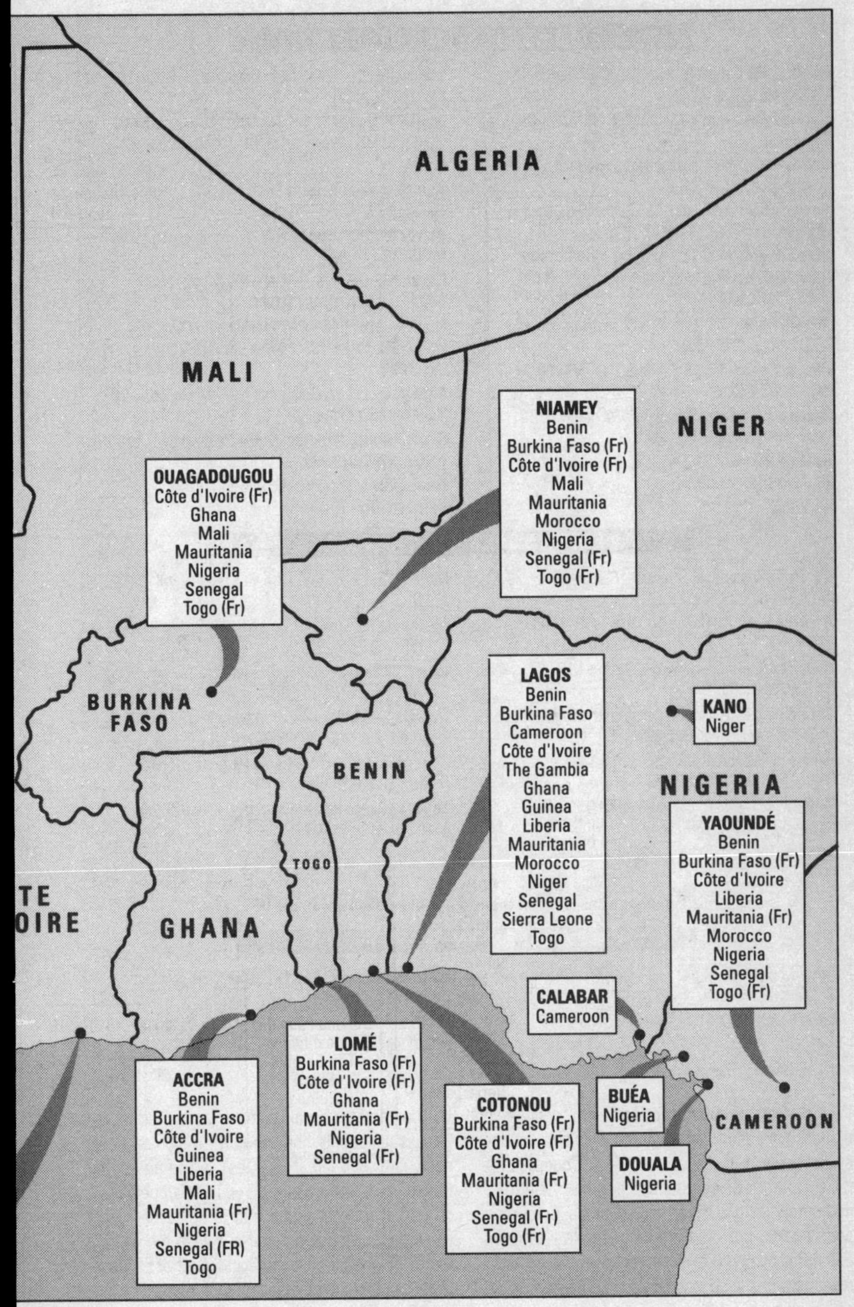
ALGERIA
MALI
NIGER
NIAMEY
Benin
Burkina Faso (Fr)
Côte d'Ivoire (Fr)
Mali
Mauritania
Morocco
Nigeria
Senegal (Fr)
Togo (Fr)
OUAGADOUGOU
Côte d'Ivoire (Fr)
Ghana
Mali
Mauritania
Nigeria
Senegal
Togo (Fr)
BURKINA FASO
LAGOS
Benin
Burkina Faso
Cameroon
Côte d'Ivoire
The Gambia
Ghana
Guinea
Liberia
Mauritania
Morocco
Niger
Senegal
Sierra Leone
Togo
KANO
Niger
BENIN
NIGERIA
YAOUNDÉ
Benin
Burkina Faso (Fr)
Côte d'Ivoire
Liberia
Mauritania (Fr)
Morocco
Nigeria
Senegal
Togo (Fr)
TOGO
TE
OIRE
GHANA
CALABAR
Cameroon
LOMÉ
Burkina Faso (Fr)
Côte d'Ivoire (Fr)
Ghana
Mauritania (Fr)
Nigeria
Senegal (Fr)
ACCRA
Benin
Burkina Faso
Côte d'Ivoire
Guinea
Liberia
Mali
Mauritania (Fr)
Nigeria
Senegal (FR)
Togo
COTONOU
Burkina Faso (Fr)
Côte d'Ivoire (Fr)
Ghana
Mauritania (Fr)
Nigeria
Senegal (Fr)
Togo (Fr)
BUÉA
Nigeria
DOUALA
Nigeria
CAMEROON

EMBASSIES IN THE USA

Benin, 2737 Cathedral Ave NW, Washington, DC 20008 (☎202/232-6656).

Burkina Faso, 115 E 73rd St, NY, NY 10021 (☎212/288-7575).

Cameroon, 2349 Massachusetts Ave NW, Washington, DC 20008.

Cape Verde (Consulate), 535 Boylston St, Boston, MA 02116 (☎617/353-0014).

Côte d'Ivoire, 46 E 74th St, NY, NY 10021; 2424 Massachusetts Ave NW, Washington, DC 20008 (☎202/797-0300).

The Gambia, 1030 15th St NW, Washington, DC 20005 (☎202/842-1356).

Ghana (Consulate), 19 E 47th St, NY, NY 10017 (☎212/832-1300).

Guinea, 2112 Leroy Place NW, Washington, DC 20008 (☎202/483-9420).

Guinea-Bissau, 211 E 43rd St, Suite 604, NY, NY, 10017 (☎212/661-3977).

Liberia, 5201 16th St NW, Washington, DC 20011 (☎202/291-0761).

Mali, 111 E 69th St, NY, NY 10021 (☎212/737-4150); 2130 R St NW, Washington, DC 20008 (☎202/332-2249).

Mauritania, 2129 Leroy Place NW, Washington, DC 20008 (☎202/232-5700).

Morocco, 1601 21st St NW, Washington, DC 20009 (☎202/462-7979).

Niger, 417 E 50th St, NY, NY 10022 (☎212/421-3260).

Nigeria, 2201 M St NW, Washington, DC, 20037 (☎202/822-1500); 733 3rd Ave, NY, NY 10017 (☎212/953-9130).

Senegal, 2112 Wyoming Ave NW, Washington, DC 20008 (☎202/234-0540).

Sierra Leone, 1701 19th St NW, Washington, DC 20009 (☎202/939-9261).

Togo, 2208 Massachesetts Ave NW, Washington, DC 20008 (☎202/234-4212).

EMBASSIES IN CANADA

Benin, 58 Glebe Ave, Ottawa K1S 2C3 (☎613/233-4429; Fax 613/233 8952).

Burkina Faso, 48 Range Rd, Ottawa K1N 8J4 (☎613/238-4796).

Cameroon, 170 Clemow Ave, Ottawa K1S 2B4 (☎613/236-1522).

Côte d'Ivoire, 9 Marlborough Ave, Ottawa K1N 8E6 (☎613/236-9910; Fax 613/563-8287).

Ghana, 1 Clemow Ave, Ottawa K1S 2A9 (☎613/236-0871; Fax 613/236 0874).

Guinea, 483 Willbrod St, Ottawa K1N 6N1 (☎613/232-1133; Fax 613/230 7560).

Liberia, 160 Elgin St, Suite 2600, Ottawa K1N 8S3 (☎613/232-1781).

Mali, 50 Goulburn Ave, Ottawa K1N 8C8 (☎613/232 1501).

Morocco, 38 Range Rd, Ottawa K1N 8J4 (☎613/236-7391; Fax 613/236-6164).

Niger, 38 Blackburn Ave, Ottawa K1N 8A2 (☎613/232-4291; Fax 613/230-9808).

Nigeria, 295 Metcalfe St, Ottawa K2P 1R9 (☎613/236-0521; Fax 613/236-0529).

Senegal, 57 Marlborough Ave, Ottawa K1N 8E8 (☎613/238-6392).

Togo, 12 Range Rd, Ottawa K1N 8J3 (☎613/238-5916; Fax 613/235 6425).

For other visas, contact the appropriate embassies in the US.

EMBASSIES IN AUSTRALIA

Côte d'Ivoire, Senegal and **Togo,** French Embassy, 31 Market St, Sydney (☎02/261-5779).

Liberia 34 Hunter St, Sydney (☎02/233-1155).

Morocco 2 Phillis Lane, North Curl Curl, Sydney (☎02/649-6019).

Nigeria 7 Terrigal Crescent, O'Malley, Canberra (☎06/286-1322).

A **letter of introduction** from your own embassy is sometimes required (this can usually be provided on the spot, for a fee). Countries for which a letter of introduction is either helpful or mandatory include Mauritania, Guinea, Cameroon and Nigeria, but it's hard to generalize as rules and norms vary greatly from embassy to embassy. Ask about this in advance if you're unsure.

The person whose signature is required for the visa is invariably the **consul**. If you're being delayed or messed around, ask to see him or her in person. Never give up. If you get stonewalled, or you're in a hurry and told to come back next week, try putting in an hour or two in the waiting room. This often has miraculous effects, especially combined with persistent whining.

BRITISH EMBASSIES AND CONSULATES IN NORTH AND WEST AFRICA

For general enquiries, the Consular Department at the Foreign and Commonwealth Office, Clive House, Petty France, London SW1H 9HD (☎0171/270-4129) can be helpful. In the following listing, where there is only an honorary consul, cities in brackets indicate the location of the embassy or high commission in authority.

Algeria British Embassy, Résidence Cassiopée, Batiment B, Chemin des Glycines, Algiers (BP 43 Alger-Gare 16000; ☎2/60.56.01; Fax 2/60.44.10).

Benin (LAGOS) CM Barnes, Honorary Consul, Lot 24, Patte d'Oie, Cotonou (☎30.11.20).

Burkina Faso (ABIDJAN) AC Bessey, Honorary Consul, BP 1918, Ouagadougou (☎33.63.63).

Cameroon British Embassy, av Winston Churchill, Yaoundé (BP 547, Yaoundé; ☎22.05.45; Fax 22.01.48).

Cape Verde (DAKAR) A Canuto, Honorary Consul, *Shell Cabo Verde*, Avda Amilcar Cabral, Mindelo (☎31.41.32; Fax 31.47.55).

Côte d'Ivoire British Embassy, Immeuble "Les Harmonies", 3rd Floor, corner bd Carde and av Dr Jamot, Plateau, Abidjan (01 BP 2581, Abidjan; ☎22.68 50; Fax 22.32.21).

The Gambia British High Commission, 48 Atlantic Rd, Fajara (PO Box 507, Banjul; ☎495133; Fax 496134).

Ghana British High Commission, Osu Link, off Gamel Abdul Nasser Ave, Accra (PO Box 296, Accra; ☎021/22.16.65; Fax 21/66.46.52).

Guinea (DAKAR) Mrs VA Treitlein, Honorary Consul, BP 834, Conakry (☎46.17.34; Fax 44.42.15).

Guinea-Bissau (DAKAR) J Van Maanen, Honorary Consul, *Mavegro*, Bissau (CP 100, Bissau; ☎21.15.29).

Mali (DAKAR) J Chaloner, Honorary Consul, Plan International, Bamako (BP 1598, Bamako; ☎23.05.83; Fax 22.28.78).

Mauritania (RABAT) Mrs N Abeiderrahmane, Unofficial British Representative, Nouakchott (☎02/52337).

Morocco British Embassy, 17 bd de la Tour Hassan, Rabat (BP 45, Rabat; ☎07/72.09.05; Fax 07/70.45.31).

Niger (ABIDJAN) B Niandou, Honorary Vice Consul, BP 11168, Niamey (☎73.20.15 or 73.25.29).

Nigeria British High Commission, Chellaram Building, 54 Marina, Lagos (PMB 12136, Lagos; ☎01/266-7061 or 01/266-6413; Fax 01/266-6909).

Senegal British Embassy, 20 rue du Docteur Guillet (BP 6025 Dakar; ☎23 73 92; Fax 23 27 66).

Sierra Leone British High Commission, Standard Chartered Bank Building, Lightfoot Boston St, Freetown (☎223961).

Togo (ACCRA) Mrs JA Sayer, Honorary Consul, British School of Lomé (BP 20050, Lomé; ☎21.46.06; Fax 21.49.89).

AMERICAN EMBASSIES IN NORTH AND WEST AFRICA

Algeria 4 Chemin Cheikh Brahimi, Alger-Gare 16000 Algiers (☎2/60.11.86).

Benin rue Caporal Anani Bernard, Cotonou (BP 2012, Cotonou; ☎30.17.92; Fax 30.19.74).

Burkina Faso BP 35 Ouagadougou (☎30.67.23).

Cameroon rue Nachtigal, Yaoundé (BP817, Yaoundé; ☎23.40.14).

Cape Verde Rua Hoji Ya Yenna, Praia (CP 201 Praia; ☎61.43.63; Fax 61.13.55).

Côte d'Ivoire rue Jesse Owens, Abidjan (01 BP 1712, Abidjan; ☎21.09.79; Fax 22.32.59).

The Gambia Kairaba Ave, Fajara (PO Box 19, Banjul; ☎492858; Fax 492475).

Ghana Ring Road East, Accra (PO Box 194, Accra; ☎021/77.53.46).

Guinea corner of 2nd bd and 9th av, Conakry (BP 603, Conakry; ☎44.15.20; Fax 44.15.22).

Guinea Bissau Avda Domingos Ramos, Bissau (☎20.11.39; Fax 20.11.59).

Liberia 111 United Nations Drive, Mamba Point, Monrovia (BP 98 Monrovia; ☎222994).

Mali rue Rochester NY, Bamako (BP 34, Bamako; ☎22.54.70; Fax 22.37.12).

Mauritania rue Abadallaye, Nouakchott (BP 232, Nouakchott; ☎02/52660; Fax 02/52589).

Morocco 2 Charia Marrakech, Rabat (☎07/76.22.65).

Niger bd des Ambassades, Niamey (BP 11201, Niamey; ☎72.26.61).

Nigeria 2 Eleke Crescent, Lagos (☎01/610 097).

Senegal av Jean XXIII, Dakar (BP 49, Dakar; ☎23 42 96; Fax 22 29 91).

Sierra Leone Walpole St, Freetown (☎22.64.81).

Togo rue Vauban, Lomé (BP 852, Lomé; ☎21.29.91; Fax 21.79.52).

Tunisia 144 av de Liberté, Tunis (☎78.25.56).

Visa fees can be high (up to £25/$40 equivalent or more) and they sometimes vary mysteriously from one applicant to the next, not always depending on different nationalities. Visas are often issued with fiscal stamps stuck in your passport, or a handwritten sum of money.

CANADIAN EMBASSIES IN NORTH AND WEST AFRICA

Algeria 27 bis rue Ali Massoudi, Alger-Gare 16000 Algiers (☎2/60.59.20).

Cameroon Immeuble Stamatiade, Yaoundé (BP 572, Yaoundé; ☎23.02.03).

Côte d'Ivoire Immeuble Trade Centre, Abidjan (01 BP 3387, Abidjan; ☎32.20.09).

Ghana 46 Independence Ave, Accra (PO Box 1639, Accra; ☎021/22.85.66).

Guinea Corniche Sud, Quartier Coléah, Conakry (BP 99, Coléah; ☎46.36.26).

Mali rue de Koulikoro, BP 198, Bamako (☎22.22.36).

Morocco 13 bis rue Jaafar as-Sadik, Rabat (BP 709, Rabat; ☎07/77.28.80; Fax 07/77.28.87).

Niger Immeuble Sonara 1, Niamey (☎73.36.86).

Nigeria 4 Idowu Taylor St, Victoria Island, Lagos (PO Box 54506, Lagos; ☎01/612 195).

Senegal Immeuble Daniel Sorano, 45 bd de la République, Dakar (BP 3373, Dakar; ☎23 92 90; Fax 23 87 49).

Tunisia 3 rue du Sénégal, Tunis (BP 31; ☎28.65.57).

The value should be what you paid. If it differs, it's worth complaining and asking for a receipt. There may have been an accidental overpayment…

In cities where there's no direct representation, visas for Mauritania, Senegal, Burkina Faso, Côte d'Ivoire and Togo are often available from the **French embassy**. There's one in pretty well every country in the region. Where Niger has no embassy, Côte d'Ivoire embassies process Niger visas. **British embassies** in Rabat, Algiers, Tunis, Dakar, Abidjan and Yaoundé provide a similar service, in principle, for unrepresented Commonwealth countries (including The Gambia, Sierra Leone, Ghana and Nigeria) though in practice this has often fallen into abeyance. British High Commissions (the mutual embassies of Commonwealth countries) cannot do this.

Lastly, as noted before, a few West African countries issue, or have an official policy to issue (which is slightly different) **visas on arrival** at the airport, particularly in cases where the passenger is arriving from a country with no embassy. Details are given in the relevant country chapters. Don't risk it unless you have to – it always delays the arrival formalities.

WEST AFRICAN EMBASSIES AND CONSULATES

FRANCE

Benin 89 rue de Cherche-Midi, 75006 Paris (☎1/42.22.31.91). Open 9am–12.30pm & 1.30–5pm.

Burkina Faso 159 bd Haussmann, 75008 Paris (☎1/43.59.21.85). Open 9.30am–noon & 2.30–6pm.

Cameroon 73 rue d'Auteuil, 75016 Paris (☎1/47.43.98.33); 496 rue du Paradis, 13008 Marseilles (☎1/91.71.00.40).

Cape Verde 92 bd Malesherbes, 75017 Paris (☎1/42.25.63.31).

Côte d'Ivoire 102 av R Poincaré, 75116 Paris (☎1/45.01.53.10). Open 9–11.45am & 3–5pm.

The Gambia 57 rue de Villiers, 92200 Neuilly-sur-Seine (☎1/47.57.31.60). Open 10am–noon & 2.30–4pm.

Ghana 8 Villa Said, 75116 Paris (☎1/45.00.09.50; Fax 45.00.81.95).

Guinea 51 rue de la Faisanderie, 75016 Paris (☎1/47.04.81.48). Open 9am–4pm.

Guinea-Bissau 94 rue St Lazare, 75009 Paris (☎1/45.26.18.51).

Liberia 8 rue Jacques Bingen, 75017 Paris (☎1/47.63.58.55).

Mali 89 rue Cherche-Midi, 75006 Paris (☎1/45.48.58.43). Open 9am–1pm & 2–5pm.

Mauritania 89 rue Cherche-Midi, 75006 Paris (☎1/45.48.23.88). Open 9am–1pm.

Morocco 3–5 rue Le Tasse, 75016 Paris (☎1/45.20.69.35).

Niger 154 rue de Longchamp, 75116 Paris (☎1/45.04.80.60). Open 9am–12.30pm.

Nigeria 173 av Victor Hugo, 75116 Paris (☎1/47.04.68.65).

Senegal 22 rue Hamelin, 75016 Paris (☎1/44.05.38.44; Fax 44.55.99.40). Open 9am–1pm & 2–5pm.

Sierra Leone 16 av Hoche, 75008 Paris (☎1/45.56.14.73).

Togo 8 rue Alfred-Roll, 75017 Paris (☎1/43.80.12.13) 9–1pm & 3–6pm.

BOX CONTINUES

WEST AFRICAN EMBASSIES AND CONSULATES

GERMANY

Benin Rudigerstrasse10, Postsech 228, 5300 Bonn Mehlem (☎0228/344031; Fax 0228/85 71 92).

Burkina Faso Wendelstrasse 18, 5300 Bonn 2 (☎0228/ 332063).

Cameroon Rheinallee 76, 5300 Bonn 2 (☎0228/ 356037).

Cape Verde Meckenheimerallee 113, 5300 Bonn 1 (☎0228/651604).

Côte d'Ivoire Konigstrasse 93, 5300 Bonn 1 (☎0228/ 63 05 88; Fax 0228/217313).

The Gambia Kurfürstendamm 103, 1000 Berlin (☎30/ 892-3121; Fax 30/891-1401).

Ghana 2 Rheinallee 58, 5300 Bonn 2 (☎0228/ 363498).

Guinea Rochusweg 50, 5300 Bonn 1 (☎0228/231097).

Liberia Mainzerstrasse 259, 5300 Bonn 2 (☎0228/ 340827).

Mali 2 Bastei 86, 5300 Bonn (☎0228/357048).

Mauritania Bonner 48, 5300 Bonn 2 (☎0228/364024; Fax 0228/3617888).

Morocco Gotenstrasse 7, 5300 Bonn 2 (☎0228/ 355044; Fax 0228/357894).

Niger Durenstrasse 9, 5300 Bonn 2 (☎0228/356057; Fax 0228/363246).

Nigeria Goldbergweg 13, 5300 Bonn 2 (☎0228/ 322071).

Senegal Argelanderstrasse 3, 5300 Bonn 1 (☎0228/ 218008; Fax 0228/717815).

Sierra Leone 2 Rheinallee 20, 5300 Bonn (☎0228/ 352001; Fax 0228/364269).

Togo Beethovenallee 13, 5300 Bonn 2 (☎0228/ 355091; Fax 0228/351639).

ITALY

Burkina Faso 26 v. Alessandria, Rome (☎061/ 86. 31. 94).

Cameroon 82a v. di Pieta, 00186 Rome (☎061/ 678.3546).

Côte d'Ivoire v. Lazzarro Spallanzani 4–6, 00161 Rome (☎061/86.80.40).

Ghana 4 v. Ostriana, 00199 Rome (☎061/839.1200; Fax 061/831.9204).

Guinea 9/13 v. Ristori, 00198 Rome (☎061/87.89.89).

Liberia 64 v. Buozzi, 00197 Rome (☎061/80.58.10).

Morocco 8/10 v. Spallanzani, 00196 Rome (☎061/ 884.8653).

Nigeria 14/16/18 v. Orazio, 00196 Rome (☎061/ 653.1048).

Senegal 3 v. Lisbona, 00198 Rome (☎061/85.94.97).

Togo 18 Corso Vitt. Emmanuele, Turin (☎11/87.17.19).

THE BENELUX COUNTRIES

BRUSSELS

Benin av Observatoire 5, B1180 (☎02/354 94 71).

Burkina Faso pl G. d'Arezzo 16, B1060 (☎02/345 99 12). Open 9am–12.30pm & 2.30–6pm.

Cameroon av Brugmann 131, B1060 (☎02/345 18 70).

Côte d'Ivoire av Franklin Roosevelt 234, B1050 (☎02/ 672 23 57).

The Gambia av Franklin Roosevelt 126, B5 (☎02/640 10 49).

Ghana 7 bd Général Wamis, B1030 (☎02/245 82 20; Fax 02 245 64 53).

Guinea av R Vanderdriessche 75, B15 (☎02/771 01 26; Fax 02 762 60 36).

Guinea-Bissau av Franklin Roosevelt 70, B5 (☎02/ 647 08 90; Fax 02 640 43 12).

Liberia 18 av des Touristes, 1640 Rhode St, Genèse (☎02/358 45 39).

Mali av Molière 487, B1060 (☎02/345 75 89).

Mauritania rue de Colombie 6, B1050 (☎02/672 47 47).

Morocco bd St Michel 29, B1040 (☎02/736 11 00).

Niger av Franklin Roosevelt 78, B1050 (☎02/648 61 40).

Nigeria av Tervueren 288, B15 (☎02/762 98 31; Fax 02 762 37 63).

Senegal av Franklin Roosevelt 196, B1050 (☎02/230 39 11).

Sierra Leone av Tervueren 264, B1150 (☎02/770 17 91).

Togo av Tervueren 264, B1150 (☎02/771 50 75).

THE HAGUE

Cameroon Amaliastr. 14 (☎070/360 1572).

Cape Verde Koninginnegr. 44, 2514 AD (☎070/ 346 9623; Fax 070/346 7702).

Morocco Oranjestr. 9, 2514 JB (☎070/346 9617; Fax 070/361 4503).

Nigeria Wagenaarwg. 5 (☎070/350 1703; Fax 070/ 361 4503).

ROTTERDAM

Cape Verde Consulate Mathenesserin 326 (☎010/ 477 8977).

BOX CONTINUES

WEST AFRICAN EMBASSIES AND CONSULATES

SCANDINAVIA

COPENHAGEN

Burkina Faso Svanemøllevej 20, DK2100 (☎31 18 40 22; Fax 39 27 18 86).

Côte d'Ivoire Gersonssvej 8, Hellerup, DK2900 (☎31 62 88 22; Fax 31 62 01 62).

Ghana Egebjerg Allé 13, 2900 Hellerup (☎31 62 82 22; Fax 31 62 16 52).

Guinea Holmemarksvej 6, Tastrup, DK2630 (☎02 99 32 42).

Liberia Storekongensgade 114, DK1264 (☎31 13 98 00).

Mali Skodsborgvej 188, Naerum, DK2850 (☎02 80 53 33).

Morocco Øregårds Allé 19, 2900 Hellerup (☎31 62 45 11; Fax 31 62 24 49).

Senegal Valkendorfsgade 22, DK1151 (☎31 13 61 88).

STOCKHOLM

Morocco Kungsholmstorg 16, 11221 (☎08/654 43 88; Fax 08/651 97 96).

Nigeria Tyrgt. 8, POB 628, 11427 (☎08/24 63 90).

Senegal Strandvagen 7B, POB 14025, 11456 (☎08/662 58 10).

SPAIN AND PORTUGAL

MADRID

Cameroon Rosario Pino 3, 28020 (☎91/571 11 60).

Côte d'Ivoire Serrano 154, 28006 (☎91/261 16 07).

Mauritania Velazquez 90, 28006 (☎91/575 70 07; Fax 91/435 95 31).

Morocco Serrano 179, 28002 (☎91/563 1090; Fax 91/561 78 87).

Nigeria Segre 23, Aptdo 14287, 28002 (☎91/563 09 11; Fax 91/563 63 20).

LAS PALMAS, CANARY ISLES

Mauritania Italia 8 (☎928/23 45 00).

Morocco av Mesa y Lopez 8, 35007 (☎928/26 28 59).

Sierra Leone Guarnateme 5 (☎928/26 09 50).

LISBON

Cape Verde 33 Avda Restelo, 1400 (☎01/301 5271; Fax 01/301 5308).

Guinea-Bissau Rua de Alconena 17–17a, 1400 (☎01/301 5371; Fax 01/301 7040).

Morocco Rua Borges Carneiro 32, 1200 (☎01/397 9193; Fax 01/397 0309).

Nigeria Rua Fernão Mendes, Pinto 50 (Restelo), 1400 (☎01/301 6189; Fax 01/301 8152).

MOROCCO

Côte d'Ivoire 21 Zankat Tiddas, Rabat (BP 192, Rabat; ☎07/76.31.51).

France 3 rue Sahnoun, Rabat (☎07/77.78.22). Issues various West African visas.

Guinea 2 Zankat Mokla, Orangers, Rabat (☎07/73.27.06).

Mali, 58 Cité Olm, Souissi, behind Hôtel Hyatt Regency (☎07/76.49.13).

Mauritania 1 rue de Normandie, Souissi, Rabat (☎07/75.68.28).

Nigeria 70 av Omar ibn al-Khattab, Agdal, Rabat (BP 347, Rabat; ☎07/63.78.56).

Senegal 17 rue Cadi ben Hamadi Senhaji, Souissi (BP 365, Rabat (☎07.75.92); visas only from Casablanca consulate, near the *Hôtel Almohades* (☎07/75.41.38).

MONEY AND COSTS

Eleven different currencies are used in West Africa, and it pays to know what the score is wherever you are. Even where sophisticated banking systems operate you may not be able to change certain foreign currencies. And in some countries a parallel "black market" in hard currencies still thrives.

CURRENCIES

The currency of all the **Francophone countries** in West Africa, with the exceptions of Mauritania and Guinea, is the **CFA franc**. CFA stands for *Communauté Financière Africaine*. Cameroon's currency is also CFA, but of a different regional grouping – the *Coopération Financière en Afrique Centrale* – which includes Chad, Central African Republic, Gabon, Equatorial Guinea and Congo. CFA francs are guaranteed by the French treasury and, since devaluation in early 1994, have a fixed value of 100:1 against the French franc (FF).

The two types of CFA can't be spent outside their own region but are easily exchanged in a bank. In Europe, major banks will sometimes exchange CFA francs at their French franc equivalent. Because of the French backing, the CFA (commonly pronounced "Sefa") is a relatively hard currency and currency laws in the countries which use it are generally relaxed. In theory there are limits to the value of CFA you can export, even from one CFA state to another, but in practice these limits are very rarely enforced. CFA comes in 1, 5, 10, 25, 50, 100 and 250 coins and notes of 500, 1000, 2500, 5000 and 10,000, making it easily the most convenient African currency.

The countries outside the franc zone have their own, usually weaker ("soft") currencies. Mauritania uses the **Ouguiya**; Cape Verde the Cape Verdean **Escudo**; The Gambia the **Dalasi**; Guinea-Bissau the **Peso**; Guinea the **Guinean franc**; Sierra Leone the **Leone**; Liberia the **Liberian Dollar**; Ghana the **Cedi**; and Nigeria the **Naira**.

MONEY

If you're travelling widely in West Africa, you're best off carrying a large part of your funds in **French franc travellers cheques**. Apart from any commission on exchanging them for cash, if you're using them in CFA countries, you've already effectively made the exchange when you bought them. In the CFA zone you'll always know how much you've got in local currency and your funds won't vary in value as you travel.

You generally end up better off if you have French francs to convert to CFA, rather than going straight from, say, $US or £sterling to CFA, because the national banks of the CFA zone normally set their own rates for exchanges with non-franc currencies. Indeed, in some towns in the CFA zone, banks will not deal in non-franc currencies – frustrating in a business-minded place like Côte d'Ivoire. Hotels and some shops and traders will take French franc travellers cheques but it's essential to have some **French francs in cash** as a standby.

Where CFA countries border non-CFA countries, your surplus CFA cash can generally be changed with ease as it's commonly used by people crossing the borders to buy goods (though note the details below on declaring your currency). But if you're heading directly for one of the **soft currency countries**, or intending to spend most of your time there, then either **US dollars** (US$) or **pounds sterling** (£) is probably the best currency to take. Again, carry some in cash – you'll often need it at borders and airports for your first food or transport.

Denominations of travellers cheques and cash should be as small as you can manage, bearing in mind the bulk that a large sum of exchange will amount to. If you take mostly

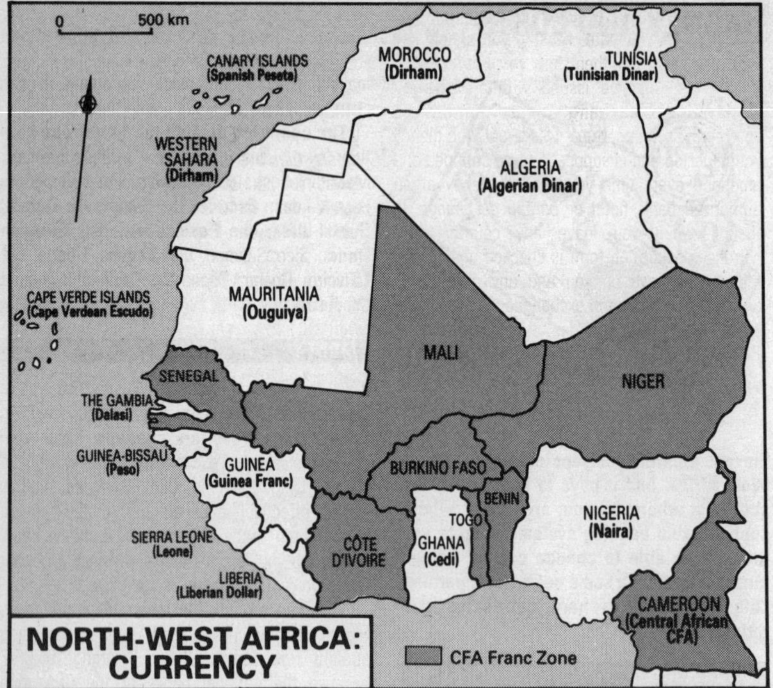

NORTH-WEST AFRICA: CURRENCY

US$50 or FF500 denominations for convenience, make sure you have plenty of US$10 and 20 or FF100 and 200 as well. A small stash of really low value hard currency notes (US$1 and 2) is always useful.

Travelling through the CFA zone, the issuing authority of your travellers cheques isn't of much consequence. Outside the CFA countries, however, *American Express* is by far the most widely recognized brand and, should the need arise, also the fastest to supply replacements for lost cheques.

Always keep the original **receipt** when you buy travellers cheques. Most banks outside the major cities won't cash your cheque without it.

CARRYING AND KEEPING MONEY

How you carry your funds around is something to which you should give serious consideration, especially if you're travelling for a long time. In certain cities, travellers are vulnerable and it only takes one piece of bad luck (or simple carelessness) to terminate your trip prematurely.

It's wise to carry valuable hard currency cash (as opposed to local soft currency) in a very safe place, ideally in a soft **leather pouch** under your waistband, hanging from a loop around your belt. This is comfortable and virtually impregnable to ordinary theft – even in the unlikely event it's noticed. It's probably worth wearing shorts, skirts or jeans with strong waistbands and a belt just for this purpose. Larger, strong, leather belt-pouches worn on the outside are good for passport, local money, travellers cheques and anything replaceable. Hanging **neck pouches** worn beneath a shirt are vulnerable, but fairly safe if the loop is strong. Nylon **money belts** are painfully hot and bulky.

Bank notes and travellers cheques (and airline tickets) need protecting from sweat in small plastic bags. Defaced, they can become worthless.

DECLARATIONS

On arrival in many soft currency countries you'll have to make a **declaration** of the money you're carrying in cash and travellers cheques. This may be accompanied by a search, varying from the cursory to the intimate. Mostly, you simply say what you've got and then show some of it.

You may also be issued with a **currency declaration** or **exchange control form**, which you retain until departure. This shows the money you imported and is supposed to be stamped and amended every time you change money at an authorized bank, hotel or *bureau de change*. In theory, when you leave any country, your currency declaration form is checked against the money you have on you and any discrepancy (which must have been exchanged unofficially, or lost, or given away . . .) has to be accounted for. In practice, CD forms are taken much more seriously on arrival than on departure. It's wise to assume, however, that your experience will turn out to be the exception.

None of this applies if you're travelling to, or within, **CFA zone countries only**. Here the fiscal arrangements commonly leave you feeling you're merely in an overseas French *departement* and there's rarely any interest in the money you have on you (apart from a purely private interest), nor any currency declaration forms or concern about where you change your money.

BANKS

West African **banking systems** are generally slow and limited. The capital cities are by far the best, if not the only, place to change money. Always try to arrive early in the day and remember your passport. Never start the transaction without checking the rate of exchange, the commission and any other charges. It's best to establish how much you'll receive in advance, before the paperwork starts. In the CFA zone there can be marked differences in the rates offered by different banks: their scales of commission and rates are often well behind the latest American and European swings.

WIRING

Try to avoid **sending home for money**. It's expensive and even faxed or telexed draft orders can take weeks to reach you at the counter – even though the normal delay should be only four or five working days. Note that Western Union does not offer its (normally swift) services in the region. You probably won't be able to receive hard currency except in the CFA zone, and not necessarily then. It's far better to have all you'll need, and more, in travellers cheques. If you do ask someone to send you money, give them several banks to choose from, as the bank at the other end may only correspond with one of them.

CREDIT CARDS

VISA, *American Express*, *Access-Mastercard* and *Diners' Club* are of some use in cities and large towns for tourist services such as upmarket hotels and restaurants, flights, tours and car rental. **American Express** has offices or agents in Morocco, Senegal, Sierra Leone, Liberia, Côte d'Ivoire, Ghana, Togo, Nigeria and Cameroon. You can buy hard currency travellers cheques with an *Amex* card – very useful. **Visa** and **Mastercard** have offices or agents in Morocco, Senegal, Sierra Leone, Côte d'Ivoire, Ghana, Nigeria and Cameroon. *Visa* also has facilities in The Gambia.

Don't count on **cash advances** against credit cards outside the CFA zone, and even in Francophone capitals you'll have to find the right local bank.

BLACK MARKETS

An unofficial, **parallel exchange rate** (the "black market") exists wherever there's a local demand for hard, foreign currency that can't be met through official channels. Except in the CFA zone, you can't usually walk into a bank and buy dollars, sterling, or other hard currency over the counter. Hard currency is kept in state control and sold to private citizens only reluctantly and with all sorts of conditions. Local currencies are worthless beyond these countries' borders and local people have enormous difficulty in obtaining hard currency to travel abroad, conduct business or support relatives.

In most of the non-CFA countries, you can exchange your hard currency for local money at higher-than-bank rates. **Black market rates** can vary from a few percentage points to several *hundred* percent better than the bank rate.

It may seem unfair on strangled economies to squeeze even harder for the sake of cheap local currency by depriving the banks of foreign exchange. But on the other hand it's naïve to hold exaggerated views of the importance of your hard currency to the national development of the country you're in, or of the net benefit to local people of putting your money into a bank rather than private hands. Sometimes the official exchange rate is simply set at an unrealistically high level that makes the place swingeingly expensive. It's worth noting that most prices tend to adjust to black market levels and that some services (especially hotels) may, in any case, be payable only in hard currency at the official rate of exchange. Questions of altruism and morality apart, it needs to be said, whatever else you do on your travels, *never change money on the street*. You run a high risk of being skilfully ripped off in public, even if the police informer scenario rarely comes to pass. Always take five minutes out to sit down in a shop or somewhere similar and count everything before handing over your cash.

COSTS AND BARGAINING

It's perhaps surprising to find that, in general, West Africa is an expensive part of the world, though the CFA countries are now much cheaper since the dramatic 50 percent devaluation of 1994. Mere survival can be dirt cheap, but anything like a Euro-American lifestyle costs as much, if not more, than in Europe or America. In between these extremes you can use the cheapest transport, eat market food and spend nights either camping in the bush, staying with people or in budget hotels. Travelling like this it's possible to get by on **£300/$450 a month** (though £600/$900 split between two gets you more value for money). It's clearly much harder to keep costs down in cities such as Dakar and Abidjan, where a panoply of tempting comforts and consumables is available in every direction and where it's hard to avoid staying in **hotels** – likely to be your biggest single expense.

The best way to keep costs *really* low is to **cycle**, which not only gives you free transport but also enables you to seek out inexpensive or free accommodation or tent space. A cycle tour of West Africa need not cost more than £5/$7.50 a day.

As a very general guideline to budget planning, a twin room in a **cheap hotel** can usually be had for under £10 ($15), often under £7 ($11) but rarely under £5 ($7.50). Long-distance **road transport** works out, on average, at about £2–3 ($3–5) per 100km, though it varies with the quality and speed of the vehicle. Train travel, if it's an option where you are, tends to be cheaper, river trips more expensive. As for **food**, you can always fill yourself with calories for under £1 ($1.50) if you eat street food or sit at a market or lorry park chop house.

Travelling on a different budget, **car rental** rates are some of the highest in the world (in a number of countries it's not difficult to work up bills of £130/$200 a day or more *without* taking the air-conditioned Range Rover). In most cities, too, top flight **international standard hotels**, are very expensive.

BARGAINING

You'll need to get into **bargaining** quickly. It's expected and is the normal way of conducting business. Moreover every time you pay an unreasonable price for goods or services you contribute to local inflation. **In markets** there's generally a "fixed price" which the seller has in mind. You can assume the one you're quoted is more, but a few good natured offers will establish the fact. Try offering a bulk price for several items at once, or add some "presents" to the thing you're negotiating over. Loads of good humour counts for much.

EXCHANGE RATES

As we go to press the following official exchange rates (approximate) apply:

	£1	$1
BENIN *CFA Franc*	800	520
BURKINA FASO *CFA Franc*	800	520
CAMEROON *Central African CFA Franc*	800	520
CAPE VERDE *Escudo*	120	83
CÔTE D'IVOIRE *CFA Franc*	800	520
THE GAMBIA *Dalasi*	15	10
GHANA *Cedi*	2000	1300
GUINEA *Guinean Franc*	2000	1300
GUINEA-BISSAU *Guinea-Bissauan Peso*	25,000	16,000
LIBERIA *Liberian Dollar*	70	50
MALI *CFA Franc*	800	500
MAURITANIA *Ouguiya*	200	130
NIGER *CFA Franc*	800	520
NIGERIA *Naira*	130	85
SENEGAL *CFA Franc*	800	520
SIERRA LEONE *Leone*	1200	800
TOGO *CFA Franc*	800	520

General stores, groceries and supermarkets invariably have **fixed prices**. Transport costs are usually subject to state control and almost always fixed, but baggage can be haggled over. Pretty well every other service (including budget hotel rooms in some countries) can and should be bargained for. This is often just a case of showing reluctance to pay what you're told is the going rate and getting some sort of **"discount"**.

It's in **buying major items** – particularly **crafts** – that you'll have the most fun bargaining. There's enormous flexibility around a few immutable rules. The most important is never to engage in bargaining if you've no intention of buying the item at any price. To offer what you thought was a silly price and then refuse to pay can cause grave offence. Nor should you embark on negotiations when you're in a hurry, or if you are feeling less than one hundred percent – it's an exhausting business.

When negotiating, don't automatically assume you're in the clutches of a rip-off artist. Concepts of **honour** are very important, and stalls are often minded by friends and relatives with whom, if you're quick and convincing, you can sometimes strike *real* bargains. Don't forget, from the trader's point of view, you're selling *money*.

Most importantly, men should make **physical contact** – hand-clasping is usually enough to emphasize a point. Be as jocular as possible and don't be shy of making a big scene – the bluffing and mock outrage on both sides is part of the fun. Women can't pursue these negotiating tactics in quite the same way, except when buying from women – invariably much tougher anyway.

Getting down to figures, try to **delay the moment when you have to name your price**. When you hear "One hundred how much you pay?", say nothing. It's amazing how often the seller's price drops way below your expectation before you've made any offer, so forget the standard "offer-a-third-come-up-to-a-half" formulae. If you do arrive at an unbridgeable gap you can always drop the matter and come by later. With stalemates, a **disinterested companion** tugging your sleeve is always a help.

HEALTH

Those who perspire readily, feel fittest in the tropics . . . If the right food is bought, prepared and served thoroughly clean and fresh, water boiled and filtered, insects kept out of homes, the usual prophylactics and daily exercise taken, sensible light clothes worn and strong alcohol avoided or drunk in moderation, then anyone with normal blood pressure should keep very fit.

R J Harrison Church, *West Africa* (1957)

It's not easy, of course, to maintain such zealous standards when you're on the move, though this old handbook advice holds good in principle. There's no reason to expect to get ill in West Africa, but plenty of opportunities to do so if you're unlucky or careless. The most likely hazards are stomach problems and malaria. Health details for each country, with a brief rundown on local problems and issues, are given in each chapter.

The only officially required *International Vaccination Certificates* are yellow fever and cholera. A **yellow fever vaccination certificate** is *always* a requirement, even if you're flying in direct from Europe, in Benin, Burkina Faso, Cameroon, Côte d'Ivoire, Ghana, Niger, Senegal and Togo. Several others require to see the yellow fever certificate if you're staying for longer than two weeks. All West African countries require the certificate if you've arrived by way of an infected area – in practice *any other sub-Saharan country*.

The **cholera certificate** is a bureaucratic, rather than a health issue. These days, many doctors who keep up with tropical medicine advances don't recommend the cholera jab for the reasons given below and some will quite willingly provide a cholera certificate discretely indicating you *haven't* had the jab. It seems to do the job at borders and airports.

If you lose a vaccination certificate, you can buy blank ones in many stationery stores. Explain your situation at a hospital or clinic and have it stamped and signed by someone (there'll probably be a small charge).

VACCINATIONS

Plan ahead. A first-time cholera inoculation needs at least two weeks between the two injections of the course, while a yellow fever certificate only becomes valid ten days after you've had the shot.

The validity of a **cholera inoculation** is a nominal six months, and it doesn't provide a great deal of protection against the disease. In fact the risks of contracting cholera are negligible unless you're living in the middle of an epidemic. The most recent epidemics have been in Conakry, parts of Guinea-Bissau and in Mindelo in the Cape Verde islands.

Yellow fever jabs are good for ten years and confer high immunity. Yellow fever is a monkey disease but it can be spread by mosquitoes to humans. Once contracted, there are no specific drugs to cure the illness, which takes a few days to develop into liver failure and kills about 50 percent of its victims. Outbreaks are very rare, but the jab is nonetheless essential.

You shouldn't consider major travels without a **typhoid vaccination** (which lasts three years) or **polio** and **tetanus** boosters. Nor is there any reason not to get **Havrix** shots which protect you for up to ten years against the common form of **hepatitis** ("A") spread by contaminated food and water. It's a lot nicer having the jabs than catching the disease, which seriously damages your liver and can leave it permanently scarred. The only problem with Havrix is its cost and the fact that you need to have the first shot at least 4 weeks before departure. Hepatitis "B", like HIV, is caught through the transfer of blood products, usually from dirty needles.

Whether you have the hepatitis "A" shots or not, be extra careful about cleanliness and in particular about contamination of water – a serious problem where, for example, a single water tank or barrel holds the whole water supply in a cockroach-infested toilet-cum-bathroom.

MALARIA

Protection against **malaria** (*le paludisme* or *"palu"* in French) is absolutely essential. The disease, caused by a parasite carried in the saliva of *Anopheles* mosquitos, is endemic in tropical Africa: many people carry it in their bloodstream and get occasional bouts of fever. It has a variable **incubation period** of a few days to several weeks so you can become ill long after being bitten. If you go down with malaria, you'll probably know. The fever, shivering and headaches are something like severe flu and come in waves, usually beginning in the early evening. Malaria is not infectious but it can be dangerous and even fatal if not treated quickly.

Female *Anopheles* mosquitos – the aggressors – prefer to bite in the evening. They can be distinguished by their rather eager head-down position. As well as a few common-sense measures – covering up after dark and using repellant – it's vital to be prepared with a course of tablets.

TABLETS

When taking **preventative tablets** it's important to keep a routine and cover the period before and after your trip with doses. Doctors can advise on which kind to take – it's generally the latest anti-resistant creation (currently halofantrine, sold as *Halfan*) but you can buy most of them at a pharmacy without a prescription.

Once in West Africa, the chloroquine-based tablets (such as *Nivaquin*, *Aralen* and *Resochin*), proguanil-based *Paludrin* and pyrimethamine-based *Daraprim* can be bought in small shops and from street drug stalls all over, but the newer drugs to which **falciparum** malaria – the common African strain – is less often resistant, are only available in big towns. Chloroquine-resistant malaria has now been reported all over West Africa, so complacency isn't in order, although even moderately resistant malaria is held at bay by proguanil and chloroquine.

Common preventative combinations are a small daily dose of proguanil and a weekly dose of chloroquine, or chloroquine alone with a supply of *Fansidar* to be used immediately if chloroquine-resistant malaria is suspected and you can't get to a doctor.

Chloroquine is safe **during pregnancy** but *Maloprim* and *Fansidar* sometimes have side effects and the latter isn't recommended (whether you're pregnant or not) as a prophylaxis. *Mefloquine*, a safer variation on *Fansidar*, which is only taken once a week, is worth asking your doctor about, but it's not recommended for stays of longer than three weeks. Some pills give some people mouth ulcers – you might want to be prepared with a suitable remedy.

In various parts of West Africa, the local or seasonal malaria risk is low but you shouldn't break your course of pills as it's vital to keep your parasite-fighting level as high as possible.

NETS AND REPELLANTS

Sleep under a **mosquito net** when possible – they're not expensive to buy locally – and burn **mosquito coils** (which you can buy everywhere) for a peaceful night. Don't use *Cock Brand* or *Lion Brand*, however, which are said to contain DDT and are banned in many countries. Whenever the mosquitos are particularly bad (and that's not often) cover your exposed parts with something strong. So-called **"Neat Deet"** (the insecticide diethyltoluamide) works well, and you could try soaking wrist and ankle bands in the stuff, diluted 1:9 with water. Beware: *Deet* is very corrosive and will chew through plastics and artificial fibres. Electric **mosquito destroyers**, which you fit with a pad every night, are less pungent than mosquito coils but more expensive – and you need electricity. Mosquito **"buzzers"** were a fad of the 1980s that proved to be completely useless.

IF YOU GO DOWN WITH MALARIA

Don't compare yourself with local people who may have considerable immunity. The priority, if you think you might be getting a fever, is **treatment**. Delay is potentially risky. Overly casual travellers die of the disease every year.

Ideally, confirm your diagnosis by getting to a doctor and having a blood test to identify the strain. If this isn't possible take 2 **quinine** tablets (600mg) twice daily for 5 days and then 3 *Fansidar* tablets. This should clear up any strain. If you don't have quinine tablets (you'd probably need to have obtained them abroad) then take ordinary **chloroquine** tablets at the rate of 10mg per kilo body weight up to a maximum of 600mg (usually 4 tablets) immediately, then half as much (usually 2 tablets) 8 hours later.

Assuming you feel an improvement, take this second dose again on the second and third days. If you notice no improvement after the *initial* dose, try again to see a doctor or take 3 **Fansidar** tablets if you have them – *your malaria is chloroquine resistant*. The *Fansidar* should clear it up within a few hours.

Strangely, the best mosquito repellant of all is said to be Avon bath oil (not that they sell it as such). Lastly, some people swear by the effects of Vitamin B in deterring mosquitos.

OTHER DISEASES

BILHARZIA

Bilharzia – also known as **schistosomiasis** – is potentially very nasty, though easily curable. The usual recommendation is never to swim in, wash with, drink or even touch lake or river water that's not been vouched for. On a long trip out in the bush, this isn't always possible, particularly if you're drinking with local people. Snail-free water that's stood for two days, or has been boiled or chlorinated, is safe, as is salt or brackish water.

Bilharzia comes from tiny flukes that live in freshwater snails and which, as part of their life cycle, leave their hosts and burrow into animal (or human) skin to multiply in the bloodstream. The snails themselves favour only stagnant water, though the flukes can be swept downstream. While it's possible to pick it up from one brief contact, the risk of contracting bilharzia is fairly low unless you repeatedly come into contact with infected water. If infected, you'll get a slightly itchy rash an hour or two later where the flukes have entered the skin.

Bilharzia is most prevalent in the **Sahelian regions** and particularly in **artificial lakes and dams**. If you have severe abdominal pains and pass blood – the first symptoms after 4–6 weeks – see a doctor.

SLEEPING SICKNESS

Sleeping sickness – trypanosomiasis – is mainly a disease of wild animals, but it also affects cattle and horses and to a much lesser extent people. It's carried by tse-tse ("setsy") flies that crowd streams and riverbanks in deep bush areas. They're determined, brutish insects with a painful bite, attracted to large moving objects such as elephants or Land Rovers. They tend to fly in the windows of vehicles driving through game parks.

Infection is extremely uncommon among travellers – fortunately, because the drugs used to treat it aren't very sophisticated. But a boil which suddenly appears, several *days* after a tse-tse fly bite, *might* indicate an infection you should get examined. Untreated, sleeping sickness results in

MEDICINE BAG

There's no need to take a mass of drugs and remedies you'll probably never use – and best not to plan a pharmaceutical relief number and give away a lot of miscellaneous pills. Various items, however, are immensely useful, especially on a long trip, and well worth buying in advance.

On a local level, if you're interested in herbal and other natural remedies, you'll find a wealth of natural cures in markets. Intuition, common sense and persistent enquries are all you need to judge whether they're worth trying.

Paracetamol Safer than aspirin for pain and fever relief.

Water purifying (chlorine) tablets Taste foul but do the trick.

Anti-malaria tablets Enough for prophylactic use plus several courses of *Fansidar* and/or quinine tablets in case of attack.

Codeine phosphate This is the preferred emergency anti-diarrhoeal pill but is on prescription only. Some GPs may oblige. *Lomotil* (*Co-phenotrope*) is second best.

Antibiotics *Amoxil* (*amoxycillin*) is a broad spectrum antibacterial drug useful against many infections. *Ciproxin* (*ciprofloxacin*) can feel like a life-saver in a bowel crisis. Both should only be used as a last resort when you cannot see a doctor. Again these are normally prescription drugs only.

Zinc oxide powder Useful anti-fungal powder (*Canestan*) for sweaty crevices.

Antiseptic *Cicatrin* is good, but creams in metal tubes invariably squeeze out messily sooner or later. Bright red or purple *mercurochrome* liquid dries wounds.

Alcohol swabs Paper *Medi-swabs* are invaluable for cleaning wounds, insect bites and infections.

Sticking plaster, steri-strip wound closures, sterile gauze dressing, micropore tape You don't need much of this stuff, and you can buy it in most capital cities.

Lip balm Invaluable.

Thermometer Very useful. Ideally you'll be 37.5°C. A *Feverscan* forehead thermometer is unbreakable and gives a ready reckoning (from pharmacies).

Lens solution If you wear contact lenses you'll need a good supply of solution.

infections of the central nervous system and drowsiness. Not amusing.

RIVER BLINDNESS

Though it's alarmingly common among West Africans, travellers virtually never pick up **river blindness** – onchocerciasis – a disease common along several river systems. It's spread by tiny **blackflies**, which have a vicious bite and pass on minute worms, which in turn move to the eyes and can eventually cause blindness. If you find yourself suffering from impaired vision, it may well be caused by long-term use of chloroquine against malaria – nothing to do with onchocerciasis.

SEXUALLY TRANSMITTED DISEASES AND AIDS

The only other real likelihood of your encountering a serious disease in West Africa is if it's **sexually transmitted**. Assorted venereal diseases are widespread, particularly in the larger towns, and the HIV virus which causes **AIDS** – known as SIDA in Francophone countries – is alarmingly prevalent and spreading all the time. It's very easily passed between people suffering relatively minor, but ulcerous, sexually transmitted dieseases, and the very high prevalence of these is thought to account for the high incidence of heterosexually transmitted HIV. So there you have it: not exactly an incitement to throw caution to the winds.

On the associated topic of receiving **blood transfusions** or injections in an emergency, you might want to carry a sterile emergency kit to be used by a doctor if you get into trouble. Usually, however, such treatment can only be offered in a hospital environment where most staff are familiar with the need for sterile equipment and fresh needles.

WATER AND BUGS

In many places in West Africa, the **water** you drink will have come from a tap and is likely to be clean. Since bad water is the most likely cause of **diarrhoea**, you should be cautious of drinking rain or well water.

In truth, **stomach upsets** don't plague many travellers badly. If you're visiting for a short time only, it makes sense to be scrupulous – purifying tablets and/or boiling kill most things. If you want to be absolutely safe, **purification**, a two-stage process involving both filtration and sterilization, gives the most complete treatment. Portable water purifiers range from pocket-size units weighing 60 grams, up to 800 grams. Some of the best water purifiers on the market are made in Britain by **PreMac**; for suppliers, contact: **Pre-Mac (Kent) Ltd** ☎01892/534361; 40 Holden Park Rd, Southborough, Tunbridge Wells, Kent TN4 0ER, England. **All Water Systems Ltd** ☎01/456-4933; Unit 12, Western Parkway Business Centre, Lr. Ballymount Rd, Dublin 12, Ireland. **Outbound Products** ☎800/663-9262 1580; Zephyr Ave, Box 56148, Hayward CA 9454, USA. **Outbound Products** ☎604/321-5464 8585 Fraser St, Vancouver, BC V5X 3Y1, Canada.

For longer stays, and especially if you're travelling widely, think of re-educating your stomach rather than fortifying it. It's virtually impossible to travel around the region without exposing yourself to strange bugs from time to time. Take it easy at first, don't overdo the fruit (and wash it in **clean**, safe water before peeling), don't keep food too long and be very wary of salads. If you travel across the **desert**, particularly if you hitch or use public transport, gradually acclimatizing, you'll probably find you can survive without ill effect most of the bugs you must be consuming. Ironically, perhaps, if you're travelling on a shoestring budget and rarely eat restaurant meals, your chances of picking up stomach bugs are considerably reduced.

If you do have **a serious attack**, 24 hours of nothing but plain tea (or just boiled water) may rinse it out. The important thing is to replace lost fluids. If you feel in need you can make up a **rehydration mix** with four heaped teaspoons of sugar or honey and half a teaspoon of salt in a litre of water, but most upsets resolve themselves. If the diarrhoea seems to be getting worse – or, horrifically, you have to travel a long distance while stricken – any pharmacy should have name brand anti-diarrhoea remedies. These (*Lomotil*, codeine phosphate etc) shouldn't be over-used. A day's worth of doses is about the most you should take.

GENERAL HEALTH TIPS

Some people **sweat** heavily and lose a lot of salt. Salt tablets, however, are unnecessary. Sprinkle extra salt on your food. Even if you're not a great perspirer it's important to keep a healthy salt balance. The body can't function without it and it's not uncommon to experience sudden exhaustion and collapse a few days after arrival in a hot climate.

Pawpaws (papaya), and their seeds – which taste like watercress – can be eaten as a kind of tonic. They contain excellent supplies of invigorating minerals and vitamins and are reckoned to help the healing process and to aid digestion. The smaller and more fragrant mountain varieties are delicious but in many parts of West Africa, pawpaws aren't even regarded as worth selling. They grow as giant weeds, left for the children, and not relished as proper fruit at all. If you don't see them for sale, approach the people of a house where they're growing in the compound and ask to buy one.

MEDICAL TREATMENT

If you need **medical treatment** in West Africa, you'll discover a frightening lack of well-equipped **hospitals**. In each country, we've tried to indicate which are the best and to give general practitioners and dentists in city "Listings". For serious treatment you're almost certain to want to come home. Blood and urine tests can be performed locally but needles and other instruments may not be fresh from a sealed package. If in doubt, insist on paying for new ones.

Moderate injuries can be treated locally. In remote areas, **missions** are usually the first recourse. If you require treatment, it's normally proficient and the charges low, though comforts fairly rudimentary.

CONTRACEPTIVES

Condoms are available from most pharmacies, or alternatively from some clinics and dispensaries. But they tend to be expensive or of dubious manufacture. Take some with you. If you use **oral contraceptives**, get your doctor to prescribe a supply. And don't forget an alternative method to fall back on if you have a stomach upset or take a course of antibiotics, as either can leave you unprotected for the rest of the month.

IMMUNIZATIONS AND ADVICE

North American travellers should not immediately head for expensive specialist travel clinics, where the cost of various jabs can easily run into hundreds of dollars. Health departments in most cities offer inoculations at a far lower rate. For general advice and information, 24 hours a day, contact the **Center for Disease Control and Prevention** (☎404/332-4565; easier to get through on Fax 404/332-4559).

For British travellers, the first source of advice and probable supplier of jabs and prescriptions is your GP. Family doctors are often well-informed and some won't charge you for routine injections. For yellow fever and other exotic shots you'll normally have to visit a specialist clinic, often in a county town health authority headquarters.

In London, advice and low-cost **inoculations** are available from the Travel Clinic of the **Hospital for Tropical Diseases**, 180–182 Tottenham Court Rd, London W1P 9LE (☎0171/636-6099; Fax 0171/637-9717; Mon–Fri 9am–4.40pm). They produce a series of useful fact sheets and you can get most jabs without prior appointment any weekday morning. With a referral from your GP, the Hospital for Tropical Diseases will also give you a complete **check-up** on your return if you think it may be worth it.

Also in London, the *British Airways Travel Clinic*, 156 Regent St, London W1 (☎0171/439-9584 or 439-9585; Mon–Fri 9am–4.15pm, Sat 10am–4pm) can provide a wide variety of unusual shots like plague, anthrax and rabies as well as the usual ones, anti-malarial tablets and various hardware.

Call **MASTA** (*Medical Advisory Services for Travellers Abroad*; premium rate ☎0891/224100) based at the London School of Hygiene and Tropical Diseases, Keppel St, London WC1E 7HT, who will provide the latest information by post. For a fee they also offer very detailed, personalized "Health Briefs" for whichever countries you're visiting (☎01705/553 933). They advise on inoculations, give rundowns on all the diseases you're likely (or not) to fall victim to and include up-to-date health news from the countries concerned. MASTA also sell sterile emergency packs and other items.

Nomad, 3–4 Turnpike Lane, London N8 0PX (☎0181/889-7014; Fax 0181/889-9529; (shop open Mon–Sat 9am–5.30pm; pharmacy open Wed and Thurs 2–5.30pm, Sat 9am–5.30pm; vaccinations only Sat 9am–5.30pm) is an adventure equipment supplier also offering health advice and an inoculation service for travellers.

Other tropical disease centres in the UK include:

Department of Communicable and Tropical Diseases, Birmingham Heartland Hospital, Bordesley Green Rd, Birmingham B9 5ST (☎0121/766-6611).

Liverpool School of Tropical Medicine, Pembroke Place, Liverpool L3 5QA (☎0151/708-9393).

Communicable Diseases Unit, Ruchill Hospital, Glasgow G20 9NB (☎0141/946-7120).

Avoid jumping for **antibiotics** at the first sign of trouble. They annihilate what's nicely known as your gut flora (most of which you want to keep) and will not work on viruses. By the time you're considering their use, you should really seek a doctor. If you've definitely got blood in your diarrhoea and *it's impossible to see a doctor*, then this is the time to take a course of metronidazole (*Flagyl*). You'd have to arrange this on prescription with your physician or GP before your trip. Antibiotics and anti-diarrhoeal drugs shouldn't be used as preventatives – this is potentially very dangerous. Women using **contraceptive pills** have another reason to fear diarrhoea – it reduces hormone absorption and can leave you unprotected.

Lastly, two common gynecological problems. **Cystitis** can be relieved, if not eradicated, with acidy fruit juice: oranges and pineapples are available in abundance over much of the region. Don't fail to get medical treatment as soon as possible however, as cystitis can be very dangerous in a hot climate. **Thrush** responds well to a good dose of yoghurt (both eaten and applied).

INJURIES, RASHES AND ATTACKS

Take more care than usual over minor **cuts and scrapes** – the most trivial scratch can become a throbbing infection if you ignore it. Otherwise, there are all sorts of potential **bites**, **stings** and **rashes** that rarely, if ever materialize.

Many people get a bout of **prickly heat** rash at first, before they've acclimatized. It's an infection of the sweat ducts caused by excessive perspiration which doesn't dry off. A cool shower, **zinc oxide powder** and cotton clothes should help. On the subject of heat, it's important not to overdose on **sunshine** – at least in the first week or two. The powerful heat and bright light can mess up your system. A **hat** and sunglasses are necessities.

As for animal attacks, West African **dogs** are usually sad and skulking and pose little threat, though like captive **monkeys** they may carry rabies. **Scorpions** and **spiders** abound but are hardly ever seen unless you go turning over rocks or logs. Scorpion stings are painful but almost never fatal – and scorpions usually need considerable goading before they'll bring their tail into attack. Spiders are mostly quite harmless. The large, terrifyingly fast and active **solifugids** (also known as camel spiders or wind scorpions) do sometimes have a painful bite, but you're not likely to sit around and find out. **Snakes** are common but, again, the vast majority are harmless and to see one at all you'll need to search stealthily – walk heavily and they obligingly disappear. For reassurance about larger beasts, see "Wildlife and National Parks" on p.77.

TEETH

Make sure that you have a thorough **dental check-up** before leaving and take extra care of your teeth while in West Africa. Stringy meat, acid fruit and too many soft drinks are some of the hazards. Floss and brush at least once in the middle of each day. You could, too, get into the habit of using a fresh "toothbrush stick" cut from a branch, as many locals do. Some varieties (for sale at markets) contain a plaque-destroying enzyme. Get into the habit of chewing gum after eating – even sweet varieties quickly lose their sugar and are soon performing a useful function on your teeth.

If you lose a filling and aren't inclined to see a dentist locally, try and get hold of some *gutta percha* – a natural, rubbery substance – which is available from some pharmacies. You heat it and then pack it in the hole as a temporary filling. Your dentist could get you some to take with you. **Emergency dental packs** are available from many vaccination centres.

For a book on your health in tropical countries, you couldn't do better than Dr Richard Dawood's *Traveller's Health* (Oxford University Press, 1992). Exceptionally sane, detailed and well-written, it covers just about every imaginable symptom. If you're living in West Africa, especially if you need to treat yourself or others, get hold of the brilliant classic *Where There is No Doctor* by David Werner (Oxfam and Macmillan, 1977)

INSURANCE

Insurance, in the light of the potential health risks, is too important to ignore. In addition to covering medical expenses and emergency repatriation, it also insures your money and belongings against loss and theft.

In Britain *ISIS* travel insurance – available to everyone up to the age of 65 through branches of *STA Travel* or *Endsleigh*, 97–107 Southampton Row, London WC1 (☎0171/436-4451) – is one of the least expensive. *Frizzell Insurance*, Frizzell House, County Gates, Bournemouth, Dorset BH1 2NF (☎01202/292333) or *Columbus Travel Insurance*, 17 Devonshire Square, London EC2 (☎0171/375-0011), are good value too. *Campbell Irving*, 48 Earl's Court Rd, London W8 6EJ (☎0171/937-6981) is known for being helpful and having a customer-centred approach to travel in more offbeat parts of the world. An outlay of £30 ($45) per month will cover you against all sorts of calamities as well as lost baggage, flight cancellations and hospital charges. Some activities (climbing for example) are usually specifically excluded but can often be included as a supplement; ask your insurers for advice. Ask them to include bicycle and motorbike travel, as you may well find yourself a passenger, if not the "driver".

Whatever insurance you decide on, make sure you're not paying a high premium for cover you don't need – too much baggage cover, or a huge sum for personal liability – and make sure you *are* covered for what you intend to do. **If you need to claim**, you *must* have a police report in the case of theft or loss, and supporting evidence in the case of hospital and medication bills. Keep photocopies of everything before you send it to the insurer and write immediately to tell them what's happened. You can usually claim later.

NORTH AMERICAN INSURANCE

In the **US and Canada**, insurance tends to be much more expensive, and may be medical cover only. Before buying a policy, check that you're not already covered by existing insurance plans. **Canadians** are usually covered by their provincial health plans; holders of **ISIC cards** and some other student/teacher/youth cards are entitled to $3000 worth of accident coverage and sixty days ($100 per diem) of hospital in-patient benefits for the period during which the card is valid. **Students** will often find that their student health coverage extends during the vacations and for one term beyond the date of last enrolment. Bank and credit cards (particularly *American Express*) often have certain levels of medical or other insurance included, and travel insurance may also be included if you use a major credit or charge card to pay for your trip. **Homeowners' or renters'** insurance often covers theft or loss of documents, money and valuables while overseas, though conditions and maximum amounts vary from company to company.

Only after exhausting the possibilities above might you want to contact a specialist travel insurance company such as *STA Travel*; or try any of

INSURANCE AGENCIES IN NORTH AMERICA

Europ Assistance Worldwide Services, 1331 F St NW, Washington DC 20004 (☎1-800/821-2828).

International Association for Medical Assistance to Travelers (IAMAT) 736 Center St, Lewiston, NY 14092 (☎716/754-4883).

Travel Assistance International, Suite 400, 1133 15th St NW, Washington DC 20008 (☎1-800/821-2828).

Travel Guard International,1100 Center Point Dr, Stevens Point WI 54481 (☎1-800/782-5151).

Travel Insurance Services, Box 299, Walnut Creek, CA 94596 (☎ 1-800/937-1387).

those listed below. **Premiums** vary widely, from the very reasonable ones offered primarily through student/youth agencies (*STA*'s policies range from about $50–70 for 15 days to $500–700 for a year), to those so expensive that the cost for anything more than two months will probably equal the cost of the worst possible combination of disasters. If you're engaging in any high-risk outdoor activity while in West Africa, you'll need to take out an additional rider – this will add an extra 30–50 percent to the premium.

Most of these American policies do not insure against **theft** while overseas. North American travel policies apply only to items **lost** from, or **damaged** in, the custody of an identifiable, responsible third party – hotel porter, airline, luggage consignment, etc. Even in these cases you will have to contact the local police to have a complete report made out so that your insurer can process the claim.

If you are travelling via London it might be a lot better to take out a **British policy**, available instantly and easily.

One thing to check: if you enter a country against the official advice of your government, your policy may become invalid (see p.43).

MAPS AND INFORMATION

Although you will find maps of individual countries, and even certain cities, when you get to West Africa, they're almost always expensive and hard to obtain. Buy those you need in advance. As for tourist offices, those few that exist are usually attached to embassies or airlines and rarely offer more than vague leaflets.

MAPS

The single most useful item to take is the **Michelin map #953** *Africa North and West*. It covers all of northwest Africa with the exception of southern Cameroon (which appears on the #955 *Africa Central and South*). The latest (1993) edition of the #953 takes account of most new roads, showing water and fuel sources, roads liable to flood, ferry crossings and a mass of other details at a scale of 40km:1cm (63 miles:1inch). The only serious competition is *Kummerly & Frey*'s "Africa North & West" map – on the same scale but less detailed and altogether less user-friendly.

For individual countries, the French **Institut Géographique National** (*IGN*, 136bis, rue de Grenelle, 75700 Paris) has maps for a number of Francophone countries (plus Guinea-Bissau), many of which have been recently updated. There's also a good *Michelin* map of Côte d'Ivoire, a number of road maps of Nigeria, and a good one of Cameroon by *Macmillan*. Other maps, where they exist, are hard to obtain abroad. Again, details for each country are given in their individual "Practical Information" sections at the beginning of each chapter.

TRAVEL AND TOURIST INFORMATION

Few countries in West Africa have money to promote tourism abroad. Those that have tourist offices can offer little more than uninspiring leaflets and brochures. Specialist **bookshops** and **libraries** are the best sources of information about West Africa. For general pre-departure

MAP RETAILERS AND TRAVEL BOOKSHOPS IN THE UK

LONDON

Africa Bookcentre, 38 King St, WC2E 8JT (☎0171/240-6649; Fax 0171/379-4929). Located in the Africa Centre. A very wide selection of books from and about the continent, with an emphasis on African writers and academic works. Mon–Fri 11am–5.30pm, Sat until 5pm.

Daunt Books for Travellers, 83 Marylebone High St, W1M 4AL (☎0171/224-2295). Superb place to browse, with indigenous fiction and travel literature rubbing shoulders with the Roughs and Lonelys.

Stanfords, 12 Long Acre, WC2E 9LP (☎0171/836-1321; Fax 0171/836-0189). The best travel book and map store in the world, with wide coverage. Mail order. *IGN* agent.

The Travel Bookshop, 13 Blenheim Crescent, W11 2EE (☎0171/229-5260; Fax 0171/243-1552). Very good new and second-hand section on Africa, with some French-language guides. Mon–Sat 10am–6pm.

The Travellers Bookshop, 25 Cecil Court, WC2 (☎0171/836-9132; Fax 0171/379-4929). Excellent, small bookseller, popular with keen travellers, with buy-back policy on used books and notice boards.

EDINBURGH

Thomas Nelson and Sons Ltd, 51 York Place, EH1 3JD (☎0131/557-3011).

GLASGOW

John Smith & Sons, 57–61 St Vincent St (☎0141/221-7472).

MAP RETAILERS AND TRAVEL BOOKSHOPS IN PARIS

Astrolabe, 46 rue de Provence, 75009 (☎1/42.85.42.95). Paris's largest travel books and map store.

Ulysse, 26 rue St-Louis-en-l'Île, 75004 (☎1/43.25.17.35). Crammed full of guides, old books and maps.

NORTH AMERICAN MAP RETAILERS AND TRAVEL BOOKSHOPS

CHICAGO

Rand McNally, 444 N Michigan Ave, IL 60611 (☎312/321-1751). 24 stores across the US; call ☎1-800/333-0136 (ext 2111) for the address of your nearest store, or for mail order.

Savvy Traveler, 50 E Washington St, IL 60602 (☎312/321-1751).

LOS ANGELES

Travel Bookcase, 8375 W 3rd St, LA (☎213/655-0575).

The Travel Gallery, 1007 Manhattan Ave, Manhattan Beach (☎310/379-9199).

MINNEAPOLIS

Latitudes Map & Travel Store, Calhoun Sq, 3001 Hennpin Ave S, MN 55408 (☎612/823-3742).

MONTRÉAL

Ulysses Travel Bookshop, 4176 St-Denis (☎514/289-0993).

NEW YORK

British Travel Bookshop, 551 5th Ave, NY 10176 (☎1-800/448-3039 or 212/490-6688).

The Complete Traveler Bookstore, 199 Madison Ave, NY 10016 (☎212/685-9007).

Liberation Bookstore, 421 Lenox Ave (☎212/281-4615).

Rand McNally, 150 East 52nd St, NY 10022 (☎212/758-7488).

Traveler's Bookstore, 22 West 52nd St, NY 10019 (☎212/664-0995).

PALO ALTO

Phileas Foggs, 87 Stanford Shopping Center, Palo Alto (☎1-800/533-3644).

PASADENA

Distant Lands, 62 South Raymond St, CA 91105 (☎818/449-320 or 1-800/310-3220).

SAN FRANCISCO

The Complete Traveler Bookstore, 3207 Filmore St, CA 92123 (☎415/923-1511).

Rand McNally, 595 Market St, CA 94105 (☎415/777-3131).

Travel Market, 130 Pacific Ave Mall, Golden Gateway Commons, San Francisco (☎415/421-4080).

SANTA BARBARA

Map Link, 25 E Mason St, CA 93101 (☎805/965-4402). Mail order supply.

Pacific Travellers' Supply, 529 State St. Map Link's shop.

SANTA MONICA

California Map and Travel Center, 3211 Pico Blvd (☎310/829-6277).

SEATTLE

Elliot Bay Book Company, 101 South Main St, WA 98104 (☎206/624-6600).

NORTH AMERICAN MAP AND TRAVEL BOOKSHOPS contd.

TORONTO

Open Air Books and Maps, 25 Toronto St, M5R 2C1 (☎416/363-0719).

VANCOUVER

World Wide Books and Maps, 1247 Granville St (☎604/687-3320).

WASHINGTON DC

The Map Store, 1636 I St NW (☎202/628-2608).

Rand McNally, 1201 Connecticut Ave NW, Washington DC 20036 (☎202/223-6751).

MAP RETAILERS AND TRAVEL BOOKSHOPS IN AUSTRALASIA

ADELAIDE

The Map Shop, 16a Peel St, SA 5000 (☎08/231-2033).

BRISBANE

Hema, 239 George St, QLD 4000 (☎07/221-4330).

MELBOURNE

Bowyangs, 372 Little Bourke St, VIC 3000 (☎03/670-4383).

PERTH

Perth Map Centre, 891 Hay St, WA 6000 (☎09/322-5733).

SYDNEY

Travel Bookshop, 20 Bridge St, NSW 2000 (☎02 241-3554).

reading have a look at the "Books" section in *Contexts*. For the official line from the British Foreign and Commonwealth Office Travel Advice Unit, tune to Ceefax p.564–568 and trawl through the notices, or call them on ☎0171/270-4129. For the same thing in the US, call the Department of State Travel Advisory Dept, 2201 C ST NW, Washington DC 20520 (☎202/647-5225).

The best source of up-to-the-minute news about conditions in West Africa are the various **Africa-centred magazines**. These are patchily available in major West African cities. They include:

Africa Confidential (73 Farringdon Rd, London EC1M 3TB; ☎0171/831-3511; Fax 0171/831-6778). Fortnightly 8-page newsletter with solid inside info. Subscription only (£150, £50 students).

Africa Report (833 UN Plaza, New York, NY 10017; ☎212/949-5666). Bi-monthly American heavyweight newsmag, with good analyses and in-depth reporting, published by the African-American Institute.

African Business (IC Publications, PO Box 261, Carlton House, 69 Great Queen St, London WC2B 5BN; ☎0171/713-7711). Good general coverage.

Focus on Africa (Bush House, PO Box 76, Strand, London WC2B 4PH; ☎0171/257-2906; Fax 0171/379-0519). The BBC World Service's colour quarterly retrospective of news and reportage.

Jeune Afrique (51 av des Ternes, 75017 Paris; ☎1/47.66.52.42). Influential weekly in the style of *Newsweek*, with African and international news.

New African (IC Publications, 7 Coldbath Sq, London EC1R 4LQ; ☎0171/713-771). Well edited news magazine with good sports coverage.

West Africa (43–45 Coldharbour Lane, London SE5 9NR; ☎0171/737-2946; Fax 0171/978-8334). Widely available Nigerian-owned weekly news magazine. Although you should be wise to the fact of its ownership, this is still the most useful regular source of news for West Africa.

LIBRARIES AND RESOURCE CENTRES IN THE UK

Africa Centre, 38 King St, London WC2E 8JT (☎0171/836-1973). Office and reading room open Mon–Fri 9.30am–6pm. The UK's best independent charity institute for African affairs, open to all – reading room with magazines and newspapers, exhibitions, music, theatre, cinema, language teaching. Bar and restaurant open seven days. A good place to meet people.

Commonwealth Institute, Kensington High Street, London W8 6NQ (☎0171/603-4535). Large centre offering library and resource services, shop, exhibitions, workshops and a performance venue.

Royal Geographical Society, 1 Kensington Gore, London SW7 2AR. Helpful *Expedition Advisory Service* (☎0171/581-2057) provides a wealth of information, including maps and technical guides.

School of Oriental and African Studies Library, Thornhaugh St, Russell Square, London WC1H 0XG (☎0171/637-2388). Open Mon–Thurs 9am–8.45pm, Fri 9am–7pm, Sat 9.30am–5pm; summer vacation Mon–Sat 9am–5pm. A vast collection of book, journals and maps – probably the world's foremost African studies library.

LIBRARIES AND RESOURCE CENTRES IN THE US

African American Institute, 833 UN Plaza, NY 10017 (☎212/949-5666).

Africa Studies Association, Emory University, Credit Union Building, Atlanta, GA 30322 (☎404/329-6410).

Boston University African Studies Center, 270 Bay State Rd, Boston, MA 02215 (☎617/353-7303).

Hoover Institute, Stanford, CA 94305 (☎408/723-2072).

Howard University African Studies, Sixth St Howard Place NW, Washington, DC 20059 (☎202/636-7115).

Institute of African Affairs, Columbia University, 1103 School of International Affairs, 420 West 118th St, NY 10027 (☎212/280-4633).

Michigan State University Africa Studies Center, 100 International Center, East Lansing, MI 48823 (☎310/825-6552).

Ohio University African Studies Program, 56 E Union St, Athens, Ohio 45701 (☎614/594-5542).

University of Illinois African Studies Center, 910 S 5th St, room 210, Champaign, IL 61820 (☎217/333-6335).

University of Wisconsin African Studies, 1454 Van Hise Hall, 1220 Linden Dr, Madison, WI 53706 (☎608/262-2380).

Yale University Council on African Studies, 89 Trumbull St, New Haven, CT 06520 (☎203/432-3436).

LIBRARIES AND RESOURCE CENTRES IN CANADA

Carleton University African Studies Committee, Ottawa K1S 5B6 (☎613/564-3816).

Centre for African Studies, Dalhousie University, Halifax, Nova Scotia B3H 4H6 (☎902/424-3814).

GETTING AROUND

Information about local route and transport conditions in each country is given under "Arrival" and "Getting Around" in the practical information at the beginning of each chapter. Specific transport practicalities are also detailed in the coverage of each capital city and in "Moving On" details throughout. What follows here is a general user's guide to West African transport.

BUSH TAXIS

The classic form of West African public transport is the **bush taxi** (*taxi brousse* in French, plus numerous local terms). This can vary from a reasonably comfortable Peugeot **station wagon** seating five or six plus driver, to the same thing seating nine or ten in discomfort, to a converted **Japanese pick-up** with slat-wood benches and a canvas awning jammed with fifteen people or more. A basket of chickens stuffed under the bench, and maybe a goat or two tied to the roof are regular fare-paying additions. Larger French **box vans**, increasingly replaced by Japanese and Korean **minibuses**, are no less zoo-like, though padded benches or seats help, as does the extra ventilation. Most vehicles have roof-rack luggage carriers and a more expensive seat or two at the front, next to the driver.

The **chaos** that seems to accompany bush taxi journeys is an illusion. They are nearly all licensed passenger vehicles, serving approved routes at fixed rates. Many even have notional schedules, though these are never published and rarely adhered to.

Peugeot taxis generally sell their places and drive straight from A to B, if possible without stopping. They often do the trip in half the time it takes a more beat-up bush taxi, which may drop people off and take fares en route. But the converted pick-ups (*bâchés* in French, after their tarpaulins) are often the only way to get to more obscure destinations, or to travel on the roughest roads. Not surprisingly they're cheaper.

Beware of inadvertently **chartering** a bush taxi for private rental (a *déplacement* in French). Once you've done it, there's no way of avoiding paying for *all the seats*.

TAXI PARKS

Most towns have a **taxi park** ("station", "stand", *gare routière, autogare*) where vehicles assemble to fill with passengers. Larger towns may have several, each serving different routes and usually located on the relevant road out, at the edge of town.

Practice varies slightly from country to country, but generally when you go to the taxi park, you'll find you're quickly surrounded by **taxi scouts** trying to get you into their vehicle. This can be trying and sometimes unnerving – when there's lots of competition and you're physically mobbed. It pays to behave robustly and to know exactly where you're going, and the names of any towns en route or beyond. It's often the case that your destination is not where all the vehicles are headed. You may have to change, or get out earlier. The ideal **time to travel** is early in the morning. By a couple of hours after sunrise the best vehicles have gone. In many parts there won't be another until the next day.

BUSH TAXI SURVIVAL

Bush taxis are probably the most dangerous vehicles on the roads so don't be afraid to make a very big fuss if the driver appears to have lost all sense. Ask and then shout at him to **"Slow down!"** ("*Ralentir!*" in French) and try to enlist the support of fellow travellers – though this is rarely forthcoming. In Peugeots it's nice to have a couple of **cassettes** for the stereo. In any vehicle, and in most parts of West Africa, sharing some **kola nuts** goes down well (see p.64). Lastly, if you're in a van with an engine mounted behind the front cab, be sure not to sit near it – you'll melt.

Before long on your travels, you'll run into a situation where you seem to be **the only passenger** in a vehicle you were assured was about to leave. Beware of this. It's true your presence will encourage others to join you – which is why they wanted you there in the first place. But sometimes it's better to forget over-ambitious travel plans (especially any time after noon) or to take a shorter journey with a vehicle that's nearly ready to go. Taxi parks are full of interest for up to an hour or so. But a half day spent in one acting as passenger bait is a waste of time.

As for **fares**: in order to guarantee you'll stay and attract others, drivers, owners and scouts will often try to get you to pay up front. Again, practice varies from country to country. Your luggage tied on the roof generally ought to be sufficient sign of your good faith and, unless you see others paying, it's always best to delay. Make sure you pay the right person when you do.

Over-charging is almost unheard of. It's your **luggage** that will cost you if you don't argue. You'll often have to argue fiercely about how small, light and streamlined it is. Fellow passengers are just as likely to suffer but aren't in such a good position to create a scene. Shout, compare and contrast; tell the crowd how he's trying to kill you with his grasping ways. Make them laugh; make him happy to give you a good price. If you get nowhere, go to one side with him and be conspiratorial – this sometimes works because people like to show off business acumen and it draws attention again. You shouldn't have to pay more than **one third** of your fare for a back pack or large bag. It's normally much less. Remember, you can argue forever about what you're *going* to pay, but once you've paid it, the argument is over.

During **long waits** it's a good idea to keep an eye on your luggage. Anything tied on the roof is safe, but taxi parks are notorious haunts for thieves, and bags sometimes get grabbed through open windows. Keep valuables round your neck. Don't worry unduly, however, if the vehicle, while waiting to fill, and with booked passengers scattered around, suddenly takes off with all your gear on top. While it's obviously a good idea to make a discreet mental note of the vehicle registration, you should avoid offence by appearing suspicious. Make friends with other passengers and relax. Maybe nobody knows where they've gone (probably to fill up with fuel), but they'll be back.

BUSES

Bus travel, when you've the option, is usually more comfortable and less expensive, though certain manifestations are little better than gigantic bush taxis and not always much faster. Niger, Burkina Faso, The Gambia, Sierra Leone, Côte d'Ivoire, Ghana and Nigeria have quite well-developed bus services. Ghana's state-run service is particularly good, and not expensive. Côte d'Ivoire even has "video coaches".

The big advantage of most buses is having your own seat (even Peugeot bush taxis usually sell more places than there are seats) and being able to buy tickets in advance for a departure at a set time. There's still some room for discussion over the cost of transporting your luggage, but it's rarely a big issue.

Whether travelling by bus or bush taxi, it's worth considering your general direction through the trip and **which side to sit on for the shadiest ride**. This is especially important on dirt roads when the combination of slow, bumpy ride, dust and fierce sun can be horrible. If you're travelling on a *busy* dirt road with lots of other traffic, you don't want to be seated on the left of the vehicle in any case.

TRUCKS

Although it's usually against the law, on all main routes – and in the remotest regions too – you'll be able to travel by **lorry**. Pick up a lift in small villages or along the road: because of its illegality, you'll rarely find a truck ride in a large town. Once aboard, you can expect the lorry to stop at every checkpoint to pay bribes – slow progress.

There's sometimes a spare seat or two in the cab, but more often space in the back.

POLICE AND ARMY CHECKPOINTS

You should pay some attention to the condition of driver and vehicle before deciding to give him your custom. It's rare to undertake any journey over 20km in West Africa without encountering a posse of uniforms at the side of the road. A neatly turned-out Peugeot with a well-tied load and quite possibly some persons of influence inside is likely to pause for a greeting and move on. Conversely, a bruised and shaken *camion bâché* with 19 passengers, no lights and the contents of someone's house on the roof may be detained for some hours. For more details see "Trouble and Personal Safety".

Travelling in the back of panelled vehicles is pretty miserable, but many older trucks are open at the back with wood frame sides. When loaded with suitable cargo, these can be a delight to travel in. You get great views and even, on occasions, a comfortable ride in a recumbent position. Do bear in mind your safety however (look out for low branches) and avoid getting the driver in trouble with the police by being conspicuous or foolhardy.

Travelling in an empty goods lorry on bad roads can be close to intolerable. They go much faster unladen and you're typically forced to stand and clasp the sides as the vehicle smashes through the pot holes, causing severe discomfort to loose parts of the anatomy. For truck travel, you need to know the equivalent bush taxi or bus fares and distances or you'll find yourself paying over the odds. Lorries often drive late into the night too – if you're being carried outside, be sure to have **something warm to wear** for later.

HITCHING

The majority of rural people in West Africa get around by **waving down a vehicle**, but they invariably pay, whether on public transport, a truck or in a private car with a spare place. Private vehicles are still comparatively rare and usually full. **Travelling for free** is often considered to be rather improper and most people will assume your car has broken down. There's some sense, however, in hitching in and out of large cities, especially if you're stuck for money or can't find a bus or taxi. The kinds of drivers who respond positively are usually foreign-educated business types or expats.

Hitching **techniques** need to be exuberant. A modest thumb-in-the-air is more likely to be interpreted as a friendly, or rude, gesture than a request. Beckon the driver to stop with your palm. You'll feel like a policeman but that doesn't matter. Always explain first if you can't – or won't – pay, and don't be surprised if you're left at the side of the road.

Best chances for conventional hitch-hiking are in Senegal, Côte d'Ivoire, Ghana, Nigeria and Cameroon. Hitching with overland tourists can be a good change of pace, and – more calculatingly – if you're in the right vicinity it can throw you in with people visiting game parks, which tend otherwise to be inaccessible to those without their own transport.

TRAINS

For many (colonial) years there was a French plan to push a **railway** across the Sahara, linking Algiers with Dakar. Had it succeeded, it might have have altered today's network, in which only two of the eight West African railway systems cross borders. And of those systems most are no more than single lines running from the coast to the interior.

In practice only three lines are much used by travellers: in Cameroon between **Douala and Ngaoundéré**; the **Océan-Niger** line between **Bamako and Dakar**; and the line between **Abidjan and Ouagadougou**. Timed right, you could do a trip as short as two or three weeks, substantially by train, through Senegal, Mali, Burkina Faso and Côte d'Ivoire.

Details are given on all these railways through the chapters. Although **other railway lines** exist, not all of them are running and some are freight only. The ones marked on our map of the region on p.viii currently operate passenger services. Some offer student discounts, though these are usually intended for nationals.

Travelling by train in West Africa is usually slower than road and while you can always get street food through the windows at stations, you should take your own drinking water for the duration. **Toilets** are rarely usable by the time you've left the city – prepare in advance for that too.

FERRIES

There are still hundreds of small, hand-hauled or spluttering diesel ferries pulling people and vehicles across the rivers of West Africa. But river transport upstream or down is very limited. The most attractive **ferry services** run on the Niger River in Mali, from the height of the rainy season to a couple of months after it finishes. Apart from the Ghanaian services on Lake Volta, there are few other significant car ferries operating in the region. The Senegal River no longer has a ferry service. The Gambia's river transport is reduced to a couple of launches ferrying tourists up to Georgetown.

On the Niger, more or less anywhere between Kouroussa in Guinea and Niamey in the Republic of Niger, you can usually negotiate a passage in a **pirogue** (a dug-out/plank canoe) or a **pinasse** (a larger, motorized freight-carrying vessel) at any time of year, but in parts of Mali this has now become prohibitively expensive.

There's virtually no scheduled regional **sea transport**. Ferries connect the Cape Verde islands with each other and Dakar and there's minor shipping on the coasts of Senegal, Sierra Leone, Guinea-Bissau, and Nigeria.

REGIONAL AND DOMESTIC FLIGHTS

West African inter-state flights are expensive, and travel by air not automatically the quickest option. On several coast connections the combination of flying time, formalities and transfers to and from the airports are enough to counteract any advantage over fast road transport. Abidjan–Accra can be done in a day and Dakar–Banjul, and hops between Accra–Cotonou–Lagos in a few hours. In most cases, however, **flying** is the best way to go if you're in a hurry.

Aviation in West Africa is in financial trouble and changes happen often. Currently the big West African inter-state **airlines** are *Air Afrique*, owned by a consortium of Francophone governments, and *Ghana Airways*. Together they more or less cover the region. Others (the larger of which operate inter-state services) include *Nigeria Airways*, *Cameroon Airlines*, *Air Burkina*, *Air Ivoire*, *Air Sénégal*, *Air Mauritanie* and *TACV* of Cape Verde. Airlines in a less certain state of repair include *TAGB* of Guinea-Bissau and *Air Guinée*. Several "national airlines" are virtually defunct and everywhere, with the new market-economic thrust of recent years, private entrepreneurs are setting up small airlines of light and medium-sized planes. Most flights on the private airlines are operated on a charter basis, though sometimes with regularity, so you can buy a seat, in effect, from the charterer.

You can expect domestic flights to **cost** in the order of twice the surface transport rate. Also, beware of lower-than-expected baggage allowances on some internal flights.

AIR TICKET TACTICS

The air ticket set-up in West Africa is quite different from that in Europe or North America. There's little unofficial discounting of **fares**. Most tickets get sold at the approved rate, though some airlines operate anomalously, in which case you'll find it hard to discover what those fares are. If you possess an **ISIC student card** it's always worth requesting a student reduction.

You can expect some problems in **getting a reservation**, further problems at the airport getting a boarding pass and (occasionally) problems yet again in exchanging the boarding pass for a seat. Many domestic and regional flights in West Africa are heavily and permanently block-booked by government and not-so-government departments. Only when the actual number of required seats is notified to the airline can they open normal reservations to the public. In many cases notification comes, if at all, on the day of departure, in the airport.

There's little you can do about all this. Obviously, book as soon as you can and re-book if plans change, rather than wait until you're certain. This anyway gives you leverage in terms of personal recognition at the airline office, and airline bookings don't require a deposit as a rule. Be utterly sceptical of a "confirmed seat" until you're sitting in it. Arrive at the airport long before the flight if you've any doubt about your status, and use every angle and pull every string you can to improve your chances. Clearly this is a worst-case scenario, but even when there appears to be no problem and no question of not getting on, always **re-confirm your seat** in person two days before the flight.

CAR RENTAL

Car rental is available in nearly every capital city, at most of the larger airports and in one or two provincial towns in a number of countries. *Hertz*, *Avis* and *Europcar* have a fair network, enabling you to pre-book. Countries covered by *Hertz*, for example, include Benin, Cameroon, Côte d'Ivoire, Nigeria, Niger, Senegal and Togo. Outlets are local licensed firms and, apart from being more expensive, not necessarily much different from others which don't have the international trademark. Where possible we've given details in city "Listings" to enable advance booking of those too.

There are several general **points to bear in mind**. Firstly, rented cars cannot as a rule, be driven into **neighbouring countries**. In a number of countries, private self-drive car rental is a novelty and authorities feel uneasy about it beyond the city limits. You may be obliged to take a **driver** with the car and this inevitably puts the price up, though it isn't always a bad arrangement in itself – and can work out brilliantly. Some firms insist on four-wheel drive (4WD) if you'll be departing from surfaced highways. The **costs** can be astronomical and you may spend in a day what would pay for a week's self-drive in Europe or North America.

An alternative is to consider simply renting a **taxi** on a daily basis. Buy the fuel separately or you'll never get anywhere and settle every other question – the driver's bed, board, cigarettes – in advance too. However good the price, don't take on a vehicle that's unsafe, or a driver you don't like and can't communicate with.

Whether you're driving or being driven, you should have your **national driving licence** with you and an **international licence** too. At delicate moments, some American, and all British, driving licences count for little as they lack the important identity photo. Minimum age for renting a car varies from 21 to 25 (18 for Nigeria) with one or two year's experience.

DRIVING

Don't automatically assume the vehicle is roadworthy. **Before setting off**, have a look at the engine and tyres and don't leave without checking water, battery and spare tyre (preferably two and the means to change them) and making sure you've a few tools. Except on certain main highways, it's important to keep jerry cans of water and fuel on board. As for breakdowns, local mechanics are usually excellent and can apply creative ingenuity to the most disastrous situations. But spare parts, tools and proper equipment are rare away from the *Michelin* map's red highways – and not really common along them.

When **driving**, beware of unexpected rocks and ditches – not to mention animals and people – on the road. It's accepted practice to honk your horn stridently to warn pedestrians, though be cautious of doing so in built-up areas which may have local laws you'd quickly fall foul of.

All of West Africa **drives on the right**, though in reality vehicles keep to the best part of the road until they have to pass each other (fatefully positioned potholes account for many head-on collisions). Right- and left-hand **signals** are conventionally used to say "Please overtake" or "Don't overtake!", but you shouldn't assume the driver in front can see. In fact, **never assume anything** about the behaviour of other drivers. Road death statistics are horrifying – Nigeria, famously, taking the lead in this respect.

You're unlikely to be kept for long by **police** or other security forces at the roadside, but you should *never* pass a check-point or barrier without stopping and waiting to be waved on. Nor should you ever drive anywhere without all your documents.

MOTORBIKING

Motorcycle rental is less common than car rental, but available in some cities. However, if you have some experience, it is well worth considering buying a machine in West Africa, avoiding the expense and paperwork of riding or shipping a bike all the way from Europe: in Mali, for example, reliable and economical Honda CG 125s are widely available, and make ideal machines, if not overloaded.

CYCLING

In many ways **cycling** is the ideal form of transport in West Africa, giving you total independence. You can camp out all the time if you wish, or take your bike into hotel rooms with you. When in rural areas you can often leave the bike unattended for a while if you're eating in a chop house or visiting a market – a crowd of onlookers will make sure no one touches it. If you get tired of pedalling you've the simple option of transporting your bike on top of a bush taxi or bus (reckon on paying about half-fare) or even "cycle-hitching".

A bike gives scope for exploring off the beaten track and getting round cities. Routes that can't be used by motor vehicles – even motorbikes – because they're too rough, or involve crossing rivers, are all accessible. With a tough bike, you can explore off the roads altogether, using bush paths – though remember to give ample verbal warning to people walking in your direction ahead of you, who may otherwise be seriously frightened by your sudden arrival behind them.

On busy roads a rear-view **mirror** is close to essential.

BIKE PRACTICALITIES

Apart from the commonest parts, **spares for mountain bikes** are rare in West Africa. But take only what you're sure to need – spare tubes, spare spokes and a good tool kit. If you need to do anything major, you can always borrow large spanners and other heavy equipment. Don't bother with spare tyres if you're going for under six months. On a long trip, it's worth depositing some money with a reputable dealer before you leave so that, in an emergency, you could fax from a public fax office and have a part sent out by a courier service like *DHL*.

You can forgo these hassles by buying one of the heavyweight **roadsters** on sale locally. There are bike shops and market areas devoted to cycling in most large towns. Ouagadougou in Burkina Faso has long been one of the cheapest places to buy, with a vast area devoted to bikes and good second-hand possibilities from about £60 ($90). You should be able to get a new bike for under £140 ($210). Bikes with three-speed hub gears (usually Raleighs or Peugeots) come somewhat more expensive. If you go for the gearless mount, console yourself with the fact that hub gears are fiddly to adjust and almost impossible to mend if anything packs up inside.

If you're taking a bike with you, then you'll probably want to **carry your gear** in panniers. These are fiendishly inconvenient when not attached to the bike, however, and you might consider sacrificing ideal load-bearing and streamlining technology for a backpack you can lash down on the rear carrier; you'll probably have to do this anyway if you buy a bike locally having travelled out to West Africa by more conventional means. Using the kind of cane that is used for cane furniture, plus lashings of inner tube rubber strips, you can create your own highly un-aerodynamic **carrier**, with room for a box of food and a gallon of water underneath.

With a bike from home, remember to take a battery **lighting system** (dynamo lighting is a pain) – it's surprising how often you'll need it. The front light doubles as a torch and getting batteries is no problem.

Take a **U-bolt cycle lock**. In situations where you have to lock the bike, you'll always find something to lock it to. Out in the bush it's less important. Local bikes can be locked with a padlock and chain in a hose which you can buy and fix up in any market.

Finding and carrying **water** is a daily chore on a long cycle trip. You'll need at least one five-litre container per person (more if you're camping out and want to wash) but you shouldn't often need to carry it full. Empty plastic oil jars and jerry cans, available all over North and West Africa, are convenient.

Lastly, **distances**: depending on your fitness and enthusiasm, expect to cycle around 1000km a month, including at least two days off for every three on the road. During periods when you're basically cycling from A to B (often on a paved road, which is somewhat slow on a mountain-bike), you'll find 40–50km in the early morning and 20–30km more in the afternoon is plenty.

BIKE RENTAL

You can **rent bicycles and mopeds** in a number of places, including The Gambia, Basse Casamance (Senegal) and Ouagadougou (Burkina Faso). But they're not usually well-adapted for touring, although they often have carriers. Anywhere you fancy cycling, however, you can often make informal arrangements to lease a bike for a few days.

OTHER FORMS OF LOCOMOTION

Clearly, if you're hardy and not tied to any schedule, you can simply **walk**. All over the region, you'll come across local people walking vast distances because they have no money at all to pay for transport. If you're hiking for a few days you can fall in with them (if you manage to keep up), but they'll rarely speak any French or English.

From a more recreational angle, we've covered a number of **hiking possibilities** throughout West Africa. These are mostly in upland and mountainous regions. You need good footwear – heat, sweat and water take a heavy toll.

Using a **beast of burden** for your travels is an attractive idea. Unfortunately, **horses** succumb quickly in the more southern tse-tse fly regions and a horse in good shape is expensive. If you know what to look for and how to a look after a horse, the most promising districts are sub-Sahelian – most of southern Mali, Burkina, southern Niger, northern Nigeria and further south into highland Cameroon. If you ride south towards the coast, however, and sell your animal, it's likely to end up in a pot.

Donkeys are a lot tougher, cheaper and will happily go further south in the dry season. They're used to long treks. You'd need three donkeys between two with luggage, however. Then there are **camels** (dromedaries: *méharis* or *chameaux* in French). It's not impossible to join a caravan in the desert or northern Sahel, though fewer and fewer such journeys are made these days. But buying, equipping and travelling with your own animals is not to be undertaken lightly even by the most qualified romantics. For salutary advice read Michael Asher's *Impossible Journey* (Viking, 1988).

ACCOMMODATION

There's not a huge diversity of accommodation options in West Africa. A good range of hotels is found only in the cities, and in several countries even hotels are rather uncommon outside the capital. Hostels of various kinds are usually an urban phenomenon, often permanently full and not to be relied upon, and there are no IYHA youth hostels. In some countries you'll find government rest houses and in remote parts where tourists are rare you may be able to stay in volunteer rest houses and missions.

Campsites, too, are very rare. Campements (not the same), in several of the French-speaking countries, are more typical: these are basically rustic motels, usually in the bush. The options of staying with local people or camping in the bush are usually there depending on how you travel.

HOTELS

In large towns, and specifically capitals, you'll want and probably have to stay in **hotels**. There tends to be a gap between the expensive places and the dives and you sometimes need to look hard to find something good at a reasonable price. If you're splurging there's usually a clutch of **international establishments** bookable from abroad. Local star ratings are not much used and in any case about as hopeless an indication of value for money as anywhere.

There's not much local market for western-style hotels (with reception, bars, restaurant) except in countries with a mobile, salaried middle class. The few **mid-range hotels** are usually

ACCOMMODATION PRICE CODES

All hotel prices in this book are coded according to the following scales. Prices refer to the rate you can expect to pay for a room with two beds. Single rooms, or single occupancy, will normally cost at least two-thirds of the twin-occupancy rate. Bear in mind that only the most expensive establishments have a set rate for every room and there's often a chance to negotiate a better deal. In most countries, for a simple but decent twin room with clean sheets, air-conditioning and bathroom, expect to pay upwards of £10–15 ($15–22). You can often get a fairly mediocre place, usually without AC and certainly without hot water, for about £5–10 ($7.50–15). The CFA countries generally have the cheapest hotels. Mauritania and Cape Verde are expensive and you'll find little if anything below the ③ bracket in those countries. The Gambia, Ghana and Nigeria fall somewhere in between. The range of facilities you can expect across the seven price bands is given separately for each country in the "Practical Information" section at the beginning of each chapter.

① under £5/ under $7.50
② £5–10/$7.50–15
③ £10–20/$15–30
④ £20–30/$30–45
⑤ £30–40/$45–60
⑥ £40–50/$60–75
⑦ over £50/over $75

ACCOMMODATION ABBREVIATIONS

AC Air-conditioning, air-conditioned

S/C Self-contained, with private shower or bath, and toilet

B&B Bed and breakfast

HB Half board, meaning dinner, bed and breakfast

FB Full board, meaning all meals included

CHEAP HOTEL PRACTICALITIES

- Always ask to **see the room** first and don't be surprised if it looks like a tornado's passed through, especially in the morning before it's been cleaned.
- Unless there's a proper tariff sheet, it's always worth haggling over the **price** of a room. If there's air conditioning or a fan but no electricity, ask for a discount. Check there'll be no **tax** on top.
- In highland regions or during the *Harmattan* it's normally expected you'll ask for a bucket of **hot water** to supplement the cold tap – but it may not be offered.
- You usually **pay** on taking the room and may have to leave your **passport** with the person in charge if there's no registration card to fill out.
- Always ask for fresh clean sheets and towel if you're not happy with them.
- Use discretion about leaving your **keys** with the management and, if your door locks by padlock, use your own and check the fixture.
- If you suspect **bedbugs** may lurk behind the plaster, pull the beds away from the wall. Keeping the light on deters them.

well-run and nice enough places to stay. But **small town hotels** – and of course the cheapest joints in the cities – are usually equated with drinking and prostitution. Rooms are often taken for a few hours only, and there may well be a gang of women and toddlers permanently in residence. Don't be put off unduly. These can be fun places to stay – and by no means all are intimidating places for female travellers – though you may have to pick a room carefully (not easy) for anything like a quiet night.

HOSTELS

Although there are no internationally affiliated youth hostels in West Africa, you'll find **YMCA** and **YWCA** hostels in several Anglophone cities (notably Freetown, Accra and Lagos) which are usually permanently full of students and single professionals. If you can get in they're great places to meet people and, though they're generally run by slightly pious types, there are few limiting restrictions on what you do and when.

CAMPEMENTS AND REST HOUSES

For non-camping travellers, alternative types of "hotel" accommodation are popular options in the rural areas. **Campements**, in French-speaking countries, have a fairly loose definition. They're certainly not camping sites, though you can sometimes camp at them, but they represent more the modern equivalent of a colonial caravanserai or "encampment" in the bush, often associated with game parks and areas of natural beauty. They tend to consist of huts or small room blocks made of local materials (often mud bricks and thatch) with shared washing and toilet facilities – at the top end they're effectively hotels. But at their most innovative, in Senegal, where some are known as *CTRIs* – *campements touristiques rurals integrés* ("rurally integrated") – they are built with government loans by the people of a village in order to host independent travellers.

In the English-speaking countries a network of **government rest houses**, for the use of officials on tour, is theoretically at the disposal of travellers when rooms aren't occupied. There's a similar *réseau* of government *villas* in Guinea. In fact, these places are very often unused for long periods and need a good airing. Water and electricity are often turned off or disconnected. First, in any case, you have to find the caretaker to open up.

And lastly there are the **aid and development organization rest houses** and rest houses of voluntary organizations like the United States Peace Corps (some 1400 of whose graduate volunteers are on placements in thirteen West African countries at any one time) and, somewhat thinly these days, **missions**. If you're travelling extensively, you may find these alternatives helpful and generous. In some cases – a few of the Peace Corps rest houses for example – there's a special tariff for "outsiders". But in general you'll be staying explicitly as a guest, using facilities intended for others. Where such arrangements are based on informal invitations and strictly word-of-mouth, we've usually kept them that way and not included them in this book. It would be unfair to suggest that such accommodation is universally open to all, and it's sometimes abused.

CAMPING

The few **campsites** that exist in West Africa are covered in the main country chapters. There are several in Mali and Niger, one or two on the coast in Togo and virtually no others.

Bring the lightest **tent** you can afford; there are lots of good geodesic models around these days with snap-together aluminium frames. *Long Road*, in Berkeley, California (☎510/540-4763; Fax 510/540-0652) makes some superb models. Or, if the prices put you off, consider making your own with ripstop nylon and fine nylon netting. The basic tent is nylon netting, zipped at the front, with a sewn-on groundsheet; the flysheet is a separate roof, for when you need privacy. The whole thing is supported by external poles, front and back, tensioned by pegged out guys. You'll probably resort to using convenient trees wherever possible.

Camping rough depends much on your style of travel. Clearly, if you're driving your own vehicle it's only necessary to find a good spot for the night. Don't assume you can always do this anonymously. A vehicle in the deep bush is unusual and noisy and people will flock round to watch you.

Bush-camping is easier **if you're cycling or walking**. For safety's sake, always get right away from the main road to avoid being accidentally run over or exciting the interest of occasional motorized pirates. You may still be visited by delegations of machete-wielding villagers, especially if you light a fire, but satisfaction that you're harmless is usually their first concern. Some cigarettes or a cup of tea breaks any ice.

If you're travelling by public transport, it's a lot harder to camp effectively night after night. Vehicles go from town to town and it's rare to be dropped off at just the right spot in between, all ready and supplied for a night under the stars. **Walking out of town** in search of a place to camp is an exercise which soon palls, and it can be miles.

STAYING WITH PEOPLE

In this context there's not much to be said. Experiences vary enormously and depend as much on the guest as the host. But all over the region you'll run into **people who want to put you up for the night**. A warm, but more noticeably, a *dutiful* hospitality characterizes most of these contacts. The visitors most open to them are single travellers who get into conversation on public transport. Your hosts are typically a low-income family with ambitions whose son has been away and has brought you home. You'll be expected to correspond later and send photographs.

It's sometimes difficult to know how to repay such hospitality, particularly since it often seems so disruptive of family life, with you set up in the master bedroom and kids sent running for special things for the guest. While it's impossible to generalize, for female guests a trip to the market with the woman/women of the household is an opportunity to pay for everything. Men can't do this, but buying a sack of rice or a big bundle of yams (get it delivered by barrow or porter) makes a generous gift.

CAMPING MATTERS

In more **heavily populated** or farmed districts it's usually best to ask someone before pitching a tent. Out in **the wilds**, hard or thorny ground is likely to be the only obstacle. Fill your water bottles from a village before looking for a site. During the dry seasons, you'll rarely have trouble finding wood for a small fire so a stove isn't absolutely necessary. But it's very useful for wet or barren conditions. You can find *camping gaz* butane cartridges in most capital cities. Petrol stoves are more convenient once you've shelled out for them. If you're cycle-camping, a small kerosene lamp is perfectly feasible. Be sure to buy kerosene (*pétrole* in French) however, and not petrol/gasoline (*essence*) . . . **Wild animals** pose little threat (see "Wildlife and National Parks" further on). Night-time noises, especially in forest regions – some spectularly eerie and sinister shrieks and calls – merely add to the atmosphere.

EATING AND DRINKING

While West Africa has little in the way of well-defined cuisines this is in large part because supplies are erratic, recipes aren't written down, and no two meals ever taste quite the same. Nevertheless, there's a considerable variety of culinary pleasures and a probably infinite range of intoxicating drinks. Describing it all is complicated by the variety of terms used for common ingredients. Indigenous food and drink was one area in which colonial interests were limited. As far as possible, "Food and Drink" sections in the practical information section for each country chapter give an indication of what you can expect, and describe the local specialities.

FOOD

The great thing about West African food is its massive calorific value. Although less bulky alternatives are usually available, most meals consist of a pile of the staple diet plus a sauce or stew often called "soup".

The **staple** varies geographically. **Rice** predominates everywhere from Mauritania to Liberia and across the Sahel and is expanding as a commercial staple. **Root crops** (varieties of yam and cassava) and **plantains** figure heavily along the coast from Côte d'Ivoire through Nigeria to Cameroon. In the Sahara, **couscous**, tiny grains of durum wheat flour, is common.

Sauces can be based on **palm oil** (thick and copper-coloured, all along the coast from The Gambia south and eastwards), on **groundnut paste** (peanut butter, found mostly in Sahelian regions), **okra** ("gumbo" or "ladies' fingers" – five-sided, green pods with a high slime content which is much appreciated), various **beans** and the **leaves** of sweet potatoes and cassava among others. All of them are usually heavily spiced, often with chillies – "hot pepper" – though the emphasis on this ingredient tends to be exaggerated. It's rarely too much and only southern Nigeria is really dangerous territory for tender mouths. Whatever else they consist of, sauces are made with *bouillon* cubes – invaribly *Maggi* cubes. *Maggi* sauce, too, is ubiquitous in every cheap restaurant.

The more expensive, or festive, "sauces" have an emphasis on their **animal protein** content. **Fish** and **mutton** are probably the most common. **Eggs** are rarely very popular (they're sometimes attributed with contraceptive powers) but they're always available. **Beef** tends to be reserved for special occasions. **Chicken** is pricey, but a favourite meat for guests. **Pork** is very localized and hogs foraging at the roadside are a sure sign you're in a non-Islamic district. Various kinds of **"bush meat"** are widely eaten except in the most devoutly Muslim regions, and often bought and sold. Large, herbivorous rodents ("bush rat", "cutting grass", "agouti") are the commonest and usually delicious, but antelopes, monkeys, even cats, dogs and giant snails are eaten in various parts of West Africa.

WHERE TO EAT

If you're lucky enough to be staying **with a family**, you're likely to experience consistently well-prepared and tasty food – though according to their means this may depend on how much you contribute. In homes, or when travelling on long-distance trucks, or by trading canoe, people eat around a **communal dish** (in strictly Islamic regions always males at one, females at another – you generally finish in order of age, the eldest first). Because of this, restaurants, where someone goes and buys a meal for themselves, are not all that common.

But it's wrong to assume you can't eat well at the cheapest **street food stalls** and roadside or **market restaurants**. The secret is to eat early – this means late morning (11am–noon) and dusk (5–6pm), when most people eat and food is fresh. Street food isn't usually a take-away – there's

WEST AFRICAN FOOD PLANTS

There's a multitude of names in different languages for the same few food plants. Some of the names appear in the "Food and Drink" sections in the practical information at the beginning of each chapter. This section is an attempt to clarify things a little (botanical and French names in brackets).

Aubergine/Eggplant (*Solanum*). Grown on garden plots all over and come in many shapes and colours (round, white, yellow, red) but rarely in the familiar large, purple variety. Known variously as garden eggs or bitter balls, they can be identified as aubergines by the star-shaped, leathery, leafy bits at the stalk end.

Cassava (*Manihot*; *Manioc* in French). Spindly 2-metre shrub from South America, with hand-like leaves, seen growing all over. The tubers, which tend to have a bitter taste, are large and coarse and have to be boiled and then usually pounded in a mortar to reduce them to an edible glob of nearly pure starch (*fufu*/*foufou*/*eba*). Cassava leaves taste much nicer and are full of vitamins. They're finely shredded and used like spinach. *Gari* is cassava flour (from which tapioca is made), but the word gets used quite broadly.

Cocoyam (*Colocasia*). Tastier than yams or cassava, but easily confused. Grown mostly in wet forest regions, the plants have unmistakably huge, heart-shaped, edible leaves. Tubers are rounded with a fleshy stalk and commonly known as "koko", "mankani", "taro", "eddo" or "dasheen". Similar names are often given to the introduced **Tannia** (*Xanthosoma*). This "new cocoyam" has giant arrow-shaped leaves and tasty, smaller, dark, hairy tubers.

Cowpeas (*Vigna*). The commonest type of bean ("black-eye beans"), cowpeas come in many varieties and are grown throughout the region. They're usually dried and stored for use, or made into flour, but you often see them freshly harvested in their long, pale pods. Mashed cowpeas are used for *akara* – "deep-fried balls" sold nearly everywhere. Common names include *wake* and *niebe*.

Groundnut (*Arachis*; *Arachide* or *cacahouètes* in French). Groundnuts (peanuts, monkey nuts) are grown widely to be used as the basis of sauces, and you'll see little dollops of peanut butter on leaves, for sale in markets everywhere.

Maize (*Zea*; *Maïs* in French). Grown a lot in forest region clearings, this is exactly the same as "corn" and "sweetcorn" and used widely on the cob as a stop-gap and a roasted or boiled snack. Maize flour is used quite extensively in some parts as a staple – in Ghana for fermented corn dough (*kenkey*) for example.

Melon seeds (*Cucumeropsis*). Certain types of melon are good only for their large, oily seeds, commonly known by the Yoruba name, *egusi*, and widely used when crushed to flavour soups.

Millet (*Pennisetum*). Looks like bullrushes, with a maize-like stalk, grown mostly in the Sahel. *Gero* in Hausa. Used for porridge, gruel and making beer.

Plantain (*Musa*). These mega-bananas are found all over the rainier southern part of West Africa. They're not eaten raw, but cooked (fried when ripe, boiled and sometimes pounded to a tasty *fufu* when hard).

Potatoes (*Ipomoea*; *Patate* in French). Unless specified as "Irish", these are always the *sweet* variety with pink skins, known in America, confusingly, as "yams". They're grown in mounds and ridges and have a mass of creeping vines. They tend to be something of a luxury, used to add flavour to stews and sauces. The leaves are good and widely used. Irish potatoes (*Solanum*) only grow in West Africa above an altitude of about 1200 metres.

Sorghum (*Sorghum*; *Sorgho* in French). Tall plants (2 to 4 metres) similar to maize but with feathery, white or red grained flower heads. Also known as "guinea corn" and "giant millet", sorghum is grown mainly in the savannah zone, and is made into porridge or pap and, outstandingly, "millet beer".

Yam (*Dioscorea*; *Ignames* in French). Massive tubers that grow singly beneath a climbing, vine-like plant with spade-shaped leaves, commonly seen in southern parts of the region, especially in Nigeria. They come in white (which is preferred) and yellow varieties and are used like cassava to make pounded yam *fufu*, but they have a better flavour.

Other common food plants include **onions** and **tomatoes** (available everywhere, even in the driest districts, but often tiny and sold in piles of four), **lettuces** (wash very carefully), short but tasty **cucumbers**, **avocados** (wonderful, huge specimens in Cameroon), **tiger nuts** (*chufa* – tiny coconut-flavoured tubers like shrivelled beans), **pigeon peas** (small, round, brown and white beans), **white haricot**, **lima** and **butter beans**, and various kinds of **gourd**, **pumpkin** and **squash**.

VEGETARIAN WEST AFRICA

West Africa makes no concessions to vegetarians. Eating ready-prepared food, whether on the street, or in any category of restaurant, is unrewarding: animal protein is the focus of most dishes, and even where it's apparently absent there's likely to be some stock somewhere (rice is often cooked in it, or fat is added to the vegetables). This means, if you're strictly vegetarian, you're mostly going to have to stick to market fruit and veg and any food you cook for yourself. Peanuts and locally ground **peanut butter** are a good source of vegetable protein. Groundnuts can be found boiled as well as roasted.

Milk in various forms (and milk powder) and **hard-boiled eggs** are usually obtainable. Cheese is largely unheard of, except in its processed and E-supplemented, foil-packaged variety. **Bread** and canned **margarine** are available everywhere.

Vegetarians who are the guests of African families have a hard time – with such status attached to meat, vegetarianism is regarded as an untenable philosophy. Avoiding meat is particularly trying if you consent to have eggs with every meal instead, as you can find yourself presented with six or more, specially prepared for you, every day.

often a table and benches, plastic bowls, spoons and cold water. Anything extra you want – soft drinks, instant coffee – can be fetched for you from nearby.

If you want to eat in more privacy, most towns, even the smallest, have at least one or two **basic restaurants**. Much of the menu or blackboard is likely to be unavailable, however, and there's probably more cause for hesitation over what you eat in small restaurants where you can't be certain of the freshness or provenance of your food, than there is from street stalls where it all has to be cooked – or has just been cooked – before your eyes.

Large towns have more restaurants and, in general, less street food options. Eating chop house cooking at inflated prices in a silver service restaurant seems odd at first, but can be a real treat. The eating out alternative to African food, in cities, is usually **French** or vaguely European, **Chinese**, or **Middle Eastern**. **Lebanese fast food joints**, providing snacks and sandwiches, especially **chawarma** (sometimes *shwarma*) – mutton in French or pita bread – are as common as burger franchises in the United States.

STREET FOOD

Street food varies widely from country to country and regionally too, and is covered in more detail for each country. One snack that's pretty well universal is the **brochette** (*suya* in Hausa) – a tiny stick of kebabed meat. This is often eaten as a sandwich in a piece of French bread.

Although common, bread isn't a staple food in West Africa, but more of a luxury, often something to eat on long journeys. Different kinds tend to conform to the colonial recipes. In the Francophone countries it's a *baguette* – a French stick – though rarely as long or as crunchy as the real thing. In the Anglophone countries you have to search hard to find good bread. Mostly it's spongey white stuff, far worse than anything pumped out of supermarkets, sometimes very sweet, and often dyed a horrid yellow, or pink.

In the French-speaking countries you're likely to adopt the habit of eating **breakfast in the street**. Practice and adroitness vary, but in several countries you'll get excellent hot, whipped *Nescafé* with *pain beurre* (and real butter) for a set price of about 60p ($1). But be ready with appropriate French if you want your coffee black or – big shock to local people – without sugar. As it's sometimes made with sweetened condensed milk, white-no-sugar can be a problem.

DRINKING

Probably the most widely consumed beverage in the region – after water – is **green tea** (in reality yellow). In the Sahel, from Senegal to northern Cameroon, it's an essential part of every day and no long journey is completed without it. It's common further south, too, in all regions where Islam predominates. Rock sugar in huge lumps, China tea leaves and water are brought to the boil in a little kettle on a handful of coals, then poured out repeatedly to infuse and froth the brew. It's traditional to drink three glasses – strong and bitter, sweet and full-bodied, and sweet and mild – and considered rude to refuse. But like everything, form isn't always followed. The tea has to be *Green Gunpowder*, however – a tin of which makes a very good little gift.

COMMON WEST AFRICAN FRUIT AND NUTS

The most satisfying eating in West Africa is **fruit**. There's a magnificent variety in the markets south of the Sahel, though even in the drier regions you'll find citrus most of the year, mangoes in season and the odd pawpaw. The main ones to watch out for are:

Banana. If you spend long in West Africa, you may never be able to face a banana again. But local varieties are often wonderfully flavoured compared to the imported, white-fleshed supermarket type. Look out for very thin-skinned dwarf bananas in huge bunches, and for very fat, squat varieties with pale orange flesh and sometimes red skins.

Cashew. Not just a nut, the cashew also has a fruit attached. The arrangement of the nut at the apex of the cashew "apple" is hard to believe when you first see it. You can't eat the apple because the fibrous flesh is bitter, but curiously you can *chew* it to extract the delicious, light juice. In some parts this stuff is made into a potent hooch. Beware of feasting off cashew trees. They only have a small number of valuable nuts each and owners get very upset.

Coconut. The familiar brown "nuts" of coconut shies are contained within a thick husk and the whole thing is green and about the size of a football. Coconuts are very hard to open without a machete, but all along the coast (they're not happy above 500 metres) you'll have the opportunity to try them in several, satisfying conditions as the flesh changes from a thin jelly to a thick layer of coconut. They're not seasonal.

Grapefruit. African varieties are often exceptionally sweet and really big. Leave the segments to dry for a while and peel off the inner skins to reveal hundreds of little packets of grapefruit juice. A fine pleasure.

Guava. Don't buy unripe ones. They should have a very strongly perfumed scent. The best ones have pink flesh.

Mango. A royal fruit this; available and rightly esteemed everywhere, it comes in hundreds of varieties. The mango season coincides with the end of the dry season and the first rains (roughly March–June depending on where you are). They're expensive at first and rapidly drop in price until they're two a penny (sometimes literally). Whole villages devote themselves to eating and selling the fruit. The very best, found in southern Cameroon, are long and narrow with bright green skins and very firm, orange, stringless flesh.

Oranges and tangerines. These – often bright green – are the main juicy fruits of West Africa. Oranges are always available for a few pence from girls and women with trays and sharp knives. The peel is shaved off, leaving the orange in its pith, then the top is lopped off and you squeeze the juice into your mouth and discard the emptied orange. You can easily go through a dozen or twenty in a day like this – diabolical on the front teeth.

Pawpaw. Not much eaten but widely obtainable. Very good (and good for you) with lime juice. Non-seasonal. See "Health".

Pineapple. Pineapples grow on the ground, with a spikey fringe of long sisal-like leaves around them. Commonest in coastal districts of Côte d'Ivoire and eastwards to Cameroon. Available throughout the dry season.

Sugar cane. Sometimes sold in markets, you simply strip off the shiny outside and chomp on the pith, which oozes sucrose. Another dental nightmare.

You'll also come across **starfruit** (attractively shaped but tasteless), **custard apples** or **soursops** (lovely pear-drop flavour in the roughly heart-shaped, green fruit) and **mangosteens** (amazing taste inside the small, round, brownish fruit with very thick skin). Towards the Sahara you get **dates** in all their different grades and, lastly, at certain times and places, quite a variety of **wild-collected fruit**, some of which (like the *ditak* in Senegal) is particularly good.

Apart from *Nescafé*, **coffee** is less popular, and real coffee rare except in big hotels. Various **infusions** are locally common. One which has wide popularity in the western part of West Africa (as a base for mixing in a lot of *lait concentré sucré)* is *kenkeliba* (also spelled "quinceliba" and various other ways). It's reasonable on its own straight from the hot bucket or kettle, but don't mistake it for water and have *Nescafé* added.

When you can't get cold water, **soft drinks** – especially fizzy orange and lemonade and *Coke* – are permanent standbys and in remote areas any establishment with electricity is almost bound to have a fridge of battered bottles (bottles are always returned to the wholesaler: *never* take the bottle away – this is serious theft!). **Soda water** (*eau gazeuse*), however, is rare. In the Francophone countries, supermarkets and some general stores carry large bottles of French-style **mineral water** but, like soda water, you'll rarely find this in roadside fridges. On the street, however, you'll often see **locally made fruit juices**, cold water and ices, in plastic bags, sold by children from buckets of ice. Ginger is refreshing, as too is the white sherbet made from baobab fruits. Don't assume the soft drinks bottling plant necessarily applies any more hygienic methods of manufacture than local outlets. The water they use is almost certainly the same as what comes out of the village pump.

BEER AND SPIRITS

The most obvious drink in the region is **beer**. Almost every country has a brewery. Nigeria has many, and a whole host of competing brands. Only the Islamic Republic of Mauritania is dry. Beer, usually in half-litre bottles, is mostly strong, gassy, sometimes quite bitter in flavour and, most of the time, cold – including *Guinness*, brewed under licence.

You can sample **home-made beer** under many different names. It's as varied in taste and colour as its ingredients – basically a fermented mash of sugar and cereal, usually sorghum or millet, sometimes with herbs and roots for flavouring. The results are cloudy, frothy and deceptively strong. Home-made beer is usually drunk in the round, each person taking their turn with the dipper, from a central calabash. It's always made by women.

In coastal parts, **palm wine** is produced from oil palms, tapped for their sap, which ferments in a day or two from a pleasant, mildly intoxicating juice to a ripe and pungent brew with seriously destabilizing qualities. The flavour is aromatic and slightly acidic. There are usually laws controlling tapping because it hinders the production of the palm nuts used in vital palm oil manufacture, but it's available wherever you see the stumpy, dark green palms. Taller *borassus* and coconut palms can also be tapped, but rarely are.

Spirits distilled from beer, palm wine or sugar cane are locally much in evidence (in Ghana, Sierra Leone, Burkina Faso and Cape Verde for example) and normally only alcoholically dangerous, rather than actually denatured with unknown toxic additives, as in other parts of Africa. But nevertheless, beware.

Imported spirits are excessively expensive. **Imported beer**, too, is rarely worth the price. Cheap French **wine**, on the other hand, is fairly affordable in Senegal and Côte d'Ivoire (unless you're French when it'll seem extortionate) where you can often buy it from ordinary general stores.

MEDIA

Local press and broadcasting in West Africa isn't likely to give you much of an idea of what's going on in the rest of world – though we've tried to uncover the best and most intrepid of the output in the "Communications" details in the practical information at the beginning of each country chapter. The availability of imported English-language newspapers and magazines is slowly improving. If you're travelling for any length of time, it's a good idea to invest in a pocket-sized short-wave radio in order to listen to the BBC World Service – quite an institution in West Africa.

THE PRESS

There has been a rebirth of the **press** in West Africa since the advent of "democracy" in the early 1990s. Countries which formerly had almost no newspapers, now have a thriving press, though critical and independent editors can still find themselves in serious trouble with governments – or government figures – uncomfortable with the results of their own policies. At the time of writing, the Nigerian press was severely restricted and several other governments are actively engaged in trying to muffle freedom of speech.

If you want a more international view of events, assuming you're in a big city, some **British and European newspapers**, plus the *Herald Tribune* and *USA Today*, are often available in the more expensive hotel lobbies together with *Time*, *Newsweek*, *Jeune Afrique* and *West Africa*. You'll find some of them, too, for sale, a few days later, from street vendors.

RADIO AND TV

Apart from general BBC World Service coverage several excellent Africa Service programmes to listen out for include the morning magazine **Network Africa** from 6 to 7am GMT, the vital **Focus on Africa** repeated three times every afternoon Monday to Friday, the Tuesday evening **Jive Zone** music show and the Friday evening news review **The Week in Africa**. You can also listen to the BBC in French, Hausa and Portuguese. Write to BBC African Service, PO Box 76, Bush House, London WC2B 4PH, for full schedules.

The best frequencies for the BBC are 6.005MHz (49.96m), 9.600MHz (31.25m) and 15.400MHz (19.48m) in the morning, and 17.790MHz (16.86m) in the afternoon and evening. Generally, you'll get the best signal on a lower frequency (higher wavelength) early and late, and on a higher frequency (lower wavelength) during the middle of the day.

Voice of America broadcasts for shorter hours. It has a less interesting output and not such good reception.

National and local radio stations have blossomed in recent years, along with the print media. It's now common to have a local FM station or two, though, as with the press, they're frequently subject to all sorts of harassment.

Most West African countries have **TV stations**, usually with a rather uninspired mix of deeds and words from government ministers and imported soaps and movies. A few, like The Gambia, still manage without their own TV. Video rental has swept across the region in any case.

MAIL AND TELEPHONE

Mail and telecommunications have improved enormously over the last ten years. Ordinary letters sent from main post offices rarely go astray if they're carefully addressed. Receiving mail is a little more variable. As for phoning, all the West African countries are now theoretically on International Direct Dialling. Specifics for each country are covered in each case under the practical information at the start of each chapter.

MAIL

In French-speaking countries the post office is called the **PTT** (*Postes, Télécommunications et Télédiffusion*), in English-speaking ones, the **GPO** and in Portuguese-speaking territories the **Correio** or **CTT**. Post offices in Francophone countries usually have **separate counters** (*guichets*) for different services, so make sure you're in the right line.

SENDING MAIL

It's easiest and most secure to use **aerograms** for writing home. Although these are often in high demand and forever going out of stock, they're usually postage pre-paid, so you don't have to worry about weighing and handing over letters.

If you have **urgent mail** to send, the best place is usually not the main post office, but the airport, whence mail is often sent on the next flight out. There may not be much of a post office, just a mail box. For similar reasons, if you're sending slightly heavy, or valuable items, it's worth doing so with a friend or contact who's flying. A lot of ordinary mail is sent this way too. It's always quicker. Leave it unsealed for customs.

If you're travelling widely, look ahead to the next country before sending your mail. **Postal rates** vary widely, especially between CFA and non-CFA countries – the latter are often cheaper.

POSTE RESTANTE

It's not wise to have mail sent anywhere except **capital cities**, not just in order to maximize your chances of getting it, but to speed up the delivery (Kano, Nigeria is an exception). Note, too, that some post offices only hold mail for a few weeks before returning it to the sender. From Europe, allow two weeks for post to be received and one week, or at most ten days, to mail out. For the rest of the world allow three days longer.

Post office staff are often remarkably uncivil, even rude, so be prepared to smile and plead. To collect mail, write your name on a piece of paper as you'd expect it to appear on the letter, and go armed with your passport, without which you'll rarely be allowed to receive mail.

For clarity's sake, ask people to write your address in this form:

DRIVER, Teresa
Poste Restante
PTT
Ouagadougou
BURKINA FASO,

and to put their own address on the back.

Alternatives to public Poste Restante are your embassy or high commission (some of which will hold mail for up to three months) or **American Express** offices, all of which will hold mail for customers, even if you only have their travellers' cheques. Local addresses are given throughout the book.

TELEPHONES

Despite IDD, most international phone calls from West Africa take a while to fix up. There always seems to be someone "occupying" the line, or an operator in the ether somewhere. If you have to go through an operator, always insist on "station to station" (number to number) rather than a personal call. The latter costs more and will only connect you if the person you name is available. Increasingly, **phone cards** are replacing cumbersome counter procedures for making international calls and the phone booths are set up in many cities. Unfortunately, the cards, manufactured outside of West Africa, are often unavailable for months on end.

Reverse charge or collect calls ("PCV" – *pay say vay* – in French) are possible from most countries, but not easy to make. In principle, there should be no problem, but you may have some pleading to do. It's often easier, if you want to have a phone conversation, but aren't up to the very high likely cost, to arrange in advance to *receive* a call at a certain time and number.

To **call home** from West Africa, you dial the international access code, which is usually 00, followed by your country code, then the area code (without the initial "0" if there is one) and then the number:

UK: 00+44+area code+number

USA and Canada: 00+1+area code+number

WEST AFRICAN IDD COUNTRY CODES

Benin 229 plus six-digit number
Burkina Faso 226 plus six-digit number
Cameroon 237 plus six-digit number
Cape Verde 238 plus six-digit number
Côte d'Ivoire 225 plus six-digit number
The Gambia 220 plus five-digit number
Ghana 233 plus area code plus number
Guinea 224 plus six-digit number
Guinea-Bissau 245 plus six-digit number
Liberia 231 plus six-digit number
Mali 223 plus area code and number totalling six-digits
Mauritania 222 plus area code and number totalling six digits
Niger 227 plus six-digit number
Nigeria 234 plus area code plus number
Senegal 221 plus six-digit number
Sierra Leone 232 plus area code plus number plus luck
Togo 228 plus six-digit number

Australia: 00+61+area code+number

New Zealand: 00+64+area code+number

It's very useful to have access to a **fax** number at home through which urgent messages can be relayed to friends or family. Fax is more flexible than telephone – and usually works out cheaper. You might contact a local fax bureau before you leave home to establish you can fax through them. Every capital in West Africa has a public fax office at which you can send and receive messages (the cost of receiving a fax is nominal). Most large hotels have fax services, too, at slightly more expensive rates.

HOLIDAYS, FESTIVALS AND TIME

In addition to the main Christian and Islamic religious festivals, each country in West Africa has its own national holidays, listed in the practical information at the start of each country chapter. These are rarely as established as you would find, for example, in Europe. Some, commemorating no longer respected events, are quietly ignored. In one or two countries, the practice of mounting national celebrations for the president's birthday and similar anniversaries adds a bizarre and unfamiliar quality. Traditional, community festivals, connected either to annual agricultural cycles or to life cycle events, are more attractive but less accessible. Details are given chapter by chapter wherever possible.

ISLAMIC HOLIDAYS

Each West African country, with the exception of Cape Verde, has a significant Muslim population. Islam is the dominant religion in most, but Mauritania is the only nation to dub itself an Islamic Republic. In other countries, Muslim holy days are variably observed – devoutly in strictly Muslim districts, perhaps only vaguely in the capital city.

The **principal events** of which to be aware are the ten days of the Muslim New Year which starts with the month of Moharem (**Ashoura** on the 10th of Moharem celebrates, among other events, Adam and Eve's first meeting after leaving Paradise), the **Prophet Muhammad's birthday** (known as *Mouloud*, or *Maulidi*), the month-

NATIONAL INDEPENDENCE DAYS

Benin Aug 1, 1960	**Ghana** March 20, 1956	**Morocco** March 2, 1956
Burkina Faso Aug 5, 1960	**Guinea** March 6, 1957	**Niger** Aug 3, 1960
Cameroon Jan 1, 1960	**Guinea-Bissau** Sept 10, 1974	**Nigeria** Oct 1, 1960
Cape Verde July 5, 1975	**Liberia** July 26, 1847	**Senegal** June 20, 1960
Côte d'Ivoire Aug 7, 1960	**Mali** June 20, 1960	**Sierra Leone** April 27, 1961
The Gambia Feb 18, 1965	**Mauritania** Nov 28, 1960	**Togo** April 27, 1960

long fast of **Ramadan** and the feast of relief which follows immediately after (known as *Id al-Fitr* or *Id al-Sighir*), and the **Feast of the Sacrifice** or *Tabaski*, which coincides with the annual *Hajj* pilgrimage to Mecca, when every Muslim family with the means to do so slaughters a sheep.

The last of these festivals (known as the *fête des moutons* in French) can be a lot of fun. **Ramadan** isn't an entirely miserable time either. Fasting applies throughout the daylight hours, and covers every pleasure (food, drink, tobacco and sex); while non-Muslims are not expected to observe the fast, it's highly affronting in strict Muslim areas to contravene publicly. Instead, switch to the night shift, as everyone else does, with special soup to break the fast at dusk, and applied eating and entertainment through the night.

The **Islamic calendar** is lunar, divided into twelve months of 29 or 30 days (totalling 354 days). The twelfth month has 29 days and a thirtieth day 11 times every thirty years. The calendar dates from 622 AD, the "Year of the *Hijra*" (AH), when the prophet fled from Mecca to Medina. The Islamic year 1416 AH began on May 30, 1995.

CHRISTIAN HOLIDAYS

Christmas, and to a much lesser extent, Easter are observed as religious ceremonies in Christian areas and, on a more or less secular, national basis, in every country. But if you can't find a bank or post office open, you'll have no trouble finding street food and some transport.

Christmas and New Year are the occasion of street parades and carnival festivities in a number of cities. On the downside, Christmas is a time to avoid contact, as far as possible, with people in uniform. This most applies to the police in the English-speaking countries, where a misappropriated tradition of "Christmas Boxes" survives and is relentlessly cultivated from mid-December to the middle of January.

Lastly, both Guinea-Bissau and Cape Verde have inherited and elaborated upon the Portuguese-Brazilian institution of **Carnaval** and host float parades and street festivals in February or March.

TIME IN WEST AFRICA

Most of West Africa is on Greenwich Mean Time (**GMT**). Cape Verde is two hours earlier (10am when it's 12.00 GMT), Guinea-Bissau is one hour earlier (11am), while Benin, Niger, Nigeria and Cameroon are all one hour later (1pm). The 24-hour clock is widely used in the French and Portuguese-speaking countries. The 12-hour system is usual in the English-speaking countries.

Although all of West Africa lies north of the equator, the coastal region from Monrovia to Douala, just a few degrees north, has roughly the equatorial twelve hours of **daylight** – a little more in summer, a little less in winter. Sunrise comes earlier in the west (about 05.00 GMT) and later in the east (about 07.00 GMT). Latitudes further north experience greater seasonal variation, with slightly longer summer days, though it's almost always going to be light by the time you wake, and dusk still comes before 20.00 GMT.

The notion that the **tropical dusk** is extraordinarily brief is true. With the sun tracing a nearly perfect arc through ninety degrees most of the year, it plunges vertically below the horizon and is lost in minutes. In more extreme latitudes it slides obliquely into night leaving the long period of twilight familiar in Europe and North America.

ISLAMIC FESTIVALS – APPROXIMATE DATES

	1996	**1997**	**1998**
Beginning of Ramadan (1st Ramadan)	Jan 21	Jan 10	Dec 31
Id al-Fitr/Id al-Sighir (1st Shawwal)	Feb 20	Feb 9	Jan 30
Tabaski/Id al-Kabir (10th Dhu'l Hijja)	April 7	April 28	April 18
New Year's Day (1st Moharem)	May 18	May 7	April 27
Ashoura (10th Moharem)	May 27	May 16	May 6
Mouloud/Maulidi (12th Rabia)	July 27	July 16	July 6

Islamic dates in brackets

TIME-KEEPING

People and things in West Africa are usually late. That said, if you try to anticipate **delays** you'll be caught out. Scheduled transport does leave on time at least some of the time. More importantly, transport may leave *early* if it's full. Even planes have been known to take off before schedule.

Although many people wear digital watches – which have flooded the region in the last twenty years – they're essentially jewellery. Notions of time and duration are pretty hazy. Outside the cities, dusk and dawn are the significant markers. You'll soon find you, too, are judging time by the sun, and reckoning how long before dark.

Note that in remote areas, if a driver tells you he's going somewhere "today", it doesn't necessarily mean he expects to *reach* there today. Always allow extra time. There's no better way to ruin West African travel than to attempt to rush it.

WARRI, WOLE, OURIL – THE GAME OF HOLES AND SEEDS

There's an ancient game for two people played all over Africa with two opposing rows of holes and a handful each of seeds, cowries or pebbles. It goes under dozens of different names and the rules vary locally. But the principle is always the same. Seeds are deposited in each hole and then the players take turns to pick up a pile from one of their holes and "sow" them, usually one by one, around the board. Depending on the rules, the hole the last seed is sown into determines the continuation of play, and, if it makes up a certain number of seeds in that hole, then they're captured. The player with the most seeds at the end, wins. It's a game that's, devastatingly simple and, at the same time, mathematically highly complex in its endless chain of cause and effect – financial analysts love it.

GREETINGS, BODY LANGUAGE AND SOCIAL NORMS

You can't hope to avoid social gaffes on a West African stay, but humour and tolerance aren't lacking, so you won't be left to stew in embarrassment. Getting it right really takes an upbringing, but people are delighted when you make the effort.

GREETINGS

Greetings are fundamental. No conversation starts without one. This means a handshake followed by polite enquiries, even as you enter a shop. Traditionally, such exchanges can last a minute or two, and you'll often hear them, performed in a formal, incantatory manner between two men. Long greetings help subsequent negotiations. In French or English you can swop something like "How are you?" "Fine, How's the day?" "Fine, How's business?" "Fine, How's the family?", "Fine, Thank God". It's usually considered polite, while someone is speaking to you at length, to grunt in the affirmative, or say thank you at short intervals. Breaks in conversation are filled with more greetings.

Shaking hands is normal between all men present, on arrival and departure. Women shake hands with each other, but with men only in more sophisticated milieux. Soul brother handshakes and variations on the finger snap are popular among young males. Less natural for Westerners (certainly for men) is an unconscious ease in physical contact. Male visitors need to get used to holding hands with strangers as they're shown around the house, or guided down the street, and, on public transport, to hands and limbs draped naturally wherever's most comfortable.

SOCIAL NORMS

Be aware of the **left hand rule**. Traditionally the left hand is reserved for unhygienic acts and the right for eating and touching, or passing things to others. Like many "rules" it's very often broken. Don't think about it then.

Unless you wan't a serious confrontation, never **point** with your finger. It's equivalent to an obscene gesture. For similar reasons, beckoning is done with the palm down, not up.

KOLA NUTS

Giving and receiving kola nuts is a traditional exchange of friendship. Kola nuts are the chestnut-sized fruit from the pods of an indigenous tree, cultivated widely all over the forest belt and traded on a grand scale throughout West Africa. Before the arrival of tobacco, cannabis, tea and coffee, kola was the main non-alcoholic drug of the region, an appetite depressant and a mild stimulant. It comes in dark red, pink and white varieties, of which the latter are the best and more expensive. Kola should be fresh and hard, not old and rubbery, and you chew it – don't swallow – for the bitter juice. Buy a handful for long journeys, as much to share among fellow passengers as to stay awake.

Don't be put off by apparent shiftiness in **eye contact**, especially if you're talking to someone much younger than you. It's fairly normal for those deferring to others to avoid direct looks.

Hissing ("Tsss!") is an ordinary way to attract a stranger's attention. You'll get a fair bit of it, and it's quite in order to hiss at the waiter in a restaurant.

Answering anything in the negative is often considered impolite. If you're asking questions, don't ask yes-no ones. And try not to phrase things in the negative ("Isn't the lorry leaving?") because the answer will often be "Yes..." ("...it isn't leaving").

Be on the look out too, for a host of **unexpected turns of phrase** which often pop up into West African English. "I am coming", for example, is often said by someone just as they leave your company – which means they're going, but coming back.

TROUBLE AND PERSONAL SAFETY

It's easy to exaggerate the potential hassles and disasters of travel in West Africa. Keep in mind while reading this section that bad experiences are unusual. True, there is a scattering of urban locations, easily enough pinpointed, where snatch robberies and muggings are common. But most of the region carries minimal risk to personal safety compared with Europe and North America. The main problems are sneak thieving and corrupt people in uniforms. The first can be avoided. And dealing with the second can become a game once you know the rules.

AVOIDING TROUBLE

Obviously, if you flaunt the trappings of wealth where there's **urban poverty**, somebody will want to remove them. There's always less risk in leaving your valuables in a securely locked hotel room or, judiciously, with the management. If you clearly have nothing on you (this means not wearing jewellery or a wrist watch), you're unlikely to feel, or be, threatened.

Public transport rarely produces scare stories. Apart from the standard of driving, which is another matter, you haven't much to worry about on the roads – except in Lagos, which is acquiring a certain notoriety for hold-ups (exaggerated, even so). Trains provide thieves with more opportunities, however. People fall asleep and robbers have been known to climb aboard and steam through the carriages. Establish a rapport with your fellow passengers as soon as possible.

If you're flying into West Africa, or arriving overland in your **first big city**, it's obviously wise to be particularly cautious for the first day or two. There's always a lot going on and it's important to distinguish harmlessly robust, up-front interaction (commonly part of the public transport scene) from more dangerous preludes. At the risk of sensationalism, the box below outlines some good strategies for big city survival in Dakar, Abidjan, Lagos or Douala – the most difficult to deal with. Praia, Bissau, Nouakchott, Banjul and Ouagaadougou are more relaxed, while Lomé, Bamako and Niamey fall somewhere in between.

Don't feel unnecessarily victimized, but be rationally suspicious of everyone until you've caught your breath. It doesn't take long. Every rural immigrant coming to the city for the first time goes through exactly the same process, and many are considerably less streetwise than you, easier pickings for never having been in a big town before.

In one or two cities, scams which play on your conscience have begun to appear: a favourite is the "student agitator" routine, in which you get chatting to a friendly young person and either give him a little money, or exchange addresses. As soon as they have gone, a group of heavies arrives, claiming to be undercover police and informing you that you have been observed planning seditious activities. You could be arrested, or pay a fine now . . . Make a big fuss and insist on going to the police station with someone in uniform. They will disappear.

Lastly, don't forget that impoverished fellow travellers are as likely – or as unlikely – to rip you off as anyone else. None of this is meant to induce paranoia. But a controlled rise in your adrenalin level is a good thing. New York, London, Paris, Rome – if you can cope with any of them, you can handle a West African city.

THIEF GRIEF

Hotel room **burglaries** and car break-ins do occur. If you get **mugged**, it will be over in an instant and you're not likely to be hurt. But the hassles, and worse, that gather as soon as you try to do something about it, make it doubly imperative not to let it happen in the first place. Robbers and pickpockets caught red-handed are usually dealt with summarily by the crowd – often killed – so when you shout "Thief!" (or "Voleur!" in French), be swift to intercede once you've retrieved your belongings.

Usually you'll have no chance, or desire, to catch your assailant(s), and the first reaction is to go to the **police**. Unless, however, you've lost a lot of money (and cash is virtually irretrievable) or irreplaceable property, think twice about doing this. The police rarely do something for nothing – even stamping an insurance form may cost you – and you should consider the ramifications if you and they set off to try to catch the culprits. If you're not certain of their identities, pointing the finger of suspicion at people is the worst possible thing to do. If they're arrested, as they probably will be, a night in the cells usually means a beating and confiscation of possessions.

In smaller towns, or where you have some contacts, a workable alternative to police involvement is to enlist **traditional help** in searching for your stolen belongings. Various diviners and traditional doctors operate nearly everywhere. If the culprits get to hear of what you're doing you're likely to get some of your stuff back. Or

BIG CITY SURVIVAL

Pickpocketing can happen anywhere – usually the work of pocket-high thieves, hanging around in markets or other crowded places. Make sure your valuables are secure.

Heavier attacks usually take place in specific areas of the city – downtown shopping streets, docks and waterfront, city centre parks and central markets. Less threatening districts include transport parks (full of tough young men with jobs who tend to be on the lookout for threats to their passengers) and, surprisingly perhaps, the lower income suburbs and slums away from the city centre, where people just aren't used to travellers.

When walking – assuming you have money or valuables on you – have a destination in mind and stay alert. Be aware of what's going on around you. Scan ahead. Don't dawdle or dream. Keep your hands to yourself. Loose hands are likely to be caught: in heavy places, a handshake from a stranger in the street, or a knicknack pressed into your hand, or some murmured offer or suggestion can foreshadow a more aggressive act. If you want to give off strong defensive vibes, hands in pockets or round the straps of a backpack are effective.

Steer clear of creepy-looking street sharks in jeans and running shoes (every robbery ends in a sprint). And never allow yourself to be steered down an alley or between parked cars.

you could offer a reward. Local people will often go out of their way to help.

DEALING WITH THE POLICE

Police in West Africa are probably no worse than most around the world. But badly paid and poorly educated as they often are, it's wise to avoid them as far as possible. You will inevitably come into a fair amount of **contact**. Even in the vast majority of countries where you're no longer obliged to check in at the local police station in every town, the notion of "control" remains highly developed. Checks on the movement of people (police and security services) and goods (customs, *douanes*) take place at junctions and along highways in most countries. Many capital cities have major checkpoints on their access roads.

Police forces vary considerably from one country to the next. For example, in Côte d'Ivoire they're not excessively corrupt but can be unnervingly conscientious and pedantic, while in Guinea they're outrageously on the make and seemingly unfazed by the question of upholding actual laws. Most police forces constitute a separate entity from the rest of the people: they have their own compounds and staff villages and receive – or procure – subsidized rations and services.

In **unofficial dealings**, the police, especially in remote outposts, can sometimes go out of their way to help you with food, transportation and accommodation. Try to reciprocate. Police salaries are always low and often months overdue and they rely on unofficial income to get by. Only brand new police forces and realistic salaries could alter the entrenched situation which now exists in most countries.

If you have **official business** with the police, smiles and handshakes always help, as do terms of address like "Sir", "Officer" or (in a French-speaking country) "*Mon Commandant*". If you're expected to give a bribe – as you often are – wait for it to be hinted at and haggle over it as you would any payment. A pound or two (say \$2 or \$3) is often enough to oil small wheels. If you're driving, you'll rarely be forced to pay sweeteners, except sometimes on entry to and exit from the country. If you're travelling by lorry or bush taxi, it's the driver who pays. If you're singled out, *remind them* it's the driver who pays. Avoid any show of temper. Aggressive travellers always have the worst police stories.

Having said all that, note that currency smuggling or drug possession can easily land you a large fine or worse, and possibly deportation. Don't expect to buy yourself easily out of this kind of trouble.

BRIBERY AND CORRUPTION

Bribery is indeed a way of life. But probably not yours. If you find yourself confronting an implacable person in uniform, you don't have to give in to tacit demands for gifts or money. The golden rule is to **keep talking**. Most laws, including imaginary ones about the importation of backpacks, the possession of two cameras or the writing of diaries, are there to be discussed rather than enforced. If you haven't got all day, a *dash* or **"small present"** – couched in exactly those terms – is all it usually takes. If you can't, or won't give gifts to officials, give words. On extensive West African travels, you have literally hundreds of police, army, customs, immigration and security checkpoints to cross and you'll sail through ninety percent of them. With patience and good humour, the other ten percent can be negotiated relatively painlessly too. When you know they know your "infraction" is bogus, keep

DRUGS

Grass (marijuana, cannabis) is the biggest illegal drug in the region, much cultivated (clandestinely) and as much object of confused opprobrium and fascination as anywhere else in the world. Many social problems are routinely attributed to smoking the "grass that kills" and it's widely believed to cause insanity. In practice, if you indulge discreetly, it's not likely to get you into trouble. The usual result of a fortuitous bust is on-the-spot fines all round.

An altogether different state of affairs exists with **heroin** and **cocaine**, which are smuggled though West African airports en route to Europe (often inside hapless female "swallowers"). Some of the consignments get on to the streets of capitals like Accra and Lagos, together with the associated tensions and paranoia. Stay well clear. Very long prison sentences and the death penalty are not unknown for those involved.

joking, keep pleading and hang on. If you think you may be in breach of a law (or someone's interpretation of it) you might suggest paying the "fine" (*amende*) immediately, or "coming to an agreement" (*faire arrangement* or *s'arranger* in French).

BEHAVIOUR

- Never go out without identification. You don't have to carry a passport at all times, but a photocopy of the first few pages in a plastic wallet is very useful. Not carrying an ID (*carte d'identité, papiers* or *pièces* in French) is usually against the law.
- If you're heading for remote regions, to hike for example, it's worth leaving some details behind with your embassy or the honorary consul.
- Be warned that failure to observe the following points of **public etiquette** can get you arrested or force you to pay a bribe:

  Stand still on any occasion a national anthem is played or a flag raised or lowered. If you see others suddenly cease all activity, do the same.

  Pull off the road completely if motorcycle outriders and limos appear, or stand still.

  Never destroy banknotes, no matter how worthless they may be.

  And don't urinate in public.

TRAVELLERS' FRENCH

Apart from some specialized vocabulary, there's little that non-fluent speakers will find characteristic about West African French beyond the accent. It's generally a lot easier to understand than French as spoken in France, because it's more vigorously pronounced. And the French colonists encouraged the use of French far more than the British, so that, assuming you have at least some French, there are fewer language problems in the *pays francophones.*

As with English spoken as a second language, West African French will have the rhythmic and tonal colouring of the speaker's mother tongue.

WEST AFRICAN FRENCH: A TRAVELLER'S GLOSSARY

This is a mix of pertinent words and expressions together with some French and West African street slang and a few historical terms that have found their way into West African French.

amende fine, penalty
atelier workshop, studio
bâché pick-up van, (lit. "tarpaulined")
balise beacon or cairn, usually in the desert
banco mud and straw mixture for building
barrage road block, barrier
barraquer to stop, rest awhile, camp
berline saloon car
bic disposable pen
biche doe, gazelle, pet
bidonville slum, shanty town
bonne arrivée favoured greeting in francophone Africa
bord fortress (Arabic)
bordelle prostitute, pick-up
borne kilometre marker, "kilometre"
bouffer to eat
break estate car, station wagon
bricolage the art of preserving equipment or making something out of nothing
brousse countryside, the bush
buvette outside bar, refreshments stall
cadeauter to give a present; children may tell you, "*il faut me cadeauter*"
caféman coffee, bread and omelette man
campement budget motel or country guest house
canari clay pot for storing cool water
carte d'identité identity card
carte routière road map
case hut, small house
chef boss, chief
chômer to be unemployed.
cinq cent quatre Peugeot 504
climatisée air conditioned (room)
colon a colonial
commander ask someone to do something
contrôle checkpoint
coupe-coupe machete
dancing dance floor, disco
depuis a long time
devises money or (hard) currency
dépannage breakdown service
discuter to discuss, negotiate
doux good (even a hot pepper soup, far from mild, can be *doux*)
eau potable drinking water
en panne out of order, broken down
escalier washboard road surface
escroc swindler, con-man
exigé required, demanded
faisable feasible, do-able
féticheur religious man with a knowledge of the ways of the spirits
fiche form, document to fill in
flic cop, policeman
fréquenter to go to school

BASIC FRENCH WORDS AND PHRASES

today	*aujourd'hui*	this one	*ceci*
yesterday	*hier*	that one	*celà*
tomorrow	*demain*	open	*ouvert*
in the morning	*le matin*	closed	*fermé*
in the afternoon	*l'après-midi*	big	*grand*
in the evening	*le soir*	small	*petit*
now	*maintenant*	more	*plus*
later	*plus tard*	less	*moins*
at one o'clock	*à une heure*	a little	*un peu*
at three o'clock	*à trois heures*	a lot	*beaucoup*
at ten-thirty	*à dix heures et demie*	cheap	*bon marché*
at midday	*à midi*	expensive	*cher*
man	*un homme*	good	*bon*
woman	*une femme*	bad	*mauvais*
here	*ici*	hot	*chaud*
there	*là*	cold	*froid*

fric cash, dosh
frequenter to go to school
fromager silk-cotton (kapok) tree
garé parked, not in use
gare routière motor transport station
gare ferroviaire railway station
gargote cheap restaurant or chop-house
gaté spoiled, broken, needing repair
gênant bothersome, a hassle
gîte (d'étape) boarding house, inn (staging post)
goudron tar, tarmac
gri-gri charm, amulet, juju
griot traditional musician, storyteller, court minstrel
hivernage rainy season
HLM "low rent housing" (council flats)
Immeuble (Imm.) Building
insh'allah if God wills it (hopefully)
intéressant good, enjoyable; eg a film or the food you're eating.
lampe tempête hurricane lamp, kerosene lamp
livres sterling pounds sterling
machin thingimajig, whatsitsname
mairie town hall, city hall
maison de passage boarding house used as a brothel
marigot creek
marque make or brand (eg vehicle or spare part)
mec guy, fellow
moustiquaire mosquito net/mosquito screen
occasion a seat or place in a bush taxi
ornières wheel ruts
paillote straw hut, sunshade, thatched awning
palétuviers mangroves
palu/paludisme malaria
patron boss, chief, mister
phacochère warthog
pièces identity papers
pirogue dugout canoe
piste track, trail
préfet/sous-préfet administrative prefect/assistant prefect (equivalent of District Commissioner and assistant)
quatre-quatre four-wheel drive
récolte harvest
régler to sort out, settle up, pay up
renseignements information, details
route bitumée surfaced road
sapeur one who is well dressed-up, usually for discos and hanging out; from Sape, the fictitious Société des ambianceurs et persons élégants
sofa Nineteenth-century Muslim cavalry
source (d'eau) spring, water source
sous money
sucrerie mineral or soft drink
sympa/sympathique nice, friendly
tampon rubber stamp
tata fortress (Mande)
tôle ondulée corrugated iron, washboard road
tourner to go out, go dancing, hang out
triptyque triptych; a document in three folds
trop more often means "very" than "too much"
truc thing, whatsit
ventilée "ventilated" – a room with a fan

TALKING TO PEOPLE

Excuse me	*Pardon*	please	*s'il vous plaît*
Do you speak English ?	*Vous parlez anglais ?*	thank you	*merci*
How do you say it in French ?	*Comment ça se dit en Français ?*	hello	*bonjour*
What's your name ?	*Comment vous appelez-vous ?*	goodbye	*au revoir*
My name is . . .	*Je m'appelle . . .*	good morning/ afternoon	*bonjour*
I'm English/ Irish/Scottish Welsh/American/ Australian/ Canadian/ a New Zealander	*Je suis anglais[e]/ irlandais[e]/écossais[e]/ gallois[e]/américain[e]/ australien[ne]/ canadien[ne]/ néo-zélandais[e]*	good evening	*bonsoir*
yes	*oui*	good night	*bonne nuit*
no	*non*	How are you ?	*Comment allez-vous ?/ Ça va ?*
I understand	*Je comprends*	Fine, thanks	*Très bien, merci*
I don't understand	*Je ne comprends pas*	I don't know	*Je ne sais pas*
Can you speak slower ?	*s'il vous plaît, parlez moins vite*	Let's go	*Allons-y*
OK/agreed	*d'accord*	See you tomorrow	*à demain*
		See you soon	*à bientôt*
		Sorry	*Pardon, Madame/ je m'excuse*
		Leave me alone (aggressive)	*Fichez-moi la paix!*
		Please help me	*Aidez-moi, s'il vous plaît*

FINDING THE WAY

bus	*autobus, bus, car*	I want to get off at . . .	*Je voudrais descendre à . . .*
car	*voiture*	the road to . . .	*la route pour . . .*
train/taxi/ferry	*train/taxi/ferry*	near	*près/pas loin*
boat	*bâteau*	far	*loin*
plane	*avion*	left	*à gauche*
What time does it leave ?	*Il part à quelle heure ?*	right	*à droite*
What time does it arrive ?	*Il arrive à quelle heure ?*	straight on	*tout droit*
a ticket to . . .	*un billet pour . . .*	on the other side of	*l'autre côté de*
ticket office	*vente de billets*	on the corner of	*à l'angle de*
how many kilometres ?	*combien de kilomètres ?*	next to	*à côté de*
how many hours ?	*combien d'heures ?*	behind	*derrière*
on foot	*à pied*	in front of	*devant*
Where are you going ?	*Vous allez où ?*	before	*avant*
I'm going to . . .	*Je vais à . . .*	after	*après*
		under	*sous*
		to cross	*traverser*
		bridge	*pont*

OTHER NEEDS

doctor	*médecin*	chemist	*pharmacie*
I don't feel well	*Je ne me sens pas bien*	bakery	*boulangerie*
medicines	*médicaments*	food shop	*alimentation*
prescription	*ordonnance*	supermarket	*supermarché*
I feel sick	*Je suis malade*	to eat	*manger*
headache	*J'ai mal à la tête*	to drink	*boire*
stomach ache	*mal à l'estomac*	bank	*banque*
period	*règles*	money	*argent*
pain	*douleur*	with	*avec*
it hurts	*ça fait mal*	without	*sans*

QUESTIONS AND REQUESTS

The simplest way of asking a question is to start with *s'il vous plaît* (please), then name the thing you want in an interrogative tone of voice. For example:

Where is there a bakery ?	*S'il vous plaît, la boulangerie ?*
Which way is it to Bobo ?	*S'il vous plaît, la route pour Bobo ?*

Similarly with requests:

We'd like a room for two	*S'il vous plaît, une chambre pour deux*
Can I have a kilo of oranges	*S'il vous plaît, un kilo d'oranges*

Question words

Where ?	*où ?*	When ?	*quand ?*
How ?	*comment ?*	Why ?	*pourquoi ?*
How many/how much ?	*combien ?*	At what time ?	*à quelle heure ?*
		What is/which is ?	*quel est ?*

ACCOMMODATION

a room for one/two people	*une chambre pour une/deux personnes*	second floor	*deuxième étage*
		with a view	*avec vue*
a double bed	*un lit double*	key	*clef*
a room with a shower	*une chambre avec douche*	to iron	*repasser*
		do laundry	*faire la lessive*
Can I see it ?	*Je peux la voir ?*	sheets	*draps*
a room on the courtyard	*une chambre sur la cour*	quiet	*calme*
		noisy	*bruyant*
a room over the street	*une chambre sur la rue*	hot water	*eau chaude*
		cold water	*eau froide*
first floor	*premier étage*	breakfast	*le petit déjeuner*

DAYS AND DATES

January	*janvier*	November	*novembre*	August 1	*le premier août*
February	*février*	December	*décembre*	March 2	*le deux mars*
March	*mars*			July 14	*le quatorze juillet*
April	*avril*	Sunday	*dimanche*	November 23	*le vingt-trois novembre*
May	*mai*	Monday	*lundi*		
June	*juin*	Tuesday	*mardi*		
July	*juillet*	Wednesday	*mercredi*	1991	*dix-neuf-cent-quatre-vingt-onze*
August	*août*	Thursday	*jeudi*		
September	*septembre*	Friday	*vendredi*	1992	*dix-neuf-cent-quatre-vingt-douze*
October	*octobre*	Saturday	*samedi*		

NUMBERS

1	*un*	11	*onze*	21	*vingt-et-un*	95	*quatre-vingt-quinze*
2	*deux*	12	*douze*	22	*vingt-deux*	100	*cent*
3	*trois*	13	*treize*	30	*trente*	101	*cent-et-un*
4	*quatre*	14	*quatorze*	40	*quarante*	200	*deux cents*
5	*cinq*	15	*quinze*	50	*cinquante*	300	*trois cents*
6	*six*	16	*seize*	60	*soixante*	500	*cinq cents*
7	*sept*	17	*dix-sept*	70	*soixante-dix*	1000	*mille*
8	*huit*	18	*dix-huit*	75	*soixante-quinze*	2000	*deux milles*
9	*neuf*	19	*dix-neuf*	80	*quatre-vingts*	5000	*cinq milles*
10	*dix*	20	*vingt*	90	*quatre-vingt-dix*	1,000,000	*un million*

TRAVELLERS WITH DISABILITIES

Although by no means easy, travelling around West Africa does not pose insurmountable problems for people with disabilities. For wheelchair or frame users, facilities are non-existent (and wheelchairs virtually unknown), but most hotels are single storey or have ground-floor rooms. Access ramps are rare, however, and travel within and between cities requires even more time and determination than usual. You'll at least have no problems recruiting local help and you can expect overwhelming consideration.

When **choosing a flight**, there are a number of factors to consider and you end up, as usual, having to compromise. By preference go for a flight with *KLM*, *Lufthansa* or *Swissair* – the best airlines for disabled passengers with a wide choice of routes. But you might want to travel overnight, to avoid the hassle of arriving after dark. In that case, you'll probably end up flying *Air Afrique* or *Air France* via Paris. On the other hand you might place greater priority on the convenience of a non-stop flight, in which case, from London, *Air Afrique* non-stop to Abidjan or *BA* to Ghana or Nigeria would probably be your best bets. From New York, the only direct flights are *Air Afrique*'s service to Dakar (continuing to Abidjan) or *Nigeria Airways'* and *American Trans Air's* flights to Lagos.

From North America to Europe, *Virgin* and *Air Canada* come out tops in terms of disability awareness (and seating arrangements) and may be worth contacting first for any information they can provide.

Once in West Africa, attitudes to disabled people are generally good, though government provision for disabled needs is almost completely absent. **Getting around** in a wheelchair on half-paved or unpaved roads, or over soft sandy streets, is extremely hard work, while cabs are typically European or Japanese compacts. Inter-city travel is even tougher, though in some countries (Côte d'Ivoire stands out), the quality of long-distance buses can be well up to international standards.

Visiting **game parks and historical sites** is problematic unless you have private transport. Historical and archaeological sites are often barely maintained, or at least require some climbing of steps or hiking through a bit of bush. In the case of the parks, it's not only difficult to reach them, but hard to figure out how to get around them when you arrive. Guided tours in safari vehicles with good springs are rare: in Nigeria's Yankari Reserve, visitors are thrown in the back of a lorry with wooden benches for game-viewing. On a positive note, most game lodges are accessible for wheelchair users and safaris can be arranged in advance in the capital – at a price.

CONTACT ADDRESSES FOR DISABLED TRAVELLERS

ACROD, PO Box 60, Curtain ACT 2605, Australia (☎06/682-4333).

Barrier Free Travel, 36 Wheatley St, North Bellingen, NSW 2454, Australia (☎066/551 733).

Disabled Persons Assembly, PO Box 10-138, The Terrace, Wellington, New Zealand (☎04/472-2626).

Holiday Care Service, 2 Old Bank Chambers, Station Rd, Horley, Surrey RH6 9HW, UK (☎01293/774535). Information on all aspects of travel with a disability.

Kéroul, 4545 av Pierre de Coubertin, CP 1000, succ.M Montréal, PQ H1V 3R2, Canada (☎514/2523104). Specializes in travel for mobility-impaired people.

Mobility International USA, PO Box 3551, Eugene, OR 97403, USA (☎503/343-1248). Information, access guides, tours and exchange programme.

RADAR (Royal Association for Disability and Rehabilitation), 25 Mortimer St, London W1N 8AB, UK (☎0171/637-5400; Minicom ☎0171/637-5315). Good source of information on all aspects of travel.

Travel Information Center, Moss Rehabilitation Hospital, 1200 W Tabor Rd, Philadelphia, PA 19141, USA (☎215/329-5715 x2233). Write for access information.

TRIPSCOPE, 63 Esmond Rd, London W4 1JE, UK (☎0181/994-9294). Phone-in travel information and advice service.

Despite the difficulties, the effort is worthwhile if you count yourself a very outgoing individual, and are prepared to be carried repeatedly. **The Gambia** and **Burkina Faso** are sufficiently low-key, accessible and accustomed to visitors to make the hassles bearable.

Campbell Irvine Ltd, 48 Earl's Court Rd, London W8 6EJ (☎0171/937-6981) is one company offering insurance for disabled travellers. For further information, together with first-hand accounts by travellers with disabilities of their experiences in Africa, see *Nothing Ventured: Disabled People Travel the World* (a Rough Guide special, distributed by Penguin). In the US and Canada it is published as *Able to Travel* (Rough Guides).

WOMEN TRAVELLERS

Machismo, in its fully fledged Latin varieties, is rare in West Africa. Male egos are softened by reserves of humour and women travel widely on their own or with each other, without the major problems sometimes experienced in parts of Asia and Latin America. Women's groups flourish in some countries, occasionally under the aegis of a government ministry – though in several they've hardly taken off. Where they exist, they're concerned more with improvement of incomes, education, health and nutrition than with social or political emancipation.

TRAVELLING ALONE

Travelling on your own or with a woman companion is by turns frustrating and rewarding. You'll usually be welcomed with generous hospitality, though occasionally you'll seem to get a run of harassment and hassles because of your gender. It's well to know, if you're overlanding from Europe, that the biggest difficulties will occur in North Africa – especially Morocco – and that Muslim regions south of the Sahara are altogether different.

On **public transport** a single woman traveller causes quite a stir and fellow passengers don't want to see you badly treated. They'll speak up on your behalf and get you a good seat or argue with the driver over your baggage payments. You can speak your mind, be open and direct and nobody takes offence. Fellow male passengers always assume protective roles. This can be helpful but is sometimes annoyingly restrictive and occasionally leads to misunderstandings (see "Sexual Attitudes" below).

Women get offers of **accommodation** in people's homes more often than male travellers (and most of them without strings attached). And, if you're staying in less reputable hotels, there'll often be female company – employees, family, residents – to look after you.

The **clothes** you wear and the way you look and behave get noticed by everyone and they're more important if you don't appear to have a male escort. Your **head** and everything from **waist to ankles** are the sensitive zones, particularly in Islamic regions. Long, loose hair is seen as extraordinarily provocative; doubly so if blonde. Pay attention to these areas by keeping your hair fairly short or tied up (or by wearing a scarf) and wearing long skirts or, at a pinch, very baggy pants.

In the heat it can be hard to be that disciplined, however, so if you have to wear **shorts** try to make them long ones. If you find it's too hot to wear a **bra**, it's not going to interest anybody. Breasts aren't an important issue and topless bathing is rarely offensive. If you'll be travelling much on rough roads, however, you'll need a bra for support. Seriously.

Teresa Driver writes:

I relished the opportunity to be with women but they continually made me feel dowdy. While gara *(indigo tie-dyed damask) is becoming more fashionable, traditional West African dresses are made from brilliantly colourful printed cloth, used in vast quantities.*

Senegalese women have to be the best dressers in the world. Their clothes are amazing, off-the-shoulder creations tailored to accentuate slim waists and sexy bottoms, and to show off long necks and broad backs (working backs). With towering head-dresses the whole ensemble has an impressive, swaying grace. Or else they wear flowing, embroidered boubous. *At parties and on festive occasions the women look stunning – decked in jewellery and flower-scented gowns and often wearing high heels that just add to the total effect. Even in the villages, women change into their best clothes to go market-shopping. The importance of your "look" can't be over-emphasized. If you make the effort to dress up it won't go unappreciated.*

I took earrings and necklaces as small presents to give away (every woman has pierced ears). Body Shop *cosmetics in small containers make excellent gifts, too.*

MEETING OTHER WOMEN

It's often very difficult **getting to know women** in West Africa. Most contact is mediated, at least initially, through their male relatives, with whom you'll take on the role of honorary man, at least in the way you're treated socially. In the small towns and villages women are usually less educated than men and rarely speak English or French. They don't hang out in bars and restaurants either and are much more often to be found in their compounds working hard. Their fortitude as **housewives** is something to behold – always in total control of the family's food and comfort, from chopping wood to selling home-made produce in order to make ends meet. Even school-educated professional women dominate their household affairs and make sure everything runs smoothly. The extended family and the use of the younger girls as helpers is a major contribution. Men are away a great deal of the time.

For their part, West African women will try to picture themselves in your position, traipsing around *your* homeland – a scenario that most find hard to imagine. Family obligations are everything. Conveying the fact that you, too, have a family and a home is a good way of reducing the barriers of incomprehension but, assuming you're over fifteen, explaining the absence of **husband and children** is normally impossible. You can either invent some or expect sympathy instead – and perhaps the offer of fertility medicine.

BROADER ISSUES

Despite widespread paper commitments to **women's rights**, West Africa remains a powerfully male-dominated part of the world. Women do the large proportion of productive labour and most subsistence agriculture is in their hands, though this varies among different ethnic groups. Women have the explicit support of government ministries (for what it's worth) in very few countries. In other countries there's often a non-governmental women's organization working to improve the lot of mothers, agricultural labourers and crafts workers. Professional market women usually run their own informal unions in the cities.

Matrilineal cultures, which once held sway over large parts of the region, are on the decline, under joint assault by paternalistic Islam and Christianity. Matrilineal inheritance doesn't, in any case, necessarily imply *matriarchal* social structures but simply inheritance by a man from his mother's brother rather than his own father.

Current major **women's issues** in West Africa are primarily concerned with rights over women's bodies – contraception, abortion and the practices of genital mutilation, known, in a classic bit of male "anthropologese" as "female circumcision".

Few West African countries have successful **family planning** programmes, though there may be substantial improvements in the near future. Men are unwilling to co-operate by using condoms and women are pushed out-of-date pills at market stalls (sold singly if they prefer...). **Abortion** is virtually a taboo subject in some parts, though abortions by traditional methods (and less traditional backstreet operations) are believed to be widely performed. Few governments permit abortion on demand.

Genital mutilation is widespread and occurs to some degree in every mainland West African country. It's traditionally carried out by female practitioners on the occasion of a girl's initiation into womanhood. Today, although on the decline, it's also performed under anaesthetic in hospital and often at an early age. It varies from clitoridectomy, to excision of the inner labia, to excision of most of the outer labia as well (a major operation known as infibulation nearly confined, in West Africa, to Mali).

All these issues are complex. Both contraception and abortion (especially as encouraged by Rich World development agencies) are topics which can incense women as well as men, so be wary of crashing into conversation. In the case of genital mutilation, women campaigning to eradicate the practices have met resistance from traditionalist women. And mutilations can't be analysed just in terms of male sexual demands (a tighter vagina, loss of sexual response and consequent presumed fidelity). Unfortunately, it's an issue that many governments would prefer not to address.

SEXUAL ATTITUDES

Don't make any assumptions about puritanism on the basis of Islamic society in West Africa. It's the church which has successfully repressed sexuality. Otherwise, sexual attitudes are liberal (though you'll rarely see open displays of affection between men and women) and sex is openly discussed except in the presence of children. It's rarely the subject of personal hang-ups either, though sexual violence is surely as prevalent in families as it is anywhere. You'll be treated as a sexual person wherever you go. If you travel with a companion of the opposite sex, you'll find the relationship tends to insulate you – but not completely.

WOMEN TRAVELLERS

Flirting is universal in West Africa and in order to avoid it you'd have to be perspicacious about where you go in towns. This is particularly true for white travellers; the fantasy inventory of black–white sexual relations tends to get played out whenever you find yourself in a bar, or on a dance floor. If a man asks you to "come and see where I live", he means you should come and see where he and you are going to sleep together. You'll have no shortage of offers. They're usually easy to turn down if you refuse as frankly as you're asked. Unwanted physical advances are rare. But it always helps to avoid offence and preserve a friendship if you make your intentions (or lack of them) clear from the outset. If you're not with a man, a fictitious husband in the background, much as you might prefer to avoid the ploy, is always useful; though it may well be met with such responses as "Tell your husband you have to go outside for some air". . .

If you're in a certain mood, all this can be fun. There's no reason you can't spend an evening dancing and talking and still go back to your bed alone and unharassed.

ADVICE FOR WOMEN TRAVELLERS

- Carry pictures of your family.
- Beware of big men in small towns. Don't accept an invitation to the disco from the local commandant unless you're on very firm ground.
- Never meet someone as arranged if you're uncomfortable about it.
- Always lock your door at night.
- Take a supply of condoms. Don't tell yourself it will never happen. Be prepared, because he will never have any.
- And three useful French phrases for persistent clingers: *J'en ai marre de toi* (I've just about had enough of you), *Laisse-moi tranquille!* (Leave me alone!), or, in a crisis, *Va te faire foutre!* (Go and fuck yourself!).

MALE TRAVELLERS

Much of what applies to women travellers in West Africa applies equally to men, though of course questions of personal safety and intimidation don't arise in the same way. It's common enough for women, and especially unmarried girls, to flirt with strangers. And many town bars and hotels are patronized by women who more or less make a living from **prostitution**. This is not the secretive and exploitative transaction of the West and pimps are generally unknown.

Unfortunately, **sexually transmitted disease**, and the AIDS virus, are rife. Attitudes in West Africa have woken up to this new reality, but you should be aware of the very real risks – and prepared for the occasion – if you accept one of the many propositions which, travelling alone, or with a male friend, you're likely to receive. Always carry, and use, condoms.

GAY LIFE

Beyond the big cities, **homosexuality** is more or less invisible. People from a more traditional African background almost always deny it exists, find the notion laughable or childish, or describe it as a phase or a harmless peculiarity. As for the legality of gay sex, it's not *illegal* in Burkina Faso. Most countries, however, including all the Anglophone ex-colonies, inherited the laws of 1950s Europe and have hardly changed – though in practice prosecutions are almost unheard of.

For gay male visitors, the only parts of the region you'll find like-minded company are the big capital cities and the resort areas. Contacts, however, tend to be rather exploitative on both sides. Gay women can't hope to find any hint of a lesbian community anywhere.

The expatriate community has a statistically high gay constituency, and the Lebanese community, too, has a visible proportion of gay men.

WORKING IN WEST AFRICA

Exceptions are noted in one or two places in the book, but in general there's no way you can work your way through West Africa. Bed and board in return for your help is sometimes available on development projects, in schools or through voluntary agencies, but such arrangements are entirely informal and word-of-mouth. Teachers and engineers have the best chances. Direct, personal approach to the appropriate ministry might open some doors. But under-employment is a serious problem and work permit regulations everywhere make your getting a wage nearly impossible without pulling strings. You usually sign a declaration that you won't seek work when you obtain the visa or fill in the arrival card.

Voluntary work is more likely. **Peace Corps** accepts applications from US citizens over the age of 18 for field work in some 60 areas of speciality. Mostly commonly, they recruit people with a background in agriculture, education, engineering or health care, but volunteers with diverse experience in other fields also serve. The organization tries to respect applicants' geographical preferences, however, in order to be sent to a specific country, you must have skills currently being requested by the country. If you are willing to serve only in one region of the world, such as West Africa, your chances of being accepted are limited. The length of service is two years, following a three month orientation. Peace Corps currently has programs either in operation or in development for most of West Africa, with the exception of Burkina Faso and Liberia. For more details, contact 1-800-424-8580, or write to Peace Corps, room 9320, Washington, DC 20526.

In Britain, **VSO** (Voluntary Service Overseas) accepts applications from people with useful qualifications and, usually, who have appropriate work experience, to work on local salaries in The Gambia, Guinea-Bissau, Ghana, Nigeria and Sierra Leone (where the programme is currently suspended). Teachers and health professionals are primarily in demand. You do get the opportunity to state your preferred country. VSO is at 317 Putney Bridge Rd, London SW1J 2PN (☎0181 780-2266).

WILDLIFE AND NATIONAL PARKS

West Africa doesn't have the game reserves and wildlife concentrations of East or Southern Africa. But it offers a number of major national parks that are worth taking in if you're an enthusiastic naturalist. Outside them, too, it's possible to see a good variety of Africa's birds and mammals in habitats ranging from desert to swamp and floodland, savannah, dry woodland and dense, moist forest – both lowland and mountain. Travelling by public transport, it always pays to spend a little more on a seat in the front. That way you can reckon on seeing a lot more creatures, mostly crossing or flying over the road – or squashed upon it.

WILDLIFE

The large animals you'll see most often out on the road, or in the bush, are **monkeys** and **baboons**. **Gazelles** and other small antelope are also quite common, especially in the Sahel. Larger grazing animals are localized and unusual sights. Along the Niger north of Niamey there are **giraffes**, and **buffalo** inhabit pockets of forest and bush thicket in various parts.

Elephants hang on in dwindling numbers in a surprising number of countries – most in fact – but the recent discovery of quite large herds north of Timbuktu (and the fact that they could just as easily be slaughtered into extinction) highlights just how difficult it is to assess their status. The **black rhino** has never inhabited more than the far east of the region: you can still see a few of them in Cameroonian parks.

None of these animals, even outside the confines of the parks, poses any threat to you as a traveller, even if you choose to camp out and hike or cycle. More threatening wildlife – the big cats, crocodiles, hippos – are very localized. You're extremely unlikely to see any large predators outside the parks. And even in a national park, seeing a **lion**, **cheetah** or **leopard** in West Africa is cause for some celebration. **Crocodiles** are hard to spot and are mercilessly hunted where they live because they do occasionally grab people at the water's edge. Be somewhat

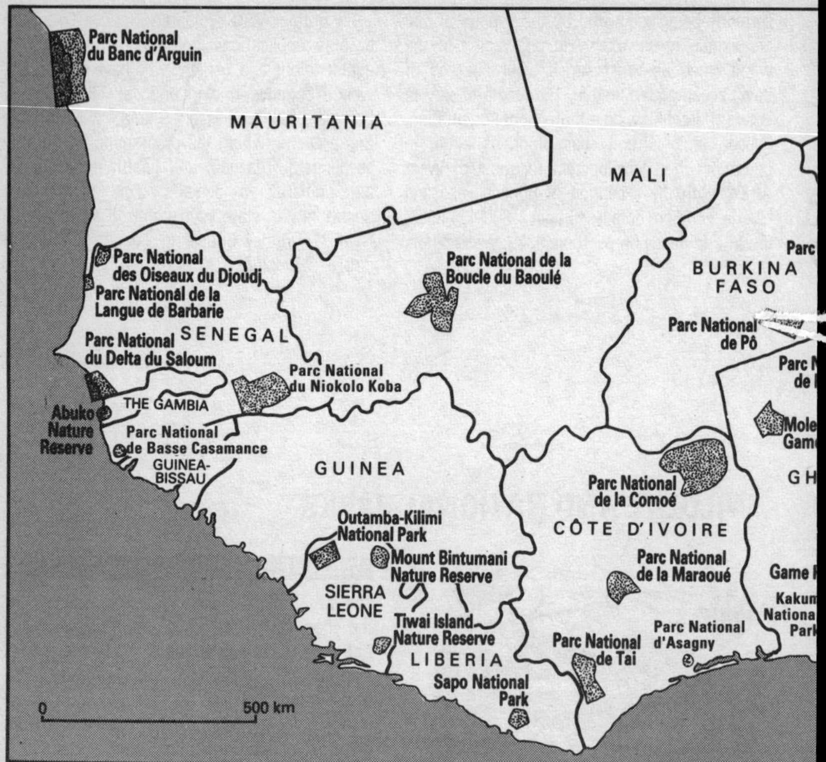

cautious by rivers and lakes. **Hippos**, too, have a justified dangerous reputation, especially when accidentally trapped on dry land or panicked in the water while dozing. You're quite likely to see them from a boat on the Niger in Mali, along the upper Gambia, along the Comoé in Côte d'Ivoire, or in Cameroon.

Another supposedly dangerous animal – the **gorilla** – is really very timid. It lives in the remote, southern forests of Cameroon and has recently been rediscovered across the border in Nigeria, where the Oban Reserve is being established to protect it (full details in those chapters). **Chimpanzees** also survive here, as well as much further to the west, in patches of remote forest from Senegal to Côte d'Ivoire, but their existence is threatened by deforestation and the pet and laboratory trade.

Spiders and scorpions and various other multi-legged invertebrates are less often encountered than you might expect, or fear. The **butterflies** – as many as a thousand different species in some districts – are extensive and colourful, especially in the lowland forests.

Lizards are common everywhere. You'll soon become familiar with the vigorous push-ups of the red-headed male **rock agama**. Some towns seem to be positively swarming with them, no doubt in proportion to the insect supply. Large lizards (all species are quite harmless) include the **monitors**, of which the grey and yellow Nile monitor grows to an impressive two metres. They live near water, but you can often see them dashing across the road. **Chameleons** too, are often seen making painfully slow progress across the road, or wafer-thin, squashed on the tarmac. In some areas, at night, little **house geckos** come out like translucent aliens from who knows where to scuttle usefully across the ceiling and walls in pursuit of moths and mosquitos.

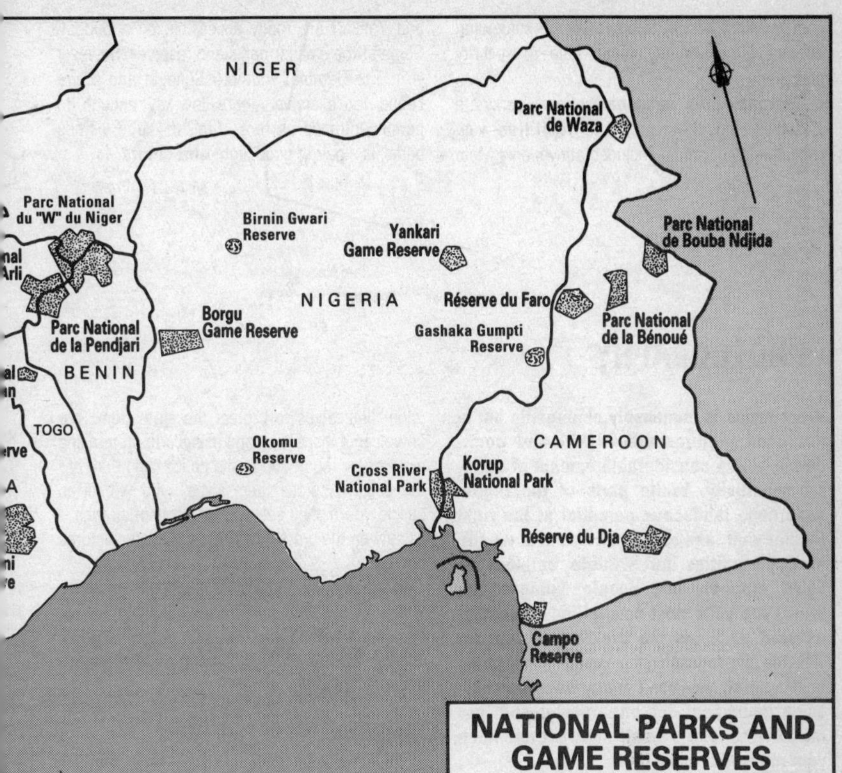

West Africa's **birdlife** is astonishingly diverse – nearly eleven hundred species ranging from the diminutive pygmy woodpecker to the ostrich. Characteristic sights are the urbanite **pied crows** of the Sahel and savannah, electric blue **Abyssinian rollers**, perched on telephone wires in the grasslands, the marvellous, lurching flight of **hornbills** swooping across the road in forest areas, and quite unmistakeable flocks of **grey parrots** in dense bush along the coast.

NATIONAL PARKS

Most countries have some sort of national park network, though in several it consists of just the one park. The most important in the west are Mauritania's **Banc d'Arguin** (sea and migratory birds), Senegal's **Niokolo-Koba** (large mammals of savannah and forest), Sierra Leone's **Outamba-Kilimi** (bush thicket and swamp forest), Mali's **Boucle du Baoulé** and **Bafing** (savannah and riverine forest with large mammals), and Côte d'Ivoire's **Comoé** (savannah mammals).

In central West Africa there's Ghana's surprisingly good **Mole Game Reserve**, Benin's **Pendjari** (excellent game-viewing), and the **Parc National du "W" du Niger**, which extends across the borders of Benin, Burkina and Niger.

Nigeria and **Cameroon** have probably the best parks in West Africa. Nigeria's **Borgu** is bush thicket while the smaller **Yankari** has well-organized game-viewing and quantities of animals. The new **Oban** is a remote rain forest gorilla refuge bordering **Korup National Park** in Cameroon. Cameroon's other parks include some fine, highland savannah reserves in the north – **Faro**, **Bénoué** and **Bouba Ndjida** – and **Waza** in the floodlands near Lake Chad, which for faunal diversity and large herds of elephant is the best in West Africa, though may be somewhat difficult of access at present due to security problems.

Entrance fees, **seasonality** (many parks are closed during the rains) and **facilities** vary considerably. Of those included above, only Mole and Yankari are really accessible on a budget. Some of the smaller parks and reserves, however – in The Gambia, southern Senegal and Sierra Leone for example – are low-key enough to permit entrance on foot. Vital, if you're visiting parks, is a pair of good, light **binoculars**.

PHOTOGRAPHY

West Africa is immensely photogenic but to get good pictures takes skill and confidence, and a considerable amount of cultural sensitivity. While parts of the region have huge landscape potential at the right time of year, and there's obviously a wealth of opportunities for wildlife enthusiasts, you'll probably find people, villages and towns are your most compelling subjects – as well as being the trickiest. Except for wildlife photography, for which a telephoto is essential, you don't really need cumbersome equipment. It's often easier and less intrusive to take a small compact and keep your money for extra film.

Whatever you decide, if you take a camera, **insure it** and make sure you've a dust-proof bag to keep it in – film in the camera gets scratched otherwise. Take spare batteries, too – miniatures are hard to obtain.

Film tends to be very pricey so bring all you'll need. Try to keep it cool by stuffing it inside a sleeping bag. If you'll be away for some time, posting it home, or preferably sending it with someone flying back, is a good idea. Local print processing is available but tends to be hit and miss. The opportunity to process **slides** is rare.

CAMERAS, PEOPLE AND THE STATE

At the risk of generalizing, West Africa is hostile to the camera's probing eye. **Mistrust of your motives** comes from three main sectors. Firstly, the people in markets, along the road and in the villages may, justifiably, resent you photographing them uninvited. Secondly, there are others, often teachers or civil servants, who may take it upon themselves to protect the state from your unwelcome inspection and ask you to stop taking pictures, or report you to the police. And third are the security forces themselves, who will often hassle you if they see you taking photographs – usually on the pretext that you are taking pictures of them.

None of this advice is intended to cause alarm, and plenty of travellers complete their trips with not a film confiscated or a camera opened. Nonetheless, disturbing encounters are not infrequent.

TAKING PHOTOS OF PEOPLE

There are two options if you want to get **photos of people**. Firstly, you can adopt a gleefully robust (or blithely arrogant) approach, take pictures before anyone knows it's happened and deal with the problems after the event. But this is the kind of crass behaviour that will almost inevitably get you into trouble and spread bad feeling in your wake. Some travellers – few – seem to get away with it. Go to a busy market place at home and try the same thing. It's difficult.

Far better is a more interactive approach. **Ask people first.** Summoning the confidence and grace to ask to take people's portraits, and to accept refusal with equanimity, is at least half the affair. If they insist on posing, so be it. Try to come to terms with the reality of your position: you can't be a fly on the wall. As for shooting with a telephoto in crowded streets or a market, or using a sneaky right-angle fitting, they're almost always a failure.

Be prepared to **pay** something or to send a print if your subjects have addresses. If you're motivated to take a lot of pictures of people, you

VIDEO CAMERAS

Everything that applies to still photography applies ten-fold to camcorders. More and more people are wandering around with them, but it would be well worth asking permission in advance through the nearest embassy and trying hard to get something in writing from the country's Ministry of Information. Most of the laws allowing amateur filming apply to non-broadcast quality 8mm filming and haven't yet caught up with videos.

should seriously consider lugging along a **Polaroid** camera and as much film as you can muster, in order to offer a portrait on-the-spot. Very few people have a photo of themselves. Or you could have a lot of photos of you and your family printed up with your address on the back, which should raise a few laughs at least when you try the exchange. The exchange is what counts. A family you've stayed with is unlikely to refuse a photo session and they may even ask for it. The same people might be furious if you jumped off the bus and immediately started taking photos. Or worse, if you stayed on the bus and did it through the window. Photos from Africa are full of examples of people who didn't want to be photographed. That you might have taken some of their soul is not an explanation, but it's a good metaphor.

SECURITY

You shouldn't take photos of anything that could be construed as strategic or military – including any kind of army or police building, police or military vehicles and uniforms, prisons, airports, harbours, ferries, bridges, broadcasting installations, national flags and, of course, presidents. Officially, this is seen as a "risk to state security", but some countries are specifically ill-disposed to tourists taking photographs of scenes reflecting poverty. With this kind of discretionary caveat, you can more or less rule out photography in the towns. It all depends on who sees you of course. Protesting your innocence won't appease small-minded officials. The Gambia, Senegal and Cape Verde are the least uptight about these subjects. Cameroon and Nigeria are notoriously touchy.

One or two countries still require you to have "**photography permits**". Details are given in the, practical information section for each country.

TECHNICAL BUSINESS

Getting (slightly) **technical**, use skylight or UV filters to block haze and protect your lens. Take several speeds of film – don't let anyone tell you it's unnecessary to have fast film. Unless you intend to do some bird or game park photography (and you have to be quite determined about this, tracking and patiently setting up your prey) it's probably not worth taking a telephoto or zoom lens. Long lenses are very difficult to use in public places. But if you feel it's worth taking a camera bag of lenses for your SLR, then it really makes no sense not to take two camera bodies as well – less lens changing and two film speeds available. Or take two compact cameras.

Early morning and late afternoon are the **best times for photography**. At midday, with the sun almost directly overhead, the light is flat and everything is lost in a formless glare. In the morning and evening the contrast between light and shade can be huge, so be careful to expose for the subject and not the general scene. A flash is very useful to fill in shade, even in bright sun. Remember too, as you frame your next master portrait, that dark skin needs extra exposure or you won't see people's faces: think of people as always back-lit – a half stop is normally enough.

The **rainy season** is perhaps the most rewarding time, especially when the first rains break. Months of dust are settled, greenery sprouts in a few hours, the countryside has a lush, bold sheen and the sky is magnificent.

PEOPLE AND LANGUAGE

Whether called peoples, ethnic groups, nations or tribes, West Africans have a multiplicity of racial and cultural origins. Distinctions would be simple if similarities in physical appearance were shared by those who speak the same language and share a common culture. The term "tribe" tends to imply this kind of banal stereotype. But "tribes" have never been closed units and appearance, speech and culture have always overlapped. Even in the past, families often contained members of different ethnic groups. Over the last fifty years or so, "tribal" identities have broken down still further in many parts, replaced by broader class, political and national ones.

The most enduring and meaningful ethnic distinction is **language**. A person's "mother tongue" is still important as an index of social identity. A *tribe*, if the word means anything, is best defined as a group of people sharing a common first language. But in the towns and among affluent families, even language is increasingly unimportant. Many people speak two or three languages (their own, French or English and sometimes a third or even fourth lingua franca like Hausa, Bamana or Krio). And for a few, the old metropolitan languages – French, English or Portuguese – have become a first language.

NAMES AND GROUPS

West Africa is the most linguistically complex region in the world. There are dozens of **major languages** and literally hundreds of less important languages and distinct dialects. Some 400 of these are spoken in Nigeria alone. Most of West Africa's languages are viable and thriving and very few are in any danger of extinction.

For an outsider, the confusion is exacerbated by the fact that, until European colonization, almost none of these languages was written. Today, many are written, in the Roman alphabet, sometimes with additional phonetic symbols. But in the early days, even the language and ethnic **names** first recorded varied according to the nationality and ear of the researchers and the identity of the person asked. Often enough in West Africa the name of the language and of the people who speak it are genuinely distinct.

We have tried to be as consistent and simple as possible in this book, without sweeping distinctions away. Generally, we've used the **names** used locally (for example Mandingo in Liberia, Malinké in Guinea, Mandinka in The Gambia). On the other hand, varieties of names for the people and language often called *Fulani* are so diverse that we've gone for simple *Fula* throughout except in Nigeria, where "Fulani" is in common usage.

Some understanding of differences and relatedness is worth achieving in order, at the very least, to come to grips with what can otherwise seem an incomprehensible and unfathomable cultural region. Most West Africans speak languages of one of **three great groups** – "Niger-Congo" (now re-named the Southern area of wider affinity – Sawa), "Afro-Asiatic" (the Northern area of wider affinity – Nawa) and Mande. African language classification (the attempt to assess the way the languages are presumed to have evolved from common ancestral languages) is immensely complicated and linguists have recently tried to get away from the notion of "families" of languages, in case it turns out they have things in common through long association rather than common ancestry.

In trying to work out where everyone fits in, it helps, especially when reading different sources, to keep a flexible attitude to **spellings** (try pronouncing the word in as many ways as possible). Two sets of much interchanged sounds are the p, b, v, f, w set and the d, gh, r, l set. And of course anything spelled "qu" might just as well be spelt "kw" or, for that matter, "cou" or "kou".

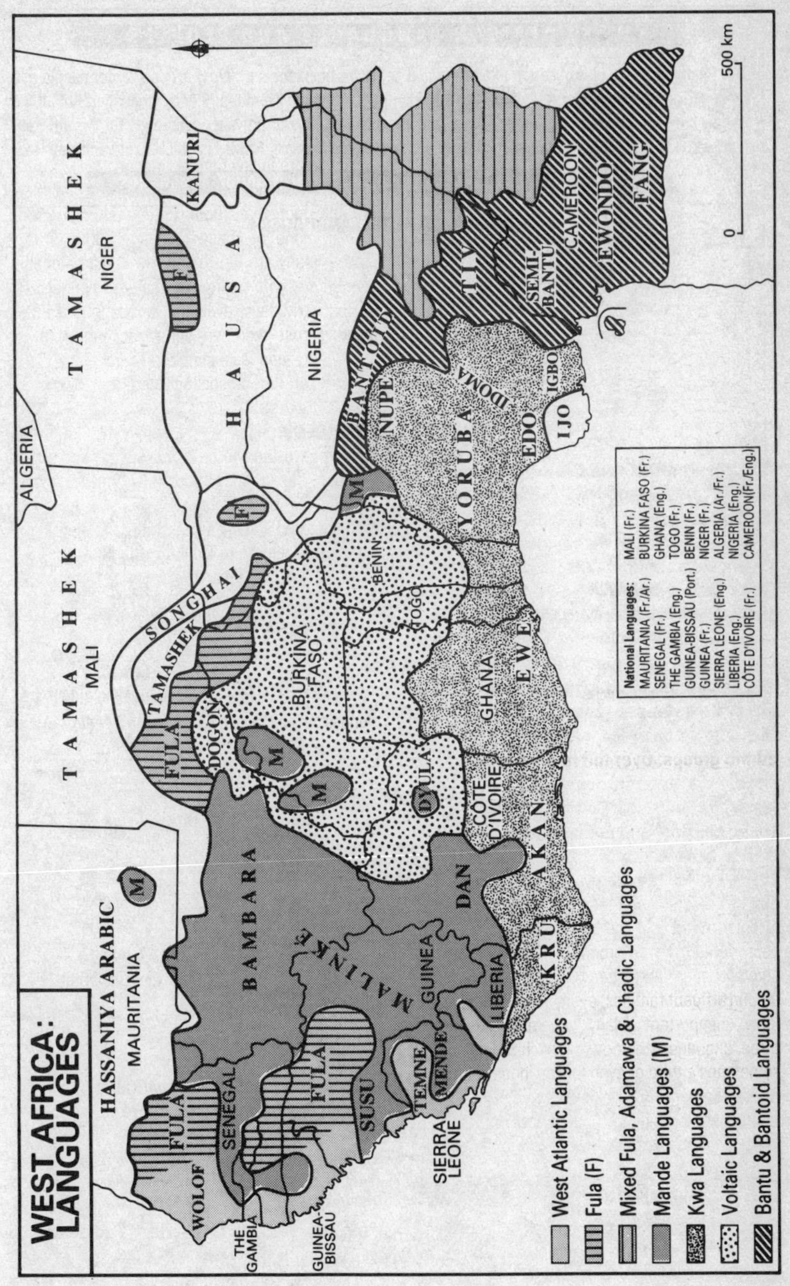
WEST AFRICA: LANGUAGES
HASSANIYA ARABIC
MAURITANIA
TAMASHEK
MALI
TAMASHEK
NIGER
ALGERIA
KANURI
HAUSA
NIGERIA
SONGHAI
TAMASHEK
FULA
DOGON
BURKINA FASO
BENIN
TOGO
M
F
WOLOF
FULA
SENEGAL
THE GAMBIA
GUINEA-BISSAU
FULA
SUSU
TEMNE
MENDE
SIERRA LEONE
BAMBARA
MALINKE
GUINEA
LIBERIA
DAN
DYULA
KRU
AKAN
CÔTE D'IVOIRE
GHANA
EWE
YORUBA
NUPE
EDO
IDOMA
IGBO
IJO
BANTOID
TIV
SEMI-BANTU
CAMEROON
EWONDO
FANG
0
500 km
West Atlantic Languages
Fula (F)
Mixed Fula, Adamawa & Chadic Languages
Mande Languages (M)
Kwa Languages
Voltaic Languages
Bantu & Bantoid Languages
National Languages:
MAURITANIA (Fr./Ar.)
SENEGAL (Fr.)
THE GAMBIA (Eng.)
GUINEA-BISSAU (Port.)
GUINEA (Fr.)
SIERRA LEONE (Eng.)
LIBERIA (Eng.)
CÔTE D'IVOIRE (Fr.)
MALI (Fr.)
BURKINA FASO (Fr.)
GHANA (Eng.)
TOGO (Fr.)
BENIN (Fr.)
NIGER (Fr.)
ALGERIA (Ar./Fr.)
NIGERIA (Eng.)
CAMEROON (Fr./Eng.)

WEST AFRICAN LANGUAGES AND PEOPLES

The following loose classification is a broad and selective breakdown of West Africa's larger people and language groups into separate ethno-linguistic identities. Although listed together by languages, not all the names here are distinct languages. These lists are intended only to provide anchorages for the different names you'll encounter. Additional names are closely related dialects. Names in brackets are alternatives.

Southern Area of Wider Affinity – "Niger–Congo" Languages

• WEST-ATLANTIC LANGUAGES •

Fula (Fulani, Peul, Fulbe), Tukulor, Bororo
Wolof
Temne
Serer
Sherbro, Bulom
Kissi
Limba

Jola (Diola), Fogny, Banjal
Balante
Pepel, Manjak
Gola
Baga
Tenda, Basari
Bijago (Bidyago)

• VOLTAIC LANGUAGES •

MORE/MOLE
Mossi
Dagomba
Mamprusi
Wala

SENUFO
Senoufo, Djimini, Karaboro
Minianka

GURMA
Gourmantché
Bassari, Tchamba
Moba

GRUSI
Gourounsi, Kassena, Sissala
Dagara (Dagarti)
Lilse, Fulse (Kurumba)
Frafra
Builsa
Wagala

TEM
Kabré (Kabyé) Logba, Tamberma, Lamba
Tem (Kotokoli, Cotocoli)

LOBI
Loron
Nabe
Gan
Koulango

HABE
Bobo, Bwaba, Kos, Siby
Dogon

BARGU
Somba (Betammaribe)
Bargu (Bariba)
Yowa

• KWA LANGUAGES •

KRU
Bete
Dida
Grebo
Krahn
Bakwe
Bassa

EDO
Edo
Bini
Isoko, Urhobo (Sobo)
Kukuruku

NUPE
Nupe
Igbira
Gwari, Koro

YORUBA
Yoruba, Oyo
Egba
Ijebu
Ekiti
Ife
Bunu
Itsekiri
Ana

IDOMA
Idoma
Igala
Egede
Iyala

IGBO
Igbo (Ibo), Onitsha

TWI LANGUAGES

AKAN
Twi (Asante)
Baulé
Fante
Agni
Abron
Akwapim
Guang

EWE
Fon, Adja, Xwala, Xuéda, Maxi
Ewe, Ang-lo
Ga-Adangme
Mina, Popo
Gun, Tofinu

CENTRAL TOGO
Akposso

LAGOON
Abé
Ajukru
Abidji
Alladian
Assini, Nzima
Ebrie

• EASTERN NIGRITIC LANGUAGES •

Fali	Mbum	Namshi	Longuda	Vere
Massa	Mundang	Chamba	Mumuye	Yungur

• IJO LANGUAGES •

Ijo (Ijaw) · Brass · Kalabari

• BANTOID LANGUAGES •

Ibibio, Efik, Anang	Birom	Jerawa
Mada	Ekoi, Oban	Anyang
Katab	Orri, Ukelle	Basa-Kaduna
Boki	Korup	Yergum
Kamberi	Dukakari	Jukun

MACRO-BANTU

Tiv · Jarawa · Mambila

NORTH-WESTERN BANTU

Ewondo (Yaoundé)	Duala (Douala)
Bulu, Fang, Eton	Bassa, Bakoko
Gbaya	Batanga
Sango-Ngbandi	Bakweri, Bimbia
Bakundu	

CAMEROON HIGHLANDS BANTU ("SEMI-BANTU")'

Ba-Miléké, -Djou, -Fang, -Foussam, -Mendjou, -Ngangté

Ba-	Ba-Fut
Moun (Bamoum, Bamum)	Tikar
Fia (Bafia)	Widekum
Nso (Bansaw)	Fungom
Li (Bali)	Ndop

Northern Area of Wider Affinity – "Afro–Asiatic" Languages

• ARABIC •

HASSANIYA

Berabish
Imragen
Kunta (Kounta)
Regeibat, Rehian
Tajakant, Arosien
Trarza
Zenaga, Chorfa, Tichit
Choa (Shoa)

• CHADIC LANGUAGES •

Hausa, Adrawa, Tazarawa	Wakura
Angas	Toupouri (Tuburi)
Bura	Wajawa
Kotoko (Longone)	Gude
Tangale	Gerawa
Mandara (Wandala)	Guizica, Mofou
Kapsiki (Margi)	Podoko
Matakam (Mafa)	Bata
Mauri	Mousgoum (Musgu)

• BERBER LANGUAGES •

Tamashek (Tuareg, Touareg)

• SAHARAN LANGUAGES •

Kanouri (Kanuri, Beriberi)

Songhaic Languages

Songhai (Sonray) · Dendi · Djerma (Zerma)

Mande Languages

NUCLEAR MANDE		***PERIPHERAL MANDE***	
Malinké (Mandinka, Mandingo)	Kuranko	Mende	Bussa (Busa)
Bambara	Diallonke (Yalunka)	Kpelle (Gerse)	Ngere (Guerze)
Soninke (Sarakolé)	Kasonke	Vai (Gallinas)	Kono
Susu (Sousou)	Konyanke	Dan, Gio, Mano, Guro	Sia
Dyula	Bozo	Loma (Toma), Buzi	Loko
	Kagoro	Samo	Gbande

Likewise, "j" is commonly spelt "dy" or "di" in French transcription. The French are keen on apostrophes everywhere, too. They don't usually mean any more than that someone found the word hard to pronounce. Finally, look out for prefixes or suffixes that may mean "people" ("Ba-" in the Bantu languages for example, or "-nke" in the Mande languages).

THE "SOUTHERN AREA OF WIDER AFFINITY"

The **Sawa group** includes the 400 **Bantu** languages that are spoken all over Central and Southern Africa. In West Africa, Bantu languages are only spoken in parts of southern Cameroon. Further west, the picture is much more complicated. The so-called **"West Atlantic"** languages, which include Wolof, Temne and Fula, are part of this grouping, though fairly distantly related to Bantu. Also part of the Sawa group is the **Kwa sub-family** of language clusters, which include the **Akan languages** (of which the Asante are the most famous speakers), the **Ewe languages** of Ghana and Togo and the **Yoruba** and **Igbo** language groups of Benin and Nigeria. To the north, the **Voltaic sub-family** of language clusters includes the **Senoufo**, **More** and **Lobi** groups of Côte d'Ivoire, Ghana and Burkina.

Many of the languages in the Sawa group have **class systems** (something like genders in French in that everything must agree) with up to 20 or more classes – Bantu languages are the classic examples. Many Sawa languages, too, are **tonal** – in which the pitch of a spoken word determines its meaning – and extra notations are often necessary when writing them properly.

THE "NORTHERN AREA OF WIDER AFFINITY"

The **Nawa group** includes most of the languages of North Africa, and the Middle East, including Hebrew, Arabic, Berber and Tamashek (the language of the Tuaregs). The most important languages in the area as far as West Africa is concerned are known as "Chadic", the biggest of which is **Hausa**, spoken by some twenty million people as a first language. Nawa languages are mostly non-tonal and classless, though many have masculine and feminine genders.

UNRELATED LANGUAGE GROUPS

The **Mande cluster of languages** doesn't belong to either area of wider affinity and, linguistically, it's on a classification level with both of them. The languages in this group are closely related and very old. Geographically, they're quite compact and appear to be centred in the Mali–Guinea border region – which, historically, was the heartland of the old Mande/Manding/Mali empire. From the linguistic point of view, the "nuclear Mande" family includes **Bamana**, **Malinke** (Mandinka), **Susu** and **Dyula**. This group is also known as "Mande-Tan" (after their word for "ten"). The languages of "Peripheral Mande" (or "Mande-Fu"), which deviate much more from the heartland languages, and from each other, include languages of Guinea, Sierra Leone and Liberia, such as **Mende**, **Dan-Gio** and **Vai**. Tones are important in this southern section, less so in the more mainstream Mande languages.

The **Songhai** of the middle Niger River are another old imperial people, with a language quite distinct from any other in Africa.

DIRECTORY

ADDRESSES The postman never comes in West Africa. Mail is sorted into PO Boxes (BP in French, CP in Portuguese) or sometimes into Private Mail Bags (PMB). The lower the number, usually, the older the address – sometimes a useful indication of credentials when making bookings or enquiries. Street addresses are often buildings, or blocks –*Immeuble*, often abbreviated to *Imm*, in French. *Your* address is likely to be much in demand – a stack of small address labels is very useful.

BEGGARS Beggars are part of town life, though not as much as you might realistically expect. Most are visibly destitute and many are blind, or victims of polio or accidents, or lepers or homeless mothers and children. Some have established pitches, others keep on the move. They are harassed by the police and often rounded up. Many people give to the same beggar on a regular basis and, of course, alms-giving is a requirement of Islam supposed to benefit the donor. Keep small change handy all the time – it will hardly dent your expenses.

There's no question of confusing real beggars with the incessant demands – in the more touristy parts of several of the Francophone countries – for "*cadeaux*", usually from children. These you simply have to devise strategies to deal with. Like heat and mosquitos, they seem to trouble new arrivals most.

CLOTHES Cotton is obviously the best material. Dirty-looking colours are best and clothes should be tough enough to stand repeated hand washing. Mostly you'll want to wear the minimum, but pack at least one warm jacket or sweater. Though you can buy clothes as you go, they'll rarely be less expensive than at home. Even "junk clothes" – "deadmen's clothes" shipped in bulk from Europe and the USA – which you'll find in every town, may be less pricey bought nearer to source. If you fancy kitting yourself up in local style, both cloth and tailoring are inexpensive.

People are generally very clothes-conscious. Ragged clothes and long hair on men don't go down well. Avoid absolutely any military-style, or army surplus, gear. Camouflage prints are out. And, however you dress, pack a set of "smart" clothes for difficult embassies and other important occasions.

Take the lightest, toughest, airiest footwear you can afford. Forget about waterproofs: all that plastic and nylon is too hot. You won't go out in the rain, and if you do, you'll get wet anyway.

ELECTRICITY When there is some, it is usually 220V AC 50Hz. Niger has 220V/380V AC 50Hz and Liberia 110V AC 60Hz. Only top hotels have shaver points or outlets in the rooms.

GIFTS It's very useful to have some tokens to give to people. Postcards of sights from home are appreciated by people who have little or no chance of possessing colour pictures. Pictures of you and your family are of tremendous value, too, while school kids are also delighted with ballpoint pens. However, you might consider visiting a school more formally, rather than just handing them out.

IVORY The elephants of West Africa are in such a dire predicament that little international effort is being made to save those isolated pockets still hanging on in remote bush against the poachers. Park boundaries aren't always much safeguard. Ivory is for sale in many West African cities, much of it carved in Hong Kong. And bracelets and bangles are widely touted. Tragically, it seems it's still a viable way to earn a living and will likely remain so as long as ivory itself remains unstigmatized. Although the following estimate of elephant numbers is now five years old, it's a frightening indication of the situation. Mauritania – 30, Guinea – 50, Senegal – 54, Sierra Leone – 100, Liberia – 100, Mali – 1000,

Niger – 400, Benin – 500, Ghana – 600, Nigeria – 1500, Burkina Faso – 1500, Côte d'Ivoire – 1600, Cameroon 17,000.

LAUNDRY Washing is always done by hand, in a stream with flat rocks by preference. You won't find laundromats, but there are plenty of people willing to do the job. Even the smallest hotel can arrange it. If you have any choice, dry your clothes indoors. Avoid spreading them on the ground if you can – they may be infested by the Tumbu fly which lays its eggs on wet clothes. Ironing kills the eggs.

STUDENT CARDS If you're 32 or under, do what you can to obtain an International Student Identity Card (ISIC) before you go. Student unions and a number of student-minded travel agents sell them. They're valid from the start of the autumn term until December 31 the following year. They're no guarantee of cheap deals, but are worth waving for many payments (airlines, railways, museum entrance fees) you may make. If you are a student it's useful also to have a rubber-stamped letter substantiating the fact.

TOILET PAPER This is usually provided by the user of the facilities rather than the owner. Never run out – using a jug of water and your hand takes more time to get used to than most people have.

WHAT TO TAKE: A FEW FINAL SUGGESTIONS

- A **pocket French dictionary** or phrase book is extremely useful. Try the new *Rough Guide to French* (£3.50/$5).
- **Binoculars** (the small, fold-up ones) are invaluable for game- and bird-watching.
- A multi-purpose **penknife** is essential, but avoid ones with blades longer than a palm-width which are sometimes confiscated.
- A **torch.**
- A **padlock** – vital in cheap hotels where doors don't lock properly.
- **Plastic bags** are invaluable – bin liners to keep dust off clothes, small sealable ones to protect cameras and film.
- If driving or hiking in remote areas, take a **compass**.
- **Camping gas stoves** are light and useful even if you're not camping. The cylinders are sold somewhere in every capital city.
- You might want to take your own pair of **flip flops** for hotel bathrooms and generally padding about, but these can be bought cheaply locally.
- A **sheet sleeping bag** (sew up a sheet) is essential for budget travel.
- A **mosquito net** – but don't spend a fortune: they're cheap to buy locally.
- A **sleeping bag** isn't much use since you'll sleep on top of it nine times out of ten anyway. If you do take one, get the best, most compressible bag you can afford – very useful for keeping film cool.
- If you shave, bring disposable **razors** (available only at import supermarkets) or preferably an old fashioned razor blade holder.
- **Tampons** are expensive and only available in big cities. Bring as many as you can be both-

PART TWO

THE GUIDE

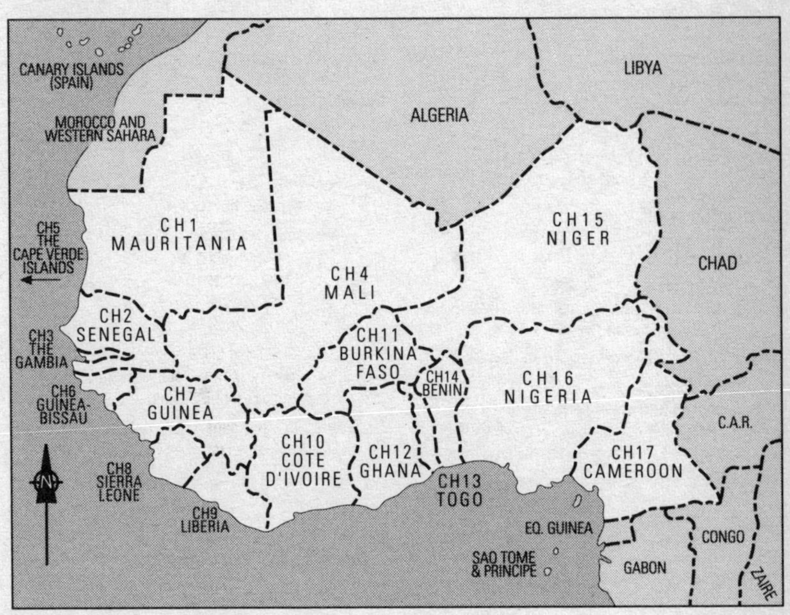

CHAPTER ONE

MAURITANIA

MAURITANIA

Scanning a map of West Africa, it's easy to see the vast obscurity of **Mauritania** as nothing but sand. Simple, too, to turn scraps of information on the country into preconceptions – of an austere, almost medieval nation, powered by Işlam, riven by racial hatred and flayed by drought. These stark images certainly have some foundation in reality, yet Mauritania comes as a revelation to most travellers: pleasantly laid-back, spacious and physically comfortable because of its dry climate, scenically dramatic in several regions and culturally complex, with its rock paintings, thousand-year-old mosques and deep-rooted class structure.

Although the southernmost region of the country – made up of the **Chemama** flood plain along the river and the hilly savannah triangle of **Gorgol-Guidimaka** – extends south to the same latitude as Dakar, this anomalous "green" region covers less than five percent of the territory and is progressively being nibbled away by the advancing desert. Apart from the rocky uplands of the north and centre – the **Adrar**, **Tagant** and **Assaba** massifs – the rest of Mauritania is indeed largely sand, and harsh, challenging territory in which to travel.

People

The country's name comes from its dominant ethnic group, the traditionally nomadic **Moors**, who speak the **Hassaniya** dialect of Arabic. The Moors are broadly divided into "white" **Bidan**, who claim ancestors from north of the Sahara, and "black" **Haratin**, whose physical ancestry lies in Saharan and sub-Saharan Africa and who were subjugated and "Arabized" by the Bidan. Traditionally, the Haratin were vassals to the noble classes, but some Haratin elevated themselves into an independent caste which owed no tribute. The formal abolition of slavery in 1980 decreed that all "ex-slaves" (usually called Abid) were henceforth to be known as "Haratin" – a source of offence to "real Haratin" and of confusion to outsiders.

This characterization oversimplifies the make-up of a very diverse and multifaceted population. **Social status** in Mauritania is considerably more than a question of skin colour. The white Moor community is divided broadly into Hassanes (noble families), Zouaya (or Tolba, the pious maraboutic caste) and Zenaga vassals (herders and cultivators). Status among black Moor families tends to be determined by their length of association and degree of intermarriage with white Moors. Within Hassaniya-speaking Moorish society, intermarriage has blurred racial distinctions and skin colour is ignored in many social contexts anyway.

FACTS AND FIGURES

The **République Islamique de Mauritanie** (often shortened to R.I.M.) covers over a million square kilometres, more than four times the size of Britain and nearly as big as California and Texas combined. The **population** of a little over two million gives it the lowest density in the world, but the eastern third of Mauritania is designated as *zone vide* (empty quarter) and there's heavy migration to the towns, to the south, and abroad. Mauritania's **foreign debt** is currently over £1.5 billion ($2.5 billion) – nearly five times the value of its annual earnings from the export of goods and services. The **government** is led by President Maawiya Ould Taya and his *Parti Républicain Démocratique et Social* (PRDS), which came to power after elections marred by fraud in 1991 and 1992.

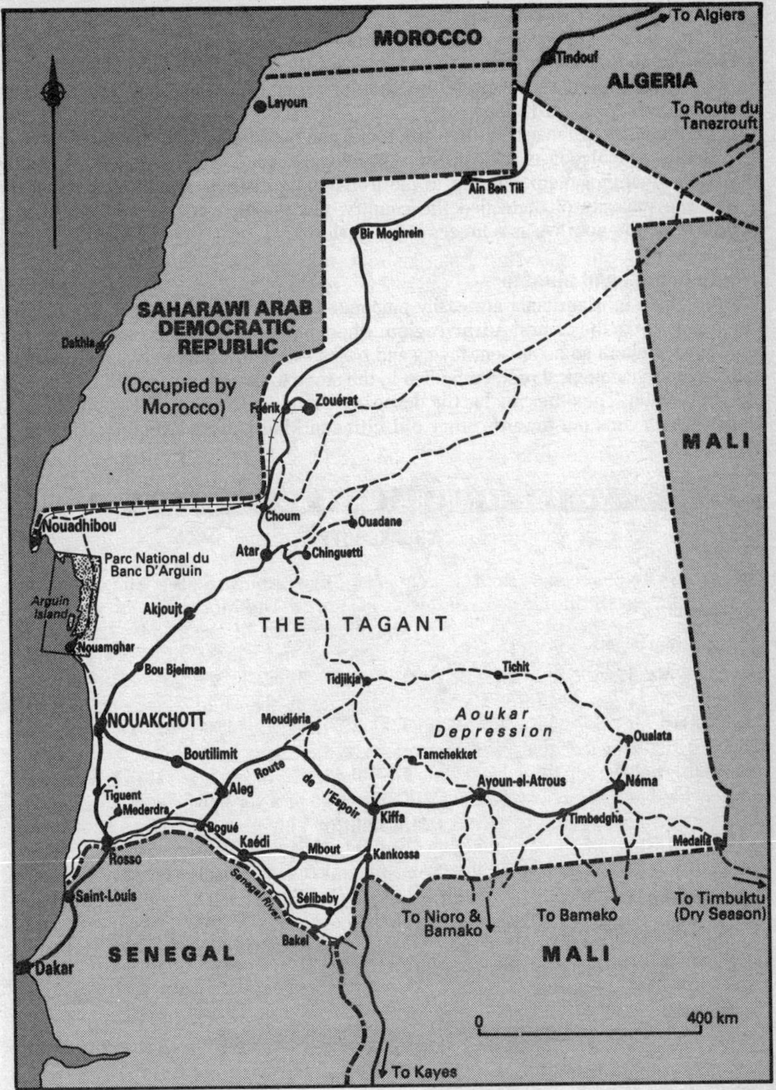

You can get an initial fix on the social complexities of Moorish society from the **position of women**, which is less rigidly defined than in most Arabic-speaking countries. Women may travel alone, drink tea with men, take an active part in male-dominated conversations and breast-feed their children in public; they rarely cover their faces, though they always cover their hair. The Berber and African heritage is apparent in these freedoms, which indicate the relative superficiality of the country's Arabic culture. In matters economic and political, however, women's freedom to act is widely curtailed.

Outside the Moorish community, the remaining forty percent of the population are southerners – *Soudaniens* in Mauritanian phraseology – speaking **Fula** (Pulaar), **Wolof** or **Soninke** and mostly farming and herding near the Senegalese and Malian borders. In Mauritania, the Fula-speakers of the Tukulor (Toucouleur) and Fula ethnic groups are known jointly as **Hal-Pulaar**.

In addition, Mauritania had, until the racial conflict of 1989 and the early 1990s, a considerable population of African **immigrant workers**, from as far afield as Guinea and Niger, many of them working in the iron-mining districts around Zouérat in the north. The majority of them fled the country, along with some 70,000 Mauritanian southerners who now live as refugees in Senegal.

Where to go – and climate

Travel targets in Mauritania are easily pinpointed. Two roads cut across the country. The first leads to the central **Adrar region**, where a rugged landscape softened by rolling dunes shelters some ancient towns and oases – Oujeft, Chinguetti and Ouadane – and a rich archaeological past, embodied in the stone tools and rock paintings found all over the region. The other road is the desperate-sounding **Route de l'Espoir** (Road of Hope), which runs out towards other **old cities** in Mauritania's inventory: Tidjikja, in

AVERAGE TEMPERATURES AND RAINFALL

NOUAKCHOTT

	Jan	Feb	Mar	Apr	May	June	July	Aug	Sept	Oct	Nov	Dec
Temperatures °C												
Min (night)	14	15	17	18	21	23	23	24	24	22	18	13
Max (day)	29	31	32	32	34	33	32	32	34	33	32	28
Rainfall mm	0	3	0	0	0	3	13	104	23	10	3	0
Days with rainfall	0	1	0	0	0	1	1	3	3	1	1	0

NOUADHIBOU

	Jan	Feb	Mar	Apr	May	June	July	Aug	Sept	Oct	Nov	Dec
Temperatures °C												
Min (night)	12	13	14	14	15	16	18	20	20	19	16	14
Max (day)	26	28	27	27	28	30	27	30	33	30	28	25
Rainfall mm	0	0	0	0	0	0	0	0	8	12	3	10

ATAR

	Jan	Feb	Mar	Apr	May	June	July	Aug	Sept	Oct	Nov	Dec
Temperatures °C												
Min (night)	12	13	17	19	22	27	25	26	26	23	17	13
Max (day)	31	33	34	39	40	42	43	42	42	38	33	29
Rainfall mm	3	0	0	0	0	3	8	30	28	3	3	0

the **Tagant region**, and Tichit and Oualata, further east on the fringe of the country's empty quarter. Dotted with ragged, newer, settlements on its way, the Route de l'Espoir is tarred its full eleven hundred kilometres, and provides an alternative route to Mali if you're driving from Senegal.

Nouakchott, the capital, is a nearly inevitable but unremarkable transit point, while **Nouadhibou**, the second largest town, is finding new significance as the point of entry to West Africa for overland vehicles since the closure of the Algerian trans-Sahara routes. Ships and flights between Nouadhibou and the **Canary Islands** are not excessively expensive, while the rail line linking Nouadhibou with central Mauritania makes for an unusual trip. Nouakchott and Nouadhibou, incidentally, both have **beaches** that seem to go on forever.

Wherever you go in Mauritania, you'll find a release from the freneticism of lands further south, and **travel conditions** generally more peaceful than elsewhere in West Africa. The worthwhile goals make travelling around attractive, and the desert journeys are a fair substitute for actually crossing the Sahara. Alcohol is effectively banned, though one or two hotels serve drinks. Throughout the country, other travellers are fairly rare.

When to visit is conditioned more by burning temperatures than disruptive rainfall. The coast is cooled by sea breezes, but you'd probably want to avoid the interior between April and October – see the climate table for Atar, and remember these daytime figures are averages: the thermometer often pips 50°C in the shade. The **southwest** gets oppressive humidity and occasional cloudbursts between July and October. At this time dirt roads can be cut – especially near the Senegal River – and transport off the paved highway can be very difficult. Nouadhibou and the **north** get an occasional shower during the European winter, and very occasionally a summer torrent if the clouds drift far enough north. Otherwise rain is a very scarce commodity.

Arrivals

The land route from Morocco, which for many years was closed because of the war in Western Sahara, has recently reopened and is now the only viable way of entering West Africa overland from North Africa.

■ Flights from Africa

Apart from *Air Gambia* (CK) and *Air Mauritanie* (MR), which link Nouakchott with **Banjul** every Fri & Sun and Sat, respectively, and the Thurs & Sun links with **Dakar** on MR, the only airline flying to Nouakchott from the rest of West Africa is *Air Afrique* (RK), which flies in from Dakar on Tues & Fri and usually operates a flight from **Niamey**, **Abidjan**, **Ouagadougou** and **Bamako** on Thurs. *Air Algérie* (AH) flies every Wed from Algiers via **Casablanca** to Nouakchott and back. Also from Casablanca is a Thurs flight on *Royal Air Maroc* (AT) and a Mon flight via Nouadhibou on MR.

■ Overland

You'll generally find Mauritanian **border officials** straight dealing, if occasionally pedantic, but not often ostentatiously corrupt. There's a gauntlet of police and customs checks along the Rosso–Nouakchott highway but they rarely bother tourists. Across the rest of the country, *postes de contrôle* are relatively few.

From Morocco

Since late 1992, the Moroccan authorities have been allowing convoys of overland vehicles to continue south of Dakhla to the Mauritanian border (see "Red Tape" overleaf for the details). At least twice a week (Tuesdays and Fridays on current information) a convoy of anything up to sixty vehicles makes the trip south along the **Atlantic route** with a soldier to escort them. Mauritania's official line on this is that the area immediately north of their frontier is too dangerous for travel because of unexploded land mines.

The details in these practical information pages are essentially for use on the ground in West Africa and in Mauritania itself: for full practical coverage on preparing for a trip, getting here from outside the region, paperwork, health, information sources and more, see *Basics* pp.3–88

They therefore allow entry to anyone arriving from Morocco, rather than sending them back across the "minefield", by the same token, they have not so far allowed any travel in the other direction, north into Morocco.

The southbound **route** itself is straightforward – you'll even see confident-looking distance signs for "Dakar". There's a regular overlanders' camping spot 28km north of Dakhla, or, in the town try the good-value *Hôtel Doubs* on the left as you arrive. From Dakhla, the first ninety percent of the 450-kilometre road south to Nouadhibou is in reasonable condition, much of it hard-surfaced. At the Moroccan frontier itself, you enter the "minefield" with some bad sand and rough bitumen, followed by the Moroccans' sand wall defensive works, which you can only cross on sand mats. After exit formalities there's more or less a day's travel to negotiate only 35km of sandy *piste* to the Mauritanian border post, a few kilometres north of Nouadhibou.

From Mali

From Mali, routes into Mauritania are only from **the south**: there are no official border crossings on Mauritania's long eastern frontier. The principal crossing is Bamako–Nioro–Ayoun, with a less-used route running Bamako–Nara–Néma (or Timbedgha). Few travellers use these, and you'll find little preparedness for nationals of countries other than Mali and Mauritania. You should therefore hasten to a police *commissariat* at Néma, Timbedgha or Ayoun and make sure you get the stamp you need. The Tuareg conflict has affected the southeast of Mauritania to some degree and there have been clashes and raids. Keep your ears open and don't proceed without being sure the route is safe. The lack of banks in eastern Mauritania makes it hard to operate the closed economy, so you will have to change money unofficially one way or another (see "Money and Costs", below).

From Senegal

The main crossing point **from Senegal** is Rosso, near the mouth of the Senegal river. The car ferry makes the five-minute crossing throughout the day, except between noon and 3pm, when the crew take a lunch break – as does the small currency exchange booth on the Mauritanian side. If you're on foot, you can take a *pirogue* at any time of the day. Other possible border crossings from Senegal are covered in that chapter.

Red Tape

Visas to enter Mauritania are required by most nationalities except West Africans, French and Italians. If you apply for a visa after you've left your own country, you'll probably have to provide a letter of introduction from your local embassy before one will be issued. Some Mauritanian embassies will direct you to get a visa from the "country of embarkation" (in other words the one you'll be leaving immediately before entering Mauritania).

Visa prices and durations vary considerably from embassy to embassy and even from one applicant to the next, but they are generally valid from the date of issue for a limited period only. Ask the price, get a receipt, and check what you've paid against the fiscal stamps stuck into your passport. In several embassies, a little discussion about Mauritania's historic sites can quickly break the ice and you may find some room for manoeuvre over the price of the visa, which otherwise can easily run to CFA2000 per day of your stay.

Mauritanian paperwork in Morocco

If you're planning to travel south along the Atlantic coast of Morocco and enter Mauritania at Nouadhibou, you're best advised to obtain your visa *before* arriving in Morocco. You might be able to get one from the Mauritanian embassy in Rabat but policy on issuing them varies – you might instead, be directed to their embassy in Algiers a city you should avoid at present. If Rabat is issuing visas, you'll need the usual letter from your embassy (Australians should get letters of recommendation from the Canadian embassy in Rabat) – and try to apply for the visa on a Monday morning, as it can take several days.

You also need authorization to travel south of Dakhla. You may either get this from the Ministry of the Interior in Rabat, or be told to get it on arrival in Dakhla.

Mauritanian embassies in West Africa

There are **Mauritanian embassies** in West Africa in Dakar, Bamako, Abidjan, Lagos (or Abuja) and Banjul. It's useful to know, however, that wherever there's no Mauritanian embassy, **French embassies' visa services** are usually authorized to cover Mauritania. In this case, the whole procedure is generally cheaper and quicker.

Visas for onward travel

There's **no Malian embassy** in Nouakchott. If you're heading straight for Mali but not equipped with a visa, it's probably worth trying the border anyway – which is unsophisticated – with the intention of sorting things out when you get to Bamako. Otherwise, you'd have to detour to Dakar first. The **French embassy** in Nouakchott issues visas on behalf of a number of other Francophone countries, and there is also a **Senegal Embassy**.

Money and Costs

Mauritania's currency is the Ouguiya (or Uguiya) Mauritanien (UM, Oug, Ug), divided into 5 khoums (which you never see). It gradually lost value against the CFA franc, on which it was originally based (1 khoum to 1 franc CFA), but with the 1994 devaluation of the CFA it's now virtually back to the old parity again: UM200 = £1; UM130 = $1. Although the economy is closed, prohibiting the export and import of Ouguiya, there's only a limited black market. Notes come in denominations of UM100, UM200 and UM1000, with coins of UM1, UM5, UM10 and UM20.

At the airports and main land entry points you'll be given a **currency declaration form** to complete, which usually has to be handed in on departure. At minor borders you may not be given one, and it's best to straighten your affairs at the first large town rather than risk a potential problem on departure. Fortunately the forms are rarely checked.

Notionally, there is also a UM4000 minimum daily expenditure requirement: a sign at the airport bank in Nouakchott stipulates that any shortfall in expenditure may be forfeited on departure. Again, this seems to be hardly ever enforced.

Outside of Nouakchott, **banks** are few and very far between. Nouadhibou, Atar, Rosso, Bogué, Kaédi, Kiffa, Ayoun el Atrous and Néma all have banks. The biggest network, with six branches, is the *Banque Internationale pour la Mauritanie* (*BIMA*), the Mauritanian division of the West African *BIAO*. Banks are free to set their own exchange rates, so it's worth shopping around: the *Banque Nationale de Mauritanie* tends to give the best. You can also change hard currency on the fairly open black market, at least in Nouadhibou, where a few changers hang around outside the police station. Although there's little premium over the banks rates, it takes five minutes instead of more than an hour in the bank.

There has only recently been any *American Express* representation (see Nouakchott and Nouadhibou listings) and **credit cards** are accepted only by a few airlines and hotels in the capital. You can't get credit card cash advances.

Note that the **CFA franc** is no longer a convertible currency and is **not accepted** by banks or hotels, though you may still be able to change CFA unofficially.

■ Costs

Daily living costs are somewhat higher than in Senegal or Mali. With distances long, travel can be costly, and there are virtually no cheap hotels. If you're content to sleep on a mattress under the stars, in a tea house or, most obviously, in someone's home, you'll find costs bearable. For more on accommodation, see below.

There's no avoiding high **transport costs**, though these may fluctuate with the cycle of date harvests and pastoral migration. (Prices generally escalate if you travel *away* from the attraction.) You can quite easily spend £20 (US$30) on a day's travel. As a broad guide, expect to pay around UM300 per 100km on tarred roads and up to two to three times as much on dirt roads and desert *pistes*. Prices are fixed on what could be considered "scheduled runs", and you won't be overcharged. Baggage, as usual, is another matter. And if you want to get to out-of-the-way sites and towns, transport costs can quickly become exorbitant. The cheapest option is to wait for a vehicle that's going anyway.

Health

Mauritanian officials are quite keen on health certificates and may ask you to show your yellow fever certificate at checkpoints.

The most critical feature of travel in Mauritania from a health aspect, however, is the size of the country and the **isolation** of most towns and villages. You'll often be *very* far off the beaten track, and here, more than anywhere else in West Africa, you must have **repatriation insurance** in case of accident or sudden illness.

Beware of **dangerous vehicles** being used for relatively rough desert and mountain passages. In the north and east, spare parts for vehicles are very hard to obtain and the scarcity of vehicles keeps many in use long after their safe life.

Treat **water** with suspicion – reserves are usually low, and domestic animals depend on them too. It's good practice to carry a five-litre container and refill it at every opportunity.

Fresh camel or goat's **milk** (*zrig*) is often offered to guests and it's probably best to limit your consumption: although tuberculosis is a very minor risk (even in the case of fresh Zebu cow's milk), brucellosis and hepatitis A can be contracted from infected milk. Your hosts' health is probably the best criterion for deciding.

The **malaria** risk is generally slight, except along the Senegal river, where it's as high as anywhere in West Africa. Roughly north of a line from Nouakchott to Tidjikja it's not reckoned to occur at all, but unless you're based in the north for a long period, there's no point in breaking your course of anti-malarial pills.

Hospitals and treatment facilities outside Nouakchott are strapped. Some of the southern towns have regional hospitals/health centres, but the north, apart from Atar and Nouadhibou, has almost no public health provision.

Pharmacies, however, are a major growth industry in Nouakchott and in the interior. These days they're often well stocked with a range of items, including medicines that most European doctors would hesitate to prescribe. Sanitary towels and disposable nappies are also on sale everywhere in Nouakchott and up-country.

Maps and Information

The *IGN* 1:2,500,000 (1993) map of Mauritania is too small a scale to be useful for serious exploration, and not really much better than the *Michelin* 953. However, the *IGN* 1:1,000,000 topographical surveys published in the 1960s are still available from their French headquarters (136 bis, rue de Grenelle, 75700, Paris) and might be obtained, or ordered, through one of the map suppliers listed in *Basics* on p.42.

There are no Mauritanian tourist offices, indeed no ministry that ever holds responsibility for tourism for more than a year or two. The current *Direction du Tourisme* (BP 246

Nouakchott; ☎53337) at the Ministry of Commerce, Small Industries and Tourism offers a "guide touristique" with perfunctory paragraphs in English. There's also a *Mauritanie* guide in the full-colour *Aujourd'hui* series from Editions Jeune Afrique – more mouth-watering than practical.

Getting Around

Most transport in Mauritania is by Land Rover, though *taxis brousse* operate on the few main highways. Otherwise, air travel is a useful option. The railway system – a single line for the iron ore train in the far north – is more of an adventure than an ordinary form of transport, but still a useful link between Nouadhibou and the rest of the country.

Road transport

The main **public transport** – between Rosso and Nouakchott, along the *Route de l'Espoir* to Néma, and north to Atar – is **Peugeot 504**, carrying nine passengers (six to Rosso). Be prepared for long, dust-blown journeys, frequent breakdowns, lack of water, and no toilet stops. Riding in the back of trucks, along these same routes, is slower, but scarcely any less comfortable, and a good deal cheaper. Fares are normally paid in advance, so if there's a breakdown you have to stick with the vehicle until it's fixed or the driver buys a place for you in another.

Between Nouakchott and Nouadhibou, trucks and Land Rovers run along the shore to Nouamghar, then turn inland to follow the railway line for the last 100km.

South of the paved *Route de l'Espoir*, in the far south, a conventional *taxi brousse* network operates on most roads, most of the year. The vehicles are generally *404 bâchés*, but Peugeot 504 drivers work on some routes, especially between Rosso and Kaédi. The new tarred road from Aleg to Bogué is transforming that part of the river's flood plain.

Road journeys **off the main routes** are arduous, with soft sand the recurring problem. Conditions are detailed in the main guide section. If you're driving yourself, you should treat Mauritania north of the *Route de l'Espoir* exactly as you would a trans-Saharan *piste*. In many respects, because of the scarcity of other travellers, the routes are tougher and more dangerous.

PUBLIC TRANSPORT ROUTES

Nouakchott–Rosso: frequent, 3–5hr

Nouakchott–Atar: up to 12 daily, 8–12hr

Atar–Choum: 3–6 daily, 4–5hr

Atar–Chinguetti (4WD and trucks only): 3–6 weekly, 4–7hr

Nouakchott–Kaédi: several daily, 7–8hr

Nouakchott–Ayoun el Atrous: 1 or more daily, 16–20hr

Nouakchott–Nouadhibou (4WD and trucks only): 2–6 weekly, 30–50hr

The *piste* between the Tagant plateau and the Adrar (connecting Tidjikja with Atar), and the myriad tracks along the coast, are notorious. If you've no room to carry local people to guide you (never a problem to find), don't set off on little-trodden trails into the desert. The Mauritanians are not used to tourists' follies and nobody may think to prevent you from going – or search for you if you don't arrive.

Car rental, available only in Nouakchott, is as expensive as you'd expect. Since there's pressure to take a driver at little extra cost, it's often indistinguishable from a personalized "safari" arrangement. Keep your fuel tanks and spare jerry cans full. Off the main routes, **petrol**, when available, is around European prices, at about UM80–100 per litre (UM320–400 per US gallon).

Rail and air

Alternatives to road travel are worth using if the opportunity arises. If your point of arrival in Mauritania is Nouadhibou, the **train** from there to Zouérat is a good way into the country, and you can hop off in Choum, only 100km short of the Adrar plateau and a further day's travel down to Nouakchott. You can take vehicles on this train at reasonable rates (details on p.138).

Air travel makes sense if time is short (the longest flight is under 2hr), and fares are surprisingly reasonable. *Air Mauritanie*'s current domestic schedule, using the same two Fokker F-28 jets that are used on its international services, includes either one or two round-trip flights every day between Nouakchott (NKC) to Nouadhibou (NDB), plus:

Mon: NKC–**Atar**–NDB–**Atar**–NKC

Tues: NKC–**Tidjikja**–NKC NKC–NDB–**Zouérat**–NDB–NKC

Wed: NKC–**Sélibaby**–**Kaédi**–**Sélibaby**–NKC
Thurs: NKC–**Atar**–**Zouérat**–**Atar**–NKC
Fri: NKC–**Néma**–(Ayoun el Atrous)*–NKC
Sat: NKC–NDB–**Atar**–NKC
Sun: NKC–**Sélibaby**–(Kiffa)*–NKC

*Note that calls at Ayoun el Atrous and Kiffa are provisional and depend on demand.

Examples of **fares** from Nouakchott are: Atar UM5400, Kaédi UM4600, Néma UM8900, Nouadhibou UM6120 and Tidjikja UM5300.

Accommodation

Mauritania's hotels generally resemble Moroccan or Middle Eastern establishments and are fine if you're not short of money. The minimum price you can expect to pay for a room is about UM1500, with most hotels charging upwards of UM2500. Payment is always in advance, and you leave your passport with reception. Nouakchott has about a dozen hotels, and there's a handful in Nouadhibou, but most other large towns have just one or two, if that.

Travellers tend to rely on the **hospitality** of Mauritanians or expatriate residents. Moorish hospitality is legendary and you'll be well looked after by taxi drivers and other casual acquaintances across the country. Money will rarely be accepted as a gift, so you may want to carry cigarettes and lighters, pens and watches, tea and instant coffee.

Several Catholic **missions** have, in the past, been exceptionally helpful to travellers, and one or two are still generous, but many are pulling out of the country. The American **Peace Corps** may put you up. Several of their *Maisons de Passage* are open to outsiders, at slightly higher prices than to volunteers (still extremely cheap), on the understanding that they aren't hotels and volunteers always have preference.

Camping out, as long as you have access to water, is always a fine option. A tent is rarely necessary.

Eating and Drinking

Mauritania doesn't come up with much food that's memorable, but food is much more widely available than a few years ago. A number of small supermarkets and comestibles are well stocked with a range of consumables and household commodities,

ACCOMMODATION PRICE CODES

Hotel prices in this chapter are coded according to the following scales – the same scales in terms of their pound/dollar equivalents as are used throughout the book. Prices refer to the rate you can expect to pay for a room with two beds. Single rooms, or single occupancy, will normally cost at least two-thirds of the twin-occupancy rate. For further details see *Basics*, p.51.

① **Under UM1000 (under £5/$7.50)**. In practice, you're unlikely to find anything as cheap as this in Mauritania.

② **UM1000–2000 (£5–10/$7.50–15).** Rudimentary lodging, perhaps with some rooms self-contained (S/C: private shower, or bath, and toilet).

③ **UM2000–4000 (£10–20/$15–30).** Basic lodging, usually offering S/C rooms, maybe some with AC (air-conditioning); breakfast included.

④ **UM4000–6000 (£20–30/$30–45).** Mod-est, but adequate hotel with S/C, AC rooms, breakfast included.

⑤ **UM6000–8000 (£30–£40/$45–60).** Tourist or business-class establishment.

⑥ **UM8000–10,000 (£40–50/$60–75).** Up-market, with close to international standards and facilities.

⑦ **Over UM10,000 (over £50/$75).** Luxury, cosmopolitan establishment.

ACCOMMODATION ABBREVIATIONS

AC Air-conditioning, air-conditioned
S/C Self-contained, with private shower or bath, and toilet
B&B Bed and breakfast
HB Half board, meaning dinner, bed and breakfast
FB Full board, meaning all meals included

even in regional centres in the interior – although the choice there is much more limited. There's no need to worry about stocking up with food supplies before a trip to Mauritania, but within the country, you'd certainly want to take in some provisions for longer trips off the beaten track.

Restaurants don't exist much outside Nouakchott and Nouadhibou, though there are chop-house eateries in most towns, sometimes run by immigrants from other parts of West Africa.

Bread (French style) is usually in good supply. Main meals are invariably **rice**-based. Towns with flourishing gardens often have potatoes, carrots and onions. **Mutton**, **camel meat** and **chicken** are standard fare, as too is **fish**, usually dried and re-cooked. Lebanese-style grilled *chawarma* (pressed mutton slices) is quite common. More expensive eating houses tend towards Moroccan *couscous* dishes and *tajine* stews. If you eat with Mauritanians, **milk** (fresh, known as *zrig* – often diluted and sweetened – or curdled) often figures prominently.

As for fruit, **dates** are cheapest after the August and September harvest; Middle Eastern imports are generally better quality, and more expensive. Other fruit is limited to what comes over the border from Senegal or Mali (seasonal shipments of mangoes and more frequent truckloads of oranges) and what's grown in the far south of Mauritania itself – the whole range of tropical fruit from bananas to papaya and sugar cane. Nouakchott now has many fruit stalls with a good selection of local and European fruit, though you'll pay around UM250/kg for the former and perhaps UM600 for the latter.

Vegetarian travellers in Mauritania have quite a hard time of it – quantities of **eggs** are served to non-flesh-eaters in homes and restaurants.

Drinking is a serious business – not alcohol, which has ceased to be sold in public places, but **tea**. Moors take their green tea often and seriously. Even more than in Mali or Niger, a few small glasses of scalding, bitter-sweet yellow froth are part of the daily round. There's invariably a shortage of glasses: throw yours back to the tea-maker as soon as you've drained it. Despite the insistence of the tourist literature, it's only rarely taken with mint. Travelling by taxi, the driver will usually foot the small tea bill for his passengers at rest-stops.

Communications – Post, Phones, Languages & Media

The main PTTs are in Nouakchott and Nouadhibou (Nouakchott's PTT is open every day), and there's not much of a telecommunications service outside these towns – Zouérat, Atar and Kaédi are passable exceptions. Poste restante is reliable but slow.

Phoning or faxing abroad is reasonably efficient: there is now IDD to the whole world. But communication is expensive even by Francophone standards and even with the plethora of public telephone and fax shops that have sprung up over the last two years. Britain and the USA may be difficult to contact for long periods from inside Mauritania but there is no trouble getting Mauritania from abroad. Rates are roughly UM300/minute to Francophone West Africa and the USA and UM400/minute to Europe.

Mauritania's IDD code is ☎222. Note that "2" is technically the town code for all Mauritanian towns. As it is not used within the country, however, the country code is effectively 2222.

Languages

Mauritania's most widespread languages are Hassaniya Arabic and French, though the latter is less popular – and slightly less widely acceptable – than formerly. Other languages are mostly concentrated in the non-Moorish regions of the far south and include Fula or Fulfulde, Wolof and the old Mande tongue known as Soninke or Sarakole.

The media

Just a few years ago, the *Bulletin of the Chamber of Commerce* was listed as one of the four main national periodicals and *Chaab*, the only daily paper, was eight pages of dull African and world news and rambling articles about Mauritanian development. Since free elections in 1992 the press has been liberalized and there are now a good half-dozen **daily papers**. Most still tend to serve up the same bland mix of news and articles about drought and the doings of the élite, but one or two are startlingly anti-Establishment. Look

HASSANIYA – SOME BASICS

Hassaniya, the language of the Hassanes and the sole language of the Moors, is a strongly Berberized form of Arabic. It's recently, and controversially, become the official language of the country, usurping less divisive French for many purposes.

Moorish Mauritanians have an elaborate greeting ritual which they go through with resignation or enthusiasm depending on their mood. Farewells, on the other hand, are brief and free of sentiment.

GREETINGS

Lyak la bas – Hope you have no bad.

La bas – I have no bad, usually followed by numerous *lyaks*, eg *Lyak mo a vin* – Hope you have no sickness. If you want to end the *lyak* sequence try:

Mar Abah – So be it.

Mah Salaam – Goodbye.

Sh'halak is an informal "How are you?" that doesn't lead to anything much.

Il hum did illai – Praise be to God. (Stick it on the end of sentences – something like *Insh Allah* when talking about the future. *Il hum did illai* rolls off the tongue. You'll hear it a lot if you listen out.)

Salaam Alaikum – Peace be with you.

Alaikum Salaam – And also with you.

Sho'kran – Thank you (hardly used).

A phrase for "Please" is never used.

OTHER PHRASES

Where is?	*Mynayn?*
What time is it?	*Waqt shin hoo?*
That's OK/enough (if someone's serving you something for example)	*Kavi*
In the name of God (said before eating or starting something)	*Bismalai*
Yes	*Ahey*
No	*Abdei*
No, by God!	*Walahi!* or *Man Allah!*
Come here	*Wahai*
Tomorrow	*Subh*
Yesterday	*Yemes*
Today	*Ilyom*
I am going to Nouakchott	*Ana nymshee shawr Nouakchott*
I am going to the market	*Ana nymshee shawr Ana min Ingletra*
I am English	*Vondeg*
Hotel	*An dak?*
Do you have?	*Halig?*
Is there?	*Ilma*
Water	*Lukil*
Food	*Nasrani*
White person/tourist	*Zaiyn*
Good	*Hutt zaiyn*
Very good	*Mal zaiyn*
Not good	*Kem?*
How much is?	*Ingus shwei*
A little less (to knock down the price)	*Shwei shwei*
A little (or "slowly")	*Ana stuk fai*
I am full	*Ana v'tran*
I am tired (male)	*Ana v'trana*
I am tired (female)	*Beshar*
Take it easy	*marsa*

If you're very displeased with something or someone, try *Gassa Ramarak* ("May God shorten your life"); use carefully, it's used a lot with disobedient kids.

Ski (with a short "i") is an expression of satisfaction, usually followed by a hand slap.

NUMBERS

1	*Wahid*	3	*Ethnayn*	5	*Hamsa*	7	*Seb'a*	9	*Tesa'a*
2	*Athlath*	4	*Arba'a*	6	*Setta*	8	*Thimayna*	10	*Ashara*

out for *Mauritanie Demain*, *Mauritanie Nouvelle*, *Al Bayane* and *Eveille Hebdo*.

You'll find French newspapers and magazines around Nouakchott and Nouadhibou, but only second-hand copies of English-language ones. The *Novotel* in Nouakchott may carry them.

The state-run *ORTM* radio and TV network broadcasts **radio** in French and Hassaniya with some programmes in Fula, Wolof and Sarakole/Soninke. **Television** has exploded in recent years, and even the current-starved *bidonvilles* around Nouakchott have

A MAURITANIAN GLOSSARY

Aftout Seasonal water course or flood zone

Aklé Zone of jumbled, live dunes

Barkane Moving, crescent-shaped dune with characteristic "crest"

Barrad Teapot

Boubou Loose cotton shirt or cloak

Chemama Flood plain of the Senegal River

Dahr/dhar Fault line (cliffs or escarpment)

Darrah Boubou (see above)

Erg District of shifting ("live") sand dunes

Girba Goatskin waterbag

Guelb Isolated mountain or peak

Guetna Date harvest

Hal-Pulaar Fula-speaking people, including Fula and Tukulor

Houli Man's headscarf, turban

Kas Drinking glass

Kedia Long tableland, mesa

L'msal Prayer ground

Mehlafa Women's long upper wrap/headscarf

Nsara Nazarene/Christian: white person (pl. *Nsarani*)

Reg Flat gravel, windblown sand plain

Rifi Hot wind from the north

Sebkha Dry, salt plain

Sirwal Loose, cotton pantaloons

Tabel Tea tray

Tishtar Dried meat, usually gazelle

Tell Hill covering the ruins of a former settlement

Zrig Sweet, diluted milk

battery-driven sets. Mauritanian TV's style of presentation is distinctively national – no jackets and ties on these presenters. The news and "cultural" programmes you'd expect are interrupted by the occasional French soccer match. Most hotels, even down-market ones, have a satellite dish, though blurred *Canal France International* – hour-long interviews with the French prime minister and puerile game shows – isn't likely to occupy you for long.

Arts and Culture

Independent artistic expression is rather rare in Mauritania, where "culture" is expected to reflect state religion (hence the Ministry of Culture and Islamic Orientation).

Cinema has a beacon in the shape of exiled director **Med Hondo**. His 1969 film *Soleil Ô* was a bleak and somewhat plodding mix of *cinema verité* and weird set pieces, dealing with African immigrants in France; more recently, with Burkinabe backing, he made the impressive historical epic *Sarraounia*, about a queen who resisted both the colonialists and the Muslims.

Theatre is non-existent, as is any accessible **literature** (certainly none in English translation). There's a little more hope for **musical culture**, though at present it's not a lively scene. At best, it combines soulful, Arab singing with complicated picking and rapid clapping that makes the Berber antecedents of flamenco music clear. One of the best-known groups is headed by **Dimi Mint Abba** and **Khalifa Ould Eide** – they've made several foreign tours – but you'd have to be unusually lucky to catch a show in Mauritania itself. **Malouma** is another famous woman singer – she supported Ahmed Ould Daddah in his failed presidential bid in 1992.

Wildlife and National Parks

Mauritania's **wildlife** has been depleted by hunting and the spread of the desert. Formerly, the south had a good cross-section of West African savannah animals, including elephants, giraffes, cheetahs, leopards, lions, and several species of antelope. The giraffes, cheetahs and lions have gone, but there are still a few **leopards** and there are said to be small numbers of **elephants** (small in stature too), hiding out in the hilly bush country between Kaédi and Ayoun el Atrous.

The uninhabited eastern desert is one of the last refuges of the endangered **addax antelope**, an extraordinary survivor – which, with careful husbandry could become a source of domestic protein in an otherwise empty environment. Other species include **mouflon** (wild sheep) in the Adrar, and gazelles and oryx antelope scattered through the north; the occasional family of **ostriches** in the southeast; and very rare **monk seals** at Nouadhibou. You'll see plenty of

camels, but these, like all of Africa's dromedaries, are domesticated.

For naturalists, the country's biggest potential attraction is the migratory **birdlife** of the isolated sandbanks and seashore in the country's only national park – the **Parc National du Banc d'Arguin**, south of Nouadhibou. This is one of the world's great bird breeding sites, with millions of water birds nesting and raising their chicks here from April to July and October to January. The migrants include greater (and, uncommonly, lesser) **flamingos**, both grey and white **pelicans**, white-breasted **cormorants**, several species of **heron** and **egret**, European **spoonbills**, grey-headed and unusual slender-billed **gulls**, Caspian, royal and gull-billed **terns** and several species of waders. **Turnstones** come here in winter to scavenge the eggs of tropical birds. Fortunately for the birds (regrettably for birders) the national park is highly inaccessible and requires a major outlay in funds for the 4WD vehicles, boats and guides necessary to visit it. If you're really determined, contact M. Ahmed Ould Ghanallah, Ministre de la Pêche et de l'Économie Maritime, BP 137 Nouakchott (☎52476) or M. Mahfoud Ould Dach, Ministre du Développement Rural, BP 170 Nouakchott (☎51836). The park is administered from Nouadhibou where there's a permit-issuing office for the suitably equipped.

Directory

AIRPORT DEPARTURE TAX None.

CRAFTS AND MARKETS Mauritania is famous for stylishly refined **carpets**, woven in Nouakchott. Sadly these are impractical purchases for most travellers, as are the brass-fitted, dark stained **wooden chests** and **camel saddles**. But there's quite a desirable selection of **jewellery** in silver (cheap) and amber (not so), tobacco **pipes** and pouches, **sandals**, and printed cotton **cloth** (good value). In the Adrar and Tagant, children and market sellers hawk neolithic stone **arrow heads** and tools. You can turn up medieval glass **trading beads** as well, though these are becoming internationally sought after and increasingly rare. Be prepared to find bargaining hard work: jocularity doesn't always hit the right mark.

HOLIDAYS Apart from those decreed by the **Islamic lunar calendar**, which are followed everywhere, Mauritania's public holidays are: **January 1**, **February 26** (National Reunification day), **May 1** (Labour day), **May 25** (African Liberation day), **July 10** (Army day), **November 28** (National day) and **December 12** (anniversary of the 1984 coup). **December 25** is an office holiday, but you'll find most commercial doors open. Don't forget the week starts on Sunday, with Friday and Saturday the weekend.

NAMES You'll quickly notice almost all Moors retain traditional names. *Ould* and *Mint* mean "son of" and "daughter of" in Hassaniya: hence Mokhtar Ould Daddah, Dimi Mint Abba.

OPENING HOURS The office day is usually 7.30 or 8am–1.30 or 2pm. Banks are open for changing money Sunday to Thursday only until 12.30pm. Other businesses close at 2.30pm. Shops close for a long break and open again in the late afternoon, until about 7.30pm.

PHOTOGRAPHY There is no photography permit. People tend to be suspicious of cameras and prefer not to have their pictures taken, but the reaction is not normally heavy. Be especially careful in Nouakchott, check before snapping and avoid all broad, street scenes – there's often an upset. Film in Nouakchott is expensive and unreliably stored.

POLICE AND TROUBLE Mauritania is **report-to-the-police** territory. Large towns have control posts on the entrance roads where your particulars will be recorded. Smaller places don't, and it's up to you to find the man on duty and proffer your *pièce*. If you fail to do so, you could have an uncomfortable dressing down when they apprehend you. If you're **driving**, you may have your vehicle very thoroughly searched; searches are otherwise rare. If you're travelling in the far south, bear in mind that nobody seems to have told the posts on the Senegal river road that the troubles between Mauritania and Senegal are over – getting past these posts can still be trying and time-consuming. **Alcohol** is theoretically illegal, except in controlled upmarket bars and hotels. **Drugs** aren't much of an issue though some expensive grass finds its way in from Mali.

SEXUAL ATTITUDES In the Moorish community, there is more openness than you might at first expect. Younger women are rapidly shaking off old values, if not always traditional costume. Urban men, too, are beginning to accept a realignment of sexual attitudes. Affairs and "love-marriages" are increasingly common in

Nouakchott, and the bride price (paid to the woman or her family) is less often stipulated. Clitoridectomy is still practised, though more in the far south. Male travellers aren't very likely to be hustled by prostitutes.

WOMEN TRAVELLERS Women travellers can expect a combination of chivalry and pestering, though not too much of the latter. Covering your hair is an effective way of cooling ardour: Moorish women never let their scarves slip. Fatness in women is considered desirable by older men, though younger men insist it's no longer important to them. Sex is openly discussed among women: if you find yourself among French-speaking Moorish women, or you speak a little Hassaniya yourself, the conversation can take remarkable turns. There is no organized women's movement in Mauritania, though Mrs Khadija Ahmed was appointed "Minister in Charge of Women, Handicrafts and Tourism" in 1988.

It's natural that you'll spend a fair amount of time, like everyone else in Mauritania, lying on mattresses on the ground. Useful to know, then, that lying either on your back or your stomach is considered highly suggestive: Moor women, you'll notice, invariably lie on their sides, supporting their head with a hand. There's reportedly a high incidence of arthritis of the elbow.

A Brief History of Mauritania

Contemporary Mauritania doesn't coincide with the ancient "Mauretania Tingitana", a region confined to present-day Morocco and Western Algeria, and annexed to the Roman Empire by Claudius in 42 AD. The events and processes that led to the creation of the République Islamique de Mauritanie are taken up below in the fifteenth century with the arrival of the first mercantile Europeans. Accounts of some of the little-known early history of the region are scattered throughout this chapter.

■ European contact

Direct contact with Europeans began in 1445, when **Portuguese traders** set up a small *factoria* – a trading base – at the raised, southern tip of Arguin island.

At about the same time, the **Hassane Arabs** from upper Egypt were moving into the northern parts of the territory, subjugating the largely Berber-speaking population, spreading the use of the Hassaniya language, and creating the cultural complex that became **Moorish society**.

Early Portuguese efforts to conduct a trade in slaves and gold were not hugely successful. Instead, acacia tree gum used in the manufacture of food and drugs (called "gum arabic" because it was originally exported to Europe by Red Sea Arabs) soon became the main item of commerce, most of it coming from the southwest region, near the mouth of the Senegal River.

When Portuguese commercial influence waned in the seventeenth century, the **gum trade** fuelled intense rivalry between French, Dutch and English trading houses. The Dutch pulled out in 1727, but Anglo-French competition (and war) continued until 1857, when the British withdrew from the region in exchange for the French ceding them Albreda island in the Gambia River. Even alone, the **French** had forcibly to impress their control over the gum trade on the Moors in order to hold a profit.

Throughout the seventeenth and eighteenth centuries, the French had also been more successful than the Portuguese in whipping up the slave trade. From their main base at **St-Louis** at the mouth of the Senegal River, they sent foreign goods up-river, ensuring a supply of slaves from the feuding and rigidly class-stratified societies of the interior. Mauritania's involvement in this trade was heavy, and the class structure of the southern agricultural districts was set in aspic by the culling of non-Arabic-speaking peoples, who were sold down the river by their captors in exchange for fire-arms, cloth and sugar.

But the slave trade didn't account for the slow **decline in trans-Saharan commerce**. This came about through the increasing imposition of Arab (later Arab-Berber) rule throughout the terri-

WESTERN SAHARA AND THE POLISARIO WAR

The colony of Spanish Sahara was acquired by Spain in a succession of Franco-Spanish conventions between 1886 and 1912. The motivation for coveting this 266,000-square-kilometre wedge of gravel plains and low hills (about the size of Britain) sprang from a desire to join in the "scramble for Africa", a sense of wounded imperialist pride at the loss of the South American colonies, and the proximity of the Spanish Canary Islands.

Villa Cisneros (Dakhla) and La Guera were the only Spanish bases until 1934, when the first foothold was established in the interior. **Smara**, an abandoned Arab town, was reoccupied, at France's behest, to help control nomadic anti-colonial resistance still swirling around the region at the time.

Africa Occidental Española had no apparent economic potential and **General Franco** didn't waste money on it. By 1952 there were only 216 civilian employees, 24 telephones and 366 school children in the entire territory. Until Franco's death, the **Provincia de Sahara** (as it became) with its capital El Ayoun (built in 1940), was ruled as a military colony where, as in Spain, independent political expression was ruthlessly crushed.

In 1966, the United Nations insisted on the right to self-determination for the colony. But a survey of Spanish Sahara's **phosphate reserves** in the early 1960s had indicated vast deposits of up to ten billion tonnes, and Spain was soon digging in.

Although there had been armed resistance to Spanish occupation in the late 1950s in the wake of Morocco's independence, **urban anti-colonial demonstrations** began only in June 1970, when troops fired on marchers in El Ayoun and hundreds more were arrested – and subsequently disappeared.

THE POLISARIO

The **Polisario Front** was born in Zouérat in Mauritania, on May 10, 1973, spurred into existence not just by Spain's continued occupation, but also by the threats posed by competing claims from Mauritania and Morocco. For two years Polisario acted as self-sufficient guerillas, with no outside support, but then in May 1975 thousands of Polisario supporters emerged in the Sahara to meet the United Nations mission of inquiry.

Meanwhile, as the world witnessed the break-up of Portugal's African empire in 1974, Spain was planning a process of decolonization and independence to thwart Polisario's growing influence, with blueprints for limited self-rule, a referendum, and a state-sponsored Sahrawi National Unity Party of Sahrawi moderates. But King Hassan put pressure on Spain to reconsider, came to an agreement with Mauritania over partitioning the territory, and then managed to persuade the International Court of Justice to consider some rather arcane questions of nineteenth-century Saharan history. This last plea was turned down and the ICJ upheld the right to self-determination. Within three weeks, 350,000 Moroccans were marching, Korans in hand, into the Western Sahara, to claim their country's historical right to the territory.

After Franco's death, Spain agreed to **pull out** of Western Sahara, leaving the territory to Morocco, Mauritania and the Spanish-installed **Djemaa** council – a body of conservative, urban Sahrawis through whom they had ruled. Although the UN continued to uphold the resolutions on Western Sahara, a UN visit in early 1976 decided that the scale of upheaval was so great that there was no way the Sahrawis could be properly consulted. The guerrilla war now began in earnest, and more than half the population fled the country – old people, women and children to Algerian refugee camps around Tindouf, and men to join Polisario. The **Sahrawi Arab Democratic Republic** (SADR) was proclaimed – in exile in Tindouf – on February 27, 1976.

MAURITANIA AT WAR

Mauritania was never an enthusiastic ruler of the desert plain it called **Tiris el Gharbia**, nor was it prepared for a long and costly war. From the beginning Polisario concentrated on knocking

tory during the seventeenth century. By 1800, most of today's Mauritania was divided into competing **"Emirates"** – Trarza, Brakna, Adrar and Tagant – highly organized internally, but with little in the way of constructive foreign relations, and inimical to commercial links between their domains. The French at St-Louis were thus able to take advantage of the divisions, and actively promoted **civil war** in order to divert ordinary trade, as well as the slave victims of battle, in their direction.

French expansion up the Senegal River (the fort at Bakel in Senegal was built in 1818) and gathering French interest in Morocco and Algeria

Mauritania out of the picture, thus breaking the Morocco-Mauritania alliance. Mauritania's army was never sufficient to look after the new territory, let alone defend the bulk of the country from highly motivated Polisario incursions. There were repeated, humiliating losses: the iron ore railway was under constant threat; foreigners working at the mines were kidnapped; and twice, in June 1976 and July 1977, Polisario mounted daring **raids on the outskirts of Nouakchott** itself, and shelled the Ipresidential palace. n 1978 a desperate President Ould Daddah agreed to the stationing of 9000 **Moroccan troops** in the Saharan territory, and they were soon routinely skirmishing with Polisario in Mauritanian terrain. France too was heavily involved in defending Mauritania, President Giscard d'Estaing sending Jaguar bombers to blitz Polisario encampments and a steady stream of personnel to shore up Mauritania's flagging army. Mauritania was crippled by debt, doubt and drought, and its war was an undignified fiasco. For President Ould Daddah, the situation had become untenable, and he was relieved of his post in July 1978. The **new regime** sued for peace with Polisario the following year.

STALEMATE

The war between Morocco and Polisario has now lasted over twenty years. Arms-dealing nations (including France, Britain and the USA) continue to supply Morocco; while maintaining token support for the UN resolutions on the Sahrawis' rights to self-determination. Despite this military support, Morocco has been increasingly stretched and, since the early 1980s, has pulled back its front line to **Dakhla** and the **northwest** area of Western Sahara (the so-called "useful triangle" containing the phosphate fields), while building immensely long, defensive, earthworks that now enclose almost 90 percent of the territory. Polisario chips away, but a stalemate has now dragged on since 1986.

Meanwhile, the **Tindouf refugee zone** has grown into a state-in-exile, a stable and relatively prosperous mini-republic which, though heavily dependent on international donations, has built a reputation for its agricultural efforts and welfare services.

After the resumption of diplomatic relations between **Algeria and Morocco** in 1988 King Hassan is no longer calling the Polisario "Algerian puppet terrorists" and there still seems a possibility of a **referendum** for the people of the territory (including the 200,000 refugees living in the four Tindouf camps). But the UN-monitored process of identifying who is eligible to vote has been lengthy and inconclusive. Moreover, Morocco has "West Banked" the sectors of the Western Sahara it holds, pumping resources – and 150,000 **Moroccan settlers** – into the region, in order to outwit a democratic solution for the indigenous people.

Meanwhile, the 300 UN peacekeepers in the **Minurso** force (deployed at a cost of £25 million/ $40 million per year) have noted dozens of ceasefire violations by Morocco and just a handful by the Sahrawis.

Not only are the Sahrawis very low in UN priorities, but King Hassan's stance on Western Sahara has widespread support in Morocco itself. The UN security council is loathe to do anything to upset the stability of the kingdom, fearing the potential for Algeria-style civil war between the state and the fundamentalist supporters of an Islamic greater Morocco. In response to the lack of progress, the Sahrawis have repeatedly threatened a resumption of full-scale hostilities, as much to draw the world's attention as to achieve any tangible advantage on the ground. They argue that there is a real possibility that without war, their plight might slip into obscurity as the second generation of camp-dwellers grows up and the Moroccan settlers become increasingly established.There have been several high-level defections from the SADR government-in-waiting to the Moroccan side.

In 1995, the referendum was again delayed, partly as a result of the chaotic conditions in Western Sahara following serious floods at the end of 1994.

led, towards the end of the nineteenth century, to the strategic penetration of the Mauritanian interior, with "protection" and "pacification" sounded as the key-notes to local people. The **assassination of Xavier Coppolani**, a French commander and Arabist, at Tidjikja in 1905, ended a period of relatively peaceful expansion and brought down a five-year reign of terror in the territory. The Adrar was occupied in 1908, the Hodh (in the southeast) in 1911. The next year, France reached an agreement with Spain over respective spheres of influence in the western Saharan region, and in 1920 **la Mauritanie** became a colony of French West Africa. "Police actions" against nomadic guerilla resistance continued throughout the north up until 1933, when complete "pacification" was finally achieved.

The path to independence

Mauritania was used by the French as a **buffer zone** protecting their more valuable assets in Senegal and Soudan (Mali), and as a place of internal exile for political agitators from their other colonies. Since the end of commercial slavery in 1820, only gum arabic and potential mineral wealth had provided any economic justification for occupying the territory. The French invested almost nothing in Mauritania's future, administering it as a part of Senegal and counting on nomadic conservatism to look after the population in traditional ways.

As late as 1946 there was still no political party in Mauritania. In that year, administrative apathy seems to have allowed **Horma Ould Babana**, a socialist, to become the first Mauritanian deputy to the National Assembly in Paris. In the view of the French administration, he was a dangerous radical whose presence on the National Assembly was intolerable.

Blatant interference in the 1951 National Assembly elections duly secured support for the pro-French nomadic chiefs from the 26 percent of the population who were registered to vote (one polling station controller declared "if a dog had come before me with a voter's card I'd have made him vote"). **Sidi el Mokhtar**, a member of the Gaullist *Rassemblement du Peuple Français*, and a puppet candidate of the white Moors, was duly appointed deputy.

In the Territorial Assembly elections of 1952, the Mauritanian representatives were still not seeking independence from France. Indeed Mauritania, still party-less, had no effective branch of the *Rassemblement Démocratique Africaine* – the affiliation of French West African parties led by Houphouët-Boigny of Côte d'Ivoire which was in the forefront of nationalist demands.

Although the 1956 National Assembly elections were free of administrative interference, and many French territories elected nationalist deputies, Mauritania again elected Sidi el Mokhtar, who stood with Gaullist support but then transferred his allegiance to the *Mouvement Républicaine Populaire*, a French Christian Democrat party.

In the same year, significantly, **Morocco** achieved independence. King Hassan V's ruling group was opposed in Morocco principally by *Istiqlal*, a party of conservative expansionists who wanted to see the reconstruction of a "greater Morocco" that included much of Mauritania. The king outflanked *Istiqlal* by taking up the expansionist cause himself. The claims naturally had repercussions in Mauritania, where an extreme, Moorish, irredentist movement took shape, fighting to hive off part, if not all, of Mauritania to Morocco which it believed was the true homeland of all Moors.

In the 1957 Territorial Assembly elections (the first with universal suffrage), the unaffiliated *Union Progressiste Mauritanienne*, Mauritania's first indigenous political party, won 33 out of 34 seats. **Mokhtar Ould Daddah**, a young, white Moor lawyer with considerable French support (he was de Gaulle's son-in-law), was elected vice-president of Mauritania's first governing council (the French governor was president). Ould Daddah, too, was territorially ambitious, calling on the people of the **Spanish Sahara** to unite with his own in a "great economic and spiritual Mauritania".

On November 28, 1958, Mauritania became an autonomous republic within the French community and the **République Islamique de Mauritanie** (the R.I.M.) was proclaimed. A national election held in 1959 gave Ould Daddah the post of prime minister, after his party (the *Parti du Regroupement Mauritanien*) won every seat in the new National Assembly, and on November 28, 1960, Mauritania became an independent nation state, with Ould Daddah as president. Its entry into the United Nations, however, was vetoed by the Soviet Union, because Morocco (which at the time had a pro-Communist foreign policy) still claimed Mauritania as its own.

Ould Daddah's presidency

With the founding of the new capital of Nouakchott, the development of the Fdérik iron ore mines and the completion of the railway to Nouadhibou in 1963, Mauritania's economic future looked fairly bright. But at the same time Ould Daddah set about eliminating **political opponents**. In December 1961, the four main political parties became one, the *Parti du Peuple Mauritanien* (**PPM**). Within three years, the *de facto* one-party state had been enshrined in law.

In the south and among the **black, non-Arabic-speaking population**, expectations raised by independence from France gave way to resentment and indignation. In 1966, Arabic was made the compulsory teaching medium in schools. Ensuing **riots in Nouakchott** were summarily suppressed and laws swiftly enacted to ban all discussion of racial conflict. The country had come close to civil war, but Arabization continued, with a 1968 law putting **Hassaniya** on a co-footing with French as dual official languages.

The government was intent on integrating the trade union movement into the PPM, a move which angered **teachers** and **miners** particularly, and led to strikes and demonstrations in 1968, 1969 and 1971. For two months in 1971 there was a complete shut-down of iron ore production. The force of government repression, and the determination of the ruling party to silence the opposition led to the creation of clandestine political movements and a simmering groundswell of anti-government feeling. Through much of this first decade of independence, however, foreign affairs issues served to dampen the opposition.

Through the 1960s, support from the **other Arab states** for Morocco's claim over Mauritania had resulted in very few of them recognizing the R.I.M. Ould Daddah's hope that the country would be seen as a bridge between Africa and the Arab world failed to materialize as his dependency on French military and economic support increased. Thus, with the isolation of Mauritania from the Arab world, the southerners' deepest fears had been partly abated during the first decade of independence.

But in 1969 came **Morocco's formal recognition of Mauritania**. Increasing Islamic radicalization, a slackening of ties with France coupled with growing Algerian support, and a clear state socialist programme were the natural consequences. The huge MIFERMA (*Mines de Fer de Mauritanie*) iron ore complex at Fdérik/Zouérat was nationalized and the country withdrew from the CFA franc zone to bring in its own currency, supported by the Arab banks, the Ouguiya. There was wide backing for these moves in the Arabic-speaking community and, by 1975, broad government confidence. Although the **drought** of the early 1970s had left the country reeling, the worst affected people were the Arabic-speaking nomads of the north and centre. Now, with trade unions and students in Nouakchott appeased, the problem of the disenfranchized southerners, who had found some voice through these groups, was less urgent.

Spain's decision to withdraw its garrisons from the Western Sahara plunged Mauritania into a **war with the Polisario** (Popular Front for the Liberation of Sagia el Hamra and Rio de Oro; see box). The war, over the small and economically worthless piece of territory ceded to Mauritania by Spain, proved the downfall of Ould Daddah. Even with a massive increase in military spending, accompanied by a tenfold expansion of the army, popular support for the war was so low in Mauritania that it was clearly unwinnable.

■ The Lieutenant-Colonels

On the night of July 9, 1978, a quiet and bloodless **coup** ousted Mokhtar Ould Daddah. The coup's leaders dissolved the PPM party and announced the formation of a **Comité Militaire de Redressement National** (**CMRN**) – "to save the country from ruin and dismemberment" – under the chairmanship of Chief of Staff Lt-Col **Moustapha Ould Salek**.

Ould Salek tried to bring Polisario and Morocco together for a negotiated settlement, but the terms suited neither party. When Polisario's kidnapping of a Mauritanian prefect pushed Mauritania into a **peace treaty** with Polisario in August 1979, Morocco immediately moved into the territory vacated by Mauritanian troops. Morocco and Mauritania have had an uneasy relationship ever since as a consequence. Meanwhile, at home, Ould Salek was confronted by outbreaks of racial conflict, student agitation, and factional strife in the CMRN – upgraded, desperately, in April 1979, to the Military Committee for National Salvation (CMSN). Ould Salek resigned and was replaced as president by Lt-Col **Mohammed Louly**, whose prime minister, Lt-Col **Mohamed Khouna Haidalla**, in turn staged another palace coup in January 1980, to take control of government.

Haidalla's five years as head of state saw an overall improvement in foreign relations, but a deterioration in the domestic situation. The continuing war between Polisario and Morocco repeatedly spilled onto Mauritanian soil, hindering rapprochement with Morocco and delaying Mauritania's recognition of the state of the Sahrawi Arab Democratic Republic.

Internally, Mauritania's most dramatic event – as far as the rest of the world was concerned – was the formal **abolition of slavery** in 1980. This may have been intended to forestall links between the Dakar-based black opposition and supporters of exiled white Moor groups in Paris, and also to divert attention away from the increasingly blatant racial discrimination against the *Soudanien* southerners, but the effect of the pronouncement was to focus world attention on a brutal military dictatorship. Mauritania's law did indeed guarantee freedom from chatteldom, but not freedom from hunger, dispossession or political repression.

For a short time in 1980–81, President Haidalla experimented with **political relaxation**. He formed a civilian government led by prime minister Ahmed Ould Bneijara, and drew up a draft constitution recommending a democratic multi-party system. But rumours of a **Libyan-backed plot** (part of the ripple of Libyan-inspired insecurity that passed through West Africa at that time), and then a genuine **coup attempt** by the **Parti Islamique** of former government ministers operating from Morocco, shook the democracy idea apart. Having executed the coup leaders, the CMSN appointed a new prime minister, Lt-Col **Maawiya Sid'Ahmed Ould Taya**, and re-militarized the government.

Despite this clampdown, another **military coup** was foiled in February 1982, involving Ould Salek and the just-deposed Ould Bneijara. In a surprise display of clemency, the instigators were given ten-year jail sentences.

Through the early 1980s, Mauritania's prospects failed to improve. Severe drought in 1983 brought tens of thousands of famine-struck nomads virtually to the door of the Presidential Palace in Nouakchott; opposition groups continued to fight a war of words in France, Morocco and Senegal; and Haidalla's recognition of the Sahrawi Arab Democratic Republic early in 1984 brought further insecurity to the country as Morocco seemed more than ever determined to oppose any referendum in the Western Sahara – increasing the tension between Morocco and Mauritania. In August, Morocco entered a bizarre pact of union with Libya, unsettling the Mauritanians. The prime minister, Ould Taya, who was already concerned about government corruption and inaction, deposed President Haidalla on December 12, 1984, in yet another, gentlemanly palace coup.

■ Ould Taya: progress and reaction

President Ould Taya wasted no time. With World Bank and IMF support he adopted a programme of economic recovery with heavy emphasis on fishing and agriculture. Targets were set, and reached, and creditors were evidently impressed by Ould Taya's abandonment of some of the capital-intensive industrial schemes set up by Haidalla to the detriment of basic infrastucture and rural development. Iron ore is still a major source of foreign exchange (reserves have been variously estimated at between 500 and 2000 million tonnes, which at the present rate of extraction would last up to 200 years), but in the late 1980s **fish** came to be seen as a more flexible resource, and was briefly the country's biggest earner.

But the government's agenda was being set by political concerns, rather than economic ones. In 1986, a tract in French entitled *Manifesto of the Oppressed Black Mauritanian: From Civil War to National Liberation Struggle, 1966–86* made the rounds among students and staff at the National Language Institute. It was the work of the Dakar-based **African Liberation Forces of Mauritania** (FLAM). Twenty prominent southerners were arrested and jailed on charges of "undermining national unity". Widespread rioting and destruction subsequently took place in Nouakchott and Nouadhibou, and thirteen of those involved were also jailed, in March 1987. Strict **Islamic law** was subsequently introduced.

In October 1987, 51 Fula-speaking Tukulor officers were arrested on charges of insurrection. According to the Interior Minister, "this plot was more than an attempt to overthrow the government, it was a crime against the whole nation". Three officers were executed (the first death sentences imposed by Ould Taya's regime) and 41 more were given long prison terms. This blow against the southerners was followed by a **purge of Tukulor army officers**, with over 500 dismissals. Tension continued through 1988, with racial killings in Nouakchott. In connection, FLAM pointed out that the "sensitization programme" being carried out by the government in the **Senegal River flood plain** region wasn't appeasing local people, who bitterly resented the new influx of Moorish and Arab land-buyers and the pressures on them to make way for alien **development projects**.

Towards the end of 1988, a number of southerners serving terms for political crimes, including the author of the "Black Manifesto", died in **Oualata prison**, an allegation denied by the government, who sent the Mauritanian League of Human Rights to investigate. The league found several Oualata inmates were, indeed, still alive.

The 1990 race riots

Events finally boiled over in April 1989, triggered by a minor incident on an island in the Senegal River, near Bakel, in which Mauritanian camels were supposed to have plundered Senegalese vegetable gardens – the sort of dispute that would normally be settled by compensation. During an argument, Mauritanian border guards opened fire on Senegalese onlookers, killing two people. Thirteen Senegalese were then captured and taken to Sélibaby in Mauritania, where they were effectively kept hostage, which led to attacks on Mauritanian shops in Bakel on the Senegalese side.

Within days, violence had spread to other Senegalese towns, resulting in the deaths of dozens of Mauritanians, while thousands more were driven out as their shops and homes were ransacked. In Dakar, the entire Mauritanian community sheltered in the Grande Mosquée and the Mauritanian embassy. In Mauritania there were even more savage attacks on Senegalese and other black Africans as security forces and lynch mobs of Haratins hunted for southerners. Both governments were quick to condemn killings by the other side, but neither took decisive action to control the violence.

A massive dual **evacuation by air**, with international assistance, began, as it emerged that at least two hundred Senegalese had died in Nouakchott. In Senegal, the army remained on the streets of Dakar and President Ould Taya was accused of declaring war on Senegal and of supplying arms to the Casamance rebels in southern Senegal.

As the exodus from Mauritania went on (in the event, there was only a limited flight of Mauritanians from Senegal), it became clear that among those leaving Mauritania was a large proportion of indigenous southern Mauritanians – whom the regime now routinely refers to as "Senegalese" but who are largely **Hal-Pulaar** (Fula-speakers) – many of whom were being forcibly expelled. The government was taking the opportunity to banish up to twenty thousand potential opponents, to reduce the impact of the returning Moors and to lessen the numbers of non-Moorish Mauritanians, who had been claiming for several years that they were in the majority. The climax of this period came in November 1990, when the government announced there had been a coup attempt, fostered by Senegal. Over three hundred southerners were picked up by the authorities, and never seen again. Most southerners remaining in any positions of responsibility in the civil service were sacked over the next few months.

The 1990–91 **Gulf War** drew the world's attention away from the horrors of Mauritania's human rights record. But Mauritania's military rulers had long been allies of Iraq (Iraqi military advisors are believed to have helped organize the pogroms against Fula villages in the south), and the government stood behind Saddam Hussein throughout the conflict. This alliance put severe strains on Mauritania's relations with Morocco and, of more immediate economic consequence, France. Thus Ould Taya's pragmatic move to adopt a democratic constitution, when faced with the possibility of complete isolation, was hardly questioned: every other Francophone state in West Africa was undergoing the same process.

The multi-party era

Southerner political groups (and Muslim fundamentalists) boycotted the **referendum** on a multi-party constitution, arguing they hadn't been consulted in drawing up the document. But, despite only a twenty percent turnout, the "yes" vote was carried into practice, and Mauritania became a multi-party state on July 20, 1991, with a president as head of state and a prime minister running the country's affairs for him. In 1992, the country's first "free" **presidential election** since 1960 was marred by fraud. The post of president was won by the uninspiring former military leader, Ould Taya, despite the best efforts of his main rival, Ahmed Ould Daddah (half-brother of the country's first president, Mokhtar Ould Daddah) to have the results annulled by the supreme court. The general elections, later in the year, were boycotted by the opposition parties, and there was widespread vote-rigging, including the effective ruse of leaving candidates' names off electoral lists.

The flavour of the present political configuration is very much business as usual – a civilian incarnation of the military dictatorships of 1978–91. There is a large number of registered political parties, either allied with the ruling *Parti*

Républicain Démocratique et Social (PRDS) or in opposition to it. The two main opposition groupings – the *Union pour la Démocratie et le Progrès* (UDP) led by **Hamdi Ould Mouknass** and the *Union des Forces Démocratiques* (UFD) led by **Ahmed Ould Daddah** – have found it hard to form a united front to challenge the PRDS. President Ould Taya's main rival, leader Ahmed Ould Daddah has lost much of his shine since the dawn of the "democratic" era, and while he certainly appears a preferable figure to the international community, and claims to support the wronged masses of the country, especially the southerners, few Mauritanians any longer believe he has any true agenda other than the pursuit of power – like his brother the late dictator.

On the streets, life is as hard as ever, though punctuated frequently enough by **demonstrations and riots** in the otherwise somnolent city of Nouakchott. In January 1990, the government stage-managed protests against American attacks on Iraq. In June 1991, there were demonstrations by the wives and mothers of men who had "disappeared" after the November 1990 coup attempt. In October 1992, the city was hit by riots over price increases and the falling value of the Ouguiya. Bread price riots in January 1995 led to the arrest of Ould Daddah and Ould Mouknass, accused of organizing unrest.

After these most recent riots, government TV broadcasts warned the youth not to follow a "treasonous" path or have any truck with foreign organizations, a tacit reference to fundamentalist agitators. Despite the country's "Islamic Republic" label, and a legal system strongly influenced by the *sharia* (the body of Muslim doctrines), the government has been distancing itself from fundamentalist causes. In October 1994, the work of a number of Islamic groups in the country was curtailed and up to sixty Islamic leaders were arrested for belonging to "secret foreign organizations".

Meanwhile, the border with Senegal is open, and officially all 70,000-odd Mauritanian refugees in Senegal are encouraged to return home. In practice, few have any papers, job or land to return to. In 1993, the government declared an amnesty for perpetrators of the 1989–90 racial violence, which is hardly an inducement to the victims to return. Those who do risk returning are subject to indiscriminate attacks by Haratins.

■ The future

On the surface a certain stability is apparent, but **the future** for Mauritania looks very difficult. Economically, Ould Taya's support for Saddam during the Gulf War lost the country much credibility with foreign lenders and investors, which was further strained during the three-year rift with Senegal. Income from fishing has declined markedly and iron ore output has dropped too as the world market for it shrinks. The recent bread riots, although sparked by VAT increases, reflect real concern about the ability of the country to feed itself – there's an annual cereal deficit of around 100,000 tonnes which amounts to nearly a kilo missing from each Mauritanian's weekly food requirements.

One quite likely result of current **racial policies** is civil war, and perhaps attempted secession by the south. Although Senegal and Mauritania are now on speaking terms again, hope over this issue can only lie in the sort of far-reaching government concessions to black opposition demands which at present seem remote and unlikely.

The final and most alarming difficulty is **Islamic fundamentalism**. While it would appear that Mauritania does not possess a large, marginalized, urban constituency in which support for fundamentalism can breed (like the slum-dwellers of Egypt; the young and poor of Algeria, or the working class of Iran under the Shah), the mere threat posed by fundamentalist activists, combined with the legal opposition's frustration, power-hunger and disunity, might lead the opposition parties into unholy alliance with the PRDS government against the fundamentalists. And thus the present government's ungodly, undemocratic, corrupt apparatus could trundle on for years. On the other hand, if the fundamentalists prove they do indeed have widespread grassroots support – and present evidence suggests they're only likely to gather more as the years go by – the crisis they are bound to precipitate will make the status quo seem admirable in comparison. The most promising scenario would be for the PRDS, while condemning fundamentalism, to initiate some dynamic social and economic policies of its own, and thus develop some healthy support. On present evidence, again, that seems very unlikely.

NOUAKCHOTT

Whipped by dust storms for nine months of the year, Mauritania's capital, **NOUAKCHOTT**, seems to be drowning under a sea of sand. This is the biggest city in the Sahara, a modern, sprawling place of over half a million inhabitants – nearly a third of the country's population. Once you're settled in, it's hard to dislike; you can wander around more or less unhassled, and there's a certain ease in the wide, tree-lined streets paved with crushed sea-shells, and half obscured by drifts of sand. Yet there's something soulless about this commercial and self-interested city, with its brutally severe state buildings and its dearth of things to do. For most itinerants, a couple of nights are enough before moving on.

A short history

The site of the new city of Nouakchott – whose name may mean "Place of Wind" or "Place of Floating Seashells" – was nominated by Bidan elders in 1957, who chose to raise it near a French military post on the **Piste Impériale**, the old imperial road. The buildings were constructed on fixed dunes, in an attempt to give protection from the flooding of the Aftout es-Saheli seasonal watercourse, which nearly surrounds it – the original Ksar ("fortified village") settlement having been seriously damaged by floods in 1950. With funds limited and formal independence pressing, the city was hastily planned and constructed – medina, residential blocks, schools, ministries – for an anticipated population of 15,000. It was already 20,000 by 1969, when the first great Sahel drought tipped the country into crisis. By 1980 the immigrant influx had pushed it past 150,000, and since then it has quadrupled again.

Arrival and orientation

Arriving at the **gare routière**, 3km northeast of the centre on rue Ghary, by *taxi brousse* from Senegal or landing at the **airport**, on the opposite side of rue Ghary, are the usual introductions to the capital. The airport's new international terminal is a big improvement on the warehouse that used to serve (and still does for domestic flights). Officially badged "welcome" personnel will politely guide you through immigration and currency formalities and get you a taxi (on the understanding they can expect a UM500 tip). There's a small bank, and car rental available, but few other facilities. Ordinary **taxis** from the airport charge around UM500–600 to the *centreville*, possibly less if you haggle. There's no airport bus, and Nouakchott city bus services extend to about two blue *STPN* (*Société des transports publics de Nouakchott*) vehicles. Best is to share a taxi for UM50–150 or find a green and yellow *Transports Urbaines* minibus (UM20–30).

At the airport exit, the scene of scruffy lanes, wind-blown rubbish, wasted palm trees and perfunctory shops seems to confirm worst fears. The *gare routière* and airport are actually in the old part of town, Le Ksar, in a slightly sleazy area where most of the car dealers and service stations are located (see "Listings"). Once in the real city centre, and assuming the dust has settled, impressions do improve. Note, however, that you'll find the city lifeless if you arrive between noon and 3pm. And during Ramadan, that's the normal condition during daylight hours.

Orientation

The **layout** of Nouakchott can be confusing at first, and there are no heights from which to get your bearings. **Le Ksar** is on the east side of town, from where the slums spread north along the Atar highway and east along the Route de l'Espoir. From the paved roads, there's no indication of their vast extent.

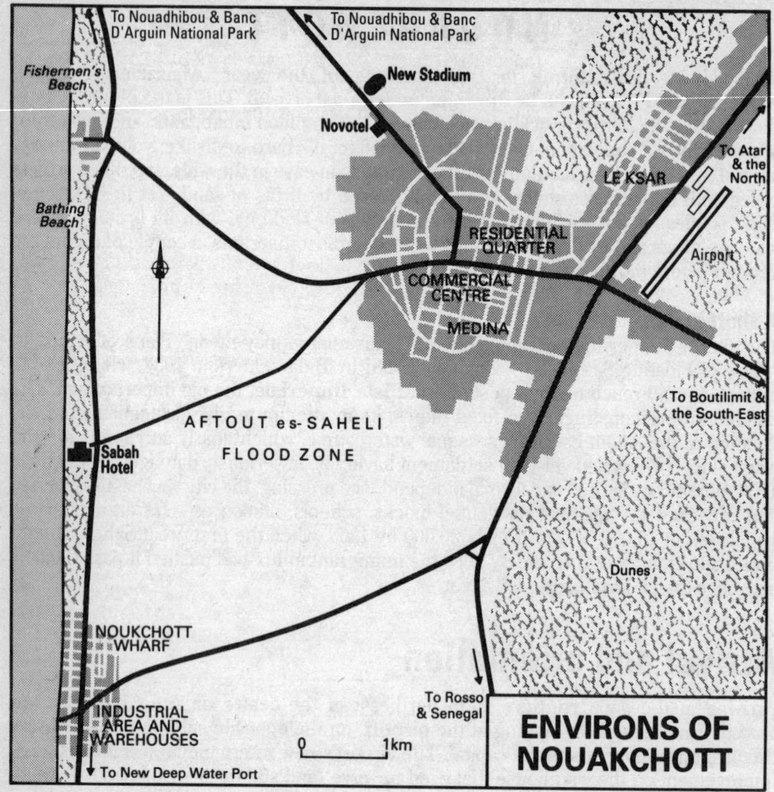

The city's main street, **Avenue Abd El Nasser**, runs east–west from just south of Le Ksar, through the new town, **La Capitale**, and out to the beach, 5km away. Cutting across it at right angles is **Avenue Kennedy**, which connects the affluent, ambassadorial and ex-pat quarter of **Tavrak Zeina** on the northern edge of La Capitale to the **Medina** and the extensive commercial districts of the *cinquième arrondissement* in the south (Nouakchott is divided into numbered **arrondissements**, subdivided into alphabetical blocks called **îlots**).

Most hotels, restaurants and shops are within a short walking distance of the Kennedy-Nasser intersection and this district is likely to be the main focus for the time you're in town.

Accommodation

The cheapest **rooms** in Nouakchott are at the basic *Adrar* (③), but there's nothing budget-priced otherwise and generally poor value for money all round. The Catholic Mission has gone, and the Peace Corps' *Maison de Passage* doesn't put up travellers. All the places listed below are in the Capitale apart from the *Sabah Hôtel*, though there are a couple of basic lodgings near the *autogare* in Ksar.

ACCOMMODATION PRICE CODES

① Under UM1000 (under £5/$7.50) ② UM1000–2000 (£5–10/$7.50–15)
③ UM2000–4000 (£10–20/$15–30) ④ UM4000–6000 (£20–30/$30–45)
⑤ UM6000–8000 (£30–40/$45–60) ⑥ UM8000–10,000 (£40–50/$60–75)
⑦ Over UM10,000 (over £50/$75)

For further details turn to "Accommodation" in the Practical Information at the beginning of this chapter.

Camping by the seaside is relatively safe and is now officially sanctioned, with a campsite by the *Sabah*, plus the option of overpriced beach huts (③) and a Mauritanian restaurant.

Hôtel Adrar, south of Grand Marché. Travellers' focus and flophouse bordello, scruffy and unhygienic, but convenient and friendly. Nominally S/C rooms with a small supplement for AC. ③.

Hôtel el Amanne, BP 1147 (☎52178; Fax 53765). Probably the best downtown hotel in Nouakchott, usually packed with Arab businessmen. Pretty courtyard restaurant. ⑤.

Hôtel du Complexe Olympique, BP 646 (☎53609). About 2km out of town, past the *Novotel*. Formerly just "Le Stade" (the sports stadium), now a fully-fledged hotel and restaurant – at least in theory. Large AC, S/C rooms, with two beds. Somewhat hostel-like, and not very clean. ④.

Hôtel Marhaba, BP 2391 (☎51686/51838; Fax 57854). Nominally upmarket haunt of most visiting UN consultants now that expense allowances no longer run to the *Novotel*. Lashings of hot water and friendly staff but no alcohol served. Swimming pool. Visit the stamp seller if philately interests you – amazing old stock. Amex accepted. ⑥.

Novotel "El Barka", BP 1366 (☎53526; Fax 51831). Architecturally Nouakchott's most interesting, which is not much of a blessing (in spite of its Arab pseudonym), at nearly US$150 a room. Standard orange *Novotel* fittings but less than standard service. Takes major credit cards. ⑦.

Hôtel Oasis, BP 4 (☎52011). Adequate, but nothing about it merits the price – at the bottom of this price bracket (breakfast not included), with a small surcharge for AC. The restaurant is cheaper than others in the Capitale area but the service is reluctant. Expensive booze at the bar. ④.

Hôtel Park BP 50 (☎51444). Modest-sized, nice enough place with S/C, AC rooms. ④.

Sabah Hôtel BP452; (☎51552) On the beach, but moribund and uninspiring. ④.

The Town

It's quickly apparent that Nouakchott doesn't spill over with things to see and do. Apart from checking out the **markets** and various **artisanal centres**, the only obvious destination is the **beach**.

There are several spots around the city where you can study tourist bric-a-brac and while away some hours in bargaining – such as outside the *El Amanne* and *Novotel* hotels. The main **Centre Artisanal**, however, is a walk or taxi ride out of town on the Rosso road. Although the place is occasionally rather empty, there's usually an impressive array of camel saddles, silver-inlaid chests and carpets. The jewelry and good-value silverware is worth close inspection, but don't buy stone arrow heads here: they're much cheaper in the regions where they're found (see "The Adrar", below). Avoid the nearby **zoo**: the less support this disastrous menagerie receives, the sooner it will close – and the animals' suffering cease.

Set up as a womens' income development initiative, the **Centre National du Tapis**, in the Ksar quarter, produces finely woven **rugs and carpets** in subtle, desert colours with rigorous geometrical patterns – sadly, they are out of range of most pockets. There's another women's centre in the Capitale, behind the Grand Marché, where the speciality is **embroidery**.

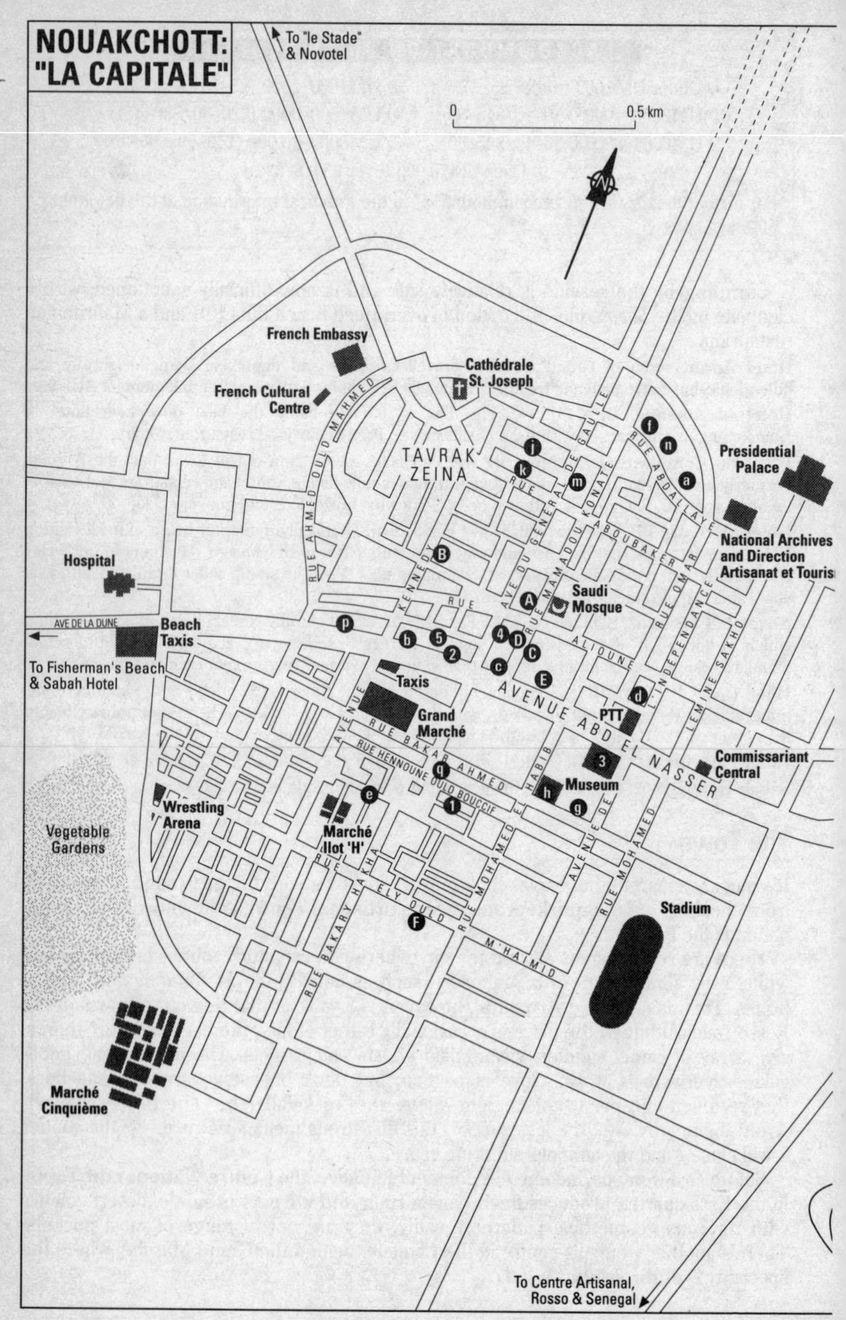
NOUAKCHOTT:
"LA CAPITALE"
To "le Stade" & Novotel
0
0.5 km
French Embassy
Cathédrale St. Joseph
French Cultural Centre
TAVRAK ZEINA
Presidential Palace
National Archives and Direction Artisanat et Touris
Hospital
Saudi Mosque
AVE DE LA DUNE
Beach Taxis
To Fisherman's Beach & Sabah Hotel
Taxis
Grand Marché
PTT
Commissariant Central
Museum
Wrestling Arena
Vegetable Gardens
Marché Ilot 'H'
Stadium
Marché Cinquième
To Centre Artisanal, Rosso & Senegal
RUE AHMED OULD MAHMED
RUE DU GÉNÉRAL DE GAULLE
RUE ABDALLAYE
RUE MAMADOU KONATE
ABOUBAKER
RUE OMAR
RUE KENNEDY
AVE DU GÉNÉRAL
RUE ALIOUNE
L'INDÉPENDANCE
LEMINE SAKHO
AVENUE ABD EL NASSER
AVENUE
RUE BAKAR AHMED
RUE HENNOUNE OULD BOUCCIF
EL HABIB
AVENUE DE
RUE MOHAMED
RUE MOHAMED
RUE BAKARY HAKHA
RUE ELY OULD M'HAIMID
RUE

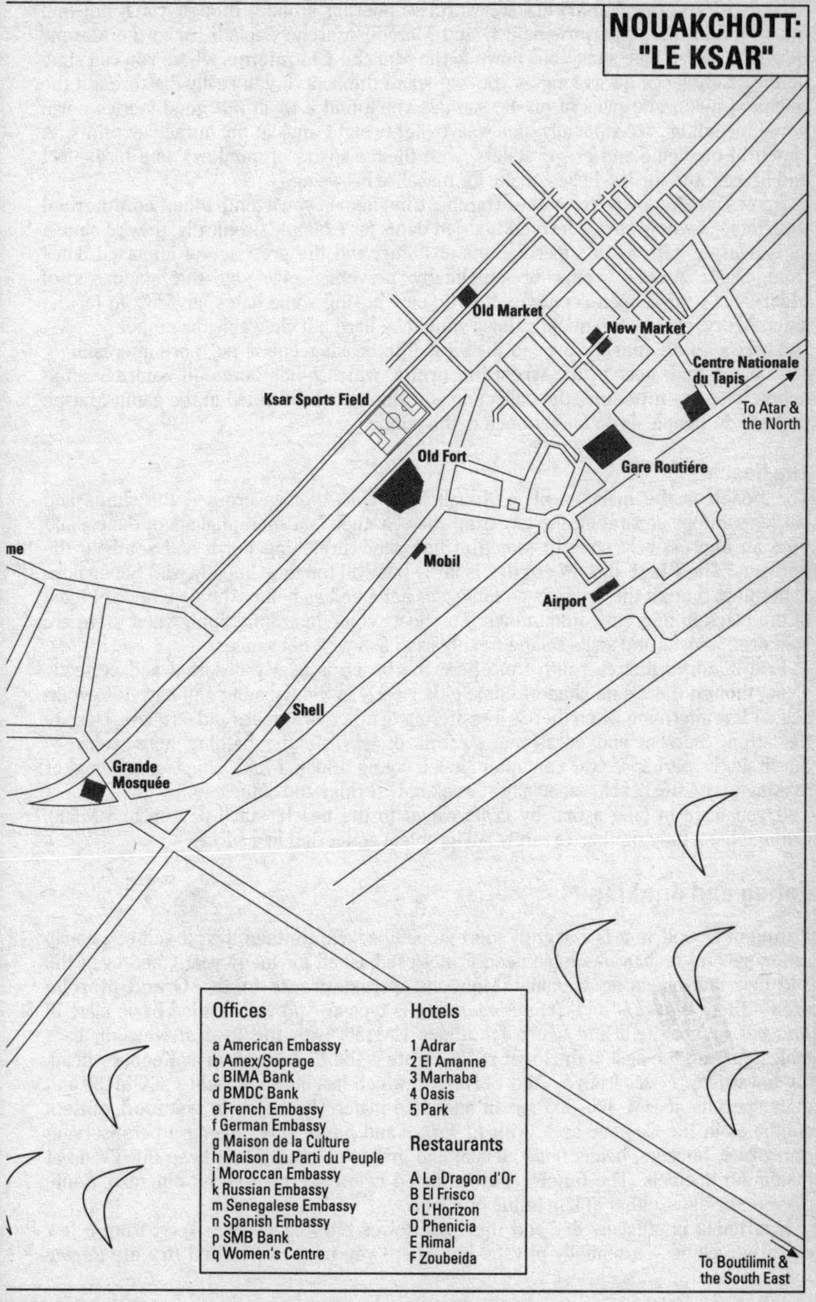
NOUAKCHOTT:
"LE KSAR"
Old Market
New Market
Centre Nationale du Tapis
To Atar & the North
Ksar Sports Field
Old Fort
Gare Routiére
me
Mobil
Airport
Shell
Grande Mosquée
Offices
a American Embassy
b Amex/Soprage
c BIMA Bank
d BMDC Bank
e French Embassy
f German Embassy
g Maison de la Culture
h Maison du Parti du Peuple
j Moroccan Embassy
k Russian Embassy
m Senegalese Embassy
n Spanish Embassy
p SMB Bank
q Women's Centre
Hotels
1 Adrar
2 El Amanne
3 Marhaba
4 Oasis
5 Park
Restaurants
A Le Dragon d'Or
B El Frisco
C L'Horizon
D Phenicia
E Rimal
F Zoubeida
To Boutilimit & the South East

The city's **general markets** are worth wandering around, though you'll not find much of note in the purpose-built Grand Marché/Marché Capitale, or in the Marché Ilot "H". Instead take a taxi/bus down to the **Marché Cinquième**, where you can shuffle the sandy lanes for as long as you can stand the heat. If you really dig through the reams of nylon and piles of plastic sandals you'll find a wealth of good fabrics down here, including exceptionally fine-weave lightweight muslin in attractive prints. A clutch of medicine and *gri-gri* sellers, with their displays of monkeys' and birds' feet and lizards' and turtles' heads, make for macabre browsing.

Across av Kennedy from the Marché Cinquième, you'll find other **commercial districts** – a whole street devoted to dried dates for example. Ironically, they're almost as expensive here as in supermarkets at home, and the presence of imported dates from Saudi Arabia seems breathtakingly perverse, even by the standards of Mauritania's misshapen economy. If you fancy buying some dates anyway, go for the smooth, dry, pale brown quality: these should be hard but chewable, like toffee.

There's a **fish market** over to the west (the beach scene is far more interesting – see below) and, near it, the **wrestling arena**, which holds bouts on Saturday afternoons. The city **museum**, the collections of which are assembled in the gaunt Maison du Parti du Peuple, is no longer open to the public.

The beach

The **beach** is the main event in Nouakchott. Once you've crossed the slums and garbage dumps separating the city from the sea, there's a solid phalanx of dunes, and then an impressively straight sweep of fine sand stretching north and south to the horizons. The **Plage des Pêcheurs** is fairly busy all the time, mostly with Senegalese fishermen, though the scene is no longer as animated as before the departure of most of the black immigrant communities. The boats come in around 5pm, when there are cold drink kiosks and stalls selling freshly fried fish with hot sauce.

Five hundred metres south from here the beach is nearly deserted and perfectly clean, though there's no shade – come either early in the morning and have it to yourself, or late afternoon when there's a scattering of other swimmers and strollers. Despite the strong current and occasional swarms of jellyfish, the bathing here is lovely. Surprisingly perhaps, you can often meet young Bidan Moor couples strolling or making tea on the beach, especially at weekends (Friday and Saturday).

If you have to take a **taxi** by *déplacement* to the beach, you'll pay up to UM500. Coming back though, there's rarely any problem squeezing in a *bâché*.

Eating and drinking

Eating in Nouakchott is a slightly more hopeful adventure than the pursuit of a cheap room: several restaurants have been firmly established for many years, and even the odd new one opens occasionally. Many cheap **restaurants in the Grand Marché area** – the *Restaurant de l'Unité Maghrebien* is typical – provide a good basic plate of *couscous* or spaghetti and sauce for under UM150, with the food arriving on bare tables. Among the best of the **local restaurants** is the *El-Zourrah* on av Kennedy heading towards *El Frisco* from av Abd El Nasser, which has big sandwiches at UM150 and daily specials at UM 400–500 for an adequate plate. The boom in **fast-food outlets** continues in the Capitale area, with *El Prince* and *Snack Irak*, among others, serving *chawarma*, burgers, beans (*foul*), felafal and grilled chicken. Most keep the TV on at maximum decibels. The **fancier places** listed below are marked on our map. Some close on Fridays, either at lunchtime or all day.

Mauritania is officially dry and there are fewer **bars** each year. Apart from a few expatriate clubs – essentially private, but where you might be invited (try the *Racing*

Club ☎/52418) – the capital's only boozers are at the *Novotel* and the *Hôtel Oasis* (see *Accommodation*).

Le Dragon d'Or, rue Mamadou Konaté opposite the Saudi mosque (☎53211). Chinese and Vietnamese specialities as well as French cuisine from a Vietnamese cook who knows what it's all about. Soups UM400-500, entrées UM600-800, main dishes UM700-1000: all prices exclude a 16% tax which can come as a nasty surprise.

El Frisco, av Kennedy (☎55909). Established place, popular with expats and trendy Mauritanians. A variety of meals in the UM500–800 range, and smallish pizzas. Good ice cream.

L'Horizon, rue Mamadou Konaté, right opposite *Phenicia*. Newly reopened under Egyptian management. More limited menu but about half the price, with pleasant, but inefficient service.

Phenicia, rue Mamadou Konaté (☎52775). Lebanese family atmosphere with good menu, most of which is available, and decent service. Main dishes around UM600, omelettes UM350-500.

Rimal, av Abd El Nasser (☎53544). Lebanese, not quite as good as *Phenicia*, but a little cheaper. Small supplement for the AC back room where you can escape the TV. Excellent *steack cordon bleu* – without the ham, evidently.

Zoubeida, rue Ely Ould M'haimid. Moroccan restaurant, hugely popular with less well-connected people, recommended for an evening out. The set-up here is piles of cushions and carpets, shoes off, TV in the corner, conversational opportunities – and endless food. Wonderful value.

Listings

Airlines The following have offices in Nouakchott:

Air Afrique, off av Abd El Nasser just west of the PTT (☎52081 or 52084); major credit cards.

Air Algérie, av Abd El Nasser, west of the PTT (☎52059).

Air France, immeuble SMAR, av Abd El Nasser, east of the PTT near the new Palais de Justice (☎53916). All major credit cards.

Air Mauritanie, av Abd El Nasser east of the PTT (☎52211 or 52212; Fax 53815).

Libyan Arab Airlines, near *Air Algérie* on av Abd El Nasser, east of the PTT (☎55390 or 55406).

Royal Air Maroc, immeuble SMAR, av Abd El Nasser, east of the PTT near the new Palais de Justice (☎53648).

American Express Represented by *SOPRAGE*, av Abd El Nasser.

Banc d'Arguin National Park To make a visit from Nouakchott, first visit the travel agents (see below). The park is most easily visited from Nouadhibou, where guides are available.

Banks The *Société Mauritanienne de Banque* (BP 614; ☎52602), the *Union des Banques de Développement* (BP 219; ☎52061), and the *Banque Internationale pour la Mauritanie* (BP 210; ☎52363) seem the surest, but they can take ages. All are open Sun–Thurs 7.30am–12.30pm; out of hours, your best bet is the airport bank or the *Novotel*.

Bookshops *Gralicoma*, near the Grande Marché between av Kennedy and av de Gaulle, is the best bet in town, open Sun–Thurs 8am–noon & 3–6pm. Alternatively, check the *Novotel* shop's more tourist-oriented offerings.

Car parts and main dealers include *Nosoco* for Land Rover (☎52352) and *Lacombe* for Citroën and VW (☎52194), both in the Ksar. *Peyrissac* for Peugeot and Nissan (☎52213) is on av Abd El Nasser in Capitale.

Church services The sizeable Catholic community holds regular mass at the Cathedral. The small Protestant community has a service every Friday at 9.30am in a room at the side of the Cathedral.

Cinemas The *Oasis* and the *El Mouna* show Westerns, Kung Fu and occasional French and Egyptian movies. There's a couple more screens in the Ksar – the *El Jouad* and the *Sahara*.

Embassies and visas The consulates of **Switzerland** (on the road to the beach, near the hospital) and the **UK** (across the ring road from the French embassy, ☎52337) may have lapsed. Britain has unofficial representation c/o Mrs N Abeiderrahmane (BP 2069; ☎51756 fax 57192); but the nearest diplomatic help is the US embassy, or the British embassy in Dakar, though Britain's Mauritanian interests are looked after by the embassy in Rabat. There is a new consulate for **Belgium** on av Abd El-Nasser near the corner with av Kennedy. Main embassies include **France**, rue Ahmed Ould Mahmed (BP 231; ☎51740); **Germany**, rue Abdallaye (BP 372; ☎51729); **Morocco**, (BP 621

☎51411); **Russia**, rue Abdou Baker (BP 251; ☎51973); **Senegal**, av du Général de Gaulle (BP 611; ☎52106); **Spain**, rue Abdallaye (BP 232; ☎51028); **USA**, rue Abdallaye (BP 222; ☎52660; Fax 52589). Note that there is no Malian embassy in Nouakchott. The visa service at the **French embassy** handles visas for **Côte d'Ivoire**, **Burkina Faso**, **Chad**, **Togo** and **Centrafrique**.

Emergencies Police ☎17, Hospital ☎52135. The hospital is helpful and not too expensive.

Fax bureaux Scattered all over the town centre.

French Cultural Centre, rue Ahmed Ould Mahmed, is the usual pleasant, chauvinistic retreat.

Post Office The PTT on av Abd El Nasser is theoretically open daily 8am–12.30pm & 2–6.30pm (Fri am). Delivery times to and from Europe average seven to eight days. Collecting mail from Poste restante depends on the availability of the bureau clerk but is otherwise efficient and costs UM24/item.

Swimming pools Only at the *Hôtel Marhaba* and the *Novotel*. The former is open only to annual subscription holders; brazen entry has the best chance of success at the latter.

Telephoning Calls abroad are most easily made from the numerous "phone shops" around town, where you can also fax and photocopy. Don't use the *Novotel*; it's incredibly expensive.

Tourist office Make enquiries direct with the *Direction Artisanat et Tourisme* (BP 246), near the Présidence.

Travel agents and car rental A number of small outfits can arrange air bookings, organize tours and rent out vehicles. Prices per day for the smallest town-car runabouts are UM6000 plus UM32/km, plus 16 percent tax; 4WD double-pick-ups and land cruisers go for around UM8500 plus UM40/km, plus 16 percent tax. Naturally, you should bargain your mouth off.

Adrar Voyages (BP 926; ☎51717; Fax 53210) is amongst the best of the new crop.

ATV (BP 861; ☎51575 or 54749) is also recommended.

Europcar (BP 791; ☎51136; Fax 52285) has an office at *Hôtel Marhaba* and a branch at the old airport terminal (☎52408).

Visas Visa "prolongation" is possible at the *Commissariat Central*, av Abd El Nasser, east of the PTT.

SOUTHERN MAURITANIA

Southern Mauritania is the most densely populated part of the country, its major settlements connected by the Brazilian-built **Route de l'Espoir**. The one thousand and ninety-nine kilometres of paved *transmauritanienne* highway have certainly opened up the isolated southeast, bringing the far-flung regional capital of **Néma** within less than three days' drive of Nouakchott. There's a grim irony to the name, though. Instead of spreading wealth to the provinces, the "Road of Hope" has sucked them dry, offering swift escape from the parched countryside to the even less hopeful Nouakchott shanties – where the nomads and impoverished farmers can only sit and wait.

South of the Route de l'Espoir the population is largely non-Arabic-speaking and the land is dry savannah and bush, with irrigated rice and millet lands near the river. Shabby **Rosso** is a first glimpse of Mauritania for most travellers arriving from Senegal, but **Bogué** and **Kaédi**, further up-river are more interesting towns. Along the road, **Boutilimit** is worth a stop, as are **Ayoun el Atrous**, **Timbedgha** and Néma itself. Off the road to the **north**, the Moorish citadels of **Tidjikja** and **Tichit** are spectacularly isolated and tough destinations – Tichit up to five days' travel from Nouakchott. **Oualata**, north of Néma, is also highly recommended if you have plenty of time. Making for Bamako in Mali, the *piste* to the border crossing south of Timbedgha passes near the site of **Koumbi Saleh**, probable capital of the ancient kingdom of Ghana.

Rosso and north to Nouakchott

Arriving on the north bank of the Senegal River, there's nothing to hold you in **ROSSO** but the encouragingly named *Hôtel Union* (☎69029; Fax 69139; AC, S/C rooms; ④), whose service and facilities are fairly basic. Rarely would you be stuck for **transport to Nouakchott** however. Rosso's *gare routière* is 500m out of town, an arrangement that seems to have been designed to allow the *calèche* drivers the opportunity of giving you a ride in their horse-drawn buggies. Peugeots do the run up to Nouakchott in three to four hours along a coastal highway which for most of the year runs through dry dunes and sand hills with a scattering of trees. With rain, the dunes become gentle, grass-spiked hills, dotted with goats and camels and planted with the flapping white tents of nomads.

If you have your own 4WD, you could deviate from the highway some 20km north of Rosso to visit **Mederdra**, an old gum arabic centre at the heart of the defunct kingdom of Trarza, now renowned for wood and silver craftsmanship.

Boutilimit

A less than engrossing two-hour drive from Nouakchott, **BOUTILIMIT** is the first major settlement along the Route de l'Espoir, a Moorish caravanserai and also the site of one of the earliest French military bases in the country, with a large, permanent **market**. Perhaps it's major claim to fame is as the birthplace of Mokhtar Ould Daddah, Mauritania's first president. The religious capital of the country, Boutilimit is renowned for the literary collection of its *medrassa* (Islamic college), and for its crafts – goat and camel hair rugs, and silverware. Nowadays the town is very much under economic thrall to Nouakchott.

To Kaédi

From the anonymous town of **Aleg**, a brand new paved road leads 60km down to the river and the Chemama (flood plain) town of **Bogué**. You can get across the river by *pirogue* to the Isle à Morfil in Senegal from here, but the car ferry may no longer be operating.

The tarmac now extends from Aleg via Bogué all the way to Kaédi on a new, and seemingly solid embankment. **KAÉDI** is Mauritania's third largest town, and a major market centre – it's a good place to buy cloth. In the late 1970s a meat-freezing plant was built here, with the intention of culling some of the over-grazing herds of the south and air-freighting the meat to Europe. But the land immediately around Kaédi is barren, and offers no grazing at all to cattle driven there, so the herders continue to drive their cattle for slaughter down to the coast. The meat plant has gone the way of many such in Africa and is slowly crumbling to dust. But Kaédi is progressing in other ways, being the first regional capital to be equipped with electricity. A high percentage of Kaédi's people are settled, or semi-settled, Tukulor, whose white, long-horn zebu cattle can be seen roaming everywhere in the Gorgol and Guidimaka districts, to the southeast.

The hotel in Kaédi has closed in the face of the unfair competition from the **Base des Nations Unies** way out on the eastern edge of town. It's officially intended for UN personnel, but if rooms are available (AC, S/C with hot water; ④), they're worth arguing for. The cooking is excellent and they have a swimming pool. The *case de passage* of *SONADER* (*Societé National pour le Développement Rural*) is less accessible, although nearer to the centre of town, cheaper (AC; ③), but you have to share facilities at the end of the corridor with the rest of the crowd.

Getting east from Kaédi towards **Sélibaby**, Mauritania's southernmost and least typical town, is difficult in the dry season and usually impossible if it rains, although several *taxis brousse* try to maintain stages between one flooded river tributary and another. The journey is not made any easier by the impressive number of checkpoints along this "border" road.

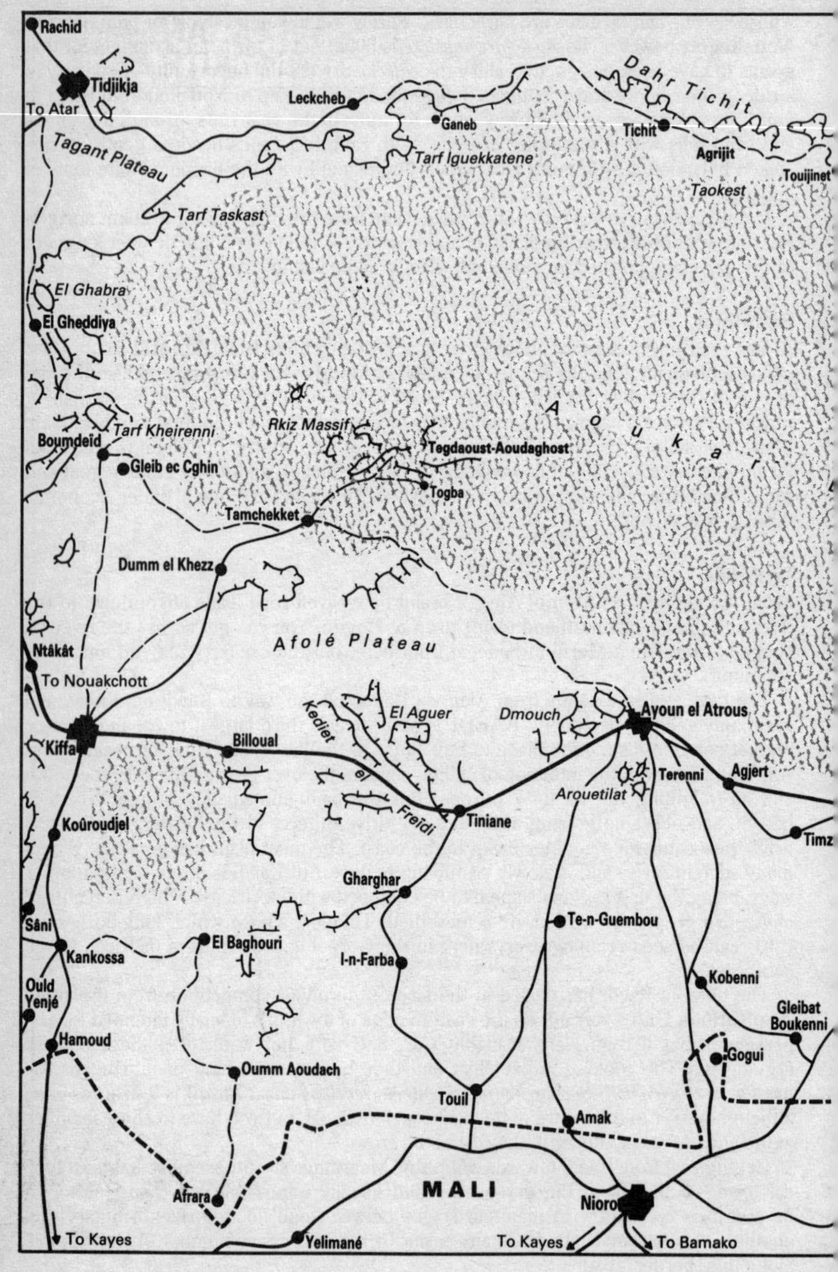
Rachid
Tidjikja
To Atar
Leckcheb
Ganeb
Dahr Tichit
Tichit
Agrijit
Touijinet
Taokest
Tagant Plateau
Tarf Iguekkatene
Tarf Taskast
El Ghabra
El Gheddiya
Aoukar
Rkiz Massif
Tarf Kheirenni
Boumdeïd
Tegdaoust-Aoudaghost
Gleib ec Cghin
Togba
Tamchekket
Dumm el Khezz
Afolé Plateau
Ntâkât
To Nouakchott
Kediet el Freïdi
El Aguer
Dmouch
Ayoun el Atrous
Kiffa
Billoual
Terenni
Agjert
Arouetilat
Tiniane
Timz
Koûroudjel
Gharghar
Te-n-Guembou
Sâni
Kankossa
El Baghouri
I-n-Farba
Kobenni
Ould Yenjé
Gleibat Boukenni
Hamoud
Gogui
Oumm Aoudach
Touil
Amak
MALI
Afrara
Nioro
To Kayes
Yelimané
To Kayes
To Bamako

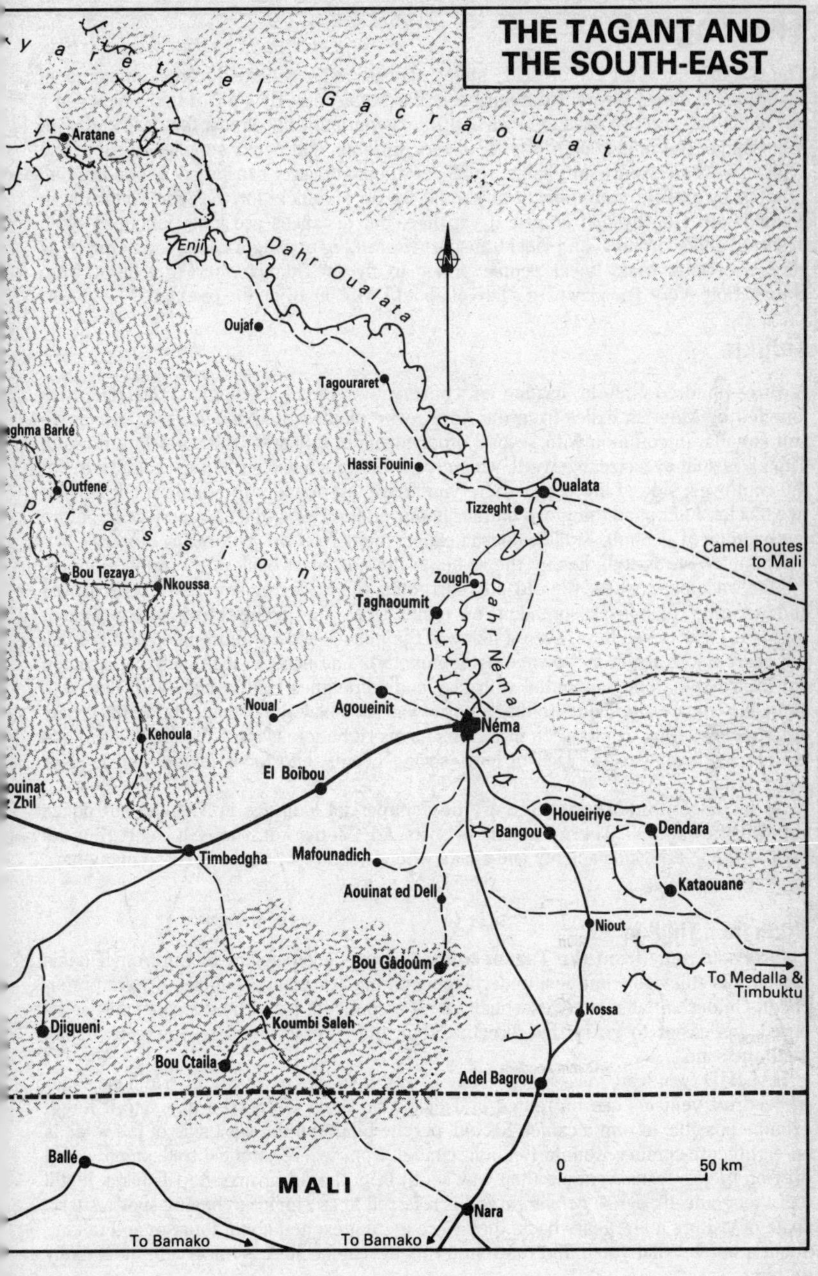
THE TAGANT AND THE SOUTH-EAST
el Gacraouat
Aratane
Enji
Dahr Oualata
Oujaf
Tagouraret
Hassi Fouini
Oualata
Tizzeght
Outfene
Bou Tezaya
Nkoussa
Camel Routes to Mali
Zough
Taghaoumit
Dahr Néma
Noual
Agoueinit
Néma
Kehoula
El Boïbou
Houeiriye
Dendara
Bangou
Timbedgha
Mafounadich
Kataouane
Aouinat ed Dell
Niout
Bou Gâdoûm
To Medalla & Timbuktu
Kossa
Djigueni
Koumbi Saleh
Bou Ctaila
Adel Bagrou
Ballé
MALI
0
50 km
Nara
To Bamako
To Bamako

The Tagant

The **Tagant** is a region of sear, stony plateaux, the remote location of some of Mauritania's oldest towns and notoriously hard of access. By 4WD it takes between a day and a half and two days to reach **Tidjikja**, geographically almost the dead centre of Mauritania. The final 200km of *piste* is very variable, and petrol supplies north of the *transmauritanienne* are unreliable, so fill your tank and jerry cans at every opportunity. Coming by **public transport**, you should fix up a vehicle for the whole journey in Nouakchott. Hop by *taxi brousse* if you like, but distances are long, junctions often deserted and scorching, and local transport (from Aleg or Magta Lahja, for example) is very uncertain. Many local people prefer to fly to Tidjikja: there's a flight from Nouakchott every Tuesday with a fare of about UM5300, twice the road fare.

Tidjikja

A three-hundred-year-old bastion of conservative Bidan ideology, **TIDJIKJA** was founded by Moorish exiles from the Adrar, who planted the *palmeraies* for which it's still famous. In common with several other towns in this area, the sprawling mess of Tidjikja is split by a sizeable **wadi**, which runs wet for a few days at most each year. On the southwest side of the town, where you arrive, are most of the modern administrative blocks. After something of a tourist "boom" in the 1970s (dozens every year, before the banning of alcohol), Tidjikja doesn't expect many *Nsarani* visitors any more.

The interest, though, lies up the slope on the northeast bank of the wadi, a fifteen-minute walk away, where the **old city** surrounds the Friday mosque, with palm groves and a jumble of houses spreading on either side. The **architecture** of the Tagant region is clear to see here, even if many of the houses appear unoccupied and are falling apart (most are in fact owned by somebody). The houses, massively constructed out of dressed stone, cemented with clay and sometimes clad in clay, with flat roofs and palm-trunk waterspouts to drain storm water, display the ornamental *kefya* – triangular niches – that can be seen in various forms right across the Sahelian belt. Rooms are narrow, owing to the lack of long, strong beams, and focus inwards on interior courtyards.

As for **accommodation**, there are no commercial lodgings in Tidjikja, but police and drivers will help. There's a bank of sorts, a PTT, market, shops, a smart Kuwaiti-built hospital, fuel, kids aplenty and a lake where nobody swims because so many have drowned.

North from Tidjikja

The caravan route **from the Tagant to the Adrar** – a journey of 470km from Tidjikja to Atar – is still viable but best undertaken with high-clearance vehicles (two in preference). Guides are absolutely essential: on no account set off without local expertise on board. It's easier to go in this direction than the reverse, because you're travelling "with the sand".

RACHID you can visit more easily – it's only 35km north of Tidjikja. Four-wheel-drive vehicles can be rented in Tidjikja for about UM8000 a day, and it might even be possible to rent a camel. Rachid, perched high on the west side of the wadi, is an eighteenth-century Kounta Bedouin citadel, from where piratical tradesmen would prey on the caravans wending their way south from the Adrar massif to Tidjikja. It still has a magnificent, dense *palmeraie* and is referred to as Tidjikja's "beauty spot". After a spate of visitors a few years back, they were getting excited about tourism and talking about a hotel. What you'll find there in terms of real facilities is uncertain: most likely nothing.

Tichit

TICHIT, too, is radically unprepared for tourism, which doesn't prevent them having piles of gear ready to sell, just in case. Such is the consuming nature of the dunes that swamp the town, however, there's every likelihood the old part will cease to exist as a viable community before the end of this century. Meanwhile, if you have the means to get there, Tichit is one of Mauritania's most interesting sites: dramatically located at the foot of the Tichit escarpment, the town has some of the finest **Tagant architecture**, and also preserves the remnants of a complex ethnic division in its town plan.

Only two or three dozen **houses** in the whole town are in reasonable condition, but these display a more elaborate and purer architecture than that seen in Tidjikja. Local stone of three different colours is used – greenish stone for the Chorfa quarter of town in the north; more crumbly, red stone used in the ruinous Masena quarter on the south side; and finely cut, hard, white stone, used only for the most prestigious buildings. The *kefya* ornamental niches are intricate, and the doors of a few of the old residences are still marvellously solid, with heavy, hob-nailed bolts and latches made of wood from Mali. Sadly the skills necessary to maintain the buildings are fading, and few people are prepared to invest the time and energy. The red clay that was once used to plaster interior walls is hardly ever seen today, and only the mosque is regularly repaired.

PEOPLE OF TICHIT

Founded around 1150 AD, Tichit once had a population variously estimated at between six thousand and one hundred thousand. Tichit's inhabitants now number about five hundred, as more families leave each year, and more houses are smothered by the sand. But the basic ethnic divisions are still visible, and encapsulate, though in an atypical way, the complexity of Mauritania.

The biggest and most economically active group, who call themselves **Masena**, are concentrated on the south side of the town, towards the modern administrative quarter. The Masena traditionally speak Aser, a Mande language closely related to the Soninke spoken in eastern Senegal. They're probably descendants of the black peoples who lived all over the Sahara in earlier, more prosperous times, and who were pushed south into oases like Tichit (and Oualata) by the expansion of the desert – and by the Berbers. Masena society has absorbed Berber immigrants and, like the Berber Tuareg, wealthy Masena families still keep slaves (*captifs*), whom they call **Abid** or **Bella**. Despite the formal freeing of the slaves in 1980, most *captifs* chose to hang on to their traditional way of life, working six days a week in the owner's gardens or household, in return for their basic needs. In comparison with an independent life in the Nouakchott slums, this kind of captivity seems less onerous. Today the Abid form a separate group in Tichit, living in their own quarter. Many Abid have mixed to some extent with Tichit's **Haratin** Moors, though the Haratins' status as free black ex-slaves is much longer established. Their reputation for piety and their long association with the Bidan Moors continues to endow them with superior social status.

The **Bidan** Moors in Tichit are called **Chorfa** – from *Sharif*, those families who believe themselves to be direct descendants of the prophet. Arabized Berbers who had established themselves in these parts by the ninth century, the Chorfa were originally part of the **Zenaga** group of Berber-speaking peoples from whose name the word Senegal is thought to have derived. The Chorfa are concentrated on the north side of Tichit.

The final group is the **Rehian**, nomadic Bedouin Arabs who pass through the town occasionally, to sell meat or take part in the date harvest. They move their tents around with the grazing, as much as 200km either way along the escarpment.

Despite this ethno-linguistic complexity, census returns from Tichit record 99 percent of the population as "Moor", meaning Hassaniya-speaking – a reflection, perhaps, of the assumption that to identify oneself with any other ethnic group is politically suspect.

The best time to be in Tichit, if you can bear the heat, is shortly before or during the July **date harvest**. The palm groves extend south of the town, between the houses and the ancient lake bed of Aoukar. Until about 1000 BC this was a vast reed-covered lake of some 50,000 square kilometres, supporting a large population of farmers, hunters and fishers on its shores. Today, the surface near the town is encrusted with **salt** which blows into the palm groves and coats the dates, making them inedible – and so the people of Tichit spend the last two months of the ripening season painstakingly washing the crop with well-water. The consequent joy and relief of the actual harvest make Tichit one of the best places to be at that time.

Travel practicalities

If you're **driving to Tichit**, you must take a **guide**. Heading out of Tidjikja, the route is clear enough to the Rehian stronghold of **Leckcheb** (a few windblown huts, some tents and a military post), but then the *piste* deteriorates. To the west of Tichit, the line of cliffs fades away and there's a waste of dunes in which to get stuck and lost. Eventually the track descends to the prehistoric lake floor of the **Aoukar depression**, where it winds along the base of the scarp.

Alternatives to your own 4WD vehicle are chancy. Getting a lift from Tidjikja isn't likely, except possibly after the plane from Nouakchott arrives on a Tuesday. And renting a vehicle for this expedition is an expensive business, even in a group – allow up to UM25,000, but bargain furiously. *Air Mauritanie* has ceased operating scheduled flights to Tichit, but at the prices you're liable to pay for surface transport, it would be worth enquiring about a chartered continuation of the Nouakchott–Tidjikja flight on a Tuesday. Obviously, you've every chance of getting stranded in Tichit, unless you go there by 4WD vehicle. You couldn't ask for much more adventure.

Unless, that is, you're determined to go further and make a full circle by taking on the three days and 400km of *piste*-driving **from Tichit to Oualata** (see p.128). This represents a major desert crossing, and the police in Tichit will make sure you take a guide. The *piste* follows the old caravan route around the Tichit and Oualata escarpments, with good wells at fairly regular intervals – Toujinet, Aratâne, Oujaf, Tagourâret, Hâssi Fouîni. The *piste* is mostly sandy, occasionally ascending the scarp to a kind of "Lost World" scene on top. You're unlikely to see other vehicles along the way and there are barely any wrecks to indicate much traffic in the past.

A less daunting forty-kilometre run east of Tichit leads to the nearly deserted and sand-swamped ruins of **Agrijit** – showing what Tichit itself is doomed to become.

The far southeast

East of the Route de l'Espoir's high point on the Tagant plateau – the Passe de Djouk – is the scrappy administrative town of **KIFFA**, where you can stay at the Peace Corps' *Maison de Passage*. The worn sign in the town centre for the *Hôtel de l'Amitié* claims it has electricity and water. In fact it's unfriendly and often has neither. The rooms are simple cubicles with thin floor mattresses (common showers and toilets are at the far end next to the kitchen). At the prices they charge (③), try to get in at the Peace Corps place or find somewhere – anywhere – else. If you're desperate to escape, it's worth knowing the Sunday morning flight from Sélibaby back to Nouakchott often stops at Kiffa (UM5500 to the capital).

Deviating northeastwards from Kiffa, there's 120km of *piste* to another post, **Tamchekket** (transport most days), enticing only if archaeological dedication drives you to find the ruins of **Aoudaghost** (see box), poking from the rocky ground in the **Massif du Rkiz**, some 40km further east. This is one for motorized travellers only.

AOUDAGHOST AND GHANA

Aoudaghost (modern name Tegdaoust) was once a great trans-Saharan trade city on the edge of what was then grassland. Its inhabitants were probably speakers of a Mande language like Soninke. From perhaps 500 BC, caravans of horses and bullocks used to arrive from Marrakech and the Roman Empire's Mediterranean shores. By the third century AD, the domestication of the **camel** had improved the viability of the trans-Saharan trade and Aoudaghost flourished on the commerce through most of the first millennium AD, in later years repulsing Berber Almoravid attempts to subjugate and convert it to Islam. The rapidly expanding empire of Ghana – focused on Oualata and Koumbi Saleh – captured the town around 1050, but within a decade Ghana's Muslim western neighbour, **Tekrur**, had helped the Berber Almoravids to invade and convert Ghana. By early in the twelfth century, the Berbers were leaving again, and over the next century both Tekrur and Ghana were swallowed by the mightier empire of Mali to the east. Aoudaghost was rebuilt in the sixteenth and seventeenth centuries, and then finally deserted. Today, it's only as interesting as the most recent excavations, and not easily visited (being so hard to find), unless a dig is in progress.

Ayoun el Atrous

Little **AYOUN EL ATROUS** is a more interesting town than most others along the road, but its economy is dead and even the caravanserai at the western town limits has had to shut down. Still, the buildings of red, dressed sandstone plus a nice hotel make it an attractive place to stop. And if you're into collecting old trade beads, you'll enjoy the **market**. If the sand-sweepers on the highway have been doing their stuff, **getting there** with your own transport (800km) from Nouakchott might be possible in one long, dawn-till-late day; public transport takes two days. The first of the three principal *pistes* to **Mali** starts at Ayoun, a two-day trip to Bamako by *taxi brousse*.

The *Aïoun Hôtel* doesn't get much business. You can get an ordinary room here with ambient-temperature water (S/C; ③), or pay twice as much if you want air-conditioning (④), but it only operates from 7pm to midnight – if the generator doesn't run out of fuel before. Food is available but expensive, out of cans and takes a long time to come. Ayoun's bank should be able to change money but may not have a clear idea of the current exchange rate and will charge you for their call to Nouakchott.

Timbedgha and Koumbi Saleh

If you're bent on visiting the ruins of Koumbi Saleh, and can find someone who knows exactly where they are, press on to **Timbedgha** (Timbedra) and then aim for the Malian town of Nara from there. The site is some 65km south of Timbedgha, close to the main route to Mali, and there seems to be a good chance of getting there by ordinary *taxi brousse* bound for the border, as long as you're prepared to pay a little extra for the diversion.

KOUMBI SALEH, the putative capital of the Ghana empire, is the most important medieval site in West Africa. Archeologists have barely scratched its huge extent. The town is estimated to have had a population of about 30,000, which would have made it one of the largest cities in the world at the time. The Arab geographer Al-Bakri, writing in 1067, described a conurbation of two towns, a northern one with twelve mosques, and, 10km to the south, the royal town of **al-Ghala**, with huts arranged concentrically around a palace. Between the two, along the royal road, was a continuous "suburb" of houses. Curiously, although traces of the royal part of Koumbi Saleh have been found, the royal quarter doesn't appear to have been constructed in stone. The main part of town is more impressive, successive excavations having uncovered massive stone houses, an enormous mosque and flagstone floors covering a more ancient layer of buildings.

Néma and Oualata

The *transmauritanienne* ends with a whimper at **NÉMA**, where the architecture – stone clad with clay – intimates that of Oualata, 90km north. Vegetable gardens, like Ayoun's, prettify Néma at the end of the brief rainy season, but for some reason hospitality here tends to be perfunctory. If you have your own 4WD vehicle, a guide can be hired for the deep desert drive from Néma to Tidjikja (4–5 days), and right up to Chinguetti (10 days) for a fee of around UM25,000–30,000 plus UM3000–4000 for his travel costs home again. A quarter of the fee is payable up front to his family.

There are fairly frequent vehicles from Néma to **OUALATA**, though not every day. The best chance of transport is on a Friday when there's a flight from Nouakchott to Néma; if you're in Néma by 8am, you may strike lucky with vehicles collecting plane passengers for Oualata. The plane returns to Nouakchott the same morning, often calling at Ayoun el Atrous en route.

Oualata's superficial glamour comes from the amazingly beautiful bas-relief **ornamentation** of its house walls. The decorations, of gypsum, white and red clay, and indigo, are designed and applied by the women, and although they're all unique, personal works, they share certain motifs and a thorough-going exuberance. The old town is partly abandoned and fewer and fewer households bother with decorating outside. Inside the houses, if you get the opportunity to look, the effects created can be stunning. Oualata's **doors** are highly stylized as well – the best ones studded with copper and silver.

Oualata's past is a fairly glorious one, and its present momentum as a viable community rests on its worldwide eminence as a centre of **Islamic scholarship**, the basis of long-term rivalry with Timbuktu. There are only twenty places in its Koranic school, creating a permanent waiting list of anything up to ten years. Less illustriously, Oualata, like Tichit, is also known as a place of internal exile, where outspoken political dissidents are detained.

You don't just show up in Oualata and wander around. Much as you'll have come to expect, a **visit to the police** is important, more so here than elsewhere. The Oualatans don't take kindly to Land-Rovies using their town as a photo backdrop, but allow some time for introductions and tea-drinking, and a day or two here can be rewarding. Such formalities are necessary, in any case, if you want somewhere to stay.

THE ADRAR

Breaking through the sands of the Sahara, the **Adrar Plateau** is Mauritania's most outstanding region. Though nowhere higher than 1000m, the gaunt, multi-brown scenery is strikingly clawed into deep **gorges** and sheer, cliff-edged mesas. In the southern parts, wind-carried **live dunes** stream ceaselessly across the landscape. The town of **Atar**, plus a handful of villages, and the ancient settlements of **Chinguetti** and **Ouadane**, account for almost all the population; camels and oases of date palms determine the economy.

Although the options are fairly limited unless you devote considerable time, the wildness of the desert, the isolation of the towns and the somewhat precarious feasibility of getting to them, make it a rewarding area to explore. The ubiquity of **neolithic stone tools** – some of them remarkably small and beautiful – adds further, acquisitive interest.

There are direct **flights** from Nouakchott to Atar on Mondays and Thursdays and flights via Nouadhibou on Saturdays. If you're taking a Peugeot **taxi** to Atar from Nouakchott's *autogare*, get to the Ksar early in the morning to secure a seat, preferably before dawn; you could otherwise be forced to wait until much later, even until the following day. Daily taxis run **from Atar to Choum** to connect with the ore train to Nouadhibou (see p.135).

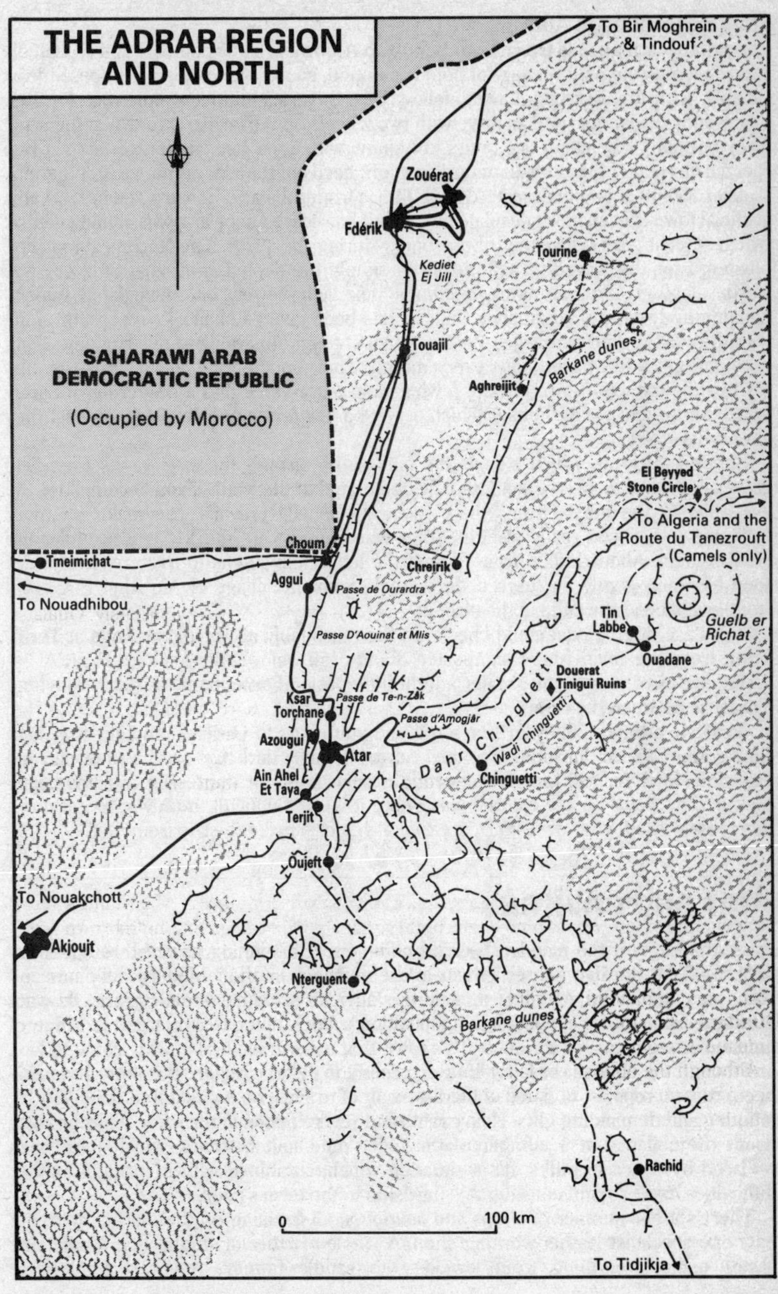
THE ADRAR REGION AND NORTH
To Bir Moghrein & Tindouf
Zouérat
Fdérik
Kediet Ej Jill
Tourine
Touajil
Barkane dunes
Aghreijit
SAHARAWI ARAB DEMOCRATIC REPUBLIC
(Occupied by Morocco)
El Beyyed Stone Circle
To Algeria and the Route du Tanezrouft (Camels only)
Choum
Tmeimichat
Chreirik
Aggui
Passe de Ourardra
To Nouadhibou
Tin Labbe
Guelb er Richat
Passe D'Aouinat et Mlis
Ouadane
Douerat Tinigui Ruins
Ksar Torchane
Passe de Te-n-Zak
Passe d'Amogjâr
Dahr Chinguetti
Wadi Chinguetti
Azougui
Atar
Ain Ahel Et Taya
Chinguetti
Terjit
Oujeft
To Nouakchott
Akjoujt
Nterguent
Barkane dunes
Rachid
0
100 km
To Tidjikja

From Nouakchott to Atar

Though the tarmac road **from Nouakchott to Akjoujt** is badly potholed and repeatedly sand-covered (the only scenery of note is plentiful, snowy white dunes), it does at least reliably mark the route you have to follow. Taxi drivers tend to leave the road for their own, sandy deviations, or else drive with two wheels on the tarmac and two in the sand. They normally take about five hours to Akjoujt, with a tea, pee, and prayer stop at Bou Rjeimat en route. More careful motorists might need eight hours or more to get there.

After 250km of empty desert, **AKJOUJT** is a frightful place. Constructed in 1949, this artificial town is even more desolate now that it has ceased to be a copper-mining centre, which at least gave it a veneer of prosperity during the 1970s. The "technical reasons" blustered for the failure turned out to be simply the depletion of what little ore was worth digging. Old mud-brick buildings mix with newer, but dilapidated miners' housing in desert-utilitarian style. Akjoujt has been given a shallow new breath of life with the start of **gold-mining** in 1992: a bunch of tough Australians are struggling along here and get a few dozen kilos every month. Their concrete cricket pitch is the only worthwhile attraction. Around the town's main *place* you'll find a scattering of barely awake shops and eating houses which service a few dozen people a day. At least they always have fuel.

Beyond Akjoujt, which signals the end of the tarmac, the *piste* varies from firm gravel and rocks to swervy sand, rapidly obliterated in the wind. If you become lost, the low relief to the north, from where the wind usually prevails, can make for more excitement than you really want as other wheel marks are quickly erased under the blowing dust. About 130km from Akjoujt the landscape begins to fracture, and you're soon climbing gently on the redefined track, with the village of Ain Ahel Et Taya a stony rest stop at the edge of the plateau.

If you are driving, you could check out the reasonably accessible **springs** at **Terjit**, 12km from the main route, signposted about 5km before Ain Ahel Et Taya. A hot spring and several cool ones water a tight little oasis of exceptional beauty, crouching like moss between the cliffs.

Continue a tough 35km further south and you come to **Oujeft** – another very lush oasis. Like many localities in the Adrar, Oujeft harbours archaeological and palaeontological relics: there's a gigantic human footprint impressed in a mudstone rock nearby (local people can tell you where it is). It's difficult, however, to get down this route without your own 4WD; occasional vehicles make the trip from Atar.

Atar and environs

From the edge of the plateau the road commences a winding ascent through rocky hills to **ATAR**, the largest settlement in the northern interior. Modern buildings and offices are fairly few, but this is a surprisingly large and energetic place, drawing business from the deepest parts of the desert. With lively markets and a fringe of *palmeraies* and irrigated gardens, it's a town that many travellers quickly come to like, and it can be a pleasant base for looking around the Adrar region. But there have also been recent reports of intense harassment of travellers by children and youths, taunting and demanding gifts. Heavy rains and severe floods in the early 1990s brought about the collapse of a number of the older mud-built quarters, which have been replaced by concrete hulks. It's a situation which, combined with Mauritania's other difficulties, has brought considerable hardship to the town's poor.

There's a fair number of shops and *boutiques*, all focusing on the market area, but only one specialist leather-working shop. A whole *quartier* of smiths (the Maalemine caste) make everything from jewellery to saddle fittings. Atar's reputation for handicrafts at first seems exaggerated, but you can find a fair amount of interesting stuff if you nose around. Much of it – Moorish clothing, camel saddles, pipe holders, belts and sandals – is designed and manufactured for local use. Apart from browsing, the standard thing to do is take a walk before sunset along the dike that separates the town from the gardens and *palmeraie* and holds back the rushing waters of the Séguélil wadi, which flow once a year at most.

Arrivals into Atar are often after dark. The main option for a **bed** for the rest of the night is the newish *Hôtel el Mourabitine*, in a converted French fort, with decent-value AC, S/C rooms (④). You can also stay in one or two restaurants in town, or find Salima Ould Sleimane, an exceptionally helpful Land Rover owner who runs trips for tourists. His house is close to the big roundabout in downtown Atar (at the roundabout, facing the bread stands, you take the Chinguetti road, the largest on the right, for about 100m: Sleimane's place is distinguished by a cluster of Land Rovers).

In the **food** line, you'll find a number of cheap eateries in the older part of town where a bowl of rice and dried fish comes for around UM150, and camel steak and chips for under UM300. Fix your price in advance; some establishments will take advantage otherwise.

Excursions around Atar

There are various good excursions out of Atar. Salima Ould Sleimane is highly recommended. You can write to him in advance (BP9, Atar): his price is usually UM18,000 per day for a large, enclosed Land Rover, which includes fuel, and will take four to six passengers. You can go pretty well anywhere with him and the price is negotiable to some extent if you're going to need him for several days.

Ten kilometres east of Atar there are **stone circles**, and 20km north of the town, on the road to Choum, is Ksar Torchane, an attractive oasis. But the best local trip is up to the ruins of **AZOUGUI**, the old Almoravid capital of the Adrar, about 15km northwest of Atar beyond the Tarazi pass, in the Tayaret wadi. During the winter, it's not too far to walk in a day if you fix up a guide in Atar, though unless you make a really early start you need to reckon on spending the night under the stars. Otherwise, it's a 4WD trip.

Azougui (the "Azokka" of medieval Arab writers) was the eleventh-century Berber base from which the Almoravidholy warriors launched raids on the Ghana empire satellite of Aoudaghost, and the Ghana cities of Oualata and Koumbi Saleh. Having swept through the southern fringes of the desert, they turned north for their second great invasion, into Morocco and decadent Andalusian Iberia.

The remains of the main stronghold are still visible today, a relatively small **citadel** (about 50 metres square) within whose walls the social framework of medieval southern Europe and North Africa was, in large part, determined. A couple of hundred metres to the west of the fort is the **necropolis** of Imam Hadrami, one of the eleventh-century holy warriors. Imam Hadrami's mausoleum, surrounded by tombstones, continues to be venerated by many Mauritanians.

Chinguetti and Ouadane

Chinguetti is probably the single most visited site in the country, though tourists in the broadest sense are still counted in handfuls each month. In itself, the town's mosque and jealously guarded library hardly add up to a compelling draw, yet the town does have picturesque qualities and the journey, through a landscape stripped to essentials, is emphatically worthwhile. **Ouadane**, which is possibly more interesting, bears comparison with Tichit in its remoteness. Neither is particularly easy to get to, and the upper *piste* to Ouadane reportedly still harbours Polisario mines.

From Atar to Chinguetti

It's about 120km from Atar to Chinguetti and the trip takes anything from three to seven hours, depending on your vehicle and any stops along the way. Occasional **supply trucks** trudge through the sand and up the passes, but their departures are barely advertised and by no means regular. More likely, a lift will come in the shape of one of the battered **Land Rovers** that whirl around Atar. If you join a vehicle that's making the trip, the fare will be around UM1500, depending on whether you sit in the cab or bounce in the back. If you rent a vehicle to get you there and back, allow up to UM20,000, returning the next day; you're best advised to take along someone who knows the route, as several sections are hard to follow – there'll be no shortage of demand for a free lift.

There are two alternatives, with the new "road" following a less scenic but safer and more direct course. The **old route** runs first through flat, grey rock and sand; then for several kilometres past steep, yellow dunes above a *palmeraie* tucked into a wadi; then between high, dry mesas and finally, in a steeply twisting series of hairpins to the head of the Amogjar wadi, a gorge which gives out to a further incline and the **Amogjar Pass**. In the interest of safety, it's common practice to get out and walk the steepest ascents and descents: don't hesitate to ask the driver to stop. Among the sandstone massifs you can see gun emplacements and the remains of military posts from the Polisario war. Up at the top squats the incongruous shell of the fake "Fort Sagane", built for the movie of that name in 1985.

Rock paintings – and lizards

Up at around 800m, a couple of kilometres after the final climb, you pass a conical rock stack on the left, fifty metres or so in height. Under an overhang near the top of the stack there are some intriguing **rock paintings** (ask for the *gravures rupestres* or *les dessins*), which are not hard to find, even unguided. While they're not up to Algerian or southern African standards in terms of size or confidence of execution, and give little more than hints about the people who sketched them, they're worth stopping for, and photographing. There are several red-coloured lanky figures, though it's not possible to make out the animals that some books refer to. The curious circular design on the left, with its four inner circles and radiating strokes, looks like Von Daniken spaceship material – but the Paris–Dakar rally has passed this way, so it's perhaps unwise to assume authenticity.

More figures are to be found on rocks directly by the road, on the right, about 6km further on, but these have been disfigured by Arabic graffiti. The figures are different from those on the hill: the frog-like heads (or headdresses) and massive thighs, could mean anything, though several resemble pygmies most of all. Thousands of examples of such rock art exist in the Adrar: only those near the roads have been seen, or disturbed, by outsiders.

The road now levels out and ploughs once again through soft sand. Look out for the heavily built, tortoise-headed, half-metre-long black Dhub (or Dhab) **lizards**, which scamper into their holes and crevices as you pass. Harmless vegetarians, they subsist between rainfalls by drawing on reserves of fat in their spiky, club-like tails, which they use to guard their tunnels. If you find yourself with an hour or so in the desert, they adore the colour yellow, and bananas send them.

Chinguetti

The route passes the turning for the upper route to Ouadane, 10km before entering the "modern quarter" of **CHINGUETTI**. On this side of the town, the main building – in fact Chinguetti's most striking – is the abandoned Foreign Legion **fortress**, used in the movie *Fort Sagane*, starring Gérard Dépardieu, about the Legion's exploits in Algeria. The fort doubled as set and film crew accommodation, and the air-conditioning and other facilities they installed made it the best hotel outside Nouakchott for a while. All is now deserted, but you can still climb onto the ramparts for fine views across the town (beware some very fragile sections). Other notable buildings on this side of town are the Gendarmerie, where you should check in on arrival, a Polisario-shot-up generator house hard by (electricity may have been restored by now) and a defunct solar water pump.

The best **place to stay** is on this side of town, and the new and the very appealing *Auberge des Caravanes*. You can sleep in the rooms, or out in tents, in Mauritanian style, with clean facilities laid on (②–③). They do very reasonably priced meals by request (UM300–500). A day out by camel can be arranged for about UM2000.

The oldest parts of the town lie across the broad football-kicked and goat-trailed wadi to the south, and to the west, where you'll also find the *Maison de Bien Être*, which may still offer a basic spot to set down for the night (②). The *Auberge des Caravanes* aside, **eating** in Chinguetti is a matter of luck at the market, and one or two perfunctory shops. There seem to be no eating houses, but you will find cold cokes at one or two *boutiques* with fridges.

Chinguetti's most venerable quarter, on the west side, dates from at least as far back as the thirteenth century. The town was established rather quickly, by exiles from the oasis of Abweir, just 4km down the wadi. Most of the buildings are made of stone, including the fine old **mosque**, off-limits to Nazarenes. Fortunately you can still get good views of it – complete with the five ostrich eggs atop its squat minaret and much of the interior courtyard – from surrounding dunes and piles of rubble. The "donnez-moi un cadeau" brigade are out in some force in the neighbourhood, and will show you to the *Maison de Bien Être* and the main **Koranic library**. The latter has been the object of some conservation work, and the most prized manuscripts are now contained in filing cabinets, opened only on payment of rather large sums. Families round about may have kept some of their own documentary heirlooms, and it's worth asking if you're interested. Chinguetti is the most venerated city in Mauritania, and was once rated as one of Islam's holiest cities, along with Jerusalem, Mecca and Medina.

Relics of a much more ancient history can be bought in the **market**. Extraordinarily fine, small **flint arrow heads** seem to be two a penny, as do the **barbs** that may have been used for fishing in a long-ago Adrar of forests and streams. They are apparently collected by children in the dunes. Weightier implements – beautifully shaped and much-worn cleavers and scrapers, for butchering meat and preparing skins – also appear occasionally. But they too are curiously small, and must have been used by small hands.

To Ouadane

The main route **to OUADANE** branches off the Atar–Chinguetti road, 12km outside Chinguetti; most transport between Atar and Ouadane calls at Chinguetti. Vehicles to and from Ouadane are few, so unless you have loads of time you're best advised to get a lift that's coming back again. The southern route to Ouadane, marked on the *IGN* map of Mauritania, is a sandy, wadi-course for high-clearance 4WDs only – but recently favoured after the discovery of land mines on the other route. If you're driving, neither route should be undertaken without a local guide.

Ouadane is a town of stones camouflaged in a landscape of stones. The place is quite extraordinary, collapsing in ruins amid the jumble of rocks from which it was constructed eight hundred years ago. So complete is the chaos that, arriving in the middle of the day, with no shadows to define the buildings, you don't even notice them stacked along the steep scarp until you're almost among them. Modern Ouadane – not a lot of it – perches above, on the plateau's edge. There was a rest house some years ago, but it's fallen into disuse, and you'll probably have to rely on hospitality, or maybe camp in the *palmeraie* beneath the town.

Ouadane was founded in the twelfth century by **Berbers** of the Ida-u-el-Hadj tribe, and some of the present-day inhabitants still speak Berber rather than Hassaniya Arabic. Its huge reputation – secure beyond the limits of the West African empires – as a **caravan crossroads** and trading centre for gold, salt and dates lasted nearly four hundred years. There was even a **Portuguese trading post** here at the end of the fifteenth century, busily intercepting the trade for the main Portuguese base on the coast at Arguin island. Ouadane's fortunes waned, unevenly, as first it succumbed to the onslaught of the sixteenth-century Saadian prince, Ahmed el Mansour of Morocco, who took control of the trans-Saharan trade and diluted much of the town's influence, and then lost its remaining economic power when the Alaouites invaded, also from the north, two centuries later.

Tin Labbé

Only 7km northwest of Ouadane, on the *piste* that curls round the mountain of Guelb er Richat, lies the semi-troglodyte village of **TIN LABBÉ**, where natural rock shelters and crevices have been incorporated into the cluster of stone and mud houses. If you've made it all the way to Ouadane, it would seem a shame not to walk up the wadi to see it. Among the tumble of huge boulders down by the vegetable gardens you can find rock paintings, and writing too, both in Arabic script and in the archaic Tifinar script of the Tuareg, a writing that traces its roots to a Libyan alphabet of the fourth century BC.

THE NORTH

For travellers flying in from Europe or the Canary Isles, or arriving by land from Morocco, **Nouadhibou**, Mauritania's second city, comes as an unlikely first taste of West Africa, and it's not a place on which to base any firm ideas of the region. Coming from the south, only plans to fly on to Morocco or the Canaries, or take a ship to Las Palmas, could really provide motivation for heading so far out of the way (overland travel to Morocco is currently prohibited, though just about possible using your own vehicle). The immensely long **iron ore trains** do at least offer a straightforward way of getting to Nouadhibou, which has no road connections with the rest of the country. If you're in the Adrar region, with a few days in hand before returning to Nouakchott, you can make a satisfyingly complete circuit by catching the train and then either flying from Nouadhibou to Nouakchott, or joining a truck convoy through the desert, the last third of which follows the sandy Atlantic shore.

Choum and Zouérat

The main draw of this region for travellers is the **iron ore railway** from Zouérat via Choum, which provides the best transport link to Nouadhibou. Taxis run daily from Atar to Choum in four or five hours, a fine trip with beautiful scenery much of the way. The Choum taxi drivers in Atar keep abreast of the news and will get you to the train on time. Before setting off from Atar, buy food for the journey, and take as much fresh water as you can – supplies on the train vary from limited to non-existent and the water at Choum itself is unpalatably salty. There's a habitual tea stop – a cool and friendly place of massive rocky outcroppings where camels are watered – halfway between Atar and Choum.

THE ORE TRAINS

The **iron ore trains** carry thousands of tons of crushed rock in a chain of wagons up to three kilometres long. Their schedules and frequencies depend partly on the speed of extraction at the mines, and on unpredictable hold-ups – damaged rails, engine failure and even, in the past, attacks by Polisario guerillas from over the border in Western Sahara.

One or more trains go from Zouérat to Nouadhibou every day, the most convenient west-bound one passing through Choum at about 5.30–6pm. The usual journey time from Choum to Nouadhibou is around twelve hours. Two others may come through late at night, or early in the morning.

The **fare** in the passenger wagon is UM1 per kilometre (so UM460 Choum–Nouadhibou or vice versa, and UM650 Zouérat–Nouadhibou), with a supplement for a fold-down bunk. Riding on the ore wagons is free – and you'll discover why, as the dust works its way into your soul. If you do go for this option, take a *houli* to wrap round your head, and have something warm for later in the night, when it can get remarkably cool.

The journey generally passes without incident these days, and there are no police checks. Restful dune scenery accompanies the trip for the last hour or two of daylight. There's generally one stop at Tmeimichatt (or *trois cents dix neuf* – kilometre post 319), to allow the empty train going the other way to pass. If you pick the right compartment you can find yourself sharing endless cups of tea and learning Hassaniya. At this point the interest outside the carriage, even on a clear moonlit night, is nil, and daylight brings no improvement, except hints of the sea as you approach the Nouadhibou peninsula. For information about taking the train **from Nouadhibou**, see p.138.

CHOUM, on the border of Western Sahara, consists of a string of restaurants and crash-out houses where Nouadhibou-bound passengers snooze through the afternoon, waiting for the train's arrival. When you arrive in Choum, leave your bags in the taxi: when the train arrives, you'll be driven alongside to meet the passenger wagon at the end of the train (a necessary taxi ride when the train may be over 2km long and it often sets off again within minutes).

If you're travelling with your own vehicle, there is the possibility of loading it aboard the train, but this cannot be done in Choum unless you have somehow been able to advise the *SNIM* (mining and railway office) in Zouérat of your requirement.

Zouérat

The *route impériale* continues north from Choum to what is now the purely military town of Fdérik. East of Fdérik it's tarmac to **ZOUÉRAT**, the economic and political heart of the far north. If you're driving, drive on the left on this section of road until the town boundary, then change again to the right. There are two round-trip flights a week between Nouakchott and Zouérat – on Tuesdays via Nouadhibou and on Thursdays via Atar (Zouérat to Atar is UM3500). Apart from the usual small shops, the *SOMASERT* supermarket is virtually the only place to buy anything in Zouérat. Tours of the spectacular mining operations can be arranged relatively easily from the *Hôtel Oasian*, which is essentially a company rest house, with all the food in the restaurant imported from the Canary Isles (BP 42; ☎49042 or 49043; Fax 49043; AC, S/C rooms with kitchen; ④).

Nouadhibou

Set on the eastern side of the Cap Blanc peninsula, a finger of desert pointing into the sea, **NOUADHIBOU** ("Jackal's Well") is fittingly colourless, a pale, flat, industrial city-satellite of Mauritania, where bars are permitted (or rather, alcohol is blind-eyed) and the mix on the streets is heavily European, Oriental, and Mediterranean. In French

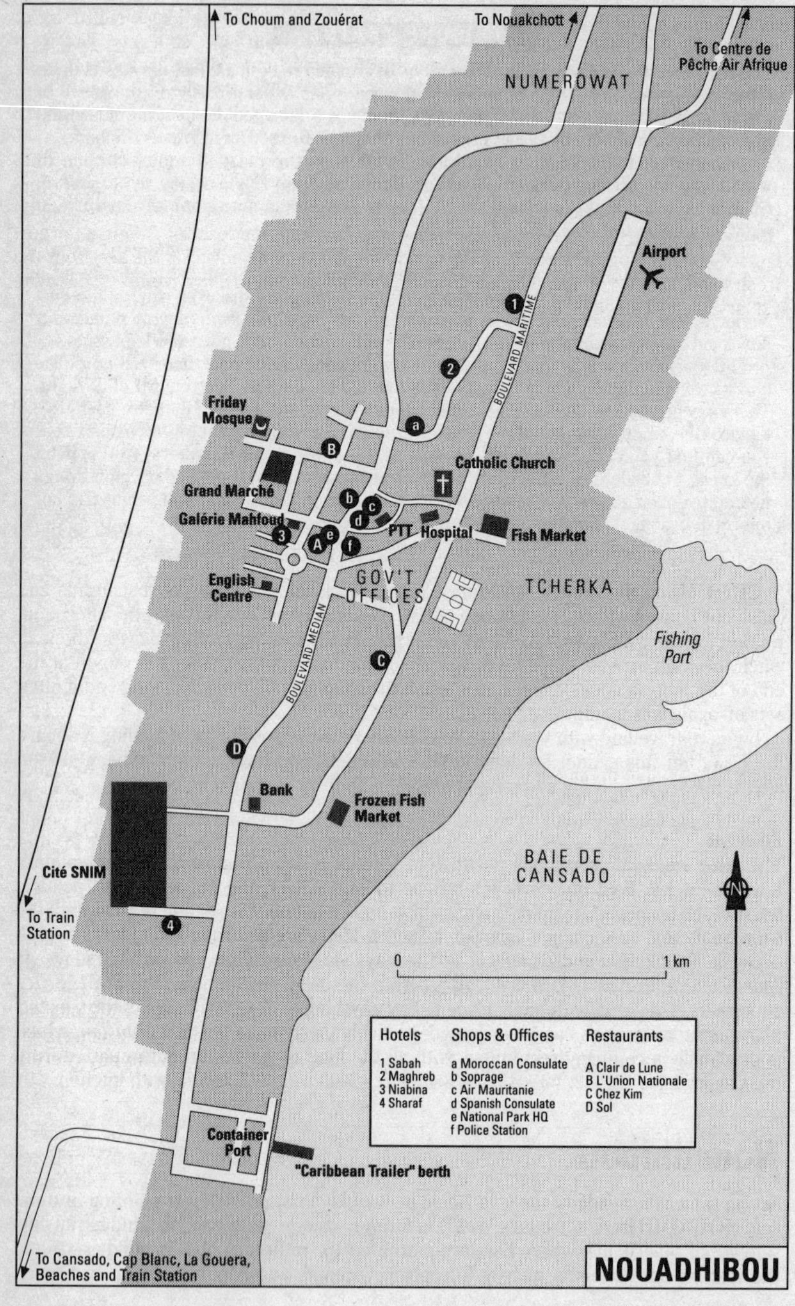
To Choum and Zouérat
To Nouakchott
To Centre de Pêche Air Afrique
NUMEROWAT
Airport
BOULEVARD MARITIME
Friday Mosque
Catholic Church
Grand Marché
Galérie Mahfoud
PTT
Hospital
Fish Market
English Centre
GOV'T OFFICES
TCHERKA
Fishing Port
BOULEVARD MEDIAN
Bank
Frozen Fish Market
Cité SNIM
To Train Station
BAIE DE CANSADO
0
1 km
Hotels
1 Sabah
2 Maghreb
3 Niabina
4 Sharaf
Shops & Offices
a Moroccan Consulate
b Soprage
c Air Mauritanie
d Spanish Consulate
e National Park HQ
f Police Station
Restaurants
A Clair de Lune
B L'Union Nationale
C Chez Kim
D Sol
Container Port
"Caribbean Trailer" berth
To Cansado, Cap Blanc, La Gouera, Beaches and Train Station
NOUADHIBOU

colonial times, this was Port Etienne ("Port Stephen") and many locals still think of themselves as "Stephanois". Nouadhibou's wealth, and purpose, come not just from shipping iron ore, but also from **fishing**, with Russian, Chinese and Korean fleets especially active. The southward sweep of the chill Canary current makes the waters here among the best fishing grounds in the world, and foreign fishing vessels are obliged to land and process a percentage of their catch in Mauritania.

The most obvious visit in Nouadhibou itself is to the **central market**, open until 10pm daily, which teems with cloth sellers, tailors and silversmiths. You may find, however, that you can get most of the artisanal works cheaper in Nouakchott. Close to the town centre, the wind-sculpted **table remarquable**, just east of the main airport runway, is a geological formation worth investigation. Down towards the sea from the fresh fish market, you can wander through what's left of the *village canarien*, once the Canary islanders' settlement of **Tcherka** or **Thiarka**.

Practicalities

Finding your way round Nouadhibou should not be difficult, and there's a wide choice of places to eat, but the paucity of decent hotels means that a tent might be useful. The options for leaving town are detailed in the box overleaf.

Arrival

Arriving by train, the passenger wagon stops at the "station" (an old shipping container) on the way south out of downtown Nouadhibou. The *gendarmes* can be difficult, so be prepared for a hostile reception. They're closed from noon to 3pm, but don't let them keep your passport: tell them you'll return in the afternoon. The **airport** is 700m from the *Hôtel Sabah*; to the town centre, it's or a twenty-minute walk, or a UM50 taxi ride (UM300 if you charter the whole vehicle). There is a bank at the airport, probably never open, although the telephone office does work. Three or four wooden shacks sell stale biscuits and imported sardines.

Orientation

Nouadhibou, like many desert cities, is immodestly large, and it comes in three parts. The first is the new quarter of **Numerowat** in the north, with its mess of construction sites, fading into shantytown on the north side. This is where the majority of people now live. The various quarters of Numerowat are identified by *robinets* ("Premier Robinet", "Deuxième Robinet", etc) according to the nearest public water standpipe, which come at 500-metre intervals along the tarmac road to downtown Nouadhibou. Downtown is **ville**, with all the usual services and shops and the city's main market. On the south side of town, a full 10km from the city centre, is the iron ore company's dormitory town of **Cansado** ("Sleepy" in Spanish). Since nationalization, this area is almost entirely occupied by Mauritanians.

Everyone travels around town by taxi and prices are fixed. Fares are UM25 for any journey in the downtown area or up the tarmac to Numerowat; UM40 in the same areas, but leaving the tarmac; UM30 town to port or vice versa; and UM50 to anywhere in Cansado.

Accommodation

If you're going to be staying in Nouadhibou, the problem is where. There's only one cheap hotel and, if those in the following list are full, or don't suit, you're pretty much down to meeting up with residents of the city or seeking suitable shade for your tent. Overland groups, newly arrived in Mauritania from Morocco, usually camp out on the beach, where it tends to be windy at night and baking hot by day. You can also camp at the station, waiting for the train to Choum and the *Clair de Lune* (see *Eating and*

Nightlife) is another possibility. You may get parties of gawping sightseers from town – not a bother but irritating.

Centre de Pêche Air Afrique, 14km north of Nouadhibou at the Baie d'Étoile (☎45571). Surf-casting is the big affair here, and you won't feel one of the boys if fishing is not your bag. FB ⑦.

Hôtel Maghreb (formerly the *Imraguens*), off bd Maritime (BP 160; ☎45544). Respectable hotel with bar and restaurant. ④.

Hôtel Niabina, town centre (BP 146; ☎45983; Fax 45835). Small, well run and good value for money. The only problem is finding the place (see map). ②–③.

Hôtel Oasian, 10km south of town at Cansado, overlooking the sea (BP 42; ☎45174; Fax 49043). Satellite TV, AC and mini-bars: this state-run establishment is the best hotel in Nouadhibou. If you reserve ahead, a courtesy bus will meet you at the airport. ⑤.

Hôtel Sabah, airport road, corner of bd Maritime and bd Médian (BP 285; ☎45317; Fax 45499). Received wisdom has it that this is the best place in town, but its standards are not up to those of the *Oasian*. ④.

Hôtel Sharaf (Foyer des Marins), 300m south of the town centre towards the main port (☎45522). A decent place though, as you'd expect, usually bursting with seamen. ④.

Eating and nightlife

There are several quite good **supermarkets** along the main tarmac road, bd Médian, and you can buy fish in the old fishing port area behind the stadium. There's a fair number of cheap **restaurants** near the central market. Standard lunchtime fare is rice and fish, with perhaps *couscous* and camel meat in the evening. The only "**nightlife**" that

MOVING ON FROM NOUADHIBOU

Leaving Nouadhibou by sea, it's still possible to do the run between Nouadhibou and Las Palmas. The *Aramas* shipping company operates two cargo vessels, the *Caribbean Trailer* and the *Cap Blanc*, that dock in Nouadhibou weekly. The easiest procedure is to visit the relevant berth and speak directly to the captain – unless you have an obscure passport (or children in tow), permission should be forthcoming. Officers are Spanish, crew Ghanaian, the food good and the cabins quite adequate. The fare is just UM3000 (less than £17 or $25) and the voyage takes about 36 hours. Some nationalities will need a Spanish visa: the address of the Spanish consulate in Nouadhibou is given in "Listings" above.

Leaving Nouadhibou by land, the train for Choum (taxi connection on to Atar) and Zouérat is detailed on p.135. For further information, contact *SNIM*, Nouadhibou BP 42 (☎45174 ext.1700; Fax 45396), the state organization that runs the iron ore mines and the railway. Departure from Nouadhibou is generally about 2–3pm, arriving at Choum about midnight and at Zouérat about 6am. Note that if you arrange things in advance with *SNIM* at their offices in Nouadhibou, you can unload your car at Choum; the cost for the Nouadhibou–Choum leg is between UM5000 and UM8000 depending on make.

If you have arrived in Nouadhibou with your own vehicle, another option is to link up with a Nouakchott-bound desert convoy. Or, if you're travelling by public transport, you can buy a ride for this adventurous desert trip. Land Rovers and trucks make the journey each day, departing from *Garage Nouakchott* next to the market. It costs UM2500 to UM4000 depending on the vehicle. If you're driving, hook up with one of these *chauffeurs*, who will certainly try to charge a fat fee. Negotiate hard, and leave it that you will pay on safe arrival and that you'll be charging them if they break down and require your help. The trip normally takes about 36 hours on the move (it's actually quicker – about 24 hours – but much farther, via Choum) and the route is never quite the same twice in a row. The last third at least is along the shoreline. By driving day and night, it's not uncommon to complete this trip inside 24 hours, but it makes much more sense to allow two to three days. Be aware that you should have police permission to do this trip, and you will almost certainly have to pay entry fees for the Banc d'Arguin National Park, merits the term is *La Sirène* disco, in the traditional fishing port by the beach, which serves alcohol, but only to foreigners.

Restaurant El Ahrem, town centre, next to the Grand Marché. A large, Egyptian-run restaurant, currently the most popular in town.

Restaurant Cap Blanc, bd Médian, next to *Air Mauritanie*. African and Western food in relaxing surroundings.

Centre de Peche, Baie d'Étoile. Fixed menu, always fish, always excellent. Never less than expensive.

Restaurant Chez Kim, bd Maritime, next to the Gendarmerie Nationale. International menu.

Clair de Lune, off bd Médian. Pleasant tea-room retreat with snack meals and inexpensive ice-cream.

Maimouna's Restaurant, Marché Premier Robinet, Numerowat (in an unmarked shack at the downtown end of the *marché*, away from the tarmac). As cheap as anywhere in town: Maimouna prepares the real Mauritanian food herself.

Restaurant Marhaba, bd Médian, opposite the *BNM* bank. Small restaurant but a good ambience. International cooking.

Restaurant Miade, next to *Galérie Mahfoud*. A little cramped, but a pleasant atmosphere.

Restaurant de Sol, bd Maritime, opposite the Chinguetti bank. Very clean place, and probably the best deal in town for upmarket eating (expect to pay about UM1000/head). Korean and global cuisine, and beer and wine.

Restaurant L'Union Nationale. One of a number of places that do chicken and chips and Mauritanian staples for a fixed price.

whether you plan to stop and "visit" or simply drive through unavoidably (see "Around Nouadhibou" for details). If you have a big enough vehicle and group, find a guide who has been vouched for, and set off alone; expect to pay him about UM25,000 for the trip, which should buy you the services of an assistant guide as well.

There are one or two flights each day to and from Nouakchott; **flights** every Monday to and from Casablanca (about £200/$300); and twice-weekly flights (Sun & Thurs) to and from Las Palmas (about £220/$330, but only £130/$200 if you can fix it to pay in UM).

GOING NORTH TO MOROCCO

Driving north from the Nouadhibou region into Moroccan-occupied Western Sahara is difficult and somewhat risky, but fairly frequently done by local and overland vehicles. The crossing is prohibited by the Mauritanians, so the key to success is avoiding Mauritanian officialdom. By far the best plan is to hire a good guide well in advance (in Nouakchott for example) and have him show you a safe route. The price will be around UM15,000, best paid in two or three payments. Travellers have crossed the border close to Boû Lanouâr, a village about 120km east of Nouadhibou (not 95km as marked on the Michelin map). Another "crossing point" is kilometre post PK71 (71km east of Nouadhibou), 3km west of the point where the *piste* crosses the railway to follow it on the north side. There's a major Mauritanian checkpoint at PK55: if you run into that, you've gone too far. If you find yourself in Mauritanian hands when obviously trying to cross, you will have some explaining to do.

Alternatively, rather than trying to avoid Nouadhibou, you can go into the town to assess the situation, but you then run the risk of being escorted back out of the vicinity of the border altogether, or paying large bribes. You can find guides in Nouadhibou, however, and they are cheaper than those from Nouakchott. Your official story will need to be that you're returning to Nouakchott.

The border is said to be mined along its length, but the consensus of opinion is that following tyre tracks is safe. Assuming you make it into Morocco, the reception at the first checkpoint you meet will depend partly on your nationality. You can expect to be detained for a day or two, though the soldiers can be very hospitable.

Listings

Airline offices *Air Mauritanie* (☎45011 or 45450).

Airport flight info ☎45147.

Amex office Try the *SOPRAGE* travel agency (BP 307; ☎45280).

Banks *BMCI* (BP 324; ☎45106; Fax 45628); *BNM*, bd Médian (BP 228; ☎45045; Fax 45573), usually gives the best rates.

Consulates Spanish, bd Médian (☎45371); Moroccan, off bd Médian, towards *Hôtel Maghreb* (☎45084); French honorary (☎45248).

Emergencies Police ☎45072; hospital ☎45288.

Tennis Courts by the *Hôtel Oasian*.

Around Nouadhibou, and the Banc D'Arguin National Park

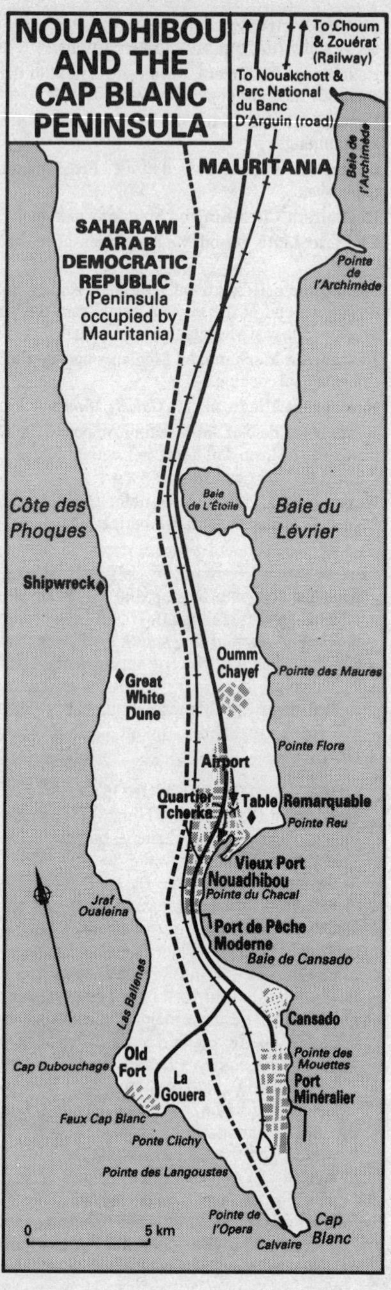

The area's wonderful **beaches** and extraordinary wave- and wind-formed **scenery**, on both sides of the peninsula, are the most obvious attractions **around Nouadhibou**. Thirteen kilometres north of town, on the east side of the peninsula, there's delightful, sheltered swimming in the almost enclosed **Baie de l'Étoile**. The *Air Afrique*-operated game fishing lodge is here, and you can get a drink or a meal.

On the western side of the peninsula, **La Gouera** (Laguéra, La Guera), a run-down Spanish fishing town almost swamped by sand, is technically part of Moroccan-occupied Western Sahara, but is now administered by Mauritania – a head-scratching arrangement that applies to the whole west side of the peninsula. There's good swimming in the sheltered bay behind **Faux Cap Blanc** but no entry to La Gouera itself.

The Nouadhibou area is the home of a colony of very rare Mediterranean **monk seals** (*phoques moines*), the lone males of which you're likely to see if you go down to the lighthouse at Cap Blanc. In appearance they resemble young elephant seals, growing to over two-and-a-half metres in length. Their valuable oil and skin has led to widespread extermination, but hunting them is now forbidden.

Intrepid birders should call at the head office of the **Banc d'Arguin National**

THE IMRAGEN – LIFE IN THE DESERT WITH DOLPHINS

The Banc d'Arguin National Park contains the seven villages of the **Imragen**, an isolated group of five hundred **fishing people**. Their traditional harvest of yellow mullet is caught in November – the period when huge shoals of fish spawn amid the sea grass in the warm shallows. By what appears to be a remarkable feat of cooperation between humans and animals, the catch is brought to shore with the assistance of dolphins. Summoned by the Imragen beating the water surface from the shore, the dolphins drive the fish to the beach, where the mullet provide a feast for them and a tremendous haul for the villagers. Recent research suggests that yellow mullet may actually *like* swimming underneath pods of dolphins, so that the only human intervention is to signal to the dolphins the fish trap that is at their disposal. In any event, it's an extraordinary occasion, a spectacular chaos of leaping fish, thrashing cetaceans and ducking fishermen. Other Imragen fishing methods are less successful: they aren't skilled boatbuilders and they only have a few small vessels. Their survival on this barren shore is entirely dependent on an extractive economy, and even water has to be trucked into the villages from Nouakchott or Nouadhibou. The best windfalls are provided by ships scuppered offshore for insurance purposes. There are literally hundreds of these, providing fuel, building materials and occasionally more interesting bounty for the Imragen.

Park, on bd Médian near the PTT, in Nouadhibou (☎45085; see also "Wildlife and National Parks" on p.104). The entry fee is UM800 per person per day but check the possibilities out with them; trips can be arranged or guides provided if you have your own 4WD vehicle. This will only get you to the right area, however – the main Imragen villages of **Iouîk**, 200km south, or **Nouamghar**, about 250km south of Nouadhibou. To do some birdwatching you'll need to rent a boat and go out among the shallow seas and sand shoals.

index

CHAPTER TWO

SENEGAL

SENEGAL

Senegal is the most French-influenced of all West Africa's Francophone countries. In 1658 the island of St-Louis became the first part of the continent to be colonized by the French, and there's an enduring relationship between the two countries. Partly as a result of this pervasive Europeanism – and in recent years a growing American cultural influence – you could breeze through Senegal and hardly notice anything distinctive about it. It is one of West Africa's biggest holiday destinations, with a fair number of beach hotels and holiday clubs, and until the Casamance conflict of the early 1990s slowed the growth, attracted 200,000 visitors a year.

As soon as you start scraping away the French skin, however, a far more fascinating creature is revealed. The **Muslim marabouts** wield exceptional power in Senegal, commanding block votes at elections and even directing the course of the economy by their injunctions to followers. Although Islam in Senegal is quite different from its North African counterpart, the idea of a future Islamic state doesn't seem wholly fanciful. The name of **Touba**, the holy city of one of the most powerful Muslim brotherhoods, is one you'll see all over the country, incorporated into numerous names and signs.

French style and deeply felt Islam coexist with extraordinary success, though both elements are relatively recent introductions to most of Senegal. Islam did not have a wide reach until the end of the nineteenth century, while the French, although long-established in key towns on the coast, finally subdued parts of the interior as recently as the 1920s.

People

The people of Senegal are dominated by the biggest language group, the **Wolof**, who figure prominently in government and business and control the Mouride brotherhood. A clutch of Wolof kingdoms used to cover the heart of Senegal – an area now largely under fields of all-important **groundnuts** – in a highly stratified society based on class and caste differences. The first Muslims were the **Tukulor** and closely related **Fula** – people whose kingdom was in the northeast, which is still their heartland. The **Mandinka**, too, were widely converted to Islam before the Wolof. In the southwest, the **Serer** (Sérère) and **Jola** resisted Islam until the twentieth century – in parts they still do, preferring their indigenous religions – and they maintained more egalitarian, clan-based societies than the Wolof or the Muslim peoples. Christian missions have had a limited impact.

Today, most language groups are increasingly subject to **"Wolofization"** and a national Senegalese identity is emerging as people move to Dakar and other towns. More resilient have been the people of the south – the Jola and other scattered, largely non-Muslim, communities of Bassari, Bainuk, Konyagi and Jalonke.

Where to go

Senegal is better organized than its neighbours: a country that's easy to get around, and one that's familiar with, and officially supportive of **independent travel**. Since the devaluation of the CFA franc in 1994, it is one of the less expensive countries in West Africa for visitors. It is also one of the freest countries with one of the region's best human rights records. But a land of contrasts it is not – flat and pale isn't unfair – and

FACTS AND FIGURES

The Wolof have an apocryphal account of the derivation of the **name** *Senegal*, in which a witless explorer points across the Senegal River and asks some fishermen what it is called. "That's our boat" they reply – *li suñu gal le*. In fact the name probably derives from the **Sanhaja** Berbers who frequently raided the river region and were known by the early Portuguese explorers as *Azanaga*.

Senegal is one of the **flattest** countries in West Africa, rising to barely 500m in the Fouta Djalon foothills. Two main rivers, the Senegal and the Casamance, roughly mark the country's north and south limits, and the southern region is sliced through by The Gambia – the result of a colonial carve-up in the 1890s that was seen as asinine even then.

Today **La République du Sénégal** has a **population** of about seven million and an **area** of 196,000 square kilometres – roughly the size of England and Scotland combined, or half as big as California. The country's **foreign debt** totals over £2.5 billion ($4 billion), a colossal figure in the West African context, and three times the annual value of its exports, but less than half the value of Bill Gates' Microsoft software empire. Senegal's **political system**, a presidential democracy, is the longest practising multi-party democracy in West Africa – though the ruling moderate *Parti Socialiste* has never been defeated. The on-off **Senegambia confederation**, a political pact between Senegal and the tiny country it surrounds, is currently off.

while there's some scenic variety to be sure, the country is most interesting at the cultural level.

The south, effectively screened from Dakar by The Gambia, provides the biggest attraction for travellers. The forests and mangrove creeks of the **Basse Casamance**, and the exceptional **beaches** of the short southern coastline, are the biggest pull – these combined with the largely non-Muslim culture of the Jola. The conflict between Casamance separatists and the government had not posed a major threat to travellers until the disappearance (and presumed kidnap) of four French tourists in 1995. Travellers to the region should keep abreast of the situation. In the southeast, **Niokolo-Koba National Park** is one of the best game reserves in West Africa, from where it is well worth the effort to push on into the remote southeast corner of the country.

The attractions further **north** are round the edges: along the coast or up the Senegal River. **Dakar** – probably unavoidable, definitely two-faced – is a place to enter with some degree of caution. Yet for all its tough character, there are rewards in the city itself, and a number of good trips round about. **St-Louis** is another ambiguous case, charged with atmosphere or depressingly run down, as it strikes you. The upriver towns, small outposts along the Mauritanian border, are stopovers rather than ends in themselves.

Climate

Senegal's **climate** is one of the best in West Africa, with a short rainy season (*l'hivernage*) between June and September – or October in the south – and a dry period between December and April. The winds turn with the seasons, tending to blow warm and humid from the southwest, then at times fiercely hot, dry and dusty from the northeast and the Sahara (the *Harmattan*). Early in the dry season, in December and January, Dakar and St-Louis can be surprisingly cool, especially at night. Through the rains however, Dakar's combination of high humidity and city pollution can be pretty oppressive.

The weather needn't alter your travel plans as a rule, but you'll find some of the **National Parks** closed during the wet season until tracks become passable.

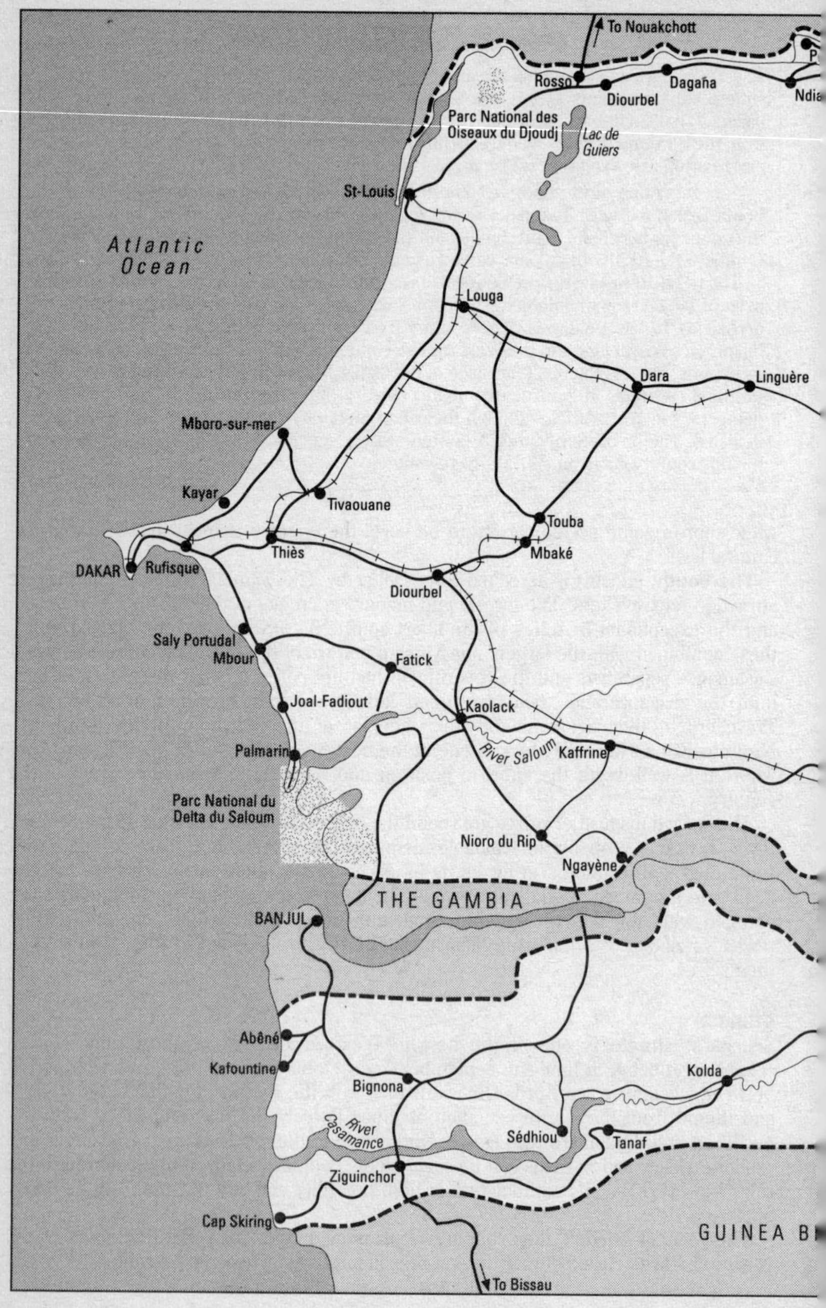
To Nouakchott
Rosso
Diourbel
Dagana
Parc National des
Oiseaux du Djoudj
Lac de
Guiers
St-Louis
Atlantic
Ocean
Louga
Dara
Linguère
Mboro-sur-mer
Kayar
Tivaouane
Touba
Mbaké
DAKAR
Rufisque
Thiès
Diourbel
Saly Portudal
Mbour
Fatick
Joal-Fadiout
Kaolack
River Saloum
Kaffrine
Palmarin
Parc National du
Delta du Saloum
Nioro du Rip
Ngayène
THE GAMBIA
BANJUL
Abéné
Kafountine
Bignona
Kolda
River
Casamance
Sédhiou
Tanaf
Ziguinchor
Cap Skiring
To Bissau

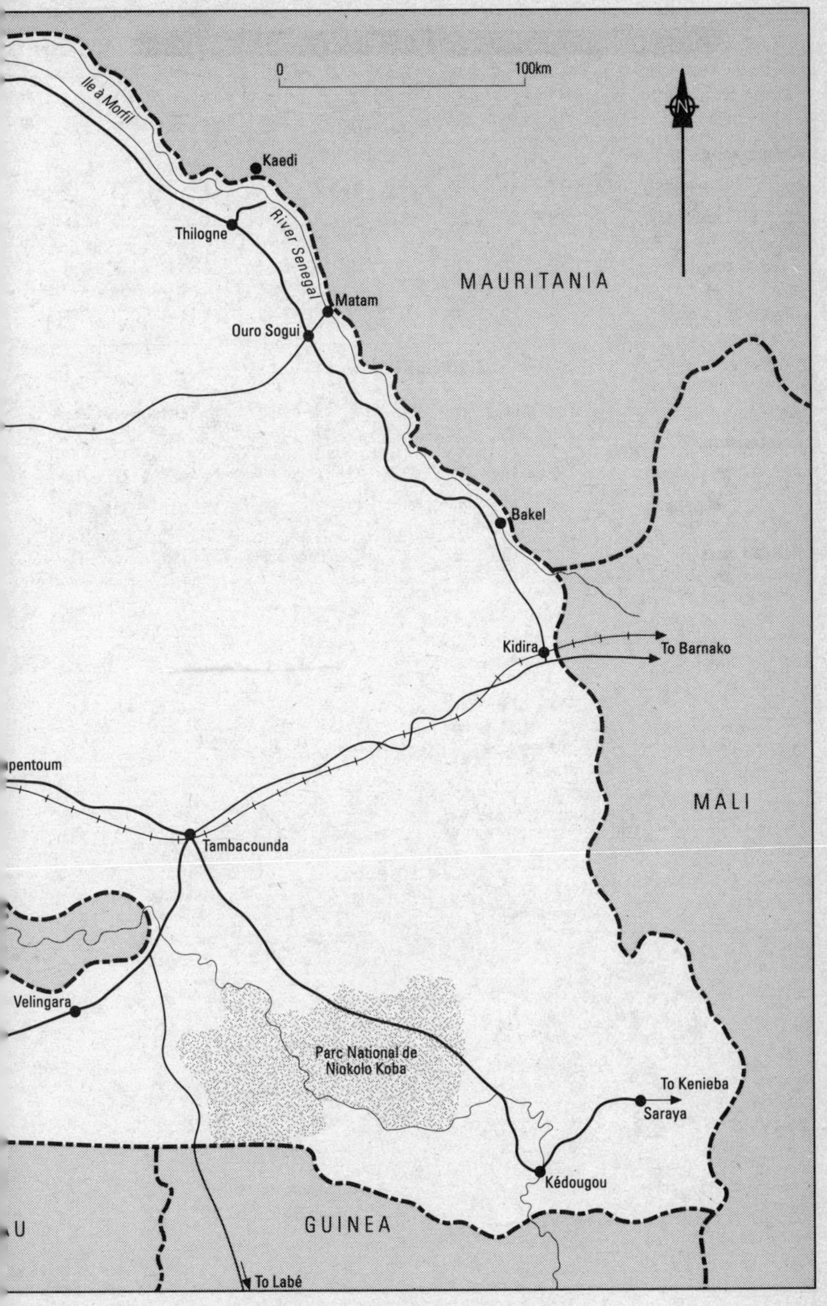
0
100km
N
Ile à Morfil
Kaedi
Thilogne
River Senegal
MAURITANIA
Matam
Ouro Sogui
Bakel
Kidira
To Barnako
pentoum
MALI
Tambacounda
Velingara
Parc National de
Niokolo Koba
To Kenieba
Saraya
Kédougou
U
GUINEA
To Labé

AVERAGE TEMPERATURES AND RAINFALL

DAKAR

	Jan	Feb	Mar	Apr	May	June	July	Aug	Sept	Oct	Nov	Dec
Temperatures °C												
Min (night)	18	17	18	18	20	23	24	24	24	24	23	19
Max (day)	26	27	27	27	29	31	31	31	32	32	30	27
Rainfall mm	0	0	0	0	0	18	89	254	132	38	3	8
Days with rainfall	0	0	0	0	0	2	7	13	11	3	0	1

ZIGUINCHOR

	Jan	Feb	Mar	Apr	May	June	July	Aug	Sept	Oct	Nov	Dec
Temperatures °C												
Min (night)	17	17	19	20	22	24	23	23	23	23	21	18
Max (day)	33	34	35	35	35	33	31	30	31	31	32	31
Rainfall mm	0	3	0	0	12	142	406	559	338	160	8	0

Arrivals

Dakar is a common starting and finishing post for overland travels, and in many ways the city feels like a stepping stone between Europe/America and Africa.

The details in these practical information pages are essentially for use on the ground in West Africa and in Senegal itself: for full practical coverage on preparing for a trip, getting here from outside the region, paperwork, health, information sources and more, see *Basics* pp.3–88.

■ Flights from Africa

The most useful flights from **North Africa** are direct flights from Tunis on *Tunis Air* (TU) via Casablanca, and from Casablanca via Nouakchott on *Royal Air Maroc* (AT).

There are direct flights to Dakar from every capital city in **West Africa**, with most of the few non-stop ones on *Air Afrique* (RK): daily or almost daily from Abidjan, Banjul and Conakry; and at least weekly from the other cities, including Praia on the Cape Verde Islands, which has four flights a week.

There are also good weekly connections from Nairobi and Johannesburg, both via Abidjan.

■ Overland

Senegal has for a number of years been a major overland terminus and departure point. These days, with the opening of the Atlantic route it is more of a crossroads.

The Atlantic Route via Mauritania

Since the early 1990s the **Atlantic Route** across the Sahara via the Moroccan-held Western Sahara to Mauritania has been open to all traffic. Military convoys depart twice a week (Tues & Fri) from **Dakhla** (1400km south of Rabat) escorting all vehicles through the sandy minefields just north of the Mauritanian port of **Nouadhibou**. From here an ore train can carry cars and passengers inland to the highway (14hr), or guides can lead suitable vehicles along the beach to the capital, **Nouakchott** (1–2 days). From Nouakchott it's just over 200km of reasonable tarmac to the Senegalese border at **Rosso** where a motor barge transports vehicles across the Senegal River. Other, less formal *pirogue*-crossings are possible upriver at Kaédi or Sélibaby.

From Mali by train

Most overland travellers arrive **from Mali** on the *Océan-Niger* **train**. Departures from Bamako are scheduled for **9.15am Wed & Sat**. It's a gruelling 30-to-36 hour journey. Scheduled arrival time into Dakar is 2.30pm the following day, but the usual delays mean you're likely to arrive after dark.

Beware that **Muslim holidays**, and particularly the *Magal* (see the Islamic calendar on p.62), can alter train timetables.

An alternative is to take the train from Bamako only as far as **Tambacounda** (where it should arrive at 3am or 4am), from where it's a hot, uninteresting, but quicker journey **by road** to Dakar. Getting off the train at this point also gives the option of going down to Basse Casamance or The Gambia before confronting Dakar.

Fares to Dakar range from around CFA21,000 2nd class to CFA28,000 1st class, to CFA45,000 sleeper. The Sat train from Bamako is air-conditioned; for which 1st and sleeper-class passengers pay a CFA4000 supplement. There are small **student reductions** in second class: it's worth paying the difference only if you want more leg-room and fewer companions. Once you're on the train, it's possible to upgrade to **sleeper class** assuming there are berths available (double cabins only), but the protracted border formalities take place during the night and require you to disembark, so you don't get much sleep in any case. There's a buffet car, serving snacks and drinks, and you can buy **street food** and drink from station vendors day and night.

From Mali by road

Driving from Bamako to Dakar is a feat of skill and endurance: the section from Bamako to Kayes via **Nioro** is notoriously sandy and the "direct route" via **Kita** requires a high-clearance vehicle. You can put your vehicle on the **train** to Dakar, but the hassle and expense makes the *piste* a far more interesting proposition for suitably prepared vehicles. There's a bridge, now, over the Falémé River on the Mali-Senegal border, where formerly the ford was regularly deeply flooded.

From Guinea-Bissau and Guinea

The principle route, now fully sealed, crosses into Senegal **from Guinea-Bissau** at **São Domingos**, direction Ziguinchor. Lesser crossings include Farim to Tanaf and Bafatá to Kolda.

Entering Senegal **from Guinea**, Koundara to Tambacounda is the usual route. A couple of spidery routes further east make the Labé to Kédougou crossing increasingly viable for suitable vehicles. You can expect daily transport except in the rainy season, when road problems will cause lengthy delays.

From The Gambia

To Dakar, there's little or no through traffic from Banjul. Consequently, there's a succession of vehicle changes to be made if you're travelling by public transport from Banjul (or rather from Barra on the north side of the Gambia River, facing Banjul). These are described in more detail in the practical information section in the Gambia chapter.

From The Gambia **to Ziguinchor**, a variety of bush taxis leave from the main taxi park in Serekunda market – 4hr by Peugeot 504, including a vehicle change and border formalities at **Séléti** where there's usually little hassle. Make sure the Gambian officials stamp you in the right direction though – *Arrival* or *Departure*. If you're trying to visit the Casamance in a day trip from a Gambian hotel, most taxi drivers will oblige – the fares to Ziguinchor and Cap Skiring are posted up. But Cap Skiring is really too far to do in a day: you'd be driving most of the time.

Red Tape

US citizens need no visa to visit Senegal. Similarly, British, Irish, French, Italian and German passport holders do not need visas. Other EC passport holders too, should be exempt, but some officials may not be aware of this, and may try to insist you have a visa – in which case buy one at the airport or border.

Non-EC passport holders definitely need visas, but they're usually for multiple entry (ask) and can be issued quickly. Visa requirements are normally minimal and they can be obtained from Senegalese embassies or consulates in virtually every country in West Africa (see map on p.22).

A yellow fever **health certificate** is obligatory (and you're advised to have the cholera certificate) even if you're flying in direct from Europe, though there's sometimes a negotiable line between what's stipulated by the Ministry of Health and what's demanded by the official at the arrivals desk.

Duty free allowances don't include any spirits, though, again, in practice this may be overlooked.

For visas for **onward travel**, Dakar has embassies for most West African countries. Addresses and visa information are given in the Dakar "Listings".

Money and Costs

Senegal's currency is the CFA franc (CFA100 always equals 1 French franc; approx CFA750–800 = £1; approx CFA500 = US$1). Changing money in Senegal can be very difficult, so be sure to have French francs on you. Fortunately for visitors, since devaluation, the country is no longer expensive.

Hotels will cost you from around CFA10,000/day in Dakar (about £12, or less than US$20), and even less outside the capital. Travelling costs, when you've taken baggage into account, are usually around CFA1500 per100km. A further boon for travellers in Casamance is the region's system of *campements touristiques rurals integrés* (*CTRI*), for more on which see "Accommodation". Camping is also feasible in many places. An *ISIC* student card is useful for reduced entry fees to sites and museums and worth trying for possible discounts on trains and planes.

■ Money

As in other CFA countries, carrying your money in **French franc travellers' cheques** makes most sense, but carrying some francs in cash is useful too – banks are scarce outside the capital and clerks are unfamiliar with most other foreign currencies. Since devaluation, even French francs are commissionable when changed at some banks. There should be fewer problems in Dakar, as the city is one of the region's main financial centres.

If you're staying in Senegal for some time, or basing yourself in Dakar, opening a **bank account** with one of the main banks is effective, though not simple. It's better to have your bank open an account for you in advance – then you can take your account number to the bank in Senegal on their letter.

Apart from Dakar airport's **24-hour exchange counter** (which is, in reality, sometimes closed), the only other out-of-hours exchange facilities are the normally exploitative hotel desks. Banks tend be closed from 11.30am until 2.30 or 3pm.

Credit cards are of more use than in other countries, with *Visa* and *Mastercard/Access* leading the field for tourist services, car rental, fancy restaurants and flashier shops. **Cash advances** on *Visa* can be arranged through the *SGBS* and *BICIS* banks; *Amex* advances through one or two Dakar travel agents (see Dakar "Listings").

Health

One of the most comfortable countries in West Africa, Senegal doesn't pose too many health problems. It's mostly dry, seasonally mild (at least along the coast), and has a relatively well-developed healthcare infrastructure.

Dakar used to be the place to convalesce from the diseases of the interior. Nowadays, however, if you're getting over something, perhaps you should find a resting-up spot away from the city. Many Dakarois have year-round colds and the city has the country's highest typhoid levels – attributed to exhaust fumes, industrial air pollution and the city has the 1400 tonnes of garbage produced every day.

If you're basing yourself – or staying some time – in the Dakar area, especially during the cool, dry season from December to March, you may prefer to forget about **malaria** prophylaxis. Local doctors often insist it's more harmful than beneficial, and many expat residents don't bother – certainly the mosquito problem is minimal at this time of year. However, as soon as you move on, heading into the back country, especially in forested or watered areas, you expose yourself to risk again, a risk that is higher if you've broken your course.

Town **water** from taps is normally fine, though the Senegalese have taken to *Evian* and their own *Montrolland* bottled water with enthusiasm. From shops it's not too expensive; from hotels and bars usually much more. As in the other Sahel countries, seasonal drought means insufficient washing water. Away from large towns try to check on the provenance of the water used (if any) to wash your plate and glass in eating houses.

Water-borne schistosomiasis (**bilharzia**) poses no threat in the brackish tidal waters of the lower Casamance, Saloum and Senegal river (though the lower reaches of the Senegal are much less brackish, and thus more dangerous, since dams came into operation upstream). Make sure, nevertheless, that you're sufficiently downriver for it to be salty before plunging in.

Senegal has a higher than usual incidence of **diphtheria**. If you're not sure whether you were immunized as a child (possibly not if you were born after 1970), check with your doctor before leaving home.

In the north along the river, especially around Rosso, there are occasional outbreaks of **"arbovirus"** diseases – similar to yellow fever but with no antivirus available. Check locally. All you can do is try to avoid being bitten by insects.

Like much of West Africa, Senegal has become fully aware of the threat of **AIDS** and there's a massive anti-*Sida* campaign. Needless to say, use prudence, and never have unprotected sex.

Maps and Information

Before you go, you can collect maps and information from your nearest Senegalese embassy; the Paris office is the big one. As well as a variety of tourist brochures, they may also have copies of the free monthly listings and adverts pamphlet *Le Dakarois*, also available in Dakar itself. For sources of information before you go, see p.41.

You're best advised to stock up on **maps** before you arrive in Senegal, where they're hard to find and expensive. The *IGN* **Senegal** map at

OVERSEAS TOURIST OFFICES

France
Office du Tourisme,
22 rue Hamelin,
75016 Paris ☎1/47.04.24.50
Fax 1/47.04.33.38

Germany
Fremdenverkehrsamt-Senegal,
Münchener Strasse 7,
D-6000 Frankfurt/M ☎069/23 26 91

Italy
Ufficio di Promozione Turistica del Senegal,
Centro di Cooperazione Internazionale,
Largo Africa,
20145 Milano ☎02/49 97 450

United Kingdom
Senegalese Embassy,
11 Phillimore Gardens,
London W8 7QG ☎0171/937-0925

1cm:10km is useful, and its companion 1cm:100m **Dakar** is invaluable in the city. There are also some moderately useful **regional survey maps** that you'll only find in specialist shops.

Getting Around

Compared with many parts of West Africa, Senegal is easy to get around: bush taxis will get you nearly everywhere; plane, train and even boat are all viable options, and hitching is possible in some areas. With over 4000km of blacktop, Senegal has one of West Africa's better tarred road networks. For the rest, flat landscapes make for lots of passable, if monotonous and dusty, *pistes*.

Bush taxis and buses

Most **public transport** is by bush taxi (**taxi brousse**). This may be (in descending order of price) a 7-seat Peugeot 504, a Japanese minibus, a *camion bâché* (covered pick-up van) or a *car rapide* (an ageing blue and yellow Saviem minibus). You'll travel fastest in a 504 and most comfortably in a minibus.

Autogares, or **gares routières** are usually well organized, and the drivers (or their assistants) will always find you before you find them. Most of the motorable roads on the *IGN* map of Senegal get at least one vehicle of some description every day.

Real 40-plus-seater **buses** are few and, apart from in Dakar, where there's an excellent bus system, they are not likely to figure much in your travels.

Fares, routes and frequencies

What follows is a **summary** of transport availability out of the capital and around Senegal.

The busiest road in the country is the **Dakar–Kaolack–Ziguinchor** route, part of which forms the *transgambienne* highway. For years this has been bedevilled with chronically unreliable **ferries** over the Gambia River between Farafenni and Soma, but now there are two new ferries and the crossing is effected in five minutes. Droves of *taxis brousses* use this route (departure is before noon, journey time 7hr plus).

The old route to **Ziguinchor via Barra and Banjul** (4 ferries daily each way; approx. 9am, 11am, 3pm & 7pm from Barra; 30min) is much less important as a transit route.

FARES

Current Peugeot fares from Dakar:
Karang (for Banjul) CFA3100; Kédougou CFA10,100; Kolda CFA6000; Mbour CFA900; St-Louis CFA2900; Tambacounda CFA6300; Thiès CFA800; Touba CFA2200; Ziguinchor CFA5400.

Ziguinchor to:
Séléti (for Serekunda) CFA1400.

12-seater **minibuses** are about 15 percent cheaper; 25-seater minibuses about 30 percent cheaper.

In Senegal it's usual to pay the bush taxi before the journey has finished, and often before it's even started. Don't pay, however, unless it's at least half full and other passengers have done so. Baggage supplements, which should be haggled over vigorously, can add about 25 percent per large item.

Thiès is an important transport hub, with a constant stream of vehicles running up from Dakar (1hr) until late in the day. With a morning departure from Dakar you can also go straight through to **St-Louis** (3hr plus) and **Rosso** (5hr plus).

St-Louis is the transport focus of the north. There are departures all day for **Rosso**, **Richard Toll** and **Dakar**, but destinations further upriver are served only by a few early morning departures and require vehicle changes in each major town.

Eastwards, a good number of vehicles make a living on the **Tambacounda** road, despite the train. You can easily make it there in a day if you get down to the Dakar *autogare* early. Continuing to the **Kédougou** district in far southeastern Senegal, you'll be relying mostly on Tambacounda-based vehicles, which are few and far between.

The **Tambacounda–Ziguinchor** road is mostly quiet – and on this route too you'll need to make an early start.

Car rental

Spectacularly expensive for leisure travel, **car rental** in Senegal is really only worth considering for special targets which might otherwise be inaccessible (national parks, for example), and even then most realistically as a group of three or four travellers. The **main agents** for *Avis* (the biggest), *Hertz* and *Europcar* (one or more in Dakar, Ziguinchor, Cap Skiring and St-Louis) provide the guarantee of a reputable name and the chance to pay by plastic, but the all-in cost for a Renault 5 or something similar, assuming 1000km and including fuel, will work out around **£500 ($800) per week** and isn't negotiable. Daily rates are fractionally more than *pro rata*, a weekend's rental costs slightly less. There's a ban on driving off the sealed highways and a minimum age of 25. National driving licences held for one year are sufficient, but don't be surprised if an **international drivers' licence** is specifically demanded if you're stopped.

If you're not concerned about going with a big-name firm, it's worth checking out some of the **local car rental places** which are usually willing to negotiate, can be persuaded to give you unlimited mileage and aren't so fussy about off-road driving. They may work out less than half the price of the big agencies. A weekend is frequently the best deal, and a convenient length of time for many trips. Don't forget possible extras (*frais non-inclus*), such as collision damage waiver and 20 percent tax.

■ Trains

There are two main railway lines: the northern Dakar to St-Louis route and the eastern *Océan-Niger* line.

The daily Mon–Sat run **between Dakar and St-Louis** departs Dakar at 3pm, arrives St-Louis 8pm, and departs St-Louis 7am, arriving Dakar at noon. Extra trains are often laid on during holidays. The route goes via Rufisque, Thiès, Tivaouane and Louga. It's the best way of getting between the towns, with immaculate first class AC seats under CFA3000 and second class less than CFA2000. Keep away from the rear wagons which get very dusty. Only the fastest bush taxis (comparable prices) cover the distance more quickly.

Dakar has its own Mon–Sat commuter service now (**le petit train bleu**) running to and from **Tiaroye** and **Rufisque** several times during morning and evening rush hours (30min).

In addition to the *Océan-Niger* service via Thiès, Diourbel and Tambacounda (covered under "Arrivals: From Mali by train", above), there's a daily **"express"** service from Kaolack to Dakar at 6.15am, arriving Dakar 11am; departing Dakar 4.50pm, arriving Thiès 5.50pm, Diourbel 7.50pm, and Kaolack 9.35pm. There's also a Friday **slow train** for irredeemable enthusiasts only, departing Dakar at 7.35am to Thiès, Diourbel, and branching to Touba (arr. 12.25pm); returning to Dakar the same evening.

■ Hitching

Because of the number of private vehicles and expats in Senegal, and a relatively high volume of tourist traffic, **hitching** on some of the main routes is an option worth trying. Moreover, if you're stuck on a minor turn-off, trying to wave down passing vehicles is less frustrating than simply waiting for the day's bush taxi service.

In decreasing order of feasibility, there are reasonable chances of lifts around the Dakar suburbs, to destinations on the coasts south and north of Dakar; in the Basse Casamance district; and from Tambacounda to Dakar and into Niokolo-Koba National Park.

■ Internal flights

Air Sénégal operates a few flights round the country from Dakar, but it's not a frequent enough service to be much competition for bush travel. Most flights depart from Dakar between 8am and 9am. Services include daily flights to and from **Ziguinchor**, sometimes via Banjul, and weekend flights to **Cap Skiring**, either non-stop, or via Ziguinchor. Every Saturday, there's a flight to **Tambacounda** and **Kédougou** which sometimes calls at **Simenti** in the Niokolo-Koba National Park.

There is also an occasional (in theory weekly) service along the Senegal River calling at **St-Louis**, **Richard Toll**, **Podor**, **Matam** and **Bakel**, and returning the same way.

Fares are roughly: Ziguinchor CFA20,000; Cap Skiring (during the season) CFA39,000. *Air Sénégal* has a whole range of percentage discounts for students, old people, groups, residents and so on.

■ Other options

The MV *Joola* **steamer** operates twice a week between Dakar and Ziguinchor (see p.191). Smaller and more exclusive pleasure boats ply the waters of the Saloum and Senegal deltas; if you're interested, staying in the right hotels in those areas will give you rapid access. There's no steamer service higher up the Senegal or the Casamance rivers, though you can usually cross by *pirogue* and there's ample opportunity to arrange your own **river transport** locally. The Senegal is navigable all year by small boats as far as Kidira; the Casamance beyond Sédhiou.

A characteristically Senegalese form of transport is the horse- or mule-drawn two-wheel buggy called a **calèche**, which you'll see all over the north and centre but not south of The Gambia (because of tsetse fly). They're often used as town taxis in smaller places, ferrying goods and people from the *autogare*.

At several *campements* in Basse Casamance you can rent **bicycles** – not very rideable ones, admittedly, and most don't have refinements such as gears, but they make a welcome change of pace. Buying the commonly seen blue single-speed bicycles, complete with dynamo lights, mudguards, side stand, a chunky steel rack and a huge sprung saddle, will cost the equivalent of around £130 ($200). You can also rent (or buy) mobylettes in some towns in Casamance.

Accommodation

For the most part, accommodation in Senegal is sophisticated and wide-ranging. With the exception of youth hostels, most overnight options are available.

■ Hotels

Most large towns have several decent **hotels**. Coming overland from one of its neighbours, Senegalese establishments seem, on the whole, plush and heavily Europeanized. In the higher price brackets, if they're not actually part of a chain, they're very often French- or Lebanese-owned or managed. And a surprising number of quite modest places turn out to have French hands behind the scenes.

CFA8000 is about the bottom line for the most basic lodging and CFA15,000 a typical price for often unremarkable amenities. There is a **tourist tax** too, of CFA400 per person per night, sometimes included in the room charge, more often added to the bill afterwards.

■ Campements Touristiques Rurals Integrés

An important and gratifying exception to the ordinary hotels is the Senegalese network of **campements touristiques rurals integrés** (*CTRIs*) established by the Ministry of Tourism over the last fifteen years to cater for smaller budgets and less mainstream requirements. Built by villagers with loans from central funds, often in a traditional architectural style, the *campements* theoretically bring tourist money into parts of the rural economy that don't usually benefit.

Facilities at the *CTRIs*, though basic, are adequate, and include European plumbing, cold running water, kerosene lighting, three-course meals, and cold drinks from a gas fridge. They provide mosquito nets and foam mattresses and sheets. At night some *CTRIs* can be uncomfortably hot as the mud brick walls release the day's

ACCOMMODATION PRICE CODES

All hotel prices in this chapter – the same scales in terms of their pound/dollar equivalents as used throughout the book – are coded according to the following scales. Prices refer to the rate you can expect to pay for a room with two beds. Single rooms, or single occupancy, will normally cost at least two-thirds of the twin-occupancy rate. For further details see p.51

① **Under CFA4000 (under £5/$7.50)**. Simplest private *campement* accommodation, or rudimentary, small-town hotel.

② **CFA4000–8000 (£5–10/$7.50–15).** CTRI *campements*, basic town hotel, or better quality provincial hotel. Some self-contained rooms (S/C) and possibly some with AC.

③ **CFA8000–16,000 (£10–20/$15–30).** Decent hotel, usually with S/C rooms, some with AC.

④ **CFA16,000–24,000 (£20–30/$30–45).** Good business or tourist-class hotel with better than adequate facilities, including a restaurant.

⑤ **CFA24,000–32,000 (£30–40/$45–60).** S/C, AC rooms are the norm, with extra facilities such as a pool and restaurant likely.

⑥ **CFA32,000–40,000 (£40–50/$60–75).** First-class hotel, with good range of facilities.

⑦ **Over CFA40,000 (over £50/$75).** Luxury establishment (prices up to £150/$230 in some cases).

Some resort hotels have two rates – high season from November to Easter, and low season roughly from May to October. Price codes are for the higher rate.

heat. For the same charge you can always camp outside. Prices are the same at all *CTRIs* and you can pay for accommodation only, or as many meals as you want. New prices were set in 1994 after devaluation, and should stick for a couple of years: FB at CFA7700, bed only CFA2300, breakfast CFA900, each meal CFA2200. Many *CTRIs* fill up over the Nov–Feb peak season, so it's wealth worth booking in advance. Contact: Coordinateur régional, Centre Artisanal, BP 567 Ziguinchor (☎911374). In recent years the laudable aims and popularity of the *CTRI* system have taken a beating from near-identical *campements* set up by private (and often more motivated) owners. These *campements* offer similar or often better facilities at a slightly lower price.

■ Other accommodation

Camping out in the bush is normally feasible in Senegal, where there's a fairly indulgent attitude to the eccentricities of foreigners: the French community has been doing it for years. Be sure, though, that you're out of any urban "zone of influence" where you might conceivably be putting yourself at risk of robbery. The Dakar region, and the towns in the groundnut basin – Thiès, Diourbel and Kaolack – are areas to avoid, as are the beaches. Senegal has no formal campsites.

Staying with people frequently comes out of efforts to camp on their land – even if it's not demarcated. Rewarding areas for such contacts lie throughout southern Senegal east of Ziguinchor – a region which, except for the Niokolo-Koba park, gets very few visitors, and virtually none who stay.

Eating and Drinking

Senegal has some of West Africa's best food, giving opportunities for everything from serious dining to snacking on street food. Drinks are equally diverse.

■ Restaurants

Restaurants in the larger towns and main hotels incline towards French style, offering a *menu* (three courses or more, and usually a choice) and a *plat du jour* (main dish only). Predictably there's lots of tough steak and chips, heavy sauces, imported canned food. For a *menu* expect to pay CFA4500–6000, and upward of CFA3500 for the *plat*. There are some decent French restaurants, and a few other exotic eating houses as well, but with a few exceptions they're an unmemorable lot. The better value venues are covered in the chapter.

■ Dishes

Indigenous Senegalese food is the most interesting: you can often eat best – certainly in Dakar – by going to one of the cheapest places, and simply eating what's offered. Most of what you'll find has heavy North African and Middle Eastern influence, with lots of seafood, mutton and Lebanese snacks. If you've been travelling elsewhere in West Africa you'll notice the near absence of plantains and root crops, and palm oil is used much less than in the southern coastal countries. The **basics**, though, as everywhere, are starch – usually rice – and spicy sauces, though the key word is aroma rather than pungency.

The national dish, eaten every day by millions of Senegalese, is **chep-bu-jen** (spelled variously as *cep-bou-dien* and *tiéboudienne*), Wolof for "rice-with-fish". This can be anything from plain rice with boiled fish and a few carrots to a glorious kind of paella with spiced rice and half a dozen vegetables. There's no fixed recipe, but it's virtually the only common meal that usually comes with vegetables.

Stuffed fish (**poisson farci**), which is an ingredient of the best *chep-bu-jen*, is associated with St-Louis and sometimes denoted *à la saint-louisienne*. Done properly, the result can be delicious. The mullet (the variety usually used) is filleted and flayed, leaving the skin whole: the flesh is then chopped finely, spiced and herbed, sewn up inside the skin and the whole package baked.

Varieties of **yassa** – a Casamançais dish – are characteristic of most menus too. Traditionally it uses **chicken**, but any animal ingredient qualifies so long as it is marinated at length in lemon juice, pepper and onions.

Riz Jollof – a mound of vegetables and meat in an oily tomato sauce on rice, named after the old Wolof kingdom – is common here, as it is all over West Africa.

Other sauces include **Mafé** and **Domodah** based loosely around tomatoes and groundnuts. The latter, so peanutty in The Gambia, is sometimes nut-less in Senegal. Both are best with beef or fish. **Soupe kanje** is a sauce made from okra (gumbo, ladies' fingers) with fish and palm oil.

You'll come across lots of places serving **couscous** (or *basi-salete*), though this is traditionally considered a festive meal and eaten at the Muslim New Year. Comprising steamed grains of millet flour with a smothering of vegetables, mutton and gravy, it's best by far when you're very hungry.

Méchoui, a whole roast sheep, is one for *Tabaski* – the *Fête des moutons.*

Away from the main growing areas in the south, **fruit** tends to be expensive: oranges imported from Morocco, Ivoirian pineapples and French apples. The best stuff is found in the Casamance, where you should look for unusual wild fruits.

■ Breakfast and snacks

The great French bequest, as always, is their **bread**, consumed in vast quantities. *Pain beurre* and *café au lait* is the ubiquitous **breakfast** and roadside snack, often with real butter. Be warned, though, in some places the *Nescafé* is often unrelated to what you'll find in, say, Mali, Burkina or Niger, as it's made with an infusion like weak tea, from a shrub called **kenkeliba** (or *quinceliba*). Mild and indifferently nutty when mixed with sweet milk or just on its own, *kenkeliba* acquires a revolting flavour when mixed with *Nescafé*. Specify "made with water" if you want *Nescafé* proper. *Kenkeliba* bars are known as **tangana** – which literally means "It's hot".

For **snacks** in towns you'll often end up in a **chawarma bar**. *Chawarma*, like doner kebabs, are shreds of barbecued compressed mutton cut from a roll, wrapped in a *pita* bread. They're normally a dependable standby, and very cheap. Alternatives include *merguez* (spicy sausage), *kofta* (meat balls), *fataya* (mince and onion pies), *nems* (like a pancake roll made of vermicelli pastry) and of course **brochettes** of grilled meat.

In the suburbs and countryside the **dibiterie** takes over. Roadside or market stalls, *dibiteries* are really butcher's shops, where you can choose your flank of flesh which is then chopped and barbecued on the spot and served with a few slithers of raw onion. It's said that flies are attracted to the best cuts, so take their choice as a recommendation.

■ Drinking

Flag is Senegal's **beer**, and not at all bad. It comes in two-thirds and third-litre bottles, and the price depends on where you buy it – any bar that sells only the small size is going to be expensive. A quite acceptable alternative, assuming you're in need of refreshment rather than intoxication, is

WOLOF FOOD TERMS

The list below will help you ask for and identify food in out of the way places. For more Wolof, see overleaf.

bey/siket	goat	*lem*	honey	*nxar*	mutton
chep/malo	rice	*lemnad*	soft drink	*nyam dunde*	food
chwi/genar	chicken	*makande*	corn	*nyebe*	beans
darr	butter	*mar*	thirst	*sangara*	alcohol, spirits
dom/garap	fruit	*mbam*	pork	*sobele*	onions
dugup	millet	*mbum*	spinach/boiled leaves	*sohu*	sour milk
gejieu	dried fish			*sukar*	sugar
gerte	groundnuts	*mburu*	bread	*suna*	bulrush millet
jen	fish	*mehu*	fresh milk	*tomat*	tomato
jeo	water	*nak*	beef	*xif*	hunger
jere	couscous/millet	*nene*	egg	*xorom*	salt
jernat	sorghum millet	*nex-na*	good (referring to food)	*yap*	meat
kani	hot pepper				

There are various **wild fruits**, sold seasonally in the markets:

ditak	oval, pebble-like fruit, with thin, dry skin and aromatic, acid green flesh surrounding a fibrous seed, sometimes made into a drink: very common in Casamance	*solom*	brown, pea-sized berry, with furry (edible) skin and a black seed
		cerise	tart, green "cherry"
		nyul	"black", a small black fruit
		dimbu	small, black, soft fruit with a vegetable taste and staining red flesh

the far less alcoholic *Gazelle* (large size only), which tends to be one of the cheapest bottled drinks you can buy.

Wine is available in groceries in most town centres, and tends to be about twice the French price. **Palm wine** costs next to nothing but you need to be in Casamance and friendly with the owner of a tree.

Non-alcoholic alternatives to bottled sodas and mineral water are plastic bags of **iced fruit drinks**: hibiscus syrup (*bisap*), ginger water, **bouille** (sherbety baobab juice) or tamarind juice. If you're interested in unusual tastes, seek out *njamban* – a concoction of tamarind juice, smoked fish, salt and cayenne pepper. Mellower are **thiacry**, a mixture of couscous, sour milk and sugar that's closer to a dessert than a drink, and **lakh** – millet, sour milk, sugar and orange water. In many parts Sahelian **tea** – tongue-liftingly strong and sweet – is a much loved refreshment.

Communications – Post, Phones, Languages and Media

Post offices (*PTT*), normally open Mon–Fri 7.30am–4pm plus Sat morning, operate with grinding, morose efficiency. Senegalese mail is expensive, and overseas delivery from Dakar (where the central *PTT* has long hours) is slow.

Getting mail at **poste restante** may require infinite patience: letters commonly take two to three weeks to find their box in the Dakar poste restante, and are then only held for a month.

Phoning home is costly, often around £10 for three minutes to Britain and US$20 to the USA, with extra minutes *pro rata*. But shop around – some of the *télécentres* are much cheaper than others (off-peak to Britain as little as CFA500/minute). Americans, in common with several other nationalities, can make collect calls (*PCV*) – a service not available to Britain.

Centres téléphoniques – where you make your call from a metered booth and pay for it at the end – are are now found in even the smallest towns. **Fax machines** are also often available for receipt and transmission at the same *centres*.

Senegal's IDD code is ☎221.

■ Languages

Though only twenty percent of the population has any fluency in the colonial tongue, communication will rarely be a problem if you speak French to some degree. (English alone won't get you far.) You'll have a far better time, however, if you know some **Wolof**. It's not an easy language, but making the effort to say even a few simple greetings will gratify people out of all proportion to your ability.

Wolof is not the whole story. Important minority vernaculars include: **Fula** (Pulaar), spoken by the Tukulor and Fula (or Peul); **Serer**, spoken by the partly Christianized people of the same name; **Kriyol**, a Portuguese creole spoken by up to 50,000 people along the coast south of Dakar; **Jola**, spoken in various dialects in the Casamance region; the **Mande** languages (Mandinka/Malinké, Bamana and Sarakolé/Soninké, spoken in scattered communities across the south and east; and the languages of the **Tenda** group – Konyagi, Bedik, Bassari. All are a major component of ethnic identity, especially so in the case of Jola (for a **Jola glossary** see p.220).

■ The media

Language politics are reflected in Senegalese government **radio** which is divided into two *chaines* – a French-language station, and a vernacular station broadcasting in Wolof with extra transmissions in Fula, Serer, Mandinka, Jola and Sarakolé/Soninke. **TV**, exclusively in French, is watched mostly in Dakar and, apart from the government station, *RTS*, there are are also pay-TV channels such as the local *Canal Horizons* and French satellite channel *TV5*.

Radio Sénégal, on about 750m MW, carries Dakar information and, on Friday afternoons, news about music and shows. You can also pick up *FM92* (a *Radio France/Radio Sénégal* station) *Sud-FM*, and *Dakar FM* on 94m FM.

The paltry Senegalese **press** seems extraordinarily undeveloped given the country's record on freedom of speech. *Le Soleil* – the "independent" paper of the *Parti Socialiste* but effectively the voice of government – is the country's only true daily and always short on readable news, though not for lack of newsprint. Most of the dozen or more political parties publish their own sheets more or less regularly, but they tend towards the turgid.

For something oppositional, look out for the weekly *Sopi*, published by the *PDS*. If your French

ELEMENTARY WOLOF

Wolof (sometimes *Ouolof* or *Volof* to the French) is understood by an estimated fifty percent of Senegalese. Perhaps two-thirds of these are ethnic Wolof, the rest are mother tongue speakers of other languages, all of which are losing ground. Wolof is growing in importance all the time and there are regular calls for it to be adopted as the official national language. Wolof is classified as a "West Atlantic" language, in the same large basket of "class languages" as Fula and Serer, quite different from the "non-class" Mande languages like Mandinka, Bambara and Dyula. The main criterion for this classification is the grammatical system of Wolof, which groups nouns into fairly arbitrary classes something like genders. There's the usual confusion over **spellings** created by British and French transcribers using their own norms, but the following selection should be quite pronounceable. The letter "x" denotes a throaty sound like the ch in loch, but even rougher.

GREETINGS

All purpose greeting...	*Salam malekum*	How are you all?	*Naka waa keur ga?*
...and response	*Malekum salam*	(formal) How are your family/home/people?	*Ana sa wa ker?*
How are you? (literally: Do you have peace?)	*Nanga def? Jam ngaam?*	(very informal)	
I'm just around here (Nothing but peace)	*Mangi fi rek/Jamarek*	Well, thank you (all purpose)	*Jam dal*
Thank God	*al xamdulilay*	What's your name?	*Naka nga sant?*
Good morning (lit. did you sleep well?)	*Jamanga fanan?*	My name is Dave Warne	*Tuda Dave santa Warne*
		Goodbye (I'm off)	*Mangi dem*

GENERAL PRACTICALITIES

I don't speak Wolof/French	*Man deguma Wolof/Faranse*	Where are you going?	*Fanga dem nil?*	Please	*Su la nexe*
Please repeat	*Wahat ko del*	The road to . . .	*Di yon wi demi . . .*	I don't mind/I don't care	*Ana sema yon*
Yes	*Wow*	Right	*Chamong*	When?	*Sar?*
No	*Dedet*	Left	*Ndejor*	No problem	*Du problème*
Perhaps	*Xey na*	Far	*Sore*	(No) thank you	*Jere jef*
Where is . . .?	*An na. . .?*	Slowly	*Ndank*	Wife	*Djabar*

PLACES

Market	*Jebe*	Room	*Neg*	Field	*Toll*
Village	*Deuke*	Bed	*Lale*	Forest/bush	*Alle*
House	*Ker*				

DAYS

Today	*Tei*	Monday	*Altine*	Thursday	*Alxemes*
Saturday	*Aser*	Tuesday	*Telata*	Friday	*Ajuma*
Sunday	*Diber*	Wednesday	*Alarba*		

NUMBERS

1	*bena*	7	*jerom nyar*	21	*nyar fuka bena* (etc)	80	*jerom nyeta fuka*
2	*nyar*	8	*jerom nyeta*	30	*nyet fuka/fanver*		
3	*nyeta*	9	*jerom nyenent*	40	*nyenent fuka*	90	*jerom nyenent fuka*
4	*nyenent*	10	*fuka*	50	*jerom fuka*		
5	*jerom*	11	*fuka bena* (etc)	60	*jerom bena fuka*	100	*temer*
6	*jerom bena*	20	*nyar fuka/nit*	70	*jerom nyar fuka*	1000	*june*

BUYING

Give me/sell me...	*Mai man/jai man*	Cheap	*Yombe na*
I want.../I don't want...	*Bugema.../buguma ...*	Expensive	*Jafe*
Enough	*Doi na*	Not...	*Do...*
More, again	*Ati*	Money	*Xalis*
A little	*Sin tut*	Lower the price (a little)	*Wanil ko (tuti)*
Lots of	*Lol/bare*	You're killing me!	*Hey! Yangi ma rey!*
Full	*Fes*	Leave me alone, I'm fed up/tired	*Baye ma, dama son*
That's all	*Mom rek*	Gift	*Nexeul*
How much is that?	*Bi nyata le?*		
It's too much	*Defa jafe torop.*		

OTHER NEEDS

Please give me some water	*Mai man ndox su la nexe*	I've got a stomach ache	*Suma biir day metti*
I'm hungry	*Damaa xiif*	Show me the way to the post office	*Won ma post bi*
What would you like to eat?	*Loo begga lekk?*	What would you like?	*Lan nga bugg?*
I'm sleepy	*Damaa gemmeentu*	Do you have a little bit of aspirin?	*Amuloo tutti aspirin?*
I'm going to sleep (now)	*Maangi nelawi waay*	Do you smoke?	*Dinga toox?*
Where are you going?	*Foo jem?*	Do you drink palm wine?	*Dinga naan sung?*
Are you going to the market?	*Dangay dem marse?*	I don't have any money	*Awma xalis*
I feel ill	*Damaa feebar*	Someone's waiting for me	*Am naa ku may xaar*

EMERGENCIES

Thief!	*Sachu kat!*	Call the police/ a doctor quickly!	*Uho police/medecin gahu!*
S/he's ill!	*Dafa fun ope!*		

TREES

Baobab	*Gui*	Raffia palm	*Bari*	kola Oil	*Netetu*
Silk-cotton (kapok)	*Bentenki*	Locust bean	*Tir*	palm	*Tabu*
		Mandingo	*Jorut*	Custard apple	

ANIMALS

Horse	*Fas*	Monkey	*Golo*	Pelican	*Jagabar*
Camel	*Gwilem*	Elephant	*Nye*	Crocodile	*Jasik*
Goat	*Bei*	Hippopotamus	*Leber*	Chameleon	*Kakatar*
Pig	*Mbam*	Large antelope	*Koba*	Monitor lizard	*Mbeta*
Cow	*Nak*	Hyena	*Buki*	Gecko	*Onka*
Bull	*Yek*	Porcupine	*Sav*	Snake	*Jan*
Lion	*Gawnde/daba*	Ostrich	*Baa*	Tortoise	*Mbonat*
Leopard	*Tenev*				

SIMPLE SERER

Hello	*Nafio*	Thank you	*Dkoka djal*
I'm fine	*Miheme*	Yes	*Io*
Does your family live in peace?	*Fambina?*	No	*Buhi*
Yes, they have peace	*Wamaha*	Coconut	*Koko*
Goodbye	*Mereda*	Rice	*Tju*

SENEGALESE TERMS – A GLOSSARY

Common words and expressions, French and Wolof.

Bana Bana wandering street vendor

Baye Fall zealous disciples of Mouridism, dressed in brilliantly coloured patchwork cloaks, often seen collecting money for their marabout

Bolong mangrove creek (Casamance)

Borom *patron*, chief, owner

Boubou long gown worn by men and women

Ceddo traditional Wolof warrior caste

Clando clandestine bar for Muslim hypocrites

Damel pre-Islamic Wolof kings

Dara pioneering settlements of Mouride disciples

Dibiterie roadside butcher and barbecue artist

Djigeen woman

Fatou somewhat derogatory as it's a woman's name: means domestic servant or "girl"

Filao casuarina tree; a kind of weeping fir

La Fleuve "The River" – the Senegal River

Fromager silk-cotton tree or kapok

Gewel griot; praise singer, musician storyteller

Goor man/male

Gue ford, river crossing

Hajj/El Hajj the pilgrimage to Mecca/one who has been on the pilgrimage

Herbe Qui Tu grass, cannabis

HLM "Habitations à Loyer Modérés" – council flats, housing projects

Jeu de Dames draughts, checkers; a more competitive game than *wure*

Keur/kerr/ker place, home

Magal annual mass pilgrimage to Touba on the occasion of Cheikh Amadou Bamba's birthday

Maquis cheap place to eat

Marabout enormously powerful religious leader accredited with magical powers

Mbalax music – modern expression of traditional roots rhythms

Mouridiya one of the two most powerful Islamic orders; headquarters at Touba

PDS *Parti Démocratique Senegalaise*, the main opposition party

Planton orderly, watchman, dogsbody

PS *Parti Socialiste*, the ruling party; curious name

Radio Kankan public rumour

Sandarma *gendarme*

Sayisayi playboy

Sopi "Change", the slogan of the main political opposition alliance

Talibe disciple of a marabout

Teranga hospitality, generosity; sums up the Wolof code of behaviour to strangers

Tijaniya numerically the largest Islamic brotherhood divided into dynasties, some of which are fundamentalist in nature; headquarters at Tivaouane

Touba the holy city east of Dakar; also means "happiness"

Toubab foreigner, usually white; from the Wolof "to convert"; you'll hear it a lot from kids.

Wure game of pebbles/seeds and holes

Yamba cannabis

is up to it, *Le Politicien* is a monthly breath of fresher air – nicknamed *Le Cafard Enchaîné* after the Parisian satirical mag. For an angle on the Islamic brotherhoods pick up the Islamic weekly *Wal Fadjri* (in French).

Entertainment

Unlike a number of countries where organized entertainments can be somewhat inaccessible to outsiders, Senegal has plenty of spectator sport, in addition to musical performers, theatre and cinema.

■ Sport

Although **football** is big in Senegal, **la lutte** – wrestling – is the most popular sport countrywide, and consists of furious jostling of oiled and charm-laden poseurs trying to get each other down in the dust: fun to watch, but best at a small venue. Casamançais style is less violent than the Wolof brawls.

■ Music

Senegalese **music** is a revelation after the foreign imports heard in other countries. While traditional **griots** are less and less to be seen, many Senegalese musicians are internationally known. **Youssou N'dour**, for the complex **mbalax** style he developed with his band **Super Etoile de Dakar**, and for his singular presence in the World Music firmament, is the biggest name, but he's just one of very many. **Baaba Maal**, a conservatoire-trained Tukulor singer from Podor, is also internationally renowned. Major stadium **gigs** are held in Dakar, Ziguinchor and elsewhere, and you can pick up on even the big names in the Dakar clubs. There's much more in the music article in *Contexts* at the back of the book.

■ Cinema

Cinema is mostly imported. Senegal's own directors, notably Ousmane Sembène, Pape B. Seck, Djibril Diop Mambety and Safi Faye, struggle for funds despite – in Sembène's, and to a lesser extent Faye's case – international critical acclaim.

■ Theatre

Theatre doesn't make much impression outside Dakar, where there is a small, active theatre community based around the Senegal National Theatre Company and the institutional *Théâtre Daniel Sorano*. Foreign cultural centres in Dakar, St-Louis and Ziguinchor may have something worth a look; where appropriate we've listed them in the chapter.

Holidays and Festivals

Apart from international Christian and Islamic holidays, during which all official and most business doors will be closed (see p.62), Senegal also has holidays on April 4 (National day, when independence as part of the Mali Federation was declared), May 5 (Labour day) and June 20 (Independence day).

There's also considerable unofficial disruption to normal hours and services at the time of **Magal** – the annual Mouride pilgrimage to Touba, which falls on the 18th of Safar, 48 days after the Islamic new year – ie on approximately July 5 1996, June 24 1997 and June 14 1998 (these dates are estimated on the early side: check the Muslim calendar closer to the time). Public transport all over Senegal is severely affected in the days before and after *Magal* with many drivers preferring to do pilgrim business only.

■ Traditional festivals

One St-Louis and Gorée institution is the **Fanals** parade, featuring the decorated lanterns (*fanals*) that slaves used to carry in front of wealthy mixed-race women (*signares*) on their way to Christmas mass. Competition developed between

TRADITIONAL FESTIVALS

Olugu March: jubilant entry of Bassari initiates who underwent *Nit* the previous year, signifying their reintegration as adults.

Fityay March–April: ritual appeasement of the spirit Beliba, supplicated to look after the people of Essil (the region around Enampore) through the dry months.

Nit end of April: ritual battle in the Bassari villages of Ebarak, Etiolo and Kote, with masked attackers (*lukuta*) of boys undergoing initiation.

Ufulung Dyendena May: throughout the kingdom of Essil this ritual propitiation of rain spirits takes place before and after rice planting.

Synaaka May: "circumcision" of Jola girls, during which the initiates are instructed in retreat for a week; widespread partying.

Zulane May–June: festival of the royal priest of Oussouye.

Futampaf May–June: initiation of adolescent Jola boys into adulthood; lasts two to three weeks, commencing and concluding with major celebrations.

Kunyalen May–June: three days of ritual performed to ensure Jola female fertility and the protection of new-born infants.

Ekonkon June: traditional dances in Oussouye.

Bukut June: takes place in each Jola village roughly every twenty years.

Wrestling June–July: takes place all year, but the start of the rains is a traditional time in Essil.

Homebel October: after the rains, girls' wrestling bouts around Oussouye.

Beweng or **Epit** November–December: a two-day harvest festival in Basse Casamance when the spirits are asked to sanction the transfer of the rice crop to the granaries. Each head of household donates a sheaf.

Ebunay every two years: a festival in the Oussouye district involving all the women of the village; female (*Bugureb*) dances in the first week, followed by the enthronement of a ritual priestess.

quartiers to produce the most elaborate lamp, the rivalry becoming so intense that the parades were banned in 1953 after violence between the teams. But they were revived in St-Louis in 1970, and you should be able to see them around Christmas. Impressive **pirogue races** also take place from time to time, notably in St-Louis.

In **the south**, in Basse Casamance and in the Bassari country beyond Niokolo-Koba park, a **seasonal cycle of festivals** and ritual events still dominates the cultural sphere, though to a diminishing extent. The events in the following box are all worth checking out if you can; most take place towards the end of the dry season.

Directory

AIRPORT DEPARTURE TAX CFA2000 domestic flights; CFA4000 African flights; CFA5000 intercontinental flights.

CRAFTS AND OTHER PURCHASES Senegal doesn't stand out as a country to buy handicrafts, but you'll find a number of hole-in-the-wall **curio shops** in Dakar, where some musty old relics can be unearthed and argued over. Officially sanctioned **centres artisanals** tend to be touristic set-ups, where you can see the stuff being made (carved statues and masks, model *pirogues*, paintings on glass, sand paintings) but where you might not want to buy it. **Cloth** *pagnes* are generally cheaper than in The Gambia, with Dakar's suburban markets being the best places for a good deal – watch out for *Sotiba's* superb range of designs. Jewellery, in variety and notably in silver, is usually a good buy. There's detailed advice on shopping in Dakar in the account of the city.

OPENING HOURS Shop opening hours are Mon–Fri 8am–noon & 2.30/3–6pm, Sat 8–11am/noon. Banks usually follow the same hours. Most other offices are now open Mon–Fri 7.30am–4pm without a break, but closed on Sat. The long lunch break is popular. Many establishments, including some restaurants, also close one day a week – museums usually Mon all day & Wed morning.

PARIS–DAKAR RALLY Since the late 1970s the annual Paris–Dakar Rally has torn across the Sahara and West Africa, covering up to 10,000km in around three weeks. The Rally, which usually sets off from the Champs Elysées on a New Year's dawn, was once hugely popular, but this has been tempered by frequent deaths among participants and onlookers and the questionable ethics of a multi-million-pound spectacle hurtling through the poverty stricken Sahel. Although still followed nightly on French TV, the inevitable loss of the Rally's early amateur spirit and the necessary elimination of the politically insecure central Saharan sections, where the Rally earned its reputation as the world's toughest trial for bikes, cars and trucks, have removed some of the Dakar's sex-appeal. These days it follows a less demanding route through Morocco and Mauritania, to Senegal, though in 1995 it added a circuit through Guinea's Fouta Djalon highlands. If you're in Dakar at the right time, don't expect to see much more than huge crowds and champagne-soaked desert racers parading through the Place de l'Indépendance. The Rally does, however, bring enormous accommodation problems to every town on the route, and Dakar especially.

PHOTOGRAPHY Officially there are few problems: you can even take pictures of the presidential guards and palace, though you should ask first. But you'll certainly hurt people's feelings if you take their pictures without permission. In many areas, high prices will be demanded.

POLICE Law enforcers are of two main types – machine-gun-toting, brown-uniformed *gendarmes* and blue-togged *agents de police* who operate the occasional countryside road blocks. The latter, though generally not into bothering tourists, will pull you in if you're not carrying any identification. You can be held for 24 hours and fined – it happens, often. If you're out at night and would rather not take your passport, keep a photocopy and another piece of ID with you.

SEXUAL ATTITUDES The Wolof tend to be exceptionally beautiful people, and unafraid of marrying out of their own communities, which tends to strengthen their already dominant position. **Prostitution** has a rather lower profile than, for example, in The Gambia. **Gay attitudes** seem relaxed, in Dakar at least: av Georges Pompidou and Ngor beach to the north are well-known cruising areas for *gor-digen*.

TROUBLE Be **security-conscious** on first arriving in Dakar. Although it's spelt out in detail in the Dakar section of the chapter, it can't be overstressed that this is a city where too many new arrivals are robbed – usually in a snatch and run attack. (The rest of the country is as safe as anywhere.) Don't aggravate street pedlars by looking at their gear if you're really not interested, or by bargaining for fun when you've no intention of buying. In Dakar this can give rise to serious offence. *Always* ignore the guy who gets an item out of his pocket to sell you; this is a set-up for a mugging. ☎17 seems to be the best bet if you require the **police** in a hurry.

On a wider front, despite some political detentions, Senegal prides itself on **freedom of speech**: domestic politics aren't taboo and you can converse openly without fear of offending or unnerving anyone.

WILDLIFE AND NATIONAL PARKS Senegal isn't well endowed with **large animals**. In **Basse Casamance National Park** you're not likely to see anything bigger than a monkey. In the **north**, however, there may still be elephants along remoter parts of the river, and large numbers of camels. In **Niokolo-Koba National Park** you can see elephants, lions, buffalos and western giant elands, plus several troupes of chimpanzees at the northernmost point of their range, and quantities of crocs and hippos. Senegalese **birdlife** is satisfying: the coast boasts some of the best spots in the world for watching palearctic migrants in the winter.

WOMEN'S MOVEMENT Long-standing and continued French influence has been superficially helpful to women in terms of career opportunities. Dakar's fairly active **movement** is coordinated through the *Fédération Sénégalaise des Groupements Féminins*. The central issue of institutional female genital mutilation – still performed in some communities – is being tackled by a pan-African organization who have their headquarters in Dakar – the *Commission Internationale pour l'abolition des mutilations sexuelles*, Villa 811, SICAP Baobabs, Dakar.

WORK Although it's getting harder by the month, Dakar is one place in West Africa where you'll quite possibly find a job if you're prepared to settle in for a while. The most likely openings are English **teaching** (approach the British-Senegalese Institute) and – if you have very good French – secretarial and other office jobs, or working in upmarket stores. All are strictly unofficial – making friends with the expat communities will help.

A Brief History of Senegal

The earliest deducible history of Senegal, from about 1300 AD, comes from the oral accounts of the aristocracy of the Wolof kingdom of Jolof, in the centre of the country. Jolof fragmented into a number of small Wolof kingdoms which, together with Casamance, had frequent contacts with Portuguese traders after 1500. In 1658, the French settled on an island at the mouth of the Senegal river, which they named St-Louis, after Louis XIV. This account picks up the story from there. For the history of Islam in Senegal, see the feature box on p.168.

■ French inroads

By 1659 the trading fort of **St-Louis** was established, buying in **slaves** and **gum arabic** – the first a product of up-river raids, the second a valuable extract from acacia trees, used in medicine and textile manufacture.

The permanent French presence at St-Louis stimulated the slave trade to a level at which it began to dominate the Senegal valley's economy, prompting a frenzy of warfare for profit in the region's indigenous states. Wolof rulers (the *damel*) and their warriors (the *ceddo*) were spurred to raid their own peasantry for slaves. In the 1670s a popular ***jihad*** by Muslim marabouts, rebelling against the social cannibalism of the traditionalist Wolof elite, was suppressed with the help of French soldiers and guns. Henceforth Wolof of all classes found themselves trapped between Islamic reformers and mercenary Europeans.

St-Louis in the eighteenth century

Through the eighteenth century St-Louis thrived and increasingly absorbed the Wolof people of Walo state, which occupied the area between Richard Toll and the coast. The Wolof had not been converted to Islam: on the contrary, the intermarriage of Wolof women and French

Catholics created an exclusive miniature society, to a large extent run by the mixed race matriarchs known as **signares**.

By the time of the French Revolution, St-Louis had a population of 7000, of whom a large proportion, including the mayor, were *métis* (mixed race). In deference to French blood, but also to post-revolutionary notions of the rights of man, the people of St-Louis and Gorée were accorded most of the privileges of **French citizenship**, including, after 1848, the right to elect a deputy to the National Assembly in Paris – a right later extended to the mainland *communes* of Rufisque and Dakar.

Futa Toro and Omar Tall

In the interior, developments were underway that would shape the future of the modern state. In 1776 a league of **Tukulor marabouts** from north of the river overthrew the Fula dynasty of Denianke in **Futa Toro** on the south bank, a region the dynasty had ruled for more than 250 years. They were replaced by a reforming government of Muslim clerics (known as *almamys*) who, with fundamentalist zeal, dispatched warrior-missionaries to spread Islam across the western part of the subcontinent.

The greatest of these expansionists was **Omar Tall**. On his way to Mecca in the 1820s Tall was initiated into the **Tijaniya brotherhood**, which was founded in Morocco in the late eighteenth century. He was appointed the Tijani chief khalif for the region and travelled extensively, gathering a huge following. By the early 1850s Tall had carved out a vast **empire** centred on **Ségou** in present-day Mali and stretching as far east as Timbuktu. Westwards, his ambitions to expand to the coast were soon thwarted by the French.

■ French conquest

In the 1820s, after the abolition of slavery, Governor Baron Roger had tried unsuccesfully to develop agriculture up-river at Richard Toll with a view to French settlement. **Louis Faidherbe**, appointed governor in 1854, saw no mileage in that approach to imperialism. Instead he annexed the Wolof kingdom of **Walo**, and brutally subjugated the Mauritanians of Trarza, who had long frustrated French ambitions to control the gum trade. To pay for the military campaigns, the first harvests of **groundnuts** were shipped to French soap and oil factories. In 1857 a deal was struck with the head man of the Lebu village of **Daxar** (Dakar) – which became the administrative capital of French West Africa for the next 100 years – and further settlements were established along the coast at Rufisque and elsewhere. Faidherbe founded the *Tirailleurs sénégalais* (West African Infantry), who became the firepower of France's "civilizing mission" across West Africa. He also strengthened the forts along the river at **Podor**, **Matam** and **Bakel**, which repulsed El Hadj Omar Tall's repeated attacks and provided bases for the French expansion across the Sahel.

Omar Tall was killed in 1864, besieged in the Bandiagara escarpment in present day Mali, his empire still land-locked and Ségou itself lost to the French. His son **Amadu Sefu** continued his reign.

Muslim conquest

After Omar Tall's death, **Ma Ba** – a senior disciple – carried on the work of the Tijaniya with a clutch of Soninke (Sarakole) followers. They led and sponsored *jihads* against non-Muslim Mandinka along the river Gambia (see **"The Soninke-Marabout Wars"**, p.254), and also converted most of the Wolof kings to Islam, goading them into individual armed resistance against the French. But a united front of Wolof states proved impossible to achieve. In 1867 Ma Ba died in a battle with the **Serer**-speaking state of Sine, marking a temporary halt in the advance of Islam and leaving the Serer to a different evangelical fate with the Christian missions.

As Wolof leaders were converted, however, pushing their people – or sometimes pushed by them – into accepting Islam, so **conflict with the French** became, with increasing clarity, a conflict between Muslims and infidels. Humiliated by their 1871 defeat in the Franco-Prussian war, the French found new reserves of aggression. And despite the marabouts' powers of mobilization, the French grip on the territory grew tighter every year through the 1880s. The Wolof armies were defeated one by one, and the old authority structures – already weakened by the imposition of Islam – were dismantled as each kingdom was annexed to France.

Wolof collapse

By now the French were irreversibly committed to making Senegal pay for itself and to directly administering the whole of their West African territory. When **Lat Dior**, the ruler of **Kayor**, appealed to the French not to build the Dakar to

St-Louis railway through his kingdom, he was ignored, and the railway was opened in 1885, despite sabotage by Lat Dior and his *ceddo*. The same year the **Berlin congress** divided the African spoils among the European powers, splitting Senegal by the creation of The Gambia and formally ratifying France's sovereignty over her possessions. Lat Dior was killed at Dekhlé the following year, and became one of the country's folk heroes.

Another Wolof *damel*, **Alboury Ndiaye** (Alboury of Jolof), at first allied himself with the French at St-Louis against Amadu Sefu's empire to the east, even undertaking to facilitate the building of the ambitious, and never-completed, railway to Bakel. But, along with his distant cousin Lat Dior, Alboury had been converted to Islam in 1864, and he was secretly in contact with Amadu Sefu. He later became violently opposed to French expansion, allying his kingdom with the Ségou empire, leading fanatical attacks and trying to expand Ségou even farther to the east. His own kingdom, whose capital was Yang Yang, was formally annexed by the French in 1889 – the last Wolof kingdom to lose its independence; Ségou fell in 1893, and Alboury died in Dosso, Niger in 1902.

French administration

As everywhere in the early years of *Afrique Occidentale Française* (AOF) the French stressed their **mission civilatrice** – their peaceful aim to bring French civilization to black Africa. It was only in Senegal that this was this accompanied by any real manifestation of assimilationist ideals. And even here, it was only in the four *communes* that French citizenship was available. Through the rest of Senegal and AOF, most people had the status of *sujet* – subject – and were at the mercy of the hated **indigénat** "native justice" code, under which they were ruled by the local *commandant* – the equivalent of a district commissioner – who could impose summary fines and imprisonment. The *indigénat* and a mass of oppressive legislation, including tax provisions, compulsory labour and restrictions on movement, were mostly operated through *chefs de canton* ("district chiefs") nominated by, and answerable to, the *commandant*. The chiefs were frequently corrupt and almost always regarded as collaborators. The only legitimate leadership in the countryside came from the **marabouts** (see p.168).

Blaise Diagne and the Marabouts

In marked contrast, Dakar, Gorée, Rufisque and St-Louis elected a territorial assembly – the **conseil général**, which controlled the budget for the whole of Senegal – and a deputy to the Paris National Assembly. In 1914 **Blaise Diagne**, a customs official from Gorée, became the first black deputy (previous deputies had been mixed race), a post he was to hold until his death in 1934.

The tone of Diagne's career was set early on when he offered to recruit Senegalese soldiers for the French war effort in exchange for legislation guaranteeing the political rights of the black *commune* residents – rights which the colonial administration was keen to erode. Laws were passed confirming that they were in fact full citizens of France. As far as Diagne was concerned, only further **assimilation** could better the lot of the Africans. He saw Senegal's fate as inextricably linked to France's.

Outside the *communes* the Senegalese still had hopes of redemption through their marabouts, but the warrior evangelists of the nineteenth century were gone. In their place, men like **Amadou Bamba** – founder of the Mourid brotherhood – and **Malick Sy** – leader of the biggest Wolof dynasty of the Tijaniya – bought their religious independence by co-opting their followers in the colonial process, organizing recruitment drives and providing support to Senegalese politicians in the *communes*: Blaise Diagne's election owed much to support from the Mourid brotherhood, who counted on him to raise his voice on their behalf. The marabouts also encouraged the **cultivation of groundnuts**, a crop that quickly exhausted the soil, was totally dependent on the rains, forced farmers to buy food they would otherwise have grown for themselves and – as groundnut prices fell while others rose – led to falling living standards. In return the marabouts were given the administration's support in their land disputes with Fula cattle herders. By the end of the 1930s a system of **reciprocal patronage** betwen marabouts and government was established, and two out of three *sujets* were growing groundnuts.

Political developments

Diagne was succeeded as deputy by Galandou Diouf, a less enthusiastic assimilationist. His main rival was **Amadou Lamine Guèye**, Africa's first black lawyer, who came to prominence by demanding the extension of citizenhood to the *sujets*. Already elected mayor of St-Louis in 1925, he forged strong links with the French Socialist party and, in 1936, founded the Senegalese branch of the *Section Française de l'Internationale Ouvrière* (*SFIO*), Africa's first modern political party. When the French Socialists came to power and conceded some limited rights to non-citizens – the right to form trade unions for example – he began organizing among *sujets* in the back-country towns.

■ World War II

With the outbreak of **World War II**, political life virtually ceased as the citizens' rights in the *communes* were abrogated, the country was scoured for supplies and the social advances of the pre-war government were swiftly negated. The Allies blockaded Vichy-ruled Dakar as Churchill and de Gaulle's **"Operation Menace"** attempted to rally the AOF to the war. Senegal was starved of imports, causing enormous suffering in the groundnut regions. Peasants were forced to switch to subsistence crops, and for the first time were encouraged by the colonial administration to do so.

After two years of Vichy control, the colonial administration did turn to the Allies and for the rest of the war the country was an important logistical base for the Free French – though political rights were not restored until 1945. During the Allied occupation an agricultural campaign – **"Battle for Groundnuts"** – was launched, which extracted more from the country, economically, than Vichy had.

Promises and blunders

The **Brazzaville Conference** of 1944 prepared the ground for major changes in France's relations with its colonies. A fairer deal for Africans, allowing them more administrative involvement, was the main theme, partly in recognition of the part played by them during the war, partly because France's credibility as a great and munificent nation was in question. The underlying aim was the reconstruction of postwar France and the incorporation of all its territories as integral parts of the Republic. The possibility of independence was explicitly ruled out.

Yet there was a clear call for "Equal Rights for Equal Sacrifices", a reference to the 200,000 Africans who were recruited to the war, the 100,000 who fought and the 25,000 who died.

Events in Senegal brought citizens and *sujets* closer together. At the end of 1944 at **Camp Thiaroye**, outside Dakar, demobilized West African soldiers just returned from Europe refused to be transported to Bamako without their back pay. When a general was taken hostage, French soldiers were ordered to open fire. Forty Senegalese were killed, many more were injured and a number of survivors sentenced to long jail terms.

Then, in 1945, the **vote for women** was finally won in France, but in the four *communes* only white women were enfranchised, a discrimination that under Blaise Diagne's 1915 guarantee should have been impossible.

Although the woman's vote decision was shortly repealed, both these events sullied relations with France and added fuel to growing demands for radical reforms.

■ The rise of Senghor

To speak of independence is to reason with the head on the ground and the feet in the air; it is not to reason at all. It is to advance a false problem.

L.S.Senghor, Strasbourg, 1950.

Early in 1945 a commission was set up to look into ways of organizing a new Constituent Assembly for the French colonies. One of the two black Africans to sit on it was a 38-year-old Catholic Senegalese, **Leopold Sédar Senghor**, who was chosen because, despite having lived almost continuously in France since 1928, he was the first African to achieve the rank of *agrégé*, (the highest teaching qualification) and was in addition a war veteran and a *sujet*. Moreover, he was a Christian Serer rather than a Wolof and had close contacts with the French administration.

In October 1945 **elections** were held to two electoral colleges of the Assembly, one for citizens and one for *sujets*. **Lamine Guèye**, now mayor of Dakar and seen as the most experienced black politician in AOF, successfully rallied various political groups to form a popular front and was elected to the first electoral college. **Senghor**, fresh back from France, was easily voted to the second college – even though few Senegalese knew who he was.

Reforms and advances

Though not without hindrance, **reforms** were rapidly pushed through: the *indigénat* was abolished, as was forced labour. Even more significant, Lamine Guèye succeeded in raising the status of all *sujets* to that of citizen.

Senghor meanwhile was emerging from Lamine Guèye's political tutelage within the *SFIO*, campaigning to extend the role of the peasants in the interior, for increased financial credits and improvements in health and education in the overseas territories, and supporting the 1947–48 **railway workers' strike** for non-racial pay differentials on the Dakar-Bamako line. In 1948 Senghor formed his own party, the **Bloc democratique sénégalais**, and became leader of an association of African deputies – the *Indépendents d'Outre-Mer*.

The postwar reforms and the rise to power of the *BDS* in the early 1950s soon transformed Senegalese **politics**, even if the economy remained heavily dependent on the fickleness of the groundnut harvest. Senghor's party capitalized greatly on its leader's ex-*sujet* status and the credibility this brought him with the newly politicized peasantry. Senghor also took advantage of maraboutic favour to impress on business interests his influence over the groundnut economy. The **marabouts**, formerly an important behind-the-scenes factor, were becoming political focal points themselves. Lamine Guèye's *SFIO* meanwhile struggled for support in the urban centres beyond the four *communes* and continued to ignore the countryside, to his party's cost.

The third political grouping, a loose association of **Marxist intellectuals**, trade unionists and students, tended to see the established politicians as too closely wedded to Paris. Their calls for independence were drowned by the clamour for fairer assimilation.

The **Loi Cadre** ("Blueprint law") of 1956 was a step in both directions. Self-government was instituted for each of the overseas territories. But there was not to be the widely desired **federation** of territories with a capital in Dakar. And defence, higher education and currency would still be issues debated in Paris.

This was transparently an attempt to **balkanize** French Africa. It's been argued, and was at the time, that it gave more Africans the chance to participate in government than would have been the case had they been answerable to Dakar instead of their own capitals. In that sense it was a device to cloud over the real issue – independence.

The UPS and the 1958 referendum

Senghor continued to build a power base, drawing his support from the marabouts, the business community and **Mamadou Dia**'s socialist movement. He also attempted to make an alliance with Felix Houphouët-Boigny's *Rassemblement Démocratique Africain* in Côte d'Ivoire, arguing the need for federation. When this was blocked by Houphouët, the *BDS* moved left and changed its name to *Bloc populaire sénégalais*, taking with it the *Mouvement autonome de Casamance* – the regional independence movement for Casamance which had grown out of the final "pacification" in the region little more than a decade earlier. Mamadou Dia became prime minister in the new territorial government of 1957 after the defeat of Lamine Guèye's *SFIO*. His party subsequently merged with the *BPS* and the *Union Progressiste Sénégalaise* was born.

The *UPS* was soon split by **de Gaulle's coming to power** in 1958 and his intransigent offer of either immediate independence and severance from the French Union or continued self-government within the French Union. It was a critical choice and one that Senghor was unwilling to make. Mindful of French economic clout as well his support among the marabouts and their mistrust of the party left wing, he ultimately sacrificed a section of young *UPS* radicals (who immediately formed their own party) and made sure that Senegal's vote to continue the Union was **Yes**. With this Lamine Guèye and even Mamadou Dia were in accord. But trade unionists, intellectuals and Casamance separatists were mostly alienated and disappointed at the submission to de Gaulle. Modern opposition politics have their roots in the 1958 referendum.

Independence

Senghor still favoured an independent, Dakar-led federation of states. Working with the ex-territory of Soudan (now Mali) and others, the **Mali Federation** was formed to further this end; but by the time it was constituted in April 1959, the federation's members were reduced to Mali and Senegal – an unworkable alliance given the influence of Dakar. But it was pursued nonetheless.

Lamine Guèye was now elected president of the new territorial assembly. Modibo Keita of Mali was elected president of the Federal Government and Mamadou Dia vice-president. In September, inspired by Guinea's secession, the Mali Federation lobbied France for independence.

ISLAM IN SENEGAL

Ligey si top, yala la bok – "Work is part of religion"

Amadou Bamba, founder of Mouridism

Any insight into modern Senegal requires an understanding of the country's extraordinarily influential **Muslim brotherhoods**. You won't stay here long without noticing – in the names on the bush taxis, the signs on the village shops and the flocks of multicoloured Hare Krisna-like disciples – that something very unusual lies in the dusty heart of Senegalese society.

ORIGINS

The Muslim **brotherhoods** are in conflict with original, Arabian Islam, which says everyone has a direct relationship with God. They resulted from the religion's spread to the Berber peoples of northwest Africa, the brotherhoods flourishing in these class-based societies, where it was natural to think that certain men should be gifted with divine insight, able to perform miracles and bestow blessings.

One of the earliest dynasties of Moroccan Muslims to make permanent contact with the people south of the desert was the ***Almoravid*** (whence marabout: holy leader/saint) who, in the twelfth century, made conversions in the kingdom of **Tekrur** in northeast Senegal. In the fifteenth century, the **Qadiriya** brotherhood was introduced south of the Sahara and, by the end of the eighteenth century, was firmly based near Timbuktu. Stressing **charity**, **humility** and **piety**, Qadirism made no exclusive demands of its followers and recruited from all ethnic groups. A local Qadiri offshoot, the **Layen** brotherhood, was founded in the late nineteenth century as an exclusively Lebu-speaking order in the Cap Vert district near Dakar.

Another order, the **Tijaniya**, crossed the desert early in the nineteenth century and was spread over Senegal by the proselytizing warlord Omar Tall. Tijaniya laid less stress on humility than earlier orders. Indeed, its Moroccan founder Al-Tijani had claimed direct contact with the Prophet Muhammad and, as a consequence, his followers were forbidden allegiance to any other orders. The brotherhood rapidly recruited the mass of Tukulor speakers in northeast Senegal. Tukulor marabouts – notably the forefathers of the hugely influential **Sy** and **Mbacke** families – were largely responsible for the later conversion of the Wolof.

MARABOUTS AND THE FRENCH

The interplay between **the brotherhoods and the French** was complicated. Allegiances often cut through ties of birth and language, so that, typically, peasants found themselves in alliance with the marabouts against their own, traditional rulers who tended to conspire with the French. Moreover, "pacification" by the French often resulted in more fertile ground for the spread of Islam. By the early 1900s, with the conversion to Islam of even the most resistant traditional rulers, a new establishment of **vested interests** had been founded, uniting the French and the marabouts. Although the Tijaniya traditionally had a core of fundamentalist, anti-French sentiment, the order soon adjusted to the material realities of colonialism. The latest and greatest brotherhood, the **Mouridiya** – exclusively rural and Senegalese – came, in practice, to be a bastion of the status quo.

MOURIDISM

The Mouridiya was founded in 1887 by **Amadou Bamba**, nephew of the Wolof king Lat Dior, and a member of the influential Mbacke family. An offshoot of the Qadiriya brotherhood, Mouridiya initially attracted many former anti-colonial fighters inspired by its discipline and dynamism, and by the charisma of Bamba.

Rumours of an armed insurrection from his court at Touba terrified the French ("We cannot tolerate a state within a state") and Bamba was twice exiled by the authorities – though these banishments served only to increase his standing at home.

Mouride folk history places great emphasis on Bamba's anti-colonial credentials, but soon after his return to Senegal in 1907 (a return celebrated in the annual *Magal* pilgrimage), he was striking deals with the authorities and trusting in the slow wheels of political reform. He was also amassing a personal fortune.

One of Bamba's early disciples, **Ibra Fall**, was personally devoted to the marabout, but he was a poor Koranic student. Bamba gave him an axe and told him to work for God with that. Sheikh Ibra Fall went on to found the fanatically slavish ***Baye Fall***. Today, these dreadlocked devotees in patchwork robes now have their own khalif but are exempt from study and even from fasting at Ramadan.

The founding of *Baye Fall* signalled a radical shift in religious thought, making **labour** a virtue and bringing Mouridism into the very heart of contemporary life. Among Mourides (whose name means "the hopeful") there's a universal belief that hard work is the key to paradise. Bamba is credited with announcing "If you work for me I shall pray for you" and even the five daily prayers are less important than toiling in the groundnut fields. The colonial authorities and the Mouride marabouts – mostly from wealthy, landed families – soon found areas of agreement.

THE BROTHERHOODS TODAY

Many senior and middle-ranking Mouride disciples today form a **new business class**. Even French-educated businessmen would rather become disciples of respected marabouts than short-cut the system. Over a dozen Mourides are multi-billionaires in CFA francs (worth up to £100 million/$150million) and Lebanese entrepreneurs find that business is increasingly out of their hands.

Illegal traffic has been profitable too, not least in the Mouride capital **Touba** itself, where the absence of government agents brought **racketeering** on a grand scale. All the hardware of Western consumerism, and even alcohol and arms, was widely available until the chief khalif, under pressure from Dakar, admitted that Mouridism was in danger of losing its soul, and allowed *gendarmes* into the holy city. The black market is clandestine again, but still funnels huge quantities of money and goods between Senegal and The Gambia.

Cooperation between the government and the brotherhoods – and more pointedly between the ruling *Parti Socialiste* and the Mourides – has continued, seamlessly, into the independent era. Yet the relationship remains one of latent mistrust, and even if many of those involved profit through it, the potential for a reactionary and anti-secular revolt against the government has always been there, as the Mouride brotherhood is conservative, overwhelmingly Wolof-speaking and rigorously hierarchical. The former chief khalif, **Abdoul Ahad Mbacke**, presided over a firmly united brotherhood from 1968 until his death in June1989.

Successions to the position of chief khalif are times of crisis in all the brotherhoods, since the relationship between the voters and the elected government hangs very heavily on the words of the marabouts. The current Mouride chief khalif, **Serigne Saliou Mbacke** is considered to be less interested in worldly matters and therefore less likely to throw his weight behind the government's posturing and campaigning. This is a worry for the government, which is voicing a growing concern about the rise of a more **fundamentalist** strand of Islam in Senegal.

Economically, the Mouride-groundnut connection remains solid, with the **religious elite** supported by the harvest and the boundless offerings of their followers. With marginal exceptions the brotherhoods have rooted firmly in the safest political ground. The government, while insisting that the state and political process is strictly secular, lavishes publicity and patronage on the marabouts for delivering votes. In 1968 the chief khalif instructed Mouride university students to disobey the strike call. Twenty years later, the **general election** was won overwhelmingly by Diouf after the usual maraboutic injunctions; the same happened in 1993.

The ***Magal*** pilgrimage to Touba looks set to continue as the occasion when the state president reiterates his support for the Mourides and his appreciation of the benefits they've brought Senegal. In turn the chief khalif emphasizes to his two million followers the sanctity of the groundnut harvest, the importance of not rocking the boat and their duty to support stable government, implying that a vote against the *Parti Socialiste* would be a vote against him, and therefore against God. The Tijaniya ***Gamou*** gatherings in Tivaouane and Kaolack are smaller-scale versions of the *Magal*, and similar back-slapping is the order of the day.

It has long been an irony of Senegalese politics – and frustrating for the country's left wing – that Senegal, with its highly developed democratic structures, should find democracy repeatedly brushed aside by the mass of its people in exchange for the grace of God.

And in a *volte-face* that amazed most observers, de Gaulle conceded that total independence should not, after all, deny a country the right to remain within the French Union. On April 4, 1960 (now "National Day") the principle of independence for the Mali Federation was declared; and on June 20, 1960 **independence** was proclaimed.

On August 20, 1960, the Mali Federation suddenly broke down over the election of a president. The Senegalese had insisted on Senghor for this role, having begun to distrust Bamako's rigorous Marxist policies. Senegal proclaimed its **independence from Mali** the same day, arresting Modibo Keita and sending him back to Bamako in a sealed train wagon. Mali refused to recognize the new **Republic of Senegal** and for three years the Dakar–Bamako railway was unused.

The Senghor years

Senghor took the presidency of the new republic, keeping Mamadou Dia as his prime minister. Senghor's formulation of **négritude**, Senegal's nationalism, blended with his motto "Assimiler, pas être assimilés", urging Africans to assimilate European culture, not be assimilated by it. On this foundation, Senghor and the *UPS* built the ideology of **African socialism**, which amounted to a tacit defence of the status quo in its emphasis on consensus. Dia, whose own politics remained to the left of Senghor, failed to find a balance between the business community and the radical left, and succeeded only in irritating the French. In 1962, Senghor had him arrested (he was sentenced to life imprisonment after an alleged coup attempt in which the army came to Senghor's rescue), and relations with France began to prosper.

The one party state

The rest of the decade saw the government growing increasingly right-wing. In 1963 a **revised constitution** was approved, strengthening the role of the president and effectively forcing radical opposition underground. Cheikh Anta Diop's *Bloc des masses sénégalaises* was the most powerful group the opposition could legally muster and this was smashed by a massive and disputed *UPS* victory in the elections of that year. **Riots** in their aftermath were put down by troops, with many deaths – the first serious smear on Senegal's hitherto spotless reputation. The *BMS* was banned; the remaining opposition had by 1966 been forced into the *UPS* or harassed out of existence.

Farmers were badly hit by the abolition of French subsidies for groundnut prices in 1967, while most town dwellers were no better off than they had been before independence. In May 1968 **trade unionists** and **students protested** at the government's complacency, confronting it with the charge of neo-imperialism. Senghor confronted the protesters with the **army**. Further strikes were followed by some concessions, then the government tried to force the unions into its own muzzled national confederation of workers (the *CNTS*). Some, like the teachers, resisted.

Repeated crises slackened off at the end of the decade when Senghor revived the post of prime minister – given to Abdou Diouf in 1970 – and, after further university unrest in 1973, banned the teacher's union and jailed some of the activists. The party was renamed the *Parti socialiste*, a cosmetic alteration that convinced few.

Democratic reforms

In 1974, a cautious new liberalism was initiated with the release of ex-PM Mamadou Dia from twelve years in detention. Soon after, the **Parti démocratique sénégalais** (*PDS*) led by lawyer **Maître Abdoulaye Wade** was allowed to register and by 1976 various brands of liberal and social democracy were on offer, as well as a legal Marxist-Leninist party, which attracted a small number of radicals. A flood of political handouts and news sheets hit the streets. Anta Diop and Mamadou Dia were banned from forming parties, but not excluded from discussion.

By 1978, Senghor – now in his late sixties – was spending more time on poetry and the *Académie française* than running Senegal, and he began to groom his vice-president, **Abdou Diouf**, for leadership. Diouf was already taking responsibility for executive decisions and his status grew as he gained support from the major aid institutions for his austerity management of the economy .

A sideshow in the late 1970s was the **militant Tijaniya dynasty** of Ahmet Khalif Niasse. Niasse went into exile in Libya allegedly intending to organize for an Islamic state in Senegal, which led to the cutting of diplomatic relations. The Libyan connection resurfaced across the border in The Gambia, where the "coup attempt" of November 1980 reportedly had the same roots.

President Jawara invoked the two countries' historic relationship, and Senegalese troops were sent in.

■ Diouf in power

Senghor, the first African president to retire voluntarily, passed the presidency to Diouf on January 1, 1981. At first it was feared that Diouf's uncharismatic style would be insufficient to carry him, but **opposition groups** were hopeful he would lift remaining restrictions on political activities and their hopes were soon fulfilled. Cheikh Anta Diop's *Rassemblement national démocratique* (*RND*) was legalized, Dia founded the *Mouvement démocratique populaire* (*MDP*), and there were several others. Wade's *PDS* relinquished its role as the focal point of opposition and actually lost a few members in a purge of pro-Libyan sympathizers.

Diouf increased his popularity by launching an **anti-corruption drive** focusing on his own cabinet and firing Senghor's "barons". And traditional supporters of the government – the moderate Muslim masses – were gratified to have a president at last who spoke Wolof as his mother tongue and peppered his speeches with Koranic references.

The July 1981 coup in **The Gambia** was the most severe test of Diouf's nerve in his first year in office. President Jawara called him from London to ask Senegal to restore him to power, which the Senegalese army accomplished with considerable bloodshed. A detachment stayed in The Gambia until the late 1980s.

However, the spectre of an unfriendly and destabilizing power taking control in The Gambia galvanized Diouf to do something about the dormant **Senegambia confederation**. In December 1981 an agreement was ratified and a Senegambian parliament met for its first session in 1983. The Gambia, with no army and little to offer Senegal except a headache and its river, was always likely to be the passive partner in a relationship that finally collapsed in 1989.

The **economy**, meanwhile, continued to decline. Although the state groundnut-buying monopoly was dissolved in 1980 after years of corruption and inefficiency, low prices and disastrous harvests that year and in 1984 meant no perceptible improvement for the peasant farmers. **Fishing** was pushed into first place as a foreign exchange earner, with **tourism** second and groundnuts third. Agricultural diversification is desperately needed: as subsidies on fertilizer and seed are phased out, soil exhaustion and poor harvests are the prospect for the future.

The **1988 election** saw the first display of really serious political and social unrest during Diouf's presidency: an ominously quiet polling day was followed by the most violent riots in Dakar since the "Mamadou Dia affair" in 1963. Diouf declared a **state of emergency**; tanks and tear gas came onto the streets; a dusk to dawn curfew was in force for three weeks, and **Abdoulaye Wade**, who claimed to have been defeated by a rigged poll, was arrested. His trial and conviction on charges of incitement to subvert the state triggered further unrest, which was later quelled by his own, characteristically conciliatory, remarks.

Diouf, however, later withdrew any inference of a pact between him and Wade and set about making **changes to the electoral system**, ostensibly to guarantee fairer elections. In practice these adjustments delayed local elections and enraged Wade and the main opposition alliance, **Sopi** ("Change"), who accused Diouf of perpetuating the distortion of the democratic process by vested interests and vote-buying.

Even the intense dissatisfaction with the political scene was overshadowed during the **Senegal-Mauritania crisis** of April 1989 to October 1990. Triggered by a land dispute on the border, local fighting flared into racial conflict as Mauritanian shopkeepers (the 300,000-strong mainstay of Senegal's retail trade) were hounded out of Senegal, hundreds killed and their stores looted. An international operation assited refugees to return to Nouakchott, while Senegalese immigrants in Mauritania (who were even more violently, and systematically, attacked) returned to Senegal. The borders closed and a cloud of deep mutual mistrust hung over the two governments, fuelled by their opposed positions during the Gulf conflict: Mauritania remained a guarded ally of Iraq, while Senegalese troops were sent to Saudi Arabia to assist in "Operation Desert Storm".

■ Recent events

Despite its troubles, Senegal is generally viewed as one of the most stable and democratic countries in West Africa. On the political front, the dominant theme of the 1990s has been a low-level, grumbling discontent with the inertia of the

Parti Socialiste, which has several times boiled up into riots.

The **elections of February 1993** were again the subject of condemnation by Wade over alleged photocopied registration papers, multiple voting and other ploys. In the presidental ballot, Wade came out in front in the main urban areas of Dakar and Thiès but Diouf won overall, taking 58 percent of the votes against Wade's 32 percent (in a 52 percent turnout). Three months later in the national assembly elections, Wade's *PDS* only obtained 27 seats, while Diouf's *PS* took 84 seats of the remaining 93 (in a turnout on this occasion of just 40 percent of the electorate). Wade claimed that the election, had it been conducted without impropriety, would have returned 63 *PDS* deputies, and only 48 for the *PS*. The frustration of the opposition was cited as the likely cause of the assassination of the vice-chief of the electoral commission, **Babacar Sèye**, days after his announcement of the disappointing results. The perpetrators remain unknown, and while a previously unheard of "Armée du Peuple" claimed to have carried out the attack, it was Abdoulaye Wade and three associates who were arrested without charge. One, **Mody Sy**, was kept in jail for more than a year.

The **devaluation of the CFA franc** in February 1994, believed to have been firmly supported by Diouf, and quite likely engineered partly by him, was particularly hard on the poor. Just a few months earlier, however, the government had imposed cruel **austerity wage cuts** across the economy (15 percent off the public sector, 5 percent off the private). These were then rescinded after the devaluation, in what seems to have been a premeditated attempt to soften the blow of huge price increases.

In a mass rally for democracy in Dakar on February 16, led by the **Tijaniya brotherhood**'s youth organization *Daira al Moustarchidines wal Moustarchidates*, militant protestors precipitated a riot and then rounded on the security forces, killing six policemen in a frenzied attack that left the country stunned.

Wade and six senior opposition figures on the march were among a group of 177 people arrested for incitement to violence. Most were eventually released. A new opposition alliance, *Bokk Sopi Sénégal* ("Uniting to Change Senegal") – formed in September 1994 from Wade's *PDS*, **Landing Savané**'s communist *And-Jëf – Parti Africaine pour la Démocratie et le Socialisme* (*AJ–PADS*), and Mamadou Dia's *Mouvement pour le Socialisme et l'Unité* (*MSU*) – seems to have emerged as a result of the experience.

Remarkably, in March 1995 Wade and six *PDS* colleagues took **cabinet posts** in the national government on the invitation of Abdou Diouf. This is almost certainly a containment measure as far as Diouf is concerned – better to deal with the charismatic and outspoken Wade behind closed doors than across the barricades. How much it will blunt Wade's campaigning style remains to be seen: he has only to snap his fingers and the youth are out on the streets. But he has served briefly under Diouf before, in 1991, and has so far resisted temptation to call the shots in this way. There's a mood of cynicism growing about Wade, however, and his credentials as a man of the people are beginning to wear thin as the political operator shows through.

■ Threats and prospects

Industry is in steep decline, relying, as it does so heavily, on imported raw materials. **Education** is in a shambles after years of class boycotts, strikes and abrogated school years. Senegalese **society** is increasingly divided into those who have access to a state salary from a family member and those who rely on the private sector and the informal and subsistence economy. The average state employee's salary is ten times the national average income.

The polarization is easily exploited, and the most enthusiastic fishers in this river of discontent – at least in the northern part of Senegal – are **Muslim fundamentalists**. The government, acutely aware of the dangers, deports known foreign agitators while juggling the less dangerous demands of secular radicals like Wade and of its conservative marabout supporters and their followers in the countryside. The rift with Mauritania was an uncomfortable period as that country is also the subject of firm fundamentalist pressures and, for a while, it appeared Nouakchott was acting to destabilize Senegal by arming the Casamance rebels. A pragmatic patching up of differences has taken place, shoring up central government in both countries against rebellion.

The new government in **The Gambia** is a wild card, but Senegal is not looking too hard at recent history – that is, when it waded in to support ex-president Jawara, who is now living in exile in Senegal. Relations between Banjul and Dakar are cool, but correct.

THE CASAMANCE CONFLICT

Demonstrations in **Casamance** in December 1982 signalled the reawakening of the Casamance separatist movement and resulted in a number of detentions without trial. The region is poorly developed and substantially non-Muslim: the charge that it's ignored because it produces less groundnuts than the north and can't muster heavyweight marabouts is not baseless. The Casamançais resent the snub, because it is Casamance rice that goes a substantial way towards feeding the country. Elections won by Abdou Diouf's *Parti Socialiste* have left in fragmented disarray the opposition parties with powerbases in Casamance.

Violently suppressed separatist demonstrations in Casamance in December 1983 left over 100 people dead and hundreds more in detention. Similar incidents continued sporadically in the Casamance through the 1980s, but it was only in 1990 that the violence errupted into serious armed conflict as the MFDC's military wing, *Attika* ("Fighter" in Jola) went into action. The government in Dakar believed the separatists were getting arms from Mauritania, channelled through Jola sympathizers in Guinea-Bissau. By early 1993, in advance of the presidential and legislative elections (boycotted by the MFDC), there were 5000 troops in the Casamance and the region was under military control.

The MFDC wants independence from the rest of Senegal and claims that Casamance existed as a separate territory before the French colonial era. The movement is split into the *Front nord*, based around Baila and Bignona, and the more extreme *Front sud* led by brothers Augustine and Bertrand Diamacouné Senghor, focussed on Oussouye and the villages to the south, along the Guinea-Bissau border. After a ceasefire agreement and the release of many prisoners by the government in mid-1993, there was an eighteen-month lull in fighting. But hostilities flared up again in the southern districts at the end of 1994 and the army and airforce went on the offensive with manhunts through the forest and bombing raids (including two that hit villages in Guinea-Bissau).

How much support the MFDC has is hard to gauge: many Jola feel marginalized by the Dakar government and do support greater autonomy. But a struggle for independence would almost certainly wipe out the **tourism** on which the region is heavily dependent for foreign exchange. In April 1995, four French tourists in a rented car disappeared, believed kidnapped. As this book goes to press (August 1995), the tourists still have not been traced, the conflict continues and the MFDC appears to be fragmenting. A recent statement by Bertrand Senghor claimed he stands by the ceasefire.

DAKAR, CAP VERT AND CENTRAL SENEGAL

West Africa's westernmost point and one of its most westernized capital cities, **Dakar** wields a powerful influence. Its pull extends well beyond Senegal's borders, drawing in migrants from across the Sahel and expatriates from overseas – especially, still, France. The city swarms with newcomers caught up in the neocolonial whirlpool, and its attractions are tempered by all this hustle and by the sheer size of the place. But the physical setting is striking, and the city has undeniable style, epitomizing the residue of French colonialism in Africa.

Out of Dakar, **Gorée island** is a major draw, while the peninsula of **Cap Vert** offers beaches and out-of-town amusements. A more sheltered coast is **La Petite Côte** to the south of the city, which, beyond the dubious tourist magnet of **Joal-Fadiout**, merges into the bird-flocked creeks and islands of the **Sine-Saloum** region, adjoining the Gambian border.

Inland, the travel options from Dakar are harsher and the attractions scarcer, the focal points being the shady rail network hub of **Thiès** and the much more distant Islamic hot-house of **Touba**. If you're interested in the culture of the **Islamic brotherhoods**, some suggestions are made at the end of this section, along with details on the Sine-Saloum **stone circles** complex.

Dakar

A giant of a city in African terms, with over a million inhabitants, **DAKAR** is hard work. The shock of arriving can be intense: it's incredibly dynamic, sophisticated and wretched in equal measure and, despite the devaluation of the CFA franc, a test of will if your budget is tight. **French** influence is everywhere, especially in the downtown **Plateau** area, where the architecture and the whole feel of the place is more evocative of southern France than Africa. The results can be quite beautiful, without question. Between sprouting skyscrapers, the terracotta rooftops and shady, tree-lined avenues of the older quarters give Dakar an elegant maturity shared by few other African capitals.

Unfortunately some of the most attractive parts of the centre swarm with vendors, hustlers and hostile, hooting traffic, though this frenetic pace thankfully subsides on Saturdays, and on Sundays disappears altogether. At this time people hang out on shady shopfronts, kids play football in the streets and even the *colons* forsake their cars and taxis for a stroll out to Sunday lunch. During the week the **Isle de Gorée**, **Hann Park**, and the beaches at **Ngor** and **Yof** all provide degrees of space and seclusion, and if, rather than retreat, you'd prefer a more human participation, most of Dakar's teeming **suburbs** are a lot more open and easy-going than experiences in the city centre might lead you to imagine.

Some history

Gorée island was first settled by European merchant adventurers in the fifteenth century, though the fortress-like peninsula of **Dakar** – the oldest European city in West Africa – was not established until 1857. The name Dakar was first used in the eighteenth century and is supposed to derive from the Wolof for tamarind tree – *daxar* – or refuge – *dekraw*.

The town's development really began towards the end of the last century, with the decline of St-Louis as a port, and the opening of the Dakar to St-Louis **railway** in 1885 (the first in West Africa), which gave a boost to groundnut farmers along its route. By

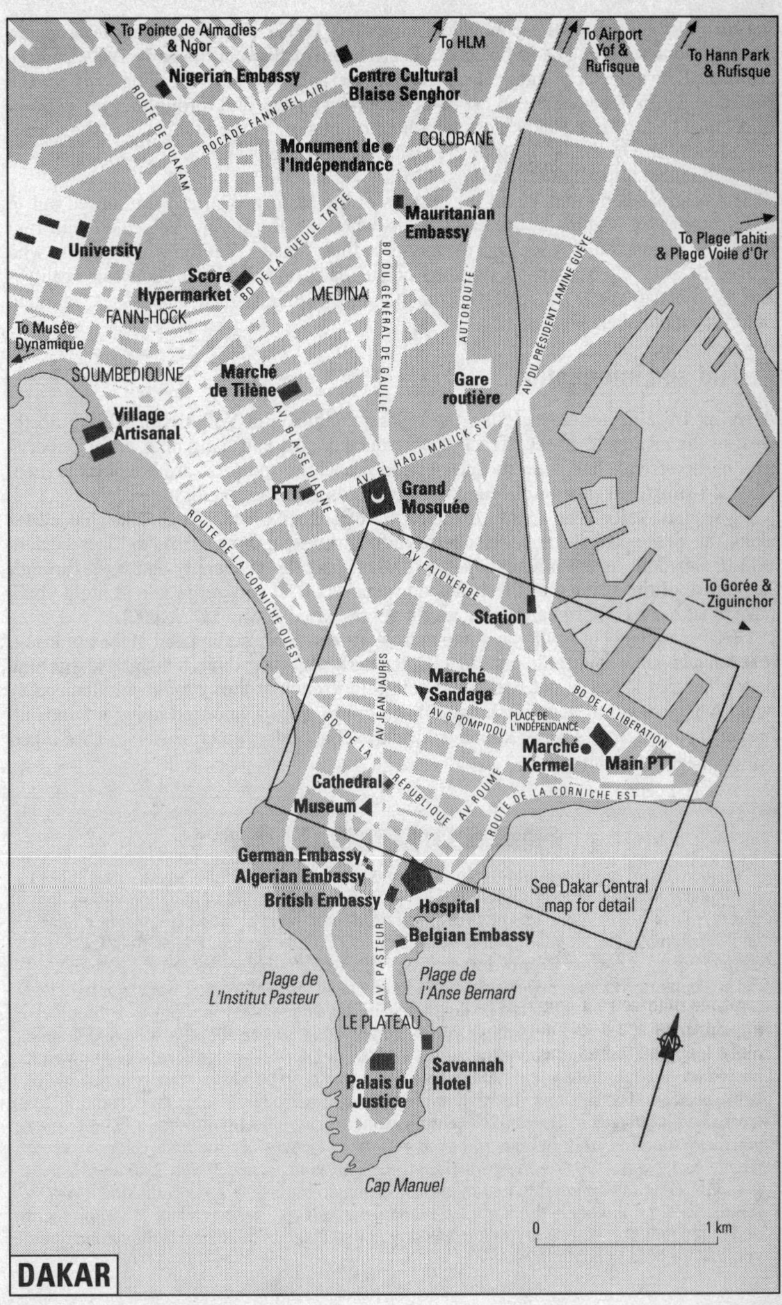
To Pointe de Almadies & Ngor
To HLM
To Airport Yof & Rufisque
To Hann Park & Rufisque
Nigerian Embassy
Centre Cultural Blaise Senghor
ROUTE DE OUAKAM
ROCADE FANN BEL AIR
Monument de l'Indépendance
COLOBANE
BD DE LA GUEULE TAPEE
Mauritanian Embassy
University
To Plage Tahiti & Plage Voile d'Or
Score Hypermarket
MEDINA
BD DU GÉNÉRAL DE GAULLE
AUTOROUTE
AV DU PRÉSIDENT LAMINE GUEYE
FANN-HOCK
To Musée Dynamique
SOUMBEDIOUNE
Marché de Tilène
Gare routière
Village Artisanal
AV BLAISE DIAGNE
AV. EL HADJ MALICK SY
PTT
Grand Mosquée
ROUTE DE LA CORNICHE OUEST
AV FAIDHERBE
Station
To Gorée & Ziguinchor
AV JEAN JAURES
Marché Sandaga
BD DE LA LIBERATION
AV G POMPIDOU
PLACE DE L'INDÉPENDANCE
BD DE LA RÉPUBLIQUE
Marché Kermel
Main PTT
Cathedral
Museum
AV ROUME
ROUTE DE LA CORNICHE EST
German Embassy
Algerian Embassy
British Embassy
Hospital
See Dakar Central map for detail
Belgian Embassy
AV. PASTEUR
Plage de L'Institut Pasteur
Plage de l'Anse Bernard
LE PLATEAU
Savannah Hotel
Palais du Justice
Cap Manuel
N
0
1 km
DAKAR

the turn of the century the population numbered 15,000. With considerable dredging and port construction, Dakar became a **French naval base** in the early 1900s and the **capital** of Afrique Occidentale Française in 1904. It was also a calling port on the routes to South America and West and South Africa runs, and throughout the century of colonial occupation, Dakar's cosmopolitan reputation as the first call on "the Coast" went before it. On the opening of the Dakar–Bamako railway line in 1923, Dakar was easily the most important city in West Africa.

The original Lebu and Wolof inhabitants of the Plateau district were forced out to the new town of Medina in the early 1930s, when the Depression coincided with rent increases imposed to pay for improvements to their houses. Yet the white settlers who moved in were often poor – a rigorous colour bar prevailing over economic reality – and even today you'll see elderly French, some running small businesses, hanging onto very modest existences.

Arrival and information

Arriving by air, you emerge into the milling confusion of **Yof Airport**, 12km northwest of the city (☎22 40 60). Track down your luggage and hang onto it: the supervision of the arrivals hall is pretty relaxed and not all the "porters" are honourable men. The **"24-hour bureau de change"** usually closes after the last flight.

Until 9pm, you've the option of *SOTRAC* **buses** #7 or #8, which take you either along the west coast of the peninsula through fairly exclusive suburbs to Place Leclerc (#7) or through the mishmash of Grand Dakar, past the University and right through the centre of the Plateau to the Palais de Justice (#8). If you get in late at night you'll have to take a taxi (hard bargaining might get the price down to CFA4000).

Dakar is unusual in having just one main **gare routière**, at the head of the autoroute that funnels suburban traffic into the city. It's fairly together, though not any less intimidating for that if you're not used to shouting in French at four people simultaneously while beggars pull at your clothing and the fumes from a hundred idling engines fill the air. From here it's a two-kilometre walk to the centre: much easier to take a taxi (CFA500–800) or a bus.

SECURITY IN DAKAR

The question of **personal safety in Dakar** is one you can't afford to be casual about, particularly when you first arrive. Decide quickly on an initial destination rather than wandering in hope. A few gangs of organized **thieves** operate with extraordinary daring and, burdened with luggage, you're an easy and valuable trophy. **Place de l'Indépendance** and **av Georges Pompidou** are notorious trouble-spots, especially the *place* itself during banking hours – remain alert and keep valuables, purses and wallets completely out of sight. Don't be deflected or distracted by anything or anyone, however friendly – keep a steady pace and get where you're going. Once you've found a base you'll soon make up your own mind about the relative safety of Dakar. As a **general rule** however, avoid carrying anything you'd hate to lose and *never* keep purses or wallets in outside or back pockets. Distractions, be they words or a touch, should always be ignored or treated with suspicion. One group **technique** is to stop you by offering a bangle, hold your legs together from behind and grab your shirt sleeves. By the time you've realized what's happening, they're off down the street with your wallet. If you lose anything of personal value (as opposed to just money or expensive items), it's worth making a visit to the market in Colobane – the so-called *marché aux voleurs* – 500m east of the Monument de l'Indépendance, where, if you keep asking and manage to make the right connections, you may be able to buy it back.

Trains come in at the old Art Deco station, north of the centre and just ten minutes from the closest budget hotels. The train from Bamako usually gets in after dark, so make sure you've looked at the map and know exactly where you're heading.

For **tourist information**, the *Délégation au Tourisme*, Place de l'Indépendance, is pretty washed up. Visit the **ministry** itself in the defunct *Village des Arts* on rue du Docteur Calmette, just off av André Peytavin (BP 4029; ☎22 22 26): they have various leaflets.

Orientation and city transport

Dakar is built on the twin-pronged **Cap Vert peninsula**. The southern spur contains the city's heart, with cliffs and coves along the ocean side and Cap Manuel, and the main port area along the sheltered eastern flank. The suburbs spread north and west towards the **airport** and the other prong of **Pointe des Almadies**, Africa's most westerly point.

Despite Dakar's size, the **city centre** is a relatively manageable two square kilometres of tightly gridded streets, with the **train station** to the north, the **museum** to the south, **avénue Jean Jaurès** on the west and the **Kermel market** and **PTT** to the east. In the middle of it all stands the big, sloping centrepiece of **Place de l'Indépendance**, from where **avénue Georges Pompidou** cuts the district into a northern, heavily commercial quarter and a southern, more affluent, residential one – the **Plateau**. Most of the grand buildings of state and several important embassies are south of this central district, where the street pattern breaks into graciously radiating avenues and looping clifftop corniches.

City transport

One of Dakar's great pluses is its excellent **bus system**. The *Société des Transports en Commun du Cap Vert* runs fast, frequent and cheap buses from dawn till late evening. They're numbered and carry destination signs, and all charge a flat fare of CFA140 (within Dakar *ville*) or CFA180 (out as far as Bargny, 5km east of Rufisque). You can get anywhere by bus, though during rush hours the squeeze – and the heat – are sapping. For long stays you'd do well to obtain a copy of the *SOTRAC* route map from the small *SOTRAC* **information office** (☎23 37 05) at the bus station at the north end of av Jean Jaurès.

Cars rapides – boxy Saviem buses, usually sporting marabout monikers ("Touba") – are a poorer, and mostly private, version. Destinations are shouted by the fare collector, and although they're more erratic than the buses and confusing to newcomers, there's no standing allowed, so you're at least guaranteed a seat – and an insight into the street life of Dakar (CFA85–120). Big white ones leave from Cinéma Malick Sy, Marché Sandaga for the route de Ouakam, Yof and Ngor, while slightly smaller yellow and blue ones jostle together up a nearby street for Grand Dakar, HLM and Colobane.

As for **taxis**, supply is ahead of demand so you can always argue about the fare. In theory most operate meters, but nobody uses or trusts them any more, so agree the price up front. Daytime journeys in the town centre should cost no more than CFA500 and trips to the suburbs roughly CFA300/km; after dark (officially from midnight to 4am) the tariff doubles. Keep some change and small notes handy for drivers who often deny having any.

The **train** isn't a very functional way of getting in or out of the city, although it is at least comprehensible. There's a commuter service to Tiaroye and Rufisque, a suburb 28km east of the centre, both sometimes used by travellers as bases. Called *les petits trains bleus*, these trains run about three times each morning and evening in both directions.

To Médina, Grand Dakar & HLM
To Gare routière
AV FAIDHERBE
To Médina
RUE ALFRED GOUX
RUE ESCARFAIT
Cour des Orfèvres (Keur Jean Thiam)
AV DU SENEGAL
AV BLAISE DIAGNE
AV V O PETERSEN
RUE GRASLAND
RUE ELI MANEL FALL
RUE DE VALMY
RUE ROBERT BRUN
RUE RAFFENEL
RUE BLANCHOT
RUE VINCENS
RUE WAGANE DIOUF
Sand Paintings
RUE AMAND ANGRAND
RUE GALANDOU DIOUF
RUE DE FLEURS
RUE DE TOLBIAC
RUE DES DARDANELLES
Sotrac Bus Station
RUE EL HADJ ABDOUKARIM BOURGI
AV EMILE BADIANE
RUE PAUL HOLLE
RUE DE LA SOMME
RUE SANDINIERI
RUE DE THONG
Marché Sandaga
AV G POMPIDOU
Ministry of Tourism
To Corniche Ouest
AV A PEYTAVIN
AV JEAN JAURES
RUE DU DOCTEUR CALMETTE
RUE DE DENAIN
AV DU PRESIDENT LAMINE GUEYE
RUE EL HADJ AMADOU ASSANE NDOYE (RUE A A
RUE CARNOT
RUE JOSEPH GOMIS
RUE FELIX FAURE
Cinema
Bookshop
RUE MOHAMED V
BD DE LA REPUBLIQUE
AV PRESIDENT F D ROOSEVELT
RUE EL HADJ SEYDOU NOUROU TALL
Théâtre Daniel Sorano
PLACE WASHINGTON DC
RUE JULES FERRY
RUE MOUSSE DIOP
RUE VICTOR HUGO
RUE RENE NDIAYE
AV CARDE
Cathedral
Supermarket
AV JEAN XXIII
RUE KLEBER
IFAN Museum
AV COURBET (NELSON MANDELA)
RUE DE 18 JUIN
PLACE SOWETO
Le Building Administratif
To Cap Manuel
To Cap

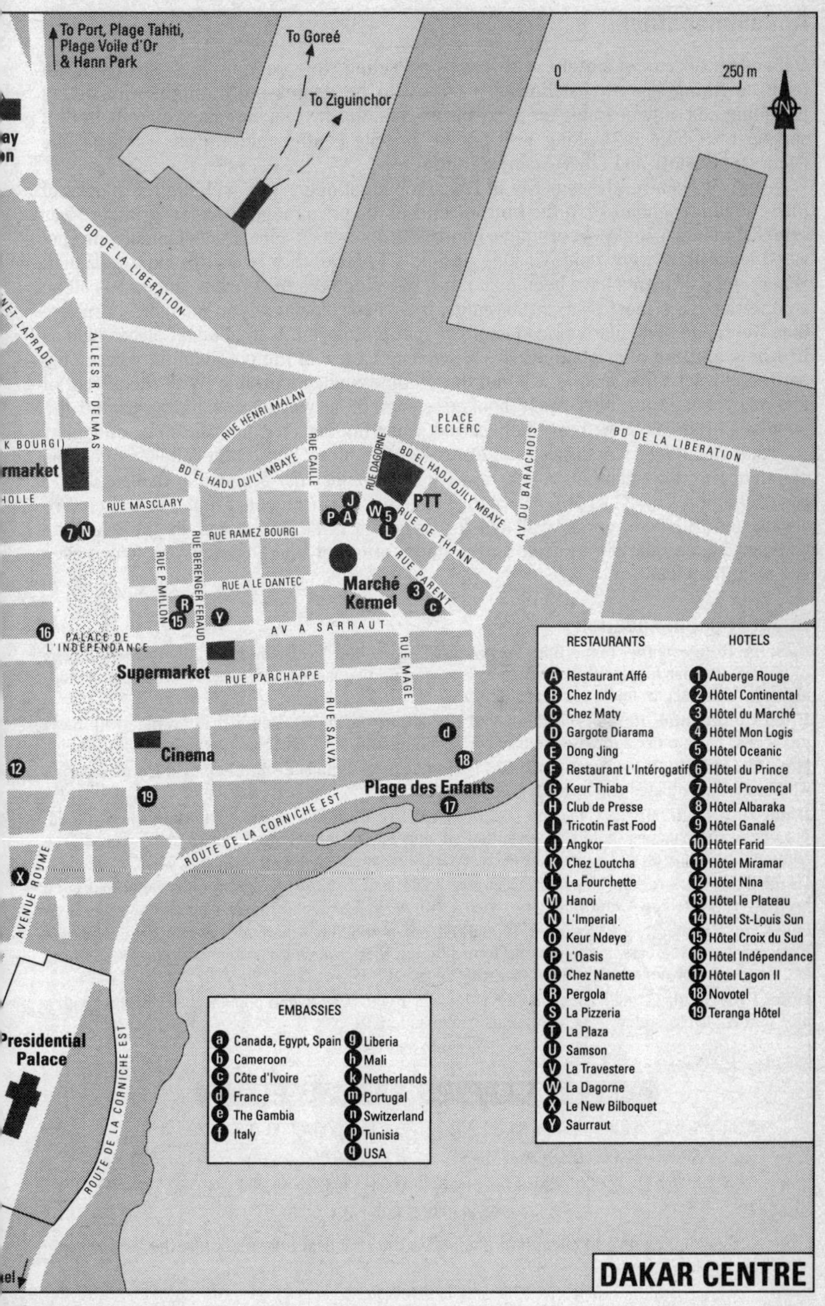

To Port, Plage Tahiti, Plage Voile d'Or & Hann Park
To Goreé
To Ziguinchor
0
250 m
N
BD DE LA LIBERATION
ALLEES R. DELMAS
RUE HENRI MALAN
RUE CAILLE
RUE DAGORNE
PLACE LECLERC
AV DU BARACHOIS
BD EL HADJ DJILY MBAYE
PTT
RUE MASCLARY
RUE RAMEZ BOURGI
RUE DE THANN
RUE PARENT
RUE P MILLON
RUE BERENGER FERAUD
RUE A LE DANTEC
Marché Kermel
AV A SARRAUT
PALACE DE L'INDEPENDANCE
Supermarket
RUE PARCHAPPE
RUE MAGE
RUE SALVA
Cinema
Plage des Enfants
ROUTE DE LA CORNICHE EST
AVENUE ROUME
Presidential Palace
RESTAURANTS
A Restaurant Affé
B Chez Indy
C Chez Maty
D Gargote Diarama
E Dong Jing
F Restaurant L'Intérogatif
G Keur Thiaba
H Club de Presse
I Tricotin Fast Food
J Angkor
K Chez Loutcha
L La Fourchette
M Hanoi
N L'Imperial
O Keur Ndeye
P L'Oasis
Q Chez Nanette
R Pergola
S La Pizzeria
T La Plaza
U Samson
V La Travestere
W La Dagorne
X Le New Bilboquet
Y Saurraut
HOTELS
1 Auberge Rouge
2 Hôtel Continental
3 Hôtel du Marché
4 Hôtel Mon Logis
5 Hôtel Oceanic
6 Hôtel du Prince
7 Hôtel Provençal
8 Hôtel Albaraka
9 Hôtel Ganalé
10 Hôtel Farid
11 Hôtel Miramar
12 Hôtel Nina
13 Hôtel le Plateau
14 Hôtel St-Louis Sun
15 Hôtel Croix du Sud
16 Hôtel Indépendance
17 Hôtel Lagon II
18 Novotel
19 Teranga Hôtel
EMBASSIES
a Canada, Egypt, Spain
b Cameroon
c Côte d'Ivoire
d France
e The Gambia
f Italy
g Liberia
h Mali
k Netherlands
m Portugal
n Switzerland
p Tunisia
q USA
DAKAR CENTRE

Accommodation

Dakar has dozens of **hotels**, with prices reflecting the generally high standards. In town, anything less than CFA6000 is likely to be depressingly rough, with dodgy plumbing and only bearable for a day or two, and for the real bargains you're better off staying on Gorée or looking well out of the city centre: middle-class suburbs like Dieupeul, Castors and Liberté can be fruitful.

In the city centre, the majority of Dakar's budget options lie within a few blocks of Place de l'Indépendance. At the **bottom end** of the price range are a few grim, pre-war establishments, usually set around a courtyard, and which appear substantially unrenovated since they were built. Costing around CFA5000, they're worth about half that. Where improvements have been made they move into the **mid-price** range and can be among the city's most pleasant lodgings, their neo-colonial charm far more attractive than the range of similarly priced anodyne modern blocks. Many budget places twin as **brothels** and can offer good value – we've listed a few of the possibilities, where only particularly sensitive visitors will find the seediness uncomfortable. With the advent of **fax** many hotels are now easily booked – something worth considering around the popular Christmas/New Year/Rally period, when finding a room at all can be difficult.

Dakar makes few concessions to **apartment** hunters. Some hotels below offer this option or if you are planning a long stay try *Regie Immobilier Mugnièr et Compagnie*, 11 rue Mohamed V (☎23 23 76). Alternatively, if your requirements are modest, there are always unfurnished rooms available for around CFA20,000/month in the Medina/Gueuele Tapée quartiers: knock on the doors of larger buildings and ask "Vous avez des chambres à louer?"

Budget accommodation

Auberge Rouge, corner of rue Jules Ferry/rue Mousse Diop ex-Blanchot (BP 1033; ☎23 55 98; Fax 23 35 05). Popular hotel with budget travellers offering two fanned and three AC rooms, although all pretty basic, set around a courtyard. ②–③.

Hôtel Continental, 10 rue Galandou Diouf (BP 2324; ☎22 38 77). Better than average with basic mod cons. The annexe at 57 rue Mousse Diop is better still; airy, light rooms with balconies. ③.

Hôtel du Marché, 3 rue Parent (☎21 57 71). An old stand-by (albeit a brothel) near Kermel market with large, unventilated and inexpensive S/C rooms. ②.

Hôtel Mon Logis, 67 rue Galandou Diouf (☎22 85 25). Hard to find and depressing when you do, but one of the cheapest hotels in town, and adequate as a last resort. Down an alley opposite the Nintendo boutique on av Lamine Gueye, past a mosque and then left up the stairs. ②.

Hôtel Oceanic, 9 rue du Thann (BP 219; ☎22 20 44; Fax 21 52 28). Pleasant old-style hotel, (*not* a brothel) with clued-up owners and clean rooms with AC and S/C, plus four-bed apartments. ②–③.

Hôtel du Prince, 49 rue Raffenel. Unmarked but numbered – behind the iron gate. *Midnight Express* without the bars, and plumbing to match, but there's a slim possibility of off-street parking and a laid-back owner who's open to long-stay deals. ②.

Hôtel Provençal, 17 rue Malenfant (BP 1375; ☎22 10 69). Cheap and popular hotel/brothel with a nice garden, five minutes' walk south of the train station. ②.

ACCOMMODATION PRICE CODES

① Under CFA4000 (under £5/$7.50) ② CFA4000–8000 (£5–10/$8–15)
③ CFA8000–16,000 (£10–20/$15–30) ④ CFA16,000–24,000 (£20–30/$30–45)
⑤ CFA24,000–32,000 (£30–40/$45–60) ⑥ CFA32,000–40,000 (£40–50/$60–75)
⑦ Over CFA40,000 (over £50/$75)

For further details turn to "Accommodation" in the Practical Information at the beginning of this chapter.

Mid-range accommodation

Hôtel Albaraka, 35 rue El Hadj Abdoukarim Bourgi (BP 578; ☎22 55 32; Fax 21 75 41). Central place offering modern and clean rooms with TVs. All credit cards. ⑤.

Hôtel Farid, 51 rue de Vincens (☎21 61 27; Fax 21 04 94). Great-value modern, clean rooms (TV; fridge) with showroom-like bathrooms and balconies. There's an excellent Lebanese restaurant downstairs. Credit cards accepted. ④.

Hôtel Ganalé, 38 rue El Hadj AA Ndoye (☎21 58 54; Fax 22 34 30). The former *de la Paix*, now one of central Dakar's newest refurbishments offering spotless motel-like rooms with TV, some apartments and a popular jazz bar and restaurant. Breakfast CFA1200. ④–⑥.

Hôtel Miramar, 25–27 rue Felix Faure (BP 973; ☎23 55 98; Fax 23 35 05). Slightly ageing S/C, AC rooms with TV. Afro-kitsch spaceship decor in communal areas and the *Soninké Bar* downstairs add eccentric character. Good breakfast served. ⑤.

Hôtel Nina, 43 rue de Docteur Thèze (☎/Fax 21 41 81). Central hotel with all mod cons. Pricey, though, and a bit bland. All credit cards. ④.

Hôtel le Plateau, 62 rue Jules Ferry (BP 2906; ☎23 44 20; Fax 22 50 24). Unprepossessing block situated right behind the Malian embassy with reasonable-value rooms and a good place to drink, the *Bar Americaine*. ④.

Hôtel St-Louis Sun, 68 rue Felix Faure (☎22 25 70). A charismatic choice, renovated in the *Louisienne*–style with an attractive patio and restaurant and tidy AC, S/C rooms. *Mastercard* accepted. ④.

Luxury accommodation

Hotel Croix du Sud, 20 av Albert Sarraut (BP 232; ☎23 29 47; Fax 23 26 55). Renovated 1950s hotel, centrally located but with little character. ⑥.

Hôtel Indépendance, Place de l'Indépendance (BP 221; ☎23 10 19; Fax 22 11 17). Dakar's earliest modern four-star flagship towerblock is overpriced but does have a great view from the rooftop pool. Breakfast extra. ⑥–⑦.

Hôtel Lagon II, rte de la Corniche Est (BP 3115; ☎23 74 42; Fax 23 77 27). Popular, French-run hotel right on the shore looking towards Gorée. ⑦.

Novotel, av Abdoulaye Fadiga (BP 2073; ☎23 88 49; Fax 23 89 29). Bland four-star high-rise with possible sea views from renovated rooms with modern facilities. ⑦.

Savana Pullman, rte de la Corniche Est (BP 1015; ☎23 60 23; Fax 23 73 06). Luxuriously landscaped tourist hotel – the best place in Dakar to spend gratuitously in genuine comfort. ⑦.

Teranga Hôtel, Place de l'Indépendance (BP 3380; ☎23 10 44; Fax 23 50 01). Not much *teranga* offered at Dakar's priciest hotel – the preferred abode of visiting statesmen. Well into the top price scale. ⑦.

The Town

Dakar is every inch a capitalist capital with **consumption** as conspicuous and contradictory as you'd expect. Lepers, polio victims and various other beggars are a common sight, and you may find the contrasts repugnant. Unless you're going to do your necessary business as fast as possible and get out, you might as well resign yourself to participation and expenditure. Once you've learnt to deal with the inevitable hassle, the two central markets of **Sandaga** and **Kermel** are worth a visit, and you'll find the irrepressible *commerçants* spilling out onto any traffic-free surface in the surrounding area. Of interest too are the superb and highly buyable offerings of the artisans at **Keur Jean Thiam**, a few minutes north of Sandaga.

There's more to do in Dakar than shop, from visiting the IFAN **museum** to merely walking the avenues and exploring the backstreets, especially during the comfortable winter months. For a wonderful **bird's-eye view** of the city, go up to the seventeenth-floor swimming pool and roof terrace of the *Hôtel Indépendance* – just buy a soft drink to get access. From this height the old red-tiled quarters and the main avenues of dark green foliage stand out clearly.

The central markets

Down towards the port stand the circular remains of the **Marché Kermel** which burned down in 1993 – a fate which, oddly enough, has befallen several metropolitan West African markets. For the time being, trading continues in earnest outside the periphery of its boarded-up ruin. Offerings include stacks of basketry, faddish fashions, carvings and other **souvenirs**, plus a cornucopia of expensive produce for the old-style *colons* still living in the quarter. Beware of dastardly sales psychology – don't accept "gifts" or, if you do, insist on paying. Repeated visits improve the atmosphere as the pushers get used to your face, but it takes courage to leave without buying something – if you do, you may hear *"libanais"* hissed after you in contempt. You should experience less aggressive merchandising, and far less interesting merchandise, below Kermel, along the portside **boulevard de la Libération**, where a grubby street market has operated for some years. Don't come down here after dark though, as it's dodgy territory.

More workaday than the now emaciated Kermel is the **Marché Sandaga** at the end of av Georges Pompidou. This is Dakar's big *centreville* market, an unpretentious two-storey emporium with a tremendous variety of fruit, vegetables and dry foods, and lots of wonderful fish in the morning. You can buy just about anything here and in the surrounding streets, from avocados to bootleg cassettes and attaché cases made of beer cans. Hassles are fewer than at Kermel, but the enormous crush does encourage pickpockets, and you should take care around the fringes of the building, where there's still a certain amount of hustle. Sandaga has been almost completely taken over by Mouride traders.

The former Mauritanian silversmiths' yard, the *cour des orfèvres,* now renamed **Keur Jean Thiam** (after an early and renowned Senegalese artisan), has long been located at 69 av Blaise Diagne – 500m downhill from Sandaga. Mauritanian artisans are steadily returning to Dakar following the conflict of the early 1990s, and their superb **silver jewellery** and **wooden chests** (the latter are "authentic copies" no matter what story they spin you) are worth bargaining for. Senegalese carved **wooden masks** and figures as well as other ornaments, are also made and sold here – if you're serious about making a purchase, be prepared to discuss the matter over a couple of hours or, better still, a couple of visits.

Nearly next door, at no. 65, there's a **sand painters' yard** where various grades and tones of sand are artfully used to depict some rather tacky tropical images of the "pouting silhouette" genre.

Medina, Bène Tali and Castors

You can't miss the **Grande Mosquée**, over to the northwest of Sandaga (bus #2 or #4). Finished in 1964 and built after the style of the Mohamed V mosque in Casablanca, it's truly impressive, with seventy-metre minarets standing out above the low rooftops of the **Medina** quarter. Non-believers are strictly barred most of the time, so your only option is to peer in through the windows. One day they'll put in the lawn that's crying out to be sown around it. The **Marché de Tilène**, a short distance north, brings you down to earth with its football-pitch-sized food market serving a massive array of **produce**. This is the place to come to absorb ordinary Dakar life.

Going a good deal further north, there's a vast array of **cloth** at the best possible prices in the market in the old African quarter of **Bène Tali** (bus #3 from Sandaga, #13 from Place de l'Indépendance), and more textiles at the less traditional **HLM V** (pronounced "ash-el-em-cinq" meaning "Council Flats 5") market in the middle-class suburbs out between Grand Dakar and the autoroute (bus #3 or #13 again).

Lastly, if you go out further to the suburb of **Castors**, there's a humdrum general market (buses #3, #13, #18, #6) where you can wander in complete tranquillity. A place to buy food, spices, traditional remedies, cheap cassettes, second-hand clothes and so on, it's somewhat cheaper than the central markets and easier to bargain.

SHOPPING IN DAKAR

You can buy nearly anything at any time in Dakar from a haircut to bootleg cassettes. The following list gives some pointers.

Barbers Men can get their hair cut cheaply at the outdoor stalls on av Jean Jaurès (corner of av André Peytavin), though the barbers aren't too familiar with straight hair.

Books *Librairie aux Quatre Vents* (Tues–Sat 8.30am–12.30pm and 3–6.30pm) on rue Felix Faure, between rue Mohamed V and rue Blanchot, is probably the best bookshop in West Africa. They also sell a few books in English, a surprisingly rare commodity. Also try *Clairafrique*, 2 rue Sandiniéri, place de l'Indépendance, next to the Chamber of Commerce.

Cassettes Stacks of bootlegs at stalls around Sandaga market and from street sellers in the vicinity. Beware of buying from the pavement cruisers down av Georges Pompidou. Prices should be close to CFA1000 – if you buy for CFA500 the quality will be dreadful. For "legitimate" recordings expect to pay up to CFA2000. For browsing and listening in a more controlled and relaxing atmosphere, head out to a suburban market such as Castors.

Curios For the real thing, visit *El Hadj Traoré*, rue Mohamed V, between rue Carnot and rue Felix Faure – a fine musty collection. There are more further north on Mohamed V, on the left before av Pompidou. Avoid flashy "galleries"– unreasonably expensive and not special.

Supermarkets *Hypersam*, the city's biggest hypermarket (closed Mon), is out on route de Ouakam/bd de la Gueule Tapée. More convenient but pricier are *Au Ranche Filfili* on bd de la République/rue Mousse Diop; *Le Supermarché* just north of the Place de l'Indépendance, and *Score* just east, on av Albert Saurraut. Many supermarket exits have notice boards for buying or selling – cameras, cars, whatever.

Tailoring For a job done well and not too expensively, try Ndiaga Ndiaye at Marché Sandaga no. A119, av Emile Badiane (☎22 97 84). The best bargains are out at Marché HLM, where they will often run something up for you while you wait.

The IFAN Museum and the Plateau

In truth, Dakar's cultural showpiece, the **IFAN (Institut Fondamental d'Afrique Noir) Museum** (Tues–Sun 8am–12.30pm & 2–6.30pm; CFA200), does not make a great first impression. Although they have recently done some renovation on the collection, it's basically thousands of objects from all over West Africa, many of them visibly decaying, pinned to the walls or lying in glass cases with little in the way of background information. You can happily spend an hour here – longer if you're intrigued.

On the **ground floor** look out for the **white man mask**, obviously modelled on a moustachioed colonial officer with a wrinkly neck. **Circumcision instruments**, the giant thighbone of an unidentified but hopefully prehistoric animal, and a large assortment of **Senoufo** (Côte d'Ivoire) initiation and ancestor ethnographia compete for attention, along with games of pebbles-and-holes (called here *Dodoi* and *Aji*), hundreds of **ancestor figures** and some fine **cattle and hippo masks** from Guinea-Bissau. There's a fascinating account too, presented through a collection of printing blocks, of the development of a kind of African swastika, a stylized lizard or crocodile motif.

The **first floor** collections are slightly easier to distinguish, though there are **masks** everywhere. In the three central halls you'll see examples of **bark cloth** and the instruments used to beat it out, dyed and woven **strip cloth**, an entire case of spindles, whorls and looms, and the **costumes** of kings and lesser mortals. One especially striking outfit is the Guerzé mask-wearer's costume from southeastern Guinea, with its all-in-one gloves and feet: notice how worn and red-mudded the feet are. The Fula (*Peul*) **circumcision costume** also stands out: it's virtually identical to the white "Phrygian caps" worn by newly circumcised boys on the streets of Dakar, especially in July.

Dogon headdresses from Mali, now a commonplace image of West African art, are on show at the far right-hand end. Their remarkable geometric appearance, as if constructed from set squares, looks like the result of a stylistic evolution when compared with the more representational masks from Mali in the middle hall (first entry on the right as you come upstairs). The latter look much more like four-legged animals and the common "swastika" motif is clear.

Chairs and tableaux from the **Benin courts** (Nigeria) and illustrations of the arrival of the Europeans fill the central hall. Over in the big room on the right, notice the **sewn canoes**, and play the lovely **balafons** – they make a glorious sound.

Outside, you can see all the main state buildings of the **Plateau** – if you want to – in an hour or so, by wandering around the Parisian quarter centering on Place Tascher. On the *place* itself, across from the museum, is the **Assemblée Nationale**; along avenue Courbet stands the appalling **"Building Administratif"** a mega-block of ministries crowned with scores of vultures; and then on the right, down avenue Roume is the high-profile **Presidential Palace**, with its be-fezzed and unfazed presidential guards.

The beaches, corniches and Hann Park

There are plenty of opportunities for physical pursuits around Dakar. The best town **beaches** are Tahiti and Voile d'Or on the sheltered Pointe de Bel-Air, on the east side of the city; bus #6 passes the sign to *Tahiti plage*, from where it's a five-minute walk to the entrance gates. Unfortunately the whole of Bel-Air is a French military base, whose only saving grace is that they make the beaches as safe as you could wish (CFA500 entry fee, less with a student card). With the *militaires* on one side and chemical and groundnut plants fuming on the other, the scene could be prettier, but the sand and sea are clean enough, and palms and sunshades provide additional compensation. You can rent windsurfers, too, for around CFA5000 per hour. **Tahiti** is the nearer and smaller of the two beaches; the adjoining **Voile d'Or** is definitely the better, stretching out to rocks at the point, and has beach cabins for around CFA10,000 per day (S/C with electricity). Both beaches get crowded at weekends; come early and bring a bite to eat and water – the bars here are expensive. The *Tahiti Plage* club of old is now the *Monaco Plage* (reasonable entrance and drinks prices) – a faintly pretentious and restrained set-up, but with an unbeatable "chill-out area" under the palms.

Other possible beaches are south of the port along the corniches (see below) – the pretty *plage des enfants*; the deep cove at Anse Bernard (crowded with local kids at weekends); and the *plage de l'Institut Pasteur*, on the rougher Atlantic side of Cap Manuel. All of these are to some extent unsafe, but if you have no valuables on you there's little to worry about.

The corniches

Walking the corniches carries some risk, as both have reputations for bag snatching and various kinds of assault. Violent attacks are in fact rare, but you shouldn't go alone and under no circumstances carry valuables. Both the Corniche Est, from the end of bd de la Libération to Cap Manuel, and the Corniche Ouest, from the Ministry of Tourism right up to Mermoz, are fine walks, mostly on the clifftop, with some stunning views.

The **Corniche Est** (4km) runs through dense vegetation, past the back gardens of various embassies and diplomatic residences and the front gate of the German ambassador's bizarre house, a kind of Sudanic-Teutonic construction. It then climbs to **Cap Manuel** via Dakar's most picture-postcard viewpoints over the city and Gorée. You pass the self-consciously tropical *Hôtel Savanna* – a good place for a break and a drink – and from the forbidding yellow slab of the nearby **Palais du Justice** you can bus back into town. As you go, look out for the beautiful **Aristide le Dantec maternity hospital** – Sudanic architectural influences in two shades of baby pink.

The eight-kilometre-long **Corniche Ouest** has a far less intimate feel – windswept, wave-ripped and racing with traffic and joggers. There's free use of jogging trails and weight-training equipment, courtesy of the Commune de Dakar. City tours come out here for the **Village Artisanal** on Soumbedioune bay, but it's frankly not up to much, with high prices and loads of pressure. However, as long as you're not carrying anything of value it's fun to go down on the ant's-nest-busy **beach** to watch the world go by in **Lebu** style. From mid-afternoon it's full of returning Lebu fishermen and women selling a fascinatingly diverse catch. The Lebu are related to the Wolof, from whom they broke away at the end of the eighteenth century. Most belong to the Tijaniya brotherhood rather than the Mourides, but a few are Layen, a largely Lebu fraternity.

The **Musée Dynamique**, on the far side of the bay, is not especially dynamic but occasionally hosts art exhibitions. Beyond, you come to the suburb of **Fann**: more diplomatic and expat residences with guard dogs and iron gates, and armies of Dakarois youth working out on the skyline – the **University** is nearby, and physical fitness is a big thing these days. Any time you get tired of walking, bus #10 follows this whole route back to the centre.

Hann Park

One part of the city that doesn't yet appear to suffer the problems of the corniches – though you should be cautious nonetheless – is **Hann Park**, eighty hectares of woodland and swamp with a **zoo** and a network of paths. It's a pleasant place for a stroll, again full of joggers and keep-fit fanatics in the hour before dark, and a good complement to the beaches at Bel-Air (bus #6). It's quite attractive to ornithologists, too, who can find several different habitats here. The **Parc Zoologique** (Tues–Sun 10am–noon & 3–6.30pm), on the other hand, is not a happy place, a small collection of listless mammals (lions, gorillas, chimps, hippos, warthogs) and a large one of birds – not counting the vultures perching ominously on the trees outside. If you want to do it the Dakar way, go armed with sweets and groundnuts and feed everything; but it's probably best avoided.

Eating and drinking

Dakar has a blaze of **restaurants**, and some that are even affordable. Don't be misled by the charmless parlours along av Georges Pompidou, though – you need to explore the safer side streets to find good food at sensible prices. Dozens of **chawarma joints** are scattered across the city, and in the suburbs you'll find roadside **stalls** selling fruit, bread, cakes, groundnuts and boiled eggs. Some stalls are more elaborate **snack bars** – one such is the *Diamelaye* near the Monument de l'Indépendance, opposite the Mauritanian embassy.

If you're really short of cash, you could *survive* on streetside snacks and fruit for under CFA1000 a day. At the top of Sandaga market you'll find a very basic food hall selling the kind of nourishing breakfast foods sold around the suburbs of Dakar, like sour milk *thiacry* (*chagry*), with millet grains and sugar, or millet porridge *fondé*, all at about CFA50–100 a bowl. The cheapest sit-down meals are found in the distinctly functional **hole-in-the-wall cafés**, or *gargotes*, sometimes unsigned, but distinguishable behind the multi-coloured ribbons over the doorways. These offer a daily Senegalese staple or an omelette, served with bread and water, for less than CFA500. For about the same price you can get a *chawarma* or other Lebanese snacks from any of the take-away bars found along av Pompidou. Pay twice that and you'll get a tablecloth, less austere suroundings, service with a smile and a genuine choice; in the exotic or better African restaurants a meal costs from around CFA2000.

UNDER CFA1500

Restaurant Affé, rue Dagorne, Kermel end. Plain Senegalese restaurant with hole-in-the-wall prices; *poisson riz* or *mafé*, for example at rock-bottom rates. Mon–Sat 7am–9pm.

Chez Amy Diongue, rue Victor Hugo, near the corner with rue Blanchot. Excellent value Senegalese food – *tiéboudienne* and one other rice dish – in a spotless, pink and blue room. CFA500.

Chez Indy, 63 rue Felix Faure. Small and friendly "tablecloth" café down an alley, offering Euro-Senegalese dishes with a smile. Daily 7am–6pm.

Chez Maty, rue Mohamed V, just south of av G Pompidou. One of the many Senegalese restaurants in this area where you can fill your stomach for less than CFA1000. Daily 8am–midnight.

Gargote Diarama, 56 rue Felix Faure. Cheap, popular and with a moderately smart interior offering full meals. Daily 7am–6pm.

Dong Jing, 58 rue Felix Faure. Dakar's cheapest Chinese place.

Restaurant le ? ("Restaurant l'Intérogatif"), rue El Hadj AA Ndoye. Two excellent venues with the same name and owner, both on the same street. Long menus of Senegalese, and more expensive European, food at outstanding value. Usually open.

Keur Thiaba, rue Jules Ferry, east of Mohamed V. Standard hole in the wall, just off the *place*, with Senegalese specialities for around CFA1000.

Club de Presse, Place Soweto. Daily dishes in the dining room, around CFA700, and cheap beer in a bar frequented by Senegalese journalists.

Touba Restaurant, corner of rue de Denain and rue El Hadj AA Ndoye. Busy, clean lunchtime eatery with generous helpings of Senegalese staples. Highly recommended mafé. CFA500.

Tricotin Fast Food, rue Thann. Not exactly *McDonalds* but a selection of sandwiches and snacks such as *crevettes pekinoise*, as well as *Flags* beer. Mon–Sat 9am–10pm.

CFA1500–4000

Angkor, rue Dagorne, opposite *La Dagorne*. Pleasant Chinese restaurant just north of the Marché Kermel, specializing in Szechuan dishes. Daily noon–2pm & 6–11pm.

Chez Loutcha, 100 rue Mousse-Diop (☎21 03 02). An exceptional Cape Verdean restaurant. Typically enormous meals; wonderful tuna salad and insurmountable three-course *menu*. Good breakfasts too. Closed Sun.

Farid, *Hôtel Farid*, 51 rue Vincens. Dakar's best Lebanese restaurant with dishes from CFA3000 and daily non-Lebanese specials for a little less. Daily noon–10pm.

La Fourchette, rue Parent. Italian *trattoria* close to the *Hôtel du Marché* with all your favourite pastas as well as veal and fish dishes.

Hanoi, corner of rues Carnot and Joseph Gomis. Vietnamese food at good prices. Daily noon–late.

L'Impériale (aka "Robert's Bar"), north end of Place de l'Indépendance, corner of Allée R Delmas. Pleasant restaurant/bar retreat, away from *place* hustlers, serving meat or fish dishes and a good value *menu*. Expensive fresh fruit juices.

Le Kermel, opposite Marché Kermel. French and continental food and a very French atmosphere on Sun mornings.

Keur Ndeye, corner of rue Sandinieri/rue de Vincens (☎21 49 73). Upmarket Senegalese with kora minstrels; meals (including vegetarian and a wine list) are nicely served but contents much the same as in a *gargote*, for twice the price.

L'Oasis, 8 rue Ramez Bourgi. Inexpensive restaurant-bar right by the Kermel Marché, offering *plats* such as boudin and chips, as well as three-course meals and *Flag*. Mon–Sat 9am–10.30pm.

Chez Nanette, rue du Dr Thèze, near rue El Hadj AA Ndoye. Portuguese-run bar with a restaurant upstairs featuring a shaded terrace at the back and a garrulous mynah bird.

Pergola, 15 rue Dantec. Cosy and intimate Belgian-owned restaurant behind the *Croix du Sud* hotel and including some fine seafood dishes. Daily 9.30am–midnight.

La Pizzeria, 47 rue de Thiong (☎21 09 26). Franco-Italian take-out concoctions over a pizza base available round the clock – try the better-looking *La Pizzalina* just opposite to eat in. Both offer pizzas and meat dishes.

La Plaza, 14 rue Raffenel, just north of Pompidou. Pizza-to-go.

Sam-son, 61 rue El Hadj AA Ndoye. Vietnamese restaurant with good-value menus.

La Travestere, 26 rue Mohamed V, corner of rue Carnot. Italian dishes and a bar serving *Flag*.

OVER CFA4000

La Dagorne, 11 rue Dagorne. Ever-popular mid-range French restaurant that has been drawing them in for years with a great *menu*. Tues–Sun 7am–7.30.

Lagon I, in the hotel of the same name, rte de la Corniche Est. Great location, set on a small pier looking out to sea and popular with the French expat crowd. Seafood dishes pricey, but the *menu* is always good value. Daily noon–late.

Macombo, Corniche Ouest, behind the *Novotel*. Beautiful views – on the best tables you're sitting over the waves. French cuisine.

Mayoti, Point E. Nice Zairean restaurant, with dancing. Very evocative for Congophiles.

Le New Bilboquet, 19 av Roume. Plush, air-conditioned French restaurant with impressive style. Grills are great value, full meals a bit pricier. Drinks – the beers are large – come with hors d'oeuvres. Mon–Sat 11am–midnight.

Le Sarraut, av Albert Sarraut. Classy French restaurant a couple of minutes' walk east of the Place de l'Indépendance and popular with the expat community. An al fresco terrace cordoned by a thick herbaceous wall makes for a relaxing meal with *plats* and a *menu*. Daily 7am–11pm.

Nightlife

Despite the city's impeccably cosmopolitan credentials, Dakar's **nightlife** is less exotic than one might expect. If you want a fairly unpredictable night out, most of the bars and clubs we have listed will do the business. Most places play a cosmopolitan mix of high and low energy Senegalese, Central African, Cuban and Western music (from Whitney Houston to Shabba Ranks). For real action at a price, try one of the **big discos** or **music clubs**, which warm up around midnight (the "soirée"), but may also have an earlier session, from 7 to 11pm (the "matinée") that can be just as hot. If you're going to check out several places and move by taxi, anticipate spending at least CFA30,000 between two, and that's without many drinks – which may be as much as CFA2–3000 after your first drink, included in the cover of CFA2–5000. Going in a group works out cheaper and is more fun. Take IDs but leave all valuables behind.

For **theatre,** *Théatre Daniel Sorano* on bd de la République is the place, though shows – which sometimes feature big name music stars – are not held nightly.

Bars

Claudel, corner of rue de Thiong/rue Wagane Diouf. Pleasant bar.

Le Colisée, av Lamine Guèye. Quiet, French family-style bar. Fairly expensive, but a regular setting-off point.

La Dakaroise, rue Ramez Bourgi, near the PTT and Marché Kermel. Always thronging with sailors and prostitutes, this does good French and continental food, with African nights at weekends.

Le Hadong, behind the cinema in Gueule Tapée, corner of rue 6 and bd de la Gueule Tapée. For a cheap drink in a relaxed African bar, try the courtyard here.

Jazz Bar Tamango, bd de l'Est, Pointe E. Could be in Paris. Clean in all senses, with occasional live jazz but otherwise discreet background piping and civilized ambience. Rarely any cover, beers not expensive. May be closed for refurbishment.

La Petite Côte Bar, Ouageniaye, near Bène Tali market. Wonderful local bar.

Keur Samba, 13 rue Felix Faure. Small, *centreville* jazz club, with comfy chairs and live music.

Le Soninké, at the *Hôtel Miramar*, 25–27 rue Felix Faure. Colourful, cosy, happy-hour type of bar.

Waw Waw Waw, rte de Ouakam, near the University. Chic bar-resto and tapas joint owned by Youssou N'dour.

Clubs and discos

Africa Star, 42 rue Docteur Thèze. Good *dancing*. Expensive.

Broadway, at the *Méridien Présidentiel* hotel, Almadies. Managed by Youssou N'dour, this is one of Dakar's hottest clubs. Don't go Mon, Tues. Expensive.

Metropolis, corner of bd de la République and rue Joseph Gomis (☎22 82 40). Dakar's biggest dance floor, this was the place of the moment as this book went to press. Cape Verdean music on Sun; Senegalese drums and dancing on Fri.

Ngalam, bd de l'Est, Pointe E (☎23 02 27). Covers CFA2500 Mon–Thurs, CFA3000 weekends; drinks the same price.

Les Rubois, rue Nani, Fann-Hock (☎21 51 53). Continuing past Soumbedioune, there's a park on the left and the smallish *Les Rubois* is opposite, behind the *Boulangerie Moderne Fann-Hock*. Busiest on Mon & Thurs (women free), with a lively student crowd. Drink in the *Bar Americain* before the club gets going.

Le Sahel, Route de Ouakam/bd de la Gueule Tapée (☎21 21 18). Taxi drivers know it as "Sam", because it's next to the *Hypersam* supermarket. A flashy place, used for fashion shows and pop video recordings.

La Siege de Gorée, corner of allées R. Delmas and bd de la Libération, behind the Dakar Hôtel de Ville. A massive open-air dance floor with mixed Western/African music. Free entrance, cheap beer, packed with people. Go early – by 10pm – as the place quietens down at 1am and closes at 2am.

Timi's, Ngor, just behind the *Hôtel Méridien* (☎23 10 05). Caters more for a tourist crowd, with more Western, less African music. If you're in the vicinity, well worth calling in on, otherwise the town clubs are better.

Live music venues

These are the places to hit at weekends – or even around which to plan a stay in Dakar.

Kilimandjaro, Corniche Ouest, Soumbedioune (☎21 62 55). Formerly the best-looking nightclub in Dakar, with a hot sound system and chic clientele. Much diminished in stature of late.

Liberté Bar, av Bourguiba. Adjoining the right side of the *Liberté Theatre*, the regular Fri night venue for the re-formed *Orchestre Baobab*. Balla Sidibé, the host, mixes a mellow and friendly atmosphere to match a less pretentious crowd than most of the competition, reflected in relatively low prices.

L T Horoscope, av Bourguiba. A cracking place, though at first inspection not very promising. Four "venues" consist of a fast food outlet at street level, an upstairs bar-restaurant with "traditional" *balafon* serenades, a sleazy *American Bar* video lounge, and a tiny but red-hot night club with a formidable twelve-piece house band who play every night from midnight till 4am. An unusual, tiered stage crams the artists in the corner.

Relais, Route de Ouakam, near the university. A student venue with cheap drinks and an open-air dance area. Small outside stage (check press for gigs) and good sound system encourage a lively young crowd paying more attention to moves than clothes. Not to miss if there's a band playing.

Stade Demba Diop, Liberté. If there's a concert at Dakar's big venue, the posters all over town will be pretty obvious. Get there on time, but be prepared for it to start two hours late and for gangs of robbers inside and out (take no valuables and get a taxi when you leave). But go!

Thiossane, rue E H D Coulibaly, ex Dial Diop (☎24 35 10). Recently bought and refurbished by Youssou N'dour, who usually plays Wed, Fri and Sat. If he's touring, or busy, Kine Lam or the superb group *Lemzo Diamono* take over.

Le Warref, route de Rufisque, Dagoudane-Pikine. A long taxi ride – this place is miles away – but a cheap club at last when you get there. Live music and perspiration – try it.

Listings

American Express Agents include *Senegal Tours*, place de l'Indépendance (☎23 40 40), who can arrange a cash advance of up to $1000 on an *Amex* card, and *SOCOPAO Voyages*, 51 rue Albert Sarraut (☎22 22 79/22 24 16).

Banks Most head offices are on Place de l'Indépendance west: *CBAO*, bad rates; *BICIS*, efficient, but poor rates; *CBAO*, no commission on FF travellers' cheques, but slow; *Citibank*, good rates. *SGBS*, on av Roume, is a *Thomas Cook* agent. There's also a bit of currency black market around rue Raffenal and rue Sandiniéri (10 percent mark-up).

Car Rental Main agents are: *Avis*, 71 rue Mousse Diop (☎23 33 00); *Europcar*, bd Libération (☎21 38 49); *Hertz*, 64 rue Felix Faure (☎/Fax 21 17 21). Best value for money is at *AutoTeranga Location*

AIRLINE OFFICES IN DAKAR

Flight information Yof Airport	☎22 40 60
Aeroflot, 2 bd de la République, next to *Nouvelles Frontières*	☎22 48 15
Air Afrique, place de l'Indépendance	☎23 80 22 or 39 42 10
Air Algérie, 2 place de l'Indépendance	☎23 80 81
Air France, 47 av Albert Sarraut	☎22 49 49 or 23 29 41
Air Gabon, 5 av Georges Pompidou	☎22 24 05
Air Sénégal, 45 av Albert Sarraut	☎23 62 29
Air Zaire, 2 place de l'Indépendance	☎21 12 79
Alitalia, 5 av Georges Pompidou	☎23 31 29
American Airlines, office in av André Peytavin	
Ethiopian Airlines, 16 av Roume	☎21 32 98
Gambia Airways, place de l'Indépendance	☎22 19 47
Ghana Airways, rue Ramez Bourgi	☎22 28 20
Iberia, 2 place de l'Indépendance	☎23 34 77
Nigeria Airways, 27 av Roume	☎23 60 68
Royal Air Maroc, 1 place de l'Indépendance	☎22 32 67
Sabena, 2 place de l'Indépendance	☎23 27 73
Saudia, 12 av Georges Pompidou	☎23 52 00
Swissair, 3 place de l'Indépendance	☎23 48 48
TACV (Cape Verde), 105 rue Mousse Diop	☎22 82 85
TAP Air Portugal, 3 rue El Hadj AA Ndoye	☎21 01 13

Voitures, 47 rue Felix Faure (☎22 59 99; Fax 22 16 24): a Peugeot 205 costs CFA93,000 a week (unlimited mileage); Suzuki 4WD CFA136,000 a week; all credit cards accepted.

Cinemas The *Paris* on Place de l'Indépendance, and the *Vog* and *Plaza* on av Georges Pompidou show familiar American or European movies either *v.o.* (*version originale* with subtitles if not in French) or *v.f.* (*version française* with French soundtrack). Smaller and/or suburban cinemas show mostly martial arts films.

Cultural Centres The **American cultural centre**, av Roume, is an air-conditioned retreat for looking at the *Herald Tribune* and a selection of mags; good library; CNN news at 5pm Mon, Wed, Fri (Mon–Fri 8am–noon & 2.30–6pm; ☎23 11 85). The **British Council** is at Immeuble Sonatel, 34/376 bd de la République (☎22 20 15; Fax 11 81 36). The **British-Senegalese Institute**, 18 rue de 18 Juin (off av Courbet), caters to the small British community; library and free film shows (Mon–Fri 9am–noon & 3.30–6.30pm; Sat 10am–noon; closed Mon am; ☎22 28 70). The **Centre culturel Blaise Senghor**, rue 10, Place de l'ONU, Cerf Volante (buses #2 & #9), named after the film director and UNESCO ambassador, hosts arty events and shows movies; closed in the summer vacation. **French cultural centre**, 36 rue El Hadj AA Ndoye (☎21 64 27); **Goethe Institute** (and German Cultural Centre – ☎22 34 82), 2 av Albert Sarraut (☎22 50 04).

Doctors If you need an emergency consultation try one of the following practitioners: Dr Chignara (gynaecologist), 5 rue Parchappe (☎22 15 66); Dr Benoît Marie Louise Correa, 25 av Georges Pompidou (☎22 00 59); Dr F Coulibaly (Mme), 69 rue Mousse Diop (☎22 19 78); Dr M Kaouk, 144 rue Joseph Gomis (☎23 46 79).

Language courses Private and group courses in French and Wolof (100hr; CFA70,000) at the *Alliance Franco-Senegalaise*, 2 rue El Hadj AA Ndoye (☎21 08 22).

Maps For large maps of Dakar and Senegal, *Directeur des Traveaux Géographique et Cartographique*, Hann BP 740 (☎32 11 81). Up the autoroute to the Hann exit and 1km on the right.

Newspapers If you can't read French you'll have to make do with the *Herald Tribune*, *Time* or *Newsweek* from newsstands along av Georges Pompidou and the Place de l'Indépendance end of Albert Sarraut. *West Africa* magazine is usually in by Friday. Also try the British-Senegalese Institute (see "Cultural centres").

EMBASSIES IN DAKAR

Algeria, 5 rue Mermoz (BP 3233) ☎22 35 09; Fax 21 16 84

Belgium, route de la Corniche Est (BP 524) ☎22 47 20; Fax 21 63 45

Cameroon, 157–159 rue Joseph Gomis (BP 4165) ☎22 34 14; Fax 24 33 96

Canada, 45 bd de la République (BP 3373) ☎23 92 90; Fax 23 87 49

Cape Verde, Imm. Fahd, near the port, in the same building as SudFM – look for the flag (BP 2319) ☎21 18 73 or 21 29 91
You should be able to get a visa (CFA5000) in a matter of hours, with three passport photos. Be sure to check when you're supposed to come back, as the office (in theoryMon–Fri 8am–noon & 3–5pm)keeps slightly irregular hours.

Côte d'Ivoire, 2 av Albert Sarraut (BP 359) ☎21 01 63
Allow 48hr to clear visa for up to 3 months' stay; CFA3500 single entry, CFA5000 multiple entry. Mon–Fri 8am–1pm & 4–6pm.

Egypt, 45 bd de la République (BP 474) ☎21 24 75; Fax 21 89 93

Ethiopia, 26 bd El Hadj D Mbaye (BP 379) ☎21 75 73

France, 1 rue El Hadj AA Ndoye (BP 4035) ☎23 43 71; Fax 22 18 05

Gabon, Km5 av Cheikh Anta Diop ☎24 15 29

The Gambia, 11 rue de Thiong (BP 3248) ☎21 72 30
Immediate processing of visas; ask for multiple entry. They are valid for up to 6 months' stay and cost CFA10,000. Mon–Thurs 8am–3pm, Fri & Sat 8am–1pm.

Guinea, rue 7, Point E ☎24 86 06
Getting a visa is no longer a problem, though you need a letter of introduction from your own diplomatic representative in Dakar. Cost: CFA20,000. Mon–Fri 9am–3pm.

Guinea-Bissau, rue 6, Pointe E (BP 2319) ☎21 59 22; Fax 25 29 46
24hr to process; CFA5000 single entry (cheaper and less fuss in Banjul, or Ziguinchor). Mon–Fri 8am–noon & 4–6pm (visas mornings only).

Italy, rue El Hadj Seydou Nourou Tall (BP 348) ☎22 05 78; Fax 21 75 80

Liberia, 20 bd de la République ☎22 53 72

Mali, 46 bd de la République (BP 478) ☎22 04 73
48hr wait for visas; 20 days' stay, valid three months; CFA5000. Mon–Thurs 8am–2pm, Fri–Sat 8am–noon.

Mauritania, 37 bd Général De Gaulle ☎21 43 43
Introductory letter required from your own embassy for a visa; 24–48hr to process; prices vary with status and length of projected visit, and should be negotiated. Mon–Thurs 8.30am–12.30pm & 3.30–6.30pm, Sat 8.30am–12.30pm.

Morocco, Av Cheikh Anta Diop ☎24 38 36

Netherlands, 37 rue Kléber (BP 3262) ☎23 94 83; Fax 21 70 84

Nigeria, rue 1, Pointe E (BP 3129) ☎24 43 97
"Issue of visas all depends on circumstances"; 3 days to process; prices vary according to nationality; one month stay. Mon–Fri 8am–2.30pm.

Portugal, 5 av Carde (BP 281) ☎21 58 22; Fax 23 50 96

Sierra Leone, consul at the *Clinique Croix Bleu*, rue 13 Castors ☎24 50 32
24hr to process visas; CFA3000. Mon–Fri 8.30am–noon.

Spain, 45 bd de la République (BP 2091) ☎21 81 78; Fax 21 68 45

Switzerland, rue René Ndiaye (BP 1772) ☎22 58 48

Tunisia, rue El Hadj Seydou Nourou Tall (BP 3127) ☎23 47 47; Fax 23 72 04

United Kingdom, 20 rue du Dr Gillet (BP 6025) ☎23 73 92; Fax 23 27 26
Letter of recommendation for certain visas costs CFA5000. Closed Fri afternoon.

USA, av Jean XXIII (BP 49) ☎23 42 96

Zaire, Fann Residence (BP 2251) ☎25 19 79

Zimbabwe, km6, Route de Ouakam (BP 2762) ☎25 21 35

Passport Photos Booths in various locations but cheapest on the corner of av André Peytavin and av Blaise Diagne.

Pharmacies *Pharmacie Nelson Mandela*, corner of rue Gomia and av Nelson Mandela (☎21 21 72); each day's 24-hour pharmacy is given on the information page of *Le Soleil*.

Photo processing Try *Fina Photo*, corner of av Ponty and rue Raffenal.

Police Commissariat Central, rue de Docteur Thèze/rue Sandinièri (☎22 23 33).

Post Main PTT, corner of bd El Hadj Djily Mbaye. Open Mon–Sat 7am–7pm. For poste restante you must present your passport or other ID. Large parcels can be sent from *Colis Postaux* office at Place d'Oran, at the junction of av El Hadj Malick Sy and av Blaise Diagne.

Swimming pools Roof terrace at *Hôtel Indépendance*; fee-paying, Olympic-sized and thoroughly tropical at the *Savana*, Cap Manuel; chic but slightly cheaper at the *Afritel*, av Faidherbe/rue Raffenel.

Telephones International calls are cheapest from phone boxes, but amassing the necessary pile of coins is a hassle. You're probably best off at the numerous *télécentres* located all over town. Don't use the one at Place de l'Indépendance, however (you have to pay a vastly inflated tariff). Private *télécentres* are mostly reasonably priced. You can also call internationally at the PTT 7.30am–10pm daily.

Wrestling *La lutte* can be seen all over the city, with regular Sun evening shows at the *Stade Demba Diop* attracting the big stars. Wandering around Medina and Grand Dakar at weekends you can find amateur – and kids' – bouts. Around the Monument de l'Indépendance seems a popular venue. Wrestling is also televised on *RTS* every Saturday afternoon.

MOVING ON FROM DAKAR

Moving on from Dakar, the obvious choices are bus or taxi, for which you need the main *gare routière*, or train, with the latest details available at the station. If you're going to Banjul by public transport don't take one of the big 30-seater buses – they take 12 hours. Train tickets from Dakar to Bamako go on sale at 3pm the day before departure – though first-class reservations can be made from 8am 2 days before. Second-class is always crowded. For full details see p.299.

For a summary of **flight connections**, check the practical information at the beginning of this chapter. If you're flying from Dakar to Europe, check out *Aeroflot* (cheap tickets; with a few nights at their expense in Moscow, but expect a few days' wait for the visa). For African destinations, *Air Afrique* offer good discounts. The main airlines are listed above; others include *Air Guinea* (☎21 44 22); *Air Mauritanie* (☎22 81 88); and *Tunis Air*, 24 av Roume (☎23 14 35). NB: *American Airlines* have an office in Dakar, on av André Peytavin, which is useful for smooth US connections. Note, however, they don't operate flights.

Boats to Casamance are operated by *COSENAM*, 1 rue Galandou Diouf (☎22 54 43; Fax 21 08 95) or ask at the office down at Gorée wharf. The *MV Joola* leaves Dakar on Tuesday and Friday at 8pm, arriving at Ziguinchor the next day between 11am and 2pm, depending on the tides. Hard seats cost CFA4000; comfortable seats cost CFA7500; four-berth cabins CFA15,000 per person; twin share cabins CFA18,000; and a cabin to yourself CFA22,000. Cars cost CFA11,000. Reserve well ahead: Dakar to Ziguinchor road connections have been disrupted by the imposition of huge price increases on the Farafenni ferry crossing over the Gambia River, making the *MV Joola* a very attractive alternative.

For **boats to Europe**, *Smith et Kraft* at *Somicoa*, 17 rue Huart (BP 55; ☎23 39 83; Fax 21 49 11), are port agents for the *Grimaldi Line*, which runs regular passenger-carrying cargo ships to Europe.

For **general bookings and tours** in Senegal itself, try the good *Senegal Tours*, place de l'Indépendance (☎21 40 40 and 23 31 81); or *SOCOPAO Voyages*, 47 rue Albert Sarraut (☎23 10 01; Fax 23 56 14); or *Sénégambie Voyages*, 42 rue Victor Hugo (☎21 68 31), who can organize piroguing in the Saloum delta. Also try the established *Nouvelles Frontières*, 1 bd de la République (☎23 34 34).

Ile de Gorée

Just twenty minutes by *chaloupe* from Dakar lies the tiny **Ile de Gorée**, a mere 800m end to end and 300m across at its widest point. Its **slave-trading** history makes it more or less a required visit, and UNESCO has declared the island one of its World Heritage Sites, but it's a compelling retreat in any case, and many people come back repeatedly. The island bristles with old buildings. Apart from the famous **House of Slaves**, there's the excellent **IFAN Historical Museum of the Diaspora** in the horseshoe-shaped Fort d'Estrées, and the less impressive **Maritime Museum**, the old **church** of St Charles Barromée, and, at the southern end, the **castle** topping a warren of bunkers and underground passages from where there are colourful views over the island and across to Dakar.

Some history

The first Europeans on Gorée were the **Portuguese**, who used the island as a trading base in the mid-fifteenth century. **Dutch** adventurers captured it in 1588 – naming it *Goede reede* (good roadstead) – but the Portuguese regained control, before again losing the island, this time to the **French**, in 1678. This date marked the beginning of the golden age of the **signares.** Daughters of white colonists and slave women, the *signares* of Gorée wielded extraordinary power in a largely matriarchal, slave-worked society.

Gorée was fought over by the French and the **English**, who repeatedly captured and recaptured Gorée from each other – the score for the eighteenth century being France 5, England 4. The island prospered despite the changes of ownership: by the 1850s there was a population of 6000 – ten times the present figure. The first fortifications of Dakar in 1857 signalled the start of Gorée's slow, graceful demise.

Around the island

For a day trip from Dakar, it's best to take an early *chaloupe* to beat the crowds, and you should try to avoid weekends, especially in the high season; Mondays are quiet, but the museums are closed. Early in the morning – when the pastel colours of the old buildings and the bougainvillea draped through the narrow alleys make it particularly beautiful – you may be the only visitor. Perhaps inevitably, pushy "guides" have found their way onto the island – their services are barely necessary but if you stay over, they'll probably leave you alone.

The **Maison des Esclaves**, or **House of Slaves** (Tues–Sat 10.30am–noon & 2.30–6pm; donation requested) is the sole survivor of a number of buildings once used to store "pieces of ebony" before they were shipped to the New World. A visit could be anticlimactic, though – especially if you've ever seen film of weeping black Americans visiting it. Until recently, the walls were smothered with the impressions of various showbiz and political luminaries (not to mention the director) felt-penned onto pieces of paper. Fortunately, the festoon of posters has been removed, allowing the walls, dark chambers and slit windows to speak for themselves once again. This is a mournful and numbing reminder of the first major phase in the European exploitation of Africa. Scarcely believable though it seems, the white traders lived in some style above the warehouse, where there are well-proportioned rooms, a balcony and a reconstructed eighteenth-century Dutch kitchen.

The cleverly designed **IFAN Historical Museum of the Diaspora** (Tues–Sat 10am–1pm & 2.30–5pm; CFA200) takes you on an instructive tour through Senegal's history to the present day, while the **Marine Museum** (same hours and price) makes a more singular contribution, being in large part devoted to the life cycle of the dogfish

– note the human foot in a preserved fish stomach. Gorée's oldest building is the seventeenth-century police station, believed to be built on the site of a Portuguese church dating from 1482.

In the town, dozens of flaking **houses** are virtually concealed from the street behind high walls and wrought iron: the president and the Aga Khan both have villas here. There's a cluster of fine and more easily viewed Gorée houses at the northern end. The sheltered harbour **beach**, backed by a row of low-key **restaurants** and bars, is a draw in itself, but the real pleasure of the island is just wandering the sandy, quiet lanes and soaking the place up.

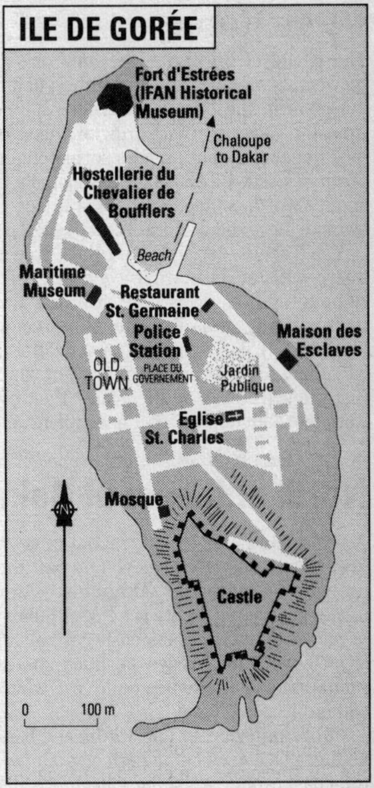

Practicalities

The *chaloupe* makes up to a dozen journeys daily from Dakar's Embarcadère de Gorée, off bd de la Libération; with very few exceptions, the return departure time from Gorée is thirty minutes later than departure from Dakar. The boat runs from 6.35am to 12.30am with a quiet period between noon and 2pm; a return ticket (valid overnight) costs CFA2000. If you're bold enough (or if it applies), ask for a "billet resident", the half-price ticket for Senegalese and expats.

Commercial **accommodation** on Gorée seems to be limited to the often heavily booked *Hostellerie du Chevalier de Boufflers* (☎22 53 64; ④), which has rooms with fan and breakfast, and a good seafood menu. An alternative is to ask around town or at the many **restaurants** facing the jetty about the possibility of **private rooms** (①). These restaurants are all pleasant, al fresco affairs with meals around CFA2000. *Restaurant St Germaine* offers a particularly warm welcome, a menu from CFA2000 and a couple of twin rooms (②).

Iles des Madeleines

Thirty minutes by motor *pirogue* from Soumbedioune Bay, the trip to the uninhabited **Iles des Madeleines** is highly recommended for naturalists. Now designated a National Park, the Madeleines are the habitat of a number of interesting **plants** – including a dwarf baobab and American wild coffee – and many species of indigenous and migratory **birds**: the tropic bird (*Phaëton aethereus*), recognized by its bright red bill and immensely long pointed tail, is found only here. There's little in the way of coral to be found in the surrounding seas, but the clear waters harbour a rich variety of **fish**.

Sarpan

The island of **Sarpan** – the only one at which a boat can anchor – is best visited between September and November, before the seas become too rough and the anchoring point in the cove inaccessible. It's necessary to obtain a park permit (CFA1000) from the office on the Corniche Ouest past the Musée Dynamique. **Pirogue rental**, best done in a group, can be sorted out on Soumbedioune beach. You should get them down to below CFA20,000. Occasionally the British-Senegalese Institute arranges a trip and it's worth contacting them first (see Dakar "Listings"). Take food and drink as well as binoculars and a snorkel and mask if possible.

You'll almost certainly have the Gorée-sized island to yourselves. It slopes from thirty-metre cliffs at its northern end to a gentler southern shore where the boats moor. Although no one lives here, it hasn't always been completely deserted, as occasional finds of **stone tools** indicate. More recently however it's acquired a malevolent reputation, and "L'ilot Sarpan" (named after a French soldier banished here) was soon corrupted to "L'île aux Serpents", of which it has none. The Lebu traditionally believe that sea spirits live on the island: their own efforts to settle on it several centuries ago were met with odd weather and violent seismic effects and they chose Gorée instead.

North and east of Dakar

An easy and much-hyped trip out of town is the ride to the beaches of **Ngor** and **Yof**. From Dakar, bus #7 takes you up past the two rounded hills of **Les Mamelles** and the turn-off to **Pointe des Almadies** – Africa's Land's End – which manages not to be totally smothered by its *Club Med* holiday camp. The new *Hôtel Méridien Présidentiel* here is about twice as expensive as any other hotel in the country (☎20 21 22; Fax 20 18 62; ⑦), with impressive facilities and standards if you can afford the CFA150,000 rooms. Bus #7 then goes on to Yof, while bus #8 heads direct to Yof up the autoroute, without passing Ngor.

Public transport to **Lac Retba** and **Keur Moussa** can be unpredictable, and in truth neither place need come high on your list. At the bottom of the list is **Kayar**, further up the coast – once a fishing village, it's now a tourist-trap of the most oppressive kind, where groups are brought to see the fishermen coming in. You can see the same thing, less intrusively, all along the West African coast.

Ngor

NGOR has blown away any charm it may once have had with the hideous *Méridien Hotel* (temporarily closed) and a rash of beach clubs, restaurants and sporting facilities between here and Yof airport. The hassles are obvious and tedious. Unless the *Méridien*'s refurbishing is complete and you choose to hide in its secure zone, the only escape is to take a *pirogue* (now with mandatory lifejackets) out to the **Ile du Ngor**, which is probably the best reason to come here.

The **island** is mostly divided into small plots for private beach houses, pretty enough retreats between the casuarina trees, but hardly idyllic. An old military assault course adds nothing to the cliff tops on the island's northern side. There's a couple of small beaches on the landward shore, but not much space when the tide comes in. There's not much **accommodation**, but the Italian restaurant rents out a couple of rooms and off-season you might get a bungalow (③).

Yof

The village of **YOF** – a maze of houses, boats on the beach, children everywhere – has a sense of community that Ngor has lost. The beach is the start of a continuous strand

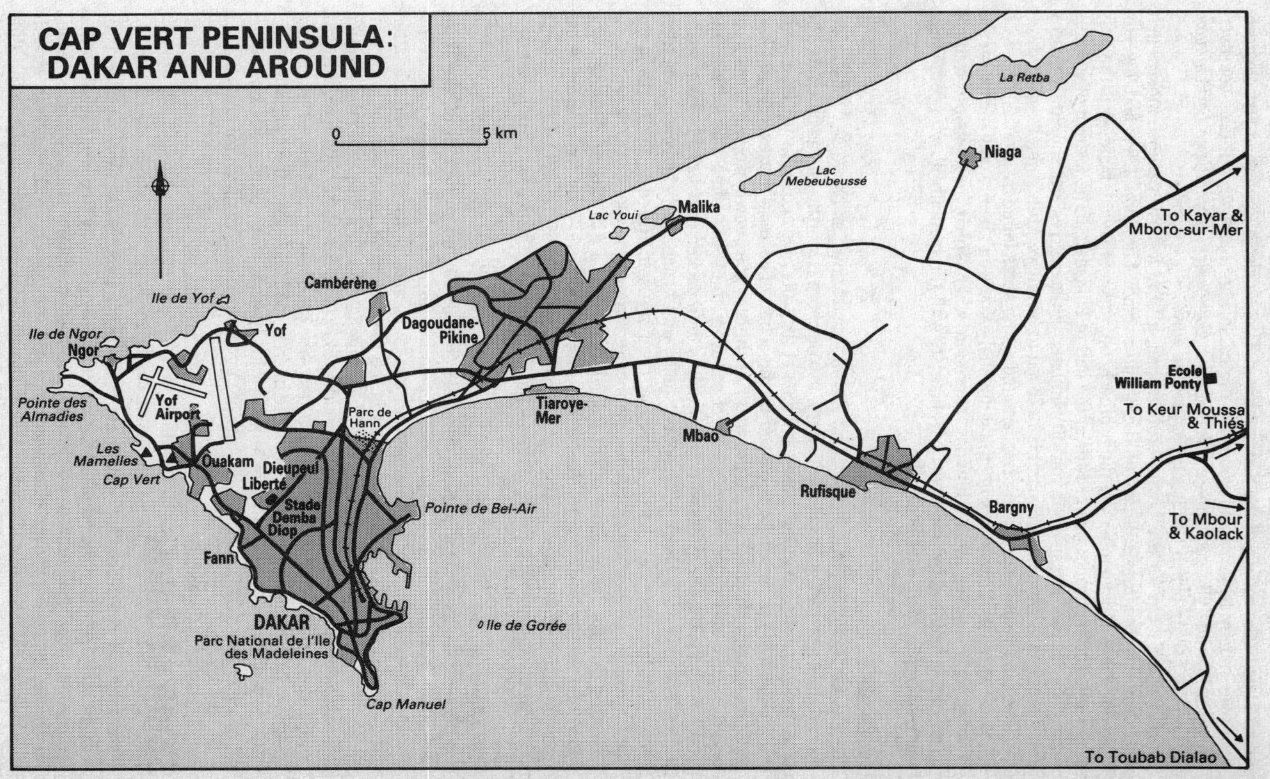
CAP VERT PENINSULA: DAKAR AND AROUND
0
5 km
La Retba
Niaga
Lac Mebeubeussé
Lac Youi
Malika
To Kayar & Mboro-sur-Mer
Cambérène
Ile de Yof
Yof
Dagoudane-Pikine
Ile de Ngor
Ngor
Ecole William Ponty
Pointe des Almadies
Yof Airport
Parc de Hann
Tiaroye-Mer
To Keur Moussa & Thiés
Mbao
Les Mamelles
Cap Vert
Ouakam
Dieupeul
Liberté
Stade Demba Diop
Rufisque
Pointe de Bel-Air
Bargny
To Mbour & Kaolack
Fann
DAKAR
Parc National de l'Ile des Madeleines
Ile de Gorée
Cap Manuel
To Toubab Dialao

that reaches to the mouth of the Senegal River. There's also a tiny island just offshore, given over mostly to goats but yours for the exploring: a *pirogue* will take you over, though at low tide you can almost wade across. *Campement Touristique Le Poulagon*, right on the fishing beach (③) is a great place to stay.

Yof is also a focus for the **Layen** brotherhood, a Lebu fraternity whose most venerated shrine is the **mausoleum** of the founder Saidi Limamou Laye and his son Mandione Laye. For members of the brotherhood, this temple-like building is the holiest of sites, and it attracts vast crowds at the end of Ramadan; if the festoon of vultures perched on its roof doesn't put you off climbing the steps, respect should. A nearby grotto contains perfumed sands and is believed to be where Muhammad's spirit dwelt for a thousand years before being reincarnated as the sect's founder.

If you want to participate in something unusual – you won't be the only tourist on the scene – come to Yof on a Thursday afternoon when **spirit possession dances** (*ndeup*) are organized by traditional psychiatrists with the mentally ill, who come with their relatives from all over Senegal.

Lac Retba

The popular Dakarois picnic spot of **Lac Retba** – also known as Lac Rose, "Pink Lake" – is certainly a remarkable spectacle, but a trip out here is worthwhile as much for the opportunity to get right out of Dakar and look at the Côte Sauvage as for the lake itself. The pinkness of the soda lake is caused by the action of bacteria that excrete red iron oxide; for maximum effect, watch the water as the sun goes down, when it turns from coral to mauve and violet. Women collect salt from the lake – almost as salty as the Dead Sea and just as hard to swim in – which is then packed into sacks by men at the far end. The shore is a beach of bleached shells, with banana plots and casuarina trees greening up an otherwise harsh landscape. Over the soft **dunes** to the north is the Atlantic, rough and swirling and definitely only for strong swimmers.

Getting to the lake, about 40km from Dakar, take a #15 bus to Rufisque (see below) and then a bush taxi to **Niaga**. The *campement* here – the *Keur Kanni* – has concrete thatched huts and a nice, local atmosphere (☎36 55 17; S/C, B&B; ③). It's then a twenty-minute walk to the lakeside and another, more expensive, *campement*.

Keur Moussa

The Benedictine monastery of **Keur Moussa** (☎36 39 09), up in the hills off the Thiès road 50km from Dakar, has acquired a reputation for its touristy *messes africaines* – African masses – with koras, balafons and tam-tams, and plenty of stuff for sale afterwards. Sunday ☎morning mass at 10am is the best. **Getting here** without your own car, you'll need early transport towards Thiès (hitchable) and a drop-off at the junction 5km past Sebhikotane, from where it's another 5km to the monastery. You can also get the #15 bus to Rufisque, then charter a taxi – or save money and spend more time taking two *cars rapides* to be dropped at the nearest road, 1km from the monastery.

Incidentally, don't confuse Keur Moussa with Keur Massar, on the #21 bus route, and much closer to Dakar. The similarity of the names results in much frustration.

South of Dakar

Beyond the city centre, on the busy **coast road** heading southeast, there's still forty or more kilometres before the edges of the capital finally give way to open, baobab-dotted countryside. Road and railway go through the agglomeration of Dagoudane-Pikine/Guediyawe, a huge spill-over of city workers and refugees from the interior: already larger in area than the rest of greater Dakar, the sprawl is fast encroaching on the shifting dunes of the north Cap Vert coast. At **Thiaroye-Mer**, 14km from Dakar, there's a pleasant small hotel just a kilometre from the beach; *Chez Charlie* on the Route de Rufisque (bus #15) offers S/C twin rooms (☎34 07 42; ②).

RUFISQUE – the Portuguese fifteenth-century Rio Fresco – is the last Dakar suburb, and is already provincial in feel. A scruffy seafront town with a couple of hotels, it's more human in scale than anything closer to the city (you'll see *calèches* here, for example). Several wholesalers of **exotic birds** line the road – middle men between the poverty-stricken peasants and a market in the west which will pay the equivalent of a year's labour for a parrot.

If you're beach-hunting, there's little difficulty in travelling down this way by bush taxi, and it's one area you might **hitch** successfully. It's worth making the slight extra effort to get to **Palmarin**'s near deserted shore – especially if **Fadiout** leaves a sour taste in your mouth. Before reaching Mbour, check out the "**Serer pyramids**" in the Bandia forest, 63km from Dakar just off the main highway south to Kaolack.

La Petite Côte

At the small resort of Bargny (just CFA180 and an hour or so from Dakar, at the outer limit of the city's municipal bus system), the **Petite Côte** begins and both road and railway turn inland to the junction for Thiès, Touba and St-Louis. You'll notice a Portuguese influence in some of the region's architecture, and a strong Catholic presence, not unlike parts of the Casamance. Pope John Paul visited both districts during his hugely popular 1992 Senegalese tour – watch out for wonderful outfits made from the material designed to commemorate the visit, adorned with the benign papal countenance.

Popenguine, Sali-Portudal and the Forêt de Bandia

Turning southeast onto the N1, 12km beyond Bargny, you pass several minor roads leading to **resort beaches** along the sandy, palm-fringed coastline. Toubab Dialao and **Popenguine** are both around 10km off the N1 and reachable by bush taxis or hitching: at the latter *Chez Ginette*'s (☎57 71 10; ②–③) is a good place to stay, right on the beach, with a couple of twin rooms, self-catering bungalows sleeping up to ten and especially fine cooking. There are more bungalows available for rent in the village. Back on the N1, at the village of Nguekokh, a road leads southwest to the sea and the resorts of Somone, Ngaparou and **Sali-Portudal**, which has similar accommodation options. Saly, as it's known, is an especially attractive resort village with everything from *Savana* (☎57 11 13; Fax 57 10 45 ⑦) and *Palm Beach* (☎57 11 37; ⑦) hotels to less extravagant lodgings, although in season you'd be better off in the small villages along the coast.

Away from this coastal swing, the scrub-and-baobab **Forêt de Bandia**, to the east of the main highway to Kaolack (1km south of Sindia, 23km from the Thiès junction), contains an interesting archeological site: the **burial mounds** of the vanished Serer village of Tay, and a **burial baobab**, where Serer griots were once entombed. A collection of skulls and bones still lie at the baobab's small entrance. Guided tours may be available; don't miss the **replicas** of the burial huts which lie beneath the hardened earth mounds.

Mbour and Nianing

Though dusty, unattractive and crammed with tourists in season, **MBOUR**, 83km southeast of Dakar, is the obvious base for this part of the coast. For **accommodation**, the most affordable of the touristy places, though nothing special, is *Relais 82* (③)at the turn-off to the town centre. The main alternative in town, a kilometre or so down the road, is the *Centre Touristique de la Petite Côte*, right on the shore next to the Préfecture (☎57 10 04), which at twice the price is unlikely to be money better spent.

Take a look instead at *Le Filao* pizzeria, which has a few rooms (③) – the drawback here is that they give onto the Jardin des Rêves, which gets noisier as the evening progresses.

Mbour has a fair number of bars and small restaurants: *Restaurant d'Islam* is an old favourite. The town has a PTT and a *BICIS* bank, and there's even a bit of a tourist office along av El Hadj Malick Sy. But the town depends first on fishing, not tourism; the beach is littered with fishy remains and associated odours, and the sea is uninviting anyway – usually calm and tending to weediness. The *gare routière* is in front of the tree-shaded marketplace.

The road continues south past **NIANING** and a couple of exclusive holiday villages – *Domaine de Nianing* for the French on the landward side (☎57 10 85; ⑦), and *Club Aldiana* (☎57 10 84; ⑦) on the sands, catering for German packagers. Closer to the village itself are two far less expensive **campements**: the *Auberge des Coquillages* (☎57 14 28; ③) with a wonderful beachside position and *Le Bintegnier* (③) with great food and a lovely garden. There's also an inexpensive **café** in the village offering meals under CFA600 and beers for about half that. Substantial **birdlife**, to be seen among the remains of the **Forêt de Nianing**, keeps the whole area pleasant, and the shore scene, with scattered palm trees, is certainly pretty.

Joal-Fadiout

Next stop is **JOAL**, where Senegal's great statesman, Léopold Senghor, was born in 1906. Another former Portuguese settlement, with a few old houses still standing – including the Senghors' – it is today a fishing village. The hauling-in of the fish at the end of the day is as enjoyable to watch as anywhere.

But apart from a visit to Chez Senghor and a pat delivery of its history from the *gardien*, the big draw is a wander over to **FADIOUT**, the fishing village on the shell-bank **island** in the estuary facing Joal. By virtue of a wicked combination of attractive features – proximity to the tourist camps up the coast, houses built of crushed shells, granary huts on stilts like a field of mushrooms, and a fishermen's cemetery on a neighbouring island – Fadiout is one of the most aggressive hustler haunts in Senegal. Down at the bridge to the island there's a gauntlet of obnoxious teenage "guides" to be overcome: if you spurn their *pirogues* and persist in walking over, they'll follow you waving sea and turtle shells for sale and making uninviting offers of cheap *logements*. If you would actually like to do a **pirogue trip**, get into top bargaining gear and make sure you know how long you're going to get. Note, too, that the grain store island, a few hundred metres to the southeast of Fadiout, is virtually empty and not very impressive before the harvest.

All this notwithstanding, Fadiout is a fascinating place, a **"shell midden"** entirely composed of the refuse from centuries of shellfish consumption. It takes about an hour to trail around the houses and Serer cemetery, which is about as long as you'll be able to sustain resistance to all the pestering.

For **food and accommodation**, look to Joal. Probably you'll want to avoid the tour-group oriented *Hôtel le Finnio* (☎57 61 12; ⑦) right by the bridge. Leave the Catholic mission alone too, even if you're broke: they have absolutely no interest in putting you up. Instead, make for the centre of town and check out the well-signposted *Relais 114* (☎57 16 14; ②), run by a Guinean family who insist on having nothing to do with "guides". They offer clean non-S/C doubles and a pleasant balcony with hammocks. The *Relais* makes a big thing of its lobster; if you want to eat more cheaply, head for the many omelette and *chawarma* bars around town. **Beaches** in this area are all too crowded and hustly for abandonment to the sun, sea and sand. On the fishing beach near the town centre you can mingle with the masses at the end of the day and normally be ignored, but about the only place you might consider for a peaceful **swim** is the sandy, casuarina-covered bar to the south, past the school and football pitch.

The Saloum delta

Situated between Dakar and The Gambia, the delta of Senegal's third river – the **Saloum** – is growing in popularity as a weekend destination from Dakar and a bird-watching district for foreign visitors. Visiting the maze of islands and creeks by *pirogue* from the landward side – the usual way – can work out expensive, but there are lots of choices, including organized tours by *Sénégambie Voyages* (see "Moving on from Dakar" at the end of the Dakar "Listings"). The less expensive option is to organize your own *balade;* get a vehicle down from Joal to **Palmarin**, 20km to the south – but be prepared to wait several hours and possibly to change vehicles at Keur Samba Dia. Going back again is harder, but there's always space when a vehicle comes: as one

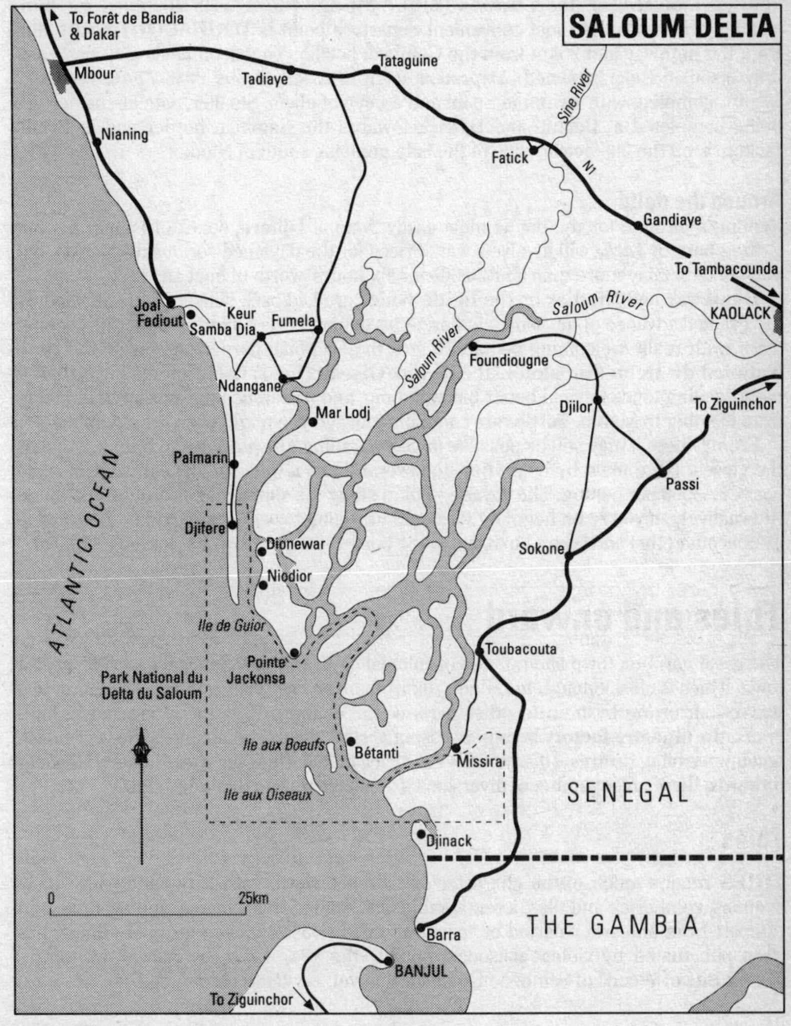

passer-by commented, cryptically, "La voiture du sous-développement est jamais pleine". And if rains have washed the road out completely, you'll hear of it.

Palmarin has a good, if basic **campement** (③) right on the beach, a short distance from the village itself. An outpost of Casamance's system of *campements touristiques rurals intégrés*, it offers thatched, twin-bed huts among the palms – gas refrigerators, kerosene lamps, shared ablutions and all your meals are included. The owner can give advice on *pirogue* rental (see below).

Other **departure points for the delta** are **Foundiougne**, west of Kaolack, 33km from the main highway at Passi (also accessible by road from Fatick and then a ferry) and **Ndangane**, reachable from Joal or from the main highway east of Thiadaye. You can take a *pirogue* from Ndangane to the island of Mar-Lothie which has a pleasant low-key hotel-*campement*, the *Limboko* (BP167 Mbour; ☎57 14 41; ③), good for bird-watching. Perhaps the most convenient departure point is **TOUBACOUTA**, just 2km from the highway and 25km from the Gambian border. Toubacouta has a recent, carefully installed Belgian-owned *campement* set-up, *Les Paletuviers* (☎48 77 76, fax 48 77 77; ④), complete with swimming pool and a bevy of chefs. Smaller, satellite camps are being completed at Bétanti and Djinack towards the Gambian border and at Pointe Jackonsa, on the far (ocean) side of the Saloum delta, south of Niodior.

Around the delta

Renting a pirogue for the day is most easily done at **Djifere**, south of Palmarin – but getting here by *bâché* will involve a wait. Prices for the day need serious discussion, but you shouldn't pay more than CFA20,000 for six hours' worth of boat and crew.

Dionewar and **Niodior** on the **Ile de Guior** are laid-back villages, little affected by the gradual advance of tourism. Niodior, in particular, is very alluring under its coconut trees, with really welcoming people. Nearer the Gambian border and inside the **Parc National du Delta du Saloum**, the **Ile aux Oiseaux** has variably interesting birdlife – early evening tends to yield better birdwatching, and palearctic migrants swell numbers from October to March. Turtles are common, too, and you might even see a dolphin.

From Djifere it may still be possible to take a trading *pirogue* down to Banjul, which is the closest large town by boat; they go several times a week (daily, some claim), and cost CFA3000 per person. The voyage – 60km along the shore – takes around six hours. Alternatively, if you're on haggling form and unwilling to wait, you could be *pirogued* to Toubacouta (4hr) and take a bush taxi to the border – expect to pay at least CFA15,000.

Thiès and onward

The great garrison town and rail hub of colonial days, and now Senegal's second largest town, Thiès is close enough to Dakar (70km) to be an easy visit, and also lies en route if you're journeying by train to other parts of the country. If you're interested in local crafts, the **tapestry factory** here is an essential stop; the workmanship is the very finest, and few weaving centres – if any – in West Africa match Thiès for sheer impact. Heading onwards, there are a number of diversions if you have time to do things slowly.

Thiès

THIÈS retains much of the character of a French town, with parks and wide shady avenues, solid brick and tiles, a remarkable old Sudanic-style cinema, and even the odd rampart from an earlier period of "pacification". Its history, even in recent times, has been punctuated by violent episodes, notably the 1947 strike by railway workers – "God's Bits of Wood" of Sembène Ousmane's novel, *Les Bouts de Bois de Dieu*.

The Tapestry factory and the Museum

Main points of interest if you're passing through are the small **museum** and the very impressive **tapestry factory**, both reached from the centre of town by following the railway (on your right) in the St-Louis direction. At the junction by the level crossing (fortifications on your left), head off left.

The **Manufactures Sénégalaises des Arts Decoratifs** (☎51 22 81; Mon–Fri 8am–12.30pm & 3–6.30pm, Sat 8am–12.30pm; admission charged), opened in 1966, focuses the output of many of Senegal's artists and has an enormous influence on younger painters. Having work painstakingly redrawn and fabricated into glowing tapestries – many for exhibition and sale abroad – is an accolade providing a rare incentive.

Since its foundation, the Thiès school has produced fewer than 500 pieces: its annual output works out at around 300 square metres, each tapestry produced in an exclusive edition of eight. Prices are accordingly high – around £500 ($750) per square metre. Common themes are village life, nature, history and myth, executed in dazzling, graphic style. Look out for the stunning *Rendezvous au Soleil* by Jacob Yacouba, a giant ten-metre version of which was purchased by Atlanta airport. However, a lot of the designs suggest some fresh ideas are needed, and as more commercially oriented foreign painters begin commissioning the Thiès workshops to weave their own work for them, there's a danger the centre will lose its creative edge.

Try to get to see all the stages of work, from drawing up the original paintings to dyeing the wool and the rapid but careful process of weaving itself. You should be allowed to take photos in the workshops, but perhaps not in the exhibition hall.

Across the way is the **Museum** (same hours), housed in the fort, first built in 1871. Aside from a number of interesting photos and a good deal of commentary on Senegalese history, there's a special concentration on the role of the marabouts. Near the museum a number of artists work and sell their paintings at a small **art workshop**.

Practicalities

Arriving in Thiès by bus or taxi you'll almost certainly be left at the *gare routière*, 3km out of town – a good reason to come by train and get delivered to the *centreville*. The railway is still the pivot of much of the town's life, its rhythms adjusted to the comings and goings on the track. Thiès's **restaurants** are mostly found along Avenue Senghor south of the tracks or in the town centre north of the station. As for **places to stay** you have the *Hôtel du Rail* (☎51 10 13; ③), opposite the station on rue Faidherbe, which has comfortable AC, S/C rooms; the centrally located *Hôtel Rex* (②) three blocks north, offering fanned rooms for about as cheap as they get in Thiès; and, as a last resort, the *Hôtel du Thiès Man Gan* (☎51 15 26; ③), on the east edge of town, which doesn't really offer good value for the price.

Inland from Thiès

Moving north, you might visit **Tivaouane** if you're gripped by the fascination of the Islamic brotherhoods. Or, heading south, you could go to **Kaolack** via **Diourbel**, from where you might strike out to **Touba**, the big Mouride stronghold with the country's most impressive mosque. From Touba there's the option of following the dusty N3 highway northeast, onwards via **Linguère** to **Matam** on the Senegal River. Lastly, if you're heading through the **Sine-Saloum region**, either south on the *transgambienne* or east on the N1 to Tambacounda, you might take time out to look at some of the Iron Age **stone circles**.

Independent transport is the best way to visit these places, though with the possible exception of the stone circles and Touba during *Magal*, you'll normally find public transport to the towns.

Tivaouane, Mboro and the Grande Côte

Tivaouane, 5km off the main N2 to St-Louis, is the seat of the **Sy** dynasty of the **Tijaniya** brotherhood, the largest in Senegal. The grand North African-style mosque is best seen during *Gamou*, the Tijani pilgrimage, or *Maulidi*, the prophet's birthday, when thousands of believers pour into the town. Accommodation, which seems pretty minimal at the best of times, is impossible to find during these periods.

Just north of Tivaouane, on the N2 highway, a road leads northwest 28km to the fishing village of **Mboro-sur-mer** on what is known as the **Grande Côte**, a 150-kilometre unbroken sweep of sand linking St-Louis to Dakar, along which the Paris–Dakar Rally traditionally hurtles towards the capital. Despite the reforestation along this coastline, the *côte*'s exposure makes it a far less popular holiday destination than the Petite Côte south of Dakar, which may be all the reason you need to come here. The *Hotel du Lac* (BP 9; ☎55 77 69; ③) offers a pool, palm-wine, excursions and comfortable **rooms**, with **meals** at around CFA3000. The nearby lake, after which the hotel takes its name, is an excellent place for birdwatching at the end of the day.

Diourbel and Touba

Diourbel, with its huge domed mosque, is one of the principal saintly towns of the Mourides, and capital of the region of the same name, the heart of the groundnut basin. Fifty kilometres east, following the Sine valley, lies **TOUBA**, the burial place of the founder of Mouridism, **Cheikh Amadou Bamba Mbacke** (1850–1927), and thus the high holy place of the brotherhood. The extraordinary 87-metre-high mosque – built over the family tomb in 1963 and visible for miles across the flat plain – is the largest and one of the finest in West Africa, and the most important religious shrine in Senegal.

Amadou Bamba's triumphal return home in 1907, after years of detention by the French, is celebrated annually in the festival of **Magal** (see the Muslim calendar on p.62 for dates). Up to half a million pilgrims flock here from all over Senegal and The Gambia, and public transport is virtually suspended on routes to and from Touba. *Magal* is the manifestation of a religious fervour whose only equal in Africa is found in northern Nigeria.

Senegalese authority is minimal here: the **maraboutic militia** is responsible for law and order, which includes absolute bans on tobacco and alcohol anywhere in the town precincts. Searches – especially of *toubabs* – aren't uncommon, and you will be fined and your drugs confiscated if found out. Photography, too, isn't likely to please many. Despite this, Touba can be an irresistible challenge. If you're going there for *Magal*, expect to spend the night awake with the crowd of disciples: you'll almost certainly have found companions on the journey.

Be warned, though, that **accommodation** is impossible to find in Touba if you don't get invited to stay at someone's house. Rooms might be available 10km away in **Mbacke**, a kind of secular counterpoint to Touba, where the maraboutic laws don't apply. You could get stranded there for the big night anyway, as Mbacke goes into partying hyperdrive, diverting attention from the devotions at Touba and increasingly reducing *Magal* to a Christmas-style commercialism.

If you're driving in, you may end up jammed in pedestrian traffic or directed to leave your vehicle in a designated zone and walk. However you manage it, don't confuse piety with honesty. Touba has plenty of "guides" and during *Magal* a nimble army of hustlers and pickpockets filters the crowds.

To Linguère

With stamina you could continue by road from Touba or better still, Mbacke, to Linguère and from there on to Ouro Sogui/Matam. This route, the N3, goes right through the heart of the Fula **Réserves Sylvo-Pastorales** (wild grazing reserves), a fragmented cluster of badlands (virtually tribal reserves), glumly conceded to the pastoralists and always under threat from the expanding Mouride groundnut enterprises. With improved irrigation and increases in population, agriculture encroaches on all sides except the east, where the *Réserves de Faune du Ferlo-Nord* and *Ferlo-Sud* – areas in which no grazing is permitted – create a barrier between the cattle herds and the potentially rich Senegal River valley.

LINGUÈRE is the main town of this region, accessible by train from Louga and surrounded by the reserves, but nevertheless a bit of a dead end and rarely used by travellers. **Accommodation** is limited to the *campement*-style *Hotel Touristique* (☎68 10 30; ④); informal enquires may elicit less expensive lodgings. If you've transport, or a dogged persistence coupled with a devotion to obscure archeological sites, you might move down the Ferlo river course from Linguère to the ruined **fortress** of Alboury Ndiaye – the last independent ruler of the Wolof kingdom of Jolof. The site is north of the road before the village of Yang-Yang.

From Linguère a rough track to the Senegal River near Ourossogui follows the normally dry upper course of the Ferlo, between the faunal reserves. Transport is limited and vehicles depart early – you'll almost certainly be the only tourist on board.

Kaolack

A big, noisy interchange town, hub of five road routes (but not on the main railway line), **KAOLACK** is not a place where you'll want to linger. There's little to see here but the **mosque**, a splendid creation, paid for partly by Saddam Hussein. The Niasse dynasty of the Tijaniya brotherhood – based here – is bent on founding an Islamic republic, a movement which is also reportedly funded by Libya. Kaolack has a venerable and bustling market and a couple of **hotels**: *Hôtel Napoleon*, east of the market, offers dirty, fanned rooms (②) and cheap food; the *Hotel de Paris* (☎41 24 70; ③–④) is your only decent choice for a S/C room. The Dakar *gare routière* near the market offers a number of **inexpensive food** outlets.

Sine-Saloum stone circles

Part of the same cultural complex as the circles in The Gambia (see "Wassu"), the **megaliths** scattered across the plain between Nioro du Rip on the *transgambienne* N4 and Tambacounda are vestiges of a prehistoric society about which virtually nothing is known. Including some unimpressive circles that you'd not glance twice at, they number approximately a thousand in this region. Associated with them are burial sites which have yielded a number of skeletons and a certain amount of weaponry, pots and copper ornaments. Seeming to date from before the twelfth century, they bear no sign of any Islamic impact.

Most impressive is the site known as **Djalloumbéré**, at **Ngayène**, hard against the Gambian border. Over eleven hundred individual pillars here make up 52 stone circles – some of them the sites of mass burials. It's virtually impossible to get here without your own transport – turn left 9km south of Nioro du Rip to Kaymor (17km) on a decent track, then continue southeast another 15km via Tène Peul and Keur Bakari to Ngayène. From here you can head straight back to the main road at Medina Sabak, 28km from Nioro. In the middle of this "circuit", 10km due south of Kaymor, is the village of **Payoma**, where stones from the local circles have been uprooted to support the buildings – including the mosque. Numerous other circles are visible at various points along these tracks.

Assuming you've got transport or you're using a *taxi brousse*, there are more sites along the Tambacounda highway, at **Malème Hodar** (right by the road) and **Keur Albé** and **Sali**, respectively 9km and 20km southwest of Kongheul on a minor road to The Gambia. This road crosses the border just north of Wassu: if you're enraptured by the circles and your papers are in order, you could cross over for further observations and stay in Kuntaur or Georgetown.

THE NORTH AND EAST

Northern Senegal is the least populated part of the country, with few large towns and a landscape whose main interest derives from its harsh marginality. Northeast of Dakar stretches the **Sahel**, where the desert's southward advance is ever apparent. But there are two conspicuous attractions in the north: the **Senegal River**, forming the border with Mauritania and feeding a flood plain up to 30km wide; and the old French colonial capital of **St-Louis**, tucked behind the bar at the mouth of the river. Two **national parks** – the Djoudj and the Langue de Barbarie – are mainly visited by keen birdwatchers.

Should you be **heading north** to Mauritania and the Atlantic route across the Sahara, St-Louis is a natural break in the journey, a few hours by *taxi brousse* from Dakar, slightly longer by train. To **follow the river**, however, you have to be a little more determined and transport-hop your way inland to **Richard Toll**, **Ouro Sogui/Matam** and **Bakel** where the tarmac ends. Continuing south through the hills, you'll intercept the Dakar–Bamako train at **Kidira**, on the border, where there'll be a crush to find space on board. Coming in the other direction, into Senegal from Mali, the river course is a marginally preferable route towards the coast: the alternative, following the direct line of the railway has very little to detain you.

St-Louis

The oldest French settlement in West Africa and capital of Senegal and Mauritania until 1958, **ST-LOUIS** is something of a world apart. In later colonial times its *commune* status – shared with Gorée, Rufisque and Dakar – meant its inhabitants were considered citizens of France; today the town's crumbling eighteenth- and nineteenth-century European architecture and its white- and blue-draped Wolof and Moorish inhabitants maintain the culture clash. Like Gorée too, St-Louis is a UNESCO-protected World Heritage Site. If decay, abandonment and the ghosts of slaves and fishermen attract you then you'll enjoy this town. Taking advantage of the Casamance's recent woes, beachside *campements* have sprung up along the Langue de Barbarie and, with its warm winters, dry summers and national parks nearby, it all adds up to a worthwhile few days' stay.

Arrival and orientation

St-Louis' wonderfully ornate **train station** is in the mainland quarter of **Sor**, close to the end of the iron Pont de Faidherbe; the **gare routière** is right by the tracks. It's a hectic area, thronged with stalls and vendors – and of course dark by the time the train gets in. The oldest part of St-Louis is the **island** of the same name, a ten-minute walk away across the bridge (which, incidentally, spanned the Danube until 1897).

Accommodation

St-Louis offers an excellent range of **accommodation** for its size, with the old colonial-era hotels situated on the island itself, more places to stay on the mainland, and *campements* strung out along the spit of the Langue, south of Guet Ndar.

Auberge de Jeunesse, "L'Atlantide", north end of av Jean Mermoz, corner of rue Bouet (☎61 24 09). Best place in town to lodge cheaply and commune with other travellers. Segregated dorms and twins – with shared ablutions and a modest breakfast included. Also offers *plats* for CFA1500, bike rental and trips to the national parks. ①–②.

Campement de Hydrobase, on the beach/river 4km south of Guet Ndar. Windblown *campement* run by the *Hôtel du Palais* (see below; lifts offered). Basic palm huts, shady *paillotes*, and a restau-

The main **ethno-linguistic groups** of north Senegal are **Wolof**, concentrated around St-Louis and along the lower reaches of the river, and **Tukulor** higher up, who speak a dialect of Fula. In the far east, around Bakel, there are **Sarakolé** (Soninké/Serahuli) speakers, while communities of semi-nomadic **Fula** live in the scorched region of Fouta Toro.

rant/bar. Windsurfers and horse rental extra; if you fancy a little more luxury, go for FB with all beach activities thrown in. ①–③.

Campement Langue de Barbarie, 16km down the spit. Plusher and more established version of the above (4WD only), run by the *Hôtel de la Poste* who will drive you down there (and on to the National Park). *Pirogue* and fishing excursions offered. Lowest rates include breakfast, higher rate is for FB and all beach toys. ③–④.

Hôtel du Palais, rue Ababacar Sy (BP 92; ☎61 17 72; Fax 61 30 08). Friendly, co-operative and least expensive of the old-style hotels offering clean AC, S/C rooms. Adjacent restaurant/patisserie has good croissants and coffee. Inexpensive excursions organized to regional attractions. Accepts credit cards – at a premium. ④.

Hôtel de la Poste, by Pont Faidherbe, opposite the post office and on the waterfront (BP 48; ☎61 11 18; Fax 61 23 13). The island's definitive, authentic colonial-era hotel where the likes of aviator Mermoz reposed on their way to Caracas. Splendid rooms and ambience and a hunter-themed bar. Car rental, and all the usual excursions including day runs down the beach to their *campement* on the Langue (see above). ④.

Hôtel le Walo, 500m south of Pont Faidherbe (☎61 18 31). Less accomplished and less expensive (though still *too* expensive) version of the *Coumba Bang* (see next) with huts and a lively nightclub. ④.

Hôtel Mame Coumba Bang, Bois des Amoureux, 6.5km south of town on the mainland near the village of Gandiol (BP 214; ☎61 18 50; Fax 61 19 02). St-Louis' luxury tourist hotel including a pool, an excellent restaurant and trips into the surrounding countryside. ⑤.

Hôtel de la Résidence, av Blaise Diagne (BP 254; ☎61 12 60; Fax 61 12 59). The town's most comfortable hotel, recently renovated with lots of white paint and clever colonial details. ⑤.

Maison de Lille, bd Lamine Gueye (BP 457; ☎61 11 35). Fifteen minutes' walk south of the *gare routière*. Plain place with little to offer other than the cheapest bed in town, a working mens' hostel feel and a spanking new bathroom. ①.

Mission Catholique, unmarked wooden door (no. 8) at the west end of rue Duret (☎61 10 04). Possibly still taking travellers but will more likely direct you to the *Atlantide*. ①.

The Town

There's an excellent bird's eye view **sketch map** (CFA1000) of St-Louis and its environs available from some hotels and bookshops which makes an informative companion for your wandering in and around town as well as making a great memento when you leave. *Hôtel de la Poste*, as the longest established tourist venue in town, offers **tours** all around St-Louis. They'll also take you down to the beach in the morning and pick you up at the end of the day – at a price. You can make cheaper arrangements through the *Hôtel du Palais*.

The island

You can walk round the **island** – *Ndar* in Wolof – in about an hour and a half. Shuttered windows, occasional balconies and flaking yellow paint are the abiding impressions. Some of the best houses – which, as in Gorée, tend to conceal their interiors from snooping strangers – are around and just north of the hotels, especially along rue Blanchot and rue Pierre Loti. *Maurel et Prom* was a slave market, and the *Hôtel de la Poste* started as a gum arabic warehouse. The old houses characteristically have interior courtyards, warehouses on the ground floor (mostly now converted) and first-floor, inward-facing living quarters.

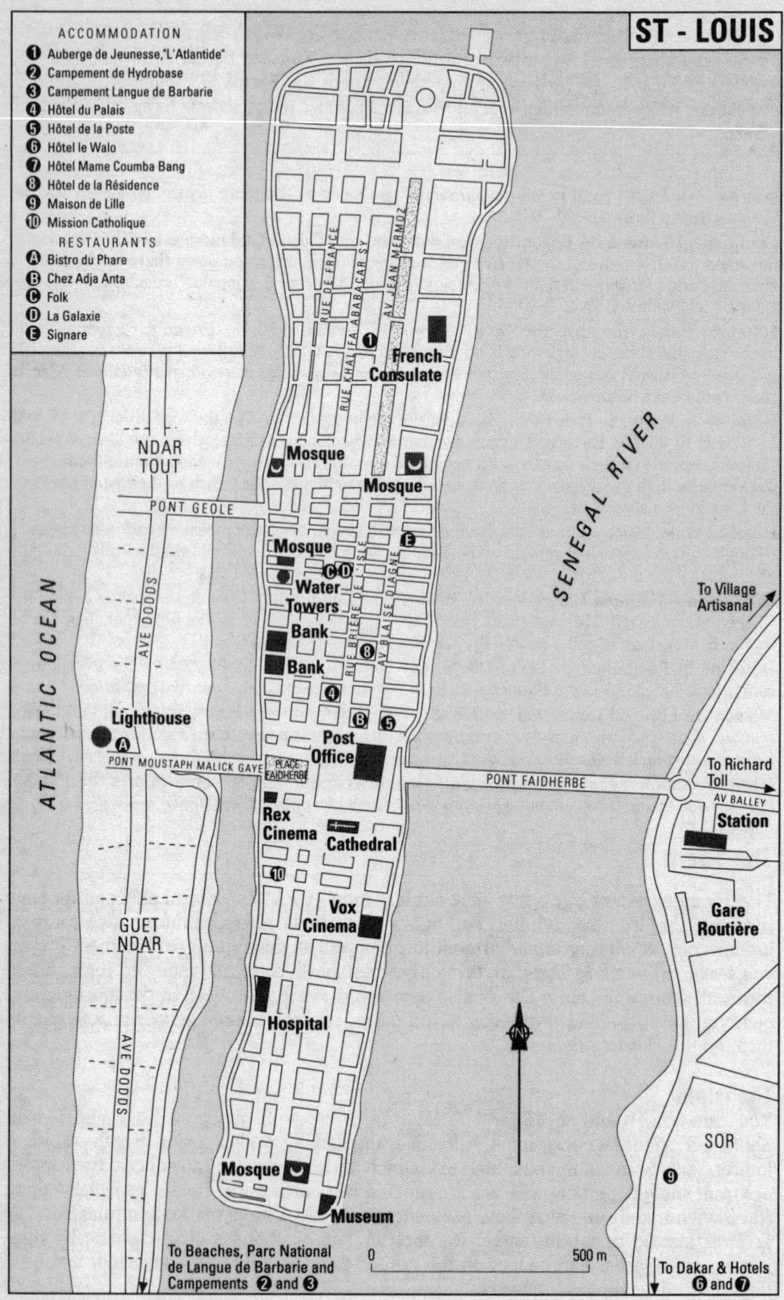
ST - LOUIS
ACCOMMODATION
1 Auberge de Jeunesse,"L'Atlantide"
2 Campement de Hydrobase
3 Campement Langue de Barbarie
4 Hôtel du Palais
5 Hôtel de la Poste
6 Hôtel le Walo
7 Hôtel Mame Coumba Bang
8 Hôtel de la Résidence
9 Maison de Lille
10 Mission Catholique
RESTAURANTS
A Bistro du Phare
B Chez Adja Anta
C Folk
D La Galaxie
E Signare
RUE DE FRANCE
RUE KHALIFA ABABACAR SY
AV JEAN MERMOZ
French Consulate
SENEGAL RIVER
NDAR TOUT
Mosque
Mosque
PONT GEOLE
Mosque
Water Towers
RUE BRIÈRE DE L'ISLE
AV BLAISE DIAGNE
Bank
Bank
ATLANTIC OCEAN
AVE DODDS
Lighthouse
Post Office
PONT MOUSTAPH MALICK GAYE
PLACE FAIDHERBE
PONT FAIDHERBE
To Village Artisanal
To Richard Toll
AV BALLEY
Station
Rex Cinema
Cathedral
Vox Cinema
Gare Routière
GUET NDAR
Hospital
AVE DODDS
SOR
Mosque
Museum
To Beaches, Parc National de Langue de Barbarie and Campements 2 and 3
0
500 m
To Dakar & Hotels 6 and 7

At the Place de Lille, named after St-Louis's twin city, notice the plaque commemorating the town's most celebrated citizen, Mbarick Fall, who as **Battling Siki** became the first world professional boxing champion in 1925. Heading south round the corner from here, beneath a wonderful old silk-cotton tree, you come to the **Place Faidherbe**, centering on a bust of the eponymous French governor, and surrounded by government and military buildings.

At the southern tip of the island, the **Museum** is worth a look (in theory, daily 9am–noon & 3–6pm; CFA200). The palm trees outside have been beheaded and carved – an appropriately bizarre introduction to a collection which, in line with the town's renaissance, is being systematically renovated. When this book was being researched the first floor was nearly completed, with displays of local ethnographia from neolithic times to the coming of the *colons,* the pre-war trans-Atlantic aviators and up to the present. By now there can only be more and even if you can't read French the cool interior will absorb you for an hour or more.

From the museum, if you head up the eastern side of the island, you pass the **Maison des Signares**, a particularly impressive example of St-Louisienne architecture. Back at the **north end** of the island, don't miss the **Palais de Justice** on rue Brière de l'Ile, with its massive staircase.

Ndar Tout and Guet Ndar

Across the other arm of the river on the spit of the Langue de Barbarie, the scene is much more animated. Turn right across either of the bridges and you're strolling on Avenue Dodds, main drag of the **Ndar Tout** quarter. With its tall, gracious houses rising behind the pavement palm trees, it is easy to picture this as the Champs Elysées of the local *signares* set, at a time when there were 4000 French *colons* and military based in St-Louis. At the far north end, ruination sets in – skeletal buff and red remains of French army buildings and then a marker pillar designating the **Mauritanian frontier** (no official border crossing).

Action in Ndar Tout focuses on the **market** and sandy **Place de la République**, which gives out straight onto the Atlantic down Avenue Servatius, itself ankle deep in sand. From here you can walk south along the shore into the fishing quarter of **Guet Ndar** – rewarding, if odoriferous in the late afternoon – and down as far as the Islamic fishermen's cemetery, a net-and-stake graveyard with the familiar and disquieting vulture retinue.

Sor

The **mainland** area of St-Louis – **Sor** – is the part of town whose population swells with every downward cycle of drought in the interior. On the whole it's an anonymous district, though there are some old buildings, and there's a lively African feel by night which the weary island can't match. On the route de Corniche at Sor's northern end is the **Village Artisanal** where you might pick up a wider and less expensive range of Senegalese and Mauritanian artefacts than those you'll be offered outside the island's better hotels.

Eating, drinking and nightlife

St-Louis has a few reliable and economical places to eat: *Dibiterie-Restaurant St-Louis* (supposedly daily 9am–3am) is a friendly but ultra-basic mainland place ten minutes along rue de Gen de Gaulle, just past the *Shell;* in the other direction *Le Diama* (daily 7am–late), just by the monument on Ndar Tout, is also a good spot for cheap **street food**. For greater expense and quality take your pick from the better hotels such as the *Poste*'s or *Residence*'s restaurants.

MOVING ON FROM ST LOUIS

Trains to Dakar leave Mon–Sat at 7am, arriving at noon. If you need a **travel agent** head for *Agence Voyages Sovet,* corner of rue de France by the water towers (☎/Fax 61 29 85); all the usual services as well as expensive car rental, the price of which you should negotiate – aim for CFA40,000 a day for a Peugeot 504 to the Djoudj Park and back, plus fuel.

The hotels are probably your best bet for **drinking**, too, though the jazzy *Le Mayo* on the southeast of the island is worth a try. There's also *La Chaumière* in Ndar Tout, owned by the *Hôtel de la Poste* (free to all guests), a classy **nightclub** charging around CFA2000 at the door and with ordinary bar prices, but it only gets into gear after midnight. Or simply cut east across the Servatius bridge to the mainland and let your ears track down the action: community events are easily located.

Restaurants and snack bars

Bistro du Phare, by the lighthouse on Ndar Tout. Great, well-prepared food and wonderful views over the Atlantic.

Chez Adja Anta, rue Bisson. The island's customary "hole-in-the-wall" serving *plats de jour* for CFA600 in unpretentious surroundings. Daily 7am–midnight.

Folk, rue Ababacar Sy. *Chawarma* joint. Daily 9am–midnight, except Thurs afternoon.

La Galaxie, rue Briere de l'Isle. About the best deal in town: friendly service and, for once, a pleasant interior plus entrées for CFA800. Daily 11am–3pm & 7–11pm.

Linguère, next to *Hôtel de la Résidence*. Good food at around the CFA1000 mark. Closed Thurs.

Signare, rue Blaise Diagne. A plush non-hotel option – when it's open.

Listings

Air Afrique place Franchet-d'Espérey (☎61 13 63).

Bank *BICIS,* on rue de France/rue Blanchot (9.30–11.30am & 2.30–4.30pm), seem able to change money in the afternoon only.

Car Rental *Hôtel de la Résidence* is the *Avis* agent (☎61 12 59). The *Hôtel de la Poste* can also arrange rental by the day. See also "Moving on from St-Louis" below.

Cinemas Kung Fu and Indian epics dubbed into French are shown at the open-air *Vox* and *Rex*. A good laugh, with the bonus of armchairs.

Mechanics Puncture repairs available for cars and bikes at the garages just south of the *gare routière.*

The Langue de Barbarie and its Parc National

With 4WD you can drive the entire length of the **Langue de Barbarie**, dodging the waves and hundreds of thousands of crabs as you go. The trip starts in Guet Ndar, passing the remains of the **Hydrobase**, the seaplane centre used as a staging post by the early airmail service between Europe and South America. The first South Atlantic crossing took off from here in 1930; the *Hôtel de la Poste* in town is full of mementoes.

Many of the casuarina trees planted here by Governor Faidherbe when the Langue was called *La Piste des Cavaliers,* have since perished, and it's an often melancholy beachscape populated by new *campements* in various stages of completion. At the tip of the spit you look across the estuary to the area protected by the National Park, where there's a good chance of seeing cormorants, pelicans and turtles.

The **Parc National de la Langue de Barbarie** (daily 7am–6pm; CFA2000) covers twenty square kilometres of estuarine islands and waterways around the southern end of the Langue. Its main entrance is on the landward side, after the village of Gandiol, which is accessible by bush taxi from the Sor *autogare* at St-Louis or on **tours** organized by the main hotels in town. The quantity of birds depends on the time of year and on an element of luck: flamingos and pelicans are the obvious species – rarer ones require more patience. On firmer ground you can see warthogs and, in a fenced enclosure, a pair of giant tortoises and a herd of deer – gift of King Juan Carlos of Spain.

In a 4WD vehicle it's possible to **follow the beach** the entire distance from Gandiol to Dakar, a 150-kilometre drive of four hours plus, depending on tides. If you need to get back on the main N2 highway, six routes lead up from the shore along the way.

Parc National des Oiseaux du Djoudj

Situated in the heart of the Walo delta of the Senegal River, and considerably bigger than the Langue de Barbarie park, the **Parc National des Oiseaux du Djoudj** (daily 7am–7pm; CFA2000) is Senegal's ornithological showcase, rated the third most important **bird reserve** in the world. If you're at all into birds and are here during the palearctic migrants' season between October and April, you should make the effort to get in. The track into the park is signposted to the left off the Rosso/Richard Toll road near the village of Ndiol; once in the park, however, restricting yourself to the tracks gives only half the picture. Try to get a good price for a *pirogue* **trip** (aim for CFA2000 per person per hour) across the shallow expanses, for it's here that you'll get close enough to the wildlife to take good pictures.

The Djoudj is West Africa's best bird reserve, its estimated 100,000 **flamingos** and 10,000 **white pelicans** among the world's largest concentrations. January is probably the ideal time to visit, with the migrants in residence but the water levels already receding. Flamingos prefer the high alkalinity – and the reduced water surface tends to concentrate the birds, making them easier to spot. Crowned cranes are among the park's more ostentatious inhabitants. You should also keep a look out on the water surface for the eyes and snouts of **crocodiles**, especially visible in the dry season.

Those without their own transport can arrange **trips to the Djoudj** with *Hôtel de la Poste* (around CFA25,000 each for the day, minimum four people; cheaper en masse), or with the owners of the *Hôtel du Palais*, who do a similar trip for around CFA15,000 per person, which includes entrance fees, a two- or three-hour *pirogue* ride and unlimited stops en route. Taxis can also be persuaded to spend the rest of the day taking you there and back, but you'll pay at least CFA20,000, and you've little room to protest if the trip is cut short. At the park entrance, the *Campement du Djoudj* (☎23 85 43; Fax 23 88 33; ④) offers overpriced S/C huts.

Along the Senegal River

From St-Louis there is frequent **transport upriver** to **Rosso** (for Mauritania) and Richard Toll. Thereafter, vehicles from St-Louis are scarcer, so you'll have to hop your way along the highway from town to town, and as the heat rises noticeably inland it can be a long slog in the back of a crowded *bâche* to Kidira, two long days and nearly 600km from St-Louis. There's little of interest to see along this route other than glimpses of the Senegal River and rural, upcountry communities getting on with life, although you'll find the former trading outpost of **Bakel**, just north of Kidira, a charismatic stopover. The only banks along this route are the shores of the Senegal River so make sure you have enough CFA, or at least French francs, to get you to Tambacounda or Kayes in Mali.

The Lower River

Between St-Louis and Richard Toll, the scene varies sharply with the time of year: in the dry season from November to May, you'll see the oblong, wicker huts of migrant Fula herders who've moved from the higher, drier lands of the interior. Signs of human habitation include the practice of planting old car tyres in the mud to stake a land claim – common all over West Africa.

Around the turn-off to Rosso, and all along the 6km causeway road to it, you see thousands of hectares of rice, along with **sugar cane**, intended not only to feed Senegal's considerable sugar consumption but also, eventually, to produce fuel alcohol to offset the high cost of oil imports. In the irrigation ditches, **nile monitor lizards** abound, growing enormous – up to two metres long – on a diet of insects, frogs and rodents.

Rosso

With the re-opening of the frontier with Mauritania, **ROSSO** (about 90min from St-Louis by minibus) is now bustling again, with black marketeers trading Ouguiya, the Mauritanian currency, and a minor **smuggling** industry – not from relatively thriving Senegal into drought-stricken Mauritania, but the reverse, from aid-saturated Mauritania into IMF-austere Senegal. If you're heading for Mauritania you're likely to be offered Ouguiya at about 10 percent above the going rate.

As you approach the town the road curls through desperate shacks and official buildings to a tongue of land from where a barge regularly crosses the brown flow to **Rosso–Mauritania**. If you're **crossing the river** – and there's little point in coming up here if you're not (there's even a local "Taxe sur les personnes Etrangères" of CFA250) – ask the driver to drop you at the first flag-poled white building on the left, where your passport gets stamped out of Senegal. If you're on foot you can get across the river easily enough using *pirogues* for about CFA100. Between noon and 2 or 3pm this is the only way to cross – it's lunchtime for the barge crew. The border closes at 6pm.

Richard Toll

Meaning "Richard's Field", **RICHARD TOLL** is named after the ambitious regional development planned by the French planter Claude Richard in the 1820s. The town's only notable building is Baron Jaques Roger's **colonial mansion**, built on an island in the River Taouey – which flows into the Senegal on the east side of town. It's surrounded by the remains of his ornamental park – now a dusty and overgrown jungle and nothing special. For **accommodation** you've one or two options: directly north of the *gare routière* is the *Gîte d'Etape* (☎63 32 40; ④), a great spot to rest up if you've had a tiring few days, with its lovely riverside setting, restaurant, Saturday-night disco and, most usefully, a swimming pool (CFA1500 for non-residents). Otherwise, ask around for the far less luxurious *Hôtel Keur Massada* (③) in the town centre, a kilometre or so to the east. Along the town's long main drag you'll also spot plenty of **street food** snack bars. If you're moving on east and there's nothing remotely full in the *gare routière*, you might prefer to walk a couple of kilometres to the edge of town, and wait there for a passing vehicle.

If you stay in this dreary town, and get up early enough, they say you can see mermaids from the bridge: that would liven things up a bit. Or perhaps they're serious, and mean manatees. It's certainly no place to join the sirens in the water, as around 90 percent of local people are reckoned to be carrying schistosome worms (the flukes that cause **bilharzia**). In 1994–95 Richard Toll had a full-blown epidemic of this nasty disease, blamed by some scientists on the abundance of fresh water snails due to the new dams upstream, where previously the river here was brackish.

Lac de Guiers

The **Lac de Guiers**, some 30km southwest of Richard Toll, has a more attractive scene. This is a wild area, and swarms with most of the birds present in the Djoudj, with the exception of flamingos. Warthogs are common and if you find a way to get out on the water you might even see **manatees** – strange, aquatic mammals which hold onto a precarious existence here. **People** of the area include Tukulor and Black Moor fishermen, and Fula herders at certain times of year. Protected from the Senegal River's brackish contamination by a dam in the River Taouey at Richard Toll, the lake supplies much of Dakar's drinking water, which is purified at Gnit on the western shore and piped 300km to the capital. You can't get right round the lake – it's best seen from the village of Mbane, on the eastern shore. The reedy western shore is accessible only from the St-Louis–Dakar road or a track which leads off south from the N2, 10km west of the Rosso junction.

The Middle River

Beyond Richard Toll, the road rises out of the valley bypassing the town of **Dagana** – an old gum arabic entrepôt on the Senegal, with colonial buildings and semi-intact nineteenth-century fort. Just east of town you get a tempting flash of the river (a good spot for lunch, but stay out of the water) and from here you leave traditional Wolof country. East of here most of the people you'll see are **Tukulor** or **Fula**, and the atmosphere is more laid-back – the friendliness no longer verging on aggressiveness, and commerce no longer quite such a feature.

Moving upriver you pass various villages – some traditional mud and grass affairs, others agglomerations of concrete blocks. At the spartan settlement of **Ndiayène** you can change into a clapped-out Peugeot 504 for the 24km run north to **PODOR**, Senegal's northernmost town right by the river, passing twin-towered mosques along the way. Despite the town's notable history – the name comes from its gold (*or*)-trading past and there's the remains of an 1854 French fort – and the fact that it's singing star Baaba Maal's home town, there is little to recommend a diversion off the highway. If you end up staying, the *Projet Integré de Podor* runs a beautiful guest house (②).

Podor is situated on the western tip of the **Ile à Morfil** (Island of Ivory), a long slug of floodlands (120km by 10km) between the main course of the river and the meandering Doué. At one time the island had a large population of **elephants**, supported by the covering of dense, silt-fed woodland. It's still a good wildlife district, with monkeys, crocodiles and a proliferation of birdlife, but elephants haven't been regularly seen since the 1960s and it's doubtful if any survive.

THE STATE OF TEKRUR

The Ile à Morfil lay at the heart of the **state of Tekrur** (whence *Tukulor* and the misleading French spelling *Toucouleur*), which was at its most powerful in the eleventh century, when it became a major sub-Saharan trading partner with the Almoravid Arabs of North Africa. The Tukulor claim, as a result, that they were the first West Africans to adopt Islam, and went on to evangelize, among others, the Fula – with whom they share a common language and much else. Their own state was annexed by ancient Ghana, with its power base to the east at Koumbi Saleh, in present-day Mauritania. When the Almoravids attacked Ghana, Tekrur helped the invaders, only to fall shortly afterwards to the Mali empire.

There's a fair number of villages with Sudanic-style **mosques** scattered along the island's one main track as far as **Salde**, the furthest east, where you can ferry back to the main road 90km short of Matam. If you can find transport the length of the island, it's a far preferable alternative to following the main N2, which is unremittingly dull.

The Upper River

Further inland, the next town of note is **Ouro Sogui**, the biggest settlement along the *haute fleuve* and around 280km and a hot and dusty four hours by car from Ndiayène or a long day from St-Louis (with a couple of vehicle changes). Along the way various routes to the river give access **into Mauritania** at Kaédi; branching north at **Thilogne**, 51km before Ouro Sogui, is the best bet. From Kaédi, there's regular transport around southeast Mauritania, and up to Nouakchott. Travellers frequently mistake the large highway town of Ouro Sogui with the former Tukulor **slave trading** station of Matam, a fading town 10km northeast of the highway, and still featured as the larger settlement on most maps.

At Ouro Sogui, turning south from the *Elf* station leads 1km along the main street to the town centre and market, passing cheap *dibiteries* such as *Chez Oussan* and the *Dibiterie d'Islam* next door. If you're being driven to the *gare routière* on the south side of town, keep an eye out for the two-storey *Auberge Sogui* (☎66 11 98; ②–③) on the right, the town's only regular **accommodation**, with large fanned or AC rooms, some S/C, and *plats* in the restaurant for CFA2000. There's a rooftop terrace on which to rest when the *Harmattan* isn't tearing in from Mauritania. You might also be offered a less expensive bed, along with cheap platefuls of whatever's in the pot, at the friendly unnamed restaurant a few minutes beyond the *auberge*. The *gare routière*, nearby, is the customary spot for basic nourishment and the place you want to get to early the next day for the run on to Bakel and Kidira.

Bakel and Kidira

Moving south from Ouro Sogui, brace yourself for a rough and dusty ride as the N2 highway to **Semmé**, 80km away, is badly potholed and often washed out completely by run-off from the surrounding hills. After Semmé you can release your grip on any fixed part of the vehicle and enjoy the rest of the run through the better-watered country hill-scapes up to Bakel, on a spur north of the highway and at the end of the tarmac.

Tucked in a bend in the river among a knot of hills, **BAKEL**'s narrow streets and colonial architectural relics make it perhaps the only place to linger a couple of days in the northeast, while possibly waiting to intercept the twice weekly Dakar–Bamako train at Kidira. The hills around evoke a sense of isolation similar to the dunes surrounding Timbuktu – indeed René Caillié stayed here and later took the post as prefect of Bakel on his return from the legendary city. The old French **fort**, regrettably still a military emplacement and out of bounds to visitors (though a *Centre René Caillié* exists in theory in one of its towers), overlooks the river where *piroguiers* ply for fish, onto an uncharacteristically verdant corner of Mauritania.

Bakel's *gare routière* is a few minutes' walk from the town centre, where the cheapest **place to stay** is the rather crumby *Hôtel d'Islam* (①), across from the *boulangerie*, with a few fanned rooms, or mat space on the roof terrace. There's a **restaurant** here too, when there are enough guests; otherwise you could try the *Linguère Buvette* in the *Télécentre*, just past the *gare routière* turn-off on the main road, a friendly sandwich bar with a small patio and undiluted *bissap* by the pint. For more luxury, check out the AC rooms in the *Hôtel de Boudon* (②–③), on the river bank a little north of town. There's also a *campement*, *Campement d'Apt* (Bakel's twin city; ①), with ordinary little huts, some with fans, but a lively weekend dancing scene.

Twin-town projects are common in the area and the whole district is surprisingly full of emigré money: many of the Soninké villagers in the district live in France, remitting savings which in turn become impressive houses. If you want to visit the villages, ideally if you have transport, **Golmy**, **Kongany** and **Ballor** are all to the north. You can also cross to the Mauritanian village of **Gouray**, or to the Malian village of **Guthurbé**. Most of the Soninké villages organize *journées culturelles* every couple of years, during which traditional Soninké ways are dusted off and presented to the community – occasions well worth planning to be here for.

Minibuses leave for the 63-kilometre run to **KIDIRA** daily (2hr) from the *gare routière*, along a rough track that certainly deserves the green, *parcours pittoresque* designation of the Michelin maps, but may be impassable at the height of the rainy season. On arrival in Kidira the bus delivers passengers to the *surête* at the west end of town, where you should get stamped out of Senegal if heading for Mali. Whatever time you arrive, plan on spending some time here, as both the east- and west-bound **trains** come through on Wednesday and Saturday evenings around midnight. Unfortunately, however, the town has nothing to offer the visitor apart from some street food by the Kidira railway crossing; but the Falemé River (follow the tracks 1km east) is a good place to pass the time and maybe catch up on your washing. You could also **buy a *pirogue*** here, for the week's punt down to St-Louis, bureaucracy and other variables permitting.

Those passing through Kidira **by road** will find a new bridge spanning the Falémé River just south of the rail bridge, while a notoriously rough track leads southwest 180km to Tambacounda, with a less demanding continuation on the Malian side passing through light baobab woodlands to Kayes, just over 100km to the east. Both tracks may prove impassable in the wet season.

NIOKOLO-KOBA AND THE SOUTHEAST

Senegal's number one **National Park** and the flag-bearer for the country's conservation policies, **Niokolo-Koba** covers 8000 square kilometres – a little smaller than the area of The Gambia – of savannah, forest and swamp. It's an undulating wilderness, straddling the Gambia River and two major tributaries in the gentle uplands of **Sénégal Oriental**.

Niokolo-Koba is open only during the **December to June** dry season (exact dates fixed according to the weather), when animals gather along the water courses, and if you check in the right places – detailed in the text and on the map – you've a chance of seeing most of the larger species. For the rest of the year tracks are cut by rising water and large areas flooded.

Aside from the park, which is visited by around 5000 people a year, **southeast Senegal** is on the whole little affected by tourism. You'll find strongly traditional ways enduring, although hunting as a livelihood took a severe blow when the park opened, displacing a large, scattered population of Mandinka, Bassari and Fula. Tourist excursions to **Bassari country**, beyond the park, have been running in a small way from Tambacounda for some years, but to reap the high rewards of this part of the country, you must be prepared to hike or make your own informal arrangements in Kédougou.

Tambacounda

Getting to Niokolo-Koba can be difficult, feasible without your own transport only if you're prepared to put in considerable time waiting for a ride, probably at **TAMBACOUNDA**, 80km from the park entrance. The town is eastern Senegal's major transport hub, the big station on the Dakar–Bamako railway after Kayes in Mali. Situated in the flat, dreary scrub, a rough 180km from the Malian border and 460km from Dakar, the town has little of interest to detain you, but if you're using public transport you will almost inevitably have to spend time here.

Practicalities

The centre of Tamba is bunched around the station, where **trains** from Bamako arrive around 7am on Thursdays and Sundays, and those from Dakar around 7pm the same days. Trains are usually packed by this stage, whichever way you're going, so don't expect a seat or bearable toilets. Being friendly with the station master is a good idea. In theory, there are fourteen seats reserved for passengers embarking in Tamba.

For **accommodation** you've a limited choice, all a kilometre or so down the main street, Avenue Leopold Senghor, which runs south of the tracks. The *Hôtel Niji* (☎81 12 50; Fax 81 17 44; ③) is first left after the *Elf* and offers an adequate selection of fanned, AC and S/C options, as well as organizing *soirées folkloriques* (CFA50,000, minimum 5 people) and piroguing along the Gambia River (same price); the very comfortable *Asta Kebé* (☎81 10 28; Fax 81 12 15; ⑤), signed another 500m down the road, gives you the works, including a pool; and the charmingly off-the-wall and unmarked *Chez Dessert* (②–③), behind the wicker fence opposite the *Asta Kebé* sign, has bed or floor space and even meals with advance notice – all assuming that the *Niji*'s furious owner hasn't succeeded in having the joint shut down yet.

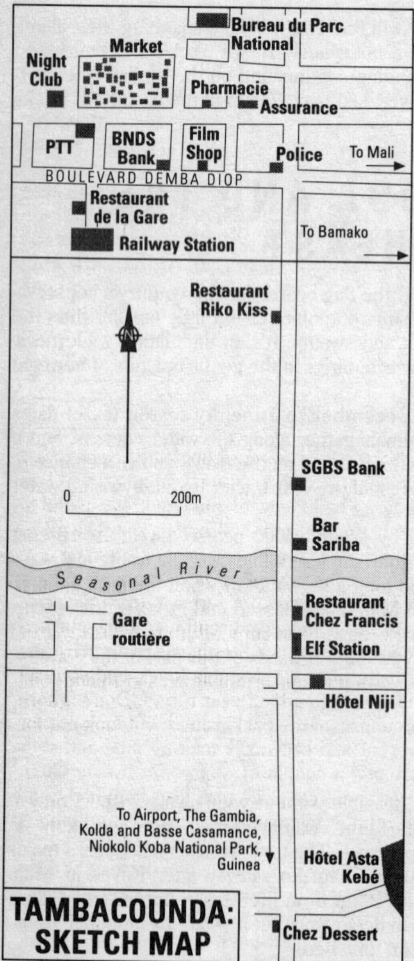

TAMBACOUNDA: SKETCH MAP

You can **eat** cheaply at *Chez Francis* (allegedly 24hr), just north of the *Elf* station, or at the marginally more pleasant – at least when the TV isn't on – terrace at the back of *Restaurant Riko Kiss* (daily 8am–11pm) up the road on the left, just south of the tracks. The *Niji* does a *ménu* for CFA4000 – at the *Asta Kebé* you'll pay CFA4000 just for a *plat*. If you just want a drink, check out the *Bar Sariba*, the usual bare walls and a coloured light bulb, just north of the creek bed.

If you're heading for the park, stock up on **supplies** in Tamba, as there's really nothing but a handful of restaurants in the park itself. The *SGBS* **bank**, av Senghor (Mon–Fri 8.15–11.30am & 3.15–5.15pm) might just be able to cough up a *Visa* or *Mastercard* cash advance. There's a couple of well-stocked *épiceries* along av Senghor and another shop selling film on bd Demba Diop, near the station. The *BNDS* bank, **PTT**, **pharmacy** and a market are also grouped here, and the **national park office** (Mon–Fri 7.30am–4pm) just a little further behind, with park **maps** for CFA1500. You can buy park entry permits here in advance at the same price as on the gate (CFA2000 per person per day, plus CFA5000 per car per day).

Moving on from Tamba, the **train** (book ahead) takes 20 hours to Bamako or 13 hours to Dakar, the latter journey quicker and cheaper **by road.** The *gare routière* whence you can get daily Peugeot 504s and minibuses to Dakar, is located in the town's southeastern corner. There is also a daily bus to Dakar from opposite the train station on bd Demba Diop. For Zinguinchor details see the section "To Guinea-Bissau and the Casamance", below.

Into the park from Tambacounda

The one-day **organized excursions** from the *Asta Kebé* are too brief to be worthwhile. Cost is the main drawback of their other deals: a two-day safari costs CFA35,000 each for a minimum group of ten, or a day's chauffered 4WD for CFA50,000 plus fuel and entrance fees, although the *Niji* offers less expensive day trips at CFA70,000 between six people.

Alternatively, you can always find a **taxi** driver who's willing to spend the day – possibly even longer – driving you round. The advantage is the price – negotiable down to realistic levels of CFA20,000 per day, plus expenses. But be sure the driver knows what he's about, that the vehicle is sound and has spares, and that you pay for fuel separately, otherwise your game-viewing is going to be limited indeed. Four people simply sharing a taxi from Tamba down to Simenti can expect to pay around CFA10,000 each.

One or two daily **taxis brousses** serve villages down the road to the park entrance at Dar Salam, but moving on from there can prove virtually impossible. Should you manage to get as far as the park headquarters at Simenti you'll find half-day game drives bookable at the hotel there. Finally, one option for a **free lift to the park** from Tamba is to make a CFA1500 investment for a day at the *Asta Kebé*'s swimming pool, where there's usually a contingent of tourists about to make their way there whom you could ask.

Parc National de Niokolo-Koba

Niokolo-Koba's tracks are mostly well maintained, and good signposting ensures you won't have much trouble getting around; the only area where you might need a 4WD is around Mont Assirik. **Where to go** is a matter of hunches and good luck. It's useful to have some French names: where they differ markedly from the English, they are given below. The park fee is CFA2000 per person.

Commonest large species include buffalos, hartebeeste (*bubale*; uniquely ugly with their long faces and hooked horns), shaggy Defassa waterbuck (*cobe defassa*), timid and fast-moving bushbuck (*antilope harnaché* or *guib*; beautifully white-marked on russet coat), warthogs (*phacochère*), of course, and crocodiles in the rivers. **Hippos** are sometimes visible from the authorized halts along the Gambia River, and you can see them in many areas where the water is deep enough all year round. Don't ignore the commoner species, which quickly become part of the background, but look out for the large, maned **roan antelope**, (*hippotrague*) and especially for the huge and very uncommon **western giant eland** which stands a couple of metres at the shoulder. Baboons and other monkeys, notably vervet and red patas, are also common. The park's **chimpanzees** are exceedingly rare, numbering around 150; they can be seen east of Assirik, the most northerly chimpanzee outpost in Africa.

Sighting **lions** is rare; with patience, though, you might see them in pockets of deep shade at the base of trees, or in hollows, especially around the confluence of tracks known as Patte d'Oie – "Crow's foot". **Elephants** are said to gather in a broad zone around Mont Assirik, and in the months before the rains (March–May) are often found

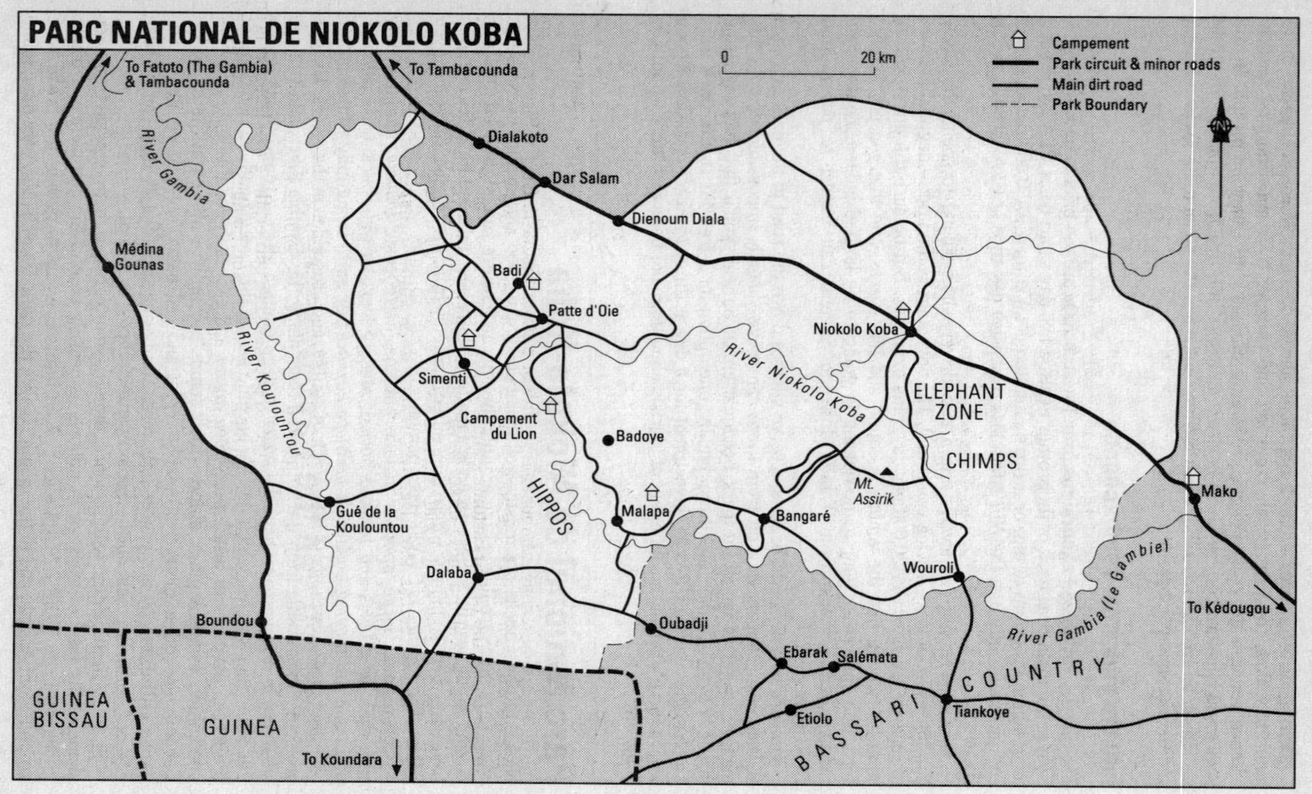
PARC NATIONAL DE NIOKOLO KOBA
To Fatoto (The Gambia) & Tambacounda
To Tambacounda
0
20 km
Campement
Park circuit & minor roads
Main dirt road
Park Boundary
Dialakoto
Dar Salam
Dienoum Diala
River Gambia
Médina Gounas
Badi
Patte d'Oie
Simenti
Campement du Lion
River Koulountou
Niokolo Koba
River Niokolo Koba
ELEPHANT ZONE
CHIMPS
Mt. Assirik
Badoye
HIPPOS
Malapa
Bangaré
Mako
Gué de la Kouloutou
Dalaba
Wouroli
To Kédougou
River Gambia (Le Gambie)
Boundou
Oubadji
Ebarak
Salémata
COUNTRY
BASSARI
Tiankoye
Etiolo
GUINEA BISSAU
GUINEA
To Koundara

in the south of this area – a drive between Bangaré ford and Worouli could be successful. **Leopards**, like lions, can range outside the park's confines and are probably Africa's most under-counted large predator; very rarely seen, they are most likely to be spotted high in a tree.

It's not a bad idea to **rent a guide** from Simenti, as they can often show you things you would never have found alone.

Practicalities

You enter Niokolo-Koba at Dar Salam, where there's a *campement*-style hotel (②). Note that driving isn't allowed after dark. Within the park, **accommodation** at the main centres of **Simenti** and **Niokolo-Koba** is expensive, the *campements* almost indistinguishable from hotels, with restaurants, fuel supplies and swimming pools (non-guests can pay a fee for a swim). *Simenti Hôtel* (③; meals CFA3500) has an excellent location above the Gambia River and a good game-viewing **hide**, while *Badi* (②), not far from Simenti in the western part of the park, has a much more basic set-up. For a prolonged stay, check out the *Campement du Lion* (②), one of the park's most tranquil spots, 8km east of Simenti. You can **camp** for free at Badi, Malapa and Bafoutabé.

To Guinea-Bissau and the Casamance from Tambacounda

Heading from Tamba by public transport for the full-day's ride to Ziguinchor (CFA4500) you want to be sure you catch a pre-8am minibus or you'll be waiting till noon. Few people slow down on their southwesterly way through the increasingly luxuriant **Haute** and **Moyenne Casamance**, and to be honest the small town of **Velingara** has little to offer other than a *campement*.

Accommodation in the regional centre of **KOLDA** is limited to the *Hotel Moya* (BP 14; ☎96 11 75; ③), a cosy nest of en suite chalets with huge beds, located by the riverside 400m south of the *gare routière* and *Elf* station. For **something to eat**, there's a cheaper alternative to the *Moya*'s restaurant: two blocks west of the hotel the *Restaurant Moussa Miop* serves a heap of *tiéboudienne* and a couple of bananas for under CFA600.

From Kolda a daily minibus takes a minor *piste* to Bafatá in Guinea-Bissau, a four-hour journey which includes border formalities – expect to have your baggage turned inside out by the Bissau customs – and a walk across a rickety bridge spanning the Rio Gêba. There's also a more direct bush taxi option to Bissau (via Farim) from Tanaf, 70km west of Kolda. At Tanaf you can also take a ferry from Sandenièr, 10km northwest of town, across the River Casamance to **Sedhiou** (*campement*) in the Haute Casamance region.

Kédougou and the Pays Bassari

Set in Senegal's verdant and rarely visited southeastern corner, the **Pays Bassari** is an area of low hills watered by the run-off from Fouta Djalon highlands to the south and the perennial Gambia River. This is the least known part of the country, ethnically diverse and very different from the Wolof-Franco Senegal to the north and west. Living in hill villages at the foot of the Fouta Djalon mountains, the ancient Bassari people have stood against the tide of Islam that over the centuries has swept around them on the plains. Matrilineal and divided into age groups, they traditionally subsist on farming and hunting (though some still pan for gold). Major initiation ceremonies are held every few years, and there's an annual **festival** before the rains in April or May, notably at the village of Etiolo, a few kilometres from the Guinean frontier.

KÉDOUGOU is the only major settlement, a bit of a dead-end to all but the very few pushing on to Guinea or Mali, or for those using it as an alternative base for exploring the Niokolo-Koba Park, though the road from Tambacounda is now all but tarmacked the whole way. The town has a post office, pharmacies and fuel as well as two **accommodation** options: *Le Relais* by the river at the west end of town (☎85 10 62; Fax 85 11 26; ④) is popular with tour groups and hunters (and offers several excursions); a better choice is *Chez Diao*'s *campement* (☎85 11 24; ②) 500m east of the *gare routière* in the town centre, with all the same services for half the price and a warm welcome for free. It's your best bet for **something to eat** too – you can safely give the overpriced and underportioned *plats* at *Chez Sory Diallo*'s (next to the *Elf*) a miss.

If you've just turned up from Mali or Guinea, get your passport stamped at the **police** post, 500m up the Tamba road just past the phone box.

Routes into Guinea and Mali

The main route from Tambacounda into **Guinea** parts from the Tambacounda–Ziguinchor road where it scrapes the Gambian border. From here the route goes via Medina-Gounas (a devout community of the Tijaniya brotherhood, where the women are veiled) to the Senegalese post at Boundou, whence an extremely rough *piste* leads 55km to Koundara on the Guinean side.

Getting transport via Niokolo-Koba into Guinea is fairly hit and miss. You should try hard in Tambacounda to find something going the whole way (keep an eye out for the all-terrain Russian lorries heading for Mali, a small town in northern Guinea, 120km south of Kédougou) rather than setting off on a series of bush taxi hops. The first of two possible minor routes passes 11km to the west of Kédougou, and heads up into the Fouta Djalon highlands, a ride you won't forget in a hurry and from which even experienced 4WD drivers have turned back. Another route, 11km east of Kédougou, winds for over 200km to the major town of **Labé**, right in the heart of the Fouta Djalon. You might be lucky with transport on the first route, which is also by far the most scenic. On the second, the Gambia River crossing in Guinea is particularly uncertain. Both are supposed to have Guinean entrance formalities on the border itself, but expect to have to check in again at Mali or Labé. In your own vehicle you might prefer the less arduous crossing to the Guinea town of Youkounkoun, 100km west of Kédougou.

From Kédougou, Land Rovers serve Saraya, 60km to the northeast, and occasionally continue another 70km along a maze of minor bush tracks to Kéniéba in the Republic of **Mali** (a rough half-day to two days' drive). This is not a regular route and is dependent on demand as well as the depth of the Falémé River which denotes the unmanned frontier – it's usually fordable from January until the rains come. Expect to pay CFA8000 each – if the car is full – for this unusual and rarely-used back route into Mali.

BASSE CASAMANCE

Despite its recent troubles (see opposite, top), **Basse Casamance** – the lower reaches of the Casamance River – is still the most seductive part of Senegal. Wonderfully tropical, with dense forest, winding creeks, rice fields and quiet back roads shaded by massive silk-cottons, the district seems to have little in common with the Senegal of Islamic brotherhoods, groundnuts, cattle and dust.

For centuries the mostly **Jola**-speaking population of Basse Casamance resisted the push of Islam (most successfully on the south bank of the river), while the Portuguese maintained a typically torpid presence. The ceding of the region to the French in 1886 didn't precipitate any great social shifts. Changes are under way, despite an isolation in which villages and language groups are cut off even from each other, but there's a

THE MFDC

In late 1992 the murder of three undercover policemen investigating *MFDC* (*Mouvement des Forces Démocratiques de la Casamance*) activities and the ensuing torching of the fishing village at **Cap Skiring** led to a swift escalation of hostilities which snuffed out tourism in Casamance for nearly two years, although tourists were not themselves a target. Today armoured cars are sited in strategic positions throughout the Casamance while the *MFDC*, hiding out in the swampy borderlands along the Bissau frontier, consider their next move. Although most places have got back to normal, the situation is still potentially explosive, especially around Cap Skiring and the **Basse Casamance National Park**. Early in 1995, four French tourists were kidnapped. Keep your ear to the ground and stay tuned to the travellers' grapevine.

resolve to maintain some degree of self-determination. Since independence, the **Casamance question** and the apparent threat to Wolof-speaking, French-abetted metropolitan Senegal, has been a prickly one. Casamance provides the bulk of the country's rice crop and, furthermore, without its full participation in national affairs, the issue of confederation with The Gambia – an even more troublesome thorn in Senegal's side – will never be resolved. Nevertheless, the region has many diversions for travellers. Allow a couple of weeks here if at all possible – it's likely to be a highlight.

Getting to and around Basse Casamance

There are three **main roads** to Basse Casamance: from **Banjul**; from **Dakar** on the faster *transgambienne* route; and from far-off **Tambacounda** in the east. If you're coming from Mali on the train, this third route makes a much better introduction to Senegal than an after-dark arrival in Dakar. Two, or maybe three, minibuses depart daily from Tambacounda for Ziguinchor, all leaving early; a late start will mean changing in **Kolda**, making a full day on the road.

Getting around Basse Casamance is generally simple. You can **rent bikes** in Ziguinchor, Oussouye, Cap Skiring and a number of other places, making cycling around the popular southern part of Basse Casamance a practical option. Unless you have lots of time, it's perhaps best to rent in Oussouye or Cap Skiring, rather than Ziguinchor, as you'll probably spend your first day cycling straight to Oussouye

BASSE CASAMANCE CAMPEMENTS

While Basse Casamance still gets thousands of French **holiday-makers** flying in for winter sun on the Cap Skiring beaches, there's more off-beat appeal in the network of **campements touristiques rurals integrés** and similar private set-ups. **Ziguinchor** is a natural base for visiting the *campements*, many of which are attractions in themselves, set in wonderful locations and of great architectural interest. All ten of the Casamançais *CTRIs* charge the same low rates (bed CFA2300; breakfast CFA900; meal CFA2200) and are bookable in Ziguinchor. Rates and facilities are at least as good, if not better at the twenty or so **privately run** *campements* in the Casamance region, but the dearth of even the more adventurous independent tourists in the last couple of years has left many virtually deserted. Note, however, that without your own transport, getting to some *campements* requires patience. It's more than 100km from Ziguinchor to the furthest *CTRI* in the Casamance network – at Sitokoto, near Kafountine.

Advance booking is highly recommended in high season; contact Coordinateur régional, Centre Artisanal, Ziguinchor (BP 567; ☎91 13 74).

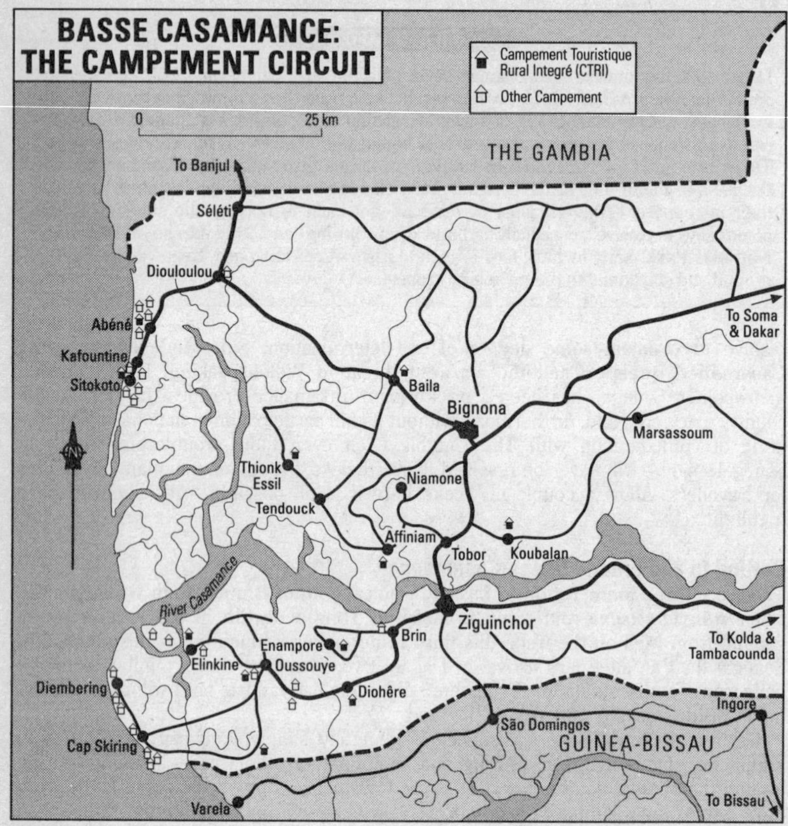

anyway, and it's not the most exciting bike ride in the area. Ziguinchor is the main transport hub with daily transport to most sites of interest.

Because Basse Casamance is so affected by tides, no two **maps** of it ever look the same: much of what appears to be virtually underwater on some maps is actually firm ground most of the time.

Ziguinchor

Something of **ZIGUINCHOR**'s appeal comes through in its exotic name, pronounced "Sigichor" by most Jola. There's a luxuriant sense of repose here, found in no other Senegalese town of its size and life here is a good deal cheaper than in Dakar or The Gambia. Surprisingly, you need reminding that Ziguinchor is on the river: its colonial trading houses don't stand out, and the river port isn't likely to figure prominently in your meanderings. It's a town of trees and avenues, roosting birds, orchestral crickets and fluttering bats at dusk, with a strong flavour of the Guineas. Less pleasant is the attention lavished by local mosquitoes from March to October – and sporadically by highly persistent hustlers, vendors and hangers-on.

THE JOLA

The people of Basse Casamance are predominantly **Jola** (or Diola; no relation to the Diola/Dyula of Côte d'Ivoire) – broadly divided by the river into Buluf and Fonyi on the north bank and Huluf (or Fulup) on the south. From around the sixteenth century they gradually displaced earlier Casamance inhabitants called the Banyun, who used to be great traders and still live among them. Where the Jola came from nobody seems to know, but their dialects are closely related to the Manjak spoken in Guinea-Bissau, and indeed the Jola generally claim to come from the south. They never developed a unified state, and their fragmentation has resulted in some **Jola dialects** being mutually unintelligible. In fact the idea of a Jola "tribe" is mostly a colonial one: only contact with outsiders has given the term any meaning for the people themselves. The word is supposed to derive from the Manding *jor la* – "he who avenges himself".

A distinctive style of **wet rice farming** has been practised for at least 600 years in the reclaimed land between the creeks. **Dikes** are built around new fields so that the rains will flood them and leach out the sea salt, which runs away through hollow tree trunks in the dikes while the fields lie fallow. Once the field is flooded, the drains are blocked and the rice plants brought out from the nurseries and planted, one by one, in the mud. After three or four months of weeding and dike care by the men, the women gather the **harvest** in November or December. For the first half of the year, though, there's little work in the rice fields and increasingly this is a time when young people drift away to Ziguinchor, The Gambia or Dakar. Many don't return for the next season. Later in the year, you'll see villagers walking to the fields early in the morning with the amazingly long, iron-tipped hoes called **kayendos**.

Traditionally, rice was never sold. Having huge numbers of granaries full of it, often for years, brought the kind of **prestige** every Jola man wanted. Consequently, conflicts over **land rights** have always been close to the surface and still occasionally erupt, as in 1976, when troops were sent in to crush a "rice war" that was being settled with guns and machetes in Affiniam and Diatok, across the river from Ziguinchor.

Islam has made little headway among the Jola, but an erosion of traditional values has been brought about by **groundnuts**. Introduced to the region in the early nineteenth century, the crop provided a commercial alternative to rice that could earn ready money, with relatively little labour, on land that had hitherto been unplanted bush. Now grown on raised ground all over the region, the groundnut crop has resulted in deforestation, soil degradation and reliance on imported food. "He who wears a *boubou* can't work in the rice fields" goes the Jola saying, ironically excusing the way things increasingly are in terms of Islam's stress on the individual.

JOLA WORDLIST

Jola is a diverse language, comprising several dialects: the following words and phrases could be helpful in Basse Casamance, but may not all provoke immediate recognition.

Gasumai?	Hello, welcome
Gasumaikep	universal response to *Gasumai?*
Yo	Yes
Eilat/Hani	No
Safi	Bonjour, hello
Oukatora	Goodbye
Karessy bou?	What is your name?
Karessom…	My name is…
Sabari	Please
Al Barka	Thank you
Ça gasse?	How is it? Ça va?
Iman jut	I don't understand
Ounomono	Sell me
Soumsoum	This is good
Diacoutte	This is not good
Katr-me	-Stop
Emano	Rice
Niankatang	Rice cooked in palm oil
Siwolassou	Fish
Bunuk	Palm wine
Bulago bara ...?	Which way to ...?
Boussana	*Pirogue*
Sibeurassou	Trees
Karambacou	Forest
Falafou	River

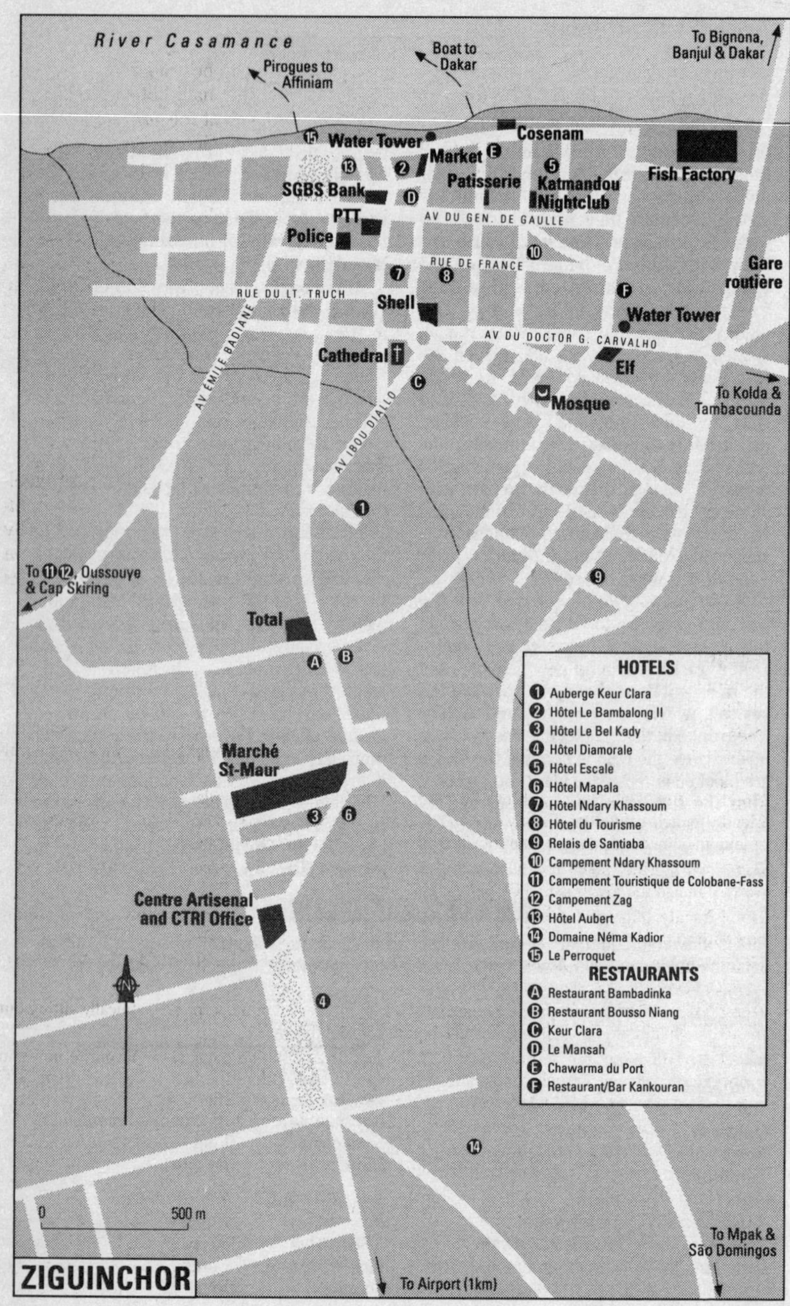
River Casamance
Pirogues to Affiniam
Boat to Dakar
To Bignona, Banjul & Dakar
Water Tower
Cosenam
Market
Patisserie
Katmandou Nightclub
Fish Factory
SGBS Bank
PTT
Police
AV DU GEN. DE GAULLE
RUE DE FRANCE
RUE DU LT. TRUCH
Gare routière
Shell
Water Tower
AV DU DOCTOR G. CARVALHO
Cathedral
Elf
Mosque
To Kolda & Tambacounda
AV EMILE BADIANE
AV IBOU DIALLO
To 11 12, Oussouye & Cap Skiring
Total
Marché St-Maur
Centre Artisenal and CTRI Office
0
500 m
ZIGUINCHOR
To Airport (1km)
To Mpak & São Domingos
HOTELS
1 Auberge Keur Clara
2 Hôtel Le Bambalong II
3 Hôtel Le Bel Kady
4 Hôtel Diamorale
5 Hôtel Escale
6 Hôtel Mapala
7 Hôtel Ndary Khassoum
8 Hôtel du Tourisme
9 Relais de Santiaba
10 Campement Ndary Khassoum
11 Campement Touristique de Colobane-Fass
12 Campement Zag
13 Hôtel Aubert
14 Domaine Néma Kadior
15 Le Perroquet
RESTAURANTS
A Restaurant Bambadinka
B Restaurant Bousso Niang
C Keur Clara
D Le Mansah
E Chawarma du Port
F Restaurant/Bar Kankouran

Arrival and orientation

Coming into Ziguinchor **up the river** on the MV *Joola* is the best approach; the ship deposits you at the heart of the town, a few minutes from the main hotels. Arriving **by road** from the north or from Tambacounda, you'll be dropped at the *gare routière*, 1km east of town, just south of the bridge. If you've come up from Guinea-Bissau, you may be dropped off on the new, wide, sealed road, just east of the Marché St-Maur and close to a few cheap accommodation options.

The old part of town is a comprehensible one-by-half-a-kilometre grid of streets extending south of the river to **Avenue du Docteur Gabriel** on which is situated the **Rond Point** (roundabout). Within this area you'll find the banks, post office, main hotels and other services as well as the small portside market, good for fresh fruit, vegetables and early morning fish. South of the Rond Point, Avenue Ibou Diallo leads past the cathedral a kilometre or two to the more animated quarter of town around the **Marché St-Maur**. If you arrive by air you're a kilometre further south on the same road.

Accommodation

Being close to the heart of Senegal's main holiday region, Ziguinchor offers an excellent and inexpensive range of **accommodation** – basic, central rooms, *campement*-style set-ups, and a few plusher alternatives. This latter category has suffered badly from the recent drop in tourist numbers, though the better establishments have remained popular – always a good sign. In the following listings, numbers in brackets denote positions on the map.

Budget lodgings and mid-range hotels

Auberge Keur Clara, off av Ibou Diallo. Set in a quiet side-street with a great restaurant/bar upstairs (a weekly jazz venue) and basic singles or S/C twins. ②–③.

Hôtel Le Bambalong II (☎91 14 75; Fax 91 11 46). Surprisingly good value S/C, AC rooms but lacking much ambience. Home of the *Bar Americaine* and, on a good night, the town's best nightclub (free to guests). ③.

Hôtel Le Bel Kady, just south of Marché St Maur (☎91 11 22). Popular budget option run by a friendly bunch of youths. Faintly bordello-ish with non-S/C rooms (some with AC) and dubious ablutions but a good-value restaurant. Also offers inexpensive *pirogue* trips. ②.

Hôtel Diamorale, 300m south of the *Centre Artisanal*. Friendly welcome but ultra-basic cells, worth it only if the *Relais* is full. Cheap food too. ①.

Hôtel Escale, off av du Général du Gaulle (☎91 12 04). On its last legs and possibly closed down by now with a couple of cells *de passage* and less austere S/C, AC options. ②–③.

Hôtel Mapala, opposite *Le Bel Kady*. Newly converted two-storey hotel with decent fanned S/C doubles plus a cheap restaurant and bar. ③.

Hôtel Ndary Khassoum, rue de France (☎91 14 72). Deserted and overpriced; stoically sitting out the tourist slump. Rooms with a slight touch of decor, but dingy. ④.

Hôtel du Tourisme, rue de France (☎91 22 23; Fax 91 22 22). Old colonial-era favourite now run by a dedicated young French couple and their tuned-in staff. Offers the best value mid-range S/C rooms in town, an excellent restaurant and a level of service rare elsewhere. ③.

Relais de Santiaba, quartier Santiaba (☎91 11 99). The town's best value *chambres de passage* up on the roof; plain but not rough, with decent, shared ablutions and breakfast included. Also some S/C rooms, a bar/restaurant and mountain bike rental. ①–③.

Campements

Campement Ndary Khassoum, rue de France (☎91 11 89). Centrally located, a bit rough round the edges but with a shady courtyard and large plain rooms, with huge bathrooms but shared toilets (fully S/C options available). *Pirogue* excursions and notably cheap beers too. ②.

RIVER TRIPS AND RIVER CROSSINGS

You can take a *pirogue* to the **Ile aux Oiseaux**, across the river to **Dilapao** and continue up the serpentine Marigot de Bignona to **Affiniam**. At Dilapao you'll see two-storey mud brick houses and can taste palm wine, while Affiniam's large **case à impluvium** is one of the oldest and nicest *campements* in the *rural integré* circuit. Just about every hotel offers this popular day trip; prices start around CFA10,000 for a motor *pirogue* to yourself, supposedly less per person with a group, but can vary wildly from place to place. Ask around at the cheaper *campements* or hotels.

For **less touristy** travels, there's a cheap, regular *pirogue* service to Affiniam, leaving on Mon, Wed and Fri at 9.30am from the jetty by the *Perroquet*; it returns from Affiniam at around noon. At other times you can try to reach an agreement with the *piroguiers* on the waterfront. This is a good way of starting a tour round the north bank region of **Buluf**, as an alternative to taxi-ing straight out of Ziguinchor.

Campement Touristique de Colobane-Fass, signed 2.5km down the Oussouye road (☎91 12 68). Standard prices for a bed or FB but poorly located and in need of a few guests. ①–②.

Campement Zag, signed 3km down the Oussouye road (☎91 15 57). Similar to the *Colobane-Fass* but a little less dingy; also adds CFA400 to the price in tax. An inexpensive option if you have your own transport. "Standard" *pirogue* excursion offered for around CFA7000. ①.

Luxury hotels

Hôtel Aubert, off av de Boucotte (☎91 13 79; Fax 91 10 15). The only luxury hotel to successfully survive the tourism crash of 1993, and deservedly so. Immaculate rooms with all mod cons and the only pool in town. ⑤.

Domaine Néma Kadior, 3km south of town on the airport road (☎91 18 24; Fax 91 10 55). Possibly re-opened following a shutdown during the troubles; a luxury hotel-reserve in its own landscaped grounds and popular with tour groups. ⑤.

Le Perroquet, rue de Commerce (☎91 23 29). Riverside French-run establishment very popular with jet-setters. Doesn't claim to be a hotel but offers neat, small S/C, AC rooms around a garden and a bar/restaurant with a great view from which to regard your bobbing yacht. ④.

The Town

There's not a great deal to keep you in Ziguinchor, but just hanging out is pleasure enough. In the old quarter of the town centre, there's a string of public gardens, heavily shaded, with park benches and – sign of a non-Islamic region – rootling piglets. Pelicans and storks congregate in the trees, however, making this a sometimes noisy and unpredictable place to relax.

Both **markets** – the **artisanal** and the **St-Maur-des-Fossés** (named after the southeast Paris suburb with which Ziguinchor is twinned) – are relatively hassle-free and well worth visiting. The municipal St-Maur, divided into merchandise zones, heaves with activity, while the *artisanal*, where the stall holders really are working at their crafts, is a relaxing place to get all your souvenirs in one go and offers real bargains for hardened hagglers. The *CTRI* office is here too, where you can make *campement* reservations (☎91 13 74; especially recommended in the high season).

For cooling-off, try the *Hôtel Aubert*'s **swimming pool** and busy terrace – non-guests are allowed in for a fee, unless it's very busy or they don't like your appearance.

Eating

With a few exceptions noted below, **food** in Ziguinchor is unremarkable. Street food is generally limited to fruit and nuts (cashews make a pleasingly inexpensive treat) or portside bread and coffee stalls. You'll find numerous nondescript restaurants, offering a low-priced daily *plat*, on the way to Marché St-Maur along av Lycée Guignabo, south of the *Total* station/taxi park; there's more sophisticated eating in town, especially at the hotels. For sweet neo-cream **pastries** check out the *patisserie* on av du Général de Gaulle, and for ice creams, head for *Fast Food Mamy,* just south of the Rond Point.

Restaurant Bambadinka, south of the *Total*, opposite the *Bousso* side street. A marginally better bet than the *Bousso Niang* for a decent feed.

Hôtel Le Bel Kady, one block south of the Marché St-Maur. Ziguinchor's best place for an inexpensive meal, offering a fair selection for under CFA1250 as well as drinks and beers.

Restaurant Bousso Niang, down a side road just southeast of the *Total* station. No table cloths, napkins or drinks other than water, just dirt-cheap heapfuls of staple-based stodge that you couldn't finish if you tried, although their interpretation of *viande* errs towards offaldom.

Chawarma du Port, down by the port. Wonderful Lebanaese snacks for CFA750 or less. Daily 7am–10pm.

Hôtel de Tourisme, rue de France. Charming restaurant offering excellent Franco-Senegalese three-course menus and pricier *à la carte* options.

Restaurant/Bar Kankouran, on the east side of town. A drab interior, but serves oriental dishes, with a Vietnamese accent on Fri and Sat. Full meals cost around CFA3000. Daily 11.30am–2.30pm & 7.30–10.30pm.

Keur Clara, 100m south of the Rond Point. Looks good from outside but dingy within. The unusual *crevettes riz* are worth it though.

Le Mansah, rue de Capitaine Javelier. Right in the town centre and well worth a visit for great value three-course meals. Check out the huge carved masks up on the walls too – they're the real thing.

Le Perroquet, rue de Commerce. Franco-Senegalese meals for around CFA5000. Great location, but bring some mosquito spray.

Nightlife

After dark, Ziguinchor smoulders. *Le Bombolong* and *Katmandou* have been *the* places to visit for a number of years, both repaying the entrance fee with hot music – lots of *zouk* – and as many chance encounters as you want. *Le Bombolong* scores highly with the French community, as well as passing *toubabs*, while *Katmandou* has a greater head of steam and a largely local crowd: the patio behind is a vital cooling-off area. Expect the drinks at *Le Bombolong II* to be marginally pricier than those at *Katmandou*.

Listings

Banks There are five banks in town but the *CBAO* (Mon–Fri 7.30–noon & 1.15–2.30pm) and the *SGBS* (Mon–Thurs 8–11.15am & 2.30–4.30pm, Fri 8–11am & 3.15–5pm) are your best bets for foreign exchange. The latter provides *Visa* or *Mastercard* cash advances (with ID) on the spot. Avoid *SGBS*, who charge 20 percent commission on traveller's cheques.

Bicycles One-speed bikes available for **rent** from the *Hôtel du Tourisme* and *Relais de Santiaba* for CFA2500 a day. The *Relais* also has some bearable – providing they've changed the unpadded saddles – 12-speed MTBs (*VTT*s), and at least one lightweight 21-speed jewel; these are the bikes for getting out to the countryside *campements*. Try to arrange a weekly rate. Blue Peugeots with mudguards, dynamo lighting, sprung saddles, a rack and a sidestand are **for sale** at several locations.

Car Rental *La Pirogue* in Cap Skiring (☎ 93 51 76; Fax 91 13 76) seems to be the only outfit in the region renting cars. Mini-Moke-like Citroen Meharis make very economical run-abouts from around CFA20,000 a day (unlimited milaege) and they'll provide you with a chauffeur virtually for free.

Doctor Dr Simon Tendang (consultations Mon–Fri 8am–2pm & 4.30–6pm; CFA4500 charge; ☎91 13 85, emergency ☎91 17 75); a minute north of the Rond Point opposite the *Sonatel* on rue de Capt Javelier.

Police ☎17.

MOVING ON FROM ZIGUINCHOR

There's a daily **Air Sénégal** (☎91 10 81) flight to Dakar (Mon–Wed 9.45am, Thurs & Sat 9.30am, Fri 10.45am, Sun 5pm; CFA24,000), and flights to Bissau (Mon & Fri 9.30am; CFA20,000).

You can get on a **boat** from Ziguinchor **to Dakar**: the *Joola* leaves promptly on Thurs and Sun at 1pm for the seventeen-hour voyage. Prices range from CFA9000 for a comfy seat to CFA22,500 for a cabin to yourself. Meals cost around CFA4500. Book tickets at the *COSENAM* office, on rue de Commerce in the port area (☎91 22 01).

For **Guinea-Bissau**, the Senegalese border post is at Mpak (18km); the Guinea-Bissau post is at São Domingos (25km). Plan for an early start from the *gare routière*. You can get Guinea-Bissau **visas** from the consulate, next to *Hôtel du Tourisme* (Mon–Fri 8/9am–noon & 2/4–6pm; ☎91 10 46). Three-month multiple entry visas are delivered in 24hr; photographs cost CFA5000. Due to strained relations between Senegal and Guinea-Bissau visas are sometimes unobtainable, and the *sûreté* in Ziguinchor may refuse to extend Senegalese visas.

Local transport for destinations in rural Casamance includes: a daily or twice daily bus to Enampore (large green vehicle leaving early morning and sometimes also 3pm; 90 mins); a daily afternoon bus to Mlomp and Elinkine; and frequent transport to Oussouye and Cap Skiring.

Northern Basse Casamance

Coming over **the border from the Gambia** at Séléti is a straightforward business – many tourists visiting The Gambia take the plunge into Casamance for a few days and are rewarded by a more leisurely pace of life, reasonable transport, and some idyllic and inexpensive lodgings.

It's a short taxi ride from Séléti to **DIOULOULOU**, the first Senegalese town, where you swop vehicles to head for the as yet unspoilt resorts of Abéné and Kafountine. Diouloulou has a good *campement* in the shape of *Relais Myriam* (②), a short way north of the main roundabout on the Gambia road, with helpful management.

The potholed N5 continues southeast across the tidal mudflats to Ziguinchor 80km away, passing through the underwhelming regional centre of **BIGNONA**, a two-kilometre string of roadside stalls at which point the N5 joins the *transgambienne* N4. In this area various tracks lead southwest into the often overlooked **Buluf** district of the northern Basse Casamance, served by a couple of *CTRI*s. Still less visited is the **Yassine** region to the east, sandwiched between the Soungrougrou and Casamance rivers.

The coast: Abéné and Kafountine

Southwest of Diouloulou a road heads seaward to unbroken beaches running down to the spit of the **Presque Ile aux Oiseaux** at which point the coastline breaks up into mangrove inlets and the mouth of the Casamance. The sealed road passes a turn-off to the village of Abéné (18km) and ends at the small town of Kafountine (24km) where a track continues to nowhere in particular. Waiting at the roundabout in Diouloulou for transport may take an hour or two, less in the high season.

From the main road a sandy track leads 2km to **ABÉNÉ**, hard work on a bike but passable in a car. The sandy-laned village is 1km from the sea and has a charmingly isolated and relaxed feel as well as a number of places to stay. In the village are two **campements**: *La Belle Danielle* (②) down a side track and the *Bantan Waro* (②) on the main road. Both are similar, offering inexpensive restaurants, excursions and bike rental; the *Belle Danielle*'s tap-operated showers and pleasant garden gives it the edge even though it's a little further to the beach. Continuing to the sea the track leads left to the *Samaba CTRI* (②) while a right turn ends at the delightful *Le Kossey*, a superior, dunebound *campement* offering S/C huts set in a lovely garden with HB or FB options (③). This is the place to head if you're looking for beachside seclusion rather than company. There are a few places to eat in the village, but most people take full board at the *campements*. Up the coast, 2km from Abéné village, the altogether different *Hôtel Village Kalissai* (⑤), run by the *Aubert* in Ziguinchor, is beautifully sited right by the beach with a landscaped mangrove creek. Even at the price, this beats much of what's on offer in the fast lane at Cap Skiring, but it's not exactly *integré*.

Continuing south down the sealed road another 6km brings you to the small fishing village of **KAFOUNTINE**, served by daily buses to and from Ziguinchor via Diouloulou. More animated than sleepy Abéné, Kafountine has a market, shops, a car rental outfit and a couple of **restaurants**: the *Africa* and opposite *Chez Mama Kendo*, both offer inexpensive and wholesome Senegalese dishes using local fish.

All **accommodation** is at least 1km south of town. On the inland side you'll see the new *Campement Africa*, with shared toilets and the rest *en suite* (HB minimum; ②); as yet this place lacks a lived-in feel. Right opposite is a turning to the *Sitokoto CTRI* (②) which, despite its beachside location, lacks the charm of Abéné's *campements*. A very pleasant, privately run *campement* is *Kunja*, which offers simple, comfortably furnished rooms (②) and good home cooking. The larger, long-established *Campement Filao* (②), set in a grove of casuarinas a couple of kilometres further south, offers a large restaurant/bar and good value S/C huts as well as beachside access and the usual excursions. Also recommended is the English-run

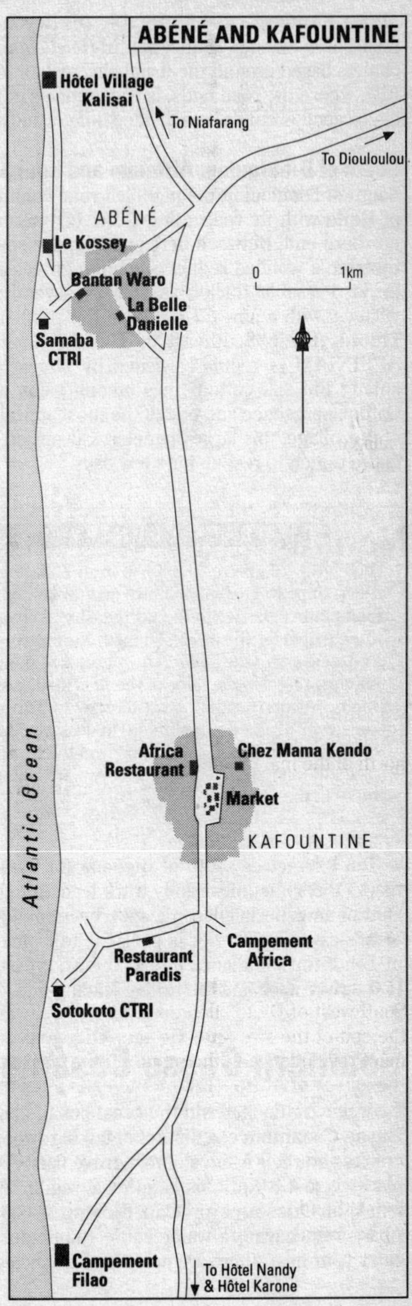

Mama Karamba (☎94 55 28; ①– ②). Beyond here are two new developments as the resort area extends further south: *Hotel Nandy* (③) is a selection of scattered upmarket chalets based around the usual bar/restaurant, and *Hôtel Karone* (BP 85; ☎94 55 25; ⑤ FB), where the road ends, is Kafountine's most luxurious *campement:* secluded huts in landscaped grounds, beachside *paillotes* and a plush restaurant/bar.

South of Diouloulou: Affiniam and Koubalan

South of Diouloulou the potholed road continues across a *marigot* or two to the village of **Baila** with its welcoming *CTRI* (②) set in a grove of mango trees at the village's northern end. Between here and Bignona several tracks lead southwest into the **Buluf district**, a wooded region of mango groves as well as orange and palm trees and rice fields. Passable tracks, as well as several minor, cycleable routes, lead to all the villages, with a new *CTRI* (②) at the southern end of the unremarkable settlement of **Thionk Essil**. Southeast of Thionk, along a rough track, the peaceful village of **AFFINIAM** is regularly visited by *pirogue* excursions from Ziguinchor. Spread out among the silk cotton trees among webs of sandy tracks, the village has a strong Catholic presence and one of the most appealling *CTRI*s in the network. Situated south of the village, this large-diameter, galvanized *case à impluvium* is one of the best spots in the region to rest up for a few days.

A BACK-COUNTRY CYCLE TRIP TO AFFINIAM

The eighty-kilometre round trip from Ziguinchor to Affiniam is more feasible than it may at first appear. Our map shows an embankment damming a tidal creek and leading to a flood control barrier to the northeast of Affiniam. This is the continuation (unmarked on other maps) of the track (signed **Niamone** – a Banyun-speaking village, the regional predecessors to the Jola) 2km south of Bignona. Crossing the embankment on a bicycle, the gleaming white edifice of the tidal station shimmers in the haze like a Grecian palace. Don't consider heading back directly to **Tobor** on the N5 (signed Diagobel at the junction north of the embankment) unless you have a couple of hours to spare and a few "Gasumai – bulago bara à Tobor?" on the tip of your tongue. The route is a maze of sandy tracks linking small villages and you are bound to get disorientated, although it's fun if you're in the mood.

Ten kilometres south of Bignona (or 3km north of Tobor) on the N5, a large sign marks the sometimes sandy track leading to the *CTRI* at **KOUBALAN**. While not situated in an especially scenic spot, overlooking a cleared mangrove swamp, the *campement*'s cave-like interior is cool, the welcome warm and the food excellent (②). South of Tobor the woodlands end as the N5 crosses the dreary tidal expanse of Casamance to the river itself and the bridge leading into Ziguinchor.

Southern Basse Casamance

Between Ziguinchor and the coast lies the boxing-glove-shaped heart of the **southern Basse Casamance**: a district of tall hardwood forest and rice fields cut by three major creeks and their fringes of mangrove flats. As the longest distance between significant places is just 34km, this is an ideal region for **cycling**;. You can rent bikes, or mobylettes, at **Oussouye** or **Cap Skiring** if you haven't already done so in Ziguinchor. Apart from having a water bottle (minimum capacity 2 litres) and devising a way to carry your gear, there are no special practical problems in cycling around.

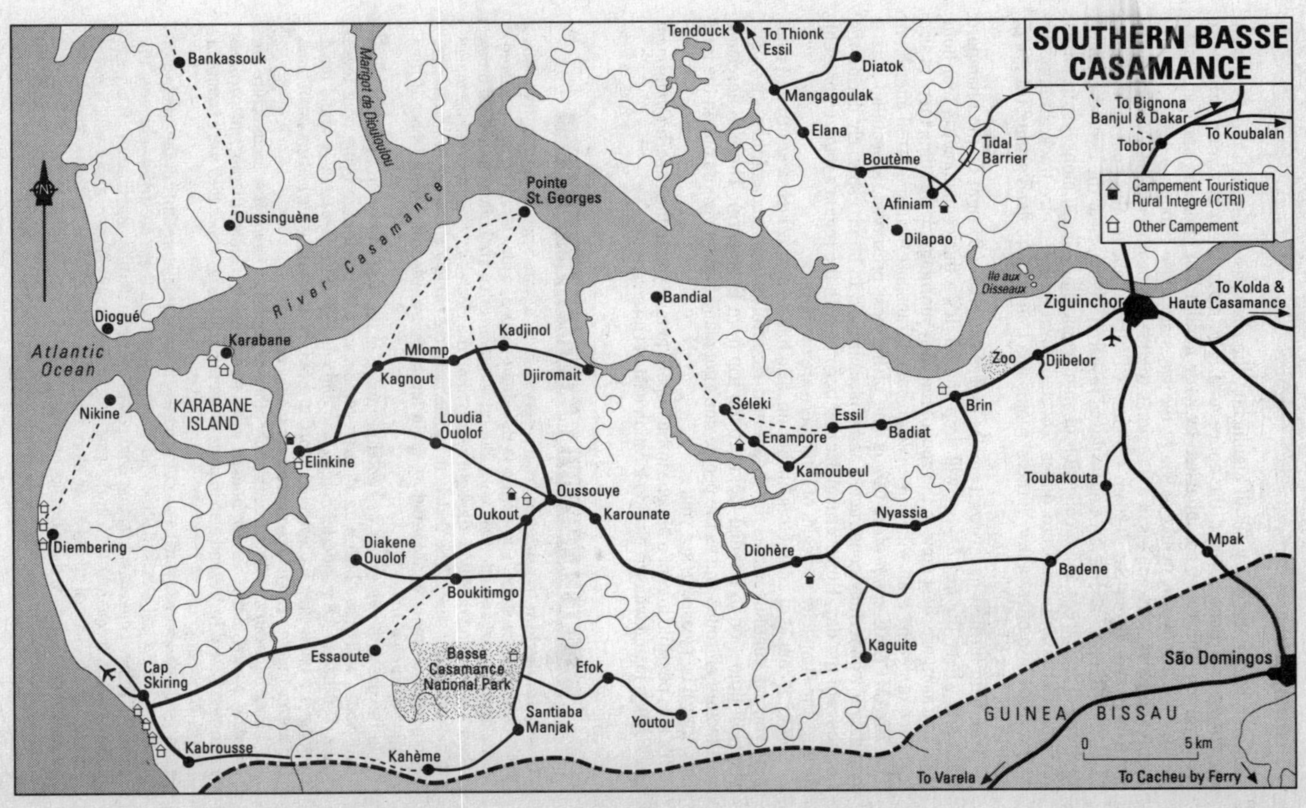
SOUTHERN BASSE CASAMANCE
Campement Touristique Rural Integré (CTRI)
Other Campement
Tendouck
To Thionk Essil
Diatok
Mangagoulak
Elana
Boutème
Tidal Barrier
Afiniam
Dilapao
To Bignona Banjul & Dakar
To Koubalan
Tobor
Ile aux Oiseaux
Ziguinchor
To Kolda & Haute Casamance
Bankassouk
Marigot de Diouloulou
Oussinguène
River Casamance
Pointe St. Georges
Bandial
Diogué
Atlantic Ocean
Karabane
KARABANE ISLAND
Nikine
Mlomp
Kadjinol
Kagnout
Djiromait
Loudia Ouolof
Elinkine
Séleki
Essil
Badiat
Enampore
Kamoubeul
Zoo
Djibelor
Brin
Oussouye
Oukout
Karounate
Toubakouta
Nyassia
Diembering
Diakene Ouolof
Boukitimgo
Diohère
Mpak
Badene
Essaoute
Basse Casamance National Park
Efok
Kaguite
São Domingos
Cap Skiring
Santiaba Manjak
Youtou
GUINEA BISSAU
0
5 km
Kabrousse
Kahème
To Varela
To Cacheu by Ferry
N

To Enampore

Climbing the gentle valley out of Ziguinchor, the road passes through the remains of the **forest** that once covered the entire area. The magnificent thirty- or forty-metre trees, strung with vines, are inhabited by large numbers of birds and small animals – though you'll only see monkeys where the trees are close enough together to form arboreal highways. Examples of the region's wildlife can be observed at the signposted **farm/orchard** (Mon–Sat 9.30am–6.30pm; CFA1000) about 4km out of town at **DJIBELOR**, opposite the *ISRA* agricultural research station. Near the river are several hectares of fruit trees and a collection of animals including lions, monkeys, tortoises, monitor lizards and dwarf crocodiles. Located down an 800-metre track through the forest, *ISRA* also offers a few workers' rooms in a tranquil woodland setting (AC, S/C; ☎91 12 05; Fax 91 12 93; ③).

Brin, 6km further, has its own small *Campement Filao* (①) right by the Enampore track and where the *taxi brousse* will drop you off. It's a thirteen-kilometre, four-hour walk to Enampore, best done in the cool of the early morning – at this time there is also a chance of getting a lift with some village-bound transport – passing Essil after 6km. The **ENAMPORE** *campement* (②) is one of the best preserved, a beautiful *case à impluvium* wonderfully constructed and a pleasure just to be in, especially during the hot hours of the day. However familiar you become with the region's *impluvium* architecture, the simplicity and calm of Enampore are memorable.

Séléki, a couple of kilometres further on, also has its own *campement* (①) and from here you can continue across the **dykes and rice fields** to Etama and then – if you've plenty of time – on to Bandial (15km round trip from Enampore). There's interesting architecture en route, and as the people don't get many foreign visitors out on the mud flats, they'll be pleased to see you.

It's also possible to rent a *pirogue* in Enampore to take you to the superb *Campement aux Bolongs* in an idyllic creek-side location east of Oussouye (③).

CASES À IMPLUVIUM AND FETISH SHRINES

Case à impluvium translates as "rain reservoir hut", a somewhat demeaning term that tells only half the story. The design is doughnut-shaped, with entrances into a shared, circular courtyard and internal doors into private rooms that are built as individual units. There's a stunning quality to the light reflected off the clean-swept courtyard floor to illuminate the living space. The thatched, saddleback roof circling above the living quarters is built like a funnel to allow rain to drain into a central reservoir, from where it runs outside through a drain.

In the past the *impluvium* was good insurance in times of war or drought, but since pure water wells have been dug all over, few *impluvium* houses are being built these days. Yet they make wonderful homes, and undoubtedly more Jola families would build new *cases à impluvium* if they could afford to – but the increasing nuclearization of families means that few can find the necessary money or labour.

Although it's often written that the only other examples of *impluvium* architecture are found in New Guinea, similar houses were traditional in Guinea-Bissau and parts of southwest Côte d'Ivoire, and also in parts of southern Nigeria, where they were square in plan.

In the bush around, you'll also come across isolated miniature huts in the briefest of clearings. Often just a forked stick under a thatched roof, these are **fetish shrines**, the earthly visiting rooms of spirits that hold power over rain, fertility and illnesses. They are consulted less frequently than in the past, but there are still matters about which many Jola feel the traditional spirits know more than modern science or medicine. You should be careful not to disturb them or take photos.

To Oussouye

From Brin, the road turns south, looping away from the river to cross the **Kamobeul Bolong** creek on a new bridge. Oussouye, the next major focus, is 34km from Ziguinchor, across scrub, open mangrove flats and more scrub – good for birds west of the bridge, otherwise unenthralling.

The rurally integrated *Campement Diohère* (②), signposted 14km from Brin, is rarely visited and so appears rather neglected. For mountain-bikers, the eastward route back to Ziguinchor from Diohère through farms and forest to the Ziguinchor–Guinea-Bissau road is idyllic, but you'll have to ask around to locate the right turn-off.

Another 10km down the main road to Oussouye you come to the **Case à Impluvium chez Theodore Balousa** (①), signposted left a little after a sign for "Niambalang"; go 800m along the track and it's just after the well. A *case à impluvium* built in 1980, it has a lived-in feel – although the interior is now decorated with locally made dolls and other souvenirs – and the family charge less than the going rate for the two rooms offered, although they'll need advance warning if you want a meal. Busy with children and scuttling chickens, the house itself is a lot livelier than Enampore's, for example, and it's well worth a passing look.

Just before Oussouye you'll pass the small village of Edioungou with a winding track leading to its *Campement de Bolong* (☎93 10 01; ②) offering creek-side views from its bar as well as the customary excursions. Another kilometre brings you to **OUSSOUYE**, sitting on the largest patch of dry land around. Once the seat of a line of Jola **priest-kings**, royalty is no longer much in evidence, but the town is still an important and growing place and has several times been on the frontline in *MFDC* skirmishes with the Senegalese army. Although the market here is pretty dull, there are one or two good shops, the usual colourful plasticware emporia, and an intriguing **wooden church** on the road out to Cap Skiring, a good example of Jola architectural innovation.

The road leading to the roundabout has a couple of inexpensive **restaurants** should you choose to turn down the full-board options of the town's *campements*. Check out the sprightly *Chez Mata – Restaurant 2000*; there may be an impressive chalkboard menu but you eat what's in the pot, always good value.

A track from the roundabout leads to a couple of **campements**, the first of which is the small and exceptionally friendly *Auberge de Routard* (①), run by Goula Diallo – his wife prepares great food and a vat of palm wine is passed around afterwards. Continuing another 600m up the track you may see men hanging beneath the crowns of the palm trees tapping the wine for the day. Oussouye's unusual two-storey mud- brick *CTRI* (②) is on the left, the biggest in the network and popular with tour groups. Day excursions into the Basse Casamance National Park are organized here (assuming the park is open), costing around CFA10,000 a day per person for a group of four or more.

Moving on from Oussouye, there's a daily minibus from Ziguinchor to Mlomp and Elinkine which passes through Oussouye around 4pm while Cap Skiring-bound vehicles pass through town every couple of hours. If you're biking into the surrounding countryside (notably the park), you might want to make use of the **bike rental** and repair shop in Oussouye right by the roundabout, close to the small market.

Mlomp and Pointe St-Georges

From Oussouye the road swoops through the forest to **MLOMP**, often crowded with tourists, come for the most part to see the pair of two-storey *banco* **cottages** with their amazing grove of silk-cotton trees. Two-storey buildings are uncommon in traditional African architecture, and nobody knows why Mlomp should have them: they're reminiscent of Ashanti houses from Ghana and it's possible that the earlier Banyun traders of Casamance brought the innovation back from their travels. The *patron* will show you round one of them, and a postcard from home is much appreciated: pictures of the Empire State Building, Windsor Castle and the Arc de Triomphe adorn the walls.

From the village a sandy footpath leads directly north to **Pointe St-Georges,** the Casamance River's last elbow before it reaches the sea. There's not much to the place – it's just a flat, densely wooded stretch of land, and the upmarket *Village-Hôtel* was burned down by the *MFDC* in 1992 – but the Pointe is reportedly getting its own *campement.* Access will remain a problem as the only driveable track (and 4WD at that) starts from the village of Kagnout, 5km west of Mlomp. A few kilometres east of Mlomp near the village of Djiromait, a huge tourist complex is being built. Involving the clearing and damming of mangrove creeks and set in an oddly beachless location, it is said the new resort will make Cap Skiring's *Club Med* look like a downmarket holiday camp.

Elinkine and Karabane Island

Beyond Kagnout, the turning to Pointe St-Georges, several stands of huge silk-cottons give way to monotonous, open country as a flat, straight route leads to the fishing village of **ELINKINE**, 10km from Mlomp. Little more than a tiny naval base and a collection of creek-side buildings, Elinkine makes an enjoyable stopover, with two great *campements,* both of which provide bike or canoe rental and *pirogue* excursions up and down the *bolongs.*

The more secluded accommodation is the *CTRI* (②) 700m to the right as you enter the village from the east. A spacious *campement* by a sandy beach, this place has been improved much in recent years, and has a tropical postcard view through the palms across the creek. Alternatively, the daily bus from Ziguinchor stops right outside the *Fromager* (②) in the town centre, a smaller and more animated *case à impluvium* with energetic hosts. Styling themselves as the village's *centre nautique,* they offer *pirogue* trips to Karabane, fishing, and so forth. A small **café** nearby provides budget food.

Karabane Island

At Elinkine the done thing is to take a trip to the history-laden island of **Karabane** in the river mouth. Expect to pay around CFA 7000 for a *pirogue* for a small group, for the thirty-minute voyage; you might also be able to negotiate a motorized boat to yourself. Karabane, or rather its headland, was an early offshore trading base with the interior, and the first French toehold in the Kasa Mansa – the kingdom of the Kasa, one of the ancestral Jola peoples. Slaves, ivory, gum and hides were exported from here, paid for with cloth, alcohol and iron bars. There's a large Breton-style church, partly in ruins, dating back to the earliest days of the Holy Ghost Fathers, and a number of crumbling merchant houses. The beach is beautiful, with 10km of salty River Casamance in front and coconuts behind, but in truth, on a short visit, the whole place can feel slack with isolation and irrelevance.

Staying the night, the trip becomes more worthwhile. Once everyone else has left and you can walk along the beach in peace, Karabane quickly becomes a place that's hard to leave. The *campements* of *Chez Amathe* (②) in the village or *Chez Badji,* owned by a painter(②), out towards the beach, are both preferable to the *Hôtel Karabane* (③), a dull mission money-earner.

Cap Skiring and around

Despite its status as Senegal's foremost holiday resort – with The Gambia and the coast of Côte d'Ivoire, one of the top three in West Africa – the straggling and undistinguished village of **CAP SKIRING** has little to recommend it: a minimal market, a few small shops, a couple of snack bars. There's a *Club Med* here, too, with high barbed wire and soldiers guarding its *plage privé*, discouraging anyone from roving outside the tourist reserve. The sands, however, are undeniably pretty – spectacular, even, along the more deserted stretches – and the sea is warm and safe. This is hedonistic territory and lacks much of deeper interest. Find a room, peel off your clothes and get down to the beach.

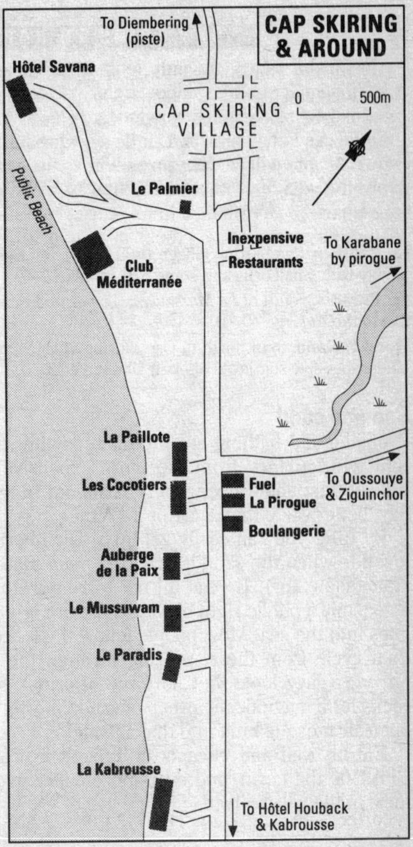

Orientation

Arriving from Oussouye at the T-junction, the village itself is to the north, *La Paillote* hotel is directly ahead and the cheaper accommodation opportunities are 1km to the south. Right on the junction is the recently reopened *La Pirogue* bar/restaurant, also offering the region's only **car rental** service (☎93 51 76). It was here in November 1992 that the three undercover policemen investigating separatist activities were murdered, starting off the conflict that killed off tourism here for nearly two years.

Accommodation

During the 1994/95 season the area was only just recovering from a disastrous two years of army–*MFDC* conflict, but **accommodation** options remain plentiful. You won't be faced with gleaming white high-rises, either; Cap Skiring's luxury hotels are modest constructions, while budget lodgings are low-key affairs, and variations to a greater or lesser extent on the *CTRI* theme.

Auberge de la Paix, just south of the T-junction (☎93 51 45). Offering the same great views and beach as its neighbours on either side for far less money. Good food and a choice of plain rooms or some with shower and basin *en suite*. ①–② .

Les Cocotiers, just south of *La Paillote* (☎93 51 51; Fax 93 51 17). Set in its own grounds and similar to *La Paillote* (of which it seems to be part) but offering better value in the mid-range. ⑤.

Hôtel Houback, 3km south of the T-junction between Kabrousse and Cap Skiring(☎93 51 36). Sub-*Savana* comforts popular with tour groups. ⑤.

La Kabrousse, 2km south of the T-junction (☎93 51 26). Plush hotel with cabins set in landscaped greenery, similar to *La Paillote*, and with a pool, giant chess and the beach just a stone's throw away. ⑥.

Le Mussuwam, next to *Auberge de la Paix* (☎93 51 84; Fax 93 51 25). Established *campement* owned by Ziguinchor's *Bel Kady* with a good range of AC, S/C rooms. Also has a small collection of captive wildlife, evening music sessions, bike rental and land and sea excursions. ②.

La Paillote, opposite the Oussuye road junction (☎93 51 51; Fax 93 51 17). Virtually identical to the less expensive *Cocotiers* next door. Very comfortable beachside huts, plus a private golf course, fine restaurant and souvenir shop. ⑦.

DAY TRIPS TO KARABANE ISLAND

Day trips to **Karabane Island**, arranged by most hotels in Cap Skiring, leave from the creek behind the village (9am–5.30pm) – around CFA7000 from *Le Paradis* or *Mussuwam* and maybe twice as much from *La Paillote*. Trips normally take in Elinkine, Karabane, the Ile des Feticheurs, and an Ile aux Oiseaux or two. That's a lot of messing around on the river among low mangroves, which cast little shade, so make sure you wear a hat. It's not a bad way, incidentally, of getting to Elinkine.

Le Palmier, Cap Skiring village (☎93 51 09). Set right in the village, this is more a place to eat than to stay with small cells and some S/C rooms. ②–③.

Le Paradis, south of *Le Mussuwam*. Lower mid-range *campement* with a *case à impluvium* alternative to the *Auberge*. ②–③.

Hôtel Savana, 3km north of Cap Skiring village (☎93 15 52; Fax 93 14 92). The Cap's beautifully landscaped five-star jewel offers it all – at a cost. ⑦.

Sea and sand

Bronzing and bathing are the main daytime occupations in Cap Skiring, and you can rent **windsurfers** from the more expensive hotels – there's almost always a good breeze. Just about everywhere rents out **bicycles** for a few thousand CFA francs per day, better value than a car or a 4WD.

By **bike** you can easily get up to Diembering in an hour or two along the beach at low tide when the sand is firm; the main motorable track through the bush is a sandy 8km (allow 1hr). Be careful not to venture onto the *Club Med*'s stretch: though it is ostensibly a public right of way, there are armed *militaires* at each end where the fence goes into the sea. Most people follow the fence down to the beach on its northern side then cycle from there, passing through the sunbed obstacle course in front of the *Savana* (dirty looks but no force of arms), and then climbing over a jumble of low rocks for a magnificent sweep of sand. Shortly after this point there's what looks like an open-air mosque built into the cliffside.

Eating well and cheaply is difficult in Cap Skiring, with stodgy fish and rice at CFA2500 the norm, and even more expensive ordinary fare pushed as an "authentic" meal in the village itself.

Diembering

An ideal excursion from Cap Skiring, **DIEMBERING** lies deep behind the dunes, 8.5km north. If you don't want to walk or cycle, there's a daily bus, about 6pm, returning to Cap Skiring in the morning. It's a traditional village, its economy based on fishing and livestock, and by no means entirely dependent on its three privately owned *campements*. The most striking thing about Diembering is the hill that rises from its centre, a steep and ancient dune crowned and stabilized by a grove of venerable silk-cotton trees. It's no more than thirty metres high, but in Basse Casamance it looks like a mountain, and there's no escaping the strong and mysterious sense of place.

On your left as you come into town along the *piste* from Cap Skiring is the first **place to stay**; the *Asseb campement* (☎93 31 06; ②): nothing special but the only one that's accessible by car. You'll need the help of the boys who hang out under the mother of all *fromagers* (silk-cottons) to search out the other two accommodation options. The *Campement Aten-Elou* (☎93 31 05; ②) named after a local priestess, is situated at the top of the hill, just past a fallen tree trunk. Closer to the beach along a maze of fence-bound footpaths is *Albert's campement* (①), a *case à impluvium* set on the far side of the village, and probably the best place to stay (albeit with basic ablutions), undercutting *CTRI* rates and just ten minutes' walk over the dunes to the sea. You'll do well to memorize the lefts and rights between the village and the *campement* or you're bound to get lost – the guide who leads the nightly lamplit procession through the village to the evening meal at Albert's **restaurant** is indispensable.

If you're craving true isolation, you could walk or cycle – again, preferably at low tide – up to **Nyikine**, a village at the very mouth of the Casamance. It's a place of coconuts and seclusion, recommended by some of the boys hanging around in Diembering, and possibly worth visiting in their company.

South of Cap Skiring

South of Cap Skiring, the road turns through the village of **KABROUSSE**, a scattered community of farmers. There's one last tourist hotel here (*La Kabrousse*; see above), and nothing in the way of *campements* until you get to the Basse Casamance National Park (see below). It was here that a major anti-colonial rebellion was instigated during World War II under the leadership of Alinsitoé, a famous Jola visionary from Kabrousse. Aged only twenty, she spearheaded a revolt provoked by the tax burden placed on the Jola peasantry by the government. After a vicious battle at Efok, Alinsitoé was arrested and exiled to St-Louis, then to Timbuktu, where she died. Her name is evoked whenever the question is raised of Casamance secession from northern Senegal.

The area inland and south of Cap Skiring is a refuge for the **separatist** *MFDC* rebels and the track east of the creek to the National Park gate described below is presently **closed**. We have retained the description from this book's first edition, however, in the event of the path being re-opened, as on a bike it's well worth the effort. For the moment the undemanding ride down to the creek is Cap Skiring's most satisfying bike excursion.

The forest path from Kabrousse to the Basse Casamance National Park

The tarmac goes into Kabrousse but fails to come out again, so make sure you pick the right path. It's rare for a motor vehicle to head out across these fields, understandably when you get to the creek, 6km on, and see the remains of the car ferry. But a bike can make it easily. A *mobylette* is less suitable, because you may have to load it onto a *pirogue* for the creek crossing, and take it through patches of deep sand later.

On the eastern side of the creek the path continues along the Guinea-Bissau border, clear enough but frequently bicycle-width only, and sometimes degenerating into sandy oblivion, where you'll have to push. Although the total distance to the Basse Casamance National Park gate is only some 22km from Kabrousse, it can feel longer. Not that it's a pain, as long as you allow a full half-day, because the entire route is blissfully peaceful, passing through family hamlets where frank stares of astonishment meet you. Much of the way is heavily overgrown, with thickets of bamboo and forest filling the gaps between farm plots and compounds.

Santiaba Manjak is the largest village you pass through before the park gate; 2km further, a right turning leads off to the Alinsitoé battle village of **Efok** (5km) and equally isolated **Youtou** (10km). Efok's main public place has a huge war drum, confiscated during the World War II rebellion, while at Youtou similar drums are apparently still being made.

Parc National de Basse Casamance

Hard up against the Guinea-Bissau border, the **Parc National de Basse Casamance** comprises forty square kilometres of streams, marshy savannah, and partly untouched primary forest. Large mammals such as forest buffalo, leopard, hippo and bushbuck are rarely seen here; but there's wonderful **monkey-spotting** from several of the paths

At the time this book went to press, there was some doubt whether the park – used as a hideout by the insurgent *MFDC* – was open. **Oussouye** is the place to try and find out the latest news, as the track beyond the creek east of Kabrousse along the Guinea-Bissau border is closed. The park itself was certainly closed for most of 1993 and 1994 and the park rangers (all members of the armed forces and thus MFDC targets) had abandoned it.

and lookout towers (*miradors*), **crocs** in the creeks, and the deep forest harbours species of **birds and insects** you're unlikely to come across anywhere else in Senegal. The best time to visit is well into the dry season, when, even in this relatively moist part of the country, waterholes dry up and sources become good spots to watch animals.

Park practicalities

Getting to the park by public transport is difficult at the best of times. Unless you make your own way there on foot or bicycle, the only other possibility is an organized trip from the Oussouye *CTRI*, but this generally means a bit of a rush.

The park (modest entrance fees) is not a place to visit in a single day: in order to get anything from it you'll need to stay for at least one dusk and dawn. The only **accommodation**, currently trashed, was a formerly very pleasant *case à impluvium* (②) near the entrance; it's not a *CTRI*, but used to charge similar rates and did excellent meals. You could also camp here if you wished.

Around the park

To maximize your chances of seeing animals, get out on the forest paths by about 6am. For animal-watching at the end of the day, come out at 4pm, install yourself somewhere comfortable, and wait. You can also look around at night, preferably in a vehicle or using a powerful torch. The hot, middle part of the day is quiet and often unrewarding.

The **Mirador du Buffle**, one of six observation platforms scattered through the park, is the best spot in the dry season, but only if you get there early. The 2.5km of the *Circuit Houssiou*, which runs past it, meanders into tall grass and near its end reaches the *Mirador des Oiseaux*, on the main track; this circuit is only negotiable by bike (just) or on foot.

Monkeys are everywhere, especially in certain trees during their fruiting seasons – they adore the tart *ditak* fruits. Lined with high trees, the *Circuit Djiban Epor*, which terminates in a rangers' encampment, is a good path for monkey-spotting.

Assuming the park has re-opened and is safe, you need not be alarmed by noises in the undergrowth – they're most often caused by small **duiker antelope** and occasionally by **bushbuck**. Noisier – and heavier – movements are forest buffalo, relatively small and not dangerous; you're more likely to see their dung. **Leopards** are exceedingly shy and silent, and you would be fortunate indeed to see one; there are no records of any attacks. Crocodiles, particularly the dwarf (one-metre) species, are common enough if you're patient at the waterfront *miradors*. The *Mirador des Crocodiles* is easily reached off the main track, which terminates about 7km from the park entrance on the creek shore – with a jetty and picnic site.

index

CHAPTER THREE

THE GAMBIA

THE GAMBIA

The Gambia could easily be dismissed as an inconsequential little tourist trap. A tiny and frail country, eking out its existence along the banks of the Gambia River, it relies heavily on the October to April influx of British and European visitors taking a step beyond Spain and the Canaries. Out of season most of the **beach resort** hotels go to sleep or close down, and Gambians turn their attentions inland to the groundnut – peanut – harvest. The feeling of nothing much happening can be acute, and if you've already travelled widely in West Africa, The Gambia isn't going to knock you out.

But after a major overland trip it's a congenial enough place to rest up. Equally, it's an easy **access point** from which to embark on more extensive African wanderings, with the flight from Europe taking less than six hours. Should you want to stay put, you can spend a week or two here in **package-holiday** style for less than what you'd pay in many European resorts – and of course you can do it in mid-winter. The beaches are good – though they get a lot better the further you go from the hotels – and the sea is unfailingly warm.

The Gambia's surest appeal lies in its **smallness**: with a population about the same size as Berkshire's or Delaware's, there's a rapidly acquired feeling of knowing everyone. Pomp and exclusivity are hard to maintain and you can find yourself in conversation with government ministers without even realising it.

Where and when to go

While a surprising drabness characterizes the capital **Banjul**, and organized excursions can be unrewarding, West Africa does reveal itself if you make an effort to leave the crowds and visit the interior. Dominated by the daily cycle of tides and the annual swing of flood and drought, the **Gambia River** has a compelling life of its own. Once you get beyond **Brikama**, the villages and the main "up-country" centres of

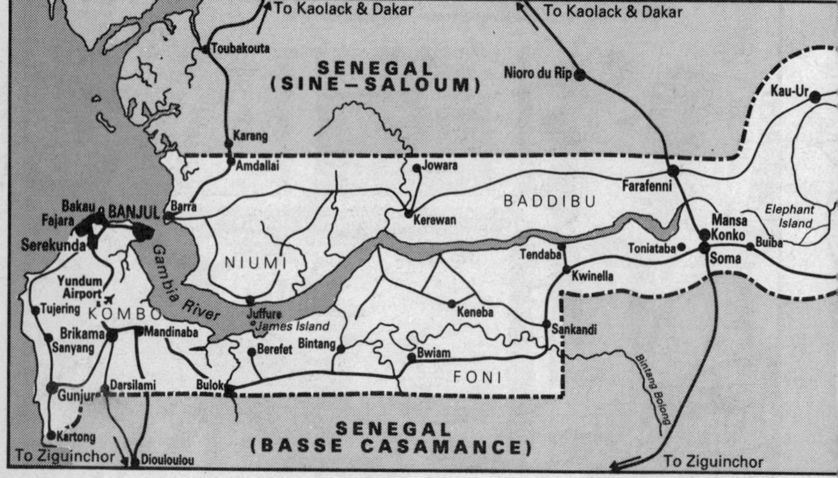

FACTS AND FIGURES

The country is officially designated *The* Gambia, a device that has a certain cachet but only tends to emphasize the fact that the Gambia River is all there is to it. The politically expedient "Senegambia Confederation", which linked the country with Senegal, came to an end in 1989 when Senegalese troops were withdrawn.

The Gambia's population, rising steadily towards one million, lives in a strip of only 10,700 square kilometres of river bank, making it one of the smallest and most densely populated countries in Africa. From independence in 1965 until 1994, the country's leader was Sir Dawda Jawara – head of the ruling People's Progressive Party and president of a nominally multi-party democracy (there were regular elections, but no other party had ever held power). Then in 1994 a coup brought in a military government, the Armed Forces Provisional Ruling Council, led by Lieutenant (later Captain) Yahya Jammeh. As this book went to press, a return to civilian rule was scheduled for 1996.

The Gambia's entire national debt is approximately £250M ($400M), about the same as the annual municipal budget of a British or American city of 100,000 people, such as Cambridge, England or Cambridge, Massachusetts. However the debt is equivalent to nearly twice the value of The Gambia's annual exports of goods and services.

Georgetown, **Bansang** and **Basse Santa Su** are little affected by the coast's tourism. Animal and birdlife is diverse and exotic (ornithologists will recognise many wintering migrants from Europe); there are coconut trees, rice fields and mangrove swamps, and creeks plied by dugout canoes. And the country's borders need not limit your explorations: encircling **Senegal**, vast in comparison, is accessible without a visa for many nationalities.

Deciding **when to go** is governed, for most people, by the rainy season. If you're going on a package you'll quickly see that there's a much reduced choice of hotels from **June to October**, the period when The Gambia gets up to 1300 millimetres of rain – about fifty percent more than Britain's annual average. However, there is a degree of regional variation. On the coast the rains don't begin in earnest much before July, but inland they can start in May; upriver they may finish by the end of August, down at Banjul often not until October. August is usually the wettest month, making

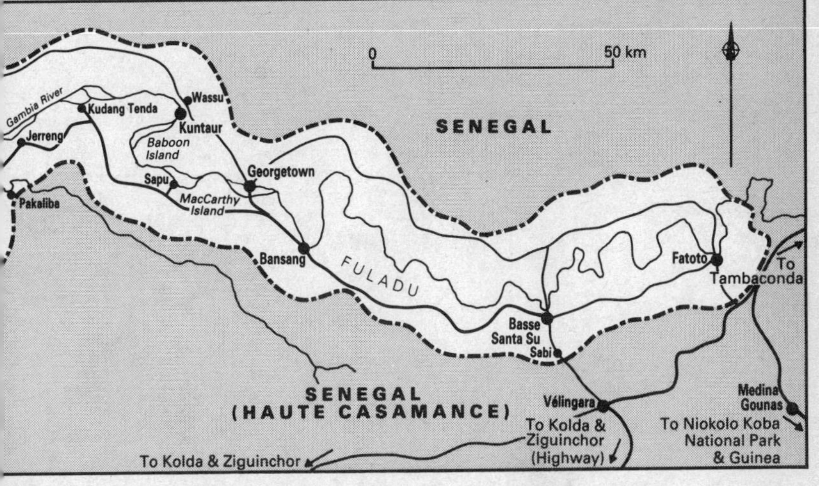

north bank roads impassable for days on end. The period from **March to May** is normally rainless, but dust and wind from across the Sahara can be a torment, and the haze can even block out the sun. Although year-round tourism has been promoted since the early 1990s, and going in the low season can mean feeling less part of a herd, the ideal period for a visit is **December or January**, when you can expect dry, hot days and mild – even cool – nights.

BANJUL: AVERAGE TEMPERATURE AND RAINFALL

	Jan	Feb	Mar	Apr	May	June	July	Aug	Sept	Oct	Nov	Dec
Temperatures °C												
Min	15	16	17	18	19	23	23	23	23	22	18	16
Max	31	32	34	33	32	32	30	29	31	32	32	31
Rainfall mm	3	3	0	0	10	58	282	500	310	109	18	3
Days with rainfall	0	0	0	0	1	5	16	19	19	8	1	0

Arrivals

As a taste of West Africa, The Gambia is an easy arrival point. It's the first choice for a fair number of expatriate workers in the region looking for a short holiday. There is a good range of flights from other cities in the region, and straightforward overland travel connections.

■ Flights from Africa

Gambia Airways (CK), the small national carrier, flies every afternoon except Fri & Sun from Banjul to **Dakar** and back (this service may be currently suspended). CK also operates a Thurs flight from Banjul to **Bamako** and back to Banjul; Mon, Wed and Sat flights to **Freetown** and back to Banjul, sometimes via **Conakry**; Fri & Sun flights to **Nouakchott** and back; and Tues & Fri flights to and from **Praia**.

The main regional airline into Banjul is *Ghana Airways* (GH), with three flights a week from **Accra:** via **Abidjan** and **Freetown** on Mon; via **Abidjan**, **Freetown** and **Conakry** on Wed; and via **Freetown** and **Conakry** on Sat. GH continues to Dakar on Mon and Sat and returns from **Dakar** to Banjul on Tues & Sun.

Nigeria Airways (WT) operates, at least in theory, a weekly service from **Lagos** to Banjul via **Lomé**, **Abidjan**, and **Dakar**.

Air Sénégal (DS) flies three or four times a week between **Dakar** and Banjul (reservations can only be made locally).

Guinée Air Service offers the cheapest flights from Guinea, flying in from **Conakry** via **Labé** every Tues and Thurs morning, and turning round swiftly at Yundum airport, Banjul, to make the return flight to Guinea.

The Belgian airline *Sabena* (SN) flies into Banjul via **Bamako** on Mon, Wed and Fri, but it may prove impossible to buy a ticket in Mali for the intra-African leg only.

To round up the smaller regional airlines that call at Banjul: a new service, *Air Teranga* (JG), flies **Freetown** to Banjul on Mon, and **Dakar** to Banjul on Tues; *Air Mauritanie* (MR) flies from **Nouakchott** to Banjul and back on Sat, via Dakar; the Guinea-Bissau national airline, *TAGB* (YZ), flies from **Bissau** to Banjul and back on Tues and Fri; and finally *Air Guinée* (GI) flies **Conakry** to Banjul on Thurs, Sat & Sun, routing via **Labé** on the Sun flight.

The details in these practical information pages are essentially for use on the ground in West Africa and in The Gambia itself: for full practical coverage on preparing for a trip, getting here from outside the region, paperwork, health, information sources and more, see *Basics* pp.3–88.

■ Overland

Whichever way you travel overland, you'll arrive first in **Senegal**. If you're heading south to The Gambia from the Saloum delta, you might want to allow time for the *pirogue* journey from Djifere to Banjul (see the Senegal chapter).

If you're travelling by bus or bush taxi from **Dakar to Banjul**, avoid taking one of the big 30-seater buses as they take 12 hours. With luck you can do it in 5–6 hours, despite the annoying succession of stops and vehicle changes to be made. Senegalese vehicles stop at the last village before the border, **Karang**. From here there's a short taxi hop (CFA100) to the border at **Amdallai**, where there are routine, everyone-out baggage searches by customs. You then have to pick up transport to Barra and hope you coincide with a ferry to Banjul – otherwise, you may have to wait up to two hours for the next crossing (last ferry around 6.30pm).

From **Ziguinchor to Serekunda** (outside Banjul) a batch of Peugeot 504 bush taxis run every morning and the border is less of a hassle.

Coming from Mali, you're unlikely to save time or money by coming direct **from Bamako** and entering The Gambia at its eastern end, but this route to Banjul is more enjoyable than the dreary highway through Senegal to Dakar. Break your journey at Tambacounda, then make your way to the Gambian border crossing at Fatoto and pick up a Gambian bus from there to Banjul (two each morning); then either bush taxi-hop your way down the river, or link up with the scheduled tourist *pirogue* service running between Banjul and Georgetown (see "Getting Around", below).

Red Tape and Visas

Most Commonwealth and European Community passport holders don't require a visa. Irish, French, Belgian, Swiss, US and Japanese nationals are among those who do – in theory. In practice, if nationals of these countries fly in without a visa, they

are routinely given a visitor's pass at the airport. If you're simply traversing the country, from northern to southern Senegal or vice versa, visas aren't required by any nationality.

For all visitors, the important document is a **full passport**, valid at least six months past your stay. You will only be asked for a Yellow Fever vaccination certificate if you are visiting other countries in the region. For package-tour visitors from Britain, a yellow fever certificate is no longer needed. **Flying in** you'll normally be given permission to stay for as long as you request – up to three months if you have a return ticket. If your flight is one-way only, you might be required to show evidence of sufficient funds, though this isn't common.

Immigration is somewhat different at the **land borders**, where most overland entrants are given a two-week stay. If you want to stay longer, visit the police or Immigration Office in Banjul to apply for an extension.

For **onward travel** from The Gambia, you can obtain visas in Banjul for Mauritania, Senegal, Guinea-Bissau, Guinea, and Sierra Leone. Visas for Nigeria may be available too, if harder to obtain. There is sporadic Malian representation. Full details are given in the "Banjul and Area Listings". There's no French embassy – only a French honorary consul – so no visa service for Francophone countries.

Money and Costs

Gambian currency is the *dalasi* (D), divided into 100 *bututs* (approximately D16 = £1/D11 = US$1). Notes come in denominations of D5, D10, D25 and D50, with coins of D1, and 5, 10, 25 and 50 bututs. Bear in mind that Gambian dalasis aren't officially convertible abroad, so go easy and only change what you think you'll need. There is no currency declaration form.

If you're arriving in the country from Senegal, it's a good idea to spend all your CFA francs before reaching The Gambia. It's not legal to export them from Senegal and Gambian banks won't exchange them. If you do have any CFA francs left, you will get approximately the right rate (D90:CFA5000) changing them in most Gambian markets – not a transaction that's likely to interest the Gambian police – and may even be able to spend them in some places.

There are **banks** in Banjul, Bakau, Serekunda and Basse, usually open Mon–Thurs 8am–1pm, Fri 8–11am. The *Standard Chartered* in Banjul will cash personal cheques on British bank accounts with a cheque guarantee card. There is normally no commission at banks.

There is no longer any black market, but forex bureaux and street hustlers offer perhaps a 5% better rate than the banks for £UK, US$ and major European currencies. Avoid changing money at the hotels if you can – they do a brisk trade with their captive clients at poor rates.

Credit cards

Credit cards (notably *Amex*, but *Visa* and *Access/Mastercard* to some extent also) are handy if you're staying in one of the main beach hotels, but they're not of much use in Banjul itself, or anywhere else in the country. Cash advances are problematic, if not impossible, to obtain – details in "Banjul and Area Listings".

■ Costs

Costs tend to be somewhat lower than northern Senegal's and overall rather higher than in the Basse Casamance region of southern Senegal. But the two countries are not really comparable: away from Banjul and the coast there simply isn't much to spend your cash on. Ordinary market produce and grocery store fare isn't going to break the bank. If you're staying on the coast, you'll soon discover which hotels charge D20 for a beer and where you can find one for less than half that.

Beer and soft drinks get pricey upriver and away from main centres. The same broad rule applies to petrol (gasoline), which varies from around D8 or D9 per litre from pumps at licensed stations to D60 per "gallon" from jerry cans upriver.

Health

The Gambia poses no special health risks. Many doctors will recommend nothing more than anti-malaria tablets, though you should certainly consider a hepatitis jab if your travels are likely to take you off the beaten track. For information about yellow fever vaccination certificates, see "Red Tape and Visas" above.

You *must* take **anti-malaria tablets** even if you're holidaying for a week. The disease is more resistant in areas like The Gambia, where malarial parasites have long been combatted with the drugs used by tourists. Given the greater virulence of the parasites here, the risks if you don't bother with tablets – including fatal cerebral malaria – are consequently higher. That said, while Banjul and the river are mosquito-prone all year round, the hotel areas on the Atlantic coast are mostly free by the middle of the season – Christmas. And the insects themselves aren't often a persistent menace. Full malaria details are given on p.34.

As for health care, the country has two principal **hospitals**: the Royal Victoria in Banjul, with its crowded wards and mosquito-netted patients visible from Marina Parade, and the more reputable Bansang Hospital, 300km upriver. If you're seriously ill, contact a hotel or, upriver, the nearest dispensary or foreign aid worker. Emergency services are rudimentary. Of a range of private clinics, the Lamtoro clinic (see "Banjul and Area Listings") is considered one of the best.

Water in The Gambia is considered safe when it comes from taps or pumps. You needn't hesitate to drink tap water in your hotel, but plastic bottled water is very widely available. If you buy it, get it in bulk from one of the supermarkets at a fraction of the hotel price.

A health concern of some importance in the Banjul area is the **sewage** system – or rather the lack of one. An EC-aided project has been digging up the capital for some time to install a plumbed-in service to households on the rates register. This means about one in five, but it's expected that many more will connect themselves unofficially, resulting in a chronic overload and the prospect of two or three times more raw sewage flowing out into the estuary than planned for. Hotels on the north-facing section of coastline will suffer most unless a solution is found.

Lastly, the **AIDS** position. The latest reported figures, at the end of 1992, showed over 300 people were suffering, or had died from AIDS and there are at least 25,000 carriers. Male and female prostitutes work in the Banjul region, though prostitution is principally a diversion of the beach hotels, some of which are fairly lax about their policy on visits by non-guests. One of military leader Jammeh's first acts was to declare "war" on prostitution. On a more positive note, HIV research on long-term infected patients in The Gambia has recently suggested some strains of the disease may never actually cause AIDS.

Information, Maps and Books

It's worth visiting a Gambia National Tourist Office before you leave. The London office (at the High Commission; see address in *Basics*) is usually efficient and helpful. Good, free maps of the country are available plus ideas on packages, flights and the rest.

In The Gambia itself things are a bit different. There is no tourist office, but you should be able to pick up the annual 70-page Gambia Visitors' Guide, well put together by the *Kololi Beach Club*, which contains a lot of useful information.

For **detailed maps**, you need to visit the Survey Department in the ominously named "Half Die" quarter of Banjul, open weekday office hours. The 1:250,000 sheet (1980) covers the country but there's also a nice 1:50,000 series (1981) based on aerial photographs that seems to show every compound. They're all hard to obtain outside the country. Some maps may have to be copied up for you, which takes time and isn't cheap.

■ Books

There are some **guidebooks** to The Gambia. Michael Tomkinson's *Gambia* (1987, Michael Tomkinson Publishing) contains nice pics and a wealth of interesting detail, but little of practical utility. *The Gambia and Senegal* (1990, Insight Guides) is solid on both countries but, again, not very practical for on-the-ground use. Terry Palmer's *Discover The Gambia* (4th edition April 1993, Heritage House, UK) is a very detailed practical guide, but a little confusing in layout.

As for general works on The Gambia, and fiction by Gambian writers, the in-print choice is very limited. There is a selection in "Books" in the *Contexts* section at the back of this book.

Getting Around

The Gambia's internal transport system is not complicated by air or rail routes, and the river is barely a significant means of transport. There are ferry services across it but only two tourist launches that run upriver (details in the "Upriver Gambia" section later in this chapter). What ought to be viewed as an asset is seen as a hindrance to north–south communications. The principal car ferry crossings are at Banjul–Barra

and Yelitenda–Bambatenda – the trans-Gambian highway crossing between Soma and Farafenni.

The Banjul–Barra and Yelitenda–Bambatenda ferries are fairly reliable, but the Georgetown–north bank and Basse ferries remain unpredictable, as does the one across Jowara Bolong at Kerewan on the north bank. Other ferries are for passengers only.

As to **roads**, there's one main, hard-surfaced artery from Banjul to Basse Santa Su ("Basse"), along the south bank of the river. It's in excellent condition as far as Serekunda, then deteriorates rapidly and becomes really appalling as far as Soma. East of Soma the road is quieter, and the surface not too bad. North bank roads are made entirely of laterite, mud, sand or rock, apart from the short stretch from Barra into Senegal.

The country is held together by the efforts of the **GPTC** (*Gambia Public Transport Corporation*), recently much improved by a fleet of new buses. The main route, **between Serekunda bus depot and Basse**, has at least six services daily, departing between 6.45am and noon and usally requiring a change at Soma. Departures and schedules depend somewhat on demand. The express service aims to roar into Basse at 3pm. In addition there's a "Super Express" which is sitting only (no standing), and comfortable. On the north bank, the *GPTC* services (three daily in each direction) concentrate on linking the villages between Barra and Georgetown with the transport hub of **Farafenni**.

In addition to the buses, privately operated **bush taxis** known as "cars" (mostly Japanese vans, pick-ups, a few saloons and goods trucks) fill in the gaps (especially in the coastal hinterland) and feed the bus routes, and can often get you out of a corner. You'll find them at "garages" – the equivalent of *gares routières* in the Francophone countries.

Around the touristy parts, ordinary **taxis** are touted by their drivers. They can be recognised by their yellow number plates. Fares to various local points are usually displayed outside the main hotels. "Local taxis" run along set routes, cramming as many passengers as they can at D1–3 per person per hop.

■ Car rental

Car rental is undeveloped, with the international agencies barely represented and just a handful of local operations meeting demand – and often preferring to provide drivers. Self-drive deals are generally only available in the Banjul/resorts area, and start from around £30 ($50) per day all-in, in the low season. Some suggestions are included in the "Banjul and Area Listings" section. Petrol costs from D8 a litre (£2.50/$4 per gallon) for "Super".

■ Motorbikes and cycling

Motorbikes can be rented from several coast hotels, as can **bicycles**. If you'd prefer to bring your own wheels, The Gambia is quiet, safe and offers very flat terrain for a first try at cycling in Africa, with ample opportunity for leisurely side-tracking to the river. In the dry season, a complete circuit of the country (inland on the south bank, back to Banjul on the north) would take a couple of weeks assuming about 75km a day. Mountain bikes would be best, but you'd get away with well set-up ordinary tourers on a short trip.

Accommodation

The vast majority of visitors have hotels pre-booked for the duration of their stays, which works out relatively cheaply.

None of the tourist hotels – except those block-booked by tour operators – is closed to you if you arrive by independent means and feel the urge to splurge (or even just the need for some decent comfort, which is all that most of them offer). But the outlay is likely to be heavy unless you turn up a special deal or visit out of season when the tourist hotels operate lower tariffs. The hotels ignored by the tour operators are of course more affordable, and there is a small but growing number of tourist lodges and local hotels upriver. Options at the budget end are limited but it is at least feasible, if you're really travelling on a shoestring, to find informal lodgings with local people.

Camping makes a lot of sense. There are no campsites as such, but, away from the coastal resorts, pitching a tent is unproblematic if you have your own transport: despite a fairly high population density, you're likely to find secluded spots off the main road where you can peg out for a night and enjoy the bush. If you're using public transport, there's less opportunity, as always, to find that good pitching place. You're going to have to ask to camp on people's land – which will often lead to invitations to stay with them instead.

ACCOMMODATION PRICE CODES

Hotel prices in this chapter are coded according to the following scales – the same scales in terms of their pound/dollar equivalents as used throughout the book. Prices refer to the rate you can expect to pay for a room with two beds. Single rooms, or single occupancy, will normally cost at least two-thirds of the twin-occupancy rate. For further details see p.51.

① **Under D75 (under £5/$7.50).** Rudimentary accommodation.

② **D75–150 (£5–10/$$7.50–15).** Basic lodging, perhaps with some rooms self-contained (S/C: shower en suite).

③ **D150–300 (£10–20/$15–30).** Reasonable lodging, usually with S/C rooms, some with AC (air-conditioning) and breakfast usually included.

④ **D300–450 (£20–30/$30–45).** Modest business or tourist-class hotel with simple facilities, breakfast included.

⑤ **D450–600 (£30–40/$45–60).** Better than adequate tourist-class.

⑥ **D600–750 (£40–50/$60–75).** Tourist-class with good facilities.

⑦ **Over 750 (over 50/$75).** Luxury establishment (prices up to £120/$180 in one or two cases).

The resort hotels have two rates – high season roughly from the end of October to Easter, and low season roughly from Easter to October. Where seasonal rates are indicated, you can expect the low-season rate to give a more accurate reflection of facilities.

Eating and Drinking

Restaurants are no more numerous than hotels – even the sort of chop-house establishments you may have come to expect from wider travels in West Africa are largely absent. With everything on such a tiny scale it's not altogether remarkable that no significant national cuisine has emerged.

Gambian dishes tend to be spicier than Senegalese. The tourist hotels' Gambian "standard" is **Yassa Chicken**, delicious when prepared well, but often just casseroled fowl with a searing sauce of lemon, chile and onions. **Domodah**, if you like groundnuts, is invariably good (the thicker the better), usually with chicken, sometimes beef, always rice. **Mafe** is another peanutty variation.

"Jollof Rice" is usually served with beef (or sometimes fish), tomato puree and vegetables – sweet peppers, aubergine, carrots and squash. The emphasis is on the palm oil that stains the rice red and goes down your chin.

Benachin is like the *tiéboudienne* you get in Senegal, essentially fish and rice, sometimes with vegetables.

Plasas (palava sauce) is an okra and palm oil sauce with dried fish and sometimes meat.

The best feature on the coast is quantities of fresh **seafood**: shrimps, ladyfish (like sole), barracuda if you're in luck, and excellent chowders and bisques in a few places. But this is effectively to recommend a clutch of decent eating houses near Banjul and the resorts. If you leave the coast and head upriver, you will find virtually no restaurants until you reach Basse.

Fortunately, you'll find quite good French-style **bread** all over. **Pies** – resembling Britain's Cornish pasties – seem to be a leftover of colonial influence: found in meat and fish varieties, they are often surprisingly tasty. And **fruit** you can get just about everywhere – especially bananas and papayas at any time (though the latter aren't often sold and you'll have to ask in the countryside), and mangoes, guavas, avocados, water melons and oranges in season – the last often imported from Morocco.

Drinking

For **drinking**, you'll have to get used to The Gambia's **lager** – *Julbrew* – which is fairly strong but not one of West Africa's better-tasting beers, and fizzy drinks (**"softs"**) from the same enterprise. Imported beers are increasingly common in the resorts. Bottled Guinness is a colonial relic, sold quite widely, but rarely cold and perhaps verging on the medicinal in the eyes of most Gambians. Soda water is usually obtainable in larger places. Plastic-bottled "spring" or "mineral" water is catching on fast, but it's a pricey way of avoiding contamination (D10/litre or more). Tap water is generally very healthy and attacks of "Banjul belly" that affect so many are more easily attributed to the assaults of heat and

MANDINKA FOOD AND DRINK TERMS

[illegible]	*mburo*	groundnut oil	*dulino*	hibiscus tea	*honjo*
[illegible]	*mano*	palm oil	*tulussy*	green tea	*ataya*
[illegible]	*subo*	onion	*jabo*	soft drink	*lemnato*
[illegible]	*nye*	aubergine	*patanse*	palm wine	*tenkuolo*
millet (g[illegible]	*nyo*	orange	*lemuno*	alcohol	*dolo*
groundnut (peanut)	*teo*	water melon	*sarro*		
groundnut paste	*dege*	water	*jio*		

unusual food – or sometimes to incautious freezing and re-heating in hotel kitchens.

If you're drinking tap water, try the homemade plastic-bag **juices**, or ices, which are popular because they're so cheap, and are on sale wherever people can get hold of plastic bags. Tasty but sticky sweet, they come in three main kinds – white, brown and red – made from baobab fruit (*bwi/bouille*), ginger and hibiscus-like *bissap* flowers (*wonjo*). Breakfast-time coffee from roadside stalls isn't as common as in the French-speaking countries. Green tea – known here as *attaya* – is fairly widespread though, especially in Fula areas upriver.

Palm wine – which of course you'll be told is a Gambian speciality – is usually tapped from oil palms and is pretty well universal: the speciality lies in getting the tourists plastered on it during "bush and beach" excursions. As everywhere it varies considerably in taste and strength depending on when it was tapped and what it's been stored in. As usual, too, it's tolerated but not strictly legal.

Communications – Post, Phones, Language & Media

The Gambia's main language is English, fairly widely spoken in Banjul and the resorts, but often not understood outside the metropolitan areas or upriver. Krio, still spoken by the descendants of freed slaves who moved from Freetown, is heard less and less. The African language you'll most often hear around Banjul is Wolof (see the Senegal chapter for some words and phrases), but the language with the strongest claim to be the country's traditional tongue is the Mande tongue, Mandinka, which is very widespread upriver, especially on the south bank.

There's a large **Fula**-speaking contingent also, particularly on the north bank. Other languages you may come across include **Jola** towards the Casamance in the south and **Serahuli/ Sarakole**, originally from far to the northeast. Around the Bakau and Fajara resort areas many young people are Senegalese and speak **French**, and many young men in the tourist resorts speak a smattering of German and Swedish.

Radio comes in three versions. Firstly, there's *Radio Gambia*, broadcasting in English and the main national languages on 670m MW. It offers news, announcements ("Will all members of the national football squad please get in touch with the coach . . .") and endless request shows – it sometimes seems there can be very few Gambians who haven't said hello to everyone who knows them. *Radio 1 FM*, based in Fajara and flourishing, is the most popular station, with an excellent selection of reggae and ragga, the favourite music of young Gambians, though it can only be picked up as far as Brikama. Thirdly, *Radio Syd* (329m and 900m MW; PO Box 279, ☎226490) is a privately owned commercial station operating from premises on the Serekunda highway at the end of Bund Road, Banjul. Started by a Swede, it specializes in good music and mundane adverts – "Remember *Chellarams* for all your beer and soft drink requirements...we are best".

If you want to tune in to what's really going on you need the BBC on short wave. There's no TV in The Gambia, but there are television sets: *RTV Sénégal* is partly responsible for the growing Francophone element in national life. There are also plenty of video stores.

As for the print media, Gambian **newspapers** are a little hard to track down. The best development in recent years was the *Gambian Observer*, though its status as a free critic was threatened in 1994 by the expulsion of its Liberian publisher, Kenneth Best, by the military authorities. *The Point* (twice weekly), *New Citizen*, and *The*

MINIMAL MANDINKA

The Mandinka of The Gambia is a fairly mainstream dialect of the large **Mande** language group. As usual in languages of Islamic peoples, there's a scattering of Arabic. Mandinka is not difficult to get your tongue round, though grammatically, of course, it's unfamiliar. The "kh" sound is the "ch" of loch. A characteristic of spoken Mandinka is the omitted final vowel, lending a "clipped" quality to the language.

GREETINGS AND USEFUL PHRASES

How are you? (do you have peace?)	*Khaira be?*	Where do you come from?	*I bota min to ley?*
		Sit down	*Si gang*
How are you all?	*Al be khairato?*	White person	*Toubab*
I'm well (I've peace)	*Khaira dorong*	Black person	*Morfingoh*
How is everyone in the compound?	*Sumo ley?*	Where are you going?	*Kata min?*
		I'm going to Basse	*Nkata Basse*
They're well	*Ibi jay*	Let's go	*Alingata*
All OK? (general, further greeting)	*Kortanante?*	Goodbye (sing./pl.)	*I si kontong/Al si kontong*
All OK	*Tanante*	Clear off! (to cheeky children)	*A cha!*
How's the work? (if you're passing by)	*Nimbara?* (pl. *Alnimbara?*)	I'll beat you! (beware!)	*Be bute la!*
The work's OK	*Nimbara, nimbara*		
Thank you	*Abaraka*	I want some bananas	*Banano sanye*
Is Musa at home?	*Musa ley?*	Five dalasis	*Dalasi lulu*
Yes (I'm here)	*Naam*	Too much!	*Alcoleata!/ Adajaweata!*
What's your name?	*Ito ndi?*		
My name is Kaba	*N tomo Kaba leti*	Lower the price!	*Atala/Njauiata*

NUMBERS

1	*kiling*	5	*lulu*	9	*kononto*	20	*moang*
2	*fula*	6	*woro*	10	*tang*	35	*tang saba ning lulu*
3	*saba*	7	*worowula*	11	*tang ning kiling*	100	*kemi*
4	*nani*	8	*sei*				

Gambia Daily (thrice weekly) have survived, as has the leftish sheet *Foroyaa*. "Political" papers are banned by the AFPRC government.

British papers, from *The Sun* to the *Financial Times*, are available in several of the supermarkets on Kairaba Avenue. *Time* and *Newsweek* are obtainable if you want them, though often late. *West Africa* magazine is available the week after its UK publication.

■ Post and phones

Keeping in contact with home is relatively easy. Aerograms are the cheapest way of writing, if the Banjul GPO has any, but ordinary post isn't expensive. **Poste restante** facilities at Banjul are not especially efficient compared to, say, Dakar. There's a small charge. If you plan on posting souvenirs home, it's worth knowing that there is no surface mail from The Gambia, making the mailing of large items (by airmail) very expensive.

Phoning home, on West Africa's best international telecom system, is good value, especially to the UK. Dialling is direct and you phone from the new call boxes – reputedly solar powered! – dotted around the country, using D45 phone cards. For international calls, dial 00, then the country code (or 01 and no country code in the case of calls to Senegal). Reverse charge (collect) calls can be made to the UK by dialling 00044 and asking for the operator. The same service is available to the USA on 00111, Sweden on 00666 and Norway on 00047. For AT&T dial ☎00111.

All *Gamtel* offices around the coastal district have public **fax** machines, also very cheap to use to the UK. You can also fax from abroad to these public machines, and your recipient will pay a nominal fee to receive the fax.

The Gambia's IDD code is ☎220.

A GLOSSARY OF GAMBIAN TERMS

This list includes Wolof and Mandinka terms and a number of suffixes used in place names.

AFPRC Armed Forces Provisional Ruling Council

Alkali Village elder

Ba Big, as in Tenda-ba (big wharf)

Bantaba Men's communal siesta platform in every village and in many compounds

Banto faro River flood lands

Bengdula/la Craft market/s

Bolong Creek

Bumster Beach boy, hustler

Car Minibus

Duma Lower

Fodi Teacher/marabout

Kafo Traditional "youth club"

Kerr/Keur Place or compound

Koto Old

Kunda Place

Kuta New

Lumo Weekly (or regular) rural market

MOJA-G A proscribed organization – the Movement for Justice in Africa-Gambia

Nding Small

PPP People's Progressive Party (ex-President Jawara's party, now banned)

Santa Upper

Su Home

Tenda Port, wharf

Tesito Self-reliance, a government slogan

Entertainment

While for the majority of visitors entertainment means the hotel formula-mix of "folkloric dance troupes" and homestyle discos, it's easy enough to escape the dross and find real Gambian musical entertainment. To be fair, the hotels do sometimes host worthwhile gigs – the country's kora players (see below) have all played to tourist audiences.

The best time to be in the Banjul area for **music on stage** is the end of the month, when people can afford tickets for the bands that occasionally visit from abroad, usually Senegal. There are normally two or three gigs – the first a more expensive **"dance"** at the Banjul City Council on Independence Drive (D40 or more, starting around 11pm and going on to 3 or 4am) and the next night a more proletarian **"show"** at the big Bakau stadium (tickets from D15; hordes of people). Arrive early to get a seat or you'll never see the musicians.

Most Gambian groups gravitate inevitably to Dakar, if not to Europe, as soon as they reap a measure of success. Musically, Dakar is The Gambia's real nerve centre.

Currently the biggest vogue is for **reggae and raggamuffin**, which a number of local groups play. The Gambia however is more distinguished for its Mandinka-speaking **kora musicians**. The most famous talents – **Dembo Konteh**, his brother-in-law **Kausu Kouyaté**, **Foday Musa Suso**, **Jaliba Kuyateh**, **Malamini Jobarteh**, **Ebrima Jobarteh** and junior **Pa Jobarteh** – are as likely to be playing in a British folk festival or with American musicians, as in a compound in Brikama or at a wedding in Serekunda.

Wolof drummers often perform at "private" functions too. Keep your ears open and drop in politely. If you're into the idea of participation, rather than merely being part of the audience, there's a box of details at the end of the Banjul section. And for pre-departure inspiration, there's a growing list of Gambian kora records available in Britain, including most of the artists above. *The Rough Guide to World Music* has good coverage.

Lastly, with no national film industry (though of course imported kung fu, Hindi movies and the like are enjoyed on video and screen all over) and theatre not happening at all (a national theatre is planned on the southern outskirts of Serekunda), spectator sports are the other principal entertainment in the country. Football is popular and even cricket gets played once in a while, but the big sport is **wrestling**, an exciting way of spending a few hours (see the box in the Serekunda section).

Women Travellers

Sexual hassles in the resort areas are generally not a problem – certainly no more so than in neighbouring countries – though you may find the frank scrutiny unnerving. And of

DRESS SENSE

While topless bathing is fine on most of the beaches, appearing elsewhere less than well-covered, particularly from the waist down, is provocative. An idea of the prevailing conservative morality can be inferred from this 1985 letter from the *Women's Bureau* to the National Tourist Organization:

Dear Sirs,

A BRIEF COUNSEL ABOUT THE APPEARANCE OF TOURISTS IN THE GAMBIA

The staff of the Women's Bureau would like to express its concern about the effects of the tourist season on citizens and residents of The Gambia. While walking through Banjul or Kombos area it is apparent that many of the tourists are unaware of the local dress stàndards. Scantily clad men and women walking into public places can be an embarrassment for both Gambians and expatriates living and working in The Gambia. Perhaps if the tourists were made aware of cultural and religious customs they would not mind wearing more discreet clothing away from the confines of their hotel. We would therefore urge that some information be presented to the tourists either at the hotels or at the airport, so that they could be informed in a nonoffensive way about local standards of dress. Perhaps a poster could express the message (ie cover up a bit when you're about in the town), and allow the tourists to make an informed choice on how to dress. It would still be their choice, of course, but once they are made aware of Gambian customs they may be less likely to walk around in outfits that elicit stares and whispers, tempt young boys to approach unaccompanied women, and contribute to the more negative impact of tourism.

Welcome to The Gambia and thank you for your kind consideration of this matter.

Yours sincerely,

The National Women's Bureau

Which really seems the height of reasonableness.

course sexual interest is by no means exclusively one-sided – which can make life harder for women not in search of adventures. See "Women Travellers" in *Basics*.

If you find your freedom is being seriously compromised by the ubiquitous presence of **"hustlers" and "bumsters"**, one strategy is actually to give in – to *one* of them; you may need to be ruthless in your choice and should be frank about your intentions. He'll act as your chaperone and, if you occasionally tip him or offer the odd souvenir or present from home, may become a real friend for the duration.

Upriver, foreign **women travelling alone** are a rare sight and arouse enormous curiosity. Disappointingly, your contacts with Gambian women may not prove any more fruitful than if you were to travel in male company.

The *Women's Bureau*, located just inside the gates of State House in Banjul, is the main organ of the Gambian **women's movement**. It's concerned primarily with establishing financial stability for women and developing non-traditional income sources, especially crafts cooperatives. Emancipation is a long way off, with polygamy still the norm and six children commonly planned (even in middle-class marriages). Clitoridectomies, performed not infrequently at the Royal Victoria Hospital in Banjul, are common. **Contraception**, for those men or women who want it and make the effort, is free, and campaigning for family planning quite extensive, but few people take notice.

Directory

AIRPORT DEPARTURE TAX Inter-continental departure tax of £15 ($22) or equivalent is payable in hard currency.

"ANY PEN?" In the 1960s the first Swedish tour groups brought **biros** with them to help The Gambia's education system. Children now teach toddlers the catch phrase. It does no harm to take some Bics yourself – there's no accounting for what happens to them all. Ideally, give them direct to a school.

FESTIVALS AND HOLIDAYS The Gambia is predominantly Muslim and, with the exception of tourist services, everything comes to a halt on Muslim holidays (see p.62). Christmas and Easter are also observed, with banks, offices and most shops closed around Banjul and the coast and a few other places. Otherwise, the principal annual days off are January 1, February 18 (Independence Day) and May 1 (Labour Day). The biggest **festival** of the year is the Christmas day **Lantern Parade** in Banjul – a competitive float festival with many similarities to the parades held in Freetown, St-Louis and Bissau.

Other times to know about include the December/January groundnut sales that put money in farmers' pockets once a year, and the miserable April/May "hungry season" that follows.

GAY LIFE Since even the straightest Gambian men customarily dance together and walk hand in hand, gay men may feel quite at home. Although there's nothing in the way of a gay scene as such (and The Gambia's laws on homosexuality are the fossilized edicts inherited from the British at independence in 1965) there's a broad acceptance of gay male visitors and several very low-key haunts in the resort area. Gay women won't find the same.

GRATUITIES AND TIPS It's a bit of a problem in the resorts to know when and how much you should give in recognition of services: you somehow have to reconcile what you give a waiter or tour guide with the fact that many staff will only be paid a wage of D20 to D50 per day, while those in business for themselves, such as taxi drivers (no tipping), might make several hundred. D1 isn't much use to anyone, but D5 is a decent tip, while D10 or D20 would be very generous. Holiday reps are always good at suggesting how much you should give hotel staff at the end of a stay.

OPENING HOURS Most places open at 8am and close at noon or 1pm. Shops and some offices (but not banks) reopen in the afternoon at 2pm or 3pm. Shops tend to close at 5pm. Fri and Sat are half-days. Most doors are closed on Sun. If you want to get things done, start doing them by 9am: the small scale of everything in The Gambia can slow business down as most operations depend on the right person being in the right place at the right time.

PHOTOGRAPHY You'll have very few problems. Gambians don't, in general, mind being in the viewfinder, and cameras aren't objects of suspicion in the Banjul and resort areas. Video cameras can arouse more hostility as people feel they are perhaps being exploited for commercial purposes. The "security" angle is rarely played up by police – though, as usual, you should avoid photographing them without their permission, or snapping anything to do with "the state". Up-country attitudes vary from clear hostility to enthusiasm. Just ask. There's good-quality colour processing in Banjul.

SHOPS AND CRAFTS Banjul, the Kombo district and Brikama are the only areas you'll find either. The crafts tradition isn't a spectacular one. "Ebony" carvings rarely are, and, as with dry land mahogany, the trade encourages deforestation. At the *bengdulala* crafts stalls, go for cheaper softwood carvings, gaudy cloth (including batik clothing), jewellery, leather and basketwork.

TROUBLE Trouble with the police – who are unarmed and among the nicest in West Africa – is unusual, though overlanders with vehicles occasionally report problems over vehicle import duty, which strictly speaking you're not liable to pay. If you're going to smoke grass (*djamba*), be extremely discreet as there have been some hefty fines and prison sentences recently.

The most trouble you're likely to encounter is with "tourist guides" whom you fail to shake off and who later expect payment for the services you didn't want. Tell them you're not going to pay at the very beginning and they'll soon give up.

The Banjul/resorts area, although still very safe on the whole, is increasingly experiencing muggings at night, and pickpockets are common in the markets.

WILDLIFE AND NATIONAL PARKS The Gambia is wonderful for ornithologists, but a disappointment to anyone hoping for big game. Despite President Jawara's much-vaunted "Banjul Declaration" in support of wildlife conservation, the faunal heritage diminishes while the human population expands. But monkeys and baboons are common enough; there are hippos upriver and small crocs in the streams; warthog are common but overhunted; hyenas, aardvarks and leopards are nocturnal, their status uncertain. Many southern Senegalese animals occasionally range towards the river.

The Abuko Nature Reserve includes a small collection of imported, caged big beasts. Baboon Island National Park was formerly a rehabilitation centre for chimpanzees rescued from Spanish street photographers, though recent reports suggest the chimps are no longer there. The park has always been closed to the public, but serious naturalists might like to try contacting the Ministry of Natural Resources and the Environment, 5 Marina Parade, Banjul (☎227431) for information. Speak to these people, too, if you want to find out more about the new, and evidently more public Kiang West National Park.

A Brief History of The Gambia

The earliest people of the Gambia valley may have been the Jola, who by tradition keep very limited oral history. By the fifteenth century, most of the valley was under the control of small Mandinka kingdoms founded by immigrants from the Mali empire. The first European settlers of the late fifteenth and sixteenth centuries were mostly Portuguese and tended to set themselves up in partnership with headmen of the locality, marrying their daughters and trading cloth for slaves. The descendants of the mixed unions were important figures. From the mid-seventeenth century, English, Dutch, French and Baltic merchant adventurers shared and fought over trading rights from the restricted, neighbouring bases of Fort James Island and Albreda. The British won lasting influence after the Napoleonic wars, declaring a Protectorate along the river in the 1820s and in 1888 establishing a Crown Colony that comprised Banjul Island, the district of Kombo St. Mary and MacCarthy island (Georgetown). In the same year, the territory ceased to be governed from Freetown (Sierra Leone) and was given its own government.

■ Colony and Protectorate

In the second half of the nineteenth century, while the British hesitated and focused their attentions elsewhere, the French were battling their way deep into the Soudan, actively engaged in a mission to conquer (see the Senegal chapter). From 1850 to 1890 the whole of the Gambia region was in a state of social chaos as the **"Soninke-Marabout Wars"** repeatedly flared up (see box), eventually forcing the British to consolidate in the region or else lose it to France.

The Gambia's acquisition by Britain, which was formally agreed at the Paris conference of 1889, stemmed less from commercial ambitions than from **imperial strategy**. The intention was to pawn the country off in exchange for some better French territory; Gabon was one chunk favoured by the British – they'd already turned down the offer of the Ivory Coast sea forts. But the temporary expedient of holding the river became permanent when, having failed to agree on an exchange, the British succeeded merely in delimiting a narrow strip of land on each side of the Gambia, into the heart of French territory. Yet Britain wasn't really reconciled to its responsibilities along the Gambia River until after World War I – thus The Gambia's era of effective colonialism lasted little more than forty years.

The imposition of **British hegemony** wasn't impressive. Beyond the limits of the Colony, the country's headmen and chiefs, some of whom were appointed by the Crown, were allowed to rule their people little disturbed by the two "travelling commissioners" to whom they were answerable. Two or three African representatives from Bathurst (the future Banjul) were nominated to the Legislative Council after 1915, but there was no representation of the 85 percent of the population who lived in the Protectorate.

The main relationship between **the people and the government** devolved around the issue of **taxes**. Yet two-thirds of the Gambia's revenue was accounted for in the salaries of the colonial administration. The remainder was insufficient to develop the country's infrastructure, education or health systems. "Benign neglect" is about the best that can be said of the administration's performance. It started to improve only after World War II, though the government was gravely embarrassed by the financially disastrous **Yundum egg scheme,** which fowl pest made an unredeemable fiasco costing £500,000. **Groundnuts** (peanuts) have been the country's main export crop since the middle of the nineteenth century – The Gambia is a classic monoculture – and until the 1970s it was also self-sufficient in food. There were minor advances in education and medical services: by 1961 for example, the country had five doctors and there were 37 up-country primary schools.

Financial pressures on the Colonial Office in the 1950s, and mounting international demands for decolonization were as much instrumental in **the push to independence** as Gambian nationalism. Britain was at least as anxious to rid itself of the financial liability as the country's own senior figures (they were barely yet leaders) were to take power. From Britain's point of view, there was no reason to delay the country's return to independence – except, perhaps, a measure of concern over the fate of such a small and unprotected nation. Colonial civil servants were in

THE SONINKE-MARABOUT WARS

Mandinka civil war along both banks of the Gambia River began in the 1850s. Local holy leaders – the **marabouts** – influenced by the great Muslim expansionist Omar Tall, called for the overthrow of the traditional Mandinka kings known as **Soninkes**, whose adherence to Islam was greatly tempered by indigenous religion and alcohol. The marabouts aimed to install a puritanical Islam and to capture local states (best described as manors) and trading networks.

Most of the "wars" consisted of battles, skirmishes and feuds between villages, which disrupted trade and agriculture year after year. Serer and Jola mercenaries were bought in on both sides to bulk out the limited armies. The main areas of unrest were: **Kombo**, south of the tiny British enclave at Bathurst, where a wild young marabout called **Fodi Kabba**, spread serious anarchy; **Baddibu** and **Niumi** on the north bank, where a renegade Soninke-turned-marabout, **Ma Ba**, caused massive destruction; and **Fuladu**, upriver on the south bank, where **Fula marabouts** from the southeast, right outside the region, swept the local Mandinka aside with great savagery.

By the mid-1870s, the whole of the Kombo district was under maraboutic control. Religious imperatives had been forgotten as purely political and economic considerations pitted one leader against another. Acting under financial constraints laid down in London the **British** avoided interference whenever possible, refused requests for protection from besieged Soninke leaders and only went into battle to defend the Colony or British subjects. Only when there seemed to be a risk that the fighting might jeopardize British commercial interests did the governor try to impose a truce.

But in the **1880s**, the British were unable to avoid being drawn into the conflicts. In Baddibu the wars had now become an internal affair between competing marabouts, and they spilled over into French-occupied Senegal. The French, in hot pursuit on behalf of their Sine-Saloum chiefs (the French were much more actively involved in protection than the British), chased the marabout army back into "British" territory as far as Barra. The British were forced to arrest the marabout in question, **Said Mati**, to forestall any further French advances. Mati's removal led to a power vacuum in Baddibu, which the French began to fill with their own appointees. The British had no choice but to enter into binding protection agreements with as many Gambian chiefs as possible.

A period of relative peace broke out, but in the Kombo and Foni regions Fodi Silla and Fodi Kabba kept up **continued resistance** against the now-expanding British. With the country's borders fixed and support at last from London, the British moved against **Fodi Silla** in 1894, occupying all the towns of Kombo – Gunjur, Sukuta, Brikama – and pushing Silla into Senegal, where he was captured and exiled to St-Louis.

Fodi Kabba pursued the struggle, killing a travelling commissioner and his entourage at Sankandi on the border in 1901. The British and French moved swiftly and in concert, "pacifying" the region in imperial style and killing Fodi Kabba, a campaign which marked the end of the Soninke-Marabout Wars.

broad agreement that The Gambia would be forced to merge with Senegal, but chose to defer the move.

The road to independence

The progression to independence was not a heroic one. In a manner similar to that of many other countries in West Africa, the men who led The Gambia into the neo-colonial era were not so much nationalists as pragmatic and ambitious politicians.

Although the **Bathurst Trade Union** had been founded in 1928 and struck successfully for workers' rights, the first **political party** wasn't formed until shortly before the Legislative Council elections of 1951. Through most of the 1950s, the Gambian parties were reactive, personality-led interest groups rather than campaigning, policy-making, issue-led organizations. The Rev. John Fye founded the **Democratic Party** as a vehicle for the civic ambitions of his Bathurst coterie; IM Garba-Jahumpa founded the **Muslim Congress Party** in an attempt to align religious consensus behind a political movement; and Pierre S N'Jie founded his largely Catholic **United Party**, which maintained close relations with up-country chiefs. All these early-1950s parties were Wolof- and Colony-based and highly sectional. Gambia had to wait until 1960 before a party with a genuinely grassroots programme emerged. This was the Protectorate People's Party (quickly relabelled **People's Progressive Party**), led by an ex-veterinary officer from the MacCarthy Island Division, **David Jawara**. The PPP looked to the

Protectorate for support, but was distinctly anti-chief. It spoke for the rural Mandinka and others in their resentment against corrupt chiefdoms, and for disenfranchized and younger Wolof of the Colony.

The administration overhauled the constitution in 1951 and finally, after consultation with senior Gambian figures, produced a complicated new constitution in 1954. This gave real representation to the Protectorate peoples for the first time, but precipitated sharpened demands for greater responsibility for Gambian ministers in the government. It also put extraordinary power in the hands of the chiefs, who were, for the most part, supporters of the colonial status quo. To avoid a crisis, another constitution was formulated in 1959 which abolished the Legislative Council and provided for a parliament – the House of Representatives.

In the run-up to the **1960 elections**, the Democratic and Muslim Congress parties merged as the **Democratic Congress Alliance**, but couldn't shake off the popular impression that their nominees were all puppets of the administration. As a result the DCA took only three seats, while the United Party of PS N'Jie (with whom the governor had recently fallen out) and David Jawara's PPP took eight seats each. The governor, in a move to placate the Protectorate chiefs, offered the post of prime minister to PS N'Jie, to the consternation of Jawara, who became education minister. But the 1959 constitution was bound to give rise to further indecisive election results. More talks resulted in yet another constitution, providing for a 36-seat House of Representatives with 32 elected seats and just four chiefs nominated by the Chiefs' Assembly.

The balance of power now shifted against the United Party. Jawara and the Democratic Congress Alliance found room for cooperation and, in the **1962 elections** – which were to determine the political configuration for full self-government – the two parties contested seats in concert to squeeze out the United Party. The results of this electoral alliance were highly successful for the PPP, who won 17 out of the 25 Protectorate seats and one of the 7 Colony seats. The DCA, however, managed to gain only one seat in the Colony, and couldn't shift the UP from its urban power base. As a result, with the support of the DCA's two elected members, Jawara had an absolute majority in parliament and his party remained in control until the coup of 1994.

Subsequently, Jawara entered into a coalition with the experienced PS N'Jie to form the first fully independent government. Independence Day came on 18 February 1965, with **The Gambia** admitted to the Commonwealth as a constitutional monarchy with the Queen as titular Head of State.

■ Independent Gambia

In 1966 N'Jie took his United Party out of government to lead the opposition. Four years later, on April 24, **The Gambia** became a republic and prime minister Dawda Jawara (now using his Muslim name) became president. At every election, the PPP continued to win the vast majority of seats, and at every election PS N'Jie claimed that the vote was rigged. The PPP, however, despite its roots in the Mandinka villages, managed to establish credible support across the country.

The **first fifteen years of independence** were peaceful, and the groundnut economy fared better than expected thanks to high prices on the world markets. But by 1976 prospects for the government were less favourable. Two new opposition parties had formed: the somewhat Mandinka-chauvinist **National Convention Party**, led by dismissed vice-president Sherif Mustapha Dibba, and the more left-wing **National Liberation Party** of Pap Cheyassin Secka. And as groundnut prices fell in the late 1970s, The Gambia experienced a string of disastrous harvests.

This economic recession, and political opposition to the government – perceived increasingly as incompetent and corrupt – partly account for the conditions that led to the formation of two new **Marxist groupings** in 1980 and an **attempted coup** in October of that year. Senegalese troops were flown in under a defence agreement and the leaders of the **Gambia Socialist Revolutionary Party** and the transnational **Movement for Justice in Africa-Gambia** (MOJA-G) were arrested and their organizations banned.

A far more **serious coup attempt** on July 30, 1981 (while Jawara was at a royal wedding in London), resulted in a force of 3000 Senegalese troops arriving with a group of SAS soldiers from Britain, to put down sporadic, bloody fighting and disorder around Banjul. The trouble lasted a week and cost up to a thousand lives. **Kukoi Samba Sanyang**, the self-styled revolutionary who led the plot – "we do not believe in elections, we wanted a radical transformation of the entire socio-economic system" – escaped to Guinea-Bissau and thence to Libya.

■ The Senegambia Confederation

The insurrection shook the government and immediate steps were taken to maintain Senegal's support. The subsequent **Senegambia Confederation**, ratified on December 29, 1981, assured The Gambia of Senegal's protection while ostensibly assuring Senegal of The Gambia's commitment to political union. **Treason trials** in the wake of the attempted coup led to long terms of imprisonment but, with the increasingly important tourist industry to consider and international opinion reminding the country of its reputation, there were no executions.

A popular **presidential election** in 1982 gave Jawara a personal vote of 137,000 and Sherif Mustapha Dibba, who was in detention at the time, 52,000. A 1984 cabinet reshuffle brought in some popular, reformist MPs, and in the following year public opinion was heeded in the dismissal of several ministers after allegations of corruption.

With Dibba released, the National Convention Party mounted a serious challenge at the 1987 general and presidential elections. However, it was a new opposition grouping, the **Gambia People's Party**, led by the respected former vice-president **Hassan Musa Camara**, that made the most impact on the government. President Jawara's own vote was reduced from 72 percent to 59, but though his party's share of the vote was also reduced, the PPP still managed to win 31 of the 36 elected seats in the House, with the NCP holding the remaining five. Supporters of the GPP, particularly in its Fula- and Serahuli-speaking strongholds upriver, were left frustrated, as were supporters of the new socialist party, the **People's Democratic Organization for Independence and Socialism**, a party with close ties to the banned MOJA-G.

Another **coup plot** – really a long-running, conspiratorial rumble – was uncovered a year after the elections, in February 1988. The conspiracy involved both Gambian leftists and Casamance separatists from Senegal. It was suggested at the trials that the Senegalese opposition leader, **Abdoulaye Wade**, had been involved in planning it, along with Kukoi Samba Sanyang, but attempts to implicate Libya directly were treated with scepticism abroad.

In 1985, the government embarked on an **Economic Recovery Programme** designed to encourage aid donors. The privatization of various state enterprises, a public expenditure squeeze and cutbacks in subsidies to farmers led to increasing hardship in the countryside. At the Independence Day celebrations in Banjul in 1986, a teenager, **Baboucar Langley**, staged a solitary protest before the presidential platform declaring that "the people are dying of starvation". He was arrested and sentenced to eighteen months' imprisonment.

Throughout the end of the 1980s and the first years of the 1990s, with the ERP still grinding through its measures, the country faced widespread malnutrition, insufficient schools for enrolled students and mounting evidence of high levels of corruption and mismanagement. Senior ministers, bankers, customs officials and heads of the Produce Marketing Board (GPMB) and the Utilities Corporation responsible for the intermittent electricity supply were all investigated. President Jawara routinely "cleaned out" public offices, but accountability was not enforced with tough sanctions, and a prevailing sense of stagnation and recycled rhetoric hung over Banjul.

On the broad economic front, the **liberalization of groundnut sales** removed the GPMB's monopoly and allowed farmers to sell their harvest to the highest bidding private trader. Although this risked forcing *down* the price in remote areas, the net effect was to keep more of the crop from being smuggled to high-paying Senegal. Tourism, too, benefitted from the sale of the state's hotel interests and an increased profile abroad, with more than 100,000 tourists visiting every year.

But the wider future was marred by the **breakdown of the Senegambia Confederation** (officially dissolved on September 30, 1989), as a result of Senegal's frustration at the slow pace of moves towards union. Senegal, in its latent conflict with Mauritania, withdrew the troops which provided The Gambia's security (and indeed President Jawara's personal security), saying they were needed at home.

The end of the Senegambia Confederation left a huge question mark over The Gambia. It had been the national controversy for the best part of a decade, supported by the mostly urban Wolof but generally mistrusted by the Mandinka, whose dominant position in the country was always threatened by a powerful Senegal. For The

Gambia's opposition parties and minorities of all ethnic groupings, the prospect of a greater Senegambia was always a provocative one which left many doors open. Those doors were now closed.

Attention was focussed in 1990 on Liberia, with numbers of Liberian refugees making their way to safe haven in The Gambia and Jawara sending a small detachment of Gambian troops to support the West African ECOMOG forces trying to maintain the peace in Liberia – The Gambia's first overseas military expedition. Administrative failures resulted in the soldiers not being paid and a dangerous confrontation was narrowly averted when they returned to Banjul. The chief of the armed forces resigned, admitting he'd lost the confidence of his men, and was replaced by a Nigerian officer. It was a warning of changes to come.

President Jawara was re-elected for a sixth term in April 1992, after being persuaded to stand, despite his wish to retire. He polled 58 percent of the vote; his nearest rival Mustapha Dibba 22 percent. Jawara softened his stance against MOJA-G and the Gambian Socialist Revolutionary Party, announcing an amnesty for all members of the previously proscribed organizations. He also began again to make noises about corruption in public life.

■ Military rule

The corruption issue boiled up quickly through the end of the 1994 dry season. In April there were protests in Brikama – the country's third largest town, close to the coast but not benefitting from tourism – over the unaffordable cost of public utilities. Then, on July 22, after returning ECOMOG soldiers had been rudely treated by Nigerian commanding officers at Banjul airport, their widespread anger and demands for unpaid salaries coalesced through the day into a successful **coup** led by **Lt Yahya Jammeh** with the support of a hastily assembled **Armed Forces Provisional Ruling Council (AFPRC)**. Jawara and some of his cabinet fled to the sanctuary of an American ship, coincidentally docked at Banjul, and received asylum in Senegal. Others were arrested.

Jammeh, a young, uncharismatic figure in painfully dark glasses, made a poor impression on the international community. Casual observers had long harboured the illusion that Jawara's Gambia was one of the few admirable political cultures in West Africa. Indeed, it appeared hard at first to find an altruistic justification for a coup in The Gambia. Though the country's human rights record was not unblemished, the fundamental fairness of its multi-party system had not seemed open to question. Opposition parties were consistently frustrated at elections but the evidence for vote-rigging was limited. Jawara won because he commanded a popular following.

However, the AFPRC has been able to convince sceptics that, fair or not, the political system was shoring up a Gambian state riddled with **corruption** from bottom to top: President Jawara himself was said to have spent the equivalent of the annual health care budget in a six-day shopping trip to Switzerland just weeks before the coup. Jammeh insisted his administration, which included some civilian members, would seek the return of stolen state property.

Jammeh's announcement, however, that the AFPRC would not step down to an elected civilian government until 1998, was greeted with disbelief. After an unsuccessful counter-coup, in which several soldiers were killed, and a reported threat by Jammeh to the safety of citizens of countries planning the forcible reinstatement of Jawara, the British government warned tourists the country was unsafe to visit. The **tour operators** and charter airlines pulled out and tourism plummeted to 20 percent of normal levels, precipitating a genuine crisis.

The response was pragmatic: Jammeh brought the date of transition forward to July 1996, which led to the withdrawal of the Foreign Office's travel advisory notice. As this book went to press it was expected that, with the lifting of the travel warning, tour operators would resume selling Gambian holidays for the winter 1995–96 season.

Jammeh has considerable grassroots support from a population who largely haven't noticed a downswing in their fortunes since his coup, and who are anticipating some results from the AFPRC's efforts to return looted Gambian funds. They may be disappointed: ministers previously sacked by Jawara for corruption have been given posts by Jammeh and there are rumours that the AFPRC itself is not squeaky-clean. The test for Jammeh will come in the dry season of 1996 as the country prepares for his departure and the return of an elected government. Indications are that he will try to make his 22 July Movement into a political party and, taking his example from Jerry Rawlings in Ghana, make every effort to stay in power as a civilian president.

BANJUL AND THE KOMBO PENINSULA

Banjul and its hinterland, fronted by 50km of broad beaches, are all that most visitors to The Gambia ever see. A good number of the country's best points and virtually all the hotels are located here.

The **beaches** are naturally the big attraction for the tour operators, with good ones in the **Bakau**, **Fajara**, **Kotu** and **Kololi** resort areas and some truly spectacular strands as you head south. Inland, in **Kombo North**, **Kombo South** and **Kombo Central** districts, dozens of small, back-country villages set in the random patchwork of forest, savannah and farmland, are accessible on foot, by bicycle or rented car, or by bush taxi or bus.

For **naturalists**, and especially ornithologists, the region is a rewarding one. The maze of mangrove-festooned **creeks** behind Banjul and the justly popular **Abuko Nature Reserve** have great appeal, and even walks in the bush near the hotels can yield delightful discoveries such as monkeys, parrots, chameleons and tortoises.

A large and expanding proportion of the population of The Gambia lives in this district, but **Banjul** itself, sited on a flat island jutting into the mouth of the **Gambia River**, is sleepy and unfocussed, and increasingly a daytime city only. At dusk, workers by the truck- and bus-load pour back over Denton bridge and down the new highway to the relative metropolis of **Serekunda** and the leafier districts around **Bakau**, behind the hotels. There's not a lot to draw you to Banjul and nothing in the line of recreation that could hold you longer than a day. Arriving overland from Senegal, however, or flying in to start a trip through West Africa, the capital is likely to figure to some extent in your plans, and if you're on a strict budget, it offers the only choice of cheap hotels within walking distance of key offices and shops. Details of places to stay and eat are included below, with a few ideas on how to pass the time if you're picking up visas, booking flights, waiting for mail or money, or otherwise treading water. But you may prefer to mingle with the sun-worshippers out by the hotels and commute into town if necessary.

Transport around the Banjul area

Between Banjul, Serekunda and the resorts you've got the choice of licensed charter taxis or local transport. A clutch of **licensed cabs** can usually be found outside every hotel, or group of hotels, with the fixed fares displayed. In the resorts, and especially in high season, there's more competition among the drivers and some may be prepared to offer you better prices. But note that the rules forbid taxi drivers to under-

ARRIVING BY AIR

Air arrivals are low-key and straightforward. Little **Yundum airport** is 24km south of Banjul and 18km from the resorts. If you arrive by charter flight you may be met by a dance troupe who entertain you as you stand in line for formalities and broil under the sun. Once you've identified your luggage and passed customs, zealous porters whisk away your bags to waiting buses. If you're not on a package, hold onto them. The *Meridien Bank* exchange counter is usually open, but offers rather below-average rates. Fixed **taxi** fares from the airport are posted on a board outside the arrivals area – D150 is the rate for either Banjul or the resorts. Otherwise it's a three-kilometre walk to the main road where, during the day, you can pick up a bus or bush taxi, either straight into Banjul or just as far as **Serekunda**, where you can get another up **Kairaba Avenue** to the beaches.

cut the agreed rates, and you can cause confrontations if you persuade an unlicensed cab to carry you when licensed cabs are waiting nearby.

Local transport comes in the shape of beat-up shared taxis and modern minibuses, which of course cost a small fraction of the price of charter taxis. For trips **from Banjul** to the resorts, Serekunda, or as far as **Brikama**, take a minibus or Peugeot taxi from the Serekunda or Brikama taxi stands off Albion Place. The main taxi stand for local services **from Serekunda** to the beaches at Kotu and Kololi is at "London Corner", near the market.

For journeys from Banjul south **along the Atlantic coast**, get a *GPTC* bus from the depot in the Half Die district in the southern part of town. It's worth the walk to be sure of a seat, as, by the time buses reach the northern part of Banjul, they're invariably full.

Banjul

At no time of year is **BANJUL** a prepossessing place. Although most of the main streets have recently been surfaced, it can still be chokingly dusty in the dry season, and the alleys become a chaos of red mud and puddles during the rains. The dilapidated architecture of corrugated iron and peeling paint, and a lattice of open drains – with no slopes to drain them – complete a somewhat melancholy picture.

As a national capital, Banjul (or Bathurst as it was known to the colonial British) was doomed to failure by its site. It was acquired by Britain in 1816 to defend the river from slavers and to control trade with the interior, but its size was restricted to the area of land that could be kept free of flooding from the creeks and swamps behind. **Bund Road** dykes the city on its present small patch, and further expansion is impossible. Hot, confined and seething with mosquitoes, Banjul is not a town where many choose to live. The exodus after business hours is understandable, and nightlife all but nonexistent.

If you have to be here, compensations are scant. With a population of barely 50,000 and shrinking, Banjul is too small to offer any of the ordinary facilities and diversions of a capital – though at least whatever you need to accomplish can usually be done in reasonable safety, and on foot. Walking gets you anywhere and the paranoia of some West African capitals is absent.

Orientation and accommodation

There are two **approaches** to Banjul. If you're coming from Senegal, you'll arrive on the north bank of the Gambia River, at the small port of Barra (see p.280). From here the regular ferry brings you straight to the wharf in Banjul town centre. The second, more stately approach is from the south bank, along the Banjul–Serekunda highway, which forks into **Independence Avenue** and **Marina Parade**. The latter is one of Banjul's pleasanter and shadier streets, fringed with somnolent wooden government buildings and terminating, after the hospital and the *Atlantic Hotel*, at the guarded gates of **State House**. Independence Avenue, widened and resurfaced, is graced with the new and impressive, boat-shaped Court House.

Despite its compactness, Banjul's layout can be initially confusing as all the streets look much the same, though a few street-name plates give some assistance. Note that Leman St has had its name officially changed to OAU Bd, and Cameron St to Nelson Mandela St, though both are usually still known by their old names. Most of your movements are likely to be around **MacCarthy Square** (where they sometimes play cricket) and down the waterfront on Wellington Street, with the **Albert market**, post office and banks.

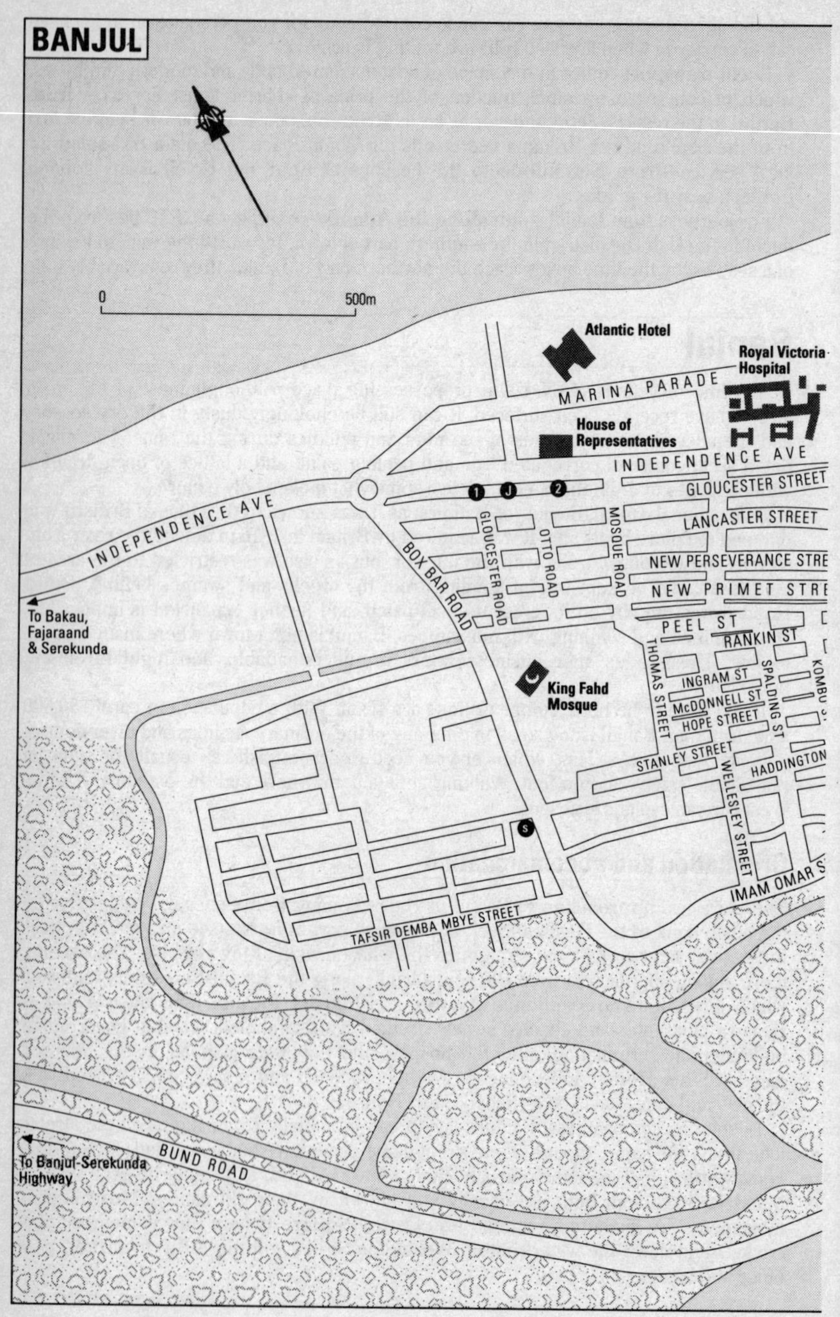
BANJUL
0
500m
Atlantic Hotel
Royal Victoria Hospital
MARINA PARADE
House of Representatives
INDEPENDENCE AVE
GLOUCESTER STREET
LANCASTER STREET
NEW PERSEVERANCE STRE
NEW PRIMET STRE
INDEPENDENCE AVE
BOX BAR ROAD
GLOUCESTER ROAD
OTTO ROAD
MOSQUE ROAD
PEEL ST
RANKIN ST
THOMAS STREET
INGRAM ST
McDONNELL ST
HOPE STREET
SPALDING ST
KOMBU S
STANLEY STREET
HADDINGTON
WELLESLEY STREET
IMAM OMAR S
King Fahd Mosque
To Bakau, Fajaraand & Serekunda
TAFSIR DEMBA MBYE STREET
BUND ROAD
To Banjul-Serekunda Highway

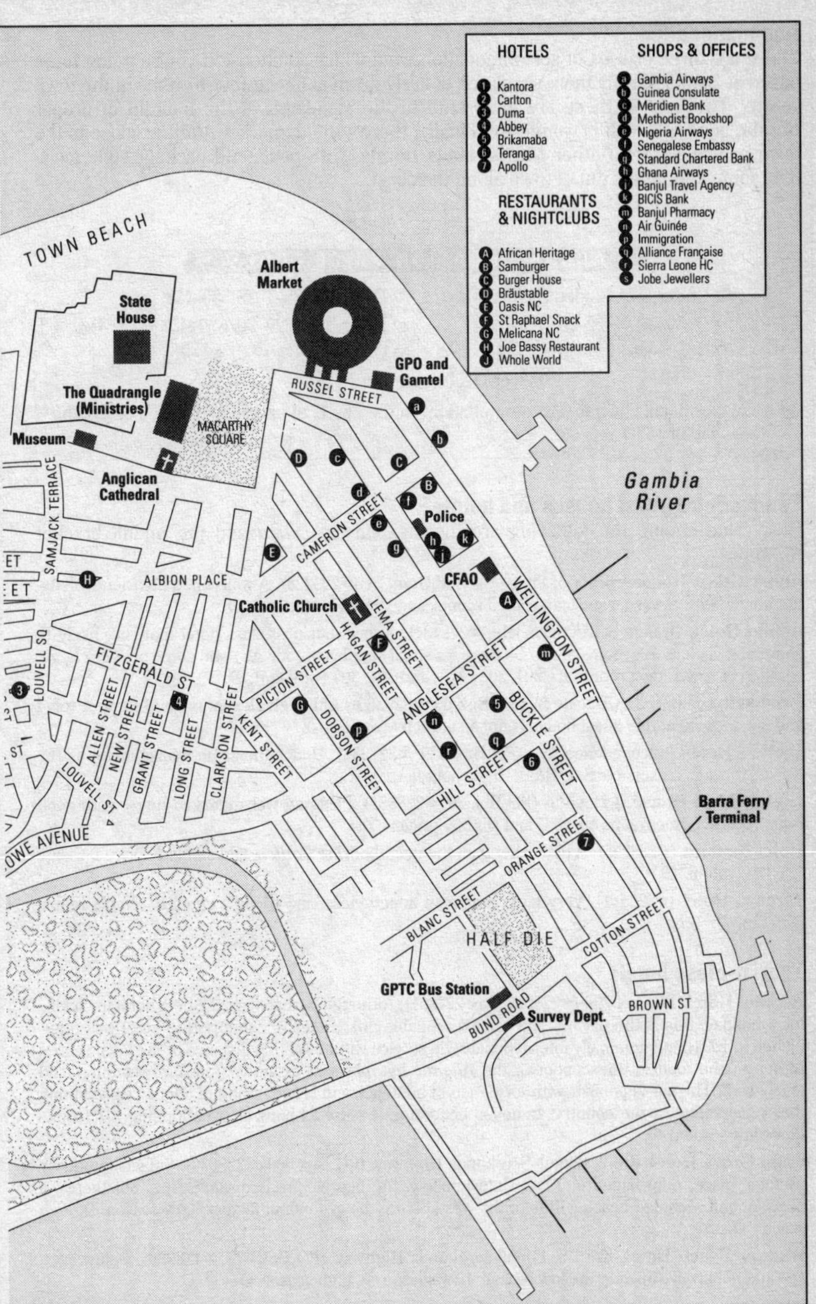
HOTELS
1 Kantora
2 Carlton
3 Duma
4 Abbey
5 Brikamaba
6 Teranga
7 Apollo
RESTAURANTS & NIGHTCLUBS
A African Heritage
B Samburger
C Burger House
D Bräustable
E Oasis NC
F St Raphael Snack
G Melicana NC
H Joe Bassy Restaurant
J Whole World
SHOPS & OFFICES
a Gambia Airways
b Guinea Consulate
c Meridien Bank
d Methodist Bookshop
e Nigeria Airways
f Senegalese Embassy
g Standard Chartered Bank
h Ghana Airways
j Banjul Travel Agency
k BICIS Bank
m Banjul Pharmacy
n Air Guinée
p Immigration
q Alliance Française
r Sierra Leone HC
s Jobe Jewellers
TOWN BEACH
State House
Albert Market
GPO and Gamtel
RUSSEL STREET
The Quadrangle (Ministries)
MACARTHY SQUARE
Museum
Anglican Cathedral
SAMJACK TERRACE
Gambia River
CAMERON STREET
Police
ALBION PLACE
CFAO
Catholic Church
WELLINGTON STREET
LEMA STREET
HAGAN STREET
FITZGERALD ST
LOUVELL SQ
PICTON STREET
ANGLESEA STREET
BUCKLE STREET
KENT STREET
DOBSON STREET
ALLEN STREET
NEW STREET
GRANT STREET
LONG STREET
CLARKSON STREET
LOUVELL ST
HILL STREET
Barra Ferry Terminal
OWE AVENUE
ORANGE STREET
BLANC STREET
HALF DIE
COTTON STREET
GPTC Bus Station
BUND ROAD
Survey Dept.
BROWN ST

Accommodation

There are three classes of accommodation from which to choose if you're going to be based at Banjul. Firstly there's a clutch of fairly down-at-heel **guest houses** in the town centre. The best of these are almost up to the standards of the handful of proper **hotels**, none of which is wonderful. Finally, there's the upmarket *Atlantic*, close to the town centre, and two other **tourist-class hotels**, with pools and package-style facilities, some kilometres out of town along the coast.

ACCOMMODATION PRICE CODES

① Under D75 (under £5/$7.50) ② D75–150 (£5–10/$7.50–15)
③ D150–300 (£10–20/$15–30) ④ D300–450 (£20–30/$30–45)
⑤ D450–600 (£30–40/$45–60) ⑥ D600–750 (£40–50/$60–75)
⑦ Over D750 (over £50/$75)

For further details turn to "Accommodation" in the Practical Information at the beginning of this chapter.

Town centre guest houses and hotels

Best value among the following are the inexpensive *Duma* and the middle-bracket *Kantora*.

Abbey Guest House, corner of Fitzgerald and Grant St (☎225228). A well-run, quite friendly lodging house, with airy, spacious, fan-cooled rooms, and shared bathrooms. ②.

Apollo Hotel, Orange St (PO Box 419; ☎228184). A local business-class hotel that isn't likely to suit many visitors. All rooms are S/C (there's a small supplement for AC) and some are very large, with street views. Best rooms are 201, 202 (AC), and 301, 302 (with fan). ④.

Brikamaba Hotel, 24A Buckle St (PO Box 60; ☎229380). Although all rooms have shower, toilet and fan, lodging at this guest house is not an attractive option. ②.

Carlton Hotel, Independence Ave (PO Box 639; ☎227258). Under the same management as the *Apollo*, this has reasonable S/C B&B. ③, without fan, ④ AC.

Duma Guest House, 1 Hope St (PO Box 39; ☎228381). Pleasant, well-managed house with good rates (B&B). Some rooms are S/C and slightly pricier. ②.

Hotel Kantora (☎228715). A better bet than the neighbouring *Carlton*, and similarly priced. Clean, S/C, AC rooms. ③.

Teranga Hotel (☎225641). Very tatty, but clean nonetheless, and friendly enough. Simple rooms with fan. ②.

Tourist-class hotels

Atlantic Hotel, PO Box 296 (☎228601; Fax 227861). Although perhaps not the best hotel to choose for a holiday, this is the place if you want reasonable guarantees of comfort (the hotel was refurbished in 1994) and nominally international-style service within walking distance of the town centre. Although the food is unexceptional, the *Atlantic* has pleasant grounds (fine birdwatching) and lovely staff. The bar is popular with local men of influence and is something of a focus for anything that's happening in the country. In-house generators ensure 24-hour air conditioning. ⑦ (sometimes low-season) ④.

Palm Grove Hotel, Km 2, Banjul–Serekunda Highway (PO Box 600; ☎228630). Smallish, unfussy package place, refurbished in 1994. Unfortunately, the beach here is disappearing, but there's a pleasant and secluded beach a little to the west, before the groundnut factory. Low season ④, high season ⑥.

Wadner Beach Hotel, Km 2.5, Banjul-Serekunda Highway (PO Box 377; ☎428239). Below average and not always open in the low season. Low season ④, high season ⑥.

The Town

The **Museum** (Mon–Thurs 8.30am–4pm, Fri & Sat 8.30am–12.30pm; D10) doesn't contain a wildly exciting display, but they haven't the funds to keep up the present collection, let alone improve it. A great deal of mouldering ethnographia – mostly the remains of private collections and not all of it Gambian – and a lot of old anthropological "type" photos are the predominant features. But there are a few discoveries to be made if you take time to peer into some of the dark corners. Excellent *warri* boards (a traditional game; see p.63), fascinating maps and documents and generally informative stuff about the wars and migrations of the Senegambia region are all worth going for. There's an impressive array of palm wine tapping and drinking equipment, and don't leave without a look at the early Iron Age wood drill with its modern-looking bit. The curator, Mr Sidibe, is interesting if you both have time.

African Heritage on Wellington Street (see "Restaurants") has a **gallery** housing miscellaneous *objets d'art*, carvings, paintings and more, all for sale, including some amazing old guns.

Albert Market

Market business is one of Banjul's big pluses. After the fire which gutted the old **Albert Market** in 1986, the art of bargaining has regained its spark in the resurrected marketplace (Mon–Sat). As a relatively laid-back and rather sanitized version of what you find everywhere in West Africa the Albert is not bad – and you won't get lost. The highly enjoyable **tourist market** is currently to be found on a patch of waste ground west of the *Atlantic Hotel*, where Independence Avenue meets Marina Parade (after its "temporary" relocation here, however, it will eventually move back to its old spot by Albert Market). Take a pocketful of dalasis and argue your head off. While you're busy bargaining for D2 bangles you can eye up the better merchandise and come back later if it appeals. There are some great bargains, especially in cloth and clothing: Chinese-made clothes are especially cheap, as import duty in The Gambia is very low. If you're not into parting with money at all then you're likely to feel uneasy – and free gifts of the very thing you didn't want are all part of the wearing-down process. Go in a bright mood.

Walks out of town

While the beach hotels will set you off on an organized minibus "city tour" – which really seems a little pointless – there are a number of manageable and more gratifying **walks** you can do near the town. A big one for bird-watchers is the morning or evening stroll along **Bund Road**, best at high tide when the birds are very prolific and the smelly mudbanks water-covered. Allow a couple of hours, but don't take unnecessary valuables, and ascertain the current safety of the excursion or go in a group: there have been several muggings in recent years.

From Banjul, Bund Road joins the Serekunda road between the prison and *Radio Syd*: turn left here and there's a short walk to the *Palm Grove* and *Wadner Beach Hotel*, the latter with really cheap beer. Walking back to town, there are Muslim and Christian cemeteries if you're interested – the epitaphs on some of the Christian tombstones are recommended reading – though much of the Muslim cemetery has been eroded by the waves, occasionally producing macabre beach-combings. The Scout HQ and – curious find – Masonic Hall are also out here on the seafront.

If you walk **along the beach** between the *Atlantic* and the markets, go in company or carry just the bare essentials – if you're going to get robbed anywhere it might be here. Which is a shame, as it's a fine walk, especially in the early evening when hundreds of boys are out doing exercises, playing football, developing their Kung Fu skills and jogging. Between the shore and Albert Market, fishing boats smother the beach: this is where to come to negotiate a private creek trip.

Eating and nightlife

The opportunities for **eating and drinking** are unexciting. Looking for cheap eats is a strangely thankless task, though the Albert Market has plenty of basic, stand-and-stuff fare. If you're looking for a decent evening meal you'll quickly gravitate to *Bräustüble*, while probably the nicest lunchtime retreat is *African Heritage*, though it's very remote from the life of Banjul.

Restaurants

African Heritage, 16 Wellington St (☎226906). A cool waterfront place, great for watching street life, with a daily menu, cold beer and soft drinks, but on the expensive side, as you'd expect. Danish-run, it has a gallery and crafts shop where you can sometimes find interesting works and ethnographic bits and pieces.

Bräustüble, 77 Leman St (☎228371). The only convincing restaurant in town, offering well-prepared but not notably Germanic dishes – excellent *domodah* (often unavailable in the cheaper places that advertise it) and fish soups. Sandwiches at lunchtime from around D15. Main dishes from about D40.

Burger House, Cameron St. *Chawarmas*, burgers and ice cream. Modest prices.

Joe Bassy Restaurant, off Albion Place. Small chop house brightened by magazine pages on the walls. Cheap soft drinks, and *domodah* D5, meat and onion sandwiches about D15.

Oasis, Clarkson St. *Chawarmas* round the clock from the street side of the nightclub.

St Raphael Snack Bar, Picton St. Cheap and homely cafe, open from 7am for breakfast and snacks and dishes in the day and evening. Cold beer.

Samburger, 10 Cameron St. Senegalese-style *chawarma* joint. Fair prices.

Whole World Bar & Restaurant, Independence Ave. Pick-up joint crammed with television sets, serving grills and snacks.

Nightlife

Nightlife in Banjul hardly sparkles, and you should be careful wandering around after dark with valuables. The long-established *Oasis* **nightclub** is lively in the high season though it's not always worth the D30–40 entrance. Also check out the *Melicana Nightclub* on the corner of Dobson and Picton streets, which has a nice atmosphere and is certainly a contender, with cheap *Julbrew*. At least one new club springs up each season in Banjul, but few survive and prospects aren't good. You could check if anything watchable is showing at either of the two **cinemas**, the *Eros* or the *Ritz* – they show mostly Indian movies.

The resorts – and Serekunda

The Gambia's tourist strip runs for some 10km along the sandy low cliffs to the Atlantic coast, barely twenty hotels accounting for virtually the whole package industry. Although the industry is small in international terms, the population here has hugely expanded since the first plane loads of tourists arrived from Sweden less than thirty years ago. The old rural economy of planting, fishing and palm wine tapping is fading fast and, when the tourist industry suffers a crash, as it did after the coup in 1994, it is clear how much the district depends upon it.

Tourism has transformed the area utterly. It's only remarkable that the Gambians who live here have retained such an equable regard for visitors who generally pay them such scant attention. As always where the poor world meets the holidaying rich, the stories of locals who made good by marrying abroad fuel hopes and dampen the inevitable resentment. More positively there's considerable enthusiasm for having a good time and it's not impossible to meet local people in the bars and discos or on the beach without the question of patronage creeping in.

There are four main **resorts**. **BAKAU**, the most significant coastal community after Banjul itself, is the longest-established resort, its "old town", east of Sait Matty Road a swarming village of dirt streets and noisy compounds, home to many of the hotel staff, while the "new town", west of Sait Matty Road, is more villas and lawns. **FAJARA**, down the coast, is hard to define, and merges into **KOTU**, with a clump of established hotels, at the debouchment of the small Kotu stream. Finally, further south, there's **KOLOLI**, separated from the suburban sprawl, and the location of the most upmarket hotels.

If you're interested in staying close to the heart of Gambian life, **SEREKUNDA**, the country's largest town, a couple of kilometres inland from the resorts, is the place. The Gambia's energy is concentrated here and it can give you (even if you're travelling nowhere else) a strong flavour of modern, urban West Africa – a choking racket of diesel engines, half-collapsed wooden trolleys, bricollaged stalls selling a riot of dust-covered imports, and music blaring from the hundreds of cassette players and radios. The focus of all this is the town's central lorry/taxi park and market. It's a lot of fun, and not unsafe, to wander round here, though avoid dangling your valuables.

If you stay in Serekunda, you can commute to the beaches in ten minutes and get the best of both worlds; the beach bars and restaurants on the coast and the chop houses and local dives in Serekunda. The thoroughfare that links the resorts and Serekunda is **Kairaba Avenue**, the former Pipeline Road that, until just a few years ago was a rutted track running through fields and orchards. Today, Kairaba's three-kilometre length is dotted, and increasingly lined, with shops, bars, restaurants and offices, and commands the highest rents in the country.

Accommodation

By international standards most of the **tourist hotels** along the coastal strip are quite basic, though they all have pools. The rates below, unless otherwise indicated, are for S/C rooms, breakfast included. In season, the Kotu to Kololi stretch becomes the heartbeat of the tourist industry, while Bakau hotels are somewhat quieter.

If you've travelling independently and looking for somewhere reasonably cheap to flop out for a few days, you'll find there are few **budget lodgings in the resort area** and, in the high season, you'll need to persevere to find a good-value room – assuming you find any space at all. Alternatives are provided by several friendly, non-package establishments in the **countryside**, a few kilometres south of the Kololi beach hotels. Located just north of Bijilo, these are good for longer stays and, in season, are often full of guests who come each year. Another option is to stay in the hinterland town of **Serekunda**, which has its complement of standard lodgings and eating houses, ranging from fairly squalid to quite decent, but none of them "tourist hotels". If you're looking for a deeper immersion in local life than the coast can provide, try any of these. Finally, if you are interested in staying as a **house guest in a Gambian compound** (something which many in Bakau and Serekunda are happy to offer as they can charge daily the equivalent of a week's wages), then just ask around and take pot luck: you should expect to be asked anything from D75 to D150 per day, with meals included, depending on the season. It's usually easiest to find this kind of arrangment by staying first in a cheap hotel.

STREET NAMES IN BAKAU

A number of roads in Bakau have either recently had their names changed or carry the burden of more than one. Atlantic Rd and Atlantic Ave are one and the same; New Town Rd is now officially Garba Jahumpa Rd; Kairaba Ave used to be known as Pipeline Rd, and often still is; and the main road from Kairaba Ave to Kotu and Kololi is officially known as Badala Highway.

Tourist hotels – Bakau

African Village, PO Box 604 Banjul, (☎495307; Fax 496042). Perched on low cliffs, this is an old favourite with a brilliant pool bar. Recommended, despite the lack of beach (an artificial slab substitutes), partly because of its convenient location in the heart of Bakau, partly because of its warm, Gambian atmosphere. Not all rooms have AC. Low season ④, high season ⑥.

Amies Beach Hotel & Apartments, Cape Point, Bakau (PO Box 600 Banjul; ☎495035; Fax ☎496484). Not on the best beach, this is, strictly speaking, at the mouth of the estuary. Opened in 1989 and beginning to mellow, it remains fairly basic, but is good for families, with a large, shady pool, decent bar prices and spacious accommodation. Low season ③–④, high season ⑤–⑥.

Cape Point Hotel, Cape Point, Bakau (PO Box 2294 Serekunda; ☎495005; Fax 495375). Modest and low-key, but rather nice, with a small pool. Again, the beach isn't up to much. Low season ③, high season ④.

Sunwing Gambia, Cape Point, Bakau (PO Box 2638 Serekunda; ☎495428; Fax 496102). Right on the headland, with both estuary and oceanside beachfronts (beware currents). Excellent reputation, with lots to do, and well organized. Rooms are simple, but pleasant, all with fans and AC. Best are those in blocks 100, 200, 300. Low season ⑤, high season ⑥.

Tourist hotels – Fajara

Fajara, Atlantic Rd, Fajara (PO Box 2489 Serekunda; ☎495605). Unattractive shambles, set amid shaved lawns and struggling shrubs, and in need of a complete refurbishment. Way overpriced. Low season ④, high season ⑦.

Francisco's, Atlantic Rd, Fajara (PO Box 2609 Serekunda; ☎495332). Popular tropical garden restaurant with a clutch of pleasant rooms in a nice setting, 5min from a quiet stretch of beach. Low season ④, high season ⑤–⑥.

Tourist hotels – Kotu

Badala Park, PMB 467 Serekunda (☎460400; Fax 460402). For such a new hotel (1992), everything looks pretty rough, but, on the plus side, some rooms (fans only) are a good size, and the gardens are attractive. Cross the road to the beach. Low season ⑤, high season ⑥.

Bakotu Hotel, PO Box 532 Banjul (☎465555). High season only. Swedish-run and informal, with relaxed service and keen prices. An attactive, intimately designed place back from the coast with no beach of its own (avoid a room overlooking the road). ⑥.

Bungalow Beach, PO Box 2637 Serekunda (☎465288; Fax 466180). Pricey apartment hotel with loyal clientele but no outstanding features. Right on a good beach, it's peaceful, but charmless. Monthly low-season rates about ⑤, high season ⑦.

Kombo Beach Hotel, PO Box 694 Banjul (☎465466; Fax 465490). One of the French *Novotel* chain, this is a mature establishment, with a strong French accent. Busy, always lively, with plenty of activities, and right on an excellent beach. Low season ⑤–⑥, high season ⑦.

Kotu Strand Village Hotel, PO Box 957 Banjul (☎465609). Not a smart place, with dull grounds and an unappealing pool, but, in compensation, the rooms are well maintained and the beach is just 20m away. Low season ④, high season ⑥.

Tourist hotels – Kololi

Holiday Beach Club, PO Box 312 (☎460419; Fax 460418). Very downmarket establishment on a poor site, with little shade. Discounts are available on the set rates – low season ⑤, high season ⑥.

Kairaba Hotel, PMB 390 Serekunda (☎462940; Fax 462947). Splendid place for a beach holiday if you can afford it, this is The Gambia's top hotel, with wide-ranging facilities. Pleasant rooms, with direct dial phones, excellent bathrooms, safe, TV – the lot. Honeymoon territory. Low and high seasons ⑦.

Kololi Beach Club, PMB 241 Serekunda (☎463255; Fax 463182). Rather barren timeshare site, but well run by cheery staff. Peaceful beach and simple restaurant are open to non-residents, and empty units are sometimes available to rent.

Palma Rima Hotel, PMB 350 Serekunda (☎463380; Fax 460002). With its main-block rooms simply functional and those in the bungalow annexes only slightly better, a vast pool (largest in The Gambia) but little shade around it, and a 5min walk to the beach past building sites, this doesn't make a great impression overall. Low season ⑤, high season ⑦.

Senegambia Beach Hotel, PO Box 2373 Serekunda (☎462717; Fax 461839). Gigantic but recommended for its impressive tropical gardens and good beach, generally high standards and excellent food. Cool, clean rooms, with either AC or fans. 50D entry fee for non-guests. Low season ⑥, high season ⑦.

Budget lodgings in Bakau, Fajara and Kololi

Atlantic Guest House, 78 Atlantic Rd, Fajara (☎496237). *The* travellers' haunt on the coastal strip, a scruffy but likeable old mansion, nearly falling off the cliff top, with its own, nearly hustler-free beach. Large rooms with shared facilities in the main house, and overflow rooms in a separate block. Owners run a drum-making business. Breakfast and other meals available. Overpriced but substantial discounts in the low season. ③.

Fajara Guest House, 23rd St West (off Atlantic Rd), Fajara (PMB 347 Serekunda; ☎496122). Friendly management and slightly better appointed rooms (with fans) than the nearby *Safari Garden*. The negotiable rates vary seasonally. ③.

Friendship Hotel, Bakau Stadium (☎495829). Functional and impersonal and too far from the beach to be really useful without transport. Tennis court. Rooms with fan or AC. ③.

Kekoi's Happy Guest House, Kololi village (Fax 465544, at *Gamtel's* public office, Kotu). Very cosy atmosphere in a Gambian family compound. Clean rooms, with fans and toilets. Chatting with the owner and friends will quickly introduce you to The Gambia. Fax in advance for an airport pick-up. ①–②.

Kololi Inn & Tavern, Kololi village (PMB 273 Serekunda; ☎463410; Fax 229572). A great place to unwind in cool, African surroundings, though about 1km from the coast. Workshops in drumming and dancing, tie-dye and Gambian cooking are available in high season. ③.

Leybato Guest House, off Kairaba Ave, about 1km from the beach (PO Box 2180; ☎390275). Get to it by going round the back of the big Pipeline Mosque and then a further 200m from the road. Big compound with a number of rooms around it, each effectively a small apartment with living room, twin bedroom, kitchen and bathroom. Basic, but ideal for long budget stays (under D1500 month). ①–②.

Mango Tree Guest House, Kololi, 15 minutes walk from the *Palma Rima* crossroads (☎460895). Pleasant, well-run guest house, with a good breakfast included. New "backpackers' block" is cheaper. Bar and restaurant. ③.

New Town Guest House, JJ Bakar Ave, off Garba Jahumpa Ave, Bakau (PMB 495 Serekunda; ☎496930). Formerly the *Malawi*, this is a good budget option, popular with volunteers, with basic, clean rooms (fan or AC), simple dining room, and communal kitchen available. ②–③.

Safari Garden Hotel, off Atlantic Rd, Fajara (PO Box 604 Serekunda; ☎495887). Pleasant place with a small pool and rooms with fans only. Shady garden and patios. B&B, ③ low season, ④ high season.

Sambou's, Old Cape Road, Bakau (☎495237). Noisy, convivial drinking place with a few rooms. ③.

Countryside accommodation

Adjis, near Kololi and *Boucarabou* (c/o PO Box 933 Serekunda; Fax 460023, at the *Gamtel* public office, Kololi). Purpose-built small guesthouse, with pleasant rooms, though less privacy than *Montrose*. Fax for airport pickup. Rates are very negotiable. ③.

Boucarabou Hotel, Ker Serigne Njaga, midway between Kololi village and Bijilo (PO Box 2491 Serekunda; no tel). An innovative hotel offering simple accommodation, exploiting renewable resources (vegetable gardens and fruit orchards, solar panels) in a delightful environment, with two *bantabas* for relaxing and enjoying the cultural focus of the place – music teaching and appreciation (see box on p.281). Closed out of season. ③.

Montrose Holidays, Bijilo village (PO Box 2436 Serekunda; mobile ☎994844; Fax 460023, at the *Gamtel* public office, Kololi). Very small, low-key homestay set-up, a real get-away; thatched huts and self-catering cottages in the garden of a Gambian-Scottish couple. Fax them in advance to be collected from the airport. Meals are available and the beach is 10min away. B&B rates are based on a weekly tariff, with reductions out of season and for each extra week. ③.

Serekunda accommodation

Gambisara Hotel, 1 Kairaba Ave (PO Box 269 Serekunda; ☎393114). Pleasant garden, but the non-S/C rooms are no great shakes and have standing fans only. There's some connection with the small mosque on the premises ("No alcohol, no prostitution"). ③.

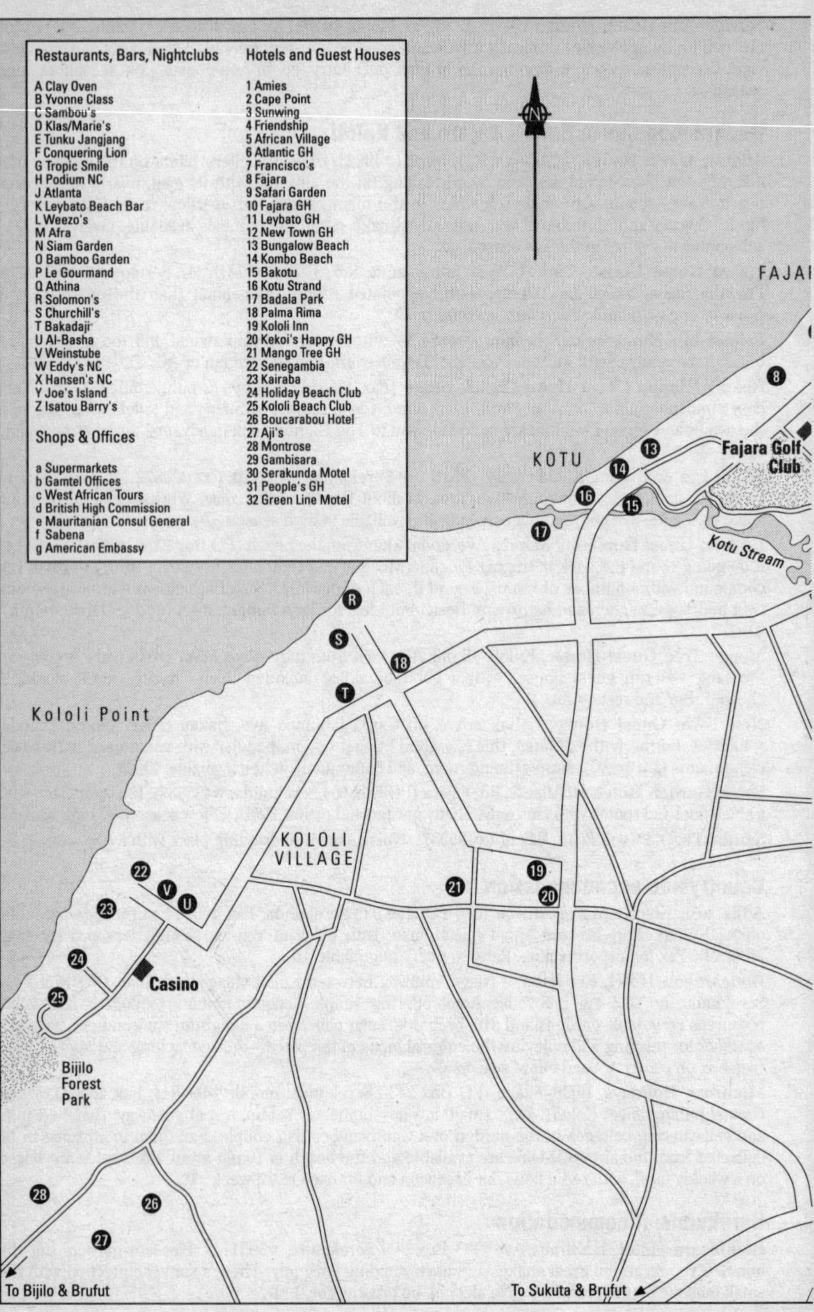
Restaurants, Bars, Nightclubs
A Clay Oven
B Yvonne Class
C Sambou's
D Klas/Marie's
E Tunku Jangjang
F Conquering Lion
G Tropic Smile
H Podium NC
J Atlanta
K Leybato Beach Bar
L Weezo's
M Afra
N Siam Garden
O Bamboo Garden
P Le Gourmand
Q Athina
R Solomon's
S Churchill's
T Bakadaji
U Al-Basha
V Weinstube
W Eddy's NC
X Hansen's NC
Y Joe's Island
Z Isatou Barry's
Shops & Offices
a Supermarkets
b Gamtel Offices
c West African Tours
d British High Commission
e Mauritanian Consul General
f Sabena
g American Embassy
Hotels and Guest Houses
1 Amies
2 Cape Point
3 Sunwing
4 Friendship
5 African Village
6 Atlantic GH
7 Francisco's
8 Fajara
9 Safari Garden
10 Fajara GH
11 Leybato GH
12 New Town GH
13 Bungalow Beach
14 Kombo Beach
15 Bakotu
16 Kotu Strand
17 Badala Park
18 Palma Rima
19 Kololi Inn
20 Kekoi's Happy GH
21 Mango Tree GH
22 Senegambia
23 Kairaba
24 Holiday Beach Club
25 Kololi Beach Club
26 Boucarabou Hotel
27 Aji's
28 Montrose
29 Gambisara
30 Serakunda Motel
31 People's GH
32 Green Line Motel
N
FAJA
KOTU
Fajara Golf Club
Kotu Stream
Kololi Point
KOLOLI VILLAGE
Casino
Bijilo Forest Park
To Bijilo & Brufut
To Sukuta & Brufut

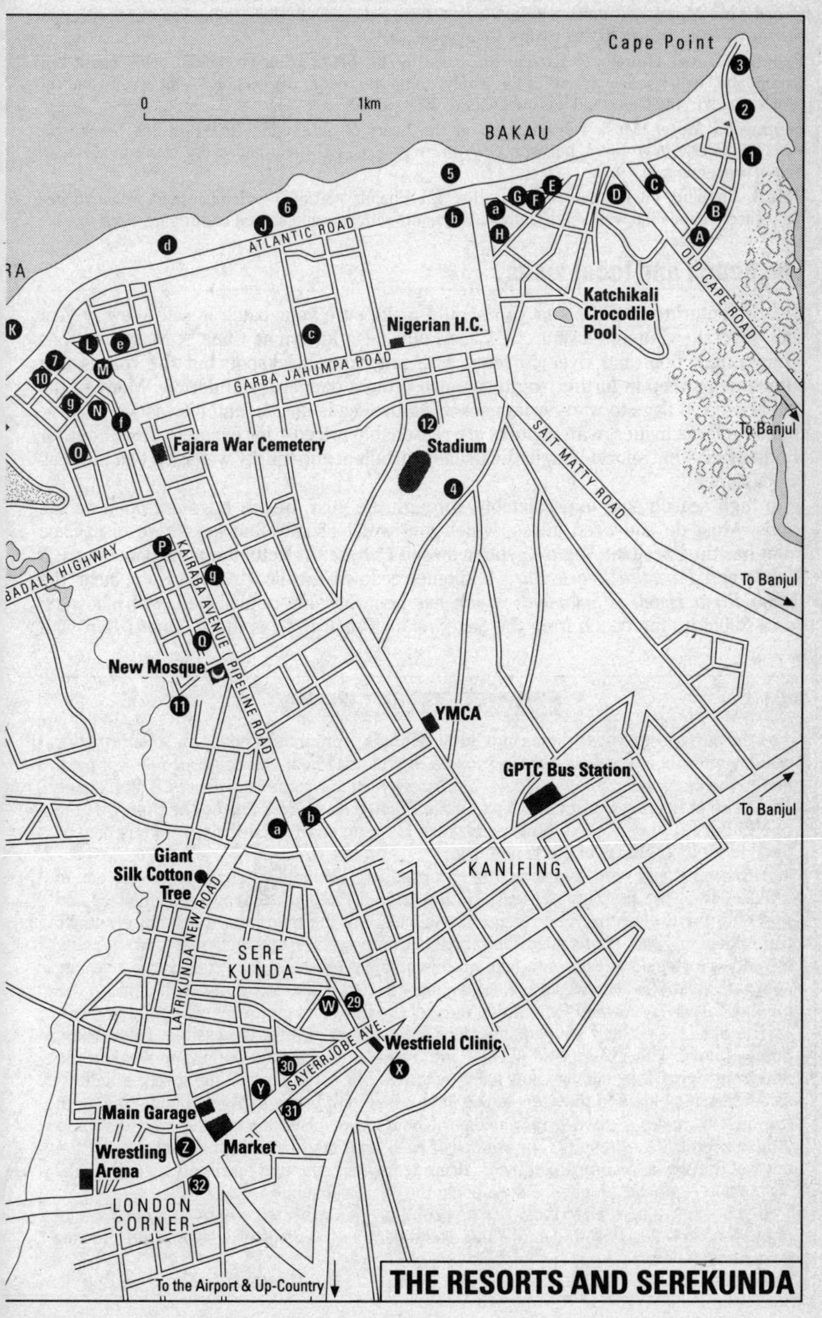

Cape Point
BAKAU
0
1km
ATLANTIC ROAD
OLD CAPE ROAD
Katchikali
Crocodile
Pool
Nigerian H.C.
GARBA JAHUMPA ROAD
SAIT MATTY ROAD
To Banjul
Fajara War Cemetery
Stadium
BADALA HIGHWAY
KAIRABA AVENUE (PIPELINE ROAD)
To Banjul
New Mosque
YMCA
GPTC Bus Station
To Banjul
KANIFING
Giant
Silk Cotton
Tree
LATRIKUNDA NEW ROAD
SERE
KUNDA
SAYERRJOBE AVE.
Westfield Clinic
Main Garage
Market
Wrestling
Arena
LONDON
CORNER
To the Airport & Up-Country
THE RESORTS AND SEREKUNDA

Green Line Motel, downtown Serekunda (☎394245; Fax 463382). Right in the heart of town, opposite the cinema. Clean S/C, AC rooms. Good value. ③.

People's Guest House, 12 Kwame Rd, close to the *BICIS* bank (☎391965). This has a real "compound" feel: you live as part of the family, go on the roof in the evening. A bit scruffy, but the people are extremely nice and it is inexpensive. B&B ②–③.

Serakunda Motel, Musa Dukureh Rd, in the heart of Serekunda (PO Box 384 Serekunda; ☎392780). Basic town hotel, but with *CNN* in every S/C, AC room and every convenience apart from a peaceful night. ③.

YMCA, Kanifing, off Kairaba Ave (PO Box 421 Banjul; ☎392647). Adequate and well-managed hostel accommodation with single and double rooms with fans and shared bathrooms. B&B ②–③.

The beach and local visits

Before venturing into the **sea** you should make sure your patch is safe – every year sees several swimmers swept out. Cape Point (also known as Cape St Mary), with its cross-cutting tidal and river currents, is a notorious blackspot, but the rollers that sometimes sweep in further south can also bring a dangerous undertow. Many of the hotels use red flags to warn swimmers when the sea is unsafe, and it's wise to observe them. As for activities, **watersports** are reasonably priced – for example, D60/hour for windsurfing – but snorkelling in the usually turbulent and murky water isn't an interesting pastime.

In high season and, unpredictably, through the year, **beach bars** are open on the sands. Most do squeezed juices, which you won't usually find anywhere else. Cape Point has the excellent Anglo-Egyptian-owned *Calypso*. At Kotu, the most popular are *Il Mondo* and *Paradise Beach Bar*. A kilometre down the beach from Kotu, near the *Palma Rima Hotel*, is *Solomon's* which has been lavishly refurbished, with showers. Some 200m up the beach from the *Senegambia Beach Hotel* is the *Bahamas Bar*, with

WRESTLING

To add purpose to your wanderings in Serekunda, you should head, on a Saturday or Sunday afternoon, for the **wrestling arena**. If you can't hear the noise, people will point you to the place when you get close – ask for *nyororu* in Mandinka, *boreh* in Wolof. It's on Mussa St, at London Corner in Dippa Kunda: if you pass *Marie's Pub* on the right (not the one in Bakau) you've gone too far. Entrance is cheap and the advertised time is usually 5pm, though nothing ever starts until later.

Drumming and whistling teams keep up steady competitive rhythms as the action builds slowly, the first few wrestlers pacing around the court flexing their muscles and psyching themselves up. The referee starts whistling the men into order and gradually the opponents pair off to start their bouts. Contestants are evenly matched, it being forbidden for small wrestlers to take on bigger men, however much the crowd roars its approval. At the Serekunda arena, teams are effectively divided along ethnic lines. The chunky Jola are renowned for winning most of the time, and for losing with good grace.

The object is to land your opponent on his back as cleanly as possible. Dust flying, bodies bound with *gri-gris* and slicked with sweat and charmed potions to weaken the opponent's grip, this usually takes a few seconds. But bouts can last for several minutes, as contestants bluff and threaten, facing each other with backs bent and hands trailing in the dust to make a good grip. Dozens of bouts take place during the afternoon and judges keep track of results. The winner of each bout takes a triumphal turn around the edge of the arena, accompanied by his drum team, and counting on collecting a few dalasis in appreciation as he goes. Take a pocketful of small change.

If you want to take **photos** there's no problem – it's expected – but you'll need a telephoto lens and fast film to capture the excitement as the contest develops and the sun goes down.

beautiful wooden carvings and good loos. The *Black and White* next door has excellent seafood. Close to *Francisco's Hotel* in Fajara is *Leybato Beach Bar* – a substantial place, which does good food. Also in Fajara is the *Fajara Club*, an old establishment that's seen much better days. With its main rooms a cross between a church hall and a rundown golf club, it's not an appealing prospect at first glance. But drinks are cheap and the clean pool at the back, with slides, is a big hit with children (temporary membership D75/day or D250/week; for golf details, see "Banjul and Area Listings").

Local visits

Bicycles can be rented at several hotels and at the main taxi and hustler focuses at Cape Point, Kotu, and Kololi (outside the *Senegambia* and *Kairaba* hotels). There's a lot you can do with wheels of your own – trundle down the coast in search of better beaches, explore the back-country between the coast and the airport, visit Serekunda for the shopping or to watch the wrestling (see box) – even get across to the north bank of The Gambia on the first ferry. You can forgo the benefits of exercise under a hot sun by renting a small **motorbike**, available from a number of places, for about D250/day. **Car rental** is available too (see "Banjul and Area Listings").

The small **botanical garden** in Bakau (daily, dawn to dusk) is a shady and rather beautiful hideaway just off the main road, naturally greenest and most impressive after the rains. The gardener will show you round, enthusiastically naming plants and offering scents to your nose. Note the fairy-tale teak tree and the prehistoric cycads.

The **crocodile pool** of Katchikali is just a ten-minute walk from here in the heart of Bakau, a path leading almost straight to it from the junction of Atlantic and Old Cape roads. Ask for "crocodiles" or, more determinedly, *bambo*, the Mandinka name. There's usually a small payment to visit the poolside to see the crocodiles – none too big and strangely white among the dense covering of lilies. No-one fears these crocs: you can approach quite close even when they're out of the water and they are believed to have a magical effect on the pool, ensuring pregnancy for women who wash in it. Not that there's very often much water: every few seasons it's necessary to call a work party together to dig a little deeper, and sometimes to introduce new crocodiles.

Bijilo Forest is a newly gazetted forest reserve at the south end of Kololi beach, accessible from opposite the *Kololi Beach Club*. Containing one of the country's last remaining stands of striking **rhun palms**, it's managed by the Gambian-German Forestry Project. In its half a square kilometre extent, there are good chances of seeing red colobus and green monkeys, squirrels, large monitor lizards and a galaxy of birds. The rangers like to accompany visitors to impart some local wisdom about fauna and flora (though the clearly marked trails make a simple visit easy enough). Although the entry fees are small (D15), an escorted visit costs extra, and you should agree how much in advance – D50 would be generous for a couple of hours unless you're in a large group.

Eating, drinking and nightlife

In addition to the bars and restaurants of the main hotels, there are several dozen independent places, whose number increases – like the prices – in season.

Restaurants

The following restaurants are recommended year-round standbys (though some close one day a week out of season, usually Sun), priced per head without drinks.

Afra, Kairaba Ave north. Unpredictable, with limited choice, but on a good night pleasantly atmospheric, with tasty grills – chicken, steak brochettes. D25–50.

Al-Basha, Kololi, outside the *Senegambia* (☎463300). Large, stylish, AC Lebanese restaurant with good food but quite high prices and somewhat uncomfortable staff. D70–150.

Athina, 41 Kairaba Ave (☎392638). Recommended Leb-Greek restaurant with good *meze*. D150.

Bakadaji, Kololi, past the *Palma Rima* towards the *Senegambia* (☎462307). Recommended, if touristy, Gambian restaurant with good-value buffets on Sat and Thurs (and Mon in high season) for around D80. Energetic dance performance most nights.

Bamboo, Kairaba Ave north (☎495764). Good Chinese restaurant. D100.

The Clay Oven, Cape Point (☎496600). Popular and expensive international-style Indian restaurant. D100–150.

Francisco's, Atlantic Rd, Fajara (☎495332). Consistently good European menu, though not cheap. Worth it for the exotic garden setting. D150–200.

Isatou Barry's Restaurant, downtown Serekunda. A cheap chophouse, clean and spacious.

Joe's Island Restaurant, downtown Serekunda, on the high street, right behind Christ Church. A bit of a Serekunda institution, featuring interesting decor, original food and good company. D20–50.

Klas Fastfood, Old Cape Rd, Bakau. Very reasonable chicken/fish/burger/fries standby, with outdoor seating. If you're budgeting it's really quite a nice place to eat a proper meal. D25–50.

Siam Garden, Kairaba Ave north (☎496141). Busy open-air Thai restaurant. People book in droves for the overrated Mon and Fri BBQ buffet. Good seafood reputation. D100–200.

Tunku Jangjang Bolong, Atlantic Rd, Bakau, 300m east of the *African Village Hotel*. Excellent, freshly prepared fish and chips (much more of a refined meal than either the name or the ambience would suggest) and good veg. Around D20 or less.

Weinstube, Kololi, outside the *Senegambia* (☎463469). Continental food. D150–200.

Yvonne Class, Cape Point (☎496222). First, forget which country you're in; then relax and forget about the impending bill. This is a first-class, French restaurant – the best (imported) eating house in the country by far – and costs half of London or Paris prices. D200–400.

Bars

The "Happy Hour" is well established: some bars post two periods of half-price drinking every day, in season. If you want to hold your own party, there's palm wine for sale by the grove of tall palm trees on the landward side of Fajara golf course; take a bottle and you'll pay around D10 for a litre.

Atlanta, Atlantic Rd, Bakau, next to the *Atlantic Guest House*. Pleasant, local-style bar with a pool table and evening grills.

Churchill's, Kotu Beach, close to the *Palma Rima*. Very British pub and restaurant, with the canned *Boddingtons* an attraction to those for whom *Julbrew* can never be joyful.

Conquering Lion, Old Bakau, opposite the *Mandela Cinema*. Hangout favoured by Bakau's coolest, with excellent music and a happening atmosphere.

Le Gourmand, Kairaba Ave, at the Kotu Rd junction. Lebanese restaurant in high season, operating year-round as a café (no alcohol). Excellent Turkish coffee.

Marie's, Old Cape Rd, Bakau. Long-established hole in the wall with a congenial atmosphere and cheap beer.

Sambou's, Old Cape Rd, Bakau. Perennially popular, somewhat serious-drinking parlour, noted for its prices.

Tropic Smile, Atlantic Rd, Bakau, 200m towards Cape Point from the *CFAO* supermarket. Just about hanging on, an English-run bar in a ramshackle garden setting.

Nightlife

In season, the after-dark action can be lively along the coastal strip and down Kairaba Avenue to Serekunda. Recommended **hotel night clubs** are the *Moonlight* at the *Palma Rima*, the highly rated *Bellengo Disco* at the *Kombo Beach*, *Musu's* at *Amies Beach*, the *Tam Tam* by the *Badala Park Hotel*, and especially the *Tropicana* outside the *Senegambia Hotel*, which draws big crowds of Gambians as well as tourists. But don't be afraid of trying strictly Gambian nightspots, such as the cheap, steamy, reggae-booming *City Pub*, between Latrikunda New Rd and Kairaba Ave, or the similar *Superbar*, by the main road, 500m south of the Westfield Clinic junction in Serekunda (neither is marked on our map). For night-time mobility, unless you have your own vehicle, you'll need to rely on charter **taxis**. It's often easiest to get a group together and rent one for the whole evening. This is usually cheaper than renting a taxi for each trip, and you may get a taxi driver who's willing to be a guide, sharing his local knowledge and the fun.

Eddy's, Finding Dailey St, downtown Serekunda. The main live music venue, with regular Fri and Sat bands playing Manding tunes, *mbalax*, *soukous* and reggae. Pool table at the back. Reasonably priced beer, dire food. Modest entrance charges.

Hansen's Restaurant, in Serekunda, on the main junction of Kairaba Ave with the Banjul–Yundum road (☎390875). More of a nightspot than a restaurant, with live music on Mon, Wed and Fri.

Kololi Casino, Kololi. Great espresso in air-conditioned comfort – with a fairly well stocked bar and a clutch of roulette and blackjack tables. No cover.

Podium, in Bakau, behind the *Elf* service station. Downtown Bakau's most highly rated joint.

Scandals, Kairaba Ave north, opposite the US Embassy. Popular nightspot for middle-class Gambians and a scattering of tourists. Good atmosphere and fairly up-to-date western sounds, *mbalax* and *soukous* recommend it. D25 entrance.

Weezo's, Kairaba Ave north. Smart, uncluttered, nicely air-conditioned bar and dance floor catering to an upmarket crowd of Gambians, expats and tourists. Good CD collection, with soca, salsa and Mexican sounds predominating, and Mexican snacks (about D40) to soak up the booze. Recommended – from about 11pm. No cover.

Banjul and area listings

Air freight *DHL*, Buckle St; around D400 per package plus D75 (UK), D90 (USA) per 500g. Alternatively, take your items, unwrapped, to Yundum airport well before a flight, where you should pay US$4.50/kg up to 45kg and US$3.20/kg thereafter (plus 10% tax) on flights to London.

Airline offices *Air Guinée*, 17 Leman St (☎227585); *Atlantic Airways*, at the supermarkets, corner of Kairaba Ave/Latrikunda New Rd (☎390460; Fax 390062); *Gambia Airways*, 16/17 Wellington St (☎227778; Fax 229339) and at the supermarkets, corner of Kairaba Ave/Latrikunda New Rd (☎472817); *Ghana Airways*, 61 Buckle St (☎228245); *Nigeria Airways*, 11–12 Buckle St (☎227438; offers 40 percent student discount); *Sabena*, 97 Kairaba Ave north, Fajara (☎496301).

Alliance Française, 2 Hill Street. Operates as a cultural exchange and exhibition centre as well as promoting francophilia. Film shows on Tuesdays; video library; library. Membership D100.

American Express, c/o *Gambia National Tours*, Kanifing Industrial Estate, Serakunda (PO Box 101 Serakunda; ☎392259).

Banks and foreign exchange *Standard Chartered*, 8 Buckle St, Banjul (Mon–Thurs 8am–1.30pm, Fri 8–11am; ☎2218681; Fax 227714) will cash personal cheques drawn on UK bank accounts, with a bank card, and you can receive funds from a UK bank within 72 hours of your bank telexing them (telex 2210 SBGL GV). *BICIS* in Banjul has good rates (Mon–Thurs 8am–1.30pm, Fri 8–11am; ☎228145; Fax 229312). *BICIS* in Bakau (☎492120) is open late. *Boule Financial Services*, 1/3 Wellington St, Banjul, and *Arrow Holdings*, 68 Wellington St, Banjul are forex dealers offering better rates than the banks: both companies have branches at Cape Point, Kotu and Kololi (different branches may offer different rates so it's worth shopping around). Street changers' rates are about 10% higher; sit down with them somewhere and count every dalasi before handing over your hard currency. For credit cash advances, see below.

Batiks Visit the brilliant batik workshop, *Gena Bes*, on Bakau Salong St in Bakau (☎495068). See the whole process in action under the supervision of owner Queen Amie. Batiks and crafts for sale.

Bicycles and mopeds Hotels rent them out at around D40/half day, D70/day. You can also buy them in town, but they're expensive at D1200–3000. Mopeds cost around D12,000.

Birdwatching The Gambia Ornithological Society (PO Box 757, Banjul) runs slide evenings and bird walks and excursions for members; temporary membership is available.

Books The *Methodist Bookshop*, corner of Cameron and Buckle streets, (Mon–Fri 8.30am–noon & 2–4.30pm, Sat 8.30am–noon) has a few imported books and magazines, plus some local publications.

Car rental and excursions The international agencies aren't properly represented and self-drive isn't common. Land Rovers with driver start at around D600/day. If you're staying in a resort hotel, ask at their excursions office. Try *Kombo Safari Landrover* at the *Paradise Beach Bar, West African Tours*, JJ Baker Ave, Bakau (☎495258; Fax 496118); *The Gambia Experience* at the *Kairaba Hotel* (☎460317; Fax 464788); *Black & White Safaris*, 55 Sayerr Jobe Ave, Serekunda or the Kanifing Industrial Estate (☎392815 or 393174); or *Gamtours*, Kanifing Industrial Estate (☎391479 or 392505).

Cassettes and music contacts The best cassette supplier in The Gambia is *Daruwari Recording Studio* in Mosque Rd, near Serekunda market, behind the taxi garage. A good point of contact is 1km up the same street – the *Sakura Arts Studio*, at 23 Mosque Rd, Latrikunda (opposite the big silk-cotton tree). It's a busy weekend hangout for local artists and musicians (☎393293). A great place for serious reggae collectors is *Studio One* on the main road in Talinding, south of Serekunda. There's a vast collection of old discs here, going back to early Sixties stuff, and all of it can be recorded for you to order.

Crafts and clothes First call in Banjul is the Tourist Market, ostensibly near Albert Market, but possibly still waiting to relocate from its temporary site at the west end of Marina Parade. Otherwise, try the *bengdulala* around the hotel entrances at Cape Point, Kotu and Kololi, or along Atlantic Road at Bakau. The best value, as Senegalese women know, is in cloth and tailoring, and there's no shortage of importers and exponents in Banjul. There's a charity shop worth supporting at 4 Anglesea St, Banjul. Also see "Batiks", above.

Credit card cash advances The *Atlantic Hotel* sometimes helps guests with *Visa* cards, but no bank offers *Visa* advances; the *Meridien Bank*, Buckle St may accommodate you, eventually, with *Access/Mastercard*. Alternatively, make a day trip to Ziguinchor in Senegal where the *SGBS* will advance you cash on the spot.

Doctors The *Lamtoro Clinic*, near the *Senegambia Beach Hotel*, is highly rated. Royal Victoria Hospital, Banjul (☎228223 or 228227); Westfield Clinic, Westfield Rd, Serekunda (☎392213).

Embassies and other diplomatic missions

Belgian and French Honorary Consulates, 14 Wellington St (*CFAO* supermarket), Banjul (☎227473); Belgian honorary consulate also has an office at the *Kairaba Hotel*.

British High Commission, 48 Atlantic Rd, Fajara (PO Box 507; ☎495133).

Côte d'Ivoire Consulate, 1A Hill St, Banjul (☎227168).

Guinea Consulate, Wellington St, south of *Gambia Airways* (☎226862). One-month visas require two photos and photocopied passport pages, ready in 24hr (D300).

Guinea-Bissau Consulate, 16 Wellington St, Banjul (*African Heritage* building; ☎228134). Mon–Thurs 8am–3pm, Fri 8am–12.30pm; visas issued on the spot, one photo (100D).

Malian Consul The post is held by Mr Panjie of *VM (Gambia)* in Half Die, Banjul (☎226947), who should be able to issue visas.

Mauritanian Embassy, off Kairaba Ave north, Section 7, Fajara (☎494098 or 496518). Visas issued the same day (D150).

Nigerian High Commission, 52 Garba Jahumpa Rd, Bakau (☎495804); visas can be issued only with a letter from your embassy.

Senegalese Embassy, 10 Cameron St, Banjul (☎227469). Mon–Thurs 8am–4pm, Fri 8–11.30am; visas take at least two working days.

Sierra Leonean High Commission, 67 Hagan St, Banjul (☎228206). Visas are expensive (UK nationals from D240).

United States Embassy, Kairaba Ave, Fajara (PO Box 596; ☎391970).

Emergencies Ambulance ☎16; Fire service ☎18; Police ☎17 (or try ☎227222).

Film processing *Mansong* has several locations around Banjul and Serekunda – about D200 for 36 prints.

Golf The Fajara Club has an 18-hole course, with nine par 4s, seven par 3s and two par 5s. Early morning weekdays are the best times. Temporary membership, clubs and a caddy cost about D200.

Immigration Ministry of the Interior, 71 Dobson St (☎227285).

Jewellery Try *Jobe*, Box Bar Rd, Banjul, which is a reputable place with nice gold.

Maps Survey maps of The Gambia are available from the Survey Dept, Cotton St, Half Die, Banjul.

Pharmacy The main pharmacy is *Banjul Pharmacy* on Independence Ave, Banjul (☎227470), with a branch on Wellington St (☎227648).

Post office Russel St, Banjul (Mon–Fri 8.30am–noon & 2–4pm, Sat 8.30am–noon) is the country's main GPO and the best place to have mail sent to you poste restante.

MOVING ON FROM BANJUL AND SEREKUNDA

The provisional timetable for the **Banjul–Barra ferry**, across the mouth of the Gambia River, is: depart Banjul 8am, 10am, 2pm and 4pm; depart Barra 9am, 11am, 3pm and 7pm (usually early, around 6.30pm). In high season, there may be extra midday sailings. Passenger fares are nominal. Large *pirogues* also operate between ferries, but they have an unsafe reputation. Note that because the river bed badly needs dredging, the end of the dry season in May and June can see the river too shallow for the ferry at low tide. From Barra there is regular transport to **Amdallai**, the Senegalese border crossing, where you can get a lift to **Karang**, the first Senegalese village, and from there a bus or *taxi brousse* to Dakar.

For *GPTC* buses **up-country**, see "Getting Around" in the practical information at the beginning of this chapter. It's preferable to start long-distance trips from the main *GPTC* bus station in Serekunda, where you're more likely to get a seat. Taxis and minibuses (no buses) to **Casamance** in southern Senegal, commence in Serekunda, at the "Main Garage" behind the market.

Supermarkets The *CFAO* chain has main stores at 14 Wellington St, Banjul and at the main T-junction in Bakau (Mon–Thurs 9am–12.30pm & 2.30–5.30pm, Fri 9am–1pm & 3–5.30pm, Sat 9am–1.30pm). Several newish, relatively smart supermarkets, full of British goods (*Atson's*, *A&K*, *Kairaba*) can be found on Kairaba Ave, and there's also *St Mary's* at Cape Point.

Taxis Main private taxi ranks are outside the big hotels. In Banjul go to the *Atlantic Hotel*, where a fares list is displayed.

Telephone and fax The *Gamtel* offices in Russel St, Banjul, Atlantic Rd, Bakau (opposite the *African Village Hotel*) and at the bottom of Kairaba Ave, Serekunda, are all open around the clock. The *Gamtel* at the airport is open while flights are arriving and departing. There are public fax booths at *Gamtel* in Banjul (Fax 226300); Bakau (Fax 496042); Kotu (Fax 465544); Kololi (Fax 460023); and Serekunda (Fax 392866).

Tourist office There's no high-street information centre, only the Ministry of Information and Tourism, New Admin Building, The Quadrangle, Banjul (☎227181 or 227182).

Travel agents *Banjul Travel Agency*, corner of Buckle and Picton streets (☎228473), is the best in the capital for flight bookings and general information. If you're staying in the resorts area, try any of the firms listed under "Car Rental", above. For a one-way charter flight to London, try *The Gambia Experience* at the *Kairaba Hotel* (☎460317; Fax 464788).

Worship Church services include St Mary's Anglican Cathedral, Banjul: Sun matins 9am; Our Lady of the Assumption Catholic Church, Banjul: masses Mon–Sat 6.45am, Sun 7am & 9.30am; and Bakau Catholic Church: Sun 9am.

Trips around Banjul

In the high season half-day **boat trips** up the mangrove creeks behind Banjul (usually dubbed "River Adventure") can be arranged in just about any hotel lobby for around D250 per person. Many hotel guests also end up on organized excursions to the other places detailed in this section, with titles like "Gambian Safari" (Abuko Nature Reserve), "Bush 'n' Beach", (the southern coast) and "Roots" (Juffure). However, it's easy enough and considerably more satisfying to take off on your own explorations in the coastal region.

Up the creeks

Lamin Lodge, reached up the snaking Lamin *bolong*, is the usual destination for creek trips. It's a large, triple-storey wooden pile built over the water at the creek head, which does food and refreshments (no rooms) for visitors – though if you arrive unexpectedly

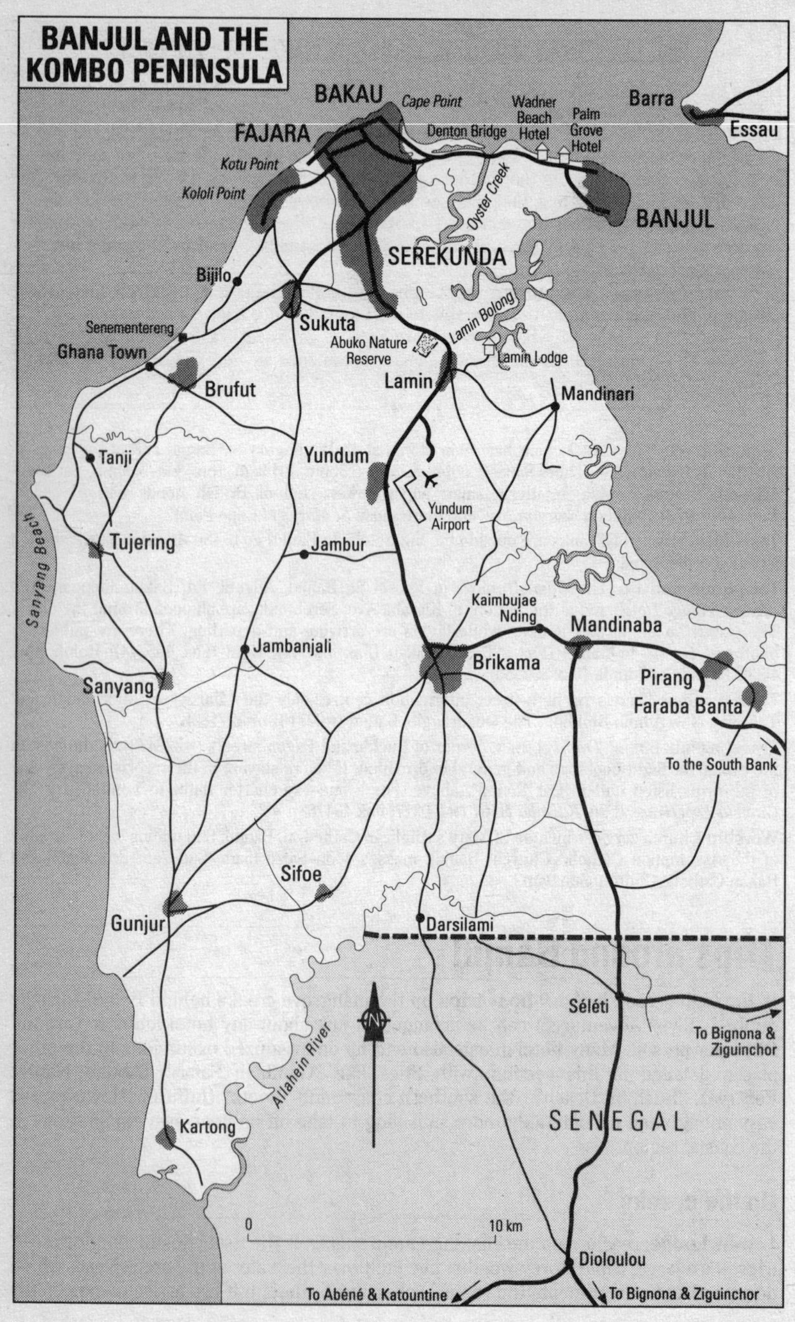
BANJUL AND THE KOMBO PENINSULA
BAKAU
Cape Point
Wadner Beach Hotel
Palm Grove Hotel
Barra
Essau
FAJARA
Denton Bridge
Kotu Point
Koloni Point
Oyster Creek
BANJUL
SEREKUNDA
Bijilo
Lamin Bolong
Sukuta
Senementereng
Abuko Nature Reserve
Lamin Lodge
Ghana Town
Brufut
Lamin
Mandinari
Tanji
Yundum
Yundum Airport
Sanyang Beach
Tujering
Jambur
Kaimbujae Nding
Mandinaba
Jambanjali
Brikama
Pirang
Sanyang
Faraba Banta
To the South Bank
Sifoe
Gunjur
Darsilami
Séléti
To Bignona & Ziguinchor
Allahein River
SENEGAL
Kartong
0
10 km
Dioloulou
To Abéné & Katountine
To Bignona & Ziguinchor

this may take some time to prepare. *Lamin Lodge* is a fine place to come by road, too, early in the morning, when you can watch the comings and goings of bird and human life in the *bolong*, and perhaps rent a *pirogue* by the hour to nose round the waterways. Another nearby base is the village of **Mandinari**. Excursion operators have recently ceased bringing groups here because of the high expectations about what the visitors might bring and the consequent hassles from crowds of kids.

The creeks' **mangroves** are beautiful, eerie and surprisingly tall – up to 20m – and their birdlife is quite prolific if unspectacular. Fiddler **crabs** beckon maniacally on every mudbank, gathering in silent, jostling droves as the boat approaches. The quicksilver, dun-coloured hopping things are **mud-skippers** – fish seemingly intent on becoming terrestrial – which always seem to have gone by the time you've noticed them. Occasional, and odder, inhabitants of the mangroves are **monkeys**, bounding through the foliage, presumably taking refuge from persecutors on the farm plots inland. Hippos, incidentally, don't circulate this far downstream – though this isn't because the brine interferes with their buoyancy control (hippos live in salt water off the coast of Guinea-Bissau), but because of over-hunting in the past.

Getting there

The cheapest way of doing a **boat trip** up the creeks is to get a group together and fix up boat rental yourself with the fishermen on the shore behind the Albert Market in Banjul. Prices depend on demand and what the boatmen reckon they could earn from a day with the nets, but don't expect much of an outing for less than D400, and maybe substantially more in the high season. While it's always useful to have a guide acting as intermediary, try to establish exactly what is going to be provided and make sure the crew know what they're about. Being stranded up a dead-end *bolong* at low tide, miles from anywhere, in the middle of the day – or worse, with the sun going down – may give you more of the mangrove experience than you want. Take plenty of water and food, clothes and hats to cover up with, and binoculars. Boats go all the way to *Lamin Lodge*, but Mandinari is more isolated. Although it has one or two small shops where you can get warm soft drinks and something to eat, it's a thirty-minute walk from the head of the Mandinari *bolong* where boats usually tie up: the path goes through rice fields and seasonally lush jungle foliage, jewelled with a mass of birdlife that makes the creek look dead in comparison.

By road, *Lamin Lodge* is signposted down a two-kilometre dirt track off the main Yundum Airport–Banjul road, close to Abuko Nature Reserve and the village of Lamin. Bush taxis run to Mandinari, which is about 10km from Lamin village and the main road, from Banjul.

Abuko Nature Reserve

Certainly one of The Gambia's best bits, the celebrated **ABUKO NATURE RESERVE** (daily, dawn to dusk; D80; reductions out of season) is barely two square kilometres in extent, but within its carefully protected confines it preserves a patch of tropical riverine woodland that's becoming increasingly rare in West Africa. For Gambia holidaymakers it's an unmissable visit and is still very worthwhile for overlanders. Most attractively, you have to walk through it: vehicles aren't allowed in.

The **Lamin stream** and its remarkable necklace of rainforest was noticed in 1967 by Eddie Brewer, father of The Gambia's conservation movement, and was fenced the following year. The barrier is there to keep domestic animals and hunters out, rather than anything in – Abuko's 200-odd bird species and dozens of varieties of small mammals and reptiles need no encouragement to stay. Apart from pond-dredging, path-clearing and hide-building, the reserve is left more or less natural, and the strongest impression is imposed by the magnificent **forest trees** themselves, spiralling up from the webbed fingers of their buttress roots through a canopy of trailing creepers and epiphytes to create dark cathedrals of vegetation.

Practicalities

Organized excursions tend to destroy the sense of place. Go alone, in the early morning or late afternoon, and the forest exerts real fascination. Abuko is situated right by the main road from Serekunda to Brikama and you can take a Brikama **minibus** from Banjul or Serekunda or any passing **bush taxi** to the reserve front gate easily enough. The **office** by the front gate has some good booklets and leaflets about plant and wildlife, and you can leave bags safely – or even camp the night if you're keen to be in the woods at the crack of dawn. Take drinks and food – there's nothing much in this line at Abuko – and bring mosquito repellent, as they can be a serious menace. If you have a bona fide interest in wildlife and conservation you can, for the purposes of research, stay overnight in the reserve in a sparsely equipped wooden hut known as the Tree House, in return for a donation to Field Centre funds. Field Centre staff are on hand to provide water and advice: contact Njagga Njie at the Conservation Department Field Centre, adjacent to the reserve exit gate.

The park

The whole walk around the marked trail through the reserve takes a couple of hours, but it could easily turn into half a day depending on your interest in the various bird species (more often heard than seen) and your curiosity about the more bizarre life forms of the forest floor. Don't count on spending long at the Animal Orphanage at the top of the circuit, though; it's a smelly adjunct for penned lions, hyenas and apes, all brought here. It's easy to work out how far you've gone: there are numbered markers on the trees at twenty-metre intervals.

From the primate world you can expect to see **patas** and **green monkeys** and beautiful, acrobatic **western red colobus**. You'll also be delighted, or else unnerved, by the amazing numbers of – harmless – **monitor lizards** which dart across the path and claw their way through the undergrowth. Most are small, but they can grow as long as two metres. There's normally a number of **crocodiles** to be seen at the Bambo Pool, from the Education Centre look-out. Watch for two distinct species: the larger, pale Nile crocodile and the small, darker dwarf crocodile, a threatened species. **Snakes** are very rarely observed, though the fact there has never been a single incident involving a tourist isn't likely to convince snake phobics, especially after reading the slightly gloating notes on sale at the office.

BIRDS OF ABUKO

Well over **two hundred species of birds** are the chief animal delight of Abuko. This is the closest patch of tropical forest to Europe, and each winter it attracts thousands of bird-watchers as well as a host of **palearctic migrants** (willow warblers, chiff chaffs, black caps, melodious warblers) to swell the numbers of its native species. Most obvious are the water birds – a couple of photo hides overlooking the stream and pools are usually occupied by murmuring birders. Look out for **kingfishers** (blue-breasted, Senegal, malachite and pied), the "umbrella fishing" **black heron** and two great bird-watcher's sights – the **painted snipe** (the male, remarkably, incubates the eggs) and the stunning **red-bellied paradise flycatcher**, with its thirty-centimetre tail feathers. You can generally see **hammerkops** around the Bambo Pool at the start of the trail; in flight, their swept-back crest of feathers and pointed beaks make them look exactly like miniature pterodactyls. In the clearings, wait to see **Fanti rough-winged swallows** flitting through the light and, above the forest canopy, **hooded vultures**, **black kites**, **palm nut vultures** and swooping **bee-eaters**.

The southern coast

Given transport, preferably 4WD, you could get to virtually any part of **the coast** between Cape Point and the mouth of the Allahein (San Pedro) River, where anglo-Gambia finishes and franco-Senegal takes over. And equipped for a few days' self-sufficiency, it's perfectly possible to walk the entire length of the Gambian coastline – less than 50km from Fajara to **Kartong**, The Gambia's southernmost village. More realistically, most people will have to rely on rented cars or taxis, or buses and lifts, or some vigorous leg-work on bicycle. There's a daily *GPTC* bus direct from the Bund Road station in Banjul via Brikama to the main southern town of **Gunjur** and on to Kartong.

It makes sense to head directly for Kartong first, and then work your way slowly back up the coast, according to how much time you have. If you're driving down south from a resort hotel, allow a long day for the trip, starting early (allow about two hours to get to Kartong), and equip yourself with a good map, plenty of water and preferably two spare wheels. It's not a difficult or in any way dangerous excursion, and the people just seem to get nicer the further you go, but there's little in the way of supplies down here and, unless you're prepared for a night away from your hotel, you'll probably want to be able to get back again for dinner.

Kartong

Kartong's main attractions are a crocodile pool – similar to the Katchikali pool at Bakau – and a fantastic beach. You can **stay** at the entrance to the village at the simple *Follonko Guest House* – a British VSO language-learning and orientation centre (bookable through the VSO at PO Box 677, Banjul; ①–②). From the guest house it's a fifteen-minute walk across dunes and pasture to the beach. To the **Falonko crocodile pool** you're likely to find instant guidance from local boys. If you don't, look for the St Martin's primary school signboard on the way through Kartong and turn right. About 100m down this track, there's a place to park outside the red gates, and then 100m to walk to the pool in its deep, shady grove. This pool is a deal more atmospheric and sacred-looking than Katchikali (there's no money to pay for a start) and there are reputed to be a fair number of crocs – though why they stay in this lily-choked swamp is hard to imagine. Women from both Kartong's communities – Muslim Mandinka and Christian Karoninka (Karoninka is a Mandinka dialect) – visit to pray and ask favours on Monday and Friday mornings.

If you have your own transport, you'll be able to drive **south of Kartong** to the last extremity of Gambian territory, a police checkpoint near the mouth of the Allahein River, on the other side of which is Senegal. A short drive from the checkpoint, at the end of the road, you can reach a busy fishing beach via a winding track.

Other beaches

Working back northwards towards Banjul and the resorts, the biggest focus of Kombo South District, is **Gunjur beach** – a messy, active seafront where fish are more important than tourists and you'll probably be ignored. For serenity continue north on the pretty track towards **Sanyang** village (wonderful baobabs on its southern side) and **beach** – a broad, smooth sweep of firm sand backed by coconut palms (water is available from the well of a farm plot nearby). **Tujering**, some 4km inland, is a pleasant old village that owes nothing of its character to tourism or colonialism: whitewashed mudstone houses, and a central crossroads with meeting place, mosque and market.

Along the forested and palm-planted stretch of track north of Tujering between Tanji and Ghana Town, you're likely to see several species of monkeys – saving the harvest from them is a nightmare for farmers. There's a recently created **forest reserve** at Tanji, with fine ornithological attractions. **Ghana Town** is a community of Ghanaian fish driers and smokers, not an uncommon coastal phenomenon in many parts of West Africa. If you're curious you can stoop inside the long, low huts where the racks of blackening fish cure over smouldering wood. The finished product – *bonga fish*, basically kippers, and often good – can be seen all over.

Finally, the holy site at **Senementereng** is a marvellously meditative spot around a craggy old baobab tree on the clifftop, the air wafting with incense burned by the incumbent marabout. Local people come here for cures, consultations and peace; it's a good place to visit at sundown. A steep path leads to another superb beach. Here you're only a few minutes' drive from the southernmost hotels.

Barra, Juffure, Albreda and James Island

The visit to **Juffure** used to be an inevitable business, when the *Roots* industry was at its peak and thousands of African Americans made the pilgrimage to see the village they believed **Alex Haley** had been describing. So convincing was the hype that the author himself seems to have believed the same thing – pictures of Haley with an elderly Kinte descendant are part of the myth of modern Gambia, used to boost the small country's respectability on the world stage. As an excuse for a trip to the **north bank**, the visit to the supposed birthplace of Kunta Kinte is still an enjoyable day, but unless you do one of the organized *Roots* tours you'll find **transport** problematic. Cycling is a possibility, but the 70-odd kilometres there and back can be hard work, despite the flat earth roads, and well-nigh impossible if the roads are wet (if you rent a car, be sure it's 4WD if there's any chance it's going to rain). On a Wednesday, you could aim to get to Juffure from *Lamin Lodge* on one of the river boats heading up to Georgetown (see p.287), though you would still need to find transport back again.

Barra

If you're travelling under your own steam, your initial target is the 8am **ferry** from Banjul to Barra (see the box on p.275 for full details), a wonderful crossing at this time of day, with dolphins often plunging in the bow-wave. **BARRA**, the old capital of the Mandinka kingdom of the same name, no longer has much of interest except for the squat hulk of **Fort Bullen**, neglected on the grassy shore. In the time of Mungo Park, the indefatigable eighteenth-century Scottish explorer, the kingdom produced "great plenty of the necessaries of life". Times change. Near the fort is the unspeakable *Rest House*, which unlucky travellers have been known to resort to if they miss the last ferry to Banjul, at around 6.30pm. A much safer bet if you're overnighting in Barra is the *Lingaire Hotel* by the ferry dock. They do good food here, and the rooms are reasonable (②).

Albreda and Juffure

Two *GPTC* **buses** from Barra call each day at Juffure en route to north bank points further up-country and you can usually count on one or two bush taxis. But for the most part the red ribbon of the road is empty, a swathe of well-graded laterite through quiet farm and savannah lands, with women (and men) in the fields and, before the harvest, small boys armed with bows and catapults in the monkey watchtowers.

You come first to **Albreda**, down on the shore. The settlement, also known as Albadarr, still has its old trading house with dangerously leaning walls and an immovable cannon pointing fiercely out over the river. **JUFFURE**, a short walk away from the river, isn't distinguished by any such monuments and, apart from a very basic sign, looks much like any other Mandinka village – a gathering of thatched, mud-brick cottages, *bantabas* and goat pens.

On entering the village your requirements are clear enough as far as local people are concerned: "You want to meet the Kintes and get some photos right?" Speak now if you

MUSICAL HOLIDAYS

In recent years, as **West African music** has made increasing impact abroad, enthusiasts are now travelling to hear and study the traditional **kora**, **drums**, **guitar**, **balafon**, **singing** and **dancing**. You can make music the whole point of a trip by taking a music workshop package at a number of smaller hotels.

The longest established is the innovative German operator *Cool Running Tours* (Kiesstrasse 9, D-6000 Frankfurt 90; ☎069/70 86 75). *Cool Running Tours* have helped build the *Boucarabou Hotel and Music School* at **Ker Serigne Njaga**, about 2km south of Kololi see p.267. You can stay here as a straightforward guest (③) or take music tuition as well (around D200/day). It naturally helps if you speak some German, though most of the German guests speak English. Tuition is partly by Malamini Jobarteh, artistic director of the Gambian National Troupe and renowned kora player and recording artist – see below.

Also check out the Jasseys' place in **Fajikunda**, a village off the main Serekunda to Yundum road. They spend some of the year in Yorkshire, England and the rest of the time here, hosting paying visitors and running arts and music workshops and courses. The UK contact address is 18 Highfield Crescent, Halifax, West Yorkshire HX7 8LA (☎01422/845977).

In **Brikama** (overleaf), there are several compounds where you can stay on a house guest basis, learning as much about Mandinka music and culture as you want. Malamini Jobarteh (☎484143; Fax 484100; both c/o *Gamtel*) has a particularly pleasant and peaceful compound in Brikama and relations are very good-humoured (FB, including all lessons ②). Malamini, his son Tata Din Din and other members of the large family all participate. Note that if you're not musically inclined, you'll be very welcome to stay without trying to learn anything: there's a small reduction. Write to forewarn them to: Jobarteh Kunda, Sanchaba, Brikama Town, Western Division, The Gambia. On arrival in Brikama, follow the path along the left side of the mosque until you pass the communal tap on the right. Turn right here and the Jobarteh compound is 300 metres on the left.

don't. First you pay a few dalasis to the guardian of the Juffure maintenance fund. Accompanied by a gang of children you then proceed on a brief tour, winding up at the **Kintes' compound** to meet whoever's in, usually the senior lady, Binta Kinte, and various sons, daughters and grandchildren. Photos are allowed, but you pay for the right to take them, and to do just about anything in this village.

It's hard to understand why this particular Juffure (a widespread place name) or these Kintes (a common Mandinka family name) should have been chosen by Haley as his roots. According to the book, the griot he met here told the same story as the one passed down through his family. But it was a simple and familiar history. It seems Haley had already written his Africa passages when he came here, and his account of Juffure appears to be unrelated to the location of today's village. In the book, Kunta Kinte is surprised by a slave-raiding party, yet Juffure is only a few hundred metres from the Gambia River and close by the sites of the trading stations of Albreda and Fort James, which would have been there throughout his childhood. On the other hand, villages can move of course: eight or ten generations have passed since the young Kunta Kinte went out to collect firewood and never came back.

You can't be sure who is taking whom for a ride – the story has been a winner for both Haley and the Juffure griots – but it's worthwhile participating in the pretence if you've read *Roots'* six hundred pages to the line "That baby was me!".

James Island

Less questionable history is out mid-river on **James Island**, but the *pirogue* ride from the shore costs at least D100 per person, and the very ruined ruins of **Fort James** are probably only for enthusiasts. Originally constructed in 1651 by agents of the Duke of Courland (now Latvia and Lithuania), Fort James rode the usual roller-coaster of occupations, routings, sackings, desertions and rebuildings. It was seized by **Britain** in 1661 when the Royal Adventurers Of England Trading Into Africa bundled out the Baltic occupants and set themselves up under the Royal Patent of Charles II, buying gold, ivory, peppers, hides and of course **slaves** for the American colonies – Britain's first imperial exploit in Africa. In one mercantile guise or another, the British and the **French** fought over the fort for more than a century. France held the trading "factory" of Albreda on the shore and continued slaving long after the British had opted for a new role as anti-slavers at the end of the eighteenth century. After 1779 James Island was rarely inhabited. Today the remains of the old walls and the strewn cannon are dominated by a grove of large baobabs.

Brikama

Leaving the Serekunda conurbation behind on the south bank road into the interior, the first town you hit is The Gambia's third largest, **BRIKAMA**. An extremely religious town, Brikama is also very poor: indeed the water and electricity price riots in Brikama in April 1994 were widely seen as triggering the decision by the military to oust President Jawara in July of that year.

Excursion groups are often brought here to visit the **wood-carving centre**, to be charged up to ten times the going rate for carvings at this, the country's main source. If you visit independently you'll generally get a much better deal. There are good deals to be had in bespoke **clothes** too – bring your chosen cloth from Serekunda and there are several tailors' shops who will make up almost any pattern very cheaply. They line the road from the garage to the main mosque.

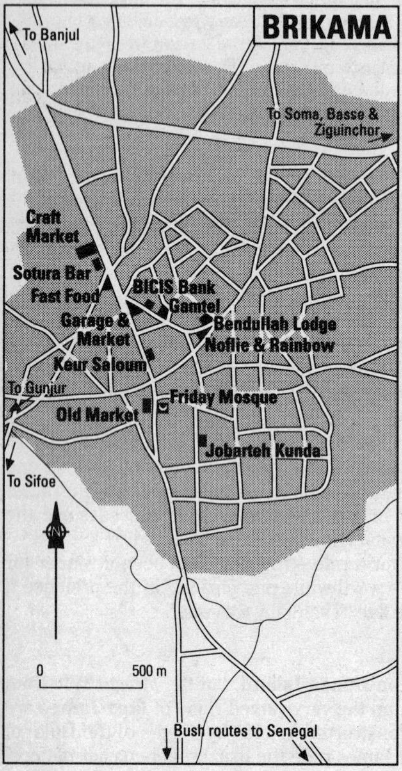

The other major attraction of Brikama is the large number of celebrated **kora musicians** who live here and are happy to receive visitors and give tuition (see box). One kora player, Malamini Jobarteh, can also arrange a visit to Brikama's "historical site", **Santangba**. Now an undistinguished area marked by a tree where a local madman lives, it was first settled by Malinké fugitives from the collapse of the ancient Mali empire. They were instructed by a scholar to seek a place such as this in the Gambia valley, so here they founded the town. It's not an exciting visit, but it makes an interesting excuse for a walk away from the bustle.

Practicalities

The only regular **lodgings** in Brikama are at *Bendullah Disco & Travellers' Lodge* (①), where there are usually a few rooms available not occupied by prostitutes. The disco is very lively and worth staying over for at the weekend.

As for **food**, try the *Rainbow Cake and Coffee Centre*, opposite the *Bendullah*, which is the most Europeanized café in Brikama, offering meat sandwiches as well as coffee and cakes, in an air-conditioned room. The *Noflie*, next door, has *domodah* for about D4, but is more notable for its wonderful murals. *Keur Saloum*, another cheap chop house, is just off the main thoroughfare, while the small *Fast Food Restaurant*, centrally located, offers basic chicken, steak and rice plates. If you need a **bank**, the *BICIS* is open from 9am to 2pm, but you can certainly change currency with the crafts merchants.

Moving on from Brikama

There's a fifteen-kilometre track from Brikama down to the Senegalese **border** at Darsilami, while the new main road to Senegal branches off right at Mandinaba, a small place distinguished by a large, four-towered mosque.

UPRIVER GAMBIA

To travel **up-country** is to travel upriver: the **Gambia River** is the national lifeline and the country's very definition. With its headwaters 500km from Banjul in the Fouta Djalon highlands of Guinea, it snakes down in typically West African fashion, heading any direction but seawards most of the way.

The river's course is paralleled by the **Senegalese frontier**, which was drawn by compass at a cannon shot's distance from the river bank. Inland, this extraordinary artificiality is madly apparent. Senegal, never more than 10km from the highway – the only tarred road going up-country – breathes all around the country, creating an increasing osmosis of Francophone language, customs, food and music. At one point in the country's thin form the Dakar–Ziguinchor highway cuts clean across it – a traverse that, but for border formalities, would take only twenty minutes. Whether the Gambians like it or not, Senegal's influence looks set to increase.

While you might expect a frontier feel along the length of the country, there are plenty of short **sidetracks** off the main road, which quickly get you into traditional village life – districts of creeks and bushland where the concerns of fuel smuggling into Senegal and black market currency are still secondary.

The principal **towns** of Brikama (see opposite), Soma/Mansa Konko, Bansang and Basse are all on the south bank. Georgetown is on MacCarthy Island in mid-river. The **north bank** is altogether bushier, with no hard-surface roads apart from the two that cross the country into Senegal, little transport or electricity, and only a couple of important centres at Kerewan and Farafenni. If you've time to explore, it's interesting territory, with much to be discovered and bearable walking distances. The site most often visited on the north bank is **Wassu**, with its strange **stone circles**, reached easily from Georgetown and the south bank highway.

Transport

Unless you're heading for Tambacounda and the Niokolo-Koba National Park in Senegal, or else down into eastern Guinea, the interior of The Gambia is a bit of a cul-de-sac. Still, it's a relatively easy – and easy-going – district, and if you're just starting your travels in West Africa, not a daunting introduction to the region.

As for **river transport**, if you visit the country at the right time of year you might be lucky with a groundnut barge or even a small private launch, but such vessels are few and, apart from the rusting ferries at the main crossing points, the Gambia River is not a busy waterway. However, while the steamers of colonial times are long gone (the *Lady Chilel Jawara*, last in a long line, has been wedged in the mud off Banjul for over a decade), there is a regular **tourist boat service** between *Lamin Lodge* and

Georgetown. The *Jamond* and the *Alhagie* depart *Lamin Lodge* at 8am on Wednesdays, getting to *Tendaba Camp* in the early evening via stops at Juffure and Kemoto. On Thursdays they motor from Tendaba, via Farafenni to Pakaliba; and on Fridays from Pakaliba to Kaur, Kudang, Kuntaur and Barajally, arriving at *Janjangbureh Camp* in Georgetown at about 8pm. The down-river trip is quicker, leaving Georgetown on a Saturday morning, going straight to Farafenni, where they dock overnight, and then sailing to *Lamin Lodge* on the Sunday, via stops at Tendaba and Kemoto. You can embark and disembark at any point on the boat's route (*Lamin Lodge* to Kemoto, for example, is D185) or cruise the whole stretch (D800). Nights en route are either spent ashore, or on board with mattresses and mosquito nets (D50 to rent). The boats have bars and limited catering services. Altogether it's a highly recommended experience – details from *Gambia River Excursion* (PO Box 664, Banjul; ☎495526).

If the timings don't work for you, **road travel** up the main tarred route along the south bank is the only straightforward option. The road is in a decrepit state until you reach Soma (it's been resurfaced from there to Basse), and there's not much transport (as the paucity of dead animals on the road tends to suggest); you'll need to rely mostly on the *GPTC* buses (see "Getting Around" in the practical information section on p.246). If you have the money, renting a car for a few days will get you just about anywhere, though you'll need 4WD during the wet season. Otherwise, to do any sort of diversion you have to hope for an occasional bush taxi – or walk.

The Lower River

The Gambia is divided into five regions known as Divisions. Furthest east is Upper River Division (URD), downriver from which is MacCarthy Island Division, followed by North Bank Division, Lower River Division (on the south bank) and finally Western Division, which includes the Atlantic coast and districts inland as far as the Bintang Bolong creek.

Villages in Western Division

The ruins at **Berefet**, mentioned in some tourist literature, are all but obscured by vegetation much of the year, and there's nothing to see of the "long-abandoned European trading post" which supposedly exists. Local people know of the site and call it "Marco", but they'll be pretty surprised if you make the six-kilometre effort down the sandy track (turn off about 30km from Brikama) to look for it. More ruins at **Bintang** (turn off at Sibanor, 15km further) are equally invisible. Either place however, is a good excuse to get down to the river – or rather creeks off it. They're building a rather grand mosque at Bintang and are delighted to have visitors.

Bwiam, just off the main road, 75km from Brikama, amid a superb grove of silk-cotton (*bantango*) trees, has a real curiosity in the form of its *karelo*. The word is Mandinka for "cooking pot", but Bwiam's inverted **iron cauldron** resembles nothing so much as a gun turret poking out of the ground. By all accounts it is quite unmovable (Europeans of course have tried), and its origins and function are obscure. It's considered good luck to leave something on the pot and take something away.

In the wet season or after the rains, brilliant emerald **rice fields** mark the shallow wooded valleys inland. At the end of the growing season in August and September, anti-monkey watchtowers are dotted among the rows of groundnuts and bush on the ridges between. As you move eastwards, the large concrete block and corrugated-iron houses that set the scene on the coast are increasingly replaced with more attractive straw thatch and mud-brick compounds. And the tripod water pumps supplied by Saudi Arabia over German bore-holes become a familiar sight in every village.

Kiang West District

As the road turns north over the head of **Bintang Bolong** creek, you're passing to the west the region newly designated as the **Kiang West National Park**. The 750 square kilometres between river and *bolong*, of which the park has a quarter share, is the wildest, least-explored region in the country. Well supplied for a few days in the bush, you could head off on foot down the track to the left, just after the village of Jataba. There are further hamlets scattered an hour's walk or so apart along the path that follows the low ridge through the district. In the middle, at **Keneba**, the Medical Research Council has a tropical disease field station (Keneba was the site of Mark Hudson's strange and fascinating Gambian sojourn, described in *Our Grandmother's Drums*; see "Books" in "Contexts"). Frustratingly, while the national park may harbour representatives of most of The Gambia's dwindling fauna, getting in to see them doesn't look very practical. At least the park now exists on the ground, as well as on paper, but construction of a lodge and viewing facilities is still going on.

People are currently using Tendaba (see below) as a base for Kiang West visits, but there's an alternative in the shape of *Kemoto Hotel* (enquiries and bookings on ☎496634; ⑦ FB), at Mootah Point, on an isolated meander of the river and at the far western end of the track referred to above. The pleasantly laid-back Spanish-run hotel, has panoramic views of the river and is located close to some of its most interesting creeks. Rooms are clean and comfortable, with fans and basic facilities but no hot water, and there's a swimming pool.

Tendaba Camp

One place where you might see a fair bit of wildlife – or at least have fun trying – is **Tendaba Camp**. About 125km from Brikama, this is one of the few tourist-class hotels upriver and it's close enough to the Kiang district for monkeys, crocodiles, hyenas and even – they insist – leopards to be around.

The Swedish owners never let their whisky bar drop below eighty varieties; they shoot warthog for dinner; and their idea of a "creek trip" is a dawn speedboat race through the mangroves, fortified with schnapps. If hunting, fishing and drinking appeal, you'll probably love it, though the slightly Viking atmosphere, briney outside showers and various caged animals put some people off. The setting on a bluff over the river is fine, however, and the bird-watching really something.

The mosquito-netted, S/C chalets (③) and meals at D60–80 are fair value out here, and if you were to turn up with a bottle of *Hankie-Bonnister* or *Sheep Dip* to add to their collection you might well be given a special discount. Evenings are not formal: staff and guests crowd round the video on the patio and when there's sufficient enthusiasm, women from the village put on a dancing show or someone sets up a disco. There might be a certain tackiness to it, but with so many types of booze, it's not a persistent worry.

Without you own wheels, there's a five-kilometre walk from the main road to Tendaba and little chance of a lift. For ornithological encouragement, a group of silk-cotton trees at Kwinella, near the main road, is the habitual roost and nesting site of hundreds of **pelicans** – a cacophonous and extraordinary sight close up.

Toniataba, Soma and Farafenni

Before the trans-Gambian highway's halfway mark at **Soma/Mansa Konko**, you pass the unremarkable village of **TONIATABA**: unremarkable that is, except for the grass-thatched and enormous **circular house** in the compound of Fatikunda ("Fati's place"). Fatikunda is the home of the Fati family, and the family head, Alhaji Fodali Fati, is one of the district's most senior religious leaders, or marabouts. First constructed in the nineteenth century by Fodali's father Sheikh Othman, the house is believed to be one of the largest traditional homes in The Gambia, at around sixty metres in circumference. It's not exactly unknown, but nor are the Alhaji's family or his house a tourist attraction, and unless you speak Mandinka you'll probably feel easier with a guide to introduce you. Take your shoes off if you're invited in, and come with some gifts – postcards or other souvenirs from home are very welcome. The old man is generally delighted to get visitors. The house itself is of unusual design, its outer wall surrounding an interior house divided into separate rooms. In the middle is an inner sanctum, a private area reserved for family prayers.

A few minutes further down the road you're hit by the trashy, sprawling contrast of **SOMA**, about 160km from Brikama, where there's the opportunity to turn either left over the river into northern Senegal for Kaolack and Dakar or south into the Casamance district. You can also escape southwards further upriver, but this is the furthest point at which you can easily turn north into Senegal. Soma is just a bustling truck stop, a charmless string of gas stations, cheap restaurants, bars and shops where you can get all sorts of Senegalese imports. Buses stop here, and bush taxis whirl up the dust, collecting passengers for the short ride down to the ferry crossing for the north bank and Farafenni. **Mansa Konko** ("King's Hill"), a couple of kilometres away, is the administrative quarter, quiet and uncommercial in exact proportion to Soma's racket. Neither centre has any special interest, but if you're driving, it's important to know that Soma is about the last **guaranteed source of fuel** – certainly of pumped petrol – up-country.

Crossing the river northwards, **FARAFENNI**'s big day is Sunday, when the weekly *lumo* is held. The S/C rooms at *Eddie's Hotel*, some with AC, if not always the electricity to run it, are reasonably priced (②–③), and the best on The Gambia's north bank. *Eddie's* also does appetizing food and is an evening focus for the whole district.

The Upper River

Back on the south bank, the road's condition improves dramatically beyond Soma, from potholed oyster-shell mix to hot black macadam, as you pass through a fairly wild stretch of bush where you're likely to see baboons and other monkeys. If you're on the water, you can start looking out for **hippos** from this point on, where the estuarine part of the river ceases and the mangroves peter out. The no longer appropriately named Elephant Island in mid-stream appears to be the hippos' lowest grazing ground.

The village of **Buiba** is the site of a long-established traditional curing centre for the mentally ill, but the first real punctuation in the new up-river scene is **Pakaliba**, 50km from Soma, a village by the Sofanyama Bolong on the district boundary between Lower River and MacCarthy Island Divisions. It's an attractive place – a scheduled river boat stop –marked by a ridge of small rocky hills that are surprising in the undulating savannah. Pakaliba is the source of a fable about a crocodile hunter called Bambo Bojang, who learned to control the Sofanyama crocodiles after being attacked by them; he's now the patron saint of the *bambo*, and his descendants live in the area. If you've time, you could track down Lalo Kebba, a famous kora player, and persuade him to sing the whole story.

Heading on through mostly flat and open grasslands, the only place you're likely to be detained is **Jerreng**, 12km further, where they make an impressive – and very cheap – range of palm beds, chairs and other furniture.

For a telling insight into The Gambia's economy, you could sidetrack 3km down to **KUDANG TENDA** (riverboat stop 85km from Soma), where giant sheds hold hundreds of tonnes of groundnuts. Under the hot corrugated-iron roofs thousands of birds and rats fatten themselves on another wasted harvest, abandoned for lack of barges to get it down to the coast.

There's a convenient and quite good place to stay in this area – the Gambia Agricultural Research and Diversification Rest House at **Sapu**, on the river bank some 3km down the slope from the road village of Brikamaba (110km from Soma). With air-conditioning, fans, a kitchen and only eight beds, it often gets booked up. Spare beds are normally available to outsiders only after 8pm, but they're unlikely to turn you away; if you manage to get in, you can look forward to some interesting development conversations.

Across the river is **Barajali**, birthplace of ex-President Jawara, for which reason it was declared a national monument in 1985. A few kilometres downstream is the off-limits **Baboon Island National Park**, where chimpanzees were once reintroduced to the wild. It's by no means certain the chimps are still there, but if you're really intent on getting there (and by travellers' accounts it's worthwhile), you'll need to contact the Ministry of Water Resources, Fisheries, Forestry and Wildlife (5 Marina Parade, Banjul; ☎227431) and convince them of your impeccable motives. How you actually get there is another matter – it's only feasible if you've made contacts.

Georgetown

GEORGETOWN, although it's located midstream on MacCarthy (Janjangbure) Island, suffers no problem of access: the southern arm of the river is barely 100m wide, and is crossed by a hand-hauled ferry from the south bank. During the steamboat era, Georgetown was The Gambia's second town, a relatively thriving administrative outpost and a major up-river trading centre. The prestigious Armitage High School is still in business, but dismiss any notions of nostalgic, tropical languor conjured up by the colonial names: backwaters don't come much further back than this. On the north side there's a whole quarter of the town that's like an open museum of the old trading days, with tiled floors and ornate plaster work disintegrating behind an onslaught of tropical vegetation. The big roofless barn usually labelled a "slave house" was probably no such thing, more likely a warehouse for perishable goods. Much of Georgetown's significance was lost in the 1970s after the completion of the main south bank highway and its fate was sealed by the closure of the riverboat service. Judging by the closed shops and clubs, it's obvious that the islanders are continuing to leave. Georgetown remains the site of the country's main **prison**, a place so grim that a number of prisoners died of malnutrition a few years back.

Fortunately, Georgetown's useful mix of **accommodation** makes it a viable and laid-back place to unwind. It's the site of The Gambia's most upmarket up-country tourist lodge, *Janjangbureh Camp*, built in a beautiful grove of trees at Lamin Koto on the north bank of the river facing the island, and with excellent bird-watching (④). If you're going there, the regular ferry is a much cheaper means of access than the direct launch to the camp. Other lodgings include *Baobolong Camp*, a good, compound-style Gambian camp (③) with a pleasant atmosphere, though very small rooms; *Allah Kabung Lodge* on the main street, a cheap place with shower and fan in your room (②); and the similarly priced *Dreambird*, just opposite, which has a good bar. Another watering hole, *Tida's Bar*, usually has warm company and cold beer.

Lastly, you might also check out the inexpensive *Government Rest House*, which has intermittent electricity powering its fans and AC, somebody to cook (if you provide the food) and a fine location beneath large shady trees (①). You may be required to "book" your room there at the Divisional Commissioner's office opposite – a tedious operation.

Wassu stone circles

You'll probably need to pass through Georgetown if you're interested in getting to the Wassu stone circles, 20km from Georetowm on the north bank. With your own transport, of course, you just wait for the ferry to Lamin Koto on the north bank of the river and drive thirty minutes – in theory. In fact, the ferry is sublimely unpredictable, breaking down all the time, running out of fuel in mid-channel, snapping its rudder cable and spinning helplessly, or simply running aground. Anticipation of disaster runs high, and it seems a shame when the crossing goes smoothly. By **public transport**, from the north bank landing, there are *GPTC* buses two or three times a day, connecting Georgetown with Farafenni, and while they will drop and collect you at Wassu, their timings are very unpredictable. For a return day trip from Georgetown to Wassu therefore, an early start by bush taxi is essential.

A bush taxi is likely to drop you at **Kuntaur**, the nearest small town to Wassu, approached down a low earth causeway across the rice fields of a broad *banto faros* – good bird country, but a murderous road after rain. It's a busy little town, purring with mosquitoes and set low by the water's edge, with a new Italian-aid-supported health centre. From Kuntaur you cut back to the main road for Wassu – a walk of an hour or so on tracks over the marsh.

In the dry season, with the bush thin, you may see the reddish pillars of **WASSU** on the north side of the road from a distance; otherwise ask for "stone circles". Wassu is The Gambia's prehistory lesson, but it's no Stonehenge, so adjust your expectations accordingly. The hardened laterite pillars, clustered in loose rings, vary from mere stumps to veritable menhirs weighing several tonnes and standing three metres high. They were apparently levered into place and then jammed upright with packed earth, hence their tendency to fall out of the circle. The burial places of senior personages, they have obscure cultural origins. Carbon dating has pinpointed some of them to 750 AD, but recent research indicates that the burials had taken place long before the circles were erected, suggesting the sites themselves were sacred. You're not likely to illuminate the mystery by asking local people – nobody seems to know anything. It's considered good form to leave rocks on top of the pillars, though again, no-one knows why.

The white huts at Wassu are a rest house. While it's not really operational, you could probably camp here and use it as a base. One hut is given over to a very half-hearted attempt at an information centre. If you're captivated by the antiquity of Wassu, you may want to go on to explore **other stone circle sites** on the north bank: there are stones on each side of the road at Niani Maru, the largest stones (up to ten tonnes) at Njai Kunda, and nine circles of pillars, including a bizarre V-shaped one, at Kerr Batch. And you could pursue the quest for the stones into the Sine–Saloum region of Senegal (see that chapter).

A different kind of pillar sits in isolation on the river bank at **Karantaba Tenda**. A large obelisk marks the site of the former village of Pisania, whence Mungo Park set out on his last adventure, in the course of which nearly everyone (including Park) either died or went missing. It's really not worth the struggle to get there unless you're passing by anyway. One reason you might be is in search of the so-called Monkey Court, a natural rocky amphitheatre on the north bank, and a favourite socializing spot for baboons.

The eastern bends: Bansang and Basse

Before getting into the eastern tail end of The Gambia – Upper River Division – you pass through **BANSANG**, where the main highway cuts within sight of the river for the first and only time between Banjul and Basse. Bansang is located on a magnificent bend, with easily accessible low hills behind the town providing excellent views. To Gambians, Bansang means the **hospital**, The Gambia's second and the only one upriver (and apparently the one to choose), which largely determines the town's character. If you're staying the night here – and not in a ward – try the *Bunyadu Hotel* at the

Basse end of town, scruffy but reasonable enough (①). A favourite volunteers' hang-out is *Carew's Bar*, located next to the police station and the best place to watch the life of the town go by, with cold beers and softs always on hand. Bansang's **silversmiths** have a good reputation – worth checking out if you're in the market for silver and know what to look for.

Basse

BASSE – Basse Santa Su, in full – is The Gambia's last town, a surprisingly animated centre that gets its energy from its proximity to Senegal. Only 20km from Velingara across the border, its shops tend to be full and there's usually some bottled petrol available. It's a major Peace Corps and VSO posting, and a popular one, with banks, bars and hotels. In the dry season, try to be in Basse on a Thursday morning when a major *lumo* is held, mostly of earthenware from the nearby villages of Alunghari and Sotuma.

Accommodation choices are less limited than you might expect. The *Apollo 2* on the main street isn't bad, with fans or AC in the rooms (①–②), but like the rest of the town centre its electricity is sporadic. For administrative reasons, electricity is only guaranteed in the administrative quarter of Mansajang, 1km out of town near the junction for Sabi and Fatoto. Here you can get a bed at the pleasant and roomy Government Rest House (①/②), where they may be surprised to see you; take food along and someone will do the cooking. The problem here is the walk back into town if you want to take refreshment at the locally famous *Uncle Peacock's Fuladu Bar* ("a bar of principle no music" he says enigmatically) and *Finch's Nightclub*. Or, if you want to sample "one of the largest and best discos in The Gambia", the *London Club*, at the *Jem Hotel*. This has cornered the market in Gambianized tourist comfort at a sensible price (☎668356; ②–③). It's just out of town on the Fatoto side (turn left at the filling station, and then right).

Beyond Basse, it's just dirt track to Fatoto, with its derelict trading station on the higher than usual river bank. For a big change of tempo, bustling **Tambacounda**, in Senegal, lies an hour or two to the east by bush taxi. Or if you're determined – and lucky – there's the passenger **ferry** to the north bank and the return loop to Banjul by whatever transport you can find, which might take several days.

index

CHAPTER FOUR

MALI

MALI

Historically, geographically and from the point of view of the traveller, **Mali** is West Africa's centrepiece. Long a bridge between the north and the south, the area outlined by the butterfly shape of the present country formed the meat of three great **empires**, the oldest of which was **Ancient Ghana** which flourished as early as the third century. The region's location on the main **caravan routes** and the banks of the **River Niger** later fuelled the rise of the powerful **Mali** and **Songhai** states, which lasted until the sixteenth-century invasion by Morocco. The political stability and unity of previous centuries was never recovered thereafter.

Reminders of its great past are remarkably intact. Camel caravans still make their way from salt mines in the Sahara to **Timbuktu**, where you can visit a fourteenth-century mosque built when the town was one of the world's most prestigious centres of learning and culture. Wooden *pinasses* continue to carry their cargo along the river from here to **Djenné** – a great commercial town that spawned numerous technical innovations including the Sudanic style of architecture now common throughout the region. Boats also ply the river to the Sahelian town of **Gao** – formerly the capital of the Songhai Empire and final resting place of the **Askia kings**.

The outstanding geographical feature of Mali is the **River Niger**. Known to the Greeks and Romans (who called it *Nigris*, a conflation of *niger* – "black" – and a Berber expression, *gher nigheren*, meaning "river of rivers"), the Niger long fascinated Europeans. But it took them nearly 2000 years – until the nineteenth-century exploits of Mungo Park, Gordon Laing, René Caillié and Heinrich Barth – to figure out its source and the place where the river emptied into the ocean. Today, 1300km of the river, from Koulikoro near Bamako to Gao, is navigable, and most of the population lives on or near the Niger's banks.

Tempering the romance of the country's opulent past is the more immediate spectre of **poverty**, evident even in the shabby capital, **Bamako**. Mali lacks substantial mineral resources and is almost wholly dependent on its agricultural and animal production, rendering the recent droughts all the more devastating. In the early 1980s harvests failed almost entirely, and as much as three-quarters of the livestock was lost. People swarmed from the countryside to already crowded towns and, having lost everything, nomads were forced into a sedentary lifestyle and a cruelly inadequate wage economy. Faced with a growing crisis, the government took pragmatic steps to increase production and denationalize state enterprises – only one of which was profitable in the early 1980s. The long-maintained socialist veneer was rubbed off; the rains returned in 1985; and by 1987, Mali was achieving a small grain surplus.

Despite this, the effects of drought are still visible today and the country's position remains extremely precarious. A popular uprising led to the ousting of the military government in 1991, but the more democratic government that followed the elections has been struggling with a serious conflict over Tuareg autonomy in the north and east. Mali is still faced with a staggering and seemingly irreducible debt and, every year, the Sahara creeps south, converting arable land, barely twenty percent of which is cultivable even now, to dust.

People

Numbering roughly a million, the Mande-speaking **Bamana** (also known as Bambara) are the largest linguistic community in Mali. Though concentrated in the region of Bamako and Ségou, their influence spreads much further, due in large part to their language, which is one of the most widely spoken in West Africa. To the west, the

FACTS AND FIGURES

The **Republic of Mali** was known as **Soudan Français** – the French Sudan – during the colonial period. The name Mali was chosen for its historical resonance and significance for the Mande (or Malinké) speaking people of the region. The largest country in West Africa, it spreads across nearly 1,240,000 square kilometres, an **area** five times the size of the UK and three times as big as California, but with a **population** of less than nine million. President Alpha Oumar Konaré leads the ADEMA party (*Alliance pour la démocratie au Mali*) which holds more than half the seats in the multi-party National Assembly. Mali's crippling **foreign debt** stands in excess of £1.8 billion (US$2.7 billion), more than six times the value of its annual exports of goods and services. Looked at from a global perspective, however, this is just about one-eighth of the cost of building the cross-channel tunnel between Britain and France.

Despite the **River Niger**, and the headwaters of the **Senegal River** which flow through the western tip of the country, much of Mali lies in the **Sahara**. The extreme north is desert, empty except for a few stranded oases and Tuareg camps. Between the desert and the river stretches the **Sahel zone**, mostly flat plains with scruffy bush and thin trees that are especially resistant to the arid climate.

Only a few ripples interrupt the overall impression of flatness across the country. West of Bamako, the **Manding Highlands** provide a rare hilly spectacle as they rise to heights of 500–1000m, and the **Bandiagara escarpment**, which winds across the landscape east of Mopti for some 200km, is striking for the sheer cliffs that drop some 500–600m to the plain. Other formations include the striking outcrops of the **Hombori Hills** a little further east, towering sheer to heights of nearly 1200m, and north of Gao, the inaccessible **Adrar des Iforhas** mountains astride the trans-Saharan chariot route of classical times.

Malinké are closely related and share a similar language and customs. Living from the Manding Highlands to the Senegal River, many Malinké have retained traditional religions, despite Islam's early penetration in the region and repeated jihads. The **Senoufo** live near the Côte d'Ivoire border in the region of Sikasso. In the sixteenth century, they formed small kingdoms at Kong, Korhogo and Odienné (now in Côte d'Ivoire), and when the Songhai Empire collapsed they began expanding northward. Their social structure is strongly influenced by the *poro* – an initiation rite that lasts 21 years, during which time the men learn the secrets of Senoufo religion and philosophy.

The **Dogon** occupy the Bandiagara escarpment east of Mopti. There's reason to believe these people may have originated from the Nile Valley, but migrated to the isolated cliffs near the Burkina Faso border in the twelfth century. Here, they kept at bay the waves of Muslim invasions that swept through Mali over the centuries and, thanks to their tight social and religious organization, have been remarkably successful at maintaining ancient traditions. They speak a Voltaic language related to Senoufo.

Several peoples live in the north. The **Songhai** concentrate in the region of Gao where they migrated in waves after the seventh century, probably from northern Benin. **Fula**-speaking herders – after the Bamana, one of the most populous groups in Mali – traverse the country but are concentrated in the delta region between the Niger and the northwestern border with Mauritania – a historical region known as Masina (Massina is the contemporary town). The **Tuareg**, of Berber origin, were pushed southward into present-day Mali after the Arabs came to North Africa from Arabia. The Tuareg mixed with sub-Saharan peoples and formed numerous independent, and often warring, clans. They still cling to their nomadic traditions, though recent droughts and conflict with the state (not just in Mali, but also in Niger and southern Algeria) have forced many Tuareg to settle. Mali is also home to a sizeable population of **Moors**, localized in the north between Timbuktu and Nioro. They too are of Berber origin, but adopted the Hassaniya Arabic language through their contact with the Moroccans.

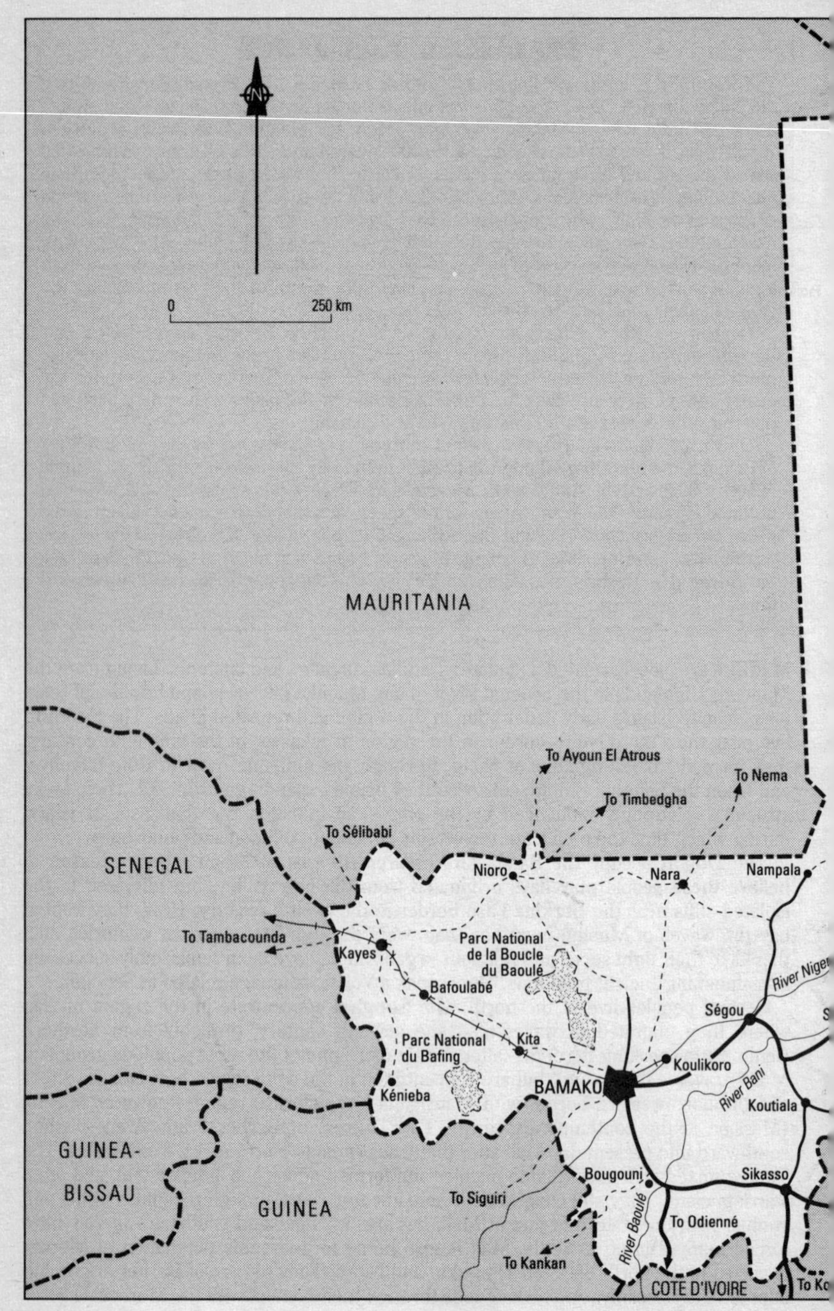
0
250 km
MAURITANIA
To Ayoun El Atrous
To Nema
To Timbedgha
To Sélibabi
SENEGAL
Nioro
Nara
Nampala
To Tambacounda
Kayes
Parc National
de la Boucle
du Baoulé
Bafoulabé
Ségou
Parc National
du Bafing
Kita
Koulikoro
River Bani
BAMAKO
Kénieba
Koutiala
GUINEA-
BISSAU
GUINEA
Bougouni
Sikasso
To Siguiri
River Baoulé
To Odienné
To Kankan
COTE D'IVOIRE

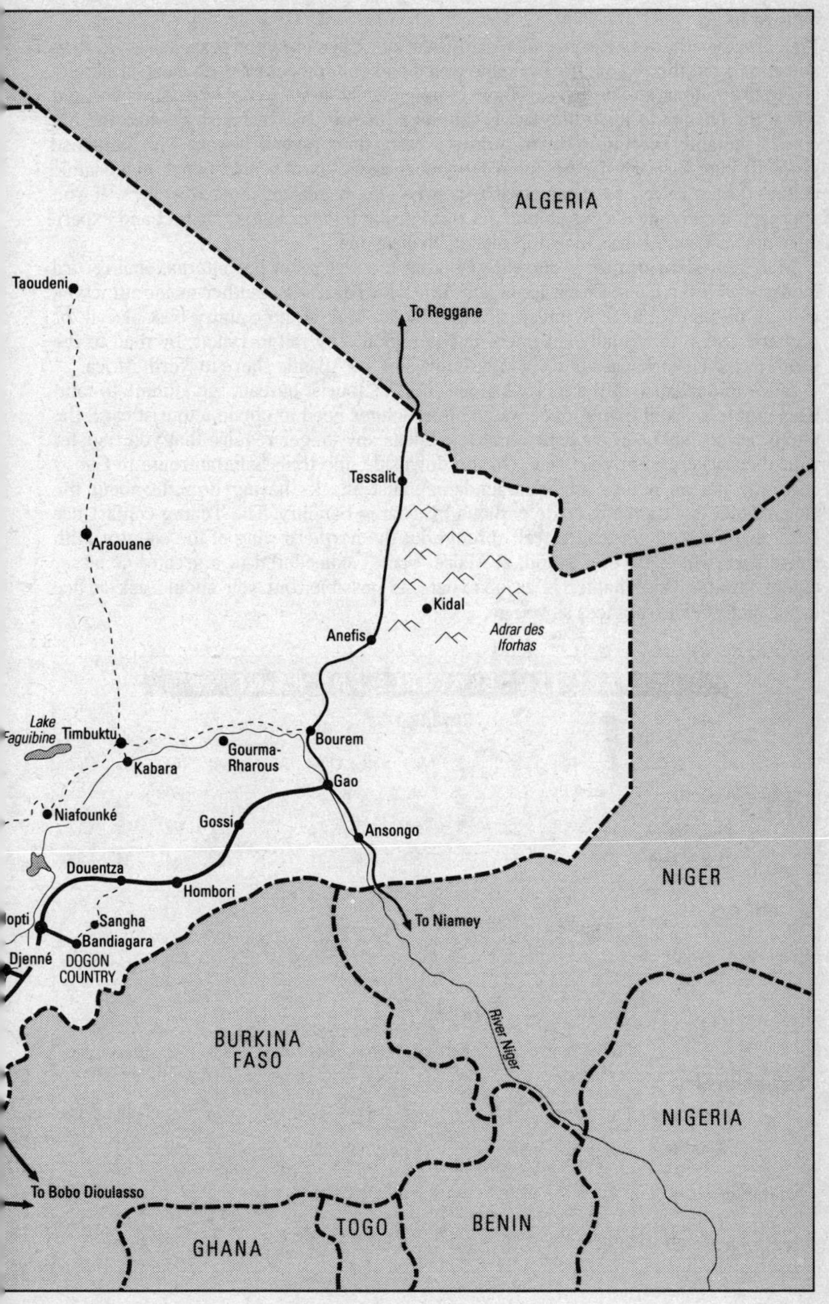
ALGERIA
Taoudeni
To Reggane
Tessalit
Araouane
Kidal
Anefis
Adrar des Iforhas
Lake Faguibine
Timbuktu
Gourma-Rharous
Bourem
Kabara
Gao
Niafounké
Gossi
Ansongo
Douentza
Hombori
NIGER
Mopti
Sangha
Bandiagara
To Niamey
Djenné
DOGON COUNTRY
River Niger
BURKINA FASO
NIGERIA
To Bobo Dioulasso
TOGO
BENIN
GHANA

Where to go

Mali breathes the very essence of West Africa, and has more good reasons to visit than any country in the region. Remarkable visual and cultural contrasts in close proximity are Mali's hallmark. The **River Niger** is magnificent (unforgettably so at dawn) and offers the chance to make the last great **river journey** in West Africa, while the old cities – notably **Djenné** and **Timbuktu** – carry their ragged history with immense grace. Hiking through the fractured **Dogon country** – where traditional, non-Islamic culture has survived to a remarkable degree – is a goal of most travellers. If you approach it carefully it's possible to get right inside this fascinating district and experience one of West Africa's most interesting civilizations.

Mali's **musical output** – currently stoking the pistons of the international record industry with the likes of Salif Keita and Ali Farka Touré – is another major attraction, enough on its own to draw music lovers. Finally, Mali is the country best placed for **onward travel** to virtually anywhere in the region – by rail to Dakar, by road to the south-facing coastal states and via Mauritania and the Atlantic shore to North Africa.

Since the collapse of the heavy-handed *SMERT* tourist bureau, the attitude to tourists is more relaxed than it once was. You no longer need to obtain a tourist card, the photo permit has been abolished and few towns any longer require that you register with the police during your stay. On the downside, the trans-Saharan route to Gao is currently not an option, Algerian fundamentalist attacks having brought about the closure of a track already made perilous by Tuareg banditry. The Tuareg conflict has severely disrupted life (and travel) throughout the northern wing of the country, with travel everywhere beyond Mopti, at Mali's "waist", considered to a greater or lesser extent unsafe. This chapter is as up-to-date as possible, but you should ask advice locally and seek assurances as you go.

AVERAGE TEMPERATURES AND RAINFALL

BAMAKO

	Jan	Feb	Mar	Apr	May	June	July	Aug	Sept	Oct	Nov	Dec
Temperatures °C												
Min (night)	16	19	22	24	24	23	22	22	22	22	18	17
Max (day)	33	36	39	39	39	34	31	30	32	34	34	33
Rainfall mm	0	0	3	15	74	137	279	348	206	43	15	0
Days with rainfall	0	0	1	2	5	10	16	17	12	6	1	0

TIMBUKTU

	Jan	Feb	Mar	Apr	May	June	July	Aug	Sept	Oct	Nov	Dec
Temperatures °C												
Min (night)	13	14	19	22	26	27	25	24	24	23	18	13
Max (day)	31	34	38	42	43	43	39	36	39	40	37	32
Rainfall mm	0	0	3	0	5	23	79	81	38	3	0	0
Days with rainfall	0	0	1	0	2	5	9	9	5	2	0	0

Climate

Without taking into account seasonal variations, it's tempting to sum up Mali's climate in two words – gaspingly hot. **Rains** generally last from June to September in the southwest. In the northeast, they may arrive at any time during that period, either for a prolonged wet season or in a few unpredictable cloudbursts. The dry season takes over the rest of the year. Between October and February the **Harmattan** can blow for days at a time causing temperatures to drop quite low in the evenings. Climate-wise, this is probably the best time to plan a trip, and it's also the period when the Niger is most easily navigable.

Arrivals

Despite being positioned at the heart of the region, Mali's surface links with other parts of West Africa aren't brilliant: from Senegal, a twice-weekly rail link or a rough *piste*; from Burkina and Niger more rough *pistes*; and only from Côte d'Ivoire a good highway.

Flights from Africa

Air Afrique (RK) handles most of the traffic from other capitals in West Africa, nearly all of it routed through **Abidjan**, which has daily flights (non-stop, except on Fri). The Fri RK flight to Bamako originates in **Lagos**, flying via **Lomé**, Abidjan, **Niamey** and **Ouagadougou**. From **Cotonou** you can connect through Abidjan on Mon, Thurs and Fri; from **Accra** through Abidjan on Sat (with *Ghana Airways*); and from Lagos, in addition to the long zig-zag of the Fri flight, you can connect straight through Abidjan on Mon and via Lomé and Abidjan on Thurs. There are also RK flights to Bamako on Mon from **Dakar** (non-stop) and on Wed from Dakar via **Conakry**; and a non-stop flight on Wed via **Niamey** on Sat. *Ethiopian Airlines* also flies in via Niamey on Sat (see below). *Air Ivoire* flies non-stop from Abidjan to Bamako on Thurs and Sun and via **Bouaké** on Tues.

Other West African connections include the following: *Gambia Airways* flies non-stop from **Banjul** to Bamako on Thurs; *Air Burkina* flies **Ouaga**–Bamako on Wed; and *Air Gabon* flies in from Libreville and **Douala** via Lomé on Wed.

As for **flights from other parts of Africa**, *Royal Air Maroc* has a non-stop flight from **Casablanca** to Bamako on Tues; *Aeroflot* offers a non-stop **Tunis**–Bamako service on alternate Thursdays; *Ethiopian Airlines* flies into Bamako from **Addis**, **Ndjamena** and Niamey on Sat; and finally *Air Afrique/South African Airways* connects (without too much of a layover) for the RK flight to Bamako at Abidjan on Mon, having flown in from **Jo'burg** and **Brazzaville**.

The details in these practical information pages are essentially for use on the ground in West Africa and in Mali itself: for full details on preparing for a trip, getting here from outside the region, paperwork, health, information sources and more, see *Basics* pp.3–88.

Overland

Coming from the north, the trans-Saharan Tanezrouft route from southern **Algeria** ends in eastern Mali at **Gao** on the Niger River, from where a paved road leads all the way to Bamako. Unfortunately a combination of civil strife in Algeria and attacks by Tuareg rebels has seen this desolate 1500-kilometre piste closed since the early 1990s.

From Niger

From **Niamey** the main route to Mali follows the Niger River to Tillabéri (where the tarmac ends) and continues through numerous villages and increasingly frequent patches of soft sand to Gao. The growing insecurity of Gao in recent years has meant that ordinary transport along this route has all but dried up and it is currently not recommended, although protected convoys and military vehicles do make the run. The alternative is to travel through Burkina Faso, via Fada Ngourma and Ouagadougou.

From Burkina Faso

The quickest **routes linking Burkina and Mali** originate in **Bobo-Dioulasso**. From here, you can travel either to **Sikasso** (tracks are extremely rough on the Burkinabe side, especially during the rains) or to **Ségou** on a paved road. You can also get direct transport **from Bobo to Mopti via San**.

Burkinabe border posts close at 6pm. Malian formalities should present no special problem, but the Tuareg conflict has spilled into northeastern Burkina in a minor way (it's a difficult area for the Burkinabe authorities to control and has been used by Tuareg rebels to launch attacks across the border into Mali), so the Malian officials along this border may be unusually zealous. The *agents* seem particularly keen on checking your health documents, anyway, so make sure you're up to date on cholera and yellow fever.

In the dry season it's possible to go directly into the **Dogon country** from Burkina – setting out from **Ouahigouya** and passing through Tiou and then Koro. Vehicles rarely pass along this stretch, so if you are relying on available transport, you may face long waits for the occasional goods truck or tourist. To compensate, this is one of the most rewarding ways of entering the Dogon country through one of the few corners not fairly saturated with tourists.

From Côte d'Ivoire

The main point of entry from **Côte d'Ivoire** is along the road from Korhogo and Ferkessédougou to Sikasso, linked by daily buses. The stretch of sealed highway from the Pogo/Zégoua border to Sikasso has been resurfaced and is in good condition. Traffic between Odienné and Bougouni (from where a good paved road continues to Bamako) is far less frequent and you may make better time from that side of the country first heading east to join the main artery north.

From Guinea

After the Niger has swelled with seasonal rains (roughly August to December) it's possible to travel down the Milo – a tributary of the Niger – by barge from **Kankan to Bamako**. The 385-kilometre trip takes you past Niandakoro, where the Milo joins the Niger, and Siguiri, before terminating some five days later at Bamako. This is an adventure, but it's no pleasure cruise: you sleep on mats and share mediocre toilets; food is provided. The boats leave about every two weeks (when water levels permit) and reservations can be made, in theory, through the *CMN* in Kankan. See also the Koroussa ferry possibility (p.512).

In the dry season, the main alternatives are by **bush taxi** from Kankan or Kouroussa, the latter an especially pretty route. Malian formalities are less of a hassle than Guinean.

From Senegal and The Gambia

Most overland travellers arrive from Senegal on the *Océan-Niger* **train from Dakar**. Departures are scheduled for 10am Wed and Sat, though it's wise to be there by 8am. You should reserve seats two days before. The Wed train is the Senegalese one – more comfortable, with AC, and more expensive. However, it's a gruelling 30- to 36-hour journey whichever train you choose. Scheduled arrival time into Bamako is 4pm the following day, but the usual delays mean you're likely to arrive after dark.

Fares to Bamako on the Sat train range from around CFA21,000 2nd class, CFA28,000 1st class to CFA45,000 sleeper (*wagon lit*). On the Wed train, all fares carry a CFA4000 supplement. Second class is not very dissimilar from first, and it's worth paying the difference only if you want more leg-room and fewer companions. Once you're on the train, it's possible to upgrade to sleeper class assuming there are berths available (double cabins only), but the protracted border formalities take place during the night and you have to disembark, so you don't get much sleep in any case. There's a limited buffet car for snacks and drinks (the best part of the train to watch the scenery incidentally), and you can buy **street food** from station vendors around the clock.

There are small **student reductions** in second class at the beginning and end of term.

As an alternative to taking the train the whole way from Dakar, you could travel by road as far as Tambacounda, picking up the train to Bamako from there. Don't expect a seat or other comforts by this stage in its journey, however.

Finally, if you have your own vehicle, you *can* transport it by the train, though after all the complexities involved, not to mention the time – allow a full week altogether – and the expense – no less than CFA150,000 – you will wish you had driven instead. Unless your vehicle cannot be driven, forget it.

From Mauritania

The main overland route from Mauritania to Bamako starts at **Néma** (sealed road all the way from **Nouakchott**) and passes through **Nara** and **Kolokani**. The tracks between Néma and Nara may be impassable during the rainy season. It's best to get up-to-date information from other travellers before heading out.

From **Ayoun el Atrous**, you may also be able to get transport to **Nioro** from which point you can continue to Bamako, or to **Kayes** along difficult *pistes*. Again, rains can make this route impassable and even in other seasons the frequency of vehicles may not add up to much. Another option is to get down to **Sélibabi**, just 60km from the Mali border from where you can try to make your way to Kayes.

Red Tape

Basically, everyone needs a visa for Mali except the French. There's no embassy in London, the closest being Paris or Brussels. Embassy addresses, including those in the US are given in *Basics*, pp.24–28.

Mali was formerly notorious for its red tape and tourists were subject to the scrutiny and control of the dramatically named *SMERT* tourist organization – now defunct. Most of the official hassles such as photography permits and tourist cards have been abolished; however the area north and east of Mopti is still a *zone securité* where you must report to the police and get your passport stamped in every town on arrival. You'll find the police, sometimes unpaid for months at a time, attempting a little mischievous extortion on these occasions.

If you're driving, you'll need to get Malian insurance and a "tourist visa" (*carnet de passage* or *laissez-passer*) for your vehicle, on arrival, without which you may find your car threatened with being impounded. You will need to get this extended, too, in Bamako, unless you're driving straight through the country.

■ Visas

Coming overland, travellers without visas are often let into the country anyhow and allowed to obtain them upon arrival in the nearest *préfecture* (this most likely means Sikasso, Kayes or Bamako). But it's a risk – although a bribe of some kind is the most likely hurdle, you never know when you'll happen on an unbending immigration officer. Unless you're flying into Bamako, it's advisable to pick up your visa en route in one of the neighbouring West African countries (there are Malian embassies or consulates in Dakar, Conakry, Freetown, Abidjan, Accra, Niamey, possibly Banjul and soon, or recently, Ouagadougou) as they're usually issued with less fuss and are much less expensive than visas issued outside Africa.

Visas for onward travel

You can get visas in Bamako for Burkina, Guinea, Mauritania, Morocco, Nigeria and Senegal; Côte d'Ivoire and Togo entry permits are available at the French embassy. **Niger** is a problem since there's no representation, and the ease with which visas for **Guinea** are obtained seems to be arbitrary and variable. The Guinean embassy in Bamako has a reputation as one of the least troublesome places to get a visa – usually valid for a single entry of fifteen days, though you may persuade them to give you longer.

■ Photography permits

Permits are no longer required to take photographs in Mali, but as elsewhere discretion and good sense should be used before snapping away. In certain areas, such as the **Dogon country**, there are still many taboos associated with taking pictures. Taking shots of people bathing in the river is a good way to get your camera confiscated: such voyeurism is not appreciated.

Money and Costs

Mali's currency is the CFA franc (CFA100 always equals 1 French franc; approx CFA750–800 = £1; approx CFA500 = US$1). Foreign visitors on a tight budget have benefited most from the 50 percent devaluation of 1994 as prices of goods and services consumed locally have risen only moderately in response, making the country cheaper for foreign visitors than at any time since independence. However, if you're booking luxury hotels, tours, or car rental – items largely consumed by those with access to foreign currency – you'll find prices still high.

Banks are rare throughout the country so you have to plan ahead. The *Banque de Développement du Mali* (BDM) has the most branches – in Bamako, Kayes, Sikasso, Ségou, Nioro, Mopti and Gao – but commission outside Bamako can be as high as 20 percent. Outside these towns, you can't expect to change money other than French francs – easily converted on the street at the fixed rate of CFA100:1FF or even useable as currency.

Health

The only vaccination certificate normally required to enter Mali is yellow fever. Outbreaks of cholera occur from time to time, in which case this certificate is necessary too, even though the cholera vaccine has been acknowledged as ineffective by the WHO for many years.

Bilharzia is another disease that remains all too common, especially in rural areas with slow streams and brackish water. Don't swim in such areas, especially if they're bordered by grass. Even stretches of the Niger can be dubious, notably in the dry season when the low waters become stagnant in many places. Along the entire course of the river, you'll see people bathing, doing their washing and bringing their animals to drink. Swimming in the river is, in fact, usually safe, and you'll probably find yourself doing it at some point, but if you come to a place where no one from the area goes into the water, stop and ask yourself why.

Tap **water** is heavily chlorinated and drinkable in Bamako and other big towns. In distant villages, wells and river water are commonly used for drinking and the purity may be suspect. Bottled water is available in the large towns. In places like the Dogon country, which receive a lot of foreign visitors, you can also find it, though the price of a 1.5-litre bottle is usually high. Purifying tablets or filters are a cheaper alternative.

Hospitals tend to be under-equipped and overcrowded. For a serious problem, your best bet is either the *Hôpital du Point G* or the *Hôpital Gabriel Touré*, both in **Bamako**. Anything requiring surgery or setting may prompt ideas of repatriation. Consult your embassy (or the American embassy) for advice.

Maps and Information

There's little information about Mali available abroad and no tourist offices. The best map of the country is IGN's 1:2 million "3165" series map of Mali published in 1993. Still rare in the country, it's a covetable item to some border guards – keep it out of sight.

With *SMERT*'s demise there is no longer an official tourist presence in Mali. Instead several independent **travel agencies** have sprung up in Bamako principally concerned with offering excursions along the Niger River, into the Manding Highlands northwest of the capital and to the country's primary tourist attractions: the Dogon country and Timbuktu. They can usually provide a few leaflets.

Getting Around

The longest navigable stretch of the Niger flows through Mali, and it's possible to travel by boat virtually from one end of the country to the other, stopping along the way at historic towns like Ségou, Mopti, Timbuktu and Gao. It's an exciting – if at times tiring and uncomfortable – way to see the country, and the regular steamer service is almost unique in West Africa. To take advantage of the boats, however, it's crucial to time your trip with the rains (see below). If you can't schedule it, Mali does have alternatives to get you around the country, including a regular train service from Bamako to Dakar, flights linking the main towns and, of course, bush taxis. Car rental is available from Bamako's more expensive hotels, but is very expensive.

■ Bush taxis and buses

Most Malians rely on **taxis brousse** to get around the country. If you're without your own transport you will too, especially in the dry season when the river boats don't operate. Vehicles aren't quite as plush as in some neighbouring countries and prices are relatively high – CFA30-50 per kilometre. In addition, drivers tend to charge quite steeply for baggage and you'll have to bargain hard.

The *Compagnie Malienne de Transports Routiers* (*CMTR*; ☎22.33.64) covers a limited number of routes by **bus** – notably Bamako to Ségou and Mopti. Although slightly cheaper than taxis, their buses tend to be old clunkers that go slowly and take forever to fill at the motor parks. You often see them broken down on the road. *SOMATRA* and *COMATRA* buses (the latter serving Côte d'Ivoire) are faster and better.

A final note of warning: on some imported air-conditioned buses the windows are not designed to be opened. If the AC doesn't work, you're in for an uncomfortable ride to say the least: get a seat at the front.

■ Trains

The *Régie des Chemins de Fer du Mali* (☎22.29.68; Fax 22.83.88) provides the **rail link from Dakar to Bamako**, described in "Arrivals" above. There are also trains from Bamako to **Kayes** (Sun 7.20am & 11pm; Mon, Tues & Thurs 7.20am; Wed 9.15am & 11pm; Fri 7.20am & 7.30pm; Sat 9.15am; 12hr; fares from CFA7000–10,000) and to **Koulikoro**, the upper terminus of the Niger River boats (daily at 6pm; 2hr).

Student reductions apply on train fares at the beginning and end of term.

■ River travel

It's possible to travel over 1300km **along the River Niger**, between Koulikoro (60km from Bamako) and Gao. Such a trip can only be made, however, in the period during and just after the rains – roughly from August to December between Gao and Koulikoro or from July to January/February downstream between Mopti

> Note that in recent years there have been Tuareg attacks on river transport and you should not expect the river boats to be operating downriver of Korioumé, Timbuktu's port; possibly not even downriver of Mopti.

and Gao – when waters are high enough for the steamers. The exact dates vary each year with the timing and volume of the rains. Aim for months in the middle if you want to be sure of travelling by boat.

Three **boats**, in theory, ply the waters: the *Général A Soumaré*, and the *Tombouctou* are the most comfortable while the *Kankou Moussa* (the youngest vessel, operative since 1982) is reportedly overdue for refurbishment, or actually out of service. Reservations for the trip can be made through the *Compagnie Malienne de Navigation* (*CMN*) in each of the port towns.

Boat schedules

According to the schedule, one boat leaves weekly in each direction, from Koulikoro on Friday evening and from Gao Thursday evening. In practice this only happens if at least two out of the three vessels are operable, which is not often. The only fairly predictable elements of the service are the **approximate journey times** between ports if there are no delays. The entire stretch takes five days from Koulikoro to Gao (downstream) and six days back again. Services from Mopti to Korioumé (the actual port for the now high-and-dry port town of Kabara, and Timbuktu's nearest port) should depart Sun evening and arrive Tues morning. In the other direction, boats should leave Korioumé Sat evening and reach Mopti Mon morning; but these are indications only, not to be planned around.

Fares and facilities

There's a choice of **six classes** of accommodation: *Luxe*, a single or double cabin with (sometimes non-functioning) extras like a fridge, AC and hot showers; 1st class A, a double cabin with beds and wash basin; 1st class B, the same as A, but with bunks; 2nd class, four people to a cabin with two bunks; 3rd class, rather cramped cabins with eight to twelve people but permission to sleep on the cooler upper deck; and 4th class, floor space (if you're lucky) on the lower deck with the cargo. The last option is a hot, dirty, completely miserable way to travel.

Approximate 3rd class **fares** from Koulikoro are CFA16,000 to Mopti, CFA20,000 to Timbuktu and CFA31,000 to Gao. 1st class A fares are CFA62,000 to Mopti, CFA79,000 to Timbuktu and CFA126,000 to Gao. *Luxe* fares sharing a twin cabin are nearly double the 1st class A fares (eg Koulikoro to Timbuktu CFA144,000), while single *luxe* fares carry a 30 percent supplement on top of that (Koulikoro to Timbuktu CFA192,000).

Food, of different qualities in different dining rooms is included in 1st, 2nd and – hardly any worse – 3rd class. 3rd class is probably the best option if you're budgeting, and some cabins have fans. You can generally use the 2nd class showers and toilets, which is a big plus. If you take 4th class, you fend entirely for yourself, buying whatever's available (and it's often not much) in the ports of call and suffering the appalling toilets. On board each boat, a bar serves **cold drinks**, but in theory 4th class passengers don't have the right to use it. **Drinking water** is a problem: only in the 1st and 2nd class dining rooms is there any alternative to river water.

Smaller vessels

Anywhere along the Niger, and virtually year-round, you can find local **pirogues** to get you from A to B. These are rowed – or poled much of the time – and sometimes venture quite long distances with large consignments of rock salt or other goods. Details are given through the chapter, but after protracted negotiations you can expect to pay from CFA2000 per person per day (50–100km) with shared food. They provide the most rewarding, if basic, means of seeing the Niger – from a few inches above its surface.

It's also possible to get **pinasses** along certain stretches of the river. These are large handmade motorized boats covered with a type of matted overhang. They operate mostly in the area around **Mopti** and you can get them from here to **Djenné** and sometimes as far as **Gao**.

Although comfort is rudimentary, there's a nostalgic sort of attraction to this type of transport which has been operating for centuries along the Niger. Some people even arrange to travel along the river in **barges** used to carry goods (especially grain) and pile their vehicle on board. This last option is spur of the moment, however, and can't be counted on.

■ Internal flights

For domestic air travel, **Air Mali** operates flights from Bamako to: **Mopti**, **Goundam** and **Timbuktu** (Sat); **Mopti**, **Timbuktu** and **Gao** (Tues); **Kayes** and **Yélimané** (Tues, Sat); and **Nioro** (Mon, Thurs). They use an old Antonov 24 on the "Route Niger" and a smaller plane on the "Route Sahel". Schedules are frequently interrupted by delayed or cancelled flights, but in theory flights depart Bamako in the morning and return at the end of the day by the same route. It can take Herculean efforts to get seats. Fares from Bamako are approximately: CFA45,000 to Mopti, CFA57,000 to Goundam, CFA63,000 to Timbuktu, CFA81,000 to Gao, CFA41,000 to Kayes and Yelimané, and CFA43,000 to Nioro.

Accommodation

Mali has few luxury lodgings, and devaluation of the CFA franc has generally lowered the price in real terms of most hotels for foreign visitors. In any case, your choice is usually limited to simple *campements*.

In Timbuktu, for example, rooms in the shabby *campement* start at CFA10,000, and the only alternative is the top-range *Sofitel*. Private *pensions* do exist in some of the small towns, but it's rare to find anything for much under CFA5000. Some towns have *campings* (not to be confused with *campements*) where you can sleep quite cheaply on mats in the courtyard or in simple rooms.

Note that the "Rail" hotels in railway towns tend to be sold on half-board (HB) basis, including dinner and breakfast.

Eating and Drinking

Mali's main staple is rice, often eaten with a thin beef broth mixed with tomatoes – *riz gras*. There are numerous regional variations on this common standby.

In the Dogon country, **millet**, or *petit mil*, provides the basis of nearly every meal and is prepared in hundreds of ways. Most commonly, it's served in a boiled mush called **tô**, and eaten with sauce. The Senoufo tend more towards tubers (**yams** and **cassava**), supplementing the rice and millet dishes which they eat less frequently than other peoples.

Food in Djenné has retained a strong Moroccan flavour. A type of **couscous** is eaten here, as is a noodle-like dish, known as **kata**, which is accompanied by meat. **Nempti** is a type of *beignet* (fritter) mixed with hot peppers, while **fitati** is a kind of thin pancake. During special celebrations the people make a pastry called **tsnein-achra** from rice flour and honey. The Tuareg, too, make a variant of *couscous* from a wild grain known as *fonio* or "hungry rice".

All along the river, of course, the people eat **fish**. One of the most common varieties is *capitaine* (Nile perch) – a boney little creature that's quite good when deep fried in oil or grilled over coals. In the northern regions of the Fula herders, beef, mutton and goat outsell fish, although for many people red meat is still a luxury.

■ Drinking

The main **Malian beer** is *Castel*, expensive (and too rarely cold) relative to other countries. Beer and soft drinks – called *sucreries* – are worth a small fortune in the remoter parts of the north and east. **Home-brewed beer**, made from corn or millet, is common to many different peoples – especially non-Muslims like many Dogon and

ACCOMMODATION PRICE CODES

Hotel prices in this chapter are coded according to the following scales – the same scales in terms of their pound/dollar equivalents as used throughout the book. Prices refer to the rate you can expect to pay for a room with two beds. Single rooms, or single occupancy, will normally cost at least two-thirds of the twin-occupancy rate, for further details see p.51.

① **Under CFA4000 (under £5/$7.50)**. Very rudimentary lodgings, with primitive facilities.

② **CFA4000–8000 (£5–10/$7.50–15).** Basic hotel with few frills. Some self-contained rooms (S/C) and possibly some with AC.

③ **CFA8000–16000 (£10–20/$15–30).** Modest hotel, usually with S/C rooms and a choice of rooms with fans, or a premium for AC.

④ **CFA16,000–24,000 (£20–30/$30–45).** Reasonable business or tourist-class hotel with S/C, AC rooms and a restaurant.

⑤ **CFA24,000–32,000 (£30–40/$45–60).** Similar to the previous code band, but extra facilities such as a pool are likely.

⑥ **CFA32,000–40,000 (£40–50/$60–75).** Comfortable, first-class hotel, with good facilities.

⑦ **Over CFA40,000 (over £50/$75).** Luxury, establishment – top prices around CFA60,000.

Senoufo – and is known variously as *konjo*, *dolo* or *chakalo*. Lastly, sweet, yellow China **tea** is drunk all over the country, but with particular devotion in the north, and above all by the Tuareg.

Communications – Post, Phones, Language and Media

Contact with Europe and the rest of the world can be slow even out of Bamako. Though letters are inexpensive to send, they usually take their time arriving; estimate two weeks from the capital, as much as a month from the provinces. The PTT in Bamako has a poste restante service which seems to work relatively well.

Although Mali is connected to the IDD system, only in Bamako can you guarantee international direct dialling. From the rest of the country you can only make operator-assisted calls to Europe and **phones** are rare. It takes a while to get through, and it's often easier to call from the big hotels rather than small post offices, where queues tend to be long and obstructions many. As elsewhere in West Africa, many larger towns have *centres téléphoniques*, where you can make your call from a private, metered booth and pay on completion. However, for overseas calls this still depends on getting a line out of the country.

Mali's IDD code is ☎223.

Languages

Though a very small percentage of the population speaks it fluently, **French** is the official language in Mali and the one you'll have to deal with for all administrative preoccupations.

The most widely spoken national language is **Bamana** (similar to Malinké), used throughout the country, but especially in the region around Bamako. Other languages include Pulaar (Fula), Senoufo, Songhai and Dogon.

The media

The Malian **press** is improving. There's a daily French-language newspaper, *l'Essor – la Voix du Peuple*, a weekly culture and sports journal called *Podium*, and a couple of interesting fortnightly revues, *Les Echos* and *l'Aurore*. *Mali Muso* ("Women of Mali") published quarterly by the *Union des Femmes du Mali*, is of particular interest to women. There are several dozen other occasional magazines, any of which is worth

BASIC BAMANA

Compare these with the "Minimal Mandinka" words and phrases in Chapter Three "The Gambia".

GREETINGS

Hello	*Aye ni ké*	How's the family?	*Den Baya ka kendé?*
Good morning	*Aye ni sogoma*	How's it going?	*Hera bé?*
Good afternoon	*Aye ni télé*	See you later	*An bé sogoma*

NUMBERS

1	*kélén*	6	*woro*	20	*mugan*	100	*kémé*
2	*fila*	7	*woronfila*	25	*mugan ni lolu*	120	*kémé ni mugan*
3	*saaba*	8	*seguin*	30	*bi sabi*	150	*kémé ni bi lolu*
4	*nani*	9	*konondo*	40	*bi nani*	200	*kémé fila*
5	*lolu*	10	*tan*	50	*bi lolu*	five franc piece	*dorem*

USEFUL EXPRESSIONS

How much?	*Jeli/joli?*	Where are you going?	*I bi taa min?*
I'll take it (give it to me)	*A di yan*	I don't know	*N'ta lou*
It's too expensive	*A songo ka gbélé*	I don't understand	*N'ma fahamuya*
Do you know of a cheap restaurant?	*I bi resitoran da duman don wa?*	Excuse me	*Ya fan ma*
Where's the bank?	*Bank bé min fan?*	What did you say? (please repeat)	*Aw kodi*
Show me the way	*Sila jira kan na*	Thank you	*I ni se*

MALIAN TERMS: A GLOSSARY

ADEMA *Alliance pour la démocratie au Mali.* The leading political party.

AEEM *Association des Élèves et Étudiants du Mali.* The national students union.

Azalaï Desert caravans that formerly dominated Saharan trade. They continue today in small numbers, notably between the salt mines of Taoudenni and Timbuktu.

Cadeauter Transformation of the French word *cadeau* meaning "gift", into a verb. Sometimes used by children in the expression: *il faut me cadeauter*, meaning "give me something".

CNID *Congrès national d'initiative démocratique.* One of the biggest opposition parties.

Dourou-dourouni *Camion bâché*, pick-up or bush taxi.

Ghana In the historical context, usually refers to Ancient Ghana, the earliest Mande-speaking kingdom (precursor of Mali), the ruined capital of which, Koumbi Saleh, is located in southeast Mauritania. The name "Ghana" was the title used by its Soninke rulers.

Hogon Dogon priests who live in isolation. These elderly men represent the highest spiritual authority in the Dogon country.

Mali An old empire (based southwest of Bamako) as well as the modern state, "Mali" is synonymous with "Manding" just as the language Malinké is basically the same one as Mandinka. Mali in Malinké means "hippo".

Oued Pronounced "wed"; French version of Arabic word designating a rocky river bed, dry except in the rainy season. The English equivalent is "wadi".

Pinasse Large wooden boat originally invented in Djenné to carry cargo. Though the basic covered design hasn't changed over the centuries, motors are added today.

Sudan/Soudan Former colonial name for the territory encompassing Senegal, Mali and Burkina Faso. Sometimes used today to refer to the same basic area. Sudanic architecture refers to the style that originated in Djenné and has nothing to do with the modern state of Sudan.

supporting to get a feel for what's going on in the country. *Nouvel Horizon*, for example, is an outspoken publication, regularly in trouble with the authorities for speaking its mind.

Government-controlled **radio** goes out in nine languages. **TV** is broadcast for five or six hours a day. The big new development, as everywhere in the region, is a plethora of small FM stations operating from various *quartiers* in Bamako: *Bamakan*, for example is pro-government. *Radio France Inter* and *Africa No. 1* (the Libreville-based station) are both available on FM.

Holidays and Festivals

Muslim holidays are celebrated with fervour in Mali, and during the month of Ramadan virtually everything closes down during the daytime – though night-time feasts redress the balance. **See p.62 for approximate dates.**

Christian celebrations – Christmas Day and Easter – are also public holidays as are New Year's Day and Labour Day (May 1). **National holidays** include January 20, the *Fête de l'Armée*; Africa Day on May 25 and Independence Day on September 22.

Directory

AIRPORT DEPARTURE TAX In theory CFA1000 domestic, CFA2500 African and CFA4500 intercontinental. In practice it depends on who deals with you. Some people have paid nothing, others up to CFA6000.

BARGAINING The first price on tourist items in Mali is invariably huge. If you make a dismissive offer expecting it to be turned down, you can be caught out. Beware: it's easy to cause offence if, in the end, you refuse to buy the item.

ENTERTAINMENT Mali is world-famous for its music with the names of singer Salif Keita and guitarist/bluesy phenomenon Ali Farka Touré outstanding, and a major part of the *Contexts* section on music is devoted to it. Malian cinema is also thriving and, likewise takes up a large proportion of the article on film, also in *Contexts*. The most famous name in Malian cinema is that of Souleymane Cissé, who made his international name with the memorable *Yeelen* (1986).

NAMES The same ones crop up all the time and it doesn't mean everyone is related; these are great, clan branches incorporating many strands and complex class and caste-like hierarchies.

Classic Manding names are **Diabaté/Jobarteh** and **Traoré** (which are historically related); **Keita** (with its royal associations); **Kanté/Konté/Kondé**; and **Kouyaté**. Fula names include **Bari/Barry**, **Diallo/Jalo** and **Cissé**. Many people have at least one Arabic name – Fatima, Moussa, Ali, etc.

OPENING HOURS Businesses tend to open Mon–Fri 8am–noon & 3–6/7pm. Many are closed on Friday afternoons, most on Saturday afternoons. Government offices are open Mon–Fri 7am–2pm & Sat 7am–noon.

WILDLIFE Mali's vast expanses of bush and swamp provide a major sanctuary for West African wildlife, with large predators and many other mammals present in significant numbers. Hippos are still relatively common all along the course of the Niger. The Parc National de la Boucle du Baoulé is a good, but very inaccessible reserve. Mali's elephants appear to be surviving, even increasing in numbers. Apart from the Baoulé elephants, a herd of 600 or more lives near Gossi, between Gao and Mopti, protected in part by the presence of the Tuareg who traditionally don't hunt them.

WOMEN'S ISSUES Women travellers don't find Mali a special hassle (at least no more so than male travellers as, for both sexes, parts of the country can try you with hustlers and vendors). In the West African context, there's a good deal of proud, feminine freedom in the country, coupled paradoxically with the highest incidence of initiatory **genital mutilation**, including the brutal practice of infibulation.

Recent History of Mali

The outstanding features of Mali's history are the old empires. Much of the modern country was part of the ancient Mali (or Manding) empire during its maximum extent in the thirteenth and fourteenth centuries. When the Moroccans crushed the Askia dynasty of the Songhai Empire in 1591, they left Mali with a political vacuum, partially filled from time to time by the rapid rise and fall of mini-empires. The first was the kingdom of Ségou (written "Segu" in many histories), founded in the early eighteenth century and almost immediately eclipsed by the Fula jihad that spread from Masina (Macina). This kingdom was founded in 1818 by Cheikou Ahmadou Hammadi Lobbo – a religious zealot inspired by Dan Fodio's religious war that had spread from Sokoto in present-day Nigeria. And from Senegal, the Tukulor marabout El Hadj Omar Tall launched his own holy war, setting out in 1852 to conquer animist Mandinka districts to the east.

■ Arrival of the French

The Tukulor cavalry spread across the Niger belt with lightning speed, carving out an empire headquartered at **Ségou** that extended from Masina to Bandiagara. Increasingly, it came to be seen as a threatening obstacle to the designs of French colonials in St-Louis, Senegal, bent on commercial and military penetration into the Soudanese interior.

The governor of Senegal, **General Louis Faidherbe**, opted in the first instance for a diplomatic response to Tukulor expansion and sent an expeditionary mission to Ségou. Arriving in 1868, the French signed a treaty with the new ruler **Ahmadou**, son of Omar who had been killed in battle in 1864. By 1880, the French were back to renew the treaty, but, although Ahmadou was increasingly suspicious of their motives and this time had the emissary locked up, it was too little too late. **French forces** had now advanced as far east as Kita and brought with them the parts of an armed gunboat which they assembled and launched at Koulikoro. They thus managed to control the river as far down as Mopti. But the Tukulor Empire based at Ségou refused to cede. Finally, the capital fell in 1890 and the other towns in the interior toppled like dominos in their turn – Djenné and Bandiagara in 1893, and, after fierce Tuareg resistance, Timbuktu in 1894.

Tieba and Samory

Meanwhile, resistance was fomenting in the Senoufo country around Sikasso. The Malinké chief **Samory Touré** had been carving out his own small empire since 1861 and had taken the Senoufo strongholds of Kong, Korhogo and Ferkessédougou. He ran into conflict with **Tieba**, king of Sikasso. Samory attacked Sikasso in 1887 and beseiged it for fifteen months, but the town resisted. The French, under Lieutenant Binger, watched the rivalry with close attention and eventually allied themselves with Tieba, helping him reinforce his regional power. Tieba died in battle in 1893 and was replaced by his son **Ba Bemba**. The new king, however, mistrusted the French and refused to follow through on the kingdom's commitment to help the colonials destroy Samory's influence. In May 1898 the French attacked and took Sikasso, and the king committed suicide, escaping the fate of Samory, who was captured in September as he dashed southwest towards Liberia, hoping to get more weapons from the British. The same year, El Hadj Omar's son Ahmadou died in exile in Sokoto. France was now the sole power in the region.

■ The French Soudan

Confident of eventual victory, the French had already declared the **Soudan** an autonomous colony in 1890. Later it was incorporated into the colony of **Haut Sénégal-Niger**, of which **Bamako** was made the capital in 1908. The railway had been extended from Dakar to Koulikoro in 1904 and, with the creation of the *Office du Niger* – a national agricultural agency based in Ségou – the French hoped to turn Mali into the bread-basket of West Africa and even make the colony turn a profit through the production of cash crops like groundnuts and cotton. *Pistes* were traced through the interior to facilitate the transportation of crops and, in 1932, a dam was built near Ségou in the hope of turning hundreds of thousands of square kilometres into irrigable land.

From the beginning, however, the ambitious designs were frustrated. In the first place, the colonial authorities soon ran into a shortage of labour which they solved by forcibly recruiting volunteers from neighbouring countries, notably the region of the Upper Volta (Burkina Faso). In addition, much of the soil in the Soudan turned out to be too poor to support cotton production and rice was substituted. Finally, the *Office du Niger* had restrictive financial limitations. As a result, only a small fraction of the territory destined to become an agricultural miracle was ever exploited. Not that it made much difference to Malians at the time, since the production was almost exclusively destined for export to France.

World Wars I and II – African participation

Of all the colonies in the AOF (*Afrique Occidentale Française*), Mali paid the highest price with the outbreak of World War I. The Bambara, especially, were recruited in large numbers to fill the ranks of the famous *Tirailleurs Sénégalais* – the **Senegalese Infantry**. These troops had already experienced European war as early as 1908 when they had been used by France to "pacify" Morocco. After 1914, tens of thousands of Africans were sent to Verdun where one in three died in the muddy war of attrition. Back in the Soudan, uprisings that sprouted to protest the draft of native soliders for a foreign war were brutally suppressed by the French authorities.

As if the price wasn't high enough, when the war was over, the new colonial governor, Just Van Vollenhoven, began mobilizing civilians in the Soudan to develop agricultural production and the regional infrastructure. It was a move he deemed necessary to make the colony profitable after the stagnant period during the war.

Parallel to this, the French made minimal concessions to give Africans an extended role in the **politics** of their countries. By 1925, Africans could be elected to sit on the governor's advisory councils, although this of course gave them no direct political power. From the 1930s, laws were made to facilitate access to **French nationality** – a status considered by the government to be a great honour despite the sacrifices Africans had made during the war. But by 1937 only some 70,000 people in the entire AOF had been granted French citizenship and the vast majority of these were Senegalese. World War II had the effect of nipping political and social development in the bud.

Postwar political developments

World War II acted as a catalyst that gave rise to a new political consciousness in Africa and a determination to achieve political rights. Independence was still only envisaged by a very few, and de Gaulle himself ruled out this possibility at the 1944 **Brazzaville conference**, although he did say France was willing to make concessions, including greater African involvement in the respective governments.

In the aftermath of Brazzaville, three **political parties** were formed in Mali: the *Parti Soudanais du Progres* (PSP) headed by **Fily Dabo Cissoko**; a Soudanese affiliate of the *Section Française de l'Internationale Ouvrière* (SFIO) with **Mamadou Konaté** at the helm; and the *Parti Démocratique du Soudan* (PDS) founded by French Communists living in Mali. Though Cissoko came out ahead in elections to a constituent assembly in 1945, the first year of government was characterized by infighting among the parties – notably the PSP and the SFIO. In 1946, Bamako hosted the **Rassemblement Démocratique Africain** – a vast political convention that brought together over 800 delegates from Senegal, Côte d'Ivoire, Guinea, Benin, Togo, Cameroon, Chad and Mali. The main theme was **union**: so that West Africa could speak with one voice, it was imperative the Soudan have a single voice within the RDA. To the surprise of everyone, the three parties agreed to form a single *Union Soudanaise* within the RDA (USRDA). But within a couple of days, Cissoko announced that a bloc with what he called "unrepentant communists" was impossible and he reformed the PSP.

The Soudan swings left

The next decade saw an intense **rivalry** between the PSP and the USRDA but, by 1957, the latter had clearly won the upper hand. This was in large part because the USRDA had more effectively distanced itself from Paris and had better grassroots organization in Mali. After the elections of 1959, in which the PSP had fared so badly, they were constrained to join forces with the USRDA. On the eve of independence, there was no effective opposition to this party.

Changes had occurred within the USRDA when Konaté died in 1956. A moderate voice on the left, Konaté had advocated union of all the peoples of Mali. The void he left in the party ranks was quickly filled by more radical elements headed by **Modibo Keita**.

In the same year, the **Loi Cadre** drafted in Paris had opened the door to semi-autonomous governments in each of the territories of AOF. This led to divisions in the formerly united RDA as a cleavage arose between leaders like Sekou Touré and Leopold Senghor – who advocated the maintenance of a federal government in Dakar – and those such as Houphouët-Boigny, who advocated the maximum autonomy for each of the territories.

Federalists and federation

Modibo Keita stood firmly in the camp of the Federalists, mainly because, as a poor country, the Soudan had a lot to gain from uniting itself with other territories (many of the country's colonial projects had been financed by AOF funds that originated outside Mali). Senghor's motives were more ideological, and he pleaded for a politically united West Africa that would maintain good relations with France. It became more pressing to decide on the pros and cons of a federation after the **1958 referendum** where AOF nations voted to continue self-government within the French Union.

Sekou Touré was the only African leader who, for better or worse, had the courage to storm out of the French Union. Guinea was therefore excluded from any West African federation as well. Côte d'Ivoire was also out since Houphouët-Boigny had already stated loud and clear that he wouldn't have his country become "the milk cow" to feed the mouths of hungry neighbours.

In January, 1959, the four remaining members of the former AOF – Soudan, Senegal, Upper Volta and Dahomey – met in Dakar and drew up the constitution for a **federation** of their territories. Under pressure from Côte d'Ivoire, Upper Volta eventually backed out of its commitment and Dahomey followed suit. Hopes for a broad-based political union in the region had been pared down to two nations, but it was still an important step for pan-African ideals. The **Mali Federation** of Mali and Senegal was born.

Unhappy union with Senegal

From the beginning, the alliance was uneasy. Keita was eager that Mali be granted independence. Senghor was more methodical, less hurried. De Gaulle himself helped sort out this problem by recognizing in 1959 that it was possible for the federation to be granted **independence** while staying in the French Community. The Mali Federation did, in fact, become independent – on April 4, 1960 – but the honeymoon between Senghor and Keita lasted barely two months.

Although numerous social and economic inequalities existed between the two former territories (which without doubt had an adverse effect on the union), the most glaring divergences were political and symbolized by the **clash of personalities** of the two leaders. Keita championed a Marxist approach to "African socialism". He was a man of (often admirable) principles who liked decisive action and who was unused to compromise. Senghor's approach was more measured and tended to favour dialogue and diplomatic action. He was especially cautious and pragmatic in his attitude to France which he hoped to keep as a friend and ally.

The stand-off between the two men – and as a consequence the territories they presided over – came to a head during the 1960 elections for President of the Federation, a powerful office that the Soudanese were wary of Senghor occupying. Senegal ruled out any alternative nominee and the brief federal arrangement collapsed.

■ Birth of the Mali Republic

After the failure of the Federation, Keita set about creating the basis of the independent Malian state – a task of Promethean proportions at such short notice. He was helped, however, by the wave of **nationalist pride** and unity that swept the country, now destined to stand alone. Even Keita's former opponent, Cissoko, threw his support behind the USRDA in the name of the national cause. In September 1960, a special congress of the USRDA announced the implementation of a **planned socialist economy**. Shortly afterwards, Keita closed French military bases in Mali. He then set up state enterprises, starting with SOMIEX. This company had a monopoly on all imports and exports of primary products – an advantage French companies operating in the country hardly appreciated. In 1962, Keita pushed his country further into **isolation** by taking it out of the franc zone and creating a national currency, the Franc Malien. In the same year, a **Tuareg revolt** in the Adrar des Iforhas mountains northeast of Gao was savagely repressed by the army.

It was a difficult start, made even worse by the fact that Senegal stopped trains to Bamako for three years after the rupture and closed its borders with Mali. As Keita continued down his radical path (and he was sincere in his belief that Mali could be the spearhead of a new brand of "African socialism", though his conception of what this meant differed from that of other regional leaders) he distanced himself from other African nations. And the West, too, turned an icy shoulder as, in the middle of the Cold War, he chose to ally his country with the Soviet Union. Opposition mounted grimly at home as the business community saw their economic privileges being eroded into state assets.

By the **mid-1960s**, Keita had created a heavy state machinery that dragged mercilessly on the nation's already fragile economy. The situation was characterized by numerous national enterprises (almost all of them running a deficit), a plethora of civil servants clogging the administrative machinery, a soaring balance of trade deficit and foreign debt, and a rapid weakening of the currency. Inflation soared and wages were frozen – a combination that wasn't calculated to enthuse Malians. By 1967, taking his cue from Peking, Keita was engaged in a **"cultural revolution"** to purge the nation of enemies within. He was supported in this by radical students, some of the unions, and by some lower grades in the civil service who resented the corruption of senior officials and business profiteers. But in the same year, Keita was obliged to devalue the Malian franc by fifty percent. The public outcry was immediate; the government's entire direction came under attack from all sides.

The coup

Keita seemed not to notice that opposition was sprouting up all around him. Believing the monumental role he'd played in his country's development absolved him from criticism by a populace faced with a deepening economic crisis, he was apparently surprised and aggrieved when a group of young military officers staged a **bloodless coup** in 1968.

The **Comité Militaire de Libération Nationale** (CMLN) was quickly formed, headed by a 32-year-old lieutenant, **Moussa Traoré**. Keita and senior members of his government were arrested and the former president died in prison ten years later.

Initially the military didn't challenge the nation's socialist orientation. The officers did, however, recognize the need to correct certain errors committed by the previous regime, to bring new order to the management of the economy and to boost production. To this end, Traoré continued to rely on Soviet and Chinese technical aid.

■ The Traoré years

The first years of military rule brought little relief to the country. Overnight revival of the economy was impracticable, and the **drought** that ravaged the nation in 1973 and 1974 had a disastrous effect on agriculture. Industrial development didn't fare much better and the **border war** with Burkina Faso, in 1974, put an extra drain on human and financial resources. Despite discouraging signs in the political and economic spheres, the military drew up a new constitution in 1974 that was approved in a plebiscite by what the government claimed was 99.7 percent of the population.

The new constitution, however, didn't go into effect until 1979 when a single party, the **Union Démocratique du Peuple Malien** (UDPM) was charged with running the country. Traoré remained at the head of government.

This symbolic transformation to civilian rule (cosmetic as it may be) was accompanied by a softening of the rigid socialist philosophy. This trend was accelerated after a second drought devastated the country from 1983 to 1985. In an effort to assure continued foreign aid, Traoré worked hard to improve relations with the West, notably with France. Most of the state organizations and companies that were a tremendous financial burden were privatized in an effort to dynamize the economy. Additionally, Traoré brought Mali into the CFA fold in 1985 which encouraged investment.

■ Democracy and the Third Republic

Through such steps Traoré thought he could bring his country out of the quarter century of political and economic isolation into which it had retreated after the so-called Balkanization of French West Africa on the eve of independence, and especially after the final rupture with Senegal. But, intentionally or otherwise, he also opened Mali to the **pressure for democratic reform** which was sweeping the region by 1990 and which was increasingly a condition of foreign aid.

At first, Traoré tried to contain the pressure within the party framework. Opposition leaders from the *Alliance pour la Démocratie au Mali* (ADEMA) wanted more and published an article in one of the new newspapers, *Les Echos*, calling for a national conference to draft a new constitution and lead the **transition to multi-party politics**. Soon after, a series of independent parties came into being, including the *Comité National d'Initiative Démocratique* (CNID) which has large support from the legal profession, and the *Union Soudanaise – Rassemblement Démocratique Africain* (US-RDA), the re-formed pre-independence party – these two remain the two most important opposition parties.

By December 1990, dissent was trickling down to the streets: the government tried to evict street vendors from downtown Bamako, provoking a **mass demonstration** that coincided with the anniversary of the Universal Declaration of Human Rights. On New Year's Eve, another pro-democracy demonstration attracted 15,000 marchers and, on January 8 1991, a **general strike** for better wages was called – the first in Mali since independence 30 years before. **Student protestors** jumped into the fray, organizing a demonstration that was brutally suppressed by the police and resulted in a number of deaths, the first in the pro-democracy movement.

The government wasted no time in demanding that political parties and student organizations cease all activity. It closed the country's schools, and deployed heavy weapons on the streets of Bamako. In the **mass arrests** which followed, Amnesty International reported widespread torture in the prisons, sometimes of schoolchildren as young as twelve.

Malians barely had time to recover from these incidents when a more concerted round of **rioting** broke out in March. In three days of intense fighting, police and *gendarmes* had killed some 150 people, and injured nearly a thousand. Wave after wave of protestors swelled through the city, however, failing to be intimidated by the government's show of strength. In the face of a failed policy of violent suppression, coupled with international disapproval and complete disruption of the economy, Traoré made plans to flee, but promised elections, and said shortly after that he would not resign and that his troops were loyal.

The new era

The next day the military responded by arresting Traoré. The **coup** leader, Lt-Col Amado Toumani Touré announced the dissolution of the government, the constitution and the ruling party – the UDPM – saying it would work with the pro-democracy movement. Within days, a multi-party committee had been formed to oversee the democratization of Mali. **Soumana Sacko**, a former finance minister sacked by Traoré when he tried a little too diligently to crack down on corruption, was appointed interim prime minister.

More arrests followed, with ex-government ministers charged with corruption and murder. Soon after the announcement that Traoré himself was to be tried on, among other charges, defrauding the national coffers, an unsuccessful **coup attempt** was mounted by officers loyal to the ex-president. A jubilant crowd swarmed through the streets of Bamako when it was learned the putsch had failed.

The people seemed less enthusiastic at voting time, however. Less than half of those eligible exercised their right to vote in the constitutional referendum, and in the first free municipal and presidential elections in 1992, the figure was barely 20 percent. The ADEMA party secured large majorities, however, and their man, **Alpha Oumar Konaré** was sworn in as president of the Third Republic on June 8, 1992.

Traoré and several members of his disgraced government were convicted of murder and sentenced to death, but they have not, so far, been executed and the sentences are not expected to be carried out (Mali has had no judicial executions since 1980). Their legacy has haunted the first three years of the new Mali – the economic crimes they are widely believed to have committed have not been presented before the courts, to the disgust of many Malians.

Meanwhile, the potential of the **school and student population** to provoke unrest is rarely far from the surface. The new order has provoked rather than satisfied demands, and demonstrations by the *Association des Élèves et Étudiants du Mali* (AEEM) on a range of issues have been quite frequent. Devaluation of the CFA franc in February 1994 sparked violent protests. The AEEM has also been associated by some observers with a shadowy group threatening European and other Western commercial interests in Mali, which distributed scare-leaflets in the aftermath of the devaluation.

Political life is dominated by the issue of ADEMA's overwhelming control of government, and of the council of ministers acting unilaterally with President Konaré outside the jurisdiction of the National Assembly.

The Tuareg rebellion

The biggest single issue facing Mali and Konaré's government is the **Tuareg rebellion**. Increasingly, the issues surrounding the rebellion boil down to one: **race**. The Tuareg view themselves, and are viewed as, "whites" and former lords or oppressors, while the sedentary population consider themselves "blacks", newly enfranchised by democratic reforms.

An estimated 160,000 people have been displaced by the war and are living in refugee camps in Algeria, Mauritania and Burkina. The Tuareg fighters pursuing it probably number no more than several hundred. Each new atrocity digs each side into a deeper hatred of the other. The war is unwinnable. Only increased help to the economically beleaguered population can ease the tensions by giving the predominantly young

ANATOMY OF A REBELLION

The roots of the rebellion were in place after France's abortive attempt to form a Tuareg state – "Azaouad" – in 1958, on the eve of independence. The current revolt began in 1990 with an attack on a military post at Ménaka, 300km east of Gao, followed up by a much bigger attack in September on Bouressa, which left at least 300 dead on both sides. Gao was placed under curfew. The rebellion coincided with the return from Algeria of **drought refugees** who were unhappy with their reception in Mali, and was framed in terms of overthrowing Moussa Traoré and improving development aid to their regions. But as the democracy movement in Bamako took hold and Traoré was deposed, the Tuareg rebellion made more specific demands for, at the very least, greater autonomy for the desert regions.

A ceasefire agreement was signed in Tamanrasset in Algeria in January 1991. The rebels' signatory was **Iyad Ag Galli**, leader of the *Azouad Popular Movement* (MPA) whose agenda listed a better deal for the Tuareg above greater autonomy and specifically excluded the ideal of independence for a Tuareg state.

The accord was rejected by other Tuareg militia – including the *Islamic Arab Front of the Azaouad* (FIAA), the *Azaouad Popular Liberation Front* (FPLA) and the *Revolutionary Army for the Liberation of Azaouad* (ARLA) – which continued a campaign of armed attacks, usually by small groups of rebels, on police stations and government buildings, invariably followed by brutal military reprisals on the most obvious Tuareg target in the district. Tens of thousands of refugees, mostly Tuareg, fled the affected areas to southern Algeria and Mauritania.

The rebels had Libyan support, and many of their military leaders had fought in various conflicts in the Middle East, including the Iran–Iraq war, Lebanon and Afghanistan.

Despite what appeared to be a fragmentation of any coordination between the different groups, a second peace agreement – the **national pact** – was signed in April 1992, with a new umbrella organization of the Tuareg in Mali, the *Unified Fronts and Movements of the Azaouad* (MFUA), claiming to represent at least four of them. During the course of the year, 600 ex-rebels were integrated into the Malian army, 300 were given civil service posts and joint Tuareg-army patrols were instituted.

But the FPLA split from the MFUA, and continued fighting until mid-1993, launching about ten attacks each month in its campaign for independence from Mali. There was a general breakdown of the umbrella MFUA in early 1994, with the FPLA fighting the FIAA and the MPA and ARLA at war with each other, the ARLA claiming that the MPA, with its demands for full Tuareg integration into Malian national life, had sold out. There were also clashes between regular soldiers of the Malian army and "integrated" Tuareg troops. The National Pact had failed.

Resentment at the Tuaregs' comparative success at achieving their aims through violence, led in early 1994 to the formation of a largely Songhai resistance militia, **Ganda Koi** ("Owners of the Land"), which has launched vicious attacks on Tuareg camps and whose members are apt to compare the conflict with the overthrow of apartheid in South Africa. Another militia, **Alert des Bella** ("Bella Awakening"), is a reprisal force formed by the Bella community – the Tuaregs' former slaves. **Lafia** is a Fula group.

In October 1994 came the worst violence so far. FIAA rebels killed 13 and injured 17 in a raid on Gao, and also stormed a Niger river steamer docked in Gao harbour. Subsequently, the army and the *Ganda Koi* went to **Kel Essouk**, 5km outside Gao, and slaughtered every light-skinned person they could find – a massacre variously estimated at between 60 and 300 people. Those who fled in time walked for two weeks across the desert to a Tuareg refugee camp in Burkina Faso.

fighters reasons to engage in civilian life. Genuine reconciliation, however, is a long-term goal.

As this book goes to press (August 1995), the unwieldy confederation of Tuareg rebel groups appears to have broken down completely. Some are still fighting; others are building on concessions won from Bamako to improve their lot. Gao is still imperilled by the threat of raids, but, in the delta region, there have been no serious incidents since the beginning of 1995. Talks are continuing and, encouragingly, the impressive peace accord in Niger is holding.

BAMAKO

Although **BAMAKO** has grown quickly since independence, evidence of modernization is only slowly penetrating the dusty city centre. Here, the mix of day-long crowds, hostile traffic and sludge-filled sewers add up to an oppressive combination for visitors just in from the *brousse*, although arrivals from Dakar welcome Bamako's less aggressive hustlers – debilitated, no doubt, by the perennial heat. At dusk the dust settles down like a pink fog as the centre expels its torrid activity into the suburbs where the conspicuous aid community reposes in air-conditioned comfort.

Architecturally, ostentatious modern developments like the Saudi-built **Pont du Roi Fahd** and nearby, the neo-Sudanic **Tour BCEAO** – the city's stunning showpiece – emerge from amid the medieval sanitation and dreary Soviet-funded blocks of the early 1960s. Compared with Mali's undeniable rural attractions, the capital is just too hot, dirty and crowded to be immediately appealing and for most, the few days taken to obtain the next visa, go to the supermarket, write a few letters or catch the train will be long enough.

Some history

As rock paintings (notably at the **Point G caves**) attest, Bamako is the site of ancient settlements, peopled as early as the African Paleolithic and Neolithic ages. Oral history traces the roots of the present town back to **Seribadian Niaré**, who sought refuge in the Bamana empire after being chased from the region of Nioro du Sahel in the seventeenth century. Upon arrival in the capital town of **Ségou**, Niaré married the sister of the king, **Soumba Coulibaly**. The couple had a son, **Diamoussadian Niaré**, and moved to the region around the present capital of Mali. A hunter of heroic dimensions, the son eventually killed a giant crocodile that had long terrorized the people of the area, thus fulfilling a prophecy and laying the basis for the establishment of a dynasty (also prophesied) that would grow up on the site. The Niarés thereby became rulers of the chiefdom at Bama-ko (crocodile-river).

The alternative opening recounts how a hunter from Kong in Côte d'Ivoire, Bamba Sanogo, killed an elephant here on the north bank of the Niger and received permission from the local lord to found a town, which he named Bamba-Kong after himself and his city of origin. Leaving no heirs on his death, the town's chieftaincy went to Diamoussadian Niaré.

Whichever its origin, Bamako grew to be a prosperous trading centre. By the time the Scots explorer **Mungo Park** arrived in the early nineteenth century the population had grown to about 6000. By 1883 the French had built a fort here and soon afterwards colonized the region. In 1904 the railway line was pushed through from Kayes and in 1908 the town was made capital of the colony of **Haut Sénégal-Niger**. When independence was returned to the country in 1960, Bamako became the Malian capital. At the time, the town's population was some 160,000, but in the following years of rapid growth that figure has risen five fold.

Arrival, orientation and transport

Note that if you're coming from Mopti or beyond by river boat you'll get only as far as Koulikoro, the port 60km east of Bamako, which has a rail link to the capital as well as road traffic. If you arrive by **bush taxi** chances are you'll be let off at the **gare routière de Sogoniko**, about 8km from the centre on the south side of the Niger River. You can either take a taxi from here to town, catch a northbound *BAMABUS* for a fraction of the cost, or hop on a Peugeot *bâché*. Whichever way you'll cross the overworked **Pont des Martyrs** which spans the Niger. Once over the bridge and in the centre, either

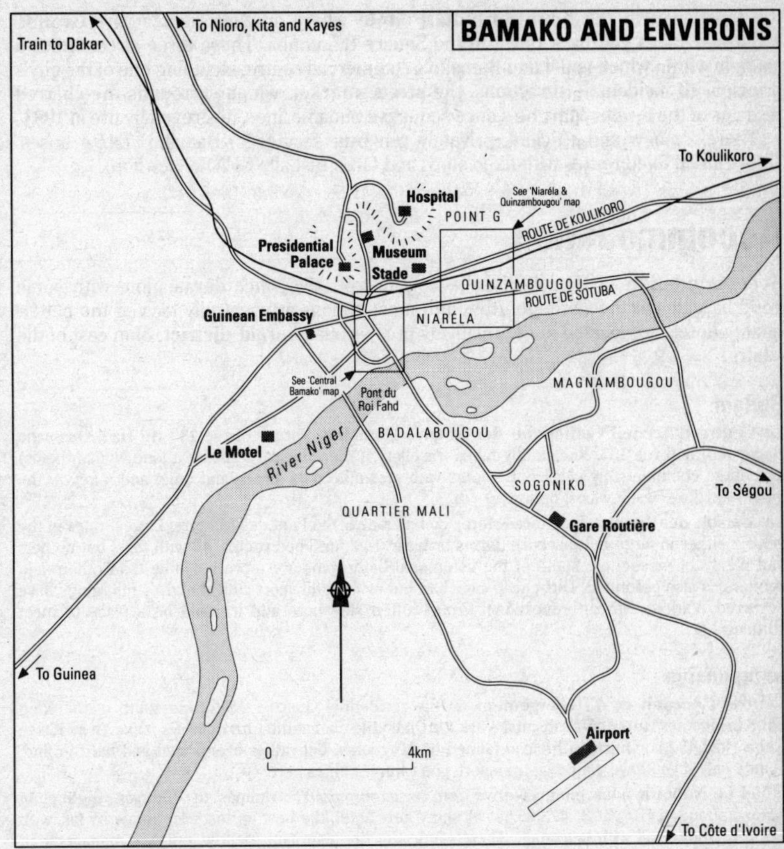

walk to a hotel or take another taxi if you want to lodge in the outskirts. **Arriving by train**, the station is walking distance from many accommodation options.

Bamako's **airport** is 15km south of town at **Senou**. After going through formalities, you'll have to catch a taxi to town as no bus service exists: check the tariff with someone who looks knowledgeable – it shouldn't exceed CFA5000, except after midnight.

Orientation and transport

Although Bamako's compact centre makes it an easy town to walk around, orientation can be difficult as one market-thronged street can look very much like another, especially at night. To get your bearings, the prominent *Hôtel de l'Amitié* and bat-eared **Tour BCEAO** serve as useful reference points: they are by the river and either side of the main thoroughfare which leads from the **Pont des Martyrs** to **Square Lumumba**, with the large French embassy and airline offices alongside. The **avenue du Fleuve**, leading north from this square towards the cliffs of **Point G**, is one of the town's main streets, lined with banks, restaurants and stores. If you follow this street all the way to the end, you'll run into the **rue Baba Diarra** running parallel to the railway tracks. Turning right, you'll pass the **train station** and American embassy before arriving at the junction with the **boulevard du Peuple** where another right at the **Grande Mosquée** takes you back down to the Square Lumumba. These three streets form a triangle within which you'll find Bamako's commercial centre, including one of the city's principal (if incidental) attractions, the **street market**, which surrounds the charred remains of the former **Marché**'s once seductive Sudanic lines, destroyed by fire in 1993.

There's a new and efficient, privately run **bus service** in Bamako, *TABA* buses. They run on fixed routes with fixed stops and fares (usually CFA100 per hop).

Accommodation

Accommodation in Bamako is relatively inexpensive since devaluation, with some good bargains in the ③ range. Although most options are centrally located the better-quality hotels are located in the relatively prosperous **Niaréla district**, 3km east of the centre.

Budget

Le Centre d'Accueil Catholique des Soeurs Blanches, corner of rue 130 (El Hadj Ousmane Bagayoko) and rue 133. Reluctantly takes travellers if there is space (being a lone woman helps) and offers commendably clean S/C rooms with mosquito nets, peace and quiet and a key to the gate. Bamako's best low-cost option. ①–②.

La Maison des Jeunes, blue three-storey complex near the Pont des Martyrs. Lowest rates in the centre: either in large but insecure dorms or basic 1-, 2- or 3-bed rooms, all with fans, but no nets and plenty of mosquitos. Some of the communal bathrooms are more bearable than others and camping is also permitted. Dirt cheap café/bar, but avoid unlit short cuts at night – muggings have occurred. Various African educational groups often stay here and it could be a place to meet students. ①.

Inexpensive

Centre d'Accueil et d'Hebergement, in the residential Quartier Mali 1km south of the King Fahd bridge next to a dental hospital – ask for Diallo the chef at the *Carrefour des Jeunes* in av Kasse Keita (☎22.43.11). Quiet, with clean fanned or AC rooms, but rather over-priced and hard to find. Handy only if you have your own transport; you can rent bikes here. ③.

Hôtel Le Naboun, a few minutes' drive from the *gare routière*, 200m past the *Hexagone* night club, Magnambougou (BP 8023; ☎22.06.88). A shiny new hotel, the best in this price range by far, with S/C, AC rooms, all with balconies. There's a decent bar-resto and friendly, efficient management. Only possible drawback is its south bank location. ③.

Mission Libanais, ("Mission Père Francis"), rue Poincaré 200m west of av de Fleuve (look out for the cross on the roof). Secure haven with off-street parking, a few fanned and netted twin bedrooms and a shared bathroom/toilet. ③.

Pension MS No 1, rue Mohammed V north of rue Archinard (BP 2244; shop next door ☎22.05.97). Formerly the *Djoliba*, and conveniently close to the train station, with large bare rooms with fans, and timely improvements to some bathrooms. No nets. Noisy disco/bar downstairs. Although breakfast is included, still overpriced. ③.

ACCOMMODATION PRICE CODES

① Under CFA4000 (under £5/$7.50) ② CFA4000–8000 (£5–10/$7.50–15)
③ CFA8000–16,000 (£10–20/$15–30) ④ CFA16,000–24,000 (£20–30/$30–45)
⑤ CFA24,000–32,000 (£30–40/$45–60) ⑥ CFA32,000–40,000 (£40–50/$60–75)
⑦ Over CFA40,000 (Over £50/$75)

For further details turn to "Accommodation" in the Practical Information at the beginning of this chapter.

Moderate

Hôtel Buffet de la Gare, next to the train station (BP 466; ☎23.19.10). Fanned or AC rooms, some S/C. *The* place to stay for committed Rail Band fans. Live music on Sat nights and plenty of shunting and hooting at other times. Rates are HB. ③–⑤.

Hôtel Dakan, Niaréla District (BP 1385; ☎22.91.96). The pleasant and old-fashioned *Jardins de Niaréla* reverts to its original name and offers a cluster of S/C, AC rooms with TVs around shady gardens. Breakfast is included and it also has its own bar/restaurant. ④.

Hôtel Le Fleuve, next to the Senegalese embassy off av de l'Yser. Pleasant small hotel with clean AC rooms and a recommended restaurant in a quiet area west of Square Lumumba. ④.

Hôtel Jamana, rte de Sotuba, next to Malibú nightclub in Niaréla (BP 1686; ☎22.34.56). Brand-new, with very clean S/C, AC rooms. Discounts available for stays of more than a night or two.④.

Hôtel Lac Debo, av du Fleuve, corner of av de la Nation (BP 2938; ☎22.96.35). The old *Majestic* with a facelifted foyer. Decent AC or fanned, S/C rooms upstairs, some with balconies. Handy central position and a small restaurant/bar. ④.

Le Motel, av Follereau (BP 911; ☎22.56.22). Another hotel with a large garden and setting near the river, though about 4km from the centre. The distance aside, the S/C rooms aren't bad value. Top of this price range. ③.

Expensive

Hôtel de l'Amitié, av de la Marne (BP 1720; ☎22.43.21; Fax 22.43.85). Ugly Soviet-built landmark offering service with a sneer unless you turn up with gold cards. Rooftop pool, fine restaurant and the priciest rooms in town: for many NGO workers this is home. ⑦.

Grand Hôtel, av Van Vollenhoven (BP 104; ☎22.24.81; Fax 22.36.26). Unexceptional international class hotel just north of the station with pool, tennis courts and organized tours. ⑤–⑥.

Hôtel Hirondelle, rte de Koulikoro, 3km east of station (BP 1026; ☎22.88.40; Fax 23.19.64). Lebanese-run hotel with an anodyne, business-like atmosphere but well-appointed S/C rooms with AC which are the least expensive in this category. ⑤.

Hôtel Le Rabelais, rte de Sotuba, 3km east of station (BP 2126; ☎22.52.98; Fax 22.27.86). A warm welcome at this cosy and very popular French-run hotel, the best choice in this category for genuine comfort and hospitality. ⑤.

Hôtel Tennessee, Niaréla district (☎22.36.77; Fax 22.61.26). Modern new hotel with a pool and other comforts patronized by aid workers. ⑥.

The Town

Bamako's bustle, filth and especially its heat make it a tiring place to enjoy at a leisurely walking pace unless, of course, you happen to thrive in sub-Saharan urban settings. In that case the **street market** around the gutted ruins of the Marché Central is the place for you. You should also head a few blocks east of here to the new Grande Marché at **N'Golonina** where all the crafts and souvenir stalls have moved since 1994. North of the **Centre Artisanal** along bd du Peuple, you'll find a good selection of **fetish stalls** with an impressive array of decomposing animal parts. And to the north of the railway tracks, the other main north–south avenue – av de la Liberté – leads through the diplomatic district past the **museum** – if you do nothing else in Bamako, be sure to spend some time here – and the **zoo**, continuing up to the cliffs of **Point G** overlooking the city.

The Centre Artisanal and Grande Mosquée

Built by the French in the 1930s in the same Sudanic style as the burned-down market, the **Centre Artisanal** or **Maison des Artisans** (at the corner of bd du Peuple and rue Karamoko Diaby) was designed to promote traditional Malian art. Today it's a rather sad, run-down place, mostly devoted to the sale of gold and silver ware. But you'll also find various **crafts** produced here – leatherwork, weaving, woodcarving and so on. Prices are reasonable.

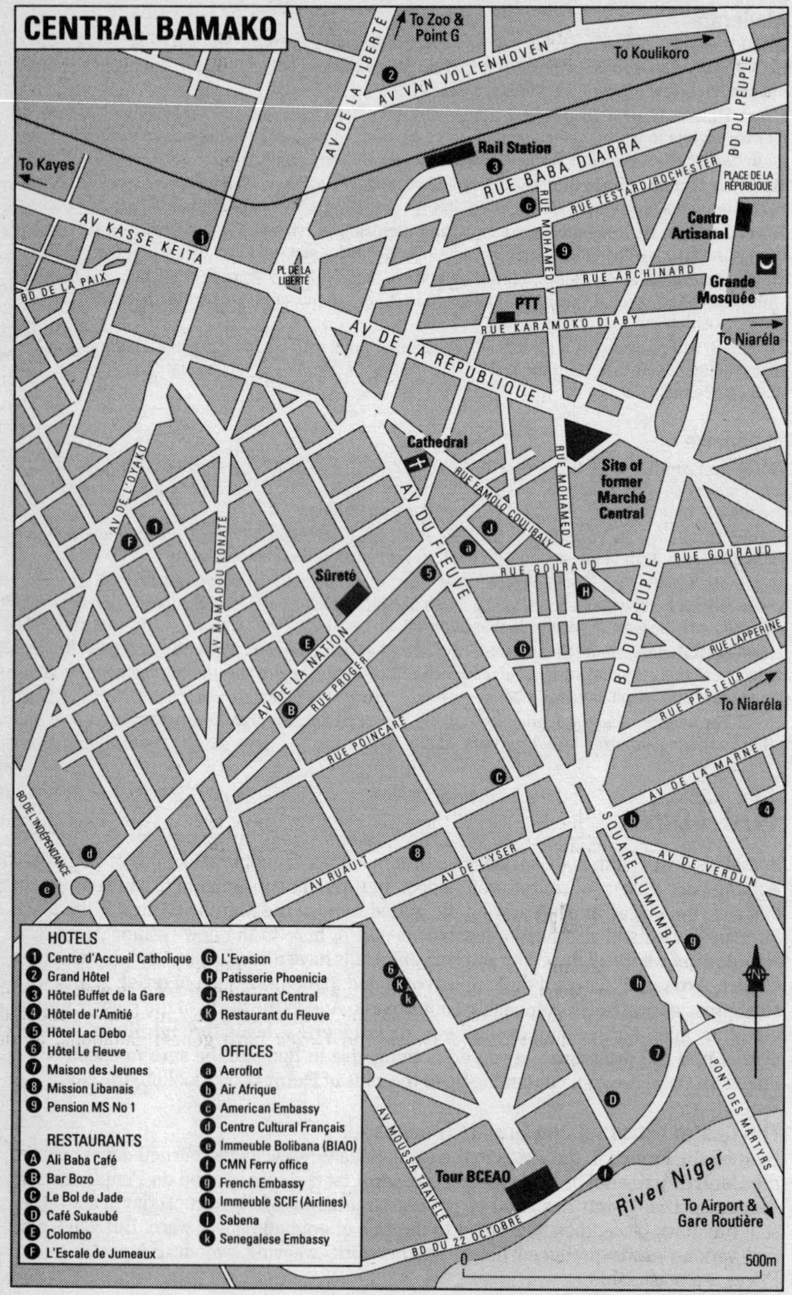
CENTRAL BAMAKO
To Zoo & Point G
To Koulikoro
AV VAN VOLLENHOVEN
AV DE LA LIBERTÉ
BD DU PEUPLE
To Kayes
Rail Station
RUE BABA DIARRA
RUE TESTARD/ROCHESTER
PLACE DE LA RÉPUBLIQUE
Centre Artisanal
RUE MOHAMED V
AV KASSE KEITA
PL DE LA LIBERTÉ
BD DE LA PAIX
RUE ARCHINARD
Grande Mosquée
PTT
RUE KARAMOKO DIABY
To Niaréla
AV DE LA RÉPUBLIQUE
Cathedral
Site of former Marché Central
AV DE L'OYAKO
RUE FAMOLO COULIBALY
AV DU FLEUVE
RUE GOURAUD
Sûreté
AV MAMADOU KONATÉ
AV DE LA NATION
RUE PROGER
RUE LAPPERINE
RUE PASTEUR
RUE POINCARÉ
AV DE LA MARNE
BD DE L'INDÉPENDANCE
SQUARE LUMUMBA
AV DE L'YSER
AV RUAULT
AV DE VERDUN
PONT DES MARTYRS
AV MOUSSA TRAVELÉ
Tour BCEAO
River Niger
To Airport & Gare Routière
BD DU 22 OCTOBRE
0
500m
HOTELS
1 Centre d'Accueil Catholique
2 Grand Hôtel
3 Hôtel Buffet de la Gare
4 Hôtel de l'Amitié
5 Hôtel Lac Debo
6 Hôtel Le Fleuve
7 Maison des Jeunes
8 Mission Libanais
9 Pension MS No 1
RESTAURANTS
A Ali Baba Café
B Bar Bozo
C Le Bol de Jade
D Café Sukaubé
E Colombo
F L'Escale de Jumeaux
G L'Evasion
H Patisserie Phoenicia
J Restaurant Central
K Restaurant du Fleuve
OFFICES
a Aeroflot
b Air Afrique
c American Embassy
d Centre Cultural Français
e Immeuble Bolibana (BIAO)
f CMN Ferry office
g French Embassy
h Immeuble SCIF (Airlines)
j Sabena
k Senegalese Embassy

Across the street from the crafts market, the **Grande Mosquée** was a gift to Bamako from Saudi Arabia. It's not one they can have been too enthralled by – an imposing twin-minareted dome lacking the grace of the country's indigenous Sudanic architecture.

The museum

Bamako's **museum** (Tues–Sun 9am–6pm; CFA500 including tour; easily visited in a couple of hours) is housed in a low-rise building inspired by the smooth lines of Djenné's architecture and contains some remarkable masterpieces of African art. Inside, objects are beautifully displayed, with photographs discreetly lining the walls, putting the exhibits in a broader context. Lighting is subtle and the museum comfortably air-conditioned – in short, it's more than you might expect.

Something of a pioneering institution, the museum is engaged in efforts to repatriate some of the vast treasure-store of artefacts taken abroad in colonial times. They conduct research here and perodically round up materials from different parts of the country. Part of the museum concentrates on domestic objects, including those used in **forging** and **weaving** – and a large, particularly strong, section is dedicated to the techniques involved in making some of the many types of **cloth** for which the region has a wide reputation; spinning, weaving, tie-dyeing and preparation of dyes. A separate section displays religious objects from Mali's various ethnic groups. Highlights include the stylized antelope **tyiwara** (chiwara) masks of the Bamana; various **Senoufo statuary**; and, of course, the world-renowned antique **Dogon sculptures**.

The zoo and botanical gardens

Bamako's **zoo** was a good idea whose time has passed. In theory, the cages and enclosures are designed to resemble closely the animals' natural habitats, but the whole place is so neglected and run-down that the best the keeper can normally do is identify cages whose inhabitants have long since expired. The surrounding **botanical gardens** are vast and, with a little attention, could provide a beautiful retreat from the city. But these too are suffering from neglect.

Point G

From the museum and zoo, you can walk up to the **north of the city** and to the hill known as **Point G**, the location of the main hospital. There are wonderful views from here, and some abandoned cliff dwellings featuring old **rock paintings**.

Eating and drinking

Street food is abundant in central Bamako but it's nice to get to know the locations of roadside stalls or *cafémen* who serve *Nescafé* and baguette breakfasts as well as meat-based snacks at other times of day. Most of the town's better **restaurants** – almost all French – are in the hotels (the *Rabelais* and *Grand* have good reputations, as do *l'Amitié* 's three restaurants).

Budget food

Ali Baba Café, opposite US embassy on rue Mohammed V. Breakfast and snack bar, (and bar) with a pizzeria next door featuring live kora music on Sun evenings.

Restaurant Central, rue Loveran. Popular formica-and-vinyl place with a small terrace outside and reasonably priced daily *plats*. Open late in the evening for meals or drinks.

Coeur d'Afrique, rte de Sotuba opposite *Shell* station. Cheap meals in a courtyard and very popular with Peace Corps volunteers.

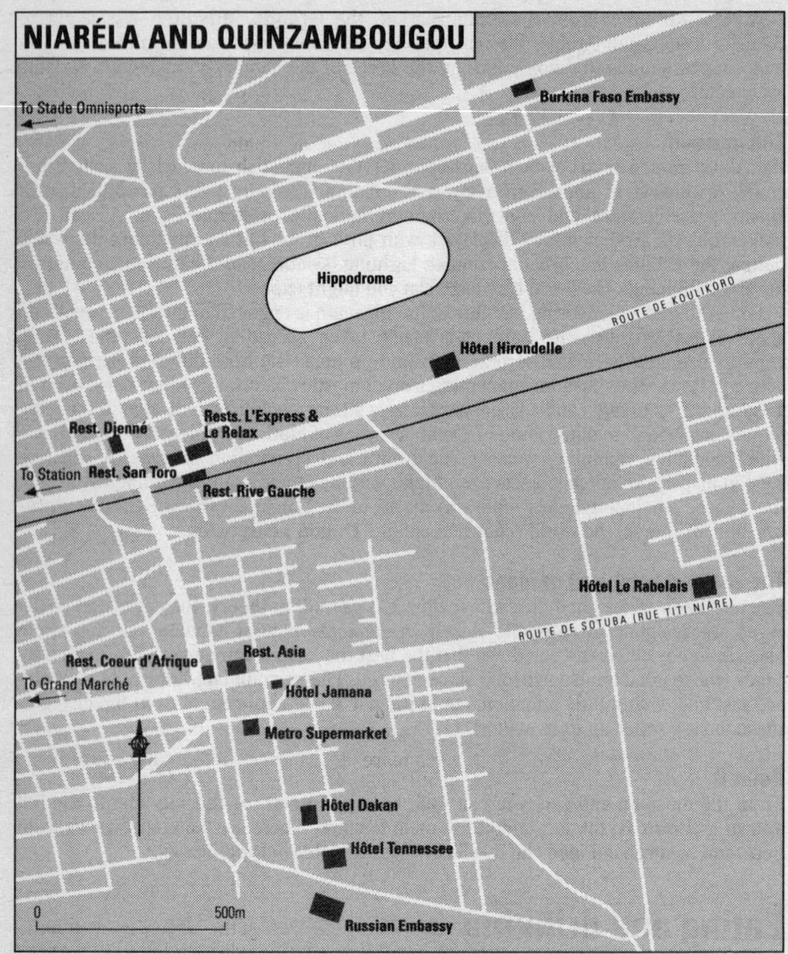

L'Escale de Jumeaux, rue 133. Cheap and friendly little shack right opposite the Catholic hostel with the affable owner offering good breakfasts and a heap of *riz gras* for just CFA600.

L'Express, rte de Koulikoro, near the Hippodrome. Upmarket French and Lebanese food. Daily till late.

Patisserie Phoenicia, rue Mohammed V. Spacious Lebanese-owned *salon de thé* and snack bar with fresh croissants and other pastries as well as pizzas, burgers, *chawarmas,* ice cream and soft drinks. Daily 6am–midnight.

Restaurant Le Relax, rte de Koulikoro near the Hippodrome. Airy patisserie/*salon du thé*/ restaurant popular with the expat community. Fresh croissants and juice, lots of cold snacks and full meals.

Café Sukaubé, opposite *Maison des Jeunes*. A long shaded hut serving pots of whatever's going. There's a cheap beer and whiskey bar too, but the scampering rats and evening mosquitoes may limit its appeal.

Restaurants

Restaurant Asia, rte de Sotuba, Quinzambougou District (☎22.22.48). High quality Vietnamese cooking in plush surroundings from the owner of Mopti's *Nuits de Chine*. Meals from CFA3500.

Le Bol de Jade, av Ruault. Well-established restaurant just west of Square Lumumba offering good value Chinese and Vietnamese dishes.

Restaurant Djenné, off rte de Koulikoro. Classy Malian restaurant with excellent reputation and meals from CFA3000 upwards plus kora and balafon accompaniment each evening. No alcohol.

Restaurant du Fleuve, next to Senegalese embassy off av de l'Yser. One of Bamako's nicest restaurants, offering Franco-Antillean specialities at good rates. Daily noon–10pm.

Restaurant La Pizzeria, in front of the American embassy (☎22.87.88). Good selection of pizzas and other Italian dishes from about CFA4000. Carry-out and delivery available.

Restaurant Rive Gauche, rte de Koulikoro, opposite the *San Toro*. Corsican-run place with a garden and affordable French food. Live music on Fri evenings.

San Toro, rte de Koulikoro. Slightly less expensive but no less agreeable Malian alternatives from the owners of the *Djenné*. Interior is decorated with authentic Malian artefacts. No alcohol.

Nightlife

Bamako has a satisfying nightlife, though the action only really gets going late. The town's most famous nightspot used to be the *Buffet Hôtel de la Gare*, an early showcase for the **Rail Band**, a government-sponsored group that went on to massive stardom and launched Mali's first international superstar, **Salif Keita**. Nowadays, however, the Rail Band only plays on Saturdays. In the same area, near the US embassy, the former *Cotton Club* has always been a great venue for live African music and cheap drinks, with no cover charge. It's gone through a couple of name changes – most recently *Manhattan* and *Le Cactus Bleu* – but was closed at the time of writing. Rumoured to be re-opening soon, it's well worth checking out. Right next door is the *37.2°* disco with a CFA2500 cover charge (including a free drink) and similarily priced drinks thereafter.

In the centre near the cathedral, the *Black and White* packs them in almost every night and just off av du Fleuve is an upmarket disco, *L'Evasion*, a crowded weekend venue for hard-core zouk. Sleazier but much more fun, especially in the early hours, are the *Bar Bozo* and *Disco Colombo* along av de la Nation, probably the capital's best night out. They have Malian bands on Friday and Saturday nights and there's street food and taxis outside – the latter is a better option to staggering home as muggers around here prey on the inebriated and, increasingly, on the wide awake. *Antipodes* on bd de L'Indépendance is part of the French cultural centre complex, with a bar and occasional music to add to its mainly theatrical output.

Among the hotel discos, *Le Village* at the *Grand Hôtel* draws the largest crowds and features a good mix of music. East of the centre in the Niaréla district, the *Blue Notes*, on the rte du Sotuba/rue Titi Niare, and the laser-lit *Métropolis* disco near the *Métro* supermarket are favoured hang-outs for young Bamakois and French volunteers. To the south of the river, *Le Select* is a new club near the Nigerian embassy in Badalabougou.

Listings

Airline offices

Aeroflot, rue Loveran (BP 93) ☎22.54.78

Air Afrique, Square Lumumba ☎22.58.02

Air France, Immeuble SCIF, Square Lumumba ☎22.22.12; Fax 22.47.34
Offers a town check-in service.

Air Mali, Immeuble SCIF, Square Lumumba ☎22.93.94; Fax 22.23.49

Ethiopian Airlines, Immeuble SCIF, Square Lumumba ☎22.60.36

Sabena, 6 av Kasse Keita (BP 2056) ☎22.63.61 or 22.37.92

American Express, *Afric Trans Services*, av du Fleuve (BP 2917; ☎22.44.35).

Banks Hours are short: Mon–Fri 8am–noon. The best bank for changing money or travellers' cheques is the *BIAO* on bd de l'Indépendance, corner of av de la Nation; quick service and no problem, especially for FF, but remember to take original receipts if changing TCs. The other three banks – the *BDM* and the *BCEAO* (opposite one another on av du Fleuve), and the *BMCD* (av du Fleuve) are less useful.

Car rental *Europcar* at the *Grand Hôtel* (☎22.24.81) and *Falaye Keita* at the *Hôtel de l'Amitié* (☎22.43.25). Expect to pay dearly.

Cinemas The nicest cinemas are at the *Hôtel de l'Amitié* and the newer cultural centre on the south side of the Niger. Apart from being the most comfortable, they also have screenings of recent releases.

Cultural centres The *Centre Culturel Français*, off the bd de l'Indépendance, has a good library including French newspapers and magazines. They also organize sporadic exhibitions, shows and movies. Similar activities are arranged at the *USIS* – the American cultural centre opposite the embassy.

Maps The *Direction Nationale de Cartographie*, av de la Nation, is the place to go for 1:200,000 survey maps.

Post and telephones The *poste centrale* is on rue Karamoko Diaby, not far from the market. There's a reliable poste restante service here. A couple of hundred metres east is a *centre téléphonique* where you can attempt to make calls abroad from a booth and pay on completion of your call. There are card phones here too.

Supermarkets At the eastern end of the city, where most of the expat community live. The *Metro* is 2.5km along rte de Sotuba, in Niaréla, next to the *Shell* station, and the *Fourmi* is an agonizingly similar distance from town along the rte de Koulikoro. There's a newer supermarket, *Azar Libre Service*, next to *Le Relax* restaurant near the Hippodrome.

EMBASSIES AND CONSULATES IN BAMAKO

Algeria, Badalabougou district, 4km south of the river	☎22.51.76
Belgium (BP 187)	☎22.51.44
Burkina Faso, Consulate, north of the route de Koulikoro just past the *Hôtel Hirondelle*, (BP 9022). Visas CFA9000, available while you wait (now handles Ghana visas also).	☎22.31.77
Canada, rte de Koulikoro (BP 198)	☎22.22.36
Egypt, Badalabougou district, south of the river (BP 44)	☎22.35.03
France, Square Lumumba (BP17)	☎22.31.41; Fax 22.03.29
Germany, av de Farako, Badalabougou (BP100)	☎22.32.99; Fax 22.96.50
Guinea (BP 118)	☎22.29.75
Italy	☎22.35.40
Mauritania, rue Titi Niare, Bagadadji (BP 135)	☎22.48.15
Morocco, south of the Pont des Martyrs (BP 2013)	☎22.21.23
Netherlands, Bureau de Coopération Néerlandais (BP 2220)	☎22.43.27; Fax 22.36.17
Nigeria, south of the Pont des Martyrs (BP 57)	☎22.57.71
Senegal, south of av de l'Yser next to *Restaurant du Fleuve*. Visas CFA2500, available next day.	
United Kingdom, Honorary Consul, Mr Harvey Smith (BP 2069)	☎22.20.64
USA, north end of rue Mohammed V (BP34)	☎22.58.34; Fax 22.37.12

Swimming pools *L'Amitié* has the nicest pool in the centre of town, but it costs – there's a Sunday buffet here at noon, too, for around CFA3000. The one at the *Grand* is small, but okay for cooling off and only half the price of *L'Amitié*.

Visa extensions These are available at the *Sûreté Nationale* on the av de la Nation (Mon–Thurs 8am–2pm, Fri & Sat 7.30am–12.30pm). Note that they may require a couple of days to deliver.

MOVING ON FROM BAMAKO

By road

SOMATRA buses leave from their own terminal near the *gare routière* in Sogoniko. There are two smaller *autogares* in Bamako; one, which serves **Nara**, behind the Grande Mosquée, and another at the Nouveau Marché by the Stade Omnisport for **Nioro**. For **bus** schedules, call the *Compagnie Malienne de Transports Routiers* (BP 208; ☎22.33.64).

By train

The **train to Dakar** leaves Bamako on Wednesday and Saturday mornings at 9.15am, though it's wise to be there at 7am. Saturdays are preferable, since this is when the marginally more comfortable Senegalese train runs. The trip takes 36hr. You can get sleeping berths, but it's barely worth it due to disturbances at the border in the dead of night. It's also possible to put cars on a goods train to avoid the *pistes* that link Mali and Senegal but this is an expensive and complicated way to go about things.

Daily trains also leave for **Kayes** in the west (11hr express, 12hr "local" service), and **Koulikoro** to the east of Bamako (90min) – the main embarkation point for the Niger River ferries.

For the latest schedules and price information stop by the train station, or call the *Régie du Chemin de Fer de Mali* (*RCFM*), rue Kasse Keïta (BP 260; ☎22.29.67).

By boat

Ferries to Gao depart from Koulikoro, 60km from Bamako. Rapids between the two towns make it impossible to travel directly by water from the capital and you must take the train or a taxi to get around them. Boats from Koulikoro operate roughly from late July or early August until December, when the rains swell the river to a suitable level, (for further details, see "Getting Around" in the practical information section at the beginning of this chapter). For reservations (get them early, especially for 2nd and 3rd class) and up-to-date information on departures, contact the office of the *Compagnie Malienne de Navigation* (Mon–Thurs 7.30am–2.30pm, Sat 7.30am–12.30pm) on bd du 22 Octobre 1946, on the river bank across from the Tour BCEAO. You could also try calling the head office in Koulikoro on ☎26. 20.34 (BP 10 Koulikoro).

CMN can also give you information on **barges to Guinea**, which leave Bamako about once every two weeks between August and December (or when the water level permits). The 385-kilometre trip to Kankan lasts about five days – a period entirely devoid of creature comforts since the boats were designed to transport cargo, not people. If you can put yourself in the right frame of mind, however, it's a cheap and exciting way to travel.

By plane

Theoretically, Mopti, Goundam, Timbuktu and Gao (in one direction) and Kayes, Yelimané and Nioro (in the other) are served by at least one *Air Mali* **flight** a week, though these are frequently delayed or cancelled, and schedules should be taken with a pinch of salt (contact *Air Mali*, address in "Listings").

Travel agents

Agents in Bamako aren't much use unless you're looking to rent a 4WD vehicle and driver. Common destinations for organized tours include the Manding Highlands, Dogon country, Timbuktu and Djenné. Try *Manding Voyages* (BP 2224; ☎22.47.36) and *Dogon Voyages*, near the cathedral (BP 2442), or *TAM*, also nearby in rue de Nolly (BP 932; ☎22.56.93; Fax 22.05.47; Mon–Sat 8am–4pm).

KAYES AND THE WEST

Often ignored by travellers due to its poor transport connections, rough roads and inaccessibility during the rainy season, **western Mali** contains some of the country's most beautiful scenery and easily rewards travellers with their own robust vehicles or footloose adventurers with time and patience on their hands. It's a region of remote villages, wooded escarpments and rivers where the Baoulé, Bakoye and Bafing rivers rush from the **Manding Highlands** through the hilly landscapes of the **Malinké country** before joining forces to form the **Senegal River**. It's also the best place to encounter some of Mali's **wildlife**: warthogs, baboons and irridescent blue kingfishers prosper in this isolated but prolific district. The region is also historically significant, for it was the heartland of the thirteenth-century **Mali kingdom** which expanded into a vast empire incorporating Djenné, Timbuktu and distant Gao.

The Senegal flows through the realm of the Fula-speaking **Tukulor** people, which extends west from **Kayes** – the regional capital and an isolated commercial centre of 50,000 people serving the region's mining ventures. The rough *piste* from Kayes to Bamako passes through the town of **Nioro du Sahel** close to the Mauritanian border, after which it deteriorates still further, skirting the **Boucle du Baoulé** national park – a virtually unvisited reserve with the nation's best game viewing.

South of Kayes, **Keniéba** is a remote outpost serving local gold mining activities and a dead end unless you plan to undertake the infrequently used backcountry crossings into Guinea or Senegal.

Kayes

KAYES is an agreeable riverside town and western Mali's principal administrative centre, which until the early part of this century served as capital of the Haut Sénégal-Niger colony, until the seat was transferred to Bamako when the train line pushed through from Dakar. Today it has the dubious honour of being Africa's hottest town, with afternoon temperatures between March and May crackling into the high forties Celsius.

Kayes is of most use as a transportation hub, with a **daily train** link to Bamako which slowly crosses the scenic west Manding Highlands in daylight. It is also the best place to seek out transport into parts of the region not served by the train.

Practicalities

The train station is on a rise southeast of the town centre. If you have arrived on the train from Dakar, you should head straight for the **Commissariat Special** next to the station to get your passport stamped (and possibly your first taste of Mali's shifty rural officialdom in the process). Several taxis greet the train's 3am arrival, but unless you're planning to catch the 8am slow train to Bamako (in which case bed down on the platform with the rest) you've only a couple of **accommodation** options. The *Hôtel du Rail* (☎53.18.98; HB ④) directly opposite the station may have passed its colonial-era heyday but still offers a certain splendour with spacious and well-appointed S/C rooms, a restaurant/bar and another bar set in the garden out front. The rooms at the newer *Hôtel Calderon*, also right by the station, aren't bad (②). At the adequate *L'Amical Campement* close to the market in the town centre (get a taxi the 2km there; ②), rooms have nets and a fan, and there's also a shared bathroom, a shaded garden and a food stall across the road.

Except for the *Hôtel du Rail*'s mediocre restaurant, budget restaurants are either thin on the ground or very inconspicuous – **street food** is the easiest alternative to feeding yourself at the large **market**. Kayes has a post office, airport, several pharmacies and three banks: the *BIAO* (Mon–Thurs 7.30–11.30am & 1.15–2.30pm, Fri 7.30–

11.30am) by the ferry ramp can change French francs but anything else will be a problem.

Moving on from Kayes

The obvious form of transport out of Kayes is the **train** to Bamako (daily express and local trains take 11 or 12 hours; fares CFA7000–10,000) or Dakar. If heading **towards Senegal**, you may consider taking the train only as far as **Tambacounda** (6hr) from where travel to the coast by bush taxi is quicker and cheaper. If you're **driving**, it's just over 100km through light baobab woodlands to the border post at **Diboli** where a new road bridge spans the Faléme River and leads straight into the flyblown Senegalese town of **Kidira**.

Because of the lamentable state of the "main road" between Kayes and Bamako via **Nioro du Sahel**, few people make the journey in a bush taxi. The rarely used track following the railway line **direct to Bamako** is occasionally rocky rather than sandy. If Mauritania is your destination, ask around in **Kayes Ndi market** for vehicles heading for **Sélibabi**, just 160km to the northwest, or **Kiffa** on the Nouakchott highway.

Kéniéba

South of Kayes, a corrugated *piste* follows the **Falaise de Tambaoura** for 240km to the small town of **Kéniéba**, caught in a suntrap by a bend in the Tambaoura's towering cliffs. As this is the jumping-off point for the joint Russo-Malian **mining ventures** nearby, the kids here are more likely to greet a white face with a cry of "Russe!" than the usual "toubab!"

The women in this region have collected **gold** from the bush for centuries – local legends tell of their ostensibly destitute husbands having amassed several kilos of gold during a lifetime, preferring to hoard their cache rather than convert it into tangible wealth. These days Russian technicians stop at Kéniéba to purchase booze and other services available at the town's bar before heading out to the mining camps near Dombia. Keniéba's frontier-town isolation and proximity to the Senegalese and Guinean borders make it something of a smuggling entrepôt for duty free cigarettes and alcohol coming in from Guinea, just 60km away.

Practicalities

Getting to Kéniéba from Kayes may take a bit of perseverance. Your best bet is to ask around in Kayes for any Russian trucks which make the bumpy, six-hour journey every few days. You'll have to pay, but if you're lucky enough to be offered a front seat rather than a sack in the back, you'll enjoy some fine views on the way down.

The friendly and informal Ghanaian-run *Bar Mandela* (①) on the town's main street provides inexpensive, *campement*-style accommodation with "draw-your-own" well water, lanterns at night and not-so-cheap meals, depending on what's available at the small **market** at the end of the road. Down here you'll find a post office, some small stores and another, unmarked, hotel. The town also has a regional hospital, an airstrip and a couple of petrol stations.

Ask at the *Total* station, or the Land Rover garage around the back, if you're interested in lifts to **Guinea and Senegal**. Every Tuesday a truck is said to leave from the *centre transportique* opposite the post office for some illicit trading at Kali on the Guinea border, returning on Friday. If you head this way expect the unexpected on the Guinean side and have money, *cadeaux* and time to spare.

Rides to **Kédougou** in Senegal are dependent on enough passengers to fill up a Land Rover and the depth of the Falémé River (usually crossable from January till the rains resume) which marks the unstaffed frontier. If nothing turns up after a couple of days' wait in Kéniéba and you don't want to head back to Kayes, consider renting a

motorbike (plus rider; ask for the mechanics near the market). Although twice the price of a shared 4WD, it's a memorable if no less uncomfortable six-hour ride along winding bush tracks into Senegal's Pays Bassari region.

Between Kayes and Bamako

In the dry season, the route to Bamako via **Nioro**, close to the Mauritanian border, is more travelled than the direct route via Kita, but both routes, and particularly the one via Nioro, are frequently impassable in the rainy season.

To Bamako via Nioro du Sahel

Between Kayes and Nioro lies a great region for exploration in your own suitably equipped vehicle. The whole district is beautiful, with impressive baobabs, roamed through by Fula herders. But the rough bush tracks are in a state of advanced disrepair and any kind of transport and facilities almost non-existent.

In recent years, there has been an emerald rush in the area of **Sandaré** (144km east of Kayes on the main *piste*), with hundreds of hopeful miners flocking to the area of Angoulá, living in improvized camps near the mines. You are certain to be offered emeralds for sale here. The most worthwhile diversion, however, is to **Yélimané**, turning left off the main *piste* 83km east of Kayes, and driving 68km north. Twenty kilometres or so before reaching Yelimané, there's a marshy area called **Goumbogo** that is highly recommended if you're interested in wildlife. From Yelimané you can make a 45-kilometre trip to the **Mare de Toya**, a spectacular geological rift and lake forming part of the Mauritanian frontier. There are twice-weekly flights from Yelimané to Bamako if you need civilization quickly.

From Yélimané, enquire about the condition of the 134-kilometre direct route from there to Nioro. Back on the main Kayes–Nioro *piste*, it's 168km from the Yélimané junction to Nioro, via Sandaré.

NIORO DU SAHEL is a seventeenth-century town built on a plateau and is famed for its **mosque**, one of the most important in Mali. Nioro has a police and customs post, petrol stations, a hospital and an airport but **accommodation** is limited to a frugal *campement* (①). Nioro is a common departure point for **Mauritania**, but traffic along the 212-kilometre *piste* to Ayoun el Atrous is thin at the best of times and can dwindle to nothing in the rainy season between July and October. Check for trucks around the market place. If you're driving to Bamako, you can bypass Nioro and save nearly 100km by forking east at Sandaré for Diéma, but ask at Sandaré about road conditions before taking this deviation.

There is a significant deterioration in the road for the last 430km from Nioro to the capital and if you are in a low clearance vehicle expect plenty of deviations and some digging. Just after Diéma the *piste* passes through the **Vallée du Serpent** named for the **Baoulé River**'s tortuous course as it snakes down from the Manding Mountains. The route marked on the Michelin map from Diéma to Didiéni can be very difficult, and you may need to go via Dioumara, 50km to the east of Diéma.

To Bamako via Kita

The railway line **between Kayes and Bamako** passes through a scenic area of hills and wooded escarpments – a welcome change from the bleak Senegalese plains. The west-flowing **Bakoye** and **Senegal rivers** run parallel to the tracks for a good part of the journey, thrashing into rough rapids at several points along their courses. The lowest of these rapids are the **Chutes de Felou**, just 10km east of Kayes, but slightly disappointing since a hydroelectric dam was built by the French further upriver. The more spectacular **Chutes de Gouina** are 65km further upstream, towards Bamako, but even with a 4WD can be hard to get to.

The Bafing and Bakoye rivers converge to form the Senegal at **BAFOULABÉ,** about 130km east of Kayes. The town, 3km north of **Mahina** where the train stops, has a small market and a *campement* (②). Leaving Bafoulabé, drivers share the long rail bridge across the Bafing river and continue 200km east to Kita. Just east of **Bafoulabé** are the **Chutes de Kale**, followed in turn by the **Chutes de Billy**, 270km short of Bamako. Unfortunately, none of these rapids is visible from the train, and you do need your own transport to get off the road that criss-crosses the railway line to get near them. If you're on the train, you'll welcome the extended lunch stop at **Toukoto**, 67km short of Kita, where plenty of cooked and fresh food is brought to the train.

Roughly midway between Kayes and Bamako, **KITA** is one of the former capitals of Sundiata Keita's medieval Mali empire, and if you're into Malian **music** it's a good place to stop over a night or two as many traditional griots hail from around here. Ask around for *Le Chat Rouge campement* (BP 43; ☎57.30.45; ②). **Mont Kita Kourou,** with caves decorated with rock paintings, rises impressively west of Kita. For the adventurous and independently mobile, a deteriorating track leads 140km southwest to the newly gazetted **Bafing National Park**, close to the Guinean border.

If you're driving from Kita to Bamako, expect some confusion in correctly locating the main *piste*, especially when entering and leaving small villages with their various secondary tracks.

The Parc National de la Boucle du Baoulé

The **Parc National de la Boucle du Baoulé** (Nov–May) covers 3300 square kilometres, part of a larger natural preserve that covers more than 7700 square kilometres of wooded savannah, just 100km from Bamako as the crow flies.

The most common **entrance** from the Bamako–Kita road is via Négala, a small village 61km northwest from Bamako, from where a *piste* branches north to Faladyé. Before arriving at this latter village, another *piste* leads westward to the *campement* at the entrance to the park on the Baoulé River. On entering the park, the tracks lead to another *campement* at the village of Madina. From here, *pistes* head out in all directions for game viewing. There's a third, less visited *campement* in the northeast of the park at the village of Missira.

The Boucle du Baoulé derives its name from a huge bend, or "buckle", in the **Baoulé River** as it heads north from the Manding Mountains before making a sharp turn south to join the Bakoye. The course of the river forms the northern borders of the park and contains a forested area harbouring numerous Bamana villages and a significant animal population. Common among the wildlife are a variety of **antelope** species, **buffalo** and **warthogs**. You might spot **giraffe** and possibly **lions** as well, though these latter beasts have been victims of widespread poaching. Boucle du Baoulé is also the home of half of Mali's estimated 1000 surviving **elephants**. If you don't have your own transport, travel agents in Bamako (see Bamako "Listings") operate 4WD **excursions** to the park – at a price.

SÉGOU AND AROUND

Between Bamako and the Delta Region lies a broad expanse of territory where numerous kingdoms rose to power after the demise of the Songhai Empire. Most important were the **Bamana Empire** of Ségou and the **Kénédougou Empire** in the **Senoufo country**, with **Sikasso** its capital. Although they were eclipsed almost as quickly as they sprang up, these towns have remained commercially important thanks to their positions on well-travelled routes, and all are interlinked with daily bus or bush taxi services.

Ségou

The second largest town in Mali, **SÉGOU**, 240km northeast of Bamako, makes a very pleasant stopover between Bamako and Mopti. It was capital of a vast empire in the eighteenth century, and more recently became an important French outpost and headquarters of the *Office du Niger* – an irrigation scheme originally planned for the exploitation of cotton. Reminders of the colonial period still stand out in graceful administrative buildings in the neo-Sudanic style, especially at the west end of town. Traditional Bamana architecture has also held its own against more modern and easily maintained cement buildings, and today whole districts of this quiet tree-lined town are filled with rust-coloured *banco* houses. Away from the busy **market** (the main day is Monday), much of the modern activity focuses on the banks of the **Niger**, with its *pirogues* and crowds.

Some history

The **kingdom of Ségou** had its roots in the seventeenth century, when a Bamana chief, Kaldian Coulibaly, brought his people to settle in the area. In 1620 his son established the village of Ségou-Koro (old Ségou), about 10km from the present town. In 1712 the able and despotic **Biton Coulibaly**, widely considered the true founder of the kingdom, became *fama* (king). The army he formed carved out a huge kingdom stretching from Timbuktu to the banks of the Senegal River, and the enemy soldiers captured during the conquests were marched to ports in Senegal and Ghana where they were traded with slavers for firearms. Along with the Songhai to the north, the Ségou Empire was one of the earliest in the Sahara to obtain guns, which were used effectively to subdue rival powers.

The Ségou rulers developed a **nationalist policy** where all rights were accorded to loyal Bamana subjects but the conquered peoples were excluded from the system altogether. It was a tenuous situation based purely on force of arms, and when the Fula empire of Masina arose in the northeast, disgruntled elements in the Bamana country rallied to it, assuring the demise of Ségou. In 1861, El Hadj Omar conquered Ségou and forced the inhabitants – who had remained one of the few **non-Muslim** groups in the Sahel – to convert to **Islam**. The French took the city in 1892.

Practicalities

The customary place for inexpensive **accommodation** in Ségou has been the *Office du Niger Campement* (☎32.03.92; ②), 3km from the *gare routière* at the west end of town. However, with the end of the *Office*'s government subsidies in 1994 there is some doubt whether the great-value, fanned, S/C rooms will still be available. Ask around in town before heading out there or check out the *Maison du Peuple* (①) east of town, which also has fanned rooms.

The *Hôtel Bakaridjana*, between the *BDM* and the river (☎32.03.15; ④) has a rather seedy reputation and you're better off staying elsewhere. Near the river the friendly, Lebanese-owned *L'Auberge* (☎32.01.45; Fax 32.03.55; ③–④) is your best choice in the town centre, providing clean S/C rooms (some with AC and satellite TV). Its restaurant and bar are popular with expats. A couple of kilometres away at the east end of town are two more accommodation possibilities: the new *Motel Mivéra* (☎/Fax 32.03.31; ⑤) with all the charisma of motels worldwide, and another kilometre east, the *Hôtel du 22 Septembre 1960* (☎32.04.62; ⑤), useful only if you have your own transport.

For an inexpensive **meal** with the workers you can't beat *Au Bon Coin* (8am–3am) or *Tantie J'ai Faim*, directly opposite, for hefty servings of basic stodge. Still cheap at twice the price – and without the audience of beggars – are meals at the *Snack Golfe* near the Petit Marché. A little further west towards the mosque, *Madame Chez Halima*

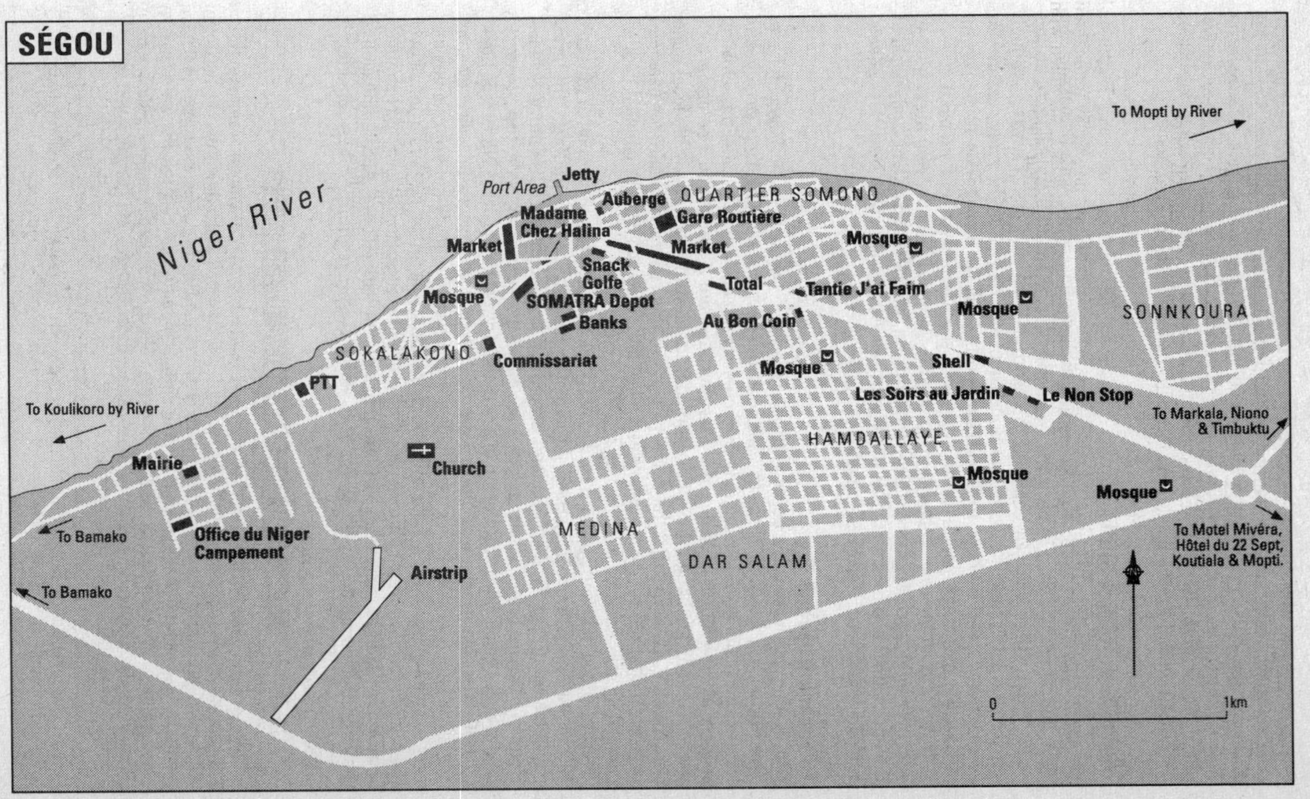
SÉGOU
To Mopti by River
Niger River
Port Area
Jetty
Auberge
QUARTIER SOMONO
Madame
Chez Halina
Gare Routière
Market
Market
Mosque
Snack
Golfe
Total
Tantie J'ai Faim
Mosque
SOMATRA Depot
Banks
Au Bon Coin
Mosque
SONNKOURA
SOKALAKONO
Commissariat
Mosque
Shell
PTT
Les Soirs au Jardin
Le Non Stop
To Koulikoro by River
To Markala, Niono & Timbuktu
HAMDALLAYE
Mairie
Church
Mosque
Mosque
To Bamako
Office du Niger
Campement
MEDINA
To Motel Mivéra, Hôtel du 22 Sept, Koutiala & Mopti.
DAR SALAM
Airstrip
To Bamako
0
1km

is a small *gargote* with down-to-earth dishes for next to nothing. Ségou's best independent restaurant with notably fine pizzas and friendly service is the *Non Stop* (6.30–12.30am) about 1500m down the Mopti road just past the *Shell* station. The *Soirs au Jardin* almost next door offers similar prices but lacks the *Non Stop*'s congenial atmosphere. As for **nightlife**, around the corner from *L'Auberge*, the *Beau Rivage* bar boasts a nice garden and a disco inside, and the *Hôtel Bakaridjana* has a nightclub.

Moving on from Ségou

Frequent **bush taxis** along Mali's principal highway link Ségou with Bamako in the west, and Mopti (via San) in the east. Taxis also head to Koutiala and Sikasso, further south, from where you can continue to **Burkina Faso** or **Côte d'Ivoire**, although you'll make better time if you head to Bobo-Dioulasso via San. In the rainy season, you can of course travel **by boat to Koulikoro** (port of call for Bamako) or all the way up to **Gao**. For more information on the river boats, see "Getting Around" on p.301.

If you're en route from Ségou south or east in your own vehicle, you might want to stop overnight some 40km from Ségou at **Zinzana**, where the excellent *campement* at the agricultural research station is a haven of peace and tranquillity – spotless sheets, vine-shaded terrace, cold beer and good food (②–③).

To Timbuktu by road

During the dry season, it's possible to zig-zag all the way across the Niger delta **to Timbuktu** by a network of tracks. Although this involves tackling long stretches of tortuous *piste* and occasional muddy river crossings, it allows you to take in fascinating scenery along a little-travelled route. This short account assumes you'll be using your own 4WD vehicle, though given time you could achieve this with available local transport. Beware, however, that the northern parts of this route (Niafounké for example) have been attacked by Tuareg rebels in the last few years and can't be counted upon as completely safe: seek local advice before setting off.

From Ségou, take the northern road to Markala, and then follow the road to Massina, 105km further. This route passes through the old city of **Sansanding**, "the great marketplace of the Western Sudan" according to the nineteenth-century scholar, Heinrich Barth. From Massina, you can make an interesting side trip, 44km to **Diafarabé**, a small village located on one of the narrowest points of the Niger (see box).

From Massina, tracks lead north towards Nampala, also accessible directly from Ségou via Niono passing lush green fields of **irrigated rice**. It's 90km from Nampala to Léré, a small village with a Friday **livestock market** that unites herders from all over the region – and another 136km across mud-cracked lagoons to the town of Niafounké, whose most famous resident is virtuoso musician Ali Farka Touré. Accommodation is available at Niafounké's small *campement*. A ferry crosses the river here, making it

THE DIAFARABÉ CATTLE CROSSING

In December, **Fula herders** descend en masse on the village of Diafarabé – and several others at narrow crossing points in the vicinity – as they lead their cattle from the northern Sahel grazing grounds to the southern banks of the Niger to await the return of the rains in May or June. The spectacle of of thousands of **cattle** crashing into the water and swimming to the other side as herders prod them along is memorable indeed. Music and festivities accompany the event, but there's no set date. Ask around in Ségou if you think you might be there about the right time.

Diafarabé is190km northeast of Ségou on the north bank. There's a very small ferry here. The town has an interesting old quarter between the market and the river, with an attractive, modern, Sudanic-style mosque. You can stay at the basic *campement* (①).

possible to connect with the road leading to Korientze and back south to Mopti. Alternatively, you can continue 90km northeast to the Songhai town of Goundam. An increasingly sandy track requiring 4WD then leads over the remaining 100km to the dunes surrounding **Timbuktu**.

San and Sikasso

Set on the banks of the Bani River (a major branch of the Niger), **SAN** is an important commercial crossroads on the main road to Burkina Faso and Côte d'Ivoire, and a chief departure point for both places. The town **market** (best on Monday) is the largest in the region, trading in everything from livestock to agricultural produce and imported goods. If you need to **stay**, try the basic rooms at the *campement* (③).

SIKASSO, Mali's southernmost town, was the last capital of the **Kénédougou Empire**, a kingdom founded by Dioula traders in the seventeenth century. Sikasso itself wasn't founded until the nineteenth century, and is traditionally a largely Senoufo town. A warrior named **Tieba** became ruler of the mini-empire in 1876, and he transformed Sikasso – his mother's birthplace – from a tiny agricultural village into a fortified capital, expanding his empire and developing trade. During the same period, the Malinké warlord **Samory Touré** was expanding his influence in the region, and thus came into conflict with the Senoufo, destroying the town of Kong and Senoufo strongholds in present-day Côte d'Ivoire, like Korhogo and Ferkessédougou. Samory laid siege to Sikasso in 1887 but fifteen months later the city had not fallen, and soon after Tieba received support from a new invasion force, the French, under Binger. Tieba died in battle in 1893, leaving his son, Ba Bemba, as ruler. But Ba Bemba fell out with the French and they attacked and routed Sikasso in 1898. Ba Bemba committed suicide; his erstwhile enemy, Samory Touré, was captured by the French and sent into captivity in Gabon where he died.

The town grew to become a colonial outpost, as the decaying administrative buildings from that era attest. Few reminders are left of the bloodier history, but you can still see remnants of the fortifications – known as *tata* – that, despite their impressive size, couldn't hold out against the onslaught of the French.

Sikasso practicalities

Today, this evergreen town drips with a humid tropical languor in which cotton and market produce flourish. Its proximity to Côte d'Ivoire assures a good deal of international activity, centred around the Sunday market. But for the passing traveller Sikasso offers few intrinsic attractions other than a possible change of vehicle on the way south. The **autogare** is 1500m south of the town centre on the road to Ferkessédougou in Côte d'Ivoire. Basic *chambres de passage* are available here (①) or over the road at the *Solo Khan Hôtel* (☎62.00.52; ①). The *Awa Sikasso* or *Keneya* **restaurants** nearby provide inexpensive meals.

In town the *Hôtel Mamelon* (☎62.00.44; ④) behind the *Shell* station offers more comfortable S/C, AC rooms with *La Vieille Marmite* in the main street presenting an alternative to the hotel's restaurant. Sikasso also has two banks and 24-hour fuel at the *Total* station.

Onwards from Sikasso

Three *COMATRA* **buses** come and go to **Bamako** every day, hammering along the badly broken road between Sikasso and Bougouni before continuing south to **Abidjan** via **Ferkessédougou**. From the *autogare* you'll need to get an early bush taxi the 140 kilometres north from Sikasso to **Koutiala** (at least this is now a good road), where vehicle changes ensure it's a full day's journey on to Mopti, Ségou or Bobo-Dioulasso in Burkina. If you overnight it in Koutiala, you can stay comfortably at *Le Cotonnier*(③).

MOPTI AND THE DELTA REGION

The Niger's extraordinary **inland delta** is one of the most compelling places in West Africa, and bound to leave a lasting impression. As the Niger slows and spreads into hundreds of channels and lagoons it passes near medieval towns like **Djenné** and **Timbuktu** – once renowned as centres of commercial prosperity and Islamic piety. Today their economic importance has been overshadowed by the more accessible and frequently visited **Mopti**, with its bustling port at the confluence of the Bani and Niger rivers. If you are prepared to explore away from these three towns by chartered *pirogue* or *pinasse*, you'll find the experience very worthwhile. There are several other towns with superb **architecture** between Ségou and Mopti that are hardly known to outsiders: try **Toa**, about 100km upstream from Mopti (two huge mosques), or **Kouakourou**, 45km upstream from Mopti (a busy Monday market and some stunning façades and interiors).

Mopti

MOPTI isn't immediately gripping. Its **old town** lacks aesthetic harmony, the **new town** is neither modern nor impressive, and the hustlers are legion. However, the more time you spend wandering through Mopti – built on three islands connected by dykes, at the confluence of the Bani and Niger rivers – the more the place grows on you, and the port and canals, busy with the traffic of wooden *pinasses* and smaller canoe-like *pirogues*, begin to work their magic.

As a consequence of its setting on the water, Mopti has become the country's major route intersection, pulling together all the peoples of Mali – Bamana, Songhai, Fula, Tuareg, Moor, Bozo and Dogon. The mix of cultures and the town's buoyant pace add to the charm, making this one of the most fascinating and popular stopovers anywhere in Mali. If you can, aim to be here on market day – Thursday.

Some history

Originally a cluster of islands inhabited by **Bozo fishing people**, Mopti became an important site early in the nineteenth century when, with the jihad proclaimed by the Fula scholar and ascetic **Cheikou Ahmadou Lobbo**, it gained strategic significance as an outpost of his Masina Empire, centred on Djenné and the Fula pasturelands around. Mopti was later captured by the Tukulor warmonger **El Hadj Omar** who turned the settlement into his principal military base, from where he launched attacks against his

STEAMER TRAVEL ON THE NIGER

By far the most fascinating way to travel through the region is **by steamer**, an option that requires a bit of planning. Ferries operate only after the rains – roughly from July to January or February between Mopti and Gao.

Along the river, the *gares routières* are replaced as the centres of trade by **steamer ports**, and wherever you arrive it will be amid a rush of activity as merchants from throughout the country scramble to buy whatever goods are available before the boat pulls out and continues its ponderous journey.

Small towns and villages dot the river bank, ground-hugging mud buildings towered over by the traditional Sudanic-style mosques. Occasionally, fields of rice and other cereals can be seen from the decks of the boat – evidence of government attempts to irrigate large portions of the delta before they are irretrievably claimed by the advancing Sahara. Although Fula and Tuareg nomads still lead their flocks and herds through the region, vegetation is relatively sparse and the landscapes often flat and barren.

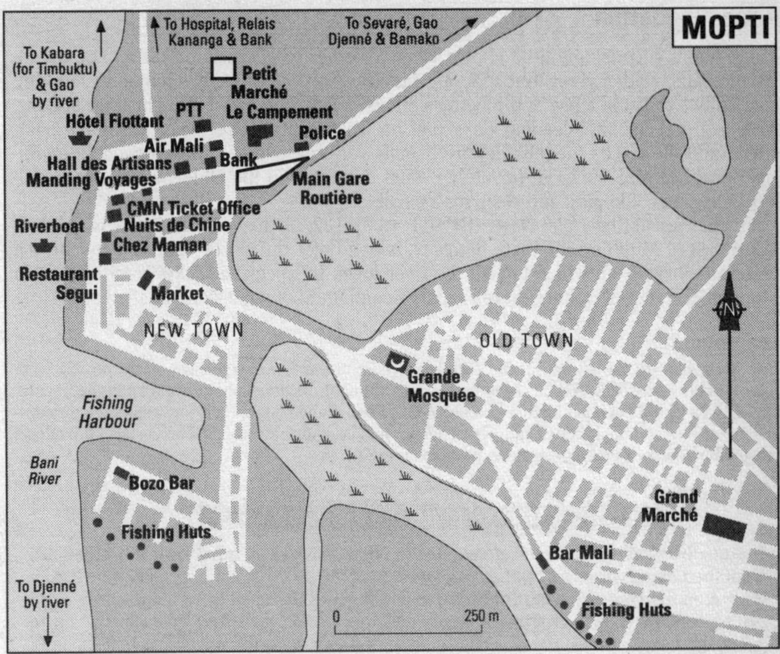

Fula rivals. A small town grew up around the site, but Mopti remained largely overshadowed by Djenné.

It wasn't until the beginning of this century that the town found commercial importance – at first with the export of white egret feathers to the *belle époque* couturiers of Paris. Indeed, economic development was largely due to the French, who exploited Mopti's position at the confluence of the Bani and the Niger and its accessibility from the main overland routes. When the railway line connecting Bamako to Dakar was built, Mopti became the largest river port in the **French Sudan**. Its population has grown steadily and today, with around 70,000 people, it rivals Ségou as Mali's second town.

Police formalities and other headaches

Assuming you plan to spend the night in Mopti, one of the first orders of business is to stop by the **police headquarters** near the *campement* to get your passport stamped. You'll need a passport photo and will be charged CFA1000, though if you say you work for an international aid agency and need a receipt, the tax may be waived. Some people skip this formality with no apparent consequence, but if you stay long in town, the police will catch up with you sooner or later (surprisingly, they *can* be helpful and even friendly). Visa extensions for 30 days cost CFA5000.

Mopti's heavy tourist influx has also resulted in another headache – that of pestering kids who try to earn a living **guiding** people through town. Mopti is straightforward enough not to need that kind of assistance, but you need to be firm with the persistent and sometimes aggressive candidates: having made your views clear, they won't usually waste their time with you.

One piece of positive practical information: the **PTT** in Mopti is open 24 hours and international calls are easily made.

Accommodation

Mopti offers surprisingly little choice when it comes to **accommodation**. The dreadful, mosquito-ridden **riverboat** (①) opposite the *Nuits de Chine* has hopefully sunk by now but we've listed a few of the better options below. You could also consider **staying with people**, usually sleeping on a mat on a rooftop terrace. Kids will make such offers, and the prices (negotiable) are usually very reasonable. There's even an unofficial **camping site** – a large privately owned courtyard in the Old Town where travellers with cars could park and sleep for a small fee.

Further afield, the *Hôtel Oasis* (BP 911; ☎22.50.22; ③) near the *autogare* in **Sevaré**, 12km east of Mopti on the main highway, is handy for the airport and in many ways a preferable base from which to visit the river town. Inexpensive *bâchés* come and go to Mopti all day, but even here there is a large contingent of guides and hustlers.

Lodgings

Bar Mali, next to the swamp in the Old Town. One of the few inexpensive places on dry land. Although it's a bit seedy and has seen better days, at night the atmosphere heats up in the popular bar, with its crowds of unambiguous *femmes libres*. Food in the restaurant is inexpensive, but notoriously bad (there's much better and even cheaper just around the corner). The bar also provides a reasonably safe lock-up luggage store, payable on return. ②.

MOVING ON FROM MOPTI

Besides being the major port of call on the **Niger Rive11 A ute**(tickets and schedules from the *Compagnie de Navigation Malienne*, near the port), Mopti is also just 12km from Sevaré on the **Bamako–Gao highway**. In addition, it's the most convenient springboard for trips to **Djenné** (via river or road) and the **Dogon country**: get a bush taxi to Bandiagara or Bankass and proceed by foot, donkey cart or bicycle. Note that for both Bandiagara and Bankass, Mopti transport will normally go only as far as Somadougou on the tarmac: after that you take your chance with anything passing, though on Monday you might find vehicles going through to Bankass's market.

By boat

Downstream, from July to January or February (depending on the rains), you can travel by steamer to **Gao**. During this period, boats also provide the quickest link to **Korioumé**, the port of call for **Timbuktu**. Mopti–Timbuktu fares are approximately CFA4000 4th class, CFA12,000 3rd, CFA20,000 2nd, CFA27,000 1st class B and CFA29,000 1st class A. Upstream, to **Koulikoro** (port of call for **Bamako**), they usually stop running in November due to the low waters. You may also be able to get a *pinasse* to Korioumé. When enquiring at the port, specify that you want a place on a goods boat, otherwise they'll think you want to rent the whole *pinasse* to yourself, a rather pricey alternative (say CFA300,000 to Timbuktu). Non-motorized *pinasses* or *pirogues* to Timbuktu should charge around CFA10,000 for the four-day voyage, but even these don't operate much after February. The journey varies from spell-binding (when you push off at dawn) to alarmingly uncomfortable (early afternoon out on the river), and it's fair to say the romance can wear thin given the restricted space and unpredictable nature of the whole trip. But, in retrospect at least, it's a wonderful adventure, and birdlife is prolific and hippos easily seen.

It's also possible to travel **up the Bani to Djenné**. *Pinasses* leave from the harbour on Friday evening for the overnight journey (local price around CFA4000). Chartering a motor *pinasse* for your group, count on about CFA100,000 for the trip of about a day, using a boat with *two* engines (an important point, if you're not going to end up spending the night on board); non-motorized charters go for as little as CFA40,000, but it can take up to three days to pole and paddle to Djenné. Motor *pinasses* also operate up the Niger to **Ségou** – a three-day journey. You can usually arrange to have your food prepared for you on these wooden boats – otherwise bring your own provisions. Try contacting the *Bureau de Location Le Bani* in advance (Fax 43.00.06).

Le Campement, near the *autogare*. Attractive, simple colonial-style accommodation, though a little overpriced. The restaurant serves good European food. If you have transport, you can camp on the grounds, but again, the price per person and per vehicle is high. The *Air Mali* office is here. ③.

Hôtel Flottant, just north of the riverboat. Inexpensive, if stuffy cabins on the river. ②.

Relais Kananga Mopti (reservations in Bamako, BP 2473; ☎22.33.18), near the waterfront in the new town. Comfortable but overpriced AC rooms with showers. ⑥.

The Town

Mopti has a great energy and variety of things to do. Most of the sights centre around the **harbour**, from where you can rent *pirogues* to take you to various Bozo or Tuareg camps. **Markets** in Mopti are colourful and famous for a wide range of crafts, including hand-woven Sahelian blankets.

The harbour

Mopti's *raison d'être*, the harbour, built by the French in the early part of the century, is always the centre of life in town. Large wooden *pinasses* with their canvas covers and colourful flags waving in the breeze tie up regularly to unload cargo and passengers, while *pirogues* taxi people back and forth from different points on the islands that make up the town.

By road

Bush taxis to Djenné leave from the station across from the *campement* and take about 3hr for the 130-kilometre trip (the bad road from the *route national* to the Bani River, where you cross to Djenné, is now hard-surfaced). Your best chance of finding taxis is on Sunday and early Monday morning – Djenné's market day. Other times there may be nothing, and during the rains the overland route may be out altogether. The main **motor park** for Gao, San, Ségou, Bamako and other destinations is opposite the *Bozo Bar* near the harbour. In addition, a slightly cheaper mail **bus**, the *courier postal*, leaves Saturday mornings for Gao. Ask at the post office.

The *Bureau de Location Le Bani* (Fax 43.00.06) has **Toyota land-cruisers** with driver available to rent from CFA50,000 per day.

By plane

From the **airport** in Sevaré, *Air Mali* operates flights once or twice a week to Goundam (CFA25,000), Timbuktu (CFA32,000), Gao (CFA45,000) and Bamako on the return leg (CFA45,000). If you're in town during the late dry season, this may be your only hope of getting to Timbuktu. Note, however, that flights out of Timbuktu are rare and you could find yourself stranded for several days. Get full details of schedules – including those out of Timbuktu – from the *Air Mali* office in Mopti at the *Hôtel Le Campement* (☎22.94.00).

Travel agents and tours

Mopti's travel agency, *Manding Voyages*, organizes two-day **tours to the Dogon country** – Bandiagara, Songo and Sanga – and to **Djenné**. Excursions include Land Rover, chauffeur and accommodation, and cost at least CFA100,000.

Countless young kids in Mopti, Bandiagara and Bankass also lead guided tours through the Dogon country, all claiming to be from there. If you select a guide, you normally pay his transport to and from Mopti and a negotiable daily fee. Although most of the youngsters turn out to be quite informative and work hard, leading you on foot through the villages and down the escarpment, there are no guarantees, and when you get there, you may discover your guide knows little about the area, or that he can't arrange to get you to places he promised. Either way, it will cost you a fraction of organized excursions. It's often wise to agree a payment for your trip fully-inclusive before setting out to include transport, accommodation, food and the guide's fee. Pay part before leaving and the rest when you return.

A **fish market** occupies the southern edge of the port near the *Bozo Bar*. Behind it is a large open-air **"factory"** where craftsmen build the traditional *pinasses* from large planks imported from the south. On the northern edge of the harbour, Moorish traders mill around stacks of marble-like **salt slabs**, brought by camel caravan from the desert to Timbuktu and then transported by boat to Mopti. Formerly one of the desert's great riches, salt is still a precious commodity for herders who need it for their livestock.

The harbour is the place to get boats to take you along the river to see the **Bozo and Tuareg "camps"**. Kids will find you and propose the trip (just hang around the *Bozo Bar*); their brothers or uncles are inevitably **boatmen** who will give you a "special rate" – the going rate is CFA1000 per hour per boat, and no more, though the first price will be many times this. Although interesting, these trips are ultimately rather voyeuristic and artificial experiences, but the boat ride is enjoyable and gives an interesting perspective of the town.

The **Bozo** are a fishing people who build circular thatched huts, clustered in small *campements*, around Mopti during the rainy season when the catch is most prolific. If you take a *pirogue* to one of these communities, you'll see them repairing their boats and nets and engaged in other piscatorial activities.

The **Tuareg camp** is nothing more than a few huts where women sell **crafts** – bracelets, necklaces and leather goods – at elevated prices. Buying brings twinges of conscience as you deliberate whether you're being stupid to pay so much or stingy for trying to beat down the price – especially considering the economic and social upheaval the Tuareg have undergone since the recent Sahelian droughts.

The Old Town and markets

From the harbour, the **Grande Mosquée** is easily visible to the east. As you cross over the dyke leading to it, you enter the **old town** with its narrow pedestrian streets and grey *banco* houses. The mosque itself is a relatively recent construction, but faithful to the regional style that originated in nearby Djenné. Unfortunately, the interior is off limits to non-Muslims.

Also in the Old Town is the **grand marché**, southeast of the mosque in the Komuguel district. There's also a large covered **fish market**. More intimate is the **petit marché** in the New Town near the bank. You'll find more food here, plus various household items like **pottery** or **calabash** utensils.

The best place for **crafts** is the *Hall des Artisans* near the *petit marché*. Blankets are a regional speciality and Mopti has a wide selection at relatively low prices – costs vary according to the quality of the wool or cotton threads. Here you'll find weaves of local peoples including the Dogons, the Fula and the Songhai. Each of these peoples also has characteristic **jewellery** handcrafted in gold, silver, copper and bronze.

Eating

Street food is plentiful in Mopti, especially near the harbour and the motor park. **Tea stalls** are open mornings and evenings for omelettes and bread with *Nescafé* or tea. A popular **restaurant** is the *Nuits de Chine* near the *BP* filling station at the harbour. The decor and name may be oriental but food is of the *steack frites* or braised chicken variety – well prepared and not overpriced, although the similar *Chez Davide* nearby offers slightly better service and a chance to sit outside. Just down the road towards the harbour, the *Restaurant Segui* provides inexpensive food also in an outdoor setting and the coffee and croissants at the French **bakery** make a great spot for breakfast. A favourite haunt is the *Bozo Bar*, an outdoor terrace restaurant nicely located on the harbour overlooking the activity of the riverside. There's nothing particularly fancy about the rice and fish dishes, but it's good value. If you don't want to eat, you can come just for a beer and watch the *pirogues* slopping between the port and surrounding islands. Much less classy is the *Restaurant N'Benida* offering rice and chicken or *capitaine* (fish) – a whole meal for about CFA500. Lastly, check out *Chez Maman* opposite the *Nuits de Chine* for fresh dairy produce.

Djenné

DJENNÉ is unquestionably the most beautiful town in the Sahel and, despite the incessant attention of unnecessary "guides", a superb place to visit. On an island for most of the year, the buildings are shaped in the smooth lines of the Sudanic style, moulded from the grey clay of the surrounding flood plains. In the main square, the famous **Grande Mosquée** dominates the townscape. People from throughout the region gather in town for the festive market day on Monday – the best time to plan a trip (transport to or from Djenné on other days is difficult). In Djenné you can easily imagine what life in the Sahel must have been like a century or more ago.

Originally a **Bozo settlement**, the town was founded around 800 AD, according to the *Tarikh es-Soudain* – one of the earliest written records of the Sahel. The original site was at a place called Djoboro, but it may have moved to the present location as early as 1043 (other sources put the date two centuries later). In the reign of the Soninke king **Koï Kounboro**, Djenné converted to Islam: the king himself dutifully raised his palace to make room for the town's first mosque in the thirteenth century. The town became a way-station for gold, ivory, lead, wool, kola nuts and other precious items from the south. Merchants had their depots in Djenné, and sold from outlets they operated throughout the region, notably in Timbuktu. They developed a large flotilla of boats – some up to twenty metres long – capable of transporting tens of tons of these goods to Timbuktu from where they made their way to the north.

In 1325, Djenné was incorporated into the **Mali Empire** under which it enjoyed a period of stability and continued prosperity. In 1473 – after a seige that purportedly lasted seven years, seven months and seven days – it was conquered by the **Songhai Empire**. The intellectual and commercial exchanges with Timbuktu were reinforced during this period until, in 1591, Djenné fell to the Moroccans, under whose domination it remained until the nineteenth century. The town went into a slow decline that successive invasions were powerless to stop. **Cheikou Ahmadou** – a religious zealot from Masina – ousted the Moroccans in 1810, and destroyed Djenné's famous mosque. The **Tukulor Empire** briefly swallowed up the town in 1862, but held it only until 1893 when **French troops** arrived and took control.

The Town

Arriving by road, you'll see Djenné's **Grande Mosquée** from some distance as you travel over the dyke leading to town. This architectural masterpiece only dates from 1905, but was built in the style of the original mosque constructed in the reign of the Soninke king Kounboro. The rounded lines of the facade are dominated by three towers, each eleven metres high and topped with an ostrich egg. Protruding from the edifice, the beams serve more than an aesthetic function; like scaffolding they are essential for the upkeep of the building. Each year rains wash away the building's smooth *banco* outer layer and the people from town work to restore it in the dry season. Inside is a forest of pillars connected by sturdy arches. The mosque is said to hold up to 5000 worshippers – not bad when you consider that Djenné's total population is barely double that number. Regrettably, due to abuses of the site by insensitive visitors, the fascinating interior and rooftop are now off limits to non-Muslims. You can get a fairly good exterior view from the roof of the market (climb up the left hand corner wall; as you walk into the market it's the wall nearest the mosque).

The weekly **market** is the other main sight, and it's worth making every effort to time your trip for a Monday when traders from throughout the region make a commercial pilgrimage to town. They spread their wares on the main square in front of the mosque in much the same way that French explorer **René Caillié** described in the nineteenth century in his *Travels through Central Africa to Timbuktu*. There are few if any markets as animated, as colourful and as *rich* – those colossal swaying earrings are solid gold – as Djenné on a Monday morning. After you've finished at the market it's satisfying to leave the crowds and wander through the dusty streets on your own, looking at the architecture and soaking up the way of life.

Sites around Djenné

A number of **villages** surround Djenné, built on small elevations in the flood plains. One of the most interesting is **Sennissa** – peopled mainly by Fula and just 4km from Djenné as the crow flies (ask a kid to take you there). The village boasts two beautiful **mosques** and an abundance of artisans working along the small streets lined with single-storey *banco* homes. You're likely to see women here wearing the huge gold heirloom earrings that were once common in the region. The biggest ones may be the size of a rugby ball and hang down to the woman's breasts; some are so heavy they have to be strung from a cord that passes over the woman's head.

In the late 1970s, a team of American archeologists discovered an ancient village 2km from town at a spot now called **Djenné-Djeno** (old Djenné). The foundations of buildings they uncovered here, along with terracotta statues, utensils and jewellery, date back as far as the third century BC and prick holes in a blanket of ignorance about archaic Africa – a highly developed, commercial society (the town counted over 10,000 inhabitants) that existed long before the arrival of Islam. For reasons still unclear, the town went into decline in the early Middle Ages and was abandoned by the fourteenth century. You're supposed to get permission from the police to visit the site, although kids will sometimes agree to take you there. In practice you can just go: keep your eyes on the ground and you'll see the pottery sherds everywhere.

Djenné practicalities

It is usually still necessary to **register with the police** in Djenné. **Guides** are not necessary to get around town, but CFA1000–2000 will give you a companion with some knowledge for a few hours, allow you to explore unhesitatingly, and keep the others away.

Accommodation is limited. *Le Campement* (②), well sited near the Grande Mosquée, seems the obvious choice. Rooms are nothing fancy, but at least there's running water and light until 11pm. It tends to be stuffed with fellow tourists on Mondays. Prices, at least, aren't excessive, and you can even sleep on the rooftop

MOVING ON FROM DJENNÉ

There's now a hard-surfaced road from the landing stage on the other side of the Bani River to the *route national*. **Taxis** run from Djenné to Mopti on Monday afternoons when the market closes down. Alternatively, you can take one of the motor *pinasses* which leave early Tuesday morning and arrive in Mopti in the evening, transporting goods in time for Mopti's market day on Thursdays. Any kid in town can take you to the water's edge from where the boat departs. The *piroguier* will sell you a ticket (even a couple of days in advance if you like) that includes the price of transport plus food if you specify. The low-lying boats hug the water's edge, passing numerous villages on the river. The landscape, however, is remarkably flat and unvaried. Outside these two possibilities, there's no guaranteed transport out of Djenné. And it's a full, long day's hike along the dyke to the main road.

terrace or **camp** (①). Order in advance for meals from the **restaurant**. It's not the best food you'll eat in West Africa, and overall the service and food at Baba's *Restaurant Cuisine du Mali* (*Chez Baba*) in a sidestreet east of the Palais de Justice is far better – though again, you have to call in an hour or two beforehand to place your order. You can sleep at Baba's too (①–②). Kids may also offer to put you up on the terrace of their homes. Some try to charge as much, or more than the *campement*, so check the price.

Timbuktu (Tombouctou)

If I told you why it is mysterious then it would not be mysterious
Minister of Sports, Art and Culture

Is that it?
Bob Geldof, after looking around

Long associated with mysterious beauty, learning and above all wealth, **TIMBUKTU**, "the forbidden city", has always fascinated outsiders. From the time of the crusades, it was one of the main entrepôts through which came the West African **gold** on which European finance relied. From the fourteenth century, when Mansa Musa, Emperor of Mali, passed through Cairo on his way to Mecca (stunning the city with his fabulous entourage and selling so much gold that its price slumped for decades), to the sixteenth, when Leo Africanus from Granada in Spain visited and described Timbuktu's opulent royal court, to as late as the eighteenth century when a lemming-like "explorers' rush" broke out to settle the enigma of the city roofed with gold, Timbuktu has achieved a near-legendary reputation. "Going to Timbuctoo" is still synonymous with going to the ends of the earth – or to hell – and only in the last few years has a more prosaic recognition forced itself into popular awareness.

Of course the town couldn't live up to the myths which disguised it so long and any illusions of grandeur you harbour are bound to be frustrated. As long ago as 1828, Rèné Caillié wrote:

> *I found it neither as big nor as populated as I had expected. Commerce was much less active than it was famed to be . . . Everything was enveloped in a great sadness. I was amazed by the lack of energy, by the inertia that hung over the town . . . a jumble of badly built houses . . . ruled over by a heavy silence.*

This frank assessment rings true today and, walking through the sandy streets, lined with pale grey stucco-covered mud-brick houses, you're more likely to be struck by the poverty and sense of despair than by the historical monuments evoking a prouder past.

A long and turbulent history

Towards the end of the eleventh century, a group of **Tuareg** who came to the Niger to graze their herds discovered a small oasis on the north bank where they set up a permanent camp. When they went off to pasture their animals, they left the settlement in the care of an old woman named Tomboutou – "the woman with the large belly button". Other versions have it that the woman's name was Buktu (or alternatively *bouctou* may derive from the Arabic for "dune") while *tim* in Berber signifies "place of".

> Note that **road access to Timbuktu** has periodically been closed in recent years due to ongoing conflict between government forces and the Tuareg. Access by air or river had not been affected as this book went to press, but cannot be assumed.

The camp quickly developed into an important commercial centre where merchants from Djenné set up as middlemen between the salt caravans coming down from the north (and general dealers from across the Sahara) and the river traffic bringing goods downriver from the south. Although the Tuareg herders didn't live permanently in the town, they continued to control it, levying heavy and arbitrary taxes from the increasingly wealthy traders. Eventually, in response, the inhabitants invited the great Mali ruler **Mansa Musa** to liberate the town from Tuareg domination and he annexed it in 1330. To commemorate the occasion, the king visited Timbuktu and built a palace and the **Djinguereber mosque**.

Under the hegemony of the **Mali Empire**, Timbuktu enjoyed a period of stability and prosperity, but as the kingdom declined in the fifteenth century, the town again slipped into Tuareg control. Extortions began again, and by the sixteenth century the merchants turned to the Songhai ruler **Sonni Ali** who chased the Tuaregs west to the desert post of Oualata. Ali laid the foundations of the **Songhai Empire** which grew under the impetus of **Askia Mohammed**. Timbuktu reached its zenith at this point and became one of the Sahel's principal centres of commerce and learning. Reports of unimaginable wealth trickled back to Europe. The **Moroccan invasion** of 1591, however, when firearms were used in the Sahel for the first time, was a catastrophe for Timbuktu. The expedition's Andalucian leader, Djouder Pasha, had a number of senior scholars executed, exiled most of the others to Fez, and caravanned out the bulk of the city's wealth. Under the descendants of marriages between the invaders (some of whom were conscripted Scots, Irish and Spanish soldiers) and Songhai women – a group who came to be known as the **Arma**, after their guns – Timbuktu went into a steady decline that lasted throughout the seventeenth and eighteenth centuries. At different times it was attacked by the Mossi, the Fula, the Tukulor and the Tuareg. Subjected to pillage and oppression, the townspeople retreated behind the heavy, metal-studded wooden doors characteristic of Timbuktu houses. These were one of the few symbols of the city's former wealth that endured until the final arrival of the Europeans in the nineteenth century.

The European explorers

On the strength of a few translated books and a skein of rumours, Europeans set about uncovering Timbuktu's fabled riches. Between the late sixteenth century (by which time the city was, unknown to them, already nearly destitute) and 1853, at least 43 travellers attempted to reach it, of whom just four succeeded.

THE RACE BEGINS

The race really began in 1824, when the Geographical Society of Paris offered a prize of 10,000 francs for the first explorer to return with a verifiable account of the city. The earliest first-hand account by a non-Muslim, however, had already been given, not by an explorer, but by an illiterate American sailor, **Robert Adams**, who had been sold into slavery after his ship was wrecked off Mauritania, and who almost certainly spent several months in Timbuktu in 1811. But the story he related to the British Consul in Morocco in 1813 wasn't given much credibility, as Adams wasn't aware of the mystique surrounding the city and his dreary description was too flat to be believed – except by Moroccan Muslims who themselves had been there. Whether or not Adams did get to Timbuktu is still a matter of some argument.

GORDON LAING

The first explorer to succeed conclusively – a prudish Scot named **Gordon Laing** – reached Timbuktu on August 13, 1826, after a hazardous desert crossing from Tripoli in which he was almost slashed to death by Tuareg robbers. The squalid slaving town was a bitter disappointment, but Laing was apparently greeted warmly by the sheikh of

Timbuktu and by the townspeople. On hearing of the arrival of a Christian, however, the Fula sultan who claimed authority over the town ordered Laing to either get out or be killed. Worried for his guest's safety, the sheikh sent Laing off towards Ségou (he was hoping to reach Sierra Leone) with an armed guide. Unfortunately, the latter turned out to be in the service of the sultan, and Laing and most of his servants were killed one night, 50km out of Timbuktu. One trailed back to Tripoli with Laing's notes and letters, two years later.

RENÉ CAILLIÉ

The first European to return from Timbuktu to write about the adventure himself was a Frenchman named **René Caillié** whose fantastic journey started on the West Coast on the Rio Nunez (now in northwest Guinea). Prior to taking off for Timbuktu, Caillié had lived in a Moorish village further north, learning Arabic and immersing himself in Muslim culture. Amazingly, he was sponsored by no government or association, and set off alone to the unexplored interior, disguised as an Egyptian. After making his way through the Fouta Djalon hills, he reached the Niger at Kouroussa, then continued to Tiémé (Côte d'Ivoire), where he fell gravely ill. After recovering, he pushed on to Tangrela and then to the devoutly Muslim town of Djenné where he made a deep and favourable impression on the sheikh – who would have had him instantly executed had his disguise been discovered. Caillié arrived in Timbuktu on April 20, 1828 and was received by Sidi Abdallahi Chebir. Two weeks later, the adventurer joined a camel caravan and headed across the Sahara to Tangiers. In eighteen months, he had crossed 4500km alone.

HEINRICH BARTH

Caillié's book wasn't considered the last word on Timbuktu, however, and in Britain, especially, it was judged to be bogus. The person who finally convinced the world was the German polyglot and explorer **Heinrich Barth**, who left Tripoli in 1850 on an expedition financed by the British government. He survived the desert crossing to Agadez, then worked his way down to the Hausa country, his two companions dying en route. With delays and long residences in various towns, including diversions into Dogon country, he finally made it into Timbuktu on September 7, 1853. Like Caillié, he originally disguised himself as an Arab, but it didn't take long for the townspeople to discover he was Christian, after which his life was in danger. Barth, phlegmatic and undeterred, stayed eight months under the protection of Sheikh El Backay and collected the most detailed information known at the time. El Backay was virtually beseiged by his Fula overlords and only after long negotiations was Barth at last able to escape, following the river back east to Gao before continuing to Sokoto, Kano and on to Lake Chad. From here, he again set out across the Sahara, arriving in Tripoli in 1855. His explorations had lasted nearly six years and had taken him over 16,000km: the five-volume book he published at last overturned some of the myths.

RECENT TIMES

Apart from a lucky young German, **Oskar Lenz**, who skipped through Timbuktu in 1880 and apparently had a wonderful time, the next European visitors were French: they came through the 1890s, little doubting success, to conquer and colonize.

Recently Timbuktu has yet again suffered the traditional depredations of the Tuareg who, threatened by the continuing suppression of their nomadic lifestyle, and increasingly supportive of a movement to create their own state from parts of Mali, Niger and Algeria, rebelled against the agents of Bamako in the early 1990s. At one point history repeated itself as the Tuareg held the town in a state of virtual siege; it was their disruption which contributed to the dictator Moussa Traoré's fall and to subsequent reforms. For Timbuktu, however, the conflict continues, and these events have forced the moribund city still further into decline.

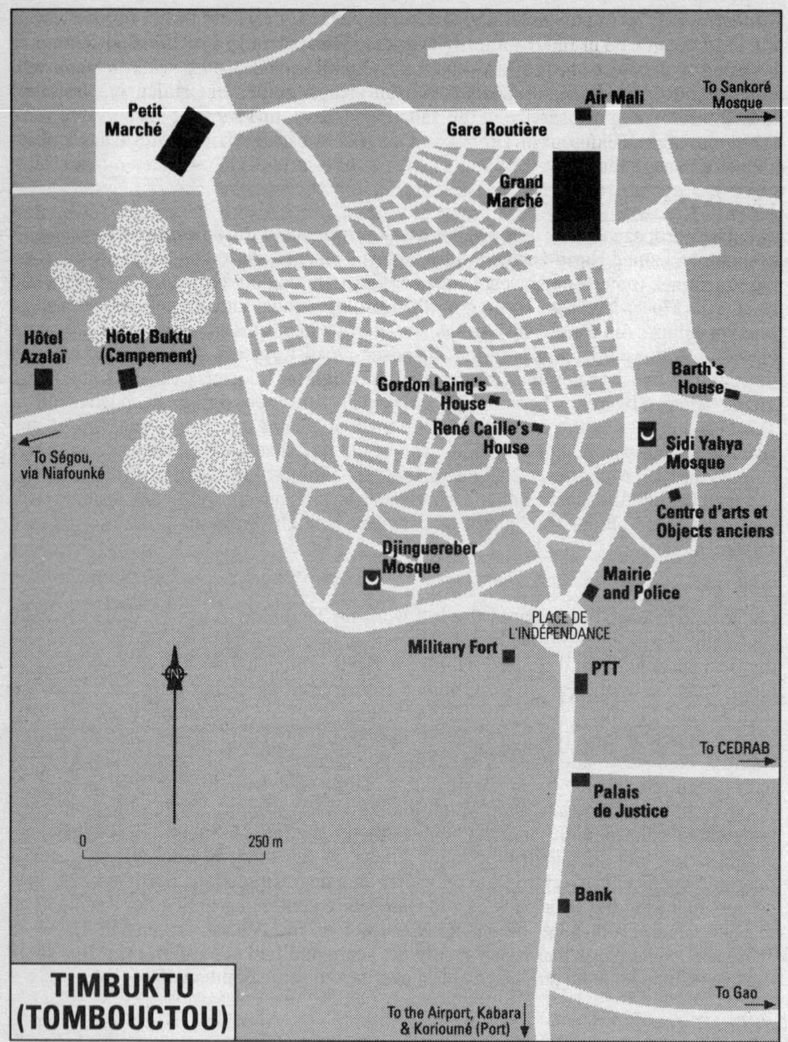

The Town

The oldest and most famous mosque in Timbuktu is the Friday **Djinguereber mosque**. It was first built in 1327 by El Saheli – an Andalucian architect whom Mansa Musa met in Cairo during his pilgrimage to Mecca – who is credited with the invention of mud bricks. Before bricks, all building was done using mud and straw, slapped on a wooden framework. Appropriately covered up and respectful, you may be able to climb the minaret here – but permission isn't always granted. The **Sankore** mosque dates from the fifteenth century. During Timbuktu's golden era, this mosque doubled as a **university**, renowned throughout the Muslim world, that specialized in law and theology. Up to

25,000 students were studying here in the sixteenth century. The **Sidi Yahya** mosque was first constructed in 1400 by a marabout named El-Moktar Hamalla and was intended to serve a saint whose imminent arrival had been prophesied. Four decades later, Sherif Sidi Yahya crossed the desert and asked for the keys to the mosque. He was declared *imam*, and is today one of the most revered of the town's **333 saints**.

Though the mosques are today the main sights, it's really more rewarding to spend some time walking through the confusion of narrow streets to take in the unique **architecture**. The finest homes – usually owned by Moorish merchants – are made of carved limestone brought from a desert quarry. Again, the basic design of these homes may date to El Saheli; the columns of square pilasters that decorate the facades are reminiscent of those in Egyptian temples, an element he may have picked up in Cairo. The small shuttered windows and heavy wooden doors with geometric ironwork designs also bear an Arabic stamp, though they seem to hark back to the Moroccan invasion of the late sixteenth century. Plaques still mark the homes where **Laing**, **Caillié** and **Barth** stayed during their exploits in Timbuktu. The first two were on the same street in the **Sankore district**; and any kid can point them out to you. Heavy rains occasionally reduce one or other of the houses to rubble, but they're regularly repaired again for the sake of Timbuktu's precarious tourist industry – building in mud guarantees an authentic, weathered, historical look.

More modest houses are made of *banco* in a style that originated in Djenné. Along the streets you'll also notice dome-shaped **clay ovens** where women bake round loaves of bread – a speciality of the town, traditionally made from wheat grown near Lake Faguibine. The outskirts of Timbuktu are bordered by circular straw huts – the domain of Tuareg, Bella and Fula nomads. Walk out past the *Hôtel Azalaï* in the west to see them, or climb one of the **dunes** at dawn to watch the sun rising above the town: the city looks best in silhouette. Also near the *Hôtel Azalaï* on the west side of town, **terraced gardens** challenge the intense heat. Looking something like Greek amphitheatres, they're built around large craters dug deep into the earth, at the bottom of which stands a pond of brackish water.

To the north of the CEDRAB centre (see box) is the **Abaradio district** where the *azalaï* or camel caravans formerly arrived in great numbers (even when the first

CENTRE DES RECHERCHES HISTORIQUES AHMED BABA

One of the greatest remaining legacies of Timbuktu's former glory is the wealth of Islamic literature that was produced here. Traditionally, families wrote their histories in chronicles known as *tarikh* – one of the most important of which was the *Tarikh es-Soudan*, written by El Sadi in the seventeenth century. These and other related writings have provided invaluable information about the scientific, legal and social practices of the seventeenth, eighteenth and nineteenth centuries throughout the region, and indeed the entire Muslim world. In addition, they've helped trace Mali's history back to the empire of ancient Ghana. Countless volumes remain in private family collections, where, exposed to damp, dust and insects, the works (some of which may be four hundred years old or more) could soon be lost for ever. Timbuktu's **Centre des Recherches Historiques Ahmed Baba** (CEDRAB) is trying to persuade reluctant families to part with these priceless documents – at least long enough for them to be restored and copied on microfilm. To date, over 2500 volumes have been collected and copies have been made of 600 others. About eighty percent of these are written in Arabic, most of the rest in Songhai and a few in unknown scripts.

The centre is on the south side of town, down the airport road and left after the PTT. It's very much worth a visit. You can leave a donation against an official receipt. Ask the staff to show you some of the older, handwritten documents, the most beautiful of which contain geometric artwork and gold lettering.

European explorers arrived, as many as 60,000 camels a year unloaded their goods here). Apart from goods from North Africa and the Mediterranean, the Sahara's biggest prize was salt from the oasis of **Taoudenni**. This ultra-remote desert post, 700km due north of Timbuktu, is famous for its salt mines – a Malian Siberia where the former president Modibo Keita was detained until his death and political undesirables were, until the 1980s, still banished. The occasional caravan of salt slabs still makes its way down to Timbuktu, but in 1989 Taoudenni ceased to be a prison camp.

Practicalities

Budget **accommodation** has become a real problem in Timbuktu, since the dilapidated government-run *campement*, the *Hôtel Buktu* (BP 49; ③), has squeezed out most competition. Otherwise, if you get stuck with no transport out of town for a couple of days, Timbuktu the mysterious can be a severe financial drain. As a possible alterna-

MOVING ON FROM TIMBUKTU

If you weren't impressed by Timbuktu's isolation during your stay, you will be when you try to leave. Unless you're travelling with your own vehicle, the options for **onward travel** are pretty much limited to river craft or the plane. The **river journey** from Timbuktu (Koriomé port) to Gao is beautiful – the Niger snakes between high yellow dunes – and hippos are often seen along the way. The current **flight schedule** consists, on paper, of a Tuesday flight to Gao and flights on Tuesday back to Mopti and Bamako and on Saturday back to Mopti, Goundam and Bamako. For up-to-date information, check at *Air Mali* (☎92.11.09) near the *grand marché*.

Note that a *bâché* from Timbuktu to the port, or vice versa, should be no more than CFA500, even with luggage – about half of what you'll be asked.

The piste to Gao

A very demanding – and presently closed, due to Tuareg attacks – *piste* follows the Niger's north bank 420km to Gao. Along the route, deep sandy ruts winding through acacia bush make a 4WD or maneagable trail bike essential. It's 195km to **Bamba**, one of the first major villages along the route – a difficult stretch with deep soft sand. Sandwiched between the road and the river, the town is said to have been founded by the Moroccan invaders of the 1590s. It has been particularly vulnerable in the Tuareg conflict of recent years. Another 135km brings you to **Bourem** on the River Niger, a Songhai village with characteristic *banco* homes and a large market – and also the southern terminus of the trans-Saharan Tanezrouft route. From here, the road continues along the river to Gao, 95km away. If you don't have your own transport, it's sometimes possible to pay for a place on a lorry. Traffic, however, is very irregular and you can't count on this alternative.

It's worth noting, however, that a feasible route exists from Gourma-Rharous, (about 100km east of Timbuktu on the south bank), to the new, paved, Gao-Bamako road. There's a basic car ferry across the river at Gourma-Rharous, though unless you're driving you won't need to worry much about the crossing as *pirogues* cross on demand. Again, this route from the river to the road is currently closed.

North to Araouane

Because of the rebellion, you can no longer travel north of Timbuktu, but for a couple of years in the early 1990s, an innovative tree-planting and green tourism initiative was in development at the tiny, formerly almost deserted oasis of **Araouane**, 250km north of the town, on the old salt route to Taoudenni. The privately funded American *Arbres Pour Araouane* project had solar-generated power, S/C rooms with furniture carved from salt blocks, a restaurant and great support from local people – who were as interested in the gardening and tree-planting initiatives as in the prospect of tourists arriving by Land Rover (8hr) or camel (5–7 days). Tuareg attacks in 1992 led to the abandonment of the project.

tive, the owner of *Le Sénégalais* restaurant – Abdoulah Arafa – has in the past lodged travellers in his home for a reasonable fee (①–②). He seems to have an arrangement with the police, and you can try tracking him down at his restaurant, across the street from *SONATAM* (the national tobacco company) in the main market building. If you pay a little more, Abdoulah will provide your day's meals. Otherwise, **staying with people** is risky indeed. Most people are reluctant, since there are now too many kids in cahoots with the *campement* manager. They'll alert him if they see you staying elsewhere, and he'll alert the police. There's no longer any law in Mali about staying with *indigènes*, but there *was* a law, formerly, and it proved a lucrative one for its "enforcers" in towns like Timbuktu.

The *Relais Azalaï* (reservations in Bamako, BP 2473; ☎22.33.18; ⑥), part of the French *Sofitel* chain, is the best option if you can afford it. They offer comfortable AC rooms (with power from their own generator) and have a restaurant with decent French food.

There's surprisingly little in the way of other **eating-houses** or bars. Apart from *Le Sénégalais*, try *Bar du Nord*. The market doesn't offer a great deal either, but as you'll either be staying in one of the hotels, or unofficially with a family who will provide meals in any case, it's not a big problem.

Lake Faguibine and Goundam

Lake Faguibine is a beautiful stretch of water surrounded by soft sand dunes, 100km west of Timbuktu. Though its size varies greatly with the seasons, the lake can swell to 120km long by 25km wide, making it one of the largest natural lakes in West Africa. In 1984, however, it dried up completely. The approach is via **GOUNDAM** – an important agricultural town in the middle of a region considered to be the breadbasket of Mali (there are weekly flights connecting it with Timbuktu and Bamako). Rice, millet, corn and, remarkably, wheat, are all grown in the area. Situated on the much smaller **Lake Télé**, Goundam has a *campement* (②) and is linked to the river by a 34-kilometre road from Diré, a sizeable port on the Niger, 100km upstream from Timbuktu. From Goundam, continue to Lake Faguibine via the *piste* that passes through the village of Bintagoungou.

To get to these places using local transport you'd need luck or money to make much headway.

THE DOGON COUNTRY

Until the end of the colonial era, the **Dogon** were one of the African peoples who had most successfully retained their culture and traditional way of life. This was in large part due to the isolation of their territory in the remarkable and picturesque **cliffside villages** they built along the **Bandiagara escarpment** (the *falaise*) east of Mopti – a 150-kilometre-long wedge of sandstone, pushed up by movements of the earth's plates in prehistoric times.

They're still dogged defenders of their customs, religion and art, but in more recent years they have become the object of an intense **touristic exploitation**. Although much of the Dogon country can only be visited on foot or at best with a donkey cart – the area you can cover with a 4WD is limited – the place can be swarming with travellers, especially over Christmas. Off the main circuit you can often pay kids to take you around the villages, but you'll have to fork out a lot of cash even for this alternative. With patience and a lot of time, you can still manage to get completely **off the beaten track**, but only the most intrepid and persistent travellers can today hope to discover the real beauty of the Dogon people's outstanding civilization.

Some history

Recent **archeological research** has uncovered caves dug into the cliffs around the Dogon town of **Sanga** that date to around the third century BC. The Dutch scientists who discovered these caves called the people who made them the **Toloy**, but there seems to be a rather large gap between this culture and the next known inhabitants of the escarpment, the **Tellem**, who arrived in the eleventh century. The Tellem were small people, often said to have been "pygmies", although they probably weren't related to the contemporary Central African people of small stature. They're generally thought to have shared the escarpment for a couple of centuries with the **Dogon**, who arrived in the fifteenth century. Some time around the seventeenth century, the Tellem were pushed out of the Dogon country and migrated to Burkina Faso.

The Dogon may originally have come from the region of the Nile, but before moving to the Bandiagara escarpment they lived in the Mande country to the west. Determined to preserve their traditional religion in the face of Muslim expansionism and religious jihads, they migrated to the safety of the *falaise* in the fifteenth century. Even with this natural shelter as a homeland, they had to fight off numerous aggressors over the centuries. In the 1470s the country was invaded by the **Songhai**, and in the early eighteenth century it was attacked by the **Ségou kingdom**. Much later, in 1830, the Fula from **Masina** marched on the region and, in 1860, the Tukulor ruler **El Hadj Omar** brought his holy war to the escarpment, making Bandiagara his capital; he died in

SEX, SPEECH AND WEAVING: DOGON COSMOLOGY

The Dogon believe in a single God, **Amma**, who created the sun, moon and stars. Afterwards, he created the earth by throwing a ball of clay into space. The ball spread to the four points of the horizon and took on the shape of a woman with an anthole for her vagina and a termite mound for her clitoris. Alone in the universe, Amma attempted to make love to the earth, but the termite mound blocked his path and he tore it out. Because of this violence, the earth could not bear the twins that would have resulted from a happy union and instead gave birth to a jackal.

Amma again had intercourse with the earth, and a pair of twins resulted, known as **nommo**. They were born of divine semen, the precious water found in everything in the universe. Green in colour, their upper bodies were human and their lower bodies like snakes. The *nommo* are present in all water. Living in the heavens with their father, the *nommo* looked down on their mother and, seeing her naked, made a **skirt** into which they wove the **first language**. Thus the earth was the first to possess speech.

Meanwhile, the jackal was running loose. His mother was the only woman, and he raped her. The earth bled and became impure in the sight of Amma. It's for this reason that today, menstruating women are considered impure in Dogon society – as they are in nearly all African cultures. When he forced himself upon the earth, the jackal also touched her skirt and thus stole language.

Having turned from his wife, Amma decided to create a human couple from clay. The couple had elements of both sexes – the foreskin being the feminine part of the man, and the clitoris the masculine part of the woman. Foreseeing that problems would arise from this ambiguity, the *nommo* circumcised the male and later an invisible hand removed the clitoris from the woman (circumcision of men and clitoridectomy of women is still an important step into adulthood for the Dogon). The couple was thus free to procreate and produced eight children, the original **Dogon ancestors**. After creating **eight descendants** of their own, the ancestors were purified and transformed into *nommo,* then went to join Amma in the sky. But before his ascension, the seventh ancestor was charged with giving the **second language** to humans. Using his mouth as a loom, he spat out a cotton strip from which the new speech was transmitted to humanity.

The eight ancestors didn't get along with Amma and the *nommo* and were eventually sent back to earth. On the way, the eighth ancestor came down before the seventh, who

Deguembere near Bandiagara. The **French** occupied the region of Sanga in 1893, but it wasn't until the battle of Tabi in 1920 that the colonial army finally "pacified" the Dogon people.

In the 1930s Reverend Francis McKinney, an American, established the first **Christian mission** in Sanga. Several years later Marcel Griaule, a French anthropologist, came to the same town to study traditional Dogon religion and customs. He spent a quarter of a century living in Dogon country and helped them to set up dams for irrigation and introduced the onion crop that's now one of the only exports of the region to the rest of Mali and Burkina. Respected by the Dogon, he also helped open the eyes of the rest of the world to the complexity and integrity of a civilization that had long been regarded by Muslim and Christian invaders as merely primitive.

Travelling around Dogon country

A trip to the Dogon country involves hours of trekking in the sweltering sun, and is likely to entail climbing up and down the 300-metre escarpment and walking over rocky terrain. You'll want to travel as light as possible, and you're recommended to leave all but the essentials behind before making the trip. Most people use Mopti (see p.332) as their base for exploring Dogon country: for a small daily fee the *Bar Mali* there will guard your baggage while you're away.

was angry as a result. He turned himself into a snake and set about disturbing the work of the other ancestors. They told the people to kill the snake – which they did. But this seventh ancestor – whose name was Lebe – held the **third language**, needed for mankind, since the second wasn't adequate. The oldest of the eight original descendants thus had to be sacrificed and was buried with the head of Lebe the snake. Humans then received the third language in the form of a drum.

Traditional religion has a profound effect on Dogon art and **symbolism** to this day, and is incorporated into the smallest item. Villages are laid out in human shape. They're frequently divided into twin parts – as in Sanga which incorporates Ogol-du-haut and Ogol-du-bas and Sanga-du-haut and Sanga-du-bas – that signify the original twin ancestors. Facades of the characteristic **Dogon houses** contain niches as reminders of primitive ancestors and **granaries** are divided into a complex series of inner compartments that represent the cosmos. The villages are filled with **"temples"** – maybe a simple rock or a clay pilaster, covered with sacrifices of chicken blood or millet paste. Carvings (such as on Dogon doors or locks), clothes and skin markings are all charged with meaning. It was formerly common to file the teeth in the shape of a weaver's comb, since speech is an action that weaves the world and should thus pass through a worthy loom. Even the baskets used by the Dogon are symbolic, the square bases representing the four cardinal points and the round top the celestial dome of the sky.

Symbolism from the story of creation also carries over into **Dogon dances**. **Masks** are an important element of the dances and the Dogon use over eighty different varieties according to the celebration. The biggest ceremony is the **Sigui**, celebrated every sixty years to commemorate the passing of a generation. The frequency of Sigui is calculated by the periodicity of an invisible satellite of the "dog star", Sirius. Sirius itself appears brightly between mountain peaks exactly when expected, suggesting a level of astronomical knowledge which has long baffled outsiders. The event serves to venerate the Big Mask, made in the shape of a serpent in reference to **Lebe**, who is credited with leading the Dogon to the Bandiagara escarpment as well as bringing them speech and, simultaneously, death. The last Sigui festival was held in the 1960s; the next – without undue optimism – should be in the 2020s.

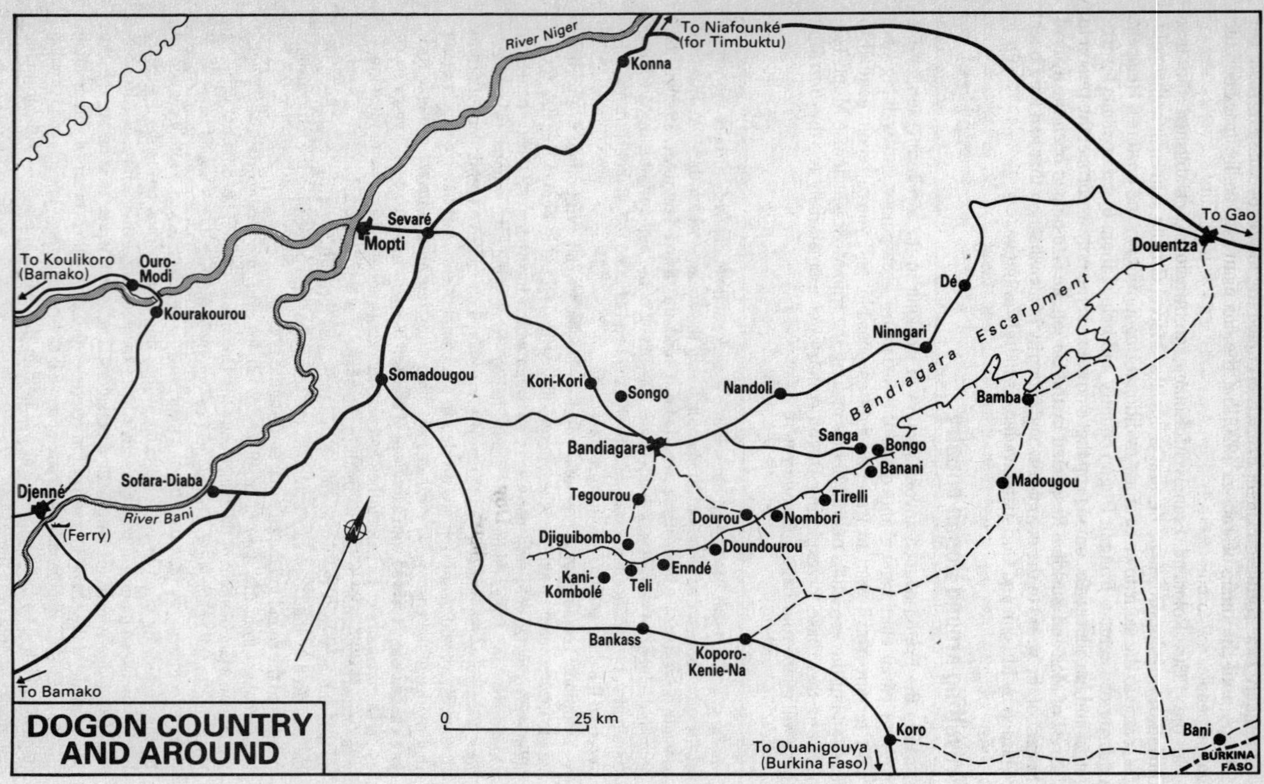
River Niger
To Niafounké (for Timbuktu)
Konna
To Koulikoro (Bamako)
Ouro-Modi
Kourakourou
Sevaré
Mopti
Somadougou
Kori-Kori
Songo
Nandoli
Ninngari
Dé
Douentza
To Gao
Bandiagara Escarpment
Bamba
Djenné
(Ferry)
River Bani
Sofara-Diaba
Bandiagara
Sanga
Bongo
Banani
Tegourou
Tirelli
Madougou
Dourou
Nombori
Djiguibombo
Doundourou
Kani-Kombolé
Teli
Enndé
Bankass
Koporo-Kenie-Na
To Bamako
0
25 km
Koro
To Ouahigouya (Burkina Faso)
Bani
BURKINA FASO
DOGON COUNTRY AND AROUND

Bring a **water bottle** or canteen for the long hot stretches between villages. Dogon villages have no running water, and you'll be drinking from local wells. It's a good idea in principle to try to boil or purify it: when stocks are low in the dry season, water can take on a murky colour that's more than enough persuasion. Guinea worm is a severe problem, though crude filtering (through a T-shirt for example) removes the parasites. You can take some fruit or light snacks with you, but most of your **food** will be bought in Dogon villages.

Although the terrain is rough, you won't need any special **walking shoes**. Tennis shoes or even sandals should be fine but you'll definitely need some form of **head-wear**. If you have your own **vehicle**, you're better off leaving it in Mopti, unless it's a 4WD. At some point in the Dogon country, you're likely to have to abandon it in order to visit villages hanging on the cliffs of the escarpment and it's best to leave it where you know it'll be safe. Despite the temptation, avoid renting a **mobylette** (moped). Few go really well even in the best conditions. Around here you'll spend all your time fixing it, and then, when you return it, arguing about who should pay for the necessary parts.

Notwithstanding your experiences in Mali's other towns, **guides** are essential in Dogon country. Without one, you'll have real problems just communicating, since few of the people here speak French. Additionally, you'll have trouble locating villages and the quickest footpaths between them, or those that lead up and down the escarpment. Guides will also help when it comes to figuring out village market days, and they can make arrangements for sleeping and eating in isolated places where, unaided, you might not make your intentions clear. Except in the most remote communities you will in any case be expected to have a local escort: it says something for Dogon cohesion that such an understanding, with its long-term benefits for all concerned, has been achieved. As a rough indication, you should expect **private guides** (who know all too well that their services are indispensable) to want a minimum of CFA5000 per day. Alone, you've most bargaining power, though it's usually cheaper per person in a group.

As you go through the villages outlined here, you'll encounter numerous **expenses** in addition to what you pay your guide. Many Dogon villages now charge a flat entry fee for visitors, usually CFA500 or CFA1000, rarely more. The same rate is generally applied for a meal and for sleeping the night, while for breakfast, half the rate is normal.

One point to note: a lot of Dogon harvest **fêtes** take place around mid-December. It's a great time to be in the district, with much dancing, drumming and drinking to do.

Circuits from Bandiagara

Although commercial tours are convenient if you want a perfunctory overview of Dogon territory, you may prefer less organization and the flexibility of following your own plans and pace. In that case it's usually best to head directly to **BANDIAGARA**, a seventy-kilometre taxi ride from Mopti over decent tracks. A sizeable administrative town, Bandiagara is nothing like more traditional villages in the region (as the large mosque testifies) although the population is sixty percent Dogon. There's a good deal of commerce by Dogon standards, plus a hospital, mission and police headquarters. It's a convenient point of entry, where you can arrange to visit villages on the plateau, the escarpment face and on the plain below. It's a pleasant enough town, but brace yourself for kids swarming around you from the minute you arrive, offering their services as **guides**.

Practicalities

At some point during your stay in Bandiagara, if not immediately on arrival, you'll be expected to **register with the police** at their post just outside town on the Sanga road. They'll want to see a **stamp from Mopti** in your passport before letting you loose in

Dogon country. As for **somewhere to stay**, there's a government-run *campement* (②) and some *auberges* and bars in town also offer cheap accommodation. The most popular is the *Hôtel Kansaye* (②) at the town exit, just before the bridge. Sadly the cleanliness and atmosphere have deteriorated in recent years, but they can fix you up with a guide and will let you leave baggage while you're hiking.

From Bandiagara to Djiguibombo

Twenty-five kilometres of walkable tracks separate Bandiagara from Djiguibombo at the edge of the *falaise*. This relatively flat road over the plateau passes through sparse vegetation of bush savannah with the occasional baobab rising up to dominate the rocky landscape. After about 12km you pass the village of **Tegourou**. Nearby is a dammed stream and the terraced fields of the Dogon's famous onions. Before continuing the trip down the escarpment most guides will stop at **Djiguibombo**, the last village on the plateau and a charming and friendly place. It stands in an extremely rocky area near the cliff: a stone wall surrounds it and many of the houses use stone in their construction.

Along the plain from Kani-Kombolé to Teli

A couple of kilometres south of Djiguibombo, you finally arrive at the cliff: from the edge of the plateau, there's a sweeping vista onto the plains below. Although the cliff drops suddenly, your guide will lead you along walkable paths down it, and the 300-metre descent poses no special problem. Once on the plain, **Kani-Kombolé** – with a reasonable little *bar-resto* and somewhere to stay if you need it – isn't too far off.

Following the *falaise* eastwards, you come next to **Teli**, a four-kilometre walk over a flat, sandy stretch bordered by millet fields. If you don't manage to get to Sanga (see opposite), Teli is a satisfying substitute that is still a lot less visited, with some of the most spectacular **cliffside houses** along this part of the escarpment. If you take this route, it's worth coming at least this far. Some guides are better than others at getting you permission to climb up to the cliff-dwellings. An old lady used to live among the remains of Tellem ancestors in caves on the rock face, but she died in 1992 and latest reports suggest nobody has replaced her as *gardien*. Go in your lowest key and make polite enquiries if you're interested to see the skulls and bones.

Enndé to Bandiagara via Dourou

Having reached Teli, you can consider you've had a pretty good overview of the Dogon country and will have seen villages on the plateau, in the cliffs and on the plains. At this point, you could either return to Bandiagara retracing the route described above, or continue east to **Enndé**. Here, you can spend the night on the roof of the house of the village chief's son, who's quite accustomed to putting up travellers. You can also pay to have meals of chicken and rice prepared and wash it down with home-brewed millet beer. In the rainy season you can swim in the waterfall pool near the village.

After Enndé, the road continues through a number of villages on the plain. One of the more picturesque is **Doundouru**, known for the spectacular homes carved in the cliff. Still following the escarpment to the east, you next come to **Konsagou**, and finally **Gimini**. After this village, you can climb back up the *falaise* and walk along the edge of the plateau to **Dourou**.

Dourou has one of the most important **markets** so near the escarpment, and a **motorable** road from Bandiagara. Every five days, vehicles arrive here from Bandiagara and Mopti bringing traders and goods to the heart of Dogon country. In addition to ubiquitous Dogon onions, grown nearby and sold in large quantities, you'll find cereals, Fula milk and rough cotton weaves of indigo-dyed material, a common element in Dogon dress. If you time your visit to coincide with **market day**, you can hope to get a ride back to Bandiagara, 25km to the north.

YAMBO OUOLOGUEM – A POEM

Yambo Ouologuem, who is Dogon, is Mali's best-known writer (see "Books" in *Contexts*).

WHEN NEGRO TEETH SPEAK

People think I'm a cannibal
But you know what people say

People see I've got red gums but who has
White ones
Up the tomatoes

People say there are not nearly so many tourists
Now
But you know
This isn't America and nobody
Has the money

People think it's my fault and
are scared
But look
My teeth are white not red
I've not eaten anybody
People are rotten they say I scoff
Baked tourists
Or maybe grilled
Baked or grilled I asked
They didn't say anything just kept
looking uneasily at my gums
Up the tomatoes

Everyone knows in an agricultural country
there's agriculture
Up the vegetables

Everyone knows that vegetables
Well you can't live on the vegetables
you grow
And that I'm quite well developed
for someone underdeveloped
Miserable scum living off the tourists
Down with my teeth

People suddenly surrounded me
Tied me up
Threw me down
At the feet of justice

Cannibal or not cannibal
Answer
Ah you think you're so clever
So proud of yourself

Well, we'll see I'm going to settle
your account
Have you anything to say
Before you are sentenced to death

I shouted Up the tomatoes

People are rotten and women curious
you know
There was one of these in the
curious circle
In her rasping voice sort of bubbling like
a saucepan
With a hole in it
Shrieked
Slit open his belly
I'm sure father is still inside

There weren't any knives
Naturally enough among the vegetarians
Of the western world
So they got a Gillette blade
And carefully
Slit
Slat
Plop
Slit open my belly

Inside flourishing rows of tomatoes
Watered by streams of palm wine
Up the tomatoes

Translated from the French by Clive Wake and John Reed in *A New Book of African Verse* (Heinemann 1988) and reproduced with permission of the translators.

Circuits from Sanga

Much has been written about **SANGA**, a striking example of a classic Dogon village with traditional homes and granaries, sited on the plateau above the escarpment. This is where Reverend McKinney set up the first mission in the Dogon country in the 1930s and where, soon after, Marcel Griaule lived and studied. Overflowing down the cliffs of the Bandiagara escarpment, the town was too picturesque to go unnoticed for long and some of the best and most popular **walking tours** through Dogon country start here.

A FEW WORDS OF DOGON

Most Dogon, especially younger people, speak some French. A few words in the Dogon language, however, are bound to help comunication.

Hello	*Po*	1	*Ti*	5	*Noonay*	9	*Tuwa*
Boy	*Ah*	2	*Loy*	6	*Kuray*	10	*Peo*
Girl	*Ñe*	3	*Tahnu*	7	*So*	And, of course	
God	*Amma*	4	*Nay*	8	*Sira*	millet beer	*Konjo*

(Not that you'll be able to say "Hello, boy, girl, God" and count to ten after a couple of bowls of *Konjo*.)

Practicalities

If you don't sign up for an organized excursion in Mopti, you can get to Sanga by taking a bush taxi to Bandiagara. From here, it's possible to get transport to Sanga, notably on the town's market day. Markets in the Dogon country are held every five days so try and find out when Sanga's will be before leaving Mopti.

Sanga is actually a conglomeration of small villages, the most useful of which is **Ogol-du-haut**, where you'll find the Gendarmerie and the government-run *campement* (③). You can hook up here with a guide for a walking tour. There's more comfortable lodgings near the Protestant church at the *Bar de la Dogonne*, which also has a good **restaurant** and cold beer.

Tours around Sanga

You may be offered three different **day trips** from Sanga, ranging from seven to fifteen kilometres in length. The first includes a tour of Sanga and a **seven-kilometre** roundtrip trek to Gogoli. A **ten-kilometre** tour continues from these villages to Banani, located partly on the *falaise* and partly on the plain below. The descent from the plateau takes you through a strange tunnel carved into the cliff near the village of Bongo. All along the escarpment, you see caves – originally used by the Tellem as granaries or for defence in case of attack – cut into the rocky face. The **fifteen-kilometre** tour extends the loop to include Tirelli, another village located both on the cliff and the plain. These treks last roughly between three and ten hours, and you could also arrange longer walking trips that last anything up to a week. Along the way, guides point out important aspects of Dogon village structure: the *toguna* open air "huts" covered with millet stalks where elders meet to chat and confer; the round huts where women stay during their periods; and the *gina*, a type of sanctuary reserved to honour the ancestors. At some point, you're bound to stop for a calabash full of *konjo* – bittersweet millet beer.

Bankass

An alternative route into Dogon country from Mopti and Sevaré bypasses Bandiagara altogether, entering the Dogon region via **BANKASS**, reached from the road that passes through Somadougou. This way you start the trek from down on the plains, and approach the escarpment from below. Bankass is a large market village with a mixed population, less centrally placed than Bandiagara for visits to the traditional villages. Hiking access to the *falaise* is more difficult from here, but in the dry season it's just about possible to go by 4WD (or rent a horse and cart) to Kani-Kombolé, Enndé and Teli. Although this is easier, the visit from Bandiagara is really more interesting and, approaching the scarp edge from above, certainly more impressive.

Practicalities

Accommodation in Bankass is limited to the *Hôtel Les Arbres* which offers overpriced S/C but unventilated rooms with nets (③; or you can camp). You can leave baggage here while hiking and the bar has a list of a dozen or so guides. If you're without transport, ask here about the possibility of reting a **mobylette** to Kani-Kombolé. However, most machines have seen better days so you may prefer the proven **donkey and cart** (*calèche*) option. Once you reach Kani-Kombolé, you can visit other villages along the escarpment by following the routes described on p.350.

Koro

Coming **from Burkina Faso**, you can also enter the Dogon country by taking the road from Ouahigouya to the border post at Tiou. From here a very bad *piste* (often impassable during the rains) leads some 55km to **KORO**, where you go through Malian police and **customs formalities**. Although Koro has a large **market** and beautiful **mosque**, it's far from the heart of the Dogon country and sees few tourists. The town could reasonably be used as a springboard for a trip through some of the less-visited Dogon villages, but you'll have to allow yourself extra time to work out transport and other details.

Practicalities

For **accommodation**, the *Tolo Bar,* across from the market, puts up travellers cheaply (①). They'll fix you up with meals and cold drinks and, while facilities are rudimentary, the reception is very warm. If you're heading out of the Dogon country towards Burkina, it can come as a welcome relief. Near the Gendarmerie, the *campement* (①–②) is more comfortable than *Tolo*, and if you catch the owner on a good day he can be very helpful. You can also find a bed at the *Le Point* bar or the *Bar de la Jeunesse* near the mosque.

To visit the *falaise* from Koro, you could head up to Bankass and follow the routes outlined above. Alternatively, you could make for **Douentza** in the northeast (see p.359). This last route is virtually untravelled by foreigners and passes through the Dogon villages of **Madougou** and **Bamba** and a wild, duney area. You will receive very genuine hospitality, with none of the commercialism of the villages further west. **Everi**, a seven-kilometre hike from Douentza, is built on a high mesa at the end of the escarpment. Infrequent vehicles link these villages on market days. Talk to people at the *Tolo Bar,* in Koro for ideas of other places to visit along this road – they may be able to get you through the entire Dogon country without ever running into the police or other officials.

If you're heading to Gao with your own vehicle, the Douentza *piste* provides a kind of "rear view" of the Dogon country. The tracks, however, are very difficult (with taxing stretches of soft sand and boulders) and it's hard to follow their endless branches. Peugeot 404 taxis do ply between Douentza and Madougou for the market, so you should be able to go by normal car, although a *quatre-quatre*, (a 4WD vehicle) is obvi-

MOVING ON FROM BANKASS AND KORO

Transport out of Bankass towards Burkina is most likely on a Monday, market day in Bankass. Koro is somewhat problematic. Taxis head fairly frequently to Bankass (at least every couple of days), but are extremely rare to the border at Tiou and into Burkina Faso. Even in the dry season you may be stranded several days in Koro waiting for the occasional goods truck or tourist heading south. During the rains, the road may be impassable for weeks on end.

ously preferable. It would probably prove just as quick to follow the longer but more obvious route via Somadougou and the main Bamako–Gao highway.

GAO AND THE NORTHEAST

Arid and inhospitable, northeastern Mali is only habitable at all thanks to the River Niger, along which life in the area concentrates. The riverside town of **Gao**, formerly the capital of a great kingdom, is now the administrative and commercial centre for the region. From here you can follow the river south **to Niamey** (in Niger) along a difficult but scenic *piste* leading through small fishing villages; head upstream, along even more difficult tracks, **to Timbuktu** in the west; or go west the easy way, on the paved road **to Mopti and Bamako**. Alternatively **the river** itself can serve as your highway, certainly a more memorable way to travel – providing you time your travels to coincide with the rains.

Like Timbuktu, Gao has suffered badly from the effects of the Tuareg rebellion of recent years, with both Tuareg fighters and government forces accused of civilian massacres and other atrocities, while Algeria's continuing civil strife has dried up the overland route and much trade from the north.

Warning: the Tanezrouft trans-Sahara route from Algeria is closed as is the piste between Gao and Timbuktu along the north bank of the Niger. Access to Gao from Mopti by road, with an armed escort, is feasible, but tourists are not encouraged and it's doubtful you would be allowed through as long as the war between the Tuareg and the state continues. Similarly, the riverside route between Niamey and Gao is all but closed as far as tourists are concerned. Note, too, that when this book went to press, there was some doubt about which places in Gao had survived the recent troubles: a curfew is still enforced from time to time. If you're at home, check with your government's foreign affairs travel advisory department for update information. In West Africa, *radio trottoir* will keep you informed.

Stop Press: Sept 14th 1995. Latest news claims the Gao–Mopti road is open.

Gao

In the repertoire of campfire travel talk, **GAO** was always one of the most romantic cities. As you arrived from the void of the Sahara, it seemed like a small miracle of civilization emerging from the wasteland. Passing the last stretch of soft sand thrown up by the desert around the town, and entering its dusty tree-lined avenues, fringed by busy shops and thronging with crowds, stirred certain exhilaration. Traditionally, desert-crossers would celebrate their arrival in West Africa by heading straight to the *Hôtel Atlantide* – a tatty colonial pile that might as well be the Ritz out here – and downing a few cold beers. Behind the hotel lies the source of all the vigour, the **River Niger**.

If you've come up from the south you get a rather different view of the place. The river, which from this direction is neither new nor unusual, is unlikely to stir much excitement, while the town itself resembles any other Sahelian city, bigger than most but neither especially beautiful nor unusually dynamic. All is relative.

Formalities and bureaucracy

You must **register with the police** on arrival. Their office is next to the market and central mosque. You'll be given forms on which you must state date of arrival and departure and your address in Gao, and your passport is then stamped.

There's hours more fun to be had in the **bank** if you need to change money. The system here hasn't changed for years and involves repeated visits to various *guichets* for different signatures. The place is always stacked full of money and full of back-country people trying to perform once-yearly transactions before it closes at noon.

And lastly, there's more time-wasting if you had the presence of mind to suggest people write to you at **Poste Restante**, Gao. Delays generally run to three weeks from posting overseas and you need exceptional powers of diplomacy if you plan on going in there every morning to repeat your request.

Some history

The original founders of Gao, known in its early days as Kawkaw, were **Sorko fishermen** who migrated from Benin between the sixth and eleventh centuries. They mingled with the rural Gabili peoples living along the banks of the Niger, and eventually this mixture evolved into a people known as the Songhai. The first **Songhai** monarch at Gao was Kanda, who founded the **Za (or Dia) dynasty** in the seventh century. He quickly opened the town to trans-Saharan trade and to Berbers who wanted to settle there for commercial reasons.

The fifteenth king of Songhai, Za Kossoi, converted to **Islam** in 1009. The town prospered to the point where it rivalled all the great regional trading centres in power and wealth, even surpassing the capitals of Ancient Ghana and later Mali. Rulers of the Mali Empire coveted Gao's success and potential and annexed the town in 1325, although the Songhai princes managed to flee from their clutches. One of them, **Ali Golon**, went on to found the **Sonni dynasty** still based at Gao. The greatest of the Sonni rulers was the despotic Sonni Ali Ber, or **Ali the Great.** It was he who, towards the end of the fifteenth century, expanded the kingdom at Gao to the dimensions of an empire (see below). The capital continued to flourish under the reign of the **Askias**, founders of a new dynasty that lasted throughout the sixteenth century. At the time, Gao had 70,000 inhabitants and in the busy harbour were crowded over 1000 war boats from the Askias' flotilla, 400 barges and thousands of *pirogues*.

With the **Moroccan invasion** of Songhai in 1591, the empire collapsed and Gao was virtually rased. The town never recovered and when the German explorer **Heinrich Barth** arrived in 1854, he described the once ostentatious city as "a desolate abode with a small and miserable population". Much of the town's present look dates to the beginning of this century. The **French** built up the port, traced new streets (which explains the rather uniform grid layout) and established an administrative district with characteristic colonial buildings still used by the present government. With a population of some 20,000, Gao still hasn't returned to its former grandeur and in its current economic and political predicament it is struggling.

Accommodation

Gao's only **hotel** is the *Atlantide* (③–④). Despite its impression of grandeur, the comforts turn out to be something of an illusion: some of the rooms have AC, but in general they're uninviting. There's no other permanent, cheap place to stay in the town centre, though one or other of the restaurants periodically risks letting out rooms – until police demands become excessive. The fact is that Gao has been in a vague state of siege since before the advent of Mali's democratic era in 1992 and the administration here has yet to catch up.

The best-value place to stay in the locality is at *Tizi Mizi Camping* (①–②), about 4km down the Niamey road. Rooms are comfortable and impeccably clean; you can pitch a tent here, too, or sleep on the rooftop terrace. They have a pleasant outdoor bar and restaurant as well as a disco. The long-established *Camping Yarga* is also about 4km from the centre, off the paved road leading to the Mopti road ferry, with buildings

THE SONGHAI EMPIRE

Towards the end of the fourteenth century, Mali's influence and power had diminished greatly and the stage was set for **Sonni Ali Ber** – nineteenth ruler in the Sonni dynasty and the effective founder of Songhai as an empire – to embark on his great conquests. A shrewd administrator, Ali was also a brilliant and ruthless strategist and it is said he never lost a battle. A half-hearted Muslim, Ali quickly set about terrorizing the Fula and Tuareg nomads – his bitter enemies in the region. His expansionist designs were greatly facilitated in 1468 when he was invited by the governor of **Timbuktu** to liberate that town from Tuareg domination.

Historians of the period reported that Ali's conquest of Timbuktu was brutal, and many townspeople who had longed for the Songhai "liberation" fled north to Oualata for fear of persecution. After an initial period of purging religious leaders who stood in his path, however, Ali brought stability to the town which once again prospered under his rule. At the same time, he managed to neutralize the **religious influence** of Timbuktu's powerful marabouts who exercised considerable political power over the entire region.

Ali next turned his sights on **Djenné**, which proved a harder target. The Sonnis besieged the town for seven years, seven months and seven days before it finally fell in 1423. Rather than wreaking vengeance on the ruling class as he had in Timbuktu, Ali married his fortunes with those of Djenné by taking the queen mother to be his wife. **Masina** was his next objective, and he conquered this Fula stronghold shortly afterwards.

All the chief strategic points of the Niger and the delta region were now in Songhai control. The nation's military strength was founded in its **navy** and Ali depended so heavily on his flotilla that, at one point, he envisaged digging a canal from the port town of Ras al-Ma to the desert oasis of Oualata in order to attack the Tuareg there. Although work started, the plan was eventually abandoned as Ali extended his control southwards to the villages of Bandiagara, Bariba and Gourma.

After he died, Sonni Ali was succeeded by his son Bakari, but the new king followed his father's example of keeping a distance from the faith and thus incited religious disapproval. He was overthrown by Mohammed Torodo, the governor of Hombori, who formed a new dynasty known as the **Askia** or "usurper".

Though he had no hereditary claim to the throne, Askia Mohammed legitimized his rule through religious channels, soliciting the backing of powerful **marabouts**. He received the ultimate benediction to his rule after making the pilgrimage to Mecca with 500 horsemen and 1000 footsoldiers. There he was granted the title of Khalif for the entire Sudan. Returning to Mali, he set about expanding his empire into Mossi country, then pushed eastward to Hausaland and into the Aïr as far as Agadez.

While away on a campaign, Mohammed was forced out of power in 1528. Internal intrigue followed and a number of Askias succeeded one another until the reign of **Ishak I** who ruled from 1539 to 1549 – a decade which marked the Songhai Empire's apogee. The country now extended from Senegal to the Aïr mountains and from the Taghaza salt mines in the desert to the Hausaland in what is today Nigeria.

Meanwhile **Morocco** far to the north was in a period of crisis. Ejected from Andalucía and hemmed in to the east by the Turks, the Moroccan sultan turned his sights towards the south, where he sought to gain control of the salt and gold trade. In 1591 he sent an army to wrest the Sudan from Songhai control. Thanks to a combination of Moroccan firearms and the disarray of the Askia rulers, the Sultan's army won a decisive battle at **Tondibi**, 60km north of Gao: Gao, Djenné and Timbuktu all fell soon afterwards.

El Sadi, writing in the *Tarikh es-Soudan*, described the invasion in these terms: "Everything changed after the Moroccan conquest. It signalled the beginning of anarchy, theft, pillage and general disorganization". And indeed the entire Sahelian region suffered a blow from which it never recovered.

of traditional mud bricks or *banco*. You can have meals prepared, and prices are slightly lower than those at *Tizi Mizi*, but the rooms are less comfortable. *Yarga* is close to good swimming beaches along the Niger – the river is considered bilharzia-free in these parts.

The Town

Considering the centuries of history through which Gao has played a leading role, the **Musée du Sahel** on the north side of town is disappointingly small, dedicated to the different **peoples of the Sahel**, with displays of their art and domestic implements. You'll see farming and fishing tools (some rather impressive harpoons), musical instruments, and household items used by the **Tuareg**, **Fula**, **Chamba** and **Arma** (descendants of Moroccan-Songhai marriages). Guided tours cost a little extra: the guides are extremely enthusiastic and their personal comments make it worthwhile, but if you want to go it alone you'll find that most of the exhibits are explained relatively well.

In the town centre, Gao boasts two outstanding **markets**. The *grand marché*, just opposite the *Hôtel Atlantide*, has an entire section devoted to **crafts**, for which the region is well known. The most common items are Tuareg **leather boxes**, knives and swords; on sale too are numerous examples of **Sahelian sandals** – flat and wide to facilitate walking on the sands. Some pairs incorporate intricate weaving and green or red dyed leather in the design. Fula and Tuareg **jewellery** can also be a good buy here, but vendors generally set astronomically high starting prices: bargaining tends to be more of a headache than the good-humoured exchange you're hopefully used to.

Behind the crafts section, women bunch around desert wares – anonymous spices, dollops of peanut butter, sour milk, fish and meat, pyramids of miniature tomatoes, onions, peppers and lettuces carefully washed (in the river) – and, in season if you're lucky, the full range of tropical fruits and vegetables. The *petit marché*, next to the police, specializes in **cloth**. Dozens of tailors – all men of course – treadle ancient sewing machines and will take orders if you want to have loose-fitting Sahelian clothes made to measure.

In physical terms, Gao has few reminders of its glorious past. The **mosque** in the centre of town near the police station was initially built by Kankan Moussa after he annexed the town in the fourteenth century but, its origins apart, it's unimpressive compared even with those in Timbuktu and certainly in comparison with the mosque at Djenné.

Following the boulevard des Askias to the northeast brings you to the **Askia tomb** – a fifteen-minute walk from the centre. Now used as a mosque, you can visit this strange fifteenth-century mud structure and climb to the top of the odd-shaped pyramid with wild wooden crossbeams sticking out porcupine style from the facade: from the top, you get a good view of town and of the river. You should tip the guardian something for the visit.

Eating, drinking and nightlife

Gao doesn't boast very classy **restaurants** except, with a stretch of imagination, the *Atlantide*'s where you can sit down to French-style *steack frites* or *poulet* and vegetables – unexciting and rather pricey. A cheaper alternative, the *Restaurant Sénégalais*, near the Place de l'Indépendance, serves copious plates of jollof rice on their patio. Cheaper still is a string of chop houses on the road running parallel to the principal boulevard des Askias – two blocks east as you walk away from the river. The *Blackpool* is a long-established and recommended place for local food such as Nile perch and *riz sauce*, while just across the street the *Restaurant Dikou* has an almost identical menu and price list. Down the street towards the Place de l'Indépendance, the *Oasis* is another popular place. And be sure to sample Gao's delicious, long spicy sausages – always a reliable evening street food fallback.

MOVING ON FROM GAO

Now that the road has been paved **from Gao to Bamako**, getting out of town is much easier – security concerns notwithstanding. During and after the rains, you can also take advantage of the **steamers** that pass along one of the most interesting stretches of the **Niger** between here (their terminus) and Mopti. The following details are theoretical – in many cases these services and transport options will not be operating for fear of attack.

By river

In addition to the main August–November steamer services, most of the year it's possible to use smaller river craft for transport. Upstream, poled *pirogues* set off for **Bourem** (all day and half the next), **Bamba** (3–4 days), **Gourma-Rharous** (4–5 days) and Timbuktu (one week). Downstream, *pirogues* rarely go much beyond **Gargouna** (one day away; Tuesday market) or **Ansongo**, two days away (splendid Thursday market). This latter trip, below Gao, is especially rewarding from a natural history viewpoint, as the boats crush through marvelous deep reedbeds harbouring a wealth of **birdlife**, and then break onto open water where they regularly pass several herds of snorting **hippos**. *Pirogue* fares have increased enormously in recent years, but a place on an ordinary transport vessel shouldn't cost you more than CFA3000 per day, including communal rice and fish.

By air

Air Mali operates one **flight** a week from Gao airfield (7km from the centre) to Timbuktu (CFA34,000), Mopti (CFA45,000) and Bamako (CFA81,000). For more details, check out the *Air Mali* office which is in the centre of town next to the *Hôtel Atlantide.*

By road to Mopti and Bamako

Regular buses leave Gao for Bamako, although schedules are frequently disrupted by the requirement that they travel only with armed escorts in convoy: this route has been a target for Tuareg rebels.

By piste to Niamey

This service was suspended at the time of publication.

The Nigérien *SNTN* **bus** leaves every Monday, Wednesday and Friday morning. It's wise to book the day before as it's often full. The bus leaves Gao around 11am and gets into Niamey the following afternoon.

Trans-Sahara and Timbuktu

At the time of publication both these pistes *were closed.*

Overlanders driving north across the Sahara are rare, so your best bet for transport is with truckers. The owner of the *Tizi Mizi* often seems to know what's going north, or you can ask at the *Atlantide*. Kids can also be a help finding out about transport through the desert if you give them a small *cadeau* (after you've scored a ride, of course). You can expect to pay in the order of CFA50,000 for the crossing to Adrar, meals included (take this option; it's a poor idea to be excluded at meal times). If you want to save money, you should head out with the first vehicle you find, even if the driver quotes you an unusually high price: in certain seasons, you can wait a long time to find transport and if you're paying out for a hotel and food, it adds up quickly.

The strategy of checking at the hotels and with children also applies for tracking down exceedingly rare vehicles heading **to Timbuktu**. This destination involves the longest wait from Gao and at times there's nothing at all heading in that direction. If you get fed up, take a vehicle to Bourem and try waiting there. Some traffic crosses the desert and turns right to Timbuktu.

Along the Mopti Road

Heading out of Gao, the only way to reach the paved road to Bamako is by taking the **ferry** across the Niger, a regular service with fixed prices. The departure point is 7km south of Gao, but boats stop running at nightfall.

THE MOPTI ROAD

In recent years the Gao to Mopti road has been the scene of attacks by Tuareg rebels. Bear in mind that your freedom to travel independently – and the public transport schedules – are likely to be determined by the latest incident. See box on p.354.

The early stages of the Mopti road are dull, with long stretches of monotonous Sahelian landscape. After 90km you arrive at **Doro**, a small town in a region where lions are said to exist. If these reports are true, you'd have to follow tracks a good 40km south of town to have any hope of seeing them. Ask in Doro if any have been spotted recently and enquire about the possibility of taking someone along as a guide.

Gossi is the next large Songhai village along the road, 160km from Gao. It's on the shore of a muddy lake and is the site of a sizeable reforestation and agricultural project headed by a Norwegian church fund. It also has a wildlife claim, one spectacularly authenticated by the BBC in a film documentary made in 1994. A herd of some 600 **elephants** lives in the district, protected partly by the traditional **Tuareg** resistance to hunting these animals. Many Tuareg are making the uneasy transition to a sedentary lifestyle in this area, however, and their crops are threatened by the *elouan*. Tuareg efforts to get official help in dealing with the elephantine crop damage aren't helped by the ongoing rebellion. Gossi has no accommodation but it's a pleasant place to stop off for a lukewarm drink and bite to eat. Reasonably priced grilled meat is sold in large quantities at the market.

After Gossi, the scenery shifts from neutral into top gear, with unexpectedly large **rock formations** in the vicinity of **Hombori**, 250km from Gao. A strikingly situated village, Hombori is built partially on the rocky slopes of **Hombori Tondo** – a flat-topped mountain that rises to 1150m. Many of the homes here are built of stone, a rarity in West Africa, and there are a couple of small **restaurants** and bars. Then, 11km out of Hombori, the road passes the dramatic formation known as **La Main de Fatima**, since it resembles the symbolic hand – with outstretched thumb and finger – of the prophet's daughter. European rock climbers used to do their stuff on these faces until the troubles interfered with such adventures.

Just under 400km from Gao, **Douentza** is a town with an important market and an impressive **mosque**, poised at the northeastern periphery of the **Bandiagara escarpment** which stretches some 200km south through the Dogon country. Just before arriving at Douentza, a signboard marks the turning for Koro. If you have transport, this *piste* provides an excellent means of getting to the Dogon villages of Amba, Bamba and Madougou. From here you can head back up to Bandiagara, and will have visited a good chunk of the Dogon country without ever running into police or tourist guides. Few people take this route, however, and with good reason. The tracks can be hard work in a low-slung car, though battered Peugeot 404 bush taxis do make the trip out from Douentza.

Back on the main paved road to Mopti, **Boré** (458km from Gao) boasts an unusually large and beautiful **mosque** for such a small place. A further 56km and you arrive at **Konna**, a market town on the junction of the road to Niafounké and Timbuktu. From here, it's a quick jog to Sevaré – the highway junction for Mopti.

South to Niamey

Although only 443km separate Gao and Niamey, the trip involves a very long day's drive – longer in the rains or if you to take it easy and stop off at the numerous fishing villages. The road hugs the banks of the **Niger** through some exceptionally beautiful scenery. It's a well-travelled route, but full of sandy pitfalls and thorn trees whose spines work their way through hot, soft rubber. And again, it hasn't escaped the general insecurity that besets the northeast, with the Nigérien *SNTN* bus company currently suspending its service on the route, and tourist vehicles either strongly advised against or prevented from using it.

The initial 95km presents few problems until you arrive at **Ansongo** – a picturesque village with an important **market** on Thursdays. The town is essentially Songhai, but you'll also see numerous Tuareg who make their way through the entire region. After Ansongo, the road becomes progressively worse, with stretches of treacherous sand that may become impassable during the rains. Despite the difficulties, it's a beautiful stretch that the government has officially classified as a protected natural area. Your chances are good of seeing **hippos** at some point along the river: in many instances they come quite close to the villages and the areas where people swim. **Giraffes** and numerous varieties of **gazelle** also roam through the region, though you're unlikely to spot them from the *piste*.

Fafa is the next village, 140km from Gao. There's a pleasant *campement – Chez Fafa* (②) – with a restaurant, and *pirogue* trips to the hippos on offer, though it's closed from the end of July to the end of August – and realistically is likely to have closed indefinitely as of 1995.

The road continues tortuously until you arrive at Labbenzanga, 191km from Gao, the Mali-Niger **border post** where you'll be subjected to protracted formalities. There's a bar and **restaurant** near the customs post. It's another 44km to Ayorou, a large market town where you pass through Niger customs, and 132km to Tillabéri where the **surfaced road** picks up the rest of the way to Niamey.

index

CHAPTER FIVE

THE CAPE VERDE ISLANDS

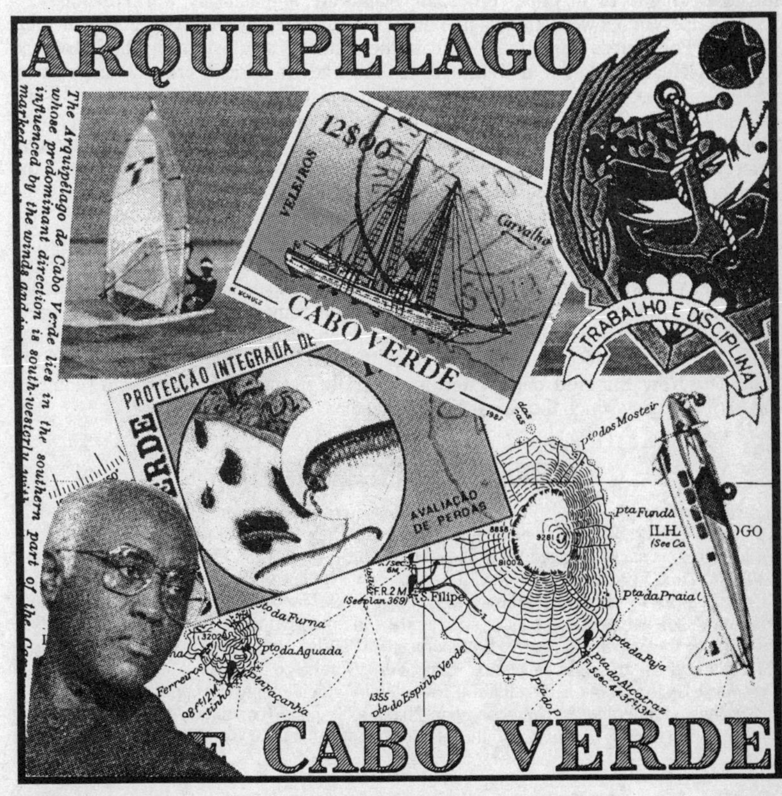

THE CAPE VERDE ISLANDS

From a traveller's viewpoint, and indeed a West African one, the **Cape Verde Islands** are barely on the map. If you ever hear of the archipelago, it's usually as an offshore supplement to the grim process of desertification on the African mainland, 500km away. An Atlantic world apart, the Cape Verdes fall in more neatly with the Azores, or even the Canary Islands. They consist of nine main islands in two groups, the **Barlaventos** (Windwards) and the **Sotaventos** (Leewards). Six of them – **Santiago**, **Fogo**, **Brava**, **São Nicolau**, **São Vicente** and **Santo Antão** – are volcanic and inspiringly scenic, while the three to the east – **Maio**, **Boa Vista** and **Sal** – are flat and sandy. Although the islands are isolated, once you've arrived, they are are not difficult to get around, using the good ferries and internal air service. There's usually somewhere to stay, a small hotel or *pensão*, and prices are reasonable. Despite the **cost** of flights to the Cape Verdes, the islands are, emphatically, worth the hassle.

The Cape Verdes were uninhabited until first colonized by the **Portuguese** in 1462. The first Portuguese immigrants, who in the sixteenth century made the islands an Atlantic victualling station and entrepôt for the trade in African produce and **slaves**, were a mixed population of landless peasants, banished malefactors, adventurers and exiles. The islands were soon being cultivated by the slaves and freed slaves who rapidly made up the bulk of the population. But while the mixed race population that emerged was considered "assimilated" – accepted as Portuguese by Lisbon – the islanders suffered in various degrees from oppressive and racist policies. In Cape Verdean society there was great emphasis on skin colour, the criterion by which "real Portugueseness" was measured.

Commercial planting was mostly of cotton, woven into the *panos* prized along the Guinea coastlands. Catastrophic **droughts** brought despair and neglect however; for nearly the whole of their colonial period the islands remained a largely ignored backwater of the Portuguese empire. Over the last 150 years, tens of thousands of Cape Verdeans have left the islands for São Tome, Guinea-Bissau, Senegal, Europe and the USA. The **New England connection** is especially strong, with *americanos* remitting the hard currency which the island families need.

FACTS AND FIGURES

The islands' **name – Cabo Verde** in Portuguese – is derived from their geographical position off Cap Vert, the Dakar peninsula of Senegal. Their total **land area**, just 4000 square kilometres, is about the same size as Kent or a little larger than Rhode Island. Less than 400,000 Cape Verdeans (under half the total) now live on the islands, with the remainder living or working abroad. In January 1991, Cape Verde was one of the first countries in the region to see democratic elections with a peaceful transition from the PAICV single party regime to the Movimento para a Democracia (MPD) led by lawyer Dr Carlos Veiga. The MPD's politics are right of centre. Cape Verde's **foreign debt** is a severe test of its resources, yet at about £100 million ($150 million) – incidentally the annual sum spent on services and amenities in Kingston-upon-Thames, England (population 150,000) – is only half its annual gross domestic product of about £200 million ($300 million).

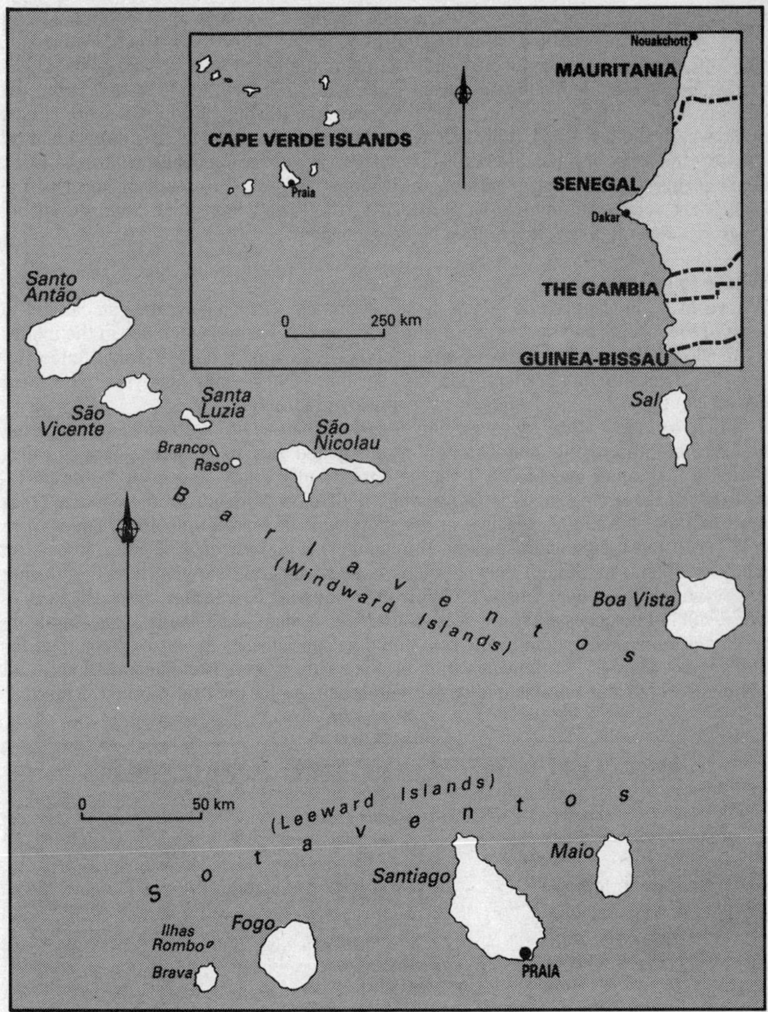

Visiting the islands

The **feel** of the Cape Verde Islands is unplaceable – not quite African, scarcely European, but Portuguese mannered and Kriolu-speaking (an African/Portuguese creole). The islands are no tropical paradise: banish any Caribbean associations. The most recent **drought**, which lasted from the early 1970s to 1985, brought malnutrition and hardships which only worsened the country's economic plight in the first decade of independence. But some good rainy seasons in recent years have seen the islands increasingly green – especially on their northern windward slopes. Several have interiors resembling anything but deserts, with towering, cloud-drenched peaks and ravines choked with vegetation. The **coasts** vary from white sands against metallic azure blue to full-tempered, Atlantic seas on black cliffs. Inland, the **roads** are for the most part steep, winding and cobbled, as if harking back to pre-motor days; **trees** are baobab, silk cotton and breadfruit, coconut and date palm; the **livestock** pigs and goats, ducks and chickens. **People** distil *grogue* from sugar cane, fish for huge tuna, and strum out laments in mournful *mornas* on the right occasions. Rip-offs and hustle seem almost unknown. In the few small, tidily colonial-style **towns**, each clustered around a central square – the *praça* – you'll find restless teenagers perched on mopeds, widows in black going to mass and potted plants on the window ledges. The towns on most of the islands are referred to simply as *povoação* – "the town". Except on Santiago island, which has several towns, there could be no confusion.

Where to go and when

Where to go in Cape Verde is a fairly simple matter – in a few weeks you can get to most of the islands and see a good deal of each one. If you've any choice in the matter try to allow for unplanned delays. Some islands – Santiago for its size, Santo Antão and Fogo for their stunning scenery, Boa Vista for its beaches – may hold you longer than others; but they're all small enough to be quickly graspable.

When to visit can be more specific. You'd want to avoid, if possible, a trip in the first five months of the year before the anticipated July to October summer rains. Between December and March it can be unpleasantly windy, especially in the northeast part of the archipelago, as *Harmattan* winds blow across from the Sahara. From April to June, the higher reaches of the mountainous islands are often blanketed in cold fog. If the rains come, splendid thunderstorms and torrents of water across the roads are the norm, though they shouldn't hinder your travels if you're visiting during this season. But the best time is probably **October and November**, when the vegetative results of a successful rainy season are truly verdant, the islands' name suddenly no longer ironic. Exceptions to the rule would be special visits to São Vicente either for the annual Mindelo *Carnaval*, a riot of Rio-style street entertainment, floats and costumes which takes over the town every February, or for the August music festival.

AVERAGE TEMPERATURES AND RAINFALL

PRAIA

	Jan	Feb	Mar	Apr	May	June	July	Aug	Sept	Oct	Nov	Dec
Temperatures °C												
Min (night)	20	19	19	20	21	22	23	23	24	23	22	20
Max (day)	27	28	29	29	30	30	30	30	31	31	30	27
Rainfall mm	2	0	0	0	0	1	8	76	102	30	10	2

Arrivals

The Cape Verde Islands are remote. Apart from the monthly ferry service from Dakar, flying to the islands is the only way of reaching them – unless you have an ocean-going yacht.

■ Flights from Africa

The only flights from the African mainland are to the capital, Praia, on Santiago island. The fifty-seater flights from **Dakar to Praia** are usually full and routinely overbooked. Operated by *Air Sénégal* (DS) and the Cape Verdean airline *TACV* (VR), they leave Dakar Mon, Wed and Thurs at noon or 1pm, and at 6pm on Sun, returning from Praia on Mon, Wed and Sat at 2pm or 3pm, and on Thurs at 8am. The cheapest official round-trip fare is CFA99,000, though you may find the *Air Sénégal* flights more expensive. Make a reservation as soon as you can and be sure to reconfirm your seat a couple of days before – or to make a strong impression in the office in Dakar. If you're not confirmed, you'll have to hustle hard at the airport on the day of the flight. Note that because of an unreliable reservations system for these flights, "confirmed" seats on a ticket purchased in Europe are no guarantee. Check again when you get to Dakar.

On Wed morning, it's possible to fly from **Bissau to Praia** on *TAGB* (YZ) at comparable prices; though you may find that Guinea-Bissau's weak currency makes it cheaper than flying out of Senegal.

Gambia Airways (CK) flies from **Banjul to Praia** every Tues and Fri am.

■ Ferries

The *Companhia Nacional de Navegação Arca Verde* runs (in theory) a **monthly ferry service** from **Dakar** to Praia. Departures are normally first Saturday of the month and fares are CFA68,000: tickets from 18 rue Rafenel, Dakar. They also run a service from **Las Palmas** in the Canary Islands. Both are often out of commission for months at a time.

There are further possibilities (though fairly remote ones) of getting a berth on board a merchant vessel out of Europe. There's at least one merchant vessel a month from **Lisbon**, **Las Palmas** and **Rotterdam** to Mindelo, on the Cape Verde Islands. If you're interested try: *Joaquim Pio & Martins Lda*, Rua da Vitoria 7–0, 1100 Lisbon (☎877181 or 877182); *Yuba de D. Juan Cardenas Guerra*, Arco 16, Las Palmas, Gran Canaria (☎243704); or *Viagens Cabo Verde B.V.*, Rochussenstraat 395, 3023 DK Rotterdam, Netherlands (☎258054).

Finally, if you're in Las Palmas, in the Canary Islands, you might check around the yachts for anyone headed to the Cape Verdes. During the east–west transatlantic crossing season, roughly from October to March, hundreds make the journey and they invariably call at the "Verdes". Even without experience, it's possible to get a berth in exchange for some basic crewing and boat chores. Expect to pay the skipper around £4–6 ($7–10) per day for your keep.

The details in these practical information pages are essentially for use on the ground in West Africa and on the Cape Verde Islands themselves: for full practical coverage on preparing for a trip, getting here from outside the region, paperwork, health, information sources and more, see Basics, pp.3–88.

Visas and Red Tape

All nationalities require visas. There are few Cape Verdean consulates and no diplomatic representation in Britain. The easiest place in Europe to get a visa is Lisbon. In West Africa the only consulate is in Senegal, at 1 rue de Denain, Dakar (☎21 18 73).

Once you've found a consulate, visas are no problem. In Dakar, you should be able to get one in a matter of hours, with three passport photos. Be sure to check when you're supposed to come back, as the rue de Denain office keeps slightly irregular hours. If you arrive on the islands without a visa, experience suggests you're unlikely to be turned away as your immediate point of departure probably had no Cape Verde consulate in any case (airlines in cities with consulates will normally ask to see your visa before issuing a ticket). If you fly in on an unusual route, or arrive by sea, you can invariably obtain a visa quickly and simply at the immigration desk.

There's a simple rule on **duty-free allowances** of alcohol and tobacco; none. The principle is not rigorously adhered to however and reasonable personal quantities are probably fine. There's rarely much of a customs check anyway.

Money and Costs

Cape Verde is not a cheap destination and if you travel widely, you'll find you can spend alarmingly fast. Cape Verde's currency is the Cape Verdean escudo (CV$) which on the islands you'll normally see written thus – 500$00 – meaning 500 escudos. Centavos account for the zeros but you're not likely to see smaller than a 50 centavo piece. The exchange rate is fairly stable, currently about CV$125 = £1, CV$83 = $1.

A *conto* is 1000 escudos. Escudos are not convertible outside Cape Verde but you should be able to buy some in Dakar. Arriving at Praia there's no bank at the airport; Sal airport has one. The *Banco Comercial do Atlântico* is the only bank and most towns – and all island capitals – have a branch. They normally take travellers' cheques in all major currencies and service is efficient. Larger hotels also accept travellers' cheques, and you don't lose much in commission. The **black market** which is said to exist isn't worth bothering yourself (or Cape Verde's balance of payments) over, in order to add ten percent to your spending power.

You won't save much by **bargaining** either; the practice is considered a little unworthy and most people prefer to stick by their starting price even if it means losing the sale. This is hard to accept at first if you've grown accustomed to a noisy exchange of mock outrage every time you buy something. But it makes life more relaxed and seems entirely appropriate in Cape Verde's almost hassle-free environment.

Credit cards don't help much on the islands. The three or four top hotels take Amex, but they're about the only establishments that will.

■ Costs

Your **outlay** will very much depend on how and how much you travel between islands. The flight network is not inexpensive (£30–£65, or $45–$100, for most of the short hops between islands) and travel costs can quickly break out of even fairly generous budgets. Ferries are cheaper but they don't offer the same flexibility. Road travel is inexpensive; but the cost of exploring those islands which don't have much public transport can soon mount up unless you have time to do a lot of walking. A basic room in a *pensão* will cost upwards of £7 ($10) and a straightforward three-course meal from about £3 ($5), with individual dishes in fancier establishments for about the same.

In three weeks, visiting half a dozen islands and keeping flights to a minimum, staying in the cheapest *pensões* and restricting yourself to one restaurant meal a day, a rough estimate of spending would be around £700 ($1050), somewhat less if you're sharing and much less if you spend any time hiking and camping. **Prices** vary considerably from island to island and of course are much lower outside the few main towns; reading through you'll get a good idea of where is most expensive. Prices tend to be lower where much food is locally produced (Santiago, Santo Antão), and higher where there are international connections or a whiff of tourism (Sal, Praia itself, São Vicente, Fogo).

Health

Arriving direct from outside Africa, you don't need any inoculations. Coming from the mainland, cholera and yellow fever certificates are routinely demanded, though you may get away without a yellow fever certificate if you're connecting straight through to São Vicente, Sal, Maio or Boa Vista.

One of the health successes of Cape Verde has been the virtual elimination of **malaria.** Until the nineteenth century a posting to the islands from Portugal was viewed as one step short of a death sentence. Now, all planes arriving from Africa get insect-sprayed before any passengers are allowed off and all visitors are issued with a health card asking them to report any fever they get on the islands. Only parts of Santiago have a malaria risk and few people use anti-malaria pills. If you're on Cape Verde for a short time only, however, and planning to return to the mainland, you shouldn't break your course.

Water from the tap is almost always good but water shortages mean that you'll sometimes be drinking water that's been stored or sold, so beware (80 people died of **cholera** in Mindelo in 1995). And be sparing too: islanders pay for tap water, which is metered, and big price increases are common during droughts. Bottled brands are widely available.

Health care on the islands isn't bad and while infant mortality is still high, life expectancy, at 63, is impressive. **Leprosy** is still a big problem on Fogo, but not one that will affect your own health. Surprisingly few people **smoke** –

though it's a habit enjoyed in pipes by elderly ladies in rural Santiago. Litter bins and enjoinments to **social responsibility** are features of urban life and Praia is a refreshingly clean capital. If, on your travels, you had the misfortune to get hepatitis, Cape Verde would be a fine place to **convalesce**. Low humidity, sea breezes and clear skies are the norm.

There are **hospitals** in Praia and Mindelo with adequate facilities for ordinary problems. Dispensaries, cottage hospitals and pharmacies (*farmacia*) in most towns or, failing these, *postos venda medicamentos*, should fulfil basic needs.

Information and Maps

Cape Verde has no tourist offices abroad and the few embassies and consulates have either nothing or the most limited leaflets. To cover every angle, contact the National Tourism Institute, INATUR, CP 292 Praia, Cape Verde (☎238/63.11.73; Fax 238/61.44.75), and ask them to send you what they have.

As for **maps** there's a good general travel sheet of the whole archipelago – which you may come across on office walls in Cape Verde. A British Admiralty naval chart based on nineteenth-century soundings (available from *Stanfords* in London; see p.42) shows quite a lot of topographical detail but is hopelessly out of date – despite twentieth-century updating – on roads and villages.

Single island sheets published in 1982 for a *Food Strategy* survey are still available in one or two bookshops in Praia and Mindelo – but stocks are mostly limited to the less interesting islands like Maio and Sal. If you can get hold of them, they're useful, particularly for hiking, as they show contours. Town plans of Praia and Mindelo are still in print, and worth obtaining.

Getting Around

The most important inter-island connections are by plane, with ferries providing a good alternative if you have more time. Except on Santiago, road transport on the islands is very limited.

■ Domestic flights

All the inhabited islands are linked by **internal flights** run by *Transportes Aereos de Cabo Verde*. Fares range from CV$4000–9000 (£32–72 or $48–108). If you're reading this before arrival in Cape Verde, you can buy a *Cabo Verde Air Pass* (must be purchased abroad in conjunction with a ticket to the islands] either of three flight coupons ($195) or, much better value, five coupons ($280).

It's important to reserve seats as far ahead as possible, as flights are usually full (though sometimes cancelled), and always to reconfirm your seat if it's been booked for more than 24 hours. It's often possible, even when there's no direct flight, to get where you want to on the same day with a little island hopping. Note however that international arrivals delayed into Sal airport can sometimes knock the whole domestic service out of joint, as planes are taken off minor routes to deal with inbound passengers. There are likely to be major changes to schedules and frequencies when the new international airport opens in Praia (scheduled for the end of 1997).

There's a helicopter service, *Cabovimo*, operating out of Praia, connecting Santiago with Fogo, Brava and Maio.

■ Ferries

Two new German-built **ferries**, *Barlavento* and *Sotavento*, run weekly schedules through the islands on a four-weekly cycle. The home port is Mindelo on São Vicente, and the itinerary is either from Mindelo to São Nicolau, Sal, Praia, Fogo and back to Mindelo or in the other direction from Mindelo to Fogo, Praia, Sal, São Nicolau and Mindelo. On this latter route, the ferries also call on alternate voyages at Brava and Boa Vista.

The voyages start in Mindelo on Mondays and terminate there on a Friday or Saturday. The big question is which itinerary is operating in any given week. If you want to plan ahead before arriving in Cape Verde, the *Companhia Nacional de Navegação Arca Verde* (CP 41 Praia; ☎31.13.49; Fax 31.35.16) are good at providing their latest details, but even they may not know which itinerary will be in force more than a month in advance.

Practicalities

Deck berths are cheap and insalubrious. Cape Verdeans are surprisingly poor sailors and the seas usually rough, leading to results which keep the crew occupied with mops and buckets. For a small supplement, there are comfortable four-berth **cabins** with basins and secure lockers. You'll find that cabin berths are often left unsold, giving you a private cabin and, in effect, a budget cruise. With a little planning you can spend the days visiting islands and nights aboard the pitching, rolling vessel. This kind of travel doesn't give you much time ashore but its great advantage is cheapness and – assuming you can handle the seas – an unexpected degree of luxury.

A few considerations: there's not much **food** for sale on board the ferries (though you can usually buy cold beers from the crew), no recommended **drinking water** (make provision) and **no showers**, so be inventive with the hand basins.

Other principal ferries

The *Porto Novo* and *Mar Azul* sail at least daily between **Mindelo** (São Vicente) and **Porto Novo** (Santo Antão). The *Furna* operates the rather impenetrable timetable shown in the box between **Praia, Porto de Vale** (Fogo) and **Furna** (Brava).

FURNA TIMETABLE

Mon	dep. Brava noon	**Thurs**	dep. Praia 9.30pm
	arr. Fogo 1pm		arr. Brava 6am
	dep. Fogo 6pm	**Fri**	dep. Brava noon
Tues	arr. Praia 2am		arr. Fogo 1pm
	dep. Praia 9.30pm		dep. Fogo 5pm
Wed	arr. Fogo 6am		arr. Brava 6pm.
	dep. Fogo 5pm		dep. Brava 8pm
	arr. Brava 6pm		
	arr. Praia 6am		

■ Buses and taxis – and hitching

Compared with getting between them, **getting around each island** is relatively straightforward: the longest land journey is less than 100km, on Santiago, and in practice most trips take under an hour.

On Santiago there's a fairly well developed **bus** network. São Vicente and Santo Antão also have buses but services are fewer. On other islands, buses usually tie in with plane and boat arrivals and are unpredictable at other times. Prices, except for local runs, are very low, around CV$2–3 per kilometre.

Minibuses called **carrinhos** (but usually known simply as "Hiace," after the popular Japanese make) are gradually replacing large buses. The minibuses operate wherever there's sufficient demand and usually carry a sign in red marked **aluguer** – "for hire". Prices tend to be fixed at fifty percent or more above the bus fare.

Particular ("private") taxis or cars are expensive, but the drivers are usually willing to bargain. For inaccessible places on the smaller islands they can be a viable option.

Hitching, when there are any vehicles, is easy and drivers *simpatico* – though habitually reckless. The lack of traffic gives some drivers a vivid sense of immortality, but the combination of tortuous bends and precipices with cobbled roads is perilous. Be confident in saying "devagar" ("slow down") if you start shaking with fear. It's normal to pay for lifts when hitching, though it won't always be expected – agree in advance.

■ Car rental – and bringing your own vehicle

The one or two local **car rental** places in Cape Verde are not very impressive, but at least they're not overpriced; the international companies haven't yet heard of the country. The only outlets are in Praia and Mindelo – unfortunately there's no motorcycle or moped rental, which would be really useful here.

It's possible of course to **bring your own bike** by ferry from Dakar, a recommended option if you have one with you on the mainland. Local ferries are used to loading and unloading motorbikes, but do check that fuel is available before crossing over to the next island – some of the less populous ones have very few vehicles and unreliable fuel supplies. Lastly, Cape Verde is wonderful **cycling** territory for the fit and fanatical and, in view of the gradients, not to mention the cobblestone roads, obviously suited to mountain bikes.

Accommodation

Putting your head down for the night is a simple business. You will usually find a Portuguese-style "pension" or *pensão* (*pensões* in the plural) offering clean, down-to-earth accommodation – often with a fan – for CV$1000–1500 for a room.

Ask to see several rooms and perhaps ask *Tem um quarto mais barato?* (which slips off the tongue and means "Do you have a cheaper room?"). Full-scale **hotels** – with hot water, private bath, air conditioning and restaurants – are restricted to Praia, Sal, Mindelo and São Filipe, with rooms starting from around CV$2500 and rising to CV$6000 or more.

ACCOMMODATION PRICE CODES

Hotel prices in this chapter are coded according to the following scales – the same scales in terms of their pound/dollar equivalents as used throughout the book. Prices refer to the rate you can expect to pay for a room with two beds. Single rooms, or single occupancy, will normally cost at least two-thirds of the twin-occupancy rate, for further details see p.51.

① **Under CV$625 (under £5/$7.50).** In practice, you will rarely find anything as cheap as this in Cape Verde, except perhaps the odd municipal resthouse.

② **CV$625–1250 (£5–10/$7.50–15).** Rudimentary lodging, perhaps with some rooms S/C.

③ **CV$1250–2500 (£10–20/$15–30).** Basic lodging, often offering S/C rooms, and breakfast included.

④ **CV$2500–3750 (£20–30/$30–45).** Decent, better than adequate hotel with S/C rooms and breakfast included.

⑤ **CV$3750–5000 (£30–40/$45–60**). Tourist/business-class establishment with good facilities.

⑥ **CV$5000–6250 (£40–50/$60–75).** Up-market, with close to international standards and facilities, including AC.

⑦ **Over CV$6250 (over £50/$75).** Luxury, cosmopolitan establishment.

It is often assumed that you'll know about the **twelve o'clock checkout rule**, sometimes applied quite ruthlessly. Hotels, especially, will try hard to make you pay an extra half or whole day if you've not vacated on time.

In smaller towns you may have to ask to locate your accommodation: tourism is still of such minor importance that everyone knows where the lodgings are, and elementary signs are often missing. This may apply particularly in the case of the local **pousada municipal** – the town resthouse – where you may need to track down the landlord for the key. Such places are usually very basic and cheap.

If you want to spend a while in one place, there should be little difficulty in arranging **private accommodation**.

Cape Verde has no youth hostels and only one camping site, at Tarrafal on Santiago. Surprisingly perhaps, truly wild country suitable for **camping** – as opposed to marginal agricultural land – isn't plentiful. Still, as an eccentric foreigner you'll be happily tolerated if you camp in the neighbourhood. You're likely, anyway, to have an opportunity to ask permission when you collect water.

Eating and Drinking

It would be surprising if Cape Verde had an extensive and flourishing cuisine: with severe malnutrition and famines that killed thousands still remembered, the question of food has tended to concentrate on the number of calories – and in respect of variety most mainland countries can do a lot better than the islands. Still, the dishes on offer are a wholesome and always filling selection, probably little changed since the sixteenth century.

Apart from the big hotels in Sal, Praia and Mindelo, and a handful of restaurants where you'll get a decent variety of unremarkable international fare as well as local dishes, the choice is always strictly limited. In smaller towns the *pensões* usually serve meals somewhere in the building, but a **casa de pasto** (dining room, diner) is the standard, and often unmarked, place to eat. You eat what they have, which as often as not will be *cachupa* (see box), the national dish, the name of which is believed to derive from the same African term that resulted in "catsup" and "ketchup".

Staples include rice, potatoes (ordinary and sweet), beans, maize, squash, pork and – inevitably – tuna. Meals always start with a solid vegetable broth and finish with fruit, occasionally *pudim* (crème caramel).

■ Drinking

When it comes to drinking, Cape Verdeans usually think first of **grog** or *canna* (sugar cane distillates known collectively with other spirits as *aguardente*), which get consumed – and apparently made at home – in large quantities. A cautious approach is recommended when trying a *copa* (glass): liquor often comes from anonymous bottles and sacking-wrapped jars and you're never quite sure what the effect will be. There are "new" (*novo*) and "old" (*velho*) varieties and different degrees of smoothness. It's usually clean, but even so can be quite deadly, gasping stuff. *"Punch"* – a concoction of dark rum, honey and lemonade – is, like *aguardente*, often on sale over the counter in rural shops. It's not an ideal midday quencher.

Beer (*cerveja*) is still largely imported from Portugal – *Sagres* and *Superbock* – but Praia has its first brewery and bottles of *Ceris* are now available in the bars and cafés. Some establishements serve draught *Ceris* – ask for a *cleps* (a glass of beer). *Ceris* also makes soft drinks. For juices ask for **sumo** – *de laranja, limão*, etc.

Wine has some potential on the islands as a significant industry, but the lethally dry, red product of Fogo's volcanic slopes doesn't inspire much enthusiasm just yet. Unreasonably expensive **imports** of Portugal's favourites can be found in most bars and groceries.

Coffee, when it's not instant, is usually terrible, either utterly tasteless or swimming with over-roasted grounds. Angola once supplied a lot, but Fogo's own more recent contribution isn't that great; often it just seems to be stale or mixed with chicory.

PORTUGUESE AND KRIOLU FOOD TERMS

Beans	*Feijões*	Jam/ marmalade	*Marmelade*	Shellfish	*Sopa*
Bread	*Pão*			Soup/broth	*Abóbora*
Bread roll	*Bolho*	Maize/corn	*Milho*	Squash	*Açúcar*
Butter	*Manteiga*	Meat	*Carne*	Sugar	*Chá*
Cheese	*Queijo* (always goat)	Milk	*Leite*	Tea	*Atum*
		Pork	*Carne de Porco*	Tuna	*Legumes*
Coffee	*Café*			Vegetables	*Agua*
Eggs	*Ovos*	Potatoes	*Batatas*	Water	*Inhames*
Fish	*Peixe*	Rice	*Arroz*	Yams	*Sal*
Food	*Comida*	Salt	*Mariscos*		

DISHES

Cachupa	A mash of beans and maize, sometimes with bacon and sausage, eaten at breakfast.	*Frango*	Chicken
		Langosta	"Lobster"; strictly crayfish
Cachupinha	Similar to *cachupa*, with green bits	*Lapas*	Tiny mussels, usually in a spicy sauce
		Licuda/linguiça	Sausage
Caldeirada de Peixe	Fish stew	*Linguado*	Sole
Carne de Vaca	Beef	*Polvo*	Octopus
Coelho	Rabbit	*Prato do Dia*	Dish of the day
Espadarte	Swordfish	*Tubarão*	Shark
Feijoada	Beans and salt pork		

TERMS

Assado	Roasted	*Frito*	Fried
Bife	Steak or cutlet, as in *Bife de Atum*	*Molho*	Sauce
		Piri piri	Hot sauce
Cozido	Boiled		

FRUIT AND SNACKS

Banana	Banana	*Melão*	Melon	*Croquetes*	Fish cakes
Goyaba	Guava	*Papaya*	Pawpaw	*Doce*	Dessert/sweet
Laranja	Orange	*Tãmaras*	Dates	*Gelado*	Ice cream
Manga	Mango	*Toranja*	Grapefruit	*Iorgurte/Yaourt*	Yoghurt
Melancia	Watermelon	*Frutapão*	Breadfruit	*Pasteles*	Pies – usually savoury

Communications – Post, Phones, Language & Media

The day-to-day language of Cape Verde is Kriolu ("Creole"), quite distinct in structure and in much of its vocabulary from Portuguese (Cape Verde's official language): the two are not mutually intelligible. Kriolu contains many elements of Fula and Mandinka and a wide range of adopted vocabulary from archaic sea-faring Portuguese and other European languages including English.

If you speak **Portuguese** – and it's one of the easiest languages to pick up, particularly if you're familiar with Spanish or Italian – you'll find you can get by easily everywhere. Even in rural areas everyone speaks some: papers, signs and radio are all in Portuguese and education is largely conducted in it. Learning Kriolu is another matter: Cape Verdeans tend to slip in and out of Kriolu and Portuguese, and Kriolu takes some time to tune into.

A BEGINNER'S GUIDE TO KRIOLU

BASICS

Hello	*Bon dia*	God go with you	*Deus ta kunpaño-lo*
How are you?	*Kuma ño sta?*	Please	*pur fabor*
I'm fine	*N sta ben*	Thank you	*brigod*
What's your name?	*Kali e bo nómi?*	Today	*oshi*
[or more formally] What is your (masc./fem.) name?	*Kal e nómi di ño/di ña?*	Tomorrow	*mañan*
		Yesterday	*ónti*
My name is Caroline	*Ña nómi é Caroline*	Before	*ántis*
Do you have/is there any...?	*Ño ten...?*	After	*dipos*
		Near	*pértu*
Goodbye	*Bon dia/te lóg*	Far	*lonzi*
See you soon/sometime	*Te lóg/te dipos di mañan*	Here	*li*
		There	*la*

TRAVELLING

I'd like some water	*N kre agu*	Is there a cheap hotel near here?	*Ten penson li pértu?*
How do I get to Tarrafal?	*Kma N pode bai pa Tarrafal?*	I'd like a room for one person/two people	*N kreba kuartu pa un psoa/dos psoa*
Is this the bus stop for Tarrafal?	*Undi e paraza di otukaru pa Tarrafal?*	Is there a toilet/ bathroom?	*Ten kasa di bañu li?*
What time does the plane leave/arrive?	*Ki óra avion ta sai/ tchga?*	What is it?	*Kuse e es?*
Where are you (masc./ fem.) going?	*Undi ño/ña ta bai?*	I don't know	*N ka sabe*
		We don't speak Kriolu	*Nu ka ta papia kriolu*
We're going to Praia	*Nu ta bai pa Praia*	Open	*abert*
How much is it?	*Kal e presu?*	Closed	*fetchod*

NUMBERS AND DAYS

1	*un*	11	*ónzi*	21	*vinti y un*	200	*duzéntus*		
2	*dos*	12	*dozi*	30	*trinta*	500	*kiñéntus*		
3	*tres*	13	*trezi*	40	*korenta*	1000	*mil*		
4	*kuatu*	14	*katorzi*	50	*sinkuenta*	Monday	*segunda-feira* (2ªF)		
5	*sinku*	15	*kinzi*	60	*sasenta*	Tuesday	*terça-feira* (3ªF)		
6	*sais*	16	*dizasais*	70	*satenta*	Wednesday	*quarta-feira* (4ªF)		
7	*séti*	17	*dizaséti*	80	*oitenta*	Thursday	*quinta-feira* (5ªF)		
8	*oitu*	18	*dizóitu*	90	*novénta*	Friday	*sexta-feira* (6ªF)		
9	*nóvi*	19	*dizanóvi*	100	*sén*	Saturday	*sábado* (S)		
10	*dés*	20	*vinti*	101	*sén-t y un*	Sunday	*domingo* (D)		

A GLOSSARY OF CAPE VERDEAN TERMS

Americano Cape Verdean living in America
Badiu peasant from rural Santiago descended, according to tradition, from runaway slaves
Bairro suburb, outskirts of town
Branco white – or wealthy – person
Camâra town hall
Cidade city, town
Conto one thousand escudos
Criança child
Crise drought, community crisis
EMPA *Empresa Publica do Abastecimento*, the public provisions company, like a nationalized wholesale grocers
Festa feast, festival, party
Funco round, stone, thatched house
Grog, Grogo, Grogue sugar-cane firewater, *aguardente*
Igreja church
Lenço traditional headscarf worn differently by women of each island
Liceu secondary school
Morabeza kindness, gentleness, considered to be a peculiarly Cape Verdean quality
Morna the heavy-hearted music of the islands, sweet-sounding, nostalgic and very characteristic
MPD Movement for Democracy
PAICV African Party for the Independence of Cape Verde
Pano cloth, *pagne*
Paragem bus stop
Pelourinho pillory, the slave auction post
Povoação "town", the local town
Praça square, *place*
Praia beach
Quinta estate, owned by a landlord; rare today
Quintal courtyard of a house
Ribeira stream, river or rivercourse
Seca drought
Vila town

While a little Portuguese goes a long way, if you don't have any you'll be falling back on **French** and **English**, neither of which is spoken very widely outside the main towns. In most places, though, you'll run into younger people who've learned them at school as well as returnee emigrants from Europe, Senegal or the USA who speak them fluently.

The media

Radio and TV are important in Cape Verdean culture, and while you're not likely to see much of the latter (an eclectic mix of Brazilian soap operas and right-on documentaries broadcasting for a few hours each day), *Radio Nacional de Cabo Verde* is a good FM station, with an insidiously catchy signature tune and an enlightened play list. There's also a government-run *Voz de São Vicente*. The BBC World Service is hard to get hold of in mid-Atlantic and signals wander.

The **press** consists of several party and economic sheets, plus the two-year-old *Novo Jornal Cabo Verde*, published three times a week, which has by far the biggest circulation. Portuguese is easier to read than to speak; just as well, as foreign papers are virtually unobtainable.

Post and phones

Both post and telephones in Cape Verde are run by the **CTT**, or simply *Correio*, now privatized as two companies – *Correios de Cabo Verde* and *Telecomunicações de Cabo Verde*. There's at least one CTT on each island, open Monday to Friday 8am to noon and 2.30 to 5.30pm, and sometimes Saturday and even Sunday mornings. **Post**, both outgoing and incoming, is generally efficient and honest though not especially swift. For poste restante have your mail marked "Lista da Correios".

If you have **urgent mail** for home to post from one of the more isolated islands try taking it to the local airstrip for the next flight to Sal, or even ask them at the local *TACV* office if someone could give it to the pilot: people are usually understanding.

Telephoning locally isn't likely to crop up much during your stay: until recently there were two phone booths in Mindelo, three in Praia, and just one telephone on São Nicolau. **Phoning abroad**, the IDD automatic system is now available to most countries. You dial ☎0 then the country code. Phone cards are available from certain shops, bars and restaurants in values of CV$1000 and CV$2000 and you use the cardphone booths usually located conveniently nearby. Off-peak

Cape Verde's IDD code is ☎238.

rates (8pm to 7am and all weekend) are CV$240 per minute to France and the Netherlands and CV$340 elsewhere in Europe and to North America. The international operator is on ☎111. You can't normally make reverse charges/collect calls. For AT&T dial ☎112.

Entertainment

There's little in the way of an organized leisure industry – less than a handful of cinemas in Praia and Mindelo and no theatre to speak of. Bull-fighting didn't travel from Portugal. The game of *orzil* or *oril* (the hole and pebble mindbender common all over Africa in different versions, see p.63) is popular everywhere, as is draughts or chequers.

The commonest entertainments are homespun – births, baptisms, confirmations, marriages and funerals providing occasions for gathering together. In the evenings it's quite the thing for young people to meet in the town square (*praça*) with a guitar or two.

■ Music

There are a number of nightclubs (*boites*), and a clutch of them are regular venues for **live music** (*musica ao vivo*). The best-known Cape Verdean forms are guitar and fiddle songs – the **morna**, a mournful lament reminiscent of Portuguese *fado*, and the more upbeat and very danceable **coladeira**, music with a wonderful muscular rhythm. Many songs are love songs – addressed to the islands – and powerfully sentimental. **Cesaria Evora**, who has released a number of superb CDs, is the foremost musical emissary of the isles, now based in Paris.

In the past, in smaller towns and rural areas, you might have heard someone playing the *cimbó* or the *berimbau*, old **one-stringed instruments** of African origin producing plangent, ancient sounds – either with a bow on the *cimbó*, or plucked and resonating in a sound box, or the mouth, with a *berimbau*. Both have virtually fallen into the realm of folklore, though in parts of Santiago you might still be lucky.

Directory

AIRPORT DEPARTURE TAX CV$2000 on international departures.

CONTRACEPTIVES You can get condoms (*preservativas* or, more colourfully, *camisas de vênus*) from most pharmacies and *postos venda medicamentos*.

EMERGENCIES These are fortunately rare in Cape Verde. If you can find a phone you can call the police on ☎132. Medical emergencies require a hospital: ☎130.

OPENING HOURS Most shops and businesses are open from about 8am to noon and again from 3 to 7 or 8pm. Lunch hours are long and lazy and *everything* closes, even – curiously and frustratingly – many bars and cafés.

PHOTOGRAPHY doesn't usually pose any problems. There are very few subjects which would get you in trouble and most people are uninterested where you choose to point your camera. When taking pictures of Cape Verdeans, ordinary courtesy is your only restraint: you'll rarely be asked for payment.

PLACE NAMES AND RIVALRIES On the islands, Cape Verde is called Cabo Verde – or Cáu Berde in Kriolu – the people Cauberdianos. It's not uncommon on Santiago, however, to hear people referring to "Cabo Verde" when they mean Santiago, as if it was the mainland, while referring somewhat dismissively to the other Cape Verdes as "as Ilhas" – the islands. There's a good deal of **rivalry** between the islands, with competition between the people of the Barlaventos – who see themselves as more urbane and metropolitan – and the Sotaventos where, in Santiago particularly, a larger proportion of the population are descended from slaves. There are subtle cultural variations from island to island too, with differences in the local form of Kriolu. Look out too, as you travel, for the characteristic women's headscarf style – tied differently on each island.

Many towns and villages are called Ribeira something, which just means River – understandable where fresh water is so important. Tarrafal is another common name. Every island seems to have its Tarrafal – which makes it useful to know which one's being referred to.

PUBLIC HOLIDAYS Cape Verde follows the main **Christian holidays** with some exotic addi tions (Dec 8, Immaculate Conception; Jan 1, Circumcision of Our Lord; Aug 15, Assumption; Nov 1, All Saints' Day) plus Jan 20, National Heroes' Day; May 1, Labour Day; July 5, Independence Day. There's a whole host of other days off – including any number of saints' days and a major **Carnaval** every February in Mindelo, emulated in the same month by Praia.

In addition, annual festivals take place on many islands, with horse and mule races, discos, bands and more than the usual grog consumption. They generally last about a week, and include:

Boa Vista: June 24
Brava: June 24
Fogo: April 20
Maio: early May
Sal: Sept 15
Santo Antão: early June
São Vicente: May 3, June 13 and August (music festival)

RELIGION Mostly Catholic, although American Protestant churches have made some headway since independence. There's probably quite a lot to be learned about the process of Islam's arrival and spread in West Africa from the fact that it's completely unknown in the Cape Verdes. It's likely that Islam hadn't made much impression in the African peasant communities from which slaves were commonly taken between the fifteenth and eighteenth centuries.

TAMPONS Usually available from larger general stores, but not on the smaller islands or outside the main towns.

TROUBLE It's hard to imagine getting into any in Cape Verde. Cape Verde is a tolerant country and etiquette has grown out of the combination of Latin manners and Wolof, Fula and Mandinka social convention that you'd expect. Drug use, in the close-knit island communities, carries a strong stigma and doesn't go unnoticed. While quite a few youngish men smoke home-grown weed, you could expect a barrel-load of trouble if seen by the wrong people. Nudity and topless bathing are pretty well out of the question and particularly ill-advised for unaccompanied women. You're just as unlikely to be a victim of trouble. While theft is not unknown, the islands are one of the safest places in the world for absent-minded travellers. Even long-term expatriates agree on this, which must say something – though they tend to single out Praia as an exception.

WATERSPORTS There's some good **snorkelling** in places and exciting **diving** in a number of wreck-strewn shallows, notably off Boa Vista and Sal. Cape Verde's **windsurfing** is some of the ocean's most challenging. The big centre (though not, in fact, big at all) is Santa Maria on Sal island – details there. Addresses are also given in the Praia "Listings".

WILDLIFE Cape Verde's native fauna is a meagre show, with no large mammals and few outstanding birds. Herpetologists are excited by *Tarentola giganta* (the giant gecko) and the Cape Verde Island skink (another relative giant) but disappointed at the total absence of snakes. Birdwatchers might want to go out of their way to spot the Razo Island lark but it's fairly uninteresting for non-specialists. The seas are more rewarding, with good chances of seeing dolphins, whales, turtles and amazing flying fish.

WOMEN TRAVELLERS AND THE WOMEN'S MOVEMENT Women travellers will find the Cape Verde Islands relaxed after mainland West Africa. While **sexual attitudes** do contain an element of machismo, it's normally expressed as nothing much stronger than winks, whistles, stares and strong expectations that you *will* dance. It can also come across as almostly absurdly innocent: heavy sexual pestering is unusual. Younger women, travelling without men, may find that their "unmarried condition" gives them almost adolescent social status, which can be frustrating. But, with the possible exception of Praia, the towns are too small for problems to last long.

As for the lives of **Cape Verdean women**, little seems to have changed despite the government's on-paper commitments to reducing sex discrimination and promoting their rights and welfare. Yet there are good reasons why change is needed: the continued emigration involves mostly men, and there are now 108 women for every 100 men, leaving many rural women *de facto* household heads. The *Organização das Mulheres de Cabo Verde* (Rua Unidade Guiné-Cabo Verde, Praia; ☎61.24.55) is quite active and the main contact-making body; otherwise, it's quite difficult for women visitors to meet Cape Verdean women.

A Brief History of the Cape Verde Islands

The Cape Verde Islands blew out of the Atlantic in a series of volcanic eruptions during the Miocene period some 60 million years ago – though Maio, Sal and Boa Vista may be a geological extension of the African mainland. The islands were uninhabited (so far as is known) until 1462, making the country unique in West Africa. In the gloriously clumsy eloquence of Adriano Moreira, Portugal's Overseas Minister from 1961–2, the Cape Verdes were "islands asleep since the eve of time, waiting to be able to be Portugal". After five centuries of such paternalism, the turn of recent events has been remarkably peaceful.

■ Discovery and colonization

Although African sailors may have visited the islands in earlier centuries, it was a Genoese navigator, **Antonio da Noli**, working for Prince Henry of Portugal, who discovered and first documented Santiago (which he called São Tiago – St James) and four other islands, some 500km off Africa's Cap Vert, in 1455. Three more in the northwest (Santo Antão, São Nicolau and São Vicente) were reached by Diogo Afonso in 1461. Santiago, by far the biggest prize, was split between the two navigators, who were granted a captaincy each: da Noli set himself up at **Ribeira Grande** in the south and Afonso made his headquarters in the northwest. Slaves were brought from the African mainland to work the parcels of land allotted the handful of immigrants and in the capital, Ribeira Grande, work began on a cathedral. The Portuguese crown viewed the new extension of empire – 2500km from Lisbon – with indifference; but the archipelago could serve as a stepping stone to exotic riches, and it would certainly do as a penal colony.

Fogo was settled in the 1480s and its western region was singled out as one of the most likely productive areas on the islands – rolling, partly wooded country, with substantial rainfall in most years. But Fogo islanders were forbidden to trade with foreign ships – a right reserved by Santiago – and the island was considered a hardship post for the Portuguese officials sent there. By the end of the sixteenth century its population had barely reached 2000 and there were appeals to Lisbon for more settlers – petitions which were met with the arrival of convicts and political undesirables (*degredados*) from Portugal and the internal banishment, from nearby Santiago, of certain offenders.

The tiny volcanic pimple of **Brava** attracted its first colonists in the early 1540s. They kept much to themselves: climatically the island was one of the easiest to survive on, yet it was very remote. It was only when large numbers of families escaped here from Fogo in 1680, after volcanic eruptions and an earthquake, that Brava became heavily populated. It has had the densest population of the islands ever since.

The big island of the far northwest, **Santo Antão**, got its first inhabitants in 1548 but its large size, with remote and rugged interior valleys and craters, and its distance from the main shipping lanes, kept it very isolated and little known for at least 200 years. Among its settlers were Jewish families fleeing the Inquisition and subsequent European persecutions. The village of Sinagoga is a reminder.

São Nicolau offered fewer opportunities to adventurous migrants and only its northwest valleys – even these with uncertain rainfall – made colonization viable in the middle of the sixteenth century. The town of Ribeira Brava became an important literary and ecclesiastical centre and was the seat of the Cape Verdean bishopric from the end of the eighteenth century until the beginning of the twentieth.

São Vicente, one of the driest islands, was virtually uninhabited until the start of the nineteenth century when the sheltered bay at Porto Grande (the best harbour in the islands) was chosen as the site of a British coal bunkering station for steamships on the Brazil and East Indies runs.

The "flat islands", **Boa Vista**, **Maio** and **Sal**, were also late in being fully colonized. Maio and Boa Vista had small numbers of herders and poor farmers, most of them freed or escaped slaves, and Maio eventually became the virtual private fiefdom of a freed slave family, the Evoras.

An early plan, conceived by Genoese merchant adventurers, was to create on Santiago a major **sugar** industry, following its success in Madeira. With the conquest and colonization of tropical lands, Europe could begin to grow the crop for itself instead of relying on expensive imports. But

THE CAPE VERDEAN SLAVE TRADE

As the New World opened across the Atlantic in the sixteenth century, the **trade in slaves** gathered momentum and the islands – now important stepping stones to Brazil and the Caribbean – became an emporium for their trans-shipment and taxation.

Although they were more expensive, slaves at **Ribeira Grande** (the main entrepôt) were better value than those bought directly on the Guinea coast: they tended to be healthier, as the sick had already perished; they spoke some Portuguese and some had even been baptized (the Portuguese were keen on finding religious justifications for their slave-trading, safeguarding the captives from purgatory). And for the slave ships, buying at Ribeira Grande was a much safer option than sailing directly into the creeks of Guinea to barter for slaves.

Roughly between 1600 and 1760 (the peak years) anything from a few dozen to several thousand slaves were sold annually through Ribeira Grande, most of them exported to the Spanish West Indies and Colombia. Large numbers were shipped off in years of bad drought on Santiago, when planters would sell their **farm slaves** to traders when they couldn't afford to feed them. This was prohibited in law: the only slaves supposed to be exported from Cape Verde were those just imported from the coast under licence.

From the earliest years of the colony, Lisbon had passed a succession of **trade laws**, ruling that the resale of slaves and foreign trade partnerships were illegal. In 1497 the sale of iron to Africans was banned, and between 1512 and 1519 further crushing edicts – equally unenforceable – were issued: outlawing the much-in-demand Indian and Dutch cloth from the islands; banning the commissioning of *lançado* adventurers to trade on the mainland; and ruling that all legally contracted slave ships bound for the Americas should first detour to Lisbon because Ribeira Grande could not be trusted to extract duty honestly.

The people involved as **trading partners** in the complex mesh of buying, selling and bartering were a mix of European merchant adventurers (sometimes merely pirates) and various mixed race labourers and entrepreneurs (see below) as well as bona fide licensed contractors waving charters from Lisbon or Madrid. But the trading networks rarely operated in a free market. For most of the time, Portugal tried to ensure that as many profits and tariffs as possible accrued to the crown, even if that meant making ordinary trade illegal and relegating much business to the status of **smuggling** – from which the crown received nothing.

Successive **governors** of the islands, who generally viewed their postings with misgivings if not actual horror, succumbed to the inevitability of **corruption** (if they survived malaria and other diseases long enough to care). Some succumbed too enthusiastically for the likes of the islands' clergy, aldermen, court and treasury officials – whose own commercial interests they threatened – but most governors managed to amass reasonable wealth while leaving space for smaller operators to do business.

The banes of Lisbon – the **lançados** – eventually became totally estranged from Portugal and even at times from Santiago. Once fully acculturated in Guinea, and unable to return to Portugal (on pain of death), they had no need to worry about the rules, as the contract holders were obliged to, and could trade with the Dutch, English and French boats which sailed around the Atlantic in growing numbers. In this way they kept a good selection of merchandise for purchasing slaves and other African goods, while contract holders were obliged to buy the limited range of goods for resale and barter offered by the state supply monopoly.

LANÇADOS, TANGOMAUS, GRUMETES AND LADINOS

A number of distinctly defined groupings were involved in the slave trade:

- **Tangomaus** (dragomans); cosmopolitan Africans who traded in the Guinea interior and did much of the initial negotiating for slaves but who were familiar with Portuguese ways.
- **Lançados** ("sent outs"); originally white or part-white Cape Verdeans who had familiarized themselves with African ways on the mainland and had settled in African communities to trade and transport goods along the coast. They eventually became indistinguishable from *tangomaus*.
- **Grumetes**; African or mixed race deckhands and carriers working for the traders.
- **Ladinos**; slaves or other Africans who could speak Portuguese or Kriolu.

the Cape Verdean climate proved unsuitably dry and, although the **rum** which normally came as a by-product of sugar production was found to be useful for **slave trading** along the Guinea coast, the sugar farms at Ribeira Grande never really took off and by the late sixteenth century were already eclipsed by the vast quantities being produced in Brazil.

Instead, the Cape Verde Islands found themselves in the middle of a growing network of **trade routes** – between Europe and India, between West Africa and the Spanish American colonies and between Portugal and Brazil. They took on the function of **victualling stations** for the trading vessels, supplying fresh water, fruit, salted and dried meat, and carrying on a trade of their own in commercial goods – salt, hides, cotton *pagnes* and slaves.

■ 1640–1775: cloth and the crown monopolies

With the **break-up of the union between Portugal and Spain** in 1640 business went into the doldrums for a number of years. Several governors were denounced to Lisbon after they monopolized what trade there was or even started applying the rule of law in order to confiscate and penalize foreign trading ships for their own gain. The islands were at a severe disadvantage because international demand for slaves had saturated the Guinea coastlands with **iron bars**, the principal currency, causing huge increases in the price of slaves. Portugal, which produced very little iron and forbade its export, was unable to compete.

Cotton, though, had become Cape Verde's main commercial crop, grown especially on the estates of Fogo. Slave women spun it; men wove it into strip cloth, dyed it with cultivated indigo and native *orchilla*, and sewed the strips together into *pagnes*. Some of the material found its way to Brazil but most was traded – generally for more slaves – on the Guinea coast. Throughout the sixteenth and seventeenth century and for much of the eighteenth – until slave trading began to be threatened by abolitionists – Cape Verdean cotton **panos**, in a multiplicity of inventive designs, were the prized dress material of the West African coast, traded as far east as Accra and as valuable as iron bars in many districts. The value of Cape Verde cloth became so universal in the region that it was also the usual currency of the archipelago: administrative officials were commonly paid with it and accumulated vast hordes of the stuff, a soft currency which only had real value locally, not in Portugal.

In the **second half of the seventeenth century**, after the split with Spain, the private contracts system fell out of use. Portugal's African territory and trade routes were seriously depleted and for some years only the most recklessly optimistic merchants had been willing to purchase the expensive rights on slaving in those parts. With wily Cape Verdeans stealing the trade from under their noses and the price of slaves going up all the time it was difficult to make contracts pay.

Instead, in 1675 the first of the **Crown Monopolies** – the **Companhia de Cacheu** – was set up, reserving for itself sole rights to trade in foreign goods with the coast and outlawing (again) the trans-shipment of slaves through Santiago. Cape Verdeans were only allowed to export their own produce. Bitter feelings were aroused in Santiago. When a new company, **The Company of the Islands of Cape Verde and Guinea**, was formed, and bought a fat contract to supply 4000 slaves a year to the Spanish West Indies, the governor of the islands was placed on the company payroll. His salary was doubled and he was expressly forbidden from engaging in any commercial activities. With their governor now effectively playing for the opposition, the islanders were more disguntled than usual. And true to form, the new company did nothing for their prosperity, stockpiling goods to inflate prices, undersupplying vital commodities and levying high freight charges for their meagre exports.

With the **War of the Spanish Succession** (1701–13), which Portugal was pulled into against Spain and France, the company's valuable slaving contract was lost and in 1712 Ribeira Grande itself was comprehensively sacked and plundered by a French force. The **cathedral**, a century and a half in the building, had only been completed nineteen years earlier. About this time, serious attention began to be given to creating a new and better fortified capital at Praia. Ribeira Grande was in steep decline from the middle of the eighteenth century and **Praia** was eventually dedicated as the seat of island government in 1774.

The first half of the eighteenth century had witnessed a great **relaxation of trade embar-**

goes. But Lisbon's persistent and neurotic attempts to prevent the trans-shipment of slaves and the sale to non-Portuguese of Cape Verdean cloth (which in the economic climate amounted to much the same thing) mystified foreign traders, especially English and Americans, who broke the laws without compunction. Apart from its triumphant (but peaking) textiles industry, the archipelago was in a state of **economic ruin** and the population too poor and too isolated to worry much about Lisbon's laws even if some did carry the death penalty.

With the foundation in 1757 of the **Companhia de Grão Para e Marnahão**, which had the sole purpose of providing slave labour to the states of the new Brazilian empire, a twenty-year era of unparalleled cruelty and hardship began for the islands. The **annexation of political control** which had begun with the last company was taken to its logical conclusion, so that the Company now effectively *owned* the islands; while in Lisbon, a clique of English gentlemen maintained discreet but weighty capital interest in its enterprises.

Apart from the utter destitution which the enforced **bypassing of trade** brought to the archipelago, a severe **drought** struck from 1772 to 1775. By this point in the islands' history the population had grown too big to be able to survive such disasters on whatever came to hand – as they had during the famine of 1689 in Santiago when they ate horses and dogs. In the face of **starvation** throughout the islands, the Company was implacable – it held back food supplies, pushed up prices and milked the islanders of every last resource. In return for food, hundreds were abducted abroad and forced into slavery by English and French traders. Smuggling, of course, had never been so essential nor so profitable. The famine left an estimated 22,000 dead – out of a total population of less than 60,000.

■ Into the nineteenth century: famine and emigration

By the time the rains returned in 1777, the Company's charter had expired and it went into merciful liquidation. At the beginning of the **nineteenth century** the Cape Verdes faced a quite different future. The harsh Company regime had battered the textile industry with enforced low prices while drought had extinguished the cotton crop as well as many of the field slaves and textile workers. The emergence of the newly independent **USA** as a major economic power began to be more important than the distant historical links which tied the islands to Portugal. Lisbon, in any case, was too distracted by Napoleonic strife at home, and tail-and-dog upsets with Brazil about who ruled who, to be much concerned with the insignificant islands and their irrepressible flouting of trade laws. Moreover Angola and Mozambique held far more promise.

New England whalers began calling at the Cape Verdes from the end of the eighteenth century, to take on supplies and crew and to do a little trading. Goatskins were a profitable sideline back in the States and, once the practice had become established, the Americans arrived each year with holds full of merchandise. Brava, Fogo and São Vicente were the main islands of contact and from these a steady trickle of impoverished Cape Verdeans escaped to New England through the closing decades of the nineteenth century.

Slavery in the nineteenth century was contained by the British and (ironically) by the American presence. While the trade in slaves from the Guinea coast was forbidden from 1815, slaves were still sold, by weight, well into the 1840s. Only with the end of the American Civil War and with pressure from Britain (to whom Portugal owed a debt going back to the Napoleonic era) was an abolition process set up on the islands. Slaves were not formally emancipated until 1869 and then they had to work for their ex-owners as indentured labourers for a further ten years.

Drought and the Cape Verdean diaspora

A series of disastrous **famines** hit the islands during the nineteenth century. In the first of these, from 1830–33, an estimated 30,000 people died. No relief of any kind came from Lisbon, but America, on this and several other occasions, sent large consignments of relief aid, though towards the end of the century it was generally wealthy emigré Cape Verdeans who organized it.

While the dispossessed of the Sotaventos moved to Praia or tried to emigrate, the poor of the Barlaventos headed to the new "city" of **Porto Grande** (Mindelo) on São Vicente to find work at the British-run **coaling station** or in the shops, bars and bordellos.

At the peak of its importance at the end of the nineteenth century the port of Mindelo was

CAPE VERDEAN SOCIETY TO 1950: THE POTENTIAL FOR REVOLT

The **slave estates** had varied in size from small landholdings run on paternalistic lines, where landlord and slave led similar lives, to extensive plantations (especially on Santiago) where wealth differences were extreme. The traditional *morgadio* system of land tenure, in which inheritance was strictly by **primogeniture** (inheritance by the eldest son), produced a growing population of landless aristocrats and tenant farmers on marginal land. Under the system, land could not be bought or sold. The **estate slaves** were often tied closely to the landlord's family, occasionally by blood. Over the centuries, intermarriage blurred the distinction between slaves and share-cropping peasants, the only practical difference being that the share-croppers were always in debt to the landlords, a life in many ways as arduous as slavery. Freedom for slaves – an act of "charity" periodically undertaken by some landlords, or else an economic necessity when food supplies were exhausted in a famine – was no release from the cycle. If they ran into debt as share-croppers, freed slaves lived on the sufferance of the landlord.

This, together with the fact that the islands are too small to offer much refuge, meant that **slave rebellions** were rare and provoked only by the most savage treatment. Among the landed families there were real fears, principally because they themselves were divided (the *morgadio* system created bitter feuds) and sometimes engaged in fierce vendettas with their rivals. At one time many slaves were armed by their masters and gangs of pistol-toting slaves are known to have clashed on occasions, even in Praia. There was a certain insecurity about what might happen if the arms were turned against the elite. In the Santiago interior there was a large underclass of freed and escaped slaves, the **badius**, partly independent of the estates. And on Santiago relations were less paternalistic and the estates often owned by absentee landlords. A group of slaves did organize a stand against their particularly oppressive landlord in 1822 and there was anaborted general **slave revolt** in Santiago in 1835 (given passive encouragement by the administration's ragged armed forces). But that was about the extent of resistance, and it was largely brought about by anticipation in the run-up to the abolition of slavery.

As for **political resistance** which might eventually culminate in an independence movement, there isn't a great deal of early evidence for that either. Conditions on the estates in the **twentieth century** became worse. With the old *morgadio* system discredited and abandoned, and the landlords themselves in debt to the *National Overseas Bank*, much of the land was bought up by a new class of absentee landlords, often returned United States emigrants. Coaling labourers mounted **strikes** for increased pay at Mindelo in 1910 and again in 1911, but they were defeated.

Opportunities for **dissent** on the islands in the fascist **"New State"** of Portugal's prime minister Salazar (1932–68) were limited to the private publication and distribution, among a small intellectual circle, of poetry and subtly nationalistic Kriolu **literature**. Organized demonstrations of opposition were impossible, and even further ruled out by the chronic plight of the islands during the famine years of World War II and the labour migrations of the early Fifties. Debtor peasants were treated as criminals and could claim nothing from the state until their debts had been repaid. **Political dissidents** found themselves imprisoned in the notorious detention centre at Tarrafal, alongside victims ejected from Portugal, and interrogated by the Gestapo-modelled **PIDE** political police.

To make the possibility of grass roots resistance even less likely, Cape Verde has an **alcoholism** problem going back to the earliest years of the sugar industry. Never viable as a major export, cane was still grown in vast quantities for distilling *grogue*, on land that could otherwise have provided food crops. The national addiction to *grogue* was such that in the drought years of the 1960s sugar was imported to satisfy demand.

servicing over 1300 ships every year – and tens of thousands of sailors. The latter industry had a far-reaching effect on the culture of the islands, introducing even more of a racial mixture and enriching Kriolu with words like *ariope* (hurry up), *fulope* (full up) and *troba* (trouble).

Meanwhile, Portugal's first efforts at "humanitarian relief" took place during the drought of 1863–5 (another 30,000 death toll). It seemed an ideal time to profit from the availability of labour eager for food by engaging the people in civil engineering projects. The islands' first **cobbled roads** date from this famine, when peasants were rounded up to work for starvation wages. A more sinister method of dealing with famine was **enforced migration** to the "Cacao Islands" of São Tomé and Principe. For a number of reasons, the abolition of slavery in São Tomé and Principe led to serious labour shortages. In the Cape Verdes the shortages were of land. Offered apparently huge bonuses by the recruiting agencies when (and if) they returned, thousands of poverty-stricken Cape Verdeans were persuaded to "go south" over the next ninety years to a system of equatorial plantation labour that was little better than ordinary chattel slavery. Like the monopoly companies of a century before, Portugal's **cocoa industry** found drought on the Cape Verdes was easily turned to its advantage.

Right from the first use of this system, measures were taken to limit the number of Cape Verdeans emigrating to a life of relative security in the USA: a heavy departure tax was imposed, beyond the means of those who desperately needed to go, and travel permits and passports were made almost impossible to obtain. Nevertheless, the trickle of emigrants to New England became a flood between 1910 and 1930 when an estimated 34,000 people left the islands. This mass exodus was to become enormously significant after World War II when the emigrants were able to send back substantial **remittances** to the islands and after independence when the economy became largely dependent on them. The USA however began to make literacy a condition for emigration from 1913 and after 1922 the door to new immigrants was progressively closed.

Drought in the twentieth century has continued to be the single most important factor shaping the lives of Cape Verdeans. Only following the drought of 1959–61 were genuinely compassionate measures taken to alleviate the suffering and these seem likely to have been initiated mostly by international outrage at the colonial labour migration policies. Earlier, there were four big *crises*: 1902–4 (15,000 dead), 1920–22 (17,000), 1940–43 (25,000) and 1947–48 (21,000 lives lost). The drought of the Second World War was probably the worst catastrophe in Cape Verde's history. Brava and Fogo suffered appallingly when they had to cope with a surge of re-emigrants returning from the American depression, because the "rainy" years of the Thirties had lulled islanders into a false sense of security. And during the war years remittances from American relatives dried up completely. Older people of Furna and São Filipe remember walking into town and finding corpses fallen at the roadside.

When the last major wave of **emigration** took place as a result of these famines, the authorities were ruthless in their efforts to prevent flight to the USA. As a result, sixty percent of applicants ended up in São Tomé and Angola. There was a small number, however, who emigrated to **Guinea-Bissau**, not out of destitution, but with ambitions. Since the opening of *liceus* (the colleges of São Nicolau in 1866 and São Vicente in 1917), about two-thirds of mainland Portuguese Guinea's teachers and civil servants were Cape Verdeans. It was principally from their ranks that organized **agitation and resistance** to Portuguese rule first germinated.

■ Organized resistance and the Portuguese revolution

In response to what they described as a "wall of silence" around the islands, a group of mostly Cape Verdean intellectuals led by **Amilcar Cabral** – and including Luiz Cabral and **Aristides Pereira** – met secretly in Bissau in 1956 to form the **PAIGC** (*Partido Africana da Independencia da Guine e Cabo Verde*). When peaceful representations to the colonial government were met with indifference and more repression (culminating in the massacre of striking dockers in Bissau – see p.436), the PAIGC began planning for a **guerrilla war on the mainland**, with the declared aim of liberating both Guinea-Bissau and Cape Verde. After four years of preparation and fairly continuous efforts to negotiate a peaceful alternative, war began in 1963. The Cape Verdes became a massive Portuguese military base, swarming with Portuguese troops drafted to the front in Guinea-Bissau – and in Angola and Mozambique, where wars of independence had also begun.

On the Cape Verdes themselves, the question of a violent uprising was purely academic. The small, barren and isolated islands are unpromising ground for guerilla warfare. Yet the island government and police force (with help from the military and the PIDE) were acutely sensitive to the possibility of open revolt: every subversive indication was examined and squashed, and activists sent to Tarrafal or worse places in Angola. On Santiago, a *badiu* religious cult movement, known as the **rebelados**, was labelled communist for criticizing the corrupt, state-run Catholic church, advocating the hands-together system of community help (the *juntamão*) and resisting outside interference, especially the anti-malaria campaign, which tried to spray members' homes. The movement virtually deified Amilcar Cabral. Its leaders were brutally interrogated and deported to other islands. But their threat was no more politically coordinated or potentially subversive than that posed by the **Nazarene church**, whose American-led, puritan-inspired clergy were also subject to repression for their denunciations of the Salazarist church. Cultural opposition was the only kind available and cultural repression the inevitable response. **Kriolu**, unintelligible to ordinary Portuguese-speakers, was considered subversive in itself and its use banned from state property.

Thousands of **women** emigrated in the early 1970s to find work as domestics in Portugal, France and Italy. But the sex ratio on the islands remained unbalanced, with women far outnumbering men.

On the mainland, **the war** was drawn-out but successful. Only the **assassination of Amilcar Cabral** at his headquarters in Conakry on January 20, 1973 (partly inspired by jealousy of the Cape Verdean role in Guinea-Bissau's revolution) deflected it from a well-planned and predictable course. In September 1973, with most of the the territory controlled by the PAIGC, the party proclaimed *de facto* independence. Portugal withdrew from Bissau the following year after the MFA's (Armed Forces Movement) **overthrow of the dictatorship** in Lisbon on April 25, 1974.

On the islands, the pre-coup government continued in office, even after the MFA had swept away the basis of their power. But the tide was coming in fast. In less than a week, the clandestine fragments of Cape Verde's own PAIGC cells had coalesced, and a **public meeting** was held in Praia on May 1. The Tarrafal detainees were released and the PAIGC took its message around the islands, agitating semi-legally for the independence that was almost at hand. The "wall of silence" had caved in. There were other parties, hatched and nurtured by the administration, which tried to promote the idea of some kind of "shared independence" between the islands and Portugal. They were maintained by small groups of wealthy activists and had supporters in Senegal, who mistrusted the aims of the PAIGC. None of them convinced many islanders.

Lisbon sent a new governor in August 1974, charged with asserting Portuguese **continuity** in Cape Verde. He was shouted out of Praia and back to Lisbon within a month. Another arrived with a heavier hand. His troops shot into a demonstration in Mindelo in September. But with Guinea-Bissau already independent, the **demonstrations** only grew larger. By October, with "continuity" sounding increasingly hollow, the Portuguese were negotiating with PAIGC leaders. In December, a meeting in Lisbon agreed on a transitional government consisting of three PAIGC members and two from the MFA. The Portuguese capitulated by allowing a general election the following June. With a landslide of votes, **Aristides Pereira** took office on **July 5, 1975** as president of the new republic.

■ Independence and the split with Guinea-Bissau

Cape Verde and Guinea-Bissau were united by a common colonial experience. The war which began in Bissau culminated in the **liberation** of all Portugal's colonies and the emergence of democracy in Portugal itself. Amilcar Cabral had been obsessive about the importance of **Cape Verde–Guinea unity** and Aristides Pereira continued to emphasize it. But the most significant political event in the first twenty years of Cape Verdean independence has been the 1980 **coup** in Bissau which overthrew **President Luiz Cabral**, Amilcar's half brother, and led to the formal separation of the two countries.

After the liberation war there was a lingering unease within the PAIGC in Guinea-Bissau. Luiz Cabral, though a close friend of party leader Aristides Pereira, was not a statesman of the same rank, and he became an increasingly isolated figure, mistrustful of his own ministers and – it seemed to them – unwilling to discuss economic and social questions outside a clique in which Pereira figured too prominently. Suspicions grew that policy in Guinea-Bissau was being constructed by the two presidents in secret and that Cape Verde, which had achieved independence relatively painlessly – though at the cost of Guinean lives – was seeking to dominate the union. Furthermore, while Cape Verdeans had been instrumental in starting the independence movement, they had also formed a large proportion of the colonial civil service in Guinea-Bissau, most of whom had passively collaborated with the Portuguese. The charge of **neo-colonialism** didn't have to be made explicit.

Against Pereira's advice, Cabral modified the Guinea-Bissauan constitution to give himself more power and his nationalistic prime minister, **Nino Vieira**, less. It was Vieira who subsequently led the coup of November 14, 1980, putting himself in the Bissau presidency. Pereira, in condemning the coup, pointed out that the party constitution provided the means for dealing with factional problems. On January 20, 1981 (the eighth anniversary of the assassination of Amilcar Cabral) the Cape Verdean arm of the party renamed itself the **PAICV** and, at a summit in Maputo in 1982, a formal division of the two countries' assets ratified the split. A vague ideological union of the two countries still exists, but rapprochement has tended to come from the Cape Verdean corner.

One immediate effect of the events of 1980 was the fright it gave to **international aid donors** and partners. Since the early 1960s, support for the independence struggles against Portugal in the international community had been broad-based and confident. The high-profile style and actions of the PAIGC leadership were applauded and, after independence, both countries quickly came to rely on aid to rebuild their wrecked economies. After the 1980 coup, Pereira moved fast to allay fears about the region, successfully pursuing a diplomatic course to maintain international support not just for the islands, but for Guinea-Bissau – efforts which showed surprising good grace under the circumstances.

■ The PAICV era

After 1981, with the union of the two countries a fast fading dream, Cape Verde at least had a chance to address purely **national problems**. The question of the very habitability of the islands was raised, but the **economy** was made viable, a result of careful and sensitive development and a remarkable absence of corruption.

The PAICV govenment answered OAU demands that it apply the **sanctions policy on South Africa** and refuse refuelling rights to *South African Airways* with the response that it could not afford to commit suicide by solidarity. It also increased the level of **aid** coming into the country and used it on local projects of direct utility. Non-governmental aid, channelled through the *National Development Fund*, matched foreign interests to Cape Verdean requirements. By leaving the door open for *americanos* to return, it encourged **private investment** and maintained a high level of goodwill amongst the vast majority of the Cape Verdean diaspora whose remittances continued to be the number one economic pillar.

Agrarian reform was patient, seeking to avoid alienating landlords, to persuade and cajole them rather than to force change and always to avoid damaging the country's overseas image of independence and openness. The worst effects of **drought** and flash floods were combated with tree-planting programmes on all the islands, and further measures like dyke building and better terracing.

Health was a priority for the PAICV government, which reckoned to spend three times as much per person as the average developing country. Mother and Child Protection and Family Planning programmes had a high profile, and were operated by the PAICV at a community level, with theatre shows and public demonstrations organized to mobilize people on the issues – including breast feeding, contraception and nutrition. The off-loading of unwanted First World drugs, so common in underdeveloped countries, was avoided by setting up a national pharmaceuticals industry.

One hundred percent **adult literacy** as well as free and compulsory **primary education** are goals that the PAICV pretty well achieved (though adult literacy rates tend to improve naturally with the demise of illiterate senior citizens).

Even under one-party rule, the **legal system** in Cape Verde was one of the most progressive in Africa. There were no political prisoners – indeed there are still few of any kind – and there is no death sentence. The country has an almost spotless record on **human rights**: since independence there has been only one seriously violent incident involving the military when a soldier accompanying the Agrarian Reform Commission lost his nerve in a noisy crowd on Santo Antão and opened fire, killing a man in the ensuing panic.

Respect abroad for the development of the Cape Verdean republic found a new dimension with the country's hosting of multilateral talks on Angola. Cape Verde's location and relative insignificance look likely to encourage this role as provider of neutral territory for delicate meetings.

Despite the successes, there remained several lurking problems which would not fade away. **Alcoholism**, especially in the rural areas, has been an ongoing problem for centuries. At root a strictly male issue, it is triply destructive where it not only wastes productive land on sugar cane but hard earnings as well, and reduces the workforce.

A more pointed issue in the late 1980s was the battle between church and state over the issue of **abortion** on demand which the PAICV supported. Although 80 percent of children are brought up in mother-only families, the position of **women** in Cape Verdean society has never had as much attention focused on it as the male-formulated charter of the Organization of Cape Verdean Women – OMCV – would suggest. The division of views was by no means straightforward: there were OMCV members among those taking part in the anti-abortion campaign. Violent anti-abortion demonstrations were led by church activists and the Catholic journal *Terra Nova* was, as a result of its anti-government stance on the issue, labelled an "opposition newspaper" by the foreign press.

Good **rainy seasons** in the late 1980s broke a drought that had persisted on some islands virtually throughout the years of independence. But the PAICV was not equipped to ride out the inevitable wave of rising expectations that came with better harvests and the end of the Cold War. It never properly examined its own renewal mechanisms, thus allowing the ex-guerillas of the party to grow old and stagnant together.

■ All change: the democratic era

At the PAICV party congress in 1988, there were discussions led by younger members about ending its status as the country's sole political party. The new **Movimento para a Democracia** (MPD) held its first meeting in June 1990 and demands were made for sweeping reforms to Cape Verde's "revolutionary" constitution and the established political culture in which the PAICV held such sway.

Under a tide of mounting pressure, especially from the church, the prime minister Pedro Pires took over as PAICV party secretary from Aristides Pereira (who saw himself as state president, outside politics), in preparation for the introduction of a multi-party system.

In Portuguese-speaking Africa's first ever multi-party legislative elections, held in January 1991, lawyer **Carlos Veiga**'s MPD swept to power, taking more than two-thirds of National Assembly seats. They had the support of the US emigrés' biggest party, the **UCID**, formerly the party of the opposition in exile (long-term emigrés, however, were prevented at the last minute from voting). Carlos Veiga was subseqently elected prime minister – though not without opposition from within his own ranks – and former supreme court judge **António Mascarenhas** won the presidential election, soundly defeating ex-president Pereira. The MPD also won most of the seats in local council elections held later in the year, with PAICV wins only on the home islands of PAICV dignitaries. The loss of support for the veterans of the liberation struggle indicated the large proportion of the population too young to remember it.

Economically, the MPD government has put great efforts into making the country investor-friendly, with emphases on its tourism and fishing potential. The scrapping of the PAICV's last major initiative, the agrarian reform laws, was a popular move at home, and was judged to have signalled the right messages to overseas investors. The civil service payroll was reduced by half and investigations carried out on embezzlement of state funds by former PAICV officials.

But despite the peaceful and widely approved transition to multi-party politics, there remains widespread **dissatisfaction** with the lack of progress and economic improvement on the islands. The MPD has been repeatedly torn by splits, resignations and defections. One ex-MPD official has formed a new party, the **Partido da Convergência Democrática**, which intends to fight the MPD head on at the 1996 elections.

The first half of the 1990s saw a return to extreme **drought** conditions, resulting in a shortfall of 85 percent of the country's food requirements and the need for emergency food aid, principally paid for by the European Community. Assuming the occasional good rainy season, prospects for the future look reasonably healthy, but they depend on the MPD keeping its house in order and maintaining a stable environment for indigenous development and foreign investment.

THE SOTAVENTOS

Santiago, **Fogo**, **Brava** and **Maio** make up the **Sotaventos**, the leeward group of islands, with two-thirds of the population, more of the rainfall (which arrives from the south) and a good deal of the wealth.

If you're coming from Dakar, your first port of call on the islands will be **Praia** on Santiago island, Cape Verde's capital and the nation's largest town. It's a pleasant enough place but there are no gripping reasons to spend time here: if you're stuck for a few days, your time is better spent enjoying one of the easy and satisfying short **trips out of town**. The rest of Santiago offers more enticing attractions in the mountainous **central region** and the beaches in the northwest. But although it has a sizeable mountainous interior, Santiago's scenery doesn't compare with that of the Barlavento islands of São Nicolau and, outstandingly, Santo Antão.

Fogo island is a vast, dormant volcano, nearly 3000m high, whose last eruption was in 1951. There's a magnificent road tracking along the lava-covered eastern slopes, fine walking country in the gentler western parts, and a formidable hike into the old crater itself, now a domain of citrus orchards and farm plots.

The smallest of the inhabited islands is **Brava**. Cape Verdeans often rate it the most beautiful island and, with the 1992 opening of the airport and twice-weekly flights from Praia, it's no longer hard to visit. Brava is certainly the most cultivated island, with a relatively benign climate – and it's long been a sanctuary for those families who could afford to flee the droughts on other islands.

Maio, one of the *ilhas rasas* or "flat islands", is duller and drier. Locally famous for its cattle, which provide the country's limited milk supply, other attempts to drum up interest seem a little desperate. As one Portuguese brochure of 1970 put it: "The desolation of its landscape contrasts with the warm welcome of its people and the fine flavour of its fresh lobsters". So there you have it.

Santiago

With half the cultivable land and half the population, **SANTIAGO** is the **agricultural backbone** of Cape Verde. And, unusual among the islands, it takes a few hours to get from one end to the other, switchbacking through the mountains or along the jagged eastern coast. Santiago's main focus is the capital, **Praia**, at the southern tip. From here one main road snakes through the interior, sending secondary roads like suckers down to the coast; another forks off it to the northeast to link up the east coast fishing villages before meeting with the main route again at **Tarrafal** in the northwest – site of the best beaches. There are dozens of hamlets and villages scattered across the island, and any number of hidden coves and *ribeiras*. We've covered a few travel possibilities below, but Santiago, in common with all the islands, is little known outside the archipelago. Most of your discoveries will be very much your own.

Praia and around

The best way to arrive at **PRAIA** – and by far the most likely – is by plane. Clean air, bright sunlight and wind are constant reminders of the Atlantic: a couple of windmills rotating on the brown hills across the *ribeira*, the extraordinary tranquillity of the little town on its small proud plateau, everything about Cape Verde, you can see, is going to be quite different. Cape Verdeans – and foreign residents too – tend to complain that Praia is soulless, thinks of nothing but money and has no *joie de vivre*. If you're already tuned to Cape Verde's gentle sensibilities this may be relatively true (though it's certainly livelier than a few years back). But after Dakar it all comes as a welcome drop in tension and the nicest possible culture shock.

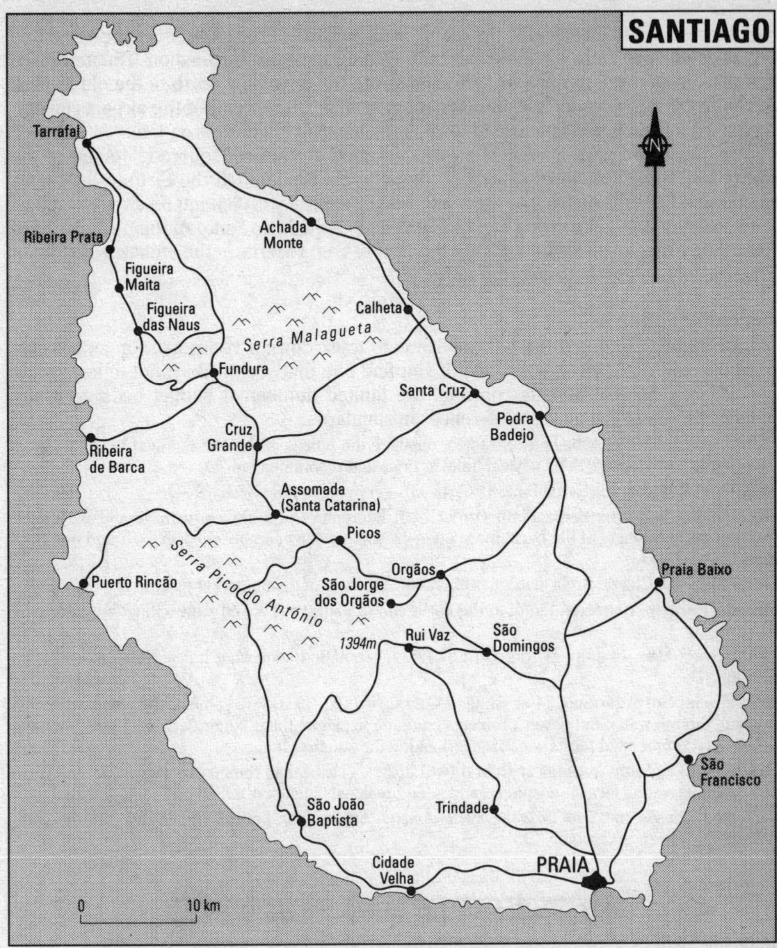

The village of Ribeira Grande (Cidade Velha), west of Praia, was the first settlement on the islands and remained the effective administrative centre until early in the eighteenth century. Praia then took over the role of capital, growing from village to town through the nineteenth century.

Arrival and orientation

Arrival, by sea or air, and orientation – on foot – couldn't be simpler. **Gago Coutinho airport** at Praia is small and has basic facilities – a small terminal building with a bar and toilets. You walk from the arrivals room to the front door and out onto the forecourt. Below is the manageable muddle of the capital, five minutes away by taxi (about CV$200). Arriving from Senegal, you may find it hard to persuade a taxi driver to accept CFA francs, but – you can't change money (of any currency) at the airport – dollars, deutschmarks or French francs would almost certainly be acceptable. Most people head for one of the more modest *pensões*, but unless you're loaded down with luggage you might just ask for the main *praça* in Platô – Praça Alberquerque – and hop out when you get there – it's cheaper than naming a specific destination. The new international airport, due to open in 1997, is close to the town, just north of the old airport. **Arriving by sea** you dock at the pier roughly beneath the end of the airport runway. Again, it's a five-minute taxi ride to town, or a couple of kilometres on foot.

The downtown part of Praia is all concentrated on the half square kilometre of the **Platô**, a neat grid of streets, simplicity itself to get around. Off the Platô to the northwest is the Fazenda district; to the southwest is Várzea, with the impressive new ministries building, the Palácio do Governo; beyond is Achada do Santo António (Achada Sto António); while further south, facing the islet of Santa-Maria, is the embassy district of Prainha, location of the *Hotel Praia-Mar*.

Accommodation

If your budget is limited the best advice is to track down a **room** as soon as possible from one of Praia's few *pensões* and, if you find one that seems okay, not to keep looking. When planes and boats come in, the limited number of budget beds go pretty quickly and there are no vast differences in standards.

Hotel Americano, in Achada Sto António, opposite the offices of the EC and next to the *Galerias* supermarket (☎61.13.20). The newest hotel in Praia and recommended. ⑥.

Residêncial Anjos, rua Serpa Pinto (☎61.42.95). Very presentable B&B. ③–④.

Hotel Felicidade, rua Serpa Pinto (☎61.21.22). Everyone's first choice, with verandah'd street-front rooms and others at the back, more often vacant and considerably cheaper. S/C and non S/C. Room only. ③–④.

Hotel Marisol, Chã de Areia district (☎61.34.60). The best of the upmarket places. ⑥.

Pensão Paraiso, rua Serpa Pinto, at the north end of Platô (☎61.35.39). Unexciting, but adequate. ②.

Hotel Praia-Mar, Prainha district (☎61.37.77). A reputation somewhat inflated by its beachfront position. ⑦.

Residêncial Sol Atlantico, 24 av Amílcar Cabral (☎61.28.72). Offers some of the cheapest rooms in Platô, though water and power problems continue to plague them. Room 1, despite being hot and noisy, is recommended for its window overlooking the square. ③.

Residêncial Solmar, av Amílcar Cabral (☎61.36.39). Pricier than the nearby *Felicidade*, but clean and spacious, with a local atmosphere, and good breakfasts included. ④.

Unnamed Pensão, next to *Casa de Pasto Amelia*, av Amílcar Cabral. Clean and friendly, with remarkably cheap S/C rooms. ②.

ACCOMMODATION PRICE CODES

① Under CV$625 (under £5/$7.50) ② CV$625–1250 (£5–10/$7.50–15)

③ CV$1250–2500 (£10–20/$15–30) ④ CV$2500–3750 (£20–30/$30–45)

⑤ CV$3750–5000 (£30–40/$45–60) ⑥ CV$5000–b6250 (£40–50/$60–75)

⑦ Over CV$6250 (over £50/$75)

For further details turn to "Accommodation" in the Practical Information at the beginning of this chapter.

Around town

It takes about twenty minutes to realize that Praia has almost nothing to offer in terms of sights or entertainment. Not that this is an alarming revelation – this is a capital where just being here is enjoyable: the streets are friendly; the *praça* has benches and a bandstand where visiting naval bands sometimes play on Sundays; and there are good views from the edge of the Platô, particularly from a couple of *pensões* on the western side.

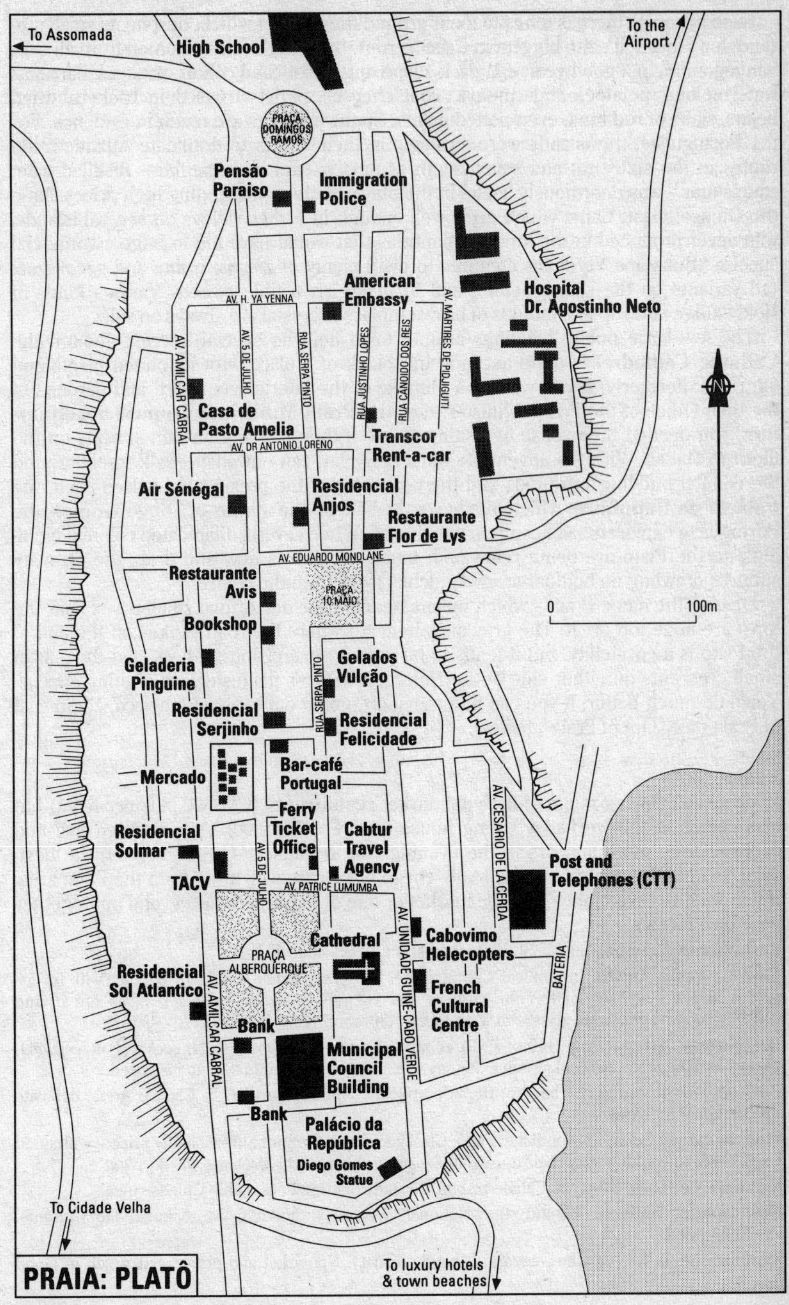
To Assomada
High School
To the Airport
PRAÇA DOMINGOS RAMOS
Pensão Paraiso
Immigration Police
American Embassy
Hospital Dr. Agostinho Neto
AV. H. YA YENNA
AV. 5 DE JULHO
RUA SERPA PINTO
RUA JUSTINHO LOPES
RUA CANDIDO DOS REIS
AV. MARTIRES DE PIDJIGUITI
AV. AMILCAR CABRAL
Casa de Pasto Amelia
AV. DR ANTONIO LORENO
Transcor Rent-a-car
Air Sénégal
Residencial Anjos
Restaurante Flor de Lys
AV. EDUARDO MONDLANE
Restaurante Avis
PRAÇA 10 MAIO
0
100m
Bookshop
Geladeria Pinguine
Gelados Vulção
Residencial Serjinho
RUA SERPA PINTO
Residencial Felicidade
Bar-café Portugal
Mercado
AV. CESARIO DE LA CERDA
Ferry Ticket Office
Cabtur Travel Agency
Residencial Solmar
TACV
AV. 5 DE JULHO
Post and Telephones (CTT)
AV. PATRICE LUMUMBA
AV. UNIDADE GUINE-CABO VERDE
Cathedral
Cabovimo Helecopters
PRAÇA ALBERQUERQUE
BATERIA
Residencial Sol Atlantico
French Cultural Centre
Bank
Municipal Council Building
AV. AMILCAR CABRAL
Bank
Palácio da República
Diego Gomes Statue
To Cidade Velha
To luxury hotels & town beaches
PRAIA: PLATÔ

Such action as there is tends to focus around the **market** which, despite its small size (and don't forget it's the biggest in Cape Verde), brings in country women from all over Santiago and, in a good year, can pack surprising variety and colour; papayas, bananas, watermelons, potatoes and cassava, goat cheeses, piglets trussed in baskets, dried beans, slabs of red tuna, even potted palms. **Sugar** products are much in evidence. For the Portuguese, the islands were strategic in their efforts to dominate Atlantic trade routes in the sixteenth and seventeenth centuries: rum in particular – distilled from cane sugar – was enormously useful in the **slave trade**, commanding high prices along the Guinea coast. Cane, which grew well enough in lusher valleys on several islands, was never produced in the kind of quantities that would have led to huge commercial success. But Cape Verdeans continue to distil plenty of *grogue*, *canna* and *aguardente* (all variants on the same theme), and to make irresistible sweets. Various kinds of sickly fudge and cup-like moulds of brown molasses crystal are always on sale.

The few large public buildings around town hold no special interest, though the **Catholic Cathedral** is quite an imposing block of a place with its potted plants and figurines. Formerly, if you wanted a glimpse of the interior courtyard and gardens of the then Office of the Prime Minister, now the **Praia Municipal Council headquarters**, you needed the excuse of visiting to see if they had any unwanted seats on the flight to Dakar. With the advent of democracy, you can nowadays walk freely around the council building's grounds and the perimeter of the presidential palace itself, the **Palácio da República**, which overlooks the beach. The **statue of Diogo Gomes**, the Portuguese explorer, has been reinstated here. While several dilapidated colonial buildings on the Platô are being renovated, much of Praia is new and drab, the scrawny suburbs crawling up boulder-strewn gulches away from the centre.

Despite the name Praia – which means **beach** – the one or two small coves near the town are none too great. The grey strip beneath where the road snakes off the end of the Platô is a possibility, but it tends to be used by exercising soldiers, and the pair of small crescents on either side of the *Hotel Praia-Mar*'s peninsula are nothing special. You'll do much better, if you can find transport, going out to São Francisco, 13km east of Praia (see "Out of Praia", below).

Restaurants

Praia has a growing range of fairly upmarket **restaurants** (CV$800 plus per head) but less choice at the workaday eating house end (CV$100–200). A basic fried fish and *cachupa* shop often appears in the evenings on av Amílcar Cabral, serving the best-value food in the centre, but the really cheap places are well away from the Platô area. If you want to save money, use the market or one of the supermarkets and put together your own picnics.

Restaurante A Bolha, Achada Sto António district. Good-value dishes.

Casa de Pasto Amelia, av Amílcar Cabral, Platô. Long established and justly popular with townspeople and a scattering of foreign workers and volunteers for its solid set meals for around CV$200–300 and generous glasses of wine (open 7.30–8am, 12.30–2pm and 7.30–9pm).

Restaurante Avis, av 5 de Julho, Platô. A favourite for breakfast – eggs, *cachupa*, *marmelada*, papaya and the rest – particularly on a Sunday when other restaurants tend to be closed.

Barbecue-Grill, round the back of the "Complexo Gymnodesportivo" in Chã de Areia, opposite *Alucar*. Good for carnivores.

Flor de Lys, av Eduardo Mondlane, Platô. Classy for Praia, but not unreasonably priced, with good Cape Verdean cooking – try their mussel-like *lapas* and very tasty *Molho de São Nicolau*.

Restaurante Hong Kong, av Cidade Lisboa, Fazenda district. Reasonable Chinese meals.

Restaurante Italiana, behind the National Assembly building in Achada Sto António. Recommended.

Restaurante Jade, rua Che-Guevara, Fazenda district. Upmarket and pricey, but worth it. Good fish.

Hotel Marisol, Chã de Areia district. Has a deserved reputation – order the rabbit if they have it – but it's expensive (around CV$2000 for two) and not exactly overflowing with character.

Restaurante Panda, Prainha district, near the *Hotel Praia-Mar*. Chinese food.

Restaurante Panorama, rua Serpa Pinto, on the *Hotel Felicidade* rooftop, Platô. Though its rooftop position is perhaps the main attraction, this does passable food, and also runs a couple of excellent caravan snack bars – in the main *praça* and down by the *Hotel Marisol*.

Restaurante O Paris, av Cidade Lisboa, Fazenda district. New and recommended.

Geladeria Pinguine, av Amílcar Cabral, Platô. Some of the best ice cream in Praia.

Restaurante Poeta, Achada Sto António. Bland establishment, but rather a good sea view.

Bar-Cafe Portugal, off the market square on av 5 de Julho, Platô. Basic eating house with one or two dishes.

Cantinha de São Tomé, Terra Branca district. A good barbecue-grill.

Restaurante Só Comer, Achada Sto António, near the *Galerias* supermarket. Probably the best restaurant in Praia, serving Cape Verdean and international food, and not markedly pricier than others.

Gelados Vulcão, rua Serpa Pinto, Platô. A good place to start the day, with excellent homemade yoghurt, drinkable coffee, cakes and sandwiches, and of course ice cream.

Nightlife

Evening is when the town is at its most delightfully unhurried. Plenty of people – whole families it seems – spend an entire evening lounging in the *praça*, playing with their children or strolling past the few shops, all of which stay open (the café-bar here is open until 10.30pm). Recent years have seen a flurry of new **nightclubs**, often hosting live music at weekends. The main club scene is around the Prainha district to the south of the town centre: none have opened in the restrictive streets of the Platô, though there are a number of friendly **bars** here. The offering at the **cinema** is rarely very interesting.

CLUBS

O Atlântico, overlooking Quebra Canela from the ridge of Achada Sto António. Part open-air, with nifty straw conical roof. CV$300.

Discoteca Dallas, Pensamento district, on the road out towards Trindade. A broad mix of music, highly recommended.

Dí Nôs, Achada Sto António. Partly open-air and one of the best clubs in town. Os Tubrarões ("The Sharks") often play here. CV$500.

Clube Nautica, Chã de Areia, by the beach.

Discoteca Prisma, rua Cápela, Achada Sto António. An indoors club, unpretentious. CV$300.

Quebra Coco, at the *Hotel Praia-Mar*. Hotel club, but not bad for that.

Complexe A Teia, rua Che-Guevara, Fazenda district. Grand and flashy: you'll need to dress up a bit. CV$500.

Clube 21 ("Clube Vinte e um"), Quebra Canela district. Open-air complex on the sea front, with centre stage set amid swimming pools. CV$500.

Zéro Horas, Achada Grande, between the port and the airport. Probably the most cosmopolitan musical mix of any of Praia's big clubs. CV$500.

BARS

Bar O Aquário, rua Serpa Pinto, opposite the *Residêncial Anjos*, Platô. Nautical-style pub/bar, with an aquarium, open lunch and evenings.

Casa do Pasto Amelia, av Amílcar Cabral, Platô. You'll usually find a good atmosphere here if you're simply into knocking back a few *copas*.

Flor de Lys, av Eduardo Mondlane, Platô. Like the *Amelia*, a popular local hangout.

Casa Inês, on the "embassy road" in Prainha, between the hotels *Praia-Mar* and *Marisol*. Trendy, cosmopolitan café bar, popular with young emigrés.

Hotel Marisol, Chã de Areia district. Attractive outdoor bar.

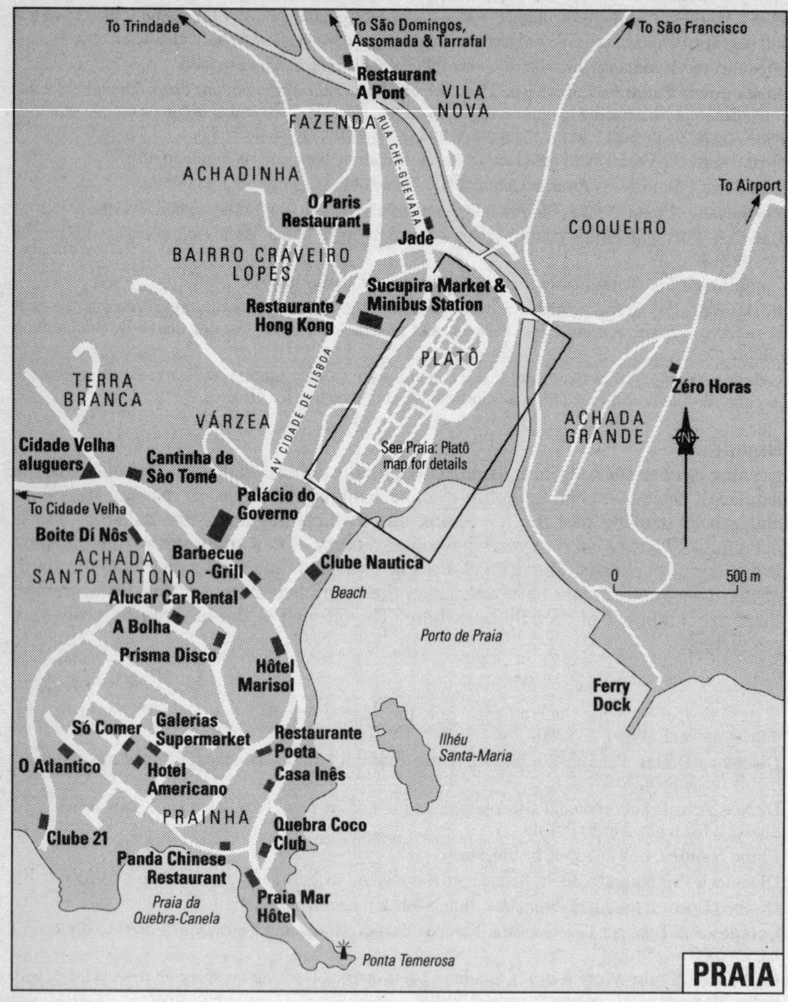

Restaurante Poeta, Achada Sto António. A better place to drink than eat. Pleasant bar.

Cantina do São Tomé, Terra Branca district. A Latin bar atmosphere, lively until the early hours.

Unnamed bar, opposite the post office, av Cesário de la Cerda, Platô. Local bands sometimes play downstairs. Recommended.

Listings

Airline offices *TACV*, av Amílcar Cabral (☎61.32.15 or 61.33.89; Mon–Fri 8am–noon & 2.30–6pm, Sat 8–11.30am). The *Air Sénégal* office is open irregular hours and is closed while the Dakar plane is on the tarmac and the staff are at the airport hustling seats.

Airport information There's no official airport information service – the *TACV* office in town knows as much as anyone.

Bank The *Banco Comercial do Atlântico* is open Mon–Fri, 8am–2.30pm.

Bookshop The best – nearly the only one – is the *Instituto Caboverdiano do Livro*, av 5 de Julho (Mon–Fri 8.30am–noon & 3.30–6pm, Sat am only), which often carries whatever maps are available.

Buses Private Hiace minibuses run from a depot next to the main "Sucupira" market west of the Platô. Cidade Velha *aluguers* go from a parking area in Terra Branca, southwest of the Platô.

Car rental *Alucar* (☎61.58.01), in Chã d'Areia, south of the Platô, offers newish Toyota Corollas for CV$3000/day. *Transcor Rent-a-Car* (☎61.18.53), on av Justino Lopes, on the Platô, have cars for around CV$2500/day. A cash deposit of CV$10,000 is required.

Embassies and visas Brazil, Cuba, China, Russia, Portugal, France, Germany and the USA are the only countries with embassies in Cape Verde. Britain's honorary consul is in Mindelo. The long-established American embassy, rua Hoj ya Yenna (☎61.43.63), is generally helpful to Anglophone travellers. The Senegalese embassy is next door (☎61.56.21). The French embassy in Prainha has a visa service for a number of Francophone states including Burkina, Côte d'Ivoire and Togo. You may get a Guinea-Bissau visa with the help of the Cape Verdean Ministry of Foreign Affairs, Praça 10 de Maio.

Emergencies Police ☎132; medical ☎130.

Ferries The ferry ticket office, the *Agencia Nacional de Viagens*, in rua Serpa Pinto, has all the details and even some slightly cryptic timetables. There's also a shipping office at the top of av 5 de Julho, *Companhia Nacional de Navegação Arca Verde* (CP 41 Praia; ☎31.13.49; Fax 31.35.16).

Film You have the choice of an unnamed shop next to the *mini-mercado* at the junction of rua 5 de Julho and Praça Alberquerque on the Platô, or *Sodifoto*, rua Serpa Pinto, opposite the *Residêncial Anjos*.

French cultural centre, av Unidade Guiné-Cabo Verde. Does the things which all *Centres Culturel Français* do, offering a French library, videos and news broadcasts and French cultural programmes.

Helicopters *Cabovimo*, in av Unidade Guiné-Cabo Verde on the Platô, and at Prédio Atlantic Trading, 2º Dto, Largo da Assembleia Nacional, Achada Sto António (☎61.21.47; Fax 61.21.49), has operated an air-ambulance service for several years, but at the time of writing was planning to set up scheduled inter-island flights once again.

Hospital If you need treatment the Agostinho Neto Hospital is adequately equipped and able to perform tests for malaria, amoebas and so on. It's worth trying to see a medically qualified person via one of the embassies first.

Immigration If you need to extend your visa, visit the police station on rua Serpa Pinto near the high school at the north end of the Platô.

Pharmacy *Farmácia Africana*, 36/8 av Amílcar Cabral, Platô, is one of the best stocked. Other reasonable pharmacies include *Central* on rua Justino Lopes, Platô, and *Higiene*, av Amílcar Cabral on the *praça*.

Post Office (Correio) Mon–Fri 8am–noon & 2.30–5.30pm.

Supermarkets The new *Galerias* in Achada Sto António is the biggest department store in Cape Verde, with a good selection. The *Supermercado do Hotel Felicidade* and the *Minimercado Carlos Veiga* in Prainha are useful standbys.

Taxis They often don't have change, so it's worth being prepared. Prices are more or less fixed.

Telephones The telephone office is open Mon–Fri 8am–noon & 3–5.30pm, Sat 9–11am. Phonecard calls in the new booths are cheapest between 8pm and 7am.

Tourist offices and travel agents Try *Cabtur* (☎61.55.51; Fax ☎61.37.54), 4 rua Serpa Pinto, or *Orbitur* (CP 161; ☎61.27.40), corner of av Amílcar Cabral and rua Eduardo Mondlane. For sub-aqua information, check out *Dive Cape Verde* (CP 294; ☎61.26.63).

INTER-ISLAND FLIGHTS FROM PRAIA

Boa Vista: 2 flights weekly, 45min.
Brava: 2 flights weekly, 45min.
Fogo (Mosteiros): 1–2 flights daily (not Sun).
Maio: 5 flights weekly, 20min.
Sal: 1–5 flights daily, 50min.
Santo Antão (Ponta do Sol): Thursday, 80min.

TACV in Praia ☎61.58.20

Out of Praia – Southern Santiago

All the following trips from Praia are feasible within a day, or even half a day if necessary. The São Francisco area has been earmarked as a tourism development zone and, with the opening of Praia's international airport scheduled for late 1997, is likely to change substantially. Cidade Velha is less likely to alter much in the near future, while developments in the Assomada district are more likely to be to do with agriculture and forestry than tourism.

São Francisco beaches

Although there are a couple of half-decent beaches near the *Praia-Mar Hotel*, the string of coves at **SÃO FRANCISCO**, about 13km from Praia, is worth the effort required to get there, to escape the odd bit of pollution and occasional hassles at the town beaches. There's no public transport, so, unless you have your own transport, head in the direction of the airport, turn left just over the bridge, walk through the *bairro* and try hitching. This is most likely to be successful on a Saturday or Sunday morning. Take food and drink; there's nothing at the beach. The track from Praia scrapes across the island's southern corner, steep and rocky, and tips you out onto a flat sandy plain by the sea. There are several **beaches** to choose from. The first you reach on the track is the biggest, dotted with palms and a couple of villas built further back, but the furthest to the south is the best, with steps for the arthritic ex-President Pereira to climb down for his swims. There's clean sand, good waves and ten thousand kilometres of South Atlantic to gaze across.

Cidade Velha

Heading out of town for 10km in the opposite direction brings you to the old capital – **Ribeira Grande** – now known simply as **CIDADE VELHA**, "Old City". *Aluguers* leave regularly from the parking area southwest of the Platô.

Cidade Velha is just about Cape Verde's only ancient site and in truth, while the landscape around is magnificent, the ruins aren't wildly interesting. After the dry moors on the way from Praia, you round the last bend and the village is down below. The **setting** is everything – a living, moving sea, awash with foam, thundering against the black crags.

Ribeira Grande was the site of the **first Portuguese base** in Africa, founded to create a slave-trading entrepôt, selling labour to the Spanish West Indies. The most notable building today is the **Cathedral**, finished in 1693, a century and a half after the foundation of the diocese. For a few years Ribeira Grande reached a peak of prestige, until its eventual defeat by a French force in 1712 led to a rethink on the part of the Portuguese and the more considered development of the new capital of Praia. The cathedral at Ribeira Grande was already falling apart by 1735 and, when a new bishop was appointed in 1754, he quickly left Santiago and spent the rest of his life on Santo Antão.

Nowadays Cidade Velha is badly neglected, a village of fishing people and farmers living among the ruins of sixteenth- and seventeenth-century Portugal. As the Praia town plan points out in its notes: "Birthplace of our nationality, one can find valuable patrimonial witnesses still in ruins, thus deserving restoration, good keeping and consolidation". Deserving or not, it seems that in sad reality what Drake started will be finished off within twenty years if nothing is done to prevent further collapse: pigs and goats forage amid the fallen masonry of the cathedral and you're quite free to wander with them between the massive, roofless walls. Fortunately a team of UNESCO archaeologists and restorers are currently working on the ruins at Cidade Velha and a museum is planned.

RIBEIRA GRANDE – SOME HISTORY

A relatively good anchorage – there was nothing safer in Madeira or the Azores – **Ribeira Grande** rapidly became the main mid-Atlantic victualling point for European merchant vessels in the sixteenth century. The *ribeira* almost never dried up and was dammed at its mouth to provide a permanent pool of **fresh water**. The town became a "city" in 1533 when a papal bull made it the seat of a diocese extending along half the West African coast.

In Atlantic trading circles Ribeira Grande's reputation soon spread. The English sea dog **Sir Francis Drake** caught the scent in 1585 and attacked the settlement with a force of 1000. It was not an unplanned assault – the union of Spain and Portugal meant that Cape Verde was considered enemy territory by the English – and Drake landed at Praia to sneak overland and attack Ribeira Grande from behind. The town was deserted; the inhabitants had sensibly fled inland. Drake's crew stayed a fortnight, plundering what little there was and foraying into the interior without reward. One of the force was killed and mutilated by African slaves and Drake torched Ribeira Grande in reprisal, sparing only the hospital – the Casa Misericorde – whose ruins are still visible to the right as you descend into the centre of the present-day village.

It's worth going down to the *ribeira* and up the other side, through cane and corn and under mango trees, to further, less explored ruins – the church of **Nossa Senhora do Rosário** which served as a cathedral in miniature when the diocese was first created, and the Capuchin **Monastery of São Francisco** higher up the valley. Once up there, you can admire the palm-filled valley and muse on what five centuries of Portuguese rule have brought, and taken from, the islands. When the first buildings were put up the treeless scene must have had much the barren cast of a tropical Iona: all the trees have been established since that time. Today, you're likely to come across sugar cane presses and *grogue* stills as you climb through the jungly allotments – the aroma is unmissable.

Out on the southernmost cliffs, the boldest attempt at preserving the religious and military ruins in their dramatic settings was made a few years back by a restaurateur: the one-time Forte São João became the very picturesque *Mirimar Restaurant* with haphazard cannons on the terraces.

Down in the town *praça* stands Cidade Velha's most famous relic, the **pelourinho** or pillory, where captives were shackled on display. Today the village is mostly populated by grizzled old rustics: there are one or two general shops but no signs of anything to do with *turismo*. Though the large fleet of red fishing boats on the beach indicates more activity than you'd at first think, most of the young have moved to the mini-metropolis of Praia only twenty minutes away.

Getting back yourself can be a little problematic if you don't feel like waiting for the next *alugner*. But you can easily fill the time drinking *grogue* with the elders down in one of the village stores or, if you manage to avoid that, hiking back up the rather magnificent descent into town and cutting back to the left, to look over the extensive remains of the **Fortaleza Real de São Filipe** which dominates the whole of Cidade Velha from on high. A vast empty shell, but in surprisingly good condition, it offers stunning views of the *ribeira* and, behind, of the Serra do Pico de Santo António towering up in the interior.

São Domingos

There's no great reason to visit **SÃO DOMINGOS**, but it's worth it for the immensely pretty **journey** – only half an hour from Praia by Hiace – which takes you rapidly from the trashy outskirts of the capital into the heartland of rural Santiago. The minibus plunges into deep valleys, dodging low-hanging trees. Straight-backed women grind corn with a boulder against a flat rock (a *pilão*); pigs root at the roadside; be-satchelled children walk home from school. São Domingos itself is one of the earliest settlements on the island, over 450 years old: its church has a famous boat-shaped pulpit. Drake ventured this far in 1585 and, finding the settlement abandoned like Ribeira Grande, thought better of continuing into the wild interior. There's a *pousada* here – the *Bela Vista* – which might be open for your visit. It's a delightful place to stay, in the floor of the valley and surrounded by irrigated cultivation. Check out also the *Morenas* bar and restaurant.

North and east Santiago

The main reason to go north is to visit **Tarrafal**, a beautiful fishing village that makes an ideal spot to rest up for a few days. It's right at the opposite end of Santiago from Praia, and there are two different minibus routes that go there – one over the rugged spine of the island, the other along the indented east coast. The journey can make a very satisfying round trip.

The mountain route

The mountain route goes straight across an unexpectedly fairy-tale interior – peaks and rocky needles, soaring valleys, narrow terraces and ridges – a fine journey, especially during or after the rains. There are steep climbs and some great views before Assomada, then higher passes in the Malagueta range, rising to over 1300m.

The highest point of the island, the 1394-metre Pico de Santo António – with the only monkeys in Cape Verde on its slopes – rises above the town of **São Jorge dos Orgãos**, a few kilometres south of the main road. **Picos**, a few kilometres further north, is the site of the INIDA, the National Horticultural Institute, which has a *miradouro* ("special panoramic viewpoint") overlooking the year-round-green plantations, and a flourishing National Botanical Garden where you can see Cape Verdean flora and birdlife. If you want to stay, try the dramatically sited *Pensão Sossego* (☎61.36.37; ③).

Shortly before you reach Assomada, you come to the small town of **Picos** perched on a crag on the right next to a huge basaltic outcrop looking out over a wide, deep valley. In season, the blooms of jacaranda and frangipani bubble around the small *praça* and church.

The Assomada Silk Cotton Tree

En route to Tarrafal, if you've time and inclination, you can break your journey at **ASSOMADA**. The town is the second largest on the island – an interesting, lively place with a fine market and some quaint old architecture – and there should be no problem finding a place for the night here if you decide to stay. If you've only an hour or two, though, take a short walk out of town (north) and a turning right, then a steep path down into the *ribeira* to see what must be a contender for the biggest **silk cotton tree** in the world – though it's always referred to locally as a "baobab". Ask for **Boa Entrada**, the village tucked in the *ribeira*. You can't fail to see the tree standing on the slope across the valley: it's a monster.

Occasionally you'll come across postcards of this colossal silk cotton which make it look impossibly huge, with tiny doll-like figures at the base of a thing the size of a cathedral. It really is gargantuan. The trunk – over fifty metres round at the base – is a maze of contorted buttresses, and the massive branches are themselves the size of large trees. Towering two or three times as high as anything else, it would stand out anywhere, but in Cape Verde, land of limited leafiness, it's a fantastic sight. The tree has a venerable significance that surpasses mere size, and must be as old as the first generation of settlers. In 1855, according to a Rev. Thomas, chaplain to the African

Squadron of the US Navy, it was "forty feet in circumference" and had been "standing where it now stands when the island was first discovered". It's frustratingly hard to get a photo that does justice to its mighty bulk.

The east coast route

Heading north by the **east coast route** you follow the same road out of Praia, then cut right at the Ribeirão Chiqueiro junction, with the village of **Praia Baixo** tantalizingly visible out on the coast (three buses a day go there from Praia: it rates *Interesse Turisitico* and *Beach* symbols on the Santiago tourist map but the road is terrible, the beach uninviting and the whole area depressing). The first village you come to on the road is **Pedra Badejo**, with a magnificent **coconut** grove marking the entrance to the settlement and gigantic bananas on sale – if you're lucky – when the bus briefly stops. You can see *pedreiros* making cobbles here, each shaded under a banana leaf on the cliff top. It's all very floral and pleasant, with good beaches and caves, but there are no **pensões**. If you want to stay, make first for the *Restaurante Falucho*, order some *mariscos*, and take it from there.

Calheta, the next stop, has a big old church on the hilltop. The dependence on rainfall in the Cape Verdes comes home to you as the road repeatedly drops to cross stoney *ribeiras* where women wash clothes in the narrow streams: when water is about, the flanks of the gulches are dense with crops – bananas, papayas, cane and cassava – and heavy rains can also bring floods that smash the cobbles in many places.

Tarrafal

TARRAFAL doesn't look much at first. You have to go right through the small town to discover the wonderful, clean white **beach** below its gentle cliffs. Once the site of a political prison under the Portuguese, Tarrafal's main claim to fame is now this **beach**. A restaurant sits, more or less perfectly, on a bluff above it, with palms and discreet beach houses to one side and a working fishing town atmosphere on the other. You're bound to want to stay.

Accommodation is easily fixed. Speak to the people at the restaurant and you can stay in one of the bungalows (*Bungalows do Tarrafal*; ☎61.32.32; ③–④). They have big bed-living rooms with basic furniture, kitchens and bathrooms, plus electricity, water and gas – though these may well not be working. If the bungalows are full you can try the *Ta-Ta Pensão* – to the left of the town centre, south of the market – which is perfectly okay but not half as attractive ③, or the row of rooms on the cliff top above the fishing beach, which some people prefer (keys for these from the *Secretaria*, the green building opposite the *mercado* on the main *praça*; ②). A new, and recommended hotel is the *Marazal* (☎66.12.89; ③). Once installed in Tarrafal it's all too easy to pass a few days – or even much longer – swimming and lounging, watching the fishing boats coming in and the children playing, drinking cold beers, and eating slabs of fresh tuna on the restaurant terrace.

The **town** has an attractive hibiscus-filled *praça* with church and marketplace (and bank, Mon–Fri 8am–noon) set traditionally around. There are one or two bars where you can drink *grogue* and play *oril*. And check out the *Casa de Dona Cesário*, for discos and seafood. With the mountainous interior of the island looming behind, Tarrafal can seem incredibly isolated; yet a boy shooting down the cobbled hill on his shiny new American mountain bike is a reminder of close and important ties with the outside world. Except at weekends though, when Cape Verdean tourists and expatriate beach hunters zone in, it's marvellously peaceful. Walk south and you come to **further beaches** – of black sand – and more coconuts. Head north and a fine **coastal path** leads up over the cliffs above the crashing surf for as far as you like, with terrific views back. There are some tiny coves along here, with great natural swimming pools.

Fogo

First impressions of **FOGO** are of its tremendous mass – a brooding volcanic cone rising forbiddingly 2829m out of the sea. Arriving at **Mosteiros airstrip** on the dark northeast coast, the plane lands like a fly picking a spot on a black wall: the airstrip, about the size of two football pitches joined end to end, seems to occupy almost the only flattish space between the thrashing sea and sheer lava walls rising through clouds to the peak. The other airstrip, at São Filipe on the west coast (out of use for several years now), is equally precarious, perched high on the dunnish cliffs. Below it, a striking beach of baking black sand drops straight into ultramarine sea.

Although all the islands have their own distinguishing marks, it's Fogo which stands out as the great character of the Cape Verdes. It's impossible to forget you're on a **volcano**: menacing vapours still drift from the crater. Fogo – which means "fire" – had an eruption in 1995, when deluges of molten laval rock streamed down the slopes and 4000 people were evacuated. To the west, the land is gentler, the old volcanic base undisturbed by fresh explosions and cloaked, when there's been rain, under a pastoral blanket of wild flowers, low trees, farms and plantations. **People** on Fogo are often startlingly kind, accommodating hikers, showing you directions miles out of their way and doing everything possible to help.

Around the island to São Filipe

Transport on Fogo depends on *aluguers* and the odd private vehicle. The south road between Mosteiros and São Filipe is the only one on which you're likely to get transport.

If you arrive by air at **Mosteiros** ("Monastery"), transport on to São Filipe is normally included in the fare. Otherwise, you'll probably have to walk a couple of kilometres to **Igreja** ("Church") which is the nearest thing to a town centre in this part of the island. An ordinary *carrinho* ride to São Filipe shouldn't cost more than CV$600, but it's as well to know that a *particular* could cost ten times as much. If the airstrip there is open, it's probably easier to arrive and depart from São Filipe, but try to catch the spectacular eastern side of Fogo at some time if you can.

Heading **anticlockwise** out of Mosteiros, there's a breathtaking road up to the hamlet of **Ribeira Ilheu**, terrifyingly steep if you're in a vehicle. Scarcity of lifts aside, this is really worth a walk – allow a day to climb the 15km – which rewards you with stunning views, sheltered and overgrown little valleys, and a village where your arrival will cause a minor sensation. Once committed, you'll probably have to continue on foot, covering the worst portion of the round-island road, another 10km or so, as far as São Jorge, where you might (with luck) find transport on to São Filipe.

Travelling clockwise, you climb quickly from Mosteiros and skirt beneath the crater walls over a battlefield of strewn lava. The road runs high in places (looking out to sea there are clouds below the horizon) and, with a fast driver, it's not a journey you'll ever forget: the cobbled highway traverses the cinder slopes in an unnerving series of undefended loops hundreds of metres above the waves. The isolated **settlements** of lava block houses have a temporary look about them – there's a menacing slag-heap darkness here. Surprisingly, it's high up on this eastern side that most of Fogo's famous (but dreadful) **coffee** is grown. And at **Achada Grande** there's a new experiment in cooperative **viticulture**; but the red wine they produce, although potent, is rather acidic and said not to be very commercial just yet.

Once the road curves **west** the countryside opens out to more relaxing dimensions; a mellow, rolling landscape of maize and agave takes over and there's a surprising amount of tree cover, mostly acacias. In the pockets of fertile volcanic soil that haven't been rainwashed there are beans growing around the maize stalks, with squash, sweet potatoes and cucumbers between. Bananas, a Santiago speciality, are much scarcer.

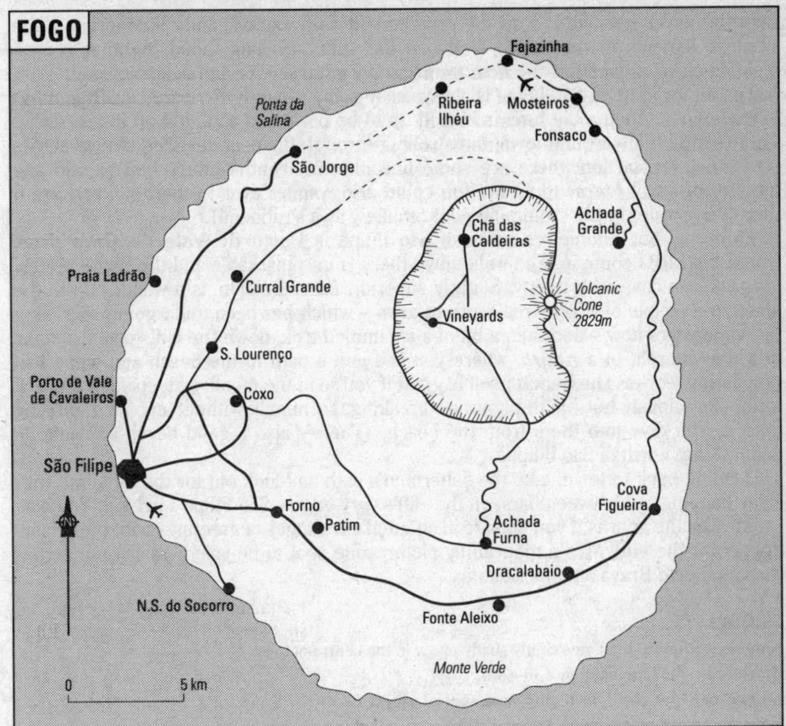

São Filipe and around

SÃO FILIPE, Fogo's capital, has an orderly civility which sits oddly with its steeply sloping cliff-top location, high above the black beach. The streets link a number of small squares and gardens and a promenade along the cliffs. All São Filipe seems to lack to be one of Cape Verde's most attractive towns is sufficient population. It is deathly quiet, the streets almost deserted even on an ordinary weekday morning. After dark everyone's inside, apparently watching TV: through every open doorway there's a blue glow and a stack of silhouetted backs. At least this is an improvement on the 1930s when an English visitor, Archibald Lyall, reported a community in the grip of diabolical poverty, isolated from Praia, let alone Lisbon, and totally without electricity or transport – small, shaggy horses were the only way to get about.

The lack of hotels and eating houses that Lyall suffered hasn't altogether been put to rights. The one **hotel**, the *Xaguate* (☎81.12.22; ④), is reasonably well organized, but more expensive than you'd hope for out here. They've found a good spot for it, though, over on the other side of the *ribeira* from the town centre, with good views across the channel to Brava – which blocks the setting sun. A pleasant, more recent option is the New England-style B&B at *Pensão Las Vegas* (③), which has recently become a bit of a traveller's focus with noisy Saturday nights. You can normally stay at the *Restaurant Vulção* too, which is definitely preferable to the *Xaguate* and perhaps the best value on the island (②). The **restaurant** here provides enormous heaps of Cape Verdean food – heavy vegetable soups, rice, beans and squash, pork or tuna, and sweet potatoes. A big cassette player gets turned on for your benefit with extravagantly appropriate Cape Verdean laments to match the food and the sultry evening mood. Another recommended place to eat out is the *Restaurant Leila* – good service and delicious food.

The atmosphere in São Filipe is always easy-going, though there are usually scuffles of excitement when a big tuna is hauled up to be portioned and sold off in the street. There's little to do around town, but strolling through the near-deserted streets has its own quiet satisfaction: there are some fine old nineteenth-century houses and any number of small *praças* to sit in. You could also wander over to the hotel and see if there's any water in the swimming pool (unlikely as it's rationed).

Three or four kilometres north of São Filipe is **Porto de Vale de Cavaleiros**, where the boats come in. The walk down there is unremarkable and the "port" merely consists of a cove with a jetty. Slightly superior, for recreation, is a wander up to the **airstrip** a couple of kilometres south of town – which has been undergoing regrading for some years now – and then a bit of a scrambled trek, down the cliffs past the ruins of a tiny church, to a *ribeira*, where you can join a path to the beach and some fish processing works. The **beach** itself is great if you're in the mood: a steep shelf of black sand – ferociously hot – with big waves breaking, seemingly without any fetch, directly onto it. You dive into them from the beach. (There's also a good beach at Ponta da Salina 17km north of São Filipe.)

Heading back to town, take the fishermen's path and look out for the building, with arms hanging out between bars, on the cliff's very edge – São Filipe's **prison**. You'll be scolded by the guards if you engage in shouted exchanges of greetings with the prisoners across the gully. It's a mournfully picturesque spot to be jailed, gazing out across the channel to Brava and the Atlantic.

Listings

Aluguers From a small, mercifully shady *praça* in the centre of town.

Bank Mon–Fri 8am–noon & 2.30–4pm.

Discoteca Open Saturday nights or on special occasions.

Electricity and water None after midnight.

Mercado Municipal A very small all-purpose market selection.

Police ☎81.11.32.

Post office (Correio) Similar hours to the bank.

TACV The office (☎81.12.28) is often open during the day. Don't forget to reconfirm your flight back 48 hours before flying – it's easy to get stranded on Fogo.

Exploring the volcano

The **volcano** is a dominant and time-filling lure, though it's hard to reach the crater, both for traveller's and for the islanders who live in it. Although there are daily *aluguers*, from Sáo Filipe, right into the crater (identified by the wording "Chã das Caldeiras" and a painting of the volcano) they are not super-abundant. If you ask taxi drivers about *particular* hire for the day you'll usually get quoted colossal figures because they genuinely don't want to do the trip: it's tremendously steep. The best plan is probably just to set off with some supplies and the time necessary to walk up if you have to. The main points of departure are **Curral Grande** on the northwest slope and **Achada Furna** on the south side of the crater (you should be able to get an *aluguer* easily enough from the

INTER-ISLAND FLIGHTS FROM FOGO (MOSTEIROS)

Praia: 1–2 flights daily (not Sun), 30min.

TACV in São Filipe ☎81.12.28

latter). From Achada Furna the crater rim is about 6km as the crow flies, but it's a 1500-metre climb (that's a gradient of one in four) and a good five or six hours' hike. Routes on the north side of the volcano are even less trafficked, if that's possible, the thirty-kilometre hike from São Filipe rolling up over some beautiful countryside, through eucalyptus and conifer plantations to Curral Grande and the crater rim.

At the rim you may be lucky and have the whole eight-kilometre wide, 900-metre deep crater spread clearly before you, or you – and it – may be blotted out by thick cloud. Either way you'll now want to go down **into the crater**, which is partly cultivated – the area known as **Chã das Caldeiras**. Many families in this district trace their descent from a Duc de Montrond who is said to have fled France in the nineteenth century after a duel – and thoughtfully brought some vines with him. This moonscape of lava and scattered mini-craters is surmounted by the current **main cone** which rises in a cindery heap to the east, several hundred metres above the large crater floor. It's an exhausting scramble to the summit, worth the effort if you have more than half a day of light left: views from the top in the right conditions can include the entire archipelago. You should be able to find a local guide to show you the way to the top of the main cone; if you're asked to pay, CV$1000 is probably the most that's fair.

Brava

BRAVA, the smallest inhabited island, has always been the most isolated of the Cape Verdes, properly settled only at the end of the seventeenth century after a major eruption of Fogo in 1675. Its capital, **Vila Nova Sintra** (Vila) – named after the royal resort of Sintra outside Lisbon – is one of the archipelago's loveliest towns, sedately arranged in a long-extinct crater high above the shoreline. The island's stone walls overflow with lobelia and vines, and clouds drift through even when the rest of the archipelago is parched with drought. Brava has lots of motorbikes and Cape Verde's best sunsets. Although its name means "wild", the island has long enjoyed a remarkable degree of domestication, with virtually all the land under neatly tended cultivation, supporting the archipelago's highest population density. Bravans have a long sea-faring tradition: the American **whalers** called at this island more than any other, and the largest contingent of *americanos* comes from Brava. Sadly, much of Brava's infrastructure was destroyed in 1982 by Hurricane Beryl.

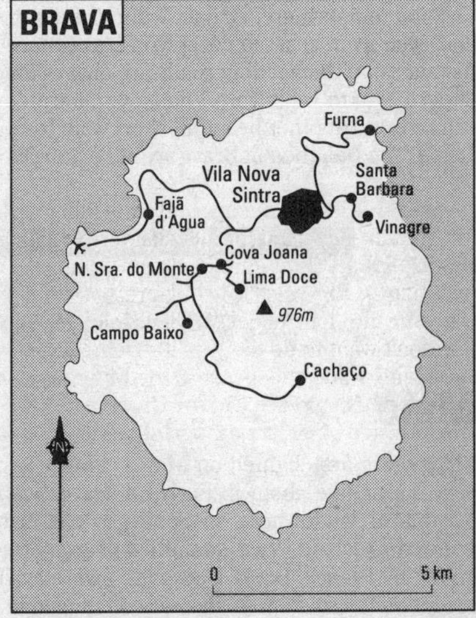

Small enough to walk all over, but precipitous too, Brava is worth the few days' visit you'll have to devote to it between ferry or plane connections. If you don't opt for the expensive **flight** from Praia (CV$6000), the **ferry** connections are inconvenient: a boat leaves Praia Tuesday and Thursday night (Tuesday via São Filipe, Thursday direct to Brava) and Wednesday evening (direct), docking at **Furna**, five winding kilometres northeast of Vila. The channel between Fogo and Brava is notoriously rough – you may well need seasickness pills.

TAVARES, WRITER OF MORNAS

Eugénio Tavares was a native of Brava, born in 1867. Tavares, a romanticized figure in Cape Verdean lore, was the country's best-known writer of the *morna* song form, the distinctive Cape Verdean music, equivalent to Argentina's tango or Portugal's fado. The fado comparison is appropriate, as, like fado, the *morna* has a minor-key melody and both may have originated in the Portuguese slave islands of São Tomé. But the heart of a *morna* is its lyric. *Mornas* evoke an unmistakably Cape Verdean feeling of *sodade* – yearning, longing, homesickness – and the classic examples are all by Eugénio Tavares. Tavares worked most of his life as a journalist and civil servant, achieving his huge popularity through his use of the Kriolu language, rather than colonial Portuguese. Tavares' *mornas* deal with the pain of love and loss. One of his best-known is "O Mar Eterno", inspired by his affair with an American woman visiting Brava by yacht. Her disapproving father set sail one night and the two never met again. Another famous composition, "Hora di Bai" ("The Hour of Leaving") was traditionally sung on the dock at Furna as relatives boarded America-bound ships. Tavares died in 1930. You can hear a recent set of his songs on a CD by the singer Saozinha, *Saozinha Canta Eugenio Tavares*, on the American label MB Records.

There's a bank in Vila and **accommodation** is easy. Stay at the clean and quiet little state-run *Pousada Municipal* (☎81.12.20; if there's nobody about, ask for keys in the *Camara Municipal*; ③) or at *Pensão Paulo Sena* (②–③), a very welcoming place, the owner of which is one of Vila's characters and a great entertainer at holiday times. On the northwest side of the island, at **Fajã d'Agua**, there's *Burgo's Pensão* (②–③), and the exclusive *Hotel Blue Merlin* (⑥). As for **restaurants in Vila**, apart from those at the *pensões*, try the *Esplanada* and the bar-restaurant run by the women's organization, OMCV. If you're looking for action on Brava, the main **boites** are the *Kananga do Japão* in Vila (Saturday nights and Sunday afternoons) and one in Nossa Senhora do Monte near the *Polyvalente* community centre.

There's little in the way of regular **transport** on Brava but seats in *aluguers* rarely cost more than CV$50. If you charter the vehicle as a *particular*, you're looking at about CV$600 to anywhere. Or just **walk**: there are wonderful hikes and strolls everywhere, and even from coast to coast won't take more than half a day. Be aware, however, that distances on the winding roads are always longer than they look on the map. There's a superb 3–4km walk from Vila Nova Sintra down to Santa Barbara and the fountain at Vinagre and another beautiful short walk from Nossa Senhora do Monte to nearby Cova Joana. The **beaches** of Brava are stony or rocky, but nice at Tantum and Fajã d'Agua.

INTER-ISLAND FLIGHTS FROM BRAVA

Praia: 2 flights weekly, 45min.

TACV on Brava: check at the office in Vila

Maio

MAIO was first sighted on May 1, 1460 – hence its name – but there's really nothing very spring-like about it. Early on, slaves were taken there to look after the livestock surplus of landowners on Santiago, but historically, Maio was important as a **salt collecting** island. Vast quantities of evaporated sea salt – "huge heaps like drifts of snow" by Francis Drake's account – were available for the cost of the labour needed to load it on board ship. As that was often paid in old clothes or other unwanted items, the

INTER-ISLAND FLIGHTS FROM MAIO

Praia: 5 flights weekly, 20min.

TACV ☎55.12.56

trade was a lucrative one. The English were largely in control of it and for a period Maio, by Portuguese default, was in English hands.

Today, Maio is a godforsaken place, poor in agriculture, a neglected neighbour of weighty Santiago – where most of its young people soon migrate – and touristically a dead loss. It's not likely to be high on your list, but if you do take the **flight** from Praia (five a week: a CV$3600, twenty-minute hop) you're likely to be fêted as the first traveller they've seen for a while, and you'll find a place with a very distinct flavour, perhaps the least European of the Cape Verdes, with a relatively wooded, savannah-esque interior and long, white, desolate beaches. However, the *Pousada Municipal* (☎51.13.34; ③) in **Vila do Maio** – commonly known as Porto Inglês – is the only obvious **accommodation**, though you could look for private lodgings or camp. To contact the *TACV* about flights back, phone Maio ☎55.12.56.

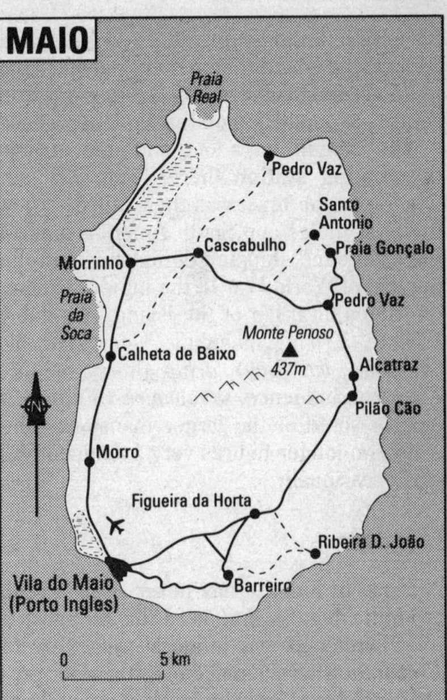

THE BARLAVENTOS

Internationally – at least in the English-speaking world – it's the **Barlaventos** that have drawn most attention to the Cape Verde Islands. Among them, **São Vicente** stands out, the location of a British coal supply depot for over 100 years. Its capital, **Mindelo**, is now the travel hub of the Barlaventos and focus of most of what's happening culturally in the Cape Verdes. While the interior of the island is unbelievably waterless and barren, the town has a self-contained appeal that draws much on its evident cosmopolitanism and clear rivalry for civic pre-eminence with Praia.

To see the Cape Verde Islands at their most naturally glorious, hop across the channel from Mindelo for restorative **hiking** among the magnificent *ribeiras* of **Santo Antão**. The most northerly isle, Santo Antão is a splendid massif – comparable to Fogo but no longer volcanically active – with an awesomely rugged interior.

São Nicolau is like a poor relation of Antão: its 400 years of human habitation seem to have been a dirge of destitution and fruitless toil and yet its town has the oldest educational and literary tradition in the country. It also offers breathtaking scenery, as well as opportunities similar to Santo Antão's for determined walkers.

Sal, the aptly named "Salt" island, is now the site of Cape Verde's main international airport, which is the only real reason to come here, but if you happen to have time to kill there's a wonderful **beach** on the southern shore. The last of the windward islands is **Boa Vista**, a flat island in the east of the archipelago. Boats call here so you may too, but once again the only possible reason to stop is for some excellent **beaches**.

São Vicente

It's hard to avoid identifying **SÃO VICENTE** with its main town and indeed there's not a lot on the island that matters outside **Mindelo**. The one or two unexceptional things to do are best achieved by striking out from the town – there are no other significant centres of population on this hulk of moonscape.

The **British** had a long and influential connection with Mindelo as the operators of the **coaling station** there. From 1838 until the 1950s, Mindelo – or rather Porto Grande as the town was then called – grew from nothing to a major supply depot on the East Indies and South America runs. With the opening of the Suez canal in 1869 the eastbound shipping diminished and diesel eventually took over from coal. But by the end of World War II, the hundred years of British presence had made some impact on the cultural life of the island. A number of English words were adopted into São Vicente Kriolu, including *blaqyefela* (blackfellow), *trôsa, ovacôte* (trousers and overcoat), *boi* (boy), *ariup* (hurry up), *djob* (job), *ovataime* (overtime) and, under American influence, *sanababiche*. English influence is still discernible in the architecture of some of the larger mansions. The British also introduced **cricket**, a game which no longer figures very prominently. There's still a team, however, and they still play occasionally.

Mindelo

A sense of identity has never been a problem for **MINDELO**. "Taken as a whole," thought Major A B Ellis of the 1st West India Regiment in 1873, "it is, perhaps, the most wretched and immoral town that I have ever seen". He stayed in the *Hotel Brasiliero* where a notice over the door proclaimed "Ici on parl Frances, Man spreucht Deutsch, Man spiks Ingleesh, Aqui se habla Español, Sabe American", and where his room was invaded by a French farce of characters during the night. By the end of the nineteenth century, Mindelo's importance as a coaling and victualling station was at its peak, and less reputable ancillary industries were in top gear.

Today, while only the faintest traces of the bawdiness remain, this is the liveliest town in the Cape Verdes – and no longer especially wretched. Relatively well-provided with hotels, restaurants and bars, it buzzes contentedly after dark, its *praça* a noisy hang-out zone, its streets cheerfully animated. It's still a small town, but it provokes good feelings in most visitors. Don't be surprised to find the atmosphere here tainted with hustle around the edges: yachts and cruise ships are intermittent and not infrequent callers (even the QE2 makes a stop once or twice a year) and the boys on the waterfront are still making escudos out of naïve travellers in time-honoured ways.

Arrival

Flying in, the airstrip is 11km from town on a bleak flat at São Pedro. For CV$500 a taxi gets you to Mindelo past brave acres of **reafforestation** where windswept acacias struggle for a foothold, protected by rusty oil drums. With the *Shell* fuel-holding tanks and a strong scent of desert and trash, first appearances aren't encouraging, but these soon recede as you get into the town with its Portuguese buildings, restored pink Governor's residence and a palmy esplanade.

Arriving **by boat**, there's a twenty-minute walk along the seafront to the town centre.

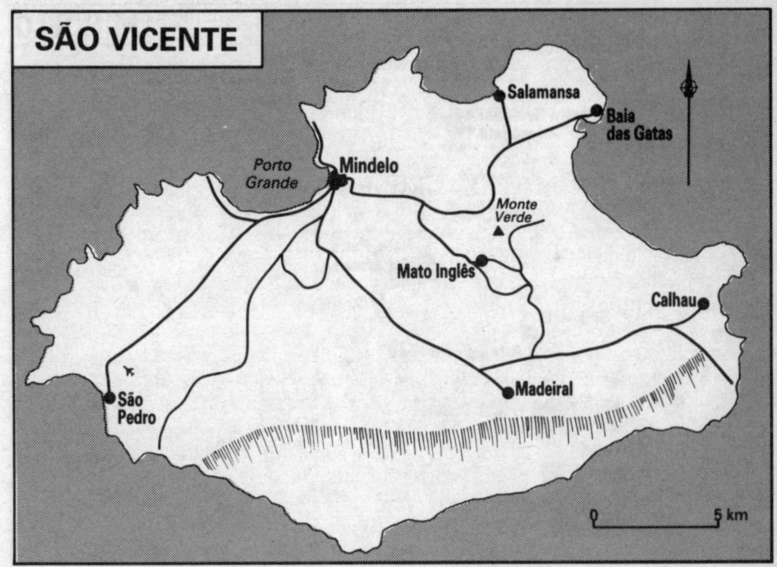

Accommodation

Hotels are a simple matter, with the *Avenida* the best-kept of the more upmarket places and *Chez Loutcha* the best of the relatively cheap ones. Most are marked on our map.

Pensão Atlantico, near the *Agencia Nacional de Viagens*, on the corner of rua de Santo António. Clean and good value. ②–③.

Aparthotel Avenida, av 5 de Julho (☎31.44.97). Soulless apartment-style hotel with mod cons. ④.

Pensão Chave d'Ouro, av 5 de Julho (☎31.10.50). Right on the main street, the "Golden Key" is a long-established budget focus, but it's getting somewhat run-down. Tiny top floor rooms and big airy rooms on the 1st floor, all non-S/C. ②–③.

Pensão Chez Loutcha, rua de Coco (☎31.16.36). High standards and wonderful staff. ③.

Residêncial Sôdade, rua Franz Fanon (☎31.35.56). Good-quality lodging house. ③.

Residêncial Novo Horizonte, 62 rua Senador Vera Cruz (☎31.20.24). Adequate guest house.②–③.

Hotel Porto Grande, Praça Amílcar Cabral (☎31.31.13 or 31.38.38). Recently renovated. Beware: the front rooms are notoriously noisy, especially at weekends. ③–④.

Hotel Rialto, 26 rua N'Krumah. A fairly new, recommended establishment. ③.

The Town

Mindelo is the town that Cape Verdeans resident abroad always go on about – perhaps because so many Cape Verde expatriates come from here – and compared with Praia it does have a more animated, less official feel. Helped along by the bay with its twin headlands, its esplanade and its clutter of backstreets, Mindelo feels like a holiday. The *carnaval* in February infects the town for the entire year, so it never entirely stops partying.

Exploring for yourself is the main daytime pursuit and the seafront provides an obvious anchor point. The unusual eagle-topped **monument** commemorates the first Lisbon–Rio air crossing, in 1922, by aviators Cabral and Coutinho, who spent a number of days recuperating in Mindelo after their 80mph leg from the Canaries in the airboat *Lusitania*. Nearby, the curious ornate little castle is the **Torre de Belem**, a copy of the

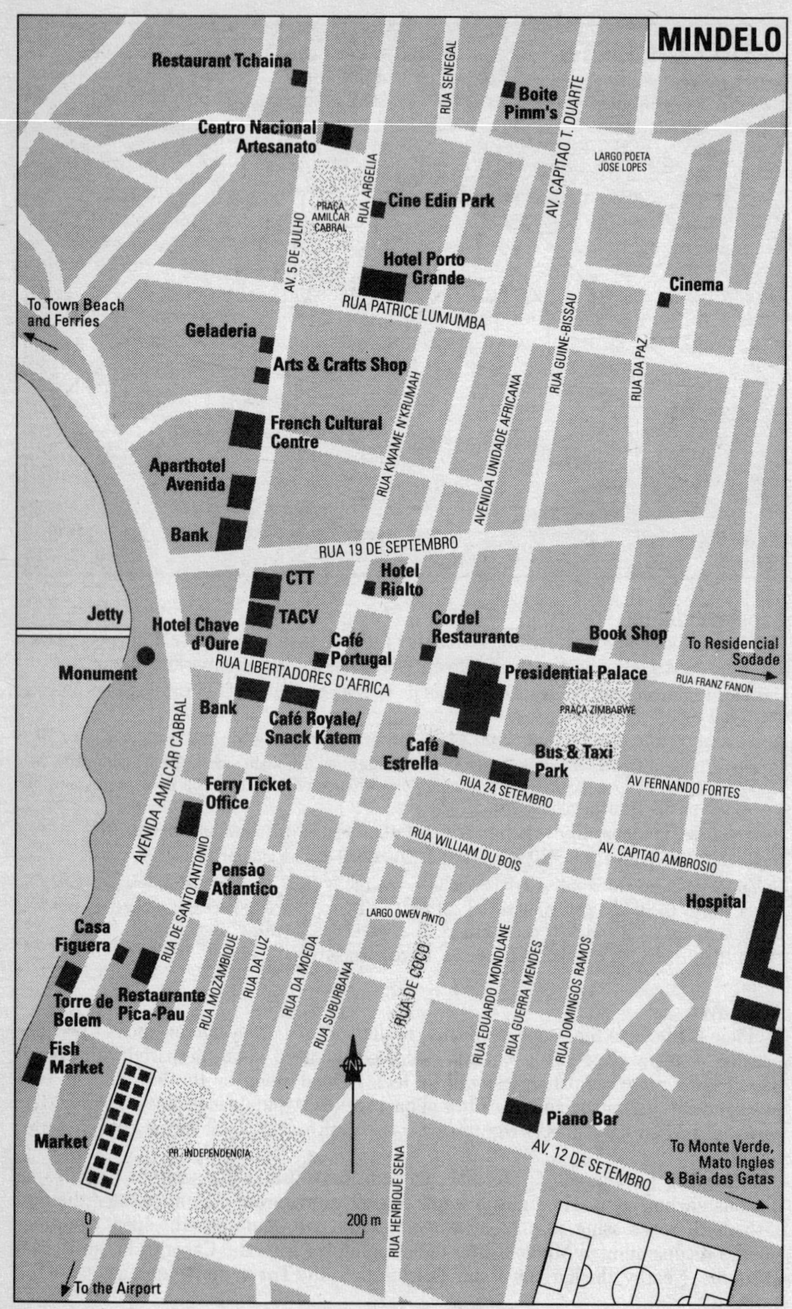
MINDELO
Restaurant Tchaina
Boite Pimm's
Centro Nacional Artesanato
RUA SENEGAL
AV. CAPITAO T. DUARTE
LARGO POETA JOSE LOPES
PRAÇA AMILCAR CABRAL
RUA ARGELIA
Cine Edin Park
AV. 5 DE JULHO
Hotel Porto Grande
Cinema
To Town Beach and Ferries
RUA PATRICE LUMUMBA
Geladeria
Arts & Crafts Shop
RUA GUINE-BISSAU
RUA DA PAZ
French Cultural Centre
RUA KWAME N'KRUMAH
AVENIDA UNIDADE AFRICANA
Aparthotel Avenida
Bank
RUA 19 DE SEPTEMBRO
CTT
Hotel Rialto
TACV
Jetty
Hotel Chave d'Oure
Cordel Restaurante
Book Shop
Café Portugal
To Residencial Sodade
Monument
RUA LIBERTADORES D'AFRICA
Presidential Palace
RUA FRANZ FANON
Bank
PRAÇA ZIMBABWE
Café Royale/ Snack Katem
AVENIDA AMILCAR CABRAL
Café Estrella
Bus & Taxi Park
Ferry Ticket Office
RUA 24 SETEMBRO
AV FERNANDO FORTES
RUA WILLIAM DU BOIS
AV. CAPITAO AMBROSIO
Pensào Atlantico
RUA DE SANTO ANTONIO
Hospital
LARGO OWEN PINTO
Casa Figuera
RUA MOZAMBIQUE
RUA DA LUZ
RUA DA MOEDA
RUA SUBURBANA
RUA DE COCO
RUA EDUARDO MONDLANE
RUA GUERRA MENDES
RUA DOMINGOS RAMOS
Torre de Belem
Restaurante Pica-Pau
Fish Market
N
Piano Bar
Market
PR. INDEPENDENCIA
AV. 12 DE SETEMBRO
To Monte Verde, Mato Ingles & Baia das Gatas
0
200 m
RUA HENRIQUE SENA
To the Airport

tower of the same name outside Lisbon; the latter was built in the early sixteenth century, the Cape Verdean replica in the 1920s. For many years the Torre at Mindelo was the seat of the Portuguese administrator of São Vicente, but even before independence it had been abandoned. For years a shored-up and rat-infested structure which looked as if it had been deliberately ignored, it has recently been renovated. Back in town a short way, the old **Governor's palace** has been well looked after and was recently restored in pale pink. Now the headquarters of São Vicente island council, it's clearly the object of considerable civic pride.

The closest you'll come to a museum in Cape Verde is a visit to the **Centro Nacional Artesanato** (open daily but closed for lunch, small entry fee). The place is divided into a display area and a shop, and there's also a workshop at the back where you're generally allowed to nose around the weaving looms: doubtless this depends on the behaviour of the last batch of cruise passengers or shore-leave sailors. The knick-knacks on sale aren't hugely appealing, but the items on display, particularly some of the pottery and tapestries, do seem old and of genuine interest. If you're drawn to **crafts and paintings**, you should pay a visit to a couple of other addresses. The arts and crafts shop on av 5 de Julho, close to the French cultural centre has some good ceramics and prices are lower than the Centro Artesanato's. *Casa Figueira*, near the Torre de Belem, is a private gallery of canvases by a father and son team, who also run a café on the ground floor.

Mindelo's **beach** is one scruffy kilometre out of town on the north side. Backed by rumbling industrial plant, the dark sands are somehow appropriate and it's altogether thoroughly unattractive. But it's a beach, and a reasonably clean one, and the sea is warm and clear.

For concerns of a consuming nature, Mindelo is not as well equipped as Praia. There's a scattering of small **shops**, but only a poorly stocked and expensive produce market, hopeless on Saturdays and closed on Sundays.

Restaurants and cafés

There are a few decent restaurants and snack bars – though it's well to remember that many of them close once a week, usually on a Sunday. Most of the following are marked on the map.

Café Estrela Negra, av Fernando Fortes, by the palace. Top-value meals and snacks.

Snack Bar Katem, rua Libertadores d'Africa. Ground floor of the club of the same name – a good breakfast address.

Restaurant O Cordel, av Unidade Africana. One of Mindelo's best restaurants; from about CV$600.

Pica Pau, rua de Santo António. For evening meals, the "Woodpecker" is one of the best-value restaurants. Go for seafood, not meat, or order the *feijoada* in advance.

Cafe Portugal and **Cafe Royale**, rua Libertadores d'Africa. These two competing hang-out spots are the principal downtown cafés – unfussy, fast places where business types read the *Novo Jornal*, and much coffee, beer and *aguardente* is consumed.

Restaurant Sodade, rua Franz Fanon. The restaurant of the *pensão* of the same name. Great view, but you may not be sold on the food, which isn't cheap.

Restaurant Tchaina, av 5 de Julho. Chinese restaurant with good fish dishes.

Nightlife

After dark, social gravity sooner or later draws most people down to **Praça Amílcar Cabral** where there's always a lot of excitement and somehow very Mediterranean courting and flirting going on, accompanied by enormous volumes of noise. Although Mindelo's youth are steadily deserting the town for Praia and further, it still holds a racy and sophisticated reputation for the young people of the Barlavento country hamlets. Sitting in the square is really fun: you'll quickly find yourself in some kind of conversation, tuning in to the evening grapevine.

Mindelo has a number of **boites and nightclubs**, though they're generally discos rather than live music venues. Apart from Cape Verdean *morna*, *coladeira* and *funana*, you're most likely to come across variants of zouk, often with Senegalese influences. Not surprisingly, successful singers and bands don't wait long before flying out to Lisbon, Paris, Holland or New England, where the Cape Verdean audience (and certainly the market for CDs) is often larger than in Mindelo itself.

CLUBS AND MUSIC BARS

Pub-Dancing A Cave, Alto São Nicolau (☎31.18.64).

Discoteca Histep, 98 Fte Inês (☎31.35.81). Busy disco.

Katem, av Libertadores d'Africa. A reasonably lively town-centre club.

Piano Bar, av 12 de Setembro. A recommended haunt that launched, among others, the much loved Cesaria Evora.

Boite Pimm's, rua Senador Vera Cruz (☎31.45.97). Always hot and crowded.

Xê Nu Bar, rua Senador Vera Cruz (☎31.24.03). Worth checking out.

Listings

Banks There are two: for changing money you want the one in the old building on rua de Santo António, south of rua Libertadores d'Africa, open usual hours.

Boats The travel agency on the corner of rua de Santo António has tickets, timetables and a fair degree of patience while you struggle to understand.

Bookshops Try rua Franz Fanon, rua da Luz/rua N'Krumah and rua 19 de Setembro.

Car rental São Vicente is a good place to explore for a day by car. Daily rates are around CV$3000. Try *Alucar*, Monte Dji Sal (☎31.11.50); *Holiday Cars*, Monte Mindelo (☎31.45.70); *Turicar* (☎31.28.47), on rua do Douro, just south of the town centre; or *Africar*, rua Domingos Ramos (☎31.54.81).

Centre Culturel Français The French do work hard at their culture, even with no consulate. Worth visiting for books, mags, movies and events.

Consulates The British honorary consul is A. Canuto, at *Shell Cabo Verde* in av Amílcar Cabral (☎31.41.32; Fax 31.47.55). Otherwise, the team from Europe includes: Belgium, av Marginal on the way to the port; Denmark, Cais Acostavel near the port; Netherlands, Norway and Portugal all in rua N'Krumah; Germany, Alto Matiota past the beach; Spain and Switzerland, av 5 de Julho.

Film/processing *Foto Express*, 14 av 5 de Julho.

Post office (Correio) Mon–Fri 8am–noon & 2.30–5pm; Sat 8–11am & 3–5pm; Sun 9–11am.

TACV A busy office on av 5 de Julho (☎31.18.69, 31.16.54 or 31.15.24). Availability on flights to Sal and Praia, notably those connecting with international departures, is often very bad. Plan ahead and remember to reconfirm everything.

Taxis Main ranks are in the obvious centre of town near the church (*igreja*). Town rates are reasonable, island trips come much more expensive, but still not utterly unrealistic.

Out of town trips

If you don't venture **beyond Mindelo** you'll not be in a minority. The rest of the island is desperately arid, for the most part treeless and largely uninhabited – 95 percent of the 40,000 inhabitants live in the *povoação*.

INTER-ISLAND FLIGHTS FROM SÃO VICENTE (MINDELO)

Praia: 1–2 flights daily (not Sun), 60min.
Sal: 1–2 flights daily (not Mon), 55min.
Santo Antão (Ponta do Sol): 2 flights weekly, 25 min.
São Nicolau: 4 flights weekly, 30 min.

TACV in Mindelo ☎31.24.65

Baia das Gatas

For a break however, and really quite a nice **beach**, the twenty-minute drive to **Baia das Gatas** is a good trip. Transport is limited on São Vicente and you'll almost certainly have to rent a taxi unless you strike lucky, perhaps at the weekend, with a lift (walk out the length of av 12 de Setembro and wait where it bends). The cost of a taxi to Baia will depend on waiting time, as little as CV$1000 for a quick dip, the best part of CV$2000 for a prolonged lounge. It's something which is obviously cheaper and more fun if you can make up a group. On Sundays, too, there's usually a bus that leaves at 9.30am and returns at 5.30pm. Baia, as it's commonly known (the reason for the *gatas* – cats – is unknown), is protected by a concrete mole and black boulders to break the thrashing surf. In the **lagoon**, the water is calm and delightfully transparent, though even with a mask there's not a lot to see. Beyond its confines the sea is more challenging and the combination of urchin-covered rocks and the threat of sharks should be enough to put you off. There's a Sunday beach bar, weekend bungalows and, in August, an annual international **festival** with a party atmosphere and plenty of music and side shows.

Monte Verde

The road to Baia climbs steeply past the junction for **Monte Verde**, the dark mass commonly wreathed in clouds that rears up behind Mindelo, and the island's highest point. This too is worth an outing but it'll cost more because of the strain on the taxi: you'll need to set aside a full morning or afternoon of your time. The last section, rough in parts, gets to within a few hundred metres of the summit. It is, truly, a "green mountain", covered in the once commercially important *orchil* lichen, used to produce brilliant scarlet and purple dyes. There can be stunning views down over Mindelo and Baia, but they're not to be counted on.

Southern beaches

Difficult roads lead southeast to **Calhau** (the direct route from Mindelo is easier than the one via Monte Verde) and south to the island's most dramatic and isolated region, a fifteen-kilometre ridge (altitude 500–700m) paralleling the southern coast at a distance of just two or three kilometres, from which *ribeiras* plunge down to the sea. There's a good beach and a restaurant at Calhau – *Chez Loutcha* – open weekends only (sometimes only on Sun).

Another worthwhile beach, somewhat easier to get to (by taxi), lies just beyond the airport at **Praia de São Pedro**, an area that seems set for touristic development.

Santo Antão

SANTO ANTÃO, the second largest of the Cape Verdes, is rugged and exciting – a tortoise shape cut into deep, arcing **ribeiras**, with the savage grandeur of a much bigger land mass. The island is also the last to suffer whenever a prolonged drought ravages the country, the northern slopes and valleys retaining a perennial verdure which is hard to believe after the desolation of Santiago and São Vicente.

However, communications have always been difficult. The story goes that Bishop Jacinto Valente visited Santo Antão from Santiago in 1755, and set off to cross the island on foot. Having been hauled up several precipices dangling from a rope, he eventually lost his nerve and had to stay put between a cliff and a chasm. The islanders went ahead, sent him back a tent and supplies, and began to construct a road for his rescue. A single **highway** now snakes up over the barren south face to edge between the peaks and abysses to the island's capital, Ribeira Grande on the north coast. Even as late as 1869, three hundred years after it was first colonized, the Portuguese minister of colo-

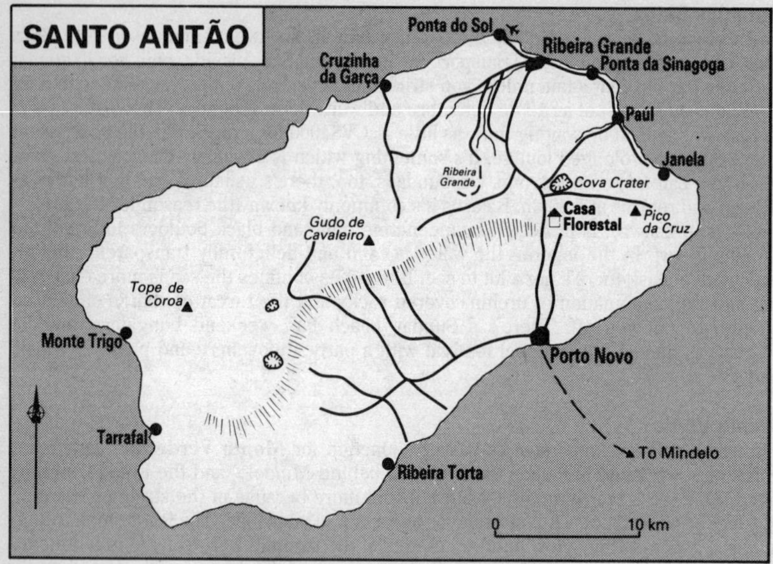

nies remarked that Santo Antão had "the appearance of an island that had only been discovered months ago".

Getting here today, you can fly from Praia and Mindelo to the airport at Ponta do Sol near Ribeira Grande. Much cheaper are the ferries – the *Porto Novo* and the *Mare Azul* – across the deep, shark-infested channel from Mindelo to Porto Novo. As the crossing between the islands can be surprisingly rough, you'd be wise to take seasickness tablets if you've ever suffered.

From Porto Novo to Ribeira Grande

Porto Novo itself is an uneventful place which clearly subsists on the daily contact with Mindelo across the channel: a crowd is always down on the quay to welcome the boat. In times not so long past, it was from Santo Antão that Mindelo got almost all its drinking water – a lucrative trade that dried up with the withering of the coaling industry on São Vicente and the opening there of a desalination plant to provide fresh water.

A fleet of Hiace **minibuses** meets the ferry and most head over the island's back to Ribeira Grande; try to get a front seat on the right for the most heart-stopping views. Leaving Porto Novo (and, it appears, almost the only trees on this side of Santo Antão), the haul up the south slope of the island presents a bleak picture to begin with: the neat, cobbled road snakes steeply through a lifeless mountain desert of tumbled volcanic rocks, bleached pale in the afternoon sun, the only vegetation the rows of cacti planted at the roadside. As the bus climbs, temperatures drop, views over Porto Novo become dramatic and, if it's a clear day, you can see São Vicente – a black mountain hanging, strangely, below the horizon.

But save your enthusiasm – and your film if you're snapping out of the window – for the descent down the northern side of the island. Approaching the crest, the road's contours relax as groves of coniferous trees and low herbage make an appearance. The **Casa Florestal** (Forest Station) is a sort of halfway house and, if you intend getting straight on with some serious hiking through the magnificent landscape further on, a convenient place to hop out.

INTER-ISLAND FLIGHTS FROM SANTO ANTÃO (PONTA DO SOL)

Praia: Tuesday, 80min. São Vicente: 2 flights weekly, 25min.

TACV in Ponta do Sol ☎21.18.14

Continuing by minibus to the *povoação*, the landscape becomes one of competing superlatives as you sweep over the island's twisted spine and skirt the magnificent circumference of **Cova crater**. Clouds drift below the road, over the houses and sugar cane plots patched into the crater's colossal scoop. Repeatedly from this point on the bus veers over chasms of hundreds of sheer metres: immense volumes of sky and cloud open out beneath, with steep terraced slopes all around. Bishop Valente's vertigo was understandable; the scenery is awesome and even Cape Verdeans on the bus stand to gaze down – and cross themselves at the hairpins. Glimpsing the sea through the crags, it seems impossible the road can get down to Ribeira Grande in such a short distance. Indeed, even a few kilometres from the town, it tracks several hundred metres above the floor of the *ribeira*.

Ribeira Grande town

With fortress-like cliffs and narrow streets, **RIBEIRA GRANDE** feels like a mountain town lost in a huge range, the slightly forbidding atmosphere quickly compelling and not easily forgotten. The town perches at the *ribeira*'s mouth, a cluster of close and shady houses, hemmed in by cliffs rising behind and the dark sea lashing a shingly beach. A broad *praça* fronts the **Igreja de Nossa Senhora do Rosário**, the formidable church intended, at one time in the eighteenth century, to be the cathedral of Cape Verde. There's a scattering of *pensões*, one or two restaurants, as well as a post office, bank and even a disco.

Finding a **place to stay** is simple, with several inexpensive *pensões*, including the presentable and clean if rather gloomy *Residêncial 5 de Julho* (☎21.13.45; ③), the cheap and charmless *Residêncial Aliança* (☎21.12.46; ②) and the better than adequate *Pousada Municipal* (☎21.13.54; ②). For **food**, the town doesn't have a lot to offer, but check out the *Progreso*, which has a very solicitous owner and a nice patio dining area. Meals there are CV$400–500 with lobster at CV$700. Or visit the *Cantinho* near the *Aliança*, which sometimes has live music.

After dark you'll quickly track down the disco if it's still operating – and if that one isn't then another is bound to be, such is the enthusiasm of the town's teenagers. The place may well be a converted front room but the entrance fee is small, the music eminently danceable and the atmosphere ringing. A balcony gives out over the street, where you may well find a couple of wandering guitarists carousing under a breadfruit tree. On a moonlit night it's delightfully atmospheric and fun.

Hiking the ribeiras

The most compelling objectives on the island are rural, not urban. Ideally, with time and energy for several days' **hiking**, you'll have the chance to explore the three big **ribeiras** of eastern Santo Antão – Grande, Paúl and Janela ("Big", "Swamp" and "Window").

The **hike up Ribeira Grande**, a solid morning's worth (see box), deserves an early start and a minimum of gear – if possible simply drinking water and camera. If you're heading back to Porto Novo for the same day's ferry, then in the dry season you should take the **bus** which rattles up the *ribeira* for a few kilometres: during or after the rains, only the occasional *paragem* (bus stop) signs painted on the rocks indicate a bus ever comes this way, and the route has to be rebuilt every season. Somebody from one of the *pensões* in Ribeira Grande is usually happy to rent their car as a *taxi particular* for the day, loading your gear in the back to meet you on the road at the head of the *ribeira* and then driving you down to Porto Novo, or just running you back to Ribeira Grande town. You should expect to pay upwards of CV$2500 for this. You might also want to hire a guide for the day – CV$800 is a fair price. If you're lucky you will see the *ribeira* cloaked in green, but unfortunately it can't be guaranteed.

Ribeira do Paúl is the most beautiful and densely planted of the three. Get there by finding a lift, 10km along the coast road (watch out for falling rocks). **Accommodation** can be fixed up through the bar-shopkeeper in Paúl, whose wife will send down very good local cooking from the kitchen higher up the *ribeira*. There's also the *Pensão Vila do Paúl* (③), and *Hotel Solnur* (③). You can arrange a car (or, if you're lucky, a free lift) up the *ribeira*, but walking is wonderful. It's a riot of vegetation and, at Passagem, some 4km from Paúl, there's a kind of tropical garden with a **swimming pool** and café open at weekends (CV$100). Alternatively you can walk down the Ribeira Paúl by getting dropped off on the main trans-island road above the Cova crater, then, with guidance, walking down across the crater and down to Paúl from the other side.

There are possible hiking routes all over Santo Antão. One, a particularly dramatic route in its later stages, heads from Ribeira Grande to Ponta do Sol, thence to the precarious village of **Fontainas** and on to **Cruzinha da Garça** via a cliff-face footpath that is at times barely 50cm wide.

RIBEIRA GRANDE: A PERSONAL ACCOUNT

We hiked up the Ribeira Grande in October, after recent heavy rains. The dirt road was slashed by a fast flowing stream; big enough pools had collected for children to play diving and jumping games, possibly their one brief opportunity in the year. Up both sides of the valley, a hothouse jungle of cultivation steamed in the morning sun, broken by grey stone and pastel-painted houses: on the lower slopes grew sugar cane and coconut palms, cassava, bananas, breadfruit and papaya trees; higher up on table-sized terraces there were plots of maize, beans and sweet and Irish potatoes.

This route towards the trans-island road takes a left turn after a couple of flat kilometres and begins a gentle ascent. An hour from town a cobbled road drives up the valley side away from the floor and the real climb begins. A hamlet of cliff-clinging farmhouses begins around here; there's a small shop with cold drinks and we replenished our supply from a water pipe (something you can only count on if there's been recent rain). For an hour the path creeps higher, through the same, elongated village, a riot of poinsettia and potted plants. People are amused to see hikers, though not completely unused to the idea.

As the heat built up, our route became increasingly tough and, leaving the last houses of the village behind, we finally trekked up a near vertical salient of cliff at the head of the *ribeira*. A slog, but an awe-inspiring one, followed, as every twenty paces gave new and better views across the breathless vista beneath. Houses on the lower slopes lost their dimensions as the distant contours flattened and then disappeared.

Towards the top the air chilled. Clouds formed and drifted across the canyon. There are a few animals about up here – nimble goats and the odd piglet – but we saw no wildlife apart from small lizards flashing over the rocks and the occasional wheeling black and white eagle. Cape Verdeans, often barefoot and with heads loaded, hurried past in both directions. One old man paused to inspect us and to offer hunks of sugar cane from his dual purpose snack and staff: a rod of the stuff, freshly cut, is probably the best sustenance to take with you. From the impressive summit, where the curved horizon on the sea seems way below you, the path leads clearly on, over a rounded hillocky landscape, until it meets a dirt road leading to the tarmac an hour or so beyond.

This hike requires the best part of a day but, if you leave Ribeira Grande town by 8am and don't break too often, you can be up at the road by early afternoon – as you'll need to be if you're to have any hope of catching the ferry back to Mindelo.

Deserted islets: Santa Luzia, Ilhéu Branco and Ilhéu Razo

Three desert islands line up in the lee of São Vicente. The biggest, **Santa Luzia**, had a bit of a population towards the end of the eighteenth century – mostly destitute farmers from São Nicolau – but successive droughts and an impossibly harsh terrain expelled them. A more recent inhabitant was the "Governor of Santa Luzia", Francisco Antonio da Cruz, who fled there from his wife and eighteen offspring and lived as a hermit for a number of years. It's now deserted again and, unless you make special efforts by boat, out of reach. Charles Darwin called here in "The Beagle"; herpetologists know Santa Luzia as the only habitat of a large, herbivorous lizard – though it seems likely that it's extinct.

Ilhéu Branco is more of a rock than an island, white (hence the name) from the guano deposits of generations of seabirds, and rising sheer from the sea in a shape supposed to resemble a ship at anchor. Ships stay well clear of its dangerous approaches. If you're sailing between Mindelo and São Nicolau, you're likely to get a good view of the **dolphins** which frequent this leg. **Flying fish** are common too – skittering things the size of a seagull which streak above the surface for several seconds at amazingly high speed.

By the time you reach **Ilhéu Razo**, you can see the jagged, cloud-protected silhouette of São Nicolau. Razo is famous – among ornithologists and conservationists – for the **Razo Island Lark**, a dun, ordinary-looking lark that, perversely, nests only on this barren slab, making it an exceedingly rare species. The Razo lark has an extra strong beak for digging up the drought-resistant grubs it feeds on. It should survive until population pressure and a solution to the problem of drought bring the first human colonists to the island.

São Nicolau

Like the peaks of a submerged mountain, **SÃO NICOLAU** rises from the ocean between São Vicente and Sal. Of its **beauty** – an elegant, hatchet-shaped trio of ridges meeting in spectacular summits above the hidden capital of **Ribeira Brava** – there's no doubt. But the cruelly desolate slopes (this is the driest of the "agricultural" islands) testify to a history of extraordinary hardship – eternal isolation, migration and desertion. The problem, as ever, is water, or chronic lack of it. In recent years, efforts have been made to tap the deep underground water table – notably with the help of French *cooperants* – and a number of dams are planned, but the legacy of centuries of neglect lives on and the drift away from the island is continuous. Driving through the countryside, you notice that virtually every other house is abandoned, and between the deserted shacks lie the ruins of older dwellings, left in earlier famines. However there have been a few good rainy seasons in the last decade; corn, planted every year, actually grows to maturity some seasons, and water has flowed again from village pumps.

São Nicolau is a good place to have **transport** of your own. If, as is likely enough, you haven't – and don't have unlimited time on the island either – you should make efforts to fix something up straight away; there's virtually no public transport. **Arriving by ship** at Tarrafal, the island's main port, you should aim to get the first transport up to Ribeira Brava. Shared *carrinhos* charge about CV$200, chartered taxis about CV$3000. **Flying in**, the airstrip is just 4km from Ribeira Brava (midway between the town and the minor port of Preguiça), and you're likely to be able to find a taxi into town (CV$500). There are flights to São Nicolau from Sal (Wed, Fri, Sat, Sun), and from Praia via Mindelo (Wed, Fri, Sat).

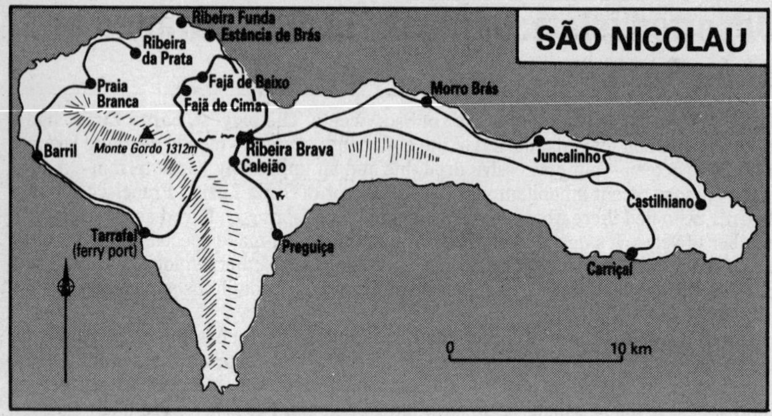

Tarrafal

At **Tarrafal**, on the southwest coast, none of the island's meld of destitution and scenic splendour is immediately obvious. The shallow bay (giving you the chance to help the local economy by paying exorbitantly to be ferried ashore by lighter) gives on to the largest region of relatively gentle terrain on São Nicolau, from where the spectacle of the interior isn't apparent.

Tarrafal's main activity is **tuna fishing**, supplying the important canning plant of the *Sociedade Ultrmarine de Conservas*. While you'll see the great beasts hauled up on many a Cape Verdean beach, the evening business at Tarrafal seems to yield some particularly spectacular specimens, many as big as a person. People are quite happy to have you watching as the fish are wheeled into the co-op on wagons, to reappear in cans. You can also join the kids on the **swimming beach** – the hot grey sands of which are said to be good for rheumatism. A few kilometres further north, towards Barril, there are much better beaches, safe and worth snorkelling, among them the little white sand cove of Praia das Francêses.

If you get stuck at Tarrafal, you'll soon locate the good *casa de pasto* along the shore to the left of the jetty, where the welcome is warm and the meals generous. **Rooms** are also available, at the *Pensão Alice* (②).

Over the island spine

The 26km of nearly deserted cobblestone between Tarrafal and Ribeira Brava is another of Cape Verde's scenically outstanding routes. After a steady and satisfying pull away from the broad, southwest bay and up to around 800m, the road takes a sudden and breathtaking swing to the left and within seconds is skating above the fractured bowl of the island's north side. Going by foot from here is a good plan: there's a steep track down to the nest of the town, an hour or two's knee-wobbling on foot – negotiable also by bike they say – or, with the day before you, take the gentler descent along the main road, incised into the cliff, with the soaring needle peaks of **Monte Gordo** dominating the skyline to the southwest. During the late summer months this – the *Fajãs* – can be a fabulously beautiful valley, spilling with green from the concerted efforts of farmers and hydrologists, dashed with colour from briefly flowering plants, spiked with the strange shapes of **dragon trees** – drought-resistant Nicolauan peculiarities. Behind, trailers of cloud – higher, thinner, pointier and more Gothic than anywhere else – float past the spires of Monte Gordo. In front, the road winds down past the hamlets and farm plots towards a deep blue North Atlantic. The walk, about 15km from the peaks down to the town via a swerving series of deep rents along the north coast, is enchanting.

Ribeira Brava

RIBEIRA BRAVA, facing out to sea on the north side, is firmly Portuguese in feel. A delightfully pretty mesh of narrow streets and whitewash, nestled deep between towering crags, it was established in the seventeenth century, about as far inland as possible, in order to resist the attacks of pirates.

The big, sky-blue **parish church** here, the Igreja Matriz, was the Cape Verdean see until the twentieth century. It's supposed to hold a small museum of religious bits and pieces, among them a valuable and unusual sixteenth-century golden chalice, but it rarely seems to be open. You've a better chance at the **seminary**, a little way up the *ribeira*, which once provided a classical education for students from all over the islands. Here there's a library and reliquary attached to the chapel, and you should be able to persuade the priest to let you in. Back in town there's a fine *praça* and town hall with neatly tended gardens in front, and a memorial bust (1876) to a much loved doctor – Júlio José Dias. The site of the town hall was the birthplace in 1872 of José Lopes da Silva, a leading Cape Verdean poet. Down on the bank of the *ribeira* a shady, second *praça* hides a café and tables for serious draughts-playing and *grogue*-imbibing.

All rather obscure attractions perhaps, but they're central to the town's appeal: Ribeira Brava, once the flourishing centre of academic and literary life in Cape Verde, quickly establishes its remote, insular identity and is a rewarding place to **stay** for a few days. Check out the large but rather scruffy *Pensão da Cruz* (☎35.12.28; ②), the simple, and cheaper *Residêncial Sila* (☎35.11.88; ②), or the little *Pousada Municipal* (①–②). Ribeira Brava also has a bank, post office (Correio), a small *mercado* and two or three basic general stores. You may even stumble across a workshop manufacturing cups and utensils – functional and miniature – out of bamboo; a tiny part of a tiny souvenir industry. It's not enough to keep many younger people here and the drift to Mindelo, Praia and abroad is unceasing.

The rest of the island

To get to the **rest of the island** you'll need to find someone who's driving. One of the few available Land Rovers is sometimes rented out (with owner) for around CV$5000 per day: it's almost worth the expense for the pleasure of being able to offer lifts to dozens of otherwise stranded Nicolauans as you go.

The communities of the north-west – **Barril**, **Praia Branca** and **Ribeira de Prata** – are only accessible by track back through Tarrafal, though you could explore the possibility of hiking round via the north coast fishing villages of Estancia de Brás and Ribeira Funda, only a few kilometres from the main road. The western road is planned to become a complete loop in the near future.

Looking east, the long axis of the island stretches 30km, narrowing at one point to less than three kilometres across. There are two principal tracks – a "ridgeway" and a north coast path – which meet high above the harbour of **Carriçal**. You'll need to be fit and determined to hike out here – supplies are very few and far between.

INTER-ISLAND FLIGHTS FROM SÃO NICOLAU

Praia: Sunday, 55min.

São Vicente: 4 flights weekly, 30min.

Sal: 4 flights weekly, 40min.

TACV in Ribeira Brava ☎31.47.24

Sal

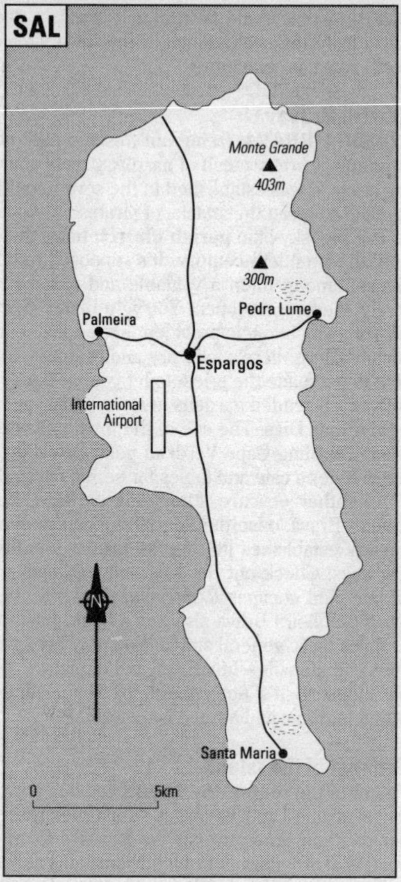

SAL, the "island of salt" – a piece of Sahara in the middle of the ocean – is the least inviting of the archipelago. Relentlessly windy and mostly flat, it's a good location for Cape Verde's main international **airport**. The majority of islanders seem to be involved with this in some way – or in the military base nearby – and the old salt-based economy looks pretty defunct. Whether you fly in from Europe or just pass through during a boat or plane connection, there's a high chance you'll sample Sal sooner or later. Attractions are simple to list – one beautiful white **beach**, which you're recommended to aim for without delay. There's almost nothing else worth a pause. On a positive note, if Sal is your first stop in Cape Verde, you can at least be sure that everywhere else you go will be more interesting.

Sal was one of the last islands to be colonized, early in the nineteenth century, when the Portuguese began to exploit its **salt** ponds properly and introduced purification techniques. In earlier centuries, vast heaps of salt could be loaded onto ships for the cost of the labour alone, though since it was full of donkey dung it was considered low-grade even then. Sal's salt was picked up by trawlers from England on their way to North Atlantic fishing grounds, and exported to the Newfoundland fishing towns and later to Brazil for beef preservation.

The tourist hotels and water sports for which the island is beginning to acquire a reputation are down at at the beach **Santa Maria**, at the southern tip of the island. **Espargos**, the capital, is the business end of things, with all the island's low-budget accommodation. Surprisingly modern as the **airport** is, it only bursts into life when an international flight is in. Airline offices – *South African Airlines*, *Aeroflot* (☎41.11.80), *TAP Air Portugal* (☎41.12.55) and *TACV* – are scattered around the tarmac. **Car rental** is available from *Transcor* (☎41.14.39) or *Alucar* (☎41.10.89).

INTER-ISLAND FLIGHTS FROM SAL

Boa Vista: 5 flights weekly, 20min.
Praia: 1–4 flights daily, 50min.
São Nicolau: 5–6 flights weekly, 45min.
São Vicente: 1–2 flights daily, 60min.

TACV in Espargos ☎41.13.05

Espargos

Arriving by boat you enter a drab grey bay – **Palmeira harbour** – and have to wait for a lift to **ESPARGOS**, the main urbanization (town sounds too characterful) on the island, 4km away. If nothing shows you might as well start walking; it's all pretty forlorn and there's unlikely to be a vehicle around anyway (except twice a week when the lobster boats come in amid great excitement and the live captives are whisked to the airport for export to Europe). If you fly into Sal, Espargos is barely 2km north up the road from the **airport** – you could probably walk there in twenty minutes. Taxis charge CV$100 or CV$150 into town, with a thirty percent surcharge at night.

Little Espargos is uninspiring – a post office in an unmarked pink mansion in the middle of town, a small market, a few groceries, two or three *pensões* and a couple of bar/cafés. Sand whistles across the half-dozen nameless streets. It's hard to believe that anyone would choose to live here.

Accommodation and eating

Pensão Doña Angela. The plain and simple rooms here are your best target and Angela herself a good-humoured hostess. Decent evening meals for CV$500 or so. ②–③.

Restaurante Arcada. Good new bar-restaurant, opposite the *Atlantico*, with a terrace and a surprisingly lively atmosphere.

Hotel Atlantico (☎41.12.10). A big, new place with the sort of airport-style facilities you'd expect; *TACV* sometimes lodge passengers here when connections are overbooked. ④–⑤.

Residêncial Central (☎41.13.66). Decent place with fairly priced food – and you may get a good cup of coffee in the bar. ③.

Out of town

For whatever reason you're here, it's nice to get out of the town. You can do this quickly (and perhaps illicitly, so don't stop to ask anyone) by climbing to the summit of the **telecommunications hill** just five minutes' walk from the *praça*. From up there behind the dishes you have a good view of the entire, drab island; to the north a number of old volcanic hills; southwards the bleak brown wastelands fading away to the fringe of white beach at Santa Maria.

If you have several hours on your hands, go further, to **Pedra da Lume**, on the east coast of Sal, about 6km from Espargos. Any vehicle that passes is almost certain to stop for you. Pedra da Lume itself is an old salt port, comprising an apologetic set of bleak apartment blocks, a tiny harbour too shallow for any but the smallest vessels, and mounds of rock-hard, dirty salt. The ship repair yard still functions and the harbour is also home to a bizarre ship runway used to haul out small boats for loading and a set of rickety nineteenth-century pulleys and loading equipment. It resembles nothing so much as the mine set in a cowboy film. Follow the creaking overhead pulley system uphill for a kilometre and you reach the rim of a gigantic, shallow, crater, awesome in extent. It seems to lie below sea level – perfect for salt production as the sea water is simply allowed to flood in and evaporate. People will tell you it's all still in use, but it certainly doesn't look that way.

Santa Maria

To **get to Santa Maria**, you might catch an *aluguer* from Espargos, or likely as not a free lift if you take time to walk down to the turn-off for the **airport**. Taxis from the airport charge CV$ 750 to get to the resort. The short trip down to the south coast is a journey through a real desert, where encirclement by sea, rather than offering relief, merely seems to stress the land's dessication. Goats, apparently surviving off rubbish, are about the only animals you'll see: their introduction in the seventeenth and eighteenth century, before any significant human settlement, began a process of **soil**

destruction which is now virtually complete. Nothing really grows, wild or cultivated. It all looks as if it was scoured by bulldozers the day before.

SANTA MARIA DAS DORES (St Mary of Sorrows) is practically a ghost town, though not without a desolate fascination. Ruined timber buildings in ornate style are scattered across the flats, linked by the twisted remains of narrow gauge rail track which once shifted tuna for the Portuguese and still goes out to the end of the thoroughly unsafe jetty. The historical interest, however, is slight. Santa Maria's pull is the stunning flex of white sand dipping into blue-green waves of scintillatingly clear water, and the heady shade of the hotels by the beach. When you're hungry, the hotels do decent (if relatively expensive) **meals**, and there are several small eateries in Santa Maria, including a French-style café and *Américo's*, which does good grilled fish. Most of the small crowd stay by the hotel pools, which is fine, giving you a perfect, private beach much of the time and some of the best swimming in the Cape Verdes.

Hotels

Hotel Aeroflot (aka *Albatroz*; ☎41.14.76). Neither of its names do it any favours, but this is the most affordable of the three "international" hotels on Sal and comes with a salt-water swimming pool, Russian cable TV and a fully equipped gym. Forget the restaurant. ⑤.

Hotel Belorizonte (formerly part of the *Novotel* chain; ☎41.14.45). A couple of hundred metres west of the *Morabeza*, this seems superfluous and much less appealing. ⑤–⑥.

Hotel Morabeza (☎41.14.20). Not a cheap place to stay but this is the best resort. It has a good restaurant with a variety of fresh salads and other surprising edibles (all flown in; CV$500 and up) and there's a wide range of water sports including windsurfing. ⑥.

Motor-Inn (☎42.11.38). Strange name, considering how few motorists might decide to call it a day and stop here for the night, but it's a really good place to stay, with an excellent restaurant. ④.

Boa Vista

Boa Vista is said to have been productive at one time; at present it is almost a desert. Its people, of whom there are four thousand, are almost always hungry, and the lean cattle, with sad faces and tears in their eyes, walk solemnly in cudless rumination over grassless fields. In the valleys there is some vegetation. Fishing, salt-making and going to funerals are the chief amusements and employments of the people.

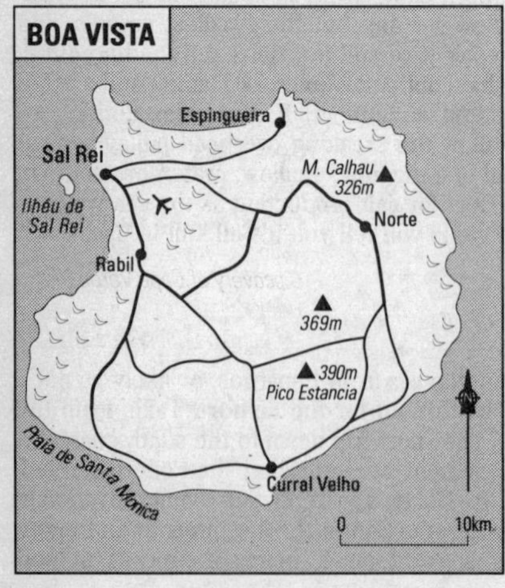

Life was not easy when the Rev. Charles Thomas went to **BOA VISTA** in the 1850s, but things have improved a little, at least for the cattle. The rains of recent years have made the hillocky pancake of an island greener than in living memory, though it still retains large areas of spectacular shifting **sand dunes**, notably in the west.

The island's struggling economy long depended on salt, but that industry has died out and now dates – there are large palm groves near the airstrip – supplemented by fishing and some livestock grazing, provide the main alternatives to emigration. Boavistans seem to have made best use too of the **shipwrecks** which frequently took place in the treacherous rocky shallows on the north and northeast coasts. There are judged to be about a hundred, some quite old; the last big one was a Spanish freighter in 1968 whose cargo of car parts, garlic, rosemary and pornographic magazines was rapidly traded across the island. The wreck of the *Cabo de Santa Maria* is still rusting off the beach, 8km northeast of Sal Rei, and items from the cargo can still be found in many Boavistan homes. **Turtles** were grist to the Boavistan mill as well, and unfortunately still are. There are precious egg-laying sites on many beaches.

Few travellers ever make it here and, apart from a necklace of spectacular white **beaches** all around (the one at Santa Monica is the most beautiful), there's little incentive, unless you're a diver and have your own gear, or hire the necessary on Sal. Boa Vista is a good place to explore under your own steam, however, with undemanding hills and a network of rural roads. If you don't have a bicycle or motorbike, you'll find the *aluguers* reasonably plentiful. Outside the only small town, accommodation is primitive but cheap, and people graciously welcoming, with a high proportion of English-speakers who've spent years at sea. The traditional *mornas* (folksongs) of the island are rated the most cheerful and upbeat in Cape Verde.

Sal Rei

SAL REI, the capital, is grubby and uninteresting, its own beach mutilated by a municipal dump. If you can find a boat, a trip out to the **Ilhéu de Sal Rei**, an islet opposite the town, is interesting: it holds the ruins of an old fort (Fortaleza Duque de Braganza) and the waters are good for snorkelling. Around the month of August you may even see turtles here.

As for a **place to stay**, the small *Residêncial Boa Esperança* (☎51.11.70; ②) is your only option for a cheapish bed. The quite new *Hotel Dunas* on the front (☎51.12.25; ③) has more appealing rooms. Pay some attention to the lobsters, which are ridiculously cheap and plentiful away from the hotels. To please you, people will cook special potato dinners with expensive spuds imported from other islands, while they make do with the local staple of lobster. So insist you want ordinary food – "Queria comida comum".

INTER-ISLAND FLIGHTS FROM BOA VISTA

Praia: 3 flights weekly, 45min.

Sal: 4 flights weekly, 20min.

TACV in Sal Rei ☎51.11.37

index

CHAPTER SIX

GUINEA-BISSAU

GUINEA-BISSAU

One of the smallest and least-known countries in West Africa, **Guinea-Bissau** was also the last on the mainland to regain its independence – from Portugal, in 1974 – and it entered the world's consciousness as a highly charged symbol of colonial repression. Guinea-Bissau's revolutionary **war of liberation** helped overthrow the dictatorship in Portugal and its revolution persisted after independence. Until the end of the 1970s, the country's struggle for national survival inspired progressive movements in Europe and North America, as Nicaragua did in the 1980s. But political rigidity set in with economic failure, and enthusiasm for the revolution waned both in Guinea-Bissau and overseas.

Geographically, Guinea-Bissau is spread across a region of low-lying jungle and grassland, meandering rivers, mangrove forest, estuarine flats and offshore islands. To the north lies Senegal, and to the east and south the Republic of Guinea.

The country's **economic situation** has improved a good deal in the past few years – gone are the days of unobtainable food supplies and bananas being exchanged for unearthly sums. The indigenous Fula community is in the vanguard of the commercial renaissance; Mauritanian traders have moved in; and Fula traders from the Republic of Guinea are mostly choosing to continue their voluntary exile in Guinea-Bissau, despite political improvements in their homeland.

The **Guinea-Bissauans** are generally effortless company and very laid-back. Gentle manners (men spend much time with their children for example) and a sense of personal security feature in your travels wherever you go. The agreeable atmosphere is partly explained by the country's unusual history. Although colonial rule was repressive and the war very bitter, the relationship between the peoples of Guinea-Bissau and Portugal began in the mid-fifteenth century and was generally good. From the earliest contact, Portuguese settlers married local women. The result has been a widespread creolization of culture in mainland Guinea-Bissau – outward looking, self-confident and somewhat cosmopolitan. The islands, as you'll discover if you visit them, are no less friendly, but very different.

Where to go

Travelling would be incredibly difficult were the country not so small: most journeys require at least one ferry ride, often more, and the tides determine when the ferries operate. The most worthwhile destinations are the admirably languid, dream-like **Bijagós islands**. Getting to them isn't that easily accomplished, however, and you need to allow for some discomfort and inconvenience, especially if you want to see more than the two most frequently visited islands – Bolama and Bubaque.

For the present, with the exception of one or two special, local attractions and a lovely absence of hustle, it's perhaps unfair to recommend **the mainland** very highly. What stands out is the poverty and inadequacy of most communities – including Bissau, the capital – despite a super-abundance of greenery and unexploited agricultural potential. You'll see families eating meals that consist of nothing more than plain white rice (often imported) and parts of the country still have an atmosphere of decay and abandon. The war's toll accounts for much, even twenty years on. Yet despite this downside, it is rare for visitors to have bad experiences in Guinea-Bissau and you may find you like the country immensely.

FACTS AND FIGURES

La Republica da Guiné-Bissau covers 36,000 square kilometres, barely half the size of Scotland or Maine. The population is about one million, but the rate of growth is slower than in most African countries. The country's **foreign debt** amounts to some £450 million ($750 million), a massive figure until compared with just the annual profit of the electrical goods company *Philips*, for example, which is rather more. Yet the debt amounts to nearly twenty times the value of the country's annual exports of goods and services (this is analogous to living on the breadline and having debts amounting to twenty times your annual income). After democratic elections in 1994, the **government**, under the presidency of Commander João "Nino" Vieira, is run by the*PAIGC* party, which has nearly two-thirds of the seats in the national assembly.

The people

The biggest of Guinea-Bissau's two dozen ethnic groups is the **Balante**, people of the southern coastal creeks and forests. Much of the area under rice cultivation has been cleared by them over the centuries. In the northwest, the smaller population of **Fulup** (part of the Jola group from southern Senegal) are also great rice farmers. **Pepel** and **Manjak** farmers from the Bissau region are heavily dependent on the city as a market, and operate a more diverse economy. In contrast, the **Bijagó** people, on the islands, are mostly self-sufficient (principally through fishing and palm nut-gathering), though men increasingly find work on the mainland or abroad. The Bijagós (a population of less than 40,000) have been under little pressure to change over the last 200 years. They've easily resisted Islam and Chrisitianity, and remain very attached to traditional ways. Women have relatively greater economic power than is usually the case, as they are the traditional owners of houses.

In the mainland interior, the biggest contingents are **Fula**- and **Mandinka**-speaking, and there's greater mixing and wider social horizons in the mostly Muslim towns and villages of the east and north. The Fula (the country's second largest language group) are, as ever, powerful players in local politics: their conservative, feudal roots can't be ignored by the government in Bissau.

A noticeable proportion of Guinea-Bissauans are mixed-race **Kriolu**-speakers; mostly from the Cape Verde Islands (much of whose population was composed originally of slaves from Portuguese Guinea), but also descendants of the small number of settlers and traders who came direct from Portugal. A fragmented Portuguese settler community still exists, bolstered by more recent expat arrivals from Lisbon, now being encouraged by the government.

When to go

The **best time to visit** is December and January. During these months, the islands are really pleasant. The *carnaval* season in Bissau (February) is a good time to be in the capital. **Bad times**, particularly in Bissau itself, are the end of the rains (November), as the sun evaporates the moisture into the leaden air, and the nerve-fraying run-up to the rains in April and May when breathing seems an impossibility. In the five very wet months, from June to October, the air is dripping wet all the time – whether it's raining or not.

For a climate chart for Bissau, see p.426.

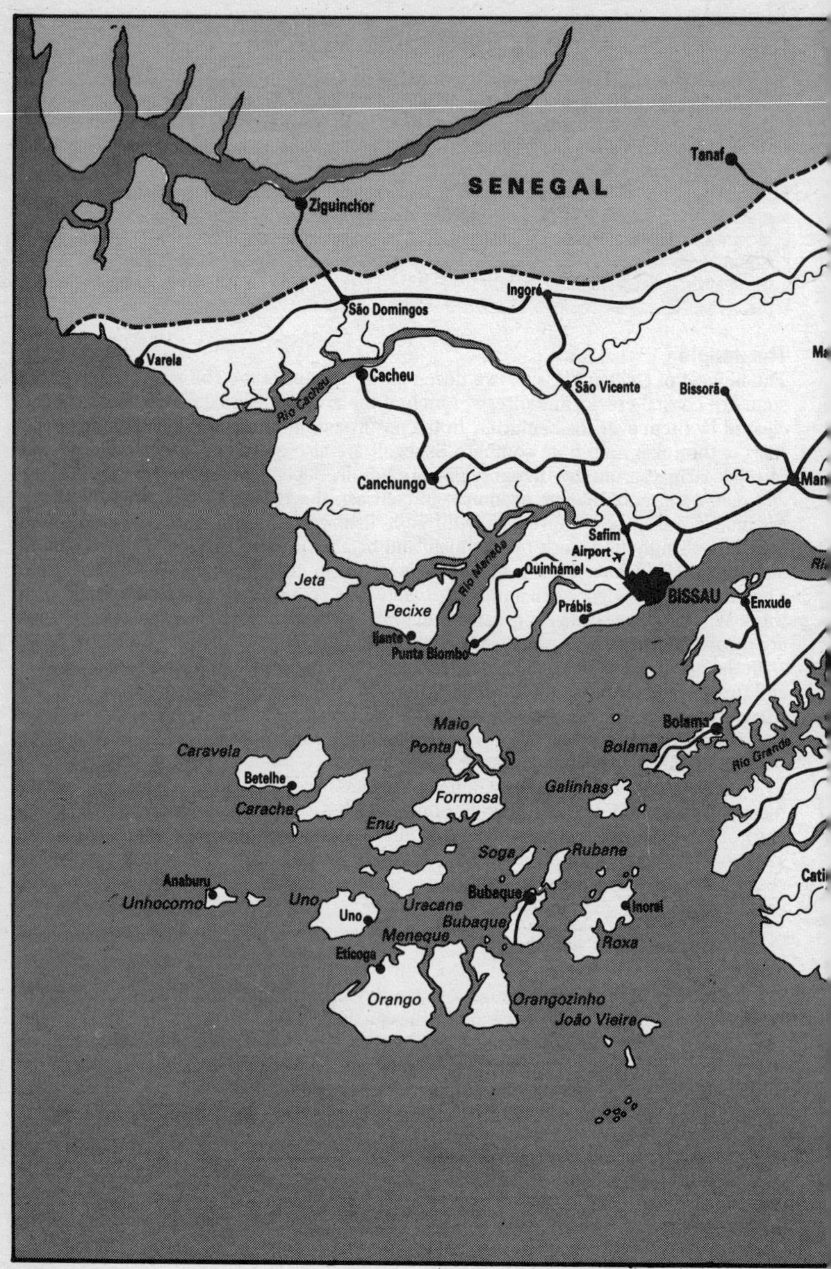
SENEGAL
Tanaf
Ziguinchor
Ingoré
São Domingos
Varela
Cacheu
Rio Cacheu
São Vicente
Bissorã
Canchungo
Safim
Airport
Quinhámel
Rio Mansôa
BISSAU
Enxude
Prábis
Jeta
Pecixe
Ijante
Punta Biombo
Maio
Ponta
Bolama
Bolama
Rio Grande
Caravela
Betelhe
Carache
Formosa
Galinhas
Enu
Soga
Rubane
Anaburu
Unhocomo
Uno
Uno
Uracane
Bubaque
Bubaque
Inorei
Roxa
Meneque
Eticoga
Orango
Orangozinho
João Vieira

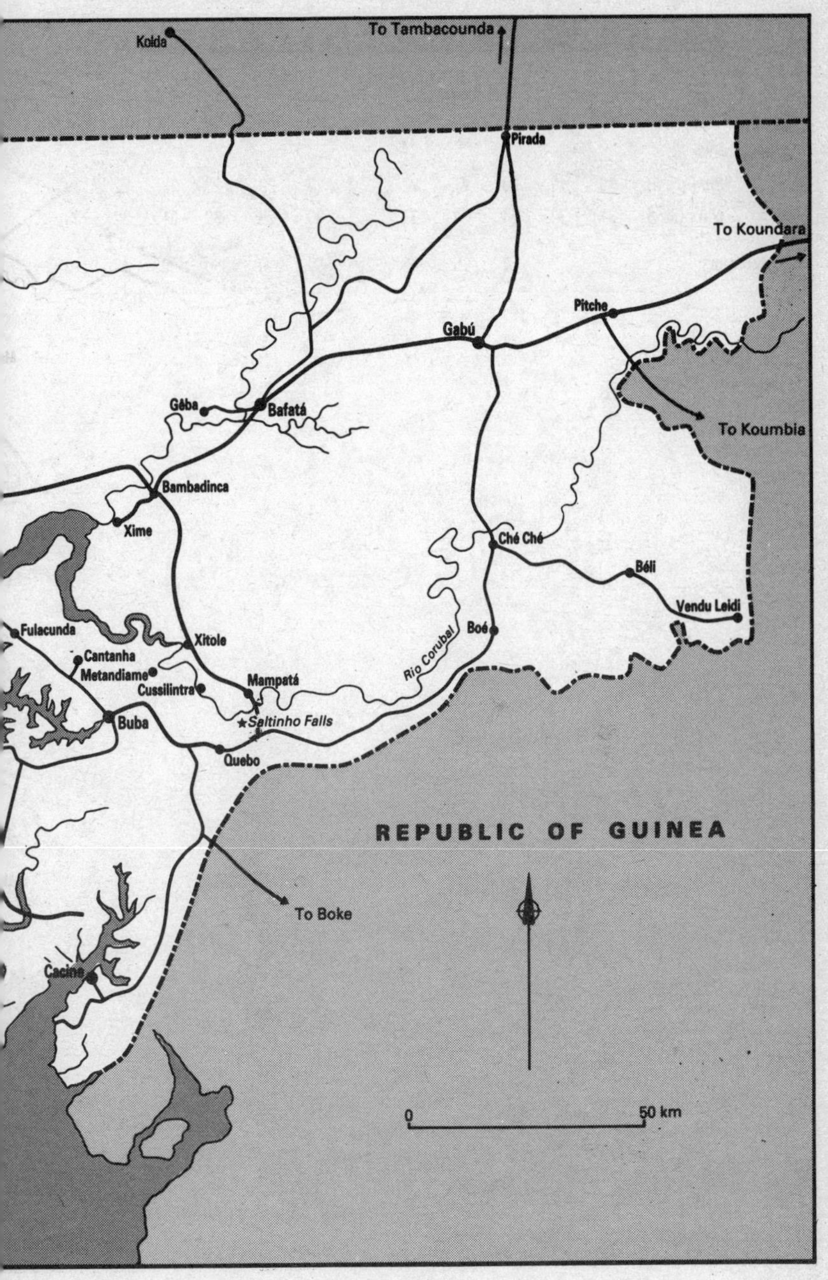
To Tambacounda
Kolda
Pirada
To Koundara
Pitche
Gabú
Géba
Bafatá
To Koumbia
Bambadinca
Xime
Ché Ché
Béli
Vendu Leidi
Boé
Fulacunda
Xitole
Rio Corubal
Cantanha
Metandiame
Cussilintra
Mampatá
Saltinho Falls
Buba
Quebo
REPUBLIC OF GUINEA
To Boke
Cacine
0
50 km

AVERAGE TEMPERATURES AND RAINFALL

BISSAU

	Jan	Feb	Mar	Apr	May	June	July	Aug	Sept	Oct	Nov	Dec
Temperatures °C												
Min (night)	18	19	20	21	22	23	23	23	23	23	22	19
Max (day)	31	33	34	34	33	31	30	29	30	31	32	30
Rainfall mm	2	2	7	15	45	200	850	900	390	180	40	5

Arrivals

Most visitors to Guinea-Bissau either fly in or cross the border from Senegal, though a few European yachts make it down here from the Canaries.

■ Flights from Africa

If you are planning to fly to Bissau **from another African capital**, you'll find your options are extremely limited. Senegal, The Gambia, Guinea and Cape Verde are the only countries with direct services.

Flights come **from Dakar** via **Ziguinchor** on *Air Sénégal* (DS) on Mon and Fri; and from Dakar on *Air Afrique* (RK) on Thurs, and on the Guinea-Bissau airline *TAGB* (YZ) on Tues and Sat.

TAGB also flies non-stop **from Banjul** on Tues and Thurs; **from Conakry** on Mon; and **from Praia** on Wed.

Lastly, *Guinea Air Service* links **Conakry** with Bissau via **Boké** every Thurs.

All other African flights are routed through Dakar, or use *Air Afrique* from **Abidjan** to connect with the *TAGB* flights out of Dakar.

■ Overland from Senegal or The Gambia

Because of limitations on flights from Europe, many visitors fly into Dakar or Banjul and then travel **overland by public transport**; a journey which is straightforward despite its complicated appearance on the map. Peugeot 504s go direct from Dakar to Ziguinchor, in southern Senegal. You'll have to accept an obligatory night in Ziguinchor, and take another bush taxi on to Bissau in the morning, crossing the border at **São Domingos**. Most of the road down to the Senegalese border at Mpak is an excellent highway. At São Domingos, the road to Bissau turns left and is paved all the way to the capital, via Ingoré, allowing you, if you're lucky with speedy border formalities and the two short ferry crossings, to do Zinguinchor–Bissau in as little as four hours.

The alternative route from São Domingos is to use the car ferry through the creeks **from São Domingos to Cacheu**. It's an interesting way of covering kilometres, but only when tides and ferries permit will you get from Ziguinchor to Cacheu in time to connect with transport on to Bissau on the same day.

The details in these practical information pages are essentially for use on the ground in West Africa and in Guinea-Bissau itself: for full practical coverage on preparing for a trip, getting here from outside the region, paperwork, health, information sources and more, see *Basics*.

Less commonly used routes from Senegal into the country exist from Tanaf to **Farim**, from Velingara to **Gabú** and from Kolda, 70km east of Tanaf, to **Bafatá** in central Guinea-Bissau; Farim, Gabú and Bafatá all have regular connections to Bissau.

From The Gambia, via Ziguinchor, you might be able to make the trip to Bissau in one long day, though you're better to plan for an overnight stop in Ziguinchor and an early start next day.

■ Overland from Guinea

Driving **from Guinea** in your own vehicle, you have a choice betwen two main routes. The first takes the tarmac road to **Labé** via Mamou, battles up to **Koundara** (a stretch that can be reasonable during the dry season), then crosses the border at Kandika, and follows the bush track to Gabú, from where it's smooth tarmac all the way to Bissau. This is a two- or three-day trip.

The second route goes from Conakry north to Boké, through **Koumbia and Foula-Mori**, then takes the ferry crossing at the border and joins the main road to Bissau at Pitche. Normal driving time between the capitals in the dry season is not much less than 22 hours on this route. With a dawn start from Conakry in a tough vehicle you might just make it to the border in time to catch the ferry man at dusk, and so be in Gabú or Bafatá late at night; but planning on a two-day journey is much more feasible.

On **public transport**, the route via Labé and Koundara is the only one with regular connections, allowing three long days for the journey. On the route via Koumbia and Foula-Mori, you'll be delayed waiting for vehicles in the border area.

The third, more obvious-looking route **following the coast** is an arduous trek, not recommended unless you have bags of time. From Boké it goes via a new bridge and Sansalé to Buba in Guinea-Bissau, thence to Enxude and by ferry or *pirogue* to Bissau.

Red Tape

Visas, generally easy to obtain, are required by nearly all nationalities apart from West Africans. Some, but not all Guinea-Bissau consulates in Europe issue visas for overland entry. At the consulates in Banjul and Ziguinchor, they're cheap and normally issued while you wait. The embassies in Dakar, Abidjan and Conakry are more formal.

The consulate in Ziguinchor, Senegal, issues thirty-day **single entry visas** on the spot. These are useful if you're in doubt about whether you'll subsequently be allowed into the Republic of Guinea for, if there's any question, Guinea-Bissau border guards won't let you leave their country without a visa allowing you to re-enter.

If you're flying into Bissau from one of the many countries with no Guinea-Bissau embassy or consulate, you can get a visa at the airport in Bissau, though you're strongly advised to try to get one beforehand.

Extending your visa, once in the country, is not difficult (ask at the main police station), but allowing it to expire and overstaying can lead to surprisingly serious problems if detected.

■ Visas for onward travel

Don't count on getting many stamps in Bissau. **Nigeria**, **Senegal**, **Mauritania** and **Guinea** are the West African states with diplomatic missions here and the French embassy can help with several others. Although there's a weekly flight to Praia, there's no Cape Verde embassy.

Money, Banks and Costs

The Guinea-Bissau *peso* (GB$) is a weak currency, valueless outside the country. There's still an unofficial market in foreign currency (*devisas*), principally CFA francs, French francs and US dollars: you should have some of one of these three currencies when you arrive. Inflation is running at 50–100 percent, but the official rate of exchange as this book is published is approximately GB$25,000 = £1, GB$16,000 = $1. Prices in pesos tend to be adjusted to the prevailing rate of exchange.

The **free market rate** (it's tolerated and no longer "black") is higher by ten percent and you can change legally at private forex bureaux. The best deal seems to be to cash travellers' cheques for hard currency at one of the forex bureaux, then use that to change small denominations with private individuals on the free market as you need *pesos*.

CFA francs can be used quite widely for payment and a number of hotels are licensed to accept – and will insist on payment in – hard currency, while setting their tariffs in pesos. Prices are commonly quoted in **contos**, equal to GB$1000: *três contos* is GB$3000. The largest *peso* note is GB$10,000, worth about £0.40 or $0.60.

On entering the country you may be asked to change some hard currency into *pesos* at the official rate of exchange. At the airport, it's normally a fixed value. At São Domingos the requirement has been dropped and at many land borders it amounts more to a gift of cheap *devisas* to the man in charge. Only very scrupulous travellers will declare all their cash. A few thousand CFA (exchanged at an often fictitious rate actually *below* that of the banks) normally satisfies.

Changing in **banks** – the main commercial bank is the *Banco Internacional da Guiné Bissau* – is a generally inefficient process that can take all morning. The new forex bureaux in Bissau are much faster as well as offering better rates. Outside of Bissau, the only banks with exchange facilities are in **Canchungo**, **Bafatá** and **Gabú** and on the Senegalese border at **Pirada**.

Credit cards are virtually useless except in Bissau – and then only for guests in Bissau's top hotel. The *BIGB* bank can arrange credit card **cash advances**.

■ Costs

Costs aren't easily reckoned in advance and we give the best current estimates. Outside of Bissau, there's very little to spend your money on, so the cost of a stay in the country is generally low, and can be minimal. Hotels are clearly the main expense, and even many of the less expensive ones now charge in CFA, and insist you pay on checking in. A cheap room costs GB$125,000–250,000 (say CFA5000–10,000) in Bissau but less on Bubaque or up country. Meals are usually excellent value. Transport costs, paid in *pesos*, are low in hard currency terms.

Health

Unless you fly straight in from Europe, you must show your yellow fever certificate on

arrival. You should take extra care to avoid catching malaria – easily done here – and be aware of the potential hazards of going down with the disease in some isolated corner of the country, especially on a remote island. There was a moderately serious epidemic of cholera in the country in 1994/95.

The only **hospitals** are in Bissau (which has 80 of the country's 150 doctors), Bafatá, Canchungo and Bolama. Bubaque has some medical infrastructure. Out on the other islands and in the south, your health problems are largely your own to deal with.

Bilharzia is a menace on sluggish inland waters, but the rivers are tidal far into the interior (the Rio Gêba as far upstream as Bafatá, the Cacheu past Farim and the Corubal as far as the Saltinho Falls) and the schistosome worms can't survive in brackish water.

Unofficial reports suggest that the country has one of the worst **Aids** problems in the region; many people are infected with the long incubation HIV II virus.

Maps and Information

Tourist information on Guinea-Bissau in English is almost non-existent. There are no official tourist offices, nor much of an organized government department dealing with this minor industry.

If you want to exhaust all possibilities, write (preferably in Portuguese, or at least French) to the *Centro do Informacão e Turismo*, CP 294, Bissau, Guinea-Bissau.

The 1:500,000, 3615 series *IGN* **map** of the country, updated in 1993, is reasonable – and the only one available.

Getting Around

Most travel in Guinea-Bissau is ruled by the tides. On the coast there's a tidal range of over five metres, more than twice the world average. Many communities are cut off except at high tide when ferries can reach them. Departure times are therefore unpredictable, unless you've got local tide tables. Add in frequent breakdowns and the potential for delay is almost unlimited.

■ Ferries

The main ferry operator is the state line *Rodofluvial*. Their office in Bissau supplies monthly lists of dates and estimated departure times for the various routes. Approximate frequencies and journey times (one-way) are:

Bissau–Enxude–Bissau: daily Mon–Fri (1hr 15 min).

Bissau–Bolama–Bissau: out Fri/Sat, back Sun (3hr).

Bissau–Bolama–Catió–Bolama–Bissau: out Tues, back Fri (9hr).

Bissau–Bubaque–Bissau: out Fri, back Sun (4–5hr).

Bissau–Biombo–Pecixe–Biombo–Bissau: out Sat, back Sun (4–5hr).

Cacheu–São Domingos–Cacheu:daily (2–4hr).

Other destinations with at least twice-monthly service include **Empada**, **Xime** and **Cacine**.

Departures can be any time from 5am to 7pm (or the middle of the night for Pecixe), though the first daylight high tide is the usual one.

Tickets, which are quoted at two rates ("ticket office" and "on board"), are usually charged at the lower rate anyway; but if you have the chance, get them in advance. Bolama is around GB$50,000 one way, Bubaque GB$60,000, Enxude GB$30,000. Argue like crazy about paying for your bags: as usual, they're negotiable. Bicycles are charged at a fixed rate around two-thirds of the full fare. Note that none of these regular diesel ferries are built to transport cars.

In addition to the *Rodofluvial* ferries, there are dozens of small hand-hauled ferry bridges and *pirogue* services around the country.

■ Road transport

The **bush taxi** network is improving all the time, but you generally have to be out and about first thing in the morning to get anywhere as there are relatively few vehicles. Conversely, later departures can take forever to fill up. Bush taxis are known as **kandongas** and sometimes marked **"aluguer"** ("for rent").

Renting a car won't help you see the islands, but car rental possibilities do exist in Bissau – usually with a driver. Expect to pay at least US$60 a day, in one currency or another, plus fuel.

If you are riding a **motorbike** or **mobylette**, note that, unlike in neighbouring countries, helmets must be worn.

Hitching around might seem a hopeless task, but unless you devote your days to arranging the next bush taxi trip, you'll find you often end up walking out of the town or village and waiting for a passing vehicle as a preferable alternative to waiting in the taxi park. Aid worker and volunteer vehicles comprise a high proportion of traffic.

Cycling through Guinea-Bissau, so long as you choose your season, is an attractive option. The 500-odd kilometres of sealed road are pleasantly quiet, flat or gently undulating, and often flanked by dense foliage and grass pouring over the road. With a week or two to spare you could explore the south and east, well off the beaten track, quite extensively. If you don't have your own bike, renting one privately in Bissau isn't too difficult. You should also try to do this if you're visiting the islands as, with the exception of Bubaque, transport is hard to come by.

Planes

TAGB keeps up regular flights to **Bubaque** (usually Mon at 7.30am and Fri at 5pm) but it has suspended the air links between Bissau and **Cacine** and **Catió**.

Accommodation

There are very few **hotels** in Guinea-Bissau and the difficulty of getting an inexpensive room, especially in Bissau itself, is a routine feature of travel here. During *carnaval* and possibly also during football's Amílcar Cabral Cup Final in May, you'll have extra trouble finding a room. Your best bet is a **pensão** (plural *pensões*) – a family-run establishment along Portuguese lines. In most of the older, Portuguese-built towns – Canchungo, Bafatá, Gabú – you'll find one or two, but in more out-of-the-way places there is not much call for hotel accommodation and basic, sleazy, bar-restaurant establishments with a few rooms are the norm.

Camping is a tolerated and useful alternative: a tent is particularly helpful on the islands. But getting food and water supplies if you're in a good camping spot is always something of a problem. There are no campsites.

It's not uncommon for travellers to find **private lodging** with Guinea-Bissauans met travelling on public transport. This can be rewarding and illuminating, but most people are very poor and will appreciate your contributions to the evening meal.

Eating and Drinking

In a small country as poor and battered as this, it's no surprise to find little attention paid to gastronomy. White rice is the staple diet of nearly everyone and, for the majority, something to accompany it once or twice a week is the best they can expect.

ACCOMMODATION PRICE CODES

Hotel prices in this chapter are coded according to the following scales – the same scales in terms of their pound/dollar equivalents as are used throughout the book. Prices refer to the rate you can expect to pay for a room with two beds. Single rooms, or single occupancy, will normally cost at least two-thirds of the twin-occupancy rate. In Guinea-Bissau there are not enough hotels to make any more than the simplest generalizations about the facilities you can expect in each price bracket. The higher price brackets normally require payment in hard currency.

① **Under GB$125,000 (under £5/$7.50).** Rudimentary lodgings, with primitive facilities.

② **GB$125,000–250,000 (£5–10/$7.50–15).** Basic hotel.

③ **GB$250,000–500,000 (£10–20/$15–30).** Modest hotel, usually with S/C rooms and sometimes AC.

④ **GB$500,000–750,000 (£20–30/$30–45).** Reasonable business or tourist-class *pensão*, with S/C, AC rooms and a restaurant.

⑤ **GB$750,000–1M (£30–40/$45–60).** Similar to the above.

⑥ **GB$1M–1.25M (£40–50/$60–75).** Comfortable, first-class hotel.

⑦ **Over GB$1.25M (over £50/$75).** Luxury establishment with pool and other special features.

This is unlikely to be your diet, at least not in Bissau itself. Restaurants in the capital (virtually the only town to have them) make the most of **seafood** and whatever else is available, and hotel dining rooms usually manage to produce enormous four-course meals in rustic **Portuguese style**. Rice soup, fish, chicken, tough beef or pork and potatoes are standard fare with, invariably, a banana to finish.

If you're used to eating **bananas** all day, then Guinea-Bissau will be less of a shock to your system. They, together with oranges, cashew nuts and small loaves, are obtainable just about everywhere. Although small supermarkets and corner shops exist, they carry less range than you'd find in, say, Zinguinchor or Conakry, and you'll turn to the markets for basic food requirements. Incidentally, if you are given unshelled cashew nuts, do not try to crack them open with your teeth: the shell contains an intense irritant that will inflame your mouth for days.

There are few Guinea-Bissauan **specialities**. *Cachupa*, the beans, corn and pork dish characteristic of the Cape Verde Islands, is a meal for special occasions. **Monkey meat** (*carne de mono*) is common everywhere and very variable: Bissau is one of the few West African capitals where it's regularly served, though be certain it's well-cooked to avoid the possibility of catching a dangerous virus. Seafood is good in Bissau. Delicious **gambas** – king prawns – are the stock in trade of the European-style restaurants. **Oysters** and other shellfish are often on Bissau menus too.

Locally made *Sagres* **beer** is the national brew. Soft drinks, all imported, are in short supply but local plastic bag juices – lime and lemon juice and wonderful **cashew juice** – can all be found for about GB$250 a bottle. Cashews are very widespread (something like 40 percent of export earnings comes from cashew nuts), and a lethal **hooch** – *canna de cajeu* – is made from the cashew apples which are otherwise inedible and have no other value. The nuts themselves, as well as magnificent mangoes and a tart but not unpleasant little plum unfairly called *miseria*, help to make the end of the dry season bearable.

> **THE BEER RULE**
>
> In older-style restaurants and dining rooms, **beer** is traditionally served only with meals. If you want to drink, eat. And if you've not ordered more beer by the time you get your banana, you may have missed your chance.

Communications – Post, Phones, Language and Media

Guinea-Bissau's mail, in and out, is remarkably efficient and reliable. Very little is ever lost or tampered with, and it's therefore one of the best places to post items home. But mail is remarkably expensive. Faxing and telephoning are pricey, too.

For **poste restante**, you can have letters marked *Lista da Correios* or *Poste Restante*, CTT, Bissau. Be exceptionally pleasant to the *funcionário* in charge.

The main place to do all this business with confidence is the **main post office in Bissau** itself. There are functioning branches in provincial towns, but you should be prepared for considerable delays.

Check out the **stamps** of Guinea-Bissau while you're there. The Portuguese may have left only fifty US cents in the government coffers when they withdrew, but they bequeathed a huge stockpile of postage stamps: "Portuguese Province of Guiné", triangular and garish, denominated in *escudos*, now overprinted in *pesos*. They are collectable philately, and usually sold as such (ordinary mail is paid for and franked without a stamp). At the post office, you may also be able to get some of the classic armed forces **postcards** produced after the war.

Though the telephone system is a good one and you can phone Guinea-Bissau direct from abroad, IDD dialling out of the country is still difficult and you will usually end up talking to the operator to place a call. Note that reverse charge (collect) calls cannot be made.

> **Guinea-Bissau's IDD code is ☎245.**

Language

Although the official language of Guinea-Bissau is **Portuguese**, the widely used, street-friendly vernacular is **Kriolu** (or **Crioulo**). An old amalgam of seafarers' Portuguese with various African languages, this is very similar to Cape Verdean Kriolu (see p.373), but significantly different from

Portuguese. If you speak some Portuguese, Kriolu becomes semi-intelligible. Other important languages include **Bijagós**, on the islands of the same name, **Balante**, the related **Manjak** and **Pepel**, **Mandinka** and **Fula**.

■ The media

Broadcasting is mainly radio, and only in Portuguese. Television broadcasting was introduced in 1989, and the national station now shows programmes every evening from 7pm, but there are still very few TV sets in the country.

Looking to **the press** for news, you'll occasionally see a copy of *Nô Pintcha* (the revolutionary slogan), which is published three times a week in an edition of 6,000, only in Bissau. Look out too for *Baguerra*, published by the PCD opposition party, and the independent *Espresso-Bissau*.

There are a few **foreign papers** on sale around Bissau. If you read Portuguese, popular tabloids from Lisbon are sometimes available. And if you're desperate, the two luxury hotels should have the *Herald Tribune*, *Time* and *Newsweek*.

Directory

AIRPORT DEPARTURE TAX For international departures US$12, but this is somewhat flexible in application.

ART AND ENTERTAINMENT Main artistic event of the year is the *carnaval* in February. Indigenous theatre and cinema are dormant. Music (see below) shows a little more promise.

BARGAINING Haggling over purchases is a brief business: few market traders will discuss for long. The last price is the last price, and quickly reached.

CRAFTS AND THINGS TO BUY A couple of spots in Bissau sell wood-carvings: the main one, the *Centro Artistico Juvenil* (see p.446) is rather good. Because of the lazy-sell attitude of most craft-sellers, you can mull over a fair range without being hassled. Animal skins – crocodile, python, even leopard and serval – are openly displayed too. The government applies no effective sanctions, though the problem is a small one at present.

DUTY FREE GOODS Strictly speaking, all alcohol brought into the country is dutiable.

HOLIDAYS **New Year's Day** is a big event; **January 20** Heroes' Day (assassination of Amílcar Cabral); **February** (variable dates) Bissau carnival; **March 8** International Women's Day; **August 3** National Day (Pidjiguiti Massacre); **September 24** Independence Day (the proclamation of the republic in the liberated zone of Boé in 1973); **November 14** Redemption Day of the Republic (1980 coup that brought the present clique to power); **Christmas Day and December 26** (a family occasion in Bissau).

Throughout the northeast, the **Islamic calendar** is observed, but a few closures and holidays aren't likely to have much noticeable effect on your travels.

MUSIC In Bissau there are several working groups who play live at the clubs. On the international stage, **Kaba Mane** and **Ramiro Naka** have both done what successful African artists tend to do and left the country for the big venues of Europe – in the case of these two, Paris. Upbeat kora-player Kaba Mane sings mostly in Balante, many of his

GLOSSARY

Assimilado In colonial times, an indigenous Guinean who, through education and connections had achieved the status of Portuguese citizen.

Bairro Suburb, slum.

Devisas Hard currency.

Feitoria "Factory" in the historical sense of a trading post.

Fermanza Local name for the dry, dusty *Harmattan* wind from the north.

Kana Sugar cane alcohol.

Kandonga Bush taxi.

Kirintim A fence of woven brushwood (like wattle) often surrounding and identifying a bar.

Navetanes Seasonal migrant workers.

PAIGC The Partido Africano da Independência da Guiné e Cabo Verde, the country's biggest political party.

Ponta Small land concession or trading post in Portuguese Guinea.

RGB–MB The Resistência da Guiné-Bissau – Movimento Bafatá, the leading opposition grouping.

Tabanka Rural village.

songs still firmly based in the *koussounde* style of his roots. Guitarist Ramiro Naka puts on a flamboyant stage show. His songs are in Kriolu, with rhythms derived from traditional *gumbe* drumming – the sound that accompanies big occasions like weddings and funerals.

OPENING HOURS There is very little consistency. Few offices and businesses have more than one location, and that's usually in Bissau. A long lunch break is common, however, usually from 11.30am or noon to 3pm.

PETROL Even in the capital, fuel is often in short supply, or overpriced, so always plan ahead with full jerry cans if you're driving. The price is around GB$10,000/litre.

PHOTOGRAPHY Officialdom is very suspicious of cameras. A permit is required, in theory, but nobody can tell you where to obtain it. In Bissau, avoid the port, presidential palace and most other places with your camera. In country areas, people aren't much concerned and may even ask you to take pictures of them. Photography on the islands is relaxed. Video, and photography in general, is much easier if you're part of an aid project, or connected to one, rather than a "tourist".

PIGS Some of the scrawniest, most long-legged and hirsute hogs you'll ever see live in Guinea-Bissau: many look like dogs. It's possible the breed is a survival of the ancient pig culture of northern Africa that's mostly been obliterated by Islam. Widespread outside the Muslim regions, they perform the street-cleaning functions normally associated with goats.

SPORT African wrestling doesn't carry much kudos in Guinea-Bissau. The big sport is soccer, encouraged by the cultural ties with soccer-mad Portugal and Brazil. There are even two women's teams. Village football is often played at dusk, but the most exciting games take place at the impressive stadium outside Bissau, especially recommended if it's an international match. The Amílcar Cabral Cup Final in May is the major national sporting event.

TROUBLE Guinea-Bissau is one of the least uptight countries in the region, with few roadblocks, and you can easily spend several weeks here without crossing the path of a uniformed official. If you're out on the street at 8am or 6pm, however, remember that the official flag-raising and lowering, accompanied by a bugle, requires you to stand still in silence. The same rule applies when VIP convoys pass you on the road, or when a funeral procession goes by.

The laws on **drug possession** are very tough: possession of a few joints normally leads to deportation, but quite often only after a spell in jail. The maximum sentence for this offence is 25 years.

WILDLIFE Much of the indigenous wildlife was hunted out during the war years or lost its habitat to defoliants or subsequent land clearance. Still, for such a small country, the fauna can be rewarding and it's likely that thorough investigations would turn up a few species unsuspected in this part of the continent. The best areas to look are the hilly southeast, parts of the forested centre, and the outer islands. The large terrestrial mammals are no longer found anywhere, but many species of monkeys and antelopes and some unusual coast dwellers – **manatees**, saltwater-dwelling **hippos** in the Bijagós islands, and large **sea turtles** – compensate for this. Reptile life is prolific. Guinea-Bissau has no national parks or wildlife reserves.

WOMEN TRAVELLERS AND THE WOMEN'S MOVEMENT Men and women can mix freely in Guinea-Bissau, without their association carrying implicit sexual connotations. For women travellers, this makes the country one of the most relaxed in West Africa. Guinean women fought in the war and their presence in the ranks of the revolutionary cadres made a lasting impression in the traditionally conservative and Islamic parts of the country. In these areas, the issues of female emancipation are still fairly hot ones. But the signals received by the rest of the world – that a sexual revolution was taking place in the country – have never been convincingly borne out in the communities. The movement's momentum slowed down in the 1980s, though the structures remain. Contact the *União Democrática das Mulheres* (*UDEMU*) if you're interested (☎21 40 81/21 27 40).

A Brief History Of Guinea-Bissau

Guinea-Bissau was first visited by Europeans in 1456, when Cadamosto, an Italian navigator working for the Portuguese crown, sailed as far as the Rio Mansôa and the Bijagos islands looking for the gold which figured so hugely in the trans-Saharan trade. Other sailors settled on the uninhabited Cape Verde islands over the following decades. By 1500, these communities had sprouted sub-colonies on the Guinean mainland: groups of Portuguese or mixed-race immigrants, partly absorbed into African society, trading with the interior and looking to the ocean. More about this early history of European contact is detailed in the Cape Verde chapter. The emphasis here is on the period of Portuguese colonialism and the brief era of independence since its demise. The story of the region's more ancient past – and of influences from within West Africa – is virtually unknown, except that it didn't result in powerful states or dynasties.

■ Kriolu society

Through the first half of the sixteenth century, the region traded out to Europe an average of over 200,000 grammes of West African **gold** every year. But with the opening up of the "New World", from the later years of the sixteenth century onwards, much of the region which is now Guinea-Bissau, was drawn into the Atlantic **slave-trading network** which linked West Africa with Europe, the Caribbean, South and North America through the Cape Verde archipelago.

Cacheu was the headquarters: by 1600 it had as many as 1000 Kriolu (mixed-race) slave traders and employees. Portugal established a military garrison in 1616 in order to guarantee the maximum revenue to the crown, charging duty on exported slaves and sending cargoes on to the Cape Verdes where they paid further duty. Other towns were established at Farim, Ziguinchor and, later, Bissau and Bolama. But despite Portugal's efforts, the benefits of trade tended to bypass Lisbon. French and English ships could offer better trade goods and more choice. Repeated efforts by the Portuguese government to enforce **trading monopolies** in their area of influence simply pushed traders into illegal commerce. The state administrators charged with extracting taxes and levies invariably exploited their positions, so that **corruption**, **smuggling** and **state control** became inextricably tangled.

The **slaves** tended to come from the least stratified ethnic groups of farmers, fishers and hunters; Fulup and Jola, Manjak and Pepel. The main **slavers** were Mandinka and, later, Fula. The Bijagos were notorious slave-hunters too, launching lethal canoe raids against the mainland. It was a circular business, however. Who was slave and who slaver depended much more on economic strength or vulnerability and on family contacts and position, than on "tribal identity". It wasn't unusual for a king or headman to sell off people under his own rule, such was the attraction of cloth and other imported goods. **Firearms** were available from the early eighteenth century to those who could afford them.

With the general **abolition of slavery** in the early nineteenth century, the slave trade from Guinea continued illicitly, given new life by the needs of Cuba's plantations. Domestic slavery (which was not abolished) was commonly used as a cover. The last big shipments, however, crossed the Atlantic in the 1840s.

Meanwhile, using labour locally, rather than selling it off unproductively, became significant with the introduction of **groundnuts**, first grown along the Gambia River at the end of the eighteenth century. Philip Beaver's attempt to start an English colony of groundnut planters on Bolama had been a disaster (see box on p.452), but local Kriolu landowners had more success. Agreements were made with Bijagos elders on Galinhas and Bolama, from where the crop was spread to the shores of the Rio Grande on the mainland. On the islands, the plantations used slaves. On the shores of the Rio Grande they called them contract labourers, with tools, transport, food, clothes and accommodation charged to the plantation workers out of their share of the crop, usually leaving nothing for wages. Portugal, however, even more than before, benefited little from the exploitation of its colonies. As much as 80 percent of the crop was sold to French trading concerns.

In 1879, Portugal's Guinean territory was separated from Cape Verde administration. The French had occupied Ziguinchor and, following a brief British occupation, **Bolama** became the **first capital** of "Portuguese Guinea".

The Portuguese province

The emptiness of Portugal's pride in its "colonial empire" – at least in the case of Guinea – continued through the end of the nineteenth century, and the formal carving-up of the continent. The **partition of Africa** after 1885 left Portugal with a scattering of territories; of which Guinea-Bissau was perhaps the least promising. Portuguese settlers weren't interested in going there for fear of the climate; and there appeared to be no attractive natural resources. Then, **Fula aggression** – jihads against non-Muslim plantation workers and raids on the foreign-run *feitoria* groundnut stations along the Rio Grande – soon led to a slump in the country's only viable export. With the region now formally annexed to Portugal, only Bolama (the capital from 1890), and the fort-towns of Bissau, Cacheu, Farim and Gêba, were in any sense under colonial rule.

Military campaigns of "pacification" took fifty years to subdue the state of general **revolt** which ensued in the 1890s. And in that time there was precious little thought in Lisbon about the administration of Guinea or the other African territories. It was somehow understood that they had always been a part of Portugal, so there was no specific colonial service, and no consideration of the purposes of colonialism, beyond furthering the greatness of Portugal and extending its benefits to those Africans who could demonstrate their "civilization". The republican government in Portugal, wracked as it was by one military intervention after another, and by costly involvement in World War I, continued virtually to ignore Guinea.

Hut taxes were imposed and labour conscripted to help maintain the colony with as little support from Portugal as possible. Almost the entire African population was classified as **indígena** – disenfranchised, second-class noncitizens. Opportunities for education were very limited, and in practice most urbanites with prospects were Cape Verdeans, or the descendants of Cape Verdean marriages. They, together with mixed race Kriolus and a tiny proportion of **assimilado** mainlanders (less than one in 300, often Fula), formed the bulk of the civil service, as government agents and tax collectors. Cape Verdeans held many professional posts as well.

It was from this small middle class that the first calls were heard for political reform. Before World War I, a political group called the **Liga Guineense** campaigned for the interests of small traders and landowners, highlighting the abuse of powers by government agents and calling for a change in the laws favouring the big commercial enterprises. The *Liga* was outlawed in 1915 without making much impact, but it provided a background – the only indigenous political example – for the radical demands of the *PAIGC* that emerged forty years later.

The **groundnut trade** began to pick up after about 1910, though it crashed again in 1918 when a law came into force prohibiting peasant farmers from trading their crop to foreign buyers. The law was repealed, and by the 1920s, the central parts of the country, particularly around Bafatá, had become the groundnut heartland. The pressure to sell all surpluses to agents of Portugal, however, only tended to stifle production.

Despite the heavy exploitation and inequalities, there was a looseness in governing the overseas territories that failed to suppress the freedom of expression completely. The paternalistic idea of **"colonial trusteeship"** was taken seriously by some: Portuguese culture allowed a vague and distant respect for Africans stemming partly from its own infusion of African culture during the medieval Moorish occupation. But these sentiments were smothered after 1926.

Guinea under the Portuguese "New State"

The military intervention in Lisbon in 1926 was unexpectedly different from previous ones. Instead of installing a new government and withdrawing, **General Carmona** presided over the installation of a military dictatorship which was to last until 1974, holding Portugal back and crippling her overseas territories. **António de Salazar**, a monetarist economics professor, was prime minister from 1932 until 1968. He promulgated the *Estado Novo*, or "**New State**", and ran Portugal on strictly authoritarian lines. The "Province of Guinea", along with the other parts of "Overseas Portugal" were brought to heel. The last pockets of resistance to the colonial invasion were finally "pacified" in 1936 and any chinks of progressive light from republican days were

"SINCE PIDJIGUITI WE NEVER LOOKED BACK"

Jose Emilio Costa now works for the Bissau Port Administration. In 1959 he took part in the Bissau dockworkers' strike that ended in a bloody massacre at the small Pidjiguiti pier. Fifty workers were killed and over a hundred wounded.

When I started working at the docks in 1949, conditions in Guinea were difficult. Many people were without work and food was always short. Our wages were almost nothing and the work hard, but we were glad not to be starving and accepted it, more or less.

This began to change after several years. More and more Africans became aware of what colonialism was doing to our country and tried to improve the situation. At the dock we formed a club to collect money and send youngsters to study in Portugal. But the Portuguese didn't like it and one administrator, Augusto Lima, tried to stop our activities. There was also an African worker by the name of João Vaz who always spoke against what we were doing. Some people in the club weren't dockers; Rafael Barbosa, for instance, was a construction worker and Jose Francisco a sugar cane worker. They were both active in the Party and so were Caesare Fernandes, Jose de Pina and Paulo Fernandes who worked with me. But this was something very few people knew at the time.

Most of us worked for the big Casa Gouvea company [part of the giant *Companhia União Fabril*'s empire], either on the dock or on boats taking goods to and from company shops all over the country. But with our low wages, life was becoming more and more difficult. The basic wage was only ten escudos [approximately 15 pence/23US cents] a day. In 1959, after much discussion in the club and at work, we finally decided to ask for higher wages.

The manager was Antonio Carreia who had just left his post as colonial administrator to work with Gouvea. Well, he refused even to listen. Of course, this was the first time in Guinea's history that workers united to confront their boss. So, Barbosa and Augusto Laserde said that we had to go on strike and show them we were serious.

On 3 August we all gathered at Pidjiguiti, about 500 men. Nobody worked, neither on the dock nor on the boats. Carreia came down and shouted and swore, but we just looked at him without moving. At about 4.30 in the afternoon several trucks of armed police arrived. First they sealed off the gate to the street, then they ordered us back to work. When no one obeyed, they began moving slowly down the pier, now packed with striking workers.

This old captain friend of mine, Ocante Atobo, was leaning against the wall of the office shed. When the line of police reached the spot where he was, an officer suddenly raised his gun and shot

blacked out by the quasi-fascist curtain now drawn across the country.

Guinea was forced into becoming one giant groundnut and oil palm plantation with **compulsory planting and purchases**. Small traders were banned from dealing in cloth and alcohol, while Portuguese commercial agents tried vainly to interest the people in Portuguese wine and cotton clothing.

With economic repression, pass-book laws and a continuation of forced labour (reduced to only five days a year after World War II) came an unwieldy and over-staffed **bureaucracy**. All potential sources of opposition were organized into officially sanctioned associations, from within which their members could be scrutinized by the *PIDE* – Salazar's political police force. For over four decades, there was an almost total suspension of political life.

In the 1950s, **Amílcar Cabral**, an agronomist of mixed Cape Verdean and Guinean parentage, was working in the colonial service, conducting agricultural censuses across the country. He analysed his remarkably detailed land use surveys in Marxist terms of modes of production. His conclusions convinced him that mechanization, collectivization, a rejection of the groundnut mono-culture and a return to mixed farming could transform Guinean society and set the country on a path to socialism. His reputation as a subversive assured, he quit the service and left the country.

■ The war of liberation

In Bissau, the capital since 1941, a small coterie of African tradesmen and Lisbon-educated civil servants began gently agitating for independence from Portugal. On September 12, 1956 Cabral (briefly back from work in Angola) and five others met secretly and formed the *Partido Africano da Independência da Guiné e Cabo Verde* (**PAIGC**). With painstaking discretion and patience they him point-blank in the chest. Ocante collapsed in a pool of blood. For a split second everyone froze – it was as if time stood still. Then hell broke loose. The police moved down the pier, shooting like crazy into the crowd. Men were screaming and running in all directions. I was over by my cousin Augusto Fernandes' boat, the *Alio Sulemane*. Augusto, who was standing next to me, had his chest shot wide open; it was like his whole inside was coming out. He was crying: "Oh God, João kill me, please". But it wasn't necessary; when I lifted his head from the ground he was already dead.

Now all the men were running for the end of the pier. The tide was out so all the boats and *pirogues* were resting on the beach. To hide there, however, was impossible since the police, standing high up on the dock, were shooting right into them. One officer was kneeling on the edge firing at those trying to get away in the water. All around me people were shouting "Run, run!", but I stayed beside my dead cousin. "No, if they want to kill me, let them do it right here".

I don't know how long this lasted when a *PIDE* inspector named Emmanuel Correia arrived and ordered the firing to stop. The last one to die was a boatman hiding in the mud under his *pirogue*, out of sight of the police. A Portuguese merchant, however, spotted him from his apartment window and shot him in the back with his hunting rifle just after Correia had arrived. One Portuguese, Romeo Martins, always a friend of the Africans, had been trying to keep the police from shooting, but all by himself he couldn't do much.

When the massacre finally ended I saw dead and wounded men all over: on the dock, on the beach, in the boats, in the water – everywhere. Among the dead were Caesare Fernandes and Jose de Pina who had worked for the Party. Afterwards we were taken to the police for interrogation. For three straight days I had to report to the administrator, Guerra Ribeiro, who wanted to know who had organized the strike. My answer was always the same: "We all organized it; our wages were so bad we had no choice". Later, when Ribeiro had finished his enquiry, the wage went up to 14 escudos a day.

Soon after the massacre a message from Amílcar Cabral was secretly circulated among us. It said that August 3 would never be forgotten and that now we had to organize to win our independence from Portuguese colonialism. Since then we never looked back. Many other workers and I joined the Party and started the difficult work of political mobilization here in Bissau. With experience of Pidjiguiti behind us, we knew that we had to accept the risks and sacrifices of an armed revolution to win freedom for our people.

Reprinted from *Sowing the First Harvest: National Reconstruction in Guinea-Bissau* (1978), LSM Press, California.

recruited people to their ranks. Within three years they had about fifty members.

The spark for armed conflict came with a **dockworkers' strike** for a living wage in 1959. On August 3, police confronted the strikers on the **Pidjiguiti** waterfront in Bissau (see box). When they refused to go back to work the police opened fire at point-blank range, killing fifty men and wounding more than a hundred. The massacre and subsequent police interrogations, convinced Cabral and the party leadership that peaceful attempts in the towns to bring about independence would be fruitless. Cabral, his half-brother Luiz, and Aristides Pereira went to Conakry (newly independent from France) to set up a party headquarters and training school. In Guinea-Bissau, others began organizing, clandestinely, in the countryside, for **social revolution** and a **war of liberation** against the Portuguese.

Other nationalist groups were forming at the time, both inside Bissau and in Senegal. Their ideologies tended to be less well-honed than *PAIGC*'s. They were prepared to accept a transfer of political power without a transformation in the economy, and they didn't work on behalf of the Cape Verde Islands. Nor did they approve of the Cape Verdean intellectuals who characterized *PAIGC*'s executive. These other groups coalesced into the Front for the Liberation and Independence of Portuguese Guinea (*FLING*) based in Dakar under Leopold Senghor's sponsorship.

Morocco was the first country to supply the *PAIGC*, based in Dakar, with arms. There had been scattered attacks by the *PAIGC* from 1961, but military action began in earnest in January 1963. Senghor and Touré reluctantly allowed the guerillas to launch operations from Senegal and the Republic of Guinea. In Europe, the Scandinavian countries voiced their solidarity. Internally, the most enthusiastic insurgents were the brutally exploited, rice-planting **Balante** of the southwest, around Catió. But coordination of their sabotage attacks with *PAIGC* strategy was often tenuous. At the other extreme, many **Fula** communities in the north and east – long established in a feudal framework which had Islamic sanction, and positively supported by the Portuguese – resisted subversion, or tried to prevent their peasants from being politicized.

As large stretches of bush and countryside became liberated, and then the first few towns, the guerillas of the *PAIGC* became consolidated into an effective, mobile army, clearing the way for a network of **"people's stores"**, **new schools**, **medical services** and **political institutions**. Portugal attacked their bases with weaponry purchased from **NATO**: West Germany played a key role in supporting the airforce. Napalm was used and the fighting, at times, was as intense as in Vietnam. In retaliation, the guerilla army – the People's Revolutionary Armed Forces (*FARP*) – persuaded the Soviet Union to deliver arms on a regular basis.

While the war continued with relentless success for the liberationists, the first **internal cracks** were being felt in their upper ranks. All *PAIGC* decisions were now being taken in Conakry by the Cape Verdean leadership. Increasingly the need to coordinate a national policy came into conflict with democratic imperatives. Although Cabral enjoyed enormous support and trust, his growing stature as a world leader physically distanced him from his half million followers. In many liberated areas, there were very few democratically elected representatives between the top leadership and the people. Only at the village level were local committees elected, and then only to discuss how to implement party strategy, not to consider the strategy itself. Beyond the villages, the exigencies of war stalled and diverted elections. Party cadres with regional responsibilities were often unaccountable.

Cabral was conscious of these difficulties. In 1970, the war could have been won in a few months as heavy armaments had just been delivered from Eastern Europe. But Cabral decided to hold off the final assault on Bissau because the weapons were only usable by Soviet-trained Cape Verdeans. He thought it would only reinforce the unpopular high profile of Cape Verdean power-holders. After seven years of fighting, however, all the indications were that the mass of the people were fed up with the war and popularity would have been more likely to follow a swift end to it.

External factors intervened. In November 1970, an **invasion force of Portuguese troops** and African collaborators set off from Soga island in the Bijagós to attack Conakry, in the Republic of Guinea, with the intention of assassinating President Sekou Touré and Amílcar Cabral. They failed, and retreated in chaos (see p.482). But two years later, a more carefully planned action in Conakry, involving *PAIGC* traitors, led to the **assassination of Amílcar Cabral** on January 20, 1973. This was only partially successful because the party, nurtured for so long by one of Africa's most radical and humane political thinkers, did not disintegrate. Portugal's plan to install a puppet "liberation government" in Guinea-Bissau had no chance of success. Nonetheless, the damage to morale was serious and the leadership vacuum plain to see. Aristides Pereira took over as party chief and Luiz Cabral as president-in-waiting.

Major weaponry (heat-seeking SAM–7 missiles) came straight into play after Cabral's assassination. One aircraft after another was shot down. The Portuguese, in a hundred or so military camps across the country, were increasingly besieged by a confident People's Army under the general command of **João "Nino" Vieira** (later to succeed Luiz Cabral as president). In four months, through the end of the dry season of 1973, the Portuguese lost the war. With their airforce demoralized and growing discontent among their conscripted troops, rumbles of revolution began in Portugal itself.

On September 24, 1973, in the liberated village of Lugajole in the southeast, the People's National Assembly (elected the previous year in ballots held throughout the liberated zones) declared the **independence** of Guinea-Bissau. It only remained to kick out the enemy. Around the world, dozens of countries recognized the new republic and the United Nations passed a resolution demanding Portuguese withdrawal. The **coup in Lisbon** on April 25 1974, by army officers of the Armed Forces Movement (*MFA*), made withdrawal inevitable. Despite a summer of political crises in Portugal, and repeated efforts by the right wing to find a way of hanging on, Portugal and the *PAIGC* signed a treaty on September 10 and the last Portuguese troops were gone within a month. **Luiz Cabral** became the new head of state, while the party leader and senior ideologue, Aristides Pereira, became president of the new sister republic of Cape Verde.

Independence: the first six years

The *PAIGC* took over a centralized and autocratic administration. Far from Amílcar Cabral's optimistic ideas of a decentralized state – of ministries scattered across a nation devoid of the usual top-heavy capital city – the party's preoccupations were almost all in **Bissau**. Realistically, with a population of 90,000 (many of whom had worked with the Portuguese to the end) the domination of Bissau city was inevitable. The urgency of the takeover, the shortage of resources (material and human) and the refugee problem in the capital, all led to government by crisis-management. The peasants of the liberated zones, who had supported the party and the war for so long and at such cost, were hardly consulted: nor were the minor-ranking party cadres who now expected to receive the fruits of independence.

THE COLONIAL BEQUEST

In October 1974, when real independence was achieved, Guinea-Bissau had only a handful of graduates and doctors, and only two percent of its population, at most, were literate. The country's industrial base consisted of one brewery: there was no other manufacturing plant. There was almost no energy production. Earnings from exports barely covered a tenth of the cost of imports. And the Portuguese had left a colossal national debt.

Apart from national reconstruction, there was **political work** to do in Bissau. Compared with the peasants of the liberated zones, some of whom had lived under *PAIGC* government for ten years, not only were the Bissauans the least influenced by the war's ravages, they also tended to be the most cosmopolitan, the most educated and the most cynical. Now that the *PAIGC* was in control, they had to come to terms with it, but not necessarily support it down the line.

There were national **"elections"** in 1976, with voting consisting of a "for" or "against" to candidates nominated to the Regional Councils (who themselves elected the members of the National Assembly). There were no alternative candidates. Results showed the widest dissent in the traditionally suspicious and anti-*PAIGC* northern and eastern regions, a fifteen percent opposition in Bissau, but over ninety percent support everywhere else.

The broad approval seems surprising in light of the **difficulties** the party was having in delivering on its independence promises to build a new society. Bissau city, for example, received over half the country's resources – justified by Luiz Cabral in terms of attracting foreign aid agencies (who poured funds into the country between 1976 and 1979) and investors. **Drought** damaged the prospects of new agricultural projects and efforts to become self-sufficient in food made no progress. A joint fisheries enterprise with Algeria was a flop. The ludicrous N'Haye car assembly plant was a grotesque waste of money, as was the over-massive and never finished agricultural processing plant at Cumeré near Bissau. Salaries in the wallowing state sector were eating away (in fact *exceeded*) the national budget. The currency was kept overvalued, and inflation soared while in real terms agricultural production and exports declined. In a remarkable echo of the fascist "New State" policy, the government tried to control the marketing of produce, setting prices at levels too low to be worth selling at and perforce encouraging a black market economy. People in the rural areas could no longer afford basic imported goods like soap and matches.

The persistent street rumour was that all this was the fault of the Guinea-Bissauans of Cape Verdean origin who, in many cases, had kept civil service positions since Portuguese times. Many of the "People's Stores" were run by them, too, and often corruptly. But it was their visibility, as part of the self-interested and irrepressible middle class, that made them popular scapegoats for a **failing economy**.

In November 1980, an "Extraordinary Session of the National Assembly" had discussed the unification of Guinea-Bissau and the Cape Verde Islands. Luiz Cabral, having increasingly isolated himself, refused to budge on the issue, or on the misallocation of state funds to Bissau city and prestige projects. Four days later, came the largely bloodless **coup of November 14**, which toppled his government.

Guinea-Bissau in the 1980s

The Commissioner for the Armed Forces, **Nino Vieira**, revoked the constitution and took control of the country. Luiz Cabral was detained on Bubaque, then allowed to fly to Cuba. Guinea-

Bissau remained in the charge of the military for four years. Despite popular anti-Cape Verdean sentiment, the new "Provisional Government", formed in 1981, looked much like a rearranged version of Luiz Cabral's. Several of Cabral's Cape Verdean ministers had fled, but Vieira was adamant in his speeches that Cape Verdeans were welcome in Guinea-Bissau, and that the two countries' destinies remained linked.

One of the first announcements of the new government, was the disclosure of a series of **mass graves**, containing up to five hundred bodies, in the Oio region northeast of Bissau. The story was taken up by the foreign press. Vieira's intention was to point out the summary justice meted out by his predecessor's govenment to dissidents and those who had collaborated with the Portuguese. But counter-claims by a furious **Aristides Pereira** (the president of Cape Verde) who believed Vieira had sabotaged any chance of unification, said that Vieira had known about the murders and was even implicated. Cape Verde set up its own party, and broke relations.

As it entered its second decade of independence, prospects for Guinea-Bissau had hardly improved. And by 1982 Vieira was already repeating history, closing himself off in a tight cabal of close advisers, shuffling his cabinet according to the dictates of his personal security. **Coup attempts**, allegations of plans for coup attempts and widespread repression characterized the early 1980s. In 1984, however, there was a shift to a freer climate with new elections (of the same type as before), a rewritten constitution and a return to civilian power. But still the plots continued. Despite international appeals, (by Amnesty International and the Pope among others), **Paulo Correia** (vice-president) and five co-accused, were executed in July 1986 after a trial of over fifty people, mostly Balante, for an attempted coup the year before. Six more of the accused were said to have died in prison.

None of this, of course, helped the government to run the country effectively. Although the **IMF** and the **World Bank** had given loans, the **austerity measures** on which they were conditional were hardly followed through and, despite debt rescheduling, the country's economic plight continued to worsen. The heady years of progress in the liberated times of the 1960s seemed light years away.

In August 1986, however, the government finally agreed to the **abolition of trade laws** that had reserved all import and export licences for state monopolies. The *peso* was massively devalued, knocking the life out of the black market and encouraging potential investors. Support for Vieira's government was suddenly stronger as exports rose impressively and the domestic economy began to revive. Within a year, Guinea-Bissau was entering into long-term agreements with the IMF and World Bank to **restructure the economy**, prune the state payroll by a third, reduce fuel subsidies and boost agriculture, fisheries and technical training. In the mid-1990s, although the countryside still lags behind Bissau, the economic future is looking a little brighter. **Cashew nuts** are the most valuable export, with many farmers paying for their cashew crop in rice. The negative side-effect of this policy is a serious alcohol problem from the widespread distillation of cashew juice from the fruits, which have no other use.

■ The democratic era

In the late 1980s and into the early 1990s, political opposition to the one-party state increased. The banned **Movimento Bafatá**, with offices abroad, upped the pressure in 1990 with demands that the PAIGC should hold talks with it or face unspecified consequences. At the same time, and in common with other African partners of the World Bank and IMF, Guinea-Bissau was asked to reform its political institutions as a condition of further aid.

By the beginning of 1991, Vieira had set a schedule for **multi-party elections**, and cut the link between the PAIGC and the military, which had nurtured the party in its early years (and still feels betrayed by the two decades of independence from which it has received so little benefit).

Over a dozen small political parties were formed and recognized between 1991 and 1994. Among the most important were FLING, the old *Frente da Luta para a Libertação da Guiné* (banned for 30 years and exiled in Senegal until 1992), the new *Frente Democrática Social* (FDS) and an FDS breakaway group, the *Resistência da Guiné-Bissau–Movimento Bafatá* (RGB-MB) formed from the *Bafatá* movement and the *Partido para a Renovação Social* (PRS) headed by Dr Kumba Iala. Safeguards in the registration process ensured that none had an entirely ethnic or regional basis, though as preparations for democratic elections got underway, the special interests of each group became clear. The PRS, for example, is dominated by the Balante, from which language group the 20,000-strong army draws most of its troops and which had long been loyal to Nino Vieira, a Pepel. The RGB-MB began as a vague right-wing movement of business interests with Mandinka and Fula support, opposed to the Marxist rhetoric of the PAIGC in the late 1980s. Now that the PAIGC has shed every vestige of socialism from its agenda, it's hard to see how it differs from a party like RGB-MB, except in its membership.

While there were efforts on all sides to preserve the ethnic harmony which characterizes Guinea-Bissau, the brief campaigns mounted by the parties before the elections were mostly personality-led and ignored the big issues facing the country. At least Kumba Iala's PRS campaigned for the restoration of state property presently in private hands – an open threat to the PAIGC elite about which they have been remarkably phlegmatic.

Meanwhile **coup rumours** continue, with at least one attempt reported most years. **João da Costa**, a former minister in the PAIGC government and now the leader of the Renovation and Development Party (PRD), has been implicated several times in coup attempts against the government, allegations which have so far come to nought.

Kumba Iala: a luta continua

The **elections**, when they were finally held on July 3 1994 were surprisingly trouble-free. Despite the torrential rain, power cuts and general muddle – with ballot boxes and papers arriving late due to lack of transport – the turnout was high, the mood good-humoured and the results widely judged to reflect a fair poll. The PAIGC won just under half the votes for seats in the national assembly (which, however, gave it 64 of the 100 seats), while Nino Vieira, the incumbent president and leader of the PAIGC, won a similar proportion of votes for president. To win, Vieira needed an outright majority, which he obtained a month later in a run-off against his closest rival, leader of the PRS, **Kumba Iala**, winning 52 percent of the vote against Iala's 48 percent.

Iala, Guinea-Bissau's most charismatic and trenchantly outspoken politician, complained, not unreasonably, that the PAIGC had been able to use the resources of the state, particularly in the remotest areas, to weigh the dice in Vieira's favour. Tactics included heavy-handed campaigning among largely illiterate communities and the denial of seats to Iala's poll-observers on the only helicopter flying to outlying islands. In fact, in the capital the votes were 53 percent to 47 in favour of Iala.

Nevertheless, Iala's acceptance of his defeat bodes well for the future stability of the country, and it may be only a question of time before he and his party obtain power. Whether he would be better able than Vieira to address the country's paralyzing **$750 million debt** is another matter. But when the figure is so small at the global level, and yet so gargantuan in domestic terms – Guinea-Bissau earns less than $40 million a year in foreign exchange – the plan to wrest back the state assets allegedly stolen by Vieira and members of his party looks like the most obvious and popular step. Some of Amílcar Cabral's message to the people "to live better and in peace, to see their lives go forward" might still come to be realized.

THE NORTHWEST AND BISSAU

The majority of overland travellers approach the city of Bissau from the north, using one of several overland routes from southern Senegal to travel for a day or so through **northwest Guinea-Bissau** to the capital.

The Northwest

Northwestern Guinea-Bissau has little to offer with the exception of the important routes between Senegal and Bissau. The vast beach along the coast at **Varela**, however, represents one the best reasons to come to the country.

São Domingos and the road to Bissau

SÃO DOMINGOS is right at the head of a creek from where a good **ferry** serves Cacheu, leaving once a day, on a high tide, and taking a couple of hours. Now that the tarred road to Bissau via Ingore has been completed, it would seem that the Cacheu route should only be for the obstinately curious with plenty of time. In practice, however, if you're on a morning ferry departure to Cacheu, you'll easily be in Bissau by nightfall, while the Ingore route has its own measure of unpredictability in a couple of short creek crossings. If you're driving your own (small) vehicle, the Cacheu ferry may even enable you to make a faster journey to Bissau, as queues for the creek crossings on the new route can delay you for hours.

If you're stuck in São Domingos there's a **restaurant** where they'll always rustle up a solid meal, run by one Titiche, and, just opposite, a dirt-cheap **pensão** the *São Felipe*; (②), as well as a small market offering imported delicacies from Senegal.

The new route to Bissau

The new, sealed route involves two **ferry crossings**, one at São Vincente and another across the Rio Mansôa north of Safim. Neither of the ageing ferries can carry more than six cars, both may give low-slung vehicles problems on the ramp at low tide and the Rio Mansôa ferry has a two-metre height limit. To save the expense and difficulties of boarding vehicles onto the ferries, three different sets of minibuses and bush taxis cover the three sections of the route, divided by the rivers, between Bissau and São Domingos, throughout the day; a few **small motor canoes** transport impatient individuals unwilling to wait for the ferries.

The old route: Cacheu and Canchungo

CACHEU, 100km from Bissau, has nothing much to offer, but you'll have to stay the night here if the São Domingos ferry arrives after 5pm: your only options are camping somewhere in the town or finding an accommodating local. There are no restaurants and little indeed in the way of shops or food. A traditional "fair" or market is held every eight days.

Cacheu is the site of a sixteenth-century fort, the whitewashed substance of which (only twenty metres square) is still in place, along with its guns, and more ruins to the right, down on the shore. Notice the unusual material used on the roads in Cacheu: broken oil-palm kernel pits which are very hard-wearing, like vegetable gravel.

The next main town along the way to Bissau is **CANCHUNGO**, to which several vehicles a day run from Cacheu. It looks promising from the outskirts, with a fine avenue of trees running into town, but, again, it's maddeningly listless. The central *praça* is at least moderately alive with people waiting for transport, a renascent market area with sellers of boiled starch and oranges, and, just off the square a few places where beer, meals and rooms are available. There's a daily afternoon **bus** from Canchungo to **Safim**, just 16km from Bissau, which has regular *kandonga* connections with the city.

Varela

The beach here is better than those across the border in the tourist ghettos of Cap Skiring, and largely empty but for local people. As a place to come for the weekend, Varela is a favourite among Guinea-Bissau's small expatriate community; a wonderful place with gorgeous swimming, pine trees and low cliffs.

Accommodation is available at the *Jordani Hotel*, which offers pleasantly tiled AC, S/C rooms on the stepped cliffside, and good, though not inexpensive, food (pay in US$ or CFA; HB; ⑥). It's co-owned with the *Jordani* in Bissau, where phone enquiries can be made (☎20 17 19). The same hotelier also has a house with small annexed huts, a *pensão* really, which is pretty basic, with shared facilities (②). A new Italian hotel was due to open at the end of 1995, so the area is gradually being developed for tourism. As yet, however, there are no restaurants and virtually no shops.

Getting to Varela can be difficult, necessitating a fifty-kilometre earth-road journey west of **São Domingos**, the principal entry point from Senegal. This road can be very muddy after rain, but it's a beautiful route and very unaffected by tourism. Monkeys are a common prey here, their black forms slung from sticks over the hunters' shoulders.

Bissau and around

BISSAU itself isn't a sightseeing city, but there are one or two visits worth making and the city is not without architectural interest in its narrow nineteenth-century houses with their wrought-iron balustrades. More memorably, however, you can wander around Bissau virtually hassle-free: it's very safe, even at night. This absence of tension and clamour defines the city's peculiar appeal and comes as quite a surprise if you've just arrived from one of the adjacent Francophone countries. It quickly grows on you.

Every year in November, after the rains, when the ground is steaming off its last sops and the sun begins to burn through, Bissau is struck by a swarm of flying crickets (*grilos*). At night they zoom into lights and batter against the walls as a handful of municipal sweepers come out with hoses and brooms. In the morning they litter the pavements and float in their millions down the gutters. After decades of neglect, Bissau is still one of the most impoverished of West African capitals, but it's on the move again: imported cars dodge the rusting shells of abandoned vehicles and new offices sprout between derelict buildings. The annual plague of *grilos* seems like a hideous goad in the right direction.

Arrival and transport

There's one main road into Bissau. If your **arrival** is by bush taxi you'll end up at the **Mercado Bandim**, a busy market in a low-rent commercial quarter of the same name. The **airport** at Bissalanca is only 11km from the centre, but too insignificant to have much in the way of facilities. Private charter taxis meet all flights, but you can get shared transport too, or walk down to the main Safim–Bissau road and pick up a ride there: it's not far.

Tourist information Don't run around town looking for long defunct addresses. The only official place with any information is the *Ministério do Comércio e Turismo* on av do 3 de Agosto near the fort. Ask to see the *Secretaria de Estado do Turismo* – Secretary of State for Tourism (morning and afternoon ☎21 32 82) – who may be helpful.

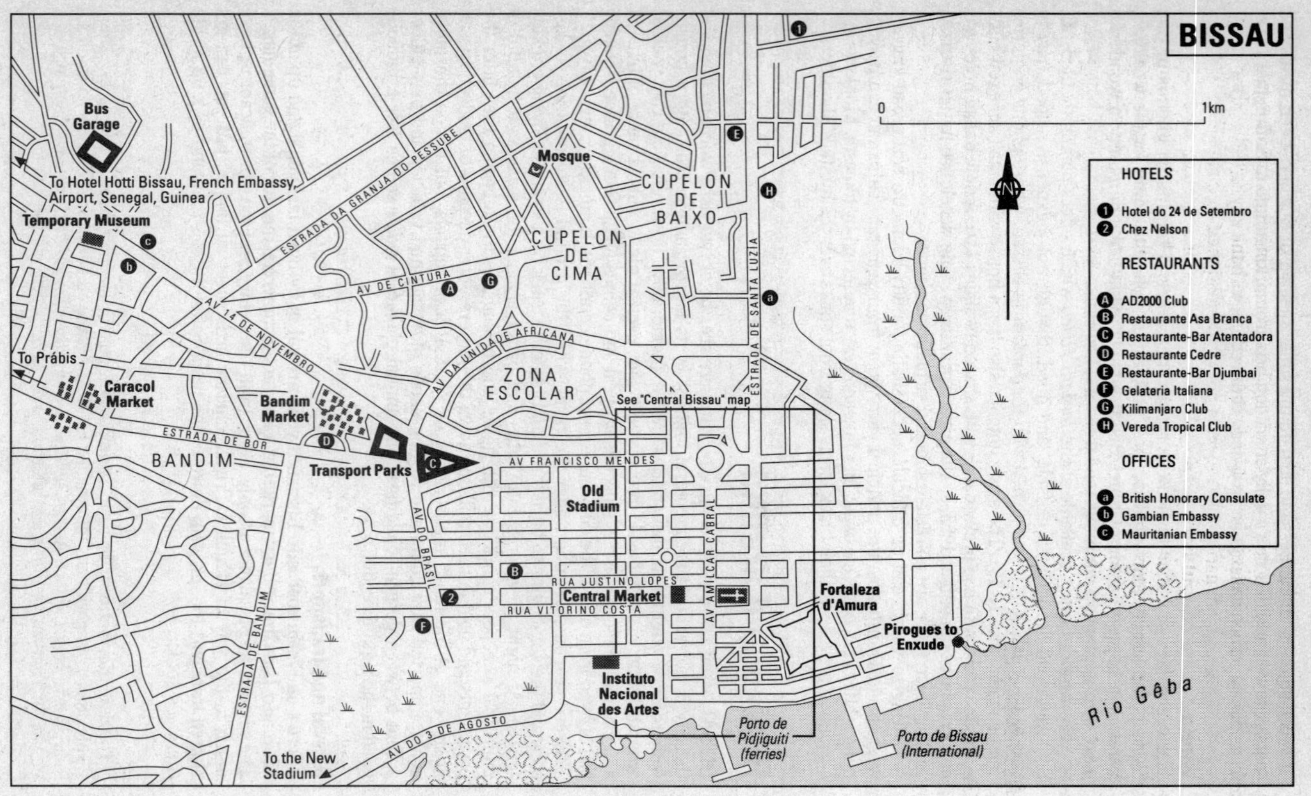
BISSAU
0
1km
HOTELS
1 Hotel do 24 de Setembro
2 Chez Nelson
RESTAURANTS
A AD2000 Club
B Restaurante Asa Branca
C Restaurante-Bar Atentadora
D Restaurante Cedre
E Restaurante-Bar Djumbai
F Gelateria Italiana
G Kilimanjaro Club
H Vereda Tropical Club
OFFICES
a British Honorary Consulate
b Gambian Embassy
c Mauritanian Embassy
Bus Garage
To Hotel Hotti Bissau, French Embassy, Airport, Senegal, Guinea
Temporary Museum
ESTRADA DA GRANJA DO PESSUBE
Mosque
CUPELON DE BAIXO
CUPELON DE CIMA
AV DE CINTURA
ESTRADA DE SANTA LUZIA
AV 14 DE NOVEMBRO
AV DA UNIDADE AFRICANA
ZONA ESCOLAR
To Prábis
Caracol Market
Bandim Market
See "Central Bissau" map
ESTRADA DE BOR
BANDIM
Transport Parks
AV FRANCISCO MENDES
Old Stadium
AV DO BRASIL
RUA JUSTINO LOPES
Central Market
RUA VITORINO COSTA
AV AMÍLCAR CABRAL
Fortaleza d'Amura
Pirogues to Enxude
ESTRADA DE BANDIM
Instituto Nacional des Artes
Rio Gêba
AV DO 3 DE AGOSTO
Porto de Pidjiguiti (ferries)
Porto de Bissau (International)
To the New Stadium

If you happen to arrive **by sea**, your timing is a question of tides. If you're sailing, you should find the Ilheu de Caio light, off Jeta island, working and other navigational aids are quite reliable. Bissau is sprawled across the right bank of the Gêba River and channels to the port are narrow. The town is directly behind the two main piers.

Bissau's municipal **public transport system** consists of a fleet of small, green and white buses – most numerous along the avenida do 14 de Novembro – and a network of bus stops (marked *Paragem* - "bus stop"). Bus routes may not be clear to newcomers but most of Bissau's needs are within walking range. In any case there are masses of blue and white **taxis** and fares are low: expect to pay around GB$5000 a ride.

Accommodation

The choice of **accommodation** in Bissau has actually deteriorated in the last few years and now offers little of good value, even if you can find a hotel that's not full. If you're travelling on a budget, you'll find you spend more on lodgings here than you're accustomed to. You could try hanging out at the *Imperio* (see "Eating, drinking, entertainment and nightlife") where one or two friendly, multi-lingual hustlers are usually helpful with cheap, private rooms.

ACCOMMODATION PRICE CODES

① Under GB$125,000 (under £5/$7.50) ② GB$125,000–250,000 (£5–10/$7.50–15)
③ GB$250,000–500,000 (£10–20/$15–30) ④ GB$500,000–750,000 (£20–30/$30–45)
⑤ GB$750,000–1M (£30–40/$45–60) ⑥ GB$1M–1.25M (£40–50/$60–75)
⑦ Over GB$1.25M (over £50/$75)

For more information, see the "Accommodation" section in the Practical Information pages at the beginning of this chapter.

Inexpensive lodgings

Hotel Caracol, near Caracol market, about 2km from the city centre. Secure, stiflingly hot rooms, with portable fan (but no guarantee their generator will be on) and basic shared facilities. Cheapest hotel in town. ②–③.

Pensão Centrale, av Amílcar Cabral (up the blue stairs; ☎20 12 32). Undoubtedly *the* place to make for, with solid S/C rooms, strictly on FB basis. Unfortunately, the rooms are often rented to long-stayers and you'll need to win the heart of the Portuguese matron who runs it to have any chance of getting in. ③.

Grande Hotel, av Pansau Na Isna (☎21 34 57). A long-standing, but run-down alternative to the *Pensão Centrale* but more likely to have a vacancy – mostly AC, non-S/C twins. ④.

Chez Nelson, rua Justino Lopes. Private accommodation – some of the cheapest in Bissau. ①.

Pensão Proquil, on rua 2 (☎21 26 29). Residential apartment block which could be in Portugal, with a few clean AC, S/C rooms, some with balconies. Payment in hard currency. ③.

Mid-range and luxury hotels

Hotel Apartmentos Jordani, tucked in a quiet street behind the *Grande Hotel* (☎20 17 19). A recent, well-managed, mid-range addition to Bissau's hotels, with pleasant rooms. ⑤–⑥.

Hotel do 24 de Setembro, Estrada de Santa Luzia (☎21 52 22; Fax 21 19 55). Established and spacious luxury complex 2km north of the centre, with a pool and car rental agency. Payment in hard currency only. ⑥–⑦.

Hotti Bissau, av 14 de Novembro (CP 107; ☎21 12 24; Fax 21 54 13). Located near the airport, the ex-*Sheraton* is, even more than the *24 Setembro*, a place where contracts are signed between flights

– a focal point for everything that's happening in the country. Payment in hard currency only. Amex and Visa cards accepted. ⑦.

Pensão Sergio Centeio, 16 rua Antonio Mbana (☎21 29 66). Poorly advertised, and also known as *Pensão Lunar*, this has secure rooms around a courtyard and relatively good prices. ④.

Hotel Tamar, corner of rua 12 and av 12 de Septembro (☎21 48 76). Renovated to quite a high standard and no longer the budget *pensão* of old. Pleasant S/C rooms. ④–⑤.

The City

If you're in Bissau at the time of the **carnaval** – February – you'll get a lopsided view of the city's entertainment value as an endless stream of floats and elaborate *papier mâché* masks is paraded through the streets. You can see the best creations (there's usually a theme, and winners) all year at the *Instituto Nacional des Artes*. Otherwise, there's little to see in Bissau. The covered **central market** is an obvious attraction, but its range of produce and other goods isn't huge and bargaining less of a custom here than you may be used to, which can keep prices frustratingly high.

There isn't a museum at present but the national collections, including modern ethic artefacts from around the country, can be seen out on the avenida do 14 de Novembro in a large school near the *Hotel Hotti Bissau*. The building marked on the *IGN* map as the museum is in fact the *UNTG* (National Workers' Union) building which does, at least, have some gloriously lurid and intense paintings in the entrance hall and up the stairs.

Down by the port, you won't miss the impressive **Pidjiguiti Memorial** to the striking dockers massacred here on August 3, 1959 (see p.436); and on a wall at the bottom of avenida Pansau Na Isna you'll easily find a beautiful and unprotected tiled mural from colonial days. Regrettably, the imposing **Fortaleza d'Amura** is still a military barracks and there's no way you'll get in to look around. The **mausoleum** of Amilcar Cabral is located within, but even Guineans only get to pay their respects on rare occasions – reportedly on September 24.

Crafts

There has been an enormous resurgence of **strip-woven cloth** in the last few years, with Pepel- and Manjak-speakers the main weavers. You'll find a decent selection at the Mercado Bandim, prices for a single *pagne* around GB$200,000 and for heavier weaves perhaps twice as much. Popular patterns include *kassave* (a check) and *volta de Bissau* (bands).

You'll usually find a spread of **carvings** and similar souvenirs opposite the bank by the *Pensão Centrale* and on Praça Che Guevara, and there are always one or two stalls of artefacts at the central market. However the recommended place to browse is the **Centro Artistico Juvenil** (also known as the *Centro Padre Batista*; daily 9am–1pm & 3–7pm), located 3km from the centre on the north side of avenida do 14 de Novembro. This boys' centre produces carvings of varying quality but there is some fine craftsmanship here and many pieces have real flair. Look out for telling family statuary – woman supporting kids and husband – and beautiful, cowrie-inlaid stools. Watch the carvers for as long as you like: there's no pressure to buy although prices are reasonable and there's a mass of small items as well.

Beaches around Bissau

If you have transport, you can explore beyond Bissau – but renting a bicycle from a private owner is a good plan and not difficult. Don't bother struggling to get to the beach unless you know you'll be there at **high tide**. Tide tables are available from the offices of *Guinémar*, 4 rua Guerra Mendes, Bissau. The nearest **sea swimming** is at **Perfilis**, near Prabis, where there's a bit of artificial beach – 18km from Bissau and reached by follow-

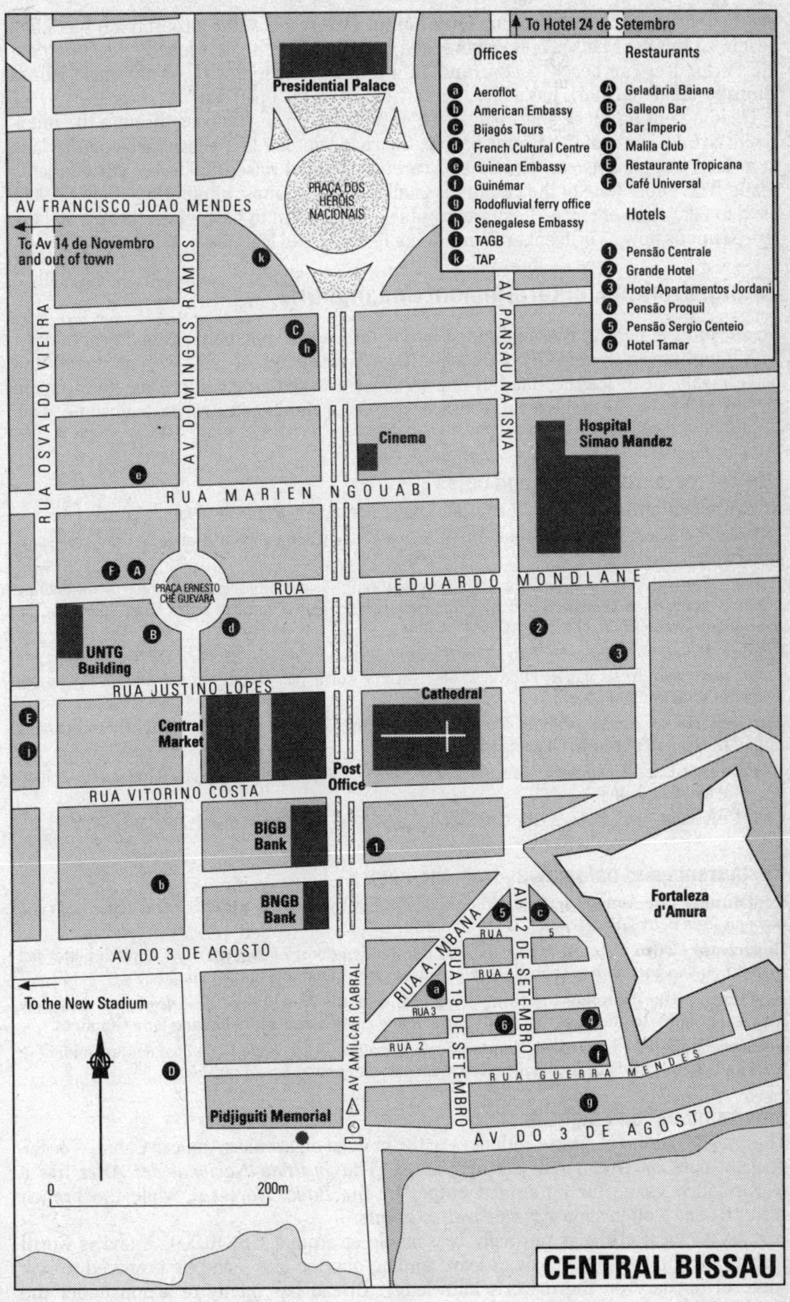
To Hotel 24 de Setembro
Offices
a Aeroflot
b American Embassy
c Bijagós Tours
d French Cultural Centre
e Guinean Embassy
f Guinémar
g Rodofluvial ferry office
h Senegalese Embassy
i TAGB
k TAP
Restaurants
A Geladaria Baiana
B Galleon Bar
C Bar Imperio
D Malila Club
E Restaurante Tropicana
F Café Universal
Hotels
1 Pensão Centrale
2 Grande Hotel
3 Hotel Apartamentos Jordani
4 Pensão Proquil
5 Pensão Sergio Centeio
6 Hotel Tamar
Presidential Palace
PRAÇA DOS HERÓIS NACIONAIS
AV FRANCISCO JOAO MENDES
To Av 14 de Novembro and out of town
AV DOMINGOS RAMOS
RUA OSVALDO VIEIRA
AV PANSAU NA ISNA
Cinema
Hospital Simao Mandez
RUA MARIEN NGOUABI
PRAÇA ERNESTO CHÉ GUEVARA
RUA EDUARDO MONDLANE
UNTG Building
RUA JUSTINO LOPES
Central Market
Cathedral
Post Office
RUA VITORINO COSTA
BIGB Bank
BNGB Bank
Fortaleza d'Amura
AV 12 DE SETEMBRO
RUA A. MBANA
RUA 19 DE SETEMBRO
RUA 5
RUA 4
RUA 3
RUA 2
AV DO 3 DE AGOSTO
AV AMÍLCAR CABRAL
To the New Stadium
RUA GUERRA MENDES
Pidjiguiti Memorial
0
200m
CENTRAL BISSAU

ing the road past the new stadium. **Quinhámel** (39km; follow the airport road) has a fine beach, on the Rio Mansôa creek shore, and quite possibly the best food in the country at the Portuguese-run beach **restaurant**, 1km from the town down a shady track. **Punta Biombo** (22km further), has a nice, but tiny beach on the open sea.

Heading out on these short trips west of the city centre you pass through the intensively farmed lands of the **Pepel** people, the road winding like an English country lane in a deep trough between fenced and carefully tended raised fields – a curious landscape. The Pepel (one of the country's smaller ethnic groups, numbering about 60,000) used to take slain enemies' heads as trophies. They seem to have given that up and are more famous now as brilliant artisans, doing fine iron and leatherwork.

Eating, drinking, entertainment and nightlife

Street food is poor in Bissau, limited to ubiquitous oranges, bananas and groundnuts, with doughnuts a treat at GB$1000 a go. If you're in search of cafés with no names and basic meals, head for the Bandim quarter, where avenida de Cintura meets the main airport road. In the centre there are a couple of new **restaurants** and some well-established favourites.

Central restaurants, bars and cafés

Restaurante-Bar Asa Branca, rua Justino Lopes. Portuguese and African fare. Upmarket.

Geladaria Baiana, Praça Che Guevara. An ostentatious place to write postcards over croissants and coffee.

Pensão Centrale, av Amílcar Cabral (1–3pm; 8–10pm). A reliable lunch and dinner spot, dishing out three courses and a banana in a style that can't have changed in thirty years. They still apply the beer-only-with-food rule. GB$40,000.

Grande Hotel, av Pansau Na Isna. The *Grande*'s terrace is one of Bissau's few rendezvous and there's generally fresh lemon juice and sandwiches worth patronizing (the *Grande*'s restaurant proper is something of a joke).

Bar Imperio, av Amílcar Cabral. For watching the world go by, putting it to rights, and playing draughts, this can't be beat. Snacks are available.

Restaurante-Bar Tropicana, near the *TAGB* office on av Osvaldo do Vieira. Moderately upmarket meat and fish dishes.

Café Universal, just off Praça Che Guevara. Plain cooking in proletarian surroundings.

Restaurants and cafés away from the centre

Restaurante-Bar Atentadora, located on wasteland by the water tower at Bandim. Offers fish and bananas for a hefty GB$180,000.

Restaurant Cedre, Estrada de Bor (behind the wooden door; 7.30pm till late). A much better bet than the *Atentadora*, with excellent Lebanese dishes in comfortable surroundings.

Restaurante-Bar Djumbai, north of the centre near the *Hotel do 24 de Setembro*. A modestly priced alternative to guests of that establishment and anyone else who's longing for a Guinness.

Gelataria Italiana, corner of rua Vitorino Costa and av do Brasil (daily 9am–3pm & 4pm–midnight; open until 2am Fri & Sat). Real Italian ice cream and other dairy-based rarities.

Entertainment and nightlife

The *UDIB* – a kind of sports club next to the cinema on avenida Amílcar Cabral – occasionally puts on **theatrical performances**. The *Instituto Nacional des Artes* has a performance venue for infrequent output by the *Ballet Nacional*, while the French cultural centre often sponsors worthwhile events.

Entry to local **clubs** is normally reasonable at around GB$40,000. A taxi is worth renting for the evening but don't leave finding one too late – and be prepared to risk some of the fare on the driver's knowledge: Bissau has plenty of action under the surface. For a popular, unpretentious and very youthful disco check out the *Vereda Tropical Club* which occasionally hosts live sounds. *Malila* is a considerably flashier nightclub, with its own restaurant, but no live music.

You can **drink** after dark in the centre, with no danger of disturbance by sweaty bodies, at the nameless *kirintim* bar across from the *Imperio* at Praça dos Hérois Nacionais, or the flamboyant *Galleon* which is open very late and keeps its AC high and its vibes as sophisticated as possible.

There are also some worthwhile nightspots out of the town centre. In the lively district of **Cupelon de Cima**, you can follow your ears, or try the *AD2000* or the nearby *Bar-Restaurante Kilimanjaro*, unpretentious *bairro* dance clubs along avenida de Cintura.

Listings

Airlines *Air Afrique* and *Air Sénégal* have desks at the airport. The following have offices in Bissau:

Aeroflot 6a rua 19 de Setembro (☎20 13 10);

Europe Aero Service (in association with *TAGB*);

TAGB (*Transportes Aereas da Guiné-Bissau*), corner of rua Vitorino Costa and av Osvaldo Vieira (☎20 12 77);

TAP (*Air Portugal*) 14 Praça dos Hérois Nacionais (☎20 13 59).

American Express No proper agent in town. The *Hotel Hotti Bissau* is most likely to offer help.

Banks and exchange The *Banco Internacional da Guiné-Bissau*, on av Amílcar Cabral, will change your travellers' cheques and cash, after considerable delay. It's possible, according to them, to have money sent out and received in hard currency. You can also change at the forex bureau by the *Pensão Centrale* or with street changers outside the main post office or in the market.

Bookshop *Pama Papeleria*, at the south end of av Domingos Ramos, sells books and magazines in Portuguese, French and English, plus maps, postcards and an excellent range of stationery.

Car rental *Tupi Car Rental* at the *Hotel do 24 de Setembro* is the only place in town to rent cars. For private charter, a city taxi should cost around GB$300,000–400,000 per day, without petrol.

Cultural centres The French cultural centre, on avenida Domingos Ramos, is worth checking out if you're in town for any length of time. The American cultural centre located at the embassy (see below) is less interesting. The Portuguese equivalent up in the Zona Escolar has a good library – all Portuguese.

Doctors Ask your embassy or consulate. Cuban doctors, resident at the *Grande Hotel*, have in the past been helpful to travellers with routine stomach and malaria problems.

Embassies and consulates include: **France**, av do 14 de Novembro, near *Hotel Hotti Bissau*, (☎25 10 31; see "Visas" below); **The Gambia**, av do 14 de Novembro (see "Visas" below); **Germany**, 28 av Osvaldo Vieira (☎21 29 92); (CP 100; ☎21 15 29 and 21 16 76); **Guinea**, Ua Marien Ngouabi (CP 396; ☎21 26 81; see "Visas" below); **Mauritania**, near the *Centro Artistico Juvenil* in Chapa (see "Visas" below); **Netherlands**, same honorary consul as Great Britain; **Portugal**, 6 rua de Lisboa (☎21 12 61; Fax 20 12 69); **Russia**, av do 14 de Novembro (☎25 10 36)**Senegal**, near the *Presidência do Conselho de Estado* (☎21 26 36); **Sweden**, 16 rua 13 (☎21 44 22); **UK**, Jan van Maanen, Honorary Consul, *Mavegro*, Estrada de Santa Luzía **USA**, av Domingos Ramos (CP 297; ☎/Fax 20 11 59).

Flight information From *TAGB* at the airport (☎21 32 04) or from the control tower (☎21 52 72) who presumably know as much as anybody.

Hospital Hospital Simão Mendes, av Pansau na Isna, just north of the *Grande Hotel*.

Immigration If you need to renew your visa, you do so at the immigration office at the airport at Bissalanca, 11km from the city centre.

Visas Although a Cape Verdean ambassador is accredited to Guinea-Bissau, there's no trace of a Cape Verde embassy: see if the Portuguese embassy can help, or ask at the *TAGB* office. Visas for Guinea are usually issued without difficulty: expect to pay around $45 for a one-month visa. A letter of introduction is not normally required although a small extra "fee" is customary. Mauritanian visas are easy to get in a day or so. Gambian visas are issued more or less while you wait. The French embassy issues visas on behalf of a number of countries.

MOVING ON FROM BISSAU

Bissau is the centre of all transport activity in the country: refer to the Practical Information pages at the beginning of the chapter ("Getting Around") for all information on road transport, flights to Bubaque, and ferries to Bubaque, the other Bijagós Islands and along the coast.

If you're heading for Bolama or the south, your first target is Enxude and it's worth knowing you can go there by *pirogue* from the shore east of the city centre.

Road transport

Most public transport goes from the big motor park off av. do 14 de Novembro (see map).

Ferries and ships

Details and tickets from *Rodofluvial*, av do 3 de Agosto. Their office is on the left-hand side of the entrance to the port. For a summary see the "Practical Information" section, p.429. For information about international shipping check out *Guinémar* on rua Guerra Mendes. Bissau is a port where you might, with time and luck, find a passage: Conakry two days, Lisbon six days, Hamburg eight days.

THE BIJAGÓS ISLANDS

The **Bijagós archipelago** is the largest along the West African coast; at least sixteen inhabited islands in the main cluster – principal of which is **Bubaque** – plus the inshore islands of **Bolama**, **Pecixe** and **Jeta** and dozens of smaller islets.

The islands are mostly covered in dense forest, with large stands of oil palm and cashew groves, less impressive patches of cultivation and necklaces of white sand or mangroves along the seashore. The islanders – predominantly Bijagó-speakers who've lived surrounded by these calm, warm waters for centuries – are remarkably autonomous: you'll see women in palm fibre skirts (*saiya*), who've never left their own island. Many of the more remote islands felt little effect from the centuries of Portuguese presence in the region (several were never, officially, "pacified" at the end of the last century when the rest of the country was being shot into line). And several still have only the most tenuous of links with the government and the outside world.

Paradise the islands are, in a way – there are even snakes in some abundance to fit – but the cost in practical terms is inconvenient **ferry connections** and an almost complete lack of facilities outside the two very small towns of Bubaque and Bolama. To these two islands come 99 percent of the few travellers who make it out here. Bolama, so close to the coast, is relatively straightforward to visit, though as ex-capital, the complete absence of hotels is mystifying. Bubaque has the distinction of being the country's only "tourist resort" – don't be misled by that – and its range of accommodation has increasd in recent years. Certainly getting a seat on one of the four flights a week to Bubaque from Bissau is easier than it used to be.

Bolama

A warped sliver of jungle and farm plots, 25km long by 5km wide, pressed in on most sides by dense mangroves, **BOLAMA** is the easiest island to visit. In the past it exercised the imaginations of the British as well as the Portuguese, and was the subject of a protracted colonial dispute in the nineteenth century. Today, where the jungle has been cleared, cashew trees for the export crop sprout between scattered termite mounds. The town of Bolama is a pleasant, quiet place facing the mainland and there are several super beaches on the south coast.

There are **ferries from Bissau** to Bolama on the first high tide every Tuesday and Saturday, returning on Friday and Sunday. Otherwise, you can get to or from the island any weekday via **Enxude**, opposite Bissau on the mainland. From Enxude, it's a 33-kilometre bush taxi trip to São João, facing Bolama town, whence a short *pirogue* ride relays you across the channel to Bolama.

Facilities for visitors on the island are virtually nil. There's no hotel, though the swimming pool, right by the harbour, does have a **restaurant** of sorts, and you can normally spend a night or two here under a *paillote* – on the understanding you buy the odd meal. Should this possibility not pan out, you may find aid workers or missionaries willing to put you up. And if you arrive on the Friday/Saturday boat, you can usually sleep on the deck (because, unlike the Tuesday ferry, it goes no further, returning to Bissau the next day). But you're better off with your own **tent**, and better off still with some wheels of your own. It's really worth tracking down **bicycles** to rent in Bissau and bringing them with you. Exploring the island otherwise, unless on foot over an extended period, is difficult. There's no more than a handful of vehicles.

On the question of **food**, the only shops are in Bolama itself, and they don't amount to much at all. There's a limited market (in a large, walled marketplace) where a small selection of fruit and vegetables, fish, peanut butter and bread is usually available. Bring with you what you can from Bissau. What you don't use will find eager recipients.

Some history

Curiously, the first colonial adventure attempted on Bolama was conducted by the **British** in 1792 (see box) and they tried again in 1814. But the agreements with local **Bijagó** elders on which these incursions were based were no more binding than the treaties the Bijagós had also signed with the **Portuguese**. And it was the latter – particularly the mixed-race Cape Verde islanders – who survived both Bolama's fevers and

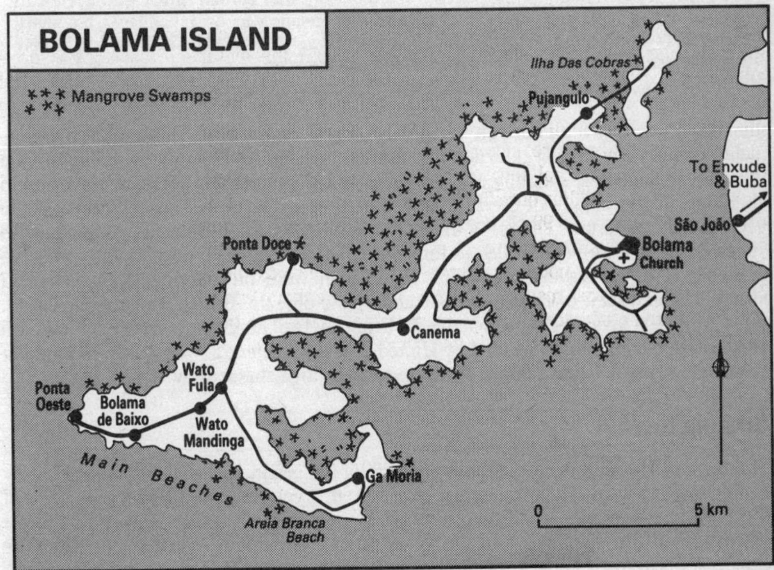

BEAVER'S COLONY

If the **British expedition to Bolama** had resulted in a successful colony, the map of West Africa might today be radically different. **Phillip Beaver**, 26, set sail from Gravesend on April 4, 1792 with 274 prospective settlers. Included among them were a ready-made Legislative Council and Governor, chosen in the Globe Tavern, London.

The first deaths occurred through smallpox before they had reached the Isle of Wight, and by the time the two ships, *Hankey* and *Calypso*, were nosing through the Bijagós islands six weeks later, half the passengers had malarial fever. Bolama, at first, seemed perfect and uninhabited, and those colonists who were well enough went ashore to chase elephants and butterflies, lie in the sun and collect oysters. Beaver was irritated at their lack of industry. They saw a Bijagó war canoe but Beaver insisted "the inhabitants were thought to be of peaceable disposition, well-inclined towards the English culture". A week later the warriors attacked, surprisingly well-armed with muskets and Solingen swords, killing and wounding a dozen people and kidnapping several women and children. The settlers' cannons had never even been unpacked.

The colony looked doomed from then on. Although the captives were released when Bolama was "bought" for £77 worth of iron bars from a pair of local headmen, over half the emigrants chose to continue to Sierra Leone in the *Calypso* in July. As the rains set in, the remaining 91 died of malaria at a remarkably even rate until by the end of the year there were only thirteen survivors. A typically laconic entry in Beavers' journal reads:

Sun 2nd Dec. Killed a bullock for the colony. Died and was buried Mr. Webster. Thermometer 92. Three men well.

Beaver and five others survived the rains of the following year and he and a companion sailed back to England in May 1794. "An ill-contrived and badly executed, though well intended expedition", he mused. The timing, arriving at the start of the rains, could not have been worse. His book was entitled "African Memoranda: Relative to an Attempt to Establish a British Settlement on the Island of Bulama on the Western Coast of Africa in the year 1792, with a Brief Notice of the Neighbouring Tribes, Soils, Productions Etc., and some Observations on the Facility of Colonising that part of Africa with a View to Cultivation; and the Introduction of Letters and Religion to its Inhabitants but more particularly as the means of gradually Abolishing Slavery". Published in 1805, and hugely readable, it's worth scanning the antiquarian bookshops for.

the Bijagó warriors long enough to establish a real community. Throughout the nineteenth century the British returned periodically to claim sovereignty by pulling up the Portuguese flagpoles, shouting at the settlers and shipping their domestic slaves off to liberation in the colony of Sierra Leone. But they made no serious efforts to settle permanently, or to take charge of the island, until 1860, when Bolama was annexed to Sierra Leone, hundreds of miles to the south. The Portuguese, desperate to preserve their stake in the slave trade which the British were busy trying to abolish, had formally lodged their own claim in 1830 and by the time the British annexed the island, there were 700 loyal Portuguese subjects living there. The dispute wasn't settled until 1870, when a commission headed by United States President Ulysses S Grant found in favour of Portugal. Grant's efforts were rewarded with a statue in the town square.

Bolama town

The town of **Bolama** is on the landward side of the island, facing the mainland barely two kilometres away. Hollow, and partly deserted, it echoes with the past grandeurs of the Portuguese empire. Solid mansions attest a century of trading in ivory and forest products and the opening up of the West African groundnut industry, but since the capital of Portuguese Guinea was transferred to Bissau in 1941, Bolama has been steadily crumbling away. The town is still the seat of government of Bolama Region, however, which includes most of the islands and a little chunk of mainland. It has its own regional president, a hospital, a nurses' school and a teacher training college.

Walking around the town will take you all of forty minutes. Down by the port you'll not miss the ugly **sculpture** bestowed on the island by Mussolini after an Italian seaplane crashed here in 1931 (Bolama used to be a "hydrobase" on the Rome to Rio de Janeiro seaplane route). The solid construction of the monument means it hasn't fallen victim to the tide of nationalism which knocked Ulysses Grant off his pedestal near the bandstand in the overgrown main praça, a few minutes' walk from the seafront. The grandest buildings in town surround this main *praça*, and include the colonnaded **Governor's Palace**, the **post office** and the abandoned, Manueline-style **Hotel de Turismo**. This upper part of town reeks of post-colonial decay, though in fact most of the buildings are still in use. The only reminder of Britain's ephemeral presence on Bolama is down to the left behind the church: the reddish two-storey ruin almost throttled by rank undergrowth is the **Casa Inglesa**, a monstrous edifice built entirely of corrugated iron. Architecturally, at any rate, the Portuguese deserved to win the island.

There's a pleasant evening stroll out of town past the secondary school and down an attractive, sandy avenue of trees, with compounds set back on both sides – surely a colonial conception, but one that's endured. Out this way too, at the start of the avenue on the left, there's a rather Gothic graveyard which is worth a look: a curious assembly of souls, including a number of middle Europeans and even one or two Britons. Rapid brown snakes shimmer out of the way as you walk.

Around the island

Fork right at the end of the avenue out of the town and you soon find yourself on a delightful, narrow lane, twisting through cashew groves. There are no beaches down here, but you do pass a **cashew jam factory** which is open a few days every year – they make more deadly cashew wine than jam (out of the fruits, not the nuts) – and a cloth manufacturing plant that evidently hasn't been open from the day the looms were delivered. Passing through the hamlet of Pujangulo, the path becomes a muddy track through the mangroves at low tide, at which time it joins the main island to the **Ilha das Cobras** – an uninhabited islet. Exciting stuff, but watch out for snakes on the other side and don't get stranded by the tide. The walk is about 15km there and back.

There are other, shorter walks you could do in the peninsula immediately south of Bolama town. But the main interest lies **further south across the island**. Down here, unless you're prepared to set off early with food and water sufficient for a couple of days, you're really going to need transport. The dirt road cuts through pretty forest, farm and plantation lands, following the central ridge of the island (maximum elevation just 26m), never far from the sea. The people you'll meet are mostly Bijagós, though it's the women who stand out (many men are away labouring) and whose apparel is so distinctive. Although bras and cotton *pagnes* have arrived, the traditional costume of palm fibre kilt (*saya*) is still the standard wear for most women, though officially banned from the town and frowned on by missionaries. For rural Bijagós, tourists are a sensational novelty and you'll occasionally find children for whom such a meeting is a first.

Hamlets and clusters of compounds are, in many cases, named after ethnic groups. Some 17km from Bolama you turn left at Wato Fula and plunge into a tunnel of cashews. **Areia Branca beach** is a further 7km down here, a narrow lip of white sand dipping beneath the coconuts into a milky blue sea. It's said to be the best spot, and you're unlikely to find it anything but deserted, but there are other beaches along the southern coast. This corner of the island is very sparsely populated and you can nose around for hours completely alone. Remember, however, if you're tempted to knock off a few coconuts for their milk and flesh, all the trees are individually owned.

Bubaque

In Guinea-Bissau, tourism begins and ends in **BUBAQUE**. In colonial days the island was a Portuguese favourite, and after independence Swedish aid provided a hotel (to which excursionists from The Gambia were flown for several seasons in the late 1970s) and a tarmac road to the beach. The trips from The Gambia ceased but these days the island is regularly visited by French tourists who fly in for the renowned game fishing of the waters nearby.

Getting there

There are at least two weekly **flights** with *TAGB* ($48 one-way, $88 round trip; bookings with *TAGB* in Bissau or with the pilot, who lives on Bubaque). The alternative involves taking the weekly *Rodofluvial* **ferry** to Bubaque on Friday, returning Sunday (4–5hr; GB$40,000), which is barely enough time for a flying visit. There are also less formal possibilities such as the *Vitoria*, a vessel belonging to the *Estrela do Mar* fisheries department, or small motorized **pirogues** operated by aid agencies and missions, although these latter craft are notoriously unstable in the frequently choppy channel and are not recommended. Prices should be the same as, or less than, ordinary ferry services, but comfort may be even more rudimentary. Take your own food, water and headwear for the hot and exhausting voyage.

On the outward voyage from Bissau, until you have cleared the **Ilha das Galinhas** (a midway stop where disembarking passengers are offloaded to a lighter), a dirty, spume-laden sea as flat as a millpond is the normal view. But as you approach the isle of Rubane, the mood improves. The intense tropicality of the green, horizontal islands leaves a strong sense of place, reinforced as you enter the channel between Bubaque and Rubane and see the red tin roofs of Bubaque with its high pier. By this stage of the voyage, it will be low tide. The scene – children picking in the mud, the viridescent foliage of the two islands tumbling to the water, the tranquillity after the racket of the diesel and what seems like bustle in Bissau – is all a bit magic.

Bubaque town

Over the last few years Bubaque's popularity with overseas visitors has increased substantially and the town now offers a number of **places to stay**. The *Pensão Cadjoco*, run by a friendly Franco-Italian couple has rooms with fans or inexpensive tents, both with full board options and excellent cooking (room only ①–②). *Pesos* or hard currency are accepted and they can also direct you to locals happy to **rent bikes** (about GB$50,000 per day). More recently established budget bases include one known simply as "Chez Paulino Cruzponte" (②) and another, *Campini* ("Chez Nattie la Cubanne"; ②), which is getting an excellent reputation for its atmosphere and management. There are also a couple of more expensive *campements* which offer a good degree of comfort – *La Maina* and *Le Dauphin* (both ⑤). All seem to quote their rates in French francs and to have French money and behind-the-scenes influence. As does the renovated, but much older *Hotel Bijagós*, formerly the *Estancia Balnear* of the Swedish tourist years, a 25-minute walk from the town, near the airstrip, which offers simple, S/C AC rooms of two different standards (☎82 11 44; ③–④).

As for **something to eat**, a good alternative to the expensive *Hotel Bijagós* and the *Cadjoco*, which caters for vegetarians and features local sauces and garnishes, is *L'Escale*, a French restaurant by the jetty which offers a warm welcome and specialities based on locally caught seafood. You should also try the inexpensive and friendly *Chez Raoul.*

Looking around Bubaque village is nice in the early morning and late afternoon. Immensely picturesque seascapes flicker through the mango boughs; oil palms in massive stands, many around the hotel, are covered in the nit-like nests of weaver birds, and resound with their chatter; lizards and butterflies dart everywhere; and mambas are occasionally seen. In the village a **produce market** sets up every morning and a growing number of **shops** sell all sorts of things. The **post office's** reliability is uncertain but you can make international phone calls easily enough.

Praia da Bruce

There's a fleet of Citröen 2CVs at the hotel which, if there are enough guests, do morning and evening runs to **PRAIA DA BRUCE**, 15km south of the hotel. Non-guests pay a rather expensive charge so it's better instead to fix something up with one of the village's few drivers. Ideally, you'd bring a bike from Bissau or rent or borrow one on the island.

It's certainly worth getting down to the beach on the south coast for at least one day as it's practically deserted and very appealing. The heavily overgrown tarred road is dead flat; a one-hour cycle ride. There are some tall stands of wild forest still to be seen and signs, too, of old Portuguese estates and villas. The only other road users seem to be women and naked children.

All that's left of the hotel's former annexe on Bruce beach are rotting stools around a derelict bar, half-bald *paillotes*, ruined toilet blocks and evidence of bygone picnics. There's also a beautiful pond of lilies with intriguing rustles and plenty of birdlife. The isolation down here is palpable – one or two fishermen may come by, stationing themselves in the waves with their throwing nets for hours on end to provide a garnish for the evening rice.

The beach offers shady cashew trees and as much clean sand as you could wish for. Try to be here when the tide is high, and bring drinking water – lots of it.

Other islands

Visiting the **other islands** is very much a trip into the unknown. Information is hard to obtain in Bissau; there are only regular *Rodofluvial* ferries to the inshore isle of **Pecixe** (see "Getting Around" in the Practical Information pages), which has a long coastline of beaches facing the open Atlantic, usefully close to its main village, Ijante. Getting to the other islands in the main Bijagós group, Bubaque is the best place to look for **local fishing boats**, and getting from one island to another is often fastest via the hub of Bubaque, rather than direct. Wherever you go, be aware of the fact that the price you pay to get out – and the ease with which you do so – may not be the same on the return trip. The staightforward alternative is to book up a trip with one of the **French outfits** in Bubaque, who charge around £20/$30, on the basis of a four-person group, for a daytrip, and around £25/$38 per 24 hours (all inclusive). You can go as far as time and money permit.

Recognized **accommodation on other islands** consists of two extremely expensive French *campements* on Rubane (*Club Ajaca* and another; both ⑦), a recommended Guinean bungalow development on Galinhas (⑥) and an Italian resort on Maio (⑥). Apart from these possibilities, you're at the mercy of Bijagó hospitality – usually profound – and your own ability to join in without offending people. The question of money is unlikely to be raised, except of course when travelling by boat, but you should be prepared with gifts of food and other small items when occasion demands some reciprocity. There is little experience of tourism out here and any generosity you show is unlikely to be exploited. The Bijagós have very severe sanctions in cases of stealing.

Central and northern isles

Rubane and **Soga** (the latter is the island from which the 1970 Portuguese invasion of the Republic of Guinea was launched) are close to Bubaque and not hard to get to.

Punta Biombo, 60km west of Bissau, is a reasonable place to get a *pirogue* passage the thirty kilometres to relatively populated and forested **Formosa** island (GB$30,000 or less). Ask to be dropped at **Nago** in the creek between **Maio** island and Formosa. If you disembark on the beautiful north-facing beach on Maio, be prepared for a most unwelcome reception if you walk across the island to Formosa (7km): the Italian hotel on Maio has done a first-rate job of alienating the island's entire population. **Catende** is Formosa's main town, with an avenue of mango trees leading to a fine old Portuguese mansion, now occupied by the island's council.

On the archipelago's northwest periphery the string of stunning beaches and crystal-clear water surrounding **Caravela** are said to be the jewel in the Bijagós' crown: the island is visited by cruises from Senegal and The Gambia. If you're in a group, the presence of an airstrip at Caravela suggests it might be worth enquiring about chartering a plane from *TAGB* in Bissau: the distance from Bissau is only 80km.

Southern and western isles

The wilder islands are on the archipelago's seaward, southwestern edge and will take a concerted effort to reach with the probability of several days' wait for a return passage. All make Bubaque look cosmopolitan by comparison and offer tremendous rewards to adventurous and flexible travellers. You'll find no shops, police or *pensões*, almost no motor vehicles and negligible outside influence. The tenuous **missionary presence** succeeds only superficially in subduing the islanders' traditional values: clandestine **initiation ceremonies** incorporating the use of *irãn* (fetishes), combine freely with Christian beliefs and practices. You're almost certain to witness the rich cultural life of the islanders, expressed through drumming and dancing.

The marine and terrestrial **wildlife** on these remoter islands is extraordinarily prolific. Exploratory walks through the bush will reveal hornbills, monkeys and even green mambas; sharks and stringrays patrol the shallows. While the mamba's bite has no remedy (just don't get bitten), a ray's excruciating sting is soothed by the islanders with a slice of fresh papaya and a few cow-hornfuls of *canna*.

Eticoga, the principal settlement on **Ilha de Orango**, has an unusual population of saltwater-dwelling **hippos** in the creek east of town (ask if any have been seen

USEFUL BIJAGO

Bijagó dialects don't vary much. These phrases are from Orango. Some of them are recognizably Kriolu in derivation. Accented letters are stressed syllables.

How are you?	*Ména?*	Good, beautiful	*Ngoséney*
I am fine	*Ñekagobo*	Bad, ugly	*Odéyney*
Thank you/ expression of agreement	*Eséyta*	1	*Mudíge*
Yes	*Eng*	2	*Asóge*
No	*Ñidóku*	3	*Oñyóko*
What is your name?	*Amenáwe?*	4	*Ngoyagáne*
My name is John	*Aynáme John*	5	*Modevokóko*
White person	*Ororá*	6	*Modevokóko na mudíge*
Black person	*Utúngko*	7	*Modevokóko na asóge*
Where are you going?	*Mindánewe?*	8	*Modevokóko na oñyóko*
See you later	*Ñibóy*	9	*Modevokóko na ngoyagáne*
Rice	*Omán*	10	*Muranáko* (with a handclap)
Fish	*Ngokáto*		
Water	*Ño*		

Numbers after 10 are expressed with a combination of claps and the numbers 1 to 9.

recently). The hippos are able to swim between the islands, and are held in some fear by the islanders owing to their penchant for ruining crops and exhibiting menacing behaviour in defence of their young. Local legends on Orango refer to an ancient Queen Pampa: artefacts dating back centuries have been found here.

The islands of **Uracane** (with its colony of flamingos outnumbering the residents a hundredfold), **Uno** and **Unhocomo** take some getting to – and the seas become rough Atlantic swell on the other side of the furthest island, Unhocomo, which is the sea route that must be followed to reach the main settlement, Anaburu. It is therefore, even more important to be sure your boat is safe.

THE SOUTH AND EAST

Reserves of enthusiasm for the **Bissau interior** – a patchwork of low ridges, divided by the country's creeks and rivers – run pretty low once you've visited the capital and the islands. From the travel perspective, the rest of the country divides into two: **the south**, a relatively inaccessible and little-known region, fronting up against the Republic of Guinea; and the **east**, hardly explored by travellers either, but Guinea-Bissau's main road runs out this way, with a number of large towns and villages along the line of travel.

The south

The gateway to the south is **Enxude**, across the Rio Gêba from Bissau. A ferry links the town to the capital once a day on weekdays, and *pirogue* crossings are negotiable any time from the creek shore behind the main cemetery in Bissau. This southern region is really isolated and there's little to draw you down here unless you're determined to follow the coast as near as possible into the Republic of Guinea.

The main town of the south, **BUBA**, has almost nothing – a small hotel (①–②) and a sprinkling of eating houses. Nearby there are swimming beaches and waterfalls along the Rio Corubal, which separates the south from the rest of Guinea-Bissau, but even these are most easily reached from the northern part of the country via **Bambadinca** (117km east of Bissau) and the new tarmac road down from there to Buba (111km). The falls (mere rapids in the dry season) are at **Saltinho**, near **Mampatá**, the only bridge over the Corubal. A French-run *campement*, *Samba Loba* (③), is located on the north bank of the Corubal, 5km from Mampatá (signposted), down a track. Beautifully situated, it's usually packed to the gills at weekends and school holidays with rich Bissauans and ex-pats. But it's a fair bet you'd have it to yourself at other times. The only potential drawback is the fact that you are more or less obliged to eat there too (generous and excellent French cooking, but the FB rate puts it into the ⑤ bracket). **Cussilintra**, a dozen kilometres downstream and closer to Xitole, was a colonial beauty spot, like Saltinho, and is still a popular weekend excursion with good swimming nearby; a hotel and restaurant are being built there. South of the Corubal, the villages of Metandiame and Cantanha are, for some unspecified and undivinable reason, marked on the *IGN* map as "notable sites".

Boé, 90km east of the waterfalls along a track which skims the Guinean border, is famous as the first town to be liberated from the Portuguese by the *PAIGC*, back in 1967. It's a false reputation, though, as the first town to be liberated was in fact in Boé *district*, a place called **Lugajole** in the deep southeast. A small plaque and hut there commemorate the occasion. Strange, hilly landscapes around Lugajole – the outliers of the Fouta Djalon – are a change from the maze of mangroves and mud nearer the coast.

The east

The two main towns of the interior, **Bafatá** and **Gabú**, are located along Guinea-Bissau's one, main highway. You'll find **transport** fairly easily along here with several daily bus and *aluguer* departures between both towns and Bissau, and even reasonable hitching prospects.

It's a good road most of the way, with unremarkable scenery of tall grass and charcoal-burning villages. Before Mansôa, the road forks: right for the east, and left (north) over the Rio Mansôa for the town. **Mansôa** has nowhere to stay, but there are a couple of restaurants: one, on the way into town, is run by a helpful Cape Verdean; the other, bang in the town centre, is a circular, thatched affair where you can drink beer, eat monkey and meet locals. The road on to **Farim** (check out the *Pensão Pic-Nic*) and the Senegalese border town of **Tanaf**, is a decent one. Farim's ferry seems to be running well these days, as much as twice an hour from dawn till dusk.

Bafatá and around

Continuing east over the old trading river, the Rio Gêba, **Bambadinca** marks the start of the new road south to Xitole and the riverine attractions mentioned above. The nearby port of **Xime** is the furthest into the interior that regular ferries (at least twice monthly) run from Bissau.

BAFATÁ comes as a surprise, its street lights offering an optimistic welcome, its brick factory apparently turning the red dust that smothers everything into the neat, tiled houses you see all round. It's an orderly, appealing town, perched on a low rise, with an atmosphere as placid as the river which, laced with fishing lines and teeming with fish, winds its graceful course below the town to the west. If you're **staying**, there are two very basic *pensões* to be found in the maze of compounds east of the main road from Bissau: *Apartamentos Gloria* (①) which is attached to a lively night spot; and *Pensão Fa*, which is cleaner, quieter and even cheaper (①). For **food**, the town has two flourishing markets and a couple of restaurants, or you could ask around in the compound area for someone willing to prepare you a meal. Behind the covered market and right on the river bank, the *Piscina Café/Bar* has serene views: here armchair fishermen can cast a line over the parapet while enjoying a quiet drink on the terrace.

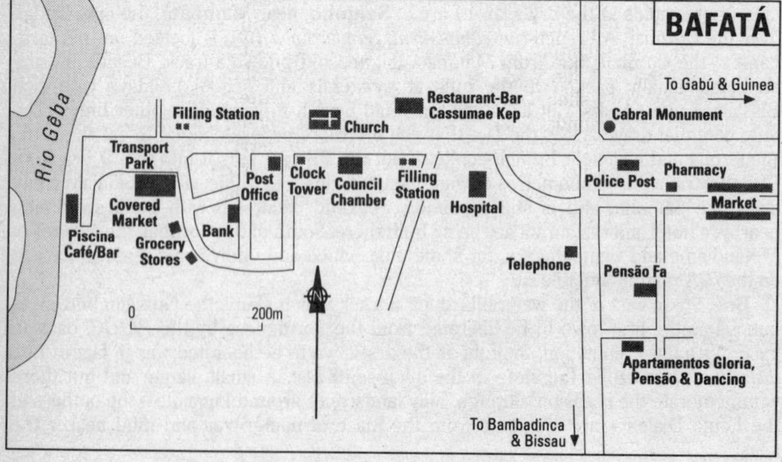

The most thriving up-country trading post of the Portuguese province of Guinea in the late nineteenth century was **Gêba**, 12km west of Bafatá down a side road off the highway on the Bissau side of town. Now virtually a ghost town, Gêba's overgrown **ruins** are supposed to be worth a look if you're drawn to such places.

Northeast of Bafatá, there's a well-maintained dirt road to the **Senegalese border** at **Pirada**, while a fork crosses a rickety bridge and continues along a deteriorating track to the frontier at Cambaju and on to **Kolda** on the Ziguinchor–Tambacounda road. From Bafatá to Gabú, unusual tall stands of bamboo flank the road.

Gabú

The country's eastern capital, **GABÚ** is the Fula and Muslim capital too, an animated commercial centre prospering from its triangular trade with nearby Senegal and Guinea. The town itself has little of interest to offer visitors, but it's a convenient stopping place en route to or from Basse, Tambacounda or Koundara and it's used as a base for French-run hunting expeditions into the nearby bush.

There are **three places to stay**: *Mariama Sadje Djaló's*, an unmarked *pensão* with a bar-restaurant, not far from the market (①); *Oasis Hotel*, on the southwestern edge of town (there's a sign on the main road and it's ten minutes' walk from there), which has pleasant, S/C accommodation in small thatched rondavels (②); and the *Hotel Suitte*, a rather upmarket tourist hotel/hunting lodge with an excellent restaurant, centrally located between the transport park and the Catholic Church (☎51 12 55; ③). Near the market are a bank, a telephone office, a handful of chophouses, and several butchers, where you can choose a piece of meat and have it char-grilled on the spot.

Gabú has good **transport** connections with all points along the road to Bissau, and vehicles heading for Senegal, The Gambia and Guinea pass through with some regularity. The northern route out of Gabú to Pirada and Senegal is a reasonable, maintained track, where you may even have luck hitching.

Into Guinea

The surfaced highway continues east to **Pitche**, and from here the **main road into Guinea** is a rough earth track which winds and bumps its way through the bush – chokingly dusty in the dry season, barely passable in the rains. Direct bush taxis bound for **Koundara** via Pitche, Kandika and Sareboïdo leave Gabú two or three times a week (around GF8000, or GB$120,000), and Sareboïdo's Sunday market generates commercial traffic. It's best to expect the unexpected on this route (east of Pitche the road is truly appalling) and bear in mind that the Guinea-Bissauan frontier at Buruntuma closes for lunch. If you stop in the tiny village of Pitche, or if you have your own transport, you should certainly check out the **route south into Guinea** via **Foula-Mori**. On a Monday (market day in Pitche) you should find transport down this narrow track. At the river border, there's a hand-hauled ferry large enough for a small truck. The route is not marked on the maps, but it's a recognized border frontier (further details on p.467) and a journey you won't forget in a hurry.

index

CHAPTER SEVEN

GUINEA

GUINEA

Between 1958, when it reclaimed its total independence and effectively cut itself off from France, and 1984 on the death of dictator Sekou Touré, the **Republic of Guinea** was an isolated and secretive country. Only in the late 1980s did it begin, hesitantly, to open its borders to tourists.

Today, Guinea holds massive appeal as a place to **travel**. It sprawls in a great arc of mountains and plains from the creeks and mudbanks of the mangrove coast to the savannah of the Niger source-lands and the montane forests on the border with Côte d'Ivoire. The great rivers of West Africa – the Gambia, the Senegal and the Niger – all rise in Guinea. The *Michelin* map shows more green-bordered roads (*parcours pittoresques*) in Guinea than any other country – always a promising indication.

Guinea's best-known attraction is the **Fouta Djalon** highlands, populated by settled, largely Muslim, Fula herders and farmers; a plateau region dramatically dissected into myriad hills and valleys, spouting waterfalls like a colossal rock garden. The length of time needed to explore the area is the only negative consideration.

Further to the east, on **the plains** where the streams flow away from the sea, where you feel the cultural resonances of the Niger valley's medieval empires, scattered **historical reminders** – and towns, rather than the sparse countryside – are the focus. To the south, another great highland region – **Guinée forestière** – fronts up against the coastal states in a zone of wet forest and remote peoples, where liana bridges cross the rivers and pre-Islamic tradition survives. One of the biggest weekly markets in West Africa is held up here, at **Guéckédou**.

Guinea's people share a wide cultural diversity. No single language predominates and there's considerable regional variation. **Susu**, the main language of the coastal region, is currently in ascendance and is the language of most of President Conté's government. Susu, as a Mande language, is related to **Kouranko** and **Malinké** (Sekou Touré's mother tongue, widely spoken in the northeast), as well as to **Kpelle** and **Loma** – minority languages of the highland forests – and to the market lingua franca known as **Dyula.**

Fula, the predominant language of the Fouta Djalon, continues to be under-represented in national life, as it was – maliciously – under the repressive regime of Sekou Touré. There's still deep bitterness among the Fula-speaking community who, with forty percent of the population, are the largest single ethnic group.

Overall, Guinea has extraordinary vitality and newly unleashed confidence – an energy debased only in the capital, **Conakry**, about which it's sometimes hard to be positive. The years of dictatorship were harrowing, yet they've resulted in a strong

FACTS AND FIGURES

The **République de Guinée** is often called Guinea-Conakry, to distinguish it from other Guineas – reflection too of the colonial preoccupation with capitals. The population at the last count (1983) was 5.4 million, with over ten percent in Conakry. The area (246,000 square kilometres) is about the same as Great Britain or Oregon. Guinea has a colossal foreign debt, estimated to be nearly £2 billion ($3 billion), which is more than four times its annual earnings from the export of goods and services, yet roughly equivalent to only a month's expenditure by the British Ministry of Defence. The government is the *Comité Transitoire de Redressement National* (CTRN) – a military-civilian grouping led by President General Lansana Conté. There are at least four dozen official political parties.

political consciousness. And outside the capital, the veneer of European culture which frequently obscures the other ex-colonies is hardly noticeable: Africa shines through very brightly.

Climate

When you visit Guinea – and where you go – is likely to be determined in large degree by the **seasons**. Off the limited runs of main, surfaced highway, most of the countryside is isolated during the rains which are concentrated between June and October. Many minor routes are completely impassable for days or weeks on end, due to flooding. Be prepared for plans to go awry, though you may find that the spectacular storms, gushing waterfalls and brilliant abundance of greenery are more than adequate compensation.

In the weeks following the rainy season, which is shorter and lighter as you head north to Labé, the Fouta Djalon can be truly delightful. The southeast highlands, too, have a good spell of fine weather, though conditions vary greatly. Away from the coast, and especially in the mountains, temperatures can plummet at night: you need some warm clothes and perhaps a sleeping bag.

As the dry season progresses, travel in the Fouta Djalon and the Malinké plains becomes increasingly dusty and hot. The *Harmattan* winds from the north can bring

AVERAGE TEMPERATURES AND RAINFALL

CONAKRY

	Jan	Feb	Mar	Apr	May	June	July	Aug	Sept	Oct	Nov	Dec
Temperatures °C												
Min (night)	22	23	23	23	24	23	22	22	23	23	24	23
Max (day)	31	31	32	32	32	30	28	28	29	31	31	31
Rainfall mm	3	3	10	23	158	559	1298	1054	683	371	122	10
Days with rainfall	0	0	1	2	11	22	29	27	24	19	8	1

KOUROUSSA

	Jan	Feb	Mar	Apr	May	June	July	Aug	Sept	Oct	Nov	Dec
Temperatures °C												
Min (night)	14	17	22	23	23	22	21	21	21	21	19	15
Max (day)	33	36	37	37	35	32	30	30	31	32	33	33
Rainfall mm	10	8	22	71	135	246	297	345	340	168	33	10

MAMOU

	Jan	Feb	Mar	Apr	May	June	July	Aug	Sept	Oct	Nov	Dec
Temperatures °C												
Min (night)	13	15	18	19	20	18	19	19	19	18	17	13
Max (day)	33	34	35	34	31	29	27	25	28	29	30	31
Rainfall mm	8	10	46	127	203	257	335	401	340	203	61	8

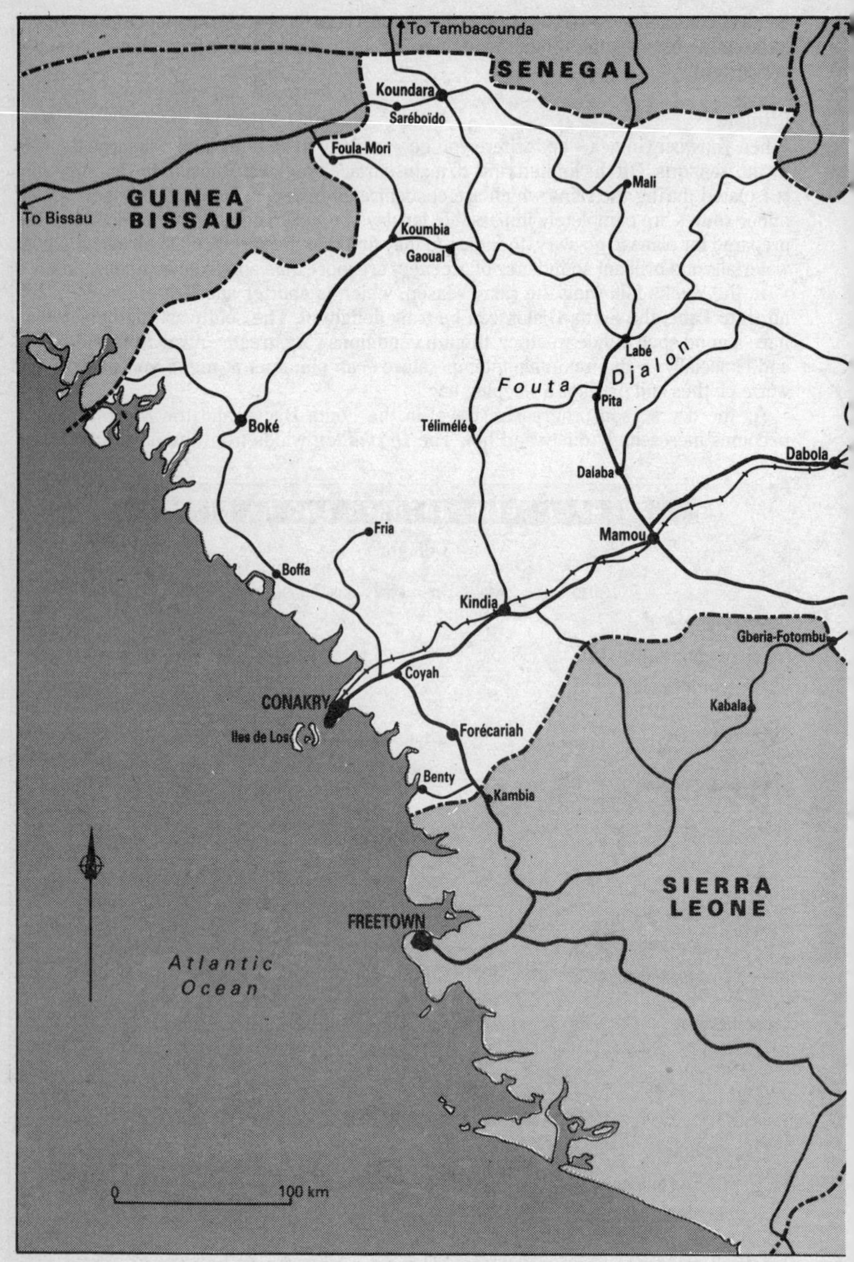
To Tambacounda
SENEGAL
Koundara
Saréboïdo
Foula-Mori
Mali
GUINEA
BISSAU
To Bissau
Koumbia
Gaoual
Labé
Fouta Djalon
Pita
Boké
Télimélé
Dalaba
Dabola
Fria
Mamou
Boffa
Kindia
Gberia-Fotombu
Coyah
CONAKRY
Kabala
Iles de Los
Forécariah
Benty
Kambia
SIERRA
LEONE
FREETOWN
Atlantic
Ocean
0
100 km

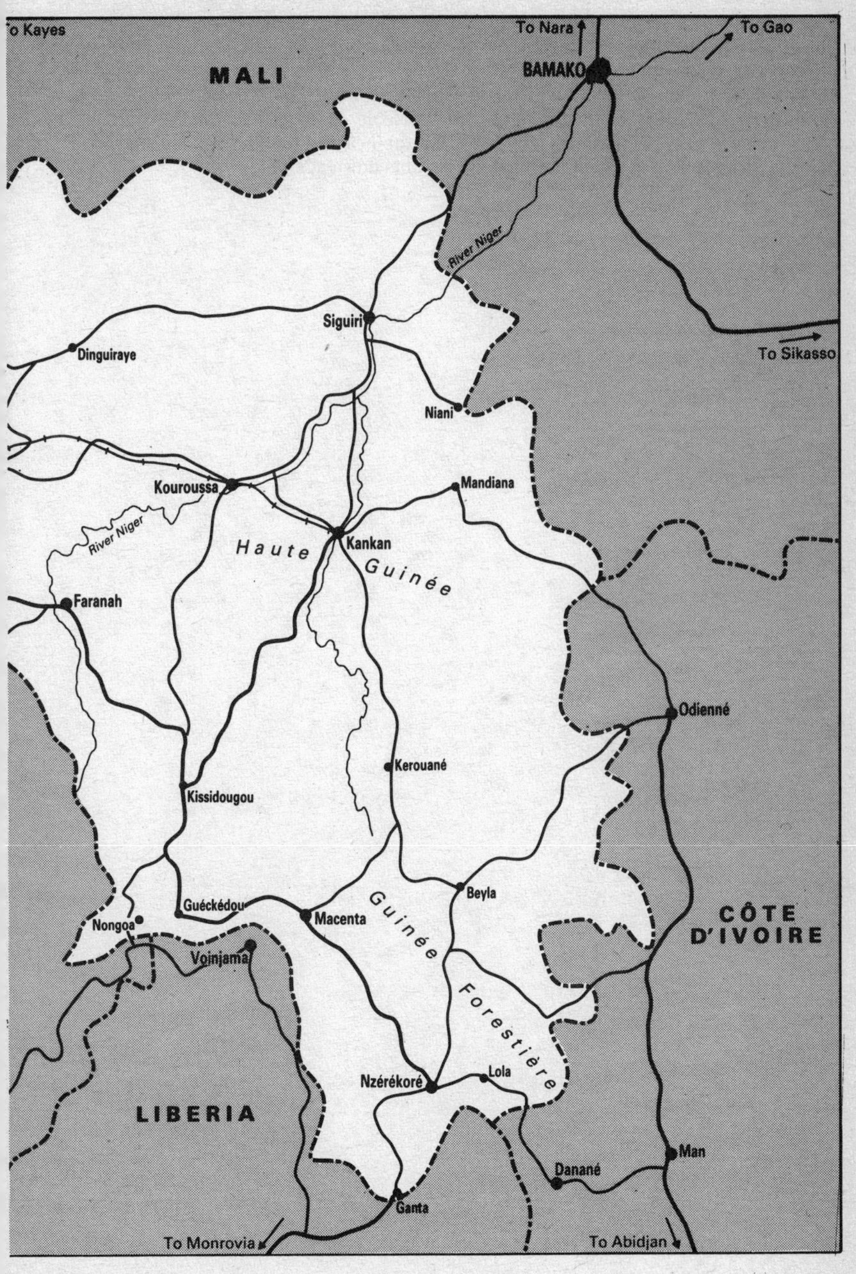

To Kayes
MALI
To Nara
BAMAKO
To Gao
River Niger
Siguiri
Dinguiraye
To Sikasso
Niani
Kouroussa
Mandiana
River Niger
Kankan
Haute
Guinée
Faranah
Odienné
Kerouané
Kissidougou
Beyla
Guéckédou
Nongoa
Macenta
Guinée
Forestière
CÔTE D'IVOIRE
Voinjama
Nzérékoré
Lola
LIBERIA
Man
Danané
Ganta
To Monrovia
To Abidjan

haze and dust as early as December, and by January landscape photographers are likely to be disappointed by the flatness of the light, but poor visibility doesn't always affect regions outside the northeast.

Overall, the easiest time to travel in Guinea is from late November to March. Conakry, at the best of times, has an insupportable climate, with relative humidity rarely below eighty percent and July delivering the heaviest month's rainfall anywhere in West Africa, much of which, fortunately, torrents down at night.

Arrivals

If you're not planning to fly in, there are overland routes into Guinea from all the surrounding countries. Most of these are endurance tests of one sort or another, but most also provide fine scenery and wild, little-travelled districts along the way.

Flights from Africa

There are flights to Conakry from most **West African capitals**. *Air Afrique* (RK) provides the widest-ranging service with non-stop flights from **Abidjan** on Tues and Thurs, from **Bamako** on Wed, and from **Dakar** on Wed, Fri, Sat and Sun. There are RK flights connecting through Abidjan from **Niamey** and **Lomé** on Tues, from **Lagos** on Thurs and from **Cotonou** on Tues and Thurs.

Air Guinée (GI) itself flies in from **Monrovia** via **Freetown** on Tues and Fri; from **Abidjan** via **Freetown** on Thurs; from **Bamako** on Sat; from **Dakar** non-stop on Mon and from Dakar via **Banjul** on Thurs and Sat; and from Banjul via **Labé** on Sun.

Guinée Air Service flies from **Monrovia** via **Nzérékoré** and **Kissidougou** to Conakry on Mon and Wed; from Monrovia via Nzérékoré and **Kankan** on Fri; from **Banjul** via **Labé** on Tues and Thurs; from **Bissau** via **Boké** on Thurs; and from **Bamako** via Kankan on Sun.

Ghana Airways (GH) is useful too, with flights from **Accra** on Wed (via **Abidjan** and **Freetown**) and on Sat (via Freetown); and flights from **Las Palmas** via **Banjul** on Thurs and **Dakar** via Banjul on Sun. There are GH flights connecting through **Accra** from **Lagos** on Wed and Sat.

Nigeria Airways (WT) flies from **Lagos** non-stop on Fri and Sun, and via **Cotonou** and **Abidjan** on Thurs.

Of the less important airlines, *Air Ivoire* (VU) flies non-stop from **Abidjan** on Wed, and via **Bouaké** on Mon and Fri; *Gambia Airways* (CK) flies **Banjul** to Conakry via **Freetown** on Mon, Wed and Sat; *Air Gabon* (GN) flies in from **Lagos** via **Abidjan** on Mon and from Dakar on Fri; *Air France* (AF) flies from **Bamako** on Sun; *TAGB* (YZ) flies from **Bissau** on Mon; *KLM* (KL) flies from **Freetown** on Mon, Thurs and Sat; and *Royal Air Maroc* (AT) flies in from **Casablanca** via Dakar on Mon.

The details in these practical information pages are essentially for use on the ground in West Africa and in Guinea itself; for full details on preparing for a trip, getting here from outside the region, paperwork, health, information sources and more, see *Basics*, pp.3–88.

Overland from Mali

There are two main possibilities from Bamako. The first involves taking a **bush taxi** to Kankan (a long day, even assuming nothing goes wrong). The border itself seems usually to be hassle-free. The second option, when the River Niger is high enough, is the **ferry to Siguiri and Kouroussa**, and sometimes **Kankan**. This service – operated by the *Compagnie Malienne de Navigation* – usually runs from August to January and does, at most, a weekly voyage.

Overland from Guinea-Bissau

Bissau to Conakry is one of the region's toughest international journeys, liable to be cut by floods and mud pools during the rains. Public transport along the various routes, especially in the border region, is tenuous. If you can arrange a ride in advance you'll save a lot of waiting en route.

The "direct" coastal route to Conakry, over the creeks **from Buba and Cacine to Boké**, is really not a viable option except at the end of the dry season – and in any case the places along the way constitute little incentive to make the attempt. There is, at least, now a bridge over the Kogon River, east of Sansalé (20km inside Guinea after crossing the border from Cacine) where formerly there was often a long delay for the ferry.

The usual route follows the tarmac through Guinea-Bissau via **Gabú** and **Pitche** (in Guinea); thence via **Koundara** and back onto tarmac at **Labé**. Bush taxis for Koundara leave Gabú two or three times a week; the road between Pitche and the border (which closes for lunch on the Guinea-Bissau side) is little more than a bush track and can be empty of passing transport as far as Saréboido (in Guinea), though Saréboido's Sunday market generates commercial traffic. From Koundara there are daily departures for Labé, through the beautiful northern Fouta Djalon. Note that officials at Koundara will try to persuade you to change money with them, but their rates are poor. Change a note or two only. A regular **Gabú to Conakry** service is supposed to depart Gabú every Friday at 8am, arriving in the small hours.

You can also cross the border into Guinea **between Pitche and Foula-Mori**, connected in the dry season by a driveable 30km track and a hauled ferry over the Koliba River. There's some transport along the way on Monday – Pitche's market day. You go through Guinea-Bissau (in)formalities at the ferry and Guinea formalities at the friendly Foula-Mori post. Although not marked on the maps, this is a recognized border crossing. **Koumbia**, 80km further on, is then the first town of any size and from here there's limited transport to the coast or up into the Fouta Djalon. If you're heading to Conakry, the road from Koumbia to **Boké** is gradually being improved; though it remains dire in many parts. The coastal forest is heady compensation and, if you have the means, a deviation out to the beaches at **Cap Verga** is well worthwhile.

Driving yourself, in good conditions – and coinciding with the ferry across the wide Fatala River at Boffa – you can do the trip from Koumbia to Conakry in under twelve hours. By **public transport** – in these parts, mostly overstacked bush taxi wagons – allow a couple of days.

■ Overland from The Gambia and Senegal

The choice is between two main routes: firstly the fairly straightforward bush taxi route through **Medina-Gounas** (see p.218) to **Koundara** (see above). If you're coming from **Basse** in The Gambia or **Tambacounda** in Senegal, this makes the most sense. Secondly, there's the more interesting but very tough route from **Kédougou** in Senegal up into the Fouta Djalon to the village of **Mali** and on to **Labé** (for route details see p.218). The large trucks which ply this route take up to *three days* to cover the 120km of boulder-strewn *piste*. It's not really one for your average off-road Land Rover-type vehicle.

■ Overland from Sierra Leone

In ordinary times, the relatively busy main route via Kambia and Pamelap connects **Freetown** with **Conakry** in a day's travel. As this book goes to press, there is little traffic, but in theory there are one or more buses to the border every day and no shortage of Peugeots and other vehicles to take you on to the pretty town of **Forécariah** and Conakry. There are numerous checkpoints along the way and while the border is normally fairly hassle-free for foreign travellers, lengthy searches and questioning are not unknown. Local people often have a hard time of it and you can expect delays on the buses.

> As of mid-1995, with the war in Sierra Leone escalating, travel outside Freetown was not advisable. The following summaries and suggestions are retained in the hope of a return to better times.

If you've had enough travel by the time you get into Guinea along this route, you might be intrigued to make a side trip down to **Benti** – the country's old banana port and a colonial settlement predating Conakry.

A second important route connects the highland region in eastern Sierra Leone with **Guéckédou**, part of the fastest overland route between Freetown and Bamako (normally four days by public transport, ferries permitting). The point to make for in Sierra Leone is **Koindu**, two days out from Freetown, from where you cross to **Nongoa** in Guinea and get transport to the tarmac at Guéckédou. Guinean visas may be obtainable in Nongoa – a useful back-up but not to be relied upon. Ask the policeman at the *pirogue* wharf on the Guinean side of the river. The *pirogues* on this river border take bicycles and motorbikes; other vehicles have to pass through Liberia. Note that Guéckédou has no bank.

A third route from Sierra Leone to Guinea is the northern road via **Kabala** to **Faranah**. In the past, formalities at **Gberia Fotombu** on the Sierra Leonean side have been sweetly perfunctory and the police hospitable, with a similar welcome at **Hérèmakono**, the first village in Guinea. You might walk this border gap – about 12km – and it's attractive, breezy country, but you'll be lucky to find transport until you hit the main road, 15km west of Faranah which might mean a walk of 60km in total. Like Guéckédou, Faranah has no bank.

A fourth possibility is to find transport heading north from **Kamakwie** to **Madina-Oula**, and from here to Kindia or Mamou.

There's also the possibility of a **ferry service from Freetown** to Conakry. See the "Moving On" details at the end of the Conakry section (p.497).

■ Overland from Liberia

There's a spread of crossing points along the watershed frontier between Liberia and Guinea. But with the amount of smuggling that goes on and the legacy of the two countries' historic mutual distrust, not to mention the more recent refugee problem resulting from the Liberian civil war, it's no surprise to find these borders troublesome. **Main frontiers** are at Foya–Guéckédou (ferry), Voinjama–Macenta, Ganta–Diécké, and Yekepa–Yalézou/Bossou (for Nzérékoré).

There's also the possibility of a **ferry service from Monrovia** to Conakry. See the "Moving On" details at the end of the Conakry section (p.497).

> As of mid-1995, with widespread insecurity and conflict throughout the country, travel outside Monrovia was not advisable. Even before the war, the border was an uncomfortable one.

Overland from Côte d'Ivoire

There are three main routes from Côte d'Ivoire. The first from **Odienné** to **Kankan** is better than it looks on most maps, but it's still an extremely tough drive and customs checks at the border are rigorous. The *Régroupement de Transporteurs Africain de Côte d'Ivoire* (*RTACI*) runs a weekly bus service between Bouaké and Kankan, departing Friday at 4pm, going via Odienné, arriving Saturday night or Sunday morning (around CFA20,000).

The second route – handy if you can't catch the bus – is from **Odienné to Sinko** and Beyla. There's a huge market in Sinko (Guinea) on Fri, for which vehicles leave Odienné early Thurs morning.

The third important route is the lovely forest road from **Danané** to **Nzérékoré**. Sometimes you'll find taxis along here and there's always transport on a Tuesday for Nzérékoré's big weekly market. The road is normally passable throughout the year. But it can be surprisingly difficult to find transport to **Gbapleu** – where Ivoirian formalities are conducted – and from there to the Guinean frontier near **Nzo**. You might, with reason, give up a day to walk through the forest; it's magnificent.

Red Tape

Guinean visas – required by all – used to be notoriously difficult to obtain. The situation has changed completely in recent years, with visas obtainable in a number of African cities and officials in Guinea genuinely welcoming to tourists.

Depending on where you apply for a visa, you may simply be required to present your passport with a photocopy of the ID pages, photos and a fee of around CFA20,000; but some embassies still ask for a letter from a resident inviting you, or a **letter of accreditation** from your own embassy. The embassies at **Accra**, **Banjul**, **Bissau**, **Bamako**, **Dakar** and **Freetown** have lately been fairly easy; the embassy in **Abidjan** less certain. Thirty-day single-entry visas are the norm, but you can get more if you plead a little and extend again in Conakry. There are also embassies in **Monrovia** and **Lagos**.

There's no embassy in London but in Europe, the embassy in **Bonn** reportedly issues visas without demur, and not only to people with return air tickets. The embassy in **Paris** is less helpful. Enlist the services of a visa agent if you want to get your visa in advance.

Visas for onward travel

Apart from the embassies of the six **neighbouring countries**, other useful African embassies in Conakry include **Ghana**, **Morocco**, **Nigeria**, **Togo** and **Zaire**. There is no representative for **Côte d'Ivoire**. The **French embassy** routinely handles visas for **Mauritania** and **Burkina Faso**. There's a full list of addresses on p.497.

Other bureaucratic business

The only **health certificate** formally required is yellow fever but it's best, as usual, to have a cholera certificate too. You are likely to be asked for both and not just at the point of entry.

If you're flying in, you may well be given a **currency declaration form**; though you may not be asked to complete one if you declare less than £2000 ($3000); it is unlikely that you will be given one at land borders. If you'll be leaving the country by air you may be required to hand the form in, in which case it must indicate bank transactions.

The **photography permit** has been withdrawn, but you should still be very discreet.

Other official business in Guinea has been much reduced: the security police in provincial towns generally expect you to present yourself and your passport to them on arrival, but otherwise you'll be left alone most of the time. However, some hotels will still try to hold your passport until you check out, even if you pay first; it's best not to allow this.

Money, Banks and Costs

Guinea uses its own *Franc Guinéen* (FG), a soft currency intended to lead the way to the country's eventual inclusion in the CFA zone. With the abolition of Sekou Touré's *syli* currency, the Guinean franc was reintroduced at the same value as the CFA franc. It has slipped to a free market rate of FG12,000 to CFA5000. In August 1995, the official exchange rate for the US dollar was approximately FG1350, so for the pound sterling you could expect about FG2000.

Information about currency declaration forms is given in "Red Tape" above. Although exchange controls have been relaxed, there is still a low-level **black market** in CFA, FF and US$, generally ignored by the police and offering around ten percent better rates than the banks. If you have CFA or FF you'll often be able to use them for accommodation and transport.

The lack of **banks** may force you to change money unofficially. The *Banque Internationale pour le Commerce et l'Industrie de la Guinée* (*BICIGUI*) is the main, and generally efficient bank (UK£ travellers' cheques are no problem), with branches in **Conakry**, **Boké**, **Fria**, **Kankan**, **Kamsar**, **Kissidougou**, **Labé**, **Macenta** and **Nzérékoré**. Don't count on finding banks anywhere else. If you don't have FF or CFA francs in cash you need to plan ahead.

Plan ahead with your FG cash too, once you've got it. Guinean franc coins are practically redundant, their values too small. It's the notes that are used, from filthy, damp twenty-five-franc bills to FG10,000 notes which are almost unusable except in large towns – change them down to FG5000 and FG1000. Convert only as much as you'll need: you can buy CFA or other currencies with your remaining FG, in border towns – though usually at marked-up prices. Any remaining FG will be confiscated when you leave the country.

The utility of **credit cards**, even in Conakry, is strictly limited to a few of the larger hotels and car rental and air ticket payments.

■ Costs

Guinean **prices** generally compare favourably with those of neighbouring countries. Cheap hotels in most towns will be from FG4000–10,000 a room; rice and sauce doesn't normally cost over FG500; and you can readily get several of most kinds of fruit for FG50 or FG100. Conakry, however, is very much more expensive than the provinces, particularly for accommodation. **Transport costs** are high, however, and can push up expenditure enormously. Seat prices are fixed on the main routes but depend on road conditions and vehicle – expect FG25–30 per kilometre on tarred roads in the west and anything up to FG80 per kilometre on rough roads in the east and northwest, especially those leading to borders.

Health

Guinea provides some of West Africa's roughest travelling and it's this, rather than any intrinsic unhealthiness, which can lead to problems. Out in the wilds, the basic health infrastructure is too limited to be a safety net.

Guinea is largely mountainous, and temperatures drop quickly after dark in the higher parts. Travelling by public transport, it makes good sense to keep something warm close at hand: your vehicle may roll for hours into the night with your luggage stowed in some inaccessible corner.

Water, as usual, is a major consideration. Although bottled *Coyah* water is increasingly available in the provinces, much of what you drink, outside a few main towns, will originate from pumped boreholes, which provide clean drinking water. The huge number of rivers and streams in Guinea means you'll likely end up wading through some of them. But try to limit this and particularly avoid slow-flowing waters and dry-season pools: there's a high incidence of bilharzia. There was a significant outbreak of cholera in Conakry during the 1994/5 dry season.

Maps and Information

There are no tourist offices, and no up-to-date official tourist information of any kind is available. As for maps, the IGN map of Guinea at 1cm:10km (new edition published 1992) is definitely worth obtaining before you go, and vital if you intend doing any hiking or trail beating.

There are some colonial survey maps around (1cm:1km), but you're only likely to track them down in university libraries. For long stays in Conakry, the IGN map of the capital, although published in 1982, is also worth getting in advance; it's only occasionally available at the *Novotel* in the city.

Getting Around

Most travellers find Guinea the toughest country to get around in West Africa: journeys are frequently long and often follow equally long waits while seats are being filled. Surfaced roads account for only 1500km or so and alternative means of surface transport – the remains of the railway system and the odd river boat – don't add up to much.

There has, however, been a proliferation of **domestic air services,** with at least three companies offering, between them, several flights a week between Conakry and provincial towns.

Bush taxis, trucks and buses

Transport on Guinea's main routes is ordinarily by **Peugeot 504** with between eight and ten passengers. In the hills, they're very much faster than the clapped-out *cars* and *bâchés* with up to twenty passengers, but there are some newer **minibuses** appearing on the roads. 504s tend to stick to surfaced and well-maintained earth roads. Travelling along the country's less comfortable byways is down to valiant and incredibly slow open-backed **goods lorries** – *gros camions* – and, to a lesser extent, elderly jeeps and Land Rovers. You should take some notice of the vehicle's condition and opt for the one least likely to break down or kill you. Price can be an uncanny indicator of speed and reliability.

The "head" price – the **fare** – is payable at the end of the trip – or often just before arrival. Be certain of your fare, especially if you're setting down en route when it can be very hard to argue if you feel you're being robbed. The price of baggage is normally discussed in advance of departure and paid then.

The *Société Générale des Transports de Guinée* (**SOGETRAG**) runs a number of bus services out of Conakry, but these appear to be declining in spread and frequency. They're recommended if you can coincide with a service, some of which are only weekly. Details are given at the end of the Conakry section on p.497.

Routes and frequencies

The busiest route is from **Conakry to Mamou** with departures until early afternoon (5hr); the Conakry–Kindia section (3hr) is now smooth and regraded and too fast for comfort. **Mamou to Labé** (3hr) is another relatively busy and newly resurfaced road: much of the transport is local to the Fouta Djalon. **Mamou to Faranah** is fairly quiet with few local vehicles. **Conakry to Kankan** or **Guéckédou** (14hr plus) tends to be an all-night trip but it's perfectly possible to make a late arrival if you start early enough. **Conakry to Nzérékoré** though (20hr or more, until the tarmac road is finished), is best contemplated with a night stop somewhere en route.

In the eastern and northwestern fringes of the country, most transport is long distance. You can wait days for a vehicle away from the main routes, especially during the rains.

Trains

The **Conakry–Kankan line** has not operated as a regular passenger service for many years – a pity, as the scenery along the way reputedly makes the road look dull by comparison. Technically the service is merely "suspended", but there are no immediate prospects of it being

SAMPLE ROAD TRANSPORT FARES

Conakry–Kindia (135km) FG3000 by SOGETRAG;
Conakry–Mamou (285km) FG8000 by 504, FG6000 by SOGETRAG;
Conakry–Télimélé (265km) FG6000 by *bâché*;
Conakry–Labé (437km) FG12,000 by minibus;
Conakry–Faranah (475km) FG13,000 by 504;
Conakry–Kankan (804km) FG30,000 by 504, FG20,000 by SOGETRAG;
Mamou–Dalaba (59km) FG2000 by 504;
Dalaba–Pita (53km) FG3000 by 504;
Pita–Labé (40km) FG1500 by 504;
Mamou–Labé (152km) FG6000 by 504;
Labé–Koundara (244km) FG13,000 by 504;
Koundara–Gaoual (111km) FG7000 by Land Rover;
Kissidougou–Kankan (190km) FG5000 by 504;
Kankan–Kérouané (175km) FG7500 by 504;
Kankan–Nzérékoré (383km) FG15,000 by lorry;
Kankan–Malian border (217km) FG16,000 by 504;
Kankan–Côte d'Ivoire border (250km) FG10,000 by 504.

revived. In theory, freight trains still run once or twice a month. Lines also go from Conakry to the bauxite works at Fria (freight only) and from Kamsar on the northwest coast to **Boké** and **Sangaredi** (freight/passenger service).

■ Planes

There has been a recent expansion of air services with *Guinée Air Service* and *Guinée Inter Air* competing with *Air Guinée* on domestic runs and some cross-border hops. Towns linked with Conakry (and in some cases with each other) include: Boké, Faranah, Kankan, Kissidougou, Labé, Nzérékoré, Sambailo (for Koundara) and Siguiri. Details are given at the end of the Conakry section (p.497) and in "Moving On" boxes throughout the chapter.

■ Other forms of transport

Car rental rates are extortionate. There are some outlets in Conakry, at the airport and the *Novotel*, but none up-country. You're unlikely to find it worthwhile except for specific targets, and there still seem to be some niggling security doubts over driving rented cars beyond the 36km city limits. Whether you like it or not, you might find it impossible to rent a car without being obliged to hire a driver as well. From pumps, *essence* (petrol/gasoline) costs around FG750/litre, while *gasoil* (diesel) is FG450/litre. Both are cheaper by the jerry can from market traders.

A **ferry-barge** still runs occasionally at high water times (roughly August to December) from Kankan, down a tributary of the Niger, to Siguiri and Bamako – though details vary season by season. There's another boat, from Kouroussa, that also makes a regular voyage via Siguiri to Bamako and back during the high water season.

Guinea has several possible **canoeing** rivers, including the upper Niger which is probably the best. Full details of obtaining a boat and paddling downstream are given on p.513. You need to be fully self-sufficient and also have tough, waterproof bags for your belongings.

The country is wonderful territory for **hiking**, **cycling** and **motorbiking**. During the French occupation, Guinea supported an enthusiastic fraternity of hunting and outdoor-pursuit fans with an infrastructure of *campements* and guides. Today there's little back-up and, as with canoeing, you need to be self-supporting if you want to make the most of the wild country. Main requirements are a tent and cooking equipment, water bottles, spares if you're cycling (even locally bought bikes are poorly serviced), and as much time as possible.

Accommodation

The recent recovery from economic coma has so far precipitated a boom in hotel building only in Conakry, and in the provinces there are just a few hotels above the level of bordellos and basic lodgings. There are no hostels or campsites.

Cheap places (from FG4000–10,000 in the provinces; generally much more in Conakry) are usually primitive – electricity sporadic, and water generally in buckets, though sometimes warmed for you. There is, however, a scattering of hotels and guest houses in the Fouta Djalon and the east with a certain idiosyncratic appeal, all detailed in the town-by-town coverage.

In smaller towns and villages you can always ask to see the *sous-préfet* (the district officer) with a view to a night at the **villa** – accommodation for visiting government employees. Some larger towns, prefectoral capitals, also have *villas*. These places are often good, though they may need an airing and a broom, and you may, or may not, be asked for payment. Always leave something for the caretaker.

On the question of **private accommodation**, Guineans are most hospitable, aware to the point of angst of the country's shortcomings. But they may assume your needs can't be met and not think to offer an ordinary room. Once it's understood you need a roof, you'll repeatedly be offered places to stay in people's compounds; the only difficulty is in moving on without causing offence.

Camping, in the bush, shouldn't be a problem. Doing so near large towns is bound to cause suspicion. The law against it could be reawakened by zealous police.

Eating and Drinking

Guinean food is based overwhelmingly on three ingredients – rice, leaves and groundnuts – but there's a terrific variety of tastes and much that's delicious. Very strongly spiced food isn't common.

International or French restaurant fare is almost restricted to Conakry, which does have a few excellent and costly establishments. For the rest of the country, although you'll find simple

ACCOMMODATION PRICE CODES

All hotel prices in this chapter are coded according to the following scales, and throughout the book in the equivalent in UK£ and US$. Prices refer to the rate you can expect to pay for a room with two beds. Single rooms, or single occupancy, will normally cost at least two-thirds of the twin-occupancy rate, for further details see p.51.

① **Under FG10,000 (under £5/$7.50).** Rudimentary lodgings, with primitive facilities. No guarantees of electricity or hot water.

② **FG10,000–20,000 (£5–10/$7.50–15).** Basic hotel with few frills. Some **S/C**.

③ **FG20,000–40,000(£10–20/$15–30).** Modest hotel, usually with S/C rooms and a choice of rooms with fans, or a premium for AC.

④ **FG40,000–60,000 (£20–30/$30–45).** Reasonable business or tourist-class hotel with S/C, AC rooms and a restaurant.

⑤ **FG60,000–80,000 (£30–40/$45–60).** As for the previous bracket but smarter. Usually a new hotel.

⑥ **FG80,000–100,000 (£40–50/$60–75).** Com-fortable, first-class hotel, with good facilities.

⑦ **Over FG100,000 (over £50/$75).** Luxury establishment with pool and other special features, but not necessarily excellent in international terms.

restaurants, it's street food that prevails. **Mafé** is the standard term for groundnut sauce: **atieké** or **tô** is steamed, grated cassava stodge, a less common alternative to rice as a staple.

Street food is a serious business, with big pots of rice, sauces, chipped yams, potatoes and bananas hiding under an awning where you squat on a bench to eat. Choose what you want and, if you're not alone, order for one person at a time and share – servings are on the gigantic side. Beware of going to eat too late. The main meal of the day usually comes around 11am and by midday most street eats are finished.

Consistently delicious – and usually meatless – is **sauce de feuilles**, best made with the finely chopped young cassava or sweet potato leaves you see being cut in the markets. If you order **riz-sauce**, it comes with chunks of meat and gristle. Order the rice only (usually home-grown and tasty) and it will be doused with thin sauce anyway. **Bouillon** is usually a beef or mutton stew made with offal. **Brochettes** (little kebabs) are common everywhere. **Bush meat** of various kinds is mostly found in off-the-road villages: if it's monkey you should be certain it has been very well cooked before eating it.

Avocados are surprisingly popular in the southeast highlands. **Taro** (cocoyams), **salads** of lettuce and tomato (something of a health risk – go by first impressions), **beans** and other garden produce are common in some parts of the country.

Oranges are the biggest **fruit** crop. In the Fouta Djalon from November to April they're abundant and cheap enough to buy all day as a drink. **Bananas** in various shapes and sizes are everywhere much in evidence, especially around Kindia. Many towns have streets luxuriantly shaded by **mango** trees.

Beer drinkers can choose between locally brewed *Skol* (FG1000 for a half-litre) and *Guiluxe*, Guinea's "national beer". **Palm wine** is common in small villages, especially in non-Muslim areas. There are all the usual bottled **soft drinks**.

White **coffee** (*Nescafé/café au lait*) is served as a rule with *pain beurre*, not drunk on its own. Unless *Nescafé* is specified, however, you may, if you order *café*, be served *lait concentré sucré* with weak *lipton* poured on top – sweet tea, in other words, not coffee at all. *Café fort*, on the other hand, is what it says and is even occasionally made with ground coffee beans rather than instant powder. Guinea's *kinkeliba* infusion is better tasting than Senegal's. **Sour milk**, laced with sugar and usually bulked out with starchy cassava flour, is more of a meal than a drink.

Communications: Post, Phones, Language & Media

Guinea's telecommunications network isn't one of the best in the region. Conakry's *PTT* leaves the worst impression of all. Forget about poste restante there: Kankan's is probably safer. If you must use facilities in Conakry, you're probably best off visiting the *Novotel* (phones and fax) and using your

> **Guinea's IDD code is ☎224.**

embassy or consulate for mail-holding. Telephone calls to Europe cost FG 15,000 for three minutes.

PTT hours vary (Mon–Sat 8am–2pm in **Conakry**, 7.30am–4pm in **Kankan** and **Nzérékoré**). Other main post offices are at **Boké**, **Kindia**, **Labé** and **Faranah**. From any of these provincial capitals you can theoretically phone or fax abroad.

The media

Radios are prized possessions in Guinea. *Radiodiffusion-Télévision Guinéenne* broadcasts **radio** in French, English, Portuguese, Kriol, Susu, Malinké and Fula and puts out evening **TV** in French with news in six Guinean languages. Cultural programming (most shows made in Guinea) is a priority. Recently **local radio** stations have been introduced in Kankan, Kindia, Labé and Nzérékoré. The national **press** used to consist only of *Horoya* ("Dignity") – a weekly rag of inspired awfulness carrying limited African news. These days there are several other newspapers but the press still hasn't taken off. *L'Evenement de Guinée* is published monthly; *La Guinéenne* is a monthly women's journal; and look out for the independent *L'Observateur*.

If you're famished for *actualités*, foreign papers and magazines are becoming more available in Conakry. In Guinea, though, more than most countries, a **short-wave radio** is worth a lot.

Language

The most important languages are the Mande tongue, **Susu**, (mostly spoken in the west), **Fula**, (spoken in the densely populated Fouta Djalon), and **Malinké** (spoken in the eastern plains). English is becoming increasingly important in the Fouta Djalon, where mainly refugees from Sierra Leone and Liberia have sought refuge.

SIMPLE SUSU

Susu is more straightforward in many respects, than Fula, but somewhat tonal, so that (like Chinese) the meaning of what you say depends on the tone of your voice when you say it. It bears comparison with Bamana (see p.305) and Mandinka (see p.249).

GREETINGS

Hello	*Inwali* (to one person) *Wo inwali* (two or more people)	Good afternoon/ evening	*Tana mogegné*
Good day	*Wo mamabé*	How's the family?	*Tanamodinbayama*
Good morning	*Tana mokhi* (literally, "did nothing bad happen in the night?")	See you later/good bye	*Won je segué*

NUMBERS

1	*keren*	5	*suli*	9	*solomanani*	40	*tongonani*
2	*firin*	6	*senné*	10	*fu*	50	*tongosuli*
3	*sakhan*	7	*soloferé*	20	*mokhein*	60	*tongosenné*
4	*nani*	8	*solomasakham*	25	*mokhein nu suli*	100	*kémé*
				30	*tongosakhan*	200	*kémé firin*

USEFUL EXPRESSIONS

How much?	*Yéri?*	I don't know.	*M'ma kolon*
I'll take it (give it to me)	*A sun nyi*	I don't understand	*M'ma fahamukhi*
		Excuse me	*Diyema*
It's too expensive	*Asaré khorokho*	Please repeat it	*Nakhadi*
Show me the way.	*Kira ma sembé*	Where's the bank?	*Banque na mindé?*

These words and phrases are intended only as a way into further communication. Guinean women, especially, rarely speak French. For Malinké look at the Bamana language section in Chapter Four "Mali" (p.305).

Although **French** is the country's official language, Sekou Touré virtually eliminated its teaching so that a broad generation of people speak it very badly or not at all. Since 1984 French lessons have been reintroduced into primary education.

FUNDAMENTAL FULA

Fula (technically *Fulfulde*, and sometimes called *Pulaar*) is a **class language** with 21 classes, implying the usual agreement between nouns, demonstratives, adjectives and so on. There's no tonal system. A little problematically the class agreements "mutate"; the class suffix can actually change in sound within the same class depending on the noun's root. It's all a rather complicated jump from European languages and unless you've tried learning a relatively easy class language like Swahili, probably too much trouble. There's little instructional material in English. Note that the following is based on the Fula of Fouta Djalon and the language spoken in other parts of West Africa – for example the Fouta Toro in Senegal, Massina in Mali or in Nigeria or Cameroon, can differ markedly, especially in respect of greetings.

GREETINGS

How are you?	*On djarama?*
Are you fine?	*Tanalaton?*
[response– fine]	*Djamtum*
How's the family?	*Bengure mandin?*
[response– fine]	*Bengure nden no djam*
How's the work?	*Gollednen?*
[response– fine]	*Gollednen no marsude*
Sorry	*A tjana khake*
Please	*A tju hake*

CONVERSATION

Do you speak Fula?	*A volaj Fula?*
Yes	*Hiji*
No	*Oo*
I don't know	*Mi anda*
I don't understand	*Mi famali*
Please repeat it	*Hondu buiyu da*
Welcome!	*On njuti edjam!*
Nice to meet you	*Minko sadjo minete*
What's your name?	*Kohono vjeteda?*
My name is Michael	*Kohono mi vjete Michael*
Where are you from?	*Kvonto ole kamo?*
I'm from Guinea	*Govena mjuri*

TRAVEL

Where are you going?	*Konto jato?*
Where is Dalaba?	*Konto ole Dalaba?*
Straight ahead	*Jee so mara*
Right	*Sengo njamo*
Left	*Sengo nano*
Far away	*Uwanto diri*
Village	*Hodho*
Big	*Non djardi*
Small	*No fandi*
Hill	*Fello*
Waterfall	*Djurnde*
Mosque	*Djulirde*

SHOPPING AND FOOD

It's too expensive	*No sati*
Where's the bank?	*Hon to bank?*
How much?	*Jelu?*
Food	*Njamete*
Rice	*Maro*
Potatoes	*Pute*
Meat	*Deo*
Milk	*Birada*
Water	*Dija*
Tea	*Dute*
It's excellent (food)!	*No mo i!*

NUMBERS

1	*goo*
2	*didi*
3	*tati*
4	*nayi*
5	*joyi*
6	*jegoo*
7	*jedidi*
8	*jetati*
9	*jenayi*
10	*saapo*
11	*sappo e goo*
20	*no gayi*
25	*no gayi joyi*
100	*témédéré*
200	*témédéré didi*

GUINEAN GLOSSARY

Alfa King (Fula).

Bowe Eroded Fouta Djalon hill (pl. Bowal).

CTRN Transitional Committee for National Redress.

Dougou Place (Mande languages).

FLING The anti-Touré Front for the National Liberation of Guinea.

Foté White person (corruption of "Portuguese").

Fouta Place (Fula).

Koro Old (as in Dabolakoro – old Dabola).

Lumo Market held weekly or sometimes every four or five days.

PDG Democatic Party of Guinea, the party of the old regime.

PUP Unity and Progress Party, the ruling party of Lansana Conté.

RPG Guinean People's Assembly, the main opposition party.

Sofa Malinké chief (nineteenth century).

Syli Elephant (and defunct Guinean currency).

Woro Kola (Mande languages).

Gara Indigo (and indigo cloth).

Public Holidays

Aside from New Year's Day, May 1 (Labour Day) and the usual shifting Islamic calendar, the principal Guinean holidays are April 3 (anniversary of the 1984 coup), October 2 (Independence Day), and November 22 ("Victory Day"; anniversary of the repulsed 1970 Portuguese invasion). Christian holidays are observed more haphazardly – in the main by large businesses and government offices.

The commemoration of other landmarks in Guinea's history depends on more ephemeral political considerations: May 14, the anniversary of the founding of the *PDG* party; September 28, the anniversary of the "No" vote; February 9, National Women's Day; and August 27, the day in 1977 when the market women revolted and forced Sekou Touré to change tack.

Regional and local **non-Islamic festivals** were attacked as sectarian and unproductive during the Touré dictatorship and for many the generation-long repression destroyed their viability. You can still come across them if you're well-placed and well-timed – January to March is the most propitious season.

Arts and Entertainment

In 1969, Guinea won the *Grand Prix* at the first Pan-African Cultural Festival (FESPAC) held in Algiers. Conakry's annual *Quinzaine artistique* (Arts Fortnight) used to attract visitors from across the continent. It looks like the new regime is trying to build on the reservoir of talent with its cultural season (October to June); details at the museum in Conakry.

■ Music

Travelling by Peugeot 504 across the country, you're accompanied most of the time by **music**. Driver and passengers take turns with the cassette deck and much of what you hear is Guinean – though Antillean *zouk* is increasingly popular even if only poor-quality recordings are made locally. Guinea has nurtured some of Africa's most talented and original musicians and singers. Many are now based abroad, in Côte d'Ivoire or France. There are more details and background in the article on music in *Contexts* at the back of the book.

Mory Kante in particular has expanded into international stardom – arguably dishing his music for the sake of Europe's high-street record shops – but his audience at home is still huge. Enthusiasm for some of the names that became legends in Guinea and abroad before 1984 – **Bembeya Jazz**, **Les Amazones** – is less noticeable now. Tastes in Guinea are often quite local: put on a cassette by the Fula musician **Dourah Barry** in Malinké country and you risk offending all the passengers. Music is a good way into Guinea's cultural complexities.

Live music on stage is mostly a pleasure of Conakry's clubs. Up-country, local bands play occasionally, but the big national *orchestres* with overseas recording contracts don't play much at home.

The **griots** retain a major role as entertainers in the countryside, and koras and guitars and a few beers are a common evening combination. In

Guinea you can still have your praises sung for small change.

Other entertainments

For other cultural affairs, the best place to check what might be going on is the National Museum in Conakry which houses the "Office of National Heritage". **Theatre** is getting some encouragement with the formation of a *Théâtre National d'Enfants* and promotion of the *Théâtre National* and the *Ballet National*, but there's a lack of decent venues, even in Conakry. **Cinema** seems to be absolutely defunct, though as a creative force it never really began, and is totally disabled through lack of film stock, equipment and, perhaps, nerve. Those who wanted to create cinema – as opposed to those content with making ideologically sound documentaries – left the country long ago. Imported movies today are predictable – French, the occasional Hollywood blockbuster, and lots of cheap, cheerful violence.

In sport, African wrestling is less important than in the countries further north. **Football** is hugely popular and Guinea's national team is moderately distinguished.

Directory

AIRPORT TAX FG3000 domestic, FG5000 Africa and FG10,000 inter-continental. Only Guinean francs are accepted.

CASSETTES Guinea's street and market vendors offer the best music deal in West Africa – about FG1000 each for copies.

GREETINGS Taken even more seriously in Guinea than in the rest of West Africa, traditional forms of greeting have been little diluted by European abruptness. Even in French you're expected to rattle off a few polite enquiries about family and life in general – particularly on official business. These phrases may pepper the whole conversation.

KOLA Kola nuts are a big crop in the southeast and very popular all over. Guinea is a country in which it's worth acquiring the taste. On long journeys a pocketful of white nuts (sweeter and speedier) keeps you from nodding off and is good to share.

MUSEUMS There's a residual national structure, with museums in Conakry, Boké, and Kissidougou, and there may be others. Four new regional museums are planned.

PHOTOGRAPHY Most of the pictures you take in Guinea will be of people you know and their families, or of unpopulated landscapes when no-one is looking. Don't assume you can get out your camera as you might in neighbouring countries and snap away. You will cause a scene and you're quite likely to have your camera confiscated, for which a large *amende* will be payable. In Conakry you should be very careful with your camera. The permis de photo, while no such thing actually exists any longer, may still be demanded.

POLITICS Not completely taboo, but Guineans are often sensitive about the fact that Sekou Touré was tolerated so long; and at the same time quick to denounce neocolonialism in any form.

RELIGION As usual, the pig is a fair indication of the boundaries of **Islam**. You won't see many between the jungles of the northwest and the hilly forests in the southeast. Islam continues to consolidate and displace the indigenous religions, and its international dimension is increasingly important in shaping Guinean society. The vast majority of practising Muslims (about three-quarters of the population) are members of the Tijaniya brotherhood. Christianity is a minority religion, only significant locally around Conakry and in the southeast.

SEXUAL ATTITUDES Guinea under the old regime was moralistic and prying. Prostitution was brutally suppressed and polygamy outlawed – both in the cause of social justice. Things have changed, and prostitution is now as widespread as anywhere in West Africa. Homosexuality is presumably a crime: discretion is advised.

TOILET PAPER Hard to obtain except in major towns.

TROUBLE Much of the pre-1984 security fabric is still, doggedly, in place and trumped-up accusations and suspicions can only be resolved in the traditional ways. Driving in your own vehicle, you will experience repeated efforts at extortion from the police and military, ranging from mildly humorous (and irritating) to hysterical (and contemptible). Even if you're in a taxi or other public transport, these can affect you, though in theory the driver himself is meant to soothe thirsty tempers and meet the incessant roadblock demands for a few hundred francs. The current state of affairs – especially in and around Conakry and as far up the highway as Mamou – is greatly resented, not so much because money is taken, but because the demands are deemed excessive. Most transport drivers lose a full fare on every trip.

If you genuinely break the law, you can ordinarily buy yourself out. Treat the police with caution, force out some humour, defuse them with cigarettes.

WILDLIFE Guinea has **no national parks** or game reserves as such, but there is a large number of newly gazetted *forêts classées* which help to preserve the environment – in theory. Guinea is one of the few West African countries which has preserved, largely intact, a diverse indigenous fauna. Most large species – including chimpanzees, hippos, elephants, lions and buffalo – hang on, unprotected and rarely seen. It's been forty years since any field surveys were carried out and the current position is hazy. Hunting appears to be as much of a threat as environmental destruction. Regionally, the best wildlife zones are the hilly acacia savannah in the northeast, between the Tinkisso River and the Malian border; the undulating bush and grassland between Mamou and Faranah where the Fouta Djalon slopes down to Sierra Leone; and the southeast highlands, particularly east of the Macenta–Nzérékoré road.

WOMEN TRAVELLERS AND THE WOMEN'S MOVEMENT Women travellers have a reasonably easy time in Guinea, sheltered from some of the hassles of Mali, Senegal or Côte d'Ivoire by the lack of tourists, and frequently escorted along the way. So long as your French is adequate you'll find quick access to people's homes and lives wherever you go. Be prepared for – normally low-key – sexual harassment. You might prefer to describe yourself as something other than a tourist, which carries slightly pejorative connotations.

Progressive women's organizations in Guinea suffered a setback though their association with Sekou Touré's deformed "socialism". Genital mutilation is still practised in many districts.

La Guinéenne is a monthly women's journal which may have items of interest.

A Brief History of Guinea

The first French expeditions into the hinterland of the Guinea coast took place from Boké, a creek-head base in contact with Europeans since the fifteenth century. Following the expansion initiated by Colonel Faidherbe across the Sahel – and to prevent the British linking The Gambia with Sierra Leone – the French commanders in "the rivers of the south" (as the Guinea region was known) forced protection treaties with dozens of small rulers through the middle of the nineteenth century. In the 1880s they came up against the first serious resistance to their invasion in the shape of the guerilla army of the Almamy Samory Touré, a man who won headlines in the French press for two decades and became Guinea's national hero. This account follows the country's history from his defeat to the present day. Some earlier historical background can be found throughout the guide and on p.509 and p.516.

■ The French occupation

Once Samory had been deported to Gabon in 1898, there was only relatively minor resistance to the French incursion. The **forest communities** put up a fight, and were aided by the hilly jungle in which the French couldn't use cavalry, but their political organization was weak and the villages submitted one after another in the years leading up to the First World War.

In the early days, wild **rubber** was Guinea's main crop. By 1905 the commerce was supporting a 700-stong Lebanese community in Conakry. But the export declined after 1913 as plantation markets opened in southeast Asia.

By 1914, the French had driven a **railway** over 600km through mountain terrain to the river port of Kankan, thus linking Conakry with Bamako. This, however, was a strategic railway rather than a commercial one. Apart from limited gold and diamonds, upper Guinea didn't appear to offer much return. Better prospects lay in the forest regions to the south where **coffee** and other tropical crops were developed on French-owned plantations, and near the coast and southern foothills of the Fouta Djalon, where **bananas** – increasingly popular as an exotic fruit – flourished.

Guinea's biggest prize, though, was **bauxite** – aluminium ore – of which its vast high-grade deposits form nearly a third of the world's reserves. But the French only began to exploit them systematically in the 1950s and for most of their occupation the necessary investment wasn't attracted.

French rule in Guinea followed standard patterns except that, more so than elsewhere, the opportunities to become a privileged **evolué** were desperately few: until 1935 there was no secondary education in Guinea and, on the eve of independence, only 1.3 percent of Guinean children were receiving even primary schooling. With one singular exception, almost all the prominent Guineans before independence came from wealthy families who had sent them to the *Ecole Normale William Ponty* near Dakar.

■ The rise of nationalism

Ahmed Sekou Touré, a Malinké speaker from Faranah, first came to attention as a disruptive and perspicacious schoolboy in the late 1930s and then as founder of Guinea's first union – the Post and Telecommunications Workers – in 1946. In 1947 Touré and others formed the Guinean section of the *Rassemblement Démocratique Africain* (the broad alliance of French West African political groupings) and named it the **Parti Démocratique de Guinée**.

In the election for deputies to the new Constituent Assembly in 1945, the Guinean "subject" elected was **Yacine Diallo** – a Fula-speaker with the support of the Islamic old guard in the Fouta Djalon.

Guinea made huge strides after the war with major investment in the bauxite industry at last and a rapidly urbanizing workforce. Touré meanwhile was making his name as a politician and unionist. He was a delegate to the 1947 Communist French Trade Unions (*CGT*) Congress in Dakar and, with support from the French Communist party, he backed several **strikes** in the early 1950s and produced a labour newspaper – *L'Ouvrier*.

The most trenchant strike was the ten-week action in 1953 over the demand for a **twenty percent wage rise** to accompany a reform in the labour laws stipulating a 40-hour instead of a 48-hour week. During the strike, telegrams of instructions from Paris and Dakar to the Governor of Guinea were intercepted by radical telecommunications workers, and the strike resulted in a victory which made a lasting impression on the Guinean public and across French West Africa.

Sekou Touré's rise to power

By the time of the strike, Sekou Touré was the territorial assembly member for Beyla. From this platform, he and other trade unionists began a campaign to disaffiliate and Africanize the Guinean sections from the parent French unions.

Touré's career took a knock in 1954 when the Guinean **deputyship to the French assembly** came up on the death of Yacine Diallo. Convinced of his outright popularity, Touré was equally convinced that the election had been rigged when he was heavily beaten by a Fula candidate, Barry Diawadou (the Fouta Djalon was inimical territory for a Marxist Malinké). There had indeed been gross tampering by the French, and voters had even been struck off the register in areas of strong *PDG* support. The Minister for Overseas Territories came to Conakry to assure Guineans it wouldn't happen again. It was a debacle which many Fula had cause to regret after independence.

Instead, Touré became **mayor of Conakry** in 1955. He was just thirty-three. By 1956, with over 40,000 members in the *CGT-Guinée*, the break with the French unions was achieved and a new, African federation of labour unions created – the *Union Générale des Travailleurs d'Afrique Noire* (*UGTAN*) with Touré its first secretary general. Uniquely, in West Africa, Touré now succeeded in marrying the *PDG* party with the labour federation – an amalgam that was ratified in March 1958.

Touré's **second bid for deputy** was successful in 1956 in an election apparently free of abuses: his vote was up 200 percent on 1954 while Diawadou's was almost identical. Sekou Touré became **vice-president** of the new Territorial Council of Government in 1957, effectively prime minister of Guinea under the low-profile Governor Jean Ramadier. Touré firmly advocated an independent West African federation of states and denounced Senghor of Senegal and Houphouët-Boigny of Côte d'Ivoire as puppets for wanting to consolidate the French connection.

One of Touré's first major acts was the **abolition of chiefs** and their replacement by party cadres. The move was particularly resented in the Fouta Djalon, where chiefdoms had some traditional legitimacy. It was accompanied by some bloody settling of scores: the groundwork for the Guinean state security network was being prepared.

With **de Gaulle's return to power** in France Sekou Touré was soon given the chance to wield full power. The new constitution of the French Fifth Republic was unacceptable to him, and the idea of a free federation of completely independent states wasn't acceptable to de Gaulle – who insisted on their giving up some of their sovereignty to the federal government.

De Gaulle's visit to Conakry to put his case was a waste of time. He would "raise no obstacles" in Guinea's path if the country chose to "secede" from the community of French states – but he would "draw conclusions". Sekou Touré replied **"We prefer poverty in freedom to riches in slavery"** and the two leaders snubbed each other at every opportunity for the rest of the visit. "Good Luck to Guinea" sneered de Gaulle on his departure.

■ Guinea under Sekou Touré

While other Francophone leaders thought at first he was bluffing, Sekou Touré prepared his country to go it alone. On September 28 1958 there was a 95 percent **"No"** vote to the referendum on staying in the French community. And on October 2, **independence** was declared.

The example of Ghana under Nkrumah was an inspiration while the swift **reaction of the French** in Guinea – flight with the booty, sabotage of the infrastructure, burning of files and cancellation of all cooperation and investment – was made to seem like good riddance by the party, though the severity of the withdrawal was a vindictive blow.

The country had virtually no technical expertise and a total of six graduates. It started work from scratch, with aid from **Czechoslovakia**, the **Soviet Union** and seven other Eastern-bloc countries, and solid support from the European and Third World left. Morale was high and the *PDG* organization initially effective.

France excluded Guinea from the CFA franc zone of the newly independent Francophone nations. Guinea adopted its own franc (and later the *syli*) which isolated it further from neighbouring states, and hindered what little (non-French) trade remained, but at least stemmed the drain of capital to France.

Despite Nato fears that Guinea might become a West African Cuba, United States **President Eisenhower** waited six months before even sending an ambassador to Conakry, for fear of offending de Gaulle. In 1962, a substantial American aid package was finally worked out and the Peace Corps went in. Revolution aside, **American aid and investment**, particularly in the bauxite industry, has been firm ever since.

The Teachers' Plot

The **Soviet Union** quickly fell out with Sekou Touré at the time of the Cuban missile crisis. Misjudging his prevailing ideology – which was more committedly anti-capitalist than pro-communist – the Soviet mission was accused of "interference" when left-wing students demonstrated for a firm espousal of socialism and the dumping of Touré's "positive neutrality" (a refusal to be anyone's puppet). As a result of this **"Teachers' Plot"**, the Soviet ambassador was expelled. Diplomatic ties continued, however, and aid and expertise from the Soviet Union was never turned away – even if its usefulness was sometimes in doubt, such as in the case of the submarine base planned for the Los islands or the famous import of snow ploughs (possibly a malicious rumour as they're not much different from earth graders).

Poverty in slavery

As the first few years of independence unrolled, Sekou Touré, the **Pan-African** ideologue and co-author of the **OAU** charter, began to be seen in a less glamorous light as his extreme policies started to bite, and the popular enthusiasm of 1959–60 sloughed away. A planned economy without planners was taking shape (or rather not), state enterprises were extended, private business curtailed and a small but growing **middle class** was reaping illicit benefits from mismanagement and fraud.

The results of the first **three year plan** weren't encouraging. Critics in the *PDG* complained the party was out of its depth in trying to control the market economy, and mistaken in extending power to the illiterate masses. Sekou Touré scolded them in a twelve-hour speech designed to weed out the party faithful from the conspirators. He wrote later "Everything became rotten, the elite enjoyed riding in cars and building villas".

There was a massive **market crackdown** in November 1964, with widespread harassment of traders and confiscation of assets. Limits were set on the number of traders allowed outside the state sphere and arrests, interrogations and arbitrary punishments grew in frequency. The party was moulded in Touré's image and political life stagnated. The very freedoms which lay at the heart of party policy (on paper anyway) were savagely suppressed. To many, it was clear the government was at war with the people; thousands fled the country.

In 1965 a group of opposition exiles – the *Front pour la Libération de Guinée* (*FLING*) – began to organize outside the country with tacit support from Senegal and Côte d'Ivoire and less discreet help from France. The **"traders' plot"** of 1966 – an apparent attempt to install a liberal government with capitalist leanings – resulted in the complete rupture of diplomatic relations with Paris.

But denouncing conspiracies – imagined or otherwise – couldn't improve the economy. There were chronic **shortages** and production and distribution methods failed. As American aid continued to pour in, world opinion began to see Guinea as an American stooge and – perversely – relations with the United States turned sour.

■ The Terror

Guinea now entered a dark period of isolationism and widespread **terror**. At the end of 1967 the eighth party congress had **radicalization of the revolution** at the top of the agenda. To shore up its bankrupt ideology, the party formally adopted a path of "Socialism". Local revolutionary authorities (the *Pouvoirs Révolutionnaires Locals*, *PRLs*) were set up in every village – ostensibly to allow power to flow from the base up; in reality to extend the security blanket to every corner of the country. In the leadership, the picture suddenly became hazier, with the inauguration of a seven-member Politburo – the *Bureau Politique National* – in place of Sekou Touré alone. And as China was promulgating its bloody Cultural Revolution, Guinea – one of China's biggest African aid recipients – started its own campaign against "degenerate intellectuals".

Remarkably, in view of his political agility, the inflexible ideology which Sekou Touré carried before him wasn't abandoned for another ten years. And the elaborate and cruelly anti-human **security apparatus** that continued its triffid-like growth lost any trace of even Kafkaesque rationale. Touré was not totally insulated from the misery of his people. Huge sums were certainly creamed off by the Touré family's **"Faranah clan"** (see box), but ostentatious displays of wealth were avoided. The funds – and particularly hoards of **diamonds** – were siphoned

THE PERMANENT PLOT

The idea that there was a permanent, **anti-Guinea plot** obsessed the party hierarchy. The first plots had been exposed even before independence, but the climate of conspiracy thickened until virtually any action could be read as suspicious. At the height of Guinea's isolation, "citizen" and "suspect" became virtually synonymous.

For the first decade of independence, most of the "plots" originated outside the country and the party skilfully manipulated them to maintain control, timing announcements to coordinate with national events. Internal dissent was simply annihilated wherever it first breathed, usually before any chance of genuine conspiracy.

In 1969, however, the focus was shifted squarely to **internal opposition** and the Fula came under increasingly harsh attack. Touré was convinced that the densely populated Fouta Djalon was trying to secede, with the help of Senegal. Army units at Labé were purged and after the Portuguese invasion, it was the Fula who bore the brunt of his revenge.

In 1973 Sekou Touré announced the discovery of a "fifth column active in all walks of life". Again, the Fula came under concerted attack with waves of arrests, executions and disappearances. This ethnic repression culminated in 1976 with the announcement of the **"Fula Plot"** and Touré's declaration that the Fula-speaking peoples were "enemies of socialism". Diallo Telli, the first OAU secretary general, was accused of leading a CIA-backed conspiracy. He was arrested and starved to death.

If there was any real "permanent plot" during Sekou Touré's tyrannical rule – apart from mass discontent – it would appear to have been his own genocidal one against the Fula. The atrocities perpetrated fuelled the outrage of exiles: stories about human sacrifice and barbarities soon became commonplace and, true or exaggerated, eventually forced the ruling clique into a defensive posture. For the present regime of Lansana Conté, as unevenly Susu as Touré's was Malinké, the rehabilitation of Fula confidence remains a priority.

abroad, while the party hierarchy lived in relatively modest style.

The **army** was kept under constant surveillance by a network of junior officers. Early in 1969 came the first big **purge** of figures close to the party leadership. Chief of Staff Kamara Diaby and the soldier-poet Fodeba Keita were the two most senior victims. Keita met his death in the prison camp he himself had built. There was an assassination attempt on Touré and more arrests in Labé the following year. As a result, the army was radically reorganized: each soldier was made a civil servant, effectively militarizing a civilian regime.

The invasion

Although Sekou Touré had been predicting an "aggression" with more than customary conviction, the country was unprepared for the **invasion** of November 22, 1970. Four hundred troops landed from ships at night and attacked Conakry and the peninsula. This was supposed to trigger a general uprising of Guinean dissidents and the overthrow of Sekou Touré. But although three hundred defenders were killed, and a number of prisoners released by the attackers, none of the key targets (the presidential palace, radio station or airport) was taken. When the landing ships moved away 48 hours later they left behind large numbers of stranded troops who were rounded up and subjected to people's justice.

Reactions to the invasion proved a crucial test of party loyalty and provided the **military victory** over the forces of imperialism that Sekou Touré had always craved. It was, he wrote, "one of those sublime moments of exaltation and patriotism . . . the affirmation of collective dignity".

The **United Nations** sent a fact-finding mission. They ascertained that most of the force had been composed of Guinean exiles of *FLING* and loyalist African soldiers from Portuguese Guinea, commanded by Portuguese officers from the Caetano fascist regime, with West German logistical support. The real aim of the invasion was to destroy the base in Guinea of the *PAIGC* guerillas fighting for independence from Portugal. It was to the lasting humiliation of the Guinea-Conakry opposition that their alliance with Caetano's fascist forces failed.

The **purge** which followed was predictably brutal. In truth, there was grass roots opposition to the Nato-backed invaders – though considerably more support for the internal rebels. Ninety-one people were sentenced to death and hundreds of others imprisoned and tortured. The hundred-stong German technical mission was expelled and dozens of Europeans spent time in jail in the aftermath.

But the popular rage whipped up by the party against imperialist aggression clouded the question of how much positive support the government still had, and obscured the **mass violations of human rights** – torture, disappearances, summary executions and detention without trial – that ravaged Guinea through the early 1970s. An *Amnesty International* report in 1978 estimated there were between 500 and 1500 political prisoners in fifteen prison camps. In six months in 1974, however, over 250 people are believed to have been executed in Conakry's Camp Boiro alone. Tens of thousands of Guineans, particularly Fula-speakers, continued to flee the country every year.

Hanging on

As the pressures – internal and external – mounted against his regime, Sekou Touré resorted to increasingly desperate measures. **Food shortages** were worsened by the effect of

THE FARANAH CLAN

Sekou Touré's quarter-century in power witnessed flagrant **favouritism** to members of his own **Malinké**-speaking ethnic group. Yet this was more a case of **nepotism** than chauvinist tribalism – indeed his wife was half Fula. The family clung jealously to their privileges. Threats from those connected to the clan by marriage were sometimes dealt with internally, but outsiders who interfered were condemned to the Boiro death camp, or simply disappeared. Sekou Touré encouraged the clan to intermarry and foresaw a long dynasty. But the paranoia that eventually touched even the president was such that the clan split into two opposing factions – the **Tourés** and the **Keitas** – each practising its own nepotism. Ismael Touré, leader of the first faction, was Sekou's half-brother and a descendant of the warlord Samory Touré (a claim also made, but vainly, by Sekou Touré himself). The Keitas were led by Mamadi Keita, the president's brother-in-law. Despite the name, the Keitas seem to have won the battle for influence with the president in his last years. The clan's reach was legendary, and supporters and beneficiaries have not all been eliminated by the new regime.

the security network in hampering the normal functioning of lines of supply and communication. There was nothing to encourage farmers. Obstinately, Touré authorized the local revolutionary authorities to handle all the production and marketing of commodities. Then early in 1975 came the **banning of all private trade** and at the same time the setting up of agricultural production brigades. The borders were closed and Touré declared a **"holy war" against smugglers** who were shot if caught. In the north of the country, the **Sahel drought** added to deteriorating prospects.

Guinea struggled for two-and-a-half years, going through another purge in 1976 in response to the **"Fula Plot"** (see p.481). **Relations with France** (broken for a decade) were patched up through the new president Giscard d'Estaing, who agreed to ban Guinean dissident propaganda there. But the exodus from Guinea continued and by the end of the 1970s as many as a million Guineans were believed to be living abroad.

ACHIEVEMENTS

The litany of denunciations of Sekou Touré's regime, amongst which the 1978 Amnesty report is outstanding, has silenced most of his erstwhile supporters. In retrospect the first quarter-century of independence was a tragic waste. Yet there were one or two significant **achievements** which can't be overlooked. Despite extraordinary biases in education and its own brutality, the party instilled an astute **political consciousness**: Guineans talk about "exploitation", "imperialism", "racism" and "freedom" with real feeling. There's a sense that ordinary people have political opinions about the way the country should be run. Despite that proliferation of isms, there's genuine national pride among rural people and an awareness – that can feel like touchiness – on a host of fairly abstract subjects. Sekou Touré also encouraged artistic expression in Guinea and was particularly responsible for the early creation of a proud musical tradition with the likes of the women police orchestra **Les Amazones** and the groundbreaking **Bembeya Jazz National.**

■ The turnaround

The country's commercial paralysis, supervised by – and unashamedly for the benefit of – the **"economic police"** couldn't be maintained. In August 1977 **market women** in Conakry and other towns spontaneously rose up against the intolerable market situation, which made it impossible for them to afford the produce of their own harvests. It was a turning point. **Riots** flared across the country and several provincial governors were killed. Sekou Touré's resolve collapsed. He began a slow process of **economic liberalization**. This coincided with a more pragmatic approach to government, a reduction of revolutionary rhetoric and – in response to outspoken criticism abroad – cosmetic improvements in democratic practices and human rights.

In his last few years, Touré left the running of the party and state more and more to a leading clique of ministers while devoting himself to the cultivation of an image as the grand old man of Pan-Africanism. 1982 saw the grotesque spectacle of Touré in Washington hailed by President Reagan as "a champion of human rights".

Progressive ideas were forgotten, however, as he forged close links with King Hassan of **Morocco** – whose side he took in the dispute over Western Sahara – and other bastions of the rigid right. Hassan provided money needed desperately by Touré to tide him over after the collapse of IMF negotiations in 1983, and arranged with conservative Arab states for Guinea to be the largest recipient of petro-dollar aid in sub-Saharan Africa. Touré was set to take his seat as 21st OAU chairman and had a special OAU village built (by Saudi Arabia) in Conakry, when, for administrative reasons, the summit was postponed to 1984.

In January and February of that year, groups of **soldiers** were arrested near the Senegalese border and accused of plotting against the government. At the time of **Sekou Touré's death** on March 26 1984 in a private clinic in Cleveland (whence he'd been flown in Hassan's jet), it appears that sections of the army had indeed been planning a *coup d'état*.

■ The new regime

Colonels **Lansana Conté** (president) and **Diara Traoré** (prime minister) waited several days after the lavish funeral before announcing, after an almost peaceful takeover, the **dissolution of the constitution and the party**, the freeing of political prisoners, the unbanning of trade unions and the **reopening of Guinea** to private investment. Judicial reforms began and French was reintroduced as the main language of education. Most of the old party structures swiftly disintegrated. Asked why the military hadn't acted years earlier, Conté said "the spirit of the Guinean was such that he would not think. Some Guineans behaved like imbeciles. They were remote-controlled".

The *Comité Militaire de Redressement National* was given an enthusiastic welcome and ministers went on foreign tours to introduce the new Guinea and cultivate aid donors. But apart from a general liberalization, it was hard to pinpoint the direction of the new government. Conté is a low-profile leader and his speeches have been conciliatory in tone. There was soon a split with prime minister Traoré however, and his post was abolished. Predictably, perhaps, in July 1985 Traoré and fellow Malinké officers attempted a coup against Conté.

In 1987, almost two years later, it was announced that those involved, together with a number of detainees from Sekou Touré's government, – sixty people in all – had been given **secret trials** and were to be executed. It was widely presumed, however, that most of them had died extra-judicially long before and Conté was merely setting the record straight – a presumption that hinted how close a return to state terrorism might be and, perhaps, how little Conté might be able to do to prevent it.

■ Guinea wakes up

On the economic front, Conakry was soon full of French technical advisors and business people. One of the **IMF**'s structural adjustment programmes was put in operation which, coupled with general **austerity**, state sector **job losses** and widespread civil service **corruption** and ostentation, was not warmly received. Conakry boiled over in January 1988 with **street riots** over **price rises** – which, yet again, had outstripped huge wage increases designed to control the black market. The riots forced the government to back down, and commodity prices were reduced. Foreign aid, unfortunately, has not poured into Guinea in the quantities hoped for, and there's clearly still suspicion about the country's direction.

Senegal, and especially **Côte d'Ivoire** have both been cautious in their relations with Guinea and apprehensive about its return to the French economic fold. Guinea is itching to flex its muscles. With almost limitless agricultural potential, plus its bauxite, iron and other mineral reserves, the country has the potential to become the most prosperous state in West Africa and the region's dominant Francophone nation.

Political developments

Politically, the initiative Conté lost after abolishing the post of prime minister, and the subsequent coup attempt, was recovered when he increased **civilian representation** in the government – though some of his rivals were banished from Conakry in the process. **Malinké** speakers have been particularly under-represented since the demise of the old regime and they, together with thousands of returned **Fula** exiles, are now regarded as the unofficial opposition to Conté's – predominantly **Susu** – military leadership.

By the end of 1990, serious protests were emerging from schools and the university in Conakry, in protest at conditions, educational standards, and the slowness with which democratic reforms were to be instituted. A number of students were killed by police or army gunfire during demonstrations.

Conté maintained his slow pace, setting up the *Comité Transitoire de Redressement National* (the CTRN; the "Transitional Commitee for National Redress"), which he ensured had some recently departed members of his own cabinet sitting on it. Meanwhile, the demonstrations, and then strikes too, continued.

In 1991, **Alpha Condé**, long-exiled Malinké opposition leader and Secretary General of the *Rassemblement du Peuple Guinéen* (RPG), considered the time right to return home, but his plan to stay had to be aborted when the security forces fired on a crowd of his supporters. He took refuge in the Senegalese ambassador's home, before fleeing the country again.

Within less than a year, it looked as if Lansana Conté's government was becoming used to the idea of a democratic opposition: Alpha Condé's RPG was formerly registered in April 1992 and Condé returned to Guinea.

But events soon proved that Lansana Conté was panic-stricken at the prospect of losing power to one or other of the opposition parties (or an alliance of them). A puppet party was formed as a front for the CTRN. Called the *Parti de l'Unité et du Progrès* (PUP), it focused on the parts of the country where the CTRN was providing development funds. Rumours began to circulate of death squads, set up to assassinate key opposition figures.

Despite intimidating the opposition and operating with state support and government money, Conté's PUP was insufficiently confident of its electoral strengths to keep to the election dates scheduled for the end of 1992. The CTRN deferred the presidential and legislative elections for another year, during which Guinea saw some of the most savage **political violence** of the post-Touré era, with dozens of deaths from security forces' gunfire, and hundreds of injuries in two separate mass demonstrations in Conakry.

In the run-up to the **presidential election**, finally held in December 1993, the PUP held public meetings unhindered (despite the CTRN's banning of them and the fact that no other party was able to flout the "law") and every tool at the government's disposal was put into service to pump up votes for the PUP.

As a result, Conté, standing for the PUP, polled just over 51 percent. The votes from two massively anti-Conté (pro-Condé) prefectures, Kankan and Siguri, were disallowed for reasons of the RPG's "malpractice", and Alpha Condé thus received barely 20 percent of the votes for president, with the other main opposition leaders, both Fula – **Mamadou Bâ** (*Union pour la Nouvelle République*) and the publisher of *Jeune Afrique* magazine, **Siradiou Diallo** (*Parti pour le Renouveau et le Progrès*) – getting twelve and thirteen percent of the vote each. As it became clear that the opposition had been cheated, there were chaotic scenes at polling stations. Several Guinean embassies, acting as polling stations for Guinean emigrés in other parts of West Africa, were ransacked.

As "democratic" presidential elections in West Africa go, Guinea's was one of the most dishonest and unimpressive. Foreign observers were all but excluded. In its wake, Condé's RPG and Diallo's PRP formed an alliance to contest the legislative elections. In response to this and other signs of opposition strength, the government disenfranchised Guineans overseas, thus excluding some three million potential voters from future elections.

Meanwhile, 1994 saw senior military officers getting increasingly agitated by the prospect of their gradual forced withdrawal from public life, as it became clear that civilian rule could not be permanently forestalled. There were rumours of a coup attempt and arrests in May 1994.

The multi-party **general elections** to the legislative assembly were finally held on June 11 1995. But in the preceding three weeks, opposition rallies throughout Guinea were disrupted by the security forces on the orders, it would appear, of the powerful interior minister, **René Aseny Gomez**. Condé and Diallo, having earlier said they would not boycott the elections despite the PUP's flagrant rigging, ultimately pulled out on the day, declaring the results null and void. Although the coalition won about a quarter of the seats (the PUP took 71 out of 114 seats and the RPG/PRP coalition 28), as this book goes to press in August 1995, they were still boycotting the national assembly.

President Lansana Conté evidently believes he has a mandate to rule and his PUP national assembly members the right to govern. The Guinean people, in large part, do not. The wait for the next presidential and legislative elections, due in 1998 and 1999, implies a degree of patience that many people – facing growing unemployment, low salaries and inflation – may not be prepared to display. And the army remains dissatisfied.

CONAKRY

CONAKRY, once "the Paris of Africa", is today a city of few graces. A continuous sprawl of urbanization claws its way off the **peninsula** and up into the hills behind the city centre. Away from the downtown districts, the elongated conurbation is animated, but morbidly dirty – with refuse, mud, dust and slicks of motor oil – and heavy with the raw noise and choking exhaust fumes of endless lines of jammed traffic trying to get from one end of town to another. Vehicle carcasses rot on the verges; a scrap metal business would make a fortune. Conakry has matured into one of West Africa's least user-friendly capitals and you may spend much of your time here planning your escape. The city drives most people away to the sweet fabled hills and grasslands of the Guinea interior.

On the positive side, downtown Conakry is a lot more pleasant than even a few years ago, easily walked around, and with offices and businesses not far apart. The main **market** – the Marché du Niger – is bountiful and growing all the time. Conakry may be expensive and palpably soulless, but at least the restaurants, cafés and other hideaways that were so thin on the ground in the early 1990s are now plentiful. And the nightlife – in this most climatically exhausting of cities by day – is still first-rate. Lastly, the **Iles de Los** are strikingly pretty and easily accessible.

Some history

Conakry was itself an **island** – as you can still see from the narrow causeway between the Palais du Peuple and the motorway bridge. For many years known as **Tumbo**, the island was the closest to the shore of the archipelago that provided safe haven for slavers and merchant vessels trading along the Guinea coasts.

The Portuguese adventurer, Pedro da Sintra, first set foot here around 1460 and named it Cap de Sagres, after Prince Henry the Navigator's residence in Portugal (until then the furthest point in the known world). At this time the inhabitants of Conakry were idol-worshipping, skin-wearing farmers, cultivating indigenous African dry-land rice and millet.

Early in the sixteenth century, the Portuguese began to anchor in the deep water on the southeast side of the island, but over succeeding centuries they and the Dutch, English and French all took turns to occupy the site and trade in slaves. By the end of the eighteenth century the Los islands were equipped as entrepôts for the transfer of slaves from the smaller coastal vessels to ocean-going merchant ships.

Yet by the time Britain, the principal contender, ceded rights over the fledgling colony to France in 1887, Tumbo island still only had four tiny settlements – Bulbinay and Konakiri and the non-native African toeholds of Krootown and Tumbo – with a total of just a few hundred inhabitants. A road into the interior was started and the channel between Tumbo and the Kaloum peninsula on the mainland was filled in. By 1904, and Britain's handing over of the Los islands, Conakry – the new capital of *Guinée française* – had its present grid pattern and a population of 10,000. The **railway** to Kankan was completed in 1914 and bananas from Kindia became the biggest export. Major developments came in the brief post-war colonial period, and concentrated on improving the port for the shipping of newly discovered iron ore and bauxite. The last ten years have seen massive growth and a major transformation into the consumer economy. The city – whose population numbers over a million – will soon cover the entire peninsula.

Arrival, transport and accommodation

Conakry is built twenty kilometres out to sea on a **promontory**. Most of what you'll want in the way of banks, embassies, post office, hotels and restaurants is right at the end, on the two square kilometres of **city centre** where all the old parts of the town are

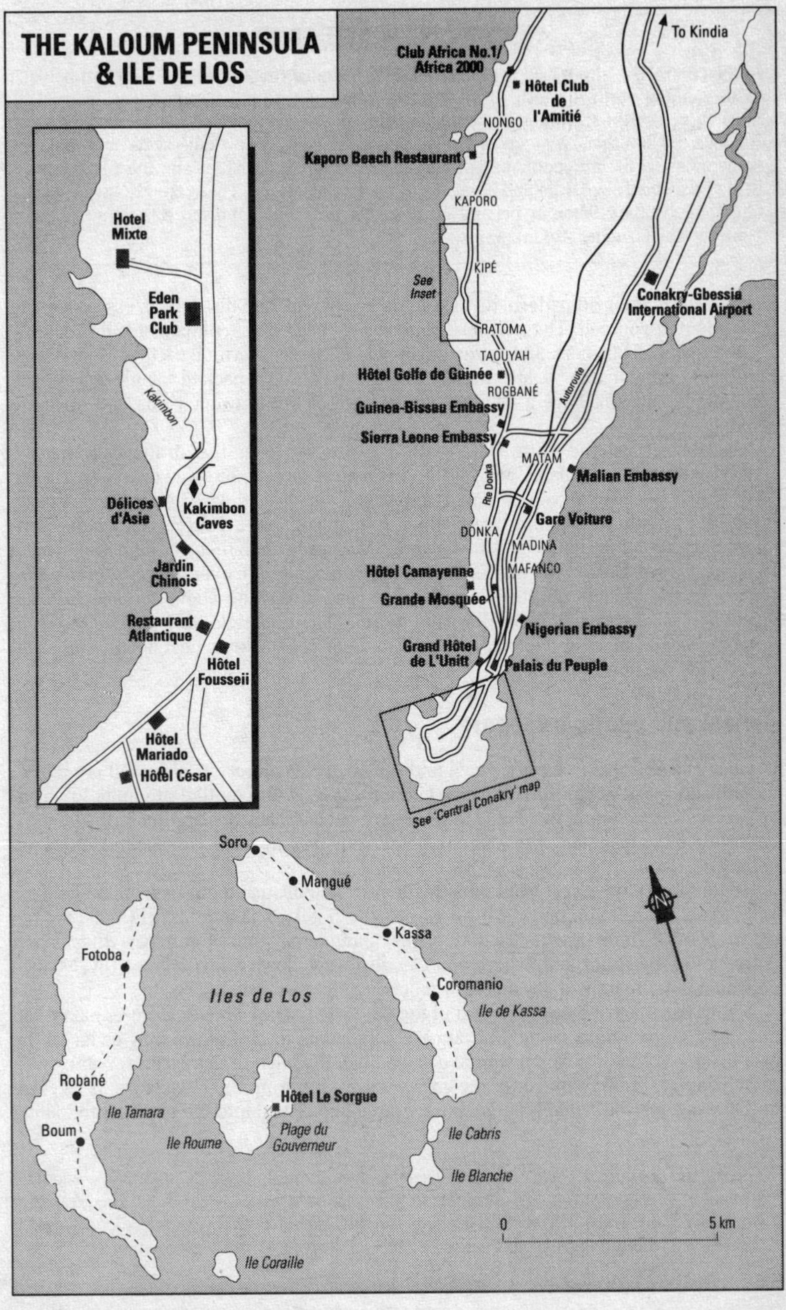
THE KALOUM PENINSULA & ILE DE LOS
To Kindia
Club Africa No.1/ Africa 2000
Hôtel Club de l'Amitié
NONGO
Kaporo Beach Restaurant
KAPORO
KIPÉ
See Inset
Conakry-Gbessia International Airport
RATOMA
TAOUYAH
Hôtel Golfe de Guinée
ROGBANÉ
Autoroute
Guinea-Bissau Embassy
Sierra Leone Embassy
MATAM
Malian Embassy
Rte Donka
Gare Voiture
DONKA
MADINA
MAFANCO
Hôtel Camayenne
Grande Mosquée
Nigerian Embassy
Grand Hôtel de L'Unitt
Palais du Peuple
See 'Central Conakry' map
Hotel Mixte
Eden Park Club
Kakimbon
Délices d'Asie
Kakimbon Caves
Jardin Chinois
Restaurant Atlantique
Hôtel Fousseii
Hôtel Mariado
Hôtel César
Soro
Mangué
Kassa
Coromanio
Ile de Kassa
Fotoba
Iles de Los
Robané
Ile Tamara
Boum
Hôtel Le Sorgue
Ile Roume
Plage du Gouverneur
Ile Cabris
Ile Blanche
Ile Coraille
0
5 km

STREET NAMES

In the centre, the street grid is numbered, with avenues running east to west and boulevards running north to south. "1ère av" and "4ème bd" are the common local abbreviations we've used, but in English-language publications you may see 1st Avenue and 4th Boulevard. Note that 10ème av is also known as av de la Gare, 8ème av as av Tubman, 6ème av as av de la République (which leads into Route du Niger and the Autoroute), 6ème bd as bd Telly Diallo and 3ème bd as bd du Commerce. There are also two important "bis" avenues: 9ème av bis and 7ème av bis, not to be confused with 9ème av and 7ème av which run next to them.

located. Here, the grid pattern, divided into closely bunched districts, is easy once you have oriented yourself. The northern *quartiers* of the centre – Almamya and Kaloum – are the focus of business and bureaucracy while the southern districts – Manquépas, Boulbinet, Sandervalia – are mostly made up of tight-packed single-storey city compounds and still have a villagey atmosphere of brush-swept yards and open-fire cooking.

Landwards, past the huge **Palais du Peuple** and over the strategically narrow causeway onto the mainland, you hit the **Autoroute** (not a motorway or freeway in the usual sense, because all vehicles, and pedestrians use it) and pass under the notorious bridge at Place du 8 Novembre from which so many of Sekou Touré's condemned prisoners were publicly hanged. The **Grande Mosquée** and then, behind the Donka Hospital, **Camp Boiro** (the main Touré-era prison camp) are over on the left. The *gare voiture*, in the Madina quarter, is further out, and stretching above the shore to the north, you hit the rapidly expanding and more affluent districts of Rogbané, Taouyah, Ratoma, Kipé, Kaporo and Nongo, where a number of Conakry's best hotels, clubs and restaurants are now to be found.

Arrival and public transport

If you arrive at Conakry **by air**, you'll find the open-plan airport is fairly well organized, though the introduction to Guinea is getting worse, with plentiful attempts to solicit bribes. It's worth noting that some airlines give out currency declaration forms: if you'll be flying out again it's advisable to obtain one in any case, to avoid hassles on departure.

Getting into town direct from outside the arrivals hall, use the *Novotel* minibus if it's still in use, even if you don't plan to stay at the hotel, or take a taxi (FG5000 for the *déplacement*). There are no airport buses, though city buses run past the airport entrance on the Autoroute, where you can also wave down a *taxi brousse* (FG200–500 depending on the time of day and how much luggage you have).

If your flight arrives early enough in the day, you may be able to leave Conakry and head up-country immediately. In that case, take a taxi towards town only as far as the *gare voiture* in Madina, which should cost you half the full fare to the centre.

Arriving at Conakry **by road**, the *gare voiture*, 6km from the city centre, is as close to the centre as you're likely to fetch up. Find a bus or taxi into the town centre, along

Tourist information *Djeli* and *Tam Tam* are free monthly "What's On" mags, widely available. If you want to go straight to the top, you could visit the Ministère du Commerce, du Transport et du Tourisme, at the Ancien Petit Lycée, Corniche Ouest (☎44.26.06), though there is no guarantee they will have any useful information.

the Autoroute, or walk across the railway tracks and a few hundred metres further to the junction with Route Donka where you can try hitching a lift: a surprising number of expatriates, most of whom live on the north side of the peninsula, will oblige.

Public transport

Conakry has reasonable **bus services** – basically running the length of the peninsula – but at peak hours (7–11am and 4–8pm) it can take literally hours to get from one end of the city to the other. The main city centre terminus is the roundabout in the port area; the big depot is 6km up the peninsula at the Madina *gare voiture*. State-owned SOGETRAG buses are increasingly a rare sight, their place being taken by the private *Melia* line and others. Minimum fares are FG100 (per route sector) and only rise to FG250 to get out as far as Ratoma.

Taxis (allow one hour between city centre and airport) are exasperatingly hard to find off the main thoroughfares, from which they only occasionally deviate. The main routes for shared taxis are "Route Donka" (north side of the peninsula), "Autoroute" (Autoroute bridge to airport) and "Route du Niger" joining with "Autoroute". Taxis are unmetered, but at least not too expensive, charging FG200 for short, shared journeys in town, and FG200–300 per kilometre for a private *déplacement*.

SECURITY

Elsewhere, people may tell you that Conakry is a den of thieves (and certainly you should be on your guard, in the ordinary way, for pickpockets and the like). But in comparison with, say, Dakar, it's relatively peaceful in that respect and the real hassles come from the police who can be quite inventive in trying to extract a bribe. Carry some ID, if not your passport, at all times.

Accommodation

Conakry has an increasing number of mid-range and expensive **hotels**, but if you're on a tight budget, you'll find the options very limited. You might even prefer to stay out of town, in Coyah (see p.499), on the way to Kindia, and commute into the city. There are no hostels or travellers' haunts and anything under FG20,000, even for a single room, is likely to be a basic brothel. Electricity and water are both unreliable and the really cheap places are usually in a disgusting state: we've selected just two – one of which, the *Djoliba*, is highly recommended. Climate has a lot to do with the tendency for all of Conakry's hotels to decline rapidly: only the places that can afford regular refurbishing survive more than a few years before going into a period of dormancy, or just closing for good.

There are a few church and aid organization guesthouses which have, in the past, been very welcoming to unexpected guests. There have been gentle complaints that directing readers to them in travel guides is exploiting the hospitality. Hence, they're not included here.

City centre hotels

Bar-Restaurant Djoliba, 9ème av (☎44.15.60). A *centre d'application*, where students in tourism gain work experience, this is a friendly, relaxed place to be a guinea pig, and extremely good value too. Good restaurant, animated bar, sometimes very busy club. ②.

Hôtel Kaloum, av de la République (☎41.33.08). Numbingly average and undesirable, this six-floor, Touré-era block has no lifts. The spacious, dilapidated S/C apartments are always full of long-term renters. ④.

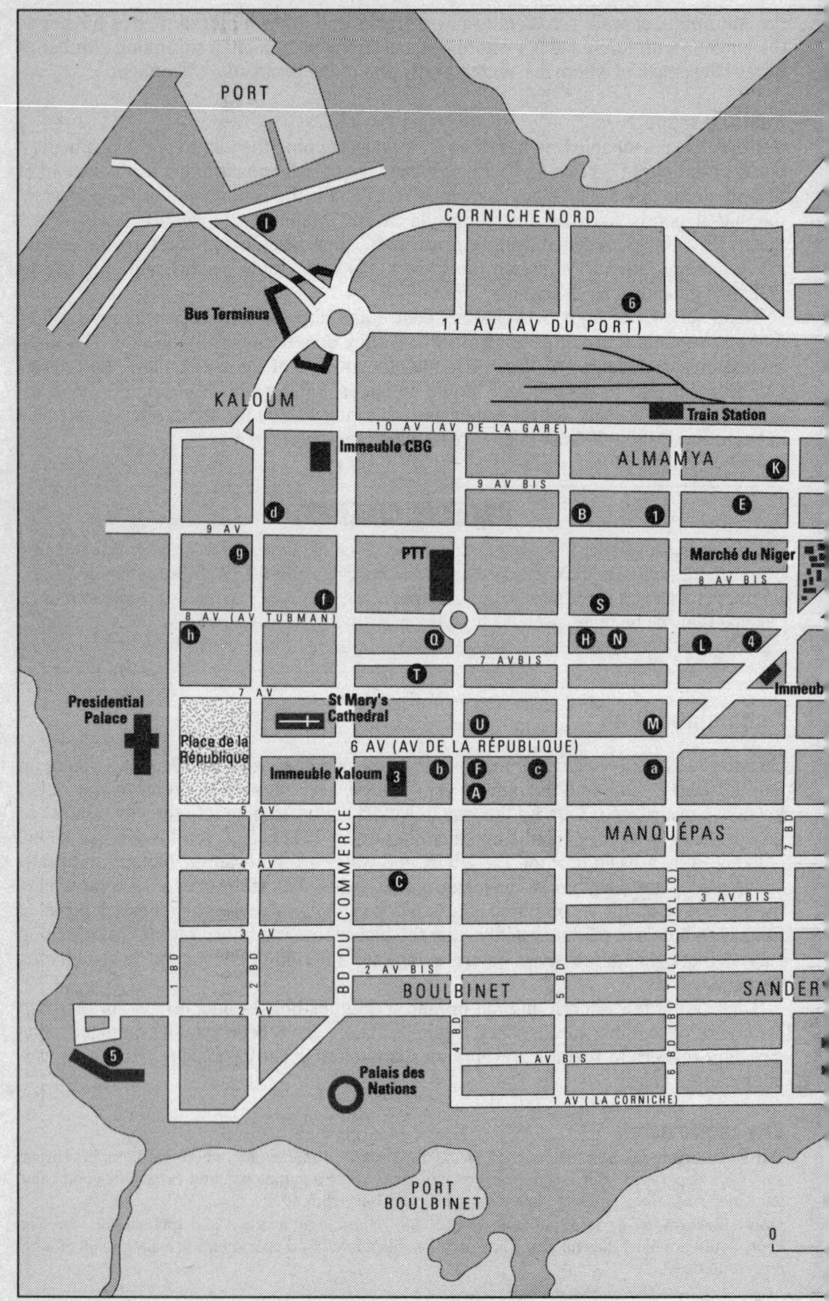
PORT
CORNICHENORD
Bus Terminus
11 AV (AV DU PORT)
KALOUM
Train Station
10 AV (AV DE LA GARE)
Immeuble CBG
ALMAMYA
9 AV BIS
9 AV
PTT
Marché du Niger
8 AV BIS
8 AV (AV TUBMAN)
7 AV BIS
7 AV
Presidential Palace
St Mary's Cathedral
Place de la République
6 AV (AV DE LA RÉPUBLIQUE)
Immeuble Kaloum
5 AV
MANQUÉPAS
BD DU COMMERCE
4 AV
3 AV BIS
3 AV
1 BD
2 BD
2 AV BIS
BOULBINET
5 BD
BD (BD TELLY DIALLO)
SANDER
2 AV
4 BD
1 AV BIS
Palais des Nations
1 AV (LA CORNICHE)
PORT BOULBINET
7 BD
6 BD
0

CENTRAL CONAKRY
To Hôtel de l'Unité (500m)
Airport & Suburbs
9 BD
10 BD
11 BD
12 AV
RTE DU NIGER
10 BD BIS
Sonia
8 BD
9 BD
Hospital
Ignace Deen
CORNICHE SUD
ALIA
Museum
N
500m
HOTELS
1 Bar-Restaurant Djoliba
2 Pension Doherty
3 Hôtel Kaloum
4 Hôtel du Niger
5 Novotel
6 Motel du Port
RESTAURANTS
A L'African Queen
B Escale de Guinée
C Le Conakry
D Le Damier
E Le Gentilhommière
F La Gondole
G Lamp Fall
H La Palmeraie
I Bar-restaurant Port Autonome
J Le Refuge
K Le Restaurant Sénégalais
L Oncle Sam's
M Patisserie Centrale
N Tyros
CLUBS
P B52
Q Bembeya Club
R Lips
S Metro Club
T Mistral Club
U Le Palais
V Le Grand Muraille
OFFICES
a Aeroflot, KLM & Royal Maroc
b Air Afrique & Sabena
c Air France, Air Guinée & Nigeria Airways
d American Embassy
e BICIGUI Bank
f French Embassy
g German Embassy
h Immigration Office

ACCOMMODATION PRICE CODES

① Under FG10,000 (under £5/$7.50) ② FG10,000–20,000 (£5–10/$7.50–15)
③ FG20,000–40,000 (£10–20/$15–30) ④ FG40,000–60,000 (£20–30/$30–45).
⑤ FG60,000–80,000 (£30–40/$45–60) ⑥ FG80,000–100,000 (£40–50/$60–75).
⑦ Over FG100,000 (over £50/$75).

For full details, see the "Accommodation" section in the Practical Information pages at the beginning of this chapter.

Hôtel du Niger, rte du Niger, close to the market BP, 14 (☎44.41.30; Fax 44.12.36). Clean, fairly secure and in a good position for downtown, this is always a safe bet. Rooms with fan or AC. ③–④.

Novotel Grand Hôtel de l'Indépendance BP 287 (☎41.50.21). Stylish example of the genre, insulated from Conakry's fickle utility cuts, with everything you could possibly need and much you probably don't. Amex, Visa, Mastercard, and crumpled FG all accepted. ⑦.

Pension Doherty, 5ème av BP 3671 (☎44.17.64; Fax 44.38.75). Although central, this is in a residential quarter, full of kids and ordinary streetlife. Good pavement area. Various rooms and variable standards. ③–④.

Motel du Port, av du Port (☎44.17.64). Why waste a good Portakabin? Approached through a courtyard thronged with children, this former German port engineers' housing offers a complex of double-decker cabins, with a pool, video room, bar and restaurant. AC, S/C rooms equipped with fridges. ⑤.

Hotels away from the centre

Hôtel Camayenne BP 2818, (☎41.40.89; Fax 44.29.95). Conakry's most expensive hotel, fully refurbished and managed by *Sabena*. Rooms with satellite TV and every other facility. Right by the sea. All cards. ⑦.

Hôtel César, Taouyah. Take the rte de Donka past Rogbané, turn left at the *Mariador* hotels sign, and then left again. Italian, family-run, with a restaurant and swimming pool, big among the expat community. The AC, S/C rooms, with mosquito-netted beds are good value. ④.

Hôtel Club de l'Amitié, about 13km from the centre, in Nongo. Take the left fork after Kaporo Port for about 1500m; there's a sign on the right. Clean sheets, fans, bucket shower in your room. Pleasant bar and simple restaurant. ②.

Hôtel Foussein, opposite the sign for the *Atlantique Restaurant*, rte de Donka, Ratoma. One of the cheapest lodgings in Conakry, pretty awful but bearable if you're really pressed for funds. ①.

Hôtel Golfe de Guinée, rte de Donka, Quartier Minière, Rogbané (☎46.43.10). Somewhat sterile place, with reasonable-value AC, S/C rooms, some with sea view. ④.

Hôtel Mariador, Rogbané, massively signposted (☎46.40.70). New and high quality, with immaculate rooms equipped with fridge and satellite TV. Swimming pool. Shares facilities with the *Résidence Mariador*. ⑥.

Résidence Mariador, adjoining the hotel of the same name (☎44.27.52). Larger and right above the rocky shore. Tennis. All cards. ⑦.

Hôtel Mixte, Kipé district. Turn left down a dirt track just after the *New Eden Park* nightclub, directly opposite a mosque; then 500m on the right. A *maquis* and *maison de passage*, popular with civil servants. Dirty walls, clean sheets, fans or AC. ②.

Grand Hôtel de L'Unité, opposite the Palais du Peuple (BP 683; ☎41.15.98; Fax 44.15.93). Various repair and renovation contracts have long been in the pipeline. Too expensive. ⑦.

The City and around

There are many more interesting West African capitals to fill the days while you wait for friends, visas, money or whatever. If you find yourself laden with spare time, you'll do best to visit the **Iles de Los**, or to get out of Conakry altogether and explore inland.

The National Museum

The **National Museum** – an unexceptional hour's worth – is down in the Sandervalia quarter off the Corniche Sud (Tues–Sat 9am–3pm & 4–6pm, Sun 4–6pm; free). The buildings, or at least part of them, were the home of the explorer Olivier de Sanderval. You might aim to come here at midday for a snack at the café and take in whatever exhibits are on display. The permanent collection consists of masks and other carvings, instruments and a few weapons. Most of the site – which has considerable potential – is little more than a large, expensive curio shop.

The Kakimbon caves

Visiting the **Kakimbon caves** is more an excuse for a look along the peninsula than a very worthwhile adventure in itself. These *grottes préhistoriques* are outside the village of Ratoma, now a suburb of Conakry at the end of the Taouyah road (north coast of the peninsula) – if you stop on the bridge between Ratoma and Kipé, you'll find them just upstream from here. There used to be a sacred forest here, a waterfall and a small lake as well as the caves. Until well after World War II, the site was held in considerable awe and annual appeasement rituals to the spirit inhabitants of the caves were held. It still retains religious significance for the district's Baga people, who perform fertility sacrifices, and good luck and curative spells here; but it doesn't stop them – or their neighbours – using it as a rubbish tip and general laundry and toilet too.

One theory suggests that the site was used by slavers and acquired its fearsome reputation as the result of the disappearance of inquisitive locals. But several **excavations** at the end of the nineteenth century – the first such in French West Africa – yielded quantities of stone tools, arrow heads and pottery sherds.

The Iles de Los

The **Iles de Los** are well worth a visit and have become quite a magnet, especially at weekends when half the expatriate community of Conakry seems to be on Roume. The islands have a colourful, enigmatic past. They were inhabited from the earliest times by idol-worshipping farmers, which earned them the Portuguese label *"idolos"*, transmuted by the French into *Iles de Los*. Roume itself – a lavishly picturesque pair of jungle-swathed hillocks joined by a sandy-shored isthmus – was once a slaving base, the site of the 1850 execution of a notorious slaver, Crawford, whose name the island carried until the end of the nineteenth century. Tales of the buried loot of Crawford and his men are supposed to have been the inspiration for Robert Louis Stevenson's *Treasure Island*.

There are two options for **getting to the islands**: using a regular service of one of the large, motorized *pirogues* and paying the local rate, or – much more expensive – chartering a *pirogue* for the day. At weekends the picture is distorted by the expat market and pressure is put on you to make up a party to charter a boat for the whole day rather than use the regular services. Most days there are several **"scheduled" runs** from Port Boulbinet to Ile de Kassa village and Koromandjo, both on Kassa, for about FG300 per person. At least once a day there's also a *pirogue* to Fotoba on Ile Tamara. On Sundays there are usually "scheduled" *pirogue* services to Soro beach on Kassa (don't pay more than FG1000 per person).

While there's never any problem **renting a pirogue** – ask around in Port Boulbinet or on the beach by the *Novotel* – agreeing the price is harder. You're likely to hear some very high starting figures but you shouldn't pay more than around FG15,000 to Soro (Ile de Kassa) or FG20–25,000 to Ile Roume or Fotoba. And that's to charter the boat for the whole day for a reasonable number of passengers: unless there's a herd of you, there shouldn't be any extra surcharge for passengers.

Ile de Kassa

Sandy, palm-fringed **Soro beach** is the largest on the islands, but its popularity makes it extremely crowded on Sundays in the dry season. Fortunately it's kept clean during this season and has the added advantage of huts to escape the sun. There's an access fee of FG1000 and an expensive *bar-resto* and *campement* (④), both only open during the dry season. It's wise for guests at the *campement* to order food a day in advance as nearly everything has to be brought over from Conakry. Spending a few days on eight-kilometre long Kassa will give you the opportunity to explore the secluded and largely rockless beaches along the west shore, and several settlements among its lovely forests. It only takes an hour or so to walk to Kassa village from Soro beach and you're likely to see monkeys and birds along the way.

Ile Roume and Ile Tamara

The small, central **Ile Roume** is best on a weekday when it's very quiet. It has always been favoured by the expatriate community and is the most expensive island to visit, with pricey accommodation in the *Hôtel le Sogue* on the south shore (open early October to the end of June), which has its own, sheltered and private **plage du Gouverneur** (reservations through *Karou Voyages*; 44.20.42; ⑥). There's an extensive, and still public, beach on the north shore.

Ile Tamara – also known as Ile Fotoba – used to be a penal colony and was for many years strictly off-limits. The old penitentiary near Fotoba village is worth visiting if you're on the island, but as on Roume and Kassa, the main attractions are the forests and seashore.

Eating, drinking and nightlife

Eating in Conakry used to be either expensive and mediocre or just poor value for money. These days, there are dozens of restaurants – the best, admittedly, still very expensive – while street food, after years of savage austerity ("we have no potatoes, we have no rice . . ."), is once again great. Fast-food joints, specializing in *chawarma*, burgers and chicken, are opening all the time, while rice dishes at FG300 and grilled meat sandwiches at FG400 can be had on many street corners or in the markets.

Basic meals and snacks

Keur Bamba, near the *camp militaire*, between the market and Ignace Deen Hospital. Very cheap Senegalese food: *riz gras* for FG300.

Lamp Fall, 7ème bd. No sign indicates this Senegalese *gargote*, but it is easily recognized by the red, yellow and green striped walls. Huge portions of nutritious, tasty food from about FG2500.

Oncle Sam's, 7ème av, Almamya. Reasonable-value Lebanese-American "specialities": burgers, *chawarma*, falafel etc. From FG2000.

La Palmeraie, 8ème av. Guinean businessmen's haunt with cheap coffee and snacks.

Bar-restaurant Port Autonome, at the port across from the bus terminus. Excellent breakfasts and lunches until about 3pm, cold beer until dusk.

Poulet Frit à la Texas, Immeuble Sonia, rte du Niger, opposite the *Hôtel du Niger*. Leb/Greek international fast food: pizzas, roast chicken, burgers, all for around FG3000.

Le Restaurant Sénégalais, corner of 10ème av and 7ème bd. You won't find better rice and fish in Dakar, and they also have *mafé*, *poulet yassa* and *steack frites*. Around FG1500.

Restaurants

L'African Queen, 4ème av, Manquépas. Good reputation, but expensive. Weekday lunchtimes only, with pizza and pasta specialities from FG6–10,000 and a FG9000 *menu*.

L'Atlantique, rte de Donka, Ratoma (☎42.10.03; Tues–Sat evenings & Sun lunch). Long-established and excellent seafood restaurant on the clifftop. Expensive.

Comme Chez Soi, Taouyah, near the *Mariador* hotels. Franco-Zairean cooking. Pricey.

Le Conakry, 4ème av, by the Ministry of Finance (☎44.26.82; closed Sun). Solid, Guinean business-class restaurant, with a French chef, a lunchtime *menu* (FG8000), and a *carte* (dishes FG6000 plus).

Le Cyprien, off rte de Donka, in Quartier Cameroun. Zairean/Swiss cuisine. Recommended. Around FG10,000 per head.

Le Cyrkano, Ratoma, near the *Mariador* hotels (closed Tues). Good restaurant/bar which regularly has live music on Thurs and Sat.

Délices d'Asie, rte de Donka, opposite the *commissariat* in Ratoma (closed Mon & Tues). Reasonable food, but a superb terrace. Dishes at FG10,000 from the *carte*.

Bar-Restaurant Djoliba, 9ème av. An affordable retreat with steak or *riz gras* for under FG2000 and *sauce de feuilles* or *sauce d'arachides* for FG1000.

Escale de Guinée, corner of 5ème bd and 9ème av bis. Looks like it's been doing a quiet lunch trade on the same corner since the 1930s. As worthwhile for the company of the folks who run it as for the homestyle French cooking. FG5–6000 for the *menu*.

Le Gentilhommière, 9ème av bis, Almamya (☎44.26.24; closed Sun). Bamboo everywhere suggests Chinese, but this serves mostly French and Antillean food. *Menu* at FG7000, with *carte* dishes from FG5000.

Restaurant des Iles, 1ère av, Boulbinet (☎44.27.64; closed Mon night). French and African cuisine, with a deservedly good reputation and not unreasonably priced.

Jardin Chinois, rte de Donka, Ratoma (dinner Tues–Sun; lunch Sun only). Good Chinese food, and relatively good prices.

Les Jardins de Guinée, near the Grande Mosquée on rte du Niger, opposite the *Super-V* supermarket (☎46.12.79). Great pizzas, swimming pool, frequent live music.

Restaurant de Kaloum, av de la République. French-owned, this lacks atmosphere and is way overpriced, with pizzas from FG9000 and a steak around FG15,000.

Kaporo Beach, overlooking the sea at Kaporo, well signposted (☎46.35.82; open Tues–Fri evenings, all day Sat & Sun). Miles out of town, but a favourite weekend haunt of expats, with a good reputation for French, especially *Niçoise*, food and pizzas, and a pool.

Le Natraj, Quartier Coléah, Matam, behind the "54 logements" (☎44.49.57; closed Sun lunch). The only full-blown Indian restaurant in Guinea.

Le Refuge, Corniche Sud, Boulbinet, near the museum. Senegalese-owned, but strictly French cuisine. Sea views.

Le Rustique, Quartier Minière. European, and particularly German, cooking. Evenings only (closed Mon). Very expensive and always busy. Dishes from the *carte* FG8–10,000.

Tyros, 8ème av, behind the Marché du Niger (closed Sun lunch). Classy Lebanese with a good selection of dishes from FG5–7000.

Le Wonderful, rte de Donka, Ratoma. Lives up to its name. The best choice among Conakry's Asian restaurants.

Patisseries

Le Damier, opposite Marché du Niger (also at *Super-V* supermarket in Ratoma). Good cakes and pastries, coffee, snacks (open Mon–Sat until dusk).

La Gondole, av de la République, opposite the *La Palace* leisure complex. Expensive, but excellent ice cream.

Patisserie Centrale, av de la République, opposite the *KLM* building. Good place for ice cream, snacks, patisserie and coffee.

Nightlife

Conakry **nightlife** is an enjoyable scene, and an ever-changing one. The testing climate means that many clubs are in a poor state of repair by the end of the rainy season and don't always survive the consequent decline in business through the next dry season. The following selection, therefore, is likely to include one or two which have already gone for good and others temporarily *hors de combat*.

City centre clubs

B52, 5ème av, a couple of doors from *Pension Doherty*. Recommended watering hole.

Bembeya Club, av Tubman/4ème bd. Newly refurbished old-timer, with good prospects of making a comeback.

Djoliba, 9ème av. A lively bar which was blossoming into a regular club when last visited.

Grand Muraille, 7ème au bis (closed Mon). Popular karaoke club, even on Sat, when entrance is FG5000.

Keur de Kaloum, next to the *Hôtel du Niger*. Very overtly a pick-up joint. If you don't want to pick up, don't visit.

Lips, opposite the *BICIGUI* bank on rte du Niger. Usually offers two sessions: 5–10pm and 11pm–dawn. Great, young atmosphere if you like to dance.

Metro Club, 7ème av bis, Almamya. Approachable, middle-class club full of Guinean townies and their girlfriends. Cosy atmosphere, which livens up at weekends. Small cover.

Mistral Club, 7ème av. Cheap and seedy, but enjoyable.

Le Palace, av de la République. A flashy disco, mostly patronized by sailors, its atmosphere depending on the ships in port. Entrance FG3000 (free on weekdays). Upstairs bar is inexpensive, dark and full of women.

Studio 4, behind the Anglican cathedral. Senegalese club with a good range of music, but the jazz-bar style and decor feel rather self-conscious. FG3000 Thurs, Fri; FG5000 Sat.

Clubs along the peninsula

In recent years, many new clubs have sprung up in Conakry's burgeoning north-peninsula development. Rogbané, Taouyah, Ratoma and Kipé are the main suburbs to head for: in many cases the clubs in these districts are livelier than the older places in town.

Africa No.1, after the sign for *Hôtel Club de l'Amitié*, in Nongo. Exciting new club.

Eden Park, Kipé. FG8000 cover.

Futura Club, at *Grand Hôtel de l'Unité*.

King's Club, Taouyah, near *Cinéma Rogbané*. FG3000 cover.

Safari Club, Autoroute, near the 8 Novembre bridge. FG3000 cover.

Listings

Airline offices Unless otherwise noted, the following are all clustered along av de la République: *Aeroflot*, Imm Banque Islamique (☎44.41.43); *Air Afrique* (☎44.47.70, 44.47.71 or 44.47.72); *Air Bissau (TAGB)*; *Air France* (☎44.36.57; Fax 41.47.27); *Air Guinée* (☎44.46.14); *Air Ivoire* (☎44.30.64); *Air Zaire* (☎44.40.98); *Gambia Airways*, opposite Imm CBG, bd du Commerce (☎44.46.14); *Ghana Airways* (☎44.48.13); *Guinée Air Service*, opposite Imm CBG, bd du Commerce (☎44.17.47; Fax 44.27.61); *KLM*, Imm Banque Islamique, (☎44.31.07; Fax 41.32.27); *Nigeria Airways* (☎44.40.82); *Royal Air Maroc*, Imm Banque Islamique (☎44.38.96); *Sabena* (☎41.34.40; Fax 41.42.94).

American Express No representative. The *Novotel* may help.

Banks and money-changing *BICIGUI* on av de la République (☎41.50.11; Fax 44.39.62; Mon–Thurs 8.30am–12.30pm & 2.30–4.30pm; Fri 8.30am–12.45pm) is the main branch for foreign exchange in Conakry, and quite efficient. The black market money traders are mostly to be found outside the airport, around the port area and near the PTT. Rates are at least ten percent better than the bank, and police seem unfussed.

Car rental The rate for a small saloon car, assuming 100km per day and including obligatory, expensive insurance starts at around FG40,000/day or FG200,000/week. There's a 16 percent tax on top. For a capable, off-road vehicle, you'd be looking at three times these figures. One of the cheaper outlets is *Guinée Cars* (☎44.39.26) in av de la République. Also try *Locagui*, by the Cité Douanes, rte du Niger, Quartier Coléah, Matam (☎41.35.24) which rents out Toyotas, with or without driver. Local franchisees of the international companies have offices at the airport and *Novotel*, but they may insist on you hiring a driver (around FG10,000/day) for trips inland from Conakry.

Cassettes Some of the cheapest in West Africa are available from the Marché du Niger. Make up a job lot and bargain your heart out: around FG1000 each for old titles, FG1500 for new releases, about half what you'd pay in Dakar or Abidjan.

Cinemas Of the ten or more in the city, the *Rogbané* in Taouyah – a fairly upmarket district – is the best, with the newish *Liberté*, by the Autoroute bridge, also quite good. They're beginning to show watchable movies too.

Crafts and curios A listless selection on the whole. The expensive hotels have a selection in their shops or on the forecourt, but they're expensive. Visit the market, and check out 4ème bd between av de la République and av de la Gare, near the post office.

Cultural centres Americans and others can visit the American Cultural Centre on the Corniche Sud, near the Autoroute bridge, for its library, periodicals, English- and French-language movies and American satellite TV (Mon, Tues & Thurs–Fri 9am–12.30pm & 2–6pm; Wed 2–6pm; Sat 9am–12.30pm).

Embassies, consulates and honorary consulates include: **Belgium**, near *La Cigale* bar in Quartier Coléah, Matam (BP 871; ☎46.24.30); **Canada**, near Cité Douanes, Corniche Sud, Matam (BP 99; ☎46.27.21); **Cape Verde**, Palais du Peuple, Corniche Sud entrance (BP 1248; ☎44.40.11); **Denmark**, c/o SOGUICOM, 10ème av (BP 3115; ☎41.32.84); **Egypt**, near the abbatoirs, Corniche Sud, Matam (BP 389; ☎46.14.25); **France**, bd du Commerce, entry on 8ème av (BP 570; ☎ 44.16.05; issues visas for Burkina and Mauritania); **Germany**, 2ème bd (BP 540; ☎44.15.06 or 44.15.08); **Ghana**, Imm Kaloum, av de la République (BP 732; ☎44.15.10); **Great Britain** Hon. Consul Mrs Val Treitlein, opposite the Coléah Lycéem, Quartier Mafanco (BP 834; ☎46.17.34; Fax 44.42.15); **Guinea-Bissau**, rte de Taouyah, Quartier Minière (BP 298; ☎46.21.36); **Italy**, Pace Villa, Camayenne (BP 84; ☎44.35.88); **Japan**, near Cité Douanes, Corniche Sud, Matam (BP 895; ☎41.25.75); **Liberia**, Cité Ministérielle, near *Hôtel Camayenne*, Donka (BP 18; ☎46.26.71); **Mali**, Corniche Sud, Madina-Port (BP 299; ☎46.14.18); **Morocco**, Villa 12, Cité des Nations, Corniche Nord, near the port (BP 193; ☎44.37.10); **Netherlands**, Imm Banque Islamique, 6ème av (BP 1604; ☎44.31.07; Fax 44.32.27); **Nigeria**, Corniche Sud, Quartier Coléah, Matam (BP 54; ☎41.35.87); **Russia/CIS**, rte du Niger, Matam (BP 329; ☎46.14.59); **Senegal**, Corniche Sud, Madina-Port (BP 842; ☎46.28.34); **Sierra Leone**, Bellevue junction (BP 695; ☎46.14.39); **Spain**, Imm FRIGUIA, 2ème bd, opposite the French Embassy (BP 794; ☎44.48.46); **Sweden**, Imm CDE, rte du Niger, Matam

MOVING ON FROM CONAKRY

Flights to the interior are handled (in descending order of reliability) by *Guinée Air Service*, *Guinée Inter Air* and *Air Guinée*. *Guinée Air Service* fly to Boké on Thurs; Kankan on Tues, Fri and Sun; Kissidougou on Wed and Fri; Labé on Mon, Tues and Thurs; Nzérékoré on Mon, Wed and Fri; Sambailo on Mon; and Siguiri on Fri. *Guinée Inter Air* fly to Kankan on Mon, Wed, Thurs and Sat (FG51,000); Siguiri on Mon and Sat (FG52,000); Kissidougou on Tues and Sun (FG45,000); and Nzérékoré on Tues and Sun (FG61,000). *Air Guinée*, whose prices undercut *GIA*'s and *GAS*'s by a few thousand FG, flies to Kissidougou and Nzérékoré on Mon and Thurs; Kankan on Mon, Wed and Sat; Labé daily except Tues and Thurs; and Boké, Sambailo and Siguiri on Wed and Sat.

There are limited possibilities for **sea travel** to other parts of West Africa: contact SOGUICOM, the main shipping agents (10ème av; BP 3115; ☎41.32.84). A service called Sierra Link connected Freetown with Conakry in the early 1990s (about FG40,000) but is currently suspended. The MV *Remvi's* regular service to Monrovia is more likely to be operating, but not particularly useful for most travellers.

All up-country **road transport** leaves from the Madina *gare voiture* which, unless you flew in, is almost certainly where you arrived in the city. SOGETRAG runs a regular bus service to a number of towns, including frequent runs to Dubreka, Coyah and Kindia; daily at 8am and 3pm to Mamou; and weekly or more frequent services to Pita, Labé, Kissidougou and Kankan. Services to Guéckédou may also be operating: for this and the other less frequent services, you should ideally reserve seats the day before. The buses are much more comfortable and no more expensive than the principal alternative, Peugeot 504s. For the latter, you simply need to be at the *gare voiture* early to secure a place for practically anywhere in the country. They also offer more flexibility in price than the buses if you're getting out before the eventual destination.

(BP 1180; ☎44.30.16); **Switzerland**, Corniche Sud, Madina (BP 720; ☎44.30.16); **Togo**, Imm Kaloum, av de la République (BP 3633; ☎44.47.72); **Tunisia**, Imm Banque Islamique, 6ème av de la République (BP 1247; ☎44.50.71); **USA**, opposite Imm FRIGUIA, 2ème bd (BP 603; ☎44.15.21); **Zaire**, 10ème av de la Gare (BP 880; ☎44.15.02).

Film processing For one-hour developing and printing, try *Amina Photo*, Imm Sonia, rte du Niger, opposite the *Texas Poulet Frit*.

Medical/dental attention For emergencies, go to Hôpital Ignace Deen (☎44.20.53) or Hôpital Donka (☎44.19.33). For private consultations, Dr Sureau in Taouyah is recommended by many expat clients. The French dentist at the university's *centre medicaire* is good.

Pharmacies Check a copy of *Djeli* or *Tam Tam* for *pharmacies de garde* (out-of-hours pharmacy rota).

Photo permits These are more a theoretical than a mandatory requirement. If you're feeling frivolous enough to want to take on Guinean bureaucracy, check them out at ONACIG, by the *Cinéma Liberté* at Place du 8 Novembre. Otherwise, keep your lenses capped in Conakry.

Post and telephones The main PTT is open Mon–Fri 8am–2pm. The telephone section stays open until 10pm, with stamps for sale. Poste restante is neither stunningly secure nor organized. The public fax number is 44.32.18.

Supermarkets The big ones are *Superbobo* on rte de Donka in Camayenne and *Super-V* in Quartier Coléah, Matam.

Travel agents The airlines often act as general agents. Independent travel agents include *Karou Voyages*, on av de la République (☎44.20.42) and at the *Novotel* (☎44.32.65), and *SDV Guinée* (☎44.43.92).

Visa extensions Available from the immigration office at the Ministry of the Interior, corner of 8ème av and 1er bd, at a cost of FG40,000 for three months.

Worship St Mary's Catholic Cathedral has masses at 6pm on Sat and 10am on Sun; the Anglican All Saints Cathedral has prayer services at 6am and 5.30pm Mon–Fri, Sun mass at 10am, and Sun prayer service at 5.30pm.

THE FOUTA DJALON

Raising some spectacular cliffs just a short journey inland from Conakry and covering the greater part of the western interior, the **Fouta Djalon highlands** are Guinea's major attraction. Cut into innumerable, chocolate-bar plateaux – some denuded to *mesa*-like outcrops – the sandstone massif is the source of hundreds of **rivers**, including the Gambia and the Senegal, major tributaries of the Niger and a lattice of streams running down to the Guinea coast. After the rains, **waterfalls** spume everywhere.

Populated by **Fula** (Peul) herders and the remnants of the indigenous agricultural groups whose territory they invaded, the region has a fascinating ethnic history and an extraordinary variety of landscape. Lushly cultivated or **jungle-filled valleys** rise – sometimes with **sheer cliffs** – to scrubby high ground, bare and rocky wastelands or lightly wooded **plateaux**. Wherever the contours are gentle enough to retain the soil, swathes of **grassland** roll in the wind. It's fabulous country and needs only time, and average determination, to explore – wanderings which can be immensely satisfying.

The approach: Kindia and Mamou

You can get to the major Fouta Djalon centres – Dalaba, Pita and Labé – in a day's travel from Conakry on a good, surfaced road, but you will have to be at Conakry's Madina taxi park early. If you're in no hurry, start the trip with the short journey up to Coyah (50km). Leaving Conakry, you follow the smog-laden fast lane, and the oily squalor and vitality of the city immigrants' highway-side *ateliers*, manufacturing every conceivable kind of item. You pass also through a string of tedious **checkpoints**, the last of which, Kilometre 36, at the Kindia-Dubreka junction, is an outlandish scene of strutting and loafing khaki where delays, particularly heading *into* the city, are commonplace.

HIKING, BIKING AND RELATED PRACTICALITIES

The Fouta Djalon is one of the best regions in West Africa for serious, stimulating **off-the-beaten-track travel**. Assuming you're armed with at least the *IGN* map of the country (the *Michelin* 953 isn't enough), there are hundreds of kilometres of, sometimes optimistically labelled, "motorable tracks" and footpaths throughout the region (see p.505 for an account of cycling along one of them). **Mountain bikes** are ideal, and on the main routes you'll have little trouble loading them onto vehicles whenever your enthusiasm for pedalling wanes. **Motorbikes**, preferably trail bikes, would also be fine. **Cars and off-road vehicles** however – even 4WD ones – will run into repeated difficulties on steep and rugged terrain and you'd need the most agile and powerful machine to negotiate more than the most often-used of the minor routes. The option open to all is **footing it** and the only consideration then is whether your visa allows you the time.

You should ensure minimal levels of **survivability** in the event of a breakdown or an accident. If you're cycling, or on a motorbike, take obsessive care: roads which seem relatively good can turn a bend and disappear without warning into a river, or lose themselves in a jumble of rocks and gullies. Have purifying tablets for water which often comes straight from the local stream; and carry some back-up **rations** for emergencies.

This is the most densely populated part of the country. The **people** of the Fouta Djalon are, in general, wonderfully kind and show a disinterested concern for the welfare of wayward *porto* (white people). There's a growing population of English-speaking refugees from the wars in Liberia and Sierra Leone, too. People will nearly always get water for you when you need it. The highlands, moreover, are a major citrus-growing area and during the early dry season you'll be able to rely on oranges in their hundreds as a cheap source of fluid. Remember of course to stock up on **essentials** like toilet paper and batteries which don't grow on trees. Remember too that temperatures at night can drop below 10°C and you'll need something warm.

COYAH (Guinea's source of bottled water) is surrounded by dense green forest and plantation, and innumerable food stalls throng its main street. There's a nice hotel here if you're in need – the *Mariani*, signposted off the main road, with good facilities, including S/C rooms (②–③).

Out of Coyah, pale dramatic **cliffs** rise to the south from a broken plain of bush and palms. Crowned with bubbling greenery, these isolated tablelands – more or less separated from the plains by rock faces on all sides, and apparently uninhabited on top – would likely repay investigation by fairly intrepid naturalists. If you're interested and ready for a hike, stop at the village of **Tabili** and follow the left bank of the Badi upstream between the cliffs. It rises on top of the plateau.

Kindia

Born on the railway line in the early 1900s, **KINDIA** (135km from Conakry) is now a bustling, workaday place dramatically located beneath the hulk of Mont Gangan. The railway barely functions any more and there aren't any obvious attractions in town apart from the huge **market** – a large section of which is devoted to local cloth, where the vendors shout to be heard over the whirring of sewing machines. Shaded by innumerable **mango trees** (Kindia is a wonderful place to fetch up the mango in season, boasting many different varieties – *chocolat, fini pas*, etc), the town has a number of decent eateries along the main road and several places to stay if you arrive late in the day.

Practicalities

If you have to stop over in Kindia (the hotel at La Voile de la Mariée falls, 18km further east is much nicer), the best **accommodation** is probably the recently refurbished

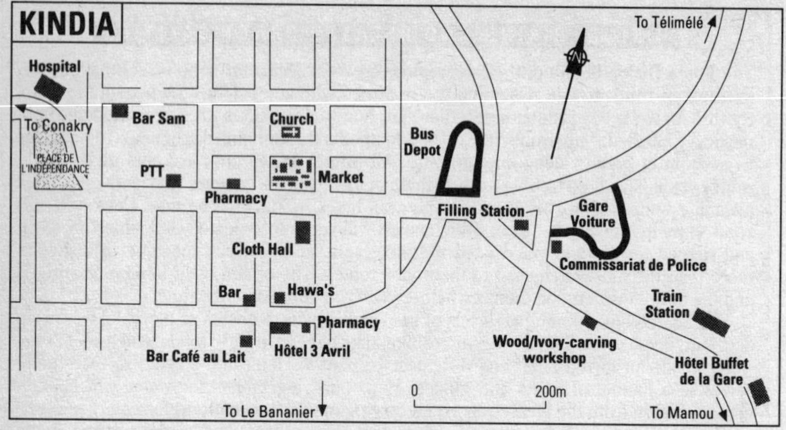

Buffet de la Gare, which has enthusiastic staff, several nearby cafés and large S/C rooms around a pleasant courtyard (②). It incorporates the *La Paillotte* nightclub, the noise potential of which you should consider when choosing a room. The most central hotel is the adequate, if grubby, *3 Avril* (①). Otherwise, choose between the hotel/dance bar, *Phare de Guinée*, 2km out of town on the road to Coyah (left hand side; ②), or the neighbouring Vietnamese-run boarding house (①).

The few **eating** options in Kindia are quite diverse. *Le Relax* is always pleasant, with basic rice dishes, or omelettes or salad to order, and ice-cold drinks. *Hawa's* is good for *mafé*, and you can get *atieké* on the street, always served with fish. For Lebanese food, check out *Bar Sam*: they serve *houmous, taboule*, french fries and the like, accompanied by beer if you want. For a broadly international menu (chicken, fish, steak) the *Buffet de la Gare* or *Le Bananier* will provide, though it's wise to go in advance to be sure of getting what you want. *Le Bananier* is also one of Kindia's main **night spots**, particularly good on Thursday and Saturday nights, when they charge a FG2000 entrance. At weekends, the *Buffet* can also be lively.

There are good purchases to be made in Kindia, especially in **cloth**, *tissus*. A pair of batik *pagnes* (two-metre lengths of printed cloth) goes for FG5000–6000, indigo dyed cloth (*gara*) for not much more and beaten damask (*lepi*) for around FG15,000 a pair. There's a large covered area devoted to cloth – the *marché aux tissus* – in the main market. Various beads and leather work are on offer across the street from it. You might also visit the woodworkers near the old station: expect to be offered ivory as well as wood carvings.

Around Kindia

There are several worthwhile day trips in the Kindia area: **Mont Gangan**, rising above the town to the north; **Pastoria**, the birthplace of TB immunization; and the **Voile de la Mariée falls**, where you might even be tempted to stay a few days.

Mont Gangan

The massif of **Mont Gangan** is one of the highest peaks (1117m) in the southern Fouta Djalon and relatively easily climbed. The big plateau halfway up offers brilliant views over Kindia, especially after the rains. Just be careful not to stroll through the military camp on the way.

Pastoria

If you'd like to have a look at **Pastoria** – the "Institut Pasteur" – which is 6km up the road to Télimélé from Kindia, you'll probably have to *déplace* a town taxi for the trip, or take a long walk in hope. The institute was founded in 1925 as a primate research centre, principally with the aim of developing various vaccines for human use. We have their consumptive **chimps** to thank for the BCG (Bacillus Calmette-Guerin) anti-tuberculosis jab. The Pasteur Institute in Paris later charged Pastoria with the collection of snake venom for anti-venene preparations. It's still open for visits if you call first on the director. They have a large collection of primates and snakes.

La Voile de la Mariée

The best known of Kindia's local excursion is to **La Voile de la Mariée**, the "Bridal Veil" falls, a five-kilometre diversion off the road to Mamou, 13km from Kindia. Here, the Santa River leaps from a black and yellow cliff in two streams to crash against the rockface and break into a broad fan, a total drop of some sixty metres. It's a year-round phenomenon, but most impressive during and shortly after the rains. The area is looked after by a hotelier who manages 15 spacious concrete huts (built by order of Sekou Touré for his weekly visits), now converted into a pleasant *campement*, set amid the jungle (S/C twin rooms in huts of two or three rooms; ②–③). You can also camp here. Meals are available, but you do need to order well in advance. If you stay several days, the hotel manager will be pleased to escort you into the nearby hills for a jungle trek and bird's-eye views of the district.

If you just visit for the day out of Kindia, you'll pay FG2000 parking fee and whatever you agree with your taxi driver (FG4000 round trip is about right). An alternative means of getting here would be to take a minibus *taxi brousse* as far as Segueya (FG400) and then walk the final couple of kilometres down the track to the falls. If you arrive on foot, the entrance fee is FG1000.

MOVING ON FROM KINDIA

A minor route into the Fouta Djalon winds out of Kindia to **Télimélé**, with onward possibilities to Pita and the far north. There's a handful of vehicles each day and the road condition is kept up fairly well. There's a continuous flow of transport shuttling between **Kindia and Mamou**. For travellers heading for **Sierra Leone**, Kindia has occasional bush taxi departures for Madina Oula, whence it's possible to reach the Outamba-Kilimi National Park and Kamakwie, as well as direct buses to the border town of Pamelap.

Mamou

From Kindia, the steep, hairpinning 130-kilometre climb up to Mamou offers a sweeping panorama back over the broad tributary basins of the Kolente (or Great Scarcies) River, the border with Sierra Leone. Twenty or thirty kilometres before Mamou you'll find a couple of hamlets which have developed into sizeable "service stations" for the passing bush taxi trade, providing roadside food and prayer stalls day and night. **Madine** is the first; **Hafiya** the second and more important one.

If you're in the mood for more waterfalls – and have your own vehicle – take a side trip, 5km to the right, to the village and falls of **Konkouré**, some 25km before Mamou. There's an old sacred wood here, containing remnant examples of trees from the ancient forest which once covered large parts of the Fouta Djalon.

MAMOU, piled on the hillside, strikes a surprisingly low-key note with its sprawl of houses and compounds. Before the building of the railway, the religious and political

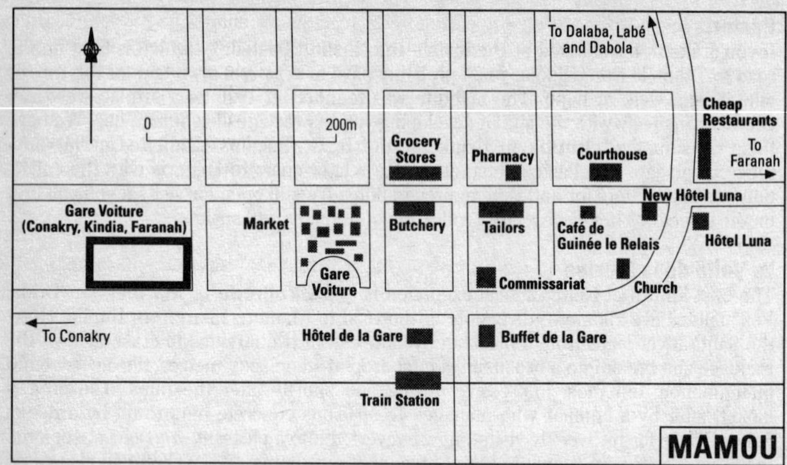

centre of the Fouta Djalon *almamys* (Islamic leaders) was **Timbo** – now just a village 50km northeast of Mamou (see opposite). Despite considerable local opposition, the French decided to bypass Timbo and set up a new railway halt and fuel depot at the hamlet of Mamou. The Fula chieftaincy was transferred and, until after World War II, Mamou was the chief administrative centre for much of the highlands. Today this unappetizing crossroads town has an agricultural college and a meat-processing industry. It also has perhaps the worst reputation for crime of any town in Guinea – though it's by no means evident and Mamouans will insist that Conakry is worse.

Accommodation options are few and simple. The *Hôtel Luna* (②) has thirty nominally S/C rooms around a large courtyard: mobilize the *patron* to organize water if you find none in your shower/toilet. The *Luna*'s terrace, in the older part of the hotel across the street, is popular among local teachers and *fonctionnaires*, and can be quite a scene. Musicians and griots come here and compete against the radio in the bar – pay them FG100–200 to sing someone's praises and you'll go down a treat. The *Hôtel Buffet de la Gare* usually looks closed, but ask in the "restaurant" (which serves drinks but no food) for someone to show you one of their large, decent S/C rooms (②). A more attractive option is the *Clos St Cathérine*, a few kilometres out on the Conakry road (③). There's plenty of street **food** in Mamou, and a good number of basic *gargotes*: try the *Café de Guinée le Relais*.

MOVING ON FROM MAMOU

Mamou is such a major transport hub that moving on is rarely a problem. The town's three taxi and bus parks, each surrounded by cheap little eateries, are hives of activity from dawn to dusk. The two in the town centre handle the Conakry–Faranah axis; the one on the road out of town towards Labé handles Fouta Djalon traffic and transport on the less busy routes to Timbo, Dabola and Dinguiraye.

Mamou to Faranah

For some distance out of town, the rough road from **Mamou to Faranah** (see p.512) drops through forest and hilly bush with views to pass the time. Then the highlands are shed, the road flattens and the scenery breaks into quickly monotonous **elephant**

grass and bush savannah for the rest of the journey to Faranah. The road, built after independence, arrows and loops determinedly through the flat wilderness, at times just a dozen kilometres from the Sierra Leone border. With time, Kouranko compounds and hamlets may gradually gather along it but for now it is still largely empty land. **At night**, this is one of the country's most soporific journeys, with little to enliven it but the cassettes on the driver's stereo. It's worth knowing, however, that the district is one of the richest faunal areas in Guinea and your chances of seeing exciting large wild animals quite high.

Mamou to Dabola

The road from **Mamou to Dabola** (see p.511), which by now should be hard-surfaced, cuts through impressive scenery: sheer rocky outcrops and forest populated by chimpanzees and other primates.

Timbo, 50km along the road, is the old capital of the Fula *almamys*. Timbo still has an eighteenth-century mosque – much restored – and there's a European cemetery dating back to the end of the last century when a French administrative *résident* was installed here to breathe down rebellious Fula necks. You'll also come across traditional Fouta Djalon houses out here; senior figures construct fine conical beehive affairs, with solid tiers of thatching to exclude the cold.

The central Fouta Djalon

The central Fouta Djalon – including the ancient settlements of **Dalaba**, **Pita** and **Télimélé** – offers some of Guinea's most beautiful countryside. The main road north from Mamou has fairly recently been resurfaced which is on the whole a dangerously speedy improvement. About 15km out of Mamou, the eastward-flowing stream you cross is the Bafing, first headwater of the Senegal; its source is in the hills a few kilometres off the road to the west. The road steepens after Bouliwel (which has a Saturday *lumo*), then drops to enter Dalaba, hidden in a conifer-carpeted valley.

Dalaba

DALABA has a beautiful setting in the hills at 1200m (though why it's called *Dalaba* – "big pond" in Malinké – is a mystery), and the French considered the site so therapeutic that they built a sixty-room sanatorium, now in ruins. The South African jazz singer, Miriam Makeba, spent time in Dalaba, in the large white house with the strange roof (near the ruined sanatorium) during her period of exile from the USA in the 1970s.

Dalaba's layout is easy to grasp. The limited market – greatly enlarged on Sunday, when it hosts the district *lumo* – and a couple of streets around comprise the town centre, with a row of cheap eating and drinking places on the street along the bottom of the market. Market produce includes, from the end of December to March, cultivated **strawberries** – a colonial bequest. For **drinks or food**, try the *Renaissance Bar*, tiny but absurdly well stocked; or the *Bar Le Relais 55*, which sometimes converts to a *dancing*. There's a **post office** but no bank.

Away across the valley and behind the hill to the west (a thirty-minute walk) is the administrative quarter of Etaconval – rural in feel and spread among the woods – and the two best **places to stay**. The *Hôtel Tangama* is a new place run by a French-Guinean couple, one of the best up-country hotels in Guinea, with an excellent restaurant (more like a French family dining room) and hot showers in some rooms, some of which also have electricity (BP 26 Dalaba; ☎ c/o PTT, Dalaba, 61.04.00; ①–③). Wonderful breakfasts are FG4000, main meals around FG10,000 and the dish of the day about FG5000. Dalaba's *villa* is run-down these days – a cluster of bare houses on the hillside with the main compensation being the infinite views (②). Occasionally it's booked for a conference, but you can always **camp** under the pines and use the limited facilities and a lock-up storage room. The caretaker's wife will cook for you if you order in advance – it's all pretty informal. Back towards the town centre is the *Etoile de Fouta* – a restaurant and sometime *boîte* which also has rooms to let (②). Unless they're busy, however, it's a mournful barn of a place (ex-French officers' club) with underwhelming appeal.

Whether you're staying at the *villa* or not, have a look at the odd house out among those on the hillside; a remarkable Fula chiefs' **assembly hall** – a *case de palabre* – built in the 1930s, with an inscribed floor and exceptional carving on its interior walls.

Dalaba to Pita

Moving on to Pita from Dalaba by public transport can sometimes prove difficult: most vehicles are either coming full from Mamou and going on to Labé, or vice versa. An early start might get you a ride without having to pay the fare the whole way to Labé.

While it's not inconceivable as a **walk** – and worth it for the stunning **scenery** which at last really opens up – fifty-two kilometres is a long way for unadjusted muscles. The first half of the route from Dalaba to Pita plunges down through various stages of gorgeous forest – conifer, broad leaf jungle, more open bush – and this section you might consider walking in the realistic hope of getting a lift further along the way.

If you have your own transport, consider a diversion down the steep grade to Tinka (right, 5km outside Dalaba). The colonial, ornamental garden here – **Le Jardin de Professeur Chevallier** – is still just about kept up, and worth a visit. The **Chutes de Ditinn**, some 30km further at the village of Ditinn, are accessible and you can swim in the plunge pool. When there's sufficient flow, the eighty-metre falls, dropping from a perfectly vertical cliff, are very impressive.

Back on the main highway about 15km from Dalaba, look out for the **Chutes de Piké**, hard by the road on the left, just after the bridge over the stream of the same name. The falls are easily accessible down a couple of short paths, one of which leads to the pool at the top where you can stand at the precipice, the other to the ledges at the bottom where you can see the cascade, a pretty ten-metre drop, though unimpressive in the dry season.

The Fouta Djalon spurts pandemically with waterfalls, but some are more easily seen from a distance than reached: **Bomboli**'s *chutes*, for example, are very difficult to get to, but clearly visible about 15km before Pita, several kilometres over on the right.

Pita and around

As a place of beauty and repose, **PITA** can't match Dalaba. But they share the same zesty atmosphere and you'll quickly grow to like it. Market day is Thursday. Pita figures in most travel plans as a place to get the necessary permission (usually free, but not always) to visit the **Kinkon Falls** – a simple matter of calling at the *commissariat* on the north side of town.

Most people who want to **stay** get directed to a fading hotel, the *Hôtel Kinkon*, in a quiet area near the school on the northwestern edge of town. It's very basic but just about adequate and quite *sympa* (①). Warm water can be ordered for the self-contained washing cubicles. It's also possible to stay at the *Centre d'Acceuil*, the imposing complex near the *commissariat*, which has spotless, very reasonably priced rooms (①).

In town there are various **eating** places, of which the *Café/Restaurant Montréal* is probably the best, and streetside bars, including the *Buenos Aires*, good for *café noir*. For added entertainment, there's a nightclub, *Le Sapin*, which hosts regular video evenings, and big screen action at the *Cinéma Rex*, with twice-daily showings of American movies.

If you're heading straight to Conakry from Pita, the SOGETRAG bus is scheduled to run on Tuesdays, Thursdays and Sundays.

The Chutes de Kinkon

The **Chutes de Kinkon** are the Fouta Djalon's best falls, a fairly easy cycle ride but a longish walk – 11km from Pita (you might be lucky and get a lift with a vehicle going to Dongol-Touma, leaving you just a kilometre to walk). A sign two or three kilometres along the road out to Labé sends you left (direction "Touma and Télimélé") and after a mostly downhill 7km you arrive at a control post where you hand in your *laissez-passer*. Here you'll be told it's 500m down to the right if you desire to inspect the dam (an unimpressive bridge across the lake; the reason for the piece of paper) and about a kilometre left for the main falls.

You can stand directly on the **rock platform** above the falls which – before the dam was built – would have surged with water, and possibly does still during the rains. There's evidence of colonial safety measures in the broken stumps of cliff-edge railings, but nothing to stop present-day visitors plunging dramatically to their deaths – take care, as the flow is powerful. Behind, on the cliffs, is a scrappy but just about legible list of various heads of state, with the dates of their visits. You can follow the path down below the falls to the power station on the river bank – but there's little point, apart from good exercise, since there's nothing to be seen.

Pita to Télimélé

Exceptionally beautiful in parts, the Pita–Télimélé "road" was formerly a tough route, with some very challenging sections. Since the surface was re-graded in the early 1990s it's now a relatively straightforward drive and ideal for **mountain bikes** (two days), **motorbikes** or **4WD vehicles** (eight hours plus) or **hiking** (four to six days). The Paris–Dakar rally came this way in January 1995, but it's still little used by public transport. The route in reverse is considerably less attractive as the rewards are mostly westwards (eastbound you face a continuous thirty-kilometre climb from Léi-Mîro to Dongol-Touma).

If you're cycling or hiking, you may want to deviate from the road to take the short cuts in the company of local people. A walking route follows, roughly, the course of the Fétoré River, which flows westwards, a few kilometres north of the road. Alternatively, you might try to get a lift as far as **Dongol-Touma**, where the thrills begin. There's at least daily transport from Pita to Dongol, though you'll probably have less of a wait if you go to the junction 3km north of Pita, where vehicles from Labé, as well as Pita or Mamou, turn off westwards towards Télimélé.

The people of the area, who live in immaculate mud-moulded compounds, are happy – once they've got over their disbelief and exchanged greetings – to bring water from their wells or the local stream, and will just as soon give you handfuls of oranges and bananas as sell them. Children in this isolated region may be just a little scared of white people.

Over the bowe

A signpost 3km up the Pita–Labé road marks the turn-off to Télimélé, which at first brings you to a confusion of tracks. Bear right where another sign points left to the Chutes de Kinkon, (see above), which, given an early start, could be easily appended to this route. The correct **track** soon starts bucking and twisting unmistakably, with many descents to narrow streams and many wearing climbs to short level ridges. There's a fair number of Fula people about, invariably surprised to see any strangers, let alone foreign travellers. The track heads northwest, southwest, east and south before establishing a more or less westerly course on a barren hogsback of rocky land discernible on the *IGN* map. In truth, this part of the journey, across the **bowe** – the Fula name for these high, sear plateaux – isn't scenically enthralling. In December smoke from burning grass obscures any views and the hazy dust brought by the *Harmattan* wind normally fogs the horizon between January and April. The path runs over unrelenting bare rock in places, and then begins a gentle descent, with occasional wooded intervals. The village of **Tulal** has an enormous mosque and, an hour's walk further west you reach **Combouroh**, where a remarkable country market takes place every Tuesday. Hundreds of Fula women converge to buy and sell a little, but mainly to share news and find men. The miracle of hairstyles and print patterns is stunning and happily typical. At the end of the *bowe*, you reach the strung-out village of **Dongol-Touma**, 55km from the Pita junction, site of a Wednesday *lumo*. If you see the *sous-préfet* you'll likely be able to **stay the night** in Dongol's *villa*, superbly sited on a high bluff with 270 degrees of panorama. The *villa* is rarely needed for official purposes and you may receive a royal welcome and repeated donations of food and drink (something in return is appreciated the next morning). It's strange to think that dictator Sekou Touré stayed in these rooms – and may well have slept in these very beds if their condition gives any indication of age.

Downhill to the Kakrima River

The road snakes out of Dongol-Touma and starts a **steep descent**, with inspiring sweeps of Fouta Djalon visible through the trees now shading it. If you're cycling or motorbiking, the only effort for 26km is in keeping the brakes on. Driving a car or truck, exercise extreme caution: parts of the route are likely to have succumbed to erosion and you could turn a bend and run into a jumble of boulders and bedrock. When you're not watching the surface ahead, however, this is a breathtaking ride, zig-zagging down a long spine and throwing up striking views of the bush country to the south, the fortress-like hills – Télimélé among them – rising in a ridge to the west, and plunging valleys right below. Streams, flecked with butterflies and overshot by parrots and hornbills, cut across the road and are quickly left behind hundreds of metres above. Giant leaves litter the ground and lianas strew overhead. Occasionally a hunter or a woodcutter emerges – usually to stand still, nonplussed, on seeing you. Monkeys, the hunters' main targets, are common.

At last the gradients relax and the road unwinds, through more cultivated country, towards the Kakrima River. The village of **Djounkoun** leaves little impression, but **Léi-Mîro**, 4km east of the river, is the second large settlement along the route. You'll find rice and other street food if you turn up early enough, or bread and sandwich ingredients if not. Léi-Mîro's *lumo* takes place every Thursday.

The winch-ferry across the **Kakrima River** has an engine, but it's not far across (either hauling the ferry's line or renting a *pirogue*) in the event of breakdown. **Koussi** is just beyond, where people know a good short cut, useful if you're walking to Télimélé. The main route beyond Koussi is hard work on a bicycle, mostly flat – and sandy in parts – with tall elephant grass jamming any view.

Sixty-one kilometres after Dongol-Touma the route hits the broad, red sweep of the Kindia–Télimélé road where you'll find a lift easily enough. The final gruelling fifteen kilometres to Télimélé up the soaring flank of **Mont Louba** is noted for gut-churning accidents on the hairpins.

Télimélé

A pleasing, well-kept town, perched as if to admire its grand views, **TÉLIMÉLÉ** sees very few visitors. In the area lies **Gueme Sangan**, the ruined **fortress** of Koli Tengela, the fifteenth-century Fula warlord who laid the foundations of the kingdom of Fouta Djalon. Télimélé – "the place where the *téli* grows" – is a town of pine trees, citrus orchards and fresh air, surrounded by imposing mountain flanks and trench-like valleys. If you're staying, there's an adequate **hotel** (②), up near the administrative quarter at the Kindia end of town, which has a formidable vista over the town from its terrace.

When you're ready to leave Télimélé there are two or three jeep or Land Rover departures per week **to Gaoual**, 130km along a beautiful route to the north. The road down **to Kindia** isn't too bad and transport is reasonably frequent, but it's worth investing a little extra for a place in a Peugeot rather than one of the minibuses. Stay awake for the last half-hour before Kindia; there are some outstanding tabular massifs, rearing like lost worlds across the valley.

Labé and the northern Fouta Djalon

Heading north from Pita, the **road to Labé**, 38km away, loops across a mellow, pastoral landscape of undulating grass, scattered with boulders and copses of oak-like *koura* trees, and fringed with lines of forest along the watercourses. The district, one of the highest in the Fouta Djalon, is a watershed between the streams that flow west and the Gambia and Senegal tributaries pouring off northwards.

Labé

LABÉ, the historic Fula stronghold and capital of the Fouta Djalon, is, by contrast with the surrounding landscape, a disappointment. Strategically situated in the middle of the highlands, it's a misshapen and unappealing, though evidently prosperous, town. Sizeable, and ranged confusingly over a number of hills, Labé is a growing centre, absorbing people from the regions of Guinea and not a few from neighbouring countries. All of which delivers a rather metropolitan jolt after the surrounding horizons and makes Labé a somewhat unsatisfactory place to stay.

Labé's pretty limited appeal arises from its status as the Fouta Djalon's largest market town and the area's main artisanal centre. If you venture a kilometre or so into

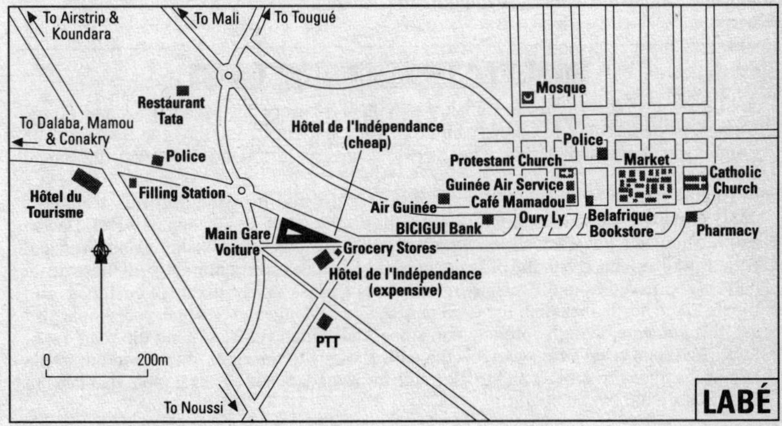

the streets that lie to the right of the airport road – a district known as Taba – you'll come to the yards of a couple of **weaving** guilds. You might do well to enlist someone to guide you to the *tisserands* if you're interested in seeing the weaving in progress. Also on the way to the airport, you pass the National Apiculture Centre, with local potted **honey** for sale.

For something a little more substantial in the way of food, the **market** in the town centre – huge, vibrant and teeming – is one of Labé's strong points, though even more of a tight squeeze to walk around than usual. There's a remarkable variety of groundnut pastes on offer, and all the usual Fouta Djalon profusion of produce. Look out for exquisite **gara** cloth, which is made from Czechoslovakian damask, tie-dyed with local indigo and beaten with clubs to a shine; it's sold, as usual, only in pairs of *pagnes*.

If you're in Labé long enough to want to do a day out fix up with a taxi to visit the **Chutes de la Sala**, near the road to Lélouma. These falls, some 37km from Labé, are some of the most impressive in Guinea – a series of small cascades tumbling above one enormous waterfall.

Practicalities

Arriving from Pita, you enter Labé past the dominating hulk of the *Hôtel de Tourisme* – clearly a once grand place in vaguely Swiss-chalet style, but now, despite its newly painted exterior, somewhat decrepit. There's no running water, but the **rooms** are very reasonably priced (②), the large *bar-resto* serves meals all day and the *Tinkisso* club downstairs comes alive at weekends. A good, and cheaper, alternative is the clean and very friendly *Hôtel de l'Indépendance* at the lower end of the gare voiture (①). Across the road, the jointly owned *Grand Hôtel de l'Indépendance*, offers clean, modern rooms and a reasonable restaurant (③).

A good bar/café is the *Café Mamadou Oury Ly* which you'll find opposite the bookshop. The Italian *Restaurant Tata*, signposted in town, does recommended homemade pizzas and pasta (closed on Tues). Another on Labé's short eating-out list is the *Café Tropical* across from the *Hôtel de Tourisme*, which has a multilingual owner and offers various interesting dishes.

Miscellaneous *renseignements* in the centre include the only **bank** in the Fouta Djalon, *BICIGUI* (open Mon–Fri 8.30am–12.30pm, 2.30–4pm; ☎51.09.47); the **PTT** (Mon–Sat 7.30am–4pm); and the *Bel Afrique* **bookshop** – owned by *Jeune Afrique* magazine, but no stronger in reading matter for that.

MOVING ON FROM LABÉ

Air Guinée operates **flights** to Conakry – in theory – every day except Tues and Thurs. *Guinée Air Service* flies to Conakry on Mon, Tues and Thurs; and direct to Banjul in The Gambia on Tues and Thurs. The fare to Conakry is around FG40,000, to Banjul FG80,000.

Labé is something of a cul-de-sac as far as regular **taxi brousse and bus transport** goes. There are plenty of transport options down the Fouta Djalon spine to Pita, Dalaba and Mamou, and in theory, thrice-weekly SOGETRAG buses to Conakry (Mon, Wed and Sat), as well as a good handful of Peugeot 504s to Conakry every morning. All these destinations are served from the main *gare voiture*. For a less steady stream of bush taxis and trucks to the north, including the town of Mali and Kédougou in Senegal, you should also use this *autogare*, though you may find some Mali-bound vehicles along the road out of Labé. A second main *gare voiture* – the gare Dakar – to the right of the road out to the airport, handles *taxi brousse* and truck traffic for Koundara and Senegal (note that taxis to Dakar take a full day and night).

LOCAL HISTORY: THE RISE OF THE JIHAD STATE

The original inhabitants of the highlands were Jalonke, Baga, Nalo and **Puli** (sedentary, animist, Fula speakers). They all coexisted in relative harmony, herding on the hills and farming the valleys. The region was known then as **Jalonkadougou**, after its dominant inhabitants, and was subject to the Mali empire.

The first ripples of tension through this rural idyll were felt during the thirteenth century, when **Fula immigrants** – the superficially Muslim clans of Ba, Sow, Diallo and Bari – arrived piecemeal, in search of pasture, from Tekrur on the Senegal River and Djenné on the River Niger. By the fifteenth century, they were sufficiently established for one of their kings, **Koli Tengela**, to shake off Mali's rule and raid widely to expand the Fula zone of influence. He later withdrew north to found the Denianke dynasty back in Tekrur.

This early Fula Muslim rule in the highlands wasn't especially zealous in its promulgation of Islam. With the demise of the Tengela dynasty, however, the increasingly fervent **Diallos** came up the Bafing and Tinkisso valleys and moved into the Labé region, spreading the faith among the Puli animists and quasi-Muslims who held local political power. Further migrations from outside the region quickened resentment of the incumbent infidel overlords. By the early eighteenth century, there was enough support for King **Karamoko Alfa Bari** to declare a jihad against the non-believers. He won a breakthrough military victory against them at Talansan in 1730.

The **Muslim Kingdom of Fouta Djalon** emerged, with Karamoko Alfa Bari as its *almamy* and its capital at **Timbo**. Karamoko's nephew, Ibrahima Sory, took power when his uncle went insane in 1767 and thereafter the **jihad state** was rapidly consolidated. The kingdom was divided into nine provinces, one of which, **Labé**, became a noted centre of learning. Labé was also a hotbed of *Alfaya* (supporters of Alfa Bari), unhappy with the rule of the nephew's line.

There were **conversions** among the animists, but many fled to less intense pastures, mostly coastwards. Those who stayed were either **"bush Fula"**, employed as herders by the Muslim aristos, or **slaves** of non-Fula origin who worked partly for their landlords and partly on their own account.

Throughout the nineteenth century, Labé drew apart from Timbo. Labé's ruler, **Alfa Yaya**, the great-grandson of Karamoko Alfa Bari, achieved his position through ruthless assassinations of his opponents. By the 1890s, with his territory extended over most of northwest Guinea, Labé constituted as powerful a state as the Timbo-based kingdom of Fouta Djalon itself. With the arrival of the French, separate treaties were entered into with both realms. Today Alfa Yaya – or Alfa Labé as he's known – is a folk hero: his **tomb** lies behind the mosque near the airport.

In the 1970s, the Fula population suffered heavy **repression** at the hands of Sekou Touré's terrorist dictatorship. He labelled ethnic Fula "enemies of socialism", and many thousands were killed or fled into exile.

The northern Fouta Djalon

If you've come up to Labé from the south, the most obvious onward option is to continue, off-tarmac, to the town of Mali and then to Kédougou in Senegal, though on average there's only one vehicle per day on this route, even in the dry season; the least obvious option is to head eastwards towards Kankan (see below).

Alternatives include the direct route **from Labé to Koundara** – much easier than the Mali–Koundara road, but still a full day's worth by bush taxi, even in the dry season. Don't be deceived by the tarmac leading out of Labé on this route – it only extends a few kilometres. In **KOUNDARA**, the *Hôtel du Kankan* is okay (①), or try the *Mamadou Boiro* (①), which is no worse, and hosts Saturday night parties free for residents, with great music.

The fabulously picturesque route from **Labé to Gaoual** is an alternative for people heading for Guinea-Bissau and Senegal's Basse Casamance region. On this route you're almost certain to have to take a Koundara vehicle and change at Kounsitel to local vehicles for Gaoual, Koumbia and north to Guinea-Bissau. **GAOUAL** is a friendly little town, with a wide avenue of trees and an old colonial PTT. The only hotel in town, off the same avenue, is overpriced (②–③) and doubles as Gaoual's disco.

Mali

The route from Labé to the small town of Mali switchbacks through the Fouta's loftiest parts, with a number of fair-sized villages on the way. Fourteen kilometres north of Labé, **Tountouroun** may still have its beautiful Fula houses and might be worth an exploratory excursion, even as a special trip out of Labé. Just a kilometre or so further, the small stream running east, which the road crosses, is the River Gambia –its source is nearby to the west. Further villages include Sarékali at 35km; the pretty hamlet of Pellal off to the left at 65km; and Yambéring, the largest, at 74km.

MALI has a small, primitive hotel, *La Dame de Mali* (①), and the slightly better *Villa/Centre d'Accueil* a few minutes away on an outcrop of rock (①). At 1460m, the town is the highest Fouta Djalon settlement, renowned for low temperatures (down to 3°C) and **views** at the end of the rains. These are particularly good from the summit of Mont Loura (1538m), the highest peak in the Fouta Djalon, 7km northeast of the village. The local *curiosité* – not necessarily worth a major effort to get to – is **La Dame de Mali**, a cliff eroded into "a well-proportioned feminine profile", on Mont Loura's eastern flank.

If you're trying to get **from Mali to Koundara**, Mali's market day, Sunday, offers the best opportunities. Otherwise, you might have to wait days for a vehicle. When you finally get one, be prepared for a diabolical road with one-in-four gradients, some dangerous hairpins and several skeletal bridges.

East of Labé

If you're heading **eastwards** for the Republic of Mali or Côte d'Ivoire, and feeling very expeditionary, then seek out transport to Tougué and work your way off the Fouta Djalon into the Malinké savannah region and Kankan. Generally the hills east of the main Labé–Mamou axis are more sparsely populated and even tougher travelling than those to the west, though for the most part not as steep.

THE MALINKÉ PLAINS

The great **plains** of the northeast – *Haute Guinée* – stretch, immensely vast and flat, over more than a hundred thousand square kilometres, big enough to swallow The Gambia ten times over. In this huge expanse, the few towns – Kankan the biggest, Kouroussa, Faranah, Siguiri – seem lost amid yellow grass, thorn trees and termite spires. In contrast to the Fouta Djalon to the west and the highlands further south, the population is sparse: most people live along the the meandering **tributaries of the Niger** which pull together in a fan in the most populous part of the region around Kankan and Kouroussa.

Getting around

Without your own means of transport you're mostly restricted to a clutch of main routes tracking through the territory. If you leave them on foot or bicycle, distances between habitations with supplies are often too long for comfort – you can go miles without seeing a soul even on the main roads. An option, for the more adventurous is to buy a boat and paddle down the Niger River, but for this you need to be completely self-sufficient (see p.513).

THE MANDE PEOPLES

The agricultural and trading **Mande**-speaking peoples are cultural heirs to the medieval empire of **Mali**, whose capital from the thirteenth to the fourteenth century was Niani, northeast of Kankan. More recently, the self-styled *almamy*, **Samory Touré**, founded and burned out two "Dyula empires" at the end of the nineteenth century and caused the French considerable grief with his determined jihad against their invasion.

The traditional Mande **names**, Touré, Traoré, Camara, Konté, Keita and Kouyaté are still the most common. Various Mande **languages** are spoken – including Bamana, Dyula and Koranko – as well as mainstream Mandinka/Malinké.

Dabola, Kouroussa and Dinguiraye

Dabola and **Kouroussa** are essentially **railway towns** whose appeal lies in a certain just-past nostalgia. Dabola, in particular, was a major centre during the French occupation and carried the Conakry–Kankan road, until the Mamou–Faranah link was built. Kouroussa, at a rail bridge over the Niger, was also once an important centre but is now somewhat cut off. It was the birthplace of Guinea's best-known author, Camara Laye. **Dinguiraye** is a remote Muslim centre well to the north.

Dabola

DABOLA grew up after 1910 as a staging post, and it retains a slightly Wild-West feel, hemmed in by gaunt plateaux rising directly behind the town and keeping those passing through well fed and entertained. It's not an unattractive place: in Dabolakoro ("old Dabola") neat compounds surround the small commercial centre. There's no longer a hotel here, but there is a pleasant bar (*La Paillotte*) and locals may be able to help with accommodation. Market day is Tuesday.

The **Tinkisso Falls** are well worth a short detour. A gentle six-kilometre climb on the road to Mamou brings you to a track (left) which drops over the railway line through a teak plantation – with drifts of huge, crunching leaves underfoot – and, forking right, to the top of the **dam** and a mass of bird life. (An alternative route just follows the power lines from town straight to the falls.) The **falls** themselves – which must have been impressive indeed before the dam was built – cascade over rocky shelves below (except at the end of the dry season, when there's no flow). The path descends steeply to the power station and its Chinese retinue, with views back to the falls. Continue on the same footpath downstream and you reach an immaculate Fula village and, eventually, the Dabola–Faranah road. Persistent hikers will want to do the circle – it makes a good day, whether or not the falls are falling, for the landscape and bird life.

MOVING ON FROM DABOLA

Dabola has daily transport connections to Mamou, Faranah, Dinguiraye, and Kankan via Kouroussa. The 110-kilometre earth road to Faranah, which descend gradually from Dabola before running past irrigated rice fields and along the stripling Niger valley into Faranah, is in rough condition. The road from Dabola via Kouroussa to Kankan is also tough-going: an uncomfortable six or seven hours by *taxi brousse*, soon to be much shortened when the tarmac from Dabola reaches Kouroussa. Take note that the ferry over the Niger at Kouroussa is often out of action, requiring a long diversion.

Kouroussa

KOUROUSSA is in a beautiful area, although owing to a lack of transport it's somewhat hard to get to (a situation that the new road from Dabola will ameliorate). The house of **Camara Laye**'s family, near the station, is quite well known and you'll have no difficulty tracking it down if you want to pay homage. The town is pleasant and leafy, and lodgings are available at *Bar La Baobab* (①), the *Hôtel Bob Marley* (①), near the French-built church or the new *Sabari* (①). *Café Savane*, near the market, is friendly.

René Caillié, the indomitable French traveller who by disguising himself and mumbling in Arabic became the first European to return from Timbuktu, arrived in Kouroussa with a bout of malaria in June 1827:

> *We crossed the river in canoes... A great number of people were going across, and they were all disputing, some about the fare that was demanded, some about who should go first. They all talked at once and made a most terrible uproar.*

The ferry crossing on the Kankan road, 26km east of the town, has apparently changed little. When the ferry breaks down in the dry season, some truckers risk fording the shallows but most Peugeot drivers won't.

An alternative means of transport in the right season (usually from mid-July until about November or December) is a weekly **ferry from Kouroussa to Bamako** in Mali.

Dinguiraye

DINGUIRAYE, isolated out in the back country to the north, was founded by Al Hadj Omar Tall in 1850 and became an important religious centre in the second half of the nineteenth century. The French post here, dating from 1896, was one of the earliest in Upper Guinea.

Omar Tall's **mosque**, an elaborate Fula-style thatched construction, has survived in good condition. What else you'll come across however, in terms of facilities, is uncertain: *Chez Cissé* is worth trying for accommodation. The town lies on a somewhat tenuous route connecting the Fouta Djalon, Siguiri and Bamako – an untouched and thinly populated part of the country, renowned for its wildlife and massive granite mounds looming from the plains. Daily transport to or from Dabola cannot be relied upon.

Faranah

After the long, nearly uninhabited void beyond Mamou – of which a hot, breezy yellowness is the enduring recollection – arrival at **FARANAH** makes some impact. A parade of mighty street lights lines up to greet you on the highway into town, and the **Niger River**, which flows beneath a rattling iron bridge, looks impressive already, with 4000km of meandering still to go before it reaches the sea. The Tinkisso dam at Dabola provides electricity: a Chinese team has been improving the system to give some juice in the dry season too.

Until independence in 1958, Faranah was an unimportant village on the old road from Dabola to Kissidougou. **Sekou Touré** pumped money into his native village, building a large mosque, as well as the *Cité du Niger* conference centre in 1981 and a massive block of a villa for himself, now a hotel. It's a town you're bound to pass through and although it's adequate for most practical needs (it lacks a bank), there's little of interest to hold you.

Practicalities

Definitely worth looking around, whether or not you take a **room**, is the Touré mansion, now the *Hôtel de Ville*, a repellently ostentatious four-storey pile stuffed with hideous presidential furniture, including the largest pouffe in the world and an absurd desk of solid marble. Musty with neglect and tumbling rapidly into decrepitude, this shrine to kitsch is still reasonable value as a place to stay and doubles as an informal "Museum of the President's Presents" – which is what most of the trappings are. You should aim to secure an interesting room over the street by pointing out that they're all unoccupied – as they are almost certain to be (②). For rather more conventionally comfortable accommodation, head up the hill to the southeast of the town to the *Cité du Niger*, whose furnished S/C, AC rondavels command fabulous views over the river valley (③).

Back in the town centre, cheap **eateries** compete at one end of the main *gare voiture*, serving high-quality street food all day, and – at least – some of them at night too. For more extended meals the excellent *Restaurant Le Regal* (around FG3000) has a varying menu and a fair selection, including wine. When satisfied, spill into the next door nightclub, *Club Winston*, which has reasonably cheap beers and lots of lively clients. Other watering holes worth visiting include the *Bar Pelican* and the *Club Savane*, while you might give the *Café les Jumeaux* a try for breakfast. Finally, if you need to **phone or fax** abroad, Faranah has an "external telecommunications centre" which makes it relatively easy to do so.

CANOEING DOWN THE RIVER

If you're looking for high adventure, and have a full life-support system (tent and cooking equipment essential), Faranah is a good place to acquire a boat and **canoe down the Niger**, either as far as Kouroussa, or all the way to Bamako, Mali. A four-metre plank boat, adequate for one, can be made to order for about FG50,000. A six- or seven-metre boat, big enough for two, will cost up to FG150,000. The wood is the main expense, and while a plank boat is slightly more expensive than a dugout, it is lighter, faster and more maneuverable.

It's not necessary to be an experienced canoeist for the trip. You need to take sufficient **food** (rice and canned food) to last the whole journey if necessary as you cannot rely on the occasional fishing camps having smoked or fresh fish for sale (there are no villages). Money and precious items need to be protected in waterproof bags as you're almost certain to capsize sooner or later.

From Faranah to Kouroussa, a 350-kilometre trip which should take between ten and fourteen days, the river winds through **forest** which looms out from the banks. There are several sections of **rapids** along the way, but only at two points are they hard – any fisherman will give you advice. **Wildlife** is abundant and interesting: you'll see beautiful birds, monkeys and baboons, antelope, warthogs, snakes, small crocodiles and several groups of hippos. Because they are hunted, hippos tend to stay well clear of boats but you should give them a wide berth anyway as they can be dangerous. There are some larger crocodiles (up to four metres) but you are very unlikely to see them and are safe in a boat. Bilharzia is not a problem and the swimming, hippos permitting, is fine nearly everywhere.

Downstream from Kouroussa, the riverscape opens out. The channel is well over a kilometre wide in places and the scenery is farmland and savannah. There are plenty of villages to restock your supplies, but the journey is less interesting, with no rapids, no crocs, and few hippos. From Kouroussa to Bamako by river is about 400km.

The **best time** to do this trip is after the rains (they usually finish in October) and before the end of the dry season (March–April). At the end of the dry season, parts of the river are very shallow indeed, making progress slow, and the rainy season is a bad time because the water level fluctuates and camping on the banks is unsafe.

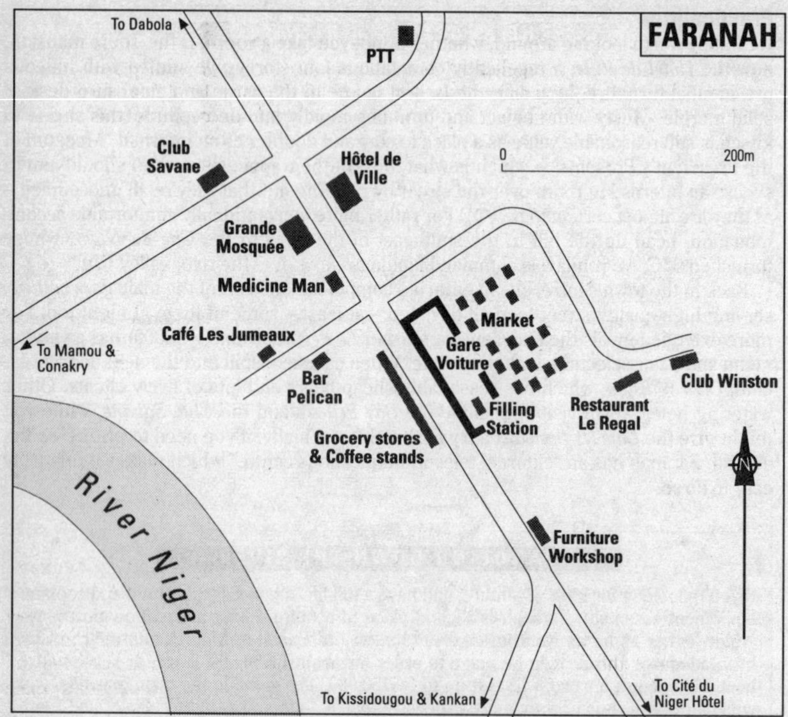

MOVING ON FROM FARANAH

Mamou- and Kissidougou-bound vehicles cluster at the main *gare voiture* below the market. It's easy to reach Conakry, Labé, Kankan or Nzérékoré in a day, though it's worth noting that the highway from Faranah to Kissidougou is in bad shape. The *gare voiture* for Dabola and Kouroussa is at the opposite end of town, its only landmark being a blue house.

Some 15km west of Faranah, a big sign on the left says "Direction Sierra Leone", and that's the way across the border to Kabala. Before the war in Sierra Leone became intense at the end of 1994, there was at least one vehicle to Kabala every Wednesday: as this book goes to print, however, there is no transport and you are strongly advised not to use the route.

Flights out of Faranah are operated by *Guinée Air Service* who fly to Conakry every Sunday.

Kissidougou

KISSIDOUGOU ("Kissi") is composed of three no longer easily distinguishable villages. **Kenéma Pompo** is the oldest, a Kissi village which goes back to the eighteenth century, when it was tucked in its sacred forest, the head of a small federation of Kissi settlements. The second, **Hérèmakono** (which means roughly "Home Sweet Home"), is the administrative and commercial district built away from

THE SOURCE OF THE NIGER

If you're curious about the **source of the Niger**, it's not difficult to get to, given a couple of days out of Kissidougou or Faranah. It rises at 9° 5' 0" North, 10° 47' 14" West, at an altitude of 74 metres. This puts it 93 metres north-northeast of a frontier marker post on the border between Guinea and Sierra Leone. First base is the village of **Bambaya**, northwest of Kissidougou, accessible up a rocky road, signposted "Kobikoro", off the Kissi–Faranah highway. USAID are improving the Kobikoro road, so it should be accessible by taxi before long. For the present only the toughest, high-clearance trucks – and the odd motorbike – can make it. There's a Friday market at Baleya, 3km from Bambaya. Second base is **Kobikoro**, 12km further up, where the *chef* and *sous-préfet* are both welcoming and you should leave your luggage if it's heavy. In theory you need the *sous-préfet* 's permission to visit the source. From there on the route gets tough for walkers and the scenery interesting as you head up to third base, **Forokonia**, 20km from Kobikoro. There are magnificent forest trees up here, though cutting is going on all over. Forokonia has a Thursday market. You need a guide (quite often this will be a soldier) on reaching Forokonia, to show you the actual source, a three- or four-hour walk. The source itself is not impressive but the surrounding scenery is beautiful.

The best chance of **a lift from Faranah or Kissidougou** is on a Thursday or Friday to Baleya market; or from Kissdougou on a Tuesday, when two trucks go to Forokonia's Thursday market, returning to Baleya on Thursday afternoon for the Friday market there.

the forest. And the third **Dioulabou** – the "Dyula town" established by Samory's vanquished lieutenants in 1893 – lies on the east side. Kissi Kaba Keita, the ruler of the town at the time of French penetration, put up a notional resistance. Today, this may seem just another fairly unremarkable town, but it borders the largest zone of forest in West Africa and the sense of transition is apparent in the patches of tropical woodland around the town. Kissidougou is also notable as the centre of Guinea's main coffee-growing area.

Spacious and unusually flat, the town isn't a bad place at all to be dumped after one of Upper Guinea's arduous taxi rides. A tiny **museum**, opposite the old police post, contains two or three dozen local objects of some interest, including a young elephant's and a repulsive hippo's skull – both bereft of their ivory – various bits of Kissi and Kouranko ethnographia and some contemporary domestic items. Fading black and white photos show meaningless scenes from French colonial days. The *gardien* may extract a small charge.

There's an interesting local visit you can make, to Kissidougou's **pont artisanal**, a liana bridge (well, not entirely lianas) about 2km east of the town centre off the road to Kankan. Take the second turning on the right after the roundabout and keep walking towards the water supply building, often to be seen emitting smoke.

Practicalities

Central options for a **place to stay** include the large, dingy and long-established *Le Kissi Hôtel*, which is frequented by prostitutes and truck drivers but is at least cheap enough for a basic non-S/C room (①). Cold beers, steaks, omelettes, chips and the like can normally be ordered. You can also stay at the *Bar Destin*, nearby (①). The best hotel in town is the *Hôtel de la Paix*, a few hundred metres round the road to the north, which offers decent S/C rooms and good food (②). Well out of Kissidougou on the Faranah road is the surprisingly good *Hôtel Savannah*, with well-appointed AC rooms and others with fans (③). Lastly – again if you have your own transport, or don't mind a walk – go and check out the quite fancy *Le Palmier*, nearly 2km from the centre on the Guéckédou road (③–④).

THE KISSI

The **Kissi** are the long-established indigenous people who live across the wide swathe of territory from the southern Niger headwaters to the foothills of the southeast highlands. Adroit farmers (it's their swamp rice which you'll see along the Kissidougou–Guéckédou road), they traditionally worship their ancestors, on whose benevolence they depend for the success of their crops, and maintain strong beliefs in witchcraft. Until recently, nearly all Kissi villages had their own witch-hunters (the *wulumo*) whose skills were called upon to divine the evil-minded whenever misfortune struck.

Kissi people still venerate small stone figures, each imbued with the spirit of an ancestor. These sculptures, usually in soapstone and called **pomdo** ("the dead"), are dug up in the fields, or found in the forest, but never carved today. The Kissi traditionally believe the sculptures are the physical essence of their ancestors, but their origin is an enigma. Like the *nomoli* of Sierra Leone (see p.564) they were certainly carved by an ancient culture, probably before the fifteenth century, but it's not certain that they were produced by the ancestors of the people who now revere them.

The daily, **covered market**, in the quarter behind the central silk-cotton tree, is worth exploration. You'll find a fair selection, at fair prices, of the kind of imported stuff (Sierra Leone country cloth, Malian blankets, printed *pagnes*) that's found in greater quantities at the international markets of Guéckédou, Nzérékoré and Kankan. Goods from Mali for example, often inflated in markets there, are offered at knock-down prices. If you want **music cassettes**, look out for Kissi's main cassette merchant, a lab called *Africa No. 2* on the Faranah road, with a veritable recording industry going on and a very wide choice. You can order special selections *en copie* and if prices are a little higher than usual, quality may be better too. You'll know you've missed it if you pass the **hospital** – a reassuring place to fall ill if the care lavished on the immaculate gardens extends to the patients. The **post office** and *BICIGUI* **bank** (☎81.02.86) face each other across the curve of the main street.

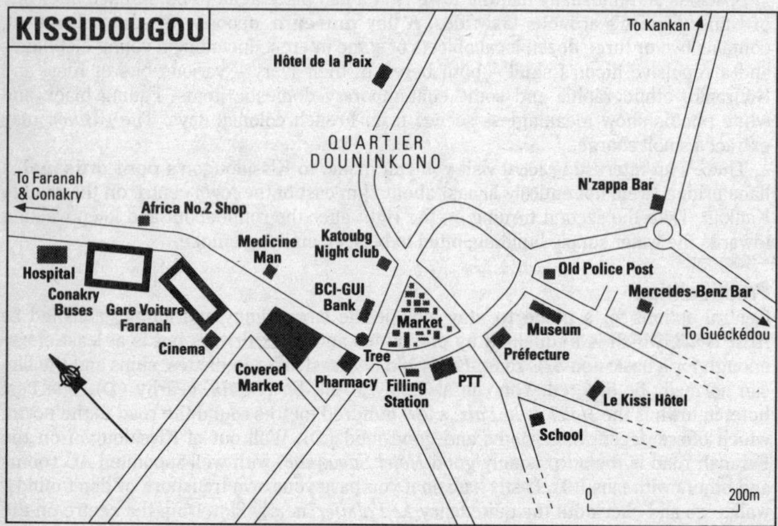

Strolling out on the Faranah road you'll find the largest selection of *gargotes* for street **food**. There are few proper restaurants in town – althought you could try the *Escale Cosmos* near the banks – but plenty of enjoyable **bars**: *N'Zappa*, at the Kankan/Guéckédou roundabout, *Bar Union* (on the Guéckédou road) and *Mercedes-Benz* (aka *Chez Madame Sow*), behind the *Kissi Hôtel* all have food as well as booze. There's a good number of **clubs**, too, including *Djamo*, on the Kankan road, *Africana*, close behind the *Kissi Hôtel*, and *Katouba* by the market, which has a twin in the courtyard of the *Hôtel Savannah*.

MOVING ON FROM KISSIDOUGOU

The road surface from Kissi to Faranah has badly deteriorated. Slightly better surfaced roads to Kankan and Guéckédou mean you should be able to make time on these journeys – though the latter sometimes snarls up at **Yende-Milimou** when the village beneath the giant granite mound (great views from the top of that) has its Thursday *lumo*. A scenic place to stop on the way to Kankan is **Tokounou**, crowded beneath a mountain escarpment. There's a hotel here, eating places and a balafon workshop, where you can buy the instruments and watch them being made.

The SOGETRAG **bus** should operate from Kissidougou back to Conakry on Sundays.

Flights from Kissidougou to Conakry are operated in theory daily by one or other of the domestic airlines with a fare of around FG45,000.

Kankan

Its name alone is enough to make you want to come here: **KANKAN** sounds remarkably exotic and, although the town is mostly very ordinary, the notion doesn't dissolve once you've arrived. There's a sense of place here, a depth of history that knocks spots off every other town in the country, making it by far the most alluring in Guinea.

Some history

The spell it casts arises largely from the fact that Kankan was originally a **Malinké town**, one of the oldest and probably the biggest in the Mande region. Kankan is, in fact, composed of a loose federation of villages which have grown into each other over time – a fact which goes some way to explaining its very laid-back and open atmosphere.

It was Muslim warrior-traders, the "Soninke", speaking Sarakolé (a northern Mande tongue from the upper Senegal), who are credited with the foundation of a mini-empire centred on Kankan. They arrived at the end of the seventeenth century and set themselves up in a dozen villages stretched out along the banks of the Milo River, including the embryonic – and at that time non-Muslim – Kankan. This trading empire, which was also a hub of Muslim propaganda under the rule of marabouts, was known as **Baté** (Baté Nafadj, 40km north of Kankan, is a reminder). Kankan grew to become its capital and by 1850 had been walled and was already sizeable: its fleets of *pirogues* were plying the Milo and Niger rivers as far as Gao in Mali. Caravans arrived from the Sahel and the desert. From the highland forests in the south, which it largely controlled, came kola nuts, palm oil and slaves. Another reason for Kankan's ascendancy was gold, from the Bure goldfields, which extended from north of Siguiri to far up the Milo.

Kankan's apogee didn't last long: Samory smashed the hegemony of the city in 1879 after a ten-month siege, and twelve years later the French were in occupation.

The Town

Kankan has a beguiling ambiance. Its generous plan and long, mango-shaded avenues cast a different light; a woman on a bicycle is a rare sight in most of West Africa, common enough here. There's a university and *lycées* and lots of students, two hospitals and a considerable, scholarly, Islamic presence. The presidential palace no longer has hippos in the swimming pool, but the building itself is still there and, just across the avenue, so is the fountain where crocodiles once disported themselves.

The **markets** are well worthwhile, for the traders at least as much as for the goods on offer. The covered *marché central* sells mostly clothes: a lot of trashy imports and "dead men's" but also brilliantly coloured local confections that look great but would require lots of guts to wear; plus myriad selections of *pagnes*, and items imported from Mali and Niger, mostly rugs and blankets. There are also a couple of stalls specializing in old bits of carving, *gri-gris*, amulets and mystical substances. If you're interested, by the way, in receiving some supernatural aid, then Kankan is the place to ask:

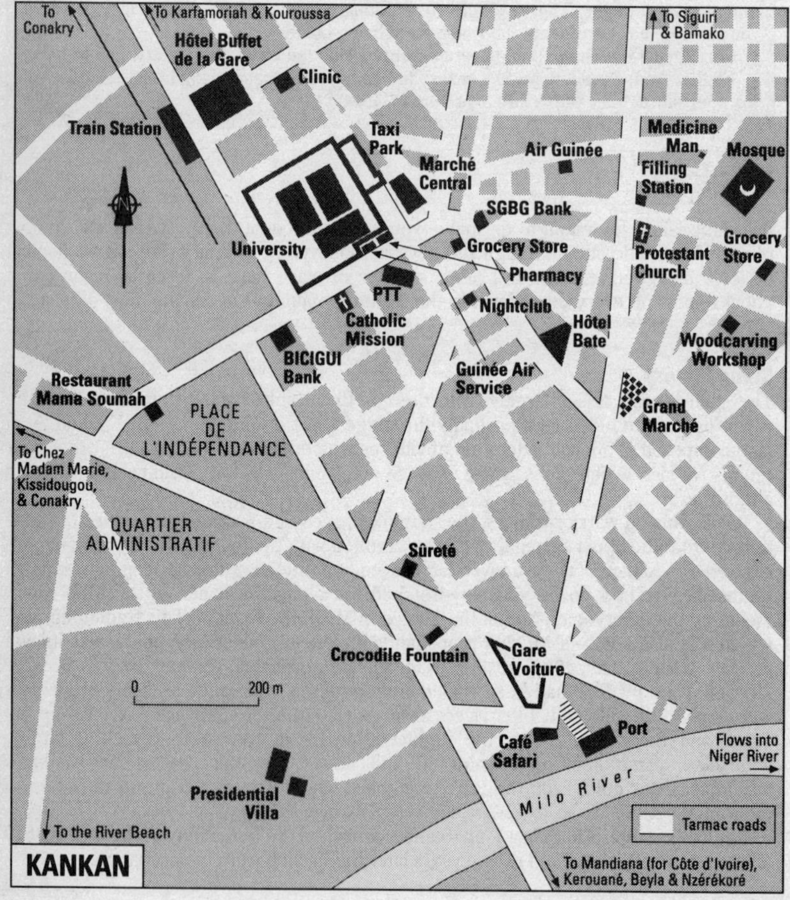

marabouts here are considered some of the most powerful in West Africa and inscriptions and potions can be obtained easily, for a fee – you don't have to be a Muslim.

The other, larger market sells mostly spices, vegetables and fruit. If you're in Kankan in the mango season (March to April) you're in for a real treat – the town is full of mango trees.

Practicalities

The main *gare voiture* is a shady patch of dust down by the river at the edge of town, but you may well find yourself dropped off at one of the minor taxi parks near the town's access roads.

Opposite the railway station, you'll find the dark and unappetizing hulk of the *Buffet de la Gare*. They have a lousy reputation here, bucket water and intermittent power, but it's clean and secure, and seems to be holding its own (②). The main budget-level competition is *Chez Madame Marie*, also known as *Le Refuge* (②) – an interesting guest house about a kilometre from the centre, off the Kissidougou road, roughly opposite the barracks and on the right as you come into town. It's not obvious, but ask and you'll find it; most people find the effort is worth it. The Madame in question is a Vietnamese lady who is something of a Kankan institution. The place is her home and while rooms around the courtyard aren't always available at first, patience will find you somewhere. Women travellers are warmly welcomed, though if your French isn't up to Mme Marie's conversation, you may not find your stay particularly relaxing. *Marie*'s has occasional discos – join in or move out – good meals (FG2000–4000; but order hours in advance) and wine and beer in the fridge. A large new hotel is apparently being built in Kankan, but for the moment, the *Hôtel Bate*, is the usual option for well-heeled tourists

MOVING ON FROM KANKAN

From the time when the rains have begun in earnest (usually mid- to late July) until about the end of November, you can, in theory, take a **steamer** out of Kankan, down to the confluence of the Milo with the Niger and on to Siguiri and Bamako. How much longer this will be possible depends on whether the water levels continue to drop as they have in recent years (down at the harbour you can see the remarkable effects of desertification – a new, lower landing has been built and a series of steps shows the progress of the drought).

If you're planning on travelling **by road** from **Kankan to Bamako** in one journey, be sure you know what you're paying for when you set off: many vehicles bound for "Bamako" turn out to be going as far as the border only, whence you're forced to pay for another ride to the capital. Kankan to Bamako should be FG28,000. A ride to the border only should cost slightly more than half this; a seat to Siguiri just under half. As this book goes to press, there is no car ferry across the Niger at Diélibakoro on the Kankan–Siguiri route. While large *pirogues* lashed together do carry some vehicles across, most Kankan taxis currently shuttle passengers as far as Diélibakoro only for around FG3000.

For **Côte d'Ivoire** there's a scheduled *RTACI* country bus service to Bouaké every Monday at 7am, arriving Tuesday night (about FG40,000). Ask at the *gare voiture* the day before – the bus should be in by early Sunday morning. If you're not going to Bouaké, you should find the *taxis brousse* that run the rough road to the border once or twice a week a better bet at FG10,000.

The SOGETRAG bus may still be operating a Tuesday service back to **Conakry**.

Flights are available from Kankan to Conakry, more or less daily, in theory, on one or other of the domestic air services. The fare is about FG50,000. There are also weekly flights on *Guinée Air Service* from Kankan to Nzérékoré (Fri) and Bamako (Sun).

and business travellers; it has a good restaurant and bar, and, although the S/C rooms aren't inexpensive (③), you get a decent place to stay for your money, and you may even be able to negotiate a deal on the rate.

There's a host of little **cafés and bars** around the centre – give *Mama Soumah*'s courtyard restaurant a try – and also a couple of thinly stocked **supermarkets** where you can splash out on luxuries like marmalade and soft toilet paper. **Breakfast** in Kankan, as if by some magic Malian influence, is delivered with a flourish.

The **PTT** which handles poste restante, is open Mon–Sat 7.30am–4pm; the *BICIGUI* **bank** is open 8.30am–12.30pm and 2–4pm (☎71.24.89); and there's a branch of *SGBG* as well.

Siguiri and Niani

At **SIGUIRI** you may find the remains of the **French post**, established in 1888 on the hilltop over the river, at the height of the campaign against Samory Touré. At independence, parts of the original defences were still standing around the administrative district of the town. A strong factor in Siguiri's favour lies in the presence of several decent **places to stay** if you're stopping over – *Hôtel Indépendance* (②) or, even better, *Hôtel Tamtam*, near the airstrip (②). If you need a **flight** to Conakry, one or other of the domestic air services supposedly operate connections on Monday, Wednesday, Friday and Saturday, often via Kankan (fare around FG50,000).

NIANI is a village on the Sankarani River (which forms the border with Mali), 80km on a very rough track southeast of Siguiri. It was here, as excavations among the baobabs have proved, that **Sundiata Keita**, the legendary founding king of the Mali Empire (aka, most probably, Mansa Mari-Djata, *c.* 1205–55), installed his capital. Sites of foundries and cemeteries are dotted around the town wall alignments. If you're motivated by this kind of historical charge – and more basically if you have your own transport, plenty of time and some imagination – it's unmissable.

Towards Nzérékoré: Kérouané, Beyla and Boola

Out of Kankan, Kérouané is the main town on the route southwards, which runs alongside the gaunt whaleback of the **Chaîne du Going** ridge and up into the remote and rugged region beyond Beyla.

This is a richly historical route. On the way down to Kérouané you pass by **Bissandougou**, the recruiting point and eventual capital of **Almamy Samory Touré**'s first empire; people in your vehicle will point it out to you. Whether the small cemetery with its *banco* wall surround is still there, is hard to tell, but the nineteenth-century fort has definitely returned to the soil.

Samory signed a treaty with the French at Bissandougou in 1887, hoping to keep them to the left bank of the Niger, but new French commanders swept the agreements aside and moved on Kankan and Bissandougou in 1890. Samory adopted scorched-earth tactics and retreated south, burning villages in his path. At Kérouané he had a fort constructed on the hilltop and from here his forces harassed the French while the holy warrior planned his next move. Samory was probably the most important indigenous figure of nineteenth-century West Africa: other fragments of his story (which ended with capture in Côte d'Ivoire and exile to Gabon where he died in 1900) can be found on p.307 and in the Côte d'Ivoire chapter.

Kérouané

Today, the small prefecture of **KÉROUANÉ** barely hints at its place in history. The remains (and very little remains) of the **Tata de Samory** fortress on a low hill are now the site of the "Villa" – the administrative quarter. Archaeologically the interest is thin: a huge block of laterite bricks – part of the massive old wall of the fort which measured 170 metres across – and what looks like a gate house – a hollow hut like a honey pot near the entrance. Alongside, on the new wall, there's a faded portrait of Samory. The French **conquest cemetery** – final resting place of a number of troops of the Third Republic – is hard to find; it may have succumbed after independence.

With table-top hills rising around and the steep, bluish ridge of Going soaring to over 1300m, it's a fine setting. Kérouané is surprisingly lively and, although the attractions are hard to pinpoint, it does have appeal. Because of the transport situation, you may well be **staying** a night here, at the so-called *caravanserai* or *chambres de passage*: at one time a rather cute little *gîte* called *La Chaumière* with open-air restaurant and courtyard, it's now a primitive and dingy night stop, with terrible security (①). There's an outside toilet and shower (watch the world go by as you scrub off the dust); staff will warm water only on request.

For **meals and food**, there's a large market and some good rice and sauce in the street leading away from the police station. Nice *café fort* and *thé vert* can be had at a couple of licensed cafés up here on the left, with pleasant patios to loaf and meet people. From here, through the dry season, you can watch the progress of bush fires on Mont Going – a sombre spectacle on December and January nights as giant orange tongues leap from its flanks.

After dark, try *Djigbe's Night Club*, where special dancing *soirées* on Wednesday and Saturday bring in a fair crowd, or one of the several video clubs.

MOVING ON FROM KÉROUANÉ

There's normally a truck or two out of Kérouané to **Nzérékoré** early each morning – and perhaps something a great deal more comfortable if you make eager enquiries. Open-back lorries, as long as they're loaded, aren't the worst travelling, but on this voyage it's important to have **warm clothes** and anticipate a very slow trip – fifteen to twenty hours – and late arrival.

THE DIAMOND ROUTE

From **Konsankoro**, there's a highly rated hundred-kilometre track over the ranges to Macenta through rarely visited diamond-mining country. You could wait a long time for a ride, but there's usually a vehicle out of Kérouané on Thursday. It's reputedly a beautiful route – massive granite sugarloaf mountains and mesas pushing from the bush – which later enters the forest.

Beyla and Boola

From Kérouané the route south winds up over a col and into **BEYLA**, a town favoured by the French and subject of all sorts of brief colonial enthusiasms in the 1950s – "the best climate in French West Africa with 230 sunny days each year and moderate temperatures". Beyla's expatriate residents were particularly proud of their church – "adapted for the climate, it is a very good example of modern architecture with quite remarkable siting and decoration". To read colonial accounts you'd never know that Beyla was founded in the thirteenth century by Mande-speaking kola traders. If you've a tough vehicle of your own, the Beyla region is unquestionably one of Guinea's most worthwhile – a number of tracks run through the Kourandou mountains, just northeast of town. For **accommodation**, the grubby *Hôtel Simadou* is about your only option (①).

If you're heading **from Beyla to Côte d'Ivoire**, make for **Sinko** on a Friday – its market day – and stay at the *Soumanso* (①) or the preferable *Hôtel du Nord* (①). Early Saturday is about the only day to find transport onwards for the long, rough journey to Odienné, the big town over the border.

South of Beyla the road roughens considerably. **BOOLA** lies at the foot of a bosky mountain and seems to be a regular truck stop with lots of street food. The route on to Nzérékoré passes patches of thickening forest and numerous streams – a couple of hours by car, four or five by goods lorry.

THE SOUTHEAST HIGHLANDS

The highland chains of the southeast, piling into the fractured border region where Guinea meets Sierra Leone, Liberia and Côte d'Ivoire, provide inducements to match the Fouta Djalon. Against their absence of towering cliffs and waterfalls, and their generally lower altitudes, the highlands of **Guinée forestière** – the common name – weigh in with **ridges** still partly covered by evergreen **rainforest**, **routes** which are just as tough as the Fouta's – and remarkably muddy outside the dry seasons – and a largely non-Islamic ethnic configuration.

Climatically this is perhaps the most appealing part of the country, even if travel can be stubbornly difficult between April and November. Altitude and clouds keep it mild or warm most of the year, and while the rains are torrential, storms are accompanied by impressive electrical phenomena. There also tends to be a drier spell in the rainy season, between the end of April and mid-June. The forest harbours significant numbers of **wild animals**, if you've the energy and resources to go looking; chimpanzees, leopards, forest elephant and buffalo, and hippos and crocs in the rivers.

Sadly the pleasures of being in the region are overshadowed by the all too obvious effects of the civil wars in Liberia and Sierra Leone on a large proportion of the people here – the half million or so, often English-speaking, **refugees** who have fled the fighting. In the Guinea highlands, they scrape together a precarious, semi-nomadic existence against the confusing and terrifying background of murder, reprisal and social disintegration in their homelands. Guinea has so far absorbed the shock with little protest on the international scene. The refugees' arrival is broadly tolerated and there have been relatively few violent incidents as a result of the turmoil. But you should be aware of the potential dangers as you travel in this region and alert to any news on the grapevine.

The cultural background

Ethnically, this is singular territory. The region's predominant **Kissi**, **Toma** and **Guerzé** inhabitants are linguistically diverse and resolutely independent. Ancestor worship, totemism and *forêts sacrés* ("sacred forests": usually a clearing within the forest where ritual is performed) are all important cultural elements. Islamic influences are far less pronounced than elsewhere and the stamp of colonialism was lightly impressed. Colonial subjugation – a gruelling village-by-village war of invasion – wasn't complete until 1920, having persisted bloodily since Samory's demise in 1898.

Most of the **towns** in the forest region are recent creations, dating back no further than the first French post at a suitable source of food, water and labour. Once victorious, the French maintained a thin and rather miserable presence. During the reign of Sekou Touré, many Guineans sought refuge in the relatively unpoliticized highlands, and tens of thousands more fled the country from here, especially to Côte d'Ivoire.

Guéckédou

Large but somewhat ignored, **GUÉCKÉDOU** sprawls between jungle-tufted hills. A short walk from the Liberian border and only slightly further from Sierra Leone, this proximity provides most of the town's livelihood and ninety percent of its character. The vast **market** which floods the town every Wednesday is famous throughout Guinea, as the biggest in the country and one of West Africa's great commercial exchanges.

Main participants in the sales jamboree spilling along every street are Guineans, Sierra Leoneans, Liberians and Ivoirians, but you'll come across Malians, Senegalese and Gambians as well as a few Mauritanians. It's not surprising – but still a disappointment – to find how little of the merchandise is in any way traditional or locally made. Apart from the agricultural produce and some domestic ware, most of the rest consists of cheap imports – Philippino clothing, Taiwanese toys, Korean radios, Greek cigarettes, Japanese cloth and Chinese tools. Despite the throng, hustlers and thieves seem uncommon, though ordinary tricksters, like the card shark with his *cherchez la dame*, clean up.

For a **view** of the townscape – which at times of clear visibility is quite attractive – head up to a vantage point near the hilltop mosque, by crossing the Boya River on the Kissidougou road at the edge of town.

Down on the north bank of the Moa (Makona) River, whose left – south – bank forms the frontier, the **Plage de Keno** is an attractive beach with safe swimming (at least in terms of bilharzia – security is another matter so talk to people before going).

Practicalities

The best day to visit Guéckédou for the market is Wednesday, but if you can manage it, go ahead of the crowds and find a room on Monday or, possibly, Tuesday morning. There are several likely **lodgings**: the *Stadium Hotel*, near the bamboo-walled football ground on the road leading out to Kissidougou (①–②); the *Terminus* (①–②) on the same road; and the marginally preferable *Escale de Makona* (in the same quarter Sandia, but more central, behind some prefectural offices), which has a few S/C rooms (②) and a terrace where you can flop out with a cold beer. There's also a more upmarket hotel, the *Hibiscus* (②), with a good restaurant. The best place of the lot, albeit a little out of town, is the clean *Hôtel Mafissa* (①), on the hillside overlooking Guéckédou near the road to Sierra Leone.

The town is full of **food**. Try the coffee house at the lorry park – good *café au lait* and *espresso* and excellent evening meals of steak, salad and potatoes. In the same vicinity you may still find a couple of excellent, cheap **cassette** booths. Guéckédou has a **post office** but no *BICIGUI* bank (the new *BICIC* bank is invariably closed): on market days you're likely to find *commerçants* willing to change money, but the nearest *BICIGUI* banks are at Nzérékoré and Kissidougou.

MOVING ON FROM GUECKEDOU

The easiest way into Sierra Leone from here is via **Nongoa**, from where *pirogues* large enough to carry motorbikes or bicycles ply the Moa River. This border closes at dusk. Cars and trucks have to go either via **Foya** in Liberia, or – an altogether easier crossing – from Macenta to **Voinjama**. Because of civil war in both countries, none of these crossings is advisable at the time of writing.

SOGETRAG **buses** may still be operating a Thursday and Saturday service back to Conakry.

Via Macenta to Nzérékoré

The route southeast from Guéckédou to Nzérékoré is a rough and exciting, though expensive fare. The orange ribbon of the road buckles and falters for much of the way, and sometimes tunnels through towering green **jungle**.

Over the years parts of the road have been improved, but the latest development is a new, tarred **highway** being raised through the felled forest to link Guéckédou with Nzérékoré in three or four hours instead of the current eight to twenty. The project – slashing through the jungle, cutting villages and, bizarrely, houses in half, bulldozing massive earthworks to canopy level – is pursued by the rains which destroy so much of the foundations each year. By 1995 they had reached Sérédou. When it's completed the voyage through the forest will have lost most of its romance.

Up to Macenta

Once out of Guéckédou, the serious forest starts with the climb on the new road from the bridge over the Makona, just beyond **Bofosso** – a large village and military post dating back to 1905. It's a steep haul up what's known, somewhat mysteriously, as the *descente des cochons*. Whether pigs or nefarious humans are being referred to, you do indeed begin to see small hairy swine poking around at the roadside – signs of a strong non-Muslim presence.

Around 44km from Guéckédou the new tarmac road passes through **Niagézazou**, tucked in the forest near a **liana bridge** over the Makona. Then, some 5km beyond the road bridge over the Makona River, you might check out the village of **Niogbozou** up a sidetrack shortly after the old mission centre of Balouma. Niogbozou, built on a rocky platform and apparently encircled with lianas, used to have a famous troupe of acrobats, dancers and stilt walkers who toured Europe several times before independence.

Passing from Kissi country into the lands of the Toma you arrive in **MACENTA**. This used to be the most important town in the highlands, chosen for its central position as a supply base for the "pacification columns" sent to the remote areas. Free

THE TOMA

The oldest inhabitants of the Macenta district, the **Toma**, earned respect from the French "pacification" troops for their resilience against raid upon raid on their isolated villages. Of all the highland peoples, it was the Toma who most harried the French invaders. Their last stronghold, the fortified village of Boussedou, was attacked by two French expeditions and numerous cannon before it finally succumbed in 1907.

Once battered into submission, the Toma found favour with the French for being good scouts and solid soldiers, utterly at home in the forest. They're fairly small people and they may have distant pygmy ancestors: oral history in the forest regions recounts stories of ancient inhabitants of small stature who were decimated by the taller invaders from the north. What's certain is that the Toma lost ground to the Malinké and ultimately mixed with Dyula Malinké to form the Toma-Manian. Today, their language – Loma – is a Mande tongue, related to Malinké.

You should look out for highly impressive **dancing** while you're in the Toma region; but you'll be lucky indeed to have the opportunity to witness one of the major **life-cycle celebrations**. Traditionally at circumcisions, female mutilations, marriages, births and funerals, "bird men" – the *onilégagi* – danced, dressed in feathers and painted with kaolin; *lanebogué* pranced and hopped on their stilts; and *akorogi* swirled and bounded in their raffia-leaf costumes and haunted masks. Similar dances take place in Côte d'Ivoire, but generally with your attendance and money in mind.

Liberian troops attacked Macenta in 1906 but were fended off: it was only in 1908 that the limits of the two territories were set. The French tried to grow tea in Macenta, not very successfully. They had much more luck with **coffee**, which remains important, though much of the crop is smuggled out of the country. The biggest indigenous cash crop is **kola**.

Today, Macenta is only a moderate-sized place and is quite dwarfed by Guéckédou and Nzérékoré. It's a pleasing town, set amid a tumble of hills with fine views all around, and still composed of hundreds of thatched, round house compounds. If you find yourself **staying** in town, there's a lovely *villa* (①), or try the *Palm Hôtel* in the centre (running water but no electricity; ②), or the *Hôtel Sapin* on the south side of town towards Nzérékoré (②). There are several decent eateries and a recent branch of the *BICIGUI* bank (☎91.06.28).

Out of Macenta through the Malinké quarter, commences a wild and wonderful **route to Kérouané** and, ultimately, Kankan. For several years it's been virtually impassable, but this needn't necessarily stop you trying with your own vehicle, or pestering drivers at the *gare voiture* in Macenta for information about transport – or just setting off in comfortable shoes with three days' supplies on your back (see box, p.521).

Through the forest to Nzérékoré

As you burrow through the jungle and over the ridges, there's a string of minor but interesting stop-offs if you have your own transport. Unfortunately, unless you pull off a ride with a very sympathetic driver, most of you won't catch these by truck or Peugeot.

One place where trucks and Peugeots often stop to stock up on palm wine or food, is **Sérédou**. At 800m it straddles a col through the moist, jungly Ziama hills and most vehicles need the rest. This is also where, at the time of writing, the tarmac from Guéckédou ends. Church bells are heard ringing here: it's an old mission and quinine research station.

The stretch of road from Sérédou to Irié is renowned for its lepidoptera, including the giant swallowtail *Papillio antimachus*, Africa's largest **butterfly**, with a wingspan of up to 23cm. The males are occasionally seen around the treetops and, very rarely, sipping moisture at muddy puddles; female giant swallowtails, however, are elusive in the extreme.

Irié itself isn't much, but the side road that heads off southwest from here 100km to the border takes you to **Koyama**, the biggest kola market in Guinea and the frontier town for **Zorzor** in Liberia.

Nzébéla is a traditional music centre, though whether you've much chance of hearing *divogi* drums and *pouvogi* trumpets it's hard to tell. Immediately down the road, however, if you can just stop awhile at the ferry across the Diani, there's a really enormous *pont de lianes* – a **liana bridge** – some 70m long. During the dry season, local men spend a lot of time mending this construction – when it was the only means of crossing, repairing it was a focal event of the year. The bridge retains a grudging mystery: women are not allowed to witness the repairs (once even cows were banned) but the dramatic dusk-to-dawn communal effort that used to see the bridge serviceable after one night's work (thus proving the industry of the forest spirits) has been replaced with a slower and more alcoholic routine which takes some days. You'll have to make a generous contribution to the bridge fund if you want to take photos at this time.

Shortly after the village of **Samoé**, a path leads left to a small hamlet where a group of sacred tortoises are kept by the community. Different groups of people throughout the forest region identify with a wide range of animals; the tortoise is a simple and popular totem. If you can't find them, you could try asking the White Fathers in Samoé.

Nzérékoré

With a very large Wednesday market and an atmosphere of thriving commerce, **NZÉRÉKORÉ** is the big town of Guinée forestière. Set amid the forest and traced through by tributary streams which feed the Mani river border with Liberia, the town's shack-lined dirt streets straggle stylelessly over hillocky ground. Yet for a backwoods agglomeration with no discernible centre, so far from anywhere (it's closer to Monrovia and even Abidjan than to Conakry) and so dependent on smuggling as a way of life, Nzérékoré is really rather an enjoyable place to be, making a good-natured exit or entrance to Guinea. Despite its size there's a more open, less cluttered feel than in Guéckédou – though there are lots of UN diplomats and NGO officials here now, involved in trying to control the refugees crises from neighbouring Sierra Leone and Liberia.

Nzérékoré just has to be visited on **market day**; in which case it's a tough choice between here and Guéckédou. From the permanent market, stalls overflow onto the main street and the activity stretches from the hospital to the roundabout. Liberians and Ivoirians are prominent; women show off their best wraps and the atmosphere vibrates with the racket of trade – everything from multifarious qualities of palm oil and a riot of local produce to clothes (some cotton shirt bargains), Liberian plastic trinkets, prints and indigo *gara*. Crafts, unless you count fabrics, are fewer, but there are good lines in leather sandals, wallets and some beautifully worked and relatively inexpensive silver. And of course you can add to your cassette collection. Lastly, and by no means unique to Nzérékoré, but unmissable if you've not seen them before, are the traditional pharmacists who set up on market day with a festoon of graphic boards, illustrating their range of treatments for complaints ranging from worms to impotence.

Practicalities

Much of the impression of the town depends on where you find **lodgings**. The best-value places to stay, on the road out to Yomou, are usually full. The first, the *Bakuli Annexe* (①–②), is a popular truck drivers' haunt run by a Vietnamese lady, with all the noise and distractions you'd expect. The second – *Bar Hanoi* – is further out, but more recommendable: it's clean, safe, with both well and generator, and again run by a Vietnamese, Madame Moe (②). Call in early to see if there's space: at the last check all rooms were rented out indefinitely to Liberian refugees. If you arrive late in the town centre, the police should help out. Otherwise, out of town on the Guéckédou road, try

SOME LOCAL HISTORY

The people of the Nzérékoré district and eastwards are **Kpelle** or **Guerzé** – related by language and some cultural elements to the Toma, and distantly to the other Mande-speaking ethnic groups. They are profoundly animist by tradition and rather resistant to Islamic influence; their mythic ancestor descended from the sky, married a local woman and settled east of Nzérékoré. Tradition relates that a man called Yegu, with a number of followers, populated the Nzérékoré district late in the nineteenth century, and these headmen were the ones in power at the time of the French arrival. It's hard to unravel the veracity of stories like these – they can easily be read as apologetics for subsequent French actions – but it seems more likely that the Guerzé had been around for rather longer than the French wanted to believe, and that colonial chiefs were not often pre-invasion notables.

There's no doubt about the Guerzé revolt in 1911 – abetted by free Guerzé forces from Liberia – which was put down by a Captain Hecquet. His life was abruptly ended during the campaign by a poisoned arrow.

the *Hôtel Orly*, a quiet, bucket-shower sort of place (①); the livelier *Case Idéale* (②) with a *bar-resto* and **dancing**; and the *Resto le Carrefour*, which is a wonderful place to have a French meal with all the trimmings for around FG7000. They also run a shop which sells imported goods, including foreign newspapers. A fair number of other **eating houses** are scattered around town. It's worth mentioning *Gargote Chez Mohammed Djouldé Baldé* at the Yomou *gare voiture* in the Quartier Goniah, where the *patron* puts together wonderful avocado salads with inimitable style.

The *BICIGUI* **bank** is open Mon–Fri 8.30am–12.30pm and 2.30–4pm, and provides efficient service (☎91.06.07). The **PTT**, opens Mon–Sat 8am–4pm.

MOVING ON FROM NZÉRÉKORÉ

The main route out of Guinea from Nzérékoré is east via **Lola** and the foot of the Monts Nimba to the Côte d'Ivoire border and **Danané**. Make an early start or you'll get stuck in Lola (excellent Monday market and several hotels). Note that the traffic through Nzérékoré comes close to a standstill on Wednesday, though there's no shortage of transport onwards after market day.

Assuming peace prevails when you're in the area, there are several **routes to Liberia**. You can go southwest towards Yomou and turn off for Diécké and Ganta on the border. East of Nzérékoré you can make a right turn on the reasonably fast Lola road, 6km out of Nzérékoré (signposted), which a number of taxis use to Yekepa and Sanniquellie; and there's a third option – the track from Bossou to Yekepa.

Flights to Conakry (in theory) include *Guinea Air Service* on Mon & Wed via Kissidougou and on Fri via Kankan; *Guinea Inter Air* on Tues and Sun; and *Air Guinée* on Mon and Thurs. The fare to Conakry is about FG61,000. *Guinée Air Service* also advertises flights to Monrovia on Mon and Wed.

The Monts Nimba and around

East of Nzérékoré, the scenery along the way is nothing special until you reach **Nzo**, from where you start to get good views of the **Monts Nimba** – the highest peak of which, at 1752m, is Guinea's highest point. The road tunnels through impressive thickets of **giant bamboo** and tracks over precarious wooden bridges in the forest.

If you have time, or your own transport, you might be interested in visiting the village of **Bossou** (turn right 5km east of Lola at Gogota, then continue 15km south), where "sacred chimpanzees" are under research by Japanese and Guinean primatologists. Ask around in Lola if you'd like to visit.

Lola is also the place to get permission to visit the Monts Nimba Reserve, which you should be able to get without much hassle from the *préfecture*. The reserve entrance is at **Gbakoré**, some 15km from Lola on the way to Côte d'Ivoire, where your *permis* is stamped by the *chef du village*. There's a **research project** based halfway up, between the reserve entrance and the peaks area, that can sometimes offer transport from Gbakoré, but if you don't find any vehicles, you may have to hike there (a two-hour walk). You can sleep at the research station (small apartment with kitchen; ②). From here, the ridge formed by the Monts Nimba peaks – all above 1600m, which is above the tree line – can be reached in a further two hours. There are some fine views from up here on a clear day. The summit, straddling the Ivoirian border 8km to the south, is a further two- to three-hour hike.

index

CHAPTER EIGHT

SIERRA LEONE

SIERRA LEONE

Sierra Leone is on the brink of collapse. The young officers who threw out the corrupt regime of Joseph Momoh in April 1992 have been unable to bring the war with rebels in the east to a conclusion. It has spread to every region and devastated most of the country, as village after village and town after town have been attacked, terrorized and looted. The economy, dependent on the export of cocoa, coffee, palm products, titanium ore and diamonds, has virtually come to a standstill with the abandonment of the harvest and the closure of mines. Foreign development assistance has ceased. Overseas aid organizations such as Peace Corps, VSO and Action Aid, have quit the country under threat of murder and kidnap. And 30,000 of the 38,000-strong Lebanese community – the mainstay of the retail sector – have emigrated to Beirut or pastures new.

If the war comes to an end, Sierra Leone is worth going out of your way to visit. Some of West Africa's best **beaches** are tucked along the mountain-flanked Freetown peninsula coast. Based on their appeal, a small tourist industry, with a clutch of reasonably good hotels primarily patronized by French holiday-makers, had been established by 1992 – and has now faded. Like the British colonials, the winter vacationers extended their interests little beyond the peninsula, leaving the interior of the country ripe for exploration by adventurous travellers. **Outamba-Kilimi National Park** in the north, **Tiwai Island Nature Reserve** in the south, and some unusually high hills and mountains in the east (including the almost spectacular **Mount Bintumani**) were all worthy goals, while along the remote southern coast, beyond Freetown, the **beaches and islands** beat even the peninsula's lotus-eating shores.

For now, all such possibilities are on hold. While Freetown itself has so far been safe, **rebel attacks** have occurred in nearly every other part of the country, and have reached right to the peninsula, where there's a justified fear that if the rebels capture Lungi airport, the capital would be cut off from the outside world. In Freetown, hotels, restaurants and other services continue to function, after a fashion; embassies and high commissions remain open; and external telecommunications work reasonably well. But nobody leaves the town limits any longer: public transport up-country has ceased and all travel is in military convoy, with the strong likelihood of attack. Consequently, visiting the besieged or overrun up-country towns – **Makeni** and **Kabala** in the north, **Bo** in the south, and **Kenema** and **Koidu** in the east – is out of the question.

FACTS AND FIGURES

Sierra Leone's **area**, about 72,000 square kilometres, is a little smaller than Scotland or Maine. The **population** is approaching five million, which gives it quite a high density. The **name** "Sierra Leone" (*Salon* in Krio, pronounced "Salone") has various etymologies. The idea that the first Portuguese visitors were referring to the Freetown peninsula as "Lion-like Mountain", when they called the country *Serra Leão*, seems unlikely, as nothing in the topography resembles the shape of a lion, and suggestions to do with the sound of roaring surf seem equally fanciful. The possibility that the area swarmed with lions in the fifteenth century is the most likely. Sierra Leone's **foreign debt** is around £870 million ($1.4 billion), more than *eight times* the insignificant sum earned from the export of goods and services in 1994–95. The country is currently ruled by a military-civilian junta – the **National Provisional Ruling Council**, led by **Captain Valentine Strasser** – which is waging a civil war with the **Revolutionary United Front** of **Foday Sankoh**.

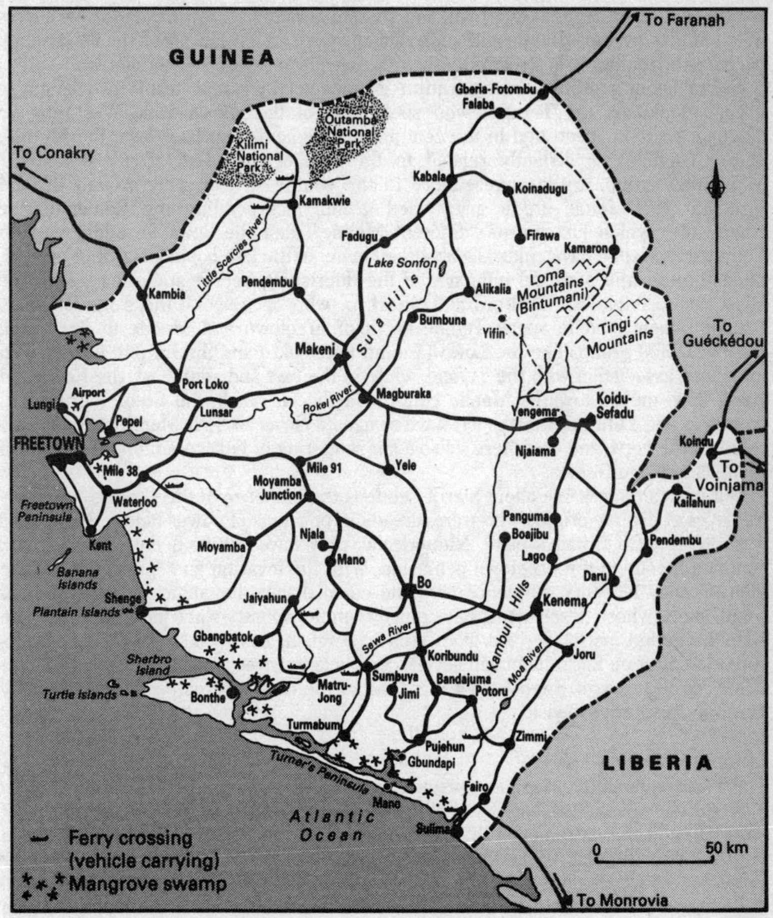

This chapter does not constitute a recommendation to visit Sierra Leone (Britain and a number of other countries advise against it), but it assumes you are there anyway. Some background coverage of the interior is included in this chapter, for use in the event of the country's return to stability during the lifetime of this edition. But practical information outside Freetown has been rendered obsolete by the trashing of the infrastructure since the beginning of 1994.

Geography and people

Geographically, Sierra Leone is surprisingly diverse. A steep indented coast at Freetown, and shallow sand banks and mangrove swamps elsewhere, are backed by tidal creeks that penetrate far inland and make a mess of the road system in the south and west. Further up-country, the land rises through dense forest (most of it now cleared) to rolling savannah hills, rocky outcrops and mountains. The remaining patches of **rainforest**, mostly in the far southeast, beyond the Moa River, are nowadays islands in a sea of secondary growth and shifting agriculture. **Swamp rice** now covers much of the lowlands. But despite high rainfall, there are critical problems for farming, because the multitude of streams on the ridges leads to severe soil erosion.

Sierra Leone's **ethnic configuration** is unusual. In simple terms two language groups dominate: the **Temne**, who speak one of the idiosyncratic West Atlantic languages, are concentrated in the central north, inland from Freetown; the **Mende**, whose language is distantly related to the rest of the great Mande (Malinke/Mandinka) group, are strongest more to the southeast, especially around Bo and Kenema. The Mende are a many-sided group, incorporating the Komende, the Gbamende (which just means "different Mende") and the Sewa. In addition, both Temne and Mende have culturally absorbed many of the less populous groups around, often through the powerful influence of the flourishing **secret societies**. Along the coast, for example, the **Bullom** and **Sherbro**, who once spoke the same language (Bullom), now tend to speak Temne north of Freetown and Mende to the south. Smaller inland groups like the **Loko** (around Port Loko) and the **Limba**, have moved into close association with the Temne, while in the east and southeast, the **Kono** and **Kissi** have moved towards Mende culture. In the far north, the **Susu** (northwest), **Koranko** and **Yalunka** (northeast) have remained closer to their Mande (with an "a") roots. In the north and east there's also a fair scattering of Fula communities – many of them exiles from Guinea.

But what's remarkable about Sierra Leone is the influence of the Creoles – **Krios** – ex-slaves of diverse origins who were already in positions of power before the interior was carved onto Britain's plate. Numerically, they have always been a small group, confined mostly to the Freetown peninsula. With the invasion and "protection" of the interior, they lost their influence with the colonial government to British-appointed tribal chiefs, whose descendants have mostly run the country since independence. The **Krio language**, partly derived from archaic English, has made a lasting and widespread imprint on Sierra Leonean society, and is largely responsible for making Sierra Leone, to the ears of English speakers, one of the most interactive and absorbingly humorous countries to visit.

Climate

There are dominating climatic constraints on travel in Sierra Leone. From **May to November**, most of the country gets heavy and prolonged **monsoon rain** on most days. Only in the extreme south, around Sulima, is there a short break in the rains during July or August. While temperatures aren't extremely high, humidity is usually excessive, above all along the coast. The lowest night-time temperature ever recorded in Freetown (19°C) is actually the *highest* record minimum temperature for any African country – indication of Freetown's altogether very uncomfortable climate much of the year.

The risk of visiting in May or November is repaid, if you're lucky, with brilliant collages of green, wonderful skies and tolerable road conditions; but between these months, travel off the hard-surfaced routes varies from slow and gruelling to impossible. And the beaches never dry out sufficiently to be much fun.

In the **dry season**, a *Harmattan* wind from the northeast can bring slightly cooler, dusty weather even to the coast. It's very difficult to predict clear blue skies and good visibility.

AVERAGE TEMPERATURES AND RAINFALL

FREETOWN

	Jan	Feb	Mar	Apr	May	June	July	Aug	Sept	Oct	Nov	Dec
Temperatures °C												
Min (night)	24	24	25	25	25	24	23	23	23	23	24	24
Max (day)	29	30	30	31	30	30	32	31	32	29	29	29
Rainfall mm	13	3	13	56	160	302	894	902	610	310	132	41
Days with rainfall	1	1	2	6	15	23	27	28	25	23	12	4

BO

	Jan	Feb	Mar	Apr	May	June	July	Aug	Sept	Oct	Nov	Dec
Temperatures °C												
Min (night)	20	21	21	22	22	21	21	21	21	21	21	20
Max (day)	32	34	35	34	32	31	28	28	30	31	31	31
Rainfall mm	8	16	76	130	252	368	406	536	419	325	170	38

SEFADU

	Jan	Feb	Mar	Apr	May	June	July	Aug	Sept	Oct	Nov	Dec
Temperatures °C												
Min (night)	14	17	19	20	21	20	20	20	20	20	19	17
Max (day)	32	34	35	34	33	31	29	29	31	32	31	31
Rainfall mm	10	20	96	160	228	282	269	411	401	292	145	41

The details in these practical information pages are essentially for use on the ground in West Africa and in Sierra Leone itself: for full practical coverage on preparing for a trip, getting here from outside the region, paperwork, health, information sources and more, see *Basics*.

Arrivals

Currently, and for several years now, practically all visitors arrive in Sierra Leone by air. The fast sea link with Conakry has been discontinued. All land border crossings are dangerous or inconvenient – or both.

Overland travel between Liberia and Sierra Leone has been out of the question since 1990. The summary (below) of details for travel from Guinea is retained in the hope of a return to better times permitting the routes to be used.

■ Flights from Africa

The couple of dozen flights each week into Freetown from West African cities (the only other flights come from outside the continent) arrive at **Lungi International airport**, across the Sierra Leone River estuary from the capital (see the "Getting into Freetown" section). Allow plenty of time to get into the city.

The west coast routes of *Ghana Airways* (GH) keep several of the coastal capitals connected to Freetown – from **Accra** non-stop on Sat; from Accra via **Abidjan** on Mon, Wed and Sat; from **Gran Canaria** via **Banjul** and **Conakry** on Thurs; from **Dakar** via Banjul on Tues; and from Dakar via Banjul and Conakry on Sun.

Middle East Airlines (ME) flies to Freetown every alternate Sun from Beirut, via **Lagos** and **Accra**.

Gambia Airways (CK) flies down non-stop from **Banjul** every Mon, Wed and Sat.

Sierra National Airlines (LJ) flies, in theory, non-stop from **Lagos** on Fri and via **Accra** on Tues.

And lastly, *Air Guinée* (GI) flies to Freetown from **Accra** via **Abidjan** on Thurs; non-stop from **Conakry** on Tues, Thurs and Fri; and non-stop from **Monrovia**'s temporary Spriggs-Payne airport on Tues and Fri.

■ Overland routes from Guinea

From Guinea the principal overland route connects Conakry with Freetown, on a mostly tarred road via Pamelap, the new bridge over the Great Scarcies River and **Kambia**. By private vehicle, assuming no border delays, this route is about a seven- to eight-hour drive. By public transport, usually involving a change of vehicle at the Guinean side, followed by bus or *poda poda*, it's a long day's journey into night.

Less-trodden routes into Sierra Leone include the track off the Conakry–Mamou road east of Kindia, to Madina-Oula for access to the **Outamba-Kilimi National Park** and Kamakwie; the canoe crossing from Nongoa to **Koindu wharf** in the far east (not a motor vehicle route, though small motorbikes can be carried); and the very little-used route from Faranah to **Falaba** in the northeast (there's a good chance you'll have to walk the ten no-man's-land kilometres in the middle).

Red Tape

Visas are required by all nationalities except for ECOWAS (Economic Community of West African States) nationals. Most countries which have a travel advisory service are currently advising against visiting Sierra Leone. You should register with your embassy on arrival. If your country appears to have no representation, check, before travelling, which embassy is looking after your national interests in Sierra Leone.

Visa charges vary on a seemingly tit-for-tat basis: nationals of countries which charge Sierra Leoneans a high visa fee (such as the UK) are charged a high rate; nationals of countries which make no charge to visiting Sierra Leoneans (such as Australia and New Zealand) are entitled to receive visas free of charge. Americans who obtain a visa in the USA get it free.

The **validity** of visas varies, but stays of longer than a month are rarely granted in advance, though you can extend your stay at the immigration office in Freetown.

In West Africa, Sierra Leone has embassies, high commissions, or representatives in **Dakar** (consular representative), **Banjul**, **Conakry**, **Accra** and **Lagos**. The status of Sierra Leonean representation at British embassies and high commissions is unclear.

Once you're in Sierra Leone, you can obtain visas in Freetown for all West African countries except Guinea-Bissau, Benin and Cameroon. There are no North African consulates.

Money and Costs

Sierra Leone's currency, devised in 1964, is called the *leone* (Le). Like the Ghanaian *cedi*, it was introduced on par with the British pound sterling at a rate of Le2 = £1 (prices are often still given in "pounds", worth two leones each), but after 1978, the link was broken. By 1990 the rate of exchange was down to Le300 = £1 and by late 1995 over Le1200 = £1 (approx. Le800 = $1). Because of the steep and steady decline in the value of the leone, most prices in this chapter are given in pounds and dollars.

Notes of Le50, Le100, Le500, Le1000 and Le5000 are in circulation. The leone has little value outside Sierra Leone, and although it is illegal to import or export the currency, there is virtually no black market. On arrival at Lungi Airport you are no longer required to change US$100 into leones. Foreigners are allowed to carry any amount of foreign currency up to $5000 without declaring it. If you have more than $5000, it is advisable to ask for a declaration form at the airport to avoid hassles on departure.

In Freetown, there are about a dozen commercial **exchange bureaux**, which offer slightly better rates than the banks if you have cash in large denominations to change (small bills and travellers' cheques are changed at lower rates). Big hotels in Freetown will also exchange hard currency, though rarely for non-guests. Meanwhile, the **banks** are usually able to exchange dollars and major currencies in cash and travellers' cheques. Banks in provincial towns have been unreliable for years. The biggest networks are *Barclays* and the *Standard Chartered*.

Access, *VISA* and *Amex* cards are accepted only in a few establishments in Freetown.

■ Costs and bargaining

Freetown is not expensive. Modest hotels charge around £3–15 ($4.50–$22.50) for a twin room, with a few more comfortable places in the £20–30 ($30–45) bracket. Basic chop-house meals can be had for the equivalent of £0.65 ($1) and more Western-style food, when offered, for perhaps £1–3 ($1.50–4.50).

Bargaining in Sierra Leone is important. Skill at it pays dividends. This is a country where foreigners are quite often and humorously deceived into paying unreasonable prices.

Health

Sierra Leone is distinguished by being the only country in the world where life expectancy has been on the *decrease* over the last twenty years, due to the collapse of the once-famous health service. It used to be 44 years; it's now 42 – bottom in the world.

Schistosomiasis (bilharzia) and river blindness (onchocerciasis) are both common in the countryside. But apart from a high incidence of malaria, Sierra Leone's main **health problems** for travellers revolve around water. The lack of clean supplies is especially acute towards the end of the dry season in the north. Population densities are relatively high, and even piped water may come straight from an open tank or dam. Freetown's water supplies are reckoned to be exceptionally healthy, as they're squeezed through porous rock before reaching the city taps. *Coyah* bottled water from Guinea is usually available in Freetown.

■ Hospitals

Medical treatment in Sierra Leone is best avoided, but in any kind of emergency, where you have a choice, the best hospital in Freetown is Netland hospital in Murray Town. Connaught Hospital is getting better and has some American doctors who have improved its appearance and infrastructure.

Maps and Information

Information for visitors is almost nonexistent. Embassies and high commissions sometimes have a few leaflets, but they are invariably years old. There are no tourist offices in Sierra Leone, though the Ministry of Tourism in Freetown might be worth a visit.

Obtaining fairly up-to-date **maps** of Sierra Leone is equally difficult. *Shell Sierra Leone* publish the only tourist map of the country (1:396,000), with a fanciful rash of "tarmac roads" all over the south of the country, and reliable Freetown street plans on the reverse. It seems to be unobtainable outside Sierra Leone: you might try writing to the printers *Cook, Hammond and Kell Ltd*, 35 Eveline Rd, Mitcham, Surrey, UK.

The last sheet to cover the country was published in 1976 (Sierra Leone Government, 1:500,000), an Ordnance Survey type map, at 1cm:5km, with vague roads and some odd place names. It would be indispensable, however, if you were spending some time in the country. The *Tourist Map of Freetown and Peninsula* (1cm:500m) would be very useful for exploring the peninsula (despite its antiquity: 1969). The best chance of finding this map is from foreign map specialists, notably in Britain.

Getting Around

If you're based in – or visiting – Freetown, there isn't much much getting around to be done. Even in the relatively peaceful days in the late 1980s and early 1990s, travel was difficult off the two or three main highways. At the time of writing (August 1995), travel outside the capital was all but impossible. Petrol (gasoline) is around £1.60 ($2.40) per gallon.

■ Travelling by road

The fleet of white, state-run buses is largely out of service at the time of writing. *Tilda's Atlantic* has bus routes throughout most of the country – in theory – but, again, it's unlikely you'll find any of them operating during the war. Schedules are hard to pin down and you should arrive early in the day to be sure of a seat, especially at the bus station in Freetown. It's not usually possible to book in advance. *Poda podas* are the beat-up urban taxi-vans you'll find around Freetown.

You pay at the end of the trip, except in the big long-distance buses. Prices agreed in advance are always honoured. Bus fares on the main routes are fixed, though you can get ripped off on the price of your baggage, which can virtually double the fare if you don't fix the price on departure.

Hitching

Hitching is pretty easy in and around Freetown. There are acknowledged transport problems and private drivers are usually sympathetic. Much of the time you'll be expected to pay.

MILES, KILOMETRES AND OTHER MEASUREMENTS

Although distances in this chapter are given in **kilometres**, Sierra Leone is hanging onto its **miles**. Where distances are given on signposts, they are usually only in miles. Signposts are rare (about as likely as getting an accurate estimate of distance) so it matters little. If you want to convert kilometres to miles, multiply by five, then divide by eight. To convert to kilometres from a signpost, multiply by eight and divide by five. Most measurements in Sierra Leone are still given in old "Imperial" units – yards, feet and inches, pounds and ounces, gallons and pints.

Car rental

Freetown's handful of **local car rental agencies** (the big internationals aren't represented) normally prefer you to take one of their drivers with you. Prices are high, despite devaluation, and you may have to pay in hard currency.

Accommodation

Freetown has a number of cheap lodgings and several expensive places, with not much in between. Until the war engulfed the whole country, Bo, Makeni, Kenema and Kono all had a handful of basic boarding houses, and one or two more comfortable addresses, but nothing luxurious. It's hard to say whether any of them will emerge to do business as usual after the war is over.

Arriving at dusk in a strange village, it's better to ask to see the chief (who could be a paramount, section or village chief), and explain to him your "mission" and your needs. Customarily, you'll be accommodated somewhere, and your food will be cooked (see the next section). Graciousness and small return favours – kola nuts, coffee, sugar – are important.

Eating and Drinking

There's an excellent range of local food in Sierra Leone. "Chop" – people's food built around rice and palm oil – is very often tasty, always fresh and filling, and only occasionally too hot to handle. Ordinary chop houses generally provide one late morning meal each day for their customers. They rarely have anything left by the afternoon.

ACCOMMODATION PRICE CODES

Hotel prices in this chapter are coded according to the following scales – the same scales in terms of their pound/dollar equivalents as are used throughout the book. Prices refer to the rate you can expect to pay for a room with two beds. Single rooms, or single occupancy, will normally cost at least two-thirds of the twin-occupancy rate. For further details see p.51.

① **Under Le6000 (under £5/$7.50)**. Basic lodging – often very unappealing, sometimes well cared for.

② **Le6000–12,000 (£5–10/$7.50–15)**. Simple amenities but adequate comfort – S/C rooms with fans and sometimes AC.

③ **Le12,000–24,000 (£10–20/$15–30)**. Reasonable business/tourist-class hotel with S/C, AC rooms, and often a restaurant.

④ **Le24,000–36,000 (£20–30/$30–45)**. Similar standards to the previous code band but more comfortable, and often newer.

⑤ **Le36,000–48,000 (£30–40/$45–60)**. Comfortable, first-class hotel, with good facilities.

⑥ **Le48,000–60,000 (£40–50/$60–75)**. Luxury establishment.

⑦ **Over Le60,000 (over £50/$75)**. Luxury establishment with pretensions.

■ Street food

If you're in a hurry to eat in Freetown, there's a good range of **street food**: rice *akara* (rice cake), fried dough (doughnuts), roast meat, egg sandwiches, boiled cassava, yams, plantains, fry soup and sandwiches. A popular snack is the "steak sandwich" – slivers of kebabed meat, with palm oil in bread, known as *rosbif* in Krio. Be sure your sandwich really is "steak", unless you like grilled tripe: at night, it can be hard to see what's cooking.

■ Staple chop

More substantial food is taken more seriously. At its simplest, **chop** can be just a bowl of rice with a splash of bright orange **palm oil** (impossible to keep from dribbling down your chin). But the commonest sauce – **plasas** ("palava sauce") – is made with finely shredded leaves of potato or cassava, gelatinous okra ("gumbo", "ladies' fingers"), dried fish and hot pepper, all cooked in palm oil. *Plasas* based on groundnuts is most common in the north. There are numerous variations on *plasas* and it's often served with meat (either domestic or bush meat). **Plantains** are another common staple, used in place of rice.

Fufu (fermented, mashed cassava stodge) and **agidi** (heavy, maizemeal stodge) are also eaten as the main meal, though not often prepared in chop-houses. You may also get **egusi** sauces or soups, based on crushed squash seed. Along the coast, **fish stew** is very common.

If you're far **off the beaten track**, you won't find chop for sale, as every woman prepares her own family's. In these areas, it's quite acceptable – and quite the custom – to carry rice, palm oil, Maggi cubes and other Sierra Leonean kitchen paraphernalia around with you and have meals cooked for you, in exchange for some of the food, or perhaps for some leones. The family meal is usually prepared late afternoon.

Stay long in Sierra Leone and you'll begin to appreciate significant differences in taste and texture between the **rice of different regions.** Upland "hill rice" is the more traditional short grain variety; the red-speckled Mende kind is the best and can be delicious. "Swamp rice" is a twentieth-century introduction that needs more work in its cultivation. But indigenous varieties always taste better than imported rice.

■ Other food

Yebe is a good and popular breakfast dish, a kind of stew made of potato or cassava – or mangoes when in season. You buy it by the ladle in markets and truck parks between 6.30 and 8am. **Pap**, a sweet rice broth, is also nice for chilly, early starts.

There are two kinds of **bread** sold almost everywhere, sweet bread (the sugar-laden variety) and fresh bread (a basic, non-sweet, white bread). Specify which kind you want; otherwise the seller will probably give you sweet.

Of the wide variety of fruit you'd expect, **oranges** are probably the cheapest; in the north, in season, they'll cost you a penny each. Mandarins, misleadingly, are called lemons in Krio.

■ Drinks

As for drinking, it all comes down to *Star* **beer**, one of West Africa's best. Imported beer costs about £1.50 ($2.25) a bottle – twice the price of *Star*. **Palm wine** (generally from oil palms) is socially and commercially very important, and a

KRIO FOOD AND DRINK TERMS

Krio	English	Krio	English	Krio	English
agidi	corn stodge	*fresh*	new palm wine	*omole*	hooch
airish petehteh	potato	*frut*	fruit	*orinch*	orange
akara	rice and banana cake	*funde*	millet	*oriri*	seasoning
aweful	kind of fish	*gari*	cassava meal	*pamai*	red, banga nut oil
behni	sesame seed	*golik*	garlic	*panapul*	pineapple
bia	*Star* for example	*granat*	groundnut	*pap*	porridge
bif	meat, animal	*grepfrut*	grapefruit	*petete*	sweet potato
binch	beans, peas	*grin*	greens, used in *plasas*	*pia*	pear (avocado)
biskit	biscuit	*jibloks/ kobokobo*	aubergine	*plantan*	plantain
bita	bitter leaf for sauces	*jolof*	rice in tomato paste served with beef, goat or fish stew	*plasas*	(palava) sauce
bolgoh	bulgar wheat	*kabej*	cabbage	*plet*	plate
bonga	dried fish	*kasada*	cassava	*pongki*	pumpkin
bota	butter, margarine	*kek*	cake	*popoh*	pawpaw, papaya
brefos	breakfast	*kenda*	seasoning	*rehs*	rice
brefrut	breadfruit	*kohn*	corn, maize	*sawa-sawa*	*plasas* made of sour leaves
buli	jug for palm wine	*kondo*	basic chop	*sof*	soft drink
bush bif	game meat	*krain-krain*	slimy leaf sauce	*sol*	salt
chak	drunk	*letu*	lettuce	*stek*	beef
egusi	squash seeds used in sauces	*lif*	leaf	*stu*	stew
fis	fish	*magi*	Maggi cube	*suga*	sugar
fohl	chicken	*mampama*	palm wine	*sup*	soup
fud/chop/yit	food	*okroh*	okra	*tamatis*	tomato, tomato purée
				ti	tea
				yabas	onion
				yams	yam

pleasant way to while away an afternoon. Sierra Leonean **liquor** from Freetown distilleries, on the other hand, is a more self-destructive commodity; *Daddy Kool* gin and *Man Pickin* rum are names to beware.

Non-alcoholic, home-made **ginger beer** is popular in Freetown and normally sold in small plastic bottles.

Lastly, while Sierra Leone is more or less outside the green tea zone, **coffee**, which is quite often both freshly ground and Sierra Leonean (and invariably served with *Peak* evaporated milk), is a pleasant surprise.

Communications – Post, Phones, Language and Media

The most useful thing you can do to keep in touch with events around you in Sierra Leone, is learn some Krio. Unless you have lessons, however, this isn't as easy as it might appear. Krio isn't a pidgin, so you can't guess it. As for staying in touch with home, recent years have seen dramatic improvements in Sierra Leone's mail and telephone services.

■ Post

The Sierra Leone **mail system** (*Salpost*) usually takes 7 days between Sierra Leone and the UK and 10 days to the USA. Aerograms are fastest and safest. Up-country mail – incoming as well as outgoing – is unreliable. For receiving mail, there's a **poste restante** counter in the Freetown post office.

Salpost has introduced *EMS Express Mail* which is very reliable and quick and competes directly with *DHL*. Letters cost approximately £13 ($20) to the USA, and slightly less to Europe.

There's no surface mail, but **airmail parcels** are cheap to send. Everything has to be checked and packed at the parcels office and, so long as it's of no value, should be safe enough. For valuable items you'd be wise to use an air freight courier like *EMS* or *DHL* (see Freetown "Listings").

KRIO BASICS

Krio is written phonetically. Vowels are open. Although many words look familiar (and numbers are the same as in English) it's a different matter to get them right in speech, and to structure your sentences correctly. Remember, too, that even with reasonable Krio, you'll still be speaking a foreign language to the nine people out of ten who are more likely to speak Mende or Temne.

Aw di bohdi?	How are you?
No bad, bohdi fine	Not bad, fine
Mohnin-o!	Good morning!
Ivinin-o!	Good evening!
Kushe-o!	Hello
A no sabi tok Krio	I don't speak Krio
Usai yu kohmot?	Where are you from?
A kohmot London	I'm from London
Wi go si bak	Goodbye/ see you again
Dehn geht hotel na dis tohn?	Is there a hotel in this town?
A ebul slip naya?	Can I sleep here?
Dehn get chop os naya?	Is there a chop house here?
Wetin na yu nem?	What's your name?
A nem Kelly	My name is Kelly
Usai yu de go?	Where are you going?
A de go na Bo	I'm going to Bo
Wan naya!/Lef me naya	Let me off!/Drop me here
Tap!	Stop!
A wan wata/Gi mi wata	Can I have some water
Ohmos foh di panapul?	How much is the pineapple?
Ten-ten lion	Ten leones
(Duya) lehs mi smohl	(Please) lower your price a little
Ustehm wi de go?	When are we leaving?
Wi de go jisnoh	We're going now
Bai gohd in powa	By the grace of god/ Insh'allah
Aw foh du?	What can a person do? (rhetorical)
Nafoh bia nomoh	Just bear it, nothing can be done

A KRIO GLOSSARY

Alagba	Bigwig, personage
Ambohg	"Humbug"; bother or pester someone
Bafa	Shelter made of thatch or leaves
Bohboh	Small boy
Bruk	To wash clothes
Bundu	Generic term for secret societies
Cora	Lebanese or Syrian, after the coral they used to sell
Gara	"Indigo", usually refers to dyed cloth
Johnks	Used clothes, "deadmen's clothes"
"Kola"	Tip or inducement, not always of kola
Lorry	Often a minibus or converted pick-up
Pikin	Child
Porto	European, white person
Pumwe	European (Mende)
Salone	Sierra Leone
Siraman	Lebanese, or other white
Titi	Small girl
Turntable	Roundabout, traffic circle
Wetman	"White man", can apply to anyone with a European lifestyle

SOME MENDE PHRASES

Mende, one of the Mande languages, is related to Susu and Mandinka. It's somewhat "tonal", so that meaning varies with the pitch of voice.

Buae! (pl.)/ *Wuae!* (sing.)	Hello there! (response the same)
Bisye! (sing.)/ *Wusye!* (pl.)	Thanks, greetings (said as you pass through the village)
O bi gahui?	How are you? ("Your bones?")
Kaye Ngewo ma	Response ("God can't be blamed")
Ngi ya le	I am leaving
Mm, ta mia, ma lo-o	Yes, OK, see you again
Bi lei?	What's your name?
Nya la a Kevin	My name is Kevin
Pelei ji a li mi?	Where does this road go?
A li Joru	It goes to Joru
Sao	No
Li lele!	Go slowly!
Gbe jongo lo a ji?	How much is this?
Na bagbango, ba mayeilo?	It's too much, can you lessen it?
Kulungoi	All right

1	*Yila*	4	*Nani*	7	*Wofela*	10	*Pu*	20	*Nu yila gboyongo* (lit. "one man finished" ie ten fingers and ten toes)
2	*Fele*	5	*Lolu*	8	*Wayakpa*	15	*Pu mahu lolu*		
3	*Sawa*	6	*Woita*	9	*Talu*				

■ Phones and fax

The **telephone system** has improved dramatically in recent years. Telephones are now working throughout Freetown and in many up-country towns, including Bo, Kenema and Makeni. There are cardphones throughout Freetown.

Overseas calls can be easily made from *Sierra Leone External Telecommunications* (SLET) in Freetown, or at any cardphone by calling the international operator at SLET on ☎017. For the USA you can call AT&T directly on ☎1100. Calls are usually clear due to the direct satellite linkage. Reverse-charge (collect) calls can be made. The charge for paid calls to the US or Europe is Le6000, or approximately £5 ($7.5), for three minutes. Internal lines are continually down in the rainy season due to flooding.

Fax is a reliable way to send messages, with international faxes Le4000 (£3/$4.50) per page to send and Le800 (£0.70/$1.05) per page to receive.

IDD AND AREA CODES

Sierra Leone's IDD code is ☎232.

Freetown ☎**022**
Bo ☎**032**
Wellington ☎**023**
Kenema ☎**042**
Juba ☎**024**
Magburaka ☎**054**
Makeni ☎**052**
Lungi ☎**025**
Kono/Koidu ☎**053**

■ The media

There are about twelve weekly **papers** (the *Daily Mail* and the *Concord Times* publish twice a week). By far the best is the *New Breed*, followed by *Unity Now* and the *New Citizen*. Most of the others offer a mix of insight, incomprehensible feature articles and glimpses (sometimes hilarious) of Sierra Leonean life. Most are in English.

In February 1993 there were 31 newspapers in print, but the NPRC instituted press regulations that closed 19 papers, thus silencing some of their harshest critics. The regulations require a paper to have approximately $5000 in a bank account and an editor with journalism training from an accredited college or university. The *New Breed* was able to meet the requirements, but its whole staff was jailed in October 1993.

West Africa magazine is usually out on sale in Freetown the week after its Friday publication in the UK.

The **television** station (SLTV) has resumed operations for the first time since 1987, broadcasting, in the evenings, local football games, cheap imported documentary fillers and CNN news. The Sierra Leone Broadcasting System – SLBS, the main tool of NPRC propaganda – is now on the air daily at 99.9 FM. In Kenema, there is a private FM radio station and a private station has opened in Bo. Some of the missions in Makeni and Freetown also have private radio stations.

Entertainment

Music in Sierra Leone is currently struggling through a recession. Cinema is, no surprise, dormant if not extinct, as a result of the economic crisis and a lack of any resources. Miserable imported movies – and of course increasingly video – are all you'll see. Film could perhaps be great in Sierra Leone, if the country's record in the field of drama is any indication.

■ Music

Popular local musicians include the **Kabba Brothers**, **Steady Bongo**, **Olayinka MacCauley**, and **Sierra Afrique**. The Kabba Brothers and Steady Bongo are influenced by reggae and soukous, while Olayinka and Sierra Afrique have a 1970s disco sound. **Dr Olo**, the leading exponent of Milo Jazz (a largely percussive music that requires no imported instruments or amplified sound) is still around, but makes few public appearances.

■ Theatre

Freetown has a remarkable tradition of **popular theatre**. Quite a few theatrical groups are currently functioning, and all of them write, or translate, their own scripts.

The 1979 banning of *Poyotong Wahala*, about high-level corruption, led to routine censorship of scripts. In their attempts to outwit the censors, playwrights have moved increasingly from concert party to exuberant **farce and satire**. Shows are uproarious, even rowdy. In Krio, especially, there's a strong blend of comedy and social comment in the East End "tough guys" *Rari Boys* school of theatre. Remember, however, that you just won't understand the dialogue if you don't speak any Krio.

The best and most professional theatre group in the country is **Spence Productions**, directed by Dr Julius Spencer, a theatre professor at Fourah Bay College and editor of the *New Breed* newspaper. The **Freetown Players** are also very popular: more details in Freetown "Listings", p.574.

Forthcoming events are usually well advertised; look out for banners, especially around Freetown's Cotton Tree and Law Courts. The best plays are often performed at the British Council Library.

Opening Hours and Public Holidays

Offices are open Monday to Friday (rarely Saturday morning), usually 8am–noon and 2–5pm. Banks and some embassies operate a long morning with no break, closing early in the afternoon. Shops usually close by 5pm, but are open Saturday morning. Many restaurants and other establishments are closed all day Sunday. The last Saturday of every month is "National Cleaning Day", enforced by the army. People are expected to clean up their neighbourhood, and businesses remain closed until late morning.

Sierra Leone's **public holidays** follow the Christian calendar. The Islamic calendar only affects business and office opening at the end of Ramadan (see below). The somewhat unpredictable secular holidays include **April 19** (Republic Day), **April 27** (Independence Day), and **April 29** (anniversary of the revolution; see below).

The **Lantern Parade** takes place on **Watch Night** at the end of Ramadan, when the new moon is due to be sighted. It follows similar lines to the *fanals* of Senegal, and absorbs a complete cross-section of Freetown's different language groups. Some thirty **"lantern associations"** compete to produce the best float. They set off around 3am from "Up Gun" roundabout in the East End, to walk past the Law Courts (where the floats are judged) and spill onto Lumley Beach at dawn.

If the north is safe, don't miss the New Year's Day "outing" in Kabala. If you are in the Freetown area around that time, go to Lumley Beach, Goderich Beach or River No. 2 on **Boxing Day** or New Year's Day, when literally thousands of people come to dance, swim and party.

April 29 has been a national holiday since the coup and celebrated with parades and dancing in the streets. With the transition to democracy expected in 1996, it is unclear what will happen to April 29, or the date of the lantern parade.

Trouble

The whole country, outside of Freetown, is a major trouble spot: the following advice has to be read with the country's ongoing civil war in mind. The smuggling of what's considered the country's biggest asset – diamonds – is a major problem and you should dismiss tempting offers. As for drugs, grass (*dhambi, yamba*) is widely smoked, but not in public. Police entrapments are more likely to lead to a bribe than the pressing of charges.

The **police** of the blue-uniformed SLP (Sierra Leone Police) vary from the utterly charming to the unspeakable. Provincial police in tan uniforms are **chiefdom police** – inheritors of the much-maligned colonial "court messenger" service with civil duties, answerable to the local paramount chief.

Bigger difficulties might occur when encountering the **army**. Since the war began, the army has expanded rapidly and its level of professionalism has dropped considerably. Nevertheless, as long as you are friendly, forthright, and willing to pay a small bribe if necessary, you shouldn't have too much trouble. However, beware that there are random military checkpoints in Freetown. Always carry some form of identification and be friendly, but be careful of soldiers who are drunk or high. Military checkpoints in the interior require everyone to exit their vehicles and have their belongings and identification checked, though under present circumstances, you are unlikely to travel upcountry.

■ "Tifing"

If you're living in the country for some time, you might as well resign yourself to the problem of **"tifing"** – thieving. Everyone reckons their neck of the woods is the very worst. Unless you're prepared to live in a permanent state of paranoia, there's nothing you can do to stop small items vanishing. If you lose something precious, however, before calling in the *kopas*, make some more discreet enquiries, perhaps offer a reward and see if there's a local **"look-ground man"** (diviner) who might help. Spread the word you're going to "swear" the culprits by putting a curse on them. This only works if you have suspicions.

Women Travellers and Sexual Attitudes

When the foreign aid organizations were in the country in strength, women travelling alone were often assumed to be *Piskoh* (Peace Corps). Consequently, shorts and T-shirts don't raise too many eyebrows. With exception made for Lumley Beach – where beach boys of all descriptions gather – Sierra Leone, in peacetime, is probably one of the safest and friendliest countries for the lone female traveller.

Settle in one place to stay, or work, though, and you're bound to be persistently discomfited by inflamed egos. "When can we meet to do some loving?" is the kind of question that Sierra Leonean women have to field all the time, though the perceived cultural gap and your potential as a source of funds too, make you more vulnerable. It's possibly unfair in individual cases, but broadly true, to expect more posturing in the north and less arrogant attitudes in the south.

■ Sexual attitudes

In the wider field of **sexual attitudes**, public boyfriend-girlfriend **relationships** – holding hands and walking together – are more acceptable in Sierra Leone than in most countries. But that doesn't mean husbands reserve the "right" to beat up their wives any the less. In certain Krio quarters of Freetown, conservative "Victorian values" are still prevalent. Female genital mutilation is widely practised within the framework of the traditional women's *Sande* society.

■ Organizations

Modern **women's organizations** are mostly Krio, and based in Freetown, which gives their concerns a slightly lopsided, Women's-Institute feel. The main umbrella organization is the National Organization for Women. Power for women in the provinces tends to be determined by ethnic affiliation. While there are a number of women paramount chiefs in the Mende chiefdoms, a Temne female paramount chief would be unheard of.

Directory

AIRPORT TAX US$20 payable in hard currency.

CHIEFS If you manage to travel in Sierra Leone you're likely to meet quite a few chiefs. These men (and women) will often be your introduction to a small town or village. Local government in the three **Provinces** (Northern, Southern and Eastern) is organized around the 169 **paramount chiefdoms**, which have local council status. These were consolidated – and invented where necessary – by the British. They're not waterproof ethnic divisions, though most have a dominant group. Beneath the paramount chiefs come section chiefs and village chiefs. Appointments are by slightly arbitrary popular vote. The **Western Area** of Freetown and the peninsula has district councils, not chiefs.

CRAFTS Sierra Leone's best buys are **cloth** (indigo tie-dyed *gara*, rusty red and black block-printed *ronko*, soft and heavy strip-woven country cloth – single weave *barri* and double weave *kpokpoi* – and batik); **leather goods** (especially slot-together neck bags and purses); **masks** connected with the secret societies (but the made-for-tourists ones are over-priced and often crude, while the real thing is seriously expensive and requires permission to export from the museum); and *nomoli* **soapstone figurines** (which, strictly speaking, cannot be exported if they're authentic – see p.564).

PARKS AND WILDLIFE Sierra Leone has two important faunal reserves. The big one is the Outamba-Kilimi National Park in the north, which was well on its way to becoming a fully operational park with visitor facilities and an active research programme when the Peace Corps workers based there left the country. The other is the Tiwai Island Primate Reserve, a jungle-covered island in the Moa River near the Liberian border, where the facilities and endangered monkey inhabitants have almost certainly been wiped out by the war. Sierra Leone's fauna still includes **elephants** (in the Outamba-Kilimi National Park), **chimpanzees** (also in the park, but widely if thinly dispersed across the whole country) and **pygmy hippos** which are so solitary and secretive that it's hard to know what their status is. If you're an enthusiastic naturalist, you'll want to visit the Conservation Society of Sierra Leone in Freetown (see p.572).

PHOTOGRAPHY Freetown itself has a tough attitude to cameras, and on just about every street corner where you frame a scene, someone is sure to demand that you stop taking photographs – the result of acute sensitivity over the city's shabbiness. There's no permit necessary, however, and so long as you avoid getting uniforms, banks and government buildings in the viewfinder and apply due respect, you'll find that, in peacetime, most of the country is easier than usual for photography. Often enough, people will line up enthusiastically for group portraits ("Mek yu snap wi"). Colour print film is available in Freetown, and you can get your pictures developed at reasonable prices.

RELIGION Krio influence has given a broadly Christian colouration to the whole country, especially the south and west, but most deeply ingrained in and around Freetown. You'll see more mosques around the northern and eastern fringes. Indigenous religion, however, is deep-rooted and widely practised, with the powerful **secret societies** (see p.580) playing a major role in keeping it alive.

A Brief History of Sierra Leone

Sierra Leone has one of the longest "modern histories" of any West African nation. The American slave trade was effectively started at the watering station by the present site of the King Jimmy market in Freetown, by Sir John Hawkins in the 1560s. Inland, at Port Loko, Afro-Portuguese *lançado* traders settled and flourished through the seventeenth century. Early British colonists gravitated to the slaving "factory" of Bunce Island (downriver from Port Loko) and the coasts of Sherbro and the other islands further south. Here, the more adventurous married into local royalty and seeded new, Creole dynasties. At the end of the eighteenth century, the first free black settlers arrived to colonize the Freetown peninsula.

■ The Province of Freedom

There were tens of thousands of **freed slaves** in Bristol, Liverpool and London in the late eighteenth century. After the outbreak of the American War of Independence in 1775, many slaves deserted to the British side from their southern plantation owners, and later made their way to London. And as early as 1772, a legal test case had ruled that, once freed, a slave could not be returned to captivity.

In 1787, the **first settlers** arrived in Sierra Leone. They were a group of 411 people, mostly "black poor" immigrants but including some sixty deported white women – "wives" for the freed slaves. Their patron, Granville Sharp, declared the mountainous shore of the peninsula "The Province of Freedom". The expedition was nearly a disaster. Sierra Leone had been chosen on the recommendation of a botanist, Henry Smeathman, who'd lived there for some years and whose private intention had been to set up plantations – using slave labour. He died before the expedition set off, but many of the putative settlers had second thoughts at the last minute and backed out. The expedition was badly managed – some of the government funding for it was misallocated or siphoned off – and much delayed, so that the ships finally arrived just before the onset of the rains. The colonists had tents, and built makeshift huts, but within three months of living through the rainy season on the sodden hillside, a third of them were dead, of malaria or other diseases.

They bought the area of what's now Freetown from **King Tom**, a Temne headman and tributary of **King Naimbama**. But Naimbama hadn't been consulted and the area had to be bought again from him (the treaty can be seen at the Public Archives in Fourah Bay College). Tom was succeeded by **King Jimmy** who resented and harassed the Bunce Island slave trading operation that was still going on. A British naval vessel, which had by coincidence arrived with new supplies for the flagging colony, torched one of Jimmy's towns – with the approval of the settlers, who had also been in dispute with him.

And there ended the "Province of Freedom". King Jimmy evicted the settlers from their homes and burnt their little colony to the ground. Those colonists that remained (it was now 1790) were absorbed into surrounding Temne villages.

Nova Scotians, Maroons and Temne defeat

A new consortium, the **Sierra Leone Company**, was formed to take over the assets of the defunct Province of Freedom and make a second attempt to establish a colony. Its members were **Granville Sharp** (the driving force), the liberal lord **William Wilberforce**, and a young radical, **Thomas Clarkson**.

They soon found a new group of colonists – some twelve hundred **"Nova Scotians"** – for their philanthropic experiment. These were freed slave refugees from the United States whom the British had fobbed off with a dead-end resettlement scheme in the Canadian colony. One of them went to London, where Sierra Leone was suggested to him as an alternative. The small hill farms the new settlers were allocated were not much of an improvement on Canada, but the Nova Scotians formed a viable community. They brought strong churches, and some of them became Company administrators. There were further vicissitudes. French Revolutionary forces caught the ill-defended British off-guard in 1794 and ransacked Freetown. But the Nova Scotians rebuilt. The colony of Sierra Leone (as it became in 1808) owed its existence to them.

In 1795, five hundred escaped Asante slaves – the **Maroons** – who had set up an independent state in the mountains of Jamaica, were tricked into negotiations, leading to their capture and deportation, once again to Nova Scotia, and then eventually to Sierra Leone. The Maroon settlers arrived at Freetown in 1800, just as a group of Nova Scotians, in an attempt to form their own government, were in the middle of Sierra Leone's first **rebellion**. The Maroons, and a detachment of soldiers accompanying them, came to Governor Thomas Ludlam's rescue. The Nova Scotian rebels were captured; two were hanged and the rest banished. From the beginning of the nineteenth century, the settlers were given no voice in the government of Sierra Leone. Britain ruled directly.

Pushing home their new strength, the Sierra Leone Company refused to countenance claims by members of the **Temne** ethnic group that a new treaty be negotiated whenever there was a new Temne king as landlord. For the governor, the treaty of 1788 was good in perpetuity. To make the point, the British garrison built a **stone fort**, now part of State House. The Temne, led by a new King Tom, and encouraged by a partisan Nova Scotian named Wansey, attacked it in November 1801 and were quickly repulsed. In a counteroffensive, the British ousted the Temne and their Bullom relatives from most of the peninsula and carried out savage punitive raids on many villages in King Tom's dominion. While the Temne prepared a new plan, a Susu ally of theirs arrived with his retinue to settle in Freetown. This sell-out turned the tide against the Temne. They gave up the peninsula.

The Crown Colony and the recaptives

On January 1, 1808, the Sierra Leone Company, by now deeply in debt, handed over the running of the settlement to the British government and Sierra Leone became a **Crown Colony**. In the same year, Westminster passed the Abolition Act and the anti-slavery movement at last had some teeth – although the last slave ships weren't intercepted until 1864. Bunce Island ceased slave-trading and the Temne country inland turned to **timber** (another non-renewable resource) to maintain its economic strength. Freetown had a naval base, charged with intercepting slave ships and **"recapturing" the slaves**. Although never precisely intended, it soon became clear that few of them could be returned to their original homes, and they were simply released at Freetown to found new villages.

Between 1808 and 1864, some 70,000 **"recaptives"** were resettled in the Sierra Leone colony. Leicester was founded by Wolof and Bambara people, Kissy by freed slaves from the "Scarcies" river and Congo Town by Congolese recaptives. In the 1820s, in war-torn Yorubaland (Nigeria), thousands of slaves of war were shipped west, in Cuban, Brazilian or American vessels, many of them to be quickly recaptured by the Freetown frigates. The "Aku", as they were called, formed the first significant **Muslim** community in the colony.

Slave-trading also continued along the southern coasts of the Sierra Leone region. Many recaptives, far from being complete strangers to the region, had roots in the territory that later became Sierra Leone the country.

After peace was achieved with the French in 1815, many of the **African soldiers** who had served in British regiments were pensioned off to the colony, where they founded villages with pugnacious names like Waterloo, Hastings and Wellington. From the interior came determined **Fula** and **Mandinka** traders who settled in Foulah Town. And much of the town's heavy labour was done by the Kru (or Kroo), who came to the coast on long residences from their homes in southeast Liberia.

In this melting pot of people, many of them traumatized by their experiences, the Church Missionary Society made headway through the early decades of the nineteenth century. Many who felt that the **Bible** had saved them from slavery were converted to Christianity. The Nova Scotians, too, were an example; African and yet European in their ways; prosperous, literate, worldly and Christian. Many recaptives adopted European names and, with intermarriage and the inevitable breakdown of many ethnic barriers, there was the gradual moulding of a new configuration – the **Creoles**, or **Krios**.

In the **interior**, the British paid kings and headmen annual stipends to try to guarantee peace between peoples whose economies had been damaged by the termination of the slave trade. Centuries of dependence upon it had left many **Temne** families, and whole districts, in disarray; while the farming peoples, like the **Limba** and the **Loko**, whom the Temne had exploited for so long, were now attacked and harassed by them. By the 1820s, the Temne had emerged as the dominant language group northeast of Freetown.

On the peninsula, recaptives began moving to Freetown from their villages. Captured cargos of **European goods** for slave-trading were auctioned off and a number of recaptive traders took advantage, selling inland, even setting themselves up in business in the interior, under the patronage of village headmen, who called them "white men". The timber trade declined with the introduction of iron steamships and a more easily undertaken trade in wild-collected **palm nuts**, for the burgeoning industries of Europe and the USA, spread across the country.

Further afield, the first **recaptive missionaries** began to follow the traders, not just inland from Freetown, but along the coast, and especially to Nigeria. From the 1850s onwards, the advent of steamships made Freetown the hub of the whole coast. With the return of peace in Yorubaland, large numbers of Krios returned there and went on to colonize the coast of Cameroon.

■ Expansion and consolidation

Expansion of the Freetown colony in the 1860s took in parts of Sherbro Island and the southern coast. Treaties were signed by local chiefs, forced to choose the lesser evil of British overlordship, when French traders made clear their designs on the region. Inland from the peninsula, a minor incident was used to force the "leasing" (in reality annexation) of the low-lying Koya Temne farming district around Songo – about as far inland as present-day Mile 38. Loko and Mende mercenary allies of the British helped clear the area of recalcitrant Temne.

The **end of the slave trade** in 1865 was in fact just the end of transatlantic shipments. In the interior of the country, slaves continued to be traded, for domestic work and for labour on export crops. As the pace of trade and competition increased, the British in Freetown made no effort to control slavery beyond the border of the Freetown colony, if anything recognizing its usefulness and the dangers of upsetting the chiefs who profited from it.

Alongside these developments, missionaries, in particular those of the American **United Baptist Church**, aimed to create conditions in the interior that would result in the gradual dismantling of traditional ways. They spread the gospels, of course, and set a lot of store in conversions. But more significantly, they taught **new economic techniques** in their boys' schools and offered substantial credit to their graduates to set them up as traders. As more and more traders left the colony to trade outside the British customs area, so Freetown Krios, complaining of unfair competition and price wars, demanded an extension of British control to annex the whole coast. London, however, explicitly prohibited any further annexations. Indeed a parliamentary committee of 1865 had already laid out a general principal of eventual withdrawal and self-government for the West African colonies.

In 1882, the borders of separate **spheres of influence** with Liberia and France were settled along the coast, and Britain found itself operating a **customs area** that extended from the Great Scarcies in the north to the Mano River in the south. The purely exploitative nature of this arrangement, in which no responsibility for internal affairs was taken by the British, led to the beginning of a draining of Krio confidence in the colonial government. One incident that incensed them was the **execution of William Caulker** in 1888 for the murder of his half-brother, the disputed king of Shenge (the coast between Freetown and Sherbro). Although the king had the government's support for his succession, his enthronement had been unpopular. Krio opinion had it that such affairs could be avoided if Britain were to annex and administer the whole country, rather than simply extract duty.

The creation of the new customs area also coincided with a general recession in trade in the 1880s and repeated confrontations and battles between the trading chiefdoms along the coast and in the interior. A number of statelets, which managed to stay on the right side of the British, emerged supremely powerful in Mende country – among them **Senehun**, under Madam (Mammy) Yoko, **Panguma**, under Nyagua, **Pujehun**, run jointly by Momo Ja and Momo Kai Kai and, in the east, **Kailahun**, a new Mende-Kissi confederation under Kai Lundu.

■ Partition

With the recognition of Freetown's importance as a **coaling station** for British shipping, and a sense of urgency in Europe's attitude to Africa, a new pragmatism overcame the colonial government in the closing years of the nineteenth century. The French were chasing Samory Touré's giant *sofa* army (which was supplied with weapons from Freetown) across territory in the British zone of influence. A war between Britain and France in the region couldn't be discounted.

Hastily, the British began formulating exclusive friendship treaties with as many chiefs as would entertain them, hoping to set up a buffer zone of allies between the French and Freetown. Boundary agreements were signed with the French in 1895, a partition that forced the British to accept the **Protectorate** of Sierra Leone. The domineering governor Frederic Cardew initiated a system of **indirect rule** through local chiefs under European District Commissioners – a system that was later followed in northern Nigeria. All kings and queens became paramount chiefs (under Queen Victoria) and their sovereignty over their peoples strictly limited to whatever their district commissioner considered appropriate. The "treaties of friendship" they'd signed were reinterpreted as surrenders of power in the new Protectorate.

Cardew's decision to build a **railway**, based on the need to encourage trade, and the requirement that the Protectorate's administration should not be paid for by the colony, led unavoidably to the invention of ways of paying for it. It was the first ever built and run by the British government: all previous lines had been private. Trading licences were introduced and a tax imposed of five shillings per year on every house in the Protectorate. Payments had to be forced out of people. The undisciplined **Frontier Police** force (initially mainly Krio, later largely up-country men) smashed their way across the country, effectively robbing the people to pay for the administration they had never asked for. People of the Protectorate regarded the white man's **"hut tax"** as an inversion of the proper order of things, which should have had them extracting payment from the newcomers. They assumed they were being charged rent on their houses, which had been stolen from them.

The Hut Tax War and the Mende Revolt

In the north, the Loko chief **Bai Burreh** resisted demands for the hut tax and fought a protracted **guerilla war** against better-equipped but untrained Caribbean troops. There was support for Bai Burreh's action from the Krio, whose views about taxes concurred with his and who detested governor Cardew's arrogance.

At the beginning of the rainy season in 1898, as the collection of taxes got under way in **Mende country** and the first few lives were lost to the Frontier Police, there was a massive organized **uprising**, planned through secret society meetings. Hut tax and trading licences were the main grudges, but decades of resentment were released in unprecedented violence directed against "every man in trousers and every woman in a dress". Hundreds of administrators, traders and missionaries were hacked and bludgeoned to death. Atrocities were widespread and few escaped. The Krio traders in the Protectorate suffered most. Although there was panic in Freetown, the colony was not invaded.

Pro-British chiefs helped the government resume control in the Protectorate, although there were fierce skirmishes in several districts. Over 200 arrests were made and 96 people were hanged. Many others, including, eventually, Bai Burreh, were deported to the Gold Coast. With a new West African regiment having replaced the West Indians, Cardew followed the crushing of the resistance with a military victory tour around the country. The Krio community was sickened. The hut tax was not repealed.

Krio disaffection – the Lebanese and the rise of nationalism

The beginning of the **twentieth century** saw a new, more complex Sierra Leone. The Krios were demoralized – ignored by the government and mistrusted by the people of the Protectorate. The Protectorate people had been defeated by the government and now found themselves paying allegiance (and corruptly inflated taxes in many cases) to increasingly alienated chiefs in the pay of the British. At least the Frontier force was disbanded. Chiefdom "court messengers" were given the job of policing the Protectorate.

British policy in general moved right away from the benevolence of a century earlier. In concordance with the new authoritarian order, **racial discrimination** became policy. Blacks – whether "natives" or "creoles" – were kept in subordinate positions no matter how highly qualified. Social mixing between the races became rare and, with the discovery that mosquitoes transmitted malaria, a new whites-only suburb was created on the high ground above Freetown, Hill Station, served by its own railway. Once malaria became less of a deterrent, more and more European companies came to trade in Sierra Leone, buying out the less prosperous Krio traders and bringing venture capital with them. But it was the arrival of **Lebanese traders** in the 1890s (many, it's said, brought by unscrupulous ships' captains who told them West Africa was America) which really did for the Krio traders at the smaller end of business.

World War I and the influenza epidemic and food shortages which followed, stalled the political advances that might otherwise have taken place. Predictably, perhaps, the Lebanese (who never seemed to go short) were accused of hoarding and profiteering. Anti-Lebanese demonstrations took place and their shops were looted. Railway workers went on strike in 1919 and again in 1926, but their demands for improved pay and conditions were not met. Although an increased quota of Africans was nominated to the Sierra Leone Legislative Council, only three were elected, and then only by restricted suffrage for the literate and propertied. The voices of Africans were timid and restrained. The **abolition of slavery** as an institution came only in 1927, when the outrage from abroad became impossible to ignore. Slave-owners lost little, as most slaves preferred to stay with them as employees.

Apart from an isolated Islamic resistance movement led by a marabout, **Idara** (who was killed near Kambia in 1931, and his followers jailed), there wasn't much motion on the political scene. But the radical propaganda of **I. T. A. Wallace-Johnson** represented a break from conservative reformism. Organizing a mass consciousness nationalist movement in the Gold Coast and Sierra Leone, he formed the West African Youth League and outspokenly denounced the government of Sir Douglas Jardine. Wallace-Johnson's use of Krio, a language more widely understood than English, was especially provocative. He was imprisoned on a charge of criminal libel, followed by years of detention though World War II, on the spurious pretext of his threat to security.

The road to independence

Only **World War II** broke the numbing spell of repression which had settled on the country since partition. By the time peace was declared in Asia and the black veterans of the Burma campaign and RAF were coming home to Sierra Leone, it was clear that profound changes could not be held off much longer.

To begin with, the colour bar was removed, opening senior civil service posts to Africans. And there was a major change in budgetary policy too, with British tax payers now funding colonial development. Independence at some point in the future was explicitly stated to be the goal. The **new constitution** of 1947 gave the Protectorate fourteen seats on the Legislative Council, and the Colony just seven, which was still a gross under-representation of Protectorate interests, despite Krio complaints that the Colony should have held a majority of seats. Wallace-Johnson bitterly opposed the new order and, making a clear distinction between Colony and Protectorate, reminded the government of the 1865 proposals to allow for self-government in the Colony, now being swept aside.

Surprised at the vehemence of the Krio attacks, the government stalled in implementing the new constitution. In the Protectorate, meanwhile, the **Sierra Leone People's Party** was being formed, the country's first. It was led by **Milton Margai**, a doctor (the first Protectorate man to receive a medical qualification) from a Bonthe business family, related to the powerful and pro-British Banta Mende chiefdom. His brother, **Albert Margai** (the first lawyer from the Protectorate), and **Siaka Stevens**, a Vai-Limba man with a union background, were also founder members. The SLPP insisted on the introduction of the new constitution. Elections held in 1951 gave them a huge majority over the Krio-based party of the **National Council of Sierra Leone**.

The People's Party gradually took over power from colonial appointees. Margai became Chief Minister in 1954, but was in no hurry to form a government to run the country independently. "It will come," he said, "but we are not ready yet. We have not got the men to run it. We want our friends to go on helping us for some time to come."

Throughout the 1950s prosperity and confidence grew. The diamond fields in the east were opened to private licensees and there was considerable investment in health and education, as well as general infrastructure. There were also signals of rumbling discontent at the way political reforms lagged behind growth. In 1955, price riots in Freetown and anti-chief demonstrations throughout the north drew little response from Margai, whose conservative and parochial leanings were becoming increasingly apparent.

The creation of a House of Representatives (the Sierra Leonean parliament) in 1956 replaced the Legislative Council. There was a general election, in which all tax-paying men were eligible to vote, in 1957, which returned the SLPP to power with a slightly reduced majority.

■ Independence

Albert Margai and Siaka Stevens, unhappy with Milton (Sir Milton in 1959) Margai's record, left his cabinet to form **opposition parties**. Although there was brief, ritualistic, all-party unity in the **United Front** for the **independence talks** held in London in 1960, there was a rapid fission of interests in the final, faster-than-expected, lead-up to independence. Stevens formed the **All-Peoples' Congress** (APC). Sir Milton Margai, now the prime minister, refused his demands for a general election before independence and went further by detaining Stevens and several others for over a month, throughout the transition, on the pretext that they posed a risk to the country's stability. Sierra Leone's Independence Day came on April 27, 1961. A **general election** held the following year, under universal suffrage for the first time, reaffirmed SLPP dominance, but also confirmed mass opposition support for the APC.

Dissatisfaction with the SLPP was spreading, but the death of Sir Milton Margai in 1964, and the return to the fold of his brother Albert (soon Sir Albert) increased popular resentment of the government, especially in the north. The party appeared to be squandering the foreign funds that were poured into the country. It still showed scant concern to reform the corrupt and antiquated system of local government by chiefs, and too much interest in its own, Mende, power base. In **Freetown**, however, important developments were under way. Siaka Stevens was elected **mayor** from 1964 to 1965 and he built up solid support among the disenchanted Krios, for whom independence had so far been disappointing. The general election in 1967 was a turning point. It ousted the SLPP and ushered in a period of intense instability, arguably unchanged to the present day.

■ The coups, and Siaka Stevens

As soon as Siaka Stevens (elected leader of the victorious APC) had been sworn in as prime minister, a chauvinistic army brigadier, **David Lansana** – an eastern Mende whom Albert Margai had been grooming in a push for regional dominance – attempted a coup to retain Margai. The following day, Lansana's own officers usurped him and seized power, eventually succeeding in nominating **Andrew Juxson-Smith** to chair their army and police **National Redemption Council** (NRC).

Stevens went into exile in Guinea, with his senior supporters. At first, they had to restrain him from launching an armed invasion of Sierra Leone, with the help of Sekou Touré (Guinean president). Instead, he waited a year in exile, while the NRC's popular promises to restore the flagging economy, clean up corruption and then return the country to civilian rule came to nothing. In April 1968 a mutiny in the lower ranks, aided by junior officers, led to the arrest of the members of the NRC and the call for Stevens' return to power.

Stevens in power

Stone wey dey botam wata, no no say wen rain de cam.

A stone under the water doesn't know when it's raining.

Krio proverb

Siaka Stevens' first decade in power was characterized by a growing alienation from his political roots and the jettisoning of virtually all objectives with the exception of **"national unity"**. Publicly, he quickly ceased to be the champion of Freetown's interests. His former outward adherence to socialist principles was ploughed under by the need constantly to retrench his power base. At the same time, he was careful to shed those of his supporters who became dangerously close. He avoided clear ethnic affiliation, using his mixed background to adopt a succession of tribal identities. And all the time, he continued to accumulate a massive personal fortune.

Early after the return to civilian rule, senior ministers in Stevens' government – Mohammed Funna and Ibrahim Bash-Taqi – resigned to form the **United Democratic Party** (the UDP, banned in 1973). A **coup attempt** by the army commander, John Bangura, and two **assassination attempts** on Stevens, all led to executions and to the arrival of detachments of **Guinean troops** to protect Stevens from his own military. Repeatedly, too, **states of emergency** were imposed, which paralysed the country's fragile "democracy" and brought despair among left-leaning politicians. Sierra Leone became a republic in 1971, with Stevens, now president, replacing Queen Elizabeth as head of state.

Such was the political climate by 1972 that there was no further effective opposition for nearly five years, and the House of Representatives became a discussion forum for APC members, in which the pronouncements of Pa Siaka (old man Siaka) were aired and approved. A **bomb explosion** in April 1974 at the home of the finance minister gave Stevens an opportunity to smash home his dominance. Eight opponents of the regime, including the ex-APC members, Funna and Bash-Taqi, were hanged in public and their bodies desecrated.

The general election of 1977 came in the wake of student- and school pupil-led **demonstrations** across the country, amid mounting **economic disarray**. Despite vote-rigging, and violence that resulted in more than a hundred deaths, the SLPP gained fifteen seats at the expense of Siaka's supporters and, for a short period, the opposition was bolstered with new confidence. This lapsed again with Siaka's announcement that he was "obliged" to hold a referendum on the question of a **one-party state**, to save Sierra Leone from tribalist chaos. The results of this poll (officially, more than 97 percent in favour) led to the absorption of the SLPP in the ranks of the APC and the formalization of one-party rule.

To seal his control, Siaka was lavish with his political patronage. But his appointment of the chief of the armed forces, **Major General Joseph Momoh** (from the minority northern Limba-speaking group), to the House of Representatives and the Cabinet itself as president-in-waiting – as a prelude to Stevens' retirement from politics – was a strategic bequest to the country. His two vice-presidents, Francis Minah and Sorie Koroma, were ignored.

The hosting of the 1980 **OAU conference**, which cost an estimated US$100 million, marked the end of the era of mere stagnation and corruption. Food shortages, price rises and non-payment of salaries led to huge and general discontent in the towns, while in the rural areas production was depressed by, among other factors, low prices paid to producers – kept down in efforts to prevent urban protest. The black economy was tolerated, and even thrived under the bankrupt official system. A government handbook to mark the OAU conference remarked that "the nation's aims of self-sufficiency and country-wide prosperity are now on the verge of achievement". By 1985 Sierra Leone's economy was apparently on the verge of total collapse – where it was to teeter for four years.

■ Momoh in power: "The New Order"

Siaka Stevens retired in November 1985. (He died, in his mansion overlooking Freetown, on May 29, 1988, after a long and painful illness.)

The **transfer of power** to Major General Joseph Momoh was peaceful. After seventeen years of Siaka's stale and hollow rhetoric, the new man was welcomed with enthusiasm. Elections in 1986 saw many of the old guard lose their seats and some 150 new APC members installed in the House of Representatives. A number of political prisoners were released, including twelve convicted after the bomb attack of April 1974.

Momoh's **economic strategy** was to cut back on public spending, in line with IMF-imposed financial conditions. Fearful of the results of austerity measures in the already hard-pressed towns, however, he declined to follow through with a full implementation that might have satisfied the IMF. In **agriculture**, a "Green Revolution" was promulgated but, from lack of consultation with subsistence farmers, it never had much chance of success. Farmers were deserting their plots for diamond and gold prospecting in the east. And, despite an economy dominated, in human terms, by **rice** farms, self-sufficiency in rice was far from being achieved and imported sacks were hoarded to raise prices. Escalating prices resulted, early in 1987, in **student-led demonstrations and riots** and several deaths, sparked by those on government bursaries with not enough money for food. Three colleges at Bo were closed, and government-funded students were dismissed and told to re-apply. Non-academic student "activities" were banned, and remained so for three years.

The causes of growing **public disillusion** with the new government were easy to fathom. While the "New Order" tag was lauded, there was no clean sweep; a number of Stevens' old cabinet cronies were retained in senior positions. **Corruption** blazed in all corners of society, allowing the **black market** to tap the leaky system virtually unchecked. The government's economic measures bit deep, yet apparently had little effect, as Momoh still fell out with the IMF for refusing a comprehensive devaluation of the leone and insisting on retaining the petrol subsidy. Sierra Leone was working itself into a deep mire.

Political events distracted attention from the economic situation and worsened it by absorbing the government's energies. The first big crisis for Momoh's presidency came in March 1987 with the arrest of sixty people on treason charges and large seizures of arms. Among those arrested was first vice-president, **Francis Minah**. After a trial of inordinate length, eighteen of the alleged coup plotters were sentenced to death.

Economically, by the end of 1987, all other problems were overshadowed by the treasury's predicament in finding itself quite unable to pay the salaries of government employees, due to the hoarding of money and a consequent severe shortage of currency in the banks. Declaring a **state of economic emergency**, Momoh beefed up border controls, announced severe measures against diamond and foreign currency smugglers, slapped limits on the amounts of Sierra Leonean currency that could be privately held, and gave Sierra Leoneans a deadline to deposit their cash in the banks.

The emergency measures – notably efforts to get leones back in the banks – had some success. But economic performance hardly altered: indeed it continued to decline. By the end of 1988, the economy seemed to have bottomed out. It couldn't get worse. Many employees on the government payroll had not been paid for months. There was even a kind of nostalgia for the Siaka Stevens era.

In May 1989, in an effort to prevent national breakdown, the government made the long-awaited **devaluation of the leone** to a realistic level and followed this by **removal of the petrol subsidy**. At the same time, **"ghost workers"** on government payrolls were exorcized with the help of computerization. Average **pay rises** of seventy percent were thus awarded with an actual *cut* in costs. Tax thresholds were raised, many agricultural export taxes scrapped and the "state of economic emergency" repealed. **Sales of diamonds and gold** to the state monopoly improved with the higher leone prices being paid.

President Momoh's record was improving; yet despite his sober and perservering style, his term in office lacked conviction. Massive corruption, combined with a total lack of will to treat as criminals those who abused their positions was compounded by the skill and dedication of the **Lebanese** community who manipulated and organized the running of the economy, making use of overseas contacts and siphoning funds to the Middle East, Britain and the USA.

In March 1991, Momoh finally announced he was accepting a constitutional commission report recommending a return to **multi-party politics**. A number of parties were formed or revived, but little headway was made in formulating policies. By the beginning of 1992 hardly any independent parties (as opposed to those that broadly supported the APC) had been registered, and it appeared Momoh was reconsidering his commitment to elections in October of that year.

At the same time, Momoh's 5000-strong army was wallowing in the east of the country in efforts to contain incursions by Charles Taylor's forces from Liberia and **Sierra Leonean rebels** – many of them teenagers or even children – under the leadership of one **Foday Sankoh**, a former army photographer. The army was undersupplied and, crucially, was not being paid on time.

■ The NPRC

The **coup of April 29, 1992**, when it came, was not unexpected – and it was certainly not unwelcome. A group of exasperated young officers (most in their twenties) fresh back from the front, led by **Captain Valentine Strasser**, 26, stormed into the president's office to claim back-pay and demand more support for the war. The president wasn't there, and they appeared to be in control. Momoh then broadcast messages intended to be reassuring from the SLBS station, while Strasser, speaking on 99.9FM, claimed he was in charge of the country and, to a backing of "Ain't No Stopping Us Now, We're On The Move!", made a string of pronouncements about the price of foodstuffs, unpaid company taxes and the cancelling of diamond-export licences. The whole country seemed to be cheering. Momoh went into exile in Guinea.

The honeymoon for the coup-leaders was relatively brief. Sober behaviour soon gave way to high living and excess and popular cynicism set in just as quickly. As the ebb and flow of the war in the provinces gradually turned more and more against the government troops, now led by Strasser, Foday Sankoh's home-grown **Revolutionary United Front** (RUF) rather than Liberian rebels was identified as the main enemy.

Within months of the coup, the government had reorganized themselves so that the **National Provisional Ruling Council** (NPRC), henceforth known as the Supreme Council of State (the SCS), could get on with the war, while a partly civilian Council of Secretaries would run the country. Strange rumours started to circulate about soldiers fighting for the other side, about an exaggerated war and about a lack of interest in resolving the conflict.

Support for the NPRC turned to fear and resentment in some quarters after the **summary executions** of 26 alleged coup-plotters at River No. 2 beach: two of them, at least, had been languishing in Pademba Road jail when the plotting was supposed to have taken place, while sixteen others appear to have been just a rowdy group of drinkers arrested by nervous soldiers. Any residual support from the international community for an ideological young government facing huge odds now evaporated.

Yet grassroots support for "The Redeemer", as Strasser is known – comparing him with the young Jerry Rawlings of Ghana – seemed widespread. The long-awaited results of the Commissions of Enquiry set up to investigate fraud and corruption in Momoh's government pleased the whole country. And support for Strasser was further rejuvenated by the sacking of his increasingly domineering right-hand man, **Soloman "SAJ" Musa**, who was politely dispatched to England to study at Birmingham University. Musa was widely believed to have been behind the hasty executions on the beach. After his departure, Strasser's pragmatic style put him in control again; he released most political prisoners, thus freeing up promised debt relief from overseas and casting a different light on his government from the viewpoint of foreign donors.

Strasser legalized political activity in April 1995 and is going ahead with preparations for elections in 1995 or 1996. Presidential candidates have to be at least 40, thus eliminating Strasser and his colleagues from the running.

■ The state of Sierra Leone

There's a Sierra Leonean joke that when God created the world, he endowed the country with such a wealth of natural resources that the angels protested at the unfairness of his distribution. "Oh that's nothing", God replied. "Just wait and see the people I put there."

The country does have an exceptional wealth of natural resources. Diamonds and gold head the list of valuable exports, but iron ore, titanium (rutile), chrome, coffee and cocoa, palm oil and rice could all create the conditions for a country as prosperous as any in West Africa.

By the beginning of 1994, it was becoming clear that the civil war had degenerated into a muddled and many-sided conflict, the only rational principles in which were ones of self-interest economics. The principal cause of alarm is **"sobels"** – soldiers turned rebel. And the real fear – as troops sent to defend a town disappear to "catch" the rebels on the night of a raid and are never seen again – is that the situation is completely out of control; that it will only be resolved when there is nothing left to loot in the provinces and the military elite in Freetown faces a desperate ragtag army massing at the neck of the peninsula.

As well as the RUF, which is opposed not only by the Sierra Leonean army but by the anti-Taylor

ULIMO forces in Liberia, a new rebel group, which aims to reinstate Joseph Momoh – the **National Front for the Restoration of Democracy** (NAFORD) – is fighting Strasser's troops from bases in Guinea. Meanwhile, the **secret societies** – with their huge membership – are being co-opted into the war as self-defence units on the government side.

Strasser's NPRC has only survived with continued military support from Nigeria and Guinea, fresh troops from The Gambia and Ghana and mercenaries from Britain (Gurkhas) and South Africa. Nobody knows what demands Foday Sankoh is fighting to achieve except the removal of foreign troops from Sierra Leone. War deaths are running at 300 a month, and over a million of Sierra Leone's population of 4.5 million have been displaced.

Looking back, it seems clear that at least some of the civil war that started in 1991 was fabricated as a front for **diamond smuggling** by the APC. The funnel of wealth thus created – from Kono to Freetown and thence to London and safe bank accounts – bypassed the troops on the ground and the vast majority of Sierra Leoneans. The inescapable conclusion in 1995 is that exactly the same mechanism is still in operation, but in different hands.

FREETOWN

FREETOWN's dilapidation is extravagant. An aged and decaying tumble of sagging streets, clapboard and cement block buildings, with a population now in excess of half a million, it fills the level areas and spreads up the steep hillsides of the otherwise vegetation-flanked peninsula. Granted there are some newer, multi-storey buildings, but rot and collapse are ubiquitous among the palms and mango trees, and the prevailing sense is one of teetering on the edge of chaos. Flying in fresh from Europe the impact of so much mutant tropicality can shock temperate sensibilities.

Yet, if you're arriving from almost anywhere else in West Africa, Freetown's overall effect is enchanting, and its name appropriate. The town (and it feels like a town, not a city) gurgles with twice as much atmosphere as any other West African capital. The hilly relief gives constantly changing points of view and there are photogenic street prospects in every direction.

Architecture and a real depth of **history** have much to do with it. Run-down, pastel-painted Creole houses, with rusty-red tin roofs, often propped-up on posts against steeply scaling streets, are preserved even in the town centre. The anonymous apartment blocks and broad thoroughfares of many cities are largely absent from Freetown, their place still taken by an intimate, almost nineteenth-century hubbub, instantly recognizable to anyone who's travelled in the Caribbean. After dark you catch domestic glimpses, through the burglar bars and tatty curtains, of murky interiors lit by dim light bulbs – or by kerosene lamps. For many years, Freetown's **electricity** supply has been notoriously unruly, the short and long power cuts, and sudden runs of success, as unpredictable as downpours in the rainy season.

In practical terms, the town is mostly easy-going; the sheer good humour of the place compensates for high humidity and shambolic inconvenience. There's a fair choice of places to stay and eat, and the business and embassy districts are compact and central. Sierra Leone's best **beaches** are all nearby – far enough away to ensure clean water and tranquillity, but still a cheap taxi ride from the town centre and exceptionally beautiful.

Arrival and accommodation

Arriving by air and getting into town can be complicated. **Lungi International Airport** provides an unpredictable reception, and formalities can take ages. The airport bank closed in 1994; there's a reasonable **hotel** nearby, if you need somewhere to stay (see under "Accommodation" below).

The airport is cut off from Freetown by the mouth of the Sierra Leone River, which has to be crossed from **Tagrin Point Ferry Terminal**, 16km from Lungi. Ferries cross from here either to **Government Wharf** in the heart of Freetown, or to the old **Kissy Ferry Terminal** about 4km east of the centre. The former option (£7/$11 for foot passengers; £20/$30 for cars) is faster and more reliable, using a fairly new ferry, the *Bunce Island*, that runs to a schedule drawn up to coincide with aircraft arrivals and departures. Taking the Kissy route (passengers about £0.35/$0.55), the journey from the airport to the town centre takes a minimum of ninety minutes and can easily stretch to three hours depending on the health of the ferry.

TOURIST INFORMATION

There is no tourist office, so the next best thing is to visit the Ministry of Tourism and Cultural Affairs itself, down on Government Wharf, and pick up whatever info they have (☎022/225950).

KLM, *Ghana Airways* and *Sabena* run their own **airport buses**. The cost varies between airlines, but is around £20/$30 and includes the ferry fare. The advantage is that the airline buses are assured entry onto the ferry. Otherwise, the main transport from the airport is **taxis**. You've a couple of options here: one is to **charter** a taxi for the whole trip from the airport to your destination in Freetown (around £35/$53 including all luggage, but not counting your passenger fares on the Government Wharf ferry); alternatively, hop in a **shared taxi** at the airport exit going to the ferry dock at Tagrin Point (£1/$1.50 plus baggage charge), then charter a taxi at Kissy on the Freetown side to take you to your destination. In the daytime, this is really no problem, so long as you're not loaded with luggage. But beware the taxi drivers at the Kissy Ferry Terminal itself, who like to charge five or ten times the fair fare. If you're trying to save money, you may as well walk a few hundred metres from Kissy Ferry Terminal up to the main road into town, where ample numbers of shared taxis will be heading your way.

Arriving by road

There's only one main road into Freetown. In peacetime, government buses arrive at the **central bus station**, close to the heart of the town, in the old railway station building. Most of the smaller, privately owned **minibuses and "lorries"** have drop-off/pick-up points to the east of here. The main location for those serving the north of the country (Makeni, Kono and points north) is **"Ashoebi Corner"** on Blackhall Road at the Upgun turntable (roundabout), a taxi ride from the centre. Up-country vehicles also park at the **Dan Street bus park** (just off Kissy Road to the west of Upgun turntable) and at the **Shell filling station** in Kissy on the new road to Waterloo. Conakry vehicles park in **Free Street**, a couple of hundred metres uphill from PZ turntable at the eastern end of the town centre.

Orientation and city transport

Freetown's wonderful hilly layout is sprawling and confusing at first, and its north-facing aspect curiously disorientating. The town begins in the east at **Wellington**, and stretches into the poor residential areas of **Kissy**, **Cline Town**, **Fourah Bay**, **Kossa Town** and **Foulah Town** (together known as East End) and the half square kilometre of the main **commercial and business district**, which roughly coincides with the historical centre.

It's no longer possible to differentiate **quarters** of the town centre according to the origins of their inhabitants. But it's worth knowing that the oldest and most established blocks are roughly within a triangle formed by **Siaka Stevens Street** (the town's major thoroughfare), Pademba Road and Waterloo Street, with its apex the famous, huge **Cotton Tree**. This triangle was home to the freed slave Nova Scotians and the Maroons from Jamaica. The unfortunate English immigrants of 1787 settled a few hundred metres to the north of here on the peninsula of **Kingtom**.

The **East End "towns"** were originally mostly developed by immigrants from the interior and neighbouring parts of West Africa (Temne, Mende, Limba, Kissi, Fula, Yoruba and Bamana). Some arrived in the nineteenth century looking for commercial opportunities, but many, like the Kissi and the influxes of Muslim Yoruba from Nigeria, were recaptured slaves, saved from the Atlantic crossing. The character of this side of the town thus has a less creolized flavour. Many of its founding families were traders, and a great deal of trade still goes on in the East End.

West of the centre, through a jungle of ravines, streams and sprawling shanties, stretch the more residential, less commercial areas of **Congo Town**, **Murray Town**, **Wilberforce** and other nineteenth-century freed slave settlements. Down by the shore near the centre, **Kroo Town** is an area still largely inhabited by Kru fishing people from Liberia. A new road (Motor Main/Wilkinson/Aberdeen Road) cuts west out of the town, down the steep hillside to the sea and over a bridge to the Aberdeen Peninsula, on the far side of which lies the five-kilometre sweep of **Lumley Beach** and the head of the road that runs south along the peninsula shore.

City transport

There's no bus service in town but you can generally walk between most points in the centre. For slightly longer trips, wave down one of the **minibuses** or **route taxis** (unmetered, yellow licence plates) going in your direction (£0.10–0.15/$0.15–0.23 for short hops; about Le150 per mile). These run on agreed routes, dropping off and picking up anywhere. If you want to hire a **private cab**, you'll find that few do private business only and you'll pay roughly equivalent to the value of the journey to the driver, estimated on the pick-up basis (which normally adds up to around £3/$4.50 for most places in Freetown, and about £6/$9 to Lumley Beach). The main private cab park is at the *Paramount Hotel*. Alternatively, don't hesitate to try **hitching** a ride, especially if you're heading out to the beaches; many drivers will oblige. You can offer to pay (say twice the shared-taxi seat fare), but you'll often get free lifts. Siaka Stevens Street at the Cotton Tree roundabout is a likely spot.

Accommodation

Electricity ("light") is the limiting factor at all **hotels**. Often enough, you'll have to put up with power cuts that last most of the night, ruling out electric fans and air conditioning and necessitating hot kerosene lamps for lighting.

Basic lodgings

There are no campsites in Freetown and sleeping out at Lumley Beach is unsafe. The following cheap and mid-range places include an assortment of styles and tastes from the notorious *City* to the holier-than-thou *YMCA*.

Ambassador Hotel, 38 East St (☎022/228482). Cheerfully chaotic, with bright AC rooms and shared facilities. ③.

Andy's Apartments, 32 Rawdon St, opposite the *Golden Bay* restaurant. Large, comfortable S/C rooms, secure and very central. ③.

City Hotel, Lightfoot Boston St. A nocturnal institution (immortalized as the cockroach-infested *Bedford* in Graham Greene's *The Heart of the Matter*), to which access, surprisingly, seems to be reserved. "Always full", it's nonetheless worth trying to get one of the extremely cheap rooms. The often recumbent manager, and far from upright main bar and lobby, present an impression of spectacular seediness. ①.

Dabo Hotel, 18 Fourah Bay Rd (☎022/225910). Dank rooms, but cheap. ①.

Diplomat Hotel, Pipeline Rd, off Wilkinson Rd. Perhaps the best choice in the mid-range bracket. S/C, AC rooms and use of kitchen. TV-video lounge and ten minutes' drive from the beach. ③.

Hotel El Basha, East St. Rooms are available by the hour, or you can pay for a whole night. It's clean, and they do good food. ③.

Leona Hotel, 1 Back St (☎022/223587). Reasonable S/C rooms. ②.

SK Hotel, 59 Fourah Bay Rd. Poky and dark, but possible. ①.

Sonna Guest House, 66 Sanders St (☎022/223538). Comfortable enough, but overpriced. ③.

Tropic of Cancer, Gloucester St. For some years the cheapest hotel in town, with a few baking hot garret rooms and one or two lower down. Separate toilet and shower and uncertain security. Good chop and cheap beer at street level. ①.

YMCA, Fort St (PO Box 243; ☎022/223608). Remarkably good – elevated location with views, safe and squeaky clean and open to all. Single and twin rooms with fans and shared facilities. Often full; if you can book ahead, do so. Cheap beer and good meals (around £1–2/$1.50–3). ②.

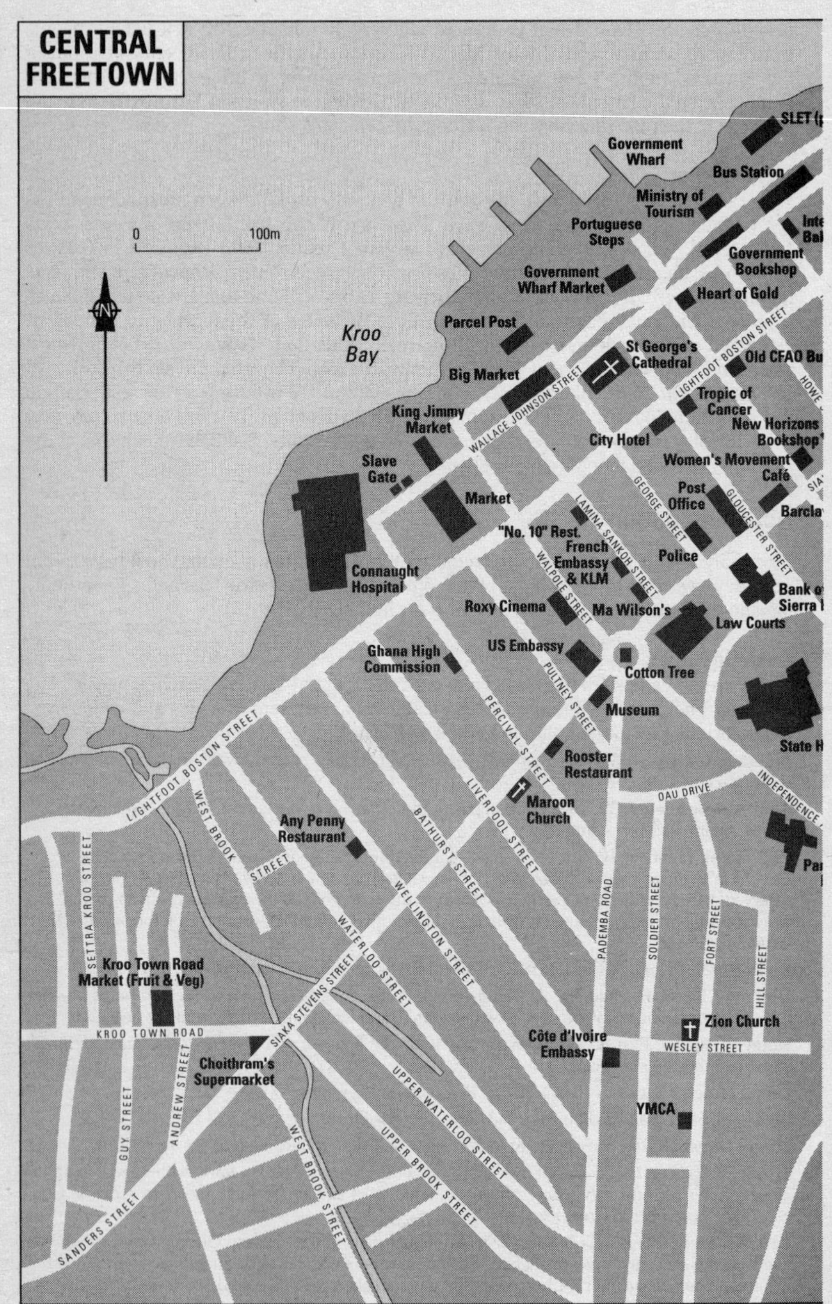
CENTRAL FREETOWN
0
100m
Kroo Bay
Government Wharf
Bus Station
Ministry of Tourism
Portuguese Steps
Government Bookshop
Government Wharf Market
Heart of Gold
Parcel Post
St George's Cathedral
LIGHTFOOT BOSTON STREET
Old CFAO Bu
Big Market
WALLACE JOHNSON STREET
Tropic of Cancer
King Jimmy Market
New Horizons Bookshop
City Hotel
Slave Gate
Women's Movement Café
Market
GEORGE STREET
Post Office
LAMINA SANKOH STREET
GLOUCESTER STREET
"No. 10" Rest.
French Embassy & KLM
Police
WALPOLE STREET
Connaught Hospital
Roxy Cinema
Ma Wilson's
Law Courts
Ghana High Commission
US Embassy
Cotton Tree
PULTNEY STREET
Museum
PERCIVAL STREET
Rooster Restaurant
LIGHTFOOT BOSTON STREET
WEST BROOK STREET
LIVERPOOL STREET
Maroon Church
OAU DRIVE
INDEPENDENCE
Any Penny Restaurant
BATHURST STREET
SETTRA KROO STREET
WELLINGTON STREET
PADEMBA ROAD
SOLDIER STREET
FORT STREET
HILL STREET
WATERLOO STREET
Kroo Town Road Market (Fruit & Veg)
SIAKA STEVENS STREET
Zion Church
KROO TOWN ROAD
Côte d'Ivoire Embassy
WESLEY STREET
Choithram's Supermarket
ANDREW STREET
GUY STREET
UPPER WATERLOO STREET
YMCA
WEST BROOK STREET
UPPER BROOK STREET
SANDERS STREET

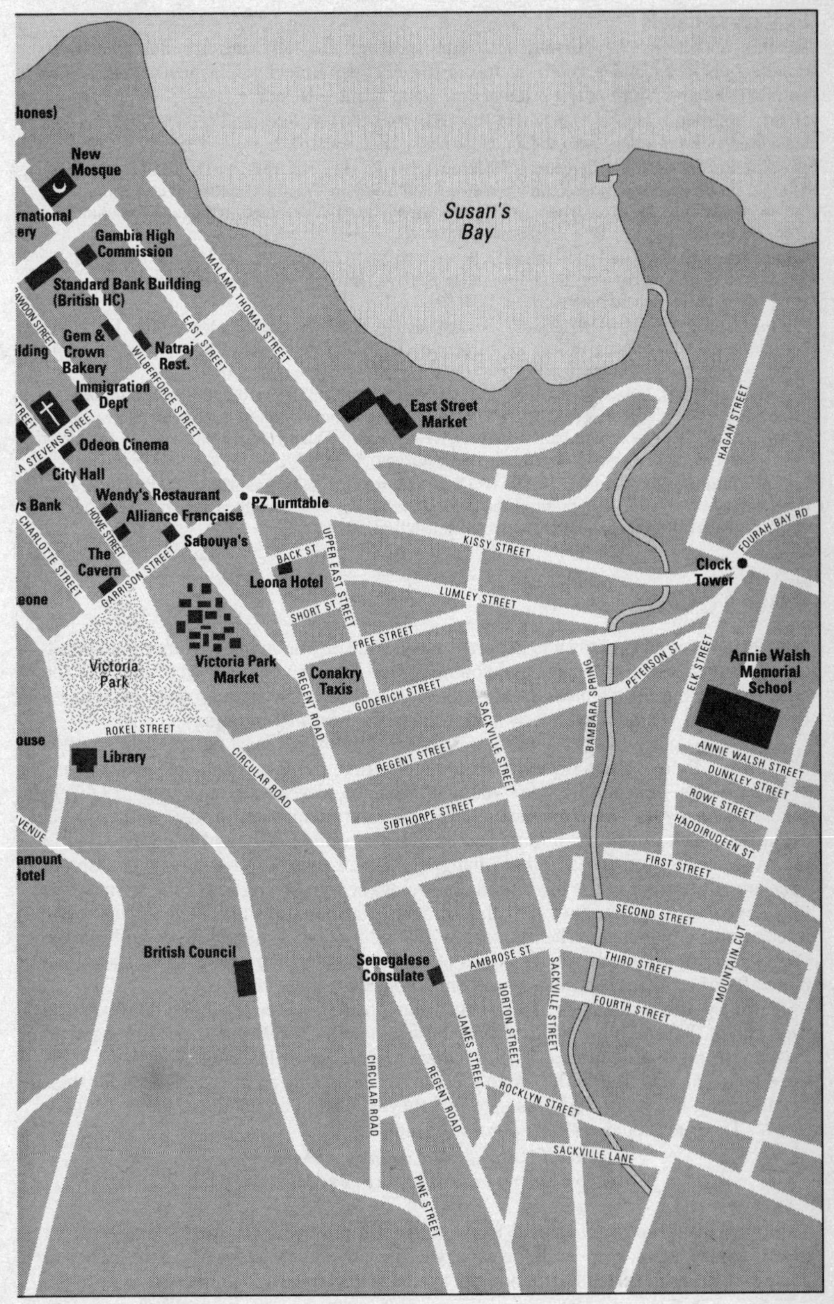

hones)
New Mosque
rnational ery
Gambia High Commission
Standard Bank Building (British HC)
Susan's Bay
MALAMA THOMAS STREET
EAST STREET
WILBERFORCE STREET
RAWDON STREET
Gem & Crown Bakery
Natraj Rest.
ilding
Immigration Dept
East Street Market
Odeon Cinema
STEVENS STREET
City Hall
Wendy's Restaurant
PZ Turntable
s Bank
Alliance Française
Sabouya's
CHARLOTTE STREET
HOWE STREET
The Cavern
GARRISON STREET
BACK ST
UPPER EAST STREET
Leona Hotel
KISSY STREET
HAGAN STREET
FOURAH BAY RD
Clock Tower
LUMLEY STREET
SHORT ST
eone
FREE STREET
Victoria Park
Victoria Park Market
Conakry Taxis
REGENT ROAD
GODERICH STREET
SACKVILLE STREET
BAMBARA SPRING
PETERSON ST
ELK STREET
Annie Walsh Memorial School
ROKEL STREET
ouse
Library
CIRCULAR ROAD
REGENT STREET
ANNIE WALSH STREET
DUNKLEY STREET
ROWE STREET
HADDIRUDEEN ST
SIBTHORPE STREET
VENUE
amount Hotel
FIRST STREET
SECOND STREET
British Council
Senegalese Consulate
AMBROSE ST
THIRD STREET
FOURTH STREET
MOUNTAIN CUT
HORTON STREET
JAMES STREET
CIRCULAR ROAD
REGENT ROAD
ROCKLYN STREET
SACKVILLE LANE
PINE STREET

Expensive hotels

Despite appearances, you may find that some of the following are not all they're cracked up to be and a room at one of the cheaper hotels would have been just as comfortable and a fifth of the price of one out at Lumley Beach.

Hotel Bintumani, Lumley Beach (PO Box 655; ☎022/231122; Fax 022/272197). Good location, but a tired, unloved atmosphere and a run-down pool area. B&B ⑦.

Brookfields Hotel, Jomo Kenyatta Rd/Mereweather Rd (PO Box 1193; ☎022/241860 or 240875). The old government resthouse (now the Hotel and Tourism Training Centre) gets much abused but still tends to be the place where expats stay when in town. Live music on Sun and sometimes on Wed. B&B ⑥.

Cape Sierra Hotel, Lumley Beach (PO Box 54; ☎022/272266 or 272269). Of the three Lumley Beach hotels, this is the one to choose. Nice S/C, AC bungalows, rooms and suites, a pleasant atmosphere and excellent management. B&B ⑦.

Lungi Airport Hotel (☎022/025345). Self-explanatory and not exactly adventurous, but worth considering if you're flying in late (or flying out early), and much better than you've reason to expect – lovely garden and pool, and even a decent beach on the doorstep. B&B ⑦.

Paramount Hotel, Independence Ave (PO Box 574; ☎022/224531; Fax 022/224533). Comfortable, establishment, town-centre stand-by with large S/C, AC rooms (with discounts for Sierra Leone residents) and big restaurant, bars and (usually) electricity. Quietly seedy (the *YMCA*, one block away, is just as good, if you don't mind sharing bathrooms). B&B ⑥.

Sofitel Mammy Yoko, Lumley Beach (PO Box 563; ☎022/272445; Fax 022/272511). The pretentious atmosphere here is off-putting, the prices doubly so. Surprisingly run-down. Pools, tennis courts and a private beach, but the rooms are small. B&B ⑦.

The Town

Wandering around Freetown is generally easy. True, it can be murderously uncomfortable outside the cooler season, and you may not delay long before migrating out to the beaches, but the town's pleasant decrepitude conceals a few sights to see, including a **museum** and, remarkably, nearly a hundred **churches and mosques**.

An obvious place to start a walking tour, and Freetown's most famous landmark, is the **Cotton Tree**, a magnificent silk-cotton older than the town itself and as tall as any of its buildings. Beneath the tree's younger branches, slaves were once sold; in 1787, in the same place, the first colonists from England are supposed to have gathered – a group of "Black Poor" immigrants and sixty white women who had been deported to Sierra Leone. Notice the large **bats** hanging, in their tens of thousands, in the Cotton Tree and other trees in the town centre, sleeping, or squabbling, above the town traffic: every evening at sunset, they set off, in dramatic fashion, for their feeding sites in the interior of the peninsula. The statuesque 1920s **law courts** nearby were built on the spot where the trials and adjudications of captured slave ship captains and crew took place after the British parliament had banned the slave trade in 1808.

Down **by the waterfront**, there's a meagre pair of historical monuments. At the west end of Wallace Johnson Road, the entrance to what's now the lower dispensary of Connaught hospital is formed by the "**Slave Gate**". Slaves liberated from slave ships were detained behind it in the "King's Yards" while arrangements were made for their resettlement. It was through this gate that they walked to an unknown future in "Free Town". The sanctimonious inscription still reads:

Royal Hospital and Asylum for Africans
Freed from Slavery by British Valour and Philanthropy
A.D. 1817

The quite inappropriately named **Portuguese Steps**, below Wallace Johnson Street near the bus station, were built the same year by Governor Charles McCarthy. They're a handsome flight, certainly, but nowadays utterly neglected and unnoticed.

Street art

In January 1993, there was a spontaneous outburst of nationalism that resulted in Freetown being painted over. Throughout the streets of the town you will see **murals** of the NPRC leadership, historical figures such as Bai Burreh and Sengbe Pieh, and depictions of morality. It was an incredible three months that saw the streets transformed. Unfortunately, some of the artwork has washed away with the rains, but there are still some excellent murals of historical figures at the Central Prisons on Pademba Road and some fascinating depictions of moral behaviour along Syke Street by the National Stadium.

In addition to the wall murals, the youth built flower boxes and sculpted some crude figures that appear at turntables (roundabouts) and down the central reservations of a number of streets. Some of the more fascinating cement **sculptures** are on Fourah Bay Road in front of PCMH (Cottage) Hospital – if you are heading out to the old Fourah Bay College, you will have an opportunity to see them.

Old Fourah Bay College

Freetown's most famous institution is **Fourah Bay College**, the oldest university in West Africa. The modern (though atrophied) university is located up at Mount Aureol, south of the town centre and is worth a visit itself, partly for the stunning view. But it's interesting to go and see the **original Fourah Bay building**, founded in 1827 by the Church Missionary Society, and now a Magistrate's Court, and it makes a good excuse for an exploration of one of the town's poorer, older and much-bypassed East End quarters. The old four-storey building at the end of College Road in Cline Town dates from 1845, and is made of red laterite bricks and decorated with iron fretwork. **Samuel Adjai Crowther**, the college's first student, later became the first home-grown Bishop of West Africa.

Churches and mosques

Of eighty **churches** and nearly two dozen **mosques**, the oldest place of worship is **St. John's Maroon Church**, a diminutive white chapel on the south side of Siaka Stevens Street two blocks west of the Cotton Tree. It was founded by the first freed slave settlers from Jamaica in about 1820. In construction around the same time was the colonial high temple of **St. George's Cathedral** on Lightfoot Boston Street, completed in 1828 and dedicated in 1852. Memorial plaques inside commemorate British administra-

THE REVEREND KOELLE AND HIS POLYGLOTTA AFRICANA

It was at Fourah Bay College, in 1852, that a young German pastor, the **Rev. S.W. Koelle**, published an extraordinary collection of vocabularies from nearly 200 West and Central African languages, the **Polyglotta Africana**. Working with immense speed he interviewed 205 informants – most of them freed slaves – and recorded the translations of about 300 words and phrases in their natal languages. He got some curious replies: one man apparently replied "Gud-bai" when Koelle asked him to give the phrase for "I am going". But the finished book is a remarkable achievement, far in advance of anything produced until then, and still useful to linguists, and interesting to look through, today; there are copies in the university library and recent editions available abroad. Apart from giving clues about the relatedness of different West African languages, the *Polyglotta* also gives interesting cultural information. Less than a third of the informants, for example, could come up with words in their mother tongues for "butter" or "ink" and there were problems too with "book", "hell" and "soap". Missionaries must have found the blanks provocative.

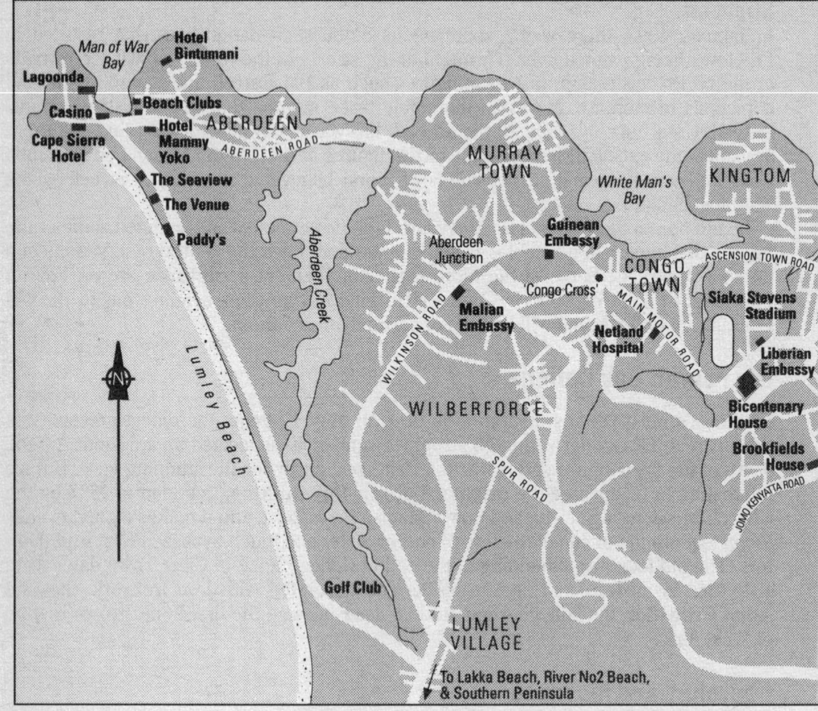

tors and traders who didn't survive the "White Man's Grave" to return home. The **Zion Church** on Fort Street is one to check out during a service; it's very audible every Sunday morning from the *YMCA*. The Catholic community, much smaller than the reforming churches, has its relatively modest **Sacred Heart Cathedral** on Siaka Stevens Street, on the corner of Howe Street.

Sunday is the day when you can't fail to notice the importance of Freetown's churches, as thousands of people, and especially the Krio community, dress in their **Sunday best** – classically, men in dark suits and homburgs, women in frocks and creative hats, boys in sailor suits and girls in virginal white frills. Services are long and enthusiastic.

The oldest mosque is the **Foulah Town Mosque** on Mountain Cut, just off Kissy Road in the East End. It's surprisingly church-like in its design, possibly in deference to the concerns of colonial and Creole ruling groups in the mid-nineteenth century – there was considerable opposition to Islam from Christian freed slaves. The freed Yoruba slaves from Nigeria (known as "**Aku**" or "Oku") were predominantly Muslims. In 1832, a British lawyer, **William Henry Savage**, was persuaded by his Aku servant to press for the release of a group of Aku who had been jailed for practising "Muhammedanism". In gratitude, several took the name Savage, and a mosque was built near his house, in the street now called Savage Square. Encouraged by this, other Aku built the Foulah Town Mosque a kilometre further west. But opposition to Islam, and a low-key conflict between the Creoles and the Aku (who came to be considered "Muslim creoles") has kept mosques out of the commercial town centre – a quarter containing no less than sixteen churches – to this day.

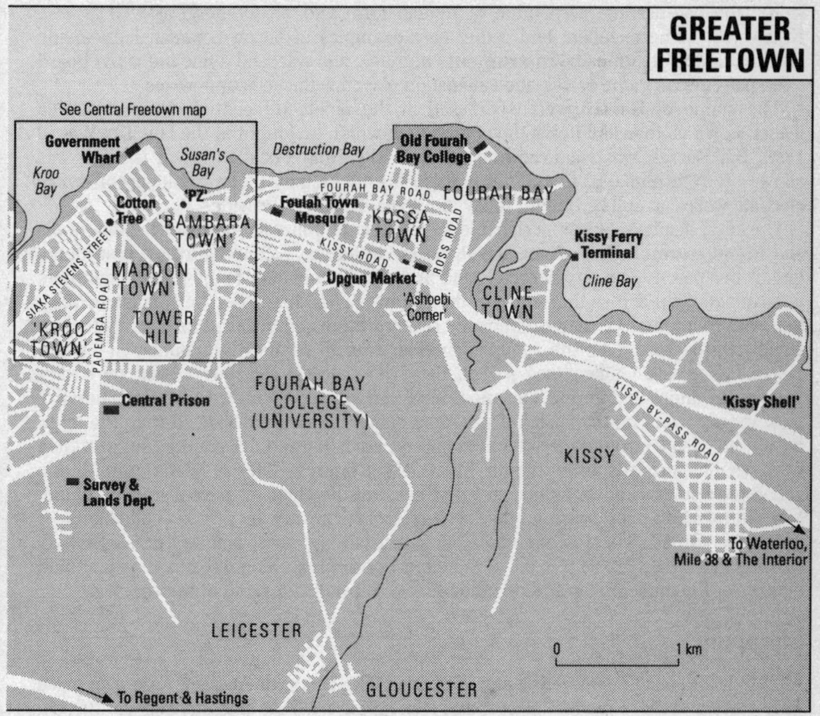

Sierra Leone museum

The newly refurbished **museum** (Mon–Fri 10am–4pm; entry by donation; curator ☎022/223555) was, until 1929, a railway terminus ("Cotton Tree Station") at the foot of the "Hill railway" up to Wilberforce and Hill Station. The diminutive white building then saw service as a school, a soft drinks factory and a telephone exchange before becoming the repository of Sierra Leonean cultural heritage in 1957. The collections are emphatically worth a visit: this is Sierra Leone's only museum. There aren't many visitors and you're likely to get a guided tour of some kind.

The **Ruiter stone** replica takes pride of place in the museum. This 1664 rock graffito, scratched by bored Dutch sea captains during a lull in a military expedition against the English, was discovered in the course of drainage work on the waterfront in 1923. It's the oldest archaeological evidence of a European presence on the peninsula. A rubbing of the names and date ("M. A. Ruiter, I. C. Meppell, Vice Admiralen, Van Hollant en Westfriesland, AD 1664") was made and the stone was then reburied "six feet below the ground just above the high water mark at King Jimmy Market, to protect it from the weather". Potentially more interesting is another stone, yet to be uncovered, but referred to by Richard Burton in 1862, which is supposed to carry the initials of Francis Drake and Richard Hawkins.

The museum's main interest, though, lies in the **ethnographic pieces** from around the country. There's an interesting mask corner where some of the regalia from Sierra Leone's still lively **secret societies** is fearlessly displayed. Look out for the figure of "**Mammy Wata**", the transmogrifying Medusa-like sea goddess (a widespread coastal icon) who can assume serpentine or human form and act for good as well as evil. Notice too, some excellent and rather rare examples of Sierra Leonean home-made **country cloth**, the unusual **instruments** of music and war, and a fine old *warri* board – the pan-African game of risk and calculation played with seeds or cowries.

The statue of **Bai Burreh** is dressed in the nineteenth-century Temne guerilla leader's own clothes and holds the cutlass with which he fought in the Hut Tax War of 1898. Bai Burreh was captured and taken to the Gold Coast to rot in jail, but was allowed to return in 1905 to end his years in his old kingdom. The "bullet-proof" *ronko* cloth he wore can still be bought today in Kabala, Northern Province.

Upstairs, displays of less perishable items include minerals, prehistoric stone tools and Mende **nomoli**. *Nomoli* are small, rather arcane soapstone figurines, first identified from a pair dug up on Sherbro Island in the 1880s and later found in huge numbers in farmland right across the centre of the country. The Mende don't claim any connection with them, though they traditionally revered them and believed they protected the fertility of the land. Like the *pomtan* (singular *pomdo*) of the Kissi country in eastern Sierra Leone and Guinea (see p.516), they were almost certainly carved by earlier peoples as ancestor figures. The most likely artists are thought to be the **Sherbro**. Now mostly living on the island of the same name, they were displaced from the interior by the Mende around the fifteenth century. Early Portuguese sources suggest they were the best artisans in the region. Much larger figures – lifesize heads from Mende and Kono country known as *mahen yafe* ("spirit of the chief") – have also been found. Like the *nomoli* and *pomtan*, the best ones are mostly in private collections or museums abroad. Sierra Leone has a fairly flourishing tourist industry in fake *nomoli* (pay no more than £3/$4.50): since the export of the real thing is banned, you should enquire at the museum for authorization to take reproductions out of the country.

Shopping

Although it doesn't have the big stores of a city like Dakar or Abidjan, Freetown has a wide variety of more modest places, and a shopping tradition that still reflects British, Indian and Mediterranean tastes.

Arts and crafts

All the way up Howe Street, as far as the entrance to Victoria Park, you'll find a succession of street traders where, if you can hang on long enough, you're almost bound to get good prices. For **musical instruments** – *balangis*, shake-shakes and so on – try down at Lumley Beach.

Charlie's No.1 Shop, at the *Paramount Hotel*. Not all curios, and not all the items are as expensive as you might imagine – a good place for protracted bargaining over gear from all over Africa.

Francis Johnson's Shop, at the *Paramount Hotel*. Johnson is the best batik artist in the country. Ask for his best batiks (from about £25/$38), otherwise they may only show you the cheap ones.

Gaga Studios, Main Motor Rd. Gallery of paintings by Sierra Leonean artists. Some of the works are interesting and desirable: expect to pay £70–140/$100–200. In addition to the paintings there are more reasonably priced crafts.

King Jimmy Cultural Centre, Lamina Sankoh St. A good bet for little presents, postcards and cheap crafts.

Mama Khadi Al-Haja Tejan Kamara, 3A Main Motor Rd (take Aberdeen junction transport and get off 500m past the stadium at Brookfields). Good batiks can sometimes be found here but, more importantly, Mama Khadi is the best *gara* artisan in Freetown. Her work is high quality and more expensive than in the market and she often has designs that can't be found there.

Tailors

If you like the idea of having **clothes** made to measure, it's possible to find skilled, cheap and astoundingly rapid workmanship all over Freetown. As ever, the ideal way of

FREETOWN MARKETS

Freetown's **markets** are an animated lot and you can spend many enjoyable hours just pushing though them with no definite object in mind. For specific bargaining and purchases, try the following:

King Jimmy Market Tuesday and Thursday for fruit, vegetables and fish.

Government Wharf Market Daily, for general goods from pomade to potato peelers, including lots of "dead men's clothes".

Big Market ("Basket Market") Daily, a covered market for a range of crafts, tourist bric-a-brac, traditional medicines and mystical materials. There are good baskets (*shuku*, *blai*), some nice musical instruments, and rather a lot of small animal skins, but you need to spend some time at the stalls to discover interesting bargains that you'd actually want to take home.

Victoria Park Tourist Market Can be fun, but keep your wits about you: a lot of people are after your custom. This is the best market in Freetown for Sierra Leonean "country cloth" and locally made-up dresses and shirts.

Kroo Town Road Fruit and vegetables, open every day.

East Street/Kissy Road Market A place of some commotion. There's a good fruit and veg market, open every day, and numbers of small stores trading in cloth and other merchandise.

Upgun/Kennedy Street Market On the left, 1500 metres further east down Kissy Road from the East Street Market, immediately before the Upgun roundabout.

Bombay Street Market In Kossa Town, the old Bamana (Bambara) quarter, not far from the shore.

being sure that you get what you want is to take along an item of your own clothing for use as a pattern. One of the very best spots is next to *Paladio* in Rawdon Street, but there are many others along Sackville Street and Pademba Road.

Zanasu, 56 Pademba Road, and **Mayaima**, 54 Pademba Road, are tailors noted for their embroidery work or "planting".

Kadie's Zodiac Boutique, 3 Locust St, off Patton St, off Kissy Road. Features unisex styles and fashion designs, and "sewing the seams of your dreams".

Groceries

There are rather frequent and unpredictable shortages of various foodstuffs. Listed below are some of the more central shops but for a huge number of African stores, head out to the East End.

Atson's, Wilkinson Rd, just before "Texaco" (the Aberdeen junction). For fancier tastes and home-food-sickness, most cravings can be remedied here. There's a large selection, plus toys.

China Store, Lightfoot Boston St. Noodles and canned food.

Choithrams, corner of Siaka Stevens St and Krootown Rd. If you can't find what you want elsewhere, this is a good, all-round, air-conditioned supermarket; and there are several smaller grocery shops stacked with food and drink nearby.

Cold Point, Murray Town Road, Congo Cross. Imported ice cream.

Dina's, Siaka Stevens St, on the corner of Wilberforce St. Greek food, imported cheese, chocolates and imported fruit.

First Choice, 21A East St. Chocolate and wines.

The Food Store, Howe St. Delicatessen selling cold meat, sausages and dairy produce.

Eating and drinking

The town is well endowed with **eating places**. While a number of them have depended heavily on resident volunteers and aid workers, there are some good Lebanese and more authentic African chop-houses and snackeries too. Many restaurants close on

Sunday. There's good **street food** at night at St. John's Corner – the intersection of Campbell Street and Sanders Street. Here you will find roast meat, chicken, fish, oysters, beans, bean and rice *akara*, and other fried foods. At the Aberdeen Road–Wilkinson Road junction, you'll find a less extensive selection. There are several decent restaurants and bars out at Lumley Beach (see p.568).

Chop

Best Foods, Victoria Park. A nice little snack/chop house in a pleasant setting. Opening hours are irregular – usually open for lunch, until 4pm. Occasionally open in the evenings.

The Cavern, 31 Garrison St. Good Sierra Leonean chop in a real sit-down restaurant. Blander international dishes too. Cold beer. Meals from £2 ($3).

Heart of Gold, 1 Charlotte St across from City Hall. For lunch a very wide selection of Sierra Leonean food (decent, but not the best in town). Bar/nightclub in the evening.

Ma Wilson's Cookery Shop, 7 Lamina Sankoh St. Wonderful cheap place for good chop, big breakfasts, bean sandwiches and more. Beer and crafts too, and a good atmosphere. Daytime only.

Number 10 (aka *Monica's*), Lamina Sankoh St next to *KLM*. Top-quality chop in a restaurant setting. You might meet politicians here: it's owned by Desmond Luke, foreign minister in the early 1970s.

Paladio, 4 Rawdon St. Recommended chop house which becomes a lively club in the evening.

Romie's, 10 Wallace Johnson St. Stays open until 7pm for good *plasas*.

Sabouya's, Garrison St, entrance on Rawdon St. Really popular for its nicely positioned first-floor dining rooms. Less to rave about with the food – decent enough but, most notably, cheap.

Sierra Leone Women's Movement Cafe, 15 Charlotte St. Good chop.

Snacks and fried food

Any Penny, 25 Wellington St. Inexpensive, small and friendly, selling above-average burgers, chicken, steak, plus home-made yoghurt.

Burgerland, 69 Siaka Stevens St. Dance floor and beer inside, sit-down and beer outside. And burgers. The street food stalls outside and round about (especially after dark) are lively competition.

Crown Bakery, Wilberforce St next to the *Gem*. Clean, AC, and well run, with the best pastries in town and decent food for lunch – fried chicken, sandwiches, pizza. Only open during the day.

International Bakery, Rawdon St. Croissants and *pain au chocolat* for breakfast; coffee, ice cream, fresh bread. Closes 5pm Mon–Fri, Sat 1pm; Sun closed all day.

Ready Foods, East St. The best take-away Lebanese sandwiches.

Rooster Restaurant, Electricity House, Siaka Stevens St. Great fried chicken (£3–5/$4.50–7.50) and sandwiches.

Shupa Burger, 9 Gloucester St, across from *Salpost*. Good burgers and cold soft drinks – nothing else. Really is a take-away place since it only has two benches. Second branch at the Clock Tower.

Snack House Fast Food, 16 Rawdon St. Air-conditioned snack bar and beer parlour with burgers and ice-cream.

Wendy's Restaurant, 24 Howe St. Lunches, and a lively bar at night.

Lebanese and international

Afroditis (aka *Khadra's*), 26 Walpole St. An American-flavour Lebanese, with fried foods, salads and sandwiches, good *merguez* sausages, *kebeh*, beer. Rather expensive. Club behind.

Balmaya Arts and Snacks, Main Motor Rd, just before Congo Cross. One of the best restaurants, with tasty, expensive Sierra Leonean food and good and reasonably priced continental fare. It can take a while to come: spend the time browsing the art gallery off to the side.

Chung Hwa, Wilkinson Rd. A very European Chinese, but the only one in town.

Country Kitchen, Main Motor Rd, Congo Cross. Notoriously bad service, but good sandwiches and cold drinks, if you have the patience to wait.

Gem, 7 Wilberforce St (☎022/223644). Big and busy, this is Freetown's best Lebanese restaurant, with an extensive menu and really good coffee. From about £17 ($25) for two (on a Visa card if you like). Open daily except Sun, 8am–10.30pm.

Marianne Salvador, Pultney St. Classy continental eating house, with quasi-pizza, paella and shrimps. Accordingly expensive. The good-value Thursday lunch buffet is the biggest attraction.

Natraj, 18 Wilberforce St. Great Indian food and good value, though you may have to wait an hour after ordering.

Provilac, Wilkinson Rd. Long-established African lunch buffet (closed evenings). Expensive and nearly worth it.

Nightlife

Sadly, the frequent power failures that leave Freetown in the dark after dark disrupt the town's **nightlife**. The surest – and blandest – **music and dance** scene is out at Lumley Beach (see overleaf), where many places have generators. Of the **town clubs** that follow, many are really only bars for most of the time. Although some town-centre clubs have survived many years, others tend to be sporadic and short-lived venues. Always carry a torch (*tochlait*), or you'll end up in a storm drain. For clubs in the East End, hire a taxi for the whole evening from the *Paramount Hotel*.

Town clubs

In addition to the following selection, note that many daytime restaurants (see "Eating and drinking", above) become bars and places of entertainment in the evenings.

Afroditis, Walpole St. Rear-of-restaurant club.

All Nations, Main Motor Rd, next to *Provilac*.

Brookfields Hotel, Jomo Kenyatta Rd. On Sun night there's a popular happy hour and polite dance; small entry charge and resident band – currently Sierra Afrique.

Countdown, Sanders St. A very lively club.

Eruption, Liverpool St, off Pademba Rd. Small, friendly club, tiny dance floor.

Kaselle, Wellington St. Can feel heavy, like other bars nearby. Fun if you're in the mood.

Midnight Mary Bar & Restaurant, Sandurst St.

Paladio, Rawdon St. A good chophouse by day, this has great music and dancing and a regular strip show – performed in the dark.

Storm, Ross Rd, Cline Town. Sometimes offers live music.

Taiwo Chandis, Blackhall Rd, Kissy. A club that really moves, with a good restaurant.

The Beaches

The **beaches** of the Freetown Peninsula are arguably the finest in West Africa, and certainly only those in western Côte d'Ivoire offer any competition. Lumley, the closest to central Freetown, is usually the busiest, and one of the less perfect. **Single women** – lone men too – should beware, as there's a general increase in bag-snatchings and other encounters to be avoided on Lumley Beach. Bring nothing of value, and your camera only if you're going to take pictures. Ideally, go in a group. Of Sierra Leone's handful of beach **hotels**, the three main ones (*Bintumani*, *Cape Sierra* and *Mammy Yoko*; see p.560) are on or near Lumley Beach; several others nestle on isolated strands further south.

Lumley Beach

Getting to the beach from downtown Freetown, you can share a taxi from the Cotton Tree to take you the 5km to "Texaco" (the garage of that name at the junction for Lumley village/Aberdeen) from where there are slightly cheaper shared vehicles to Aberdeen and the beach. But unless the heat is overpowering, it's worth walking some of the way, at least from "Texaco" onwards – about an hour's walk in the unlikely event of your not getting a lift.

At Lumley Beach's first roundabout, the *Hotel Bintumani* is up on the right. Continue west and the entrance on the right leads to the small, sheltered, north-facing beach of Man O'War Bay and some beach bars and restaurants. On the left is the *Sofitel Mammy Yoko* (named after the powerful nineteenth-century queen), that used to rely heavily on French package tourists and is now rather in decline.

A second roundabout sends you, to the right, up to Cape Sierra and the hotel of the same name, to the headland **lighthouse**, and to the *Lagoonda* entertainment complex, with its bright lights glittering across Man O'War Bay after sunset. In front of you starts the great sweep of **Lumley Beach**, dotted with the odd coconut tree, but backed mostly by scrub and grass. In season, there's a cluster of **beach bars** and snack restaurants, detailed below. The beach here is pleasant, sloping gently, with little undertow and, on occasions, half-pint waves. Late in the afternoon, the beach road from the hotels down to Lumley village makes a nice walk, and, if you've got the equipment, an equally good run or cycle ride (it's exactly 5km from Lumley Beach North to Lumley centre). A lift back again should be easy to find.

Beach bars, clubs and restaurants

Atlantic Beach Bar, Lumley Beach. At the southern end of the beach, this is well run with a quiet ambience and excellent food.

Blue Dolphin, at the *Cape Sierra Hotel*, north end of Lumley Beach. An excellent restaurant with good food at moderate prices, brunch on Saturdays and a band in the evenings.

Casino Leone, Lumley Beach. Free entry, but not in beach wear. Slots plus blackjack and roulette.

Lagon Bleu, Aberdeen Bridge (☎022/272282). Nightclub in a French chalet hotel.

Lagoonda The country's major entertainment complex, next to the *Cape Sierra Hotel*, includes a perfectly reasonable, air-conditioned disco palace with recent international sounds and a well-behaved, largely Lebanese and European crowd. Also has two new restaurants and a cinema.

Paddy's Beach Bar, just south of the *Venue*, Lumley Beach. Genial owner-manager and excellent food make this the most popular beach bar. Background music is mostly gruesome 1970s, except at weekends, when there's usually a band.

Sans Souci, right on the beach by the Aberdeen/Lumley roundabout near *Blue Dolphin*. Wonderful ice cream at decent prices.

Sea View Beach Bar, Lumley Beach. Has a fitness centre, with gym equipment.

Venue Beach Bar, Lumley Beach. The most northerly of the Lumley beach bars, this is the least friendly, the least clean, the least maintained and the most expensive and paradoxically the most popular, probably because it's also a pick-up joint. The owner recently returned to Lebanon so its status is in doubt.

Where Else?, *Bintumani Hotel*, Aberdeen. Open Wed to Sun. Band on Fri. Sat nights are college nights, and the place is usually packed. No cover charge and a more laid-back atmosphere than some of the beach bars.

The southern beaches

For committed sun and sand devotees, the **southern reaches of the peninsula** harbour some spectacular shores. If you go as far as **Tombo**, there may be an occasional ferry south via the Plantain Islands to **Shenge**, which, in peacetime, is an attractive means of heading on down the coast.

SECURITY

Before setting off down the peninsula, be sure that your destination is safe. Rebel incursions in 1995 came very close to the peninsula itself.

While it's useful to have wheels of your own for **getting around the peninsula**, it's not absolutely necessary, so long as you don't mind hitching, or muddling along in whatever "public" transport comes your way. *Poda podas* go down this way several times a day, though not beyond York. You're more likely to score a lift at the roundabout in Lumley village, with weekenders or expatriates. On weekdays, the sand lorries that scour certain beaches for Freetown's building requirements often give lifts. Be prepared for some walking; it's a badly maintained road, but pretty for most of its length. Road signs, distances and directions aren't always clear: those included below, unless indicated otherwise, are road distances from Lumley roundabout.

Goderich

Out of **Lumley village**, past the quaint red-brick St Mary's Church, and Siaka Stevens' distant mansion perched high above, you cross Lumley Creek and pass the *Let's Live Hospital*. After Juba Beach, which is somewhat cluttered, **Goderich** (3km from Lumley and 1km off the road) is the first beach, a perfectly good place to see an archetypal West African event late every afternoon – the **return of the fishing boats** – but not one to go out of your way for otherwise. Goderich village sits behind the yellow kilometre of steeply shelving sand.

Lakka

From here on, the coast road steadily deteriorates. In places the tar surface gives up completely; if you're driving, beware some dastardly potholes. A sign (4km) for the "Milton Margai Training College" indicates one access to the first really wonderful beach, **Lakka Beach**, which consists of a pair of long, gently shelving bays punctuated by a minuscule, rocky peninsula, two-thirds of the way down. There's little to spoil it at present. At the far north end the bay curves to face the south, beneath a riot of vegetation. Beyond the rocky promontory, the second bay crescents down towards Hamilton, with a cascade of coconut jungle behind it and the select *Cotton Club* (⑦) at its southern end.

If you don't get down to Lakka beach from "Milton Margai", continue, past the ancient colonial **Adonkia police station**, to Lakka junction (8km: if you pass the wretched-looking Lakka Isolation Hospital for TB and leprosy victims, you'll know you've gone too far). Lakka village is just down here, the beach itself ten minutes' walk away.

River No. 2

The main road, meanwhile, climbs through the foothills, past the Guma Dam turn-off/checkpoint (14km) and down to **Sussex** (16km). There's another rocky cove at Sussex, and a pleasant beach a kilometre further at **Bawbaw**, but most people head on, close to the shore, to **River No. 2** (19km) and the much-hyped beach of the same name. This is magnificent, Rousseau-esque country – dense, green jungle hills rising steeply behind a beach of brilliant white sand, constantly modified and redesigned by the River No. 2 (Guma River) which flows behind and around it, and whose headwaters are stemmed by the Guma Dam, a few kilometres inland. No. 2 beach, however, while great to look at, has unstable swimming conditions, and a very steep shelf. On weekends in season, and on public holidays, it also gets busy, with "car park attendants", food stalls, even crafts, set up among the village houses behind.

Tokey

While at low tide you can get across the river from No. 2 beach to the much longer stretch of **Tokey Beach**, you're then stuck until the next low tide, unless you walk the 3km or so to Tokey village to find the track up to the main road. Tokey Beach (27km)

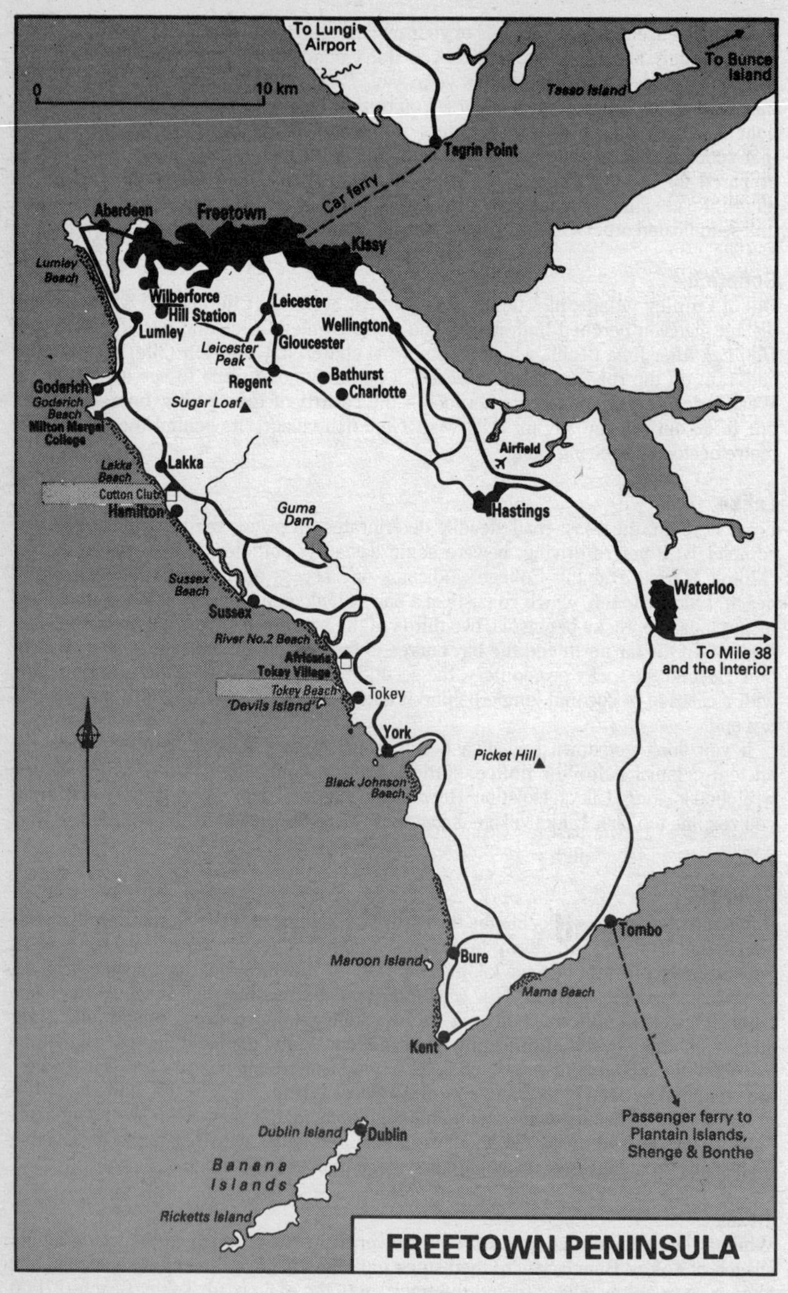
To Lungi Airport
To Bunce Island
Tasso Island
0
10 km
Tagrin Point
Car ferry
Aberdeen
Freetown
Kissy
Lumley Beach
Wilberforce
Hill Station
Lumley
Leicester
Wellington
Leicester Peak
Gloucester
Regent
Bathurst
Charlotte
Goderich
Goderich Beach
Milton Margai College
Sugar Loaf
Airfield
Lakka
Lakka Beach
Cotton Club
Hamilton
Hastings
Guma Dam
Sussex Beach
Sussex
Waterloo
River No.2 Beach
Africana Tokey Village
To Mile 38 and the Interior
Tokey Beach
Tokey
'Devils Island'
York
Picket Hill
Black Johnson Beach
Tombo
Maroon Island
Bure
Mama Beach
Kent
Passenger ferry to Plantain Islands, Shenge & Bonthe
Dublin Island
Dublin
Banana Islands
Ricketts Island
FREETOWN PENINSULA

has, among a number of private chalets and villas, the *Africana Tokey Village*, on a marvellous stretch of safe beach, where the forest comes right to the sands. A kilometre off Tokey Beach, **Devils Island** is reputed to be a meeting place of male *Poro* society members.

York and Black Johnson

Four kilometres beyond Tokey junction, you come to the village of **York** (31km) at the mouth of Whale River creek. There's an **old fort** (at one time a rest house) on the other side of the village, with glorious views. From here south, all semblance of surfaced road ceases, and transport becomes very difficult.

If you're fairly self-sufficient, and don't expect to get back anywhere the same day, you could walk on to **Black Johnson Beach** (36km), on Whale Bay, five hilly kilometres round the creek from York. You might also find a boat to take you the relatively short distance across the creek. Palm-fringed, remote and quite undeveloped, with clear sea, Black Johnson is an excellent area for snorkelling or diving.

Kent and the Banana Islands

At the southern extremities of the peninsula, and off the main dirt road, are **Bure** (48km) and **Kent** (52km), both of which have beaches several kilometres long. Kent's reputation for sharks in the water and cannibals inland is worth bearing in mind, though the former are the more likely contemporary worry, and even then rarely encountered. The forested Maroon Island, just 300m from the shore, lies between Bure and Kent beaches. The main point of coming down to Kent, though, is to find a boat across to the **Banana Islands** 5km offshore. Prepare yourself for some vigorous bargaining. Dublin Island and Ricketts Island are joined by a causeway and have villages of the same names at opposite ends connected by an eight-kilometre footpath. Dublin has a couple of small beaches (limpid water and some coral) on its northwest coast; Ricketts is steeper (233m high) and more densely forested. Neither has any real facilities, so take supplies and adaptability. Mes-Meheux, an uninhabited island, lies southwest, just off Ricketts' shore.

Back on the mainland, east of Kent, on the peninsula's south-facing coastline, there's a chain of coves and small bays, with a tourist/weekender base at **Mama Beach**. Heading back to Freetown or Lumley Beach from this far south, it's quicker to make for Waterloo (20km past the turn-off for Bure and Kent), where you can pick up the reasonably surfaced highway into Freetown.

Bunce Island

Much mentioned but less often visited – and strangely omitted or mis-sited on most maps – **Bunce Island** (pronounced Buncey) in the Sierra Leone River, is definitely worth a visit if you can find transport. *Yazbeck*'s sometimes offers day trips in the winter season, or you might be lucky on the ferry quay at Kissy, and find a motor boat willing to make the voyage. But beware the distance, over 20km, and make sure the vessel is seaworthy and the fuel, shade and water supplies sufficient. It's physically easier to get to Bunce from the village of **Pepel**, on the north bank, from where it's only a couple of kilometres offshore. Pepel, however, is more than 160km by road from Freetown.

Bunce, the country's first certified historical monument, is looked after by the Sierra Leone Monuments Commission. They kept a caretaker there for several years until his house collapsed and there was no money to rehouse him. The flat, rocky islet is now deserted. It was first occupied early in the seventeenth century, by British traders in slaves, ivory and camwood – a local timber used to make red dye. They used the much larger Tasso Island, downstream, as an annexe, for farming. As on James Island in the Gambia River, a fort was built on Bunce, and several times rebuilt – it offered only token protection from determined sea attack. In the 1780s, Fort Bunce was supplying an average of 3000 **slaves** a year from the interior to Danish traders alone, who sold them to the new American rice plantations of South Carolina. Today, the ruins are almost entirely overgrown, covered in creepers and fig trees and rather eerie to wander around.

Listings

Airfreight *DHL*, Delco House, 15 Rawdon St (☎022/225800).

Airline offices *Aeroflot*, corner of Lightfoot Boston St and Charlotte St (☎022/223328); *Afrik Airlink*, 11 Charlotte St (☎022/224428); *Air Guinée*, Rawdon St, by the *International Bakery* (☎022/225534); *Air Mali*, 15 Wallace Johnson St (☎022/224433); *Ghana Airways*, 15 Siaka Stevens St (☎022/225493 or 230835); *KLM*, Bishop Building, Lamina Sankoh St (☎022/224444 or 225254); *Sabena*, 12 Wilberforce St (☎022/226077 or 226078); *Sierra National Airlines*, 25 Pultney St (☎022/222075).

American Express Agents are *Yazbeck Tours*, 22 Siaka Stevens St (PO Box 485; ☎022/224423 or 222063).

Banks include: *Barclays Bank of Sierra Leone*, 25–27 Siaka Stevens St (PO Box 12; ☎022/222501; Fax 022/222563); *Sierra Leone Commercial Bank*, 29–31 Siaka Stevens St (☎022/225264; Fax 022/225292); and *Standard Chartered Bank Sierra Leone*, 9–11 Lightfoot Boston St (PO Box 1155; ☎022/225021; Fax 022/225760).

Books European and American titles are somewhat hard to find, though occasionally you'll come across bargains which have been sitting on the shelf a year or two. Try the *Ahmadiyya Bookshop*, Back St, near the East St market (☎022/222617) or *New Horizons*, 13 Howe St (☎022/226288). If you're searching for something, or up at Fourah Bay College, check out the possibly surviving *College Bookshop* (☎022/227226), traditionally the best in the country.

Car rental Try *IPC Travel* or *City Travel* (addresses under "Travel Agents", below), or the *Apex Automobile Corporation*, 11 Regent Rd (PO Box 618; ☎022/224478 or 224431). The *Diplomat Hotel* offers cars, with driver, for Freetown use for £60/$90 per day all-inclusive. The *Mammy Yoko* offers 4WD vehicles with driver and unlimited mileage (but not including fuel) for £120/$180 per day. Or contact JS Lisk, Damba Rd, north shore of Murray Town (PO Box 1314; ☎022/231325) who offers a Land Rover for under £60/$90 per day.

Cassettes Buy your own tapes from *New Horizons*, and have an LP recorded for less than £1 ($1.50). Try *Aba Tapes* in Goderich St, *Tapes International* in Regent Rd, or another, opposite *Sabouya's* in Garrison St. There's a good selection, not all of them pirated, at a number of places.

Cinemas The *Odeon* on Siaka Stevens St, the slightly better *Roxy* on Walpole and the *Strand* on Waterloo St are the three town centre cinemas. Fuzzy videos are increasingly replacing celluloid. And electricity cuts are increasingly closing everything down. If there is a show, there are good opportunities to meet people on the streets outside. If you want Euro-quality cinema and ice-cold AC (take something warm to wear) check out the night's offering at the *Lagoonda* cinema (about £2/$3) at Lumley Beach.

Conservation Society of Sierra Leone 1st floor, left, 1 Walpole St (☎022/229716). Run with the support of prominent citizens and the Royal Society for the Protection of Birds, to preserve and encourage enthusiasm for the country's natural heritage. Has the latest information about Outamba Kilimi, Tiwai Island and other reserves.

Dentists Top recommendation for Dr Norman Wright, 45 Percival St. Also: Drs MA Rekab and R Holst-Roness, 8 Siaka Stevens St (☎022/222671), or Dr George B Morgan, 30A Wallace Johnson St (☎022/226536).

Doctors The embassies are helpful with suggestions, because medical facilities are generally under strain. In an emergency, however, the Netland Hospital, Motor Main Rd, Congo Town is certainly preferable to the Connaught Hospital. Dr Mary Hodges has a clinic on Bathurst St (private clinics on Mon, Wed and Fri afternoons) and is very good. A specialist in cardiology and internal medicine is Dr RH Eleady-Cole, 1 East St (☎022/224438). Dr Bernard Frazer, 11 Gloucester St (☎022/226788), is a kind gynaecologist.

Embassies and consulates include: **Austria** (Hon Consulate), King St, south of Congo Cross; **Belgium** (Hon Consulate) c/o *SCOA*, 27 Blackhall Rd, Kissy (☎022/250143 or 223941); **Côte d'Ivoire**, 1 Wesley St (☎022/223983); **Denmark** (Hon Consulate), c/o Delco House, Lightfoot Boston St (☎022/226220 or 225021); **Egypt**, *Pademba Laundry*, 37 Percival St (☎022/222224); **France**, 13 Lamina Sankoh St (PO Box 510; ☎022/222477; Mon–Fri 10am–noon; handles visas for Burkina Faso, Central African Republic, Mauritania and Togo); **The Gambia**, 6 Wilberforce St (☎022/225191); **Ghana**, Percival St (☎022/223461; Mon–Fri 8am–4pm; visas available within 24 hours); **Germany**, Santanno House, 10 Howe St (PO Box 728; ☎022/222511; Fax 022/226213); **Greece** (Hon Consulate), c/o *P Z*, 24 Wilberforce St (☎022/223087); **Guinea**, Wilkinson Rd, between Congo Cross and Aberdeen junction (☎022/223080 or 222331; Mon–Thurs 8am–2pm, Fri 8am–noon; visas about £15/$22.50); **Ireland** (Hon Consulate), 8 Rawdon St (☎022/222017); **Italy**, 32A Wilkinson Rd (PO Box 749; ☎022/230995); **Japan** (Hon Consulate), 3 Upper East St (☎022/226256); **Lebanon**, 22 Wilberforce St (PO Box 727; ☎022/223513); **Liberia**, 30 Brookfields Rd (PO Box 276; ☎022/240322; Mon–Fri 9am–3pm; you have to present cholera and yellow fever innoculation certificates; visas valid for six months cost £47/$70); **Mali**, left-hand side of Wilkinson Rd, west of Aberdeen junction (☎022/231781); **Netherlands** (Hon Consulate), c/o *KLM*, Bishop Building, Lamina Sankoh St (☎022/224444 or 225254); **Niger**, c/o Côte d'Ivoire embassy; **Nigeria**, 21 Pultney St (☎022/236098; Fax 022/224219; Tues–Fri 11am–2pm; as a rule, you need a ticket out of Nigeria before the visa can be issued, unless you're resident of Sierra Leone); **Norway** (Hon Consulate), 1 College Rd, Cline Town (☎022/225124); **Senegal** (Hon Consulate), 9 Upper East St; **Sweden** (Hon Consulate), Wilberforce St; **Switzerland**, c/o *Freetown Cold Storage*, 14 Howe St (PO Box 451); **UK**, Standard Chartered Bank Building, Lightfoot Boston St (☎022/223961; Fax 022/1445251; Mon–Fri 9am–1pm; mail-holding service, but no visa service for any other country); **USA**, Walpole St (Private Mail Bag; ☎022/226481; Fax 022/225471).

Foreign Exchange Bureaux (FEBs) include *African FEB*, 40 Siaka Stevens St; *Citizens FEB*, 1 Kissy St; *First FEB*, 26 Siaka Stevens St; *Nimo FEB*, 47 Siaka Stevens St; *Paramount FEB*, 9 Rawdon St; and *Sierra Forex Bureau Ltd*, 18 Siaka Stevens St.

Immigration To extend your visa or visitor's permit, go to the Passport and Immigration Office, Rawdon St, near the junction with Siaka Stevens St (☎022/223034). It's normally necessary to register here within 48hr of arrival. A little "kola" never hurts in this office.

Libraries and cultural centres The Sierra Leone Library (☎022/223848), corner of Rokel and Gloucester streets, near Victoria Park, is open Mon to Fri 9am–1pm.The American cultural centre is at the American embassy, with air-conditioning, cold water, a library (open 9am–4pm) and free showings of ABC news Mon, Wed, Fri, at noon and Mon, Fri at 3pm. The British Council is another nice retreat to beat the heat, with videos, BBC broadcasts, library and regular events – and a very un-Sierra Leonean café called the *BBC Room*.

Maps Try *New Horizons*, 13 Howe St. The place to look for a more detailed map than the *Shell* map is the Survey and Lands Department, New England, near *Brookfields Hotel* on Jomo Kenyatta Rd.

Newspapers and magazines The British Council has some of the London dailies, as does the British High Commission. To buy them, check at *New Horizons*, Howe St. The *Daily Mail*, 29 Rawdon St, may have some titles too. *West Africa* magazine is fairly widely available and should be sold for the price printed on the cover (unless you want to do a street boy a favour). Copies of *Time* and *Newsweek* are sometimes available too.

Pharmacies *City Pharmacy*, at 20 Siaka Stevens St (☎022/226868) and 2 Regent Rd (☎022/223838) is Freetown's best. Most pharmacies now have a current stock of drugs and a fairly wide selection.

Phones and faxes Sierra Leone External Telecommunications (SLET) is down on the waterfront. Phone cards are available at a few restaurants and businesses. Just ask, and someone will be able to direct you to a place to buy a card and where the phones are. If you are in central Freetown, head to the *Paramount Hotel* to make a call. The public fax number at SLET which can be faxed from abroad to be collected is (232) 22/224439.

Photos *Suncolor Photo Labs*, 24 Wilberforce St, *Hope Photo*, 24 Siaka Stevens St, and *Lion Photo*, 55 Siaka Stevens St, all give about the same prices and quality and charge to develop a roll and then per photo to print.

Police Headquarters is in George St (☎022/225896).

Post office For posting letters and cards, *Salpost* on Siaka Stevens St is open Mon–Fri 8am–4.30pm, Sat 8am–2pm. *EMS* is *Salpost*'s express airmail courier service. There's a free poste restante service, though it's not renowned for its security. Items mailed to *American Express* (see separate listing) are only held for clients. Parcel post is airmail only.

Swimming pools The relatively new public pool at the Siaka Stevens Stadium is the obvious one, though the town's water supply can't always keep it healthy and it may be closed for repairs.

Theatre The British Council (see "Libraries and cultural centres", above) frequently stages local productions. Freetown Players are very popular and will let you watch their daily practice at their compound at 57 Dundas St. From the Cotton Tree take Pademba Road until you reach the UN filling station and take a right. Walk two blocks and you'll be there. The director of the group, Charlie Hafner, is a friendly, creative man. Buy one of their cassettes when you visit.

Travel agents *Yazbeck Tours*, 22 Siaka Stevens St (PO Box 485; ☎022/224423 or 222063) are the best known, and the ones to visit first. They take most credit cards. A spin-off of theirs, now in competition, is *IPC Travel*, 19 Siaka Stevens St (PO Box 1434; ☎022/226244 or 223551; Fax 022/227470). *City Travel*, 14 Rawdon St (☎022/225493), is recommended, as is *Lion Travel*, 13 Howe St (☎022/226617), particularly for fiddly air routes round West Africa. If you book a flight through an agent, be sure to reconfirm the reservation with the airline's own booking system.

Worship St. George's Cathedral, corner of George St and Wallace Johnson St (services Sun 9am); Wesley Methodist Church, corner of Lamina Sankoh St and Lightfoot Boston St (services Sun 9am); St. John's Maroon Methodist Church, Siaka Stevens St (services Fri, Sun); Samaria WAM Church, corner of Siaka Stevens St and Waterloo St (services Sun 7.30am & 9.30am); St. Anthony's Catholic Church, corner of Syke St and Hannah Ben Coker St (services Sun 7.30am).

THE INTERIOR

While Freetown and surrounding districts have up to two centuries of history behind their present, Creole appearance, this influence has hardly rubbed off on the **up-country towns** – of which the principal are **Makeni**, **Kabala**, **Bo**, **Kenema** and **Kono**. These have all grown from small seeds early this century. With the exception of the diamond centre, Kono (also called Koidu and Sefadu), they reached some sort of zenith of development shortly after independence, since when they've increased in size, but not in stature.

The limited coverage of the interior given here is based on pre-war travels: it highlights the best of the country in the hope that stable conditions for travel will prevail again soon.

SECURITY

The whole of up-country Sierra Leone, inland from Waterloo, a peninsula village just 25km from the centre of Freetown, is deeply insecure. There are, however, variations in the security situation. The war only came to the **Northern Province** in 1994, but the kidnapping of two VSO workers from Kabala at the end of the year and of nuns and around a hundred schoolchildren from Kambia soon after, made it clear that the region could no longer be visited with confidence.

Southern Province has been brutalized by the war. The Bo–Kenema highway is particularly vulnerable; much of Bo itself has been destroyed; and dozens of small towns and villages have been devastated. The region is a confusion of battle fronts and, as of late 1995, emphatically out of bounds.

Eastern Province is where the Sierra Leonean civil war began, in 1990. The whole of the province, between the Moa River and the Liberian border, has been the primary battle front, with most towns and villages destroyed or seriously damaged and many having gone through the trauma of repeatedly changing hands between rebels and government troops. No part of the province is safe and the northeast corner (the towns of Kailahun and Koindu), wedged between Guinea and Liberia, has been unvisitable for five years.

The North

The **Northern Province**'s best specific attraction is **Outamba-Kilimi National Park**. Pressed around the foot of the Kuru Hills, and hard up against the Guinean border, the park is the only one in this part of West Africa and, in normal times, worth the effort to visit, even without your own vehicle.

Heading northwest to Conakry, across the creek heads, the diversions are limited, though **Port Loko** is a pleasant stop, split by tumbling streams and positioned on steep slopes above Port Loko creek. It was a strategic town in the eighteenth century, when there was a significant Portuguese-speaking community. Loko slaves, from three days march to the east, were shipped from here to Bunce Island. For ornithologists with their own transport, the creeks and flats to the west offer exceptional birding.

The provincial capital of the north, **Makeni**, is animated and relatively well provided, with a famously good market, but until you head beyond Makeni for the **far north** and the town of **Kabala**, the scenic and cultural distractions aren't numerous. From Kabala, there are adventurous possibilities on wonderful mountainous backroads, including the trail to the top of **Mount Bintumani**.

Outamba-Kilimi National Park

The joint **Outamba-Kilimi National Park** was set up in 1980 after the International Union for the Conservation of Nature and Natural Resources singled the region out for urgent protection. Sensitive work with the people of the Tambakha chiefdom (or at least with their paramount chief) led to agreements to cede land for the park and give up hunting rights. For over a decade, there was steady progress, with major Peace Corps involvement and the Worldwide Fund for Nature supporting the energetic work of the people on the ground. The Peace Corps have now left and the park is vulnerable to poaching.

The park's thousand-odd square kilometres cover two great slabs of untouched, uninhabited, undulating **savannah and jungle**, in the basins of the Great and Little Scarcies rivers. Here lives a rich diversity of animal species, including **elephants** and most of the other large West African savannah mammals (lions and giraffes excepted), and featuring a solid population of **chimpanzees** (perhaps the biggest concentration in West Africa), and twelve other primates, amomg them **red colobus, black-and-white colobus** and **sooty mangabey**. In the deepest sections of forest there are rare and scattered **bongo antelope** – magnificent, heavily built animals. And in the overgrown water margins there are **pygmy hippos**.

Makeni

Like Sierra Leone's other provincial centres, **MAKENI** can make few credible touristic claims. It was once the terminus of the northern branch railway line, and quite a boom-town in the 1920s. Today, though still a busy **Temne** trade exchange, the momentum has largely vanished.

THE TAMBAKHA CHIEFDOM

The **Tambakha chiefdom** (which formerly occupied most of Outamba-Kilimi) is named after the *Tamba* – "leader" – of a successful nineteenth-century slave revolt. Slave-owning Susu were massacred by their captives, who moved to this region and set up their own, very mixed, kingdom. Susu, the slaves' customary language, was retained.

Off the main highway, a spider's web of dust-clouded streets focuses noisily on what used to be a roundabout at the centre of town. The big four-minareted mosque is here, and a number of two- and three-storeyed colonial shop fronts. Most vehicles drop off at the downtown turntable, or in the lorry park itself.

By day, Makeni's best asset is the large and heaving **market**, from which it's practically impossible to escape without buying something. The attraction is the availability, at very good prices, of reams of beautiful *gara* cloth, in a multiplicity of blue and green hues, and a huge variety of weights and finishes.

Kabala

Beyond Makeni, the architectural interest improves greatly, with small steeply conical houses of the Temne pattern, topped with an extra tuft of thatch and an entrance lobby at the front. Praying circles are to be seen all over, though sometimes, as reserved areas, they're used for drying rice or other grain.

Ringed by a circle of hills, the highest of which leap, bold and bare, right above it to the west, **KABALA** is an attractive "highland" town. It splits roughly into two: on the way in from Makeni, the town centre is dominated by the Koranko people; across the stream on the northwest side of town, the district is more Limba. Try to buy some

THE KORANKO

More than most of Sierra Leone's ethnic groups, the **Koranko** of the northeast have maintained a fairly distinct cultural integrity. Koranko is a Mande language, very close to the most mainstream Mande tongue, the Malinké of Guinea and Mali, and only distantly related to the more peripheral Mende of southern Sierra Leone. The Koranko are great **rice** farmers, filling the valleys with an emerald green carpet, and they grow a fair amount of **cotton**, too, for their famous *ronko* cloth.

The Koranko are also **hunters** of some repute (and have always supplied most of the troops for the Sierra Leone armed forces). Traditionally, they belonged to totemic **clans**, known as "houses", each called by a "surname" and symbolized by taboo animals that were never eaten. For example, the Fona clan's totem was the royal python, the Mensereng had the monitor lizard and the lion, the Kamara's were the hippo and the chimpanzee, the Kagbo's and Sise's the crocodile and the Mara's (the most distinguished) was the leopard; not that all these animals were commonly eaten by members of other clans.

Today, an increasing contingent of the Koranko community is **Muslim**, and the old clan divisions are less significant. But the **Bundu** society initiations (*Biriye* in Koranko) are still important for young people in rural areas, with girls in seclusion for a few weeks' instruction during the rains and boys going off in the dry season. Circumcision and clitoridectomy usually take place at the same time. Another pre-Islamic activity that's pursued with enthusiasm is the making of *kamakuli* – **bamboo wine**. It's not always available, but you should try to get a taste if you're in the territory for a few days; talk to the youth of the village rather than the big men.

CURSORY KORANKO

Greetings, thanks, goodbye	*N-weli*	Yes	*Ohn* (pronounced like French "non")
Greetings (pl)	*Wa-n-wali*	No	*Oh-oh*
Good morning	*Tanamase*	Thank you	*Kubaraka*
Good day	*Tanamatale*	Bamboo wine	*Kamakole*
Good evening	*Inoor-agh*	What's your name?	*Eh tu kama?*

ronko cloth, when you're in Kabala. Made by the Koranko, it's a deep rusty red-coloured country cloth, patterned in black block prints, sewn together from narrow strips, soft and durable and formerly vested with bullet-proof powers

Kabala is famous throughout Sierra Leone for the New Year's Day **mass picnic** that normally takes place on the gaunt inselberg summit at the edge of the Wara Wara range, west of town (it didn't take place in 1995 and is unlikely to again until peace resumes). No-one seems to know how this started, but several hundred people spend New Year's afternoon up there, eating, drinking and dancing. It's a steep climb, but not difficult or long; other than on New Year's Day, these heights are usually deserted, but always worth the hike up.

Mount Bintumani

Midway between Kabala and Kono-Koidu-Sefadu in the east, **Mount Bintumani** in the Loma Mountains is the highest peak in Sierra Leone, and the highest mountain in West Africa west of Mount Cameroon. The mountain is best climbed at the beginning or end of the rainy season (either in April–May or October–November). Dry season dust will limit visibility. Whenever you go, it can get very cool at night near the summit (1945m) and you should take some warm clothes, as well as a sleeping bag.

There are no tarred roads nearby, and climbing Bintumani of necessity involves some trekking from the end of the nearest motorable road. Kabala is probably the easiest base from which to go. You need transport to **Firawa** (51km from Kabala), from where a five-day hike will get you to the top and back again. The small town of **Koinadugu** (28km) is the most likely destination of vehicles heading this way, but your best chance of a vehicle right through to Firawa is Tuesday, when there's a major market in **Bumbukoro** (misplaced on most maps), 22km along the road, from which vehicles often go on to Firawa afterwards. Of course, if you're taking a couple of weeks or more to climb Bintumani, you may want to walk the whole way from Kabala. Koinadugu's hill-top location and venerable silk-cotton trees make it a great place to stay. **Yirafilaia Badala** (36km) is another nice village, located above a rocky bend of the Seli River. There's a sandy beach, wonderful for swimming, fishing and washing clothes. Just beware of the current if you're here at the height of the rains.

All the villages along the Bintumani trail are Koranko (for whom the mountain is **Loma Mansa** – King of the Lomas) and you'll find charming hospitality. If you want to stay in a village, ask to speak to the headman, who'll arrange overnight accommodation for you. It's important to carry some **basic provisions** – rice, palm oil, onions, salt and pepper – as supplies along the way can be short, especially in the "hungry season" before the rice harvest (August and September). Don't worry about cooking, this will be fixed for you; naturally you'll be expected to share some food. For snacks on the move (don't forget most people only cook once a day) take fruit and groundnut or benniseed cakes from Kabala. Take a supply of the freshest kola you can find, as well. This is the traditional gift in return for hospitality, though you can give leones instead. You may also want to give kola to the woman who cooks for you.

After Firawa, you'll need a **guide** to find your way down the maze of footpaths to **Banda-Karafaia**, about 19km distant. This day's hike is where the trip becomes exciting and the scenery spectacular. There are usually several former students in Firawa who know some English (assuming your Koranko is limited) and are more than willing to hike up the mountain with you.

At Banda-Karafaia, you have to sign the headman's **register** of people climbing the mountain. A cash gift is expected for this service; while there's no fixed fee, it will be made clear if it's too small. About 13km further is **Yalembe**, a small village at the foot of the mountain, where you hire a guide for the final ascent.

The South

The frustrating thing about the geography of **southern Sierra Leone**, as of much of West Africa's southwest-facing shores, is that the **coast** itself tends to be indistinct and often miles from the nearest road. The sea lies beyond vast expanses of mud, marsh and mangroves, only accessible down narrow ridges of slightly higher ground between the maze of creeks. The coast here seems to be separating entirely from the mainland and, indeed, **Sherbro** (with its town of **Bonthe**) and the Turtle Islands are already adrift in the Atlantic. Southeast of Sherbro, the surf hits a tremendous, unbroken **beach**, which stretches 110km to the little port of **Sulima** on the Liberian border. Backed by small fishing villages, this is, in times of peace, a highly recommended week-long walk.

Inland, much of the south is sticky, palm- and bush-specked grassland, which makes for uninspiring travel. But the higher, forest areas are another matter. In the southeast, the hills come to within 50km of the sea and here, south of the provincial capital, **Bo**, there are opportunities for some of the country's most rewarding exploring. The trip to **Tiwai Island Primate Reserve**, blanketed in rainforest in a crook of the surging **Moa River**, is impressive and hugely enjoyable, though not feasible at the time of writing.

Bo

Long established as the most important town in the colonial "Protectorate" of up-country Sierra Leone, **BO** was overtaken in size some years ago by the burgeoning diamond-fed Kono-Koidu-Sefadu conurbation in the northeast. Bo holds a big, spread-out population of fifty or sixty thousand people – mostly Mende, but with a heavy Krio presence. The town's best-known institution, the **"Chief's School"** (now Bo School) north of the old railway yards, was founded in 1906, for the education of chiefs' sons from the Protectorate. It was a curious amalgam of English public school and extended traditional instruction, intended to lend weight to the position of the chiefs, through whom the British ruled the country. The boys, divided into "houses" of Liverpool, Manchester, London and Paris, were expected to wear the customary dress of their fathers, learn improved farming and building methods, adopt "good manners" and speak "good English". The use of Krio was forbidden. Fees, of £10 a year, were extraordinarily high. The school is still a prestigious government-run establishment and the elitism and patronage remain. Coming into Bo from Freetown, the highway is a couple of kilometres from the centre. On the way in, you pass the wasteland of the old railway yards and station on the left, and skirt the town's only (indescribably ugly) landmark, the **Clock Tower**.

Tiwai Island Nature Reserve

The **Tiwai Island Project** – run by Njala University College and the Peace Corps until the war engulfed the district – transformed a considerable island in the Moa River into a *de facto* national park. Although only covering about twelve square kilometres, the largely pristine, forest-cloaked island shelters an extraordinarily rich fauna, including chimps and ten other primates, pygmy hippos, red river hogs, crocodiles and electric fish. The Tiwai island office is at **Kambama**, 16km northeast of the small town of Potoru, which is an hour's drive southeast of Bo. Before the war came to this region, the chief would arrange the **river crossing** and there were visitors' facilities on the other side.

Tiwai is the Africa of imagination. The air is saturated with sound – the rattle, squeak and vibrato incessance of a billion insects (listen out for the eerily ventriloqual mole cricket), the squawks and yelps of birds, monkeys, tree hyraxes, squirrels, chimpanzees and hundreds of others. The island has the world's third-highest biomass of monkeys, and it must hold some kind of record for its termites, too. In the background is the dim rush of the rapids on the Moa River, where it splits to roar around Tiwai through rocks and channels. To be sure of seeing chimps, you used to need to devote a few days. In the dry season, they can migrate freely across the river into the Gola forest reserve to the east. Increasingly, however, even before the war, they were spending more time on the island as they came to appreciate its security (the local paramount chiefs had a voluntary no-hunting agreement). At the local level, much prestige was attached to the reserve's successful operation by the people on the mainland west of the island, while the people on the east side remained unconvinced. How much damage has been done over the past two years is unclear, but the visitor and research facilities are bound to have been ransacked and many animals must have been hunted for food.

Sulima and the south coast

SULIMA was a trading station in the nineteenth century. The first Englishman here was John Myer Harris, a Jewish trader who arrived in 1855. Harris soon creamed off much of the Moa River trade, which had previously been controlled by the Liberian government, thus pushing the effective frontier back to the Mano River. A number of the old colonial buildings are still standing and there's a freshwater **lagoon**, where you can swim and wash. Sulima used to gather a community of holidaying volunteers every Christmas, building *baffas* (shelters) and sitting round fires on the beach; now, there are thousands of Liberian refugees in the area.

In theory it's possible to follow the unbroken beach west from Sulima (110km) in a walk that takes from five days to a week without strain. This is **Turner's Peninsula**, a strip of land ceded to the British as long ago as 1825. The people are Vai, Krim and Sherbro but, increasingly, everyone speaks Mende first, Krio second and English a poor third. Houses are made from entirely natural materials – woven palmfrond walls with thatched roofs.

Most of Turner's Peninsula is backed by low scrub, but towards the western end, coconut palms start to appear. The most attractive stretches of coast, however, are on Sherbro and the nearby Turtle Islands.

Sherbro Island

Though very much in ruins these days – and attacked several times during the war – **BONTHE**, the main town on **Sherbro Island**, is one of Sierra Leone's most appealing towns. When Frederick William Hugh Migeod (Colonial Service, retired) visited in 1924 while writing his *View of Sierra Leone*, he found "about forty Europeans there, including those on York Island, and a big gathering at tennis every evening". The atmosphere has changed somewhat in the intervening years, but Bonthe is still very pleasant. Wide sandy lanes cross the town, and many of the great old run-down buildings of the glory days are still upright. The secondary school is magnificent and the people of Bonthe charming. The *Bonthe Holiday Complex* may still be in one piece.

Eastern Province

Diamonds and cross-border trade have made **Eastern Province** the country's most densely populated region. **Kono-Koidu-Sefadu** is now the biggest provincial town and shows an unexpected side of the country. It would be a good jumping-off point for Mount Bintumani (see p.577) and, closer but rather inaccessible, the **Tingi Mountains** and the source of the Niger. **Kenema** is busy, but unexceptional: it used to be the common embarkation point for Liberia and southern Guinea.

THE MENDE AND SECRET SOCIETIES

There is a thing passing in the sky; some thick clouds surround it; the uninitiated see nothing.

Opaque Mende proverb

The **Mende** language – the biggest language group in Sierra Leone – is supposed to have arrived from the northeast, either with people fleeing the chaotic conditions in sixteenth-century Songhai, or perhaps before the creation of the Mali empire in the thirteenth century. Ptolemy's second-century map even indicates *Purrus Campus* in about the place where the ancient Mende might have had a **"Poro Bush"** – a secret society grove. The Mende are skilled and very long-established **farmers**, to whom trading and hunting are low priorities. Rice, sorghum and millet, root crops, oil palms and kola are the big crops. Women **fish** the streams, too, with circular nets, as much for relaxation as for the meal.

Along classic "divide and rule" principles, the British split the **Mende kingdoms** into dozens of "paramount chiefdoms", introducing a new tribal identity. The Mende chiefs came to see themselves as natural successors of the British, in competition – or association – with the powerful **Temne**. But the upper-class Krio families of Freetown had the same idea. The most serious of the **anti-tax revolts**, in Mende country in 1898, resulted in the deaths of hundreds of Krio traders and deepened a rift, never completely bridged, between the indigenous Protectorate peoples and the non-native Krios of the Colony. The Bo school for chiefs gave an incentive to Protectorate ambitions. Later, Mende politicians from a pro-British family of Bonthe – **Milton Margai** and his brother **Albert** – became the country's first and second prime ministers. Krio opponents attributed much of the second Margai's attachment to power to membership of the secret *Poro* society.

You can't spend more than a week in the country without hearing mysterious rumours about the **secret societies**. Among older or more traditional Mende people, enquiries get a hostile response, and the few books on the subject tend to disappear from libraries. Society graduates are sworn to secrecy and the arcane details remain hidden. But they're perhaps less sinister institutions than their reputation would suggest. It's worth knowing

Kenema

Basically a one-street town, **KENEMA**'s main life stretches from the old railway station area north up Hangha Road, and out of town on the road to Tongu and Kono. Originally a Mende settlement, Kenema grew fast on the strength of the railway and burst into development after the discovery, in 1931, of **diamonds** a few kilometres to the east, and the opening up of the Tongo diamond field to the north. Kenema's main industry, however, is logging and carpentry, with a large **Forest Industries Department**.

Kono-Koidu-Sefadu and around

Koidu and Sefadu are the official alternative names for this town, but most locals refer to **KONO** (the district of which it's capital) when they mean the town. And the old settlement was called Sembehun, so New Sembehun is a fourth, pedantic, possibility. Over one hundred thousand people live around here. It's the one place in the country where people can make the big time without connections – through illegal diamond mining in the area. The results used to be plain to see in the **town centre**, where piles of goods (children's bikes, ghetto blasters, televisions sets) were on sale in the wide and dusty main street. At night the streets were illuminated as if for a special occasion and villas – tightly guarded and burglar-barred – hummed smugly with air-conditioning. Not surprisingly, over the last few years, Kono has been repeatedly ransacked and it's hard to say what sort of impression you will get when it's finally safe to return to this distant corner of the country.

about them in general, because they still dominate life in Sierra Leone. Even Christians don't exclude themselves, and Islam, while opposing them, makes no purist insistence.

The general name for the societies is **Bundu**, actually a Krio word. **Poro** is the men's society (the same name is found elsewhere in West Africa, for example among the Senoufo in Côte d'Ivoire) and is by far the most powerful; the women's is called **Sande**. They're followed in almost all communities, as secret brotherhoods and sisterhoods, cutting across the family and clan divisions, maintaining stability and marking life-cycle events. *Poro* and *Sande* provide the framework for **traditional instruction** to adolescents about sex, adult behaviour and folk knowledge. Traditionally, too, the period of seclusion and endurance in the bush was when **circumcision and clitoridectomy** were performed. Boys of the same age group go through the school in the dry season, girls in the rains. Beyond the teenage rites of passage, membership of *Poro* proceeds by different stages. In addition to *Poro* and *Sande*, there's a kind of high *Poro* society called *Wunde*, and a number of other societies, some operating as professional associations of medical, psychiatric and social welfare specialists – *Humo*, *Toma*, *Njaye* – and some of entertainers and conjurers, the *Njoso*.

As an outsider, beware of "No Entry" signs in the bush, indicating a society grove, and fenced compounds outside villages. It's acceptable to witness youngsters with whitened faces, however, celebrating their new names and status.

Heavy black **Bundu masks** worn by women in the *Sande* society (and called *Sowo* by the Mende) are the most visible signs of the societies' active existence. They tell a lot about Mende ideals of feminine beauty – high-domed foreheads, elaborately braided hair, fine-pointed features, eyes that see nothing, mouths closed. They're carved by men.

"Animal societies" – "Baboon" (chimpanzee), "Boa" (python), "Alligator" (crocodile) and "Leopard" – were always uncommon, though sensationalized. Intended to imitate attacks by wild animals, they were created in order to obtain human organs for **witchcraft**. They've tended to die out along with the animals imitated; nobody would believe a chimpanzee murder in Bo anymore.

Witchcraft is another matter.

Sakanbiaiwa Botanical Sanctuary

Sakanbiaiwa, in the Tingi Mountains, is Sierra Leone's second highest peak (1709m) – a **botanical sanctuary** for its orchids, especially at the end of the dry season, but more remote and much less visited even than Bintumani. First step is transport to Jegbwema, 18km east of Kono, where you turn left into the mountains. The villages to head for are Kundundu and Yengema (respectively, 38km and 44km from Jegbwema), along a really rough road.

Koindu

KOINDU (not to be confused with Koidu) was originally a **Kissi** settlement, but it's been swelling with immigrants from a wide reach for decades. The town is a sort of tradesman's entrance to Sierra Leone. Everything from rice and sugar to diamonds and human sacrifices is rumoured to pass through the town – and most of the rumours are verifiable on a Sunday. There's locally made cloth in the market (cotton is sown in with the rice and harvested afterwards), along with excellent silversmiths who specialize in filigree earrings and pendants. And you can still buy **"Kissi pennies"** here, the regional currency of pre-Protectorate days, that continued to be used until World War II – pieces of twisted iron rod, about 30cm long, with the ends flattened out into a T-shape. All of this, of course, in theory: Koindu has been rebel leader Foday Sankoh's base since 1991 and visitors are not welcome.

index

CHAPTER NINE

LIBERIA

LIBERIA

The love of liberty brought us here

Liberian National Motto

Even early in the nineteenth century, when black settlers first arrived from America, motives less virtuous than love of liberty were also at work. Today, 150 years after the declaration of independence, Liberia has disintegrated. A savage, aimless, slow-burning civil war has charred the nation to the point where its existence as a sovereign country begins to look like the first goal that any government of national reconciliation needs to achieve. This is not a part of West Africa you visit for a holiday: half a dozen separate militias, some including boy "soldiers" as young as eight, control various parts of the country and continue to kill each other. Up to 200,000 Liberian civilians have died at their hands; perhaps a million have been displaced from their homes and are living in exile, either within Liberia or in sprawling refugee camps in Côte d'Ivoire or Guinea.

As in the case of Sierra Leone, this chapter does not constitute a recommendation to visit the country (which your government is almost certain to strongly advise against), but assumes you are going there on necessary business. While security in the capital, Monrovia, is reasonably good, with life returning to a semblance of normality, supplies of food and consumer products flowing in, and many services functioning adequately, the coverage which follows is brief. The interior cannot be visited except on pre-approved, official business and is not treated in this edition.

The country

Liberia is divided into **counties**, like a US state, each with its "county seat". Nine small counties along the coast – Bomi, Grand Bassa, Grand Cape Mount, Grand Kru, Margibi, Maryland, Montserrado, River Cess and Sinoe – reflect the old centres of settler power. The four large ones in the interior – Lofa, Bong, Nimba and Grand Gedeh (pronounced Jeddah) – are the stronghold of indigenous Liberian culture.

If **Monrovia** was formerly the headquarters for American interests in Africa, with the sort of Kool-aid/burger culture you might have anticipated, the pre-war impression of the other **coastal towns** was usually of gone-to-seed backwaters, sleepily reminiscent of their African-American roots. Perched on rocky promontories on a coast of creeks and mangroves, they were always redeemed, from the travel angle, by splendid nearby beaches.

FACTS AND FIGURES

The **Republic of Liberia** took its name from the Latin, *liber*, meaning "free". The country has an **area** of 111,000 square kilometres – somewhat smaller than England or New York state – and a **population** of some 2.8 million. Until 1980, Liberia was ruled oligarchically by a narrow elite composed mostly of the descendants of coastal settler families. The coup of that year brought to power Master Sergeant Samuel Doe, an up-country man who presided until 1990 over a purely nominal multi-party system through the all-powerful National Democratic Party of Liberia. Monrovia is currently the only part of the country with an internationally recognized government – a Transitional Ruling Council overseeing the run-up to national elections (assuming the warlords stop fighting) under the leadership of three civilians and three rebel leaders.

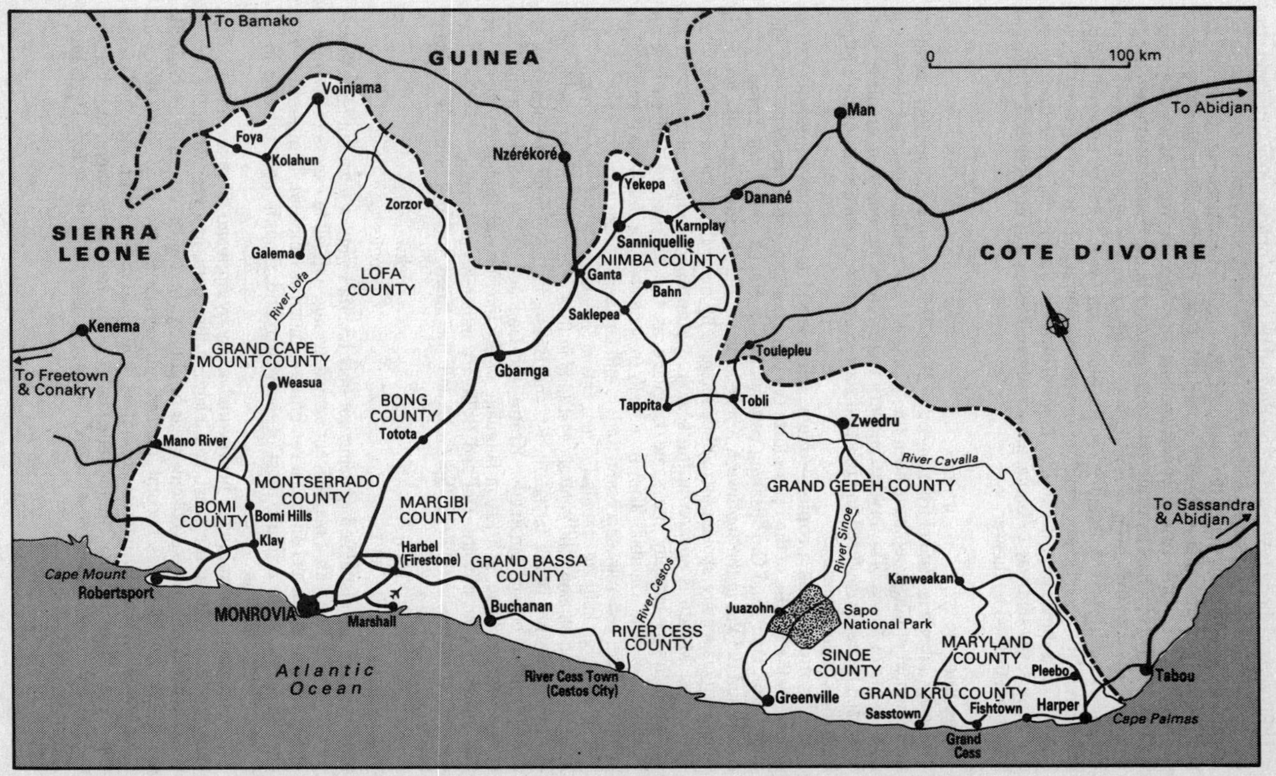
To Bamako
GUINEA
0
100 km
To Abidjan
Man
Voinjama
Foya
Kolahun
Nzérékoré
Yekepa
Danané
Zorzor
Karnplay
Sanniquellie
SIERRA LEONE
Galema
NIMBA COUNTY
COTE D'IVOIRE
Ganta
LOFA COUNTY
Bahn
River Lofa
Saklepea
Kenema
Toulepleu
GRAND CAPE MOUNT COUNTY
Gbarnga
To Freetown & Conakry
Weasua
BONG COUNTY
Tappita
Tobli
Totota
Zwedru
Mano River
River Cavalla
MONTSERRADO COUNTY
GRAND GEDEH COUNTY
MARGIBI COUNTY
BOMI COUNTY
Bomi Hills
To Sassandra & Abidjan
River Sinoe
Klay
Harbel (Firestone)
GRAND BASSA COUNTY
Cape Mount
Robertsport
River Cestos
Kanweakan
Sapo National Park
Juazohn
Buchanan
MONROVIA
Marshall
RIVER CESS COUNTY
MARYLAND COUNTY
SINOE COUNTY
Atlantic Ocean
River Cess Town (Cestos City)
Pleebo
Tabou
GRAND KRU COUNTY
Greenville
Fishtown
Harper
Sasstown
Cape Palmas
Grand Cess

Up-country Liberia is very different. Beyond the maze of tidal creeks, the land rises onto rolling forested plateaux, split by rivers which head, surprisingly straight, to the sea. On the Guinean border in the far north, the highlands poke above 1000m and just about qualify as mountains. Nearly one fifth of the country has a dense cover of **primary forest** – the largest concentrations anywhere in West Africa. The **Sapo National Park**, Liberia's only one, on the Sinoe River in the remote southeast, used to be one of the country's major attractions for hardy travellers and determined naturalists and canoe trips were organized up the Sinoe every year between between January and March. It's unclear how much of the park's natural habitat has survived since it was last open to visitors, in the late 1980s. **Towns** in the interior, apart from several along the paved highway to Ganta, are mostly very small and undeveloped. Almost all have been trashed by the war.

The people

Ethnically, Liberia is distinct from any other West African country. Since its foundation, the dominant ethnic group have been the **"Congos"**– descendants of freed slaves from other parts of Africa. The original settlers were American, but their numbers were increased by newly captured and released slaves taken from slave ships (many of them from the Congo region).

Of the **indigenous peoples** – often still referred to as "the tribes" (or "tribal people") – the **Kpelle** of the centre form the biggest group, some twenty percent. Like the **Mano-**, **Dan-**, and **Gio**-speaking communities of Nimba county, the **Loma** of Lofa county and the **Vai** in the southwest, Kpelle is part of the **Mande linguistic grouping** whose languages are spoken as mother tongues by more than one in two Liberians. The purest Mande is spoken in the scattered **Mandingo** communities all over the north. Theirs is virtually the same language as the Malinké of Guinea and the Mandinka of The Gambia. They're usually responsible for bush taxi transport in Liberia and are generally successful traders and business people, too.

The other big language family (35 percent) is "Kruan", of which the main language, **Kru**, is spoken all along the central coast (and in fishing communities in neighbouring countries). **Grebo**, in the far southeast, and **Bassa**, in the vicinity of Buchanan, are closely related coastal languages. **Krahn**, the language of the late President Doe's ruling military clique, is a Kruan language of the interior with affiliated dialects over the border in Côte d'Ivoire. **Dei** and **Belle** are minor Kruan languages of the northwest. Also in the northwest, the **Gola** and the **Kissi** speak less easily classified languages.

The climate

Monrovia has the distinction of being not only Liberia's wettest town but also Africa's wettest capital city, with a magnificent annual average rainfall in excess of five metres (eight times as much as London, seven times as much as Chicago). **Temperatures** are high throughout the country, most of the year round, though more extreme in the central plateau regions.

In most parts, **the rains** are heavily under way by April and there are few dry days until November. Along the coast, and inland in the south, in a year when the pattern behaves itself, you can expect some clear bright days in August, known as the **"middle dries"**. The middle dries become increasingly certain as you head south down the coast. Conditions in the interior are not as moist but, in the north, the middle dries don't come to the rescue. The unpredictability of the rains everywhere, together with the appalling condition of most "roads", put constraints on travel before December 1 and after April 15.

AVERAGE TEMPERATURES AND RAINFALL

MONROVIA

	Jan	Feb	Mar	Apr	May	June	July	Aug	Sept	Oct	Nov	Dec
Temperatures °C												
Min (night)	23	23	23	23	22	23	22	23	22	22	23	23
Max (day)	30	29	31	31	30	27	27	27	27	28	29	30
Rainfall mm	31	56	97	216	516	973	996	373	744	772	236	130
Days with rainfall	5	5	10	17	21	26	24	20	26	22	19	12

GANTA

	Jan	Feb	Mar	Apr	May	June	July	Aug	Sept	Oct	Nov	Dec
Rainfall mm	16	57	123	150	199	278	259	298	422	266	132	35
Days with rainfall	2	5	10	12	15	18	18	19	21	17	10	3

HARPER

	Jan	Feb	Mar	Apr	May	June	July	Aug	Sept	Oct	Nov	Dec
Rainfall mm	149	111	146	219	543	530	147	96	234	299	285	288
Days with rainfall	12	9	12	16	22	22	12	8	16	19	18	18

Arrivals

Overland routes into Liberia are closed. The only option is to fly from Abidjan, Conakry or Freetown.

■ Flights from Africa

There are presently four scheduled flights each week into Spriggs Payne Airport. *Air Ivoire* (VU) flies in non-stop from **Abidjan** on Wed and Fri. Air Guinée (GI) flies in from **Conakry**, via **Freetown**, on Tues and Fri.

There are no other flights fom African cities and no intercontinental flights. The main international airport, Roberts Field, trashed in 1992, is closed.

Red Tape

All nationalities, apart from West Africans, need visas. You will need a letter explaining the purpose of your visit – and most likely some documentary evidence of being invited or needing to visit Monrovia. Liberian embassies also require a letter from a doctor confirming you don't have any communicable diseases and are not HIV-positive.

Regardless of the length of stay recorded on your visa, **registration at the Immigration Office** in Monrovia is normally required *within 48 hours*, at which time you can get an extension of your stay permit *past* your anticipated visit; 60 days is standard.

Before leaving Liberia, you'll have to apply for an **exit visa**, seven days or less prior to your intended date of departure.

Photography permits are mandatory (see the "Photography" section in the Directory, below).

■ Embassies in Liberia

The British embassy closed in March 1991 and the French embassy is also closed. The US embassy in Monrovia is open. There were formerly embassies for Cameroon, Ghana, Mali, Guinea, Sierra Leone, Côte d'Ivoire and Nigeria, of which the last-mentioned four are supposed to be open.

Money

Financially, the country's position is parlous. Officially, the Liberian dollar is at par with the US dollar; on the well-organized and open black market, the rate is L$50=US$1.

The details in these practical information pages are essentially for use on the ground in West Africa and in Liberia itself: for full practical coverage on preparing for a trip, getting here from outside the region, paperwork, health, information sources and more, see *Basics*.

The largest denomination of Liberian currency is the L$5 note, worth 10¢. Cash is the only form of payment in Monrovia and, for most purchases, US dollars are much preferred. You can, and should, bargain for most things.

Health

Liberian embassies require to see your yellow fever and cholera certificates before they'll issue a visa (see "Red Tape").

Liberia doesn't have any **health problems** that you wouldn't predict from its climate and economic situation. Water-borne diseases (especially **schistosomiasis**) are a serious menace and outbreaks of **cholera** routine. Rabies is prevalent. **Health care facilities** are completely unreliable.

Information and Maps

Despite being an Anglophone country, independent since the middle of the nineteenth century, Liberia is very little known outside its own borders. There is no tourist industry and scant tourist information.

The Ministry of Information, Culture and Tourism at 110 United Nations Drive (PO Box 9021, Monrovia) may have some literature, and the National Bureau of Culture and Tourism (see p.601) may be open.

There is no reasonable **map** of the country: the best widely available coverage is contained on the Michelin 953 sheet. You might still find copies of *A Tourist Map of Liberia* (published in 1980) in overseas map specialists.

Getting Around

Travel in Liberia beyond the Monrovia city limits is out of the question. Monrovia itself has some old taxis and minbuses.

Car rental is feasible, but entirely down to ad hoc arrangements with car owners. The international companies are not represented.

Missionaries and mining engineers used to get around **by plane** before the roads were developed, and there are as many as 100 airfields across the country. But *Air Liberia* and the private charter company *Weasua Air Transport* don't offer domestic services, though planes can be chartered from Spriggs Payne to neighbouring countries.

Eating and Drinking

The national dish of Liberia is *pepper soup*, eaten all over the country. Imported food is important in Monrovia, where timid palates can stick to many familiar brands and dishes, mostly American. But there is also locally grown backyard produce on sale in the city.

Various forms of **cassava stodge** are the familiar staples. Fermented **fufu** is the commonest, while unfermented **G.B.** is coarser, and unfermented **dumboy** comes somewhere between in texture. **Rice** is another important staple, either prepared into a *jollof*-style dish with meat, vegetables, spices, and sometimes shellfish (known as *jala*), or made with chicken (*pela*).

Palm butter, the thick oily gravy strained from the pounded pulp of palm nuts, is one of Liberia's more distinctive dishes, usually mixed with pepper (chilli), meat, *bitter ball* (a small round aubergine) and onions – or whatever's available – and eaten as a relish with a starch base.

Among the other flavours to help the starch down, ground **cassava leaves**, boiled to death with Maggi stock cubes, palm oil, onions and meat, are widespread, and **potato greens**, from sweet, rather than Irish, potatoes, likewise. **Ground pea soup** is the Liberian version of groundnut sauce/ *sauce d'arachides*, based on peanut butter. **Bean gravy** is self-explanatory, and usually tasty.

■ Drinking

Liberia's **beer** is *Club*. There's also lethal **palm wine** (usually to accompany a smoke of grass) and **"cane juice"** rum.

Communications, Language and the Media

Due to the near-absence of international flights, there is no proper postal service to the outside world. People based in Monrovia rely on phone, fax and e-mail.

For *AT&T* dial ☎797-797.

Liberia's IDD code is ☎231.

■ Language

Liberia's official language is English. It sounds like nothing you've ever heard before – in one

A LIBERIAN GLOSSARY

The trick is to recognize that correctly hearing what's said is no instant route to comprehension. Many words and phrases have different meanings from those in American or British English. You'll soon find yourself slipping into it.

A seh, my maa Excuse me my man (common)
Car Bus, motorbike, any kind of motor transport
Cheap-o Cheap ("-o" is a characteristic suffix)
Congos Descendants of freed slaves
Dash Tip, bribe (from Portuguese, *dar-se*)
Donkahfleh Used clothes (lit. "Try it on; if you like it, buy it" – Mandingo)
Du Kor Monrovia peninsula, as referred to by inland peoples
French/French side Guinea or Côte d'Ivoire
In the bush A private matter, settled privately, sometimes a chance sexual encounter
Kwi Foreign, or a foreigner/white person (eg "Kwi food")
Merico "Americo-Liberian" or "AL"; less common these days
Money bus Converted pick-up van or lorry with inward-facing bench seats
Of course Maybe, yes . . .
Palava Discussion, argument
Pekin Child
Reach Arrive, get to, stretch, be sufficient
Rogue A thief, or to steal
Straight Straight away, immediately
Sumangama Illicit sexual behaviour
Thank you (*Thanky ya*) Congratulations!/you're welcome/I'm glad

traveller's opinion, "as if a punch-drunk Brando of *On the Waterfront* taught to drop all the final sounds of each word and slur the rest". You'll be understood, but you may not always understand. Liberian English is not a proper creole, however, like Krio in Sierra Leone.

Up-country people are more likely to speak one of the country's twenty or so indigenous languages first, though all but the elderly speak some English. The two largest language groups speak peripheral languages of the Mande family: **Kpelle**, concentrated in Bong county and **Dan/Gio/Mano** in Nimba county. **Kru**-speakers and the linguistically-related **Bassa** in Grand Bassa county and **Grebo** in Maryland have a high profile along the coast.

■ The media

As for keeping in touch with events, **radio** is your best source of information, with the BBC World Service the most useful station. **ELBC** ("The Voice of Peace, Harmony and Reconciliation") broadcasts in Liberian English, French and indigenous languages. The Sudan Interior Mission's station – ELWA – may still be broadcasting in English and French and forty-two African languages. **Television** is transmitted for five hours a day during the week and nine hours a day at weekends.

The best **newspaper** is the independent *Daily Observer*, edited by the resilient Reuters correspondent Stanton B. Peabody, which commands a relatively handsome 30,000 daily circulation (five issues a week).

Trouble

Monrovia's crime rate, in view of its circumstances, is surprisingly low and, pickpockets aside, you'll have few problems with ordinary people.

The ubiquitous soldiers of the ECOMOG peace-keeping force have roadblocks all over the city and are keen on making money. There is a strictly enforced curfew from 7pm to 7am. UN staff have curfew passes. If you're picked up without one you'll be frightened half to death and kept behind bars for 24 hours.

Directory

AIRPORT TAX US$20 on departure.

CLOTHES Liberians are very clothes-conscious and treat dress as a mark of respect. You will cause offence all over if you dress below your perceived wealth and status. Shorts are pretty unacceptable for women except on the beach.

CRAFTS AND SHOPPING Liberia is not renowned for crafts. You can buy **masks** in Monrovia (best are the **Dan/Gio** ones from the northeast, the archetypal style of which is remarkably beautiful) but most are tacky imports from all over Africa. **Tailoring** is the best deal. Two good shirt styles are "Vai" and "Paramount Chief".

ELECTRICITY When you can find some it's a mix of American-style 110v, AC 60Hz, and European 220–240v, AC 50Hz.

HANDSHAKES The classic Liberian handshake ends with both parties making a deft snap of the fingers. This custom is supposed to derive from the missing fingers of freed slaves.

PHOTOGRAPHY Leave the VCR behind; ordinary cameras are hassle enough. Official attitudes to photography tend to treat it as a serious crime. There is a photo permit, which you can obtain, in theory, from the Tourist Office there. In practice, it's best simply to avoid displaying your camera.

WILDLIFE Liberia's huge tracts of primary forest remain (for the time being) one of its great natural resources, but are fast being slashed and burned for farm plots and plundered by logging, and the war has wreaked great destruction. Forest **elephants**, which are thought to have numbered 2000 in the early 1980s, are almost certainly extinct. The **pygmy hippo**, although rarely seen, may not be threatened. It was discovered here in 1913 and Liberia is its stonghold. Another pygmy, a **"pygmy rhino"**, was reputed to live in the mountain jungle but its existence has never been proved.

A Brief History of Liberia

The very reasons that led to Liberia being chosen for the resettlement of American freed slaves mean that its "pre-modern" history is scantily recorded and still barely known. Until the time of American colonization, large regions were virtually stateless territory and, before the demographic shock waves set off by the collapse of the Niger River's Songhai empire in the sixteenth century, it's likely that much of what is now Liberia was dense, uninhabited rainforest. True, in the northwest, where people were influenced by the urban culture of Mandingo immigrants, some fairly state-like features did emerge – and there was even a large Kpelle confederation called Kondo in the southern Lofa region north of Monrovia. But life mostly revolved around family and clan; nothing larger. Trade in the interior was largely conducted by the Mandingos. Some of the earliest overseas contacts, from before 1700, were between European merchant adventurers and Vai- and Kru-speaking coastal people. The Vai were a Mande-speaking group from the north; the Kru had probably migrated along the coast from the east.

■ The colonization

The motives that brought **freed American slaves** to the "Grain Coast" from 1822 onwards were more mixed than those that inspired the settlement of Freetown in Sierra Leone. The drive behind the repatriation of Africans was as confusedly racist as it was humanitarian, and for every Bible-inspired philanthropist there was a plantation owner with a mistrust of America's growing free black population.

The white patrons of the **American Colonization Society** succeeded in raising funds and in getting Congress to support their scheme. In 1822 the first emigrants were landed on a tiny island – Providence Island, now under the road bridge in Monrovia – at the mouth of the Mesurado River. Protracted negotiations with local Bassa and Dei headmen eventually secured the "right" (for $300 worth of trading goods) for the Americans to occupy the Du Kor peninsula on which Monrovia now stands. As in Freetown, there was a mixture of resentment of the settlers and anticipation of the material benefits they might bring.

The power of **firearms**, however, was often used to put the final seal on settlement and "protection" agreements, as the colonists continued to arrive, their numbers swelled by slaves freed from illegal slave ships in West African ports. With the approval of the white agents of the ACS, and later the first white governor of the "Commonwealth of Liberia" (Thomas Buchanan), followed by the first black governor and president (JJ Roberts), the settlers expanded into the coastal hinterland and extended their control over communal, trust-held African land. Concepts of ownership of territory were, as in most of Africa, quite alien; there was often no immediate indigenous response to what appeared, from the local viewpoint, to be meaningless posturing on the part of the black Americans.

Through the 1820s and 1830s, Washington shirked any responsibility and refused to recognize Liberia as an American colony, despite the industry of the ACS branches in New York, Pennsylvania, Mississippi and Maryland. In 1847, when British interests in Sierra Leone directly conflicted with those of the Liberian settlers, three of the Liberian colonies issued a **"Declaration of Independence"**, drawn up on American lines and establishing Africa's first republic under the presidency of **Joseph J Roberts**. Maryland-in-Liberia, the colony in the southeast, at Cape Palmas, was annexed by the republic ten years later, but it was only in 1862 that Abraham Lincoln's government finally recognized the Liberian republic.

During its first century of existence, Liberia's main **trading partners** were not American but British, Dutch and German. The republic used British currency until 1943. The United States provided mostly symbolic support – and a stream of earnest missionaries, black and white. America made Liberia its first major loan in 1871, but high interest and embezzlement frittered it away. Serious economic development of the country was, in any case, not viable if it was to be based only on the small coastal enclaves.

■ Nineteenth-century colonial society

The **class system** of nineteenth-century Liberia bore a remarkable resemblance to that of the

United States. Established **free black families** formed the social and economic elite. **Slaves emancipated** in order to go to Liberia were next in status, followed at some remove by the **"Congos"** – displaced Africans from captured slave ships who had never been to America. The Congos' position was at first marginal, but their indoctrination in American ways and the determination of the churches to keep them from returning to "barbarism" saw them rapidly assimilated into the ranks of the Americo-Liberians, a merging that was further aided by the formation of the True Whig Party in 1869. At the bottom of the social heap were the **indigenous population** – the "tribes of savages" who were the target of missionary zeal and who outnumbered the colonists by twenty to one. The "tribes", as they were called, were ruled as a protectorate, in strictly colonial fashion. Slightly adrift of this quite rigid order was a small group of **Caribbean blacks** who had emigrated from the British empire for political reasons and who were to become highly influential in government.

This social order only existed to begin with in the colonial pockets along the coast. In the interior, Americo-Liberian traders and missionaries were at the mercy of local sympathies. And until after World War I missionaries (whether white or black) were prohibited by the government from establishing churches and schools more than fifty miles into the interior, for fear of indigenous insurrection. In places there was deep hostility towards the Americo-Liberians. Right up until the 1920s parts of Kru-land openly resisted tax payments and the judicial authority of Monrovia.

But in the late nineteenth century, as the Republic of Liberia became a fact on the ground as well as on paper, the biggest threats were external. Liberia had to concede large areas of disputed territory in the 1890s and early 1900s to the French and British.

■ Forced labour: the Firestone Republic

Where they were in complete control, the **economic practices** of the Americo-Liberians were mostly repressive. Labour was purchased from compliant chiefs; various forms of debt-slavery and "apprenticeship" served the interests of plantation owners; and in the 1920s a full-scale trade in **forced labourers**, captured at gunpoint, flourished with the Spanish-ruled island of Fernando Po in Central Africa. The **League of Nations** commissioned an enquiry which found evidence of high-level government complicity in the commercial activities of the Liberian armed forces.

President King and his vice-president were forced to resign and diplomatic relations with Britain and the USA were suspended for five years. During this period, international discussions over Liberia's future tended to favour the placing of the country under a League of Nations mandate (without any admission that practices as illiberal as Liberia's continued in many European-held territories). At the same time, Colonel Elwood Davis of the **Liberian army** was engaged in brutally putting down the last outbursts of anti-settler resistance from the Kru in the Grand Bassa district – a resistance emboldened by the League report.

But what had first focused world attention on Liberia was the arrival of the **Firestone rubber company** in 1926. Firestone was granted, on give-away terms, a concession of a million acres (4000 square kilometres) of which it still hasn't planted more than one third. Firestone, in boosting rubber to the country's principal commodity, turned the economy round, soaked up Monrovia's unemployed (and in the early years at least, participated in the use of forced labour) and encouraged the arrival of an array of peripheral industries. The United States, which had no small interest in the fortunes of Firestone, began taking a strategic commercial view of Liberia. Under the Firestone loan agreement in 1927, Liberia came under American financial supervision. By the outbreak of World War II (in which Liberia was used as an allied seaplane base and communications centre), the "Firestone Republic" was clearly established. The fall of Malaya and consequent extra demand for Liberian rubber – followed, in 1943 by the adoption of US currency – confirmed Africa's first neo-colonial state.

■ Tubman: 1944–71

President William V Tubman was elected into West Africa's period of most rapid change. The nationalist demands across the borders couldn't be ignored in Liberia, and small measures of democratization were enacted. Although paper citizenship had been granted to all Liberians in 1904, it meant little to the "tribal" majority until 1946, when they finally got the **right to vote** – or rather their chiefs did on their behalf. Even then, a property clause kept anyone who didn't own land disenfranchised.

Tubman, a lawyer by training and an astute politician, promulgated two major new policies: an **"open-door policy"** to encourage foreign investment throughout the country (foreign capital had previously been restricted to the coast in a crude economic repression of the interior); and a **"unification policy"** to improve domestic relations between the Americo-Liberians, who were beginning to see favour in African names and culture, and the peoples of the interior, who were less often labelled "the tribes". These apparently progressive moves signalled a new era in Liberia. Yet their effect was to raise expectations without delivering any substantial improvements in most peoples' lives. When foreign companies began to arrive in large numbers in the 1960s, the prizes for the elite were plain to see, but there was little to benefit the rural poor. While some advantages did come along the new roads being cut through the forests, improved communications also heralded a **land grab** that ranks with the most blatant in African history. Tens of thousands of peasant farmers were forced to sell ancestral land, or simply lost it to Americo-Liberian interests they were powerless to resist. Monrovia and other towns swelled with rural migrants forced into the coastal cash economy, while agricultural land lay fallow, or was turned over to export crops – coffee, cocoa and rubber.

Even the new **political structures** were very heavily biased towards the interests of the Americo-Liberians. The coastal counties, with less than half the population, had over half the seats in the upper house or Senate and no less than four-fifths of the seats in the House of Representatives. The new migrants to the towns and coastal plantations held no land and were therefore not entitled to vote in any case. Needless to add, the opportunities to occupy senior posts for anyone not connected to a leading Americo-Liberian family were nil. Moreover, freedom of the (government-owned) press, like political freedom, was severely curtailed.

Tubman's efforts to appear reformist were further belittled by the deep-rooted influence of **freemasonry**. Almost every important and influential figure in Liberian society was a mason, and Tubman and several senior ministers took turns in office as Worshipful Grand Masters. Masonry was the medium through which flowed almost unrestricted corruption, though Tubman was diligent in keeping his family's activities as quiet as possible.

Yet President Tubman had a large following. He was lauded among settler families and in the first two decades of his presidency there was some showing of a genuine popularity among the indigenous peoples, more so than any previous incumbent – which is perhaps not to say a great deal. While it was recognized that the lid couldn't be kept on forever (and there were a number of assassination attempts), Tubman had no popular opposition to contend with (either from within the Whig party or from outside) and there was no alternative agenda to compare with his.

But as Tubman's post-war reforms began to lose their shine, his genuine popularity became an increasingly insincere, fearful and costly **cult of adulation** (for example, workers on state payrolls found their salaries docked to pay for annual birthday presents) and he lost credibility. By the mid-1960s an elaborate security apparatus of "public relations officers" was informing on every disgruntled conversation; "popular" public support had to be underpinned by government inducements; and libel and slander laws were interpreted in ways which made any criticism very expensive.

■ Tolbert: 1971–80

Tubman died during surgery in a London hospital in 1971. His successor, long-time vice-president **William Tolbert**, was a career politician, unable in the long term to camouflage his elite background. His family were enormously influential and rapacious in business, and his style was ostentatious.

On first becoming president, however, Tolbert acted the part with determination, abandoning New York fashion for sober Kaunda suits and even putting on a special country accent for his up-country tours. Although he had a knack for coining platitudinous slogans ("total involvement for higher heights", "lifting the people from mats to mattresses"), he picked up Tubman's "unification policy" with more enthusiasm than the old man himself – releasing political prisoners, freeing the press and touring the country in a VW Beetle instead of the executive Mercedes.

Tolbert surprised the country. For the first few years of his rule he was frequently given the benefit of any doubts. But he had none of Tubman's charisma, counted on less support within the True Whig Party, and was evidently fearful throughout his life of the fate he was finally to meet, for his public appearances, once the honeymoon period was over, became few and shy. Bullet-proof limousines and a mix of paranoia and self-glorification once again became the order of the day. He spent a good deal of time, and vast sums of public money, at the presidential "city" of **Bentol**, the renamed and reconstructed Bensonville of his birth.

Liberia in the 1970s was a country open to American cultural influence, but also with its own internal momentum for social change. The customary barriers that had set the settler families against native Liberians had less and less meaning, and a new constituency of disaffected, often foreign-educated, Liberians of all backgrounds was beginning to make known its demands for root-and-branch reform and its repugnance for the status quo. Four percent of the population owned more than sixty percent of the land. **Opposition groups** began to form – the Movement for Justice in Africa (MOJA) and the Progressive Alliance of Liberians (PAL).

The year of ferment

By the end of the 1970s, Tolbert had lost any sense of purpose in his presidency beyond the expansion of the Tolbert family empire. His **chairmanship of the OAU** in 1979 climaxed with a Monrovia summit of preposterous expense. At the same time, a deepening domestic crisis over the price of rice caused him to vacillate dangerously between the clear need for reforms and family pressure to carry on with business as usual. In his indecision, he became increasingly alienated from even his True Whig backers and lost any vestige of support from the young dissidents and students.

Rice production, unlike that of most export crops, was not government-subsidized. The state offered no marketing help and co-operative marketing was officially discouraged for political reasons. Cash-hungry farmers were therefore forced to sell their rice harvest at a crippling discount to Lebanese wholesalers, who would later sell it back to them at the much higher government-approved price. In April 1979, at the end of the "hungry season", when the whole country was having to buy rice, Tolbert announced a hike of fifty percent in the price of a sack of rice, to encourage local planting and decrease the bill for imported rice.

He could hardly have been more provocative. The PAL called a **demonstration** to protest the increase and, on April 14, two thousand people led by students marched through Monrovia. The troops who'd been ordered onto the streets included many sympathizers, and they let the crowd pass peacefully. But the police lost their nerve and opened fire. In the panic, the shooting became indiscriminate and the demonstration turned into a full-scale riot which blazed through Monrovia for the whole day. Lebanese shops were particularly singled out by the crowd. President Tolbert called frantically for Guinean president Sekou Touré's help and, later in the day, MIG fighter planes from Conakry made passes over the city.

Over a hundred people were killed in the **"rice riots"**, and buried en masse without ceremony. Hundreds more were arrested in the aftermath and thirty were convicted on the capital charge of treason. Press and personal freedoms that Tolbert had introduced eight years earlier were suspended, the universities were shut down, and the army increasingly found itself the tool of True Whig repression. High-profile foreign policy and Tolbert's OAU chairmanship kept international attention on Liberia, to the president's unease.

The "rice riots" marked a watershed in Liberian politics. The Old Guard was squarely on the defensive. Tolbert had become a pathetic, dithering figure. In October, MOJA's leader, **Togba-Nah Tipoteh**, challenged the True Whig incumbent in the election for the Mayor of Monrovia, and would have won but for the cancellation of the poll. The PAL was recognized as a party and then later banned and its leaders detained. In March 1980 there was a series of arrests of army officers and ordinary soldiers.

■ The April 12 coup and the PRC

A military takeover by the largely Americo-Liberian officers' ranks had long been thought likely. They were competent, educated men, known to be frustrated at the lack of political will on the part of the government. However, as Tolbert himself appeared to be toying with permitting an opposition, the establishment was actually more fearful of a *right-wing* putsch by hard-line reactionaries close to the president.

Instead, when **the coup** came, in the early hours of April 12, it was the army's senior enlisted soldier, 28-year-old **Master Sergeant Samuel Doe**, a Krahn from Tuzon in Grand Gedeh, who with sixteen others stormed into the Executive Mansion in Monrovia, slashed and shot to death President Tolbert and killed and mutilated his 26-strong executive guard. As daylight dawned and key communications centres and arsenals were captured, the entire century-old True Whig edifice collapsed across the country. Some ninety senior Tolbert officials were detained and many others were placed under house arrest or threatened.

It was not an elegant coup. By mid-morning Monrovians were dancing in the streets and rejoicing over Tolbert's body, displayed at the Kennedy Hospital. Two days later, the body, along with the remains of the murdered presidential guards, was dumped in a swampy area near the Palm Grove cemetery (the same spot where victims of the rice riots had been buried a year earlier). Across Liberia, **revenge attacks** were raging, mostly by ill-disciplined troops, on Americo-Liberian persons and property. The Masonic temple in Monrovia was ransacked. The town of Bentol was demolished. An estimated 200 people were killed.

Doe's **People's Redemption Council** (PRC), largely composed of Krahn-speaking soldiers, set up a military-civilian cabinet, partly of released PAL and MOJA leaders, and made the usual promises about a swift resumption of civilian rule. Meanwhile, all political activity was banned and the constitution of 1847 suspended. There was support from "revolutionary" governments abroad and silence or protests from West African neighbours and the West. But the broad popularity of the coup within Liberia wasn't in doubt. The PRC "tried" most of its prisoners in a hastily convened "People's Court" and, ten days after the coup, thirteen senior figures were executed.

The trials and the summary nature of **the executions on the beach** bore no significant difference from practices conducted with less fanfare under the regimes of Tubman and Tolbert. But Doe made the colossal public relations mistake of inviting the **press and foreign TV crews**. The film of the brutal shootings, dispatched with total contempt for suffering, in an atmosphere of drunkenness and confusion, has become an indelible image of inhumanity in modern Africa.

Europe and the United States reacted to the executions with horrified hypocrisy. But after Doe's brief flirtation with the Soviet Union, the USA recognized the new regime. President Carter's defeat by **Ronald Reagan** in October could hardly have been better timed from Doe's point of view. The United States swiftly moved to increase its aid package to Liberia tenfold, making it a larger recipient of US aid than all other African nations put together.

The end of the PRC's "radical phase" (not that it had ever clearly expressed any ideology) was marked by the departure from the cabinet in July 1982 of MOJA's Tipoteh and Baccus Matthews of the PPP (the successor to the PAL) and by the execution in August of five PRC radicals who had earned Doe's distrust, including the vice-chairman **Thomas Weh Syen**. Meanwhile, on a more positive note, a broad-based commission worked intensively to devise a **new constitution** with the mandate of all Liberians. It was accepted by referendum in 1984.

But by mid-1983, with an unbanning of political parties to look forward to, and elections scheduled for a return to civilian rule, the PRC was already turning back towards the **True Whig model of government**. All the traditional trappings of power had long been taken on by the revolutionaries; now, disgraced figures from the Tubman and Tolbert era were gradually allowed back into public life. Striking workers found the PRC dealt with them just as Tolbert would have done, with violence and intimidation. There were **high school student riots** in Sanniquellie, Nimba county, and, in October, army commander **Thomas Quiwonkpa** (a Nimba man credited with pulling the armed forces into line since the coup) refused a downgrading and went into voluntary exile in Côte d'Ivoire, pursued by Doe's accusations that he had tried to stage a coup.

■ The road to "civilian government"

When political rights were restored in July 1984, severe restrictions were placed on the **new parties** that emerged – including the requirement of a $150,000 deposit in order to contest the elections. The university's **Dr Amos Sawyer** resuscitated MOJA in the form of the Liberian People's Party (LPP), but it was banned. So, too, was **Baccus Matthews**' United Peoples' Party (successor to the PPP and PAL who had organized the 1979 rice protest). Doe's own National Democratic Party of Liberia was immediately registered, and three less influential opposition parties, led by a headmaster, **Gabriel Kpolleh**, and former Whig ministers with "tribal" links, **Edward Kesselly** and **Jackson Doe**, were eventually registered weeks before the elections.

Attack on the university

The most restless proponents of change and reform, **the students**, had waited four years in virtual silence, patiently enduring intimidation and arrest for the least contentious remarks about the PRC's rule. They justifiably felt their pressure had weakened the Tolbert regime and paved the way for the success of the 1980 coup.

The spark for the **attack on the university** was a press interview given by Amos Sawyer, Dean of Social Science, in which he criticized Doe for preempting the democratic process and bending his own rules. On August 22, Sawyer was arrested and the students mounted a demonstration on campus. Eye-witnesses reported that a 200-strong detachment of the Executive Mansion guard stormed the University, firing into the backs of fleeing students. No official enquiry has ever been held into the attack though the government admitted 74 people had been wounded. Judging by the number of students missing afterwards, dozens must have been killed. Many women were raped and horrifically tortured. The soldiers looted and destroyed some two million dollars' worth of property. The campus was subsequently sealed off for five days.

The process of return to civilian rule, from this point on, was little more than going through the motions. The credibility of the coup leaders of 1980 had been shattered. Finally, Doe's right-hand man, Major-General **Nicholas Podier**, was arrested on suspicion of treason, and then retired from the military (he was reported killed after a failed "invasion attempt" two years later). This left Doe the sole survivor of the original PRC executive.

The elections

The run-up to the **elections** of October 15, 1985 made nonsense of the claim that they were to be "free and fair". The NDPL was able to pull the whole government apparatus into serving its campaign before opposition parties had even been legalized. There was widespread intimidation and coercion. The elections themselves went off peacefully, with a large turnout (though not without serious malpractice, including a bonfire of ballot papers outside Monrovia). But when early counting indicated a large vote for Jackson Doe's **Action Party**, the NDPL-partisan "Special Elections Commission", in charge of running the election, found spurious arguments to justify ordering all ballots to be transported to Monrovia. They were counted there by an overwhelmingly biased committee of citizens, "hand-picked by the Commission", consisting of Samuel Doe's aids, Krahn civilians and NDPL supporters.

Two weeks later it was announced that Doe's party had won with a 51 percent share of the vote. The only voice that sounded a credulous note in response to this "result" was that of the US Department of State. In Liberia, the victorious government banned demonstations in the aftermath "out of fear that the jubilation might get out of hand".

■ The Second Republic

The **Second Republic** got off to a bad start, with the refusal of the elected opposition to take their seats in the Legislature on the grounds that this would legitimize the fraudulent elections.

This shaky beginning was crippled by the serious **coup attempt** of November 12, 1985, led by the respected ex-PRC man **Thomas Quiwonkpa**. He arrived from Sierra Leone with two dozen heavily armed soldiers. The tragedy of the coup lay in the premature radio announcement that Doe had been toppled. There was mass jubilation on the streets of Monrovia. But Quiwonkpa's small force failed to strike hard enough. Doe kept control, recaptured the radio station, and set about rounding up those who had celebrated his end.

Retribution was frenzied and, for the first time, unmistakably **tribalist** in nature. Quiwonkpa himself was caught and killed, and his body taken to central Monrovia where onlookers and a TV crew witnessed hysterical soldiers tearing it apart with bayonets. The soldiers, mostly Krahn, arbitrarily subjected non-Krahn speakers to extortion, beatings and murder. For a week, truckloads of mutilated corpses passed through Monrovia to be buried in mass graves on isolated beaches. Upcountry, in Doe's Krahn homeland of **Grand Gedeh county** and in **Nimba county**, the Dan/Gio-speaking ethnic group of both Quiwonkpa and Jackson Doe was viciously harassed. A reign of terror descended, and hundreds were killed over the ensuing months. The iron-mining town of Yekepa was a particular target. Officials of the part-foreign-owned mining company that operated there refused to speak to human rights investigators about reports that company staff and vehicles were involved in summary arrests and executions.

The **United States**, Liberia's prop, refused to notice what was happening – or perhaps was too ill-informed to see – and the Liberian opposition, at home and in exile, was bitter over the administration's official "satisfaction" with Doe's performance and the conduct and outcome of the elections. Only Congress resolved that the aid package should be contingent on honest elections and an improvement in human rights.

After Doe's lavish inauguration as president on January 6, 1986, there was a remarkable strengthening of nerve. The new constitution was technically now in force and the press began to speak up again. While most of the opposition seats in the Legislature were finally filled, the three opposition parties found scope for a united front in **the Grand Coalition** which served as a platform for all dissenting voices in the country. The Coalition was banned and its three leaders (Jackson Doe, Kesselly and Kpolleh) sent to the notorious **Belle Yella** prison camp in Lofa county on charges of "contempt of court" for referring to themselves as members of what was not an officially recognized body.

1987 saw Doe requesting American expertise in running his shambolic and corrupt economy. His shameless admission of failure ("I don't know who to trust any more") was, he knew, the only way to keep the funds coming in. The **seventeen accountancy "experts"** stayed most of 1988, acting virtually as a parallel government, limiting the diversion of US aid to private accounts, overseeing tax collection and sorting out salary backlogs. But they were not empowered to veto cheques signed by Doe himself. Following a US Congressional freeze on aid, they left Monrovia before time, shaking their heads. The IMF and World Bank had by now given up on Liberia addressing its debts and pulled out.

On the political front, a number of **opposition figures** fled to the USA where they continued their campaign to remove Samuel Doe. Liberian "justice" could claim a catalogue of abuses and deliberate misinterpretations of the law by corrupt senior judges. It was even made explicit that the new constitution was to be seen as no more than a framework on which the government might, or might not, hang its decisions.

The "Grand Coalitionists" were released from Belle Yella, but **Gabriel Kpolleh** was detained again in March 1988 and given a ten-year jail sentence on treason charges in June.

■ Outbreak of war and Doe's death

Liberia's ill-founded distinction as West Africa's oldest independent republic disguises the fact that, until 1980, it was simply a **colony** whose rulers had *declared* their independence. Had they been white Americans, it seems doubtful whether Washington would have permitted this (any more than Britain did Rhodesia in 1965). Liberia, ruled as a colony by a small elite caste, still retained, at the time of Samuel Doe's coup, a property restriction on voting rights. Economic development was entirely colonial in nature. To make some sense of what has happened in the country, it's necessary to see Liberia as the newest independent nation in West Africa, not the oldest.

Under Doe, the Liberian armed forces were overwhelmingly Krahn-speaking (a minority group from Grand Gedeh accounting for some five percent of the population). Virtually all the key military leaders were Krahn. Disproportionately, so too were the non-Americo-Liberian holders of high government office. Ordinary Krahn people of Grand Gedeh lived in fear of eventual retaliation on their ethnic community.

The **United States administration** has much to answer for in the support, both military and economic, which it extended to Samuel Doe. The US claimed it did not want to jeopardize the **"special relationship"** it had with Liberia – a relationship based on outdated Cold War strategy, allowing the virtually free use of a giant military-commercial **"Omega"** navigation station outside Monrovia, as well as **Voice of America** transmitters broadcasting to the whole continent, and the largest American embassy and American community in Africa. America's failure to drop its support for one of Africa's most entrenched and tribalistic military dictatorships is partly responsible for the current civil war.

On Christmas Eve, 1989, several hundred rebels under the leadership of Charles Taylor, invaded Liberia from Côte d'Ivoire (Houphouët-Boigny of Côte d'Ivoire was keen to see the ousting of Doe, who had been responsible for the murder of his neice's husband, William Tolbert: she later married Blaise Compaoré of Burkina). Government troops – accompanied by US military advisors – soon lashed back in Nimba county, burning suspected rebel villages. Hundreds of **Gio and Mano civilians** were murdered by troops and thousands fled to Côte d'Ivoire and Guinea. **Mandingos and Krahns** were viciti-mized by the rebels. By early January 1990, the rebels had overrun Karnplay and they were soon in control of most of Nimba county and gathering strength all the time.

Charles Taylor, leader of the National Patriotic Front of Liberia (NPFL), had been a little-known minister under Doe. He is still wanted by the FBI for jumping bail in Boston while waiting to be extradited to Monrovia to face charges of embezzlement. In February 1990 he fell out with one of his senior commanders, **Prince Yormie Johnson**, who moved his breakaway group – the Independent PFL – into the northwest.

For three months, the main NPFL consolidated and continued its invasion across the country, but leaving much of Grand Gedeh county and the southeast in the control of government forces. At the end of May they took the major sea port of **Buchanan**.

In June 1990, as foreign governments scrambled to make evacuation plans for their nationals, the country entered a phase of desperation. In **Monrovia**, Doe and several hundred of his Israeli-trained presidential guards holed themselves up in the Executive Mansion. Businesses closed, stocks of food ran down, city life came to a halt, and the people fled – many to Sierra Leone. Those who stayed, especially any who couldn't prove their unrelatedness to Gio or Mano (the commonest language groups of the rebels), risked summary execution by **Armed Forces of Liberia** (AFL) troops who terrorized the city under cover of the curfew. Massacres and starvation became commonplace.

As the **Economic Community of West African States**, led by Nigeria, tried to arrange negotiations, and then a peacekeeping force, Charles Taylor's rebels moved into the eastern suburbs of Monrovia – and Prince Yormie Johnson's into the north of the city. A three-sided street battle ensued around the city centre. **American marines** were sent in by helicopter in August 1990 to rescue remaining American citizens and protect the embassy.

The long-awaited **West African peacekeeping force**, ECOMOG, finally arrived at the end of August. It proved quite incapable of separating the rebels or imposing any ceasefire and lost credibility early on when, on September 10, Samuel Doe, who ventured out of his mansion to speak to Prince Johnson at ECOMOG headquarters, was captured from under the noses of the "peacekeepers" by Johnson's men and tortured to death, in a now infamous incident recorded on video.

■ The war since Doe's death

The pattern of the war since Doe's death has been a steady fragmentation of rebel groups and militias into smaller units. These are mostly unstable in composition; loyalty to their leaders is fickle; none of them has a public agenda or a clear set of policies; and they rarely enjoy grass-roots support that extends beyond the fear of the protection racket.

The 1990 Banjul conference handed the job of president in the optimistically named Interim Government of National Unity (IGNU), to **Dr Amos Sawyer**, while the commander of ECOMOG, a Ghanaian, was replaced with a Nigerian – and Nigeria henceforth assumed a dominant role. Despite conference agreements, the fighting continued and, in March 1991, a Sierra Leonean dissident, Foday Sankoh, and his band of rebels, joined forces with NPFL rebels in northwest Liberia and attacked Sierra Leonean villages across the border.

The All-Liberia conference in Monrovia on March 15, 1991, made no progress at all, but confirmed an unbridgeable rift between two factions *within* the Independent PFL. Charles Taylor, meanwhile, was too afraid to come to Monrovia for the conference because of security difficulties – ECOMOG guarantees of safety for faction leaders in Monrovia were not taken seriously after Doe's death.

The United Liberation Movement for Democracy (**ULIMO**), a ragtag army of Doe loyalists, was formed in northern Liberia late in 1991. Led by Raleigh Seekie, and supported by Sierra Leonean president Joseph Momoh, ULIMO fought Foday Sankoh's rebels to the west and Charles Taylor's to the southeast. By the middle of the rains in 1992, however, Seekie had been sidelined by a tougher ULIMO warlord, **Alhaji GV Kromah**. This new development changed the nature of the war, introducing a third rebel force, and making the job of "peacekeeping" virtually impossible for the ECOMOG soldiers.

ULIMO's successes against the NPFL led Taylor to talk with some outward enthusiasm about peace and good relations with ECOMOG, which he tended normally to characterize as Nigerian colonialists. Meanwhile, as he went about proclaiming himself President of Greater Liberia, old "Congo" interests began to be reasserted in the central and coastal regions he controlled, to the dismay and anger of many of his erstwhile supporters. During the lull while Taylor was outwardly exploring peace options, he rearmed, and business continued as usual out of **Buchanan**, his main export port, through which he was selling iron ore, timber and other goods.

In October 1992, the country saw some of the worst fighting of the war, with ULIMO and NPFL battles raging in several areas and the NPFL pounding Monrovia, which, for a few weeks, was widely expected to fall. Meanwhile, Prince Yormie Johnson's INPFL quietly surrendered to ECOMOG on October 17, 1992. ECOMOG's performance in defence of the capital was not brilliant, and they seemed to know nothing about NPFL troop movements, while Taylor's intelligence about ECOMOG was excellent. ECOMOG, no longer even pretending to be involved in "peacekeeping", joined forces with the "armies" of ULIMO, the AFL and the IGNU force, the Black Berets, to prosecute a **full-scale war** against the NPFL.

By the beginning of 1993, Taylor had lost most of his grassroots support, even among those who had feared and hated Doe the most – the NPFL had massacred too many. There was great fear among the NPFL's largely Dan and Gio forces of being captured by the Mandingo and Krahn men of the AFL and ULIMO, which are not controlled by ECOMOG. May 1993 saw Taylor on the run. He lost Roberts Field airport, control of the Firestone rubber plantation (from which he had been getting protection money) and the port of Buchanan.

However, in response to what looked like terminal setbacks, Taylor started putting infiltrators into Monrovia, spreading fear and insecurity and tying up the ECOMOG troops in house-to-house searches and operating the curfew – causing resentment among Monrovians about foreign troops in their city. A succession of agreements signed at **Yamoussoukro** collapsed as Taylor adhered to none of them – to the irritation of Côte d'Ivoire, who only seemed to be supporting Taylor now because of the support for him from President Compaoré of Burkina. Every ceasefire agreement was used by Taylor as an opportunity to rearm.

Yet by the end of 1993, peace was really beginning to seem a possibility. Disarmament was in the air after the **Cotonou peace accord**. UNOMIL (the UN monitoring force) were now in the country too. However, there was a lack of harmony between them and ECOMOG as they attempted to disarm the warring factions. So far only around 3000 of the 30,000–60,000 armed men and boys have given up their guns in the **School-for-Guns** programme worked out by the self-help aid agency *Susukuu*, led by **Togba-Nah Tipoteh**. Taylor had always claimed that ECOMOG was a front for a Nigerian colonization of Liberia. Financially, at any rate, the Nigerian soldiers have done very well. Buchanan has been stripped bare by them, and there is no shortage of evidence that for hundreds, if not thousands of Nigerian soldiers, their ECOMOG posting has been first and foremost a business exercise.

In September 1994, Taylor's "capital", Gbarnga, was almost totally destroyed by his own dissidents in coalition with other forces, while Taylor and his "cabinet" were away in Ghana at the Akosombo conference. The **Akosombo accord** which resulted from the conference took equal account of the AFL, the ULIMO and the NPFL (giving them one seat each together with two seats for civilians, on the Monrovia State Council), but no account of the NPFL dissidents led by **Tom Woewiyu** and **Lavell Supuwood**, the Krahn faction of ULIMO led by **Roosevelt Johnson** and the Liberian Peace Council of **George Boley**, all of whom rejected the accord.

In Liberia itself, the third major period of fighting broke out in October 1994, this time between NPFL loyalists stranded in the southeast and the coalition of NPFL dissidents, ULIMO Krahns and the LPC. This went on right through the 1994–95 dry season and well into the rains of 1995 and squeezed the NPFL in the east into tiny pockets and over the border into Côte d'Ivoire.

Taylor eventually won back his Gbarnga base, after months of fighting and, politically, he came out on top, with support from Rawlings, Abacha and other west African leaders.

■ Prospects

The silence of the international community on Liberia is deafening. **Jimmy Carter** has worked earnestly, shuttling between Monrovia and other capitals, but to little avail. There are no obvious leaders with a broad power base. As early as October 1992, Côte d'Ivoire and the USA were acknowledging their desire to see Taylor president of Liberia. Nigeria's dictator, Sani Abacha, is increasingly keen to escape from the Liberian mess. The disarmament programme having so far failed, he and Ghana's Jerry Rawlings have been trying to rescue the ECOMOG from ignominy. A wild card in the analysis is **France** which has so far not sought to prevent Burkina and Côte d'Ivoire from meddling in Liberia.

Charles Taylor is a survivor. While it would seem he doesn't have the necessary means, competence or support to lead Liberia legitimately (and he still has the tricky problem of being wanted by the FBI), participants in the peace process – including Jerry Rawlings and Nigerian negotiators – prefer to deal with the devil they know, and he may yet become president. But Taylor's chances of long-term survival – until the end of August 1995 he hadn't dared set foot in Monrovia since the start of the war – seem slim.

After at least a dozen failed peace agreements, the **Abuja accord**, signed in the Nigerian capital on August 19, 1995, seems the most promising to date. A ceasefire was declared a week later and the six-member **Transitional Ruling Council** (weightiest of whom is Taylor) met in Monrovia for the first time on September 1. Elections have been scheduled for August 20, 1996. Peace may last, and there's optimism in the air, but experience suggests there may be more setbacks, failures and bloodshed before eventual peace and stability.

Meanwhile, out of the glare of the media spotlight, a rotten wound in Africa's side continues to brutalize the Liberian people and to infect neighbouring countries. The town of Tai, in Côte d'Ivoire – long considered safe for Liberian refugees – was attacked by Ivoirian troops at the end of July 1995, leaving dozens dead.

WHO'S WHO IN LIBERIA – 1995

THE MONROVIA GOVERNMENT

IGNU – Interim Government of National Unity. The legitimate government of the early war years, now supplanted by the LNTG.

LNTG – Liberian National Transitional Government. Created in March 1995 as a government of national unity, based in Monrovia. Its new, six-member executive body, the Transitional Ruling Council, consists of Charles Taylor, Alhaji Kromah (ULIMO), George Boley (LPC) and three civilians – academic Wilton Sankawulo, politician Oscar Quiah and the elderly parmount chief of the Kissi, Tamba Tailor.

THE FOREIGN TROOPS

ECOMOG – the ECOWAS (Economic Community of West African States) Monitoring Group. After five years in the field, ostensibly as a peacekeeping force, ECOMOG is the major belligerent and the biggest "army", with at least 10,000 Nigerian troops, and 3000 from Guinea, Ghana, Sierra Leone and The Gambia. Supports the LNTG. Based in Monrovia, Buchanan and along the north coast and Sierra Leonean border.

OAU Troops – 2000 soldiers from Uganda and Tanzania supporting ECOMOG.

UNOMIL – United Nations Observer Mission in Liberia. 600 troops from around the world, mostly cooling their heels in Monrovia.

THE REBELS AND MILITIAS

AFL – Armed Forces of Liberia. The rump of Samuel Doe's army, still based in Monrovia.

NPFL – National Patriotic Front of Liberia. The original 1989 invasion force, led by Charles Taylor, with headquarters in Gbarnga. Supported by Burkina Faso, Libya, and Côte d'Ivoire. Taylor split early on with Prince Yormie Johnson, whose Independent PFL achieved notoriety for murdering Samuel Doe. A more recent dissident NPFL army led by Tom Woewiyu and Lavell Supuwood is based in the east, along the Côte d'Ivoire border and around Zwedru.

ULIMO – United Liberation Movement for Democracy, based in the far north with its headquarters in Voinjama. Formed by Doe loyalists in 1991 to attack the NPFL, and, with Sierra Leonean support, to prevent cooperation between the NPFL and anti-government rebels in Sierra Leone. Now split into ULIMO Mandingos under Alhaji Kromah and ULIMO Krahns under Roosevelt Johnson. The latter faction is tending to be absorbed into the AFL. Secret societies and powerful local commanders play major roles within ULIMO, making the forces especially unstable.

LPC – Liberian Peace Council. Largely Krahn-speaking guerilla group, harassing Taylor's NPFL forces. Based in Greenville and led by George Boley.

"Coalition Forces" – An ad hoc, anti-Taylor grouping, consisting of several of the forces mentioned above: NPFL dissidents, the ULIMO Krahn faction, the AFL and the LPC. It controls a large swathe of central Liberia, inland from ECOMOG, and part of the central coast.

MONROVIA

Monrovia was named after US President James Monroe, and grew up on the hilly peninsula at the mouth of the Mesurado River as a home from home for American freed slaves. A slightly skewed emulation of southern architecture and plantation manners was inevitable, so you find the relics of antebellum-style grandeur amid decaying 1960s multi-storey optimism. A city with a population approaching three quarters of a million people, it used to come across like a dull southern-states American town you'd barely leave the interstate to see – until 1992. Then the suburbs were mostly destroyed when Charles Taylor's rebels almost took the city. Only the city centre escaped the pummelling. The utter dilapidation of the central grid of downtown Monrovia is more to do with years of neglect than war damage.

The city spreads widely, north past the Free Port to the teeming slums of **Bushrod island** and southeast through the main suburb of **Sinkor**, the older quarter of **Congotown** ("Congo" referred to the presumed embarkation point of captured slave ships) out to the **beaches** and, eventually, the mortar-blasted international airport.

TOURIST INFORMATION

The **National Bureau of Culture and Tourism** (PO Box 3223; ☎262989) on 14th St and Cheesman Ave in Sinkor may be open.

The Town

Monrovia's sightseeing interest is limited and the place is so infernally humid most of the year that traipsing about isn't high on many people's list of priorities. Tiny **Providence Island**, in the Mesurado River on the north side of the city centre, is the site of the first settlers' landings in 1822. It's overflown by a road bridge, but the squat grey hulks of various military edifices remain at one end.

The **National Museum** on Broad Street at Buchanan Street – housed in the mid-nineteenth-century building that was once the seat of the State Legislature – formerly had modest collections of historical and ethnographic items, and various photos and archaeological pieces. Next door, on the corner of Center Street, the **Providence Baptist Church**, founded in 1839, is the city's oldest. One block north and two west, the **Executive Pavillion** on the corner of Randall and Ashmun streets was built by the first president of the republic, JJ Roberts.

Down at **Waterside market** you soon realize where all Monrovia's action is concentrated. In the market and along the top of Mechlin and Randall streets is all the downmarket city centre commercialism. Head off into the thick of things beyond the market and you're on **West Point**, an extraordinary bottleneck of a slum and more crowded than you'd believe possible. Pickpockets are everywhere. Be prudent.

Shopping

Monrovia is surprisingly well supplied with imported consumer goods, and is also one of the best cities in West Africa for **cloth and clothing**, combined result of the Free Port and large numbers of self-exiled Fula tailors from Guinea. The main garment district is **Benson Street**: the entire avenue is lined with clothing and shoe shops. For *lappas* (cloth *pagnes*), go down to the Waterside end of Mechlin Street, and for lengths of cloth cut from bolts, to Water Street at the Gurley Street junction. **Randall Street** is a good, general shopping street (as well as being the main foreign exchange street),

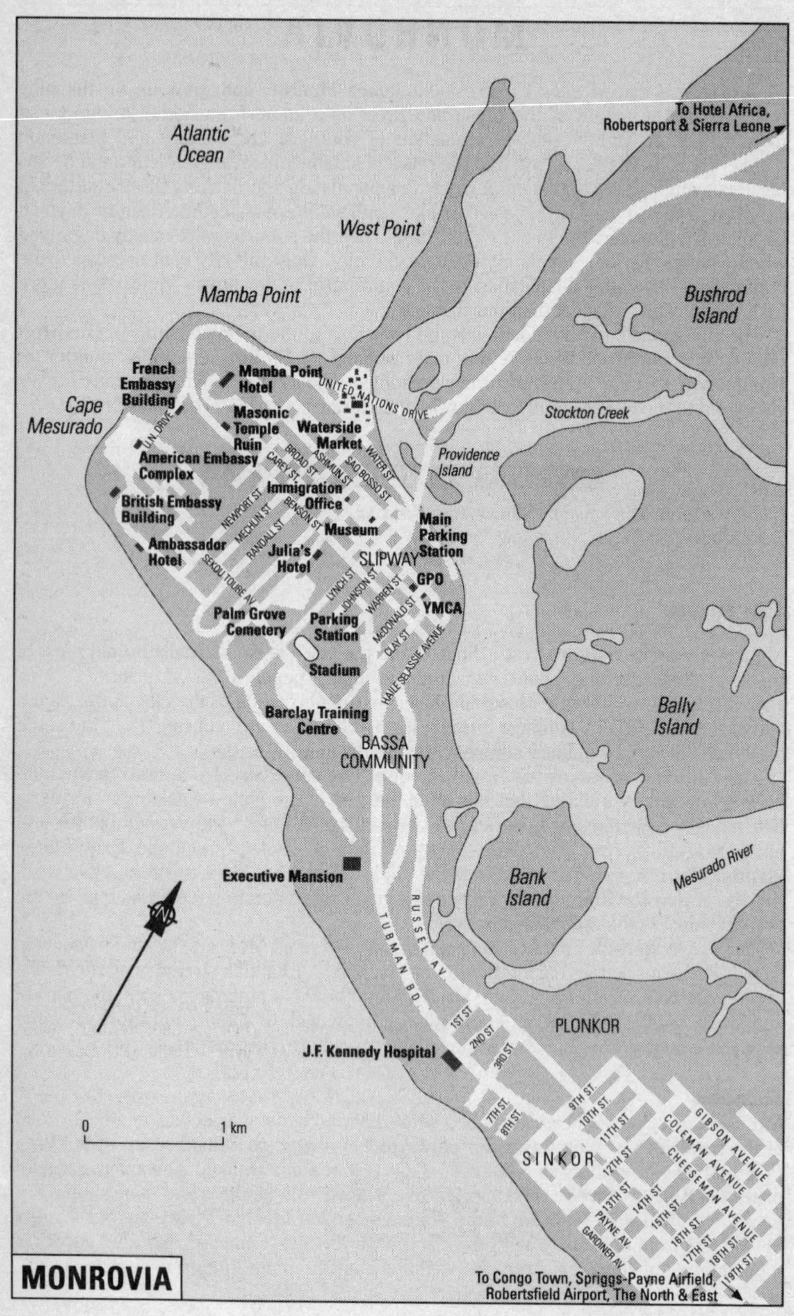

Atlantic Ocean
West Point
Mamba Point
Bushrod Island
To Hotel Africa, Robertsport & Sierra Leone
French Embassy Building
Mamba Point Hotel
UNITED NATIONS DRIVE
Cape Mesurado
Masonic Temple Ruin
Waterside Market
Stockton Creek
Providence Island
U.N. DRIVE
American Embassy Complex
BROAD ST
CAREY ST
ASHMUN ST
SAO BOSSO ST
WATER ST
Immigration Office
British Embassy Building
NEWPORT ST
MECHLIN ST
BENSON ST
Museum
Main Parking Station
Ambassador Hotel
RANDALL ST
Julia's Hotel
SLIPWAY
GPO
SEKOU TOURE AV
LYNCH ST
JOHNSON ST
WARREN ST
McDONALD ST
YMCA
Palm Grove Cemetery
Parking Station
CLAY ST
HAILE SELASSIE AVENUE
Stadium
Barclay Training Centre
Bally Island
BASSA COMMUNITY
Executive Mansion
Bank Island
Mesurado River
RUSSEL AV.
TUBMAN BD.
N
PLONKOR
1ST ST
2ND ST
3RD ST
J.F. Kennedy Hospital
7TH ST.
8TH ST.
9TH ST.
10TH ST.
11TH ST
12TH ST
13TH ST
14TH ST
15TH ST.
16TH ST.
17TH ST.
18TH ST.
19TH ST.
GIBSON AVENUE
COLEMAN AVENUE
CHEESEMAN AVENUE
PAYNE AV.
GARDINER AV.
0
1 km
SINKOR
MONROVIA
To Congo Town, Spriggs-Payne Airfield, Robertsfield Airport, The North & East

with a number of supermarkets and grocers and several gold dealers, where you might get a good deal with hard bargaining.

Beaches

It's important to note that most of the beaches along this part of the coast are very dangerous, with tugging **rip tides**. **Bangor Beach** at the *Hotel Africa* has safe swimming – and safe lounging because it's only open to hotel residents and their guests. The rest of Monrovia's beaches string along the coastline by the road to Roberts Field International Airport but most are out of bounds.

Practicalities

Slowly the city's infrastructure is returning to some kind of normality. Public utilities have still to recover, however: electricity, in particular, is mostly a privately supplied commodity, dependent upon a reliable generator. As for eating and drinking, the city puts on a relatively good show under the circumstances: there are **cook shops** everywhere and **bars** in quantity. Nightlife is severely restricted by the 7pm–7am curfew, which limits night-time discos, bars and clubs to those with UN curfew passes (of whom there seem to be hundreds). Assuming you don't fall into this category, many clubs are now open in the afternoon, and charge around US$2.

Accommodation

Hotel Africa, OAU village, off the Bomi Hills road, 10km north of the city (PO Box 1515; ☎223992 or 224519). The best hotel in Monrovia. Safe sea swimming at Bangor Beach, 500m north of the hotel. US$130 for a twin room.

Ambassador Hotel, UN Drive (PO Box 889; ☎223147). On the beach beneath the British embassy. US$125 for a twin room.

El Meson, 83 Carey St (PO Box 67; ☎222154). US$80 for a twin room.

Hotel Holiday Inn, 100 Carey St (PO Box 996; ☎222342). Not part of the international chain. US$100 for a twin room.

Mamba Point Hotel (ex-Ducor Palace), Broad St (PO Box 86; ☎224200 or 224301). Occupies the highest point on the peninsula but, prices considered, deserves a less elevated position in Monrovia's hotel listings. US$120 for a twin room.

YMCA, corner of Broad and McDonald streets. Cheap and usually full. Around US$5–10 for a bed.

Listings

American Express No representation.

Banks If you're trying to make a transaction with your own bank, the following may be the most useful: *Citibank (Liberia)*, Ashmun St (PO Box 280; ☎224991); *Meridien BIAO Bank Liberia*, corner of Randall and Ashmun streets (PO Box 408; ☎221500; Fax 224087).

Embassies and consulates Diplomatic missions currently open include: **Côte d'Ivoire**, Tubman Blvd, Congotown (PO Box 126; ☎261284); **Nigeria**, Tubman Blvd (PO Box 366; ☎261093, telex 44278); **Sierra Leone**, Tubman Blvd, Congotown, past Spriggs Payne Airfield (PO Box 575; ☎261301 or 261203); **USA**, 111 UN Drive, Mamba Point (PO Box 98; ☎222992).

Immigration Bureau of Immigration and Naturalization, Broad St (Mon–Fri 8am–4pm, Sat 8am–3pm).

Newspapers Nowhere in town sells foreign newspapers. You might find something at the *Hotel Africa*.

Pharmacy *Charif's*, on Randall St, has a very good range of drugs and medicaments.

Phones and fax The Telecom office is off Broad St. Reverse-charge (collect) calls can be made only after 9pm, or on Sun. You can send and receive faxes.

Post offices There are two post offices. The main one is on the corner of Carey and McDonald streets. The other is on Randall St at Ashmun. Hours are 8am–4pm Mon–Fri and 9am–noon on Sat.

index

CHAPTER TEN

COTE D'IVOIRE

COTE D'IVOIRE

Surrounded by countries whose economic circumstances have ranged from hopeful to desperate, Côte d'Ivoire long stood out as an example of **pragmatic capitalism** at work in independent Africa. Politically, too, it was viewed as a close ally of the West, maintaining "stability" without the kind of outright repression the word usually implies. Côte d'Ivoire had, until recently, a generous press in Europe and America, where it was called everything from the "African Miracle" to the "Land of Welcome". Most of this impression hung on a single factor – **Houphouët-Boigny**. The diminutive and soberly engaging president's word and work determined much of the course of Côte d'Ivoire's thirty-year independent history. He never passed up an opportunity to profile his country as a place where new meets old and Western economic principles got along famously with African values. It's easy to apply scorn to this *National Geographic* approach to foreign relations – the coupling of images of **skyscrapers** with shots of local **folklore** such as Dan dancers or Akan kings – but glitzy development did seem to encourage investors, and the three decades of Houphouët's reign were marked by widespread prosperity and no coups or major ethnic conflicts. Under his tutelage, Côte d'Ivoire was close to becoming an emergent industrial nation, comparable, in its atmosphere of feverish transformation, to Brazil.

Much of the country's optimism faded in 1993 when Houphouët died and a new era of uncertainty settled in. Many of the forty thousand **French people** who formerly lived in Abidjan (running businesses, hotels, restaurants, and even taking positions of high office in the government and civil service) abandoned ship. Thousands of others who worked on French government overseas salaries across the country also left. What appeared to be formal integration suddenly looked more like an overextended vacation, and when check-out time came, Ivoirians were left to tackle serious economic and political problems on their own.

The widespread prosperity never had deep roots and, as successful at generating wealth as the country has been – largely on the principle that if you allow virtually unlimited foreign exploitation without closing any doors, a proportion of the cash will stay behind and multiply – some of the very worst **malnutrition** in West Africa still affects parts of northern Côte d'Ivoire, while contrasts between rich and poor in Abidjan are as stark as can be found anywhere in the world.

Viewed from the villages, **Abidjan** is still the glittering capital, though the tarnish is very evident to new arrivals from Europe. Its highly developed service infrastructure, most of which works, still persuades rural Ivoirians to take the bus there in search of jobs and dreams. But well-off Abidjanis who once considered Paris to be the country's real capital have been spurned by the "metropolis" and France's desire to relinquish the responsibility of its "special relationship" with Côte d'Ivoire.

For these slightly voyeuristic reasons, Côte d'Ivoire is an interesting place to visit – a stage on which you can see the traditional and the modern clashing in a drama intensified by heavy capital investment and industrialization. **Tourism** here is probably the most developed in West Africa. The government actively encourages the industry through advertising campaigns emphasizing the exotic and mysterious aspects of traditional culture – images Ivoirians themselves tend to eschew. The cultural heritage is undeniably rich, but Senoufo initiation dances or funeral ceremonies are best witnessed in the bush, as an invited guest, rather than after dinner on a hotel patio.

People

There are over sixty different peoples (*ethnies*, in French, sounds better) living in Côte d'Ivoire. Though their languages, customs and religious practices differ locally – and of course there's been wide intermarriage and blurring of difference – the diversity makes most sense if they're considered as four major groups with distinct historical origins. One of the largest is the **Akan**, to which the Asante in neighbouring Ghana belong. The **Baoulé** (centered around Bouaké), **Agni** (Indénié) and **Abron** (in the east) are all Akan-speaking, though the languages are only partially mutually intelligible. They're also related to peoples who settled around the lagoons – including the **Abé** (Agboville), **Akies** (Adzopé) and **Ebrié** (Abidjan).

Another large group is the **Mande**, who migrated from the north in large-scale waves from around the fourteenth century onwards. Peoples of this group include the **Malinké** (around Odienné), **Dyula** or Dioula (Kong) and **Bamana**. Southern Mande-speaking groups like the **Dan** (near Man) and **Gouro** (Bouaflé) also belong in this ethnic configuration. **Voltaic**-speaking peoples – the **Senoufo** (focused around

Korhogo), the **Lobi** (Bouna), and **Koulango** (Bondoukou) – were already living in the north by the time the Mande speakers arrived.

In the southwest and west, the **Krou** (or Kru, or even **Krumen**) migrated from Liberia and Guinea from some time in the seventeenth century onwards. The name is supposed to derive from the common occupation of crewman on sixteenth- and seventeenth-century English ships. The **Bété** (Gagnoa), **Krou** (Bereby, Tabou), and **Dida** (Lakota) are part of this family of languages.

Côte d'Ivoire has a very large **immigrant population**, most of whom come from Burkina Faso, Mali and Guinea. These immigrants are frequently blamed for urban problems such as unemployment and crime. In addition to these African "strange workers", the **French** and around 120,000 **Lebanese** (traditionally Maronite Christians but including an increasingly high proportion of Shia Muslims) are especially conspicuous minorities because of their economic clout.

Roughly half the population practises traditional African **religions**, though many people – not just the other half – profess Christian or Islamic beliefs. As you'd expect, Muslims predominate in the north while smaller concentrations of various Christian sects are mainly in the south. **Harrism** – founded by William Wade Harris, a Liberian born at the turn of the century – is the oldest of these, and most developed in the Bingerville district. Other indigenous churches have also started to flourish on the preaching of a number of coastal prophets.

Where to go

Despite being publicized as a holiday paradise, most of Côte d'Ivoire is disappointingly monotonous – a uniform plateau with few variations in altitude. The highest peak, **Mont Tonkoui**, rises to a modest 1189m in the country's most mountainous region, the far west. Waterfalls and streams in this district make for some of the country's most scenic hikes and drives.

Côte d'Ivoire's **forests**, which fifty years ago covered most of the southern half of the country, are now hugely reduced – through logging, shifting agriculture and road building which opens up remote jungle to settlement. If you're looking for adventure, the far **southwest** still contains vast districts of primary forest. Anywhere between Guiglo and San-Pédro can yield barely explored valleys and ridges.

An obvious target is the **coast**, where a major system of **lagoons** around Abidjan is separated from the ocean by long chains of sand banks. But swimming tends to be dangerous: when the French say *Attention à la barre!* they're warning about a strong tidal race that claims many lives. For the best beaches, some with safe swimming, too, you really have to make for the **far west coast**, where West Africa's most idyllic palm-rustled strands and coves are still almost untouched. Sassandra isn't too far from Abidjan and makes a good base.

Abidjan is itself part of the lagoon system. The snaking fingers of the Ebrié lagoon wind through the heart of the city, dividing a Manhattanesque urban landscape into manageable districts. If you're flying in from overseas, the only shock you're likely to face upon this first encounter with Africa is how familiar it all seems. Côte d'Ivoire, as showcased by Abidjan's glass and concrete, seems the least culturally disorientating country in West Africa. Even passing through the city on long African travels can feel like a quick trip to Europe.

While still the Ivoirian metropolis, Abidjan is technically no longer the capital. That mantle has been passed to **Yamoussoukro** which, virtually overnight, changed from a colourless village to a colourless administrative centre. Home of the former president, this burgeoning city with its monstrous **Catholic Basilica** lies in the heart of Côte d'Ivoire. This is the **Baoulé country**, settled in the eighteenth century by refugees from the Asante Empire. Their customs and art – in which gold plays an important symbolic role – still resemble those of their neighbours in Ghana.

FACTS AND FIGURES

The **République de Côte d'Ivoire** (often shortened there to *RCI*) is a sizeable country of 323,000 square kilometres – more than twice the area of England and Wales combined, or about the same size as New Mexico. Although long called Ivory Coast in English, Elfenbeinküste in German, Costa de Marfil in Spanish, and so on, the French name is now the official one in all languages. The **population** is estimated at over 13 million, of whom roughly a quarter are migrants from neighbouring states. Many Ivoirians live in urban centres – Côte d'Ivoire has ten towns with populations of more than 100,000.

Despite its image as a wealthy, progressive country, Côte d'Ivoire's **national debt** is the biggest in Africa after Nigeria's, currently amounting to some £12.5 billion ($19 billion) – a somewhat smaller figure than the final cost of building the Anglo-French Channel tunnel. This represents over £1000 for every Ivoirian citizen, which is by far the heaviest per capita debt burden on any African country. Moreover, Côte d'Ivoire's debt is equivalent to six times its annual export earnings, making the prospects for paying off the debt, or even a small fraction of it, negligible. Nearly one billion dollars is spent each year just servicing it.

The **north**, despite the heat and the endless flat grasslands, has its share of interesting sites. There's a number of moderately old Islamic centres, which relate culturally to the medieval empires of the Niger River region. Towns are fewer and further apart up here and the pace slower, while the French influence, so pervasive on the coast, is much less entrenched. This is the home of some of the country's longest-settled ethnic groups; people like the **Senoufo**, whose elaborate system of education and initiation – the **poro** – served as the social glue that held them together in the face of colonialism, and more recently has preserved their identity against the onslaught of tourism.

Also in the north is West Africa's biggest game reserve, the **Comoé National Park**, where you stand a good chance of seeing some of Côte d'Ivoire's remaining ivory.

Climate

Côte d'Ivoire has **two climatic zones**, a fact which complicates any efforts to time your travels to miss the rains. In the **south**, a **long rainy season** from late April to July is followed by **short rains** in October and November, separated by a **long dry season** from December to late April, and a **short dry** in August and September. Dividing the seasons into months like this only gives an approximate idea of when to expect dry weather; "dry" seasons in the south include days of rain and dense clouds blowing in off the coast. Temperature-wise, the coast varies little through the year, neither does it cool down much at night.

The **north** has only two seasons. Rains usually last from late May to early November. Because of the mountains, the northwest receives more rain and is generally cooler than the northeast.

The **best time** to visit, especially the north, is probably between February and April, late enough in the season to avoid the *Harmattan* winds that may adversely affect travel (and dust that makes photos drearily flat). Remember, too, if you're intent on visiting the **game parks**, that they close during the rains, though the dates of closure vary from year to year.

AVERAGE TEMPERATURES AND RAINFALL

ABIDJAN

	Jan	Feb	Mar	Apr	May	June	July	Aug	Sept	Oct	Nov	Dec
Temperatures °C												
Min (night)	23	23	24	25	24	23	23	21	22	23	24	24
Max (day)	30	31	31	32	31	29	28	27	28	29	31	31
Rainfall mm	41	53	99	125	361	495	213	53	71	168	201	79
Days with rainfall	3	4	6	9	16	18	8	7	8	13	13	6

FERKESSÉDOUGOU

	Jan	Feb	Mar	Apr	May	June	July	Aug	Sept	Oct	Nov	Dec
Temperatures °C												
Min (night)	16	19	22	23	23	22	21	21	21	21	20	25
Max (day)	35	36	36	36	34	32	30	30	31	33	34	34

MAN

	Jan	Feb	Mar	Apr	May	June	July	Aug	Sept	Oct	Nov	Dec
Temperatures °C												
Min (night)	19	20	21	21	21	21	20	20	20	20	20	19
Max (day)	32	33	33	32	31	29	27	27	29	30	31	31

Arrivals

Abidjan, as the economic capital of Côte d'Ivoire, plays a pivotal role in the region, and is consequently well connected to the rest of Africa. Flights in are easy, and land connections excellent – relatively speaking.

The details in these practical information pages are essentially for use on the ground in West Africa and in Côte d'Ivoire itself: for full practical coverage on preparing for a trip, getting here from outside the region, paperwork, health, information sources and more, see *Basics*.

■ Flights from Africa

Abidjan, the home of *Air Afrique*, is one of the region's busiest air hubs, with direct connections from every capital city in West Africa except Bissau, Monrovia and Praia, many links with East and Central Africa and regular flights from Johannesburg.

From West Africa

Air France (AF) and *Air Afrique* (RK) handle most of the traffic **from other West African cities**. Their near-daily flights from Europe to Abidjan are routed via **Bamako** (RK, Mon and Sat), via **Cotonou** (RK, Wed and Sun), via **Lagos** (AF, Fri), via **Lomé** (AF, Sat), via **Niamey** (AF, Thurs; RK, Thurs), via **Nouackchott** (AF, Sun) and via **Ouagadougou** (AF, Tues).

Air Afrique's regional services to Abidjan are:

From Accra: two flights, non-stop, on Sun.

From Bamako: via Niamey and Ouagadougou on Sat.

From Conakry: non-stop on Tues.

From Cotonou: via Accra on Fri.

From Dakar: non-stop on Tues and Thurs; via Accra on Sun; via Conakry on Fri and Sun; and via Bamako and Ouagadougou on Mon.

From Douala: non-stop on Mon and Sat; via Lagos and Cotonou on Thurs.

From Lagos: non-stop on Tues and Thurs; and via Lomé on Mon, Fri, Sat and Sun.

From Niamey: via Lomé and Cotonou on Tues.

Cameroon Airlines (UY) flies from **Douala** via Lagos on Tues, Wed and Sun; and via Cotonou and Lagos (in that order) on Fri.

Air Guinée (GI) flies from **Conakry** via Freetown on Thurs.

Ghana Airways (GH) flies non-stop from **Accra** on Mon, Wed, Thurs and Sat; from **Dakar** via Banjul and Freetown on Tues and Sun (also calling at Conakry on Sun); and non-stop from **Freetown** on Sat.

Nigeria Airways (WT) flies from **Lagos** non-stop on Wed; via Cotonou on Tues and Thurs; via Lomé on Mon and Fri; and via Accra on Fri and Sun.

Air Ivoire (VU) flies non-stop from **Accra** on Wed, Fri and Sun; non-stop from **Bamako** on Thurs and Sun and via Bouaké on Tues; non-stop from **Ouagadougou** on Mon, Thurs and Sat; non-stop from **Conakry** on Wed and Fri and via Bouaké on Mon; and non-stop from **Monrovia** on Wed and Sun.

Air Burkina (VH) flies from **Ouagadougou** via Bobo-Dioulasso on Tues, Fri and Sun.

Lastly, *Air Gabon* (GN) flies from **Conakry** non-stop on Fri and from **Cotonou** non-stop on Sat.

From the rest of Africa

Ethiopian Airlines (ET) flies from **Addis Ababa** via Lagos and Lomé on Tues; via Nairobi and Accra on Wed; via Lagos and Accra on Thurs; via Nairobi, Kinshasa and Lomé on Fri; via Nairobi, Brazzaville and Lagos on Sat; and via Nairobi and Lagos on Sun.

Royal Air Maroc (AT) flies from **Casablanca** non-stop on Tues.

Egyptair (MS) flies from **Cairo** via Kano, Lagos and Accra on Wed.

South African Airways (SA) shares the route from **Johannesburg** with *Air Afrique*, with flights via Brazzaville on Mon and Thurs.

■ Overland

Overland routes are good from Mali and Burkina – with the option of the train service from Ouagadougou to Abidjan – and from Ghana. Coming overland from Guinea, conditions are

DRIVING INTO CÔTE D'IVOIRE

If you're coming in with your own vehicle, you'll usually be given a fifteen-day *vignette de passage* by customs, which has to be extended in Abidjan. Don't ignore this if you're not going to Abidjan; be sure to sort the matter out before you leave the border.

rougher, while travelling by land from Liberia – which always was slow-going – is not likely to be on your itinerary.

From Mali

The easiest way into the country **from Mali** is via Sikasso, crossing the border at Pogo. The road has recently been resurfaced, and this gives you the possibility of joining Côte d'Ivoire's main north–south road at Ouangolodougou.

From Bamako, heading for western Côte d'Ivoire, you can also cut down to Bougouni at which point a *piste* leads directly to Odienné, although public transport along this stretch is unreliable and especially bad during the rains.

From Burkina Faso

From Burkina, a main highway runs **from Ouagadougou** to Abidjan and is in pretty good shape. The border post stays open 24 hours a day. Back-country *pistes* through the **Lobi country** are in bad condition. Very little traffic connects the towns of **Gaoua** and **Bouna**.

The **train** from Ouagadougou or Bobo-Dioulasso to Abidjan is still relatively popular (see p.721 & 742).

From Ghana

The principal route **from Accra** is paved through the border town of Elubo, meaning you no longer have to catch a ferry across the Ehi Lagoon dividing the two countries. Besides the normal formalities, there are no special difficulties at this border and the crossing is generally quick. The road **from Kumasi** is also frequently travelled and in decent condition, except for the border stretch between Takikroum in Ghana and Agnibilékrou in Côte d'Ivoire.

From Guinea

Travelling from Guinea is somewhat problematic, owing to the bad condition of the roads. Rains and ferry breakdowns may bring traffic to a standstill. The two most common routes run from **Kankan** and **Beyla** to **Odienné**, from where regular buses head through to Bouaké. There is a stubbornly regular Ivoirian bus service from Kankan to Bouaké. A third route, **Nzérékoré to Man**, skirts uncomfortably close to the Liberian border and has been less often used in recent years, although no reports have been received of travellers having problems related to the Liberian civil war.

From Liberia

> As of mid-1995, with widespread insecurity and conflict throughout Liberia, travel outside Monrovia was not feasible. Even before the war, the border was an uncomfortable one.

The road is paved between Monrovia and Ganta, leaving about 90km of tracks until you arrive at Danané, in Côte d'Ivoire. An alternative, along the coast via Harper and Tabou, may take days if the weather is bad, but once you're at Tabou the road is tarred all the way to Abidjan.

Visas and Red Tape

Passport holders of most EC states (except France and the Benelux countries), Americans and Australians can stay up to three months in Côte d'Ivoire without requiring a visa. Other nationals must obtain a visa before entering (they're not available at the border or the airport). Visas are generally easy to obtain and are often issued at French consulates in those countries where Côte d'Ivoire lacks representation.

An international **vaccination card** proving you have an up-to-date yellow fever inoculation is required at the border. Be sure your arrival formalities are completed. At some borders you're expected to complete things at the first main police station, but you may not be told this – if in doubt, ask, because it may save you having to make a long trip back to the relevant police station later on. Ivoirian bureaucracy has a reputation for being extremely officious.

■ Visas for other countries

All neighbouring countries – Guinea, Liberia, Mali, Burkina Faso and Ghana – are represented in Abidjan. Malian and Ghanaian visas are easily obtained, although the latter take up to 48 hours to be issued. Embassies' addresses are listed at the end of the Abidjan section.

Money and Costs

Ivoirian currency is the CFA franc (CFA100 always equals 1 French franc; approx. CFA750–800 = £1; approx. CFA500 = US$1). If you are travelling cheaply, you will get the

most benefit from the 50 percent devaluation of 1994: prices of goods and services consumed locally have risen only moderately since then. If you're booking expensive hotels and tours, or car rental, however, you'll find prices very high.

In towns across the country there are branches of the *Société Générale de Banques en Côte d'Ivoire* (*SGBCI*), *Banque Internationale pour le Commerce et l'Industrie de Côte d'Ivoire* (*BICICI*), the *Afribail/Banque Internationale de l'Afrique Occidentale* (*BIAO*) and *Société Ivoirienne de Banques* (*SIB*). Be aware, however, that they are often unwilling to change UK£, US$ or DM, especially in travellers' cheques issued by a company with whom they do not have arrangements (it's worth noting that *SGBCI* appears to have an understanding with *Thomas Cook* that means you can change *Thomas Cook* TCs in most branches). The only place you can routinely change non-franc currencies is Abidjan, where *Barclays* and *Citibank* have branches and many banks work in conjunction with European banks.

French franc travellers' cheques are the easiest and safest form of money. The exception might be if you come into the country from Ghana, Guinea or Liberia and think you may have trouble changing money straight away at the border. In that case, French **notes** could come in handy and are usually accepted by taxi drivers, hotel operators and merchants in lieu of CFA. If you arrive by plane, the *bureau de change* at the airport theoretically opens for incoming flights.

Credit cards have made some headway, and are more use here than in any other West African country. Most big hotels now take Amex and often Visa, as do car rental and travel agencies. In Abidjan, they can be used in some of the fancier restaurants and in banks for cash advances. Access/Mastercard is uncommon.

■ Costs

A sluggish economy has brought **costs** in Côte d'Ivoire in line with other West African countries. Prices in Abidjan are certainly high, but other towns no longer seem prohibitively expensive.

Your major expense will be **accommodation**. Staying in the cheapest places, you should plan on averaging CFA5000–8000 per day on twin rooms in hotels, slightly less if you're travelling on your own. Decent hotels tend to be more in the CFA12,000–20,000 range. **Transport** also adds up, though the excellent bus system is no more expensive and a lot more comfortable than the battered bush taxis of other countries. The average trip costs around CFA15 per km. Car rental is unbelievably expensive. **Food** is still affordable; a meal in a market or *gare routière* comes to only a few hundred CFA, though sit-down *maquis* are slightly more expensive – CFA1000–2000. Ordinary meals in mid-range hotel restaurants cost a little less than what you'd pay for *le menu* in an average hotel in France – in other words about CFA5000–6000. Indulging at a foreign restaurant in Abidjan or Yamoussoukro, however, could easily set you back CFA30,000 per person.

Health

Notwithstanding some shocking malnutrition, Côte d'Ivoire has the best record in the region in terms of percentages of people affected by disease. You'll generally find adequately treated water supplies, Ivoirian bottled water everywhere, and soda water stocked in shop fridges.

Health care facilities, in the main towns at least, are pretty much up to international standards and, for long-term residents, there's not much that could befall you that would require evacuation abroad.

Aids figures, however, are alarming; some estimates of HIV carriers run as high as 10 percent of the population and 70 percent of prostitutes. While the Ministry of Health figures are lower, the problem is undeniable and a huge Aids prevention programme is now under way. Blood screening facilities have been introduced, condoms are readily available and billboards in town promote safe-sex: *Confiance d'accord, mais prudence d'abord.*

Maps and Information

Despite its high profile in the French-speaking world, Côte d'Ivoire is little known in Anglophone countries. It's worth contacting their tourist offices abroad, which put out some very attractive material, though sometimes lacking in detail.

For **tourist information in Europe** contact the Délégation du Tourisme de Côte d'Ivoire, 24 bd Suchet, 75016 Paris (☎45.24.43.28); **in the USA**, DTCI, 117 E 55 St, New York, NY 10022 (☎212/355 6975).

As for **maps**, the best one currently available, regularly updated to take account of an active road-building programme, is the *Michelin 975 Côte d'Ivoire* which shows the country in satisfying detail at 1cm:8km and gives all *Michelin*'s usual supplementary information.

Getting Around

Côte d'Ivoire is one of the easiest West African countries to travel around, thanks to good internal road and air connections and the Abidjan–Ouagadougou railway. Off the beaten track you can still get stuck, but rarely for long, even during the rains. There's no serious river transport.

■ Bush taxis and buses

Every city or town has its lorry park, or *gare routière*. 22-seater *"mille kilos"* minibuses and Peugeot taxis have almost been made obsolete by air-conditioned buses, which are more comfortable and cheaper, and run to regular schedules. There's not much need to consider Peugeots an option, unless you're in a *piste*-ridden area where buses don't run, or you're in a hurry and have missed the scheduled departure.

You may occasionally run into problems in the bush trying to pick up between "fare stages". Transport syndicates force vehicles to keep to set routes; no overlapping is allowed; and only vehicles in the syndicate are allowed to carry passengers.

■ By car

Côte d'Ivoire boasts eight-lane super highways – rarely seen in this part of the world. If you stick to the motorway linking Abidjan with Yamoussoukro, or the big highway running near the coastal lagoons to Ghana, you'll have a very favourable impression of the road network. In all, however, there are barely 5000km of paved roads, and in the north and southwest dirt tracks are the rule.

■ Hitching

There's a lot of private traffic on the roads in Côte d'Ivoire and you've a reasonable chance of success in **hitching** on the main routes: Abidjan–Man, Abidjan–Ferkessédougou or along the coast. You *might* strike lucky on the approach roads to the game parks, but your timing needs to be impeccable (public holidays, weekends) to really make it worth a try. In any case, with such good public transport, hitching in Côte d'Ivoire may well take more time than it's worth.

■ Trains

The *Société Ivoirienne des Chemins de Fer* (**SICF**) runs 1173km of track between Abidjan and Ouagadougou, 655km of which are in Côte d'Ivoire. With a daily train in both directions (in theory), this would be a convenient way to cover the country, were it not for the fact that the whole service has been going downhill for years. It's common for the nominally thirty-hour journey to take forty hours or more, which means two nights on board. Agreement has recently been reached with a French company to manage the line privately; it's certainly hard to see how the system can get any worse. The first-class carriages are in reasonable condition while second is rather trashed, but not too bad considering the volume of passengers. Prices are higher than road transport – even second class is more expensive than going by bus unless you qualify for a student discount (at the start of Côte d'Ivoire's school term, an ISIC card may get you up to 50 percent discount on second-class fares).

For more information, see "Moving on from Abidjan" (p.640).

■ Internal flights

Air Ivoire links Abidjan to major towns in the interior; for example, Bouaké, Bouna, Korhogo, Man, Odienné, San-Pédro, Touba and Yamoussoukro. Most of these places are served by several flights a week, with most fares falling in the CFA21,000–27,000 range. Note that there are some student and youth reductions on *Air Ivoire*. You have to be under 32, and you need an ISIC card if you're over 26.

Accommodation

Hotels in Côte d'Ivoire are generally very good and in most sizeable towns you'll find something affordable with air-conditioning and self-contained rooms.

Unsurprisingly, **Abidjan** is the most expensive place to stay, though prices are better in other major towns. In the extreme north prices are generally lower than in the rest of the country, and at least comparable to those in neighbouring countries.

Côte d'Ivoire has a star-classified **rating system** for hotels. Five stars, the maximum, are given to luxurious places like the *Ivoire* in Abidjan

ACCOMMODATION PRICE CODES

Hotel prices in this chapter are coded according to the following scales – the same scales in terms of their pound/dollar equivalents as are used throughout the book. Prices refer to the rate you can expect to pay for a room with two beds. Single rooms, or single occupancy, will normally cost at least two-thirds of the twin-occupancy rate. For further details see p.51.

① **Under CFA4000 (under £5/$7.50).** Very rudimentary hotel with no frills at all – often a *chambre de passage* rented to the average guest by the hour.

② **CFA4000–8000 (£5–10/$7.50–15).** Basic hotel with simple amenities and some S/C rooms.

③ **CFA8000–16,000 (£10–20/$15–30).** Modest hotel, with S/C rooms the norm, either with fans, or with AC – for a premium.

④ **CFA16,000–24,000 (£20–30/$30–45).** Reasonable business or tourist-class hotel with S/C, AC rooms and often a good restaurant.

⑤ **CFA24,000–32,000 (£30–40/$45–60).** Similar standards to the previous code band but extra facilities such as a pool are usual.

⑥ **CFA32,000–40,000 (£40–50/$60–75).** Comfortable, first-class hotel, with good facilities.

⑦ **Over CFA40,000 (over £50/$75).** Luxury establishment – top prices around CFA80,000–100,000.

or the *Président* in Yamoussoukro – both of which have state-of-the-art gadgets in the rooms and splendid facilities. A night in one of these places starts in the neighbourhood of CFA60,000. At the other end of the scale, one-star hotels usually have S/C rooms with AC and not a lot more. They cost from around CFA8000 per night for a double.

Unclassified hotels are the least expensive option. You'll find many throughout the country, their prices varying according to the region. The less respectable of these are known as *chambres de passage*, and although they're often rented out by the hour and not really intended for travellers, you can stay in them, usually quite cheaply, for the night. Some take their social responsibilities quite seriously and provide clients with clean bathrooms and towels.

Staying with people is perfectly feasible. However, Ivoirians see a lot of travellers and tourists, most of whom appear to be in a hurry, and you're not likely get a lot of spontaneous invitations. This shouldn't be mistaken for a lack of hospitality.

Camping out is possible in many areas, particularly in the more open and sparsely populated north. If you're anywhere near the big highways, or in the vicinity of one of the country's large towns, however, security may be a problem.

Eating and Drinking

Côte d'Ivoire has a variety of more or less unique dishes. In the south, you'll find usual varieties of tubers – yams, cassava (manioc) – which, along with plantains, make up a large part of the diet. They are often pounded into *foutou* and eaten with a clear sauce.

Around Abidjan, cassava or manioc is commonly dried, grated and steamed. The result, called **atieké** (occasionally spelled here and in other countries *achéké*), is often compared to couscous, although the steam makes the manioc grains stick together in a large lump. It's a heavy meal served with **poisson braisé** and, for some reason, it seems to induce sleep. You can buy *atieké* ready-made in the markets – all wrapped in large leaves. Another staple is **aloko**, the local name for sliced, deep-fried plantains. In other countries this is more of a snack, but in the RCI it's the basis of a meal served with a bit of *piment* and fish.

Rice is grown in the northwest and is the main staple there, although you now find it throughout the country. In the northeast, millet and increasingly corn make up the basis of the diet. **Kedjenou**, which originates in the north, has caught on throughout the country and is commonly served in the *maquis* of Abidjan. It's made from chicken, steamed together with vegetables – aubergines, tomatoes and onions – and served on rice.

Foreign restaurants catering to the big expat community are commonplace in Côte d'Ivoire, and this is where you'll find some of the best European eating in West Africa. In Abidjan, dining in a French restaurant costs substantially more than in Paris, but the quality compares well.

Drinking

Local **liquid refreshments** include palm wine – *banqui/bangi* – commonly found in the south. *Chapalo* (or *tchapalo*) is the millet beer favoured by northerners: Ivoirians usually drink it *pimenté*, adding hot peppers to give it an extra kick. *Mouroudji*, a non-alcoholic drink based on lemon and ginger, is sold throughout the country, notably in town markets and *gares routières*. Staple internationals – *Coke* and other soft drinks, notably soda water – are supplemented by Ivoirian **beer**. The thought of a giant, litre bottle of ice-cold *Bock* (*grand modèle*) has encouraged many a dusty traveller. Other popular brands are *Flag* and *Mamba* and locally brewed *Stella Artois* and *Tuborg*. A small, 33cl beer is known as a "Flagette".

Communications – Post, Phones, Language and Media

Côte d'Ivoire has a well-developed telephone system and good mail service, though you pay a lot for both. Poste restante tends to be held for a limited period only – better to use a private box number or the Amex representative in Abidjan. If you're travelling widely in West Africa, don't count on the Abidjan PTT as a major mail and telephone point: it's an exasperating place to deal with.

Côte d'Ivoire's IDD code is ☎225.

Internal, let alone international, **phone calls** can be fiendishly expensive. Card phones have been established in various towns – cards cost from CFA1000–10,000. Also common throughout the country, and handy after hours are *cabines téléphoniques* – not public booths, but private phones in small stores. Rates are determined by impulses, and compare well with the PTT. International calls go through quickly; if your funds are limited, say how much you want to pay and you'll be cut off at the appropriate point.

The *AT&T* access number is ☎00 111 11, though you need coins or a phone card first.

Language

The official **language** of Côte d'Ivoire (and God forbid you should call it Ivory Coast) is French. In addition there are numerous national languages the most widespread of which is **Dyula** (often spelled *Dioula*), a Mande language of commerce very closely related to Bamana and Malinké (in fact the three are virtually dialects, to a large extent mutually intelligible). The Akan language

A SHORT GLOSSARY OF IVOIRIAN TERMS

A mix of French and Ivoirian language words.

Akwaba Welcome in Baoulé, and the name of numerous hotels, restaurants and bars

Apatam Men's meeting shelter, palava house.

Barre The surf barrier; on the landward side, the tidal race is often too much to swim against.

Bia The thrones of the Akan-speaking kingdoms.

Deguerpi Meaning "he who had to get out", it refers to people displaced by development projects, notably those forced to move when the Kossou Dam flooded the region west of Yamoussoukro.

Maquis A French word meaning scrub or bush, and hence the French underground resistance in World War II. Formerly, local drinking places couldn't operate without authorisation so they moved to hidden courtyards, gaining the name *maquis*. Today it refers to small restaurants – now legal – that serve drinks with inexpensive Ivoirian food.

Mille kilos 22-seater, one tonne mini-buses, generally the type of vehicle to avoid at a motor park.

Papo Palm fronds woven into roofs or fences, common along the coast.

Yacouba Name commonly given to the Dan people. A misnomer, it supposedly stuck when one of the first Europeans asked what the people were called and someone responded with a sentence that started "*yacouba*", meaning "he says". Frequently the area around Man is referred to as the Yacouba country.

Baoulé is also widespread; Baoulé people (Houphouët-Boigny's community) account for a large chunk of the total population (fifteen percent) and are well represented in the admin-istration. The Kru language, **Bété**, is the most widely spoken language in the southwest, while the Voltaic tongue **Senoufo** is spoken in a number of dialects across a substantial region in the north.

■ The media

Two major dailies, the news sheet *Fraternité Matin* (commonly referred to as "Frat-Mat") and sports and entertainments organ *Ivoir'Soir* keep Ivoirians abreast of national and regional news, but neither has extensive international coverage and both are owned by the ruling conservative political party, the PDCI. The main opposition party, FPI, puts out the daily *La Voie*, although their weekly *Nouvel Horizon* has a better reputation as a non-government paper. *Le Jour* is a good new independent paper and *Ivoire Dimanche* a weekly magazine with in-depth articles and popular comic strips. Another new paper, *La Patrie*, takes an oppositional stance and was briefly banned in 1995 – for writing "defamatory articles" about President Bédié.

Côte d'Ivoire has one of the most together and user-friendly TV and radio services in West Africa. Colour transmissions in French on *Télévision Ivoirienne* go out eleven hours daily on two channels. *Radiodiffusion Ivoirienne* broadcasts mostly in French, plus English and several Ivoirian languages. There are several FM radio stations, of which the most innovative is the new *BBC Afrique*, the British corporation's first venture into FM broadcasting in Africa.

Entertainment

Soccer is Côte d'Ivoire's national sport, and seeing a match in the Abidjan stadium is recommended. Considering the fairly elaborate recording facilities and relative availability of instruments, the Abidjan music scene is none too exciting.

■ Sport

Half a dozen Ivoirian footballers play for French clubs, but the domestic game is well worth a look, especially if you have the chance to see either of the two pre-eminent sides – **ASEC** and **Africa Sports** – in action. The country's star players are the captain of the national squad, midfielder **Serge Maguy**, goalkeeper **Alain Gouamene**, and **Abdoulaye Traoré** (aka Ben Badi).

■ Music

Live gigs are infrequent. Reggae superstar **Alpha Blondy** has lost some of his more politically aware fans abroad and opted for comfortable sell-out; crooner **Daouda** continues his gush of bilious sweet-soukous tunes; and **Ismaela Isaac et les Frères Keita** provide Blondy-esque wallpaper-music. **Aïcha Koné** also records and tours overseas, but has preserved a fine style of her own.

Look and listen out for **Meiway**, a local band who play a dance beat called *zouglou* or *dance des jeunes*; **Gnaoré Djimi**, whose fourteen-member band play the amazingly fast *polihet* sound, which is a variation on the traditional *zigli-bithy* rhythm; and **Zagazougou**, a percussion and accordions group who play at a rare lick.

Holidays and Festivals

The usual Christian holidays are official, while moveable Muslim feasts affect local services only. Beyond these are New Year's Day, Labour Day (May 2), Ascension Day and Assumption Day (both variable), All Saints Day (November 1), and Independence Day (December 7).

■ Festivals

Numerous **regional festivals** include:

January: Ancestral festival in **Tiagba**; harvest festival in **Dabou**; yam festival in **Abengourou**.

March: Carnival in **Bouaké** – Mardi Gras-like celebration.

April: Dipre festival of the sacrifice in **Gomon**, north of Abidjan (self-mutilation and trances); mask festival in **Behoua**.

June: Lagoon festival in **Yassap** near Dabou.

July: Circumcision festival in **Man**.

August: Generation festival in **Blokosso**; yam festival in **Sikensi**.

November: Abissa festival of the dead in **Grand Bassam**; Prophet Atcho festival in **Bregbo** (Harrist celebration); yam festival in **Bondoukou**; mask festival in **Man**.

Directory

AIRPORT TAX None.

OPENING HOURS **Banks** open Mon–Fri 8–11.30am & 2.30–4.30pm. **Government offices** operate Mon–Fri 8am–noon & 2.30–5pm, Sat 8am–noon.

PHOTOGRAPHY No permit is required and people are generally unperturbed by picture taking. In some areas where tourism is popular, artists, dancers or local chiefs may ask for money before being photographed. Either comply or don't take the shot. Other than that, the only real restriction concerns pictures of military installations, airports, bridges and the like.

TROUBLE You're less likely than usual to get into misunderstandings in Côte d'Ivoire. The manners and customs of tourists – especially young ones – are well recognized. That said, police and customs officers can be surprisingly prickly and in the roadside encounters you'll have with extraordinary frequency (especially in the east towards the Ghana border) they can be hostile and humourless – though not especially corrupt. It's as well to know that the official line on **illegal drugs** (in response to the threat of heroin and cocaine trans-shipments) is severe.

Situations where you're clearly a victim occur most often in **Abidjan**, only rarely elsewhere, and some advice is given in that section. The worst pickpocketing goes on at the end of the month, when Ivoirians are carrying their salaries home. Beware, too, in this very mobile society, of being robbed as you get off a night bus half asleep.

WILDLIFE AND NATIONAL PARKS You'd be forgiven for thinking Côte d'Ivoire has little to offer in terms of natural history: much of the countryside is dedicated to plantations or subsistence farming and it's fairly rare to see wild animals from the road. But the two main national parks – **Comoé** in the north and **Maraoué** in the central region – harbour good numbers of animals, including buffalos, hippos, lions, elephants and many species of antelope. In the far southwest, the Parc National de Taï is a little-visited rainforest reserve which protects chimps and pygmy hippos and a wealth of other forest species in a region with a relatively low human population.

A Brief History of Côte d'Ivoire

The early history of Côte d'Ivoire is perhaps better known than that of many other West African countries because its northern fringes were part of the vast, literate, Mande cultural domain. Several towns are estimated to have been founded as far back as the twelfth or thirteenth centuries – including Kong, Bouna and Bondoukou – though not by Mande speakers, who arrived later. By the sixteenth century, the early European presence was being felt along the coast, but trading posts were strictly temporary affairs, dependent on the supplies of ivory, hides, gold and slaves that could be extracted from the people of the interior. Early slaving "factories" – but not stone forts – were set up at São Andreas (Sassandra), Grand Lahou, Jaqueville and Assinie. During the eighteenth century, the interior was transformed with the arrival and establishment of an Akan-speaking offshoot, the Baoulé, who set up a successful planting and trading economy in the forest and savannah lands of central Côte d'Ivoire, and became the country's most important people.

■ Arrival of the French

Apart from a brief contact at Assinie around 1700, the **French** only became interested in the coast after the Napoleonic wars, when they began to buy "treaties" with local kings and chiefs along the coast. In the 1840s, they built **forts at Assinie, Bassam and Dabou**, which during the 1860s and again in 1875 the French government tried to exchange with Britain for the Gambia colony. But the French "resident" at Bassam, **Arthur Verdier**, had his own plans for the future of the settlements and resisted the idea, a relatively minor obstinacy that did much to set the shape of West Africa. Verdier had already estab-

SAMORY TOURÉ

Pressured by the French advance from the west in the 1880s, the Malinké warmongerer, jihadist and empire-builder **Almamy Samory Touré** organized a systematic scorched-earth retreat to the northern part of Côte d'Ivoire, where he set up a temporary second Dyula Empire stretching from Séguéla to the Upper Volta. In the process, Kong was largely destroyed (in 1897) and Bondoukou sacked. Thousands of people, especially Senoufo farmers, fled their homes, and several seasons' worth of crops were lost. Samory was planning to hold a heavily defended mini-empire based at Katiola, against the French on one side and the British on the other. But he altered strategy on learning of the defeat by the French in a single day of the well-fortified town of Sikasso (now in Mali) and the death of his ally there, Ba Bemba. He fled west again, only to be captured at Guéoulé, near Man, on September 29, 1898. He was exiled to Gabon, where he died of pneumonia on June 21, 1900.

lished *la Compagnie de Kong*, trading French goods far into the interior, via Bondoukou. A young director of the French school at Assinie, **Marcel Treich-Laplène**, was persuaded by the governor of Senegal to make an expedition to the northeast to consolidate the districts threatened by British expansion from the Gold Coast. Treich-Laplène's, and then Louis Binger's, expeditions effectively laid claim to most of the area of today's Côte d'Ivoire. It became a colony of France in 1893, with Grand-Bassam its capital.

■ "Pacification" and anti-colonial resistance

After the **1885 Berlin conference**, France had aggressive competitors for African territory in Britain, Belgium and Germany. With the commencement of the Abidjan–Niger railway and the building (after Grand-Bassam's yellow fever epidemic) of the new capital, **Bingerville**, the French adopted a vigorous imperialism which stressed their "mission to civilize". The exploits of Samory against the French had featured off and on in the French headlines for some years and "pacification" now became a violent series of repressions against poorly armed insurgents. Governor **Angoulvant**, whose name is still remembered in an Abidjan street name, had a reputation for using strong-arm tactics, and he made a deeper impression on colonized Ivoirians than any other Frenchman.

There were uprisings all over the country; the Agni kingdom revolted from 1895–96, sections of the Baoulé in 1899 and the Dida and Wobe groups of Kru-speakers in 1913. But the **Abé revolt** of January 8, 1910 was one of the most violent and well organized.

The Abé, from the area around Agboville, were directly in the line of the railway. Traditionally chauvinistic, the Abé were independent to the point of hostility; but, forced to pay taxes, intimidated into labouring on the railway construction, and press-ganged from their families and villages to walk for days through the forest carrying iron rails and sleepers, they prepared secret plans for an uprising. On the chosen day, the line to the coast was destroyed in several places and every non-Abé whom the rebels encountered was killed, including a number of French settlers and engineers.

Angoulvant reacted with characteristic swift brutality, bringing in troop reinforcements and organizing **manhunts** through the forest. But the Abé's guerilla war against the railway line – and against the creeping usurpation of Abé dominance in their homeland by other groups, some of whom actively collaborated with the French – continued for several years.

■ The Côte d'Ivoire Colony

Because of Angoulvant's energetic methods, the people of southern Côte d'Ivoire had to contend, in the early colonial years, with even worse treatment than was common in West Africa. Not unconnected with this, their country was also viewed as the most economically promising in French West Africa. Trade routes deep into the interior were well-established, the railway gradually drew more wealth to the coast and, most important, two crops of massive significance on the world markets – **coffee and cocoa** – flourished. Although their cultivation was at first forced on farmers, the value of coffee and cocoa wasn't lost on them and they soon began to devote most of their land to cash crops. By the 1920s, families with large holdings on coffee or cocoa land had become an incipient middle class. Côte d'Ivoire also exported rubber, palm oil, timber and fruit crops.

Meanwhile, Bingerville had been dismissed as a permanent economic capital and surveying and initial work at the site of Abidjan had begun in 1903, the same year the railway started its journey north. De facto capital and economic lynchpin since the early 1920s, Abidjan finally became official capital in 1934.

Côte d'Ivoire was governed by decree, from Paris and Dakar. Its very attractiveness brought hardships for those who found themselves "Ivoirians" under colonial rule. Forced labour, "for the development of the country", was extracted through chiefs as part payment of dues and taxes. But subjects (the status of nearly all Ivoirians) were also forced to work on private plantations where corporal punishment and privation were normal practice. Such forced labour wasn't always a local matter, either; thousands of labourers were rounded up in the Upper Volta region and trucked south.

Chiefs were co-opted into the lower ranks of French administration, doing the dirty work of recruitment, tax collection, crop and livestock requisition (common during both World Wars) and enforcing compulsory cultivation. In large measure, too, the chiefs increased their customary **judicial power**, now with higher authority. Where districts were quiet and taxes and harvests flowed in, the French senior administrators did little to interfere with the running, smooth or otherwise, of colonized society. The corrupting effects of the system were almost immediately apparent.

Nationalist stirrings

It was injustice at a level above the grassroots that led to the earliest clear signs of nationalist aspirations. **French plantation-owners** benefited from both a cheap labour supply and the market rate for their coffee and cocoa. **African farmers** had to rely on their own kin and community networks for labour and were forced to accept low prices for their harvests, even though the differences in quality, compared with French produce, were negligible.

Nevertheless, African unions and associations were permitted and flourished, though at this stage (the 1930s) calls for more equality and faster assimilation were heard considerably more often than demands for self-government or independence. **Felix Houphouët-Boigny**, a Baoulé doctor, trained in Dakar, became involved in the question of cocoa prices in 1932, when he first lobbied on behalf of farmers in Abengourou.

World War II delayed political progress, and also marked a threshold. De Gaulle's appearance on the scene, and the 1944 Brazzaville declaration that ended forced labour and accepted the need to overhaul administrative methods, utterly transformed future possibilities in Côte d'Ivoire. Houphouët-Boigny had been given the job of *chef du canton* for Akoué in 1939. Now he set up, with several other wealthy farmers, the *Syndicat Agricole Africain* (African Farmers' Union), which had the support of the progressive French governor. The planters persuaded northern chiefs, including the Moro Naba in Upper Volta, to send labourers for their own plantations, to be paid four times the rate paid by French planters *and* to receive a share of the crop. In the climate of conflict between settlers and *indigènes*, this was a serious, political step; it also put the white tribe of Côte d'Ivoire on the defensive, and pitted them against their own liberal governor, **André Latrille**.

Postwar politics

In the **1946 elections** to the French Constituent Assembly, Houphouët-Boigny was elected as people's deputy for Côte d'Ivoire. He won by a narrow margin: there were other important candidates, one of whom received support from settlers trying to keep the African planters out of power. Houphouët's first act was to ensure that the Brazzaville recommendation on forced labour was followed through. The law that abolished forced labour was quickly coined the **loi Houphouët-Boigny** and the reputation of the planter from Yamoussoukro reached a new peak.

In response to clear messages of antagonism from postwar France, however, and especially to the French Socialist and Christian Democrat parties' failure to support the African cause, Houphouët, and several other African deputies (including those from Senegal and Soudan – later Mali), formed the *Rassemblement Démocratique Africaine* (RDA) in October 1946 to act as an umbrella negotiating body for local political parties in French West and Equatorial Africa – in Côte d'Ivoire, for the *Parti Démocratique de la Côte d'Ivoire* (PDCI). The settlers in Côte d'Ivoire finally succeeded in getting rid of the pro-Houphouët governor Latrille, whom they distrusted intensely. And, spreading the belief that the RDA was a hotbed of Soviet-backed agitators, the next colonial administration in Abidjan managed to break the ties between the Mossi chiefs in Upper Volta and Houphouët's new political power base.

Reactionary responses to political developments continued, however. During 1949 and 1950 a series of **"incidents"** across the country involved quarrels started by anti-RDA *provocateurs*, which provided the colonial government with pretexts to bully and arrest Houphouët's followers. In many of the disturbances dozens of people died, most of them innocent villagers killed when troops opened fire. And in several cases, cold-blooded extra-judicial executions took place. Most leaders of the RDA except Houphouët were arrested and imprisoned in Grand Bassam. A year of ferment ended when troops in Dimbokro shot thirteen people on January 30, 1950. A decree banning all RDA activity was issued two days later.

But the momentum for change couldn't be held back. Despite the predictable formation, under colonial auspices, of parties like the *Parti Progressiste de Côte d'Ivoire* and the *Bloc Démocratique Eburnéen*, vehemently opposed to the relatively mild and reformist goals of the PDCI-RDA, the movement made progress. Through the "dark years" of 1948–50, when over 3000 supporters were arrested, they staged **strikes and protests**, culminating in a 1950 boycott of European goods. To drive home the message of the PDCI's independence to anyone who still believed its actions were being orchestrated in Moscow, Houphouët-Boigny broke off his party's alliance with the French Communists which had given his critics so much political ammunition. Houphouët the Marxist had never sounded very credible.

■ Independence

The constitution of the PDCI declared its "struggle for the unity of the native people of Côte d'Ivoire with the French people, for political, economic and social progress following a programme of democratic claims". It didn't sound revolutionary, and when moves **towards independence** came after the 1956 *Loi cadre* (blueprint law) established local government for each of the French colonies (but expressly headed off calls for federalism), it was clear that Houphouët favoured close ties with France over the kind of West or pan-African federation that Nkrumah (of newly independent Ghana), Senghor of Senegal and Sekou Touré of Guinea each envisaged in his own way.

When, in 1958, **de Gaulle** returned to power, established the "French Community", and made his famous Yes or No offer to the colonies (self-government within the French union or complete independence outside it), there was never much doubt that Houphouët wanted the country to plump for the first option. The idea of a French West African federation with its capital in Dakar had never appealed to the Ivoirians, whose country, already the richest in the group, stood to gain little. On the other hand, Houphouët would certainly have countenanced a federation of states which included France on equal terms.

By 1960, with de Gaulle suddenly prepared to see independence (which really meant control over currency and defence) *within* the French union, a scramble began in some territories to salvage the federal ideal. Houphouët prevented Côte d'Ivoire's involvement by unilaterally declaring **independence** on August 7, 1960. At the same time he formed the *Conseil de l'Entente*, consisting of Côte d'Ivoire, Niger, Haute Volta (now Burkina) and Dahomey (now Benin), to loosely pull together those economies which relied upon Abidjan, and further to hinder any West African federation which might seek to draw them away.

■ Independent Côte d'Ivoire: "Economic Miracle" – and crisis

The **first twenty years** of independence bore out the hyperbole pretty well; in comparison with every other West African country, Côte d'Ivoire made staggering progress. Economic growth rates were remarkably high, though everything depended on coffee and cocoa. There were strong developments in manufacturing, too, and the country moved into the "middle bracket" of under-developed nations.

By the late 1970s, however, Côte d'Ivoire's long and complacent record of success began to erode, and cutbacks in public expenditure were necessary as the country slid into serious debt. For nearly every year since the early 1980s the country has been the world's largest cocoa producer, but a glut on the world market forced cocoa and coffee prices down. At first Houphouët tried to hold up the producer price paid to the farmers, and stockpile the crop in an attempt to raise world market prices. But the ploy was unsuccessful and, ultimately, Côte d'Ivoire had to agree to World Bank and IMF adjustment plans in 1988 as the country was unable to service its foreign debts. As a result, cocoa farmers were paid in the early 1990s roughly half what they received in 1989.

On the **political scene**, events – or the lack of them – in the 1960s and 70s seemed to mirror the stability of the republic. Houphouët-Boigny took personal control of the country's transformation from colony to regional power, directing the French-dominated economy and avoiding confrontation with political opponents by a skilful mix of stick and carrot.

As the country slipped into economic crisis, criticism of the president or of government policies was rarely tolerated and strikes often resulted in the temporary banning of the union involved. Denunciation of the top-heavy role of **French expatriates** in administration and senior management, on the other hand, was an escape valve generally sanctioned. Periodic reductions of their numbers, in drives for **Ivoirianization**, were greeted with applause.

The earliest clear opposition came in the 1960s, when Kragbe Gnagbe tried to set up an alternative party with support from his Bété ethnic community around Gagnoa. This led to **mass arrests** of alleged coup plotters in 1963 – and the death in detention of one of them, **Ernest Boka**, a former head of the supreme court. The perceived threat to the government led inexorably to the bloody **Bété revolt** in 1970 in which Gnagbe was banished to his village and several hundred people died in clashes with troops.

Côte d'Ivoire's relationship with its four neighbours and their leaders have sometimes been strained. Relations with **Liberia** and **Ghana** have long been soured by the presence in Côte d'Ivoire of political exiles and the country's relations with Blaise Compaoré of **Burkina** (who is married to Houphouët's niece) were not helped by an article in *Jeune Afrique* magazine which suggested that Côte d'Ivoire had played a role in overthrowing Thomas Sankara.

■ The Growth of Opposition

> *There's no number two, three or four in Côte d'Ivoire; there's only number one . . . and that's me.*
>
> Felix Houphouët-Boigny, July 1987

From the outside, Houphouët-Boigny seemed to signal dependable neo-colonialism – at least until 1990 – with enough wealth trickling down and enough progress being made to keep the pot from boiling over. But **opposition** to the president's espousal of pro-Western, capitalist values – mostly from students and teachers' unions – resulted in several of the one-on-one *dialogues* for which the old man was famous, and which temporarily served to defuse the issues – or at least defer them – with large dollops of Houphouët charisma.

As long ago as 1975, with Houphouet-Boigny starting his fourth unchallenged term in office and already at least seventy years old, Ivoirians were beginning to wonder when (or if) he might step down, and who might replace him. The names of several senior figures were trailed before the public. By the early 1980s, however, the post of vice-president was vacant – and abolished in 1985 – and public debate on the question of **succession** was considered almost treasonable.

In 1987, another in the growing tradition of Bété critics of the government, **Robert Gbai Tagro**, took on the establishment in his own *Parti Républicain de la Côte d'Ivoire* by apparently pitting himself as a future president against Houphouët. His party was never banned, but nor would Houphouët recognize it. Its first major attempt to rally support – at the proposed first congress of the party in April 1987 – was crushed and its leaders detained.

A more outspoken thorn in Houphouët's side was **Laurent Gbagbo** (another Bété from Gagnoa). Long self-exiled to France and leader of the *Front Populaire Ivoirien*, he insisted he wouldn't return until a framework for multi-party democracy was established. Houphouët managed to woo him back in September 1988 and, although the president was supposed to have offered him a ministerial post to absorb his political ambitions, he turned it down.

The closest the Houphouët government may have come to falling was in the spring of 1988, when rumours surfaced of a plot within Houphouët's PDCI party by a clique of Dyula businessmen from Touba. With stories circulating that he was importing arms, **Lamine Fadika**, the navy minister from Touba, was dismissed. Armed forces Chief of Staff **Zeze Baroan** was given the job of ambassador to Brazil. And the Ivoirian representative in Hamburg of the government shipping organization *SITRAM* (who was supposed to be the arms supplier) was murdered on a visit home – according to the rumours, for informing the government about the plot. Houphouët went to his funeral.

■ The 1990s

By the early 1990s the country was in the grip of **austerity measures** under an imposed "structural adjustment programme" of the kind which most of Côte d'Ivoire's neighbours had had to put up with for some years. Power worker strikes led to blackouts in February. 1990. These in turn pushed **students** into marching on Abidjan city centre and finally led to the violent arrest of 150 students who had barricaded themselves in the Abidjan cathedral. They were demanding **Houphouët's resignation**, an **end to one-party rule** and better grants and conditions on campus. **Marcel Ette** of the lecturers' union *SYNARES* (which has always been vocal in support of democratic reforms) spoke out eloquently and with some courage against the "deep malaise afflicting Ivoirian society".

National turmoil

Houphouët's oft-repeated claim that "not a single drop of blood has been spilled in this country since I've been President" was conclusively sunk in April 1990, when a schoolboy was shot dead as police tried to disperse a crowd of demonstrators in Adzopé, north of Abidjan. Amid rumours that Houphouët was shortly to resign, **protests** flared in a number of towns and doctors went on strike.

Under siege, the government dropped the massive **tax increases** (effectively pay cuts) due to be implemented in 1990. Although peace was restored for a few weeks, there was an unprecedented **army rebellion** in May of that year, led by hundreds of young conscripts demanding improved conditions. They took over a radio station in Abidjan, and were soon emulated by air force personnel who staged an **occupation of Abidjan airport**. There was a further army uprising the next day, and a state of general panic and confusion reigned in the Plateau district of Abidjan as soldiers tore through the streets in commandeered cars. Dozens of other disturbances occurred in garrison towns around the country, most of them contained by the police, who remained loyal throughout. The 1000-strong contingent of **French troops**, based at Port Bouet, was placed on alert by Paris, but not deployed.

During this period of instability, Houphouët appeared to backtrack. He agreed to **legalize opposition** parties and scheduled legislative and **presidential elections** for 1990. Still, he refused to implement a transitional government or to convene a national conference of the type sweeping reform into other West African countries.

The campaign was kept short and the president was accused of adeptly wielding government powers to stymie the opposition. Access to the state-owned media was jealously guarded, particularly for the most serious threat, **Laurent Gbagbo**, running on the FPI ticket. The president won a seventh term in the country's first contested elections, though the FPI was quick to point out voting irregularities and tried unsuccessfully to have the Supreme Court annul the results.

Despite the political jockeying, calm prevailed and significant constitutional changes were implemented. The first allowed for the president of the national assembly, **Jean Henri Konan Bédié**, to assume the presidency should the office become vacant, an indication that the ageing president was planning his own succession. The second allowed for the appointment of a prime minister, a post assigned to **Allasane Ouattara**, the former governor of the Banque Centrale de l'Afrique de l'Ouest, who had implemented the nation's economic reforms.

The post-election quiet broke down in May, 1991. As students and teachers began a campaign to protest poor conditions in the education system, security forces violently disrupted a meeting at Abidjan university. Troops swept through residency halls to round up ringleaders and killed four students, injuring and raping dozens of others. Though 180 people were arrested, the government denied deaths had occurred and expelled the bureau chief of Agence France Presse for reporting otherwise.

The incident carried over into 1992 when the commission set up to investigate it implicated high-ranking military officials. Although the army chief of staff was found to be directly responsible for the violence, the president refused to take disciplinary action, saying it would be bad for military morale.

Violent **demonstrations** immediately erupted as students and teacher's unions took to the street. They were soon joined by the FPI which organized a march that attracted 20,000 supporters who demanded the government step down. A hundred people were arrested as the protest turned violent; among them, Gbagbo and the president of the national human rights organization.

Despite the gravity of the situation, Houphouët never saw fit (or was physically unable) to leave the serenity of his mansions in France and Switzerland where he remained for five months. He only returned to Côte d'Ivoire in June 1992, and soon after, granted amnesty to opposition leaders who had been detained during his absence. Gbagbo was released in August and received a hero's welcome from thousands of supporters.

The tumultuous final years of Houphouët-Boigny's fifty-year political career ended on December 7, 1993, when the president died and an entire era of West African politics ended. Bédié assumed the presidency as prescribed by the constitution, but was soon challenged by Ouattara, who was forced to resign as prime minister. He was replaced by **Daniel Kablan Duncan**, the former finance minister.

The **succession crisis** thus fizzled out fairly quickly, yet the era of uncertainty has only just begun. As the nation now finally faces the problems of debt, poverty and ethnic tensions that its neighbours have been grappling with for years, it does so on a very shaky political foundation.

None of this is helped by **France's rapid political retreat** from the region, as it abdicates economic influence to Washington-based institutions like the World Bank and IMF. The eagerness to end post-colonial dependency in the region was symbolized most dramatically in the devaluation of the CFA franc, which was announced only days after the president died. And Paris' permanent promise of *petits fins du mois* (monthly bailouts to help pay salary arrears) has also dried up. No current national leader has the clout formerly wielded by Houphouët to foster the "special relationship" with France, bring in the army of *coopérants* to stimulate the economy, and call on the French military to keep the opposition at bay.

A new and uncertain era

As this book goes to press, all attention is focused on the presidential, legislative and local **elections of October–December 1995**. Whatever their results, the political stability and economic confidence secured by Houphouët-Boigny seem to have evaporated with his passing, opening a void that looks like taking much time and sacrifice to fill. Attempting to fill it, the main contenders in the 1995 polls seem likely to dominate the Ivoirian political scene for years to come.

Politics in Côte d'Ivoire is increasingly divisive and played out along ethnic and religious grounds relatively unfamiliar to Ivoirians. There is wide scope for legitimate, as well as mischievous, undermining of political figures: politicians of all shades, as well as the media, are citing the widely detested "parenthood rule" (part of the electoral code that stipulates candidates' parents must both have been born in the country), another part of the code requiring continuous residence in Côte d'Ivoire for five years before the candidacy, and the pervasive fear of Islamic fundamentalism. The 1995 election line-up of front-runners consists of the incumbent PDCI president **Konan Bédié** (who, say the opposition press, has a Ghanaian father), breakaway PDCI candidate Alassane Ouattara (rumoured in PDCI quarters to have a Burkinabe father), who is expected to stand for the **Rassemblement des Républicains** (RDR) formed of disaffected PDCI members in 1994, and Laurent Gbagbo of the FPI. Gbagbo's FPI and Ouattara's RDR have joined forces as the *Front Républicain* – an alliance which, if it were to field just one candidate, would probably knock Bédié out of the picture and give the opposition its first taste of power.

But the *Front*'s effectiveness could be limited by a lack of consensus over power-sharing and regional conflicts of interest – not to mention the parenthood and residency rules. The FPI draws its primary support from the Christian/Animist south and west, while the RDR is strongest in the Muslim north. The PDCI media have been trying to split the alliance and deter voters, by suggesting that voting for the opposition encourages fundamentalists.

On a more positive note, Côte d'Ivoire is considered to be the West African country that most benefitted from the CFA devaluation: **exports of cocoa and coffee** are doing well, to the satisfaction of famers. Yet these upbeat signs have done little to allay the concerns of urban Ivoirians, especially the unemployed. And growing evidence of human rights suppression and paranoia about press freedom, as well as renewed reports of government corruption – widely believed to have diminished during the Ouattara premiership – do not bode well.

ABIDJAN AND AROUND

ABIDJAN's wide **avenues** have names like de Gaulle, Marseille and République; **pavement cafés** and **billboards** push *Orangina* and *L'Express* – it is all one big monumental tribute to the heady days when it appeared the honeymoon between France and Côte d'Ivoire would never end. Downtown Abidjan looks like the work of a mad urban planner who dropped the Little Manhattan quarter of Paris' 15th arrondissement onto the set of the *Blue Lagoon*. But even if the coconut trees, red flamboyants and frangipanis lining the city's financial centre lend an exotic air to its supermarkets, **skyscrapers** and **traffic jams**, they barely camouflage the increasing signs of urban paranoia.

Now the second largest city in West Africa, Abidjan has grown from nothing in less than sixty years, and at an astounding pace since independence. Considering the number of **rural migrants** and **foreign workers** who've come in hope of easy money, the city has done a fair job of absorbing the influx – certainly much better than its nearest rival, Lagos. On first glance, this is a well laid-out and aesthetically appealing city. For many, it's the very model of what **prosperity** can bring to Africa. But you don't have to go far outside the centre to find shocking examples of poverty and **overcrowding**. In a scenario that has played itself out repeatedly around the world, the jobless and displaced turn to illicit survival tactics. Violent crime, prostitution and drug trafficking now taint the image of the "pearl of the lagoon". A few years ago, you could have spent a good deal of time in the city without encountering its dark side. That's hard to imagine today.

Some history

The French abandoned their first capital, Grand-Bassam, in 1900 because of disease. The hilly location of the new capital, Bingerville, away from the sea, posed transport problems that limited its economic future. In 1934, the governor moved to a new mansion 17km to the southwest, in a spot then known as **Abidjan**.

The **European district** thus grew up on the Plateau peninsula, where administrative buildings sprang up beside trading depots, shops and villas. It was surrounded by two African suburbs – Adjamé to the north and Treichville across the lagoon to the south – although in the early days the collective population of these three districts was barely 20,000.

After 1950, however, Abidjan began to grow apace, and quickly took on the dimensions of a capital city. The catalyst was the **Vridi canal** which opened the Ebrié lagoon to the Atlantic and gave Abidjan the capacity to become an international **port**. Five years later, the railway line was extended from Treichville all the way to Ouagadougou, 1156km to the north. People started flocking to the town as new commercial possibilities developed. The population has jumped from 60,000 in the early 1950s to somewhere in the neighbourhood of three million today, and although Yamoussoukro became the country's administrative capital in the mid-1980s, Abidjan remains the undisputed economic nerve centre.

Orientation and Information

Abidjan's most striking physical feature is the **Ebrié Lagoon**, as one piece of tourist blurb attempts to describe: "With its capricious tentacles the lagoon spreads as it were its silvery arms into the surrounding country offering Abidjan to the gaze of the overwhelmed traveller". They are rather murky fingers these days, dividing the city into distinct land masses, quarters which have evolved into large distinct neighbourhoods,

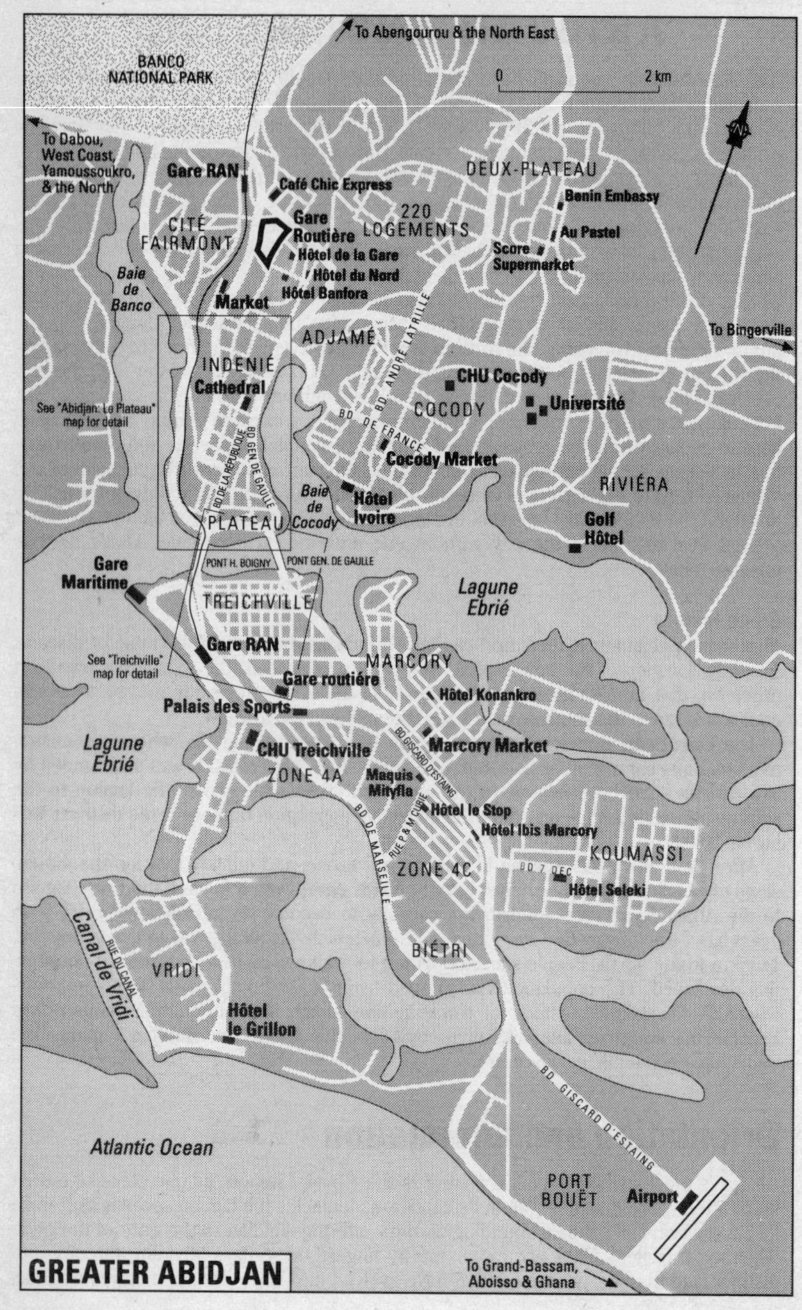
To Abengourou & the North East
BANCO NATIONAL PARK
0 2 km
To Dabou, West Coast, Yamoussoukro, & the North
Gare RAN
Café Chic Express
DEUX-PLATEAU
Benin Embassy
220 LOGEMENTS
CITÉ FAIRMONT
Gare Routière
Au Pastel
Score Supermarket
Hôtel de la Gare
Hôtel du Nord
Hôtel Banfora
Baie de Banco
Market
ADJAMÉ
To Bingerville
INDENIÉ
Cathedral
CHU Cocody
BD. ANDRÉ LATRILLE
Université
See "Abidjan: Le Plateau" map for detail
COCODY
BD. DE FRANCE
BD DE LA RÉPUBLIQUE
BD GEN DE GAULLE
Cocody Market
RIVIÉRA
Baie de Cocody
Hôtel Ivoire
PLATEAU
Golf Hôtel
PONT H. BOIGNY
PONT GEN. DE GAULLE
Gare Maritime
TREICHVILLE
Lagune Ebrié
Gare RAN
MARCORY
See "Treichville" map for detail
Gare routiére
Hôtel Konankro
Palais des Sports
Lagune Ebrié
CHU Treichville
BD GISCARD D'ESTAING
Marcory Market
ZONE 4A
Maquis Mityfla
Hôtel le Stop
BD DE MARSEILLE
RUE P & M CURIE
Hôtel Ibis Marcory
KOUMASSI
ZONE 4C
BD 7 DEC
Hôtel Seleki
BIÉTRI
RUE DU CANAL
Canal de Vridi
VRIDI
Hôtel le Grillon
BD. GISCARD D'ESTAING
Atlantic Ocean
PORT BOUËT
Airport
GREATER ABIDJAN
To Grand-Bassam, Aboisso & Ghana

SECURITY IN ABIDJAN

It's not a surprise to find Abidjan one of the **least secure cities** in West Africa. As usual, stories get repeated and recycled, and the true incidence of attacks on tourists has to be related to the high number of tourists and expatriates passing through. Having said that, Abidjan can be a dangerous city and violent robberies – usually at knife point – do occur, in Treichville and Adjamé, but also on the Plateau. Simply leave all your valuables behind when going out and you'll feel less threatened and be less intimidated. The notorious **blackspots** are the bridges from Treichville to the Plateau, especially the eastern one – Pont Général de Gaulle. An emphatic warning: **do not cross on foot**. But one last thing – don't let anyone put you off going to Treichville market; it's brilliant.

each with its own flavour. Although there are officially ten such districts, only four are likely to figure prominently in your plans – **Plateau**, **Treichville**, **Cocody** and **Adjamé**.

The main **points of arrival** are the **airport**, close to the city at Port Bouët on the ocean-front, **Treichville gare routière** if you're coming from Ghana or the east coast, and **Adjamé gare routière** if you're arriving by road from anywhere else. Passenger trains terminate at **Treichville's Gare RAN**.

Note that if you're arriving in the city at the end of the week with business to attend to, you might just as well shoot out again to somewhere less expensive and more relaxing like **Bingerville** (p.641), **Grand-Bassam** (p.652) or **Jacqueville** (p.644) and come back bright and early on Monday morning.

Plateau

This futuristic financial district is the showcase of Côte d'Ivoire's economic capital. The quarter's main thoroughfare, the **Boulevard de la République**, stretches from the **Houphouët-Boigny Bridge** in the south up to the **Palais de Justice**. Along its way, it passes the Post Office, the food and crafts markets and the stadium. The main **banking district** is on the Avenue Joseph Anoma north of the Post Office. Nearby, Abidjan's most famous skyscraper, **La Pyramide**, commands a view of **Cocody Bay**. The city's most recent architectural curiosity, the stunning **Cathédrale St-Paul**, lies on the northern fringe of the Plateau, off the Avenue Jean Paul II. Intimidating **administrative towers** loom up west of the church near the Boulevard Angoulvant, dwarfing the **National Museum**.

Treichville, Marcory, Koumassi and Zone 4C

Two bridges, Houphouët-Boigny and de Gaulle, lead from the Plateau to **Treichville**. Described by those who don't live here as Abidjan's "most African" quarter, Treichville is the city centre's least expensive and poorest district. It's divided into 25

TOURIST INFORMATION

For **tourist information**, the travel agencies listed in "Moving on from Abidjan", p.640, are better prepared to field questions, and make travel arrangements, than the **Office Ivoirien du Tourisme et de l'Hôtelerie**, across from the post office on the Plateau (☎20 65 00; Fax 22 59 24). There are a couple of useful listings and entertainment magazines you might want to obtain – *Abidjan 7 Jours* and *Le Guido*.

"wards", each with its own character; in **Quartier Arras**, one of the poorest, you'll find an amazing mix of nationalities and ethnic groups – Ghanaian, Gambian, Sierra Leonean, Hausa, Yoruba, Wolof – and "blocks" mostly consisting of a compound with a gate onto the street. What Treichville lacks in high-cost high-rises, it makes up for in its level of activity. When the Plateau is fast asleep, this neighbourhood still moves at a frenzied clip. Treichville's grid layout, with numbered **rues** running north–south. and numbered **avenues** going east–west, is dominated by the Boulevard du 6 Fevrier – a popular shopping street that leads south from Treichville's **main market**. The Avenue de la Reine Pokou, which cuts the district from west to east, is another main artery, with a heavy concentration of shops and restaurants. Abidjan's **train station** faces the port on the Boulevard de Marseille, and off the Boulevard Giscard d'Estaing in the southwest is the *gare routière* serving destinations to the east of Abidjan.

Bordering Treichville to the east is the middle-class **Marcory** district, where you might venture in search of a moderately priced hotel. Between Treichville and the airport is the similar district of **Koumassi**, again with some worthwhile hotels and, like Marcory, a safer atmosphere than Treichville proper. **Zone 4C**, across the bd Giscard d'Estaing from Koumassi is a comfortably-off district, with corner shops, bars and a scattering of places to stay and eat.

Cocody and Deux-Plateaux

The Boulevard de la Corniche snakes around Cocody Bay, leading from the Plateau to the tropical opulence of Abidjan's foremost **residential neighbourhood**. Whatever Ivoirian reggae star Alpha Blondy may sing in his former hit song, **Cocody** does not rock, nor is it even vaguely rasta. The neatly landscaped streets and villas set a decidedly bourgeois tone, improved a little by the presence of the university. Cocody's major stake in tourism is the *Ivoire*, the city's biggest and most expensive hotel. An architectural extravaganza when it was inaugurated in 1963, this towering high-rise is today something of a dinosaur, but it still has the best views of the Plateau's skyline; a good place for taking photos.

Deux-Plateaux is a predominantly middle-class residential district that merges imperceptibly with Cocody (Cocody Les Deux Plateaux was the earlier appellation for the two districts). It's commercial life revolves around a good number of restaurants and bars.

Adjamé

North of the Plateau, **Adjamé** is another *quartier populaire*, swarming with recent immigrants and, because it's on the mainland in the north, expanding and evolving unchecked. The neighbourhood **market** is Abidjan's biggest, and surrounded by a multitude of boutiques where you can find the widest selection of bric-à-brac imaginable. The district's **gare routière** is also the busiest in the city and services the entire country, with the exception of towns along the route to Ghana.

City transport

Abidjan's four main districts, and the six others surrounding them, are connected by an overworked **bus service**, *SOTRA*. The main terminus, the **Gare du Sud**, is located on the Plateau, at the foot of the Houphouët-Boigny Bridge. It's a vast system and maps are unavailable. Buses cost CFA100–300 a ride and can get you virtually anywhere in

ABIDJAN PLATEAU BUS ROUTES

A large number of bus routes run through the Plateau. The following selection is useful:
#05 Gare du Sud – Treichville – Koumassi
#06 Aeroport – Gare du Sud (daily 6am–9.20pm; every 10–15min)
#10 Gare du Sud – Cathédrale St-Paul
#12 Gare du Sud – Cathédrale St-Paul
#15 Gare du Sud – Gare Abobo
#18 Gare du Sud – Treichville market and *gare routière* – Vridi Plage
#20 Gare du Sud – Banco National Park (Cité Fairmont)
#28 Gare du Sud – Cocody market – Golf Hôtel
#75 or #76 Gare du Sud – Zoo
#86 Gare du Sud – Musée National – Adjamé *gare routière* – Blokosso (Cocody)

the greater Abidjan area; that is if you can squeeze on. Keep your ticket until the end, as controllers make random checks, and note that the buses are notorious for pickpockets.

As an alternative, the city boasts a large fleet of orange **metered taxis** – one of the best in West Africa. Remarkably fast, they can, however, work out expensive. They operate on meters with a daytime tariff (*Tarif 1*; CFA150 plus CFA100 per km) from 6am to midnight, and a higher night-time tariff after midnight – check you're on the right tariff. Fares from the airport to anywhere in Treichville or the southern half of the city shouldn't exceed CFA1200, to Plateau no more than CFA1600, to Cocody maximum CFA2100. Don't get into any car painted *like* a taxi, that doesn't have a meter; they hang around the airport, hotels and other likely tourist traps and try to overcharge.

SOTRA also operates a **ferry service**, *bateaux bus*, to various points around the lagoon. The main *gare lagunaire* (☎32 17 37) is on the southern tip of the Plateau, near the Gare du Sud bus station and Houphouët-Boigny Bridge. From here to Abobo-Doumé and Treichville, the ferry goes every ten minutes, a much safer alternative to walking across the Houphouët-Boigny Bridge.

Accommodation

Abidjan boasts a good choice of comfortable **accommodation** in the middle-to-upmarket price range, but budget lodgings are extremely hard to come by. Not surprisingly, the closer you are to the centre, the more expensive things are – places on the Plateau are geared mainly to business travellers and wealthy tourists.

ACCOMMODATION PRICE CODES

① Under CFA4000 (under £5/$7.50).
② CFA4000–8000 (£5–10/$7.50–15).
③ CFA8000–16,000 (£10–20/$15–30).
④ CFA16,000–24,000 (£20–30/$30–45).
⑤ CFA24,000–32,000 (£30–40/$45–60).
⑥ CFA32,000–40,000 (£40–50/$60–75).
⑦ Over CFA40,000 (over £50/$75).

For further information see the "Accommodation" section in the Practical Information pages at the beginning of this chapter.

Camping, budget and mid-range hotels

At the very bottom of the scale, the campsites are preferable to *chambres de passage*. Respectable accommodation can be reasonably priced, but there's no guarantee of value for money; it's recommended that you look at a number of places if you're going to be in town for a while. Be sure to ask for the best room: you'll often be fobbed off with some fleapit in the hope they can keep the nicer accommodation for choosier guests.

Plateau

Grand Hôtel, off the av du Général de Gaulle/rue Montigny (01 BP 1785; ☎32 12 00 or 33 21 09). Near the lagoon, looking out onto Treichville. Newer and showier hotels have forced the *Grand* to keep its prices low in order to remain competitive. ③–④.

Hôtel des Sports, av du Général de Gaulle (☎32 71 97). The only hotel in the Plateau that approaches the inexpensive range, the *Sports* has dingy but acceptable AC rooms. ③.

Treichville

Hôtel Argiegeois, bd de Marseille. Virtually next door to the *France* and not bad for the price. ②.

Hôtel Atlanta, corner av 15 and rue 15 (☎33 24 69). Fairly unrefined, but friendly and quite good value. ②.

Hôtel de France, bd de Marseille (☎25 25 00). An older hotel that has some charm and is reasonably well maintained. ③.

Hôtel Fraternité, corner av 21 and rue 44 (behind the *Cinéma l'Entente*). Musty rooms though not too bad for a brothel. ①.

Hôtel le Prince, corner av 20 and rue 19 (☎32 71 27). Good value and fairly clean. S/C rooms: those without AC are suitable for budget travellers. Take bus #3 from Plateau. ①.

Hôtel de Succès, corner av 14 and rue 25 (☎32 18 39). Basic but reasonable and quite friendly. Top-floor front rooms with AC are good value; *rez de chaussée* (ground-floor) rooms on the wrong side are dismal, mostly used for *passages*. ①–②.

Hôtel Terminus, bd Jean Delafosse (01 BP 790; ☎32 11 98). Large rooms, each with fan and corner kitchen. Located across from the *RAN* train station, this one's convenient if you get into town late. ③.

Hôtel Tourbouroux, corner rue 8 and av 13 (☎32 64 48). Unmarked and sleazy. A last resort. ①.

Treichotel, 45 av de la Reine Pokou (☎24 05 59). This tall hotel is well situated and not too pricey, with mod cons. S/C, AC rooms. Safe parking. ②–③.

Marcory

Hôtel Konankro, av de la TSF (BP 4237; ☎26 13 28). Small S/C rooms with AC in a busy part of the district, near the Église Sainte Thérèse. ②.

Adjamé

Hôtel Banfora, off av 13 (☎37 02 52). Recent hotel near the *gare routière* and Adjamé market – popular with merchants. Friendly service. ②.

Hôtel de la Gare, off rue 13, across from Gare UTB (the *Union des Transports de Bouaké* bus station). Convenient location and very clean rooms, some with AC. ①–②.

Hôtel du Nord, 220 Logements area of Adjamé (09 BP 230; ☎37 04 63). Conveniently situated just north of the Plateau. Good-value, well-maintained AC rooms. ②–③.

Koumassi and Zone 4C

Hôtel Seleki, bd 7 Dec. A nice, no-nonsense hotel in a quieter part of town, not far from the airport. Clean S/C, AC rooms. ②.

Hôtel le Stop, 38 rue Pierre et Marie Curie, Zone 4C (01 BP 1947; ☎35 40 18). Smartish place in an upmarket neighbourhood, convenient for the airport. S/C, AC. ③.

Vridi Plage

Beach Camping, rue de l'Ocean, near the *Palm Beach* (☎24 84 50). Popular spot for overlanders; clean and without frills (rooms available for those without tents), not too far from the centre. Take buses #07, #17 or #18. ①.

Hôtel Le Grillon, Vridi Plage, near the SIR refinery (01 BP 2393; ☎ 27 52 60). Clean, quiet and convenient for the airport, but a long way from town. S/C rooms with AC on the beach. ②.

Out-of-town camping

Camping Coppa Cabana, rte de Grand-Bassam, 15km from Abidjan. A bit far from the centre, but accessible from Treichville; take bus #17 or a collective taxi from the *gare routière*. Reasonable value, it also has a restaurant serving meals for CFA2000. ①.

Hôtel du Baron, rte de Grand-Bassam. A popular haunt of expats and affluent Abidjanis. Camping includes use of the pool. ①.

Luxury hotels

There's generally a very high standard in the luxury bracket, with a number of hotels of international standards (or close), catering mostly to expense-account business travellers, and visitors on large budgets.

Plateau

Hôtel Ibis Plateau, 7 bd Roume (☎32 01 57; Fax 21 78 75). Affordable luxury and one of the better bargains among the international-class options. Rooms with TV, video and phone. ⑤–⑥.

Novotel, av du Général de Gaulle (01 BP 3718; ☎21 23 23; Fax 33 26 36). An imposing hotel and a great location (rooms with all the amenities). Swimming pool. ⑦.

Sofitel Abidjan, av Delafosse (01 BP 2185; ☎22 11 22; Fax 33 22 18). Posh and relatively new with famous service and lagoon views. Very convenient for the city centre and much more personal than you might expect. Pool, sauna and massage parlour count among the perks. ⑦.

Hôtel Tiama, 22 bd de la République (04 BP 643; ☎21 08 22; Fax 21 64 60). Located in the ministerial district and favoured by journalists and business people. Rooms on the upper floors look out onto the lagoon. Restaurant, brasserie, shops and car rental. ⑥.

Cocody

Golf Hôtel, Riviera (08 BP 18; ☎43 10 44; Fax 43 05 44). Just east of Cocody near the golf course and lagoon. More intimate than the *Ivoire* but almost as classy. An attractive residential setting; well-cropped lawns sweep down to meet the clear pool. Garden *terrasse-bar*, restaurant and water skiing in the lagoon. ⑦.

Hôtel Ivoire, bd de la Corniche (08 BP 8001; ☎44 10 45; Fax 44 00 50). Abidjan's pride and joy, this *Intercontinental* hotel is really a city within the city, with everything from a bowling alley and car rent to West Africa's only **ice rink**. Cinema, sauna, casino, nightclub, swimming pool and tennis courts add to the razzle-dazzle, but jaded business travellers find it all a bit much. Numerous restaurants include the *Toit d'Abidjan* (☎44 10 45) on top of the tower – elegant and expensive French dining with the city's best view. Incidentally, the public areas of the *Ivoire* are probably the city's biggest pick-up and cruising spots. ⑦.

Marcory

Ibis Marcory, bd Giscard d'Estaing 15 (BP 594; ☎24 92 55; Fax 35 89 10). Comfortable AC rooms convenient for the airport. Pleasant garden restaurant under *paillotes*, and a swimming pool. ⑤.

Vridi Plage

Palm Beach, rue de l'Ocean, Vridi (01 BP 2704; ☎27 42 16; Fax 27 30 16). Beachfront hotel with AC bungalows and AC rooms. One of Abidjan's older establishments, with a certain charm. Substantial savings on upstairs rooms with showers instead of baths. Saltwater pool, excellent restaurant, and a satellite disc to hook you up with CNN. ④–⑤.

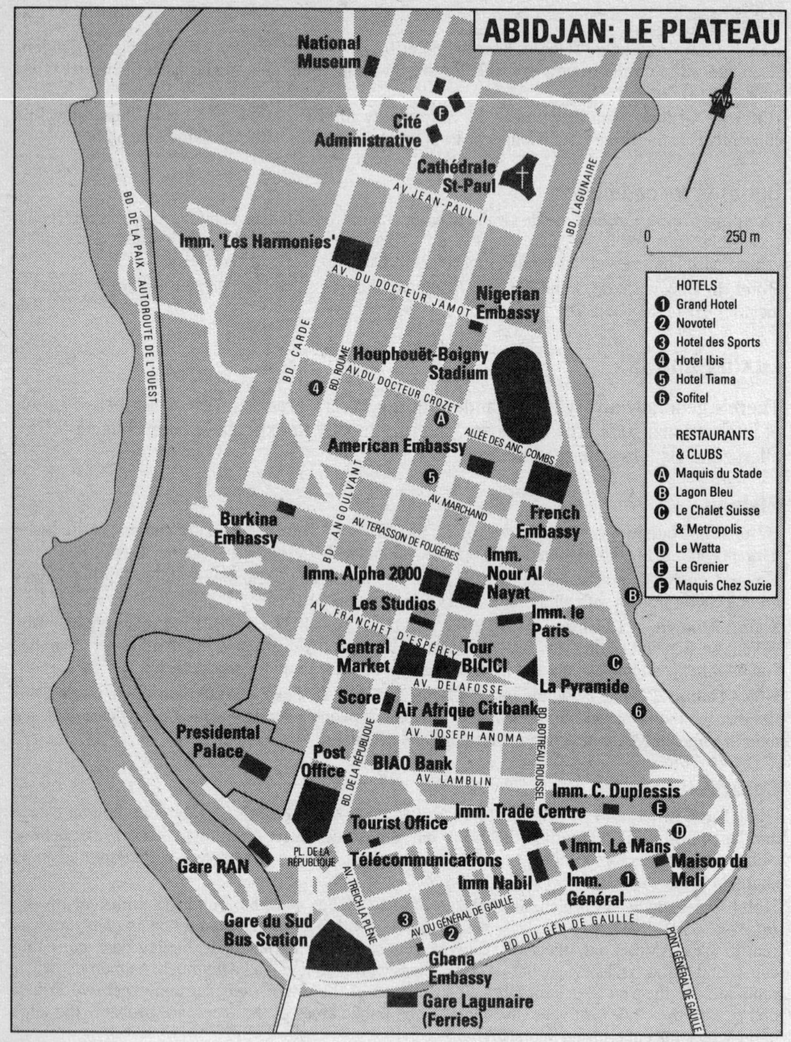

The Town

There's not a lot of **sightseeing** to do in Abidjan. You may be satisfied simply to absorb the energy of one of West Africa's busiest urban centres and, if your heart is gladdened by concrete and glass, to contemplate the merits of some of the city's more daring high-rises on the Plateau.

One of the first of these was the **Nour al Hayat** building, built in 1966 on the av Chardy. A landmark of sorts, the modest tower has since been humbled by more recent skyscrapers, like the **Alpha 2000** building, whose 21 floors filled with shopping galleries, offices and the headquarters of the **Société Ivoirienne de Banque**, made it the largest commercial centre in West Africa when it opened in 1977. Other additions include the **BICICI Tower** with its fifteen storeys of tinted glass and, of course, **La Pyramide**, on the corner of the av Franchet d'Espérey and av Botreau-Roussel. Designed by Italian architect Olivieri, this building caused some stir when it opened in 1973; today it is more of an embarrassment with its broken windows, aged curtains and lack of activity inside. The modernist trend continues in the form of the **Cathédrale St-Paul**, erected in the north of the Plateau in 1985 with the futuristic towers of the **Cité Administrative** serving as a backdrop.

Abidjani cosmopolitanism hasn't obliterated one or two other distractions. The **National Museum** houses a fine collection of Ivoirian art, and the district **markets** make for interesting shopping. You could even get back to nature with a quick trip to the **Banco National Park** or the **Parc Zoologique** (see p.641), both of which are just a short distance from the city centre, north of Adjamé.

The National Museum

Set in the shadows of Abidjan's sparkling ministerial towers, the **National Museum** (daily except Mon 9am–noon & 3–6pm; free, donations anticipated) holds a fantastic collection of Ivoirian art containing several thousand pieces. Expanded and improved, it reopened in late 1994 with thoughtfully organized displays shown off with careful lighting.

Many of the works in the museum are **woodcarvings**, including religious statuary, Senoufo sculpted doors, and the symbolic sceptres of the Agni chiefs. An impressive group of **masks** spreads over the walls, representing the ritualistic art of nearly every ethnic group in the country. **Musical instruments** from throughout Côte d'Ivoire make up a sizeable portion of the collection, along with sacred objects used in various ancestral cults and **pottery**, including vases, water containers and Agni figurines. Also on display are beautiful **bronze weights** used for measuring gold and other bronze objects made by the Akan-speaking peoples (especially the Baoulé) using the *cire perdue* or lost wax method (see the box on p.654).

After the renovation, the collection previously housed in Grand-Bassam's museum was moved here, and now presents a good variety of current Ivoirian **national dress** as well as genuinely old and handmade bark and raffia cloth, painted Senoufo cloths, and several serious hunters' outfits bedecked with *gri-gris*. The Yacouba, Malinké, Senoufo and Baoulé costumes are mostly *pagnes* in variations of blue, grey and black, sometimes made from broad strips.

On the walls, old **photos** of Côte d'Ivoire reveal life in the country in colonial times, including scenes of suavely reclining moustachioed young officers with their boots up, surrounded by crowds of bemused *indigènes*. There are pictures, too, of the Abidjan–Niger railway in construction, which was prevented by the Abé revolt from reaching Bouaké until 1912.

The markets

The **Central Market** on the bd de la République provides a burst of traditional colour in the heart of the Plateau high-rises. It's a great place to visit; not only for food shopping, but also to take a break in one of the bars or restaurants housed in the market building – a relaxing vantage point from which to watch the lively commerce. Nearby, the **Marché Artisanal** (also called *marché sénégalais*) targets tourists and is expensive. This doesn't mean you can't find well-made sculptures, bronze objects or cloth, but you'll have to brave the aggressive salesmen. One place you might visit for crafts is the *Fraternité des Artisans Handicapés* on the corner of bd de la République and av

Docteur Jamot (open Mon–Fri 9am–noon & 3–5pm, Sat 9am–noon). Ultimately, however, towns such as Man, Bouaké or Korhogo offer the best buys and the most interesting selection when it comes to Ivoirian crafts.

Much bigger than the Central Market is the excellent **Treichville Market**, which displays myriad goods from throughout West Africa on its two milling floors: hand-woven and dyed cloth; traditional sandals and leather bags; basketwork and pottery. Locally made goods still occupy as much space as electronic equipment from Japan and European imports.

Larger still, the **Adjamé Market** spreads over several blocks near the train station. Cocody too has a good **food market** located near the intersection of the bd de France and the bd Latrille.

The Cathédrale St-Paul

When the **Cathédrale St-Paul** (Mass: Mon–Thurs 7pm, Fri 12.15pm & 7pm, Sun 8am, 9.30am, 11.15am & 7pm) was inaugurated on August 10, 1985 by Pope John-Paul II, nearly 100,000 Ivoirians turned up for the event. At the time, it was one of the largest cathedrals in the world (though now there's also the Basilica in Yamoussoukro . . .). You really need to be standing over on the waterfront in Cocody to grasp the significance of its extraordinary design: it's a human figure, presumably representing St Paul himself, arms outstretched to the north, his robe trailing lavishly behind to accommodate 3500 seated worshippers and another 1500 standing.

If its construction endures, the Italian architect Aldo Spirito's cathedral will one day rate as classic twentieth-century church architecture. You enter under the back of the robe and it would be hard not to be impressed; the ceiling cleaves away and upwards with stunning grace. The lines pull you into the heart of the building, soaring 50m or more above the altar. Breathtaking **stained glass tableaux** depict Paul's conversion on the road to Damascus, black slaves in his retinue; and, on the right, the arrival of the paddle steamer *Dahomey* with its contingent of French fathers come to spread the gospels in Africa. The picture is glorious, if naive, portraying unrealistically enthusiastic pagans rushing to the shore with welcoming smiles and baskets of fruit. For CFA500, you can take an elevator up the towers for more views of the town.

Eating, drinking and nightlife

Abidjan has carved out a deserved reputation for good eating, and you can find cuisine from just about any corner of the world: the following **restaurants** are just a small selection. Some of the classier Asian, European and African restaurants are prohibitively expensive; to save money, eat the **street food** at the markets of Treichville, Adjamé, Cocody and even on the Plateau – Senegalese rice with a thick vegetable sauce is good. Also inexpensive are the many **maquis** scattered about town. The chain of *Opéra* croissanteries is recommended too.

Budget

Abidjan's expensive reputation obscures a lot of reasonable places to fill up, where the competition helps keep prices down.

Le Bar du Marché, off rue Gourgas in the market, Plateau. Wonderful place right in the Central Market, that serves African and European dishes.

Chic Café Express, north of Adjamé *gare routière*. Sidewalk café covered by large green canopy where you'll find petit pois with steak in the afternoons, *café complet* in the mornings. Espresso made with real coffee and excellent *lait caillé* (sweetened curds); a favourite of drivers from the *gare routière*.

George V, opposite *Score* supermarket, Deux-Plateaux. Inexpensive houmous and tabouleh; a popular Peace Corps hang-out.

L'Impeccable, off bd de Marseille, Vridi. *Maquis* near the port featuring excellent and inexpensive prawns.

Maquis Chez Suzie, Cité Administrative, Plateau. Restaurant under the breezeways of the administrative towers where civil servants mingle with neighbourhood hawkers for *aloko* or *atieké* with deep fried fish and piment.

Maquis Chez Willy, opposite the Commissariat de Police, Deux-Plateaux. Bar serving street food. Good place to meet expats on a Wednesday night when Americans come for happy hour.

Maquis Harmonie, av Laurent Clouzet, Treichville. One of a whole clutch of inexpensive places to eat surrounding the *Whiskey A-Go-Go*. The grilled fish is good. Down the street, you can order a drink at the popular *Café des Arts* and have it with street food prepared by women at the front.

Maquis du Stade, av du Docteur Crozet, Plateau (☎32 21 49). Excellent lunchtime *maquis*, shady and convenient. The service is slow, but when the food finally arrives it's delicious, from the plantain *foutou*, rice, meat and fish to the quite excellent *kedjenou*.

Restaurant de Bah, av de la Reine Pokou, Treichville, opposite the *Treichotel*. One of a string of inexpensive restos on the same street: clean, tasty and unpretentious.

Snackorama, adjoining the bowling alley of the *Hôtel Ivoire*, Cocody. Burgers, milk-shakes and sundaes served to the sounds of crashing pins. Inexpensive Americana.

Southern Fried Chicken, av Anoma, Plateau, near *Air France*. Colonel Sanders meets Ronald McDonald – real fast food ranging from chicken to burgers.

Moderate

In addition to the many **moderately priced African restaurants** representing cooking from across the continent, you can also eat **international-style snack food** without breaking the bank. Though mid-range restaurants are scattered all over the city, there's a concentration of them around Cocody market.

Chez Babouya, corner av 7 and rue 7, Treichville (☎32 39 28). Thoroughly enjoyable experience with Mauritanian specialities. Set-price dinner might be *pigeon aux dattes* or excellent *couscous*. Babouya's incomparable self is the extra attraction. Around CFA10,000.

Dolce Vita, Cocody market. Possibly the best pizza in West Africa.

Maison des Anciens Combatants, allée des Anciens Combatants, off rue Jesse Owens, near the Stadium, Plateau (☎22 77 24). Very popular four-course set lunches – healthy servings of French and African dishes and nice service and atmosphere.

Le Mechoui, Cocody market. Diverse selection of Lebanese specialities.

Au Pastel, av des Jardins, Deux-Plateaux (☎41 35 80). French and Italian specialities, and home deliveries for pizza orders.

Pizza di Sorrento, bd de Marseille, Km 6, Zone 4 (☎35 57 75). Popular pizza place that's been around for 30 years.

Reine de Saba, bd Latrille, Plateau. Ethiopian eating experience with tea ceremonies taken at round tables from undersized chairs.

Shanghai, Cocody market. Good Chinese specialities; try the Beef Shanghai.

Le Vatican, near Eglise Ste Thérèse, Marcory (☎35 71 14). Very well-known *maquis* on upper level with views on the street. Grilled fish and chicken, atieké and the like.

Le Watta, rue du Commerce, Plateau. Airy terrace overlooking the lagoon. *Pintade*, or *agouti* served with style.

Expensive

At the expense-account end of the scale, Abidjan tends to lay on the style very thick. The best of these restaurants are usually excellent by any measure, but it's always wise to hear the latest reports on the grapevine before risking any of them for an important occasion – especially in view of the fact that a meal for two is not likely to cost less than CFA40,000.

African

Chez Cakpo, rue du Canal, Vridi (☎35 29 78). African specialities served by the waterfront. Excellent lobster and grilled prawns.

Maquis Mityfla, bd Giscard d'Estaing, at rue P & M Curie, near Zone 4 (☎24 93 34). Huge *paillote* entrance and fancy African specialities plus a piano bar.

European

Brasserie Abidjanaise, bd de la République, Plateau (☎32 92 35). Long rated one of the best French restaurants in town. Correspondingly high prices. The menu changes weekly.

Le Chalet Suisse, bd Lagunaire, Plateau (☎21 54 80). Popular spot for fondue or interesting French and Swiss specialities. Less expensive than many upmarket restaurants; book a table.

L'Etable, av Botreau-Roussel, Plateau (☎22 23 93).Very upmarket steak house, currently quite in.

Le Grenier, av Crosson Duplessis, Plateau (☎32 34 94). Refined French cuisine, like *riz de veau bordelaise* and seasoned escargots. Closed Sun.

Lagon Bleu, bd Lagunaire at av Chardy, in the lagoon (☎32 84 68). Seafood at sea: a nice idea if you don't mind the slight motion.

Asian

Le Maharaja, 30 av Chardy, Plateau (☎22 73 73). The town's classiest Indian restaurant.

Tuan, bd Lagunaire, Plateau (☎21 63 80). Posh lacquered interior with fancy napkins and hovering waiters, but considered one of the town's better Vietnamese restaurants.

Nightlife

Dinner over, there's the nightlife to look forward to. Abidjan has a busy scene, though as you might expect, most places only get lively towards the end of the week and closure from Sunday to Tuesday is common. Be safety conscious: you need to look after yourself, especially in Treichville, so be sure that at least one of your group stays fairly sober (less of a problem when you start counting the bills). Go out on the town with only as much cash as you need, no jewellery and no watch. You can get around easily by **taxi**, and you may even be lucky with a well-informed driver, but don't try to go clubbing on foot. The cover charge usually includes a drink and should be around CFA3000–5000. Drinks thereafter cost about CFA1000–3000.

The **Plateau clubs** are good if you need softening up. Currently, one of the most popular is the *Bastring* on the bd de la République, near *Les Studios* cinema, where African yuppies create a safe but satisfying ambiance (it is possible). Near the *Sofitel*, the *Metropolis* attracts a more middle-aged clientele, while the young and restless head for the *Blue Note* – probably the Plateau's liveliest club with good music and loose dancing. You're now ready for **Treichville**. Try any of those in the following listing, or, for something a little cheaper and rather unstructured, ask the driver to suggest a club along **rue 12** – the famously sleazy Treichville street. *Jannick* is the best known.

Treichville clubs

La Cabane Bambou, av Laurent Clouzet, Quartier Arras. A popular spot for years, still packing in the crowds.

La Canne à Sucre, corner of bd Delafosse and av 6, Quartier Akpopa. Another long-established club. Flashy and expensive though it only warms up after midnight, Thurs–Sun.

Hit Parade, bd Delafosse, near the *Hôtel Terminus*, Quartier France-Amerique. Likened by people of the neighbourhood to an American disco. Recommended – showy and fun. Again, top money to get in.

Midnight Express. Another popular Treichville club in the Quartier France-Amerique.

Whiskey A-Go-Go, av Laurent Clouzet, Quartier Arras. Opposite the *Cabane*, this provides some stiff competition; young, lively and raunchy.

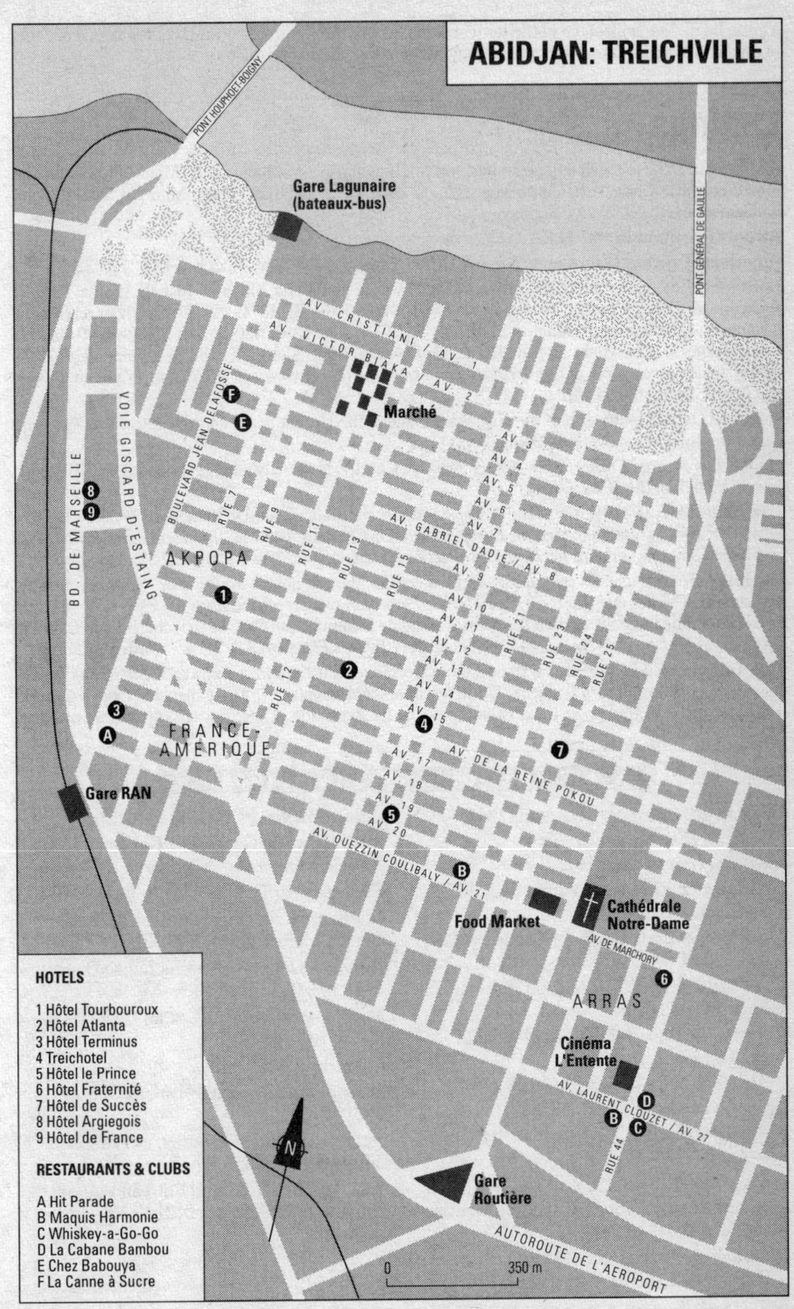
ABIDJAN: TREICHVILLE
PONT HOUPHOET-BOIGNY
Gare Lagunaire (bateaux-bus)
PONT GÉNÉRAL DE GAULLE
AV. CRISTIANI / AV. 1
AV. VICTOR BIAKA / AV. 2
Marché
AV. 3
AV. 4
AV. 5
AV. 6
AV. 7
AV. GABRIEL DADIE / AV. 8
AV. 9
AV. 10
AV. 11
AV. 12
AV. 13
AV. 14
AV. 15
AV. 17
AV. 18
AV. 19
AV. 20
AV. DE LA REINE POKOU
AV. OUEZZIN COULIBALY / AV. 21
BOULEVARD JEAN DELAFOSSE
VOIE GISCARD D'ESTAING
BD. DE MARSEILLE
RUE 7
RUE 9
RUE 11
RUE 13
RUE 15
RUE 12
RUE 21
RUE 23
RUE 24
RUE 25
AKPOPA
FRANCE-AMERIQUE
Gare RAN
Food Market
Cathédrale Notre-Dame
AV. DE MARCHORY
ARRAS
Cinéma L'Entente
AV. LAURENT CLOUZET / AV. 27
RUE 44
Gare Routière
AUTOROUTE DE L'AEROPORT
0
350 m
N
HOTELS
1 Hôtel Tourbouroux
2 Hôtel Atlanta
3 Hôtel Terminus
4 Treichotel
5 Hôtel le Prince
6 Hôtel Fraternité
7 Hôtel de Succès
8 Hôtel Argiegois
9 Hôtel de France
RESTAURANTS & CLUBS
A Hit Parade
B Maquis Harmonie
C Whiskey-a-Go-Go
D La Cabane Bambou
E Chez Babouya
F La Canne à Sucre

Yams, bd de Marseille. One of the hottest clubs, where the Central African DJs play an eclectic mix of music with all the latest light technology. Expensive, but no-one minds.

Listings

Air freight *DHL* are efficient, whether you're shipping in or shipping out. Main office is on rue Pierre et Marie Curie, near bd de Marseille, in Zone 4C (☎35 90 39). Open Mon–Fri 8am–6.30pm, Sat 8am–noon.

Airport information ☎27 71 83.

American Express Main agents are *SOCOPAO Voyages*, bd de Marseille, Km 1 (☎24 23 52).

Banks The Plateau is the main banking district where you'll find, all on av Joseph Anoma: *Banque Africaine de Développement* (☎20 44 44); *Afribail/BIAO* (01 BP 1274; ☎22 07 22; Mastercard cash advances); *Citibank*, Imm. Amci (☎21 46 10); *SGBCI* (01 BP 1355; ☎20 12 34); *SIB* (☎20 00 00; Visa cash advances). Elsewhere on the Plateau are *Barclays*, Imm. Alpha 2000, bd de la République (☎21 28 04), which gives some of the best rates for non-franc currencies, and *BICICI*, av Franchet d'Espérey (01 BP 1298; ☎20 16 00).

Beaches On the south side of the city, Vridi Plage is the closest beach to the centre. Bus #18 runs here from the Plateau Gare du Sud.

Books *Librairie de France*, Imm. Alpha 2000, av Chardy, is the city's biggest bookshop. They also have a branch in the *Hôtel Ivoire*.

Car rental *Avis* (☎32 04 57) at the *Novotel* and airport; *Budget*, rue Dr Blanchard (☎25 60 11; Fax 25 45 09), *Hôtel Tiama* and airport; *Europcar*, rue Dr Colmette (☎25 11 35), agencies at *Sofitel*, *Golf* and *Sebroko* hotels and airport; *Hertz*, bd Giscard d'Estaing (☎25 77 47; Fax 25 82 52) and airport.

Cinemas There's usually something worth watching, though not always in "v.o." (*version originale*, undubbed). The big ones on the Plateau are *Le Paris* with two screens in Imm. Le Paris on av Chardy (☎32 64 96); the huge five-screen *Les Studios* on bd de la République (☎32 38 97); and *Le Sphinx* on rue du Commerce. Cocody's *Ivoire* (☎44 10 45) and Treichville's *Plaza* (☎22 20 21) are worth a try, too.

Cultural centres In Cocody on the bd de la Corniche, the *American Cultural Center* (☎44 05 97) has an AC reading library featuring US newspapers and magazines. The expansive *Centre Culturel Français* (☎21 15 99) is on the Plateau, next to La Pyramide. There's a strong flavour of Paris'

AIRLINE ADDRESSES IN ABIDJAN

Air Afrique, 3 av Joseph Anoma (☎20 30 00 or 20 33 89).

Air Burkina (☎32 89 19).

Air France, av Joseph Anoma (☎21 12 78; Fax 21 12 94).

Air Gabon, Imm. Nabil, av Noguès (☎32 55 06 or 32 74 29).

Air Guinée, Imm. Général, bd Botreau Roussel (☎32 60 64).

Air Ivoire, Imm. SIDAM, av Houdaille (☎21 34 29).

Air Mali, Imm. Maison du Mali, av du Général de Gaulle (☎22 62 96).

Air Zaire, Imm. BNDA, av Joseph Anoma (☎22 42 27).

American Airlines (☎22 13 15).

British Airways, Tour BICICI, rue Gourgas (04 BP 827; ☎32 11 40).

Cameroon Airlines, Imm. Pyramide, av Franchet d'Espérey (☎21 19 19).

Cathay Pacific (☎22 62 43 or 22 62 46).

Egyptair, av du Général de Gaulle, next to *Nigerian Airways*

Ethiopian Airlines, av Chardy (☎21 93 32).

Ghana Airways, Imm. Général, av du Général de Gaulle (☎32 27 93).

Iberia, av Delafosse, rue Alphonse Daudet (☎33 19 91).

Nigeria Airways, 28/40, av du Général de Gaulle (☎32 26 14).

Royal Air Maroc (☎21 20 38).

Sabena, Imm. Nour al Hayat, av Chardy (☎21 29 36).

Swissair, Imm. F d'Espérey, av Franchet d'Espérey (☎21 55 72).

TAP Air Portugal, Imm. Botreau Roussel, 25 bd Botreau Roussel (☎21 17 55).

EMBASSIES IN ABIDJAN

Algeria, 53 bd Clozel (01 BP 1015; ☎21 23 40).

Benin, rue des Jardins, Deux-Plateaux (09 BP 238; ☎41 44 84).

Burkina Faso, 2 av Terrasson de Fougères (01 BP 908; ☎32 13 13).

Cameroon, Imm. Général, bd Botreau Roussel (01 BP 2886; ☎32 33 31).

Canada, Imm. Trade Center, av Noguès (01 BP 4104; ☎32 20 09).

Central African Republic, rue des Combattants (01 BP 3387; ☎32 36 46).

Denmark, Imm. Le Mans, bd Botreau Roussel, av Noguès (01 BP 4569; ☎33 17 65).

France, rue Lecoeur/rue Jesse Owens (17 BP 175; ☎20 04 04).

Visas available for Togo and Chad among others.

Gabon, Imm. Les Hévéas, bd Carde (01 BP 3765; ☎44 51 54).

Germany, Imm. Le Mans, bd Botreau Roussel (01 BP 1900; ☎21 47 27).

Ghana, Résidence de la Corniche, bd du Général de Gaulle (01 BP 1871; ☎33 11 24).

Apply 8.30am–noon, Tues–Fri, collect 1–2pm two days later (closed Mon).

Guinea, Imm. C Duplessis, av Crosson Duplesis (08 BP 2280; ☎32 86 00).

Allow two days for visas.

Israel, Imm. Nour al Hayat (01 BP 1877; ☎21 49 53; Fax 21 87 04).

Italy, 16 rue de la Canebière, Cocody (01 BP 1905; ☎44 61 70).

Liberia, Imm. Général, bd Botreau Roussel (BP 2514; ☎22 23 59).

Mali, Imm. Maison du Mali, rue du Commerce (01 BP 2746; ☎32 31 47).

Mauritania, rue Pierre et Marie Curie, Zone 4C (01 BP 2275; ☎41 16 43).

Netherlands, Imm. Les Harmonies, bd Carde (☎21 31 10).

Niger, 23 bd Angoulvant (01 BP 2743; ☎26 50 98).

Nigeria, 35 bd de la République (01 BP 1906; ☎21 19 82).

Norway, Imm. N'Zarama, bd Général de Gaulle (01 BP 607; ☎22 25 34).

Senegal, Résidence Nabil, av du Général de Gaulle (08 BP 2165; ☎33 28 76).

South Africa, Villa Marc André, rue Monseigneur Réné Kouassi, Cocody Président 08 (☎44 59 63; Fax 44 74 50)

Switzerland, Imm. Alpha 2000, rue Gourgas (01 BP 1914; ☎21 17 21)

United Kingdom, 3rd floor, Imm. Les Harmonies, av Dr Jamot/bd Carde (01 BP 2581; ☎22 68 50 or 32 82 09; Fax 22 32 21).

USA, 5 rue Jesse Owens (01 BP 1712; ☎21 09 79)

Beaubourg about its high-tech interior design and sunken front courtyard. Relax amid shade and plants and simply sit. There's a library, conference centre and cinema, and the centre is a live performance venue with plenty going on.

Emergencies Police ☎170; Ambulance ☎35 36 88; Fire Service ☎180.

Hospitals University Hospital Cocody ("CHU Cocody"; ☎43 90 24); University Hospital Treichville ("CHU Triechville"; ☎24 91 22). Best place to be ill is the Polyclinique Internationale Ste Anne-Marie ("La Pisam") on av J Blohorn near *Hôtel Ivoire*, Deux-Plateaux district (BP 1453; ☎44 32 39 or 44 51 32; outpatients' clinic ☎44 62 83 or 44 62 84), which has a near-legendary reputation among sick expats in West Africa – though it has recently come in for criticism for being too commercial. The Clinique Aricène in Marcory is a highly recommended alternative.

Lagoon trips The *Promenade* excursion gives you ninety minutes on the lagoons with a stop on l'Ile Boulay (departs Wed 3pm, Thurs 9am & 3pm, Sat, Sun and holidays 11am & 3pm).

Newspapers and magazines There are various outlets for foreign journals and papers, including the large hotels. On the Plateau, head to the *Librarie de France* (see "Books").

Post and telephones The post office is on the Place de la République in Plateau. A trip here won't be your most pleasant as the *fonctionaires* are generally obnoxious. Poste restante costs CFA300 per letter and those not collected within three weeks are returned or destroyed. The Telecom office is around the corner on the av Houdaille, where you'll find booths for local or international calling; or you can go through the operator. They sell phone cards here.

Swimming pools The big hotels all have pools, including the *Ivoire*, the *Sofitel*, the *Novotel*, and the *Palm Beach*; the *Golfs* is probably the most alluring. Most of them charge about CFA2000 for non-residents.

Weather forecast ☎36 71 71.

MOVING ON FROM ABIDJAN

BY ROAD

The **main gare routière** is in **Adjamé** at the junction of the roads to Dabou, Abobo and Bingerville on the northern edge of the Plateau. **Buses** here service the entire interior of the country – Abengourou, Bouaké, Yamoussoukro, San-Pédro, Korhogo – and through to Mali and Burkina Faso. Those heading to towns along the railway line are generally cheaper than the trains and much quicker. Owing to the labyrinthine nature of the Adjamé *gare* and the alarmingly robust approach of some ticket touts, you're best advised to get a taxi directly to the part of the gare from where buses to your destination depart. The **gare routière** in **Treichville** handles eastbound traffic to Grand-Bassam, Assinié, Aboisso and coastal towns in Ghana.

BY TRAIN

The *RAN* railway company (☎32 02 45; schedule and booking information ☎21 02 45) runs a daily train from Abidjan to Ouagadougou, calling at Dimbokro, Bouaké, Ferkessédougou, Ouangolodougou, Niangoloko, Banfora, Bobo-Dioulasso and Koudougou. In theory it leaves Treichville at 7.30am and arrives the next day in Ouaga at 1.30pm; in practice you may spend a second night on board. An afternoon train leaves at 4.45pm and terminates in Bouaké. Prices to Ouaga are CFA16,000 first class, CFA11,000 second class. First-class ticket holders can pay a supplement for a couchette. Remember that at certain times of the year (before school starts) an International Student ID card may get you up to 50 percent discount on second-class fares.

BY AIR

Air Ivoire, Imm. SIDAM, av Hondaille (☎21 34 29) connects Abidjan to major cities in the interior, including Bouaké (daily flights), Korhogo, Man, Odienné, San-Pédro, Touba and Yamoussoukro.

Travel Agents

Afric-Voyages, Imm. Le Paris, av Chardy (01 BP 3984; ☎21 21 11; Fax 21 28 88).

Expace Voyages, av Houdaille (☎21 26 46; Fax 21 29 44).

Haury Tours, Imm. Le Chardy, 23 av Chardy (☎22 16 94; Fax 22 17 68). Good for arranging trips within Côte d'Ivoire.

SAGA-CI Voyages, rue de Senateur Lagarosse (01 BP 1727; ☎32 75 03; Fax 24 25 06).

SITRAM (*Société Ivoirienne de Transports Maritimes*), rue des Pétroliers, Vridi (☎27 00 26; Fax 27 23 93). Offers berths on freighters to Europe via West Africa ports.

SOCOPAO Voyages, bd de Marseille, Km 1 (☎24 14 55).

Around Abidjan

You don't need to spend much time in Abidjan to feel like getting **out of the city** – a little goes a long way. The **zoo** isn't exactly a big escape, but **Banco National Park** can be a good breather. Getting further out of town, **Bingerville**, on the shore of the Ebrié lagoon, 17km east of Adjamé, makes a pleasant break. A former colonial town now settled into comfortable obscurity, it's an interesting place for a slow-paced day trip and, whether you have your own transport or not, can lead to an easy weekend round trip if you include Grand-Bassam on the way back.

The Parc Zoologique

Just north of town on the Williamsville Road is Abidjan's **Parc Zoologique** (daily 8am–noon & 2.30–6.30pm; small entrance fee). Though now quite extensive, the town zoo was started many years ago by a French animal lover who raised chimpanzees in his backyard and crocodiles in his bathtub. Gradually his collection of beasts grew and was taken over by the state's National Park Service. Today you'll find hippos, crocodiles and tortoises, as well as lions, buffaloes, elephants, monkeys and various birds. This is one of Africa's better zoos and some attempt has been made to create a natural environment for the luckier animals. Others sit in bare cages. Take bus #75 or #76 from the Plateau.

Parc National du Banco

Just 3km from the noise and traffic of the city, the **Parc National du Banco** comprises thirty square kilometres of dense forest which have been set aside as a natural reserve. Though it's said that a wide variety of animals still lives in the park, they stay well hidden in the woodlands and you're likely to see no more than perhaps a monkey or two skirting along the main paved road leading to the lake in the middle.

Despite this, Banco's **towering trees**, over-sized **ferns** and **hanging vines** make for a satisfying day trip – a reminder of the thick rainforests that once spread along the entire coast. The best way to visit the park is by car; to get there, take the road towards Dabou from Adjamé. Or you can catch a #3 bus to Cité Fairmont and walk the last few hundred metres to the entrance. Ideally, take a mountain bike. The main road criss-crosses the river as it leads to the lake in the heart of the park. From here various **foot trails** lead through the forest, passing through small villages which survive in the park interior.

Early morning at the park entrance there are unlimited opportunities for photographing one of Abidjan's classic scenes, the *fanicos*, or **Banco washer men** (if you're taking a taxi, ask for "Banco lavage"). The small Banco River runs by the park entrance, and along it hundreds of immigrant workers squeak out a living thrashing clothes against their rocks jammed in truck tyres in the stream. There's a lot of competition for this work. If you want to take photos, you're likely to find large members of the "syndicate" blocking your way and demanding CFA1000 for each visitor and each camera. It's best not to refuse.

Bingerville

Set in the hills that rise between the Ebrié and Aguien lagoons, **BINGERVILLE** is today a quiet town in a rich agricultural region (bananas, pineapple, oil palms). This was an early capital of the French colony, but you'll find surprisingly few vestiges of that era. Today, the town has been utterly eclipsed by Abidjan (a mere 20-minute drive away) and, with its *lycée*, military academy, psychiatric hospital and Catholic seminary, almost has the feeling of a distant suburb. It's an appealing, intriguing place, lapsed and restful.

One of Bingerville's most striking old buildings is the beautifully restored **Governor's Palace**, which now serves as an orphanage. Near the palace is the *jardin d'essaie* – a vast **botanical garden** where the French carried out agricultural experiments. Entering through a walk with giant bamboos forming a natural archway, you discover a wide variety of regional plants, trees and spices in the gardens, though the original layout today is rather overgrown and unkempt.

At the bottom of the steep grade that shelves to the lagoon (following the Eloka Road) is the small **Musée Charles-Combes**. Combes was a French merchant who founded the *Ecole d'Art Moderne Africain* in Bingerville, where he taught until his death in 1968. The giant **sculptures** he left behind consist mainly of idealized busts of

BINGERVILLE'S HISTORY

Bingerville – named after Côte d'Ivoire's first colonial governor, Louis-Gustave Binger – was known as Adjamé-Santey when it was an **Ebrié settlement** in the early part of the nineteenth century. Around 1850, the villagers first came into contact with Europeans, and by the end of the century they had signed a treaty with the French which paved the way for the creation of a colonial post. The first government buildings went up in 1901, after disease drove the French out of Grand-Bassam.

Bingerville thus became the colony's second political capital, but due to its hilly inland setting it never attained the economic importance of Grand-Bassam. In 1931, a new wharf was built at Port Bouët and, from then on, Abidjan grew to become Côte d'Ivoire's major town. The capital was transferred in 1934.

Ivoirian women from various ethnic groups. They're a bit much really and not very African, suggesting rather more about the artist than his subjects. There's no charge to visit the museum, but donations are appreciated. In the grounds, students chisel out copies of Combes' works as well as more original creations.

Practicalities

Frequent shared **taxis** to Bingerville leave from the Adjamé *gare routière*. To continue by transport to Grand-Bassam you need a ride, 15km further, to the **Eloka ferry** where you cross the Ebrié lagoon, with another 10km to Grand-Bassam on the other side.

There's not much here in the way of **accommodation**. The main place to stay is the *Bakona Hôtel* (②), a short distance from the *gare routière* as you walk towards the botanical gardens. It has simply furnished rooms, some with AC, and a restaurant that serves French and African food. The clean non-S/C rooms at the *Hôtel Obounon* (①) are less expensive. Find it by heading down to the museum, turning left at the junction just before the housing blocks and continuing about 200m.

Women prepare *foutou*, rice and other local dishes in small **restaurants** grouped around the *gare routière*. You'll also find stalls for **bangi** (palm wine) here, tapped freshly in the district. There's a string of good *maquis* in the **Quartier Sans Loi**, along the "rue 12" – not the street's real name, but coined, because of its lively reputation, in imitation of rue 12 in Treichville, Abidjan.

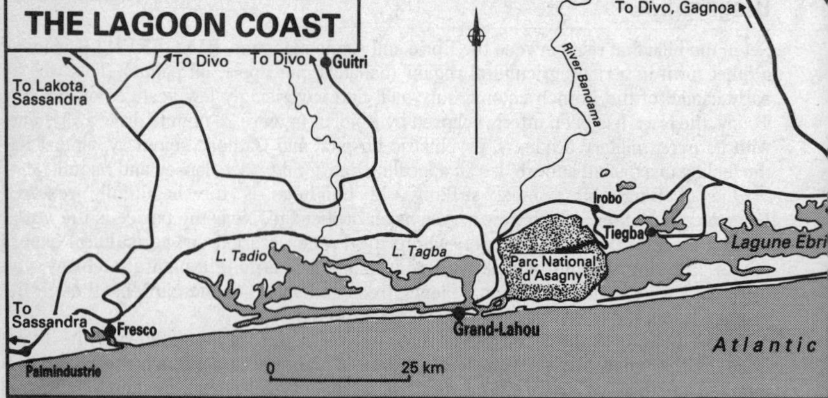

THE WEST COAST

Côte d'Ivoire's longest and most unexploited stretches of coast reach **westward from Abidjan**, and curve south to the remote Liberian border at Cape Palmas. Along the way, the string of **lagoons and sand bars**, scattered with the vestiges of old trading stations, gives out to a solid, forest-backed strand. Here, **Sassandra** is the first of the accessible towns; **San-Pédro** and **Tabou** lie beyond, offering some of West Africa's very best beaches if you're prepared to make a little effort.

Inland, in the far west, lies the country's remotest region and one of West Africa's most secure zones of primary **tropical forest**.

West of Abidjan: the lagoon coast

West of Abidjan, the coast shatters into a string of **lagoons and canals** for nearly 200km. You can find *pétrolettes* (boats holding 30 to 50 passengers and odoriferous fish baskets) in Treichville to take you along here, to **Jacqueville**, **Tiegba** and **Grand Lahou**. The departure point is next to the *bateaux bus* station on the northern shore of Treichville. A less romantic option is to go by road; now that the coastal highway has been completed, all these towns are easily reached this way, as is **Fresco**, further along the coast and inaccessible by boat.

Dabou

DABOU, the first main junction if you're heading out this way by road, isn't interesting. But as you survey the bucolic passing scene of oil palm plantations and banana groves, consider the local legend of red hairy dwarves. As recently as the 1940s, there were reports of "little men with long reddish fur", rarely seen in the daytime. One sighting – of a small, hairy figure between the roots of a silk-cotton – took place in 1947 at the science research station at Adiopodoumé, just a few kilometres from Abidjan. More reports of sightings, and stories of captures, come from further west, especially in the high forest now within Taï National Park and northwards. It's something to ponder as you lie on the beach; excitable scientists like to dwell on the possibility of ape-men surviving into the modern era.

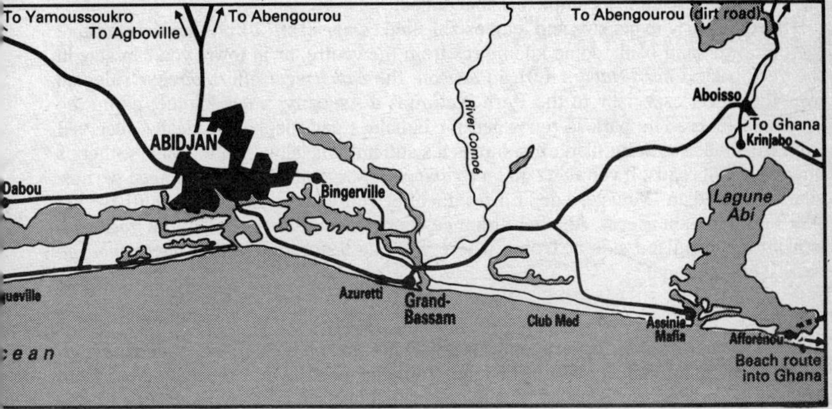

Jacqueville

Something of a resort in the style of Grand-Bassam, **JACQUEVILLE** (once "Grand Jack" – an English slaving port) is out on the ocean-front sandbar which encloses the Ebrié lagoon, some 50km west of Abidjan. You can get here by *pétrolette* from Treichville, or by taking a bush taxi from Adjamé and then a ferry for the last 500m from the mainland.

There's little sense of history in the modern town. Old buildings have been left to collapse. The *Hôtel M'koa* (BP 4375 Abidjan; ☎22 74 74; ③) is nice enough and not over-priced, set on the shore of a small pretty lagoon now sealed off behind the town on the sandbar. More modest is the *Campement de Jacqueville* (☎31 51 21; ②) with comfortable bungalows scattered about the coconut trees (they allow camping, too) and a seafood restaurant. Close to the *gare routière*, the *Hôtel Relax* (②) has less expensive, basic lodgings which, along with those at the *Cocoteraie du Lac* (☎37 45 83; ②), are among the town's cheapest. **Toukouzou**, 44km west along the beach, is the headquarters of one of the coast's most famous **Harrist** bible prophets – Papa Novo. Ask if anything by way of celebration is going on while you're in Jacqueville; a visit is quite something.

Tiegba

On an island in the northwest corner of the Ebrié lagoon, **TIEGBA** is a **stilt village** – or used to be, many people having moved to the mainland. As with similar places, like Fadiout in Senegal or Ganvié in Benin, you're likely to be so overcome by pestering children that any appreciation of the village is flattened in the effort to survive without losing your temper. Go in an organized group and you might as well forget the whole point of the visit; try an individual approach and things seem a lot different. Tiegba is accessible by *pétrolette* from Treichville, and by *taxis-brousse* from Dabou. On the mainland, *Aux Pilotis de l'Ébrié* has **rooms** (①), near where the *pirogues* take you over the hundred-metre channel.

Grand Lahou and Parc National d'Assagny

Like other places on the lagoon, **GRAND LAHOU**'s old town is on the narrow strip of a sand bank, a short ferry ride from the new and developing modern town on the mainland proper. Grand Lahou is similar in many ways to Grand-Bassam (both were trading stations at the mouths of major rivers), but the old sea-front buildings here, in a variety of styles according to the nationality of the owners – Dutch, English, German and only later French – are almost completely abandoned.

There's a fairly expensive and long-established *campement* (③) on the eastern tip of the old town sand bank, some kilometres from the centre, or in town, you can stay in the very basic *Chez l'Habitat* (①). In season, the *campement* offers *pirogue* rides all over the place, especially to the **Parc National d'Assagny**, a few kilometres up the Bandama River. The park is renowned for buffaloes and elephants, ideally observed from tree-house viewing platforms, but as it's still not officially open to visitors, there's no network of roads. If you don't go on a *campement*-organized trip, you'll need permission from Abidjan (Ministère de l'Environment et Tourisme, av Jean Paul II, 01 BP V6; ☎29 13 67) to gain access. Another entrance, more practical if you've got the go-ahead, is from the mainland side at **Irobo**, where you might get a lift with rangers *into* the park, if not around it.

Fresco

Another former trading "factory", old **FRESCO** is completely deserted, under the high **cliffs** (rich in fossils) across the lagoon from the new town. Since the road from Abidjan to San-Pédro was paved, this once isolated enclave is easily accessible by bus from both Abidjan and Sassandra.

FLATTERY WILL GET YOU ROUND THE WORLD!

"The excellence of the TV series is only surpassed by the books. All who have had any involvement in Rough Guides deserve accolades heaped upon them and free beer for life."
Diane Evans, Ontario, Canada

"I've yet to find a presentation style that can match the Rough Guide's. I was very impressed with the amount of detail, ease of reference and the smooth way it swapped from giving sound advice to being entertaining."
Ruth Higginbotham, Bedford, UK

"What an excellent book the Rough Guide was, like having a local showing us round for our first few days."
Andy Leadham, Stoke, UK

"Thank you for putting together such an excellent guidebook. In terms of accuracy and historical/cultural information, it is head and shoulders above the other books."
John Speyer, Yorba Linda, California

"We were absolutely amazed at the mass of detail which the Rough Guide contains. I imagine the word Rough is a deliberate misnomer!"
Rev. Peter McEachran, Aylesbury, UK

"I have rarely, if ever, come across a travel guide quite so informative, practical and accurate! Bravo!"
Alan Dempster, Dublin, Ireland

"The Rough Guide proved to be a very popular and useful book and was often scanned by other travellers whose own guides were not quite so thorough."
Helen Jones, Avon, UK

"My husband and I enjoyed the Rough Guide very much. Not only was it informative, but very helpful and great fun!"
Felice Pomeranz, Massachusetts, USA

"I found the Rough Guide the most valuable thing I took with me – it was fun to read and completely honest about everywhere we visited."
Matthew Rodda, Oxford, UK

"Congratulations on your bible – well worth the money!"
Jenny Angel, New South Wales, Australia

"Our Rough Guide has been as indispensable as the other Rough Guides we have used on our previous journeys."
Enric Torres, Barcelona, Spain

We don't promise the earth, but if your letter is really useful (criticism is welcome as well as praise!), we'll certainly send you a free copy of a Rough Guide. Legibility is a big help and, if you're writing about more than one country, please keep the updates on separate pages. All letters are acknowledged and forwarded to the authors.

Please write, indicating which book you're updating, to:

Rough Guides, 1 Mercer St, London WC2H 9QJ, England,
or
Rough Guides, 3rd floor, 375 Hudson St, New York, NY 10014-3657, USA

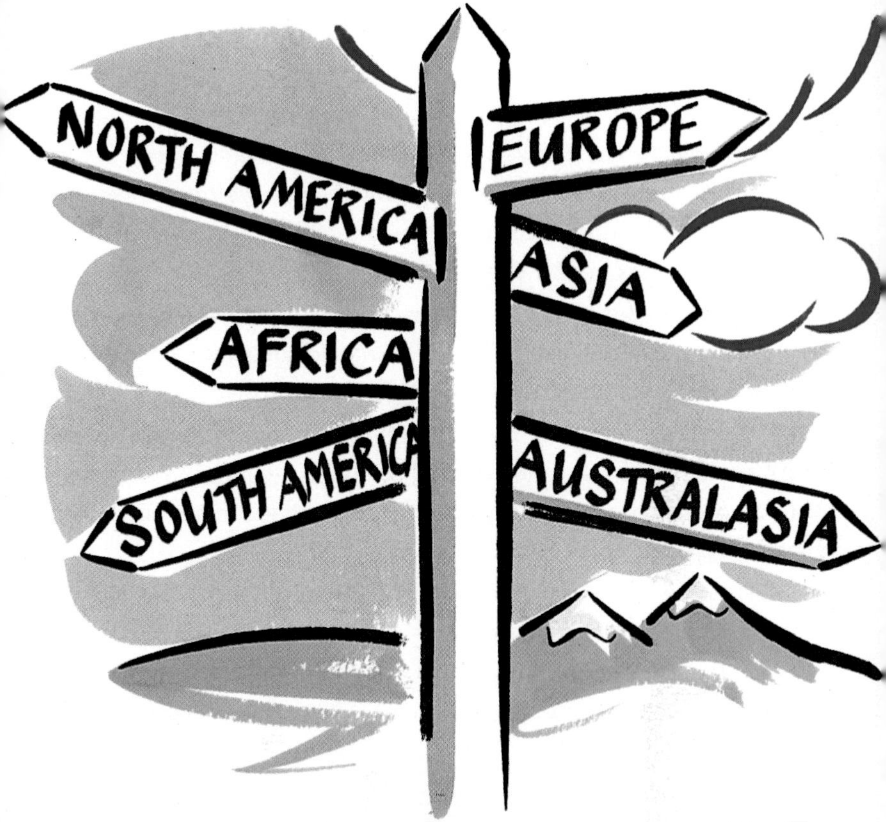

NORTH AMERICA
EUROPE
ASIA
AFRICA
SOUTH AMERICA
AUSTRALASIA

Travel the world HIV *Safe*

Travel *Safe*

Sassandra and around

SASSANDRA has *really* beautiful **beaches** nearby – the best, if not quite the only, reason for coming here. Unusually for the West African coast, there's also some topographical relief in the form of low cliffs that extend most of the way to the Liberian border.

The town itself is built at the mouth of the Sassandra River, so what with rivermouth islands and lagoons there's lots of water about and pretty views in every direction. The **best beaches** are out west, the first – Batelébré I, II and III – about 2km from town, further ones – Yeseko, Grand-Dréwin, Lateko, Poli-Plage and Niega – requiring transport and defined only by the roads and tracks that lead to them. One desirable option is to make Sassandra a base and spend a few days beach-hopping. Sleeping out on the sand is quite viable and for sustenance there are always coconuts . . .

Getting to the town from Abidjan is no problem, and now that the coastal road is completed, can be done in a few hours. Three daily buses (*cars*) leave Adjamé as well as 22-place Renaults and more expensive 504s.

Accommodation

Accommodation in Sassandra is reasonably priced, if basic; many places have superb tropical settings.

La Cachette du Warf, 50m from the *gare routière* next to the old wharf. The least expensive accommodation in town, in palm-frond huts with cement floors and fans. Coconut trees, fishing boats and the sound of waves make for budget paradise. ①.

Chez Tanty Youyou, at the mouth of the Sassandra. Clean bungalows in a range of categories. Budget non-S/C rooms available, though most accommodation has AC and private toilets. Idyllic location. ②.

Hôtel Campement, on the seashore near the river's embouchure (☎72 05 15). Colonial hotel, fixed up and not lacking charm, though it doesn't see a lot of guests these days, perhaps due to the relatively steep prices (S/C, AC rooms). ③.

Hôtel Eden, rte de San-Pédro, 1200m from centre (BP 349; ☎72 04 64). Rooms verging on the clean with shower and occasional water. ②.

Hôtel Grau, rte de San-Pédro (☎BP 168; ☎72 05 20). Clean fanned or AC rooms and one of the town's best restaurants. ③.

The Town

The **Portuguese** named the site of **São Andrea** at the mouth of the same-named river and there was a permanent French settlement here after 1730. The town became really important, though, only in the years leading up to independence, when it was the main port used by Soudan Français (later Mali) and a timber port for the forests of the Ivoirian southwest.

A relaxed stroll around Sassandra is a pleasant enough way to pass an hour or two. You can't miss the tall yellow **waterfront monument** to the British victims of the SS *Oumana*, sunk by a German submarine on Christmas Day 1943. A visit to the hospital, high above the river mouth, is recommended for the **view** – especially really early in the morning to watch local Neyo and migrant Fante fishermen pushing out to sea. To get there, go up the hill past the Ghanaian fish-smokers.

Numerous **pirogue trips** ply the Sassandra and can be arranged through any of the guides that hang out at all the hotels. Longer rides (3hr plus) usually include spottings of hippos and monkeys, though they can be quite expensive. If you are interested in seeing hippos, try to take a motor *pirogue*, as boatmen will not approach closer than 100 metres in rowing boats. More affordable **taxi-bateaux** leave from behind *Tanty Youyou* and ferry townspeople across the river to the Neyo fishing village of **Glodjé**. The trip takes only a couple of minutes and upon arrival, you'll find there's absolutely nothing to do except watch the fishermen reel in their nets.

Eating

Unsurprisingly, the focus in Sassandra is on **seafood**, although most places expect you to order your lobster, swordfish or sole in advance. The row of **maquis** behind the market is the place for budget food, where you can fill up on *foutou* or rice with sauce.

La Croisière. Popular *maquis* with grilled fish and *atieké*. Also a good place for night-time drinking; the dance floor can get busy.

Maquis Tanty Jeanne, next to *Garage Henri Kéké*, near the cultural centre. Grilled fish or chicken *kedjenou*, reputed by those in the neighbourhood to be one of the town's best *maquis*.

Le Safari (aka *Chez Francis*), directly behind the *gare routière*. One of the town's best addresses for moderately priced African and European dishes. The upstairs terrace overlooks the busy motor-park and the ocean, and the Nigerian owner is happy to take orders in English.

La Terrasse du Phare, up the hill, 50m from the lighthouse. German-run restaurant with breath-taking view on the fishing port, ocean and mouth of the river.

Beaches around Sassandra

You can sleep out along the beach near the village of **Niezeko**, about forty minutes' walk west from the centre along the coast. Here, a Robinson Crusoe affair of basic huts and shelters costs about CFA1000 per person (you'll need to be suitably equipped). The beach is pretty and the sea safe, so it's an ideal spot. Though it's popular at the weekend, on other nights you'll have the beach to yourself. Check the latest situation regarding water supplies and staff at the site. Nearby, the **lac au caïmans** is a sacred lake of sorts where the crocodiles apparently don't harm the townspeople – outsiders, though, need beware.

If you're mobile, opportunities for beach-hunting are limitless. If you're not, you can fix up a trip anywhere along the coast with the taxi drivers in Sassandra. If you have to make this (necessarily expensive) choice, then **Poli-Plage**, 16km from Sassandra, is the one to go for. Fares are settled by agreement, not meter; out and back shouldn't cost more than CFA10,000. Most drivers will return to town and come back for you later, but you need to be specific – and very firm – about your return time. For substantially less money and more effort, you can catch a collective taxi from the Sassandra *autogare* to Bassa and walk the remaining 6km.

There's a village at **POLI-CRIQUE**, and rustic, well-managed bungalows (①) to sleep in at the popular *Farafina* restaurant at the beach. This place seems to be more

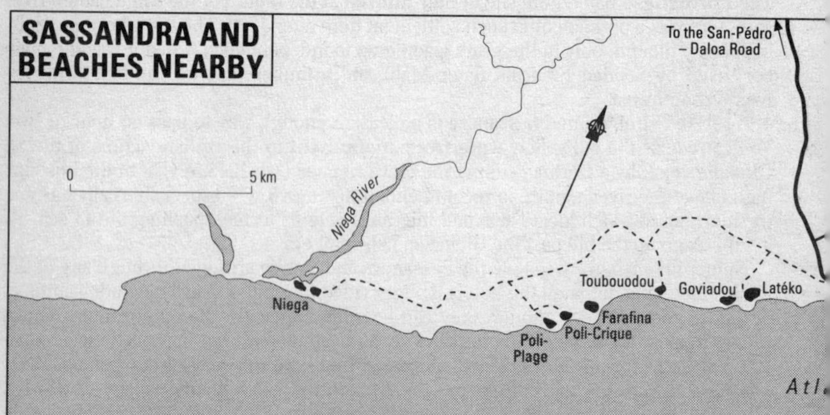

permanent than other beach accommodation that pops up from time to time, but it's still best to check in town before heading out – any kid can update you. If you're self-sufficient, then nearby beaches are heaven to camp out at – beautiful sand and coconut palms; hot rocks and a clear blue sea; tropical vegetation, dugout canoe-makers, total peace.

Niega, some 3 or 4km beyond Poli, is as far as the rough road from Sassandra goes. If you start getting into private *déplacements* to points much further down the coast you're talking about a lot of money. Instead, arrange a **daily rate**, pay for the fuel yourself, and try and get a group together. One popular destination is the stunning, sheltered cove at **MONOGAGA**, 65km away via the San-Pédro road, where the *Langouste d'Or* (☎24 84 80; Fax 24 81 97; ③) has fifteen beachfront bungalows that fill up fast at the weekend. Reserve in advance.

San-Pédro and beyond

Until a decade or so ago, **SAN-PÉDRO** was earmarked for serious development as a timber exporting port. Thousands of immigrant farmers moved here to a vast shanty area called **Le Village** on the north side of the town. These days, San-Pédro is just about ticking over, and much of the energy devoted to its expansion remains fixed on the ground among the unfinished building sites and semi-deserted timber yards. Despite the sprawl it's still a relatively attractive place, with hills and a good bit of forest pressing in all around. Yet for a town of such grandiose proportions, San-Pédro seems strangely empty. Although it has a lot of good infrastructure, there's not much to do here but hang out and listen to stories of dashed hopes. On the plus side, the **beaches** are very under-rated and often passed up by travellers who prefer the more tranquil coastal oases near Sassandra.

Some history

Forty years ago there was little in the region around the mouth of the San Pédro River save scattered Krou villages in a dense and otherwise uninhabited rain forest. The promise of something more significant, however, already began taking shape in 1959, when the government started to buy huge chunks of land amounting to some 3000

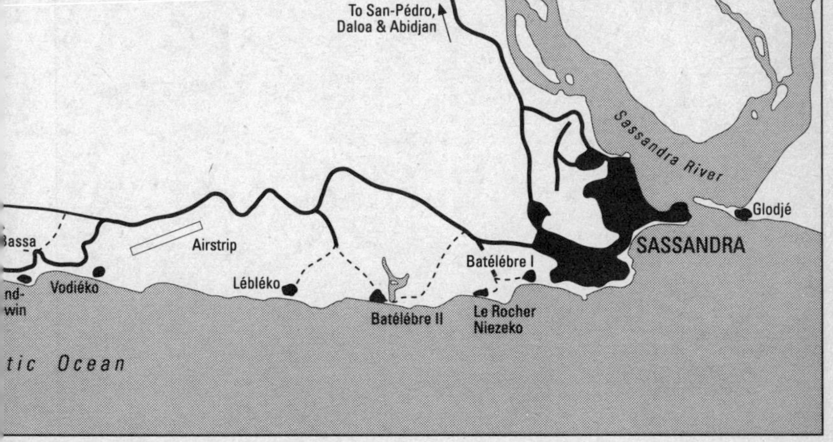

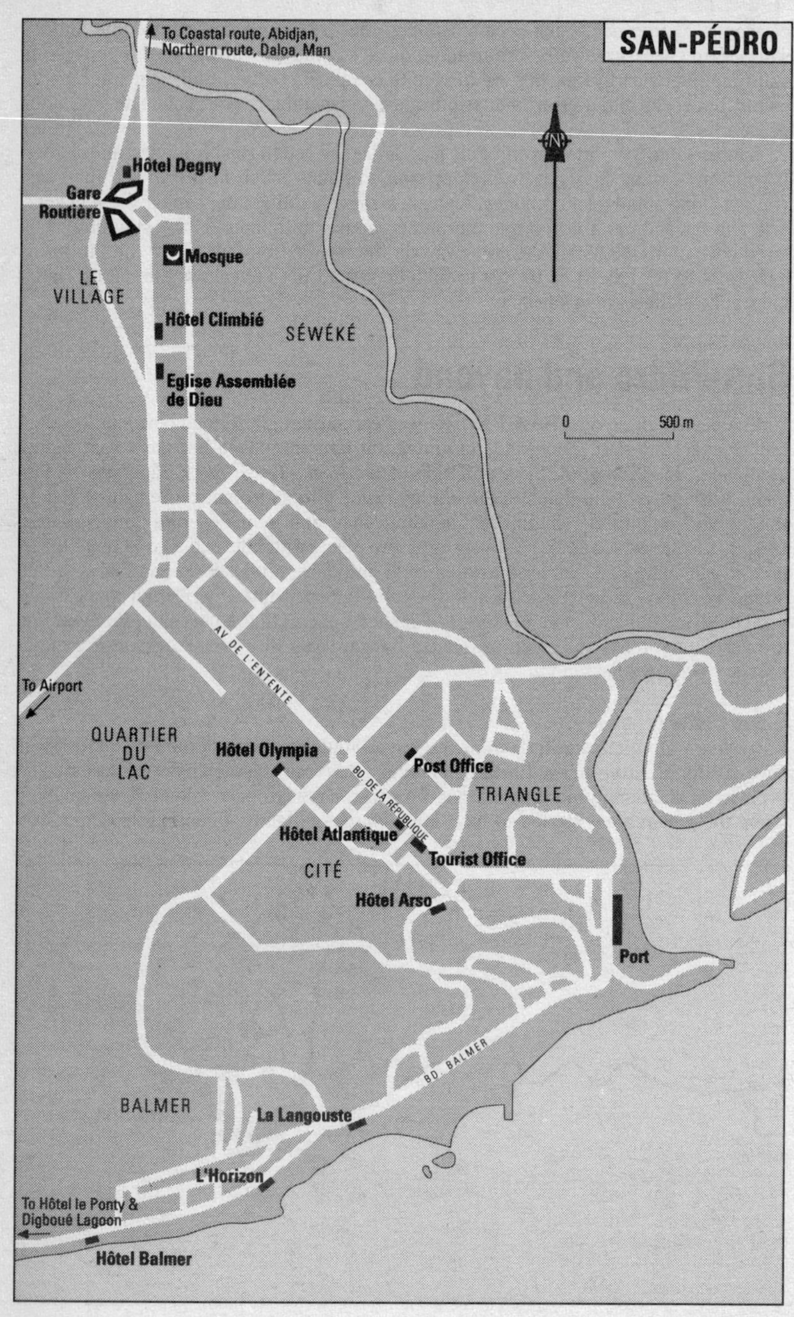
SAN-PÉDRO
To Coastal route, Abidjan, Northern route, Daloa, Man
N
0 500 m
Hôtel Degny
Gare Routière
Mosque
LE VILLAGE
Hôtel Climbié
SÉWÉKÉ
Eglise Assemblée de Dieu
AV DE L'ENTENTE
To Airport
QUARTIER DU LAC
Hôtel Olympia
Post Office
BD. DE LA RÉPUBLIQUE
TRIANGLE
Hôtel Atlantique
Tourist Office
CITÉ
Hôtel Arso
Port
BD. BALMER
BALMER
La Langouste
L'Horizon
To Hôtel le Ponty & Digboué Lagoon
Hôtel Balmer

square kilometres. The river mouth was the natural site for a port, and, when Abidjan became too busy to handle increasing sea freight, the new port, with its hinterland of timber forests, seemed the ideal way of launching the far-western economy on the back of the timber industry. In 1969, with German, French and Italian loans, the state-operated *Société pour l'Aménagement de la Region Sud-Ouest* (*ARSO*) began construction of the port and town layout. Within two years, the first ship had pulled out with a full cargo and for fifteen years, San-Pédro experienced an economic boom in its isolated corner. By the end of the 1980s, however, the forests were already being over-logged, and the drop in price of cocoa pushed the region into recession.

San-Pédro was initially settled in large part by people displaced by another massive construction project, the Kossou Dam (see p.661), which flooded a good portion of the interior and left 100,000 homeless. San-Pédro's population grew steadily through the 1980s, as other rural migrants and foreigners came in search of work; more recently, the town has seen an influx of Liberian refugees from war-torn Maryland County.

Arrival, orientation and accommodation

If you come in by public transport, you'll arrive at the *gare routière* in the northern **Séwéké** quarter, 4 or 5km from the town centre. It's a pretty bleak place to be dropped off, though the town livens up considerably as you get closer to the commercial heart, the **Cité**. Branches of all the main banks line the main paved road – known along this stretch as the bd de la République – but none change travellers' cheques. Along the strip, among the pharmacies and photo shops (where the Vietnamese and Lebanese merchants sometimes *do* change travellers' cheques) is a good supermarket, *La Côtière*. The **national tourist board** has an office next to the landmark *Hôtel Atlantic*, and while they give only sketchy information on local sites, they can hook you up with options for car rental. Nearby is the animated **quartier triangle**, a neighbourhood packed with inexpensive *maquis* and clubs and the only sensible place to head for evening entertainment, while west of the Cité lies the residential **quartier du Lac**, a stylish area with all the pretensions of Abidjan's Cocody.

The bd de la République terminates in the south of town at the impressively large port, where the cargo ships and containers completely obliterate the **quartier Balmer** whose string of tempting beaches, upmarket hotels and fancy seafood restaurants hug the strand. North of the bd Balmer is the **airport**, which sees regular flights to Abidjan.

Accommodation

There's no shortage of **hotels** in San-Pédro, and something for every price range. Some of the beach-front restaurants even allow for camping if you have your own gear.

Hôtel Arso, off bd de la République, just south of Cité (☎71 24 74 or 71 20 26). One of the centre's nicer hotels with AC bungalows and rooms around an expansive courtyard, a swimming pool and restaurant. ④.

Hôtel Atlantique, bd de la République, Cité (☎71 18 25). Older and well-established venue dominating the city's main commercial street. AC rooms throughout – those on the top floors have views of downtown and the surrounding hills. Restaurants and nightclub. ③.

Hôtel Balmer, qtr Balmer (☎71 22 75 or 71 25 03). Resort-like hotel with newly renovated AC bungalows built on the rocks jutting out over the beach. Excellent restaurant, and at 3km from the centre, a good place for quiet isolation. ④.

Hôtel Le Climbié, Séwéké II, on the main road near Assemblée de Dieux Church (☎71 41 54). Friendly and clean with inexpensive non-S/C rooms. Rules forbidding hourly rental strictly enforced; a respite from low-budget sleaze. ①.

Hôtel Degny, directly on the *gare routière* (☎71 22 53). A depressing exterior belies a small flowering courtyard with impressively carved doors leading to attractive furnished rooms. AC available, or fans for the budget-minded. ②.

Hôtel Olympia, qtr du Lac (BP 325; ☎71 10 10). Pleasant, well-run hotel with S/C, AC rooms and a restaurant. ③.

Hôtel le Ponty, qtr Balmer (☎71 23 46). Popular beach retreat, French-run with tidy bungalows, a good restaurant and camping facilities. ③.

Hôtel Poro, qtr Triangle (☎71 22 60). In the heart of one of the town's liveliest neighbourhoods, an attractive and quiet hotel with clean S/C rooms that have fans or AC. ②.

Hôtel le Relais, qtr Triangle (☎73 23 11). Unassuming hotel set back from, but within walking distance of, the high energy of the Triangle district. Spotless rooms with fan or AC. ②.

Eating

San-Pédro is bursting with **restaurants** and bars. The *gare routière* and markets are the obvious targets for inexpensive stalls serving *riz sauce* or pounded plantains. Inexpensive **maquis** line the main street from the *gare routière* almost to the port, and in certain areas, such as Triangle, restaurants are literally wall to wall. The fancier seafood and European restaurants are concentrated in the Balmer and Cité districts.

La Belle Vie, qtr Triangle. One of the countless *maquis* in the neighbourhood serving up inexpensive *atieké* and grilled fish smothered in a sauce of chopped tomatoes, onions, cucumbers and spices.

Le Caulally, qtr Nitoro, Cité. French-style *salon de thé* serving sandwiches, salads and ice cream.

L'Horizon, qtr Balmer. Popular beach-front restaurant specializing in moderately priced Vietnamese and African dishes.

La Langouste, qtr Balmer (☎71.19.00). Pricey seafood served on the terrace overlooking the ocean.

Maquis Amenan, Cité, near the police station. A good address in the centre for inexpensive dishes of rice or *foutou* and grilled chicken.

Super Maquis Elole, qtr du Lac. Slightly upmarket *maquis* with grilled chicken and fish heading the menu.

AN IVOIRIAN MYSTERY – THE RED HAIRY DWARVES

The huge area of almost uninhabited forest south of the road from Guiglo to Toulépleu (northwest of Taï National Park) is the most frequently mentioned haunt of mysterious, half-legendary, **ape-men** creatures inhabiting the twilight zone between animals unknown to science and mythical human ancestors. The Ngere (or Guere) people of the district used to call these beings **Séhité**, and told how they had a system of barter with them, in which they left cultivated food and manufactured goods in the forest and received forest fruits in exchange. The Ngere claimed hardly to know who the Séhité were themselves. Anthropologists have suggested the stories may be part of a folkore about the pygmy people who are presumed to have lived throughout West Africa several thousand years ago. And the cultural memory may have been mixed with the existence until quite recently (possibly still) of a large, sometime bipedal primate with a superficially human appearance. This was not a chimpanzee mistaken for something else, but it may have been an animal that died out before it was ever given a formal zoological identification.

Tabou, Boubélé and Grand-Bérébi

Now joined to San-Pédro – and thus to Abidjan – by tarmac, **TABOU** is reachable in a day from the capital (and there are 2 or 3 flights a week). The *hôtel campement* on the beach has plain S/C rooms (①), but the water supply can be problematic. More upmarket accommodation is found in the village of **BOUBÉLÉ**, 18km west of Tabou, where the *Hôtel Village de Boubélé* (reservations from Abidjan; ☎43 01 74; ④) has stylish AC bungalows overlooking the ocean and a club-like ambiance. Beaches round about are good, of course, but rough and dangerous for swimming. For that, visit **GRAND-BÉRÉBI** midway between Tabou and San-Pédro – a wonderful east-facing beach with an expensive expat-favoured hotel and restaurant, *La Baie des Sirènes* (☎71 29 94 or 71 15 20; ④).

The Parc National de Taï

There are no official facilities for visiting the **Parc National de Taï**. It's a conservation area, at present, rather than a wildlife park, and strictly not open to visitors without permission from the Ministère de l'Environment et Tourisme in Abidjan (av Jean Paul II, 01 BP V6; ☎29 13 67). Poaching is a serious problem and the government response has been to keep people out as much as possible. Assuming you have permission, the most promising approach is from the west and the small town of **Taï** itself, 202 rough kilometres north of Tabou, following the Cavally River frontier with Liberia through thick forest most of the way. The road is hardly used, and if you're relying on public transport, you'll need a lot of luck (and a pocketful of money: taxis charge around CFA20,000 to the research station). It's best to plan on a week or more for the trip and expect to hop from village to village with whatever vehicles you can pick up. A track leads into the park from **Pauléoula**, a village 10km before Taï. Guards may or may not stop you to check your authorization.

The Taï forest is rated highly as a natural heritage site: human pressures on it are relatively light and it contains all the essentials to be West Africa's most important rainforest reserve. Unfortunately, the many animals here – forest elephants, leopards, pygmy hippos and buffalo – are notoriously difficult to spot. Even researchers living at the station rarely see more than duikers and various monkeys. The famous monkey-hunting chimps that featured in David Attenborough's BBC documentary series *The Trials of Life* live in the Taï reserve, but they're an uncommon sight. Furthermore, the scientists who've been studying the animals for the past fifteen years are not employed as hosts and you'll need reserves of tact and plenty of time if you're hoping that someone might show you around: this park isn't a "green tourism" resort just yet.

The Réserve de faune de N'Zo

An easier way to get a feel of the rainforest, without the need for authorization, is to head to the **Réserve de faune de N'Zo**, which borders the Taï reserve to the north. Although this isn't a pristine reserve like Taï, it's still pretty exciting country for the average visitor and virtually all the mammals and birds found in Taï are found – and can often be seen more easily – here. You'll need your own transport: access is quickest from Daloa, taking the road from Zakué (near Buyo) to Zro. Near Zakué, the **barrage de Buyo** provides a good vantage point for spotting some of the numerous species of birds inhabiting the area, including jacanas, egrets, palm nut vultures and different types of heron – though it also gives a plain view of the savage habitat destruction wreaked by the dam.

THE EAST COAST

East of Abidjan, the coastal highway runs through fine coconut groves broken by the occasional fishing village. Curio and crafts stalls dot this touristy stretch of road and become particularly dense just before **Grand-Bassam** – a picturesque weekend retreat popular with Abidjanis. Further east, towards the Ghanaian border, **Assini** lies in another resort area renowned for its **beaches** and exclusive holiday clubs. **Crossing into Ghana** is straightforward if you use the obvious route: more adventurous travellers can experiment with shoreline hikes and obscure lagoons.

Grand-Bassam

Easily the most attractive settlement on the Ivoirian coast, **GRAND-BASSAM** is a simple day trip from Abidjan, and makes an excellent excuse to get out of town. And if you're leaving Abidjan for Ghana, or you've just arrived from there, it's a great place to spend the night. Some travellers, too, find Abidjan's pace so frenetic that they use Grand-Bassam as a base, and go into the city as they need or want to.

Founded in the early nineteenth century by the Nzima people, the original village derived its name from the word **bassam**, meaning "coastal settlement". Grand-Bassam is one of the oldest settlements of the European era and was the **first capital** of the colony of Côte d'Ivoire from 1893 to 1900. Yellow fever decimated the town in 1898–99; the French evacuated, almost overnight, and the capital was transferred to Bingerville, considered healthier. For three more decades, Grand-Bassam survived and developed as an active commercial centre and the country's number one port. But the cutting of the Vridi canal opened Port Bouët and Abidjan in 1950, and the old centre of Grand-Bassam has been in decline ever since. Many of the town's graceful administrative buildings remain, however, and the hotels and seafood restaurants bask in the derelict elegance of their surroundings. In contrast, the mainland part of the town gets livelier every year.

Arrival: the Route de Bassam

From Abidjan, there's a good paved road to Grand-Bassam. Taxis leave frequently from the Treichville *gare routière*; the journey takes little more than thirty minutes. Less frequent buses also make the trip from Adjamé. The route also makes a great half-day **bike ride** – with the exception of Togo, the only strip of main highway actually **on the shore** along the entire West African coast.

The **Route de Bassam** is a seemingly endless coconut *bidonville* jammed with **artisans' stalls**, "motels", bars and hotels (some offering "room service"). Stalls sell a wonderful variety of useful and useless crafts – toys, ships, gaudy model motorbikes, basket-work, in fact everything from table mats to double beds. Further on, the shacks fade and the coconut trees begin to rustle in earnest. Between them **concessions** of *guérisseurs traditionnels* (healers) offer guaranteed cures, long-distance witchcraft and divine inspiration and support: "*La Maison du Tout Puissant*" (the House of the All Mighty) is a popular epithet.

You enter Grand-Bassam down a gauntlet of souvenir and craft shops. Arriving by taxi, you'll be let down at the *gare routière* in Grand-Bassam's modern district, **Nouveau Bassam**. The market is down on the right. From here, follow the bridge that spans the lagoon to the **old town**, and the **Quartier France**.

Accommodation

Most people come to Bassam to lie on the beach, and the majority of the **hotels** face the seafront. Generally accommodation is clean and comfortable, often European-run and catering to European tastes, with obligatory HB in the high season. The budget possibilities are limited (search out *Le Village*, on the beach, for basic camping), but some of the town's *maquis*, notably *Le Quai*, *Lou Lou* and *Balafon*, also have an odd room or two for little money (see "Eating").

Chez Antoinette, qtr France. The old town's least expensive choice, once you've found it. The price will depend on you and Antoinette but it's bound to be reasonable. Only a few rooms, none with private bath. ①.

Hôtel Assoyam Beach (☎30 15 57). Comfortable S/C rooms with AC, a private beach, saltwater pool and restaurant. Horses to rent for a seaside trot. ④.

Auberge Koral Beach (☎30 16 26; Fax 30 12 63). Fancy beachfront hotel with pool (CFA1000 for non-guests), bar, restaurant and rather posh rooms. ③.

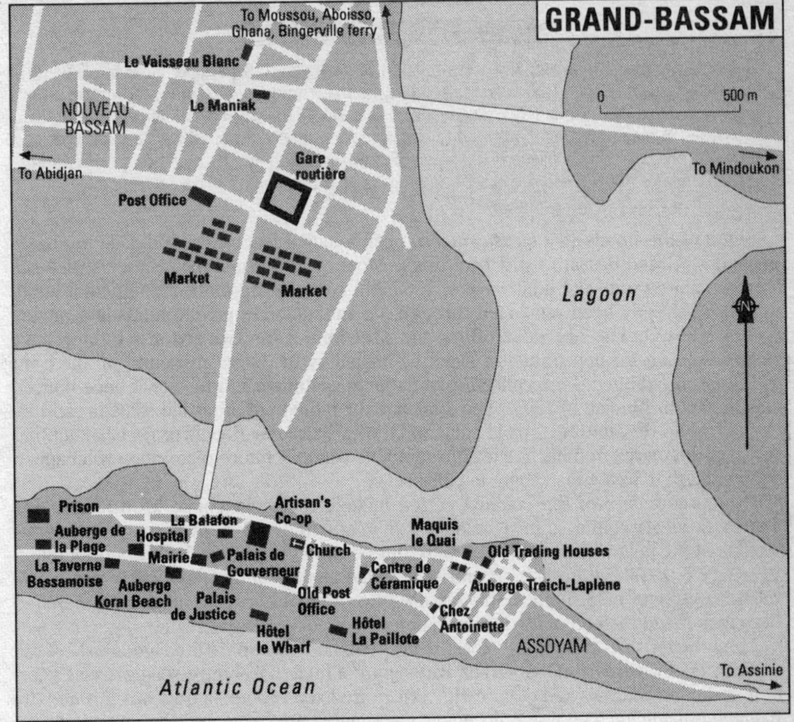

Auberge de la Plage (☎30 14 40). Restored colonial building with wooden porches and courtyard full of archways and balustrades. Rooms are spacious but drab. Still, it's one of the town's least expensive lodgings and good value. ③.

Chez Loulou, opposite *L'Auberge Koral Beach*. Very pleasant, simple rooms in this well-run *maquis*. Very helpful staff. ②.

Hôtel La Madrague (☎30 15 64; Fax 30 14 59). Stiff competition for the better-known *Bassamoise* (see below) with 12 AC bungalows, a private beach and pool. Excellent seaside restaurant. ④.

Hôtel La Paillote (☎30 10 76). Very ordinary S/C, AC rooms, but one of the least expensive on the beachfront. They also have a saltwater pool and good restaurant. ③.

La Taverne Bassamoise (☎30 10 62; Fax 30 12 96). The town's most luxurious lodgings and an Ivoirian institution. Colonial-style set-up including gardens, bungalows, a swimming pool and a terrace restaurant overlooking the ocean. ⑥.

Auberge le Treich-Laplène, in the French quarter (BP 590; ☎30 17 31). A restored colonial mansion with stunning hardwood staircase and balconies gracing the main hall. Comfortable AC rooms with TV, some overlooking the lagoon. Excellent value. ③–④.

Hôtel Le Wharf (☎30 15 33). Chintzy double rooms and an excellent seafood restaurant. ③.

The Town

Although **the beach** is Bassam's main draw, swimming isn't really recommended on this part of the coast (people who think otherwise are swept out all the time) so the town itself is likely to occupy most of your active hours.

> **CIRE PERDUE**
>
> The **cire perdue** ("lost wax") process used in the artisans' co-operative at Grand-Bassam for metal-casting is one of West Africa's oldest crafts techniques. Everything from the intricately ornate to the mundanely obscene starts as a model in wax. This is dipped repeatedly in washes of clay-water, each allowed to dry, and then finally wrapped with a thick coat of clay and fired, in which process the wax exits through a hole. Through this same hole, molten metal is poured and the clay "wrapping" is later chipped off to reveal the cast.

Some of the hotels (try *La Bassamoise*) sell a useful leaflet which details the background of Grand-Bassam's **old buildings**. Most of the turn-of-the-century structures were inhabited until the tidal wave of 1965 and some of the more monumental buildings have already been renovated through a combination of private funds and money from UNESCO. The **old post office**, the **Mairie** and the **Governor's Palace** have recovered their former grandeur. Don't be misled by the sign "museum" on the front of the last-mentioned – the collection of national costumes and history it once housed was moved to Abidjan in 1993. The dilapidated condition of other old structures, such as the **Palais de Justice**, the old bank and the early trading depots projects a haunting sense of the march of time, and it's questionable whether future restoration will happen soon enough to save those about to collapse.

Other reminders of the colonial period include the melancholic **Monument des Morts** (a weary white France holding her dead), the **old cemetery** (where many victims of the yellow fever epidemic were buried) and the **prison**. Following rioting on February 6, 1949, the French arbitrarily arrested leaders of the *Parti Démocratique de Côte d'Ivoire* and held them in this prison. In protest, the women of Abidjan marched here to demand the end of the incarceration and of political oppression.

Much better than you might expect is the **Artisans' Co-op** on the lagoon side of the town (Mon–Fri 8am–5pm, Sat & Sun 8am–6pm); a huge warehouse selling a vast selection of carvings, fabrics and other crafts. Prices are fixed and not outrageous. Around the hall and outside you can watch dozens of co-op members fashioning their merchandise. Nearby, there's a **memorial pillar** to Marcel Treich-Laplène (1860–90), founder of the colony of Côte d'Ivoire. Treich-Laplène was also first **explorateur** of Indenié in 1887 and of Abron and Bondoukou in 1888 – an active young fellow in his short lifetime.

The **Centre de Céramique** co-operative (Mon–Sat 8am–noon & 3–6pm, Sun 9am–noon & 3–6pm) offers an uninteresting selection of pots and plates. Unfortunately they've got the measure of the ceramics market with their globby little pottery fishes. To get out of colonial (or neocolonial) France and find Africa again, strike off east of this quarter, through the heart of the old commercial district with its rambling trading houses, and you'll enter **Assoyam**, a fairly traditional fishing quarter.

Before leaving Bassam, take a look at an old Ivoirian quarter of the town – **Moosou** – once a village and 4km inland from the France quarter. There are a few budget places to eat here, and as for sights, an elaborate, angel-topped mausoleum in the main street. If you're on foot, you don't have to walk all the way back: climb up onto the highway and wave down a vehicle.

Eating

Dining is an extravaganza in Bassam and generally expensive. Low-budget *maquis* are pretty much limited to Nouveau Bassam, especially around the market and *gare routière*. The following are all in the old town.

Maquis le Balafon, near the bridge. Grilled *capitaine* or barracuda served in a quiet garden.

Maquis Chez Suzie, near *Chez Antoinette*. One of the few places in the old district where you can eat for about CFA1000. Grilled chicken and fish or pepper soup.

Maquis Loulou, opposite *L'Auberge Koral Beach*. A slightly pricey restaurant specializing in seafood and superb breakfasts. Highly recommended.

La Pirogue Almico, near the Artisans' Co-op. Lobster and crevettes under a *paillote* overlooking the lagoon.

Le Quai, opposite *Auberge Treich-Laplène*. French-style *maquis* with tomato and cream sauces to accompany calamari or crevettes. Popular expat meeting place and a good source of information for further travels.

Restaurant le Saigon, near the bridge. Eclectic selection ranging from Vietnamese to pizza.

Entertainment

Nightlife in Bassam is low-key, but among places worth checking in the new town, *Le Maniak* is run by a former Ivoirian DJ who kept an extensive collection of records from his radio days and now boasts the best stock of oldies in all Côte d'Ivoire. Friday is jazz night; other evenings it might be funk or soul. A more classic nightclub, *Le Vaisseau Blanc* is also popular (cover CFA1500 at weekends).

MOVING ON FROM GRAND-BASSAM

For excursions along the lagoon, you can rent a **motorboat** from opposite the *Auberge Treich-Laplène*. It travels all the way to **Assini** and could presumably drop you there. After the rains, however, pretty purple waterlilies completely clog up the waterway and make this option impossible.

If returning to **Abidjan**, you can make your way (9km north) to the ferry across the Ebrié lagoon for the track to Bingerville (18km on the other side), and return that way, rather than using the coast highway; you should find transport every morning. Taxis and other transport leave town all the time for **Aboisso**, the last main town before **Ghana**.

On to Assini

East from Grand-Bassam, it's all **pineapples** and **coconuts**, pockets of secondary forest, a few old trees still standing, plantations of wispy, temperate-looking **rubber trees**, punctilious police and rather more military *gendarmes*.

At the town of **Abrobakro**, a secondary road leads down to the **Assini canal**, which stretches along the coast to connect the Ebrié and Abi lagoons. On the other side of the canal, **ASSINI** has gained fame for its **unspoiled beaches**.

The coast here tends to be exclusive. Many wealthy Abidjanis own private bungalows along the seafront for use as weekend getaways. This is package-tour country, too, with a number of resorts as luxurious as they're antiseptic. *Club Méditerranée* (Abidjan ☎30 07 17; ⑤) has a "village" in a coconut grove, with 200 AC rooms, the usual combination of sports facilities, a disco, boutiques and organized excursions. *Les Palétuviers* (BP 4375; Abidjan ☎30 08 48; ⑤) is even more ambitious, a club complex (with a gay emphasis, though not exclusively) with 338 luxury AC rooms and facilities from water skiing to riding. Open from October to April, it's mostly filled with tour groups flown in direct from Europe. Should you want to, you can only stay at the *Club Méditerranée* or *Palétuviers* by booking in advance via the above reservation numbers in Abidjan.

Into Ghana

Most travellers and nearly all vehicles enter Ghana via **Aboisso** and **Elubo**. For the sake of a more interesting route, turn off the main *route nationale* to **Frambo**, down a beautiful road in pitiful condition; then check out of Côte d'Ivoire in the customs and immigration shed by the wharf, before picking up a launch across the lagoon to **Jewi-Wharf** in Ghana.

It's also feasible to take a small ferry-*pirogue* across **from Assini-Mafia** on the Abri lagoon (22km east of Assini-Terminal) to a huge sand bar which, although part of Côte d'Ivoire, is connected by land only to Ghana. There's fairly frequent transport from Abrobakro to Assini-Mafia via Assini-Terminal (where the *Club Med* crowd cross the lagoon to their private paradise). Once on the sand bar, you can find transport east into Ghana. It's likely, however, that you'll be picked up by Ghanaian officials from **Newtown Post** (not, as marked on maps, a village as such), politely searched, escorted to Jewi-Wharf and sent on the launch to Frambo to complete Ivoirian exit formalities properly.

THE BAOULÉ COUNTRY

The **Baoulé** live in the centre of Côte d'Ivoire, where the northern savannahs meet the southern forests. Related by language and culture to the other Akan-speaking peoples of the east and Ghana, their prosperity formerly derived from trade in **gold**. Ancient mines can still be seen at **Orumbo Boka** (south of Toumodi) – the Baoulé's **sacred mountain**.

In the south of the Baoulé country, **Yamoussoukro** recently became the nation's administrative **capital**, a slice of architectural artifice that now just needs a couple of hundred thousand more inhabitants to lend it a real sense of city. Further north, the country's second largest town, **Bouaké**, is a bustling centre of trade and industry that attracts a diverse mix of people from throughout the country.

In addition to these **urban centres**, the Baoulé region also contains much unspoilt countryside. Though flat and unvaried landscapes are normally not cause for excitement, they lend themselves well to **game viewing**. The **Maraoué National Park** near the town of Bouaflé could be a chance to take in wildlife ranging from elephant to antelope. But Houphouët-Boigny's safari land, **Abokouamikro National Park**, within limo distance of Yamoussoukro, is a more likely bet, if it's up and running – and if the animals (imported at huge cost from South Africa) are settled in.

Yamoussoukro

In the 1950s, few people had heard of the small village of **Ngokro** except for the 500 or so who lived there. One of those residents was Nana Yamoussou, whose son Felix became the president of Côte d'Ivoire. That fact permanently altered the hamlet's history, since Houphouët-Boigny tirelessly used his influence to turn his birthplace into a present for his family and ancestors. In honour of his mother, he changed its name to **YAMOUSSOUKRO** and devised a plan to transform the town into a glittering metropolis. Many of the **monumental buildings** now dotting the cityscape are indeed impressive. Besides the imposing **Hôtel Président**, Yamoussoukro boasts modern college **campuses**, government buildings like the **Maison du Parti**, the **Hôtel de Ville** and, completed in 1990, a colossal **basilica** – a virtual replica of Saint Peter's in Rome and just a fraction smaller.

But in between these isolated pockets of pomp are vast stretches of nothingness – large open fields and vacant lots waiting for people to breathe some life into them. The vast layout is confusing and impersonal and the splendid dimensions of the futuristic buildings further diminish the human scale. The place is worth visiting as a phenomenon, but don't expect warmth or spontaneity, and don't expect to want to stick around.

Orientation

With a population now estimated at 100,000, Yamoussoukro comprises four main neighbourhoods. In the southeast part of town, **la Résidence** was the private domain of the former president. The town's main **market** is held in **l'Habitat** – the one part of town that feels really lived in – alive with the activity of merchants, restaurants and clubs. South of here, beyond the town's lake, lies **Dioulakro**, a residential *quartier populaire*, while **N'Zuessy**, to the northeast, is a slightly upmarket neighbourhood. The **banks**, PTT and the *gare routière* are on **Boulevard Houphouët-Boigny**, the major road dividing these two districts.

Accommodation

Yamoussoukro has a reasonably good choice of **rooms**. For a long time, much of the budget accommodation was grubby and unenticing – hole-in-the-wall hotels or *chambres de passage* – but it's becoming increasingly possible to find inexpensive, respectable places to stay, especially in the Habitat district.

Budget and mid-range accommodation

Hôtel AGIP (BP 9; ☎64 00 39). One of the plainest of the mid-priced hotels surrounding the *gare routière* though S/C rooms are clean and have AC. The restaurant looks curiously like a Norman Rockwell painting of an American diner. ③.

Hôtel Akwaba, Habitat, facing the lake (☎64 07 61). Good location a short walk from the *gare routière* and surrounded by *maquis*. Clean rooms with fan or AC and amiable staff. ③.

Hôtel Bonheure I, opposite the *gare routière* (☎64 00 61). Basic place, recently restored and good value. Bar and restaurant. ③.

Hôtel Bonheure II, opposite the *gare routière* (☎64 00 31; Fax 64 09 42). Same ownership as the above. Revamped hotel with furnished AC rooms and, if you like, minibars and TV. Some suites available. Pool, bar, pizzeria and *salon de thé*. ④.

Hôtel la Découverte, opposite the *gare routière*. Clean rooms, if small, with shower but no WC. Some AC available. ①–②.

Hôtel Las Palmas, Habitat, opposite *Maquis Le Jardin* (☎64 02 73). Very popular with overlanders and in a good location near Habitat's market, *maquis* and clubs. Inexpensive rooms with shower and fan. AC costs a bit more. Very friendly management. ①–②.

Hôtel de la Paix, directly behind the *gare routière*. Inexpensive squalor. A lot of hourly rentals, but you can't find much cheaper. ①.

Hôtel le Repos, Habitat (☎64 03 27). Small but well-maintained hotel where even AC and video are affordable. Some simple rooms with fan. ②.

Hôtel Résidence, La Résidence (BP 84; ☎64 01 48). A cut above the others, the *Résidence* has spacious AC rooms with TV, plus its own bar, restaurant and nightclub. ④.

Luxury accommodation

Hôtel Président (BP 1024; ☎64 01 81; Fax 64 05 78). Part of the *Sofitel* chain, this is one of Côte d'Ivoire's poshest hotels – 284 rooms (including 18 suites), all with colour TV and telephone. Here you can get a sauna, play squash and tennis, and cool off in one of the two pools. The 18-hole golf course adjoining the hotel is rated one of the best in West Africa. There are 3 restaurants and 4 bars, including one on the top floor with striking **panoramic views** of the city. All this, plus the disco, cinema and shops, just for you and the management (or so it may seem). ⑦.

The Town

As early as the 1960s, Houphouët-Boigny already planned to convert Yamoussoukro into the nation's capital, moving ahead cautiously, however, so as not to incite criticism. One of the first moves was to build a system of roads capable of handling traffic for a

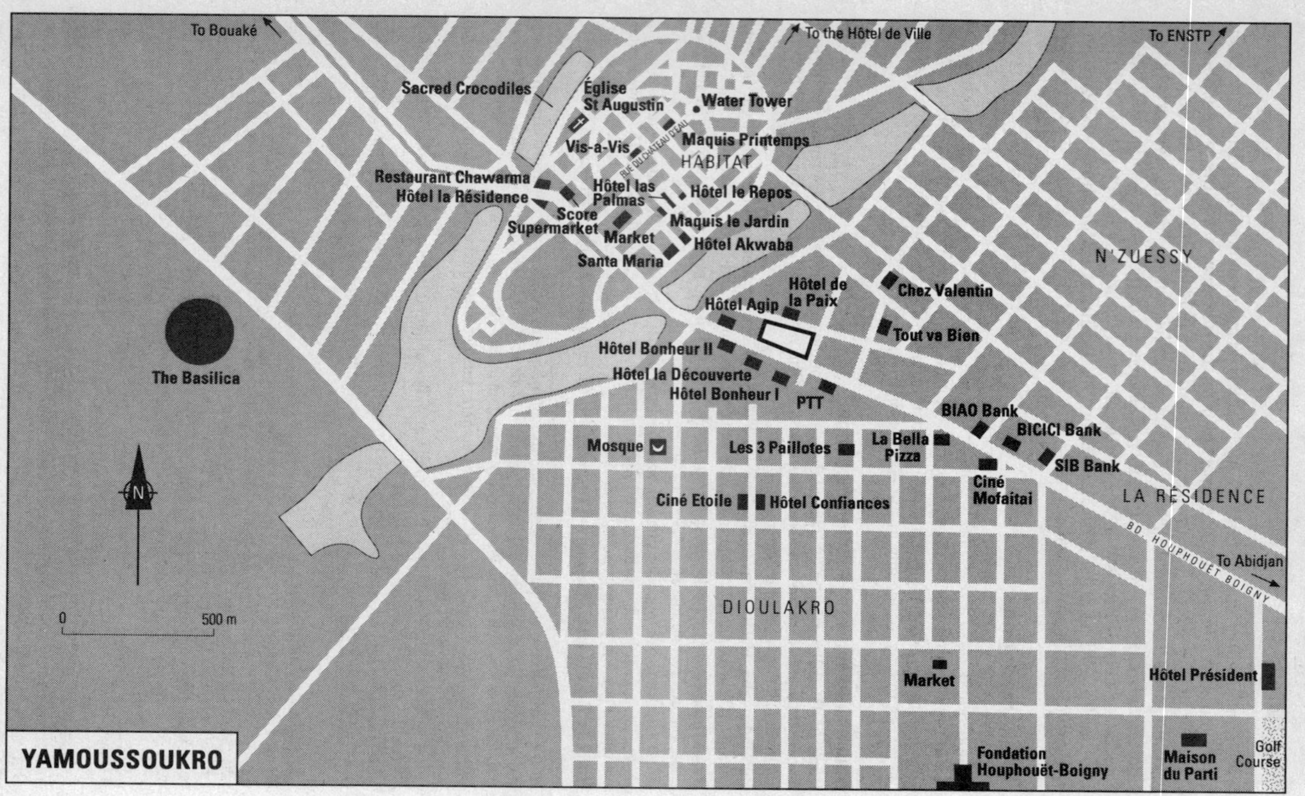
To Bouaké
To the Hôtel de Ville
To ENSTP
Sacred Crocodiles
Église St Augustin
Water Tower
Maquis Printemps
Vis-a-Vis
RUE DU CHATEAU D'EAU
HABITAT
Restaurant Chawarma
Hôtel la Résidence
Hôtel las Palmas
Hôtel le Repos
Score Supermarket
Maquis le Jardin
Market
Hôtel Akwaba
Santa Maria
N'ZUESSY
Hôtel de la Paix
Chez Valentin
Hôtel Agip
Tout va Bien
The Basilica
Hôtel Bonheur II
Hôtel la Découverte
Hôtel Bonheur I
PTT
BIAO Bank
BICICI Bank
Mosque
Les 3 Paillotes
La Bella Pizza
SIB Bank
Ciné Mofaitai
LA RÉSIDENCE
Ciné Etoile
Hôtel Confiances
BD. HOUPHOUET BOIGNY
To Abidjan
N
0
500 m
DIOULAKRO
Market
Hôtel Président
YAMOUSSOUKRO
Fondation Houphouët-Boigny
Maison du Parti
Golf Course

vast metropolis. Wide **paved avenues** were traced through the empty countryside and **multi-laned highways** laid out, linking the village to Abidjan, Bouaké and Man. By the mid-1970s, the incandescence of 10,500 streetlights flooded the quiet nights of the burgeoning town whose population was still only around 30,000.

Prestige projects followed. The lavish *Hôtel Président*, a brash combination of reinforced concrete and marble, shot up and was surrounded by what must be the continent's most-watered **golf course**. Dominating a nearby hill, the gilded **Maison du Parti** became a showy symbol representing the power and grandeur of what was at the time the nation's only political party. (For a tip, you can be shown around the various assembly rooms.) Houphouët-Boigny then set out to create in Yamoussoukro the nation's **educational centre**. No expense was spared on the town's three outstanding **écoles superieures** – the INSET, ENSTP and the ENSA – blessed with beautiful **campuses** of inspired architecture and state-of-the-art facilities (permission to visit obtainable at the *Hôtel de Ville*). A Moroccan-style mosque established a sense of religious legitimacy as did the Neoclassical Saint Augustine church – built in honour of one of the president's brothers. By 1983, Yamoussoukro had sufficient trappings to back up its international pretensions. The president's private dream became a public reality when the National Assembly voted to transfer the political capital here from Abidjan and it became Côte d'Ivoire's fourth capital.

The crowning glory is the granite and marble **Basilique de Notre Dame de la Paix**, planned to be the largest cathedral in the world and entirely financed out of the president's own pocket – a claim far from politic, even were it true, in a country as poor as this. It can be visited (daily 9am–noon & 3–6pm; free) if you're suitably attired and preferably if you're prepared to buy some of the nick-nacks offered by the nuns in charge of guiding visitors. To visit the cupola by escalator there's a nominal charge. Public mass is held on Sundays at 10.30am.

THE BASILICA: H-B'S "DEAL WITH GOD"

When they built St Peter's, were there no hungry people in Rome? When England after the Great Fire built itself St Paul's, were there no poor or homeless in London?

Ivoirian craftsman, quoted in the UK's *Sunday Times*, December 2, 1989

On a clear day, **the Basilique de Notre Dame de la Paix** stands out from miles away on every approach road to Yamoussoukro. It was built between September 1986 and January 1990, in conditions of immense secrecy, by a labour force of **1500 men**, working continuously in two shifts a day between 7am and 2am. It cost an estimated **£100 million** ($150 million). Among other barely comprehensible statistics, the basilica required the equivalent of an entire year's output of French white cement; each of its **7000 seats** has individual air-conditioning; it can hold another 12,000 people standing; and on its "piazza" and surrounding areas of Italian marble, there's space, in theory, for 300,000 more – a theory that's unlikely ever to be tested as the figure surely exceeds the country's Catholic population. There are 36 **stained glass windows**, in 4000 shades, each 30m high, covering an acreage of glass greater than that at Chartres cathedral. And, although the dome is a little lower than St Peter's in Rome – which the whole enterprise has so slavishly imitated – it is surmounted by an immense cross of gold soaring to **168m** above the savannah, which makes the whole edifice 23 metres taller than St Peter's.

In September 1990, **Pope John-Paul II** finally consecrated the basilica – though with evident unease, and only after receiving assurances (hollow ones, it would now appear) that a new hospital would be built too. Far from being a resounding success, the Pope's visit triggered a wave of protest and only served to increase Côte d'Ivoire's domestic political crisis and foment rumours of financial scandal. Houphouët claimed the basilica was inspired and made possible because "I did a deal with God, and you wouldn't expect me to discuss God's business in public, would you?"

While spending on his hometown, the late president didn't neglect his own fancies. The large **presidential palace** imposes itself on the city centre, but is enclosed and off-limits to visitors. Bordering the palace are the man-made **sacred crocodile ponds** filled with snappers – a gift from the former president of Niger. You can watch the reptiles being fed each evening. Behind the palace, the president's private **plantation** spreads out over 2000 hectares, making it one of the largest in West Africa. Experimental methods of farming national crops like rubber, coffee, cocoa, pineapples, avocadoes and yams are carried out here.

A further enhancement to personal glory was the **Fondation Houphouët-Boigny** – a vast historical and cultural complex in the south of town not far from the *Maison du Parti*. But to visit you'll need authorization from the *Garde Républicaine* (*GR*) and the *Direction et Contrôle des Grands Travaux* (*DCGTX*).

Eating

While Yamoussoukro has its share of stylish **African restaurants** (and some very average European-style ones, which you should avoid) there are also numerous *maquis* – especially in Habitat and around the *gare routière* – where you can get tasty Ivoirian food without spending too much.

Budget food

Restaurant Chawarma, Habitat, opposite the crocodile pond. Reasonably priced salads, sandwiches and *chawarma*.

Le Ravin, Dioulakro. A good choice among a whole clutch of *maquis* opposite the *gare routière*. Grilled chicken with *atieké* on the menu or *agouti*. You could also try *Les 3 Youhous* or *Le Soleil* next door.

Santa Maria, Habitat. Excellent Ivoirian food served evenings along the street overlooking the lake. Grilled chicken and fish head the menu. Next door, *Les Alizes* and *La Paillote* are not as good.

Tchong Fa, Habitat. Small Chinese restaurant with very moderate prices and an eclectic menu.

Les Trois Paillotes (*Chez Melissa*), Dioulakro. Along with traditional grilled chicken, interesting hors d'oeuvres and creative specialities such as *grenouille sautée persilée*.

Vis-a-Vis, Habitat. One of a string of restaurants along the rue du Chateau d'eau where you can try popular local dishes like *tête de mouton* or *pied de boeuf*.

Moderate to pricey

La Bella Pizza, Dioulakro. The town's longest-running pizzeria with red-and-white checked tablecloths and heavy wooden furniture, just like the old country. The pizza's authentic too.

La Belle Epoche, Habitat (☎64 07 76). Brasserie, bar and restaurant featuring the town's finest French cooking. Prime beef and seafood and a good wine list.

Chez Valentin, N'Zuessy. French and African cooking, served in vast outdoor eating areas separated by handsomely carved wooden railings and shaded by well-trimmed thatch. Excellent seafood includes sole and calamari.

Le Jardin, Habitat (☎64 14 22). Magnificent *paillote* for a very chic *maquis*. Along with European food, unusual African dishes such as *biche aubergines*. Recommended and reckoned the best in town.

Riviera, Habitat (☎64 15 62). Italian and French specialities. Good pizza and pasta and a couple of African dishes.

Super Maquis Tout Va Bien, N'Zuessy (☎64 20 96). Fine French cooking including killer shrimp and thick brochettes. Some African dishes thrown in for good measure.

Nightlife

Yamoussoukro's two **clubs** to be seen at are the *Masters*, near the *Ciné Mofetai*, and *Circus* in the *Hôtel Bonheure II*. Both have a cover of around CFA1000 and draw large crowds out to enjoy a good selection of music. Less expensive nightlife is concentrated in Habitat around the **rue du Chateau d'eau**. The *Maquis Printemps* has a lively bar where a very young crowd flocks nightly for energetic dancing and no cover. Nearby, *Le Marco Polo* is equally young and enthusiastic, but with a small entrance fee. Another *boîte populaire* is over in Dioulakro, where the at *Hôtel Confiances* benefits from the overflow crowd at the town's least expensive cinema, *l'Etoile*, just across the street. On the stiffer side, the *Hôtel Président*'s disco – the *Kokou* – is where moneyed hopefuls pay a CFA2000 cover only to find that few other people had the same idea. At weekends there's usually more of a crowd.

MOVING ON FROM YAMOUSSOUKRO

Frequent transport from the **gare routière** heads to Abidjan (266km), **Kossou** (43km) and **Man** (233km) – all accessible on paved roads. Taxis and *cars* also head regularly to Bouaké and Korhogo in the north.

Yamoussoukro's **airport** was designed to be large enough to receive any visiting heads of state who might need to fly in urgently by Concorde. More mundane traffic goes via *Air Ivoire* which has flights to Abidjan and Bouaké.

The Parc National de la Maraoué and Kossou Dam

Set aside in 1968 to preserve wildlife in the relatively populated area of the Baoulé country, the **Parc National de la Maraoué** spreads across a thousand square kilometres. In environmental terms, that's really not much (a fraction of the size of the Comoé Park further north) and the variety of animals you can see here isn't overwhelming. Bordered by the namesake **Maraoué River**, the park does, nonetheless, harbour various **antelope** species and different kinds of **monkeys**. The main *piste* leading off towards **Mont Saninlego** leads through a valley where you can sometimes spot **elephant** or **buffalo. Hippos** still live in the rivers.

The **park entrance** is at the village of Goazra, near **BOUAFLÉ**, 59km west of Yamoussoukro. The park has no accommodation, but you can sleep in Bouaflé at the *Campement Hôtel* (④), which has hot showers in the AC rooms and a good restaurant. For eating, the *Maquis du Centre* does good grilled fish. While in town, you can pick up an authorization to **camp** in the park at the *Eaux et Forêts* office, where you might be able to arrange a guide.

The road to the park from Yamoussoukro passes just south of the **Kossou Dam**, built where the White Bandama River joins the Maraoué (or Red Bandama). The hydroelectric dam created the nation's largest **lake**, which spreads, indented like an insect-eaten leaf, over 1700 shallow square kilometres, and which doubled the country's production of electricity when it opened in 1972. It also flooded numerous villages and displaced an estimated 100,000 people, most of whom were resettled in new towns. The paved road to Bouaflé passes near many of the sad concrete and aluminium villages which were built to replace the traditional settlements of local Baoulé fisherpeople and farmers by the *AVB* – the Bandama Valley Development Authority. In **KOSSOU**, you can stay at the **guest house** (①) of the national electrical company, the *EECI*, which has comfortable AC, S/C rooms, and a cantina.

Bouaké

The antithesis of Yamoussoukro, **BOUAKÉ** lacks glamour and a sense of overall planning. It has grown dramatically in the last fifty years, to become Côte d'Ivoire's **second**

largest city, with a population not far short of a million. As workers and traders from throughout the country flocked to this commercial crossroads on the major north–south route, neighbourhoods grew up willy-nilly, attaching themselves loosely to the districts laid out by the colonials. The diversity and dynamism of the peoples who've come together here make it an exciting place to visit, although the town is visually unappealing and there's admittedly not much to see. The highlight of any trip here is a visit to the **market** – one of the biggest and most colourful in the country.

Some history

Sometimes called the capital of the Baoulé country (a title which more accurately belongs to **Sakasso**, 42km southeast near the lake, where the successors to Baoulé **Queen Pokou** still reside), Bouaké was already an important commercial centre at the end of the nineteenth century when the French established a **military base**. It was used to launch attacks against the armies of **Almamy Samory Touré**, then sweeping into the region from the northwest. When Samory Touré finally surrendered at Guéoulé, the colonials once again sought to open up trade routes to the north. Bouaké soon regained prominence as a **centre for trade** in cloth, gold powder, indigo and tobacco.

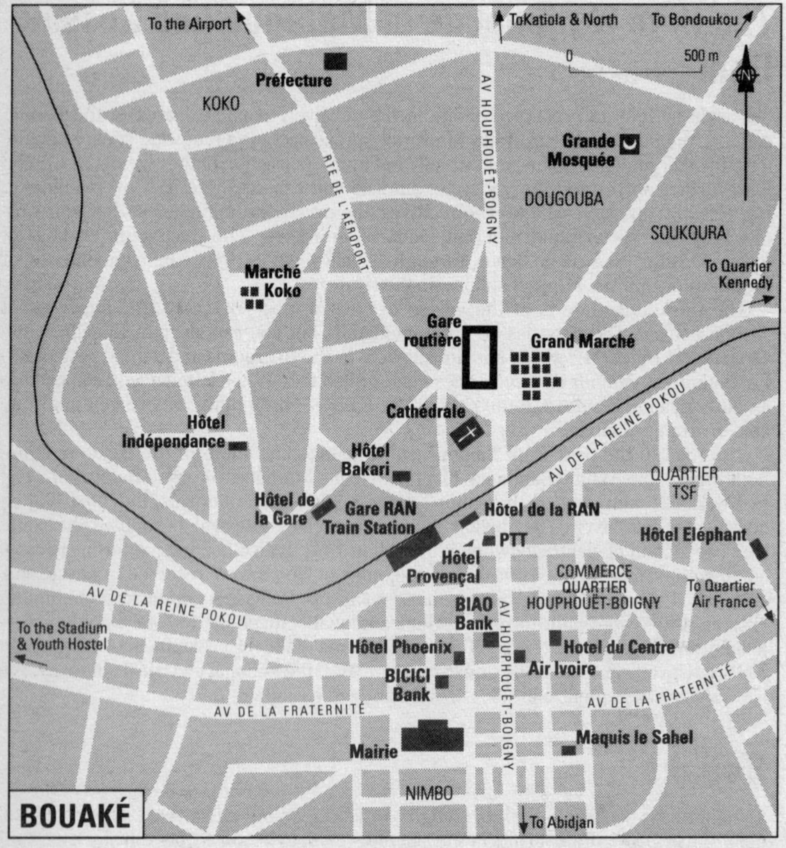

An added boost was given to commerce when the French brought the **railway** line up from Abidjan in 1912, eventually extending it all the way to Ouagadougou. That same year, **industry** was launched in the interior when a cotton seeding plant was opened in Bouaké. In 1919, Robert Gonfreville, a French agriculturalist, opened a textile factory – the first in Afrique Occidentale Française.

As maritime trade dwindled during World War II, the railway line took on added importance and Bouaké found itself in the centre of a wartime trade boom. The country's food supply rolled into this town – beef cattle from the Upper Volta, dried fish from Mali, rice from the western territories, peanuts and sheep from the north – from where it was redistributed to the regions. By the end of the war, the population had swelled beyond 25,000.

Since 1945, rural immigrants have continued to pour into Bouaké in search of work. Part of the influx was spurred by chronic rural dislocation caused by the building of the **Kossou Dam** in 1972. Though many people were resettled in villages specially created along the lake, many migrated to the towns. Today, Bouaké's wide **mix of people** includes Malinké and Sarakolé, Dyula (Dioula), Bamana, Senoufo and large numbers of Burkinabe. The original Baoulé inhabitants today only account for about a quarter of the total population.

The Town

Bouaké spreads confusingly in a thousand directions. The undisputed centre, however, is the **Commerce Quartier**, today known as the quartier Houphouët-Boigny. This is one of the oldest neighbourhoods in the modern town, which grew up between the **train station** and the **Mairie**. Here you'll find the **banks** (*BIAO*, *BICICI*), **post office** and administrative buildings. North of Commerce, the **gare routière** is located in the **Koko District**, a principally Baoulé quarter. Near the *gare routière* is one of the town's few buildings of monumental proportions, the **Saint-Michel Cathédrale**, built in a heavy modern style.

The market

Bouaké's expansive **market** spreads over three separate neighbourhoods east of Koko – **Dougouba** (site of the **grande mosquée**), **Soukoura** (also known as the quartier Dioula) and **TSF** (a residential area with large villas and shaded streets). This market is one of the most fascinating in Côte d'Ivoire and brings together over four thousand vendors from all parts of the country, guaranteeing the widest imaginable array of goods. A panoply of fruit, vegetables, cereals and spices from across the country comes together here: in season you'll find mangos from the north as available as pineapples from the south; palm oil as plentiful as *karité* butter; yams and other tubers as abundant as millet and corn. More intriguing than all this, and the sections full of hardware – everything from plastic wash bowls to handmade farming tools – are those devoted to a variety of locally made **crafts**. The Baoulé have a reputation for their **leather goods** especially snake- and lizard-skin bags and wallets (consider your conscience and be aware of import restrictions in Europe and elsewhere), but you'll also find a large selection of **jewellery** if you'd prefer to leave the reptiles in the bush. Also good value in Bouaké market are the intricate, hand-woven blankets, principally of Baoulé manufacture, but also in the distinctive styles of Agni and even Fula weavers.

Accommodation

Though Bouaké doesn't offer much in the luxury range, it has an excellent selection of moderately priced **hotels**. Overlanders will be pleased to find a **youth hostel** here (a real rarity in West Africa) and a couple of missions that sometimes take in travellers.

Budget accommodation

Auberge de la Jeunesse, near the stadium. Soft-sprung beds in communal rooms for four; showers and fans included. Recommended. Taxis to the centre are CFA100. ①.

Hôtel Bakari, Koko district (behind cathedral). Relatively cheap for the centre and not too run-down. Basic rooms with fan. ①.

Hôtel Eléphant, on the outskirts of the residential Air France district (☎63 25 24). Not bad value for AC rooms near the market. ②.

Hôtel de la Gare, near the train station. Great central location guarantees a lot of animation. S/C rooms not overly depressing. ①.

Hôtel Indépendance, Koko district. Basic accommodation, but friendly and good value. ①.

Hôtel Iroco, off av Houphouët-Boigny, Kamonikro district, in the north of Bouaké (☎63 34 95). A newer place, clean and well-run though far from the centre. S/C rooms with AC. ①–②.

Mission Catholique, Nimbo district on the Abidjan road. A very limited number of clean rooms in the *centre d'accueil*. ①.

Mid-range hotels

Hôtel de l'Aïr, rte de l'Aeroport (☎63 28 15). Twenty-two clean, comfortably furnished rooms with AC and bath. There's a good restaurant, too, but it's a taxi ride from the centre. ③.

Hôtel du Centre, Commerce (☎63 34 95). Rooms here come with AC and bath. The hotel has its own restaurant and nightclub, plus a crafts boutique. ③.

Hôtel Phoenix, rue du Commerce (☎63 17 27). A large, fully AC place in the heart of town with comfortable S/C rooms, some with TV. Popular terrace restaurant. ③.

Hôtel Provençal, Commerce, behind the PTT (☎63 34 59). Fifties-style hotel run by Belgians and conveniently located. Spacious and clean rooms with AC. The restaurant here is very good and the outdoor *terrasse* a nice place to come for a drink. ③.

RAN Hôtel, next to the train station (☎63 20 16). The town's classiest accommodation with 60 furnished rooms (TV, video, mini-bars). The *RAN* also has a popular restaurant and bar and Bouaké's best pool. ④.

Eating

Bouaké's **maquis** are some of the best and least expensive in the country, while the **Koko** district is probably the best place in town for great African food served in lively venues.

Chez Tanti Alpha, Quartier Nimbo. Huge outdoor *maquis* with healthy portions of *atieké* or *aloko* with grilled meats.

Maquis Le Sahel, off av Houphouët-Boigny, Quartier Nimbo. One of the centre's most popular places to eat with selections of "bush meat" (antelope or *agouti*), grilled chicken and fish, in an outdoor courtyard.

Le Poulet Show. Down the street from the *Sahel*, this restaurant does the town's best chicken, marinated and grilled to perfection.

La Terrace, av Houphouët-Boigny. Lebanese food including salads and *chawarma*.

MOVING ON FROM BOUAKÉ

Bouaké's **gare routière** is in the Koko district across from the market. **UTB coaches** and **taxis** head from here in all directions – Man, Abidjan, Korhogo, Odienné. For **Guinea** the *Régroupement de Transporteurs Africain de Côte d'Ivoire* (*RTACI*) runs a weekly bus service between Bouaké and Kankan, departing Friday at 4pm, arriving Saturday night or Sunday morning (around CFA20,000).

You can also go by **train**, daily, to Abidjan or Ferkessédougou (continuing to Ouagadougou).

Air Ivoire operates regular **flights** to Abidjan and other urban centres. If you're in a hurry – or suddenly get sick of the whole Ivoirian scene – weekly flights also link the town, at some considerable expense, with Ouagadougou, Bamako and Conakry. For flight information, contact *Bouaké Voyages* (☎63 34 91).

Katiola

Although small, **KATIOLA**, 50km north of Bouaké, enjoys fame throughout Côte d'Ivoire for its **pottery** – though it's a puzzle why the jugs and **canaries** made here should attract such attention when no one pays much mind to those produced elsewhere in the country. Chalk it up to a strange quirk of fate, but it's one that has drawn a lucrative **tourist trade** to the town – or at any rate capitalized on the traffic passing through.

The traditional jugs the women here turn out are, in truth, rather nice. They're almost perfectly symmetrical, but shaped without a wheel. The women smooth the surfaces with their hands and use a special tool to cut out ornamental motifs. If you want to watch them work these days, you're probably going to have to pay for it. Photos are extra and the price of the real thing – mainly sold through a co-operative – is downright expensive.

You can **stay** at the *Hôtel Hambol* (☎65 47 25; ②) – a modern place with African-style archways lining the facade. Rooms have AC and there's a good restaurant, swimming pool and nightclub. Less expensive accommodation can be found at the *Hôtel l'Amitié* (①), an affordable place in the town centre, or at the *Hôtel la Paillote* (①), with round bungalows in a quiet setting 2km outside town.

WESTERN CÔTE D'IVOIRE

The big attractions of **western Côte d'Ivoire** are high forest-strewn ridges and valleys, and the relatively intact traditional culture of the Dan (or Yacouba) speaking people. **Man** is the main town, while **Danané** – close to both Guinea and Liberia – comes a close second. **Touba** marks the northernmost fringes of the mountainous west before the road winds away from the last remaining peaks into the drier savannah lands that are the cultural domaine of the Malinké.

Although the main centres of the west are accessible enough at any time, the **rains** fall heavily in the region from March to October, and getting to some of the more out-of-the-way sites can be difficult. Lulls between showers provide fantastic conditions for photography, however; this is an area that needs clear air to be appreciated.

Daloa

The first western town you hit along the great central highway, **DALOA** is a good place to break your trip to Man. This is a coffee-growing area – which brings the district substantial wealth – and, although it doesn't figure much on the tour itineraries, Daloa is one of the country's oldest and most important towns, solid, well-planned and industrious.

Of the various **accommodation** options, *Les Ambassadeurs* (BP 754; ☎78 32 19; ③) is the most upmarket. Right on the *gare routière*, the comfortable and clean *Auberge de l'Ouest* (②) has some AC rooms. Cheaper is the *Hôtel C12* (①) with a nice restaurant-bar, or you can stay at either the *Collège Protestant* (near the *centre artisanal*; ①) or the *Mission Catholique* (①) across the street.

Man and around

MAN, a large commercial centre of some 60,000 people, is rather hideous – most of the appeal derives from its spectacular geographical setting. Often called the "town of eighteen peaks", it spreads over a valley with mountains rising up on all sides and from the end of its wide streets. There's something of an American feel here; there are

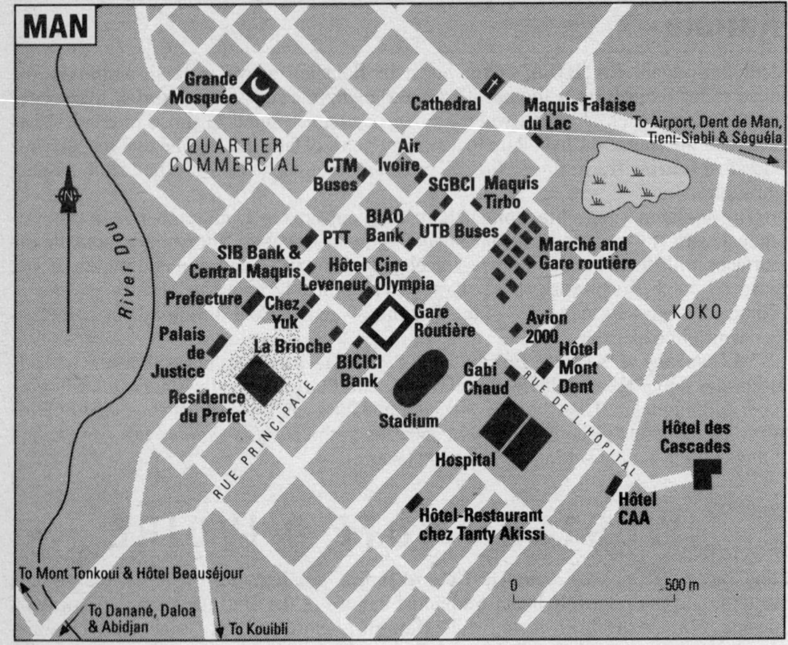

places in Colorado like Man and though the horizons inspire, the town itself is a muddled confusion of districts that leaves little impression. Still, it's lively enough, with much activity focusing around the market and adjoining *gare routière*.

It's best to use the town simply as a base for exploring the surrounding area; it consists of numerous districts, most of which you probably won't get the time to visit. The centre is occupied by the **quartier commercial**, where you'll find the large town **market** and the *gare routière*.

If you're interested in buying **masks** from the region, there's a wide selection sold on the upper level of the market along with numerous other crafts and a mass of musty fetish material. Nearby are countless shops and small businesses, and branches of the major **banks**, among which the *SGBCI* has in recent years been willing to change non-franc currencies.

On arrival in Man you're likely to be besieged by children offering their services as "guides", especially if you're driving. Many of the sites around town take a dim view of street children and will make life difficult for you if you are accompanied by one.

Practicalities

Man has a decent choice of **lodgings**, most of which are in the budget range, but there are also upmarket places with TV and pools. Lots of places near the market serve inexpensive food – there's not much in the way of upmarket African or European restaurants, but you'll find excellent cooking nonetheless.

Accommodation

Hôtel Beauséjour "Les Masques", rte de Mont Tonkoui, 3km from centre (☎79 09 91). Upmarket, popular place with bungalows (AC and TV) around an attractive courtyard. Smaller

THE MAN DISTRICT IN HISTORY

Hidden in the forests of the western mountains, the **Dan** (also known as Yacouba), lived in almost complete isolation after the beginning of their migration from the Guinea and Liberian regions in the fourteenth century. Other peoples of Côte d'Ivoire – the Akan, Senoufo and Malinké – had little contact with them, while the Europeans, who had been along the coast since the early 1700s, only made it to Man in 1897. It was largely the military victories of **Samory Touré** that drew the French to the region; they finally tracked down the most serious threat to their colonialist ambitions in 1898, capturing him in the village of Guéoulé, northwest of Man. They built a military post at Man in 1908 and used the town for regional administration.

DAN CULTURE

The Dan base their traditions and religion on a single God, **Zran**. Creator of the universe, Zran contains elements of both good and evil. Part of traditional education involves **secret societies**. After passing a first initiation, boys and girls enter these societies where they gain more profound religious instruction and learn to assume their adult roles. Members of the *gor*, for example, are charged with administering justice. They ultimately gain the power of turning themselves into animals, notably the leopard, in order to pass unnoticed as they survey the forces of good and evil at work in the community. **Masks** are important symbols in initiations and other ceremonies. Dan masks, unlike many others, characteristically have smooth, delicate lines and gentle, even sensual, human features. They're easily recognized and well known throughout the entire country.

Dance is another important element of Dan culture, and the region is famous for it. One of the most unusual is the **stilt dance** (Zekre Touli). Dressed in grass skirts and covered with cowrie shells, the masked performers make beguiling, inexplicable movements on stilts up to six metres high. Also impressive is the Menon or **juggling dance**. Young girls, about four years old, are specifically chosen for this dance and undergo a special two-year initiation. They live with the dance troupes and have no contact with their families until puberty. Their death-defying acrobatics include being tossed into the air to land on knife blades held by their adult partners. Such dances are performed in slightly sanitized form throughout the country and versions are frequently staged in large hotels.

non-AC rooms and camping available for budget travellers. Recommended, especially if you're driving. ④.

Hôtel CAA, off rue de l'Hôpital. Excellent location on top of a hill with views of the town and surrounding mountains. From this vantage point, Man looks almost attractive. Large cavern-like bar downstairs with cool stone walls and a maze of arches. High standards of cleanliness in S/C rooms with fan or AC. Great value and highly recommended. ②.

Hôtel des Cascades (BP 485; ☎79 02 51). Another hotel in a hill-top location, this three-star – Man's best – also commands a brilliant view of town and mountains. AC rooms overlook the swimming pool, gardens and tennis courts. ④.

Hôtel Leveneur, qtr commercial (☎79 00 39). Good mid-range hotel with clean AC rooms that come with TV. The French restaurant here is rated one of the town's best. Good value. ③.

Hôtel Mont Dent, rue de l'Hôpital. One of the town's least expensive places, near the market. Non-S/C rooms are very good value, and for just a bit more, you'll get a fan and your own toilet. Attractive courtyard, lively bar and relatively clean. ①.

Hôtel-Restaurant Chez Tanty Akissi, behind the stadium (☎79 04 78). Feels more like sharing a room in the Akissi family home than staying in a hotel, with cooking, washing and tressing in the courtyard. The restaurant is well known in town. ①.

Eating, drinking and nightlife

La Brioche, rue Principale across from the *gare routière*. Tasty cakes, *brioches* and ice cream on an outdoor terrace overlooking the *gare routière*. A good place for breakfast.

Central Maquis, qtr commercial, near the PTT. Drinks (no food) served in an outdoor courtyard. On Thurs and Sat there's a "rock club" where, for a small fee, you can learn the steps of the latest dances. Your chance to get in on the "*danses chocs pour gens chics*".

Chez Yuk, rue de l'Hôtel Leveneur. Excellent cheap food.

Gabi Chaud, rue de l'Hôpital. Tiny *maquis* with mudbrick oven easily seen from the street. One dish only, roasted pork with *atieké*, but they do it right. Numerous other inexpensive places line the same street; the popular *Maquis Avion 2000* is just around the corner.

Maquis Falaise du Lac, qtr du Lac. Unusual wall murals to complement unusual (and very inexpensive) dishes like *biche djoungblé* (deer with gombo sauce) or *kedjenou pintade*.

Maquis Tirbo, qtr commercial. One of the better-known inexpensive *maquis* featuring grilled fish smothered with cucumbers, tomatoes and onions. Beer, wine and a pleasant atmosphere. Across the street, the *Maquis Univers* is a bit pricier.

La Paillote, qtr commercial (☎79 08 82). Upmarket "*maquis*" run by the owner of the *Leveneur*. Fine French dining under a paillote of monumental proportions.

Resto-Chawarma, qtr commercial. Reasonably priced pizzas, pasta, hamburgers and salads. Everything from the mundane (sandwiches) to the unexpected (*lapin aux olives*).

MOVING ON FROM MAN

Several companies run **buses to Abidjan** assuring several daily departures via either Bouaké or Yamoussoukro. They are *UTB*, near the cathedral, *Les 18 Montagnes* at the *gare routière*, and *CTM* in the commercial district. Prices are competitive at around CFA3500. The bus for **Odienné** on the route to Bamako, has been discontinued, and for the meantime, taxis may be the only option. Enquire at the *gare routière*.

Peugeot 504s run north to **Touba** and south to **San-Pédro** (CFA5000), though the latter town is also covered by *UTB* buses. Heading west to **Guinea**, 504s go to Danané, whence a few taxis a day drive to Gbapleau (no shops or facilities). Going into **Liberia** from Man and Danané is not recommended.

Around Man

The bold, green mountain scenery around Man lends itself well to **day trips**. For some of the longer destinations, you'll need to go by car or taxi, but if you're feeling in shape, there are rewarding outings within hiking distance. Kids around town may approach you to offer their services as guides (some try to pass themselves off as representatives of the tourist office) and are generally quite helpful. To avoid bad feelings, come to an agreement on payment before you head off.

Some of the most popular excursions are outlined below. If you want more information, or are interested in organized tours, contact the *Délégation Régionale du Tourisme*, BP 613 Man (☎79 09 41).

The cascade

One of the easiest trips, and one you won't regret taking, is to the **cascade**, only 5km from the centre of Man along the road to Mont Tonkoui. You can drive almost the entire distance (you'll have to park nearby and walk down a steep footpath to the base of the falls), and it's perfectly feasible to hike. Depending on the mud levels, it won't take much over an hour, and the road winds its way through beautiful mountain scenery. The last stretch passes through a thick bamboo grove where the rush of the stream in the valley below can be heard but not seen through the greenery. Walk towards the top of the waterfall and continue until you see a painted sign indicating where you scale down the cliffs to the bottom of the falls. In full view for the first time, they're magnificent, with the white water crashing down a stair-like rock formation.

The **restaurant** at the base of the falls is run by the same owner as the popular *Paillote* in town. Though slightly expensive, the food is good and the setting – outdoor decks shaded by thick trees with the *cascade* thundering away behind you – is spectacular. Spanning the river near the restaurant is a **hanging bridge** – a copy of those for which the region is famous. Although real vines are woven into it, this one is supported by thick metal cables put in place by the French. From a distance it looks authentic enough for atmospheric photos, with the falls tumbling in the background.

Mont Tonkoui

Its name deriving from the Dan word *tonkpi*, meaning big mountain, **Mont Tonkoui** is the tallest mountain in Côte d'Ivoire. You can see it clearly from Man, its summit marked by an unsightly **television transmitter**. A *piste* leads northwest from town (the same tracks that pass the *cascade*) and continues about 20km to the mountain. The road winding its way up to the peak adds another 12km to the total distance. About two-thirds of the way to the top tracks lead off to a guest house – formerly the *villa du gouverneur* – used occasionally by visiting dignitaries. From here you get a magnificent panoramic view of the mountain chains and **thick forests** of the region. On a clear day, it's said you can see for 150km, beyond the **Nimba Mountains** on the Guinean border.

La Dent de Man

The bald rock formation of **La Dent de Man** rises, incisor-like, 12km northeast of Man. Aptly named, the "Tooth" is the most distinctive of the mountains visible from Man and is practically a town totem. Some say it has special protective powers – a spiritual sentinel watching over the townspeople. If you're without transport, take a taxi from town to the village of Glongouin, at the foot of the mountain. Here you can find a kid to lead you up the *dent*, guiding you through the maze of footpaths and, hopefully, finding the easiest way up the steep parts. It's a hard climb in areas – you'll get hot – but you don't have to be in spectacular shape to make it. The view from the top is worth the effort.

Tieni-Siabli and Fakobli

The village of **TIENI-SIABLI**, 14km east of Man, has become a common target for travellers, though there's nothing of essential interest. Tieni was the original settlement, built atop a cliff. Few of the old huts left on the hill are still lived in, and most of the inhabitants live below in the uninspiring new town of Siabli. To visit the dwellings on the hill, ask permission from the town chief. Authorization will cost.

Ten kilometres further down the same road, you arrive in **FAKOBLI**, a quiet town that lies at the foot of numerous mountains. A branch of the **Sassandra River** flows within a couple of kilometres, keeping the surrounding countryside especially green. Fakobli is best known as home of the *tematé* dance, performed by young girls around harvest time.

Biankouma, Zala and Touba

A paved road leads north of Man, cutting its way between the Dan and Toura mountain ranges and some of the region's most striking scenery. On first impressions, **BIANKOUMA** (47km from Man) is an unenticing *préfecture*, but away from the highway, the old town is an attractive collectivity of fifteen neighbourhoods, each with its protective *case à masques*, shrines and traditional round huts (CFA2000 is commonly demanded by the "village guide"). You can **stay** at the *Hôtel du Mont Sangbé* (①) which has modest S/C rooms and a good restaurant. Five kilometres west is the village of **Gouéssésso** where the owner of Man's *Hôtel Leveneur* has another of his string of regional hotels and restaurants, *Les Lianes de Guéssesso* (③). A *Club-Med* type resort, S/C, AC bungalows are built in a traditional fashion barely distinguishable from the village huts, with beautiful gardens around a lavish swimming pool and stunning views across the surrounding valley.

Further north, Touba was originally a Malinké town, founded in the 1870s by immigrants from Timbuktu. But the country here was Toura (people related to the Dan) before that, and the Toura, whose reputation as sorcerers has stayed with them, today live southeast of Touba, especially around the steep village of **Zala**. The tracks off the main highway stop abruptly at the village and to climb Mount Zala, you'll have to continue on foot, perhaps picking up a guide before proceeding. The pay-off is some of the best views in the entire country.

TOUBA is larger than Biankouma and has good accommodation along with other facilities like pharmacies, banks (no change), even a cinema. The most central **place to stay** is *L'Escale du Port* (☎70 70 63; ②) with comfortable AC rooms near the *petit marché*. Across the street is the more modest *Hôtel Savanne* (①), while closer to the *gare routière* on the rue de la Paix is another simple hotel, the *Belle Étoile* (①). The best accommodation in town, however, is in the south of town at the *Hôtel Le Mahou*, which has AC rooms, a restaurant and swimming pool (③).

Danané and around

If you arrive in Côte d'Ivoire from southeastern Guinea, **DANANÉ**, sprawling across a great valley, is likely to be your first stop. The **gare routière** for arrivals from the west is on the western side of town. Vehicles to Man, and on to other main towns in Côte d'Ivoire, leave from the other *gare* in the eastern quartier of Danané. On arrival from Guinea, ask your driver to drop you by the police station in the centre if possible. Here you need to get a *tampon* (stamp) from the *chef* to finish off your entry formalities. Don't go on to Man without it; you'll have to come back.

The best of the very few **places to stay** in town is the *Hôtel Tia Etienne* (①) – well out on the east side of town, but on the Man road, and only 500m from the *gare routière est*. It's a nice enough place, with simple S/C rooms (choice of AC or fan) and quite good meals for around CFA1500; arriving from either of Côte d'Ivoire's western neighbours, the prospect of so much comfort (including wine, and TV in the bar) seems positively over the top. Another good place is the *Maquis La Frontière* (①), on the road to the border, which has clean rooms with AC or fan. The bar and restaurant here are also good.

The liana bridges

So long as you have your own transport to get around, Danané's **liana bridges** are worth the trip: authentic old swinging constructions that span the Cavally River south of town at Drongouineau (15km), Lieupleu (26km) and Vatouo (30km), all off the main road to Toulépleu. Like those in Guinea and Liberia, considerable mystique attaches to these bridges (which also makes them paying attractions) and they're supposed to be reconstructed when necessary in a single night – something that women and outsiders are not allowed to witness. The bridges at **Lieupleu** and **Vatouo** are the easiest to visit by Peugeot 504 from Danané (you'll have to walk 4–5km from the main dirt road).

THE NORTH AND EAST

Northwestern Côte d'Ivoire is sparse, mostly flat country, yellow and dusty for eight months of the year. While **Odienné** may figure only as a night stop en route to or from Mali, it offers an unusual and beautiful route into Guinea via Beyla. More central, **Korhogo** is certainly worth a detour if you're heading up the country's main transport axis. You can jump train or bus at Ferkessédougou and spend a rewarding two or three days in the Senoufo country.

The **northeast**'s great attraction is the **Comoé National Park** – the largest in West Africa. For most travellers this is a fairly inaccessible reserve and doesn't always repay the expense and effort of getting there, though at the northwest corner there are opportunities for worthwhile, and just about affordable, **game-viewing trips** out of Kafolo. If you're travelling south from Burkina (or north from Abidjan), and you've some spare days, it's worth making a big loop through the northeast, calling in at the old Dyula capital of **Kong**, following the boundary of the park around its eastern side, and using an unusual back-country route through the Akan centres of **Bondoukou** and **Abengourou** – nice untouristy towns the pair of them. Or else you can cut across the border to Ghana at one of several frontier posts and make for Kumasi.

The far northeast is **Lobi country** and you'll see Lobi hunters, tracking in the bush with bows and hunting tackle. But the **Koulango**, whose language is close to Lobi, have long had a more settled farming lifestyle and are the *de facto* land holders in the region.

Eastern Côte d'Ivoire is the least touristy part of the country. The hilly central east, close to the Ghana border, is the heartland of the **Agni** and **Abron**, which, culturally and linguistically, have much in common with the Ashanti in Ghana.

Odienné

ODIENNÉ, an agricultural town of some 30,000 people, is the focus of the most scenic district in the northern grasslands. To the west, the **Dienguélé range** ripples over to the Guinean border. Another set of hills follows the road to Boundiali, peaking near Tiemé with **Mont Tougoukoli** which rises to over 800m. Although it's a historic town, Odienné has few reminders of the days when it was capital of the **Kabadougou Empire**, founded by the local hero Vakaba Touré, whose modest grave can still be seen on one of the town's main streets near the post office. In the 1970s Odienné was scheduled for radical **urbanization**, but the scheme only went far enough to give it an anonymous could-be-anywhere feeling. Though the old quarters were knocked down, the new city never came, and the former charm of the traditional houses and shady streets has long since been forgotten.

Despite the town's impressive **grande mosquée** – and the lively **market** with Dyula, Malinké and Bamana merchants from northern Côte d'Ivoire, Mali and Guinea – there's not much of interest in Odienné. But many travellers (and traders) on their way to or from Mali find it a good place to break the journey.

Some history

A Muslim fief, Odienné was originally founded by the Senoufo. But as early as the sixteenth century, Mande migrations had pushed all the way to Touba, and over the next two centuries their movements slowly displaced the Senoufo. Odienné remained in Senoufo control until the mid-eighteenth century, but eventually the native people were overwhelmed by the newcomers and made peace with the Malinké.

Soon after, the townships of **Samatiegla** and **Tiéma** became important Muslim centres along with Odienné. By the mid-nineteenth century, the town had also become a commercial stop on the **caravan routes** linking Bougouni (Mali) to Touba and Seguéla. Salt and horses from the north were traded here against gold and kola nuts from the south. And, as the town prospered, it grew to become the capital of a sizeable kingdom led by **Vakaba Touré**, who expanded his empire east to Boundiali. Vakaba's son, **Maagbé Mandou**, was later to marry one of the daughters of **Samory Touré**. Odienné thus became an important ally of Samory, whose hegemony extended over the town until it was captured by the French in 1893.

Practicalities

There's little choice when it comes to **places to stay** in Odienné; one of the best is the *Hôtel Les Frontières* (BP 135; ☎80 02 03; ③), a three-star hotel arranged in attractive S/C bungalows around a swimming pool and featuring one of the town's better restaurants. Closer to the *gare routière* you'll find the friendly, if basic *Hôtel Kao-Ka* (②), where rooms come with choice of AC or fan. Two options for those on a limited budget are the *Hotel le Refuge*, off the rte d'Abidjan (②), which although a little outside the centre is clean and does at least have running water, and the *Mission Catholique*, near the post office (①). Here you can stay in a tidy dorm, or in private S/C rooms.

As for **food**, the *Yankadi*, near the police station, does a good chicken *kedjenou*. You could run into northern-based expats here. Opposite the market, *La Bonne Auberge* is another popular *maquis* with rice and manioc dishes served with grilled beef or chicken. A little further afield, *La Villa* dishes up inexpensive food and salads, and more unusually for the region, ice cream.

If you're heading north, Odienné is a springboard **to Mali**. **Taxis** run to Bougouni, though the tracks are often bad. *Pistes* are well-maintained east as far as Korhogo where the tarmac to Abidjan begins. The road to Man is paved.

Boundiali

The short drive east from Odienné to **BOUNDIALI** passes through a hilly agricultural region before entering the flat plains of the **Senoufo country**. The town, whose name means "drum dried in the sun", was founded around the twelfth century by a Senoufo ancestor, a hunter named Nambaga Ganon. Eventually, it was incorporated into Vakaba Touré's empire, and it's said that René Caillié, the first explorer to be recognized for reaching Timbuktu and returning again to recount the tale, stayed here on his way to the "mysterious city".

The town has an attractive **hotel**, the *Dala* (BP 90; ☎82 00 41; ③), run collectively by a community association and laid out like a small village with comfortable S/C accommodation in round thatched huts. The venture has been quite successful at attracting tourism, with the villagers organizing events like dancing (troupes from throughout the region come to perform) and excursions. Less expensive accommodation is found in town at the *Hôtel Record* (①).

Korhogo

KORHOGO is capital of the Senoufo country, and the most touristy of Côte d'Ivoire's northern towns. It's famous for its rough, unusual, painted *toiles*, examples of which seem to hang in every hotel and expat home in the country. Fortunately there's more to the town and its district than this pretty, but somewhat debased, art form. **Senoufo culture** finds its firmest expression in the district and there's every possibility, if you make some effort to meet people, of witnessing some of the frequent ceremonial events that take place – worlds apart from what you might be served as after-dinner entertainment in some of the hotel lounges.

The Town

The **centre artisanal** (daily 8am–noon & 3–6.30pm) exhibits some of the best examples of Korhogo's crafts. To get there, head for the roundabout near the Préfecture and walk towards the **municipal pool**, from where you can already see the large conical thatching of the centre's rooftop. Inside, the wide selection of local artwork includes weaving, carving and basketry. The quality is strictly controlled and artists receive a take of the (non-negotiable) selling price.

You can get better buys, though, in the **Koko district**, where many craftsmen have workshops. Here you have to bargain the price of sculpted masks and wooden objects

THE PORO

Senoufo society is regulated by a process of **training** (sometimes called initiation) that may last an entire lifetime. Young men normally go through three phases of this training, known as **poro** (the same name as a similar institution found far to the west, especially in Sierra Leone), each of which lasts seven years. Girls go through an initial phase that ends when they get their first period. After their menopause, women are considered asexual and may begin the training again. If they live long enough, they become fully initiated.

Traditionally, the *poro* served as the basis of Senoufo government. Communities were led by elders who had reached the highest level of the training. These elders themselves chose the members of their ranks from the brightest and most talented initiates, thus ensuring that the governing body was composed of the most able leaders. Though effective, this system of ruling broke down somewhat when Malinké invasions sparked the need for village elders to relinquish some of their authority to a central chief – the most famous of which was **Gbon Coulibaly**.

But the initiation lived on and is today still practised throughout Senoufo country. Exactly what is learned during the seven-year cycles is unknown by outsiders, since it is a highly guarded **secret** considered vital to the survival of *poro* and thus to Senoufo society. In very general terms, initiates receive religious and professional education and learn about social obligations. Among other things, they learn to communicate in a special language. Part of the training takes place in the **sacred forest** in **Korhogo**.

Various stages in the initiation are marked by festivals – a sort of graduation ceremony. One of the better known is the **dance of the leopard-men**, celebrated after a group of initiates returns from the sacred forest having learned to master religious forces. Similar celebrations may mark a birth or a death, and since the whole community participates, the whole community takes part symbolically in the important stages of an individual's life. Many of these dances are now acted out in major regional hotels (the **Mont Korhogo** or, in Boundiali, at **Le Dala**). This may be your best shot at experiencing such an event (or at least a commercially staged version thereof), but if you stay any time in the region and get to know some people, it's not unrealistically difficult to accompany them to one of the celebrations. They leave a lasting impression.

and must be your own judge of the workmanship; it varies from good to shoddy. This district borders the fenced-off **fôret sacrée** – where *poro* initiates go through secret training (see above).

South of Koko, you'll see the **Grande Mosquée**, built in 1980 in a style similar to the mosque at Yamoussoukro. On Fridays, men turn out in large numbers for the afternoon prayer. And in the distance, the mountain looming up with its **sacrificial rocks** recalls a different religious tradition: in former days, when a chief died, his slaves were sacrificed on these rocks and he was buried on a bed of their skulls. You'll hear people insist that in remote villages the practice still continues.

Practicalities

Due to the large number of visitors, Korhogo has many services. You can **change money** at the *Société Générale*, the *BICICI* or the *Société Ivoirienne de Banques,* all located in the town centre. Sometimes, however, they have trouble getting current rates from Abidjan in which case they only change French francs.

If you haven't got transport, but want to visit some of the **surrounding villages** described on p.675, it's possible to do so by arranging an excursion through the **Délégation du Tourisme** (☎86 05 84), on the same roundabout as the Préfecture, who can arrange **car rental** or organized tours of the region. Private **tourist agencies** providing similar services are *Touraco Tours* and *Mory Voyages*, both in the *Hôtel Le*

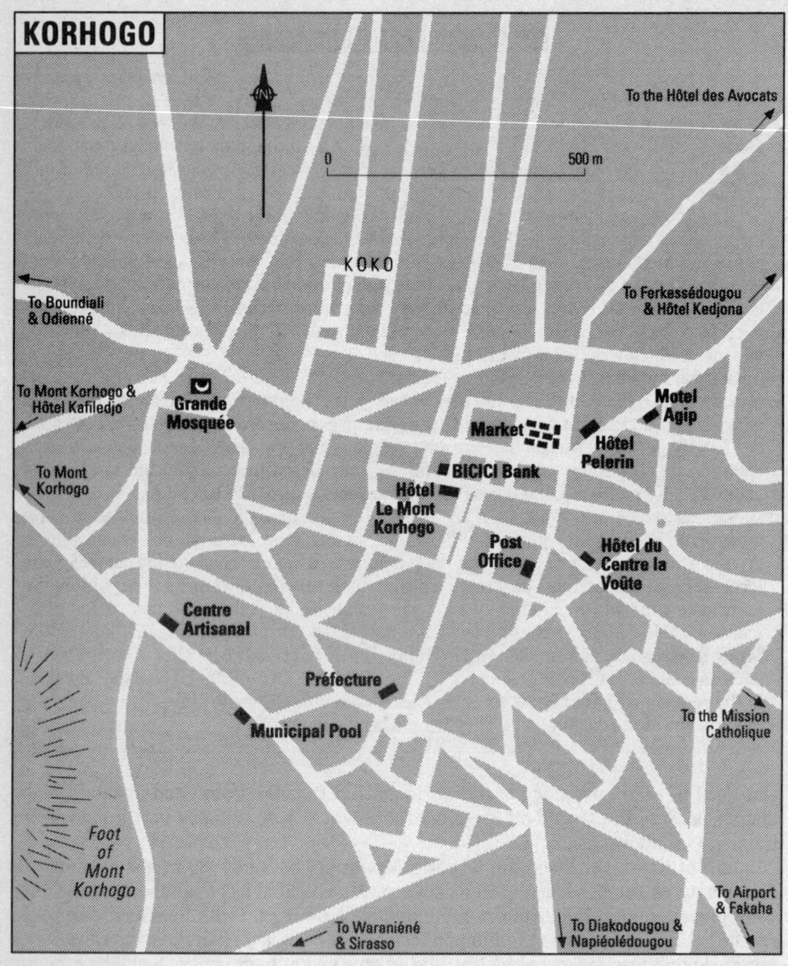

Mont Korhogo. *Air Ivoire* is represented at the *Hôtel Kedjona*, and has regular **flights** to Bouaké and Abidjan.

Accommodation

There's a wide **accommodation** choice in Korhogo, with hotels capable of handling large organized tours and individual backpackers on a budget.

Motel Agip, near the market, next to *Le Palmier* (☎86 01 13). One of the better bets in the medium price bracket and centrally located. It's a small place, with spotlessly clean rooms. The French restaurant here is one of the town's better eating places. ②.

Hôtel des Avocats, off rte de Ferké (☎86 05 69). Nicely furnished AC rooms and a pizza restaurant. A good find, though a bit far out. ②.

Motel du Centre la Voûte (☎86 08 56). Respectable S/C rooms with choice of fan or AC and a restaurant serving *chawarma*. ②.

Mission Catholique, southeast of the town centre. A limited number of well-kept rooms, with collective showers. Simple, but about the town's cheapest. ①.

Hôtel Kafiledjo, rte de Mont Korhogo (☎86 09 88). Near the foot of the mountain, this upmarket place has pleasant AC rooms, a pool, restaurant and bar. ③.

Hôtel Kedjona, rte de Ferké (☎86 03 64). Quiet garden setting for comfortable AC accommodation with pool. Popular *maquis* and *boîte*. ③.

Hôtel Le Mont Korhogo (BP 263; ☎86 04 00). The town's plushest, ideally located near the market – to which you may be dragged by one of the crafts vendors who sell their wares at the hotel entrance. S/C rooms with AC throughout. The hotel has a pool, restaurant and bar. ④.

Hôtel le Palmier, near the market. Popular with budget travellers due to the good location, friendly management and high standards of cleanliness. ①.

Hôtel Pelerin, near the market. A good buy in the budget range, with S/C rooms a cut above some of the other low-cost lodgings. ①.

Around Korhogo

Many of the crafts you see in town – at the *Mont Korhogo* hotel or the *centre artisanal* – are made in the surrounding villages, which make easy **day trips**. However, because it's a lot more interesting to see the artisans at work and was once less expensive to buy from them directly, in recent years the neighbouring villages have become suspiciously touristy and prices have risen to the point where you can probably find better buys in Korhogo itself from sellers undercutting each other.

One of the easiest villages to get to – and therefore one of the most visited – is **WARANIÉNÉ**, noted for its weavers (*tisserands*). Now, in addition to the rough handwoven cloth, you can buy embroidered tablecloths with matching napkins – one suspects tourism has affected local production. Waraniéné lies only 6km southwest of town on the road to Sirasso, close enough to take a taxi or even to try hitching if you've no other means of transport. You can **camp** in the gravel pit on the right just before you enter the village from Korhogo.

Other villages lie along the southern road which leads to Dikodougou. At Tioroniaradougou, turn left towards **Fakaha** (35km from Korhogo), where the *toiles peintes* seen all over Korhogo and, indeed, in markets throughout West Africa are produced. Originally these fabrics were made for costumes used in *poro* ceremonies and had geometric patterns – if you get the chance to go to a funeral or initiation, you'll still see dancers wearing them. Now, however, they're mostly made into wall hangings for tourists, and designs represent scenes from folklore and local legends; the colours are made from mud and vegetable dyes. Note that those in black and white retain their colours fairly well, but the multi-toned patterns fade almost immediately and the slightest moisture causes the dyes to run. Because of the demand, prices are steep. Taxis head here from Korhogo's *grand marché*. The nearby town of **Napiéolédougou** (Napié) also produces the same fabric.

Ferkessédougou

Whatever you do in **northeast Côte d'Ivoire**, you're likely to pass through **FERKESSÉDOUGOU**, an unexceptional road town, but nice enough. Ferké, as it's known, stretches a couple of dust-blown kilometres along the highway, with turnings west towards Korhogo and east to Comoé Park and Kong. The best time to come is for the **market on Thursday**, when all morning the 22-place lorries rumble in loaded with tomatoes, yams, hot peppers and whatever's in season. If you've come up by public transport from Abidjan, Ferké is about as far as you'll get in one day, and it's likely you'll have to stay the night.

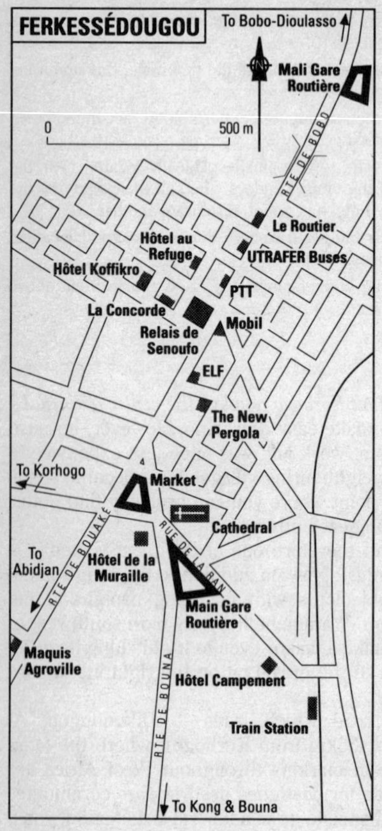

Incidentally, if you're **heading north** and have your own transport, it's worth mentioning here the lovely ancient little mosque at Kauara, 60km beyond Ferké. It's beyond **Ouangolodougou**, just off the road to the left and deserves a look.

Practicalities

Branches of the major **banks** line the rte de Bobo, but none will change travellers' cheques and even French franc notes could be difficult. The new **post office**, on the rte de Bobo, is useful for reliable but expensive international calling and faxing. On the same street, across from the *BICICI* bank, is the *Pharmacie de Ferké* and for serious medical problems, the *Hôpital Baptiste* has a good reputation.

If you arrive in Ferké by **train**, note that taxis don't serve the station after dark.

Accommodation

Auberge de la Réserve, rte de Bouaké, 2km south of the centre (☎88 01 85). A very comfortable S/C, AC place with an interesting menu if you want to splurge. A shame the pool is such an unappetizing lurid green. ③.

Hôtel Campement, opposite the train station. Basic, gloomy non-S/C rooms with fan. Though you can certainly do better in town, this may be your only option if your train arrives late. ①.

Hôtel Koffikro, off rte de Bobo, near *BICICI* bank. Down a small street bathed in the shade of mango trees, this place has simple S/C rooms around a courtyard. Friendly and good value. ①.

Hôtel de la Muraille, rue de la RAN. Inexpensive S/C rooms that are good value if unexceptional. Right next to the *gare routière est*. ①.

Hôtel La Paillote, off rte de Bobo. Curious outcropping of traditional-style round huts (fully AC) with thatched roofs. Pleasant garden and calm setting. ②.

Hôtel Refuge, off rte de Bobo, behind *Shell*. A satellite disc dominates the otherwise plain courtyard. Very reasonable AC, S/C rooms with round beds and TV. The best option in the centre. ③.

Relais de Senoufo, directly behind *Shell*. The entrance looks posh, with bright cushions on the armchairs and Korhogo prints on the wall, but the tidy S/C rooms (choice of AC or fan) are good value. Friendly staff can give information on visiting Comoé National Park and the surrounding region, and you may even hook up with a guide. ③.

Eating and drinking

La Concorde, off rte de Bobo, behind the *Relais de Senoufo*. Rather spiffy tables in a large shaded courtyard. Popular watering hole, and they serve meals too.

Maquis Agroville (*Chez Germain*), rte de Bouaké. A straw screen fences off this backyard restaurant where chickens scratch around the outdoor *paillotes*. Wild boar and rabbit smoked on the premises and grilled to taste.

Restaurant-bar Le Routier, rte de Bobo. Chicken or steak with chips or very cheap *riz-gras*.

Super Maquis "The New Pergola", rte de Bobo near *Elf*. Chicken with *foutou* or rice in courtyard with *paillote*. Good grilled fish.

Nightlife

Of the few **clubs** worth mentioning, the *Djeby,* which adjoins the *Concorde* restaurant, is the most popular. Stiff competition is provided by the newer *Le Millionaire* off the main road near the market. Both places have a cover of about CFA1000. Less expensive entertainment can be had at the new *Motel Opera*, rue de la RAN, near the intersection with rte de Bobo, which is busy most nights and especially at the weekends (no cover).

MOVING ON FROM FERKÉSSEDOUGOU

On the rte de Bobo, *UTRAFER* has clean and reliable **buses** to Abidjan (CFA3500) and Bouaké (CFA2500) with daily departures at 8pm. They also run Peugeot 504s to Bobo (CFA4000) and Ouaga (CFA8000). The **train** is less expensive (at least the one heading north), with a daily departure in each direction at around 8.30pm – though it's often late.

The **gare routière est et Abidjan** is on the rue de la RAN near the cathedral (look for the spires). Here you'll find taxis to Abidjan, Ouaga and Bobo in addition to daily transport to Kong (CFA1200) and Kafolo/Bouna (CFA2500/4500). Further out, on the rte de Bobo, the *gare routière* for **Mali** has minibuses direct to Sikosso (CFA3500) via Ouangolodougou.

Kong

Known and visited for its old Sudanic mosques – sloping *banco* walls on a wooden frame with characteristic protruding joists – **KONG** is worth a side trip from Ferkessédougou especially if you've not seen the much more impressive architecture in Mali. It's not on the way to anywhere else; occasional vehicles come up from some of the Djimini Senoufo villages to the south (from Dabakala, for example), but this means a diversion in any case; and several times a week something goes from Kong to Kafolo, up on the main Ferké–Bouna northeast axis.

Otherwise you're pretty much limited to one or two vehicles a day from Ferké, and the same back again. This isn't a bad trip (3hr), with a foretaste of Kong's architecture at Nafana, 22km before it. But you'll see some of the poorest villages in Côte d'Ivoire around here and, at the end of the dry season, when the granaries, like giant egg-cups are empty, you come face to face with the awful downside of the country's economic "miracle" – serious malnourishment. The people here are suffering partly as a result of wildlife conservation policies which have ignored their needs – they depend upon hunting to survive, and much of the local game is now protected in the Comoé Park.

The Town

Once prevalent, **"guides"** nowadays rarely approach the few visitors who make it to Kong. They're hardly needed in any case, as all there is to see is standing before you. The large **Friday mosque** dates from the seventeenth century (though most of it was rebuilt in 1905 after its destruction by Samory Touré) and the smaller one to the south, behind the houses on the main square, from the fourteenth. This latter has white painted coconuts on its turrets which you'll be told are ostrich eggs from Mecca. Both are impressive enough relics in an environment largely devoid of monuments, but neither is accessible to non-Muslims.

THE KINGDOM OF KONG

The town of **Kong** was founded, probably in the twelfth or thirteenth century, by Voltaic-speaking ancestors of the Senoufo, but was relatively unimportant until its commercial invasion by Muslim Mande-speaking **Dyula merchants** at the end of the seventeenth century. Islamic scholarship followed in the footsteps of mercantile success, and the town became the capital of a **trading empire** that stretched south and east to the Baoulé- and Akan-speaking farmers of the hills and north to the edge of Ségou's domain near the Niger River, while the **mosques and Koranic institute** extended its reputation. But, although the Dyula exerted a powerful influence in Kong, it was another hundred years before **Sekou Ouattara**, chief of one of the most influential Dyula families, seized power in a bloody coup directed against the ruling **Falafala-Senoufo** incumbents. The new kings of Kong were constantly in dispute with the Bamana of Ségou and the peoples of the south. As a political entity, Kong ceased to have much cohesion by the early nineteenth century. But it was still a prestigious centre as late as 1897, when Samory Touré swept in – and then moved on having all but destroyed the town in his scorched-earth flight from the French.

The other sites are really hardly worth bothering about. There's the rubbish-strewn grave of a certain **Voyageur Moskowitz** who succumbed here in 1894 while on Marchand's expedition, and the **Maison du Binger**, of dubious authenticity, which stands in ruin some way off as memorial to the French expansionist who based himself in Kong for a while in 1889.

If you end up **spending the night**, there are basic S/C chalet rooms at the *campement*, which is straight down the road through town about 800m and then up on the left (①). Food and drink is concentrated up by the town centre: pay a visit to the *Kiosque Patience*, on the street towards Ferké.

Parc National de la Comoé

The **Parc National de la Comoé** is the largest in West Africa – 11,500 square kilometres of rolling, tse-tse-plagued savannah and bush with patches of forest in the south. As late as the 1950s colonial maps marked the region "uninhabited". While this wasn't quite true (the Lobi and Koulango hunted and planted there, and continue to do so despite the rangers), it's basically wild animal territory. And the animals know it.

The main feature of the park (which is also known as the **Réserve de Bouna**) is the broad and twisting **Comoé River**, flanked by stretches of riverine forest. Seasonal streams flow in from the north and the generous scattering of lakes and pools across the park provides animal-viewing targets in the dry season. The zones to concentrate on are westwards; the eastern borders of the park are included more as a buffer against human encroachment than as recommended game country.

Visiting the park

The park is generally **open** from December to the end of May (but check in Ferké, Katiola or Bondoukou before setting off, just in case). **Entry** (CFA2000 per person per day) in the north is through Kafolo or Ouango Fitini, in the south Gansé or Kakpin, and in the east Bania.

The most enjoyable way to see Comoé is from a **private car**, with a ranger on board to navigate and scan for wildlife. There are no facilities inside the park, so you need to plan ahead to avoid re-tracing your route, or else aim to cross the park, most rewardingly north to south (or south to north). While the east may be worth exploring at the beginning of the park season, when the animals are dispersed, if you're here after the end of January you're best advised to stay fairly close to the main river.

If you've **no transport**, Kafolo is the place to head for. The visit is still likely to cost you dear, but there are one or two money-saving devices.

Kafolo

KAFOLO is hard by the Comoé bridge right on the park boundary. You can **stay** at the *Comoé Safari Lodge* (Dec–May only; ④); pretty good, with cool, pyramid-shaped rooms, a fine swimming pool and some imaginative, if expensive, cooking (including homemade bread). The construction of the lodge disturbed some old middens: you can find pots and other scraps of domestic Lobi life all around the perimeter. There might be less expensive accommodation at the *Maquis Chez M le Maire,* which has been known to put up travellers in rustic *chambres de passage*-type rooms (①). Kafolo has a few **snack and chop sellers** where your food may well come wrapped in the chits you signed at the lodge.

Subject to four or more takers, **game-drives** round the northwestern corner of the park run from Kafolo every morning (CFA10,000). What you see is very dependent on luck, but on a good run you should see buffalo and elephants and possibly lions. Hippos are nearly guaranteed (afternoon *pirogue* rides, arranged in the lodge, afford the best opportunities to get close up). At the very least there'll be antelope (great numbers of hartebeest), warthogs and monkeys. Persuade the driver to make a diversion to **Lake Dalandjougou** – a major dry season watering place. You'll be out from 6am until at least 11am, so take fluids and something to eat.

If you're travelling without a car, you may well strike lucky anyway and get a free lift into the park. They don't see many backpackers out here, and there's at least a good chance of a ride out again with tourists or a tour group.

Gansé and Kakpin

On the southwest perimeter of the park, **GANSÉ** and nearby **KAKPIN** are not at all easy to get to without your own vehicle. Access from the southeast is from Bondoukou, (see p.681) some 170km away, and from the southwest from Bouaké (180km; see p.661) or, with less *piste*, Katiola (160km; see p.665).

The big draw in the 150 square kilometres of bush and forest between Kakpin, Gansé and the river (known as **"Kakpin trianglé"**), is the singular presence of **lions**. There's a good network of tracks here, too. You need sharp eyes, binoculars and patience. Keep stopping to scan around (remember to look behind you) and take notice of the behaviour of prey animals like hartebeest and warthog.

Kakpin's **accommodation** is a simple *campement* (①), with S/C huts and a sometime bar-restaurant. Gansé has the *Comoé Sogetel* (④), an all-in lodge along the same lines as *Comoé Safari Lodge* and similarly priced, but styled, with cubist abandon, on local architecture. Recent reports suggest it has closed indefinitely.

The Lobi country and Bouna

In Côte d'Ivoire, **traditional Lobi territory** begins somewhere along the road from Ferkessédougou towards the Parc National de la Comoé (the people and their culture are covered in more depth in the Burkina Faso chapter). Until you reach Kafolo, however, you won't see any Lobi compounds, as the whole area is part of the Muslim domain of Kong. The easiest way to get an impression of Lobi life is to take an excursion from *Comoé Safari Lodge* up the road to **Bolé** village. The market here (on a five-day cycle) is a gathering place for a wonderful diversity of people (mostly women) who come to buy and sell. Among the Dyula, Koulango and Senoufo, you'll even meet a few Fula women – though perhaps not all year round.

But the chief purpose of the *Safari Lodge*'s four-hour *Tour Lobi* (CFA8000) is a visit to a compound – a *soukala* – on the way to Bolé, usually one where the guide has friends or family; the chance to look around the organically sculpted, rectangular, mud-built houses around a central courtyard; and the opportunity to meet some Lobi people – including elderly ladies who dutifully arrive, lip plugs in place, to sit and be photographed. You get to poke around in private homes and climb up notched tree trunks on to the roof terraces. The whole event reeks of forced welcomes, and the impression of smiling tourists hurling sweets at the naked children through the windows of the minibus (an established ritual) is hard to stomach. Nevertheless, if you're not set up for independent travel well off the beaten track between Kafolo and Bouna (the Lobi heartland), then the tour is probably worthwhile. Take a Polaroid camera if you can.

The **heartland of the Lobi region** in Côte d'Ivoire (their main districts are in Burkina) lies to the north of the Bouna road. At the park ranger post at **Téhini** (Monday market), try for a vehicle on a Wednesday, or early Thursday morning up to **Doropo**, whose Thursday market and location on a crossroads close to the Burkinabe border make it a major rural centre. It's a surprisingly active town, especially at weekends when the open-air bar on the main street jumps to the sounds of highlife. At the opposite end of the street, the *Restaurant Sénégalais* serves decent food and has *chambres de passage* (①).

The time to get the most out of a trip up here would be during the **Djoro** – the moveable initiation of boys to men which takes place every six to ten years for all the uninitiated boys who are big enough to stand the rigours. The rites of passage are fairly secret, but there's no mystery about the celebration that concludes them, when the boys return home decked in cowrie-covered costumes.

Bouna and beyond

Originally a Lobi town, **BOUNA** is nowadays a workaday mixture of Koulango, Dyula and administrators from the south. It lacks a strong ethnic or religious identity: the *Eglise Baptiste* is a stone's throw from the mosque and fetishes of the market; rows of cinderblock houses topped with corrugated metal bear the stamp of an anonymous crossroads. Bouna suffers and benefits from being the country's remotest outpost. Chokingly dusty in the dry season and so muddy in the wet it's almost cut off, it has never quite recovered from the savagery of Samory Touré's full frontal assault in 1892.

Today it's a garrison town and capital of the country's biggest *département*. Bush taxis pull into the central square surrounded by single-storey shops and **gargotes** such as *Au Sable*, which serves beer until the last vehicle of the night pulls in from Ferké. For **accommodation**, the inexpensive *Hôtel Eléphant*, 100m from the *gare routière*, has clean and fresh rooms with optional AC and S/C (①). Slightly upmarket, the *Hôtel La Réserve* (②) is over by the market, and easily distinguished by its pseudo-Sudanic tower. Rooms are clean and comfortable with AC throughout. The town's only **nightclub** is here, only open on Saturdays and holidays. The hotel also has a *maquis* that will prepare food if given advance warning. Bouna's permanent **market** is busy and interesting, spilling over with unusual trinketry and magical paraphernalia as well as the usual pots and pans and a rather limited selection of fruit and vegetables (seasonal commodities this far north).

If you're staying for a day, there are some particularly good examples of Lobi architecture at **POUON**, 18km northeast of Bouna. You should be able to get transport there several times a week, or charter a taxi. But you won't make it across the Koulda River (tributary of the Volta Noire) in the rainy season – and even if you do, you might not get back again.

South from Bouna, the road along the eastern boundary of the Comoé park (transport to Bondoukou mornings and afternoons for around CFA3000) passes through desolate regions cleared of human inhabitants. Run-down and abandoned Lobi *soukalas* seem to indicate mass migration or expulsion – or maybe, in the dry season, simply that people are away on Lobi business. Traditionally the Lobi were quite nomadic, returning to their homesteads only periodically. Between the park ranger posts at Bania and Kotouba, however, the road tracks dustily through wild bush, with never a compound.

Continuing south, the desolation of the far northeast is left behind. Beyond the village of Saleye, the land begins to rise and the road passes through fine, hilly forest and dense cultivation on the approach to Bondoukou. On the east side of the road, some 10km beyond **Yézimala**, a group of impressive **Abron tombs**, inhabited by life-size plaster figures, signals the start of a new cultural zone. If you're coming in by public transport, Bondoukou's northside *gare routière* is just a few minutes beyond here.

Bondoukou and around

Set amid rising hills which hint at the forests further south, **BONDOUKOU** has a distinctive flavour, a long-established centre of Islamic studies with an old Koranic university and now some forty mosques. The town also has a heavy Ghanaian population, who, along with the culturally related Abron community, help to knock off some of the Ivoirian brashness and also provide strong alternative religious counterpoints to the town's Islam. Despite its dust (or mud) and a real shortage of decent places to stay, it's a likeable town and worth a day or two, especially as a base for making several worthwhile **short excursions** to the surrounding countryside.

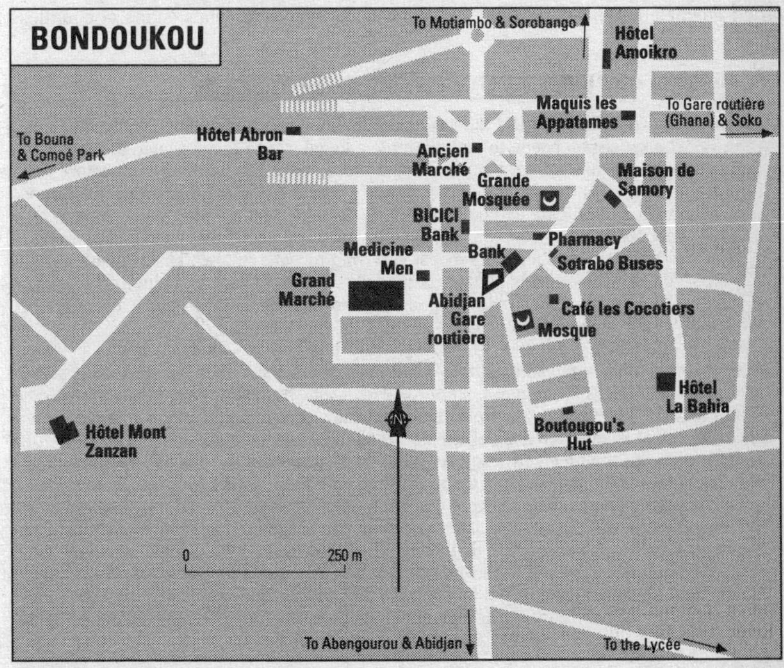

The Town

Architecturally, Bondoukou's most striking attribute is the exotically pink **Ancien Marché** building, in the centre of town and visible all the way up the approach road from Abidjan. Its appearance belies its history, however; built in the colonial *style soudanais* by the French in 1952, it served briefly as a civic museum, before the collection was moved to Abidjan, and now no one seems to know what to do with the building. They do have dance performances here periodically.

More authentic is the **Maison de Samory** (yet another) – not actually one of the leader's abodes, but it was inhabited by a fellow Touré. It has a massive, fortress-like appearance and a flat roof, reached up a flight of steep stairs (watch your step). Below, in the street, **metal workers** turn out bracelets and rings for local consumption – painstaking and surprisingly earnest labour.

Another surviving historical fragment is the hut of **Goudougou** or Boutougou, the Lobi or Loron-Koulango hunter and semi-mythical founder of Bondoukou. The hut, according to Bondoukou civic tradition, has been preserved to this day; a curious mud *case* in a large fenced compound down below the Abidjan *gare routière*.

The market

The best day to visit Bondoukou's **Grand Marché** is Sunday, when people come from the dozens of farming villages in the hills around. For the rest of the week the market, though imposing in its purpose-built two-storey hall, is like any other, except that, unusually for West Africa, it's full of the most amazing selection of secondhand clothes.

Nearby, traditional "pharmacists" (**medicine men** is probably a fair term) stand at stalls overflowing with a cornucopia of python skins, baby crocodile and viper heads, dried chameleons, baboons' feet, shrivelled bats, hyenas' genitals, skins of countless

BONDOUKOU IN HISTORY

Whatever the real date of the first settlement in Bondoukou (probably in the fifteenth century), the **mosques** began to be built quite a lot later with the arrival in the 1800s of Mande-speaking Dyula from the north. Few of those you see today were built before the turn of this century and many have gone up since World War II, as the town's **old quarters**, each with its own **gate** and built entirely in the style of the Touré house, have been progressively replaced by concrete and *tôle* (at one time, there was even a cloth-dyers' quarter, with dye pits and all). The oldest surviving mosque in town has a square minaret, a portion of which stands behind its modern-day descendant in a slumped lateritic pyramid, like a termite hill. This relic goes back to the nineteenth century and may be the last of the mosques of the Dyula era.

Also in the nineteenth century, Akan-speaking people – the **Abron** – began arriving from the east. With some administrative and military efficiency they succeeded in establishing themselves as the region's overlords. Unusually, however, many families adopted **Islam** and the language of the Koulango inhabitants and, today, the Abron kingdom is one of the most Islamicized and deracinated of all the Akan societies.

By the end of the nineteeth century, **King Ardjoumani** of the Abron was in contact with the rulers of the British Gold Coast (flushed with their victory over the Asante – see p.000). But the French, as usual, were quicker to take the initiative, and they entered into agreement with the Abron and later annexed the kingdom for France. Meanwhile, **Samory Touré**'s gale-force transit through Bondoukou in 1895 largely wrecked the district's economic stability; thousands of families fled east and south out of his way. Bondoukou never fully recovered its pre-eminent position, and was left in the economic wilderness by its proximity to the British frontier and by the new **railway**, which had reached as far as Bouaké by 1912 and which sucked trade away.

small mammals, turtle shells, bones, tails, tufts, feathers and beaks; and then leather *gri-gris*, amulets, bracelets, beads, bark, fibres, stones, crystals and powders. They even have old British coins (Victorian shillings, for example) from Gold Coast days. These traders rarely speak French, and bargaining with tourists isn't their strong point.

Practicalities

Gares routières for the north and for Ghana are several kilometres out of the town centre; take an orange taxi. Vehicles coming in from Abidjan and the south, however, will stop at the *gare routière* or the *Sotrabo* bus station right in the middle of town.

Accommodation options are strictly limited, especially since the landmark *Hôtel Mont Zanzan* closed down. In town, the budget choice seems to rest between two basic *chambres de passage, La Bahia* (①) and the *Hôtel Abron Bar* (①). The former is almost respectable, but note that the AC rooms are scruffier than the simple ventilated ones and the place is a real thrash at weekends. As for the *Abron Bar*, it's pretty dismal as the sign on front, "Entrée Interdite aux Mineurs", indicates, but it is at least centrally located and cheap (①). For a more comfortable night, the *Hôtel Amoikro*, out of town on the rte de Sorobango, is a decent place with S/C, AC rooms, bar and restaurant (BP 184; ☎92 53 80; ②).

As for **eating**, Bondoukou offers plenty of street food, but nothing more sophisticated for a sit-down meal than a clutch of *maquis*. The best of the bunch are *Les Appatames*, set in a large garden with excellent grilled chicken and *kedjenou*, and, a bit further out, *Le Lys*, on the rte d'Abidjan, opposite the *lycée*. At breakfast time, the *Café Les Cocotiers* near the Abidjan *gare routière* does bread and generous bowls of coffee.

Around Bondoukou

Most famous of the many sights clustered around Bondoukou is the village of **SOKO**, right on the Ghanaian border, 8km from town. Soko is a **monkey village**, where the local vervets are especially tame and demanding; harmed – let alone eaten – by nobody. The story goes that in 1895, with Samory's forces ransacking the district, the people of Soko turned to their fetish priest for help. He transformed them into monkeys but he himself was killed by the invaders and the monkeys were powerless to become humans again. Tradition requires that the people of Soko now treat the monkeys as their relatives. It's interesting to guess at how such a story came to be invented: the likeliest explanation is that most of the inhabitants fled the village, or were killed or sold into slavery, and the pride of survivors demanded an alternative explanation.

Take your passport to Soko, as you may have to go through part of the border control. Take some food for the monkeys, too, and try to come early in the morning, before the monkeys retreat to the forest to hide through the heat of the day. The whole place has become a bit gimmicky of late: if you're asked for lots of money to take pictures or even to wander around, simply refuse and head to the *M'Gourou Bar* at the entrance to town, where sometimes the monkeys wander into the courtyard anyhow.

Northeast from Bondoukou, **MOTIAMBO** (8km on the Sorobango road, turn right at the "lion house") is a good village to visit if you're after local pottery. The technique is the great thing; work is done by hand, not on a wheel, and they **dance** around the work to fashion it. Potting is generally done on Wednesday and Thursday and firing on Friday in time for Bondoukou's Sunday market. If you go on to **SOROBANGO** (29km from Bondoukou), you'll find more potters, Koulango weavers, an old mosque and (somewhere) plates embedded in the walls – an Islamic style rarely found in this part of Africa.

Akan country: Abengourou and beyond

The route from Bondoukou to Abengourou is along a brilliant, twisting forest road studded with the amazing figurative **Akan tombs**. There's a fine set down on the left of the road (beyond a cemetery on the right) as you leave the village of **Aprompronou**, 25km south of Agnibilekrou.

Abengourou

ABENGOUROU is solidly Akan – both culturally and linguistically. Royal capital of the **Agni** kingdom of **Indénié**, it's of the south, firmly engaged with metropolitan Côte d'Ivoire, and, if you've come from sparser northern regions, offers a first taste of a big Ivoirian town.

The Agni left the Akan homeland around Kumasi in the eighteenth century and moved west to set up a new community with its capital at Zaranou, 40km to the south of the present site. Abengourou seems to have been established by a part of the royal family about a hundred years ago in a zone of good hunting country they named **N'pekro** ("I don't like chatter") for its tranquillity, from which the present name was Frenchified.

Orientation

The town spreads widely, though its heart is compact, with many of the restaurants and most other commerce on the main paved street, **rue Principale**, which runs from the water tower to the market. **Banks** are on the east end of this street; the *BIAO* is the best hope for changing non-franc currencies, and even then you'd be amazingly lucky if they have the current rates.

Accommodation

Hôtel Forêt, rue Principale (☎51 36 16). Central location and very decent standards, some rooms with balconies overlooking the action. AC optional. ②.

Hôtel Goma, rte de Bondoukou by the *gare routière* (☎91 34 74). New and upmarket with AC rooms including TV and video. Good restaurant. ③.

Hôtel Relais Agni, rte d'Abidjan (BP 322; ☎91 35 75). The town's best value, with very friendly staff and large AC rooms. ②.

Hôtel le Relief, 200m south of rue Principale, Dioulokro (☎91 36 32). Actually respectable, though very cheap S/C rooms with fan or AC. ①.

The Town

Abengourou's **market** is great, a (never threatening) warren of tight-packed stalls and dark alleys and masses of possibilities if you're looking for crafts and locally manufactured items – from the smallest size of **daba** (digging hoe) forged virtually before your eyes to children's play-kitchen sets made of old tuna cans, and very inexpensive leatherwork.

Nearby, the **royal palace** (built 1883, restored 1988), a big oblong villa with wooden balconies running right round, isn't a remarkable sight. The large courtyard in front, however, is the scene of serious ritual and festivity each year in December or January, when the **Yam Festival** (*la fête des ignames*) takes place and astonishing quantities of gold and finery are on display. You may be able to arrange an audience with the king, though he's very old and frail now. Make an appointment, dress as smartly as possible, and take something as a gift: postcards of other royal families seem appropriate and welcome, but a bottle of Scotch goes down just as well. The best time for an audience is usually between noon and 3pm.

Another site of interest is the **museum/art gallery** (Mon–Sat 8am–noon & 3–6pm, Sun 8am–2pm), which has ambitions to be a regional showcase. However, the banality of putting masks and statues around a room strikes forcibly. Out of context they lose most of their meaning, and many of the pieces are in urgent need of woodworm treatment. Most interesting of the ethnographia are the Senoufo crime-detection statuettes with headdresses and swivelling arms for seeking out culprits, though it's not quite clear how they worked.

Eating

The best option for good street **food** is the endless string of *maquis* behind the water tower. Take your pick from the array of stalls for *foutou*, *atieké* or rice. For something fancier, head to the *Café Idéal* on the rue Principale where they serve sandwiches and salads or more substantial meals with chicken. Another step up is the highly recommended *Cave des Rois* (☎91 37 28), a large *maquis* with colourful wall murals and indoor or outdoor eating. The *poisson braisé* is great, and the **nightclub** among the town's best.

South from Abengourou

Several companies have scheduled bus departures **to Abidjan** all day from the rue Principale (4hr). Having bought your ticket, you can sit in a waiting room with a television for the next departure.

Since the road was tarmacked, the **alternative route**, via Aboisso, is no longer much used except by local traffic. But if you make an early start from Abengourou, this dirt road, which stays on the east side of the Comoé close to the Ghanaian border, feaures some exciting jungle scenery. You could stop off at the old Indénié capital of **ZARANOU**, where there's a small museum originally conceived as a memorial to Binger, who spent a total of three years here.

The nice little town of **ABOISSO** itself – site of France's earliest (late seventeenth century) base in the country – is also worth a stay. **KRINJABO**, 9km south of Aboisso on the Bia lagoon, is the capital of another Agni kingdom, **Sanwi**, whose king is often roped into packaged tourist-visit audiences. By all accounts he's as happy, if not more so, to meet independent travellers.

index

CHAPTER ELEVEN

BURKINA FASO

BURKINA FASO

There are few such unlucky countries as **Burkina Faso**. But for a twist of administrative fate in colonial times, it would never have existed. It is desperately, and famously, poor, with an almost total lack of raw materials or natural resources. Although it shares its land-locked predicament with Niger and Mali, unlike them it lacks direct access to the important trans-Saharan routes. And its experiments with radical forms of government, under young and ideological leadership, have unfortunately cost it dear in terms of foreign relations and investment.

Added to these national difficulties are several superficial disadvantages from the traveller's point of view: the country is unremittingly flat, and offers little of the natural spectacle and traditional cultural colour of its neighbours; it has a bare minimum of places to stay and roads to travel on; and it suffers from an image problem in the foreign press which acts as an unreasonable deterrent.

Despite all this, however, most visitors really enjoy Burkina. Although there are endless military checkpoints throughout the country, soldiers and customs agents treat you with respect, and even familiarity, as they venture a "Bonne arrivée, ça va?" while verifying your passport. For all the slogging poverty, there's a climate of youthful **optimism**, and you'll encounter a refreshing lack of complexes and a vital popular culture. Getting business done is perhaps no easier than anywhere else, but as a place to travel, or simply hang out, Burkina leaves a good taste with most visitors.

People

With some sixty different language groups, Burkina has the usual West African ethnolinguistic mosaic. But most Burkinabe (*Burkinabè* is also used, but not *Burkinabé*) speak languages of the large Voltaic group, and the country is unusual in having an

FACTS AND FIGURES

The country's official name, **Burkina Faso** is a hybrid of a More word meaning dignity-nobility-integrity and a Dioula word meaning homeland. The name, changed in 1984 from Haute Volta (Upper Volta), and commonly abbreviated to Burkina, thus means roughly "Land of the Honourable".

With an **area** of 275,000 square kilometres, the country is slightly larger than Great Britain and slightly smaller than the state of Nevada. Nearly all flat, most of it is swathed in semi-arid **grasslands**. The further north you go, the drier things become until you arrive at the denuded **Sahelian landscapes** of the extreme north. Only in the southern regions of Banfora and the Lobi country will you find much greenery. Around Banfora, the forests are run through by streams that fall in striking waterfalls from the cliffs. Although the Volta Blanche, Volta Rouge and Volta Noire rivers all rise in Burkina, only the Volta Noire flows in the dry season. The three meet up much further south in Ghana where they form a navigable river the Portuguese called *Rio da Volta*, or "River of Return".

Burkina's **population** numbers perhaps ten milllion people, around 500,000 of whom live in the capital, Ouagadougou. Since 1991 it has had a constitutional democracy (though political participation has not always appeared too free), which replaced the military regime. On the economic front, even with the cancellation of its French debt, Burkina's **foreign debts** total above £1.3 billion ($2 billion), which is more than double the value of its annual exports of goods and services – but it's still a piffling amount in international terms, about the cost of an aircraft carrier for example.

overwhelming majority of a single people. The More-speaking **Mossi**, who live in the central plains around Ouagadougou, make up over half the population. They are related to the **Gourmantché,** who live in the east around Fada-Ngourma, and less closely to the Grusi or Gourounsi from around Pô and Léo.

Main peoples of the north include the **Fula**, the **Hausa** and the **Bella**. Near the northwestern border with Mali, live small enclaves of **Dogon**, **Samos** and **Pana**. In the south, different **Bobo** peoples – Bwaba, Kos and Siby – populate the area around Bobo-Dioulasso. The **Senoufo** occupy the southwestern tip near Côte d'Ivoire and Mali, while the **Lobi**, towards the border with Ghana, remain one of the most isolated peoples in the country.

Burkina's population has suffered greatly over the last two or three generations. It was from the region of the Upper Volta that the French recruited much of the **labour** to work plantations in their Côte d'Ivoire colony, and the Burkinabe continue to look south for work in relatively prosperous Côte d'Ivoire as the land at home becomes impoverished. Burkina has been one of the countries most blighted by the recurrent Sahel droughts and it remains a main focus of many aid and development agencies.

Where to go

Specific targets for travel include **Bobo-Dioulasso** ("Bobo"), unquestionably one of the most attractive cities in West Africa, the hilly and prettily wooded **Banfora region**

AVERAGE TEMPERATURES AND RAINFALL

OUAGADOUGOU

	Jan	Feb	Mar	Apr	May	June	July	Aug	Sept	Oct	Nov	Dec
Temperatures °C												
Min (night)	16	20	23	26	26	24	23	22	23	23	22	17
Max (day)	33	37	40	39	38	36	33	31	32	35	36	35
Rainfall mm	0	3	13	15	84	122	203	277	145	33	0	0
Days with rainfall	0	1	1	2	6	9	12	14	11	3	0	0

BOBO-DIOULASSO

	Jan	Feb	Mar	Apr	May	June	July	Aug	Sept	Oct	Nov	Dec
Temperatures °C												
Min (night)	18	21	23	24	24	22	21	21	21	21	20	18
Max (day)	33	34	35	35	34	31	30	29	31	32	34	32
Rainfall mm	3	5	28	54	119	124	253	310	219	65	18	0

GOROM-GOROM

	Jan	Feb	Mar	Apr	May	June	July	Aug	Sept	Oct	Nov	Dec
Temperatures °C												
Min (night)	12	17	22	26	28	26	25	23	25	25	18	15
Max (day)	32	35	38	42	41	38	36	33	38	38	35	32

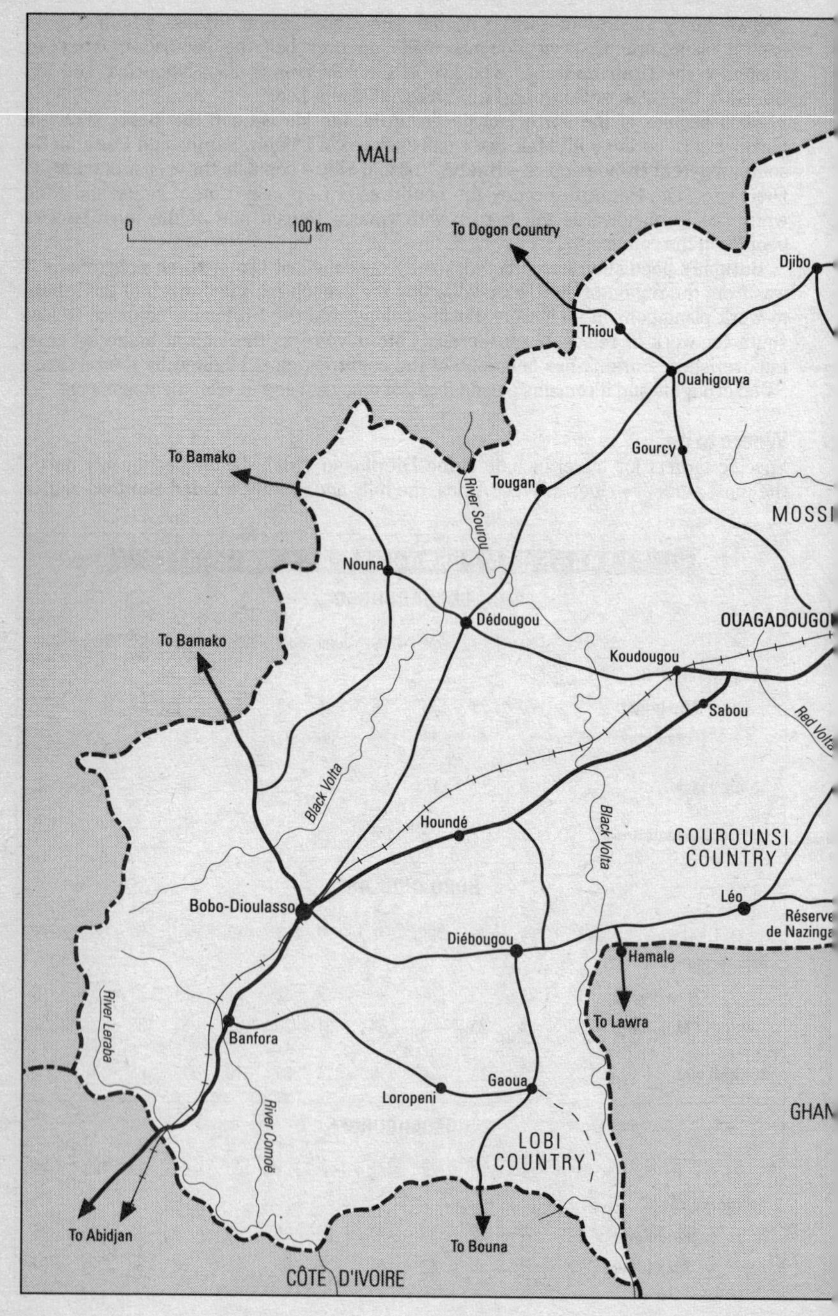
MALI
0
100 km
To Dogon Country
Djibo
Thiou
Ouahigouya
Gourcy
To Bamako
Tougan
River Sourou
MOSSI
Nouna
Dédougou
OUAGADOUGOU
To Bamako
Koudougou
Sabou
Red Volta
Black Volta
Houndé
Black Volta
GOUROUNSI
COUNTRY
Bobo-Dioulasso
Léo
Réserve
de Nazinga
Diébougou
Hamale
River Leraba
To Lawra
Banfora
River Comoé
Gaoua
Loropeni
GHAN
LOBI
COUNTRY
To Abidjan
To Bouna
CÔTE D'IVOIRE

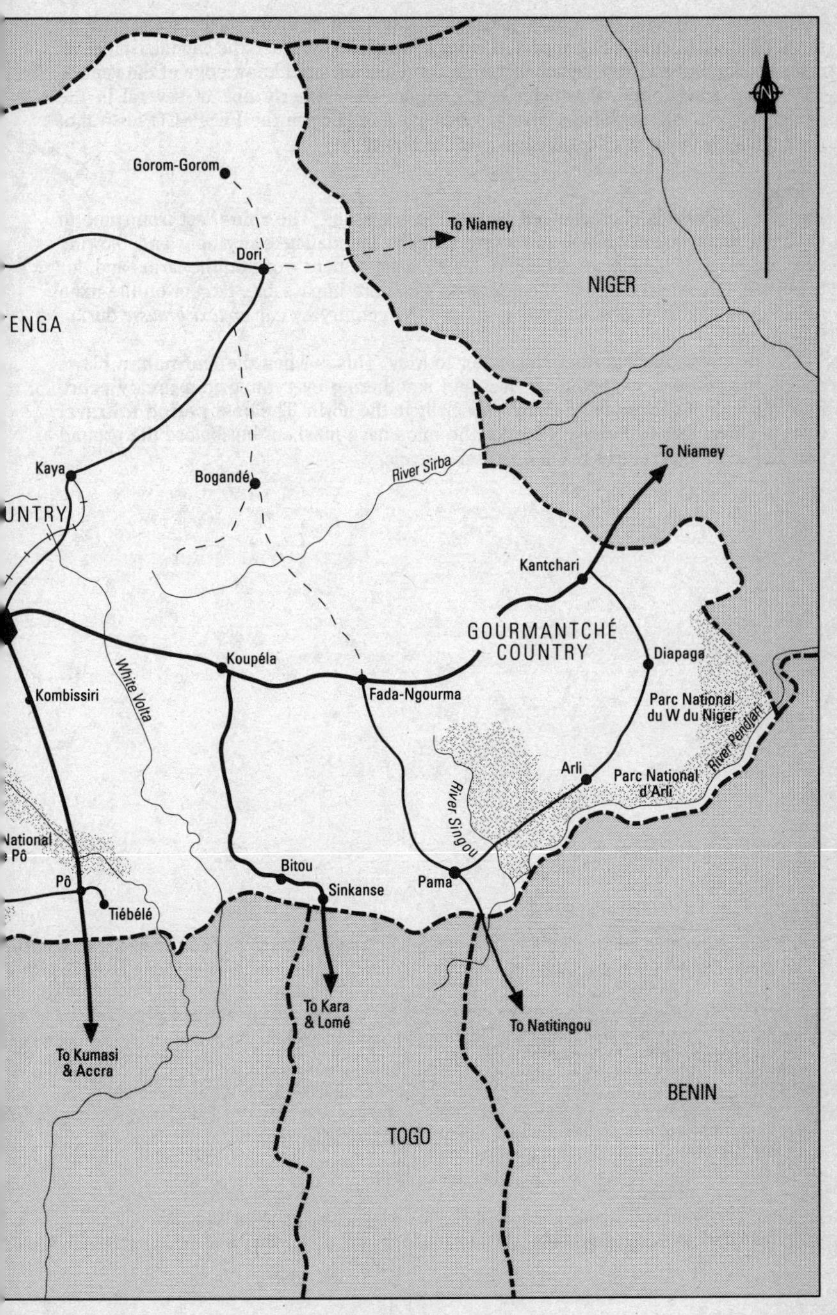
Gorom-Gorom
To Niamey
Dori
NIGER
TENGA
To Niamey
Kaya
Bogandé
River Sirba
UNTRY
Kantchari
GOURMANTCHÉ
COUNTRY
Diapaga
Koupéla
White Volta
Kombissiri
Fada-Ngourma
Parc National
du W du Niger
River Pendjari
Arli
Parc National
d'Arli
River Singou
National
e Pô
Bitou
Pô
Sinkanse
Pama
Tiébélé
To Kara
& Lomé
To Natitingou
To Kumasi
& Accra
BENIN
TOGO

in the southwest, and the remote and fascinating **Lobi country** in the south with its mysterious stone ruins. The appeal of **Ouagadougou** ("Ouaga"), the capital, isn't especially strong, but a visit here benefits from some background knowledge of the venerable **Mossi kingdoms**, of which Ouagadougou was formerly one of several in the central region. Ouagadougou also has a major attraction in the FESPACO festival of African film held every odd-numbered year in February.

Climate

Burkina's climate is characterized by two main seasons. The **rains** last from June to October, with violent storms gathering quickly, inundating everything and blowing away to leave clear blue skies behind. It's a period of hard work on the farms and, for travellers, one when many of the country's *pistes* are impassable. Except on the main routes, you can have trouble getting around the country by car or *taxi brousse* during this period.

The **dry season** lasts from November to May. This is when the **Harmattan** blows across the country, whipping up dust and smothering everything in a dreary ochre haze. At night it can get quite chilly, especially in the north. The **best period to travel** is from December to February – after the rains have finished, but before the ground gets hot and temperatures reach oppressive levels.

The details in these practical information pages are essentially for use on the ground in West Africa and in Burkina itself: for full details on preparing for a trip, getting here from outside the region, paperwork, health, information sources and more, see *Basics.*

Arrivals

Burkina is a great West African travel crossroads, with main highways from Niger, Benin, Togo and Ghana converging in Ouagadougou, and roads from Mali and Côte d'Ivoire meeting at Bobo-Dioulasso. Transport on these axes is relatively good. Air links, apart from the regular services from Abidjan, are weaker.

■ Flights from Africa

There are flights almost daily to **Ouagadougou** from Abidjan, but other West African capitals have flights only two or three times a week at most. *Air Burkina* (VH) flights usually stop at **Bobo-Dioulasso** before going on to Ouagadougou.

Air Afrique (RK) flies in from **Lagos** via Lomé, Abidjan and Niamey on Fri; and from **Bamako**, via Niamey on Sat. There are also RK flights from **Dakar** via Bamako on Mon and non-stop from **Cotonou** on Fri.

Air Burkina (VH) flies from Abidjan to Ouagadougou via **Bobo-Dioulasso** on Tues, Fri and Sun; from **Bamako** via Bobo on Wed; from **Cotonou** via Bobo on Fri; and from **Lomé** – non-stop on Wed and via Bobo on Sun.

Air France (AF) flies non-stop from **Cotonou** to Ouagadougou on Mon and Fri; and non-stop from **Abidjan** on Tues.

Air Ivoire (VU) flies non-stop from **Abidjan** to Ouagadougou on Mon, Thurs and Sat.

Aeroflot (SU), on its West Africa run, links **Bamako** with Ouagadougou twice a month on Thurs.

Lastly, *Air Gabon* (GN) flies Libreville–**Douala**–Ouagadougou every Wed.

There are no direct flights to Ouagadougou from Accra, Banjul, Bissau, Conakry, Freetown or Monrovia: in most cases Abidjan offers the best connection.

There are no direct flights from **east and southern Africa**: again, the best connections are via Abidjan.

■ Overland

Burkinabe borders, with the exception of the Côte d'Ivoire border, often close from 6pm to 7am. Otherwise these border crossings are some of the most travelled and straightforward in the region.

From Niger

A 499-kilometre surfaced road links **Niamey** with Ouagadougou via Fada-Ngourma. *Taxis brousse* and buses regularly make the trip in about 12 hours, or twice as long if you have to sleep at the border. Fares range from around CFA6000–10,000, depending on the vehicle.

From Mali

The usual routes from Mali are from **Bamako** to Bobo-Dioulasso via Sikasso, or from **Mopti** to Bobo (via San). Once a week there's a reasonably comfortable bus from Bamako to Bobo, but taxis run along each of these routes regularly and take about 12 hours in good conditions. The latter route is all surfaced; but Sikasso to Bobo (168km) is very rough *piste* in parts, and periodically washed out during the rains, when it's necessary to do a big detour north via Koutiala (345km). Fares range from around CFA5000–10,000, depending on the vehicle.

It's also possible to come down through the **Dogon country** via Koro. There's no regular *taxi brousse* service on this route, and it's often well-nigh impassable during the rains. If you don't have your own vehicle, you will be dependent on passing tourists or goods trucks. You can't rush this approach, but it gives an interesting first perspective on Burkina through Ouahigouya and the historical Yatenga region.

From Côte d'Ivoire

The privately owned *Société des Chemins de Fer du Burkina* (*SCFB*) and the *Société Ivoirienne des Chemins de Fer* (*SICF*), created out of the old consortium, the *Régie du Chemin de Fer Abidjan-Niger* (*RAN*), run the daily train from **Abidjan** to Ouagadougou via Bobo-Dioulasso. The trip is scheduled to take about 30 hours and sleeping cabins are available. With departure from Abidjan around 7.30am, you cross the border in the middle of the night to arrive in Bobo in the early morning and Ouagadougou, in theory, early afternoon.

The bus and bush taxi alternatives to the train are generally a little faster and competitive on price – and the 1224-kilometre road is in reasonable condition. Note that the routes through the Lobi country in the northeast are very lightly trafficked and transport there mostly depends on markets on five-day cycles.

From Ghana

Taxis and Ghana *State Transport Corporation* (*STC*) buses run to Ouagadougou from **Kumasi** via **Tamale**. From **Accra**, you change buses in Kumasi. The 977-kilometre road between Accra and Ouagadougou is good on the (short) Burkina stretch, but poor in Ghana. Allow 24–26 hours.

From Togo

Bush taxis ply regularly between **Lomé** and Ouagadougou. They take about 20 hours to cover the 967 kilometres and cost around CFA16,000. As usual, you'll save money by changing vehicles between countries (in this case about CFA5000), but you'll have to spend the night in Dapaong. The surfaced road is in general good as far as the Burkina border where it is in a deteriorated condition as far as Koupéla.

From Benin

The usual route from **Cotonou** is via Lomé. If you're coming from northern Benin, vehicles link Natitingou with Fada-Ngourma where you can change for Ouagadougou.

Visas and Red Tape

Unless you're from Germany, Italy or the Benelux countries, you'll need a visa to enter Burkina. Burkinabe embassies are few and far between, but in many countries where Burkina lacks representation, the French embassy can process the visa.

■ Visas for onward travel

Although there are relatively few diplomatic missions in Ouagadougou, the **French embassy** handles visas for several West and Central African countries (see Ouagadougou "Listings"). Note that they don't take care of visas for Mali, Benin, Niger, Cameroon or Guinea, none of which have representation in Ouagadougou (Mali was expected to install an embassy in 1995/6). The consulate in the Canadian embassy handles the affairs of Commonwealth citizens and may be able to issue visas for Sierra Leone and The Gambia.

■ Photography permits

In theory, before taking any pictures in Burkina you need to obtain a photo permit at the *Ministère de l'Environnement et du Tourisme* in Ouagadougou (details in Ouagadougou "Listings"). Obtaining the permit is definitely advised if you want to use your camera in the city, but you will rarely be checked for the permit except in Ouagadougou. The ONTB tourist office has a long list of scenes and places of which photos are prohibited.

Money and Costs

Burkina Faso is part of the CFA zone (CFA100 = 1 French franc; approx CFA750–800 = £1; approx CFA500 = US$1). In Ouagadougou and Bobo-Dioulasso, you'll have little trouble changing travellers' cheques or cash (French francs are best) although banks can be fussy in other towns, for example refusing to change travellers' cheques without the original receipt.

Banks in small towns in the extreme north of the country may refuse to change even cash, including FF, although if you're in a fix, you can usually pay for transport and commodities with French currency. Banks in towns throughout the country are the *Banque Internationale pour le Commerce, l'Industrie et l'Agriculture* (*BICIA*) and the *Banque Internationale du Burkina* (*BIB*).

Credit cards are not widely accepted. You will find **Visa** and Amex of some use for expensive hotels and travel services in Ouagadougou and, to an even more limited extent, in Bobo-Dioulasso. If you're taking a Visa card, it's worth knowing that to get a cash advance on it in Burkina can be very difficult (try *BICIA*). With **Access/Mastercard** you should be able to get a cash advance at the *BIB*, though it can take half a day.

■ Costs

Prices in Burkina are reasonable and even Ouagadougou is inexpensive. Rooms in budget hotels around the country will cost you from CFA3000–6000. Eating street food, you can fill up on *riz sauce* or *tô* for as little as CFA300. Transport costs are also reasonable, ranging from CFA7–20 per kilometre (rarely more), depending on whether the road is paved or *piste* and the type of vehicle.

Health

You'll need a yellow fever vaccination certificate in Burkina as elsewhere in West Africa. During outbreaks of cholera, you may (unpredictably) need that certificate too.

Tap water is treated in Bobo-Dioulasso and Ouagadougou. It smells of chlorine, but otherwise is drinkable. In the bush, progress has been made in water purity, but some supplies are still dubious. If you have any doubts, use purifying tablets. The only other real worry is **bilharzia**. Except around Bobo, where a number of bodies of water are clean, you should be careful of swimming, especially where the water is stagnant or grassy.

Note that Burkina has one of the world's highest incidences of onchocerciasis and whole villages have been evacuated where this **river blindness** has run its course (notably near streams where the simulium blackflies breed). A giant WHO project is wiping out the disease and allowing the resettlement of these areas. Oncho rarely affects short-stay visitors.

Maps and Information

In recent years, the government has promoted Burkina Faso in quite a big way. However, there are no overseas tourist offices as such. The best map of the country is that published by the *Institut Géographique du Burkina*, after the style of the French IGN maps. It's available anywhere that stocks IGN.

In Ouagadougou, the *Institut Géographique du Burkina* has good city maps of Ouaga and Bobo. For tourist information, branches of the *Office National du Tourisme Burkinabe* (*ONTB*) in Ouagadougou and Bobo-Dioulasso can be helpful. An *IGN* National Parks map, covering Burkina, Niger and Benin, is also useful.

Getting Around

With the exception of the Lobi country near the Ghanaian border, a decent road system connects Ouaga with most places in the south of Burkina. The north is still a problem area, however, and many towns are virtually impossible to get to during the rainy season.

■ Bush taxis, trucks and buses

Bush taxis are usually 504 *breaks* (estate cars/station wagons) or 404 *bâchés* with boarded-up back ends. The latter are cheaper and, given the level of comfort, rightly so. You won't see much of the countryside in them unless you arrange to have a seat in the cab – a possibility that a small supplement usually fixes.

The *Régie X9* is the largest bus company in Burkina. It's a far more comfortable option than the taxis; highway checkpoints are much less of a hassle with *X9*; and prices are competitive.

Faso Tours is one of a number of smaller companies, and partly a tour operator for the Arli National Park and other destinations. *FT* also acts as the agents for Niger's *SNTN* buses to Niamey and operates services to Koupéla, Fada-Ngourma and Kantchari along the same route.

For more details see the "Moving On" information at the end of the Ouagadougou section.

Routes, frequencies and sample fares

There's plenty of traffic along the main *route nationale* axis Banfora–Bobo–Ouagadougou–Fada-Ngourma and frequent enough vehicles north to Ouahigouya and Dori and south to Pô. It's only when trying to get to more remote northern towns – or to other isolated areas such as the Lobi country – that you might experience long waits for vehicles (several days in some cases).

Ouaga–Bobo, 360km, CFA2000, many daily (5hr);

Ouaga–Fada-Ngourma, 234km, CFA1600, three times a week (4hr);

Ouaga–Gaoua, 385km paved to Pâ (half-way), CFA4000, three times a week (8–9hr);

Ouaga–Gorom-Gorom, 300km paved as far as Dori, CFA3700, three times a week (8–9hr);

Ouaga–Ouahigouya, 182km, CFA1500, daily (4–5hr);

Ouaga–Pô, 142km, CFA1450, daily (3hr).

■ Car and bike rental

You'll find **car rental** agencies in Ouagadougou and Bobo-Dioulasso (see the "Listings" for those towns), and they are not excessively expensive.

But it's more economical, and potentially much more satisfying, to rent a **bicycle**, **mobylette** (**moped**) or **motorbike**. This is an excellent way to see the sights around Ouagadougou, Bobo-Dioulasso and Banfora: you'll find people around the market places who rent out machines.

Trains

The Ouagadougou–Abidjan *Express* train runs via Koudougou, Siby, Bobo-Dioulasso, Banfora and Niangoloko – the Burkinabe border post. There is also a separate domestic service (the "fast" *Etalon*) between Ouagadougou and Bobo-Dioulasso: see the "Moving On" information at the end of the Ouaga section. Check prices and arrival/departure times by calling the *SCFB* (in Ouagadougou ☎30.60.47 or 30.60.48) or visiting the *gare chemin de fer* in Ouaga in person. A new line now runs north from Ouaga as far as Kaya.

Internal flights

On its outward and return flights to/from Abidjan, Bamako, Cotonou and Lomé, *Air Burkina* flies five times a week between **Ouagadougou** and **Bobo** (CFA15,700). Details are given in the "Moving on" sections for Ouaga and Bobo. Other domestic *Air Burkina* routes are currently suspended. A new domestic air service, *Air Inter Burkina*, may prove a useful supplement for smaller airstrips.

Accommodation

Ouagadougou and Bobo-Dioulasso have their fair share of international class hotels, invariably full during the big festivals (see p.699). But in any town smaller than Koudougou, the country's third largest, accommodation is much more basic. In smaller towns, especially in the extreme north, electricity and running water are luxuries. Hotel rates carry VAT of 10 percent, included in our prices.

A network of **auberges populaires** has been set up by the Ministry of the Environment and Tourism, which has put at least a basic hotel in each of Burkina's thirty main towns.

Off the few beaten tracks, **staying with people** is a viable and recommended option. In the bush, so too is **camping**: much of the country is ideal.

Eating and Drinking

The staples in Burkina are rice and millet. After grinding, the rice or millet is boiled and made into a mush known as *tô*. One of the most common sauces to accompany *tô* is made from cassava (manioc) leaves with palm oil, fresh fish and seasonings. Gumbo (okra) is another common sauce base.

Despite its drought-land reputation, most towns in Burkina have an array of **street food** and throughout the country, you'll find women selling bean or banana fritters, yam chips, fried fish and *brochettes*.

Drinking

Nationally brewed **beers** include *SOBRA*, *Brakina* and *Flag*. You may be offered the unopened bottle to see if it's cold enough.

Different **homemade drinks** are enjoyed in the various regions. A national favourite is *chapalo*, locally made millet beer, also known as

ACCOMMODATION PRICE CODES

Hotel prices in this chapter are coded according to the following scales – the same scales in terms of their pound/dollar equivalents as are used throughout the book. Prices refer to the rate you can expect to pay for a room with two beds. Single rooms, or single occupancy, will normally cost at least two-thirds of the twin-occupancy rate. For further details see p.51.

① **Under CFA4000 (under £5/$7.50).** Very rudimentary hotel with no frills at all – often a *chambre de passage* rented to the average guest by the hour.

② **CFA4000–8000 (£5–10/$7.50–15).** Basic hotel with simple amenities. S/C rooms with fans are the norm, and possibly some with AC for slightly higher rates.

③ **CFA8000–16,000 (£10–20/$15–30).** Modest hotel, with S/C rooms the norm, and a choice of fans or, for a premium, AC.

④ **CFA16,000–24,000 (£20–30/$30–45).** Reasonable business or tourist-class hotel with S/C, AC rooms, and often a good restaurant.

⑤ **CFA24,000–32,000 (£30–40/$45–60).** Similar standards to the previous code band but extra facilities such as a pool are usual.

⑥ **CFA32,000–40,000 (£40–50/$60–75).** Comfortable, first-class hotel, with good facilities.

⑦ **Over CFA40,000 (over £50/$75).** Luxury establishment – top prices around CFA60,000–80,000.

pit or *dolo*. The deadly African gin, known in Burkina as *patasi* or *"qui me pousse"*, is cheap.

Around Banfora, you'll find a lot of palm wine, *banji*, which you can order by the (beer) bottle in most small bars (*cabarets*). Sweet and frothy, it goes down easily and has the added advantage of being cheap.

The usual foreign soft drinks compete against hideously coloured *Spark* (in lemon, orange and banana flavours). *Savanna* is a non-gassy bottled fruit drink in exotic flavours like mango – far too sugary. Throughout the country (especially in motor parks), you'll run into *Lemburgui*, thirstquenching homemade ginger beer frozen in small plastic bags.

Communications – Post, Phones, Language and Media

You can make direct-dial international phone calls from Burkina to the UK, North America and most of Europe. Ouagadougou's poste restante works well, although you should be careful to have your letters addressed with the exact name that appears in your passport – which you have to produce.

Burkina Faso's IDD code is ☎226.

Languages

French is the official language of Burkina, although it's estimated that only fifteen percent of the population speak it with any degree of fluency. That percentage is noticeably higher in the large towns. The most widely spoken African language is **More**, mother tongue of the Mossi and spoken by over half the population. Other widely spoken languages are **Pulaar**, spoken by the Fula herders of the north, and **Dioula** (Dyula), which has become the major commercial lingua franca spanning most of the borders in this part of West Africa.

The media

The national **press** consists of a government French-language daily, *Sidwaya* ("Truth"), and the independent dailies *Le Pays* and *L'Observateur*.

A LITTLE MORE

GREETINGS

Good morning (early)	*Neyibeogo*	Response	*Yung soab*
Response	*Yibeoog soab yeaala*	How are you?	*Yibeoog yaa laafi?/Laafi beeme?/Lafi bala?*
Further response (men)	*Naaba*		
Further response (women)	*Eyn*	Response	*Lafi bala*
		Goodbye	*Wend na tasse*
Good day	*Neywindaga*	See you later	*Wend na kodnindaare*
Response	*Windg soab yeaala*	See you tomorrow	*Wend na kodbeogo*
Good evening	*Neywungo*	Response	*Wend na kodbeogo/Ammi*

LIMITED CONVERSATION

Excuse me	*Ysugri*	Yes	*Nye*	I have no money	*Ligidi kabay*
Sorry	*Ykabre*	No	*Ayo*		
Thank you	*Barka*	How much?	*Wanwana?*	Water	*Koom*

DAYS

Today	*Dunna*	Monday	*Fene*	Friday	*Arzuma*
Tomorrow	*Beoogo*	Tuesday	*Falato*	Saturday	*Sibri*
Yesterday	*Zaame*	Wednesday	*Arba*	Sunday	*Hado*
This evening	*Zaabre*	Thursday	*Lamusa*		

NUMBERS

1	*Aye*	4	*Anaase*	7	*Yopoe*	10	*Piiga*
2	*Ayiibu*	5	*Anu*	8	*Anii*	100	*Koabga*
3	*Ataabo*	6	*Ayoobe*	9	*Awe*	1000	*Tusri*

BURKINABE GLOSSARY

Américain General term for a missionary regardless of nationality or religious affiliation. Early missionaries in the region were anglophone Protestants.

Brousse Common West African term for bush or countryside, but to the Mossi, it means anywhere outside the Mossi country, especially outside the purlieu of Ouagadougou. Thus someone who has gone to study in Côte d'Ivoire or France is said to be *en brousse*.

Burkinabe (or Burkinabè). Man or woman from Burkina Faso; there is no masculine or feminine form.

Cabaret A rural bar (especially in Lobi country).

CDR *Comités pour la défense de la Révolution* – first established by Sankara to implement government policy and organize local affairs on a regional level.

Ghanéenne A popular term for a prostitute, equally insulting to Ghanaian women and barmaids (since most are Ghanaian).

Koure Mossi funeral ceremony.

Kwara Gourounsi chief's sacred insignia, equivalent of a staff of office.

Marabout Muslim holy man who may use his spiritual powers for divination.

Mogho Naba Also spelled *Moro Naba*, traditional leader of the Mossi people who resides in Ouagadougou. *Mogho* signifies the traditional cultural realm of Ouagadougou.

Naba King of a Mossi state, and also village chief.

Nassara Common appellation for white people and other foreigners.

Ouédraogo The most common surname in Burkina, it's derived from the More *ouefo* (horse) and *raogo* (male). It is the Mogho Naba's name and that of other important political and cultural leaders.

Zaka Round house in the countryside with *banco* walls and thatched conical roof. The plural is *zaksé*.

The weekly magazine *Carrefour Africain* is another mouthpiece of the information ministry but the weeklies *Journal du Jeudi* and *L'Intrus* attempt a satirical treatment of current events and are worth a look. Among other weeklies that have sprung up in the "democratic" era, are *Le Clef*, *Regard*, *Zoom* and *Le Républicain*. Look out, also, for the sports and culture magazine, *Big Z*.

Listening to **Radio Burkina** government radio (in sixteen Burkinabe languages, on AM 705) or watching TV (one channel, with very limited transmission and audience) aren't likely to be major leisure activities. **Canal Arc-en-ciel** (FM 96.6), **Radio Energie** (FM 103.4), **Horizon FM** (FM 104.4, in Ouaga and Bobo) and **Radio Bobo-Dioulasso** are commercial stations with more promise.

Entertainment

There's a thriving, though severely underfunded, popular culture in Burkina. In Ouaga and Bobo live music is a nightly occurrence and even isolated villages come alive with the sounds of impromptu balafon bands. During the major festivals, Burkina's international stars can be counted on to make appearances. But Burkina is best known as the capital of African cinema: you have a better chance of catching an African movie here than in any other country in the region.

■ Music

Despite the ease with which you can hear local **music** in Burkina Faso, very few artists have reached a wide African or international audience. A couple of good albums of traditional music are available, including *Haute Volta* – a compilation of Mossi, Peul (Fula), Bambara, Lobi and Gan music – put out by the *Agence de Coopération Culturelle et Technique* (ACCT).

In a more popular vein, **Hamidou Ouédraogo** – the self-proclaimed *Vedette Voltaïque* – is one of the nation's better-known stars. A Fula-speaker from the region of Dori, he moved to Ouagadougou in the 1970s and formed the group **l'Orchestre Super Volta**. Popular albums from the period include *Le Vedette Voltaïque* and *Le Chanteur Voltaïque* both on Sonodisc. The best-known artists outside the country are the brilliantly watchable percussion group **Farafina**, and the very exciting **Coulibaly Twins.**

All are based, when at home, in Bobo-Dioulasso, the town to head for if you want to get to grips with Burkinabe music. The big **Semaine de la Culture** festival held each even-numbered year in February or March offers a tremendous opportunity for **dance and percussion** enthusiasts. It's attracting increasing interest from drummers around West Africa.

■ Theatre

Burkinabe drama has received a boost in recent years and the major towns (Ouagadougou, Bobo-Dioulasso, Koudougou) all have well-equipped theatres. The country has over a dozen drama troupes that give regular performances. Check out what's going on by calling in at the French cultural centres in Ouagadougou or Bobo, and if you're really keen, be sure to catch the Festival du Théâtre (see below).

Holidays and Festivals

Burkina has a growing reputation for major arts festivals, of which the best known is the big African filmfest, FESPACO. It's well worth timing a trip around one of these.

Office holidays include all the usual Muslim and Christian celebrations. Additional Christian holidays include **Ascension** Thursday, **Pentecost** and **Assumption**. **New Year's Day** is also a bank holiday. The principal **national holidays** are January 3 (1966 Revolution), May 1 (Labour Day), August 4 (Revolution Day), August 5 (Independence Day) and December 11 (Proclamation of the Republic).

■ FESPACO

The **Festival Panafricain du Cinéma** is held in Ouagadougou every odd-numbered year at the end of February. FESPACO was founded in 1969 and is dedicated to promoting African film-makers throughout the world. Thrusting Burkina to the forefront of African cinema, the festival now attracts tens of thousands of people. If you happen to be here at the time, you won't find a hotel room unless you've booked in advance, as the city fills with an international crowd of film-makers and movie hacks flocking to the ten-day extravaganza. Rooms in private homes help mop up the overflow; enquire at the festival's headquarters or at the information centre in the *Hôtel Indépendance*.

Happily, the event is open to all and CFA5000 buys you a badge that allows access to the myriad of films showing simultaneously in the capital's many theatres. If you have the stamina, you could easily take in thirty or more African films in the course of the event – substantially more than most people see in a lifetime. In addition, the badge allows access to: the opening and closing ceremonies (the president inevitably speaks); debates with the directors (including headphones for simultaneous translation); press conferences; and the Film Market at the French cultural centre, where you can view films in competition on video monitors.

This is undoubtedly the most star-studded event you'll see in Africa (besides a whole host of *vedettes* from the continent, celebrities from throughout the African diaspora, such as Tracey Chapman and Alice Walker, increasingly make the pilgrimage) and the energy is absolutely electric. Local bands play everywhere, as people crowd the streets stopping for a drink or to browse at the countless booths for traditional crafts and FESPACO merchandise. Organization is excellent; schedules are posted throughout town; a free daily festival paper lists each day's events; and hotels provide free shuttles. For more information, contact FESPACO (01 BP 2505 Ouagadougou; ☎30.75.38; Fax 31.25.09).

■ SIAO

Another biennial event (held in October in even-numbered years), the **Salon International de l'Artisanat de Ouagadougou** is touted as the largest crafts meeting on the African continent. The SIAO attracts over 300 artisans from across Africa and over 100,000 visitors, including buyers from throughout the world. Focused around the *Maison du Peuple*, the entire city centre fills with exhibitors' booths and stalls – some laid out under the traditional architecture of a specially created village. While the objectives – to promote African crafts as cultural expression while stimulating the industry – is serious, the atmosphere is festive, with music, food, fashion shows and performances of dance and theatre on every street corner. For information, contact the *secrétariat permanent*, SIAO (01 BP 3414 Ouagadougou; ☎30.20.25; Fax 30.61.16).

■ Festival du Théâtre

Recently a biennial **Festival du Théâtre** has been organized (late November in even-numbered years) – a chance to catch national troupes performing works as diverse as Greek tragedy and modern African comedies. For information, contact the *Secrétariat du Festival* (☎30.73.89).

■ Semaine de la Culture

Finally, the **Semaine de la Culture** is another biennial event (February/March) that is in theory meant to alternate between towns, though it was held in Bobo-Dioulasso in 1990, 1992 and 1994. The town turns into a fair for the event with **dance and percussion troupes** from throughout the country performing non-stop. You can also catch demonstrations of traditional **wrestling** and **archery**; booths everywhere display national crafts and regional cooking and music spreads throughout the town.

Directory

AIRPORT DEPARTURE TAX None.

CRAFTS Crafts are an important industry in Burkina, ranging from those intended for everyday use (pottery, basketwork, wooden utensils) to those used in ceremonies (masks, statues) or as tourist fodder/decoration. **Bronze statues**, cast using the lost wax method, were traditionally made for the royal court, but are now widely available in Ouagadougou. **Pottery** is the most widespread craft in Burkina and is used everywhere. Look out for **leatherwork**, too, an offshoot of the country's large livestock industry. Traditional sandals, bags and pouches are sold in village markets, and in Ouagadougou, you can see new uses for old materials at the *Société Burkinabe de Manufacture de Cuir* – check out the leather-covered chessboards.

OPENING HOURS Businesses open 8am–12.30pm and 3–6pm on weekdays. Many are open Saturday mornings too. Government offices operate 7am–12.30pm and 3–5.30pm on weekdays only.

WILDLIFE AND NATIONAL PARKS Burkina's flat, over-grazed, relatively over-populated lands offer poor refuge for the country's natural savannah fauna. A conscientious conservation programme does exist (with controlled tourist hunting part of its policy), though its best chances of success lie with the Burkinabe ethic stressing community before individual. Hippo and crocodile "pools" are recognized tourist assets. Encouraging reports indicate a relatively large elephant population in the Burkina sector of the **Parc National du W**, in the **Parc National d'Arli** (both in the remote southeast) and in the little-visited **Pô and Nazinga reserves** south of Ouagadougou. For information on the game reserves, including their opening seasons and daily fees, call the ONTB tourist office in Ouagadougou on ☎31.19.59.

Recent History of Burkina

The Mossi empires dominated the Volta region's politics until the French usurped the independence of their states in the 1890s. For two decades the colonials simply merged their new territory with the *Colonie du Haut-Sénégal Niger*, and it wasn't until 1919 that they divided this huge mass into two separate colonies – *Soudan Français* and *Haute Volta* (Upper Volta) – the latter comprising present-day Burkina Faso. In 1932, commercial considerations (primarily a need for manual labour in neighbouring colonies) led the French to divide Upper Volta again, annexing half the colony to Côte d'Ivoire and dividing the rest between the French Sudan and Niger. It wasn't until September 4, 1947 that Upper Volta re-emerged as an entity.

■ Independence

Maurice Yaméogo, the prominent figure in pre-independence politics, founded the **Union Démocratique Voltaïque** – the UDV, a local section of Félix Houphouët-Boigny's *Rassemblement Démocratique Africain* – shortly after World War II. By 1958, Upper Volta had become an autonomous territory, and Yaméogo its prime minister. When full independence was granted on August 5, 1960, he was elected the country's first president.

The French did little to upgrade the Upper Volta, or give it an infrastructure capable of spurring economic development. Admittedly,

Yaméogo had inherited a desperate situation, but he did little to reverse the trend and outside of Ouagadougou, the country had few roads or communications systems. As the economic situation deteriorated, Yaméogo introduced austerity measures unpopular with increasingly disgruntled workers and civil servants. In the face of rising opposition, he banned political parties outside the UDV and adopted an autocratic style. He was ousted, on January 3, 1966, in a coup led by the army chief of staff, **Sangoulé Lamizana**.

■ The 1970s

The army, with Lamizana at its head, ruled the country during a four-year period in which the nation was ostensibly being prepared for a **return to civilian rule**. Parties were formed and a new constitution was drafted. In 1970, a semi-civilian government was elected with the UDV winning a majority of the seats in parliament.

But the UDV's leadership was split, with a rivalry developing between **Joseph Ouédraogo** and **Gérard Ouédraogo** – both of Mossi origin though unrelated. After a period of political infighting, it was agreed that Gérard would serve as prime minister and Joseph as president of the assembly. Lamizana remained in office as head of state and the army retained real power.

By the early 1970s, drought had struck the country and the economic outlook was bleaker than ever. As parts of the north were struck with the prospect of starvation, a scandal erupted with the discovery of **food aid embezzlement** by members of the government distribution committee – confirming rumours of widespread administrative corruption. The government suffered a further crisis in 1973, when conflict developed between civilian leaders and the militant teacher's union and a **general strike** swept through the public sector. As the situation deteriorated, the national assembly refused to pass further legislation until the prime minister stepped down. Gérard Ouédraogo refused to do so and on February 8, 1974, the army took control of the country once again, dissolving the parliament and suspending the 1970 constitution.

A new crisis hit Upper Volta in 1975, when **war** broke out with Mali over the **Agacher Strip.** Their rival claims to this 150-kilometre-wide border strip in the desolate northern regions of the Sahel – believed to be rich in mineral deposits – were based on legal documents dating back to when Upper Volta had been divided and redivided between Côte d'Ivoire, the French Sudan (Mali) and Niger. Before the dispute was settled with OAU mediation, a new generation of popular military heroes had arisen, including a young officer, **Thomas Sankara**.

■ The rise of Sankara

Under pressure from the labour unions, **elections** were once again held in 1978, and on May 28 of that year, the Third Republic was proclaimed. Lamizana was elected president, but his UDV party didn't have an overall majority in parliament and his tenure was habitually challenged by the trade unions (at the time, an unusually powerful force since half of all wage earners belonged to one of the four national unions) and students. He was overthrown in a quiet palace coup on November 25, 1980, by **Colonel Saye Zerbo** who became head of the new "Military Committee for Recovery and National Progress" (CMRPN).

The coup was initially supported by the unions, but they quickly became disgruntled after the CMRPN's **banning of political activity**. Relations deteriorated utterly when the Military Committee withdrew the right to strike in 1981. Serious cleavages began to become apparent within the Military Committee, and in 1982 Sankara – whose popular appeal was growing – was removed from his influential position in the Ministry of Information.

Unrest quickened, and a coup d'état followed. On November 7, 1982, a group of military officers forced out Zerbo and set up the "Provisional People's Salvation Council" (CSP) with an army doctor named **Jean-Baptiste Ouédraogo** at its head. The new regime let fire a volley of denunciation at Zerbo's corrupt and repressive government and took a radical pro-union position, championing the right to strike. In January 1983, Sankara was named prime minister.

By early 1983, it was clear that the new government was divided between **traditionalists** – led by the army chief of staff, Colonel Gabriel Somé – and **radicals**, headed by Sankara. The two factions came into open conflict when Sankara invited Colonel Gaddafi to Upper Volta in May 1983. The day after the Libyan leader's departure, Ouédraogo ordered Sankara's arrest on the grounds that he had dangerously threatened national unity.

The arrest of the prime minister triggered a rebellion in Sankara's commando unit at Pô, a small town near the Ghanaian border. The commandos, led by **Captain Blaise Compaoré** believed the move to have been instigated by Somé and encouraged by France. They took control of Pô and refused orders from the capital until Sankara was unconditionally released. But Ouédraogo refused to dismiss Somé and gradually the rebellion spread to other commando units in the country. On the eve of the 23rd anniversary of independence – August 4, 1983 – Sankara seized power. Ouédraogo had lasted less than a year as head of state.

■ Changes: Burkina Faso

Sankara settled in as president of the new governing body, the *Conseil National de la Révolution* (CNR), and as head of state. Compaoré was nominated minister of state to the president. The country was renamed Burkina Faso. With the logistic help of the previously underground **"Patriotic Development League"** (LIPAD), the CNR quickly set about reorganizing the administrative regions of the country and ousting **traditional rulers** from their positions of power and influence. Revolutionary **"people's courts"** were established to try former public officials charged with political crimes and corruption. One of the first to be tried was Lamizana, who was acquitted. But several former ministers were convicted and sentenced to prison, as were ex-president Zerbo (who was also ordered to repay US$200,000 in public funds) and Gérard Ouédraogo, former UDV leader.

The style of Thomas Sankara

Only 34 years old when he came to power, **Sankara** symbolized a new generation of leaders with innovative ideas, but his popularity went beyond his ability to compose revolutionary music on his guitar or eloquent denunciations of capitalism and imperialism. Sankara may have had a penchant for facile rhetoric, but he could also transform words into **action**. He waged war on desertification, women's inequality and children's diseases (creating a "vaccination-commando"). When foreign investors refused to finance a railway line to magnesium deposits in the north of the country, he launched the *bataille du rail* – encouraging peasants to build the tracks themselves. (Although critics said his recruitment methods were hauntingly reminiscent of French *travaux forcé*, Sankara was too young to remember that.) But perhaps his greatest achievement was the virtual elimination of **corruption** and government waste, proving his commitment to the cause by having himself chauffeured around in the back of a Renault 4, rather than the customary black Mercedes.

In another popular move, Sankara early in his term announced free housing for all Burkinabe and called a moratorium on rents (an incautious decision from which he later had to retreat). But even though the young president seemed to prove himself as a capable, if unpredictable leader, he was gaining a long list of enemies.

Detractors – at home and abroad

By early 1984, there was growing **opposition** to Sankara's radical style, and in May of that year a plot to overthrow the government was uncovered. The leaders were hastily arrested and tried. Unlike the people's courts, these proceedings took place in secrecy and the penalties were severe. Seven of the alleged plotters were executed and five others sentenced to hard labour.

In light of these events, **relations with France** soured, and Sankara accused the French government of supporting exiled political rivals. Other Western nations also viewed the new regime with scepticism, though the fact that Sankara made efforts to distance his government from Libya and the Soviet Union was interpreted as an encouraging sign. Gradually, the "revolution" came to be identified less with Marxist ideology, and was seen more as a means of unifying a wide cross-section of society. The success of the CNR and the genuine popularity of the movement hinged primarily on the dynamic personality of its founder.

War with Mali flared up again in late 1985. Over fifty people were killed and better-armed Mali did major damage in Burkina. In December 1986, the International Court of Justice in The Hague divided the disputed Agacher Strip between the two countries and peace was restored.

But relations were also deteriorating with other West African neighbours – especially **Côte d'Ivoire** and **Togo**. Close ties between Sankara and Jerry Rawlings of Ghana were regarded suspiciously by these conservative nations – especially after 1986 when the two socialist neighbours decided to work towards political integration by the late 1990s. Relations with Togo were nearly broken off after an attempted coup in Lomé shook President Eyadema's regime in September 1986. Both Ghana and Burkina were accused of involvement and of harbouring Togolese dissidents. Despite a 1987 visit to Ouagadougou by François Mitterrand, **France** continued to treat Burkina with reserve – a wait- and-see attitude generally shared by Western powers.

At home, Sankara was frequently criticized by intellectuals, labour unions and business leaders, though he had a charismatic knack for diffusing enmity from all these groups. In January 1985, opposition to the austerity measures Sankara introduced led unions to wage a "leaflet war", but the tumult quickly died down and no major dissent ensued. Even salary cuts for civil servants and the military were accepted on the grounds that they were necessary to raise the level of social services among the poor. In the absence of serious opposition from **traditional political forces**, it was a growing lack of consensus within the governing CNR and resulting rifts that ultimately proved Sankara's downfall.

■ The new regime

Thomas Sankara was killed in a botched and bloody coup on October 15, 1987. It was precipitated by a group of soldiers loyal to **Blaise Compaoré** (Sankara's companion in arms and partner in the government), who opened fire on Sankara after arresting him. The precise nature of the overthrow is still shrouded in mystery. It did not, at any rate, take a planned course and it doesn't seem likely that Compaoré intended to come out of it looking like a murderer. He later said "Thomas confiscated the revolution and brought untold suffering to the people", and it's clear at least that Sankara had allowed himself to become fatally isolated. But Compaoré's image as a West African leader with the blood of a brother on his hands won't easily be erased.

Sankara's death sent shock waves through the region and chilled progressive movements round the world. For even if his methods were often open to question (something he never denied), he had demonstrated sincerity in his aims and proved himself a credible friend of the people. Most importantly he had managed to instil **national pride** and create a realistic **sense of hope** in one of West Africa's most brutalized countries. Most West African, and not a few Western governments seemed relieved with the change, but the Burkinabe people's response varied from mournful to muted – not a good sign for the new president.

The basis of the revolutionary system Sankara set in place remained intact, although Compaoré quickly announced that "rectification" would be made, signalling a willingness to conform to the inevitable pressure of World Bank and IMF loan negotiations.

However, the early years of the new regime were characterized by the almost continuous rumble of **rumour and incident** within the *Front Populaire* (high-level disagreements, coup attempts and a number of subsequent executions). Though by 1990 the party had been purged, by death or desertion of all members of the original 1983 revolution, events suggested considerable latent support of Sankara and serious threats to the survival of the new leadership, which could hardly have been forgiven. Compaoré therefore sought to bring disenfranchized political groupings into the fold and to achieve peace with the powerful unions.

Towards this end, a new constitution was drafted in 1990, which called for a multi-party **electoral system**. Political parties mushroomed, and a transitional government was set up with Compaoré as head of a council of ministers that contained a smattering of opposition leaders. But conflict arose quickly at a conference to discuss the constitution's implementation. The new parties decried the fact that their input was merely consultative and there was to be no sovereign national conference such as those taking place elsewhere in West Africa. Soon after, opposition leaders resigned their government posts to protest Compaoré's intransigence on the issue.

■ The Fourth Republic

As the **presidential elections** approached, opposition parties united under the banner of the **Coordination des Forces Démocratiques** (CFD) and collectively pushed for a sovereign national council. Popular demonstrations in support of opposition demands occurred throughout the second half of 1991, and, as the outcomes tended increasingly towards violence, the government banned political rallies. By the end of the year, it was clear there would be no council and no opposition: "opposition" candidates withdrew from the presidential race and called for an election boycott.

Compaoré was left as the only candidate and, naturally enough, won the election, although three out of four voters stayed away from the polls. He was sworn in as president of the "**Fourth Republic**" on December 24, 1991, but was probably no closer to having obtained wide public support than he was after the unpopular coup of 1987.

Even as the president called for **national reconciliation** following the elections, he became increasingly mistrusted when opposition leaders were attacked. One, Clément Oumarou Ouédraogo, was assassinated just outside the *Hôtel Indépendance* as he left a CFD meeting. Although Compaoré condemned the murder, there was general public cynicism, and angry crowds stoned the minister of defence when he showed up at Ouédraogo's funeral. Still, with some deft political manoeuvring, the president managed to persuade much of the opposition to participate in the upcoming **legislative elections**. By May 24 1992, the polling date, almost half of the nation's 62 political parties had decided to contest.

Although Compaoré's party, the *Organisation pour la Démocratie Populaire/Mouvement du Travail* (ODP-MT) won a majority of the parliamentary seats, the president's image suffered as a result of the popular belief that the elections had been rigged. **Youssouf Ouédraogo** – a young economist from the ruling party – was appointed prime minister and formed a cabinet that, in keeping with the theme of reconciliation, contained some opposition leaders, mostly relegated to the least important posts. Ouédraogo resigned in 1994 after failed union negotiations in the aftermath of the crippling devaluation of the CFA franc. His successor is **Roch March Christian Kaboré**, who takes a tougher line than his predecessor.

Compaoré has done much to consolidate his position as head of state, relying on a shrewd mix of carrot and stick. He has established a ruthless **security network** and remains intransigent to any opposition he cannot co-opt. In December 1992 and January 1993, troops were brought onto the streets to crush trade union protests against the savage economic restructuring imposed by the IMF. In February 1993, several students were wounded when police opened fire on a demonstration for increased allowances.

But the president has also formed a wide, if at times shaky, coalition of political support ranging from ambitious right-wing professionals to heads of the influential socialist and communist parties. Leaders from all these groups have been rewarded with ministerial posts and top-level participation in national politics. In return, they have kept criticism of the government to a minimum.

■ Prospects

Burkina Faso is most often in the headlines as the sponsor of several rebel and opposition forces in West Africa. Most notably, Blaise Compaoré has actively supported **Charles Taylor**'s military effort to win the civil war in Liberia, supplying 700 troops to assist in military operations – to the disgust of the Nigerian-led ECOMOG peacekeeping force of West African troops. Libyan arms (Gaddafi is another Compaoré ally) have been routed through Burkina to Taylor's forces. Compaoré is also said to have good relations with Yahya Jammeh in The Gambia and Gnassingbé Eyadéma in Togo (relations with Eyadéma improved considerably after the murder of Sankara, who was the political soulmate of Eyadéma's arch-enemy, Jerry Rawlings of Ghana). How much longer Compaoré can get away with playing such a destabilizing role in the region is hard to assess, but he is well-connected (his wife's uncle is the late Félix Houphouët-Boigny of Côte d'Ivoire) and keeps a low profile on the international scene – unlike his outspoken predecessor.

Meanwhile, in Ouagadougou, though Compaoré's position seems secure, he unquestionably suffers from lingering Brutus syndrome. Despite his country's status as one of the region's two outstanding examples of IMF/World Bank-imposed economic restructuring (the other is Ghana) Compaoré will always have a difficult time obtaining the genuine respect accorded to his former friend, whom most Burkinabe still credit for any positive social developments. Compaoré is recognized as perhaps the only figure who can hold the army at bay and it is clear that the economy is faring better than most in the region (even though, at the same time, it frequently fails to deliver to the country's neediest). The next presidential elections, in 1998, are likely to see Compaoré returned to power for a further seven years.

CENTRAL AND NORTHERN BURKINA

Lying in the centre of Burkina, **Ouagadougou** is an inevitable stopping point and a pleasant place to rest up for a few days before heading off to some of the country's more isolated outposts. Though relatively small for a capital city, it generates a satisfying amount of commercial and cultural activity.

Main roads head from here to all major national and international destinations. West of Ouaga, the route to Bobo-Dioulasso is lined with small Mossi towns and villages such as **Sabou**, famed for its sacred crocodile pond, while a branch road leads off to **Koudougou** – the nation's third-largest town and a centre of Burkina's textile industry. The eastern route to Niamey passes through the **Gourmantché country** and the important market town of **Fada-Ngourma**. Another busy junction along this route is **Koupéla**, where the highway to Dapaong in neighbouring Togo starts its southern course.

Possible trips to **northern Burkina** include the impressive market town of **Gorom-Gorom**, near the point where Burkina, Mali and Niger meet, and through the old **Yatenga state** to the historic town of **Ouahigouya** – an obvious overnight stop if you're heading for the Dogon country in Mali.

Ouagadougou

On the surface, **OUAGADOUGOU** – routinely abbreviated to "Ouaga" – has little to offer. Capital of one of the world's poorest countries, it seems more like a shambling provincial town. The heat is oppressive; the flat, dirt streets are filled with choking red dust in the dry season and muddy morasses during the rains; and overhead, vultures wheel on the lookout for scraps, and bats flutter from roosting sites.

Yet despite its unpromising appearance Ouaga turns out to be exceptionally animated – and there is more to attest to this than simply the clouds of exhaust that sputter from the thousands of mobylettes crushing into traffic jams at rush hour. Over the last fifteen years, drastic measures have been taken to try to improve the city's image. New roads have been paved, more efficient sewerage systems are being laid and the government has encouraged people to clear the streets of garbage and goats, both of which had come to be permanent fixtures. As the town modernizes, building projects have included the striking Grand Marché – an attractive and spacious brick complex in the city centre – and the enormous BCEAO Bank, a tower distinctive enough that a locally modernist haircut has been named after it – though on the whole there's a notable absence of the strutting skyscraper architecture so popular in many other West African capitals.

Ouaga is the traditional capital of the **Mossi empire**, but all the country's major ethnic groups, religions and languages coexist here with remarkable harmony. A good number of international organizations, and the nation's only university, are also based in Ouaga. Life moves at a brisk pace, but as a visitor, you'll find that contact with the people is much more immediate than in other West African cities.

Some history

Mossi oral literature traces the beginning of the **Mogho** or **Moro** (the Mossi empire: *Mogho* literally means "the world") to the thirteenth century and a chief named Gbewa or Nédéga who ruled over Pusiga in present-day Ghana (see overleaf). In the course of a battle, Gbewa's daughter, a horsewoman named **Yennenga**, was separated from the clan when her horse took fright and fled into the Bitou woods. She chanced upon the forest's one inhabitant, an elephant hunter named **Rialé** (a corruption of the More

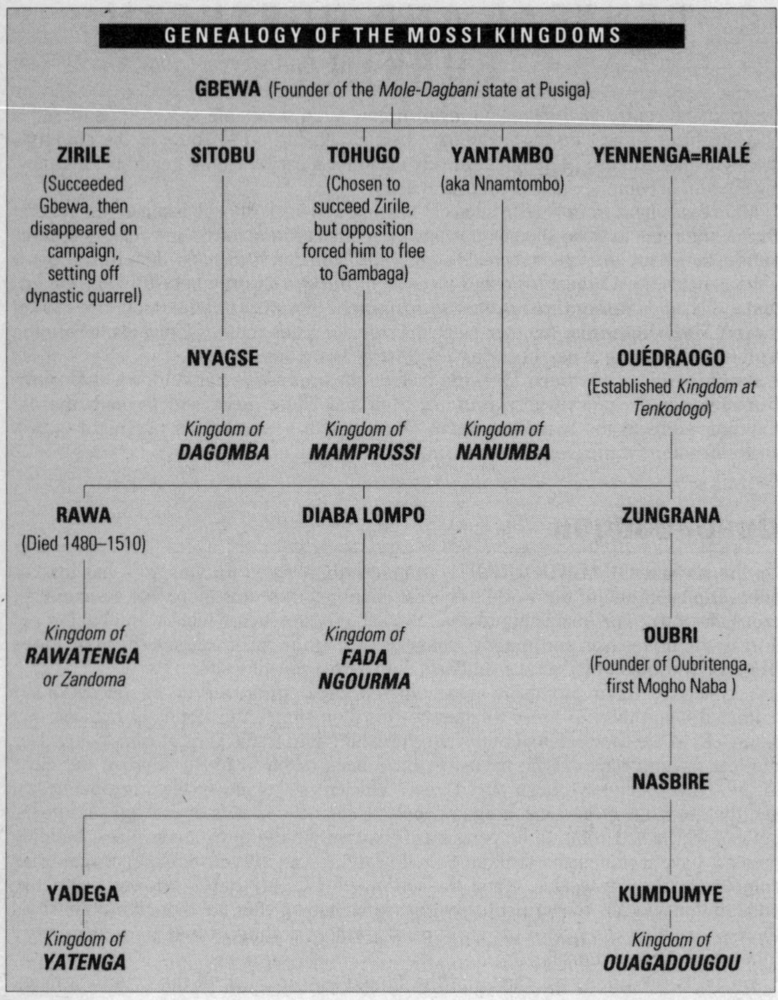

words *ri*, "to eat", and *yaré*, "anything", since bush-dwellers ate anything they found). The couple eventually returned to Gambaga and had a baby, which they named **Ouédraogo**, after Yennenga's steed – from *ouefo*, "horse", and *raogo*, "male".

But the territory of Pusiga became overpopulated and Ouédraogo set off with a company of his father's cavalry to conquer the northern territories. He established a kingdom at **Na Ten Kudugo** (Tenkodogo). Much later, Ouédraogo's grandson **Oubri** sought to conquer new territories and founded the statelet of **Oubritenga**, later known as Wogodogo or Ouagadougou. A grandson of Oubri broke off to form another small state, **Yatenga**, with Ouahigouya as its capital.

The autonomous Mossi states or kingdoms (see above for genealogy) remained remarkably stable for over four centuries, but by the end of the nineteenth century, the

French, Germans and British were pressing in on the region. In 1898, the French occupied Ouagadougou, and within a short time subjugated the surrounding empires which they integrated into their colony of *Haut-Sénégal Niger*. Today, there are still four Mossi kings, whose authority is applied in parallel with that of the Burkinabe state in the kingdoms over which they hold sway.

Arrival and information

Ouagadougou spreads across a considerable area, though the centre is fairly compact. It's officially divided into thirty *secteurs* (like the *arrondissements* of Paris), though you're likely to spend time only in the few at the centre.

The **international airport** is well within the city limits. Collecting your baggage and going through **customs and immigration** is normally an untraumatic experience, but you'll be asked your place of residence; just say the *RAN Hôtel* or any other that comes to mind. There's no bank at the airport. **Getting into town** is easy. Taxi prices are marked up outside the airport (check, and tell the driver before setting off what you're prepared to pay). A quick zip up Avenue Yennenga gets you to the centre in a matter of minutes. Alternatively you can take a #6 bus and disembark at Place des Nations Unies.

Arriving **by train** is even more straightforward as the **SCFB station** is just a stone's throw from Avenue Nelson Mandela and the *zone commerciale* in the heart of the city. You could reasonably walk to a hotel from here, but if you've got a lot of luggage bear in mind that the taxis aren't expensive.

The main *gare routière*, commonly known as **Ouagarinter**, is some 6km south of the city on the Route de Pô. If you get into town after dark, you'll have to rely on urban taxis. In the daytime, you can get buses to the centre: they stop on the Route de Pô across from the *gare routière.*

Tourist information

The **Office National du Tourisme Burkinabe** (ONTB) is on Avenue Frobenius, one and a half blocks north of Avenue Boumedienne, near the *Hôtel Indépendance* (BP 1311; ☎31.19.59 or 31.19.69; Fax 31.44.34).They have a variety of brochures, but are more useful for **game reserves** information and bookings.

Orientation and city transport

The precise centre of Ouaga could be considered the **Place des Nations Unies**, with its ironwork globe sculpture. All the major roads seem to start from this square. To the east, Boulevard de la Révolution (formerly known as the Champs Elysées) leads through the **administrative quarter** down to the *style coloniale* **Palais Présidentiel**. The Avenue d'Oubritenga leads off to the northeast, past the **hospital** and **museum**, and on to the **Zone du Bois** (formerly the Bois de Boulogne). This road then joins the main route to Niamey. West of the Place des Nations Unies, Avenue Nelson Mandela passes through the **zone commerciale** and continues to the semi-modern **Maison du Peuple** and the **Place de la Révolution** where speeches and political gatherings take

SECURITY IN OUAGADOUGOU

Ouagadougou is generally very **safe**, but incidents do happen, the most common of which is bag-snatching by thieves riding on the back of mobylettes (mopeds). If you need to have all your valuables in one bag, make sure you've a good grip on it and walk on the left-hand side of the road against the traffic. If you pay modest attention, it's very unlikely that anything will befall you.

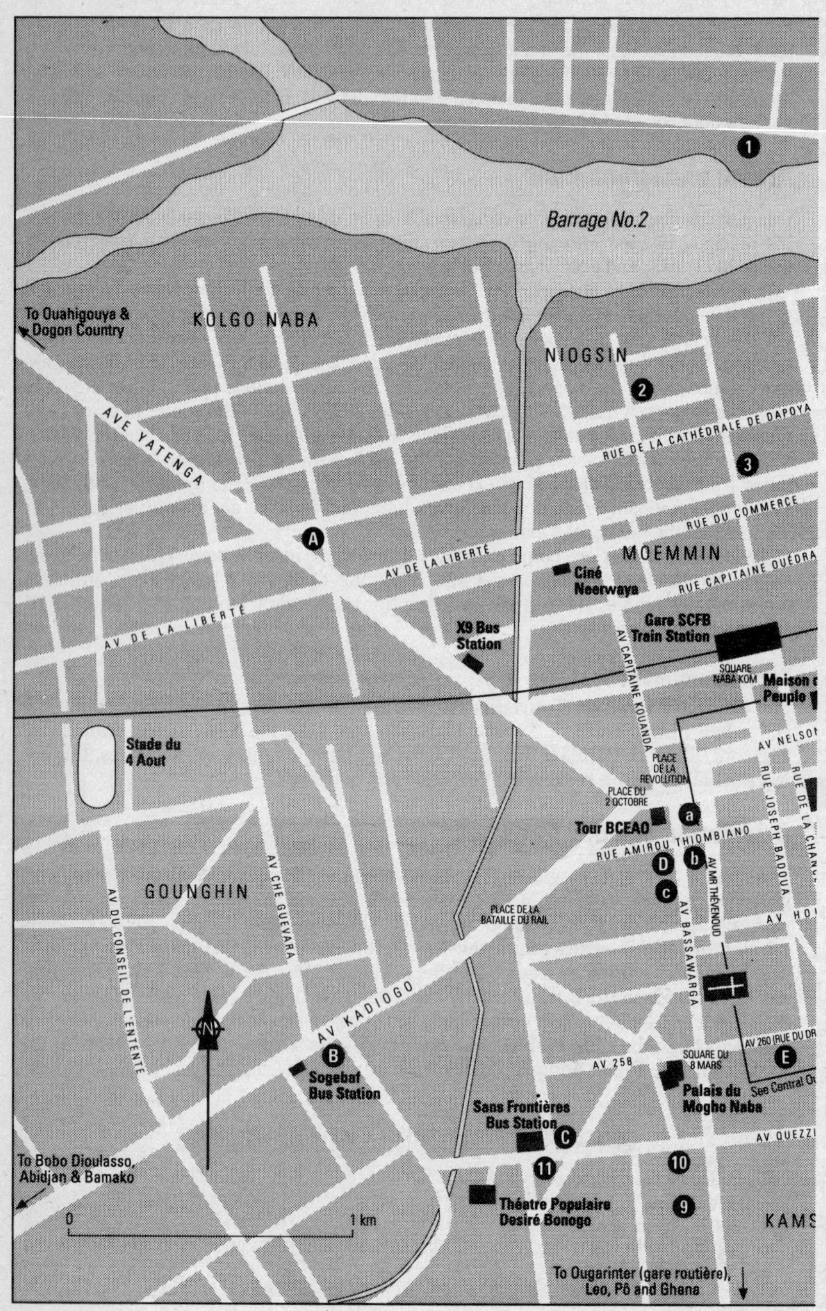

Barrage No.2
To Ouahigouya & Dogon Country
KOLGO NABA
NIOGSIN
AVE YATENGA
RUE DE LA CATHÉDRALE DE DAPOYA
RUE DU COMMERCE
MOEMMIN
AV DE LA LIBERTÉ
AV DE LA LIBERTÉ
Ciné Neerwaya
RUE CAPITAINE OUÉDRA
X9 Bus Station
Gare SCFB Train Station
SQUARE NABA KOM
AV CAPITAINE KOUANDA
Maison du Peuple
Stade du 4 Aout
AV NELSON
PLACE DE LA REVOLUTION
PLACE DU 2 OCTOBRE
Tour BCEAO
RUE AMIROU THIOMBIANO
RUE JOSEPH BADOUA
AV MR THÉVENOUD
GOUNGHIN
AV CHE GUEVARA
AV DU CONSEIL DE L'ENTENTE
PLACE DE LA BATAILLE DU RAIL
AV BASSAWARGA
AV KADIOGO
AV 260 (RUE DU DR
SQUARE DU 8 MARS
AV 258
Sogebaf Bus Station
Palais du Mogho Naba
See Central Ou
Sans Frontières Bus Station
AV QUEZZI
To Bobo Dioulasso, Abidjan & Bamako
Théatre Populaire Desiré Bonogo
0
1 km
KAMS
To Ougarinter (gare routière), Leo, Pô and Ghana

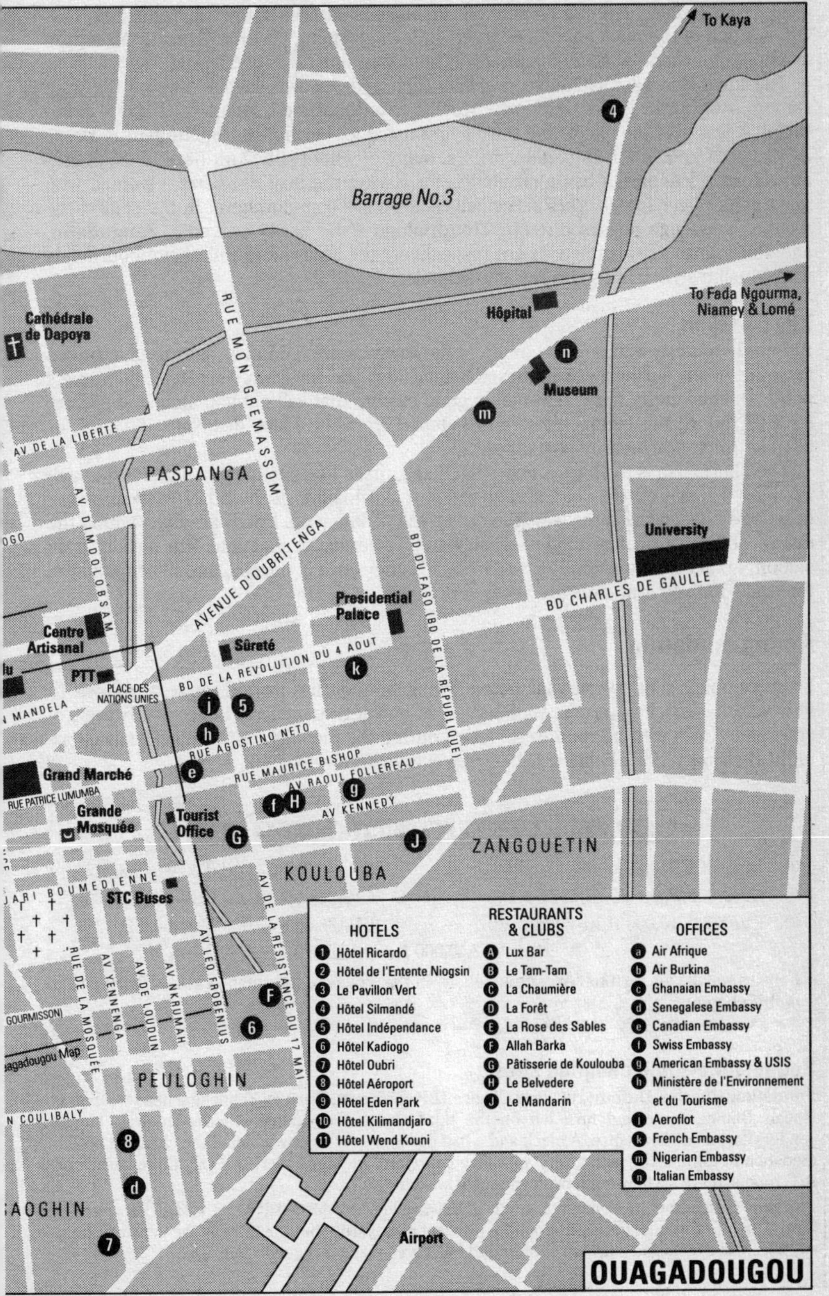

To Kaya
Barrage No.3
To Fada Ngourma, Niamey & Lomé
Hôpital
Museum
Cathédrale de Dapoya
RUE MON GREMASSOM
AV DE LA LIBERTÉ
PASPANGA
AV DIMDOLOBSAM
AVENUE D'OUBRITENGA
BD DU FASO (BD DE LA RÉPUBLIQUE)
University
BD CHARLES DE GAULLE
Presidential Palace
Centre Artisanal
Sûreté
BD DE LA REVOLUTION DU 4 AOUT
PTT
PLACE DES NATIONS UNIES
MANDELA
RUE AGOSTINO NETO
RUE MAURICE BISHOP
AV RAOUL FOLLEREAU
Grand Marché
RUE PATRICE LUMUMBA
AV KENNEDY
Grande Mosquée
Tourist Office
ZANGOUETIN
KOULOUBA
BOUMEDIENNE
STC Buses
AV LEO FROBENIUS
AV DE LA RÉSISTANCE DU 17 MAI
RUE DE LA MOSQUÉE
AV YENNENGA
AV DE LOUDUN
AV NKRUMAH
GOURMISSON
PEULOGHIN
COULIBALY
Airport
HOTELS
1 Hôtel Ricardo
2 Hôtel de l'Entente Niogsin
3 Le Pavillon Vert
4 Hôtel Silmandé
5 Hôtel Indépendance
6 Hôtel Kadiogo
7 Hôtel Oubri
8 Hôtel Aéroport
9 Hôtel Eden Park
10 Hôtel Kilimandjaro
11 Hôtel Wend Kouni
RESTAURANTS & CLUBS
A Lux Bar
B Le Tam-Tam
C La Chaumière
D La Forêt
E La Rose des Sables
F Allah Barka
G Pâtisserie de Koulouba
H Le Belvedere
J Le Mandarin
OFFICES
a Air Afrique
b Air Burkina
c Ghanaian Embassy
d Senegalese Embassy
e Canadian Embassy
f Swiss Embassy
g American Embassy & USIS
h Ministère de l'Environnement et du Tourisme
j Aeroflot
k French Embassy
m Nigerian Embassy
n Italian Embassy
OUAGADOUGOU

place. To the south, Avenue Kwame Nkrumah runs parallel to Avenue Yennenga. This latter is one of the most animated streets in town, running past the **Grande Mosquée** in a neighbourhood of small *commerçants* before ending near the **airport.**

The town also has distinctive *quartiers* each with its own flavour. Behind the train station, **Moemmin** is the traditional Muslim neighbourhood. Home of Ouaga's grand Imam, it was also the site of the town's first mosque. Further north, **Niogsin** is a residential area known for its metal workers, many of whom still work here in small *ateliers*. Nearby **Paspanga** has a reputation for having the best *dolotières* – women who make millet beer (*dolo*). Bars and small *cabarets* are common here. In the centre, the Avenue Yennenga passes through **Tiendpalogo** ("the newly arrived"), **Zangouetin**, and **Peuloghin**. The latter two are respectively the Hausa and Fula neighbourhoods with Muslim-style homes and Koranic schools.

City transport

Although you can walk around much of the town centre, you may want to take **buses** to some of the further extremities (Ouagarinter, the museum, the *Hôtel Silmandé*'s pool). Ouagadougou has a reasonably good system that will get you almost anywhere for CFA150. In the centre, most buses depart from the Place des Nations Unies, or from in front of the nearby post office.

The alternative is to share a **taxi** – in Ouaga, that's likely to mean a battered Renault 4L. Flag it down on the road and shout your destination. If the other passengers on board are headed the same way, the driver will pick you up. Prices are fixed within the centre, so find out beforehand what they are. To certain destinations (the airport, train station, luxury hotels and outer suburbs) a higher tariff is normal, and after midnight, the price doubles. But fares are never very high.

Accommodation

From camping sites to four-star hotels, Ouagadougou has a wide range of **places to stay** and backpackers are as well served as business travellers. Beware, however, of arriving in town with no room reservation during the biennial *Fespaco* film festival fortnight (February 1997, February 1999), as everywhere will be full.

ACCOMMODATION PRICE CODES

① Under CFA4000 (under £5/$7.50).
② CFA4000–8000 (£5–10/$7.50–15).
③ CFA8000–16,000 (£10–20/$15–30).
④ CFA16,000–24,000 (£20–30/$30–45).
④ CFA24,000–32,000 (£30–40/$45–60).
⑥ CFA32,000–40,000 (£40–50/$60–75).
⑦ Over CFA40,000 (over £50/$75).

For further details turn to "Accommodation" in the Practical Information at the Beginning of this chapter.

Budget hotels and camping sites

Fondation Charles Dufour, rue de la Chance (BP 2855; no☎. From av Yennenga, head west on av Houari Boumedienne and turn left on the third street, the extension (crowded with bicycle vendors) of rue de la Chance. A block and a half down to your right you'll find the cheapest accommodation in town, along with a very appealing courtyard. Although there are only three basic, non-S/C rooms, there's a fully equipped communal kitchen. ①.

Pension Guigsème, av Yennenga, south of the Grande Mosquée (BP 1135; ☎33.46.98). Nothing fancy – non-S/C rooms grouped around a pleasant courtyard – but the price is the centre's cheapest. Cleanish rooms and a decent shower and toilet area make this good value. ①.

Hôtel Idéal, av Yennenga (☎33.57.65). Not so ideal really – an older hotel with AC rooms that are run down and mainly rented by the hour. ②.

Hôtel Kadiogo, one block west of av de la Résistance and a block north of av Coulibaly (BP 716; ☎30.69.44). Simple accommodation, but pretty cheap S/C ventilated double rooms (though if you happen to be two women or two men, you'll pay a slight surcharge to share a room). ②.

Hôtel Kilimandjaro, av Coulibaly next to the *Théâtre Populaire* (01 BP 3407; ☎30.64.74). Relatively new hotel with a reputation for cleanliness and friendly service. Budget travellers won't be over-stretched by the cost of the tidy S/C rooms with fan, although AC is more expensive. ②.

Les Lauriers, in the gardens of the Catholic cathedral (BP 387; ☎30.64.90). From av Yennenga, go west on av Houari Boumedienne about 600m and turn left from the concrete roundabout into the cathedral grounds. The *centre d'accueil* for the mission offers spotless accommodation with starched sheets and mosquito nets. Mostly women-only, though four rooms in the women's building are reserved for couples. ①.

Hôtel Oubri, rue de la Mosquée, near Place Yennenga and the airport (BP 1689; ☎30.64.83). Clean AC rooms and a bar loaded with ambience – maybe more than you'd want. There's a nice airy terrace and something for every budget – from a bed in a dorm to private rooms with TV for three times the price. ①–③.

Le Pavillon Vert, av de la Liberté, 500m from av Kouanda (01 BP 4715; ☎31.06.11). A popular place with pleasant courtyard that appeals to travellers on a budget as well as those in search of comfort and basic amenities. A range from non-S/C rooms to AC apartments with private WC. For most people, the congenial atmosphere and setting make up for the distance from the centre. ②.

Hôtel de la Paix, av Yennenga, three blocks south of the Grande Mosquée (BP 882; ☎33.52.93). Recently renovated, this hotel now boasts some of the cleanest and most comfortable S/C budget rooms – with AC or fans – and friendly staff. ②.

Hôtel Wend Kouni, off av Bassawarga in the Kamasaoghin district, two blocks south of the Mogho Naba palace (BP 6356; ☎30.80.79). Basic cheap hotel that's beginning to look a little worn. Non-S/C rooms with fans count among the town's best value for money. ②.

Hôtel Yennenga, av Yennenga just south of the Grande Mosquée (☎30.73.37). Older and slightly depressing place despite what appears to be – with a little plaster and paint – real potential. Budget travellers could get by in the S/C rooms with fans, though those with AC seem a bit much. The courtyard restaurant and bar add a little spark to otherwise drab lodgings. ②.

CAMPING SITES

Ouaga Camping, on the route de Pô, 500m from Ouagarinter; signs mark the way from the *gare routière* (☎30.48.51). Quiet setting with inexpensive bungalows and plenty of space to pitch your tent. They also have a good restaurant and bar. ①.

Le Poko Club, 15km west of Ouaga on the Bobo road (BP 275; ☎30.24.06). The rooms here are slightly more expensive than at the *Ouaga*, and it's only accessible with your own transport, but the camping's cheaper, and nicer too. ①.

Mid-range hotels

Hôtel Aéroport, av Yennenga, one block south of av Coulibaly (BP 3407; ☎31.39.20). New hotel with comfortable S/C rooms – most with balconies – and fully AC. ③.

Hôtel Belle Vue, av Nkrumah, one block south of *BICIA* bank (BP 71; ☎30.84.98; Fax 31.10.32). Fairly new hotel; clean, comfortable and centrally located. Furnished S/C rooms with AC, television and phones. Also a rooftop terrace where you can look over central Ouaga as you drink or dine. ③.

Hôtel Central, rue de la Chance at northwest corner of Grande Marché (BP 56; ☎30.63.09; Fax 31.02.48). A colonial-style hotel with a great location. Recent renovations have got the place looking quite smart. The popular bar-restaurant (great pizzas) is always full of action. ③.

Hôtel Continental, av Loudun across from *Ciné Burkina* (BP 3593; ☎30.86.36). Clean and fully AC rooms, many with balconies that look onto the bustling commercial centre – usually more interesting to watch than the TV, which costs extra in your room anyway. Great location, and a popular AC dining room specializing in baked chicken. ③.

Hôtel Delwendé, rue Lumumba, half block west of Grande Marché and *BIB* bank (BP 570; ☎30.87.57). Excellent location, and since recent renovations, most rooms are looking quite good.

Streetside rooms have balconies from where you can take in the busy life around the market. Rooms with sinks, showers and fans within the reach of budget travellers. The balcony restaurant is a popular place for salads and grilled meat. AC rooms available. ③.

Hôtel de L'Entente Niogsin, one block east of av Kouanda and two blocks north of av de la Liberté (BP 558; ☎31.14.37). A little shabby, but in an interesting neighbourhood of bronze workers. Cheaper fanned rooms, or AC rooms with private WCs. ②–③.

Hôtel Nazemse, av Frobenius, one and a half blocks north of av Houari Boumedienne (BP 2397; ☎31.04.76; Fax 33.53.28). A box-like 3-star hotel with furnished accommodation including TV and phones, but devoid of any charm or atmosphere. ④.

Hôtel Ricardo, north of *barrage* no.1 (☎30.70.72). It's a shame this hotel is so far from the centre, because the comfort and friendly reception are worth the effort. Near a fishing reservoir to the north of town. Good disco and restaurant. ④.

Hôtel Tropicale, av Frobenius in the Tiendpalogo district (BP 1758; ☎31.27.38; Fax 31.08.75). Clean and comfortable, this place is in a busy neighbourhood near the centre. Brace yourself for 5am prayer calls from the nearby mosque. ④.

Tourist-class and luxury hotels

Hôtel Eden Park, av Bassawarga, three blocks south of the Mogha Naba palace (01 BP 2027; ☎31.14.86 or 31.14.90 or 31.14.91; Fax 31.14.88). A new luxury high-rise with extras such as swimming pool, night club and restaurants, including a rooftop terrace. Comfortable furnishings (colour TV, video, minibars) and some good views from the upper floors. ⑥.

Hôtel Indépendance, av Coulibaly (BP 127; ☎30.60.60; Fax 30.67.67). Top hotel in the centre, the *Indépendance* recently underwent a very necessary renovation, making its rooms and bungalows quite good value and the poolside bar a popular hangout. ⑥.

Hôtel Relax, av Mandela across from Maison du Peuple (BP 567; ☎31.32.31 or 31.32.33; Fax 30.89.08). New, quite posh hotel with swimming pool. Central location and very good value. ⑥.

Hôtel Silmandé, 3km from the centre, near the reservoir and the Bois de Boulogne (BP 4733; ☎30.01.76; Fax 30.09.71). One of the few high-rises in town, the *Silmandé* is Ouaga's luxury base with total comfort and facilities to unwind – tennis courts, pool, disco, and the rest – at prices far in excess of anywhere else. Great views and photo opportunities from the (unprotected) roof. ⑦.

OK Inn, bd Circulaire, near Ouagarinter and route de Pô (BP 5397; ☎30.40.61; Fax 30.48.11). Spacious grounds with attractive rooms and bungalows around the pool and gardens. About 6km from the centre, but with free transport to the centre and to the airport. Complete comfort (AC, colour TV, even 12-hole mini golf) in a relaxing environment. ④–⑤.

RAN Hôtel, av Mandela (BP 62; ☎30.61.06 or 30.61.07). The colonial era's best, the old station hotel has aged with a certain grace. No longer the swankiest, it still offers good service and facilities, with a pool, French restaurant and bars. ④.

The Town

A satisfying way to get to know Ouaga is to settle at a favourite *café terrasse* and simply observe the town's life as it passes by your table. Once you become known you'll find contact easy with other habitués, who are never too rushed for conversation. Ouaga has few sights to take in, though the lure of the **Grand Marché** will probably draw you to more than one visit. The small **Musée National** is also worth a look. When you're through with sightseeing, the shopping possibilities are endless.

The Grand Marché and crafts markets

After Sankara rased the old market in 1985, Ouagadougou had a gaping hole in its heart for three years. Then the **Nouveau Grand Marché** opened, and Ouaga now boasts the most modern (and perhaps the most attractive) market place in West Africa. The variety of stock ranges from Chinese bicycles to American beauty products and local *gri-gris*. This is by far the best place to shop for fresh **fruit and vegetables**, meat and poultry (live), and cereals. Basketry (of which Burkina produces some of the region's best), like

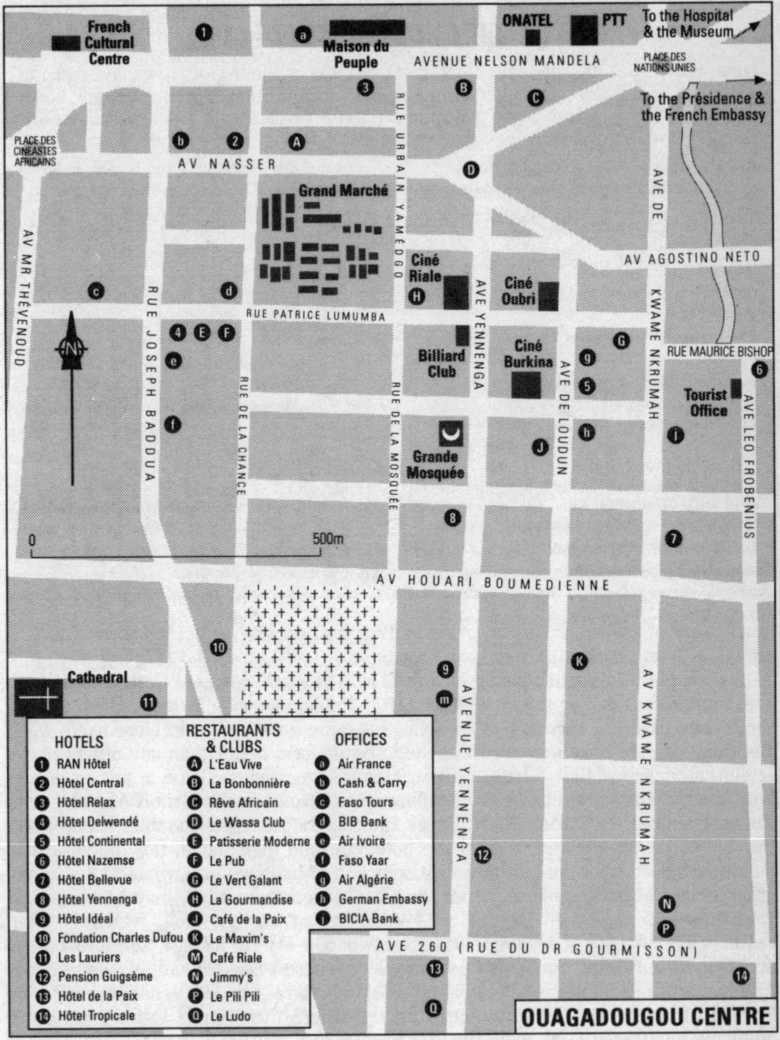

the round multi-coloured **baskets** with leather-wrapped handles, are sold beside Asian-made enamel bowls, commonly used for eating throughout Africa. Much of the market is reserved for **fabric sellers**, who sit by stacks of much-prized Holland wax prints – very often made in England. They also sell quite decent, and substantially cheaper, prints made down the road in Koudougou and Côte d'Ivoire plus a good selection of indigo tie-dyed cloth from Guinea and Mali. Tailors work inside the market to the hum of lovingly tended, foot-operated sewing machines, and will make clothes to order. They're adept at European styles (shirts, trousers, dresses) if you don't think you'll get

SHOPPING IN OUAGADOUGOU

Quite apart from its wonderful markets, Ouaga has a number of stores and emporia where you can make more mundane purchases. Selling techniques have become much more aggressive of late, so be prepared for some psychological trickery and serious discussion when bargaining for cloth and crafts.

Art The *Galerie Art et Emballage*, 51 av Yennenga, offers a good selection of masks and wooden statues, or across the street, try the *Tomos Man Galerie d'Art Africain*. A bigger selection, including paintings, carved tables, jewellery and antiques can be found at the *Galerie des Arts*, 4 av Oubritenga (☎30.78.65).

Books and Magazines The premier place for books is the *Diacfa Librarie* on the rue du Marché at the northwest corner of the market. They have a large selection of French titles and a good sampling of the foreign press, though English-language publications are mostly limited to *Herald Tribune*, *Time* and *Newsweek*. Some maps and tour guides also available. Also check out the bookstore at the *Hôtel Indépendance* for the best selection of local news and some foreign magazines plus a selection of books on Ouaga and West Africa. Used books, including a few English-language titles, are sold on the av de la Résistance, across from *Aeroflot*. Finally, try the bookstore at the *Silmandé* or the racks of the *Patisserie Koulouba*.

Supermarkets Near the Grande Marché you'll find: *Self Service*, the town's best-stocked store, a half block west of av Yennenga and a block north of rue Lumumba; *Cobodium*, on av Mandela across from the Maison du Peuple; and *Cash and Carry*, on rue du Marché at rue Badoua. The *Marina Market*, on av Yennenga across from the Grande Mosquée, is open daily until at least 10pm. Other stores include: *Super Printemps* on av Houari Boumedienne a half block west of av Nkrumah; *Mini-Alimentation* on av Follereau a half block east of av de la Résistance; and *Faso Yaar* on av Loudun across from *Ciné Burkina*.

much wear out of more African designs. But the best way to get what you want, as always, is to take along a garment to be copied.

A good place to start shopping for **crafts** is at the state-operated **Centre Artisanal**, 3 av Dimdolobsom, near the Post Office (Mon–Fri 8am–noon & 3–6pm). The quality of the bronze castings, carvings and weavings is quite good, and prices are fixed, while Burkinabe artists have mastered the exotic **batik** form better than any others in the region, mixing beautiful colours with striking village scenes. Come to get an idea of how much items should be before heading off to bargain in the **Grand Marché** or at the **antiquaires de l'Hôtel RAN**. These latter operators sell from tables set up along the av Nelson Mandela in front of the hotel. Despite their name, they don't deal in antiques, but do offer one of the widest selection of **bronzes** in town as well as many other crafts. **Masks**, imported from the Côte d'Ivoire and Mali, may be treated in workshops in Laglin or Dapoya to give them an ancient look, which is often aesthetically effective if nothing else. Other wooden objects include **Senoufo chairs** and **Dogon carvings**. You'll also find jewellery – desert crosses and terracotta beads from Niger for example, and the ubiquitous old glass trade beads. Vendors can also be found in front of the *Cobodium* supermarket, where there tends to be more of an emphasis on **Tuareg leather boxes**.

Try too, the **Centre de formation féminine et artisanale** at the exit of town on the Bobo road (Gounghin district). This is a religious-sponsored organization, where the women make a variety of crafts such as Tuareg-inspired **woollen rugs**, and less compelling tablecloths and napkins embroidered with African motifs. Finally, for **leather goods**, there's the **Centre du Tannage** on the Fada road opposite the prison.

The Musée National

Ouaga's **Musée National** (Tues–Sat 7.30am–12.30pm & 3–5.30pm) is located northeast of town in the *Lycée Bogodogo* on the av d'Oubritenga. Primarily an **ethnographic collection**, it holds various Burkinabe household utensils, tools and weapons. Numerous **clay pots** are on display, including ones made specifically to store clothing, jewellery or grain. Among the most interesting are the magic pots used for keeping medicines. Their potency was protected with sacrifices. **Basketmaking** and **weaving exhibits** from around Burkina are complemented by **regional costumes**, including a Mossi **chief's regalia** – compare it with what the Mogho Naba wears on a Friday morning at the *Nabayius Gou* ceremony. A good part of the display is dedicated to sculptures in wood, including **ancestral statues** of the Bobo, Mossi, Lobi and Gourounsi. These are accompanied by carved stools and sceptres (*kwara*) symbolizing the authority of chiefs, and a fantastic collection of **masks** showing the different regional styles: abstract and geometric in the north; exaggerated animal shapes in the Senoufo country; cylindrical helmets used by the Mossi; and horizontally shaped *masques papillon* ("butterfly masks") common among the Bobo-Bwa.

Sankara's grave

After Sankara's assassination (see p.703), his body was relegated to an **unmarked grave** outside the centre. Martyrdom made the leader an international symbol of hope, and people from throughout the continent still make the pilgrimage to his burial site. The route to the grave follows much the same path that the body took – from the presidential palace, head east along the bd Charles De Gaulle for 2.5km, turn right at the Tagui petrol station and head straight on for 1km. To the left, you'll see a large tree behind a row of *banco* houses. Fifty metres east of the tree is a row of white-washed tombs, bearing only the name and rank of those killed in the 1987 coup – among them, Thomas Sankara. Despite the isolation of the site, it's not uncommon to find mourners paying their respects, or leaving scribbled notes on the grave. An elderly woman living nearby daily fills a clay pot with fresh water – her personal homage to the man who lashed out against the system, and provided her with low-cost housing.

THE *NABAYIUS* GOU – OR FALSE CEREMONY

Ouagadougou's answer to the changing of the guard, the **Nabayius Gou** is a reenactment, every Friday at 7am by the western side of the Mogho Naba's palace, of events that took place in the early eighteenth century, in the reign of Ouarga, the twentieth Mogho Naba, when the kingdom's frontiers were under threat by raids from Yako.

The Mogho Naba's favourite wife had obtained his permission to visit her family, but she hadn't returned on the agreed date. Heartbroken, he prepared to set out and find her, but his courtiers, fearing war, begged him to stay. With a heavy heart, the king concurred that his duty to his subjects came before personal concerns and, dismounting from his horse, he returned to his palace. The ceremony reaffirms this commitment to his people.

The present-day Mogho Naba comes out of his palace dressed in red for war. His courtiers surround him, begging him to stay, and eventually he heeds their pleas and returns to the palace, to re-emerge in white. This rather solemn affair isn't a spectacle put on for tourists, and needs to be approached with some respect. Nonetheless it's a fascinating ceremony, well worth getting up early for. Photographs aren't usually allowed, but you may be able to get special permission by applying (in advance, with a normal photo permit) to the Naba's secretariat.

Eating

Finding good, reasonably priced **places to eat** is no problem in Ouaga. The town is full of small **café terrasses** separated from the dusty streets by brightly painted fences. A host of such places along av Yennenga all serve similar food – spaghetti, rice and meat sauce, *couscous*, potato stew. Most of them also do large bowls of homemade **yoghurt** – delicious, especially at breakfast when it's freshly made.

The more upmarket restaurants – and there are some very good ones, serving a range of international cuisines – are rarely overpriced, but where the city really excels is at **street food**. In the evenings, the streets fill with **brochette vendors** gathered around the glow of their charcoal fires. You can get beef and lamb, beautifully cooked, but if you want to savour the smokey flavour, be sure to ask for *sans piment*. Kerosene lamps light the tables of *les cafémans* who also emerge in the morning to whip up omelettes and sticky Nescafé concoctions. Finally, Ouaga's **patisseries** are wonderfully lively places to sit eating fattening cakes while watching the world go by.

Budget food

Resto/Maquis Le Coin, corner of av Yennenga and av Houari Boumedienne. This small restaurant has a long and varied menu, mostly of French food. Meals for about CFA2000 and the best murals in town.

L'Elephant Rose, 91 av Coulibaly. Inexpensive African specialities and a large selection of salads. Closed Wed.

Jazz Temple, av Loudun, near av Houari Boumedienne. Small African place with courtyard where you can hear live music Fri and Sat nights.

Les Lauriers, unmarked restaurant on the grounds of the Catholic cathedral. Run by the sisters, this restaurant serves home-style meals with soup, veg, meat, bread and fruit plus a dessert. Only one menu each day, and you have to sign up 90 minutes in advance. Be punctual or you will miss the noon–12.15pm and 7–7.15pm serving times. Solid meals for under CFA1000.

Café de la Paix, av Loudun near *Ciné Burkina*. Mostly African food; baked chicken a speciality (CFA1000 and up).

Café Riale, av Yennenga, one and a half blocks south of the Grande Mosquée. The best of the countless *café terrasses* in the area with a more extensive menu, including fish, than most.

La Rose des Sables, near the Mogho Naba palace. A signboard on the av Bassawarga (two blocks north of av Coulibaly) points the way to this popular restaurant. Good and inexpensive African food in a protected courtyard.

Patisseries

La Bonbonnière, av Mandela across from the Maison du Peuple. Still the most popular pastry shop in Ouaga and a great breakfast address. Fresh and flakey *croissants* to go with juices and yoghurt. The apple turnovers and meat pies are also excellent. Magazines on the tables for browsing.

La Gourmandise, southeast corner of the Grand Marché. Upstairs café with terrace overlooking the market. Popular spot for expats to wind down after the rigours of shopping. Hamburgers, hot dogs and Lebanese sandwiches to chase with juice, ice cream and pastries.

Boulangerie/Pâtisserie de Koulouba, av de la Résistance, one block north of av Houari Boumedienne. Second only to *La Bonbonnière* in popularity. Great pastries, sandwiches and omelettes. Ice cream served until 8pm.

Boulangerie/Patisserie Moderne, rue Lumumba, half a block south of rue de la Chance. Well-known bakery and a *de rigueur* breakfast joint if you're staying at the *Delwendé* upstairs.

African

Allah Barka, av de la Résistance. Moderately priced African and European specialities served in an AC dining room or in the shaded outdoor eating area.

La Forêt, av Bassawarga (☎30.72.96). Where well-heeled Ouagalais head for lunch, this restaurant, like *La Grotte*, has its own swimming pool beside which you can snack on sandwiches or order the *menu du jour*.

La Grotte, 18 rue Agostino Neto (☎31.04.45). Large courtyard shaded by trees and dotted with *paillotes*, with a swimming pool you can use while waiting for your meal.

Quatre Paillotes, av Kadiogo (☎34.04.05). Recently opened in an attractive courtyard with shady trees and flowering shrubs. Extensive choice of African and European dishes ranging from *agouti* to pigeon or rabbit. Around CFA2000.

Rêve Africain, 100m southwest of Place des Nations Unies. Disco which doubles as a popular restaurant with West African specialities. Pleasant courtyard and friendly service.

Tambarze, av de la Résistance. Well known by the expat community, this reasonably priced restaurant features excellent salads and a fine beef fondue. Desserts are recommended too.

Le Walemb, off av Coulibaly, behind *Hôtel Aeroport* (☎33.24.52). Large walled courtyard with some of the best African food in town. Try the *yassa au poulet* or *atieké au poisson*. Well worth a visit.

Wassa Club, av Yennenga (☎31.16.69). Snack bar featuring a range of moderately priced *grillades* and a rather large statue of mother and child in the courtyard.

French

La Chaumière, 106 av Coulibaly, two blocks east of the *Théâtre Populaire* (☎33.43.23). Cuisine from the south of France with a special accent on salads, fish and prime cuts of meat. Attractive setting on a terrace shaded with *paillotes*.

L'Eau Vive, Place du Marché (☎33.35.12). Most famous restaurant in Ouaga, this is an appealing place where the sister-waitresses pause mid-service to belt out the *Ave Maria*. More international than French, the daily rotating menu shifts between African, European and American specialities (from CFA5000). Closed Sun.

L'Escapade Café Théâtre, av Houari Boumedienne (☎33.23.75). French and African food served on a covered *terrasse* surrounded by trees. Friendly atmosphere and live entertainment on Wed and Fri nights.

Le Pub, rue Lumumba next to *Hôtel Delwendé* (☎31.25.25). Intimate restaurant with small wooden booths and a terrace in front. Short, reasonably priced European menu (salads, *fruits de mer*) and live music after 10pm Fri and Sat.

Le Safari, av de la Résistance. Pleasant French restaurant where you can eat in the AC dining room or outdoor courtyard.

Le Vert Galant, rue Patrice Lumumba (☎33.66.69). This restaurant features fish and meat dishes accompanied by salads and soups, crêpes and sorbets and a small wine list. Around CFA5000 and up.

Italian

Le Belvedere, av Follereau (☎33.64.21). One of Ouaga's fancier restaurants with pizza and other *cucina Italiana* complemented by African and Lebanese dishes. Shaded terrace and AC dining room.

Central Pizzeria, *Hôtel Central*. The only place in town where you can get pizza at lunchtime.

Ougarit, av Houari Boumedienne (☎31.18.60) Newly renovated, this classy pizzeria also serves well-prepared French and Middle Eastern cooking.

La Pizzeria, *Hôtel Indépendance*. In the evenings, good pizza which you can eat poolside.

Hôtel Ricardo, north of *barrage* no.1. Hotel restaurant which concocts its pizzas in a woodburning oven and offers a variety of *grillades* on the side.

Asian

Chinois Restaurant, av Lumumba, west of rue de la Chance. Ouaga's foremost Chinese restaurant with a wide selection of *à la carte* dishes.

Le Mandarin, off av Houari Boumedienne (☎33.23.75). Vietnamese food including *nem* and excellent pork ribs. Good service if a little pricey. Look for the sign near *L'Escapade*.

Diverse

Hamburger House, av Houari Boumedienne (☎30.80.92). American fast food staples served with more unusual, slightly pricier, dishes like . . . Japanese crepes? Try that with a milkshake.

Le Tam Tam, av Kadioga Gounghin at av Che Guevara (☎30.28.04). Sauerkraut, sausages, breaded veal and cordon bleu – a range of Austrian specialities you never dreamed of seeing here. Well-prepared and not overly pricey. Occasional live performances in the outdoor courtyard.

Nightlife

One of the few Sahelian towns that's predominantly non-Muslim, Ouagadougou lives for the night. Energy suppressed by the day's heavy heat is ecstatically released when the sun sets. The streets fill with thousands of Ouagalais walking to the cinema, checking out the clubs or just looking for conversation and a breath of night air (staying inside, of course, is mostly too hot). Ouaga's **bars and discos** pack out nightly and often feature live music and dancing. As an extra bonus, they're cheap (cover charges and drink prices are fixed by law and covers are never more than CFA4000). All this adds up to a good time – and some credit to the revolution.

Host city to the FESPACO (see p.699), Ouaga is full of cinephiles and, in addition to a town square dedicated to the seventh art, boasts some great movie theatres, showing some of the very best in new African **cinema**. For **theatre**, it's worth checking out the *Théâtre Populaire Desiré Bonogo* on the av Coulibaly in the southwest of town (☎30.88.09 or 30.88.06), which also hosts a theatre **festival** in early December. You might also catch a show at the *French Cultural Centre* (see listings opposite) or the *Atelier Théâtre Burkinabe ATB* (☎33.50.84).

Clubs and bars

Bar de l'an II, route de Pô. Far out from the centre, this is a well landscaped (lots of exotic plants) outdoor disco with two dance floors and tables for drinking under thatched *paillotes*.

Burkina Bar, av de la Résistance, one and a half blocks north of av Houari Boumedienne. Loud speakers blast African and western pop over the courtyard dance area every night from 9pm. Food served. Modest cover at weekends.

Harlem, Dapoya Secteur, north of av de la Liberté and east of *Hôtel Pavillon Vert*. Outside courtyard with *paillotes*. Nightly live performances and disco sounds coordinated by Zairian DJ. No cover.

Jimmy's, av Nkrumah, corner of av 260. Currently the most popular indoor disco in Ouaga and usually packed out on weekends. Cover Fri and Sat (free entrance during the week) and pricey drinks thereafter. Open from 10.30pm.

Le Ludo, half block south of *Hôtel de la Paix*. Also known as *Lido*, this is an outdoor *resto-dancing* with excellent *coq au vin* and loud music.

Lux Bar, Kologo Naba Secteur, off av Yatenga. Loud pop music nightly and occasional dance competitions. You'll need to take a taxi from the centre to get there. No cover.

La Matata, Dapoya Secteur, two blocks south of av de la Liberté and one block west of av Dimdolobsam. Courtyard bar with live music Thurs–Sat from 9pm. Modest cover.

Le Maxim's, av Loudun, half a block south of av Houari Boumedienne. Plush indoor disco with music from 10pm. Wed to Sun; weekend cover includes drink.

Le Pili Pili, av Nkrumah next to *Jimmy's*. Live music nightly. Beers are reasonably priced, and they serve pizza. No cover.

Rêve Africain, off av Yennenga near the Palais de Justice. Indoor disco aiming for chic, with blinking lights and dark corners. Heavier emphasis on American pop (driving beat essential), but African and Antillean hits are also popular. Cover charge.

Le Waguess, Cité An III, av Capt Kouanda (☎31.36.33). Pricey but popular outdoor disco shaded by *paillotes*. Thurs–Sun from 11pm. High cover.

Cinemas

Ciné Burkina, near the Grande Mosquée. Modern AC theatre with bar and the newest films.

Kadiogo, Gounghin Nord near the Lycée St Jean. Enclosed, but no AC. Foreign or "B" films.

Neerwaya, Cité An III off av Capt Kouanda. The newest AC theatre with big screen and some African films.

Ciné Oubri, rue Lumumba near the Grand Marché. Outdoor theatre, low prices and, generally, older films.

Rialé, rue Lumumba near the Grand Marché. Another inexpensive open-air theatre.

Listings

Aid agencies If you want to contact any of the agencies, there's a central bureau for all the NGOs in Burkina, the *secrétariat permanent des ONG*, on ☎30.62.63.

AIRLINE OFFICES IN OUAGA

Aeroflot, av de la Résistance at rue Neto	☎30.71.29
Air Afrique, av Bassawarga	☎30.60.20 or 21 or 22
Air Algérie, av Nkrumah	☎31.23.01 or 02
Air Burkina, off av Loudun, a block south of *Ciné Burkina*	☎30.61.44 or 30.76.76; Fax 31.02.19
Air France, 12 av Mandela	☎33.30.86
Air Ivoire, rue Badoua at rue Lumumba	☎30.62.07
Ethiopian Airlines, rue Lumumba at av Nkrumah	☎31.00.82
Sabena, av de la Résistance at av Follereau	☎30.15.95 or 96

American Express There's no official representation – the big hotels may act as unofficial representatives.

Banks Bank hours may vary. Typically they are Mon & Thurs 7.30–11am & 3–4pm, Tues, Wed & Fri 7.30–11am & 3.30–5pm. Note that there's no bank at the airport. In town, the fastest service tends to be at the *BIB*, on rue de la Chance at the southwest corner of the Grand Marché. To change money enter by the door to the right of the main entrance. You can also use *Mastercard* for cash advances here, though it may take 24hr to process. The other main choice is the *BICIA*, av Nkrumah, a block east of *Ciné Burkina*, who give *Visa* cash advances and have a separate first-floor change counter. Their branch near the *Hôtel Indépendance* can't always change money. The *BND* bank at the Place de la Révolution has no money-changing service.

Bicycles and mobylettes The best place to try is the bicycle/moped market next to the cemetery on av Houari Boumedienne, two blocks west of av Yennenga. A new bike costs about CFA100,000, or you can get one second-hand for perhaps half that. Also try the place between *SOBA* and *GEXI* on the north side of the Grand Marché (near *Hôtel Central*). You can rent too – rates are open to discussion.

Car parts and repair Repair shops clustered near the Grand Marché include: *CICA Burkina*, rue Lumumba at av Badoua (☎30.61.59) for Peugeot parts; *Codium Toyota*, next door (☎30.63.88) for Yamaha and Suzuki parts; *Diafa Honda*, across from *Hôtel Central* for Honda and Mitsubishi parts; *Kia Motors*, av Mandela, across from Maison du Peuple (☎30.63.50) for Fiat and Mazda parts; and *Renault Diacfa*, next door (☎30.62.97) for Mitsubishi and Landrover parts. For **general repairs**, try the *Garage Special Automobile*, av de la Résistance, just north of av Coulibaly (☎30.01.28).

Car rental In Ouaga, typical rates are CFA7000–10,000 per day for a small car, plus a distance charge of around CFA100/km and a 22 percent road tax. It adds up to about CFA25,000/day if you drive 100km or so. You usually won't need to get a chauffeur, but you may have to pay insurance (CFA3000/day) if you don't. A driver costs about CFA3000. The two main rental agencies are: *Burkina Auto Location* at the *Hôtel Indépendance* (☎30.68.11 or 30.64.61), and at the *Hôtel Silmandé* (☎30.01.76), and *Express Auto Location*, *Hôtel RAN* (☎30.61.06 or 07). Other agencies include *Faso Tours*, rue Lumumba (☎30.66.71), *Ouaga Auto Location*, av Frobenius across from *Hôtel Tropicale* (☎33.27.69; Fax 31.38.23), and *SOFRA Auto Location*, *Hôtel Central* (☎30.63.09). Alternatively, **taxis** can be rented in town for about CFA15,000 per eight-hour shift.

Cultural Centres The *American Cultural Centre* (*USIS*) is on av Kennedy near av Boumedienne (Mon–Fri 7.30am–noon & 1–4.30pm; ☎30.17.13). They have an exhibition space here and show videos of last week's ABC and CBS news along with various films and events. Pick up a schedule here or at the library (major newspapers, weeks out of date) located across the street from the embassy on av Follereau (Mon–Fri 9am–noon & 3.30–7pm). The *French Cultural Centre* (*Centre Culturel George Méliès*) is on av Mandela, one block west of *RAN Hôtel* (Tues–Sat 9am–noon & 3.30–7pm; ☎30.60.97). With a vast library, exhibition space, open-air theatre, indoor cinema and shaded café featuring direct broadcasts of French television, this is the most active cultural centre in Ouaga and an excellent source of information. Get the month's programme when you arrive in town.

EMBASSIES AND CONSULATES IN OUAGADOUGOU

Canada, av Agostino Neto, west of av de la Résistance (BP 548; ☎31.18.94 or 30.00.39; Fax 31.19.00). Handles the affairs of nationals of Commonwealth states in Burkina.

Egypt, BP 7042 (☎30.66.37).

France, bd de la Révolution (BP 504; ☎31.32.73 or 31.32.74; Fax 31.32.81; Consulate: ☎30.67.70). Visas issued for Côte d'Ivoire, Togo and Mauritania plus Gabon, Chad, CAR and Djibouti. Two photos required, prices vary.

Germany, rue Badoua at rue Lumumba (BP 600; ☎30.67.31 or 30.67.32).

Ghana, av Bassawarga (BP 212; ☎30.67.35).

Italy, av d'Oubritenga next to the Nigerian embassy (☎33.22.57).

Nigeria, av d'Oubritenga (BP 132; ☎30.66.67).

Senegal, off av Yenenga (☎31.28.11). At *Aeroport Hôtel*, go south; turn right at the first street, and it's one-and-a-half blocks on the left.

Spain, BP 23 (☎30.61.60).

United Kingdom, Honorary Consulate, BP/ELF, corner av Houari Boumedienne and av Nkrumah (☎30.63.19 or 30.63.20). Ask for AC Bessey or Louis Bandaogo. UK and other Commonwealth members may have more luck getting assistance at the Canadian embassy.

USA, av Raoul Follereau, 3 blocks east of av de la Résistance (BP 35; ☎30.67.23 or 30.67.24 or 30.67.25; Fax 31.23.68; Consulate: ☎30.75.41).

Film and developing Many places in the centre develop B&W or colour film – some with same- day service. One such place is *Photo Olympia* on av Loudun, across from *Ciné Burkina*. To buy film, try *Photo Vision* across from the *Hôtel Central*; *Photo Optique* off the av Loudun one block west of *Ciné Burkina*; and *Photo Lux* on av Lumumba across from the *Ciné Oubri*.

Games *Billiard Club*, av Lumumba, half a block west of av Yennenga. Pinball, video games, table hockey.

Horse riding Conyougo Polo Club, 12km south of Ouaga on the Pô road. No membership necessary to ride. Around CFA5000 an hour, and an interesting way to see some of the countryside. Polo matches Sun at 4pm. Also try *Cheval Mandingue* on ☎34.04.04.

Hospital and medical treatment The only hospital is the *Hôpital Yalgado Ouédraogo*, av d'Oubritenga (☎30.66.43; ambulance: ☎30.65.44). For a simple consultation, contact Dr Bernard André (☎33.67.79) at the Belgian embassy.

Maps The *Institut Géographique du Burkina*, 21 bd de la Révolution (☎30.68.02 or 30.68.03) has decent city maps of Ouaga and Bobo, plus a good national map with routes, and detailed topographic maps which are useful if you're heading off the beaten track.

Pharmacies Two central pharmacies are *Pharmacie du Sud* on av Yennenga (☎30.65.37 or 33.36.31) and *Pharmacie Keneya* across from the market.

Photography permits Obtainable from the *Ministère de l'Environnement et du Tourisme* on rue Agostino Neto, one block east of av de la Résistance, near the *Hôtel Indépendance* (☎33.43.15) – a process which normally takes no more than five minutes and which costs nothing.

Post Office The main PTT is open Mon–Fri 7am–12.15pm and 3–5.15pm; Sat 8–11.45am.

Swimming pools One of the cheapest pools is at *La Forêt* restaurant on av Bassawarga. Mon–Fri, 9am–6pm, they charge CFA1000; weekends it can get a little crowded and the price goes up. *La Grotte* on rue Neto a half block west of av de la Résistance costs about the same. Of the hotels, the *RAN*'s pool is inexpensive and central – CFA1000 Mon–Fri; CFA1500 on weekends. Other hotels with pools generally charge CFA2000 for non-guests. The *Hôtel Indépendance* has the longest pool.

Telephones Go to the *ONATEL–Agence* building three doors down from the main post office on av Mandela (daily 7am–10pm). They sell a magnetic *télécarte*, which can be used in booths outside the building, as well as in the *Hotel Indépendance* and *Ciné Burkina*. You can also send telexes and faxes from the *ONATEL* (Mon–Fri 7am–12.30pm & 3–5.30pm; Sat 8am–noon).

Visa extensions Processed at the *Sûreté*, on the corner of bd de la Révolution and av de la Résistance.

MOVING ON FROM OUAGA

BUSES

Many **bus companies** provide services from Ouaga to every conceivable national and international destination – except Lomé which is currently serviced only by *taxi brousse*. Major bus companies are:

Faso Tours, 3 rue Lumumba at rue Badoua (01 BP 1318; ☎30.66.71 or 30.65.13). The most central station in town, *Faso Tours* has a twice-weekly service to **Niamey** and also runs services to towns along that route.

Sogebaf, av Kadiogo at av Che Guevara (☎30.36.27). Five buses a day to **Bobo-Dioulasso** and a daily departure to **Ouahigouya.**

STC, ticket office on av Houari Boumedienne at av Nkrumah (☎30.87.50). The Ghanaian *State Transport Corporation* provides six coaches a month to **Accra** with stops at **Bolgatanga**, **Tamale** and **Kumasi**. Departure days alternate between Mon and Fri (on certain weeks buses leave on both days); call in advance. Buses depart from Ouagarinter.

Sans Frontières, av Coulibaly across from the *Théâtre Populaire* (☎30.46.75). Two buses daily to **Abidjan** via **Yamassoukro**. More expensive than the train, but usually quicker unless you don't manage to clear customs by midnight and have to sleep in your seat at the border (not unheard of). They also have two daily buses to **Bobo**, and daily service to **Ouahigouya**, **Kaya**, **Djibo** and **Kantchari** from where you can continue to **Niamey**.

Regie X9, av Yatenga, 800m northwest of the place du 2 Octobre (☎30.42.96 or 33.46.69). Weekly buses to **Niamey** (Tues) and to Tanguieta in **Benin** (Sun). The *X9* is Burkina's biggest public transport company. National destinations include: daily runs to **Bobo**; Mon, Wed and Sat departures for **Fada-Ngourma**, **Kantchari** and **Namounou**; Wed and Sat to **Tenkodogo** and **Garongo**; daily departures to **Pô** and **Tiébélé**; Sat departures to **Léo**; Mon, Wed and Sat runs to **Diébougou** and **Gaoua**; Mon, Wed and Sat trips to **Koudougou**, **Dédougou** and **Nouna**; Mon, Tues, Thurs and Sat trips to **Ouahigouya**; and Mon, Wed, and Sat trips to **Kaya**, **Dori** and **Gorom-Gorom**.

OFFICIAL TAXI BROUSSE STATIONS

Taxis from the **Ouagarinter** *gare routière* leave for: **Lomé**, **Niamey**, **Abidjan**, and Hamalé and Bolgatanga in **Ghana**. Ouagarinter also serves most destinations in Burkina.

Northern towns like **Djibo** and **Ouahigouya** are served by the **Tampouy** *gare secondaire* on av Yatenga, just north of the railway tracks and 4km from the city centre. You can even get to Bobo, Kaya and Dori from here.

UNOFFICIAL TAXI BROUSSE STATIONS

There are also several **unofficial stations** in town, which are subject to closure by the police (not that the vehicles themselves are in any way illegal). Fairly established is the station across from the *Rêve Africain* restaurant southwest of place des Nations Unies. Taxis collect fares here for **Lomé** and to the eastern towns on the road to **Fada**. For some unknown reason, Lomé taxis are about 30 percent cheaper from this station than those leaving from Ouagarinter.

If you're heading to **Bobo**, **Diebougou**, **Gaoua** and **Léo** it's worth checking the station on av Kadiogo at av de l'Entente (across from the *Elf*).

TRAINS

The *Société des Chemins de Fer Burkinabe* has trains to **Koudougou**, **Bobo**, **Banfora** and through to Abidjan in **Cote d'Ivoire**. Trains are comfortable, but often late. The faster train, *L'Etalon*, operates only the Ouaga–Bobo route, leaving at 6.30am and 5pm and arriving five hours later. A second-class ticket costs the same as the bus and the trip is about as quick. The slower *Express* is the Abidjan service, leaving at 8.30am daily and scheduled to arrive 28–30hr later. There is also a service to **Kaya**, leaving on Tues and

Continued overleaf

Moving on from Ouaga continued...

Sat at 7.30am. Since schedules do change, you should check them at the station, or call ☎30.60.47 or 30.60.48 or 30.60.49; Fax 30.77.49. At certain times of the year, for example at the beginning and end of school terms, national holidays and vacation periods, you can get a 30 percent **student discount** for one-way travel and 50 percent off a round-trip ticket by showing an ISIC card.

PLANES

Air Burkina, Air France and *Air Afrique* provide the main service to West African cities, complemented by other airlines listed on p.693. *Air Burkina* operates the only **domestic flights**, currently to **Bobo** three times a week, with departures at 9am on Tues and Sun and at 8am on Fri (40min, CFA15,000).

For **flights to Europe**, *Air Afrique* and *Air France* offer the most possibilities. *Sabena, Air Algerie* and *Aeroflot* can also get you there.

TRAVEL AGENTS

Besides national excursions to places like the Lobi country, the southern Sahel and the reserves, larger operators arrange interesting treks to the Dogon country and Timbuktu in Mali, to Togo, Cote d'Ivoire, Ghana and Benin. The major ones are:

Egi Voyages, av Frobenius, one and a half blocks north of av Houari Boumedienne (☎31.02.62).

Faso Tours, 3 rue Lumumba (BP 1318; ☎30.65.13 or 30.66.71). Specializes in trips round the country. Worth a stop for the stuffed wild animals in the storefront and a rather lively bar outside.

Le Rêve Africain (☎31.59.69; Fax 31.59.70). Has a very good reputation.

Savanna Tour, at *Hôtel Indépendance* (BP 0457; ☎30.60.61; Fax 30.67.67). Excursions with special attention to the business traveller.

Vacances OK Raid, at the *OK Inn* (see p.712). Wide range of adventure-type excursions, some short as a day, others lasting several weeks.

From Ouaga to Koudougou

West of Ouaga, the **road to Koudougou** passes through a number of villages where you could reasonably stop if you've got your own transport and aren't pressed for time. Barely out of the city, you arrive in the small town of **Tanguin-Dassouri** which has a lively market every three days. From here a *piste* leads 6km north to a friendly village renowned for its sacred crocodiles – **BESOULÉ**. When you arrive here, teenage boys collect a small fee for your visit and the cost of a chicken and will show you where the *caïmans* live. After sacrificing a chicken, you can touch and photograph the reptiles (the oldest male is the most docile). There's no public transport from Tanguin-Dassouri to Besoule, and the place is much less visited than the lake at **SABOU** – about 90km down the main road to Bobo, a staple destination for the tour operators. Sabou has become a ghastly trap, although at least it's in a pleasant setting and has a modest *campement* (②).

Koudougou

Before reaching Sabou, the main road to Bobo branches in the direction of **KOUDOUGOU**, Burkina Faso's third-largest town. It's a quiet place with wide tree-lined avenues, but a certain level of activity is assured by the country's largest textile factory, **Faso Fani**, and no less than three secondary schools (*collèges*). Koudougou is also the hometown of the first president of Upper Volta, Maurice Yaméogo.

During the day, wander around the **market** which is especially good for its fruit – mangos, pineapples, avocados, bananas – vegetables and cereal. There's a reasonable selection of **handicrafts** too; woven goods (hats and baskets), leather (handbags, wallets and shoes) and pottery (jugs and bowls of all sizes). You'll find ready-to-wear outfits made from locally handwoven and embroidered cloth. There's a superb bronze maker in Koudougou – seek out Gandema Mamadou's shop in Secteur 7 if you're interested in buying.

Evening diversions include a couple of **cinemas** – the *Nelson Mandela* on the main road to Ouaga, and a second one north of the market near the mosque. The town also boasts an impressive new **théâtre populaire** in the west beyond the *palais de justice*. Koudougou has its own troupe that puts on periodic performances (mostly in More); worth seeing if you're in town at the right moment. On other nights, the theatre doubles as an open-air cinema. Good **discos** in town include the *Okinawa* on the Old Ouaga Road near the *Photo-Luxe*; and *Au Joie du Peuple* in the north of town.

Practicalities

Koudougou boasts a variety of **places to stay**: nothing very luxurious, but several comfortable places with AC and a number of more inexpensive options. Next to the market, *Hôtel l'Oasis* (☎44.05.23; ①) has simple rooms grouped around a mango-shaded courtyard, while *Hôtel Toulourou*, in the centre near the motor park (☎44.01.70; ②–③) is convenient and comfortable with S/C rooms, some AC. It also has a European-style **restaurant** serving good, reasonably priced meals. There's another good, inexpensive restaurant in the courtyard of the friendly *Hôtel Yaleba*, on the same street as the old mosque (☎44.00.91; ②), where some rooms have AC. At the *Relais de la Gare*, 100m from the train station (☎44.01.38; ②), there's a spacious bar-restaurant and a *dancing*. Probably the nicest hotel in town, though a bit far from the centre, is the *Hôtel Photo-Luxe*, on the junction of the old and new roads to Ouaga (☎44.00.87; ④). Clean and friendly, with many S/C, AC rooms, it also has an excellent bar and small **pool** (fee for non-guests).

Apart from the hotel restaurants, plenty of **street food** is sold near the market or at the train station. A Koudougou speciality is *pintade* (guinea fowl) which you see being grilled on roadside braziers in the evening.

Changing money is far easier in Bobo or Ouaga. The Koudougou *BICIA* changes cash (FF) only and the *BIB* wants to see receipts before changing even major travellers' cheques. Moving on, two **trains** a day leave Koudougou in each direction. The **autogare** for Bobo and Côte d'Ivoire is next to the train station, while vehicles leave for Ouaga and the north from near the market.

From Ouaga east to Fada-Ngourma

The route to Niamey runs from Ouagadougou through the **Gourmantché country**. The first town of any size on this road is **Koupéla**, which, on the main road to Togo, is one large and very busy intersection.

Koupéla

The flow of traffic through **KOUPÉLA** makes for a lively scene. The town has a large daily **market** renowned for its pottery, concentrated around the southern end. There's also a small *centre artisanale* on the junction of the Ouaga and Togo roads, with a very limited selection of leather and weaving by artisans with disabilities. Across from the *centre artisanale* is a *BICIA* **bank**, though there's no guarantee you can change travellers' cheques here. If you want to take in a movie, the *Buuru Cinema* is right next to the *Calypso* on the main road; they don't show recent releases.

Practicalities

If you want to **stay the night** in Koupéla, there are several options. The *campement* (①) on the main Ouaga road has basic, non-S/C rooms; for twice the standard price they throw in a "shower" – for which read bucket, as there isn't any running water. Cleaner than the *campement*, but still quite simple, is the *Hôtel Wend Waoga* on the Togo road (①). If that's full you can try the *Bon Séjour* (②), behind the post office, though their rooms – non-S/C – tend to be dirty. **Food** is no problem in town as countless vendors line the streets waiting for taxis and buses to roll in, many after the slog of the appalling road from the Togolese border. Buy a grilled *pintade*, take it to the *Amicale Bar* on the eastern edge of the market, and wash it down with a cold *Brakina*, or buy good grilled fish from just outside the *campement* and eat it in the bar there. Next door to the *campement*, the *Calypso* is a popular bar/*dancing*.

Fada-Ngourma and beyond

Midway between Niamey and Ouagadougou, **Fada-Ngourma** is another of Burkina's junction towns, the eighth largest in the country. It was founded by Diaba Lompo, who is variously claimed to be the son, maternal uncle or cousin of Ouédraogo (see the Mossi genealogy, p.706). The town was originally called Bingo, meaning a slave settlement, but Fada-Ngourma is a Hausa appellation, mysteriously meaning "The place where you don't pay tax". It happens to be twinned with Epernay, the champagne capital of France, where the prosperous burghers certainly do pay tax. A more unlikely match is hard to imagine.

Fada is a pleasant, tranquil place, and hosts a colourful **market** with a wealth of goods from across the Sahel region. The beautifully woven **blankets** and **rugs** on sale are invariably better buys here than in Ouagadougou.

Practicalities

The *Auberge Yemmamma* (☎77.00.39; ②) at the eastern end of the market is the best **accommodation** in town; a little pricey with plain rooms (with fan) and some AC options. They do have a good restaurant however, serving grilled chicken and chips and the like. A little cheaper is the *Auberge Populaire* across from the *gare routière* (☎77.01.69; ①). It's pretty well kept, though basic, with a bucket for showers and toilets in the courtyard. Next door to *Auberge Yemmamma*, the *Restaurant de la Paix* has a peaceful courtyard eating area, and you can also eat at *Restaurant du Gourma*, north of the market.

The *BIB* **bank** in town won't change travellers' cheques unless you can show receipts; they will exchange cash. You'll find the **autogare** on the main road near the modern, particularly strange-looking cathedral. There are direct, frequent departures for Ouagadougou and Niamey.

From Fada to Benin and the Parc National d'Arli

Besides the main, paved Ouaga–Niger highway, an important *piste* to Natitingou and northern Benin leads out from Fada and past the **Parc National d'Arli** (dry season only). You can **stay** at the village of **Pama** at the western end, where there's a budget *campement*. There are fairly infrequent taxis down here. If you're driving – and there's really no other way of looking around the park independently – you might do better to continue on the Ouaga–Niamey road to Kantchari and then skirt south through **Diapaga** (where there's a *campement de chasse*) to **Arli** village and the district's pretty lodge, the *Safari Hôtel (*BP 14 Diapaga; ☎79.00.79; FB; ⑥), which is the base for game-viewing trips around the park.

Northeast from Ouaga to Gorom-Gorom

Until recently the 300 kilometres of dirt roads and tracks separating Ouaga from the remote outpost of **Gorom-Gorom** in the **Sahel** took considerable time to cover, even in the dry season. Now the road is paved as far as Dori, making it a relatively easy journey from the capital. Along the way you'll notice a change in the peoples as Mossi-speakers give way to northerners – principally Fula, Tuareg and Bella – and the Muslim influence becomes more predominant. The vast majority of the people of the north are farmers and herders, whose livelihoods are especially sensitive to the drought conditions that continue to threaten the country. The northeast has also been sporadically affected by the ongoing Tuareg rebellion in Mali: if you're thinking of adventurous border crossings in the region, you may find some of the *pistes* closed in the effort to prevent Tuareg rebels launching attacks on villages in Mali from Burkina.

MARKET DAYS IN THE BURKINABE SAHEL

Market days north of the Djibo–Dori road follow a predictable weekly pattern – useful to know about whether you're interested in coinciding with a market or simply want to use bush taxis which are usually only available on market days.

Mon – Markoye, Tongomayél
Wed – Djibo, Ti-n-Akof
Thurs – Gorom-Gorom
Fri – Dori
Sat – Aribinda, Déou, Falagountou
Sun – Oursi, Assakana

From Ouagadougou to Kaya

The route to Kaya passes a couple of villages with important roles in Mossi tradition. Whenever the Mogho Naba dies, a **blacksmith** is sent to the Muslim fief of **Loumbila**, and confined there for three years in order to cast a bronze effigy of the deceased ruler. Since the death of Ouédraogo, thirty-six sets of five statues (each representing the Mogho Naba, one of his wives, a servant and two musicians) have been cast, and are carefully guarded in the chief's compound. The other village, nearby **Guilongou**, marks the spot where, according to Mossi legend, pottery was first invented. It's still an important industry here.

Kaya

KAYA, 98km from Ouaga, is the last major Mossi town on this route. Kaya's flourishing **market** sells many of the **crafts** for which the region is widely reputed; there are weavers and tanners in town and more pour in from neighbouring villages to sell their wares. This is the place to buy leatherwork.

With a population of some 20,000 the town has a certain infrastructure, including some banks and hotels, the best of which is the *Hôtel de l'Oasis* with large S/C rooms (②). You could also try the *Mission Catholique* on the Kongoussi road, where the rooms are a sight cleaner and cheaper (①) than those at the *Oasis*. The government also runs an inexpensive *auberge* in the western part of town (①), with an outdoor **bar/restaurant** specializing in *steack frites*. Other than that there's nowhere special to eat in town, though the market has no shortage of cheap stalls.

From Kaya there's now a **train to Ouagadougou**, departing 2.30pm on Tuesday and Saturday (2hr).

From Kaya to Dori – and Djibo

Sixty-eight kilometres beyond Kaya, Tougouri marks the northern limits of the Mossi country. A short distance further, **YALOGO** is a Fula village with a large Tuesday market. And another 60km brings you to the Islamic stronghold of **BANI** with its solid, large mudbrick *mosquée* standing out among the numerous other minarets that push against the side of a hill, and an important regional market held every Wednesday.

Dori

Despite its small size, **DORI** is an important administrative centre. There's a **bank** (though they don't change travellers' cheques, only French francs) and numerous bars, but not much in the way of **rooms**. One hotel, *Le Bonbon* (③), was started up by Dutch development assistants, who moved out, leaving the place in the hands of a Burkinabe. Essentially a small house with three bedrooms, a living room and a kitchen – nice and clean with netted windows – it's a little expensive. Even sleeping on the verandah with your own bedding is no bargain. Otherwise, though, you'll have to fall back on one of the *chambres de passages* adjoining the bars. Dori's **market day** is Sunday and, just as reported by the German explorer, Heinrich Barth – who passed through in July 1853 – it's really good for blankets. They have a variety of styles and prices, those woven from camel hair being the most expensive.

From Dori, there's a rough, but pretty route through hilly bush to **DJIBO**. Founded in the sixteenth century, the town became capital of the Peul (Fula) kingdom of Djilgodji, and, in the nineteenth century, came under the control of the Muslim state of Masina, in present-day Mali. Little evidence of that remains, however, outside the handed-down memories of a few old men and women. Djibo today is a livestock market, at the mercy of the encroaching desert. It has an *Auberge Populaire* and a small hotel, *Le Massa*. It is also the site (just to the north) of a large Tuareg refugee camp, home for thousands of Tuareg from Mali, fleeing the bitter conflict between Tuareg rebel movements and the Malian state.

Getting to Djibo from Dori may be problematic if you don't have your own transport. It's accessible by public means only from Ouaga, and via a tough *piste* that passes through **KONGOUSSI**, a town that is just about capable of handling visitors. There's a hotel (①) but no electricity.

Gorom-Gorom

Fifty-three kilometres of lousy earth road separate Dori from **GOROM-GOROM**, a large Sahelian village with a **market** – one of the biggest in the north – that draws a vast array of northern peoples. Tuareg, Fula and Bella nomads trek into the mostly Songhai-run market on Wednesday, the main trading day. In addition to the foodstuffs, you'll find a variety of leather goods, jewellery and textiles, all produced locally. A short distance away, camels, goats, sheep and donkeys are bought and sold at the **animal market**. The town itself is a picturesque blend of *banco* houses and narrow dusty streets dotted with numerous mosques.

Practicalities

Gorom's best **place to stay** has to be the *Campement Hotelier*, built by the now defunct airline *Le Point* as "the cornerstone of a different kind of tourism based on dialogue and exchange." Today the villagers run the *campement* themselves (②). Contacts here are direct and motivated by the people's genuine desire to open their town to you. The complex is modelled after a Sahelian village, with houses and thatched lean-tos surrounded by a large mud wall. House interiors match the local style. There's a **bar** on the premises and a restaurant, though, admittedly, meals are slightly more expensive than you would normally expect to pay in these parts. Alternatively, you could stay at the government-run *Auberge Populaire* which is not as clean, but still good, and offers the town's cheapest accommodation (①). Eat cheaply there, or at the small café by the *X9 gare* in town.

The *campement* also offers **excursions**, including camel-rides. Among the offerings are trips to nearby Songhai villages (Korya, Zena, Ti-n-Akof) or to cave paintings near Aribinda. Emphasis is placed on getting to know regional lifestyles and the relationship between the people and the Sahel's fragile ecosystem. With the continuous threat of desertification, the **agro-ecological centre** opened in conjunction with the *campement* is designed to provide local farmers with information and technical advice with the aim of self-sufficiency in food production.

If you've got your own 4WD transport, it's very worthwhile getting to the sand dunes at **Oursi**, a two-hour drive from Gorom – or you could rent a 4WD vehicle and driver for the day for CFA30,000–40,000. The *mare d'Oursi* is a vast watering hole that attracts herders and livestock from throughout the region – an amazing sight. The dunes themselves offer a picturesque foretaste of the Sahara. Ask any of the small kids from Oursi village to direct you there.

If you're continuing **into Niger** from this corner of Burkina, further details can be found on p.972.

Ouahigouya and the Yatenga state

Sparse and mostly bone dry, but historically important, **Ouahigouya** is the capital of northern Burkina. It was founded in the eighteenth century as capital of **Yatenga**, the northernmost Mossi kingdom, which had broken away from Ouagadougou some three hundred years before. It's a relaxed and pleasant place to mooch around, perhaps dallying in its large market, or taking in some of the 37 picturesque mosques. Most of Yatenga's sights, however, lie outside the city in the villages: its former capitals at **La** and **Gourcy** in the south; the burial sites of many of its *nabas* at **Somniaga**; and the region's most impressive mosques at **Ramatoulaye** to the west, and **Yako** to the south. All these places are worth a look, but you'll be back in Ouahigouya by sunset if you value cold beer and music.

The Yatenga region is an arid, undulating **plateau**, barren for most of the year. The rains in May lay a green carpet on the earth that lasts until October, during which time the region's main crops, particularly millet and sorghum, but also maize, cotton, groundnuts and indigo, are sown and harvested. Outside this season, Yatenga reverts to a scrubby savannah of tree-dotted thornbush – shea-nut, *neré* (carob) and false mahogany trees – with tamarind and types of plum (*nobega*) and fig (*kankanga*) among the wild fruits.

The animal life is unimpressive (there was still the odd lion in the region fifty years ago, but you'd be lucky to see as much as a gazelle today) but **birds** are much in evidence – especially vultures, which seem even more overbearing here than in the rest of Burkina. A good deal more agreeable are the electric blue **Abyssinian roller birds**, perched on telegraph wires in the barren landscape, like travellers' heralds.

Ethnography

The main ethnic group in Yatenga is the Mossi, who were living around here by the end of the 1330s, when they sacked Timbuktu. They took political power probably in the second half of the fifteenth century (some claim several centuries earlier). The Dogon, then living in the north of the region, fled up to the Bandiagara escarpment in Mali, while the Samos, based in the east, stayed on and have now more or less assimilated with the Mossi.

The principal state was run by the **Kurumba** or Fulse, who claim to have come from the region of Say and Niamey some two hundred years before the Mossi, to set up the Kingdom of Lurum, with its last capital at Mengao, now in Djibo district. Just as the Dogon hadn't resisted the Kurumba invasion, so the Kurumba hardly opposed the Mossi, and the two communities have merged into the dual socio-political system largely still existent today, in which the **Mossi** hold political power (as "masters of the sky") while the Kurumba have authority over agriculture and the land (the "masters of the earth").

HISTORY OF YATENGA

The first great Mossi conqueror, **Naba Rawa**, eldest son of Ouédraogo, founded the kingdom of **Zandoma** or Rawatenga, maybe around 1470. His great nephew Ouemtanango, son of Oubri, perhaps jealous of Rawa's success, expanded his father's Oubritenga kingdom (later Ouagadougou) to the north, moving its capital from Tenkodogo to **La**.

The kingdom of Yatenga was probably founded around 1540 on the death of the fourth Mogho Naba, **Nasbire**. It happened thus. Nasbire's son and heir, **Yadega**, who was away, heard about his father's death and rode straight to La to claim the kingdom. He arrived, however, to find that his brother Kumdumye had taken power, kept the news from reaching him and moved south to Ouagadougou. Yadega followed but found Kumdumye's authority already well established. He returned angrily to La, where he was soon followed by his sister Pabre, who'd managed to seize the **royal amulets** embodying the Mogho Naba's power. With these, Yadega declared a new kingdom and had himself enthroned at La. His new state was known after him as **Yatenga** (from *Yadega tenga*, "Yadega's land"). A legacy of the dispute is the continued mutual avoidance of the holders of the offices of Mogho Naba and Yatenga Naba who to this day refuse to set eyes on each other.

Oral history is a bit confused on some of these points. Ouagadougou tradition inserts a fifth Mogho Naba between Nasbire and Kumdumye, making the latter the sixth Naba, and also claims that the royal amulets were recovered from Pabre – though Yatenga tradition says they got nothing more than her horse's droppings. It's possible that Nasbire had named Kumdumye his heir in any case. But why Yadega was away from La, and where he was, are also disputed, as is his relationship to Kumdumye, who may have been his cousin. The date of Yatenga's foundation could have been as much as four hundred years earlier.

THE RISE OF YATENGA

At first the Yatenga statelet was the runt of the Mossi litter. Consisting of the towns of **La**, its first capital and **Gourcy**, its second, plus a few surrounding villages, it lay sandwiched between Zandoma to the north and Oubritenga to the south. When Yadega's brother Kouda jumped on the bandwagon and set up his own kingdom of Risiam, to the southeast (independent until the nineteenth century), it was bigger than Yatenga. What changed this balance was a tradition of conqest and expansion that commenced with the activities of the ninth Yatenga Naba, **Vanteberegum**. He moved the Yatenga capital to **Somniaga**, extending the kingdom to do so, and his son set out on a campaign of aggrandizement that gobbled up most of Zandoma and established Yatenga as the second most powerful Mossi kingdom. However, it was the twenty-fifth *naba*, **Naba Kango**, famous for his cruelty as much as his conquests, who really fixed Yatenga in the oral histories.

Deposed almost as soon as he took power in 1754, Naba Kango returned after three years, aided by the formidable advantage of **firearms**, to retake power with an army of mercenaries. He then built a new capital at **Ouahigouya**, with an enormous **palace**, and summoned all Yatenga's chiefs (including the *naba* of Zandoma) to pay homage to him there. Those who failed to do so received a visit from his troops, who then went on to invade neighbouring territories, leading to a vast expansion of Kango's kingdom. Within it, he maintained an impressive unity, largely by burning down any villages that defied his authority. He had criminals publicly burnt to death and even massacred his own Bamana

Each village has a Kurumba "earth chief", whose functions complement those of the Mossi *naba*. There's a third element in this system, the **blacksmiths** (*saaba*), who never marry out, usually live in their own wards (*zaka*) inside Mossi villages (though they have one or two villages of their own, like Séguénéga) and have special ceremonial duties such as performing circumcisions. Only the men are smiths; women are generally potters.

Within this same system are the captives (*Yemse*). Descendants of prisoners of war, and loyal to the Yatenga Naba, they live in their own section of town called the *bingo*.

troops when they misbehaved. He was succeeded in 1787 by his nephew, **Naba Sagha**, but the large kingdom was growing unwieldy and and, within forty years, Yatenga had plunged into the series of civil wars that were to destroy it.

CIVIL WAR AND DISSOLUTION

The wars concerned the succession of Sagha's 133 sons, the first of whom, **Tougouri**, managed to succeed him in 1806. Following his death in 1825, war broke out between those of Sagha's sons who were next in line. Only after 1834 was there a lull in the strife. On the death of Naba Yende, in 1877, however, the dynastic conflicts flared up once more.

This time the dispute was between Sagha's grandsons. The sons of his first-born and successor, Tougouri, claimed that they alone were entitled to rule. The sons of Tougouri's brothers and successors disagreed, pointing out that the intended *naba*'s mother had been a concubine, and that in any case, each branch of Sagha's family should take a turn. The two groups formed opposing parties called **Sons of Tougouri** and **Sons of Sagha**.

When two Sons of Sagha were successively enthroned as *nabas*, the Sons of Tougouri went to war against them. Baogo, the incumbent *naba*, turned to the **French** – who, although new on the scene, had just taken Bandiagara, and were hovering on Yatenga's borders. **Desteneves**, the leader of the French expeditionary force, offered only to mediate. Undeterred, Baogo went into battle against the Sons of Tougouri in 1894 and was killed.

All other eligible branches of Sagha's family having had their turn, the kingdom now returned to Tougouri's family. His senior son, Naba Boulli, took the throne but predictably the Sons of Sagha refused to accept him and set up a rival *naba* in **Sissamba**. Boulli turned to the French, who this time seized the opportunity and, on May 18, 1895, declared Yatenga a protectorate, thus usurping its independence.

The French sacked Sissamba, but the Sons of Sagha successfully recaptured Ouahigouya as soon as they had left. The French bailed out Boulli and put him back on the throne twice more, by which time half Ouahigouya was in ruins. The rebellion of the Sons of Sagha wasn't put down until 1902, and violent incidents in connection with it continued as late as 1911.

MODERN YATENGA

French military occupation ended in 1909 when Yatenga passed to civilian colonial rule, and the region was generally quiet during the 1916 anti-conscription rebellion. With the 1932 division of Upper Volta, Yatenga became part of the French Sudan until the recreation of Upper Volta in 1947. The 1930s and 1940s saw the rise of **Hammalism**, a reformist Muslim cult which the French considered anti-colonial (it was). The movement was largely responsible for the spread of Islam in Yatenga (hitherto strongly resisted because of its association with hostile empires, especially Songhai to the north). This in turn became the base for opposition to the traditionalist, chief-led *Union Voltaïque* in the region. A *UV* breakaway, the *MDV* (*Mouvement Démocratique Voltaïque*), carried Yatenga in the 1957 election with a base of Muslim support.

Since independence, Yatenga has been a *département* of Burkina, divided into four *cercles*: Ouahigouya, Gourcy, Séguénéga and Titao. Yako lies outside it in the *département* of Koudougou.

Ouahigouya's *bingo* consists of half the city and captives form more than half its population. Village chiefs and court dignitaries are often captives by descent.

The **Peulh** (Fula) are the region's other main group. Although based in Djibo and outside the Mossi-Kurumba system, they've played an often major role in Yatenga's history. The **Silmi-Mossi**, descendants of a union, considered somewhat disreputable, of Fula and Mossi, live in their own villages, mainly isolated in the south and southeast of the region. Lastly, members of three Islamic trading nations, the **Songhai**, **Bamana** and Mande-speaking **Yarse**, also live in Yatenga. The Mossi themselves, despite having resisted the advances of Islam for so long, are nowadays mostly Muslim here too.

Ouahigouya

OUAHIGOUYA's wide streets and low buildings give a lazy feeling of space, especially after the dust and shimmering heat of day. The market sprawls, the *autogare* sprawls, the main square sprawls: you can't rush about here.

The town's lack of specific "sights" belies its significant **history**. Most important buildings were destroyed in the nineteenth-century **Yatenga civil wars**. Ouahigouya was founded in 1757 – the last of Yatenga's capitals – and marked the northern limit of the state's expansion. King Kango's summons to the chiefs of Yatenga to pay him homage gives the town its name (from *Waka yuguya!* – "Come and greet"). Unfortunately, the great palace where this took place was destroyed in 1825 during one of the struggles for the throne, in which the city was rased to the ground.

Kango may originally have built Ouahigouya as a salt depot; he certainly had his eye on trans-Saharan commodities (gold and kola for example) and hoped to make money by channelling more of their trade through Yatenga. Another motive in building the town could have been to escape from the power of the Mossi aristocracy which had always resented his rule and may well have been repsonsible for usurping him in the first place. At any rate, Kango populated the new city with captives and ethnic minorities, from whose number he chose many of his officials.

As well as the dynastic struggles of the 1820s and 30s, Ouahigouya suffered serious damage in the later wars between Sons of Sagha and Sons of Tougouri. By the time the French managed to secure their stooge Boulli on the throne at the end of 1896, it was half in ruins again, but they needed a base for eastward conquest and "pacification" of Yatenga, and so constructed a fort and rebuilt the town as the regional capital.

Accommodation

Ouahigouya's **hotels** range from dirt cheap and seedy to French-style deluxe.

Auberge Populaire, along the main road near the *quartier administrative*. Simple rooms with fans, showers and nets. ②.

Hôtel de l'Amitié, 500m down the Mopti road (☎55.05.21). More polished than the above with large, airy rooms, some S/C and AC. ②.

Hôtel Dunia, off the Kaya Road, east of the hospital (☎55.05.95). AC luxury and even a pool: excellent value for money. ③.

Hôtel du Nord, north of the *autogare* (☎55.01.94). Very basic place, and not that clean. The bar is a bit loose, but the management's friendly and they don't run out of cold beer (or music) till midnight. ②.

Hôtel Receuil, 2km out of town towards the *barrage*. Incredibly low-priced rooms around a shady inner courtyard. Backpackers' paradise. ①.

The Town

By day, Ouahigouya lends itself to gentle meanderings. The only sight as such is **Naba Kango's tomb**, an imposing white edifice between the Mairie and the present Naba's compound. According to popular legend, anyone who walks all the way round it will die. The **Yatenga Naba's compound** lies on the old site of Kango's palace. With luck, you may even get to meet the Naba, who's said to be an expert on Yatenga history – as well he would need to be to justify his position. On the way back, you could check out the **market**, always worth a wander. Ouahigouya also boasts no less than 37 **mosques**, built in a pretty and distinctive style. Not to be overlooked either is the atractive lake formed by the **barrage** just 100m west of *L'Amitié* (see "Accommodation"); the desert is in bloom around here and you can stroll across the *barrage*.

Eating and other practicalities

Hotel food in Ouahigouya is good; the *Amitié* serves up satisfying meals, and the *Dunia*'s excellent French-Middle Eastern food makes it the first choice of local expats. Smaller places, where you pay for the food and not the service, include the *Ciné Restaurant*, the *Restaurant du Centre* and the *Faso Benie* – rice, yam, pasta, soup, chicken, liver, beans and salad. For **picnic supplies**, there are two small supermarkets just off the market square. The *BICIA* bank in Ouahigouya will change FF travellers' cheques.

In the evenings, **cold beer and hot music** at the *Nord* and the *Populaire* take you through to midnight – and you can keep going beyond that if you move on to the *Amitié*'s disco. The *Amitié* is the main night spot in Ouahigouya and can be a bit of a thrash. For a quieter drink, the *Bar Caïman*, next door keeps a well-stocked bar and does brochettes.

Moving on

If you're **heading for Ouaga**, you have plenty of choice of vehicles, including the *Régie X9* bus (they have their own stop by the market and leave at 3pm Mon–Fri, 8am Sun, no service on Sat). The road is now paved the whole way to Ouaga; allow three hours for the trip. You should also be able to find the odd *occasion* to **Djibo**, something to **Bobo-Dioulasso** most days (weather permitting), and even the odd **Abidjan**-bound truck. **Into Mali**, however, transport is scarcer and there's no through service to Mopti, just a vehicle every couple of days or so to **Koro**, where you'll have to change. The *piste* to Koro is passable in the dry season, but be prepared for tough travelling conditions. *Taxis brousse* leave from Ouahigouya's main square, but if you end up waiting for days, try the lorries that head out on Saturday to Koro.

Around the Yatenga district

Most of Yatenga's **sites of interest** are spread around the villages. Its first capital, and the Mossi capital before Yatenga's secession, was La, now called **La-Todin**, beyond the borders of modern Yatenga, 22km west of Yako.

The fourth Yatenga Naba, Guéda, moved his capital north to **GOURCY**, where you can see the **sacred hill** on which his successors are still enthroned. Here, too, are the royal amulets stolen by Pabre on behalf of her brother Yadega. In the civil wars of the 1890s, the Sons of Sagha kidnapped the amulets, thus preventing the French from crowning Naba Boulli until they were returned at the end of 1897. Gourcy is on the main Ouagadougou–Ouahigouya road, 42km south of Ouahigouya.

The kingdom's third and penultimate capital, **SOMNIAGA** was seized from the kingdom of Zandoma by Naba Vanteberegum as part of his campaign to enlarge Yatenga. Seven kilometres south of Ouahigouya on the Ouaga road, it makes an easy walk first thing in the morning (don't forget to carry a few litres of water), or you can hitch. Most of Yatenga's *nabas* are buried here in the **royal cemetery** (*nayaado*) and looked after by the Yaogo Naba, the man to find if you want to see it. One quaint little Yatenga burial custom was the interment of the *naba's* court jesters – alive – with their dead king.

Of the capitals of neighbouring traditional states, **YAKO** is the easiest to visit. Some 70km south of Ouahigouya, it is now accessible by paved road. The most striking first impression is of its **mosque**, but its main claim to local fame goes further. Capital of a kingdom founded by Naba Yelkone – son of the same Kumdumye who split with Yadega over the question of the Mossi throne – it was a perpetual object of Yatenga-Ouagadougou rivalry, generally a fief of the latter. Naba Kango managed to force its submission and the flight of its *naba*, who was only allowed to stay on condition that he planted a sacred grove of thorn bushes (*kango* in More) outside the town. The French also found Yako a tough nut to crack. More recently, **Thomas Sankara** was born here; with some discretion, you may be able to get someone to show you exactly where.

ZANDOMA, the region's very first Mossi capital, is now a tiny village some 40km southwest of Ouahigouya, northwest of Gourcy. The chief still claims descent from **Naba Rawa**, whose tomb can be seen close to his compound.

Other places of interest in and around Yatenga include: **Ramatoulaye**, 25km east of Ouahigouya on the road to Rollo, with another impressive **mosque**, a major centre of Hammalism in colonial days; **Lago**, some 30km south of Ouahigouya (but 41km by road from Zogoré), **burial site** of the first Yatenga *nabas*; **Sissamba**, 11km southwest of Ouahigouya and en route to Lago, where the Sons of Sagha installed their pretender to the throne on Naba Boulli's accession in 1894 and which the French sacked the following year; and **Mengao**, 82km northeast of Ouahigouya on the road to Djibo (27km further), which was the last capital of the kingdom of Lurum and is still the home of the **Kurumba paramount "earth chief"**, the counterpart of the Yatenga Naba – the Mossi paramount sky chief.

THE GOUROUNSI COUNTRY

The area **around Pô** on the Ghanaian border **south of Ouagadougou** is dominated by the Grusi or **Gourounsi**, which usually includes the **Kassena**, the **Nouna** and the **Sissala** from around Léo. Their distinctive **architecture** provides the region's main attraction. Gourounsi country also boasts a couple of **national parks** – difficult to get to without your own transport – and some interesting archeological remains near Léo.

The Gourounsi build their **houses** from mud in smooth, sand-castle shapes, often painted with striking diamond patterns. Larger compounds may consist of whole labyrinths of submerged rooms and doorways through which people weave and duck. Buildings are not expected to last more than a few seasons and new houses are built around the foundations of older dwellings, resulting in a characteristic organic appearance. Also typical are the forked and notched logs, leant against the walls as ladders to the **flat roofs** where grain is commonly dried, out of goat-reach. Women gather here to chat and smoke during the day, the whole family often sleeps here, and all sorts of stuff is stored. Village chiefs usually have the largest and most impressive compounds – though not necessarily the prettiest. You can often tell the status of a family from the height of its walls.

THE GOUROUNSI

How long the people known as **Gourounsi** (originally a Mossi term of denigration) have lived in this region isn't clear, but Mossi tradition claims they were pushed back across the Red Volta River by the thirteenth Mogho Naba, Nakiem, at the end of the seventeenth century. Never united, the various strands of Gourounsi-speakers have long existed in a state of near-permanent village war. Their lack of central government has always made them vulnerable to attack from more organized groups, especially the Mossi who often made kidnapping raids for slaves. Many Mossi dissidents set themselves up as chiefs in Gourounsi-land, and their families continue to live here. Gourounsi chiefs possess sacred objects called *kwara* – insignia of office – which are handed down from generation to generation.

At the end of the nineteenth century, the Gourounsi were the targets of Djerma Muslim zealots from the Niamey region, who stormed down on horseback and engaged in heavy slave-raiding under a *jihad* banner. They converted the son of the chief of Satí and set up shop there, almost decimating the lands of the Sissala, Nouna and Kassena, before being defeated by a Gourounsi–French alliance in 1895.

On the way to **Pô**, the region's main town, from Ouagadougou, you pass through **Kombissiri**, 40km south of the capital. This town became a Muslim centre following the settlement here of a community of **Yarse** (Mande-speaking traders) in the eighteenth century. Its religious status was developed by the pro-Muslim 25th Mogho Naba, Sawadogho, who ruled from 1825–42 and had the mosque built. It's 4km east of the town: follow the *piste* from the police checkpoint at the northern end of Kombissiri.

THE GOUROUNSI LANGUAGE

If you learn no other Gourounsi, at least learn to say *Din le*, the all-purpose greeting, which means "Thank you". The following sampler comes from "Kassem", the main dialect of Gourounsi, spoken by the *Kassena*.

Good morning	*Tim paga*	1	*Kalo*	6	*Trodo*	20	*Finle*
		2	*Inle*	7	*Tirpai*	50	Finnu
Good evening	*Tim dadan*	3	*Nto*	8	*Nana*	100	*Bi*
		4	*Nna*	9	*Nogo*	500	*Bi yennu*
		5	*Unu*	10	*Fuga*	1000	*Moro*

Pô

PÔ lacks traditional architecture, but has plenty of **fountains** with revolutionary names – "Nelson Mandela", "Enver Hoxha", "Les Trois Luttes". If this is your last town in Francophone Africa, make the most of the plentiful cold beer and relative lack of petty corruption. Coming the other way, it's a gentle introduction to some of French Africa's more tiresome aspects – high prices and an obsession with *papiers*. The Pô **police** are fond of asking for these and you can expect a fair number of spot checks, but like most of the townspeople they're friendly enough and there's no big hassle. Pô is also a garrison town with a chequered recent history – though the soldiers don't obtrude.

A SHOT OF PÔ HISTORY

According to legend, Pô was founded around 1500, by a Mossi man, **Nablogo**, son of Mogho Naba Oubri. He started cultivating a field (*pô*) but got into a land rights dispute with Kassena neighbours. About this time, a certain **Gonkwora** from Kasana near Léo turned up here, having left his village after being disinherited of his rightful chiefship. He brought three magic bracelets with him (still looked after by his descendants in Pô) and fell in with Nablogo, who helped him, and in whose dispute with the Kassena he interceded. Gonkwora's brother – the ancestor of Pô's present chief – then arrived from their home village with the village *kwara*. Gonkwora meanwhile married Nablogo's daughter and they all lived happily ever after. Gonkwora's tomb is supposed to be under a sacred baobab in the Kasno quarter of town.

More recent and less halcyon history has also been made in Pô. In 1976, **Thomas Sankara** set up the *Centre Nationale d'Entrainement* here, taken over by Blaise Compaoré in 1982. The following year the Ouédraogo regime arrested Sankara and fellow officers. Pô became a radical focus for students, young workers and academics, who came to join the commandos. In August 1983, the coup that toppled Ouédraogo, fired the revolution and put Sankara in power, was launched here. And it was from Pô that Compaoré planned a second takeover in 1987, that led to Sankara's untimely death and put Compaoré in power.

Practicalities

Don't expect much comfort in Pô – all the **accommodation** is pretty basic. Arriving from northern Ghana, you'll find it pricey too, but, as a frontier town, there is at least some choice. Your most economical option is the *Bar la Montagne* opposite the customs about 1km south of the town: they have a variety of rooms and prices, from cheap and dirty to half decent, with a bucket shower and murals by a passing Ghanaian artist – but no *courant*, water off from dusk to dawn, warm beer and limited food (①). For a few luxuries, you could check out the *Hôtel Mantoro* (☎39.00.41; ②), behind the *cité* (housing development) north of the town, whose 24 aid workers' houses, built by Sankara, are looked after by an elusive caretaker.

For street **food**, try near the market and around the cinema. Every evening, there's good fried fish from the Black Volta, brochettes, guinea fowl, roast mutton and plenty more. There's a variety of sit-down places, too, dishing up *couscous*, sandwiches, omelettes, rice, spaghetti, *tô* and brochettes. Pô bursts into life in the **evenings**, despite the fact that electricity is mainly confined to the north end of town; the *Commando Woro* down near the customs post (look for the "Honte a l'Imperialisme" sign) is worth braving despite its military atmosphere (it's an army club) for the ice cold beer, music till midnight and edible food. The *Consolatrice Bar Restaurant*, opposite the *cité*, plays music till 11.30pm.

Note there's no **bank** in Pô: people in the market or around the *autogare* will change Ghana cedis, FF and dollars (but not sterling) for CFA francs.

MOVING ON FROM PÔ

Frequent *taxis brousse* to **Ouagadougou** (anything from 2–7hr) leave from the *autogare* in front of the police station. *Régie X9* goes every afternoon. South **into Ghana**, there are taxis to Paga and even as far as Bolgatanga, especially on Friday (market day in Bolga). Alternatively you could reasonably expect to hitch from the customs post just south of town. The *STC* Ouaga–Accra bus also halts in Pô and is scheduled to churn into town on Monday or Friday morning.

Vehicles to **Tiébélé** only operate on market days there (Tues, Wed, Thurs) and to Léo likewise (Sun). On other days, and to other destinations such as the wildlife reserves, you'll have to make private arrangements with taxi drivers or car or moped owners, though taxis are expensive if you want to do a *déplacement*. To rent, ask around the *autogare* or market, or see if your hotel proprietor knows anyone. Women might try the *Action Sociale* women's movement, 100m up the Léo road.

Around Pô

The best of the Gourounsi country is to be found outside the modern city of Pô and in the smaller villages along the roads parallel with the frontier on both sides. The Gourounsi traditional capital, **Tiébélé**, has the finest architecture, and the highest volume of visitors. The **Pô National Park** lies across the road from Ouaga to Pô and, south of **Nobéré**, you may see representatives of the district's elephant herd – one of the few places in West Africa where "Elephants on Road" is a delightful possibility. Finally, if you can find transport from Pô (tricky except on Sunday, market day), you could make the 126-kilometre trip to the Djerma-Gourounsi ruins near **Léo**.

Tiébélé

TIÉBÉLÉ, the traditional Gourounsi capital, 31km east of Pô, is something of a tourist attraction, and worth the visit. The chief here is the most important *chef de canton* in Gourounsi country and you should go and see him on first arriving: his compound is, in any case, the town's main attraction. Tiébélé's houses are better built and decorated than others in Kassena country and the Tiébélé chief's is a magnificent maze of mud-pie huts. For a good view of the whole compound, scale the refuse heap behind it.

Coming into town from Pô, you'll find yourself travelling down an avenue of large trees that unexpectedly cleaves off from the road, leaving you on a much more recent road. To find the chief, you want to leave the road and follow the original avenue of trees, which will take you to his compound. You have to sign the visitor's book and pay a steep fee for a guide and authorization to take photos.

Tiakané

TIAKANÉ, 7km west of Pô, is more laid-back. Its houses aren't as striking as those in Tiébélé but you'll feel more like a visitor and less like a punter. The *Cave de Binger* in the chief's compound is a mini underground labyrinth where the villagers hid the nineteenth-century French explorer from a party of Mossi who were out to kill him. Binger went on to become governor of Cote d'Ivoire. His family have evidently not forgotten Tiakané: recently they sent funds from France to build a village school. The chief provides a guide to show you round Binger's hide-out and both will expect a reasonable tip. Tiakané makes a nice early morning walk from Pô, especially after it's rained.

Parc National de Pô and Nazinga reserve

Without your own transport, you'll have to make private arrangements to get to the two **reserves** near Pô. Cycling down from Ouagadougou isn't a bad idea. To visit the **Parc**

National de Pô (main gate 31km north of Pô, 5km south of the bridge over the Volta Rouge; open Nov–May), you first need a permit from the rangers' office by the PTT in Pô town, behind the police station. The park *pistes* aren't currently in good shape and rangers have been advising moped riders against using them. The sector **east of the main road** does have a feasible circuit of about 35km however, which you could ride around, preferably in the early morning from the unstaffed south gate – some 9km north of Pô – to the north gate. Baboons and antelope are the most obvious inhabitants but the elephants are there if you keep looking, and there are buffalo and warthog too. Tracks are mostly rather sandy, the vegetation tall rank grasses, thick bush, stands of dense forest near the water courses and occasional clearings of more open country savaged by fire. Going round the park alone may be an exciting business, but if you try it by bicycle, be sure to take at least ten litres of water per person and leave word of your plans in Pô.

The **Nazinga Reserve** south of the Léo road (its north boundary runs along the road from about 15km to about 40km west of Pô) is an easier target, and you may have better luck spotting game there. Set up by the Canadians to study wildlife resource management, the place is (comparatively) bursting at the seams with **elephants**, and also harbours several species of monkeys, baboons, antelopes, gazelles and warthogs and, rather surprisingly, **lions**. You'll have to get a ranger to accompany you from the office; he'll know where you're likely to find animals. It's even possible to do a tour on foot, though entirely at your own risk. **Accommodation** is available but it's rudimentary and you'll need a mosquito net and mattress or sleeping bag.

Léo and the Djerma-Gourounsi ruins

A small border town with a couple of hotels, **LÉO**'s main attraction is the nearby **ruins** in the villages of Satí and Yoro. They date from the period of the **Djerma invasions** at the end of the nineteenth century, when the Djerma made alliances with Gourounsi Muslim chiefs. Satí became the capital of a Djerma mini-state and Yoro was fortified as a warehouse for slaves and booty acquired in raids on the local "infidel" Gourounsi. Later, the Gourounsi Muslim leaders had a change of mind about their Djerma business partners and revolted – a resistance which eventually involved collusion with a Djerma renegade called Hamaria who successfully enlisted French support to defeat the Djerma. French involvement led, as everywhere, to a colonial sell-out and the formal "protection" of the Gourounsi.

Satí, 22km northwest of Léo, should still have the remains of fortifications and battlements, especially on the eastern side, while a kilometre to the south, the chief's personal mosque and compound may still be visible. Seven kilometres back down the road to Léo are the ruins of more fortifications – including triangular loopholes and a well, used by the Djerma while besieging Satí. **Yoro**, 32km west of Léo on the way to Diébougou, still preserves a long stretch of wall, part of the Djerma treasure house.

None of this amounts to very impressive archaeology, but the search for the ruins makes a good hook from which to hang idle wanderings. And if you have your own transport, Léo is a reasonable night stop en route from Gourounsi to **Lobi country** (see p.745).

BOBO, BANFORA AND THE SOUTHWEST

Fed by the **Comoé** and other lesser rivers, the southwest is the most densely forested, and hilliest, region in Burkina and a pleasant change from the relentless grasslands covering most of the rest of the country. Rich vegetation camouflages a wealth of natu-

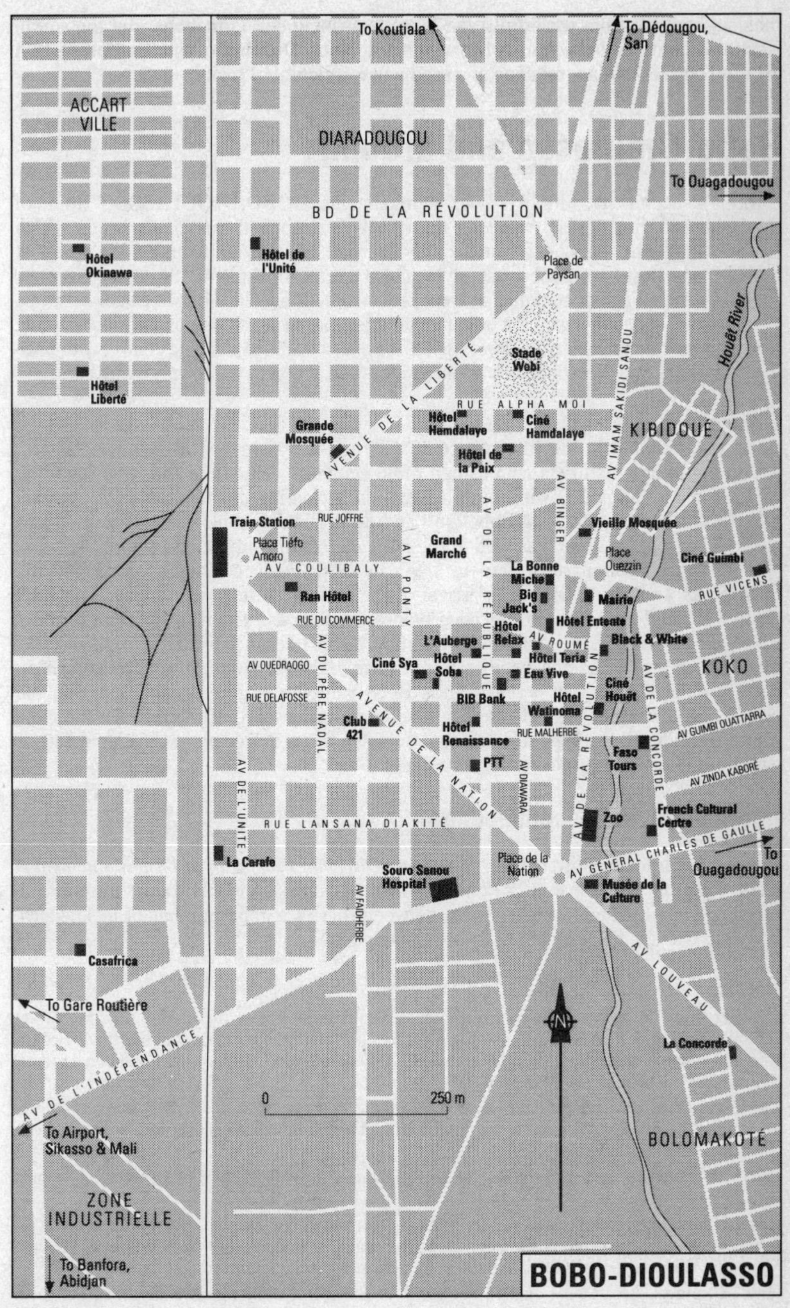

To Koutiala
To Dédougou, San
ACCART VILLE
DIARADOUGOU
To Ouagadougou
BD DE LA RÉVOLUTION
Hôtel Okinawa
Hôtel de l'Unité
Place de Paysan
Houët River
Stade Wobi
AVENUE DE LA LIBERTÉ
AV IMAM SAKIDI SANOU
Hôtel Liberté
RUE ALPHA MOI
Hôtel Hamdalaye
Ciné Hamdalaye
KIBIDOUÉ
Grande Mosquée
Hôtel de la Paix
AV BINGER
AV DE LA RÉPUBLIQUE
Train Station
RUE JOFFRE
Vieille Mosquée
Place Tiéfo Amoro
Grand Marché
Place Ouezzin
Ciné Guimbi
AV COULIBALY
AV PONTY
La Bonne Miche
Big Jack's
Mairie
RUE VICENS
Ran Hôtel
RUE DU COMMERCE
Hôtel Entente
Hôtel Relax
AV ROUMÉ
Black & White
L'Auberge
AV OUEDRAOGO
AV DU PÈRE NADAL
Ciné Sya
Hôtel Soba
Hôtel Teria
KOKO
Eau Vive
RUE DELAFOSSE
BIB Bank
Hôtel Watinoma
Ciné Houët
AV DE LA CONCORDE
AVENUE DE LA NATION
Club 421
Hôtel Renaissance
RUE MALHERBE
AV GUIMBI OUATTARRA
Faso Tours
PTT
AV DIAWARA
AV ZINDA KABORÉ
AV DE L'UNITÉ
AV DE LA RÉVOLUTION
Zoo
French Cultural Centre
RUE LANSANA DIAKITÉ
AV GÉNÉRAL CHARLES DE GAULLE
La Carafe
Place de la Nation
To Ouagadougou
Souro Sanou Hospital
Musée de la Culture
AV FAIDHERBE
AV LOUVEAU
Casafrica
To Gare Routière
AV DE L'INDÉPENDANCE
La Concorde
0
250 m
To Airport, Sikasso & Mali
BOLOMAKOTÉ
ZONE INDUSTRIELLE
To Banfora, Abidjan
BOBO-DIOULASSO

ral sites, ranging from **waterfalls** and lakes to striking cliff formations. But the southwest also contains important urban centres – **Bobo-Dioulasso** and **Banfora** – that grew up on the Abidjan train line in a productive agricultural region.

Bobo-Dioulasso and around

Burkina's second city, with over 300,000 inhabitants, **BOBO-DIOULASSO** ("Home of the Bobo and the Dioula") was long the country's economic capital, a position which has only in recent years been convincingly usurped by Ouagadougou. Yet life moves at a slow pace here, and Bobo has style and a great atmosphere. Sweeping avenues roofed by the foliage of cool mango trees, colonial buildings in the *style soudanais* and a rich mixture of peoples give it a unique character that makes it one of the most inviting places to unwind anywhere in West Africa. It's also a traditional music centre, with balafon orchestras and electric bands adding night-time action to the town's many bars.

Some history

Bobo was founded in the fifteenth century, when it was known as **Sya**, or "island". According to oral history, a man named Molo Oumarou came here and, after founding villages in Timina and Sakabi, built a house in a clearing of the woods by a stream called the Houet. A village of Bobo-Fing and Bobo-Dioula people grew up around this original home. The French arrived in the late nineteenth century, and set up their first administrative headquarters here in 1897. In 1928, Pépin Malherbe broadened the town limits as Bobo awaited the arrival of the **railway line** from Abidjan. The RAN pushed through in 1934, two decades before the line was extended to Ouaga, and a large colonial town grew up around the station, a short distance from the original settlement (the graceful Sudanic-inspired architecture of the *gare routière*, market and *palais de justice* dates from this period). Thus Bobo gained a large economic jump on the present capital, which helps to explain its commercial importance today . On the main routes to Mali and the Côte d'Ivoire, too, the town has acquired an international flavour with numerous foreign workers and students.

Information and accommodation

For tourist information, contact the *Houët Direction Provincial de l'Environnement et de la Tourisme* (BP 18; ☎98.25.12 or 98.26.09). **Lodgings** in Bobo range from dormitory beds to AC hotels with pools. In between there's a good number of inexpensive *auberges*, lacking in luxury but usually well maintained.

Hotels

L'Auberge, av de la République (☎99.01.84). Centrally located near the market, this restaurant (French cooking at a good price) also has nice, S/C, AC rooms, a clean pool in the shaded courtyard and billiards in the bar. Recently expanded, the hotel has a new wing with 30 additional rooms. The *terrasse* is a popular place for drinks. ④.

Casafrica, off av de l'Indépendance near the *Brakina* brewery (☎98.01.57). Best budget place in town, French-owned, with clean rooms ranged around a delightful shady courtyard, where you can also camp for a very low rate. ①.

Hôtel de l'Entente, corner of rue du Commerce and av Binger (☎98.15.12). Large non-S/C rooms with fans and nets or AC. Well-maintained and attractive courtyard. ②–③.

Hôtel Hamdalaye, rue Alpha Moi. Nice management and very clean, S/C, AC rooms in terraces. Only possible disadvantage is the very loud disco right next door (the music stops at 11.30pm Mon–Fri). Otherwise, top-of-the-line Bobo budget boarding. Bike rental too. ②.

Hôtel Okinawa, Accart Ville district, Secteur 9 (☎98.06.34). Simple rooms without fan but clean and friendly. The attractive courtyard hosts a nightly disco (no cover) and there's a restaurant, serving reasonably priced meals. The same management own the very similar *Hôtel Liberté* nearby. ①.

Hôtel de la Paix, next to the *gare routière*. Neither the cleanest nor the most comfortable accommodation in town, but it's the cheapest in the centre. ①.

RAN Hôtel, near the train station (☎98.18.45). This three-star place is the best in town. S/C, AC rooms and a pool. ⑤.

Relax Hôtel, av Ouédraogo (☎98.02.93). Swimming pool and S/C rooms with AC. ④.

Hôtel Renaissance, av de la République (☎98.23.31). Popular restaurant and *dancing*, brilliantly located in the very heart of town, with clean, adjoining rooms, grouped around an attractive courtyard. ②.

Hôtel Soba, rue Delafosse (BP 185; ☎99.10.48). Colonial-style place, with good rooms, some with AC, and a pleasant patio-garden. ③.

Hôtel Teria, av Roumé (☎97.19.72). Comfortable and calm with an ideal location near the market. ②.

Hôtel de l'Unité, av de l'Unité (☎98.08.42). Good-value, clean and friendly accommodation in rooms with fans. ②.

Hôtel Watinoma, corner of rue Malherbe and av Binger (☎98.21.62). Clean AC rooms. They also have an excellent restaurant with European food. ④.

The Town

In the heart of Bobo, the **grand marché** was built in 1951 in a pleasing neo-Sudanic style. It's still today the centre of activity in town and among the fruit, vegetables and manufactured goods, you'll find a wide selection of **crafts**, including woven blankets and cloth from the region. Follow the road leading out of the market's eastern end 200m to the **old town** in the **Kibidoué** district. As you arrive, you'll notice the porcupine silhouette of the **Vieille Mosquée** – a *banco* construction originally built in 1880. Except during prayers, it's possible to visit; ask the guardian and leave him a small tip after the tour, but beware of taking photographs.

From here, kids will doubtless pick you up and want to show you around the historic core of town. First on their list of worthy sites is the "Konsa", the **oldest house** in town, said to date from the fifteenth century. As you follow them through the narrow streets of the ancient neighbourhoods, they'll point out **traditional artisans** – mostly blacksmiths and weavers – and finish the tour with a stop at the **sacred fish pond** – the murky backwaters of the Houët stream where oversized mudfish peer up for food. There's no telling what makes them sacred: fishy totems are a Bobo speciality.

In the midst of your meanderings, don't miss the **Marché de Poterie**, two blocks north of the mosque, where demand is still high for earthenware vessels from remote villages like Dalgan, Tcheriba and Sikiana. Pots vary in size and shape depending on their function, but they're all quite reasonably priced, and there are striking examples of unusual water jugs painted in bright colours and bold designs.

Lastly, do take time to see the new **Musée de la Culture**, on the Place de la Nation (9am–noon & 3.30–6pm; closed Mon). Small, but pleasant to wander through, the museum boasts an interesting collection of **ethnographic artefacts** such as Bobo wooden statues and Senoufo funeral masks as well as regional clothing as worn by the Fula, Senoufo and other nationals. Outside, stroll through examples of Burkinabe housing styles – Bobo, Fula and Senoufo – beautifully decorated and furnished.

Incidentally, Bobo's **zoo**, on the av de la Révolution, is a pretty sad collection of half a dozen beasts, none faring too well in captivity. Don't bother with it.

Eating

Quite apart from the consistently good hotel restaurants, Bobo has plenty of fine **places to eat**, many of them serving up the especially delicious local **beef**. The best street snacks in town are to be had from a group of women opposite the cinema south of the market, who serve huge, tasty **avocado salad submarines** for next to nothing.

Café des Amis, av Binger. Fresh yoghurt daily and a really nice place to sit and eat.

Restaurant La Beninoise (aka *Chez Dominique*), across from the *Pharmacie du Levant* (☎98.02.02). Meat and fish with spicy vegetable sauces. Great cooking, friendly service and affordable prices.

La Bonne Miche, av Binger at av Coulibaly. Popular *patisserie* and a likely place to bump into other travellers in search of the country's best *pain au raisin*.

La Boule Verte, av Ouédraogo at av de la République (☎99.02.79). Counts among Bobo's better French restaurants.

La Carafe, near the tracks, one block west of av de l'Unité, off rue Lansana Diakité. Moderately priced Ivoirian specialities such as chicken *kedjenou* or *atieké* with grilled fish. A good place to taste *foutou*, made from pounded plantains.

La Casa, one street north of the market. A narrow leafy entrance leads into one of Bobo's hidden delights. The food is excellent (inexpensive too) and the music and ambience enjoyable in this shaded courtyard retreat.

Chez Mme Diallo, av Faidherbe, near the *Club 421*. Inexpensive African food.

La Concorde, av Loveau, across from the prison (☎98.12.59). Classic French cuisine, with a lively atmosphere. Courtyard tables grouped around a dance floor – a favourite local haunt.

L'Eau Vive, across from the *Relax Hôtel* (☎98.21.72). Sister restaurant (literally) to the *Eau Vive* in Ouaga, with similar international specialities and waitressing nuns.

Le Transfo, zone des Ecoles (☎98.17.05). Out of the centre, but well known by taxi drivers. Energetic bar/*dancing* where you can eat moderately priced European dishes including salads and a variety of grilled meats.

Le Troquet, av de la République, across from the *Auberge*. Cheap and excellent African food – a great place to hang out and watch Bobo buzz. Always crowded.

Yan Kady, av de l'Unité. A good place for inexpensive and well-prepared African food.

Restaurant Yasmine, av Binger at rue du Commerce (above *Big Jack's*). Upstairs restaurant with *paillotes* and a great view of the streets around the commercial centre. African specialities reasonably priced.

Nightlife

Like the Ouagalais, the people of Bobo are great night-timers. The percussionist **Coulibaly Twins** and **Mahama Konaté**, the founder of Farafina, are from Bobo and regularly play the town clubs when home from Paris. Some restaurants are worth a visit – including *La Concorde* and *Le Transfo*, listed under "Eating". In the excitement of the urban clubs, don't overlook the wealth of **traditional music** that vibrates from balafons and calabash drums at *dolo* bars in the Koko district just east of the city centre – by far the lowest priced entertainment in town. At the time this book was going to press, it was rumoured that one of Bobo's best venues for traditional live music, *Le Makhno*, had relocated in the secteur Sigasou-Cilla in the northwest of town. It's probably best to ask a taxi driver to help you out.

Le 421, rue Malherbe at av Faidherbe (☎98.20.03). Dark indoors hotel-disco, very frenetic and usually full despite the high cover charge.

Big Jack's, av Binger near the *Black and White*. Very hip place to hang out, dance and be seen.

Black and White, av Binger at rue du Commerce. The restaurant is bad (limited menu, dreadful service), but the disco's fine. Good music and plenty of sweaty bodies.

Le Daffra, rue Alpha Moi, next to *Hôtel Hamdalaye* (☎98.20.55). Inexpensive bar/*dancing* and notorious pick-up joint.

Le Golfe Dancing, av de la Révolution, a little north of the *Memphis*, near the Commissariat. Pleasant garden and dance floor under *paillotes*.

Memphis, av de la Révolution across from the Mairie. Bar-restaurant-disco with good food and frequent live music.

Bar-Restau-Club Nouvelle Renaissance, av de la République at rue Delafosse. Open-air bar-*dancing* with attractive *paillotes* in the courtyard and live bands almost nightly. A lot of people, and hustlers can be a hassle.

Le Rêve, opposite the PTT (☎98.04.19). Formerly *Le Makhno*: a little touristy, but with good music during the week and live bands at the weekends. Popular restaurant too.

Around Bobo

Some rewarding **side-trips** are within easy distance of Bobo. If you haven't got a car, perhaps the best way to see them is by renting a bicycle or moped from the place next to the *Total* station on the west side of the market towards the railway station.

Top on the list of Bobo excursions is a swimming hole called **La Guinguette**, 18km west of town in the **Kou Forest**. You can splash around in bilharzia-free waters, though it's sometimes crowded, especially at weekends. Some 15km further, the Sikasso (Mali) road takes you to the village of **Koumi**, with characteristic, pseudo-fortified, Bobo architecture. This is a popular spot, and your presence will surprise no one; check with the chief if you want to take pictures (whether you've a permit or not).

Dafra, 8km southeast of Bobo, boasts a **pool of sacred fish**, in beautiful surroundings, much more important than the underwhelming mud hole in Bobo. Chickens are sacrificed to the enormous catfish – some even wearing earrings ("a miracle") – who are the symbol of Bobo and reproduced on the Mairie wall in town. To get there, take a taxi most of the way, or walk along the **path** from the junction of the Ouaga road and av du Gouverneur Général Eboué, right on the edge of town. It's a tricky route to follow and you'll probably need a guide (kids en route will no doubt oblige for the customary *cadeau*) but it's worth it for the scenery. Set off early and take water. Unfortunately, there have been some recent muggings, so take no valuables. Remember, too, to wear nothing red – it's prohibited at this sacred place.

Another popular attraction, the **hippo lake** (*mare aux hippopotames*), is located some 60km from Bobo, near Satiri on the Dédougou/Ouahigouya road. It's a little far for a moped and the difficult tracks (even in the dry season) just about rule it out, so take a Dédougou-bound taxi from the main *gare routière*, or head to the *gare de Satiri* on the intersection of the bd de la Paix and the av Général Merlin. The Satiri taxi stops in small villages along the way – many of them featuring picturesque **Sahelian-style mosques** – and takes up to three hours (as opposed to less than two for the Dédougou-bound taxi) to cover the scenic route. To get to the lake from Satiri, you could hope to hitch with passing tourists at weekends, or, if you're alone, you could probably find someone to take you on the back of a bike (fix an arranged price for the return trip). Fishermen at the lakeside will take you out by *pirogues* for as close an inspection of the hippos as you're likely to want. Again, fix the fee in advance – they appreciate aspirins and cigarettes as a tip. If you're extremely lucky, they say, you may even spot elephants.

Bobo listings

Airlines *Air Afrique* is on av Ponty near the market (☎98.19.23). The office is useful for information and flight bookings only; there are no *Air Afrique* flights to/from Bobo. *Air Burkina* is on av Ouédraogo, near the *Ciné Sya* (☎98.18.87). See the "Moving on from Bobo" box for flight details.

Banks *BIB*, *BICIA* and *BND* all have branches near the central market (Secteur 1). Changing travellers' cheques is usually no problem.

Bike/mobylette rental Easy to find, in the market area, especially at the west end towards the train station.

Books, newspapers and maps International press, mostly French, available at *L'Auberge*. *Librairies* in the market area include *Socifa* and *La Sarane*, where you can also buy city maps.

Car rental *Auto-Location* has an office on the av de la Nation.

Cinemas In addition to the new and comfortable AC *Ciné Bobo 90*, rue Alpha Moi across from the stadium, are less state-of-the-art neighbourhood theatres: *Ciné Sya*, av Ouédraogo next to *Hôtel Soba*; *Ciné Houet*, av de la Révolution; and *Ciné Guimbi*, off rue Vicens.

French Cultural Centre Junction of av Géneral Charles de Gaulle and av de la Concorde, just east of the river. Good library and outdoor reading area, with magazines and newspapers. African, European and American films, several nights a week.

Hospital *Hôpital Sourou Sanou*, av Lansana Diakité at av Ponty (☎98.00.79 or 98.00.82).

Post office av de la Nation at av de la République. Functioning poste restante. International calls from the adjoining *ONATEL* office.

Supermarkets *Faso Yaar* near the market off av Ouédraogo; *Socibe*, opposite the market's eastern side on av de la République; and best of the lot is the well-plenished *Self Service* across the street on the southern end of the market.

Swimming The *Auberge*'s pool is not open to non-residents: try the pools at the *Rélax* or the *RAN*, which are likely to be less fussy about it.

Theatre Check the schedule at the *Théâtre Amitié*, on av Géneral Charles de Gaulle. Also ask at the French Cultural Centre.

MOVING ON FROM BOBO

In addition to domestic destinations, Bobo is a springboard for Mali (Mopti, Bamako) and Côte d'Ivoire. You can get fuller details on buses and flights from Bobo's travel agents: *Faso Tours* (BP 18) has an office next to the Mairie. Other agencies include *Egi Voyages* on rue Delafosse.

TRAINS

The *Etalon* has a daily 6.30am departure for **Ouaga** – five hours of Miami Vice and Bruce Lee on the video and you're there. You can also use the *Express* (up from Abidjan), which reaches Bobo around dawn, en route to Ouaga, but it's less convenient and much slower. Call the *SCFB* (☎98.29.50, 98.29.22 or 98.23.91) for schedule changes or check at the station – and buy your tickets in advance. Get to the station early: seats are not allocated. There is also the daily train to **Abidjan** (dep. 3pm), a possible means of reaching **Banfora.**

BUSH TAXIS AND BUSES

The main *gare routière* for *taxis brousse* is on the west side of town. This is the quickest means to points in **Mali** (punishing *piste* as far as Sikasso if you go that way, reasonable tarmac to Ségou if you go that) and **Côte d'Ivoire** (good sealed road) as well as to Ouagadougou and Dédougou, Banfora and Boromo. Bobo is also a possible departure point for the **Lobi country** via a difficult *piste* to Diébougou.

The *Régie X9* (station next to the Mairie; ☎99.07.86) has buses to **Ouaga**, **Gaoua**, **Ouessa** and **Hamale** (for Ghana); **Dédougou** (for Ouahigouya and the north); and **Banfora** and **Niangoloko** (for Côte d'Ivoire).

FLIGHTS

Airport information from Bobo airport on ☎98.03.68.

There are currently flights from Bobo to **Ouagadougou** on *Air Burkina* (☎98.18.87) on Tues (2.20pm), Wed (12.20pm), Fri (1.20pm and 7.20pm) and Sun (2.10pm and 8.20pm). The flight takes 40–50min and the fare is CFA15,700. Flights from Bobo to **Abidjan**, also on *Air Burkina*, go Tues, Fri and Sun mornings (1hr 10min; CFA79,000).

Banfora and around

Although the town of **Banfora** lacks the spark of Ouaga and Bobo, it lies in a beautiful region of cliffs and forests. Today, the economic importance of the region springs from

MARKET DAYS IN WESTERN BURKINA

Market days west of Bobo follow a predictable weekly pattern which can be useful in itself and for ensuring you don't get stranded somewhere remote without transport: most small villages only have *taxi brousse* connections with main towns on market days.

Mon – Koloko, Kotoura, Samorogouah, Soukouraba
Thurs – Mahon
Fri – Kangala
Sat – Orodara

the vast **sugar cane** projects that have made Burkina a net exporter of manufactured sugar. On the approach from Bobo by train or taxi, you see streams and **waterfalls** from the roadside and notice the vegetation getting denser.

Banfora

With a population of some 17,000, **BANFORA** is Burkina's fifth-largest town, developed during colonial times due to its position on the railway line. Banfora's only paved road is its main street – centre of the limited commerce in town. The market and **bank** (word has it they now change FF traveller's cheques, but it's still better to plan ahead) are along here. There are few distractions in town and wandering about won't turn up much apart from the **traditional drinking places** scattered about the backstreets, where you can guzzle *banji* (palm wine) and *chapalo*. To kill an hour or two in the afternoon, a ten-minute walk along the Sindou road takes you across the tracks to the **palm wine sellers**. Join the old men and women under the mango trees for a calabash or two. Banfora's **market day** is Sunday.

In the **evening**, you could take in a film at the *Paysan Noir* cinema or head to one of the many open-air nightclubs with garden seating and large dance areas.

Accommodation

Since the area around Banfora has become a major attraction in Burkinabe terms, enterprising young people have started **renting rooms** in their homes (you may be asked at the motor park upon arrival). A bed and bucket shower at these places usually costs less than CFA2000. There are a few reasonable official places too.

Hôtel la Canne à Sucre (☎88.01.51). Banfora's top hotel with clean and comfortable AC rooms and beautiful gardens. The restaurant dishes up excellent international cuisine – a good place for a splurge. Near the train station. ③.

Hôtel Comoé (☎88.01.51). The best address for budget accommodation with rooms (some with private bath) around a shaded courtyard that serves as restaurant, bar and nightclub. ②.

Hôtel Fara (☎88.01.17). Conveniently located near the train station,with clean S/C rooms with fan and its own restaurant and bar. ②.

Eating and drinking

Chez Djana (☎88.03.35). Well-known place on the Bobo road frequented by travellers and townspeople alike. Reasonable prices and a menu that's a bit more varied than most. Friendly service.

Le Creuset du Militant, near the police station. Popular café serving cold drinks and inexpensive food.

Le Flamboyant, just north of the market. *Restaurant-terrasse* with inexpensive meals and nighttime dancing.

L'Harmattan, behind the market. This busy place specializes in *grillades* including excellent fish, chicken and kebabs.

Maison des Femmes. An unusually large *paillote* under which you can eat cheap *riz-sauce*, salads and *couscous*. The restaurant was built by the townspeople and is run by an organization of women.

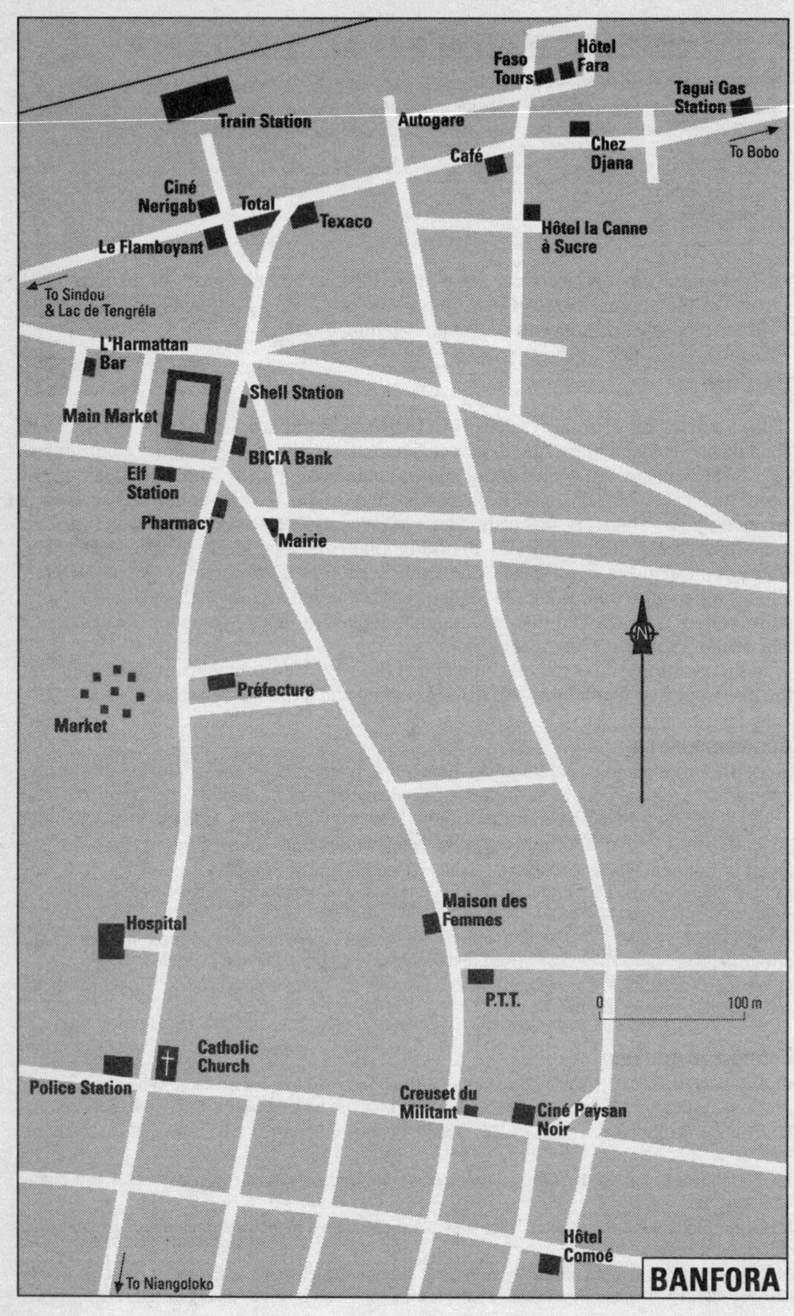
Hôtel Fara
Faso Tours
Tagui Gas Station
Train Station
Autogare
Chez Djana
To Bobo
Café
Ciné Nerigab
Total
Texaco
Hôtel la Canne à Sucre
Le Flamboyant
To Sindou & Lac de Tengréla
L'Harmattan Bar
Shell Station
Main Market
BICIA Bank
Elf Station
Pharmacy
Mairie
Préfecture
Market
Maison des Femmes
Hospital
P.T.T.
0
100 m
Catholic Church
Police Station
Creuset du Militant
Ciné Paysan Noir
Hôtel Comoé
To Niangoloko
BANFORA

Around Banfora

To see the region west of Banfora – quite richly endowed with sites of scenic beauty – it's best to rent a mobylette at the market. The **Lac de Tengréla** and **Chutes de Karfiguéla** are surprisingly difficult to find (numerous tracks lead through a tall growth of sugar cane most of the year), so you might consider taking someone from town along with you.

Lac de Tengréla

Some 10km from Banfora, Tengréla lake makes a great excursion. Take the Banfora–Sindou road west out of town. A sign about 7km from town points to the left of the lake, from where a two-kilometre-long track passes through the hamlet of Tengréla (no supplies). On arrival, you'll see fishermen along the shore who'll take you around the lake in their *pirogues*. Settle on a price before heading out. It's usually possible to spot the **hippos** that live in the waters. At the edge of the lake, an abandoned cement house provides an ideal place for **camping** if you have the equipment. Mosquitos are a problem, but if you wait around, you may be offered accommodation by one of the *piroguiers* touting for extra business.

Chutes de Karfiguéla

These waterfalls, located in a beautiful, verdant setting, are about 12km from the lake, though again, the way is difficult to find (ask the fishermen or people in the vicinity to point you to the *chutes* or *cascades*). Note that the river has been dammed as a source of irrigation for the cane plantations and be warned, too, that in the dry season, the falls are a disappointing trickle. During the rains, however, they swell to thunder impressively over the solid rock formations. From the main track, you approach the falls by means of a narrow path bordered with huge mango trees. If you're tempted to swim, take note that bilharzia is a risk here.

Sindou

SINDOU derives its fame from *les pics de Sindou*, a three-kilometre-long chain of sculpted crags forming a dramatic backdrop to the village, particularly at sunset. The sandstone has been eroded by the elements into spectacular pancake **towers** and 50-metre-high needles often topped with precarious rocky crowns. It's an excellent place to spend a day or so exploring or rock climbing. Despite the area's natural beauty, Sindou has remained little affected by the meagre trickle of tourists. Mango trees line the main street of conically thatched *banco* houses, yet to be replaced by corrugated iron shacks. Bring lots of film.

Getting to Sindou is not straightforward. Although it lies on a back route into Mali, few vehicles make the fifty-kilometre run from Banfora. Without your own transport, you have two equally feasible options: hitching with occasional local traffic (Sindou's market day is Monday), or renting a mobylette or bike in Banfora. The ride is tiring, but rewarding and not too difficult. **Supplies** are limited to street food and a couple of tiny restaurants. There is some relief, however, with tepid beer at the **bar** which also has *chambres de passage* (①). Much better is to stock up in Banfora and camp out among *les pics*.

THE LOBI COUNTRY

A green and pleasant corner of Burkina, nestling between the Ghanaian and Ivoirian frontiers, the **Lobi country** is a favourite travellers' destination and an interesting diversion en route from Bobo and the southwest into Ghana. It's all hilly, tree-

LOBI TRADITIONS

The Lobi believe in maintaining their **traditions**. Lobi men, for example, still hunt with bow and arrows for hares, guinea fowl and gazelles, and it's common to see men carrying these weapons – traditionally poison-tipped – as they walk along the road. Another notable aspect of Lobi culture is the cutlery embedded in gravestones: the Lobi are buried with their fork, spoon, plate and saucepan. Every seven years, too, the new generation of young people still take part in the **djoro** initiation ceremony. Some customs, however, are disappearing. Few Lobi women nowadays wear the disc plugs through their lips which used to be so admired. And the old-fashioned, all-in-one method of house building is giving way to easier mudbrick construction.

The traditions the Lobi maintain best are the ones with widest appeal – booze, music and markets. No Lobi town or village would be complete without its **cabarets** – not nightclubs but places where *chapalo* and *qui-me-pousse* or *patasi* (home-brewed firewater) are consumed in serious quantities and **traditional music** is often played. Many *cabarets* brew their own *chapalo*, a process that thankfully only takes three days. And it's so much cheaper than bottled beer that you could afford to shout the whole place a drink for the same price as a bottle of *Brakina* in a bar. Many *cabarets* keep a drum and a balafon handy in case anyone feels like playing, which they often do. Even in the unlikely event you don't acquire a taste for *chapalo* and Lobi music, *cabarets* are the best places to go and be sociable with the locals – there's never any shortage of welcome. The **markets** are traditionally held on a five-day cycle, though now increasingly on the same day every week. In more remote ones, you can still use cowries if you have any (you could buy some).

scattered savannah, and rich enough in wildlife for the elephant stories to be just about credible.

Although the lively town of **Gaoua** and the strange ruins of **Loropeni** are the region's only real tourist draws, the Lobi themselves, with their traditions and their *cabaret* drinking bars, not to mention their friendliness, make their corner of the country one of the best to visit, in spite of the fact that transport in the region is often difficult.

Food in the Lobi country is generally of the rice and sauce variety though there are other staples, such as fish and guinea fowl, if you look for them. More typically Lobi is millet *tô* with a sauce of baobab leaves, shea nuts or *néré* fruit.

Gaoua and around

Though the principal reasons for coming to Lobi country are to see the **ruins** and bustling **market** at **Loropeni**, the region's main town is **Gaoua** – absolutely shaking with *cabarets* – and it's here that you'll probably want to base yourself.

Gaoua

GAOUA is almost certainly the best place to get thoroughly acquainted both with *chapalo* and traditional roots music, though obviously the sounds in Bobo-Dioulasso are more refined. The main draw in town though, apart from the *cabarets*, is the magnificent Sunday **market**, a maelstrom of colour and activity. Look out for the leather workers just north of the market, spread out under a tree in front of the mosque.

On the west side of the hill, you can visit the **escarpment** with its sacred grotto, easily identified by the masses of plucked feathers from sacrificed chickens. You're supposed to have permission, and a guide (any kid in the town can take you), who will tell you spine-tingling tales of the pythons living in the caves.

LIMITED LOBI

The simplest Lobi greeting is *Me foaré* ("Hello") to which the normal response is *Monicho?* ("How are you?") and the reply to that *Michor* ("Fine thanks"). "Thank you" is *Ferehina foaré.*

FOOD

water	*ñyoñi*	meat	*nuni*	yam	*puri*	tomorrow	*kyo*
chicken	*yolo*	maize	*wologyo*	today	*ni*	yesterday	*gye ale*
egg yolo	*pala*	millet	*gyo/di*				

NUMBERS

1	*Biel*	5	*Yamoi*	9	*Nuor biri pero*	100	*Tama*
2	*Yenyo*	6	*Maado*	10	*Nuor*	1000	*Bulani*
3	*Yetter*	7	*Makonyo*	20	*Kpuele*		
4	*Yena*	8	*Makotter*	50	*Kpalanyo nuor*		

Up the hill in the administrative quarter, the *Centre Sociale* has opened a **museum** (CFA1000 including guided tour) in an old, colonial-style house with exhibits of traditional art, Lobi lifestyles, and homes typical of local ethnic groups. Plans to open an *Action sociale* welfare centre, and to run a library and crafts centre, seem to have stalled, but they're a committed lot in Gaoua, so hopefully most of this will be up and running by the time you arrive. You can stop by the *Centre Sociale* office near the PTT to enquire.

Practicalities

Gaoua has three **hotels**. The *Pony Bar* in the centre by the market, has moderately priced S/C rooms – reasonably comfortable either with or without fans but with no choice about the reggae and soukous sounds till midnight (①). The *Hôtel Hala* (1.6 km out on the Diébougou road; ③) offers a little high living in its ultra-clean, super comfortable, AC rooms with sit-down toilets, and has a laundry service if you want to make a fresh start. And lastly there's the *Hôtel 125*, which has small, dark rooms, bucket showers and no electricity, but it's the cheapest in town (①).

Food-wise you'll find plenty of stalls doing roast meat and fried fish, especially around the *X9* station and mosque, and there are several **restaurants**, including two on the road to Diébougou. The first of these, a shack selling rice in a rather salty sauce, is on the right just as you leave the market square. And two blocks further, also on the right, the *Porte Ouverte,* full of anti-malaria and anti-apartheid posters, offers an inexpensive menu of rice, beef, omelette, not very good yoghurt and the ubiquitous national slogan "*La patrie ou mort, nous vaincrons!*" Another place to try is the *Reele Wende Café* in front of the *Poni Cinema* and across from the market. The frozen

MOVING ON FROM GAOUA

Sunday is the best day for transport into or out of Gaoua, though **Loropeni** and **Nako** are best reached on their own market days, when vehicles usually leave early in the morning and return in the evening. There's usually something to **Doropo** in Côte d'Ivoire, especially on its market day, Thursday, where you'll probably have to change for other Ivoirian destinations. Often there's also a vehicle or two to **Diébougou**, where you may have to change for Bobo and Hamale. **X9** runs a thrice-weekly service to Bobo, weekly to Ouaga, all via Diébougou. Flights to Bobo and Ouaga have been suspended. If all else fails, try **hitching** from the police post 2km out of town on the Diébougou road.

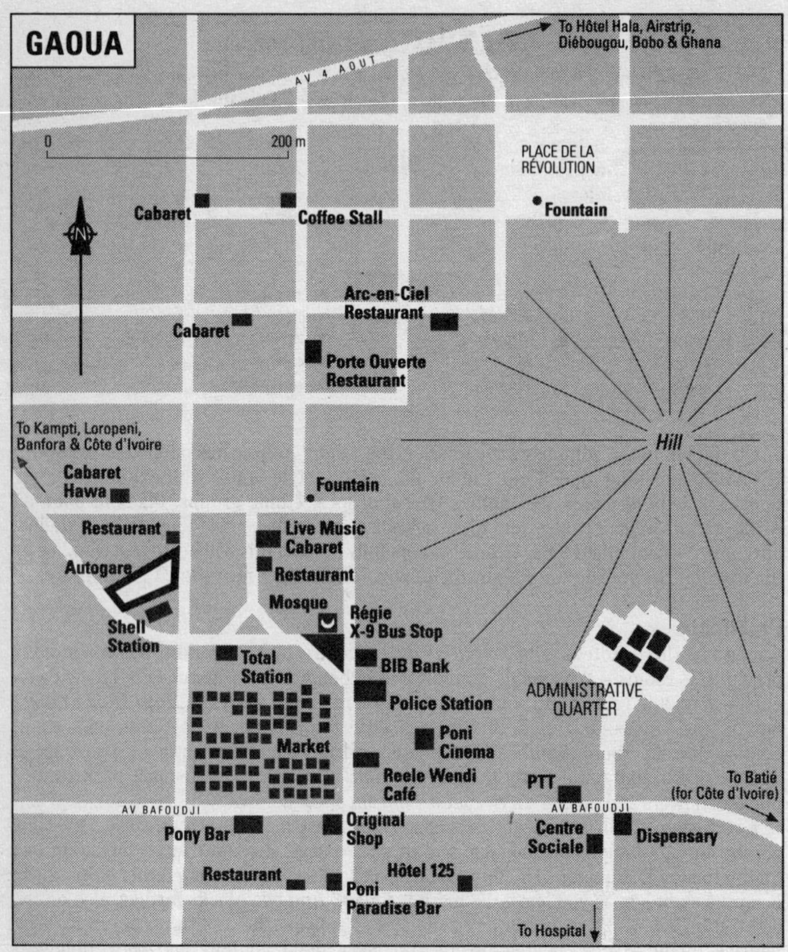

yoghurt here is more of a draw than the plates of kidney, liver or heart, and the owners are exceptionally friendly to travellers. For a splurge, make for the extravagant selection of Lebanese, African and French cuisine on offer at the *Hôtel Hala*. For **breakfast**, there's a little bar two blocks on the left, beyond the *Porte Ouverte*, that does tea, real coffee, Nescafé, omelettes and *pain beurre*.

Drinking is mainly a *cabaret* sport – the *Cabaret Pastis* and the *Cabaret Hawa* both stay open until late, or until the *chapalo* runs out, and both have sporadic live music. There are dozens of others, located by ear.

Around Gaoua

Better known for its market than its ruins, **Loropeni** is an easy excursion from Gaoua on trading day, when transport is certain – although you can get there, and back, on other days too, if you're lucky. En route from Gaoua is the mildly interesting village of **Kampti**, and you might see monkeys and gazelles, and even the odd elephant. To the north of Gaoua, **Nako** is the jumping-off point for a slow short cut into Ghana.

Kampti

KAMPTI, en route between Gaoua and Loropeni – the direct route being out of commission – isn't especially compelling, though it has its own ruins nearby. There's a mass of food stalls, about a kilometre from the *autogare*/junction, and, if you get stuck, the locals will probably put you up in the *Consolatrice*, a place sometimes used for dances.

Loropeni

LOROPENI's **market**, held every five days, is a bustling throng of colour. You can buy fruit, hot food, chillies, multi-coloured ground spices and peanut paste, and watch flip-flops being made out of old tyres, and enamel bowls being re-bottomed with bits of vegetable oil tins ("furnished by the people of the USA"). You might meet Ghanaians selling worming tablets (armed with lurid photographic displays), or Gan women, from the west, often wearing brown string mourning bands on their heads, arms, necks and ankles. You can change, and use, **cowries** here.

The only **accommodation** is in the basic places around the *autogare*. Ask around and you'll come up with something for about CFA1000. Apart from the *riz-sauce* **restaurant** in the middle of the market, there are plenty of *tabliers* along the main road doing grilled meat and soup, though tea and coffee become a scarce commodity after breakfast. Across from the car park is a *cabaret* of thatched *paillotes* shading wooden log benches and drinkers waiting for the balafon bands to start up again. Bottled drinks are available at the *buvette* behind the *autogare*, though they are no cooler than the inside temperature of the bar.

The ruins

To get to Loropeni's enigmatic **ruins**, head out of town on the Banfora road. After 3.5km you come to a small hill, at the top of which a track leads off to the right. Follow it for 500m to the ruins. Though not massively impressive, the Loropeni ruins are among West Africa's very few stone remains, rising up out of the scrub like some lost temple in a Hollywood movie. Unlike the great stone ruins of East Africa and Zimbabwe, they don't get many visitors, and since their origin and the identity of their builders are still viable mysteries, your ideas about them are as good as anyone else's. The ruins are more or less rectangular, some 50m long, by 40m wide, by (originally) 6–7m high, and noticeably lack any doors or windows. Inside, like other rectangular Lobi ruins, they're divided into two enclosures, one large and one small, connected by a door and each divided into chambers.

If you don't have transport, head to the *buvette* behind Loropeni's *autogare*. The owner has a mobylette and for a couple of litres of petrol, he'll take you out to the ruins and throw in a trip to the Gan village of **Obiré**, 8km northwest of Loropeni. The latter has no mysterious walls, but is remarkable for its round thatched huts (a thatching style very different from Lobi houses) and for the **life-size mud statues** representing ancestral kings. The chief requests CFA500 to visit.

The **Gan country** a few kilometres north and west of Loropeni harbours more archeological oddities if you can get the transport. There are ruins near **Yerifoula**, others near **Oyono** and **Lokosso**, and some large relics at **Loghi**.

Nako

NAKO has its market always the day after Loropeni's. You may find yourself here if taking the short cut **into Ghana via Lawra**: from Nako you'll need a lift 11km to

Boukéro and then a *pirogue* ride across the Black Volta, which forms the border here. It's straightforward enough to do this, and fun, but quite time-consuming, especially when you add in the fairly long walk from the Ghanaian bank of the river to the main road, and the likelihood that you will be asked to go 50km north to Hamale to be officially received into Ghana. Be sure to go to **immigration in Nako** to get stamped out of Burkina in the first place or the Ghanaians will send you back.

Diébougou and Hamale

Lying outside the Lobi country proper, **DIÉBOUGOU**'s people are mostly Lobi-Gan and Dagara (Dagarti). The place doesn't hold a lot of interest in itself, but it's friendly, full of kids and has better transport connections than Gaoua (but note that no banks change money).

There are two **hotels**, both near the *taxi brousse* and bus stops. The *Campement Danabone* has rooms in not too bad a state, some with fans (①); and it's also a bar, disco and pick-up joint with generator electricity in the evenings. There's a rather mucky shower and sink for each pair of rooms. The nearby *Relais la Bougouriba* is slightly smarter with a shower in every room and fans too – if they can fix them. Rooms are cleaner and more expensive and worth it (☎86.02.88; ②). The *Bougouriba* also has a generator, a bar and plenty of atmosphere. The only **restaurants** are at the hotels, with rice, guinea fowl, steak and the usual solid stuff. Outside there's a run of

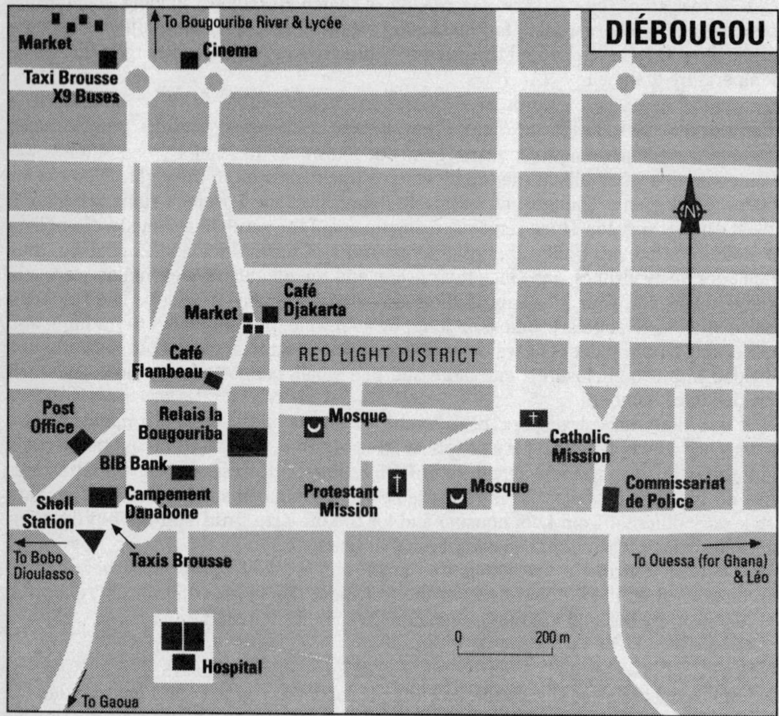

food stalls around the market and lots of *cabarets* to slake your thirst. Deserving of a mention is the *Flambeau Café*, a breakfast joint with real coffee, tea, omelettes and so forth. Passing an evening in Diébougou you'll likely gravitate to the hotel discos or possibly the cinema.

During the wet season **crocodiles** (though not, it's important to point out, sacred ones) collect in the swamp that forms at the eastern end of town. They're best observed around dawn, if you can manage it, when coolness keeps them calm and visible. Older folk can be overheard complaining that they don't have swamps like they used to; needless to say, the crocodiles are diminishing in number.

Transport out of Diébougou isn't much problem; there are **X9 buses** five times a week to Bobo, four times to Gaoua, twice to Ouessa and Hamale and once to Ouagadougou. Other transport east to Hamale often comes in late at night from Bobo.

Hamale and into Ghana

A busy border town and the main crossing point into Ghana from Bobo-Dioulasso, **HAMALE** rarely has much to offer – at least when beer supplies in Ghana are satisfying demand. When Ghana goes dry, periodically, Ghanaians, including police in uniform, pop across the border for a drink at the *Zodo Bar*. You can stay at the *Zodo*, but you might as well spend a cheaper night in Ghana.

Burkinabe border formalities take place at Ouessa, where you visit police and customs, and probably the gendarmerie too, just to be sure. Cedis are available at the ordinary (poor) border rate, a rate beaten just about everywhere else. **Transport on the Ghanaian side** almost all goes to Lawra and Wa, including the twice daily STC bus .

index

CHAPTER TWELVE

GHANA

GHANA

Ghana was the first modern African country to retrieve its independence, in 1957. At the time it was one of the richest nations on the continent – the world's leading **cocoa** exporter and producer of a tenth of the world's **gold**. But after Kwame Nkrumah's optimistic start it suffered a hornet's nest of setbacks. Repeated coups, food shortages and sapping corruption for years combined to make Ghana a place to be avoided.

No longer. Conditions have improved almost out of recognition since the terminal bottoming-out in 1979 and the country is firmly back on its feet and pursuing a vigorous course of IMF rehabilitation with the grudging approval of most Ghanaians – and so far with huge success as far as the international development agencies are concerned. From a traveller's point of view, this means low prices, but limited luxury. Compared with the other Anglophone countries in West Africa, Ghana offers a **transport and accommodation** infrastructure that's second to none; a **cultural mix**, inevitably stressing the **Asante** nation's rich and vibrant lifestyle, that's every bit as rewarding as Nigeria's (without that country's immense size or intimidating reputation); and better **beaches** than The Gambia. The Ghana government has, moreover, an enthusiastic commitment to tourism, with a number of regional tourist offices set up and plenty to engage visitors.

The country has a distinctive personality and perhaps more claim to a **national character** than any other in the region. On the other hand, Ghana has had long contact with European cultural forms. School education has had a major impact, going back four generations now, and there's a high level of literacy and an inventiveness with language – both written, on signs and in the press, and spoken, in repartee – that hints at a creativity as yet barely unleashed in Africa. Ghanaians are hospitable and generous to a fault and there's more warmth to be experienced in Ghana than in either of its coastal neighbours.

The country

Ghana is compact and mostly flat. With the exception of the striking **scarp system** that curves through the country from the Gambaga escarpment in the northeast, round to the Wenchi scarp west of Lake Volta, and southeast as the Mampong scarp through the forest, there are few striking highland regions. But there are some attractive rolling green landscapes and, in the central regions, away from the **cocoa** plantations and the

FACTS AND FIGURES

Known as the **Gold Coast** during the colonial era, **Ghana** took its present name from the former West African empire (with which it has no historical connection) located in present-day Mauritania. With a **population** of around 15 million and an **area** of 240,000 square kilometres – about the same size as Britain or Oregon – Ghana is one of the region's most densely populated states. The foreign debt stands at around £3 billion ($4.5 billion), which, for some sense of scale, is about half Britain's annual expenditure on armaments research, or, seen from another perspective, less than a quarter of the value of the Chrysler corporation. It is also, however, nearly four times the country's annual earnings from the export of goods and services. Since 1981, Ghana has been led by Flight-Lieutenant Jerry Rawlings who ruled dictatorially through the Provisional National Defence Council, until he was elected president by universal suffrage in 1993.

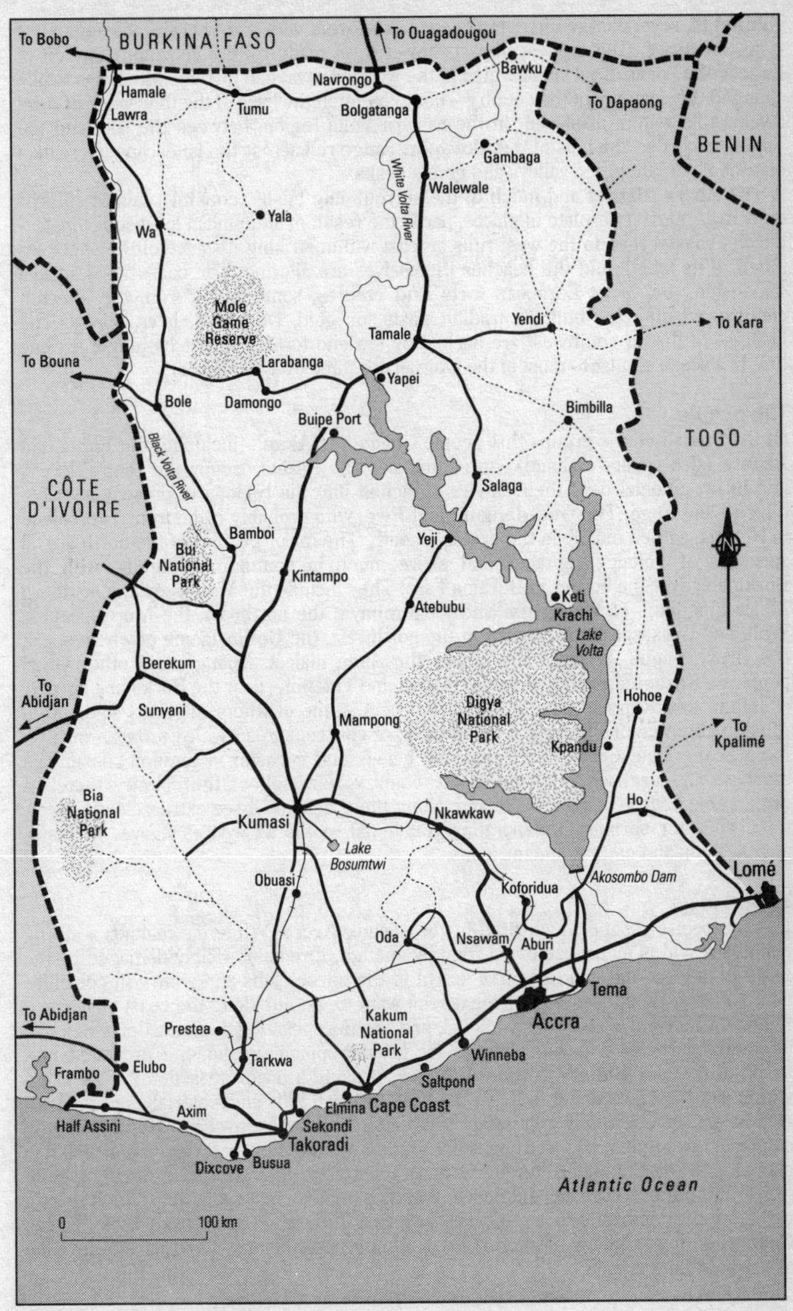
To Bobo
BURKINA FASO
To Ouagadougou
Bawku
To Dapaong
BENIN
Navrongo
Hamale
Tumu
Bolgatanga
Lawra
Gambaga
White Volta River
Walewale
Yala
Wa
Mole Game Reserve
Yendi
To Kara
Tamale
To Bouna
Larabanga
Yapei
Bole
Damongo
Buipe Port
Bimbilla
Black Volta River
TOGO
CÔTE D'IVOIRE
Salaga
Bamboi
Yeji
Bui National Park
Kintampo
Atebubu
Keti Krachi
Lake Volta
Berekum
To Abidjan
Sunyani
Digya National Park
Hohoe
Mampong
Kpandu
To Kpalimé
Bia National Park
Kumasi
Nkawkaw
Ho
Lake Bosumtwi
Lomé
Obuasi
Koforidua
Akosombo Dam
Oda
Nsawam
Aburi
Tema
Accra
To Abidjan
Kakum National Park
Prestea
Winneba
Tarkwa
Elubo
Frambo
Saltpond
Elmina
Cape Coast
Axim
Half Assini
Sekondi
Takoradi
Dixcove
Busua
Atlantic Ocean
0
100 km

goldfields, several large districts of dense **rainforest** with giant hardwoods and palms vying for space. The biggest impact, however, is made by the enormous stretch of **Lake Volta**, an artificial lake created in the wooded savannah in 1966, which has totally changed the anatomy of the country – not to mention the lives of the thousands of rural dwellers its waters displaced. In the eastern Volta region, between the lake and the Togolese border, the hills of the **Akwapim range** roll across the landscape to create a district of verdant green valleys and gentle peaks.

The **Accra district** and much of the surrounding bushy, **coastal plain** is surprisingly dry – almost desolate in places, partly the result of an unusual local sub-climate – but the coastal road to the west runs at least within striking distance of the shore for much of its length and the beaches themselves are alluring. The coast has a special dimension, too, in its European **forts and castles**, some dating from the fifteenth century, which were built as trading posts for gold, ivory and, later, slaves. The beaches of the far southwest are backed by lowland forest and patchy jungle agriculture in a scene similar to most of the Ivoirian coastline over the border.

The people

Of the myriad ethnic groups that people Ghana, the **Akan** – including the **Fante** and **Asante** (also spelled Ashanti) – predominate. The Asante occupy the central forest, and in pre-colonial days their empire stretched into the regions of present-day Côte d'Ivoire and Togo. The **Ga-Adangme** and **Ewe**, who probably came from Yorubaland in Nigeria, settled mainly in the east and south. The major peoples of the north are all speakers of Voltaic languages and share much in common, culturally, with the Burkinabe over the border in Burkina Faso. They include the More-speaking southern Mossi kingdoms of **Mamprusi** and **Dagomba** in the northeast, the More-speaking **Wala** and Grusi-speaking **Dagarti** in the northwest, the **Gonja** (some of whom speak the Grusi tongue, Wagala, and others the Akan dialect, Guang), and other Grusi peoples – **Kassena**, **Frafra**, **Sissala**, **Builsa** and **Talensi** – near the Burkinabe border.

Islam is widespread among the northerners, some of whom migrated south from Muslim communities in Mali. **Christianity**, of course, spread with European involvement in the Gold Coast, but pantheistic beliefs and ancestor veneration remain the most widely practised religions in the country. Throughout the country there's a remarkable degree of syncretism and, along the coast, you'll see extraordinarily decorated ancestor shrines, incorporating traditional motifs as well as figures of Jesus, angels, djinn and more mundane icons.

Where to go

Don't expect to spend much time in the capital, **Accra**. While it's making a strong comeback and is manageable and friendly enough, it remains visibly damaged by the years of neglect and, unless you're drawn to the music clubs and your visit coincides with some weekend live shows, you'll soon want to get out along the coast or into the interior. The **west coast** is exceptional, and the European **castles**, most of which can be visited, provide excellent focuses for beach-hopping. Inland, the protected rain forest of the new **Kakum National Park** is proving a major attraction for travellers who make the effort to get to it. To the east, the lush hills and waterfalls of the **Volta region** are also currently generating great interest among travellers. **Kumasi**, in the centre of the country, has a strong sense of identity, and the forest region of which it is capital is scenically and culturally Ghana's most appealing area. The **north** is quite different, both in landscape and people, but its climate is more tolerable and, if there's not a lot that demands to be seen as you pass through – apart from **Mole Game Reserve** – there's plenty of interest in its ethnographic history if you have more time or are based in the area.

Climate

Ghana has a lot more **climatic variation** than most of West Africa. Central and southern Ghana – south of Tamale – is unusual in having **two distinct rainy seasons**, the first lasting roughly from March to June and the second from September to October. The far southwest gets heavy rains, but in Accra they tend to be light and it's uncommon to experience day after day of torrential downpour. The central rainforest regions tend to be wetter and (though you wouldn't know it because of the high humidity) slightly cooler. The north is basically hot and dry most of the year, with a climate much like that of Ouagadougou in Burkina, and a single rainy period from June to October.

AVERAGE TEMPERATURES AND RAINFALL

ACCRA

	Jan	Feb	Mar	Apr	May	June	July	Aug	Sept	Oct	Nov	Dec
Temperatures °C												
Min (night)	23	24	24	24	24	23	23	22	23	23	24	24
Max (day)	31	31	31	31	31	29	27	27	27	29	31	31
Rainfall mm	15	33	56	81	142	178	46	15	36	64	36	23
Days with rainfall	1	2	4	6	9	10	4	3	4	6	3	2

TAMALE

	Jan	Feb	Mar	Apr	May	June	July	Aug	Sept	Oct	Nov	Dec
Temperatures °C												
Min (night)	21	23	24	24	24	22	22	22	22	22	22	20
Max (day)	36	37	37	36	33	31	29	29	30	32	34	35
Rainfall mm	3	3	53	69	104	142	135	196	226	99	10	5
Days with rainfall	1	1	1	6	10	12	14	16	19	13	1	1

The details in these practical information pages are essentially for use on the ground in West Africa and in Ghana itself: for full details on preparing for a trip, getting here from outside the region, paperwork, health, information sources and more, see *Basics*.

Arrivals

Ghana is one of the most popular countries for independent travel in West Africa and its good connections and central location make it an excellent starting point for longer travels. Ghana was notorious for the deplorable state of its roads in the 1980s, but they are now much improved. There aren't too many roadblocks and you won't be constantly asked for identity papers.

■ Flights from Africa

Accra's best air links in Africa are with **Abidjan**, a one-hour hop with flights pretty well every day, and more than one on some days, on *Ghana Airways* (GH), *Air Afrique* (RK) or *Air Ivoire* (VU).

Other flights in the region mostly emanate from further west. *Ghana Airways*' New York service flies to Accra via **Dakar** on Thurs and Sun night; RK flies Dakar to Accra on Sat night.

GH makes three long treks up the coast each week, flying the return legs to Accra on Tues, Thurs and Sun: they all call at **Banjul** and **Freetown**, having called at **Las Palmas** on Thurs, **Dakar** on Tues and Sun, and **Conakry** on Thurs and Sun. There are further flights from Freetown on Sat with GH and in theory also on Fri with *Sierra National Airlines* (LJ).

From the other direction, there are non-stop flights from **Cotonou** on Mon (GH) and Fri (RK) and non-stop flights from **Lagos** once or twice daily on GH and *Nigeria Airways* (WT).

Flights from other cities in West Africa require a plane change, usually in Abidjan. **Bamako** has reasonable connections on Tues, Thurs and Sun, using VU and GH, while the best connections from **Ouagadougou** are on Tues and Sun (same airlines). If you're flying from **Douala**, the best connections are through Lagos. There are no good connections from Nouakchott, Bissau, the Cape Verde Islands, Lomé or Niamey.

Ethiopian Airlines (ET) provides the link from **East Africa** with a flight from **Addis Ababa** and **Nairobi** every Wed afternoon and from Addis via Lagos on Thurs afternoon. There are no direct flights from North Africa.

From **Southern Africa**, *Ghana Airways* flies every Sun night from **Johannesburg** and **Harare**.

ORGANIZED STAYS IN GHANA

For details of organized stays in Ghana with *Insight Travel* of England and the *Suntaa-Nuntaa* project based in Wa, Upper West Region, see p.8. The *American Council on Educational Exchange*, 205 E 42nd St, New York (☎212/661-1414) also arrange trips to Ghana, as part of their International Workcamps programme.

■ Overland from Burkina Faso

Coming from Ouagadougou, you have several possibilities: taking a **bush taxi** or **bus** to the border at Paga, or getting transport through to Navrongo, Bolgatanga or Accra. Going by bush taxi you'll make better time on the road but the buses are more comfortable and generally get through the border and various checkpoints more quickly. If you're lucky with connections, it can sometimes work out cheapest and fastest to change transport at the border, which is generally amicable – though note that it closes at 6pm.

Other crossings include the one between Léo and Tumu and the one at Hamale. Transport is patchy on both sides of the border, and there's no direct through transport to speak of in either case – your prospects are best by far on market days.

The **fast route to Accra** goes via Tamale, Kintampo and Kumasi; the more easterly route, involving a Lake Volta ferry or canoe crossing between Makongo and Yeji, is extremely rough.

■ Overland from Togo

The road from Lomé to Accra is surfaced. The quickest way between the two capitals is by **bush taxi** but you'll save some hassle if you first get yourself to the border on the west side of the city of Lomé, cross on foot to Aflao, and then continue by bush taxi or bus – a journey of about three hours. The border closes at 6pm and, due to strained relations between the two countries, can be unpleasant. Togo has frequently closed its border with Ghana since the early 1990s charging the Ghanaian government with sending mercenaries to topple the Eyadéma regime. In practice, the Aflao border is always the most hassle (crossing points further north are usually easy), and you may have to get a laissez-passer from the Togolese *Ministère de l'Administration du Territoire et de la Sécurité* in Lomé before being allowed to enter Ghana.

■ Overland from Côte d'Ivoire

The coastal stretch between Abidjan and Accra is in good condition, and Ghanaian *STC* **buses** – not to mention fleets of **bush taxis** – connect the two capitals in a day. Buses leave from the Treichville *gare routière* in Abidjan. There's also a fast route direct to Kumasi via Abengourou – also a day's journey – from Abidjan's Adjamé *gare routière*.

Red Tape

Visas, which tend to be expensive, are required by all non-Commonwealth nationals. Commonwealth citizens need an entry permit, which amounts to the same thing. Multiple-entry visas valid for three months are now available.

Entering the country, you will be asked how long you plan on staying and your reply is noted in your passport. If you say a week, that's your limit, even if you have a one-month visa. It's wise to get the longest possible stay, since extensions are in practice only delivered in Accra and are difficult to obtain (see Accra "Listings"). You'll also be asked at the border for a Ghanaian address, so have a hotel in mind.

The form that you fill out on arrival may still indicate that you should present yourself with passport photos to the **Immigration Department** of the Ministry of the Interior in Accra within 48 hours of arrival. In fact this has not been necessary for several years (staff at the airport may tell you it's "optional", as if there might be some advantage in it for the traveller), but until they get round to printing new forms, the uncertainty will continue.

Yellow fever certificates are required for overland entry, and are closely checked at the borders.

Another piece of paper you may come across is the T5, or **currency declaration form**. If you are given one, you're very unlikely to ever have it checked.

■ Visas for onward travel

Ghana's three neighbours (Côte d'Ivoire, Burkina and Togo) issue **visas in Accra** as do most West African countries. **Nigeria** has become somewhat sticky, at times insisting you need a residency permit for Ghana in order to be issued a visa at the embassy in Accra. Although some travellers report little trouble here, the whole process is generally easier in Lomé or Cotonou. **Benin** visas are quick and inexpensive. For addresses and further details see the Accra "Listings".

Money and Costs

Ghana's currency is the cedi (C/). Formerly, one cedi was divided into 100 pesewas, but inflation long ago rose well past the point at which pesewas had any value. The biggest note is C/5000, which is worth £2.50 (roughly $4). Notes of C/50 and C/100 are being withdrawn. There are C/10, C/20, C/50 and C/100 coins.

The official **exchange rate** (currently roughly ₵2000 = £1; ₵1400 = $1) is set every week in an auction of foreign exchange in Accra. This has resulted in an annual inflation rate running at about 25 percent. There is no black market.

In other countries market women tie up their money in their skirts, but in Ghana they keep it in huge plastic bags. You'll find yourself walking around with **wads of money** that don't add up to much. But don't destroy any – a tourist was once fined ₵200,000 and jailed for a month for lighting a cigarette with a ₵100 note.

For changing money you'll find **foreign exchange (forex) bureaux** in Accra, Kumasi and other major towns, and new ones springing up all over the country, including Aflao on the Togo border. Shop around for the best rates which are always to be had for large denominations such as US$100 bills. Forex bureaux offer rates slightly higher than the banks, not all of which change money anyway.

Cash US dollars are the prime medium of exchange, with other currencies, including pounds sterling, and all travellers' cheques, worth relatively less. (Note that it can be difficult to change travellers' cheques at forex bureaux and Thomas Cook cheques are particulary unwelcome on account of their perceived forgability.) You can also buy hard currency from forex bureaux.

If you're stuck for a forex bureau the most likely banks are the *Ghana Commercial Bank* (which has over 100 branches throughout the country) and *Barclays* and *Standard Chartered*, which have several dozen branches each, covering all the main towns. **Banking hours** are Monday to Thursday 8.30am to 2pm, Friday until 3pm.

Credit cards are accepted in major hotels in Accra and Kumasi and at some travel agencies. Outside the main cities they won't get you far. *Barclays* handles *Visa* cash advances at a reasonable exchange rate, but subject to a 2 percent fee.

You can have **money sent to you** easily enough at the *Bank of Ghana*, Thorpe Road, Accra (PO Box 264; ☎021/66.69.02). In the UK you can do this through the *Ghana Commercial Bank*, 69 Cheapside, London EC2P 2BB, or *Midland Bank International*, 110–114 Cannon St, London EC4N 6AA.

■ Costs

Cedi devaluations make it difficult to gauge **costs** but in terms of foreign exchange value – even in Accra – they are dropping all the time.

Accommodation in Accra runs as low as C/5000 (£2.50/$3.75) for a twin room, and can be cheaper still up-country. Businesses which rely heavily on customers wielding foreign currency (which of course includes the more expensive hotels and restaurants, imported goods outlets and so on) tend to keep a close eye on the exchange rate and adjust their prices accordingly. Hence they often quote prices in hard currency and accept payment at prevailing rates – often skewed in their favour – in any currency.

Although Ghanaians find even street **food** expensive on their wages (the minimum wage currently provides an income equivalent to £3 or $4.50 *per week*), it will seem cheap enough to you, as you can usually eat heartily for under ₵ 1000 (£0.50/$0.75).

The other major cost, **transport**, is also cheaper in Ghana than surrounding countries, especially if you travel by *State Transport Corporation* (*STC*) buses: fares currently range from around ₵10 to ₵30 per kilometre (mostly the lower end of the scale), depending on vehicle, route and road conditions, which is roughly half the cost of travel in Burkina or Côte d'Ivoire.

Health

Yellow fever vaccinations are required before entering Ghana. Cholera epidemics occur, especially in isolated regions with limited sources of clean water. Bilharzia is another concern; stay away from stagnant ponds or slow-running streams – especially in savannah areas. Lake Volta is notorious.

In large towns, **tap water** is always drinkable. In smaller places, and villages, the well or stored rain water isn't always the purest and you may want to try some combination of boiling (not always practical), filtering or adding purifying tablets. Except in the remotest areas, bottled water is available though expensive.

The main **hospitals** are in Accra and Kumasi. Smaller hospitals and clinics can be found in towns throughout the country, but for a major medical problem you may prefer a private clinic. For a reference, consult an embassy.

Ghana has a surging **AIDS** problem, as much as any other country in the region, with thousands of cases reported and hundreds of thousands of HIV carriers. Unfortunately, there is little acknowledgement of the problem as a truly domestic one: the disease is associated with Ghanaians who travel and foreign visitors (European or African).

Maps and Information

Virtually no official tourist information is supplied outside the country. You can get to know Ghana quite well, however, through the detailed weekly coverage provided by *West Africa* magazine.

Map availability is dire, and you will not find any decent, up-to-date single sheets of the whole country. In Accra, the best place to find detailed regional and basic national maps is at the *Survey Office* (Cantonments, PO Box 191, Accra; ☎021/77.73.31) on Giffard Road near the airport – the only place in the country with a dependable supply. They sell **town maps** for a number of places outside the capital. An **Accra city map** is available here, or you can get it at the *KLM* office in town on Ring Rd, or *Shell* stations.

The **Ghana Tourist Board** has offices, in theory, in Accra and a number of other large towns throughout the country (Kumasi, Bolgatanga, Takoradi). A new office is supposed to be opening in Tamale. The office in Accra has closed, however, and it's not clear what future the service has. In the past, the tourist offices have sometimes organized tours. They are the publishers of a useful booklet, *Ghana: A Travel Guide* (₵3000), and a free brochure, *It's Great in Ghana*, plus local guides for Elmina, Cape Coast and some of the parks.

Getting Around

The government has made real improvements to the transportation system. They have resurfaced roads, bought new rolling stock for the railway system and expanded the country's now highly efficient bus service. Buses, in fact, are the most convenient means of travelling around the country and you'll find them a real luxury after the battered bush taxis you may have grown accustomed to using elsewhere.

■ Buses

The *State Transport Corporation*'s **bus service** provides a cheap and hassle-free way to get around the country with a minimum of waiting at roadside checkpoints. The buses run on fixed schedules to all towns of any size and are safe and comfortable. It's always a good idea when possible to book seats in advance with *STC*, especially if you're heading for popular destinations like Accra, Kumasi or Tamale. The *State Transport* yard in each town usually adjoins the main motor park. You will need a luggage ticket too in order to get your gear into the hold, unless you're prepared to carry it on your lap. In some parts you'll also find *Omnibus Services Authority* (*OSA*) buses. They are all now non-smoking.

■ Bush taxis and *tro-tros*

Minibuses (*tro-tros*) and **Peugeot 504s** ("caravans") are less comfortable than the coaches, but they leave more frequently and travel faster. They're notoriously overloaded and, if you're out to enjoy the ride, should be used only if you're not going far or can't get on a bus. Worse than the bush taxis are the **lorries**, or mammy wagons, which you'll only want to consider as a last resort. These squeeze as many people as can possibly fit onto wooden planks in a boarded-up truck. You'll see nothing on the way and collect lots of bruises to boot.

ROAD TRANSPORT: SAMPLE FARES AND TIMES

Accra–Kumasi, 253km, ₵3000 (*STC* bus), 4hr.
Accra–Tamale, 611km, ₵7500 (*STC* bus), 10hr.
Accra–Hohoe, 235km, ₵2400 (*STC* bus), 4hr.
Accra–Takoradi, 237km, ₵2550 (*STC* bus), 3hr.
Tamale–Bolgatanga, 191km, ₵2000 (*OSA*, poor road), 3hr.
Hamale–Wa, 115km, ₵1500 (*tro-tro*, rough track), 3hr.
Wa–Kumasi, 454km, ₵4000 (*OSA* bus, mostly bad road), 7hr.

■ Trains

Trains are the cheapest way of travelling and, since the government bought new rolling stock in the 1980s, they're actually quite comfortable, though there is still a tendency for them to derail – not that derailment usually causes a disaster, as they travel so slowly. Of the three main lines, the most useful is the stretch linking **Kumasi to Takoradi** which is a better alternative than the beaten-up roads that run through the forest and connect the Asante country to the coast. There are two trains daily, one in the morning and an overnight sleeper. The government has been repairing tracks on the other two lines connecting **Accra to Takoradi** and **Accra to Kumasi**, and passenger service is suspended. Should the service start up again, note that the Accra–Takoradi line unfortunately skirts inland, well away from the coast. In terms of scenery, therefore, the road is better along this stretch.

■ Planes

Ghana Airways no longer operates any domestic services. Instead, the Ghana Air Force now provides civilian air services linking Accra, Kumasi, Tamale Sunyani and Takoradi. *Ghana Airways* offices can't offer any scheduling details, but flights operate daily or several times a week out of civilian airports and airstrips. Details can be obtained in Ghana directly at the airports or from *M&J Travel* in Accra (see p.792). Fares from Accra are around ₵30,000 to Kumasi, ₵40,000 to Tamale.

■ Volta ferries

You can cover part of the country by boat, as a Lake Volta **ferry service** links the southern town of Akosombo (100km north of Accra) with Kpandu (213km from Accra) and Kete Krachi (520km from Accra) once a week, taking 12hr. Apart from this "scheduled" passenger service, cargo vessels also ply this route and venture further north – as far as Yapei, just 32km east of Tamale (except at the end of the dry season), a voyage which can take up to three days, depending on stops en route. For current information, check at the big hotel in Akosombo. The scenery is not as exciting as you might expect – long stretches of dead tree trunks sticking up through flooded landscapes.

■ Driving and cycling

Outlets for **car rental** are still limited, though Accra has a number of possibilities, including some licensed outlets for the big international groups. Rental normally includes a driver. **Fuel** is relatively cheap at about ₵500 per litre (£1.12 per Imperial gallon; $1.28 per US gallon).

Lastly, Ghana is a good country for **cycling**, covering a manageable area (two to three weeks from north to south) and offering immense scenic variety. You don't need to be super-fit: the hilly zones are fairly restricted. If you start in the north it's all basically downhill; or tour along the coast, slog up to Kumasi, then take the switchback route back to Accra – again a perfect trip for two to three weeks.

Accommodation

Although luxury accommodation is rare in Ghana, major towns have decent hotels – run by the government or privately – which are in general comfortable if lacking in conveniences. Running water and AC can be had in most places, but may only work sporadically. Added to your bill is a ten percent state hotel tax, which has been included in our calculations of room price codes.

Special mention should be made of the handful of forts along the coast which have been converted to rest houses. They offer exceptionally cheap and characterful accommodation, though they have limited space so are often full in high season. The museum at Cape Coast may help with bookings.

■ Staying with people

Ghanaians are generally curious to meet travellers, and if you're on your own, you may be surprised how many offers you get to **stay with people**. (For details of organized home stays with UK-based *Insight Travel*, see p.8.) It can be rewarding, but you should be extremely conscious, when accepting such offers, of the expense your stay imposes, and be aware that even for salaried government workers a bottle of beer may be a luxury in which they rarely indulge. Be as generous as your host; pay at the cinema, bars or discos, and, if you go to the market together, pay for the food. Ghana's cost of living is incredibly high relative to local wages and most people are barely scraping by, and generally doing so outside the money economy.

■ Camping

If you have your own transport, you have the freedom to get off the beaten tracks and visit many small towns and villages which don't have accommodation. **Camping** is feasible in the bush, though in practice it's most pleasant in the

ACCOMMODATION PRICE CODES

Hotel prices in this chapter are coded according to the following scales – the same scales in terms of their pound/dollar equivalents as are used throughout the book. Prices refer to the rate you can expect to pay for a room with two beds. Single rooms, or single occupancy, will normally cost at least two-thirds of the twin-occupancy rate. For further details, see p.51.

① **Under ₵10,000 (under £5/$7.50).** Anything from very rudimentary lodgings to an adequate, simple hotel with S/C rooms with fans, and possibly some with AC for slightly higher rates.

② **C/10,000–20,000 (£5–10/$7.50–15).** Modest hotel or guesthouse, usually with S/C rooms and a choice of fan ventilation, or AC for a premium. Often the best place in a small town.

③ **C/20,000–40,000 (£10–20/$15–30).** Usually a reasonable business or tourist-class hotel with S/C, AC rooms and often a good restaurant.

④ **₵40,000–60,000 (£20–30/$30–45).** Comfortable, first-class hotel, with good facilities, including phones in rooms, full AC and pool (though some city hotels in this price bracket offer poor value for money).

⑤ **₵60,000–80,000 (£30–40/$45–60).** Luxury establishment.

⑥ **₵80,000–100,000 (£40–50/$60–75).** Accra-only luxury.

⑦ **Over ₵100,000 (over £50/$75).** Accra-only luxury.

north, beyond the damp forest zone. If you arrive in a village you can ask the chief if and where you can spend the night, and he'll make the arrangements. **Camping gas** is very hard to find in Ghana; stock up in Francophone countries where it's readily available.

Eating and Drinking

In southern Ghana, the most common staple is *kenkey* – fermented maize flour balls, steamed and wrapped in maize leaves. You'll see it in markets everywhere. The sour taste takes a while to acquire, and you don't often get much sauce to help it down – just a splash of ground tomatoes, onions and peppers and deep fried fish. But it does, eventually, taste good. In the north, *tozafi* (or *TZ*) takes over – a mush made from millet (occasionally maize) flour, and commonly eaten with palm nut or okra soup.

Plantains are used a lot in Ghanaian cooking and, together with **beans**, **groundnuts**, **rice**, fresh and dried **fish**, **guinea fowl** (especially in the north) and **grasscutter** (the large, tasty rodent, also known as bush rat, hunted mainly in the south), supply the basis of one of West Africa's best national cuisines.

If you're adventurous, there are other flavours, including clay-baked **lizard** (in Dagomba country; the skin comes off with the clay) and giant forest **snails** – even bat, rat, cat and dog in various parts of the country.

Bread, as you would expect, reflects the taste and style of the British former rulers and is usually soft, white and plastic bagged. Baguette-style bread sticks and loaves made of wholemeal flour are becoming more widely available.

Ghana has a lot of good **chocolate**, available everywhere and not expensive, but it's not popular with Ghanaians.

The country's outstanding fruit is the **pineapple** – notably along the coast – cheaper in Ghana than anywhere else in West Africa. **Coconuts**, too, are incredibly cheap and surprisingly good for you.

Drinking

Ghana was the first West African country to possess a brewery and it now has a wide range of **beers**. One of the most popular, perhaps because it's got the highest alcohol content, is *Gulder*. Other brands include *Star*, *ABC*, *Club* and bottled *Guinness*. **Minerals** include the usual *Coke* and *Fanta* varieties. *Refresh* comes in orange, mango and pineapple and, with 25

GHANAIAN FOOD TERMS AND DISHES

Abenkwan	Palm nut soup (Akan)
Aduane	Food (Akan)
Akawadu	Banana (Akan)
Akokoh	Chicken (Akan)
Amadaa	Fried, ripe plantain (Ga)
Ampesi	Plantain and yam mash
Banku	Corndough, good with groundnut soup
Boflot	Doughnut (north)
Borode (kokoo)	(Ripe) plantain (Akan)
Borodo	Bread (Akan)
Ekwei bemi	Boiled, sweetened corn kernels
Enam	Meat (Akan)
Fufu	Yam mash
Gari	Cassava flour
Gari foto	Gari dish, mixed with palm oil and other ingredients
Kalawule	Spicy fried ripe plantain with stew
Khosay	Bean cakes (north)
Klaklo	Ripe plantain dough, deep-fried
Koko	Corn or millet porridge with milk and sugar
Kokonte	Cassava meal (Akan)
Kontumbre	Cocoyam leaves
Kyinkyinga	Beef with vegetable sauce (Hausa)
Momone	Sun-dried fish (Akan)
Nsuomnam	Fish (Akan)
Nuhuu	Cocoyam porridge (Akan)
Ode	Yam (Akan)
Omo tuo	Mashed rice balls with soup or stew, usually served Sundays only (also written *Emo* or *Amo tuo*)
Rice water	Rice pudding, often for breakfast
Shito	Pepper soup (Ga)
Suya	Small shish kebab
Tatare	Ripe plantain, pounded and fried
TZ (Tozafi)	Millet mush (north)
Waachi	Rice and red beans

percent juice, it's not bad. A more acquired taste is *Supermalt*, dark and sugary with a burnt caramel flavour. Homemade drinks include *Taka Beer* (a ginger drink) and *Ice Kenkey* – sweetened, fermented maize flour in water, a taste you may not acquire. **Pito** is the millet-based beer commonly drunk, from shared bowls, in the north; it varies greatly but is quite likeable. In the south, the favourite local brews are naturally fermented **palm wine** (known in Akan as *ntunkum* when it's fresh and low in alcohol and *nsa* when it's winey) and **akpeteshie**, a potent firewater distilled from palm wine, also called "VC10" or "Kill-me-quick".

Communications – Post, Phones, Languages & Media

Ghana's postal services are inexpensive and relatively efficient to Europe and America. Letters take a week to ten days to Britain and slightly longer to North America, although to neighbouring West African countries they can take up to two months. Postal pilfering used to be a problem, but has now largely disappeared. If mailing packages of crafts or souvenirs, be sure to get an export permit at the cultural centre in

TWI PHRASE LIST

Twi, pronounced somewhere between "Twee" and "Chooi", is the name commonly given to the language of the Asante and Fante people. It's a difficult tongue to master, with a complex tonal system – and anyway most people you meet will have some English – but a few words and phrases in Twi always go down well. Note that it's usually written with the somewhat impenetrable orthography mentioned **above**, but we've gone for a simple transliteration that should sound okay.

GREETINGS

Hello, you are welcome	*A kwaaba*	Good evening	*Mma adjo*
Response	*Yaa*	Response	*Ye muu*
Good morning	*Mma ache*	Anyone home?	*Ebi wo fie?*
Good afternoon	*Mma aha*		

BASIC CONVERSATION

How are you?	*Wo o te sen?*	Thank you	*Meda ase*
I'm fine	*Me ho ye*	Response (you're welcome)	*Mme enna ase*
Come here (to children)	*Bra*	Do you speak English (lit. "white language")?	*Wote Borofo anna?*
Go away (to children)	*Koh*	I don't understand	*Mnta se*
Yes	*Aan*	I'm married	*Ma ware*
No	*Dabe*	(Please) give me water	*Ma me nsuo*
Please (lit. "I beg you")	*Me pawocheo*	I want/like . . .	*Me pe . . .*
What's your name?	*Ye ferew sen?*	I'm not well	*Me nti apoh*
My name is . . .	*Ye fere me . . .*	I'm hungry	*E komdeme*
Where do you come from?	*Wo fri he?*		
I come from . . .	*Me fri . . .*		

TRAVEL

I'm going	*Me ko*	Today	*Enne*	Yesterday	*Enrah*	Lorry	*Lore*
We're going	*Ye ko*	Tomorrow	*Echina*	Tonight	*Annajoh*	Bus stop	*Bossogyinabea*

NUMBERS

1	*Biako*	7	*Asong*	30	*Aduasa*	500	*Ahannum*
2	*Abieng*	8	*Awotwe*	40	*Aduanang*, etc	600	*Ahansia*
3	*Abiesa*	9	*Akrong*	100	*Oha*	700	*Ahansong*
4	*Anang*	10	*Du*	200	*Ahannu*	800	*Ahangwotwe*
5	*Anum*	11	*Dubiako*, etc	300	*Ahasa*	900	*Ahangkron*
6	*Asia*	20	*Aduonu*	400	*Ahannang*	1000	*Apem*

Accra, even for obviously new items, such as kente cloth, or things bought in a neighbouring country (see "Crafts and Other Purchases", p.769).

Accra's poste restante service is free and reliable. Telephones are improving all the time and card-operated public phones in Accra now provide international direct dialling. AT&T's *World Connect* service can be accessed on ☎0191.

Ghana has phone numbers of three to six digits, and area codes which are three or four digits always commencing with 0 (which you omit if calling from abroad). In this chapter, the full area code and number are given, except for manual exchanges, where just the number is given.

Ghana's IDD code is ☎233.

■ Languages

Ghana's official language is English and you can use it without much trouble throughout the country, although you'll likely need a period of adjustment before completely understanding the broader **pidgin** accents. If English is not your first language, you might be misunderstood.

The two main language "families" into which Ghanaian languages fall are Kwa in the south and Voltaic in the north (see p.84).

The great **Twi group** of Kwa languages and dialects includes the **Akan languages** like **Asante-Twi**, spoken by the Asante and Fante, **Ewe** and its associate dialects (spoken in the southeast – see p.84), and **Ga**, or Ga-Adangme, the traditional language of the Accra region.

Important **Voltaic languages** include the big **More** (or Mole) cluster – including **Dagomba**

GHANAIAN TERMS – A GLOSSARY

Adinkra Cotton, funeral cloth with printed black symbols worn by Akan mourners.

Agbada Large embroidered robe, usually white, worn on special occasions.

Akan The language that includes dialects spoken by the Fante and the Asante.

Asafo Military-style "company" of the Fante

Asante Standard spelling of the Kumasi-based ethnic group.

Ashanti Popular European spelling and name of the administrative region.

Burglar Means rip-off artist in general, including con-merchant.

Chop Food, or "to eat".

Colo Ingratiating, "colonial" behaviour.

Concert party Popular entertainment that started in the villages. When people couldn't afford to go to clubs, they began "concert parties" with a theatrical performance – usually humorous – and highlife music.

Dash From Portuguese for to give, it means a gift or bribe. It can also function as a verb as in "How much you dash me?"

Durbar Not the horse rally of northern Nigeria, this is the occasion that climaxes traditional festivals when chiefs receive distinguished guests.

ERP Economic Recovery Programme.

Ghana Ancient Ghana was based in what's now southeast Mauritania. It never reached the borders of modern Ghana.

Highlife "Big Band Highlife" is Ghana's best-known dance music form, but Ghanaians use the term to refer to a much broader range of music which is no more homogenous than, say, rock.

How be? Common greeting meaning "How are you?"

Kalabule Corruption and palm greasing.

Kente Multi-coloured, woven strip fabric, sometimes silk, made by the Asante.

Kotoko Porcupine, symbol of the Asante. The animal's countless sharp quills stand for boundless Asante bravery, reflected in the saying "Kill a thousand porcupines and a thousand more will come" (*Kotoko wokum apem, apem beba*).

Obroni wawu Imported second-hand clothes (lit. "A white man has died").

Oware The game of pebbles and holes (see p.63).

Paa "Very", for example "It's expensive, paa", very expensive.

Posuban Ancestor shrine.

Silly Pejorative term implying an insult to one's intelligence – stronger term than in US or Britain.

Stool The royal throne of Akan-speaking peoples "Stooling" means enthronement.

Tro-tro Collective taxis, usually lorries, derived from the Akan for "Three pesewas, three".

Wee Marijuana.

Weeding, or Weeding-off, is the collective grave-tending ceremony that takes place some time after a funeral.

and **Mamprusi** – and various **Grusi** tongues, among them **Frafra** and **Nunumba**.

A number of Ghanaian languages have long been written with unfamiliar **orthography** and you'll see satisfyingly exotic-looking spellings used in many hand-painted signs: ɔ (pronounced "o" as in "cost"); ε (pronounced "e" as in "men"); ŋ (pronounced "ng" as in "sing"); and ɣ (pronounced as a very soft "h").

■ The media

Ghana has an established and respected press, with an enthusiastic readership. Press freedom is now a fact of everyday Ghanaian life and there are dozens of weekly papers and regular magazines.

The main **newspapers** are the *People's Daily Graphic*, the *Ghanaian Times* and the more critical Kumasi-based *Pioneer*. They stick fairly close to the government line (*Graphic* and *Times* are both government-owned), but often have interesting coverage of national and regional events. International news is barely scratched by them, but the *Graphic's* "Tit Bits" column is a bizarre collection of snippets from around the world – worth the price of the paper alone.

Since press laws were liberalized in 1991, a flurry of other papers has sprung up, mainly serving as mouthpieces for different political parties. Most are unsophisticated in their layout and tend more towards editorializing than hard journalism. The main ones are *Champion*, *The Ghanaian Voice*, *New Nation*, the *Weekly Spectator* and the *Statesman* which together have a circulation of over 800,000 a week.

As for **foreign press**, there's normally a small selection of British papers available at Accra airport and the posher hotels, and *West Africa* magazine, which provides probably the most detailed regular coverage of the country in English, is always on sale.

There's colour **TV** broadcasting (three channels including CNS) and three state-owned GBC **radio** stations, plus an external service in French and English. GBC FM plays current pop and covers news and the social scene. The short-lived pirate station, **Radio Eye**, founded by the outspoken Dr Charles Wireko-Brobby in 1994, was crushed by the government very quickly; they cited overwhelming "national security" considerations against the previously untested 1992 media freedom laws.

Holidays and Festivals

The main Christian and Muslim holidays are celebrated in Ghana, but the impact of Islam is patchy and strongest in the northwest. Shops and businesses also close down for Fourth Republic Day (January 7), Independence Day (March 6), Revolution Day (June 4), Republic Day (July 1), Farmers' Day (December 2) and the Anniversary of the Second Revolution (December 31).

Entertainment

Ghana has a satisfying cultural life, with theatre, cinema and especially music accessible. If you're in Accra in June, you'll catch notice of the annual Entertainment Critics and Reviewers Association of Ghana awards. Towards the end of even-numbered years you may find the Panafest music and arts festival in progress. November 1994 was its first, somewhat disorganized, manifestation. It is due to take place again in August 1996.

■ Theatre

Accra's fine, new, Chinese-built **National Theatre** and the **Greater Accra Centre for National Culture** are the capital's two main theatre venues. The **School of Performing Arts** at Legon University also stages occasional productions in Accra. In the country as a whole, **"Concert Party"**, a traditional type of lightly satirical musical-comedy-drama, is the theatrical form you're most likely to come across. *Akpeteshie* is the drink and the party typically goes on all night. Many itinerant bands cover the village and small town circuit. You might get a taste, if you can't attend a show, by tracking down a Concert Party cassette, like the one by the stand-up comic "Waterproof" (on the local *"Q" Production* label).

■ Cinema

Ghanaian **cinema** has a wealth of unexplored potential (there's talent in the wings, held back by financial constraints), but you're still more likely to get a helping of Bond or Stallone than something from top Ghanaian director **Kwaw Ansah**. In Accra, the Ghana Film Institute does show regular African films in between European

THE GHANAIAN FESTIVAL YEAR

In addition to the official public holidays, many **regional celebrations** or festivals (*afahye* in Twi) animate the country throughout the year. Dates often vary. This **selective listing** covers most of the country but there are very many more. Note that dates are approximate in most cases and, in some, the local name of the occasion just means "festival".

FESTIVAL (DATE)	LOCALITY
JANUARY	
Kwafie (early)	Berekum
Ntoa Fokuokese (10th)	Nkoranza, west of Ejura, Asante Region
Kpini-Kyiu (22nd)	Wa, Upper West Region
Danso Abaim Afahye (end)	Techiman, 130km north of Kumasi
Tengbana	Tongo, Upper East Region
Jimbenti A period of purification and pacification of the gods. An all-day festival, *Jimbenti* ends at sunset when burning sticks are thrown into the eastern sky to scare away unknown demons.	Tumu (Sissala people)
Adae Kese Asante festival culminating in the purification of the ancestral stools.	Kumasi and other Asante towns
FEBRUARY	
Damba	Wa, Upper West Region
Amu Harvest festival including ritual *Asafo* dances and other cultural displays.	Vane Avatime near Ho, Volta Region
MARCH	
Kotokyikyi (first Friday)	Senya Beraku, west of Accra
Kyiu Sung (7th)	Throughout Upper West and Upper East
Golgu (around Easter)	Bolgatanga
Lalue Kpledo (10th)	Prampram, east of Accra
Ogyapa (end March, early April)	Senya Beraku
Sigi Sheep and chickens are slaughtered and *pito* offered to God through the ancestors in a thanksgiving and harvest celebration that includes drumming and dancing.	Navrongo
APRIL	
Dam and ***Bugum*** festivals	Tamale and around
Godigbeza Celebrations to commemorate migration from the Ewe ancestral lands at Notse (Togo) include drumming, dancing, ceremonial costumes.	Aflao
***Aboakyer* antelope-hunt** (late April/early May) More commonly known as the Deer-Hunting Festival, this famous event involves two hunting groups competing to bring back a live antelope. The first to present it to the chief and elders is proclaimed champion.	Winneba, Central Region
MAY	
Don (14th)	Wa, Bawku and Bolgatanga
Sallah	Tamale and Tumu
Chimisi	Bawku, Upper East Region
JUNE	
Dzimbenti or ***Bugum*** (11th)	Throughout Upper West and Upper East

continues over

THE GHANAIAN FESTIVAL YEAR (cont.)

Apiba	Senya Beraku, west of Accra
Fire festival	Tamale and Bawku
Dongu	Wa, Upper West Region
JULY	
Bakatue Festival (first Friday)	Elmina, coast
Damba (last week of July or early August)	Dagomba people, Northern Region
Yam Festival	Tamale
Edjodi	Senya Beraku, west of Accra
Bugumlobre	Bongo, Upper East Region
Jimbanti	Tumu, Upper West Region
Dzumbanti	Wa, Upper West Region
AUGUST	
Asafotufiiam (first week)	Ada, coast east of Accra
Akumasi (second week)	Senya Beraku, coast west of Accra
Damba (August/September)	Tamale and surrounding region
Bontungu Five days of drumming and dancing in which villagers clear all superfluous or undesirable objects from their homes and ask God for good health and prosperity in the coming year.	Anomabu, near Saltpond, west of Accra
Homowo (Aug/Sept). Traditional festival of the Ga people including street processions of twins and offerings of ceremonial *kpokpoi* food to the gods.	Accra, Prampram and surrounding districts
SEPTEMBER	
Odwira Thanksgiving festival held any time in September.	Held throughout the Asante country and by most Akan people
Yam Festival (all month)	Volta Region
Oguaa Fetu Afahye (first Saturday) A big, dressy occasion lasting several days.	Cape Coast
Black Stool Festival (25th)	Seikwa, north of Berekum
Yam Festival (last week or early October)	Effiduasi, Asante Region
OCTOBER	
Daa (1st–12th)	Tongo, Upper East Region
***Sabre* dance** (9th)	Lawra, Upper West Region
Akonedi (9th–13th)	Larteh, 56km north of Accra
Kobina (15th)	Lawra, Upper West Region
Boaram (28th)	Tongo, Upper East Region
Yam Festival	Ejura and Effiduasi, Asante Region
Fijyiiyna/Monomene Bayere Afahye	Nkoranza, west of Ejura
NOVEMBER	
Atweaban (second week)	Ntonso, northeast of Kumasi
Yam Festival	Ejura, northeast of Kumasi
Afahye	Agogo, 100km east of Kumasi
Yango	Bawku, Upper East Region
Boaram	Tongo, Upper Region
Hotbetsotso Commemoration of the Anlos' migration from a tyrannical kingdom to their homeland.	Anloga, on the Atlantic shore southwest of Keta
DECEMBER	
Fao (1st)	Navrongo, Upper East Region
Kwafie (over the New Year)	Berekum
***Kpini* guinea fowl festival**	Dagomba and Gonja people

and American blockbusters. Video shows, in any case, are fast taking over from fleapit cinemas. There's more background in the "Cinema" piece in *Contexts* at the back of the book.

■ Music

While Ghana is famous for the urban goodtime dance music known as **highlife**, the country has an active tradition of **rural music and dance** that continues to influence urban sounds. Look out for folkloric gigs and events..

Although "big band highlife" declined in the 1970s with the frequency of coups, curfews and power cuts, these technical problems didn't really affect guitar highlife, which can still be heard all over. Concert parties and **gospel highlife**, took off in the 1970s and are still thriving.

Many "name" stars migrated to Europe, and more went to Nigeria, where they've kept the highlife flame burning. Those currently based in Ghana include **Kwame Ampadu and the African Brothers**, still one of the nation's top electric guitar bands after nearly three decades and the irrepressible **Alex Konadu** – a gig of whose you might catch just about anywhere in the country.

Some of the other prominent names in Ghanaian music, at home and abroad, are **K. K. Kabobo**, **Kwadjo Antwi** and the **Lumba Brothers**. Also see the music section in *Contexts* at the back of the book.

For concert dates in Accra, get hold of a copy of the listings mag *Ghanascope* and see the *Daily Graphic*'s "Entertainments" page every Saturday.

Wildlife and National Parks

Ghana's native fauna is not in as desperate a position as you might expect. Conservation laws ban hunting for food or sport (except as part of a traditional festival) and even trade in game meat is prohibited. Such edicts are impossible to enforce but at the very least discourage the practices. The current wave of interest in new national parks and the attraction they hold for travellers and tourists are positive signs for the future of Ghana's flora and fauna. On the downside, much of the rainforest was felled decades ago, never to return.

Along the coast, the British RSPB has been effective in helping to curb the killing of **sea birds** for sport and food – especially the very rare and now protected **roseate tern**, which migrates to these shores every winter from northern Europe. They can be contacted at the Environmental Protection Council (☎021/ 66.46.97). Ghana **Friends of the Earth** (PO Box 3794, Accra; ☎021/22.59.63; Fax 021/22.79.93) is an active group, one of the few such in Africa.

The tourist board is currently in the process of opening several new parks to exploration. Already, the **Kakum Nature Park** is receiving visitors and other places are following suit. While the long-established **Mole Game Reserve** is a functioning and well-stocked park with the full complement of bush-savannah mammals, most of the new parks don't yet provide facilities and some tracks are not maintained. This means you are limited to what you can see on foot. But the park rangers are typically very enthusiastic and helpful in organizing excursions.

Listen on the travellers' grapevine to find out if there have been any developments in the **Digya National Park** (formerly the Kujani Game Reserve). Bordering the western edge of Lake Volta, this is Ghana's largest park, harbouring elephants, various antelopes, hippo, waterbuck and a wide range of other species.

It's also worth checking whether facilities have been added to the **Bia National Park** in the rainforests of the west near the Côte d'Ivoire border. Further north, the **Bui National Park** straddles tributaries of the Black Volta in a protected woodland, and should by now have basic accommodation.

Finally, the **Kalakpe Game Production Reserve**, only 15km southwest of Ho, now provides another attraction in the Volta region, an area quickly becoming a big destination for travel. Here you'll find a proliferation of birds along with buffalo, antelope and many varieties of monkeys.

Directory

AIRPORT TAX ₵22,000, payable only in cedis.

CRAFTS AND OTHER PURCHASES Ghana has a huge variety of arts and crafts, still widely made for local consumption. Accra is good for imported printed cloth. The Asante region is a prolific producer and well known for its *kente* and *adinkra* cloths. These can be bought in villages around Kumasi or at the town's cultural centre. The region is also famed for its carvings – especially of stools made in Ahwiaa. The north specializes more in leather goods, rough cotton weaves and basketry, all of which are found at the Bolgatanga market. Perhaps the best place for selection is in Accra where art from all over the country – and from throughout West Africa – comes together at the crafts market.

Whatever you buy, including cloth, you should obtain an **export permit** from the Ghana Museum and Monuments Board declaring the item has no historical value. Take your pieces to their office in the Centre for National Culture or the National Museum and they'll sell you a certificate on the spot. This ensures your purchases won't be confiscated when you leave Ghana.

DRUGS *Wee* (**marijuana**) is illegal, though widely available. The main areas of production are around Ejura in the Asante region and Nsawam north of Accra. Generally looked upon more as a bad habit than a dangerous drug, consumers aren't likely to run into big trouble, though discretion is always advisable.

EDUCATION Ghana has traditionally been known for a relatively high level of education. The country has four universities – the University of Ghana, near Accra; the University of Science and Technology, Kumasi; the University of Cape Coast; and the new University of Development Studies, Tamale. Primary school is compulsory.

FOOTBALL Soccer is the most popular sport in Ghana and a number of Ghanaians play overseas, including Tony Yeboah and Abedi Pele. Since the mid-1980s, the most consistently top-quality team has been Kumasi Asante Kotoko: the Kotokos have won the Africa Cup three times. The oldest team is Accra Hearts of Gold, while the current bright stars are Obuasi Goldfields.

GOLD This is the country all right, but you'll be hard pressed to find much sign of the precious metal (except during major festivals, notably the *Ogua Fetu Afahye* in Cape Coast) away from the big goldfields around Tarkwa and Obuasi, southwest of Kumasi. Visits take some advance preparation (see p.815).

OPENING HOURS Government offices are open Monday to Friday 8am–12.30pm and 1.30–5pm. Most businesses operate Monday to Friday 8am or 9am–noon and 2–5.30pm. Many shops also open on Saturday, from around 8am to 1pm. Shops are closed on public holidays, without exception – it's the law.

PHOTOGRAPHY You don't need a **permit** to take pictures in Ghana, though the usual regulations against snapping military installations and strategic points are rigorously enforced. Especially sensitive is Osu Castle in Accra – the seat of government. Taking pictures anywhere in the vicinity could lead to the confiscation of camera and film, if not arrest.

SMOKING The government actively campaigns against smoking, with health warnings on packets and a smoking ban on all *Ghana Airways* domestic flights (not much of a problem while they're grounded) and *STC* buses.

STUDENT CARDS ISIC cards may entitle you to discounts on *Ghana Airways* and *STC* buses if you get a letter of certification from a Ghanaian educational institution, or possibly produce a letter from your college.

TROUBLE Muggings aren't a problem in Ghana, not even in Accra, though this may change if the city becomes a transit point for hard drugs, as seems to be happening. Ordinary pick-pocketing is probably worst in Kumasi market. Police sometimes stop travellers (and Ghanaians) and pretend to be really angry about a minor infraction (such as jaywalking, which is illegal at certain places including Kwame Nkrumah Circle in Accra). Customs and immigration officers employ similar tactics. They are almost certainly angling for "dash" (a present or bribe), and you may have to pay up, but large amounts aren't necessary and politeness and smiles will help.

WOMEN TRAVELLERS AND GHANAIAN WOMEN Most travellers experience great kindness and there are few special problems for women – indeed, many rate Ghana one of the most hassle-free countries in West Africa. However, even more than in other parts, Ghanaian men and boys are likely to respond with unrestrained lewdness to what may be seen as provocative clothing or inappropriate behaviour in a woman (riding a bicycle, for example).

As for women in Ghanaian society, the Akan-speaking people (but not all other groups) are mostly **matrilineal** – a system in which men inherit from their maternal uncles, rather than their fathers – but the impact on women's status is, if anything, reduced as a result and there is firm government pressure against this form of inheritance. Genital mutilation isn't practised much in Ghana. If you're interested in making contacts, write to the *Ghana Assembly of Women* (PO Box 459, Accra) or the *Federation of Ghanaian Women* (PO Box 6326, Accra).

A Brief History of Ghana

Though the present country has been peopled for well over two thousand years, some of the earliest migrations to the region that are known about in any detail occurred after the Ghana Empire was sacked in the eleventh century. At this time, the Ntafo, early ancestors of the Akan people, moved south to the parkland west of Gonja, in northern Ghana. About 700 years ago, they began moving further south in three waves consisting of the Guan, Fante and Asante peoples. Early trading relations existed with much of West Africa, particularly with the western Sudan. Gold and kola nuts were important products which poured out of the region, across the Sahara and into North Africa. Mande peoples from the Niger bend greatly influenced the economy and culture of the north as they established numerous trading centres alongside existing townships.

By the early nineteenth century the Gold Coast interior had developed a complicated network of northern states – Gonja, Dagomba, Mamprusi and Nanumba – and, in the south, smaller confederations (the Fante for example) and statelets (Ga, Ewe, Nzima). In the central region, the Asante confederation was rapidly mushrooming. Given time, the Asante empire might have conquered and assimilated most of the smaller political units in the surrounding territories which were later to come under French rule. Such a scenario, however, was thwarted by the colonial experience which began in earnest in the nineteenth century. European involvement in the region had begun, on a smaller scale, much earlier and provoked a shift in the emphasis of trade away from the northern routes to the southern ports.

■ European arrival

Searching out new trade routes and a way to obtain the gold of the trans-Saharan caravans closer to source, the first **Portuguese** ships came to Ghana in 1471. By 1482 they had returned to build a fort at **Elmina** ("the mine"), using a mixture of persuasion and threats to gain the consent of the local ruler. The region turned out to be rich in gold, ivory, timber and skins, and other Europeans followed the Portuguese. Over the next four hundred years, sea powers like the Dutch, Danes and British competed heavily for the trade. With the European colonization of America, this expanded to include **slaves**, in exchange for which the Europeans brought hard liquor and manufactured goods like **clothing** and **weaponry**. Guns eventually helped the **Asante** – the principal traders with the foreigners – to expand their influence over the region's interior and to apply pressure to the **Fante** middlemen through whom they'd been dealing with the British since the 1600s.

■ The British colony

By the early nineteenth century, the British had emerged as the strongest foreign power on the "Gold Coast". In 1807, they abolished the slave trade in the region and began looking for other exploitable resources. Over the next hundred years, palm oil, cocoa, rubber, gold and timber were developed as exports. These products drew the British – hitherto content to remain in their coastal forts – increasingly into the hinterland.

The stage was set for the outright **conquest** of the interior when the Asante invaded the Fante confederation in 1806. The Fante had long been able to resist the attempts of their powerful northern neighbours to dominate them, thanks in large part to their role as preferential trading partners with the Europeans. Now the British rallied to the aid of their Fante "allies", even offering them protection in one of their coastal forts.

Hostilities flared and **tenuous treaties** were reached between the two Akan factions throughout the first half of the century. But, as competition increased for the control of trade, the British decided there could be only one victor. They ultimately found the excuse they needed to invade the interior when war again broke out between the Fante and Asante in the 1870s. The British sacked the Asante capital, Kumasi, in 1874. Subsequent **Asante wars** followed in 1896 and 1900, when the ruling Asanthene was finally exiled (see p.808).

By that time Germany, France and Britain had already agreed on borders for the areas they would control. The British introduced elements of **indirect rule** in their new colony, even allowing the Asante confederation to be re-established under the Ashanti Confederacy Council – a government agency – in 1935. After World War I, part of German Togoland was integrated into the British colony.

The rise of nationalism

Nationalist movements were created early in the colonial period, with one – the Aborigines' Rights Protection Society – dating as far back as 1897. Other parties sprang up during the 1920s and 1930s and, by 1946, concessions to African demands for representation had led to an African majority in Ghana's Legislative Council, although the executive branch – and effective rule – was still in the hands of the British Governor. In 1947, **JB Danquah** formed the United Gold Coast Convention, a party which favoured the principle of a gradual shift to self-government and independence. The same year, the party invited **Kwame Nkrumah** to join its ranks as party secretary in an effort to broaden a base that consisted mainly of the educated elite – civil servants, lawyers, businessmen and doctors.

In the aftermath of the 1948 **Accra riots** (see p.779) Nkrumah lost patience with conservatives in the UGCC and split from it to form his own party, the **Convention People's Party** – campaigning slogan, *Self-government now.* He gained prominence among the masses as a result and the British detained him when he called for a national strike in 1950. The CPP, meanwhile, won the Legislative Assembly elect-ion of 1951, and the governor, Sir Charles Arden-Clarke, prudently released Nkrumah and invited him to help form a government. Thus, in 1952, Nkrumah became the first African prime minister in the Commonwealth. He went on to win the elections of 1954 and 1956 – a period during which his CPP party shared power with the British. On August 3, 1956 the Legislative Assembly passed a unanimous motion calling for complete independence.

■ Independence: heady days . . .

When **independence** was ultimately returned on March 6, 1957, the future looked bright for the first African country to break colonial bonds. Ghana was then the world's leading cocoa exporter and produced a tenth of all the world's gold. Other valuable resources, of which the country had many, included bauxite, manganese, diamonds and timber. Perhaps Ghana's greatest asset was a high percentage of educated citizens who seemed well qualified to run the new nation (25 percent of the population was literate, compared, for example, to an estimated 1 percent in Portugal's colonies).

Nkrumah became a larger than life figure, respected throughout Africa and the African diaspora and highly regarded in the West. He was an eloquent advocate of **pan-Africanism** and the **non-aligned movement**. His economic principles looked sound, too, as he sought to create an industrial base that would reduce dependence on foreign powers while improving social services throughout the country (hospitals and clinics, universities and schools were part of his legacy). The port city of **Tema**, with its smelting and other industrial plants, was constructed at this time as was the ambitious **Akosombo Dam**, built to supply hydro-electric power.

. . . and disaster

Nkrumah's economic strategy was, however, extremely costly, and with four decades of hindsight it seems painfully clear that his biggest mistake was to over-emphasize **prestige projects** at the expense of a solid agricultural base. Worse still, many of the projects held no prospect of any economic return: Accra's showy conference centre – designed to be the headquarters of the Organization of African Unity, which based itself instead in Addis Ababa – and symbolic monuments like Black Star Square and the vainglorious State House were the dizzy results of a belief in the invincible rightness of Nkrumah's ideals. Foreign currency reserves dwindled at a frightening rate and the country accumulated a debt running to hundreds of millions of pounds.

As the economic situation turned suddenly bleak, political discontent rose. Despite concern for his international reputation, Nkrumah responded with increasing repression at home where his support was dwindling. Government suppression of a 1961 workers' strike had already seriously alienated Nkrumah from the working class and the educated elite had long been disillusioned with his expensive brand of scientific socialism. When the world price of cocoa plummeted in the mid-1960s, Ghana's hopes for economic self-sufficiency – and long-term stability – were dashed.

By 1964, Ghana was legally a **one-party state.** As the CPP tried measures to stamp out opposition, the government increasingly arrested those it feared under the Preventive Detention

Act which allowed for "enemies" of the regime to be held for up to five years without trial. Public gatherings were strictly controlled, press censorship became commonplace and an extensive network of informants was developed by the party central committee. Such measures were effective in crushing opposition, or at least in driving it deeply underground, but Nkrumah still had to contend with the military. Suspicious of the army's loyalty, he lost his nerve and made policy decisions that were bound to antagonize officers – placing limits on recruitment and hedging military procurement procedures with elaborate safeguards. Isolating himself still further from the support of the military, he formed an independent **presidential guard**, accountable only to him.

In the light of such developments, Western nations increasingly criticized **governmental corruption** and recognized a **personality cult** surrounding Nkrumah, where previously they'd seen a charismatic figure. Nkrumah was forced to abandon his non-alignment and turn to the Soviet bloc for support. By then he had totally lost the backing of the military and almost every other element of society. Only a blind sense of impunity could have allowed him to travel abroad. On February 24, 1966, while on a visit to Peking, he was overthrown in a bloodless coup by British-trained officers. He died in exile in Conakry in 1972.

Coups and "kleptocrats"

Following Nkrumah's flight, Lieutenant-General **Joseph Ankrah** was appointed head of the National Liberation Council (NLC) that ruled until 1969. The conservative junta went on a witch-hunt, arresting left-wing ideologues, banning the CPP and harassing its leaders. The junta's **economic direction** seemed promising to the West, however, as they privatized many state enterprises and broke off relations with the Soviet Union and its allies. But for all the promises made to better the economy, life for most people without special connections grew steadily worse.

From its inception, the NLC viewed itself as a provisional government and much of its period of rule was spent preparing for a return to civilian democracy. A bill of rights was drawn up, and safeguards implemented to ensure the independence of the judiciary – measures intended to stop the reconstitution of an autocratic one-party state. In May 1969, political parties were legalized. The **Progress Party**, headed by Kofi Busia – an Akan who represented the traditional middle-class opposition to Nkrumah's rule – was counterbalanced by the **National Alliance of Liberals** led by Komla Gbedemah, an Ewe and one-time associate of Nkrumah who had broken with the leader and gone into exile.

In September 1969, Ghanaians gave democracy another try, and elected **Dr Kofi Busia** prime minister. But the new leader struggled to wade through the economic mess. Cocoa prices dropped again in 1971, sparking a new crisis and, at the same time, mismanagement and racketeering led to shortages in food production, supplies and foreign exchange. Under mounting pressure, Busia took the necessary but politically dangerous step of **devaluing the cedi**. Massive price increases followed and the public enthusiasm that had ushered in the new regime faded almost immediately. Busia was overthrown on January 13, 1972.

General corruption

From 1972 to 1979, Ghana was led by a series of juntas with remarkably **corrupt generals** at the helm. One of the most flagrant offenders was **General I Acheampong**, who headed the National Redemption Council (NRC) from 1972 to 1975 and then the Supreme Military Council until 1978. During his period in office, Ghanaians coined the term "kleptocracy" – rule by thieves – as the official economy moved closer and closer to complete collapse. The **black market** thrived, meanwhile, as basic goods like bread and eggs became unattainable for the poor. Production declined even further and what few agricultural goods emerged onto the market were smuggled abroad to Togo and Côte d'Ivoire, where they fetched higher, hard currency prices. The educated elite – doctors, teachers, lawyers – led a brain drain to Nigeria and overseas where they had some chance of supporting themselves.

The basis of Acheampong's economic policy was **"self-reliance"**, symbolized by programmes such as "Operation Feed Yourself", launched in 1972. Moderate successes were achieved in the early years of the NRC, but by the mid-1970s the economic outlook was so grim that the professional middle class, and especially the Ghana Bar Association, demanded a return to party politics. Acheampong sought a compromise by proposing a **"union government"** where power would be shared between civilians, the armed forces and – radically – the police. The opposition viewed UNIGOV as a mechanism to keep the military in power and reacted cynically when Acheampong pushed his idea through on the back of a trumped-up referendum held in 1978.

As criticism grew, so did **repression**, and hundreds of opposition leaders were jailed without trial. Viewed increasingly as a tyrant, Acheampong withdrew into isolation. He was quietly deposed in a coup led by **General William Akuffo** on July 5, 1978. Akuffo established the "Supreme Military Council II" and eventually set a date for elections in June 1979, but little else changed and widespread discontent in the country now spread to the ranks of the military.

A new age: Rawlings Mark I

There can be no peace where there is no justice – and there will be no justice unless everyone can be made to answer for his conduct

Jerry Rawlings, 1979

On May 15, 1979, there was a bungled uprising of junior ranks in the army, led by a 32-year-old flight lieutenant of mixed Scottish–Ghanaian parentage – **Jerry Rawlings**. He was captured and imprisoned but freed by fellow soldiers and they made a second, successful, attempt to take power on **June 4, 1979**.

Rawlings made it clear that his coup would be different, that he was out to eliminate corruption and restore national pride to an economic order neglected in fifteen years of waste. The title of his governing **Armed Forces Revolutionary Council** set the tone – Rawlings envisaged a "moral revolution" based implicitly on socialist principles of an economy for need rather than profit. He took a hard line, sending high-ranking officers to the firing squad (including Acheampong and Akuffo) and approving a purge of public figures under suspicion of fraud. At the same time he pledged that the AFRC would work quickly to restore order and return the reins of power to a civilian government.

The world community noted little more than another coup d'état in Ghana, but, in a remarkable departure (no African military ruler had ever voluntarily relinquished power before, except arguably, Eyadéma in neighbouring Togo), the promise was kept. Following elections held on June 18, 1979, the newly elected president, **Dr Hilla Limann** took office in September and the soldiers returned to their barracks barely three months after leaving them.

Limann rode in on a wave of popularity at home and in the West where his conservative politics won respect. But despite his best intentions, the economy continued to slide – production dropped further, the cedi remained overvalued (fearing unpopularity, the president refused to devalue the currency and thereby cost his country a major IMF loan) and the country's infrastructure became hopelessly eroded. And despite the moral high ground captured by the Rawlings clique, and Rawlings' own shadowy behind-the-scenes presence, **corrupt practices** had been re-established by the end of 1980 in virtually every sphere of public life.

Rawlings' second coming

On December 31, 1981, Rawlings led a **second successful coup**, toppling the Limann government, abolishing the entire "democratic" framework, and placing the government in the hands of a **Provisional National Defence Council**. As before, he justified the action by the urgent need to halt corruption and put Ghana's wrecked and abused economy in order. This time, however, no plans were made to restore the country to civilian rule. Rather, the PNDC decided to put into practice the leftist populist principles of the original coup.

Early moves were made to democratize the decision-making process and to decentralize political power. This was done through **People's Defence Committees** (PDCs), which replaced district councils and which were intended to increase local participation in the revolution while raising political consciousness at the grassroots level.

The political orientation of the second revolution proved too much for large sections of the army, particularly northerners, and there were several **coup attempts** in 1982 and 1983, including a nearly disastrous attempt mounted from Togo (see "Foreign Affairs", below). Meanwhile, the revolution itself provided excuse enough for a few hard-line radicals to undertake terrorist attacks under the guise of "popular justice". There were calls from several quarters for a complete overhaul (even abolition) of the judiciary and there was worse in June 1982 with the kidnap and **murder of three senior judges**.

Unfortunately for Rawlings, the trial and conviction of the two murderers wasn't sufficient to clear all elements of the PNDC of any involvement and it was forced into a public position of greater moderation.

Like Thomas Sankara, who arrived on the scene in Burkina Faso two years later, Rawlings initially enjoyed huge popularity among the masses fed up with government lies and excesses. With his battle cry of **"accountability"**, he proved sincere in the **war against corruption** and, although the economy continued to slide during his first years, he soon managed to produce a **turnaround** (by 1984, the economy was showing a five percent growth rate, the first upswing in ten years).

Despite Rawlings' penchant for revolutionary rhetoric, his early friendship with the Libyan leader Colonel Gaddafi and his ties with Cuba and Eastern Europe, his pragmatic economic approach – including taking the risky political step of drastically devaluing the cedi – earned him high marks with the IMF, which started once again to provide sizeable loans to the country.

Foreign affairs

Relations with **Burkina Faso** were extremely close while Sankara was alive, and at one point the countries even envisaged a common currency. Plans were also made to co-ordinate their energy, trade, transportation and education programmes which shared many similarities of emphasis.

Predictably, more conservative regimes were less receptive to Rawlings' style of government. Relations with **Britain**, **Côte d'Ivoire**, and especially **Togo** have been, at best, cool. All three countries have harboured Ghanaian exiles, some of whom have maintained links with **dissident opposition** groups in Ghana. In 1983 this secret opposition came dangerously close to toppling the government as they infiltrated Accra from Togo and took over the GBC broadcasting station before being apprehended. More recently the January 1994 coup attempt against Togo's President Eyadéma triggered new tension between the two countries. The rebels were said to have entered Lomé from Ghana. In recent years the border has frequently been closed, but a surprise meeting between Rawlings and Eyadéma in Kara, Togo, in July 1995, seemed to be heralding a new era of good relations.

Rawlings has been an eloquent critic of the world's **commodity markets**, pointing out, for example, that the tyranny of cocoa price-setting in determining Ghana's earning power (and thus the living standards of its people) quite overshadowed what he viewed as the necessary curtailments on personal freedom in a society effectively under siege.

■ The coming of the Fourth Republic

By the end of the 1980s, after a decade in power, Rawlings had made much of what seemed a hopeless situation. But he had not always had an easy time straddling diverse elements in society. Although most rural dwellers and many wage earners remained loyal, he had suffered scrapes with the ambitious middle class, who loathed his socialist rhetoric and raised the banner of human rights. Many students and academics, on the other hand, charged him with selling out to the IMF, saying he presided over a neo-colonialist state. Still, the performance of the economy (Ghana recorded the highest consistent rates of economic growth in Africa throughout much of the 1980s) seemed to shield the president from pressure to liberalize the government, whether it came from disgruntled nationals, or Western donors.

Ghana entered the 1990s against the background rumble of the **Quarshigah Affair** – apparently yet another attempt to murder Chairman Rawlings and overthrow the PNDC. Major Courage Quarshigah and six other officers were sentenced for their connection with the alleged plot. One of them was found hanged in his cell, and Amnesty International adopted the others, denouncing what they claimed was imprisonment for political dissension. Ghanaians rallied around the affair, demanding the abolition of a number of laws, particularly those allowing detention, and an end to the ban on political parties. Foreign pressure to democratize also increased.

Rather than entrenching, Rawlings surprised many when, in July 1990, he formed a **National Commission for Democracy** to review decentralization and consider Ghana's political future. Though opponents criticized the commission for being too close to the ruling party to instigate reform, changes took place quickly. By 1991 the commission was recommending a new constitution and presidential and legislative elections – recommendations approved by the PNDC which, contrary to all expectations, endorsed the restoration of a **multi-party system.**

Rawlings remained on the defensive, however, and in June 1991, had to reiterate denials that political prisoners remained behind bars. He invited Amnesty International to see for themselves, but was soon back in trouble with them when **John Ndebugre**, leader of the Movement for Freedom and Justice (MFJ) and an outspoken government critic, was jailed because he failed to stand for the national anthem.

Despite what appeared a questionable commitment to democracy, reforms continued apace. In addition to the completion of the new constitution and the unbanning of political parties, 1992 saw the emergence of a **free press** and three new human rights organizations plus the release of remaining political detainees.

As the November **presidential election** drew near, opposition parties – especially the **New Patriotic Party** (NPP), an Asante-based group in the Danquah-Busia tradition, headed by **Professor Albert Adu-Boahen** – seemed confident of success in the polls against Rawlings' National Democratic Congress (the party formed from the PNDC). **Dr Hilla Limann**, who had been overthrown in Rawlings' second coup, returned to the political arena as candidate for the **People's National Convention** (PNC).

The opposition euphoria faded fast after the elections: Rawlings took 58 percent of the vote (compared with 30 percent for Adu-Boahen), and a stunned opposition protested that the government must have rigged the vote. Some **voting irregularities** undoubtedly did take place, though the margin of victory was large enough to have ensured a win even under perfectly fair conditions. In the eyes of many Ghanaians, however, Rawlings had held onto power without a clear popular mandate. The subsequent **opposition boycott** of the ensuing legislative elections assured victory to the NDC and its affiliates, the NCP and the EGLE party, and denied the new Fourth Republic (based on the constitution devised by the National Commission for Democracy) the legitimacy it might otherwise have had. As a result, the post-democracy government looked oddly like the military dictatorship that had preceded it.

■ The present and the outlook

Rather than usher in a new era of optimism, the elections poisoned the political atmosphere which had seemed so promising at the beginning of the 1990s. Under the PNDC, Rawlings had led a bold attempt to stabilize an economy that appeared broken beyond repair, and throughout the 1980s, he had taken tough steps to restore a measure of fairness in the allocation of resources between the towns and countryside. After the elections, Ghanaians seem sceptical on whether he can also prove himself a champion of multi-party democracy.

But there are encouraging signals. In his first address to Parliament, Rawlings offered an olive branch to opposition parties, inviting them to dialogue with the legislature from which they had excluded themselves. Soon after, the NPP stated it was ready to "do business", a spokesperson adding, "we should start settling some of the crucial, outstanding issues that can only be resolved sitting down with the government, not sitting in a corner sulking." Although any opposition will be extra-parliamentary until the next elections, the deadlock between the president and his opponents seems to be loosening.

Also encouraging is the role of **the press** in providing a platform for opposition. Before and during the elections, Rawlings was generally credited with exercising restraint towards the slew of publications that emerged when the press ban was lifted, especially since many bolstered sales with the type of president-bashing articles still considered treasonous throughout much of Africa. Although the "Culture of Silence" appeared to have ended for newspapers, soon after the elections, the New Patriotic Party charged the state with **television censorship**. The complaint arose after *Talking Point*, a current affairs programme, abruptly went off the air just as an NPP spokesman was launching into an attack on Rawlings' economic policy. The Supreme Court agreed the government acted unconstitutionally and ordered it to share the airwaves. That ruling was in itself reassuring: a sign **the judiciary** would not be a rubber stamp.

Important as political issues are, however, success or failure for Rawlings' government depends ultimately on the economy, as it tries to juggle policies that maintain foreign approval while not further alienating Ghanaians at home. The IMF continues to talk about Ghana in glowing terms, and in a recent report, *Ghana in the Year 2000*, recommended an Asian-style **Accelerated Growth Strategy**. Rapid development ought to bring yet further investment, but would mean more deep cuts in the short term.

KONKOMBAS AND NUNUMBAS

A setback for Ghana that was not widely foreseen was the outbreak of an **ethnic war** in the north-east in 1994. The conflict between **Konkomba** and **Nunumba** people, in the region of Bimbilla, flared from a marketplace brawl over a chicken to widespread carnage in the space of a few days, costing the lives of over 2000 people, leaving another 150,000 homeless in refugee camps, destroying or badly damaging as many as sixty villages and small towns and paralyzing much of northern Ghana for months.

The roots of the conflict lie in the tensions between the Konkomba, who have no traditional system of chiefhood, and the chieftancy-organized Nunumba. The Nunumba have always assumed a dominant stance in areas where both groups live, claiming that the Konkomba are "newcomers" from Togo who pay them tribute in the form of work, crops and livestock, in return for the use of Nunumba land. The Konkomba, for their part, retort that this is just an arrogant take on the facts of the matter – that the Nunumba invaded their lands from the north centuries ago and have never had any rights over it. The oral histories of most ethnic groups in the region tend to support the view that the Konkomba are the "indigenous" local people.

The army was sent in to keep the fighters apart, but there was a further outbreak of violence in 1995. The government has been unable to resolve the dispute, which now focuses on the issue of paramount chieftancies. While Nunumba chiefs are influential in the **Northern Region House of Chiefs** and have some key figures in government, there is no equivalent role for Konkomba leaders. The Konkomba are thus marginalized when government spending plans are put into effect and miss out on local, and even national, decision-making. They are now demanding the creation of a Konkomba paramount chieftancy. In light of the government's unwillingness to follow this dispute-laden path, the Konkomba Youth Association has written to the United Nations asking for their intervention.

A new era of prosperity?

The prospect of prosperity just around the corner has tantalized Ghanaians for so long that many have become cynical about it. Despite the economic growth, partly measurable by the rapid expansion of the country's new **stock market**, and by populist programmes that have included rural electrification and road-building, the poor and the wage-earners are paying a heavy price for economic reform. The percentage of people living below the **poverty line** has barely decreased in the last decade; social services are all but non-existent; there are fees to attend state-run primary schools; and in many areas the only available health care is from mission-run clinics.

Equally troublesome is the fact that much of the recent expansion has been fuelled by a boom in the **gold-mining industry**, with gold surpassing cocoa as the most lucrative export of the 1990s. But local businesses complain about unfavourable policies and tight money supply: lending rates are around forty percent, which, even with high inflation, is enough to stunt the development of local manufacturing.

The first signs that the population at large had reached breaking point came in May 1995, when parliament approved a **Value Added Tax** rate of 17 percent. With a rallying cry of **Kume Preko** ("Why not just kill me?"), tens of thousands of protestors demonstrated on the streets of Accra. Five people died in the melee, including at least two who were killed by unidentified gunmen. It was the most serious display of popular opposition to date and was seized upon by detractors – many in exile overseas – who claim Ghana's human rights record is deplorable and insist that politically inspired murders and deaths in detention are commonplace.

With elections on the horizon in 1996, the government was forced to rescind the tax. Against its defensive posturing, a group of opposition parties found room for agreement. The NPP, PCP (People's Convention Party) and NDM (New Democratic Movement) formed the Alliance for Change, providing Rawlings with a serious challenge.

If the government doesn't meet its targets for cutting public spending, the World Bank may withhold loans worth £200 million ($300 million). Yet Rawlings is unlikely to satisfy the Bank without imposing new taxes, freezing government salaries and cutting public sector jobs further, all courses of action likely to lose him the presidency at the next election. In July 1995, the internationally respected Minister of Finance, **Dr Kwesi**

Botchwey – architect of the scuppered VAT policy – resigned over personal and policy disagreements with Rawlings and his feared security advisor and right-hand man **Tsatsu Tsikata**. In particular, Botchwey was frustrated at the fact that his exchequor had bailed out the Ghana National Petroleum Corportation (headed by Tsikata) to the tune of £70million, and there were no prospects of a repayment.

Encouragingly, the military has held back and few people expect a coup these days. That alone is indicative that Ghana really has turned a corner. But even those who support the principles of the present reforms are becoming less concerned about high growth than about achieving a sustainable development that can produce benefits throughout the population. And, so far, that is proving elusive.

ACCRA AND AROUND

Flat, sprawling and for the most part aesthetically nondescript, the cityscape of **ACCRA** is still blighted by heavy concrete stacks harking back to the Soviet-inspired early years of independence. But belying first impressions, Accra is an exciting city making a rapid comeback. Renewed prosperity is evidenced by a flurry of new building ranging from the Nkrumah mausoleum to the International Conference Centre, a stylish building opposite State House. Such structures symbolize a vibrancy matched by the energy of the people, including a good number of foreigners attracted to one West African capital that can look ahead with some confidence.

With a population approaching one and a half million, Accra is one of Africa's biggest cities and hasn't been spared the urban problems of traffic, noise and overcrowding, especially now that the economy is on a steady rise. Despite some uninspiring images – including open drains and sewers that hark back to the malodorous era of decay – the city's trees make it exceptionally green. Rush hours are dynamic and the streets thronged with a racket of vehicles and people, while after dark, Accra's club scene is one of the liveliest in West Africa.

THE HISTORY OF ACCRA

Accra's **Ga founders** arrived in the region some time before 1500, setting up their capital at Ayawaso ("Great Accra") some 15km inland, and building a "Small Accra" on the coast for trade with the **Portuguese**, who put up a fort here in the sixteenth century. Trade – of slaves, gold and palm oil for guns – increased over the next hundred years with the building of the Dutch **Fort Ussher**, Danish **Christiansborg** and the British **Fort James**.

Accra originally consisted of **seven quarters** – the Ga quarters of Asere, Abola, Gbese, Sempe and Akunmadzei; Otublohu, the Akwamu quarter; and Alata, which later became the core of the British-protected area of Jamestown. Other quarters placed themselves under Dutch protection and became Usshertown. Much later, in 1840, the chief of Abola was chosen as the military leader (*Ga Mantse*) for the whole city, and treated by the British as the Ga king. Nowadays he is considered the Ga paramount chief.

Akwamu expansion from the north led to victory over the Ga in 1660 (Chief Okai Koi, defeated by treachery, put a curse on Accra that it should remain disunited against its enemies ever after) and to the destruction of Ayawaso, now just a tiny village. But the Ga regained much of their independence in 1730, when Akwamu fell to the Akim state of Akwapim, which now took over control of the **"notes"** (documents issued by African rulers giving Europeans the right to trade) for the Accra forts. These "notes" later passed to the Asante, who gained control at the beginning of the nineteenth century, but gradually lost it in a series of wars with the British. Battle was averted in 1863 when British and Asante armies were both struck by dysentery and too ill to fight, but a decisive victory in 1874 led to the British taking over and setting up the Gold Coast Colony with its capital at Accra after 1877.

Since then the city has expanded considerably, despite serious earthquakes in 1862 and 1939. After the introduction of **cocoa**, Accra became a major export port, also shipping out gold, palm oil and rubber and, from 1933, boasting West Africa's first brewery (*Club*). The municipality, set up in 1896, was expanded east to include Christiansborg and, in 1943, to bring in the ancient, walled, farming and salt-producing village of Labadi.

On February 28, 1948, major **anti-colonial riots** in the city centre followed British police shootings at a demonstration at the junction of Rowe, Castle and Christiansborg roads. Twenty-nine protestors died and 237 were wounded in an outburst that caused £2 million worth of damage.

Arrival, orientation and information

At **Kotoka International Airport** there's generally a crowd of KIA porters in blue boilersuits (inscribed "Porter", with a number), trying to handle your luggage and earn a "dash". Keep cool and nominate one, or make it clear you'll do it yourself. Customs procedures tend to be slow and the currency declaration form delays matters further. You can **change money** with the officials – legally – but their rates are even worse than those at the forex bureau in the arrivals hall, which in turn are worse than at places downtown.

There's no airport bus into town and **taxi drivers** converge on you as soon as you leave the terminal building. They can be quite heavy and stories circulate about menacing demands. It's all bark: stay cool and do nothing until someone calms down enough for you to go with them. The fare into the city centre should be clearly agreed before you go, and although it's easy to be pressurized into paying ₵5000 or more, the fare to virtually anywhere should be no more than ₵3000, even at night. The city centre is only about 8km away – a ten-minute ride. Alternatively, you can walk out of the airport zone to the main road, and pick up a **shared taxi** for around ₵300 to Kwame Nkrumah Circle, or other points around the Ring Road.

If you're **arriving by road**, entering Accra can be a confusing business, with little in the way of landmarks to indicate where you are and a generally chaotic cityscape of dust (or mud) on the outskirts. Whether arriving from the direction of Takoradi, Kumasi or Lomé, the final approach into the city is from the north. If you're arriving by public transport, it's possible you will want to hop out before reaching the terminus. Check our map for likely arrival points for your vehicle.

The **train station** is in the heart of the city, a short taxi ride from just about anywhere, and will be a convenient place to arrive once work on the lines connecting the capital to Kumasi and Takoradi is completed.

Orientation

Despite the urban sprawl, downtown Accra is neatly contained by the **Ring Road**, in relation to which points of interest in the city are usually located. Lined by shops and commercial and business premises, two main thoroughfares – Nkrumah Avenue and Kojo Thompson Road – run through the city centre south to north from the old **Jamestown** district to **Kwame Nkrumah Circle** (known to taxi drivers simply as "Circle"). Shady **Independence Avenue**, sprinkled with embassies and business headquarters, also leads from the south of town, past East Ridge and North Ridge and Ringway Estate to **Sankara Circle** in the northeast and on out to the airport. **Cantonments Road** runs from the coast near **The Castle** (the seat of government) northeast through the district of **Osu** to **Danquah Circle**, and then on through the

PUBLIC TRANSPORT IN ACCRA

The main group of **parking stations** in town is at the junction of Barnes and Kinbu roads.

Taxis in Accra can be rented outright for the journey, in which case they're **"dropping"** (₵1000–4000 in town, depending on the distance, but confirm the price before setting off; fares double at night), or you can share the collective **"line taxis"** for around ₵200–500 per hop. Line taxis roll along fixed routes, often from circle (roundabout) to circle, servicing virtually the whole city. Note that "Circle" always refers to Nkrumah Circle, never Sankara or Danquah, and a circling motion of the finger means that's where you're going. *Tro-tros* (uncomfortable vans) are slower and about thirty percent less expensive than saloon car line taxis. Tourists are generally assumed to be chartering, so make it clear if you're not.

Cantonments district to the airport. Cutting east to west through the city centre are the main arteries of Castle Road, Liberia Road and Kinbu Road.

The core of Accra stretches from the banking district of **High Street** near the waterfront to the **Makola market** – a colourful hive of activity that overflows into the surrounding streets. In between, the ample proportions of the stately colonial **Parliament** and **Supreme Court** give an idea of the importance the British placed on their Gold Coast Colony.

It's worth noting – in case you were wondering – that Accra's **port** is at the separate town of **Tema**, some 30km east of the capital.

Tourist information

The Ghana Tourist Information Centre on Kojo Thompson Rd is closed. Try the Ghana Tourist Development Company on Sanchi Rd in the Airport Residential Area (PO Box 8710; ☎021/77.20.84 or 021/77.61.09; Fax 021/77.20.93). The projects officer there may be helpful and should be able to provide you with free literature. It's also worth getting a copy of the Accra listings magazine, *Ghanascope*.

Accommodation

Accommodation in Accra is relatively cheap and varies from absolutely basic dorm space for those counting every penny to luxury hotel rooms. Problems with power cuts and water shortages are diminishing. The nearest **campsite** is at Coco Beach, about 10km east of the centre on the Tema road (₵2000).

Hostels and student rooms

Accra Polytechnic, Barnes Rd opposite *Novotel*. Basic and very inexpensive rooms during the holiday season. ①.

Teacher's Hostel, Castle Rd, near the Museum. Budget accommodation open to all if they have space, which they often don't. ①.

YMCA and **YWCA**, both located on Castle Rd near the National Museum. Central and some of the cheapest dormitory rooms in town. Good places to meet Ghanaians. ①.

Cheap hotels

There's a great deal of variation in the standards of the following places. Check carefully before settling on a room and always ask first for the best room they have.

ADABRAKA

Bellview Hotel, Tudu Crescent, off Kojo Thompson Rd, behind the Accra Polytechnic (☎021/66.77.30). Good budget hotel, with S/C, fanned rooms in a convenient location. ②.

Hotel de California, Kojo Thompson Rd at Castle Rd (PO Box 7337; ☎021/22.61.99). Long a popular haunt with travellers, but now only a good prospect for that reason. The fanned rooms (shared facilities) are dirty and the whole place needs an overhaul. ①.

ACCOMMODATION PRICE CODES

① Under ₵10,000 (under £5/$7.50) ② ₵10,000–20,000 (£5–10/$7.50–15)
③ ₵20,000–40,000 (£10–20/$15–30) ④ ₵40,000–60,000 (£20–30/$30–45)
⑤ ₵60,000–80,000 (£30–40/$45–60) ⑥ ₵80,000–100,000 (£40–50/$60–75)
⑦ Over ₵100,000 (over £50/$75)

For further details see p.51 and p.762.

Crown Prince Hotel, Kojo Thompson Rd (PO Box 400; ☎021/22.53.81). The AC rooms with shared facilities aren't expensive, but the noise here never stops. Water is often off. ①–②.

The Date Hotel, Adami St (PO Box 3407; ☎021/22.82.00). One of the best-value places, with a good bar area and open space and a great restaurant for *fufu* and groundnut soup. Well managed and highly recommended. ①.

Nkrumah Memorial Hotel, Kojo Thompson Rd. Walls are thin, but the place is kept clean and the location is great. Very good food, including *omo tuo* in the restaurant. ①.

Station View Hotel, Kinbu Rd, 25m east of Kojo Thompson Rd, opposite lorry park. Nice for the location; but rooms with fans now a little seedy. Bar and restaurant with rice and *fufu* type dishes. ①.

ASYLUM DOWN

Korkdam Hotel, 18 2nd Crescent, off Mango Tree Ave, Asylum Down (PO Box 4605; ☎021/22.67.94). Range of rooms from S/C singles with hot water and fridges to "executive suites" with the works (phones, TV, AC). ②. (Note that there's a more expensive *Korkdam* in New Achimota, several kilometres north of the centre off the Kumasi road.)

Lemon Lodge, off Mango Tree Ave, near the *Korkdam Hotel* (PO Box 76 Kanda; ☎021/22.78.57). In a quiet, leafy neighbourhood, this offers good value and is usually full. Clean rooms with fan or AC; breakfast included. ①.

New Haven Hotel, east of Nkrumah Circle and north of the Ring Road Central. Good value for S/C rooms with fan. ①.

KOKOMLEMLE

Hotel Britannia, Nsawam Rd opposite Accra North P&T. Very good value with decent S/C rooms and a robust atmosphere at the in-house bar featuring slot machines and Jack Daniels. ①.

C'est Si Bon Hotel, near *Challenge* bookshop (☎021/22.03.79). Reasonable singles and doubles, clean and airy with fan or AC and private bath. ②.

Kokomlemle Guesthouse, Oroko St near ATTC (☎021/22.45.81). Excellent value, with clean S/C rooms, friendly staff and a relaxed atmosphere in the lively bar and restaurant. Well known to visiting NGO workers and travellers. ①.

Mid-range hotels

Adeshi Hotel, Ring Rd Central, 1km east of Nkrumah Circle (PO Box 11380; ☎021/22.13.07). Rooms are small but with all the amenities. Friendly staff. Breakfast included. ④.

King David's Hotel, near Nkrumah Circle, Kokomlemle (PO Box 10323; ☎021/22.98.32). Small, very clean hotel with friendly staff and large rooms, used by transiting *Ghana Airways*' passengers. Good restaurant too. ④.

Kyn's Hotel, 21 Klanaa St, Osu Ako-Adji (☎021/77.41.12). Well looked after and good value, with breakfast included. ③.

Penta Hotel, Cantonments Rd near Danquah Circle (PO Box 7354; ☎021/77.45.29; Fax 021/77.34.18). Great location for clubbing and eating out and you can nearly always get a taxi from outside at just about any hour of the day or night, but rooms with mediocre facilities are somewhat overpriced. ④.

Ringway Hotel, Ring Rd Central, 700m east of Nkrumah Circle (☎021/22.83.06). Poor value, with unreliable service, though the rooms are quite nice. ③.

Riviera Beach Hotel, Marine Drive, Victoriaborg (PO Box 4226; ☎021/66.29.90). The name suggests something exotic, but the S/C, AC rooms are run-down. Still, the beautiful views of the coastline help make up for shortcomings in comfort and a giant swimming pool that hasn't had water for decades. Excellent terrace bar and restaurant overlooking the sea; worth a detour even if you don't sleep here. ③.

St George's Hotel, Amusudai Rd, opposite Methodist School, Adabraka (☎021/22.46.99). In a restored colonial home, this hotel has charm plus conveniences like fridges, phones, TV and AC in posh S/C rooms. Clean and comfortable, with a great location near the museum. ③.

Sunrise Hotel, 7th Ave Extension, North Ridge (PO Box 2287; ☎021/22.22.01; Fax 021/22.76.56). Five minutes from the centre and in a quiet neighbourhood. Emphasis on business travellers with fax and other services available. Stylish AC rooms with fridges and TVs. Swimming pool and tennis courts in a pleasant garden. Amex accepted. ④.

Expensive hotels

Golden Tulip, Airport Rd (PO Box 16033; ☎021/77.53.60; Fax 021/77.53.61). Run by *KLM*, this luxury hotel has central AC, lots of hot water and rooms with TV and phone. The swimming pool is a draw, but otherwise the hotel lacks atmosphere. *Tulips* nightclub sees a little action at the weekend. Happy hour in the bar Thurs 7–8pm. ⑦.

Labadi Beach Hotel, La (Labadi) Beach, 5km from centre (PO Box 1 Trade Fair; ☎021/77.25.01; Fax ☎021/77.25.20). Opened in 1991, right on the beach, this is by far Ghana's most expensive and well-appointed hotel. Amenities include a health club, gym, pool and beautiful gardens. Happy hour in the bar Wed 6–7pm. Accepts most cards. ⑦.

Marriset Plaza, Agbawe St, Ako Adjei, in Osu (PO Box 0608; ☎021/77.59.92; Fax 021/77.31.54). The former *Marriot International*, with all-new AC accommodation, though there's little or no hot water in the bathrooms and the in-house video and TV doesn't work well. ⑥.

Novotel, Barnes Rd, north of Kinbu Rd (PO Box 12720; ☎021/66.75.41; Fax 021/66.75.33). Accra's first international establishment still has an antiseptic feel. Free airport shuttle for guests. Great buffet breakfast – all you can eat for ₵6000 – non-guests welcome. Happy hour in the bar Tues 5–6pm. Major credit cards accepted. ⑦.

Shangri-La, 1500m from the airport (PO Box 9201; ☎021/77.69.93 or 77.69.94; Fax 021/77.48.73). More intimate than the *Novotel* and somewhat cheaper though not lacking in facilities like tennis courts and swimming pool. The local feel makes it deservedly popular with expats. Great pizzas at reasonable prices. *Harmattan* nightclub attracts a lively crowd of young expats and rich kids on Fri nights. Accepts all major credit cards. ⑥.

The City

Accra doesn't especially lend itself to scenic walks and sightseeing and, by day, there's not much in the way of things to see. The main diversion is simply absorbing the energy of an African urban centre. Even the coast and lagoons aren't shown off to any real advantage and, from most places in town, you're barely aware that Accra lies right on the seafront – though Jamestown is an exception. A visit to the interesting **National Museum** is in order, as is a quick trip to the **WEB Dubois Memorial Centre**, and perhaps a look at the gradually improving **zoo**, on Kanda Ave, past the Ring Rd (open daily 9.30am–5.30pm). The **crafts market** offers a vast selection from all over the region, though not necessarily at the best prices.

The National Museum of Ghana

The **National Museum of Ghana**, on Barnes Rd near the junction with Castle Rd (daily 9am–6pm; ₵600), houses one of West Africa's best ethnographic, historical and art collections, with exhibits from Ghana and across the continent. You could conceivably visit the entire museum in a morning or afternoon, but because of the variety and eclecticism of the exhibits, it's perhaps best to pop in several times to avoid cultural fatigue. The exhibits are well displayed, though poorly explained – and in some cases in need of a dusting. It's worth investing in the excellent **museum handbook**, which contains numerous black and white photos and detailed descriptions.

The museum is dedicated in large measure to still-thriving **local crafts**. There are numerous examples of clay water-coolers, bowls and lamps, calabash drums, iron clappers and wooden zithers, ornamental brass pots and implements, while complementary exhibits show the **technology** of the cottage industries. You can see how iron is forged (still common in the north), how brass weights, once used for weighing gold, are cast, and how glass beads are manufactured.

Interesting, too, are the **ceremonial objects** so common among the Akan and other peoples of the country. Gilded umbrella tops, carved royal stools, metal swords of state and intricate *kente* cloth are charged with a social and religious significance that the displays help illuminate. Artefacts from further afield in Africa (Zaire, South Africa,

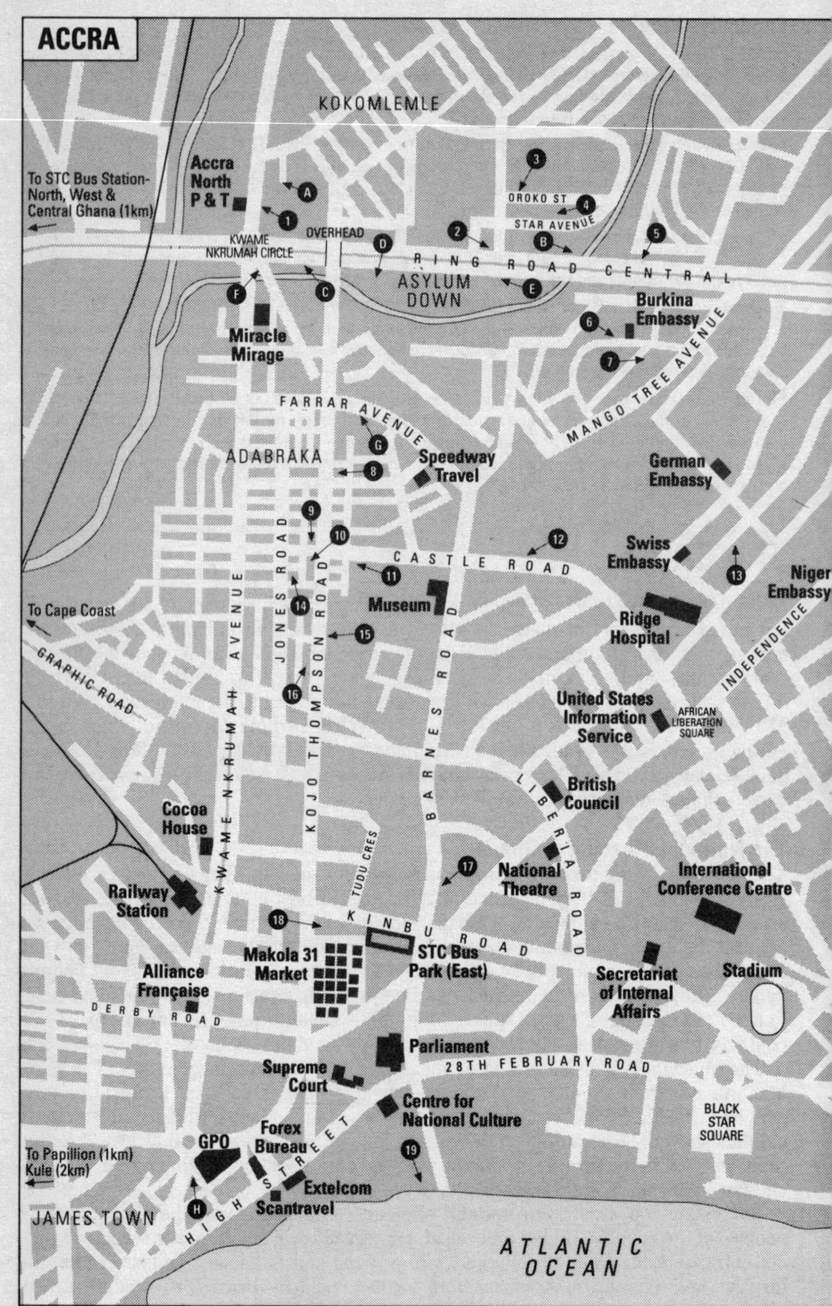

ACCRA
KOKOMLEMLE
Accra North P & T
To STC Bus Station-North, West & Central Ghana (1km)
OROKO ST
STAR AVENUE
KWAME NKRUMAH CIRCLE
OVERHEAD
RING ROAD CENTRAL
ASYLUM DOWN
Burkina Embassy
Miracle Mirage
MANGO TREE AVENUE
FARRAR AVENUE
ADABRAKA
Speedway Travel
German Embassy
CASTLE ROAD
Swiss Embassy
Niger Embassy
Museum
Ridge Hospital
To Cape Coast
GRAPHIC ROAD
KWAME NKRUMAH AVENUE
JONES ROAD
KOJO THOMPSON ROAD
BARNES ROAD
INDEPENDENCE
United States Information Service
AFRICAN LIBERATION SQUARE
LIBERIA ROAD
British Council
Cocoa House
TUDU CRES
National Theatre
International Conference Centre
Railway Station
KINBU ROAD
Makola 31 Market
STC Bus Park (East)
Alliance Française
Secretariat of Internal Affairs
Stadium
DERBY ROAD
Parliament
28TH FEBRUARY ROAD
Supreme Court
Centre for National Culture
BLACK STAR SQUARE
Forex Bureau
GPO
To Papillion (1km) Kule (2km)
HIGH STREET
Extelcom
Scantravel
JAMES TOWN
ATLANTIC OCEAN

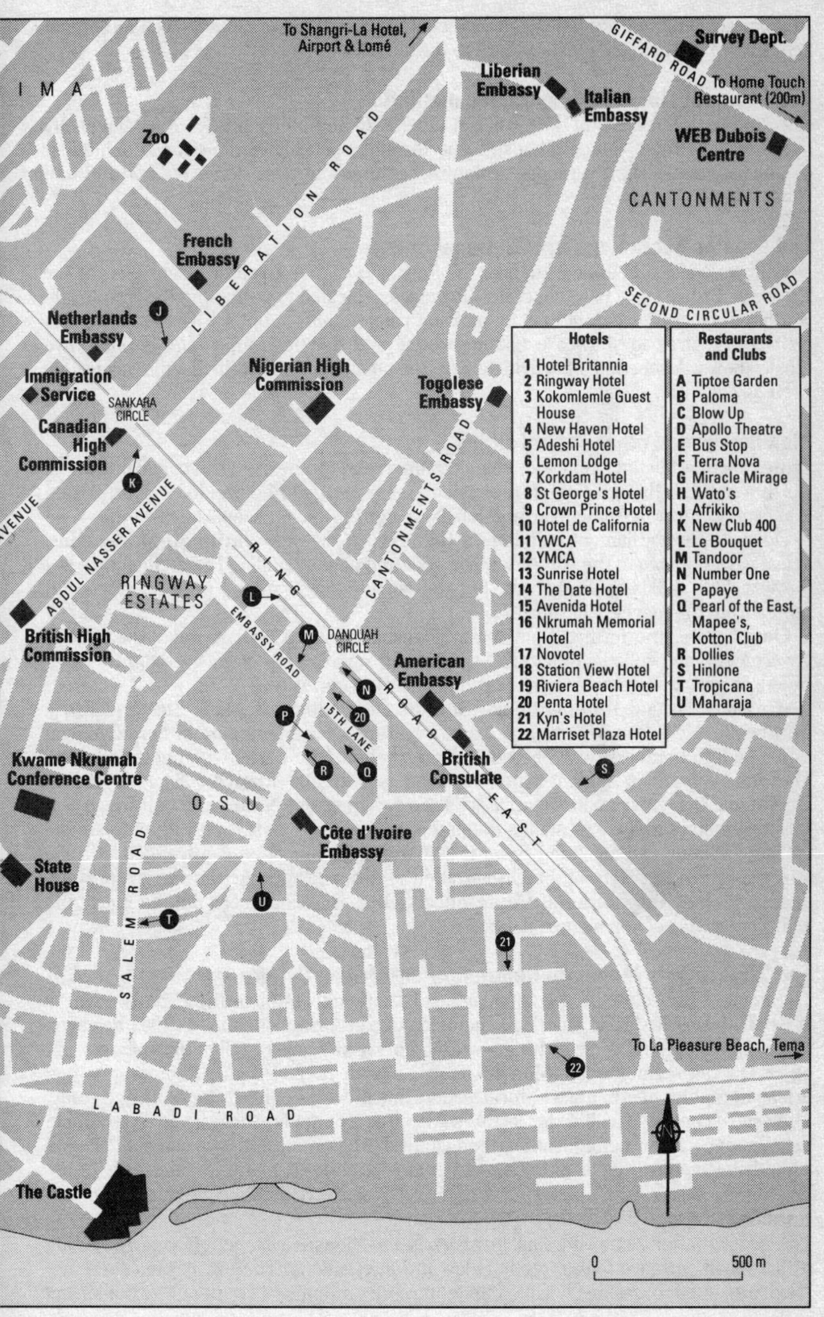
To Shangri-La Hotel, Airport & Lomé
GIFFARD ROAD
Survey Dept.
To Home Touch Restaurant (200m)
Liberian Embassy
Italian Embassy
WEB Dubois Centre
CANTONMENTS
I M A
Zoo
LIBERATION ROAD
French Embassy
SECOND CIRCULAR ROAD
Netherlands Embassy
Immigration Service
SANKARA CIRCLE
Canadian High Commission
Nigerian High Commission
Togolese Embassy
CANTONMENTS ROAD
AVENUE
ABDUL NASSER AVENUE
RINGWAY ESTATES
RING ROAD EAST
EMBASSY ROAD
DANQUAH CIRCLE
British High Commission
American Embassy
15TH LANE
British Consulate
Kwame Nkrumah Conference Centre
OSU
Côte d'Ivoire Embassy
State House
SALEM ROAD
To La Pleasure Beach, Tema
LABADI ROAD
The Castle
0
500 m
Hotels
1 Hotel Britannia
2 Ringway Hotel
3 Kokomlemle Guest House
4 New Haven Hotel
5 Adeshi Hotel
6 Lemon Lodge
7 Korkdam Hotel
8 St George's Hotel
9 Crown Prince Hotel
10 Hotel de California
11 YWCA
12 YMCA
13 Sunrise Hotel
14 The Date Hotel
15 Avenida Hotel
16 Nkrumah Memorial Hotel
17 Novotel
18 Station View Hotel
19 Riviera Beach Hotel
20 Penta Hotel
21 Kyn's Hotel
22 Marriset Plaza Hotel
Restaurants and Clubs
A Tiptoe Garden
B Paloma
C Blow Up
D Apollo Theatre
E Bus Stop
F Terra Nova
G Miracle Mirage
H Wato's
J Afrikiko
K New Club 400
L Le Bouquet
M Tandoor
N Number One
P Papaye
Q Pearl of the East, Mapee's, Kotton Club
R Dollies
S Hinlone
T Tropicana
U Maharaja

Angola) are interspersed among the national exhibits. Upstairs, dusty **archaeological relics** trace the country's history back to the late Stone Age.

The National Theatre ethnographic exhibition

The **National Theatre**, on the corner of Liberia Rd and Independence Ave, diagonally opposite the British Council, houses a permanent, specially commissioned exhibition of Ghanaian musical instruments, sculpture, carvings and other items. It's free and well worth a look.

The Greater Accra Centre for National Culture

Downtown on 28th February Rd, near the *Riviera Hotel*, the **Greater Accra Centre for National Culture** is a new concrete showpiece dedicated to promoting the arts. Inside is a large gallery for exhibitions by national painters and sculptors. The building also contains theatres to showcase national dance and theatre troupes and periodic live music shows. A schedule of activities is posted outside, or check the listings magazine, *Ghanascope*.

Monuments and other central sights

Jamestown, a bustling centre of small commerce at the heart of the colonial town, is worth a wander, though **Fort James** itself (see p.794) is to be avoided – it's a prison. You can, however, visit the nearby colonial-era **lighthouse** for scenic town views.

Opposite the Parliament building on High Street, the new **Nkrumah Mausoleum** at last pays homage to the pan-African pioneer and nation builder. The architecture is a throwback to 1960s triumphalism, but the surrounding gardens provide a peaceful refuge from the mayhem of the city.

Osu Castle, the former Danish Christiansborg (see p.794), is today the seat of government, and called simply "The Castle". All surrounding streets are tightly barricaded, so you can't get anywhere near this historical curiosity.

A wander around **Independence Square** (also known as Black Star Square) is worthwhile. Here, the **Triumphal Arch**, a Nkrumah-era monument of heroic dimensions, built to herald African liberation, looms behind The Castle – no photos allowed. The square itself is a giant parade ground, site of the Eternal Flame of African Liberation, lit by Nkrumah. Nearby are the ministries and **National Stadium**. A few hundred metres to the east stands the first president's proudest legacy, the monumental **State House** and adjoining **Kwame Nkrumah Conference Centre**, built in 1965 to serve as headquarters of the Organization of African Unity. Across the street is the impressive new **International Conference Centre**, built in record time to house the 1991 conference of non-aligned nations.

The WEB Dubois Memorial Centre for Pan-African Culture

The home – House no. 22, 1st Circular Road, Cantonments (near the airport) – where **WEB Dubois**, the black American champion of pan-Africanism, died in 1963 has been turned into a cultural centre with a research library and gallery full of manuscripts and other Dubois memorabilia (Mon–Fri 8am–12.30pm & 1.30–5pm). Photographs and brief biographies of other black world leaders line the walls of his living room and study. The centre contains facilities for lectures – keep an eye out for these if you're around in the summer – and other educational and cultural programmes. It's not ostentatious, but a highly informative and inspiring monument to pan-Africanism and its vanguard.

Beaches

The best area for sea swimming in Accra is **La Pleasure Beach** (formerly Labadi, with a small entrance fee), directly below the International Trade Fair site. There are lifeguards at La, occasionally called upon to rescue swimmers swept out by the strong undertow. This is *the* place to be on weekends when Accra's young people turn out for beach parties – and just to see and be seen. Taxis and *tro-tros* run here from Nkrumah Circle. You can also take a dip below the *Riviera Beach Hotel*, but take nothing of value (and be seen to have nothing of value). For swimming pools, see "Listings".

Markets and crafts shops

Vast **Makola market** is where you feel the city centre's retail pulse most strongly. These days it contains just about everything in the food and domestic line, including cheap glass beads. The **Kaneshi market** by the motor park on Weija Rd is also huge and an excellent place for rummaging.

Spreading out around the Centre for National Culture on 28th February Rd is the **crafts market**, a huge depot for works from throughout West Africa. On the whole, buying here isn't as satisfying or cheap as searching out such goods in the regions where they're manufactured, but if you've got no time or just like one-stop shopping, this is the place. You'll find everything from **Asante sandals** and **kente cloth** to **leatherwork** from the north, woven cotton fabric and glass beads, any of which can easily be bought more cheaply elsewhere. The wood crafts – **masks**, **carvings** and **boxes** – and the **brasswork** are somewhat harder to find. Expect heavy pressure to buy; bargaining tends to be a battle of wits here and not a great deal of fun. If you buy anything, even if it doesn't look like an antique, you must obtain an export permit, proving it has no historical value (see p.771).

The Ark crafts shop, just past the *Golden Tulip Hotel* on the way to the airport (Mon–Fri 8.30am–4pm, Sat 8.30am–1pm), is less overwhelming if you're not up to speed with your bargaining skills. *The Loom* gallery, at the top end of Kwame Nkrumah Ave, also has a good selection of crafts and jewellery.

Finally, some fifteen minutes' drive east of central Accra, on the coast road to Tema, you'll find the *Artists' Alliance*, an art gallery/shop selling artefacts, modern art, cloth, pottery and jewellery. All the goods are high quality, but most prices differ little from what you'd expect to pay for Africana in a shop at home. The most compelling items are the samples of old *kente* cloth (see p.814), which surpass anything else you're likely to come across. This is cloth with soul, and very dear – ₵200,000–300,000 a piece – and you can't help wondering how it came to be here.

Eating

In addition to the places listed below, cheap **street eats** are available in the motor parks, markets and in certain districts. Adabraka, for example, has many cheap eateries and, if you're staying in one of the neighbourhood's inexpensive hotels, you'll find numerous *kenkey* and fish vendors in back streets running between *The Date* and the *Hotel de California*.

Inexpensive

In most of the following establishments you can eat heartily for ₵2000–3000 – standard international fast food in most of them, with salads and some Ghanaian dishes also featuring.

Bus Stop, Ring Road Central, near the *Agricultural Development Bank* (☎021/22.30.90). Pavement tables and a varied menu of snacks (sandwiches, kebabs), European specialities, ice cream and cheap beer.

Dollies, Danquah Circle near the *Penta Hotel*, Osu. Basic fast-food place (one of a chain) featuring tasty burgers and chips.

Ghana National Museum Café (aka Edvy Restaurant), at the museum gate, Barnes Rd, West Ridge. Excellent Ghanaian food served at lunchtime only; liable to unpredictable closure.

Kule, Eduardo Mondlana Rd, Larte Biokorshi, west of the Korle lagoon (on the west side of Korle-Bu Hospital). Ghanaian-style fast-food joint, with "palava" huts outside. Inexpensive, and owes nothing to tourist or expat expectations.

Papaye, Cantonments Rd, Osu. *Dollies*-style but better – good chicken, burgers or fish and chips.

Papillon, Guggisberg Ave, Mamprobi, on the south side of Korle-Bu Hospital (over the Korle Lagoon bridge, 1km west of Jamestown). Ghanaian home cooking and live music at weekends.

Providence, Cantonments Rd, just off Danquah Circle. Very good, reasonably priced Ghanaian food (lunch only, open to 5pm).

Terra Nova, Nkrumah Circle (☎021/22.22.83). Outdoor drinking and cheap chop (₵1000) under thatched cover.

Western Fried Chicken, near American embassy annex. Very good southern fried chicken with coleslaw and chips. A little pricey, but worth it.

Moderate and expensive

In a moderately priced league (from about ₵4000–10,000 for a full meal), the options are more varied, with a good variety of Asian restaurants and several high-quality Middle Eastern and European-style establishments, as well as a number of very classy African places. Prices at the most expensive eating houses, which include hotel restaurants not mentioned here, run to about ₵20,000 a head.

AFRICAN

Afrikiko, Liberation Rd, near Sankara Circle. A very popular expat hangout, known for cheap beer and moderately priced African dishes in a garden bar setting. Good chicken and salads. There's often a dance at weekends, but it's worth knowing that the place has some notoriety as a pick-up joint.

Afro-Caribbean Centre, near Silvercup junction, Kokomlemle. Very trendy place owned by a Rasta couple from London. Attracts an interesting crowd of upmarket musicians and others come for the vegetarian specialities.

Country Kitchen, off Ring Rd East in Ringway Estate. Very good African cooking and soul food dishes.

Fikodar, near Obetsebi-Lamptey Circle, Kaneshi. Expensive, but a good reputation for well-prepared national specialities including "grasscutter marengo" (very fancy bush rat). Some European dishes as well.

Kikiriki, Basel St, Osu. It's worth coming a little out of your way for excellent spicy chicken (the house speciality), beers and occasional live music.

Lalibela, off Cantonments Rd, Osu, behind the *Goil* filling station. Excellent and not overpriced Ethiopian food. *Wat* stew with *njera* bread is the standard fare. Recommended.

ASIAN FOOD

Chez Lien, Senchi St, Airport Residential Area. Vietnamese restaurant with magnificent food.

Dynasty, Cantonments Rd near Danquah Circle. A newer Chinese restaurant providing stiff competition for the older venues. Clean surroundings and high-quality meals. Atmosphere tends to become smoke-filled.

Hinlone, in Labone, off Ring Road East, first left and left again 500m south of the American embassy. Wonderful fresh selections of premium quality vegetables, meat and seafood.

Kung Fu, Danquah Circle. Very good and not too expensive, with quick service. Open every day.

Maharaja, Cantonments Rd, below Danquah Circle. Accra's best Indian restaurant, excellent in terms of atmosphere and quality cooking. The "Indian prince" doorman rather sets the tone.

Pearl of the East, 15th lane, off Cantonments Rd, behind *Penta Hotel*, south of Danquah Circle (same courtyard as *Mapees* and the *Kotton Club*; ☎021/77.63.37). Perhaps the best Chinese restaurant in Accra, with authentic dishes and great vegetables (daily except Sun, noon–3pm & 7–11pm).

Regal, off Cantonments Rd, Osu. Excellent Chinese restaurant. Moderate prices.

Royal Orchid, off Cantonments Rd, Osu. Oriental cuisine, mostly Thai-based. Sometimes has live music on Fri.

Sony's, 20 Crescent Link, Asylum Down. Moderate and friendly Indian restaurant. Excellent eating in an old colonial house.

Tandoor, Embassy Rd, just off Danquah Circle. Indian tandoori cooking. There's a no-smoking section – something of a novelty in Accra.

LEBANESE

Le Bouquet, Ring Rd East, north of Danquah Circle (☎021/77.24.17). A former Chinese restaurant, with a varied menu of European dishes and Lebanese meze.

New Club 400, Ring Rd East, just south of Sankara Circle. Art gallery and restaurant with wide range of Lebanese food.

Tropicana, Salem Rd, Kuku Hill, Osu (☎021/77.66.31). Lunch and dinner service featuring Middle Eastern and European specialities.

EUROPEAN

Home Touch, Giffard Rd, near the Elwak stadium, just south of the airport. Stylish wining and dining, with European and Ghanaian dishes on the menu.

Number One, Danquah Circle. Busy, noisy spot (loud music at night), with a wide choice of pizza, salads, ice cream, all fairly good. Cheap draught beer. Slow service. Sit outside on the terrace.

Paloma, Ring Rd Central, east of Kwame Nkrumah Circle. Europeanized Ghanaian food – excellent kebabs, pizza, salads and ices. Live music at weekends.

La Pergola, on Airport Rd, just after the "37" roundabout, on the left shortly before the *Golden Tulip Hotel*. French-style European and Ghanaian food in a pleasant, partly open-air atmosphere. Around ₵5000 a head.

Nightlife

Nightlife in Accra is an ever-evolving scene. Accra's clubs and dives change hands almost as often as shifts. Many of the following venues serve food and may even present themselves as restaurants some of the time, just as certain restaurants sometimes offer live music – anything to get the punters in. From Monday to Wednesday the action – if it happens at all – starts late, though there are one or two "ladies nights", usually Wednesday, when women get free admission. Thursday, Friday, Saturday and Sunday are the big nights out. Thursday night is La beach party night. At weekends you can party most of the daytime, too, in some venues. Covers are very moderate by international standards – ₵4000 is about the most you'll pay.

African Heroes Hotel, Nima, Accra Newtown, just north of Ring Road Central. Similar to *Tip Toe* and the *Apollo*, but rougher; the African Brothers stronghold with some hardcore regulars and underworld vibes. "Now you're on the borderline of where angels fear to tread". Remember they warned you.

Apollo Theatre, Ring Road Central east of Nkrumah Circle. Similar set-up to *Tip Toe* and also open-air, so comfortable. Doesn't close till the last punters have left. A good place to meet down-to-earth local people.

Aquarius, off Cantonments Rd, south of Danquah Circle. Supposedly a "German pub" (though feels anything but), with pool tables. Expensive, but a popular starting point for a night out.

Balm Tavern, Orgle Rd near Cocoa Clinic, Kaneshi. Old residence converted to a tavern with indoor and outdoor eating. A gathering place for local society come to enjoy the roast chicken. Also a great place for dancing at weekends, with good bands.

Blow-up, Nkrumah Circle. No longer *the* place to go, but still a place to go, early, before moving on somewhere hotter.

Cave du Roi. Firmly established disco palace for couples.

Chester's Place, Gbatsuna St, Nyaniba Estates, Osu (☎021/77.75.03). Well known and well liked by expats: wide selection of chilled cocktails and light snacks plus live jazz on Wednesdays. Half-price drinks at happy hour, weekdays 5.30–7.30pm, but it gets crowded much later.

Kilimanjaro, Nkrumah Ave, Nkrumah Circle (☎021/22.68.66). A popular European restaurant (open 8pm–3am daily) and also one of the town's hotter clubs, if a bit of a pick-up joint. The action gets going after 11pm.

Kotton Club, 15th lane, off Cantonments Rd, behind *Penta Hotel*, south of Danquah Circle (same courtyard as *Pearl of the East* and *Mapees*). Busy disco. "Ladies night" is Sun (very quiet).

Macumba, Ring Rd East, near Danquah Circle. Elaborate new disco establishment with good music.

Mapees, 15th lane, off Cantonments Rd, behind *Penta Hotel*, south of Danquah Circle (same courtyard as *Pearl of the East* and the *Kotton Club*). Not a club, but a very popular pub where you'll bump into expats – if you want to. Music, but no dancing and cover only at weekends.

Matador. Central venue with a darkened interior – what's known as a "lights off" club, in other words, one not to be seen at, with whoever you take or meet there. Fri music nights are good.

Miracle Mirage, opposite the Hotel President, Farrar Ave, Adabraka. Lively night club with lots going on. No cover for women on Wed, no cover at all on Fri.

Red Onion, North Kaneshi. One of the best discos in Accra, popular with a mostly Ghanaian crowd. African and funk sounds. Reasonably priced drinks.

Tip Toe Garden, north of Nkrumah Circle. Open-air, with stage and large dance floor. Changes hands often and is frequently at the mercy of Accra trend-setters. A good, well-mixed crowd of locals and foreigners enjoys plenty of live musical variety, including highlife and "copyright bands" (playing cover versions).

Wato's, opposite the GPO in Jamestown. A serious watering hole with good ABC bubra, chicken curry with salad and a fourth-floor view of downtown.

Listings

Air freight *DHL*, C913/3 North Ridge Crescent, near *KLM* (☎021/22.16.47), will send precious items home by air courier service.

Airline offices include: *Aeroflot*, 57 Kojo Thompson Rd (PO Box 9449; ☎021/77.74.14); *Air Afrique*, Cocoa House, Kwame Nkrumah Ave (PO Box 539; ☎021/22.83.28); *Balkan Bulgarian Airlines*, 37 Kwame Nkrumah Ave (☎021/22.20.97); *British Airways*, Kojo Thompson Rd, corner of North Liberia Rd (PO Box 2087; ☎021/66.76.45; Fax 021/66.78.66); *Egyptair*, Ring Road, just south of Danquah Circle (☎021/66.79.76); *Ethiopian Airlines*, Cocoa House, Nkrumah Ave (PO Box 3600; ☎021/66.48.56); *Ghana Airways*, Ghana House, near GPO (PO Box 1636; ☎021/77.61.71); *KLM*, Ring Road Central, North Ridge (PO Box 2223; ☎021/22.40.20; Fax 021/77.57.29); *Lufthansa*, near the German embassy, North Ridge (☎021/22.10.86); *Nigeria Airways*, Danawi Building, Kojo Thompson Rd (PO Box 9068; ☎021/22.37.49 or 22.47.35); and *Swissair*, 47 Independence Ave (PO Box 1808; ☎021/22.81.65; Fax 021/66.73.41).

American Express Represented by *Scantravel*, High St (PO Box 4960; ☎021/66.31.34 or 66.42.04).

Banks Major commercial banks are on High Street near the intersection of Bank Lane and include: *Barclays Bank* (PO Box 2949; ☎021/66.49.01; Fax 021/66.74.20); *Ghana Commercial Bank* (PO Box 134; ☎021/66.49.14; Fax 021/66.21.58); and *Standard Chartered Bank* (PO Box 768; ☎021/66.45.99; Fax 021/66.77.51). Remember the private forex bureaux offer better rates.

Books Try the southeast corner of Kinbu and Kojo Thompson roads (second-hand), or the *UTC* bookstore on Nkrumah Ave.

Car rental *Avis* through *Speedway Travel and Tours*, 5 Tackie Tawia St, Adabraka (PO Box 214; ☎021/22.87.99); *Hertz* through *Allways Travel Agency* (PO Box 1638; ☎021/22.45.90), in *Kingsway* on Nkrumah Ave. Also try *Vanef* in Sobukwe/Farrar Ave, Adabraka. The big hotels can usually help, too. Note that most companies only rent out cars with drivers.

Cinemas The best place to see newish European and American films, plus Ghanaian hits, is the Ghana Film Institute north of Sankara Circle. Other theatres include the AC *Film Corporation Theatre*, off Independence Ave (near the French embassy); *Orion Cinema* on Liberation Circle; the *Globe* on Adjaben Road; and the *Rex*, behind Parliament House.

Cultural centres Among the foreign cultural centres is the *British Council*, Liberia Rd, just off Independence Ave (Mon–Wed 9am–5pm, Thurs & Fri 9am–2.30pm, Sat 9am–noon; ☎021/66.34.14; Fax 021/66.39.79), which has an excellent library and British papers and regularly hosts musical and theatrical events; the *Alliance Française*, on Derby Ave, down in the town centre, just off Kwame Nkrumah Rd, does the same in French. The *USIS* (American cultural centre) on Independence Ave and the German *Goethe-Institut* on Ring Rd also run active programmes.

EMBASSIES AND OTHER DIPLOMATIC MISSIONS

Working days are Monday to Friday, unless otherwise stated.

Australian affairs are handled by the Canadian High Commission.

Benin, 19 Volta St, corner of 2nd Close, Airport Residential Area (8am–3pm; PO Box 7871; ☎021/77.48.60; 15 day stay visas, valid 3 months, issued overnight or in two days).

Burkina Faso, 772/3 Asylum Down, off Mango Tree Ave (7.30am–2pm; PO Box 651; ☎021/22.19.88).

Canada, 46 Independence Avenue (8am–12.30pm and 1.30–4pm; PO Box 1639; ☎021/22.85.55).

Côte d'Ivoire, No. 9 18th Lane, Osu (7.30am–2.30pm; PO Box 3445; ☎021/77.46.11).

Denmark, 67 North Ridge, near the World Bank offices (☎021/22.69.72).

Egypt, 27 Noi Fetreke St, near Nyaho Clinic, Airport Residential Area (9.30am–2pm, Mon–Thurs; PO Box 2508; ☎021/77.68.54; Fax 021/77.67.01).

Ethiopia, 6 Adiembra Rd, East Cantonments (PO Box 1646; ☎021/77.59.28).

Finland, PO Box 262 (☎021/77.45.13).

France, 12th Road, off Liberation Ave (10am–1pm, except Tues 8.30am–12.30pm; PO Box 187; ☎021/22.85.71; visa service for most unrepresented Francophone countries).

Germany, Valdemosa Lodge, 7th Ave Extension, North Ridge (7.30am–2pm; PO Box 1757; ☎021/22.13.11).

Guinea, 11 Osu Badu Street, Dzorwulu, off Kwame Nkrumah Motorway (8am–3pm; PO Box 5497; ☎021/77.79.21).

Italy, Jawaharlal Nehru Rd, Cantonments (PO Box 140; ☎021/77.56.21).

Japan, 8 Tito Ave, off Switchback Rd (8.30am–2.30pm; PO Box 1637; ☎021/77.56.15).

Liberia, Switchback Close, Cantonments (8.30am–noon; PO Box 895; ☎021/77.56.41).

Mali, 14 Agostino Neto Rd, Airport Residential Area (7.30am–2pm; PO Box 1121; ☎021/77.51.60; Fax 021/77.43.39).

Netherlands, 89 Liberation Rd, Sankara Circle (8am–2pm; PO Box 3248; ☎021/22.30.92; Fax 021/77.36.55).

New Zealand affairs are handled by the British High Commission.

Niger, E 104/3 Independence Ave (☎021/22.49.62).

Nigeria, Tito Ave (8am–3pm; PO Box 1548; ☎021/77.61.58; visas delivered Tues only and quite often hard to obtain here if you're travelling abroad).

Spain, Lamptey Ave Extension, Airport Residential Area (8am–2pm; PO Box 1218; ☎021/77.40.04; Fax 021/77.62.17).

Switzerland, 9 Water Rd, North Ridge (7.30am–1.30pm; PO Box 359; ☎021/22.81.25).

Togo, Togo House, near Cantonments Circle (8.30am–2pm and 3–4.30pm; PO Box 4308; ☎021/77.79.50).

United Kingdom High Commission at Osu Link, off Abdul Nasser Ave (7.45am–3.45pm; PO Box 296; ☎021/22.16.65; Fax 021/66.46.52); Consulate on Ring Rd East.

USA, Ring Road East (7.30am–12.30pm and 1.30–4.30pm; PO Box 194; ☎021/77.53.47; Fax 021/77.60.08).

Foreign exchange bureaux Numerous and widespread.

Horse riding Bookable through the *Shangri-La Hotel*, at about ₵4000 per hour (☎021/77.21.78, ext. 269; no riding Sat pm or Wed).

Maps The *KLM* office sells an excellent city map, though it's easier to pick it up at a *Shell* station. You can also get this map at the Survey Offices on Giffard Rd near the airport, which has national and regional road maps on sale, too.

Newspapers Overseas newspapers, mostly British, can be bought at the *Novotel*, the *Labadi Beach Hotel* and the *Penta Hotel*.

Phones Main hotels are the best bet, or use the Extelcom, on the seaward side of High Street or at the North Accra PO. Shop around for phone cards as they vary in price.

Photos If you want decent quality passport photos, head to a studio (there's a 24-hour one on the corner of Kojo Thompson and South Liberia roads and another at Danquah Circle). Otherwise, you can get fuzzy wooden-box photos done more cheaply in five minutes on Kinbu Rd, across from the lorry park.

Poste restante At the GPO and open Mon–Fri 8am–4.30pm. No charge.

Shipping agents If you want to try getting a berth on a ship, *Umarco Ghana Ltd*, PO Box 215, Harbour Area, Tema (☎0221/4031 or 4035), are the port agents for *Grimaldi Lines*.

Supermarkets Many have sprung up to the south and west of Danquah Circle near the *Penta Hotel*. *Kwatsons*, for example, is expat heaven, with fresh cheese, meat and French bread. Others

MOVING ON FROM ACCRA

Buses

STC **buses** for the west and north depart from the *STC* station, on the Ring Rd north of Kaneshie Roundabout (Lamptey Circle). Kumasi-bound *STC* buses (air-conditioned and well driven) leave roughly hourly, from dawn until 4–5pm, taking 4hr. Air-conditioned *STC* buses also run direct to Abidjan, but no longer direct to Ouagadougou. For Ouaga, you need to change in Kumasi, and will have to spend the night there. *STC* runs a weekly direct service to Wa, and to Hamale in the far northwest on the Burkinabe border (departs Wed at 4pm). *STC* buses for the east go from the transport park along Kinbu Rd, between Tudu Crescent and Barnes Rd.

Ordinary bus lines to all destinations follow roughly the same division, with north- and westbound buses operating out of a transport park just to the west of Nkrumah Circle and eastbound buses departing from Kinbu Rd.

Tro-tros

Tro-tros pretty much follow the bus pattern – with less organization. Greater Accra and the coast are their main areas of operation. For the northern and eastern suburbs, get a seat at the transport park along Kinbu Rd, between Tudu Crescent and Barnes Rd. For the western suburbs go to Nkrumah Circle, and for the western coast, at least as far as Takoradi (though you really have to want to save money to go so far by *tro-tro*), go to Kaneshie.

Trains

Passenger **train** services to Kumasi and Takoradi are suspended pending the completion of line repairs.

Planes

There are currently no *Ghana Airways* domestic **flights**. The Ghana Air Force operates, in theory, regular flights to Kumasi and Tamale and occasional flights to Sunyani. Make bookings with *M&J Travels and Tours* (☎021/77.34.98 or 70.60.81). Departures for Kumasi (₵30,000; 40min) should be at 5pm on Tues, Thurs, Fri and Sun, while departures for Tamale (₵40,000; 1hr 15min) are scheduled for 8am on Mon, Wed and Fri.

Travel agents

For general agents, check out the car rental recommendations in the "Listings" above. Very helpful for a range of organized tours in the country is *Euroo Tours*, McCarthy Hill, PO Box 6937, Accra North (☎021/66.47.33; Fax 021/22.45.07); the city office is at *Hotel de California*. Also recommended are *Starline Travel & Tours* (☎021/22.96.46; Fax 021/22.29.17). Another agent worth checking out is *Silcon Travel & Tours*, Coopland House, 231 Kojo Thompson Rd, near the corner of Castle Rd (PO Box 11489; ☎021/22.85.20; Fax 021/66.26.80). For cheap flights to Europe, *Aeroflot* is likely to be most promising. You might also try the *Balkan Bulgarian* agents, *Secaps Holiday Travels Ltd*, Vanderpuye-Orgle Building, 46 Sobukwe Rd (Farrar Ave), or *Egyptair* if you can put up with a long flight.

nearby include *Quick Pick* and *Afridom. Kingsway* on Nkrumah Ave often has wholemeal bread. *UTC*, also on Nkrumah Ave, is an extensive store, with just about everything, including inexpensive books. The Lebanese supermarkets along Cantonments Rd in Osu have a big range of imported goods.

Swimming pools The best pool is the one at the *Shangri-La* which non-guests can use for a small fee. The swimming pool at the *Labadi Beach Hotel* is extremely expensive. Canadian nationals can use the bar and pool at their High Commission.

Visa extensions are arranged at the Immigration Office on Independence Ave near Sankara Circle (Mon–Fri 8am–1pm). They expect two photos, a typed letter explaining why you need the extension (typists can be found in front of the GPO), and a fee of ₵500. They may retain your passport for up to two weeks; change money first.

North and east of Accra: short excursions

Getting out of the city for a while, especially at the hottest and most humid times of the year, from January to June, can be a relief. To the north, Aburi, a former hill station whose large gardens are still well maintained, offers the best escape from the heat. The beaches to the east, and the inland Shai Hills game reserve, are less often visited than the coast west of Accra.

Legon, Aburi and Shai Hills

LEGON, 14km north of Accra, is the headquarters of the **University of Ghana**, described by the tourist board as "a showpiece of Japanese architecture" – judge for yourself! There's a good bookshop but less opportunity to meet students than you might wish.

You can visit the university's botanical garden in the grounds, but there are older, more interesting and extensive gardens at **ABURI**, on Akwapim Ridge, 23km further north, with potentially magnificent views north over the forest and south to the city when the air is clear. Aburi, several hundred metres above the plain, was a colonial hill station and site of a sanatorium (now a hotel), and the gardens still bear the well-tended hallmarks of landscaped colonial taste, with hundreds of tree specimens from all over the tropical and sub-tropical regions. There's a pleasant restaurant in the gardens as well as a snack bar. The **hotel**'s S/C bungalows (☎081/3055 ext. 22; ②) are frequently full, but an excellent alternative is the *Olyande Guesthouse*, which has very nice rooms, with tea and toast for breakfast included in the price, and a pleasant family atmosphere (①). Popular too is the little English-run place in Aburi village called *May & Lodge* with fine views from its S/C rooms (②).

Tro-tros from the Tudu Crescent/Barnes Rd station run frequently to Legon, taking half an hour or so, and **buses** from the same area take about an hour to Aburi (the last one back to Accra leaves at about 6.30pm, not at 6pm as taxi drivers may tell you). If you're driving to Aburi, you continue past the airport to Tetteh Quarshie Circle, then take the Akosombo road until it forks right; you take the left-hand fork and start climbing.

Some 60km to the northwest of Accra are the **Shai Hills**, which feature bizarre volcanic formations and a small **game reserve**. You can **stay** at an old office block/camp near the rangers' office here and guards are available to take you around the reserve (horseriding may still be available). Troops of baboons and parrots are the most likely sights, though kob antelope and ground hornbills can also be seen. There are some extensive bat-filled caves that can also be visited, which were formerly used as sites of worship by the Shai people, until they were moved out by the British in colonial times when the reserve was set up. They return annually, to perform ceremonies.

THE FORTS

Soon after the Portuguese found the maritime routes to the Gulf of Guinea in the fifteenth century, they began setting up trading posts. Rumours of the vast wealth of the region filtered back to Europe and it wasn't long before other nations established themselves on the coast, building sturdy fortresses to protect their interests in the trade of gold, ivory and, later, slaves. By the end of the eighteenth century, thirty-seven such forts dotted the coastline, eight of which have since been completely destroyed. After independence several forts started taking in travellers – it's now theoretically possible to sleep at the rest houses (marked "RH" below) in at least four of them.

Recent restoration work – including the whitewashing of slave cells – has enraged African-American visitors, who argue they have a right to a say in how these relics of their history are to be preserved. They complain that the Ghanaian Ministry of Tourism is trampling on their history for profits, sanitizing the crumbling slave forts at the behest of grant-making bodies like the "white" Smithsonian Institution and USAID. Limited catering facilities at one or two forts have had to close after vigorous protests.

Along the coast from east to west, the **major forts** include:

• **Prampram** Fort Vernon was built in 1756 by the French and taken by the British in 1806.

• **Accra** Christiansborg was built by the Danish in 1659. Earlier a Swedish fortress, which at one time had probably belonged to the Portuguese, stood on the same spot. Ussher Fort was built by the Dutch in 1642. Ten years later it was taken by the French and named "Fort Crevecoeur", then passed through the hands of the Dutch and finally the British who rebuilt it in 1868. James Fort was built by the Portuguese in the mid-sixteenth century, taken by the English, and rebuilt in 1673.

• **Senya Beraku (RH)** The last fort built by the Dutch, Fort Good Hope was erected in 1702 and extended in 1715.

• **Apam (RH)** Fort Leydsaemheyt was built in 1698 by the Dutch. Occupied by the British (who named it Fort Patience) in 1782 and retaken by the Dutch three years later, it was abandoned around 1800.

East of Accra

Looking east of Accra towards Togo, the quiet beach at **PRAMPRAM** (40km from Accra), distinguished by the French **Fort Vernon**, is reputed to be Ghana's best. Beyond Prampram, watersports resorts at **ADA** (120km from Accra), at the mouth of the Volta River, and **KETA**, out on the Volta delta (175km from Accra), are popular with Ghanaians. Both locations provide first-class bird-watching: you can rent a motorboat for around ₵20,000 an hour. **Accommodation** at Ada includes the wood and thatch *Paradise Cottage Camp* (②) and a soulless German-run watersports hotel (④–⑤).

THE COAST WEST OF ACCRA

The scenic coastline stretching from Accra to the Côte d'Ivoire border is one of the most obvious tourist targets in West Africa. The big attractions are the densest concentration of European **forts and castles** anywhere on the continent – twenty-nine of them, some over five hundred years old – and innumerable, unspoiled Fante **fishing villages** tucked between links of sandy, coconut-backed beaches. It's an irresistible combination, and not one you'll be alone in discovering. Tourism has increased dramatically since the late 1980s, and you'll have to come on a weekday or out of season to have much hope of finding your own isolated paradise. Nevertheless, few places are ever more than quietly humming with tourist business.

• **Anomabu** A Dutch lodge was founded here in the seventeenth century and taken by the British in 1665. Fort Charles was built on its site in 1674, expanded in the 1730s and renamed Fort William.

• **Mouri (Moree)** Fort Nassau was built by the Dutch in 1598. It went back and forth between the British and Dutch until it was finally abandoned in 1815. It is now in ruins.

• **Cape Coast** The original castle was founded by the Swedish then taken by the Danes and passed to the hands of the Dutch before finally being taken by the English in 1662. After a French bombardment in 1757, it was entirely reconstructed in 1760 when it lost its original design.

• **Elmina** Saint George's Castle, the oldest European monument in sub-Saharan Africa, was built by the Portuguese in 1482 with dressed stones brought from Europe. The original castle was expanded by the Dutch in 1637. Fort São Iago (**RH**), which faces it, dates from the seventeenth century and was taken by the Dutch in 1683.

• **Komenda** Fort Vredenburg was built by the Dutch in 1688, taken by the English in 1782 and abandoned three years later. Fort English, in the same town, was founded by the English in 1663. Both forts are now in ruins.

• **Shama** Fort Sebastian was founded by the Portuguese around 1560 and occupied by the Dutch in 1640.

• **Sekondi** Fort Orange was built by the Dutch in 1640; it became British after 1872.

• **Dixcove (RH)** Fort Metal Cross was built by the English in 1691, and occupied by the Dutch from 1868 to 1872.

• **Princestown (RH)** Grossfriedrichsburg was built in 1683 by the German Brandenburgers and taken by the Dutch and later British. In ruins at independence, the fort has since been restored.

• **Axim** Fort Santa Antonia (Fort St Anthony), built in the fifteenth century, was the second Portuguese fort on the coast. Taken by the Dutch in 1642 it was rebuilt on several occasions.

• **Beyin (RH)** Fort Apollonia was built by the English Committee of Merchants in 1756.

From Accra to Cape Coast

Leaving Accra, the highway at first stays well inland, running through scrubby bush and farming country, hot and unyielding. Just 16km west of Accra is the first break, at **KOKROBITE**, a beach resort with a dance and music school (*Academy of African Music and Arts Ltd*, PO Box 2923, Accra; 027/55.40) which doubles as a hotel and bar – look out for the "AAMAL" sign on the main road. The Ga master drummer Mustapha Tettey Addy, an internationally renowned percussionist with several CDs on general release, is the leader of the group and joint owner of the establishment. There are wonderfully dynamic drumming and dance displays on weekend afternoons between 2pm and 6pm, and the school offers courses in African dance and drumming. The **hotel**, though quite swanky in a Ghanaian way, isn't too expensive (②). They also allow **camping** and have an excellent **restaurant** – a foretaste of the grilled seafood that abounds further along the coast. The place has become a popular weekend retreat – despite the difficulty of getting here – partly because the beach – and for an hour's walk west and east – is not the public toilet that many other beaches only too obviously are. Take a *tro-tro* from the Kaneshi motor park in Accra and drop at the "AAMAL" sign; from there, you may find continuing transport down the minor road to Kokrobite, or else you'll have to walk the remaining 7km.

The first fort along this coast is **Fort Good Hope** at **SENYA BERAKU**. To get here from Accra, take a bush taxi to Awutu junction (not Senya junction, from where you won't easily get onward transport). From there, you can get another taxi down to the coastal village, 8km away. The village is dull, but the setting is scenic, and the trip interesting mainly for the fishing activities of the Fante inhabitants (remember, the Fante don't fish on Tuesdays). You get sweeping panoramic views from the fort which hangs over the sea, and you can **stay** the night – bucket showers included (①). Senya Beraku is the site of a number of **festivals** throughout the year (see p.767).

WINNEBA, the main town in these parts, perched on raised ground between the Muni and Oyibi lagoons, is reached from Swedru junction on the main coast highway. Although it is beginning to acquire a reputation for its **pottery**, Winneba is most famous in Ghana as the site of the *Aboakyer* or **"deer-hunting festival"** which takes place at the end of April or early May (see p.767). At other times of year, there's little to do in the town itself apart from watching canoes at work and fish being smoked, and enjoying the noise and bustle of dusk. You can **stay** right on the beach on the far west side of the town, at the *Sir Charles Tourist Centre*, which offers decent bungalows with no fans (②), and good food. There's a saltwater pool for swimmers who don't want to struggle with the dangerous sea, and their beach is very clean. An alternative is the modest *Winneba Rest House* with airy rooms looking out to the sea (①). Out on the (almost shit-free) beach you can watch **drag fishing**, with music and singing, and fifty men hauling the net rope. Between the beach and the town an amazing **posuban shrine** is watched over by a genial priest who'll go out of his way to explain his job (see box).

Some 20km west of Winneba you can stay at **Fort Patience** in **APAM** (see p.794). Getting to Apam requires taking a taxi or *tro-tro* to the Apam junction and changing. Near the junction, you can eat cheap chop at *The Hut* (along the road to the east a little) while you wait for a vehicle. It's about 8km down to Apam – too far to walk in the

THE ASAFO COMPANIES AND POSUBANS

Like other Akan states, the Fante maintain a highly formalized military institution known as **Asafo** (from *sa*, "war", and *fo*, "people"). The original function of the *Asafo* was defence of the Fante state. Although that role largely disappeared after the colonial invasion, *Asafo* companies still thrive and exercise considerable political influence. They enstool chiefs – and can destool them in certain instances – and act as royal advisors.

The companies put on at least one major festival each year and also provide community entertainment in the form of singing, dancing and drumming.

A Fante town typically has between two and twelve *Asafo* companies, each identified in a military fashion by number, name and location (for example Number 5 Company, Brofu-mba, Cape Coast), with members in ranks, easily identifiable as general, senior commander, divisional captain and so on. *Asafo* membership is patrilineal (in contrast to the chieftaincy, which is matrilineal, passing to the next man through the line of his maternal uncle).

As well as their military-ceremonial duties, the *Asafo* are active in the arts. In every Fante town there are painted cement **Asafo shrines**, known as **posuban**, for each of the town's companies. Rich with symbolism, the *posuban* evoke proverbs proclaiming one company's' superiority over its rivals. The shrine of No. 3 Company, Anomabu, for example, is guarded by two life-size cement lions, recalling the saying "A dead lion is greater than a live leopard". The rival No. 6 Company boasts a warship-shaped shrine, symbolic of its military prowess.

Similar symbolism carries over into the vibrantly coloured, appliqué **Asafo flags** made and paraded by each company. These can be seen flying over shrines or, more often, displayed throughout a company's area during town festivities. They have recently acquired serious value in European and American galleries and private collections – a phenomenon that, more than anything else, threatens to unravel the social fabric of the *Asafo* companies.

heat of the day. At the entrance to town is another imposing *posuban* shrine: colourful statues of Africans mounted on horseback decorate the three-storey affair which is topped by a white Jesus. Fort Patience is beautifully sited above the town and has well water for washing (①). Food is limited pretty much to the market. Nearby is Apam's only other **accommodation**, the *Hotel/Restaurant King Pobee* (①). The spacious rooms are a good deal, but if you're not staying at the fort, there's little point in staying in Apam.

The next town is **SALTPOND**, 42km west of Apam junction (you may have to change buses at Mankessim, 35km west of Apam junction), which offers precious little reason to call in (a bypass skirts the town) though it vies with Winneba for importance. If you fetch up here for the night, be sure to avoid the obnoxious *Nkrubem Motel*. Give the *Palm Beach* (☎101) a try instead.

A better plan is to go another six kilometres west to **ANOMABU** where the *Adaano Hotel* is recommended unreservedly, especially on a Friday when it becomes the musical focus of the village (①). Buses between Cape Coast and Accra can be hailed outside the hotel. Anomabu's fort, Fort William, is a prison, so no photos allowed – and in any case there is little to admire (see p.795).

The last place of note on this stretch is the idyllic crescent of sand and coconuts at **BIRIWA**, 3km west of Anomabu. It's right beneath the main highway, which makes it both accessible and a little too popular at weekends. Time was it sheltered various semi-resident hippies in wooden shacks at the village end of the beach, but those days have passed and there's now a restaurant on the sands – closed for renovations at the time of writing, however – and a fair-sized crowd on the beach at weekends. There's also an excellent, if somewhat pricey restaurant at the German-run *Biriwa Beach Hotel*, on the hill behind the strand. If the comfortable S/C chalets, or more modest non-S/C rooms are beyond your budget (room 201 is the nicest by far; ③–④), they allow camping for a small charge. Supplies are available in the village above the rocky bluff.

Cape Coast

British capital of the Gold Coast until 1876, **CAPE COAST** is a relatively large town with a solid infrastructure. The site of the nation's first university and major secondary schools, your chances of running into Ghanaian students here are good. The major attraction is the seventeenth-century **Cape Coast Castle** and museum. There are no recommendable beaches nearby. Note that through traffic doesn't go via the town, but round its north side on a **bypass**, off the frame of our map.

The Cape Coast Tourist Board is to be found in the basement of the *Savoy Hotel* (☎042/29.34).

Accommodation

Several of Cape Coast's recommended hotels are out of town, in particular in the village of **Pedu**, just north of the bypass on the road to Kakum National Park, about 5km from the centre of Cape Coast.

Catering Resthouse, off Residential Rd, Second Ridge (☎042/25.94). Large and comfortable S/C accommodation, though the setting is isolated and over 2km from the centre. Choice of fan or AC. Expansive courtyard and restaurant. ③.

Dan's Paradise ("Dan's Pee"), 1500m north of the town centre off the Saltpond road (PO Box 57; ☎042/18.02). A popular disco with accommodation featuring large AC rooms with double beds. A cut above the town's other inexpensive hotels. ②.

Holiday Inn, 5km from the centre in Pedu (*not* part of the international chain). Very good value for the six tidy rooms with fans, in a pleasant setting with swimming pool. ①.

Hotel Mudek, 5km from the centre in Pedu (take a shared taxi). Very modest hotel, but you get a large bed and it's much cheaper than anything in town. ①.

Palace Hotel, Aboom Rd. The cheapest lodgings in town with acceptable non-S/C rooms.

Sanaa Lodge, off the Elmina Rd (☎042/23.91). New and comfortable accommodation with AC and mini-bar in the stylish, S/C rooms. The town's best. ⑤.

Savoy Hotel, Ashanti Rd (☎042/28.66). Good value for clean rooms with fan. Centrally located near the beachfront on the east side of town, and often full. Terrible restaurant. ②.

The Town

Perched on a rocky ledge that juts out over the ocean, **Cape Coast Castle** is today a classified monument open to the public. Originally a Swedish and then a Danish fort, it was taken in 1662 by the British who made it their Gold Coast headquarters until 1876. In the nineteenth century, the building was enlarged to its present dimensions (see p.795). A guided tour (₵2000 plus a supplement if you want to take pictures) takes you through the maze of damp, suffocating **dungeons** where slaves were held before being shipped to Europe. The tour also includes a visit to the small adjoining **museum**, which contains scattered examples of Ghanaian pottery, carvings and other artistry mixed with historical exhibits documenting the slave trade – don't leave without seeing the Governor's wardrobe. Displays on local religion give a few clues about the fascinating *posuban* architecture and symbolism.

The new Cultural Centre in Cape Coast is worth seeking out – it houses a **Gramophone Records Museum** that is a must for serious devotees of highlife music and students of early West African recordings.

Food and other practicalities

Though there are plenty of cheap chop houses and bars, very few **restaurants** stand out in Cape Coast apart from those in the hotels. One central and unusual place to grab a bite is in the Law Court's canteen which is open to all. More mundane is the cafeteria

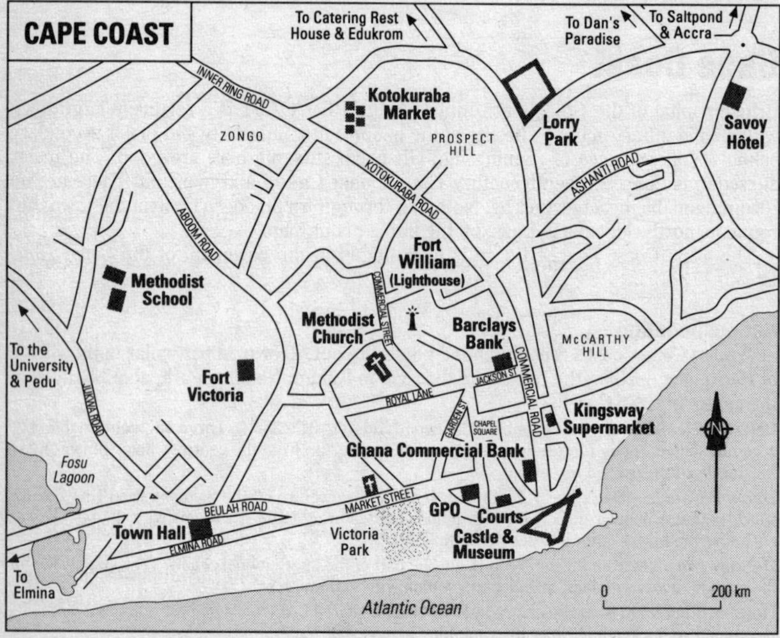

THE OGUAA FETU HARVEST FESTIVAL

Of many harvest festivals held in the region, one of the biggest is Cape Coast's **Oguaa Fetu Afahye**, which takes place on the first Saturday in September. Traditional chiefs from throughout the surrounding districts parade in sumptuous *kente*-cloth togas bedecked with gold crowns and medallions. The most important rulers are carried in canoe-like stretchers balanced on the heads of four manservants and shaded by huge parasols. They're accompanied by the queen mothers, wearing bracelets, necklaces and rings of solid gold, with more gold ornaments in their beehive coiffures. Fetish priests dance through the procession dispensing good fortune and collecting payment; palm wine flows freely. The parade lasts most of the day, terminating in **Victoria Park** for speeches by the chiefs and government representatives. Later, the streets fill up again and the party continues through the night with orchestras and dancing. This carnival atmosphere reigns for a couple of days and if you can time your trip right, it's worth making a detour. Come early and try and book a hotel in advance – most are crammed solid for the duration.

of the *Kingsway* department store which serves inexpensive chips, chicken and the like. Near the *UTC* supermarket on Tantri Road, the *New Metropolis* is a lively **bar** with inexpensive Ghanaian food. For night-time diversions, try the *Starlight* and *The Big Apple*.

When it's time to **move on**, the lorry park and *STC* yard near the castle can connect you with Accra, Takoradi or Kumasi. Peugeot pick-ups and station wagons also depart regularly for the fourteen-kilometre trip to Elmina, the nicest stretch of the coastal highway, where it runs directly above the beach through endless swaying coconut trees.

Kakum National Park

If you don't manage to get to the north and the Mole Game Reserve, you could do a little safari-ing at the superb new **KAKUM NATIONAL PARK**, 35km north of Cape Coast. The park consists of 360 square kilometres of protected forest, harbouring monkeys, elephants, antelope, warthogs and buffalo. Park facilities are very limited, though there's a good-value restaurant at the park entrance, where the views and even the animal watching are excellent. The infrastructure is improving month by month, however, and the rangers go out of their way to make a trip worthwhile. A 300-metre aerial walkway through the rainforest canopy should by now be built and a mountain bike trail is planned.

Tro-tros are fairly frequent from the Kotokuraba Market in Cape Coast to the park HQ in the village of **Abrafo** (Jukwa, or Dwokwa, the only village in the vicinity that is marked on the Michelin 953 map, is about two-thirds of the way there). When you arrive in Abrafo, ask to see the game warden who will arrange your visit (the entrance charge is nominal, but likely to increase).

For a **guided walking tour** to see the animals (price negotiable), you have to head out in the very early morning or late afternoon. A **two-day tour** of Kakum, including use of a 4WD vehicle and a night out on a tree platform, costs around ₵20,000 per person in a group of two or more. It's at night that you are most likely to see wildlife, though the chances of coming across large mammals are very slender. If you arrive at midday, they'll take you on a shorter trek to point out the wide range of flora, explaining the names and various medicinal and domestic uses of the different trees and shrubs (about ₵3000). For want of accommodation, rangers lend their **tents** to visitors and even camp out with them to ensure an early start.

For more information, contact the Senior Game Warden (PO Box 895 Cape Coast; ☎042/23.96 or 22.88; Fax 042/28.29) or contact the Cape Coast Tourist Board, at the *Savoy Hotel* (☎042/29.34). The Ghana Tourist Development Company in Accra also puts out a booklet on the park.

Five kilometres south of the park in the direction of Cape Coast, you can **stay** in the oddly named *Hans Cottage Botel* (③) which boasts a terrace on piles over a crocodile pool. The crocs are usually invisible except at feeding time, but the bird-watching is good. It's a great place for a late breakfast after an early morning park trip.

Elmina and around

ELMINA, now a small but active fishing town, was one of the first European toe-holds on the West African coast – its name is Portuguese, and means "The Mine". The principal attractions remain the **Portuguese castle and fort**, although the slow pace makes Elmina a rewarding place to relax and absorb the rhythms of a coastal town. But it's not all calm – when the fishing boats come in, Elmina can be spectacularly vibrant – and the town's unusual layout is arresting, counterposing the ocean against the lagoon and the two castles against each other. There are also a number of interesting *posuban* shrines, and this is one of the most rewarding places for photographers along the coast.

The castle and fort

One of the oldest buildings still standing in West Africa, the castle of **St George El Mina** was built by the Portuguese in 1482 – ten years before Columbus discovered America – although the original stockade was barely half the size of the present structure. It served as the **Portuguese headquarters** in West Africa for over 150 years until it was captured by soldiers of the Dutch West Indies Company in 1637. By that time, Saint George had grown roughly to its present size. In the courtyard, you'll notice a **Catholic church** built by the Portuguese. The protestant Dutch transformed this place of worship into a mess hall and **slave market** – an onerous image that poignantly drives home the barbarity of the trade. In 1872, the British bought Elmina castle, along with Holland's other possessions on the Gold Coast.

Given its age, the castle has held up well, but parts are beginning to deteriorate rapidly, notably the **Governor's kitchens** and the **officer's mess**, whose beautiful arched facade dates from the eighteenth century. Restoration work under UNESCO supervision is under way. Extremely good tours of the castle cost ₵3000 (photos extra), but you can gain entry and simply walk around on your own, communing with the baffling past, for ₵1000.

Across from the castle atop a steep, partly artificial hill, **Fort St Jago** (São Iago) dates from the seventeenth century. Built to protect Elmina, it was taken by the Dutch in 1683. Formerly a resthouse and one of the best places to stay in Ghana – if only on account of its dramatic position – it has been under renovation for several years, but should soon be open again. Again, a visit costs ₵1000, a tour ₵3000.

Accommodation and practicalities

The cheapest **place to stay** is likely to be Fort St Jago, if they *ever* finish the "renovations" which have been under way for at least ten years (②). Alternatives include the good *Nyansapow Hotel*, a family-run establishment with non-S/C rooms with electricity around a lovely courtyard (②). At the town entrance as you come from Cape Coast, the *Oyster Bay Hotel* has fairly high-standard AC accommodation, though the pool is empty and they don't serve food (③).

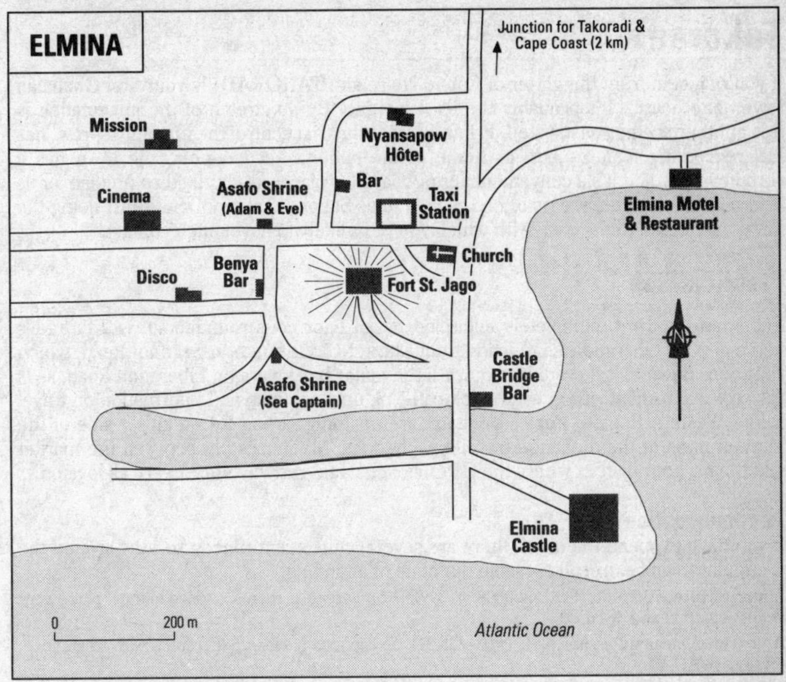

For **eating**, you generally have to rely on the streetside chop stands or hotel restaurants: *Oyster Bay*'s meals and setting are fine if you can afford it (₵5000–10,000 a head). Or try the good *Gramsdel J Bar* along the beach front, which has a big selection of Ghanaian and European dishes. The best place to park a weary body and unwind over a beer is the *Castle Bridge Bar*, built on the water by the fishing port amid all the action.

Brenu-Akyinim

Ten kilometres west of Elmina, accessible by foot along the coastal track, **BRENU-AKYINIM** has one of the most spectacularly perfect beaches on the Ghana coast, a long strip of palm-laden white sand with swimmable breakers. Part of the beach has been taken over on a private basis quite recently, where the sand is kept clean and loungers and other facilities are available. Most of the time there's almost nobody here. In the village itself, built like Elmina, between the sea and a lagoon, there are basic, clean **rooms** to be had at the *Celiamen's Hotel* (①). The cook there, Aggie, does wonderful meals of crayfish, plantain and rice.

If, rather than walk along the coast from Elmina (for which you'll need to allow a good three hours), you use **public transport**, you'll almost certainly be dropped off at the Brenu-Akyinim junction on the main highway, approximately 12km west of Elmina and 4km from Brenu and the beach. Aggie keeps a shack at the junction, *Aggie's Catering*, where you can sample her cooking if you decide to wait for a lift down to the coast.

Takoradi

If you're just in from the glitter of Côte d'Ivoire and **TAKORADI** is your first Ghanaian town, take heart – it's probably the least inviting. By no stretch of the imagination is this another scenic coastal stop. Primarily an industrial centre, the ungainly sprawl has few redeeming features but, as home of the nation's second **port**, the town has a certain vitality and it's a convenient springboard for places as far afield as Abidjan, or as near as Dixcove. Takoradi is often referred to as Sekondi-Takoradi, **Sekondi** being the naval base 10km to the east, with which you're unlikely to have much contact.

Practicalities

The **main market**, completely encircled by an enormous roundabout, is Takoradi's nerve centre. Liberation Road leads from Market Circle south to Sekondi Road, which continues down to Takoradi harbour. All the major **banks** are on Liberation Road, as is the regional **tourist office** where you can pick up a city map and information on travel in the Western Region. **Forex bureaux** are on John Sarbah Rd on either side of the market: none of them change travellers' cheques. Minibuses ply between the market and the harbour district where the **GPO**, hospital and **railway station** are all located.

Accommodation

If you have to spend the night, there are several convenient **places to stay** around the triangular town centre, all passable but none outstanding.

Ahenfie Hotel, Axim Rd (PO Box 0608; ☎031/29.66). Large AC rooms, a video lounge, plus a very good restaurant and disco. ③.

Arvo Hotel, near the motor park (☎031/35.31). Exceptionally clean S/C rooms with fresh linen; some have AC. ①.

Atlantic Hotel, near the main hospital and port (PO Box 273; ☎031/33.00). Upmarket place with everything from car rental services to a conference centre. The AC rooms, however, are run-down, and the place is famous for shortages of electricity and water. ④.

Beachway Hotel, near the *Atlantic* (☎031/47.34). Large and well-scrubbed non-S/C rooms, many with balconies. Good value on the beachfront makes it the VSO choice when staying in Takoradi. ②.

Hotel de Star, corner of Califf Ave and No 2 Rd. A well-run hotel, and recommended, if you can put up with the high-volume cassette stall opposite (choose a room carefully). Simple rooms with shared facilities. ①.

Western Palace Hotel, off Axim Rd on Chapel Hill (☎031/24.15). Airy rooms with AC or fans. ②.

Zenith Hotel, Califf Ave. Circus decor that looks like something out of a Fellini film. It's plain and a bit dirty, but a room with fan is very cheap. ①.

Food and entertainment

Street food abounds in the area around the *Zenith* between Califf Ave and Liberation Rd, if you're in need of a night-time fix of *kenkey* and fish. For more formal surroundings try the *Chez Connie* **restaurant** and bar, next to the *Arvo*, which serves moderately priced European and African food. More exciting offerings are served up at the popular *Harbour View Restaurant*, a nice place to sit outside and eat Western or Ghanaian specialities on a hill above the sea. *Twin Peaks* near the *Beachway* serves a good range of reasonably priced Chinese dishes made all the more interesting by the zealous owner's penchant for conversation. Over by the *Western Palace*, the *Shalimar* has a good selection of Indian food. The current weekend venue for **live music** is *Westline*, about 1km north of town (definitely a case for a taxi ride), where the music and atmosphere attract a smartish Ghanaian crowd.

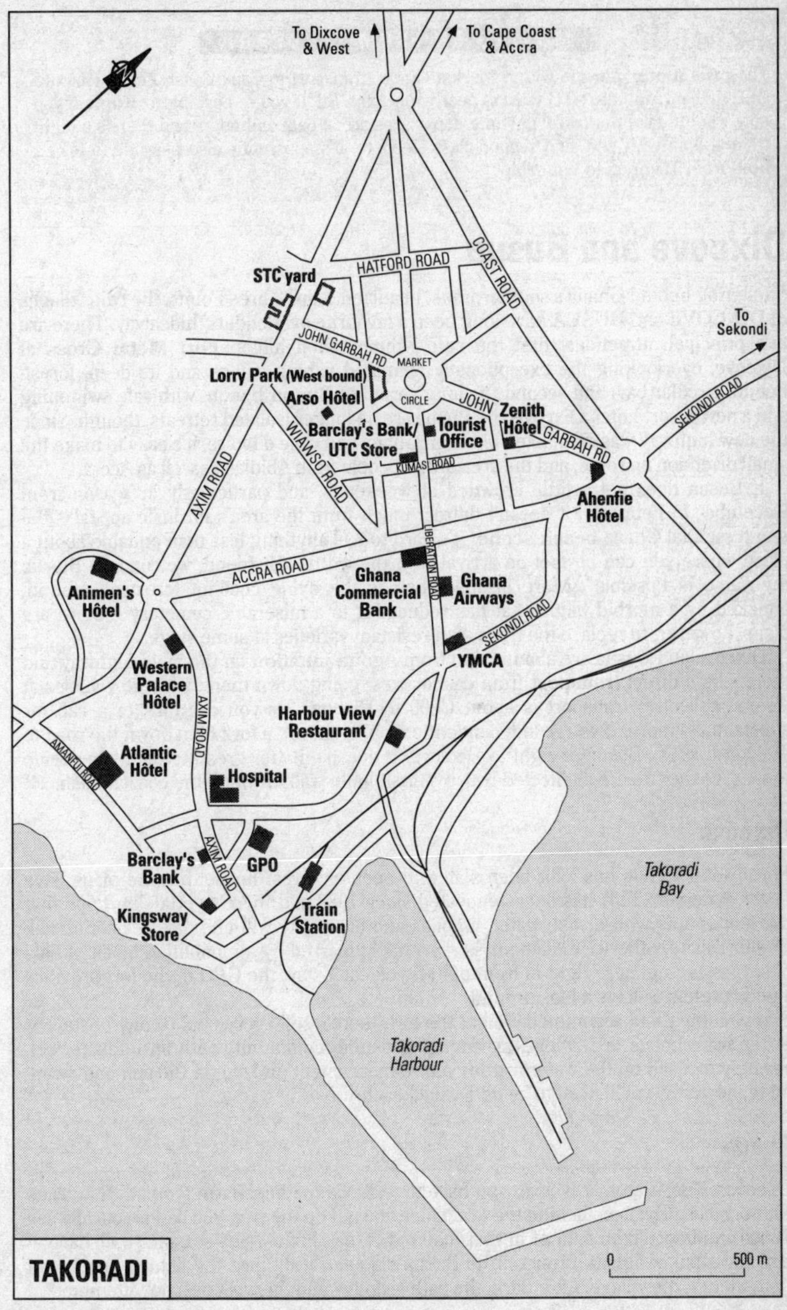
To Dixcove & West
To Cape Coast & Accra
To Sekondi
HATFORD ROAD
COAST ROAD
STC yard
JOHN GARBAH RD
MARKET
CIRCLE
Lorry Park (West bound)
Arso Hôtel
JOHN GARBAH RD
Zenith Hôtel
Barclay's Bank/ UTC Store
Tourist Office
KUMASI ROAD
SEKONDI ROAD
Ahenfie Hôtel
WIAWSO ROAD
AXIM ROAD
ACCRA ROAD
LIBERATION ROAD
Ghana Commercial Bank
Ghana Airways
Animen's Hôtel
SEKONDI ROAD
YMCA
Western Palace Hôtel
Harbour View Restaurant
AMANFUI ROAD
Atlantic Hôtel
AXIM ROAD
Hospital
GPO
AXIM ROAD
Barclay's Bank
Kingsway Store
Train Station
Takoradi Bay
Takoradi Harbour
TAKORADI
0
500 m

MOVING ON FROM TAKORADI

The main **motor park** is within Market Circle (transport to Cape Coast, Accra, Dixcove and Abidjan), and the **STC yard** is nearby on Axim Rd. If you're heading **to Kumasi** you may want to take the **train**: daytime departures are at 6am and noon, and there's a night train at 8pm with first- and second-class sleepers. It's apparently also possible to take a **boat** from Takoradi to Winneba.

Dixcove and Busua

Sheltering behind Ghana's southernmost headland, Cape Three Points, the twin villages of **DIXCOVE** and **BUSUA** have long been a favourite overlanders' hideaway. There are two principal attractions: first the cute, whitewashed hilltop **Fort Metal Cross** at Dixcove, overlooking the exceptionally animated fishing village and its deep, forest-bound, circular bay; and second the long strand of **Busua beach**, with safe swimming and a new resort hotel. Dixcove and Busua are no longer isolated retreats, though. Since the new highway was completed between Ghana and Côte d'Ivoire, it's easy to make the small diversion en route, and the area draws people from Abidjan as well as Accra.

If Busua does get a little crowded at weekends, and particularly in season from December to February, it doesn't detract much from the area's intrinsic appeal – the quintessential Ghana **beach scene**. It's hard to feel anything less than equable about a place where you can be met on arrival with the words "Hi friend, welcome to Busua, my name is Possible". More disappointing is the dying coconut forest all around, attacked by a morbid blight that has reduced it to a miserable cemetery – there are plans, however, to replace the trees with resistant varieties at some stage.

Dixcove and Busua are about 13km from **Agona junction** on the main highway and there's little direct **transport** from east or west going down there. Change vehicles at Agona: collective transport is about ₵200 to Dixcove, or you can charter a cab for substantially more. If you're independently mobile, there's a fork 6km down the road to the coast: left to Busua or right to Dixcove. It doesn't matter greatly which you decide to take, as the two are connected by a twenty-minute walk through the coastal bush.

Dixcove

Fort Metal Cross has long been slated to open as a rest house, but the plans have never materialized. It has been renovated since 1988 and there's yet a slim hope that the four rooms with erratic water supplies and electricity will one day be operational. The fort's site, otherwise eminent, is regrettably marred by a monolithic block of flats of surpassing ugliness right in front of it. If you can't stay, the GPO in the fort provides a good pretext to have a look around.

If you don't find accommodation at the fort, there's still every opportunity of staying in a private house in Dixcove, an engaging fishing community with an intimate feel, strongly focused on the waterfront. If you're more intent on lying in the sun and swimming, however, you'll need to be on Busua beach.

Busua

To reach **Busua** from Dixcove, you have to walk via the bush-farm footpath that leads off, northeasterly, from behind the fort. Once you get up the rise, you can practically see Busua and it would be difficult at this point to get lost. In the rainy season, you'll have to ford the shallow Busua River on the Busua side and walk past the fishing beach and right though the village. After dark, the path is dodgy and the walk best not attempted.

The *Busua Pleasure Beach Hotel* (PO Box 7, Dixcove) is unmissable on the sands. Rooms in the run-down hotel are cheaper than the chalets, though both have been in a state of renovation for years and ongoing development means it's hard to know for sure whether you'll be offered basic beach accommodation (②) or the long-awaited new luxury hotel (④–⑤). Camping is allowed but, because of thieving, not encouraged. There's no electricity or running water, but they have bottled water and there are drums of washing water available. They do solid meals to order on their terrace, the cook fixing whatever's for sale in the village; lobster, shark, tuna and swordfish are all readily available and not too pricey. The beautiful sands and equally clean, surfy sea are together a very big plus. It's a place to meet travellers, swap tales, and maybe find companions.

There are also **rooms** available in Busua village if the hotel is full or if you're determined to avoid the inevitable overlanders' "scene" around the chalets. Ask anyone to direct you to *Sister Elizabeth's* or *Aunt Mary's*, which, like other places, provide a bare room in a family compound (①). You can also eat very cheaply at the village street stalls, or have *fufu* and palmnut soup at the *Don't Mind Your Wife* chop bar.

A multitude of short **walks** are possible in the area, either west to Cape Three Points, 5km beyond Dixcove, or east along Busua Beach, cutting over the headland and down to **Butre**, just a kilometre beyond the beach, which used to have a fort of its own – Fort Batenstein – now completely in ruins.

Princestown and west to the Ivoirian border

The principal attractions on this stretch of coast are **Princestown** and **Axim**, the latter served by most buses along the main road towards Côte d'Ivoire. Both have fine castles and magnificent views, but neither can compete with the charms of Dixcove and Busua.

Princestown

In 1681, Prince Friedrich Wilhelm of Brandenburg sent an expedition to the area of what is now **PRINCESTOWN** (aka Prince's Town) in an effort to break the seventeenth-century Portuguese, British and Dutch hold over West African trade. This led to the founding of **Fort Grossfriedrichsburg** (see p.795), within whose walls the Brandenburgers soon fell victim to malaria and repeated attacks by the Dutch and British. They abandoned the citadel in 1708, turning it over to the Ahanta-Pokoso chief **Johnny Konny**, who earned the dubious title "Last Prussian Negro Prince". The Dutch stormed the fort in 1748 and renamed it Hollandia. It was finally abandoned around 1800.

Restored since independence, the fort has spectacular views and is open to visitors. You can also spend the night here; the caretaker is very helpful. The nearby beaches are beautiful, and for real isolation you can take a canoe trip across the river. The road down to Princestown from the highway used to be unthinkably bad and periodically impassable in the rainy season, but it has now been repaired. If it deteriorates again you may well have to walk one way or both.

Axim and Beyin

Now in the small town of **AXIM**, **Fort Santa Antonia** was built by the Portuguese, probably in the fifteenth century, and taken by the Dutch in 1642 (see p.795). Today the fort houses government offices, but if you ask politely you should be allowed to visit. There's a very basic hotel on the edge of town (*San Marco*) with no running water or electricity (①). The staff provide lanterns and buckets. *Frankfurs Guesthouse* is a good deal more expensive (①), and a lot nicer, though equally lacking in running water.

By the village of **BEYIN**, Fort Apollonia (see p.795) is the last of the forts along the Ghana coastline and has rudimentary accommodation (①). The only way to reach Beyin without a lot of walking is to head by *tro-tro* to Mpataba, then to Bonyeri down the road towards Half Assini, and finally eastwards along the shore to Beyin (36km from Mpataba).

Into Côte d'Ivoire

Onward travel into Côte d'Ivoire is simple from Axim. There are daily buses through to the border at **ELUBO**, where, if you don't cross directly, you can find accommodation with the friendly people at the *Hotel Cocoville* near the motor park. It's a comfortable place with AC, S/C rooms (②), where staff organize a number of excursions in the area, including canoe trips on the Tano River or the Juen Lagoon. Travellers who change at **Mpataba** junction to tackle the seashore route into Côte d'Ivoire report numerous problems and are often turned back. If you still want to try it, some details of this route in reverse are given on p.655. Last (or first) money changing facilities in Ghana are at a big new branch of the *Ghana Commercial Bank* in Half Assini.

KUMASI AND CENTRAL GHANA

The **central part of Ghana** is one of the country's most attractive regions. The road from Accra, skirting past the northeast fringe of the old **Asante heartland**, is scenic and hilly. Around the great hub of **Kumasi** itself, a clutch of different routes radiate through steep scarp and forest country. Much of this has long been under cultivation – especially **cocoa**, which brings a dark, gloomy silence to the woods – but plenty is still jungle-swathed, stacked with impressive, buttress-rooted forest giants, and scattered with hillside villages. These settlements, misty grey-green in the chilly mornings, sticky and brilliantly coloured in the afternoons, are the key elements in an area to savour. Travel is easy, and the cultural heritage as rich as anywhere.

Kumasi

In the main Asante city of **KUMASI**, history weighs heavily. You feel it walking through the streets where monumental **colonial buildings** – a reminder of half a century of British domination – have become worn with time and covered in water-stained layers of ochre-red dust. Foreign edifices have taken on an African look in a town that oozes with the traditions and customs of the **Asante** – one of the most powerful nations in West Africa at the end of the nineteenth century. A combination of the old order and hectic modernity makes this extremely active commercial centre one of Ghana's most satisfying cities.

Orientation and information

Even in its early days, Kumasi was an imposing capital. Today it spreads widely over the hills, and is home to close on a million people. The heart of the downtown district is marked roughly by **Kejetia Circle**, a large roundabout with a wonderfully kitsch replica of the Golden Stool (see the "Asante" box) rising from its centre. Nearby, the **central market** – the largest in Ghana and one of the very biggest in Africa – spills over the railway tracks to fill a hollow in the city centre.

Just west of the market, the **Adum district** is the commercial centre where you'll find major **banks**, supermarkets and department stores (*UTC*, *GNTC*, *UAC* and

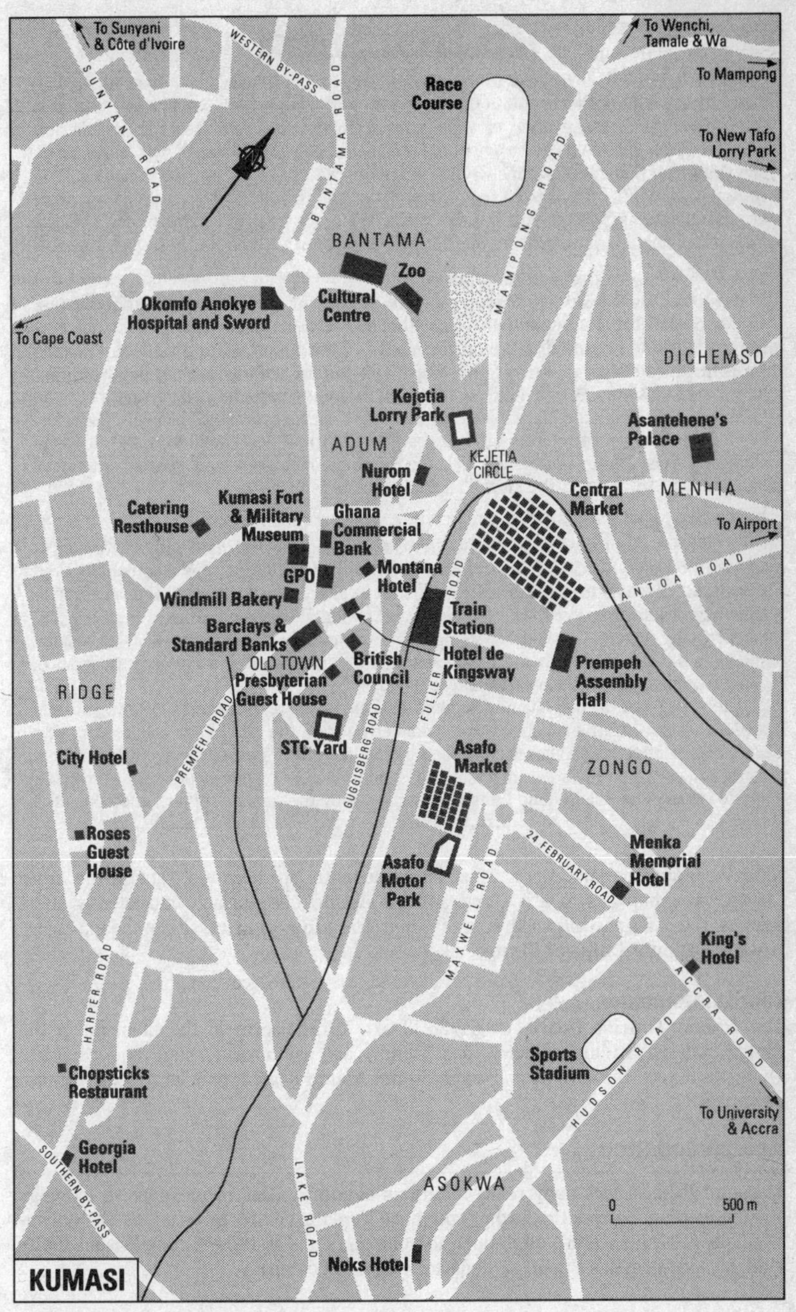
To Sunyani
& Côte d'Ivoire
WESTERN BY-PASS
To Wenchi,
Tamale & Wa
To Mampong
SUNYANI ROAD
BANTAMA ROAD
Race
Course
To New Tafo
Lorry Park
MAMPONG ROAD
BANTAMA
Zoo
Okomfo Anokye
Hospital and Sword
Cultural
Centre
To Cape Coast
DICHEMSO
Kejetia
Lorry Park
Asantehene's
Palace
ADUM
KEJETIA
CIRCLE
Nurom
Hotel
Central
Market
MENHIA
Catering
Resthouse
Kumasi Fort
& Military
Museum
Ghana
Commercial
Bank
To Airport
ANTOA ROAD
GPO
Montana
Hotel
FULLER ROAD
Windmill Bakery
Train
Station
Barclays &
Standard Banks
Hotel de
Kingsway
Prempeh
Assembly
Hall
OLD TOWN
British
Council
Presbyterian
Guest House
RIDGE
PREMPEH II ROAD
GUGGISBERG ROAD
STC Yard
Asafo
Market
ZONGO
City Hotel
Roses
Guest
House
24 FEBRUARY ROAD
Menka
Memorial
Hotel
Asafo
Motor
Park
MAXWELL ROAD
HARPER ROAD
King's
Hotel
ACCRA ROAD
Sports
Stadium
HUDSON ROAD
Chopsticks
Restaurant
To University
& Accra
Georgia
Hotel
SOUTHERN BY-PASS
LAKE ROAD
ASOKWA
0
500 m
Noks Hotel
KUMASI

THE ASANTE

The Asante trace their **origins** to the northern regions of the savannah belt. Along with other Akan peoples, they came to this region around the eleventh century and settled in the area of **Lake Bosumtwi**, carving farms from the wild rainforest. These districts contained rich gold fields and trade in the metal gradually developed, at first to the north, supplying the Saharan caravans. By the fifteenth century, however, the Akan also had commercial links with the Portuguese and, by the seventeenth century, they were organized into dozens of small states, each vying for control of the mines and the slave-supplying districts in the far interior where European merchants hadn't ventured.

The Founding of the Asante Nation

In the 1690s, **Osei Tutu** – the first great **Asante king**, or *Asantehene* – brought together a loose confederation of states into a single nation under his rule. **Kumasi** was chosen as the site of the new capital on the advice of Osei Tutu's most trusted adviser, **Okomfo Anokye**, an extremely powerful fetish priest. Okomfo planted the seeds of two *kum* trees in separate locations, one of which sprouted, indicating where the Asante seat was to be established (*kum asi* means "under the *kum* tree"). Having received this sign, the priest evoked the **Golden Stool** from the heavens. This "throne" descended from the clouds to alight upon Osei Tutu, and thereby became the single most important symbol of national unity and the authority of the king. The Asante nation was born.

Expansion and Consolidation

Osei Tutu set about expanding his empire. One of his most important early victories was against the Denkyira king, **Ntim Gyakar**, under whom the Asante had traditionally lived as vassals. They captured, tried and killed Ntim Gyakar in 1699. Other rival powers fell in their turn, each conquered state left intact, but owing allegiance and taxes in goods and labour to the Asante. Gradually the kingdom grew to include most of present-day Ghana and Côte d'Ivoire, with only the **Fante** states of the coast putting up realistic resistance, using European allies to their advantage.

The sheer size of the Asante kingdom spawned a royal **bureaucracy** and **judicial system**. Administrative functions were transferred from the hereditary nobility to a new class of appointed functionaries controlled by the king. Even **commoners** could fill lower court offices which included linguists and commissioners or governors sent to oversee vassal states. The Asantehene himself was chosen by the queen mother, who consulted

Kingsway), and the post office. Most **forex bureaux** are here too, though the *Sweet Money Forex*, between Kejetia Circle and the Asantehene's palace, consistently offers the best rates. Up the hill northwest of Adum, **Bantama district**, site of the expansive **Ghana National Cultural Centre**, takes over.

Tourist information

The **Ghana Tourist Board** (☎051/26.33 ext. 12), adjacent to the museum in the Ghana National Cultural Centre, has friendly and enthusiastic staff, and complete guides to hotels, restaurants and sights in the Asante Region, plus large-scale Kumasi city maps.

Accommodation

Although Kumasi lacks any really luxurious **accommodation**, inexpensive lodgings abound, getting cheaper the further you move from the centre. In vacations, the university halls of residence are often open to volunteers and travellers: the pleasant **Unity Hall**, for example, has a pool, gardens and no lack of company.

with advisers before making her decision (in the matrilineal system, successors were chosen from the king's brothers or his sisters' offspring). Though his power was nearly absolute, an unworthy Asantehene could be "destooled" – removed from the throne – by the royal family.

War with the British

The Asante empire had reached its apogee by the year 1800 when **Osei Bonsu** ascended to the throne. The borders of the country now extended well beyond the present-day borders of Ghana, and Kumasi was a capital with a population of 700,000. In the vast market in the heart of town, trade was so healthy that the king's servants periodically sifted the sand to collect loose gold dust. Despite the prosperity, **rebellion** was fomenting among Asante refugees who took shelter in the Fante confederation of the coast. In 1806, Osei Bonsu launched a full-scale attack against the Fante and invaded their lands. The attack marked the beginning of the last phase of the great conquests.

The coastal **Fante** had traditionally traded directly with the British, and Osei Bonsu's invasion thus led to direct **conflict between the British and the Asante**. In 1824, on the death of Osei Bonsu, the British were anxious to squash this main obstacle to the control of Gold Coast trade. Hostilities, which were to simmer throughout the nineteenth century, erupted in the **First Anglo-Asante War**. War broke out again in 1826 when the Asante were heavily defeated and Britain assumed the role of "Protector" along the coast and as far as 130km inland. A third war, in 1863, was inconclusive, though Asante history relates it as a victory, with a strong invasion force from Kumasi holding the British back for a few years. After some preparation, the British marched on Kumasi in the **Fourth Anglo-Asante War** (1874), but found the palace empty since the Asantehene and his retinue had fled to the forest. The British troops took whatever treasure they could find in the palace (most of which was later auctioned in London) and then blew it up. The rest of the city was razed to the ground.

By the end of the nineteenth century, the British had annexed the Asante country as part of their Gold Coast colony. They sought to humiliate and demoralize the nation by publicly arresting the young Asantehene, **Prempeh**, and exiling him to the Seychelles. The final slap in the face came in 1900 when the new colonial governor, Sir Frederick Hodgson, demanded the Golden Stool be handed over for him to sit on. Having foreseen such a scenario, astute royal court members had made a fake golden stool and concealed the real one, which was only discovered by accident much later, in the 1920s. Nobody, not even the Asantehene, had ever sat on it. To do so would have violated national unity.

Inexpensive

Ayigya Hotel, 24th February Rd, near the university junction (PO Box 3515). Clean rooms with common or private baths and fans. Restaurant, bar and car park. ①.

Hotel de Kingsway, Prempeh II Rd, Adum district (PO Box 178; ☎051/24.41). Handily situated in the commercial centre, this is a big favourite. The restaurant, bar and occasional nightclub assure a lot of activity here; rooms with fans. ③.

Menka Memorial Hotel, 24th February Rd, Amakom district (PO Box 3371; ☎051/64.32). Large, and very dilapidated, hotel about 2km from centre; S/C and non-S/C rooms with fans. Lively bar and restaurant. ①.

Montana Hotel, Adum district (PO Box 1416; ☎051/23.66). Smaller than the *Kingsway*, but a similarly central location, within easy walking distance of points of interest downtown. Rooms with fans – or AC for a small premium – and shared facilities. ①.

Pollux Hotel, New Tafo district opposite the motor park (PO Box 4464; ☎051/63.55). "Decent accommodation – no problem" is their motto, backed up with small, furnished S/C rooms. Bar and food "on request". ②.

Presbyterian Guest House, Mission Rd near the *STC* yard and British Council. Comfortable twin rooms in an imposing colonial building once used as the missionary's residence. The best budget place in town – a good place to meet fellow travellers – "the presby" has a low-key atmosphere that's hard to tear yourself away from. Communal cooking and eating are the norm. Camping is available if the rooms are full. ①.

Moderate

Catering Resthouse, Ridge district (PO Box 3179; ☎051/36.56). The second state-owned hotel, the *Catering Resthouse* doesn't have the *City Hotel*'s pretensions and, perhaps for that reason, is good value for money: furnished rooms, some with phone and AC. Convenient for downtown. ③.

City Hotel, Harper Rd, Ridge district (PO Box 1980; ☎051/32.98). Ostensibly the best in town, this state-owned pile is showing its age badly. All the amenities are here – casino, disco, cinema – but the sum seems less than the parts. Depressing. ④.

Georgia Hotel, Harper Rd (☎051/39.15). A stylish hotel with a pleasant bar in the gardens and amenities like TV and AC in the well-furnished rooms. Friendly management. Swimming pool. ⑤.

King's Hotel, Ahodwo district (PO Box 8803; ☎051/44.90). Small garden hotel in a quiet residential neighbourhood. S/C rooms have AC and phones and there's a car park and a bar and restaurant that "welcomes you with finger-licking meals". ③.

Noks Hotel, Asokwa district (PO Box 8556). One of the better hotels, with comfortable S/C rooms and efficient service. Some of the rooms have AC and carpets. Restaurant, bar and car park. ③.

Nurom Hotel, Suame district (PO Box 1400; ☎051/40.00). Wins the prize for best design, from the colourful statue of the chief in front, to the Asante symbols on the modern facade. S/C rooms with fan or AC. ③.

Rose's Guest House, Ridge District (PO Box 4176; ☎051/40.72). An intimate place with very comfortable and tidy S/C, AC rooms, complete with satellite TV, and a pleasant garden setting. *Rose's* restaurant is well known. ④.

The Town

Kumasi is one of the rare West African towns where you can go **sightseeing** in the formal sense. In addition to the **museums**, other historic points of interest, like the **palace** of the Asante king, dot the cityscape, and you could easily spend a few days just checking them out. The large **central market** alone merits a couple of trips to search hidden corners for unusual finds. There's a terrible "**zoo**", north of Kejetia Circle. Be kind to yourself – and potential future captives – and avoid it like the plague.

The central market

Despite the tumbledown appearance of rambling, rusty, corrugated-iron-clad stalls, the **central market** is a fantastic place to explore, and the largest market (certainly in terms of acreage) in West Africa. Traders come from all the surrounding countries, and beyond, to buy and sell here. You can while away hours just wandering by the stalls of fruit and vegetables, provisions, plastic imports and spare car parts (if you need the latter, incidentally, "Magazine", in the north of the city, is a separate, vast district entirely devoted to spare parts). You can also search out the corners filled with every kind of **Asante craft** (sandals, leather goods, pottery) and most importantly, **cloth**.

This is probably the best place in Ghana to buy *kente* cloth and it's worth paying a child to take you to the row of stalls where it's actually stored – a dedicated lane in the northwest of the market, near Kejetia lorry park – as they're easily missed otherwise. Prices are high and depend on whether you're buying single- or more expensive double-weave *kente*. To add a further complication, there's *kente* woven from imported rayon and real silk. You can sometimes buy just a small piece, or even a souvenir strip.

Prempeh II Jubilee Museum and the National Cultural Centre

In the grounds of the **Ghana National Cultural Centre**, the small **Prempeh II Jubilee Museum** (Tues–Sun 9am–6pm; nominal entrance fee) holds a rich collection of Asante artefacts housed in a reproduction of a traditional Asante regalia house, few examples of which remain since the nineteenth-century wars with the British. Such buildings served both as palaces and **shrines**; note the characteristic mural decorations on the lower walls. The designs, like those found on the **adinkra cloth** for which the region is famous, symbolize proverbs commenting on Akan moral and social values.

Among the many historical articles inside the museum is the **silver-plated stool** that the Denkyira chief Nana Ntim Gyakar was supposedly sitting on when captured in a surprise attack by the Asante in 1699. This victory marked the expansion of the Asante empire and the stool, with its intricate carving and design, became an important symbol of liberation and power. Also on display is the fake **golden stool**. The real one remains guarded in the Manhyia palace, and is only brought out for special occasions. The replica was designed at the beginning of the century to deceive the British, who demanded that the most sacred of all Asante symbols be handed over to them.

Notice, too, a **treasure bag** on display that was presented to the Agona king by the fetish priest Okomfo Anokye. No one knows what the leather sack contains, for according to tradition to open it would bring about the downfall of the Asante nation. Other articles include examples of traditional dress, jewellery, furniture and musical instruments.

In addition to the museum, the grounds of the cultural centre contain a model Asante village, a cocoa farm, a palm wine "factory", performance facilities for music and dance, and a **crafts centre** where you can see how **kente** and **adinkra fabrics**, traditional sandals, brass weights and pottery are produced. Prices are fixed and seem fair. Don't miss the centre's small **library** with numerous works dedicated to Asante civilization.

Fort Kumasi and the military museum

Housed in a British-built fort dating from 1820, the **military museum**'s collections have a heavy emphasis on modern **weaponry** captured by Ghanaian troops in World War II's East Africa and Asia campaigns. Far more interesting, but less extensive, are the exhibits documenting the **Anglo-Asante wars**, with period photographs and mementoes. **Fort Kumasi** itself is an intriguing structure where, as part of the obligatory guided tour, you'll be locked in a dark dungeon, to experience briefly the manner in which the British dealt with rabble-rousers. Those who went in rarely came out alive, and a few seconds is plenty to impart a sense of the terror the condemned must have felt.

Manhyia: the Asantehene's palace

The traditional **Asantehene's palace** was sacked by the British, and the present royal residence (Mon–Fri 9am–5pm), where the Asantehene and his family live, has a curiously colonial look to it. Completed in 1926, it first served as the residence of Nana Prempeh I when he returned from exile. Until 1956, the palace also served as the **Asantehene's court**, where criminal, civil and constitutional cases were heard. Even today a traditional council presides over customary and constitutional matters here: the Prempeh dispenses judgements on land disputes and chieftaincy matters every Monday and Thursday at the unusual hours of noon–2pm. Every sixth Sunday at noon, the chief receives visitors and welcomes a bottle of schnapps from the many nationals and foreigners who show up to pay their respects. If you sit out the lengthy speechifying, he will shake your hand as you leave. The museum can give further details.

The Okomfo Anokye sword

Across the street from the National Cultural Centre, the **Okomfo Anokye Teaching Hospital** contains another sacred Asante symbol in its grounds. This is the **Okomfo**

AKAN NAMES

People are named according to the day of the week on which they are born.

	GIRLS' NAMES	BOYS' NAMES
Monday	Ajoa	Kojo
Tuesday	Abena, Aba	Kwabena, Kobina
Wednesday	Akua	Kweku
Thursday	Yaa	Yao, Ekow
Friday	Efua	Kofi
Saturday	Ama	Kwame, Kwamena
Sunday	Esi	Kwesi

Anokye sword that Osei Tutu's fetish priest planted on the spot shortly after choosing Kumasi as the Asante capital in around 1700. According to the legend, the day this sword is pulled from the ground, the Asante nation will collapse. The deteriorating state of the heavy metal blade seems an ominous portent, but locals swear that bulldozers have tried and failed to budge it – though they don't explain why.

The University of Science and Technology

When it first opened in 1952, this university was one of the largest and most sophisticated in Africa. The beautifully landscaped grounds are still impressive even if many of the buildings and facilities are beginning to show their age. A self-contained "city of technology", the university has its own hospital, sports facilities (including an Olympic-length pool, open to the public), banks, library and a limited bookshop. *Tro-tros* to "Tech" leave from Asafo market or Kejetia lorry park.

Eating

Kumasi is a fine place for **street food**, which you'll find throughout town, notably in the motor parks and markets where numerous **chop bars** serve rice dishes, *fufu* or plantains with sauce. Streetside coffee men whip up two-egg omelettes with Nescafé and sweet Ghana bread at breakfast time. Recommended **restaurants** in town include:

Bamboo Snack Bar, near *Hotel de Kingsway*. Inexpensive samosas, hot dogs and Indian curry.

Chopsticks, Nyiaeso district, near the golf club (☎051/32.21). Chinese, and one of the best restaurants in town – usually crowded. Relatively high prices reflect the popularity (closed Mon).

Copa Cabana, Fanti New Town district. A good place if you're fed up with chop houses. Chicken, rice and salad from ₵1800.

Famale Restaurant, above the *Hotel de Kingsway*, Prempeh II Road, Adum district (☎051/24.41). European and Lebanese cuisine in the middle of the commercial district, excellent and not unreasonably priced. Book ahead if you want to start eating within an hour of arrival (lunch noon–4pm, evenings from 7pm).

Hamburger Heaven, Prempeh II Rd opposite *Hotel de Kingsway*. Good pizza, felafel, spring rolls and burgers. They cut hair too.

Hit Parade Restaurant, Ntomin Rd, Adum district (☎051/64.05). Formerly the venue of the *Golden Key Disco*, this now serves good, cheap Ghanaian food (11am–9pm).

House of Lords, Bompata district, behind Prempeh Assembly Hall. European and Oriental food served to jazz and African music. Wine available with meals (11am–11pm).

Royal Garden Chinese Restaurant, *Hotel Georgia*. Another good choice for Chinese cooking or a chance to try frog's legs. More refined though no more expensive than *Chopsticks*.

Sweet and Low Chop House, 24th February Road, near the *Menka Memorial Hotel*. Serves wonderful breakfast chop.

MOVING ON FROM KUMASI

Several major **lorry parks** service Kumasi if you're heading out by **bush taxi** or **tro-tro**. They include New Tafo park, in the north, for vehicles to Tamale, Bolgatanga, Navrongo and Yendi; Asafo park, by the Asafo market, for Konongo, Koforidua, Accra and Takoradi; and Kejetia park for Mampong, Sunyani, Berekum, Wenchi, Wa and Abidjan. It's worth knowing that the direct route to Takoradi and Cape Coast is very rough and liable to be impassable in the rains.

The new bus station on Prempeh Road, a few hundred metres south of the railway station, is the departure point for **STC buses** to Accra, Tamale, Wa and Bolgatanga. Most of these destinations have twice-daily service, though runs are commonly cancelled at the last minute. Less frequent are the buses to Ouagadougou and Abidjan. Check the boards – in theory, departure for Ouagadougou is at 9am, with a stop from midnight to 6am in Tamale.

There's a daily *City Express TATA* bus to Mole Game Reserve departing mid-afternoon from Kejetia Circle (be there by 2pm). Departure is usually about 4pm, arriving at Mole 2am.

The passenger **train** to Accra has stopped running, but there are two services down through the forest to Takoradi, leaving at 6am and 8pm – a twelve-hour trip.

Ghana Airways' domestic services are currently suspended, but may start up again, with daily flights from Kumasi to Accra, and twice weekly to Tamale. The *Ghana Airways* office is in Adum (☎051/26.33). Meanwhile, there are, in theory, regular air force flights to Accra at 6.30am on Mon, Wed, Fri and Sat. Call *M&J Travel & Tours* (☎051/62.34 or 41.32) for bookings.

Windmill Bakery and Snack Bar, opposite *Barclays Bank*. Inexpensive Ghanaian and European fare including excellent cheese toasted sandwiches, real wholemeal bread and great almond cake.

Nightlife and entertainment

Keep your eyes and ears open for **live music** in Kumasi; shows take place irregularly at the main hotels. The *City Hotel*'s *Nsadwase Disco* (☎051/62.10), for example, has occasional bands, but the best bet for a musical night out in Kumasi is the *Old Timer's Club* at the *Kingsway* (☎051/24.41). Nearby is the *Sphynx* nightclub on Prempeh II Road, which also puts on bands occasionally. The Cultural Centre hosts programmes of music, dance, poetry and drama, as well as occasional **live concerts** – often of high-life – and less recreational **choral evenings** with church choirs. Check the centre's schedule of events.

Among the **clubs**, *Berkeley's* across from the railway station (the sign can be seen from the road, but you enter from a small street in back) is currently popular and they have a good restaurant where you can eat before dancing. The *Star Nightclub*, just west of the Stadium, the *Subin* on Okomfo Anokye Rd in New Tafo, *Hedonist*, Accra Rd near the University, and *Club 600*, on Mampong Rd near Kumasi Girl's Secondary School, are all worth following up by taxi if you're in the mood to move – though bear in mind that clubs in Kumasi open up and close down as often as in Accra.

On Sunday afternoons it's worth checking if there's a **soccer match** at the Sports Stadium. When the home team (**Kotoko**, meaning porcupine, the Asante symbol) plays it's wild: tickets are very inexpensive.

The two best **cinemas** are the *Rex* near the Prempeh Assembly Hall and the *Odeon* near the cultural centre. Others include the *Roxy* in Manhyia; the *Rivoli* in Bantama; the *Royal* in Asawasi; and the *Romeo* in New Tafo. The *British Council* is on Bank Rd (☎051/34.62).

KENTE CLOTH

Kente dates from the early days of the Asante empire. The dazzling patterns are intended to enhance their owners' status as kings, queens and nobles. Court designs took on the name of the clan or individuals by which they were commissioned (a common pattern known as *mamponhema*, for example, derives its name from the Queen of Mampong). *Asasia* designates a pattern and type of cloth worn only by the Asantehene. *Kente*, like most African cloth, is woven in narrow strips, later sewn together. The highest quality pieces are made entirely of silk threads, which in former times were unavailable to the Asante. To satisfy the demands of royalty, the craftsmen therefore unravelled imported silk fabric and rewove the threads into *kente* patterns. In addition to the name denoting their owner, the most valuable cloths bore another name – *adweneasa* – a technical term indicating that the already complicated pattern contained an additional inlaid design. The word means "my skill is exhausted", indicating that the weaver had made his supreme effort.

Around Kumasi

Venturing into the rainforest hills around Kumasi, numerous villages offer a less urbanized glimpse of Asante lifestyles. Many villages – **Bonwire** to the northwest and **Pankrona**, **Ahwiaa** and **Ntonso** along the road to Mampong – are known for the **traditional crafts** industries for which the entire region is famous, and best treated as day trips. You may want to spend a night in the resthouse at the **Boabeng–Fiema Monkey Sanctuary** to the north, a hundred kilometres or so from Kumasi. **Lake Bosumtwi**, too, has a well-cared-for resthouse near the pretty shore, and makes a good retreat. If you have your own transport, even a bicycle, **the road past Mampong** to the shore of Lake Volta – once the main route through Ghana, but now very much a back road – offers some exciting travel. A more obvious excursion, though one that is seldom embarked on, is a visit to the **goldfields**.

Obuasi gold mines

The gold mines at **OBUASI**, 70km southwest of Kumasi, are a relatively easy trip from the city. The Obuasi district is interesting but not a scenic place to visit: the whole area is scarred into a lunar landscape by the open mining pits, while the toxic drainage ponds add an alarming note to what's already a rather depressing landscape.

On Thursdays and Fridays it is possible to see gold being smelted and on Sundays and Tuesdays you can go underground and witness the mining itself. Tours of the surface works, conducted at present free of charge, are enjoyably informative (call the head of public relations on ☎0582/494 to arrange one). Only those who can demonstrate commercial or technical interest will be escorted underground, however. Obuasi is full of English and Italian expat technicians and managers who may be able to advise on accommodation if you want to stay. There are one or two basic **hotels** – and if you're here for the night you might want to visit the flashy *Confidence Disco*.

Bonwire

A frequent target for tourists, **BONWIRE** is a traditional Asante village and principal home of the famous **kente cloth**. Along the streets in town you can still see weavers working hand-operated looms to turn out the long strips of intricately patterned material. *Kente* is still the usual dress of Asante people on special occasions and great significance is placed on the cloth which, because of its importance and its complex design, is very expensive – especially here. Bonwire is just over 20km from Kumasi, southeast of Ntonso on the road to Effiduasi. **Taxis** go to the town regularly from the Kejetia motor park. The quickest route if you're getting there under your own steam is down the Accra road, then turn left near Kumasi airstrip.

Boabeng–Fiema Monkey Sanctuary

An increasingly popular target, about 100km north of Kumasi, 22km north of Nkoransa off the Wa road, is the **Boabeng-Fiema Monkey Sanctuary** – a remarkably successful experiment in community conservation. The villagers of Boabeng and Fiema have a traditional veneraation for the large numbers of monkeys living in the small patch of forest nearby. The **sacred grove**, just 4.5 square kilometres, has been set aside under their guardianship and they run the guesthouse (①) as well as keeping an eye on the primates. The forest has one of the highest densities of monkeys of any forest in West Africa and inhabitants include **Lowe's mona monkey** and the strikingly beautiful **black and white colobus**. There's a threat hanging over the reserve, however, from the rapidly increasing human population and the ravages of dry season bush fires. It all comes down to the number of visitors coming: if it makes economic sense to local people (a trust fund for entrance fees and overnight charges has recently been set up), they'll continue to support it.

Lake Bosumtwi

Only 27km south of Kumasi, **Lake Bosumtwi** fills a crater surrounded by steep hills that rise nearly 400m above sea level. With a diameter of 8km, this is the largest natural lake in Ghana. You can get here by taking a Benz **bus** or **tro-tro** from the Asafo lorry park to the town of Kuntansi (a half-hour drive that costs almost nothing); from there you can either catch another vehicle (expect a long wait) or walk the remaining 5km to the village of Abono on the lakeshore, via the resthouse which overlooks it.

The lake itself lies in the midst of lush greenery, a superbly relaxing scene in which to unwind. Traditional boats are still used to fish the lake, propelled by fishermen with calabashes cupped in their hands to serve as paddles. Formerly, the spirit of the lake forbade other forms of transport but, as one villager commented, "people used to be scared, but we don't believe in that nowadays." Clearly not, because expats and rich kids from Kumasi come to water-ski and there are now motor boats buzzing over the lake. Boat trips for an hour or so cost around ₵10,000. Swimming, in the bilharzia-free waters, is fine.

The **resthouse** (②) offers fantastic views of the natural setting; unfortunately the management is less welcoming. To stay here, you have to book beforehand at the regional tourist office in Kumasi (in the grounds of the National Cultural Centre; ☎051/26.33). Another hotel, dating from 1975, was never finished and is now in ruins, though it's still possible to sit on the terrace, or camp in the vicinity.

Along the Mampong road

Within a short distance of Kumasi, the small towns along the Mampong road – which is in excellent condition – have developed reputations for artwork and handicrafts. The first you come to is **PANKRONA** (5km from Kumasi), a village known for its **pottery**, traditionally produced by the women. All kinds of clay objects, from water jugs to characteristic Asante *fufu* bowls, are piled high in front of the homes and sold at prices that are rather inflated compared with those in Kumasi.

The next stop along the road is the town of **AHWIAA**, which specializes in **wood carvings**. Numerous shops along the main road sell tables, statues and games, but the **carved stools** you'll see craftsmen sculpting in open-air workshops along the street stand out among the wares. Throughout Ghana, such stools were not merely for decoration, but were considered prime necessities. Commonly the first gift a father would give to his child was a stool, which his soul was believed to occupy until death. To this day, stools still represent one of the most important elements of a chief's regalia and symbolize his office. When he dies, a chief's stool is blackened with ash and smeared with the yolk of an egg, and this **black stool** is preserved in a special house in memory of the late owner. "Enstoolment" and "destooling" are terms often seen in Ghanaian newspapers.

The stools carved in Ahwiaa today are mostly made with an eye for tourism, and you may not admire the lacquers and shoe-polish dyes that give them a tawdry finish. Nonetheless, they contain many intricate **traditional symbols** (the carvers can explain what they mean), and there's no cause for complaint about the quality of craftsmanship. They're expensive, a result of the time involved in making them and the high demand from tourists, among whom they're extremely popular despite their weight. Ask about the types of wood used. It's worth avoiding the more expensive hardwoods – not just for the sake of the forests, but because softer wood is lighter and cheaper.

Further down the Mampong road, **NTONSO** is the famed home of **adinkra cloth**. Not quite as prestigious as *kente*, it's made of cotton material (often a deep red colour) covered with black patterns. These are produced with stamps carved from bits of calabash and dipped in a tree-bark dye. Craftsmen use a variety of such stamps, some with geometric patterns, others with stylized representations of plants or animals, but most with symbols reflecting an Asante saying. A cloth incorporating all such symbols in its pattern was known as the **Adinkrahene** and was reserved for the Asante king, but it wasn't uncommon for the ruler to wear a cloth marked by a single symbol that reflected a specific message he wanted to convey to the people. Today, you still see these cloths being worn toga-fashion throughout the Asante country, notably at funerals and on other important occasions. Unfortunately you'll be pestered to death in Ntonso. Weavers will speed up their work as you approach to give a better impression and teenagers hassle you to buy cloth at enormous prices.

Mampong and northeast to Lake Volta

MAMPONG itself is surprisingly large and busy, perched on the lip of the impressive **Mampong escarpment**. There's a number of places to stay, but a good choice is the *Midway Hotel*, a clean and welcoming place on the outskirts of town (①). Beyond Mampong, the road north curls down through formidable forest to the deep valley of the Afram River and then steeply, in a series of hairpins, up the other side to **Ejura**. The scenic beauty of this road is matched by the pleasure of being relatively off the beaten track. **Atebubu**, the next settlement, is a small, smoky town at the savannah's edge. Beyond, there's only the villages of **Prang** – which on this road, once tarred, now ragged asphalt and dirt, could hardly have a more appropriate name – and then **Yeji**, on the bleak Volta shore, where unpredictable small boats make the crossing to **Makongo**, 150km short of Tamale.

NTONSO DYE STAMPS

Nyame biribi wo soro na ma embeka mensa: "God, there is something in the sky, let me reach it"

Gye Nyame: "We have nothing to fear but God"

Dwonnin ye asise a ode n'akorana na ennye ne mben: "The heart, not the horns, leads a ram to bully"

THE EAST: AKOSOMBO, HO AND HOHOE

Eastern Ghana is home of the **Ewe**, who have traditionally been farming and fishing people. Formerly part of German Togoland, the region has periodically provided a bone of contention between the governments of Ghana and Togo and those who favour the reunification of the Ewe, who also live in Togo. The **Ewe people** are primarily involved in maize and yam farming, with cocoa plantations adding a further cash crop stimulus to the region. The administrative capital is at **Ho**, a large town in the middle of an agricultural area rich with cocoa plantations. The Akwampim mountains add to the beauty of the fertile landscapes, but the outstanding geographical feature of these parts is artificial – the vast body of **Lake Volta**, created when the ambitious dam and hydro-electric plant was built at **Akosombo** in the mid-1960s.

This region provides an interesting alternative **route to northern Ghana**, either through the remote eastern border region via **Hohoe** or straight across the great lake to Tamale Port by ferry. The forest and hills – Ghana's highest – are rapidly becoming a major draw for travellers, though transport and facilities are limited.

Akosombo

Besides generating much-needed foreign exchange for Ghana, the giant **Akosombo Dam** was also responsible for **Lake Volta**, the largest artificial lake in the world. Nkrumah's pet hydro-electric project at the once insignificant village of **AKOSOMBO** provides electricity for the greater part of Ghana (a large proportion of which goes to the Valco aluminium smelter at Tema), with some left for export to neighbouring countries. Amid the landscape of hills and water, the general interest lies more in the **scenic beauty** – and it is beautiful – than in the traditional lifestyle of the people here, who are a broadly cosmopolitan mix of employees from all over Ghana.

Note that both the Akosombo Dam and the Atimpoku Bridge are considered strategic installations and it is therefore technically illegal to photograph them. Now that tours are available of the site, so many people have done so, however, that few officials seem concerned any more.

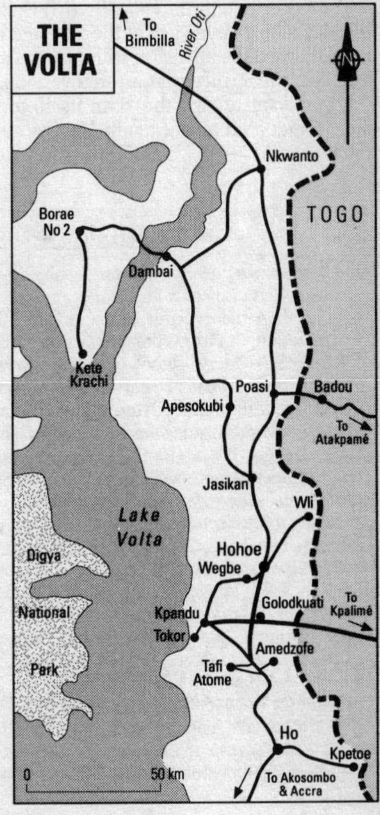

Atimpoku district

Akosombo's **lorry park** is 5km south of the town in the district of **Atimpoku**, a quiet locality on the main Accra road in the shadow of the large bridge spanning the **Volta River**. Taxis run regularly from here (or walk up the road to the fire station and get a lift) to the lower part of Akosombo town proper. Most of the **cheap accommodation**, however, is here in Atimpoku. Near the motor park, the *Benkum* is a basic hotel with the town's least expensive accommodation (①). The *Lakeside Motel* (☎0251/310) is an out- of-the-way though pleasant and slightly upmarket place just south of Atimpoku (②). **Street food** abounds: oyster kebabs and smoked shrimp to go with *abolo*, the slightly sugary, but not unpleasant, dumpling commonly eaten in the region. Across from the motor park, the *Royal Spot* chop bar and the *Delta Queen* serve inexpensive *fufu* and palm nut soup along with cold drinks.

Akosombo town

Akosombo proper consists of two communities, both of which emerged in the 1960s when workers flooded here to fill demand for labour. The first perches on a hillside, whence it commands a magnificent **view of Lake Volta** and the mountains around. The spot was too scenic to resist putting in a tourist hotel, yacht club and public **swimming pool** among the luxurious expat and executive villas. The second community, in the valley below, is a working-class neighbourhood for employees of the Volta Power Authority – no hotel, but there is a **community centre** with library, bar and the *Dam Video Theatre*. Buses run between the two districts during daylight hours.

The government-run *Volta Hotel* (PO Box 25; ☎0251/753) is ideally situated on the hill with a bird's-eye view of the lake and dam. Following recent renovations, it is now quite showy and expensive, with modern and comfortable AC rooms (④). At least have a drink in the terrace **restaurant** overlooking the lake – the views are terrific.

If you want to visit **the dam** itself, for which you need authorization, you're only likely to get a lift at weekends. Hang around at the site office down the road from the hotel.

CROSSING LAKE VOLTA

Lake transport has been unpredictable for years. This deters many travellers, but while it's true that transport is erratic and timetables unreliable (there are generally less options than theoretically available), it's also true that the trip is highly enjoyable. If you're setting out from Akosombo, there'll usually be some kind of vessel in a day or two.

The official **ferry** is the *Akosombo Queen*, which plies betwen **Akosombo** and **Kete Krachi** once a week. Departures from Akosombo have in recent years been Tuesday mornings, with arrival at Kete Krachi around twelve hours later; meals are available on board. Midweek, the vessel runs a shuttle between Kete Krachi and Kpandu. Unfortunately, it's often out of commission. Note that the ferry dock in Ketekrachi is a ten- to fifteen-minute walk from the centre of this isolated town: there is *nothing* at the dock itself in the way of services or food.

When the passenger ferry isn't running, **cargo barges** – the *Yapei Queen*, *Yeji Queen*, the excellent *Volta Queen*, and the even more modern *Buipe Queen* – also make the trip, but rarely run on fixed schedules. They sometimes go as far upriver as **Yapei** (Tamale Port) on the White Volta's course to the north, but this port is sometimes out of reach at the end of the dry season, in which case the port of **Buipe**, on the course of the Black Volta further to the west, is used as the northern terminus. En route there are usually stops at **Kpandu**, **Kete Krachi** and **Yeji**. The voyage to Yapei or Buipe takes between one and two days (and nights) and you sleep on the deck. Normally, you should stock up on **food** for the trip: water and cooking facilities are provided.

For all details, enquire at the *Volta Hotel* on arrival or make advance contact with the *Volta Lake Transport Company* in the *Ghana Commercial Bank* building in Akosombo (PO Box 75, Akosombo; ☎0251/686 ext. 204).

Ho and around

Despite its prestigious designation as the Volta Region's capital, **HO**, 50km northeast of Akosombo, remains a quiet, rural community. Set in a green valley dominated by **Mount Adaklu**, Ho is graced with a tidy tracing of narrow paved roads winding through the trees, a large hospital and banks, and even an interesting **regional museum** – some surprise in a rather remote corner like this.

Accommodation

Ho has a good choice of inexpensive **accommodation**, though little to tempt you upmarket.

Alinda Guesthouse, near the museum. Basic inexpensive accommodation. Clean and popular with travellers, it also has a decent bar and restaurant. ①.

EP Church Social Centre, 1km from the centre at the church headquarters. Very clean and inexpensive S/C rooms, or dormitory space for next to nothing. ①.

Fiave Lodge, near the central market. Clean and quiet, an intimate retreat with a friendly management. ②.

Freedom Hotel, on the main street. New hotel with good facilities. Something of a social focus, so often noisy. ②–③.

Hek Lodge, near the *STC* yard. Large rooms and basic facilities. ①.

Tarso Hotel, up the main street from the *Ghana Commercial Bank*. Recently upgraded, the hotel has pleasant and relatively inexpensive accommodation plus a popular bar. ②.

Woezor Hotel, west of the town centre (PO Box 339; ☎091/534 or 550 or 551). The town's most expensive accommodation with bar and restaurant. New "chalets" or less expensive rooms in the older and shabbier main block. ③.

YMCA, in the town centre, just north of the cathedral. The cheapest singles in town, but for men only. ①.

The Town

The road leading from Aflao, on the coastal border with Togo, constitutes the main street in town. It heads from the *Texaco* and *BP* filling stations in the south, past the regional police office, on to the **central market** and out to the main **lorry park** on the north side of town. Main **banks** are on this street but there are no forex bureaux. Changing cash or travellers' cheques is possible here but it takes ages while they phone to Accra for current rates.

Along this same road, you'll find a large roundabout near the **post office**. The road leading off west from here runs down to the hospital, behind which are the grounds of the **Volta Regional Museum** (daily except Mon 8am–6pm). Well presented and little frequented, the museum is worth a visit to see exhibits of ceremonial objects (Akan "spokesmen" staffs and swords), traditional **musical instruments,** and carved **stools** from various regions. **Colonial relics** complement the ethnic displays, including some dating to the district's German Togoland period.

Eating and entertainment

Street food is readily available near the main lorry park: a traditional Ewe dish is cat, often advertised rather graphically. For something more conventional, try the *Doris Day Restaurant* on Housing Road. In the evenings several places show **videos**, notably *Foxtrot Video Theatre* along the main drag.

North of Ho: Amedzofe, Tafi Atome, Logba Tota and Liati Wote

In addition to the verdant slopes of some of Ghana's highest hills, the road north towards Hohoe passes traditional Ewe cemeteries shaded by groves of white, pink and

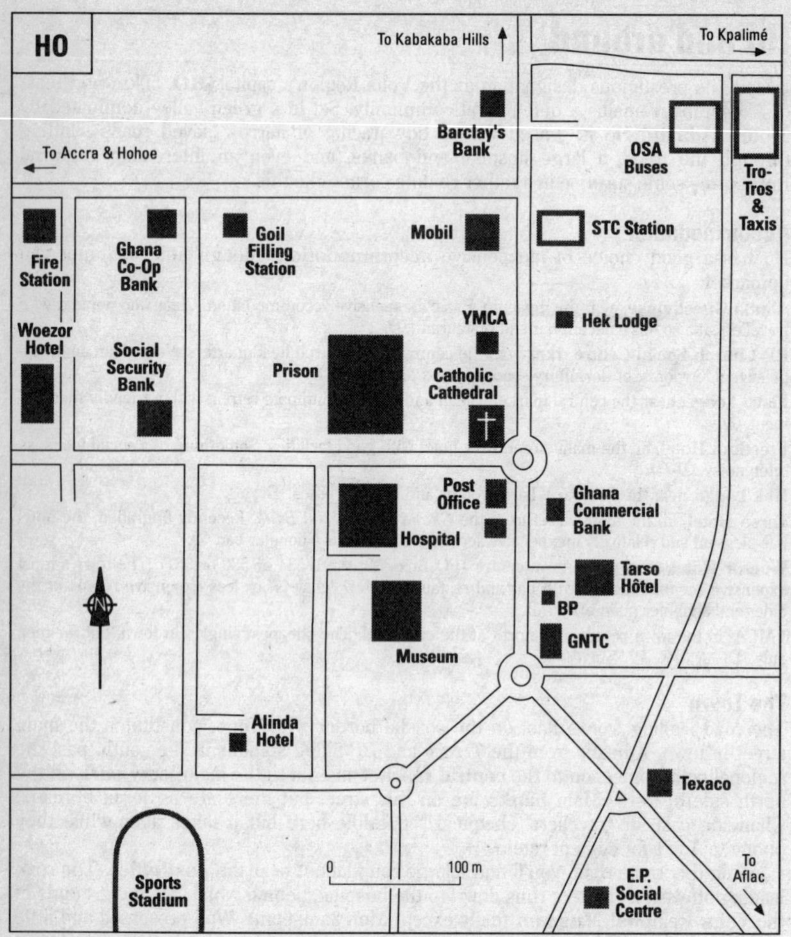

yellow frangipani. However, explorations off the main road are limited if you don't have your own transport.

Relatively easy to get to by public transport is the village of **Amedzofe**, 30km north of Ho and just east of the road at the base of **Mount Gemi**. A visit to the chief is appropriate, and a bottle of schnapps, or a small dash, very much expected. He'll fix you up with a guide to seek out the village's namesake **waterfall**, difficult to find on your own and accessible by an almost vertical leaf-strewn path. At the summit of Mount Gemi you'll find a tall iron cross erected by German missionaries in the 1930s, but more striking are the vistas stretching in every direction. From up here, the Volta stands out shimmering beyond the Biakpa hills. There's a modest **government resthouse** in Amedzofe with sporadic electricity and water provided by an outside tap. The lack of comfort is more than compensated for by the lush setting and views (①).

From the main road, you could alternatively branch westward, 25km north of Ho, towards **Tafi Atome**, a town known as a refuge for various species of **monkeys**, including the rare Mona. In the morning, they romp unhindered through the streets and courtyards looking for scraps. Later in the day, they retreat to the surrounding bush and you'll have to rely on a guide to find them.

Continuing towards Hohoe, another branch road leads west up a steep mountain road towards **Logba Tota**. The twisting hairpins make for slow driving and captivating views of the wooded valleys and Mount Gemi. Arriving at Logba Tota (500m above sea level), you'll be escorted to the district assemblyman, who is enthusiastic about visitors and about launching a small tourist centre, plans for which are already under way. Signing the guest book seems compulsory as does a guide to lead you on the 45-minute trek to the nearby **waterfall** that cascades off a vertical cliff seamed with small caves and jutting overhangs. After wading through the pool at the base, the guide will take you up a slippery ledge to the highly overrated **"town cave"**. Tiny and insignificant, with one or two limestone formations, a high chimney and a colony of bats, the cavern fails to live up to the hype the villagers give it, but the surrounding views take the edge off any disappointment.

Further north, a branch road at the Golokuati police post leads to the village of **Liati Wote** near the base of Ghana's highest peak, **Mount Afadjato** (968m), a few kilometres east of Hohoe. Residents in town will find you a guide to seek out the main village attraction, the **Tagbo Falls**. It's an easy one-hour walk through dense bush full of bright flowers and butterflies, and fields of cocoa and coffee. The falls themselves appear without warning as they flow off an almost circular cliff formation covered with moss and ferns into a pool. The resthouse in Liati Wote is now a private residence, but **accommodation** is easy to arrange with the villagers and there's always the possibility of a warm beer at *Stella's Inn*.

Hohoe and around

A town of few sights of specific interest, **HOHOE** is busier than Ho and has a number of hotels and banks, as well as a forex bureau near the post office. As a base for treks to nearby waterfalls, or as a stopping point on the eastern route to the north, it is both convenient and restful.

Accommodation

Hohoe has a number of reasonable places to stay, and your main consideration is simply one of expense.

African Unity Hotel, near the post office. Central yet quietly situated with inexpensive if slightly dingy accommodation. ①.

Grand Hotel, on the main street, opposite the *Bank of Ghana*. Very central with bright rooms and a courtyard bar. ①.

Matvin Hotel, Jasikan Rd, fifteen minutes' walk from the post office (PO Box 397; ☎091/134). Upmarket place with rooms in various categories ranging from AC chalets equipped with fridges and TV to rooms with fans and shared facilities. The good restaurant and bar have some fine views over the Danyi River. ③.

Pacific Guest House, on the south side of town, signposted off the Ho road 300m south of the post office. The nicest place to stay in Hohoe, quiet and clean with restaurant and bar. ②.

MOVING ON FROM HOHOE

The main motor park is south of the centre on the Ho road. Vehicles leave daily for points north (Kadjebi, Nkwanta and **Bimbilla**) as well as for **Ho** and **Accra**. Bush taxis also go direct to Kpalimé in **Togo**. Besides the *STC* bus that leaves daily at 4am from in front of the *Central Hotel* **to Accra**, there is a private bus that leaves from a point near the *Mobil* station at 9am.

Eating

For cheap **eating**, the area around the post office abounds with street stalls. Near the *Grand Hotel*, the *Eagle Canteen* does good and inexpensive Ghanaian dishes like *fufu* with palm nut soup. Also good is the *Winatrip* bar, a few minutes' walk from the post office, near the *Glamow* department store. Slightly upscale is the *Maryland Restaurant*, past the *Grand* as you head towards the *Matvin*. In the evening, try the ultraviolet lights and grassy lawn at the *Prestige Terrace Bar*, or seek out the *Tanoa Gardens,* off the main road near *Ghana Commercial Bank,* which has music and better food.

Wli Falls and on to Togo

The most obvious target for sightseeing around Hohoe are the **Wli Falls**, 20km to the east. *Tro-tros* are relatively frequent from the Hohoe motor park to the village of Wli which nestles at the foot of the hills forming the Togolese border. You'll be shown to the Game & Wildlife office to pay a ₵500 fee and be assigned a largely unnecessary guide. The path to the falls crosses and re-crosses a winding brook over eleven log bridges. Set in a coomb among thousands of nesting bats, the cascade plunges thirty metres into a pool just deep enough for swimming.

If you've got the gear, you can **camp** by the falls, where the tranquillity will only be disturbed by kids shooting the bats with homemade flintlocks and locally manufactured shot. If you want to try the local bat, they'll gladly sell you their catch, and even cook it up for you.

To continue **to Togo**, Ghana border formalities are casually carried out at the eastern end of Wli. From there, you must walk the half-kilometre to **Yipa-Dafo** for the Togo crossing. Transport onwards from here heads either to Dzobégan or Kpalimé, both routes tracing the scenic curves of the Danyi plateau.

West of Hohoe

Off the Kpandu road, 10km west of Hohoe, the **Tsatsudo Falls** provide another opportunity for exploration. Stop at the village of Alavanyo Abehenease and pick up a guide there. **Ferries** theoretically leave **Kpandu** Wednesdays and Fridays at 3pm to arrive in Kete Krachi six hours later. Check schedules as they are notoriously unreliable (see p.818).

The route north and Bimbilla

As the route towards Tamale continues north, cultivation declines and the road narrows noticeably. Between Jasikan and Poasi, it deteriorates into deep ruts and channels dug out by the overloaded yam lorries that ply the route. Arriving at Nkwanto, you can either continue north over the flat open landscapes that lead directly to Bimbilla, or you can branch left towards Dambai, to catch a fifteen-minute ferry across the lake. Boats leave several times daily.

BIMBILLA provides a convenient place to break up the long trip from Hohoe to Tamale. **Accommodation** can be found here at the basic *31st December Women's Movement Guest House* on Salaga Road in the town centre (①). Though there's no electricity, it's a comfortable and welcoming place. If it's full, they'll direct you to the *Teacher's Hostel* on the Yendi Road (①). For **food**, the *Kotoko Bar* near the old market is a good place to head for filling rice and meat dishes during the day, or grab a bite

MOVING ON FROM BIMBILLA

Buses leave for **Kete Krachi** (linked by ferry to Akosombo) Mon, Wed and Fri between noon and 3pm. Daily buses to **Tamale** leave between 5 and 6am or you can try to catch a seat on the Wulensi bus which passes through Bimbilla around 9am. The daily bus to **Accra** via Hohoe leaves at 11am and arrives in the late evening.

with the regulars at the *Pito Bar* near the clinic. The town's best address for a cold drink is the *Work and Happiness Bar*.

Bimbilla was where the **Konkomba-Nunumba "war"** started in 1994, sparked by an argument over a chicken. This was an outbreak of ethnic violence between local Nunumbas and Konkombas over land rights. The clashes took the lives of several thousand people, orphaned hundreds of children and cost billions of cedis in homes and businesses destroyed (see p.777).

NORTHERN GHANA

Coming either from the coast and Kumasi, or up the country's eastern fringe, you'll be struck by the changing landscape, as the central forests give way to arid, low-lying **grasslands**. Due to the harsher, unpredictable climate and the effects, to this day, of the slave trade (from which the inhabitants of the open plains and plateaux lacked natural protection), the region is sparsely populated, characterized by traditional **compound agriculture**. The few urban centres like **Tamale** or **Bolgatanga** seem more subdued than their counterparts to the south.

The main peoples of the north include the More-speaking **Dagomba**, with their capital at Yendi, and the **Mamprusi** people, based around Nalerigu. The **Gonja**, with their capital at Damongo, are an interesting ethnic group, formed partly of the remnants of sixteenth- and seventeenth-century Mande-speaking migrant invaders from Songhai in the north, and partly of local Voltaic-speaking peoples. As a result, the Gonja, who are mostly Muslim, speak different languages according to their class – the nobles using a dialect of Akan known as Guang, and the commoners speaking Wagala. **Sudanic influences** have been important in this region, reflected in architecture, customs and dress – *boubous* for the men and long veils for women, draped over their heads. In short, the north is a completely different world and, with the exception of the popular **Mole Game Reserve** – easily visited and well set up for inexpensive stays – a region where you're unlikely to run into throngs of fellow travellers.

Tamale

Capital of the **Northern Region**, **TAMALE** is a large commercial town and junction of the main roads leading from Burkina Faso in the north, Togo in the east and Accra and Kumasi in the south. Despite its size and importance, it lacks the slightest cosmopolitan spark, and you're not going to want to spend an inordinate amount of time here. Still, if you are stopping over en route to other destinations, you'll find a reasonable number of hotels and diversions. Note that the water is a constant problem in Tamale, with the taps often dry.

The **Ghana Tourist Board** may by now have opened their regional office in Tamale. It's something to keep a look out for as they envisage excursions to the Mole Game Reserve and around the region. Ask at the *STC* yard when you arrive to see what progress there has been.

Accommodation

Accommodation in Tamale tends to be basic. Some places run to S/C rooms with AC, but problems with running water are perennial.

Al Hassan Hotel, across from *Ghana Commercial Bank* (PO Box 73; ☎071/28.34). Balconied rooms, with or without showers, around a central courtyard. None too clean (especially in the shared showers) and rarely quiet. Its proximity to the motor park, plus the restaurant and video theatre, make it a bit of a caravanserai where you might run into other travellers. ①.

Atta Essibi Hotel, St Charles Seminary Rd (☎071/25.64). Reasonable if dingy rooms, some S/C, on the southern fringes of town. ①.

Catering Resthouse, off Residency Rd, 1km from centre (☎071/29.78). An older place that gets very varied reports. The restaurant, however, is still decent. ②.

Catholic Guest House, Bolgatanga road near the Agricultural Turning Point. Breakfast is included in the price of the S/C rooms in a garden setting. Very popular and often full. ②.

Christian Services Guest House, near the Agricultural Turning Point. Doubles with fans are more basic than at the *Catholic Guest House*, but it's cheaper here and the staff are friendly. ①.

Inter Royals Hotel, Kalpuni Estates (☎071/22.47). Not well kept, but rooms, some with AC, are inexpensive and there's an in-house restaurant and disco. ②.

Las Hotel, Hospital Rd (☎071/22.17). Comfortable S/C rooms with fans, plus a very popular bar and nightclub. A lively town meeting place worth a visit even if you don't stay here. ①.

Picorna Hotel (PO Box 1212; ☎071/26.72 or 20.70). Perhaps the best of the lot with S/C, AC rooms and a nice garden. ③.

The Town

The centre of town wraps around the **motor park** and *STC* station, easily recognized by the towering telephone transmitter which juts up next to it and can be seen from almost anywhere in town. The **central market** (good for locally woven cloth) and major **banks** are an easy walk away. Next to the market is a shaded **public garden** that makes a good place to read the *Daily Graphic* (usually a day or so late in these northern parts) or watch the adept draughts players who gather here daily for lightning-quick tournaments. A paved road leading out from the west of the market heads down past the *Social Security Bank* and a small market before arriving at a large **classified forest** – a rather unusual thing to find in the middle of an important administrative town. The shade of the teak trees makes for an excellent place to retreat from the afternoon heat, which reaches oppressive levels on the exposed avenues downtown.

The **National Cultural Centre**, near the central market, off the Yeji road, is in a horrific state of repair, but holds sporadic performances of **regional music and dance**; in the afternoons, you can sometimes catch a rehearsal. If nothing's going on, there are good leather stalls opposite. (Don't confuse the centre with the Tamale Institute for Trascultural Studies – where the man in charge is a mine of information on northern culture and society.) You can watch some excellent **football** on Sunday afternoons, when major Ghanaian teams play at the main stadium on Catering Rest House (CRH) Road.

It's possible to rent a **bicycle** in town (hotels seem able to help) and take it up to Education Ridge, off the northwesterly road out of town. There's a fine ride commencing behind the Polytechnic and running for about 8km through lovely villages, coming back the same way. If you need to cool down afterwards, check out the **swimming pool** at Kamina barracks (small entrance fee), about 3km out of town on the Bolgatanga road.

Eating and nightlife

There are plenty of **places to eat** in Tamale, including the hotel restaurants. All around the *Goil* station after about 6pm there's a mass of street food, especially guinea fowl. For something a little more formal, *Sparkles Restaurant* does a good chicken curry with rice and has really good salads. The *Cowrie Restaurant* (Kalpuni Estates) is another popular and straightforward spot for European and Ghanaian food, while *Vida's* and, especially, *Swingers* both do good chop. But the best place at the moment is the *Picorna* which serves great kebabs and has a popular **disco**.

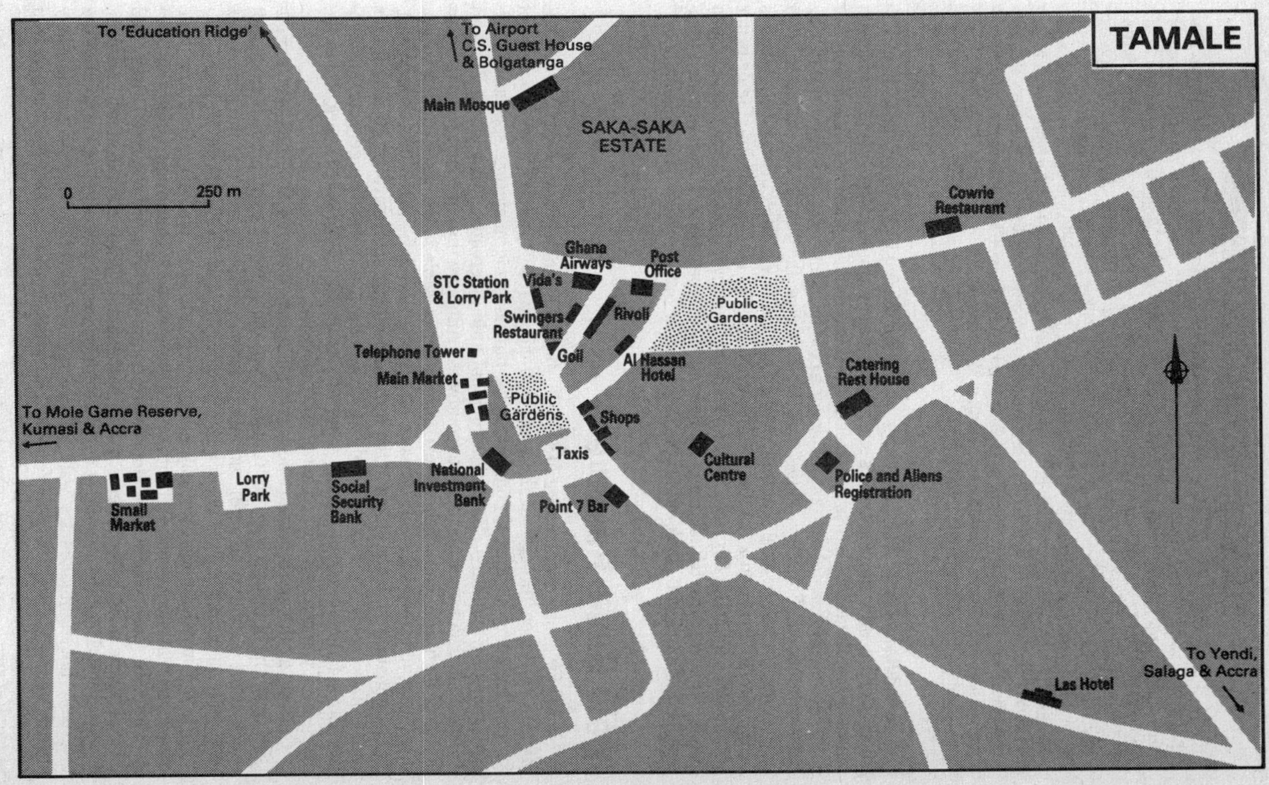
TAMALE
To 'Education Ridge'
To Airport
C.S. Guest House
& Bolgatanga
Main Mosque
SAKA-SAKA
ESTATE
0
250 m
Cowrie
Restaurant
Ghana
Airways
Post
Office
STC Station
& Lorry Park
Vida's
Swingers
Restaurant
Rivoli
Public
Gardens
Telephone Tower
Goil
Al Hassan
Hotel
Main Market
Public
Gardens
Catering
Rest House
To Mole Game Reserve,
Kumasi & Accra
Shops
Taxis
Cultural
Centre
Police and Aliens
Registration
National
Investment
Bank
Point 7 Bar
Small
Market
Lorry
Park
Social
Security
Bank
To Yendi,
Salaga & Accra
Las Hotel

MOVING ON FROM TAMALE

As the north's major city, Tamale is the springboard for **Burkina Faso** via **Bolgatanga**, though the road north is in very bad shape. Heading south, the road is paved to **Kumasi and Accra**, and passes through **Yapei** where you cross Lake Volta. On the west side of the lake the Accra highway splits from the road going west to **Sawla** in **western Ghana** via **Damongo**, which is the point of entry to **Mole Game Reserve**. *STC* and *OSA* **buses** head in all these directions as do *tro-tros* and taxis. There are also two daily buses from Tamale southeast to **Bimbilla** where you can continue to Accra via eastern Ghana and **Hohoe**. Tamale also has a **ferry** link with Akosombo and the south. The boat leaves from Tamale Port (Yapei) to which there are buses from Tamale motor park. Full ferry details are given on p.818. Daily **flights** to Accra via Kumasi on *Ghana Airways* have been suspended, but there are, in theory, regular air force flights to Accra at 10am on Mon, Wed and Fri, bookable in town through *M&J Travel & Tours* (☎071/24.26 or 24.35).

The *Giddipass* **bar** is a large set-up with rooftop seating and a huge dance area. The music has recently stopped, but it's still a good place to come for an evening drink with views out on the town. Across the street, *Point 7* (with music) and the *Continental Bar* (opposite the *Al Hassan*) are reasonable for a cold beer and you can while away a pleasant few hours on "Education Ridge" (ask for Tamasco, the Tamale Secondary School) in the *Drop In* bar, or in any of the *pito* bars around town. The *Catering Rest House* is usually worth a visit on a Saturday night, when it quite often bursts into life or better yet, try the club at the *Las Hotel*. In the evenings, the *Rivoli Theatre* attracts a big crush to see dated **movies** (Hindi, Kung-fu, Rambo). It competes with a rash of **video** theatres throughout town – look out for the street-corner blackboard announcements.

Mole Game Reserve

Set in the savannah country west of Tamale, the 2000-square-kilometre **MOLE GAME RESERVE** (open throughout the year, entrance ₵1500) protects a wide variety of fauna – including elephants, lions, leopards, buffaloes and numerous species of antelope, monkeys and birds – in an environment little differentiated but for the Konkori escarpment, which runs northeast to southwest. Although the concentration of animals is not as high as in some other West African parks, Mole's striking advantage, if you don't have your own transport, is **ease of access**. Christmas is the best time to visit, when animals are most visible and the mosquitoes least oppressive (at other times it's vital to have repellent). From the lodgings inside the park, armed rangers run inexpensive foot safaris to track the game. A network of tracks crisscross the park and in the dry season, you can also cover a lot in an ordinary car.

Getting to the park couldn't be less complicated, since an *OSA* bus leaves regularly from the transport yard in **Tamale** (2pm daily except sometimes Sunday, but check at the station to be sure) and takes passengers all the way into the park, dropping them off at the motel. There's also a daily *City Express* bus **from Kumasi** (see p.813). If you're coming from any other direction, most obviously Bouna in Côte d'Ivoire or Wa, you can connect with one of these buses at **Damongo** (other transport is extremely rare), where they stop before continuing into the reserve. Drivers and buses stay the night in the reserve, and depart again for Tamale and Kumasi at 5–6am. If you want to leave the reserve at any other time, you'll have to get to **Larabanga** (an invariably hot eight-kilometre walk for which the rather beautiful old mosque only slightly compensates). From there a local lorry can get you to Damongo, where you should be able to pick up the Wa or Sawla bus on its way back to Tamale or, if you're heading to Wa or northern Côte d'Ivoire, find transport westwards easily enough.

Accommodation and other park practicalities

At the park's entrance, the *Mole Motel* perches on a bit of a hill dominating an artificial water hole where animals gather to drink in the dry season. **Accommodation** ranges from rooms in a bunkhouse or chalets (①), to a "VIP Lodge" (②). The twin-bed chalets are spacious and clean with large bathrooms and screened verandahs overlooking the water hole. Electricity and water are fairly reliable and the whole place is great value and includes a swimming pool. The motel has its own **restaurant**, but you have to order in advance for meals and there's little choice. If you're arriving by bus in the evening, eat before leaving or bring your own food: you won't get anything much until next morning's breakfast. The motel turns its electricity off from 11pm to 6am. If you have a tent, you can camp for next to nothing near the motel buildings, using the pool's toilet block and showers.

In addition to the motel, two **camps** may still be open (no provisions; bring your own bedding and food). **Lovi** is in the centre of the park about 30km from the motel and **Konkori** is in the northeast, near the scarp (both ①).

You need your own vehicle to get to the outlying camps. The only vehicles that can be easily rented at the park are the rangers' **bicycles** (₵1000 per day) which are only suitable for the ride to Larabanga.

Reservations can be made through the Senior Game Warden, Mole National Park, PO Box 8, Damongo, Northern Region (☎071/25.63), or through The Chief Game and Wildlife Officer, Dept of Game and Wildlife, PO Box M.239, Accra. In the dry season – especially during weekends or holidays – you should be sure to reserve in advance as accommodation is often booked out. During the rains, this doesn't seem to be much of a problem. It's always worth telephoning to see if it has recently rained: if it has you're not going to see many animals.

Game viewing

When you check in at the motel, book a ranger to wake you in the morning for a **walking safari**. They expect a reasonable dash (₵1500 per hour is the standard) and are generally quite helpful and know where to find what's around. Your chances of seeing **elephant**, **antelope** and **buffalo**, at dawn near the motel water hole, are relatively good.

To have any real chance of seeing other large animals, like **lions**, you'll need a vehicle. The motel claims to offer Land Rover rental, at reasonable rates, but they're normally broken down. In the absence of other transport, you might therefore try your luck with other park visitors. You're still recommended to take a ranger to help in the quest for animals.

Note that in the **wet season** animals are dispersed, the grass much thicker and you may not see any game at all.

Wa and the Upper West Region

Capital of the Upper West Region, **WA** is predominantly Muslim as the many **mosques** dotting the townscape attest. Although noticeably poorer than towns in the south, shortages of food and other goods no longer pose the problems they did a decade ago. The **market** near the lorry park is large and well supplied.

Wa is home of the **Wala** people who migrated from Mali. Upon arrival in Ghana, they chased the resident Lobi population to the west and converted the Dagarti inhabitants to Islam. The **traditional chief**, the Wa Na, still lives in a large white **palace** built in the Sudanese style. You can visit the palace (located behind the government transport yard), but if you do so you're expected to greet the Wa Na. Courtiers outside will arrange this; ask permission before taking photos. Apart from his ceremonial role, the Wa Na still adjudicates disputes between his subjects. The small Wa museum would be worth visiting if there was anything in it: it's just a shell.

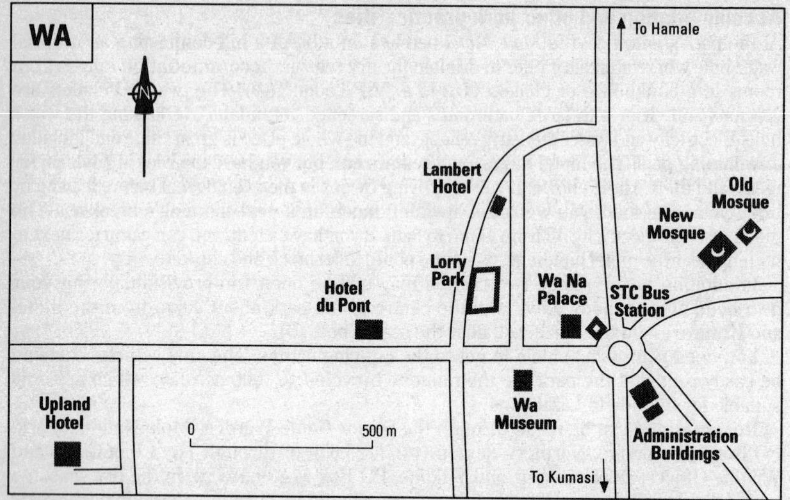

Besides local people, a number of office workers have come from outside to work in local administrative posts. Even so Wa feels remote from Accra, and even Tamale seems positively metropolitan in comparison.

Wa practicalities

The cheapest **place to stay** in town is the *Sawaba Guest House* – no electricity or water, but the plain rooms with lumpy mattresses are tidy, and they can help you get on the *STC* bus out of town again (①). Another recommended place is the *Hotel du Pont* at the west end of town, past the motor park on the road to Dorimon, with clean rooms, and a good bar with evening dancing. The restaurant does excellent fried chicken with jollof rice, and best of all, they have a laundry service (①). The *Upland Hotel* (☎180; ②–③) is the nicest in Wa and has a garden bar and restaurant, but it's way out of town.

The *Catering Rest House* no longer takes in travellers, but anyone can eat the traditional regional **food** in the dining room. Other than that, meals are pretty much limited to the many **chop bars** located around the market and transport park. Cold beers can be had at the *Meet Me There*.

If you are interested in working and staying in a development context, then contact the **Suntaa-Nuntaa project**. Located near the *Upland Hotel*, this is a tree-planting initiative, aiming to provide local women with the means to obtain regular supplies of fruit and fuel wood. Up to half a dozen overseas volunteers stay each year to help out and involve themselves in local life: you'll be expected to make a modest contribution to your keep. The address is given in *Basics*, p.8.

STC **buses** leave for Tamale twice daily, Kumasi daily, Tumu daily, Hamale via Lawra twice daily, and three times a week for Bolgatanga.

Around Wa

North of Wa, the crossroads town of **Tumu** has a couple of **places to stay**, the *Kunateh Hotel* in town (①) and the very inexpensive and rudimentary *Lim's Hotel* at Stadium Rd (①), and a few chop stalls near the bus stop. Otherwise there's little here of note, apart from a profusion of silk-cotton trees. Market cycles are mostly six days in this region – Tumu's market is held on the first day of the cycle. You can usually find transport across the border to the Burkina Faso town of **Léo**, but except on market days there's virtually no transport from here to Hamale.

Lawra, 80km north of Wa on the road to Hamale, is well known locally for its **musical instruments**, notably balafons. Lawra also hosts the culmination of the important northern harvest festival of **Kobina**, now a nationally televised event, which usually takes place in mid-October. Dancing and percussion teams come from throughout the north to take part. **Accommodation** is available at the *Catering Guest House* (①) or the *District Assembly Guest House* which is rarely used despite the running water in the bathrooms and periodic electricity (①).

Nandom, 25km north of Lawra, boasts the biggest church in the Upper West, and an animated Sunday market. There's a new **motel** adjacent to the hospital 1km south of the town, with basic, but clean rooms (①).

Hamale, in Ghana's far northwest corner, 35km north of Lawra, is a regular crossing point for Burkina and has a couple of places to stay. The one near the petrol station offers occasional highlife bands. Hamale's market is held on the second day of the six-day cycle. It's easy to visit Burkina briefly, whether you have your passport or not (much less your visa): Ghanaian and Burkinabe officials are unlikely to mind if you want to pop across the border for a few hours. There's a direct *STC* bus from Hamale to Accra on Fridays at 4.30pm.

On the Kumasi road **south of Wa**, there are interesting mosques at **Sawla**, **Maluwe**, and especially at **Bole** and **Banda Nkwanta** (one of the oldest in the district). They all date from the sixteenth-century Gonja conquest.

Navrongo and around

Coming south from Ouagadougou on the main highway, **NAVRONGO** is the first Ghanaian town. In the middle of a vast but undeveloped **agricultural region** (where crops include rice, millet and yams), it has a distinctive rural flavour. This is the second town of the Upper East region (Bolgatanga being the first). The people here are mostly **Kassena** farmers, part of the Gourounsi group of closely related language speakers.

Navrongo enjoys a reputation in the north as a centre of education because of its large secondary school. It was also one of the first towns in the region to have a church built, in around 1920. This, now a **cathedral**, was done in the traditional style with *banco*, and the interior decorations reflect regional art and cultural values. Today it's one of the few "sights" in town and definitely worth a visit, Sundays especially.

Navrongo nearly received a major commercial boost when construction began on a resplendent **"cultural centre"**, complete with cinema, hotel and Olympic-size pool. That was in 1975 when Acheampong was president. Subsequent governments decided the project was not a priority for national development, and for over twenty years the building has remained an unfinished cement carcase. Rumour has it that a scaled-down version of the centre has been approved and that work will start again. In the meantime, Navrongo remains a dusty farmers' town largely overshadowed by Bolgatanga to the south.

Navrongo practicalities

Navrongo still has very limited facilities, which make it less convenient as a stopping point than Bolgatanga, but the *Catholic Social Centre* does have good clean **rooms**. It's about 300m behind the market and any kid can show you the way (①).

Numerous **chop houses** and bars crowd around the market and adjoining motor park. *Pito* bars are also plentiful. Evenings you have your choice of several **video theatres** showing "action" and "brutal" films.

Daily *STC* **buses** link Navrongo to Bolgatanga and Tamale, and they now service Burkina's capital, Ouagadougou, several times a week as well, although **taxis** are more frequent and faster. Heading west, the buses stop at Tumu, from which point you can get onward transport to Wa and Côte d'Ivoire.

Around Navrongo

Some 6km from Navrongo, down a turning off the Tumu road, is the *Tono Guest House*, built on the edge of **Tono Lake**. Sometimes referred to as the "Akosombo of the Upper Region", the lake resulted from a dam designed to create a massive irrigation project for sugar production. There's a pool, sports facilities and first-class birdwatching on the dam lake. The **guest house** is one of the best in the north, though there's no guarantee you'll be offered a room, especially not if it's already busy (②).

Twenty kilometres further west, beyond **Chuchiliga**, are the **Chiana-Katiu caves**, 1km out of Chiana village. They feature natural rock formations that appear, eerily, to be of human construction – though no one seems to know much about them.

Paga

PAGA, only 5km north of Navrongo on the Burkina border, has become a popular destination for its **sacred crocodile pool**, which is now something of a fleecing operation. As soon as you arrive someone will offer to take you to the lake (of course expecting money), but it's in fact quite easy to find on your own, a five-minute walk east of the village. When you approach the lake, a hustler brandishing **chickens** runs up to prevent you from getting too close without paying. He'll demand at least ₵2000 (for the chicken: you may be able to beat him down a little) and, money in hand, will ask for another ₵2000 for your right to take pictures.

After you've paid, the crocs are summoned by whistling and a long clicky sound – *Nnn-kii-kikikikiki*. You pose for snaps holding their tails or squatting lightly on their backs. Finally the chicken is fed to them. Expect to feel ripped off – it's not so much the amount you pay, but the way they grab it. In spite of it all, you'll be hard pressed to get an account of what, apart from their money-making abilities, makes the crocodiles sacred.

Pick-ups run regularly up to Paga from Navrongo. In Paga there's a small **catering resthouse** – the *Paga Hotel* – if you want to spend the night.

Bolgatanga and villages of the Upper East

As capital of the Upper East Region and of the Grusi-speaking **Frafra** people, **BOLGATANGA** is much larger and faster-growing than Navrongo. Growing too fast, perhaps, for it's own good – it looks a real mess. However, if you're entering the country from Burkina it's a good place – far better than Navrongo – to take care of business, change money or find decent accommodation. The large town **market** is a good place to hunt for local **handicrafts**, especially leather, and there are a number of interesting sites nearby.

Accommodation

Most accommodation in Bolga (with the exception of the excellent *Catering Rest House*) is at the budget end of the scale, but there's plenty to choose from – and new lodgings pop up all the time.

Black Star Hotel, Tamale Rd. A reasonable stand-by, with surprisingly clean shared bathrooms, loads of good atmosphere and occasional disco nights. ①.

Catering Rest House, in the Bukere quarter (☎072/23.99). Expensive bungalow-type rooms – and a fifty-metre swimming pool which should by now be finished. ④.

Catholic social centre, Tamale Rd. Clean and secure individual non-S/C rooms, plus a welcoming management. Only slightly more expensive than the dive hotels. Dorm space also available although they often don't say so. ①.

Central Hotel, opposite the market. Ideally located as the name suggests and a little nicer than the average, with clean S/C rooms and a very friendly management. ②.

Oasis Hotel, Kumasi road. In a quiet area a couple of hundred metres from the *STC* station this reasonable hotel offers clean, S/C rooms. ①.

Super Service Hotel. Basic rooms that are dirty and, worse yet, don't have fans. They have a video theatre at night. ①.

The Town

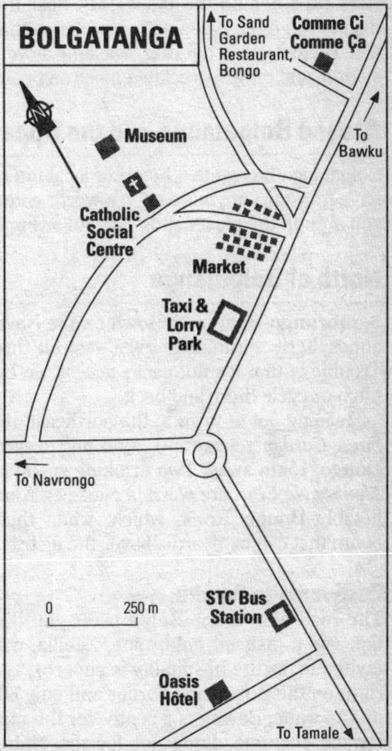

The main feature downtown is the **central market**, walled in around large boulder formations. Many goods are still hand-made in the market itself. **Leather items** (a local speciality), superb **basketwork** and clothes are all produced here and have their own sections. Beautiful examples of hand-made smocks – sewn from locally woven material and commonly worn by men throughout the region – are still sold more for local consumption than for the tourist market. The main market day is on a three-day cycle.

Bolgatanga has a new **museum** in the administrative block behind the Catholic social centre, which exhibits the region's cultural, historic and ethnographic heritage in two small rooms (small entrance charge). It's not a big draw, but an interesting way to spend an hour or two, with displays of stools, pots and musical instruments.

The **Ghana Tourist Board** has a regional office near the Catholic social centre, where the staff are extremely receptive to enquiries. They are beginning to compile information about little-known regional sights, and eventually plan to organize excursions in the north.

Look into the **Bolgatanga library** if you're dead from heat. It's a cool retreat on Navrongo Road, with a decent selection of language and cultural works – not much in the way of Ghanaian fiction though. To do something more active about cooling off, find out whether the **pool** at the Canadian Aid (CIDA) compound, opposite the Bolgatanga girl's school on Navrongo Road, has any water. If it does, it's a little oasis in the searing afternoon heat.

Eating

A pleasant garden **restaurant** is the *Comme Çi Comme Ça* where dishes like guinea-fowl with rice and salad go for around ₵2000 – a price most locals find expensive. *Top*

MOVING ON FROM BOLGATANGA

Lots of **taxis and tro-tros** leave Bolgatanga daily for Ouagadougou, Kumasi and Accra from the main taxi and lorry park. Smaller villages in the vicinity (see below) are also served. Vehicles for Tamale leave from a separate motor park near the police station. *STC* **coaches** have regular departures for Accra, Kumasi, Sunyani, Tamale and Wa from their own depot.

in Town is a smaller version of *Comme Çi Comme Ça* at the edge of town on the Navrongo road, while *Sand Garden*, in similar vein but cheaper, is behind the fire station. If you want really inexpensive eating, an alley of cheap **chop stands** and **pito bars** runs behind the *Black Star*, near the Catholic social centre. The favourite local dish is *TZ*, often eaten with *kino* sauce made from bitter green leaves. A more specialized Bolga taste is hot **dog**, available as very spicy kebabs from stalls at the Tamale taxi station, and only appreciated by strong constitutions.

Around Bolgatanga and the Upper East Region

Bolgatanga has quite a hoard of local interest if you're here for a few days. If you don't have transport of your own, it's worth enquiring in town about **renting a bicycle** to get you around the closer sites. The following destinations are ordered clockwise.

North of Bolgatanga

Sambrungo, 8km out of town on the Navrongo road, has a **night market**, offering an atmospheric – romantic even – stroll through the lanterns in the cool, evening air. Trouble is that it's not easily accessible by public transport so you may have to walk, hitch or cycle there and back.

Heading out of town to the northeast, the turning to the left (which takes you to the *Sand Garden* restaurant) runs out towards the Burkinabe border via the village of **Bongo**, 15km away. Two drinking spots on the outskirts of Bolga, *Meet Me There* and *Monkey No Fine*, are worth a pause en route. The goal at Bongo is the Bongo Hills and notably **Bongo Rock**, which, when thumped, makes an appropriately resounding boom that can be heard all over the district.

Eastwards to Bawku

The road **east from Bolga** takes you through the villages of Nangodi, with sacred fish and a disused gold mine, Zebilla, with beautifully decorated houses (try to get invited in, as the hospitality is superb), and on to the (black) market town of **Bawku**, right on the Burkinabe border and only 30km from Togo. Apart from smuggling, now on the wane, Bawku is a centre for the manufacture of *fugu* shirts, the north's characteristic costume. Look out for the **Naba's palace** and geometric designs on the houses.

Tongo and around

Southeast of Bolga, the hills around the Talensi village of **Tongo** are interesting, though not that easy to get to. Apart from their natural beauty, they're the site of **Tenzugu**, a famous religious shrine in a rocky cavern. The British destroyed it in 1911 and again in 1915, but couldn't prevent people from going there. Tongo is two **bus** rides away from Bolga – either 6km along the Bawku road to Zwerungu then 10km south, or 10km along the Tamale road, then 6km east – and has its market day on a Friday. The people are very friendly in Tongo, including the chief, who can arrange for someone to guide you on the hefty hike through the hills to Tenzugu. If you're doing this, you should take some *akpeteshie* with you.

Between Zwerungu and Tongo is the village of **Bare**, where the sacred **bat tree** makes a change from crocodile pools and holy fish ponds. The best time to visit the Tongo area would be for the **Sowing Festival** around Easter or the **Harvest Festival**, usually in September or October. Both reflect a curious blend of old and new – iron-bangled dancers shaking radios, tennis racquets and rubber dolls.

The road from Walewale to Nakpanduri

South of Bolga, **Walewale** is the site of a venerable mosque, the Nakora. **Gambaga**, 50km east of here, is famous for its scarp, stretching out towards the Togolese border and up to 300m high in places. The town is also the **ancient Mamprusi capital** and the site of current excavations investigating the origins of the Mamprusi kingdom (see the "History in the Upper East" box). The modern Mamprusi capital is **Nalerigu**, 8km east of Gambaga, with administration offices and a highly regarded mission hospital. Here you can see the palace of the Mamprusi kings as well as remains of the defensive walls built around the town when it was founded in the seventeenth century.

NAKPANDURI, 30km further east, is an unspoilt village situated high on the scarp. The **government resthouse** here is superbly sited, with a magnificent view north and some inspiring hikes nearby through rocky outcrops. Vehicles run here from Bawku, and though traffic is slow outside the market day (a three-day cycle), the relaxed and scenic atmosphere is worth a detour.

HISTORY IN THE UPPER EAST

The Upper East Region is the traditional domain of the More-speaking peoples. Their history goes back to a thirteenth-century chief named **Gbewa** who founded a kingdom at **Pusiga**, east of Bawku on the Togolese border (where his tomb can still be seen). His sons fought over their inheritance and founded a number of mini-states in the region which grew from the fourteenth century and remained essentially intact until the nineteenth – **Mamprusi**, founded at Gambaga, **Dagomba**, and the other "Mossi" kingdoms mentioned in the Burkina Faso chapter (genealogy on p.706). These nations are now the names of distinct ethnic groups speaking dialects of More. Dagomba's first *Ya Na*, or king, founded a capital at **Yendi Dabari** (Dipali), north of Tamale, where ruins were unearthed in 1962. That capital was abandoned for **Yendi** (100km east of Tamale) after the sixteenth-century Gonja invasions. The *Ya Na*'s palace is still there. At **Bagale**, in the remote country south of Gambaga, is the Dagomba kings' mausoleum. The house built over it is the abode of the spirits of all departed *Ya Nas*.

index

CHAPTER THIRTEEN

TOGO

TOGO

Although still comparatively little known outside the region, **Togo** has been in the papers often in recent years. Once considered a safe bet and an island of stability, it has had a particularly difficult time moving beyond the post-colonial era of dictators and there have been two violent **coup attempts** since the early 1990s, some involving days of shelling and shooting in the capital. Hundreds of Togolese have died and hundreds of thousands have fled to Ghana or Benin. The relaxed atmosphere – for which Togo was famous among overlanders and business travellers in the 1980s – has evaporated, leaving tension and uncertainty throughout the country. Even basic issues, such as who needs a visa, seem open to question; police and military checkpoints can turn even short trips into drawn-out nightmares; and as tourists head to more dependable spots in Ghana and Benin, a number of hotels and restaurants have closed indefinitely.

The mood of despond is not so pervasive, however, that it completely overshadows Togo's attractions. The country packs satisfyingly diverse **scenery** into a small space and has a vigorous **culture** differentiated into over a dozen linguistic and ethnic groups. While years of strikes and disinvestment have left the economy in tatters and the formerly excellent roads and service infrastructure are returning to West African norms, the fair legislative elections of 1994 were cause for some celebration. As the current calm distances the terrors of the early 1990s, the mood in Togo is cautiously optimistic, though this may be lost on the traveller.

Where to go

The country's small size makes **transport connections** relatively easy. The main *route nationale*, which shows off the country's **cultural and geographical variety**, runs from Lomé north to Dapaong, near the Burkinabe border, and even the most isolated villages lie within 100km of its path.

The capital, **Lomé**, while not without its modern districts, feels for the most part like a provincial town, tuned to the shuffling pace of crowded narrow streets, where goats and chickens share space with the occasional taxi. At the worst moments of the military madness, tens of thousands of people fled Lomé, leaving it like a ghost town. Although refugees are cautiously returning, the spark is gone.

FACTS AND FIGURES

The **République Togolaise** is a strip of a country with a 56-kilometre coastline and an area of only 57,000 square kilometres – less than half the size of England or New York state. The name Togo means "By the water" in Ewe. The **population** is officially estimated at under four million, with some 500,000 living in the capital, Lomé; during the upheaval of the early 1990s, however, hundreds of thousands of refugees fled to Ghana and Benin. Togo has a **foreign debt** of about £800 million ($1.2 billion), a relatively small sum even by modest West African standards, yet still amounting to four times the annual value of its exports. The government is theoretically democratic, although **President Gnassingbe Eyadéma** has been in power for nearly thirty years and laid claim to his present title in 1993 after the country's first elections in three decades. Most Togolese and foreign observers regarded that poll as rigged, although the elections to the national assembly in 1994, which gave a large number of seats to the opposition, were considered fair.

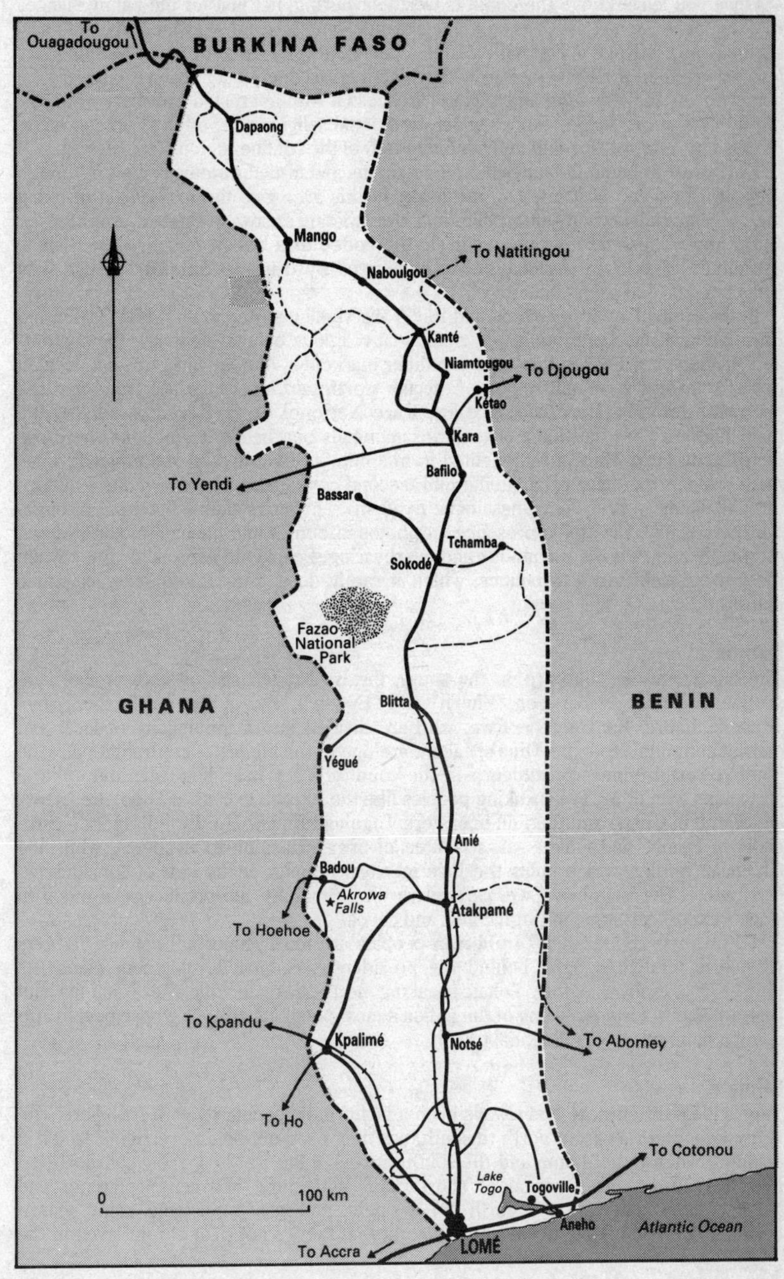
To Ouagadougou
BURKINA FASO
Dapaong
Mango
To Natitingou
Naboulgou
Kanté
Niamtougou
To Djougou
Ketao
Kara
Bafilo
To Yendi
Bassar
Tchamba
Sokodé
Fazao National Park
GHANA
BENIN
Blitta
Yégué
Anié
Badou
Akrowa Falls
Atakpamé
To Hoehoe
To Kpandu
Kpalimé
Notsé
To Abomey
To Ho
To Cotonou
Lake Togo
Togoville
0
100 km
Aneho
Atlantic Ocean
To Accra
LOMÉ

Once you leave Lomé, the **coast** is worth savouring, not just for the palmy villages rustling between the lagoons and the Atlantic, but also for **voodoo**. The fetishes, shrines and festivals of **Togoville**, **Aného** and **Glidji**, reveal a lot about a religion no less bizarre than the **Catholicism** with which it is strikingly interwoven. Followers are usually open about *vaudau* and willing to discuss it with interested travellers – surprising in view of the secrecy under which traditional religions are often shrouded – and here is one area you'll feel the unjaded strength of the continent.

Northwest of Lomé stretches the mountainous and fertile **plateau region**. Although they never exceed 1000 metres, the peaks of this area give the impression of being higher, especially when you're climbing the twisting roads to **Badou**, **Kpalimé** or **Atakpamé**. These three towns delineate the **coffee and cocoa** triangle – the richest agricultural district in the country, characterized by **thick woodland** studded with fruit orchards and palm plantations.

In the **central region**, Sokodé and Bafilo are Muslim strongholds, while Bassar and Kara have retained predominantly traditional religious beliefs (although the customs and religious practices in the latter two differ markedly). Mango and Dapaong, located in the semi-arid savannah region of the **far north**, already evoke the Sahel and the spectre of drought. Here, the once fine **Parc National de la Kéran**, straddling the main highway, has had most of its large mammals poached to extinction. The president's hometown, **Kara**, has benefited from a number of industrial and other development projects that have catapulted it into "second city" status. The enormous influence of "The Guide" – President Gnassingbe Eyadéma – is unmistakable here and throughout the country. His ample presence on photos in homes and businesses, on posters, on the TV and radio, is ubiquitous and overbearing. People are especially jumpy when the conversation turns to politics, which it rarely does, and almost never in public places.

People

The big groups in Togo are, in the south, the Ewe (often spelled Ewé or Evé, and pronounced midway between "Ehveh" and "Eyway"), and in the north, the Kabyé (Kabyié, Kabré, Kauré). The **Ewe**, who are divided into a multiplicity of local and district communities – the Mina-speakers are one of the biggest – are traditionally the most powerful ethnic constituency in the country. They have linguistic and cultural affiliations with other Twi-speaking peoples like the Akposo in central Togo, the Asante and Fante in Ghana and the Fon in eastern Togo and Benin. The Ewe diaspora – especially in France and Ghana – is a source of firm opposition to Eyadéma, while the Ghanaian border, which splits the Ewe into two regions, is the butt of considerable frustration. The Togolese Ewe, particularly the Mina, are the producers of much of Togo's export earnings, through coffee and cocoa.

The **Kabyé** and related **Tamberma** peoples are mostly poor subsistence farmers who have tended to unite behind the president's regional development plans (he himself is a Kabyé). Other Voltaic-speaking northerners include the Tchamba and Bassari, and the Kotokoli, one of the nation's most populous groups, whose people also count among the most influential traders.

Climate

Togo's pleasant **climate** has always been a factor in its popularity with travellers. The **rainy seasons** vary from north to south, but they need not be an overriding factor in deciding when to go. Lomé and the southern region has its "long rainy season" from March to June and a period of short rains some time between September and November. Sokodé and the north get a single, and less predictable, rainy season between April and September. Note, though, that there's not a lot of rain, even in the south (baobabs grow right down to within 10km of the coast) and the table for Lomé given here is an average, indicating that some years are very dry. Except in small villages off the paved road, notably in the Tamberma Country or the areas around Bassar and Tchamba – where steep muddy tracks can be demanding – the weather won't greatly hamper your travels.

AVERAGE TEMPERATURES AND RAINFALL

LOMÉ

	Jan	Feb	Mar	Apr	May	June	July	Aug	Sept	Oct	Nov	Dec
Temperatures °C												
Min (night)	23	24	25	24	24	23	23	22	23	23	23	23
Max (day)	31	31	32	31	31	29	27	27	28	30	31	31
Rainfall mm	15	24	52	118	145	224	71	8	35	61	28	10
Days with rainfall	1	2	4	8	9	12	5	1	5	9	2	1

Arrivals

Given the high degree of uncertainty about Togo's stability and safety, the country is not a common target for travel these days, and, as the border with Ghana is occasionally closed, even the freedom to cross Togo overland between Ghana and Benin cannot be guaranteed. On a more positive note, if you're entering Togo by road, you'll find the routes are mostly paved, and the frequency of public transport better than average.

Flights from Africa

Air Afrique (RK) and *Nigeria Airways* (WT) provide most of the direct flights from West African capitals to Lomé.

From **Abidjan** there are one or more flights most days on RK or WT, though note that some of RK's routings will have you doubling back via Lagos or Cotonou. Non-stop flights are mostly at weekends.

WT fly from **Banjul** via Abidjan on Tues and from **Dakar** via Banjul and Abidjan on Sat. RK's flights from Dakar are not direct – the best connection in Abidjan is on Fri.

From **Niamey**, RK has a non-stop flight on Tues and from **Ouagadougou** a non-stop flight on Wed. Also from Ouaga, *Air Burkina* (VH), flies non-stop on Sun and via **Cotonou** on Wed. Other Cotonou flights are on Mon, both with RK; one non-stop, the other inconveniently via Lagos.

From **Lagos**, there are several non-stop flights to Lomé each week: Mon with RK and WT; Wed vey unpredictably with *Air Zaire* (QC); Fri with RK and WT; Sat with RK; and Sun with RK and QC.

From **Bamako** there are non-stop flights on *Air Gabon* (GN) on Wed and Fri. GN also flies **Douala**–Lomé non-stop on Wed.

Lastly, from South Africa, there's a useful non-stop flight from **Johannesburg** to Lomé on *Aeroflot* (SU) on Fri; and from East Africa, *Ethiopian Airlines* (ET) flies on Fri from **Nairobi** to Lomé via Kinshasa.

Overland from Burkina Faso

The road from Ouagadougou is sealed all the way to Lomé (with minor exceptions in Togo where stretches are undergoing repairs). Border formalities pose no special problems on either side of this well-travelled route, although the posts close at 6pm. Coming from Ouaga **by bush taxi**, you can save money by going as far as Dapaong and changing vehicles there. This may be your only option, in fact, as the "express taxis" that used to ply the Ouaga–Lomé route appear to have suspended their service.

The details in these practical information pages are essentially for use on the ground in West Africa and in Togo itself: for full practical details on preparing for a trip, getting here from outside the region, paperwork, health, information sources and more, see *Basics*.

Overland from Ghana and Benin

The international highway along the coast is in good condition throughout the route from Abidjan to Lagos. There's a lot of traffic from both Accra and Cotonou, and in normal times, catching bush taxis from Cotonou or buses from Accra is no problem.

The **border with Ghana** was closed frequently and unexpectedly in the early 1990s, due to strained relations with Ghana, and is likely to be an unreliable crossing for the foreseeable future. Assuming it's open, get transport to the Ghanaian border town of Aflao and walk into the centre of Lomé from there. In times of peace, those taxis that drive right into Lomé to deliver you at the gare routière charge a big premium for a few extra kilometres. Even under normal conditions the border posts on both sides close at 6pm, and can be a little tense.

The Hilakondji border post between Togo and **Benin** is open 24 hours a day.

Red Tape

Nationals of the UK, the USA and Canada need no visa to enter Togo and can stay up to three months. The same holds true for nationals of Belgium, Denmark, France, West Germany, Holland, Italy, Luxembourg, Norway, Sweden and ECOWAS members. All others need a visa or transit permit before entering the country. Where Togo has no diplomatic representation, you can usually get one at the French consulate.

During the turmoil of recent years, many nationals normally exempt from the visa requirement have been told (for example by the Togolese embassy in Accra) that they are required to obtain a visa before entering Togo.

These are often not checked at the border, but the rules can quickly become very confused. If you have any doubts, get a visa.

Whether you enter by air or overland, customs and immigration officials usually give you little grief and will certainly permit the maximum stay. Sometimes you may be asked how much money you're carrying, but the amount is rarely verified. The only other piece of paper you'll need is a **yellow fever certificate**.

When leaving the country for Ghana, you may need a **laissez-passer** (see Lomé "Listings").

■ Visas for onward travel

Lomé has only a limited number of **West African embassies and consulates**. You can get visas for Nigeria here, and visas for some Francophone countries, including Burkina Faso, from the French consulate – addresses are given in the Lomé "Listings". Benin has no embassy, but visas are issued at the Hilakondji border. In 1994, a Ghanaian consular officer was arrested in Togo, and the status of the Ghanaian embassy in Lomé remains unreliable. It is therefore advisable to pick up a Ghanaian visa before arriving in Lomé. Ghana has embassies in Cotonou and Ouagadougou.

Money and Costs

Togo is part of the CFA zone (CFA100 = 1 French franc; approx. CFA750–800 = £1; approx. CFA500 = US$1). Coming overland, you're likely to have some CFA but, arriving by air from Europe, it's a good idea to bring some French francs in cash as they are generally acceptable for taxis, services and hotels. The airport banks close at 6pm: arrive later than this and you'll find it difficult to change money.

Changing other major **international currencies** (traveller's cheques or cash) is no problem in Lomé, Kara or Sokodé. (During the frequent strikes of the early 1990s, however, travellers sometimes arrived to find everything shut down, including banks.) In smaller towns, **banks** are likely to accept only francs or dollars, not pounds sterling or Deutschmarks. Banking hours are short and inconvenient: Monday to Friday 7.30–11.30am and 2.30–4pm. **Credit cards** are accepted in the major hotels, and in Lomé you can get Visa cash advances at the *UTB* or Mastercard cash advances at the *BIAO*.

■ The black market

Lomé has the biggest **currency black market** in West Africa, near the old Cotonou taxi station and Grand Marché, and all along the aptly named rue du Commerce. The quarter is notorious throughout the region and the free market operates here quite openly. You can buy **Nigerian naira** and **Ghanaian cedis** but also **CFA** (useful if you get caught without when the banks are closed) and other international currencies. Though you're not breaking any Togolese law, you should bear strongly in mind the fact that cedis and naira may not legally be exporeted or imported.

Streetwise **moneychangers** are very adept at sleight-of-hand tricks, so go with a friend, pay attention, and only carry the money you want to change. In general, it's advisable to avoid the sharks on the street who'll perform magic before your eyes, and deal with one of the bigger bosses at a shop front, doing the actual exchange inside the shop. Hand over nothing until you've verified your deal note by note. Much cooler exchanges are often to be had with resident expatriate money-dealers who have legal currency businesses and will give better-than-bank rates if you're buying CFA. Ask around.

■ Costs

The **cost of living** in Togo is substantially below that in other Francophone countries, but if you plan on living and eating *à l'européen*, you'll pay dearly for imported goods that would be cheap at home. **Hotel rooms** in Lomé run anywhere from CFA4000 to CFA100,000 but the interior of the country is less expensive and you can find good rooms for CFA5000–10,000 nearly everywhere. Ready-cooked **street food** and market produce is quite cheap, especially in the productive southwest. **Restaurants** serving European food generally do meals from about CFA2500. Beer and soft drinks are very inexpensive, although the big hotels and tourist hangouts knock the prices up as you'd expect. In a local bar, prices are the same from north to south (CFA300 for a beer, CFA100 for soft drinks). **Petrol** costs about CFA400 per litre for super but all over the south you often find it sold more cheaply in jerry cans along the roadside.

Health

In common with most of West Africa, a yellow fever vaccination certificate is

compulsory. Malaria tablets are essential. Chloroquine resistance has been reported, so extra care is needed.

Towns and large villages have either a hospital or – more likely – a **dispensary**, but these are characteristically overcrowded and lack adequate supplies. If you get seriously ill, it's best to get to your embassy (never very far in Togo) or one that speaks your language. They'll be able to refer you to a specialist or decide if you wouldn't be better off flying back home to get the help you need.

As in other countries, official reports invariably say that only a handful of **AIDS** cases have been registered in Togo and of course they're all prostitutes and foreigners; in fact, AIDS is now prevalent.

Maps and Information

The best travel map of Togo is the large 1cm:5km sheet produced by the French *IGN*, with its optimistic scattering of animal life (latest edition 1991). The Office National Togolais du Tourisme in Lomé also sells large national maps, but the single fold of the *Michelin 953* is more useful.

In Lomé, the Togolese survey office, the *Direction de la Cartographie Nationale et du Cadastre*, is responsible for large-scale (1:200,000 and 1:50,000) mapping. Whether they will sell you any sheets is another matter.

North Americans can get preliminary information from the **Togo Information Service**, 1625 K St, NW #102, Washington DC 20006 (☎202/569-4330). Europeans can try writing to the *Office National Togolais du Tourisme*, 23 rue François 1er, 75008 Paris.

Getting Around

Getting around Togo is most easily done by road. The very limited railway network in the south dates from the era of German occupation and its days are numbered. There's no domestic air service.

■ Bush taxis and car rental

There are few bus services in Togo and most of the time you'll be using privately run **taxis**. Every year Japanese vans gain ground on the traditional Peugeot 504s: the Nissans and Hiaces are new and comfortable. Laws against overloading are enforced more often than in the past – though the number of passengers a driver will take usually depends on how many policemen he thinks he'll meet on the road, and whether the fines he pays will cancel out the extra fares.

In Lomé itself, **zemidjans** (moped taxis) are common and convenient.

Togo has good roads on the whole and you can drive on **tarmac** to all the neighbouring capitals. Lomé and Kara have **car rental** agencies, but prices are prohibitive.

■ Trains

The Germans built **railway lines** to Aného (for freighting out the coconuts), Kpalimé (for coffee and cocoa) and Blitta (for cotton), an antiquated system, which is enthused over by rail buffs. However, trains stopped running to Aného some years ago, and the reduced service to Kpalimé and Blitta has frequently been out of commission during periods of unrest – there is every likelihood that these routes too will soon be completely discontinued. If the daily trains are still running and you're in no hurry, the wooden carriages with shutters and colonial styling are rather fine, and travel by train is the cheapest form of transport. Schedules are given in appropriate sections of the guide.

Accommodation

Except in Lomé and Kara, each equipped with showy, five-star hotels, Togo has little in the way of luxury accommodation. From north to south, however, it does have an adequate number of more modest lodgings, either privately owned or government-run. Accommodation is usually good value compared with neighbouring Francophone countries, although amenities like air-conditioning, TV and phones are less common.

Togo has no youth hostels and little in the way of mission accommodation, though the **Affaires Sociales** government rest houses will always put you up cheaply if they have a room free.

There's a handful of organized **camping** sites east of Lomé and a limited number of other sites throughout the country. It's also useful to know that some hotels allow campers to pitch on their grounds for CFA2000 or CFA3000 a night. In the past, it was acceptable – if you had your own

ACCOMMODATION PRICE CODES

Hotel prices in this chapter are coded according to the following scales – the same scales in terms of their pound/dollar equivalents as are used throughout the book. Prices refer to the rate you can expect to pay for a room with two beds. Single rooms, or single occupancy, will normally cost at least two-thirds of the twin-occupancy rate. For further details see p.51.

① **Under CFA4000 (under £5/$7.50).** Basic hotel ranging from rudimentary *case de passage* to decent S/C accommodation.

② **CFA4000–8000 (£5–10/$7.50–15).** S/C rooms, often with AC.

③ **CFA8000–16,000 (£10–20/$15–30).** Modest business or tourist-class hotel, often with a restaurant.

④ **CFA16,000–24,000 (£20–30/$30–45).** Comfort-able hotel with good facilities.

⑤ **CFA24,000–32,000 (£30–40/$45–60).** First-class hotel.

⑥ **CFA32,000–40,000 (£40–50/$60–75).** Luxury accommodation.

⑦ **Over CFA40,000 (over £50/$75).** Luxury accommodation.

transport and were out in the bush – to pull off the road discreetly, and camp for the night just about anywhere, especially in the centre and north. In the present security climate you should be very careful when doing this and preferably seek local permission, letting people know who you are.

Staying with people is officially frowned upon unless you make a declaration at the town *préfecture*. Lomé is big enough for you to be able to skip this formality without the authorities finding out. However, given the present tension, there seems little point in risking it. Outside the capital, police will soon learn of your whereabouts and, if you're not staying in a hotel, may drag you into headquarters to reprimand you and make you fill out endless forms. Sheer misery.

Eating and Drinking

Togo has a reputation in West Africa for some of the best cooking in the region. Small restaurants or street stands as far afield as Niamey, Bamako and Abidjan are often run by Togolese women. The secret of their success lies in their sauces, which tend to be less oily than usual and contain more vegetables. Not that you'll necessarily love Togolese food; some of it may seem unappealing at first (slimy gumbo, or okra, can be a real turn-off) and all of it is guaranteed to be heavily laced with hot peppers.

Staples vary across the country. In the south, **cassava** (manioc) predominates, along with **palm oil** and **maize**. Cassava is often grated and steamed as *atiéké*. In the plateau region, the diet contains more tubers – **yams**, **cocoyams** and **sweet potatoes** – boiled, grilled, steamed or fried. **Plantains** are another favourite staple, commonly pounded into **fufu** (which can also be made with cassava or yams). In the north, **shea-nut oil** is commoner than palm oil. Likewise, **rice**, **millet** and **sorghum** (any of them can be ground, boiled and served as a mash) are eaten more frequently than towards the coast.

Vegetables include tomatoes, gumbo, aubergines (small and yellowish), squash and beans. These are used in **sauces** with cassava, baobab or taro leaves and mixed with fish, shellfish, meat or poultry. Common **spices** are ginger, peppers, anis, garlic, basil and mustard.

The south and plateau region have the most **fruit**, although even in the extreme north you'll find a good variety. **Pineapples**, **mangoes**, **papayas**, all the **citrus fruits**, **avocados** and **guava** are plentiful in the markets (depending of course on the season) and downright cheap in the south. Supplements to the basics include **agouti** (the large and tasty herbivorous rodent known in Ghana and Nigeria as "bush rat" or "grasscutter") and **koliko** (deep fried yam chips). Togo's best-known **dishes** are **moutsella** (a spicy fish and vegetable dish), **adokouin** (shellfish with a prawn sauce known as *azidessi*), **djekoumé** (chilli chicken), and **gboma** (a spinach and seafood based dish). You're most likely to sample these at an important private gathering, or as part of the *Cuisine Togolaise* menu in one of the more expensive restaurants.

Togo has a great line in **street food** and, even in the smaller **village markets**, women sell exotic as well as fairly familiar food by the portion, from basins. The variety is huge.

If such a variety of dishes isn't already enough, the large towns all have restaurants serving **European food**, but these tend to be fairly expensive, especially if you want wine.

Drinking

Togo has its share of local drinks, similar to the other common intoxicants of West Africa. **Palm wine** is big in the south: the juice that flows from the trunks is already fermented and ready to drink, its frothiness indicating its freshness (if it's flat it will be high in alcohol). A hard liquor can be produced by distilling it. Though illegal, this highly potent "African gin", or **sodabi**, flows freely in the coastal region. Northern Togo specializes in millet beer, known locally as **choucoutou** – a taste somewhat reminiscent of dry cider. Filtering it produces **chacbalo**, which is clear and slightly sweeter than *choucoutou*.

Togo's brewery pumps out a wide selection of more familiar drinks. The **beer** here is excellent and cheap. *Bière du Bénin* (referred to as *BB*, "Bé-Bé") is the standard lager. *Eku* is more potent. *Guinness* is also available, served cold. There's a wide range of soft drinks, good *Lion Killer* lemonade, soda water, tonic and the rest – even a splendidly fruity, carbonated *Cocktail de Fruits*. They all come in large and small bottles and they're all refreshingly inexpensive.

Communications – Language, Post, Phones and Media

The official language of Togo is French. Communications with Europe are relatively good, at least from Lomé. The local media is limited, but papers and magazines are imported, and in Lomé you won't feel out of touch with the news.

French is widely spoken in Togo. Due to the commerce with Ghana and Nigeria, many traders also speak rudimentary **English**, especially in the area around Lomé.

There are some fifty African languages and dialects, the most widely spoken among them being **Mina**. Mina is spoken by thirty percent of the population in the coastal region and into Ghana. Government reports list President Eyadéma's mother tongue **Kabyé** (also known as Kabré or Kauré) as being the second most common language in the country. To arrive at this claim, they lump Kabyé together with a host of related **Tem** dialects from the Voltaic group, spoken in the Kara region. Linguistically, if not politically, **Kotokoli** – the language of Sokodé and environs; see box on p.879 – is certainly more prevalent than Kabyé. Other languages include **Bassari**, in the area around the town of Bassar, **Tchamba** in the east, **Moba** around Dapaong and scattered communities of **Hausa, Fula and Mossi** in the extreme north.

Post and phones

Post is inexpensive – CFA190 for airmail letters to Europe (except France which is slightly cheaper) and America. Surface mail packages cost about CFA2000 per kilo and a small fortune by airmail. **Phoning home**, reverse charge (collect) calls are only possible to France, and normal calls are pretty expensive (CFA1500 per minute to America and most of Europe, CFA900 to France). There are now some phone boxes in Lomé where you can phone abroad on IDD using phone cards.

Togo's IDD code is ☎228.

The media

Radio Togo, the national station, broadcasts news in French, Ewe, Kabyé and English (endless reports of telegrams the president received that day followed by a wrap-up of West African events). Libreville's **Africa Numero Un** and **Radio France Inter** are better music stations with more comprehensive international news coverage. It's not clear whether **Radio Liberté**, the station of the *COD-2* opposition alliance, is still broadcasting.

National **TV** broadcasts every evening – news in French and local languages plus old movies.

The only readily available **newspaper**, the state-owned *Togo Presse*, in French, with Ewe and Kabyé pages, has sketchy international coverage, but local news items are often interesting. A vigorous free press sprouted in the early 1990s, but bombings and other intimidation has dampened the enthusiasm of most publishers. Look out for *La Parole*, *Kpakpa Désenchanté*, and *La Tribune des Démocrates*. You'll find international **English-language press** like *The Herald Tribune*, *Time* and *Newsweek* (as well as French and German mags and papers) at the airport and the big hotels.

MINIMAL MINA AND ESSENTIAL EWE

Mina is spoken by about a third of the population in Togo, making it the most common language in the country. You'll run into it mostly along the coast, including in parts of Ghana and Benin. Unlike **Ewe**, to which it is closely related, Mina is not written. Both languages are tonal, so that meaning varies (as in Chinese for example) with the pitch of the voice. They're therefore rather hard languages for speakers of European tongues to come to grips with, and the following words and expressions can only be a very rough guide to pronunciation.

MINA GREETINGS AND BASICS

Good day	*Sobaydo*	Have a nice day	*Nkekay anenyo*
Reply	*Dosso*	Yes	*Aaaaa*
How are you?	*O foihn?*	No	*Ow*
Reply ("fine")	*aaaaa* (as in cat)	Come here (to a child)	*Va*
Thank you	*Akpay*	See you later	*Sodé* or *Sodaylo*
Thank you very (very) much	*Akpaykaka (kaka)*	Until we meet again	*Mia dogou/mia dogoulo*
		See you tomorrow	*Ayeee'soh*

MINA NUMBERS

1	*Dekaa*	5	*Ametón* (high tone)	8	*Ameni*
2	*Amevé*	6	*Amadé*	9	*Amesidiké*
3	*Ametòn* (low tone)	7	*Ameadrreh*	10	*Amewo*
4	*Amené*				

EWE GREETINGS AND BASICS

Good morning	*Nngdi*	I don't understand	*Nye mese egome o*
Good afternoon	*Nngdo*	Goodbye	*Hede nyuie*
Good evening	*Fie*	I'm a stranger	*Amedzro menye*
Good night	*Do agbe*	Please	*Taflatse*
Welcome	*Woe zo*	What is your name?	*Nko wode?*
How are you?	*E foa?/ Ale nyuie?*	My name is . . .	*Nngkonyee nye . . .*
I'm fine	*Mefo/Meli nyuie*	I am leaving Ewe land	*Mele Evegbe srom*
Pleased to meet you	*Edzo dzi nam be medo go wo*		

EWE NUMBERS

1	*Deka*	7	*Aderen*	20	*Blave*
2	*Uhve*	8	*Enyee*	30	*Blatòh* (low tone)
3	*Etoh*	9	*Asiekee*	40	*Blana*
4	*Enah*	10	*Ewo*	50	*Blatóh* (high tone)
5	*Atoh*	11	*Wedekee*	60	*Bladee*, etc
6	*Adee*	12	*Weuhve*, etc	100	*Alohfa deka*

A GLOSSARY OF TOGOLESE TERMS

Anasara In the northern parts, a white, derived from Nazarene, or Christian.

Authenticité Programme initiated by Eyadéma to instil pride in "authentic" roots, requiring French names to be exchanged for African and proficiency in Ewe, Mina or Kabyé for all school children.

Auto-suffisance alimentaire Food self-sufficiency – which, in non-drought years, Togo had nearly obtained before the unrest.

Evala The annual wrestling matches in the president's hometown of Kara.

Soukala A compound of round huts connected by a wall, found in the north.

Vaudau/Vodu Generic names for the spirit children of God – Mawu-Lisa in Ewe.

Yovo White person (Mina).

Holidays and Festivals

Both Muslim and Christian holidays – including Catholic festivals like Pentecost, Ascension and Assumption (the former two variable and the latter on August 15) – are celebrated in Togo, along with New Year's Day. National holidays are: January 13 (National Liberation); April 27 (Independence Day); May 1 (Labour Day); and a few days in July on the occasion of Evala (see below) which, with so many Kabyé employees granted leave, is increasingly a public holiday.

■ The festival year

Traditional festivals take place in the regions, many with ancient ethnic roots and corresponding celebrations in Ghana and Benin. The following are the most notable among them.

July

Evala is an initiation celebration in the Kabyé country with wrestling matches (*lutte traditionelle*). The tournaments in Kara are now televised nationally and attended by the president, said to be a former champion.

Akpema is the Kabyé young women's initiation ceremony.

August

Kpessosso is the Gun harvest festival celebrated in the region of Aného and marked by traditional dances (*Adjogbo* and *Gbékon*).

Ayize is the bean-harvest festival celebrated by the Ewe, particularly in the region of Tsevié.

September

Agbogbozan is the festival of the Ewe diaspora celebrated on the first Thursday in September and especially colourful in Notsé.

Kpessosso is an element in the week-long **Yékéyéké**, or *Yakamiakin* festival.

In Bassar, the **Dipontre**, or yam festival, is celebrated around the first week of September.

Directory

AIRPORT DEPARTURE TAX None.

CRAFTS There are numerous places throughout the country where crafts are plentiful. The principal mart in Lomé is the Passage des Arts – a small street near the market with nothing but art vendors selling sculptures, bronzes, jewellery and textiles from across West Africa. Near Kpalimé, the Centre Artisanal de Klouto is a noble attempt to keep regional crafts alive: here, traditional forms of **pottery**, **calabash decoration** and **wood carving** have taken on a modern, more commercial flavour. Kpalimé itself is a good place to buy **kente cloth** (see p.870) which is woven in the town streets. Traditional cloth is also woven in Bafilo and can be purchased directly from the *coopératives des tisserands* in the town centre. An unwelcome footnote is the presence of **ivory** in Lomé's craft shops and a flourishing ancillary trade in fake ivory bangles.

FOOTBALL A popular sport, with particularly fierce competition between **Semassi**, the team from Sokodé, and **Gomido** from Kpalimé.

MUSIC In the world of **pop music**, Togo's sole international star has been **Bella Bellow**, who was "discovered" by Cameroon's Manu Dibango and who had a successful career before her death in a car accident. Some of her cassettes can be found in Lomé. More recent musicians who've made a name for themselves include **Itadi K. Bonney** and **Afia Mala**. But one of Togo's biggest stars is **Jimmy Hope**, a rock/blues musician with a huge following who often plays around Lomé.

OPENING HOURS Offices and most **businesses** are open from 7.30am–noon and from 2.30–4.30pm. **Banking hours** vary slightly from one institution to the next, but are roughly 7.30–11am and 2.30–4pm. The more modern "journée continue" hours (roughly 8am–2pm, with no closure) are increasingly common in all institutions.

PHOTOGRAPHY No photography permit is required in Togo, though the usual restrictions apply to taking pictures of military installations and strategic points. People generally tend to be less camera-shy than in some African countries and children in particular are eager to have their pictures taken. Polaroid snaps are popular.

WILDLIFE PARKS None of the game reserves and national parks are faring well. The **Parc National de la Kéran** that once straddled the northern highway has reverted to farmland as most of the game had been killed off. The other large park, the **Parc National du Fazao**, west of the main north–south highway near Sokodé, closed its gates for rehabilitation after much of its wildlife was also decimated.

WOMEN Tradition, in rural areas especially, dictates a strict sexual division of labour, but women have considerable economic clout, particularly in the south where well-organized women merchants – known in Lomé as the *Nanas Benz* after their favourite cars – are a political force of consequence. The government recognizes and sanctions the *Union Nationale des Femmes Togolaises.* Women have access to all administrative functions and professions but the reality is that education, though compulsory in theory for all children, is less likely to be received by girls than boys (62 percent compared to 89 percent) and there are few women with high-level positions in government or business.

A Brief History of Togo

For centuries, Togo has been on the fringes of several empires – Mali, Asante, Benin, Mossi – but the centre of none. The country – which formed part of what was once called the Slave Coast – came into contact with Europeans in the fifteenth century as the Portuguese made their sweep of the African continent. Porto Seguro (Agbodrafo) and Petit Popo (Aného) evolved to become important trading posts where slaves were exchanged for European goods. By the end of the nineteenth century, trade had shifted to "legitimate" products – principally palm oil, used in soap manufacture in Europe. French and German companies competed along the coast in their dealings with the Mina people.

■ The colonial period

In 1884, **Gustav Nachtigal** sailed into Togo and signed a treaty with a village chief that made the country a **German protectorate**. In the following years, **Togoland** developed into the Reich's "model colony" as the Germans tried to force the country to produce economic miracles. Railways and roads were laid, and forests cleared for coffee and cocoa plantations. A direct radio link with Berlin was established and wharves were built.

The beginnings of an ill-defined educational system tried to create Christians and wage labourers out of reluctant farmers and fishermen. It took the Germans until 1902 to "pacify" the people of Togo, relying on forced labour and other repressive measures to push through their progress.

Despite the colony's economic importance, German military presence in Togoland was weak. When World War I broke out, the British and French easily overran the territory, forcing the Kaiser's soldiers to capitulate at **Kamina** on August 26, 1914. The tiny village was thus the site of the Entente Powers' very first victory. After the war, a **League of Nations mandate** placed a third of the territory under British administration and two-thirds (corresponding to the present country's borders) in the hands of the French.

The way to independence

Both **France and Britain** showed only half-hearted interest in their new acquisitions which technically were not colonies. The British quickly attached western Togo (today the Volta Region in Ghana) to the Gold Coast, but the French administered eastern Togo as an entity separate from its other holdings in West Africa. Thus several of Togo's peoples – the Adele, Konkomba and especially **Ewe** – suddenly found their communities divided by a border. Reunification was an early political theme, but one the European powers looked on unfavourably. A "pan-Ewe" vision, championed by early nationalist leaders like **Sylvanus Olympio**, was dealt a severe blow in 1956 when people of West Togo voted in a referendum to amalgamate with the Gold Coast, then preparing for independence.

At the same time, the French were grooming eastern Togo for independence. In 1956, Togo became an autonomous republic, with **Nicolas Grunitzky** as prime minister. Two years later,

Olympio took over the role and, when Togo became fully independent on April 27, 1960, he was elected the nation's first president.

■ A shaky start

Olympio aspired to the ideals of early nationalists such as Nkrumah, Touré and Senghor, although he never achieved their stature. In any case, even as he ushered in a new era, the stage was set for his own demise. In a scenario all too common to the former colonies, the Germans and later French had groomed a class of coastal peoples to be civil servants and the educated elite. After independence, these peoples inherited political power and, as a consequence, economic advantages. It was a formula guaranteed to result in **ethnic tension** in countries where unity should have been of primary importance.

In the case of Togo, Olympio, an Ewe from Aného, represented the **elite minority**. He tended to put reunification with the Ewe in Ghana ahead of Togolese national unity and was openly contemptuous of the northern Togolese, whom he called *petits nordistes*. Increasing repression and disregard for the poor north didn't help to broaden his already narrow political base.

Meanwhile **Nkrumah of Ghana**, who had supported Olympio's efforts for Togo's independence, had apparently intended the territory to be integrated with Ghana and, that objective thwarted, actively harassed Olympio's new government with border closures and trade sanctions. But the worst blow to Olympio's prestige came in 1963, when **returning Togolese soldiers** who had fought for France in the Algerian war of independence, were refused permission by him to join Togo's national army, since in his eyes they had betrayed the African liberation movement. For the troops, in the main Kabyé men from the north, it was a humiliating snub, and seemed to be proof that Olympio was determined to exclude northerners from participation in the new nation.

On January 13, 1963, a group of disenfranchised soldiers, including a young Kabyé sergeant named **Etienne Eyadéma**, staged the first coup in independent Africa. They stormed the president's home and, according to the official version, shot and killed Olympio while he was trying to escape by scrambling up the wall from his residence and into the grounds of the American embassy where he had hoped to seek refuge.

The soldiers set up a civilian government and placed Grunitsky, who had returned from exile, at its head. The new president lasted four ineffectual years and, as the country's increasing problems outstripped his competence to deal with them, he was replaced in a bloodless coup by Eyadéma – staged in a symbolic style that became his hallmark, on January 13, 1967, four years to the day after Olympio's assassination.

■ The Eyadéma years

After his second coup Eyadéma seized power "at the insistence of the people", suspended the constitution, dissolved political opposition and set about, much after the style of Zaire's President Mobutu, protecting his political future through the powerful mechanism of the single party he himself controlled – the *Rassemblement du Peuple Togolais* or RPT. By 1972, he was secure enough to hold a referendum on his future as president, in which voters held up one colour card to indicate a "yes" vote and a different colour for "no" as soldiers guarded the booths. A landslide 99 percent of the population thus expressed its desire for Eyadéma to remain the national leader.

Two years later, the president profited from a bizarre series of events that seemed to give supernatural backing to the demonstration of popular support. It started in 1974 with what has gone down in Togolese political legend (actively encouraged by the president) as the **"Three Glorious Days"**. On **January 10**, Eyadéma announced that a 51 percent share of the French-operated phosphate mines (one of the country's principal resources) would be nationalized. Exactly two weeks later, **January 24**, the president's private plane crashed over **Sarakawa**, but Eyadéma walked away from the wreck virtually unmarked. An international plot was suspected, and, without any real proof, the world was led to believe this was a classic case of capitalist meddling – an assassination attempt on the man who had dared to liberate his country's economy.

After recovering, the president made a drawn-out journey from Kara to Lomé, and throngs of people came to look at the man who had become a myth. On **February 2**, Eyadéma made his **triumphal return** to the capital and announced that the phosphate industry was henceforth one hundred percent in Togolese hands.

The incident turned into a political windfall that made Togo look like the mouse who roared. **Eyadéma's anti-imperialist record** was enshrined in myth. He began an **"authenticity"** campaign, again modelled closely on Mobutu's in Zaire, abolishing French names (and renaming himself Gnassingbe) and introducing Kabyé and – with a little shrewdness – Ewe into the schools as languages of instruction. Phosphate money helped build a few modern buildings in Lomé and Kara and ambitious projects like an oil refinery, steel plant (both now closed) and cement factory near Lomé. But rather than creating jobs, these simply lost money, forcing the country to bend to IMF pressure to denationalize as the economy slumped badly in the 1980s. The irony of Togo's position ever since Sarakawa is that it became one of the most pragmatically **pro-Western** countries of the Cold War era.

International affairs

Despite economic decline, Eyadéma managed to keep a high diplomatic profile and created a new larger-than-life image for himself as **West African peacemaker**. At one point he served as an intermediary between combatants in the Chadian war and helped smooth over relations between Nigeria and the Francophone countries that had backed Biafra. More recently he provided another African platform for **Israel**, with which Togo opened diplomatic relations in 1987.

On an economic level, Eyadéma has championed ECOWAS (the West African common market, known in French-speaking countries as the CEDEAO). Along with Nigeria, Togo was a major sponsor of the organization, established in 1975 when fifteen regional nations signed the Treaty of Lagos. But his proudest achievement was hosting the meeting that resulted in the signing of the **Lomé Convention**, giving Third World nations in Africa, the Caribbean and the Pacific preferential treatment from the EC and linking the name of Lomé with co-operation in development policy.

Cross-border relations

Relations with **Ghana** have traditionally been rocky, partly as a result of the pan-Ewe movement, which dates from the colonial era and continues in a more subtle form today. The ideological opposition of Rawlings' and Eyadéma's regimes has also led to serious tensions between the two neighbours. During Thomas Sankara's period in power, Togolese relations with **Burkina Faso** also chilled, but improved rapidly after Compaoré's assumption of power in 1987. Eyadéma was the first African head of state to recognize the new Burkinabe government, and he did so just hours after Sankara was overthrown.

Ideology has also been a source of conflict with **Benin** – a country periodically charged by Togo with giving refuge to politically active exiles. During the 1980s, the Togo–Benin border was frequently closed.

At home: increasing opposition

Eyadéma, who orchestrated two coups and has been witness to numbers of others in the states neighbouring his own, has been careful to nip **opposition** in the bud. Active underground dissent has long existed, and it rises to the surface in periodic **eruptions of violence**.

In 1984, when the papal visit focused international attention on Togo, a series of **bombings** rocked Lomé. A **coup attempt** occurred in a 1986 shoot-out with armed rebels who got perilously close to the presidential residence. The attempted takeover was blamed on an exiled movement led by Gilchrist Olympio (son of the former president) who was subsequently sentenced to death *in absentia*. The date of the aborted uprising – September 19 – is today celebrated as a national holiday.

In 1990, the government was again shaken when members of the **Convention Démocratique des Peuple Africains du Togo** (CDPA-T), an opposition group which had been based in Côte d'Ivoire until ousted by Houphouët-Boigny in 1989, were arrested for distributing anti-government literature. The ensuing trial led to massive demonstrations in Lomé which left many dead or injured, and which flooded the nation's prisons.

Subsequent protests forced Eyadéma to **legalize political parties**, but student unrest again erupted in April 1991. Fatalities were reported in Lomé when security forces dispersed demonstrators who demanded nothing less than Eyadéma's resignation. Afterwards, mutilated bodies began surfacing in Lomé's brackish Bé district lagoons. Twenty corpses were discovered, and the opposition blamed the **brutality** on the military. Anxious to dispel the idea that army thugs now publicly perpetrated the types of **human rights abuses** they had long been suspected of carrying out behind prison walls, Eyadéma ordered an investigation. But the opposition persisted and called a **general strike**, again demanding Eyadéma's resignation. More protests followed, and in June 1991 the government was constrained to agree on the mandate for a **national conference**, similar to the one that had brought sweeping reform to Benin.

In July 1991, delegates of newly legal political parties and the government convened, and with lightning speed, the conference proclaimed itself sovereign and suspended the constitution. By August, Eyadéma had been stripped of most of his power and the RPT had been outlawed. In an act of defiance, the president suddenly changed course and suspended the conference.

Opposition leaders refused to disband and proclaimed a provisional government under the leadership of **Joseph Kokou Koffigoh**, a lawyer and leader of the *Ligue Togolaise des Droits de l'Homme*. To stave off further unrest, Eyadéma consented to recognize Koffigoh. But within weeks of being instated, the new prime minister woke up to find soldiers had seized his house, captured the radio and television stations, and surrounded his office with tanks. Troops returned to the barracks on Eyadéma's orders, but in the following months, repeated popular protests led to bloody clashes with security forces. In November, **the army arrested Koffigoh** and demanded the transitional government be disbanded.

In prison, Koffigoh "reconsidered" his stance and consented to Eyadéma's euphemistically titled **"government of national unity"** which paved the way for the RPT's re-entry into the political scene. Although he spared the transitional government and allowed Koffigoh to remain as head, Eyadéma padded the council of ministers with close associates. With a tight grip on the council, the president allowed the appearance of reform to continue and laid plans for **new elections**.

Early 1992 was marked by repeated delays in the transitional process and by resulting protests. Trouble intensified when Olympio was shot while campaigning in Eyadéma's northern stronghold. The security forces were implicated in the **assassination attempt** and evidence even pointed to the president's son, Captain Ernest Gnassingbé. While Olympio recovered in Paris, a massive two-day general strike paralyzed Lomé as demonstrators once more flooded the streets.

Undaunted, the president cautiously took back all the power he had ceded to the national council in 1991. The sham of democratization was further highlighted in October 1992 when security forces stormed the parliament and held forty MPs hostage until the speaker pushed through a bill returning frozen funds to the RPT. In November, another **general strike** was called as opposition parties and union members demanded the creation of a politically neutral security force, a new government and free and fair elections.

The promised elections still hadn't materialized by January 1993 and the strike dragged on. A French and German delegation arrived in Lomé to help mediate the crisis, but their efforts were thwarted when security forces fired on a crowd of opposition supporters, killing at least twenty according to the French minister of cooperation who witnessed the atrocity. After two security officers were found murdered on January 30, the army went on a retaliatory **shooting and looting spree** which left hundreds dead at the hands of the military.

The new wave of violence led to a **mass exodus**, adding to the tens of thousands who had previously fled (including the wife of the prime minister, Rosaline Koffigoh). Forty thousand refugees streamed over the borders to Ghana and Benin, straining Togo's already dismal international relations. President Jerry Rawlings of Ghana condemned Eyadéma's continued denial that security forces were responsible for the slaughter and seemed to advocate sending ECOWAS troops to Togo to prevent it from becoming "another Liberia". While both Ghana and Benin mobilized troops along their borders to protect the refugees, the United States, France and Germany suspended aid to Togo.

New elections and an uncertain future

Against such a troubling backdrop, Eyadéma announced **presidential elections** would be held in August. Opposition leaders objected, demanding a recomposition of the Supreme Court and a postponement of the election date as preconditions for participating. They also called for a revised voter register and the issuance of new voter's cards. Eyadéma rejected the requests and furthermore denied the candidature of Gilchrist Olympio on the grounds that his medical examination was invalid.

Even the team of international observers monitoring the elections denounced the polls as "undemocratic", and US and German observers withdrew from the process. Candidates **Edem Kodjo** (*Union Togolaise pour la Démocratie*, UTD) and **Yao Agboyibo** *(Comité d'Action pour le*

Renouveau, CAR) pulled out of the race in protest and called for a **national boycott**. On a turnout of only 36 percent, Eyadéma garnered 96 percent of the vote and proclaimed himself victorious. The following day, fifteen CAR members who had been arrested for allegedly tampering with electoral material, died in prison.

On January 5, 1994 gunfire once again erupted near Lomé's Tokoin military base where President Eyadéma normally sleeps. Simultaneous **rocket fire** blasted a presidential motorcade, striking Eyadéma's bulletproof Mercedes and sending it skidding off the road. Soon after, the government issued a communiqué saying that the city was under a **commando attack**, but that the president and prime minister, who were in a private meeting far away from the motorcade at the time of the incident, were unscathed.

Fighting continued for four days as Loméans remained locked in their homes. When the dust had settled, Eyadéma announced that government forces had defeated the insurgents which he charged had infiltrated the capital from Ghana. Official reports put the death toll at 69 people, mostly members of the commando. Some estimates, however, ran as high as 300–500 victims, including many civilians.

The nation was shocked and demoralized as **legislative elections** were held in February. With the exception of Olympio's *Union des Forces du Changement* and a couple of lesser parties, most of the opposition decided to participate. In a tight race, Agboyibo's CAR won 36 seats in the 81member parliament, while Kodio's UTD won 7 and the RPT won 37. Though the RPT thus formed the minority in parliament, Eyadéma gained leverage by appointing Kodjo to the premiership – a move that gave the appearance of benevolence to the opposition, while effectively dividing it, since Agboyibo naturally felt he had claims to the post. As a result, CAR members refused to sit on the cabinet of ministers, which was quickly padded with Eyadéma backers, and the party began a parliamentary boycott.

By the mid-1990s, however, the worst of Togo's political crisis seemed to have abated, and people talked cautiously of a return to stability. Though 1995 began with rumours of another coup plot and the arrest of the head of Eyadéma's presidential guard, in the same year the CAR called off its boycott and resumed its representation in parliament after Eyadéma offered guarantees for a fairer approach to future elections. Earlier, the president had extended a general amnesty to the **refugees** who had fled to Ghana and Benin, prompting a slow return of emigrants.

Relations with Ghana dramatically improved when Togo surprisingly supported Jerry Rawlings' bid to become chairman of ECOWAS, a post he had sought for most of his tenure as Ghana's head of state. Soon after, the two nations opened their mutual border and began coordinating policy on security and drug-trafficking issues. Sources of tension persist, however, as hundreds of Togolese military deserters and civilian militants reportedly still remain in Ghana.

Western nations' responses to the return to calm have been mixed: the European Union agreed to lift sanctions and immediately offered CFA13 billion (£16m/$24m) in urban aid for Lomé, which had suffered badly in the worst days of unrest. The United States, however, has decided to continue its sanctions, claiming it is sceptical of recent reforms and of Togo's commitment to its very fragile democracy.

After nearly three decades in power, Eyadéma still holds the reins, but he has not emerged from the recent events unscathed. Few can forget the early years of the 1990s, when he governed through intimidation and force, the popular image he fostered of himself as a peacemaker and protector has been badly damaged at home and abroad. He stands little hope of restarting Togo's crippled economy before the next presidential elections, and even less of persuading the gaping pockets of resentment that he represents their best interests. Olympio still waits in the wings.

Meanwhile, although Eyadéma could well continue to govern for some time, his best chance of political survival depends on his ability to divide the country and silence opposing views. The chances of creating an atmosphere of national unity, economic growth and sustainable development under such conditions seem remote, and Togo's prospects for the future – once so bright – now look bleak.

LOMÉ AND THE COAST

Despite the terror of recent years, **Lomé** still manages to display the energy of a small capital – at least during the day. Most of the town's activity centres around the bustling market and surrounding commercial district – a pleasantly archaic area laid out by the French – where the pace falls far short of the frenzied tempo you find in the big cities of West Africa. The mix of urban sophistication and rural informality once combined to make Lomé West Africa's most enticing capital: for overlanders a popular respite from the rigours of travel in the bush; for the large expat community working in finance, development or as volunteers, an important centre of operations. But Lomé has been so badly hit by strikes and violence and its people so demoralized that it may take a long time for the city's spark to return.

East of the city, there are just fifty kilometres of coastline, wedged between the Ghanaian and Benin borders. The surf is notoriously rough, even dangerous at times, yet the whole **Atlantic shorefront** is picture-postcard perfect, with its coconut groves, white sand beaches and **fishing villages** – none more than an hour's journey from the capital. The towns of **Togoville**, **Anécho** and **Glidji**, with their fetishes, shrines and festivals, offer the possibility of interesting insights into local voodoo customs.

These towns also served as the spearhead for the German colonial invasion which began in 1884 – the year when Gustav Nachtigal landed in Togoville and signed a treaty placing the chief under the Kaiser's "protection". Soon after, Anécho became capital of German Togoland. Today, the coastal villages are full of colonial vestiges and, in varying states of dilapidation, they stand in sharp contrast to the dominant voodoo culture.

Lomé

Although **LOMÉ** spreads widely, the city's population (normally a manageable 500,000, though this number was nearly halved during the worst moments of unrest) is hardly enough to push it into the major metropolis category. The heart of the downtown district sweeps around the crowded, old **Grand Marché**. In the immediate vicinity, throngs of **shoppers and street vendors** press through a maze of narrow avenues and sandy streets lined with two-storey colonial buildings – the domain of Lebanese shopkeepers and small import-export businesses. The whole area is dominated by the **beach** and pervaded by an ocean breeze ambience. Only along and beyond the Boulevard Circulaire do you encounter the broad streets and high-rises that attest to the city's status – despite its troubles – as West Africa's financial capital. The city's factories are out of sight, about ten kilometres east beyond the port.

Some history

The settlement of Lomé was founded by Ewe people fleeing a tyrant ruler in their homeland of Notsé in the eighteenth century. By the end of the nineteenth century, the Germans had moved the **capital** of their newly declared colony from Anécho to Lomé. Reminders of their rule, like the **neogothic cathedral** or the **old wharf** near the Grand Marché, are still visible. Lomé remained the capital of the French protectorate after World War I, but Togo had lost its former importance, and development was minimal compared with other colonies.

Much of the infrastructure of the old part of town dates from the colonial period and has proved inadequate in coping with rapid growth. **Development** has been concentrated elsewhere. The first part of the city to be modernized was the **administrative centre** just west of the Grand Marché. Wide tree-lined avenues were traced here, and the capital's first skyscraper – the **Hôtel du 2 Février** – erected. Built in the middle of nowhere, this 37-storey marble and glass tower was part of Eyadéma's bid to have the Organization of African Unity's headquarters transferred to Lomé. The plan failed and, despite government PR, the hotel – one of the most luxurious in Africa – is virtually empty for most of the time. Nothing daunted, further, expensive symbols were built to promulgate the glory of Eyadéma and Togo's entry into the twentieth century – the **Palais de Congrès** (formerly the convention hall of the *RPT*) and the **ministries** with their gold-tinted glass.

Development of the city's northern and eastern fringes came to a virtual standstill when the troubles started. The Avenue Jean Paul II and the Boulevard Général Eyadéma lead to neighbourhoods that may still have a future of economic activity – if Lomé ever regains its position as a magnet of regional trade. For the moment, however, the Nouveau Marché, the Lomé 2000 conference centre and the new *gare routière* at Agbalepedo and Akodessewa still feel isolated from the city centre.

Arrival

Coming in by *taxi brousse*, from **Benin** or **Nigeria** (or **Ghana** if the border is open and relations not too frosty) you are most likely to be deposited at the *gare routière* at **Akodessewa**, about 3km east of the city centre. From here, you can take a shared or private taxi into town, most easily to the **Grand Marché autogare** right in the middle of things, from which you're within walking distance of a number of hotels if you're not piled down with luggage. This is where vehicles from Aflao and Aného terminate, and some international vehicles are now also using this downtown *autogare*.

From Ouagadougou and northern Togo, most vehicles terminate at the *nouvelle station* in the **Agbalepedo** neighbourhood, a good 10km from the centre. As you turn off the route d'Atakpamé, the lack of activity in the area tends to confirm first impressions – you're being dropped off in the boondocks. To get to the centre of Lomé, hire a cab (CFA500–1000), or pile into a collective taxi. These ply from the *gare routière* to the market for around CFA200.

If arriving **from Kpalimé**, you wind up (unless your driver continues to the centre) at a small *gare routière* on the route de Kpalimé in the Casablanca neighbourhood, about 5km from the central market. Again, there are collective taxis waiting to take you into town.

If you happen to be **arriving by rail**, taxis are usually waiting to meet any trains, on the rue de la Gare between the market and the bd Circulaire. If not, flag one down at the roundabout in front of the station.

Airport arrivals

Lomé's **airport** is small, but one of the most modern in West Africa and still relatively hassle-free (customs and immigration are thorough, but not intimidating). It's not far from town (7km), but there's no airport bus service, so you'll have to rely on taxis, the prices of which to various destinations are posted up. During the day, you can often get collective taxis by flagging them down on the main road outside the airport, just a few hundred metres from the arrivals hall.

Orientation

Getting around Lomé isn't difficult if you think of the Grand Marché as being the hub from which all the major roads shoot out like spokes. Hotels, restaurants, banks and shops are within walking distance. The big *SGGG* supermarket (pronounced "S-trois-jay", the *Societé Générale du Golfe du Guinée*), 500m northwest of the Grand Marché, is also something of a landmark in the town centre.

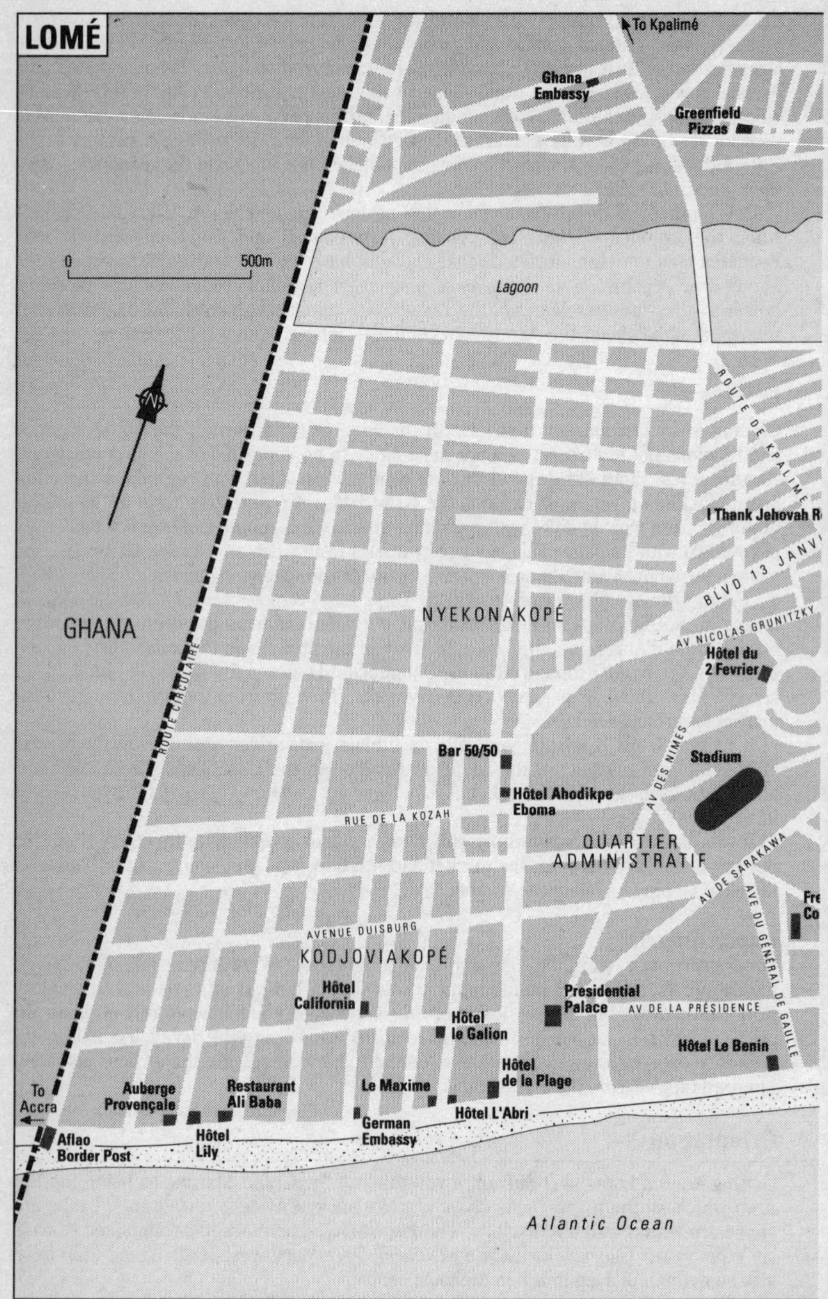
LOMÉ
To Kpalimé
Ghana Embassy
Greenfield Pizzas
0
500m
Lagoon
ROUTE DE KPALIMÉ
I Thank Jehovah R
BLVD 13 JANV
AV NICOLAS GRUNITZKY
Hôtel du 2 Fevrier
GHANA
NYEKONAKOPÉ
ROUTE CIRCULAIRE
Bar 50/50
Hôtel Ahodikpe Eboma
AV DES NIMES
Stadium
RUE DE LA KOZAH
QUARTIER ADMINISTRATIF
AV DE SARAKAWA
AVE DU GÉNÉRAL DE GAULLE
AVENUE DUISBURG
KODJOVIAKOPÉ
Hôtel California
Presidential Palace
AV DE LA PRÉSIDENCE
Hôtel le Galion
Hôtel Le Benin
Hôtel de la Plage
To Accra
Auberge Provençale
Restaurant Ali Baba
Le Maxime
Hôtel L'Abri
German Embassy
Aflao Border Post
Hôtel Lily
Atlantic Ocean

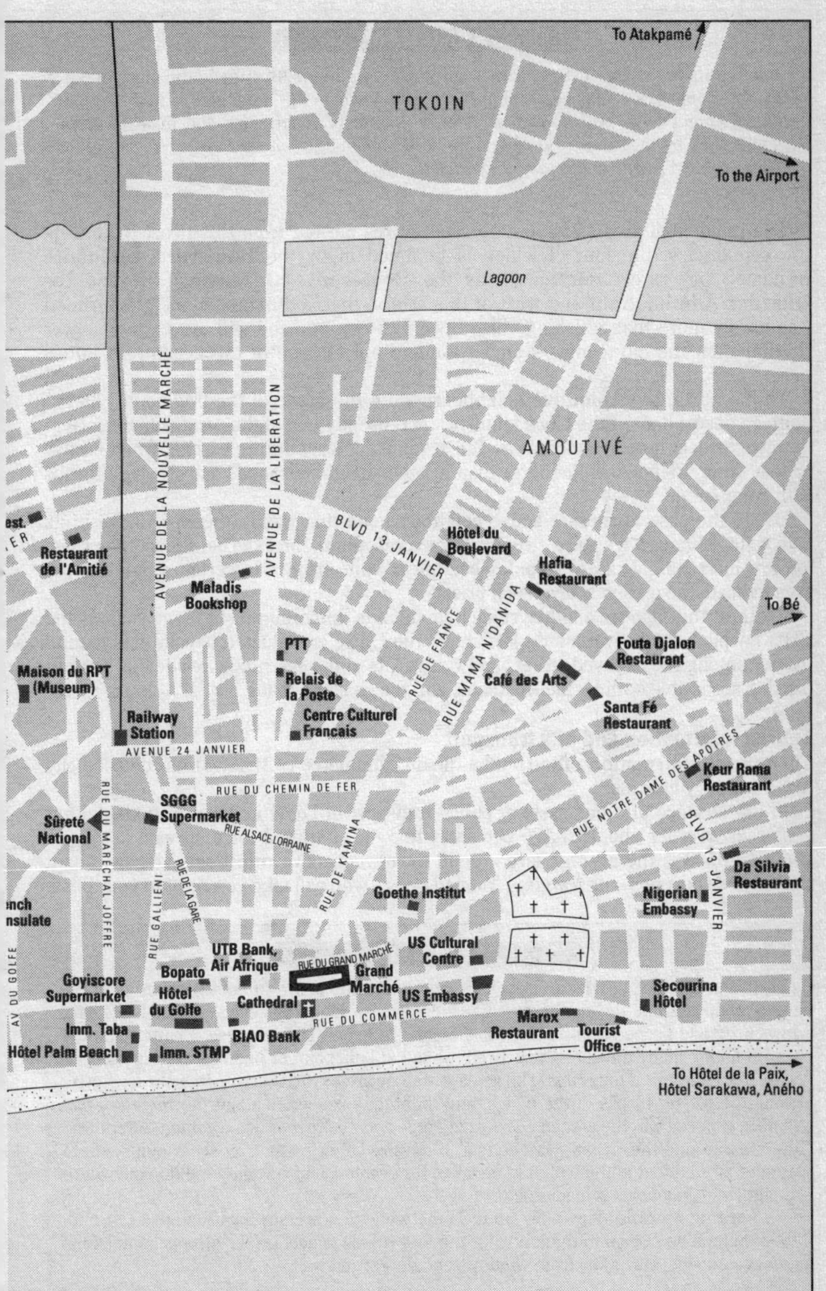
To Atakpamé
TOKOIN
To the Airport
Lagoon
AVENUE DE LA NOUVELLE MARCHÉ
AVENUE DE LA LIBERATION
AMOUTIVÉ
BLVD 13 JANVIER
Hôtel du Boulevard
Hafia Restaurant
Restaurant de l'Amitié
Maladis Bookshop
RUE MAMA N'DANIDA
RUE DE FRANCE
To Bé
PTT
Relais de la Poste
Fouta Djalon Restaurant
Café des Arts
Maison du RPT (Museum)
Santa Fé Restaurant
Centre Culturel Francais
Railway Station
AVENUE 24 JANVIER
RUE NOTRE DAME DES APOTRES
Keur Rama Restaurant
RUE DU CHEMIN DE FER
SGGG Supermarket
Sûreté National
RUE ALSACE LORRAINE
RUE DU MARÉCHAL JOFFRE
RUE DE KAMINA
RUE GALLIENI
RUE DE LA GARE
Da Silvia Restaurant
Goethe Institut
Nigerian Embassy
UTB Bank, Air Afrique
US Cultural Centre
RUE DU GRAND MARCHÉ
Grand Marché
Bopato
Goyiscore Supermarket
Hôtel du Golfe
Cathedral
US Embassy
Secourina Hôtel
AV DU GOLFE
Imm. Taba
RUE DU COMMERCE
Marox Restaurant
Tourist Office
BIAO Bank
Hôtel Palm Beach
Imm. STMP
To Hôtel de la Paix, Hôtel Sarakawa, Aného

STREET NAMES

Lomé has its fair share of street names surplus to requirements. Among the more important, the Boulevard 13 Janvier is almost always known as the Boulevard Circulaire; the route d'Amoutivé is also known as Avenue Mama N'Danida; and the main seafront avenue goes by the names Boulevard de la République, Boulevard de la Marina, route d'Aflao, route d'Aného and *route internationale*.

The residential areas and commercial centres fan out from this heart in concentric semicircles, the first of which is hemmed in by the **Boulevard Circulaire** (renamed but rarely referred to as the **Boulevard 13 Janvier**). Beyond the **Quartier Administratif** and west of this artery, the **Kodjoviakopé** neighbourhood was hardly more than a fishing village twenty years ago and still moves to a slower rhythm than the city centre. Many travellers opt for one of the beachfront hotels here.

To the north, the **Amoutivé** neighbourhood – the home of the traditional chief of Lomé, a descendant of the city's founder – is presently one of the most active quarters in town. Streets here are more crowded at night (at least during periods when curfew or fear don't drive people indoors) than in other neighbourhoods and the area throbs with commerce.

Bé, to the east, is another active neighbourhood that was formerly a village in its own right. Although it's still a stronghold of **voodooism**, the external signs of the religion are increasingly rare. Flagpoles bearing a white banner in certain homes in the area indicate the presence of a fetish priest.

North of **the lagoon**, another semicircle unfolds. Important institutions such as the CHU hospital, the Université du Benin and the Lycée are situated beyond this natural barrier among the unpaved streets and vacant lots of the essentially residential **Tokoin** district, accessible both by the Atakpamé and the Kpalimé roads.

Tourist information and city transport

The **tourist information office** on the rue du Commerce (☎21.43.13) has detailed city maps and very little else.

In the absence of a bus system, public transport in Lomé is down to **taxis** (either *taxis collectives* for about CFA75 per short hop, or chartered for a specific journey – about CFA500 is the average fare around town), collective **minibuses** (again, about CFA75 per short hop), or *zemidjan* "moped taxis", who will take you right to your desti-

SECURITY

Apart from the obvious risk to travellers who happen to arrive in Lomé during an uprising or coup attempt, the city has become increasingly dangerous even in periods of calm. Insecurity and desperation have led to a feeling of general lawlessness. **Crime** is on the rise in Lomé; many travellers have been robbed at knifepoint or been sprayed in the face with something in a mugging. Thieves are well aware of the tourist penchant for hotels along the western parts of the beach, and night-time robberies along the *route internationale*, especially in the area of *Hôtel de la Plage* and *Le Maxime* are common. After dark, the area around the Grand Marché is also unsafe. Other areas may seem quite safe to wander around, but nothing should be taken for granted, and certainly walking anywhere at night with valuables is inadvisable.

If **serious trouble** does blow up in Lomé while you are staying (though as of mid-1995 there is no reason to think it will), the first rule is to stay off the streets completely: don't go outside; stay away from windows and doors; and wait.

nation for CFA100. These are especially useful at night, when they're easier to find than taxis, though not all the moped drivers are very good.

Gares for *collectives* are scattered around the vicinity of the Grand Marché: those for Kodjoviakopé, Tokoin, Casablanca and Agbalepedo are west of the market; for Amoutivé and Lomé 2000 they are to the north on av Mama N'Danida; for Bé and Ablogamé to the east. The *collectives* run on fairly fixed routes – for example up and down the main radial thoroughfares from the Grand Marché to the bd Circulaire, or clockwise around the bd Circulaire to Bé and back again.

There are outlets for **car rental** at the airport, in the *2 Février* and *Sarakawa* hotels, and elsewhere. See "Moving On", p.865, for details.

Accommodation

Lomé has dozens of hotels, but most people head to the **beachfront** when seeking out places to stay. Along the *route internationale*, from the Ghana border to the eastern outskirts of town, you'll have no trouble finding a place to fit your taste and price range. In the present political and economic climate, hotels in all price brackets have been slashing their tariffs to lure back guests. The **camping sites**, beyond the port to the east of the centre all have rooms and/or bungalows, as well as tent pitches.

ACCOMMODATION PRICE CODES

① Under CFA4000 (under £5/$7.50).
② CFA4000–8000 (£5–10/$7.50–15).
③ CFA8000–16,000 (£10–20/$15–30).
④ CFA16,000–24,000 (£20–30/$30–45).
⑤ CFA24,000–32,000 (£30–40/$45–60).
⑥ CFA32,000–40,000 (£40–50/$60–75).
⑦ Over CFA40,000 (over £50/$75).

For further details turn to "Accommodation" in the Practical Information at the Beginning of this chapter.

Camping

If you don't have your own transport, collective taxis can get you out to the camping beaches for under CFA300. Camping rates are around CFA750–1000 per person at all three. Unfortunately, the immediate vicinities of the beach camping sites are now notorious for armed **robbery**. Take precautions if you're carrying valuables and be especially careful after dark.

Chez Alice, 14km east of the centre near the village of Baguida, a good 300m from the seashore (☎27.91.72). Something of a roadside holiday camp, with rooms and bungalows ranging from basic to moderate, as well as tent pitches. The good restaurant and bars make this a favourite overlanders' haunt. ①–②.

Ramatou Plage, 10km from the centre (BP 1256; ☎21.08.75). Places to camp or bungalows (some with private bath). This place is okay, but nothing special, particularly considering it's barely out of range of the industrial zone (the air can be smelly round here). Fairly expensive restaurant. ①.

Robinson Plage, 10km from the centre, next to *Ramatou* (BP 9149). The nicest of the lot with AC, S/C rooms around landscaped gardens on the seafront, or simpler bungalows with fan and mosquito nets. The seafood restaurant is very good, though expensive. ②.

Cheap to moderate hotels.

Hôtel l'Abri, bd de la Marina (☎21.35.84). Now probably a better bet than the popular *Hôtel de la Plage.* Same beachside location, but cleaner and friendly with a pleasant terrace and restaurant. ①.

Hôtel Ahodikpe Eboma, 45 bd Circulaire (BP 7025; ☎21.47.80). S/C rooms with AC. The big plus of this place is its location right next to the very likeable *50/50 Bar-restaurant.* ②.

Hôtel Le Bénin, on the seafront, corner of av du Général de Gaulle (BP 128; ☎21.24.85). Actually a training hotel, which is not known for stunning service and is currently not very popular, despite the good atmosphere, location and competitive prices. ④.

Hôtel California, directly behind the German embassy (☎21.18.75). The S/C rooms here are clean and have AC. Pleasant, well-stocked bar and restaurant. ②.

Hôtel Le Galion, rue Professeur Lassey, Kodjoviakopé, via rue Houndjagoh, the small street running next to *Le Maxime* (☎21.65.64). Immaculate rooms in a refurbished home with landscaped courtyard. Stylish design and attentive staff make this very popular with travellers and excellent value. ②.

Hôtel du Golfe, rue du Commerce (BP 36; ☎21.51.41). An older but well-kept establishment. Extremely central, with high standards of service. Rooms with AC and phones. ④.

Hôtel Lily, bd de la République, Kodjoviakopé, a stone's throw from the border and the beach. Spacious rooms and reasonable rates, but a bit far from the centre. ①.

Le Maxime, bd de la République, near the bd Circulaire (BP 1909; ☎21.74.48). Formerly a magnet for younger travellers attracted by the outdoor bar and restaurant, this is gradually becoming less appealing with the absence of the crowds. Still not bad if you don't mind paying a bit extra for S/C, AC comforts. ③.

Hôtel Paloma, rue du Grand Marché, corner of rue de la Gare. Scruffy and windowless cells with the merits of cheapness and a very central location. Bargain hard. ①.

Hôtel de la Plage (☎21.32.64). Right on the beach and only a short walk from the market, this hotel used to be *the* haunt of budget travellers fresh in from Ghana. These days it's on a steep decline, grubby and very insecure. ②.

Secourina Hôtel, 63 route d'Aného with annex 100 metres down the street, (☎21.60.20). Newer place with comfortable AC rooms with phones and lots of hot water. For hotels in the price range, it's good value: creature comforts without chain-hotel sterility. ③.

Upmarket hotels

Hôtel de la Paix Frantel, 3km east of the city centre, set back from the sea (BP 3452; ☎21.52.97; Fax 21.23.02). Badly run-down with chipped paint, water stains and a depressing atmosphere. Despite the attraction of its own beachfront, hard to recommend. ⑤.

Hôtel Palm Beach, bd de la Marina at rue Gallieni. A new high-rise hotel which looks promising, though it had the bad fortune to open just as tourists stopped coming to town. Comfortable rooms overlooking the beach plus a pool, nightclub and casino. ⑤.

Hôtel Sarakawa PLM, 3km east of downtown (BP 2232; ☎21.65.90; Fax 21.71.80). A huge pool dominates the grounds and you'll find TV and phones in every room. But even this once irreproachable (if perfectly predictable) international hotel has become tatty of late, though it's still the most popular with business travellers. ⑦.

Hôtel du 2 Février Sofitel, place de l'Indépendance (BP 131; ☎21.00.03; Fax 21.62.66). Not the one you'd be likely to choose, and not the most expensive, but a mad folly with nearly 400 rooms and a handful of guests knocking around inside like seeds in a calabash. Somewhat spooky really, and the impeccable views are the most it has in its favour. ⑦.

The City

There's not really a lot in Lomé to go out of your way to see, but there's plenty to take in as you wander through town. At some stage in your stay, try and have a look at the **Hôtel du 2 Février**, built to commemorate the president's miraculous escape and "Triumphal Return" after his plane crashed near Sarakawa. On clear days, you get a splendid panoramic view of Lomé, Ghana and the coastline from the top-floor restaurant and bar. Even a small drink costs a packet.

The focal point of the city, the Grand Marché, takes up a full city block near the ocean and may occupy a lot of your time. Lomé has numerous other market districts specializing in everything from bicycle parts to fetish paraphernalia.

If you're looking for a **beach** to lie on, in town you're limited to stretches of shore in front of *Hôtel de la Paix* and the old *Hôtel le Bénin*, the latter more popular, especially at weekends; however they're both dirty, prone to crime and the sea has a fearfully strong undertow. Out of town past the port, *Robinson Plage* draws a large weekend crowd and is a far better bet. The sand bar makes for safe swimming and the shipwreck adds a certain something.

The Grand Marché

Business in the **Grand Marché** is slowly picking up after the strikes, and though Lomé's market is not the regional draw it once was (formerly merchants from as far afield as Zaire would trade here), there's again a wide range of goods. It's not an attractive building but it is about the only place you need to go for provisions, presents, in fact purchases of any kind. Commerce spills over into all the surrounding streets as traders (mostly women between the ages of 3 and 103) zig-zag through the crowd to hawk everything from rat poison to greetings cards.

The **ground floor** of the building is filled with food – canned food, fruit and vegetables, meat, poultry, fish, and staples like yams, rice, cassava and pasta, spices and peanut butter. Sellers have a flare for display and fruit and vegetables are invariably arranged in eye-catching pyramids of colour. Quality is generally high, though if you're cooking it's best to buy meat first thing in the morning, for obvious reasons.

Up on the **first floor**, the celebrated, and extravagantly proportioned **"Nana Benz"** (which, roughly translated, means "Mercedes Mamas", a reference to the cars they often drive) lounge around fanning themselves in a decadent style befitting their reputation as some of the richest and most adept business people in Africa. They monopolize the sale of **cloth** and journey as far as Europe and Saudi Arabia to assure a stock that attracts buyers from the whole region. "Made in Holland" Dutch wax prints are their most expensive and prestigious wares, but you'll also find English and African prints, hand-woven *kente* cloth from Ghana, Ewe strip cloth, naturally dyed indigo wraps from Guinea and Mali and rough cotton weaves from the Sahel.

Generally you'll have to buy in relatively large quantities here (the rue du Commerce is the place for single cloths), though after recent lean years the Mamas have begun to make exceptions. Material is traditionally sold by *la pièce*, *une pièce* being six *pagnes*, and a *pagne* roughly equal to an arms-spread – or about 1.8m, the length of a wrap. The smallest length you can traditionally buy in the market is a *demi-pièce* or three pagnes' worth, the cost of which varies according to the method and place of manufacture. Prices are marked and, although you may be able to get the vendor to come down slightly, bargaining never gets you very far here.

The **second floor** at the top is a hodge-podge emporium of goods – everything from bicycle tyres to wigs, envelopes and Chinese enamel basins to plastic dolls (white as well as black). Mountains of cosmetics – lotions, shampoos, make-up – swamp an entire section. This is also where you can buy the cheapest cigarettes in town, by the carton.

Handicraft markets

Crafts from all over West Africa filter into Lomé and there are several locations in town to look for them. The main selling venue is the **Passage des Arts**, where you'll find a large selection of carvings, batiks, sculpture and other handicrafts here, although the majority come from Nigeria, Cameroon, Ghana and even Kenya; there's little in the way of typically Togolese art. Beware of "antiques": they almost never are. Prices are steep and the pressure to buy can be unpleasant, but the urgency of the vendors gradually gives way to something more bearable if you hang on for a few minutes, especially if you make a purchase, even of something small.

Opposite the cathedral on the rue du Commerce, the handmade **sandals** sold on the streetside are comfortable and sturdy, qualities that have made them popular throughout West Africa. The kind with the cushioned soles and toe loop go for about CFA2000 and are worth every franc. On the same street, you'll also find **cloth**, and you can easily buy short lengths of one or two *pagnes* here.

On the rue de la Gare, next to the *Bopato* café, you'll find the biggest selection of **batiks** and some vaguely African-looking tie-dyed dresses and shirts mixed together with carvings and other bric-a-brac.

Over on the route d'Aného, near the tourist office, you'll find brilliantly patterned **blankets** – mainly from Mali and Niger. These are handmade and expensive, but patient bargaining gets results. Something big enough to cover a double bed or look huge and striking on a wall should ultimately cost somewhere between CFA20,000 and CFA30,000, though price is determined to some extent by the state of the market, the time of year and the number of profligate punters in town. Another regular treasure trove of blankets is laid out on the pavement across from the *Goyi Score* supermarket on rue Gallieni.

On the eastern end of the rue du Commerce, the **tourist information office** has a showroom for regional crafts, including batiks, carvings and brasswork, produced mainly for aesthetic appeal – the traditional function of the masks and other objects has pretty much ceded to the desire to please souvenir-hunters. Prices are marked here, so you can get a rough idea how much things are going for.

The museum

The **National History Museum** has been relegated to a small room in the *Palais de Congrès* (formerly the party headquarters) for over a decade and since the troubles is closed indefinitely. Even if it opens again, you'll find the pickings are decidedly slim. Musical instruments and religious objects (statues, masks and ceremonial dress) give the merest glimpse into the material cultures of various ethnic groups such as the Kabyé, Mina and Ewe. One room is dedicated to the colonial period, tracing it from Nachtigal's landing in 1884 through the division of Togoland between the French and British in 1914 and ploddingly on to independence, with a succession of pictures of moustachioed governors puffing their be-medalled chests.

The Bé and Amoutivé markets

The **Bé market**, on the rue Pa de Souza, lost much of its charm when walls went up around it in the early 1980s and the adjoining fetish market was moved to Akodessewa (see below). Now Bé is mainly a neighbourhood market with food items and a scattering of pottery, calabashes (rapidly losing ground to "Made in Nigeria" plastic ware) and other household items. The **Amoutivé market**, on the rue Mama N'Danida, is similar.

Akodessewa fetish market

The **Marché des Féticheurs** at Akodessewa is a popular draw for visitors and Loméans alike, despite its distance, some 8km from the city centre. Adjoining a small food market in this northeastern suburb, it is West Africa's largest fetish market – a myriad of stalls displaying animal skulls, rotting bird carcases, statues, bells, powders and all the imaginable and unimaginable ingredients of **traditional medicine and religion**.

Children are always pestering to show you around the stalls and explain some of the charms or **gri-gris** – as usual, explain what you'll give (CFA100–200) before setting off, and make the most of what they know. Mostly they'll try to interest you in a talisman for safe travel or success in love – disarmingly inexpensive items that it's easy to take an interest in. Scorpions and dead snakes, used to make potions for ailments such as arthritis and rheumatism, have a more ghoulish and less user-friendly appeal. Though fetishers won't hesitate to make a quick sell, at times giving the feeling of a fleecing operation, it's a serious profession, still handed down jealously from generation to generation. The reputation of the Togolese for their spiritual gifts is widespread. A little time spent here listening to tales of supernatural healing and therapy will sow seeds of doubt in the most rational mind.

The powers of the *féticheurs* are sought after by all classes. In Togo, the overwhelming majority still practises traditional ("animist") religions and even the Christian and Muslim minorities commonly incorporate traditional practices into their beliefs. But the reputation of Akodessewa also attracts people from all over West Africa, and from as far away as Gabon and Zaire.

There are two ways of **getting to the market**. The first is to head out on the Nouvelle rue de Bé or the rue Notre Dame des Apôtres, which converge by the old **Fôret Sacré** ("Sacred Forest", on the left) and pass the former site of the fetish market at Bé. The forest is a remarkable little jungle, surrounded by buildings, but out of bounds to non-believers. Alternatively, you can go the more boring way, by taking the route d'Aného along the coast, past the *Hôtel Sarakawa*. At the Rond-point du port, 6km from central Lomé, turn left and follow the paved road for a kilometre and a half. If you're getting to Akodessewa by private taxi, expect to pay over the odds for the distance.

Eating

Cheap **street food** can be found – during the day only – mainly around the different markets in town. At the Grand Marché, women serve delicious salads from stands directly opposite the taxi park. They'll throw anything that strikes your fancy onto the bed of lettuce – tomatoes, macaroni, avocadoes, even grilled chicken or Guinea fowl – and top it off with a tangy vinegar sauce. It's an excellent meal, so long as your system is acclimatized to somewhat insanitary conditions. Behind these stalls, women sell *fufu*, or *akoumé* (fermented white corn mash) with different sauces and meat (beef, goat, chicken). Similar food can be found in the Amoutivé and Bé markets.

For cheap eating **after dark**, try in front of the popular *50/50 Bar-restaurant* (aka *Free Time*) on the bd Circulaire next to *Hôtel Ahodikpe Eboma*. At **breakfast** time, keep your eye out for *les caféman*. Scattered about town, they serve cheap omelettes with Nescafé and bread.

If you're looking to off-load some funds in an **upmarket restaurant**, Lomé can easily oblige. Note, however, that the drop in tourism, combined with frequent strikes, bombings and the mass exodus of residents has caused many restaurants to close and others seem to be scraping by. The once popular *Marox*, for example, on the rue du Commerce, famous among travellers for its inexpensive German deli-type meals, had to close when it was bombed in broad daylight. Places open and close their doors frequently these days and the following is an abbreviated list of the restaurants that seem to be the most stable.

Low-cost eateries

L'Amitié, bd Circulaire. A pleasant place to sit, with a bar, simple, inexpensive food and no pretentions. Local musicians often drop by.

Bopato, rue de la Gare, across from the *BIAO* bank. Sandwiches and snacks in the outdoor café. The tourist custom assures a steady flow of hawkers. Tedious, but still a good place to meet people and one of Lomé's main rendezvous.

Fouta Djalon, 238 bd Circulaire, east. A good-value Guinean restaurant where you can eat for about CFA1000.

I Thank Jehovah Dieux Merci, bd 13 Janvier, near the Kpalimé road, has a huge range of interesting bean dishes, yam stew, things fried and boiled – a diversity of tastes and incredibly inexpensive. You pay by the portion, average CFA100–200. It's not slick, but for real food, well cooked, it's one of West Africa's best eating houses.

Restaurant de la Paix, north of bd Circulaire, northeast, near the *Hôtel du Boulevard*. A third Guinean place and likewise excellent value – *steack-frites*, omelettes, *couscous, lait caillé.*

Restaurant Sénégalais, rue du Commerce. Reasonable meals on a pleasantly shaded street terrace.

Moderate restaurants and cafés

La Canne à Sucre, off bd Circulaire, east. Curious grey and pink bamboo decor, but the breezy upstairs patio is a pleasant place to enjoy good food, including pizza, at moderate prices.

Kilimandjaro, bd Circulaire near rte de Kpalimé (☎22.04.67). Ethiopian restaurant (*njera* bread "plates" served with *wat* stew) with indoor or outdoor dining and currently popular with the expat crowd. Not too expensive.

Marox restaurant, near the market, always pulls in a crowd, mainly ex-pat and showy Togolese. It's run by Germans and does a big trade in sausages and meat dishes with fries and salads from around CFA2500.

L'Orientale, bd Circulaire, south of the *50/50 Bar*. Good Lebanese restaurant with eat-in or take-out dishes.

Rabile, near the *Santa Fé*. Sandwiches and grilled meat, but the location on one of the busiest intersections in town makes for a loud and exhausting lunch.

Relais de la Poste, av de la Libération. Good French food at reasonable prices. Only 50 metres from the post office, it's also a fine place for breakfast while you read your mail.

Santa Fé Bar and Restaurant, 217 bd Circulaire (☎21.75.88). Still attracts a sprinkling of expats and travellers who enjoy excellent brochettes and French fare like steak *à la crème*, plus soups, salads and fast food. Meals cost around CFA3000 and drinks are slightly pricier than in local bars.

Expensive restaurants

All the big hotels serve French cuisine at elevated prices. There are several good, independent, French establishments, plus a number of other international restaurants worth trying.

AFRICAN

Keur Rama, 290 bd Circulaire (☎21.54.62). Delicious fricassee of bush rat ("grasscutter" or *agouti*) and a long *carte* of other African specialities. Highly recommended and shouldn't cost more than CFA6000 a head.

CHINESE/VIETNAMESE

Le Galion, off the bd de la République (see "Accommodation"). This popular hotel also has the town's best Vietnamese restaurant with a superb selection of reasonably priced specialities and very friendly service.

Golden Crown, bd du Mono, around the corner of bd Circulaire and route d'Aného. A first-class restaurant with wonderful dishes, and not over-priced, from CFA4000 a head.

Le Jade, route de Kpalimé. Superb food – around CFA5000 per head.

ITALIAN

Green Field, bd de Cebevito Tokoin-Hôpital, just east of the rte de Kpalimé. Very busy place where the chef slaps pizzas together behind the horseshoe bar and the overworked waitresses try to cope with 100 customers or more. Good atmosphere, but not the place if you're in a hurry.

Da Silvia, 298 bd Circulaire. Much more formal and expensive Italian food.

FRENCH

Ali Baba, bd de la République. Good fresh fish dishes. Accommodating owner and reasonable prices: expect to pay around CFA4000.

L'Auberge Provençale, bd de la République, at the border(☎21.16.82). A flashy place to spend a lot of money, preferably someone else's. Wonderful bouillabaisse and other seafood, plus *couscous* and paella (specialities need advance ordering).

Le Belvedere, av Duisburg in the Kodjoviakopé neighbourhood. Good French cooking in the open air for around CFA3500.

Nightlife

Sadly, after years of curfew and fear, people tend to keep indoors after dark these days. Sections of town are considered dangerous when the sun goes down, notably anywhere along the beach road or around the Grand Marché. There's still a range of **discos**, running the gamut from popular spots where you pay no entrance and drinks are hardly more expensive than in daytime bars, to flashy joints with complicated light shows and DJs hyping up the crowds. Those crowds are usually thin, however, and many of the best, cheap places towards the Ghana border in Kodjoviakopé have had to close.

Among Lomé's workaday **bars**, *Le Pajar Bar* by the *Goyi Score* supermarket stands out – exceptionally cheap draught *BB*, served in an atmosphere of advanced mayhem. For a good bar to kick the evening off, the *Free Time* (still known as the *50/50 Bar*) is perennially popular and doesn't draw an especially touristy crowd.

Bars, Clubs and discos

L'Abreuvoir, rue de la Gare, near *SGGG* (☎21.64.88). Popular with travellers.

African Queen, rte d'Atakpamé, Tokoin. Low prices and the ambience of a youthful *boîte populaire* have helped this one hang on as other clubs have closed.

Café des Arts, 229 bd Circulaire. With few volunteers, the mainstay clientele, around, no longer such a popular evening rendezvous, despite the unusual milkshakes and *pression* beer.

Domino, rue de la Gare, near *SGGG* . Popular nightspot but drinks are not cheap.

Maquina Loca, 8 av de Calais (☎21.75.55). Popular European-style dance house. Full sound and light show plus a heavy emphasis on Euro-American disco. Cover and drinks relatively expensive.

Oro Night Club, 85 rue de la Paix, 300 metres from bd Circulaire, Quartier Bé. One of the town's most expensive clubs; very high-tech, very good music and very in to be seen at.

Privilège, *Hôtel Palm Beach*. Throbbing disco atmosphere in a new and trendy venue.

Safari Club, route de Kpalimé, just north of the lagoon. Large dance area and low prices attract an exuberant crowd of young partiers.

Z, rue Kokéti near the *Abreuvoir*. Expensive club that attracts an upmarket crowd, with lights and the whole shebang.

Listings

Airline offices include: *Aeroflot*, 7 av 24 Janvier (☎21.04.80); *Air Afrique*, 12 rue du Commerce (☎21.20.42 or 21.20.44); *Air France*, 20 rue du Commerce (☎21.69.10); *Ghana Airways*, 16 rue du Commerce (☎21.56.91 or 21.72.91); *KLM*, Immeuble TABA, 1 rue du Commerce (☎21.63.30 or 21.63.31); *Nigeria Airways*, Immeuble, Vendome, rue du Maréchal Foch, by the Passage des Arts (☎58.26.32 or 58.26.54); *Sabena*, Immeuble TABA, 1 rue du Commerce (☎21.73.33 or 21.75.55) or *Swissair*, 9 rte d'Aného (☎21.31.57).

American Express The representative is upstairs in the Immeuble STMP, 2 rue du Commerce, (☎21.26.11).

Banks include: *BIAO*, on the corner of the rue du Commerce and rue de la Gare, Mon–Fri 7.30–11.30am & 2.30–4pm (☎21.32.86); *UTB*, 20 rue du Grand Marché, Mon–Fri 7.45–11.30am & 2.45–5pm; and *BTCI*, bd Circulaire near av de la Libération, Mon–Fri 7.30–11.30am & 12.30–4pm (☎21.46.41; Fax 21.32.65).

Books and magazines Foreign newspapers (though no British ones) are sold at the airport. You'll sometimes find *Time*, *Newsweek* and even *West Africa* magazine hawked around town. *Maladis* off bd de la Libération (see map) has a good selection of books and foreign newspapers – from *Jeune Afrique* to the *Herald Tribune* and *Der Spiegel*. *Librairie Bon Pasteur*, corner of rue du Commerce and av de la Libération, has a wide selection of French papers and mags plus fiction and non-fiction in French. For second-hand books in English, try the ambulant pedlars along the rue du Commerce.

Clinics and hospitals The *Centre Hospitalier Universitaire* (CHU) in the north of town in Tokoin is the main hospital (for ambulance phone numbers, see "Emergencies" below). There's a good Chinese-run clinic, the *Bon Secours*, across from the American embassy on rue du Maréchal Foch. Also worth trying is the *Clinique de L'Union* in Nyekonakpoe.

Embassies and honorary consulates include: **Belgium**, 165 rue Pelletier Caventou (BP 7643; ☎21.03.23); **Denmark**, Honorary Consulate (BP 2708; ☎21.34.45); **Egypt**, route d'Aného (☎21.24.43); **France**, 51 rue du Colonel de Roux (☎21.25.71; issues visas for Burkina Faso, Côte d'Ivoire, Mauritania and Senegal); **Gabon**, Tokoin Super-Taco (BP 9118; ☎21.47.76); **Germany**, bd de la Marina (☎21.23.38); **Ghana**, 8 rue Paulin-Eklou, Tokoin Ouest (BP 92; ☎21.31.94; plan on getting a visa before arriving in Togo as the embassy here is subject to closure); **Israel**, 159 rue de L'Ocam (BP 61187; ☎21.79.58; Fax 21.88.94); **Italy**, Honorary Consulate (BP 2105; ☎21.08.61); **Netherlands**, Honorary Consulate (BP 347; ☎21.63.31); **Nigeria**, 311 bd Circulaire (BP 1189; ☎21.39.25 or 21.34.55); **Norway/Sweden**, Honorary Consulate (BP 34; ☎21.07.13); **Switzerland**, Honorary Consulate (BP 495; ☎21.02.11); **Tunisia**, rue de Mélinas (BP 2983; ☎21.26.37); **United Kingdom**, Honorary Consul Mrs JA Sawyer, British School, Cité du Benin (BP 20050; ☎21.46.06; Fax 21.49.89); **USA**, corner of rue Pelletier Caventou and rue Vauban (BP 852; ☎21.29.91; Fax 21.79.52); **Zaire**, 325 bd Circulaire (BP 102; ☎21.51.55).

Emergencies The emergency number for the police is ☎17. For an ambulance, dial ☎21.20.42; or the hospital, ☎21.25.01.

Immigration The Sûreté National on the rue du Maréchal Joffre (near *SGGG*) handles requests for residency permits and visa extensions.

Laissez passers for Ghana Assuming the border is open you may need a *laissez passer* to cross (it depends on the state of relations between Togo and Ghana). This is obtainable from the Ministère de l'Administration du Territoire et de la Sécurité (MATS) up the street from the Palais de Justice, not far from the *Goyi Score* supermarket. You fill in the form in the morning (no need to leave your passport) and pick up the paper in the afternoon. The *laissez passer* is unlikely to be demanded if you cross at any other point, north of Lomé (eg Kpalimé or Badou).

Libraries and cultural centres The *American Cultural Centre* at the corner of rue Caventou and rue Vauban (across the street, north of the embassy) has a free library with American magazines and papers (Mon–Fri 9am–12.30pm and 3–6pm, Sat 9am–noon), ABC TV news and free movies every Fri afternoon at 3pm and 6pm respectively. The *Centre Culturel Français* on rue 24 Janvier is the most active of the cultural centres with theatre, dance, music, library and videos. The German equivalent, the *Goethe Institut* (see map), is worth visiting for shows and events.

Maps *Direction de la Cartographie Nationale*, corner of rue Maréchal Joffre and av Albert Sarraut. In theory, survey maps of the whole country at 1:50,000 and 1:200,000 are available.

Mechanics Professional and reliable service at *Turbo Garage* (☎21.16.28), rue Rhodes, Kodjoviakopé.

Notice boards and messages All the supermarkets have free notice boards – not so much used these days, but worth scanning for buying and selling, lifts, accommodation, employment and forthcoming events.

Pharmacies Ordinary hours are Mon–Fri 8.30am–noon & 3–6.30pm, Sat 8am–noon. Main ones include: *Togopharma*, towards the ocean from the Sûreté Nationale (☎21.32.47); *Pharmacie Akofa*, av Mama N'Danida (☎21.00.97); *Pharmacie du Bénin*, av de la Libération near the PTT (☎21.29.64); *Pharmacie Populaire*, 27 rue du Commerce (☎21.47.65); and *Pharmacie du Grand Marché*, 39 rue du Grand Marché (☎21.26.36). The *Pharmacie pour Tous*, route de Kpalimé, also has a clinic and can do X-rays and provide other medical attention. *Togo Presse* carries the changing list of pharmacies open out of hours (*pharmacies de garde*).

Phone Telephone and fax service behind the PTT. Calls can also be made from major hotels (more costly) and from an increasing number of phone boxes.

Photos and film Best-equipped place is *Colorama*, bd Circulaire, next to the *Santa Fé* restaurant. *Magic Photo*, rue du Commerce, offers more expensive one-hour development and on-the-spot passport photos. There's a photo booth on the rue du Commerce, next to the *Librairie Evangelique*.

Post office The main PTT (Mon–Fri 8am–noon & 2.30–5.30pm, Sat 7.30am–12.30pm) is on av de la Libération, near the bd Circulaire. Poste restante is helpful and reliable. There's a fee for each item collected.

Supermarkets include: *Goyi Score*, rue Maréchal Gallieni, near the Grand Marché, which has a good dairy department, wines, everything – just like France, but twice the price; and *SGGG*, which has several stores at the corner of rue Gallieni and rue de la Gare selling everything from plumbing fixtures to children's clothes.

Swimming pools The nicest and most expensive are at the hotels *2 Février* and *Sarakawa* (CFA2000 for non-guests). The *Hôtel de la Paix* has the cheapest pool in town.

MOVING ON FROM LOMÉ

PUBLIC TRANSPORT

The main **gare routière** is in **Agbalepedo** district 10km north of the centre, which handles northbound traffic to Atakpamé, Sokodé, Kara, Dapaong and Ouagadougou. For Kpalimé and towns along the Kpalimé road, there's a *gare routière* in the **Casablanca** neighbourhood, about 5km from the centre on the route de Kpalimé. Most taxis for Aflao, Aného, Cotonou and Lagos depart from the old **downtown** *gare routière* near the Grand Marché, but the *nouvel autogare* at **Akodessewa** also handles transport on the coastal routes, including direct taxis to Accra (when feasible; and see "Listings" above about *laissez passers*), Cotonou and Lagos.

The **train** schedules out of Lomé for **Blitta** and **Kpalimé** are very unreliable and services usually stop completely during periods of unrest – check at the station. In theory, the schedules are: dep. Lomé 5.45am daily, via Atakpamé (arr. 9.15am), arr. Blitta 11.45am; dep. Lomé 6.30am daily, arr. Kpalimé 11.30am.

CAR RENTAL AND TRAVEL AGENTS

If you're considering **renting a vehicle**, there are several outlets, including: *Africom*, 37 bd Circulaire (☎21.13.24); *Avis*, 252 bd Circulaire (☎21.10.33) and branch at airport; *Budget Rent-a-Car*, Kodjoviakopé (☎21.09.31) and at airport; *Hertz*, rue du Commerce (☎21.50.52), with branches in *Hôtel du 2 Février*, *Hôtel Sarakawa* and at the airport; and *Loc-Auto*, bd Circulaire (☎21.42.50).

With the game parks closed and the tourist industry virtually washed up, many of the **travel agents** have shut down. Perhaps the best address for finding reasonable **air tickets** is *STMP* at 2 rue du Commerce (☎21.57.93). Compare prices here with nearby agencies such as *Togo Palm Tours*, 1 rue du Commerce (☎21.57.84), or *Togo Tourisme*, 9 rue du Commerce (☎21.09.32), who are also agents for *Nouvelles Frontières* .

East of Lomé

The short drive from Lomé to the Benin border passes along the coastal highway, with alternating views of the lagoon and the Atlantic. The villages along this stretch are peopled by Mina and Gun (or Guin), who migrated from Ghana at the beginning of the nineteenth century. Today, they make their living principally from fishing, coconut planting and small-scale cultivation. Main towns like **Togoville** and **Aného** are interesting combinations of colonial relics and fetish symbolism and move to a slower rhythm than the capital.

Agbodrafo and Togoville

Perched atop a hill on the north shore of Lake Togo, Togoville is most easily reached by *pirogue* from behind the main coast road. First step is a taxi from Lomé, 30km to **AGBODRAFO**. Formerly known by its Portuguese name, Porto Seguro, this village was the site of a small coastal fort similar to those in Ghana. Today it's ruled by one **Fio**

EWE NAMES

As in the Asante country in Ghana, Ewe people usually take at least one name after the day of the week on which they were born.

	GIRLS' NAMES	BOYS' NAMES
Monday	Adzo	Kodjo
Tuesday	Abla	Komla
Wednesday	Aku	Kokou
Thursday	Ayawa	Yao
Friday	Afi	Koffi
Saturday	Ami	Komi
Sunday	Kosiwa or Essi	Kossi

Adjete Sedo Assiakoley IV who keeps the royal sceptres, thrones and weapons that have symbolized his family's authority in the region for 150 years.

Pirogues ply regularly between Agbodrafo and Togoville, leaving from a lagoon landing about 100 metres from the highway; any kid can point you there. You can rent a *pirogue* by paying the round-trip fare (at a price you negotiate) and arranging to be picked up in Togoville at a specified hour. Alternatively, you can simply wait for the boat to fill up with market women, though you will have a hard time convincing the *piroguier* to take you for the normal collective fare, and you may have a lot of hanging around on both shores.

Togoville town

Once you dock in **TOGOVILLE**, your itinerary will be pretty much determined by the boys who wait at the shorefront to be hired as semi-obligatory guides. You might as well go with the flow; they're nice enough and very adept at showing strangers the more interesting local curiosities. The first order of business, and one you can't refuse, is to **visit the chief** and advise him of your arrival. If he's in, the chief will greet you personally and show you his memorabilia, including photographs of his ancestors and copies of the famous document signed with the Germans. With great pomp you'll be asked to sign the **"Golden Book"** and a small gift is expected at this point.

The present ruler is a direct descendant of **Mlapa**, the village king who signed the treaty that made the Germans protectors of the region (at which time the town was known simply as Togo, meaning "beside the water"). The contract signed with this tiny village was the basis on which the colonial government laid claim to all of present-day Togo and much of Ghana.

Formalities completed, you can wander around Togoville at your leisure. The children take you first to the **Catholic cathedral**, built in the early part of the century by the Germans. Notice the interior murals of African martyrs being burned at the stake, and a shrine to the Virgin who was seen walking on the lake in the early 1980s. This miracle reportedly inspired the Pope's 1986 visit to Togoville.

Despite the work of the Catholic church, Togoville remains essentially animist. Walking through the narrow back streets, you'll be shown several fetishes, including two **fertility shrines** – one of a formidably endowed man and the other of a well-

THE VODU

For some background on "voodooism" and the *vodu*, see the next chapter, "Benin", and in particular, the box on p.920.

rounded woman with spikes protruding from her body. Photographs are permitted provided you leave a small offering. Beyond the small market, on the north side of town, a modern **statue** marks the centenary of the Germano-Togolese treaty, celebrated in 1984.

Practicalities

From the waterfront, the silhouette of the cathedral in Togoville stands out on the hill across the lake, while on the right, windsurfers, boaters, and swimmers disport themselves in the schistosome-free waters in front of **Agbodrafo's** *Hôtel Suisse-Castel* (☎35.00.07; ③). This is a pleasant place, with a pool, a good restaurant and watersports facilities. Another possibility is the nearby *Auberge du Lac*, which offers S/C bungalows geared to more modest budgets, with good food and an excellent setting on the lake (②–③).

In **Togoville**, even more modest accommodation can be had at the small *Auberge de l'Arbre de Palabre* or the *Hôtel Nachtigal* which offer only basic non-S/C lodgings (①).

Aného

Of all Togo's towns, the colonial presence is most strongly and most eerily felt in **ANÉHO** (10km from Agbodrafo). The Portuguese were the first to come to the spot – a pleasing natural setting with sea and lagoon vistas – which soon developed as a major slave market. Current African family names like de Souza and the light skin of the people are surprising reminders of this "Brazilian" period, further reflected in the history and culture of Ouidah in Benin (see p.918).

Many buildings, bear witness to the days when "Anecho" was the capital of Kaiser Wilhelm's prize African possession – among them, the **Peter and Paul Church** (1898), close to being washed by the ocean, the thick-walled **préfecture** near the bridge, the intereresting **German cemetery**, and the finely restored **Protestant church** (1895) on the route de Lomé. Other buildings are reminders of the French presence, including a number of grandiose villas used by colonial administrators when Aného was capital of the protectorate.

Aného has been in a slow decline for decades. Walking the streets, there's a feeling that residents are too entrapped in their daily routines of farming, fishing and trade to have any illusions of grandeur – or much opportunity to bring the old town to life. It's a small community, completely overshadowed by Lomé and with no hope of reviving its former commercial importance. All of which is a source of frustration for the young, most of whom migrate to the capital to seek their fortunes. But they leave Aného a satisfyingly moody place for travellers. The main **market** is on Tuesday and has a small fetish selection: monkey heads, crabs dead and alive, various skulls . . .

In contrast to the crumbling reminders of European occupation, Aného's **voodoo culture** thrives. Fetish priests are highly respected members of the community and are often more trusted than doctors practising Western medicine. Sacrifices are offered to shrines guarding many of the homes, and regular festivals are dedicated to the cult.

Practicalities

It isn't hard to find your way around Aného since virtually the whole of the town stretches along the **route de Lomé/Cotonou**. The market, post office, bank, *préfecture* and most shops are along this street between the Protestant church and the bridge. A more residential neighbourhood, and the area where you'll find all the major hotels and restaurants, lies across the bridge.

The first **hotel** you come to as you cross the bridge towards Cotonou is the *Oasis*, which has the best views of the sea and lagoon in town, and S/C rooms, most with AC (BP 171; ☎31.01.29; ②–③). Even if you don't stay, have a drink at the thatched terrace restaurant and watch the fishermen cast their nets into the shallow lagoon waters. Less expensive is the *Hôtel Royal Holiday*, which has very comfortable, large, carpeted S/C rooms with fan and small balcony or with AC (☎31.00.27; ②). The cheapest place to stay is the *Auberge Elmina* on the seafront near *SGGG* (①).

The market is the place for cheap **eating**; otherwise try one of the hotels listed above. For drinking, check out *La Paillotte* on the route de Lomé, which has an unremarkable bar, but good music and atmosphere. The *Jardin Mama N'Danida*, in front of the Protestant church, serves cold drinks and food during the day in its shady garden.

MOVING ON FROM ANÉHO

The main *gare routière* in Aného is across the lagoon in the east of town towards the Benin border at Hilakondji. **Taxis** run direct from here to Cotonou and Lomé. It's also possible to flag down taxis to Lomé if you stand on the main road near the market.

Glidji

On the surface, **GLIDJI**, 4km north of Aného, looks just like any other Mina village. You'll notice the same *banco* huts with thatched roofs and the same narrow sandy streets found all along the coast. Yet the town is symbolically important since the present chief is a direct descendant of **Foli-Bebe** – the first ruler of the region and the man responsible for the political organization of the Gun and Mina into independent chiefdoms after these peoples migrated from the Accra area in the early seventeenth century. Before starting off through town, you should pay a **visit to the chief**. To do so, you have to fill out a request at the royal secretariat. If the chief is around, and not otherwise occupied, he will receive you.

Glidji is also important from a religious perspective, since all the major sanctuaries to the principal **voodoo deities** are found in this town. You won't have trouble finding a boy to take you around to visit the different **fetish shrines** and voodoo **meeting places**. Ask to see the **temple of Egou**, the deity who is traditional protector of the Mina people.

THE YÉKÉYÉKÉ FESTIVAL

Because of its **historical and religious pre-eminence**, Glidji is the site of the **Yékéyéké festival**, celebrated annually on the Thursday before the second Sunday in September. Delegations arrive from all the major Mina and Gun centres to make offerings to the deities and to be blessed by the priests. Animals are sacrificed, but the climax of the ceremonies occurs when the colour of the **sacred stone** is revealed. This stone determines the fortune of the coming year. For example, a blue stone indicates abundant rain. If your stay in the area coincides with the festival, these are four days of celebrating not to be missed. Note that there's no **accommodation** in Glidji, so you have to stay in Aného. And, around *Yékéyéké* time, room availability is very tight.

THE PLATEAU REGION

Some of the country's most beautiful and fertile rural back country is located in the **plateau region** in the southwest quadrant of the country along the Ghanaian border – Togo's most agriculturally significant district. With its mountain vistas, thick vine-strewn forests and streams leaping in cascades from ragged clifftops, this corresponds to a stereotype of the jungle – especially if you've been brought up on Tarzan- type images. The wild country is as much a part of the region's scenery as the lush plantations of coffee, cocoa and fruit crops that make it so important economically.

Just a few hours from Lomé, the whole area is wonderfully accessible too, ethnically diverse and full of opportunities for hiking and discovery. The **coffee and cocoa** triangle, hemmed in by the towns of **Kpalimé**, **Badou** and **Atakpamé**, is home to several ethnic groups who came here from Ghana and the coast. Kpalimé and surrounding villages retain essentially Ewe populations but Badou and Atakpamé are melting pots of agricultural peoples.

Kpalimé and around

Capital of the *pays cacao* – the **cocoa country** – and of the entire fruit-growing region, **KPALIMÉ's** unusually busy market is your first hint of its importance. Early on in their brief rule, the Germans recognized the agricultural potential of this mild and attractive district. Once the plantations were established, they wasted no time in driving a **railway** through the forested hills to the town, and since that time Kpalimé has never been long out of the news in Togo. It was a stronghold of Olympio support in the early days after independence and even now is considered to be anti-Eyadéma.

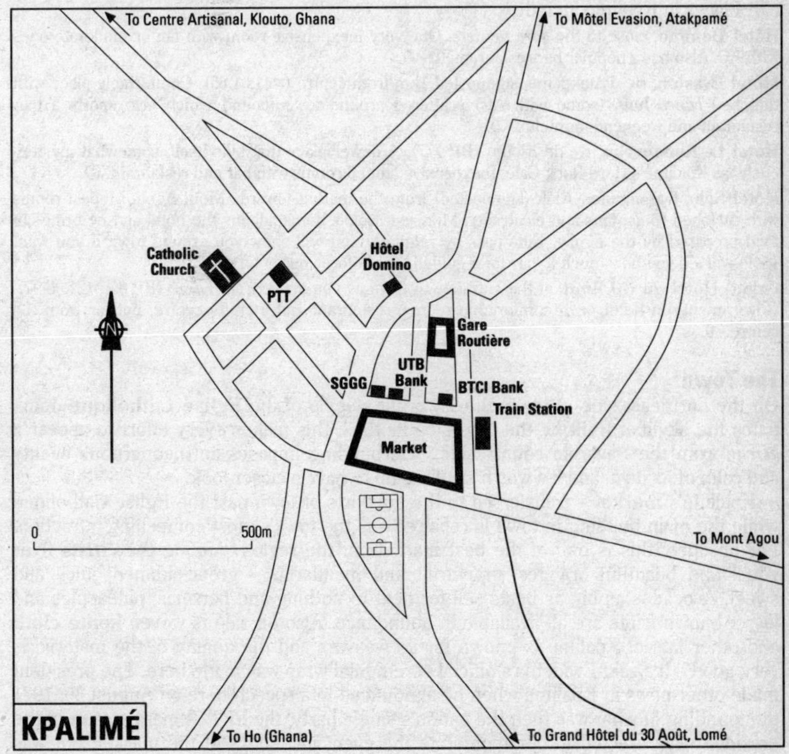

There's enough to see and do around Kpalimé to keep you busy for a couple of days – and longer if you're into **trekking** in the nearby mountains. But the town is small and, if you have less time, you can still get a good feel of the place in a day.

Arrival, orientation and accommodation

If you're **arriving by taxi**, you'll find the *autogare* is near the old market building, off the road leading to Klouto. The **train station** (this is the end of the line from Lomé) is right on the market square, on a hilltop in the town centre. Standing here, mountains rise in all directions around you. To the east, a TV tower rockets up from a distant peak to interrupt the harmony of the setting but helps you spot Togo's highest summit – Mount Agou (986m). Closer to hand, most immediate needs can be met in the area around the market. **Banks** (*UTB* and *BTCI*: Mon–Fri 7.30–11.30am & 2.30–4pm), **shops** (including an *SGGG* supermarket) and cheap **restaurants** line the streets that box in the market area. The **post office** is on the north side, towards the Catholic church, beyond which is the temporary home of the market.

Accommodation

Besides the **hotels** in Kpalimé, of which there's a good choice, you can also find accommodation around the pretty nearby town of Klouto (see opposite), but, despite the beautiful scenery, you're likely to feel stranded there if you don't have your own car. Places in Kpalimé include:

Hôtel Domino, close to the *gare routière*. One very inexpensive room with fan or moderate ones with AC. Also has a popular bar-restaurant. ①–②.

Motel Evasion, rte d'Atakpamé, signposted 1km from centre (☎41.01.85). Comfortable place with thatched *banco* huts (some with AC) scattered around a compound which also sports a bar-restaurant and weekend nightclub. ②.

Hôtel Le Renouveau, rte de Klouto (BP 177). A newer place that bills itself, somewhat mysteriously, as Kpalimé's Hard Rock Café. Inexpensive fanned rooms with bar and restaurant. ①.

Hôtel Solo, five minutes' walk (signposted) from the market towards Mont Agou. Modest rooms with thatched roofs, fans and electricity. Monsieur Solo's home adjoins the hotel and he brings in food prepared by the family. Kids pass by regularly and will show you around town if you want (Solo will tell you how much to pay for a guided tour before you set off). ①.

Grand Hôtel du 30 Août, at the entrance to town as you arrive from Lomé (BP 85; ☎21.95.97). Government-run hotel, with comfortable rooms, restaurant and a crafts centre, but far from the centre. ③.

The Town

On the northeast side of town, the towering steeple of the **Eglise Catholique** dominates the skyline. Built by the Germans in 1913, this makes every effort to appear a *kirche* from the Bavarian countryside. The building imposes an incongruous beauty and calm of its own, and it's worth strolling up to have a closer look.

Kpalimé's **market** – transferred to the outskirts of town past the Eglise Catholique while the main building in town is repaired – is the town's most compelling attraction. For produce, this is one of the best markets in the region. Among the **citrus fruit** you'll find beautiful oranges, grapefruit and mandarins – green-skinned, juicy and sweet. Avocados as big as boats sell for next to nothing and bananas, pineapples and lesser-known fruits are all available in abundance. Also on sale is woven **kente cloth** and other fabric. Kpalimé is known for its weavers and the quality of the material is very good – it's said Eyadéma's official ceremonial wrap was made here. The president made other news in Kpalimé when he announced in a speech here on August 30, 1971 the founding of what was then the nation's single party, the RPT. A giant **statue** of the president was erected to commemorate the event just south of the market, but was toppled in the riots that followed the 1991 coup attempt. Now a stronghold of anti-

Eyadéma sentiment, thousands of refugees passed through the border here into Ghana during the upheaval of the early 1990s.

Down near the stadium, **weavers** work foot-operated looms at the roadside. They'll be happy to chat if you want to stop, never breaking the rhythm of their movements in the course of conversation. It's not hard to appreciate the time involved in making cloth and why it's so expensive. You can order directly from the weavers, but you have to be prepared to wait several days (or even weeks) for bespoke products.

The **Centre Artisanal de Kpalimé** (Mon–Fri 7am–noon & 2.30–5.30pm; Sat 8.30am–noon & 3–5pm; Sun 8.30am–1pm), on the route de Klouto, a couple of kilometres from the town centre, offers more immediate fulfilment. This crafts centre is a whole complex, run by the state to encourage the arts. Much of the work consists of modern interpretations of conventional forms – calabashes carved into delicate lampshades, pottery ashtrays, and decorative statues and batiks (though the origins of the latter are completely un-African) depicting ceremonial masks or village scenes. The excellent wood carvings, such as the chairs and tables sculpted out of single tree trunks, represent a more traditional – though less portable – type of expression. *Kente* cloth is made at the centre too, but prices are well up on the market in town.

MOVING ON FROM KPALIMÉ

From the *gare routière* in Kpalimé, **taxis** run to the **Ghana border**, **Lomé** (1hr15 min) and **Atakpamé** – the latter a pretty route skirting the Danyi plateau. For Lomé, one **train**, in theory, leaves daily at 1.20pm (journey time 4hr 30min). Should you be heading to – or just arrived from Ghana – **moneychangers** openly convert CFA to cedis and vice versa – but try to get an idea of the street rate in advance.

Klouto and Mont Agou

Some 12km northwest of Kpalimé, **KLOUTO** (also spelled Kloto) is a mountain retreat and site of an old **German hospital** built before World War I. The road up here from Kpalimé is nothing short of spectacular. Carved out by the Germans, it snakes up steep slopes through cocoa plantations and burrows through the dense **Missahohé Forest** where tree branches form a complete tunnel over the road in certain areas.

Collective taxis run pretty regularly from the Kpalimé *gare routière*, but your best chances are on market days. In the village of Konda, which you pass on the way to Mont Klouto, the *Auberge des Papillons*, is managed by local celebrity, Prosper the butterfly collector. It offers basic **accommodation**, with no running water or electricity, arranged round a *paillote* and all set in fledgling jungle (①). Guided bushwalks are extra. Less rudimentary lodgings are to be found near the summit of Mont Klouto where, amid the rolling hills and forest, the old colonial buildings of the *campement* provide a rustic retreat with pretty views in every direction (②). Even if you don't sleep here, it's worth stopping at the large *paillote* where you can order food and drinks. As you follow the road leading up here, you'll see the entrance to the **Chateau Viale** – a stone fortress of medieval aspect built during World War II by a French lawyer, Francois-Raymond Viale. It became state property in 1971 and is now used by the president, so you can forget about visiting it. Photography is forbidden.

Once you've arrived at the *campement*, you'll notice a path bordered by huge mango trees that leads to the top of **Mont Klouto** (741m). Before you set off, there's a CFA1000 fee to pay to the *gardiens* who keep the paths clear. From the mountain, you can see across into Ghana and may even be able to make out the shining, artificial expanse of the dammed **Lake Volta** 35km away to the west. Numerous rural villages are hidden in the forest around the *campement*, and the kids will be happy to take you around to see any of them or other curiosities in the area, including streams, small waterfalls and palm-wine makers. Of course, you're expected to dash them something, but for finding your way around the wilds, there's really no better way.

On market days, it's also possible to catch taxis from Kpalimé to villages on **Mont Agou** and to hike around its 1000-metre peaks. For more information, ask at the *Hôtel Solo* in Kpalimé. You'll have to plan on setting off at dawn and returning early, or risk missing the last taxi back to Kpalimé. If you have a car, a good road leads all the way to Mont Agou's 986-metre summit.

From Kpalimé to Atakpamé: the Danyi plateau

The road from Kpalimé to Atakpamé runs along the base of the sheer cliffs of the **Danyi plateau**, rising up to the west. About 10km out of Kpalimé, you can see the **Kpimé falls** from the roadside, a couple of kilometres up on the left (the driver or other passengers will point them out if you're in a taxi). The results of the hydro-electric dam built in the late 1970s haven't done much for the site's aesthetic appeal and in the dry season the falls are little more than a trickle, but during or after the rains, they tumble rewardingly a hundred metres off the cliffside.

It's a picturesque drive to Atakpamé, passing through numerous Akposso villages where you could easily stop and have a look around if you have your own transport. At **Dzogbégan** (turn off the road at Adeta, 30km from Kpalimé; then it's 20km further) no one will be surprised to see you as the **Benedictine monastery** a kilometre from the town has become a local attraction. Their chapel, built entirely of local materials – teak, iroko, mahogany, bamboo – is unusual, but the real interest is more gastronomic. The monks run an orchard and produce jams from the exotic fruit as well as coffee, honey and other comestibles not so often found in these regions. The *soeurs bénédictines*, who run a convent closer to the village, sell some of the same items. Both places have clean rooms with showers for stray travellers (①). Meals are excellent and very inexpensive.

A direct road runs from Dzogbégan to **Badou** (50km): it's not paved but is kept in good condition and provides some scenic views. **Agbo Kopé**, along the way, is a welcoming, tranquil village where you can stay cheaply (*Chez Momo*; ①) and visit the local forest and waterfall.

Atakpamé and around

Situated in the mountains, **ATAKPAMÉ** has historically been a place of refuge. The **Ewe** were the first to arrive, from Notsé, in the seventeenth century. They were followed by the **Ana** – a people related to the Yoruba who came from the east in the nineteenth century – and then by the Akposso who came down from the surrounding mountains in the early part of this century to farm the **fertile plains**. Today, Atakpamé's road links with Lomé, Badou and Kpalimé and the measure of **industry** in the area – a nearby textile works, the new hydro-electric power station and a sugar refinery 20km to the north in Anié – have all helped it maintain its status as a regional hub and an ethnic melting pot.

Practicalities

The most scenic approach to Atakpamé is from Kpalimé, via Hihéatro, a couple of kilometres west of the town. After this village, vehicles winds their way up one last steep hill and, before you were aware the town was anywhere nearby, turn a bend to pull into the *autogare Kpalimé* right by Atakpamé's market place. If you're

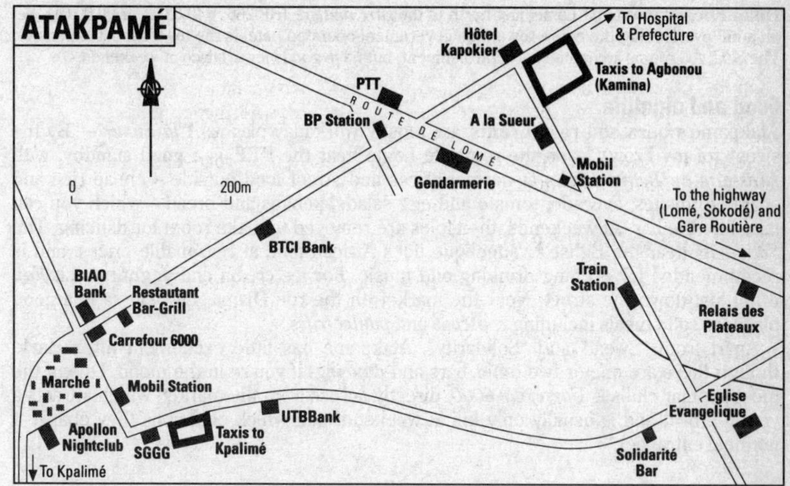

coming from Lomé or Sokodé, you'll be dropped at the main *autogare Sokodé-Lomé* across the other side of town, about 1km west of the *route nationale* junction and 1km east of the town centre. If you're planning on staying the night, most of the **hotels** are just around the latter *autogare*. The hilly topography of the town and its scattered environs are confusing. The local neighbourhoods – sprouting in the hillocky valleys or on the rocky hillsides – have grown up wherever people found it possible to build.

The **route de Lomé**, which runs northwest–southeast to meet the *route nationale*, is the major thoroughfare in town. Main hotels and the PTT are along this street, while **banks** (*BIAO* and *BTCI*: Mon–Fri 7.30–11.30am & 2.30–4pm) and **shops** cluster around the market on the west side. The **market**, although located on the edge of town, is substantial enough to be the real town centre; on Friday – market day – the commotion is sensational. If you head left down the road on the other side of the market, towards the Eglise Evangelique – whose modern bell tower can be seen for some distance – then take another left after the *Solidarité Bar*, and pass the **train station**, you'll have seen pretty well the whole of Atakpamé town centre.

Accommodation

Of **places to stay**, the cheap *chambres de passage* at the *Le Retour* bar, located very near the main *gare routière* off the route de Lomé, offer the minimum of comfort and lots of late-night noise, but it's not fair to complain given the cost (①) and central location. Another very basic alternative is to stay at the *Buvette Amou Kackpo*, 500m east of the market on the road to Kpalimé (①).

Foyer des Affaires Sociales, rte de Lomé near the main *gare routière*. Clean but spartan rooms typical of those run by the *Affaires Sociales* throughout the country. The restaurant is good value. ①.

Hôtel Chez Soi, near the *route nationale* junction. Inexpensive lodgings around a pretty garden and very friendly staff. The restaurant is good too. ②.

Hôtel Kopokier, off the rte de Lomé on the hospital road. More upmarket than *Chez Soi*, with comfortable S/C, AC rooms. ②.

Relais des Plateaux, rte de Lomé (☎40.02.32). Long a travellers' favourite with clean and comfortable S/C rooms available with or without AC. ②.

Hôtel Roc, off the rte de Lomé, just north of the *gare routière* (BP 266; ☎40.02.37 or 90.00.01). Set on a hill overlooking the entire town, this government-operated hotel is the town's most expensive. The S/C, AC rooms are in need of refurbishment, but have good views. Disco at weekends. ③.

Food and nightlife

Atakpamé's **bars** and **restaurants** are mostly workaday places. *A la Sueur* – "By the sweat (of my brow)" – on the route de Lomé near the PTT, is a good standby, with *Brasserie du Bénin* drinks at normal prices and street food outside – cheap rice and spaghetti dishes, avocado, tomato and egg salads, kebabs and bread – which you can take into the bar. At weekends, the tables are removed to make room for dancing. The *Solidarité* near the Eglise Evangelique does African food at reasonable prices, and is recommended for evening drinking and music. For ice cream and yoghurt, visit *Fan Milk*, just down the street. Near the market on the rue Djama, *La Sagesse* is a good place for solid meals including *couscous* and *poulet frites*.

Apart from "Sweat" and "Solidarity", Atakpamé has little excitement **after dark**, though there are one or two other bars and *dancings* if you're in the mood. One of the most popular clubs is *Carrefour 6000*, directly across from the market, which attracts a young crowd and is usually only full at weekends (on which occasions they charge a nominal entrance).

MOVING ON FROM ATAKPAMÉ

Taxis for Kpalimé and Badou leave from the *autogare Kpalimé*, in front of the market near the *Mobil* station. Taxis operating up and down the Lomé–Sokodé *route nationale* leave from the main *autogare* on the route de Lomé. Taxis for Agbonou (for Kamina) go from their own small *gare* just off the rte de Lomé.

The **train station** on the short Atakpamé branch line is sometimes closed to passengers. If you have your heart set on taking the train and the branch line into Atakpamé is not being used, you can get a collective taxi to Agbonou which is on the main Lomé–Blitta line. All trains on the Lomé–Blitta–Lomé run stop at Agbonou (assuming any trains are running at all). In theory, there's one train each day in each direction.

Kamina

KAMINA – a major German military post in the colonial era, complete with airstrip – is an easy excursion from Kpalimé. Today, a few buildings dating from the end of the nineteenth century are a reminder of the German occupation, one of which is now used to house a **boys' reform school**. The idea of such a school is quite revolutionary in this part of the world, and you might find it more interesting to visit than the town's historical remnants, which are hardly spectacular.

Assuming you don't have your own vehicle, the only way to get to Kamina is by collective taxi to **Agbonou** on the *route nationale* (they leave from opposite the *A la Sueur* bar). From Agbonou you can take a local taxi for the four kilometres of dirt road to Kamina.

Along the route, you'll notice the chief military officer's headquarters. Now in a ruinous state, it's still called the "first house" by locals, since it was the first cement building to go up in the area. Across the street is the grave of a German soldier dating from 1914. Apart from the barracks which are now a school and some cement pylons that once hooked up to a giant wireless transmitter linking Togo direct with Berlin, these are all that's left of the German presence. Most of the pylons have been reclaimed by the bush, but if you take a closer look at the only one visible near the school you'll see a hole chiselled into its base. Local folk history relates how the French put dynamite inside when they captured the colony and tried to blow the thing up. When the dust settled, the pylon was still standing.

Badou and around

BADOU is the smallest, most isolated and most distinctly rural of the three towns of the coffee and cocoa triangle. Most of its people are cash crop farmers and, despite the small size of the average farm, cocoa and coffee have brought a measure of prosperity to the people of the region. In neighbouring Akrowa they've even managed to pay for all their streets to be paved. But there have been setbacks in recent years with the falling price of cocoa on the world market. Recent gluts of both crops have wreaked economic havoc in the quiet forest districts around Badou, and many young people are pinning their hopes on salaried jobs in the towns.

Practicalities

You'll get your bearings pretty quickly since Badou has only one proper hotel, one bank and one restaurant, all located near the market. Taxis let you off at the town entrance at the junction of the Atakpamé and Tomegbé roads. To get to the **market**, head down the road that leads to Ghana, across a small bridge and past the *Toyota Bar*. Further along this same thoroughfare, you'll come to another fork marked by the *Carrefour 2000 bar/dancing*, Badou's liveliest place at night, which offers somewhat overpriced *chambres de passage* (①). Turning left at this junction, you pass the post office on the way to Badou's fanciest **accommodation** – the government-run *Hôtel Abuta*, with a European-style restaurant and AC rooms costing little more than those at the *Carrefour 2000* (☎91.11; ②). You can also can **camp** in the grounds here for CFA1000 per person. The **UTB bank** is right next door, but there's no guarantee they'll change foreign currency – it's best to take care of that in Atakpamé. Badou's **pharmacy** is just behind the hotel.

Young boys like to earn a few francs showing visitors round their town and its surrounds. Although Badou itself doesn't merit this treatment, you might want someone to take you to nearby hamlets. They'll sometimes even offer lodgings *en famille*, a cheaper and more enjoyable option than staying in the places in town.

Around Badou

One of the main attractions around Badou, and well worth taking the time to discover, is the **Akloa Falls**, 11km to the south. **Getting there**, you first need a taxi along the Tomegbé road to the village of Akloa (Akrowa on some maps). At its entrance, you'll see a hand-painted sign advertising the falls and a bar-restaurant. This is the official starting point for the falls hike up the mountain, and the place where you pay CFA500 for a ticket to proceed.

The **climb** to the falls is strenuous, but it requires determination rather than fitness. In any case, there's no rush; it's hard to resist dawdling through the cool, dark underbrush of the forest. After some thirty minutes of hiking through the dense vegetation, you arrive at the falls – a drop of over thirty metres from the granite cliff. You can swim in the pool at the base of the falls and it's said the waters are therapeutic. If you've come with people from the area, ask them to tell you about **Mamy Wada** – the spirit that guards the water – or about the numerous other supernatural forces in the forest. Two generations ago this whole area was sacred and off-limits to the uninitiated.

SOKODÉ AND THE CENTRAL REGION

In the semi-daze of a long and comfortless taxi ride, you could miss the many signs indicating the shifts in peoples and lifestyles as you move from the balmy south of Togo to the central and northern regions. Gradually, however, you take in the change from the traditional square buildings of the south to the round, thatch-roofed **banco huts** of the interior. Around these are fixed silos of baked earth, used to store millet and corn. North of the coffee and cocoa zone, **subsistence farming** is the major economic activity of the people, and, along the roadside, the earth is pushed up into small mounds planted with yams, groundnuts and cassava. Traditional **African religions** retain a tight hold on the inhabitants of **Bassar** and **Tchamba**, two major towns in the region. The place of the church in southern Togo, however, is increasingly taken by **Islam** as you head north. And by the time you reach **Sokodé**, a long day's travel from Lomé, the whole environment – natural, cultural, social – has changed.

The predominant ethnic group of the central region is the **Kotokoli**, a people who migrated south from Mali in the late eighteenth or early nineteenth century. They brought Islam with them and Sokodé is now the most devoutly Muslim town in the country. Numerous **mosques**, in faded pastel colours and crowned with the star and crescent moon, attest to their faith. So, too, does **dress style**, especially the flowing *boubous* (embroidered gowns) and skullcaps commonly worn by men. Women don't wear veils, but they do drape a long, transparent scarf over their heads, wrapping it around their necks and letting it fall over their backs to flap on the ground when they walk. In accordance with the strict code of manners, people bow to one another in greeting and children even go down on their knees when greeting parents or elders.

Sokodé

In terms of numbers, **SOKODÉ** is easily Togo's second largest town, with around 50,000 inhabitants. But development has been slow in coming. There are only three paved roads

FESTIVALS IN SOKODÉ

Sokodé is well known for its **festivals**, most of which revolve around Muslim religious holidays. During these occasions, the town breaks from its normal slow pace to become surprisingly animated – and even prospects of another bleak year for the economy don't seem to dampen people's spirits. One of the most important festivals is that marking the **end of Ramadan** (see p.62 for dates). The day this month-long fast ends, the entire male population of the city – decked out in embroidered *boubous* – gathers at the stadium for a collective prayer. Afterwards, the day dissolves into feasting and dancing.

The **Fête du Tabaski** – celebrating Abraham's sacrificing the lamb in place of his son – takes place two months later. Several days prior to this festival, the streets in town begin filling with sheep and goats, which on the day of *Tabaski* are slaughtered en masse, roasted and shared out among the community.

The **Knife Festival**, or *Adossa*, mixes Muslim elements with a custom that certainly pre-dates the introduction of Islam into Kotokoli society and has many parallels in other West African societies. On this occasion – marking Muhammad's birthday about three months after *Tabaski* – the men drink a potion specially prepared by a marabout which supposedly renders their skin impenetrable. In public dances, they then proceed to cut one another with knives. It's even said that babies who have been administered the potion are rolled over broken bottles with no harm coming to them.

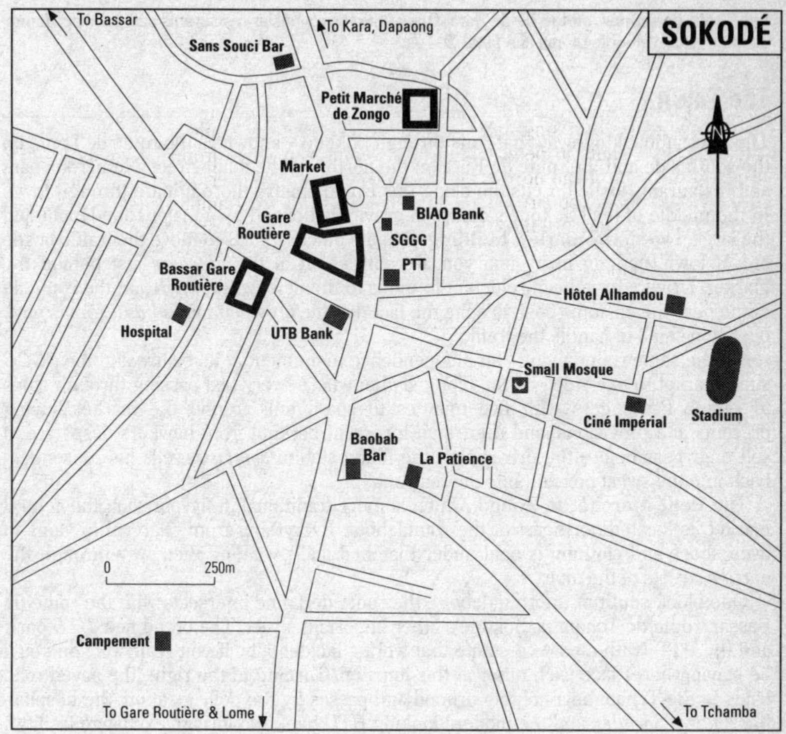

in town, including the Lomé–Dapaong *route nationale* and the road to Bassar, both of which run through the centre. Sokodé's position at the focus of the routes assures it a certain vitality despite obvious lack of government interest in stimulating the local economy. A good number of homes in the heart of town are still made of *banco* and thatch and most of the people are involved in trade and subsistence routines.

Accommodation

Sokodé has a number of possible **places to stay**, either to break a journey north or south, or if you're here for one of the festivals. If you are here during a festival, don't delay in finding a room – they can fill up quickly.

Hôtel Alhamdou, near the stadium. Among the cheapest rooms in town – with shared facilities and nothing fancier than fans, but clean and friendly. If it seems far from the centre when you take a taxi there from the *gare routière*, it's an easy walk once you get your bearings. ①.

Le Campement, off the route de Lomé near the *préfet*'s residence. An old colonial building set on a wooded hill overlooking the town. The place hasn't been kept up (they have modest rooms, or you can camp on the grounds) but it has a pleasant bar and restaurant. ①.

Hôtel Central, rte de Lomé (BP 37; ☎50.01.03) Fully S/C, AC rooms or bungalows, and formerly an expat favourite. Pleasant restaurant and bar. ③.

Le Relais de la Cigale, rte de Lomé. The AC rooms here are a cut above the rest, and those with fans are priced competitively with the town's budget hotels. Also a well-run restaurant and popular bar on a shady terrace, plus a boutique full of ethnic knick-knacks. ①–②.

Les Trois Fontaines, off the rte de Kara. One of the town's busier restaurants and good accommodation with tidy double rooms and fans. ②.

The Town

The international highway that runs through Sokodé – known as the route de Lomé on the south side and the route de Kara on the north – is the main street. Numerous bars and restaurants jostle for custom along this two-kilometre thoroughfare through town. In the middle of it all Sokodé's centre of gravity is defined by a major roundabout and the large, two-storey **market building**. Despite official efforts to move the traffic bustle out of town, coming in by taxi you are still let off in the *autogare* just behind the market. Drivers have been reluctant to move to the new *gare routière*, on the route de Lomé near the customs post, despite the fact that the crowded market *autogare* is obviously too small to handle the traffic.

On the same roundabout – an independence monument at its centre and the *SGGG* supermarket to one side – is the filling station where every taxi passing through stops to refuel. Passengers with five minutes to spare mill around the market buying presents and provisions, and there's an incessant barking from hawkers desperate to sell their gear before the driver pays the filling station *pompiste*, yells his passengers back into the sweat-box and hits the road again.

The **Petit Marché de Zongo**, which is more traditional in flavour than the central market, is located northeast of the roundabout. Everything from charcoal to yams to used shoes and clothing is sold under thatched stalls winding their way through the narrow streets of the quarter.

One block south of the roundabout, the route de Lomé intersects with the route de Bassar/route de Tchamba, Sokodé's other important street. The brand new *UTB* bank and the **PTT** (with a poste restante that works, incidentally, if you really reckon you'll be staying here) face each other at this junction. Turning to the right, the paved road leads to the Tchaoundja neighbourhood and passes by the police station, the hospital, the *Affaires Sociales*, and the modern-looking *BTD* bank (no foreign exchange facility). Turning left, the dirt road leads down to the town's main **mosques**, the **cinema** and the **stadium**. If you happen to be in town during a soccer match, be sure to get a ticket: **Semassi**, the home team, is one of the nation's best and, even if soccer isn't your bag, the enthusiasm of the crowd would give anyone a buzz.

Near the stadium is the site of Sokodé's new **Grande Mosquée**. The Saudis have been promising for years to send funds for the building's completion. The old Grande Mosquée, located a couple of streets southwest of the post office, is beautiful for its simplicity. It's completely devoid of ornamentation – you could walk right by and not even see it – but the humble architecture has a tolerant and undogmatic appeal.

Eating and nightlife

For **food**, budget travellers naturally head for the market. **Local specialities** include *watche* (rice and beans boiled together with onions and hot peppers), *kadadia* (mash made from finely ground cassava mixed with millet or corn) and *wagassi* (locally made cheese either served plain or deep-fried). In the evening you can get lamb kebabs. For snacking, be sure to try *kosse* (bean batter deep-fried in peanut oil) or *koliko* (yam chips), both local favourites.

Besides the hotel **restaurants**, a good place for casual sit-down meals is *La Patience*, located off the route de Lomé behind the *Baobab* bar where they do Europeanized dishes and salads from CFA1000; try the grilled guinea fowl – tough but tasty. Similar food – served outside under the mango trees – is also available at *Mama J'ai Faim* near the intersection of the Lomé and Tchamba roads. *Sans Souci* is a popular **bar** up on the route de Kara and they also serve some of the best kebabs in town. In the evenings, *Les Affaires Sociales* runs an outside **bar** in a courtyard giving onto the route de Bassar. There's a regular cluster of women on the street outside, serving salads and rice dishes.

Nightlife

Togo's current political and social uncertainty is especially felt in Sokodé, perhaps a consequence of the historical ill-feeling between the Kotokoli and the Kabyé. People in town speak of the dangers of going out **after dark** (unthinkable a short time ago) citing a lack of security and increase in the crime rate. It's not likely that you'll notice any clear cause for alarm, although walking in the streets after 9pm, you will probably feel quite alone. One of the only places going that late is *Les Trois Fontaines* and even here, the people don't muster much enthusiasm. You might also see what's going on at the *Relais de la Cigale*, where the nightclub once had an outstanding reputation. When things improve, other old and popular clubs like *La Gaité* in the Kpandidjio neighbourhood (off the route de Lomé near *La Patience*) and the upmarket *Zinaria*, on the rte de Bassar, may make a comeback.

MOVING ON FROM SOKODÉ

Taxis brousse head in all directions from Sokodé and most leave from the town centre or from the main *gare routière* (on the route de Lomé). Taxis heading to **Bassar** have their own *autogare* on the route de Bassar. If you're making the long haul north, there are no direct taxis to **Ouagadougou**. Direct vehicles come up from Lomé and are already full. Get as far as Dapaong and change – or preferably stop over there for the night.

North and west of Sokodé

The mountainous scenery and good roads around Sokodé provide opportunities for some easy excursions. Though the **Fazao National Park** is currently closed and being rehabilitated after much of the wildlife was exterminated, you might still, with a little luck and a helpful taxi driver, see an animal or two anyway – the hilly and forested **road to Bassar** passes right along the game park boundary, offering glimpses of shy **monkeys** scampering as soon as they hear the car coming.

A LITTLE KOTOKOLI

English/French	Kotokoli	English/French	Kotokoli
Welcome, bonne arrivée	*Nodé*	Yes	*Mmm*
		No	*Ay*
Bonjour (5–8am)	*Nyavinakozo* (pl. *Mivinekozo*)	How are you/Ça va? (" in health?")	*Alafyaweh?*
Bonjour (8am–4pm)	*Nawsé* (pl. *Minawose*)	Fine/Ça va ("fit")	*Mumumum*
		Fine / Ça marche ("the work")	*Kokani*
Bonsoir (4–7pm)	*Neda nana* (pl. *Minadananga*)	How much?	*Ngyinidé?*
Good night (may God wake you well)	*Esofesi*	Money	*Lidé*
		Five	*Byé*
See you tomorrow/later	*Blabtcheri* or *blabtesi*	Ten	*Byefu*
		Twenty-five	*Tchente*
Thankyou (for a gift),	*Eesobodi*	One hundred	*Alfa*
(for help or work completed)	*Natimaré*	Two hundred	*Alfa nolé*
		One Thousand	*Milé*

The road to **Bafilo** runs through equally striking scenery including the famous **Faille d'Aledjo** – a dramatic chasm, dynamited out of the cliff, through which the highway passes. Pictures of it help keep the Togolese postcard industry alive. Skull and crossbones warning signs line the twisting and looping road as it works its way over the mountains: if you're driving, the wrecked vehicles strewn in the valleys below are evidence they should be taken seriously. If you're a bush taxi passenger, tell the driver *allez doucement!*

Bafilo and around

Surrounded by mountains, **BAFILO** is the Kotokoli's second largest town and another Muslim fief – you'll see the large white **mosque** some distance before arrival. Bigger than any of the mosques in Sokodé, this place of worship was built by the funds of a single **alhadji** (one who's been to Mecca), a wealthy merchant and native son. Bafilo is a small town, easily visited in a day and famous for its hand-weaving industry.

The route de Kara is the only paved road and village life centres around the *gare routière* and adjoining market place. The main dirt road leads from the *gare routière* down to the mosque. About halfway between these landmarks, a small road (little more than a path) leads down to the **weavers' yards**. You can spot them easily enough by the looms they operate in the middle of the street, and by the skeins of yarn stretched out along the roadside. If you don't see these tell-tale signs, ask someone to take you *chez les tisserands*. The quality of their work has brought them distinction throughout the country, and prices, depending on your bargaining skills, are as low here as you'll find anywhere. They sell either strips of woven cloth, complete *pagnes* or ready-made clothes direct from their shops near the looms.

Accommodation

The choice is simple since there's only one hotel, the *Maza Esso* ("I thank God"). On the route de Kara, this extremely clean and well-managed establishment looks expensive, but the prices are wonderful, considering the quality (with fans and even AC available in higher-priced rooms). The restaurant does European food – for example good, reasonably priced breakfasts with coffee, toast and the works (②).

Bafilo Falls

The **Bafilo Falls** are the main attraction near the town. Located about 4km from the centre, you can get to them easily enough by continuing down the main road past the mosque. After about a kilometre, turn right through the fields of corn, groundnuts and beans and head for the mountains. You'll see villagers out tending the fields at most times of year and you can ask them to point you to *la cascade*. Small kids may even offer to accompany you, in which case a modest dash at the end (value dependent on how old they are) will bring smiles and peals of laughter – they're not too mercenary here, yet. A concrete staircase leads to the top of the falls where a small dam assures a **swimming hole** filled with fresh spring water. It's a great escape and perfect for a break in the middle of your travels. If you wanted to stay longer, there are two other waterfalls located a bit further from town to which the kids, or the hotel, can give directions.

Bassar

Culturally, the **Bassari** (no relations of the people of southeast Senegal) are worlds apart from the Kotokoli – and linguistically they belong to another cluster of Voltaic languages, **Gurma**, while the Kotokoli speak **Tem**. Unlike the Muslim Kotokoli, they maintain traditional religious beliefs, and they are known for their many festivals and powerful fetishes. Traditionally the Bassari were the iron smelters for the region – in Africa, indication enough of their special status – and traces of their smelting furnaces can still be seen in some of the villages neighbouring the town of **BASSAR**. The Bassari **fire dance** is still celebrated in the town and surrounding villages. Staged versions are sometimes organized by the hotel in town, but only spirits can determine the dates for the real thing by speaking through a member of the community, who enters the arena in trance.

Practicalities

The paved road coming in from Sokodé runs right up to the town **market place** – where it suddenly stops. A dirt road runs in a ring round the market and functions as the high street. To the right where the tarmac ends is the *école centrale* and, just after, the *BP* station with, hard behind it, the **autogare** and PTT. Continuing, you pass *Shell*, the *SGGG* and the *Cascade* bar, before coming to a huge carbuncled **baobab**, revered by the Bassari, and thus tolerated bang in the middle of the street. Beyond it there's not a lot – unless you count a couple of small bars – until you get back to the paved road, having by now completed the circle. Note that there is no bank in town.

There's a **campement** off the paved road in the Kebedipou neighbourhood (near the *préfecture*) with basic, rather run-down rooms, some of them S/C with fans (①). The friendly staff here have all sorts of ideas for things to see in the area. The *Hôtel de Bassar* on the other hand is part of the state-run network, moderately expensive and somewhat dull, but nicely sited on the hilltop overlooking the town (③).

For cheap **eating**, the market provides the best sources of tasty calories. And for unwinding after dark, two **bars** not far from here – *Le Palmier* and *Le Bassanto* – usually run spirited discos at a small charge. They face each other, a hundred metres down the dirt road that runs out, left, from the market as you enter from the Sokodé direction.

KARA AND THE NORTH

Relatively harsh geography and climate make the north **Togo's poorest region** and one where you're not likely to spend much time. Much of the area is open savannah where the ochre grass of the dry season suggests the drought conditions of the Sahel, just a few hours' travel to the north. During the rains, however, green shoots quickly cover the hilly countryside, briefly lending a lush appearance to the region.

The north used to harbour Togo's highest densities of **wild animals**, but the former **Kéran National Park** doesn't even exist as a reserve anymore; the whole area is reclaimed farmland. Further north, the lions long ago left the classified **Forêt de la Fosse aux Lions** and the elephants that once congregated at its large waterhole have been killed or have moved to less hostile conditions in Benin and Burkina. Much of the former wildlife wound up as meat in local market places when unrest cut off food supplies in the north, but papers in Ghana also reported massive military sweeps through the park, claiming that a "shoot to kill" policy was used to clear the region and that villages were bulldozed as helicopters fired on anything that moved, including many innocent villagers.

The people, mainly small farmers of the Voltaic language group, including Tamberma, Lamba, More and Kabyé, grow staple crops of millet and, in isolated areas, rice. Cotton – an important cash crop – is grown around **Dapaong**. But the only town of any size north of Sokodé is **Kara**, which is gradually becoming the nation's administrative centre. The **Kabyé country** spreads over a rocky, mountainous area where the people have acquired a reputation as renowned agriculturalists despite the hostile setting. This is the homeland of President Eyadéma – who, not unexpectedly, has made great efforts to develop his district and to transform its humble city, Kara, into the capital of the north. Other towns – **Sansanné-Mango** and **Niamtougou** – are extended villages with markets of local importance.

Despite a feeling of stagnation hanging heavy like a heat wave, the north offers a number of interesting sites. The **Tamberma country**, in the valleys around **Kandé**, is famous for its remarkable architecture, each home being built like a small fortress. Until very recently, this region remained quite isolated, and to this day certain Tamberma communities have little contact with the outside world. As a result, the traditional **folklore**, **festivals** and **customs** of the Tamberma people have changed little over time.

Kara

KARA doesn't impress as a major metropolis and, taking the town in for the first time, you start to realize why the hype about "Togo's second city" is so necessary. But even if the town retains a provincial, not to say rustic, flavour, it has come a long way in under two decades, since its days as a rural village called Lama-Kara. Crucial political considerations – it was the nearest village of any size to Eyadéma's birthplace, and hometown of his most ardent supporters – have favoured Kara's development and in the space of a few years it has become the nation's second most important centre for **administration** and **manufacturing industries**. Today, incontestably the main town of the north, its infrastructure and continued growth look like helping it maintain that position for a long time to come. Some of the institutions here are worthy of a city of international pretensions, including the four-star *Hôtel Kara*, the imposing Banque Centrale, the sophisticated radio station and especially the grandiose **Maison du RPT** – the party headquarters. The town also boasts more paved roads than anywhere outside Lomé and flashy illuminated road signs just like those in Paris. But the biggest boost has come from new regional industries (the *Brasserie du Bénin* brewery, textile mill and sheanut oil refinery) which have been the driving force behind the expansion.

Kara is a town with a lively market and pleasant setting, and a lot going on. Every July, the **Evala** initiation celebrations and wrestling contests take over the town. Traditionally a strictly Kabyé affair, *Evala* is now a national event, televised across the country, and of huge importance to the town's economy. Competitions start as neighbourhood bouts, then move on to competitions within villages, and finally competitions between villages. Champions from the first, second and third year of initiation face each other for the supreme bouts. Greased with shea nut butter (to prevent their opponent getting a firm grip), they try to grab their opponent's arms or legs to topple him over and pin him in the dust. Bouts rarely last longer than a minute or two but the atmosphere among the rival spectators is feverish.

The centre of town is marked by the **Marché Moderne** and the adjoining *gare routière* for town vehicles – the **main autogare** is to the east of town at the intersection of the main Lomé-Dapaong highway and the Kétao road. It's a chaotic area with a constant flow of passengers and traders swarming about frenetically, despite the heat. To escape this, most of your needs can be met in the immediate vicinity – banks, PTT, shops, bars and restaurants.

Near the *Hôtel Kara*, you'll find the posh **UTB bank**, a convenient place to change money. The other major bank in town is the *BIAO*, one block west of the market. At weekends you can change money at the *Hôtel Kara*'s reception desk; they usually don't ask for a receipt of purchase for traveller's cheques (as the banks often do) and the rates aren't too bad.

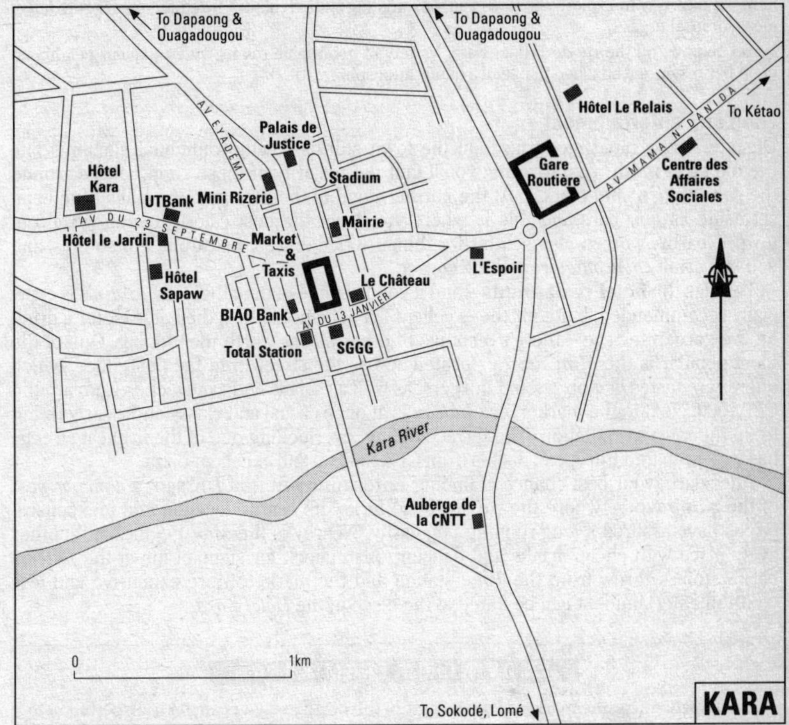

Accommodation

There's a good variety of **places to stay**, though they fill up quickly for *Evala* in July and when other important national festivities are taking place.

Centre des Affaires Sociales, rte de Kétao. Inexpensive dorm rooms with clean showers and baths down the hall, or private rooms, some with AC. Their restaurant serves inexpensive European dishes and good continental breakfasts. ①–②.

Auberge de la CNTT, rte de Lomé. Inexpensive S/C rooms, sponsored by the *Confédération Nationale des Travailleurs Togolais*, with a garden and restaurant. ①.

Hôtel-Bar Le Dacoma, off the rte de l'Hôtel Kara, past *Hôtel le Jardin* (look for signs). One of the cheapest hotels in town. The rooms with shared facilities are rather wretched, but the bar and restaurant are quite good. ①.

Hôtel Kara, west of the town centre (BP 5; ☎60.60.20 or 60.60.21). With its rough stone and beam façade vaguely reminiscent of a hunting lodge, this stands in strange contrast to the iron-roofed huts of local people in the vicinity. The hotel is as expensive as it looks, but it boasts many of the extras you'd expect – and its swimming pool (CFA2000 to visitors) is an obvious place to beat the heat. ⑤.

Hôtel le Jardin, opposite the *UTB* bank (☎60.61.91). More popular as a French-style garden restaurant, this place has comfortable AC rooms in a relaxing environment. ②.

Hôtel Le Relais, off the rte de Kétao (signposted from the *autogare*; ☎60.62.96). Reasonably clean hotel built around a courtyard with *paillotes* and exotic plants. Good value S/C rooms with fan or AC. The restaurant has a long menu of European and African meals. You can also rent bicycles here – a nice way to explore the town and surrounding Kabyé country – and the manager is full of ideas for local trips. ②.

Hôtel Sapaw, off the rte de l'Hôtel Kara. Variety of good-value rooms with a popular neighbourhood bar-restaurant attached that lend a family atmosphere. ①–②.

Food and entertainment

Despite Kara's rapid modernization the town still has many traditional elements like the old **street-side restaurants**: you'll find the majority of these chop houses around the *gare routière* and market. At the northern end of the *gare routière*, stalls have been set aside as *fufu* bars and this is where you'll get the best calorie-to-money ratio in town. Nearby, women also sell tastier things – rice, beans, macaroni and so on – and you can drink *choucoutou* round the corner.

Besides the **hotel restaurants** – and if you try none of the others, *Le Jardin*'s is especially recommended, if not for the excellent French specialities, then at least for a drink on the garden terrace – there's a couple of other places worth mentioning. One of the most popular is the *Mini Rizerie*, located across the street from the post office, which offers rare tastes like pizzas and burgers, as well as salads and sandwiches from around CFA2000. Next to the market, *Le Château* is at once casual and classy and clearly trying to up the town's reputation. The terrace dining, overlooking one of the liveliest streets, has well-prepared European dishes from CFA4000 up and excellent pizza.

After dark, your best chance of finding **entertainmen**t is at *L'Espoir*, a *dancing* west of the *gare routière* where the rte de Kétao forks. Its central location and inexpensive prices have assured a long-running popularity. Nearby is the *Mon Village* bar, another lively place with cheap drinks and dancing. Also check for signs of life at the *Détente* bar, a stone's throw from the *Total* station and the market. More expensive and less youthful entertainment can be found at the disco of the *Hôtel Kara*.

MOVING ON FROM KARA

The *autogare* near the market is the largest in the north and you can get transportation to any point between Lomé and Dapaong. If you're heading to **Bassar**, there are direct taxis that go via a good *piste*, saving you the trouble of changing in Sokodé. For international destinations, the road is good in Togo as far as Kétao and the border of **Benin**, but deteriorates after that until you arrive in **Djougou** (regular taxis from Kara) where a well-kept *piste* connects with Parakou. The road to **Ghana** is also good on the Togo side, but the border between the two countries is subject to frequent closure and there's no guarantee of finding any transport to **Tamale**.

North of Kara

The route north from Kara leads through the Kabyé country, dotted with characteristic *soukala* – round *banco* houses covered with conical thatched roofs, commonly called *tatas* by the French. The picturesque road, with its striking **mountain vistas**, continues as far as **Kandé**, the departure point for travel in the **Tamberma country**. After Kandé, it passes through the farmland that once was the **Kéran National Park** and the village of **Nouboulou**, former site of the reserve's lodgings, now abandoned. Finally the road stops at **Dapaong**, the last major town before Burkina Faso.

There's a deviation in the road that takes you around **Pya** – the president's birthplace just north of Kara. From the *piste* you've been relegated to, you can see an odd building on a distant hilltop, with monumental dimensions that might lead you to mistake it for a modern cathedral. That's the general's humble abode and the reason why you're making a detour.

Kandé and the Tamberma country

KANDÉ (also spelled Kanté) would surely have faded into obscurity had it not been on the nation's main *route nationale*. There's not much of anything in this tiny town of the Lamba people, where the surrounding countryside is hardly conducive to cultivating more than the bare staples of millet and yams. There's a small *gare routière* in the middle of town, with vehicles mostly to Kara, and one or two women selling food in the vicinity. On the north side there's also **accommodation** in the modest *campement*, recently restored and good value, with a decent restaurant (②).

Kandé would be easily overlooked if it weren't the starting point for excursions into the **Tamberma country**. The region was settled by the Tamberma (closely related to the Somba across the border in Benin) in the seventeeth century, as they sought refuge from the king of Abomey on the coast, who raided far and wide in his quest for slaves to trade with the Portuguese. This explains the amazing fortress-like construction of Tamberma houses and their deep-rooted suspicion of outsiders.

Because these people have lived so long in isolation, their customs have remained largely unadulterated by outside influences. For that reason, if you get the chance to visit one of the villages, it can be a fascinating experience. On the other hand, this region is no longer a secret and the Tamberma country has long figured on the route of tour buses driving up from Lomé. This in turn has whetted the community's appetite for tourist money and reduced their fear of foreigners. You may be invited into a Tamberma home only to find, as soon as you enter, the women pulling off their tops, inserting bones through their lips, lighting up pipes and grinding millet. Meanwhile the men are rounding up bows and arrows, clay pipes, carvings and anything else that looks like something a tourist might buy. It's all about as spontaneous as a circus performance, and probably not as traditional, but you can take pictures – as long as you pay of course.

These reservations apart, however, the **homes** are indeed remarkable, self-sufficient settlements, both aesthetic and functional, built some distance from each other with millet fields planted around each one. Their large central entrances were originally designed to store animals in case of attack, while grain was stockpiled in the towers and everything necessary for preparing and cooking food kept inside the house. The roof doubled as a look-out post, with rooms for sleeping built into those towers not being used as silos. With **fetishes** dotted around the house and built into the walls, the Tamberma had everything necessary in their homes to allow them to withstand long sieges. While the threat that led to the creation of such fortresses no longer exists, their architectural style has remained unchanged.

Transport and other practicalities in the Tamberma country

Unfortunately, if you're without your own car, **getting to the Tamberma country** can be mightily difficult, unless you **walk**. Since the first village is some 25km from Kandé that idea may not appeal – and remember this is raw bush and hotels and even *buvettes* are unheard of. The alternative is to find a **taxi** to take you in Kandé, but drivers will charge as much as they can get away with and are unlikely to take you at all for much under CFA25,000. One possibility is to hang around Kandé in the hopes of striking up a friendship with someone who'll invite you to a village – an idea that may seem implausible, but which is perfectly feasible. You'll probably end up walking anyhow, but at least you have a local companion and you'll know there's a place to sleep and eat when you arrive.

If you do have a vehicle of your own, the *piste* from Kandé leads all the way to **Natitingou** in Benin – although at times it's hard to tell if you're still on the road or in the middle of a millet field. If you see people walking along the road, don't hesitate to stop and give them a lift. It could lead to that first contact you've been waiting for. Kids flagging down cars along the roadside are invariably looking for tourists and, if you stop, they'll show you inside their homes and expect you to pay. It's a cringing notion, perhaps, but it's the easiest way to see inside a home and, as long as vast sums aren't laid out, doesn't do the Tamberma economy any harm.

MOVING ON FROM KANDÉ

In Kandé, there is no *gare routière* for **Sansanné-Mango** (also called Mango, or Nzara, and nothing to recommend it), **Dapaong** or other towns in the far north. To get there, you have to wait on the roadside by the customs post (the *douane*, where all traffic is obliged to stop) near Kandé's *campement*. The customs agents will find you a place in a vehicle if you ask. Usually, it's best to go in the early morning, because there are more cars and because this stretch is full of roadside inspections; a whole day of answering questions, showing your documents, and packing and unpacking your bags. If you're heading south, catch a taxi to **Kara** from the *place* in the centre of Kandé, and change there.

Dapaong

Togo's last town in the north, **DAPAONG** (also spelled Dapaongo and Dapango) is home to a mixture of peoples of whom the **Gourma**, immigrants from the Burkina region, are the most numerous. This is a **farming district** where cotton and rice are important crops. **Cattle ranching** is also prevalent, owing to the presence of a sizeable Fula (Peulh) population, who came down from the Mossi Country in Burkina in the mid-nineteenth century. Not many travellers show up in these parts since the closure of the Kéran National Park, which is a pity since Dapaong is a very pleasant town, a route focus and a reasonable enough stopover.

Arrivals

The **autogare** is at the entrance to Dapaong, some 2km south of the centre. Normally, if you come in by taxi, you should be let off in town, but if you do get dropped at the *gare routière* either walk north along the paved road (it leads directly into town) or get a town taxi to the centre. *Taxis brousse* coming into town usually stop where the road forks around the *douane*, with the Hôtel de Ville and hospital off to the west. From here it's an easy walk to the hotels, most of which are within a 500-metre radius.

Accommodation

There is nowhere luxurious to stay in Dapaong, but several pleasant and inexpensive hotels compete for custom.

Centre des Affaires Sociales, rte de Burkina. Typical of the *Affaires Sociales* throughout the country with clean dorm space available or private S/C rooms, some with AC. ②.

Auberge des Travailleurs, rte de Burkina. Upmarket lodgings used for conferences of the *Confédération Nationale des Travailleurs Togolais* and other groups, though it's more often used by travellers. Very clean AC rooms with private bathrooms, and a reasonable restaurant. ②.

Hôtel Campement, on the hill overlooking Dapaong (☎70.81.59). The mundane name belies very pleasant accommodation in a colonial-style building. Clean rooms with fan or AC. The courtyard bar and restaurant, shaded by thatched arcades, serves excellent French food and *pression* beer, but the swimming pool is long dry. ③.

Hôtel Chinois Vietnamien, directly on the place du Marché. Accommodation at various prices, including dorm beds and S/C rooms with AC. There's an attractive restaurant with Asian cuisine, though it's often closed. Central and excellent value. ①–②.

Hôtel Lafia, rte de Mango. Clean and friendly, and only five minutes' walk from the *autogare*, with comfortable AC rooms, or less expensive lodgings with shower and fan. ②.

Hôtel le Ronier, behind the hospital (signs indicate the way from the *douane*). Basic lodging. ①.

Eating

There is plenty of the usual street food around the market, including coffee and omelettes in the morning, but a better **place to eat** is the popular *Relais des Savanes* bar, which has great food, including tossed salads and, if you arrive at the right moment, guinea fowl with groundnut sauce – dishes from CFA1500. The terrace bar of *La Flamboyante* is another good place and a big Dapaong meeting point, where you stand a good chance of running into any travellers passing through the region.

Other practicalities

The **market** (main market days Wednesday & Saturday) is just east of the *douane*, down the dirt road opposite the Hôtel de Ville and past the *Relais des Savanes*. Besides the usual bric-a-brac, you'll find handmade farm tools, pottery and cheap woven gear like the broad-rimmed hats that are so common in the region. And there's no shortage of *choucoutou* bars where you can pause if the shopping gets too heavy. Around the market square are several small *boutiques* and the inevitable *SGGG* supermarket. On the hill behind the market, the *UTB* **bank** is the only place in town to change money.

MOVING ON FROM DAPAONG

Heading south, you can get **taxis** to Kara, Sokodé and Lomé from the main *gare* on the Mango road. If you want to get off before Kara (for example in Mango, Niamtougou or Kandé), you still have to pay the full fare to Kara. Many people up from Lomé heading for **Ouagadougou** change taxis in Dapaong because it's cheaper than going direct. In fact, you can save about 30 percent on your fare by changing vehicles here. You'll almost certainly wait several hours, however, for a Ouaga-bound vehicle – if not a day or two – which tends to cancel out any saving. There are periods when traffic is particularly slow at this depot, so even if you're planning to stay in town before moving on to Burkina

index

CHAPTER FOURTEEN

BENIN

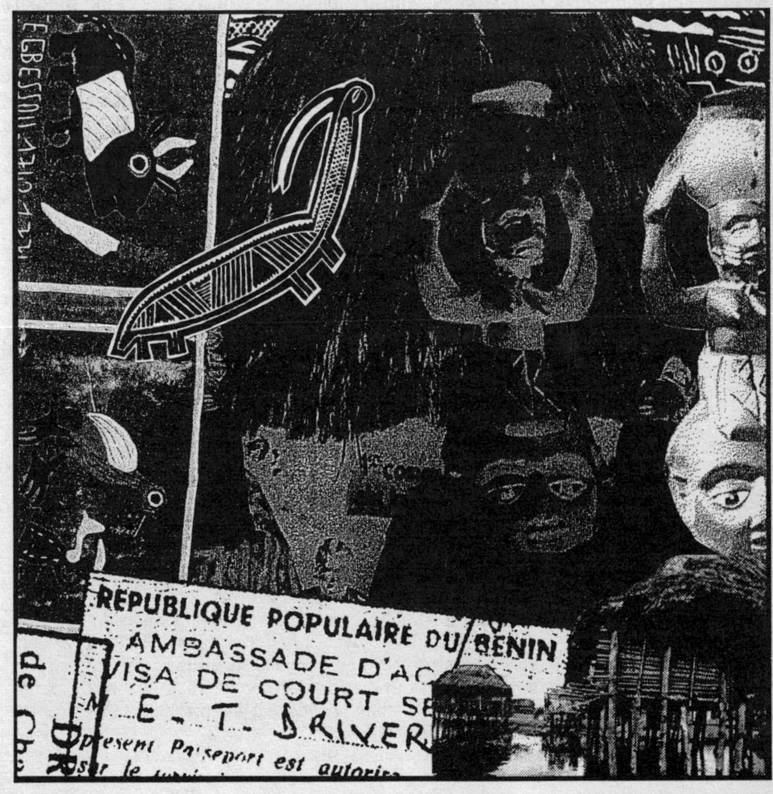

BENIN

Benin is the Gulf of Guinea's least-known nation – ignorance about it the result of seventeen reclusive years of struggle through one of West Africa's least successful and most repressive revolutions. The political climate inched towards democracy throughout the 1980s, but in 1990 the momentum rapidly increased, the revolutionary rhetoric was thrown out, and Benin leapt into the vanguard of states adjusting to new orders imposed, in part, by France. In 1991, Benin adopted a multi-party democracy and a liberal economic system. For years the government had been wary of **tourism**, never especially encouraging visitors. This attitude is changing rapidly and Benin is now a popular and pleasant place to travel, though the country still has a very limited tourist infrastructure.

Benin's years of seclusion have left it an intriguing country, considerably more open than you might suspect, its people mostly warm and mild in their dealings with outsiders but quick to strike up conversations on real issues – especially now that freedom of expression is acceptable. Several factors distinguish the country. First, a number of sophisticated indigenous states developed here, the largest and most urbane of which was the Fon kingdom of **Dan-Homey**, whose capital, in the heartlands of the southern savannah, was **Abomey**. Secondly, this well-organized and prosperous kingdom was one of Africa's biggest centres of the slave trade from the sixteenth to the nineteenth century. The trade wasn't finally ended until 1885, when the last Portuguese slave cargo steamed out of Ouidah. Already by then, a considerable amount of imported wealth had been amassed in the country. Lastly, it was in colonial Dahomey that French Catholic **mission schools** were most influential in the old empire of Afrique Occidentale Française. Thousands of highly qualified students graduated from its secondary schools, giving the country a dynamic intellectual reputation that has coloured its personality deeply.

Where to go

Benin is mostly thinly wooded savannah, part of the **open country** that comes more or less to the coast between the rain forests of Nigeria and Ghana and which partly accounts for the different shifts of history that have taken place here – easier travel and trade, more successful armies and faster conquests.

FACTS AND FIGURES

Known as **Dahomey** during the colonial period (after the Fon kingdom, Dan-Homey), the **République du Bénin** adopted the name of the ancient West African kingdom located in present-day southern Nigeria, after the 1972 coup led by northerner Mathieu Kérékou, the nation's most durable president. The **population** is around six million, a good tenth of whom live in Cotonou, the largest city and the *de facto* capital. The **official capital** remains Porto Novo, a much smaller coastal town that served as the colonial administrative centre. Benin's area is 113,000 square kilometres, approximately the size of Louisiana, or slightly smaller than England. Benin's **national debt** is around £1 billion ($1.5 billion), a figure roughly equivalent to France's annual state subsidy for the arts. In 1990 Kérékou's dictatorship collapsed as the nation began converting to a **multi-party democracy**, a process completed in 1991 when presidential and parliamentary elections were held. **Nicéphore Soglo** was elected president.

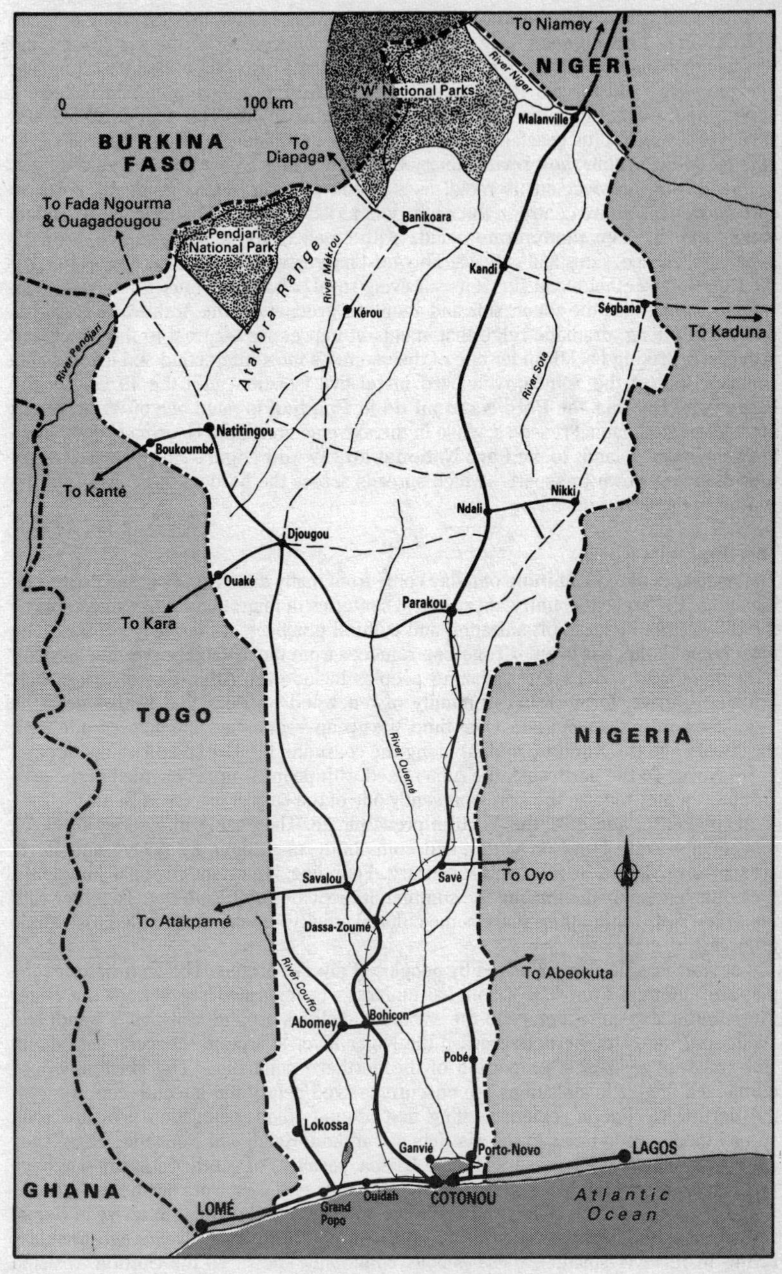

To Niamey
NIGER
River Niger
'W' National Parks
0
100 km
Malanville
BURKINA FASO
To Diapaga
To Fada Ngourma & Ouagadougou
Pendjari National Park
Banikoara
Atakora Range
River Mékrou
Kandi
Ségbana
To Kaduna
Kérou
River Pendjari
River Sota
Natitingou
Boukoumbé
To Kanté
Nikki
Ndali
Djougou
Ouaké
To Kara
Parakou
TOGO
NIGERIA
River Ouemé
Savè
To Oyo
Savalou
To Atakpamé
Dassa-Zoumé
River Couffo
To Abeokuta
Bohicon
Abomey
Pobé
Lokossa
Ganvié
Porto-Novo
LAGOS
GHANA
Ouidah
COTONOU
Atlantic Ocean
LOMÉ
Grand Popo

A flat sandy plain runs the whole length of the **coast**, broken up by a string of picturesque **lakes and lagoons**. The coast offers little enticement in the sea (rough and terrifyingly dangerous) but the **old towns** – including **Porto Novo**, Benin's crumbling official capital, and the old Brazilian quarters of **Ouidah** – have a certain flaked-out appeal, and are full of interest if you have time to explore. The over-exploited stilt village of **Ganvié** is the coastal site of which you're most likely to catch a (tourist's eye) glimpse, while grubby, post-revolutionary **Cotonou** makes a poor first impression.

Inland, the improvement is rapid, as a gentle **plateau** slopes gradually north to spread over the entire centre of the country in a rich patchwork of agriculture. Coffee, cotton and oil palm **plantations** collide with small fields of **subsistence crops** – maize, millet, rice, yams and cassava. The most interesting town is **Abomey** – capital of the Dan-Homey empire and site of its surviving royal palaces and museum.

In the northwest, the sheer cliffs and abundant greenery of the **Atakora Mountains** rear up in a long, dramatic ridge that stands in impressive contrast to the plains and provides a striking backdrop for one of the country's most interesting and inaccessible cultures, that of the Somba, who lived in relative isolation until the 1970s. On the border with Burkina, the **Parc National de la Pendjari** is rated one of West Africa's most interesting faunal reserves; while in the extreme north, the Gourma plains roll up in sweeping grasslands to the **Parc National du "W" du Niger** – not at all easy to get to without your own transport – which spreads across the borders into Niger and the southeast tip of Burkina Faso.

The Béninois

The ancestors of the **Béninois** of today come from many different areas and arrived on the site of the present country after several centuries of migrations, a fact that explains the differences in social organization and cultural practices of the many peoples. The most recent influx has been of **Togolese** refugees from the instability over the border.

In the south, various Ewe-speaking peoples include the **Adja**, one of the earliest groups to arrive, formerly a community of renowned warriors that settled near the Togolese border town of Tado. Over time, the group fragmented and dispersed to form the **Xwala** and the **Xuéda** (Ouidah) along the coast and the **Gun** a little inland around Porto Novo. To the northwest, the Adja mixed with peoples already settled in the area around Abomey to form the **Fon** – presently one of the largest groups in Benin.

In the centre and east, the **Yoruba** predominate. They came in a series of vague movements, setting out on family and community migrations from Oyo and Ife in present-day Nigeria in the twelfth century. Founding important regional kingdoms, they often ended up dominating the commercial activities of the interior. Together with the Fon – with whom they share some cultural affinity – make up an influential ethnic grouping.

The northeast is also populated by peoples of diverse origins. The **Dendi**, for example, are migrants from Mali's Songhai empire, who migrated south from the Niger River in the sixteenth century to the savannah districts around Malanville, Kandi and Djougou. **Fula** cattle herders crossed the Niger River at around the same period and still make up a sizeable proportion of the northern population. The **Bariba**, whose ethnic and linguistic affiliations are obscure, arrived before the fifteenth century from the northwest Nigeria region. Settling first around Nikki, population pressure soon spread their communities to the districts of Parakou, Kandi and Kouande, where they came to dominate predecessors like the **Bussa**, speakers of another obscure language (probably a relict Mande tongue), who had also migrated west from northern Nigeria.

In the northwest, the **Betammaribe** were one of the first peoples to arrive in Benin, settling near the Atakora range at an unknown date a thousand years ago or more. Living in relative isolation, these people, commonly known as the **Somba**, resisted changes inflicted by the spread of Islam and the French invasion. Until quite recently, they lived in the seclusion of their fortified *tatas* and farmed their lands, wearing no more than the traditional *cache sexe* of their ancestors. Although their subsistence way of life had been ignored for centuries, in the 1970s they were exposed to the raw glare of the French press – delighted to have located a rare example of "real Africa". Stung by the sensational reports of naked tribesmen, Kérékou's government ran a campaign to force the Somba to wear clothes. As a result of this humiliation and other insensitivities, the Somba remain a very private, reserved people, and outside of the main towns, such as Natitingou – where traditional ways are fast breaking down – it's difficult, and perhaps from no one's point of view very desirable, to penetrate their tight-knit communities.

Most Béninois adhere to traditional African **religious beliefs**. Along the coast, **voodooism** is common, particularly among the Ewe-speakers. **Islam** was brought from the north by Arab, Hausa and Songhai-Dendi traders. It extended as far south as Djougou, and even into the Yoruba country. Perhaps as much as fifteen percent of the population are Muslim. **Christianity** came with the Europeans and spread principally along the coast – where it was soon integrated into voodoo – and over the central plateau.

When to go

Given the generally bad condition of roads in Benin, the weather can have a very adverse effect on travel and it's best to avoid the rainy seasons, which can be prolonged and oppressive. In the **south**, there are two **rainy seasons** (a long one from April to July and a short one from October to November) and two **dry seasons** (a short one from August to September and a long one from December to March). Temperatures fluctuate little throughout the year.

In the **north**, the year divides simply into the rainy season, which lasts from late May to October, and the dry season, which lasts from November to early May. In parts of the Atakora region – Natitingou, for example – the rain falls virtually unabated from April to November. Temperatures vary more dramatically than in the south. When the northerly *Harmattan* wind blows in December, nights can be quite cool.

AVERAGE TEMPERATURES AND RAINFALL

COTONOU

	Jan	Feb	Mar	Apr	May	June	July	Aug	Sept	Oct	Nov	Dec
Temperatures °C												
Min (night)	23	25	26	26	24	23	23	23	23	24	24	24
Max (day)	27	28	28	28	27	26	26	25	26	27	28	27
Rainfall mm	33	33	117	125	254	366	89	38	66	135	58	13
Days with rainfall	2	2	5	7	11	13	7	3	6	9	6	1

Arrivals

Despite being so centrally placed in the region, Benin is not a country to which many travellers make initial flights into West Africa. Entering overland is straightforward enough from Togo or Niger, but the routes down from Burkina Faso are little used, and the way in from Nigeria can sometimes be a hectic hassle.

The details in these practical information pages are essentially for use on the ground in West Africa and in Benin itself: for full practical details on preparing for a trip, getting here from outside the region, paperwork, health, information sources and more, see *Basics*.

■ Flights from West Africa

Most **direct flights to Cotonou** from neighbouring countries in West Africa are handled by *Air Afrique* (RK). RK flies from **Abidjan** to Cotonou daily (up to three flights some days of the week).

Other West African cities have much less frequent links. RK flies from **Niamey** via **Lomé**, on Tues and also flies Lomé–Cotonou on Wed.

From **Ouagadougou**, RK flies to Cotonou on Tues night. Otherwise *Air France* (AF) flies Ouaga–Cotonou on Mon and Fri, and *Air Burkina* (VH) on Wed and Fri.

From **Lagos**, there are direct, non-stop flights to Cotonou on RK (Thurs, Fri); on *Ghana Airways* (GH) on Mon; on *Nigeria Airways* (WT) on Tues and Thurs; on *Air Gabon* (GN) on Tues; and on *Aeroflot* (SU) twice a month on Thurs.

Other cities with direct links to Cotonou include: **Accra**, on GH on Sat; **Conakry** via Abidjan, on WT on Sun; **Freetown** via Accra on SU twice a month on Thurs; and **Douala** non-stop on *Cameroon Airlines* (UY) on Tues and Fri, and via Lagos on RK on Thurs.

From **Dakar**, the only direct flight is an inconvenient one on Tues on GN via Abidjan and Lagos. There are indirect RK flights pretty well daily, all connecting in Abidjan (fastest time on Thurs). Similarly, the only flights from **Bamako** are indirect ones connecting in Abidjan (fastest time, Tues).

There are no direct links or convenient connections from Nouakchott, Banjul or Bissau to Cotonou.

■ Overland

Beninois customs and immigration rarely present any special problems, but at most border posts you must state where you plan on staying. Give the name of any hotel, whether you intend to stay there or not.

From Nigeria

The commonest point of entry has traditionally been via the **Badagri** coastal road from Lagos to **Kraké** on the Benin side. When it's open, this frontier is always crowded and it may take some time to get through the formalities. Your bags will be given a perfunctory search, but it's not likely your Nigerian currency declaration form will even be checked.

Recently, however, the Badagri route has been **closed**, and travellers have been using the border crossing from **Idiroko** in Nigeria to **Igolo** in Benin, 30km north of Porto Novo.

Roads on both routes are surfaced and in reasonable shape.

From Niger

From Niamey to Cotonou, the road is tarred the whole way. At the Gaya border post, a bridge spans the Niger River and leads to the Benin customs at **Malanville** (open daily 7am–7.30pm).

From Burkina Faso

Most people coming from Burkina take the sealed road through Togo and branch over to Benin either at Kara or Lomé, as described below. Some vehicles do, however, leave with irregular frequency from Fada-Ngourma to Natitingou. You may have to change vehicles at Pama, the last Burkinabe town of any size.

From Togo

Despite the political turmoil in Togo, taxis speed along the coastal highway from Lomé to Cotonou all day long. Although there's no Béninois embassy in Togo, **visas** are issued on the spot at the border post of **Hila Kondji**. Though customs operate here around the clock, the visa section only works during business hours (Mon–Fri 8am–12.30pm & 3–6.30pm, Sat 8am–12.30pm). Note that this is the only border post where you can expect to enter Benin without acquiring a visa beforehand.

From the north of Togo, a paved road leads from Kara to the border post at **Kétao**. Customs and immigration agents here are generally quite good-humoured and the *piste* leading on to Djougou in Benin is well maintained if a bit slippery when wet. Alternatively, if you have your own vehicle you could take a very minor and neglected *piste* that branches off the main road at Kandé and heads **through the Tamberma country**. Little traffic uses this route and you're not likely to be aware that you've crossed the border until you get to the main road to Natitingou. When you arrive at this latter town, go to the police and customs to get your passport stamped.

Red Tape

French, Germans, Danes, Swedes and Italians don't need visas to enter Benin. Most other nationalities, apart from Ecowas member states, do.

In some cases, visas are only issued for a 48-hour period. This is not a major problem if you arrive in the south, since **extensions** are easily obtained at the immigration office in Cotonou. If you arrive by road from the north, however, you'll have to rush your trip to get to the coast within two days – an obvious headache if you'd planned on taking in sights along the way.

Within the country, **spot checks** by the police are increasingly infrequent along the roadside. Though they do still occur, the police aren't very intimidating: they tend to be friendly through the formalities, provided you approach them politely.

■ Visas for onward travel

Cotonou is a good place to pick up a visa if you're going to **Nigeria**. You can generally get your stamp within 24 hours and without hassle, though usually for only a brief initial stay. The **Ghana** embassy issues visas within 48 hours, but if you're planning to do the journey by land, note that the Togo–Ghana border is often closed and likely to remain unreliable due to political tensions. Ghanaian and Nigerian visas cost around CFA10,000. **Niger** visas normally take 48 hours to issue and cost CFA15,000.

Money and Costs

Benin is part of the CFA zone (CFA100 = 1 French franc; approx. CFA750–800 = £1; approx. CFA500 = US$1). Outside of Cotonou and Parakou, changing money in Benin is next to impossible.

Although larger banks have branches in the towns of Natitingou, Bohicon and Kandi, they usually don't touch anything other than French franc notes. Bank opening hours are usually 8am–12.30pm and 3.30–7pm. The main bank is the *Banque Internationale du Bénin* (*BIB*).

■ Costs

Costs are broadly similar to those in franc-zone neighbours Niger, Burkina and Togo – though the price of fuel is a little cheaper. Except in Cotonou itself, there is little opportunity to spend much money. Public transport works out around CFA15 per kilometre.

Health

Yellow fever is currently the only vaccination required for travel to Benin. Malaria is widespread and, as in neighbouring Togo, is increasingly found to be resistant to the common chloroquine-based drugs.

Except in Cotonou, some sort of **water purification** is highly recommended. You should avoid swimming in streams and lakes in the lagoon regions of coastal Benin, and don't walk barefoot in the grass surrounding them. These areas are almost invariably infested by schistosome parasites which transmit **bilharzia**.

Hospital facilities throughout the country are meagre, with drugs and equipment in short supply. In Cotonou, the most obvious place to head for in case of medical problems is the *Centre National Hospitalier et Universitaire* in the Patte d'Oie district (☎30.01.55). The privately-run *Polyclinic* in the Cocotiers district (☎30.14.31), however, has a better reputation.

Maps and Information

The best map of Benin is the *IGN* national road map (1cm to 6km) which includes detailed *pistes* and topographical material, and is especially useful in the confusing lagoon areas along the coast. If you're not planning on staying long or travelling much off the beaten track, however, the *Michelin 953* map of West Africa is adequate.

Benin has no overseas tourist offices, but the embassy in Paris and the London honorary consulate have limited supplies of leaflets. In Cotonou, the **Ministère du Commerce et du Tourisme** has sketchy pamphlets about travel, but not much information you can sink your teeth into. Any *librairie* in the country has a hundred-page reader called *Le Bénin* which gives an overview of the nation, intended for school children.

Getting Around

Benin's road network has improved dramatically since the early 1990s and now compares favourably with that of Togo. Police checks are refreshingly infrequent. The rail system, on the other hand, dates from the colonial period: the network is down to one line between Parakou and Cotonou. There is no domestic air service.

Road transport

The main **national highway** runs for 742km from Cotonou to Malanville and is paved the entire distance. The other main road runs 114km across the country from the Nigerian border in the east to the Togolese border in the west.

The Béninois have remained faithful to the Peugeot **bush taxi** – still common despite the new, Japanese vehicles beginning to appear. Peugeot 504 *familiales* – nine-seater estate cars – are the common mode of transport for most people.

The government-run **bus service** is in a state of reorganization. Buses stop at major towns between Malanville and Cotonou, but the buses are mostly old and battered. Still, seats are cheaper than bush taxis and run on regular schedules. They usually leave from the same *gare routière* as the *taxis brousse*. Ask in advance for times and arrive early, as they tend to fill quickly.

Public transport in large towns is the preserve of **share-taxis** and **zimi-djans**. *Zimi-djans* are *mobylette* drivers who rent out the back of their scooter seats to passengers – a cheap (and negotiable) means of transport (usually identifiable by a coloured shirt – yellow in Cotonou). Note, however, that you won't be protected by a helmet.

Trains

The national **railway** company, *l'Organisation Commune Bénin-Niger des Chemins de fer et Transports*, operates the only railway line still running in Benin. Built between 1900 and 1939, the **northern line** covers the 438km from Cotonou to Parakou, via Bohicon, Dassa and Savè. Despite the time involved, many Béninois still take the train over this stretch since the price is slightly less than bush taxis. The trip to Parakou takes over ten hours; it's possible to reserve a *couchette* on a night train. Plans have been kicking about for decades to extend the line to Malanville, Dosso and Niamey: don't, however, expect anything to materialize in the immediate future.

The **eastern line** from Cotonou to Pobè, passing through Porto Novo, and the **western line** from Cotonou to Sègbohouè via Ouidah are now defunct.

Planes

Domestic **air transport** is handled only by travel agents who occasionally charter planes from Cotonou to the country's three main airports – Parakou, Kandi and Natitingou.

ACCOMMODATION PRICE CODES

Hotel prices in this chapter are coded according to the following scales – the same scales in terms of their pound/dollar equivalents as are used throughout the book. Prices refer to the rate you can expect to pay for a room with two beds. Single rooms, or single occupancy, will normally cost at least two-thirds of the twin-occupancy rate. For further details see p.51.

① **Under CFA4000 (under £5/$7.50).** Very rudimentary hotel with no frills at all – often a *chambre de passage* rented to the average guest by the hour.

② **CFA4000–8000 (£5–10/$7.50–15).** Basic hotel with simple amenities. S/C rooms with fans are the norm; some rooms may have AC for slightly higher rates.

③ **CFA8000–16,000 (£10–20/$15–30).** Modest, but adequate hotel, with S/C rooms, and a choice of rooms with fans, or for a premium AC.

④ **CFA16,000–24,000 (£20–30/$30–45).** Reasonable business or tourist-class hotel with S/C, AC rooms, and often a restaurant.

⑤ **CFA24,000–32,000 (£30–40/$45–60).** Similar standards to the previous code band but extra facilities such as a pool are usual.

⑥ **CFA32,000–40,000 (£40–50/$60–75).** Comfortable, first-class hotel, with good facilities.

⑦ **Over CFA40,000 (over £50/$75).** Luxury establishment – top prices around CFA60,000–80,000.

Accommodation

A good network of hotels hasn't yet been developed in Benin. Cotonou has its *Sheraton* and a scattering of less luxurious places, and Natitingou has a hotel in the French *PLM* chain, but such international-class establishments are the exception.

More typical accommodation is basic: sparsely furnished rooms, usually with electricity (and sometimes a fan), but not necessarily with private toilets or even running water. Outside Cotonou, accommodation is fairly inexpensive and budget travellers can usually find something for under CFA4000. Increasingly, and especially in well-travelled towns like Ouidah, Abomey, and Natitingou, a few good mid-range hotels are opening, with S/C rooms and air-conditioning.

The Béninois are hospitable and may invite travellers for meals or to stay the night – forbidden until the advent of democracy. *Camping sauvage* (pitching your tent in the bush, or on the beach) has also been legalized, beyond city limits.

Eating and Drinking

Food in Benin largely resembles that of neighbouring Togo: for background and details on local staples and popular dishes, refer to the food section in the previous chapter. Well-prepared street food sauces can be very tasty. Cotonou has no gastronomic reputation in West Africa but there is a growing variety of restaurants.

In the provinces, eating houses are usually small *buvettes* specializing in rice, *pâte* (the generic term for pounded starch based on cassava, yam or sweet potato), *moyo* (like wheat semolina) or macaroni served with sauce.

One of Benin's leading industries is the *Societé Nationale des Boissons* which produces the national beer, *La Béninoise*, and a variety of carbonated soft drinks. These are the cheapest drinks sold throughout the country. Along the coast, **palm wine** is plentiful, as is the lethal African firewater known as **sodabi**. In the north, **home-made beer** made from millet, known as *chapalo* or *tchacpalo*, is more common.

Communications – Post, Phones, Language and Media

French is the national language. Of the host of local languages none stands out as being widely useful across the country. There's little on the airwaves and few daily papers. Cotonou is the place to go for phones and post.

■ Post and phones

If you're just passing through, Cotonou is the only reliable place to receive **post**. The main PTT is fairly efficient and the poste restante service good. International **phone calls** can be made either from the PTT in Cotonou, or from the *Sheraton Hotel*, although the latter is twice as expensive and you've no way of knowing if the operator is adding an unofficial commission.

Benin's IDD code is ☎229.

■ Languages

Benin's official language is **French**. The fifty or so Béninois ethnic communities speak about as many different languages or distinct dialects. Some languages have become regional lingua francas. In the south, **Adja** and **Fon** – closely related to Ewe and Mina under the "Ewe group" umbrella – are widely spoken and are probably the most useful to know a few phrases in. In the centre and east, **Yoruba** takes over (see p.1008). **Bariba**, a Voltaic tongue, is the common language of Parakou and the northeast, while the old Songhaic language, **Dendi**, is spoken in the extreme north near the banks of the Niger. **Hausa** and **Fula** are also widely used in the north. Because of the proximity and influence of Nigeria and the importance of commerce, some Béninois speak a kind of trading **English**, though it's not likely to get you very far.

■ The media

Although not as visible as the press in other countries, there are three daily **newspapers** – *Le Matin*, *24 Heures* and *La Nation* (the government-owned paper) – and dozens of small weekly, fortnightly or monthly sheets. None of them have big circulations. The weekly *Gazette Du Golfe,* the main opposition paper under the

BÉNINOIS GLOSSARY

Amazon The name given to female Fon soldiers by visiting Europeans. In Greek mythology, it referred to a race of Scythian female warriors who supposedly underwent mastectomies to facilitate use of their longbows; the word probably derives from the Greek for "without a breast", see p.927.

Féticheur Traditional religious leader.

Tata Fortress-like houses built by the Somba in the region of Natitingou.

Vaudou/Vodu "Divinity" or "Other" (Fon). Voodoo, the religion of the coast, spread from these parts to Haiti with the exile of slaves.

Yovo "White" or "European" (Fon).

Kérékou regime, now competes with *Tam-Tam Express*, *L'Observateur* and *Le Forum de la Semaine* among others.

The state-run *Office de Radiodiffusion et de Télévision du Bénin* has **radio** broadcasts in French, English and eighteen national languages and three or four hours of TV each night.

Directory

AIRPORT DEPARTURE TAX CFA2500.

BUSINESS HOURS Most businesses are open Mon–Fri 8am–12.30pm & 3.30–7pm. Government offices are open Mon–Fri 8am–12.30pm & 3–6.30pm.

HOLIDAYS Christian holidays and New Year's Day are public holidays. Muslim celebrations are less formally observed, though everything shuts down in the north for them. (Ramadan, however, isn't conspicuously disruptive). In addition there are secular holidays on **May 1** (Labour Day), **August 1** (Independence Day), **October 26** (Armed Forces' Day), **November 30** (Benin Day) and **December 31** (Harvest Day).

MUSEUMS Benin has several museums. By far the best is housed in the former Dan-Homey palace in **Abomey**, which has undergone massive renovations with the help of UNICEF funds. **Porto Novo** also has two museums, one in the former residence of King Toffa. The museum in **Ouidah** is dedicated primarily to the voodoo religion.

MUSIC Angélique Kidjo is the one internationally known name from Benin – a hugely charismatic singing star based in Paris whose songs are heard on dance floors worldwide. In Benin itself, there's little thriving musical culture, though every indication that with economic liberalization, a less insecure government and relaxations on censorship, there'll be more musical instruments, better facilities and greater freedom of expression in the future. Listen out for the local cassette star **Stan Tohon**, whose *tchink system* percussion is interesting. See the "Music" section in *Contexts*.

PHOTOGRAPHY You need no official permit to take pictures in Benin but photographing people can be a very sensitive issue, especially in Somba country. People in touristed areas like Ganvié and Ouidah are likely to demand money, and snapping away without permission can lead to problems.

VOODOO The religion of the coast, especially among Ewe-speakers. In many ways, Ewe practices are similar to those of the Yoruba and Fon: all believe in a single supreme God who created the universe (*Mawu* in Fon). On earth, lesser divinities are charged with power over thunder (*Xebioso* or *Shango*), iron and war (*Ogun* or *Gu*), land and disease (*Sakpata* or *Cankpana*), and so on. They possess or "mount" the bodies of their devotees. Their help can be solicited through the work of fetish priests. For more details see the box on p.920.

WILDLIFE Although densely farmed and populated in their southern parts, Benin's northern regions spread into a broad zone of thinly populated savannah and uplands – one of West Africa's best game-viewing areas. There are significant concentrations of wildlife, especially in the Pendjari and "W" du Niger national parks, including several hundred – possibly a thousand – elephants.

WOMEN'S ISSUES The position of women in Benin has been little improved by the revolutionary 1970s and 80s or by democratization. In fact it appears they have even less involvement in politics and decision-making than elsewhere.

Women travellers report Béninois men generally pleasantly reserved and low-key and there's relatively little sexual harassment.

A Short History of Benin

The earliest history of the territory that is now Benin is obscure. The far north was under thrall to the Niger River's Songhai empire by the end of the fifteenth century. Meanwhile, in the south, having built the fort at El Mina in Ghana in 1482, the Portuguese continued along the coast and began trading with local rulers from the 1520s. Porto Novo and Ouidah developed through the sixteenth and seventeenth centuries into important commercial centres where slaves were traded for European cloth and guns. The British, Dutch and French, seeking labour for their American colonies, soon joined the Portuguese in the traffic, establishing their own coastal forts and commercial depots during the seventeenth century. By the 1690s, some 20,000 slaves were being shipped annually out of Ouidah and lesser ports.

■ The Slave Coast

By as early as the beginning of the eighteenth century, the **Dan-Homey kingdom** (though itself effectively a vassal of the great Yoruba Oyo empire to the east) dominated the politics of the region. One of Dan-Homey's rulers, **Agadja** (in power 1708–40), subjugated the districts south of his capital Abomey, and finally took Ouidah itself. With access to the coast, his empire was now poised to control international trade – primarily in slaves. But he had exceeded the terms of his license with Oyo and a protracted conflict ensued which resulted in Oyo's definitive conquest of Dan-Homey. There followed a period of desperate slave-hunting as the Dan-Homey king **Tegbesu** tried to rebuild his country's war-shattered economy (more background on p.927).

After the French Revolution, however, a wave of **anti-slavery sentiment** began to sweep Europe. In France, the *Decret du 16 pluviôise an II* (February 4, 1794) abolished the trade, though it was later reinstated by Napoleon. In 1802, Denmark became the first European nation to abolish the slave trade permanently. Britain followed in 1807 and from 1819 to 1867, British ships patrolled the coast, arresting slave ships and resettling the captives in Freetown, Sierra Leone. France definitively outlawed the trade in 1818.

These moves coincided with a severe shortage of slaves in the region, in large part because of excessive human sacrifices in Abomey. A Brazilian mulatto, **Francisco Felix de Souza**, whose career had been helped by **Prince Ghezo** of Dan-Homey, entered into a blood pact with the young man and supplied the guns for Ghezo to overthrow the incumbent of the stool (throne) in Abomey in 1818, in return for which he was granted a monopoly over the slave trade (and became the "Viceroy of Ouidah"; see "Books" in *Contexts*).

By the 1830s, however, the nature of most commerce in the region had fundamentally changed and **palm oil** became the primary export. The French soon gained the upper hand in the regional oil trade when representatives from Marseille soap-making companies arrived in Ouidah in 1843 and travelled to Abomey where they signed a contract with the Dan-Homey king, the same Ghezo, granting them trading rights at Ouidah. In 1861, Lagos became a British colony. **King Toffa** of Porto Novo had claims on the town of Badagary which the British now controlled. Worried that their influence would spread westward, Toffa called on the French for support and in 1863, Porto Novo became a **French protectorate**. In 1868, the new **King Glele** of Abomey ceded rights to Cotonou to the French who had by now established themselves as the most prominent European power along Benin's coast.

■ French conquest

Good relations between France and the Dan-Homey kingdom had soured by the end of the century. In December 1889, a new sovereign, **Behanzin**, was enstooled. He adopted a more combative attitude to the French who were beginning to look less like trading partners and more like a force of occupation. He refused to recognize French rights over Cotonou and was angered that the foreigners had allied themselves with one of his bitterest enemies, King Toffa of Porto Novo. After funeral ceremonies for his father Glele, Behanzin ordered an **attack on Cotonou**. On March 4, 1890, some five to six thousand Dan-Homey warriors marched on the city and withdrew only after inflicting numerous casualties. A month later, the army surrounded Porto

Novo and clashed with the French at Atchoukpa on the northern outskirts of the city.

Other skirmishes followed and in April 1892, Behanzin sent the following message to French authorities:

I warn you that if one of our villages is touched by the fire of your cannons, I will march directly to crush Porto Novo and all the villages belonging to Porto Novo. I would like to know how many independent French villages have been overtaken by me, King of Dan-Homey. I request you to keep calm and do your business in Porto Novo. That way, we can remain in peace as it was before. But if you want war, I am ready. I will not finish it. It will last a hundred years and will kill 20,000 of my men.

The threat was taken seriously by the French who knew that Behanzin possessed more than 5000 modern firearms and was still being supplied by the Germans and the British. The government in Paris sent a distinguished commander to handle the situation, **Colonel Dodds**, a mulatto from Saint Louis in Senegal.

In August 1892, Dodds began his northern march to conquer Abomey. Accompanied by Senegalese and Hausa infantry, the French went to the Oueme River and followed its course. Although the army was sporadically engaged by Dan-Homey troops, including divisions of Amazons – skilled female warriors specially trained to use the new Martini-Henry rifles – it was the Dan-Homey who received the heaviest casualties in the clashes. By November 1892, when the French arrived at Cana – the village where Dan-Homey kings were traditionally buried – Behanzin's army had lost 4000 dead and twice as many wounded.

The king prepared himself for a **last stand**. He recruited every warrior capable of carrying a gun and the massed ranks of his Amazons – even those specialised in hunting. And he got the nation's slaves to join the battle, promising them freedom in return. But the effort was in vain; the army was defeated and Behanzin was forced to retreat with meagre reserves. On November 16, 1892, Dodds marched on Abomey to find the city already in flames, torched by the retreating army. It took another two years for the French to track down and capture Behanzin (betrayed by the newly French-enstooled Fon king) and he was transported to exile in Martinique.

The Colonial Era

Their main rival in the region at last conquered, the French went on to subdue the north of the country, which they now called **Dahomey**. Colonial frontiers were drawn up in agreement with Britain to the east and Germany (which held Togo) to the west. In 1901, the present borders were fixed and, in 1904, Dahomey became part of AOF (French West Africa).

French policy in Dahomey was partly shaped by the influence of Catholic missions which sent large numbers of envoys into the territory in the 1920s and 1930s. Catholic seeds had been sown from a very early period, with the arrival in the eighteenth century of influential **Brazilian** families and Christian **freed slaves**. Moreover, the climate, open country and dominant voodoo religion of the south were not strongly antithetical to missionary activity. The result was that early in the colonial period, Dahomey acquired a reputation for mission-educated academics and administrators. By the 1950s, many middle-ranking posts in the French colonial service – right across West and Central Africa – were occupied by Dahomeyans, most of whom were Fon or Yoruba from the relatively prosperous south.

With few mineral resources – no gold or other precious metals – Dahomey's economy depended very heavily on its **oil palm plantations**. In addition, there were close commercial relations with Nigeria, both legal trade and illicit smuggling.

Independence

No single, national leader rose to pre-eminence during the fifteen-year postwar period on the road to independence. Instead, an ethnic and regional competition developed in which three prominent figures jockeyed for political prominence. They were: **Hubert Maga** representing the north, **Migan Apithy** of the southeast, and **Justin Ahomadegbe** from the southwest. On the eve of independence, the three managed to form a coalition, the *Parti Progressiste Dahoméen*, but unity was superficial. Each commanded the loyalties of about one third of the country's population and distrusted the others. After some seventy years of French rule, the **Republic of Dahomey** became independent on August 1, 1960.

In December, 1960, **elections** were held in which Maga's *Parti Dahoméen de l'Unité* won. The northerner became the nation's first president. But an uneasy dissatisfaction prevailed in the south where supporters of Apithy and Ahomadegbe suspected the new leader was trying to consolidate his position and eliminate his two most formidable rivals. By 1963, unrest had led to **political riots** as students and workers took to the streets of Cotonou. Truckloads of angry northerners descended on the town to confront the protestors.

■ Years of instability

The situation had got out of hand and it was clear that serious violence would ensue if Maga stayed in power. At the same time, it also seemed possible that the north would try to secede if either of Maga's rivals took over the presidency.

The impasse was resolved in October 1963 when Maga was deposed in a **military coup** led by **Colonel Christophe Soglo**. The takeover was not a sudden or unexpected event, however. For two days prior to the coup, Soglo met with Maga and Apithy (who was vice-president) and members of the trade unions and the army. His ascent to power seemed the only way to maintain order. Soglo never mobilized the army and no shots were ever fired. After taking over the leadership, he immediately set about restoring civilian rule. A new constitution was adopted and, in January 1964 transparently undemocratic **"elections"** took place.

During the period of military rule, **Apithy and Ahomadegbe** had formed a coalition party which received 99.8 percent of the vote. Maga had meanwhile been jailed on charges of conspiracy to assassinate the two southern leaders. Apithy thus became the new president and Ahomadegbe took on the job of prime minister. Under a false guise of unity, the two men worked against one another, each trying to consolidate his own position within the party. The **exclusion of the north** from the political process led to more riots and bloodshed in Parakou and there were more political detentions for conspiracy to overthrow the government. But what brought the two southern leaders to loggerheads was a law concerning the appointment of members to the Supreme Court – Maga happened to be on trial at the time – which placed the judiciary in conflict with the government. Ahomadegbe, with the party behind him, demanded President Apithy's resignation. The president refused. Chaos within the party was coupled with widespread public discontent from outside its ranks, which reached fever pitch with the announcement of a 25 percent salary cut for civil servants to try to reduce the country's burgeoning deficit. In its distress, the government was virtually unable to act and normal administration began to break down. The military again intervened, and Colonel Soglo forced both Apithy and Ahomadegbe to step down.

A provisional government, headed by **Tahirou Congacou**, who was president of the National Assembly, released Maga from prison and set about writing a new constitution with the joint consultation of all three leaders. Elections were to be held in January 1966, but campaigning never began as, still posturing for position, Maga and Apithy allied themselves against Ahomadegbe in a move which triggered trade union protest. On December 22, 1965, Soglo intervened for a third time, and on this occasion assumed power as the head of a **military regime**. Maga, Apithy and Ahomadegbe exiled themselves in Paris.

Soglo remained head of state for two years, but his term soon met with criticism. He was accused of mishandling Dahomey's affairs and of presiding over a military structure that was rife with **corruption**. In 1967, workers went on strike to protest against intolerable economic conditions. The subsequent and predictable ban on union activity led to yet another, equally predictable **coup**, led by **Major Maurice Kouandété**, and supported by junior officers including one Captain Mathieu Kérékou.

■ Continuing coups

After protracted disputes and negotiations, the army chief of staff **Alphonse Alley** took over as head of state, with Kouandété his prime minister. The military government had a strong, northern cast. Kouandété drew up another constitution and scheduled new elections for May 1968. Many politicians were banned from participating, however, including the elder statesmen, Maga, Apithy and Ahomadegbe. The trio, reunited in their exclusion, called for a boycott, and on the day of the elections, only 26 percent of the eligible voters turned out. An unknown doctor, **Basil Akjou Moumuni**, won the presidency, but the elections were immediately annulled, and the military instead conferred the presidency on a low-profile former Foreign Minister, **Emil Derlin Zinsou**.

In December 1969, sixteen months into his term, Zinsou was himself overthrown by the same man who had put him in power, Kouandété. The newest coup was spurred by divisions within the military and seemed to have more to do with corruption and personality differences than with ethnic tensions. Though there was no special crisis to justify the military takeover, it was the first time force had been used. Zinsou's car was sprayed with bullets in downtown Cotonou, but the president escaped with his life.

Fellow officers prevented Kouandété taking power himself. Instead, a **Military Directorate** was established with Lieutenant-Colonel **Paul Emile de Souza** in charge. Once more, elections were set and this time the three old-guard politicians were allowed to participate. Maga was set to win in his loyal Atakora region, but not to receive a majority over Apithy and Ahomadegbe combined. De Souza cancelled the Atakora poll. Declaring that the north would secede if the Military Directorate refused to accept his presidency, Maga pushed the country to the brink of civil war. Apithy upped the stakes by stating his region would attach itself to Nigeria if Maga was instated. In a last-ditch compromise to save Dahomey from self-destruction, a **Presidential Council** was formed in which the three men would rotate power every two years. Maga was the first to serve as president, replaced in 1972 by Ahomadegbe.

The system seemed to be working when, in 1972, internal rivalries within the army triggered two mutinies at the Ouidah military camp. Though they were put down, more than twenty high-ranking officers were arrested, and six of them, including Kouandété, sentenced to death. That move prompted one last coup, led by a man who, like Kouandété, was a northerner from Natitingou – **Major Mathieu Kérékou**.

■ Stability – and a step to the Left

At the time of Kérékou's takeover on **October 26, 1972**, Dahomey had suffered nine changes of government in twelve years. Administration had grown used to the notion of government by crisis control and the nation had struggled with no clear lead and almost continual uncertainty.

Although remarkable **stability** marked the next phase in the country's history, it seemed at first that the pattern of biennial coups might continue. In **1973**, the national radio, "The Voice of the Revolution" reported that top-ranking military officers had been arrested for trying to overthrow the government. Later that year, some 180 student organizations were banned following demonstrations and strikes.

1975 was another bleak year for the government. Finance Minister Janvier Assogba was arrested after it was disclosed he had documents allegedly linking the president and other important government members in a financial scandal. In March, former president Zinsou was sentenced to death *in absentia* (he had been living in Paris where he headed the outlawed *Parti Démocratique Dahoméen*) for allegedly planning to assassinate Kérékou. And in May, Captain Aikpe, the Minister of the Interior, was shot to death by a Kérékou bodyguard when the president allegedly caught him *in flagrante delicto* with Mme Kérékou.

In **1977** there was another dramatic **coup attempt** when a group of **mercenaries** landed at Cotonou airport and, after trying to shell the presidential mansion, were forced to retreat (events on which some of Frederick Forsyth's thriller *The Dogs of War* are said to have been based). Most of the mercenaries, led by the notorious thug Bob Denard, were French and, afterwards, already dismal Franco-Béninois relations sank to a new low. Morocco, Gabon and the *Mouvement de la Rénovation du Dahomey* – an exiled political party based in Brussels – were all implicated. A personal experience of the events is described by Bruce Chatwin, in typically laconic fashion, in "A Coup" (*Granta 10: Travel Writing*, Penguin, 1984).

Kérékou's revolution

Kérékou weathered all the storms. Two years after his coup, the new leader announced that Dahomey would engage in a **popular revolution**, embarking on a socialist path based on Marxism-Leninism. The country established relations with the People's Republic of China, Libya and North Korea and received the blessing of Sekou Touré of Guinea. Benin also moved closer to the Soviet Union and its tributary states.

Also in 1975, Kérékou changed the country's name from Dahomey to the **République Populaire du Benin** and launched the single political party, the *Parti de la Révolution Populaire du Benin* (PRPB). The new course instigated significant changes. Schools were nationalized, the legal system was reorganized and committees were established round the country to stimulate participation in local government. In 1977, a *Loi Fondamentale* established new political structures including the *Assemblée Nationale Révolutionnaire*. In 1979, the assembly's 336 members were selected by the party and approved by 97 percent of the voters. Later in the year, the party selected Kérékou as the sole presidential candidate and the assembly unanimously elected him in February 1980.

The 1980s

It would be hard to assert that Kérékou was ever a committed Marxist. Certainly it was a late conversion which only became clear after he took power and which was only defined in 1974. While the **centralized economy** hardly produced miracles for the nation, the revolutionary stance was a major contributing factor in maintaining stability since the 1970s. In the first place, it significantly reduced the regional disputes that continuously brought down early governments, by shifting political argument from ethnic loyalties to issues of social and economic ideology. It also helped to appease Benin's radical intelligentsia. For a long time, Benin's dissatisfied intellectual elite (the French called the country the "West African Latin Quarter") were unable to find work in the stagnant economy. Their calls for radical reforms in the early days of independence were popular with unions and student groups and helped to topple more than one president.

But while rhetorically supporting the revolution, Kérékou began gradually to embark on a path of **liberalization**. By 1982 the government was busy selling off or reforming its unproductive and corrupt state-run companies and *sociétés*. Under IMF and World Bank pressure, Cotonou also began retraining officials and adopting measures to encourage private investment. In 1985, the government asked the IMF for assistance – a policy, it said, designed to "exploit the positive factors of capitalism".

The former leaders, Maga, Apithy and Ahomadegbe had been released in 1981 and many other political prisoners were pardoned (though those implicated in the bitterly resented "mercenaries invasion" of 1977 remained behind bars). The country also began fostering **relations with the West.** The relationship with France improved after the Socialists came to power in 1981, especially following President Mitterrand's official visit to Benin in 1983. Three years later, Kérékou made a series of trips to West European nations urgently seeking more aid and better debt terms. He also moved closer to conservative African nations, repairing old rifts with Togo, Côte d'Ivoire, Cameroon and Gabon.

Most of the policy reforms of the early 1980s were prompted by the deteriorating state of the economy and a scramble to find new sources of foreign aid. **Oil**, discovered off the coast, began to be exploited in 1982. It provided some relief to the government as the country was able to produce sufficient for its own consumption and to export small quantities. Bright prospects, however, turned gloomy as the world price of oil dropped and ambitious plans for increased exploration and drilling were scrapped. With few other viable resources, the economy was still heavily reliant on the agricultural sector – cotton and, especially, palm oil. A measure of the government's desperation was the risky agreement it entered into in 1988 to import highly dangerous **toxic waste** (some of it possibly radioactive) for dumping in a two-square-kilometre landfill site near the railway line not far from Abomey. The Nigerian government, which had a problem with a private commercial agreement along the same lines in Nigerian territory, was outraged at the danger to the region and the Béninois had to renege.

Economic woes had already forced the government to devise extreme austerity measures, announcing in 1985 that it would no longer guarantee **jobs to graduates**. That decision sparked bloody rioting and widespread arrests. Kérékou quickly removed the Minister of Education, who was a Fon, thereby isolating himself from that ethnic community. When the border with Nigeria closed that year and relations with Benin's powerful neighbour deteriorated, resentment also grew among the Yoruba-speaking communities in the southeast, diminishing still further Kérékou's political stock. His resignation from the army seems to have impressed no one.

In 1987, student riots again broke out in protest at non-payment of government allowances. Further unrest, in January 1989 – when the government diverted public funds to pay the military in the wake of two coup attempts by disillusioned left-wing army officers – led to spontaneous oubursts of **violent anti-government protest** in Cotonou, where public buildings were vandalized and shops looted.

■ The democratic era

Lénin n'aura plus de chance au Bénin

Slogan of revolting students in Cotonou, December 1989

There were **demonstrations** in **December 1989**, unprecedented since Kérékou's coup of 1972, as they involved public demands for his resignation, for the adoption of a multi-party system and for a complete purging of entrenched, corrupt economic practices. Students and civil servants hadn't received allowances or pay for months, absenteeism had reached epidemic proportions and the country was in a state of muddle, discontent and stagnation not witnessed since the 1960s. Because of the **fear of coups**, most of the armed forces were no longer armed, and for several days in December 1989 anti-riot police stood by in Porto Novo and Cotonou as tens of thousands of protesters roared for Kérékou's downfall. In the middle of all this, Kérékou decided to go on a walkabout in the poor quarters of Cotonou. He got a mixed response, state radio reporting his progress at one stage as taking place "amid ovations and stone-throwing".

The events were inevitably compared to similar scenes being played out in **Eastern Europe**, and certainly the Béninois were encouraged by the limited news from there that filtered through. But it had been abundantly clear for many years that Benin's wasteful command economy was not working and that the human resources at the country's disposal – some of the best-trained **administrators, teachers and intellectuals** in West Africa – were being squandered by a top-heavy and grossly inefficient bureaucracy.

After the events of December 1989 – which coincided with an agreement by the IMF and World Bank to bale out Kérékou one more time, and pay some of the salary backlog – the Marxist-Leninist ideology was dropped: this was a condition of French economic support. By March 1990, a **multipartite national conference** had been held to establish a framework for the country's future – and to decide what role Kérékou might play. Fifty-two different political groups were represented; the conference declared itself sovereign, reduced the powers of Kérékou to that of a figurehead, and appointed a new cabinet headed by Soglo, a former official of the World Bank.

So wide-reaching were the reforms and so effective was the transitional government in replacing members of the military regime with civilian administrators, that Benin was quickly dubbed the first country in West Africa to experience a "civilian coup". Independent newspapers flourished; Amnesty International commended Benin for releasing all its political prisoners.

A giddy sense of renaissance swept the country. With the referendum of August 1990 overwhelmingly supporting the conference's draft multi-party constitution, the way forward seemed optimistic and when Soglo soundly beat Kérékou in the **presidential elections** of 1991, the nation's mood was ecstatic.

International relations improved in the aftermath of democratization, particularly with western powers such as the US and France. A new era of **cooperation** also blossomed with neighbouring Nigeria as negotiations took place over the demarcation of their common border and measures aimed at curbing smuggling were introduced. Recently, Nigeria began granting substantial financial aid to Benin.

Despite the new lines of credit that have opened to the country, however, the immediate economic outlook continues to be bleak, and the Western-imposed structural adjustment has hit wage earners especially hard, reducing Soglo's popularity. Labour unrest has continued through the early years of his administration with strikes and demonstrations causing occasional havoc in Cotonou. Several coup attempts were also reported in the early 1990s. Approval for the new president fell even further in 1994 when he accepted a regional agreement for the devaluation of the CFA, a move widely interpreted as bending to Western insistence on painful **economic remedies**.

■ Prospects

In the run-up to legislative elections in March 1995, Soglo formed, and became leader of, the **Parti de la Renaissance du Bénin** (PRB), which soon merged with another new party, the **Pan-African Union for Democracy and Solidarity**. At the elections, 31 parties fielded candidates for just 83 deputies' seats. Provisional results gave a win to the opposition alliance, but Soglo's side claimed serious irregularities had taken place, and the results in thirteen seats were invalidated by the electoral commission, giving a majority – just – to Soglo's deputies and deputies from allied parties. As the year progressed, a number of deputies belonging to other parties switched allegiance to Soglo's PRB, while the Communist Party of Benin agreed to vote with the PRB.

Such manoeuverings mean little, perhaps, to the majority of Benin's economically embattled population. Yet, while parliament and the president increasingly come in for criticism, the democratic ideal is rarely questioned. On the occasion when Soglo – worried by developments in Togo and the possibility that reforms in Benin could just as easily crumble – allowed French troops to be stationed in Benin, public opinion was behind him. International expectations are at work, too: Benin is viewed as the **barometer of democratic reform** in West Africa – a positive example for the region, and one of which its people are proud. The country's progress is thus likely to be interpreted as an omen for West Africa.

There must be cause for optimism in a climate of tolerance and security in which three former presidents are reputed to meet for drinks in Cotonou's bars, and Mathieu Kérékou himself is able publicaly to acknowledge his seventeen years were a disaster.

COTONOU AND THE COAST

On the basis of physical appearances, **COTONOU** is one of West Africa's least enticing cities. Though the population is under half a million, it spreads over a considerable reach of monotonously flat, lacustrine landscape, clogged with residential, commercial and administrative *quartiers* that run chaotically into each another. Laid out in a grid, the cratered, grubby tedium of the streets is accentuated at rush hour, when a seemingly endless tide of rattling *mobylettes* kicks up clouds of dust and exhaust fumes. You might expect the **waterfront** to add a picturesque backdrop to this bleak environment, but the harbour view is unfortunately blocked by the **modern port** – located right in the heart of the city and redolent of export produce that's waited too long in the sun. To cap it all, with not a hill or geographical landmark in the whole of Cotonou, it's difficult to get your bearings on first arriving in the smoggy clamour.

But the city is something of an African melting pot, with a still intact intellectual reputation that has only grown more visible with the government's recent liberalization. Commercially, it has gained considerable importance due to the frequent closures of Lomé's duty-free port. Most hotels here are more geared to regional traders than to tourists. And its immediate saving grace is its fantastic **markets**. For want of other things to do by day, you could spend a good deal of your time in town shopping and browsing. Cotonou **nights** are thoroughly enjoyable by any standards, buzzing with people out to enjoy the cool air, and vendors crowding through the streets. There's a clutch of good **nightclubs** where you can hear music till late.

Three of the country's best-known attractions are each less than an hour out of the city. **Ouidah**, can strike a slightly hollow note in its "fetish tourism", and the stilt village of **Ganvié** is a thorough rip-off – though none the less striking for that – but the official capital of Benin, **Porto Novo**, has a proud gravity that no amount of superficializing could rub out. It's well worth spending a day or two here, in the nicest town on the coast. Lastly, if you're heading to Lomé, or arriving from that direction, you might stop a night at the virtually derelict old trading town of **Grand Popo**, whose magnificently picturesque lagoons and coconut groves provide the backdrop for a lethargic day or two sunning on the beach.

Cotonou

Though Cotonou is a large city, you'll spend most of your time in the diamond-shaped **centre**, defined by three main thoroughfares – **Boulevard Saint Michel** in the northwest, **Avenue Steinmetz** (formerly av Sekou Touré) in the northeast and **Avenue Clozel** to the southeast. The **port** forms a natural barrier to the southwest marking the centre's fourth boundary. Many of the hotels and restaurants listed below are within the confines of these streets, as are the major **businesses**, the **post office** and the **banks**.

East of the centre, Boulevard Saint Michel extends to the Nouveau Pont, and crosses the **lagoon** that cuts Cotonou in two, linking the downtown districts with the **Akpakpa district** on the east side of the city. At the bridge's western foot spreads the

TOURIST INFORMATION

The Ministry of Commerce and Tourism, at the Carrefour des Trois Banques (☎31.54.02), is happy to hand out a slew of brochures, and maps. Otherwise, they won't be able to do much for you. To find out about renting a car or joining an organized excursion to somewere like Ganvié or the Pendjari National Park, you're best off going to a travel agent.

vast **Marché de Dan Tokpa**, one of the largest markets along the West African coast. About 1500km down the lagoon towards the ocean, Avenue Clozel, in its turn, extends over the **Ancien Pont** and continues east to join the road to Porto Novo.

West of the centre, Boulevard de la Marina follows the coast to the high-rent **Cocotiers district** near the airport. Along the way, it passes near the French and American embassies and the imposing Presidential Palace, or **Présidence**, a modern pile encircled by a seriously large fence with security cameras peering from every corner.

On the **north side of town**, Avenue de la République leads west from the Nouveau Pont up to the **Place de l'Etoile Rouge** – a monumental square (complete with torch-bearing cast-iron statue rising up from the giant red star at its centre) commemorating the country's now lapsed revolution.

Arrival and city transport

The **airport** (with a small **exchange bureau** that opens for the day's few incoming flights) is 5km from the centre and you need to take a taxi to get into town. Though the fare is officially fixed at around CFA2000, few drivers are keen to take you for this sum: try to get an idea of the going rate, and bargain strenuously. If you have little luggage, **zimi-djams** (*mobylette* drivers wearing yellow shirts with numbers stencilled on the back; pronounced, more or less "semi-john") wait in front of the airport and will take you to the centre for a fraction of a taxi's cost.

Coming in by **bush taxi**, you're most likely to be let off in the city centre. Arriving from Lomé, for example, you end up at the **Jonquet autogare** right in the heart of the downtown district. Other towns in Benin have their own *autogares* in Cotonou (see "Moving On" p.917), conveniently situated on or near one of the three main streets marking the centre – bd St-Michel, av Steinmetz or av Clozel. If you happen to arrive from the north by train, the **railway station** is also centrally located, near the port.

Within the city centre, **taxis** are shared and cost CFA200–300 for most destinations, though they are not as widely available as *zimi-djans* – by far the most frequent form of transport in the centre. These should only cost you CFA100–150, even for quite long rides in town: as you're the only passenger, they are of course completely negotiable. There are no buses.

Accommodation

From dirt-cheap *chambres de passage* to luxury money temples, Cotonou has **accommodation** for everyone. Unless you are penniless, avoid the low-budget places where levels of hygiene are about as low as the prices: there's a number of very decent mid-range lodgings which aren't expensive.

Campers are well provided for at the rustic but friendly *Camping Ma Campagne* (CFA1500 per person to camp; or simple rooms ②) 12km west of the centre on the

ACCOMMODATION PRICE CODES

① Under CFA4000 (under £5/$7.50).
② CFA4000–8000 (£5–10/$7.50–15).
③ CFA8000–16,000 (£10–20/$15–30).
④ CFA16,000–24,000 (£20–30/$30–45).
④ CFA24,000–32,000 (£30–40/$45–60).
⑥ CFA32,000–40,000 (£40–50/$60–75).
⑦ Over CFA40,000 (over £50/$75).

For further details turn to "Accommodation" in the Practical Information at the Beginning of this chapter.

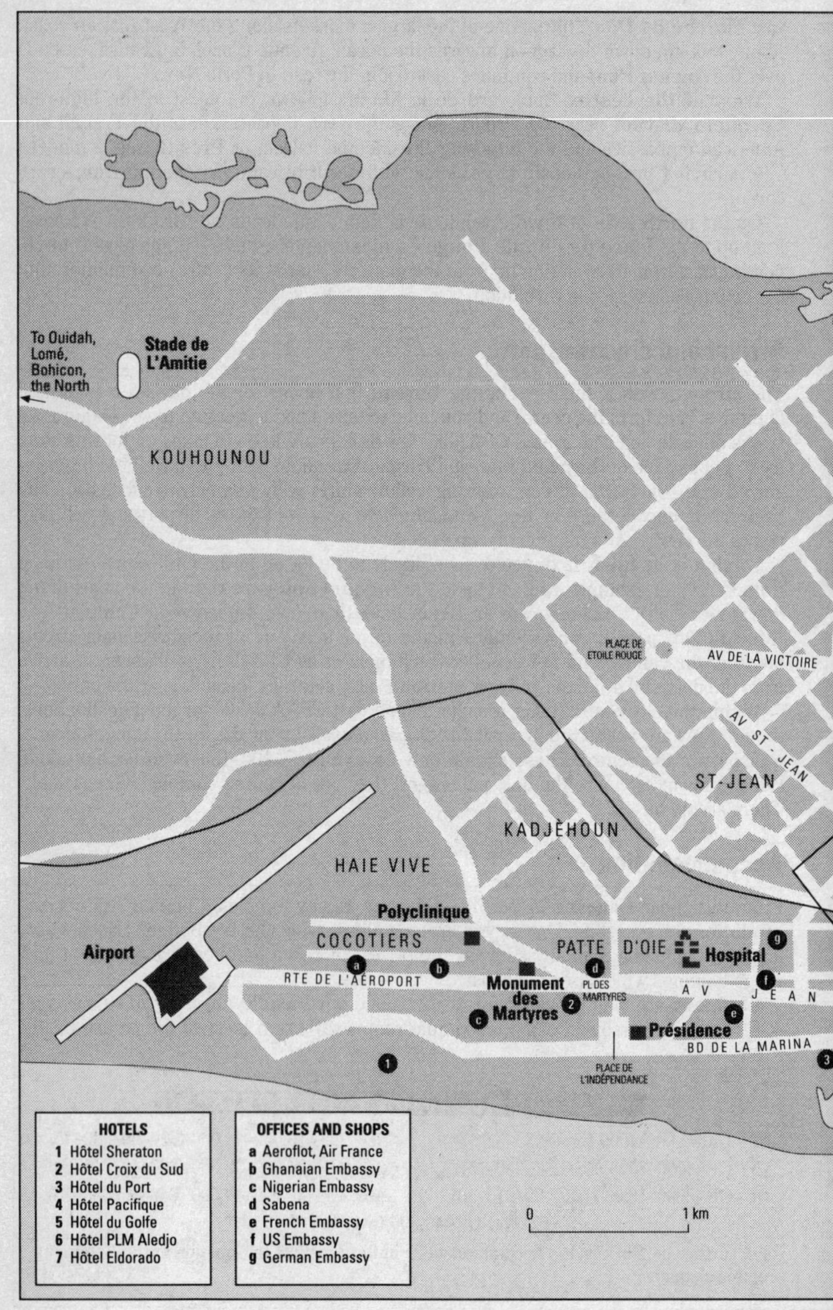
To Ouidah, Lomé, Bohicon, the North
Stade de L'Amitie
KOUHOUNOU
PLACE DE ETOILE ROUGE
AV DE LA VICTOIRE
AV ST-JEAN
ST-JEAN
KADJÈHOUN
HAIE VIVE
Polyclinique
COCOTIERS
Airport
PATTE D'OIE
Hospital
RTE DE L'AÉROPORT
Monument des Martyres
PL DES MARTYRES
AV JEAN
Présidence
BD DE LA MARINA
PLACE DE L'INDÉPENDANCE
HOTELS
1 Hôtel Sheraton
2 Hôtel Croix du Sud
3 Hôtel du Port
4 Hôtel Pacifique
5 Hôtel du Golfe
6 Hôtel PLM Aledjo
7 Hôtel Eldorado
OFFICES AND SHOPS
a Aeroflot, Air France
b Ghanaian Embassy
c Nigerian Embassy
d Sabena
e French Embassy
f US Embassy
g German Embassy
0
1 km

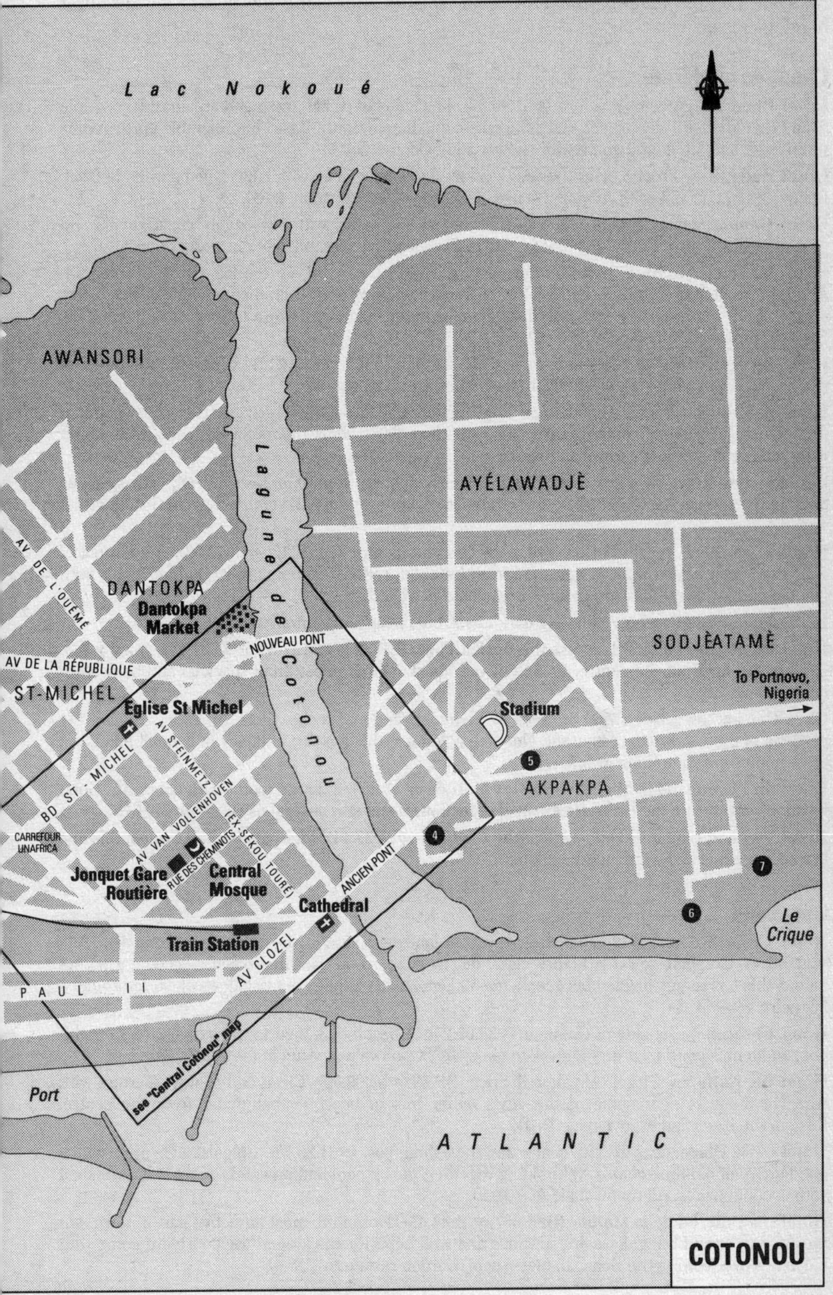

Lac Nokoué
AWANSORI
Lagune de Cotonou
AYÉLAWADJÈ
SODJÈATAMÈ
DANTOKPA
Dantokpa Market
NOUVEAU PONT
AV DE L'OUÉMÉ
AV DE LA RÉPUBLIQUE
ST-MICHEL
Eglise St Michel
To Portnovo, Nigeria
Stadium
AKPAKPA
BD ST-MICHEL
AV STEINMETZ
AV VAN VOLLENHOVEN
(EX-SEKOU TOURÉ)
CARREFOUR UNAFRICA
Jonquet Gare Routière
RUE DES CHEMINOTS
Central Mosque
ANCIEN PONT
Cathedral
Train Station
AV CLOZEL
PAUL II
Le Crique
Port
see "Central Cotonou" map
ATLANTIC
COTONOU

route de Lomé. Pitching your tent in an isolated spot along the beach, on the other hand, is unsafe.

Cheap to moderate

Hôtel Babo, rue Agbeto Amadore (☎31.46.07). In shades of pastel green and cream, this is visible from bd St-Michel (easy to spot as it's the tallest building around). Basic, but tolerable upper rooms (on the 4th and 5th floors) some with shower and balcony. ②.

Hôtel Bodega, av Proche, near the train station. Extremely clean with landscaped garden in front. Renovated S/C rooms with AC and a sense of spaciousness. Recommended. ③.

Hôtel Camair, off av Proche. One of the cheapest in town, with reasonably clean rooms and shared facilities (never mind the bloody wall stains – just one less mosquito to worry about). ①.

Hôtel la Colombe, PK 5, route de Porto-Novo, Voie Sobetex, 4th on the left (BP 156 Cotonou). Although some way from the centre (5km), this is an obliging and recommended hotel. They'll pick up free from the airport, a fifteen-minute drive at night. Share taxis into town cost only CFA200. Some S/C rooms, fanned or AC. ②.

Hôtel le Concorde, av Steinmetz near *Ciné Vog* (BP 1557; ☎31.33.13). Different categories of rooms, all AC, of which those with shared facilities are cheapest. ③.

Hôtel le Crillon, off av Steinmetz near the *Ciné Vog* (BP 03-1433; ☎31.51.58). The most central of the inexpensive hotels, and well cared for with clean S/C rooms (floors swept, beds made daily) with fans. Attentive staff – towel and bar of soap provided. ②.

Pension Familiale, av Proche (☎31.21.25). Newly opened, central and very clean, with spacious S/C rooms and overhead fans. The Cameroonian owners can give travel tips if you're heading that way. ①–②.

Hôtel Miva, PK 6, rte de Porto Novo, 6km from the centre (BP 9112; ☎33.12.08). A good place, near the beach, if you want to get away from Cotonou, rather than explore it. Budget rooms with fan, but comfortable AC accommodation available as well. ③.

Le Muguet, off av Proche. A stinking dark hovel, but cheap and central. ①.

Hôtel Pacifique, av Clozel, across the Ancien Pont (BP 423; ☎33.17.60 or 33.01.45). Good value, and not too far from the centre. Rooms of various standards, most quite spacious and some with lagoon views. ③.

Chez Patrick, on a side street between av Steinmetz and av Proche. Clean AC rooms around the gardens of the *Estaminet* restaurant. Not widely known, this has the intimacy of a small hotel, but the amenities of something grander. ③.

Hôtel de l'Union, bd St-Michel (BP 921; ☎31.27.66 or 31.55.60). Large rooms with fan or AC. Good location across from the *Halle des Arts* and reductions if you stay several days. ②–③.

Hôtel Vickenfel, off av Steinmetz near the *Ciné Vog* (☎31.38.14). Right next to the *Crillon*, this one is a little upscale and a little more expensive. ③.

Upmarket

Hôtel Croix du Sud, facing the beach on the landward side of the bd de la Marina (BP 280; ☎30.09.54). Creeping towards luxury class, but more informal than the expense-account guzzlers below, this has rooms divided between a main block and a complex of bungalows clustered round a 25-metre pool. ④–⑤.

Hôtel Eldorado, east side of Cotonou (☎33.09.23). A beach club next to the expensive *PLM* with pool and tennis courts. Large rooms with fan or AC. Good value for fun in the sun. ③–④.

Hôtel du Golfe, av Clozel, Akpakpa district (BP 37; ☎33.09.55). Clean and roomy quarters with AC. The hotel is near some of the city's better bits of beach – though far from the centre. Restaurant, disco and even a gym. ③–④.

Hôtel de la Plage, near the city centre and the fishing port (☎31.25.60). Colonial-style place with a good share of old-time charm still holding together, plus a pool and private beach nicely furnished with coconut palms. All rooms have AC. ③–④.

Hôtel du Port, bd de la Marina (BP 7067; ☎31.44.43). Not in the most attractive part of town, but the AC rooms and bungalows are spacious and well kept. Rooms around the courtyard come with balconies overlooking the clean, 25-metre pool. Garden restaurant. ③–④.

Luxury

Hôtel PLM Alédjo, on the east side of town, 4km from the centre (BP 2292; ☎33.05.61). A dull modern hotel in a twenty-hectare tropical park, the *Alédjo* found a place in history as the venue of the March 1990 democracy conference. There's a pool and the hotel offers horse riding; it's also right next to a protected ocean bay ("La Crique") with windsurfing. ⑥–⑦.

Hôtel Sheraton, bd de la Marina, 4km from the centre, near the airport (BP 1901; ☎30.01.00 or 30.12.56; Fax 30.11.55) Two hundred luxury rooms and bungalows (some with hazy ocean outlooks), all fitted out with colour TV, video and phone. The hotel is right on the beach with a popular poolside bar and a flourish of restaurants, including one with first-class breakfast buffets. There's also a disco, sauna, crafts shop, travel agency and bank. Generically international; sterile. ⑦.

The City

By way of **sights**, Cotonou is unexciting. On the western approach to the city, a striking example of revolutionary architecture, the Chinese-built **Stade de l'Amitié** ("Friendship Stadium"), dominates the district and flaunts a not typically Béninois **pagoda** at the entrance. And in the city centre, there's a **cathedral** built in an Italian neo-renaissance style. Making a special effort to see these buildings, however – or for that matter, the **central mosque** over by the Jonquet *gare routière* – seems like scraping the bottom of a very small barrel. In the end, it's really only the **markets** that will leave a lasting impression, and Cotonou boasts some very good ones.

The Dan Tokpa Market

Everyday, a steady stream of people can be seen skirting down the Boulevard Saint Michel or over the Nouveau Pont towards the **Dan Tokpa Market**. From the bridge, you can already sense the energy of the commerce as you look down on the confusion of taxis, traders, stalls and merchandise spreading out in a thousand directions near the banks of the lagoon. In the middle of it all stands the heavy cement shoe-box structure of the **market building**, inside which are the cloth boutiques and stands of merchants.

The ground level of the market building is the food hall, devoted to everything from locally grown tubers and grain to boxes of *Milo* and *Nescafé*. Other floors have their own ranges of goods. One large section is filled with Nigerian-made cosmetics – skin lotion, shampoos and hair softeners. Piles of *Savon de Marseille* crush against Chinese enamel bowls and Nigerian plastics. **Cloth** is an especially important item. Colourful Parakou prints are quite reasonable, though less prestigious than the expensive Dutch wax designs. **Clothes** and **shoes** – flip-flops, plastic sandals, *Bata*-style loafers and imitation Italian dress shoes – also have their own specialist domains and dealers.

The Dan Tokpa **Fetish Market** is worth investigating: it's up along the lagoon shore, north of the main market building. After the big open square, the pole market, the wicker market and the empty bottle market, you come to the fetish market. The usual wide assortment of animal body parts and whole dried specimens is on offer – and the usual exececssive demands for cash are made if you want to take photos.

Marché Saint Michel, the Village Artisanal and Marché Ganhi

The **Marché St-Michel**, between the church and Dan Tokpa, is a small, pleasant area, on the edge of which you'll find people selling books – in English as well as French.

The **Village Artisanal** (crafts market) on the bd St-Michel provides the best location in town to shop for Béninois handicrafts. A series of hut-like shops contain familiar specimens of traditional national art – for example, the colourful **patchwork cloths** originating from Abomey that once were used as the banners of that city's kings. Wooden carvings and **masks** from the various regions are also common, as are different varieties of drums – though the ones sold here are mainly decorative. The good collection of jewellery makes for easily portable gifts.

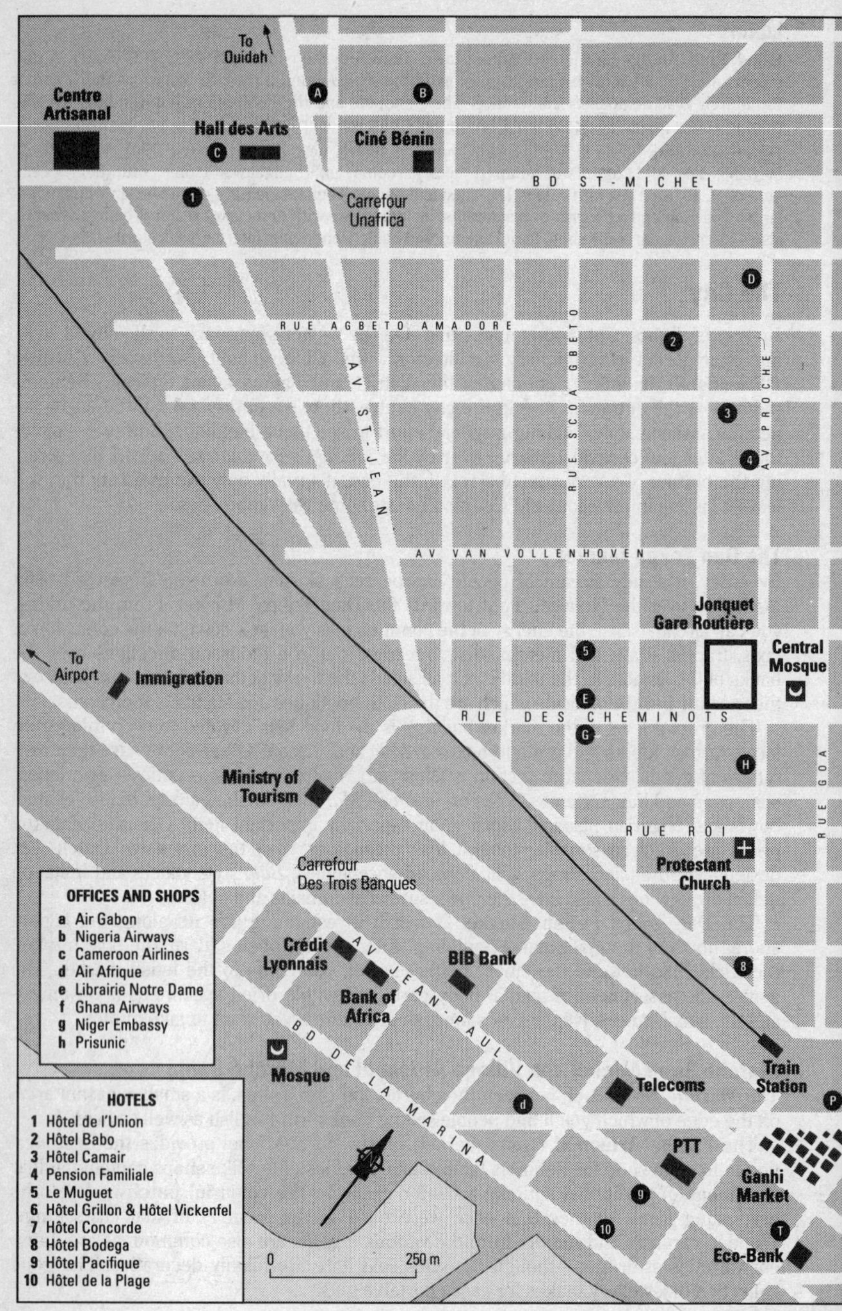
To Ouidah
Centre Artisanal
Hall des Arts
Ciné Bénin
BD ST-MICHEL
Carrefour Unafrica
RUE AGBETO AMADORE
AV ST-JEAN
RUE SCOA GBETO
AV PROCHE
AV VAN VOLLENHOVEN
Jonquet Gare Routière
Central Mosque
To Airport
Immigration
RUE DES CHEMINOTS
Ministry of Tourism
RUE GOA
RUE ROI
Protestant Church
Carrefour Des Trois Banques
Crédit Lyonnais
AV JEAN-PAUL II
BIB Bank
Bank of Africa
BD DE LA MARINA
Mosque
Telecoms
Train Station
PTT
Ganhi Market
Eco-Bank
0
250 m
OFFICES AND SHOPS
a Air Gabon
b Nigeria Airways
c Cameroon Airlines
d Air Afrique
e Librairie Notre Dame
f Ghana Airways
g Niger Embassy
h Prisunic
HOTELS
1 Hôtel de l'Union
2 Hôtel Babo
3 Hôtel Camair
4 Pension Familiale
5 Le Muguet
6 Hôtel Grillon & Hôtel Vickenfel
7 Hôtel Concorde
8 Hôtel Bodega
9 Hôtel Pacifique
10 Hôtel de la Plage

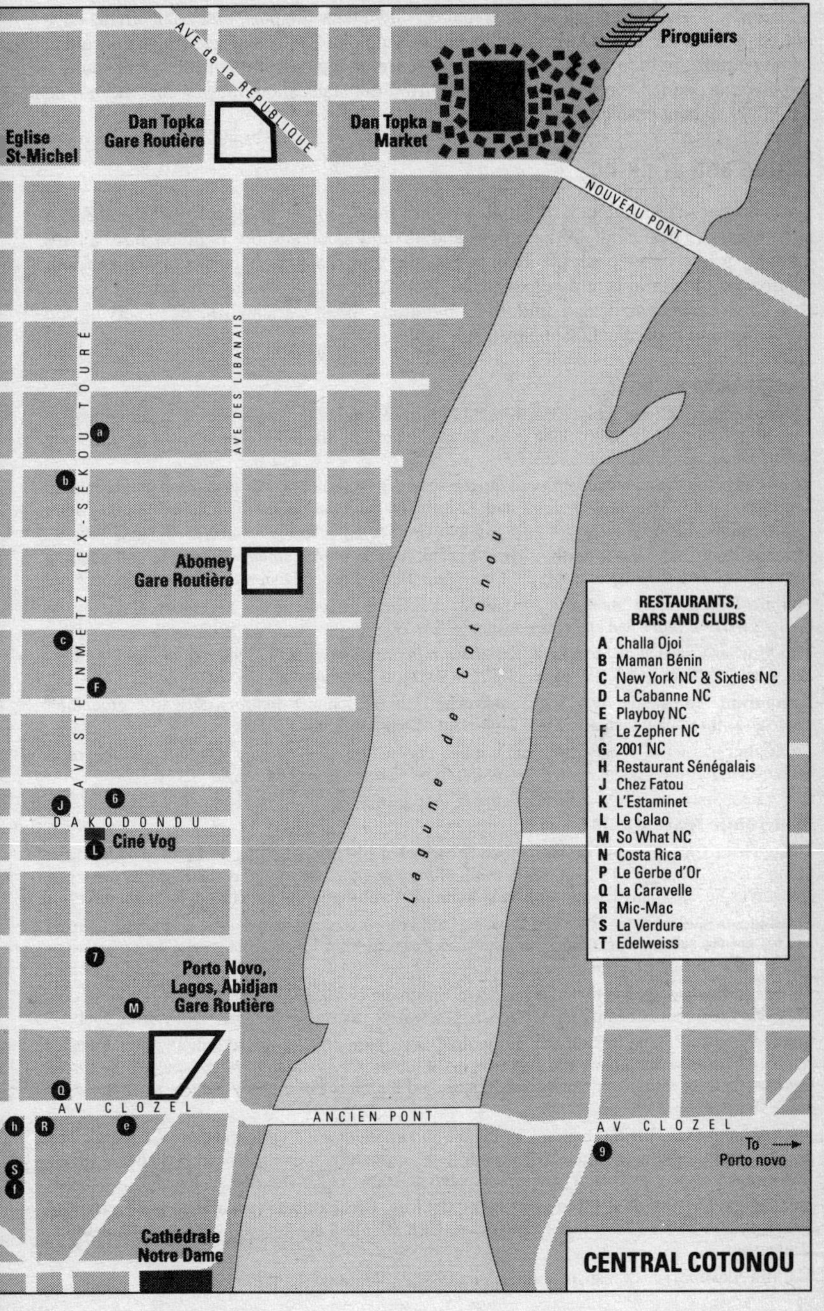

Piroguiers
AVE de la RÉPUBLIQUE
Dan Topka Gare Routière
Dan Topka Market
Eglise St-Michel
NOUVEAU PONT
AV STEINMETZ (EX-SÉKOU TOURÉ
AVE DES LIBANAIS
Abomey Gare Routière
Lagune de Cotonou
RESTAURANTS, BARS AND CLUBS
A Challa Ojoi
B Maman Bénin
C New York NC & Sixties NC
D La Cabanne NC
E Playboy NC
F Le Zepher NC
G 2001 NC
H Restaurant Sénégalais
J Chez Fatou
K L'Estaminet
L Le Calao
M So What NC
N Costa Rica
P Le Gerbe d'Or
Q La Caravelle
R Mic-Mac
S La Verdure
T Edelweiss
DAKODONDU
Ciné Vog
Porto Novo, Lagos, Abidjan Gare Routière
AV CLOZEL
ANCIEN PONT
AV CLOZEL
To Porto novo
Cathédrale Notre Dame
CENTRAL COTONOU

Marché Ganhi is a small produce market down near the port, essentially these days aimed at and used by expats and wealthy Béninois. There's a general selection of produce here, but it's also a good place to score cheap cassettes of the latest sounds. Tapes recorded for you or bought straight from the stalls should never cost more than CFA1200, except possibly Angélique Kidjo.

Eating and drinking

Cotonou doesn't have much of a high culinary reputation as far as European and Asian cuisine goes. Local food, on the other hand, is quite good and the Béninois have a flare for tasty sauces made with plenty of vegetables and seafood or meat. For **street food**, try around the markets and *autogares*. In the centre, especially the area around the rue des Cheminots, you'll also find the ubiquitous West African *cafémen*, serving up omelettes and instant coffee on streetside tables.

Inexpensive eateries

Challa-Ojoi, av St Jean, a block north of bd St-Michel. One of the city's best and least expensive open-air restaurants. Home cooking in cauldron-like pots; try the *purée d'igname* with *pied de boeuf* or fish. Good salads too. Under CFA1000.

Chez Fatou, off the av Steinmetz, opposite the *Ciné Vog* (☎31.49.78). Fair prices and good cooking. Local specialities like *sauce poisson* and Frenchified fare like rabbit in mustard sauce. Menu changes daily. Always packed as it's also a popular watering hole, with cheap beer on tap (*pression*).

Maman Bénin, one block north of bd St-Michel. A good choice among the wall-to-wall informal restaurants lining the street behind the *Ciné Bénin*. Bits of beef and fish with different types of *pâte*.

Maquis le Lagon, av Steinmetz (☎31.55.53). Excellent grilled chicken served evenings on the outdoor *terrasse* with salad and chips. Around CFA1500.

Mic-Mac, av Clozel at av Steinmetz. The *chawarma* are a safer bet than the burgers, and the fries and salads are quite good. One of the city's few fast-food joints. Around CFA2000.

Restaurant Sénégalais Awa Seck, av Proche near the Jonquet *autogare*. Rice with groundnut sauce and other filling dishes in a small, pleasant setting. Around CFA1000.

Le Zepher, corner of av Steinmetz and rue des Cheminots. Small *buvette*, with unpredictable meal each evening. Always good, always cheap, and there's always great company.

Mid-range restaurants

L'American Club Temple of Jazz, off bd St-Michel in Gbégamé, turning north immediately west of the *Village Artisanal* (it's then signposted). Not a jazz club, but a quiet restaurant that plays jazz and serves European food. Good ambiance if you want a change from street food. Not expensive.

Le Calao, av Steinmetz (☎31.21.32). Lebanese and French cooking with daily specials ranging from *boudin noir* to *couscous* or, on occasion, oysters flown in from France. Long established and very well known. Around CFA5000.

La Caravelle, intersection of av Clozel and av Steinmetz (☎31.26.56). A popular expat rendezvous, with food and beer on the upstairs terrace, and expensive pastries. Sometimes suffers from dust.

Costa Rica, av Proche (☎31.33.66). If the draft beer, *piste de pétanque* and nightly broadcasts of *Antenne 2* news wasn't enough to draw the expat crowd, the pizza and French cooking is. Across the street, *Le Backgammon* annexe has crêpes and ice cream in a shady *paillote* surrounded by crafts vendors.

l'Estaminet (*Chez Patrick*), between av Proche and av Steinmetz (same street as *Chez Fatou*). The drab bougainvillea-draped façade belies a tidy flowering garden where pizza and French specialities (the *menu du jour* is good value) are served under an attractive *paillote*. Around CFA4000.

La Gerbe d'Or, near the PTT on av Clozel (☎31.42.58). Best pastries in town since way back – rum babas, éclairs and custard slices for around CFA500. Also serves croissants and wholewheat sandwiches.

Maquis Akwaba, rue St Jean, near the prison (☎32.19.21). Good standby.

Expensive restaurants

Edelweiss, near the Marché Ganhi (☎31.31.38). Unusual combination of specialities where sauerkraut mixes with African fish dishes. Good service and pleasant atmosphere.

Le Kinkeliba, bd St-Michel in the *Village Artisanal* (☎31.27.89). Upscale African restaurant with a well-deserved reputation for excellent, if expensive, national specialities.

Hôtel du Lac, Akpakpa, near the Ancien Pont. A great terrace for a drink and maybe a meal, looking out across the lagoon as the sun goes down.

L'Oriental, in Kadjehoun. Excellent Lebanese restaurant. Superb meze dinner on Wed and Sun. About CFA7000.

Le Rufino's, Zone Residentielle, near the German embassy (☎31.39.38). Haute cuisine from China and Vietnam, served in the AC dining room or on the terrace.

La Seppe, bd St-Michel. Refined French restaurant with trellised outdoor eating area.

Le Sorrento, bd St-Michel near *Ciné Bénin* (☎31.57.79). Benin's best Italian restaurant and one of the most popular dinner addresses in Cotonou. Excellent pizza along with unusual pasta dishes.

La Terrasse, rue Goa (☎31.54.25). Large garden restaurant in the city centre, with a long list of Vietnamese specialities.

The Three Musketeers, off av Clozel next to the cement works. Colonial house converted into English pub, featuring fish 'n' chips and shepherd's pie. Downstairs drinking area with darts and snooker and a pleasant outdoor beer garden. Same owners as Grand Popo's *Auberge*.

La Verdure, off av Clozel (☎31.21.32). Casual bar-restaurant with lobster and seafood specialities. Something of a gathering point, with pinball and a small pool table.

Nightlife and entertainment

For a cheap night on the town, **rue des Cheminots**, down near the Jonquet *gare routière*, is a lively introduction. In addition to the many restaurants and boutiques that stay open late, a couple of good **clubs**, listed below, have made this one of Cotonou's most active after-dark centres.

La Cabanne, av Proche (☎31.23.75). Nice club though usually low-energy until Thursday when diverse bands come to kick off the weekend. No cover most nights.

La Case de la Musique, bd St-Michel. No cover most nights, but the price of drinks – though not unreasonable – is prohibitive for the masses (on an off-night, talented musicians work hard to enthuse an audience of three). Livens up for the weekends. Well worth checking out.

Le Golden's Club, out of the centre in the Cadjehoun district. Béninois bar and disco – lively after 10pm.

New York, New York, bd St-Michel. Currently the place to be seen among young trend-setters. CFA3000 cover, but a dependably good time, though it's not cool to come before midnight when things start getting lively.

Playboy Club, rue des Cheminots. Sleazy, but always packed out and thronging with prostitutes who reside on the premises. More a *bar populaire* than a nightclub, it's aptly enough named, as the main occupation of male customers is leering at the women as they wind their bodies around the rhythms. *Le Soweto*, just down the street, is similar in every respect.

Sixties-60s, bd St-Michel. Another swanky, trendy club that caters to the same clientele as *New York*, and is increasingly popular in its own right.

So What!, off av Clozel near the cathedral. The biggest, most popular and most expensive of the live music clubs. Musicians from Benin, Togo and Nigeria play an extraordinary range of styles from jazz to urban African pop. CFA2000 cover and CFA1000 for a drink, but consistently good music.

Le 2001, rue des Cheminots. Top of the list despite the relatively high price of drinks (CFA2000–3000) and cover (CFA3000). It attracts a younger crowd looking for music and romantic encounters.

Movies and culture

With the march of videotape, **cinemas**, in the big movie-theatre sense, are closing down. The following are currently closed: *Ciné Vog* on av Steinmetz; *Ciné Bénin* on bd

St-Michel; and the *Cocotiers* at the *Hôtel Croix du Sud*. Though they may reopen, it's currently hard to see a film except on a small video screen or at the American or French cultural centres.

The dynamic **Centre Culturel Français** is on the route de l'Aéroport (☎30.08.56; Fax 30.11.51) next to the French embassy. Besides the library with books and newspapers (Tues & Thurs 9am–noon & 3–9pm; Wed 9am–7pm; Fri & Sat 9am–noon and 3–7pm; closed Sun & Mon), they have regular art exhibitions and theatrical performances by local artists, and a good programme of film. The **American Cultural Centre**, off the bd de la Marina (☎30.03.12), has its own movie programme (mostly recent Hollywood releases) and library.

Listings

Airline offices include: *Aeroflot*, rte de l'Aéroport (BP 032014; ☎30.15.74); *Air Afrique*, av Clozel (☎31.21.07; Fax 31.53.41); *Air France*, rte de l'Aéroport (☎30.18.15); *Air Gabon*, av Steinmetz, (☎31.20.67); *Cameroon Airlines*, 119 av Steinmetz (31.52.17); *Ghana Airways*, off av Clozel (☎31.42.83); *Nigeria Airways*, av du Gouveneur Ballot (BP 221); and *Sabena*, place des Martyrs (BP 2622; ☎30.03.55).

Banks In the centre, the best bank for changing money is the *BIB* near *Air Afrique* (BP 03-2098; ☎31.55.49; Fax 31.27.07), which has good rates and takes no commission. The *Financial Bank* off av Clozel by the PTT (BP 2700; ☎31.31.00; Fax 31.31.02) is slow and takes a hefty commission but in theory they give cash advances on Visa. Other possibilities include the *Eco Bank* near the Ganhi market which can give Access/Mastercard cash advances (BP 1280; ☎31.40.23; Fax 31.33. 85).

Beaches Most of those around the city are filthy and, in any case, often have a dangerous undertow. The best strands are in front of the hotels, notably the *Sheraton* and *Croix du Sud*, which are cleaner than that of the *Hôtel du Port*. Near the *Aledjo*, the protected cove known as La Crique is popular among expats and townspeople since swimming is relatively safe. Don't take valuables on to any beach – La Crique, especially, is notorious for grab-and-runs.

Books and magazines *SONAEC*, av Clozel (☎31.22.42), has all the national papers as well as the best international selection, along with books in French – African and French literature, travel guides, etc. Also try the *Librairie Notre Dame* (☎31.40.94), near the junction of av Steinmetz and av Clozel, behind the cathedral, and *La Plume d'Or*, bd St-Michel, near the US embassy.

Car rental The major companies – *Hertz* (☎30.19.15), *Avis* (☎31.51.38), and *Europcar* (☎31.34.42) – have branches at the airport. *Hertz* is also represented at 157 av Steinmetz (BP 8128; ☎30.19.15) and at the *Sheraton*. Smaller firms often work out substantially cheaper, though their cars and conditions may not be as dependable. These include *ONATHO* (☎31.26.87), *Locar Benin* (BP 544; ☎31.38.37), *Sonatrac* (BP 870; ☎31.23.57), and *Locauto* (BP 117; ☎31.34.42).

Embassies and consulates include: **Algeria**, rte de l'Aéroport (BP 1809; ☎31.29.91); **Egypt** (BP 1215; ☎30.08.42); **France** – embassy, rte de l'Aéroport, Cocotiers district (BP 966; ☎30.08.24 or 30.08.25) or the consulate, av du Général de Gaulle, just south of *Air Afrique* (☎31.26.80 or 31.26.38) issues visas for Togo, Burkina Faso and a number of other Francophone countries; **Germany**, 7 Route Inter-Etats (BP 504; ☎31.29.67); **Ghana** BP 488 (☎30.07.46); **Niger**, behind *Hôtel de la Plage* (BP 352; ☎31.40.30); **Nigeria** Lot 21, Patte d'Oie district (☎30.11.42); **United Kingdom** Honorary Consul, M. Inchelin, *Sobepat* (BP 147; ☎31.33.42); a consular officer from the British High Commission in Lagos is also available every alternate Monday from 10am–2pm at the *Sheraton*; and **USA**, rue Caporal Anani (BP 2021; ☎30.06.50; Fax 30.19.74).

Hospitals The privately-run *Polyclinic* (☎30.14.31), in Cocotiers, has the best reputation, though the most obvious place to head for with medical problems is the *Centre National Hospitalier et Universitaire* in the Patte d'Oie district (☎30.01.55).

Maps The *Institut National de Cartographie*, on rue des Libanais, close to the av Clozel junction, has survey maps of the country in 1:50,000 and 1:200,000 series. Many are out of print.

Passport photos and film developing Passport photos for your visa extension or onward visas are done quickly at *Photo Minute*, on av Clozel near the main PTT, and *Zoom Service*, av Steinmetz near *Ciné Vog*. The price is around CFA2000 depending on speed (five minutes to two days). Across the street from *Zoom Service* is a place that does one-hour film developing.

Pharmacies Of many, the main ones are: *Pharmacie du Jonquet*, rue des Cheminots (☎31.20.49); *Pharmacie Notre Dame*, av Clozel (☎31.23.14); and *Pharmacie Camp Ghezo*, bd St-Michel (☎31.35.55).

Post and phones The main PTT is off av Clozel, near the port. The poste restante service seems reliable here. International calls can be made easily from the Telecommunications office on the av Clozel (collect calls can be made only to France). Phone cards have been introduced, though there aren't many cardphones in Benin, apart from at this PTT, that take them.

Supermarkets The three largest are all near the intersection of av Clozel and av Steinmetz. *La Pointe* is the best for imported European products, though it's now got stiff competition from the more recent *Prisunic* which carries some department store goods along with the groceries. *Benin-Self* has a more limited selection, though the hours are longer.

Swimming pools The cheapest and most central pool is at the *Hôtel du Port,* which non-guests can use for CFA1000. Though much nicer, the *Sheraton*'s pool costs a stiff CFA3000 (and it's circular, so hopeless for serious length-swimming). The *Aledjo* has a smaller but equally expensive pool.

Visa extensions From the Ministry of the Interior, av Jean Paul II.

MOVING ON FROM COTONOU

ROAD TRANSPORT

The main international *gare routière* for travel along the coast on the Cotonou–Lomé axis is the Jonquet *gare routière*, on the rue des Cheminots near the central mosque. Vehicles depart regularly for **Ouidah**, **Grand Popo** and **Lomé**. The commonest vehicles are Peugeot 504 saloon and estate cars, which fill quickly before taking off. The Itajara *gare routière* is focussed a block or so south of Jonquet on the av Proche, but in practice is almost indistinguishable from Jonquet. This is the place to get vehicles for **Parakou** and the north. For **Porto Novo**, **Lagos** and **Abidjan** head to the *autogare* near the old bridge (across from the cathedral) where, depending on the destination, you will find cars, buses and minibuses. Vehicles for Lagos also leave from the Dan Tokpa *gare routière* near the Dan Tokpa market. **Abomey** is serviced from a separate *autogare* located near the *Ciné Vog*, between av Steinmetz and the lagoon.

TRAIN

If you want to head north by train, you'll find the station is downtown, near av Clozel. Two trains leave daily for **Parakou** at 8am and 7pm and cost CFA4000 2nd class and CFA60001st class. Couchettes are available on the evening train.

TRAVEL AGENTS

One of the best organized **travel agents** is *Savanna Tours* on bd St-Michel (☎31.46.26) which has trips to national attractions like Ganvié and Pendjari as well as international tours. Also reputable are *C & C Voyages* on the route de Porto Novo near the Ancien Pont (☎33.00.15; Fax 33.01.49) and *Phimex Voyages* on av Steinmetz (☎31.21.37; Fax 31.57.13). For **car rental**, see "Listings".

Ganvié

GANVIÉ, said to be Africa's largest **lake village**, is an extraordinary sight. The entire town spreads across the shallow, grey-green waters on the northwest side of **Lac Nokoué**, opposite Cotonou, with wood and thatch houses built on tall stilts rising above the rippling surface. The lake is "grooved", as the tourist leaflet puts it, "not by gondolas like in Venice but by graceful *pirogues* or heavy boats loaded to the boards". The village is home to some 15,000 people who make their living primarily from **fishing**. In the shallow waters, they plant branches that form a network of underwater fences known as *akadja*. Trapped inside, the fish can either be caught and eaten or sold, or kept for breeding.

Ganvié is only accessible by boat, and all around the northwest part of the lake the water is crowded with bumping log jams of vessels – even the market is held on the water, women selling wares from their canoes. Not altogether surprisingly, the stilt village is overrun with tourists whose presence has encouraged a commercial free-for-all in the little town, destroying the initial impressions of a tranquil aquatic idyll. This seems to be the way with stilt or maritime villages throughout West Africa – Fadiout in Senegal and Tiegba in Côte d'Ivoire have responded to outsiders' interest in precisely the same way. If you have a low tolerance for this sort of thing, it's best to avoid Ganvié altogether.

Some history

As the **slave trade** expanded after the Portuguese arrival on the coast in the sixteenth century, armies of the Dan-Homey king swept the surrounding countryside, rounding up people to trade with the Europeans for exotic goods such as cloth, gin and guns. Insecurity led to the widespread migration of weaker communities, and it was in this manner that the ancestors of the **Tofinu people**, who now inhabit Ganvié, came to settle in the area around Lake Nokoué. The earliest may have arrived in the sixteenth century, although at the end of the seventeenth century, an exodus of peoples from Tado near the Togolese border is known to have settled at the site of the present village, where they found sufficient space for grazing and farming. More importantly, the people were safe from invasion since, for religious reasons, the Dan-Homey were forbidden to extend their attacks over water. The name Ganvié probably derives from the Tofinu words *gan*, meaning "we are saved", and *vié* or "community".

Getting there

The departure point for Ganvié is **Abomey-Calavi**, 18km north of Cotonou. **Taxis** leave from the Akpakpa market station, but the tourist demand is such that drivers may insist you take a whole vehicle for CFA12,000 or more; **collective taxis** make the trip for around CFA500 per person. Once you've arrived in Abomey-Calavi, you can find motorized boats to take you on a two-hour tour of Ganvié – at a price of CFA10,000 or so. Some of the villagers also run *pirogue* trips, through their own watery backyards, allowing people to take photos of kids standing on porches yelling "Cadeau!" A bit depressing really – you need to adopt a robust sociological approach to find it an enlivening experience. If, instead of stopping at Abomey-Calvi, you continue 5km up the northern highway to **Akassato**, you can approach Ganvié from behind and at slightly less cost. *Pirogues* punt you south 4km or so through the creeks and marshes to the edge of the lake and the stilt village.

Accommodation and food

Tourist facilities have been set up in **ABOMEY-CALAVI**, including decent lodgings at the *Ganvié Bungalow Hôtel*. It's a small place with comfortable AC rooms (☎36.00.39; ③). As an unusual, cheaper alternative, villagers often put up people in their homes. Ask around at the dock; someone will make contact. A lakeshore restaurant near the hotel, *La Pirogue* (☎36.00.40), offers an over-priced Béninois and international menu. There's a couple of bars and a crafts shop nearby.

Ouidah

Hauntingly quiet after centuries of dynamic history, **OUIDAH**, 30km west of Cotonou, and located on a back road off the main Cotonou–Togo highway, works a wonderful spell, exactly as you'd hope. This is a **voodoo** stronghold and the religion's eerie influence penetrates as deeply as the salt air blowing off the ocean. Clearly, the cult has

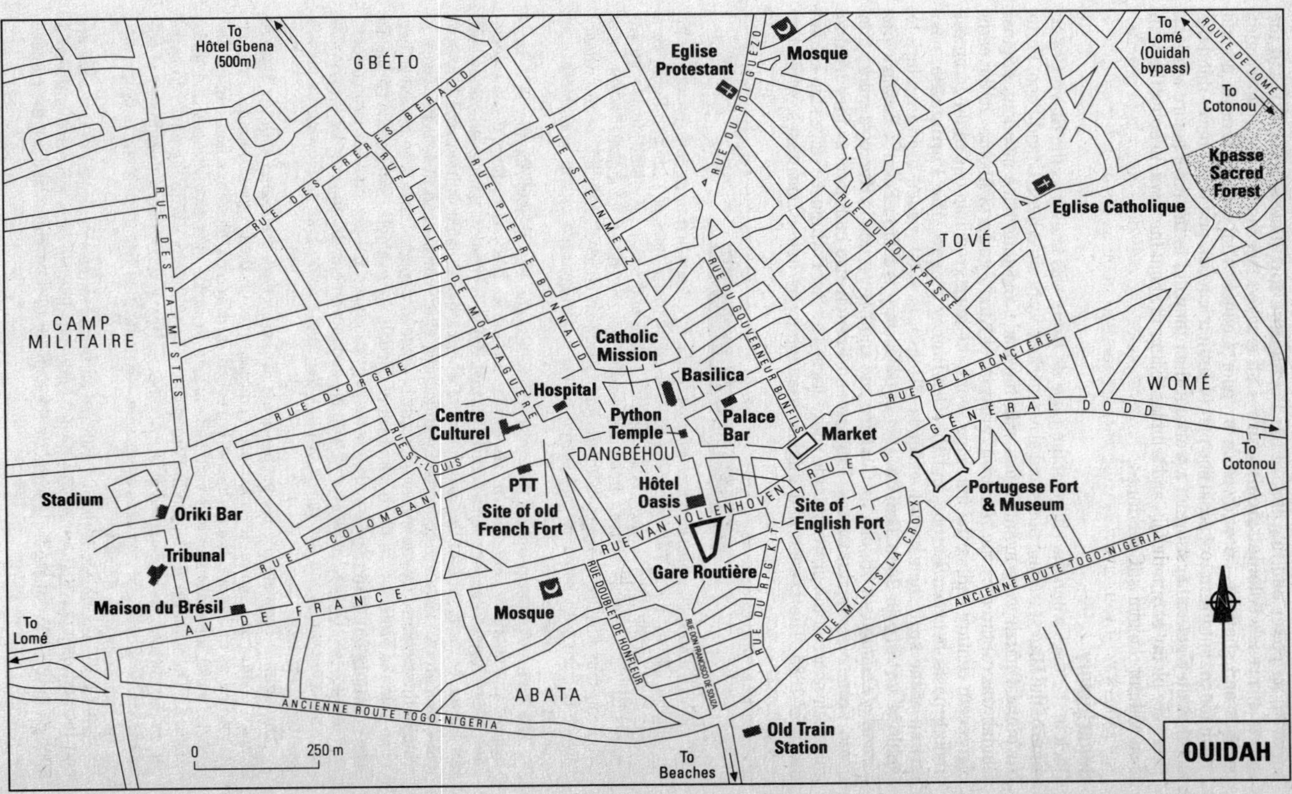
OUIDAH
To Hôtel Gbena (500m)
GBÉTO
Eglise Protestant
Mosque
To Lomé (Ouidah bypass)
ROUTE DE LOMÉ
To Cotonou
Kpasse Sacred Forest
Eglise Catholique
TOVÉ
WOMÉ
CAMP MILITAIRE
Catholic Mission
Basilica
Hospital
Python Temple
Palace Bar
Market
Centre Culturel
DANGBÉHOU
To Cotonou
PTT
Hôtel Oasis
Site of English Fort
Portugese Fort & Museum
Stadium
Oriki Bar
Site of old French Fort
Tribunal
Gare Routière
Maison du Brésil
Mosque
To Lomé
ABATA
Old Train Station
To Beaches
0
250 m
RUE DES FRÈRES BERAUD
RUE DES PALMISTES
RUE OLIVIER DE MONTAGUÈRE
RUE PIERRE BONNAUD
RUE STEINMETZ
RUE DU ROI GUEZO
RUE DU ROI KPASSE
RUE DU GOUVERNEUR BONFILS
RUE DE LA RONCIÈRE
RUE DU GÉNÉRAL DODD
RUE D'ORGRE
RUE ST-LOUIS
RUE F COLOMBANI
RUE VAN VOLLENHOVEN
RUE DU RPG KITI
RUE MILLIS LA CROIX
AV DE FRANCE
RUE DOUBLET DE HONFLEUR
RUE DON FRANCISCO DE SOUZA
ANCIENNE ROUTE TOGO-NIGERIA
ANCIENNE ROUTE TOGO-NIGERIA

survived, its power outliving that of the **Portuguese fort** (now a museum), and the streets of French **colonial architecture** – all cracked façades and sagging wooden porches and shutters – now dwelt in by poor families. The **python temple** adds a kitsch touch, but the use of snakes is part of authentic fetish practice – never mind the fact that they get rather more of a workout than they did in the days before tourism. There are plenty of other altars and temples scattered about the town, keeping the faith alive without the touristic overtones.

Some history

Back in the days when the shore of the *Golfe de Bénin* was known as the **Slave Coast**, some of the largest trading posts and slave markets were sited here. Grand Popo, Porto Novo and Ouidah were synonymous with the trade and thus have infamous origins. Ouidah was captured by the "Amazon" warriors of **King Agadja** of Abomey in the early eighteenth century and, in the following years, the town grew into one of the foremost trading posts between Europe and the Dan-Homey empire. The **Portuguese**, who arrived at the spot, then known as Ajuda ("Help"), in 1580, waited over a century to build the fort of **São João Batista**. Part of their story is told in Bruce Chatwin's *The Viceroy of Ouidah* (see "Books" in *Contexts*) and another version in Herzog's quirky film *Cobra Verde*. Nearby, the **Danes**, **English** and **French** also built forts as they tried to gain their share of the growing trade with Africa. The last Portuguese slave ship left for Brazil in 1885. The Danish and English bastions today house businesses, while the

THE *VODU*

"Voodoo", also spelt *vodu, vodun, voudou*, or *vudu*, is a confusing term. It does not signify a religion, at least not in Africa, but is a word used by the peoples of Togo and Benin for a spirit, demigod or intermediary. *Vodu* "priests", male and female, are individuals who are particularly susceptible to *vodu* influence, easily "possessed" or "mounted" by the *vodu* who can thus display their emotions through a human channel. A **fetish** is an ordinary object imbued with some of this sacred power – a token*vodu* charm available at any market.

The **Ewe** and other people of the coast – as well as the **Fon** around Abomey in Benin – believe in a supreme God, **Mawu**. Their religious stories link him or her (in some societies, Mawu is a woman, or even a couple, Mawu-Lisa) with creation. Shrines are rarely built for Mawu, however, but for the *vodu*, many of whom are associated with **natural forces** or with **ancestors**. *Vodu* are concerned with looking after humans and their benevolence is sought by offerings. Communities often pay homage to a specific *vodu* who becomes their main spiritual protector. In the Benin town of Ouidah, for example, **Dangbe** has a special place. Representd by the snake and sometimes by rainbows, curling smoke, running water, or waving grass, Dangbe is associated with life and movement. In Abomey, he is known as **Da** and is shown on the bas reliefs of the royal palace as a snake swallowing its tail – a symbol of eternity.

Throughout Togo and Benin, people honor **Buku**– a *vodu* associated with the sky. At Dassa Zoumé in Benin, townspeople dedicate one of their oldest temples to her. Renowned as an oracle, Baku's name is evoked in proverbs, blessings and curses, and people travel long distances to visit her shrines to make gifts or sacrifices and make prayers. The *vodu* **So** (Hebiosso in Fon) is the *vodu* of thunder. With the power to strike down the impious, he is depicted at the Abomey palace as a red ram with lightning shooting from his mouth and two axes at his side. **Gu**, the guardian of smithing and war, also has associations with the sky.

Sapata is more closely identified with the earth and shrines dedicated to this *vodu* are usually seen outside villages near the fields. Linked to disease, he is respected and feared. Priests devoted to Sapata are known for their ability to treat illness and for their under-

Place du Fort Français now features a small outdoor theatre. Ouidah remained an important coastal city while under French dominion, but in the early twentieth century the colonials built a new and larger port at Cotonou. From then on, the old town went into a slow decline.

The Town

The **Ouidah Museum of History** (daily 9am–noon & 4–6pm; CFA1000 "donation" includes free photography; enquiries ☎34.10.21) is housed in the Portuguese fort of **São João Batista**, built in 1721. Remarkably enough, a Portuguese flag waved symbolically over the building until the eve of Dahomey's independence in 1960, although the rest of the town was in French hands. The present museum traces the history of European exploration and exploitation of the Slave Coast region, and follows the dispersal of its people to the Caribbean and Brazil. The documentation includes displays of enlarged maps juxtaposed with period photographs and engravings. Many of the exhibits concentrate on the spread of the **voodoo religion** to Haiti, Cuba and Brazil, with examples of religious fetishes and pictures of rituals.

Another small art museum – the **Maison du Brésil** – has recently opened and contains an exhibit of contemporary art that incorporates voodoo symbols into modern forms of expression. Brilliant sculptures made from the transformed carcasses of rusty *mobylettes* highlight the collection that also includes less memorable paintings, photographs and collages. Many of the works pay tribute to Africans in the diaspora in recog-

standing of medicinal plants. **Hu** is connected with the ocean and water. His daughter, **Avlekete**, is honoured at the port of Cotonou and in nearby villages.

Legba, the trickser, whose image is distinguished by an exaggerated phallus, contains elements of good and evil. Though Legba can bring bad luck on a house, he can also chase it away. His shrines can be seen everywhere – guarding the entrance to a community or compound, in a market, in fields, or at a crossroads.

Countless other *vodu* exist, and many occupy natural niches. **Iroko trees**, for example, are often inhabited by *vodu*. The creation stories of some societies in the region tell of men and women descending to earth from the branches of an Iroko. They are associated with fertility or new life, and you will often see sacrifices among their roots.

There are many parallels between the *vodu* and the *orisa* of Yoruba religion in Nigeria and also between *vodu* and elements of Akan religion further to the west in Ghana and Côte d'Ivoire – all the result of migrations and the wax and wane of empires. A further complexity was introduced by the return of Brazilians between the seventeenth and nineteenth centuries to the land of their (partial) ancestry. They reintroduced elements of Yoruba custom when they settled on this part of the coast.

Slaves sold across the Atlantic took their religious systems to North and South America and the Caribbean. Even metropolitan areas like carry reminders: Legba statuaries made in the last fifty years can be found in New York City and Miami. But West African religions are more often identified with Brazil, Cuba and Haiti. Many Haitian slaves came from the Dahomey (Benin) coast and the names of numerous *vodu* are virtually unchanged to this day. Legba is known as Papa Legba; Sapata as Sabata; Avlekete as Aizan-Velekete. The iroko tree, known as *loko* in Fon, became Papa Loko. Only the supreme god, Mawu was given a completely new, French, name – Bondieu.

In the Americas, Catholicism and the *vodu* system were soon melded together. But even in West Africa, many elements of Catholic teaching found fertile soil in the local belief system: the pantheon of a supreme God, the Virgin Mary and saints who could be called upon for help was a similar structure to Mawa and the *vodu*. Saint Patrick, not surprisingly, was identified with the snake *vodu* Dangbe, while Saint Peter was considered to be the Catholic incarnation of the phallic Legba.

nizing the cultural connection between Africa and the Americas. The turn-of-the-century Afro-Brazilian building that houses the exhibit is itself noteworthy. Entrance is free; the guards will ask for money if you want them to explain anything.

Ouidah's large **cathedral** is a formidable monument that was upgraded to the rank of basilica during the 1989 visit of John Paul II, who also consecrated the new altar. Dating from the beginning of the century, it's recently been restored and fitted with new stained glass windows.

The cathedral attracts nowhere near as many visitors as the nearby **python temple**, however, which guards the secrets of Ouidah's snake cult. The key to the secret of the fetish serpents of Ouidah lies in the strength of your donation to open the temple doors. The demand of visitors – coupled with the open encouragement of voodoo tradition by the new government – has led to a thorough restoration of the site (with UNESCO support) and the price of admission seems to have stabilized at CFA1000. For this, you get to pose with the tame pythons – wrap-around snakes believed to give vitality and protection over your person. But on days when the reptiles are, understandably, tired, your payment may get you no more than a peek into the room where they're kept.

An interesting walk through the town's residential streets leads to the **sacred forest of Kpasse**. Tradition holds this site to be where Kpasse, a fourteenth-century chief, transformed himself into a tree in order to hide from his enemies. The ancient *iroki* tree still marks the spot and believers leave offerings by its roots. Modernistic bronze statues depicting voodoo divinities are scattered about the woods and are explained (in French) by the caretaker who meets you at the entrance. Photography is permitted and the tour is free – though a tip is appreciated. While not an extraordinary adventure, a visit here is a pleasant pretext for a tramp through some pretty woods, and the guide's enthusiastic explanations are vivid. In fact the more questions you ask, the more insightful become the answers.

Practicalities

Budget **accommodation** can be found only in a *chambre de passage* at one of the town's *bar-dancings*: very basic non-S/C rooms can be had at *l'Hermitage* for around CFA3000; try too *La Palace* and the *Soleil de Minuit*. Any kid at the *gare routière* can lead the way. More official lodgings include the following, all of which serve **food**:

Hôtel Gbena, route de Lomé (BP 36; ☎34.12.15). Long the only place in town, this government hotel is still probably the best accommodation, though far from the centre (on the main road to Togo). Good food and excellent service. ③–④.

Hôtel Oasis, across from the *gare routière* and an easy walk from the fort (BP 24; ☎34.10.91). This new hotel puts clean AC accommodation right in the heart of town. Although a little out of the range of budget travellers, it gives reasonable value for money. The hotel restaurant is a classy place for *akassa, monyo* or *agouti* – or even foreign fare, including pizza. ③.

Oriki Bar, rue Marius Moutel. This stylish *bar-resto* recently added very presentable and mostly AC rooms around the flowering gardens. Good value in the moderate range and a homely atmosphere. ②.

Grand Popo and around

At the height of the slave trade, **GRAND POPO** rivalled Porto Novo, Ouidah and Aneho (in Togo) as a major port. With the demise of the trade, however, its importance declined more dramatically than the other towns and, today, even vestiges of the more recent colonial past have literally been washed away by the advancing ocean. Villagers remember the large church, commercial depots, administrative buildings and colonial mansions that disappeared into the water as recently as the 1960s, and though a few

antiquated buildings still dot the road that leads to town from the main highway, most of the old quarter is entirely submerged.

As a result, Grand Popo looks very much like any of the other small fishing villages that stretch between Lomé and Cotonou, tucked between the lagoon and the ocean and lost in a sea of coconut trees. Though **voodoo** thrives here, few visitors even notice the snake pit, fetishes or temples and confine themselves mainly to the idyllic **beach**. In fact, there is little else to do once you get here.

The lagoon provides the possibility for excursions, however (small boys will try to recruit you from the moment you arrive), and fishermen are happy to supplement their incomes ferrying guests of the *Auberge* in their *pirogues*. The most popular destination is the **Bouches du Roy** – a vast expanse of water where the Mono River empties into the ocean. Along the way, you pass through scenic island villages.

Practicalities

Taxis from Lomé or Cotonou (85km via Comè) let you off on the main highway. There's a small bar on the intersection of the road that heads down to the strand and this is your last chance for inexpensive food and refreshment. *Zimi-djans* and taxis wait at the junction and for CFA200 will take you to the town's only **accommodation,** the English-run *Auberge* (4km). Housed in refurbished colonial buildings, the lodgings offer a refreshing combination of nostalgia and comfort; all rooms have private baths and fans or AC. Its popularity as a weekend get-away for expats, however, has led to an increase in prices that are prohibitive for budget travellers (③–④) and facilities for camping have closed. The hotel's **restaurant** terrace sits right on the waterfront – spectacular scenery for European dishes.

Lac Ahémé

The lagoon that extends for thirty kilometres inland from Grand Popo is **Lac Ahémé**. It's a highly picturesque area to visit and there's a pleasant **hotel-restaurant** on the west shore, *Village-Club Ahémé* (BP 2090 Cotonou; ☎45.02.20) – a place for lazing away a few days, with plain, comfortable S/C, AC rooms and optional excursions on the lake and around the district (③). The location is **Possotomè**, 87km from Cotonou. To reach it you turn right at Comè, the main junction village 18km north of Grand Popo, and then go 20km north on a bad road, in the direction of Bopa.

Porto Novo

Capital of Benin, but only in name, **PORTO NOVO** has two attributes Cotonou lacks – a geographical setting of some presence and a place in **history**. Sprawling over the hills surrounding a sizeable lagoon, the town was formerly the centre of a large kingdom of the Gun people, and the palace of the rulers has been restored. More recently it served as capital of the French colony of Dahomey – the **colonial buildings** are reminders of this period – and the town was, and remains, the centre of the country's intellectual life and something of a barometer of political opinion in Benin. For visitors, it's one of Benin's most interesting towns, with a strikingly good ethnographic museum.

Orientation

Porto Novo consists of four main parts. The **old town** in the centre is characterized by narrow dirt roads and *banco*-built houses. The old town runs into the **commercial centre**, with the *grand marché* and surrounding businesses that stretch down to the lagoon on the southern flanks of the town. In the east, the **administrative district** is the location of the former **Governor's Palace** as well as a couple of ministries and

office buildings while, scattered around the margins, the zone of new **residential quarters** is inhabited by those who've moved to the city in recent years.

The town

Despite a population of around 150,000, Porto Novo seems much smaller. Perhaps this is because of its coherent layout, but the narrow streets and absence of modern structures also add to the provincial, passed-by, feeling: most of the architecture in town harks back to the colonial and pre-colonial periods.

The Musée Ethnographique

Porto Novo's superb **museum of ethnography** (daily 9am–12.30pm and 3–6pm; CFA1000) contains a wealth of well-presented artefacts – material culture from all Benin's peoples, but concentrating on the southeastern Fon and Yoruba communities – each item accompanied by explanations and background. The visit kicks off at the entrance with a pair of beautifully **carved doors** from the palace of the king of Kétou, 100km north of Porto Novo. The rooms inside are each organized around cultural themes – one dedicated to **masks** and other carvings of religious significance, including fetishes used in the voodoo cult, another devoted to **local arms**, with examples of old rifles and poisoned spears, another containing a large collection of Béninois **musical instruments**. A major part of the museum is dedicated to **regional history** and the treaties signed by local rulers that led to Porto Novo's transformation into a great slave-trading centre.

Palais du Roi Toffa

East of the market, the **Palais du Roi Toffa** (or Palais Honmè) has been restored and costs CFA1000 for the obligatory guided tour. It's an impressive maze of baked mud and thatch divided into the private residences of **King Toffa** and his entourage and public assembly halls. For the moment, this *palais royale* is rather empty except for a few rare mementos of the local kings, and you have to rely on your imagination to bring to life the guide's detailed explanations of local history and court life.

The grand marché

The **market** is held every four days in Porto Novo, in keeping with the traditional calendar. It's a colourful affair that spreads over a large central square, with stalls selling agricultural goods from the surrounding countryside and fish from the nearby lagoon. Dominating the scene, the curious Brazilian-style building painted in muted pastel colours was built in the nineteenth century as a church, but is today the central mosque.

Practicalities

Although this is Benin's capital, Cotonou is the centre of business and government. Porto Novo doesn't even benefit greatly from Lagos traffic and trade as it's off the main coastal highway. There is a **hospital** (☎21.34.91) and pharmacies, but for banking (you can't change money here) and just about every other business, you'll find Porto Novo limited indeed.

Accommodation

Porto Novo has a number of hotels, but for a town of its size, the options are fairly limited.

Hôtel Beaurivage, out of the centre on the bd Lagunaire (BP 387; ☎21.23.99). Old, but well-maintained hotel with nicely planted terrace overlooking the lagoon. Extremely accommodating staff and comfortable S/C, AC rooms, but variable food. ③.

Hôtel la Capitale, in the Akron district southeast of the market (☎41.34.64). Convenient for walking, but suffers from neglect in terms of both service and upkeep. Only one fanned room; those with AC seem depressing and overpriced. ②–③.

Casa Danza, av Victor Ballot (☎21.48.12). The popular eatery now offers the town's most central accommodation. New, clean and comfortable S/C rooms are reasonably priced and come with choice of fan or AC. ②.

Hôtel La Détente, off the bd Lagunaire. The cheapest place in town and well located: panorama of the lagoon and within walking distance of the palace and market. Barren but clean rooms with fan or AC. ①–②.

Hôtel Dona, rue Catchi/bd Extérieur nord, near the water tower (BP 95; ☎21.30.52). Modern place with twenty well-furnished S/C, AC rooms, bar-restaurant and nightclub. ③.

Hôtel Malabo, bd Lagunaire. Basic low-budget accommodation that caters mainly to the guests of its lively *bar-resto*. Near the lagoon, but a bit far afield – take a *zimi-djan* to town. ①.

Eating

Apart from the street food in the markets and *gare routière*, or the pricey hotel **restaurants** at the *Dona* and *Beaurivage*, there's a surprising dearth of of places to eat. Off the bd lagunaire, near the *Beaurivage*, *Aux Ventes de la Mer,* is a good outdoor restaurant near the water. A safe choice in town is the *Casa Danza* at the corner of av no. 6 and the av Victor Ballot. Slightly upscale, they serve moderately priced European and African food in a well-manicured courtyard. More basic is the *Java Promo,* further down on av no. 6 where you can eat inexpensive meals like *moyo* with chicken or fish in the shade of the expansive patio.

Around Porto Novo

Across the lagoon from Porto Novo are a number of stilt villages that are less of a hassle to visit than Ganvié. Nearby too, is the lively market centre of Adjarra.

Adjarra

An important market – held every fourth day like Porto Novo's – takes place in **ADJARRA**, 8km northeast of Porto Novo on the Kétou road. This small village has a reputation for its **drum-makers** and produces over fifty different types of *tam-tams* varying in construction, material (wood or clay) and colour. Their quality attracts many buyers from Nigeria. Alongside fruit and vegetables, the market also sells a selection of useful fetishes, medicinal herbs and *gri-gris*, as well as locally made pottery and hand-woven cloth.

The stilt villages

Porto Novo's surrounding lagoon contains a number of stilt villages not unlike Ganvié (see p.917), though, until recently, travellers never ventured to them. The outlying area has still not become a tourist trap, though the price of a *pirogue* has become steeper in recent years. The closest, and easiest to reach is **AGUÉGUÉ**, 12km through the creeks: *piroguiers* near the bridge in Porto Novo can easily be found to take you there. There is no accommodation in the village, but just gliding through and observing makes for an interesting excursion. You may be asked for money if you want to take pictures. The *Hôtel Beaurivage* in Porto Novo also organizes trips to the villages by motorboat, which doesn't work out vastly more expensive and avoids the hassle of negotiating with the *piroguiers*.

CENTRAL BENIN

Benin's interior is a relatively homogeneous series of **plains** dominated by low, sloping hills. This was the site of early kingdoms, most notably that of the **Fon** founded at **Abomey**. The **Yoruba** also established a number of chiefdoms in the area, while further north, the **Bariba** carved out a small territory – the **Borgou country** – in the region of **Parakou**. These are still the main peoples of central Benin, an area of intensive agricultural production and small industries.

Driving north **from Cotonou to Abomey**, the road swings west, then northeast, then at Sèhouè back northwest again. For the next twenty-odd kilometres the road passes through the **Lama depression**, a low-lying swampy region of clay soils, patches of rain forest and a designated forest reserve, the **Forêt de Ko** or **Lama**. If you have your own vehicle and the will to explore, then turn off left at the **maison forestière**, 18km from Sèhouè and make for **Koto**, 5km south into the forest.

Abomey, Bohicon and north towards Djougou

Capital of one of the great West African kingdoms in pre-colonial times, **ABOMEY** boasts a fascinating history and counts as one of Benin's greatest attractions. Commercially the town is overshadowed by **BOHICON**, of which Abomey is essentially the ancient precursor, and which has benefited from its position on the rail line and main north–south highway (the French deliberately laid the railway to the east of Abomey to reduce the commercial power of the Abomey royal dynasties). Despite Bohicon's immense market, however, the town is a chaotic sprawl with little that could tempt you to stay for a prolonged period (if you stay, the *Hôtel Relais Sinnoutin*, on the main road at the south end of town, has decent rooms with shared facilities; BP 27; ☎51.00.75; ②). Most people skip Bohicon altogether and head straight out to Abomey, 9km from the highway, which is more manageable and, with the **Dan-Homey palace and museum**, infinitely more interesting.

Abomey town

Abomey is fascinating to wander through; any path off the main roads leads through twisted alleyways with *banco* houses and colourfully painted **fetish temples**. Between the museum and the *préfecture*, overgrown plots with weather-worn mud ruins are vestiges of former royal palaces.

THE DAN-HOMEY KINGDOM

From as early as the sixteenth century, much of the present territory of Benin was coalescing into small, socially stratified **states** – a string of them along the coast (including Grand Popo and Ouidah) and a cluster of less clearly defined smaller states inland. A more powerful (though still very small) city-state had developed around the town of **Allada**, just 40km from the coast, which was renowned for its slave-trading. At the end of the sixteenth century, three princes were in dispute over the rule of this little empire. The first, **Meidji**, eventually wrested power from his father. Of his two brothers, **Zozerigbe** headed south to Porto Novo where he founded the Hogbonou kingdom while **Do Aklin** went north where he founded the kingdom at **Abomey** in the early seventeenth century.

In 1654, one of the descendants of Do Aklin, **Ouegbaja**, killed the sovereign of Abomey, a king named **Dan**. Ouegbaja then built his palace over the body of the deceased monarch and his kingdom came to be known as Dan-Homey, meaning "from the belly of Dan". In the succession of kings, one of the greatest was **Agadja** who ruled from 1708–1740. He conquered the surrounding mini-states of Allada, Savi and Ouidah and, in expanding his empire to the coast, earned the title *Dé Houito*, or "man of the sea". Having gained a gateway to the Atlantic, the empire embarked on a period of direct trade with Europe, a trade dependent above all on slaves. Meanwhile, however, the powerful Yoruba state of **Oyo** (to the east, in present-day Nigeria) was increasingly bent on retaining as much as possible of the trade for its own benefit, and through the middle of the eighteenth century, repeatedly intimidated and attacked Dan-Homey, which, after 1748 was formally a vassal state of Oyo.

The Dan-Homey state became a dictatorship under the reign of **Ghezo**, who overthrew the previous king in 1818 and ruled bloodily for forty years. He ceded his monopoly rights in the slave trade to his right-hand man in Ouidah – the Brazilian **Francisco Felix de Souza** (the "viceroy" depicted in Bruce Chatwin's biographical novella and by Klaus Kinski in Werner Herzog's movie *Cobra Verde*) – and increasingly preyed on his own subject peoples. His autonomy was only limited by the duty he owed to Oyo. He reorganized the army into a powerful unit comprising 10,000 soldiers and 6000 female "Amazon" warriors, who were better armed than their male counterparts. Trained to use rifles as well as bows, they were reputed to cut off one of their breasts if it impaired their ability to shoot – an apocryphal story that probably sprang from the reactions of European visitors to the sight of well-drilled women soldiers.

The Dan-Homey kings amassed a stockpile of weapons through trade with the Europeans. By the end of the nineteenth century, the royal arsenal was full of modern weaponry and the stage was set for an intense conflict as the French started out in conquest of the interior. Hostilities were high and fighting had already broken out between the French and the Fon when **King Behanzin** led an attack against the forces of **Colonel Dodds** as they advanced on Abomey. Behanzin lost the battle, and the capital of the Dan-Homey kingdom fell to the French on November 16, 1892. Abomey was already in flames as the colonial army marched into the city.

The royal palace and museum

In the three hundred years of the Dan-Homey empire, the kings built a magnificent **palace** in the centre of Abomey. In fact, it was a vast complex of many palaces, since the sovereign never occupied the residence of his predecessor, but built a new one next to the old. By the time the French attacked the city in 1892, there was thus a honeycomb of twelve **adjoining palaces**, ten of which were soon destroyed by the invading army. Today, only two – those belonging to Ghezo and his successor Glele – remain intact, but even these have suffered badly from the effects, ultimately no less brutal, of the climate. They're being restored with the help of funds from UNESCO. Work carried out so far shows up magnificently the pomp and grandeur of the royal court – and there's no doubt that this will be a spectacular site when restoration is completed. There are even plans to rebuild the ten ruined palaces – eventually – though this would seem to require decades of work.

In the meantime, you can visit the first two renovations (CFA1500 with compulsory guided tour) though it's disappointing to find rusty corrugated iron, rather than old-style thatch, used to cover the **animist temples** (where the kings communicated with their ancestors), the **throne room** and other ceremonial buildings. It's all impressive nonetheless, with the massive walls of the complex clad in brilliantly coloured symbolic bas-relief designs, and as you walk round, the history of this powerful, energetic, brutal society comes alive. All the stools of the kings are guarded in the throne room with their individual banners – including that of Ghezo, built on top of four human skulls, a symbol of his conquests and domination over weaker peoples. The banners, which are known as the **royal tapestries**, are themselves remarkable and commonly seen in "best of Benin" type photos – vivid patchworks sewn with symbols and emblems relating the qualities of the various kings.

Part of the collection of the **museum** – housed in one of the palaces – is devoted to the **treasures of the kings**, including gifts they were offered by European royalty and merchants. Mixed in with examples of silver jewellery are wood and iron sculptures, though some of the pieces on exhibit are copies, the original works of art stored in French museums since colonial times.

Crafts outlets

Attached to the palace, the **centre artisanal** is an effort to keep alive the craftsmanship that was the pride of the Abomey kings. The artisans were formerly constrained to produce their works for the royal court only. Crafts that were popular with the kings – brightly decorated tapestries, bronze statues made by the *cire perdue*, or "lost wax", method, jewellery – are still churned out, although the quality required by tourists is rather less than that demanded by the royalty. This centre is the most obvious place to shop for crafts: though it seems expensive, prices are wide open to discussion.

Along the road running in front of the palace, notice the house with the lion and inscription painted on front. This is the residence of the **Yamedje family** – the traditional embroiderers for the king. Walking in the courtyard, you'll see members of the family still sewing the tapestries, their works strewn over the ground, all for sale. Next to the *préfecture*, a collective organization, the **artisans de Zou**, is an outlet for still more crafts. The tailors here can whip together quick African outfits.

Abomey practicalities

Despite it's importance as a tourist centre, Abomey has few services. No banks here will change money, and even in neighbouring Bohicon, the best they can do is change French francs cash.

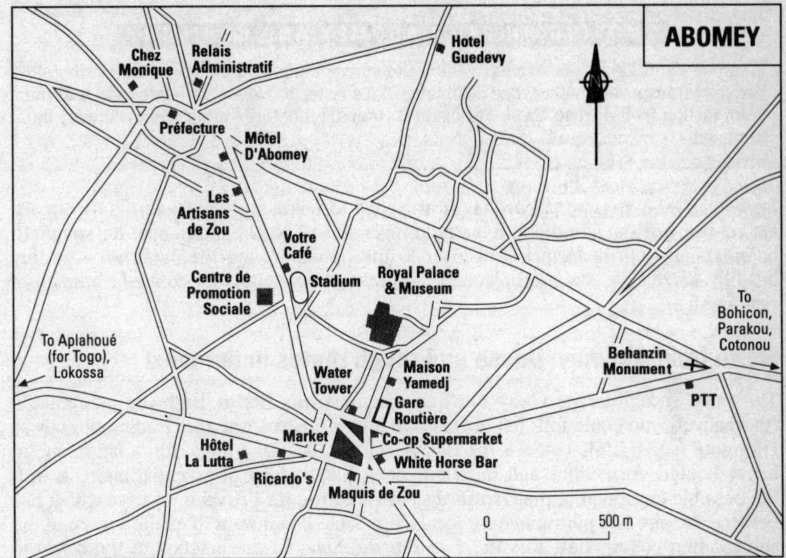

Accommodation

There's not a lot of choice in hotels, though there's something for every price range. Most accommodation is a stiff walk from the centre. *Zimi-djans* and taxis come in handy here.

Chez Monique, on a dirt side street, 200m west of the *préfecture* (☎50.01.68). Immensely popular with overlanders, Monique's is an exotic spread with pet monkeys and antelopes in the yard. Simple, but clean S/C rooms with fan are comfortable, but success has pushed prices up. Don't be afraid to bargain. ②.

Hôtel Guedevy, 3km north of the centre (☎50.03.04). Brand-new lodgings, and very pleasant, with Abomey-style bas-reliefs on the walls as you enter. Choice of fan or AC in the clean S/C rooms, plus an inexpensive restaurant and even a *bar-dancing*. Good value. ②–③.

Hôtel La Lutta, west of the centre (BP 2009; ☎50.01.41). From the centre, follow the signs to this pleasant African-style abode – Abomey's most central lodgings and a great find for budget travellers. Plain but decent twin rooms with fan and shower. The management here is very friendly and will arrange for inexpensive guided tours of the town. ①.

Motel d'Abomey, 100m from the *préfecture* (BP 2168; ☎50.00.75). The town's best hotel, to which recent renovations have brought remarkable changes. Well-heeled travellers can enjoy beautifully furnished private bungalows with TV and video and phones, while the smaller S/C rooms with AC are not out of reach of those on a budget. The restaurant is one of the town's best, and the new disco is an added draw. ②–⑥.

Relais Administratif, (formerly *Foyer du Militant*), across from the *préfecture*. Run-down colonial lodgings offering the option of pretty miserable S/C rooms (no fan) if you're in a fix. ①.

Eating

Inexpensive **street food** is available all around the market; at night, women set up tables under the awnings of the *Co-op* supermarket for the town's best cheap eats. Around the market, small **buvettes** double as chop houses where you can sit indoors or on the terrace for low-cost African meals. Among the many are the *Maquis de Zou*, the *White Horse Bar* and, a little futher out on the road to Bohicon,

MOVING ON FROM ABOMEY AND BOHICON

Abomey's small *gare routière* has vehicles to surrounding villages and Cotonou, though for road transport to most other destinations, it's faster to take a *zimi-djan* or cab to the train station in Bohicon. There are also two trains a day to Parakou and Cotonou from Bohicon.

Le 2 Fevrier. A step up, *Ricardo's*, on the road to Lokossa (☎50.02.42), is the smartest **restaurant** outside the hotels, though it's still a casual enough spot for spaghetti or inexpensive grilled chicken. Closer to the hotels around the *préfecture*, the tiny but tidy *Votre Café* is a good place for a breakfast omelette with coffee or a lunch of rice and fish.

North from Abomey: Dassa and rough routes in the west

The most straightforward way north is via the **trans-Benin highway** to Parakou. Alternatively you could fork left at Dassa to follow the western *piste* leading directly to **Djougou** (see p.935). **DASSA** (or Dassa–Zoumé), a village tucked in a landscape of heavy boulder formations and thick greenery, has nothing of essential interest, with the possible exception of the **Grotte de Notre Dame de l'Arigbo** – a cave which has become the site of a pilgrimage for local Christians. If you want to explore more of the surrounding countryside, the *Motel de Dassa-Zoumé*, on the junction of the roads to Parakou and Savalou, has inexpensive fanned **rooms** (☎53.01.71; ②). A more recent addition is the moderately priced *Auberge de Dassa*. Run by the same owners as the popular get-away in Grand Popo, it has very comfortable, clean rooms with fans or AC, and excellent food in the restaurant (③).

The western route beyond **Savalou** (30km from Dassa) is little travelled, and involves longer waits for transport. It's difficult going, too, especially the washboard-infested stretch up to **Bassila** (173km from Dassa), which is the first town along the way where you'll find **accommodation** and, perhaps more importantly, a *buvette* with the possibility of cold drinks. There's a small *chambre de passage* next to the filling station, run by a very friendly family (①).

The west is an agricultural region hemmed in by the forests of the Monts Kouffé and Agoua, and was the location of an early **Yoruba** kingdom, conquered in the eighteenth century by the **Maxi** (related to the Fon). These are still the main peoples of the area although numerous smaller groups result in a variety of regional building styles and customs. Despite the relative difficulties in getting about along this stretch it can be rewarding to travel off the beaten track, and you're likely to find contacts with people warm and immediate.

THE NORTHERN UPLANDS AND PARKS

Parakou is the last big town on the main road. Beyond it, in the **northeast**, the only main centres of activity are **Kandi** and **Malanville**, small towns bolstered by agriculture and trade. The **northwest**, though harder to travel through, is a region of striking natural beauty dominated by the country's only serious highlands, the **Atakora Range**, and populated by a relatively ancient people, the **Somba**. Two towns of some size, **Natitingou** and **Djougou**, are the bases for discovering this outback region. Lastly, northern Benin has some of West Africa's best faunal areas in the **Pendjari National**

Park and, in the extreme north, the **"W" du Niger national park**, which spreads across the frontiers of Niger and Burkina Faso. Access to Pendjari is relatively straightforward and there are several places to stay, but the Benin sector of the "W" park is extremely inaccessible (the most promising access is via Kandi) and has abundant wildlife probably as a result.

Parakou

Formerly a station on the caravan routes, **PARAKOU**, with a population of nearly 100,000, is today the largest northern town – and the first, as you go north. Its importance still derives from its position on the major roads and on the **railway** which terminates its snail-like trail here. The brewery, and sheanut oil mill have brought about rapid growth in the last couple of decades and Parakou is now the undisputed commercial centre of the interior. It's a town of little enduring interest, but abuzz with the activity of hundreds of small businesses, bars and passing traders.

Practicalities

With the burgeoning business activity, all the major **banks** – *BIB*, *Eco-Bank*, *Bank of Africa* (the best bank for changing travellers' cheques) – have branches here, making Parakou the only place outside Cotonou where you can count on changing travellers' cheques. If you're heading to towns further north, be sure to take all the money you'll need.

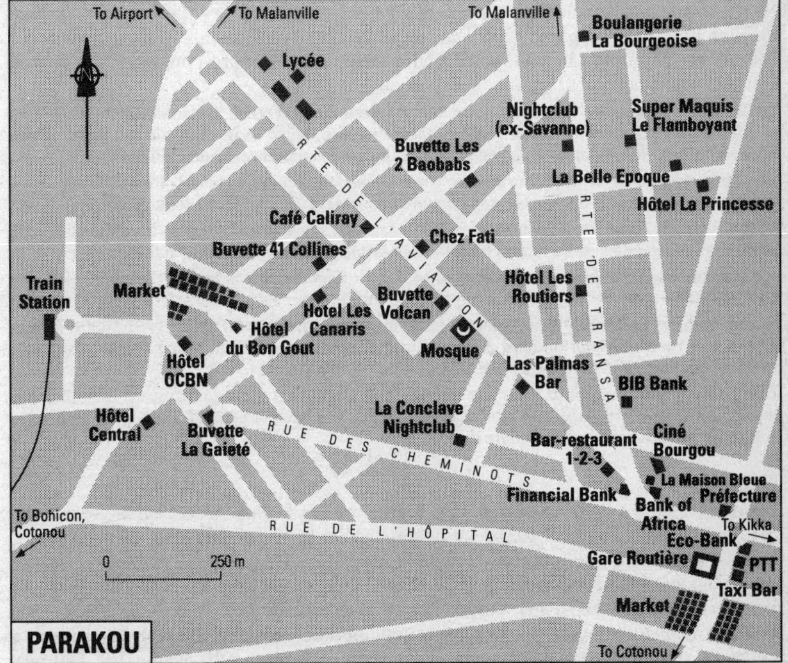

Accommodation

Parakou has nothing in the way of world-class **accommodation**, but there's plenty of small comfortable hotels that border on fancy and one or two cheaper alternatives.

Hôtel du Bon Gout, close to the station. Long-running overlanders' standby with simple accommodation and shared facilities. Beginning to look a little run-down. Cheap, but you can do better elsewhere. ①.

Hôtel les Canaris, near the station (☎61.11.69). Two shady courtyards provide a pleasant backdrop for various rooms ranging from non-S/C low-comfort quarters (among the cheapest in town) to fully furnished AC accommodation with private bath. Before the Sahara routes closed, this was the focus in Parakou for European car-sellers. ①–③.

Hôtel Central, near the station (☎61.01.24). A little far from the town centre, but arguably the best accommodation in town. Imposing building hidden behind a walled garden where you'll find a bar and restaurant. Some of the AC rooms have TV and phone. ④.

Hôtel OCBN, (☎61.11.09). A crocodile in the courtyard watches over this well-managed, colonial-style hotel. Airy rooms and great bathrooms. Reasonable restaurant and bar. ②–③.

Hôtel La Princesse, quartier Ladjifarani in the north of town (☎61.01.32). The rooms, surrounding a courtyard, are a little posher than the norm, with phones, TV and video among the extras. French and African food in the *Nafi* restaurant or snacks in the *Plantation* bar. ③–④.

Hôtel Regal, near the station. Clean and well-run basic accommodation. Good value if a bit more expensive than the *Canaris* for the same standards. ②–③.

Hôtel Les Routiers, route de Transa (BP 81; ☎61.21.27/61.04.01). Centrally located, upmarket accommodation, popular with expats. Clean and comfortable AC rooms. Very small pool; tennis courts. ④–⑤.

Eating

The prospects for good **eating** are actually better than the town's initial impression seems to suggest. In addition to some really fine **street food** (try the wonderful grilled chicken and salad prepared *Chez Fati*, on route de l'Aviation, only in the evenings, or see under "Nightlife", below), you'll find a wide range of more upmarket African and European cuisine.

Belle Epoque, quartier Ladjifarani, near the *Princesse* hotel. French restaurant with specialities ranging from *charcuterie* to *filet de boeuf au roquefort*. Also Italian lasagne, ravioli and pizza. Tables under a *paillote* with unmistakable lion statues at the garden entrance. From CFA5000.

Boulangerie-patisserie La Bourgeoise, route de Malanville, in the north of town. *Salon de thé* with sandwiches, salads and ice cream or a more filling *menu du jour*. Good rooftop bar.

Café Coulibaly, route de l'Aviation. A modest affair that's just a small step up from the streetside *caféman*, but a good place for really cheap omelettes and *nescafé*, or *riz sauce* in the evening.

La Maison Bleue, behind the *Bank of Africa*. Good range of African and international dishes at CFA2000–3000.

Super Maquis Le Flamboyant, quartier Ladjifarani, near the *Princesse* hotel (☎61.11.90). African dishes like *riz au poisson* or *couscous poulet* with Ivoirian specials, including chicken *kedjenou*. Attractive gardens and friendly service. From under CFA1000.

Las Palmas Bar Jazz Club, near the station. "Jazz Club" in this case just means they play pop music, but it's a lively place with a terrace overlooking the main street and some good brochettes and other food available from vendors in front.

Nightlife

Despite Parakou's status as second city, **nights** are low-key and street lights are noticeable only by their absence. Kerosene lamps instead light the darkness, their flickering indicating the stands of hundreds of night-time vendors. It's safe and satisfying to wander here, stopping for street food or a drink at one of the many *buvettes* – *Les 41 Collines, Le Volcan, les 2 Baobabs* . . . A karate flick or spaghetti western may be playing at the *Bourgou Cinéma* and there's a handful of good **clubs**. Currently, the popular place is *Le Conclave*, off the rue des Cheminots. It's a tight, dark place with small cover and rare appearances by music groups, although most of the time they play a good selection of urban pop. Another possibility is *Le Miel* at the *Boulangerie La Bourgeoise* which gets rolling for the weekends. Finally, you could try the former *Savane* which has reopened (the new owners were in the process of renaming this club, though any taxi driver will know the old appellation), and is as strong a draw as ever. Besides the inside disco (small cover), there's a large and lively outdoor *buvette* tucked in a forest of teak trees.

MOVING ON FROM PARAKOU

Two **trains** a day – 8am and 6pm – chug out of Parakou, arriving in Cotonou about twelve hours later. Second-class travel costs only CFA4000, making the drawn-out journey a lot cheaper than going by taxi. The night train has *couchettes* for CFA7500.

Taxis leave from the main *gare routière* by the market and head towards **Niger** via Malanville, or **Togo** via Djougou, as well as to domestic destinations. There is next to nothing direct to Natitingou and the Somba country so you will do best to catch a vehicle to Djougou and continue north from there.

Kandi, Malanville and the "W" National Park

The northeast is characterized by relatively unvaried, north-facing, woodland savannah scenery, broken by a series of small rivers (the Mékrou, Alibori and Sota) that descend gradually to join the Niger. It's the least densely populated region of the country, the principal peoples being the **Bariba**, the **Dendi** and the **Fula**. Despite the important highway running through the region linking Cotonou with Niamey, the Niger Basin remains economically undeveloped. Cotton is a big cash crop, but industrialization hasn't penetrated much beyond a cotton-seed plant in Kandi and a rice-shelling factory in Malanville.

Kandi and around

Like Parakou, **KANDI** was formerly a stopping point on the caravan routes and grew to become a sizeable chiefdom – a vassal state of Bariba rulers in Nikki, to the southeast. A small town, it relies heavily on farming, a livelihood with which young people are becoming increasingly disenchanted. They've been deserting the countryside in numbers that are unsettling to the local economy, and heading east to Nigeria, linked to Kandi by a well-travelled *piste* that heads through Segbana. You may question the attractions of a place from which even the townspeople are engaged in a mass exodus and, true enough, there's not a lot of note. Still, it's a convenient highway stopover and, with its dusty mango-shaded streets, not entirely charmless.

Practicalities

As district headquarters, Kandi has a post office, *AGP* supermarket and bank (travellers' cheques can't be changed). **Accommodation** is limited to the *Hôtel Baobab 2000*, about a kilometre from the centre on the Malanville road, where rooms come with bucket showers only if you ask ahead – a pail of warm water left by your door morning and night (①). Cheap *buvettes* for **drinking and eating** are scattered around the market place. Among them, *La Verdure bar-dancing* also has inexpensive and dirty *chambres de passage* (①).

North of Kandi: Alfa Kouara

About 40km north of Kandi, the forest rangers' post at **Alfa Kouara** is a required stopover if you have your own transport. The post is to the left of the road. Here, in the dry season, you can make simple arrangements to walk to a nearby **waterhole**, where, with a modicum of luck, you'll see plenty of **wildlife**, including on occasions dozens of elephants.

Malanville

Tucked in the northeast corner near the Nigerian and Nigérien borders, **MALANVILLE** is a trading town *par excellence* where you can run into people from all over West Africa. The **market** is Benin's largest after Cotonou and large-scale regional rice-planting attracts wage-hungry labourers from as far afield as Mali. The presence of many foreigners, mixed with the Fula and Songhai-speaking **Dendi** locals who form the base of the town's inhabitants, makes for an upbeat atmosphere, although the lack of notable sites means you're not likely to want to make an extended stay.

Practicalities

Border formalities usually present no problem here. If you're **entering the country at Malanville**, you have to state your destination and intended address. The immigration officers have a list of all hotels in the country – pick any one, there's no obligation.

Besides the rudimentary and inexpensive *campement* located near the police and customs post at the town entrance (①–②), there's new **accommodation** at the comfortable *Hôtel Rose des Sables* (☎67.01.25; ②), which is much better value. Numerous **street food** stands line the paved road near the *autogare*, churning out cheap meals for travellers. You'll also find a host of *buvettes* with cold drinks.

When **moving on**, remember that in addition to the many taxis waiting in the central *gare routière*, cheaper state-run **buses** also head south to Kandi and Parakou, but usually quite early in the morning. If you're heading north **to Niamey**, it's quicker and cheaper to catch a taxi to Gaya, on the other side of the river, and to find another vehicle there.

Parc National du "W" du Niger

The **"W" du Niger national park** (open early December to late May) spreads over 10,000 square kilometres of wild bush in Niger, Burkina Faso and Benin – an area, virtually without human habitation. The "W" (pronounced *double-vé* in French) refers to the double U-bend in the course of the Niger River at the point where the three countries all meet. Though nearly half the park is in Benin, the only real viewing trails, and all the park lodgings and *campements*, are in Niger (see map on p.975) and Burkina.

Most of the big plains game is here, however, if you can find a way in. Although the **buffalo** herds are thinning out, **elephants** can still be spotted in the Béninois sector – notably in the Mékrou valley – while in the Mékrou's waters, unmistakeable herds of snorting **hippos** are fairly plentiful. All the cats are found in the "W" as well – **serval**, **caracal**, **leopard**, **cheetah** and **lion** – but you can visit repeatedly and never see a single specimen. Most commonly encountered are a good number of **antelope** species – bushbuck (*guibs harnachés* in French), cobs or waterbucks (*cob de buffon*, *cob defassa*), reedbuck (*redunca*) and the red-fronted gazelle – and, of course, **warthogs** (*phacochères*) and **baboons** (*babouins*). Aardvarks (*oryctéropes*) are around, too, but their strictly nocturnal habits ensure they're rarely spotted.

Practicalities

You need your own 4WD vehicle to visit this park, at least on the Benin side. Even with one, there are no reliably motorable *pistes* until you cross the borders. The most common way to get to the park is up from Kandi to **Banikoara** (69km from Kandi), a small town where you'll find the last **accommodation** (a small *campement*; ②) before entering the reserve. From here, it's a short drive to **Kérémou** – one of the main gateways to the park in Benin.

The only area that's normally visited is the 400-square-kilometre triangle formed by the Kérémou–Diapaga road, the Mékrou River (which the road crosses) and the Benin–Burkina Faso border. There's a *piste* along the left bank of the Mékrou that leads up to the **Koudou Falls**. A plan is apparently under consideration to build a bridge across the Mékrou at this point and to develop tracks that would follow the Benin side of the river all the way to Pekinga near the confluence with the Niger. In the meantime, you have to cross over to Burkina Faso near the falls to keep on motorable tracks.

The Somba Country

The **northwest** is home to some of the oldest **civilizations** to migrate to Benin – a number of which groups lived for long periods with virtually no interaction. The best known are the **Somba** (more accurately the Otammari, or Betammaribe), famous for the fortress-like houses known as *Tatas-Somba* that they built to protect themselves from the slave raids of Dan-Homey warriors. They still live in largely isolated villages scattered along the base of the **Atakora Mountains** (and don't, as a rule, take kindly to foreign visitors) though the young people are increasingly inclined to migrate to urban centres such as **Natitingou** – the Atakora provincial capital. Further south, Somba give way to the Yowa, part of the same cluster of Voltaic-speaking peoples, and the Songhai-speaking Dendi who live in the region of **Djougou**, a large commercial town on the main road to Togo.

Djougou

With a population of some 30,000, **DJOUGOU** is a large town and surprisingly busy considering it's only accessible by *piste*. But the town's importance as a major regional market has been assured by its position on the main roads linking Natitingou to Savalou and Parakou to the Togolese border and through to Kara.

Practicalities

Accommodation is pretty much limited to the *Motel du Djougou*, a basic hotel that at least has fans in the rooms (☎80.01.40; ②). You could also rent a *chambre de passage* in the *Dee-Mystree* nightclub on the market square (①). Apart from the motel restaurant, the **market** is the obvious place for **eating** – besides the numerous vendors selling local staples, there's a number of small restaurants and bars surrounding the market square.

Djougou's large **gare routière** adjoins the market and you shouldn't have any problem finding transport to Natitingou and Parakou. Many vehicles also head to **Kara** in Togo, via the border post at Kétao.

Natitingou

Home town of former president, Mathieu Kérékou, **NATITINGOU** never received the degree of patronage extended to Yamoussoukro in Côte d'Ivoire or Kara in Togo, but even if Kérékou didn't go so far as to turn his birthplace into the national capital, he didn't forget it either. Though it's only a small centre, Natitingou has received the beginnings of an industrial base with the siting here of a *SONAFEL* juice factory and rice- and peanut-husking factories. You're more likely to notice other manifestations of the president's munificence in the town's modern bank, cinema and beautiful luxury hotel. But despite these surprise perks, the real draw of the town lies in the countryside that surrounds it – a magnificent region of hills dotted with the *Tata-Somba* homes that have become as famous as anything in Benin.

Accommodation

Though hotels are not numerous, Natitingou has a good range of accommodation, from budget to business-class.

Auberge Tanéka, rte de Djougou (☎82.15.52). Small budget hotel with fanned, S/C rooms and a very reasonable restaurant providing tasty fare. ①–②.

Hôtel Kantabourifa, rte de Djougou (☎82.17.66). Popular and inexpensive lodgings. Though rooms are basic, some contain AC. ②.

Hôtel Nanto, on the main road between the police and the PTT (☎82.12.40 or 82.12.42). Slightly upscale S/C rooms with fans, grouped in a courtyard around a central lobby and restaurant. ②–③.

Hôtel Tata Somba, BP 4 (☎82.11.24 or 21.65.90). A classy hotel in the French *PLM* chain with stylish AC rooms, a swimming pool and the town's swankiest restaurant. The same chain manages the *campements* in the Pendjari game park, so this is the best place for information on accommodation and vehicle rental if you're heading there. ⑤–⑥.

Eating and nightlife

In in addition to the hotel **restaurants** and the market, there's the *City Coffee*, on the main road down by the *auberge*, which is good for omelettes and fry-ups. It's also a place to meet young people from the region and possibly work out an arrangement to visit some of the Somba countryside. Another possibility is *Le Manguier* on the route de Tanguieta where they serve up well-prepared and relatively inexpensive African dishes.

Natitingou has a good **cinema** at the south end of the main street. You'll also find a couple of **discos** in town including one built into a "Somba-style" house at the *Hôtel Tata Somba*. Another popular place for dancing (less expensive and more local in flavour) is the open-air *Le Village*, located in the centre of town.

Around Natitingou

Rather than forming large communities, the Somba built their homes about five hundred metres apart from one another; the distance a man could throw a spear, you'll be told – which would surprise the current javelin world-record-holder (under 100m). Whatever the brawn of their throwing arms (it seems more likely that 500m is the maximum dangerous range of an eighteenth-century musket), this defensive safeguard was adopted during slave-raiding days and the custom has carried over. Houses are still built like fortresses with round turrets for grain storage and internal animal pens. During slave raids, families could hole up in these houses for days on end until the marauding Dan-Homey armies went off in search of easier prey (see the "Tamberma Country" section in Chapter 13, "Togo").

The **Tatas-Somba** still dot the countryside around the Atakora region and it's worth a trip through these parts to take in the unusual architecture, though contact with the people – who tend to shy away from all foreigners, and even fellow Béninois – is limited at best. Coming in by bush taxi from Djougou, you'll see some of the architecture from the roadside, notably along the stretch between **Perma** (56km from Djougou) and Natitingou. One of the highest concentrations of *Tatas-Somba* is found further west, however, along the road from Natitingou to the Togolese border town of **Boukoumbé** (43km west of Natitingou). If you have your own vehicle, you could cross the border to Togo near Boukoumbé and drive to **Kandé** in Togo, via a *piste* that leads through the region of the **Tamberma**, a people closely related to the Somba. Though difficult, it's one of the most beautiful drives in this part of West Africa.

Parc National de la Pendjari

The **PENDJARI National Park**, one of the best game-viewing reserves in West Africa, spreads over 2750 square kilometres of woody savannah north of the Atakora Range, up against the Pendjari River, which runs along the Burkinabe border. Unlike the "W" National Park, access to Pendjari is relatively straightforward.

From Natitingou, the usual route goes north through **Tanguiéta**, a village at the edge of the reserve. There's a small *campement* here and two rudimentary **hotels** – *A Petits Pas* (①) and *Chez Basille* (where basic lodgings include mosquito nets; ①). There are also two waterfalls in the area, both on the road to Batia – the **cascades de Tanguiéta** near the village of Nanèbou (6km northeast of Natitingou), and the larger **cascades de Tanougou**, near the village of the same name, 33km from Tanguiéta. Swimming at the latter, with the falls pounding your back, is a memorable experience.

At Tanguiéta, the road divides. You can aim northeast to **Batia**, where there's a park entrance, though no accommodation. However, most people continue northwest to the town of **Porga** on the Burkina border, which does have **lodgings**, and the main park entrance gate. The *Campement de Porga* has bungalows and rooms – some with AC – and dormitory space plus a bar-restaurant (①–③). If you've made it this far without your own transport, you might hope to tag along with tourists heading into the park at Porga, though your chances would be just as good if you looked for a lift at the *Hôtel Tata Somba* in Natitingou. In theory, you can rent Land Rovers here, though you may have to book before coming (check with the *Hôtel Tata Somba* or the *poste forestier* in Natitingou).

Wildlife

Lions still stalk these parts and your chances of seeing them are relatively good. Other large mammals you have a good chance of spotting include **elephants** (notably in the south of the park) and **buffalo** which roam in large herds. **Hippos** and **crocodiles** (*caïmans* in colloquial French) are widespread in the Pendjari River, while the same species of **antelope** as are found in the "W" park, plus **warthogs** and **monkeys**, are pretty sure bets. As usual, however, all the animals are most easily and abundantly seen at the end of the dry season, when their movements are restricted by the need to stay close to water.

Park practicalities

The park is only open from mid-December to the end of May. Permits to visit may be obtained from the *postes forestiers* in Porga, Batia, Kandi and Natitingou, but for complete information, contact the Ministry of Tourism in Cotonou, or the *Hôtel Tata Somba* in Natitingou.

Inside the park, **accommodation** can be found at the *Campement de la Pendjari*, located near the river. They have renovated bungalows and twin rooms plus a restaurant, bar and, miraculously, a swimming pool (③–④). If it's full you can **camp** there. Camping, under the supervision of rangers, is also permitted at the **Mare Yangouali** and the **pont d'Arli**, where you can cross the Pendjari River into Burkina Faso and the Pendjari's extension there – **Arli National Park**.

index

CHAPTER FIFTEEN

NIGER

NIGER

Vast expanses of **Niger**'s million-plus square kilometres are desert. But most visitors see only the south, where thriving commerce and relative prosperity characterize the towns and agricultural districts. The **River Niger**, flowing for over five hundred kilometres through the southwest, is one of the country's few bodies of water – an attraction in itself. The cosmopolitan capital, **Niamey**, straddling the banks of "Le Fleuve", draws a mix of local and regional traders and international aid and business visitors. Air-conditioned hotels and restaurants provide welcome relief from the Sahelian bush, but the city's modern high-rises coexist uneasily with its sprawling markets and slum neighbourhoods of mud-brick homes.

From the capital, you can travel by road along the east bank of the Niger towards the Malian border, visiting Songhai villages and the commercial centres of **Tillabéri** and **Ayorou**, which has a spectacular market that unites all the regional peoples. South of Niamey, the Niger is navigable only in short sections as it closes in on the game reserve named after the bends in the river – the **Parc National du "W" du Niger**.

A second main line of travel lies along the southern border with Nigeria and the **Hausa** towns of **Birnin-Konni**, **Maradi** and **Zinder**. These historic centres lie in the country's green belt and have been bolstered by agriculture – the region's dominant feature. The road from Zinder is paved all the way to **Nguigmi**, a Kanouri settlement near **Lake Chad**.

THE TUAREG UPRISING AND THE ALGERIAN CIVIL WAR

In the late 1980s, **Tuareg herders** fleeing drought in the deep Sahel in northern Niger and southern Algeria began returning *en masse* to central parts of Niger. Although the government had earmarked relief aid to ease resettlement, there was no actual assistance. In 1990, amid rumours that allocated funds had been embezzled by government officials, angry Tuareg – many of whom are scathing of their Nigérien citizenship – mounted a military attack against the remote Gendarmerie at Tchin-Tabaradene between Tahoua and Agadez. Government forces retaliated, killing around 100 Tuareg and arresting over 200 people, of whom some 40 were executed in jail. Tuareg resistance intensified as a united movement with an agenda to form a Tuareg homeland – the *Front de Libération de l'Aïr et l'Azaouad* – launched violent raids and took its own prisoners. By 1992, the government was admitting to a full-scale rebellion. Trans-Saharan traffic was cut as tourist vehicles were randomly commandeered by the FLAA. Outlying regions in the north were put off-limits to visitors and those overlanders who made it to the region reported **harassment** by the military and frequent delays due to searches and the confiscation of documents. The domestic situation in northern Niger has improved since 1994, when the FLAA agreed to a truce, but the region remains extremely volatile.

Problems on the **Algerian side of the border** are even more severe. Since October 1993 when they declared all non-Algerians should leave the country under threat of death, the *Groupe Islamique Armée* (GIA) – extreme fundamentalist militia – have murdered nearly 100 foreigners, not to mention tens of thousands of Algerians (the precise figure is not known). Tourism in Algeria has entirely ceased and the trans-Saharan routes are effectively closed to foreigners. There seems no obvious way to resolve the crisis: the spark for the present civil war was the secular government's cancellation of democratic elections in 1991 which would have brought the fundamentalist party, the *Front Islamique du Salud* (FIS) to power. The FIS claim not to control the GIA, who refuse all dialogue.

Given the instability in the Sahara, few visitors make it to the third great travel axis, **the north**, where the government now restricts all movement. Whether you will be allowed to travel north of **Tahoua** or Zinder depends on the latest round of negotiations with the Tuareg rebel movement – or the latest battle (see box). **Agadez** is the region's main town, an ancient desert metropolis, seat of a powerful sultanate, and one of the most important centres in the southern Sahara. For several decades, it has also been the base for determined travellers to make, usually costly, visits to more isolated oases in the **Erg du Ténéré** and the **Grand Erg du Bilma**, where occasional camel caravans still cross the shifting dunes to the salt mines of **Bilma**. Since the early 1990s, however, most of the region has been officially off-limits and even during periods when the government's travel ban has been lifted, travel advisories by foreign governments have remained in effect. This has also been the case for other, historic villages such as Timia, Iferouâne and Assodé, which lie isolated deep in the harsh volcanic mountains of the **Aïr region** and can, in any case, only be reached with special advance preparation from Agadez.

People

Nearly half the population of Niger are **Hausa**-speaking. Engaged principally in agriculture and commerce, the Hausa are mostly based in the south, where they long ago established large urban centres such as Maradi and Zinder. The overwhelming majority of Hausa are Muslim, but small splinter groups have retained traditional religious beliefs, notably in the Birnin-Konni district. If you don't have a chance to get further south to the original Hausa city states in Nigeria, you can still see the brilliant **durbar festivals** – cavalry charges, clashing costumes and all – in Zinder, which retains its sultanate and beautiful quarters of traditional architecture.

The **Djerma** and **Songhai** speak the same language and probably have common origins. Numbering about one and a half million, they're the second largest group in Niger and have been politically dominant in Niger for generations. The Songhai of today are descendants of those who fled the collapse of Gao's great Songhai empire, and live mostly along the banks of the Niger as far downstream as Tillabéri, retaining the essential class structure – nobles, commoners, slaves, and crafts people – of the old empire. The Djerma live further south in the regions of Niamey and Dosso.

Another large group, the **Fula** (Peul or Peulh in French), make up some ten percent of the population. Centuries ago they founded large kingdoms in what are now Senegal and Guinea, before spreading east. By the end of the nineteenth century, a group of town Fula (as opposed to nomads), led by Uthman Dan Fodio, had established a huge

FACTS AND FIGURES

The **République du Niger** has a confusing name for English-speakers. Pronouncing it like an unfinished "Nigeria" means nothing to Nigériens – the people of the country – who pronounce it "Nee-zhé". It is a vast country on the map, spreading over 1,270,000 square kilometres – twice the size of Texas and five times as big as Britain. In reality, however, the Sahara covers most of the northern region, making a large proportion of the country uninhabitable. A population of some eight million people is concentrated in a fairly high density, mainly along the borders with Nigeria, Mali and Benin. About 600,000 people are reckoned to live in Niamey.

Niger's foreign debt amounts to some £1.1billion ($1.7billion), and, with that being equivalent to nearly six times the value of its annual goods and services exports, the country faces bleak economic prospects. Ninety-eight percent of the population is employed in agriculture, livestock and informal trade; and mining and manufacturing continue to slump due to the unstable price of Niger's unhealthy principal export resource – uranium. In 1993, Mahamane Ousmane, leader of the MNSD–Nassara party, became the country's first president to be chosen in a multi-party election.

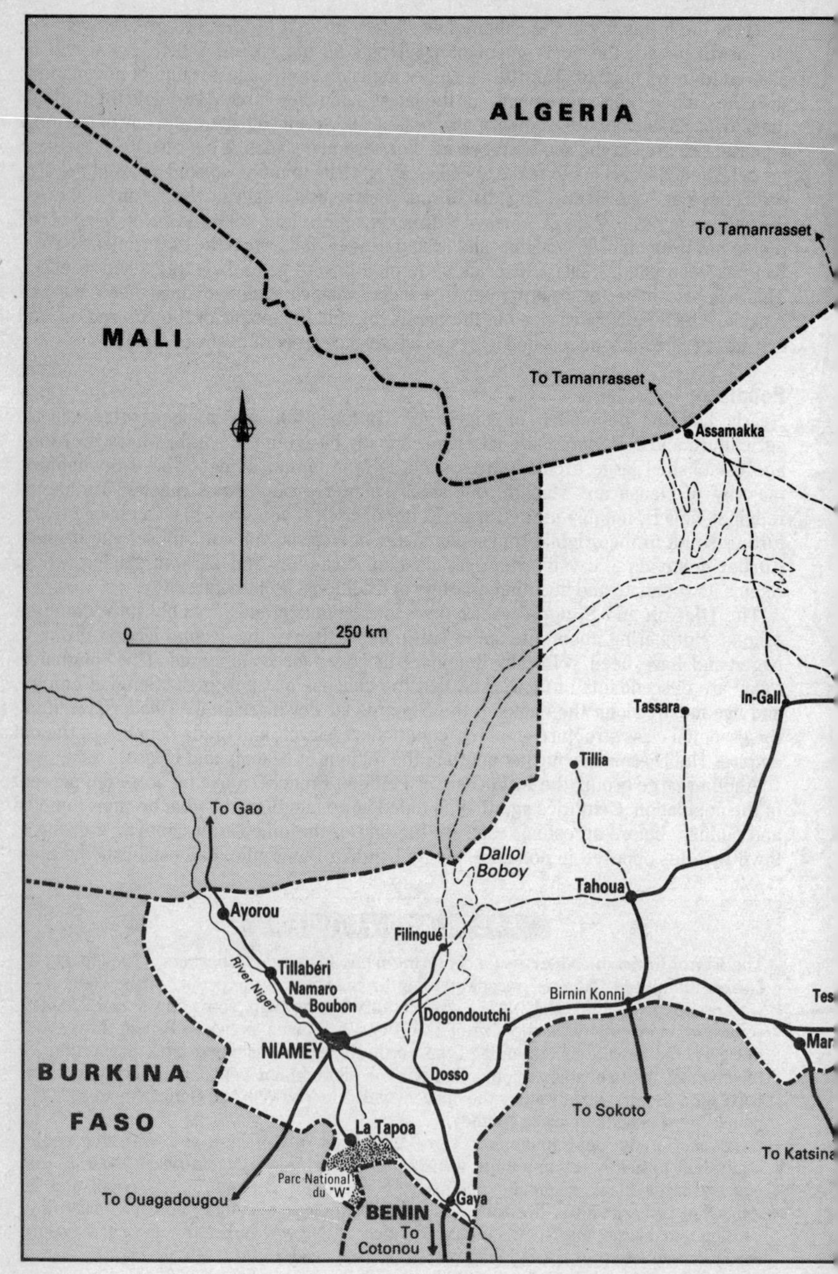
ALGERIA
MALI
To Tamanrasset
To Tamanrasset
Assamakka
0
250 km
Tassara
In-Gall
Tillia
To Gao
Dallol
Boboy
Tahoua
Ayorou
Filingué
Tillabéri
River Niger
Namaro
Boubon
Birnin Konni
Dogondoutchi
NIAMEY
BURKINA
FASO
Dosso
To Sokoto
La Tapoa
Parc National
du "W"
To Ouagadougou
Gaya
BENIN
To
Cotonou
To Katsina

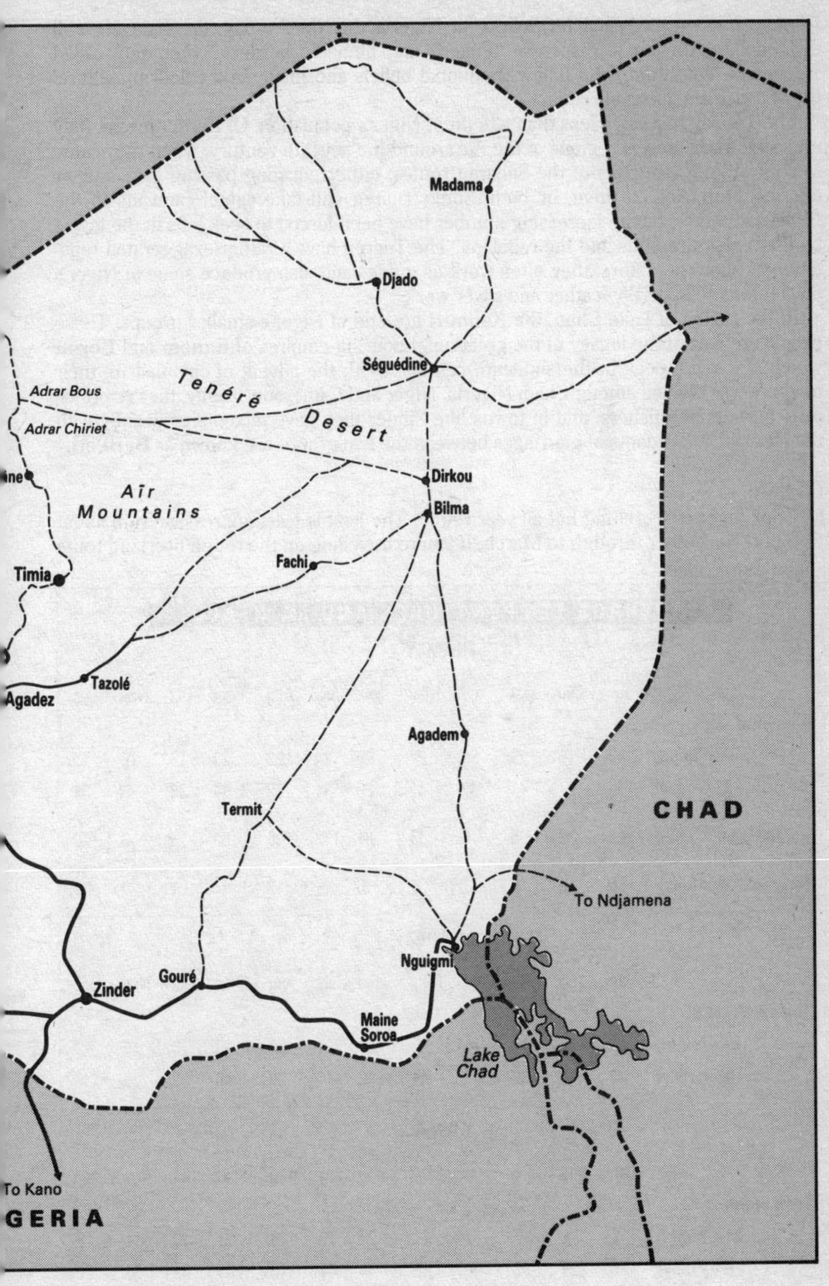
Madama
Djado
Séguédine
Adrar Bous
Adrar Chiriet
Tenéré Desert
Dirkou
Bilma
Aïr Mountains
Timia
Fachi
Tazolé
Agadez
Agadem
Termit
CHAD
To Ndjamena
Nguigmi
Gouré
Zinder
Maine Soroa
Lake Chad
To Kano
GERIA

Islamic theocracy centred on Sokoto in Nigeria. In Niger today, the Fula are still divided into Muslim townspeople (Fulani) and nomadic herders, commonly called **Bororo** or **Wodaabe**, who follow traditional beliefs and maintain a colourful cultural life of dance and life cycle ritual.

The **Tuareg** represent less than a tenth of Niger's population. Of Berber origin, they migrated to the desert regions of the Aïr around the seventh century, when they came to control long stretches of the Saharan routes, either pillaging passing caravans, or offering protection to them, or both. Some Tuareg still take camel caravans to the Bilma salt mines, but an increasing number have been forced to seek jobs in the towns by the recent droughts and the rebellion. The Tuareg have a rather exaggerated reputation as sharp operators: they often work as guides and also produce some of Niger's finest crafts – especially leather and silver work.

In the region of Lake Chad, the **Kanouri** are one of Niger's smaller groups. These people are part of the legacy of the great neighbouring empires of **Kanem** and **Bornu** which reached a peak in the sixteenth century. With the advent of colonialism, their territory was divided among Chad, Nigeria, Niger and Cameroon. Today, they're principally farmers and fishers, and in towns like Zinder they have mixed significantly with the Hausa. Descendants of marriages between the two groups are known as **Beriberi**.

Climate

Most of Niger is scorching hot all year round. The heat is least oppressive from about October/November through to March. If you're travelling on the rough overland route

AVERAGE TEMPERATURES AND RAINFALL

NIAMEY

	Jan	Feb	Mar	Apr	May	June	July	Aug	Sept	Oct	Nov	Dec
Temperatures °C												
Min (night)	14	18	22	26	27	25	24	22	23	23	19	15
Max (day)	34	37	41	42	41	38	34	32	34	38	38	34
Rainfall mm	0	0	5	8	33	81	132	188	94	13	0	0
Days with rainfall	0	0	0	1	4	6	9	12	7	1	0	0

AGADEZ

	Jan	Feb	Mar	Apr	May	June	July	Aug	Sept	Oct	Nov	Dec
Temperatures °C												
Min (night)	10	13	17	21	25	24	24	23	23	20	15	12
Max (day)	29	33	38	41	44	43	41	38	40	39	35	32

BILMA

	Jan	Feb	Mar	Apr	May	June	July	Aug	Sept	Oct	Nov	Dec
Temperatures °C												
Min (night)	6	8	13	17	21	22	23	24	21	16	11	8
Max (day)	26	29	35	40	43	44	42	40	41	39	33	28

from Gao in Mali to Niamey, it's also worth trying to avoid the **rainy season**, which falls roughly between July and September, when heavy storms can knock out the *pistes* for days. In contrast, when the *Harmattan* wind blows down from the north in November, it can kick up blinding clouds of dust and sometimes cause morning temperatures to tumble near to freezing point, especially in the north around Agadez, and in the Aïr mountains.

Arrivals

Formerly West Africa's main overland entry point (from Algeria across the Sahara), the combination of fundamentalist terrorism in Algeria and Tuareg rebellion in northern Niger has placed Niger on the extreme fringe of West African travel routes. Overland travel from Mali is effectively suspended. Meanwhile, flight connections with the rest of the region remain barely adequate.

Flights from Africa

Within **West Africa**, direct flights to Niamey are nearly all from **Abidjan**, *Air Afrique* (RK) or *Air France* (AF) providing most services. AF flies Abidjan–Niamey non-stop on Thurs, en route to Paris. Non-stop RK flights are on Fri during the day, and on Tues in the middle of the night.

RK flies Abidjan–Niamey via **Bamako** on Wed, and there are non-stop RK flights from Bamako to Niamey on Sat morning and late Sat night.

RK flies **Ouagadougou**–Niamey non-stop on Sat evening; and Abidjan–**Cotonou**–**Lomé**–Niamey on Mon night. There's also a non-stop AF flight from Cotonou to Niamey (destination Paris) on Sun.

There's nothing useful from **Lagos** – only a round-the-capitals flight on RK on Fri (via Lomé and Abidjan to Niamey), or RK connections through Abidjan on Mon and Tues (arriving after midnight). These, however, are still probably more efficient than flying on a Nigerian domestic carrier to Sokoto and taking a taxi the last 500km.

There are no direct flights from **west coast cities** (Nouakchott, Dakar, Banjul, Bissau, Conakry, Freetown), nor from Accra, and reasonable connections via Abidjan only from **Conakry**, on Tues and Fri on RK.

From **the rest of Africa** (south of the Sahara), Abidjan is the obvious hub, although there is a Sat flight to Niamey on *Ethiopian Airlines* from **Addis** via **Ndjamena**.

There are also weekly flights from **Casablanca** on *Royal Air Maroc* (AH) via Bamako on Tuesday.

Overland

As this book goes to press, the overland route through the **Algerian Sahara** is closed, as are many of the roads in northern Niger.

The details in these practical information pages are essentially for use on the ground in West Africa and in Niger itself: for full practical details on preparing for a trip, getting here from outside the region, paperwork, health, information sources and more, see *Basics*.

From Mali

Due to the Tuareg rebellion, the following overland route is not advised. Any public transport using the route is not an indication of its safety. *See p.973 for more details.*

The route follows the Niger River between Gao and Niamey. It's a difficult stretch for drivers, awash with deep soft sand and dreaded thorn trees (endless punctures), but motoring frustrations are more than compensated by Sahelian scenery at its best – dust-shrouded sunsets over the broad river and numerous fishing villages along the banks.

From Burkina

The 500-kilometre paved road linking **Ouagadougou** with Niamey is a relatively busy and straightforward route. But you need to make an early start from Ouagadougou as the border, 113km from Niamey, closes at 6pm. Formalities are pretty routine.

From Benin

The 1030-kilometre road **from Benin** is paved all the way from Cotonou. The offices on both sides of the border at Malanville (bridge over the Niger) close at 7.30pm, and present no special problems.

From Nigeria

Numerous paved roads feed into Niger **from Nigeria**, retaining a Hausa-land commercial unity despite the frontier dividing it. Main lines of entry are Sokoto to Birnin-Konni, Katsina to Maradi and Kano to Zinder. From the south, the best route is direct to Sokoto, then to the border at Birnin-Konni. If you're setting off from Kaduna or Kano, the best surfaced route is via Katsina to Maradi.

Red Tape

Niger cultivates one of the most irksome bureaucracies in the world. Although

Nigériens are subject to much more scrutiny at police and customs checkpoints throughout the country than tourists, officials have a reputation for being painfully no-nonsense. Though the situation seems to be improving, except in the restricted travel areas of the north, don't expect jocular exchanges or upbeat conversation.

■ Visas and health certificates

Visas for Niger are not required by Ecowas members and citizens of the UK, France, West Germany, Belgium, Netherlands, Luxembourg, the Scandinavian countries or Italy.

For nationals who need visas, they are most easily obtained in neighbouring West African countries – Benin; Côte d'Ivoire; Nigeria (Lagos and Kano); and Senegal. Note that French embassies don't handle visas for Niger but some Ivoirian embassies do; and that Niger has no representation in Bamako. If you're arriving from Mali and need a visa, plan ahead. In general, Niger officials are literate and well-versed in the rules and regulations. Bluffing in any situation is rarely effective.

If you apply for a visa outside Africa, Nigérien embassies may ask for a return air ticket or, at the very least, the registration details of the vehicle you'll be travelling with. To avoid these headaches, you're better off getting the visa in Africa. In either case, the visa is expensive.

To enter Niger you need a **yellow fever certificate** (except infants under 12 months).

Visas for onward travel

In Niamey, you can get visas with little problem for all neighbouring countries. Burkina Faso, Togo and Chad have no representation, but the French consulate handles their visas. There's an Algerian embassy in Niamey, and a consulate in Agadez, but they have suspended the issue of tourist visas – not that you would want one.

■ Photography permits

Formerly mandatory, the **photography permit** is no longer required and it's possible to take pictures with no problems.

■ Vehicle passes

If you're driving, the police require to see a **carnet**. If you don't have one, they'll issue you with a Temporary Importation document. You'll also be issued with a *laissez-passer*, a visa for your vehicle, with the same details as your Vehicle Registration Document (V5) or *Carte Grise* (French and West African equivalent), to be surrendered on exit. There's no charge.

Third party **insurance** is compulsory, and the police like to check it. It's not available at frontier posts, but the police allow travel without it to the nearest town. The large and efficient *Société Nigérienne d'Assurances et de Réassurances*, av de la Mairie, Niamey BP426 (☎73.55.26), has branches throughout the country and charges about CFA2000 a day.

■ Bureaucracy

Officially, you're no longer required to **report to the police station** in every town you visit. In Arlit and Agadez, however, they still like to put a stamp in your passport. If police in these towns seem keen to do so, let them. If they ask for money, don't pay. And if they don't seem concerned about stamps, you shouldn't be either.

Money and Costs

Niger is in the CFA zone (CFA100 = 1 French franc; approx. CFA750–800 = £1; approx. CFA500 = US$1). It's essential, arriving either by air or from Nigeria, to have some French francs in cash to tide you over until you reach a bank where you can change travellers' cheques.

The two main **banks** in Niger are the *BIAO* and the *BDRN*. Outside Niamey, one or the other has branches in Zinder, Tahoua, Birnin-Konni, Maradi, Agadez and Arlit. Banks will charge four percent commission for money changing.

Credit and charge cards are pretty much limited to use in Niamey, and even then only for major expenses such as car rental, luxury hotels and a handful of upmarket restaurants. Major ones that are accepted are American Express and Diner's Club. *BIAO* handles Access/Mastercard cash advances; no bank gives Visa cash advances.

As far as **costs** are concerned, Niger is **expensive** relative to other CFA countries, though still fairly cheap in real terms. You can always find street food and a basic room for the night, even if the choice is often limited. If your budget is less restricted, the biggest expense is likely to be on hotels and car rental, both of which can eat deeply into your pocket.

Health

In Niamey and other large towns, tap water is usually suitable for drinking, and the borehole water of Arlit and Agadez is noted for its purity. Cholera epidemics, however, occur frequently along the Niger and in the bush you should use purifying tablets, or boil water. In case of an epidemic, even town water is suspect.

Health care facilities are very limited. For minor ailments you can be treated at Niamey's **hospital**. If you have a medical problem, embassies will always recommend a **private clinic**. For anything serious – surgery for example – they're sure to suggest repatriation.

Maps and Information

Tourist information on Niger is virtually non-existent outside the country; there are no tourist offices abroad. In Niamey, the tourist office has a good plan of the capital, with many of the city's restaurants and hotels indicated.

Since the entire Saharan region is off-limits to travel, the tourist office in **Agadez** can't do much for you though it could be a source of current information.

The *IGN* publishes maps in scales of 1:2,500,000, 1:1,000,000, 1:500,000, 1:200,000, and 1:50,000. You're not supposed to obtain the latter three series without authorization, which you can apply for at any Niger embassy. In Niamey, maps are available at the *Direction de la Topographie*.

Getting Around

Niger has some good roads, a decent bus service, plus perfectly feasible hitching prospects at checkpoints. In the southwest of the country, you also have the limited possibility of using the Niger River.

■ Buses, bush taxis and trucks

Three main, surfaced routes cover the western parts of Niger: Niamey–Gaya, Niamey–Zinder and Birnin-Konni–Agadez. Furthermore, the *Route de l'Uranium* – from Niamey to Agadez and Arlit – and the *Route de l'Unité* – connecting Maradi, Zinder and Lake Chad in the southeast – were resurfaced in the years following the 1980s' droughts, and, as this book goes to press, are still in reasonably good condition.

The state-run *Société Nationale des Transports Nigériens* (*SNTN*) operates a scheduled **bus network** between major towns. Because of their popularity, it's imperative to book a seat in advance at the local *SNTN* office. **Taxis brousse** soak up the excess passengers; they're slightly less expensive and always overcrowded. Transport rates on main routes are about CFA12–18 per kilometre. **Trucks** also run between certain centres and often take travellers for a fee – a useful option for the stretch between Agadez and Zinder, and in other remote areas where transport is scarce.

■ Driving your own vehicle

On tarmac, experienced local drivers tank along at 150kph. If you're driving yourself you can keep up a good speed too; visibility is excellent and all bends and hazards are marked well in advance. **Night driving**, formerly banned, is now legal. Driving **off the paved roads** is still subject to police jurisdiction, though in practice they're rarely fussed about it in the south.

The entire **northeast** is a domain of tough desert *pistes* and presently closed to travellers. Restrictions on driving in various parts of the country – notably north of Niamey along the river and on the roads north of Tahoua and north of Zinder to Agadez – will only be clear on arrival.

Petrol (gasoline) and diesel are generally plentiful, but supplies can be far apart. Fuel can be bought from either a filling station – dependent on electricity – or from an entrepreneur with half a dozen fifty-gallon drums at the roadside. Maps aren't generally a good guide to fuel supplies; ask regularly. Fuel is generally expensive, except along the southern border between Birnin-Konni and Zinder, where there's a thriving black market in Nigerian petrol. North of Zinder, lubrication oils and transmission fluids can be hard to come by.

■ Hitching

Roadblocks and police checks at the entrance to every large town help to make **hitching** a viable alternative. Cars are obliged to stop at these controls and while the *gendarmes* are checking the papers you can ask drivers if they're headed your way. Often the police will help. Foreign aid workers often take hitchers for free; Nigérien drivers will usually expect you to subsidize the trip.

Hitching is fast. On the three main axes you can expect a vehicle going to one of the big towns or a neighbouring country at least once an hour, and most vehicles will stop. But lorry drivers sometimes turn off en route, so check the final destination and any detours to be made.

A hitch on a lorry usually means standing in the back for several hours under the blazing sun; hats and/or *cheches* are essential plus **at least two litres of water**. Lifts in the cab can be noisy and very hot, and get exhausting if you're also trying to make conversation in French.

■ River travel

Large steamers don't ply the Niger below Gao, in Mali, but motorized **pirogues** venture along the river between Ayorou (near Mali) and Gaya (near Benin). They operate only during and after the rainy season when the water level is high enough. Deals have to be struck on your own in the river towns. Between March and September, it may also be possible to canoe-hop downstream from Gaya to Port Harcourt in southern Nigeria but rapids and artificial barriers block the way at numerous points and prevent a continuous journey in the same vessel.

■ Internal flights

Since the closure of *Air Niger*, scheduled domestic flights in Niger are non-existent: your only recourse is to rent a light aircraft and pilot from the *Transniger* company (☎73.20.55) in Niamey.

Accommodation

Hotels tend to be relatively expensive in Niger, but at least you'll find comfortable places with toilets and air conditioning in all the major towns. Budget accommodation seems especially bad value: you'll often have to pay upwards of CFA4000, even for a room with just a fan and shared facilities.

Camping sites are an idea that's caught on in Niger and you'll find them scattered lightly throughout the country. They usually cost around CFA2000 per person plus extra for each vehicle. **Staying with people** is now officially sanctioned (it used to be banned).

Eating and Drinking

Though Niger has concentrated heavily on improving its agriculture, food shortages occur in years of bad harvest or drought. Staples tend to be less varied than in countries to the south, meals being usually based around millet, rice or *niebé* – a type of bean that has become an important crop. Along the river, these are usually eaten with sauces and fresh or smoked fish.

The Songhai often make a cornmeal stodge (or **pâte**) eaten with a baobab leaf sauce perked up with fish or meat.

Another traditional food, **foura**, is one of the most common dishes, and eaten throughout the country. It consists of small balls of ground and

ACCOMMODATION PRICE CODES

Hotel prices in this chapter are coded according to the following scales – the same scales in terms of their pound/dollar equivalents as are used throughout the book. Prices refer to the rate you can expect to pay for a room with two beds. Single rooms, or single occupancy, will normally cost at least two-thirds of the twin-occupancy rate. For further details see p.51.

① **Under CFA4000 (under £5/$7.50)**. Very rudimentary hotel – increasingly hard to find a room at this price.

② **CFA4000–8000 (£5–10/$7.50–15).** Commonest budget-price bracket in Niger, with simple amenities. S/C rooms with fans are the norm but some rooms may have AC.

③ **CFA8000–16,000 (£10–20/$15–30).** Modest, but adequate hotel, with S/C rooms, and a choice of rooms with fans, or AC for a premium.

④ **CFA16,000–24,000 (£20–30/$30–45).** Reason-able business/tourist-class hotel with S/C, AC rooms, and often a restaurant.

⑤ **CFA24,000–32,000 (£30–40/$45–60).** Similar standards to the previous code band but extra facilities such as a pool are usual.

⑥ **CFA32,000–40,000 (£40–50/$60–75).** Comfor-table, first-class hotel, with good facilities.

⑦ **Over CFA40,000 (over £50/$75).** Luxury establishment – top prices around CFA60,000–80,000.

BASIC HAUSA

Surpassing even French and English, **Hausa** is the most international language in West Africa, and is spoken by anything from 25 million to 100 million people. The language developed into a regional *lingua franca* in the fifteenth century, when Hausa traders led caravans to North Africa. Through their widespread commercial liaisons, Hausa became a trade language throughout northwest Africa and, in terms of the area over which it's spoken, Hausa is today second only to Swahili in sub-Saharan Africa. Though there are many dialects, the two most important are **Kano** and **Sokoto**. Differences are primarily phonetic and discrepancies don't prevent speakers of different dialects from understanding each other. The following words and phrases are based on the Kano dialect, which is generally considered to be "classical" Hausa.

NUMBERS

1	*daya*	8	*takwas*	30	*talatin*	90	*casa'in* (or *tamanin da goma*)
2	*biyu*	9	*tara*	40	*arba'in*		
3	*uku*	10	*goma*	50	*hamsin*	100	*dari*
4	*hudu*	11	*goma sha daya*	60	*sittin*	200	*dari biyu*
5	*biyar*	12	*goma sha biyu*	70	*saba'in*	250	*dari biyu da hamsin*
6	*shida*	20	*ashirin*	75	*saba'in da biyar*	1000	*dubu*
7	*bakwai*	25	*ashirin da biyar*	80	*tamanin*		

In Niger, money is commonly counted in multiples of CFA5 (*dela*) – which can be difficult to calculate even if you're thinking in English. For example:

CFA100	*dela ashirin*	CFA200	*dela arba'in*	CFA500	*dela dar*
CFA150	*dela talatin*	CFA450	*dela tamanin da goma*	CFA1000	*jikai*

GREETINGS

If the following list seems long and trivial, it barely gives a taste of the extended formal exchange that's so important in Hausa, as in most African languages. Just learning the three words *sanu, lafiya* and *yauwa*, will permit you to carry on a surprisingly lengthy conversation.

All purpose greeting (men)	*Salamu alaikum*
(Response)	*Alaika salamu*
Greetings	*Sanu*
(Response)	*Yauwa, sanu kadai*
Are you in good health?	*Kazo lafiya?*
(Response)	*Lafiya lau*
How's the household/your family?	*Ina gida?*
Good morning (how was the night)?	*Ina kwana?*
How are your children?	*Yaya yara?*
Fine (general response)	*Lafiya lau*
Are you tired? (how's the tiredness)	*Ina gajiya?*
No, I'm not tired	*Ba gajiya*
What's the news?	*Ina labari?*
Everything's fine	*Labari sai alheri*
Good afternoon	*Barka da yamma*
(Response)	*Barka kadai*
See you tomorrow	*Sai gobe*
Okay, see you tomorrow	*To, sai gobe*
See you later	*Sai an juma*
Okay, see you later	*To, sai an juma*

SHOPPING

How much?	*Nawa nawa ne?*
Do you have oranges?	*Akwai lemo?*
Yes I do/no I don't have them	*I, akwai/ah ah babu*
How much are your oranges?	*Lemo, nawa nawa ne?*
They're expensive!	*Kai, suna da tsada*
I'll give you CFA100	*Zan biya ka dela ashirin*
No deal (seller refusing)	*Albarka*
Give the money (offer accepted)	*Kawo kudi*

slightly fermented millet, crushed in a calabash with milk, sugar and spices added.

Beef and mutton is common in the Hausa country and the nomadic regions of the north. But brochettes are sold everywhere on the streets. Stuffed into a *demi-baguette* and doused with a bit of *Maggi* sauce, they make a quick, satisfying meal.

Niamey has a reasonable selection of **foreign restaurants**, but outside the capital, eating places tend to be much more modest, the selection of dishes usually something like grilled chicken or *steack frites*. **Street food** is common with vendors selling omelettes, salads, *riz gras* and a variety of other cheap meals.

■ Drinking

As for **drinks**, Niger's great beverage – in common with other Sahel countries – is **tea**, drunk on most occasions, especially on the road whenever a little time is available to fix up a fire. You'll also find *Flag* **beers** in most towns, though they're rather expensive.

Communications – Post, Phones, Language and Media

The official language of Niger is French, but by far the most important lingua franca is Hausa. Niamey's new PTT is quite modern and efficient, with a reliable poste restante. Phoning directly abroad with IDD is straightforward.

If you want to make a reverse-charge (collect) call, known as PCV in French, you may be told that such calls are possible only to France. But ringing ☎16 from a payphone puts you through to the foreign operator, who should be able to connect a reverse-charge (collect) call anywhere. Persistence may be needed.

Niger's IDD code is ☎227.

■ The media

There's nothing much in the way of **newspapers** in Niger: *Le Sahel*, a government-owned news-sheet, is published daily in Niamey, but has a very small circulation. There are also various new independent news magazines, including *La Marché*, *Haske*, *Horizon 2001*, *Kakaki*, *La Tribune du Peuple* and *Le Républicain*, which sprang up when the government began liberalizing, as did the weekly satirical mag *Le Pont Africain*. You can find French papers and news magazines in some of the bigger Niamey hotels and news and book stores, but little or nothing in English.

Nigérien **radio**, *La Voix du Sahel*, broadcasts in French, Hausa, Songhai-Djerma, Kanouri, Fulfuldé (Fula), Tamashek, Toubou, Gourmantché and Arabic. The **TV service**, *Télé-Sahel*, comes on air each evening for a few hours.

Entertainment

Wrestling and one-armed boxing (fist wrapped in cloth) attract big crowds, but there's not a great deal going on in terms of national "culture" in Niger – no theatre except the odd event in Niamey, and little happening musically. The film tradition, brief as it is, shows more promise.

■ Cinema

Cinema in Niger has been dominated by three film-makers, none of whose work you're very likely to come across abroad. **Oumarou Ganda** began his career as an actor in a Jean Rouch film, *Moi, un Noir*, and went on to become a director in his own right and one of the great cultural archivists of African cinema. You're more likely to see his (largely autobiographical) works at Niamey's Centre Culturel Franco-Nigérien or even abroad than in any ordinary Nigérien cinema.

A SHORT NIGÉRIEN GLOSSARY

Azalai Camel caravans.

Baba Old man, a term of respect.

Birni Hausa word meaning a formerly fortified town.

Boro Bi Black person or people.

Canaris Large clay pots for storing water.

Djoliba Malinké name for the Niger. Literally "River of Blood" since the body of water was as vital to life as blood flowing in the veins.

Erg Shifting sand dunes common in the Ténéré.

Fech-fech Soft sand hidden beneath a hard crust.

Gravures Rupestres Rock paintings, common in the Aïr and Djado regions.

Kaya-kaya Wandering salesmen.

Kori Seasonal river course or wadi (Hausa).

Razzia Slave raid.

Reg Stony wastes.

Wonki-wonki Launderers, common along the banks of the Niger in Niamey.

Zongo Section of a town or village where newly arrived strangers live.

Jean Rouch also inspired another relatively well-known director, **Moustapha Alassane**, whose most famous feature film is *Femme, Villa, Voiture, Argent* (1972), a popular comedy dealing with the issue of cultural identity.

Another film-maker to gain international acclaim is **Djingary Maïga**, producer of *l'Etoile Noire*, in which he also starred, which deals with the clash between Western and traditional values.

■ Music

In the realm of **music**, Niger remains rooted in tradition and the country has produced no international stars. In Niamey, look out for performances of the national music and dance troupe, **Karaka**. You might also catch a less worthy, mimed show that goes out on *Télé-Sahel* TV. For a taste of Nigérien music, the *Agence de Cooperation Culturelle et Technique* has put out two volumes of a record entitled *Festival de la Jeunesse Nigérienne*. Most recently, an international CD release by **Moussa Poussy** and **Saadou Bori** (*Niamey Twice*, Stern's) has put Niger on the musical map.

Holidays

As 85 percent of Niger's population is Muslim, **Islamic holidays** are of key importance (see p.62). The best place to be during festivities is Zinder. Other national holidays are: **January 1**, **April 15** (Anniversary of the 1974 coup), **August 3** (Independence Day) and **December 18** (Proclamation of the Republic). Christmas and Easter are also office holidays.

Directory

AIRPORT DEPARTURE TAX CFA3500.

CONTRACEPTION Birth control was only legalized in Niger in 1988. There's an active *planification familiale* programme now, but contraception still isn't widely available.

CRAFTS AND MARKETS Niger has a wealth of mostly inexpensive and portable crafts. Agadez is well known for its **silversmiths** who turn out some fine jewellery; popular items are the pendants known as desert crosses, particularly the *Croix d'Agadez*. The Hausa towns, and notably Zinder, specialize in **leather goods** including sandals, bags and boxes. Fula weavers (*tisserands*) are noted for their geometrically patterned **blankets**. To get a good overview, the National Museum in Niamey shows a wide range of the country's artisanal output. Best buys are in local markets, though for guaranteed quality and variety you should also check out the official *Centres Artisanales* in Niamey.

OPENING HOURS Due to the heat, business starts early in the morning and generally closes down for at least three hours in the afternoon. Banking hours vary from one institution to the next but they're approximately Mon–Fri 7.30–11.30am & 3.30–5.30pm. Government offices are open Mon–Fri 7.30am–12.30pm & 3.30–6.30pm. Most businesses are open Mon–Fri 8am–12.30pm & 3–6.30pm, plus Saturday mornings.

WILDLIFE AND NATIONAL PARKS Niger's harsh climate and terrain have preserved some rare species from the vicissitudes of habitat spoliation and hunting (which was outlawed in 1964). Even in the south, hippos can nearly always be seen in the Niger River and several herds of giraffe live in the vicinity of Tillabéri, Baleyara and Dosso (to the north, east and south of Niamey), where they're often to be seen from the road. The **Parc National du "W" du Niger** (which crosses borders into Burkina and Benin) has a good cross-section of savannah fauna, including several hundred elephants. Niger's portion of the park has the best visitor facilities.

WOMEN TRAVELLERS Though Niger is a Muslim country, women don't wear the veil and their public presence is strongly felt. Women travellers generally have few problems and female Western volunteers, for example, feel comfortable making trips across the country unaccompanied. Advances tend to be frequent but harmless and easily rebuffed.

A Brief History of Niger

After the demise of the Songhai empire, whose territory spread into western Niger, two spheres of influence predominated in the region. In the twelfth century, the Tuareg settled in the north around Agadez, and soon controlled regional trade. The Hausa spread from the original seven city-states founded in Nigeria in the tenth century to settle southern towns like Zinder and Maradi. Unlike the western Sudan, where trans-Saharan trade focused mainly on gold, slavery was the mainstay of the eastern routes and the basis of local economies.

■ Explorers on the Niger River

For centuries, news of cities like Timbuktu, Gao and Djenné (all in present-day Mali) had circulated in Europe, but although the Portuguese had been trading along the West African coast since the fifteenth century, no western power had penetrated the interior. It wasn't until the eighteenth century that expeditions were launched into a region notorious for its hostility to Christians. In 1796 Mungo Park reached the Niger near Ségou (again, in present-day Mali) and described its eastern course. Until that time, Europeans believed the river flowed west – as documented by Leo Africanus in the sixteenth century – or that it was a branch of the Nile.

It was another thirty years before the Europeans saw Timbuktu. In 1826, **Gordon Laing** became the first white man to reach it, though he didn't return from the legendary city alive. In 1850, **Heinrich Barth** led a new expedition into the interior, his route from Tripoli, in Libya, taking him south through Agadez, Zinder and the Hausa country as far as Kano. He thus became the first European to explore the region of present-day Niger – and to return to Europe.

■ Colonial conquest

The information gleaned by these expeditions opened the doors to colonial conquests. France, anxious to link colonial settlements in West and central Africa, was the most ambitious usurper of Sahelian territories. In 1854, General Louis Faidherbe became governor of Senegal and plotted the eastward expansion of France's West African empire. He sent troops up the Senegal River and east to the Niger. Following its course, they broke the resistance of such formidable adversaries as **Samory Touré** and **El Hadj Omar Tall**, who had founded the Tukulor empire of Ségou. By the end of the nineteenth century, the French had established a military presence at **Niamey**, which they quickly turned into the most important army post east of Bamako.

In 1898, spheres of influence were established between France and the United Kingdom, the principal powers vying for control of the Niger. The following year, the French sent an expedition to Lake Chad to demarcate borders between Niger and Nigeria. Led by two generals, **Voulet and Chanoine**, it was to be one of the bloodiest of the colonial missions. As the two soldiers pushed east with troops of Senegalese infantry, they embarked on a series of massacres, torching villages in their path and slaughtering the people. Birnin-Konni was virtually rased to the ground. Reports of the brutality reached France and the government sent an expedition led by Colonel Klobb to investigate. Infuriated that their tactics should be questioned, the generals went over the edge, murdered Klobb, broke with France and apparently set about conquering the territories for themselves. Their madness was only stopped when they were killed by their own infantrymen. Replacements were sent out and Lake Chad was finally reached in 1900.

■ French rule

With the territory's southern borders established, Niger became part of French West Africa in the following year. But the nature of this territory differed from that of its West African neighbours: officially, it was an **autonomous military territory**, and its importance was strategic, rather than commercial. Outside the army, the French presence was minimal: there was no French settlement and development was barely considered.

"Pacification" was a difficult process in Niger, as resistance sprouted in pockets across the country. One of the most serious **uprisings** was that of the **Kel Gress Tuareg**, who occupied Agadez from 1916 to 1917 and controlled most of the Aïr highlands. In 1919, a rebellion broke out in the region of Tahoua, which was only quelled in 1921, the same year that Niger was finally upgraded to the status of a colony.

World War II was a turning point in West African politics, and following the Brazzaville Conference of 1944, reforms were enacted which provided African representation in the national assembly, the senate and the assembly of the French Union. In 1956, the famous *Loi Cadre* was passed, establishing local government for the French colonies.

In the wake of these reforms, two political movements developed in Niger, the more radical of which was embodied in the *Union Nigérienne Democratique* – also known as **Sawaba** – which dominated political life in the 1950s. Led by **Djibo Bakary**, the party fought vigorously against close ties with France and de Gaulle's proposed constitution, the main provision of which was for a Franco-African Community with limited autonomy for individual colonies, but continued economic dependence on Paris. For a while, it seemed probable that Niger would join Guinea in saying "No" to de Gaulle's proposal and in opting for immediate independence "with all its consequences".

In the event, the new constitution was approved in the landmark **1958 referendum** – a victory for the *Parti Progressiste Nigérien* of **Hamani Diori**, who had advocated the alternative of close links with France. It's generally believed the election results were falsified. According to the official count, 370,000 people voted for the union compared to 100,000 who voted against, leaving 750,000 people who ostensibly didn't exercise their voting rights.

Despite its wide support, the *Sawaba* party was banned in 1959, and Bakary forced into exile. With the implicit backing of the French, the PPN was thus poised to dominate post-independence politics and Diori was assured the presidency of the new nation, formed in 1960.

Independence

Conservative politics prevailed in the days after independence, as Diori aligned his country with France and developed close ties with moderate neighbours, notably Côte d'Ivoire. Diori ruled with a small Council of Ministers, carefully selected to maintain the status quo. *Sawaba* tried to operate from abroad (its foreign backers included Algeria, Ghana and China), but opposition to government policies was rigorously suppressed. Various plots to overthrow Diori's regime in the early 1960s led to mass arrests and violence. When *Sawaba* was accused of leading a series of guerilla attacks near the Nigerian border in 1964, seven of the presumed assailants were publicly executed in Niamey.

By the late 1960s, the PPN – by then the only political party – was in a state of disarray and the target of mounting criticism. Diori made an effort to reorganize it, but was careful to stack the party leadership with faithful pre-independence politicians – and ensured that it remained ineffective as a forum for the discussion of opposing views. Despite his tight control over the political reigns, however, he began to loose his grip on power as the economic situation deteriorated drastically in the late 1960s.

Diori was given a political reprieve when the mining of **uranium**, discovered in 1968, gave new financial hope to a nation that had previously gained seventy percent of its export earnings from groundnuts. Eager to take advantage of the new source of revenue, Diori accepted a minimal seventeen percent share for the national mining company, *Société des mines de l'Aïr* (SOMAÏR), which was controlled by the French Atomic Energy Commission. However, 1968 also saw the start of the first great **Sahel drought**. Lasting until 1974, the natural catastrophe brought Niger to its knees.

By the early 1970s, over a million head of livestock (nearly two-thirds of the national herd) had died, and the pasturelands of the northern nomads had disappeared. International organizations helped establish emergency refugee camps and sent food supplies, but rumours began circulating that government officials were hoarding food and selling it off at hefty profits, rather than distributing it to those facing starvation. These were quickly confirmed by the discovery of **emergency food aid**, stockpiled in the homes of several of Diori's ministers.

Kountché's coup

Disillusion with the government turned to anger. When Lieutenant-Colonel **Seyni Kountché** overthrew Diori in April 1974, there was widespread satisfaction, and even the French conceded they could do business with the new order. Kountché established a *Conseil Militaire Suprême* (CMS) which made a priority of dealing with corruption and reinvesting the government with credibility. In a conciliatory move, hundreds of political prisoners were released and Djibo Bakary, *Sawaba*'s leader, returned home from exile. In 1975, Kountché pulled off an economic coup, when he managed to renegotiate the terms under which uranium was mined, raising SOMAÏR's share to 33 percent and making the national company the biggest single partner.

Fuelled by uranium revenues (prices for which soared following the oil crisis of the 1970s) and aided by the end of the drought, the economy began to pick up. Government workers received wage increases, roads were improved and prestigious building projects undertaken in Niamey. Even the agricultural sector improved dramatically. Niger, one of the countries hardest hit by the drought, was also one of the quickest to recover, and by the end of the decade, it could boast self-sufficiency in food production – no mean feat.

Niger had become something of an economic oasis in the middle of a poverty-stricken region, and that alone was enough to lend stability to Kountché's military regime. But policy and personality conflicts within the CMS threatened his authority, and he repeatedly reshuffled the ruling council and expelled critics. Following a new outbreak of political activity, Bakary was rearrested in 1975. A coup attempt the following year led to the execution of its alleged protagonists. Even as he tightened the screws, however, Kountché made a number of good-will gestures. In 1980, Diori and Bakary were granted a degree of freedom, along with many of their supporters. And by 1982, the president appeared to be making plans for a return to a constitutional government.

■ Setbacks in the 1980s

A *Conseil National de Développement* was established in 1983 as a means of granting greater participation on a local level. But the CND had barely started functioning when another coup attempt, this time led by some of Kountché's closest aides, nearly toppled the government while he was abroad.

Reforms thereafter proceeded at a slower pace, though the president eventually announced that a **National Charter**, or draft constitution, would be drawn up and submitted to a referendum. Approved by the government in 1986, the charter was submitted to voters in May 1987 – the first time elections had been held in the country since independence – and received overwhelming approval.

But even as Kountché was setting about reorganizing the government, the **economy** took an unexpected dive. Already in 1980, a combination of the world recession and cuts in nuclear power programmes had led to a drop in the price of uranium. Production in Niger has since continued to fall off and plans to mine some of the country's unexploited reserves have been scrapped. Hopes that Niger would become one of the world's leading uranium producers faded rapidly. And as revenues dwindled and the national debt grew, another drought struck the country in the early 1980s. By 1984, the number of livestock had dropped by a half and, as cereal shortages climbed to nearly 500,000 tons, the country again found itself importing vast quantities of food, depending much on the USA. At about the same time, Nigeria closed its land borders and cut off some of Niger's important markets.

The downswing was accompanied by tensions with Niger's northern neighbour, **Libya**, which claims some 300 square kilometres of territory in northern Niger, an area with certified uranium deposits. After the Libyan army occupied northern Chad in 1980, Kountché's government had become wary of possible destabilization – with some justification after Gaddafi told reporters "We consider Niger second in line". Gaddafi accused the Niger government of persecuting its **Tuareg** population – an issue about which Niamey is acutely sensitive – and may have encouraged dissent among the nomads, who have generally been sold short since independence. Many observers suspected Gaddafi of behind-the-scenes support for the 1983 coup attempt and although relations have subsequently improved between the two countries, they remain strained. Relations with other Maghreb countries – Morocco, Algeria and Tunisia – were strengthened over this period, however, and Niger has developed close ties with Saudi Arabia, Kuwait and other Arab states in the Gulf, Muslim confrères who have proved reliable sources of aid.

■ Colonel Ali Saïbou

In 1986, Kountché travelled abroad to countries that had been traditional sources of political and financial support. He made his first official trip to France, during which he suffered a brain haemorrhage and subsequently died, after an operation in Paris, in November 1987.

Kountché's chosen successor as head of state **Colonel Ali Saïbou**, the military Chief of Staff and a long-time supporter – followed the same orientation as his predecessor. In mid-1988 Saïbou announced the creation of a one-party state (the PPN and all the other parties were disbanded when Kountché came to power), a move which he said would "normalize" political expression and which was generally perceived as a step to further reforms started in the early 1980s. In 1989, the first congress was held of the military council's **National Movement for a Society of Development** (MNSD), a supra-political organization which promised great things, but within a party-state order that threatened to be elitist and almost exclusively urban-based. The government's fear of ethnic divisions in the country was so great that even acknowledging the plurality was viewed as a danger.

The IMF-ordered economy forced in austerity measures which hit poor urban dwellers very hard. Students, too, felt the full impact of rising prices and reductions in already strapped services. In 1990 the university in Niamey was the scene of large-scale **student demonstrations** that ended in a violent clash with security forces and the deaths of three students and many serious injuries. A week later a mass protest rally swept through the streets of the capital, while the Lagos-based opposition, the **Niger Movement of Revolutionary Committees** (MOUNCORE), issued statements demanding a popular uprising in Niger and the overthrow of the Saïbou clique.

Niger was put under the spotlight in June 1990, after *Le Monde* reported a **massacre** of about 200 Tuareg civilians in reprisal for a Tuareg raid on Tchin-Tabaradene, near Tahoua. Amnesty International reported other atrocities near Tchin-Tabaradene and at In-Gal, in which dozens of people were summarily executed.

■ "Democracy" and Tuareg rebellion

As the national crisis deepened, Saïbou was compelled to speed up reforms. By the end of 1990, he had legalized opposition parties and formed a **national conference** to plot the country's future. Within a year, conference delegates had reduced the president's role to a ceremonial level and voted to suspend austerity measures imposed by the IMF and World Bank, an act which effectively made the country an outcast from the international financial community.

Despite two military mutinies (during which the army not only took over state broadcasting, but also detained Saïbou's prime minister before returning to the barracks when the government agreed to pay back-wages) plans for **elections** pressed on. A majority of seats in the national assembly was ultimately won by a new group of opposition parties – the *Alliance des Forces du Changement* (*AFC*) – whose candidate for president, **Mahamane Ousmane**, won the title in the presidential elections in March 1993. A Muslim and the first Hausa head of state in a traditionally Djerma political culture, the new leader of "democratic" Niger pledged to address the country's economic and social crises. He appointed another presidential contender, **Mahamadou Issoufou**, prime minister.

But student and labour unrest continued through 1992–93, and **Tuareg resistance** in the wake of Tchin-Tabaradene grew into a full blown rebellion headed by the *Front de Libération de l'Air et l'Azaouad*. Martial law was imposed across the entire north as security forces launched a major offensive against the rebels. There were violent clashes and, by early 1993, 200 Tuaregs were in prison and the FLAA was holding some 50 government troops.

Secret negotiations in France in 1993 led to a precarious truce whereby the north was to be demilitarized and talks were to open on the principal **Tuareg demands**: greater political autonomy; assistance for the return of refugees from Algeria; and a commitment to regional development. Though the truce held into 1994, the FLAA began to splinter into more militant groups that refused to support any agreement that didn't specifically address demands for a federal system of government.

Meanwhile, President Mahamane tried to rekindle talks with Western creditors in the hopes of securing new loans and much-needed debt relief. During a 1993 visit to France, he received emergency financial assistance, which allowed him to settle some pay arrears to public sector employees, but when he conceded the government could not afford the back-pay accumulated under the transitional administration, new **strikes and mutinies** broke out in Maradi, Agadez, Tahoua and Zinder. Though the government found the funds to pay an extra month's arrears, the weakened economy continued to make the situation extremely volatile. Periodic union strikes continued into 1994 with Niamey

University closed once again when student protests over inadequate resources led to widespread rioting.

By mid-1994, the country was in a state of continual upheaval. A campaign of civil disobedience seeking proportional representation was mounted by key opposition leader (ie oppositiion against the *AFC*) **Tandja Mamadou** of the *National Movement for the Society of Development–Nassara* (*MNSD–Nassara*, which had been the sole party between 1988 and 1990). Meanwhile, trades union leaders called an indefinite strike over demands for back-pay. Although the strike soon withered, prime minister Issoufou resigned in September for party political reasons; then his successor **Souley Abdoulaye** was voted out of office on a no confidence ballot. President Mahamane, faced with the loss of two governments in a single month, shied away from nominating a third prime minister, and instead called a general election and announced the dissolution of the national assembly.

The election, held in January 1995, gave a 43 to 40 seat majority to the opposition parties grouped under the banner of the *MNSD*, whose candidate for prime minister was **Hama Amadou**. Hama's cabinet was chosen entirely from the ranks of the opposition. Two women were among them – a new departure in Niger – but no associates of President Mahamane, the figurehead of the first wave of democratic reforms in the country. The political climate had come full circle.

Niger, in 1995, however, seemed ready for reconciliation. The new government came to a back-pay agreement with the unions, and repealed anti-strike legislation.

Most significantly, in Ouagadougou on April 15 the new government and the Tuareg rebels signed what was billed as a definitive and lasting peace accord – with Algerian, Burkinabe and French mediation (to many Nigériens the French are the least attractive partners in this as they have long been suspected of promoting Tuareg nationalist ideals with the aim of creating a Francophile Saharan state). The Tuareg rebels in Niger, organized as the **Armed Resistance Organization** (*ORA*) now consist of four groups: the **Tamoust Liberation Front** (*FLT*) led by Mano Dayak; the **Aïr and Azaouak Liberation Front** (*FLAA*) led by Rissa ag Boula; the **Revolutionary Army for the Liberation of Northern Niger** (*ARLN*) led by Mohammed Abdoulmoumine; and the **Patriotic Front for the Liberation of the Sahara** (*FPLS*) led by Mohammed Anako. The groups' agendas range from a long-term desire for total independence to better treatment and more autonomy within a unitary state. Whether peace will last depends on how much Niamey can deliver to the north, and on moves towards a decentralized state. An encouraging aspect of Niger's peace is that it does not have to deal with a self-defence militia of sedentary anti-Tuareg "blacks", like Mali's *Ganda Koi* militia, where the race question is uppermost.

■ Prospects

Economically, Niger has been a classic case of a country over-dependent on a **single resource** (uranium) and held hostage to fickle world market prices. The importance of improving agriculture is critical as only three percent of the land is arable. In addition to the vast **irrigation projects** that have been undertaken in regions around Tillabéri, Birnin-Konni and Dosso, there's been a positive trend towards smaller-scale projects involving co-operatives for individual farmers. With its huge public debt and limited possibilities for further credit, the new government will have to look increasingly to Niger's untapped resources to underwrite both future development and better prospects for stability. Investment will only come if issues such as the status of the Tuareg can be resolved.

As this book goes to press in August 1995, an issue that has so far barely made any impression is beginning to attract attention – **Islamic fundamentalism**. The government is firmly secular and wedded to the ideals of material progress; it aims to ban or suppress any large-scale Muslim demonstrations. The root causes of recent **disturbances** – in Maradi, where youths ransacked bars and accosted women for wearing non-Islamic dress, and in Kalouka north of Niamey, where gendarmes tried to arrest members of a sect for extortion and intimidation and somehow ended up shooting ten of them – need urgently addressing.

NIAMEY

As uranium money showered on Niger in the 1970s, **NIAMEY** changed almost overnight. Many of its dusty roads were paved, and a Voie Triomphale was traced through town, its bright streetlights blotting the Sahelian nights from memory. Avant-garde buildings such as the Palais des Congrès and, fittingly, the Office National de Recherches Minières were built, to be joined by futuristic hotels, banks and offices.

This development, however, was nowhere near as dramatic as in Abidjan or Lagos, however, and the juxtaposition between modernity and tradition, and city and country, works remarkably well here. The sight of camel caravans crossing the Niger River on the Kennedy Bridge hardly seems incongruous, and neither does the spectacle of Fula, Hausa, Tuareg and Djerma traders gathering at the Petit Marché under the shadow of high-rise office blocks.

As a place to stay, or live, however, Niamey leaves plenty to be desired. It's bigger and more aggressive than other Sahel capitals – Bamako or Ouagadougou for example – and is developing some notoriety for muggings and other unpleasant encounters. In compensation, it offers an outstanding museum, good markets and some pleasant retreats within a short drive of the city.

Some history

Before the colonial era, Niamey was no more than a small village whose origins probably didn't predate the eighteenth century. When French troops swarmed into the desert in the 1890s, they recognized the strategic importance of this spot on the river and dug in their heels. By 1902, it had grown into one of the most important military and administrative posts east of Bamako. When Niger officially became a colony, the larger urban centre at Zinder was chosen as the new capital, but the French administrators preferred Niamey's climate, and in 1926 they transferred the capital back again.

Throughout the colonial era, Niamey never developed much beyond the **European quarter** built in the plateau district. The population in the 1930s was under two thousand, though by independence it had increased to around thirty thousand. Real growth only occurred in the 1970s, with the population surging to over a quarter of a million by 1980. A great deal of the influx was caused by the **drought** of the mid-1970s, which sparked a rural exodus of Biblical proportions. Niamey, fattened on uranium income, flourished as immigrants from the devastated provinces poured into the city where they could hope to find food, housing and work. A second drought in the mid-1980s led to a new wave of immigration, forcing the city's population still higher. Today, it's estimated nearly 700,000 people live in Niamey, and virtually every ethnic group is represented here. This rapid growth, combined with the recent fall in the world price of uranium, has put huge strains on the city. Though Niamey provides comforts for travellers and expats with cash in their pockets, the benefits of modernization are now tempered by the spectre of shantytowns, mass unemployment and urban blight.

Arrival, city transport and information

Coming in by *taxi brousse* you're most likely to be let off at the *gare routière* in the **Wadata district**, about 4km from the centre. It's not difficult or expensive to get a taxi into town: **collective taxis** cost an average of CFA150 each, though at night drivers often ask twice that. If you take a cab for yourself it will cost around CFA1000 per short trip. During daylight hours, **city buses** also operate and work out a little cheaper than shared taxis, but there are no printed schedules or map routes, and even a trip to the

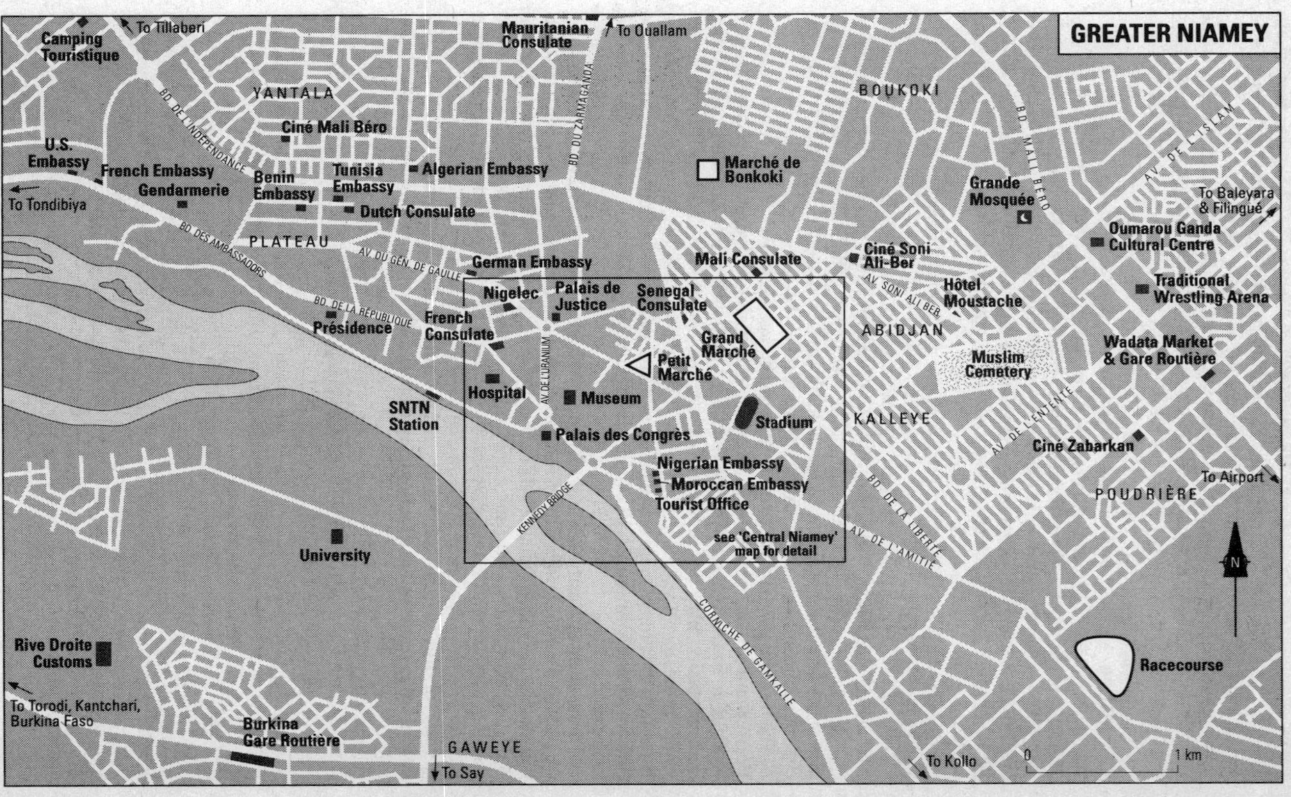
GREATER NIAMEY
Camping Touristique
To Tillaberi
Mauritanian Consulate
To Ouallam
YANTALA
BOUKOKI
BD. DE L'INDÉPENDANCE
BD. DU ZARMAGANDA
BD. MALI BÉRO
AV. DE L'ISLAM
Ciné Mali Béro
U.S. Embassy
French Embassy
Benin Embassy
Tunisia Embassy
Algerian Embassy
Marché de Bonkoki
Grande Mosquée
To Baleyara & Filingué
To Tondibiya
Gendarmerie
Dutch Consulate
Oumarou Ganda Cultural Centre
BD. DES AMBASSADORS
PLATEAU
Mali Consulate
Ciné Soni Ali-Ber
AV. DU GÉN. DE GAULLE
German Embassy
Traditional Wrestling Arena
Nigelec
Palais de Justice
Senegal Consulate
AV. SONI ALI BER
Hôtel Moustache
BD. DE LA RÉPUBLIQUE
French Consulate
Présidence
ABIDJAN
Grand Marché
Wadata Market & Gare Routière
Muslim Cemetery
Petit Marché
AV. DE L'URANIUM
Hospital
Museum
SNTN Station
Stadium
KALLEYE
AV. DE L'ENTENTE
Palais des Congrès
Ciné Zabarkan
Nigerian Embassy
Moroccan Embassy
To Airport
Tourist Office
POUDRIÈRE
KENNEDY BRIDGE
BD. DE LA LIBERTÉ
AV. DE L'AMITIÉ
see 'Central Niamey' map for detail
University
N
CORNICHE DE GAMKALLÉ
Rive Droite Customs
Racecourse
To Torodi, Kantchari, Burkina Faso
Burkina Gare Routière
GAWEYE
To Say
To Kollo
0
1 km

SNTN office on the Corniche de Yantala (☎72.30.23) may not help you sort it out. Though you'll see signs marking bus stops scattered throughout the town, there's no way of knowing where the bus is going except by asking.

Niamey's **airport** (☎73.23.81) is 12km southeast of the city centre on the bd de l'Amitié/bd du 15 Avril. Unfortunately, buses don't shuttle into the centre, so you'll have to take a cab. Expect to pay about CFA3000.

Information

While the *Office National du Tourisme* on rue Luebke (BP 612; ☎73.24.47; Fax 72.33.47) is not much help with the sort of in-Niamey tourist office enquries you might well have – apart from possibly being able to sell you a city map, and give you a few leaflets – it is useful for organizing excursions to places like the Parc National du "W" du Niger, their prices comparing favourably with those of travel agents.

Orientation

Niamey spreads along 7km of the Niger's left (north) bank, and has now expanded to the other side of the river. The size of the city makes it difficult to get an immediate grip on its layout – a problem compounded by the French-style planning, with numerous roundabouts and streets that rarely run parallel.

You'll spend virtually your whole time on the left bank. To define a centre, use the **Pont Kennedy** as a landmark. To the north of the bridge, rue de Gaweye leads straight up to the **Grand Marché**, bordered by boulevard de la Liberté. The entire **commercial centre** lies between this new market and the river, and this is where you'll come to shop, eat, change money, and visit sights such as the **Musée National**. Two important commercial buildings along rue de Gaweye are **Immeuble Sonara II** and **Immeuble El Nasr**. Many embassies and airline offices are located in them.

To the **west of Pont Kennedy**, avenue F Mitterrand runs past the impressive *Hôtel Gaweye* as it heads towards the tree-lined avenues of the **Plateau district**. This colonial-looking neighbourhood is where most government ministries are located, along with the Palais du Président and many of the embassies. Continuing west, you come to the underdeveloped **Yantala district**, which you'll become familiar with if you stay at the *camping* near the entrance to town on the Tillabéri road.

East of the bridge, the rue du Sahel leads to the residential neighbourhoods known collectively as the **Niamey Bas** district. Streets are comfortably shady in this

SECURITY

Once a traveller's haven, Niamey has in recent years acquired a rough edge. Though townspeople throw up their hands and sigh "c'est la démocratie", increasing crime probably has more to do with Niger's dismal economy, which is even more severe since the drastic decline in trans-Saharan trade.

Petty theft is commonplace, and the principal area to avoid is the **river bank on the north side**, especially the stretch along the Corniche between the *Grand Hôtel* in the east, past the Pont Kennedy, to the *SNTN* bus station in the west. Muggings at knife point, and in broad daylight, occur often here and anyone carrying a bag that seems to contain cameras, money or valuables is a target. The area around the **Petit Marché** can seem tense, though given the volume of people, the greatest danger here – and incidentally, in front of the banks – is posed by pickpockets. Apart from these areas, the town still feels quite safe even to walk at night, and by taking precautions (like leaving all bags at your hotel) you're not likely to feel, or be, threatened.

area, where you'll find a good number of hotels and restaurants. Further east, Niamey Bas gives onto the **Gamkalé district** and then to the capital's **industrial zone**.

Accommodation

Although Niamey has a number of mid-range and expensive **hotels**, there are few in the cheaper brackets. Some relief is provided by a couple of shabby places in the centre that can put you up at reasonable rates – and by the **campground** out of town.

ACCOMMODATION PRICE CODES

① Under CFA4000 (under £5/$7.50).
② CFA4000–8000 (£5–10/$7.50–15).
③ CFA8000–16,000 (£10–20/$15–30).
④ CFA16,000–24,000 (£20–30/$30–45).
⑤ CFA24,000–32,000 (£30–40/$45–60).
⑥ CFA32,000–40,000 (£40–50/$60–75).
⑦ Over CFA40,000 (over £50/$75).

For further information see the "Accommodation" section in the Practical Information pages at the beginning of this chapter.

Budget accommodation and camping

Camping Touristique, rte de Tillabéri, Yantala district. A well-run site with decent showers and toilets. Ideal if you have a car, but a little out of the way otherwise. Very noisy bar tends to stay open until late. A bus stops nearby every 10–15 minutes on its way to the centre. ①.

Hôtel Le Dé, off the bd de la Liberté and rue du Maroc. Niamey's cheapest rooms, and central enough, but it's very grimy and the downstairs bar may keep you awake. ①.

Hôtel Moustache, rue du Cameroun, north of bd de la Liberté (☎73.42.82). Another inexpensive alternative, a bit further from the centre. S/C rooms with AC; cheaper accommodation is usually reserved for hourly guests. ②.

Mid-range hotels

Hôtel Maourey, Rond-Point Maourey (☎73.28.50). A good location about halfway between the Grand Marché and the Petit Marché. Not nearly up to the standards of hotels like the *Terminus*, but its decent S/C rooms with AC are very reasonably priced. ④.

Hôtel Rivoli, rue Luebke (☎73.38.49). Once a popular place among overlanders, often seen drumming up business with local hustlers – notably car dealers – in the bar. Now it's virtually empty, and in sad decline. ③.

Les Roniers, Tondibia road, about 7km from the centre (BP 795; ☎72.31.38). Far from the centre and suffering from a lack of overlanders, which perhaps explains its good value. Bungalows are grouped around a park with swimming pool, near the river. ③.

Hôtel du Sahel, rue du Sahel (BP 627; ☎73.24.31). Well-maintained and comfortable, with 35 AC rooms (some facing the river), restaurant, disco and various crafts boutiques. ④.

Hôtel Terminus, rue du Sahel, near rue du Terminus (BP 882; ☎73.26.92). Good value, with 38 AC bungalows around a well-kept garden, swimming pool, bar and restaurant. ④.

Luxury hotels

Hôtel Gaweye Sofitel, place Kennedy, near the Palais des Congrès and the river (BP 11008; ☎72.34.00). The most distinguished and luxurious – but impersonal – of Niamey's hotels; 248 rooms, with river or town views, plus pool, tennis courts, restaurants, bars and nightclubs. ⑦.

Grand Hôtel, place de la Fraternité (BP 471; ☎73.26.41). Colonial-style hotel which holds its own against more modern competitors, partly because of its striking location overlooking the river. Comfortable rooms and 35 bungalows plus pool and restaurant. Best value in this category. ⑤–⑥.

Hôtel Ténéré, bd de la Liberté (☎73.39.20). Part of the *PLM* chain, the *Ténéré* has 55 very comfortable AC rooms, a pool, conference rooms and the usual abundance of restaurants and bars. ⑤.

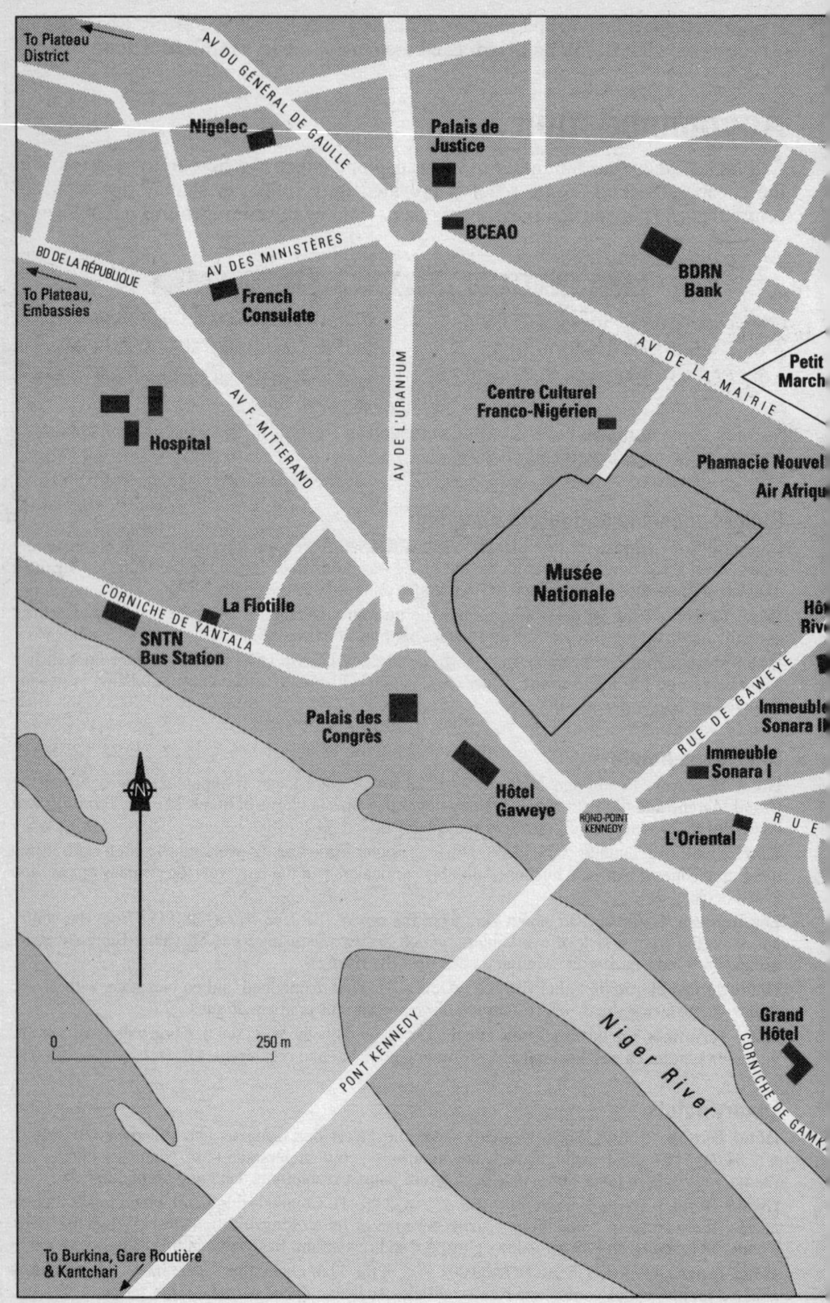
To Plateau District
AV DU GÉNÉRAL DE GAULLE
Nigelec
Palais de Justice
BCEAO
BDRN Bank
BD DE LA RÉPUBLIQUE
AV DES MINISTÈRES
To Plateau, Embassies
French Consulate
AV DE L'URANIUM
AV DE LA MAIRIE
Petit March
Centre Culturel Franco-Nigérien
AV F. MITTERAND
Hospital
Phamacie Nouvel
Air Afriq
Musée Nationale
CORNICHE DE YANTALA
La Flotille
SNTN Bus Station
Palais des Congrès
RUE DE GAWEYE
Immeubl Sonara I
Immeuble Sonara I
Hôtel Gaweye
ROND-POINT KENNEDY
L'Oriental
RUE
0
250 m
PONT KENNEDY
Niger River
Grand Hôtel
CORNICHE DE GAMK
To Burkina, Gare Routière & Kantchari

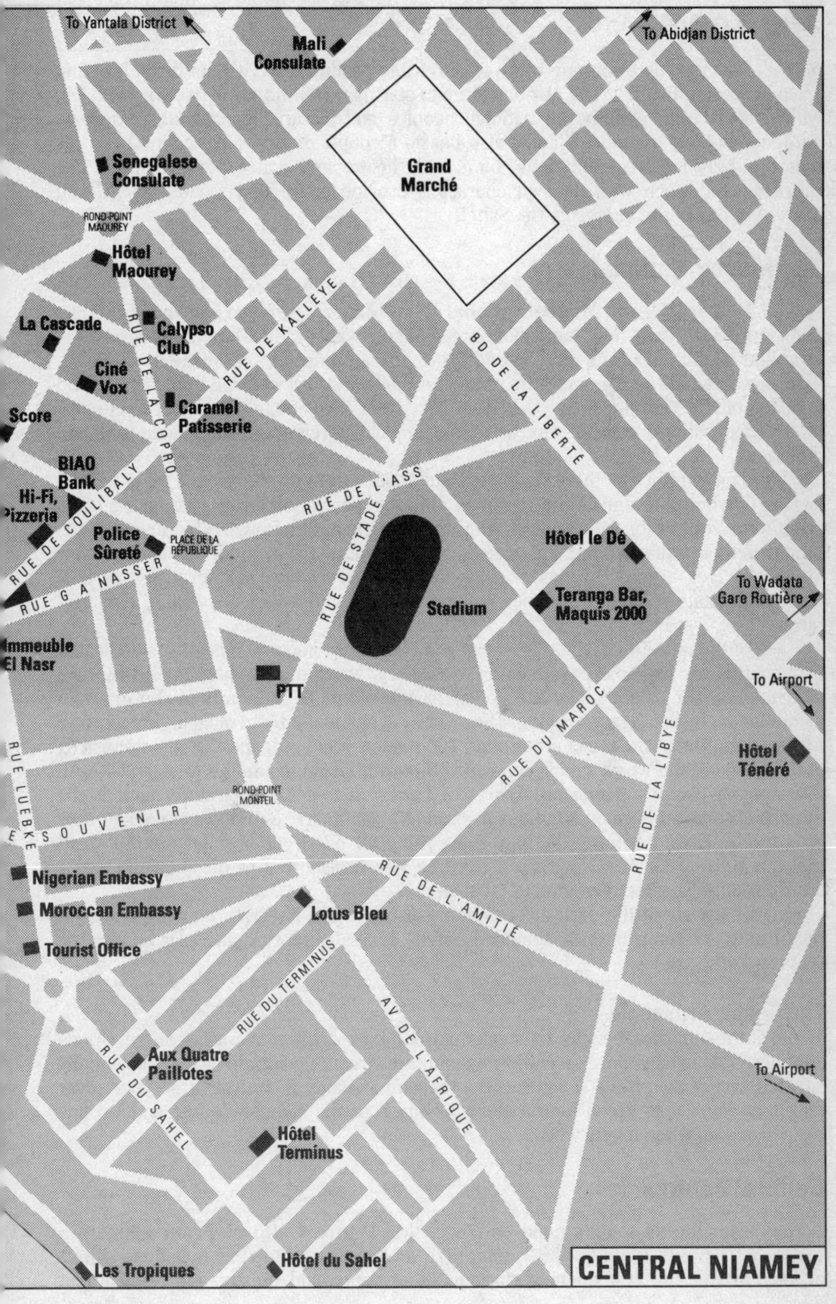
To Yantala District
To Abidjan District
Mali Consulate
Grand Marché
Senegalese Consulate
ROND-POINT MAOUREY
Hôtel Maourey
La Cascade
Calypso Club
RUE DE KALLEYE
RUE DE LA COPRO
Ciné Vox
Caramel Patisserie
Score
BD DE LA LIBERTÉ
BIAO Bank
Hi-Fi, Pizzeria
RUE DE COULIBALY
RUE DE L'ASS
Police Sûreté
PLACE DE LA RÉPUBLIQUE
RUE DE STADE
Hôtel le Dé
RUE G A NASSER
To Wadata Gare Routière
Teranga Bar, Maquis 2000
Stadium
Immeuble El Nasr
PTT
To Airport
RUE DU MAROC
Hôtel Ténéré
RUE DE LA LIBYE
RUE LUEBKE
ROND-POINT MONTEIL
SOUVENIR
RUE DE L'AMITIÉ
Nigerian Embassy
Moroccan Embassy
Lotus Bleu
Tourist Office
RUE DU TERMINUS
AV DE L'AFRIQUE
Aux Quatre Paillotes
To Airport
RUE DU SAHEL
Hôtel Terminus
Les Tropiques
Hôtel du Sahel
CENTRAL NIAMEY

The Town

Niamey isn't exactly brimming with pleasures and pastimes, but it's not difficult to find ways of passing the day. The obvious place to start is the **National Museum** complex, which, apart from exhibits on national peoples and culture, incorporates extensive gardens, a zoo and shops. Niamey also boasts a couple of innovative cultural centres that regularly feature exhibitions, films and theatre and dance performances. The **markets**, too, each with its own character, provide active diversions – the Grand Marché is one of the biggest in the Sahel.

The Musée National

Inaugurated in 1959, the **Musée National** (Nov–March, Tues–Sun 9am–noon & 3.30–6pm; April–Oct Tues–Sun 9am–noon & 4–6.30pm) was a radical breakthrough at the time and is still out on its own among West African museums. Contained within the extensive grounds are the museum exhibition halls, a zoo, a working crafts centre and a village of Nigérien housing styles. The place feels alive and, especially at weekends, is crowded with an eclectic mix of young and old, foreign and local, scholarly and illiterate.

The main entrance to the grounds is from a side street off the avenue de la Mairie. Before heading into one of the pavilions housing the exhibition spaces, take a stroll around the **zoo** – especially popular with the young kids from town. A big draw are the hippos in their artificial pond, but cages scattered around the grounds display the other fauna of Niger – lions, hyenas, various monkeys, crocodiles and tortoises, all in a reasonable state of health. Aviaries contain vultures and a variety of more colourful birds.

Each of the museum pavilions – of stylized Hausa architectural design – is dedicated to a theme: for example costumes and jewellery, weapons, handicrafts and musical instruments. The paleontology and botany pavilion contains **dinosaur skeletons** from Gadoufaoua, in the Agadez region. Discovered accidentally by geologists prospecting for uranium, these skeletons are around 100 million years old, and the remote district is today one of the world's most renowned dinosaur sites outside the western USA. In the same pavilion is the amazing **Arbre du Ténéré**, a tree that once stood alone in the Ténéré desert and became a famous overlanders' landmark, until it was knocked over by a truck driver. Formerly the only living thing for hundreds of miles around – and still marked on the *Michelin* map – the tree was transported to the museum and a sturdy steel replacement erected in the desert.

In a far corner of the park are examples of traditional Nigérien housing – a good opportunity to compare Fula thatched cones, Hausa mudbrick and plaster, Tuareg tents and other styles.

The Centre Artisanale

While at the museum, be sure to check out the *Centre Artisanale* **crafts centre**. Goods sold here are usually more expensive than on the streets (in certain cases substantially so), but part of the profits subsidizes the museum. Quality is controlled, so your silver jewellery won't turn green hours after you buy it or the camel-hide bag smell suspiciously of goat when it gets wet.

Cultural centres

Across from the museum's main entrance, the **Centre Culturel Franco-Nigérien** (Tues–Sat, 9am–12.30pm & 4.30–7.30pm) has an active schedule that includes exhibits of local artists and craftsmen, performances of dance and theatre and regular film screenings. You can stop by and pick up their events programme, or check the pages of *Le Sahel*.

Also check the paper for the schedule of the **Centre Culturel Oumarou-Ganda**, named after the late, great Nigérien film-maker and right across on the other side of town on bd Mali Bero near the Grande Mosquée. The centre has an open-air amphitheatre where concerts of traditional music, ballet and theatre are often staged.

The **Centre Culturel Americain** also sponsors events and runs American news programmes and movies. It's located near *Nigelec*, the state electricity supplier; ask a taxi to drop you there, and then follow the dirt side street behind the *Elf* station.

The markets

Niamey's **Grand Marché** (daily until sunset) – also called the Nouveau Marché – reopened in 1986 after being completely devastated by fire. The new building makes a decidedly modern statement, with monumental entrance gates and a fountain or two for show, yet the smooth lines and earth tones still respect the more traditional styles of the Sahel. Inside, paved alleys lead through a maze of merchant stalls grouped into sections according to wares – clothing and fabrics; soaps, cosmetics and pharmaceuticals; hardware; ironmongery and utensils, and so forth. Along with the main market in Ouagadougou, this is one of West Africa's finest.

Further south in the **Zongo district**, where rue du Président Luebke and avenue de la Mairie intersect, the **Petit Marché** has a more casual flavour. Merchants who can't secure a space in one of the Grand Marché stalls simply clear space on the ground and set up shop. It's primarily a **food** market, and you'll find a good selection of fruits and vegetables, meat, fish and grains. People from all over the country converge here to buy and sell – a wide mixture of Fula, Djerma, Tuareg and Hausa. Nearby streets give way to **crafts** stands, which are reasonable places to pick up jewellery, leather goods or blankets – but dealers tend to be aggressive and bargaining can turn into a battle.

There's another small market, devoted entirely to **pottery**, across from the tall *BDRN* bank down avenue de la Mairie – look for the beautiful hand-painted water pots produced in the village of Tondibia, just outside Niamey.

Several communities have their own **neighbourhood markets**, usually specializing in everyday domestic goods. At the **Marché Boukoki,** north of bd de l'Indépendance near the *Lycée*, vendors sell firewood, calabashes, mats, scrap metal and small livestock. In other districts, you'll find the **Marché Yantala** (along bd de la République) and the **Marché Gamkalé** (on the Kollo road).

Eating and drinking

Niamey has a number of upmarket restaurants, and **street vendors** are making a comeback after a period of official harassment. In the mornings there's a *caféman* on every busy corner, while evening stalls sell *fufu*, rice, macaroni or *tô* (cornmeal dough).

Inexpensive

During the day, you can get really cheap food at the Petit Marché, the Grand Marché or the *gare routière*. For street food after dark – notably beef brochettes or fried omelettes with onions, tomatoes and *Maggi* sauce – head for the places around rue de Kabekoira, especially in the general area of the *Ciné Vox*.

Calypso Club, rue de la Copro, near *Hôtel Maourey*. Typical outdoor bar where the Béninois chef cooks up, among other things, some of the tenderest brochettes you'll ever taste. Good music and quite lively at night. Recommended.

Caramel (Chez Michel), rue de la Copro. Pastry shop with decent, affordable croissants, brioches and sandwiches (homemade bread).

Snack Bar La Cloche, near the corner of rue Luebke and rue du Coulibaly. Salads, sandwiches and *chawarma* just a stone's throw from the Petit Marché. An expat haunt.

L'Islam, av de l'Arewa, near av Soni Ali Ber. No alcohol, but copious servings of a daily African *plat du jour*. Good value for money.

Le Meridian, rue Coulibaly next to *BIAO* bank. Fast-food stand serving burgers and *chawarma*.

Buvette de la Piscine, behind the *piscine olympique* on rue du Sahel, near the *Hôtel du Sahel*. Hardly a soul in the day, when it offers cheap beer and a view not to be missed – as good as that from any of the expensive hotel *terrasses*. At night this is a popular restaurant serving inexpensive grilled chicken; occasionally music and dancing. Take a cab; it's a bit dodgy to walk here after dark.

La Poêle Bleu, pl Liberté, a few blocks from the Grand Marché. Extensive menu includes omelettes, steak sandwiches, freshly made yoghurt. Very good prices.

Le Refuge, rue du Maroc, near *Hôtel Le Dé*. Courtyard African place, where the *plat du jour* will set you back little more than CFA1000.

Le Tango, opposite *Ciné Vox* near the Petit Marché. Wonderfully seedy bar with wide assortment of street food sold in front. Next door, *Le Regal* has inexpensive burgers, sandwiches and other quick eats.

Teranga Bar, one block north of rue du Maroc and two blocks south of bd de la Liberté. One of the best African restaurants in town. Meticulously maintained gardens with flowering bougainvillea. Rice, pasta or *couscous* with *capitain*, beef or tripe. Always crowded.

Bar La Terrasse, av de l'Islam. Courtyard bar with, in the evenings, rice and macaroni served with fish or mutton.

Moderate

From Italian pizza to Ivoirian *poisson braisé*, it's possible to treat yourself to something a little out of the ordinary without spending too much.

Aux Quatre Paillotes, rue du Sahel. Formerly known as *Au Feu du Bois*, this restaurant still features well-prepared African specialities in the indoor restaurant or in the large courtyard shaded by the namesake *paillotes*.

Le Croissant d'Or, av Coulibaly. *Patisserie* patronized by French expats – a good sign if you crave something sweet.

Damsi, Immeuble Sonara I. Expensive French-style fast food.

Maquis 2000, near *Hôtel le Dé* and next to *Teranga Bar*. Slightly upmarket Ivoirian food, featuring *fruits de mer* and *grillades*.

Marhaba, off rue de Kalleye, near the Grand Marché. "Discovered" by Peace Corps workers and other expats, the chop-house meals at around CFA3000 may seem pricey, but it's a good place to meet people.

Mickey's, rue du Sahel next to the *Hôtel du Sahel*. A big expat hangout (nice sunset views across the river) with beer on tap and very reasonably priced brochettes and fries.

La Pizzeria, rue du Coulibaly, next to *HiFi*. Niamey's best pizza, using real mozzarella and fresh vegetables.

Tapoa, rue du Terminus, near *Hôtel Terminus*. First drink is free with your meal. Big plates of food for around CFA2500.

Foyer Zela, rue Soni Ali Ber, directly across from *Moustache*. Ivoirian-style *maquis* in attractive courtyard. *Poisson braisé* or *poulet kedjenou* with plantains or *frites*, and *à la carte* choices also available if you have time.

Expensive

Niamey has a surprisingly good selection of upmarket places to eat, including classy restaurants specializing in exotic cuisines such as Russian or Vietnamese – with the raw ingredients usually imported direct from France.

African and Middle Eastern

Diamangou, Corniche de Gamkalé (☎73.51.43). French and African dishes served aboard a boat docked in the Niger – one of the town's more interesting venues.

L'Oriental, near the Rond-Point Kennedy, towards the rue Luebke (☎72.20.15). Niamey's best Lebanese food.

European

La Cascade, near the *Ciné Vox* (☎73.28.32). Best French restaurant in town, specializing in fish with a variety of interesting sauces. Good wine list, and reasonably priced.

La Flotille, Corniche de Yantala (☎72.32.54). Russian food cooked by a native. French specialities are also on the menu of this very good – and accordingly expensive – restaurant.

Hôtel Gaweye Sofitel, place Kennedy. Lavish Sunday breakfast buffet (8–11am), about CFA4000.

La Reserve, rue du Grand Hôtel (☎73.21.05). Delicious, upmarket French cuisine: *foie gras*, *langoustes* and *noisettes d'agneau*. Excellent desserts.

Tabakady, near the PTT (☎73.58.18). Another well-known French restaurant whose traditional cooking gets high marks from the French community, offering unusual (at least for this part of the globe) items such as oysters or salmon.

Les Tropiques, Corniche de Gamkalé. Popular with expats for the French food and the lively disco ambience. Especially crowded at weekends when you can dance under the stars until the wee hours. For safety's sake, take a cab there and back.

Oriental

Dragon d'Or, rue du Grand Hôtel (☎73.41.23). Wide variety of Chinese food including soups, spring rolls, sweet and sour pork and the like.

Lotus Bleu, av de l'Afrique (☎73.21.05). Excellent Vietnamese food; stiff competition for *Le Vietnam*.

Le Vietnam, rue du Terminus (☎73.26.46). Probably Niamey's best Vietnamese food.

Nightlife

Niamey nights are very low-key, and eating is the principal after-dark pleasure. The bigger hotels have **discos** – the *Kakaki* at the *Gaweye* and the *Fofo* at the *Sahel* – with high covers and expensive drinks; the latter is the looser of the two, and on weekends can be quite fun. Of the **downtown clubs** the *Takoubakoyé*, near the *Rivoli*, still draws an enthusiastic crowd, though its popularity is seriously challenged by the energetic – at weekends anyway – *Hi-Fi* just a block away on rue du Coulibaly. The *Pacha* (formerly *Satellite*) in the Immeuble El Nasr is another stylish disco with the typical cover that assures an upmarket, though none the less upbeat, clientele.

Less expensive entertainment can be found at the *Niamey Club* on rue du Coulibaly near the *Rivoli*. For a small cover, it has good music and occasional live bands, though locally it's known as a bar that caters to Europeans – especially tourists – and is clogged with prostitutes after dark. The *Calypso Club* near the *Hôtel Maourey* is generally more satisfying, but although this outdoor bar often breaks into dance in the evening (especially Friday and Saturday), there's no guarantee of it. Another popular spot with (mainly French) expats is *Les Tropiques* near the river on the Corniche de Gamkalé. Good music and a pleasant outdoor dance area assure a consistent crowd that really gets going at the weekend.

Listings

Banks Banks are on, or near, av de la Mairie. The two most convenient are the *BIAO* (which does Access/Mastercard cash advances) and the *BDRN*. *Citibank* also has a branch in Niamey (☎73.36.20).

AIRLINE OFFICES IN NIAMEY

Most of the following are in the area of the Petit Marché, near the *Rivoli*.

Air Afrique, Immeuble Air Afrique, rue Luebke (BP 11090; ☎73.30.11).

Air Algérie, Immeuble Rivoli (BP 10818; ☎73.38.98).

Air France, Immeuble Sonara I (BP 10935; ☎73.31.61).

Air Mali, (BP 8; ☎73.31.89).

Ethiopian Airlines, Immeuble Sonara (BP 11051; ☎73.50.52 or 73.50.53).

Nigeria Airways, Immeuble El Nasr (BP 714; ☎73.32.58).

Royal Air Maroc, Immeuble Air Afrique, rue Luebke

Sabena, Immeuble El Nasr (BP 11656; ☎73.23.20 or 73.23.21).

Books Try *Camico*, near the Score supermarket on av de la Mairie, or *Papeterie Burama*, on rue de la Copro, near the *Hôtel Maourey*.

Car rental *Hertz* is represented at the *Hôtel Gaweye* and has an office at the airport. Other options are *Niger-Car* in the Immeuble El Nasr (☎72.23.31) or *Sonauto* at the *Hôtel Terminus*. The tourist office can also set you up with a rental agency.

Cinemas The *Studio* (☎73.37.69) – an AC place with perhaps the town's newest films – and the *Vox* (☎73.32.19) – an outdoor theatre where old action films often play – are downtown near the Petit Marché. In other districts, you'll find the *Cinema Soni Ali-Ber* (Haut Niamey), the *Cinéma Zarbakan* off the av de l'Entente (Poudrière), and the *Cinema HD* (Yantala).

Maps The *Direction de la Topographie* off bd de la République in Yantala, near the French embassy, has 1:50,000 and 1:200,000 coverage of the country. Although there are restrictions on the availability of all survey maps, these are not always applied.

Newspapers and magazines A sprinkling of international papers (mostly French) and news magazines such as *Time* and *Newsweek* are sold in the *Hôtel Gaweye* bookshop. Check also the *tabac* in the Rivoli Arcade, the *Camico Papeterie*, av de la Mairie, near the *Score* supermarket, and the *Papeterie Burama*, between av Coulibaly and the *Hôtel Maourey*. For browsing, there's also the library of the American Cultural Centre.

EMBASSIES AND CONSULATES IN NIAMEY

Algeria, off av de l'Imazer (BP 142; ☎72.31.65).

Benin, Plateau district (BP 11544; ☎72.39.19).

Canada, Immeuble Sonara, II (☎73.36.86).

Egypt, Nouveau Plateau (☎73.33.55).

France, Embassy: Tillabéri road, Yantala district (BP 10660; ☎72.24.31).
Consulate: by the hospital roundabout (BP 607; ☎72.27.22 or 72.27.33).
Visas issued for Côte d'Ivoire, Togo, Burkina Faso and Chad.

Germany, av du Général de Gaulle (BP 629; ☎72.25.34).

Italy, Consulate (☎72.32.91).

Mali, bd de la Liberté next to the Grand Marché (☎72.28.83)

Mauritania, off bd Mali Béro, Yantala district (BP 12519; ☎72.38.93).

Morocco, rue Luebke (BP 12403; ☎73.40.84).

Nigeria, rue Luebke (BP 11130; ☎73.24.10).

Tunisia, av du Général de Gaulle (BP 742; ☎72.26.03).

United Kingdom, Honorary Vice Consulate, (BP 11168; ☎73.20.15 or 73.25.39).
The British honorary vice-consul, B Niandou, who speaks no English, works in the main
Elf (formerly *BP*) offices on the rte de l'Aéroport, 2km from the centre.

USA, bd des Ambassades, Yantala district (BP 11201l; ☎72.26.21).

Pharmacies Almost every *quartier* has a small neighbourhood pharmacy. Two of the most central and best stocked are: *Pharmacie Kaocen* on the rue du Coulibaly (☎73 54 54) and the *Pharmacie Nouvelle* next to *Air Afrique*.

Post office The PTT is on rue de Kabekoira, down from the *Sûreté National*, with efficient poste restante and phone services.

Supermarkets The best of the European-style supermarkets is *Score* on av de la Mairie. It's completely AC and a carbon copy of a Parisian *supermarché* – from the shopping trolleys down to the boxed Camembert. Vegetables and fruit are flown in directly from France – for which you'll pay prices two to three times higher than at source. Next door, *Peyrissac* is somewhere between a department store and discount hardware store. They may have hard-to-find camping supplies.

Swimming pools Non-guests may pay to use the pools of the three major hotels – the *Ténéré*, the *Grand* and the *Gaweye*. The last is the nicest, most central and priciest. Less expensive than any of the above is the *piscine olympique* on rue du Sahel, near the *Hôtel du Sahel*. On most days, you'll have the whole place to yourself.

MOVING ON FROM NIAMEY

BUSH TAXI AND BUS TRANSPORT FROM WADATA

Peugeot 504s and Japanese minibuses head from the main **Wadata gare routière** north to Tillabéri, south to Dosso and Gaya, east to Birnin-Konni, Maradi and Zinder and north-east to Tahoua and Agadez (the latter subject to security considerations). Private buses covering the same destinations also leave from this *autogare*. Likewise, taxis for most international destinations – Lomé, Kano or Cotonou, for example – leave from Wadata.

TRANSPORT TO BURKINA AND SAY

Taxis to Burkina leave from the Rive Droite – across the river from town, near the Douane. This is also where you can catch a *taxi brousse* to Say and possibly on to Tamou (for the Parc National du "W"). To leave quickly, it's best to break up the trip, paying for a seat for anything heading in the direction of Kantchari, the Burkinabe border town. From here, you can catch another bush taxi or, if you arrive fortuitously, the more comfortable Burkinabe *Sans Frontières* bus that leaves daily for Ouagadougou. Arrive early in the morning as traffic on this stretch is far from dense and after midday, you could wait hours for a vehicle.

SNTN BUSES

The depot for the more comfortable and expensive **SNTN buses** is on the Corniche de Yantala (☎72.30.20), west of the *Hôtel Gaweye*. Take a taxi to the "station" as muggings are frequent along this stretch of the river bank. There are three buses a week for Ouagadougou (Tues, Wed & Thurs, departure 7am) and a bus for Gao on Sundays (security permitting). Buses for Arlit – calling at Tahoua and Agadez – leave Mon, Wed, and Fri afternoons, again subject to security considerations. A further service heads to Zinder, with stops in Birnin-Konni and Maradi, on Mon, Wed and Sat. Call *SNTN* to confirm times as schedules may vary and are never printed or posted in town. Buy tickets in advance to assure a seat.

FLIGHTS AND TRAVEL AGENTS

You can often get good deals on **flights to Europe** from Niamey, notably with *Air Algérie*, and *Royal Air Maroc* has recently had $300 one-way fares **to New York**, including an overnight in Casablanca. For the most current information, contact the airlines direct. Among the **travel agents**, *Transcap Voyages* in the Immeuble El Nasr (☎73.36.36) and *Temet Voyages* (☎72.34.00), both of which formerly specialized in trips to the now off-limits Aïr Mountains and Ténéré desert, now focus mainly on the Parc National du "W" du Niger.

Visa extensions Get your stay permit extended at the Sûreté, on the corner of rue Nasser and av de la Mairie.

Wrestling Just down from the *Centre Culturel Oumarou-Ganda*, on bd Mali Bero, the *Arène des Jeux Traditionels* is a good place to check out a *lutte traditionelle*, at which Niger excels. Scan the paper for announcements.

SOUTHWEST NIGER

Southwest Niger is the greenest and most densely populated part of the country. As well as being an important crossroads for travel between Nigeria, Benin and Burkina, there are some worthwhile destinations in the region, just a few hours' travel out of Niamey, including superb markets to the northeast, and pleasant riverside excursion areas just north of the city.

North of Niamey, the scenic road to Gao in Mali, via **Tillabéri** (the end of the tarmac) and **Ayorou**, hugs the river most of the way. Beyond Ayorou, however (200km north of Niamey and 50km before the Malian border), the route is these days normally considered too dangerous to be used by travellers: most embassies strongly advise against going any further north up-river. Since the early 1990s and the Tuareg rebellion, anywhere north of Ayorou has been under threat. People still travel along the road, both on public transport and in their own vehicles, but tourist cars have been spotted limping into Niamey with bullet holes and smashed windshields, and *SNTN* buses have been hijacked, the passengers robbed and left on the road. Make careful enquiries about the situation before setting out north from Tillabéri.

The **districts south of Niamey** are not affected by the rebellion. A paved road runs the whole way down to the Niger-Nigeria-Benin border at Gaya, but it's less interesting scenically than the route north of Niamey. A second southbound route traces the west bank of the river on tarmac to **Say**, before reverting to *piste* en route to Niger's only game reserve, the **Parc National du "W" du Niger**.

Northeast of Niamey: market towns

For a change of pace and a taste of Nigérien rural life, make a trip a few hours out of the city to the northeast. Taxis head daily from Niamey along the scenic route to **Filingué**, passing through the market towns of **Baleyara** – itself worth a day trip from the capital – and **Bonkoukou**. Considerable regional commerce derives from crop and livestock production, and the paved road runs along a water-worn valley – a vestige of a river that once flowed south from the Sahara into the Niger. It's inspiring scenery, with rugged cliffs and hills, all 197 kilometres of the way to Filingué. If you're heading for Tahoua and Agadez, this route provides an alternative to the main highway via Birnin-Konni.

Baleyara

Although the name **BALEYARA** (97km from Niamey) roughly translates "where Bellah come together", it is primarily a Djerma settlement, where Tuareg, Hausa and Fula people come to trade at the gigantic **Sunday market**. The animal market is well known throughout western Niger, and for days before the market caravans can be seen wending their way towards the village. This is also one of the best places to find handwoven Fula and Djerma blankets, leather goods, and intricately carved calabashes. There's really nowhere to stay in Baleyara, but there are several bars and no shortage of street food. Unfortunately, if you're unlucky there may be several groups of Europeans out of town for the day and on such occasions the local kids can be obnoxious and the atmosphere unrelaxed.

Bonkoukou and Filingué

Beyond Baleyara, the road follows the **Dallol Bosso** – a rich valley cut out centuries ago by run-off waters from the Aïr Mountains. Another large depression, the **Dallol Boboy**, extends north of **BONKOUKOU** – a town of semi-sedentary Tuareg that holds an impressive Saturday market. You have to work hard to find crafts at Bonkoukou, but they are here.

A Hausa settlement and administrative town, with characteristic architecture (note the *chef du canton*'s house), **FILINGUÉ** boasts another important regional market, though it's less impressive than the two described above. On Sundays, the town snaps into life as traders make their way from the countryside and converge on the market square. Herds of livestock file in and are sold beside millet and other regional produce, and you'll find good buys on crafts ranging from pottery to woven blankets and mats. Filingué is the only town along the route with **accommodation** – *La Villa Verte* (①), a substandard *campement* with bucket showers and kerosene lamps. There's a filling station in town, and a pharmacy, though little else in terms of services apart from a couple of small canned goods stores.

Transport to **Tahoua**, 225km beyond Filingué, depends on demand created by local market days. The main route – subject to deviations during the rains – passes through **Talcho** (where the tarred surface ends) then veers eastward through an agricultural region dotted with Hausa villages, the largest of which are **Sanam** (market Tuesday), **Chéguénaron**, and **Tébaram**.

North of Niamey

A small village on the banks of the Niger, **BOUBON** has become a popular weekend rural getaway for Niamey's expatriates. The town is some 25km north of the capital, approached by a small *piste* leading west from the main paved road; **taxis from Niamey** leave for Boubon from in front of the Petit Marché. The village is especially known for its handmade pottery, sold in vast quantities in Niamey's markets, and is also good for bird-watching. There's **accommodation** on **Boubon Island**, reached by *pirogue* from the mainland. Here you'll find a government-run *campement* with nicely set-up huts, a swimming pool, bar and restaurant. Reservations can be made in Niamey (☎73.24.47; ②).

A WALK ALONG THE NIGER

If you've missed out on seeing riverside village life from a *pirogue*, a viable, albeit arduous, alternative is to take the four-hour **hike from Farié to Gothèye**. The path takes you close to the Niger through a series of small villages surrounded by vegetable gardens and mango orchards. After the rains, rice is grown in the shallows, but a short distance inland, the verdure soon gives way to Sahelian savannah with cattle and goats getting meagre nourishment from the gleanings of the harvest. Occasional water holes provide some good **bird-watching** opportunities: golden orioles are common.

The Djerma-speakers who inhabit the villages are unused to tourists, especially those on foot, and are keen to communicate – even if "Ça ba?" is about the limit of the conversation. The general greeting in Djerma, *Fofo* (literally "Thank you"), goes a long way in breaking the ice.

There are plenty of opportunities to **camp** along the river bank, but you'll need to bring everything with you. Supplies in the whole region are sparse. From the Niamey–Tillabéri road, it is 2km down to the vehicle ferry at Farié which crosses every hour during the day (10min). A **path** then leads upstream from the tiny market on the far side and stays roughly parallel to the road.

Continuing upstream, the *Complexe Touristique de Namaro* (☎73.21.13; ②) perches on a hilltop above the village of **NAMARO** on the west bank. Comprising bungalows, a pool and restaurant, it's reached by taking a *piste* off the main Tillabéri road and crossing by pirogue. Reservations should be made in advance: you can book at the *Office National du Tourisme* in Niamey. Namaro's market is held on Saturday – a colourful event with many traders arriving by boat.

Midway between Niamey and Tillabéri, the town of **FARIÉ** used to be an important crossroads, as the only point between Gao and Gaya where cars could cross the river. A **ferry** still links the Niger's banks, and at the end of the dry season there's usually a passable ford, but the Kennedy Bridge in Niamey has removed the crossing's main significance. Although there's nothing of specific interest here, Farié makes a base for scenic riverside meanderings.

The route to Burkina: Gothèye and Téra

A viable, if slow, alternative to the direct Niamey–Ouagadougou route is to cross the river at Farié and continue the 10km north towards **GOTHÈYE**, which has basic food supplies and a bar/restaurant, but no fuel. The Sunday market boosts the otherwise limited traffic flow. Here, the road veers "inland", away from the river towards northern Burkina Faso. The unpaved *piste* passes through occasional villages among the millet stubble and acacia, but as the road climbs away from the river, larger trees and more intensive cultivation take over. Some 40km further, **Dargol** only comes to life for the Friday market. The next stop along the route, **Bandio**, has a small Saturday market, but otherwise no facilities.

The largest town in the region, **TÉRA** is backed by an earth dam that forms a reservoir after the rains (July–Dec). Filled in the early 1980s to irrigate rice and bean fields, the reservoir and the pools below are now the focus of village life. The only **accommodation** is in the rudimentary *campement* (①), which has no water or electricity. Their bar-restaurant is one of the only places to eat apart from streetside stalls.

SNTN leave Niamey for Téra on Wednesdays and Saturdays returning the following days; minibuses go from the Wadata *gare routière*. If you're heading to Burkina Faso, leave your passport at the police checkpoint over the bridge on the way into town. They'll hold it until you leave, and stamp you out of Niger as this doubles as the border control. The *gare routière* and two filling stations are near the market on the opposite side of town to the *campement*.

Into Burkina

The most direct route to Burkina Faso from Téra is via Dori, but it may be quicker to take a back route to **Falangountou**, along a narrow track across open savannah dotted with acacia, baobab and occasional Fula villages. Burkinabe formalities are efficiently dealt with in Falangountou, and from there your route will depend on local market days. Vehicles leave either to Dori or towards Gorom-Gorom via Asakam (12km, Sunday market) and Gozé (13km further).

Until a gold mining company moved into **Gozé** five years ago, there was nothing in the village. Now, despite the company's departure, it is booming. Hundreds of ex-employees and hopeful immigrants prospect by hand, digging tunnels up to 20 metres deep and trading their gains along the dusty main street. There are few facilities in town, but it is only 25km on to Gorom-Gorom.

Tillabéri and Kokomani

A Djerma town, and an important agricultural centre surrounded by fields of rice and millet, **TILLABÉRI** was never very lively even in the days when it saw a steady stream of overlanders grateful for the paved road after enduring hundreds of miles of thundering desert *piste*. Moreover, since the drought of the 1980s, the **giraffe herds** that once roamed the wooded savannahs and provided a tourist attraction have migrated further south, and there's little to do in town besides take in the **market** – notably on the big trading days, Sunday and Wednesday.

Tillabéri is a good place for a roadside stop, however as it has a number of small **restaurants** and **bars**, some with fridges. There are modest and affordable **rooms** at the *Relais Touristique* (②), which tries to bolster tourism by offering *pirogue* rides.

A better destination than Tillabéri on Wednesday is **KOKOMANI**, a small riverside village 24km downstream, which bursts into life for its weekly market. The water's edge is littered with *pirogues* as hundreds of people squeeze into interconnected courtyards resonating with the sound of braying donkeys and the calls of calabash carvers working under low wooden shelters.

Ayorou

AYOROU, 88km north of Tillabéri, is a quiet Songhai fishing village on weekdays. But on Sundays the population is swelled by a diversity of Sahelian peoples who, having crossed the river by *pirogue* or the savannah by mule, camel or on foot, converge for the weekly **market**. Famous throughout West Africa, it's an event well worth catching.

An important element is the **animal market**, the main draw for nomads – Fula cattle herders, Tuareg with their camels, and Bello with mules. Songhai, Djerma and Sorko people bring fruits and vegetables, various grains, fish, goats and chickens, while Moorish (Mauritanian) merchants, in distinctive light blue robes and white headscarves, run their typical general stores. Traders also sell traditional medicine and a variety of **regional crafts**, especially jewellery and leather work.

Though most of Ayorou crouches along the eastern bank of the river, the oldest part of town, with traditional *banco* houses, spreads over the island of **Ayorou Goungou**. You can rent a *pirogue* to visit it, or one of the surrounding islands, at the mooring point near the market square. Your chances of seeing **hippopotamus** along this stretch of the river are good, and exotic **birds** are common, especially near the island of **Firgoun**, 12km north of town. During or shortly after the rainy season – when the river is high enough – you may even be able to rent a *pirogue* to take you as far as Niamey.

Ayorou's sole **hotel** is the *Hôtel Amenokal* (reservations through the *Hôtel Ténéré* in Niamey, ☎73.39.20; ⑥). Part of the French *PLM* chain, it's only open from November to April, but offers more than you'd expect in such a small town. Though expensive, it's got charm too, with a good location on the river bank, comfortable AC rooms, plus its own swimming pool, bar and restaurant.

If you have time for a jaunt downstream (and the security situation permits it), you might want to take a **pirogue from Ayorou to Tillabéri** after the market closes – a one-day voyage, setting off Sunday evening or Monday morning. The trip involves plenty of weaving between the rapids and manoeuvring down narrow channels and there are some particularly exciting rapids just before you enter Tillabéri. There's no fixed price.

South of Niamey

South of Niamey towards the Benin border, the main road and river separate, joining up again only Gaya. Near the town of **Kouré**, 30km down the road from the capital, the **giraffe herds** that once were the pride of Tillabéri, have found refuge from drought and poaching in the surrounding countryside. In the rainy season, this is an easy day trip from Niamey: taxis to Kouré are no problem, and there's no shortage of local kids eager to take you to the giraffes. Expect to be mobbed, but choose a guide nonetheless, as they know where the herds are located. With luck, you may walk no more than a couple of kilometres before spotting two dozen of these extraordinary animals sailing by in their slow-motion canter; however a ten-kilometre trek is not uncommon. In either case the experience is well worth it, even more so given that these are some of the last giraffes left in West Africa. In the dry season the herds migrate again, well out of walking distance from the town.

Further south, the road passes through the important trading town of **DOSSO**, which occupies a crossroads position between Niamey, Benin, Maradi and Zinder. The *gare routière* is frenetic and there's a large market (though, importantly, no bank). Dosso still has its traditional Djerma chief who lives in the *Djermakoye* – a compound built in the Sudanic style. With authorization you should be able to visit it. **Accommodation** is pretty much limited to the *Hôtel Djerma*, a rotten place with some AC rooms (☎65.02.06; ②), and the far preferable *Auberge du Carrefour*, on the rte de Niamey which has simple rooms with choice of fan or AC (☎65.00.17; ②). The town is teeming with bars and **places to eat**. One, *Chez Rita*, near the market, serves filling plates of spaghetti, great salad and a good *steack frites*.

GAYA is the last town in Niger before crossing the river into Benin. The border post closes at 6.30pm, so if you're rolling in after dark, you'll have to spend the night in town. There are rooms without electricity or water at the town's only bona fide **lodgings**, *Hôtel Dendi* (①), but you may notice people in your taxi heading to a house near the *gare routière*, where they get mats to sleep on the earth floor inside. People pay next to nothing for this privilege and there's no reason not to join them, though you'll elicit some embarrassed laughter.

Parc National du "W" du Niger

Part of the vast reserve that spreads across into Burkina Faso and Benin, the **Parc National du "W" du Niger** (pronounced *double-vé* and named after the double U-bend in the Niger River) covers 2200 square kilometres in Niger alone. It's one of West Africa's better game parks and relatively good for animal-watching, with herds of **elephant** concentrated in the Tapoa valley and **buffalo** (*buffle*) on the wooded savannahs. Reports still come in of **lions** and **leopards** roaming the park, but they stay very well hidden. Easier to spot are antelope – waterbuck (*cob de buffon* or *cob defassa*) and **duiker** especially, as well as the big roan antelope (*hippotrague*) and hartebeest (*bubale*) – and large troops of **baboons** (*babouins*) scampering through the bush, often near the camp (see below). **Warthogs** (*phacochères*) and **hippos** are also quite common. The park counts some 300 species of **birds**, with good showings of storks, herons and ibises. When the rainy season begins in June the park closes down, and doesn't usually reopen until early December, after the 400-odd kilometres of *piste* have been groomed.

The park entrance is 150km south of Niamey, via **Say** and **Tamou**. For the last 40 kilometres, after turning south at Tamou, the route runs through the **Réserve Totale de Faune de Tamou**, an appendage of the main park. If you're not driving or on an organized tour (and a visit to the park is hard to arrange otherwise), public transport from Niamey will get you as far as Say, where you may have to change to head on to Tamou. You're not likely to get down to La Tapoa without a lift from a park administration vehicle or from fellow travellers. At the park entrance you pay for a visitor's permit valid for the duration of your stay. You can also pick up a road map that is quite detailed and useful for orientation, though an accompanying guide is obligatory. The main **park accommodation** is the *Hôtel de la Tapoa*, at the village of **La Tapoa**,

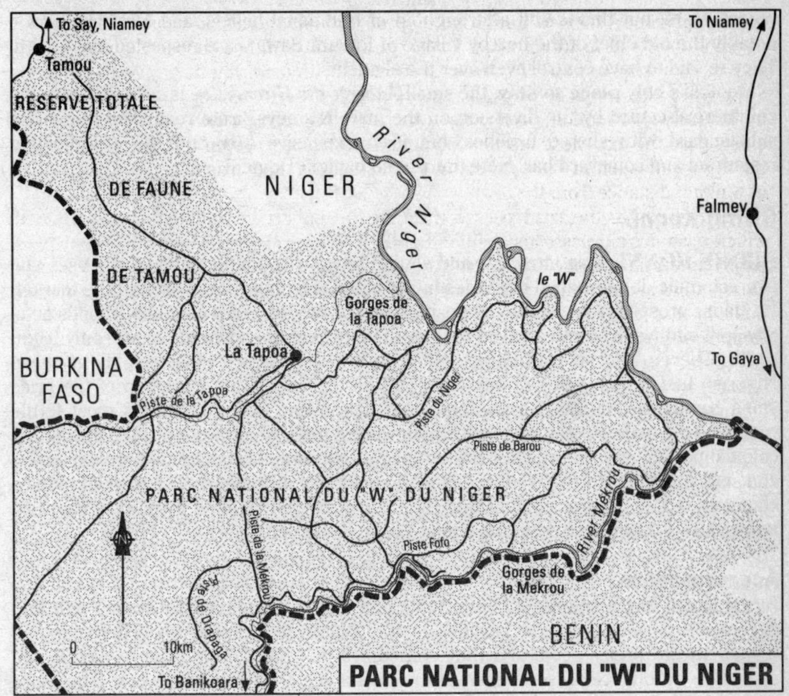

PARC NATIONAL DU "W" DU NIGER

on the edge of the reserve. It has comfortable bungalows or AC rooms (HB; ⑤–⑥), grouped around the swimming pool, and you can make reservations in Niamey at the *Office National du Tourisme*, or through any travel agent.

Nigercar Voyages has set up a true safari-style *campement* in the park with tents, folding chairs and gas lights (HB; ④).

SOUTHERN NIGER

Southern Niger is the nation's richest agricultural belt. It also contains the bulk of the country's population and is home to the biggest ethnic group, the **Hausa**. Renowned traders and leatherworkers, with a long history of regional statehood, they are energetically commercial, the vigour of their towns enhanced today by the region's proximity to Nigeria.

From Dogondoutchi to Birnin-Konni

Two hundred and thirty kilometres east of Niamey, **DOGONDOUTCHI** (commonly shortened to "Doutchi") is a small town surrounded by sculpted red cliffs reminiscent of a cowboy movie backdrop. It's inhabited by the **Maouri**, a people of Hausa origin who consistently refused to adopt Islam, even in the nineteenth century when the Sokoto jihad led to the conversion of the entire region. Islam has made some inroads in recent years, but this is still a stronghold of traditional beliefs, and local fetishers – notably the old chief of the nearby village of Baoura Bawa – are respected and feared. They're said to have control even over the elements.

Doutchi's only **place to stay**, the small *Auberge des Hirondelles*, is set away from the commercial centre by the diversion on the main Niamey–Birnin road. The rooms are substandard with shared facilities, but it's inexpensive (①), and has an adjoining restaurant and courtyard bar. Note there is no bank in Doutchi.

Birnin-Konni

BIRNIN-KONNI is an attractive and soulful town, with traditional *banco* houses and characteristic dome-shaped granaries in the older neighbourhoods around the market. Its Hausa prosperity is owed to its position on the border. Some neighbourhoods actually spill into Nigeria, and a paved road pushes through the town to Sokoto, only 93km south. There's a lot of **trafficking** going on in these parts – most notably of cheap Nigerian fuel, which you can buy from jars on the streets for a fraction of the price you'd pay at the pumps. Birnin-Konni also lies in one of the country's most fertile regions – the main streets are shaded by towering trees which were planted during the colonial period, and the **market** has a range of goods and produce that are expensive and scarce further north (Wednesday is the main day of trading). The rows of money-changers seated on grass mats along the main street surrounded by piles of Nigerian *naira* and CFA francs attest to the amount of cross-border trade.

Accommodation

Birnin-Konni has a couple of comfortable and affordable **places to stay**. You'll find decent rooms plus camping facilities at the *Relais Touristique* (①). Their bar and restaurant are pretty good, and they sometimes pull the TV onto the terrace in the evenings – a chance to see Niger's tiny TV station (*Télé-Sahel*) at work. The more upmarket *Kado Hôtel* (③) has S/C rooms (AC optional), some of which are upstairs and have interesting streetside views. The *Kado*'s restaurant does appetizing continental breakfasts and *poulet frites* at night, and across the street is a rather good **disco**. Finally, if you're broke, there's a simple *campement* with showers and fans (①), just up the road from the *Kado*.

Maradi

Sometimes dubbed Niger's "groundnut capital", as over half the country's crop is grown in the surrounding region, **MARADI** – Niger's third largest town – lies in an area of nascent industrialization. Formerly it was a province of Katsina, one of the original seven Hausa city-states, which lies over the Nigerian border, just 90km south. After the nineteenth-century Sokoto jihad, Hausa refugees fled to Maradi and eventually overthrew the Fula here. Sokoto and Maradi remained at odds for years afterwards.

Despite its historical links, Maradi has lost much of its traditional flavour (an anonymous-looking grid of streets was laid out in the 1950s) but it isn't devoid of interest. Foremost among the "sights" is the **Dan Kasswa Square**, bordered by the **Grande Mosquée** and the **Chief's Palace** – a colourful and typically Hausa confection. The **marketplace** is also impressive, spreading over a couple of blocks along the main Katsina road. You'll find a vast array of produce grown in the region or imported from Nigeria, at prices much lower than in Niamey (Monday and Friday are the main days). Over by the Hôtel de Ville there's a shady public garden, with gazebo-like bar in the middle and a church nearby.

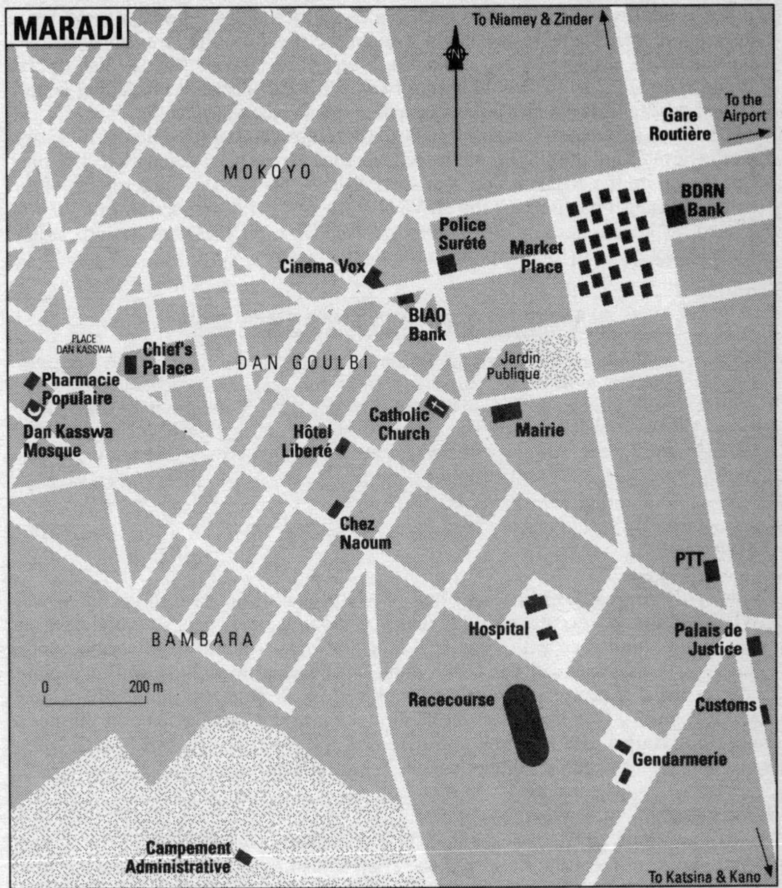

Practicalities

The town's least expensive **accommodation** is at the *Campement Administrative* (①), which has decent rooms. Other low-priced options include *Hôtel Liberté* (②), which has some S/C rooms with AC. The modest *Hôtel Niger* (☎42.02.12; ②) is not bad value, with inexpensive S/C rooms. For a little luxury, the four-star *Hôtel Jan Gorzo* (☎51.01.40; ④) on the route de l'Aéroport, has a nightclub, one of the town's better restaurants and a **pool** (open to non-guests for a fee, assuming it has water). In the same league is the Guest House (☎41.07.54; ③–④) reached by following the signs on the east side of the Kaksina road, then turning right at the old water tower. The four AC rooms, two of them S/C, are the nicest in Maradi. The European-style restaurant has a devoted following.

The best place **to eat**, apart from in the hotels, is the Afro-Lebanese *Chez Naoum*, for good and generous steaks, chicken and fish. There are loads of cheaper Nigérien eating houses in and around the market. *Le Yorumba*, just north of the *gare routière*, and the *Cercle de l'Amitié* are two good places for rice with beef scraps served in a soup, and other inexpensive regional dishes. In the evenings, the *Jardin Publique* is a popular spot for grilled chicken cooked and served in outdoor stands. Also try *Les Hirondelles* (☎41.00.85) for a cold beer served with local specialities including pepper soup and goat's head soup; it's across from the *Dan Kasswa Cinéma*.

Maradi has a number of useful facilities. There are two **banks** – the *BIAO* across from the Sûreté, and the *BDRN*, on the Katsina road across from the market. The **post office** is also on the Katsina road near the Palais de Justice. One street north of the Sûreté, you can get **car parts** at the *SONIDA* store, or try *Auto Service* near the *BDRN*. For medical needs, head to the *Pharmacie Populaire*, on the same square as the Grande Mosquée, or to the **hospital**, in the south of town.

MOVING ON FROM MARADI

Maradi's main **gare routière** is right next to the market on the Katsina road. Vehicles head off from here to all points, but note that you won't get into Nigeria without a visa and there are no issuing facilities at any of the border posts. **Taxis** generally stop at the border town of **Dan-Issa**, where you change vehicles for further travel in Nigeria. Two *SNTN* **buses** a week leave for Niamey and two for Zinder. Private buses also service these towns.

Zinder

Formerly the largest town in Niger and briefly capital of the French colony, sleepy **ZINDER** has more recently seen its influence slide. It's still Niger's second city, but much of the commerce with Nigeria – long the main source of its wealth – now bypasses it via Maradi, on the faster Kano–Niamey highway. But even in decline, Zinder remains a centre of trade, as a quick stroll through the impressive Grand Marché confirms. Nor has it lost all its former glories: it retains some of the finest **traditional Hausa architecture** anywhere, and the old town of **Birni** is even better preserved than its Nigerian counterparts in Kano, Zaria or Katsina.

Some history

The **sultanate** of Zinder was founded by the Kanouri, descendants of the Kanem Bornu empire of the Lake Chad region. They settled here after being chased from northern territories by Tuareg invaders, and mixed with the Hausa population which itself had fled the region of Sokoto under pressure from the Fulani. In the eighteenth and nineteenth centuries, the Kanouri and Hausa joined forces to found the powerful **Damagaram state**, of which Zinder was capital. The sultan is still Kanouri.

Zinder reached its apogee in the mid-nineteenth century under the reign of **Tamimoum**, who greatly enlarged the boundaries of Damagaram, introduced new crops and developed trade. Under his rule, a vast wall or *birni* was erected around the town. Originally ten metres high and fourteen deep, this wall has long since crumbled, but its ruins can still be seen around the old town. According to legend, the structure's invincibility was ensured by incorporating into the walls a number of Korans and several virgin girls. Under subsequent rulers, however, Zinder's fortunes were tied more to those of the slave trade than to magic. By the 1890s, one of the Sahel region's biggest **slave markets** was regularly held here. To support his empire, the sultan led frequent raids on vassal villages and captives were sold in town, taken to Kano and then force-marched down to the coast. The **French** captured Zinder in 1899. With a population well in excess of 20,000, it was by far the region's biggest metropolis at the time and remained the effective capital of Niger until 1927.

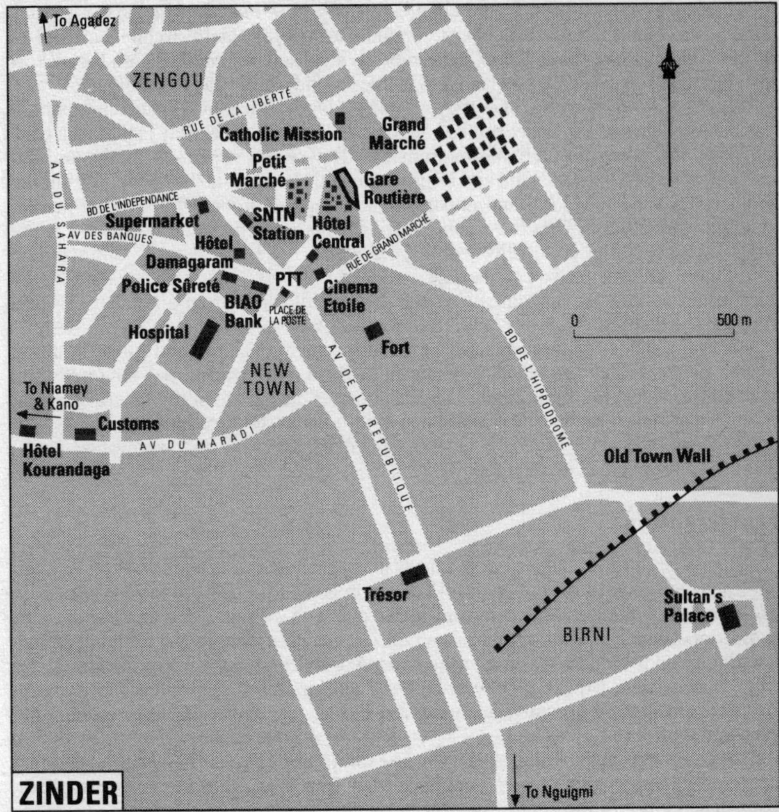

Orientation

Zinder comprises three separate districts, so distinct they're almost individual towns. To the north, **Zengou** was the original Hausa settlement, formerly a stopping point for camel caravans. **Birni** – the old fortified town and site of the sultan's palace and Grande Mosquée – lies about a kilometre to the southeast. Between the two is the **new town**, with administrative buildings laid out in characteristic French colonial style.

Services are entirely concentrated in the new town. They include the hotels and better restaurants, three **banks** (*BIAO*, *BDRN* and *BCEAO*), the **post office** and a couple of **supermarkets**. There's also an outdoor cinema, *L'Etoile*.

The Town

The most obvious attraction in town is the old quarter of **Birni**, reached from the new town by following av de la République south beyond the old French fort (still used by the Nigérien military). This will take you past the **Grande Mosquée**, the front of which gives onto a large public square facing the **Sultan's Palace**, a two-storey *banco* building set apart by its size. There are tombs of the former sultans in the grounds, which you should be able to visit with authorization from the Mairie. Another noteworthy residence is that of the Fulani chief, just east of the mosque; the façade is decorated with colourful raised motifs, a common feature of Hausa architecture. All of Birni's buildings have been left in the traditional style, and walking through the narrow streets you get a real sense of what life was like in Zinder's heyday a century ago.

Zinder's **Grand Marché**, one of the country's biggest, has long been an important way-station between the Sahel and the regions to the south. Thursday is the main trading day. Salt pillars brought down from the Ténéré are sold next to the **animal market**, with its Tuareg, Fulani and Bousou traders. Hausa and other peoples from the south sell a variety of local and imported goods in and around the arcaded market building, which dates from the colonial period. This is perhaps the best place in the country to get low-price, quality **leather**, for which the Hausa have a long-standing reputation: sandals, bags, pouffes and pouches are sold around the market or by wandering merchants. Craftsmen also sell their wares direct from a number of workshops in the district.

Although Zengou has its fair share of modern cement buildings and corrugated iron roofs – elements that are completely absent in Birni – the **traditional flavour** is still strong. The oldest house in Zinder is in this quarter, and some of the town's showiest examples of Hausa architecture have been built here by the wealthier merchants. The pride in this style of decoration is by no means dead, and new, quite innovative, examples are commissioned all the time.

Practicalities

For such a large town, Zinder doesn't have an overabundance of **hotels**. The two main ones are both located off the central Place de la Poste. The *Hôtel Central* (☎51.20.13; ②) is the cheaper alternative, a colonial-style pile with average comfort – rooms with shower and fan. The outdoor bar-restaurant is a popular place in the evening; people often hook up here before going to the cinema or out on the town. Up the street, the *Hôtel Damagaram* (☎51.06.19; ③) is bigger, nicer and correspondingly more expensive. Its furnished AC rooms are considered the best in Zinder and the restaurant is excellent too.

The **least expensive places** in town are a number of small hotel-bar-restaurants clustered in Zengou, about twenty minutes' walk past the *Central* in the Agadez direction. Heading out of the centre the other way, the Kano road leads past the Customs building (where, if you're driving, you may or may not be stopped), and on to the *Hôtel Kourandaga* (☎51.07.42; ③). Spacious Hausa-style rooms surround a courtyard, and, built over a spring, it has its own reliable water supply – there's even hot water on tap. This is where Zinder's middle classes go for a quiet drink; you might meet the chief of police or the mayor. The restaurant does good meals at slightly high prices.

Street **food** is easy to find in town, especially in the Place de la Poste, across from the *Hôtel Central*. For something a little upmarket, try *El Ali*, behind *Nigelec*, which serves good chicken and *steack frites* in an attractive garden of banana trees, papayas and formidable *paillotes*. Also reliable, the *Dan Kasina*, near the *Central*, serves inexpensive chicken and *steack frites*. Watch the hygiene everywhere, as **Zinder's water** is considered suspect and usually needs purifying.

For **night-time drinking**, the *Scotch Bar*, near the market, is popular, and the *Damagaram* and the *Central* hotels both have night clubs. Popular spots you could check out in town include the *Moulin Rouge*, well known by expats, and *La Cascade*. For something a little less local in flavour, you could – if feeling homesick, decadent, or a combination of the two – try the *Club Privé*. Besides a swimming pool, tennis, basketball and volleyball courts, it has a classy bar open until 2am weekdays and 24 hours at weekends. Officially, you can only enter upon introduction by a member; some smooth talking may be in order.

MOVING ON FROM ZINDER

SNTN buses link Zinder to Niamey (departing Tues, Thurs & Sun at dawn) and to Agadez. The *gare SNTN* is on the av de la République across from the *Hôtel Damagaram*. Private buses and bush taxis leave from the **gare routière** near the Petit Marché and connect with all major towns. **Taxis** also head regularly to Kano in Nigeria along a good road; it works out a little cheaper to take a vehicle to the border where you will easily find a taxi continuing to Kano.

Zinder to Agadez

Assuming the route is safe, the journey north **from Zinder to Agadez** (see overleaf) can be accomplished comfortably in a day. If you're driving, it's worth taking your time on this stretch, as it's a relatively narrow band of the Sahel, with sights you won't get elsewhere. The **Kel Gress Tuareg** live in the region in their huts of fibre matting. There are tall **Sodom apple trees** as well as many smaller, sometimes colourful, plants, and you might see an **ostrich** or two. Be careful walking in what appear to be tufts of grass – the seeds have a casing like a small, horse chestnut, the spikes of which draw blood.

The small town of **Tanout**, 140km north of Zinder, is a good stopping point for a cold drink, and sometimes has petrol. Several wells beyond Tanout contain water for which you'll need a forty-metre rope. At the little village of **Aderbissinat**, there's sometimes a cursory police check, and foreigners stopping here are regarded with interest and curiosity by traders in the market (leather, sweets and basic food). There's usually a fuel dump with diesel and petrol on the right of the road, as you leave the village. The road then passes near the **Falaise de Tiguidit**, an escarpment with a wonderful view back across the plain.

On to Lake Chad

Heading **towards Lake Chad** from Zinder, travel may be impeded by government travel restrictions (see box, p.940). Check the situation before heading out here: if circumstances permit eastward exploration, you'll find that road improvements have been undertaken as far as Nguigmi. The infrequently travelled route heads through a region that was part of the Kanem Bornu empire up to the nineteenth century, and today is peopled by Hausa, Kanouri, Dangara and Manga. Just 22km east of Zinder you arrive at **MIRIA**, the first **oasis** in these arid parts. The gardens here harbour date palms and groves of mango and guava. Sunday is the main **market day**; look out for local pottery.

A further 144km brings you to the small *sous-préfecture* of **GOURÉ**, and its overpriced and rudimentary *campement* (②). It's another 330km to **Maïné-Soroa**, the next place of any size, where the people make a living drawing salt from the earth. The desert looms close to the east of town, and you can see large dunes from the roadside. **DIFFA**, an administrative town on the banks of the **Komadougou River** – which sometimes flows into Lake Chad – is 75km further and has the last filling station for eastbound drivers.

Finally you arrive at **NGUIGMI**, a full 1500km from Niamey and nearly 600km from Zinder. An important town during the days of the Kanem Bornu empire, when it was home to the semi-nomadic Kanouri princes, Nguigmi became wealthy from its position on the trade routes to the **Kaourar oases** (whence salt was brought by caravans) and, of course, from its site on the shores of **Lake Chad**. Today access to the lakeshore is difficult: it has shrunk much farther south and virtually disappears in periods of drought. Indeed, at times the closest standing water to the town is 100km to the south. Nguigmi is devoid of basic facilities (including filling stations), so stock up in Diffa. A very arduous *piste* leads north of here to Bilma, but is currently off-limits to travellers. If you're heading **into Chad**, Nguigmi is where you take your official leave of Niger and drive, or find a ride, east, then south, around the lake zone to Ndjamena.

THE NIGÉRIEN SAHARA

To travel through the north of Niger takes some determination. It's a region with a stifling climate, great expanses of emptiness between the towns and very little water. From Niamey, a paved road now leads the whole way to the boomtown of **Arlit** – the northernmost major settlement – passing through the commercial centre of **Tahoua** and the historic Tuareg stronghold of **Agadez**. Due to the Tuareg rebellion, these may be the only towns of the north open to travellers. Other interesting sites are extremely hard to reach in normal times, let alone since the uprising, during which they have been placed off limits by the government.

Should the situation change, the effort is rewarded by beautiful **desert oases** which eke out a living from the **salt trade**, and the continued spectacle of **camel caravans**. Trips through the volcanic moonscapes of the **Aïr region**, or through the awesome dunes of the **Ténéré desert** also provide opportunities to visit a wealth of **prehistoric sites** – including the rock paintings near **Iferouâne** – and a number of **springs and waterfalls**.

Tahoua

Niger's fourth largest town, **TAHOUA** is a major stopping point on the main road between Niamey and Agadez. Despite a population of over 40,000 and a wide mix of peoples, the town hasn't really warmed up to travellers – indeed it was expressly closed to them until the mid-1980s, and could well be again. There's little to detain you here except the authorities – and even the rosy dunes that have settled permanently on the edge of town, while pretty examples of their kind, aren't worth a special detour.

Primarily a commercial centre, Tahoua does, however, boast a singularly animated **market** – the building is itself an attractive example of Sahel-inspired architecture. It's one of those places where everyone in Niger – Djerma, Hausa, Bororo, Fula, Tuareg, the odd tourist – comes together, notably on Sunday, the main trading day. The nomads bring salt pillars, dates, livestock and leather, which they sell to regional farmers who provide grain, cotton, spices, peanuts, tobacco and locally made indigo fabrics. Look out for the intermediaries called *dillali*, who bring together traders, help them strike a deal and even serve as translators.

Practicalities

Tahoua's most useful facilities are the two **banks** in the town centre which change traveller's cheques for a small commission. **Accommodation** is limited. On a budget, head to the shady and moderately hygienic *camping* (①) about 2km west of town, next to the *arènes des jeux traditionels*(wrestling arenas). The alternative is *Les Bungalows de la Mairie* (④), across from the town hall and surrounded by pleasant gardens. This set-up is very good, with furnished, AC bungalows, and a recommended **restaurant.**

Agadez

AGADEZ has been a major stopping point on the trans-Saharan routes for hundreds of years. You can read its history through buildings like the **Grande Mosquée** – a monument known throughout West Africa – or the more prosaic **camel market**, which has been drawing the peoples of the Sahel here for generations. While the salt caravans still come from Bilma, they do so very rarely, and since the uprisings of the early 1990s, other formerly common visitors, such as cross-Sahara travellers, tour groups and even film crews, have tapered off as well. While Agadez is still accessible, most of the rest of the north is off limits; even short walks or drives outside the city limits are prohibited, and there's an unsettling military presence in town. The discovery of uranium to the north, and the roads linking Agadez to Niamey and Zinder still offer hope of future prosperity, but for now the town seems cut off in dusty isolation.

Some history

In the fourteenth century, Agadez was a small but expanding town, a **centre of commerce** where Arabs from Tripoli traded with the Hausa from Nigeria and the Songhai from Gao. By the fifteenth century it was on its way to becoming the **capital of the Tuareg** – as far as such a thing existed for the nomads – and in 1449, a **sultanate** was established under the leadership of **Ilissaouane**. Fifty years later, the town came to be controlled by the Songhai and throughout the sixteenth century, Agadez marked the northernmost point of their great empire, with a huge population, for the time, of perhaps 30,000.

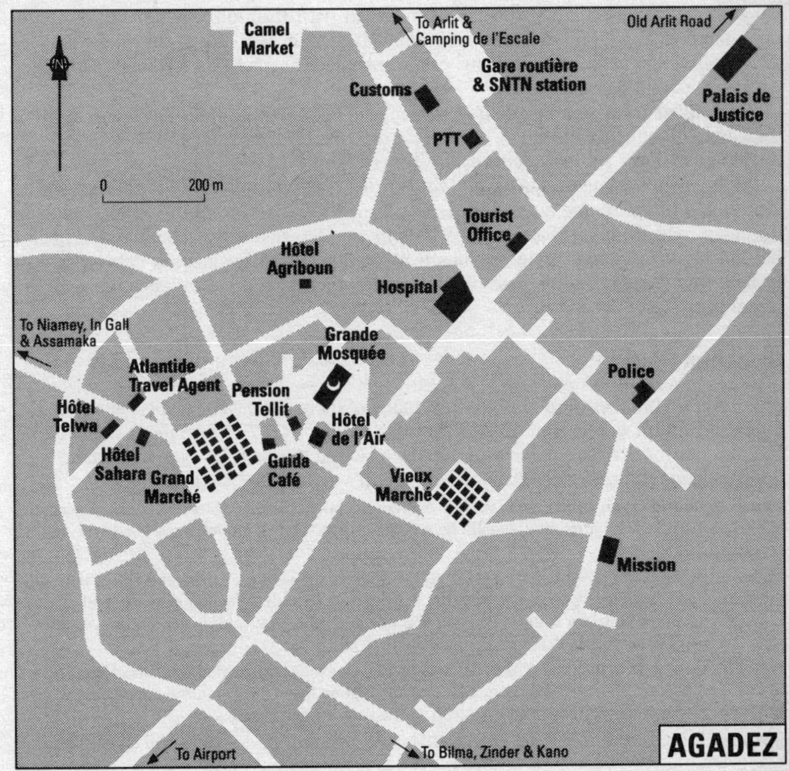

After the Songhai were defeated by the Moroccans, the Tuareg regained the town, but like other trading posts in the region it was already entering a period of long decline. Agadez fared better than most, however, thanks in large measure to its location near the salt mines of Bilma; trade continued, especially with Hausa-land to the south. Nonetheless, by the time the German explorer **Heinrich Barth** arrived in 1850, the population had dwindled to about 7000 and many of the old buildings were in ruins.

Early in the twentieth century, Agadez was incorporated into French territory, but not without resistance. One of the most serious threats to colonial rule was led by the Tuareg reformer **Kaocen Ag Mohammed**, who swooped down from Djanet to take Agadez in 1916, aiming to reunite all Muslims of the region and to terminate foreign domination. Supported in his efforts by the Germans and the Turks, Kaocen held the town for three months before being ousted by the French, who sent up emergency reinforcements from Zinder. The rebellion quelled, the colonials killed over 300 suspected conspirators and guillotined many of the town's marabouts.

Since independence, the population of Agadez has rapidly increased, in part because of the discovery of uranium in Arlit, which provided an economic boost to the entire north, and partly due to the droughts of the 1970s and 1980s, which resulted in tens of thousands of Tuareg and Bororo herders converging on the town for food and water.

Arrival and information

On arrival, you may still be expected to **check in with the police** and have your passport stamped. You'll find the *commissariat* near the main post office. They may demand a "fee"; be diplomatic but don't pay. Some travellers neglect this formality altogether with no apparent consequence.

For **tourist information**, the government-run *Office National du Tourisme*, north of the Grand Mosquée, can set you up with tours of the town and give the latest update on the situation in the Aïr mountains or the Ténéré desert.

As the main administrative town in the north, Agadez has plenty of facilities: **service stations**, a **hospital** and a small **airfield**, plus a **PTT** across from the tourist office on the main road (Mon–Fri 8am–noon & 3–5pm; poste restante service offered). Agadez has no bank to change money, though most hotels and businesses eagerly accept French franc notes, and it's possible to change other currencies (at poor rates) in the larger hotels.

Accommodation

Agadez has a number of **places to stay**, many of them good value, especially since the recent downturn in tourism. As for **camping**, *Camping de l'Escale*, about 4km out, on the new (tarmac) Arlit road, was a popular place in the days of overland traffic, with good facilities and a friendly management, but it's unlikely to be open.

Hôtel Agriboun, town centre (☎44.03.07). A recommended cheaper place, with unsophisticated S/C rooms with fans; bargaining usually gets good results. They'll let you park inside the fenced courtyard. ②.

Hotel de l'Aïr, in the town centre (☎44.01.47). Formerly the sultan's palace and still wonderfully quiet, cool and dignified. Except the bar, that is, which has a wide selection of booze and customers. Despite the architectural grandeur and the clientele, the *Aïr*'s rooms are not fancy, though some have AC. Budget travellers can sleep on the roof. ③.

Hôtel Sahara, west of the Grand Marché (☎44.01.97). Conveniently located, and a traditional haunt of overlanders, but overrated. Its rooms are looking shabby these days, and the management has a frustrating *laisser-aller* attitude. You can sleep on the roof at great savings. ②.

Pension Tellit, across from *Hôtel de l'Aïr* (☎44.02.31). Attractively decorated and spotlessly clean S/C rooms with AC. Luxurious roof patio with Italian restaurant. ③.

FESTIVALS IN THE AGADEZ REGION

The town of Agadez celebrates the Muslim holidays in style, especially the end of **Ramadan**, the **Tabaski** and the **prophet's birthday**. Festivities marking these events begin with a morning prayer led by the *imam*, who then kills a lamb according to tradition. Families return to their homes for a feast, after which the entire town reassembles along the streets between the mosque and the sultan's palace, as drummers announce the recommencement of festivities. Already men on horseback are beginning to gather, among them the sultan's guards with their bright red turbans. The event everyone's come out to see is the **cavalcades**, the highlight of celebrations that last until sundown and then pick up again the next day. When the signal is given, the riders race their horses at a frenzied pace, kicking up clouds of dust. Men, women and children all strain for a better look, pressing dangerously close to the horsemen, who halt their charge in front of the palace, where the sultan and dignitaries are gathered. The elaborate costumes, the music and the excitement of the races leave an indelible impression – you won't regret making an effort to be in town for the festivities.

THE CURE SALÉE

Along with the Muslim festivals, one of the more interesting celebrations of the nomadic Fula and Tuareg is the **Cure Salée**, a traditional homecoming that takes place some time after the rains, between July and September. Herders who have migrated to the far south in the dry season then return to the region around **In-Gall**, west of Agadez, whose large salt flats fill with water at this time. It's a period for fattening the animals and giving them the "salt cure", punctuated by festivities including music, dancing and, frequently, camel races.

During the month of September, the **Bororo** – a nomadic Fula people – stage a remarkable ceremony called the **Gerewol**, as part of their *Cure Salée* celebrations. Often likened to a beauty pageant, this is a party for unmarried men, who spend hours adorning themselves with jewellery and putting on make-up – red ochre on the face, white outlines for features like the nose and mouth, black on the lips and round the eyes. Elaborate hairpieces are also concocted with scarves, beads, braids and feathers. Having prepared themselves to emphasize Bororo ideals of male beauty – long slender bodies, bright white teeth and eyes, and straight hair – the bachelors line up in the festival arena to dance, roll their white eyes, flash their broad smiles and chant a droning melody. The young women, who also spend a considerable amount of time beautifying themselves, look on, and one by one come forward and take their choice of the most handsome man. According to custom, if a girl doesn't like the husband proposed for her by her parents, she can marry the man she desires, chosen at the *Gerewol*. A man who isn't happy with his new partner has some difficulty getting out of the social obligation to spend a night with her, but numerous weddings do take place over the course of the *Cure Salée*. Another Bororo *Cure Salée* event is the virility test known as the **Soro**. Here men stand in front of their girlfriends and allow other men to strike them several times across the chest. To show their courage to their loved one, they're expected to smile as they're beaten.

These elaborate demonstrations of manliness are part of an extensive and complex **codified social life**, which characterizes many pastoral peoples – it's similar in many respects, for example, to that of the Maasai, Samburu and Dinka in East Africa – and which finds expression in a mesh of taboos and ritual behaviour maintaining extraordinary social cohesion and group identity.

Although the events at the Bororo *Cure Salée* have been filmed and photographed often enough to make them relatively familiar images, the occasion is not a tourist spectacle and it's difficult to arrange to witness it. Increasingly, government bureaucrats are setting the agenda, however, so you might find that you can visit on an official tour. If you have time enough to be persistent, the best approach would be to make friends first in Agadez.

The Town

Agadez is a sprawling town, so taking up the offers of a young guide may be invaluable. You might find yourself invited into houses (men should avoid looking at the women within the courtyard), and you'll see all the sights you ask about.

The Grande Mosquée and around

Spiring through the one-storey skyline to a height of 27 metres, the tower of the **Grande Mosquée** is a landmark whose fame has spread beyond West Africa. Built in 1515, the mosque is a classic example of medieval Sudanic, with the wooden support beams protruding from the minaret like quills from a porcupine. Over the years the structure has been much renovated and was completely rebuilt in 1844, following the original style. In former days, the tower doubled as a sentry post, and it's worth climbing today for views of the town and surrounding countryside. Though the mosque is normally off limits to non-believers, there's a guardian who, in exchange for a *cadeau*, will lead you to the top, providing you don't arrive at prayer time. He's recently become accustomed to hefty *cadeaux* from wealthy tourists, and you may not be let in for less than several thousand CFA francs.

The nearby *Hôtel de l'Aïr* served as the **Kaocen Palace** early this century. It's a beautiful building, and even if you don't stay here you should stop by for a look. The large dining hall is where the sultan formerly received his audiences and, it's said, where subversives were hanged after the 1916 Tuareg uprising. You can go upstairs to the rooftop terrace for an interesting perspective on the mosque and town.

Also in the centre, the massive *banco* structure of the **Sultan's Palace** is the current residence of the traditional city ruler. The Nigérien government has left the basic structure of the sultanate intact, but although he's often called upon to mediate in local disputes, the sultan has at best blunted powers at the state level. Agadez's main festivals always culminate at the informal public square in front of the palace.

The markets

Not far from the mosque, the **Grand Marché**, often called the Marché Moderne, is the town's main commercial venue. Tumbledown corrugated iron sheds offer a variety of goods, loosely divided into food sections (expensive, as most fruit and vegetables have to be trucked in from the south), tools, fabrics and so on. Many traders sell **crafts** aimed at the tourist trade, and this is one of the cheapest places to get Tuareg and Fula **jewellery**. Quality is often wanting, however, since the shiny trinkets are often made from melted-down Algerian dinars or other alloys that quickly acquire a dull green patina. Leather goods – sandals, pouches and bags – also abound.

On the eastern side of the main north–south road that splits the town in two, the **Vieux Marché** is much less hectic, but worth visiting, since it lies in one of the town's oldest quarters. The dusty streets surrounding the market are tightly hemmed in by *banco* houses bearing the stamp of Sudanic and Hausa influence, with their smooth lines and decorated facades.

Most interesting, though, is the **camel market**, on the town's northwestern outskirts. In the mornings, camels, donkeys, sheep and goats are bought and sold in an open field bordered by stalls featuring nomadic goods – mostly salt pillars, rope, water containers and mats. If you've never sat on a camel, you can do so here by approaching one of the Tuareg traders. In exchange for a small tip, he'll help you into the saddle and let you circle the area – not exactly an adventure, but it gives you a taste.

Eating and nightlife

In addition to the hotel **restaurants**, Agadez has several small places dishing up inexpensive meals. Near the mosque, the *Tafadak* serves copious helpings of

SILVERSMITHS AND SADDLEMAKERS IN AGADEZ

The refined craftsmanship of the Agadez **silversmiths** has become a byword in West Africa and even in some international circles. Though these artists make a variety of innovative jewellery and other objects from precious metals, they're best known for the **desert cross** pendants, especially the renowned *Croix d'Agadez*. Other towns with their own unique crosses include Bilma, In-Gall, Iferouâne, Tahoua and Zinder.

The smiths still work out of small *ateliers*, which you won't have to seek out, as young boys make it a point to propose a **tour of the workshops** to every tourist passing through. They say there's no obligation to buy, but once you're in the shops, the pressure to do so is intense. If you're fairly certain you're not interested in making a purchase, perhaps you should decline the whole show. That said, watching the *forgerons* producing jewellery by the time-honoured **lost wax process** is genuinely interesting. A wax form of the intended object is used to make a clay mould, which is then baked in a charcoal fire until all the wax has trickled out of the holes made for that purpose; liquid silver is poured into the mould, which after cooling is broken to free the hardened metal. Detailed carving and polishing can then take place. The craftsmen are known not only for the quality of their work, but also for the honesty of their materials. Unlike the market vendors, they have a reputation for straight dealing – when they say something is pure silver, it usually is.

Other artisans specialize in the **leather work** for which Agadez is also famous. The workshops still produce *rahlas* (camel saddles), covering the wooden frames with treated hides that are then decorated. They also make colourful sandals, with red and green leather in the design, and Tuareg "wallets" – stylized pouches worn round the neck with compartments for money, tobacco and other necessities.

couscous and other regional specialities in a pleasant interior courtyard. The nearby *Restaurant Chez Nous* is also recommended – *riz sauce* and a full range of Niger dishes, along with cheap, help-yourself coffee. Behind the market near the bank, the *Restaurant Islamique* is popular for its friendly service, good salads and inexpensive main courses. For sandwich-type snacks and *gelati* there's an Italian ice cream place – *Vittorio's/Guida* near the *Hôtel de l'Aïr*. A bit further out on the route de l'Aéroport, *Le Pillier* (☎44.03.31) is a fancier restaurant run by the owner of the *Pension Tellit* and highly recommended for moderately priced Italian specialties served alongside more traditional Sahel food.

For **picnic supplies**, you can find European canned and dry goods plus a selection of wine at *Ruetsch*, across the main road from the *Hôtel Agriboun*. The main supermarket, though, is *MiniPrix*, on the main tarred road. They sell French cheese, British biscuits, Italian pasta and Mars Bars – and it's not that expensive. Incidentally, the **water** in Agadez is perfectly drinkable straight from the tap.

At **night**, you could check out the open-air *Cinéma du Sahel*, near the airfield: films are generally bad but the crowd reaction adds a little excitement to quiet Sahel nights.

MOVING ON FROM AGADEZ

The **gare routière** is on the asphalt road to Arlit, (the old *piste* to Arlit is not used any longer) across from Customs. Most of the *taxis brousse* from here seem to be heading to Niamey via Tahoua, though with patience you can also find transport to other major towns. *SNTN* **coaches** leave from nearby and can get you to Arlit (three times a week), Zinder (once), Tahoua, Maradi and Niamey (three times). Niamey in a day is just about possible, with an early start and no delays – it's a little over 900km. The 430-kilometre journey from Agadez to Zinder can be accomplished comfortably in one day.

Arlit

Overland routes from Algeria closed abruptly in 1993, and travellers today miss the spectacle of approaching **ARLIT** from the Algerian Hoggar and seeing the town appear from nowhere, like a vast aberration on the fringes of the Sahara. As little as thirty years ago there was virtually nothing here, but after the discovery of uranium in the mid-1960s a town burgeoned beside the vast complex built for the *SOMAÏR* company. Despite its recent origins, Arlit's prosperity has drawn a wide mix of people that formerly made it an attractive stopping point for desert-crossers, but it holds little appeal for travellers coming from the diverse commercial centres of the south and is today rarely visited.

Arlit is really **two towns**. The first, built entirely for the mining company and its employees, is well planned and exclusive, with villas for engineers and executives, supermarkets stocked directly from France, a well-equipped hospital, and the town's best restaurants. The obvious divisions between the African and European workers – unequal housing, salaries and living standards – make this a disturbing sight, and you won't really have access to the facilities unless you know or befriend someone working here. A more **traditional town** has grown in a chaotic fashion alongside the mining complex. The large **market** – a maze of tiny stalls covered by mats and corrugated iron – sells vegetables, fresh meat (cut before your eyes in the open-air abbatoir), and household items like decorated calabashes, pottery and basketware.

Practicalities

On arrival, you should pay your respects to the **police**. You shouldn't have to pay any money, but they might want to stamp your passport, and they may insist on keeping it for the duration of your stay in Arlit. The police station is at the north end of the main street on the east side of the older, African part of town. If you need identification to change money, go to the bank before the police. The *BDRN* and the *BIAO* provide the north's only reliable money exchanges.

Arlit has a pleasant **hotel**, the *Tamesna*, on the main street near the market (②); its rooms are nothing to write home about, but some of them have AC. The bar here is a popular place to hide from the heat (cold beer and soda with ice cubes – Arlit's **water** is perfectly pure), and the tables spill over into the shaded interior courtyard. At night this is the centre of town activity.

The town's two **campsites** are suffering badly from the dearth of overland traffic, and are unlikely to be open. The first, where facilities don't go much beyond showers,

THE ROAD NORTH FROM ARLIT TO ASSAMAKKA

The 200-kilometre drive takes three to six hours, depending on your vehicle and desert driving experience. From Arlit, the main *piste* runs – within a distance of, at most, 3km – parallel to the line of *balises* (marker drums) which have in many cases been replaced with piles of tyres or rocks. The Assamakka customs post closes at 6pm and it is forbidden to enter Assamakka after dusk. If you have to camp en route, choose a mound or a gully well off the *piste* – where you won't be hit by a night-driving smuggler's lorry.

As this book goes to press in August 1995, the *piste* between Arlit and Assamakka was **closed** to travellers due to "army manoeuvres" related to the Tuareg rebellion (see p.940 & p.956). While a solution to the problems in Niger is conceivable, travel is unlikely to be safe in Algeria for some time. Even should the road open on the Niger side to make travel there possible, Assamakka is a bleak outpost that nobody would want to visit for its own sake.

is about 3km out of town, along the road to Agadez. The second, some 3km to the north of town, is an equally basic set-up.

The **restaurant** at the *Tamesna* does reasonable European-style meals such as *poulet frites* with canned peas. Down the street the popular *Sahel* is good for inexpensive meals – *steack frites*, rice and sauce – and at night has a lively bar. Also on the main drag, the *Restaurant N'Wana* prepares good *couscous* and salads that go down well with a cold beer on the patio.

The Aïr Mountains and east of Agadez

Two classic journeys from Agadez lead through the volcanic **Aïr Mountains** and the rolling dunes of the **Ténéré Desert**. At the time of publication of this book, however, a government travel ban (see box p.940) was still in effect and both destinations were off limits to visitors. Should restrictions be lifted, *pistes* wend through both areas, but they are mostly demanding in the extreme and often get washed away during the rainy season or obliterated from sight when unheralded winds kick up a desert sandstorm. Partly because of the danger and partly because these scenic regions are potentially big earners of tourist dollars, the government in the past required all travellers to set off with an expensive official guide, assigned at the tourist office in Agadez. You couldn't forego these restrictions without running into serious problems (including arrest), and, of course, there were good reasons – possible dehydration and death – for following them meticulously. Until the region reopens, however, the following itineraries are only theoretical possibilities.

The Route de l'Aïr

The **Route de l'Aïr**, accessible from the old, unsurfaced Arlit road northeast from Agadez, is relatively good *piste* apart from the jostling washboard surface and one or two other unexpected hazards. The road forks at Teloua (take a left), and about 15km later there's the possibility of a diversion left to **Tafadek**, a deep spring that's great for swimming and diving, and believed to possess curative properties. Back on the main *piste*, 77km out of Agadez, you branch off to the right from the Arlit road, and follow the sign to Elméki, 125km from Agadez.

Just outside Elméki, you'll notice a number of tracks leading off the main route – they head to the mines and nowhere else. Follow instead the large *piste* to the village of Kreb Kreb, 72km from Elméki. (About 15km before Kreb Kreb, an alternative route leads directly north to Assodé, a short cut that bypasses Timia.) Just after Kreb Kreb, the tracks lead through the beautiful **Agalak Range** – difficult driving, as the route crosses dry river beds (*kori*) and hidden stretches of sand.

Timia to Iferouâne

Roughly 220km from Arlit and a little more from Agadez, **TIMIA** is a large Tuareg-controlled village nestled between the Agalak mountains and a wide desert *kori*. The town itself is one of the most beautiful oases in the Aïr, with extensive gardens and palms. Away from the box-like *banco* houses that spread over the valley, **Fort Timia**, built by the French colonials in the 1950s, commands a striking view of the In-Sarek *oued* and mountains. On the outskirts of town the **Cascade de Timia** grows from a trickling waterfall into something quite spectacular during the rains.

North of Timia, the road continues some 30km to the **ruins** of **ASSODÉ**. Founded as long as 1000 years ago, Assodé preceded Agadez as **capital of the Tuareg** and was once the most important town in the Aïr. As trans-Saharan trade declined, so did its fortunes and Kaocen dealt the final blow to the struggling community when he sacked it in 1917. Today the site is a ghost town – its ruins lie east of the *piste* and you'll need sharp eyes to spot them. A maze of empty streets winds through abandoned houses and squares with many of the larger buildings – including the **grande mosquée** – remarkably well preserved.

Beyond Assodé, the tracks are progressively easier. After 90km, they lead to Niger's northernmost settlement of any size, **IFEROUÂNE**, a marvellous oasis on the fringes of the striking **Tamgak Mountains**. The *kori* running through town breathes life into some of the most beautiful **gardens** in the Aïr, and there's a small *campement*, the only bona fide **accommodation** on this route.

Iferouâne is also the starting point for visiting the Aïr region's wealth of **prehistoric sites**. Just north of the town along the Zeline *kori*, neolithic rock paintings of giraffes, cattle and antelopes can be seen on a distinctive boulder outcrop. More such paintings are found in the valley of the Aouderer *kori* near Tezirek, 90km from Iferouâne.

The Ténéré

The route to Bilma leads through what's often described as the most beautiful desert in the Sahara – the **Ténéré**. This is strictly for the well-equipped; an arduous, 620-kilometre journey, with a great deal of very soft sand and hardly any supplies or water along the way. You must have a guide, and usually be in convoy, before the police will let you go (again, of course, this is subject to their allowing *any* travel). Markers along the route include the graves of victims of the crossing.

Leaving Agadez, take the Zinder road and, after a couple of kilometres, follow the eastern branch towards Bilma. The first 200-odd kilometres run through the southern Aïr, with alternating stretches of sand and rock-strewn *piste*. After 270km, you arrive at the site of the **Arbre du Ténéré**, formerly the only tree growing in a region the size of France. For over a century it served as a landmark for desert crossers, until it was knocked over by a truck driver in 1973. A scrap-metal sculpture now marks the spot.

After 500km, you arrive at **Fachi**, a small Toubou and Kanouri village with a few hundred inhabitants and cool groves of date palms. In the centre, the fortified palace (*ksar*) is built of salt blocks – you can visit the **salt mines** on the eastern outskirts of town. The road covering the remaining 110km to Bilma is the one used by the *azalai*, or camel caravans, that still ply the region. It's full of long stretches of soft sand, and can be tough going.

Bilma and the pillars of salt

With around a thousand Kanouri, Tuareg and Toubou inhabitants, the small fortified town of **BILMA** is nearly a miracle out here in the middle of nowhere. Set against the backdrop of the **Kaouar Cliffs** – and as picturesque and hospitable as you could wish – Bilma owes its existence to natural water sources, which support a sizeable *palmeraie* and gardens. People in Bilma often refer to themselves, distinctively, as **Beriberi** (or *Blibli*), a term which has various interpretations but usually implies Hausa-Kanouri. Many Beriberi are Hausa in all but name and some speak Hausa most of the time.

Bilma is best known for its **salt manufacture** (for animal, rather than human, consumption) which just about maintains the viability of one of the desert's last camel caravan routes. Perhaps twenty to forty caravans a year make the trek from Agadez, with altogether up to a thousand camels in train in each one – although in living memory the figure was sometimes 50,000 or more. In recent years, the demand for Bilma's commodity has slackened in the traditional Hausa markets of southern Niger and Nigeria, where drought has depleted so much livestock in recent years. Meanwhile Bilma is filled with unsold sixty-centimetre pillars of dirty brown, rock-hard salt. They continue to make them in moulds of saline mud, piling up vast reserves for a fatter future.

index

CHAPTER SIXTEEN

NIGERIA

NIGERIA

Listen to Nigerian leaders and you will frequently hear the phrase this great country of ours. *Nigeria is* not *a great country. It is one of the most disorderly nations in the world. It is one of the most corrupt, insensitive, inefficient places under the sun. It is dirty, callous, noisy, ostentatious, dishonest and vulgar. In short it is among the most unpleasant places on earth.*

Chinua Achebe

Nigeria is a country many people feel needs no introduction: corruption, military dictatorships and urban violence seem to be its very definition. And if Chinua Achebe – one of the country's most humane and respected writer-philosphers – can describe Nigeria thus, then seeking to defend it may seem perverse.

But in truth, Nigeria's notoriety is unduly influenced by its *de facto* capital, **Lagos** – a city of incalculable population and urban distress. If you can handle the Lagos tempo its one big compensation is fine musical opportunities – no other city in West Africa is as blessed with night energy. If not, then leave the city – for **Oyo**, **Oshogbo**, **Ife**, **Benin**, or even giant **Ibadan** – and Lagos soon seems an anomaly: other cities certainly have their share of blight and bluster, but none really compares. These hinterland towns, where growth has been less dizzying and local traditions not yet bulldozed into oblivion, still show you hints of the greatness of the old Yoruba and Benin kingdoms in their palaces and museums, festivals and sacred sites.

To the **east** – beyond the geographical and cultural dividing line of the **Niger River** – the forests and plantations of the **Igbo Country** stretch out behind the vast fan of the **river delta**. This region has made a remarkable recovery since the civil war of the late 1960s, caused by its attempted secession, and its creek and waterfront towns – **Onitsha**, **Warri**, **Port Harcourt** – have gained a new prosperity with their oil reserves. They're mostly busy, self-interested cities and faintly anonymous until you root around a little, but the engaging old trading base of **Calabar** is immediately attractive and probably the country's most easy-going city. There's a conservation focus, too, in this corner of the country, since the rediscovery in 1987 of **gorillas**, long thought to have been extinct, now protected in the wilds of the **Cross River National Park**.

Central Nigeria is a region of lower population, higher ground and some inspiring scenery, dotted with outcrops and massive stone inselbergs. It is one of the best parts of the country to travel around and its main city, **Jos**, is an old hill station with a rare line in museums. Three other **wildlife reserves** – **Borgu** in the northwest, the new **Sabon Birnin Gwari** and the long-established **Yankari** with its remarkable natural swimming pool – are all located in this central region. And the **eastern highlands** are some of the most beautiful and unexplored mountains in Africa, abutting Cameroon's much better known Rhumsiki region.

The north of the country is **Hausa-Fulani** territory, predominantly Islamic, like the neighbouring regions of the French-speaking Sahel. There's a more comfortable climate at these latitudes and the cities are manageable, but it's the region's history – embodied in the **walled old cities** of Zaria, Katsina and the big metropolis of Kano – that gives northern Nigeria a special slant. While they can't compare for flavour and historical atmosphere with the old cities of North Africa or the Middle East, these emirates do have their special character. In the afternoon crush of the **Kurmi market** in Kano, or wandering through Zaria's striking **architecture**, or witnessing any of the amazing *Sallah* **durbar** festivals at the end of Ramadan, a much bigger and more rewarding view of Nigeria begins to emerge than the one most visitors bring with them.

FACTS AND FIGURES

The **Federal Republic of Nigeria** is the most populous country in Africa, with an estimated 100 million people (there has been no census since 1963); its land area of 924,000 square kilometres is nearly four times as big as Britain and bigger than Texas and New Mexico combined. **Lagos**, the largest city (at least eight million inhabitants), is the country's economic and cultural hub; administration, however, is slowly being transferred to the Federal Capital Territory of **Abuja**, in central Nigeria, which became the country's capital in 1991. Principal **exports** are oil, cocoa, palm products, rubber, timber and tin. Nigeria's **foreign debt** is in the order of £22 billion ($33 billion) – two and a half times the value of its annual exports of goods and services – which puts the country in a major league when that's compared with the relatively small sums owed by most African nations. Even so, in global terms, it's not an unimaginable figure – merely equivalent to the annual public expenditure of the state of New Jersey (population eight million), or roughly what the British Ministry of Defence spends in a year. Nigeria is currently governed by the **Armed Forces Ruling Council**, headed by **General Sani Abacha**. Democratic elections are not envisaged.

Nigeria is a federation, like the USA, divided into thirty states (plus the Federal Capital Territory), each with its own capital and state government (the 12 states created after the civil war in 1968 were increased to 19, then 21 and finally to 30 in 1991). The states are divided into three groups, separated by the Niger River and its tributary, the Benue.

NORTH
Bauchi (capital Bauchi)
Borno (capital Maiduguri)
Jigawa (capital Dutse)
Kaduna (capital Kaduna)
Kano (capital Kano)
Katsina (capital Katsina)
Kebbi (capital Birnin Kebbi)
Niger (capital Minna)
Plateau (capital Jos)
Sokoto (capital Sokoto)
Yobe (capital Damaturu)

SOUTHEAST
Abia (capital Umuahia)
Adamawa (capital Yola)
Akwa Ibom (capital Uyo)
Benue (capital Makurdi)
Cross River (capital Calabar)
Enugu (capital Enugu)
Imo (capital Owerri)
Rivers (capital Port Harcourt)
Taraba (capital Jalingo)

SOUTHWEST
Anambra (capital Enugu)
Delta (capital Asaba)
Edo (capital Benin City)
Kogi (capital Lokoja)
Kwara (capital Ilorin)
Lagos (capital Ikeja)
Ogun (capital Abeokuta)
Ondo (capital Akure)
Osun (capital Oshogbo)
Oyo (capital Ibadan)

The people

Geographically, Nigeria has been profoundly shaped by its two great rivers – the **Niger** and the **Benue** – which flow together in a Y-shape at Lokoja. This isn't the centre of the country, but it exactly corresponds to the meeting place of the three great cultural spheres which dominate Nigerian life – the southwest (**Yorubaland**), southeast (**Igboland**) and north (**Hausaland**).

The **ethnic differentiaion** of these regions is a convenient way of coming to grips with exceptionally complex cultural and linguistic groupings, but it does the country's "minorities" – several of which number in the millions and could be in the majority elsewhere in West Africa – a profound injustice. Nigeria in fact has no fewer than 250 peoples, speaking nearly as many languages in perhaps a total of 400 dialects, making it one of the world's most linguistically complex regions.

In the central part of the **southwest**, the Nupe are a major group and are culturally somewhat assimilated to the Yoruba. Other non-Yoruba speakers include **Edo**, **Urhobo**, **Itsekeri** and **Ijaw**.

In the **southeast**, the Igbo (formerly spelt Ibo) have cultural affiliations with the **Tiv** and **Jukun**. They are almost matched in numbers by the minority peoples who speak **Ibibio**, **Efik**, **Ekoi**, **Kalabari** and **Ogoni** – among dozens of other languages.

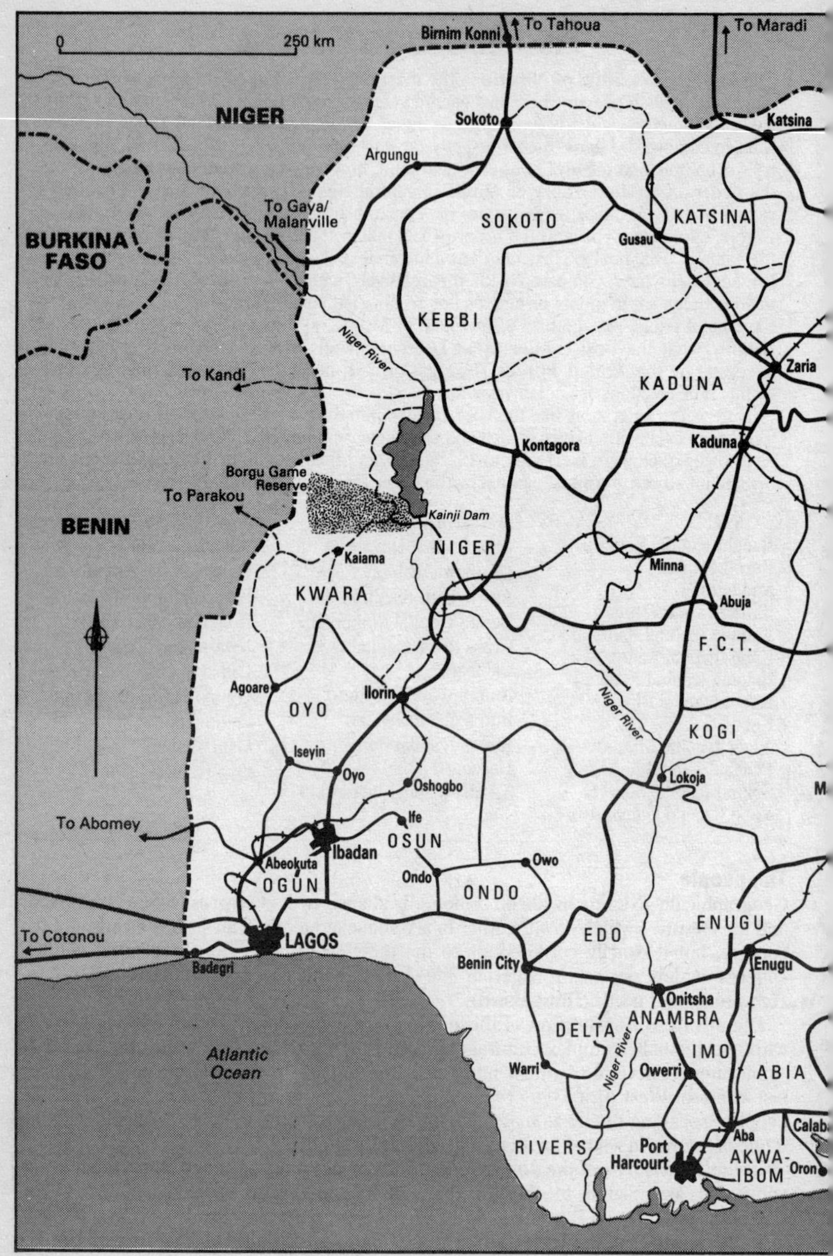
0
250 km
Birnim Konni
To Tahoua
To Maradi
NIGER
Sokoto
Katsina
Argungu
To Gaya/
Malanville
SOKOTO
KATSINA
Gusau
BURKINA
FASO
KEBBI
Niger River
To Kandi
Zaria
KADUNA
Kontagora
Kaduna
Borgu Game
Reserve
To Parakou
Kainji Dam
BENIN
NIGER
Kaiama
Minna
KWARA
Abuja
F.C.T.
Agoare
Ilorin
OYO
Niger River
KOGI
Iseyin
Oyo
Oshogbo
Lokoja
To Abomey
Ife
OSUN
Ibadan
Abeokuta
Owo
Ondo
OGUN
ONDO
ENUGU
To Cotonou
LAGOS
EDO
Badegri
Benin City
Enugu
Onitsha
ANAMBRA
DELTA
Atlantic
Ocean
IMO
Niger River
Warri
Owerri
ABIA
Aba
RIVERS
Port
Harcourt
AKWA-
IBOM
Oron

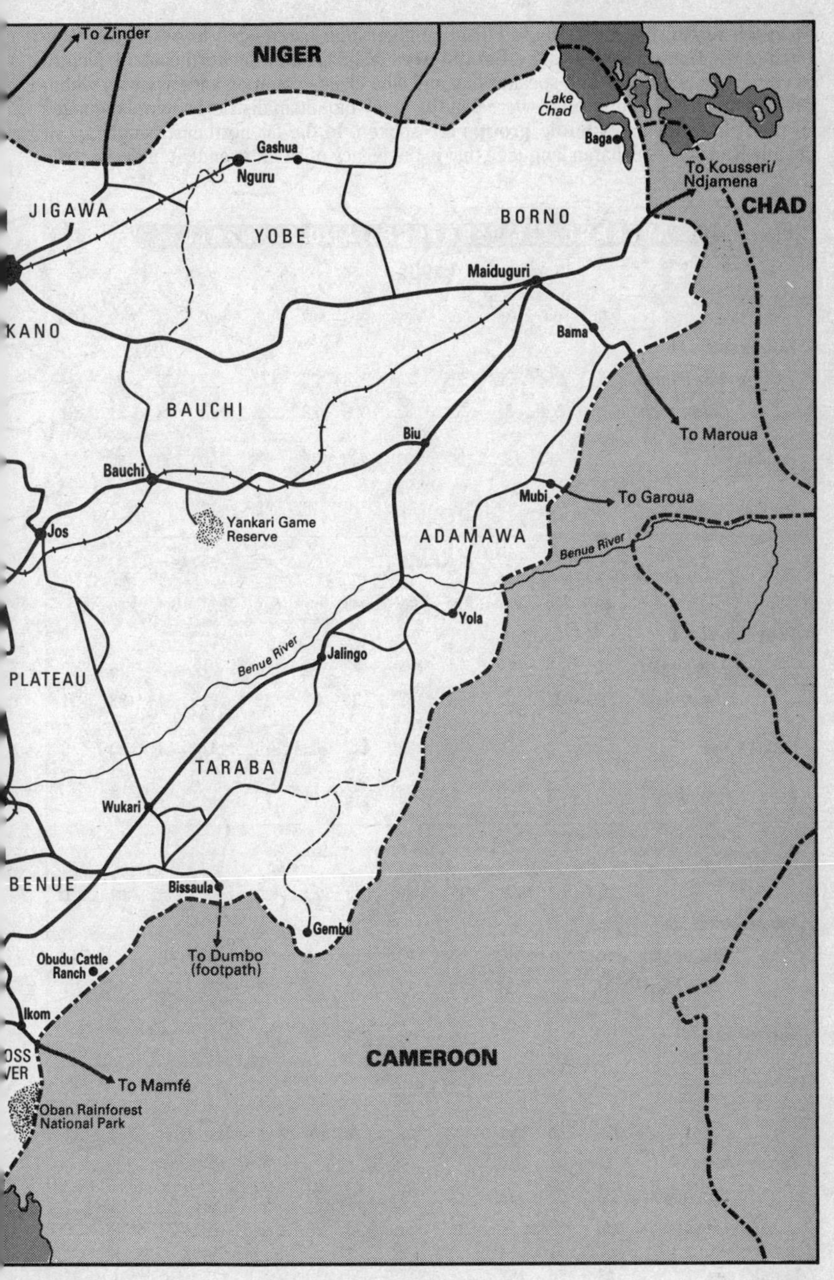
To Zinder
NIGER
Lake Chad
Baga
Gashua
Nguru
To Kousseri/ Ndjamena
CHAD
JIGAWA
YOBE
BORNO
Maiduguri
KANO
Bama
BAUCHI
Biu
To Maroua
Bauchi
Mubi
To Garoua
Yankari Game Reserve
Jos
ADAMAWA
Benue River
Yola
Jalingo
Benue River
PLATEAU
TARABA
Wukari
BENUE
Bissaula
Gembu
To Dumbo (footpath)
Obudu Cattle Ranch
Ikom
CAMEROON
To Mamfé
Oban Rainforest National Park

In the **north**, the great Hausa-Fulani configuration has tended to obscure groups such as the **Gwari**, as well as the **Bauchi area** languages. In the northeast the picture is very fragmented and who speaks what and who claims common ancestry with whom are questions still largely unanswered, in the many mountain districts where languages of the **Adamawa** and **Chadic groups** are spoken. In the far northeast people speak mainly **Kanuri** – a Saharan language that is the legacy of an independent imperial past.

AVERAGE TEMPERATURES AND RAINFALL

LAGOS

	Jan	Feb	Mar	Apr	May	June	July	Aug	Sept	Oct	Nov	Dec
Temperatures °C												
Min (night)	23	25	26	25	24	23	23	23	23	23	24	24
Max (day)	31	32	32	32	32	29	28	28	28	29	31	31
Rainfall mm	28	46	102	150	269	460	279	64	140	206	60	25
Days with rainfall	2	3	7	10	16	20	16	10	14	16	7	2

KANO

	Jan	Feb	Mar	Apr	May	June	July	Aug	Sept	Oct	Nov	Dec
Temperatures °C												
Min (night)	13	15	19	24	24	23	22	21	21	19	16	13
Max (day)	30	33	37	38	37	34	31	29	31	34	33	31
Rainfall mm	0	0	3	10	69	117	206	310	142	13	0	0
Days with rainfall	0	0	0	1	8	8	14	19	12	1	0	0

JOS

	Jan	Feb	Mar	Apr	May	June	July	Aug	Sept	Oct	Nov	Dec
Temperatures °C												
Min (night)	11	12	15	17	17	16	16	16	16	16	13	11
Max (day)	31	33	34	34	33	30	28	28	29	31	31	31
Rainfall mm	3	3	27	85	205	226	330	292	213	41	2	3

CALABAR

	Jan	Feb	Mar	Apr	May	June	July	Aug	Sept	Oct	Nov	Dec
Temperatures °C												
Min (night)	23	23	23	23	23	22	22	22	22	22	23	23
Max (day)	30	32	32	31	30	30	28	28	29	29	30	30
Rainfall mm	43	76	153	213	312	406	450	405	427	310	191	43

Climate

There's a clear climatic division between north and south and many variations within the two major zones. The most comfortable time to be in Lagos is December and January; on the Plateau, November to February; in Kano, November and December; and in Calabar, December.

Rains in **the north** fall during a single season, roughly between May and September. Usually this amounts to no more than 500mm (20 inches), most of it falling in the months of July and August. Typically the hottest months are March and April, when the *Harmattan* winds have run their course and the rains not yet begun; at this time, midday temperatures often rise above 45°C (113°F) in the shade.

In the **southwest**, the long rains bucket down from March to July with the wettest months usually May and June. There's a short lull, usually sometime in August (the "little dry"), then further heavy rain from September to October. The yearly rainfall in the southwest averages around 1800mm (72 inches).

In the **southeast**, the total annual rainfall can exceed 4000mm (160 inches – about five times the annual average of London or Minneapolis) and there is a continuous and somewhat depressing rainy season from April to October, with a brief drying-off period in the middle which is not guaranteed every year. Temperatures in the south tend to be lower than in the north despite the region's proximity to the equator, but the humidity can be really oppressive.

The details in these practical information pages are essentially for use on the ground in West Africa and in Nigeria itself: for full practical coverage on preparing for a trip, getting here from outside the region, paperwork, health, information sources and more, see *Basics*.

Arrivals

Flying into Lagos hardly provides an easy introduction to the continent (it helps to be met on arrival), but flying from London to Kano is much less intimidating and can be convenient for starting your travels in West Africa (see p.1097). Overland routes from Niger are good and there are also fast connections to Nigeria along the coast from Togo and Benin. Road links with Cameroon are poorer.

■ Flights from Africa

While Nigeria's intercontinental air links are well developed, links within **West Africa** have surprising gaps: there are no direct flights, for example, from Niamey, Nouakchott, Ouagadougou, or Bissau (the only options are on *Air Afrique*, with inconvenient connections in Abidjan). Although several Nigerian airports have international facilities, all flights from other parts of West Africa arrive in Lagos. *Nigeria Airways* (WT) handles the largest share of the traffic (it occasionally suspends certain routes), followed by *Air Afrique* (RK).

WT flies from **Dakar**, via **Banjul**, **Conakry**, **Abidjan** and **Lomé** on Tues, and operates almost the same route (commencing in Banjul) on Sat. *Air Gabon* (GN) operates a similar route (Dakar–Conakry–Abidjan–Cotonou–Lagos) on Tues and Fri.

Conakry also has non-stop flight to Lagos on Mon and Thurs with *Guinée Airlines* (G7) and a flight every Fri on *Air Guinée* (GI) via **Bamako** – which is Mali's only air link with Nigeria.

From **Freetown** to Lagos, the only reliable services are operated by *Ghana Airways* (GH), with connections in Accra. However, *Sierra National Airlines* (LJ) aims to fly non-stop to Lagos every Tues.

From **Abidjan**, there's an average of two non-stop and one or two stopping services every day. Any travel agent can fix you up with a seat.

Of the other nearby capitals, **Accra** has one to three flights daily to Lagos, nearly all of them non-stop; **Lomé** has one daily flight from Wed to Sun; and Cotonou at least one flight every day (though from Cotonou you should seriously consider going by land – it's only 120km and you'll probably get there quicker, airport delays taken into account).

Lastly, **Douala** has at least one flight each day to Lagos on RK, WT or *Cameroon Airlines* (UY). Flights with WT go via Port Harcourt on Sat and Calabar on Mon.

■ Other African air links

From **Central Africa** there are several direct flights each week to Lagos from Kinshasha (*Air Zaire* and WT), Bangui (RK), Libreville (GN, WT via Port Harcourt) and Brazzaville (*Ethiopian Airlines* and WT), and weekly flights on UY from Malabo, Equatorial Guinea, via Douala.

From **East Africa**, ET flies four times a week from Addis Ababa – non-stop to Lagos on Tues and Thurs, via Nairobi on Sun and via Nairobi and Brazzaville on Sat. UY also flies from Nairobi, but you have to get a connecting flight in Douala.

The only direct flight from **southern Africa** is *Balkan Bulgarian*'s weekly haul from Harare.

■ Overland from Cameroon – and Chad

The main frontier crossing from Cameroon is **Mamfé to Ikom**, over the Cross River bridge. Customs and immigration for Cameroon are in **Ekok**, on the east bank of the Cross (open daily 8am–7pm), whence you walk over the bridge to **Mfum**, the Nigerian post. As Nigeria and Cameroon have been close to war at several times in the last few years, over disputed offshore territories, you would do well to assume this border will be a hassle. The heaviest traffic is at dusk and dawn, when it can take hours to get through (many drivers stay overnight in Ekok), but because of the geography on the Cameroonian side it's almost impossible to time your arrival during the day. There's a less often used, but viable and more direct route from Mamfé to Calabar, turning off south (left) from the "main" Ikom road at **Eyumajok**, 48km west of Mamfé. Note also that the Mamfe–Ikom road is frequently impassable on the Cameroonian side during the rainy season. For further details see the "Moving On" box on p.1077. From Mfum, catch another taxi to **Ikom** and onwards to **Calabar** or **Enugu**.

Further north, out of the Bamenda Highlands, you can cross on foot from **Dumbo to Bissaula** (see p.1182 and p.1116), and there are minor crossings all the way along the mountainous border, though few see much traffic.

The rough route from Garoua to **Yola** is a little busier, as is the northern route from Mora to **Banki** – a village straddling the border. Customs and immigration at Banki are generally low-key, but the small post is poorly equipped and the waits can sometimes be long. Taxis are generally no problem from here to Maiduguri.

Finally, there's the northernmost crossing from **Kousseri** to **Fotokol** (Cameroon formalities) and **Gambaru** (Nigerian post). This is your likely way into Nigeria coming from Ndjamena in Chad. If you're transiting Cameroon like this, the Cameroon customs will issue you with a free one-day transit visa at the immigration post in Kousseri.

■ Overland from Niger

Coming from Niger two main routes aim for **Kano**, one from **Maradi**, the other from **Zinder**. The latter route is preferable since Zinder is a beautiful Hausa town with outstanding architecture and a giant market. Coming from Maradi, however, would allow you to take in the old Nigerian emirate of **Katsina**. You can also cross from **Birnin Konni to Sokoto**, or, further west, from **Gaya to Kamba** from where you can connect to Sokoto. All four routes have good bush taxi transport.

■ From Ghana, Togo and Benin

The **coastal route** from **Accra** (476km) and **Lomé** (275km) to **Lagos** takes in some picturesque coastal scenery of palms, creeks and beaches. By private car, the trip takes a full day (about eight hours) but it may take half as long again or more if you're travelling by public transport as the vehicle is repeatedly unloaded and reloaded at the three borders, each with customs and immigration posts on both sides.

The Benin border tends to be a hassle these days, as Benin is suspected of being a base for a "terrorist campaign" against Nigeria's military government. An extra complication is that Togo's borders have frequently been closed due to the political instability of recent years. Typically they have re-opened quickly, but if the situation arises, you may be compelled to fly from Accra to Lagos.

Barring that eventuality, you can get taxis direct to Lagos from Accra, Lomé or Cotonou. They're relatively cheap these days, but you can cut further on costs by taking the taxi to the **Kraké** frontier post and finding another vehicle on from there.

If you're intent on avoiding Lagos altogether, get yourself to **Porto Novo** in Benin, from where you can enter Nigeria 30km north at the Idioko frontier post, continuing from here on the A5-1 to meet the main A5 Lagos–Abeokuta road 10km north of Ikeja. If you're relying on public transport, however, you will end up at the Oshodi motor park in northern Lagos, where you can get onward transport without going into the city centre.

Red Tape

Visas are required by all except ECOWAS nationals. Nigerian officials are not usually familiar with the idea of foreigners visiting the country for tourism and some border crossings can be heavy. You may well be asked to pay customs duty on some of your personal belongings – up to you to prove as cheerfully as possible that they are your personal belongings, and not dutiable merchandise.

■ Nigerian visas

Nigeria has embassies or high commissions in most major capital cities. The policy is for the embassy in each country to issue **visas** only to nationals (or long-term residents) of that country, and to do so only once travel details such as date of arrival, itinerary and evidence of sufficient funds are produced (£500 is the figure commonly expected of British passport holders). For overland travel this isn't likely to be convenient and you will be obliged to pick up a visa at a Nigerian embassy in a country en route, some of which are prepared to bend the rules. In **Yaoundé** and **Lomé** for example, visas are delivered within 48 hours and are quite cheap. British passport holders, however, are at a further disadvantage. Since the imposition of harsh regulations on Nigerians visiting Britain, UK nationals are sometimes subject to deliberate bureaucratic obstruction.

■ Vehicle documents

Nigeria requires a **Carnet de Passage en Douane** issued by the AA or similar organization. Be sure to get one before arriving here as the alternative is to pay 250 percent of the value of the car in hard currency at the border and receive it back in Naira when you leave. When leaving the country, be wary of giving up your carnet, as the authorities may neglect to return their copy of the document to your national motorists' association as required, thereby holding up the release of your funds from bond.

As for **insurance documents**, you may find, as have many travellers, that the *Campbell Irvine* certificate, which specifically excludes third-party risks in Nigeria, is acceptable to the police, even though it doesn't cover you. However, as local Nigerian insurance doesn't cost much at the frontier, it seems foolhardy not to buy it. If you have already bought regional coverage in another ECOWAS member country, it is valid in Nigeria.

■ Other red tape

It's illegal to export antique works of art, and there's full scope for anything that looks old to be confiscated when you come to leave, unless you have obtained a **certificate of export** from the National Museum in Lagos. Barring that, anything you buy that looks like art or an antique is best sent home through an air or sea freight agency.

■ Visas for onward travel

Most **West African countries** have embassies in Lagos: few have yet moved to Abuja. Cape Verde and Guinea Bissau have no representatives; for these, a visit to the Portuguese embassy, one of the few in West Africa, might be worthwhile. For addresses, see Lagos "Listings".

While visas for neighbouring countries can be obtained in Lagos, it's useful to know that you can also get **Cameroon visas** at the Cameroonian consulate in **Calabar** (and generally with less hassle than in Lagos where a letter of reference from your embassy is required). **Niger visas** can be obtained at the consulate in **Kano**.

Money and Costs

Nigeria's currency is the Naira (₦), divided into 100 kobo. There are coins of 50 kobo and ₦1 (though you rarely see coins in use), and notes of ₦5, ₦10, ₦20 and ₦50. Currently, the approximate *official* rate of exchange, pegged to the fortunes of the US dollar, is ₦22 = US$1 (₦35 = £1), but on the free market (including from hotels and forex bureaux) £1 buys up to ₦130 as of mid-1995.

■ Exchange

Changing money can take ages but is rarely a problem in Lagos. In other towns, banks can be fussy about travellers' cheques, sometimes asking to see receipts from the place of issue. Privately operated **forex bureaux** (bureaux de change) are less of a hassle to deal with and give substantially higher rates than banks for cash in £ or US$. Travellers' cheques and all other currencies in cash attract much lower rates.

As regards **banks**, you'll generally have best luck changing francs at branches of *Afribank Nigeria*. The other main banks – *African Continental*, *First Bank* and *Union Bank* (ex-*Barclays*) – have branches in large towns throughout the country. You're unlikely to get a cash advance on any credit card in Nigeria – absolutely not with a *Visa* card.

■ The Black Market

You can still change hard currencies on the streets of Lagos and other cities close to the borders, but it hardly seems worth the risk and hassle as you'll get more or less the same deal from an authorized currency dealer in a forex bureau or hotel. Currency smuggling and illicit dealing is treated as a serious offence. **Export and import of Naira** is prohibited.

■ Costs

The Naira has fluctuated substantially over the last few years, and anything may happen in the future. You should generally find costs reasonable – even quite decent hotels can be found for under £10 ($15) a night, and long-distance travel is a real bargain. Recent government measures, notably lifting the subsidy on petrol (gasoline), have started an upward spiral of prices, but petrol is still no more than £0.50 ($0.75) per gallon (less than $0.20/litre). If you're buying fuel, the question is always whether to queue at filling stations to buy it at the official price, or to pick it up from roadside hawkers for two or three times the price.

Health

Vaccination certificates for yellow fever are mandatory. Immigration officials sometimes also demand cholera vaccination certificates. Malaria, however, should be your main health concern.

Water is good and drinkable from the taps in most towns across the country. In isolated rural areas, it requires filtering or purification tablets. In the dry season, rural areas are often short of water and people have to make great efforts to keep supplied, so if you're travelling in the sticks in March or April don't be surprised if there's a certain reluctance to fill your water bottles, at least for free.

Hospitals are reasonably well equipped in comparison to neighbouring countries. In Lagos, the **Eko Hospital** is one of the better places to go for treatment (see Lagos "Listings"). Also recommended is the **Sacred Heart Hospital** in Abeokuta, 100km north of Lagos. In a case of serious illness, contact your embassy.

Information, Maps and Guides

Tourist offices and local branches of the Ministry of Information can be found throughout the country – and are listed throughout this chapter. There are no overseas tourist offices.

As for **maps**, the *Michelin* #953 is largely accurate and constantly improving. This apart, there is little worth acquiring, though in Nigeria you'll find several larger scale national **road maps** – published by *Spectrum*, *Peugeot* and the *Nigeria Mapping Company* all at 1cm:15km. The *Macmillan* Nigeria map (also 1cm:15km) is disappointingly featureless and quite at odds with the *Michelin* map. The same applies to the *Bartholomew* map (1cm:15km), though it does at least have a little topographical detail.

Recently published **town plans** of a number of cities are available in bookshops and stationery stores and at their respective tourist offices.

■ Local guidebooks and streetfinders

For a **long stay in Lagos**, get hold of a copy of the annual *Guide to Lagos* by Philippe Dupriez and Jacques Soulillou (in French and English, published by the French Cultural Centre in Lagos). This has complete, map-keyed listings of hotels, nightclubs and travel details, plus considerable cultural information and masses of listings. The guide's "streetfinder" is better than adequate, but for greater legibility and real detail, get the *Winnay Lagos Street Atlas* (Macmillan, 1985), an admirable full colour A–Z.

A more general resident's guide is *Survive Lagos* by Elizabeth Cox and Erica Anderssen (Spectrum 1984), a lot blander than its title suggests and very out of date, but useful nonetheless and with some countrywide coverage. More recent and therefore more helpful is *Enjoy Nigeria: A Travel Guide* by Ian Nason (Spectrum 1991) which has good nationwide coverage and tips for travelling on your own.

Getting Around

Nigeria has some 70,000km of paved roads – a fairly remarkable figure for this part of the world. Road transport is easily the fastest in West Africa – often dangerously so. A rail network connect the northern and southern extremities of the country, but all Nigerian train services are currently suspended. Domestic air services are relatively good and reasonably priced. River travel on the Niger and Benue isn't developed commercially.

■ Bush taxis and buses

Bush taxis are quick and comfortable – though any concerns you may have about speeding are justified: be prepared to shout at the driver to slow down if you fear for your life. Fortunately, overcrowding is the exception rather than the rule. There's usually a choice between a Peugeot 504 (estate or saloon) and a 16-seat Japanese minibus. There's rarely a long wait in the motor parks of major cities. **Buses** ("luxury buses" as the companies like to call them) also link major cities and usually run to fixed schedules.

■ Getting around towns

Every Nigerian town has countless bust-up old taxis making the rounds. The usual distinction applies between those which are driving fixed routes and piling customers in for very modest fees per sector and those which hire out as private cabs and cost appreciably more for pre-agreed journeys. Whichever you choose, your progress may be extremely slow, especially at rush hours. To overcome the "go-slows" (traffic jams) a common phenomenon in most cities is that of **choba** – motorcycle taxis – which you hail at the roadside and are very cheap. Mostly, they're also very competent, but they're not much use if you are not travelling alone, or if you're weighed down with luggage.

Hitching

Hitching in Nigeria isn't especially difficult but you need to be confident of your abilities to tell a bad driver from a fast driver, and to act decisively on your conclusion – much better to be stranded on the highway than spread over it. Truck drivers are your best bet, and they'll often want payment.

Cycling

The perspective you get on the country from a **bicycle** saddle is unlike any other. Everyone you meet will think you're mad but the rewards of cycling in Nigeria are as big as the country itself and the supposed dangers fade to a manageable scale among all the pleasures – of magnificent landscapes, bush camping, village markets, small town evenings and off-road explorations.

On the road, you will never be ignored, so the fear of being hit is diminished: but you should obviously keep off the main highways as much as possible. Be sure to have a mirror, and be careful when camping en route (see below).

DRIVING IN NIGERIA

Nigerian **petrol** is very inexpensive, though filling stations often have long lines or low supplies and people often buy at the side of the road from jars or four gallon "Sunflower" cans. Much of the petrol is smuggled out of the country to be sold on the roadside in Benin or Cameroon.

Nigerian **oil** is of high quality and multigrade petrol/gasoline and diesel engine oils are readily available and cheap. Gearbox fluid (*Hypoy*) and automatic or power steering transmission fluids are harder to come by, though, and even in large towns you might need to spend several hours cruising round filling stations to find what you need. In extremis, most motor parts stores sell oils by the litre.

If you're on a long overland trip, it's worth **stocking up** with two or more complete fluid changes. You won't be taxed at the border and it'll be four times as expensive in the surrounding franc zone countries (and possibly unavailable for days or weeks in the Sahel). Beware of taking large quantities of fuel into Cameroon, where you may be accused of fuel-smuggling: there's a major trade in smuggled Nigerian petrol, which is sold, often watered down, by the roadside.

Nigerian **motor parts** are good quality and available for a wide range of Japanese, French, British and German cars. Prices are about the same as in Europe but it's well worth knowing the list price of any parts you might need, as the first price quoted may be twice what the item is worth. Small town parts traders will bargain, but usually start off with a sensible price. Original manufacturers' parts, as everywhere, carry a premium.

The main **sale and exchange of parts** (outside Lagos) is in Kano, in the streets around Ogbomosho Avenue in the Sabon Gari district. As soon as you pull up you'll be offered whatever you want by a young man who doesn't own a shop but operates on commission. It's generally quicker to go directly to a dealer in your make and check his stock personally.

ROADS

Nigerian **main roads** were superb until the early 1990s, by which time they were beginning to need more maintenance than they were getting. Since then, the neglect of the network has become an increasing problem, causing serious accidents and millions of dollars' worth of damage in a society by now very mobile and car-oriented.

In theory, collapsed sections of road ahead are flagged by signs with a skull and crossbones followed at 100m intervals by 60, 50, 40 and 30 "Slow Down" signs. But hundreds of kilometres of road surface are now in a very bad state and the warning system is becoming redundant. Drive with extreme caution.

Along all main roads there are regular roadside **marker stones** marked with the first three letters of the name of the next and previous major towns, and the distance in kilometres.

CAR RENTAL

The cost of **car rental** has gone down in recent years, but it's still quite pricey as a **driver** often comes with the vehicle. Many Lagos outlets insist on this – and it's preferable if you're new to the city; elsewhere you may be able to drive yourself. The distinction between chauffeur-driven car rental and taking a taxi is blurred; be clear that you will pay for fuel.

See also "Trouble on the road" p.1013.

■ Planes

Nigeria Airways links Lagos, Abuja, Calabar, Enugu, Jos, Kaduna, Kano, Maiduguri, Makurdi, Port Harcourt, Sokoto and Yola. Tickets are cheap and on some routes there are several flights a day to and from Lagos. Reservations normally aren't taken so get to the airport early even though your plane is likely to leave late.

Several **private airlines**, including *ADC* (currently one of the largest), *Triax, Belleview, Haco, Okada Air* and *Kabo Airlines* operate out of the domestic airport at Ikeja, Lagos. They generally offer relatively inexpensive and professional service (though flying with *Kabo* is always an adventure) and are preferred by frequent-flyers over the "flying elephant" *Nigeria Airways. ADC, Haco* and *Belleview* are probably the most reliable.

■ River transport

River transport is mainly bulk goods traffic rather than passengers. Boats operate along some 6500km of waterways in Nigeria, half of which consists of the **Niger** and **Benue** rivers. During the rainy season, boats go up the Benue all the way to Garoua in Cameroon.

Since the completion of the **Kainji Dam and Reservoir**, the Niger is apparently navigable above it to Niamey, though below it, only as far as Jebba. Whether you can get transport along these stretches is uncertain. **Onitsha**, the main river port, is the place to find out.

Boats also operate along the **creeks and lagoons** of coastal towns, details of which can be found in the Lagos, Port Harcourt and Calabar sections.

Accommodation

In the 1970s and 80s, international-style hotels started springing up everywhere from Lagos to Maiduguri, Calabar to Sokoto. Although multinational chains are represented, some of the newer hotels, notably in the *Arewa* chain, are Nigerian owned and operated, cheap by the standards of neighbouring countries and very comfortable. Two important, general points to note: all hotels levy a fifteen percent tax and require a deposit, usually at least equal to a night's lodging.

Upmarket hotels have every mod con in the rooms and some also have tennis courts and pools. Water and electricity go out often and unpredictably, but bigger places have generators to cope. Most hotels of standing have rates for residents and non-residents, the latter being substantially higher and often payable in foreign currency.

Rooms in **budget hotels** (£2–20/$3–30) may range from a bed with four walls to gadget-filled abodes cluttered with TV, rattling AC units and leaking fridges. Prices vary according to the perks, which are becoming more and more

ACCOMMODATION PRICE CODES

Hotel prices in this chapter are coded according to the following scales – the same scales in terms of their pound/dollar equivalents as are used throughout the book. Prices refer to the rate you can expect to pay for a room with two beds. Some hotels charge twice the normal rate for foreigners. Where they exist, such "non-residents" rates are the rates given in the guide. Single rooms, or single occupancy, will normally cost at least two-thirds of the twin-occupancy rate. For further details see p.51.

① **Under ₦650 (under £5/$7.50).** A range of possibilities, from the most rudimentary flophouse to a modest budget-priced hotel with good facilities.

② **₦650–1300 (£5–10/$7.50–15).** S/C rooms, (usually with some sort of AC unit), and a reasonable restaurant.

③ **₦1300–2600 (£10–20/$15–30).** Adequate, business-class establishment, often with extras, such as phones or TV in rooms.

④ **₦2600–3900 (£20–30/$30–45).** Standard, business-class hotel, with full facilities, in which the AC generally works efficiently.

⑤ **₦3900–5200 (£30–40/$45–60).** Similar standards to the previous code band but extra facilities such as a pool.

⑥ **₦5200–6500 (£40–50/$60–75).** Comfortable, first-class hotel, with good facilities.

⑦ **Over ₦6500 (over £50/$75).** Luxury, international-class hotel.

common. In towns of any size, rooms without electricity and facilities are becoming rare. The term **"single"**, incidentally, refers to the number of beds in the room. The price you pay is for the room, and you'll often find the single bed is nearly two metres wide.

If you're driving, it's essential to find a **hotel with a compound**, where the gates are locked and usually guarded through the night. There's no extra charge.

Missions

The Evangelical Church of West Africa (**ECWA**) runs a series of **mission guesthouses** throughout the country, often in association with the Sudan Inland Mission (**SIM**). They're very cheap – and VSOs and other volunteers get a further discount. Rooms are generally tidy and spartan but in the better guesthouses – as in Jos, for example – come quite well equipped.

Camping

If you have your own transport, **camping** can be a good option – but the further off the beaten track the better. You should be very wary of camping within 50km of the urban centres and it's wise to stay right away from the more congested parts of the south. Don't camp anywhere near busy roads with a car or other large vehicle, as the attention you'll attract spreads rapidly and isn't always welcome.

Eating and Drinking

European, Lebanese and Asian restaurants are found in almost any large town, and most hotels have their own restaurants for either Nigerian or European meals (often with two menus). Beware: Nigerian food in the south is usually eaten firey hot with a devotion to chilli that makes a vindaloo or the hottest salsa seem mild by comparison. Many hotels also serve English breakfasts of eggs, toast, marmalade, tea and juice – a pleasant change from the French bread and coffee of the Francophone countries.

Assuming you're eating in **local restaurants and chop houses** – *buka* in Yoruba – there's a wide range of foods and dishes you'll come across (see box). In addition, chicken and chips (fries), and omelette and chips are universally available (in cheaper places the price of an omelette includes bread and "Lipton's").

Vegetarians have a moderately difficult time in restaurants, as many apparently (even explicitly) "vegetarian" items on menus should be understood as "plus a bit of meat" – usually goat. But salad vegetables are often crisp and fresh, and delicious once you overcome any worries about them having been washed in unsterilized water. Good transport helps to provide fresh fruit and veg even to dry regions and parts of the country where they would otherwise be out of season.

If you're travelling cheaply it's easy enough to **live on the basics**. Bread with tinned Blue Band margarine, hard-boiled eggs, portions of deep-fried fish (with or without scalding chilli sauce), bananas, oranges and salted roast peanuts make for a reasonably balanced diet that's obtainable in the remotest parts of the country. While supplies of milk are less reliable than in neighbouring countries, you can find milk powder all over (pushed by the drug companies for baby feed) which mixes well with chocolate powder (also widely available). The worst aspect of this budget diet is the bread – sweet, brick-shaped, often coloured yellow or pink and plastic-bagged.

Drinking

Nigerians are great **beer** drinkers. Every state has its own breweries and their advertisement hoardings are one of the countries' most pervasive symbols. A widely available brand is **Star** – 5% alcohol. Among the other thirty-odd brands are **Rock**, **Gulder**, **Harp** and **Satzenbrau** (a new premium lager). Beware cheaper brands, which tend to provoke treacherous hangovers and, so many people maintain, diarrhoea. And be cautious with Nigerian **Guinness** – which is an impressive eight percent alcohol by volume.

Palm wine, tapped from oil palms, is drunk in the south and pasteurized bottled versions are available, although their taste is a far cry from the frothy sweetness of the bush brews. Distilled, the wine becomes potent *ogogoro*, also common but usually more discreetly sold.

Coke, Sprite, Fanta and Doctor Pepper figure prominently in a long list of minerals manufactured in Nigeria. You can find them cold from fridges – at a filling station if nowhere else – all over the country.

NIGERIAN NOSH

THE BASICS

Amala	Yams ground before boiling – the finished product has a brown colour of little initial appeal.
Eba	Moist ball of steamy *gari* (cassava flour), overwhelmingly the favourite national dish, bland on its own and extremely heavy but always eaten with a hot sauce.
Fufu	Fermented pounded cassava.
Pounded yam	Boiled yam that's been pounded to a wonderful, glazey, aerated blob – which can be delicious when you're really hungry. Commonly eaten in the south, often with a palm oil or groundnut-based soup.

THE TASTY PART

Akara	Beans (cow peas or *Ogbono*).
Begiri	Yoruba bean soup.
Bitter leaf	Not far from spinach.
Bushmeat	Any kind of game meat, including antelope, but the most valued is grass-cutter (or cutting-grass), the giant herbivorous rodent also known as cane rat and, euphemistically in French, as *agouti* (an unrelated animal).
Cowleg	Prosaic local term for shin of beef.
Dodo	Fried plantains.
Draw Soup	Igbo soup which "draws" (ie it's mucilaginous or viscous) , made from ground Ogbono seeds.
Egusi	Oily soup based on pounded melon seeds, usually containing stock fish or meat and green leaves (bitter leaf or pumpkin leaf).
Eja gbigbe	Yoruba smoked fish on a stick.
Igbin	Large forest snails; they taste rubbery and are usually eaten with an extremely hot sauce.
Jollof rice	Rice cooked with palm oil, served with vegetables and meat.
Moin-moin	A delicious steamed bean cake snack with a slightly gelatinous texture, found mainly in the south. *Kause* are the fried variety.
Okro	Gumbo, okra, ladies' fingers.
Soup	Any stew, often thick, often hot.
Stock fish	Air-dried fish, usually cod (from Norway) soaked and cooked.
Suya	Grilled kebabs of beef, mutton or occasionally camel, sold everywhere but especially in the north. In the Yoruba and Ibo countries you'll find a variation on these kebabs made from black-eye peas, or fried bean fritter.

Communications – Languages, Post, Phones and Media

Nigeria's official language is English and in the larger cities – especially those with universities – it's spoken widely and with accents you'll adapt to easily. Pidgin English, however, which is spoken as a lingua franca everywhere, especially in the smaller towns and rural areas, will initially throw you. Keep trying, though; ask people to repeat phrases, and before long most visitors find their own speech punctuated with pidgin expressions.

The three most widely spoken ethnic languages are **Hausa**, **Yoruba** and **Igbo** (see boxes overleaf and on p.950). Next to these, there are some 400 separate dialects representing twelve language families. The linguistic situation in central and southeast Nigeria is one of the most complicated in the world and on the islands of the Delta region there are villages a few kilometres apart with mutually incomprehensible tongues.

■ Post and phones

Mail is unpredictable and letters to and from Europe and North America can take anything from a couple of days to two weeks or more to arrive. The **poste restante** in Lagos, however, despite its disorganized state – all letters are thrown in a pile and tied together with string – works relatively well. Kano and Kaduna also seem reasonable places to receive mail. **To send mail out**, many people still use courier firms or friends flying abroad. The post office's **EMS Speedpost** is, however, inexpensive and reliable in addition to being quick: three days to Europe and five to Australia for parcels and letters alike.

Telephones are run by NITEL. **Phoning abroad**, you can dial directly from Lagos and a couple of other cities; the best lines are from Kaduna. Connections are usually good, but you may be cut in the middle of a conversation for no apparent reason. To make a reverse-charge (collect) call to an overseas number, dial the foreign operator (☎191).

Nigeria's IDD code is ☎234. Domestic codes are 0X or 0XX and numbers can be six digits (usually), five or four digits.

YORUBA

Yoruba is a difficult, tonal language, a cluster of close dialects in the Kwa grouping. Because meaning is so dependent on tone, messages can be easily understood with little vocalization:talking drums were (and still are) able to transmit messages, and you don't have to listen to much of Sunny Ade's music to realize how easily this is accomplished. The diacritics in the following words and phrases are not accents but indicate the tone of the sound – either rising (´), or falling (`). E is pronounced "Eh" or "Ey" and O is pronouced "Or" or "Oh". E is the plural or formal prefix.

GREETINGS

Good morning	*E káàárò*	Greeting someone just arriving or returning	*E káàbò*
Response	*E káàárò*	Greeting someone who is working	*E kúushé*
Good afternoon	*E káàsán*	Response (lit. thank you)	*Adúpé*
Response	*E káàsán*	How are you?, how's life?	*Shé alaáfià ni*
Good evening	*E káalé*	Response (lit. thank you)	*Adúpé*
Response	*E káalé*	Goodbye	*Ó dàbò*
On entering a house	*E kúulé*		
Response	*E káàbò*		

PERFUNCTORY CONVERSATION

I want	*Mo féé*	Money	*Owo*
I don't want	*Mi ò féé*	Please, reduce the price	*E dín owó lori e*
Which one?	*È wo?*	Give me	*E fún mi*
This is the one	*Eléyìí*	All right, okay	*Ó dáa*
Take (it)	*E gbà*	Please	*E jòó*
Water	*Omi*	Don't be annoyed	*E má bínú*
Meat	*Eran*	What's your name?	*Kini oruko ré?*
Palm wine	*Emmu*	My name is Dayo	*Dayo ni oruko mi*
Thank you (on receiving it)	*E sheé*	Greetings/commiserations	*Pèlé*
How much is (it)?	*Èló ní?*	I don't understand Yoruba	*Mi ò gbo Yoruba*
It's ten naira	*Naira mewa ni*	No, (not) at all	*Rárá*
To pay	*Sanwó*	My friend	*Òré mi*

NUMBERS

1	*ookan*	9	*mesan*	17	*metadinlogun*	30	*ogbon*
2	*méjì*	10	*mewa*	18	*mejidinlogun*	40	*ogoji*
3	*méta*	11	*mokanla*	19	*mokondinlogun*	50	*adota*
4	*merin*	12	*mejila*	20	*ogun*	60	*ogota*
5	*marun*	13	*metala*	21	*mokan le logun*	70	*aadorin*
6	*mefa*	14	*merinla*	22	*meji le logun*	80	*ogorin*
7	*meje*	15	*mèedogun*	25	*mèd ogbon*	90	*adorun*
8	*mejo*	16	*meridlogun*	26	*meridin logbon*	100	*ogorun*

The Media

Nigeria is a country where it's fun to read the **newspapers**. They're outspoken and informative and there are lots of them. Coming from Cameroon, Benin or Togo, the frankness of the editorials and bite of political cartoons is refreshing. Most of Nigeria's papers are privately owned ventures (though *Daily Times Publications* is a government-owned company). Of course there are limits to how far criticism can go and the new military government has put restrictions on the press, but there's still a wide range of styles and opinions.

Some fifteen percent of the population reads the news regularly, and the major dailies have circulations ranging from 100,000–400,000. New titles appear on the stands all the time, but of the 100 or more tabloids printed throughout the country, six national dailies dominate – *The Guardian, Daily Times* (top circulation), *The Punch, New Nigerian, Vanguard* and *National Concorde*. The *Guardian* and *National Concorde* provide the most complete economic and political analysis but none of the papers is very strong on international news. There are some big-circulation Sundays, too – with the *Sunday Times* weighing in with a readership of 500,000 – and some twenty weekly news magazines are also published.

Political affiliations have resulted in frequent bannings. The *Guardian* was banned in August 1994, and the *National Concorde* (owned by Muslim Yoruba millionaire Moshood Abiola,

IGBO

Igbo is also a tone language and part of the great Kwa grouping – but it is not intelligible to Yoruba speakers. Again, be prepared to squeeze your mouth a little to get an intelligible vowel sound.

GREETINGS

Hi/How are you?	*Kèdú/Kèdú ka í mère ?*	Welcome (to one who has arrived)	*Nnòo*
How are the children?	*Kèdú maka umú-àka?*	Keep up the good work/well done	*Jisie ike*
I'm fine	*Ó dì nma*	Thank you	*Daalu/Imèela*
Good morning?	*Ututu òma?*	Good bye	*Ka e mesia*
Good night	*Ka chií fò*		

BASIC CHAT

Please	*Bìkó*	How much?/How much money?	*Olé?/Egó olé?*
Sorry (commiserations)	*Ndó*	Give	*Nyé*
What's your name?	*Kèdú àha gí?*	Give me	*Nyé m*
My name is Theodora	*Áhà m bu Theodora*	Come	*Byá*
Where are you from?	*E béè ka ísì?*	Go	*Jé*
I'm from Scotland	*E sim Scotland*	Come in	*Bhàta*
Where are you going?	*E béè ka í na-ijè?*	Good	*Ézí*
I'm going to Enugu	*Á na m èje Enugu*	This soup's tasty	*Ófé tòrò èto*
I want	*Á chorò m*	It's good	*Ó dè úmá*
I want to go to the market	*Á chorò m ije ahia*	Meat	*Áné*
I want to buy	*Á chorò m ego*	Pepper	*Ose*
This one	*Nke á*	Water	*Mmírí*
How much is this?	*Nka á bù olé?*		

NUMBERS

1	*ótu*	9	*itenanì*	17	*irí na asáà*	50	*irí ìsé*
2	*abúo*	10	*irí*	18	*irí na asáto*	60	*irí ìsí*
3	*àtó*	11	*irí na ótu*	19	*irí na itenanì*	70	*irí asáà*
4	*ànó*	12	*irí na abúo*	20	*irí abúo*	80	*irí asáto*
5	*ìsé*	13	*irí na àtó*	21	*irí abúo na ótu*	90	*irí itenanì*
6	*ìsí*	14	*irí na ànó*	22	*irí abúo na abúo*	100	*nari*
7	*asáà*	15	*irí na ìsé*	30	*irí àtó*	1000	*puku*
8	*asáto*	16	*irí na ìsí*	40	*irí ànó*		

NIGERIAN TERMS – A GLOSSARY

Abule Hamlet or small village (Yoruba).

Agbada Yoruba cloak for men.

Alhaji One who has been to Mecca.

Amingo White person (from Portuguese), used in Cross River State.

Ariya Enjoyment, having a good time (Yoruba).

Babanriga Long Hausa tunic.

Batoure White person (Hausa).

Buba Yoruba shirt.

Buka Chop house (Yoruba).

Chiroma Traditional title of the far northeast.

Dash Bribe or payment for service rendered or simply a gift (verb and noun).

Durbar Staged horse gallops in which senior men pay homage to an emir in the Muslim regions.

FCT Federal Capital Territory (Abuja).

FESTAC Festival of Arts and Culture hosted in Lagos in 1977 at incredible cost. Legacies from this event include the National Theatre and the housing project of Festac Town.

Galadima Traditional title of the far northeast.

Go-slow Traffic jam.

GRA Government Reserved Area, civil servants' housing district.

Ileto Village (Yoruba).

Ilu Alade Big town (Yoruba).

Ilu Oloja Small market town (Yoruba).

Kabu kabu Unlicensed taxis.

Lappa Casual loin cloth (men and women).

Mai Traditional Kanuri ruler.

Moto Any car – a term you'll hear a lot if travelling by bush taxi.

NEPA Nigerian Electric Power Authority – also translated as *Never Electric Power Always*.

Oba Traditional Yoruba king. The Nigerian government has allowed traditional rulers to keep their titles and in some cases has even supported regional monarchies. Although the *obas* have less *de jure* power than they once did, they still enjoy considerable prestige and often mediate in local disputes. In some cases, they've taken on official government functions to complement traditional roles.

Off To turn/switch something off.

On To turn/switch something on.

Onyeocha White person (Igbo).

Oyinbo White person (Yoruba).

Sabi To know (Pidgin, from Portuguese).

Sabon Gari Foreigners' town (Hausa).

SAP Economic Structural Adjustment Programme.

Shehu Chief, big man (Hausa).

Sokoto Yoruba trousers.

Touts Hyperactive youths who take it upon themselves to escort you through customs, health, immigration and currency declaration at airports or land borders, or onto vehicles in the motor parks. Much as they can be a pain, they're usually very hard to shake off. Use them, because if you let them hang on, they'll demand payment anyway.

the jailed winner of the cancelled presidential election of 1993) is barely tolerated. The *Vanguard* is a small and committed outfit, with some excellent columnists, that somehow keeps going.

Television

There are reckoned to be about five million TVs in Nigeria. The government gave up its tight monopoly on **television** through *NTA* – the *Nigerian Television Authority* – in 1993, when the first private stations were licensed. Over thirty TV stations broadcast regional programmes, interspersed with the national programmes (news, talk shows, local soaps) and foreign productions. Programmes are in English and national languages (Igbo, Yoruba, Hausa).

Radio

Radio is organized much like television under the **FRCN** – *Federal Radio Corporation of Nigeria*. Individual stations for the different states also broadcast their own medium-wave programmes. The *FRCN* puts out three short-wave programmes in English and national languages nationwide.

You can also receive *Voice of Nigeria* transmissions – in English, French, German, Spanish, Hausa, Arabic and Swahili – abroad.

Holidays and Festivals

Nigeria's official public holidays include Christian and Muslim celebrations plus New Year's Day, May Day and Independence Day (October 1). Muslim holidays marking the

MAIN TRADITIONAL FESTIVALS

Pategi Regatta A regatta held every other year in February–March at Pategi, 100km downstream from Jebba, the big crossing point on the Niger, 70km from Ilorin. This is one of the country's best-known events, and includes horse racing, swimming, dancing and music.

Fishing festival February. Argungu, near Sokoto (see p.1109).

Egungun Usually April. A whole host of Yoruba ancestor festivals. The one at Ibadan draws huge crowds – as does the one at Okene, on the A2 between Benin City and Lokoja. Masquerades and sporting events accompanied by exhilarating dancing and drumming.

Ofala December. Festival in Onitsha and other towns along the Niger to honour the traditional ruler who appears before his people.

Ogun Between June and August. Yoruba festival in honour of the god of iron with singing, dancing and drumming. Held in numerous towns of the region.

Oshun August/September. Festival in honour of the river goddess and guardian spirit of the people of Oshogbo. Another well-known celebration, but much of the week-long event is considered too sacred to be shared with visitors.

Igue December. Procession of the Oba of Benin. The ensuing celebration lasts several days and includes traditional dancing and a lot of drinking and eating.

Sekiapu. October. Masquerades, regattas and a great deal of merriment in Rivers and Cross River States.

end of Ramadan (*Sallah*), Abraham's sacrificing of the sheep (*tabaski*) and Muhammad's birthday are based on the lunar calendar (see p.62 for dates). In the north, these often climax with spectacular "durbar" cavalry displays. A number of non-Islamic festivals are celebrated in the different regions throughout the year. In the south, the most famous of these is the terrifyingly exciting *Egungun*.

Entertainment

Nigeria has a thriving and complex cultural scene. Music, of course, is a massive industry. Theatre is lively and inventive and now benefiting from cross-fertilization with TV. Cinema is blighted by financial incapacity (see *Contexts*). Nigerian literature is of world importance – there's a clutch of great writers, including Nobel prize winner Wole Soyinka (who spends much time in the USA) and the renowned and more accessible author and opinion-moulder Chinua Achebe (who's often in Britain) as well as a new generation of writers – the most well known in Britain being Ben Okri and Adewale Maja-Pearce – who choose to live permanently abroad (see "Books" in *Contexts*). In sports, football and athletics are the big crowd-pullers.

■ Music

Lagos feels the heartbeat of Nigerian music and you can hear all the styles here and stand a good chance of seeing international stars – **Fela Kuti**, son **Femi Kuti**, **King Sunny Ade**, **Victor Uwaifor**, **Sonny Okosuns**, **Victor Olaiya** – at any of three dozen or so clubs and hotel dance floors. In other cities around the country you may be lucky, but more likely in the south – Ibadan, Benin, Enugu, Port Harcourt or Calabar. For further background and insights, see the "Music" section in *Contexts*.

■ Theatre

Nigeria has a 400-year-old theatrical tradition with the **Yoruba language** its outstanding vehicle. The **Alarinjo Theatre** was the court entertainment of sixteenth-century Oyo. Once allowed by the rulers to become a popular form, it spread and travelled from city to city among the old kingdoms. By the nineteenth century it was a major cultural influence but it waned with the penetration of Christianity, only to resurge again in the 1940s, when players performed biblical scenes before church congregations.

Duro Lapido, **Kola Ogunmola** and **Hubert Ogunde** were the most famous names in the travelling theatre genre. They took plays from town to town, giving voice to the changing social and cultural scene in southern Nigeria, right through the pre-independence era and successive federal governments since. You may be lucky and catch one of the noisy, half-improvized productions. But these days many groups are more involved with making their own **films** (see *Contexts*), which are popular well beyond southwest Nigeria.

As for **English-language drama** groups, they're mostly attached to the universities, don't attract any state or federal support and inevitably don't have a mass audience. **Wole Soyinka**, **John Pepper Clark**, **Femi Osofisan**, **Ola Rotimi** and **Bode Osanyin** are some of Nigeria's best-known playwrights. In Lagos, check how the **Pec Repertory Group** is faring. They're the first full-time professional rep group, established by John Pepper Clark.

■ Football

With 100,000 licensed players, Nigeria's footballing skills are highly respected in Africa, though the national side – **Super Eagles** – has been under a cloud of bad luck in recent years. Current star players are defenders **Emmanuel Amunike**, **George Finidi** and **Kanu Nwanko**. Many Nigerian players appear in European teams and, without them, the national side is always at a disadvantage.

Successful regional teams include **Shooting Stars** of Ibadan and **Enugu Rangers**, whose matches are often attended by enormous crowds.

Women in Nigeria

Most foreign women working in Nigeria don't feel comfortable travelling alone in the Islamic-dominated north (pay special attention here to covering arms and legs) but the southern half of the country doesn't pose any gender-related problems: flirtatious sexual harassment may occur in clubs and at parties, but not on the street.

In a country where the change from traditional to urban-industrial values is taking place remarkably quickly, women have achieved larger real gains here than elsewhere in West Africa. But while they occupy positions in business, government and increasingly in the universities, there's still a lot of ground to cover. Two groups – the **National Committee for Women and Development** formed in the early 1980s, and the **National Council of Women Societies**, twenty years older – aim to fight for more equitable integration in all spheres. A radical alternative to NCWS, **Women in Nigeria** (WIN), was founded in 1985 in the male bastion of Zaria. It now has groups nationwide. Counterposing WIN is the **Federation of Muslim Women** (FOMWAN), a northern fundamentalist grouping. And lastly there's **Nigerwives**, for foreign wives of Nigerian men (see Lagos "Listings").

Trouble

Nigeria's dreadful reputation for trouble is exaggerated, but security is not something to take lightly in Lagos and other large cities. Lagos gangs are active and well organized. Even more disturbing is the huge number of handguns and other weapons in private possession and the implication of some police in criminal activities. Though outlaws may "control" entire neighbourhoods, you're most unlikely ever to see one, or anyone out of uniform carrying a gun. Leave valuables behind when you go out and you'll be fine.

If you spend much time in expat circles in **Lagos**, you'll hear plenty of recycled gossip about the **security problems**. Despite mandatory death sentences for armed robbery, burglaries are extremely common and night watchmen are often killed. But visitors, even long-term ones, are rarely at risk. Be alert, not paranoid.

You're unlikely to get into real trouble yourself in Nigeria unless you cross someone with serious influence. There are a lot of **drugs** floating around Lagos, however, and if you become involved you could easily find yourself in deep water. **Marijuana** is cultivated in the south and commonly smoked. It became popular in the army during the civil war but its use is officially considered a serious offence. The Indian Hemp Decree of 1966 provides for ten-year jail sentences for smokers and the death sentence for cultivation or import. Lorry drivers have long used amphetamines but Lagos' pivotal position in the worldwide transportation of **hard drugs** is bringing heroin and cocaine onto the domestic market. Stay well clear.

If you're British, and considering doing business in Nigeria, you might want to check credentials with the DTI Nigeria Desk (☎0171/270 4966).

TROUBLE ON THE ROAD

If you have **your own vehicle**, be careful where you leave it. Overlanders will encounter no special problems in northern Nigeria but in the south some take a lesson from residents who carve their licence numbers on all windows and use crook locks. Never park in an unguarded area and leave nothing of value in your car at any time.

There are few **roadblocks** in central Nigeria, but they appear with increasing frequency towards the borders (seven, for example, in the last 21km before Ikom). Most have oil drums staggered across the road, or two nail-studded planks, and they're illuminated by torches at night. Very occasionally a roadblock will consist of just a piece of string. Although often privately on the make, the officials are there to maintain law and order and, sometimes only a few hundred yards apart, may be staffed 24 hours a day by police, army, customs, the Agriculture Ministry or detectives, each with their own particular interest in your documents, movements and motivations. Any of them may wave you through, but it's always advisable to slow down to be sure. When stopped, remain inside until told what to do, as half the officials will want you to stay put and the other half will want you to assemble outside: it's impossible to predict which.

The Nigerian **police and civil service** has its quota of thugs and morons but the jobs themselves are respected occupations, and many officers, even in the lower ranks, are educated and well read. You'll meet senior officers who've been to university in Britain or the USA. Often posted far from home, they may welcome a chat about books or politics. They may also be waiting for a lift and the minor inconvenience of an extra passenger is far outweighed by the ease with which one passes through subsequent roadblocks.

Nigerians' **sense of humour** varies greatly. Generally, officials in the north are restrained and courteous while in the south it seems to be a great joke for a soldier to storm up to a foreigner shouting about illegal parking, the wrong colour of number plate or some other misdemeanour. When you've been adequately embarrassed or terrified, there's a hearty thump on the back, and an invitation to share the joke (try to be polite!). It's worth pointing out that the police – and others in uniform – keep abreast of the news and know full well that expatriates and other foreigners break the law and indulge in criminal activities from time to time. Rumours circulate fast among the police. Your behaviour may be impeccable, but they don't know that. In a country as big and hard to control as this, it's important you find every last ounce of tolerance.

Lastly, it's not unknown for enterprising traders, or even highway **bandits**, to pose as a roadblock by setting up their wares on a couple of oil drums. Sometimes it's hard to tell. Nigerian detectives are always in plain clothes but they invariably show their ID as soon you pull up. Bandits really do exist. Their ingenious exploits are faithfully reported in all the tabloid newspapers and stretches of road become black spots as a result. The more you talk to locals, the more you'll hear, and the safer you'll be. Fortunately, the number of roadblocks in towns and on the roads has been officially reduced since the early 1990s, and armed robbery and road accidents have dropped significantly – surely some connection.

Wildlife and National Parks

There's still a fair bit of wildlife to be seen in Nigeria, though little in the big game league. If you go to Yankari Game Reserve, Kainji National Park or the newly created Birnin Gwari Reserve, all in the north, you can see elephants, hippos and larger antelopes, and there's the remote possibility of glimpsing lions or other big cats.

More exciting, perhaps, is the recent discovery of **gorillas** in the thick forests of the southeast, and the decision to create the **Cross River National Park**, containing the **Mbe Mountain National Park** and **Oban Rainforest Reserve** in Cross River State – an initiative that ties in with the development of the Korup National Park over the border in Cameroon. Also exciting is the **Gashaka Gumpti Reserve** in Gongola State, a huge area with terrain that varies from savannah grasslands to mountain forests. There are no elephants left here, but a variety of other wildlife including chimpanzees. Near Benin City is the tiny **Okomu Reserve**, another protected rainforest with rudimentary accommodation. The Nigerian Conservation Foundation (5 Moseley Rd, Ikoyi, Lagos; ☎01/686 163 or 687 385) is making valiant efforts to rouse Nigerians from a complacent attitude to the wildlife heritage.

Directory

AIRPORT DEPARTURE TAX US$35 on international departures. For non-residents it is only payable in dollars.

CRAFTS Nigeria has a fantastic wealth of things worth acquiring, both utilitarian and aesthetic. Jewellery (including the antique, multicoloured glass trading beads that are now getting expensive), leatherware, carved calabashes, bronze figures made with the lost wax method, handwoven cloth and woodcarvings are the most obvious. Regrettably, you're likely to be offered ivory from time to time and various other animal products – lizard, snake and crocodile skin bags and belts. Possibly the best value and longest-lasting interest is to be had from musical instruments, which you'll find if you look beyond the souvenir stands at the big hotels. Talking drums – the expressive *iyaalu* tension drums which so unerringly imitate the Yoruba voice – are particularly worth looking out for. See the "Music" section in *Contexts*.

EMERGENCIES If you run into trouble, the police emergency number is ☎199. But help doesn't always come in a hurry.

GAY LIFE Being gay in Nigeria is not easy, but there is a community, with its own advocacy group *Gentlemen Alliance* that is attempting to overturn centuries of ignorance about gay issues. AIDS awareness campaigning is important, but their ongoing priority is to educate the public at large about the existence of gays in every walk of life in Nigeria and to overcome the view that homosexuality is an imported phenomenon.

MUSEUMS Nigeria has more museums than anywhere in West Africa. The main ones are in **Lagos**, **Kano**, **Ife**, **Jos** and **Calabar**, but just about every town of any size has a museum of some sort. They tend to focus either on history, art or customs, though there's also an **oil museum** in Oloibiri (50km from Port Harcourt), a **mining museum** in Jos, and **military museums** in Zaria and Umuahia (former headquarters of Biafran military leaders).

OPENING HOURS Banks open Mon–Thurs 8am–3pm and Fri 8am–1pm. Shops usually open Mon–Sat 8am–5pm.

PHOTOGRAPHY Although no permit is required, photography is something police and security agents are extremely touchy about. You're best off not taking pictures on Lagos Island where there are many government buildings (if one of them unwittingly works its way into your picture, it's a good way to get your film and possibly camera confiscated) and only discreetly in other neighbourhoods of Lagos. Photographing people in traditional costume, at country markets and the like, is likely to incur wrath among interfering types who may report you. Unfortunately, police are usually convinced your sole intention in taking such pictures is to assault the national image.

On departure, you can expect to be quizzed by the police about photographs, although they may accept your word that you haven't taken any. Remove film from your camera, and repack it, as a precaution, before the border. If you fly out, there's no problem.

UNIVERSITIES Nigeria has far more universities – 30 in all, one in each state – than all the other countries in West Africa put together. They include the **University of Lagos** ("Unilag") and the **University of Ibadan** ("UI"), the nation's first, founded in 1946. Nsukka, Ife, Zaria and Benin are other large campuses. There's still quite a community of expat visiting scholars and teachers.

A Brief History of Nigeria

Nigerian history is the most complex and also one of the most ancient in West Africa. The earliest indications of the use of iron in the region come from the Nok Culture (named after the Jos plateau village where much of the evidence was found) and date back to 300 BC. For reasons unknown, this civilization faded, and the next discoveries date from over a millennium later. The development, by the ninth century, of mineral wealth in the Yoruba and Igbo regions of the south, led to long-lasting and sophisticated political structures. In the north, kingdoms arose at much the same time – first the Bornu Empire in the ninth century, then, not long afterwards, the Hausa City States – and they became powerful stations on the trans-Saharan caravan routes, supplying many of the exotic requirements of medieval Europe.

The slave trade and, much later, colonial invasion, wreaked havoc on these indigenous states, as well as on the weaker, stateless communities living among them. Detailed coverage of pre-colonial history is included on a regional basis throughout the main guide section of this chapter.

Since the end of the nineteenth century, the colonial protectorates, and then the federation of modern Nigerian states, have been the setting for a panoply of events and characters set against a background of poverty, booming population and almost continual crisis. Unlike most smaller West African nations, a substantial and expanding literature exists on the history, sociology and political science of Nigeria (see "Books" in *Contexts*). The following summary is only the simplest historical framework, picking out the most salient features of Nigeria's history.

The Arrival of Europeans

The **Portuguese** were the first Europeans to reach the Benin Gulf, in 1472, and within a short time they had made contact with the kingdom of **Benin**. Trade soon began, initially centred on pepper, ivory and other exotic goods. It was not until the second half of the seventeenth century, when the Americas had been widely colonized and plantations needed increasing supplies of labour, that the focus shifted to slaves.

The early Europeans had few permanent forts or settlements, basing themselves instead on offshore "hulks" near the ports. By the 1660s, these permanently moored ships were highly developed, sparking off an explosion of competitive slave-trading at ports like **Lagos**, **Warri**, **Calabar** and **Bonny**. Much of the driving force behind the trade, which was exploited by local chiefs, came from the insecurity of a West African arms race for the latest European muskets and cannon. In exchange for weaponry, the French and British, who had supplanted the Portuguese and Brazilians by the eighteenth century, were scarcely interested in buying anything except slaves.

The colonial carve-up

At the beginning of the nineteenth century, things appeared to change, as the newly republican **French** sent warships to the southeast Nigerian coast to break up the slave trade. To French cries of *Liberté, Egalité, Fraternité*, the British added their own hollow *Christianity, Commerce and Civilization*. In fact, slaves no longer made economic sense; instead, in the wake of the European industrial revolution, **markets** were needed for manufactured goods and there was a massive demand for supplies of raw materials – cotton, sugar and the rest.

In 1851, the British shelled Lagos, ostensibly to quicken the demise of the slave trade, in practice to impose a puppet regime and improve the newly important oil palm trade. The slave trade went underground, and slavers hid cut in the lagoons around Lagos from where they would sneak out their cargo to Brazil, which was still an importer. Meanwhile the British seized Lagos Island in 1861 – which then became Lagos colony, the first particle of Nigeria.

After the European Powers' **Berlin Conference** of 1885, the London-based **Royal Niger Company** was granted exclusive trading rights in the Niger River basin. With the Germans expanding to the east, and the French to the north and west, the British government took over the RNC in 1899 and began pushing it in all directions.

By 1900 they'd succeeded in drawing borders around a vast region of diverse peoples, who found themselves under the ultimate authority of northern and southern protectorates. In 1914 a federation was formed – in preference to a united colony – and named **Nigeria**, a term coined by the wife of Lord Lugard, the British colonial commander in the region.

Indirect rule

From the beginning, Nigeria was an ill-matched association and it was clear that conflict would arise between the conservative, largely Muslim and feudal **north**, and the more outward-looking **south** – with its Christian missions and, in the southeast, lack of rigid social hierarchies. At the very least, problems would be caused by the new territory's southward-looking orientation, away from the old Saharan routes and towards the ports and European trade.

The British, however, pressed ahead with their system of "**indirect rule**", which in the **north**, worked easily enough to the benefit of both the Hausa-Fulani emirs (who carried on much as before) and the British administration. Lord Lugard simply took over the role of regional overlord from the Sultan of Sokoto, whose functions were perforce purely religious and ceremonial.

But indirect rule was a disaster in the **southeast**, where decisions and judicial processes were traditionally applied by consent among groups of senior men. In **Igboland**, the "Warrant Chiefs" commissioned by the British had no mandate for their authority, and on the contrary were usually independent-minded status-seekers who had acquired a mission education.

In **Yorubaland**, another variation was imposed. The British held Yoruba traditional rulers, with British "advisors", accountable for their decisions. But the British had failed to understand the fabric of Yoruba politics and perceived in their centralized **government of obas** and the traditional ceremonial-executive titles of the **Alafin of Oyo** and the **Oni of Ife**, simple dictatorships somewhat akin to the emirates of the north. Disregarding the fact that the Yoruba offices were posts given to selected senior men by others of high rank, Lugard tried to control the selection of pliant chiefs by men who, again, had no mandate to enforce his requirements. And he actively connived to empower those Yoruba elements who posed least threat to white prestige, to turn the clock back, as far as possible, to his own avowedly racist vision of an Africa untainted by progress.

While British rule led to internal schisms in Yorubaland, the region benefited from the fastest input of technology and **modern infrastructure**. There was electricity in Lagos by 1898, bridges between the islands and a rail link with Ibadan by 1900. All of which was to prove another source of division for north and south to deal with after independence.

■ The road to independence

Nigerians became involved in the political process relatively early, by the standards of other African colonies. In 1923, the first Africans, led by **Herbert Macaulay**, a Yoruba whose father had returned from slave captivity in Sierra Leone, were elected to a legislative advisory council in Lagos. But local parties really only developed after the experience of World War II, when Nigerians returned from fighting for European ideals like "self-determination" and "liberty".

In 1944, the **National Council for Nigeria and the Cameroons** was formed by Herbert Macaulay and **Dr Nnamdi Azikwe**, an Igbo. Four years later, **Chief Obafemi Awolowo**, a Yoruba, founded a second party, the **Action Group**. By the end of the decade, the northerners also had their own party, the **Northern People's Congress**, with **Tafawa Balewa** at its head.

Predictably, these three parties came to represent the **regional interests** – the NPC for the north, the NCNC for the east, and the AG for the west. As they jockeyed for position to rule an independent nation, the parties agreed on nothing, delaying the process of reform in the process. In a dispute over the date for self-rule, suspicious northerners walked out of the colonial assembly in 1953, and bloody **riots in Kano** followed. Members from each region felt sure the other two were conspiring to dominate, and there was talk of dividing the country into several smaller political units in an effort to relieve the tension. The British argued such a measure would only stall independence further, an argument in which they were supported by the northern region, which had to have a friendly route to the sea.

Finally, in 1957, it was decided the nation would be formed of the three rival regions. **Tafawa Balewa** became the head of the new central government and Nigeria had its independence returned to it on October 1, 1960.

■ Independence: the early years

The early 1960s were characterized by an **uneasy coalition** between the **north** and the **southeast** against the powerful **southwest** region dominated by the Yoruba. The latter thus saw its worst fears realized and its leaders panicked when a bogus census in 1963 suggested the north had four million more inhabitants than the rest of the nation combined. The threat of Muslim domination in the political arena now seemed very real.

The southeast eventually slipped out of the coalition and Chief Awolowo raised angry cries against government tinkering with the country's structure. He was tried for treason and jailed. **Early chaos** seemed to be gaining momentum and in January 1966 the army toppled the government – killing Tafawa Balewa in the process – and set about trying to restore order.

Military rule

The new **military government** was headed by **General J. Aguiyi-Ironsi**, an Igbo. Northerners rioted in reaction to his radical early reforms that abolished the federation and imposed a unitary government dominated by Igbos. Fighting broke out within the army and, after only six months, Ironsi was killed in another **coup**, this time led by northern officers. As many as 7000 Igbos living in the north were massacred in the aftermath and up to half a million fled to the east.

But the military's new leader was different from his predecessors. **Yakubu Gowon** was a Christian northerner, a young and charismatic figure, who restored the tripartite federation and released Awolowo and other Action Group leaders of the west. But the southeast region, led by the military governor, **Lieutenant-Colonel C. Odumegwu-Ojukwu**, who rejected Gowon's leadership, pushed instead for a loose confederation.

In September 1966, elements of the Northern army began the systematic **killing of Igbos** who had remained in the north. Official reports placed the deaths at 5000, though Igbos claimed that as many as 30,000 were massacred. The pogrom was a decisive blow to the shaky federation. High-ranking Igbo civil servants began returning from Lagos to the regional capital at Enugu and pressuring Ojukwu to secede.

National politics in the early part of 1967 were completely dominated by the **question of the future of the Federal Republic**. The Ghanaian government attempted to mediate between the sides and, in January 1967, leaders of the federal government met with Ojukwu in Aburi. The meetings produced no acceptable compromise; nor did subsequent government moves to appease the east with conciliatory measures and guarantees.

At the last minute, Gowon announced the **division of the federation** into twelve separate states in an attempt to undermine the overweening north and disarm his critics from the ethnic minorities, especially in the southeast, who had long sought greater autonomy. It was too late. Fearing the Igbo constituency would be pushed permanently into the margins of national politics, Ojukwu unilaterally withdrew the Eastern Region from the federation and declared the independent **Republic of Biafra** on May 30, 1967.

The Biafran War

In July 1967, Biafran troops marched into the Western Region in an attempt to surround Lagos. Federal troops responded by blockading eastern ports and by attacking Biafra from the north and west. Despite a lack of manpower and resources, Biafra scored a number of military successes in the early days of the war, but by the end of 1967, the conflict had degenerated into a brutal **war of attrition**. Fighting was vicious and confused. Most of the major towns changed hands several times. Federal forces captured a number of coastal towns, reducing Biafra to an enclave in the Igbo heartland. Federal military atrocities, of which many were reported, further convinced the Igbos that they were engagaed in an all-out war for survival.

Biafra gained considerable sympathy in the international press: for the first time, public opinion in the rich world was mobilized against third world poverty. Yet few countries gave official recognition to Biafra, and French military and technical aid seemed suspiciously self-interested. The war dragged on for three years, claiming the lives of at least 100,000 soldiers, but many more Igbo civilians, of whom between half a million and two million are estimated to have perished as a result of the government's policy of **blockade and starvation**. Supported by British aid and Soviet arms, the Federal government finally captured the last rebel-held town of Owerri and quelled the rebellion in December 1969. Much of the southeast was ravaged.

■ Reconstruction

The gaping wounds of the war appeared to heal with remarkable speed. Gowon, who was still in power after four years, was careful not to humiliate the defeated and bereaved easterners or exclude them from the new federation. In fact, he offered an **amnesty** to all who had fought on the Biafran side, and vowed to rebuild the east while furthering the economic development of the entire country.

Reconstruction didn't take place overnight, but it is remarkable today how little evidence of the war remains, even in cities that were virtually destroyed. The number of roads, bridges and industries now largely exceeds pre-war levels.

Gowon was aided in the early days of reconciliation by **oil revenues** that flooded into the coffers in the early 1970s as Nigeria became one of the world's ten largest producers. But as blatant corruption became a national issue, and Gowon began dragging his feet on promises of a return to civilian rule and devoting most of his energies to international image-building, he was ousted, after nine years in power, in a bloodless coup led by **General Murtala Muhammed** in July 1975.

Murtala Muhammed

Of all Nigeria's leaders, Murtala Muhammed has been without doubt the most popular. Even today, his name is referred to with a reverence not normally reserved for politicians. Another northerner with considerable charisma, he structured all his policies around the return of power to an elected leadership and devoted himself to wiping out corruption.

Shortly after coming to power, Muhammed instigated **"Operation Deadwoods"** – a policy of forced dismissal or retirement of public officials on a whole range of charges from corruption to "infirmity". In all, more than 10,000 civil servants – police officials, senior diplomats, university professors, even military officers – were relieved of their posts. Swift action was taken against embezzlement of public funds. Assets were confiscated. Appointees were sacked for reasons as simple as a conflict of interests. It was a breath of fresh air in a stagnating and counterproductive bureaucracy and brought the government huge popularity.

By the end of 1975, Muhammed had concluded the purge and announced a four-year countdown to return the country to civilian rule. He had come to be regarded as a politician who made promises and kept them, and drew attention to the future and away from the divisive tragedy of the past. Nigerians felt they were leaders in a liberalizing movement that would sweep the continent and break the cycle of totalitarianism in Africa.

It's difficult to know if posterity would have been so kind to Muhammed had he lived to see his programmes carried out. After only six months of reshaping the country he was assassinated in a hail of bullets, by disgruntled members of the military, while his car was in a Lagos traffic jam.

■ The Second Republic

The counter-coup was effective only in eliminating Muhammed, for the plotters were rounded up and with the help of Major General Ibrahim Babangida, power was smoothly transferred to Muhammed's chief of staff, **Olusegun Obasanjo**, a Christian Yoruba.

Obasanjo pledged to adhere to Muhammed's schedule for the return to civilian government and continued reshaping the civil service. A new constitution, based on that of the USA, was drawn up, and political parties were unbanned in September 1978.

Five **political parties** were finally approved, but four were headed by familiar old names, had vague right-of-centre programmes and seemed to indicate the persistence of regional divisions. **Awolowo** and **Azikwe** (now in their seventies) headed parties largely representing the west and the east respectively, or at least their personal powerbases in those regions – the Unity Party of Nigeria and the Greater National People's Party. The National People's Party, from which the *GNPP* was a breakaway group, was led by a northern businessman, **Alhaji Waziri Ibrahim**. The National Party of Nigeria, based on Kaduna and led by **Alhaji Shehu Shagari**, claimed to cut across regional loyalties but was essentially the old NPC northern party, controlled as ever by the Fulani oligarchy. Shagari, himself a Fulani from a leading northern family, had been a member of the first civilian government and had served under Gowon's military regime. Lastly, in opposition to the NPN, another northern party had also been formed – the People's Redemption Party. Led by **Alhaji Aminu Kano**, it had radical socialist leanings and was explicitly committed to the cause of inter-ethnic cooperation.

In the complicated elections that spread over six weeks in 1979, all the parties achieved some representation, but **Shagari** won the all-important **presidential election**. He rode out his first term in Nigeria's new "Second Republic" on a wave of genuine popularity and public relief that the long period of military rule was over. But the new president didn't survive long untarnished. **Crackdowns on the press** – which had begun reporting government corruption, and even daring to point fingers at Shagari and his Kaduna clique – clearly signalled his insecurity, and he faced serious challenges from other northern parties and eastern allies in his unstable coalition.

The **economy**, too, was slipping badly. The oil boom had peaked in 1980. In December of that year serious **riots** broke out in Kano, prompted by the popular "jihadist" teachings and calls for social justice of Mai Tatsine. As foreign currency reserves dwindled and the external debt skyrocketed, the standard of living for most Nigerians rapidly declined, while government officials, cabinet ministers and the president himself made fortunes, indulging in what came to be known as "squandermania". Further, serious **riots in Maiduguri** in October 1982 were dismissed by Shagari as "religious agitation", and in February 1983, some two million immigrant workers – from Ghana, Cameroon, Chad and Niger – were expelled as economic scapegoats.

Despite these various obstacles, Shagari managed to get elected to a second term in October 1983, a sounder win, in fact, than his first, though achieved with less than sound methods.

■ Another coup: a new military regime

The inevitable happened barely three months after the 1983 elections, when another northerner – **Major-General Mohammed Buhari** – staged a bloodless takeover of power and suspended the 1979 constitution. Explaining his actions, the new leader announced shortly after the takeover: "The economic mess, the corruption and unacceptable level of unemployment could not be excused on the grounds that Nigeria was a practising democracy."

Buhari announced the "voluntary retirement" of high-ranking military officers and the inspector general of the police, all of whom were implicated in financial mismanagement and corrupt practices on a gigantic scale. Prominent members of Shagari's party were arrested, as was the president. Through such moves, Buhari sought to associate his regime with the purist popularity of Muhammed. Important elder statesmen from the martyred president's administration were brought into the new government, including former head of state Obasanjo.

The attack on graft – the **"War Against Indiscipline"** – even crossed international borders. One of the most wanted offenders was the former transport minister **Alhaji Umaru Dikko**, who was living in luxurious exile in London, from where he openly criticized the new government. In one of the more bizarre instances of abuse of diplomatic privilege, Dikko was kidnapped, drugged and bundled into a crate, ready to be shipped off as diplomatic baggage from Gatwick airport. The plot was only aborted when British customs officials queried the contents of the crate. Buhari's government quickly denied any responsibility, although the Nigerian High Commission was strongly implicated in the abduction. Diplomatic relations between the UK and Nigeria nearly broke over the incident and subsequent British immigration policy has tended to keep relations cool.

Buhari, however, seemed serious in his efforts to wipe out corruption, and as a result was initially quite popular with people fed up with government abuse. But it soon became apparent that members of Shagari's Kaduna clique were not prominent among those convicted on corruption charges. In addition to the accusation of partiality, it was not long before Buhari himself was gaining a reputation as an unbending **autocrat**. As those accused of corruption were given sentences of as much as 72 years, Buhari arrested many of his regime's critics and suppressed the Nigerian media in ways Shagari had not dared. On the discovery of an alleged coup plot in 1984, he swiftly executed a group of some forty soldiers. And two government decrees, reflecting the new hard line, proved extremely unpopular with the masses. The first, known as Decree 2, allowed for detention without trial of citizens regarded as a threat to the state. Decree 4 imposed press controls by insisting journalists verify the "truth" of their reporting.

Even more unpopular were **austerity measures** adopted by Buhari in 1984 as he sought to remedy the country's growing economic problems. Strong opposition to his rule grew as resulting price increases and shortages of consumer goods jolted the nation – especially its poorer citizens. Buhari tried to deflect criticism, as Shagari had done, by blaming the country's economic woes on foreign workers robbing Nigerians of jobs. **Mass expulsions of immigrants** were instigated and, in May 1985, up to a million foreigners – again many of them

Ghanaian – were shipped out in chaotic conditions. Relations soured with Nigeria's neighbours which, facing economic crises of their own, suddenly found a flood of displaced and unemployed refugees on their doorsteps.

None of Buhari's drastic measures worked, partly because there was virtually no popular support for the man behind them and principally because the Naira was overvalued and worthless. With the economy hardly performing any better after his two years at the top, and a foreign debt of some £12 billion ($18 billion) pulling the country down, a new coup was orchestrated, in August 1985, by close associates of Buhari in the Supreme Military Council, led by army chief of staff **Major-General Ibrahim Babangida**, born in Minna, in Niger State, but brought up in Kano.

The "Period of Transition": Ibrahim Babangida

Within a short time of taking office, **Babangida** and his new Armed Forces Ruling Council had released many of the political prisoners from Nigerian jails and a new sense of freedom began to be felt. Not without misgivings, though, for in December 1986, ten officers from Benue State, who, Babangida alleged, had been conspiring to overthrow him, were executed.

Babangida began preparing the country once again for national elections which he scheduled for 1990. Such political moves went down well at home, though his economic policies were tough and unyielding. Shortly after taking power, he declared an **economic state of emergency** and assumed control over the economy. In 1985, he broke off loan negotiations with the IMF – a move that met with popular nationalistic support. But enthusiasm waned when the president imposed austerity measures of his own. He devalued the Naira fourfold, in the hope of attracting investors, and began privatizing unprofitable public enterprises and lifting government subsidies, notably on petrol.

Periodic **demonstrations and strikes** resulted, and, although conflict tended to be sparked by economic policies, **ethnic and religious tensions** were never far away. In 1986, Babangida announced that Nigeria had joined the Organization of the Islamic Conference. Despite stressing this had been done for cultural and religious reasons – and not political ones – non-Muslim southerners feared that the government and its northern powerbase were trying to impose Islamic rule on the whole country. There were **campus protests** and a number of deaths in northern universities in 1986 and, in 1987, **religious riots** broke out between Muslims and Christians in Kaduna State, leading to the deaths of dozens of people, the arrest of over a thousand and the banning of religious organizations at schools and universities.

Adding to the political frustration, Babangida postponed the elections three times between 1990 and 1992, leaving many to question if he ever intended to step down. In April 1990, a group of junior, Christian officers attempted a coup, which was quickly put down but resulted in 300 deaths. Over the next two years, ethnic-religious clashes intensified. In April 1991, Muslim demonstrations erupted in Katsina, leading to violence and many deaths. In Bauchi, 130 people were killed when Christians slaughtered pigs in a market shared by Muslims. Later in the year, 300 people died in Kano following demonstrations provoked by a touring Christian minister.

Babangida's solution to the regional problem was to create **nine new states** in 1991, arguing they would stimulate stability and development while ensuring more equitable representation of ethnic minorities. Despite the measures, it seemed ethnic enmities remained the driving force of Nigerian politics. In February 1992, fighting broke out in Kaduna State between Hausa Muslims and Kataf Christians. In the east, a land dispute between the Tiv and Jukun peoples resulted in an estimated 5000 deaths.

The deteriorating economy put a further strain on Babangida's government. By mid-1992, **inflation** was already soaring at 50 percent and widespread rioting broke out in Lagos over a sharp increase in transport fares. There were a number of reported deaths as demonstrators, who demanded the government resign, were brutally dispersed by security forces. More protests ensued after prominent human rights activists, including Dr Beko Ransome-Kuti (brother of musician Fela Kuti) and Chief Fani Fawehinmi were arrested for accusing the government of instigating the riots so as to delay elections. In June, the Academic Staff of Nigerian Universities called a nation-wide strike in a wage dispute. Despite his stated commitment to collective bargaining, Babangida banned the union and with it, the National Association of Nigerian Students. Most of the nation's 30 universities closed as a result.

The mood of the country was therefore downbeat as Nigerians prepared for **National Assembly elections** in July 1992. Despite the vast sums of money spent on the campaign, the election sparked little excitement among voters. Babangida had insisted on a **two-party system** and created the Social Democratic Party and the National Republican Convention in order to prevent the rise of regional, ethnic or religious interest groups. But Nigerian commentators liked to call them a "Yes" party and a "Yes Sir" party. The fact that the increasingly unpopular military regime had created, funded and written the platforms of both SDP and NRC led to widespread **voter apathy**. Despite slick, state-financed media blitzes, neither party challenged the government's handling of issues such as inflation or ethnic tension. Serious opposition seemed only to come from the nation's human rights organizations, students and lawyers.

Although the SDP won majorities in both the House of Representatives and the Senate, the Armed Forces Ruling Council decided in mid-July that the legislature would not be inaugurated until after a new civilian president was sworn in.

■ Failed elections

When the **presidential elections** finally rolled around in June 1993, there were few signs of voter enthusiasm. Though Nigerians welcomed the prospect of ousting the current regime, no popular movement had evolved to give hope for a new era of civilian rule. The two candidates that emerged – **Moshood Abiola** of the SDP and **Bashir Tofa** of the NRC – stood out more for their abilities to amass huge fortunes than for any record of public service. Cynicism ran high among voters who found it hard to digest promises of prosperity in a country where yearly per capita income had fallen from $1000 to $290 in the ten years preceding the elections. Such pessimism, and the candidates' inability to distance themselves from the military regime, accounted in large part for the poor showing at the polls, with barely a third of eligible voters turning out.

The results, however, surprised observers. Abiola – a Muslim from the mainly Christian Yoruba country of the southwest – won an apparently clear victory with 58 percent of the vote. Winning in several northern states, including Tofa's own, Kano, he appeared to seal a mandate that cut across ethnic lines. Marring this seeming triumph was a deadlock created by legal wrangling over the election results. The judiciary's partisan colouration in giving judgements on the elections created an atmosphere of suspicion between the north and south. On June 23, Babangida stepped in and annulled the elections.

Human rights organizations immediately called for a campaign of civil disobedience. Mass **pro-democracy demonstrations** led to more violence and brought Lagos and much of the southwest to a standstill. Abiola declared himself winner on June 24, stating in a national broadcast, "From now on, the struggle in Nigeria is between the people and a small clique in the military determined to cling to power". But the standoff between civilians and the military also aroused old regional divisions: southerners remained convinced the military would never accept a southern president.

Babangida, who had started his presidential career as a liberal reformer, seemed, after the elections, ominously entrenched and intolerant of dissent. As troops put down anti-government riots in Lagos, the military threatened the death sentence for anyone whose words or deeds might undermine "the fabric of the nation" and shut down critical newspapers including the *Sketch*, *Observer*, *Punch* and *Concord*. Abiola fled the country.

But in August 1993, Babangida unexpectedly announced that he was stepping aside as president and commander-in-chief of the armed forces. He insisted, however, that an **interim government** backed by decree would be the most favourable alternative to military rule and appointed **Ernest Shonekan** – former chairman of the United African Company, Nigeria's largest conglomerate – to lead the country until the next elections were held.

Abiola promptly returned from abroad where he had been trying to rally foreign support for his claims to the presidency. But within weeks of taking over as head of state, Shonekan seemed to have swung public opinion behind himself. Former presidents **Nnamdi Azikwe** and **Olusegun Obasanjo** supported the interim government and the unions called off strikes. Meanwhile, Abiola isolated himself from the masses with his calls for an "economic blockade" of Nigeria and warnings of "a bloodbath" were he not sworn in. Preferring to stay in Lagos rather than tour the country to rally support, he increasingly became associated with a Yoruba, rather than a national cause.

But neither was Shonekan a credible figure. Ardent democrats labelled him a puppet of the military. Shonekan's ultimate downfall, however, was provoked when he tried to cut fuel subsidies in late 1993. As the price of gasoline increased 600 percent, rioting again broke out in Lagos and a general strike threatened economic devastation. In November, **General Sani Abacha**, who was instrumental in the coups that toppled Shagari and Buhari, seized power, and, once again, the military stepped in "to save the nation from chaos".

■ A new era of military rule

Abacha quickly set about purging the military of officers loyal to Babangida, who remained in exile after the events. He dissolved all political parties and elected institutions. By then, politically numbed Nigerians didn't seem much worried that elected governors were replaced by military appointees and that the National Assembly ceded authority to a mainly military legislative council.

Abacha has talked often of a willingness to restore multi-partyism, but Nigerians – used to over a decade of such promises from military rulers – remain profoundly sceptical. Even the new leader's decision to set up a **constitutional conference** to iron out political problems before yet again committing the country to a civilian handover (a process which could take many years to accomplish) would appear to be a pretext to remain in power indefinitely.

By mid-1994, Abacha was already being attacked from all sides. Civil liberties groups, students and unions, with the support of retired generals like Olusegun Obasanjo, publicly urged him to step down. Although political parties were banned, **political organizations** were formed and began turning up the heat. Abacha could only count on northerners for support, and even there he was losing ground. The Sultan of Sokoto, and other powerbrokers from Katsina and Maiduguri, started criticizing the military's policy, leaving the **Emir of Kano** as Abacha's only ardent supporter.

The **Campaign for Democracy** became influential, having gained credibility by organizing many of the demonstrations that led to Babangida's downfall. Meanwhile, the **National Democratic Coalition** (Nadeco) campaigned for a return to a civilian government headed by Abiola, and grew into a broad-based movement with support in the north as well as the south. On the first anniversary of the elections, Abiola was persuaded to declare himself president. He was promptly arrested. Though still a force in national politics, both organizations have lost momentum with the detention of their leaders, Abiola and Beko Ransome-Kuti. But in the face of opposition, senior military officers seem to be keeping their distance from Abacha.

Abacha hasn't fared well in terms of **international relations**. Western nations deplored the banning of parties, arbitrary detention of opposition members and tight controls on the press. Officially, it was these policies that provoked **economic sanctions** against Nigeria, although the West has been equally displeased with Abacha's resistance to IMF pressure to impose a tougher economic policy, the country's continued refusal to address the question of its £20 billion ($33 billion) debt and the new administration's tougher terms for drilling rights to Nigeria's oil reserves. London's reception of the new regime has been icy cold, and while at Nelson Mandela's inauguration, US vice-president Al Gore gave a clear indication of his country's leanings when he met with Abiola, rather than Abacha. France, which developed a cosy relationship with Babangida's government (when it worked out advantageous drilling contracts for its Elf-Aquitaine oil company), has been equally distant. African-American leaders, led by the Congressional Black Caucus, launched an active campaign against the military regime. The US government "decertified" Nigeria, making the country ineligible for aid or for US support credits from the IMF. Some leaders pushed for harder sanctions, including an oil blockade, the effects of which would be catastrophic for the Nigerian economy, already reeling from the oil-workers' strikes in the wake of the aborted elections.

The Abacha regime's inter-African relations were initially overshadowed by **conflict with Cameroon** over the Bakassi peninsula, a disputed strip of oil-rich border territory near the mouth of the Cross River. During the early part of 1994, it seemed Abacha and Cameroonian president Paul Biya might be ready to risk war, in part, perhaps, to bolster their unpopular images at home. By the middle of the year, however, both leaders appeared willing to negotiate a settlement. Nigeria remains the most influential member of the Economic Community of West African States (ECOWAS) and was instrumental in seeking a regional solution to the Liberian crisis.

Other West African states have refrained from openly criticizing the new administration, opting for a wait-and-see policy (though Fifa's decision not to hold the Junior World Cup soccer championship in Nigeria was a humiliating rebuke).

Amid the political turmoil, the economy provided no good news for Abacha. In early 1995 inflation was running at about 80 percent, exports had slumped badly and several banks looked set to collapse. Underlying this, a crisis in the oil industry had been triggered by a fall in world market prices, by repeated strikes, and by gross corruption. Billions of dollars have been stolen from the country's oil earnings over the last five years.

Not only is **fiscal mismanagement** bad for general economic recovery, it sits poorly with a frustrated populace. Nigerians have few allusions about the level of government theft, but seem more angered than during past regimes, when grand building projects and government spending at least had a trickle-down effect. Money isn't circulating any more, and the government almost seems to be baiting the people by associating with the likes of Umaru Dikko, who was held up as the very symbol of arrogant corruption (when the Buhari government tried to kidnap him from London to face charges of graft) until Abacha brought him back from exile to sit on the constitutional conference.

Dikko pushed regional tensions to boiling point when he stated soon after arrival that the north was "prepared to go to war" should Abiola ever be inaugurated as president. Resentment was already at fever pitch among southwesterners, especially the Yoruba, who have been systematically marginalized within the government and the army since Abacha's takeover.

The Ogoni affair (see box) has not encouraged **foreign investors**. Nigeria has been ranked the world's third riskiest location for business investment, after Iraq and Russia, with (to add to its unenviable human rights record) a well-established reputation for perpetrating fraud against unwary foreign investors – a notoriety of extreme concern to reputable Nigerian businesses. Although Abacha did an about-face in early 1995 and began espousing economic poli-

THE CASE OF THE OGONI

In recent years a major focus of anti-government resentment has been the oilfields of the southeast, culminating in the murder trial over the deaths of four **Ogoni people** in the Ogoni district of Rivers State. The Ogoni, one of the southeast's minority ethnic groups, number half a million. The well-known TV writer, publisher and author, **Ken Saro-Wiwa**, who leads the Movement for the Survival of the Ogoni People (**Mosop**), was charged in the affair, which soon escalated from a local incident to a national crisis, with international implications.

The case has a history of army abuses and government apathy behind it, going back three decades. The 25km by 40km strip that comprises Ogoniland, to the southeast of Port Harcourt, now contains ten oilfields, over a hundred oil wells, a petro-chemical complex, two oil refineries and seven flares burning off waste gas day and night. The land is scarred by pipelines and sludge-filled canals. When Shell Oil, which partly operates the Ogoni oilfields, was accused of neglecting its environmental reponsibilities – oil pollution has damaged crops and farmlands and caused serious health problems – **Amnesty International** and **Greenpeace** took up the cause of Saro-Wiwa and the Ogoni and were joined by celebrities and opinion-formers as diverse as British Labour MP Glenda Jackson, US presidential contender Jesse Jackson and Body Shop supremo Anita Roddick. Both Amnesty and Greenpeace have been banned from Ogoniland. As a British TV documentary showed, in 1990, in the single worst incident to date, a village was razed to the ground and 80 people massacred, when resentment among the Ogoni first exploded. Critics accuse Shell of standing by, while the government is accused of purposely stirring up ethnic tensions as a smoke screen, and of depleting the resources of the oil-rich region, while returning almost nothing to the poorly developed local infrastructure.

The Ogoni are not all united behind Saro-Wiwa, but there is no disagreement that revenues from the oil drilled from their land (some £200 billion or $300 billion in thirty years of drilling, equivalent to 80 percent of all Nigeria's foreign currency earnings) are not being fairly shared. As local militants began sabotaging drilling facilities, the region was put under the charge of a tyrannical military commander – Major Paul Okuntimo – who has publicly boasted of his murderous activities. The glare of bad publicity has more or less driven Shell out of business in Ogoniland. Meanwhile, as this book goes to press, Saro-Wiwa waits to be sentenced.

cies more in line with the wishes of the World Bank, foreign money did not flood in.

■ Prospects

Resentment of the new regime still runs high in parts of the military. Throughout Abacha's tenure, revelations of coup plots and reports of bombings near the army barracks in Abuja have led to the arrest of numerous officers, including high-ranking generals whom Abacha had considered loyal. The chief of state has called in Israeli anti-terrorist experts to shore up the regime's stability and restructure the presidential guard.

How Abacha handles the hundreds of dissenters who remain in jail – including the 24 men convicted of a supposed **coup attempt in March 1995**, one of whom is Olusegun Obasanjo – could be decisive in determining his regime's survival, even in the short term. Hardliners among Abacha's advisors argue for mass executions – a strategy which would assuredly push the country to the brink of civil war and draw down economic sanctions from major trading partners. Others envisage the creation of a military-backed transitional government, incorporating members of the former National Party of Nigeria. Though Abacha himself helped overthrow the NPN on the grounds of "corrupt leadership" in 1983, he has become chummy with its former leaders, most of whom come from the north. This scenario would at least pave the way for a return to civilian rule, but is said to be opposed by powerful forces within the military who distrust the NPN. Nor is it likely to inspire much confidence among dissenters in the south, especially the Yoruba, who are likely to be excluded from participation.

Even mild critics describe Abacha as unable to confront powerful economic interests at home or to make the tough choices needed to set his country on the right path. But a growing body of hardened cynics claim there is nothing to suggest that Abacha and his cronies have any other motive than self-enrichment, whatever the cost to Nigeria. Life, for the vast majority of people, is as bad as it has ever been – a slamming indictment of the failure of those in power to accomplish anything of value.

In response, in June 1995, the exiled Nobel laureate **Wole Soyinka** and others announced the formation of a **National Liberation Council** (NLC) of seventeen prominent opposition leaders. The NLC aims to form a government in exile to campaign for the removal of the Abacha regime. A week later, Abacha announced he was lifting the ban on political activities – though since several hundred people remain incarcerated in Nigeria's jails for taking part in political activities, this move is a hollow gesture. There have been calls to suspend Nigeria's membership of the **Commonwealth**; and Commonwealth Secretary General Chief Emeka Anyaoku is being pressed to harden his, up to now mild, criticisms of the regime in his home country.

Most analysts, both nationals and foreigners, consider Abacha's government the most incompetent and brutal military regime ever to blight Nigeria, and predict that the lot of 99 percent of Nigerians will continue to decline over the next few years. There is widespread speculation, too, that unless it becomes more skilled at walking a very thin tightrope, the current government will itself fall victim of a military takeover.

LAGOS

If you're reading nervously, you wouldn't be the first traveller to approach **Lagos** with a sinking feeling of despair and trepidation, convinced you're going to hate the place – should you live through it. A city of eight million inhabitants, Lagos has grown too big too fast. Long ago, the city overflowed from the **islands** at its heart, and the urban sprawl on the mainland has mushroomed alarmingly. Of the infrastructure – housing, roads, public transport, water, electricity and sewerage – only the new expressways show any sign of keeping up (cars, as everywhere, getting priority). Pollution, squalid overcrowding, violent crime and a 24-hour din are the inevitable results of the shortfall. There's a lot here to keep you on your toes.

But you might just be surprised. It's the **international airport** – the business of arrival or connecting planes there – that is (or was until recently) to blame for much of the terrible first impression. On approaching the city itself, you may find rather less chaos – and more to excite. For Africa's foremost metropolis is, at the very least, a city of intense, voluble personality and breathtaking dynamism. Ships from around the globe berth at its **ports** of Apapa and Tin Can Island, and the **skyscrapers** that spike Lagos Island house a swarm of international firms. A more immediate sign of "success" is the commuter traffic packing the **flyovers**, regularly grinding to a halt in rush hour "go-slow" traffic jams, to be exploited by thousands of irrepressible **street vendors** trying to sell anything from imported apples to bathroom scales. And beyond the non-stop, unrestrained commercialism on the streets, universities, museums, galleries and the national theatre all attest to a thriving **intellectual and cultural life**.

While it would definitely be misleading to downplay its problems, Lagos is no more of a hell hole than any other gigantic, seething, impoverished city with a military administration and an oppressive climate. The risks of muggings and pickpocketing are high, but most people get through their stays safely. Travel with as much confidence as you can muster and you may well have a good time . . . and debunking some myths and surviving the experience unscathed, as nearly everyone does, carry their own satisfaction.

SOME HISTORY

The swampy mangrove zone around Lagos was originally inhabited by small Ga fishing communities, but rainforest and marshes probably prevented large scale settlement. **Portuguese mariners** first arrived at the islands around Lagos in 1472 and named the place *Lago de Curamo*, but it wasn't until much later that the area became an important port of trade.

In the sixteenth century, **Yoruba settlers** came to Iddo and later moved onto Lagos Island – which they named Eko – and beyond. The settlement was eventually incorporated into the **Benin Kingdom** which at the time extended all the way to the area of Cotonou. In the early eighteenth century, the ruling Oba granted a trade monopoly to the Portuguese whose main export was, by then, **slaves**. In the early nineteenth century, the French and British governments began sending warships to break up the slave trade. Lagos was used as a hideout by profiteers who made advantage of the many creeks and rivers to conceal their human cargo. In 1851, the **British** shelled Lagos and eventually forced the Oba to abandon the slave trade. Soon after, they captured the islands and formed Lagos colony.

Early this century, Lagos grew into an important commercial centre thanks to the port and the **railway line**, begun in 1896 and opened through to Kano in 1912. It became the capital of the southern Nigerian protectorate and later of the entire Federation when north and south were merged. After independence, Lagos maintained its role as capital until 1991 when the seat of government moved to Abuja. The city is still the country's undisputed commercial, industrial, cultural and diplomatic centre, capital in all but name.

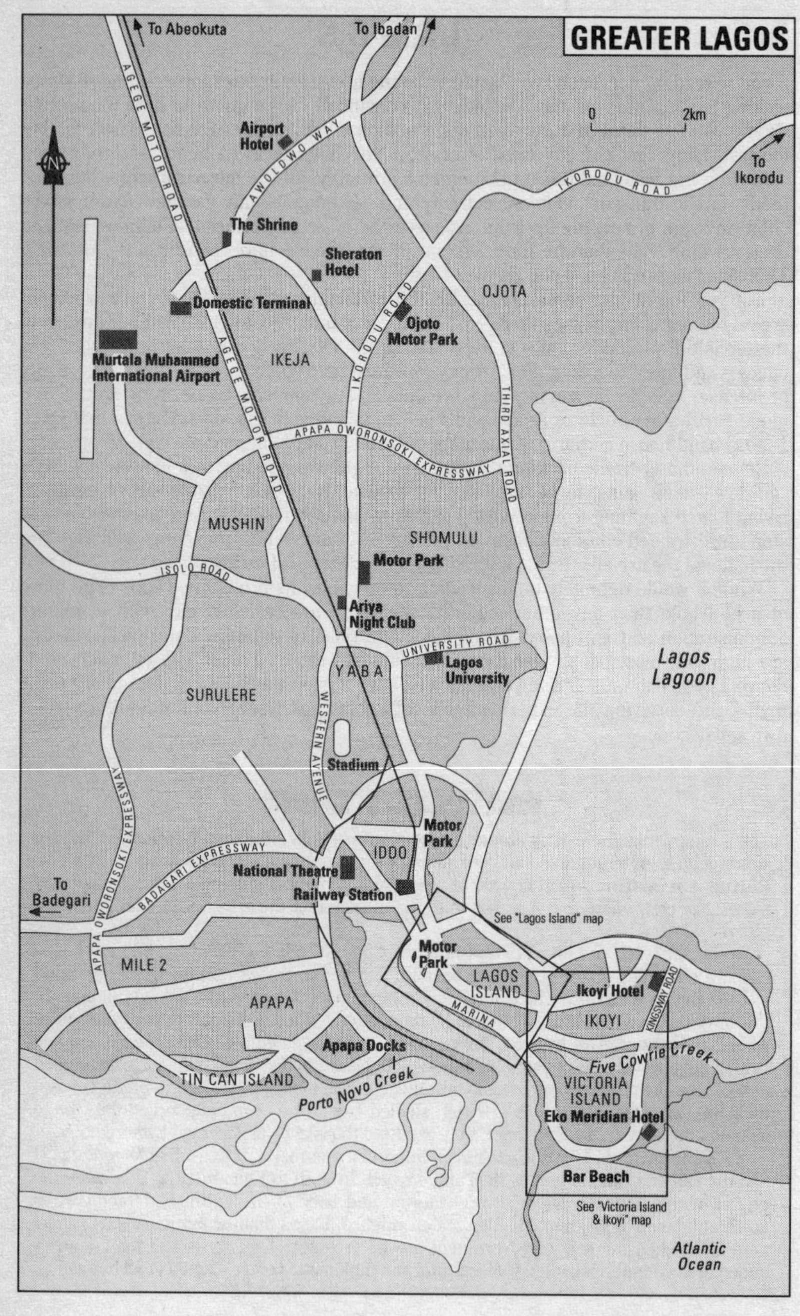
GREATER LAGOS
To Abeokuta
To Ibadan
0
2km
To Ikorodu
AGEGE MOTOR ROAD
AWOLOWO WAY
IKORODU ROAD
Airport Hotel
The Shrine
Sheraton Hotel
Domestic Terminal
Ojoto Motor Park
OJOTA
Murtala Muhammed International Airport
IKEJA
THIRD AXIAL ROAD
APAPA OWORONSOKI EXPRESSWAY
MUSHIN
SHOMULU
Motor Park
ISOLO ROAD
Ariya Night Club
UNIVERSITY ROAD
YABA
Lagos University
Lagos Lagoon
SURULERE
WESTERN AVENUE
Stadium
Motor Park
IDDO
BADAGARI EXPRESSWAY
National Theatre
Railway Station
To Badegari
See "Lagos Island" map
Motor Park
MILE 2
LAGOS ISLAND
Ikoyi Hotel
KINGSWAY ROAD
APAPA
MARINA
IKOYI
Apapa Docks
Five Cowrie Creek
TIN CAN ISLAND
Porto Novo Creek
VICTORIA ISLAND
Eko Meridian Hotel
Bar Beach
See "Victoria Island & Ikoyi" map
Atlantic Ocean

Arrival and orientation

Lagos spreads over some 200 square kilometres and comprises myriad **neighbourhoods**. But the heart of the city, where you're likely to spend most of your time, is tucked onto **Lagos and Ikoyi islands** – now merged – and **Victoria Island**, to the south.

By whatever means you come to Lagos, the **mainland** is your point of entry. Although there are bland neighbourhoods here (like the administrative district of **Ikeja**), most are populated by the city's working class and poor – and they can feel distinctly heavy. This is where many Lagos horror stories have their origins, but that's largely because most of the city's rich don't live there. As a temporary visitor you're no more likely to run into serious, violent trouble on the mainland than anywhere else in Lagos (perhaps, in truth, less).

THE TAXI DRIVERS ACTUALLY SCREAM

"Well, it's true you have to fight to pay a normal taxi fare. For women, including Nigerian women, it's harder. The taxi drivers actually scream at you if you try to pay the regular price. But the regular price is the regular price and you can pay it after a fight (verbal) and all is well. This didn't bother me, but then I spent fourteen years living in New York City. By comparison Lagos is a gentle place."

Airport arrivals

Arriving by plane at **Murtala Muhammed Airport** used to be the most harrowing experience you'd be likely to have in Lagos, with customs agents routinely aggressive and unsubtle ("What are you going to dash me?") and the whole entrance process – verification of visa and health certificate, luggage search, body search and so on *ad nauseam* – enough to put you off the city forever. The situation is improving, however, and some travellers report no problems at all.

Only limited numbers of **taxis** are licensed to trade at the airport (ask to see the driver's ID card), and there are no buses out here. You could pay much more than the going price (but there are set rates posted in the airport and on the driver's tariff card, which you should insist on seeing). If it's after dark, your main concern, rather than worrying about saving a little money on the fare, should be to get out of the airport and into a hotel. If you're lucky enough to be flying in during daylight hours, you could, alternatively, walk down the airport road about 2km and pick up a shared taxi or a bus. The best option of all is to arrange to be **met from the airport** – all of the travel agents detailed on p.1041 offer this service.

Arriving by long-distance taxi

By **long-distance taxi**, you'll arrive at one of several points on the mainland – Mile Two, Yaba, Ojota or Iddo. From these places, battered yellow private buses or state-run red and white buses (see "Getting Around") will drop you at Lagos Island, where you can get a cheap taxi to a hotel.

Arriving by ship

These days it's unusual to arrive by ship, though a number of cargo lines still offer berths. If you're interested in leaving this way, follow up the address in "Moving on from Lagos" on p.1041. Ships berth at Apapa, opposite Lagos Island.

Orientation

From a traveller's point of view, Lagos consists of four main areas: the mainland, Lagos Island, Ikoyi and Victoria Island. If your stay is going to be any longer than a day or two, it's worth getting hold of the excellent *Winnay Lagos Street Atlas*, published by Macmillan, either before you arrive, or as soon as possible in Lagos.

The mainland

A vast reach of working-class districts, industrial zones and shanty towns heaves over the mainland for miles. At its northwest edge is the **international airport** (20km from Victoria Island). Also in the far north is the industrial and administrative district of **Ikeja**. Closer to the city centre are **Shomolu** (15km from Victoria Island – a low-rent residential and small business district); **Yaba** (10km; an important schools district); **Surulere** (10km; schools and residential, home of the National Stadium and a vibrant quarter containing some of Lagos' most popular nightspots); and **Ebute Metta** (8km; site of the National Theatre complex).

Lagos Island

Lagos Island is the commercial centre and site of the towers that provide the city's striking skyline. Many of these high-rises – including most of the bank headquarters and **Nitel House**, Africa's tallest skyscraper – are on the south side of the island behind **Marina Street** (usually known simply as Marina), which used to run along the waterfront. Today, Marina is several hundred metres back from the water, shadowed by the zooming split-level expressway of **Apongbon Street**. But it retains some buildings of note, including the former **State House** – residence of the British governors – the infamous headquarters of **NEPA** (electricity corporation), with the bronze statue of Shango the thunder god before it, Lagos' **General Post Office** and the eighteenth-century **Anglican church**.

Broad Street, which runs parallel to Marina, is another well-known thoroughfare with more banks and markets and some fairly upmarket shops. It runs into **Tinubu Square**, a landscaped roundabout, with a perpetually defunct fountain, in one of the busiest parts of town. Nearby, the **markets** of **Jankara**, **Isale Eko**, **Ebute Ero** and **Balogun** all run into one another, filling the western part of the island with frenetic small-scale commerce. The **Brazilian quarter**, founded by former slaves brought back from Brazil, is concentrated in the area around Campos Square and Campbell Street, while the **Palace of the Oba** (the traditional ruler of Lagos) lies on the northern tip of the island on Upper King Street.

The eastern end of Marina is dominated by the great scar of **Tafawa Balewa Square**, with its monumental equine statues rearing up at the entrance on the south side, in memory of the old racetrack that used to be here. The north side of Tafawa Balewa is now where many of the major airlines and travel agencies have their offices. The south is mostly shops and cheap restaurants. Just up the road is the **National Museum**.

Ikoyi

The swamps that used to divide **Ikoyi** from Lagos Island have been filled in, and today the two sections of town are separated only by a tangle of motorway flyovers, but Ikoyi still retains its individual flavour. Its main artery, **Awolowo Road**, links Lagos Island with Victoria Island via the **Falomo Bridge**. Awolowo contains chic **boutiques** – many operating out of converted private homes – high-priced **restaurants**, a sprinkling of **embassies** and the **Polo Club**, a reminder of the days when Ikoyi was the posh colonial neighbourhood. The **Falomo shopping centre** crowns Awolowo Road at the junction with Kingsway Road near the bridge.

The centre of Ikoyi, dominated by the **administrative district**, includes the **Federal Secretariat**, where most of the ministries are housed, and the present State House. Further west, **Obalende** is a vibrant working-class neighbourhood with a large market, numerous chop bars (good places for authentic pepper soup or *suya*) and watering holes where locals come to drink and dance. As Dodon Barracks and the Presidential Lodge border this neighbourhood, it is well policed and one of the safest low-income areas in town. However, it's still a good idea to go accompanied at night.

Victoria Island

The principal modern residential area of Lagos, **Victoria Island** (V.I.) is divided into thousands of expensive plots, many of them taken up by foreign **embassies** and expatriate residences. Near the **Independence Bridge** to Lagos Island, **Eleke Crescent**

GETTING AROUND

Transport is a nightmare. Getting around Lagos, unless you have unlimited time or patience (or your own car and driver as many expatriates do), is basically down to **taxis**. Fares are inexpensive, and you'd need to be down on your luck (or just curious) to use the complex array of buses and minibuses. There are one or two limited boat services. The plan in the 1980s for a **metro system** that was to have come to Lagos' rescue, has been shelved.

Taxis

Lagos taxis are usually yellow Peugeot 504s with black stripes. The drivers like to "pick" people as they go, effectively running a **share-taxi** service, often on the route of their choice, and ignoring the regular fares (a table of which they're obliged to display) and the protests of passengers. You hail them by yelling out your destination.

Use some discretion over where you say you're going (be prepared to get out and walk a hundred metres) as it can affect the fare, which you should discuss and agree on first. Stand in the door till you're sure the driver knows the price is agreed. Try also to have the notes ready (if possible wave them in the driver's face) to emphasize the fare you're prepared to pay. Change is a rare thing in any case. The kinds of fares you'll end up paying vary from ₦5–10 for district-to-district hops and ₦50–100 for lengthy cross-city trips. If you want to **charter**, rather than wait for a share, shout "Drop!" to hail a taxi. You'll pay much more – ₦50 for short hops, ₦100–200 for cross-city journeys.

Minibuses and buses

Lagos public transport makes you nostalgic for Dakar or Abidjan, or even Douala. The system is fraught, exhausting and unpredictable. There's a struggling fleet of red and white, **Lagos State Transport Corporation** midibuses, minibuses and Mercedes buses (*oluwale*). But they're far outnumbered on the mainland by motley swarms of **privately owned** midi- and minibuses – either VW or Japanese *kombis*, or local Merc or Bedford conversions known as *molue* (large, with aisles) or *danfo* (small, seat only). Privately owned vehicles in this league aren't officially allowed off the mainland. Maximum fares (private or LSTC) are very low (around £0.10 or $0.15), but the discomfort and hair-pulling frustration and slowness of them can undermine the resolve of even the staunchest city survivor.

Ferries and boats

The main water route consists of an hourly ferry service in a big, hundred-seater vessel, from midway along **Marina Street** across Lagos Harbour to Apapa and **Mile Two**, on a canal west of the Apapa–Orowonsoki Expressway, about 1km south of the Badagari Expressway.

You can also get ferries from **Victoria Island** to **Tarkwa**. *Tarzan Boats* run from near the Italian embassy to Tarkwa Bay and other local beaches.

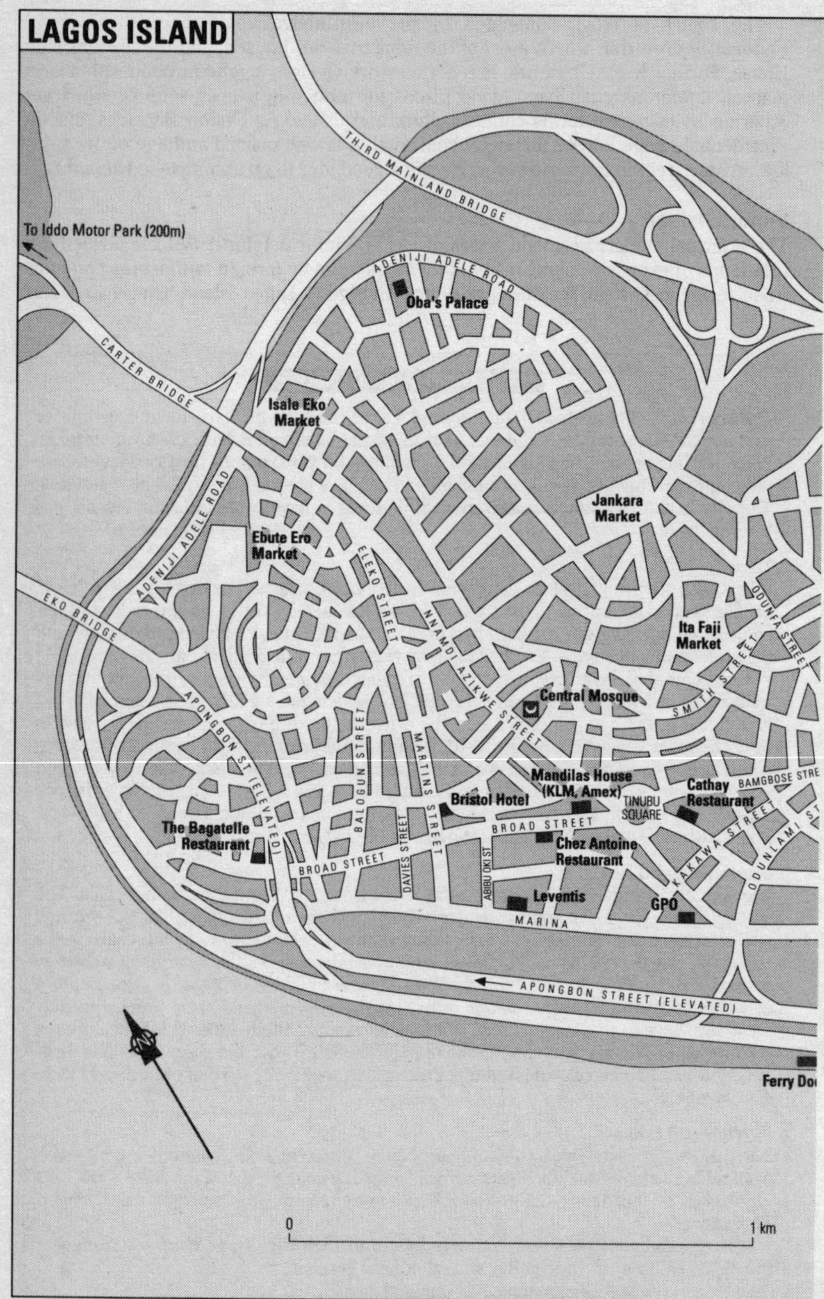
LAGOS ISLAND
THIRD MAINLAND BRIDGE
To Iddo Motor Park (200m)
ADENIJI ADELE ROAD
Oba's Palace
CARTER BRIDGE
Isale Eko Market
Jankara Market
ADENIJI ADELE ROAD
Ebute Ero Market
ELEKO STREET
EKO BRIDGE
NNAMDI AZIKWE STREET
ODUNFA STREET
Ita Faji Market
SMITH STREET
Central Mosque
APONGBON ST (ELEVATED)
BALOGUN STREET
MARTINS STREET
Mandilas House (KLM, Amex)
Cathay Restaurant
BAMGBOSE STRE
Bristol Hotel
TINUBU SQUARE
BROAD STREET
The Bagatelle Restaurant
DAVIES STREET
Chez Antoine Restaurant
KAKAWA STREET
ODUNLAMI ST
BROAD STREET
ABIBU OKI ST
Leventis
GPO
MARINA
APONGBON STREET (ELEVATED)
Ferry Do
0
1 km

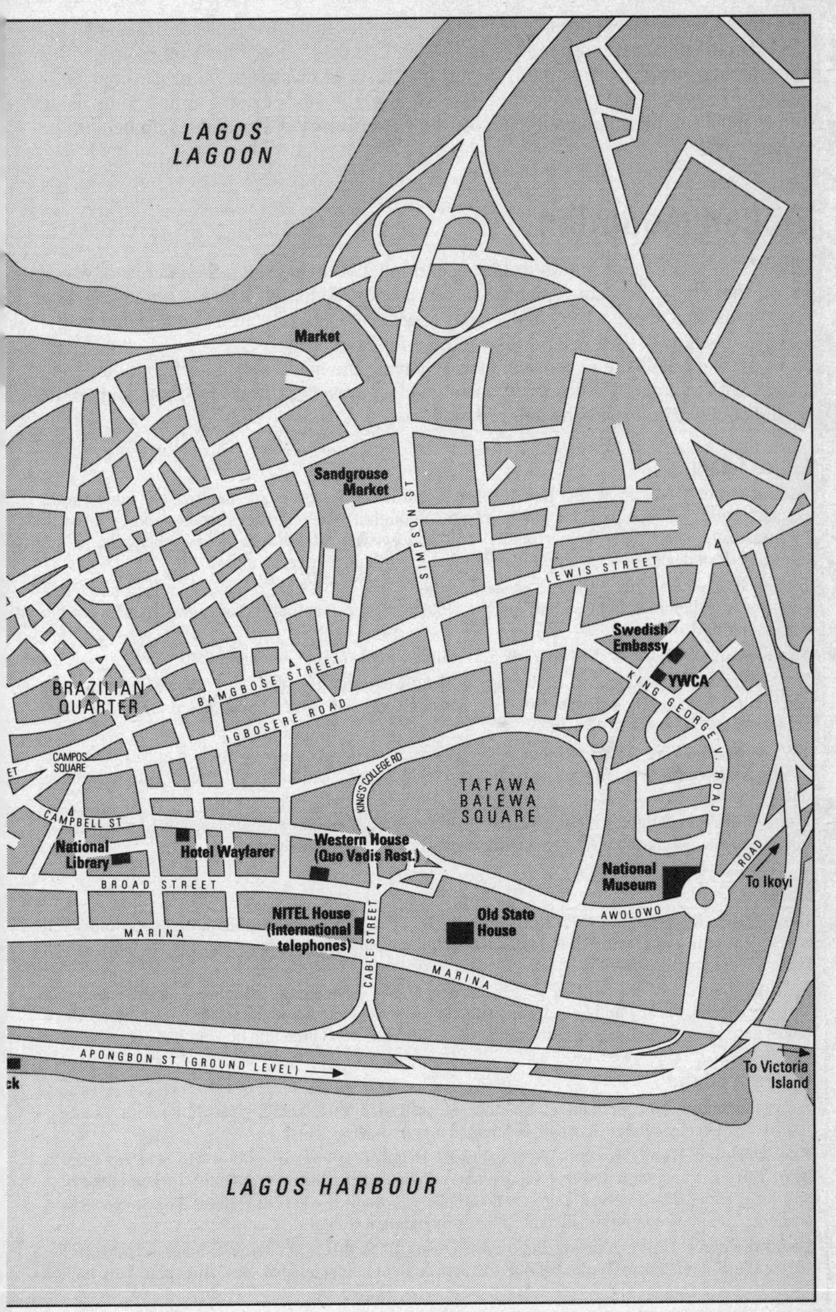
LAGOS LAGOON
Market
Sandgrouse Market
SIMPSON ST
LEWIS STREET
Swedish Embassy
YWCA
KING GEORGE V. ROAD
BRAZILIAN QUARTER
BAMGBOSE STREET
IGBOSERE ROAD
CAMPOS SQUARE
KING'S COLLEGE RD
TAFAWA BALEWA SQUARE
CAMPBELL ST
National Library
Hotel Wayfarer
Western House (Quo Vadis Rest.)
National Museum
ROAD
To Ikoyi
BROAD STREET
NITEL House (International telephones)
CABLE STREET
Old State House
AWOLOWO
MARINA
MARINA
APONGBON ST (GROUND LEVEL)
To Victoria Island
LAGOS HARBOUR

has the highest concentration of diplomatic missions, including those of Britain and the USA. On the northeast corner of Victoria Island, **"1004"**, a vast housing project with a thousand and four apartments, is Lagos' first taste of massive-scale urban housing, a maze of buildings and parking lots. **Bar Beach**, the city's closest strand, runs along the island's southern flank and, nearby, the **Eko Meridien Hotel** rises up behind the ocean front.

Accommodation

There's no shortage of **hotels** in Lagos, and most of them are on the mainland, which is, on the whole, less convenient than the islands. Although it has a reputation as a dangerous area, those who actually enjoy aspects of Lagos life aren't intimidated by the mainland – most of the music clubs are there for example.

Upmarket hotels are expensive if you're paying the non-resident tariff, but moderate places with AC and TV are good value. Budget travellers won't be disappointed, as plenty of cheap hotels and hostels are available.

Lagos Island

Bristol Hotel, 8 Martin St (PO Box 1088; ☎01/266 1204). A lapsed old standby, well known from colonial days. You could do a lot worse in Lagos, though it's moderately expensive and (along with its immediate, claustrophobic surrounds) now almost synonymous with money changers, prostitutes and drug dealers. Never a dull moment, but in truth not dangerous. ③–④.

Ishaga Inn, off Balogun St, at the western end of the island. Clean, reasonably priced hotel, in a colourful area hemmed in by a cloth market. Note, however, that this end of Lagos Island is not the safest after dark. ②.

The Regent, 23 Abibu Oki St (☎01/662 527). Similar to the *Bristol*, but darker. ③.

Hotel Wayfarer, 52 Campbell St, by Lagos Island Maternity Hospital (☎01/263 0113). Moderate and central, with simple and safe S/C, AC rooms. Good value, with a small restaurant and friendly management. Book ahead. ②–③.

YWCA, George V St, corner of Moloney St. Clean, cheap dorm rooms for women only. Convenient for the National Museum, but locks on the lockers don't lock and loud bells ring at 6am to turf you out for the day. ①.

Ziena Hotel, 11 Smith St (☎01/636 158). A rare moderately priced hotel on the islands, with a folksy feel and comfortable AC rooms. Book in advance as space is limited. ②.

Ikoyi

Ikoyi Hotel, Kingsway Rd (PO Box 895; ☎01/603 202). Once a colonial institution and top-notch hotel, now somewhat frayed at the edges. It's still reasonably good value and the amenities are all there – including a pleasant pool. ⑤.

YMCA, 77 Awolowo Rd (☎01/680 516). Men only but conveniently equidistant from Lagos and Victoria islands. Scruffy non-S/C dorms with fan. Nigerians and young men from throughout Africa board here and can be a big help showing you around the city. Often full; book ahead. ①.

Victoria Island

B-Jays Guesthouse, Sir Samuel Manuwa St (☎01/612 391). Small, clean hotel with AC, S/C rooms and friendly service, in a safe residential neighbourhood. ⑥.

Eko Meridien Hotel, Kuramo Waters (Private Bag 12724; ☎01/615 000 or 615 695; Fax 01/615 205). The sparkling white tower – rising a short distance from the open Atlantic – is one of the best and most expensive hotels in Lagos and the place to book if you're travelling on someone else's account. Complete comfort in all departments, including a crystal-clear pool. ⑦.

Federal Palace Hotel, Ahmadu Bello Rd (PO Box 1000; ☎01/610 031). *The* hotel in Lagos in the 1970s, the *Federal Palace* harks back to the first flush of independence. But faulty plumbing makes

ACCOMMODATION PRICE CODES

① Under ₦650 (under £5/$7.50). ② ₦650–1300 (£5–10/$7.50–15)
③ ₦1300–2600 (£10–20/$15–30) ④ ₦2600–3900 (£20–30/$30–45)
⑤ ₦3900–5200 (£30–40/$45–60) ⑥ ₦5200–6500 (£40–50/$60–75)
⑦ Over ₦6500 (over £50/$75)

For further details see p.51 and p.1005.

bucket showers obligatory in older rooms and while the new wing is better, the furniture is falling apart. The lagoon-side bar, accessible from the new building, offers spectacular views of the Lagos Island skyline and ships nosing into harbour. At weekends, there's poolside dancing (but no water in the pool) to live music. ⑦.

Victoria Lodge, 5 Ologun Agbaje St, off Adeola Odeku St. Very pleasant, homely and clean, with a limited restaurant, bar and TV. ⑤.

Mainland

Airport Hotel, Obafemi Awolowo Rd, Ikeja (☎01/901 001 or 932 051). Large, plush pile gone to seed, but not all bad and not expensive or anonymous compared with the competition by which it's recently been overtaken. ④.

Circular Hotel, 136 Bode Thomas St, Surulere. AC rooms with TV and phones for room service. Very helpful management goes out of its way to please guests, sometimes even showing them around town. ②.

Kolex Hotel, 3 Olufeko Close, off Fola Agoro St, Shomulu (☎01/876 575). Small, quiet, comfortable and modern, with a disco and a useful shop. Transport available. ②.

Hotel Rialto, 6 Alhaji Amoo St, Ojota. Off the beaten track in a working class neighbourhood in the far north of the city, but very inexpensive S/C lodgings with TV. Small restaurant and friendly staff. ①.

Ritalori Hotel, Animashawun St, off Eric Moore Rd, Surulere. A highly recommended Nigerian hotel in a lively area, with a pool and friendly management, though it's become rather expensive. ④.

Sheraton, 30 Airport Rd, Ikeja (PMB 21189; ☎01/900 930; Fax 01/525 953). Lagos' smartest hotel, American-run and right by the airport, catering for business people whose contacts come to them. Everything is on hand – no need even to go into the city. ⑦.

Stadium Hotel, 27–33 Iyun St, just west of the National Stadium, Surulere (☎01/833 593). Popular hotel with an exciting disco with live music performances, and comfortable AC rooms; always animated and often full. ②.

The City and nearby beaches

The effort of getting around the city is the only thing that really detracts from its worthwhile sites. It can literally take hours to accomplish journeys by car that could probably have been walked more quickly. Don't be afraid of venturing out on foot during the day: so long as you have nothing of value on you, you've nothing to fear – apart from the drivers.

Museums

Lagos is almost alone among West African cities in having more than a single museum. The **National Museum** is highly recommended and, if you've time or opportunity, make an effort to visit the **National Theatre** and see what's on view at its cultural centre and galleries; the local press will have details.

The Onikan National Museum

Nigeria's foremost museum, just east of Tafawa Balewa Square on Lagos Island (daily 9am–6pm), is a required visit, especially worthwhile if the travelling exhibition, "Treasures of Ancient Nigeria", happens to be home for a rest from world touring.

The "**Treasures**" traces 2500 years of Nigerian art from the earliest terracotta figures from **Nok** in the Jos Plateau, through extraordinarily intricate and sophisticated **Igbo-Ukwe** bronze castings from southeast Nigeria, to the almost Hellenic realism of the later **Ife and Owo** brass and terracotta busts – which provide a glimpse into Yoruba court life from the twelfth to the fifteenth century. The famous **Benin bronzes** were made exclusively for the Oba by master craftsmen working for the court, and represent some of the greatest masterpieces of West African art.

In the permanent collection, the **Ethnographic Gallery** is designed to give an overview of the cultural materials of Nigeria's diverse ethnic groups. The display of **Masquerades**, common to a range of peoples, shows off one of the oldest forms of cultural and artistic expression. In Nigeria, masquerades not only served to provide a link with the realm of the dead but were important in instigating other art forms like music, dance and drama. Other exhibits range from decorated pottery and calabashes from the different regions to shrines and household gods reflecting the importance of the supernatural in people's lives.

The **Benin Gallery** contains a selection of bronzes and ivory carvings, including the well-known waist mask that appears on the Naira note and was symbol of the FESTAC festival. Unfortunately, many masterpieces of Benin art are still held abroad, despite numerous requests for their return from the Nigerian government.

An additional permanent exhibition – **"Nigerian governments: Yesterday and Today"** – traces the political history of the country from the slave trade to the present. The post-independence section acts as a visual *aide-mémoire* in figuring out the rather complicated train of events since the days when Abubakar Tafawa Balewa became Nigeria's first prime minister. Amid the displays recounting the coups and governments that followed, President Murtala Muhammed's bullet-holed car pays menacing homage to one of Nigeria's most popular assassinated leaders.

If you're looking to buy crafts, check out the **crafts shop** in the museum, at least for an idea of how much you can expect to pay for works in Lagos – prices here are fixed. In fact, the chances are you won't find prices any cheaper outside the big hotels, where all the gear is often laid out. Lastly, you can take a break from all the culture in the very good **Museum Kitchen** (see p.1038, top).

National Theatre complex

Rising out of the district of Ebute Metta above the creeks, the **National Theatre** vaunts its modernistic architecture in a low-rent area. Built for the 1977 FESTAC cultural festival, the theatre is a classic example of high-prestige, low-reward development. It's more a cultural complex than simply a theatrical venue, which is actually a role it rarely has the chance to play. The main ancillary site is the **Centre for Black and African Arts and Civilization** (Mon–Sat 7.30am–3.30pm) which contains archives, a library and a museum with periodically changing exhibits, all dedicated to African culture – in Africa and the diaspora. The original FESTAC 1977 exhibits should still be on show.

The **National Gallery of Crafts and Design** (Mon–Fri 10am–5pm, Sat 10am–4pm; ☎01/830 200) displays traditional Nigerian handicrafts. The **National Gallery of Modern Art** at Entrance B of the theatre complex (Tues–Fri 10am–3pm, Sat & Sun noon–4pm, closed public holidays) is an exhibition space for the work of young Nigerian talents. The drinks stalls opposite the theatre are a great place to hang out in the early evening for a cheap beer and a meat pie or *moin-moin*, and watch the actors and artistes.

Brazilian-style buildings

Lagos Island is the oldest part of the city. Between the high-rises and the market shacks and the exhaust emissions and the rains, a few Brazilian-style buildings have survived. However, they're falling apart and jealously guarded against photographers. The Oba's palace is particularly unimpressive. Still, if you're keen on a hunt, the following, all on Lagos Island, may still be worthwhile: **Chief's House**, Ado St; **Ebun House**, 85 Odunfa St (300m east of Tinubu Sq), a great pile of a place dating from 1914; **Brazilian House**, 29 Kakawa St, off Marina; **Da Silva House**, Odufege St; and the comely **Shitta Mosque** on Martins St, with its Brazilian tilework.

Markets

Wherever you fetch up in Lagos, you'll find a **market** close by: there are literally dozens on the mainland, notably Tejuoso in Surulere, and the market in Apapa, which is also close to a good range of ordinary shops and supermarkets. On Lagos Island, **Jankara market** is the prime site and one of the cheapest places for new clothes or second-hand garments, general hardware, **traditional musical instruments**, cassettes, **jewellery** and **trading beads**, magical materials (jujus, skins, powders), and *aso-oke*, beautiful woven cloth which is used on special occasions. West of Jankara, between Adeniji Adele Road and Ebute Ero Street, **Isale Eko market** specializes in food, crocks and baskets; you can also find some ready-made clothes here. In the same area, near the old Carter Bridge, is an **Ogogoro market** with scorching local spirit for sale.

Focussing around the street of the same name on Lagos Island, **Balogun market** is the best place for **cloth**. In the rambling maze of alleys you'll find mostly imported material, including damasks, plus a wide range of African prints. A little to the east, around Nnamdi Azikwe Street, you can find batiks and ready-made clothes, plus records and cassettes.

Between Lewis and Simpson streets at the eastern end of Lagos Island, **Sand Grouse market** is the best bet for **food** – fresh fish, shrimps and huge snails, as well as more conventional provisions.

Another food market, **Bar Beach market**, can be found towards the end of Ahmadu Bello Road on Victoria Island. In view of all the money and expatriates on the island, it's no surprise to find some **crafts** here, too – including basketry, batiks and even Tuareg leather chests.

Beaches

Bar Beach, on Victoria Island, has always been unattractive and shadeless, but it's the closest spot to swim in the sea (and a meeting place for Christian sects). Since exceptional spring tides in 1990 and 1994 swept most of the sand away, the beach has been steeper and less enticing than ever. Still, people continue to come here because it's within walking distance of the homes on Victoria Island.

If you want good beaches, you have to go by car or boat. **Badagary**, to the west of Lagos, is a good area, but somewhat far. **Lekki Beach**, 10km east of town off the Lagos Expressway, is lined with coconut palms that improve the mood considerably. Take a taxi to Gbara village and walk 2km down the sand road leading from the Expressway to the beach, or arrange to be dropped directly at the beach; settle the cab price beforehand. You can ride horses quite cheaply here and food and drink are on sale. The Nigerian Conservation Foundation (NCF) has a fine **nature trail** at Lekki, with a well-marked route. It's a peaceful haven out of the city, and you can see monkeys and small crocodiles. The **market** at Lekki is also a good place for a wander, with a range of beads, cloth and crafts, and the usual fruit, herbs and commodities.

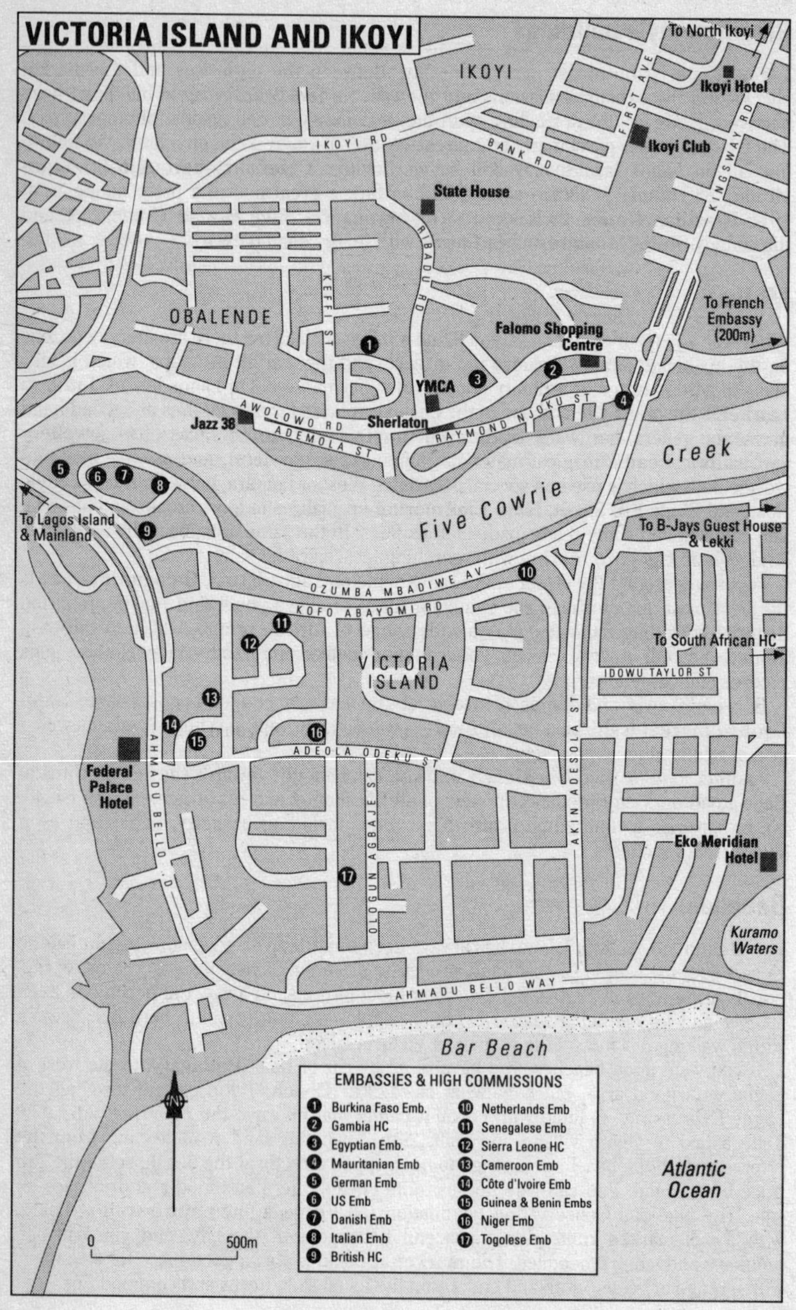
VICTORIA ISLAND AND IKOYI
To North Ikoyi
IKOYI
Ikoyi Hotel
FIRST AVE
IKOYI RD
BANK RD
Ikoyi Club
KINGSWAY RD
State House
RIBADU RD
KEFFI ST
OBALENDE
To French Embassy (200m)
Falomo Shopping Centre
YMCA
AWOLOWO RD
ADEMOLA ST
Jazz 38
Sherlaton
RAYMOND NJOKU ST
Creek
Five Cowrie
To Lagos Island & Mainland
To B-Jays Guest House & Lekki
OZUMBA MBADIWE AV
KOFO ABAYOMI RD
VICTORIA ISLAND
To South African HC
IDOWU TAYLOR ST
ADEOLA ODEKU ST
AKIN ADESOLA ST
Federal Palace Hotel
AHMADU BELLO D.
OLOGUN AGBAJE ST
Eko Meridian Hotel
Kuramo Waters
AHMADU BELLO WAY
Bar Beach
Atlantic Ocean
N
0
500m
EMBASSIES & HIGH COMMISSIONS
1 Burkina Faso Emb.
2 Gambia HC
3 Egyptian Emb.
4 Mauritanian Emb
5 German Emb
6 US Emb
7 Danish Emb
8 Italian Emb
9 British HC
10 Netherlands Emb
11 Senegalese Emb
12 Sierra Leone HC
13 Cameroon Emb
14 Côte d'Ivoire Emb
15 Guinea & Benin Embs
16 Niger Emb
17 Togolese Emb

If you have your own transport, try the much quieter **Eleko beach**, 50km further east on the Epe expressway, where many expats rent beach huts on a long-term basis, but empty ones can usually be rented by the hour.

You can also get **ferries** from Victoria Island to **Tarkwa**. *Tarzan Boats* from Eleke Crescent, by *After Hours* restaurant on the north side of V.I., run to Tarkwa Bay and other local beaches. Tarkwa is the most attractive beach near the city centre, sheltered within the harbour and safe for swimming. Lighthouse beach is beyond Tarkwa, and also attractive, but dangerous because of its strong currents.

Most boat trips out to the beaches (the best ones all to the west) tend to be a private affair. Lagos is a place where it pays to have friends, or make friends quickly: a lot of boats take off every weekend from the Motor Boat Club at the west end of Awolowo Road on Five Cowrie Creek.

Eating, drinking and nightlife

Lagos has thousands of cheap eating places, but is also geared up for splashing out a bit: flashy restaurants, bars, clubs and discos abound, as do more tacky establishments. None of these, however, will burn a big hole in your pocket: with the Naira cheap, you can have a good time on a low budget. If you think you might go out on the town later, leave all but the necessary minimum of possessions in your hotel.

Eating

By day, numerous **snack bars** line the southern edge of Tafawa Balewa Square on Lagos Island. All serve similar fare of meat pies, sausage rolls and pizza – nothing fancy, but quick and inexpensive. Over on Marina Street, the supermarkets all have cafeterias for reasonable lunches. Most of Lagos' **pricier restaurants** are on Lagos Island and Ikoyi and even the expensive places aren't unreasonable at current exchange rates. A number are quite formal, however, and you'd do well to book and dress smartly at these.

Cheap to moderate

In **Ikoyi**, there's a favourite small restaurant near the *YMCA* (left down Raymond Njoku Rd when coming from the Y, then 300m) marked only by two *7 Up* signs at the entrance. They do plain Nigerian food – *eba*, rice and beans, *dodo* and *amala* – with cold beer and minerals: the best cheap eats in the neighbourhood. The **Obalende area**, on the west side of Ikoyi, is full of inexpensive restaurants and outdoor stands where you can buy fish, *suya* (kebabs), rice and so on. Don't miss the pepper soup, a speciality of this quarter, and the wonderfully flavoured chicken, charcoal grilled to order. On **Victoria Island**, street food is available from a small side street directly opposite the *Eko Meridien*: boiled yams, beans and rice, *fufu* with meat or fried fish. Eat here and then have a drink in the *Eko* for rapid culture contrast.

Delikisis, 4 Dipeolu St, off Obafemi Awolowo Way, Ikeja. Bar and restaurant with a friendly atmosphere and music at weekends.

Josephine's restaurant, Keffi St near the junction with Awolowo Rd (also near the *YMCA*), Ikoyi. Reasonable fish-and-rice type meals at rock-bottom prices.

Leventis, Lagos Island. One of the best supermarket restaurants, serving inexpensive snacks and salads, overlooking the harbour.

Mr Biggs, in the former Kingsway building on Marina St, Lagos Island. This restaurant looks like a *McDonald's* (and is recommended for nostalgic Americans) but the meat pies are better value than the shrivelled Big Mac effigies. You'll find another branch on Tinubu St behind the post office.

Museum Kitchen, National Museum grounds, Lagos Island. Extensive selection of reasonably priced stand-bys – *eba, moin-moin, fufu, dodo, egusi, ogbono* – plus a daily regional speciality dish. Highly recommended.

Upmarket

LAGOS ISLAND

Chez Antoine, 61 Broad St (☎01/664 881). Popular restaurant with French and Lebanese cuisine and sandwiches at lunchtime. Cool and relaxing after the heat and bustle of the street.

The Bagatelle, 208 Broad St (only open on certain nights; ☎01/662 410). Old established eating house with a Middle East flavoured international menu. Fourth-floor harbour view with bar and dancing. Ties required for men.

Cathay, 88 Broad St (☎01/664 926). Quite good Chinese food, in a dodgy-looking building.

The Phoenecia, 35 Martins St, near the *Bristol Hotel* (☎01/663 156). A popular evening retreat with European food and a cover charge, African house bands and late night service.

Quo Vadis, Western House 17th floor, 8 Broad St (☎01/635 132). This restaurant has excellent seafood and Lebanese dishes and a view of the harbour. Men need a tie. Closed Sun.

Tabriz, behind the *Bristol* at 90 Breadfruit St (☎01/662 328). French and Lebanese food.

Tam Tam, 16 Market St (☎01/660 273). Another downtown restaurant with a French and Lebanese menu.

IKOYI

Al Basha, Awolowo Rd. Excellent Lebanese restaurant.

Bacchus, 57 Awolowo Rd (☎01/681 653). A popular European restaurant with music and dancing. Dress up and be ready to pay a cover.

Ciao, Awolowo Rd. Smart Italian restaurant.

Double Four, Awolowo Rd. Pizzas, Lebanese *meze* and a good range of other dishes. Tends to be crowded, with the TV blaring, but the food is tasty and not overpriced.

New Yorkers, Raymond Njoku Rd. US-diner-style place with high quality fast food and confident service.

The Sherlaton, 108 Awolowo Rd (☎01/681 914). One of Lagos' best Indian restaurants and, despite its uncomfortable name, not over-priced or ostentatious.

VICTORIA ISLAND

After Hours, Eleke Crescent. Brightly lit café downstairs, smart restaurant upstairs, piano bar on the top floor, with live music Fri & Sat. Very expensive.

The Brasserie, 52 Adetokunbo Ademola St, near the *Eko Meridien Hotel* (☎01/615 464). Complex including Indian/Chinese and European restaurants.

Calabash, Ozumba Mbadiwe Ave. Very pleasant waterside place with Nigerian dishes and live music some nights.

The Flamingo, Kofo Abayomi Rd. Good Indian and Chinese food.

The Lagoon, 1 Ozumba Mbadiwe Ave. Good meals in a relaxing and spacious environment (though again formal dress for dinner).

The Mirage, in the *Federal Palace Hotel* (☎01/614 225). The city's top-notch Chinese, with higher standards than its host establishment.

Peninsula, Plot 8, Ozumba Mbadiwe Ave, on the lagoon facing the 1004 apartments (☎01/616 911). Terrace restaurant right on the water, serving good Chinese meals in a really nice ambience. Even if you're not hungry, you can come for a drink and the view.

Shangri-La, *Eko Meridien Hotel*. Superb Chinese, but quite pricey.

MAINLAND

Club Panache, *Mainland Hotel*, 2 Murtala Muhammed Way (☎01/800 300). Good Chinese food in an extravagantly decorated setting, with music and dancing. Closed Sun.

Rambo's, Onike, Yaba. Barbecued pork, chicken and fish.

Some Place Else, Yaba. Good chicken meals.

Nightlife

Lagos is famous as a **music** centre, and the styles that have originated and evolved here – **Highlife**, **Juju**, **Fuji** and **Afrobeat** – are as legendary and international as any in Africa. Lagosians are proud of this and prefer listening to their own music than to the anodyne Anglo-American pop that's current over so much of West Africa. The daily *Evening Times* normally has details of what's on across a span of forty or fifty venues, where you can dance till dawn and often see live performances. The following clubs (mainly selected for their live show pedigrees) are mostly on the mainland. Don't be intimidated. Get a taxi and get on down.

IKOYI

City Tavern, Awolowo Rd. Dress up for this fancy joint.

Club Towers, Ikoyi. Heavy disco.

Fiki's, Ikoyi. A more relaxed version of *Koko's* (see below), with Zairean music on Fri and Sat.

Jazz 38, 38 Awolowo Rd (Fri only; ☎01/684 984). Owned by Fela Kuti's niece, Frances, and her husband, Tunde Kuboye, this open-air place is also known as the *Dental Club* (after the surgery next door).

Koko Bar, Ozumba Mbadiwe Ave. Unlicensed nightspot where you can dance to live music several nights a week. Always full of expat men and stunning "night fighters".

APAPA

Bank Hotel, 20 Achakpo St, off Kirikiri Rd, Apapa-Ajengunle district. This is something of a focus for eastern Nigerian musicians like Nico Mbarga and Sonny Okosun. Well worth checking out.

Faslak Nightclub, opposite NNPC. Orlando "Dr Ganjah" Owoh, rebel granddad inventor of the Juju-Highlife hybrid he calls *toye*, plays here every Thursday.

Filling Station, Apapa-Ajegunle. Stray over here if you're feeling very brave – it's a real low joint.

Wazobia, Apapa. Fri and Sat disco

SURULERE AND YABA

Ariya Night Club, 12 Ikorodu Rd, at Jibowu St, Yaba (no phone). Belongs to juju maestro King Sunny Ade, who plays here on Wed or Sat, when he's not touring.

Jazzville, Majaro St, Onike. Two regular bands and several guest artistes hot it up every Fri night until dawn. Friendly management and lively clientele.

Murphis Jazz, Surulere. Club and burger bar.

Neighbours, by the *Stadium Hotel*. Fri and Sat *makossa* sounds.

Satellite One, Surulere. Popular new spot.

Stadium Hotel, 27 Iyun Rd, just west of the National Stadium, Surulere (☎01/833 593). Home of Highlife supremo Victor Olaiya and boasting a fantastic floorshow with dancers and contortionists. You could of course stay at the *Stadium* afterwards (see "Accommodation").

IKEJA

Daniel's, Old Kingsway Building, GRA. Relaxed disco.

Niteshift, Opebi St. Flashy disco.

Pinto's, Allen Ave. Expensive, but very popular, this is one of the best international-style clubs, with a resident jazz band accompanying different singers. All night at weekends.

The Shrine, Pepple St (no phone) This is it, Fela Kuti's club, not far from the *Sheraton*, near the airport. It's one to rest up in preparation for. Get there no earlier than 11pm and be prepared for Fela to come on – if he does – sometime after 2am and play till 4am or later.

Virgin Cafe, Ikeja. Live music on Fri and Sat, with a great atmosphere.

Listings

Air freight *DHL* at 1 Sumbo Jibowu St, Ikoyi (☎01/681 106).

Airlines Most are on Lagos Island, either in Tafawa Balewa Sq or along Martins St. Opening hours given here are Mon–Fri, unless specified. They include: *Aeroflot*, 36 Tafawa Balewa Sq (☎01/637 223; 8am–4pm); *Air Afrique*, 18 Tafawa Balewa Sq (☎01/634 775; 8.30am–4pm); *Air France*, 1 Davies St (☎01/664 909); *Alitalia*, 2 Martins St (☎01/662 468; 8am–5pm); *Balkan Bulgarian Airlines*, 39–41 Martins St (☎01/661 974 or 661 102); *British Airways*, Unity House, 37 Marina St (☎01/662 669; Mon–Fri 8am–5pm, Sat 9am–noon), and Commerce House, 1 Idowu Taylor St, V.I. (☎01/613 004; 8.30am–5pm); *Cameroon Airlines*, 11a Tafawa Balewa Sq (☎01/630 909; 8.30am–4.30pm); *Egyptair*, 39–41 Martins St (☎01/661 974); *Ethiopian Airlines*, 20 Tafawa Balewa Sq (☎01/637 655 or 632 690); *Ghana Airways*, 17 Martins St (☎01/661 808; 8am–4.30pm); *Iberia*, 17 Tafawa Balewa Sq (☎01/636 950; 8am–5pm); *Intercontinental Airlines*, 25 Adeniyi Jones Ave, Ikeja (☎01/932 050); *Kabo Air*, Terminal Two, Domestic Airport, Ikeja (☎01/934 404); *KLM*, Mandilas House, 96 Broad St (☎01/661 452), and NUJ Building, Adeyemo Slakija St, V.I. (☎01/619 406); *Lufthansa*, 150 Broad St (☎01/664 430); *Nigeria Airways*, Tafawa Balewa Sq (☎01/631 003); *Okada Air*, Terminal Two, Domestic Airport, Ikeja (☎01/963 881); *Sabena*, 23–25 Martins St (☎01/664 133; 8am–5pm); *Swiss Air*, Hamburg House, 31–33 Martins St (☎01/662 299).

American Express *Mandilas Travel Ltd*, 33 Simpson St, Lagos Island (PO Box 35; ☎ 01/636 887).

Banks include (all open Mon–Thurs 8am–3pm, Fri 8am–1pm): *Afribank Nigeria*, 94 Broad St (☎01/266 3608; Fax 01/266 2793); *African Continental Bank*, 106–108 Broad St (☎01/266 0579; Fax 01/266 0204); *First Bank of Nigeria*, 35 Marina St (☎01/266 5900; Fax 01/266 9703); *National Bank of Nigeria*, 41–45 Broad St (☎01/266 1342; Fax 01/266 0006); *Société Générale Bank (Nigeria)*, 113 Martins St (☎01/266 1881; Fax 01/266 3731); *Union Bank*, 40 Marina St (☎01/266 5439; Fax 01/266 3822); *United Bank for Africa (Nigeria)*, 97–105 Broad St (☎01/266 7410; Fax 01/266 0884).

Bookshops Lagos has the best English-language bookshops in West Africa. Besides the hotels (reasonable selections in the *Eko Meridien* and the *Federal Palace*), try *Glendora* and *Best Seller* in the Falomo shopping centre or the bookshops on Broad St, including *C.S.S. Bookshop* at the intersection with Odunlami St. Check out also *New World Bookshop* on Tafawa Balewa Sq.

Clubs The Ikoyi Club, near the *Ikoyi Hotel*, isn't terrifically expensive for a short membership, though you have to be introduced by a member. Playing squash in Lagos feels like you've had six games before you've started.

Cultural centres and libraries include: **British Council**, 11 Kingsway Rd, Ikoyi (☎01/269 2188; Fax 269 2193); **Centre Culturel Français**, Plot PC14, off Idowu Taylor Rd, V.I. (☎01/615 592); **Goethe Institut**, next to the *Centre Culturel Français* at Plot PC14, off Idowu Taylor Rd, V.I. (☎01/610 717); **National Library**, 4 Wesley St (☎01/656 590), open Mon–Fri 7.30am–3.30pm (a reference library with books and periodicals); and **United States Information Service**, 1 Kings College Rd, near Tafawa Balewa Sq (☎01/635 665).

Embassies and consulates Most are on Victoria Island (V.I.) and are open Mon–Fri. They include : **Algeria**, 26 Maitama Sule St, Ikoyi (PO Box 7288; ☎01/683 155; 9am–2pm); **Australia**, 2 Ozumba Mbadiwe Ave, V.I. (PO Box 2427; ☎01/618 875); **Belgium**, 1A Bank Rd, Ikoyi (PO Box 149; ☎01/260 3230; 8.30am–1.30pm); **Benin**, 4 Abudu Smith St, V.I. (PO Box 5705; ☎01/614 411; 8am–3pm); **Bulgaria**, 3 Eleke Crescent, V.I. (☎01/611 931; Fax 619 879); **Burkina Faso**, 15 Norman Williams St, Ikoyi (☎01/681 001); **Cameroon**, 5 Elsie Femi Pearse St, V.I. (PMB 2476; ☎01/612 226; 8am–2.30pm); **Canada**, 4 Idowu Taylor St, V.I. (PO Box 54506; ☎01/269 2195; Fax 269 2919; 7.30am–3pm); **Central African Republic**, Plot 137, Ajao Estate, New Airport, Oshodi (☎01/682 820; 8am–noon); **Chad**, 2 Goriola St, V.I. (PMB 70662; ☎01/613 116; 8am–2pm); **Côte d'Ivoire**, 3 Abudu Smith St, V.I. (PO Box 7780; ☎01/610 963); **Denmark**, 4 Eleke Crescent, V.I. (PO Box 2390; ☎01/610 841; 8am–2pm); **Egypt**, 81 Awolowo Rd, Ikoyi (PO Box 538; ☎01/612 922; 8am–2.30pm); **Equatorial Guinea**, 7 Bank Rd, Ikoyi (PO Box 4162; ☎01/683 717; 8am–2pm); **Ethiopia**, Plot 97, Ahmadu Bello Rd, V.I. (PMB 2488; ☎01/613 198); **Finland**, 13 Eleke Crescent, V.I. (PO Box 4433; ☎01/610 916; Fax 613 158; 7.30am–2pm); **France**, 1 Queens Drive, Ikoyi (PO Box 567; ☎01/260 3300; 9am–2.30pm); **Gabon**, 8 Norman Williams St, Ikoyi (PO Box 5989; ☎01/684 673; 8.30am–2.30pm); **The Gambia**, 162 Awolowo Rd, Ikoyi (PO Box 8037; ☎01/681 018); **Germany**, 15 Eleke Crescent, V.I. (PO Box 728; ☎01/611 011; 8am–2pm); **Ghana**, 21 King George V Rd, Lagos Island (PO Box 889; ☎01/630 015; 8am–2.30pm); **Guinea**, 8 Abudu Smith St (PO Box 2826; ☎01/616 961; 8am–2pm); **Ireland**, 34 Kofo Abayomi St, V.I. (PO Box 2421; ☎01/615 224; 8am–1pm); **Italy**, 12 Eleke Crescent, V.I. (PO Box 2161; ☎01/614 066; 8am–2pm); **Japan**, 24 Apese

St, V.I. (PMB 2111; ☎01/614 929; Fax 614 035; 8am–3pm); **Kenya**, 53 Queen's Drive, Ikoyi (PO Box 6464; ☎01/682 768); **Liberia**, 3 Idejo St, off Adeola Odeku St, V.I. (PO Box 70841; ☎01/618 899); **Libya**, 465 Raymond Njoku Rd, Ikoyi (☎01/680 880); **Mauritania**, 1a Karimu Giwa Close, Ikoyi (☎01/682 971; 9am–1pm); **Morocco**, 27 Karimu Katun St, V.I. (☎01/611 682); **Netherlands**, 24 Ozumba Mbadiwe Ave, V.I. (PO Box 2426; ☎01/613 510; 8am–2.30pm); **Niger**, 15 Adeola Odeku St, V.I. (PMB 2736; ☎01/612 300; 8am–noon); **Norway**, 3 Anifowoshe St, V.I. (PMB 2431; ☎01/261 8467; 8am–2pm); **Portugal**, Plot 1677, Olukunle Bakare Close, V.I. (☎01/619 037); **Senegal**, 14 Kofo Abayomi Rd, V.I. (PMB 2197; ☎01/611 722; 8am–3pm); **Sierra Leone**, 31 Alhaji Waziri Ibrahim St, V.I. (PO Box 2821; ☎01/614 666; 8am–3pm); **South Africa**, 177B Ligali Ayorinde St, V.I. (☎01/616 160; Fax 01/269 3340); **Spain**, 21c Kofo Abayomi Rd, V.I. (PO Box 2738; ☎01/615

MOVING ON FROM LAGOS

Bush Taxis and Buses

Motor park	Destinations
Ojota motor park, on Ikorodu Road, near the junction with the airport road in the Ojota district	**The southwest**, including Ibadan, Oshogbo, Ilorin, Ife and other towns in Yorubaland.
Iddo motor park, on Murtala Muhammed Way near the train station	**The north**, including Kaduna and Jos, Zaria, Sokoto and Kano.
Oju Elegba motor park, Oju Elegba junction in Surulere district	**The east**, including Benin City, Onitsha, Enugu, Aba, Port Harcourt and Calabar.
Ebute Ero motor park, near Eko Bridge at the western tip of Lagos Island.	**International destinations**, including Lomé and Cotonou.

Trains

The **train station** is on Murtala Muhammed Way, near the Carter Bridge in Iddo. For information on whether any trains are running, call the Nigerian Railway Corporation head office (☎01/834 302).

Domestic flights

Nigeria Airways and several private airlines – *ADC* (currently one of the largest), *Triax*, *Harco*, *Okada Air* and *Kabo Airlines* – fly from the Domestic Airport at Ikeja, to the east of Murtala Muhammed Airport. There are, in theory, flights on *Nigeria Airways* at least every day to **Abuja**, **Jos**, **Kano**, **Maiduguri**, **Port Harcourt** and **Yola**, plus several flights a week to **Calabar**, **Enugu**, **Kaduna**, **Makurdi** and **Sokoto**.

Ships

Panalpina, 4 Creek Rd, Apapa (☎01/803 440; Telex 21346), are port agents for the Italian *Grimaldi Lines*, which runs some quite smart vessels on regular voyages to Europe.

Car rental

There are many agencies in Lagos but they nearly all insist on renting a driver with the vehicle. The major ones – *Hertz*, *Europcar*, *Budget* – have branches at Murtala Muhammed Airport. The main offices are *Avis*, 225 Apapa Rd, Iganmu (PMB 1155; ☎01/846 336); *Europcar* (PO Box 6569; ☎01/662 572); *Hertz* agents are *Mandilas*, 96–102 Broad St, Lagos Island (PMB 35; ☎01/663 514).

Travel agents and tour operators

Many agencies are grouped around the north side of Tafawa Balewa Square. Other important firms include: *Bitts Travel & Tours*, E7 Falomo shopping centre (☎01/684 550), who organize excursions for groups to various tourist destinations; *Tours and Trade International Limited*, 4 Adeyemo Alakija St, Victoria Island (PMB 70047; ☎01/618 665), who run trips to the game parks, Obudu Cattle Ranch and other sites; and *Transcap Travel*, CFAO Building, 1 Davies St (PO Box 2326; ☎01/660 321 or 665 063), who are agents for *Thomas Cook*.

215; Fax 618 225; 9am–2pm); **Sweden**, 26 Moloney St (PO Box 1097; ☎01/263 0688; 7.30am–2.30pm); **Switzerland**, 7 Anifowoshe St, V.I. (PO Box 536; ☎01/613 918; 7.30am–noon & 12.45–3.45pm); **Tanzania**, 45 Ademola St, Ikoyi (PO Box 6417; ☎01/613 594); **Togo**, Plot 976, Oju Olobun Close, V.I. (PO Box 1435; ☎01/617 449; 8am–3.30pm); **United Kingdom**, 11 Eleke Crescent, V.I. (PMB 12136; ☎01/619 531; 8am–3pm), consular section at Chellarams Building, 54 Marina (☎01/266 7061 or 266 6413, Fax 266 6909; 8am–3pm); **USA**, 2 Eleke Crescent, V.I. (☎01/610 097; Fax 610 257); **Zaire**, 23a Kofo Abayomi Rd, V.I. (PO Box 1216; ☎01/656 289); **Zambia**, 11 Keffi St, Ikoyi (PMB 6119; ☎01/680 991); **Zimbabwe**, 6 Kasumu Ekemode St, V.I. (PO Box 50247; ☎01/619 328).

Maps The place to go for large-scale maps is the Survey Division, Ministry of Works and Housing, Tafawa Balewa Sq north side (☎01/653 120; open Mon–Fri 7.30am–3.30pm). Almost all of Nigeria was mapped at 1:50,000 (1cm:500m) many years ago. How many sheets are in print, and whether they can be bought without special authorization are unknown.

Medical and dental treatment The best hospital is undoubtedly the *Eko Hospital* in Bank Anthony Way, Ikeja, near the *Sheraton*. Akimbola Awoliyi Memorial Hospital, 183 Bamgbose St, Lagos Island (☎01/631 520 or 930 916), is also good, with a 24-hr casualty service. Near the airport there's Maryland Clinic, Abida Close, Maryland Estate, Ikeja (☎01/962 348). Recommended general practitioners include: Dr Williams, 13 Airport Rd, Ikeja (☎01/933 482), and Dr M Semaan and Dr D Semaan, St Francis Clinic, Keffi St, Ikoyi (☎01/684 125). A recommended dentist is Dr E Solarin, Flat 2, Block D, Eko Court, Kofo Abayomi Rd, V.I. (☎01/610 917).

Newspapers International press and news magazines (*The Economist*, *Time*, *Newsweek*, *Herald Tribune*) are available at the airport and hotels, and the Nigerian-owned *West Africa Magazine* all over the city from newsstands and hawkers.

Post and telephones The GPO (Mon–Fri 8am–noon & 2–4pm, Sat 8am–noon) is on Marina St, with main branches in **Ikoyi** on Awolowo Rd and **Victoria Island** on Adeola Odeku St (branches are closed Sat). Phone calls can be made around the clock from the NITEL Building on Marina St, Lagos Island, or from 7am–8pm daily at Falomo shopping centre, Ikoyi.

Swimming pools The big hotels have pools, but those at the *Ikoyi* and *Federal Palace* (in theory open for a fee to non-guests) usually don't have water. The *Eko Meridien* has the cleanest water, but it's reserved for residents only. There's also a public pool across from the museum which has relatively grimy water.

Womens' groups The national group of the *Nigerwives* association of foreign women married to Nigerians (PO Box 54664, Falomo, Lagos) meets the last Saturday of every month at 3pm at St Saviour's Church, Tafawa Balewa Square.

YORUBALAND

The towns and rural parts of **Yorubaland** have an exceptional wealth of cultural interest and natural beauty. In pre-colonial times, the **Yoruba** created one of the most powerful empires on the West African coast – and the area is still charged with reminders. Most of the larger towns, for example, still have ruling **Obas**, or kings, who wield a good deal of political clout despite limitations imposed on them by the federal government system. The Obas continue, too, to live in **royal palaces**, many of which – including that in **Oyo**, former capital of the Yoruba empire of the same name – can be visited.

Some of what is now known about the area's more distant past is the result of excavations carried out in **Ife**. The brass and terracotta statues found here drew international attention and suggest a sophisticated civilization dating back to at least the ninth century. According to Yoruba custom, however, Ife is even older – the first place in the world to be created. It has naturally enjoyed a position as the holiest place in the Yoruba realm, a sort of Mecca of Yoruba religion. Here and throughout the region, the living wood of the **old religion** still breathes beneath a thin veneer of Islamic or occasionally Christian belief. You'll see shrines and temples in almost all the towns. At **Oshogbo** a whole **Sacred Forest** has been set aside as a reserve for worshippers, or "fetishers": the shrines here are vast and amazing and the worshippers only too eager to show visitors around – definitely a Nigerian highlight.

Abeokuta

ABEOKUTA, north of Lagos, on the old road to Ibadan, is "Ake" in Wole Soyinka's novel of the same name (the name of the royal district of the town where he grew up). The capital of Ogun State, Abeokuta was founded in the early 1800s as a site for freed Yoruba slaves, some of whom were being liberated by the British Royal Navy, and some of whom had made their own way back to their homeland from Freetown and elsewhere. It's an attractive town, with a spectacular, and easily climbable, outcrop of gigantic granite boulders overlooking it. At the summit, the **Oluma Rock Museum** traces the early settlement and history of Abeokuta, while at the base, the **Oluma Art Movement** has set up workshops and a gallery for traditional and modern art.

The town's top **hotel** is the mid-range *Ogun State Hotel* on Murtala Muhammed Way (PO Box 30; ☎039/200 130 or 231 787; ④) with TV, tennis and pool, but the *Alefin Guest House* in Oke Ilewo district, or the *Frontline* in Onikolobo are a good deal cheaper (②). In a pleasant park on Ademola Rd, Ibara, the *Gateway Motel*, is a relaxing retreat with a good restaurant and very helpful management (②).

Ibadan

Nigeria's second city, **IBADAN** (pronounced as in "pardon") is the modern capital of Oyo State – a vast metropolis that sprawls so far you think it's never going to stop. The city's horizons are marked by few Lagos-style high-rises but instead a plethora of two-storey, corrugated iron-roofed houses, spreading like an urban fungus over the low hills. People here assert Ibadan has the biggest population of any city in Africa – twenty million people, some say; the real figure is probably around five million.

Somehow the crowds, congestion and noise are especially oppressive, and as the city lacks a real centre, a shambolic, unfocused tumult is about the only lasting impression. However, coming from Lagos, this is likely to be your first stop in Yorubaland and, with its numerous hotels, banks and other facilities, it is a convenient base for visiting other sites in the region.

Some history

Originally founded by Yoruba renegades, at the end of the eighteenth century, Ibadan occupies a strategic position between the forest and the plains, its name deriving from *Eba Odan*, meaning "field between the woods and the savannah". The settlement began to grow after 1829, when it became an important Yoruba military headquarters and a refuge for people dispossessed in Fulani raids on northern Oyo. By the time the British forced it into a treaty of protection in 1893, it was already extraordinarily large for its time, with an estimated population of 120,000.

In colonial times, Ibadan went on to become an important trading centre, which it remains. It is also a major academic city: the **University of Ibadan** (UI), founded in 1948, was the first in the country and is still considered one of West Africa's best; the **University College Hospital** and the world-renowned **International Institute of Tropical Agriculture** (IITA) add to Ibadan's academic prestige.

Accommodation

Ibadan has dozens of hotels and lodging houses: the following selection includes some of the more pleasant and/or convenient among them.

Alma Guest House, 19 Oyo–Ibadan Ave, Bodija, near the customs post. (☎022/417 657). Small, quiet and clean, with a bar and restaurant. ②.

Catering Guest House, behind the train station in Jericho. Nice colonial-style building in a quiet neighbourhood, with reasonably priced AC, S/C rooms and a Nigerian-European restaurant. ②.

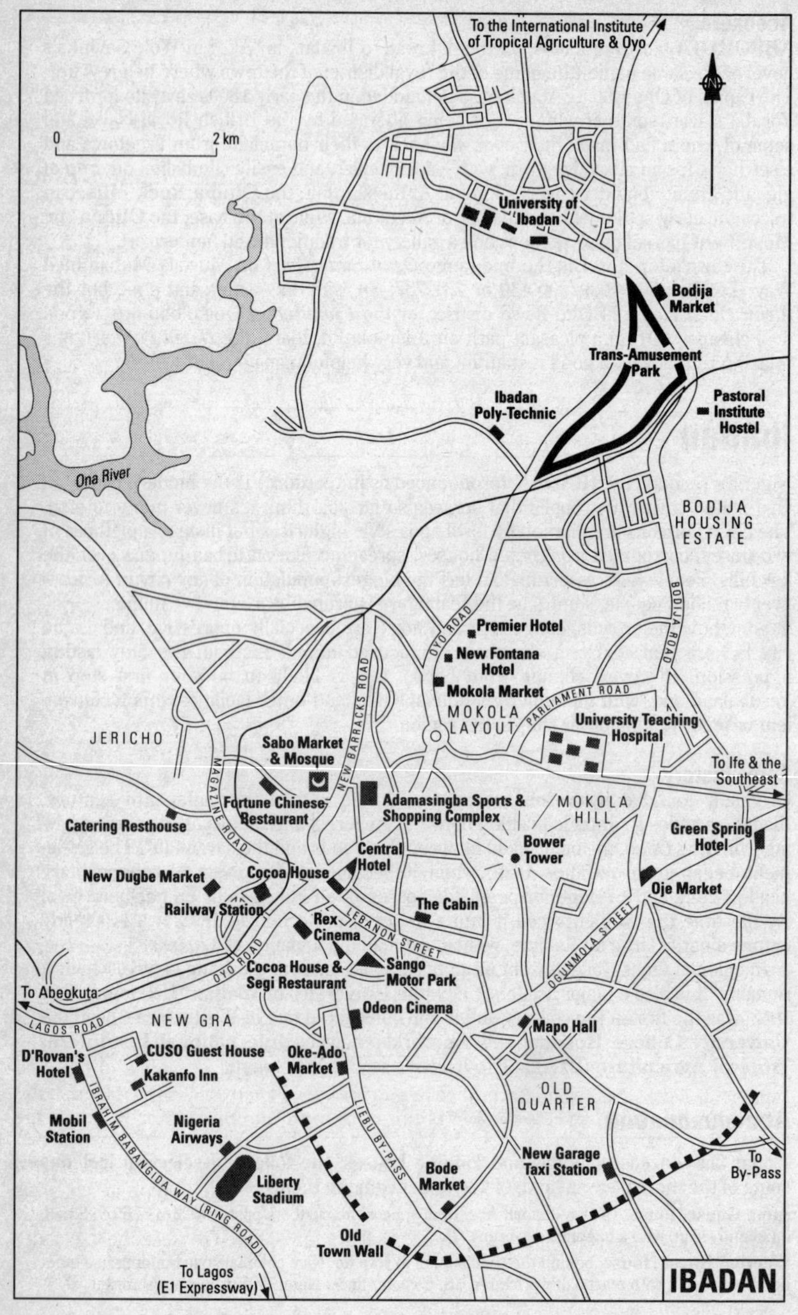
To the International Institute of Tropical Agriculture & Oyo
N
0
2 km
University of Ibadan
Bodija Market
Trans-Amusement Park
Pastoral Institute Hostel
Ibadan Poly-Technic
Ona River
BODIJA HOUSING ESTATE
BODIJA ROAD
OYO ROAD
Premier Hotel
New Fontana Hotel
Mokola Market
PARLIAMENT ROAD
MOKOLA LAYOUT
University Teaching Hospital
JERICHO
NEW BARRACKS ROAD
MAGAZINE ROAD
Sabo Market & Mosque
To Ife & the Southeast
Adamasingba Sports & Shopping Complex
MOKOLA HILL
Fortune Chinese Restaurant
Catering Resthouse
Green Spring Hotel
Bower Tower
Central Hotel
New Dugbe Market
Cocoa House
Oje Market
The Cabin
Railway Station
Rex Cinema
LEBANON STREET
OGUNMOLA STREET
Sango Motor Park
Cocoa House & Segi Restaurant
OYO ROAD
To Abeokuta
Odeon Cinema
LAGOS ROAD
NEW GRA
Mapo Hall
CUSO Guest House
D'Rovan's Hotel
Kakanfo Inn
Oke-Ado Market
OLD QUARTER
Mobil Station
Nigeria Airways
IBRAHIM BABANGIDA WAY (RING ROAD)
LIEBU BY-PASS
New Garage Taxi Station
To By-Pass
Liberty Stadium
Bode Market
Old Town Wall
To Lagos (E1 Expressway)
IBADAN

Central Hotel, Dugbe Alowo Rd. Budget accommodation in the heart of town, with basic, non-S/C rooms. ①.

CUSO guesthouse, 12 Adelabu Rd, Iyaganku GRA (PMB 5297; ☎022/315 484). The Canadian volunteers' guesthouse is open to all. It's clean, friendly and cheap, but a little hard to find. From Abeokuta Rd, take Ring Rd towards the *Challenge* bookshop. Turn left on Olaniyan Fagbemi Rd and continue past *Ring Rdoa Restaurant*. The *CUSO* office is off Olaniyan Fagbemi Rd to the right, and the guesthouse to the left. ①.

D'Rovan's Hotel, Ibrahim Babangida Way (☎022/313 617 or 313 618). New, upmarket hotel with every modern convenience in the AC rooms that range from singles to studios. There's also a night-club and music and conference hall, plus a pricey restaurant for Nigerian and European dishes. ③.

Green Spring Hotel, Old Ife Rd (☎022/713 796). An older hotel with AC, S/C bungalow-style rooms and a pool. Good bar and restaurant. ②.

Influential Hotel, towards the centre of town on Mokola Hill (☎022/414 894). Reasonably priced hotel in a very handy location. ③.

Kakanfo Inn, 1 Nihinlola St (☎022/311 471 or 311 473). Stylish hotel on the south side of town with TV in the AC doubles and mini-bars in the large suites, and one of the town's best restaurants. ④.

Lafia Hotel, Abeokuta Rd (PO Box 5353; ☎022/416 750). Boasts features like colour TV and, more desirably, a swimming pool, but at a price and some distance from the city centre in Apata Ganga. ③.

Pastoral Institute Hostel, Bodija Rd, near the University. Commonly referred to as "PI", this has non-S/C rooms, and is immaculately clean with fans and mosquito nets. Breakfast is included; other meals can be had in the cafeteria. ①.

Premier Hotel, Mokola (PO Box 1206; ☎022/623 409 or 400 340). Expensive-looking place that's not unreasonable for what it offers. You can relax in relative style here with all the amenities, including a pool – though this is rarely cleaned. There's also a Chinese restaurant – one of the few such in town. ④.

The City

Given the city's unwieldy dimensions, it's hard to pinpoint Ibadan's heart (note the very small scale of our map, more than 15km from the north, by the university, to the south by the line of the old city wall). By default, however, you'd have to say it beats around the **New Dugbe Market** – one of Nigeria's largest. Ibadan's streets seem to wind at will, so your chances of getting lost while exploring are high. Should that happen, look for the the strange **Bower Memorial Tower** on **Mokola Hill** to the east, a good viewpoint to climb and a visible reference point from virtually anywhere in the city.

The tower of **Cocoa House** is another guide for the disoriented. One of the few skyscrapers in town, and nearly lost in 1985 when it was severely damaged by fire, Cocoa House is evidence of the regional importance of a vital export crop and marks Ibadan's commercial centre. You'll find **banks** in the area (*Afribank*, *First Bank*, *Central Bank*; all Mon–Thurs 8am–3pm, Fri 8am–1pm), and, of more relevance if you're changing money, several **bureaux de change**. A good place to change French francs is *Hakasurs*, along Lebanon Street. For more predictable shopping than at the market, *Leventis* and *UTC* **supermarkets** are located nearby. A couple of hundred metres to the west of this area on Abeokuta Road is the already old-looking **New GPO** (Mon–Fri 8am–noon & 2–4pm). The obsolescent **train station** is directly across the street.

More good views are to be had in the **Old Quarter** where the British established themselves on the city's highest hill. **Mapo Hall** was built on the summit in the 1920s and served as the colonial government house. Today, the stylish building is mostly used for wedding receptions, and if it's not been rented out, you're welcome to wander around.

On the north side of town on Oyo Road, the campus of the **University of Ibadan** was designed for the most part by the distinguished British architect, Maxwell Fry (who worked with Gropius in the 1930s and with Le Corbusier on Chandigarh in India after the war). You can meet and mix with people here at the **cafeteria** or the **coffee shop** (open to all). The university **bookshop** (Mon–Fri 8am–4pm, Sat 8am–noon) used to have an excellent reputation, but is now dreary and low on stock. The Institute of African Studies building houses a small **museum** (Mon–Fri 10am–3.30pm) with bronze statues and carvings.

The **International Institute of Tropical Agriculture** (IITA) is 5km beyond the university campus on the Oyo road. With rich foreign sponsors and an international team of staff, it's a welcome respite from the hurly-burly of Ibadan. You obviously have to know someone to get in, but it's surprising how easily such contacts are made. In the grounds there's a crystal-clear pool, ice cream, hot dogs and guest chalets. If you're going to be passing through, or staying in Ibadan, you might write to the IITA (PMB 5320, Ibadan) requesting their introductory information about Ibadan, provided for newly arrived staff.

On your way to these centres of academia, you'll pass the huge new **Transwonderland Amusement Park**, an attraction as close to Disneyland as you'll find anywhere in Africa. It's a somewhat surreal experience to sample the rides and Ferris wheel in the environment of Ibadan, but it's proving a big hit in the city and, at weekends and holidays, the place is packed.

For something less active, visit the **British Council** at the Leventis Foundation Library, Magazine Road in Jericho (☎022/400 870). They have a range of reading material in the library including British and other papers and periodicals, and a full artistic and cultural programme.

Food

For cheap, quick calories, **chop bars** – serving *eba*, *amala* and pounded yam with the usual *egusi* and other soups and stews – line Magazine Street near the junction with Abeokuta Road close by the train station. And up on Mokola Hill, there are *bukas* doing *begiri* (traditional bean soup) and *amala*. If you're at the university, use the **student cafeteria** – bland but cheap food (and of course a good place to meet students if you want to).There's also the **Staff Club** here, the meeting place for people who work on campus, with a restaurant and an empty swimming pool.

IBADAN AREA MARKETS

Most of Ibadan's **markets** work on an eight-day cycle, which is fine as long as you know where you are in it: check local papers such as the weekly *Irohin Yoruba* for details.

Bode, every eight days, near Molete bridge, specializing in beads.

Mokola, daily, 3km north of Cocoa House. Food, pots and baskets.

New Dugbe, daily, near the train station. A massive general market.

Oje, every sixteen days, near Mapo Hall, east of Bere Rd. One of the biggest cloth marts in Africa, with over three million yards sold annually (they sell the *Aso-oke* strip cloth made in Iseyin and locally produced tie-dyes), plus trade beads.

Ojoo, every eight days, 2km north of UI, west of the Oyo road.

Onidundu, every eight days, 14km north of IITA, west of the Oyo road, specializing in spices, herbs, mats and baskets.

Sako, daily, near the Friday mosque. The big food and domestic market. This is the place to get a good food pounder.

University market, UI, a daily souvenir market.

MOVING ON FROM IBADAN

Long-distance taxis

Vehicles heading to Oyo and further north leave from the **Sango motor park** southeast of the GPO (get a taxi there). The **New Garage taxi station** is the departure point for Lagos, Ife and the southeast, located off Lagos Rd in the southeast of town.

Trains

In theory, trains leave for Lagos via Abeokuta and Jos via Oshogbo. Check at the station to see if there is anything running.

Flights and travel agents

Nigeria Airways has offices at Lister House, Southwest Ring Road, Agbowo Shopping Complex, Jaja Rd, and the University of Ibadan (☎022/462 550) but no scheduled flights out of Ibadan – the closest large airport is Lagos. *British Airways* is at the C. Zard Building, 6 Lagos By-Pass (☎022/413 967), and *KLM*'s representative is *Airlink Travel Agency*, Jubilee House, Ring Rd (☎022/315 098). *Tess Travels*, Leventis Building (☎022/414 406), is an excellent travel agent for arrangements in Nigeria and beyond.

The Cabin, Onireke St, off Lebanon St (☎022/414 846). Lebanese and European specialities including great steaks and ice cream.

Fortune Chinese Restaurant, 21 Kudeti Ave, Onireke (☎022/410 077). Long menu and very good food, if somewhat pricey.

Kakanfo Inn, 1 Nihinlola St (☎022/311 471). The upmarket hotel also features one of the town's best Indian restaurants with a varied menu and friendly service.

Koko-Dome Restaurant, Cocoa House premises (☎022/413 384 or 415 230). Lebanese, European and American food including cheeseburgers and fries. For a small fee, you can spend the day at the clean pool and have food brought to your patio table. Sit-down eating is upstairs and there's a good disco here at weekends; there's no cover charge, but you have to eat at the restaurant to enter.

New Fontana, Mokola. The restaurant in this hotel of the same name is one of the town's best for European and Nigerian specialities.

Segi Lebanese Restaurant, in the city centre on the 1st floor of the yellow-tinted glass skyscraper. Excellent food including an all-you-can-eat Sunday brunch from 11am. Definitely worth the splurge.

Oyo and around

OYO is a relatively small town by Nigerian standards, with only a quarter of a million inhabitants, and its characteristic rust-stained roofscape looks like an Ibadan that never quite took off. On its earlier site to the north, the town was the capital of a Yoruba-speaking empire that stretched as far as present-day Togo (including in its hegemony such vassal states as Dan-Homey). At its apogee in around 1700, Oyo was probably the most powerful state in West Africa.

The Town

Everything in Oyo centres around **Abiodun Atiba Hall** (also called Town Hall), perched high on a hilltop. If you're walking from one of the hotels, you can see this monumental ochrous building from a kilometre away. When you arrive at the Hall, you'll see the **market** spreading out before you on Palace Road. Besides the usual provisions and various household goods, you can find wonderful **leatherwork** and intricately **carved calabashes** – a local speciality, carved at the market in small ateliers. Another speciality are **"talking drums"** – *dundun* – and these too are made and sold in market workshops.

SOME HISTORY

Oyo was founded in the northern Yoruba savannah, some time between the eleventh and thirteenth centuries by **Oranmiyan**, the youngest of the Ife princes (sons of Oduduwa). It was strategically located in a part of the savannah relatively free from tse-tse flies – and so could use **horses** for transport and war.

From its old capital in **Oyo-Ile**, Oyo began to expand southwards in the sixteenth century, using its highly efficient horsemen to extend its power to the coast. Until the end of the eighteenth century, it had not been directly concerned with the slave trade on a large scale, most of its wealth coming from the control of the trade routes between the coast and the north. By the late eighteenth century, however, the courts of **Lisbon** and Oyo were increasingly involved as partners in the slave trade.

The name "Yoruba" is a corruption of "Yooba", meaning "the dialect of the Oyo people". The fact that missionaries applied the term to all the peoples of the region attests to the city's once far-reaching power. Revolt by vassal states and war with the Muslim jihadists from the north spelt the end of the empire in the nineteenth century.

The present town of Oyo was founded in the 1820s, when Oyo-Ile fell to Muslim raiders. The *alafin* attempted to re-establish the grandeur of the old capital at **Ago**, a market town south of Oyo-Ile, which he named Oyo. Now, the only hint of its grand past is a sign welcoming visitors to "The City of Warriors".

Oyo's main point of interest is the **Alafin's Palace**, situated near the market on Palace Road. Townspeople will tell you that the present ruler is still head of all the Obas of Yorubaland, although the Oni of Ife is also considered to hold the title. In fact a raging dispute – going back to colonial times when the practice of rotating the Chair of the Council of Obas was upset – has occupied attention for years and the two leaders are effectively at daggers drawn. The Oni of Ife, however, is more a spiritual leader, the descendant of Oduduwa, and thus in theory should not be open to challenge by earthly office-holders.

Whatever the respective virtues, the Alafin of Oyo is one of the nation's most influential traditional rulers. His residence is a curious compound with numerous low buildings roofed in the ubiquitous rusty corrugated iron. Some of the buildings are decorated with traditional symbols and statues and carvings line the grounds. You'll have to get a guide at the gate before visiting the grounds. Money is never discussed, but at the end of the tour you're expected to dash something. Put all thoughts of seeing inside the palace out of your head.

Practicalities

The two best-known **hotels** are located at the entrance to town as you arrive from Ibadan, and both have moderate rates. The *Labamiba* on Ibadan Road (☎038/230 443; ③) is the main one and more expensive of the two, but the *Adeshakin International Hotel* on Awe-Iwo Road is also good (②). The cheaper *Merry Time* (☎038/230 344; ②), with clean S/C rooms and optional AC, is across from the *Agip* filling station on the Ibadan road – a very convenient stopover if you arrive by taxi, as you'll probably be dropped here. It has a great bar with huge armchairs and a lively atmosphere after dark; you can order meals or snack on *moin-moin* – delicious bean cakes. For other cheap **eating**, you'll find plenty of chop bars in the market place, and you can wash down meals with frothy palm wine. Don't leave town without sampling **gbegiri** (bean soup) and **wara** (curd cheese), which you can buy in **Akesan market**.

The **post office** is directly opposite the market. There are branches of *First* and *National* **banks** on Atiba Street, though you're advised to change money in a forex bureau before arriving in Oyo.

Iseyin – and towards Benin

West of Oyo, and accessible from Abeokuta – 60km of unfinished paved road and then red washboard – the small town of **ISEYIN** is famous locally for its wonderful **night market** and cashew trees. It's also one of the main centres for **Aso-oke** strip cloth – most of its weaves come from here. If you're staying, try the *Trans-Nigeria Hotels* resthouse, on the way into Iseyin from the south.

Between Iseyin and the border of Benin, there's a wealth of beautiful countryside dotted with old Yoruba **hill forts**. If you've got your own transport visit Ado-Awaiye, 26km south of Iseyin, and Saki (Shaki) and Ogboro, respectively 87km and 105km to the north of Iseyin, both off the Agoare–Kaiama road that leads north through the Oyo and Kwara back-country to Borgu Game Reserve (see p.1078). Returning east to the main A1 highway north, much of the road from Iseyin to Oyo is rough until you cross the bridge over the Ogun river.

Ife and around

According to Yoruba legend, **IFE** (also known as **ILE IFE**) was the first Yoruba city, and indeed, the first city in creation. Custom says it was at this spot that **Olorun** – Supreme God – threw an iron chain from the heavens into the waters below. He then instructed his son **Oduduwa** to climb down the chain. Oduduwa carried with him a calabash full of sand, a chicken and an oil palm nut. He dumped the sand on the water and let the chicken loose. The bird began scratching in the sand, causing dry earth to appear, and meanwhile the palm nut produced a tree. The sixteen fronds of the palm tree represented the sixteen crowned rulers of Yorubaland.

More prosaically, **excavations** indicate that Ife was probably founded in the ninth century. They have also revealed much about the lifestyle of the royal court: many of the brass and terracotta sculptures from the digs are today on display in the **Ife museum**. Although Ife was already in political and economic decline by the early 1500s, the town remained a spiritual focus and is still an important symbol of Yoruba nationhood. In addition, it has had a post-independence renaissance as a modern cultural centre with Nigeria's most extensive university campus – the **Obafemi Awolowo University**. The thousands of students add energy to what would otherwise be a sleepy town.

Accommodation

Ife has a number of reasonable options if you're planning to stay over and there's invariably the opportunity for animated conversations here, either with students or local people.

Central Olympique Hotel, Ondo Rd. Ife's budget option with quite adequate S/C rooms. ①.

Diganga Hotel, Ibadan Rd, near the university. Videos in the S/C, AC rooms make this an expensive place, but it's not excessive. The bar-restaurant fills with students in the evening (though *Folabot*, next door, serves cheaper African meals). There are buses to the centre during the day, but at night, you'll have to rely on rare taxis. ④.

Mayfair Hotel, Ondo Rd on the corner of Ibadan Rd. A good hotel in the moderate range with comfortable AC rooms – a reasonable distance from Ife centre. ②.

Motel Royal, Ibadan Rd. Compensates for being slightly run-down by having a swimming pool and tennis courts. ③.

Transmotel, Ibadan Rd. A standard government-issue resthouse with moderate AC, S/C chalets. ②.

University Conference Centre, on the campus. AC accommodation with TV in the rooms and access to staff facilities – including a pool and tennis courts. Good value, and not too far from the centre of the campus (there's a short cut through the gardens at the back that makes it a lot closer – if you can find it). ③.

The Town

Although you won't be able to visit the residence at the **Oba's Palace** in Ife, it's easy enough to walk around the courtyard, with its statues and dignitaries milling about. One of the Oba's messengers will take you around (with a translator) to show you the **meeting hall** where local criminal cases are tried under the Yoruba penal code, and the **shrine to Ogun** where each September, a dog or goat is sacrificed.

Ife Museum

Adjacent to the royal palace, and not to be missed, although some of its collection was stolen recently, is the **Ife Museum** (daily 7am–7pm; free). As much as a millennium ago, the Oni of Ife wielded great political and spiritual powers. He commanded a whole army of servants, including indentured artists who made brass castings for him and his retinue – staffs, chest ornaments, and miniature pieces in abstract designs or animal shapes. The museum also contains terracotta works dating from the tenth to the thirteenth centuries and more recent wooden carvings. But the most precious treasures are the magnificent **brass and bronze heads** of the Oni and other senior royal figures, made by the lost wax method (although some of the best examples are in the National Museum in Lagos). The sculptors of the heads worked pure copper and copper alloys of various composition – either with more tin (to make bronze) or more zinc (to make brass) – in a realistic mode of expression that is relatively uncommon in African art. They were clearly technical virtuosos of enormous skill, producing heads of rare grace, scored with the fine lines of scarification indicating royal rank. But there is an imperious, remote, vanity about these heads, and a sense of duty and proscribed creativity, indicating the sculptors' obsession with formal ways of doing things.

The Pottery Museum and the Oranmiyan Staff

Ife also has a small **Pottery Museum**, on More Street – two floors of dusty pottery works including musical jars (like skinless drums), coolers and cooking jugs. Entrance is free, but you're encouraged to make a contribution on departure. In an unmarked garden in the middle of town, the **Oranmiyan Staff** – a carved and decorated stone monolith about five metres high – symbolizes the sword of the first Alafin of Oyo.

The university

Obafemi Awolowo University was established by the government of Western Region (the post-independence division that was later sub-divided into states including Oshun, Oyo, Ogun, Ondo, Lagos and Bendel, and further divided since) and renamed after the first premier of the region when he died in 1988 – a nametag that didn't meet with unanimous approval. The 1960s architecture looks very dated now, but the scope of the grounds and facilities (this is the third largest university campus in the world) is impressive indication of the stress laid on higher education by the governments of the early independence era.

The university has its own **Museum of Natural History** (Mon–Fri 8am–6pm, Sat & Sun 11am–6pm) and a rather unspectacular **zoo** (daily 10am–5.30pm). To get there, take one of the frequent minibuses from the town centre to "Campus" which drops you in the heart of things. If the driver lets you down at the **campus gate**, you're only halfway to the university and must catch another bus or flag down students driving into college.

Eating and Drinking

The *Samtad*, by the Ondo junction, has a garden **restaurant and bar** and features Nigerian and continental food in a relaxed atmosphere; if you're not eating it's a good place for a few beers. Over on the Ondo road, the *Beacon Disco & Restaurant* does

A GLOSSARY OF YORUBA RELIGION

Aje The malevolent and destructive aspects of womanhood.

Efe Male masks.

Egungun Masks to honour family ancestors, worn during the annual festival of the secret, male society of the same name. Some *egungun* are put on just for entertainment, to mock police, prostitutes, avaricious traders, people with deformities or anyone who unsettles the community. Many come from Abeokuta, and reflect that town's links with Sierra Leone.

Ekiti Masks of the eastern (*ekiti*) Yoruba kingdoms. Best known is the *ekiti epa* mask, a wooden helmet surmounted by a carved figure.

Eshu Messenger of the *orisha* (gods) and the divine trickster responsible for everything that goes wrong in the world. Every market place has a shrine to him, often a simple pillar of sun-baked mud, over which the priests pour daily libations to preserve harmony in the market and community. Devotees of Eshu keep wooden sculptures of him in their houses.

Gelede The Gelede society is found only in some of the western Yoruba kingdoms. Its job is to appease female witches by entertaining them.

Ibeji Twins. If a twin dies, an image is carved of the dead child.

Ifa A powerful and respected oracle, consulted by those afflicted by disease or madness, or by anyone with a problem to solve. A series of sacred texts – poetic sayings – are interpreted by the *babalawo* or "father of secrets" using the Ifa board and cowries, seeds or stones thrown in a pattern.

Ijebu masks The Ijebu kingdoms of southern Yoruba have imported some of the delta region societies – like Ekine, from the Ijo. Their masks tend toward the formalistic cubism of Ijo sculpture, quite distinct from the naturalistic lines of northern Yoruba sculpture.

Obatala Obatala (or Orishanla) is responsible for the creation of each individual human form, to which Olurun, the Supreme God, gives life and destiny. Obatala's devotees wear white beads and on ceremonial occasions dress in white cloth.

Ogboni The Ogboni society, to which all Yoruba chiefs, priests and senior men belong, is the cult of the earth. It also has a judicial role, being responsible for all cases of human bloodshed – which are an offence against the earth – and a political one, in providing a forum for discussion free of outside interference. Meetings take place in a cult house, where the society's rites and discussions are kept secret from non-members.

Ogun God of iron, whose devotees include all those who use iron or steel to make a living or who drive on roads or fly planes.

Olorun The Yoruba supreme deity.

Orisha Oko God of the farm.

Osanyin God of medicine, responsible for the magical therapeutic action of leaves, herbs and other ingredients. There's a fundamental relationship between Osanyin and all other cults since devotees use appropriate medicines in order to enter into a close relationship with their chosen *orisha* during their initiation and subsequent life in the cult.

Oshun Goddess of the river which flows through Oshogbo, the patron deity of the town and bringer of fertility to women.

Shango God of thunder and lightning, identified with one of the very earliest kings of Oyo.

inexpensive Nigerian food – including great fish pepper soup – and has been known to get lively at night.

For **cheaper eating**, try the *Modern Food Centre* at 14 Aderemi Rd (behind *Prof. Ojulari's Pool Agency*) for *eba* and pounded yam with soup, or the host of eateries on or around the **campus**. Apart from whole areas of *bukas* doing hot food all day, the student union cafeteria offers a pretty good and inexpensive greasy spoon selection, and you can also get chicken and chips in Oduduwa Hall or eat in the more expensive staff club restaurant. *Banwill* is a "Chinese" restaurant on campus in the *New Bukaria*, two rows of largely African mini-restaurants flanking a concrete yard.

Owo and Idanre

East of Ife, the usual route through the rainforest lands is via Ondo and Ore, at which point you hit the expressway to Benin City. At Ondo it's also possible to branch towards Akure and **Owo**, the easternmost Yoruba town, with its own Oba's palace and museum. Midway between Ondo and Akure, on the old road to the east, is **Idanre**, a town surrounded – extraordinarily in these sticky lowlands – by stern granite massifs with steep cliffs. Old Idanre, up on top, is a sacred site of some significance and a good base for some wonderful walks and scrambles, though you would need to allow a day or two to do it justice. There are rooms at the *Idanre Tourist Centre* in the Hilltop quarter of town.

Oshogbo

Despite a population close on half a million and an important modern sheetmetal plant, **OSHOGBO** seems somehow smaller and more traditional than either Ife or Oyo. **Traditional religion** is perhaps no more prevalent here than in other Yoruba towns, but it's more obvious. Ironically, the renaissance of the religion and art of the town was in part due to an influx of European artists and philosophers who moved here in the 1950s, the most notable of whom was **Suzanne Wenger**, an Austrian painter and sculpter. In 1991, Oshogbo became capital of the newly created Oshun state. Its new status has brought a flurry of activity and pushed up rents, but doesn't yet seem to have translated into increased prosperity for the townspeople.

The Sacred Forest

Suzanne Wenger was interested in the beliefs and language of the Yoruba as inspiration for her painting, but she soon became a follower of **Obatala** – the Yoruba God of Creation – and, as local women came to appreciate her charismatic "artistic power", became a priestess of the religion in the 1960s. She has been a prime mover in restoring Oshogbo's **Sacred Forest**, which is devoted to the female water deity **Oshun**. With the help of Nigerian artists, she set about rebuilding the broken-down shrines, places of worship and sculptures, using modern cement on wooden and steel frames and a style that combined traditional elements with her own inspiration. The results are spectacular, mysterious and unique.

The forest is on the outskirts of town. It's not far to walk – about 2km from the centre – but you're better off taking a taxi there the first time. From the roadside, you can make out various shrines and an elaborate fence confining the retreat, before arriving at the gate. Here you'll find followers waiting by the road. To visit, you have to be accompanied by one of these disciples, and it's just as well, as none of the site would make much sense otherwise.

The first place you'll be shown is the **Oshun Temple** – the main place of worship and said to be the first building of the old town (Oshogbo used to be on this site until Oshun said she couldn't live with human beings any longer and sent them off to found the new town). If you go into the temple, you'll see shrines dripping with palm oil and will be asked to make a **sacrifice**. Make sure you've plenty of small change, and don't pull out wads of bills; your guide will say something like, "Make a small contribution, you know, like N=500", when a lot less will perfectly do the trick. The money is supposedly used by **priestesses** to buy things for a sacrifice in your name. If you don't use discretion from the outset, though, you'll find yourself paying an arm and a leg for kola nuts to be "sacrificed" every time you blink. The offering taken, prayers will be made by the priestesses and your fortune told. You may be asked to kneel in front of the shrines and pray yourself: what you do at this point is up to you, though a rendering of the Lord's Prayer or any humble invocation would be quite adequate.

Afterwards, you will be taken down to the **river** – the sacred domain of Oshun, the water goddess. Having had the surrounding shrines explained, you may be handed a calabash full of murky river water. It makes a big impression if you drink it and you probably won't die if you do, but you know best how your body is likely to react. Either way, you're unlikely to cause offence.

Walking through the forest, you'll be shown shrines depicting a myriad of deities, all of whom are represented by statues on the site of the market of the old town. The god of creation, **Obatala**, is portrayed riding on an elephant. He is the moulder of human beings, but when his penchant for palm wine leads him to drink too much, he's apt to create deformed people. **Oshun** is the goddess who showed all the other deities the way down to earth when they were sent to pull the world together. Other representations at the old market place include **Ogun**, master of iron, **Shango**, who controls thunder and lightning (he's been coopted by NEPA, the electricity board), **Iyamapo**, goddess of women's crafts, including weaving and dyeing, and **Nanabuku**, who controls the wind.

Other temples in the forest include **Ontoto's Building**. Ontoto is the son of Obatala and this building is a place for prayer. Designed by Wenger, the architecture forces you into the world of the fantastic – one of the rooms is in the shape of an ear so that those who pray will have their prayers heard. The **Ontoto Conference Hall** – a meet-

THE OSHOGBO SCHOOL

Oshogbo is the site of a famous **artists' workshop**, set up as an offshoot of Ibadan's Mbari Club in the 1960s, by writer Ulli Beier (previously married to Suzanne Wenger) and artist Georgina Beier. They ran it for three years, attracting a collection of locals and performers involved in the Duro Ladipo Travelling Theatre. Nigerian artists such as Twins Seven Seven, Muraina Oyelami, Jimoh Buraimoh, Rufus Ogundele, Adebisi Fabunmi and others learnt from Georgina Beier new techniques to which they'd previously had no access. Some of these names are now world famous, and rich and influential at home.

Each of the studios can be visited and you can meet the artist and buy his work (they're almost all men), as well as batiks, which are a speciality of Oshogbo. **Twins Seven Seven** is a particularly entertaining, maverick character, who has determinedly made his art the most commercially successful (if you and he are talking money, talk hard!). **Jimoh Buraimoh** works with beaded collage, beads being traditionally a part of royal insignia on the Yoruba beaded crown. Jimoh's murals adorn public buildings all over Lagos and in 1990 he exhibited at the Africa Centre in London.

For a look at the Oshogbo School's works in general, visit the **cooperative gallery** and workshop on Station Road (you can't miss the green and white sign), where there's a permanent collection.

Lastly, Nike Davies (a former wife of Twins Seven Seven) has set up the **Nike Centre** for young artists on Iwo Road (take a taxi from the Oke Fia garage and if the driver doesn't know it ask for the Dada estate and look out for the signpost). Recently renovated and enlarged, it's booming with creativity, and heavily into batik, painting, carving and even quilt making.

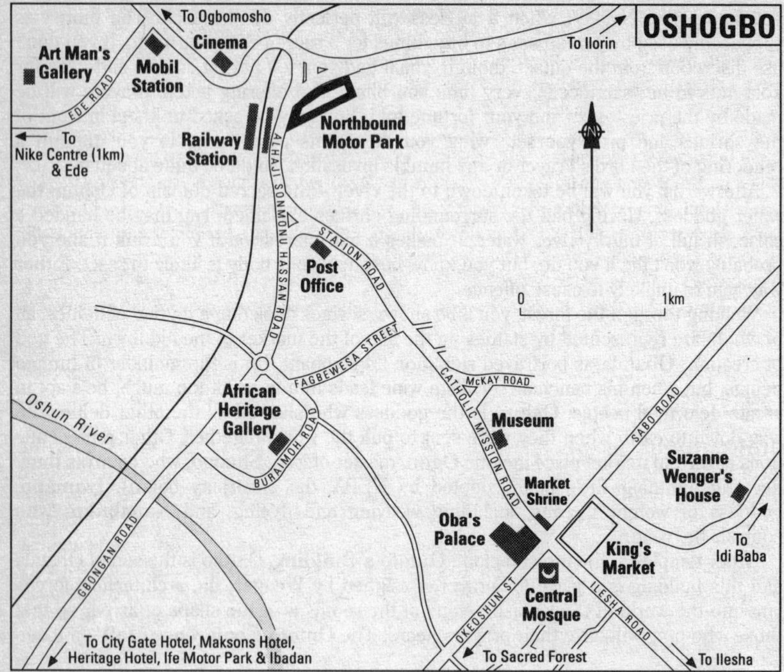

ing hall for initiates – has an entrance way consisting of a gigantic statue of Obatala on his elephant.

Around town

In Oshogbo town itself, try to visit the **Oba's Palace**, on the junction of Catholic Mission and Okeoshun streets. Besides the old and new palace buildings, the grounds contain a temple to Oshun with traditional wall paintings and sculpted wooden pillars. Aged priestesses guard the inside of the temple and will say prayers for you in exchange for an offering. To see the Oba in person, you must write in advance to: Oba's Palace (Alafin), Oshogbo.

Directly across from the palace is one of the most interesting buildings in town, the meeting place for elders and **"King Makers"**, decorated with carved wooden totems and abstract paintings at the front and with a tree growing out of the back. Flamboyant Brazilian houses with wild ornamentation and bright colours line the whole length of Catholic Mission Street.

King's Market spreads out opposite the palace. Besides the wide selection of fruit and vegetables, which grow easily in this fertile part of the country, you'll notice a lot of juju, sacred pots and other ritual articles. **Suzanne Wenger's house** is nearby on Ibokun Street and it's worth having a look at from the outside for the imaginative architecture and ornamentation replete with traditional imagery and symbolism. If Adunni (Wenger's Yoruba name) is in, you may be able to meet her. She has a shop with artefacts for sale, and will gladly sell you a copy of her book, *The Sacred Groves of Oshogbo*. For a deeper understanding of Yoruba religion, it makes interesting, if at times difficult, reading, and the photographs are beautiful.

Practicalities

The main **motor park** is outside town on the Ilesha road. If you're staying in Oshogbo, there are several reasonable hotels and the usual scattering of basic dives.

City Gate Hotel. Something of a brothel, but central and cheap. ①.

Heritage Hotel, signposted, on a small road off the Ibadan–Ife road, on the outskirts of town. Jimoh Buraimoh's place and one of the best in town with a bar, restaurant and art gallery. ②.

Maksons Hotel. A step up from *City Gate*, cleaner and with better facilities, but no bargain. ②.

Moeje Hotel, Airport Rd. Relatively modern hotel with TV in the AC rooms. ③.

Osun Presidential Hotel, Old Ikirun Rd (☎035/232 399). Oshogbo's best hotel with comfortable AC rooms, plus a nightclub, cinema and car rental facilities. ④.

Terminus Hotel, Ajegunle St (☎035/230 423). Comfortable hotel with S/C rooms with AC. ②.

Trans Motel, Ede Road. Refurbished government guesthouse from colonial days – airy and secluded, with attractive architecture. ②.

Ogbomosho and Ilorin

OGBOMOSHO, midway between Oyo and Ilorin, is a large industrial centre, the biggest town in the region after Ibadan, and variously reckoned to be the third or fourth largest town in Nigeria, with a population of about a million. It's horrible in every way: ferociously busy, massively congested and in a state of permanent commercial mayhem along its manic main road, bottlenecked with traffic, fumes and dust. But if you can bear to stop, it has a large market with a reputation for Yoruba cloth; it also boasts a very good Baptist Hospital. If you decide, or need, to stay in town, try the *Catering Resthouse*, the *California Hotel* or *Hotel Terminus* (☎710 032) at the Igbo Market. Note, if you're driving, that the Ogbomosho–Ilorin road is a notorious accident blackspot.

Ilorin

ILORIN, capital of Kwara State, lies at the edge of the Yoruba cultural domain, its strong Muslim flavour the result of Usman dan Fodio's nineteenth-century jihad. Basically a workaday trade and market centre, it's not too enticing for passing visitors. The colossal, white and blue **mosque** with its four spiring minarets and the Emir's palace make the dust and noise more bearable. The end-of-Ramadan **Sallah festival** is celebrated with a vigour that's unusual for a southern town – Ilorin is a good place to be, in fact, for any Muslim festival. The town was dramatically in the news in May 1995 when a large bomb, aimed at senior members of the military government, went off in the stadium during the launch of a government initiative, killing one person and wounding forty.

Among the **hotels**, the *White House* on Lagos Road is pleasant and reasonably priced. Others include the *Fisayo* and *Niger*, both on Niger Road, and the *Unity* on Murtala Muhammed Way. The *Kwara*, at 9 Ahmadou Bello Ave (☎031/221 490), is the best place in town, though unfortunately that's not to say very much.

THE SOUTHEAST

Once you cross over into **Edo State**, it's a short distance to **Benin**, once a formidable kingdom though already in decline by the time the British arrived. Faced with the modern town of the same name, you may be hard pressed to conjure up images of the former empire, but there are vestiges of the past, including ruins of the **great wall** that surrounded the city and numerous bronze and ivory **sculptures** housed in the city's renowned museum. Further east, you arrive in what's often called the **Igbo Country** (see box), although numerous other peoples also live in the region. The **Niger River**

THE IGBO

Igbo speakers have played an important role in the uncertain history of Nigeria. Unlike the Yoruba of the southwest, or the city-states of the centre and north, the people of the southeast forest country have traditionally maintained much more clan-based societies with fewer social hierarchies. Largely spurning slavery in their own culture, these communities fell easy prey when it was imposed from outside from the sixteenth to the nineteenth centuries. Later, having few cumbersome political structures to set up barriers, they quickly adapted to the new ideas of colonial society – its stress on personal achievement, on virtue earned through work and self-advancement, on business acumen and the creation of wealth. By the time World War II was over, the Igbo were clearly dominating the roles allowed to native Nigerians by the colonial government. Their success was partly responsible for the bloody trauma of **Biafra** – the still-born Igbo republic declared in 1967 – which resulted in civil war and a federal blockade which brought widespread starvation. And their continued dynamism is still the source of frustration among other groups in Nigeria – in particular the Hausa and Fulani Muslims of the north. It has tended to earn southeast Nigerians a reputation as survivors. After all, they have the **oil**. But, having relatively poor representation in the Federal Republic's formal political structures (and those representatives often corrupt and rarely called to account) has meant an acknowledged deficit of infrastructure and social services in the southeastern states. The image of the Igbo in Nigeria is a cruelly contradictory one which has parallels with many commercially successful peoples around the world.

passes through **Onitsha**, an industrial port city heavily damaged during the Biafran conflict. Although it has now regained a dominant commercial position in the area, you won't find much of interest and even the market – home and source of Nigeria's "market literature" and the hometown of Cyprian Ekwensi – has lost its verve. Northeast of Onitsha, **Enugu** survived the civil war largely unscathed. As capital of the fledgling republic of Biafra, however, strategically placed on the railway line, it was continually under threat and became more or less a ghost town. It has since bounced back and is now a vital economic centre and home to many international firms.

As it approaches the coast, the Niger River fans out into the endless meandering channels of the **Delta region**. The major town in the area, **Port Harcourt** is another modern town that's grown quickly since independence. You'll understand why when you see **oil flares** belching black smoke and flames on the seaward horizon: this is the heart of Nigeria's oil country. But it's also a good place for exploring **creek villages** and island towns like nearby **Bonny**. **Calabar**, relaxing and scenic, spreads over a hill overlooking the Calabar River in the very far southeast. This town, once a big slave port and now devoted to the palm oil trade, is one of Nigeria's most enjoyable.

Calabar is the natural base for visits to some of Nigeria's most exciting natural history sites – **Oban Rainforest Reserve** and **Mbe Mountain National Park**. Like the long-established **Obudu Cattle Ranch**, a little further north, gorillas live in these protected hill forests, and basic facilities are being put in place for visitors to see them.

Benin City and around

Long before Europeans arrived on the West African coast, **BENIN**, now the capital of Edo State, was capital of a powerful empire with a **divine king**. A direct descendant of this line, the **Oba**, still rules over his kingdom, even in the restrictive context of federal government. Today the city is as business-like as any in Nigeria – feverish, dirty, noisy and crowded. It has a wretched climate, no coast, and little in the way of open spaces to escape to; yet its remarkable history, traced in the **Benin National Museum**, has made the town into something of a cultural centre.

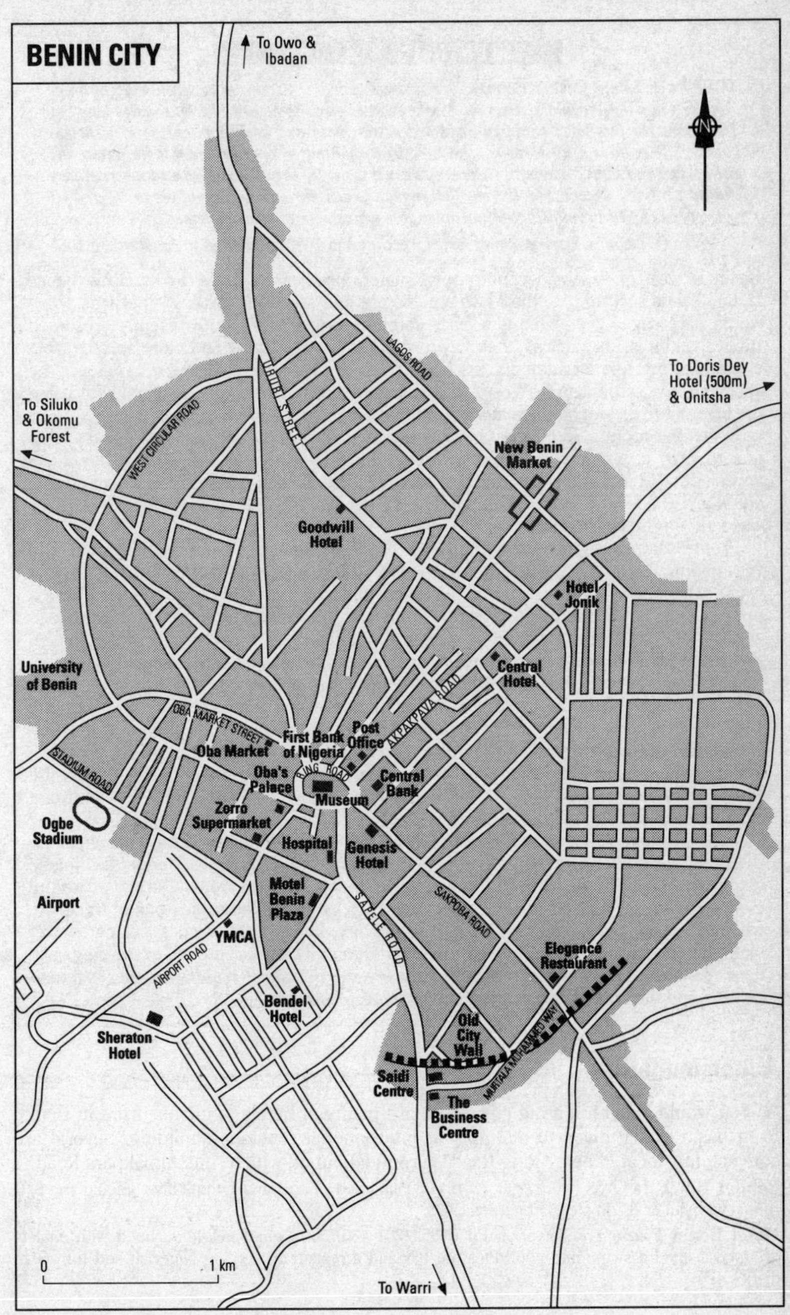
BENIN CITY
To Owo & Ibadan
LAGOS ROAD
URUBI STREET
To Doris Dey Hotel (500m) & Onitsha
To Siluko & Okomu Forest
WEST CIRCULAR ROAD
New Benin Market
Goodwill Hotel
Hotel Jonik
University of Benin
Central Hotel
AKPAKPAVA ROAD
OBA MARKET STREET
First Bank of Nigeria
Post Office
Oba Market
STADIUM ROAD
Oba's Palace
RING ROAD
Central Bank
Museum
Zerro Supermarket
Ogbe Stadium
Hospital
Genesis Hotel
Motel Benin Plaza
Airport
SAPELE ROAD
SAKPOBA ROAD
YMCA
AIRPORT ROAD
Elegance Restaurant
Bendel Hotel
Sheraton Hotel
Old City Wall
MURTALA MOHAMMED WAY
Saidi Centre
The Business Centre
0
1 km
To Warri

BENIN IN HISTORY

When you go into it you enter a great broad street, which . . . seems to be seven or eight times broader than the Warmoes street in Amsterdam . . . and thought to be four miles long . . . The houses in this town stand in good order, one close and evenly spaced with its neighbour . . . They have square rooms, sheltered by a roof that is open in the middle, where the rain, wind and light come in . . . The king's court is very great . . . built around many square shaped yards . . . I went into the court far enough to pass through four great yards . . . and yet wherever I looked I could still see gate after gate which opened into other yards.

From O. Dapper, *Description of Africa*, recorded in 1602, published in Amsterdam 1668

Benin is west of the Igbo country, and mainly peopled by the **Edo** or **Bini** (hence "Benin") who according to their own oral history migrated from the east – perhaps, some would dare say, Egypt. This is a fairly common origin myth, until recently presumed Biblical and mission-inspired, that may turn out to have a deeper and more ancient grain of truth as more is learnt about the black roots of pharaonic civilization. Whatever the case, the Edo settlement in West Africa was founded by **Ere**, a man credited with being the inventor of order and instigator of traditions.

Sometime around 1300, the chiefs impeached their king and for some years were governed by a democratically elected ruler. But this system also failed and the chiefs appealed to Ife to send over a capable monarch. The Yoruba prince **Oranmiyan** arrived and married a local woman. Their son **Eweka** became the first Oba and the royal palace was built during his reign.

From Oranmiyan's time onward, **bronze** achieved status as an important symbol. The very notion of kingship seemed to reside in this alloy of local tin and copper imported at great expense. When an Oba died, it was customary to send his head to Ife to have a portrait cast, but in the mid-fourteenth century, the Edo became bronze-workers themselves. This art form, however, was reserved strictly for the court. A smith foolish enough to waste his talent on anyone other than the Oba was quickly executed.

The kingdom enjoyed its **golden era** between the fifteenth and the seventeenth century. One of the greatest rulers was **Oba Ewuare** who ascended to the throne around 1440. He expanded the empire through conquests and his exploits brought new wealth – slaves, ivory, livestock – rolling into the city. Ewuare also greatly enlarged the capital, adding wide avenues and nine new gates each manned by a tax collector. When the **Portuguese** first arrived here, in 1485, they encountered a vast capital – the heart of a capable kingdom.

Other Europeans – English, Dutch, Florentines – quickly followed the Portuguese to the Bight of Benin. Their requirements were slaves, ivory, pepper, leather and handmade cloth. The Oba, **Ozula the Conqueror**, had plenty to offer from a string of fruitful conquests but he refused to sell slaves after 1516, after only a few seasons of trade. He willingly exchanged his stocks of pepper and ivory, however, for metals, silk and velvet cloth, mirrors and European horses – most of which quickly succumbed to sleeping sickness. Ambassadors were exchanged with several European nations in the sixteenth century and the Oba's court acquired a Portuguese cultural veneer.

Accommodation

As you would expect in a big city, there are plenty of hotels to choose from in Benin, from basic sleazy dives to attempts at international reputation-building. Several are conveniently located near "Ring Road", a roundabout off which runs Akpakpara Road.

Bendel Hotel, 1st Ave (☎052/200 120). Old-fashioned charm and competitive pricing for S/C rooms with fan or AC in pleasant gardens. ③.

Motel Benin Plaza, 1 Reservation Rd (☎052/201 430). In a quiet neighbourhood with chalets grouped around a swimming pool. Pleasant bar and a restaurant serving Nigerian and European dishes. ③.

The Oba became interested in **guns**, but the Pope had forbidden traders to sell weapons to heathens. Oba Ozula sent a son to Portugal to be converted and promised to build churches in his kingdom. He never built any, but he got the guns: the Vatican looked the other way and trade flourished. Copper and copper alloys became plentiful and the Oba could afford to commission unlimited metal plaques to line his palace walls. Heady from the booming business, the trade partners even fought side by side, as when Portuguese mercenaries aided the Edo in their war against the neighbouring kingdom of Idah to the northeast, at the end of the sixteenth century. The Portuguese did very well out of the trade, even though they only succeeded in overturning the sanction against slave-trading out of Benin's dominions in the eighteenth century. Even then, the Obas placed strict limits on the numbers sold.

By the late nineteenth century, the **British Empire** had become the Benin kingdom's principal partner and London was increasingly determined to develop new commodity sources and expand her markets for manufactured goods. The Oba's council increasingly perceived the calculating Europeans as a threat, while the Oba himself tried hard to find ways of negotiating a peaceful takeover that would allow him maximum power. His council sabotaged his plans and attacked and slaughtered a British negotiating team, though civil war was averted. Benin retreated behind the massive city walls to concentrate on metaphysical ways of dealing with the impending disaster of invasion.

Creating an image of savagery was in Britain's interest, since public opinion at home would accept relatively painless war and invasion as long as it was linked to a "civilizing mission". When the British Army launched a retaliatory "punitive expedition" to crush and seize Benin in 1897, they apparently found the Oba had made one last desperate effort to save the city in the only way he knew, and had ordered human sacrifices on a massive scale. The British reported corpses lying everywhere and the pervasive stench of death in the town. The king himself had escaped, but was captured in the forest and sent into exile. His palace was pillaged. The great art treasures were sent to England – where they remain to this day, many in the Museum of Mankind in London. Others were sold to private collections.

The stories of sacrifice undoubtedly had some basis in fact – the Oba's efforts to appease the spirits and ward off the encroaching white men were by no means extraordinary – but there was certainly sensationalist reporting too. Writing in the *Evening News* forty years after the event, Major James F. Ellison referred to a "14 hours running fight with the fleeing enemy" all around the city walls. Inside,

> *Benin ran with blood. Human sacrifices were everywhere. Some of the human beings who were in chains were still alive, speedily to be liberated. Around a huge tree in the centre of the city were erected poles on which were cross-pieces. On these were bodies, remains of those who had been sacrificed. In the Valley of the Skulls were hundreds of human heads and bones.*

After the campaign, the British press referred to Benin as the "City of Blood and Crucifixions". Whatever the magnitude of the barbarities carried out on the kingdom's own slaves and convicts, however, there was far more blood shed by the conquering British force.

Central Hotel, 76 Akpakpava Rd (☎052/200 780). A little run-down, but perfectly acceptable S/C rooms with AC, or cheaper ones with fan. Listen out for live music performances in the popular courtyard bar. ②.

Doris Dey Hotel, on the Benin–Onitsha road. New, well-appointed mid-range hotel, with S/C, AC rooms, all with CNN on the TV. ③.

Genesis Hotel, 4 Sakpoba Rd. Ideally situated near the museum and King's Square. Comfortable AC accommodation with private bath. Adjoining the hotel is the *Idubor Art Gallery*, where you can buy bulky statues, or simply watch the craftsmen. ②.

Goodwill Hotel, 23 Urubi St. Relatively clean S/C rooms with fan or AC and even a video option. ②.

Jajat Hotel, Akpakpava Rd. Well-kept and likeable accommodation with shared facilities. ①.

Hotel Jonik, 134 Akpakpava Rd. The rooms with shared facilities are a little shabby, but not bad – until you get to the WC. ①.

Saidi Centre, Murtala Muhammed Way, near the junction of Sapele Rd. Unpredictable room standards – this is one of those hotels that are constantly expanding and never quite finished – mean that you wouldn't always guess this is Benin City's best. Good Chinese-European restaurant. ③.

Sheraton Hotel, 7th Ave near the airport. A fine structure stands at the end of the golf course, but work ceased on it in 1990 and it is unlikely ever to be finished.

Victory Hotel, 2 Victory Rd off Lagos Rd. AC, S/C rooms, friendly staff, and even a car park. ②.

YWCA, Airport Rd. Budget accommodation, for women only. Central and friendly. ①.

The City

Although Benin is a big city with some 300,000 inhabitants, it's well laid out and not especially difficult to get to grips with. Everything centres around **King's Square** (popularly known as Ring Road), a roundabout at the heart of town. As the name, if not the square's various bronze statues, would suggest, this is where you'll find the **Oba's Palace**. You may have to ask someone to point it out among the various buildings along the square, because the bland exterior doesn't shout to be noticed. You can visit the modest interior of the palace but you have to write for an appointment first (addressing yourself most respectfully to The Secretary to Oba, Oba's Palace, Benin City, Edo State, Nigeria). The Oba himself never makes public appearances except for festivals or important court or civil state occasions. Since you have to state the date you want to visit and provide a return address, this seems like a real hitch if you're only passing through, but it's worthwhile if you're living in the area. By simply showing up at the palace, on the other hand, you're virtually guaranteed to find someone willing to recount the history and give a short tour of the grounds outside the palace.

The **Benin National Museum** (daily 9am–6pm; nominal entrance charge) in the middle of Ring Road – when the traffic's heavy, it's a life-risking manoeuvre getting to it – contains many sacred royal treasures and some of the legendary artworks of the former empire. Most of the kingdom's treasures were stolen and taken abroad following the British invasion of 1897, so that today Benin can claim only the world's third largest collection of Benin art – after London and Berlin. It's an impressive collection nonetheless and very well displayed: there are examples of the **bronze plaques** that lined the palace interior together with masks, ivory works and a series of heads exemplifying the three distinct periods of an art form that spanned five centuries.

Also on Ring Road is the **Oba's Market**, once one of the largest and most animated in the region. It burned down in 1983, but rebuilding is now complete. The major **banks** are also on this roundabout, as is the **post office** (though note that for international calls, you're best off going down to *The Business Centre* on Murtala Muhammed Way).

The best place for buying **crafts**, naturally including replica bronze busts, is on Igun Street. If you're interested in the vestiges of the **old city wall**, ruined morsels of it can still be seen on Sakoba Road on the outskirts of town.

Eating and nightlife

One of the best markets for street food is **New Benin Market**. You can get some of the town's best fruit here during the day and cheap finger food (*suya* for example, or grilled chicken) at night when this turns into a very active area and many shops and bars stay open late. A smaller market in a similar vein near Ring Road is the **Agbadan Market**, on Akpakpava Road, just next to the *Central Hotel*. The *Asumufoashi* **restaurant**, opposite, does inexpensive Nigerian dishes – *amala*, *eba*, *dodo*, rice. Down the street at 73 Akpakpava Rd is the *Queen's Rendezvous*, another good address for local specialities and meat pie-type snacks. The *Elegance*, on the corner of Sakpoba Road and Murtala

MOVING ON FROM BENIN CITY

Vehicles to **Onitsha and the east** leave from the Abo motor park on Ikpoba Rd out at the end of Akpakpava Rd to the northeast. To **Lagos** and the west, head to the Uselu motor park on Lagos Rd. **Buses** – cheaper and slower than taxis – leave from a row of service stations on Urubi St in the Iyaro neighbourhood. Departure times and destinations need careful advance checking.

If you're **driving**, the main A232 goes east to Onitsha, from where you branch either to Enugu by the new expressway link, or south on the A6 to Owerri and Port Harcourt. You'll hear dire warnings about this route, as it holds something of a record for accidents in Nigeria – and that says a lot. If you're going directly to Port Harcourt, you might want to consider the A2 rainforest route via Sapele and Warri. Look for palm wine sellers along the roadside, but don't even inhale near the stuff if you're behind the wheel.

Domestic **flights** are covered mainly by *Okada Airlines*, with an office at Airport Rd (☎052/244 942 or 241 504). The **travel agency** at 63 Akenzua St (☎052/222 806 or 244 724) handles Lagos bookings on *BA*, *KLM* and others.

Muhammed Way also does good Nigerian dishes. A restaurant opposite the *Zorro Supermarket*, on Airport Road, might satisfy a craving for American flavours – they also do Nigerian dishes, including snails. Over on Sapele Road, you can get decent, moderately priced **Chinese food** at the *Right Time*. And at the bottom of Sapele Rd, on Muratala Muhammed Way is the city's best restaurant, the *Saidi Centre*, with a Chinese and European menu and the energetic owner always in the background.

After all this, if you're lucky in the evening, you may catch the famous highlifer, Victor Uwaifo, at the *Paradise Nite-Club*, or any one of a number of local artists at a club called *The Difference* in the GRA. Have a taxi driver take you.

Okomu Forest Reserve

The **Okomu Forest Reserve** is a patch of indigenous forest of the kind that blanketed southern Nigeria before the nineteenth-century European invasion. It's 35km west of Benin City, near the small town of Udo and is looked after by the Nigerian Conservation Foundation. You might make it to Okomu by taxi, but most visitors drive themselves. It's possible to **stay** in the forest reserve, at the somewhat disconcertingly named *African Timber & Plywood Guest House*. This is actually a delightful old colonial cabin in a remote setting: you'll need to bring all food requirements. Despite encroaching development, a herd of **forest elephants** is hanging on at Okomu, plus various species of monkeys, an array of birdlife and the usual startling variety of reptiles and invertebrates. An observation platform in the forest canopy provides good viewing possibilities.

Onitsha

ONITSHA, about halfway between Benin City and Enugu, was almost completely destroyed during the Biafran conflict, and the town has since been rebuilt. Famous as the location of the earliest indigenously published literature in Nigeria (novels and tracts from 1949, under the label "Onitsha Market Literature"), it's still a highly energetic place, though there's no compelling reason to **stay** here except for a night stop. In that case, the very cheap and dingy *AP2 Hotel* at 30 Creek Rd near the renowned town market is budget-level (☎046/210 889; ①). More reputable places include the *Traveller's Palace Hotel*, very near the taxi park at 8 Agbu Ogbuefi St (☎046/211 013; ②), or the *Nkisi Palace*, Old Nkisi Rd, GRA (☎046/211 711 or 211 719; ②). Even better value in the middle price range is the *People's Club Guest House*, off Owerri Road (☎046/212 717; ②), where AC rooms are equipped with TV and fridge. The *Bolingo Hotel*, Zik Ave (☎046/210 877; ④), is more upmarket, and has a pool and a very good Chinese restaurant.

Igbo-Ukwu, one of the earliest Bronze-Age sites, dating from the ninth century, is southeast of Onitsha. Enormous bowls have been discovered here, only 1–2mm thick, indicating a *tour de force* of lost-wax casting at a time when other civilizations were still hammering their wares into shape. Evidence of old copper mines has now been found in the region.

Enugu

In sharp contrast to Benin City, **ENUGU**, capital of the newly formed Enugu State and the effective capital of Igboland, is a town without a long history. It was founded in 1909 when **coal deposits** were discovered in the area; some time later iron ore was also located; and when the railway came through in 1916, the town's economic future was sealed. It became capital of the Eastern Region in the 1930s (which dates most of the large government buildings) and later was the headquarters of the secessionist republic of Biafra. Although the town was all but deserted during the Civil War, it has since rediscovered its old vitality. Industry has taken off and there's even a Mercedes assembly plant, which must be some crude indicator of local prosperity. Enugu displays a certain colonial charm and has the odd, shady open space – and it's certainly better than the congested, commercial frenzy of Onitsha – but with mines, railway tracks, smoky factories and a population pushing past half a million, you'll have to work hard to really like it.

Accommodation

There's a decent selection of hotels in Enugu, making it a good stopping-off point between Calabar or the Cameroon border and the centre and north of Nigeria.

Dayspring, 178 Ogui Rd (☎042/257 591). Not special, but conveniently located on one of the town's main roads. ①.

Hotel Metropole, 13 Ogui Rd, near the train station (☎042/255 411). Flamboyant decor, inexpensive rooms and a lively nightclub. ①.

Modotel, 2 Club Rd, off Garden Ave (☎042/338 870). A sparkling, expensive, international-class set-up with a surprisingly pleasant restaurant and bar, in the heart of the administrative district. ⑤.

Nike Lake Resort Hotel, Nike Layout (☎042/337 000). Upmarket hotel with tennis courts, casino and pool, but they have also allowed camping on the grounds in the past. ③.

Hotel Pan Afric, behind the administrative district (☎042/335 248). Elegant gardens and reasonably priced rooms. ③.

Hotel Placia, 25 Edinburgh St (☎042/331 565). Well-kept hotel in the older part of town – Ogui district. Choice of rooms with S/C, AC and optional TV; good restaurant and bar, and an exceptional staff. Excellent value. ②–③.

Presidential Hotel, Independence Layout (☎042/252 065). Formerly one of the town's best, now looking slightly run-down and far from the centre, but the restaurant is nonetheless excellent, as is the bookshop. ③.

The Town

You can take care of most of your business in the area around Okpara Avenue, along which *First Bank*, *Union Bank* and *Afribank* are good for changing money. The **post office** is just off this road – on Post Office Avenue – and Enugu's vast **administrative district** straggles off behind it. Another main strip is Ogui Rd, where the train station is located. At 9 Ogui Rd, you'll find offices for the **National Museum**. Oddly enough, there's no museum as yet, but plans are in hand to build one in the future. You might stop by and check on progress. A number of **parks** dot Enugu, including the Murtala

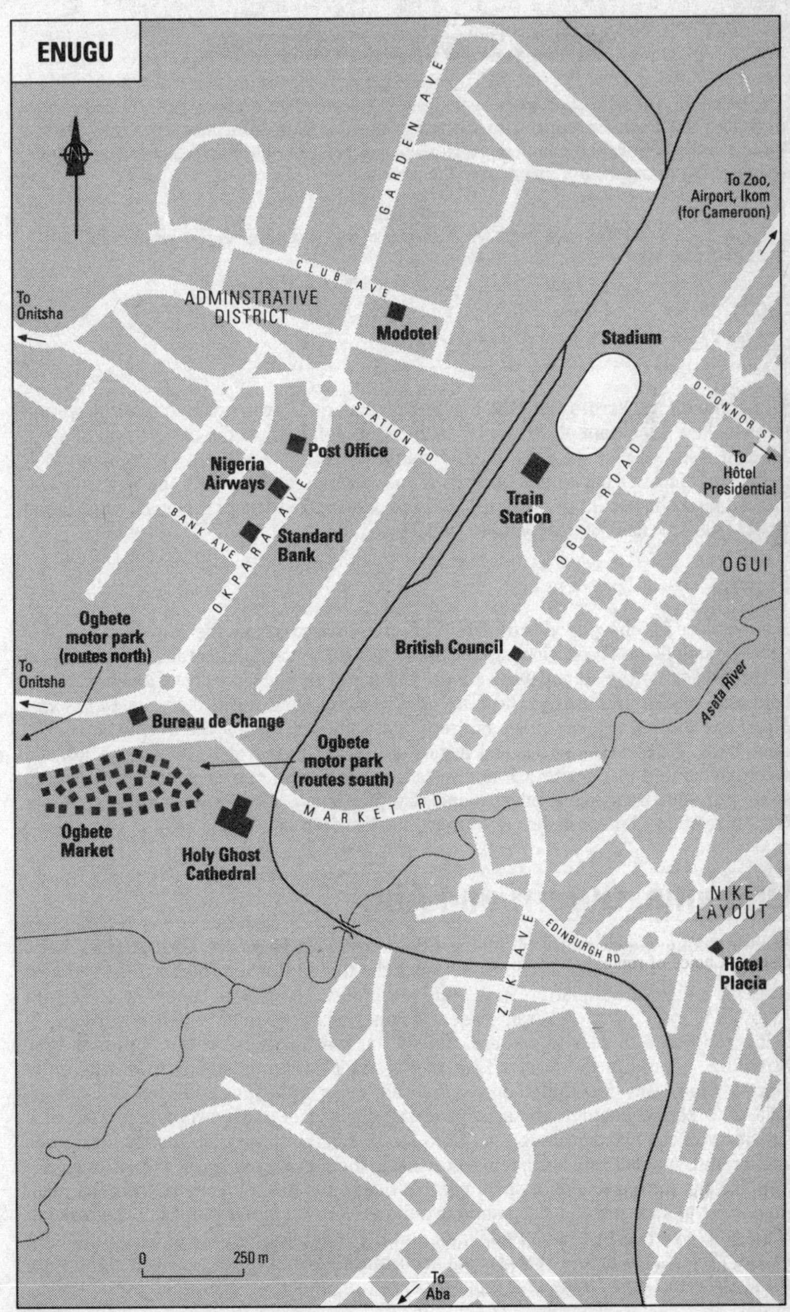
ENUGU
GARDEN AVE
CLUB AVE
To Onitsha
ADMINSTRATIVE DISTRICT
Modotel
Stadium
To Zoo, Airport, Ikom (for Cameroon)
STATION RD
O'CONNOR ST
Post Office
Nigeria Airways
BANK AVE
OKPARA AVE
Standard Bank
Train Station
OGUI ROAD
To Hôtel Presidential
OGUI
Ogbete motor park (routes north)
To Onitsha
British Council
Asata River
Bureau de Change
Ogbete motor park (routes south)
MARKET RD
Ogbete Market
Holy Ghost Cathedral
NIKE LAYOUT
ZIK AVE
EDINBURGH RD
Hôtel Placia
0
250 m
To Aba

MOVING ON FROM ENUGU

By Road

Vehicles for **Onitsha and west** leave from the New Market motor park. Southbound vehicles for **Port Harcourt** via Aba and Umuahia, leave from near the Holy Ghost Cathedral at the Ogbete motor park. Northbound vehicles, via **Nsukka**, also leave from Ogbete motor park, but from opposite the prison.

By Air

There are several **flights** a week on *Nigeria Airways* to **Lagos** and **Calabar**, with independent carriers covering other major cities.

British Airways, 5 O'Connor St, Asata (☎042/334 806).

KLM, Chuben Travel Agency, 35a Ogui Rd (☎042/339 586).

Nigeria Airways, 23 Okapara Ave (☎042/252 881).

Muhammed Park across from the bustling new market; jacaranda and other flowering trees make it a pleasant place to relax in the afternoon heat. At the eastern end of town, the **zoo** also has nice gardens, but the animals (those few of them that remain) look neither particularly happy nor healthy. If you want to catch up with the news or plug into some British culture, visit the **British Council**, Teacher's House, Ogui Road (☎042/338 456; Fax 330 158), and see what's on offer.

Eating

A good place for cheap food is the *MOWLT canteen* across from the New Market. They serve pounded yams, *eba*, rice and beans along with beer and minerals, and it's always full and noisy. In the administrative area, you might try the *Cool Spot Canteen* for cold beer and snacks. Or, next to the *Hotel Metropole* on Ogui Road, there's a *Danny Boy Fast Food* with meat pies, "mega burgers" and samosas. It's not the freshest food, but quite okay. *Chicken Danny's* is just next door. *Ideal Cuisine*, at 15 Edinburgh Rd, is a nicely decorated place with a friendly staff, serving good pepper soup, *egusi* or okra soup. For something more international, try the *Genesis Chinese Restaurant* at 36 Zik Ave for reliable Chinese dishes or burgers and fast food (☎042/336 355).

Umuahia, Owerri and Aba

Midway along the expressway linking Enugu and Port Harcourt, **UMUAHIA's** large central market and quiet tree-lined streets belie the days when this town served as a strategic military headquarters in the Biafran conflict. The private bunker, at 15 Okpara Ave, GRA, from where Biafran leader, Colonel Ojukwu, commanded his troops, is being renovated to receive visitors, but the current focus is on the **National War Museum**, housed in the former Eastern Nigeria TV relaying station from where the *Voice of Biafra* was transmitted during the war. It's an interesting collection of memorabilia, with period photographs accompanying displays of guns, swords and uniforms. Outside you can wander among the "Red Devil" Biafran troop transporters, field guns and aircraft. A small café has been set up inside the carcass of a naval ship. Entrance is free, but the museum is on a dirt track that dead-ends half a kilometre from the main road. Best to take a motor drop and have the driver wait while you visit. The *Banana Hotel* at 37 Warri Rd (☎088/220 879; ②) and the *Blue Spot Sun Inn* at 34 Ozu Item St (☎088/220 113; ②) provide reasonable **accommodation**. Less expensive lodgings are at the *Del Mar Guest House*, 25 Lagos St (①).

Some 60km west of Umuahia, and about 100km south of Onitsha, **OWERRI**, the capital of **Imo State**, is famous for its oilfields and its pottery – but it's a quiet town for its size. **Places to stay** include the *Executive* (☎083/230 100; ③) and the smaller *Ivory Hotel*, northeast of town on the Okigwi road (☎083/230 902; ②). The flashiest place in town is the *Imo Concorde* (☎083/231 111; ⑤) with restaurant, nightclub, pool and tennis courts.

Continuing south from Umuahia, the road bangs into the unprepossessing outskirts of **ABA**, an ugly commercial town (capital of Abia State) with its vast **Ariara Market** spilling onto the expressway. Even passing taxis and buses are accosted by vendors pressing their goods up to the windows. If you choose, or are obliged, to stop here, the **Museum of Colonial History** (daily 9am–6pm; small entrance fee) is only a two-minute walk from the chaos of the main motor park, on the A342 Ikot Ekpene Road (leading east out of town). A small, orderly collection, housed in a wooden British administrative building, traces the history of Nigeria through well-presented and informative photo exhibits from pre-colonial times to the 1960s.

There's a cluster of crafts shops, chop bars and weaving huts in the museum compound. Of the inexpensive **hotels** on Pound Road, in town, the *City Guest Inn* is a likeable, simple place with friendly management (①). More comfortable accommodation can be found at the *Ambassador Hotel* at 21 Park Rd (☎082/221 487; ②), while the *Crystal Park Hotel*, Crystal Park Avenue, off Port Harcourt Road (☎082/221 930; ④), and *Imo Hotel*, in the GRA (☎082/220 111; ④), are more upmarket.

Port Harcourt and around

Capital of Rivers State, **PORT HARCOURT** ("Po-ta-ko" in Pidgin) promotes itself as the **"Garden City"**. Given its location in the rainforest, it would be remarkable if it wasn't green. Port Harcourt first came to prominence during World War I as a result of military operations mounted from here against German Kamerun. But the fortunes of the modern city are thanks primarily to the **oil wells** that have sprouted throughout the region since 1956 when commercial quantities were discovered in **Oloibiri**. The first shipload of Nigerian crude was exported from Port Harcourt in 1958 and the country was launched on a new economic course that promised rapid industrial development and prosperity. As a side benefit, Port Harcourt has acquired a strikingly **modern aspect**, with wide avenues, flyovers and high-rise blocks easily outshooting the last of the giant forest trees left standing in the city limits. Yet the **"Old Township"** (founded in 1913) has survived the rapid growth and if you were to limit your time to this corner of the city, you could come away believing that Port Harcourt is still a small town with a good deal of charm.

Arrival and orientation

If you're using public transport, the main problem in the city is its sheer size. You're likely to be dropped at Diobu Mile 3 Motor Park, which is a good 5km from the most appealing parts of town. And if you have to get around a lot, then taxi fares from one end of the city to the other will soon start to eat into your pocket.

Port Harcourt is divided by the **flyover** – a freeway overpass that's something of a symbol of the town's modernity – into two distinct zones: the new town to the north and the old town to the south. The **Aba Expressway** runs clean through the new part of town, from the air force base in the northern suburbs down to the flyover. Expressway is no exaggeration since cars seem to be out to break speed records as they scream down it; pedestrian overpasses are few and far between. Banks line the expressway, as do various governmental buildings. Off the expressway, the **Kaduna**

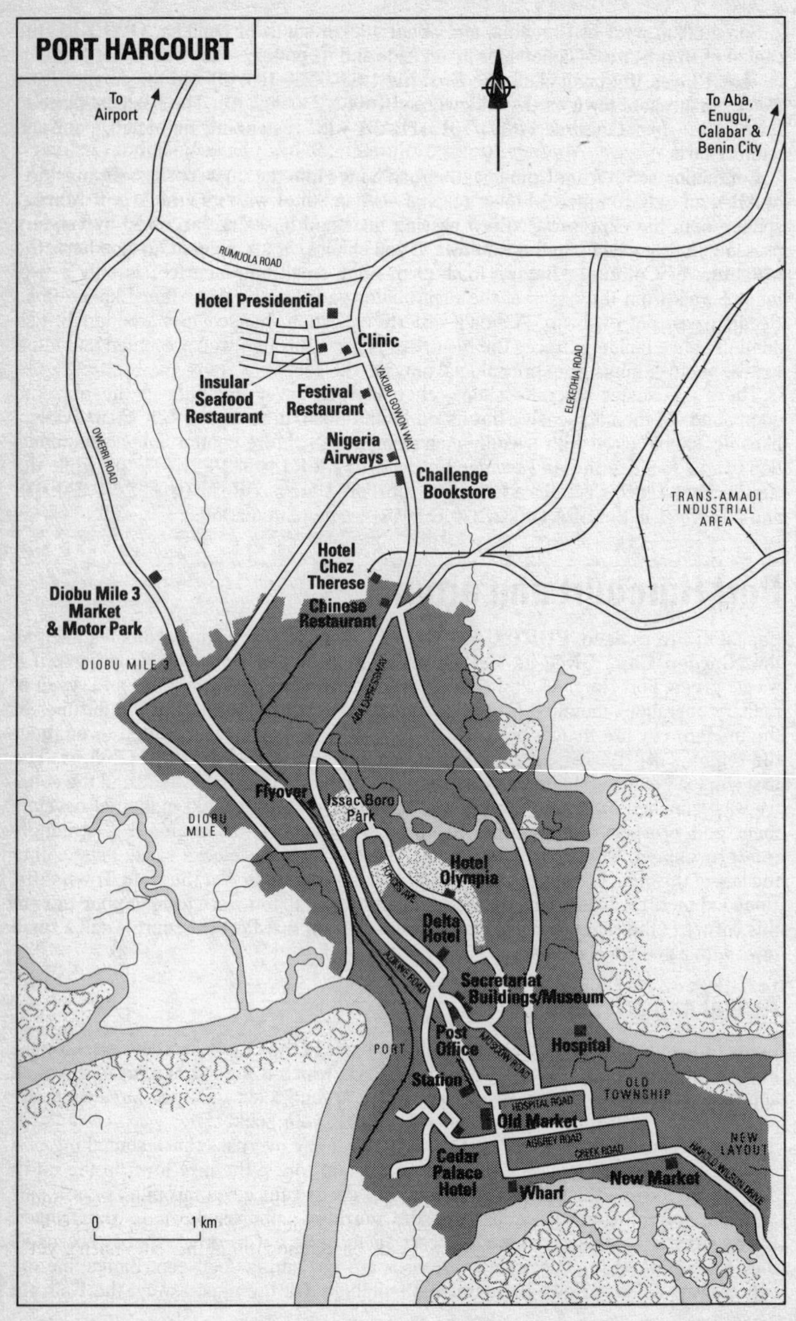
PORT HARCOURT
To Airport
To Aba, Enugu, Calabar & Benin City
RUMUOLA ROAD
Hotel Presidential
Clinic
Insular Seafood Restaurant
Festival Restaurant
YAKUBU GOWON WAY
ELEKEOHIA ROAD
OWERRI ROAD
Nigeria Airways
Challenge Bookstore
TRANS-AMADI INDUSTRIAL AREA
Hotel Chez Therese
Chinese Restaurant
Diobu Mile 3 Market & Motor Park
DIOBU MILE 3
ABA EXPRESSWAY
Flyover
Issac Boro Park
DIOBU MILE 1
Hotel Olympia
Delta Hotel
Secretariat Buildings/Museum
PORT
Post Office
Hospital
Station
OLD TOWNSHIP
HOSPITAL ROAD
Old Market
AGGREY ROAD
CREEK ROAD
NEW LAYOUT
Cedar Palace Hotel
New Market
Wharf
0
1 km

Street Public Market is a good place for food, including the fresh fish which is so plentiful around here. Other markets are in **Diobu neighbourhood** at Mile 1 and Mile 3. **Azikwe Road**, south of the flyover, is the effective city centre, where you'll see the towering state headquarters of numerous **banks** and a fine showing of **supermarkets**, including *Supabod Stores*, *Leventis*, *GB Olivant* and *UTC*.

In the **Old Township**, Aggrey Road runs through the heart and constitutes the high street. From here, in the crowded southern quarter of the city, you get striking views of the distant oil flares as you take in a wide variety of stalls, restaurants and shops lining the street. On the southern side of the township, down near the creek, you'll find two of Port Harcourt's main markets – the wonderfully chaotic **Creek Road Market**, excellent for fish, and **New Layout Market**.

Accommodation

Port Harcourt has a good cross-section of places to stay, though some are very far from the central area. The whole town is built, on oil money, for car-drivers.

Airport Hotel, Owerri Rd (40min from centre; ☎084/331 513 or 332 309). Posh business-class establishment, convenient for the airport, but isolated from the town. A wide range of amenities includes shops, restaurants and swimming pool. ⑥.

Cedar Palace, 11 Joseph Wayas Rd (☎084/300 180). Moderate hotel with AC and TV in the rooms, near the train station and port. ②.

Hotel Chez Therese, 23 Udom St, off Aba Expressway (☎084/330 820). A proper, yet slightly overpriced place with clean S/C, AC rooms. ②.

Delta Hotels Ltd, 1 Harley St (☎084/334 047). The old catering resthouse is now a scruffy AC hotel, though the twin rooms offer decent value. The restaurant has little selection and a disinterested staff. ②.

Erijoy Motel, Plot 5 Trans-Amadi Industrial Layout. Moderate hotel with reasonable standards and frequent live music performances. ③.

Ibani Castle Hotel, 31 Harold Wilson Dr (☎084/333 244). Atmospheric hotel in the Old Township with reasonable standards and accommodating staff. ③.

Mary Dok Guest House, 27 Sangana St, Diobu Mile 3. Convenient to crawl into from the motor park just across the way – an inexpensive bordello with shared bucket showers, but clean AC rooms, some with TV. ②.

Olympia Hotel, 45 Forces Ave. (☎084/334 941 or 334 936). Smart hotel, conveniently located near the post office, banks and museum, and surprisingly inexpensive. ③.

Hotel Presidential, Aba Expressway (PMB 5141; ☎084/310 400). The centre's international-class hideout, with restaurants, shops, pool, tennis and a casino. ⑦.

Zuru Hotel, 1A Rebisi St, Diobu (☎084/330 904). Good value for tidy rooms with AC and TV, and a good restaurant. ②.

The Town

The Secretariat Complex at the bottom of Azikwe Road houses the city's small **ethnographic museum**. Its examples of regional art include outstanding examples of the colourful, often bizarre local **masks**, and there are also limited and poorly displayed scatterings of domestic utensils from major ethnic groups in the area – Ijaw, Ikwerre, Etche, Ogoni, Ekpeye and Ogba. An ambitious new complex is proposed for the museum on the Aba Expressway.

Not far away, on Bonny Road, the **Cultural Centre** (Mon–Sat 7.30am–3.30pm, closed holidays) has various exhibits on handicrafts, which you can also buy here, and canoe building. A "**tourist beach**" was recently set aside down by Bonny Waterside, and though the surrounding parks are quite accommodating, the site hasn't yet sparked much interest.

TOURIST INFORMATION

The chaotic offices of the Rivers State **Ministry of Tourism** are at 35–37 Aba Expressway (☎084/334 901). The staff are friendly and helpful – within the limits of available information – and they've been putting together a Rivers State Travel Guide which may exist by now. For more information, including how to arrange trips to Bonny and Brass islands (see below), try the *Ideal Travel Agency* on Aba Expressway in the Nigeria Airways Building.

In keeping with Port Harcourt's image as a garden city, the **Isaac Boro Park**, near the flyover, adds a bit of extra green to the city centre. The park is dedicated to Major Isaac Adaka Boro, a champion of the minority peoples of the southeast, who, in defending his cause against Governor Ojukwu's Igbo domination, was killed in 1968 fighting for the Federal forces during the civil war. In the north of town the **zoo park** contributes a wild touch to the otherwise relentless **Trans-Amadi Industrial Area.**

Eating and nightlife

For **inexpensive eating** head to "Suya Street" in the Old Township. Every taxi driver is familiar with this atmospheric road lined with foodstalls and glowing with the warm light of charcoal fires in the evening. There's a wide range of chop here, more than the street's name suggests, though if *suya* is all you are interested in, it's available along with grilled corn on just about every street corner. There's not much in the way of **foreign cuisine** though a couple of Chinese restaurants stand out: *Hong Kong* at 27 Aba Expressway has a long menu at moderate prices and compares well with the *4-5-6* at the *Presidential.* Less expensive is the *Chi-Chi,* next to the nightclub of the same name. *Martinique*, in Bebbe Street, off the expressway, is currently popular for Nigerian and European eating. Moving **upmarket**, the *Insular Restaurant*, off Aba Road, a block from the *Presidential*, serves the town's best seafood in rather elegant surroundings. For hamburger type snacks, there's a number of fast-food places along Rumuola Road in the north of town, and along the same street, *Den's Bakery* has good cakes, pies and pizza.

As you would expect in a town the size of Port Harcourt, there are numerous **nightclubs** that cater, Thursday to Sunday, to all (male) tastes. Two notoriously raunchy ones are *Friends* (*Uncle Sam's*) and *Chi-Chi,* both unabashed meat markets well known in the expat and salary-earning communities. In this same, new part of town, the very stylish *Dreams*, next to the *Presidential*, and the nearby *Aquarius* at 205 Aba Expressway, have their own flashy mirror-and-lights **discos**. The clubs at the *Erijoy Motel* and the *Savannah Love Garden* have **live bands** several times a week. The best – the only – way to find out which is currently trendiest and most likely to have a group playing, is to ask around. In the old part of Port Harcourt, have a look at the *Ibani Castle Hotel*'s in-house *Orupolo Night Club* at 31 Harold Wilson Drive, or the *Tropicana* in the *Cedar Palace.* Of the numerous **cinemas** around town, the one in the *Hotel Presidential* is best.

Bonny and Brass islands

You can travel by irregular motorboat to **Bonny and Brass islands** (three and six hours respectively). Alternatively take the smaller boat "taxis" used by people of the creek villages. They depart from Bonny Waterside (at the bottom of Bonny Road by the Cultural Centre) and head to numerous destinations (Ke, Bekingkiri, etc). There are sheds for booking the ferries, but for the small boats just go to the jetty where people and cargo are loading. Expect to do hard bargaining to get the regular price: you need to be very firm.

Bonny and Brass were the first fifteenth-century Portuguese toe-holds in Nigeria, and later became missionary gateways (St Stephen's on Bonny is one of the oldest Anglican churches in the country), but are now devoted to the oil industry. There are still some wonderfully ornate Victorian tombstones and monuments and some great old houses. Local chiefs tend to wear Edwardian shirts with tucked fronts and top hats. **Accommodation** can be found at a number of hotels on Bonny. The least expensive is the *Beach Hotel* with shabby rooms with shared facilities that still cost more than anything on the mainland (②). The other town hotels are considerably more comfortable. Beware of zealous immigration officials, and be fully armed with your paperwork.

MOVING ON FROM PORT HARCOURT

The **Mile 3 motor park** has vehicles to almost everywhere – Port Harcourt is literally at the end of the road, or at least the Old Township is – and transport isn't hard to find, though a driver without suicidal inclinations may be (if you're Enugu-bound, don't forget the 270km of lethal motorway when selecting your vehicle). For Calabar, head to the **Leventis motor park** on the Aba Expressway.

As for **trains**, there was formerly a weekly service to Maiduguri, requiring a change at Kafanchan for Kano and Lagos. Since 1994 the service has been suspended.

Flights on *Nigeria Airways* to **Lagos** (two to four times daily, most via **Enugu**) continue to **London** on Thurs. *Nigeria Airways* fly direct to **Libreville** on Wed, and to **Douala** on Mon, en route from Lagos. The numerous national carriers that fly here guarantee frequent flights to Lagos and to most major cities in Nigeria; they include *Okada, ADC, Triax, Kabo,* and *Harco*. Helicopter flights run to Bonny and Brass for oil industry personnel: check at the tourist office for how to hitch a ride.

Airlines and their agents include: *British Airways*, Rivers State Tourist & Hotels Corp Building, Aba Expressway (☎084/331 986); *KLM*, Leventis Stores Building, Liberation Drive (☎084/331 055); *Nigeria Airways*, 6 Bank Rd (☎084/229 931); and *Sabena*, Mr Nwosu, 14 Udom St (☎084/333 505).

Calabar and around

It's not just its position perched high on the hills overlooking the river that makes **CALABAR** such a pleasant town to visit. There's a general good ambience created by its compact size and the outgoing nature of the Efik, Ibibio and Kalabari people. Calabar offers a fine introduction to the nicer facets of Nigerian life and, if you're heading east, is a good place to prepare for in-your-face Cameroon and the rigours of Central Africa. The waterfront sums up its elegantly run-down, colonial feel. Apart from Lagos, Calabar is the only Nigerian city near the coast, and the tension that crackles in so many other large towns is absent, as if whisked away on the ocean breeze. Calabar also has the best **culinary reputation** in the country, with lots of varied, traditional cooking. Nigerians say that if a Calabar woman cooks for you, you'll never leave the town. Lastly, a tip: visit the fascinating *Orill Ranch* **monkey sanctuary**, just off Ndideng Usang Iso Road, past the market.

If you've any choice about when you visit, opt for October, **masquerade month** in Calabar, the time when cultural values and traditional beliefs are most in evidence. The masquerades – **Sekiapu** – include not only continuous drumming and dancing, sculpted masks and elaborate and dazzlingly costumed performers, but regattas of huge, fabulously decked, competitive society canoes.

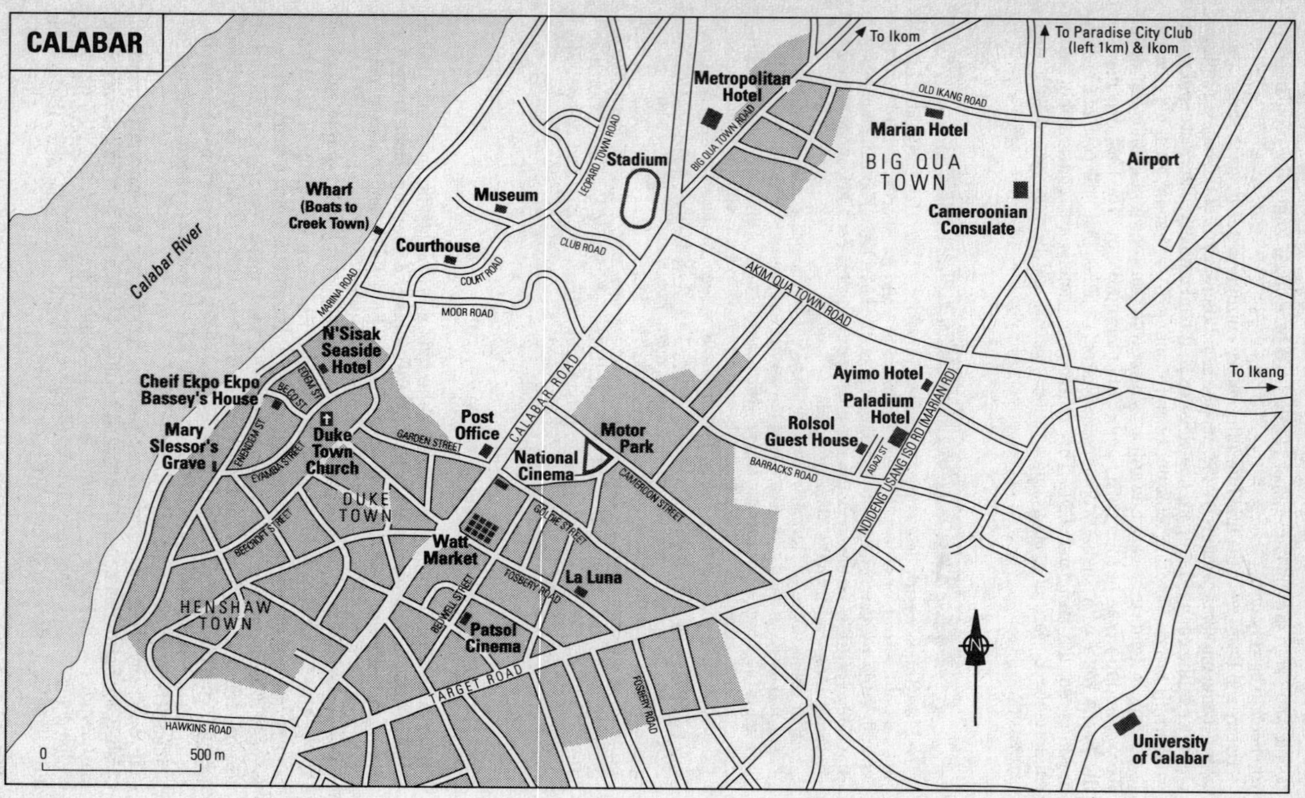
CALABAR
Calabar River
Wharf (Boats to Creek Town)
MARINA ROAD
Museum
Courthouse
COURT ROAD
MOOR ROAD
LEOPARD TOWN ROAD
CLUB ROAD
Stadium
Metropolitan Hotel
BIG QUA TOWN ROAD
To Ikom
To Paradise City Club (left 1km) & Ikom
OLD IKANG ROAD
Marian Hotel
BIG QUA TOWN
Airport
Cameroonian Consulate
AKIM QUA TOWN ROAD
To Ikang
Ayimo Hotel
Paladium Hotel
Rolsol Guest House
ADAZI ST
NDIDENG USANG ISO RD (MARIAN RD)
BARRACKS ROAD
N'Sisak Seaside Hotel
EDEM ST
BECO ST
Cheif Ekpo Ekpo Bassey's House
Mary Slessor's Grave
ENENDEM ST
EYAMBA STREET
Duke Town Church
DUKE TOWN
Post Office
GARDEN STREET
CALABAR ROAD
Motor Park
National Cinema
CAMEROON STREET
GOLDIE STREET
BECROFT STREET
Watt Market
FOSBERY ROAD
La Luna
BEDWELL STREET
Patsol Cinema
HENSHAW TOWN
TARGET ROAD
FOSBERY ROAD
HAWKINS ROAD
0
500 m
University of Calabar

TOURIST AND PARKS INFORMATION

Call at the local office of the Ministry of Tourism to pick up the informative *Cross River State Tourist Guide*. If you're heading to the forest reserves, up-to-date information can be had at the Cross River National Park Office, 3 Ebuta Crescent, Ette Agbor Layout.

City transport and orientation

Calabar is an easy town to get around. Taxis, together with even cheaper buses and motorcycle taxis, provide nearly 24-hour mobility. There's a **bus park** right by Watt Market in the centre of town where you're likely first to land up. The buses run on set routes but will usually stop if you wave them down. **Motorcycle taxis** – or "motor drops" – usually cost the same as a shared taxi for a single drop, though it may be double this for long transits across town. They're extremely polite, usually apologizing for bumps in the road and checking that the speed is okay. Like taxi fares, prices double after dark, though you may be able to negotiate a good price for two up on the bike. The busiest streets in town are the long-established **Calabar Road**, and the newer commercial street called **Ndideng Usang Iso Road**, formerly Marian Road.

Accommodation

There's a host of pleasant, small, **family-run hotels**, many of which have air conditioning and TV at affordable prices.

Hotel de Achiv, 3 Clifford Lane (unpaved alley that runs alongside the *ITC Supermarket*), off Calabar Rd. Near the market, S/C single or double rooms with fans. Not exactly of good repute, but the people are very nice and they have a bar/TV room with snacks – try the snail kebabs, a local delicacy. ①.

Ayimo Hotel, Ndideng Usang Iso Rd. An older place which has worn well, the *Ayimo*'s double rooms are quite reasonable for two, but slightly pricey if you're on your own. ②.

Marian Hotel, 125 Old Ikang Rd. New luxury hotel, challenging the *Metropolitan*. Modern chalets and suites in a quiet area away from the centre. Excellent Nigerian/European restaurant. ④.

Metropolitan Hotel, Calabar Rd (PO Box 1071; ☎087/220 911 or 222 257). Calabar's international-class place, with the usual amenities. The AC rooms *without* TV are very reasonable. Highly rated restaurant, cocktail bar, hair salon and bookshop. ④.

Neebee Guest House, 5 Dan Achibong St, off Calabar Rd. Inexpensive lodgings and a good restaurant featuring garlic steak and fish pepper soup. ②.

Nsikak Sea Side Hotel, 45 Edem St (☎087/228 443). On the waterfront, a modern-looking facade belies a faded interior with scruffy and overpriced S/C, AC rooms. The top floor bar is enclosed by huge bay windows for a beautiful view of the river and town. ②.

Paladium, 106 Ndideng Usang Iso Rd. This has been around for twenty years or more and is showing its age, but is still reasonably priced and welcoming. ①.

Resort Sophie, 151 MCC Rd. A new place with upmarket AC accommodation, swimming pool, bar and restaurant. Clean and friendly. ③.

Rolsol Guest House, 91 Palm St (☎087/220 328). Simple, but good-value doubles with fan or AC, and a nice garden. ①.

The Town

At the centre of Calabar is **Watt Market**. Calabar Road runs through the middle of the market, dividing foodstuffs on one side from cloth and household goods on the other. Also on Calabar Road, between the market roundabout and the *Metropolitan Hotel*, you'll find the **post office** and major **banks**. For really spectacular views of the town, the river and the surrounding forest, climb to the top of the **Calabar University Library** – the largest library building in Africa.

CALABAR'S HISTORICAL BACKGROUND

The **Qua** (or Ekoi), who came from the northern woodlands and were principally hunters and farmers, were the first people to settle in the Calabar area. Later migration brought the **Efik** and **Efut** – predominantly fishers and subsistence farmers. The Portuguese arrived in the closing years of the fifteenth century and the economic orientation of the local people slowly shifted to **trading**. By the seventeenth century, the Efik were in control of the lucrative export of **slaves**. Efik settlements on the estuary of the Calabar River developed into trading **city-states** that dealt with the Portuguese, Dutch, French, German and English. Rich and powerful, the rulers took European names to emphasize their importance – the Dukes, the Jameses, the Henshaws – and welcomed **missionaries** despite their opposition to the slave trade. Calabar thus became a centre of education and religion, and local rulers gained further advantages with the European trading partners, as the Efik forbade missionaries to come into contact with ethnic groups in the hinterland. With their understanding of the ways of the West, the Efik made the transition as smoothly as anyone could have expected when trade shifted from slaves to **palm oil** and later when Nigeria became a colony and the Efik were ruled "indirectly", through their chiefs. At the end of the nineteenth century, Calabar became the capital of Southern Nigeria and during the **Biafran War**, the town was recaptured from the secessionists and served as an important federal forces naval base.

There's still a good deal of **colonial architecture** in the older parts of Calabar, especially around the Henshaw Town, Duke Town and waterfront districts. The **courthouse** is a characteristic piece of period design and many other buildings are still inhabited, or in use, despite their dilapidated condition. Another good example is the nineteenth-century **house of Chief Ekpo Ekpo Bassey** at 19 Boco St, now falling into extravagant disrepair. Nearby, the **Duke Town church** is one of the oldest in Nigeria, established in the nineteenth century by Presbyterian missionaries. Continuing uphill on Eyamba Street past the church takes you to the **old cemetery** – an enchanting, if neglected, spot, with stunning views over the town and river. The tomb of one of southern Nigeria's most influential missionaries, **Mary Slessor**, from Dundee, near Edinburgh, lies here, marked by a plaque.

Calabar Museum

On the hill overlooking the waterfront, **Calabar Museum** (daily 9am–6pm; ☎087/223 476) is housed in the **Old Government House**, the former residence of the colonial governor. The building, designed and built in Glasgow and shipped over in pieces, has been beautifully restored. As a museum, it has few, if any, equals in the country.

The museum concentrates on the **history** of old Calabar, rather than on ethnography or art, and the collections are clearly documented and displayed. In fact, there's almost too much to contemplate here in one visit, with a mass of details on trading, missionary activities and colonial administration. It's a remarkable collection spanning pre-colonial days, the slave and palm oil eras, British invasion and anti-colonial resistance, to end with the path to independence. The museum also contains a **craft village** and shop and there's a good outdoor bar with wonderful views over the town. The small **bookshop** has interesting material on the history and culture of the region.

Creek Town

From the waterfront, you can catch a "fly boat" (motor boat) to nearby **Creek Town** (also spelt Greek Town: even residents seem to have lost track of the correct name), a 45-minute ride down the Calabar River, with dense mangrove greenery reminiscent of scenes from *African Queen*. On arrival, there's little specifically to visit, but you can wander around and absorb the intimate creekside village atmosphere. The people here are very proud of the **Creek Town church**, which is, indeed, a fine piece of colonial architecture, and, they claim, older than that in Duke Town. Some of the houses still have small "factories", where they produce **palm oil** using antiquated nineteenth-century mills from Britain. If you express interest, people are surprised but happy to show you their production methods. The town has a small **market** and numerous **palm wine bars** – look for the tell-tale phallic gourds that serve as cups, hung in front of the bars – where you'll find the beverage much fresher, and therefore much less alcoholic and more quaffable, than in Calabar town itself. It's often served with grilled **monkey meat** – not a bad accompaniment if you can get into the frame of mind the wine will ultimately induce anyway. Check it's been thoroughly cooked.

Eating

Calabar soup with periwinkles is famous in Nigeria. Another local delicacy is dog meat and if you walk past houses with cages full of canines, they're not there to mount the guard: these are restaurants, and the dish is not bad if you can redefine ideas of man's best friend.

Decalogue Restaurant, 14 Bedwell St. Good fried fish, plaintain and pepper soup, near the market and the centre of town.

Freddy's Restaurant, 90 Atekong Drive, opposite *Paradise City*. Upscale restaurant with specialities like houmous, pepper steak and avocadoes stuffed with shrimp. A popular choice among expats, who come around often.

High Quality Bakery, 34 Ndideng Usang Iso Rd. Fresh bread and cakes or superb meat pies and pizza. Good ice cream too.

Restaurant Sans Tache, 19 Ndideng Usang Iso Rd. Inexpensive eatery and a great place to try local specialities like *Afong soup* and *gari*.

MOVING ON FROM CALABAR

Details on crossing into Cameroon by land are given on p.1077. For details on sea crossings see p.1074.

By Road

Most vehicles go from the **Watt Market motor park**, from where there's regular transport west to **Port Harcourt**, north to **Ekang** (the route you need for Oban Rainforest Reserve and Cameroon) and north to **Ikom** (for Cameroon and northern Cross River State). *Crosslines* has its own garage in Calabar Rd, north of Watt Market and offers a daily bus to **Jos** (12–14hr) and services west to **Uyo** and **Aba**, north to **Ekang** (via Oban village) and **Obudu** (via Ikom). There's also a motor park for **Oban** at the junctions of Ekang Rd and Ndideng Usang Iso Rd.

By Air

Flights out of Calabar (on *Nigeria Airways*) include Wed and Sat flights non-stop to Lagos, Mon flights to Lagos via Port Harcourt and Sat flights to Douala originating in Lagos. *ADC* domestic airlines provides two daily flights to Lagos. Airline agents' addresses (for information, bookings and ticket alterations – in theory) include *British Airways*, 164 Ndideng Usang Iso Rd (☎087/224 466); *KLM, Tripton Travel Agency*, 1 White House St (☎087/224 488); and *Nigeria Airways*, 45 Bedwell St (☎087/222 504).

Visas for Cameroon

Even if your application for a Cameroonian visa was refused at the Lagos embassy, your chances of getting a visa at the **Cameroon Consulate**, 21 Ndideng Usang Iso Rd (any taxi driver or motorcyclist can take you there) are good, though they are very expensive for some nationalities, notably British. Bring two passport photos, and you can normally get the visa the same day.

Entertainment and nightlife

Calabar has two downtown **cinemas** – the *National* on Target Road, opposite the motor park, and the *Patsol*, 22 Bedwell St. The *Patsol* is the better of the two, as it's nearly impossible to make out the soundtrack at the *National* – not that it matters a great deal as most of the movies are Hindi dramas or Kung-fu. For the chance of something better, try the Calabar University Campus.

A number of zesty **clubs** enliven Calabar nights and, since this is one of the southern Nigerian cities where you can feel relatively safe after dark, it's fun to wander around checking them out.

Jazz Club, Target Rd. A small place, with a good music selection.

La Luna, Fosbery Rd. Regular live music at weekends and slightly cheaper than *Paradise City*.

Metropolitan Hotel, Calabar Rd (☎087/220 911 or 222 257). Although very mainstream, the *Metropolitan*'s disco always packs them in.

Paradise City, 87 Atekong Drive, off Ndideng Usang Iso Rd (☎087/221 234). Currently one of Calabar's flashiest and most popular clubs, with live music (reggae or Highlife) on Fri and Sat (modest entrance fee).

Tuxedo Junction, 147 Calabar Rd. Different theme each evening, including Makossa night (Cameroonian music and pop) and Ladies night (free entry for women). There's a small cover and doors open around 8pm, but the real excitement is between midnight and 4am.

Akwa Ibom State

UYO is the capital of the recently formed Akwa Ibom State. Taxis and buses ply the 100-kilometre highway between Uyo and the Calabar motor park, and the local airline, *ADC*, runs a shuttle from Calabar airport. It's a pretty enough town in the mangrove region of the Cross River estuary, but there's little point in making a special effort to come here. If you're passing through, inexpensive **accommodation** can be found at the *Minds Hotel* on Oron Road, where they have rooms with balconies, fans and (usually inoperative) televisions (②). A step up is the *Summit Complex* with its clean, AC rooms and friendly staff (②). Fancier still is the *Tevoli Hotel* (④–⑤), though it's not as well kept as you might expect for the rates.

Between Uyo and Aba is the more traditional town of **Ikot Ekpene**, a pleasant place to stroll around and perhaps see what's on sale at the *Carving and Raffia Weaving Multipurpose Society* (the town has quite a reputation as a crafts centre).

Oron and boats to Cameroon

While the serious territorial dispute over the Bakassi peninsula remains unresolved and Cameroonian and Nigerian troops continue to line each other up in their sights, it is uncertain whether you can cross into Cameroon by sea. Assuming normality returns, the details below are more or less what you'll find.

ORON is the departure point for **boats to Cameroon**. Ferries to Oron from Calabar (25km) leave from near the *Nsikak Hotel*. Boats ply regularly from Oron to the Cameroonian town of **Idenao**, 48km north of **Limbé** (Victoria). Motor boats are the quickest option (three to four hours) for the 150-kilometre sea voyage around the creeks and mangroves, though substantially more expensive than the fishing boats that take up to two days. The latter are commonly taken by local people, but you may be dropped on the coast almost anywhere and then run the risk of missing official entry procedures to Cameroon. Make sure your passport is stamped as soon as possible after arrival.

You'll likely have to spend the night in Oron in order to get an early boat to Cameroon, in which case, decent and affordable **accommodation** can be found at the *Maycom Guest House* (②). You'll find a brilliant collection of regional artwork at Oron's

National Museum, located right next to the ferry dock and easily visited while waiting for a boat. The Oron region is famous for its wood carvings, especially the Ekpo figures, used in ceremonies for communication with ancestors. There are some fine examples on display in the museum which is quite extensive despite the fact that it was greatly damaged in the Biafran conflict. You can pick up a copy of the *Guide to the Oron National Museum* which is full of information about the musical instruments, bronzes, pottery and carvings on display.

Upstate Cross River

The natural vegetation of **Cross River State** is almost entirely **rainforest**, though large reaches have been cleared for oil palm plantations since the turn of the century. Some of the most exciting wildlife and conservation projects in Africa are currently under development in the state: the **Oban Rainforest**, an amazingly rich biosphere, and **Mbe Mountain**, both sponsored by the World Wide Fund for Nature. On paper, these are divisions of the **Cross River National Park**, currently the focus of world attention for its recently discovered **gorilla** denizens. It was thought the gorilla had disappeared from most of West Africa in the last century, and from Nigeria and western Cameroon several decades ago, but the WWF has located at least four separate gorilla populations, mostly around Mbe Mountain, and it's thought there may be several hundred individuals in the park.

Oban Rainforest Reserve

From Calabar, irregular **public transport** to Oban (some 60km along the A4-2 to Ekang) leaves from Watt motor park or from the junction of Ekang Road and Ndideng Usang Iso Road. A more reliable option, though much more costly, would be to **rent a vehicle** and obligatory driver at the *Metropolitan* hotel. This choice gives the flexibility to turn off the road near the village of Aningeje (about 50min from Calabar, look for the sign indicating the Kwa Falls oil palm plantation), and have a wander around the dramatic **Kwa Falls**. The entire stretch to Oban is a rough one, though once you reach the village, the road improves towards the Cameroon border. Just outside Oban village, **accommodation** can be found at the *Jungle Club*, originally set up for oil palm workers. It's quite adequate with simple S/C rooms (①).

Each village between Oban and the border has a Village Liaison Assistant or VLA, a resident employee of the WWF, easily tracked down by asking around town on arrival. Besides providing up-to-date information on the state of the conservation project and how it affects their local communities, the VLAs can arrange **guided treks** in the forest for a reasonable fee. The VLA in Akor is particularly helpful. The forest trail at Mfaminyen (the last village before the border) is the best organized.

For more information, write in advance to WWF, Panda House, Weyside Park, Godalming GU7 1XR, UK, and see if you can be put in touch with field workers; or contact the Cross River National Park office in Calabar (see p.1071).

Ikom and around

The border town of **IKOM** is hardly a Cross River attraction but it's tolerable enough. If you need to stay there are two decent **hotels** both of which have compounds for safe parking – the *Unima* (①) and the *Lisbon*, at 70 Calabar Rd, which is clean but tatty, with torn mosquito netting (①). Ikom has banks (though you will not be able to buy Central African CFA, even if travellers newly arrived from Cameroon can exchange them for Naira) plus a number of shops, and the usual services. If you are making for

Cameroon and arrive early enough in Ikom, it's preferable to move straight on to the border: there are regular taxis to Mfum, 26km away.

The surrounding countryside is famous for the **Ikom Monoliths**, curious stone steles intricately carved with abstract human figures. There are some 300 of these statues spread throughout the area, but the easiest to reach are near the village of Alok, just off the A4, 50km north of Ikom. You can find a guide in the village. Though early estimates traced the monoliths to the sixteenth century, they are now believed to date as far back as 200 AD. Their origins and significance are unclear.

Mbe Mountain National Park

Hidden in the bush between Ikom and Obudu, the **Mbe Mountain National Park** consists of a breathtaking expanse of cloud-drenched mountain forest, home to a number of rare primates, including gorillas, chimpanzees and drills. Other wildlife includes duikers, mountain foxes and porcupines. There are no facilities at the park, and a trek along its trails (plan a couple of days at least) will see you crawling through thickets, forging streams, and grabbing at branches as you slip on mossy boulders. Expect to come out bruised, battered and blistered, and to have a brilliant time.

The World Wide Fund for Nature has a centre outside the town of **Kayang I**, signposted from the road. If you're relying on public transport, ask to be dropped at Kayang I or Kayang II and follow the signs to the centre, or simply ask anyone to show you to the WWF Village Liaison Assistant. Once you've hooked up, he'll take you around to the chief who extracts a fee for visitation rights. It's a solemn affair, but you'll soon be off with a guide through the forest and on your way to places with evocative names like **Gorilla Rock** and **Swimming Pool Camp** (a large splash pool formed by a waterfall cascading into a limestone gully). You camp out along the way, and you should be prepared for dampness and cold. Don't forget provisions and something to start a fire. The guides are extremely informative and seem genuinely interested.

An even less frequented means of entering is via the village of **Buanchor**, further north on the road to Obudu. By public transport, ask to be dropped at the Olum junction. Irregular vehicles pass the junction on their way to Olum village (9km from the road), from where you can walk the remaining 6km to Buanchor. Again, you'll be asked to pay the chief for permission to visit the forest and given a guide. Villagers seem amused by the few visitors that wander through these parts, offering a "you're welcome" at every turn. They'll arrange **accommodation** if you arrive late, and probably set you up with some palm wine, but once you set off through the forest, you'll be camping or sleeping in caves. The guides are good company in addition to being informative and are handy at rustling up forest snails and mushrooms to snack on. You may see gorilla tracks, gorilla nests, gorilla dung and even fruit half-eaten by gorillas, but very few people manage to see the gorillas themselves, or even many of the other monkeys that abound here. The splendid mountain scenery is compensation enough for the difficult hike, however, and any wildlife you see, an extra bonus.

For further **information**, contact the Cross River National Park Mbe Mountain Conservation Project, Kayang Field Station, Boki-Boki LGA, Cross River, or the Cross River National Park office in Calabar (see p.1071). You may be able to get a permit at the latter which would exempt you from paying the local chief, though going over his head is not likely to put you in his good books.

Obudu Cattle Ranch

The best-known attraction in Cross River is **Obudu Cattle Ranch**, in the north of the state. This hill resort-cum-cattle station is spread across the north-facing slopes of Oshie Ridge in the folds of the beautiful **Sonkwala Mountains** (1500–1900m above

CROSSING INTO CAMEROON

The most direct crossing from Calabar is between **Ekang** and **Otu**, at the end of the Oban Rainforest road. Cross River State's main crossing point, however, is southeast of Ikom, from **Mfum** to **Ekok**. Taxis from Ikom stop a few hundred metres before the Nigerian customs and immigration posts at Mfum. At the taxi park, "guides" will try to show you the way, which isn't really necesary.

You should allow a few hours for customs and immigration at Mfum (open 8am–7pm). In the past, officials here have been oppressive in the extreme – confiscating used film for example – and it may require full reserves of humour on your part to rescue the situation. "Yes sir" is important, and you'd better mean it. Once you've filled in your Nigerian exit forms and been questioned, searches are usually fairly limited. You can then be on your way across the bridge into Cameroon (see p.1166).

Ekok, the first small town in Cameroon, is a lively place to stay the night, with something of a a Wild West feel about its bright lights, loud music, hotels and burger bars. There's no bank, however, for changing money into Central African CFA. Naira are acceptable currency for the short journey to Mamfé, but the price will be a lot more than you're officially allowed to export from Nigeria. French francs are probably the best cash to have. Mamfé, Cameroon's first large town, has banks (see p.1165).

sea level). In the 1960s and 1970s Obudu Ranch was a fashionable place for oil industry expats to escape the maddening climate of the delta oil fields, as it offered a virtually European climate and exotic fresh garden produce like strawberries and cauliflowers. Today, the *Ranch* (PO Box 40, Obudu, Cross River State; ④) offers chalet **accommodation** ranging from moderate singles to executive suites, or you can rent a private lodge. The excellent restaurant still serves up home-grown vegetables, chicken and steak. An on-site shop sells necessities like soap, candles, sardines and biscuits and there's a bar. More interesting than the tennis courts (no rackets or balls), putting green and table tennis, are the **walking** opportunities in the district. A path leads from the hotel about 7km to a striking waterfall. Also in the area is a natural spring – "the grotto" – but most interesting is the **Gorilla Camp**, a thirteen-kilometre trek through dense bush, involving some arduous climbing over hills and valleys. A guide is necessary and even if you don't see gorillas (not really very likely), the lush mountain scenery is reward in itself.

The easiest way up here from Calabar is to head to Ikom (take the A4 if driving, not the A4-2). There are usually direct vehicles from Ikom to Obudu village (along the N40), or you can find transport for Ogoja, whence it's 66km to Obudu. In the village, you can rent a taxi or motorbike to the ranch. The road is good all the way and still improving, the final stretch – beset with hairpins as it snakes up to the ranch – a wonderful climax to the trip. Getting away depends on the vagaries of taxis returning to Obudu after dropping other guests, or lorries heading into town. The ranch gets busy during holidays and advance bookings are always advisable – most Nigerian travel agents can help.

CENTRAL NIGERIA

The huge area that is **"Central Nigeria"** is an artificial division, and really consists of the middle margins of the country's more natural divisions into southwest, southeast and north. However, the centre has quite a concentration of interest. If the new federal capital of **Abuja** has nothing to offer but projections for the future, the same cannot be said of one of the country's most favoured towns, **Jos**, on its fine, high plateau of almost

Mediterranean climate. **Bauchi** is less attractive, though pleasantly spacious, while **Yankari Game Reserve**, not far away, is the country's best-organized park and its **Wikki Warm Springs** a pristine attraction in their own right. On the way north, you might consider striking out to the **Borgu Game Reserve** – something that's a lot easier to do with your own vehicle.

Kainji Dam and Borgu Game Reserve

Scenically, climatically and culturally, this area feels more like a part of northern Nigeria, but it's remote and far to the west, and most commonly and easily approached from the south.

Kainji Dam and New Bussa

North of Ilorin (see p.1055) you leave Yorubaland and enter a drier and less mono-ethnic environment, populated by a mix of Nupe, Bussa, Bargu, Kamberi, Fulani and Hausa communities. After some 70km you reach Jebba (off the road to the right) and cross the Niger on a fine, low bridge. At Mokwa, 38km further, the road to the Kainji Dam, New Bussa and Borgu Game Reserve sweeps off to the northwest. There are few towns up here amid the wild bush and dry patchy farmlands. **Zugurma** (24km from Mokwa) is a pretty halt, however, with a fine, jungly stream running past and, beyond, you're sure to see some wildlife – monkeys at least.

Kainji Dam is impressive, though you probably won't be allowed to go onto it – the road runs past it, below. It was just north of here, at Old Bussa, which has now been submerged by the artificial Kainji Lake, that the Scottish explorer Mungo Park was killed in 1805 by people on the bank – who apparently thought he and his expedition was a party of raiding Fulani jihadists.

The local town, **NEW BUSSA**, is dull and scruffy, as you'd expect of a settlement created to house displaced persons whose homes and land lie under water. In town there are various basic hotels, but little of interest. The upmarket *Kainji Tourist Motel* is a modest establishment 3km out of town, with old-fashioned but comfortable S/C chalet rooms and a safari atmosphere, and a wonderful swimming pool which sometimes even contains water (③). It accommodates frazzled expats up from Lagos for the weekend and is the first base for the Borgu Game Reserve whose boundary is 20km west of here. Much cheaper beds can be had at the *Student Hostel* and the *NIFFR Guesthouse* (①) in town.

Borgu Game Reserve

Borgu Game Reserve (also known as Kainji Lake National Park) is open from December to June. It doesn't get a lot of visitors, and it's doubtful if it has a lot of wildlife – in fact it looks certain that much has been poached out. However it's uninhabited by humans, and its 4000-odd square kilometres do contain plentiful numbers of various **antelope** species and there are several families of **hippos** in the pools of the somewhat seasonal Oli River which flows through the reserve. Lions may still roam the bush too, but elephants have not been seen for years.

The roads through Borgu tend to be well maintained. Vehicles can be rented, as can rangers, compulsory companions to your game drive; they are to be found up at the guard post and headquarters in Wawa, where you also pay your entrance fee. Inside the park, on the banks of the Oli River, the *Oli River Lodge* operates during the park's open months (Dec–June) and provides simple, FB **accommodation** with AC (④).

Bida

Heading east towards Abuja from Kainji Dam, you'll pass through the old Nupe capital of **BIDA**. Nupe was an early kingdom, contemporaneous with the Hausa emirates, that lasted from around 1400 until its submission to Fulani rule after the nineteenth-century jihads. The Nupe people (who speak a Kwa language related to Yoruba) are still renowned **crafts experts** and Bida has a reputation as a place to buy locally made metal jewellery, and cylindrical coloured glass "trading beads" whose style is supposed to have originally derived from the markets of medieval Venice.

Crafts

Neither of the town markets particularly reflects Bida's reputation for crafts, but a quick walk along the **Sotamaku Road** brings you to a host of **metal workshops** heralded by a glittering array of brass and aluminum plates, bowls and ornaments. Inside the ateliers, school-age boys pump away at goatskin bellows while their elder brothers reshape old pans and scrap metal using gearbox housings, crankcases and steel rods as anvils. The same sweatshop approach is used in the **Masaga** area where **glass beads** are made from melted down beer and minerals bottles which lend an opaque lustre quite different from the trading beads found elsewhere. Steel rods are dipped into the glass and a single bead is formed as the rod is spun over a furnace. The panoply of patterned beads so formed is then strung on to necklaces or sold singly on roadside stands.

Harder to locate are the traditional Nupe **ten-legged stools** carved from a single piece of wood. Apart from their intricately patterned tops and unsurpassed stability, they are unusual because the seat is cut along the grain of the wood rather than across. Stools can still be bought in local villages, but dealers rapidly snap them up to sell in Lagos where they fetch high prices. If you're keen to buy, start asking around a hundred metres south of the *Total* station, and hopefully someone can lead you to an artisan with some unclaimed stock.

Practicalities

Arriving in Bida, you are likely to be dropped at the motor park on the Abuja–Ilorin road. Most points of interest are within walking distance of here but you may want a taxi to the **hotels** which are on the outskirts of town. The most expensive is the *Bida Guest Inn* with non-AC rooms (PO Box 105; ☎066/461 643; ②). Less costly, but preferable is the *Samola S.G. Guest Inn*, nearly 2km from the centre but with its own restaurant/bar and quite reasonable rooms with fan (PO Box 34; ①). Closest to the centre, but with little else to recommend it is the *Nasara Guest Inn* (PO Box 66; ①). The scope for **eating** is not great, but there is ordinary street food around the *Total* junction.

Abuja

ABUJA has a beautiful setting, with a backdrop of stunning stone inselbergs and a good deal of greenery. But that's about it. There are landscaped avenues with wonderful views across the savannah, an empty ring road called Ring Road 1, which skims miles from the centre in a lemon-shaped, pointless, thirty-kilometre loop, a scattering of snappy administrative and commercial buildings, spaces for city parks – and lots more spaces to be filled by new businesses – and a few uneasy international hotels writing off empty rooms against a less and less promising future. The new federal capital is Nigeria's only well-planned modern city and one day may develop into something exciting. Meanwhile, it's just a great, soulless blueprint on the plains.

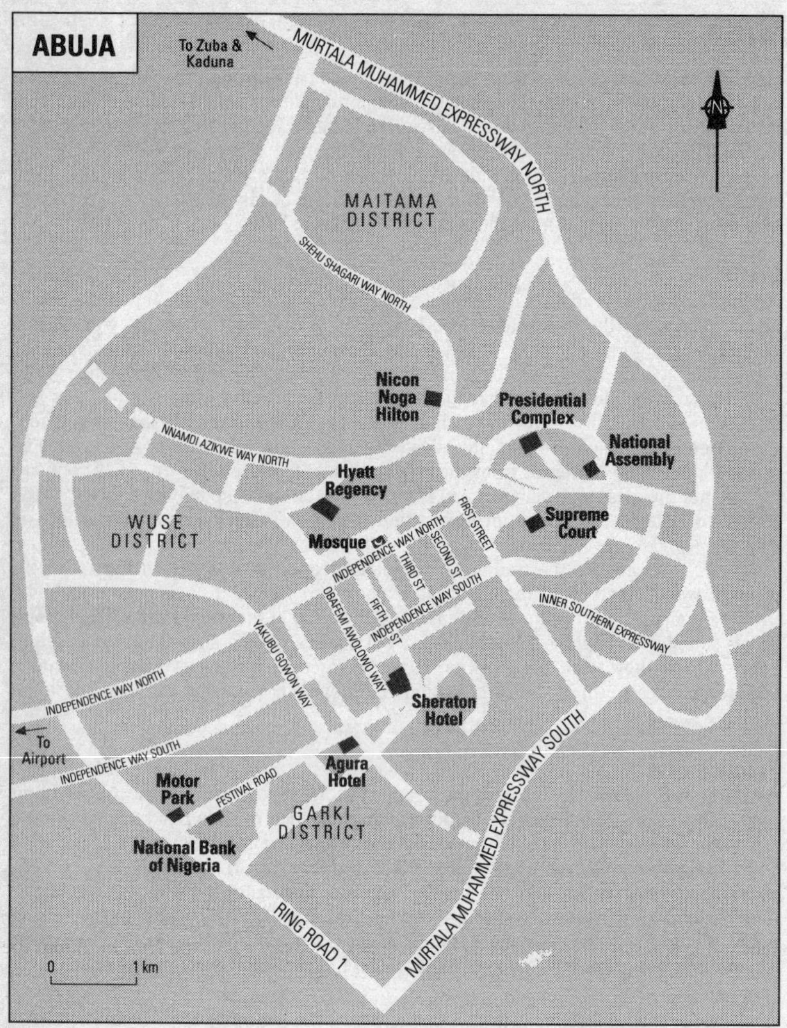

The new capital

The federal government's decision to create a new capital dates from 1976 when the experience of the civil war made it clear that Lagos, with a seventy-five percent Yoruba population, was not conducive to relieving ethnic tensions. Besides, Lagos had already outgrown its capacities. Work on the new capital began in 1981 and, almost overnight, the peaceful setting of this hitherto sparsely populated corner of the Niger State was transformed into Africa's biggest construction site. The enormous cost of creating a city from scratch, especially one with such ambitious designs and such opportunity for misappropriation, led to serious economic difficulties for the civilian presidency of

Shehu Shagari. After the 1983 coup which deposed him, the project came to an abrupt standstill. Although the capital has now officially been transferred from Lagos, Abuja remains unfinished and, in these austere times, progress continues at a snail's pace.

As a result, the city holds little appeal. You can walk for block after block in some parts of the town without passing a single building – nothing but vacant plots and stilled construction sites. The only site you might want to go out of your way to see is the **Central Mosque**, with its large golden dome and fairytale minarets. Many of the proud boulevards lead nowhere and the flyovers fail to fly right over. Indeed half the time, it's hard to believe anyone could still lay their hands on any plans. Although the city is designed with a population of three million in mind, there are as yet no signs of an influx. Few foreign countries have bothered to move their diplomatic missions to Abuja: there's a **British High Commission**, at Shehu Shagari Way (North), Maitama, (☎09/523 2010; Fax 09/523 3552), and an Israeli embassy.

Don't expect to meet an "Abuja local". People living and working here come from all parts of the country and no one considers Abuja home, except perhaps the **Gwari**, the original "sparse population". Partly village-based and partly nomadic, they were unceremoniously evicted from their ancestral lands in the cause of federal glory – which reveals both the ruthlessness of the power elite and the disregard of the urban middle classes for other Nigerians living according to traditional customs. It's sad, and ironic in view of the unifying purpose of the Abuja plan. Today, the Gwari have nearly disappeared as a distinct ethnic and linguistic (Kwa-speaking) community.

Accommodation – and golf

If you have a passion for visiting the bars of **international hotels**, you'll love Abuja. Otherwise, you'd have to be especially interested in urban planning or the sociology of development to find any reason to want to stay. In the continued absence of the projected National Museum, or any other worthy distraction, many travellers resign themselves to one of the air-conditioned cocktail lounges in the *Nicon-Noga Hilton* (PMB 200, PO Box 81; ☎09/523 1811; Fax 09/523 1839; ⑦). With 817 rooms and a huge conference centre, this is the largest hotel in Africa. They feature a happy hour from 6 to 7pm – a good pretext for people-watching. The *Sheraton* (☎09/523 0224; Fax 09/523 1570; ⑦) offers similar diversions, as will, eventually, the *Sofitel* (completed in 1994, but mothballed because of the obvious over-capacity). An alternative, at some stage in the future, may be the *Suleja International Hotel*, a building begun in the early 1980s in the shadow of the Zuma rock, a massive inselberg 50km away on the road to Kaduna: work was suspended when nearly complete, but there is again talk of finishing the job.

Cheap lodging doesn't really exist in Abuja (one of the best deals in town is a Fri and Sat two-nighter for the price of one at either the *Sheraton* or the *Hilton*). About the best you can do is the *Sunny Guest Inn* (PO Box 199; ☎09/523 1881; ③), across from the motor park, or the *Baguda Suite Hotel*, Festival Road (PMB 326; ☎09/523 1563; ③), also near the motor park, in the Garki district in the southern reaches of the city, in what looks like a run-down tenement – you could easily walk by without noticing it. Despite the air-conditioning, TV and fridges, both of these are modest places. You might also try the *Agura Hotel* in Festival Road (☎09/523 1753; ⑤), which has all the perks of the big hotels – pool, tennis, shops, nightclub – but is much cheaper and less pretentious.

Abuja's **IBB Golf Course and Country Club** has opened its first nine holes. This is Phase One (everything in Abuja has a phase number) of an ambitious development which will eventually give the city the best course in Africa. Golf enthusiasts love it – there are no "browns" at the IBB: it's an expensively managed, perfectly green course and fees for the day will set you back a mere ₦500.

MOVING ON FROM ABUJA

The main **motor park** is on Festival Road near the junction with Ring Road 1. Considering this is the federal capital, traffic is limited. Cars and buses leave pretty regularly for **Kaduna**, but departures are rare for other destinations, even Lagos. There is a regular service to **Suleja**, one of the original settlements now swamped by the Federal Capital Territory, which has a much more active motor park. It's often a good plan to go out there if you have trouble getting long-distance transport from Abuja.

If you're in a hurry, there are numeous **flights** to Lagos on various airlines (1hr) and a limited service to Port Harcourt. The two most reliable airlines are *Bellview*, with an office at the *Agura Hotel*, and *ADC*, whose office is in the *Sheraton*.

Jos and around

Set 1200m above sea level, **JOS** enjoys a mild climate that has long attracted Europeans weary of the coastal humidity or the northern heat and dust. Laid out in a beautiful, rocky landscape, the hill resort grew up around **tin mines** exploited by the British at the turn of the century – and still partly managed by expatriates. Jos's history, though, can be traced back much further to the **Nok Culture** (named after the Jos plateau village of the same name) which spread throughout central Nigeria 2500 years ago. Terracotta artefacts left behind by this civilization were discovered quite accidentally in the mines and are today housed in the **Jos Museum**.

This is only one of many sights in a town that seems to have been intentionally designed for visitors. Other diversions include the **zoo** (now slightly depressing) and the **Museum of Traditional Nigerian Architecture**, where lifesize replica buildings from Zaria, Kano, Katsina and other cities have been constructed. Here you can visit the gems of traditional architecture which have largely fallen into disrepair or disappeared altogether in their native cities.

Orientation

The **main market** is an unmistakable landmark, covering a large area in the middle of town. Built after the the old market burned down in 1975, it's a massive modern structure with a wild, colourful design – and it's well stocked to boot. From the market, **Ahmadu Bello Road**, one of the town's main thoroughfares, runs down towards the **post office**. Along this road, you'll find a number of **supermarkets** and several **banks**, although the major ones are behind the post office around Bank Road. You can make **international calls** from *Grukol Ltd* at 10 Ahmadu Bello Rd, though the cost is double that at NITEL, 3km from the centre on the road to Bukuru. Near the post office, **Beach Road** ("The Beach") runs parallel to the railway tracks, across from the main goods yard. Vendors line this street selling a variety of local crafts, with a heavy emphasis on leather and basketwork. A pedestrian bridge leads over the tracks to **Murtala Muhammed Way**, another major thoroughfare, which runs from the redundant train station back down to the main market.

Accommodation

Jos has a variety of places to stay, including several good mission-type guest houses.

COCIN guesthouse, Noad Rd. One of the town's many missionary-orientated places with clean and comfortable rooms where they'll put you up if they have space. ①.

ECWA Guest Inn, off Kano Rd – behind *Challenge Books*. Clean, inexpensive and safe, this is often used by travellers; rooms (including dorms) at various prices, some S/C with hot water. The restaurant serves solid helpings of meals like Irish stew and two veg. ①.

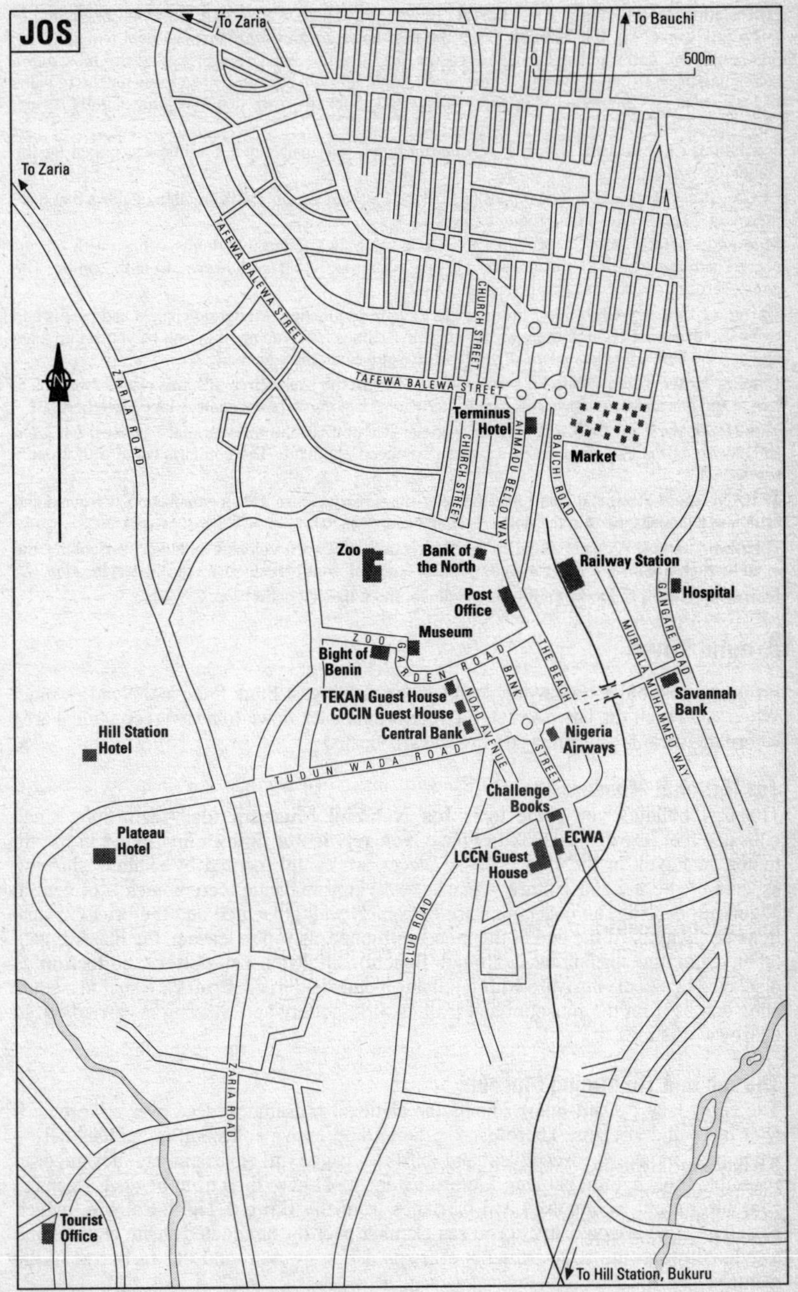
JOS
To Zaria
To Bauchi
0
500m
To Zaria
TAFEWA BALEWA STREET
CHURCH STREET
TAFEWA BALEWA STREET
ZARIA ROAD
Terminus Hotel
AHMADU BELLO WAY
CHURCH STREET
BAUCHI ROAD
Market
Zoo
Bank of the North
Railway Station
Post Office
Hospital
GANGARE ROAD
Museum
ZOO GARDEN ROAD
Bight of Benin
BANK
THE BEACH
MURTALA MUHAMMED WAY
Savannah Bank
TEKAN Guest House
COCIN Guest House
NOAD AVENUE
Central Bank
Nigeria Airways
Hill Station Hotel
TUDUN WADA ROAD
STREET
Challenge Books
Plateau Hotel
ECWA
LCCN Guest House
CLUB ROAD
ZARIA ROAD
Tourist Office
To Hill Station, Bukuru

Hill Station Hotel, Tudun Wada Rd (PO Box 72; ☎073/52808 or 55399). Although beginning to feel a little run-down, this remains easily the best hotel in town, with shops, a pool (small fee for non-residents), and satellite TV in the rooms. An attractive building overlooking the hills, and a refreshing place to come, even if just for a cold drink, it is still something of a focus for the remains of Jos's expat community – call in and you'll get a feel for the town's curious, only slightly lapsed, colonial mentality. ④.

Jos Hotel, Zaria Rd (☎073/55381). A state-run hotel, well maintained if a little overpriced for the standards. ③.

LCCN Guest House, Bank St (opposite *ECWA*). Pleasant gardens with small bungalows that have hot water. Meals in the dining room/lounge. ①.

Moonshine Hotel, Atili St (☎073/55645). Good value for comfortable rooms – those with (clean) shared bath are especially cheap – plus a decent restaurant. A bit far, however, from the centre. The annex across the street is slightly posher. ①–②.

Naraguta Country Club, Ring Rd near the Bauchi Rd junction. Moderate chalets and rooms and extensive grounds. Though there are no specific facilities for camping, they will let you set up tents and use the baths of empty rooms if available. Helpful expat management. ②.

Plateau Hotel, Tudun Wada Rd (☎073/55740). One of the state-run hotels, this place is well maintained and has a pleasant swimming pool. Occasional live music performances take place here. ③.

Tati Hotel, Zaria Rd (☎073/52554). In a pricier league than the mission guest houses, but good value, with extras like phones and a popular weekend nightclub. The comforts come with friendly service. ②.

TEKAN Guest House, 6 Noad Ave. Another missionary centre with inexpensive S/C rooms and even less expensive beds in the dorm. Friendly and clean. ①.

Terminus Hotel, Ahmadu Bello Rd. An attractive, timeworn colonial building overlooking the main market. Rooms are clean and comfortable – it's a decent bargain given the central location. ②.

Universal Hotel, 11 Pankshin Rd. Great value – and it has hot baths! ①.

Around Town

From the post office, follow the road leading uphill past Bank Road and Noad Avenue. When you reach the latter street, the road winds back down to a vast recreational area where the various museums and the zoo are located.

Jos National Museum

The first building you come to is **Jos National Museum** (daily 8am–6pm; small entrance fee), created in 1952 to house **Nok terracotta figures** first found in the tin mines near Nok in the 1920s. These pieces are complemented by exhibits showing aspects of the art and culture – masks, weaving, medicine, ceremonies – of central Nigerian peoples. The collections are extremely well presented and the brief explanations are helpful. At the end of the museum (notice, as you're leaving, the massive gate taken from the ancient wall around Bauchi), an extensive **pottery collection** is displayed in a cool courtyard with fountains, ponds and trees. **Crafts** are sold in a small shop across from the museum and leatherwork, pottery and weaving is carried out in nearby workshops.

The zoo and Tin Mining Museum

The **zoo** (daily 7.30am–6pm) adjoins the National Museum, spread over a large park with trees and streams. There used to be an impressive collection of animals here – antelopes, monkeys, crocodiles and birds – caged in environments designed to resemble their natural habitats. Unfortunately, most have died from neglect. Near the zoo, several old locomotives and carriages from the **Bauchi Light Railway** (which closed in 1959) are on display. You can clamber over the antiquated steam engines and wander through the compartments of trains dating from around the early part of the century.

Also nearby, the **Tin Mining Museum** (daily 7.30am–6pm) is dedicated to the history and technology of mining in the area. If you're minded to find out more about how the metal is extracted – it's a wet and messy, open-cast business requiring considerable land rehabilitation – try contacting the *Nigerian Tin Mining Company Ltd* (PMB 2036, Jos; ☎073/80632) for a **guided tour**.

Museum of Traditional Nigerian Architecture

Probably the most unusual museum, and one well worth spending some time to discover, is the **Museum of Traditional Nigerian Architecture** (MOTNA), which covers a vast area behind the zoo. Full-scale reproductions of the country's most impressive monuments have been built on the site. You get a better idea of the magnitude of the **Kano Wall** here than you do in its city of origin, especially if you climb the narrow staircase leading to the top. The **Zaria Friday Mosque** with its impressive vaulting reveals the highly sophisticated technical skills of the Hausa. There are also smaller copies of the **Katsina Palace** and the **Ilorin mosque**. Be sure to agree a price before entering.

Jos Wildlife Park

Not to be confused with the miserable zoo in town, the **Jos Wildlife Park**, 14km southwest of the town off the Bukuru road (daily 10am–dusk; small charge), is a more worthwhile encounter. The drive-through park, covering an area of about eight square kilometres, contains a variety of antelopes and monkeys, lions in a large enclosure, some elephants, and various other species, a few of which are in ordinary cages near the entrance. If you're in a 4WD vehicle, you should be able to make it to the observation tower at the highest point in the park, where there's a good view of Jos and the plateau. Otherwise, rent a taxi in Jos for a three-hour visit, or take Bukuru-bound public transport, which can drop you at the junction for the road to Miango to the west. The park entrance is 4km down this road: if it's a weekend, you might get a lift with other visitors.

Eating

Eating out in Jos isn't a richly satisfying experience, but you should find something reasonable among the following. The *Bight of Benin* and the *Cedar Tree* have long-established reputations.

Andalucia Restaurant, 41 Yakubu Gowon Way (☎073/56137). To add to its exotic name, this offers Lebanese dishes prepared by a Russian chef. Good food, generously served.

Bevelyns, 2 Ahmadu Bello Rd. A central place for African and European eating at fair prices.

Bight of Benin, Zoo Garden Rd, near the museum. Good cooking, in a replicated Benin noble's house. A cool place to take a break, with a limited menu of national specialities at reasonable prices.

Cedar Tree Restaurant, 17 Yakubu Gowon Way, out of the centre in the Bukuru direction. Well-prepared Lebanese and European fare at reasonable prices.

Palace Restaurant. The Chinese restaurant of the *Hill Station Hotel*, with indifferent food and poor service.

Sharazad, Yakubu Gowon Way. Near the *Cedar Tree*, this restaurant features a similar, Euro-Lebanese menu, though there's a limited range of Chinese dishes here as well.

Starbok, Bank Rd near Museum Rd. Toasted sandwiches and fish and chips type meals complement Nigerian specialities.

Jos Plateau

If you want to get into the **Jos Plateau** countryside, take a taxi or minibus out to Bukuru from the end of Tafawa Balewa Street, near the market. Get out somewhere en route and camp, or stay in the very nice *Yelwa Club* in Bukuru, which has a pool and is surprisingly cheap. For **camping**, the Vom area to the southwest of Jos is pretty, with

MOVING ON FROM JOS

The main motor park for the **east**, **northeast** and **southeast** is the Bauchi Road Motor Park, 3km north of the centre. Daily bus services to **Calabar** and **Port Harcourt** are operated by *Crosslines* and depart in the morning from here. Bus services to **Bauchi** and **Maiduguri** are run by *Yankari Express*, who park next to *Crosslines*. The main motor park for the northwest, including **Kano** and **Kaduna**, and for **Lagos**, is the Zaria Road Motor Park, out of the town centre to the northwest.

There have been no **train services** on the Jos branch line for several years.

There are daily **flights to Lagos** on *Nigeria Airways*, via Abuja on Mon, Tues, Thurs and Sat, and via Kadun on Wed, Fri and Sun. There are no international flights out of Jos, but airline offices in town include: *British Airways*, 41 Murtala Muhammed Way (☎073/53547); *KLM, Plateau Hotel* (☎073/52185); and *Nigeria Airways*, 6 Bank St (☎073/52298).

plenty of good grassy spots amid boulders and groves of gum trees. **Vom** itself has a mission and veterinary labs servicing its dairy where, on weekdays, you can sample fresh Friesian milk at next to nothing a litre and wonderful cheese. In the plateau farmland they grow apples and strawberries for export; McDonalds is planning a daily 747-load of lettuces to supply the green bits in its European burgers.

Off the plateau: routes into Cameroon

Heading south from Jos the topography is complex and travel delightful. Forests of gum trees spread around **Panyam** and from here on the road (surfaced, whatever the maps may say) drops down a breathtaking escarpment through coniferous woods and Mediterranean landscapes to **Shendam** and **Yelwa**. It's fine cycling country; otherwise, apart from one or two exhausting through bus services to big cities in the southeast, travelling by road becomes chancy as you get into this eastern part of Central Nigeria. If you're travelling south on this road into Taraba State, you're in a position to make an unusual entry into the **North West Province of Cameroon** (see p.1117). The more direct route south from the Jos Plateau follows the A3 and A4 into **southern Cameroon**, a regular driving route bringing you to Mamfé and the highway for Douala.

Makurdi

MAKURDI, the capital of Benue State, lies roughly midway between Jos and Cameroon, on the south bank of the Benue River on the fringes of Igboland. It's a fair-sized town with several small and medium **hotels**; the *Dolphin* – part of a complex of cinemas, restaurants and lodgings in Secretariat Road to the north of town – is clean, welcoming and inexpensive. If you need a **travel agent** in Makurdi, *Chuben*, 35A Bank Rd (☎044/32060) is reliable.

Bauchi and Yankari National Park

Northeast from Jos, the road drops down from the plateau in a spectacular curve, turns east and then runs across featureless plains to **BAUCHI**, capital of the state of the same name. Bauchi is a large impersonal place with wide avenues and ranks of office buildings, though it gives a more exotic first impression if approached from the north down the A3 Kano/Maiduguri route, which lines up a grand assembly of inselbergs known as the Belo Hills, shortly before you reach town.

After the Fulani jihad, in the 1840s, an Emirate was established at Bauchi. But despite the **Emir's palace** and the **old mosque**, the town has little of enduring interest. Bauchi is the nearest big centre to **Yankari National Park** and if you don't have transport you'll very likely have to spend a night here before getting to the reserve.

If you're stuck waiting for transport, you could spend an interesting half-hour at the **Mausoleum of Tafawa Balewa**, Nigeria's first prime minister, especially weekdays when you may get a chance to see a video of his Independence speech. A tour of the complex (daily 7am–6pm) takes you up a ramp through regions of dark and light symbolizing colonial repression and the hope of independence and leads to the roofless mausoleum. The concrete and stone are austere, but it remains a powerful monument to the fight for self-determination.

Bauchi practicalities

In 1991, sectarian fighting resulted in a fire that swept through the Bayan Gari district and gutted many of Bauchi's **inexpensive hotels**. Most have reopened, and there are a dozen or more all charging about the same price. The *Rendez-Vous Hotel* (pronounced "rendezz-voos"; ①) stands out because of its friendly management. The *Derkerker Lodge* on Murtala Muhammed Road is no cheaper, but a lot less appealing (①). The *Karama Hotel*, across from the **Gombe motor park**, also has reasonably priced accommodation and is conveniently located if you're planning to catch an early taxi to the national park (①). The **expensive hotels** in town are the *Awalah* (☎077/42344; ④) which has a swimming pool, tennis and AC rooms with colour TV, and the *Zaranda* (☎077/435 909; ④), featuring similar luxuries. The *Zaranda* is where you book for *Yankari Lodge* and can arrange transport to Yankari too.

For **flights** on *Nigeria Airways*, the closest airport is **Jos** – enquiries and bookings at 40 Kobi St, Bauchi (☎077/42800).

Yankari National Park

Yankari National Park (open Nov–June) was the first game reserve in Nigeria and it remains the most popular. It covers over 2200 square kilometres of protected bush, but despite the best efforts, poaching is still widespread and has taken its toll on the once abundant wildlife. You're likely to see herds of **gazelle and antelope**, and **elephants** with a little luck, but **lions**, which still hunt in the park, are getting increasingly shy and elusive. Other animals include warthogs, hippos, waterbuck, buffalos, several species of duiker, hartebeest, various monkeys and crocodiles.

In addition to the animals, **Wikki Warm Springs** provides reason of its own to come to the park. If you have any difficulty organizing game-viewing trips at the lodge, you probably won't be unhappy spending your time in its crystal-clear waters.

Getting there

There is no regular transport from Bauchi to *Wikki Warm Springs Lodge* (the main focus in Yankari). If you don't have a car you can take a **collective taxi** from the Gombe station on the east side of Bauchi. These vehicles can drop you at **Dindima** on the highway, where the Yankari road splits off south – or they sometimes go to villages along the latter road and will let you off right in front of the park gate en route. Either way, you still have to get a lift for the rest of the journey with incoming visitors (if you inform the guards at the gate you're looking for a ride into the park, they're usually pretty good about asking the cars on their way in). Note that in the middle of the week and on certain quiet weekends, the park may be devoid of visitors, in which case you could be really stuck. For that reason, avoid setting off from Bauchi in the late afternoon, hoping to make it all the way to the camp. Another way of getting to the camp is to **charter a taxi** in Bauchi and arrange a price with the driver – you'd pay around £40 ($60). If you're **cycling**, the road from Bauchi highway to Wikki is a fine and exciting day's ride in the park, with no access problems, and no serious worries about animals.

Accommodation

If you're visiting the park on a weekend or any major holiday, it's a good idea to make advance **reservations**. The lodge gets very full, particularly at Easter. You can book by contacting the *Yankari Game Reserve and Tourism Company Ltd* direct (PO Box 12, Bauchi; ☎077/42174 or 43675), by enquiring at the *Zaranda Hotel* in Bauchi, or by fixing things up several days beforehand with any local travel agency.

Yankari has recently been taken over by a private company but, although prices have gone up substantially, it's still relatively inexpensive. There's a small entrance fee at the gate, then, arriving at the camp, a range of accommodation which all turns out to be of the same mediocre standard. Still, a double chalet costs a little more than a cheap hotel in Bauchi, though water and electricity are frequently off during the day (and routinely go off at a set time late each evening).

For food, the **restaurant** near the lodge serves European meals at reasonable prices – and it could be a lot worse considering there's no alternative. To save money, bring provisions from Bauchi and do your own cooking. A pleasant **outdoor bar** overlooks the savannah, and the lodge has a small **natural history museum** (free) – well laid out and full of local tales.

Game-viewing

Morning and afternoon **game-runs** are organized at the lodge. If you don't have your own car, you can go on one of the camp vehicles (a lorry with benches in the back) for a fee, provided they get enough people together to form a worthwhile group. If you have your own vehicle, you must take one of the rangers – which isn't a bad idea anyway, as they're most likely to know where to see animals and can direct you to other sites like the **Marshall Caves**, believed to have once been inhabited, or the **Borkono Falls**. On any drive – assuming you go early in the morning, which is best, or late afternoon – you'll see antelope and gazelles of various species, and there's every likelihood you will see elephants. To see any predators at all, however, you'd need to be very lucky.

Wikki Warm Springs

Below the restaurant, a steep path leads down to **Wikki Warm Springs**. It's hard to imagine any site in West Africa more completely satisfying from a hedonistic point of view. Twelve million litres a day of perfectly clear, clean water at a steady ideal temperature of 31°C comes bubbling up from a dark hole at the bottom of a deep pool, at the base of a steep, sheltering cliff. Nothing, save perhaps the persistent hassles of monkeys and baboons, detracts from the site's beauty. From its source, the water flows out for a hundred metres or more past steep banks of overhanging foliage, over a bed of glistening sand. It's almost too pretty, especially at night when it's lit by floodlamps – like an elaborate bit of New Age interior design.

The access side of the stream is concreted over, which keeps it clean, and there are parts shallow enough for toddlers to enjoy, and deeper areas for bigger swimmers. Downstream, camp staff wash clothes and bathe. Access is free if you're staying at the camp but there's a charge if you're just here for the day – as, at weekends, rather a lot of people are. If you take food or valuables down there, watch out for those monkeys.

THE NORTH AND EAST

Formerly a conglomeration of disunited and often warring emirates, the **Hausa country** spreads over the arid **savannah** of the northern plateaux and comprises the largest geographical entity in Nigeria. In this vast region,.Hausa makes sense as a linguistic grouping rather than an ethnic one, since there are many different northern peoples. The religious and in many respects political head of all the Hausa peoples is in fact a Fulani – the **Sultan of Sokoto** – and has been for over 180 years. Thanks to the common faith of **Islam** and the *lingua franca* of Hausa, however, a bond has been created among northerners that puts them politically at an advantage over the south.

The area near **Lake Chad** in the northeast of the country is peopled by the **Kanuri**, who, around the ninth century, migrated from the northern, desert regions of Kanem to form the new empire of Bornu which grew rich on **trans-Saharan trade**. In the context of the current Federal Republic, this kingdom translates roughly into the **Borno State** with its capital in **Maiduguri**, the only major town in the rather depressed northeast. Further west, the **Hausa city states** (the *Hausa Bokwai*: Gobir, Katsina, Kano, Zaria, Daura, Rano and Biram) developed into powerful emirates from around the eleventh century and had partially converted to Islam by 1400. Old walled cities from this era still exist in **Katsina**, **Zaria** and **Kano**. Kano today is a major urban centre, with international airport and diverse industries. Development has come more slowly to the conservative Islamic stronghold of **Sokoto**, the spiritual capital of the north, while **Kaduna** is a much more anonymous, modern town neatly laid out by the British colonials as an uncontroversial administrative capital.

This section also includes the remote eastern reaches of Nigeria – the states of **Adamawa** and **Taraba** – where the moutain forests remain poorly mapped and very little travelled. Here, there are some fine opportunities for hiking and some unusual options for routes into Cameroon.

Birnin Gwari

If you're driving north towards Kaduna on the A1 and A125, you go through the town of **Birnin Gwari** (or Sabon Birnin Gwari). There's a **wildlife reserve** here with the basic *Birnin Gwari Hotel* just outside (①). It's only been open a few years and has so far allowed access only on foot. In terms of accessibility and visible game – it has a small herd of elephants and other savannah species along with a mass of birdlife – it looks set to rival Yankari.

Kaduna

With no palace (the town was formerly a fief of the Zaria Emirate), no city wall and no ancient mosque, **KADUNA** is essentially a **modern town** of broad avenues, with an oil refinery, a good smattering of industry and a bustling business environment. It's not the kind of place you'd want to spend weeks or even days discovering (indeed there's not much to find), but hitting upon this kind of cosmopolitan atmosphere, second only to Kano in the north, is not completely disagreeable either, especially if you've just arrived from the remote rural areas of Niger or Nigeria.

TOURIST INFORMATION

The **Tourist Information Centre** is near the KSBC Radio station, on Wurno Road, off Alli Akilu Road, at the northern end of town.

HAUSA ORAL HISTORY: THE ORIGIN OF THE SEVEN STATES

The Hausa have a rich oral literature outside the overweening influence of more recent Islamic tales. In folk history, the origin of their states is traced to **Bayajida**, son of the king of Baghdad, who fled his homeland afer a bitter dispute with his father. After years of wandering he arrived in Bornu and was recognized as a natural leader by the *Mai* or king, who gave one of his daughters in marriage to the boy. Bayajida fell out with his father-in-law, and fled again, with his pregnant wife, to a place called Garun Gabas. He left his Bornu wife here, where she gave birth to a son, **Biram**, who later established the first of the *Hausa Bokwai*, named after him, in the area to the east of Kano. Meanwhile Bayajida had taken off again for the west and, in the middle of the night, fetched up at Daura, a place east of Katsina that was ruled at the time by a dynasty of queens. He stopped an old woman, Ayana, to ask for water and was told it was the wrong day of the week: the snake who owned the well only allowed people to draw water on a Friday. Nobody had been able to kill the snake. Bayajida, of course, went straight to the well, woke up the snake and chopped its head off. Then he drank his fill, pocketed the head and moved on. The next day was Friday and the queen wanted to know who had killed the snake. Ayana told her about the stranger and the queen sent messengers to catch up with the restless Bayajida, who agreed to return – and then asked her to marry him as a reward. They had a son, **Bawo**. Following the death of Bayajida, Bawo's own six sons went on to found the remaining towns of the *Hausa Bokwai* – Daura, Katsina, Kano, Rano, Gobir and Zaria.

Coming up from southern Nigeria, Kaduna is usually looked on as the first town of the north. This is a slightly misleading assumption since it doesn't have much in common with the other towns in this section. It's a place, however, that on any major travels through Nigeria, you're unlikely to avoid.

A short history

Originally conceived as the capital of the Northern Region, and perhaps the entire federation, Kaduna represents one of the best examples of a town created to be the seat of government. The original **northern capital** was at Zungeru, on the Kaduna river 150km southwest of Kaduna, but when **Sir Frederick Lugard** became governor of the amalgamated colonial federation in 1912, he shifted the site to the small town of Kaduna which had the advantage of being near a good water supply and on the line of the newly constructed railway. Within easy striking range of all the former emirates, the spot was also strategically important. The West African Frontier Force moved here from Zaria in 1912, and in 1917 the civil administration was transferred from Zungeru.

Kaduna lost its role as capital of northern Nigeria when the states were created in 1967, but it has continued to thrive as a centre for the army (in 1965, 28 percent of the city's area was taken up by the armed forces) and industry. Near Nigeria's main cotton growing region, Kaduna contains several textile mills, a vast oil refinery, the Peugeot assembly plant, a brewery and an ordnance factory.

Accommodation

Kaduna has a good range of hotels for all budgets, including one of the best in the north, and a clutch of decent cheap lodgings on Constitution Road.

Central Hotel, Benue Rd. One of the centre's cheaper options if you can live with the basic rooms (shared showers and toilets) and raucous environment. ①.

Durbar Hotel, near the junction of Waff Rd and Independence Way (PMB 2218; ☎062/201 100 or 201 108). One of the nicest hotels in northern Nigeria, with 311 luxury rooms including suites; 3 restaurants, 4 bars and a nightclub; sports facilities including 50-metre pool and tennis; car rental; shops and a well-stocked bookshop. ⑤.

Durncan, 6 Katsina St. Comfortable AC rooms with TV: good value in the moderate range. ②.

ECWA Guest House, Alli Akilu Rd. Small guesthouse with dorm rooms. Although reserved for ECWA staff, they'll let you have a bed if one's available (ask at *Challenge Books*). ①.

Fina White House Hotels, Constitution Rd (☎062/216 418 or 211 852). Actually three establishments near each other, with rooms of varying degrees of comfort and sanitation. The better ones have TV and fridge. ②.

Gloria Moria Hotel, on Junction Rd, towards the Kaduna River (☎062/214 501). Clean S/C, AC rooms and a restaurant. ③.

Hamdala Hotel, Kashim Ibrahim Rd (PO Box 311; ☎062/211 005). Upmarket hotel with TV and video in newly renovated rooms, a good restaurant and a large, but somewhat cloudy, swimming pool. ④.

Kimbo Hotel, Constitution Rd. Not quite as nice as others on the street, but its AC rooms are decent enough and quite a bit cheaper. ②.

Safari Hotel, 10 Argungu St (☎062/211 838). Rooms with shared facilities. A little grubby, but inexpensive and central. ①.

The Town

Kaduna's vast and purposeful layout reflects its former function as seat of government. **Administrative buildings** line Independence Way, one of the principal tree-lined avenues, including, at the northern end, the monumental **Lugard Hall** with its impressive dome – now government offices – the GRA for senior officers, various administrative buildings and the junior staff quarters. The golf course and racecourse are nearby.

The main commercial axis, **Ahmadu Bello Way**, runs in a north–south direction parallel to Independence Way. Main offices and businesses are along this street as are most of the banks, restaurants and hotels. In the extreme north of town, Ahmadu Bello Way becomes Alli Akilu Road.

Past the State House on Alli Akilu Road, the **Kaduna National Museum** (daily 9am–6pm; free) houses a small collection of masks, musical instruments, leather and brass work and miscellaneous ethnographia. Its **Gallery of Nigerian Prehistory** traces the country's past back to neolithic times (the New Stone Age ended in parts of Nigeria, as in many other parts of West Africa, only over the last two thousand years), and examples of Nok terracotta and bronzes from Ife and Benin also figure in the exhibition. It doesn't take very long to look round the museum, but the exhibits are well presented and documented. Behind, a **Hausa village** has been recreated, and **traditional crafts** – weaving, forging, leatherwork – are carried out in the different buildings. Just north of the museum, the **Arewa House** in Rabah Road, off Alli Akilu Road, was the residence of Sir Ahmadu Bello, the Sardauna of Sokoto, when he served as Regional Premier of Northern Nigeria. It now contains a library with archives and pleasant gardens.

Kaduna's large **market** is off Ahmadu Bello Way, in the centre of the commercial area. As in many northern cities, it's a good place to get leather goods and cloth, although most of the area is dedicated to plastic ware, factory clothes and other modern goods. There's a good food section at the back of the market with a range of fruit and vegetables. Further south, Ahmadu Bello Way changes name to become Junction Road, then crosses the bridge spanning the **Kaduna River** to Kaduna South – the industrial side of town.

If you fancy getting out of town a little, the **river bank** on the northeast side of town is a recommended area, though somewhat difficult to get to. Get a town taxi and ask for Malali village – or just "village" and get out near Malali "GTC" on Rabah Road. A walk parallel to the school, then over the hill through a housing estate, brings you down to the river. You can watch fishermen and lounge around on the rocks in relative peace and quiet.

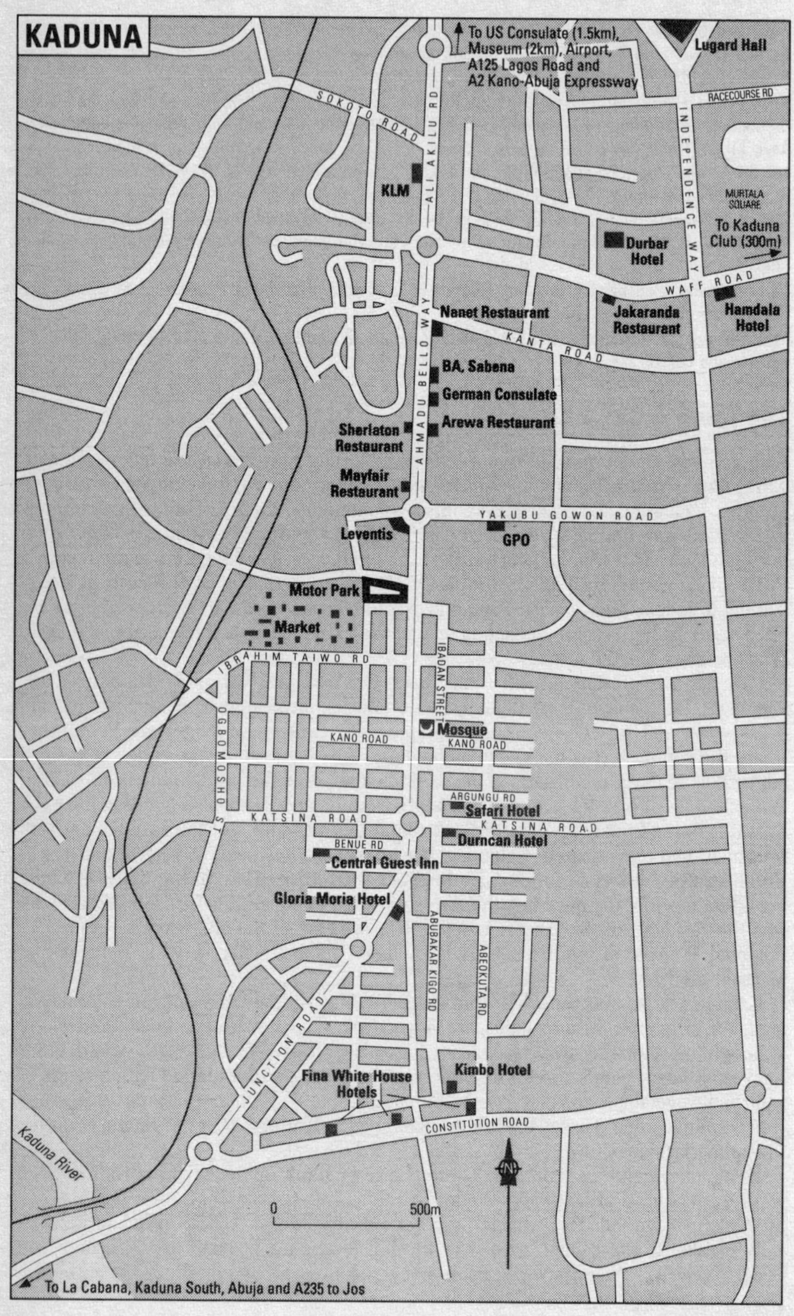
KADUNA
To US Consulate (1.5km), Museum (2km), Airport, A125 Lagos Road and A2 Kano-Abuja Expressway
Lugard Hall
RACECOURSE RD
SOKOTO ROAD
ALI AKILU RD
INDEPENDENCE WAY
KLM
MURTALA SQUARE
To Kaduna Club (300m)
Durbar Hotel
WAFF ROAD
Nanet Restaurant
Jakaranda Restaurant
Hamdala Hotel
KANTA ROAD
AHMADU BELLO WAY
BA, Sabena
German Consulate
Sherlaton Restaurant
Arewa Restaurant
Mayfair Restaurant
YAKUBU GOWON ROAD
Leventis
GPO
Motor Park
Market
IBRAHIM TAIWO RD
IBADAN STREET
OGBOMOSHO ST
Mosque
KANO ROAD
KANO ROAD
ARGUNGU RD
Safari Hotel
KATSINA ROAD
KATSINA ROAD
Durncan Hotel
BENUE RD
Central Guest Inn
Gloria Moria Hotel
ABUBAKAR KIGO RD
ABEOKUTA RD
JUNCTION ROAD
Kimbo Hotel
Fina White House Hotels
CONSTITUTION ROAD
Kaduna River
N
0
500m
To La Cabana, Kaduna South, Abuja and A235 to Jos

Restaurants

If you're a *suya* fan, there's a big spot for them and other street food outside the *Durbar Hotel*. More upmarket alternatives are scattered around the centre; the *Jakaranda Farm and Pottery* is essentially a weekend excursion.

Arabian Sweets, 5b Yakubu Ave. Turkish coffee, fresh juices and real ice cream. Sister to the restaurant of the same name in Kano.

Arewa Chinese Restaurant, Ahmadu Bello Way. Generally considered to have the best oriental food in Kaduna – if not the whole of Nigeria – and they do a splendid buffet on Sat.

La Cabana, Junction Rd opposite the train station. Lebanese and French food, popular with expats. This place also runs a good disco at nights and can be a lot of fun.

Jakaranda, Waff Rd, opposite the *Durbar Hotel*. Excellent African and European specialities including seafood.

Jakaranda Farm and Pottery, Mile 20, Katchia road, southeast of Kaduna (lunch only). Beautiful outdoor restaurant with crocodile pool, landscaped water garden and fruit orchards. Excellent African and European food (weekend buffets), and exotic cocktails. And they produce pottery, as will hardly escape your notice.

Les Boro, Rabah Rd extension, Malali village. Moderately priced Nigerian and English dishes (it's good to combine it with a visit to the riverside by taxi).

Mayfair, Ahmadu Bello Way. Slightly formal, mid-price restaurant, but recommended for a cooked breakfast of omelettes, chips and sausage.

Nanet Restaurant, 6 Ahmadu Bello Way. Up the street and across the road from *Mayfair*. Mostly African food "well-prepared and attractively served" they say, and indeed they deliver solid meals, not overpriced or overspiced, served in a large, fresh dining area.

Patisserie Francaise, 3 Kinshasa Rd (Mon–Sat 9.30am–8pm). French bread, croissants and tempting chocolate cakes.

Sherlaton Restaurant, Ahmadu Bello Way opposite the *Arewa* (☎062/210 021 or 214 488). Excellent Indian food that compares well with the sister restaurant in Lagos.

Listings

Airline offices and agents include: *British Airways*, Development House, 18 Ahmadu Bello Way (☎062/212 815 or 217 315); *Kabo Airlines*, Ahmadu Bello Way (good value for domestic flights); *KLM*, Philips House, 4 Alli Akilu Rd (☎062/212 419 or 217 228); *Nigeria Airways*, 26 Ahmadu Bello Way (☎062/210 174 or 210 298); *Sabena*, Development House, 18 Ahmadu Bello Way (☎062/210 034).

Banks The banking district is around the intersection of Ahmadu Bello Way and Yakubu Gowon Rd. You'll find main branches here and should have no trouble changing major international currencies (though preferably dollars or pounds) either in cash or travellers' cheques.

MOVING ON FROM KADUNA

The town's **main motor park** is adjacent to the market; but note that Kaduna is bypassed by the highway (A1/A125) between Lagos and the north. The motor park for Lagos is **Mando Motor Park**, for Zaria and Kano, **New Kawo Motor Park**, both at the top of Alli Akilu Rd.

Kaduna Junction **train station** is just south of the river bridge. Kaduna grew up with the railway and is Nigeria's major railway town, with services, in theory, to Maiduguri, Kano, Port Harcourt and Lagos. At the time of publication, and for over a year now, services nationwide have been suspended.

According to the (not altogether reliable) schedules there are at least daily **flights to Lagos** from Kaduna on *Nigeria Airways*. In addition, *Kabo Air*, 11 Alli Akilu Rd (☎062/242 248 or 242 249), provides domestic service to a number of cities.

British Council Yakubu Gowon Way (☎062/236 033; Fax 062/216 330). In theory you have to be a member to use the library, but if you explain that you're passing through and want to catch up on the British press, you're likely be allowed in. They also show films and run the occasional exhibition.

Consulates American Consulate, 2 Moska Rd (☎062/213 074); British Deputy High Commission, 2/4 Lamido Road (PMB 2096; ☎062/233 380; Fax 062/237 267); German Consulate, 22 Ahmadu Bello Way (☎062/223 696).

Post office The GPO is on Yakubu Gowon Rd in the heart of the banking district. The poste restante is reasonably reliable.

Supermarkets There's a large *Chellarams* and a *Leventis* on Ahmadu Bello Way near the intersection with Yakubu Gowon Rd. Also try the *Kurfi Memorial Shopping Centre* on Alkali Rd, north of the racecourse.

Zaria

One of the seven *Hausa Bokwai*, the old town of **ZARIA** has withstood the tests of time rather better than most of the other emirates. The **ancient wall** has largely crumbled away, but some of the old gates have been restored and are very impressive, and the **Emir's Palace** is a beautiful example of traditional architecture. Nearby, the **Friday Mosque** was formerly one of the most magnificent in the region, though it's now enclosed by a plain-looking modern structure. Almost all the homes in old Zaria are built in the traditional style and many display the detailed exterior decoration for which the town is famous.

After the British arrived, a new town – **Sabon Gari** – was built some 3km north of the walled city, across the **Kubani River**, and this is the quarter where you'll arrive if coming in from Sokoto or Kano. In the centre, the **train station** and the main **motor park** stand next to each other on Main Street. It was in this part of town that, early this century, Yoruba and Igbo traders settled near the tracks. The new town's **main market** is in the neighbourhood, with **banks** and major businesses nearby around Crescent Road and Park Road. Hospital Road leads south across the bridge to the **Tudan Wada** neighbourhood where most of the infrastructure is located – the hospital, schools and teacher training colleges. Zaria is noted for the **radical student life** of Ahmadu Bello University. Over the years it has been the scene of a number of violent clashes with the security forces.

Accommodation

It's quite possible to arrive in Zaria in the morning, take a look around, and then head out of town again before evening. If you want to stay, however, you'll find a number of pleasant, inexpensive hotels and one that's a cut above what you might expect.

Beauty Guest Inn, Sokoto Rd. Clean AC rooms but far from the town centre. ②.

Kongo Conference Hotel, Old Jos Rd (PO Box 1068; ☎069/32872). The town's nicest with pool, tennis courts, restaurants and bar. One of the few places in Zaria with reliable cold beer, even during Ramadan. ⑤.

Kuta Hotel, off Hospital Rd, between Zaria old town and Sabon Gari (☎069/33268). Dusty non-S/C rooms, with balconies giving onto the courtyard, have character though the AC and water no longer work. Restaurant (but no alcohol). ①.

Royal Guest House, Park Rd. Conveniently located near the motor parks and market. Not bad, and very cheap. ①.

Zaria Hotel, Sokoto Rd (☎069/32820 or 32829). Frequent buses to Zaria centre stop nearby. Clean AC rooms, restaurant and bar in a quiet neighbourhood. Friendly staff and an excellent bookstore. Good value all round. ②.

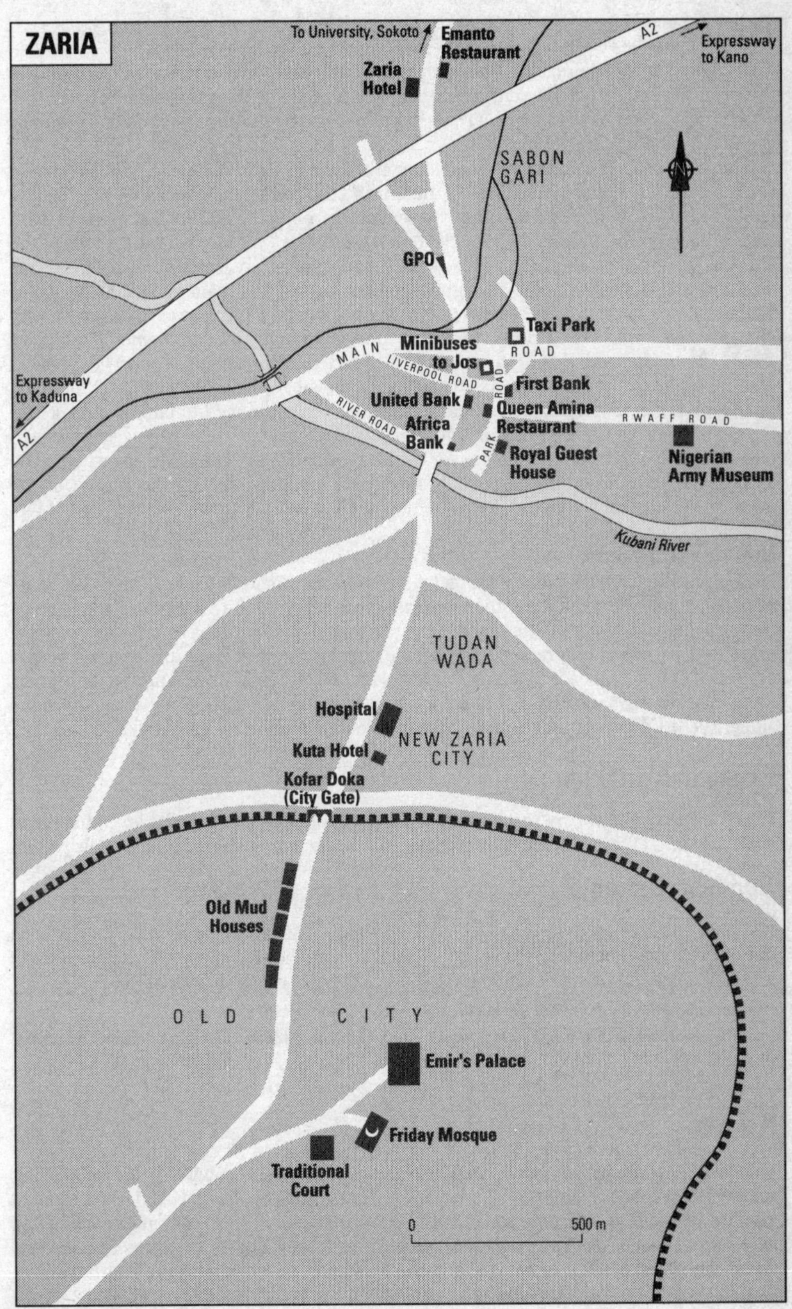
ZARIA
To University, Sokoto
Emanto Restaurant
Zaria Hotel
A2
Expressway to Kano
SABON GARI
GPO
Taxi Park
Minibuses to Jos
MAIN ROAD
LIVERPOOL ROAD
PARK ROAD
First Bank
United Bank
Queen Amina Restaurant
RWAFF ROAD
RIVER ROAD
Africa Bank
Royal Guest House
Nigerian Army Museum
Expressway to Kaduna
Kubani River
TUDAN WADA
Hospital
NEW ZARIA CITY
Kuta Hotel
Kofar Doka (City Gate)
Old Mud Houses
OLD CITY
Emir's Palace
Friday Mosque
Traditional Court
0
500 m

The Town

To explore the **old town**, the best plan is to rent a taxi for half a day with a clued-up driver or – failing that – to rent a taxi and find a guide at the same time. To visit the Emir's Palace you have to make a request at the secretary's office next door – normally granted if the Emir is at home.

The main centres of activity in the old town are the **Emir's Palace** (*Gidan Sarki*) and the **market**. The houses and stores of traders and the craftsmen's workshops (including leather-workers, tailors and dye pits) are scattered around the market and many of them can be visited. The palace, with its elaborately decorated facade, is to the south of the market (as in other northern cities, palace and market are set well apart from one another) and is surrounded by a high walled enclosure. The main entrance, the **Kofar Fada**, faces a large square where ceremonies, including the annual **durbar** cavalry charges are held. The **Friday Mosque**, disappointingly hidden behind a modern facade, dominates one side of the square, surrounded by the offices of court counsellors and the homes of leading citizens. According to the story, the architect who designed it in 1834, Babban Gwani Mallam Mikaila, was later commissioned to build a mosque for the Emir of Birnin Gwari. Immediately after it was completed, this Emir seized him and had him put to death so he would never create a more beautiful building elsewhere. The architecture is outstanding, especially the inside vaulting, though the replica of the mosque in Jos gives a better idea of what the building actually looks like.

Nigerian Army museum

Located in the Chindit military barracks, the Nigerian Army Museum (Mon–Fri 8am–2.30pm) houses a small exhibition tracing the history of the Nigerian armed forces through displays of weaponry and other assorted memorabilia (uniforms, medals, maps and period photographs). The eras of military government are covered with a degree of comradely back-slapping, but the sections on the Biafran War and the Burma Campaign during World War II make a visit worthwhile. To get there, follow the signs along RWAFF Road, or take a motorbike from Sabon Gari (it's a long walk).

Eating and drinking

There are few noteworthy restaurants in Zaria. Alcohol is rarely available, and, outside of *Sallah* time (Muslim celebrations, especially at the end of Ramadan) it's a fairly quiet town.

Blue Velvet, 5 Gaskiya Rd, off Hospital Rd. A tiny and very cheap eatery with African dishes.

Emanto Restaurant, opposite the *Zaria Hotel*. A very good, rather stylish restaurant with avant-garde photos on the wood-panelled walls.

Shagarikun, Kongo Rd, Tudun Wada. Formerly in a *banco* house, the restaurant is now in a modern "storey building" (ie with several floors), but they've thoughtfully kept a section where visitors can eat on the floor. One of the best restaurants in town and inexpensive.

Unique Restaurant, RWAFF Rd, Sabon Gari. Cheap African meals in clean, functional surroundings.

Kano

The largest town in the north, and effectively Nigeria's second city (despite being smaller than Ibadan), the thousand-year-old Hausa metropolis of **KANO** is a strange mixture of modern and traditional, with the former gaining ground and invading the latter every year. The **international airport** has daily flights to Lagos and several direct flights each week to Europe and the Middle East, while growing **industrialization** in the region continues to draw people from the countryside to a city with a popul-

FLYING IN FROM EUROPE

Kano is a good place to start West African travels – reasonably lively but not so intolerably frenetic and intimidating as to put you right off – and well placed for Niger and Mali or for Cameroon. **Aminu Kano International Airport** is only 8km from the central Sabon Gari quarter of the city, an inexpensive taxi ride. International **airlines** currently serving the airport are: *KLM* non-stop from Amsterdam (Tues & Sun, arriving early evening); *Nigeria Airways* from London (Mon, Wed & Sun, arriving at 3.15am), Rome (Thurs & Sun, arriving in the afternoon) and Jeddah (Thurs & Sun, arriving at dawn); *Sabena* from Brussels (Thurs, arriving early evening); and *Egyptair* from London via Cairo (Tues & Sat, overnight in Cairo, arriving next afternoon). All the airlines have connections from other European cities. For departures, see "Moving on from Kano" on p.1105.

tion of two million that continues to spread, apparently unchecked, over the dusty savannah. Its vehicle pollution, especially at the close of the dry season in April or May, has to be breathed to be believed.

The other side of Kano is its history. The **Gidan Makama Museum** is a beautiful effort to protect its heritage, housing historical exhibits of the city and its environs in a former Makama chief's palace, completely restored to show off the intricacy and technical excellence of the ancient architecture; qualities which can also be admired at the **Emir's Palace** and the **Central Mosque** nearby. Other reminders of the past include the **old market** and the **dye pits** where, beside a busy multi-laned avenue, cloth is still soaked in indigo in the gloriously messy way it's been done for centuries. Yet everywhere there's a distinct feeling that much more could be done to preserve the ties with Kano's past, especially maintenance of the **old city wall**, which resisted British colonial invaders with greater success than it has the elements in recent years. Although a few of the great **gates** that once protected the emirate still stand, much of the wall has now become huge lumps of rain-smoothed mud, and people still dig away at it to make bricks for new homes.

Accommodation

Kano has a wide range of places to stay, ranging from camping grounds or dorm beds to international-class hotels. Inexpensive **small hotels** are concentrated in the Sabon Gari district, but whatever your taste or means, Kano has it.

Inexpensive to moderate

A little-known option that's well worth pointing out is the AC rooms at the *Empire Peking Restaurant* (see "Eating and nightlife"), which has one of the town's most reliable water sources, and offers a ten percent reduction on meals if you stay there.

Baptist Guest House, Abuja Rd (ex-France Rd). Twin rooms (if you're alone, you may end up with a room-mate) with fan and fridge. Very simple, but clean and cheap. ①.

Criss Cross Hotel, 42 Ibrahim Taiwo Rd. Basic accommodation with fan and bucket showers, but very inexpensive. ①.

Hotel De Mikela, 29–31 Awolowo Ave (ex-Church Rd; ☎064/627 009). Excellent-value lodgings with reasonably priced rooms that include AC, TV and even a fridge. They also have a pleasant bar and restaurant. The annex across the street has simpler, cheaper accommodation. ①–②.

Kandara Palace Hotel, Unity Rd, near the old city (☎064/623 073). Nice place with clean enough AC rooms, and very kind and friendly service. ③.

Kano Tourist Transit Camp, Club Rd (☎064/626 309). Camping places, dormitory space and private rooms with showers and fans, all at reasonable rates. Safe, friendly and central with a tourist information office, travel agency and forex bureau on site. Reasonable restaurant – but beware the creative pricing policy. ①.

ACCOMMODATION PRICE CODES

① Under ₦650 (under £5/$7.50). ② ₦650–1300 (£5–10/$7.50–15)
③ ₦1300–2600 (£10–20/$15–30) ④ ₦2600–3900 (£20–30/$30–45)
⑤ ₦3900–5200 (£30–40/$45–60) ⑥ ₦5200–6500 (£40–50/$60–75)
⑦ Over ₦6500 (over £50/$75)

For further information, see the practical information pages at the beginning of this chapter.

Remco Motel, 61 New Rd, Sabon Gari (☎064/628 600). Clean rooms with AC, fridge and mini-bar. Friendly staff. ②.

Rolling Hotels, 82 Church Rd (☎064/620 097). Inexpensive option with clean S/C rooms with AC and its own restaurant. ①.

SIM/ECWA Guest House, Tafawa Balewa Rd between Mission Rd and Zaria Ave. Very clean rooms and friendly staff, but its "budget" prices are almost up to the small hotel range. Family atmosphere, but you have to be on your best behaviour. ①–②.

TYC Hotel, 44 Abuja Rd (ex-France Rd), at junction with Ibo Rd (☎064/627 491). Options range from singles to elaborate suites with colour TV and fridge. The restaurant serves full Nigerian meals – or just pepper soup or sandwiches – and the "roof garden" is nice for drinks while looking out on the lights of Sabon Gari at night. Good value and very friendly. ②–③.

Universal Hotel, 86 Awolowo Ave (ex-Church Rd). One of the cheaper small hotels in the Sabon Gari area. ①.

Upmarket hotels

Central Hotel, Club Rd (☎064/625 141). The main international-class hotel looks like it could use a new coat of paint (among other things), but has a pool (small fee for non-residents' use), tennis courts and, most alluring of all, an air-conditioned bar – a popular expat rendezvous. ⑤.

Daula Hotel (☎064/628 842). Newer than the *Central* and has its own swimming pool. ⑥.

Prince Hotel, Tamandu Close. The newest upmarket hotel with a pleasant patio restaurant and bar that's currently popular for an evening out. Efficiently run with modern facilities. ⑤.

The old city

Most of Kano's special appeal lies in the **old city**, down Kofar Mata Road from the modern centre. The fortified **town wall** has all but disappeared, but some of the original **city gates** (*Kofar*) have been restored and are worth a look. The best-preserved gates are all on B.U.K. Road – Kofar Na Isa (literally, "I have arrived"), Kofar Dan Agundi and Kofar Sabwar.

As you walk round the old city, be on the lookout for examples of **traditional Hausa exterior decorations**. Particularly beautiful is the "masque" style of house facade, but if you have the chance to travel widely, you'll notice how much dirtier the Kano houses are than similar buildings in, say, Zinder in Niger, where the destructive combination of rain, exhaust fumes and industrial pollution is that much less. There's a fine "masque" house just past the dye pits on the left as you head into the old city.

The dye pits

Inside Kofar Mata, a modern gate into the old city (small hillocks indicate where the wall used to be), you'll see the **dye pits** on the right. They soak cloth here in natural indigo as they have for hundreds of years, using great basins of dye buried in the hard ground. Kano fabrics once clothed most of the people in the Sahara region and were highly valued. You can buy material or ready-made clothes here, or even have some of your own clothes dyed. But beware: if you take a picture, you'll be asked for a dash (the demanding upturned palms are plain to see on most snaps of the dye pits). More spectacular than Kano's dye pits are those in **Kura**, a small town 30km south of Kano, just off the expressway to Zaria, in the heart of a major cloth-dyeing area.

The Central Mosque and Emir's Palace

Continuing down Kofar Mata Road, the **Central Mosque** is imposing, but not the most noteworthy building architecturally. It has, however, been of enormous importance as a focus for the Islamic nationalism that has so bedevilled successive federal governments. With proper authorization you can climb one of its two minarets for fine views over the city (enquire at the secretary's office at the entrance to the Emir's Palace). Behind the mosque, the **Emir's Palace** spreads out over a huge acreage, and approaching from this direction its traditional architecture blends easily with the buildings of the old city, albeit on a rather larger and more stately scale. The front is far more modern and obviously palatial. Unfortunately, whichever way you approach, you can't visit inside.

Kurmi market and Dala Hill

North of the Emir's Palace, **Kurmi Market** (also known as **City Market**) forms an almost impossibly tight maze of alleys and stalls. They're pressed together to exclude the heat, but there are so many people milling about, it gets claustrophobic and sweaty anyhow. The market swarms with petty hustlers and "**guides**". Come to terms with just one, accept you'll have to pay him something and be prepared for a little transparent salesmanship at certain stalls of his acquaintance. Once you've got to know each other, a guide is instructive and helpful and his presence saves you from the onslaught of other would-be assistants.

The busiest and best time to visit is the afternoon, any day except Friday. The market retains a strong traditional flavour, although certain sellers with an eye on tourist bucks turn out shoddy and not very traditional junk. As always, you have to confront the question of the "authenticity" of the goods you're buying, but it's not yet too common a dilemma, and **leather**, **cloth**, **brass**, **silverwork** and **beads** will continue to be made whether tourists buy them or not – and are still good value. Be sure to stop at the section for local riding tack, housed in the market's oldest structure, dating from the nineteenth century.

Dala Hill, site of the original settlement in Kano, rises up to the north of the Kurmi market, pretty well in the centre of the old city. You can walk up there – it involves finding your way through narrow alleys and backstreets – and can usually find a kid to take you for a dash, but remember to fix the price first.

TOURIST INFORMATION, DRESS SENSE – & TRAFFIC COPS

There's a **Tourist Information Office** at the *Kano Tourist Transit Camp* (see p.1097; it's a key trans-African travellers' haunt). They organize excursions around the city and to nearby sites. You can get **maps** and a *Kano State Hotel Guide* at the Ministry of Home Affairs and Information, New Secretariat, Zaria Rd, or at the *Tourist Information Centre* in the Airport. You can also sometimes buy maps at the bookstore of the *Central Hotel*.

Note that Kano's old city is a traditional, Muslim centre – as are all the old walled towns of the north. Men as well as women should be careful to **dress appropriately**: shorts on men and sleeveless tops, shorts or jeans on women go down very badly with more conservative citizens. Save such clothes for the modern parts of town.

If you're **driving**, you will certainly be pulled over by orange-uniformed traffic cops sooner or later. When they try to extract a bribe, explain you have no cash and will have to be arrested and charged – call their bluff. They have very few powers and you should not be intimidated.

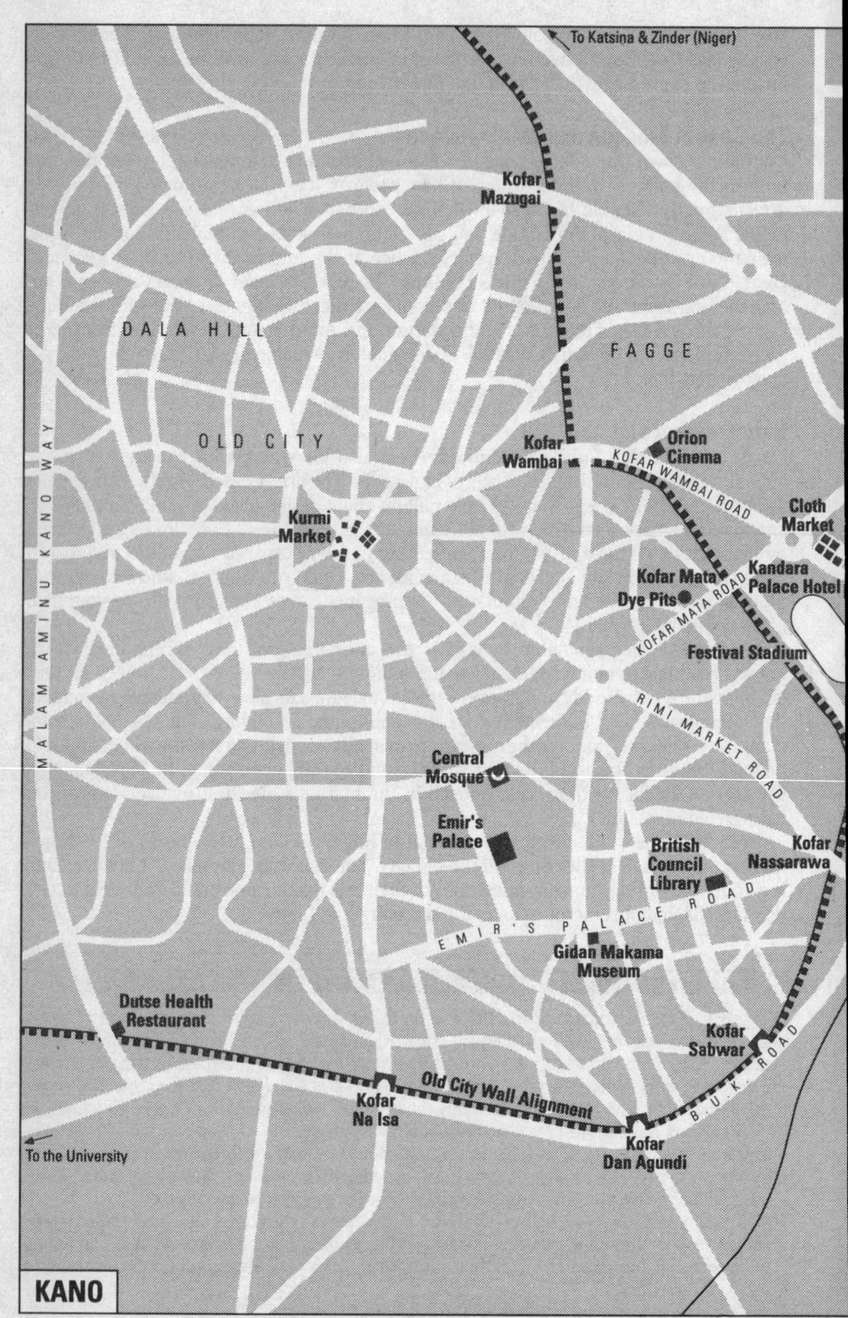
To Katsina & Zinder (Niger)
Kofar Mazugai
DALA HILL
FAGGE
OLD CITY
Kofar Wambai
Orion Cinema
KOFAR WAMBAI ROAD
Cloth Market
Kurmi Market
Kofar Mata Dye Pits
KOFAR MATA ROAD
Kandara Palace Hotel
Festival Stadium
MALAM AMINU KANO WAY
RIMI MARKET ROAD
Central Mosque
Emir's Palace
British Council Library
Kofar Nassarawa
EMIR'S PALACE ROAD
Gidan Makama Museum
Dutse Health Restaurant
Kofar Sabwar
Old City Wall Alignment
Kofar Na Isa
B.U.K. ROAD
Kofar Dan Agundi
To the University
KANO

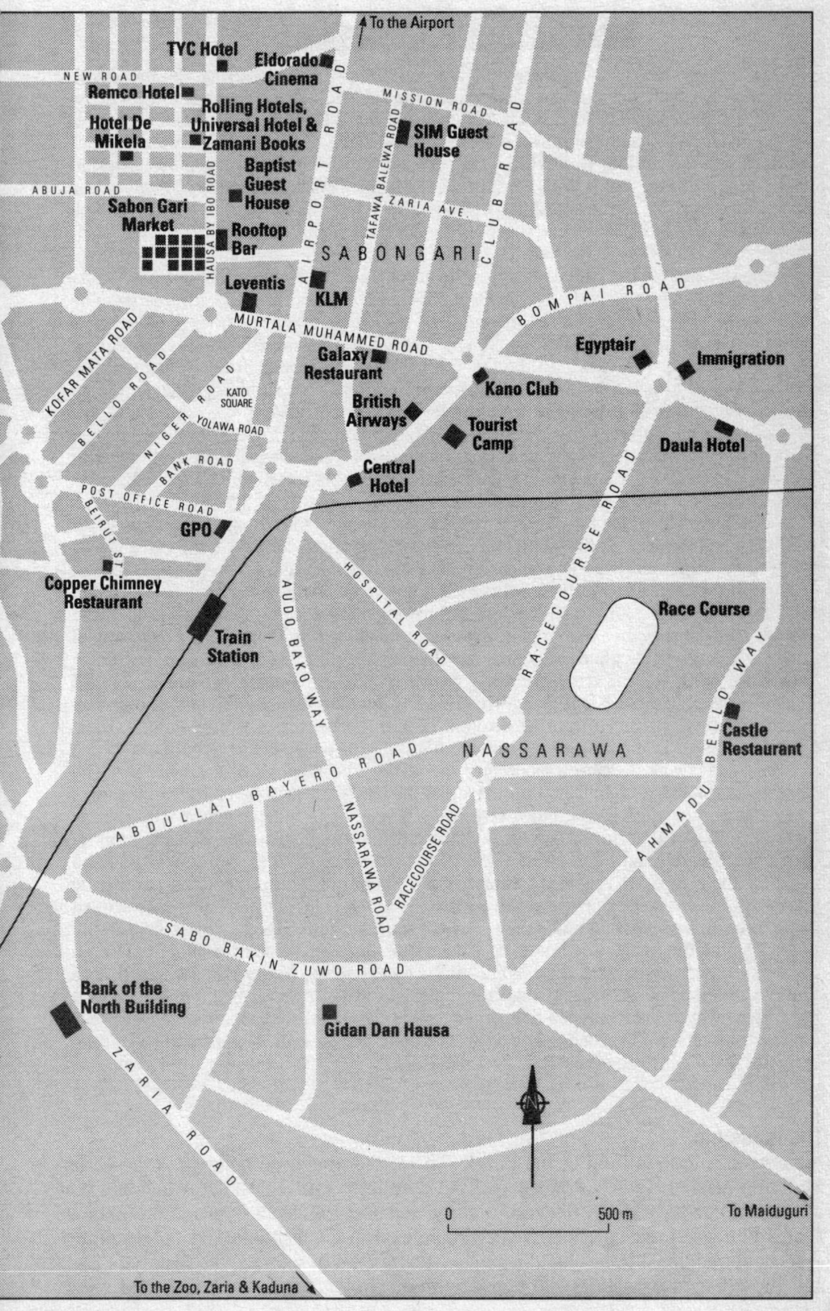
To the Airport
TYC Hotel
Eldorado Cinema
NEW ROAD
Remco Hotel
MISSION ROAD
Rolling Hotels, Universal Hotel & Zamani Books
Hotel De Mikela
SIM Guest House
TAFAWA BALEWA ROAD
CLUB ROAD
AIRPORT ROAD
Baptist Guest House
ABUJA ROAD
HAUSA BY IBO ROAD
ZARIA AVE.
Sabon Gari Market
Rooftop Bar
SABONGARI
Leventis
KLM
BOMPAI ROAD
MURTALA MUHAMMED ROAD
KOFAR MATA ROAD
BELLO ROAD
NIGER ROAD
KATO SQUARE
YOLAWA ROAD
Galaxy Restaurant
Egyptair
Immigration
Kano Club
British Airways
Tourist Camp
Daula Hotel
BANK ROAD
Central Hotel
POST OFFICE ROAD
BEIRUT ST
GPO
Copper Chimney Restaurant
HOSPITAL ROAD
RACECOURSE ROAD
Race Course
AUDO BAKO WAY
Train Station
NASSARAWA
Castle Restaurant
AHMADU BELLO WAY
ABDULLAI BAYERO ROAD
NASSARAWA ROAD
RACECOURSE ROAD
SABO BAKIN ZUWO ROAD
Bank of the North Building
Gidan Dan Hausa
ZARIA ROAD
N
0
500 m
To Maiduguri
To the Zoo, Zaria & Kaduna

KANO'S HISTORY

Kano's history (its courtly history at any rate) has been preserved in the **Kano Chronicles**, which give the most detailed account of any Sudanic nation with the exception of Songhai. A compilation of brief histories of the region, the Chronicles originated in the mid-seventh century, shortly after the introduction of Arabic. The first settlement of Kano was founded on **Dala Hill**, where archaeologists have uncovered furnaces and slag heaps indicating ironworking from as early as the sixth century; this settlement was later conquered by the descendants of **Bagauda** – one of the six sons of **Bawo** who founded the *Hausa Bokwai* – the seven legitimate Hausa states (see p.1090).

Kano was fortified at the beginning of the twelfth century during the reign of **Gijimasu**. Later, under **Yaji** (1349–85), it developed a powerful army that used new technology – quilted armour, iron helmets and chainmail – to overthrow its adversaries. The city became independent of its neighbours and gained control of the trans-Saharan trade in gold and salt. It thus acquired wealth and power to rival Timbuktu and Gao. Additions to the walled city were made in the fifteenth century under **Muhammed Rumfa**, who had converted to Islam and who transformed Kano from a local military chiefdom to an Islamic sultanate with close links across the Sahara and to Arabia.

Contact with Europe came in the mid-sixteenth century. **Portuguese** attempts to establish a trading centre were thwarted, but settlers from Ragusa (now Dubrovnik in Croatia) maintained a presence in Kano throughout the 1560s and 1570s, under the protection of the North African-based Turkish Ottoman sultan.

Over the next two centuries, Kano warred continuously with the neighbouring states of Borno and Katsina. At the same time, European maritime powers on the coast slowly undermined the trans-Saharan routes that were the basis of Kano's power and autonomy. Although the textile and leather **industries** kept the economy going (indigo-dyed cloth and soft red leather, known as "Moroccan", were exported as far afield as Europe), the state's political structure was fragile. When the Fulani, led by Usman dan Fodio, waged their religious war, or **jihad**, Kano was unable to resist: the city fell in 1807. A new era of hostilities followed, and it was during this period that **European explorers** reached Kano – Clapperton in 1824, Barth in 1853 and Monteil in 1891. By the end of the nineteenth century, **British imperial designs** posed a direct threat to the emirate. Kano refortified its walls and prepared to resist, but in 1903 the city fell to British troops.

Kano effectively became a laboratory for testing the theories of colonial rule. The British appointed a compliant Emir in order to try out a system of **indirect rule** – successful in colonial terms, but a disastrous precursor to independence. The railway was opened in 1911 and the airport in 1937 and Kano's future as the dominant city of northern Nigeria, and the biggest in the Sahel, was sealed. After World War II, Kano became the centre of a renewed **Islamic nationalism** in Nigeria, intent on resisting the power of the southern regions of the country as much as, if not more than, the British who were clearly intent on pulling out. The rift with southern Nigeria, especially with the Igbo community in the southeast, continued after independence, through the Biafran War and into recent years. In 1980, a mad Kano prophet, **Maitatsine**, whipped up a frenzy among landless peasants and unemployed townspeople against Nigerian armed forces in the city, in an uprising that left dozens of casualties. And almost every year sees at least one major disturbance arising from ethnic tensions, usually an ordinary urban murder that leads to an ethnic riot.

The museums

Across the square in front of the Emir's Palace, the grandiose building is the **Gidan Makama Museum** (daily 10am–4pm; free). Formerly a palace itself, the building is as interesting for its superb, fifteenth-century Sudanic architecture as for the exhibits inside. Fittingly, the displays in the first room explain the technological and decorative aspects of traditional Hausa building styles. Rooms two to six trace the history of Kano and the other Hausa states through drawings, photographs, documents and reconstructions spanning a thousand years – a dense and informative chronology, not for the faint-hearted. The coming of Islam to Kano and the Muslim tenets are laid out in the seventh room. Finally, rooms eight and nine are dedicated to a less demanding selection of **traditional arts** – music, weaving, brasswork and so on. Set aside a couple of hours to visit, as it's well worth the time – you may want to come back.

A new museum, the **Kano State Museum**, is slated to open in the **Gida Dan Hausa** – the first British colonial residence in Kano. Built in 1909, it's a remarkable Hausa structure with beautiful gardens, and until the exhibits are ready, you can explore at will.

The new city

The intersection of Murtala Muhammed Road and Lagos/Airport Road is the centre of modern Kano, the heart of its main commercial district, at any rate. Many **banks** – *Afribank*, *First*, *Union* and *Bank of the North* (Mon–Fri 8am–2pm, Sat 8am–noon) – are located just south of this junction around the intersection of Lagos and Bank roads. Continuing south on Lagos Road brings you to Post Office Road and the **GPO** (8am–5pm). The **train station** is nearby, on Fagge Road. Up on Club Road, the **Central Hotel** makes a good place to stop for a cold drink: even if you don't stay here, you can pay to use the pool, though the water is often murky. Across from the *Central*, vendors sell various **crafts**. The quality is not bad, and while prices start high, patient bargaining can reduce them to realistic levels.

North of Murtala Muhammed Road, the **Sabon Gari** ("New Town") neighbourhood is home to mainly Igbo and Yoruba workers and has a distinct southern Nigerian flavour, with flocks of cheap hotels and energetic bars – particularly animated after dark and something of a relief after the more austere "dry" areas of the old city. The recently rebuilt **Sabon Gari Market** always draws a lot of colour and crowds. Get your food and other odds and ends here, but for traditional crafts head to the old city.

Slightly out of town on the Zaria road, the **Audo Bako Zoo** has an exotic collection of animals, including a kangaroo – nothing to go out of your way for but a good excuse for a late afternoon stroll if you've nothing else to do. There's also a beer garden.

Eating and nightlife

If your travels have featured Kano as a significant goal for any length of time, you won't be disappointed with the variety of edible treats on offer. The whole gamut of West African food is available here, together with a full variety of imports in the supermarkets – Kano is, after all, only six hours from London.

Inexpensive food

Arabian Sweets, 4 Beirut St opposite *Chellarams*. Lebanese pastry shop – one of many on the same street – with deliciously sticky Middle Eastern sweets and Italian ice cream.

Choice Restaurant & Takeaway, 40a Niger St, by the International Clinic. Excellent simple meals – plantains, omelette and meat, for example – for a few Naira.

Danish Bakery, Beirut St. Light meals like omelettes with chips and more filling Nigerian fare including chicken with rice or pounded yam.

Dutse Health Restaurant, 604 Malam Aminu Kano Rd. A good address for inexpensive Nigerian meals if you're out near the university, and a popular meeting place for students.

El Capitan, off Beirut St. Healthy servings of chicken or fish with pounded yam, rice or plantains, or *egusi* soup with riceballs.

Galaxy Restaurant, 139 Murtala Muhammed Way, not far from the *Tourist Camp*. Good omelettes and chips for breakfast, and dishes like rice with chicken or beef stew later in the day. It's in an old cottage with an outdoor terrace for drinking at night.

Supreme Time Supermarket, Murtala Muhammed Way near *Daula Hotel*. Lebanese snacks with fresh mango and orange juice and good ice cream.

Upmarket restaurants

Castle Restaurant, 20 Ahmadu Bello Way. Lebanese and European food. Adjoining nightclub.

The Copper Chimney (formerly *Shangri-La*), 15b Beirut St. A haven for vegetarians – superb and reasonably priced Sunday brunch Indian buffets. Open other evenings for à la carte meals.

El Diwan, Hedidjia Rd. One of the classiest restaurants in Kano: Lebanese food in a stylish setting.

Empire Peking Chinese Restaurant, 2 Bompai Rd (☎064/625 146). One of the better Chinese restaurants, with rooms at the back.

Jay's Restaurant, 2b Niger St. A wide range of European food, including pizza, and an upbeat atmosphere.

La Locanda, 40 Sultan Rd, off Ahmadu Bello Way. Superb Italian food in a lively ambience. Pizzas can be ordered to go.

Nightlife

The place to be is **Sabon Gari**, the old city being pretty quiet in the evening, and the new city south of Murtala Muhammed Way hardly sparkling. **Cinemas** – including the *Plaza* on Kofar Mata Road, the *Orion* on Kofar Wambai Road, the *Eldorado* on Lagos Road near Mission Road, and the *Rex* and *Sheila* along Murtala Muhammed Way – and **bars** are the main diversions, though there's the odd **disco** too – *Lilywhite*, next to the *Galaxy Restaurant* on Murtala Muhammed at the bottom of Club Road, is a positively outrageous example. The bars of the *Central* and *Daula* hotels are usually quite animated too, but as you'd expect there are frequent and fickle shifts of favour among their regular customers. If you're looking for an evening of calm, spend it drinking on the *Rooftop Bar*, opposite Sabon Gari market.

Listings

Airline offices include: *British Airways*, Hafsatu House, 7 Bompai Rd (☎064/626 040 or 624 834); *Egyptair*, 16c Murtala Muhammed Way (☎064/624 027); *Kabo Air*, 6775 Ashton Rd (☎064/625 291); *KLM*, 17 Airport Rd (☎064/600 240); *Nigeria Airways*, 3 Bank Rd (☎064/623 891 or 623 041); and *Sabena*, *Central Hotel*, Bompai Rd (☎064/621 364).

Bookshops Used books are sold in front of the post office. *Zamani Books Ltd* at 84 Awolowo Ave, Sabon Gari, has a broad spectrum of good cheap books including novels by African writers (Mon–Fri 8am–12.30pm & 2–5pm, Sat 8am–1pm).

British Council 10 Emir's Palace Rd (Mon–Fri 10am–7pm, Sat 10am–1.30pm; ☎064/626 662; Fax 064/626 500). A good place to catch up on the news – but they've also got a dynamic cultural programme that includes theatre, film and dance.

Changing money There are many forex bureaux, notably along Bompai Rd near the *Tourist Camp*. The one in the camp itself is as good as any other.

Consulates and diplomatic assistance include a British Liaison Officer, 64 Murtala Muhammed Way, weekday mornings; *Niger Consulate*, Katsina Rd, near the army barracks; there are no consulates for Cameroon or Chad.

Dentists Dr JP Rossek, Kowa Specialist Clinic, Club Rd (Mon–Fri 8.30am–noon, Sat 9am–12.30pm); Ahmadiya Clinic, Club Rd (Mon–Fri 8.30am–12.30pm, Sat 8am–1pm).

Doctors Dr K Khouri, Club Rd (Mon–Fri 8.30am–12.30pm & 3–6pm, Sat 8.30am–12.30pm); Bompai Road Clinic (Mon–Sat 8am–8pm; 24-hr emergency cover).

History and Culture Bureau across from Governor's mansion. A good place to find out about dance performances. If the Hausa troupe, the Koroso Dancers, are in town, it's definitely worth catching a show.

Poste restante Free, reliable and relatively swift because of international air services.

Phones and faxes The town centre office for international calls is down Lagos Rd, beyond the post office, near the corner of Ibrahim Taiwa Rd. A good line is hard to get. The new *NITEL* office at the end of Zoo Rd is much more modern and comfortable; more importantly, long-distance connections are good. The *Central Hotel*'s rates for phone and fax aren't unreasonable, and the convenience wins points.

MOVING ON FROM KANO

Most long-distance taxis and minibuses leave either from the **Ngwa Uku Motor Park** (Lagos, Maiduguri, Enugu, Sokoto and Abuja) or the more distant **Nai Bawa Motor Park** (Jos, Kaduna, Zaria). Both are about 5km out on the Zaria road. Buses and minibuses towards the **Niger border**, and to Niger itself, go from the **Kofar Ruwa Motor Park**, north of the old city off the Katsina road. Vehicles heading, broadly, east – to northern parts of **Cameroon** and to **Maiduguri** and the Chad border – leave from **Murtala Muhammed Way** near the Sabon Gari market.

In theory, there are weekly **trains** to Lagos and Port Harcourt. Check at the station, as the service is suspended at the time of publication.

Nigeria Airways has at least a couple of **flights** a week to Maiduguri, Sokoto, Port Harcourt, Kaduna and **Lagos** (several flights daily). *Kabo Air* covers other domestic destinations. See "Listings" for airline addresses.

INTERNATIONAL NON-STOP FLIGHTS

KLM flies to **Amsterdam** (Mon & Wed night, arriving early morning); *Nigeria Airways* (flights originate in Lagos) to **London** (Mon & Wed, arriving evening) and **Rome** (Wed & Sat night, arriving early morning); *Sabena* to **Brussels** (Sun night, arriving early morning); *Egyptair* to **Cairo** (Mon & Thurs, arriving evening) and **Jeddah** (Thurs & Sun, arriving evening).

Katsina

Tucked in the extreme north, **KATSINA** flounders in the dry Sahelian badlands. Recent efforts to pump some life into the region, notably through the installation, in 1982, of a steel plant, have so far brought few noticeable signs of development other than the dual-laned highways that wrap around the outskirts of town. Vestiges of the once powerful **Katsina emirate** – one of the oldest of the seven Hausa states – have hardly fared better. One or two of the original city gates still stand in varying states of ruin, but the fortifications that once surrounded the town have been all but flattened. Reminders of the past remain in the **Emir's Palace** and the **Gobarau Tower** that once served as a sentry post. You can visit these, but the real pleasure of Katsina perhaps lies more in simply wandering the dusty streets, absorbing the atmosphere of a Hausa city that shows few signs of modernity.

The Town

"Downtown" Katsina spreads along Kano Road between the **Kofar Kaura**, a recent stone gate built to replace an older mudbrick one, and the **Central Mosque** with its onion domes. Along this road, you'll find the major **banks**, the post office and the big trading stores. Just beyond the mosque, Kano Road veers to the left and continues to the **Emir's Palace**. The entrance to this building looks more recent than you might expect and sports a bizarre clocktower in apparent imitation of a Central European castle. Inside, the large compound is a hodge-podge of old mudbrick and new cement buildings that pile into each other inelegantly. If you want to visit the palace, you must make advance arrangements at the Ministry of Information building on Kano Road.

Following the paved road to the west, the **Central Market** is a short way from the palace. You'll find a few fruits and vegetables here (mangoes in season, oranges, tomatoes, onions and okra), decorated calabashes and pottery with a bronzey glaze, cereals (corn and different kinds of millet) and livestock including the occasional camel. Notice the open-air "butcher's shop" and Fulani women selling milk from calabashes.

To the north of the market, you can make out the **Gobarau Tower**. To reach this minaret follow the unmarked street called Gobarau Road on the eastern edge of the market. Built in the seventeenth century as a lookout post, the tower later served as the muezzin's platform in pre-loudspeaker days. A guide will take you to the top and explain the history for a small dash. From the minaret, Hospital Road leads past a walled cemetery to the **Kofar Uku**. This gate "of the three doors" was formerly attached to **Katsina Teacher College**, the first institute of higher learning in town. Now falling into ruins, the gate was built, say the residents, in the seventeenth century. Other gates of note include the **Kofar Guga** and, at the end of Nagogo Street, the **Kofar Durbi**, where you can still see part of the old wall.

Practicalities

The old central motor park has been flattened, and you now arrive at a bright new motor park on the outskirts of town, a taxi-motorbike ride from the centre. Most of the **hotels** are on Kano Road outside the Kofar Kaura. The *Siamond Hotel* (①) and the *Abuja Guest Inn* (☎065/30319; ①) are both scruffy and uncomfortable though reasonably priced. Similar accommodation can be found at the *Darma Annex* (①), in the same area. Right near the Kofar Kaura, *Maikudi*, 3 Kano Rd (☎065/690; ②), is very clean with pleasant staff and has a good AC **restaurant** serving Nigerian and European food. In the same general area, you'll also notice signs for the *New City Hotel* and the *Liberty Hotel*. These two aren't for lodging (though they have basic rooms; ①) as much as dancing, drinking and other forms of recreation.

Sokoto and around

Until the beginning of the nineteenth century, **SOKOTO** was a small town of little significance, surrounded by the Hausa city states. It only gained its present status as **religious capital** of the north after Usman dan Fodio's Islamic jihad led to the creation of the **Sokoto Khalifate** in 1807. The present Emir is to this day leader of all other Hausa emirates and effective spiritual leader of Muslim Nigeria. Modernization came slowly to this region as development goals conflicted with the khalif's own ideas about what "civilization" should entail. Thus, at the wish of the khalif, the railway line that pushed northwards as far as Kaura Namoda in the 1920s was never extended to Sokoto. The town's isolation from corrupting outside influences was thus preserved.

The Town

Despite Sokoto's rich history and its position as spiritual capital of the north, there's little in the way of sightseeing. The city's core is the **Sultan's Palace** and the nearby **Masallachin Shehu** (Shehu's Mosque), on Sultan Bello Road. These buildings, with their Sudanic aura, are pleasant enough to look at, but you cannot go in. About halfway between the palace and the mosque is the **Hubbare**, the former home of Shehu Usman dan Fodio (located off Sultan Bello Road, it's a bit tricky to find; if you're near the mosque, ask any kid and he'll take you there). Take off your shoes before entering and be as respectful as possible. Inside the house is the **Shehu's Tomb**, where dan Fodio is buried with his companions. People from throughout the region still make pilgrimages to this spot to pay homage.

Not far from the palace as you head down Sultan Abubakar Road, the **Sokoto Museum** is housed in a small building opposite the Federal Prisons. The few exhibits are poorly maintained and you're not likely to find much of interest – unless you count some damaged musical instruments, Arabic scripts and letters from members of the ruling family. A much larger and more comprehensive **History Bureau and Museum**

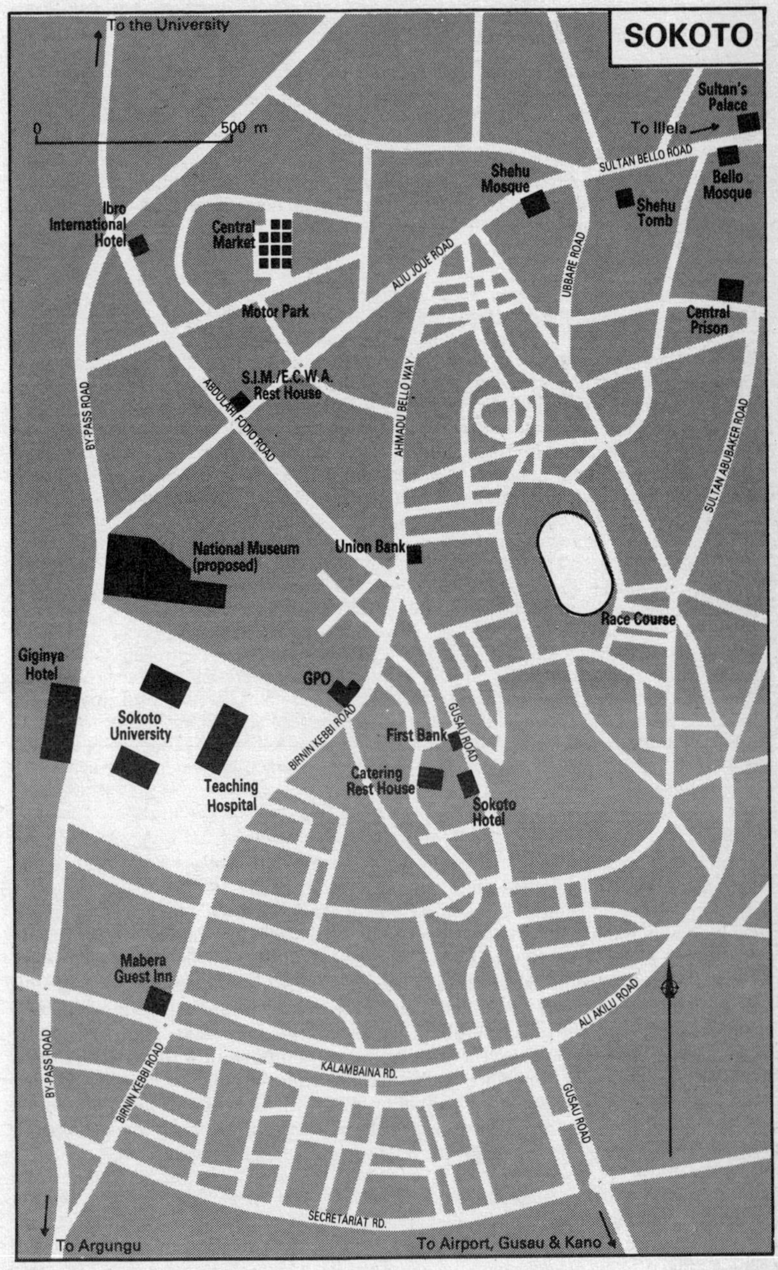
SOKOTO
To the University
0
500 m
Sultan's Palace
To Illela
SULTAN BELLO ROAD
Shehu Mosque
Bello Mosque
Shehu Tomb
Ibro International Hotel
Central Market
ALIU JOUE ROAD
UBBARE ROAD
Motor Park
Central Prison
S.I.M./E.C.W.A. Rest House
BY-PASS ROAD
ABDULAHI FODIO ROAD
AHMADU BELLO WAY
SULTAN ABUBAKER ROAD
National Museum (proposed)
Union Bank
Race Course
Giginya Hotel
GPO
Sokoto University
BIRNIN KEBBI ROAD
GUSAU ROAD
First Bank
Teaching Hospital
Catering Rest House
Sokoto Hotel
Mabera Guest Inn
ALI AKILU ROAD
BY-PASS ROAD
BIRNIN KEBBI ROAD
KALAMBAINA RD.
GUSAU ROAD
SECRETARIAT RD.
To Argungu
To Airport, Gusau & Kano

SOME SOKOTO HISTORY

The **Fulani** of Sokoto are thought to have migrated from Mali in the thirteenth century and to have settled in **Gobir**, then a powerful ancient kingdom. Known as *Fulanin Gida* (town Fulani as opposed to pastoral nomads), they were mainly traders and highly regarded Muslims. The most learned were welcomed into the Hausa Emirs' courts as advisors, where some succumbed to lives of indolence; others kept on the move and preferred a more ascetic lifestyle, teaching and speaking on behalf of the poor. **Usman dan Fodio**, from Gobir, was of the latter mould, preaching energetically against the corrupt influence of high office and the lax ways of the traditional non-Muslim (or quasi-Muslim) Hausa Emirs. There was much support for his stand, which called for the retrenchment of the widely ignored or circumvented *sharia* legal code. And naturally there was also plenty of resentment of his politicking piety from traditionalists with an interest in maintaining the status quo. By 1804, the tension had led to the birth of a radical reform movement and to civil war in Gobir, where the traditionalist Emir first used arms against the reformers. Dan Fodio was a reluctant warrior and, while he agreed to be appointed Amir al-Muminin (Commander of the Faithful), the military leadership of the **holy war**, or jihad, was handled by his brother Abdullah and son Muhammadu Bello.

Weakened from centuries of warring, the Hausa emirates fell quickly and, over the space of four years, with growing popular support, dan Fodio became the uncontested ruler of the entire north. Although often characterized as a war of pious Muslim Fulani against corrupt Hausa, the reality was considerably more complicated and very much determined by people's economic position – the jihad promised a more equitable distribution of wealth and the reduction of taxes and levies. In 1809, dan Fodio's son, **Bello**, who later became the second Sultan, established Sokoto as the *Sarkin Musulmi*, the spiritual and political capital of the empire. By the time of Bello's death in 1835, Sokoto was effectively the capital of Islam for the whole of West Africa.

The **social consequences** of the jihad were many. Dan Fodio had created, for the first time in the region, a single state with a central government controlling the entire north (with the exception of Bornu) and extending deep into present-day Cameroon and south into the Yoruba country which up to then had resisted Islam. As a result, trade was facilitated throughout the region and the Arabic language and writing spread with the teachings of the Koran. When the **British** conquered Sokoto in 1903, they took advantage of the highly stratified and unified government system to implement their policy of indirect rule.

Complex has been under construction for some time on By-Pass Road next to the Sokoto University Teaching Hospital, and may one day open.

You won't be disappointed by Sokoto's **Central Market**, adjacent to the central motor park. It's one of the biggest and best stocked in the entire Sahel Region – an amazingly well-planned, clean, modern site with a startling abundance of flowering plants and trees. And for what seems like such an isolated city there's a remarkable variety of stuff here – if you're lucky, you could find a **produce** selection ranging from pineapples, coconuts and mangoes to millet, sorghum, a mass of vegetables and all the usual proliferation of spices and condiments. There's a large **cloth emporium** with busy tailors who sew to order on the spot. And when you're tired of drifting around, a pleasant and inexpensive **outdoor restaurant** has been set up round the large, green-and-white tower that dominates the whole area. Prices, especially of the cloth, are cheap when compared with elsewhere in Nigeria and mostly fixed. There's little or no haggling here.

Practicalities

Sokoto's main commercial district runs along Gusau Road, where you'll find the major **banks** and hotels. The **GPO** is on Birnin Kebbi Road, not far away.

Accommodation

Sokoto doesn't have an overwhelming selection of hotels, especially in the lower price brackets.

Catering Rest House, Gusau Rd behind the *Shukura* (☎060/232 505). Sorely in need of an overhaul, but passable, with rooms at various prices: those with shared facilities and no AC are in the budget range; private baths are even quite affordable. ②.

Giganya Hotel, By-Pass Rd (☎060/212 263). New five-star hotel with TV, fridges and cassette decks in the spacious double rooms. The disco under the hotel is fabulous and really winds up despite the fact they sell no alcohol. ⑤.

Ibro International Hotel, Abdullahi Fodio Rd (☎060/232 510). Excellent location next to the central market and motor park, and luxuries like AC, TV and hot water. There's a good restaurant in the hotel as well, and a small supermarket across the street. Best buy in town. ②.

Mabera Guest Inn, Mabera Layout (☎060/233 205). Clean and in a lively part of town. Good value. ①.

Shukura Hotel (☎060/232 126). One of the town's best and very efficient with comfortable AC rooms. Prices are comparable to those at the *Sokoto Hotel* and the AC video bar and restaurant are popular. ④.

SIM/ECWA Rest House, close to the motor park and market. This mission house will normally let you stay quite cheaply. ①.

Sokoto Hotel, Gusau Rd (PO Box 1193; ☎060/232 412). AC rooms and swimming pool, in an ageing modern pile but there's a travel bureau and other services. ③–④.

MOVING ON FROM SOKOTO

The main **motor park** in the north of the city handles regular transport for **Kano** and **Illela** (the border town facing Birni Nkonni in Niger). Vehicles to **Argungu** (and on to the Nigeria–Niger–Benin border at Gaya/Malanville) are less frequent, as too are vehicles heading south down the A1 to **Yelwa** and **Kontagora**.

If you want to make a quick getaway, *Nigeria Airways*, Gusau Rd (☎060/232 252), flies Tues, Thurs and Sat to **Lagos** via **Kano** – always very heavily booked. For international travel arrangements, the *Sokoto Hotel* has an accredited travel agency that can make airline bookings.

Argungu

Ninety-nine kilometres southwest of Sokoto by good paved roads, **ARGUNGU** makes for an interesting excursion. Well known for its annual fishing festival in February – photo library shots of which have been reproduced on countless occasions – the town also has the excellent **Kanta Museum** with historical relics and traditional artefacts, and an impressive **Emir's Palace**. You can **stay** at the *Government Catering Resthouse* and there's a new hotel either in place or on its way – the *Grand Fishing Hotel.*

Some history

Argungu has an illustrious place in the annals of West African history. The **Kingdom of Kebbi**, which had formerly been an outlying province of the **Songhai empire**, was founded near here in the early sixteenth century by **Muhammadu Kanta**, a general in the army of the Songhai emperor Askia Muhammed. When the Songhai invaded the Hausa states between 1512 and 1517, Kanta revolted against his overlords, and established himself as an independent ruler of the area between the Niger and Sokoto rivers. The capital of his kingdom was Argungu.

Later, Argungu was one of the pockets of traditionalist resistance to the Fulani jihad led by Usman dan Fodio, and was never successfully conquered by Sokoto. An apocryphal account even derives the town's name from the Fulani moan *Ar sunyi gungu* (Oh dear, they've regrouped), since their invasions were repeatedly repulsed. The Kebbi kingdom fell to the British at the beginning of the century and became part of the Northern Nigeria protectorate.

The fishing festival

Most years, in late January or February (sometimes even as late as March), the **fishing festival** takes place on a stretch of the **Sokoto River** (the Rima to people who live here) known as *Matan Fada*, where it braids into a multitude of channels. Here, thousands of huge *giwan ruwa* fish (some weighing as much as 100kg) are penned in a confined, shallow lake. On the chosen day, the signal is given and hundreds of fishermen plunge into the waters watched by thousands of onlookers. Using only hand-held "butterfly" or clap nets called *homa*, and hollowed calabashes with an opening at the top, they thrash around among their prey. Fishing is banned for the rest of the year in this part of the river and rituals are performed to try to ensure the biggest possible catches. The fish hunt, however, is only the climax of a festival that spreads over three days and includes a long list of other sporting activities and competitions (boxing, archery, camel and donkey races), punctuated with endless speeches by commissioners of Sokoto State government, local leaders and sponsors. If you want to see the festival, it's imperative to make room reservations in advance through the Ministry of Information, Secretariat Road, Sokoto, since rooms at the available accommodation in Argungu get solidly booked.

Maiduguri

The north's closest major town to the Cameroon border, **MAIDUGURI** is the first (or last) stop in Nigeria for many overlanders. The town is incredibly flat and hot, and has that quiet, nothing-happening feeling characteristic of so many places in the arid Sahel regions. If it wasn't for the **neem trees** lining the neatly laid-out avenues and providing a bit of respite from the merciless sun, you might find it unbearable. But as capital of the **Borno State**, it has a good infrastructure and makes a reasonable resting point for further travels in the arid north. The people of Borno are largely **Kanuri**, and women, especially, are elegant dressers and hairstylists and often wear nose rings. If you spend a night here – or more – you may also come to appreciate a second level of life in Maiduguri, as experienced by the many students from all over Nigeria, who live on the Maiduguri university campus and probably feel almost as much strangers in this northwestern outpost as you do.

The Town

Thanks to its fairly modern origins, Maiduguri is a well-planned city and easy to get around. Its characteristic landmarks are the **roundabouts** which have come almost to designate neighbourhoods and are thus convenient markers for orientation. The major ones include "**West End**", with three large cast-iron fish in the middle, "**Banks**", a large spikey phallic symbol, "**Welcome**", a green and white concrete statue, "**Post Office**" near the GPO, "**NEPA**" near the market, "**Customs**" near the museum, and "**Eagle**", with a large eagle statue in the south of town. The easiest way to get around town is by collective taxi to one of these roundabouts, walking from there to your destination. For example, when going to the market, hail a cab going to the NEPA roundabout and walk up Amadu Bello Way from there.

Maiduguri doesn't have much in the way of sights, and any exploring, at almost any time of year, should be done in the early hours before the town gets intolerably hot. An

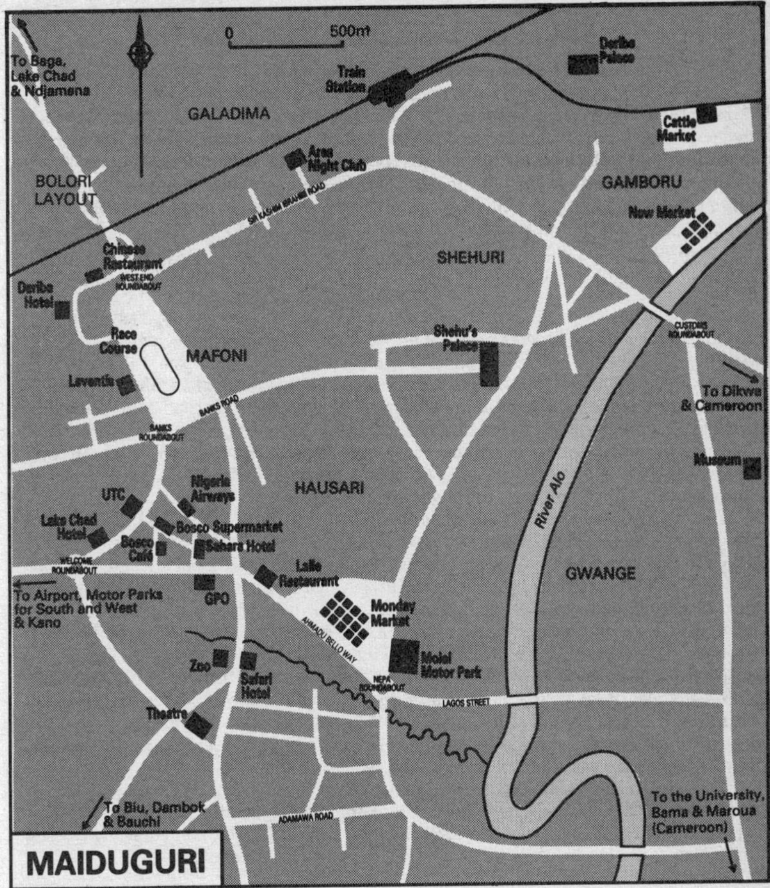

obvious place to start is at the **Shehu's Palace**. A colonial-style building with clock tower, the palace has no organized tours, but if you tell the guards in front that you're interested in visiting they usually try to arrange it. Inside, the emphasis is more on modern administration than Bornu history: after taking off your shoes, a guide trails you from one scorching patio to the next, making a point of showing you every room with a typewriter or a leatherette armchair.

Much better for a historical overview is the small **museum**, near the customs warehouse on Bama Road, which provides a useful introduction to the customs of different peoples living in Bornu State. Artefacts – pottery, jewellery, mats, utensils – are well displayed with accompanying texts. In the courtyard there's an interesting reproduction of an "Arab" tent with characteristic furnishings.

Maiduguri's colourful **Monday Market** now takes place in a covered cement building in the commercial centre of town. The **New Market** sprouted a few years back in the Gamboru district near Customs roundabout. Apart from all the usual gear, it's well known locally for its attractive handwoven **mats** made of Lake Chad reeds.

SOME MAIDUGURI HISTORY

The rise of the **Kanem-Bornu empire** was a consequence of the spreading Sahara and the subsequent migration of nomadic peoples who concentrated in the **Lake Chad** basin, in districts that had been covered in lake water in earlier times. Conflicts flared between the newcomers and established communities. The **Kanuri** (a people of distinctively Saharan origins, with a language quite unrelated to Hausa, whose distant ancestors are presumed to have farmed and hunted in the era of Saharan fertility) eventually gained the upper hand in the struggles, out of which arose the **Sefawa dynasty** which ruled over **Kanem** – the concretion of mini-states northeast of Lake Chad – from about 850 AD.

Oral history claims that the founder of the dynasty was **Sayf Dhi Yazam**, and that he was of Arabic origin. It is possible, and more likely, that the first dynastic family had Berber connections rather than Arab. Whatever the truth, the authority of the *Mai* (as the kings of the dynasty were known – they converted to Islam in the eleventh century) gradually spread over nomadic peoples, and the *Mai* came to be accepted as a divine ruler. In Mecca, a special guesthouse was built for Kanem pilgrims and in Spain, the court of El Mansur (1190–1214) in Seville, numbered renowned Kanem poets among the courtiers.

A new series of conflicts arose in the thirteenth century that incited **Mai Umar bin Idris** to emigrate west to Bornu. The new empire – now effectively Bornu, rather than Kanem – remained unstable until the end of the fifteenth century when **Mai Ali Gaji** came to power, put an end to dynastic squabbles and established a new capital at Gazargamo, the first permanent residence in more than a century.

A new golden era was thus launched that reached its peak under the best known of the Bornu rulers – **Idris Aloma** – who ruled until 1603. He was a zealous Muslim reformer under whose reign Islam became the basis of Bornu ideology and who also achieved military advances by importing Turkish mercenaries and military advisors to instruct his troops in the use of muskets. Although the empire was among the most severely affected by the decline in trans-Saharan trade, Bornu was the only northern power to repulse dan Fodio's invasion. The Fulani did manage to attack the capital city and sent the king into retreat, but a Bornu *malam* (teacher) named **Al-Kanemi** organized a counter-offensive that successfully drove out the enemy. As a result, Al-Kanemi became the Bornu ruler and his sons started a new dynasty, drawing to a close the dynasty of the Sefawa, which, with its origins in the ninth century and a final date of 1846, may have been the world's most enduring line of royal rulers.

Maiduguri gained its importance as a regional capital only after 1907 when the British reinstated the Shehu in the new town where they had established a military base. It wasn't until after independence, however, that the town was linked to Kaduna by rail and thus gained a slight advantage for its beef, leather and groundnut exports.

The **zoo**, located across from the *Safari Hotel* at the end of Shehu Lamisu Way (Mon–Fri 9am–noon & 3–6pm, Sat & Sun 9am–6pm), is actually not bad, whatever your feelings about zoos. Many of the animals are captives without cages, and are kept in place by large ditches surrounding reproductions of their habitats. Shaded in a forest of neem trees, the zoo and park are excellent places for a picnic, and the whole town seems to turn out here on Sundays.

When the afternoon sun begins to drum down, head to one of the town's two **swimming pools**. The best is at the *Deribe Hotel*, which has crystal-clear water, but unfortunately serves no beer. The more central *Lake Chad Hotel* has murkier water and more people, but there is a poolside bar. Some dilemma.

Practicalities

Maiduguri has all kinds of **accommodation** ranging from cheap bordellos to **international-standard hotels**. Among the nicest of the latter is the *Deribe Hotel*, Kashim

Ibrahim Road (☎076/232 445; ④), with pleasant AC rooms and the town's best pool. It's kept in better condition than its nearest competitor, the *Lake Chad*, Kashim Ibrahim Road (☎076/232 746; ③), which is looking slightly worn despite extras like the pool, tennis courts and TVs. The *Borno State Tourist Centre*, Talba Road (down to Eagle roundabout and turn right) has a bar, restaurant and **moderate accommodation** with fan or AC (②). Another recommendable medium-range hotel is the *Mairi Palace*, off the Bama Road near the university. In addition to their comfortable rooms (②), they allow camping on the premises.

For **inexpensive lodging** try the *Merry Joe Guest Inn*, Bolori Layout (☎076/232 872; ①), which has rooms with or without AC that start at less than half the price of the upmarket places. It's clean and pleasant and there's a good bar and inexpensive restaurant. Similar hotels in the Bolori Layout include the *Safecon Hotel* (②) behind the *Merry Joe* and the *Aceta International Hotel* (☎076/232 871; ①). Along Kashim Ibrahim Road in the Galadima area, the *Horizontal Hotel* is slightly more expensive, but more central (②). For **dirt-cheap accommodation**, there's a "hotel colony" off Kashim Ibrahim Road near the railway tracks. A lively neighbourhood known for discos and cheap restaurants in addition to the hotels, the whole quarter is seething with notoriety. If you really want to save money you'll find the *Traveller's Hotel*, the *Peace and Charity*, the *Benue Annex Hotel*, the *Rockefeller Plaza*, and the *End Well Hotel*, all squalid and all within about a four-block radius of each other (①).

Eating

There are a couple of **inexpensive restaurants** on Bama Road, east of the museum. The first you come to is the *De Bee Restaurant*, which is pleasantly AC and serves very good European and Nigerian dishes. Nearby, the *Li Sandra* is popular with students as it has AC and serves cold beer (alcohol isn't allowed on campus) and reasonably priced food. Close to the Monday market on Ahmadu Bello Way, the clean and friendly *Lalle Restaurant* also specializes in inexpensive Nigerian food. The nearby *Nefertiti 2000* has inexpensive dishes like rice and chicken or beef and boiled yams. The *Bosco Café* is another popular place for inexpensive Nigerian chop. For **Chinese** food, *Chopsticks* has a cheap takeaway service.

MOVING ON FROM MAIDUGURI: NIGERIA

There are several **motor parks** in Maiduguri. To **Kano** and Biu (the Calabar road), the motor park is just outside the town gates along Airport Road. To **Baga**, Geidam and Gashua, the park is just up from the West End, past the railway tracks. To **Bama** (the Cameroon road), the motor park is after the customs roundabout on Ring Road.

The weekly **train** departure for Kafanchan junction (change for Lagos) is suspended along with all Nigerian rail services.

There are daily early morning **flights** on *Nigeria Airways* to **Lagos** via **Yola**, with additional afternoon departures on Mon, Wed, Fri and Sun via **Kano**. *Nigeria Airways* is at 19 Hospital Rd (☎076/232 743).

MOVING ON TO CAMEROON AND CHAD

If you're making the short crossing of Cameroon to **Ndjamena**, Chad, start off by taking a vehicle from the **Gamboru motor park** on the northeast side of Maiduguri (you won't need a Cameroon visa if you're simply passing through this narrow neck of the country en route to Chad). Four- and six-seater taxis shuttle to the village of Gamboru (Nigerian exit formalities). From **Fotokol** on the Cameroonian side (where you'll have to seek out the *douaniers* and *gendarmes* 1km away, but they're pleasant enough) you take a much more expensive ride to **Kousseri**, 100km away. For Kousseri and onward details into **Chad**, see overleaf.

KANURI PHRASES

Good day	*Ndawatu*	Come in	*Are*
I'm fine	*Kalewa sule*	Sit down	*Namne*
Hello	*Wooshe* (pronounce carefully: *Wus!* is an expression of disgust in Hausa)	I have it	*Fi*
		I don't have it	*Ma fi*

Nightlife

Because of the strong Muslim influence, nights in Maiduguri tend to be tranquil. But the presence of the university, which has a large proportion of students from the less Islamic regions of the south, means there are a lot of young people out to drink and have a good time, and a few decent **clubs** to dance away the nights. One of the most popular is the *Chez Coan Nightclub* behind the Federal Lowcost Housing Estate in Galadima. It's young and lively and also features a half-decent restaurant. In addition, the *Alliance Française*, behind *Leventis* and the *Deribe Hotel*, has a regular *disco-soirée* with a good mix of music, that attracts expats and some of the university crowd.

The Far East

Although Maiduguri feels like the end of the road – and certainly most Nigerians consider the town is already at the back of beyond – it is still 100km further to the borders of Niger, Chad or Cameroon. If you're driving in far northeastern Nigeria, it's as well to know that it's an area of some political sensitivity where you should notify the authorities of your movements before setting off from each town or village.

To Lake Chad

Getting to **Lake Chad** is somewhat difficult, and police are suspicious of people who want to go to the region whether they've come by their own means or with public transport. They've apparently been known to confiscate ID cards and to generally harass travellers. An additional problem is the total retreat of the lake itself from Nigerian territory over the last few years. The place to go if you want to check out the situation is **Baga**. Taxis head here from Maiduguri. When you get into town, check in with the police, who won't take long anyhow to discover your arrival. There's a customs and immigration post at Baga and, if the water is high, foot travellers may be able to get a boat across into Chad: the village of Baga Sola is 76km away to the northwest, about three days by pole and paddle or a full day by outboard. If there's no water, there's **accommodation** at the *Baga State Hotel* and the small village of **Doro**, 2km away, is interesting.

Bama and around

Bama, on the main road from Maiduguri to Cameroon (still in Borno State), is a Kanuri town with a large market – Saturday is the big day. There's a good *Guest House* on the southern side of town, which features occasional gatherings with dancing and *brukutu*, locally made Guinea-corn beer.

If you're driving a 4WD vehicle, and want to experience the **old route to Cameroon**, it starts with a left turn down a sandy, but motorable track, 38km down the A13 Bama to Gwoza road from Maiduguri. The track soon leads into a dry river bed which you follow to **Ashigashiya** and then, out of the riverbed, along tracks to **Mora** in Cameroon – about 25km in all.

Thirty-two kilometres south of Bama, **Gwoza** lies on the western flank of the **Mandara Mountains**. It's hardly visited in comparison to the relatively touristy villages a short distance away in Cameroon, and there's little in the way of facilities ouside the government resthouse, numerous chop houses and small market. Market day in Gwoza is Sunday, and there's a trade fair in March with demonstrations of local crafts like calabash-carving and mat-weaving.

From Gwoza you can hike east through the mountains (a four-hour trek) to another village, **Ngoshe**. There's no official accommodation here though enquiries at the police station or government Girls' School will produce some sort of solution for lodging. The mountain footpath is the quickest way between the two towns, but particularly hard to find, especially if you're coming from Gwoza to Ngoshe. It's less difficult in the other direction and many people use it on market day. In either case, ask people to point it out to you. If you have time, this trip makes for a rewarding excursion: the scenery is perhaps less impressive than on the Cameroon side, but the contact with the mountain people is much less contrived. There is regular transport to both Gwoza and Ngoshe from Bama.

Northern Adamawa State

The wedge of **Adamawa State** spreads from the Sahel near Maiduguri south along the mountainous Cameroon borderlands. It's a huge and very little travelled region but, if you can devote the necessary time, offers some of Nigeria's best rewards in terms of landscapes and traditional rural communities.

As you enter the state south of Gwoza, the scenery starts to become spectacularly spiky and volcanic. There are terrific hikes up into the **Mandara Mountains** east of the A13 Madagli–Mubi road. One route starts off from **Chambula**, about 12km southwest of Madagli, and goes some 10km southeast to **Mildo Market**. About 5km further you reach a school (keep asking, young people generally speak English and there's even hope of flagging down transport, especially during the market on Tuesday) from where you can expect (or hope) to be taken around the district. Bring food and flexibility.

The payoff for such remote meanderings is **SUKUR**, the seat of a once powerful mountain kingdom. There's a remarkable stone causeway – product of ancient civil engineering – from the school up to this village. Very few travellers make it this far and the people are refreshingly welcoming. They've set up a small "**guest house**", a traditional round hut with straw mats to sleep on, and have started a regional artefacts museum. Neither is exactly a reason for coming here, but the village itself is and people are more than willing to share their guinea corn and green leaf soup and show you around their unusually constructed compounds – round huts held together with stone, mud and thatch and surrounded by a protective wall. A **visit to the king** (*heedi*) imposes itself and slow clapping to greet him meets with enthusiastic approval. Though he doesn't speak English, he's remarkably hospitable, and through translators seems eager to recount the history of Sukur, from the early slave raids to the period when this village was part of Cameroon. People don't expect payment, even, as yet, for staying in the guest house, but given the level of generosity, you'll find it hard not to reciprocate with a gift. Photos seem appropriate (a Polaroid camera would come in handy here), as do hard-to-come-by pharmaceuticals. Even food makes a good gift; it's a long way to the market.

Further south along the A13, **Kamale** is a village with an amazing **volcanic plug** nearby – accessible from Michika, 20km south of Chambula. This whole area has everything in common with its Cameroonian counterpart and mountain people don't generally draw much of a boundary line (see p.1211).

Yola and Numan

The Adamawa State capital is **YOLA**, an unexceptional, flat, spacious town near the banks of the Benue. It's fairly accommodating, but the cheaper **hotels** tend to be a little more expensive than usual. Best value are the *Ise Hotel* (☎075/24810; ②), the *Palace* (☎075/25204; ②) and the *Bridge Hotel* (③) – in that order. A recommended upmarket place is the *Yola International Hotel*, on Kashim Ibrahim Road (☎075/25739 or 24669; ⑤). Run by the *Arewa* chain it has high standards of comfort and efficiency. If you need to travel fast, there are daily **flights** out of Yola on *Nigeria Airways* to Lagos and Maiduguri: their office (☎075/24713) is on Main Street in Jimeta, the new suburb on the riverbank 7km from the city centre.

If you're travelling on the A345 **Yola–Numan–Bauchi road** be sure to do so by day, and if you're going by public transport, get a window seat on the left. Don't stay in **Numan**, 60km west of Yola and an older town somewhat left behind by the state capital's surging modernism: both its hotels are dreadful. Numan to Gombe, however, is a superb stretch of scenery and, if you've got your own transport, there are some fantastic **hikes and climbs** in the Mouri mountains. **Tangale Hill** near Kaltungo, is a steep and stunning volcanic plug and a brisk three-hour climb, but you'll need permission from the Emir of the little town and help from local men in guiding you up.

Gashaka Gumpti National Park and Gembu

Further dramatic highland regions span Adamawa and **Taraba** states – to the southeast of Yola the Atlantika range, to the southwest the Shebshi Mountains (with 1690-metre Vogel peak), and, in the far south, in the corner of Nigeria tucked into western Cameroon, the verdant Mambila plateau around the town of Gembu. Although the region is similar to Obudu (see p.1076), few travellers venture here. It comprises some of the least explored, most exciting and unknown territory in the whole of Africa.

An area of nearly 7000 square kilometres of mountain forests and savannah abutting the border – still harbouring a sizeable **chimpanzee** population and, after an absence of several decades, **elephants** – is now protected as the **Gashaka Gumpti National Park**, and is the site of a major new World Wildlife Fund project in collaboration with the Adamawa and Taraba state governments. There are now eighty rangers, and ten wildlife officers for the park, and efforts to gear it up for visitors are in progress at the park headquarters in **Serti**, a village on the "main" road between Yola and Gembu, where there is some simple **accommodation** (①). The park entrance is 15km to the south.

In **GEMBU**, the main town of the region, 137km south of Serti and 430km south of Yola (very hard and slow travel by occasional bush taxis or land rovers), or 220km southeast of Wukari (see below), there's a half-decent **hotel**, though it has only sporadic electricity and water (①). An hour's trek towards Cameroon from Gembu takes you to the red clay valley of the **Donga River**, a superb sight as it snakes through the jungle. You can cross by canoe or raft, and climb a towering rocky peak on the other side for magnificent views (two hikes/4WD routes lead up into Cameroon near here, but ascertain driving viability locally). Another excursion from Gembu takes you to the **Highland Tea Plantation** and factory, beyond Kakara (a village 30km northwest of Gembu). You'll be the first traveller the management here has seen in a while, and they'll not only give you a tour of the place, but let you stay in the club (①), watch TV and videos, eat and drink beer, before sending you off with a kilo of produce.

Wukari to Cameroon – the Dumbo Trek

From the bustling market town of **Wukari** (try the *Catering Rest House*, or *Ishaku* or *Taraba* hotels), head for **Takum**, where the highlands ahead begin to make their presence felt (the *Dadin Kowa Supper Inn*, on the Yola road, is a reasonable place to stay; ①). Takum is at the southern end of the paved road and beyond it, looping into the green hills, with bananas and fleshy jungle plants increasingly conspicuous, there is just an earth track, mostly in reasonable condition, passing over innumerable frog-filled streams up to the village of **Bissaula** (also spelled Bissuala). You'll be able to get transport as far as here, though don't miss any vehicles that are going, as they're not numerous.

The Michelin map used to mark as a "recognized track" the route that snakes from Bissaula to **Dumbo** on the Bamenda Higlands Ring Road: an optimistic gesture, as it consists only of the roughest footpath, the first few kilometres of which scale a steep, rocky, root-entangled, forest-smothered escarpment, inaccessible to any vehicle. If you are keen to do some **trekking**, though, it's a winner: a moderately tough two-day hike (about 40km) that takes in towering trees, squealing parrots, leaping monkeys, thatched-hut hamlets in smoky forest clearings, and lines of porters (mostly portering on their own accounts, beer, cigarettes and cloth). When you reach the top, it seems half of southern Nigeria is spread out below.

You shouldn't set off trekking on your own – orientation here is very difficult – but for about ₦3000 (or CFA20,000) you can hire the services of a **porter** to walk up to Dumbo with your luggage (the Nigerian immigration post will stamp you out and write "Footing" in your passport). You can carry your own luggage, of course, but you should join with a group for the initial stages of the trek. You walk for about two hours through lush forest and farm plots, then start climbing the steep scarp, which takes a couple of hours to the top. People generally leave Bissaula late afternoon, and either spend the night in a village at the foot of the scarp and then set off at 4am, or reach the top of the scarp after dark and spend the night in the village there. With an early start on day two you can be in Dumbo by the evening, but it's less exhausting to arrive mid-morning on day three. You should be aware of the fact that the Cameroonian immigration and customs post at Dumbo isn't frequently blessed with tourists and may try hard to extract presents from you. If you take photos on the trek, try to be discreet – it's a slightly sensitive border area – and remove film before you get to Dumbo.

index

CHAPTER SEVENTEEN

CAMEROON

CAMEROON

The **landscapes of Cameroon** are exceptional. The country stretches from the fringes of the Sahara in the north to the borders of Congo and Gabon in the south and takes in every African variation, from equatorial rainforest (some of the continent's most unexploited tracts) to moist, tree-scattered savannah; from dry grassy plains to bucking volcanic ranges flecked with crater lakes; from gaunt rocky massifs to the swampy basin of Lake Chad; and, to cap it all, the highest mountain on this side of the continent – the 4095 metres of Mount Cameroon – rising direct from the ocean shore to an impressive cloud-wreathed summit. For good measure, the country also has some entrancing beaches and several large parks, with rewarding quantities of wildlife, including species found nowhere else in West Africa. At the simple level of tourism, it's hard to oversell Cameroon – it's simply the most dramatic country in West Africa.

There's another side to Cameroon in its hugely stimulating cultural make-up, which exhibits some striking **ethnic distinctions**: the Muslim sultanates of the north are reminiscent of northern Nigeria and also have strong Arab connections, but exist alongside the avowedly non-Muslim people of the mountainous Rhumsiki district; in the forests of the far south, the so-called "Pygmies" – the original inhabitants – still live a hunting and gathering life largely untroubled by the concerns of the modern nation state; and in the mountains and pasturelands of the country's western "bulge", a remarkable complex of kingdoms has developed over the last four hundred years, speaking dozens of Bantoid languages (closely related to Bantu). This is the only country in West Africa with a large **Bantu-speaking** population (the Bantu languages, including Swahili and Zulu, are some of the most important in Africa), which gives the south much in common with the Central African region. Coupled with its natural diversity, it's a country that can claim to embody cultural elements of the entire continent.

Cameroon has a colonial past of German, French and British occupation. With the current division between Francophone and Anglophone in every aspect of national life, it all means that a sense of national identity is profoundly lacking – and impressions of contrast and fragmentation are never far away. Recently the old Anglo-Francophone tensions have flared up fiercely, leading to calls for secession in the west. And as the economy began faltering in the 1990s, opposition has become more vocal in the northern regions as well. Wherever your travels take you, the prospects for political debate are good, though due to widespread police harassment, people are still wary whose ears their commentary may fall on.

The increasing importance of tourism as a source of foreign exchange has led to some improvement in official attitudes to foreign visitors. The searches and controls that once dogged visitors from the moment of arrival are no longer so aggressive. There are, however, still numerous roadblocks – little havens for police and custom officials to extract dash money – throughout the country. And the **tourist industry** has upmarket expectations: backpackers who sleep in D-class hotels and cram into bush taxis are still prone to be put down as *pauvres blancs,* and may experience the disdain of local law officers. If you wander off the beaten tracks leading to selected, officially promoted sites, you may well attract suspicion.

Where to go

Cameroon's main city, **Douala**, is a seething, sweltering metropolis that wins few accolades. Fortunately, an hour's drive from Douala, the black sand beaches of **Victoria**

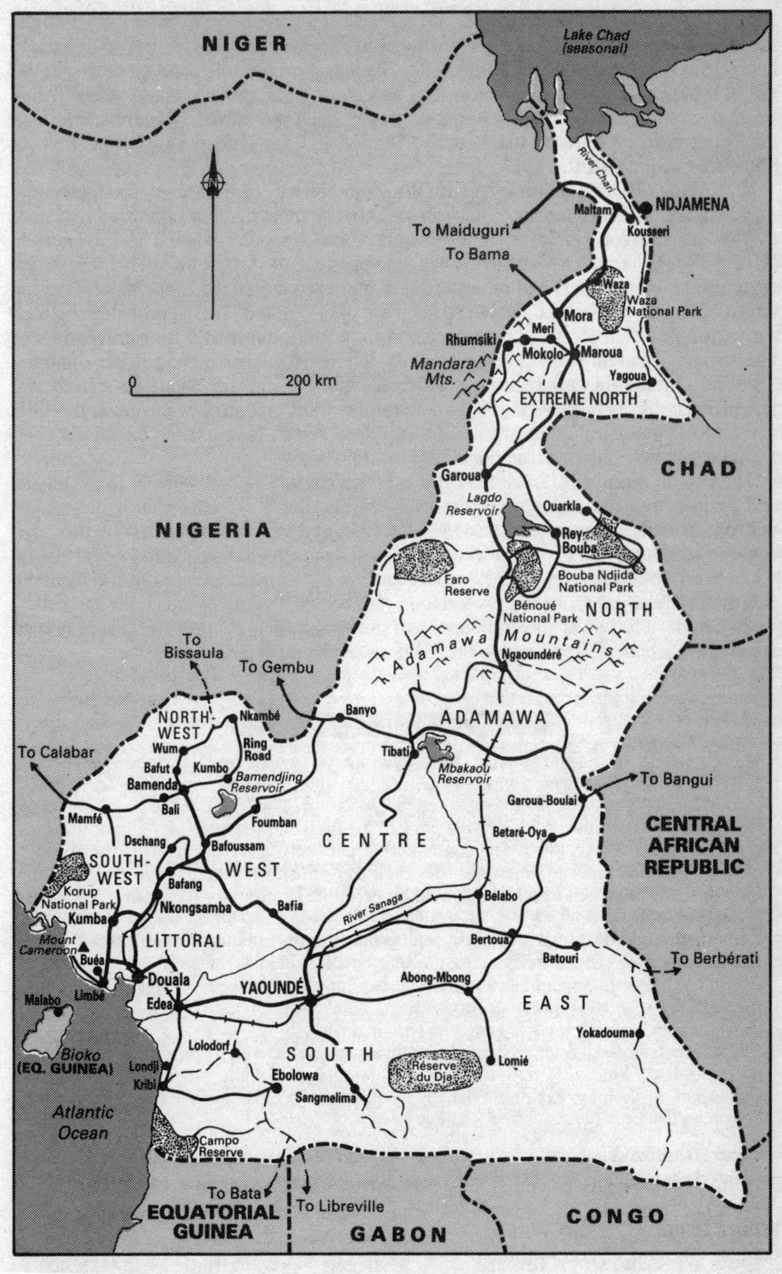
NIGER
Lake Chad (seasonal)
River Chari
NDJAMENA
Maltam
Kousseri
To Maiduguri
To Bama
Waza
Waza National Park
Mora
Meri
Rhumsiki
Mokolo
Maroua
Mandara Mts.
Yagoua
0
200 km
EXTREME NORTH
CHAD
Garoua
Lagdo Reservoir
Ouarkla
Rey Bouba
NIGERIA
Faro Reserve
Bouba Ndjida National Park
Bénoué National Park
NORTH
Adamawa Mountains
Ngaoundéré
To Bissaula
To Gembu
Banyo
NORTH-WEST
Nkambé
Wum
Ring Road
To Calabar
Bafut
Kumbo
Bamenda
Bamendjing Reservoir
ADAMAWA
Tibati
Mbakaou Reservoir
To Bangui
Garoua-Boulai
Mamfé
Bali
Foumban
Betaré-Oya
CENTRAL AFRICAN REPUBLIC
Dschang
Bafoussam
CENTRE
SOUTH-WEST
WEST
Bafang
Korup National Park
Nkongsamba
Bafia
Belabo
Kumba
River Sanaga
Mount Cameroon
LITTORAL
Bertoua
Batouri
To Berbérati
Buéa
Douala
Malabo
Limbé
Edea
YAOUNDÉ
Abong-Mbong
EAST
Yokadouma
Bioko (EQ. GUINEA)
Lolodorf
SOUTH
Londji
Kribi
Ebolowa
Réserve du Dja
Lomié
Sangmelima
Atlantic Ocean
Campo Reserve
To Bata
To Libreville
EQUATORIAL GUINEA
GABON
CONGO

(Limbé), in **South West Province**, are a good, quick getaway. Between the strands, the dense vegetation pushes right to the water's edge, although it has increasingly been cleared to create plantations of coffee, bananas, rubber trees and oil palms, in the rich soil beneath **Mount Cameroon**. The mountain, a still active volcano, offers a challenging – but perfectly feasible – trekking ascent. To the north of Mount Cameroon, the country drops towards the Nigerian border and the **Korup rainforest**, now an accessible national park.

The **West Province** and **North West Province** (the former predominantly Anglophone, the latter mostly Francophone) are the most densely populated region of Cameroon, and contain some of the country's most popular sites. The Province de l'Ouest (West Province) is relatively well-equipped for tourists, with a developed infrastructure of roads, hotels and other facilities, and even a quite cosmopolitan feel in the larger towns. Nevertheless, the landscapes are often rugged. This is probably the easiest region in which to strike out on your own, visiting the **traditional chiefdoms** of the Bamoun Tikar and others around the 400-kilometre red earth **Ring Road** – and the beautiful **Grassfields** area through which it circles – and the Bamiléké district and **Foumban**, with its Sultan's Palace and a crafts market that attracts buyers and sellers from throughout Africa. The whole of this upland region is renowned for its thatched architecture and animated traditional life.

The capital, **Yaoundé**, is, climatically, a better city to live and work in than Douala, and a more relaxed place to rest up from travels. But it remains a fairly aggressive metropolis with its share of tension. The vast **plateau** that stretches to the east, covered with huge tracts of hardwood rainforest – sapele, mahogany, iroko and obiche – has been little logged (in either sense) and renders great expanses of the **Central**, **South** and **East** provinces impenetrable. A number of **"Pygmy"** bands hunt and gather in the jungle, and this is also the domain of **gorillas**, which are quite prolific in certain areas: the Campo and Dja reserves are remote and have no facilities.

FACTS AND FIGURES

The **Republic of Cameroon** (or *République du Cameroun* to Francophones) covers 475,000 square kilometres, an area twice the size of Britain and somewhat larger than California, with a population estimated at twelve million. The name derives from *camarões*, the Portuguese for prawns, which the first European visitors found in large quantities in the Wouri River. The common reference to **"Cameroons"** is a legacy of the colonial division into two Cameroons – French and British – a dual heritage preserved in the official bilingualism (easily dominated by French). The country has been ruled since 1982 by **Paul Biya**, long the head of the *Rassemblement Démocratique du Peuple Camerounais* (RDPC), the country's sole political party until opposition parties were legalized in 1990. The country's foreign debt, at £4.5billion ($7billion), stands at more than three times the value of its annual exports of goods and services – a huge figure for the country's relatively small population, equivalent to £375 ($583) for every Cameroonian, a sum few could expect to earn in a year.

Cameroon is divided into ten administrative **provinces**, with governors appointed by the president. You may find their names confusing at first, especially in western Cameroon, in that, for example South West Province extends further north than West Province. The provinces and their capitals are:

Centre/Centre (Yaoundé)
South/Sud (Ebolowa)
East/Est (Bertoua)
Littoral/Littoral (Douala)
South West/Sud Ouest (Buéa)
West/Ouest (Bafoussam)
North West/Nord Ouest (Bamenda)
Adamawa/Adamaoua (Ngaoundéré)
North/Nord (Garoua)
Extreme North/Extrême Nord (Maroua)

North of Yaoundé, the northern sectors of Central and Eastern provinces are an immense, empty savannah, patched with forest. Together with the gaunt **Adamawa Range**, they effectively cut the country in two and hinder north–south overland travel. Further north you come into pre-Sahelian grasslands and dusty bush country. The upper tributaries of the **Bénoué** (Benue) flow through this region, where you'll find the **Bénoué National Park** and **Bouba Ndjida National Park**. They contain a wonderful richness and diversity of game including sizeable herds of elephants and buffalo, giraffes, lions and the only native rhinos in West Africa.

In the far north, **Waza National Park**, in the flat plains, is Cameroon's outstanding faunal reserve, with, at the end of the dry season, good conditions of visibility for its elephants, lions, giraffe, ostriches and a host of antelope species clustering at the waterholes. To the west, a few hours away, the other-worldly volcanic plugs of the **Mandara Mountains** are a beautiful, unsettling backdrop to the stony homeland of the non-Muslim "mountain people" (see below). The northernmost tip of the country, leading up to what's left of **Lake Chad**, is usually dry, but floods under the waters of the **Logone** and **Chari** rivers during the brief, annual rains.

The people

The oldest group of people to have lived in Cameroon are the "**Pygmies**" of the south and southeast forests. Although forced onto the defensive by the expansion of the various Bantu-speaking groups (many have settled in small villages, notably in the area around Kribi), most of these people have opted for the traditional independence of the impenetrable rainforest where they live by the hunt.

Although over the best part of two thousand years, there had been a gradual southeasterly spread of **Bantu-speaking** populations through the Cameroon region into central Africa, Bantu-speaking communities migrated in strength from the Adamawa range and settled along the coast from about the fifteenth century. The first to migrate were the **Bassa** and **Bakoko**, followed by the **Douala**. In the nineteenth century, pushed in a chain reaction by migrations engendered after the Fula Sokoto invasions in Nigeria, the **Fang**, **Ewondo** and **Eton** came from the plateaux in the east to settle in the central southern region around Yaoundé.

In the west of the country, waves of northern immigration between the sixteenth and nineteenth centuries saw the installation of "**Semi-Bantu**" peoples. The first to arrive were the **Tikar**, who probably came from the area near Ngaoundéré and who today live in semi-autonomous chiefdoms throughout the Grassfields. In the eighteenth century a splinter group broke away from the Tikar country to form the powerful **Bamoun** empire a little to the east. The **Bamiléké** – a fusion of peoples from the north, east and southwest whose arrival spread over three centuries – settled in the plateau region south of the Noun River. Now the country's largest single ethnic group, the Bamiléké are also numerous in Douala where they have come to control a good deal of the national economy.

The predominant group in the north is the **Fula** (also known as Foulbé or Peul) who settled in principalities (*lamidats*) around the early nineteenth century, bringing Islam with them. But the mountains of the far northwest are inhabited by staunchly non-Muslim groups known collectively as **Kirdi** – which just means "infidels". Pushed to these desolate extremities by the Muslim invasions of dan Fodio, they comprise numerous Adamawa- and Chadic-speaking peoples: the **Podoko**, **Fali**, **Kapsiki**, **Mafa** and **Bata**. Principally farmers, they grow millet in terraced gardens on the rocky slopes of the mountains.

The northern plains near Lake Chad are home to the **Choa**, semi-nomadic peoples of Arab origin, who share these open spaces with the **Kotoko** – descendants of the ancient Sao culture – who live from fishing and growing a few cereals. Near the Logone River live the **Toupouri**, **Massa** and **Mousgoum**, people of pre-Islamic belief who are increasingly becoming Islamized.

Climate

The region around Mount Cameroon and the western mountains has the dubious privilege of one of the highest levels of **rainfall** in the world: Debundscha, 30km west of Victoria (Limbé), is the second wettest place on earth, after Cherrapungi in India. The general pattern here and in **the south** can be divided into three approximate seasons: a period of relatively light but persistent rains from March to June; the long rainy period from July to October; and the dry season from November to February. Travel can involve great waits during the rains, especially to or from towns accessible only by track, such as Mamfé. Roads around the Grassfields are often unmotorable during the rains when even four-wheel-drive vehicles can have problems. The grasslands further north choke towards the end of the dry season with fine red laterite dust, blown up by the northerly *Harmattan*. Plants and crops turn rusty red, while cameras – and lungs – seize up.

Northern Cameroon, north of the Adamawa Plateau has a different weather pattern, characterized by a long rainy season from May to October. Although travel in

AVERAGE TEMPERATURES AND RAINFALL

YAOUNDÉ

	Jan	Feb	Mar	Apr	May	June	July	Aug	Sept	Oct	Nov	Dec
Temperatures °C												
Min (night)	19	19	19	19	19	19	19	18	19	18	19	19
Max (day)	29	29	29	29	28	27	27	27	27	27	28	28
Rainfall mm	23	66	147	170	196	152	74	79	213	295	117	23
Days with rainfall	3	5	13	15	18	17	11	10	20	24	14	4

DOUALA

	Jan	Feb	Mar	Apr	May	June	July	Aug	Sept	Oct	Nov	Dec
Temperatures °C												
Min (night)	23	23	23	23	23	22	22	22	22	22	23	23
Max (day)	30	30	30	30	30	28	27	27	27	27	29	29
Rainfall mm	46	94	203	231	300	539	742	693	531	429	155	64
Days with rainfall	4	6	12	12	16	19	24	24	21	20	10	6

KOUSSERI

	Jan	Feb	Mar	Apr	May	June	July	Aug	Sept	Oct	Nov	Dec
Temperatures °C												
Min (night)	14	16	21	23	25	24	22	22	22	21	17	14
Max (day)	34	37	40	42	40	38	33	31	33	36	36	33
Rainfall mm	0	0	0	3	31	66	170	320	119	36	0	0
Days with rainfall	0	0	0	1	6	10	15	22	13	4	0	0

the north doesn't present any special problem during this period, note that the national parks are closed, depending on the rains, roughly between May and December. Overall, the **ideal time to visit** the country, taking into account different regional patterns, is December and January.

Arrivals

Getting to Cameroon is facilitated by the fact that *Cameroon Airlines* is one of Africa's best. Flying in, however, suffers the disadvantage of arrival in the uncomfortable and rather heavy city of Douala (unless you use one of the few direct flights to Yaoundé). Arriving overland from the east, Cameroon feels like the threshold of a new region, which it is, as you leave the confines of the Central African rainforest and enter West Africa.

■ Flights from Africa

Cameroon has **international airports** at Yaoundé and Garoua, but most foreign flights still arrive in Douala. **Cameroon Airlines** (UY) has a good network, connecting African cities with Douala. West African flights to Douala on UY include: from **Abidjan** via **Lagos** (Mon, Tues, Thurs & Sat); from **Accra** via Lagos (Mon & Tues); and non-stop from **Cotonou** (Tues & Sun).

Air Afrique (RK) flies to Douala from **Dakar**, via **Conakry** and Abidjan (Fri); from Abidjan via **Cotonou** and Lagos (Wed); from Abidjan via **Lomé** (Sun); and non-stop from Lomé (also Sun).

Other flights from West Africa include the non-stop flight on *Air Gabon* (GN) on Sun; and the twice-weekly flights on *Nigeria Airways* (WT) from **Lagos**, via **Port Harcout** (Mon) and **Calabar** (Sat). From the Sahel capitals of Bamako, Ouagadougou and Niamey, the most likely reasonable connections to Douala are via Abidjan.

Close political and economic ties ensure that Cameroon has good air links with its neighbours in Central Africa. Between RK, UY and GN, direct flights originate in **Bangui** (three flights a week); **Brazzaville** (three); **Kinshasa** (three); and **Libreville** (four). UY and *Unitair* (inauspiciously coded UN) have between them four flights a week from **Ndjamena**, Chad, via two or more of Maroua, Garoua, Ngaoundéré, Bafoussam and Yaoundé. UY and Equatorial Guinea's airline, *Ecuato Guinean de Aviacon* (8Y) also operate regular flights from **Malabo**, Equatorial Guinea.

From East Africa, UY flies from **Nairobi** (always heavily booked) on Sun, via **Kigali** and **Kinshasa**, and on Wed via **Bujumbura** and Kinshasa, while from southern Africa, there's a UY flight from Johannesburg via Harare on Fri.

The details in these practical information pages are essentially for use on the ground in West Africa and in Cameroon itself: for full practical coverage on preparing for a trip, getting here from outside the region, paperwork, health, information sources and more, see *Basics*.

■ Overland from Nigeria

The two main overland routes from Nigeria lead to **Mamfé** in the west of Cameroon and to **Mora** in the north. Coming in via the north, if you don't already have a Cameroon visa, you may be forced to head south (see "Red Tape").

The southern route is straightforward and involves getting a bush taxi from **Calabar to Ikom**. From here small taxis leave regularly to the busy border, where the tarmac ends abruptly, and where, after completing Nigerian customs and immigration formalities, you walk over the bridge spanning the Cross River and up the hill to the Cameroonian post at **Ekok**. Taxis from Ekok to **Mamfé** rattle along bumpy tracks through a beautiful but tortuous mountain region. There are a couple of variations on this route, one via the Oban Rainforest National Park and one using boats through the creeks (see p.1074).

The main northern route leads from **Maiduguri to Bama** over a good flat paved road, where taxi drivers love to get up a bit of speed. Forty kilometres separate Bama from the border post at Banki. From here you can get taxis across the unpaved plains (look out for antelope) to **Mora** and on to Maroua or up to Waza National Park.

■ Overland from Central African Republic

A reasonable, graded road runs from **Bouar** in the west of CAR to the Cameroonian border post at **Garoua Boulaï**, and a rougher route leads from **Bebérati** in CAR to **Batouri**. In each case, the road deteriorates in Cameroon to become a difficult, bone-shaking track. To minimize the *piste*, either head north from Garoua Boulaï, to Meiganga and find continuing transport to Ngaoundal (273km from Garoua Boulaï) where you can take the **train** southwest to **Yaoundé** or north to **Ngaoundéré**; or take transport to Bertoua (260km from Garoua Boulai and 90km from Batouri), from where a 45-minute taxi ride will deposit you at the train station at Bélabo. For schedule details, see the relevant "Moving On" sections.

■ Overland from Equatorial Guinea and Gabon

The main road from **Bata** in **Equatorial Guinea** heads far inland to **Ebebiyin**, at the point where Gabon, Cameroon and Equatorial Guinea all meet. From here, you travel via **Ambam** to **Ebolowa** where there's the choice of heading either direct to Yaoundé or taking the roundabout but more scenic coastal route via **Kribi**.

You'll use this same arrival point (Ambam) if you come up from **Gabon**, reached from **Libreville** by heading to **Oyem**, where you can pick up transport to Ambam.

■ Overland from Chad

There is now a bridge between **Ndjamena** – the capital of Chad – and **Kousseri** in Cameroon, open from 6am to 5.30pm. Details of this border are given on p.1214.

Red Tape and Visas

All passport holders (other than certain African nationals) need visas to enter Cameroon. In the past these have been given only with reluctance at Cameroon embassies other than in the applicant's country of residence.

In West Africa, **Calabar**, **Lagos**, **Abidjan**, **Monrovia** and **Dakar** are the only places which have embassies or consulates. There are no embassies or consulates in the Sahel states. The embassies in Abidjan and Lagos have recently been refusing visa issue to transient travellers. The consulate in Calabar is more flexible and issues visas without problems for around $50, though you should try to exhaust all other options before arriving this far in case the situation changes.

Broadly, **visas** are expensive, valid for three months, and must be activated within one month of issue. They're generally issued for an initial stay of twenty days. The main requirements are either a return air ticket, or proof of your intended onward route – including any other relevant visas. Stays are not hard to extend in any of the provincial capitals, though expect some hassle in Yaoundé. More difficult is the prospect of trying to prolong your stay beyond the validity of your visa.

If you are travelling from Central or East Africa, Cameroonian embassies and consulates can be found in **Central African Republic**; **Chad** (rue des Poids Lourds, Ndjamena; ☎51.28.94); **Equatorial Guinea** (c/ de Rey Boncoro, Malabo; ☎/Fax 22.63); **Congo** (rue Bayardelle, Brazzaville; ☎83.34.04); **Zaire** (171 bd du 30 Juin, Kinshasa; ☎12/34787); and **Ethiopia** (Bole Rd, Addis Ababa). In **Kenya**, the French embassy issues Cameroonian visas.

For more on red tape, see the "Roadblocks" box see p.1131, and "Photography" on p.1136.

■ At the border

When you arrive in Cameroon – especially if you come in overland – immigration officers may well want to check that you have what they consider to be **sufficient funds** to stay in the country. If your visa is in order, you shouldn't have difficulties getting in.

Health certificates are frequently checked on the road, and must be presented at the border. A certificate for yellow fever is always obligatory, and for cholera when there are epidemics in Cameroon or neighbouring countries. It's a good idea to have this latter certificate, though the jab itself is not considered effective (see p.34).

Money and Costs

Although Cameroon uses the CFA franc (CFA100 for 1 French franc; approx. CFA750–800 = £1; approx. CFA500 = US$1), it is part of the Central African economic zone. West African CFA are exactly equivalent in value, but the bills for the two regions are different and people on the streets will refuse West African notes. The two currencies are easily exchanged in banks.

The best way to carry your money is in French franc **travellers' cheques**. There tends to be a flat fee for changing money, rather than a percentage, so it may make sense to change all your money at once. One or two banks (or possibly certain branches of them) seem to levy no commission: try *Société Commercial de Banque–Crédit Lyonnais* first, then *Banque Méridien BIAO* and *BICIC*. Pounds and dollars are easily converted in Yaoundé, Douala and one or two other big towns, but in smaller places, you are likely to encounter great difficulties changing them and may not be able to make a transaction at all.

Outside the two major cities, banks frequently run out of money, especially around payday (at the end of the month). **Credit cards** have made advances in big city hotels and some shops and restaurants. *Visa* is the most widely accepted, and the most reliable too for cash advances.

There is no limit on importation of cash in any currency. There's an **export limit** on CFA francs of CFA20,000, unless you're going to a franc zone country, in which case there's no limit. Any CFA you have left over when leaving Cameroon can, in theory, be exchanged at the fixed rate – if you can find a bank with French francs.

■ Costs

Cameroon is one of the three or four most expensive countries in West Africa. Living cheaply, and travelling on your own, you can probably expect to average CFA4000–6000 daily for **accommodation** (maybe CFA5000–8000 for two). Douala is by far the country's most expensive city for lodging and even budget accommodation here is no bargain. Fortunately, there are numerous missions throughout the country that take in travellers, especially in the Anglophone North West and South West provinces. The country's most expensive **luxury hotels** charge over CFA40,000 per night.

The cost of **bus and bush taxi travel** varies widely, depending on the remoteness of the route and the condition of the road. Expect fares to vary from CFA10 to CFA20 per kilometre.

Health

Cameroon poses no exceptional health problems. Malaria prophylaxis is essential throughout the country and there are multi-drug resistant strains. It's generally okay to drink the tap water in major towns. If you have doubts, you can find bottled water everywhere except in small villages, but it becomes increasingly expensive the further north you go.

Cameroon, like most countries in West Africa, has a serious **schistosomiasis** (bilharzia) problem though it's usually safe enough to use free-flowing stream water in the highlands, especially after recent rain. There's a major regional initiative based in Cameroon and assisted by USAID which may help to eradicate the disease from large areas of the country in the near future.

■ Health care

Medicines, well within their sell-by date, are available over the counter in most pharmacies. Dental care in Douala and Yaoundé is excellent. Hospital care is also very good in the capital, although the "polyclinics" in the rest of the country are generally poorly stocked with medicines and equipment, and often dirty. You're expected to supply your own food in hospital.

Information and Maps

Abroad, tourist leaflets and information are best obtained at the *Cameroon Airlines* offices in Europe, listed below. The embassies too, may have some information, though probably the same stuff (see pp.21–28).

CAMEROON AIRLINES

UK 44 Conduit St, London W1 (☎0171/734-7676).
France 12 bd des Capucines, Paris 7500 (☎47.42.78.17); and 55 pl de la République, Lyons (☎78.92.87.89).
Germany Langer Kornweg 19, 6092 Kelsterbach Main, Frankfurt (☎61 07 60 37).
Italy via Bissolati, Rome (☎474.51.33).
Switzerland 12 quai Gi Gruisan, Geneva (☎20.28.44).

■ Maps

It's well worth getting hold of some **maps** before arriving in Cameroon. Much the best-looking is the *Macmillan* road map of Cameroon, which has excellent city maps for Douala and Yaoundé on the flip side, but was published in 1988. The 1994 *Institut Géographique National* map is more up-to-date on newly surfaced roads, but inaccurate about the year-round viability of many others and less clearly designed. Both maps are at 1cm:15km. The *Michelin* #953 is good, though you need the #955 as well if you want coverage of the southernmost hundred kilometres of the country.

Getting Around

The main choice for travelling around Cameroon is between road and rail. The roads can be okay, though the good-

quality paved sections are often separated by endless kilometres of rough dirt track, while the trains only cover certain very limited routes – barely venturing for example into the north or the west. As for flying, *Cameroon Airlines* and *Unitair* cover a good deal of the country, though at a price.

■ By road

Although 35,000km of roads criss-cross Cameroon, only about 4000km are paved. Even those are often in decay, with sections washed out by floods or pitted with potholes. Less-used dirt roads in particular can also be blocked for several days by overturned vehicles.

That said, the roads around and between **Douala** and **Yaoundé** are always reliable, as are those from Douala to **Bamenda** or **Foumban** via Bafang and Bafoussam (though not via **Mamfé**, which some maps show as the main road).

Western Cameroon has a reasonable road network and there's a long-unrealized plan to surface the Bamenda highlands Ring Road. The north is well served by the highway which runs between **Ngaoundéré** and **Maltam**, past the four national parks in the north.

The entire **centre** of the country, however, lacks a good system, the **Adamawa Plateau** providing a formidable obstacle. Between **Yaoundé** and **Ngaoundéré**, where the dirt roads are quite appalling, you'd be wiser taking the train – in fact you can even take a car on the train, though that option has become quite expensive. In the east of the country, the dense forest is another barrier to overland travel, and there are no good paved roads.

The far **south** – pretty well everywhere south of Yaoundé apart from the paved roads to Ebolowa and Sangmélima – is held together by dirt roads and tracks through the forest, though the new paved road to **Kribi** has cut travel time to that beach resort considerably.

A couple of **dangers** are peculiar to road travel in Cameroon: firstly the law that forbids motorists involved in an accident to move their cars until the police have inspected the site – meaning that all traffic may be held up for a couple of hours (quite apart from the implicit danger of hanging around if you are the party at fault); and secondly the behaviour of Cameroonian hitch-hikers, who often attempt to stop cars by standing in the middle of the road with both arms outstretched. Stopping is an implicit offer of a lift, so they tend to stand just round a blind corner where cars will be forced to screech to a halt to avoid killing them.

Taxis and buses

In the absence of a national transport system, most Cameroonians rely on **taxis de brousse.** Beware of what seems to be the common trick of booking you onto a bush taxi journey only for the vehicle to stop before your destination and transfer you to another vehicle. You don't pay any more, of course, but it can make the journey twice as long if the second bush taxi is slow to fill up.

Increasingly, **buses** link major towns and cities. Besides being more comfortable and running on fixed schedules, they tend to pass police checkpoints quicker. Within cities, taxis cost CFA125 for most short distances – one of the few real bargains in Cameroon. Taxi drivers

ROADBLOCKS

The one hazard even the most careful driver can't avoid in Cameroon is **police roadblocks**. These are usually on the outskirts of towns, often outside a bar or café. They're not easy to spot, as they may consist of no more than a policeman fast asleep in camouflage fatigues, and a piece of string stretched across the road.

Cameroonian police are less troublesome to foreigners than they were a few years ago, but can still be drunk, abusive, surly, and alarmingly casual about pointing submachine guns at your stomach.

The best precaution you can take is always to travel with a full clutch of documents, whatever current regulations may say – better to show an International Medical Certificate ("carte jaune") than to insist that you aren't required to carry it.

As a foreigner, you're permitted to move about with a certified photocopy of your passport, which avoids the fear of having it confiscated at a police check. Take the original and copies of the first five pages (as well as your visa) to any main police station, where it will be stamped and signed for a small fee.

Recently **péages** or **toll barriers** have been set up on the highways outside many towns.

generally don't attempt to overcharge – it's hard to imagine why not.

Car rental

Car rental rates border on the outrageous. This is especially true of the main operators – ***Hertz*** and ***Avis*** – which at least back up their high prices with reliable cars and services. You will find car rental agencies only in the larger towns (Douala, Yaoundé, Garoua, Maroua, Ngaoundéré, and Kousseri); their addresses are in the "Listings" sections of the guide. Rental charges are higher in the north, and you'll be charged extra for any *piste* driving as opposed to street driving. If you rent on a daily basis, expect to pay about CFA40,000 per day for a European or Japanese compact, made up of a basic rate of around CFA15,000 per day plus CFA150/km, plus extra for taxes and insurance.

■ By rail

The **Régiefercam** operates nearly 1200km of track, along two main routes. First is the western line from **Douala to Nkongsamba** (172km, up to eight hours' travelling time), which branches to **Kumba** at Mbanga.

The substantially longer *Transcamerounais* line links the country's two major cities with Ngaoundéré in the north. **Transcam I** covers the 308-kilometre stretch from **Douala to Yaoundé** with up to four services a day in each direction (about CFA4500 first class). Given that this train takes over three hours, it's often more convenient to do the 233 kilometres by road. **Transcam II** forges on for 620km from **Yaoundé to Ngaoundéré** with a daily overnight service in each direction (about CFA15,000 first class). This is a fairly quick trip – roughly twelve hours assuming there are no delays. Certainly you couldn't expect to get through this part of the country any more quickly by road.

Carriages are relatively comfortable, with restaurant cars and air-conditioning in first class in some trains. Couchettes (linen, blankets and pillows provided) are available on the *Transcam II* route if you book the morning of the day you're leaving. Second class (roughly two-thirds of the first-class fare) has seats only and is often crowded. Food is available from vendors in the stations, but you ought to take your own water for the trip. Reductions are possible with **student cards**.

The railway authorities are extremely sensitive about foreigners taking **photographs**, and it would be wise to pack your camera deep inside your bag during the journey.

■ By air

Cameroon Airlines and *Unitair* operate a reasonably efficient domestic service connecting **Douala** and **Yaoundé** with each other and **Bafoussam**, **Bamenda**, **Batouri**, **Bertoua**, **Garoua**, **Mamfé**, **Maroua**, and **Ngaoundéré**. Details are given in the relevant town sections in the guide. The northern towns are usually linked in series, which makes the flight up to Maroua very long. Note that on the routes to Maroua, Garoua and Ngaoundéré, *Cameroon Airlines* offers **student reductions** (ISIC card or letter) and weekend excursions (available to all, out Fri or Sat, back Sun or Mon).

Five or six daily flights connect Yaoundé and Douala. Most other links have services varying from three times a week to daily. Note that flights are often overbooked: arrive early and hope for the best.

Accommodation

Hotels in Cameroon are officially classified from A to D. The luxury ones – those with air-conditioned rooms containing bath and shower and extras like swimming pool, tennis courts and the like, fall into the A category. After that, it's hard to discern how hotels are classified, especially since in the cheaper *auberges*, some rooms may have AC or fans, while others little more than four walls and a barely sleepable bed.

Ratings take into account only the facilities and not considerations like cleanliness and service, which you may find more important than finding a toilet that doesn't flush in your grimy private "vaysay". In the west and south, the most expensive regions, you can expect to pay anything from CFA4000 a night for D-class to CFA60,000 for A-class.

■ Camping and missions

If you have your own transport, **camping** away from the major urban centres is a fine alternative to hotel living. The game parks and natural reserves are restricted, but that only excludes a small chunk of the north. Elsewhere, there are tens of thousands of square kilometres of wild country you can freely pitch in. See p.53 for advice.

The **missions** scattered throughout Cameroon often put up travellers, but they don't have to – and don't always want to. In Douala and Yaoundé,

ACCOMMODATION PRICE CODES

Hotel prices in this chapter are coded according to the following scales – the same scales in terms of their pound/dollar equivalents as are used throughout the book. Prices refer to the rate you can expect to pay for a room with two beds. Single rooms, or single occupancy, will normally cost at least two-thirds of the twin-occupancy rate. For further details see p.51.

① **Under CFA4000 (under £5/$7.50).** Rudimentary hotel or *maison de passage*. Running water and electricity treated as luxuries. Not classified.

② **CFA4000–8000 (£5–10/$7.50–15).** Commonest budget-price bracket, with simple but adequate amenities. S/C rooms with fans are the norm. Some rooms may have AC. Class D.

③ **CFA8000–16,000 (£10–20/$15–30).** Modest hotel with S/C rooms. There is usually a choice: rooms with fan or rooms with AC at a small premium. Class C/B.

④ **CFA16,000–24,000 (£20–30/$30–45).** Reason-able business or tourist-class hotel with S/C, AC rooms, and often a restaurant. Class B/A.

⑤ **CFA24,000–32,000 (£30–40/$45–60).** Similar standards to the previous code band but extra facilities such as a pool are the norm. Class A.

⑥ **CFA32,000–40,000 (£40–50/$60–75).** Comfort-able, class-A hotel, with good facilities.

⑦ **Over CFA40,000 (over £50/$75).** Luxury, class-A establishment – top prices around CFA80,000.

the religious institutions are a real godsend if you're on a budget. In the face of ever-increasing demand, however, many missions are starting to turn away all who are not on church business. In recent years the government has tried to enforce this policy by decree.

■ Staying with people

There's a large European presence in Cameroon, so you won't be thought special or exotic. Travellers are treated with nonchalance and you're unlikely to receive many offers to **stay with people**. You may find exceptions in the north, where the rocketing price of accommodation in out-of-the-way villages such as Mokolo has given enterprising young people the idea of "inviting" travellers to spend the night in their homes. If you stay a couple of days, they can earn a month's income, even for a contribution that is negligible compared to what you'd pay in a hotel. You might find this blend of commerce and *camaraderie* a little difficult to handle, but it's a solution that benefits both parties. Be clear about prices before agreeing to any such arrangements.

Eating and Drinking

Cameroon has a rich and varied cuisine, with a heavy emphasis in the south on cassava, yams and plantains and in the north on maize, wheat, millet and groundnuts. Fruit and vegetables are probably the best in the whole of West Africa and the variations in climate and altitude mean you can get nearly everything all year round – except the luscious and varied types of mangoes, in which Cameroon excels and which are in season from February to May.

In common with much of Francophone West Africa, **French cuisine** dominates in the big hotels and expensive restaurants – though all the glitter is no guarantee of special food. When you're paying CFA20,000–30,000 (the price per head in many Douala and Yaoundé restaurants), you don't expect tough meat and soggy vegetables.

As for **Cameroonian cuisine**, although you're unlikely to find such specialized regional treats as fried termites, grasshoppers, dog, snake or cat in Yaoundé, you can taste a wide variety of national dishes without leaving the capital. Beware that in the city centre of Douala, and especially Yaoundé, it can be very difficult to **eat cheaply**. Even restaurants serving what seem like standard Cameroonian dishes, may be charging the earth for *plats typiques*.

In "bush bars" and country town cafés, an item such as "omelette" (about CFA700–1000) is likely to include toast or bread, a cup of tea or soft drink, chilled water, and perhaps chips or peas.

All over, especially in the north, you'll find the tasty little snack kebabs known as **soya**, exactly like the *suya* of Nigeria. With French bread they make a good meal.

■ Dishes

Cameroonian cooking varies radically by region. **Millet**, most commonly ground and made into a stodge, and **rice**, are the staples of the north.

In the equatorial south, plantains and tubers such as **yams and manioc** (cassava) dominate the diet. These can be boiled, pounded or even grilled, but invariably turn out bland – a characteristic which may put you off at first, but that complements the fiercely peppered sauces quite nicely. **Atchu** is the Grassfields version, made from small, quite tasty, cocoyams. **Bobolo**, a heavy, nearly translucent cassava preparation, comes in a miniature *baguette* shape, while **miondo** is fermented cassava served wrapped up in banana leaves. The most widely eaten southern dish is **ndolé**, made from a boiled bitter leaf pounded into a paste. Seasoned with hot oil and spices, it's eaten with fish or meat. The similar **kwem** is made from pounded cassava leaves and usually eaten with a red, palm oil sauce. Such meals are served throughout the south in small restaurants known as *chantiers* ("worksites"), run by *veuves joyeuses* ("merry widows") or *tantes* ("aunties").

■ Buying your own food

If you plan to buy food to cook for yourself, expect to pay the same for vegetables as in Europe. A wide range is available in the markets, and basic vegetables like potatoes, cereals, onions and yams are roughly the same price throughout the country, with reductions near the place of cultivation. Fruit and vegetables for export, such as pineapples and mangoes, vary enormously in price depending on growing area and season. At harvest time in a growing area you can buy a sack of ten pineapples for CFA1500; you often see the roof rack of a *taxi de brousse* with half a dozen sacks on top, perhaps to be sold in a mango-growing district down the road.

Good bread and pastries are available throughout the country at fixed prices, and there's a good selection of **supermarkets** in most major towns.

One final bargain, wherever you might be in Cameroon, is superb local **chocolate**.

■ Drinking

The *Brasseries du Cameroon* represents one of the country's most important industries. Although relatively expensive, **"La 33"** is real prestige beer, often associated with French-style affluence. Other brands include *Guinness*, *Gold Harp* and *Special*. If you're not into alcohol, the brewery also manufactures minerals (*sucreries*) in sickly-sweet orange, yellow, brown and colourless. If it's hot (and they're cold), you may even enjoy these syrupy carbonates. Mineral water can be had in the big hotels, and at most large supermarkets.

Palm wine (*mimbo*) is available throughout the south and west, where the best quality is said to come from raffia palms. After distillation, it becomes **arki**, or "African gin". Other indigenous drinks include millet beer and corn beer (*kwatcha*).

Communications – Post, Phones, Languages and Media

Cameroon has a real mixture of facilities in the communications field, with sophisticated telecom systems in the metropolitan areas and virtually no communications in parts of the far south and remote centre. Linguistically it's very diverse – easily the most complex and interesting country in Africa. In the field of the media, there's much less to be proud of, through no fault of the journalists, who've endured well-documented harassment despite the liberalization of the press laws in the 1990s.

■ Post and phones

Post offices keep the same hours as other offices, Mon–Fri 8am–noon & 2.30–5.30pm, and Sat 8am–1pm. Letters to Europe take a week to fourteen days. The **poste restante** service seems to operate well enough in Yaoundé and Douala.

Douala and Yaoundé have a sophisticated modern **telephone** system which is generally reliable between the two cities and has IDD to Europe. First-try connections are common. Phoning up-country is considerably less reliable.

Cameroon's IDD code is ☎237.

■ Language

Uniquely in Africa, Cameroon has **two official languages**, French and English, and a difficult

A CAMEROON GLOSSARY

Auberge Cheap hotel or *maison de passage.*

Ba- Means "people of" in the Bantu and Semi-Bantu languages, widely extended (by European geographers) to indicate their towns and villages. Place names are a good deal easier to remember if this prefix is mentally dropped.

Boukarou In hotel jargon, bungalow-like huts with thatched roofs.

Chantier Literally a construction site. In Yaoundé's popular jargon "street food stands".

Circuit Northern appellation for *chantier.*

Fon In western Cameroon, a chief or king.

Kirdi Collective name for the mountain people of the Mandara range. It means pagan, since most of these people are non-Muslim and non-Christian.

Lamidat In the north, equivalent to a sultanate. The sultan is the *Lamido.*

Mayo In the north, a river or dried river bed.

Ramassage "Collection" or "pick up". You take a taxi *en ramassage*, meaning you share it (and the fare) rather than rent it individually.

Saré Sudanic-style huts common in the north.

Sauvetteurs Wandering vendors, hawkers.

Stationnement Motor park.

but worthy policy of bilingualism in the civil service and education. In practice, French has always had the upper hand. The majority of the country is Francophone, and only 22 percent (corresponding to the populations of North West and South West provinces) is Anglophone. This of course does not mean that most people speak one or the other language, although you might get that impression in the big towns. In North West and South West provinces, people in major towns usually speak **Pidgin English**, which is a different language, and doesn't come easily to an outsider – though you'll recognize a few words.

Of the four generally accepted groups of **African languages** (Afro-Asiatic, Nilo-Saharan, Niger-Congo, and Khoisan – divisions that contain languages as diverse as those found within the Indo-European group) all but Khoisan-related tongues are spoken in Cameroon. In all, some 160 different dialects are spoken, representing seventeen different language families. In the face of such diversity, some languages have become lingua francas. In the south, **Douala** and **Bassa** are often used as trading languages, while in the north **Pulaar** (the Fula tongue) has taken on that role.

The media

The press looks quite limited in Cameroon, especially if you've just come from print-mad Nigeria. The *Cameroon Tribune*, a daily published in French and English editions, represents the (laconic) voice of the government – with so few lines to read between it's hard keeping informed. The independent press mushroomed in the early 1990s but has been the target of severe government harassment. *Le Messager* and *Challenge Hebdo* are two widely read opposition papers that may or may not survive. **English-language periodicals** such as *Cameroon Outlook*, the *Cameroon Post*, *Cameroon Times* and *The Gazette*, mostly published in Victoria (Limbé), account for a great deal of Cameroon's press.

Radio Cameroon, broadcasting from Yaoundé in French, English and main Cameroonian languages, repeats, between programmes of African music, everything you could have read in the paper.

Arts and Entertainment

Cameroon has produced a number of highly regarded dramatists, film-makers and novelists, of whom the best known are *cinéaste* Jean Pierre Dikongue-Pipa and writers Mongo Beti and Ferdinand Oyono (see *Contexts*). But it's the country's musicians who have most successfully put Cameroon on the map for a world audience.

By repute and commitment, **Francis Bebey** – multi-talented artist in the broadest sense – is Cameroon's honorary cultural ambassador to the world. But more familiar in the record shops is the tireless saxophonist, singer, pianist and arranger **Manu Dibango**. Dibango helped popularize the Makossa style. Makossa – the name derives from *kosa*, to strip off – is Cameroon's biggest dance music, a sexy fast-paced rhythm, now increasingly underscored by thunderous bass and, with the influence of Paris, only a squeeze away from Zouk. **Sam Fan Thomas** and **Moni Bile** are the two other best-known exponents out of hundreds (more coverage in *Contexts*).

Less enduring stars of recent years were **Les Têtes Brulées**, whose wild cross-cultural appearance (day-glo "tribal paint", shaved and sculpted hair and the clumpiest trainers they could find) and an album of the same name, stirred up a whirlwind of excitement abroad and confusion and controversy at home when they became internationally famous in 1989. If their success has now burnt itself out, their fast-paced musical style, **Bikutsi**, is still very popular, especially in Yaoundé.

Directory

AIRPORT TAX CFA5000.

ARTS AND CRAFTS It's illegal to take antiques and certain works of art out of the country without government authorization. That still leaves a wide variety of arts and crafts to choose from. The most famous region for art is the Bamoun-Bamiléké district of West and North West provinces, known for carved statues, masks and bas- reliefs. The long tobacco pipes used by the Tikar and others of the region have become popular tourist items and are widely available. Northern Cameroon is more renowned for leather and jewellery, fashioned primarily by the Fula. Samples from all the regions can be found at the *marché artisinale* in Yaoundé.

Many antiques are smuggled down the Gamana and Donga rivers from Nigeria, which has strict views about the export of its heritage, and harsh penalties for smugglers. If you are continuing north from Cameroon, don't buy anything that even looks old; it will almost certainly be confiscated by Nigerian customs officers, whether antique or not.

There's not likely to be a problem exporting artworks through Douala airport, as export rules are loosely observed. If you want to check, call the Ministry of Economic Planning Cultural Affairs Division in Douala on ☎22.51.89.

CRIME Douala, and increasingly Yaoundé, are especially dangerous after dark, and stabbings are common, with money the main motive. Cameroonian justice is rough. The death penalty exists even for minor thefts, though few get as far as the courts. They may be dealt with by a roughing-up behind the police station or, if the cry of "Voleur" is heard, by a beating from an angry crowd.

DRESS AND APPEARANCE A strong streak of puritanism runs through Cameroon's official psyche, especially in the Anglophone regions. Western men will attract the disdain of officials and many locals if they go bare-chested, or wear earrings, or have long hair – especially in dreadlocks. At best you may be regarded as a "bush man", at worst as the village idiot. Shorts are acceptable if you are engaged in some kind of sporting activity, like hiking or biking. Otherwise, Cameroon is cover-up country, unless you're prepared to put up with the sniggering.

EDUCATION Long the only university in the country, the **University of Yaoundé** now has an enrolment of 20,000 students. In the early 1990s, the specialist faculties at Douala, Dschang, Buéa and Ngaoundéré were also upgraded to university campuses. Students from South West and North West provinces commonly head to Nigeria to pursue higher education.

FOOTBALL Always a wildly popular sport in Cameroon, after the **Indomitable Lions'** mighty result in the 1990 World Cup (they reached the quarter-finals against odds of 100:1), and their qualification for the 1994 World Cup, the status of soccer is now close to religious. Cameroon certainly has some of Africa's, and the world's, finest players, though regrettably for home games, many have given their careers to European clubs. Go to a match. The big teams are **Canon** and **Tonnerre** of Yaoundé and **Union**, **FC Rail** and **Dynamo** of Douala.

HOLIDAYS AND FESTIVALS Shops and administrative services all shut down for the major **Muslim and Christian holidays**. The most important of the **official holidays**, the *Fête Nationale*, takes place every May 20. On this day, parades and speeches commemorate the 1972 approval of the referendum for a united Cameroon. Other holidays include **Labour Day** (May 1) and **Youth Day** (February 11).

OPENING HOURS Most businesses, banks and offices are open Mon–Fri 8am–noon & 2.30–5.30pm, and Sat 8am–1pm. The practice of weekday continuous opening from 7.30 or 8am until 3pm is gaining ground.

PHOTOGRAPHY Although you're theoretically allowed to take pictures openly, photography is hedged about with restrictions. These go beyond the usual military and "national security" taboos to include anywhere the president is likely to stay when travelling, parades and festivals and anything "likely to cause a decline in morality and damage the country's reputation". The interpretation of this law is left to the person who decides to take you to task for breaking it. Taking pictures in Yaoundé and Douala, all over the forest zone and in Muslim areas in general, is likely to lead to trouble unless you're very discreet or very charming.

POSTCARDS Look out for the handpainted and screenprinted cards by local artists, available in bookshops and at the *Seamen's Mission* in Douala.

RELIGION Officially, Catholics, Protestants and Muslims number about a million each, but this estimate sounds too fortuitous to be true. Given that the country's population is now about twelve million, it seems clear at least that an overwhelming majority still practises traditional African religions.

WILDLIFE Cameroon is blessed with a wonderful natural heritage, as the late Gerald Durrell discovered in the 1950s. Fortunately, it seems the government is fairly committed to saving some of it – even at the expense of lucrative logging contracts and difficult decisions over local development. There are enough national parks to validate the country's safari claims and the latest initiative, in league with the powerful World Wide Fund for Nature, is the **Korup National Park** in a remote corner of rainforest in the southwest on the Nigerian border. Details are given on p.1163. In Cameroon's other parks, you can do the closest to an East African safari available on this side of the continent. Cameroon is the only country in West Africa that has rhinos. These, along with most other African big game, including one of Africa's largest elephant counts, can be seen in several localities. Cameroon actively encourages paid-up hunting, however, as part of its conservation strategy.

WOMEN IN CAMEROON There's not been a great deal of progress for women in Cameroon, though there is a Ministry of Social Affairs and Women's Affairs in Yaoundé – which you might call (☎22.41.48) if you're keen to make contact with groups in the country.

Any foreign woman considering marriage to a Cameroonian man should be aware of the law that requires a husband's written permission for his wife to leave the country. The law applies equally to foreign nationals, and even to those with work visas. It's not strictly enforced for holders of tourist visas leaving through Douala, but an unaccompanied wife can't guarantee being able to exit the country without her husband at her side.

A Brief History of Cameroon

In the southern half of the Cameroon region, the first Bantoid-speaking peoples had moved in by 200–100BC from the Nigerian plateau, displacing the original inhabitants (the people of small stature known as "Pygmies") and pushing them deep into the forests. But the earliest clearly defined presence in Cameroon is that of the materially advanced Sao culture, which developed around Lake Chad, and left archeological evidence in the form of works in bronze and terracotta – human and animal figures – coins, dishes, jewellery and funeral jars. From the eighth century the Sao evidently began mixing with peoples pushed southward by the powerful empire then forming in Kanem (the Kotoko who live along the banks of Lake Chad and the Logone River are thought to be their descendants). Today, Cameroon is a complicated mixture of peoples, none of which is really predominant. As an archetypal example of an artificial state its present configuration derives in large part from the imposed colonial history of the last hundred years, a legacy from which it is still struggling to break free.

■ The arrival of the Portuguese

In 1472, the Portuguese navigator **Fernando Po** led an expedition around the Bay of Biafra and was the first European to penetrate the estuary of the **Wouri River**, which he called *Rio dos Camarões* ("Prawn River"). From this time on, the coastal region gained influence, taking over from such northern powers as the **Bornu Empire** (which extended down to the Benoué in the sixteenth century). The centre of trade shifted to the regions around Douala, Limbé and Bonaberi where local chiefs signed consecutive trade agreements with the Portuguese, Dutch, English, French and Germans. These chiefs rounded up slaves and ivory which they traded against cloth, metal and other European products.

Although commerce flourished over the ensuing four centuries, the Europeans didn't settle on the Cameroonian coast until the nineteenth century, when British missionaries began to protest against the **slave trade**. In 1845, an English pastor, **Alfred Saker**, founded the first European settlement in Cameroon at Douala. Although he set up churches and schools Saker was hardly a liberator. He recognized early on the strategic importance of **Douala** and **Victoria** and pushed for them to become crown colonies.

With the arrival of British, German and French **commercial houses**, trade shifted to "legitimate" exports of palm oil, ivory and gold. But the **Douala chiefs** became increasingly worried they would lose their role as middlemen between interior peoples and the Europeans and sought British guarantees that would have led to a protectorate. Queen Victoria hesitated. By the time she finally sent an envoy to make an arrangement, the Germans had beat her to it. On July 12, 1884, **Gustav Nachtigal** signed a treaty with the Douala chiefs **Bell**, **Deido** and **Akwa**, who willingly ceded their sovereignty to Kaiser Wilhelm in exchange for trade advantages.

■ The German, French and British occupations

In 1885, Baron von Soden became the first governor of *Kamerun*, and spent the next ten years trying to quell **rebellions** in the interior. He was replaced by **von Puttkamer** who relied on forced labour and brutality to carve out the colony's first **railway line** in 1907. But the promising economic results of the German activities, which included building some roads, hospitals and schools, came to an abrupt halt with the outbreak of **World War I**. In 1916, after a long, arduous and bloody campaign, the Allies wrested control of the territory from Germany and, in 1922, it was officially placed under French and British mandates – with only about one fifth of the area ceded to Britain.

The **British Cameroons** were joined to Nigeria in an administrative union, but lay outside the framework of development plans for Nigeria, and received only minimal funding. Ironically, much of the growth in the region after World War I was spurred by the **Germans** who returned as private citizens to develop the plantations around the Victoria plains. (When, in the 1930s, many of them rallied to the call of Nazism, they were expelled and their private development efforts consolidated into the *Cameroon Development Corporation*, today the country's second biggest employer.) The **French** were more active in developing the infrastructure. Cultivation of the main export commodities of cocoa, palm oil and timber increased dramatically. French plans, however, relied heavily on exacting taxes and forced labour (in lieu of tax), to extend the road network, enlarge Douala's port and build up the vast plantations. Arising from such methods, well-founded grievances grew up over French rule.

■ The beginnings of nationalism

After World War II, the United Nations renewed the French and British mandates. The **British sector** continued – essentially – to be ruled from Nigeria. On the eve of independence, two camps emerged; the first pushing to become a state within the Nigerian federation, and the second calling for reunification with "the other" Cameroon.

In the **French territory** the call for reunification was also voiced. Political parties began to form, including the **Union des Populations Camerounaises** (UPC) and the less radical **Bloc Democratique Camerounais** of northerner **Ahmadou Ahidjo**.

The UPC was the first party to call both for unification of the two separate Cameroons and for **independence from France**. Prevented by force of opposition from attaining these demands legally, it organized a **revolt** in the larger towns of the French colonies in 1955. The uprising was put down, but at the cost of hundreds of lives and huge economic waste and destruction. The UPC, using increasingly extreme and violent liberation tactics, was banned in 1956 by the French government, but its influence barely diminished, especially in the **Bamiléké country** and **Sanaga region** where rebellion continued to foment and was brutally suppressed.

The UPC's actions acted as a catalyst to Cameroonian nationalism and focused the attention of more conservative parties on developing specific policy. Its influence was felt by leaders such as Ahidjo, who was still working within the political mechanism put in place by the French. In 1958 he founded a new party, **l'Union Camerounaise** and became the Prime Minister of the *Assemblée Legislative du Cameroun*. His platform called for reunification, total independence and national reconciliation.

■ Independence

Ahidjo met his first aim when he proclaimed **independence** on January 1, 1960. The next year, his goal of reunification was also partly satisfied. Following a United Nations plebiscite, the northern half of the former British territory voted to join Nigeria, while the southern British Cameroons voted to join the Francophone territory. But national reconciliation proved more difficult as the UPC problem dragged on and it took a further twelve years before Ahidjo (with continued French assistance) prevailed over the rebels when their last members were executed. In remarkably astute political manoeuvring, he then neutralized much of the internal opposition by integrating it into his government and the enlarged party, **l'Union Nationale Camerounaise**.

As the political wrinkles were being ironed out (symbolized through the adoption of a new constitution, the dissolution of the federal system and the formation of the **United Republic of Cameroon** in 1972) progress was also being made on the economic front. Like Houphouët-Boigny in Côte d'Ivoire, Ahidjo focused first on developing agriculture and then moved on to basic industry. Thanks in part to the discovery of oil, the country's GNP nearly doubled in the first twenty years of independence. By the end of the 1970s, Cameroon was thus shaping up as one of the rare stable countries in the region. If reports of **political prisoners** and repression trickled out of the country, and **Anglophone students** (to single out just one obvious group) were supremely dissatisfied with the way Cameroon was going, the West turned a blind eye on the autocratic excesses of a reliable friend.

■ A change of regime

Yet, as the years dragged on, it looked as though Ahidjo was settling into a pattern all too familiar in post-independence Africa – that of the powerful political leader who refuses to relinquish power or look to the future. He had been president for 22 years when he rather unexpectedly stepped down in 1982, citing ill-health as his reason. Just as Senghor had done in Senegal, he passed the sceptre to a young prime minister of his own grooming, from a different background – the 49-year-old bilingual southerner, **Paul Biya**. Recognized for his honesty and competence, Biya had barely been in office a year when his reputation, and that of Cameroon, took a beating in the international press.

Trouble started in 1983 when Biya fired the prime minister and several members of his cabinet, on the grounds that he had uncovered a **treasonous plot**. Ahidjo resigned as UNC party boss and, from his residence on the French Riviera, he openly criticized his heir, claiming that Biya was turning Cameroon into a police state, and asserting that he had been tricked into relinquishing power by faked health reports (it seems the former president was resentful that Biya would not allow him to transfer his vast fortune out of Cameroon, and was sensitive to Muslim worries that the balance of power had shifted to southern Christians). The showdown had begun, but Biya seemed to have all the cards. Ahidjo was sentenced to death in absentia.

Although Biya then pardoned his predecessor, things went from bad to worse in 1984, when units of the presidential guard formed by Ahidjo (and still loyal to the ex-president) revolted in Yaoundé. They were only put down by the army after three days of **fighting in the streets** of the capital and an unknown death toll that has been estimated at as many as 1000. Ahidjo denied any involvement, but Biya cracked down on dissidents and dozens of guard members were secretly tried and executed. Calm returned and Biya consolidated his position, but the incident showed the world that, even in Cameroon, stability is fragile.

■ Consolidation of power

For months after the coup attempt, Biya rarely left the presidential palace. Indeed, many observers expected a further attempt to overthrow him, and it was widely believed an irreparable rift between the north and the rest of the country had been opened. But after a series of purges within the government, military and public sector, the president seemed to gain confidence.

As the nation prepared for the five-year congress of the UNC, in 1985, expectations ran high that Biya would announce sweeping reforms, including the revival of a multi-party system. Such hopes were disappointed when the president directed that no legal opposition to the ruling party would be allowed. Furthermore, he announced he was changing the UNC's name to the *Rassemblement Démocratique du Peuple Camerounais* (RDPC), apparently a move to distance the political body from its association with Ahidjo. At the same time, he moved towards a **cautious democratization** within the party, and in 1986, elections were held for members of RDPC bodies from the village level up to the *départements* which saw the emergence of a lot of new blood.

On an **international level**, relations improved with the West, and in 1985 Biya made a much-publicized official visit to France. This was viewed as a conciliatory move, as the two countries had been on bad terms due to the widely believed suspicion of French complicity in the attempted coup of 1984. Shortly afterwards, Biya travelled to Britain, and in 1986, to West Germany, the Vatican City and Canada. Also in 1986, Cameroon became the fourth African nation, after Zaire, Liberia and Côte d'Ivoire, to restore diplomatic relations with Israel, partly in response to the wishes of the American government, with whom Biya was seeking closer ties after the cooling of relations with France.

These events, however, were largely overshadowed by the worst **natural disaster** in the nation's history. In late 1986, an eruption of underwater volcanic gases escaped at Lake Nyos, a crater lake in the grassfields of North West Province. A cloud of deadly chemicals leaked into the atmosphere, suffocating at least 2000 people almost instantly and killing thousands of head of livestock. It caused great insecurity among local people who depend heavily on the crater lakes for fish and drinking water. Even some of the Anglophone intelligentsia persisted in the belief that a crude American or Israeli experiment in chemical warfare had been carried out at the lake site. Rumour aside, Lake Nyos served to bring Cameroon under the international spotlight once again.

At the end of 1986, Biya announced that **elections**, scheduled for early 1989, would be brought forward to April 24, 1988. The sole presidential candidate, he was "elected" to a new term by 98.75 percent of the votes, a bit of a dip since his 99.98-percent win in 1984.

■ The 1990s

At the end of the 1980s, Biya's great strength – apart from skill at political manoeuvre – lay in the relative stability of the economy. Cameroon moved to the middle-bracket status of underdeveloped nations, its gross national product per person much above West Africa's average. When coffee and cocoa prices dropped in the early 1980s, Cameroon was able to fall back on its rapidly growing oil exports, which actually pushed foreign trade into a surplus. But as the country entered its fourth decade of independence, economic and political stability were about to undergo serious challenges.

Pro-democracy – anti-people?

Not that the decade didn't start without optimism. In July 1990, Biya's address to the RDPC indicated a willingness to go down the road to a multi-party system. "One can imagine things will go quite fast in the coming months", he said. However, **Amnesty International's** much publicized concern on political detentions and torture, and steady pressure from Paris on reforms, explicitly tied to **debt relief**, made this announcement of measures to liberalize politics look like a response to unexpected events, rather than a planned programme of reform.

Two events in particular detonated the political bedrock. The first was the arrest of the former president of the Cameroonian Bar Association, **Yondo Black**. Black, from Douala, was arrested early in 1990 and sentenced to prison on charges of showing contempt for the president and planning for a multi-party political system. There was an immediate response from the **Cameroonian legal community** and 200 lawyers went on strike to demand Black's release. He was finally freed in August – significantly, after Cameroon's surprise success in the **World Cup** focused international attention on the country.

The Black affair triggered the other event that pushed Biya into talking democracy. The newly formed, but unlicenced **Social Democratic Front** – the vanguard of the pro-democracy movement – proceeded, despite a government ban, with its inaugural rally in Bamenda on May 26, 1990. In the run-up, **troops** were massed in the town. The organizers managed to get over 30,000 people onto the streets. After a peaceful demonstration, attempts to disperse the crowd met with stone-throwing and, in the ensuing rout, troops shot into fleeing marchers, killing six people and injuring dozens more. On the same day in Yaoundé, the university campus was the scene of brutal attacks on **students** supporting the rally.

Leaders of the SDF, not all of them from the Anglophone region, claimed the Anglophone districts were being treated like a colony by the Francophone. As support withered for the government in the North West and South West provinces, the Bamiléké of West Province – powerful in Cameroon commerce – also lost enthusiasm after the slaying of a senior lawyer, **Pierre Bouobda**, at a Bafoussam roadblock on the day of Black's conviction. The ill will from the west, added to continued resentment from the north about the treatment of Ahidjo and his barons, amounted to a heavy show of support for the opposition.

As pressure mounted, the national assembly adopted a draft law in December 1990 for the introduction of a multi-party political system. By early 1991, over twenty opposition parties had registered and collectively – under the banner of the **National Coordination Committee of Opposition Parties** (NCCOP) – they began calling for a **national conference** to outline the country's political future.

Biya flatly refused and seemed taken aback that the opposition, with its disparate regional, ethnic, religious and political elements, had united so quickly against him. He placed seven of Cameroon's ten provinces under military rule, lashed out at the mushrooming **independent press**, and prohibited opposition gatherings. His hardline stance led to an uneasy period of demonstrations. As security forces became increasingly violent in their crackdown on opposition rallies, the NCCOP tried a tougher tactic – a nationwide campaign of civil disobedience. **Operation Ghost Town** began in July 1991 as a highly effective strike that closed the ports and brought business and transport to a halt from Monday to Friday, allowing the public to buy food at weekends. The economic effect was crippling for the big towns and industries. Even in Douala, business slammed to a standstill.

But Biya refused to budge and the **stalemate** continued through much of 1991. The strikes dragged on until November, when the government, opposition and civilian organizations agreed on the formation of a constitutional committee. Biya consented finally to release all political prisoners, lifted the ban on opposition meetings and set legislative elections for February 1992. Not everyone was happy, however. As Biya began tailoring the process to suit RDPC aims (he insisted on a single round of voting and forbade coalitions from participating), many opposition elements – including two of the four principal parties, the SDF and the *Union Démocratique Camerounaise* – called for an **election boycott**. The RDPC won 88 of 190 seats, but although the national turnout was put at 66 percent, in the western provinces less than ten percent of eligible voters participated.

Biya's political support was clearly flagging and the president mounted an assiduous attempt to secure re-election. A secret committee was set up to control every aspect of the poll and was shameless in its bid to influence the National Vote Counting Commission and to skew the voter registrar. The domestic media were tightly controlled: the Douala-based printing house which published most of the independent newspapers was surrounded and closed; papers such as *Le Messager* and *Challenge Hebdo* were censored or banned; some opposition candidates were refused free access to public radio and television.

But the principal opposition contender – the SDF's **John Fru Ndi**, an Anglophone bookseller from Bamenda – was better organized than Biya expected and he gathered widespread support throughout the country. Internationally, he scored high marks as he travelled to Germany, Britain and the US, and Nigeria openly backed his candidacy.

The opposition's momentum, however, was no match for Biya's tight control over the election process. After the polls of October 11, 1992 the president claimed 39.9 percent of the vote to Fru Ndi's 35.9 percent. The United States' National Democratic Institute, which had monitored the elections, wrote a scathing report of wilful fraud and widespread irregularities.

Predictably, demonstrations broke out almost immediately, provoking the kind of repression reminiscent of Africa's pre-democratic dictatorships. Amnesty International reported mass arrests and related deaths as a **state of emergency** was declared in western Cameroon. Fru Ndi and other prominent leaders were placed under house arrest. Journalists were detained and tortured.

The bad press refocused international attention on Cameroon. South Africa's Nobel Prize-winning peacemaker **Desmond Tutu** tried to negotiate a settlement, but the government and opposition were too far apart to consider his proposals for a unity government. After his release, Fru Ndi, flew to Washington where he had been invited for the January 1993 inauguration of President Clinton who quickly imposed economic sanctions on the Biya government. For his part Biya flew to Paris and negotiated a loan of $115 million to help stave off IMF pressure to resolve the growing **national debt crisis**.

The current impasse

The nation has been at an impasse ever since. Biya, who had spent years cultivating the image of a humane and stable leader, came out of the fight bruised and battered. International papers described him as a degenerate autocrat – an epithet that had already been circulating inside the country for some time.

The president was effective in dividing the opposition. When western Cameroonians convened in 1993 at two **All-Anglophone Conferences**, in Buéa and Bamenda, they called for a return to a federal system of government, and more radical members advocated **secession**. Northern opponents, on the other hand, sought change within the system. Their principal party, the *Union Nationale pour la Démocratie et le Progrès* (UNDP) had participated in the elections and could therefore pursue regional aims in parliament.

Meanwhile, Fru Ndi has been only marginally successful in separating himself from the Anglophone cause and in promoting himself as a national, rather than regional, leader. His campaign for constitutional reform and a transitional government to set the stage for new elections is entirely extra-parliamentary.

Only the **threat of war** shifted the focus from the sphere of domestic politics when, in early 1994, hostilities with Nigeria flared over the long disputed border at the Bakasi peninsula. Though the conflict was limited to localized incidents, the military posturing on both sides led to speculation of a full-fledged confrontation, and the situation remains unresolved.

Addressing **the economy** is Biya's biggest task, and his first priority is to repair relations with foreign creditors. He began ousting top-ranking cabinet members in 1994, a move designed not to accommodate the opposition, but to satisfy Western pressure to reduce the size of government. Despite this move and the World Bank's acknowledgement that Cameroon's economy has declined faster than any other in the region in the last ten years, donors have virtually blocked all aid to the country, charging Cameroon with gross mismanagement and corruption. Even France has become reluctant to make credit arrangements and now publicly admits that economic assistance will not work without political liberalization.

The tightened money supply came at a time when Cameroon was feeling the bite of the **CFA devaluation**. The country has been hit harder than any other in the franc zone. Though coffee and cocoa planters reaped the benefits of increased prices, their earnings have been offset by the higher cost of imports such as fertilizer and pesticides, and by an inflation rate which was running at around 40 percent in 1995.

Biya's best hope for the near future is the project to build a thousand-kilometre **pipeline** from the oilfields of southern Chad through Cameroon to the port at Kribi. The country stands to gain $500 million annually from the pipeline which will generate thousands of new jobs. The timing is fortuitous since Cameroon's own oil industry has declined and the country is predicted to be a net oil importer by the year 2000. For now, however, the World Bank still won't commit to approving credit to build the pipeline, and even if work started immediately, it would be years before the fuel started flowing.

Though oil, coffee and self-sufficiency in food are a healthy combination, the combined effects of debt, devaluation and a political climate that has scared away private investment are real concerns. As the pressure mounts, the opposition appears to be moving closer together. The UNDP has recently begun adopting a more radical position, perhaps hoping to distance itself from the current government before the next presidential elections.

For the meantime, a dissatisfied and impatient people seems resigned to the fact that human rights and a real measure of democratization are not at the top of the government's agenda. But if the economy slips further as the World Bank continues to tighten the screws, it's hard to imagine how even a political survivor like Biya will overturn the next onslaught of mass disapproval.

DOUALA AND SOUTHWEST PROVINCE

As **economic capital** of Cameroon, **DOUALA** is a vast and energetic city. The driving force behind its growth has been the **port**, which handles ninety-five percent of the nation's maritime traffic and has stimulated regional development in trade and industry. But despite Douala's activity and relative prosperity, the cityscape is a relentless urban jungle distinguished neither by traditional flavour nor modern flashiness. Urban planners have concentrated their efforts on Yaoundé in the interior, with the result that Douala suffers from overpopulation and a worn-down and inadequate infrastructure. It's all a bit depressing – and aesthetically disastrous.

Fortunately, a variety of natural highlights are within easy reach of the metropolis. For simple rest and recuperation, you can't beat the **black sand beaches** of **Victoria**, a small town with a distinctly British flavour tucked against wooded mountains on the ocean. On a clear day in Douala, you can just about make out **Mount Cameroon** – West Africa's highest peak. The colonial town of **Buéa** is only 70km away, 1000m up the slopes of the mountain, and makes a good base for climbing expeditions. Continuing north, **Kumba**, a vibrant commercial town located near beautiful **Lake Barombi**, makes a good stopover on the way to Nigeria. Kumba is the first base for a visit to **Korup National Park**.

Douala

Despite its status as the nation's largest city, **DOUALA** is not dazzling. The architecture is dreary, with neither spectacular modern buildings nor attractive colonial remnants, and the streets in the major commercial and administrative quarters lack atmosphere. With certain exceptions, notably the lively market area around the **Lagos neighbourhood**, Douala could hardly tempt you to explore, nor to stay long enough to figure out its complex patchwork of peoples – even if it were not also a somewhat unsafe place. The population has skyrocketed in recent years and may now have passed the million mark, an influx which, in conjunction with a scarcity of jobs, has brought about acute social malaise. Crime is rampant and certain areas of the city – those around the port, for example – are just plain dangerous.

Some history

Like so many settlements on the West African coast, the Douala area was once home to small fishing communities, who first came into contact with Europe when the **Portuguese** made contact at the end of the fifteenth century. Although trade – especially in slaves – between local rulers and seafarers continued for many centuries Europeans didn't settle on the shores of the Wouri (or Cameroons) River until the nineteenth century. The first were **English missionaries** led by **Alfred Saker** who, in 1845, founded a small community at the site where the Eglise du Centenaire stands today. By that time, the **Douala people** (who probably arrived in the estuary at the beginning of the seventeenth century) were established into two groups united around the **Bell** and **Akwa** families.

German trading companies followed in the footsteps of the missionaries and quickly persuaded Bismarck to protect their interests in the region. The German chancellor thus sent **Gustav Nachtigal** to claim the lands in the name of the Kaiser. In July 1884, Nachtigal signed treaties with the chiefs Bell, Akwa and Deido. With the flick of a pen, British designs in the region were wiped out and the Douala chiefs had ceded legal

TOURIST INFORMATION

The **Service Provincial du Tourisme** (☎42.14.22) is located on avenue de Gaulle beyond the tennis club. They have **city maps** of Douala and Yaoundé and the usual pamphlets for travel in the different regions. Some bookshops sell the Douala street map for CFA2500, but many streets are unnamed both on the map and on the ground. Locals and taxi drivers give directions by landmarks – hotels, nightclubs, water towers – rather than by street names.

rights to the territory (at least they had by German law). In 1885, a German governor was appointed and **Kamerunstadt** became the capital. The name stuck until 1907 when it was changed to Douala.

After World War I, Douala became part of the French protectorate. Although it was no longer capital of the territory, the French began large-scale urban construction, and enlargement of the port. Industry followed and Douala forged ahead to become the economic engine of the whole country.

Arrival and city transport

The **airport** at Douala handles nearly all **international** flights to Cameroon. Older than the airport at Yaoundé, it's showing signs of age, and is surprisingly small. From the airport, you can get a **taxi** to the town centre for around CFA3000. Though the **bus** service to the airport is suspended, you can get **collective taxis** to town by turning left out of the airport and walking down to the local "SOTUC Terminus". The driver will drop you in the middle of the Lagos Market – a sure way to get radical culture shock if you're arriving direct from Europe.

If you happen to arrive **by train** from Yaoundé, the station is just off boulevard de la République in the northeast part of the city centre.

Coming into central Douala **by bush taxi**, the main **gares routières** are **Yabassi** (also known as **Sotuc**, after the SOTUC bus company) for Yaoundé and Kribi, and **Rondpoint Deido** (or simply **Rondpoint**) for Buéa and Victoria (Limbé). Arriving at either *gare*, it's best to take a cab to the centre. Long-distance drivers sometimes continue all the way into the centre, letting off passengers along the way. If this happens, ask to be dropped at the main PTT, which is central and within walking distance of several moderate hotels.

City transport

The quickest way to get around town is by **shared taxi** – around CFA300 for any distance within the city (even to Douala airport). Douala also has a very good **bus system**, at a flat fare (still under CFA100) and covering virtually the whole city, on eleven routes. Run by SOTUC (*Société des Transports Urbains du Cameroun*), the buses aren't as convenient as taxis – and the crowds can be murder – but they provide a reliable means of getting around town.

Accommodation

Cheap accommodation doesn't really exist in Douala – even the missions charge premium rent on rooms – though you might get lucky with a room attached to a restaurant, such as the *Restaurant du Centre* (see "Eating and drinking"). There are a number of decent hotels in the moderate category, but the city seems to belong to the international hotels.

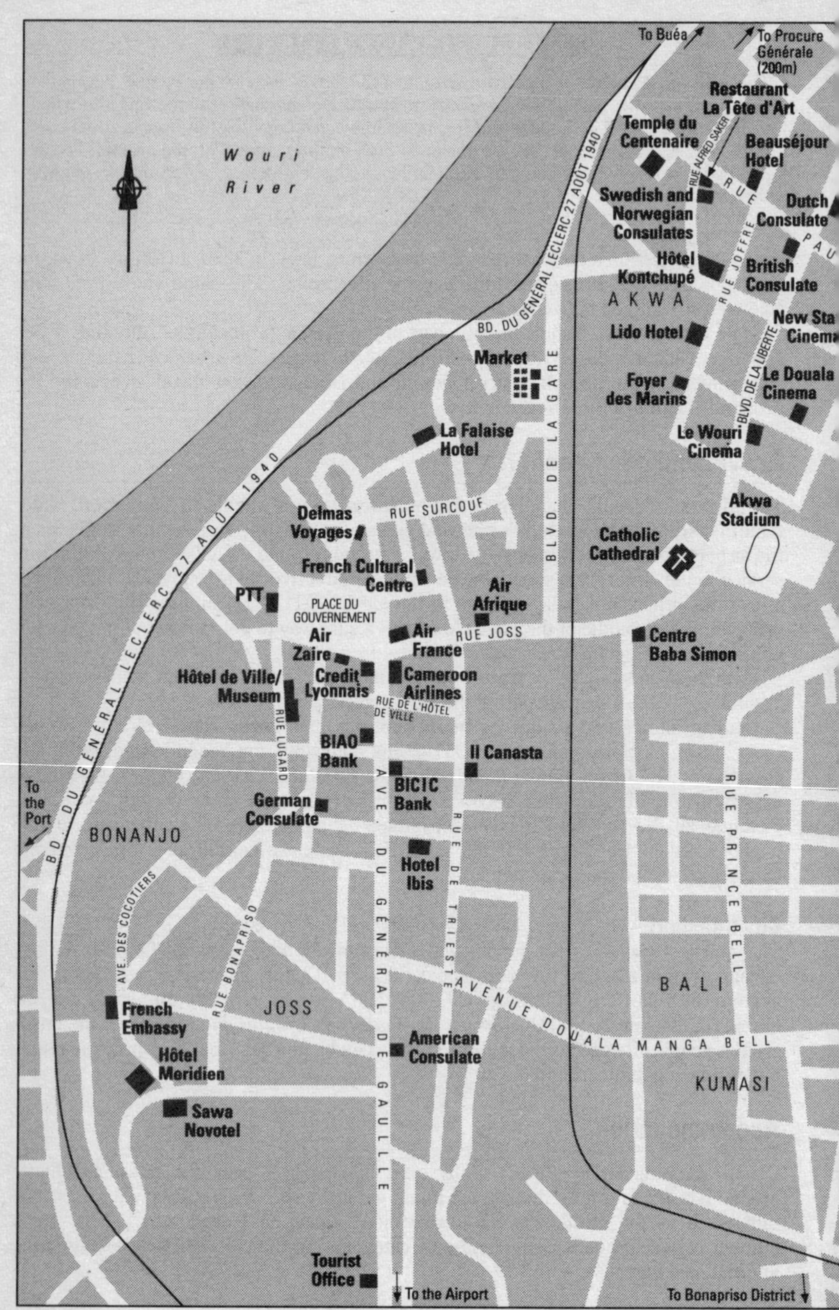

Wouri
River
To Buéa
To Procure Générale (200m)
Restaurant La Tête d'Art
Temple du Centenaire
RUE ALFRED SAKER
Beauséjour Hotel
Swedish and Norwegian Consulates
RUE JOFFRE
Dutch Consulate
Hôtel Kontchupé
British Consulate
AKWA
BD. DU GÉNÉRAL LECLERC 27 AOÛT 1940
Lido Hotel
New Sta
Cinema
BLVD. DE LA LIBERTÉ
Market
Foyer des Marins
Le Douala Cinema
La Falaise Hotel
Le Wouri Cinema
BLVD. DE LA GARE
Akwa Stadium
RUE SURCOUF
Delmas Voyages
Catholic Cathedral
French Cultural Centre
Air Afrique
PTT
PLACE DU GOUVERNEMENT
Air Zaire
Air France
RUE JOSS
Centre Baba Simon
Hôtel de Ville/ Museum
Credit Lyonnais
Cameroon Airlines
RUE DE L'HÔTEL DE VILLE
RUE LUGARD
BIAO Bank
Il Canasta
BICIC Bank
To the Port
German Consulate
BONANJO
RUE PRINCE BELL
Hotel Ibis
RUE DE TRIESTE
AVE. DES COCOTIERS
RUE BONAPRISO
AVE. DU GÉNÉRAL DE GAULLE
AVENUE DOUALA MANGA BELL
BALI
JOSS
French Embassy
American Consulate
Hôtel Meridien
KUMASI
Sawa Novotel
Tourist Office
To the Airport
To Bonapriso District

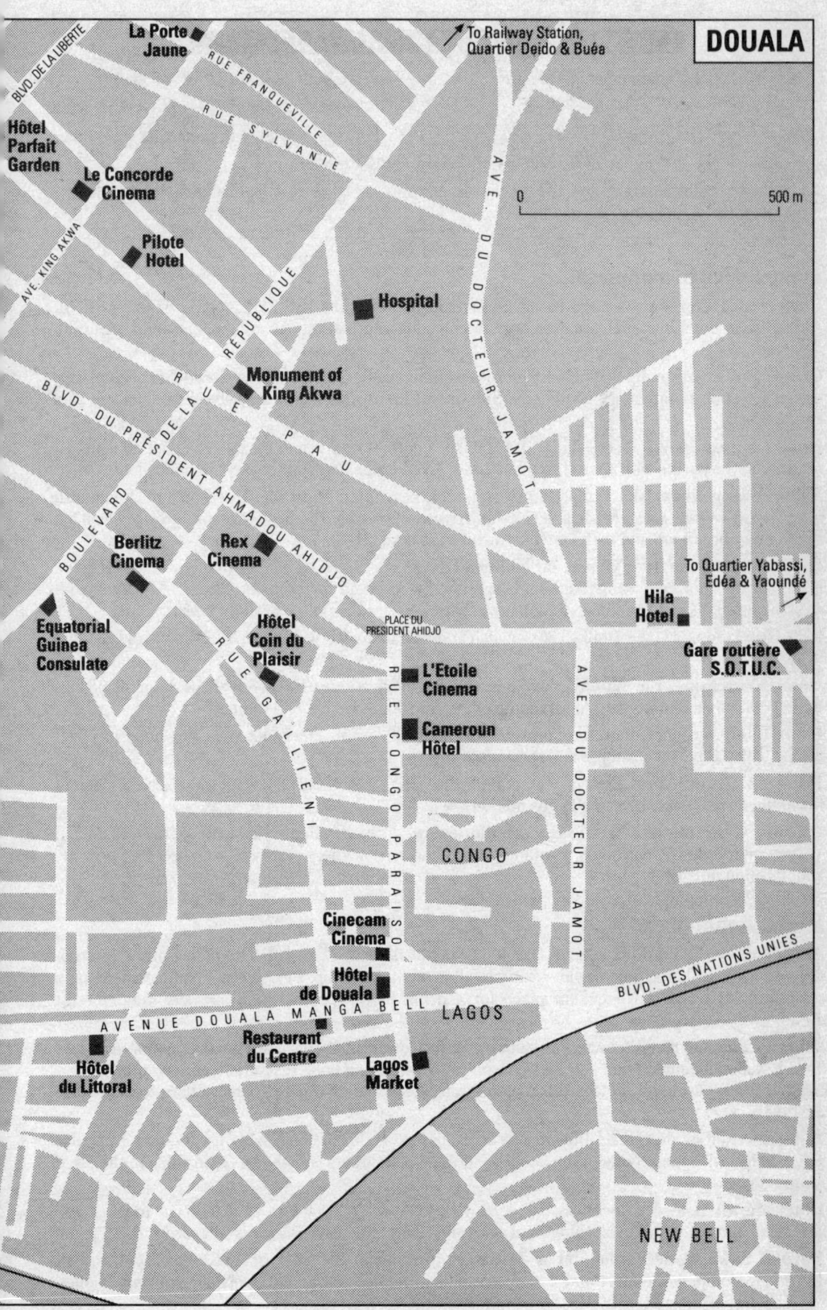
DOUALA
To Railway Station, Quartier Deido & Buéa
La Porte Jaune
BLVD. DE LA LIBERTE
RUE FRANQUEVILLE
RUE SYLVANIE
Hôtel Parfait Garden
Le Concorde Cinema
AVE. KING AKWA
Pilote Hotel
AVE. DU DOCTEUR JAMOT
0
500 m
Hospital
RUE DE LA RÉPUBLIQUE
Monument of King Akwa
RUE PAU
BLVD. DU PRÉSIDENT AHMADOU AHIDJO
BOULEVARD
Berlitz Cinema
Rex Cinema
To Quartier Yabassi, Edéa & Yaoundé
Hila Hotel
Equatorial Guinea Consulate
Hôtel Coin du Plaisir
PLACE DU PRESIDENT AHIDJO
Gare routière S.O.T.U.C.
RUE GALLIENI
L'Etoile Cinema
Cameroun Hôtel
RUE CONGO PARAISO
AVE. DU DOCTEUR JAMOT
CONGO
Cinecam Cinema
BLVD. DES NATIONS UNIES
Hôtel de Douala
AVENUE DOUALA MANGA BELL
LAGOS
Restaurant du Centre
Hôtel du Littoral
Lagos Market
NEW BELL

ACCOMMODATION PRICE CODES

① Under CFA4000 (under £5/$7.50).
② CFA4000–8000 (£5–10/$7.50–15).
③ CFA8000–16,000 (£10–20/$15–30).
④ CFA16,000–24,000 (£20–30/$30–45).
⑤ CFA24,000–32,000 (£30–40/$45–60).
⑥ CFA32,000–40,000 (£40–50/$60–75).
⑦ Over CFA40,000 (over £50/$75).

For further information see the "Accommodation" section in the Practical Information pages at the beginning of this chapter.

Inexpensive to moderate

Cameroun-Hôtel, 3 rue Congo Paraïso, Carrefour des Flèches (BP 5412; ☎42.17.67 or 42.81.53). African-style hotel in a lively quarter near the mosque and market. AC rooms, bar and restaurant. ②.

Centre Baba Simon, bd de la Liberté across from the cathedral. Dormitory space that seems overpriced for such rudimentary conditions. Still one of the town's least expensive and often full as a result. ①–②.

Hôtel Coin de Plaisir, rue Galliéni (☎42.69.70). Central location and inexpensive, but no sense of security in the rooms with shared facilities (often used for *passages*) or in the neighbourhood. ②.

Eglise Evangelique (aka Temple du Centenaire), near the port off rue Alfred Saker. The church guesthouse (*centre d'accueil*) has very clean rooms – probably the best bargain in town, but it's a tough neighbourhood and thefts are not uncommon here. ①–②.

Foyer des Marins, rue Galliéni, off bd de la Liberté (BP 1594; ☎42.27.94). One of the best-value places in the moderate range, although supposedly reserved for seamen. Clean S/C rooms with AC. Swimming pool on premises and many expats, perhaps due to the draught beer. ③.

Hila Hotel, bd de l'Unité (☎42.15.86). Stylish and well managed with clean S/C rooms and AC that works. ③.

Hôtel Kontchupé, rue Alfred Saker, near Eglise Evangelique (BP 558; ☎42.04.85 or 42.68.52). Rather run-down, but it's central and some of the AC rooms are not bad value. ②.

Lido Hôtel, rue Joffre, near the *Foyer des Marins* (☎42.04.45). In a quiet area, this hotel has S/C rooms with AC plus its own bar and restaurant. ③.

Hôtel du Littoral, 38 av Douala Manga Bell, Bali (BP 1389; ☎42.24.84). Not the classiest place in town, but decent value near the Lagos market. ②.

Procure Générale des Missions Catholiques, rue Franqueville in Akwa (BP 5280; ☎42.27.97). Very comfortable (AC in rooms, swimming pool) and reasonable, but missionaries get first priority, and it's often full. ②.

International class

Akwa Palace, 52 bd de la Liberté (BP 4007; ☎42.26.01; Fax 42.74.16). The oldest of the international hotels, still boasting an older wing in all its colonial pomp. Pleasant pool and gardens plus restaurant and bar. An excellent place for a drink in the popular *café terrasse*. Major credit cards. ⑤.

Hôtel la Falaise, rue Kitchener, Bonanjo (☎42.46.46; Fax 42.68.91). Very good value for an established, well-maintained hotel perched on a hill with swimming pool, restaurant, and AC rooms overlooking the Wouri River. In fact, this pleasant retreat isn't much more expensive than some moderate hotels. ④.

Hôtel Ibis, off av de Gaulle, Bonanjo (☎42.58.00; Fax 42.36.05). Affordable luxury, and a popular place, abuzz with the activity of the poolside terrace, restaurants and shops. Good value in the price range. ⑤.

Hôtel Méridien, av des Cocotiers (BP 3232; ☎42.46.29 or 42.90.44; Fax 42.35.07). The most expensive hotel in town. It has everything: real class and really expensive. Major credit cards. ⑦.

Novotel Sawa, av de Verdun, off av de Gaulle, in Bonanjo (BP 2345; ☎42.08.66 or 42.14.70; Fax 42.78.31). Complete comfort and extras like video, tennis, sauna, and poolside barbecue. Coffee shop and restaurant with European food, plus banks, car rental and boutiques – a whole complex. Crafts and curios and some good jewellery are sold in the foyer. Major credit cards. ⑦.

Hôtel Parfait Garden, bd de la Liberté near Akwa Palace (BP 5350; ☎42.63.57). All the services of a luxury hotel but lacking charm. Major credit cards. ⑤.

The City

Douala sprawls in every direction. Much of its industry and many of its workers are housed on the far side of the Wouri Bridge, on the right bank of the river. Nonetheless, the various distinct quarters into which the town is divided – most of them named after local ruling families – aren't too difficult to figure out. If you take the town *quartier* by *quartier*, orientation is much easier, and Douala becomes less overwhelming and more interesting.

Akwa: the modern centre

As the main commercial area, the **Akwa neighbourhood** is more or less the centre of the modern city. Its lifeline is the boulevard de la Liberté, with the **Cathédrale Catholique** something of a landmark at its southern end. Built in the 1930s, this is one of the few attractive edifices in town, even if its neo-romanesque style is a bit incongruous in this sweltering climate.

Just opposite the cathedral, the **Stand Municipal Artisanal** is a market for a wide range of **crafts**. Foumban (see p.1174) has a reputation for being the best place in Cameroon to buy authentic artefacts (and high-quality reproductions), but this rates a good second. They sell good-quality jewellery as well as both real and fake antiques. The masks, both new and old (and it's pretty hard to tell which is which), are imported from all over West Africa, and are the same as those on sale in London or Paris at ten to twenty times the price. There's more about buying and exporting crafts in the practical information pages (p.1136), and in the account of Foumban.

Continuing north, you pass the Akwa PTT (post office) and the *Wouri* cinema before arriving at the wide tree-lined **boulevard du Président Ahmadou Ahidjo**. Here, numerous department stores, supermarkets, boutiques and outdoor cafés provide an upmarket commercial backdrop for the street vendors selling clothes, shoes and accessories.

Turning towards the river on boulevard Ahidjo (away from the shops) takes you past the **Eglise Evangelique** (or Temple du Centenaire, built to commemorate the 100th anniversary of Alfred Saker's arrival) and down the hill to the **port**. The surrounding area is run-down and has a dangerous reputation, so it might be wise to skip this detour and continue north on boulevard de la Liberté to the **Akwa Palace**. This old colonial hotel was for long Cameroon's ultimate in luxury accommodation and still retains a certain charm. The outdoor café in front is a popular meeting place for expats. Beyond the hotel, businesses become more sparse on boulevard de la Liberté as it leads on to the **Wouri Bridge** and over to the industrial **Bonabéri** neighbourhood on the right bank of the Wouri River.

Bonanjo and the administrative district

Heading south from the cathedral, instead of north, the boulevard de la Liberté curves to the west and becomes rue Joss – a street that leads downhill to **place du Gouvernement**. This is the heart of the administrative quarter and the **Bonanjo** district. The **Poste Centrale**, with a large monument commemorating the World War II exploits of General Leclerc, dominates the square. On one corner, you'll see the pagoda-shaped colonial house which was once the **palace** of Prince Rudolf Manga Bell. The grandson of a Douala signatory of the German treaty, the prince was later killed by the Germans for treason. East of the square, the main branches of all the major **banks** congregate around avenue du Général de Gaulle.

The museum

Mon–Fri 8am–noon & 2.30–5.15pm, Sat 8am–1pm; CFA500 entrance.

The rather forlorn **Musée de Douala** is housed in the **Hôtel de Ville**, off rue Lugard behind place du Gouvernement. It's not marked anywhere, so don't worry about just walking into the City Hall and heading upstairs to find the museum on the first floor.

It consists of a dusty collection of national art, poorly presented, inadequately explained, and looking as if no one has paid it any attention in years. But if you're going to be travelling around the country, the museum gives a generous overview of regional art, and has one or two rare pieces. Visits start in a sort of entrance hall, framed by posts from the famous **Bandjoun chiefdom**. Here the whole **history** of the nation, from the Paleolithic (Old Stone) Age via the slave trade to the colonial era, is represented by a somewhat haphazard assortment of articles. This room also contains a couple of **Bamoun statues**, some of clay and one beautiful bronze cast, to draw your attention from the clutter.

The other four rooms of the museum are much more coherent. The **Salle du Sud** represents art from the forests of southern Cameroon. Wooden objects dominate, such as **Fang statues** and colourful sculpted Douala decorations for the bows of *pirogues*. A Basso cloak made of hammered tree bark is especially striking and there are also various musical instruments and games. The **Salle du Nord** is military, with an emphasis on Fula arms, such as a suit of mail and helmet together with spears, saddles and harnesses. In the **Salle Bamoun**, dedicated to the Bamoun culture, is a series of coloured drawings evoking the Cameroon region's history, up to the reign of the great innovator and statesman Sultan Njoya (see p.1173). Njoya created the alphabet used in the writings alongside. Numerous sculptures adorn the room, including a magnificent **bas-relief** depicting the sultan returning from war. Lastly, the **Salle Bamiléké** contains a collection of thrones, and statues representing the chief and his servants. Notice the sculpted wooden posts – a traditional part of Bamiléké architecture used to decorate the house of a chief.

Markets

From Bonanjo, avenue Douala Manga Bell leads east through the Bali quarter to the district known as **Lagos**. This area is the site of the **Marché de Lagos** – the biggest market in the country. It spreads south of the avenue Douala Manga Bell and is hemmed in by the rue Congo Pariso to the west and the avenue du Dr Jamot to the east. The northwest corner is marked by the busy place de l'Indépendance and the adjacent mosque, in front of which assorted barks, seeds and powders – the essential ingredients of the **African pharmacopoeia** – are on sale. Nearby on rue Congo, the **Marché Congo** specializes in African and imported fabrics. Across the railway tracks from place de l'Indépendance, the Lagos market further unfolds, stretching up boulevard des Nations Unies where it merges with the **Marché de Kassalafam**. The *quartiers* of Lagos and Kassalafam are two of the liveliest neighbourhoods in town, well worth visiting even if you don't want to buy anything.

Eating and drinking

Although you should find something suitable below, eating in Doula is shockingly expensive. Even if you decide you can afford them, some restaurants close in July and August when the rain comes bucketing down and people stay in. Many of the upmarket restaurants are grouped in the Bonapriso district, the town's prime residential area. The town also flaunts a number of Paris-style pavement **cafés**, where shoppers retire for a break and business people do their deals. You can relax in their air-conditioned comfort for as long as you like for the price of a coffee (which is about CFA1000). *Akwa Palace*, *le Delice* and *Gourmandaise* take turns at being the in place of the moment. If you're feeling flush or homesick, splash out CFA1500 on one of their superb pastries.

Cheap to moderate

You'll pay at most CFA10,000 a head (without drinks) to eat at these restaurants and bars, and considerably less at some of them.

Bar Express, bd de la Liberté, next to the *Wouri* cinema. A cross between an American coffee shop and a French café. Burgers, pitta sandwiches and salads for around CFA800–1500. Not a place to go if you're starving, but decent snacks.

Circuit Mado, Akwa, near the *Akwa Palace Hôtel* (150m from *Photo Prunet*). Down-home Cameroonian cooking, featuring freshly grilled sole or *Poulet DG* – a mixture of chicken and plantains in a spicy sauce.

Le Croco Club, Koumassi, near *Le Phaco* (see below). Worthwhile bar/restaurant with pool table and draft "33". Friendly management serves a good variety of reasonably priced Cameroonian dishes; the crocs laze in a small pool.

Marina 2000, off the airport road, on a jetty in the Wouri River (take a taxi, and ask the driver to come back later). A limited menu, specializing in prawn or meat brochettes. Relaxed, friendly atmosphere improved further by the evening breeze. Main courses CFA5000; drinks cheaper than in town.

Le Phaco, near the *Sonel* building on Le Circuit, Koumassi. As rumbustious as the warthog it's named after – and much friendlier. Tasty grilled fish and chicken served on wooden tables in the open air. Superb chocolate mousse. Allow CFA10,000 per person, without drinks.

Pizzeria, av de Gaulle, identified by the illuminated Fiat 500 on the roof. Authentic Italian pizzas for CFA4000 (plate-sized) to CFA10,000 (tray-sized model).

Restaurant du Centre, av Douala Manga Bell. Upstairs eatery with inexpensive home cooking. If the place appeals, they have some adjoining rooms, much cheaper than the budget hotels.

La Sanaga, next to the *Douala* cinema on rue Galliéni. Copious meals – spaghetti, rice and beans, *steack frites* or chops for CFA1000–3000. Try a bit of everything. One of the best bargains in town.

Le Touristic, bd de la République at bd de la Réunification (☎42.40.88). Outdoor restaurant serving Cameroon specialities like grilled fish or chicken. Very reasonable by Douala standards, with meals running about CFA8000.

Expensive restaurants

Il Canasta, rue de Trieste. Good Italian food for about CFA40,000 for two, with wine.

Le Coq Noir, rue Tokota, Bonapriso. White-uniformed waiters serve upmarket African food on linen tablecloths to wealthy Cameroonians and visiting French dignitaries and music stars. Elitist Parisian ambience; hundred percent African live music; Cameroonian food (crocodile and python are best ordered in advance). CFA25–40,000 a head, without drinks.

Feu de Bois, Akwa (☎42.37.78). African decor, with woodcarvings on the wall. Good solid African food and few concessions to European tastes. CFA15–30,000.

Lotus, rue Kitchener. More or less Vietnamese, as far as ingredients will allow. Excellent food, but the portions are not overgenerous. Allow CFA25,000 per person if you don't want to go home hungry.

Le Marieke, rue Tokota, off rue Bonapriso. A friendly family-run place offering hearty North French cuisine. Around CFA20,000 each.

La Porte Jaune, corner of rue Franqueville and av King Akwa (☎42.98.54). Original African cooking with dishes like crocodile, python and porcupine. Wild and well served; expect to pay around CFA20,000 per person.

La Tête de l'Art, near the British consulate in rue Pau. Lives up to its name with elegant decor and regular exhibitions of paintings. Excellent French cuisine, good wines, friendly service. CFA30,000 a head.

Nightlife

Douala's **clubs** open, close down and change hands even more frequently than the city's restaurants. However, as the clubs tend to be grouped together, it's easy to cruise around by taxi until you find a good one. The driver will be able to locate the club of your (or his) choice even if it's in an apparently derelict warehouse. Clubs usually open around 11pm or midnight and close when they get quiet, sometime between 3am and 5am.

Entry **prices** vary enormously for foreigners and locals, men and women, but once in, you rarely come under pressure to spend. Drinks cost anything from CFA3000–8000, or you can buy a bottle of whisky for about CFA20,000 to be kept for you behind the bar.

For **women**, alone or in groups, nightclubs are almost completely hassle-free and safe. The worst that can happen is a man asking you to pretend to be his wife for the evening (or sometimes the whole night).

Café des Sports, near the British consulate (☎42.09.52; also called *Le Kontchoupé*). Chart and African music, and a tiny dance floor. As the *Café* opens around 10pm, it is used mainly by those warming up for a long night. The one place where foreign women might feel threatened by the local bar girls.

Canne à Sucre, rue Sylvani. Usually has good music from a resident band.

Le "78", rue Sylvani. Popular venue run by expats, with a large expat clientele. Modern imported light and sound systems, and mainly up-to-date Western music.

Le Night Spot, av King Akwa (☎42.23.03). Western and African music, small dance floor, limited seating.

Safari, rue de la Motte Piquet, off rue Surcouf (☎42.61.99). Fairly up-to-date pop chart and African music. Generally quiet on weekdays. There's seating around a minuscule dance floor (barely larger than the enormous video screen) and a mostly white crowd – and often very young, particularly during school vacations.

St-Hilaire, rue Alfred Saker. Fairly small bar, with dancing to (not particularly up-to-date) chart music. This is something of a pick-up joint (with a gay reputation, too), and has very dark seating areas. Usually the most crowded nightspot, the last to open and the last to close.

Listings

Airfreight Precious and express items can be sent and received through *DHL*, Soms Building, rue Drouot (☎42.98.82).

Airlines Most airline offices are in the Bonanjo neighbourhood or in Akwa along bd de la Liberté. They include: *Aeroflot*, 83 bd de la Liberté (☎42.79.91); *Air Afrique*, rue Joss (☎42.42.22); *Air France*, 1 place du Gouvernement (☎42.80.20); *Air Gabon*, 3 rue Joss (☎42.49.43); *Air Zaïre*, 2 av de Gaulle (☎42.19.41); *Alitalia*, place du Gouvernement (☎42.36.08); *British Airways*, Standard Chartered building, 61 bd de la Liberté (☎42.01.47 or 42.38.73); *Cameroon Airlines*, 3 av de Gaulle (☎42.49.99); *Ethiopian Airlines*, bd de la Liberté (☎42.47.04 or 42.47.86); *Iberia* (☎42.14.50); *Lufthansa*, 82 bd de la Liberté (☎42.57.76); *Nigeria Airways*, 17 bd de la Liberté (☎42.62.34); *Sabena*, 60 av de Gaulle (☎42.05.15); *Swissair*, 33 bd de la Liberté (☎42.29.29).

American Express Represented by *Delmas Voyages*, rue Kitchener at rue Surcouf (BP 263; ☎42.11.84; Fax 42.88.51).

Banks Major branches in the Bonanjo neighbourhood include: *Banque Internationale pour le Commerce et l'Industrie du Cameroun* (*BICIC*), rue Kitchener (☎42.84.31); *Banque Méridien BIAO*, av de Gaulle (☎42.80.11); *Société Commercial de Banque–Crédit Lyonnais* (*SCB–CLC*), rue Joss (☎42.98.60); and *Standard Chartered Bank Cameroon*, 57 bd de la Liberté (☎42.36.12; Fax 42.27.89). *Crédit Lyonnais* and *Standard Chartered* usually have slightly better rates than the others, though the latter charges a high commission.

Bookstores *Aux Frères Réunis* (*Librairie Catholique*), bd de la Liberté (next to the *Akwa Palace*) is the town's largest bookstore (Mon–Fri 8am–12.30pm & 3–7pm, Sat 8am–12.30pm & 4.30–7pm), and though there's not much in English, the selection in French, including works by Africans, is good and there's a good history section. This is also the best bet for maps and travel literature. *Aux Messageries*, bd de la Liberté, between the *Akwa Palace* and the cathedral (same hours), is also good.

Car rental The major firms are at the airport and in the larger hotels: *Hertz* at the *Novotel Sawa* (☎42.99.18); *Avis* at the *Akwa Palace* (☎42.61.36 or 42.70.56; Fax 42.35.07); *Locauto* at the *Akwa*

Palace (☎42.26.01); *Europcar*, bd de la Liberté across from the *Akwa Palace* (☎42.18.79); *IVS Auto Location*, bd de la Liberté (☎42.64.09).

Cinemas The two big air-conditioned cinemas are *Le Concorde* on rue Lapeyrère and *Le Wouri* on bd de la Liberté (☎42.19.47). Smaller movie houses showing old re-runs include *Le Douala* on rue Galliéni, *The Rex* on bd Ahidjo and *Le Toula* on rue Kitchener.

Consulates The following countries maintain consular or honorary consular offices in Douala, with main embassies in Yaoundé: **Belgium**, 13 av de la Marine (BP 263; ☎42.47.50); **Equatorial Guinea**, bd de la République (BP 5544; ☎42.26.11); **Denmark** (BP 215; ☎42.64.64); **France**, rue des Cocotiers (BP 869; ☎42.62.50; Francophone country visa service); **Germany** rue Victoria near place du Gouvernement (☎42.35.00); **Italy**, rue de l'Hôtel de Ville (☎42.36.01); **Nigeria**, bd de la Liberté (BP 1553; ☎42.71.44); **Norway and Sweden**, rue Alfred Saker (BP 320; ☎42.02.88); **Spain** (BP 1102; ☎42.23.95); **United Kingdom**, 3rd Floor, Standard Chartered Building, opposite the *Akwa Palace Hotel* (BP 1016; ☎42.21.77; Fax 42.88.96); **USA**, 21 av de Gaulle (☎42.34.34).

Cultural centres *Centre Culturel Français*, rue Ivy (☎42.69.96); *Centre Culturel Africain* in the college Liberman, rue des Ecoles (☎42.28.90). The latter has African language courses. *USIS* has closed its library in Douala.

Korup National Park/World Wide Fund for Nature The main office is at 60 av de Gaulle (BP 2417; ☎/Fax 43.21.71). See p.1163.

Maps Try the main bookstores (see above). *IGN* maps are available at 36 rue Joffre in the Akwa neighbourhood (☎42.02.75).

Pharmacies The *Pharmacie du Centre*, 38 bd de la Liberté (☎42.14.30), is well stocked and central.

Post office The *Poste Centrale* is near the banks in the Bonanjo neighbourhood, on the place du Gouvernement (☎42.40.25). Branches include: *Poste d'Akwa*, bd de la Liberté (☎42.25.30); *Poste de New Bell*, av Douala Manga Bell (☎42.13.30); *Poste de Deido*, rue Dibombé (☎42.17.70).

Supermarkets *Monoprix* and *Aux Bonnes Courses* stock French delicacies flown in regularly from Paris – lobsters, caviar, champagne, pastries, and fresh European vegetables all available at something less than twice the Champs Elysées price. The *Mysan Market* supermarket has American goodies.

Swimming pools Non-guests can use the pools at the *Akwa Palace* and the *Novotel* for a fee. They're both expensive, but nice and worth it when the humidity gets too much.

MOVING ON FROM DOUALA

BY ROAD

The main motor park is the **Yabassi gare routière** at the junction of av Japoma and rue Nassif (bus #2). This *autogare* handles traffic for the West and North West provinces (Bafang, Bafoussam and Bamenda) and for Littoral, Centre and South provinces (Yaoundé, Edéa and Kribi). The smaller **Rondpoint gare routière** at Deido roundabout, near Wouri Bridge (bus #6) is for vehicles to South West Province – Victoria (Limbé) and Buéa. It's often quickest to get a vehicle to Mutengené, then change for Buéa or Victoria.

Check too the schedules of the **bus companies**, all of which are located near place Ahidjo. The buses, which are comfortable and convenient, run primarily between Douala and Yaoundé. Among the many are *Express Le Bien* (☎42.27.11), *Concorde*, and *Erko Voyages*.

BY TRAIN

The station is in the northeast part of the city centre, off the bd de la République. Enquiries should be made in advance to **Régiefercam**, BP 304, Douala (☎42.91.20), since the schedules change often. You can buy tickets to Yaoundé, and possibly still to Nkongsamba and Kumba.

Intercity

Dep. Douala 7.15am, arr. Yaoundé 10.30am.

Dep. Douala 7pm, arr. Yaoundé 11.20pm.

Continued overleaf

Moving on from Douala continued...

Express-Autorail, stopping service
Dep. Douala around 1pm, arr. Yaoundé 4.45pm, continues overnight to Ngaoundéré.

Omnibus service, all stations
Dep. Douala 8.25am, arr. Yaoundé 5.50pm.
Dep. Douala 6am, arr. Nkongsamba 12.20pm.

Douala–Edéa "shuttle" service (*Navette*)
Dep. Douala 3.30pm, arr. Edéa 6.10pm.

BY AIR
Cameroon Airlines, 3 av de Gaulle (☎42.32.22), and *Unitair* (☎43.27.52) have flights to:
Bafoussam Mon, Thurs & Sat (*Unitair*)
Bamenda Tues & Sat (*Unitair*)
Batouri and Bertoua Mon & Wed (*Unitair*)
Dschang Mon, Thurs & Sun (*Unitair*)
Garoua daily (*Unitair & CamAir*)
Mamfé Tues, Thurs, Fri & Sat
Maroua daily (*Unitair* or *CamAir*)
Ngaoundéré once or twice daily except Tues (*Unitair & CamAir*)
Yaoundé several flights each day (*Unitair & CamAir*)

BY SEA
If you're heading back to Europe, *SOCOPAO*, 30 quai de Dion Bouton (☎42.64.54), are agents for *Grimaldi Lines*, which operates regular cargo services, with comfortable cabins, to Europe. For travel to Equatorial Guinea, visit *IMCA* at the Port de Peschaud (☎42.33.18), for a place on the deck of the weekly boat, the *Doña Elvira*. Schedules are irregular so you must phone to find out the exact day of departure and schedule.

TRAVEL AGENCIES
In **Akwa**, *Emil Travel* in bd de la Liberté (BP 5393; ☎42.55.59) has a reputation for reliable bookings. Others in Akwa include: *Jully Voyages* (BP 1868; ☎42.32.09); *Camvoyages*, corner of bd de la Liberté and rue des Écoles (☎42.31.88); *Mory and Co Voyages*, rue Joffre (BP 572; ☎42.61.66 or 42.04.66). There is a further selection of travel agencies in **Bonanjo**: *Transcap Voyages*, rue de Trieste (☎42.92.91); *SATA Voyages*, rue Lugard (☎42.68.77); *SOAEM*, av de Gaulle (☎42.02.88); *Delmas Voyages*, rue Kitchener (☎42.11.84); *West African Alternatives, Meridien Hotel* (BP 3232; ☎42.46.29; Fax 42.35.07).

Victoria (Limbé)

VICTORIA is everything Douala isn't – small, scenic and restful – with the mass of Mount Cameroon looming to the north. This is the nearest town to Douala on the open ocean, and it owes its popularity primarily to the surrounding beaches along the shore of **Ambas Bay**. There's a holiday feel to it, with historical touches added in its well-preserved German and British **colonial buildings**, the distinctive Creole elements of its **Caribbean past** and its shady **botanical gardens**. Yet despite the influx of holidaying expats and weekenders, Victoria is not the expensive and overdone resort town you might expect. There's enough economic stimulus in the old **port** and the market, plus the nearby oil refinery and various agricultural projects, for the town not to rely wholly on its tourist industry, and it has retained an authentic provincial feel.

Incidentally, the Victoria area is host to a specially virulent and untreatable form of **malaria**. Avoid being bitten.

Accommodation

Most hotels are oriented to affluent Douala weekenders. However, given the standards of accommodation, prices seem reasonable if you've just come from the city. There's even budget accommodation to be had alongside the pricier places.

Hôtel Atlantic Beach (BP 63; ☎33.32.32 or 33.23.33). Once a military hospital used by the Kaiser's imperial army, now converted and restored almost to the point of luxury. AC rooms or bungalows and a sea-view restaurant that features a lunch buffet, with masses of beautifully presented Cameroonian and French food. On the downside, the pool is filled from the sea, and collects a fair amount of effluent from the oil wells up the coast, while the tennis courts look as though the last players used hand grenades. ④.

Bay Hotel, near the main roundabout. A restored colonial building commanding spectacular views of Ambas Bay. Fully S/C rooms, some with AC. ②.

Mansion Hotel, Church St. One of the cheapest in town. Dingy, rudimentary rooms (often rented by the hour) with fan and shared facilities. ①.

Park Hotel Miramar, about 2km from the centre. Co-managed with the *Atlantic Beach* (same telephone) and much cheaper. From its hilltop position it has beautiful views of Ambas Bay and its islands, and also has a pool, and a good disco. ②.

Hotel Mondial, past the Botanical Gardens. Clean rooms, and a pool. ②.

Seafarer Hotel, Idenao road at Bota Village, 3km from the centre. A perfect haven to get away from it all and maybe embark on some fishing, easily arranged with the townspeople. Clean and excellent value. ①.

The Star Haven Hotel, off the Douala road near the *Blue Whale*. Clean, inexpensive rooms and an excellent restaurant. ①.

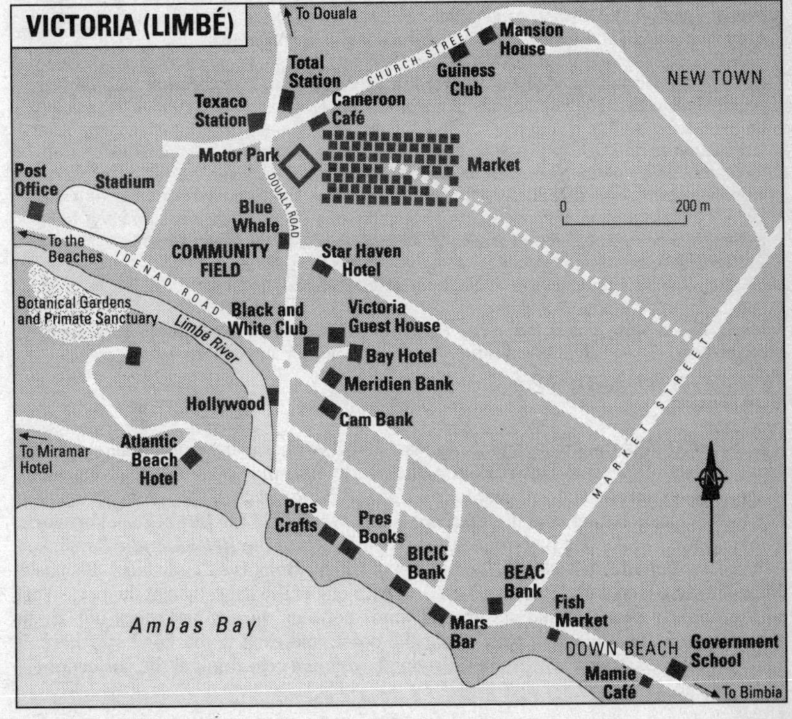

THE HISTORY OF VICTORIA

Victoria was originally created by the **London Baptist Missionary Society**, after they were chased from Fernando Po by the Spanish in the mid-1850s. The missionaries turned to **Alfred Saker** – a former navy engineer converted to missionary work – and asked him to get them a foothold on the mainland. Saker bought the lands around the **Ambas Bay** from the Isubu king, **William of Bimbia**, and, in 1858, founded Victoria.

The first inhabitants of the town were mostly **freed slaves** from Jamaica, Ghana and Liberia, and converted Bakweri and Bimbia (indigenous peoples related to the Douala). From 1859, these townspeople were governed by their own tribunal, headed first by a Jamaican and then by a Sierra Leonean recaptive, and Victoria was effectively an African Christian colony. At first, the town centred around the church, the school (established in 1860), and the missionary residences. But by the 1870s, English and German **commercial enterprises** – *John Holt*, the *Ambas Bay Trading Co.* and the *Woermann Co.* – had established their own set-ups alongside the church. Contrary to Saker's wishes, the site was neither turned into a British naval base, nor declared a colony of the British crown. It was left to the Baptists to administer.

British holdings in Cameroon were ceded to the Germans on May 7, 1875. Victoria however posed a special problem, as it belonged technically to the missionaries and not the crown. The problem was solved in 1887 when Presbyterian missionaries from Basle purchased the land, and incorporated it into the Kaiser's colony. The town then became an important urban centre surrounded by the industrial plantations of the **West Afrikanische Pflanzung Victoria**. By the beginning of the twentieth century, the Victoria–Buéa–Douala triangle had become the political and economic nerve centre of German *Kamerun*, and Victoria grew to become the colony's second port, exporting vast quantities of cocoa and other agricultural products. Although the Victoria territory became part of the British protectorate in 1915, German companies swiftly regained economic control of the district by buying back their old concessions.

With the outbreak of World War II, the Germans' lands were once again confiscated. In 1947, the British founded the **Cameroon Development Corporation**, and the vast regional plantations – dense stands of cocoa, bananas, oil palms and rubber trees still to be seen as you drive through – spurred Victoria into a new period of expansion. After independence, the CDC was partly taken over by the government, but the British government retains a commercial stake in it. The corporation remains the district's biggest employer. In recent years Victoria (renamed Limbé by the Francophone government in 1983) has become an opposition stronghold, focusing Anglophone resentment at being treated in a colonial fashion by Yaoundé. Refusal to accept the new name is a symbol of this rebellion.

Victoria Guest House, next to the *Bay Hotel* (BP 358; ☎33.24.46). Rooms with or without AC, some of them S/C, and always clean. Friendly staff and a homely atmosphere. ②.

The Town

The beachfront is the obvious place to start a visit, with a main thoroughfare running along the shoreline from **Down Beach**, the nearby **fish market** and the German colonial-era **government school**, over to the *Hôtel Atlantic Beach*. In between are many of the town's major **banks**, and the *Prescraft* centre where you can buy regional **artwork**. Looking out over Ambas Bay from either Down Beach or the *Hôtel Atlantic Beach*, you can see a group of small islands, the biggest of which, **Bota**, is still inhabited. It's possible to get across to it if you can strike a deal with one of the fishermen at the port. West of the *Atlantic Beach*, an old paved road winds between the sea and rocky hills up to the *Miramar*. It's a pleasant walk along the coast, and even if you don't stay here, it makes a nice excursion – with the satisfying payoff of a cold drink at the bar overlooking the bay.

North of the *Atlantic Beach*, the westbound road shooting out from the main roundabout leads to the **post office**, oddly remote from the centre. Across the street, the **Botanical Gardens** were originally laid out by the Germans for agricultural experimentation. Now it's a big pleasure park with hundreds of varieties of trees and the **Limbé River** flowing through the middle, a relaxing spot to spend an afternoon.

Opposite the gardens, the Limbé Zoo is being transformed into a **primate sanctuary**. The orphans of mother apes killed as bush meat are often brought here, as are household "pets" that are no longer wanted. You can see chimps, lowland gorillas, drills, mandrills red capped mangabeys, several kinds of guenon, and a number of other animals, including crocs, snakes and duikers. Although the project has a long way to go, the former dilapidated zoo may, with international support, become the focus of primate conservation work throughout Africa.

Around Victoria

Although Down Beach is a convenient place to frolic in the water and catch some sun, its proximity to the port means it gets pretty dirty; and in any case it feels a little odd to disport yourself under the gaze of the fishermen. But west of Victoria, a whole string of **beaches** awaits. Like the one in town, they all have fine **black sand** (actually, a deep bitter-chocolate colour) – result of the ocean's grinding of ancient **lava flows** from Mount Cameroon. The combination of lush tropical vegetation with sea and mountains produces a paradisiac landscape, often enriched with the brooding purple and yellow of an impending storm or the green and gold sheen left behind by a recent downpour. Furthermore, the waters around here are calm – unlike most places along the West African coast – and perfect for swimming. The beach scenes of the film *Chocolat* were shot here.

You can get **transport to the beaches** from in front of Victoria's **stadium**, near the post office. There's a small motor park and you can either hire a cab (roughly CFA1000) to your destination, or take a collective taxi (CFA200) with people heading to neighbouring villages along the coast. To get to the most popular beach, ask to be dropped at **Mile 6**, where a signboard points through 500m of palm groves to the sea. Mile 6 is a public beach with a guardian, so you have to pay a small entry charge to use it. The nearby oil refinery spoils the view a bit, but it's still not a bad place.

If you'd rather be watching fishing boats, you might head two miles further on to **Batoké**, a fishing village with a stunning (free) beach surrounded by mountains that drip with vegetation. If you have your own car, it's worth knowing the paved road continues all the way to **Idenao** and passes numerous other unspoiled beaches, including a popular public beach at **Mile 11** (small entrance fee), as well as the second wettest place on earth, **Debundscha**, 28km from Victoria (Mile 17).

Heading south from Victoria, the eleven kilometres through dense forest to **Bimbia** is a trip worth making. You can go by pick-up truck from the fish market for about CFA400 each way. Bimbia was the site of the original Camp Saker, where the missionary first landed. Today, Bimbia consists of a Baptist Church and a small holiday chalet set-up overlooking the ocean (②). The 150-odd people here are are the remnants of the kingdom of Bimbia: the grandson of the last King of Bimbia is the manager of the *BICIC* bank in town. A few kilometres beyond is Man O' War Bay, an army base (don't take a camera).

Eating and drinking

Away from the more expensive European food in Victoria's hotel restaurants, there are a few good cheap places in town. **Church Street** has many "off licence" bars and inexpensive restaurants, among which the *Blue Whale* stands out for outdoor eating and lively music. The new *Hollywood* is a good drinking spot, and the *Guinness Club* another popular outdoor bar with some of the best *soya* in town – try them grilled with a coating of ground peanuts. Another casual place on Church Street is the *Café Cameroon* by the *Agip* filling station. They serve excellent avocado salads as well as more filling dishes like rice and beans, and omelettes, coffee and fresh bread make it a good breakfast stop, too. Turning left at the *Agip* station and heading down the paved road towards the ocean, you'll come to the *Kintu Bush House* after about a hundred metres. Put together with rough planks, this has a treehouse feeling enhanced by airy windows and views over the town. You can eat cheap meals here, or simply get a cool drink.

The ocean takes regular bites out of the **shoreline** at Victoria, nowhere more so than in the corner of the esplanade where the *Mars Bar* perches precariously at the edge of the road. For as long as the building stands they aim to continue serving snacks, meals and drinks in comfortable armchairs (chicken and chips CFA2000). Further along the Bimbia road, *Mammies'* blue wooden café serves excellent grilled fish with beautiful views over the Ambas Bay. The town's best chicken is to be had at the *Limbé River Club*, in a pleasant setting 3km from the centre on the Idenao road.

MOVING ON FROM VICTORIA

The main motor park at the intersection of Douala Rd and Church St has frequent transport to **Douala** and **Buéa**. If you're inclined to try an adventurous back route to **Nigeria**, it's possible to take a taxi 48km up the coast to **Idenao** and continue to Nigeria **by boat**. Avoid the cheaper cargo vessels which are laden with smuggled goods and apt to sink quite often (June 1995, for example, with the loss of 100 lives). They tend to make clandestine entries in remote areas, leaving you with the task of finding further transport. Much worse, you'll have no official stamp in your passport and will face serious problems with immigration officials somewhere down the road. Passenger boats drop you in Oron, where official customs and immigration procedures are dealt with. Regular ferries link Oron with Calabar on the Nigerian mainland. Note that you'll be passing through waters which have been at the centre of an intense border dispute between Cameroon and Nigeria. Navy boats patrol the area and the frontiers have closed for brief periods. Pick up the latest news in Victoria, before heading out this way.

Buéa and Mount Cameroon

Once the capital of *Kamerun*, **BUÉA** is located on the slopes of **Mount Cameroon** some 70km from Douala. Perched more than 1000m above the ocean, the town breathes in a relatively cool climate – something the Germans were always keen to seek out during their colonial days. Like Victoria, it's a popular retreat for flagging city folk from Douala looking for calm and natural beauty.

In 1895, with the arrival of colonial governor **Jesco von Puttkamer**, the Germans began establishing military outposts in their new protectorate. Buéa was one such spot, and was made capital in place of Douala from 1901 until 1909. It still has many reminders of its **colonial past**, including administrative buildings, an old school, numerous villas built on piles and a magnificent **palace** built as von Puttkamer's residence. Today this German *schloss* is used by the president – you could be arrested for taking pictures.

During British rule, Buéa was under the authority of the Lieutenant Governor of the Southern Provinces of Nigeria. On the eve of independence, the town had dwindled to 3000 inhabitants and was primarily a colonial resort. But Buéa once again found its prestige as an administrative centre when it became capital of the English-speaking

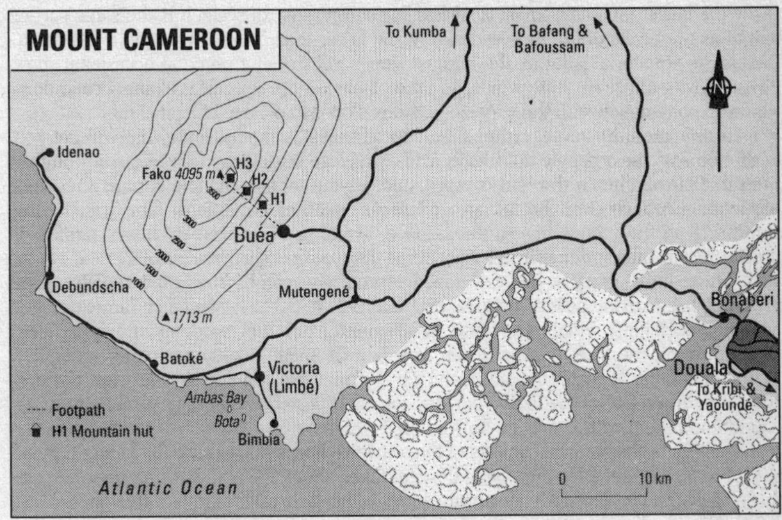

West Cameroon, in the post-independence federation. Over the next ten years, it received substantial public investment in the form of government buildings and the population grew rapidly. Since then, Buéa has been demoted to capital of South West Province only, and expansion has once more given way to calm stagnation.

Practicalities

If you're heading for Nigeria after Buéa, it's useful to know that there's a Nigerian consulate in town, where they issue visas without creating a big fuss or charging the earth. To find it, turn left at the police station roundabout as you're coming into town from Victoria, then it's around 200m past the *Mountain Hotel*, on the left. Most of the practical matters you'll want to attend to are connected with climbing the mountain, however, and this invariably requires you to spend the night in Buéa, before making an early start on the ascent. This is invariably a pleasure, however, as people are noticeably friendly and helpful in Buéa. There are several reasonably comfortable places **to stay**; check to see if the *Mermoz*, off the Victoria road to the west, is open again.

Batasof Hotel, off the Douala road. One of Buéa's cheaper hotels with simple and unexciting S/C rooms. ②.

Mountain Hotel, BP 71 (☎32.22.51). Reminiscent of an old hunting lodge with fireplace in the trophied lobby plus pool, tennis court and an excellent garden restaurant. Cosy nostalgia. ③.

Parliamentarian Flats, 250m north of the police station roundabout (☎32.24.59). Clean and comfortable accommodation overlooking the slopes of Mt Cameroon. Pleasant restaurant with alpine views. ②.

Presbyterian Mission, past the roundabout at "Prison Farm". Double rooms, excellent shower facilities and a well-equipped kitchen. ①.

Mount Cameroon

Buéa is the usual starting point for the ascent of the occasionally active volcano **Mount Cameroon** – its last, minor, eruption occurred during the filming of the Tarzan movie *Greystoke*, in 1982. At 4095m high, and rising directly from sea level, Mount Cameroon is easily the tallest mountain in West Africa. For some sense of scale, it is the same sort of height as the peaks of the Alps and barely any lower than Mount Whitney in California. Despite its equatorial latitude, the highest slopes get freezing rain and occasional snow mixed in with unusually high winds, and the climate at the summit is alpine – conditions which, in conjunction with the very steep, stony slopes make it a difficult climb.

Determination, however, rather than super-fitness, is the attribute that will get you to the top – as most people do. Ideally you should go during the "dry" season, roughly from mid-November to the end of April, and, if you get the chance, contact the Buéa Mountain Club (☎32.22.68) for an update on weather conditions. The trail to the summit is up the mountain's southeast face, avoiding the extremely heavy rainfall of the western slopes and the thunderstorms of the east and northern slopes.

A whole little industry has developed around the climb. You must register your group at the **tourist office** in Buéa (PO Box 92; ☎32.32.34; Mon–Fri 7am–2pm, Sat 7am–noon), failing which you face harassment from the wardens and stiff fines. Depending on the size of your group, you pay CFA5000–10,000 per climber per day (with reductions available for students) for permits and a guide. If you want porters, add on another CFA6000–10,000 per day for each porter (depending on how high up you intend hiking with gear, and how much it weighs).

The climb to the summit consists of ten to twelve hours of trekking (including regular short breaks), and the leg-dissolving descent takes about five hours. Along the route are three basic (and rat-infested) **mountain huts**, with a bare minimum of furnishings. Most people do the climb over two days, but, if you register and take on any porters the day before, it's possible, making a pre-dawn start, to be on the summit by mid-afternoon, and down in Buéa again shortly after dark. A major disadvantage of this high-speed approach is not having time to pause to absorb the mountain's moods and images.

Equipment requirements need not be daunting. Footwear is the most important item: ideally you should wear lightweight, waterproof hiking boots. Plenty of people tackle the mountain in running shoes, but only the sturdiest will cushion your feet from jabbing rocks. Good sleeping bags and warm, waterproof clothes are necessary if you're staying the night on the mountain. A few items can be hired in Buéa. Take supplies of dried foods (nuts, raisins and chocolate are recommended), a stove, and water, which is not available with any degree of certainty above Hut I.

The climb

The ascent starts at **Prison Farm** (also known as Upper Farm), a couple of kilometres up the mountain behind Buéa (walk or get a taxi). For the first hour of the climb, you walk through a mix of secondary forest and cultivation. For the second and third hours, the track winds through mostly primary mountain forest, with fine bird and insect life and the likelihood of seeing monkeys. Before the end of the third hour, 9km from Buéa, you reach Hut I – altitude 1830m. There's a clean spring nearby. Less than an hour after leaving Hut I, you suddenly break out of the forest and begin what feels like the ascent proper, through tussocky moorland. There are no switchbacks; the steep path is a straight shot to the top, marked by painted rocks and the occasional "Guinness Is Good For You" sign and intermittently marred by the scattered trash of previous climbers and marathon runners. Hut II, at 2860m, reached about four hours after leaving Hut I, is positioned at the end of the steepest part of the climb. It usually has supplies of firewood and, towards the end of the climbing season, rainwater in drums. A good three hours further, Hut III, at 3740m, is just 355m below the summit, less than one more hour's hike. By now you're likely to be noticing minor altitude effects – essentially shortness of breath. **Fako peak** itself is at 4095m (13,435ft) and you can sign the book (protected in an old ammunition box) to mark your triumph. Disappointingly, whatever the time of year or day it's rare to get a clear view from Fako.

THE GUINNESS MOUNTAIN MARATHON

Since its inception in 1973, the annual Guinness Mountain Marathon has achieved a reputation as one of the toughest athletic events in the world. It's held the last weekend in January with a field of about 350 runners slogging 37km over tortuous terrain from the Buéa sports stadium up the jungly lower slopes to the chilly summit and back. Although Cameroonians dominate the competition, they have been joined by an international array of athletes including Europeans and representatives of most African countries. Fifty thousand spectators watch the proceedings, with the men's winner usually completing the event in around four and a half hours and the women's winner in about five hours fifty minutes. If you want to take part in the marathon, contact Guinness in Douala (BP 1213 Douala; ☎42.28.41; Fax 42.71.82).

Kumba and around

The first of the major towns of western Cameroon that you come to heading north from Buéa or Douala is **KUMBA**, an agricultural and commercial centre. Although the town itself is large and uninspiring, with a population approaching 60,000, it's in the heart of a beautiful region. **Lake Barombi Mbo** – a picturesque crater lake just 5km out of town – is like another world.

Kumba's layout is disorientating: the town has no real centre – or rather it has too many – and single-storey, wooden-plank houses spread in all directions. But there's a very big **market** here, and if, like most travellers, you're only passing through, it's to the market that you should direct your attention. With the main **motor park** next door, the market is in a modern, covered building and specializes in goods imported from Nigeria (there's a large Igbo immigrant community in Kumba). East of the market, you'll find the **post office** and **banks**. The main **administrative quarter** is located a good 4km from the market. Another centre has grown up around the **train station**, at the terminus of a branch line from the Douala–Nkongsamba line.

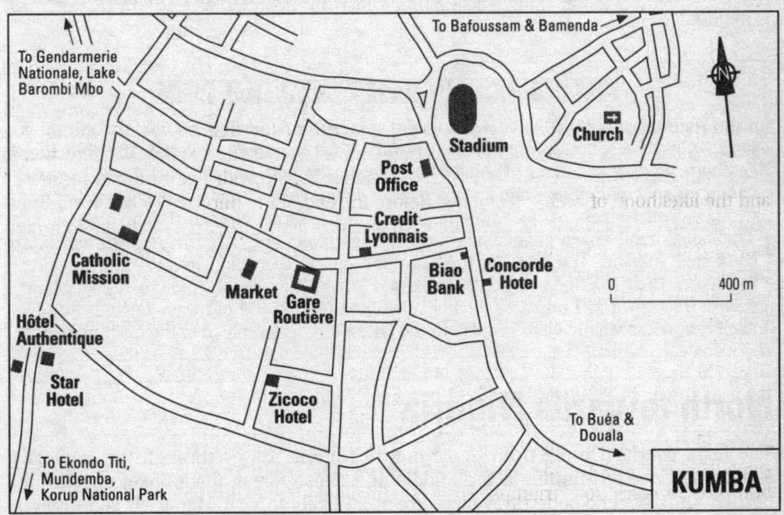

Accommodation

As you'd expect in a busy market centre such as this, there's a host of reasonably cheap hotels.

Hôtel Authentique, off the Mundemba road (☎35.44.20). An older establishment and not without charm, featuring clean S/C rooms, hot water and friendly staff. ②.

Concorde Hotel, near the market on the Buéa road. One of the pricier hotels in the centre, but clean and with comfortable S/C rooms. ②.

Lido Hotel, near the post office. The rooms, on the squalid side, have shared facilities, though the disco with occasional live music is perhaps some compensation. ①.

Hôtel Même Pilote, just south of the market. Convenient location near the motor park, helpful management and clean, if unluxurious, rooms with shared facilities. ①.

Queens Inn, Endeley St, near the market. Good-value rooms with shared facilities and fans, in a central location. ①.

Star Hotel, off the Mundemba road. One of the town's nicest hotels, with well-kept, S/C rooms, but correspondingly pricier than other mid-range lodgings. ②.

Western Inn, Kramer Ave, near the market. Very clean S/C rooms with fans. ②.

Lake Barombi Mbo

Lake Barombi Mbo is only an hour's walk from the main part of Kumba, and quite close to the administrative quarter, but there are no signs marking the way and the paths that lead there are obscure. The best way to proceed is to take a taxi from town to the *gendarmerie nationale*. From here, follow the dirt road leading past the colonial-style government buildings for about a kilometre. At this point, a small and inconspicuous footpath leads off to the left. If you have doubts, ask anyone for directions. Once on the path, you continue up and over the slippery hills for about another kilometre before arriving at the lake.

The dense forest of the area crowds right down the inside of the crater to the lakeshore, providing an unbelievable green backdrop. The lake – 2.5km across and 110m deep – is crystal clear and perfect for swimming. You'll see a couple of fishing boats when you arrive, and if their owners are around, they'll paddle you around the lake, or take you across it to the small village of Barombi on the other side. The price of the trip is negotiable.

THE ECOLOGY OF BAROMBI MBO

The **Barombi** people of the lake shores are completely dependent on the lake and seem to have lived in a harmonious symbiosis with it for hundreds of years. The **fish** they catch are an obscure series of small cichlid species (mouth-breeding fish) called *pundu*, *kululu*, *dikume* and *pingu* – and a single type of catfish. All of them live only here, some at depths scientists haven't been able to account for in terms of normal fishy physiology. Traditional hand-woven gill-nets and basket traps select only larger fish, ensuring their continued survival. Traditionally, the Barombi took further care, by actively appeasing the lake at their Ndengo cult grove. More and more young people, though, are installing themselves down in Kumba or further afield and leaving the old ways behind. Kumba itself is now drawing not just people but the lake's very water, piped to the town system.

North towards Nigeria

The main overland route from Cameroon to Nigeria passes through the somewhat isolated enclave of **Mamfé**, in the middle of a dense forest about 65km short of the border. Only Nigeria-bound travellers are at all likely to visit Mamfé. If you drive up from Douala, much the quickest way is via Nkongsamba and Dschang.

The direct road, via Kumba, is one of the most difficult in Cameroon, frequently impassable in the wet season, even to four-wheel-drive vehicles. This road has been the focus of a surfacing project for a number of years but it may still not be finished. Meanwhile, if you can cope with its difficulties, it's quite a trip. The road passes through dense rainforest, and occasionally yields spectacular views as it detours around mountains. This region has its own unique flora and fauna, and the Cameroonians are developing the district between the road and the Nigerian border as the Korup National Park, with British and European assistance. It's relatively straightforward to continue from a visit to the park at Mundemba straight into Nigeria, via the creeks, to Ikang and Calabar.

Korup National Park

The **Korup National Park**, which adjoins Nigeria's Cross River National Park (see p.1075) harbours one of the richest remaining equatorial eco-systems in Africa. The whole Korup project covers an area of about 2500 square kilometres, stretching across most of the area west of the Kumba–Mamfé road, but the core protected area, where no logging or agriculture is permitted, is just 1250 square kilometres. It contains forest elephants, 250 species of birds, 400 different kinds of tree and a quarter of all the primate species known in Africa, including chimpanzees. It was thought that gorillas lived in Korup, but it's now believed this was a misunderstanding over the Pidgin for chimpanzee (gorillas do live further north, near Eyumojok in the Takamanda Forest Reserve, contiguous with the Okwango division of the Cross River National Park). In the wild rivers flowing through the park – the **Cross**, the **Ndian** and the **Munaya** – many varieties of fish previously unknown to zoologists have recently been discovered. And new finds in natural pharmacological products are being made all the time. The governing principle of the Korup project is that the people of the area should be involved in all the decisions relating to its management, and that their own needs – hunting and gathering, farming and trading – should be respected as an integral part of the forest system.

Access

The main entrance to the park is at the village of **Mundemba** and the *piste* leading here from Kumba is well maintained and clearly signposted. **Bush taxis** run regularly between the two towns. Count on about six hours from Douala to the park via Kumba and Ekondo Titi. If you're coming **from Nigeria**, it's possible to get to the park **by boat**, as regular transport from Ikang makes the two- to three-hour trip along the Cross River to arrive at Bulu Beach near Mundemba. Customs and border controls are dealt with before proceeding into town, and are usually uncomplicated. Coming overland **from Mamfé**, the entrance to Korup is at **Baro**, which you reach via Nguti on the Mamfé–Kumba road. Transport is hard to find for the 30km from Nguti to Baro: there are occasional bush taxis and you may be able to get a ride with one of the project staff (anyone in Nguti can direct you to the WWF office there). Finally, you could make arrangements to **fly** to Mundemba, though you would have to charter a small plane through *Air Affaire Afrique*, and reserve the airstrip through *Plantations PAMOL du Cameroun Ltd*, rue Flatters, Douala, opposite *Maison de la Radio* (☎42.44.33 or 42.46.60; Fax 42.76.45 or 42.70.62).

Mundemba

On arrival in Mundemba, the **Conservation Education and Visitor's Centre** is unmissable on the left-hand side of the road as you reach the middle of town. Officially open daily 7.30am to 3.30pm, they collect a CFA5000 **park entrance fee** here and assign a guide (CFA4000/day, plus CFA3000 per porter as needed). An additional CFA1000 is collected per person for each night of camping. The guides speak good

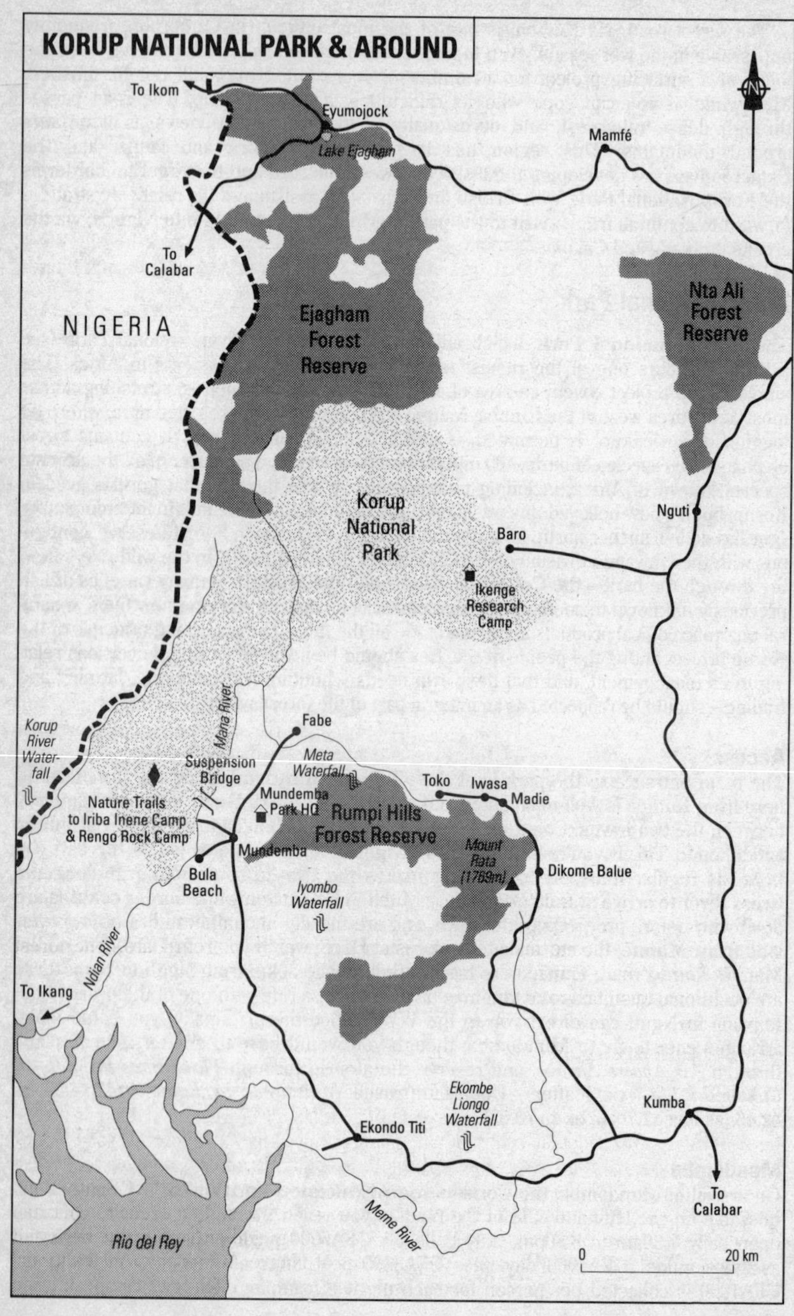
KORUP NATIONAL PARK & AROUND
To Ikom
Eyumojock
Lake Ejagham
Mamfé
To Calabar
NIGERIA
Ejagham Forest Reserve
Nta Ali Forest Reserve
Korup National Park
Nguti
Baro
Ikenge Research Camp
Mana River
Korup River Waterfall
Fabe
Meta Waterfall
Suspension Bridge
Mundemba Park HQ
Rumpi Hills Forest Reserve
Toko
Iwasa
Madie
Nature Trails to Iriba Inene Camp & Rengo Rock Camp
Mundemba
Bula Beach
Mount Rata (1769m)
Dikome Balue
Iyombo Waterfall
Ndian River
To Ikang
Ekombe Liongo Waterfall
Kumba
Ekondo Titi
To Calabar
Meme River
Rio del Rey
0
20 km

English, and are excellent company. Since they live in the forest, they know the terrain well and are enthusiastic in their explanations. Formalities out of the way, it's 8km from the Visitor's Centre to the park entrance, and you can either walk it with your guide, or rent a Land Rover.

Modest **accommodation** is to be had at the *Iyas Hotel* with clean S/C twin rooms with fan and a bar-restaurant serving *steack frites* or fish and chips (②–③). The more basic *Vista Palace* has rooms with shared facilities, though they're neat and very reasonably priced (①).

If you have a large group, special requirements, or simply want to be very organized, you might like to make arrangements before arriving at Korup by contacting the WWF representative in Douala at 60 av de Gaulle (BP 2417; ☎/Fax 43.21.71) or in Yaoundé (BP 6776; ☎20.12.91).

The park

At the park entrance, an impressive **wooden suspension bridge** (built in 1989 and officially opened by the Prince of Wales in 1990) spans the Mana River, allowing year-round access to the park. If you only have time for a **day trip**, follow the nature trail marked with indicator posts and numbers to point out interesting features of the forest – everything from termite mounds to an endless variety of plants and trees.

For longer visits, a **campsite** has been set up 10km inside the forest, with open-sided huts. There's firewood, water for drinking and bathing and latrine-type toilets. Insect repellant is a good idea as wasps sometimes swarm the camp in the day, and swimming in rivers during your hikes is likely to attract blackflies, known in French as *mout-mout* – nasty creatures with a stinging, itchy bite. Beware too of driver ants.

The possibilities for exploring are pretty well unlimited, and two or three days of hiking is not unreasonable. In the southern sector of the park, trails lead to the **Mana River Waterfall**, to the **Rengo Rock** camp (cave explorations in the area), and up to **Mount Yuhan** which peaks at 1079m. Hiking in the opposite direction leads to the **Meta Waterfall**, on the headwaters of the Mana River (half a day's trek from Mundemba), and on to the **Iyombo Waterfall**. Further east, **Mount Rata** rises to an elevation of 1769m, the highest peak in the Rumpi Hills. Despite the wealth of wildlife, your chances of seeing large animals are slim, though most people at least spot red colobus moneys scampering through the canopy, and duiker antelope in the undergrowth.

If you enter the park's northern sector at the **Baro** sub-headquarters, you penetrate the forest at the **Bake River** suspension bridge. In addition to the nature trails, you can hike to the **Ikenge Research Camp**, where a programme to tag and observe forest elephants is being coordinated. In Baro, the people are welcoming and though you'll need your own sleeping and cooking gear, there is a small hut to sleep in. Better equipped is the campsite inside the forest, a five-hour hike from Baro. The forest reserve around Nguti, outside the park, harbours a reasonable chimpanzee population, and sightings are not uncommon in the area.

Mamfé and around

MAMFÉ is basically a stopover point for travellers or traders, many of whom use the town as a base to unload goods they have smuggled from Nigeria on small boats up the **Cross River**. The constant comings and goings add energy to the otherwise sleepy town, but make it rather anonymous as well: it could be almost anywhere in West Africa. Today the administrative headquarters of the Manyu district of South West Province, Mamfé (the name is a corruption of Mansfield, the settlement's first German district officer) was later part of the British Cameroons and subject to the policy of **"indirect rule"** expressed through the creation of Native Authorities. When it was administered as part of Nigeria, it was an important town. In 1959, the town hosted the

Mamfé Conference which tried unsuccessfully to establish voting rules for the upcoming UN plebiscite. In 1961 its inhabitants voted for unification with the Cameroon Republic, since when its status has declined.

Practicalities

Considering its remoteness, Mamfé has a reasonable infrastructure – district buildings, hospital, filling station, missions. If you've just arrived from Nigeria, and have made it this far without CFA francs, you may be relieved to discover there's a *BICIC* bank here. They'll change travellers' cheques denominated in French francs or West African CFA, but don't usually have the current rates for dollars or pounds.

Fresh in from Nigeria, Cameroonian prices are rather a shock. But **accommodation** seems pretty expensive in Mamfé even if you've come from the other direction, especially once you see what you actually get for your money.

African City Hotel, near the motor park (unmarked except for the "hotel" sign). One of the town's cheaper places, with clean, basic rooms and shared facilities. At night, there are numerous small shacks nearby for cheap eating. ①.

Data Guest House, town centre (☎34.13.99). The original guest house now has a flashier hotel-cum-disco annexe, providing accommodation for a range of budgets, and with a striking view over the Cross River. Good value and friendly staff. ②–③.

Great Aim Hotel, near the motor park. Good bar-resto and rooms with shared facilities and fans. ①.

Inland Hotel, Bamenda road (☎34.11.28). A well-appointed colonial pile and top of the line in Mamfé. The pleasant garden – where you can eat or have a drink – looks onto forested hills and valleys. ③.

MOVING ON FROM MAMFÉ

Regular transport to **Kumba** and **Douala** leaves from the main motor park in the centre of town. To the **Korup National Park**, take a taxi as far as Nguti and proceed from there (see p.1163). The exciting mountain road to **Bamenda** is difficult at any time of year and can become impassable during the rains. Enquire at the motor park to see if any transport is headed in that direction, and prepare yourself to be panic-stricken for much of the trip. Wrecked vehicles strewn down the cliffsides attest to the real danger of this route.

By plane, *Unitair* flies to Bamenda on Sat, Douala on Thurs, Yaoundé on Fri and Douala via Yaoundé on Tues.

Ekok: the Nigerian border

Two or three hours west of Mamfé is the border town of **EKOK**. The gates on the Nigerian side close at 7pm; clear Cameroonian customs with ten minutes to spare unless you're willing to sleep in the muddy lorry park in no-man's-land. Otherwise, stay in Ekok – a brash, noisy place with an authentic, frontier-town feel. There are several **hotels**, almost always full of overnighters waiting for the border to open. Rock music blares from every stall, kerosene lamps dazzle and street sharks besiege you with all kinds of nefarious suggestions. Many Cameroonians visiting Nigeria come here by taxi, and the drivers hang around until 7pm or 8pm hoping to get a fare back to Mamfé (about CFA3000). Note that there's no bank in Ekok.

THE BAMENDA HIGHLANDS

The landscapes of Cameroon's mountainous west – the Bamenda Highlands – are overwhelmingly beautiful, ranging from the **volcanic hills** of the **grassfields** to sheer cliffs with **waterfalls** and **crater lakes** hidden behind dense vegetation. The area is also interesting from a cultural point of view, with many of its old chiefdoms surviving into an era when increasing agricultural prosperity has brought one of the fastest rates of development in the country. There's a wealth of sights and towns which you could spend weeks, or months, exploring.

The area divides up fairly clearly into the **Bamiléké country** in the south and the **Bamoun country** in the north. The main town in Bamiléké country – and the capital of West Province – is the rapidly growing centre of **Bafoussam**. Formerly its wealth was based on coffee production, but in recent years, industrialization has come fast and it's not a very soulful place. Situated on a junction of good paved roads, though, it's a convenient springboard for visiting other, more characterful regional towns. **Bandjoun**, for example, retains the traditional flavour of its old chiefdom, and boasts the best-preserved **palace** in the region. **Dschang**, situated in the mountains at an altitude of 1400m, has a mild, almost European climate that's led to something of a tourist boom, focused on its luxury hotel and the cultivation of a Club-Med ambience.

In Bamoun country, the cultural and historical highpoint is **Foumban**, a town with a remarkable turn-of-the-century palace, notable museums and a thriving crafts industry. For all its rich past, however, Foumban takes an economic backseat to **Bamenda**, capital of North West Province. From here, you can travel around the rough but passable **Ring Road** which dips and bends through the mountainous **Grassfields**, a district of hilly, moist savannah, passing through a number of **Tikar chiefdoms** and Fula settlements along the route.

Bafoussam

The **administrative capital** of the Western Province, with a population that has mushroomed in the last two decades to over 150,000, **BAFOUSSAM** is a noisy and unwieldy centre of commercial hyperactivity. It marks the edge of the Francophone zone (the Gallic influence is fairly unmistakable if you've just arrived from "Anglo" Bamenda). Despite its traditional **chefferie** (chiefdom) – to the southeast, off the route de Douala – the numerous crafts workshops and a tiny museum, Bafoussam lacks basic appeal. Its homogeneity (the Bamiléké may move and trade all over the country but they never sell their land so newcomers rarely integrate) means that it doesn't have the vital mix of culture and language so common in Cameroon's livelier towns.

Bafoussam owes its prosperity largely to **Arabica coffee**, which flourishes in the surrounding hills. **Industry**, spurred on by earnings from the coffee crop, has also made deep inroads in recent years. The *Union des Coopératives du Café de l'Ouest* (UCCAO) set up a coffee processing plant in the 1970s and since then, a *Brasseries du Cameroun* brewery, a cigarette factory and a printing press have all gone into operation.

The Town

Bafoussam's dual administrative and commercial functions are reflected in its layout. The broad avenues of the administrative quarter, where you'll find the Résidence du Gouverneur, Préfecture, and Mairie, are neatly gathered on a hill in the **Tamdja neighbourhood**. From the roundabout where the Mairie stands, the main **avenue Wanko** heads downhill to the north, passing the Palais de Justice as it leads to the **market**. You'll find the major **banks**, including *BIAO*, *BICIC*, and *SCB*, either on or around avenue Wanko; *Crédit Lyonnais* is at the place Félix Roland Moumie, at the junction of the rue du Marché and the route de Foumban. If you're staying a day, visit the **tourist office**, on arrival, for leaflets. It's next to the museum, *gendarmerie* and post office in the administrative district (☎44.11.89).

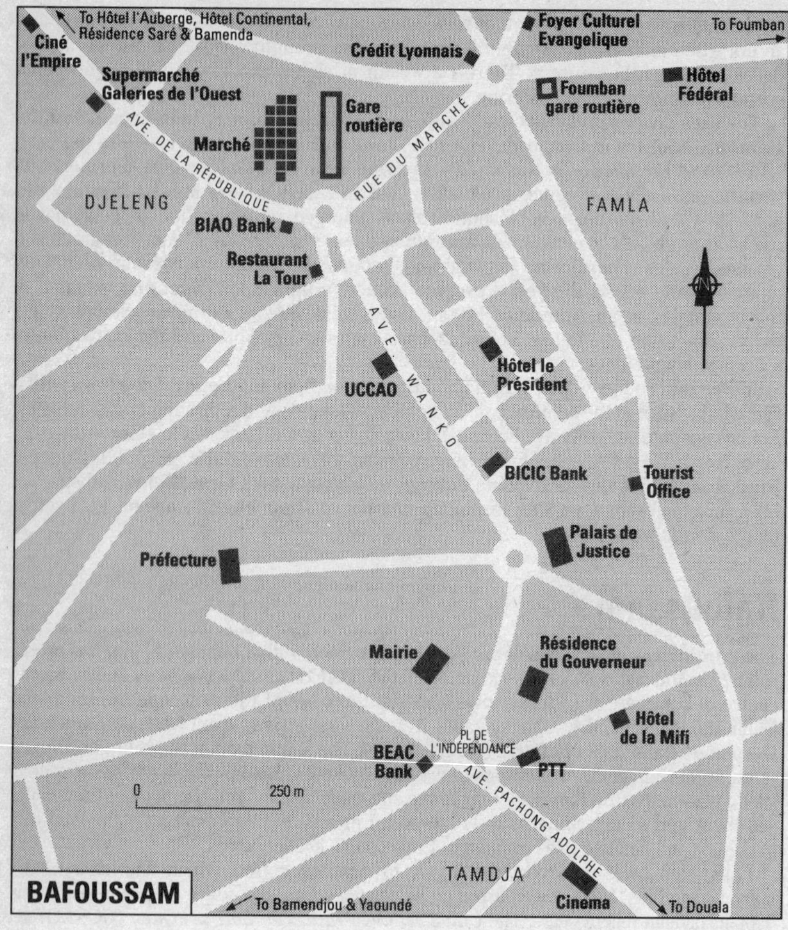

Bafoussam's **market**, which occupies a small hill, and is held every four days, is in the middle of the older commercial neighbourhoods known as Djeleng and Famla. A wide range of **crafts** can be bought in the market, although it's better to head to the street in front of *Hôtel Le Président* (parallel to av Wanko). Here you'll find numerous workshops where artists carve decorative wood panels, furniture and sculptures, and it's possible to bargain directly with them.

Practicalities

A number of cheap **eating places** line the route de Foumban near the *Hôtel Fédéral*. Try the *Relais Africain* or the *Intercontinental* for healthy portions of rice, beans and vegetables at low prices. There are similar places on the streets surrounding the market. Next to the *Relais*, the *Pâtisserie de la Paix* makes a good place to stop for fresh baked bread and pastries. *La Tour* is a popular restaurant directly opposite the market where you can get *steack frites* for around CFA3000.

Accommodation

Bafoussam has a surprisingly narrow range of accommodation for a town of its size.

Hôtel l'Auberge, av de la République. An inexpensive place with some S/C rooms, though the *Fédéral* seems better value. ①.

Hôtel Continental, av de la République (BP 136; ☎44.11.81 or 44.14.58). Relatively new and quite comfortable with expansive S/C rooms and a good restaurant and bar. ③.

Hôtel Fédéral, near the market on route de Foumban (☎44.13.74). Breakfast is included in the price of the fairly clean rooms with shared facilities. There's a good restaurant (meals at CFA2000) and a video bar – where *femmes libres* keep vigil. ①.

Foyer Culturel Evangelique, 100m north of the motor park. Dirty and run-down, but still puts up travellers – if you can find the caretaker with the only set of keys. For the price, however, you're better off in a cheap hotel. Camping here is possible – about CFA1500 each. ①.

Hôtel de la Mifi, a stone's throw from the post office and the place de l'Indépendance (☎44.11.81). A moderate place, with simple rooms. The bar and nightclub attract a younger crowd, often including overlanders. ②.

Hôtel Le Président, town centre (BP 78; ☎44.11.36). The biggest hotel in town, with AC rooms, and a nightclub. It's not new, though, and can't really be considered luxurious anymore. ③.

Résidence Saré, route de Bamenda (☎44.25.99). Well-maintained chalets around a bar-restaurant complex. Hot showers and working AC in every chalet. ④.

MOVING ON FROM BAFOUSSAM

The **gare routière** is right next to the market and has bush taxis to most destinations. An exception is **Foumban**, for which taxis leave from in front of the *Shell* station down the street (very near the *Hôtel Fédéral*). Taxis to **Bamenda** leave from the route de Bamenda near the Catholic Cathedral.

A number of **bus companies** also run scheduled services to **Yaoundé**, **Bamenda** and **Dschang**. Their offices are off the rue du Marché in the area of the *gare routière*.

To get around the region under your own steam, **car rental** can be arranged through *Avis* (☎44.13.88), located on the route de Foumban on the east side of town.

There are **flights** on Tues and Sun to Douala via Yaoundé; on Mon to Maroua via Garoua and Ngaoundéré; on Thurs to Garoua via Ngaoundéré; and on Sat non-stop to Ngaoundéré.

The Bamiléké Country

The **Bamiléké country** is roughly a triangle, delineated by the main roads that pass through **Bandjoun**, **Bangangté**, **Bafang**, **Dschang** and **Mbouda**. These towns are all accessible by taxi and have accommodation. The area has numerous **chefferies** (chiefdoms) and natural sites including **crater lakes** and **waterfalls**. Tourism is quite developed – it's an important supplementary money earner in the district – which unfortunately means things are generally expensive; B-class hotels are not uncommon even in the smaller towns.

Bandjoun

Twenty kilometres south of Bafoussam, **BANDJOUN** is the largest and best preserved of the Bamiléké chiefdoms. If you arrive by taxi, you can walk to the **chief's**

THE BAMILÉKÉ

Most populous of the Cameroon Highlanders (also called semi-Bantu, a collective term for the Bamiléké, Tikar, Bamoun and many others – peoples often associated with one another because of their similar histories and cultures), the **Bamiléké** arrived from the north in a series of migrations and settled in the plateau areas southeast of the Bamboutos Mountains probably around the early seventeenth century. The prefix "Ba-" is characteristic of Bantu, simply meaning "people of". The Bamiléké organized themselves into a multitude of chiefdoms with populations ranging from fifty to upwards of 30,000. Social organization revolved around the **chief** – the titular owner of all land, dispenser of justice, and religious leader. Under these rulers came a quite rigidly stratified hierarchy of notables, freemen and slaves. These groups were further organized into age-grade associations and **secret societies**, most of which still operate within the limitations imposed by the Cameroonian state. Admission to fraternities is controlled by the local chiefs who are themselves heads of the societies.

compound, situated on the route de Bangangté, 3km south of the *Hôtel de Bandjoun* and the *gare routière*.

Bandjoun is the ideal place to admire traditional Bamiléké architecture at its best (see box). Traditionally, the chief's compound was the largest in town, incorporating several huts encircled by a bamboo fence. Inside were rooms and granaries for the chief and each of his wives, who could be quite numerous. Larger public buildings used for assemblies, judicial gatherings and dispute settlements or meetings of secret societies also figured in the compound. Commonly, a large square preceded the entrance-way to the "palace" and served as a **market** (market day in the Bamiléké country traditionally falls every eight days).

The Bandjoun chieftaincy follows this basic pattern more faithfully than others in the region, where cement and corrugated metal sheeting are replacing traditional building materials. Even here, the chief lives in a modern palace, but the overall effect of the compound is an impressively large and harmonious ensemble of bamboo and thatch. You have to pay an **entrance fee** of CFA500–1000 to visit the grounds, and there's a further charge of CFA2000 to take photos. Included in the price of admission is a visit to the "**treasury**" where you can see the chief's collection of carved thrones, arms, pipes and other memorabilia.

The *Hôtel de Bandjoun* is near the motor park in town. Comfortable and popular, it's also very reasonable (②) and offers rooms with and without facilities. The new manager is an excellent cook.

From Bangangté to Bafang

There's a direct paved road all the way from Bafoussam to Bafang, but the road that heads south from Bandjoun via Bangangté, while making for a much more circuitous

BAMILÉKÉ ARCHITECTURE

Characteristic Bamiléké houses consist of a square room topped with a conical roof covered with a thick layer of thatch. Although the principle seems simple enough, an elaborate framework is necessary to make the conical roof sit on square walls. These walls are built of palm fronds or bamboo filled in with mud. A circular platform is then made and set on top of the walls. Finally, a pyramid-shaped frame is constructed on top of the platform and the thatch added. The exteriors of the buildings are often decorated with bamboo and intricately carved wooden boards.

route to Bafang, is worth experiencing in its own right. The most spectacular stretch comes west of Bangangté, as it passes over the **Col de Bana**, a depression in the mountains that offers panoramic views of the Bamiléké country.

BANGANGTÉ is a fairly large town, with its share of administrative buildings and a wide divided avenue that leads from the *préfecture* down to the modern Maison du Parti. The **chefferie** has recently been renovated: modern buildings have been replaced with traditional Bamiléké structures, and the complex promises eventually to rival that of Bandjoun. You can **stay** in Bangangté at the moderately expensive, partially air-conditioned, *Auberge de Ndé* (②). Next to the hotel there's a small **crafts centre** and the town also has a **post office** and **banks**.

The *piste* leading from Bangangté to Bafang is motorable for normal cars (taxis also ply regularly between the two towns) and passes by another traditional chiefdom, the **Chefferie de Bana**, located off the main road.

Bafang

A line of small businesses at a major intersection on the Foumban–Douala road marks the centre of **BAFANG**. This could be a convenient stopping point, although there's no exceptional reason to spend a long time here and **accommodation** is mostly expensive. Especially steep is the B-class *Hôtel la Falaise* (BP 143; ☎48.63.11; ④) across from the Palais de Justice. It's fully air-conditioned and has a bar, restaurant and nightclub. The *Grand Hôtel le Paradis* (☎48.63.62) has fourteen rooms without AC and, despite being cheaper than *La Falaise*, is still overpriced (③). The *Auberge du Haut-Nkam* is the place for inexpensive rooms, some of which are S/C, and it has a nightclub (①). The paved road continues directly south from Bafang to Douala, though if you're travelling by taxi you may have to change vehicles in Nkongsamba.

Around Bafang

The scenery around Bafang is striking, with numerous **waterfalls**. One of these, the **Chute de la Mouenkeu**, is only a kilometre outside the town (on the Nkongsamba road). A sign points to the falls, which you can see by walking a short way into the woods.

More spectacular (and more famous) are the **Chutes d'Ekom**, 30km further down the Nkongsamba road. The falls are not marked from the road; assuming you have your own car, you turn off the main road, heading southeast, at the sign indicating the Chefferie de Bayong. From here, it's about 10km to the falls, though you have to walk the last few kilometres. If you're unsure about the directions, you can ask at the village of Ekom Nkam; they'll know what you're looking for even before you tell them. In a beautiful forest setting, the **Nkam River** plunges dramatically eighty metres from the clifftop to the valley below.

Dschang and around

Heading north from Bafang, the quickest way to Bafoussam is via the paved road, but you can also get there via the small town of **DSCHANG** by taking the **route des Mbo** which winds its way through coffee and cocoa plantations. Dschang was founded by the Germans in 1903; in the 1940s, Europeans forced by the war to stay in Africa all year round built a **vacation colony** here, attracted by the mild climate. The resulting complex, the *Centre Climatique* (BP 40; ☎45.10.58), still attracts numerous tourists with its pool, tennis, volleyball and riding stables. The centre's hotel is the nicest in the region and consists of luxury bungalows in a landscaped garden (④). The town also has smaller **hotels** that are reasonable value. A good choice is the *Hôtel Constellation* (BP 22; ☎45.10.61; ②) which sometimes has special rates on rooms in the back courtyard. Other small hotels include the *Menoua Palace* (②) and the *Auberge de la Menoua* (②). A recommended place to eat is the *Phoenix Restaurant*, which features

Cameroonian dishes priced from CFA500 to CFA4000. After dark, *Las d'Or* nightclub is the place to head for.

Unless you've been drawn here by the hill resort facilities, Dschang doesn't have much to offer apart from its colourful **market**, one of the biggest in the area. The surrounding countryside, however, is well worth exploring if you have a car. From the place de l'Indépendance, the route to Fongo-Tongo leads through a series of hills and valleys, passing by two waterfalls. The first, the **Cascade de Lingam**, is signposted, 10km from Dschang. The more impressive **Chute de la Mamy Wata** is roughly 10km past Fongo-Tongo and is reached by a small side road that ends at the top of the falls.

Foumban

Capital of the Bamoun people and seat of their **sultan**, the town of **FOUMBAN** is charged with history and culture. You're reminded of it at every turn as you pass monuments like the outstanding **Royal Palace**, built at the beginning of the century, the **Musée des Arts et des Traditions Bamoun** or the *ateliers* of the talented **craftsmen** who churn out works in bronze, ebony and a host of other materials. These elements have given Foumban the most touristy feel of any town in the west. You get endless offers from children who want to be your guide, shouting claims to be "sons of the sultan" (with such a prolific ruler, there may be an element of truth to many of them). There's definitely an unusual pressure to spend money at every turn – "come in to my shop, just for the pleasure of your eyes". Such an atmosphere, however, shouldn't deter you from visiting Foumban. Delving into its history and culture is a rewarding step towards an understanding of the whole region.

Practicalities

For **food**, apart from the hotel restaurants, you might try *Au Mur Jaune* at the motor park and near to the *Hôtel Beau Regard*. Nearby, the *Caféteria Viva* serves enormous helpings of rice, beans and meat for about CFA500 and they do good breakfasts of

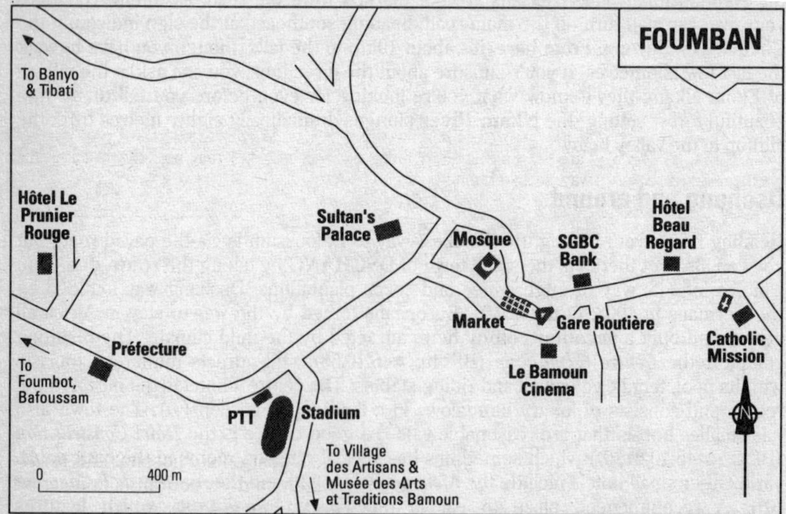

SOME FOUMBAN HISTORY

The Bamoun Empire dates from the eighteenth century and was founded by **Nshare Yen**, the first of seventeen kings in the present dynasty. Son of a Tikar chief, Nshare led a faction of rebels away from the main territory and settled in the eastern country known as Pa-Mbam. Here he consolidated his power and proclaimed himself king, establishing **Mfom-Ben** (whence Foumban) as his capital. The subsequent history has been carefully recorded, and today the accomplishments of all Nshare's successors are known in detail.

One of the most remarkable was **Mbuémbué**, a giant of a leader (he is said to have been 2.6m tall) whose first words were, "I will make the borders of the kingdom with blood and black iron; borders made with words are inevitably erased". Speaking at a normal level, his voice carried 2km, but when he shouted, he could be heard for a radius of 15km. Not surprisingly, people listened. He fortified his capital (ruins of the old walls can be seen today), withstood Fulbe (Fula) invasions and pushed back his Tikar and Bamiléké rivals, thus expanding the empire.

Of all the kings, however, the greatest was the sixteenth in the dynasty, **Ibrahim Njoya** (who reigned from 1895–1924), under whose rule Bamoun culture had a golden age. A remarkable figure, he masterminded numerous inventions, not the least of which was the **Bamoun alphabet** (one of only two in the whole West African region: the other was the Vai script in Liberia). Shumom, the language of the Bamoun, consists largely of monosyllabic roots, so Njoya's 348 original signs were easily converted, in 1909, into a syllabary and later refined into a true alphabet.

Once the alphabet was created, Njoya founded schools throughout the kingdom to teach the new writing. He also tried, less successfully, to design a printing press, and set about recording Bamoun tradition. It is thanks to his *History and Customs of the Bamouns* that so much is known about the empire (or, to be accurate, about his account of it, as related through oral tradition). Njoya also drew up a map of his kingdom, invented an electric mill and designed the outstanding **royal palace**.

Having converted to Islam he proclaimed himself Sultan of Bamoun, but with the arrival of Christian missionaries, he attempted to create a **new religion** that fused Islam, Christianity and traditional beliefs. The secular state (first colonial, later independent) tended to restrain this development, but Bamoun **court music and theatre** still reflect it and Islam, especially, is a strong influence on Bamoun sculpture. Njoya was deposed by the French in 1924, and eventually exiled to Yaoundé where he died in 1933, his pro-German views still mistrusted by the French. The present sultan is Seidou Njimoluh Njoya.

bread and coffee. Due to the heavy tourist presence, **hotels** tend to be slightly expensive in Foumban.

Hôtel Beau Regard, on the main commercial street, near the palace, museums and market (☎48.21.82). Most rooms are S/C in this dingy but central haunt. They may not tell you about the cheaper rooms straight away, so ask. Limited bar and restaurant. ②.

Hôtel le Chalet, off the route de Bafoussam (☎48.62.67). Airy rooms in a quiet setting. Clean, comfortable and good value despite the distance from the centre. ③.

Hôtel le Prunier Rouge, in the west near the *préfecture*, within walking distance of the centre (☎48.23.52). An older place with charm (though the namesake plum tree that grew through the roof of the restaurant is gone), friendly management and picturesque views from the upstairs rooms. Good value. ②.

Mission Catholique, near the *gare routière*. The cheapest accommodation in town – clean, friendly and set in a pleasant garden. ①.

The Town

While the administrative quarter – with the town hall, post office, hospital and *préfecture* – clusters on the west of town, the sites more likely to draw your attention are all in the centre, within walking distance of the **Royal Palace**. Built in 1917 by King

Njoya, the old palace (the present sultan lives in a new one) is a notable architectural achievement, unique in Africa. The townspeople may tell you the king conceived his design in a dream, but he must have done some studying to enable him to combine assorted elements of German Baroque with such pure Romanesque forms. He was greatly influenced by a visit to Buéa, where he saw the German castle.

The Palace and Sultan's Museum

You approach the palace by means of a vast **courtyard** lined with *rônier* palms, tempering its blue tones with long shadows. Constructed entirely of locally made bricks, the mass is supported by strong pillars, the walls are carried by arcades and the structure embellished with balconies worked with intricately carved wood. As you enter the building, you can't help but be impressed by the grandeur of the entrance hall, the armoury and the reception hall with its ceiling supported by four majestic columns. In the morning, at about 11.30, you can pass by to watch as the sultan holds court in the palace foyer. This is a colourful and deeply traditional event, with court musicians playing for the sultan and brilliantly dressed subjects paying their respects and seeking the sultan's advice and good offices.

Tickets are on sale in the reception hall (CFA1000) to visit the **Sultan's Museum**, upstairs on the first floor. A private collection of memorabilia from the long line of kings, this gives an interesting, very personal, overview of Bamoun history. Among the eclectic assortment of objects there are thrones decorated with beadwork, masks, shields and weapons made from hides and woven raffia palms, and a large collection of **sculptures**. One room contains the personal possessions of Mbuémbué – his pipe, shields, and dagger, and a calabash decorated with the jawbones of his enemies. Writings by Njoya are also on display – including the famous *History and Customs of the Bamouns* in the Shumom script he invented, still taught today. A less obvious exhibit is the recently acquired chunk of Berlin Wall.

The Village des Artisans

Don't listen to the small boys in Foumban's main square, who insist that the handful of little artisan shops clustered round the palace entrance constitute the town's main craft market. In fact, the real **Village des Artisans**, a major distribution centre for crafts and antiques from all over Cameroon and neighbouring countries, is about 2km away. Go west for 500m down the Bafoussam road, and turn left at the roughly scrawled signpost. At the bottom of a hill the road forks to the right. Each of the twenty or thirty

HINTS ON BUYING

The diversity of buyers who come to the Village des Artisans is such that the sellers have little idea of what prices they can get away with. An item which might sell for CFA1000 to a dealer from Douala could equally be bought for a hundred times that by a German tourist. The mainly Muslim dealers will be happy to discuss prices for an hour or three, usually in French, which is the only European tongue spoken by most artisans. The exchange of courtesies is an integral part of the process; offer a coke or a cigarette to help the process. Anything you can to do to give the impression that you're not just an ignorant foreign sucker is worth trying; local knowledge, or signs of a long-term stay such as local car number-plates, will be noted and respected. What you're hoping to achieve is to pay the *prix de brousse* – the bush, or local, price. While it's a mistake to imagine you're doing the local economy a favour by paying more than the lowest price acceptable – it's a free market and local inflation can be very damaging – still, the bottom line on buying has to be that if you like something, and can afford it, buy it for its intrinsic beauty and the hours of skilled craftmanship it represents; not because you hope to flog it at home for ten times the price.

houses lining the short road up to the village square is a workshop, where you can watch craftsmen from all over the country casting and beating metals, and carving kola wood, mahogany and, from time to time, ivory.

The biggest range of artefacts is in Ndam Ismaila's *Galerie Prince*, at the top of the hill on the left as the street widens. Don't bother with the "Exhibition Centre" in the square, which asks for an entrance fee to look at items you can see for free down the road.

Some of the finished artefacts are bright and new-looking, some tarnished to suit European tastes for elusive "authenticity", but there's little attempt to fool you that you are buying a valuable antique when you can see identical items being manufactured alongside. Nevertheless, some shops do also sell genuine antiques, mainly smuggled from Nigeria, and you need some expertise or wit to tell the difference.

Musée des Arts et des Traditions Bamoun

On the square above the Village des Artisans is the **Musée des Arts et des Traditions Bamoun** (Tues–Thurs 8am–noon & 2.30–5.30pm, Sat & Sun 8am–noon & 3–6pm). You enter through two ornate carved doors, and begin your visit in the **Salle Mosé Yeyap** (Mosé Yeyap was a patron of the arts at the time of Sultan Njoya, and this museum started off as his private collection). Along the walls, a series of intricately carved wooden plaques portray important events in Bamoun history. Beside these are jugs for heating palm wine, clay masks, and samples of naturally dyed cloth. Notice the collection of clay and bronze pipes (some up to two metres long) used by dignitaries in traditional ceremonies, as well as the engraved gongs which the sultan would present to military heroes. The **Salle du Guerrier** contains military relics recalling the many clashes between the Bamoun and their Bamiléké, Tikar and Fula neighbours. You'll see spears, engraved *coupe-coupes*, protective charms and a calabash decorated with a skull and jawbones that was used in victory celebrations. In the **Salle du Notable**, a carved bed and table, weapons for fighting and hunting, and riding gear evoke the lifestyle of the Bamoun elite. The **Salle du Danseur** is dedicated to music and dance, with costumes and unusual instruments including a xylophone with carved snake heads. The Sultan's **court orchestra** still play these instruments to accompany elaborate set theatrical pieces, and have toured abroad. The final room, the **Salle de la Cuisine Bamoun**, contains cooking utensils – pottery, baskets for smoking meat, mortars – used by Bamoun women.

The attendants at both museum and palace are welcoming and helpful, not importunate but always ready to answer any questions; and happily you're positively encouraged to take photographs.

MOVING ON FROM FOUMBAN

From the main **motor park** next to the market, vehicles head to Kumbo, Nkongsamba, Bafoussam and Bamenda. Although the route looks direct enough to **Ngaoundéré** and the north, there's no direct transport and you will have to count on two or three days of travel to get there from Foumban. To do so, first take a taxi to **Banyo**. If you miss the afternoon's taxi from here to **Tibati** you will have to spend the night (Banyo has a couple of inexpensive hotels near the market). From Tibati, get another taxi to **Ngaoundal** (paved road at last); and from Ngaoundal, trains run to Ngaoundéré twice daily.

Bamenda and around

BAMENDA, capital of North West Province, is really two towns – one administrative and the other commercial – separated by a steep scarp. The **government buildings** perch high on the clifftop in a neighbourhood known as **Upper Station** (or Supply Station). With its sweeping views and cooler air, this used to be a spot favoured by the

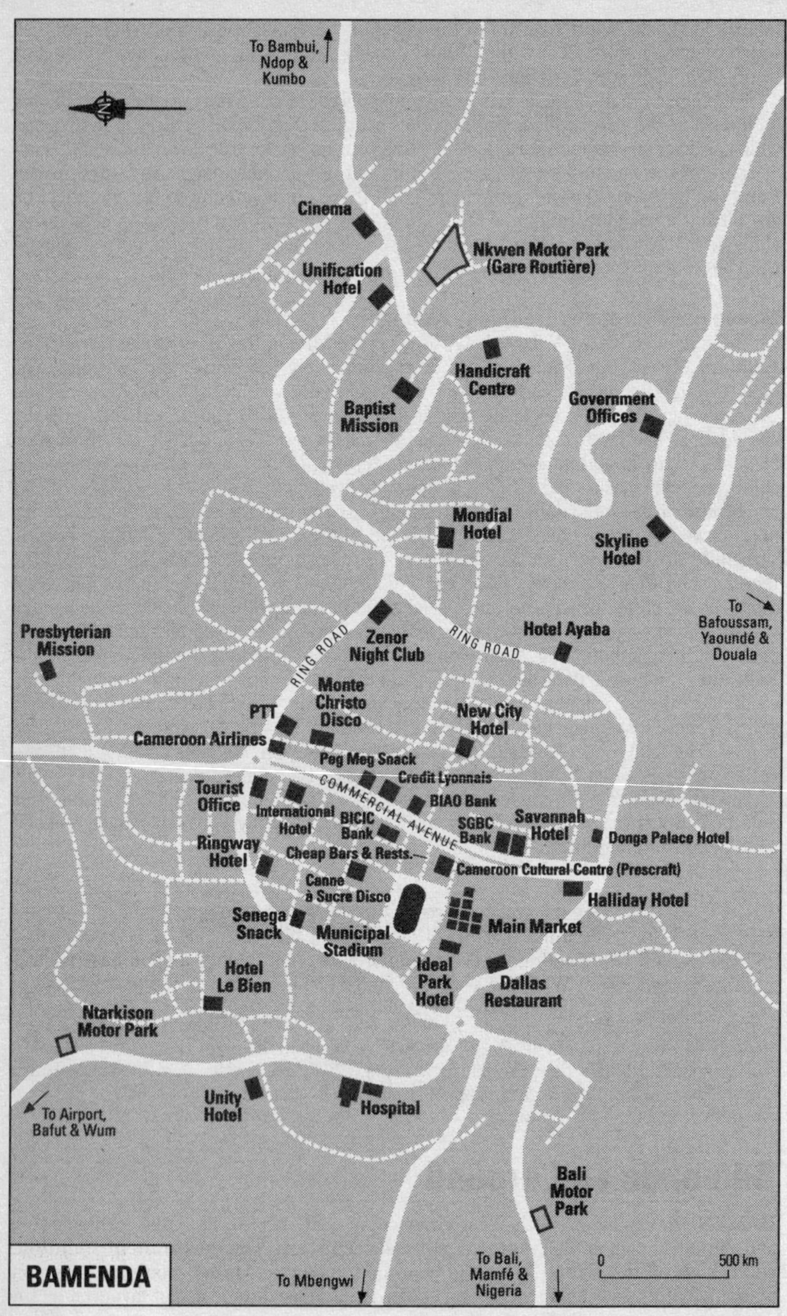

To Bambui, Ndop & Kumbo
Cinema
Nkwen Motor Park (Gare Routière)
Unification Hotel
Handicraft Centre
Baptist Mission
Government Offices
Mondial Hotel
Skyline Hotel
To Bafoussam, Yaoundé & Douala
Presbyterian Mission
Zenor Night Club
RING ROAD
RING ROAD
Hotel Ayaba
Monte Christo Disco
PTT
New City Hotel
Cameroon Airlines
Peg Meg Snack
Credit Lyonnais
Tourist Office
COMMERCIAL AVENUE
BIAO Bank
International Hotel
BICIC Bank
SGBC Bank
Savannah Hotel
Donga Palace Hotel
Ringway Hotel
Cheap Bars & Rests.
Cameroon Cultural Centre (Prescraft)
Canne à Sucre Disco
Halliday Hotel
Senega Snack
Main Market
Municipal Stadium
Hotel Le Bien
Ideal Park Hotel
Dallas Restaurant
Ntarkison Motor Park
Unity Hotel
Hospital
To Airport, Bafut & Wum
Bali Motor Park
BAMENDA
To Mbengwi
To Bali, Mamfé & Nigeria
0
500 km

Germans and British, and even today it remains a high-class **residential area**, the stomping ground of expats, civil servants and the local business elite. Arriving from the cities of the south in this part of town, Bamenda seems to be nodding off, almost suburban. From Upper Station, a tortuous road, carved out by the Germans at the beginning of the century, snakes its reluctant way to the hot valley and the main **motor park**, 300m below.

Downtown Bamenda is a vast conglomeration of small businesses and working neighbourhoods and it's here that most of the town's life happens. A mid-morning stroll down Commercial Avenue, with its dual carriageway of workshops and ghetto blasters, is as fit an introduction to the real heart of town as any. Apart from the glorious pines-and-bananas setting of the town, Bamenda stands out as being at the heart of Cameroon's opposition movement. Home of the presidential candidate, bookseller **John Fru Ndi**, it was here that the initial riots leading to multi-partyism took place after police opened fire on the inaugural rally of the Social Democratic Front. Following the elections, security forces arrived en masse in the town, surrounding Fru Ndi's compound and arresting prominent party leaders. More recently, Bamenda hosted the second All-Anglophone Conference which drafted a statement suggesting the North West and South West provinces were ready to secede from the Cameroonian union. Throughout the early 1990s Bamenda was the site of numerous violent confrontations and much local business suffered under the dual effects of government harassment and Operation Ghost Town, the Monday-to-Friday commercial strike.

The **tourist office** (☎36.13.95), at the extreme north end of Commercial Avenue, may be able to provide you with a town map and some ideas for local excursions (they organize some regional tours themselves). All the major **banks** – *BIAO*, *BICIC*, *SGBC* – line Commercial Avenue and will change travellers' cheques or cash. At the southern end of the street, the **Main Market** is one of the biggest in the west and offers cheap deals on goods smuggled in from Nigeria – nice for you, tough on Nigeria. Local crafts are also sold here, but before you get into bargaining mode you may want to check out the **Prescraft Centre** next door (Mon–Fri 8am–noon & 2.30–5pm, Sat 8am–1pm), where you'll find a good selection of fixed-price bronzes, carvings and basketwork. Another crafts centre is located at the eastern end of town, along the road that climbs to Upper Station and the popular *Skyline* **terrace restaurant**. It's worth going to Upper Station just for the views – early in the day the valley can be smothered in mist, the conifers poking though like a northern winter scene.

Practicalities

Bamenda offers **accommodation** of almost every imaginable description, from mission dorms and cheery brothels to comfortable hotels, so it's a good base for trips out to nearby districts. Whatever your budget, you'll find suitable sleeping quarters.

Baptist Mission, at the foot of the road to Upper Station, near the main motor park. Slightly pricier than the Presbyterian Mission, but bargaining sometimes helps. Excellent restaurant. ①.

Donga Palace Hotel, Ring Rd near Commercial Ave. Extremely good value for spacious rooms with shared facilities. Even the S/C ones are inexpensive. Friendly bar to hang out and chat. ①.

Halliday Hotel, at the southern end of Commercial Ave on Ring Rd (☎36.13.82). A great location, but otherwise uninspired lodgings in the moderate range. ③.

Ideal Park Hotel, off Commercial Ave, behind the market (☎36.11.66). One of the cheapest in the centre – clean and spacious rooms, some S/C. ②.

International Hotel, Commercial Ave, very near the tourist office (☎36.25.27). Central and reasonable, with spacious, carpeted rooms, some with telephone. ②.

Presbyterian Mission, on the north side of town, 1km from Commercial Ave and well signposted. Tidy rooms with clean sheets, or camping if you prefer. Well kept and friendly, but a bit far from the centre. ①.

Skyline Hotel, Upper Station (BP 11; ☎36.12.89). The tremendous cliff-edge perch overlooking downtown Bamenda makes it the favourite upmarket hotel. Despite the pool and a really good restaurant, however, business has fallen off and they now offer very good deals for comfortable AC rooms. ③–④.

Eating, drinking and nightlife

Street eating is good in Bamenda. Besides the **finger food** like *soya* and grilled corn cobs available all around town, more solid meals can be had at any of the numerous **roadside restaurants**. The heaviest concentration is along Sonac Road between the PTT and the *Zenor* nightclub. Cheaper still are the stalls behind the Ntarikon motor park on Wum Road.

Several informal sit-down restaurants offer Western and African fare at **moderate** rates. One of the best-value places is *Gracey's Restaurant* at the *Prescraft Centre*, where filling Bamiléké dishes cost under CFA1000. Also popular is the *Peemeg*, on Commercial Avenue across from the *BIAO Cameroun Bank*. They do salads, fish, steak and chips (around CFA2500) in an upstairs dining room overlooking the busiest street in town. The *Snack Concorde* near the *Roxy Cinema* is a good place for salads and the like, while *Sister Rose's,* just off Commercial Avenue behind the *Agip* station, features some of the town's best grilled fish. Finally, if none of these suit your taste or budget, on the road running from Commercial Avenue to the stadium, there's a number of cheap and noisy **bar-restaurants** with good food.

The **high-class restaurants** are in the big hotels, a notable exception being *Dallas*, on Ring Road, where European dishes and excellent grilled chicken are served on the pleasant terrace. For good food and atmosphere, you can't beat the *Skyline* in Upper Station, a taxi ride from downtown, which serves European food and the best burgers in town in the garden restaurant.

In the centre, near the municipal stadium, *Canne à Sucre* is a long-standing **club**, popular with a young clientèle. Several other clubs are attached to hotels, and attract energetic crowds for an inexpensive, unpretentious night out.

Bali

Of the region's main chiefdoms – Bafut, Bali and Nso – only **BALI** is not accessible by the Ring Road. A **Chamba** settlement (the Chamba are part of the Adamawa linguistic grouping), it was founded relatively late, around 1830. Its history has been a series of wars and conflicts, notably with the nearby kingdom of Bafut. Only 20km west of Bamenda by taxi, Bali makes for a satisfying excursion, though less for the chance to visit the ugly, modern **Fon's palace** than for the **scenery** on the way and the town's **crafts centre**. A good many of the artefacts sold in Bamenda (notably those at *Prescraft*) are made in Bali; the difference is that here you get to see the artists at work.

Lake Awing

Another possible excursion from Bamenda is to **Lake Awing**, a crater lake very similar to Lake Nyos (the lake which erupted with devastating effect in 1986 – see p.1181). Just north of Santa on the N6 Douala–Yaoundé road, a signpost to the west points to a forestry reserve open to the public. Bamenda expats come here to swim, and Cameroonians to fish, although many prefer to steer clear of it altogether. In the evening you can see will-o'-the-wisps rising from the water – miniature eruptions of methane, or possibly the still unidentified gas that erupted from Lake Nyos. By day the lake is often mirror smooth, and shows a perfect reflection of the surrounding woods. Climb for about an hour up the adjoining peak and you can take in a view of the Bamenda plateau, and of other crater lakes in various stages of geological formation.

MOVING ON FROM BAMENDA

Three motor parks serve Bamenda. The biggest is **Nkwen Park** where you get bush taxis or buses to Yaoundé, Bafoussam and Douala. In the northwest of town, **Ntarikon Park** is the place to get transport to Mankon, Bafut and Wum and where to start if you're going around the **Ring Road**. Finally, **Bali Park** has vehicles for Bali, Batibo and Mamfé.

Unitair flies from the small **airport** at Bali to **Mamfé** on Tues and to **Douala** via **Yaoundé** on Sat.

The Ring Road

The **Ring Road** comprises 360km of difficult red-earth road – in the rainy season a vicious streak of orange mud and rocks inadvisable in anything but four-wheel-drive vehicles, and tough-going even then – through some of the finest scenery in Africa. Despite the demanding road conditions (and the plan to surface the road has been on the point of realization for many years), this is a highly recommended route, bucking and swerving through the verdant pasturelands of the **Grassfields**. But don't expect rolling savannahs – for the most part the Grassfields are hilly meadows of rank herbage between stands of hardwood forest and patches of shifting agriculture. Natural sites in the region include the thundering **Menchum Falls**, a number of volcanoes such as **Mount Oku** (3008m), and nearly forty clear **crater lakes**, many of them sacred, and at least one of them (Nyos) potentially dangerous. Terraced farmlands defy the steep slopes; the mountain soils, ploughed along the contours, sustain crops like cocoyams, maize and plantains. Cash crops, such as coffee, grow at higher altitudes, and **Fula herders** roam the pastures to graze their cattle.

The best way to tour the Ring Road is by car, which allows you the freedom to stop between the route's main centres, **Bamenda**, **Wum**, **Nkambé** and **Kumbo**. Wum, Nkambé and Kumbo are all accessible by bush taxi from Bamenda and in Wum and Kumbo you can be sure of accommodation. But many of the most interesting sites outlined below are off the main road and you'll have to forego them if you're travelling by what little public transport creeps around the ring. Using bush taxis also means it's very difficult to camp as you travel, and camping in the countryside – when you can find a flat space – is one of the Ring Road's greatest pleasures. Should you choose to **cycle** some of the way round, beware that any rain will stop your machine dead in its tracks, horribly clogged with mud. In dry conditions, though, this is outstanding mountain-bike territory. Whichever way you go, try to have a larger scale **map** than the *Michelin*; there's a certain frustration in trying to follow a twisting, village-spotted route at 40km to 1cm. It's also a good idea to bring some Dutch *Key Schnapps* or even just a stash of *Becks Beers*, available in Bamenda, to present to the kings, or fons, if you visit any of the palaces in the various chiefdoms.

Bafut

The first stop along the Ring Road, heading in a clockwise direction from Bamenda, is the chiefdom of **BAFUT**, which acquired a little international fame in the 1950s and 1960s as the site of two animal-collecting trips by the naturalist, Gerald Durrell. His account of the first, *The Bafut Beagles* (a reference to the team of hunters he assembled), makes amusing reading, though Bafut today feels a far cry from those slightly mythologized days of Assistant District Commissioners and pink gins.

Bafut is a **Tikar** community – people who migrated to Bafut from the northern regions of Lake Chad. It's the most powerful of the traditional kingdoms in the Grassfields, divided into 26 **wards** in a ten-kilometre stretch of the Ring Road that trails along a ridge above the Menchum valley. The current Fon of Bafut – **Abumbi II** – is a Paramount fon, titular overlord of a large number of lesser fons in the region. Still quite young, Abumbi was chosen from his father's 100-odd offspring to ascend to the throne when the aged fon died in 1971. Although he was educated in Yaoundé, he was allowed to succeed his father – in theory, upon pain of death if he broke local tradition. In **religion**, although the Tikar have long been dominated by intrusive Fula Muslims, and thus heavily Islamized themselves, they've also (perhaps not coincidentally) been the subjects of intense Presbyterian missionary work, so you'll meet a fair few intense Christians too.

Taxis from Bamenda cost CFA600 for the sixteen-kilometre trip. A guesthouse built above the fon's compound recently opened (②), or you can arrange more informal **accommodation** when visiting the palace.

The Town

If you arrive in your own vehicle, the centre of Bafut can seem elusive. It's at the southern end of the "town" that Bafut spreads into something more than roadside compounds. The main attraction is the **Fon's Palace**, a large complex laid out in a quiet pattern of dark interiors and bright courtyards. The fon himself lives in a large villa overlooking the grounds. The most sacred building in the complex is the **Achum**, the previous fon's palace, with its striking, pyramidal thatched roof. Dedicated to the ancestors, only the fon and other notables are allowed to enter this shrine. A visit to the royal compound and grounds costs CFA2000.

Bafut's **market** is the liveliest in the Grassfields and people come from all over the region for its selection of fruits, vegetables, spices, meat and animals. Hard by the market lives a local celebrity, Peter Fu, the **snake charmer**. A magician of sorts, Peter has no fear of serpents, holding cobras and green mambas in his bare hands and keeping a wide variety in cages in his home. He's been bitten so many times (scars cover his arms and legs) that he claims he's now immune to the strongest venom. He is highly respected in the community for his power over the reptiles, and you're in for a memorable experience if you get to meet him.

More dependable, however, is the yearly **grass-gathering ceremony**, still performed much as it was in the 1950s when described by Durrell. The entire community goes into the grasslands at the end of the dry season, usually in late April, to collect bundles for rethatching the Achum and other important buildings. They troop before the fon with their offerings. It's a confirmation of community spirit and always ends with tremendous feasting and the consumption of huge quantities of palm wine – *mimbo*. A second annual Bafut festival takes place a week or so before Christmas each year, with formal, dressy presentations and much discharging of old guns followed by a noisy series of dances and musical shows. It's usually possible for outsiders to attend the festivals, though there are occasions in each when you should be prepared to step aside for local participants.

Wum and around

Travelling towards **Wum**, the last important town along the west side of the Ring Road from Bafut, the vegetation grows increasingly dense as the road follows the course of the **Menchum**. About 20km before Wum, the **Menchum Falls** plunge spectacularly down a rocky cliffside, but they're set slightly off the road (on the west side) and you could easily pass right by without noticing them. If you have your own car, start looking out about 30km north of Bafut and listen for the thundering sound of falling water. At the exact spot, you'll probably see tyre marks where cars have pulled off the road. If you ask your taxi driver to pull off for a moment here, he's likely to oblige. There are no "tourist facilities" of any kind here, nor anything to stop you boulder-hopping across the river in the dry season – except common sense; a French woman was swept over the edge in 1990s doing just this.

When you get to **WUM**, the staff at the **tourist office** have little information (in fact they barely seem to know the area), but they're eager to help and should develop more expertise as people call. Wum is effectively a roadhead: beyond the town, public transport more or less fades out. The cheapest **hotels** in town (and none are expensive) are the tumultuous *Happy Day Lodge* near *Ambassador Books* (①) and the *Morning Star Hotel* which has some S/C rooms and a restaurant (①). Slightly better are the *Lake Nyos City Hotel* (②) and the well-maintained, misleadingly named *Gay Lodge* at the entrance to town (②). The latter two have no restaurants, but you can usually arrange to have **food** prepared for you. Otherwise, try the *Peace, Unity and Hygienic* restaurant; if it's closed down, the *New Deal* near *Ambassador Books* is a popular "off-licence" where you can also buy food. If you're equipped to **camp**, enquire first at the tourist office and they'll set you up with a site at Lake Wum (you should be aware of the justified paranoia of some locals about their crater lakes: see the advice about Lake Nyos below).

Three kilometres northwest of the town centre, **Lake Wum** is a beautiful crater lake nestled in the hills, which are patchily cultivated from the peaks right down to the water's edge. Fula herders graze their cattle in the open fields and bring them down to the lake to drink. The banks are a bit muddy but you can swim here; the cool, green waters are immensely deep.

Moving on to Nkambé by collective transport, there is only one reliable vehicle a week, on Wednesday (though demand sometimes calls for a Saturday departure as well), and when the rains start in April, even that may not run. At the motor park, however, you may be able to rent a truck and driver on other days for a steep CFA40,000. When you see the condition of the road, you'll understand why the price is so expensive. Get ready for a very rough ride.

Wum to Nkambé

Northeast of Wum, the Ring Road branches at **We**, which offers the last chance until Nkambé of pumped water, market produce and chop-house food. If you head right (to the south), you get back to Bamenda via the "small ring road" and the town of **Fundong**. The left branch continues on to the wildest stretch of the road which switchbacks up from We into a broad valley.

Up here, the population diminishes drastically, and, if you're travelling under your own steam, you can go for kilometres without seeing a soul. The landscapes are astonishingly beautiful, at their pristine best when the **rains** have started in April. At this time, when the region is so inaccessible, there are complex vistas of startling colour and dimension in every direction; before an afternoon cloudburst, great swathes of reflected, glistening light bounce off the scenery in a celestial performance; the land stirs from heavy torpor to meet the deluge and clouds become magnificent, solid creations of sculpted mist like shadowy meteorites blowing through the sky.

You won't notice many villages along this part, but will understand fully why the area has acquired the name Grassfields. Frequent burning on the slopes favours the growth of grass over shrubs and bushes. It makes for excellent grazing and you're likely to see Fula and their cattle along this stretch.

Lake Nyos

The dead village of Nyos is on the Ring Road about 20km from We (not, as marked on some maps, south of the road). The notorious **Lake Nyos** is a couple of kilometres to the south. Nyos is a deep, crater lake, the site of a mysterious, natural gas eruption on August 21, 1986 which killed up to 3000 people enveloped in a cloud of suffocating fumes – perhaps carbon dioxide – that billowed off its surface, and was blown north to

Su-bum. The cause of the disaster is still unknown. There were no indications of a volcanic eruption and some scientists have postulated a weird reaction between warm and cold waters in the lake depths. Some victims appeared to have suffered chemical burns – and volcanic sulphur seems the most likely cause. Whatever the geo-chemical explanation, the people of the area suffered the worst disaster in their history, and many believe it was Western scientific experimenting that caused the phenomenon. The crater lakes are supposed to be the homes of the spirits of the fons and foreigners are regarded suspiciously by some locals, who you may have to convince of your harmless intentions before they'll let you visit, making sure you leave all bags behind. Scientists have warned that whatever caused the eruption may strike again, and a similar event could happen at any lake in the region.

SU-BUM (Soumbon) – a scattering of houses and smoke-stained compounds looped along the valley about 20km from We – is now the only settlement of any size in the Nyos area. It, too, suffered a number of casualties from the gas disaster. More happily it boasts quite spectacular avocadoes.

Kimbi River Game Reserve

Some 60km from We, you enter the **Kimbi River Game Reserve**, which straddles the road, marked by a large signboard. The most abundant animals here are said to be **waterbuck and buffalo**, though one night camped in the reserve revealed only a lone and disoriented kob antelope crossing the road. The few **leopards** that still roam the wilds here are now exceptionally rare, and you've no chance of spotting one. There's a **rest house** of doubtful standard in the reserve (①), but you have to have your own 4WD transport to head out in search of the fauna. Ask at the tourist office in Wum.

Dumbo: trekking into Nigeria

Seventy-four kilometres from We at **Msenje**, a pleasant market village, a branch road heads north to **Dumbo** (17km) and the start of an exceptional trekking route – strictly foot traffic only – into Nigeria, covered on p.1117. Customs and immigration are in Dumbo. Officials are generally friendly here, and will even help you find a porter to continue to Nigeria (about CFA15,000 for a big bag). There's a small **hotel** in town (①), where you can rest up before starting off for the 40-kilometre hike at around 3am. Until dawn you climb gently, then level out for a few hours before reaching the edge of the escarpment and the steep, beautiful descent into Nigeria. The first small town you reach is Bissaula, where customs and immigration formalities can make for an unnerving welcome to the country.

Nkambé to Kumbo

NKAMBÉ, on the northeast side of the Ring Road, is a large town by Grassfield standards, with filling stations and numerous eating and drinking houses. It signals your return from remote regions. To the south, the route continues at an altitude of between 1500 and 2000m and soon becomes more densely populated again. Among the settlements through which it passes is the chiefdom of **Mbot**, which has its own fon and palace. **Ndu**, a couple of kilometres further, is the site of Cameroon's largest tea plantation, an enterprise begun by the British in the 1950s. In Ndu, *Hillside Guest Inn* (①) is a serviceable stopover, though none too clean. A rough road leads east from Ndu to **Sabongari**, whence some sort of track allegedly connects with Gembu in Nigeria. Don't count on it being motorable.

Kumbo and the Nso

KUMBO stands on a plateau 2000m above sea level. One of the biggest towns in the Grassfields, it has no shortage of accommodation, banks and other attributes, including two of the best hospitals in the region. But it's also the seat of another powerful **chiefdom** – as important as those of Bali and Bafut. Kumbo is in the heart of the Nso-speaking (the language is called "Lamnso") region of Bui and the fon here lives in a **palace** with both old and new sections (the latter with a decidedly Muslim flavour, after his recent conversion to Islam). Though now predominantly a Catholic community, the Nso are traditionalists. Don't offer traditional office-holders your hand when greeting, nor drink in their presence, nor pass the traditional policeman (the *Ngwerong*) on his left. The Nso were defeated by the Germans in 1906, and their fon executed in Bamenda – bitter history to which they have never been completely reconciled.

There's a large **market** in Kumbo, and, every eight days, an animal market. *Guinness* has recently started sponsoring an annual **horse race**. Fula people from throughout North West Province assemble here for the event, which usually takes place in November – the Nso Cultural Week. If you can plan it right, it's exhilarating to watch their daredevil bareback ride through the streets. On a slightly more off-beat note, but just as interesting, there's a cave about half a kilometre east of Kumbo which is the resting place of a number of old skulls from long-ago traditional feuds. Find someone to take you.

As for **accommodation**, the bottom line is the *Baptist Mission Catering Rest House*, which puts up travellers for a small fee (①). Inexpensive hotels include the *Travellers Lodge* near the cathedral (①), and the *Merry Land* (PO Box 89; ☎48.10.77; ②). The *Bonni* (②) and the *Tourist Home* (☎48.12.02; ③) are just a little more expensive, while the pleasant *Central*, with its roof terrace overlooking all the action, is the town's most comfortable hotel (③).

Oku

From Kumbo, you can deviate off the Ring Road to visit **OKU**, a traditional village high on the mountain of the same name. There is a motorable road to the village, but it's a demanding hike to Mount Oku's summit (at 3011m the second highest point in West Africa after Mount Cameroon). On the slopes of Oku, you'll find pasturelands and a spectacular crater lake, below the mountain to the west, at 2200m. For the sake of protocol, you should ask the fon's permission before setting out to **Lake Oku** (which in any case is not accessible by car, and is most easily found with the help of a guide). To do so, go to the **fon's palace** at the far end of town, with its myriad of huts, many decorated with carved posts representing symbolic leopards, chameleons and soldiers. Here you will be given permission to see the lake and someone may well be assigned to lead you there. There's a very uninviting "tourist chalet" up here, though no good reason to stay in it. Below, the lake is a deep green pool, perhaps 2km wide and 3km long, encircled by splendid, dark rainforest. Lake Oku is sacred and tradition forbids fishing and swimming, though exceptions are sometimes made for foreigners. The area has diverse birdlife and, in the **Kilum Mountain Forest Project** (headquarters in Oku opposite the crafts centre), you may see the very localized and unmistakeably red-headed **Bannerman's Touraco** and the rare **Banded Wattle-Eye**. There are several private houses in Oku with rooms available to rent (all ①).

Kumbo to Bamenda

The stretch from Kumbo to Bamenda is the most populated district along the Ring Road. South to **Jakiri** it affords panoramic views of the **Ndop Plains** that stretch out to the east, forming a bed for the vast waters of the dam lake, **Lake Bamendjing**. You'll notice many **crafts** being sold along the roadside around here, including baskets. Other stands sell carved calabashes and root figures. If you want to spend the night, there's a small *Auberge Trans Afrique* in Jakiri (①) and the equally simple *Hunter's Lodge* (①). This was the headquarters of British troops from 1958 to 1961 when South

Cameroons was on the verge of independence. A spectacular range of hills rears up near the town.

From Jakiri, you can branch off on a direct road, 75km southeast to Foumban (see p.1172). The main Ring Road continues on through ravishing scenery to Ndop and Bambui whence it's a twelve-kilometre hop to Bamenda.

YAOUNDÉ AND THE SOUTH

As the capital of Cameroon, **Yaoundé** (the name is a corruption of *Ewondo*, the local language) has been consciously developed as a showcase, but remains essentially a shanty town interspersed with prestige buildings, not all of them finished. Still, you'll find most of the facilities you need, and mercifully the city's population remains comparatively low.

Only a few hours away to the southwest, spectacular beaches dot the Atlantic coastline between the fishing village of **Londji** and **Campo**, on the border of Equatorial Guinea. In between, the nation's second port, **Kribi**, has become something of a holiday centre where the well-to-do from the capital head for the weekend.

Thick rainforest covers the southern interior and there are few decent roads, making travel difficult. Even with determination and time, you could only begin to explore the forests, by heading out from towns like **Ebolowa** or **Mbalmayo** as bases.

Yaoundé

Comparisons between the rival cities of **YAOUNDÉ** and Douala are inevitable; most visitors prefer the capital. It lies amid magnificent natural surroundings, heavy with green vegetation, and with a range of peaks, including **Mont Fébé**, as a backdrop. At an altitude of some 700m (over 2000ft), Yaoundé also enjoys a cooler climate. The city's architectural attributes add to the overall visual effect; new buildings, especially in the administrative quarter, give at least a superficial feeling of upward momentum lacking in Douala. But what Yaoundé has gained in credibility, it has perhaps lost in colour and spontaneity; somehow it all seems a bit stiff. Since 1989, too, there have been chronic **water problems**, with supplies on a rota basis around the city districts five days in every week. The situation seems to be getting worse.

Arrival and city transport

The most likely place to arrive by **road** in Yaoundé is the **SOTUC bus station** and main *autogare*, on boulevard de l'OCAM about 100m south of the city's main square, place

YAOUNDÉ'S HISTORY

The site was originally founded by the **Ewondo**, whose history has them crossing the **Sanaga River** on the back of a giant snake before settling on the hilltops of the site of present-day Yaoundé. When the **Germans** criss-crossed the country at the end of the nineteenth century, setting up military posts to affirm their influence in the new protectorate, they established a small presence here. The first commercial enterprises followed in 1907. After World War I, the French chose the budding settlement as capital of what was now their territory; the British had claims to the former capital, Buéa, so Yaoundé became the administrative centre more or less by default. It has continued in that role ever since (except for a brief period during World War II), although its population and industry remain far behind Douala's.

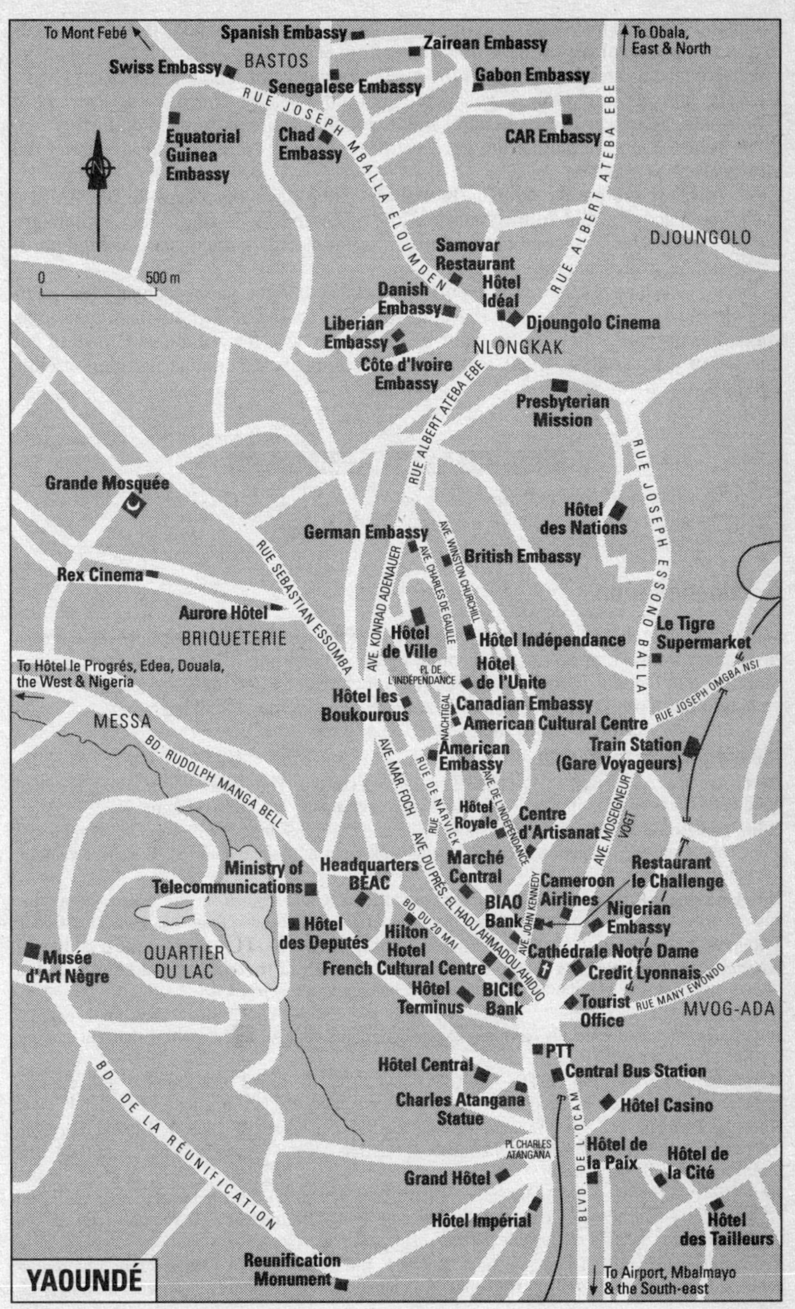

To Mont Febé
Spanish Embassy
Zairean Embassy
To Obala, East & North
Swiss Embassy
BASTOS
Senegalese Embassy
Gabon Embassy
RUE JOSEPH MBALLA ELOUMDEN
Equatorial Guinea Embassy
Chad Embassy
CAR Embassy
RUE ALBERT ATEBA EBE
DJOUNGOLO
0
500 m
Samovar Restaurant
Hôtel Idéal
Danish Embassy
Djoungolo Cinema
Liberian Embassy
NLONGKAK
Côte d'Ivoire Embassy
Presbyterian Mission
RUE ALBERT ATEBA EBE
Grande Mosquée
RUE JOSEPH ESSONO BALLA
Hôtel des Nations
German Embassy
British Embassy
RUE SEBASTIAN ESSOMBA
AVE. WINSTON CHURCHILL
AVE. CHARLES DE GAULLE
AVE. KONRAD ADENAUER
Rex Cinema
Aurore Hôtel
BRIQUETERIE
Hôtel de Ville
Hôtel Indépendance
Le Tigre Supermarket
To Hôtel le Progrés, Edea, Douala, the West & Nigeria
PL DE L'INDÉPENDANCE
Hôtel de l'Unite
Hôtel les Boukourous
Canadian Embassy
NACHTIGAL
American Cultural Centre
RUE JOSEPH OMGBA NSI
MESSA
Train Station (Gare Voyageurs)
BD. RUDOLPH MANGA BELL
American Embassy
AVE. MAR. FOCH
RUE DE NARVICK
AVE DE L'INDÉPENDANCE
AVE. MOSEIGNEUR VOGT
Hôtel Royale
Centre d'Artisanat
RUE
AVE. DU PRÉS. EL HADJ AHMADOU AHIDJO
Ministry of Telecommunications
Headquarters BEAC
Marché Central
Restaurant le Challenge
Cameroon Airlines
AVE. JOHN KENNEDY
BIAO Bank
Nigerian Embassy
Hôtel des Deputés
Hilton Hotel
BD. DU 20 MAI
Musée d'Art Nègre
QUARTIER DU LAC
Cathédrale Notre Dame
French Cultural Centre
Credit Lyonnais
Hôtel Terminus
BICIC Bank
Tourist Office
RUE MANY EWONDO
MVOG-ADA
PTT
Hôtel Central
Central Bus Station
Charles Atangana Statue
Hôtel Casino
BD. DE LA RÉUNIFICATION
PL CHARLES ATANGANA
Hôtel de la Paix
Hôtel de la Cité
BLVD. DE L'OCAM
Grand Hôtel
Hôtel Impérial
Hôtel des Tailleurs
Reunification Monument
YAOUNDÉ
To Airport, Mbalmayo & the South-east

Ahmadou Ahidjo. This throws you right into the heart of things, and is the central focus of an excellent **local bus** system which runs from 6am to 9pm; every bit as good as the one in Douala, it can get you all over town – except the furthest points, like Mont Fébé – for very little money. Only if you come in from West or North West Province – Bafoussam, Foumban and Bamenda – might you find yourself dropped off further out; these vehicles tend to stop at the **gare routière Etoudi** on the northern edge of the city, near the présidence.

The **airport** is roughly 3km south of place Ahidjo down boulevard de l'OCAM. By train, you'll arrive at the **railway station** just off place Elig-Essono, about a kilometre north of place Ahidjo; several of the cheaper accommodation options are located north of the station, away from the centre.

Unless you have your own transport or a healthy budget, you'll probably find yourself dependent on the buses for the time you're in Yaoundé. With its undulating hills spreading over an area of some eight kilometres by five, it's not an easy town to get around on foot: straight streets and square junctions are exceptional, making orientation difficult.

TOURIST INFORMATION

The **Secretariat d'Etat du Tourisme** is on place Ahidjo (☎22.44.11) and should be able to help with information about the city, leaflets and the like.

Accommodation

While Yaoundé has the luxury hotels you'd expect in a capital city, it's also got a reasonable network of moderate accommodation. Small hotels here are less expensive than those in Douala. If you're on a budget, but can't get a bed in the excellent mission, you still have a pretty good selection of inexpensive lodgings to fall back on.

Inexpensive to moderate

Hôtel Aurore, rue Sebastian Essomba (BP 152; ☎23.08.06). The central location is the selling point of this otherwise mundane hotel, with simple, reasonably priced S/C rooms. ②.

Hôtel Les Boukarous, rue Narvick, quartier du Lac (BP 1295; ☎22.47.48). A garden hotel in the quiet Lake Quarter. Attractive S/C rooms and a pleasant outdoor restaurant. Excellent value in the moderate range. ③.

Hôtel Casino, off bd de l'OCAM (BP 246; ☎22.22.03). Only 100m from the *gare routière*, this austere hotel offers S/C rooms that are cleaner and more comfortable than the dilapidated facade might suggest. ①.

Hôtel Idéal, rue Albert Ateba Ebé roundabout (☎22.03.04). The *Idéal* has a large selection of rooms, and is clean and friendly. Both #2 and #4 bus lines stop in front. ②.

Hôtel Impérial, av Charles Atangana (BP 977; ☎22.35.66). A charming older hotel, popular among overlanders, especially Germans. Nostalgic rooms with AC and a good restaurant and bar on the outdoor terrace. ③.

Hôtel de la Paix, off bd de l'OCAM (BP 106; ☎23.32.73). Lacks basic comfort and wins no hygiene awards, but it's in a good location near place Ahidjo, and is very affordable. Often full. ①.

Hôtel Le Progrès, rue Nana Tchakounté near the Messa market (BP 1005; ☎22.49.06). Far from the centre in the lively Messa neighbourhood, this has a good reputation with comfortable AC rooms and friendly service. ③.

Hôtel de l'Unité, place de l'Indépendance (BP 1034; ☎22.20.22). Ideally located, near the Hôtel de Ville, for exploring the commercial district on foot. The modest S/C rooms verge on the depressing, but there's a reasonable garden restaurant. ②.

Presbyterian Mission, Djoungolo (take bus #4 to the terminus at rue Albert Ateba Ebé roundabout, and walk 200m uphill to the east). A colonial-style guesthouse, clean and friendly with individual or shared rooms. Missionaries get first crack and so the place is often full. The town's cheapest. ①.

Expensive

Hilton Hotel, bd du 20 Mai (☎23.59.19; Fax 22.32.10). This swanky new hotel far outranks the older upmarket establishments, with modern styling based on African themes. Lavish gardens with health club, pool, shops, restaurants, tennis and casino. A variety of services is available for business travellers. Major credit cards accepted. ⑦.

Hôtel des Députés, in the administrative quarter near the lake (BP 24; ☎22.10.55; Fax 23.37.10). Bland modern hotel with AC rooms, pool, tennis courts, bar and a restaurant overlooking the lake. Major credit cards accepted. ⑦.

Hôtel Indépendance, av Winston Churchill (BP 474; ☎23.32.65). Very good hotel in a central location with 40 AC rooms. The bar and restaurant get lots of praise and the nightclub is a popular after-dark retreat. ⑥.

Hôtel Mont Fébé (BP 711; ☎21.40.02; Fax 21.15.00). Formerly the town's top A-class place, the *Mont Fébé* is still more often crowded than the *Hilton*. It has a swimming pool, 18-hole golf course, shopping boutiques, banks and car rental service. At 6km from the centre, it's a bit far, but offers peace and prime views of the capital and surrounding hills. Major credit cards accepted. ⑦.

Hôtel Royale, off av de l'Indépendance (☎23.19.53; Fax 22.41.92). A modern place lacking the pretensions of the larger hotels but with most of their amenities. Clean, comfortable and in a central location. ⑤.

The City

There are not that many specific targets to aim for in your explorations of Yaoundé, beyond the usual pleasures of pavement cafés and the main market. In the midst of all the recent building, the government has opened the new **Musée National**, housed in an impressively restored colonial building off the avenue Marchand: it should prove well worth visiting. The city's two, small private collections could hardly be more different from each other: the jumble of clobber in the **Musée d'Art Negre** and the immaculately presented **Musée d'Art Camerounais**, one of West Africa's most worthwhile museums.

The commercial centre

Despite its difficulties for pedestrians, Yaoundé does have a walkable centre, its heart at **place Ahmadou Ahidjo**. The most startling of the many buildings grouped around this square is the very 1950s **cathedral**, with a sloping roof that goes on forever. The city's main arteries shoot out from place Ahidjo. To the east, avenue Monseigneur Vogt runs uphill past many of the city's major banks. Avenue du Président El Hadj Ahidjo leads north of place Ahidjo up to the colourful **marché central**, while avenue Kennedy, off avenue Ahidjo, is one of the city's classier streets, with its **sidewalk cafés** and upmarket shops, flaunting a distinctly French flavour. This street ends in place Kennedy where you'll find the **Centre d'Artisanat**, the town's biggest crafts depot and well worth checking out. Avenue de l'Indépendance leads from place Kennedy to place de l'Indépendance, dominated by the futuristic **Hôtel de Ville** – the city hall.

The Lake Quarter and Melen

Most of the administrative buildings in town congregate to the west of place Ahidjo, between boulevard du 20 Mai and the town lake. Known as the **Quartier du Lac**, this tranquil neighbourhood, with its imposing avenues, has long been a construction site for experiments in modern architecture. Buildings such as the **Ministère des Postes et Télécommunications** or the imaginative headquarters of the **Banque des Etats**

de l'Afrique Centrale have gone a long way towards changing Yaoundé's self-image in recent years. On boulevard de la Réunification, which marks the southern fringe of this *quartier*, the **Monument de la Réunification** rises up in a helter-skelter spiral commemorating the coming together of Cameroon's French- and English-speaking components. In the middle of this neighbourhood, the **lake** itself hardly provides the serene natural backdrop you might imagine. It's more like a stagnant pond – and a perfect mosquito breeding ground.

Musée d'Art Negre

The **Musée d'Art Negre** (daily 8am–noon & 2–6pm; free entrance, but slip the caretaker a tip) is relatively close to the centre, in the Quartier du Lac. Dark and dusty and not worth making a special effort for, the works here all come from the private collection of the Jesuit founder. African odds and ends are arranged haphazardly and include masks from Zaire, a Benin bronze and Bamoun pipes, with a crown from Thailand thrown in for good measure. The museum does contain an interesting **library of African history** with archives of transcribed oral histories and some period photographs. Get there by taking bus #2 to place Melen and walking down rue de Melen. After about 100m, follow a sign reading *Centre Aumonerie Catholique Universitaire* down a small path to the right leading to the museum.

Mass at Ndjong-Melen

This is a famous tourist outing, but not done for tourists. Every Sunday from 9.30am to noon the congregation in the **Catholic church** in the quarter of Ndjong-Melen, just west of the Musée d'Art Negre, works itself into a state of high excitement during the Ewondo language service – wonderful music and dancing, high-energy drumming, and everyone in their most colourful outfits.

The northern suburbs

Yaoundé's poor and working-class districts are mostly tucked away in valleys, hidden from sight by the hill tops. Such neighbourhoods include the **Briqueterie**, with the town's **Grande Mosquée**, and **Messa**, which has one of the liveliest markets outside the centre. In the extreme north of town, the **Bastos** neighbourhood is the most exclusive residential area. Site of the nation's first factory (making the *Bastos* cigarettes which gave it its name), this quarter is now better known for its many embassies and the modern, and top-heavy présidence – the **presidential palace**.

Musée d'Art Camerounais

Situated in a Benedictine monastery on above *Hôtel Mont Fébé*, the **Musée d'Art Camerounais** (Thurs, Sat & Sun 3–6pm; free entrance, but a donation is expected) is way out of the centre and accessible by taxi; the alternative is to take bus #5 to the end of the line and hike up the mountain. A narrow flight of steps takes you up to the museum from the main road and continues to the hotel. Ring the bell when you arrive at the monastery; a monk will lead you to the exhibit.

Like a monument to minimalism, the museum's interior is completely stark, with clean whitewashed walls and appropriate lighting to force your attention onto the displays. Although the collection is small, it contains many masterpieces, notably from the western provinces. First of all is a display of pipes (in ivory, wood and terracotta) including some amazing **Bamoun bronze pipes**. Another room features **masks**, mainly from the Grassfields, and a fantastic wooden **bas-relief** depicting a market scene. Notice too a carved wooden bed for a king, and intricate wooden panels showing scenes from the hunt. A third room contains **Tikar bronzes** and includes pipes, bells used to call the ancestors, and a king's throne.

Eating, drinking and nightlife

The surest way of guaranteeing yourself **cheap eating** is to buy food supplies from the well-stocked **marché central**, or other neighbourhood markets such as that in the Messa quarter. For inexpensive snacking, the commercial area is full of *soya* sellers. Vendors also tempt you with cool pineapple slices stored on ice packs. Should you be staying at the Presbyterian Mission, there are numerous **small eateries** on rue Onembele Nkou and rue Joseph Essono Balla. They serve good breakfasts of omelettes and *Nescafé* in the morning, and filling rice and bean dishes in the afternoon and evening.

Inexpensive to moderate restaurants

Inexpensive to moderate restaurants are easy to stumble upon in the residential districts of Bastos, Messa and especially Briqueterie, though they are noticeably rarer in the centre. Some good choices in the CFA2000–3000 bracket include:

Bambou Village, off rue Albert Atebe Ebé, Bastos. Copious servings of Cameroonian specialities. Not at all fancy, but satisfying cooking in an agreeable atmosphere.

Boulangerie Calfatas, rue Nachtigal, just south of pl de l'Independence. The address for fresh pastries, croissants, pain au chocolat, and other decadent snacks including ice cream.

Le Challenge, av Kennedy. A good find in the heart of the commercial centre. Moderate prices for salads, sandwiches, and chicken or beef with chips.

Le Marseillais, av Foch. Very good value for the centre, with home-style French dishes such as *steack frites* with haricots. There are at least two other branches of the *Marseillais*.

Expensive restaurants

As in Douala, upmarket restaurants can be prohibitively expensive, but you can find well-prepared food at down-to-earth prices in some of the hotels and many of the Asian restaurants.

AFRICAN

L'Agora, qtr Nlongkak (☎22.35.96). Upmarket Cameroonian cuisine with unusual main dishes including crocodile. Less adventurous tastebuds will be tempted by the excellent fish and chicken dishes.

Les Boukarous, rue de Narvick (☎23.30.30). This hotel restaurant isn't strictly African, but there's a good choice of Cameroonian dishes thrown in with the French or Lebanese fare. Superb atmosphere in the outdoor garden and not as pricey as all that.

EUROPEAN

Le Cintra, av Kennedy (☎22.33.88). Classy *café terrasse* with Corsican cuisine, including excellent seafood, and rather elevated prices.

Le Dauphin, rte de l'Aviation (☎23.12.54). Well known and liked for excellent French food – but at a fiendish price (up to CFA20,000 a head).

Mbankolo, at the *Mont Fébé* (☎22.43.24). One of the best restaurants in town for French cooking and one of the most expensive. There is a cheaper coffee shop in the hotel and a poolside buffet.

Le Samovar, rte de Bastos (☎20.76.98). Run by a Russian couple, the *Samovar* features authentic dishes from the old country and some not-so-traditional pizza, fired up in the outdoor oven.

La Switza, av Churchill, just south of *Hôtel de l'Independance*. Fair prices for solid French meals, fine wine and creative *entrées*.

CHINESE

Grand Muraille de Chine, av Charles de Gaulle, near the German embassy. Chinese vegetables, egg rolls and so on, for as little as CFA3000. A good place for lunch.

Chez Wou, rte du Mont Fébé near the Swiss embassy. This Chinese restaurant features authentic decor and terrace eating. A good place for a special dinner, but expensive.

Nightlife

Yaoundé has little of Douala's after-dark energy. There are a few well-known clubs and of course the hotel discos. But apart from these, a number of bars and a few small places in Briqueterie and Messa are about all the city can offer. Unfortunately, idle meanderings have become dangerous after dark. Take a taxi to get around or go in the company of someone who knows the terrain well.

Le Balafon, at the *Mont Fébé*. High-tech but stuffy, as the remote location limits the clientele pretty much to the hotel guests and those that can afford to drive there.

Black and White, rue Goker, near pl Kennedy. A popular venue despite the high cover and price of drinks. The central location assures a large crowd.

Le Caveau, south of pl Ahidjo. An unpretentious *boite populaire* that throbs with the latest Central African hits. A younger crowd keeps the place lively.

Katio, av Ahidjo at rue Goker. The biggest and best in town, a flashy place with pulsating lights, good music and several dance areas. Drinks and cover among Yaoundé's most expensive, but good energy guaranteed.

Oxygene, by *Hôtel Royale*, off av de l'Indépendance. Newer club, with Western and African sounds and a middle-class clientele that includes a good number of expats.

Le Pacha, basement of Imm. Hajal Massad, av Foch. A disco palace that's been around forever and still packs them in.

Super Paquita, east of pl Ahidjo, quartier Mvog-Ada. Inexpensive dancing and high-powered music in a neighbourhood club well-frequented by local youth.

Listings

Airfreight *DHL* (☎23.13.58).

Airlines *Cameroon Airlines* is on av Monseigneur Vogt, behind the cathedral (☎23.40.01 or 22.39.74). For additional flight information, including international carriers, call the airport (☎23.06.11).

American Express There is no officially appointed international representation. *Delmas Voyages* in Douala (see p.1152) is your best port of call: or try one of Yaoundé's big hotels or major travel agents.

Banks The main banks are near place Ahidjo. Those on av Ahidjo include: *Banque Méridien BIAO* (BP 182; ☎23.41.35), which is recommended for having money sent to; and *BICIC* (BP 5; ☎23.41.30). Many others are on av Monseigneur Vogt, including: *SGBC* (BP 244; ☎23.41.25); *SCB–Crédit Lyonnais* (BP 145; ☎23.41.20; Fax 22.41.32). *Standard Chartered* is just south of the place de l'Indépendance.

Bookshops *Librairie Moderne Hachette*, av Kennedy (☎23.04.54), offers the biggest selection of international papers and magazines, books (mainly French) and some national maps. Also try *Librairie Hermes Memento* (☎22.12.39).

Car rental As reliable as it is expensive, *Hertz* has its office in the *Mont Fébé* (☎23.40.02). *Avis* is on the rte de Douala (☎30.02.85). Other agencies include: *Jully Auto*, av Ahidjo (BP 6064; ☎22.39.47); *Neuilly Auto*, av de l'Indépendance (BP 375; ☎22.15.35); *P.Z. Motors Europcar*, at the airport (☎22.33.44) and on av Ahidjo (BP 198; ☎22.11.47).

Cinemas The best movie theatres, with the most up-to-date films, are *Le Capital*, on av Ahidjo (☎22.49.77), and *L'Abbia* on rue Nachtigal (☎22.31.66). Other neighbourhood cinemas include: *Le Djoungolo*, rue Albert Ateba Ebé; *Le Fébé*, in the Messa quarter on rue Sultan Njoya; *La Mefou*, place Awae, off bd de l'OCAM; *Les Portiques*, av John Kennedy; and *Le Rex*, in the Briqueterie quarter on rue de la Briqueterie.

Cultural centres include: **British Council**, av Charles de Gaulle (office and library; BP 818; ☎21.16.96; Fax 21.56.91); **Centre Culturel Français**, av Ahidjo (☎23.40.13); **Goethe Institut**, av Kennedy (☎23.38.74); and the **United States Information Service**, av Nachtigal (☎23.16.33).

Doctors Polyclinic André-Fouda (☎22.24.64), rte de Ngousso, east of the railway tracks.

Embassies and consulates include: **Algeria** qtr Bastos (BP 1619; ☎23.06.65); **Belgium** qtr Bastos, Mban Building (BP 816; ☎22.27.88); **Benin** (☎23.34.98); **Canada** Imm. Stamatiades, av de l'Indépendance (BP 572; ☎23.02.03); **Central African Republic** off rue Albert Ateba Ebé (BP 396; ☎22.51.55); **Chad** rue Joseph Mballa Eloumden, qtr Bastos (BP 506; ☎22.06.24); **Congo** qtr Bastos (BP 1422; ☎23.24.58); **Côte d'Ivoire** Imm. Ndende, qtr Bastos (BP 203; ☎22.09.69); **Equatorial Guinea** qtr Bastos (BP 277; ☎22.41.49); **France**, av de Gaulle (BP 1631; ☎22.02.33); **Gabon** qtr Bastos off bd de l'URSS (BP 4130; ☎22.29.66); **Germany**, av de Gaulle, near the Hôtel de Ville (BP 1160; ☎23.05.66); **Israel** (BP 5934; ☎20.16.44; Fax 21.08.23); **Italy** qtr Bastos (BP 827; ☎22.33.76); **Liberia** rue Mballa Eloumden, qtr Bastos (☎23.12.96); **Morocco** qtr Bastos (BP 1629; ☎22.50.92); **Netherlands** av 27 Août, Imm Le Concorde (BP 310; ☎22.05.44); **Nigeria** off av Monseigneur Vogt (BP 448; ☎22.34.55); **Senegal** qtr Bastos (BP 176; ☎22.03.08); **Spain** qtr Bastos (BP 877; ☎22.41.89); **Sweden** bd Edjoa Mbede (BP 830; ☎23.38.54); **Switzerland** rte du Mont Fébé (BP 1169; ☎23.28.96); **Tunisia** rue de Rotary (BP 6074; ☎22.33.68); **United Kingdom** av Winston Churchill (BP 547; ☎22.07.96; Fax 22.01.48; Mon, Wed, Fri 8.30am–noon, 2.30–4.30pm, Tues & Fri 8.30am–noon; issues visas for most Commonwealth African countries); **USA** rue de Nachtigal (BP 817; ☎23.40.14; Fax 23.07.53); **Zaire** qtr Bastos (BP 632; ☎22.51.03).

Emergencies Police ☎17, Fire ☎18.

Maps The *Institut Géographique National*, on av Monseigneur Vogt (☎22.34.65), has city and national maps. For less detailed versions, try the tourist office.

Newsline English news of the day ☎22.90.00, French ☎22.80.00.

Pharmacies Among the best stocked and most central is the *Pharmacie Française* (☎22.14.76) on the corner of av Kennedy and av Ahidjo.

Post offices The main post office (Mon–Fri 8am–noon & 2.30–5.30pm) is on place Ahidjo. The poste restante service costs CFA400, but they don't hold letters very long.

Supermarkets *Prisunic*, av de l'Indépendance (near USA cultural centre), is one of the cheapest. On the same street, *Score* is well stocked, but *Tigre* in the north of town on rue Essono Bella is a mega-mart and considered the best place for one-stop shopping.

Telephones The main *Intelcam* office is on pl Ahidjo, across from the post office.

MOVING ON FROM YAOUNDÉ

BY ROAD

Most **buses** and **taxis**, including those for Douala, leave from the **bus station** on boulevard de l'OCAM. For the western towns of Bafoussam, Foumban and Bamenda, head to **gare routière Etoudi** on the north side of the city, near the présidence.

BY TRAIN

Trains leave daily to **Ngaoundéré** via **Belabo** and **Ngaoundal** (for road routes to the Central African Republic) from the railway station by place Elig-Essono (enquiries ☎23.40.03), and there's a night train with couchettes. You can also get trains to **Douala**, although for this stretch, the speed of the excellent paved road makes the train journey a bit pointless unless you're an enthusiast.

TRANSCAM I

Intercity service
Dep Yaoundé 7.15am, arr Douala 10.40am.
Dep Yaoundé 7pm, arr Douala 10.30pm.

Express Autorail stopping service
Dep Yaoundé 12.50pm, arr Douala 4.45pm.

Omnibus all stations service
Dep Yaoundé 7.30am, arr Douala 4.05pm.

TRANSCAM II

Trains couchettes service
Dep. Yaoundé 7pm, arr. Ngaoundéré 6am.

Continued overleaf

Moving on from Yaoundé continued...

BY PLANE

Flights leave from the new Nsimalen International Airport, 18km south of the centre (a CFA2500 taxi ride). Flights to northern towns invariably call at Ngaoundéré, Garoua and Maroua. There are several flights daily to Douala and flights to Bafoussam (Sat); Bamenda (Tues); Batouri via Bertoua (Wed); Dschang (Mon & Sun); Garoua (daily); Mamfé (Tues via Bamenda & Fri); Maroua (daily, via several towns; usually a 4-hour-plus flight); and Ngaoundéré (five flights a week). Domestic traffic is handled by *Cameroon Airlines* and *Unitair* both of which also operate flights to Ndjamena, Chad, via northern Cameroon. Other **international flights**, including those to Europe, leave from Douala, except *Swissair's* weekly flight to Zurich.

TRAVEL AGENCIES

Travel agencies include: *Antoniades Travel Agency* (*ATA*), place Kennedy (BP 419; ☎23.14.88); *Camvoyages*, av de l'Indépendance (BP 606; ☎23.22.12); *Cameroun Publi-Expansion* (*CPE*), Imm. Les Galeries (BP 1399; ☎23.39.21); *Intervoyages*, place Hôtel de Ville (BP 127; ☎22.03.61); *Transcap Voyages* (BP 153; ☎23.12.96).

The Province du Sud

As an escape from the swelter of Douala or the rigours of overlanding, **Kribi** and the white sand beaches of the "south coast" are hard to beat. Now that the road is paved all the way from Douala, access to this once remote corner is now no more difficult than a two-hour taxi ride.

The quickest route from Yaoundé to Kribi is via **EDÉA**. This attractive and well-provisioned town has always made a good living from the passing Douala–Yaoundé–Kribi trade at the lowest bridge over the broad **Sanaga River**, but especially since the completion of the N3 highway brought a mass of new traffic. It's also responsible for much of the country's electric power generation. If you're staying over, the *Foyer* and *Auberge* are reasonable (②), *Hôtel La Sanaga,* on the route de Douala and overlooking the river (BP 54; ☎46.43.11; ③), is better.

Alternatively, it's possible to make your way to Kribi through the forests of Le Province du Sud – South Province – along tracks which, in the dry season at any rate, are passable by normal cars. There are two main routes from the capital; in either case the first stage is to **Ebolowa**, then either via **Lolodorf** or **Akom II**. Travel can be painfully slow along these stretches, but the roads take in lush scenery punctuated with the occasional waterfall, and skirt a number of "**Pygmy**" **villages**. Note, however, that the finest beaches in the Kribi area are to the north of the town, on the Edéa road.

Mbalmayo and Sangmélima

Heading south through rich forests broken by plantations of coffee and cocoa, the N2 highway links the capital to Ebolowa, then continues to the borders of Gabon and Equatorial Guinea. The first major stop along the way is **Mbalmayo** – a prosperous logging town with accommodation, banks and post office. You can actually get as far as Mbalmayo by train, but the road is so good (and so frequently served by **taxis**) that there's little point.

From Mbalmayo, the N9 branches southeastward to **SANGMÉLIMA**, another large town in the forest region, centre of the president's Beti ethnic group (his home town is Mvomeka, 50km northeast). There's modest **accommodation** in Sangmélima at the *Hôtel Dja Bel Air,* with simple S/C rooms (②). Slightly upmarket, the *Hotel Afamba* has AC and TV in the rooms (③), but for atmosphere, you can't beat the *Jardin des Tropiques* on the route de Mbalmayo (☎28.33.39; ③), where the bungalows with TV and AC press right up to the forest's edge. The **Gabonese border** at **Nsak** is 150km away to the south. Eastward, you could strike out to the rarely visited rainforest zone of the **Réserve du Dja**.

Ebolowa

To get to the coast, or to the borders, take the road that leads from Mbalmayo via Ngoulemakong to **EBOLOWA**. This lively provincial capital in the forest is an important cocoa marketing centre. It's a pleasant stopping point with a large market that spreads out near the town's artificial **lake**. With over 40,000 inhabitants, Ebolowa also has good services, including **banks** (*BIAO, BICIC* and *Credit Lyonnais*), a **post office**, pharmacies and even a small supermarket. There's not much in the way of sights, however – you could stop by the **Hôpital Enongal** to contemplate the chair where Albert Schweitzer sat while having dental work done.

Practicalities

There are several small **hotels**, most with **restaurants** and **bar/dancings** that make for rather wild nights in the jungle. Water supplies are irregular in town, and even the best hotel can't guarantee enough pressure for a decent bath.

L'Ane Rouge, off the town's main roundabout and an easy walk from the *gare routière* (☎28.34.38). The clean S/C rooms with mosquito nets are very good value. ②.

La Cabane Bambou, north of the *gare routière*, towards the market. Inexpensive hotel and restaurant, popular with overlanders. ①.

Le Ranch (BP 670; ☎28.35.31). The town's best. Comfortable S/C rooms looking out on an attractive courtyard. ③.

Auberge de la Santé, north of the market, opposite the lake (☎28.35.17). Spotless S/C rooms. ②.

Hôtel Splendid, 200m west of the *gare routière*. Another inexpensive option though the rooms with shared facilities are none too clean. Pleasant restaurant. ①.

Moving on

From the main *gare routière*, taxis run frequently to **Yaoundé**. Check too for departures of coaches run by *Bucavoyages*, by far the most comfortable way to travel to the capital. Taxis from the *gare routière* are less frequent **to Kribi**, though there are at least a couple a day. If you're continuing to **Gabon** or **Equatorial Guinea**, you need to get to **Ambam** (see overleaf), which has its own *gare routière* to the south of Ebolowa on the route d'Ambam.

Around Ebolowa

The environs of Ebolowa harbour a number of interesting natural curiosities, though to see them you really have to have your own transport. One of the best known is the **Trou des Fantomes** (Phantoms' Cave), reached by taking the Sangmélima route out of town and following it 20km to the village of Nkoétyé. Ask there for directions to the yawning chasm, where a fabulous chained monster is reputed to live.

Given time for an even longer excursion, you could conceivably get as far as the **Menvé Elé Falls**, over 150km away towards the Campo Game Reserve. This trip leads into the heart of the Cameroonian wilds, far from the world of hotels, restaurants and filling stations (except in Méyo, and even there the pumps are sometimes dry). You therefore need to be equipped with survival provisions, and take all the fuel you'll need for the 300-odd-kilometre round trip. Although the falls are marked on the maps near **Nyabessan**, the most difficult part of the trip is yet to come. At Nyabessan, you have to ask the chief's permission to visit the area, and he'll make sure you get a guide (at this point you'll have to settle on a price, and it won't be a trifling sum). You then hike with your guide through 7km of forest (and cross two rivers by *pirogue*) to the village of Ebianemeyong. Here you again need the chief's permission (and dash some more money) to continue. There are 4km more of forest to bash your way through before you reach the **Ntem River**, once more crossed by *pirogue*. From here, follow the river up to a series of seven cascades, the highest of which crashes down from a height of fifty metres. It's the getting there that makes the falls – modestly impressive – really worthwhile.

Ambam and on to Gabon and Equatorial Guinea

The paved road stops just south of Ebolowa, making for an adventurous trip through dense forest to **Ambam**, the last major town before the borders of Equatorial Guinea and Gabon. There's a large market here with an international array of traders, and rudimentary **accommodation** at the *Auberge du Petit Calao* (①). But this is a transit town and like most people who pull in, your main objective will be to get on to somewhere else.

Taxis **to Gabon** leave from Ambam's market and take little more than an hour to reach the border. On Saturdays, they stop at **Aban Minkoo** for the eventful weekly market. Once at the border, you can take a ferry across the Ntem River, or hire a *pirogue*. Taxis on the other side assure regular transport to **Bitam**.

The station for taxis **to Equatorial Guinea** is in Ambam across from the post office. Halfway to the border, your vehicle crosses the Ntem River on a regular ferry and then pushes on to the frontier town of **Ebebiyin**. You'll be dropped on Cameroonian territory, some 2km before reaching the town. After going through customs, you can continue in a waiting taxi.

Lolodorf

From Ebolowa, it's 73km by decent *piste* to **LOLODORF** (its name about the only reminder of the German presence in the area – "Lolo's village" – as most towns were renamed by the French), where you may be able to fill up with petrol, but won't find any accommodation. Only 110km separate Lolodorf from Kribi, but the tracks that wind through the hilly tropical forest make for a long trip. As a payoff, however, this route does pass by numerous "Pygmy" villages where, unlike in the extreme east of the country, the people have adopted a sedentary lifestyle. The worst stretch of road comes in the first 34km to the village of Bidjoka, from where you can walk to the **Bidjoka Falls**. Ten kilometres further on is the larger village of Bipindi whence it's another 66km to Kribi.

Kribi

As a backdrop to the daily activity of commerce, fishing and foresting, colonial reminders abound in **KRIBI**, creating a quiet nostalgic feeling. The hometown of the Bassa, Kribi was a noted hotbed of UPC radicalism in the 1950s. The **port** at the centre of town was built by the Germans and is today too shallow for larger vessels to enter the harbour: from the nearby hillside, crowned with its colonial **cathedral**, you can see ships anchored a few kilometres offshore as their cargo is transferred by lighter. The former **German administrative buildings** lining the beachfront in the northwest of town now house government offices such as the *préfecture* and the **tourist office**.

Kribi is Cameroon's second-largest port, but has long remained in relative isolation. Since the new highway linking the town to Yaoundé and Douala opened in 1991, however, travelling time has been slashed from nine hours to less than three. The road has given a much needed economic boost to the region – though at the expense of opening the tourism floodgates. Fortunately, there are still numerous remote corners where you can escape from the weekend sun-seekers.

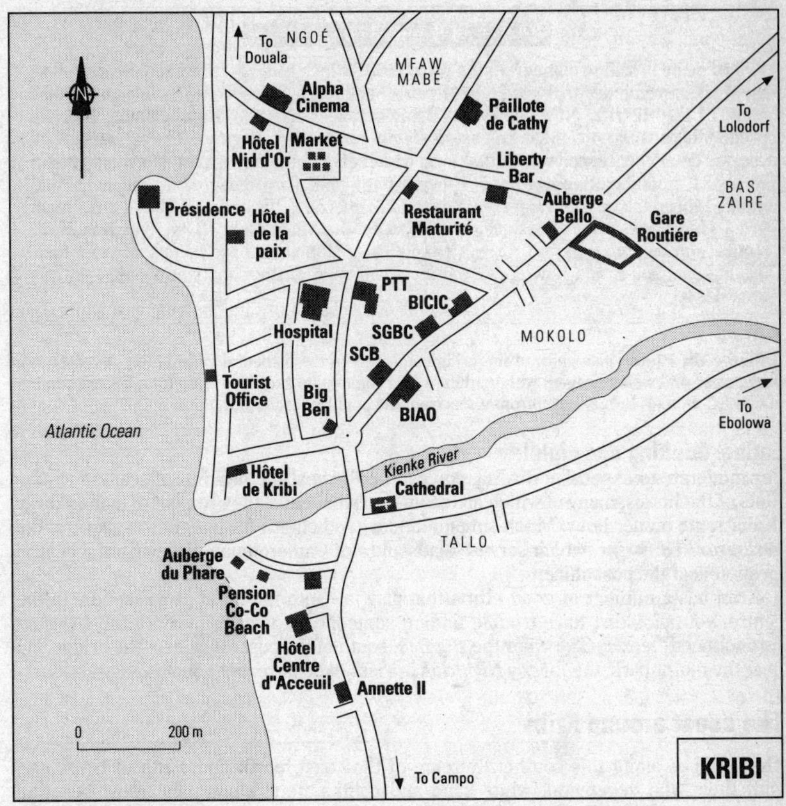

Accommodation

Because of the relatively heavy tourist influx, **accommodation** tends to be expensive in Kribi, though a number of relatively inexpensive places still do good business. In the off season, or even weekdays, bargaining gets good results, and if you're staying for an extended period, you should be able to shave 10 to 30 percent off the regular room rate.

Auberge Annette I, east of the market, near the water tower (BP 53; ☎46.10.57). Inexpensive lodgings, basic but livable and right in the centre of things. ②.

Auberge Annette II, over the bridge, 1km south of the centre (BP 53; ☎46.10.57). An ideal beachfront location that justifies relatively high prices considering it's only an *auberge*. Still one of the cheaper places on the sea. ③.

Auberge Bello, two blocks east of the *gare routière* in the New Bell neighbourhood. Near the *Annette I* and a good place to fall back on if it's full. Clean rooms, friendly management and good value. ②.

Hôtel Centre d'Accueil, rte de Lobé (BP 142; ☎46.16.35). Attractive ocean-front rooms with unnecessary AC. The fine bar-restaurant looks out on the water. ④.

Hôtel Coco Beach, south of the bridge, on the beach (☎46.15.84). Well-scrubbed AC rooms with showers and hot water, though there are only 10 and they're often full. German-run with an outstanding seafood restaurant right on the seafront. ③.

Paillote de Cathy, 200m north of the market in Afan Mabé quarter. A bit far from the centre and, more serious, the beachfront, but a fair price for presentable non-S/C accommodation. ①.

THE KIRIDI

Kribi's name is said to come from the word *kiridi*, which roughly translated means "short men". It's a reminder that you're in "**Pygmy**" country – these were the original inhabitants of the district. Now, however, Bantu-speakers like the **Batanga** and **Bakoko** predominate, and you might not see a single convincing "Pygmy". The "Pygmies", of course, don't call themselves by that term and every community is part of a small cluster of bands, traditionally nomadic, but increasingly sedentary these days, and more and more dependent on the larger economy of Cameroon, beyond the forest. The main groups of the western part of equatorial Africa are the Binga, Beku, Baka, Jelli, Koa, Kola, Kouya, Rimba and Yaga. All Africa's people of small stature have completely lost their original languages and now speak the local language of the dominant people – in this area Bassa.

Auberge du Phare, just south of the bridge and west of the cathedral (☎46.11.08). A reasonable place, clean and well managed, with moderate AC rooms (plus excellent value for a limited number of non-AC rooms). Breezy beachfront vistas from the popular restaurant. ③.

Eating, drinking and nightlife

For moderate to expensive **dining**, you can hardly beat the beachfront seafood restaurants of the hotels, many of which are so busy at weekends, they run out of food midway through the dinner hour. Much simpler, and a good choice for budget travellers, is the *Restaurant La Sirène*, which serves salads and hot Cameroonian dishes from a central location near the post office.

Kribi has a number of good **clubs** that play late into the night at weekends. In the centre, you shouldn't have trouble finding someone to point the way to the *Gin Fizz* (pronounced "feez"), *Club 45* or the *Big Ben*, south of the post office near the bridge. Up near the motor park, the *Liberty Nightclub* is a less expensive, but equally lively option.

The coast around Kribi

The beaches along this southern stretch of the coast, north and south of Kribi, are, with their wild vegetation, white sand and calm waters, among the most beautiful anywhere in Africa. They stretch over 100km, from the small village at **Londji** to the town of **Campo** on the border of Equatorial Guinea. Beach bums will be in their element, though the paradise is far from being a well-kept secret.

Londji and the beaches to the north

North of Kribi, the road to Edéa hugs the coastline as it skirts some of the most picturesque strands. It passes the village of Mpalla and, after 15km, **Cocotier Plage** (a beautiful beach where there are rudimentary bungalows for rent) before arriving at **LONDJI**. Some 25km from Kribi, this small fishing town spreads round a large bay with calm, warm water, white sands and coconut trees. A comfortable *auberge* with electricity and running water nestles on the beach offering the town's best **accommodation** (②). The Cameroonian *patronne* and her French husband are extremely friendly and operate an excellent seafood restaurant. Though it fills with expats at weekends, on other days you'll have the place and the beach to yourself. If you're on a low budget, a humbler *auberge*, without water or electricity, offers perfect repose – and you're unlikely to miss modern conveniences in the beautiful natural setting (①). You can fill up in town on fish, snail kebabs and rice and a couple of local bars sell beer, minerals and freshly tapped palm wine.

After midnight, **fishermen** set out in wooden canoes across the bay, stirring up phosphoresence in the water as they paddle towards the deeper ocean. You may be able to persuade one to take you along, though it's not always an eventful experience. On arrival *au large* – out at sea – they cast their nets, which are hundreds of metres long, and simply wait until dawn (in daylight, fish can see the nets and avoid getting caught). When they arrive at shore in the morning, buyers from surrounding villages are already waiting at the beach to see the night's catch.

Staying in Londji is as relaxing as the fishing technique, but despite its position on the main *piste* it does feel isolated and if you're looking for bars with *dancings*, restaurants and the like, this is not the place. Although Kribi isn't far, taxis there are rare and if you want to go to town for the day, you'll spend most of the time waiting for transport – with the distinct possibility of being stuck for the night in Kribi if you don't head back to Londji early enough in the afternoon.

The southern beaches to Campo

Another *piste* follows the coastline southwards from Kribi to the Ecuato-Guinean border, passing still more beaches, all exotically named – Marseilles, Océan Amérique, Azure. Seven kilometres from town, just before **Grand Batanga**, a small signpost points down to the **Chutes de la Lobé** where the river of the same name comes thrashing over a rocky descent as it plunges directly into the ocean. The force of these rapids stirs up an unappealing brownish foam in the bay, but the surrounding beaches are clean and have excellent swimming. A small and rather pricey restaurant at the foot of the falls serves grilled fish specialities under a pleasant *paillote*. You could walk down here from Kribi, but would probably want a lift back again.

You certainly need to take transport to the fishing village of **Eboundja**, 20km south of Kribi, where the local chief authorizes camping on the beach, and will arrange meals and fishing boat excursions. The more complicated trips that you may be offered up the Lobé River, however, tend to be disappointing, for while paddling upstream is not without interest, the "Pygmy" villages you've ostensibly come to visit are completely inauthentic and the "traditional" hunting trips – with people taller than you – really seem like something out of a second-rate theme park.

Some 25km further south, a rocky land formation, the **Rocher du Loup** – a photo of which is unfailingly included in all the tourism literature – rises dramatically, but not very wolf-like, from out of the water. South of here, you're getting into very remote districts: the road passes yet another fishing village, Ebodje, before petering out at the two-bit border town of **CAMPO**. You can expect customs and immigration checks in the vicinity, whether or not you're crossing. The big **Réserve du Campo**, 3000 square kilometres of gazetted but unmanaged rainforest, doesn't currently aim to attract visitors. Still, there's a network of tracks into the forest east of Campo, and, in your own vehicle, you could venture forth. The town beach stretches south out to the mouth of the **Ntem River**, on the other side of which lies Equatorial Guinea. From Ipono, 10km south of Campo, you can negotiate with a *piroguier* to take you 10km up the Ntem River to **Yengue** in Equatorial Guinea. There's a frontier post here (make sure to get your passport stamped before continuing on), and tracks leading to the road to **Bata**.

The Province de l'Est

Three hundred kilometres of *piste* separate Yaoundé from **Bertoua**, the capital of East Province and one of the few towns of any size in the region. The tracks are relatively good as they follow the **Sanaga River** to **Nanga-Eboko** (accommodation at the *Etoile d'Or de Nanga*; ①). An alternative route follows the course of the **Nyong River** between the towns of **Akonolinga** (accommodation at the *Auberge du Nyong*; ①) and **Abong Mbang**. Either of these routes provides a satisfying sense of being away from it all, but even more isolated is the magnificent forest *piste* that leads south from Abong

Mbang to the remote agricultural village of **Lomié**. Small *campements* can be found at many of the villages that dot the road, and at Lomié itself there's an *auberge* (①), where you can certainly hook up with a guide for a trek through the forest. Throughout the area, the "Pygmy" camps are more traditional than the sedentary villages around Kribi. Most travellers, however, press eastwards towards Bertoua, passing through **Doumé**, formerly the capital of the eastern region and site of some remarkable colonial vestiges, including a French cathedral and an imposing German fortress. Moving on from Bertoua to the **Central African Republic**, the main road shudders northeast to **Garoua-Boulai**, a long journey through a great swathe of jungle and grassland to a busy crossing point and marketplace on the savannah fringes of northern Cameroon. Less travelled is the route heading east to **Batouri**, a busy town on the road to Berbérati in CAR.

Bertoua

Situated on the border of the savannah and the forest, Bertoua has grown rapidly in recent years, thanks to its economic base of agriculture and livestock. Some industry has grown up around these sectors and there's an urgent sense of commerce about, but this town of some 30,000 is above all an **administrative centre**, seat of the East Province and of the Lom and Djérem *département*. Despite the **banks** (*BIAO*, *BICIC*), cinemas and bars, however, it's an uninspiring place to visit. For overland travellers, the most salient feature is likely to be the good selection of **accommodation** which makes Bertoua an obvious stopping point on the roads to and from Central Africa.

Accommodation

Auberge Beaulieu (☎24.16.93). A modest but comfortable place in the centre with box-like rooms and shared facilities. ①.

Auberge BP (☎24.10.03). Inexpensive and convenient for the Batouri motor park, but the S/C rooms are depressingly dirty. ①.

Hôtel Central, near the Batouri motor park. A good choice for budget travellers with very inexpensive rooms; private bath optional. ①.

Hôtel de l'Est (☎24.15.18). Slightly better standing than the budget hotels with spacious S/C rooms and one of the town's best restaurants. ②.

Hôtel Jenyf, opposite the Batouri *gare routière*. As pleasant as it is central: the best rooms have balcony and bath, and the hotel restaurant is good value. ①.

Mansa Hôtel (BP 285; ☎24.13.33). An A-class symbol of recent economic expansion and far and away the town's top hotel, though no longer a *Novotel*. Fully AC accommodation set on an artificial lake. Swimming pool and tennis courts. ④.

Moving on

If you're travelling by **bush taxi**, different destinations have their own *gare routières*, each in the town centre and easy to locate. The main ones are for **Yaoundé** and Belabo in the west; **Batouri** to the east; and **Garoua-Boulai** to the north. **Buses** run regularly along the 80-kilometre stretch to Belabo, the closest town on the **Transcam railway** line. Unfortunately, trains heading both north and south reach Belabo late at night. *Unitair* operates **flights** to Batouri, Yaoundé and Douala on Mondays and Wednesdays.

Batouri

East of Bertoua, the forest yields to hilly savannah broken by rivers and woodlands. Travel is difficult along the poorly maintained *piste* leading to **BATOURI**, the last main town before the border with CAR. Besides the basic *Auberge* (①) at the motor park in the centre of town, you can **stay** at the *Club des Planteurs du Tabac* (②) which has very presentable S/C accommodation at the private club, with tennis courts. The cheapest option is the *Mission Catholique* (①).

With **Mount Niong** and **Mount Pandi** flanking the town, Batouri could be the base for some interesting expeditions. The region is famous for its **gold mines** and still attracts prospectors from many parts of West and Central Africa. In Batouri, find a guide to take you to the makeshift mining village 6km from town. Seeing the river panners and the gold scales in the market (dominated by Hausa speculators), it's hard to avoid Wild West comparisons, but behind these images is the danger inherent in digging.

Moving on

Taxis usually leave from the *gare routière* before dawn to tackle the 102 kilometres of tortuous tracks leading to the frontier town of **Kenzou**. Border formalities are dealt with efficiently and connections usually quick for continuing taxis to **Berbérati** – 100km into the Central African Republic.

Garoua-Boulai

The route leading north of Bertoua to **GAROUA-BOULAI** is better maintained than the Batouri *piste*, and takes in some fine mountain scenery near Ndokayo with panoramic views over the valley of the **Lom River**. The Adamawa Mountains are not far to the north and many Fula herders pass through Garoula-Boulai. Several small *auberges* provide inexpensive **accommodation** in town, including one right in the motor park (①). Another option is the *Mission Catholique*, with rooms or dormitory space a stone's throw from the border (①).

Garoua-Boulai's main motor park is at the border, the crossing of which is relatively uncomplicated on either side. After dealing with customs in Béloko, the frontier post in the **Central African Republic**, it's another 160km to Bouar on the main road to Bangui. If you're continuing to **northern Cameroon**, taxis can be found to **Meiganga** where you can either branch westward to catch the train at Ngaoundal, or continue by road to Ngaoundéré.

NORTHERN CAMEROON

Northern Cameroon is remarkably detached from the rest of the country by a vast, almost trackless region in the centre. This huge expanse of rolling savannah and forests – as big as Scotland or Maine – is thinly populated and crossed by just three *pistes*, and the railway. On its northern edge, the **Adamawa Mountains** cut across the centre of Cameroon, and as you cross this barrier, it's striking how effectively it divides the country into two distinct parts. It's a tough journey by road from Yaoundé or Bamenda to the first town of northern Cameroon, **Ngaoundéré** – good enough reason to use the train. Beyond, a flat plateau stretches over much of the north, where light forests and grasslands replace the south's thick vegetation, indicating that the climate is harsher and nature less generous. But there's more variety to the scenery than you might detect from the mostly flat sealed highway, running from Ngaoundéré all the way to **Kousseri**, which makes the north one of the easiest regions to travel through.

No less than four **game parks** are situated in the north, ranging from the hilly **Bouba Ndjida** reserve, where there's still some chance of spotting the (increasingly rare) **black rhinoceros**, to the popular **Waza National Park**, where the flat savannahs are ideal for seeing herds of giraffe and elephant, as well as lions and numerous other species.

In the extreme northwest, the volcanic **Mandara Mountains** have been scoured by thousands of years of *Harmattan* winds and the people of the region squeeze their livelihood out of the dry rocky slopes. Although this region has been "discovered" by travel operators, you can, if you're determined enough, work your way off the more beaten tracks and away from such overrun sites as **Rhumsiki** to villages which may not be any more authentic but are at least less tainted by organized tourism.

While the mountain people of the northwest have retained traditional religious beliefs, the rest of the region bears the stamp of **Islam**, brought by Fula migrants who established principalities called **lamidats** in the eighteenth century. The Muslim influence is especially noticeable in towns such as **Garoua** and **Maroua**, which seem unusually large and dynamic in a region where you might expect climate and geography to reduce energy to a minimum.

Ngaoundéré

Coming from the south, **NGAOUNDÉRÉ**, with its mango-shaded streets and mild climate resulting from its 1400-metre elevation, proves a satisfying introduction to the north. Though rapidly growing, the **old Fula settlement** is well contained in the neighbourhood around the **Lamido's Palace**, where the architecture of the houses and mosques and the dress of the people bear witness to a Sudanic tradition that is very much alive.

TOURIST INFORMATION

The small **tourist office** on avenue Ahidjo (☎23.13.74) has enthusiastic staff with good regional travel tips. They can also recommend places to eat and sleep in town and aren't snooty about directing you to the cheaper *auberges* if you emphasize you're on a budget.

Accommodation

Auberge Centrale, near the train station (☎25.19.36). Convenient if you're arriving by train, the well-maintained S/C rooms around the courtyard cost only a little more the the town's least expensive hotels. ②.

Auberge du Château, off the rue du Petit Marché. No-frills rooms without fan or bath, but among the cheapest in the centre. Good value too at the excellent restaurant. ①.

Collège Catholique, on av Ahidjo, near the mission. The best bet for the budget traveller, especially since the mission stopped taking in guests. ①.

Auberge de la Colombe, near the Presbyterian church, in quartier Joli-Soir. Reasonably priced rooms with showers, and a bar that's a popular hang-out. ①.

Hôtel du Rail, rte de Garoua (BP 319; ☎25.10.13). Clean and very comfortable S/C rooms, costing slightly more than at *Le Relais*. Good value for moderate budgets. ②.

Hôtel le Relais, behind the *Cinéma Le Nord* (BP 47; ☎25.11.38). Optional AC in spacious rooms, convenient for the centre. ②.

Hôtel Transcam, off the rte de Garoua-Boulai (BP 179; ☎25.10.41). A showy place with TV and other perks in the AC bungalows. First-rate service, tennis courts, bar, restaurant and nightclub. ④.

The Town

The **old town** centres around the **Lamido's Palace**, which is a *saré* – the Hausa word for this style of housing, made of *banco* huts and with vast straw rooftops that swoop down nearly to the ground. A large wall surrounding the compound keeps the maze of courtyards, private dwellings and public rooms out of view from the street. For an **inside visit**, ask at the Lamido's *secretariat* at the palace entrance, or go to the **tourist**

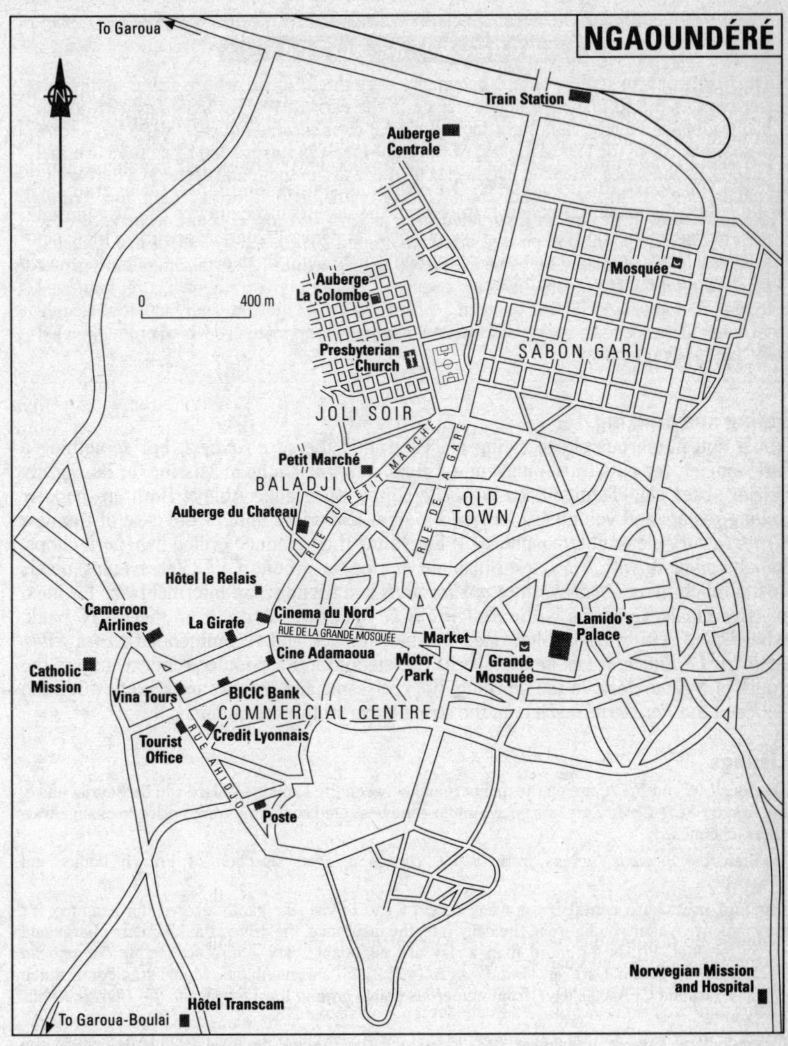

office on avenue Ahidjo. They'll phone and make a booking for you. Entrance is CFA2000.

For pageantry, come at the end of the week, in time for the **Friday prayer**. Dignitaries in brightly coloured *boubous* – magnificent accents of orange and red against the ochre tints of the town – come to pay their respects to the Lamido, who leads a procession to the mosque. Similar displays take place on Saturday and Sunday.

Ngaoundéré's **marché central** is just down the main avenue from the palace, and is surrounded by an arcaded wall. The **gare routière** adjoins the market. The main avenue from the market leads to the commercial centre, with its banks and PTT.

NGAOUNDÉRÉ HISTORY

The first people to settle around Ngaoundéré were the **Mboum**, whose claims to the area were lost to the **Fula** after a military siege in the early 1830s. By 1835, **Ardo Ndjobdji** had established the Muslim **lamidat** and the Mboum became Fula vassals. A large town of some 10,000 at the end of the last century, the city was surrounded by a protective wall in 1865; its influence extended over a vast territory to the south and east. Even during the colonial period, the traditional town changed little, and it wasn't until the **Trans-Cameroonian Railroad** was extended here in 1974 that a real boom occurred. In the early 1970s, the population paused briefly at around 20,000, but by 1983 it had rocketed to nearly 60,000 and may be close to 100,000 people by now. New *quartiers* have grown up all around the old centre – adding a sense of vitality to the traditional core. Improved transportation also facilitated economic activity that today includes an industrial slaughterhouse (livestock is a regional mainstay), a tannery, and intensive wheat production led by the *Sodeblé* company.

Eating and drinking

You'll find numerous cheap eating places around the *gare routière*. For something a little fancier, try *La Girafe*, on avenue Ahidjo, near the Catholic Mission, or its slightly pricier sister establishment, *La Nouvelle Girafe*, off avenue Ahidjo. Both are popular among expats and volunteers for good food at fair prices and, in the case of the new *Girafe*, a very pleasant atmosphere. At lunchtime they produce grilled fish, pork chops, kebabs or lamb with *frites*, fried plantain or rice for around CFA2500; evening meals cost a touch more. Nearby, the *Café des Amis* is a friendly and informal place for inexpensive meals. Good too is the *Restaurant Le Meilleure*, across from the *BICIC* bank, where they serve reasonably priced northern dishes and recommended *steack frites*. Also try *Le Snack*, a fast-food place in the station and a popular rendezvous for the youth of Ngaoundéré. In the morning, hot croissants and *gateaux* are served with fresh coffee at the *Patisserie Sagba* – on the street between the two cinemas.

Listings

Banks *BIAO* and *BICIC* are on the main avenue between the Lamido's Palace and the tourist office, but first try *SCB–Crédit Lyonnais* on av Ahidjo – the best (and sometimes only) place to change travellers' cheques.

Bookstores *Sicamax*, across from *BIAO*, carries a good selection of French books and newspapers.

Car and mobylette rental If you want to rent a car, to visit the game reserves for example, it's very expensive after you figure in the daily rate, the insurance, the driver, the kilometre charge and of course fuel. Prices for more than a day are negotiable. Try *Auto Location de l'Adamaoua* (☎25.20.30) in Sabon Gari, or *Vina Voyages* (☎25.25.25) on av Ahidjo. Mobylettes come much cheaper (around CFA5000/day), from numerous points around town – opposite the *Hôtel le Relais*, for example.

Cinemas The *Cinéma Adamaoua* (☎25.13.04) and the *Cinéma du Nord* (☎25.10.04) are in the centre of town.

Hospital If you need medical help, head first to the Norwegian Mission's hospital (☎25.11.95).

Supermarkets Wine, cheese and other imported goods are available at *Dabaji Alimentation*, across from *Le Girafe*, or *Supermarché Djiya Eli* in the Balaji district.

Around Ngaoundéré

If you have your own transport – or make yourself mobile by renting a mobylette – you're well positioned to take some easy side trips in the environs of Ngaoundéré. The nearest site of scenic interest is **Lac Tison**, just 10km from town. Take the Meiganga road south and after 6km a signpost points east to the crater lake, deep in the woods

3km further on. It's a pleasant ride along a *piste* bordered by awkward boulder formations, but forget swimming when you get there, as bilharzia is a real risk.

Back on the Meiganga road, the **Chute de la Vina** is a well-known, if rather unspectacular waterfall, just past the village of Wakwa.

Further afield, you could conceivably go as far as the **Chutes de Tello** by mobylette, although to attempt the 50-odd kilometres of track might be pushing your luck. To get there, follow the Mbalang road 22km out of Ngaoundéré to the village of Mbalang Djalingo. (A side trip from here could be the 2-kilometre deviation to **Lac Mbalang**, a crater lake around a wooded island.) The road branches after the village, and it's the right fork you need to take, towards Tourningal. After a further 28km, turn off the main tracks and follow a small side *piste* 2.5km to the Tello Falls. These are most impressive between July and November.

A popular weekend getaway for locally based expats, the **Ngaoundaba Ranch** is another possible excursion, 40km towards Meiganga on a dry season road. Perched in the mountains by a beautiful **crater lake**, the main lodge recalls a Hemingway-esque vision of Africa from where the now-deceased founder once led guests on hunting safaris. The image lives on as visitors gather for meals at a long trestle table with animal trophies on the heavy stone and wood beam walls. Most of the bougainvillea-bedecked bungalows have panoramic views of the area, which is great for **birdwatching**. Other diversions include swimming and boat trips on the lake, tennis and riding. The ranch is open from November to May (④); reservations BP 3, Ngaoundéré (Fax 25.19.05).

MOVING ON FROM NGAOUNDÉRÉ

Heading south, the best bet is the **train**. The modern **Gare de Chemin de Fer** (enquiries ☎25.13.77) is a kilometre from the centre. Couchette trains leave every evening at 7pm for **Yaoundé**. If you're heading to **eastern Cameroon**, or on to the **Central African Republic**, take the train to Bélabo, from where taxis continue to Bertoua.

The **gare routière** is next to the central market. Vehicles can take you from here to **Tibati**, on the long and rugged road to Foumban; to **Tcholliré**, between the Bénoué and Bouba Ndjida parks; to **Meiganga** on the main overland route to Yaoundé and Central Africa; and of course up the road 300km to **Garoua**.

If you want to move on fast, *Cameroon Airlines* (☎25.12.95) and *Unitair* between them have five **flights** a week to Douala via Yaoundé, and several flights a week to Garoua and Maroua, including *Unitair's* Friday flight via the northern towns, to Ndjamena, Chad. You can confirm schedules by calling the airport (☎25.12.84).

From Ngaoundéré to Garoua

Northern Cameroon has some of the best **game viewing** in West Africa, with the Waza National Park (see p.1213) heading the list of attractions, followed by the **Réserve du Faro**, the **Parc National de la Bénoué** and the **Parc National de Bouba Ndjida** off the Ngaoundéré–Garoua road. Unfortunately, you can't get around them if you don't have transport, so assuming you're not taking an air tour out of Douala or Yaoundé, you're left with the painfully expensive option of **renting a car** in one of the main towns (Ngaoundéré, Garoua or Maroua), or the painfully slow and uncertain option of hitching a lift in with mobile tourists. To stay at any of the *campements*, you should reserve in advance, especially for weekends or holidays when bed spaces fill up (contact the *Provincial Tourism Service*, BP 50, Garoua; ☎27.10.20). Note that Cameroonian conservation policy makes special provision for big game hunting, with macabre head prices on every species, from elephant down to monkey. Hunting blocks are well defined and the paths of camera- and gun-users don't cross.

Réserve du Faro

Comprising over 3000 square kilometres, **Faro** is the largest parcel of land under government protection in the north. Though slated to become a proper national park, this rugged, mountain-dotted slab of bush is currently almost impossible to visit as it has virtually no usable tracks. The only facilities are the quarters at the *Campement Hippopotames* (③), on the Faro River outside the reserve, near the village of Voko. The wildlife in Faro is reputed to be prolific and you can supposedly see much large game that's hard to see elsewhere. However, in the absence of any infrastructure, tourists or a proper ranger service, and in its location hard up against a remote sector of the Nigerian frontier, it's no surprise to hear how much poaching goes on.

Parc National de la Bénoué

Coming north from Ngaoundéré, you can enter the **Parc National de la Bénoué** (Dec 1–June 30; entrance fee CFA5000 payable at the *Buffle Noir*, obligatory guide CFA3000/day) either at Mayo Alim or Banda. From both these towns, tracks lead through the park to the *Campement du Buffle Noir* (reservations through the Garoua tourist office, BP 50, Garoua; ☎27.10.20; FB ⑥). Situated on the banks of the Bénoué River, this camp has S/C **rooms** grouped in simple and comfortable *boukarous*. With prior permission from the tourist office in Garoua, you may be able to camp on the grounds, though you won't have access to facilities. Meals at the **restaurant** run between CFA5000 and CFA7000.

Buffalo and **eland** predominate in the park, where you may well also see **waterbuck**, **reedbuck**, **hartebeeste** and other species of antelope. **Elephants** and **lions** are not as prolific as at Waza, but **hippos** and **crocodiles** are common in the river. **Hunting** is popular in the park, especially from the *Campement du Grand Capitaine*, the Bénoué's second resthouse (③) which lies on the main road leading from Guidjiba to Tcholliré.

Parc National de Bouba Ndjida

The main access to the **Parc National de Bouba Ndjida** (Dec–May; entrance fee CFA5000; obligatory guide CFA3000/day) is via Tcholliré. Cameroon's largest national park, the Bouba Ndjida was created in 1968 to protect the increasingly rare herds of **rhinoceros** and **Derby eland** which still inhabit the area. A salt lick was created to attract the rhino, but it's still much more difficult to spot them than **elephant** and **buffalo**. With luck, you could sight **lion**, which sometimes approach the resthouse and are quite plentiful. The rugged landscape, with rivers and relatively thick vegetation, makes this one of the country's most beautiful parks, but the vast space (2200 square kilometres and 450km of track) and thick bush means that the animals are more dispersed and not as visible as in Waza, for example. The *Bouba Ndjida camp* is 40km inside the park and faces the Mayo Lidi river (reservations through the Garoua Tourist Office, BP 50 Garoua; ☎27.10.20; ④).

Rey Bouba

One of the most influential and traditional of the Fula *lamidats*, **REY BOUBA**, west of the Parc National de Bouba Ndjida and north of Tcholliré, can be a worthwhile excursion, though it will prove time-consuming if you don't have your own transport. Despite its historical interest, it's only really colourful and exciting if you time your trip to coincide with one of the Muslim festivals – celebrated here with vigour; at other times, the town is uneventful.

Rey Bouba was founded by **Bouba Njida** in 1804. For thirty years, this religious zealot led a regional jihad to subdue the animist peoples of the region. While extending his authority over a vast territory, he also freed the area from domination by the powerful **Yola Emirate** (whose capital was in what is now Nigeria). By the time of Bouba Njida's death in 1864, he had created the most powerful and prestigious *lamidat* in northern Cameroon, a position Rey Bouba upholds today.

Built on the banks of the **Mayo Rey**, and only a few kilometres from the shores of the large Lagdo Reservoir, the village is a conglomeration of straw-roofed, ochre-coloured *saré*, clustered around the **Lamido's Palace**. You won't be allowed into this fortified compound, where the spiritual leader of the region lives with his concubine, counsellors and servants, without the approval of the Lamido himself, and, even if he consents, you may have to wait several days before the reception. Subjects are not allowed to look at the face of the "prince", who wears a veil in public. At night, you can sleep on a mat on the floor of a traditional resthouse reserved for travellers (①). If you do stay, you wash in the river and eat food served in a calabash.

To get here from Ngaoundéré, take a bush taxi to Tcholliré – where if necessary you can spend the night in a rudimentary **guesthouse**, the *Campement de Djiré* (①) – and then find a vehicle going on the 35km to Rey Bouba. Your best chance is on Friday – market day.

Garoua

Capital of Northern Province, **GAROUA** has grown rapidly since independence, and now has a population of over 100,000. Surprisingly, for a town situated so far into the interior, it has the country's third largest port, on the banks of the **Bénoué (Benue) River**. This has helped smooth the way for local industrialization – though being former president Ahidjo's birthplace was no hindrance: he was always ready to invest in his home town. As the principal administrative and economic focus of the north, Garoua's more traditional aspects have been eclipsed to a large extent by its heterogeneous blend of northern Cameroonians, Nigerians and Chadians. Traditional *saré* buildings – quite common up to the 1960s – have ceded to cement homes with tin roofs and the centre of town is dotted with modern blocks. Growth of course has meant increased facilities – with convenient banks, hotels and tourist information – but you're unlikely to miss its swarming crowds and oppressive heat when you leave.

THE HISTORY OF GAROUA

Fali and Bata people were the first to settle along the banks of the Bénoué, in the eighteenth century. They were followed by **Kilba Fula** – herders who came in the early nineteenth century. After dan Fodio's jihad (see p.1108) the Fula built a fortification (*ribadou*) around the town they called Ribadou-Garoua, to stave off Fali invasions. Other Muslims – Hausa, Bornu and Choa Arabs – arrived in the second half of the nineteenth century, lending an early urbanism to the settlement. The present **Lamidat** dates from 1839.

The **Germans** subjected Garoua in 1901 and set up a small port (British steamers from the *Niger Company* had been trading in ivory, salt and cloth since 1890). Enlarged in 1930, the port served as a vital link between Cameroon, Chad, and Nigeria, even though it has only ever been able to function during the rainy season, from mid-July to mid-October. Garoua became an important international focus and has always had a large expatriate community. After independence, the roads were improved, and investments increased in the various industries reliant on cotton, the regional cash crop, which were in time joined by a brewery and soapworks.

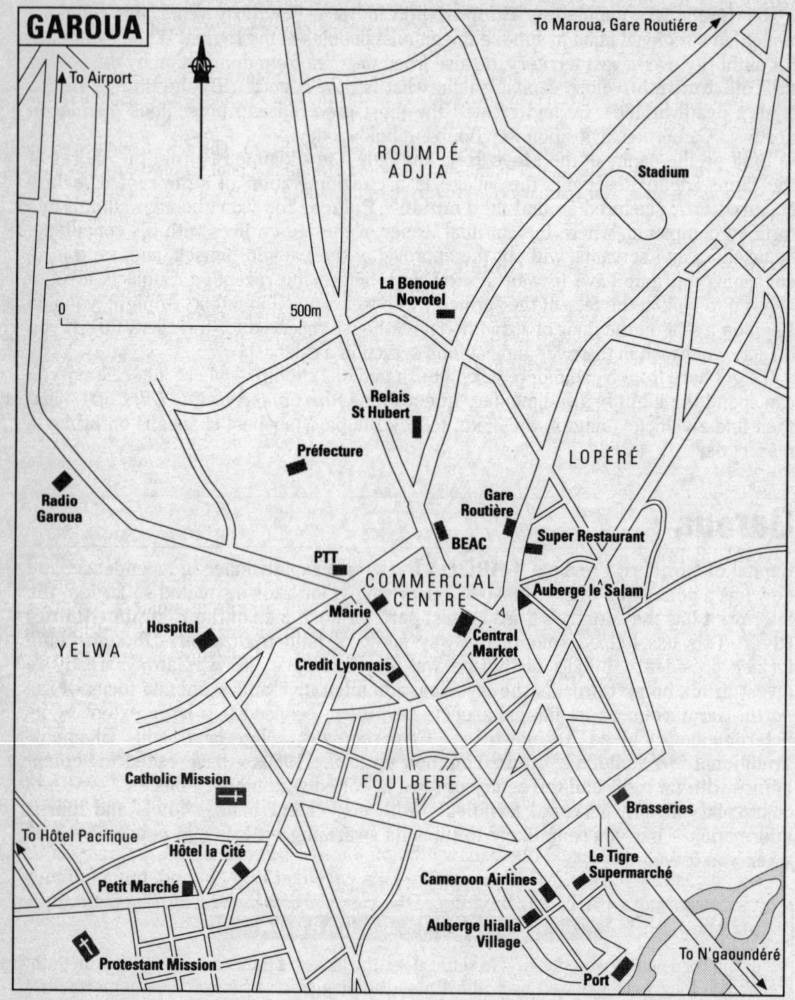

Accommodation

For a town the size of Garoua, there's surprisingly few hotels, and budget travellers in particular are left with little choice. But there is some accommodation in all price ranges, including a couple of very comfortable places in the international class.

Hôtel de la Cité, rue du Petit Marché. Good mid-range accommodation with tidy AC rooms and a recommendable restaurant. ②.

Auberge Hiaila Village, near the *Ciné Etoile*. A modest hotel with clean rooms around a courtyard. Excellent meals. ②.

Novotel La Bénoué (BP 291; ☎27.12.04). A-class comfort plus a pool, tennis courts and – for the mostly French guests – *pétanque*. In a shaded area away from the commercial centre, it also features a French restaurant and a nightclub. Major credit cards accepted. ⑥.

Relais Saint Hubert, near the commercial centre (BP 41; ☎27.13.21). Recently restored S/C *boukarous* (many with AC) in an attractive garden setting. The restaurant and bar are decent value. ③.

Auberge Salam, conveniently opposite the *gare routière* (☎27.22.16). The dingy exterior belies clean rooms in the courtyard. The outdoor showers are perfect for the hot climate, and the restaurant is good value. ①.

Tourist Motel, rte de l'aéroport (☎27.26.42 or 27.32.44; Fax 27.27.78). The newest addition in the upmarket range with phone and TV in the AC rooms and a swimming pool, tennis courts, bar and a choice of restaurants. More casual meals are served by the pool. ④.

The Town

Aside from the monumental **Grande Mosquée** on the route de Maroua – which is Cameroon's largest, but cannot be visited by non-Muslims – there's nothing around town worth going out of your way for, apart from the huge **central market**, best at weekends. Near the market is the **centre artisinale**, though the name is somewhat overstated as it merely indicates a place under the neem trees where traders spread out their wares. The masks and statuettes tend towards airport art anonymity, but this is the most concentrated place for **crafts** and some of the leather work is tempting. Depending on the time of the year, you may well find other tourists in the area, so be prepared to bargain vigorously. Across the street, bookings for game park lodgings can be made at the **tourist office**, behind which is a small, and wholly unimpressive **zoo**.

North of the market, the commercial centre encompasses **banks** (*BIAO*, *BCD*, *BICIC*, *SGBC*, *SCB–Crédit Lyonnais*, all within 100m of the **post office**), and administrative buildings such as the Mairie, with the obligatory fountain in front. It's more interesting to wander through the Yelwa district where the **petit marché** keeps things lively and where there's a good concentration of bars and *circuits*, as small chop houses in the north are called. The energy, which continues **after dark**, makes it a likeable place to seek out an evening's entertainment; or head to the clubs around the *Ciné Ribadou*, back in the commercial centre.

Eating

Cheap restaurants grouped around the taxi park include *L'Etoile*, *La Camerounaise* and *Le Bénoué*. All similar, they serve rice, plantain, yams or macaroni with beef sauce for around CFA1000. Across from the Marché Central (near the *Shell* station) the *Super Restaurant* serves the same sort of hunger-stoppers, along with freshly blended fruit juices (pineapple, banana, lemon, orange). For something upmarket, *Le Berry* (across from the *Ribadou* cinema) serves excellent French food, but a full meal costs upwards of CFA10,000. Next door, the casual *Tempête du Sahel* has affordable roasted chicken.

Listings

Bookstores Reading is limited to books and newspapers in French, the best selection of which you'll find at the *Librarie Nouvelle Moderne*, near the *mairie*.

Car rental *Hertz* is represented at the *Novotel* (☎27.12.04). Also try *Avis* (☎27.12.98); *Esgreg Voyages* (BP 210; ☎27.11.20); *Sorileges Voyages* (BP 133); *Renault Cameroon* (☎27.11.34); or *Jean Despotakis*, av du Port (☎27.12.11).

Cinema Relatively recent films are screened at the *Ciné Ribadou*. If you want karate and the like, head to the *Ciné Etoile* in the south of town.

Hospital ☎27.14.14.

Supermarkets Imported boxes, tins and produce at the *Supermarché Tigre* near the *commissariat de police*.

Tourist information Contact the *Service Provincial du Tourisme* (BP 50; ☎27.10.20). This is the place to book lodgings in the game parks.

MOVING ON FROM GAROUA

Transport out of Garoua is straightforward. The old **gare routière** near the *marché central* has regular *taxis de brousse* **to Maroua** and further north or **to Ngaoundéré** and the south. There are also less frequent *taxis de brousse* to Gaschiga (customs and immigration) and Demsa for Yola in Nigeria (a bad road). **Minibuses** tend to leave from the larger *gare routière*, 4km from the centre of town on the rte de Maroua. If you're not having much luck finding quick transport from the market, you could head out here.

Cameroon Airlines and *Unitair* between them have at least daily **flights** to Douala and Yaoundé, plus a Tues flight to Bafoussam, Tues and Thurs flights to Ngaoundéré and several flights a week to Maroua. There is also a weekly flight to Ndjamena, Chad. Precise information and reservations are available by calling *Cameroon Airlines* (☎27.10.55) or **the airport** (☎27.14.81 or 27.14.83).

Maroua

One of Cameroon's few pre-colonial cities, **MAROUA** already had a population of some 25,000 when French administrators took their first census in 1916 and 100,000 people lived in a twenty-kilometre radius of the town. Today it remains the largest northern city, and has retained a much more traditional flavour than its main rival Garoua. The old neighbourhoods of Maroua spread out on both banks of the **Mayo Kalliao**, run through with streets shaded by sweet-smelling neem trees.

Accommodation

A popular town in its own right and convenient stopping point for northern adventures, Maroua has a good selection of accommodation for all prices. Most of the inexpensive *auberges* can be found on the south side of the river near the stadium, though there is some choice near the *gare routière*. Upmarket lodgings are in the west, near the river and the Kaygama district.

Auberge le Diamaré, east of the *gare routière*. Convenient if arriving by bush taxi, and the well-kept ventilated rooms are very reasonable. Good outdoor bar-restaurant. ①.

Auberge Maidjiguilao Domayo, south of the river off the bd de Renouveau. Simple rooms with fan and showers and a helpful staff. ①.

Baptist Mission, near the market and the *SGBC*. The cheapest place in town. Clean with shower and electricity, but no fan. Very friendly. ①.

Campement Bossou, south of the river, off the bd de Diarenga. Non-S/C *boukarous* with fans and cold showers. It's clean and well known to budget travellers seeking good value. ①.

Hôtel Maroua Palace, qtr Djoudandou (☎29.12.24; Fax 29.15.25). The newest international-class hotel rises at the base of the northern hills a good kilometre from the centre. Rooms have TV, video, mini-bars and phones, plus there's a pool, travel agency, shops and restaurant. American Express and Visa accepted. ④.

Mizao Novotel (BP 205; ☎29.13.00; Fax 29.13.04). With lavish, furnished rooms plus tennis courts, video club and swimming pool, the *Novotel* makes up for in comfort what it lacks in character. The restaurant serves mostly French cuisine (CFA5000); and there's *Novotel*'s usual *boite de nuit*. American Express and Visa accepted. ④.

TOURIST INFORMATION

The **Délégation Provinciale du Tourisme** opposite the *Relais de la Porte Mayo* can help arrange excursions to the game parks or Mandara Mountains.

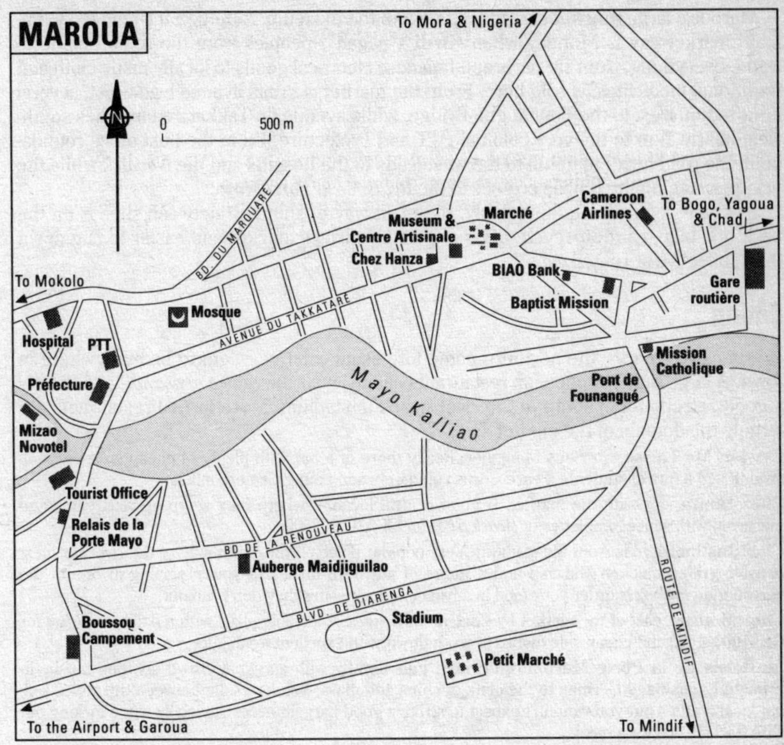

Motel Le Saré (BP 11; ☎29.12.45). As commodious as the *Novotel*, but far more likeable, in a large shaded garden with its own pool and crafts centre. The spacious rooms here are among the town's most expensive. American Express accepted. ④.

Le Relais de la Porte Mayo, near the river (BP 112; ☎29.11.98). Comfortable AC *boukarous* in a garden setting. A popular rendezvous for expatriates and volunteers with a pleasant courtyard restaurant, shops and a steady stream of crafts vendors. The best in the moderate range. ③.

The Town

The **Musée du Diamaré** (Mon–Sat 8am–noon & 2.30–5.30pm; free entrance but tip the guide) contains only a small collection of regional objects, but it's worth checking out nonetheless. It's in a rosy Sudanic-style building near the market. They don't get many visitors, so the *gardien* is usually very eager to provide thoughtful explanations of the assortment of objects from the **Sao civilization**, and artefacts collected from the Toupouri, Massa and Mousgoum peoples. The **Fula** are represented by carved calabashes, jewellery and clothing, including a beautifully crafted *boubou* worn by a *lamido* for special occasions. Notice the shield made from a dried and shaped elephant ear.

The **centre artisanal** is in a separate wing of the same building. A large crafts supermarket with innumerable stands, the emphasis is on the locally made **leather goods** for which Maroua is famous (sandals, bags, round floor cushions) but you find goods from throughout Central and West Africa as well. Jewellery and handwoven cloth can be good value here but bargain astutely and take your time choosing; there's a vast selection.

Maroua's large **market** spreads out next to the museum. Although it's held daily, the main market day is Monday when **Kirdi** ("pagan") peoples from the region come to trade. Everything, from car parts and Japanese electrical goods to locally made cloth and traditional medicines, is sold here. From the market, a broad avenue leads east, several hundred metres, to the Founangué Bridge, while avenue du Takkatare stretches southwest nearly 2km to the very colonial **PTT** and Préfecture. From the post office roundabout, the road heading uphill to the west leads to the hospital and the *Novotel*, while the bridge spanning the Kalliao crosses to the *Relais de la Porte Mayo*.

As you'll determine quite quickly, the main way of shuttling between sites is on the back of a bike, as **motorcycle-taxis** are almost always quicker and easier to flag down than collective or rented cabs.

Eating

Inexpensive *circuits*, the northern name for casual eateries, seem to be everywhere in town. A large number of cheap restaurants cluster near the *centre artisanal,* and there's a good selection too, south of the river near the stadium. More formal restaurants are largely the domain of the big hotels.

L'Avion Me Laisse, qtr Sous Manguier. Really more of a bar with plenty of cheap street eats all around and a mix of students, Peace Corps volunteers and young Cameroonians.

Chez Hanza, opposite the market. A good central location where they serve up rice, yams and macaroni with sauce, omelettes or *steack frites* for CFA1000–2500.

Chez Justine, across from the stadium. Very popular place on the south side of the river for inexpensive grilled chicken and fish and a range of northern dishes. If you're staying at one of the surrounding *auberges* order your food in advance to make sure they don't run out.

Chez Moussa, east of the market by *Cameroon Airlines.* A likeable place with a daily *menu fixe* for CFA1000–1500 and cheap side dishes to wash down with excellent fresh juice.

Le Relais de la Porte Mayo, town centre. Fills nightly with an expat crowd chatting noisily in French, English and German to the clink of china and glass. Vendors sidle between the tables selling local crafts – but you wouldn't expect to strike a good bargain here, especially when forking out CFA7000–12,000 for a meal.

Le Saré. Very good garden restaurant in the hotel, serving continental food – upwards of CFA10,000 a head.

Listings

Banks *BIAO, BICIC, SCB* and *SGBC* are in the immediate vicinity of the market. Changing money is no problem.

Car rental Contact *Auto Location Extrême Nord* (☎29.10.89) opposite the *BIAO*. You can also rent 4WD vehicles with driver from the *Relais de la Porte Mayo* at extremely fair prices.

Cinema The only choice is what's playing at the *Diamaré*, opposite the *BIAO.*

Hospital quartier Zouloum (☎29.10.48).

Swimming pools Of the big hotel pools, the closest to the centre is that at the *Novotel* which you can use for CFA1000.

MOVING ON FROM MAROUA

The **gare routière** is east of the Founangué Bridge. Regular transport heads south to Garoua and Ngaoundéré and north to Mora, Mokolo and Kousseri.

In theory either *Unitair* or *Cameroon Airlines* has a flight to **Yaoundé** and **Douala** daily, to **Garoua** daily except Sun, and to **Ngaoundéré** on Thurs and Sun. Contact *Cameroon Airlines* (☎29.10.50) or call the airport (☎29.10.21) for flight information numbers.

Mokolo, Mora and the Mandara Mountains

Beautiful and haunting, the denuded volcanic plugs of the **Mandara Mountains** rise up to the west of Maroua like stony brown fingers. They form the backdrop to some of the country's most fascinating, desolate scenery, and are home to communities who have come to be known as the "mountain people" – staunch non-Muslims who were pushed to the extremities of the inhabitable areas during the Muslim wars of the nineteenth century. Today the region highlights Cameroon's most striking contrasts in the cultural clash of Kirdi, Fula and Choa Arabs from the far north. In its ethno-linguistic complexity, highland setting and stone buildings – as well as the rise of organized adventure tourism – the Mokolo district bears superficial similarities to the Dogon country in Mali.

There is **no bank** in Mokolo nor in any of these villages and towns; change money in Maroua. Smuggled **petrol** is usually sold cheaply along the roadside, but it's not safe to set off with an empty tank without getting up-to-date information from other travellers.

Mokolo and around

The main point of entry to the region, **MOKOLO** is the capital of the **Mafa** people (also called Matakam by the Fula) – one of the most populous groups in the mountains. Mokolo, however, is a quiet town (perhaps "village" is more accurate) with round houses of stone with thatched roofs, a market, motor park and not much else.

You can **stay** at the *Rucotel* (BP 22 Mokolo; ☎29.51.16; ③) which has AC *boukarous*, and a good restaurant and bar. The *Catholic Mission* on the hill behind the motor park is putting up travellers again (①) or there's the small *Auberge Menchem* on the main paved road (②). As a cheaper solution, some people in town will put up travellers for a negotiated fee; if you want to find them, call at *Rex Photo* on the main road. The owner speaks some English and his younger employees at the *Café Mirage* next door have in the past been able to make arrangements. The **centre artisanal** in the village of **Djingliya**, 15km from Mokolo, also puts up travellers for a small fee.

Mokolo's small **museum** occupies a square off the motor park, but it keeps odd hours. Besides visiting the exhibition of **local crafts**, ask the guardian about the possibility of getting a **guide** to take you through the region. The level of tourism in the mountains to the west is such that you can't really avoid this sooner or later, and it might just as well be initiated by you. At the major attractions such as Rhumsiki you'll wind up with a guide whether you like it or not, and villages off the beaten track are unfindable (even if you do manage, you'll need someone to interpret and make arrangements for sleeping and eating). Be clear about the itinerary and price (probably not less than CFA6000/day) before setting off. A walking trip through the area could last anything from a day to a week, or it's possible to arrange excursions on **horseback**. And check out the alternative possibility of **renting a mobylette** around the market. On the highest paths, you can cross undetected and unmolested into Nigerian territory (see p.1115) but you should be wary of going further into Nigeria without making a formal exit from Cameroon.

If you're heading on to Rhumsiki, note that trucks from the **motor park** depart early in the morning. If you arrive after 8am, you are likely to have missed the day's transport.

Rhumsiki

A brief visit to **RHUMSIKI** (Roumsiki), 50km from Mokolo, is very much a standard item on Cameroon's tourist circuit. This despite the fact that it's a small and fairly ordinary village in itself. The appeal of the visit is largely to get a taste of the "real" Cameroon, and the built-in flaw is that the more people come, the more distorted and unreal life in the village becomes. However, there's one overwhelming reason why it is genuinely worth making the trip. Wherever you look, the scenery is breathtaking. Rhumsiki lies deep in the mountains, surrounded by magnificent time-worn peaks, the highest of which is much-photographed **Kapsiki**. Houses built of local stone in the traditional style blend in with the gothic backdrop, changing shades of ochre and orange to umber and russet as the sun moves over the horizon.

You have no option when arriving at Rhumsiki other than to allow the little kids who greet you to act as your guides (unless you brought a paid companion with you from Mokolo). They follow their own rigid programme in showing you what they imagine every tourist wants to see. There's no point resisting their help and trying to explore the village on your own; you'll just be made to feel like an unwelcome voyeur. So let the boys show you the **féticheur** who tells your future by watching the way a river crab moves pieces of wood; the **weavers** who make cloth by hand; the **potters** and the **blacksmiths**. They explain how the huts are made and tell you about local customs and history. The people of Rhumsiki are called **Margui**, or often **Kapsikis** – "those who have grown tall". In the evening, your guides even accompany you to a nearby peak to get a better view of the sunset. Your every question, in fact, is answered before you ask it. It's all quite interesting on a superficial level, but it's about as personal as watching a television documentary. The bottom line is definitely money, and you'll just have to accept that.

You can **stay** in the village at the new *Campement de Rhumsiki* (BP 27, Mokolo; ④–⑤) – a tastefully rustic cluster of *boukarous* with beautiful mountain views. Less expensive is the rudimentary *auberge* (no fans or self-contained facilities; ①) attached to the main restaurant. Alternatively you can arrange to sleep in people's homes. Ask the little kids, but do so before the last taxi heads back to Mokolo. Once they know you can't escape, prices rise.

Mora and around

On market days (Wednesday for Mokolo and Sunday for Mora) you can get a bush taxi from Mokolo to **MORA** via **Koza** – a picturesque track road that cuts through the heart of the **Mafa Country**. Even on these days, you will have to leave Mora very early in the afternoon to get back to Mokolo with the last taxi. Other days, you'll probably have to go by the less scenic route that passes through Maroua.

Capital of the **Wandala** (also called *Mandara*) – a people who accepted Islam in the late seventeenth century after their contact with the Bornu Empire – Mora is especially known for a **market** which attracts a wide range of peoples from throughout the region. Muslim Fula, Wandala and Choa women sell their goods alongside the traditionalist mountain people – **Podoko**, **Guizica** and **Mofou** – who retain their own firm views on suitable dress and headgear. It's a colourful mixture of cultures and produce from goat's milk to mangoes and millet. Donkeys and goats are sold in the **animal market**. You'll find also jewellery and carved calabashes. Directly across from the market, you can get cold drinks and a bite to eat at the *Bana Bar*.

The best option for budget **accommodation** is the *Auberge Mora Massif* (①), located just a couple of blocks east of the motor park. Rooms here are kept clean by the attentive staff and the bar/restaurant serves meals with inexpensive cold drinks, that make their way in from Nigeria. Similar in price, the *Hotel Podoko*, off the main road to Maroua also offers good value for its S/C bungalows with fans (①). The mid-range *Campement du Wandala,* at the northern entrance to town, has been having troubles keeping afloat, and may have closed indefinitely.

Oudjilla

Mora is the departure point for the eleven-kilometre trip to the village of **OUDJILLA** in the mountains, a spot which, like Rhumsiki, has become a magnet for tourism. You can barely set foot in Mora without a posse of gushing teenagers racing up to you on motor bikes and asking, "Mistah, tu vas où, à Oudjilla?"

Oudjilla is an authentic **Podoko village**, though once again your experience there may seem a bit contrived. You're led on arrival to the *saré* of the chief, who lives in a walled compound with over fifty wives and countless children. For an incredible price, you get to visit the chief's compound and see the hut that serves for public deliberations; another where the chief's father is buried and where jugs of millet beer are stored; and the sacrificial pen where the chosen cow awaits slaughter during the harvest festival. You're taken into the hut of one of the wives to see the kitchen and the utensils used for pounding millet, storing water and so on. At the end, you are "invited" to take pictures of the chief and some of his wives with shaved heads and bare chests. For just a little more money, the wives might even do a harvest dance. It makes for the kind of photographs that put postcards to shame, but, at the same time, is liable to leave you feeling rather empty. To get beyond the performance, however, would take more time and dedication than most people have. There's nothing to stop you putting your feelings back in balance by exploring some of the other roads in this region; or by trying, "Non, merci, Oudjilla ne m'intéresse pas, mais pourrais-tu me diriger à . . . ? " (then picking a small name from the map).

Parc National de Waza

With a minimum of vegetation, **Waza National Park** (Nov 15–June 15; entrance fee CFA 5000; obligatory guide CFA3000/day) spreads over 1700 square, and flat, kilometres, and is probably the single best site for viewing game in the whole of West Africa. The main park entrance, just outside the small town of Waza, is marked by two Mousgoum huts. Pay your fee here, before heading to the nearby *Campement de Waza* (BP 361, Maroua, ☎29.10.07, or reserve through any *Novotel;* FB ⑥). It's an excellent camp set on a hill with comfortable AC *boukarous* equipped with running water and electricity and grouped around a clean swimming pool (CFA1000 for non-guests). Expect to pay about CFA7000 for casual meals taken at the restaurant, which affords a splendid panorama of the surrounding park. If such accommodation is out of your range, you can camp for a small fee near the park entrance and there are informal options in Waza village itself. Enquire at the *buvettes* along the main town street, or ask for *Chez Suzanne*, a bar-restaurant with a limited number of box-like rooms (①). The restaurant *Allah Karim* on the main road serves good cheap food and excellent tea. Since Waza is the most popular of the game parks, it's also the one you have the best chance hitching into. Enquiries at the *campement* invariably yield good results, but if your luck is down, vehicles are available to rent by the hour.

Giraffe are quite plentiful here, and congregate near the gate. There's a substantial **elephant** population, too, which you should have no problem seeing with a decent guide. Your chances of finding **lions** are also pretty good. **Ostriches** tend to be shy but herds of **buffalo** and **antelope** fill the scene often enough.

Kousseri and the northern extremity

At the confluence of the **Logone** and **Chari** rivers, **KOUSSERI** lies directly opposite the war-scarred capital of Chad – **Ndjamena**. The new bridge and *pirogues* that link them are the main *raison d'être* for a town that otherwise would be right off the beaten track.

Principal sites in town include the **port** and **market** where, not surprisingly, fish is the mainstay (market day is Thursday). There are two **hotels**, but nowhere cheap. Outside the centre, *Le Relais du Logone* (☎29.41.57; ③) has rooms, some of which have

AC, overlooking the river. The *Hôtel Moderne* (☎29.40.91; ②) is slightly less expensive and the friendly management may be persuaded to give verandah space if you plead a good case. Neither of the two **banks** – *BICIC* and *SCB* – can be relied on to change money, not even French francs, in a hurry. A good road now links Kousseri to the south via Maroua. Boats still provide an important link with **Ndjamena** but the new bridge downstream from the centre of Kousseri is an easier crossing.

Lake Chad and the Parc National de Kalamaloué

Accommodation facilities don't exist **north of Kousseri**. In the towns along the route to **Lake Chad**, you're therefore at the mercy of the local authorities (police or sultans). Problems you may have getting to the lake, however, generally have less to do with police than with the fact that the elusive waters have receded well to the north of the bigger towns.

From Kousseri, take a taxi to **Makari**, which has a market on Wednesdays when transport is easiest to arrange. It's a scenic route that hugs the banks of the **Chari River**, then veers westward through desert landscapes to Maltam, before heading north. In Makari, you can get a taxi on to **Blangoua**, but though you'll be told the town is on the lake, it's actually on the river. Head to the market by the water's edge, where, if you're willing to shell out CFA25,000 or so, you can charter a motorized *pirogue* for the hour-long journey to Lake Chad. Transport back to Makari can be problematic as well, and you may be coerced into chartering a taxi at great cost.

Well before you reach the lake, you'll pass through the smallest and most recently created of Cameroon's northern reserves, the **Parc National de Kalamaloué**, which stretches along the road from Kousseri to Maltam. Something of a budget park, the rudimentary *campement* (①) costs only a fraction of the one at Waza and although the animals aren't as abundant, you still see herds of **elephant**. You can take guided **walking tours** to see **crocodiles** and **hippos** in the Chari River that borders the park and separates it from the outskirts of Ndjamena on the opposite bank.

MOVING ON TO CHAD, NIGERIA OR NIGER

From Kousseri, you can enter **Chad** – directly into its captial, Ndjamena – across the new bridge. Taxis across are cheap and frequent. Since the situation in Chad has calmed down, there appears to be no more than the routine drama of border formalities you'd expect to encounter anywhere.

If you're continuing into **Nigeria**, Fotokol is your last destination in Cameroon: Gamboru, over the border in Nigeria, is 140km short of Maiduguri (see pp.1110–1114). If you happen to be travelling **direct from Ndjamena to Maiduguri** in Nigeria, you shouldn't need a visa to cross the 100km or so of Cameroonian territory from Kousseri to Fotokol.

Making for **Niger** *circumventing* Nigeria, you've a number of options for where to cross the border into Chad for the short detour around the lake to **Nguigmi** (see p.981). If you're in Kousseri, cross here to Ndjamena, rather than risk going further north and finding yourself in a difficult position with nobody authorized to process your entry. If you're driving and intending heading the same way, Ndjamena is your most northerly reliable crossing point in any case.

index

PART THREE

THE CONTEXTS

BOOKS

While there's a substantial volume of reading material on West Africa, its subject matter and authorship is very unevenly distributed. By far the largest body of literature in English comes from Nigeria, with its hundreds of novelists and academics. By contrast, many of the Francophone nations have scant coverage other than in French. In the following listings, UP means University Press and o/p means out of print. If a book is recently o/p you may still find copies in some bookstores. Otherwise, check libraries.

For pre-departure reading, probably the best foretaste is provided by West African fiction – much of which is available in paperback in Heinemann's **African Writers Series** or Longman's **African Classics**.

The following recommendations are divided first by subject matter across the region, and then country-by-country in the order in which they appear in the book. French works have been included only when there is little alternative in English. One-off travel guides and similar publications are mostly covered in the "Maps and Information" section at the beginning of each chapter.

SERIES PUBLICATIONS

African Historical Dictionaries (Scarecrow Press, US & UK). If you're seriously looking to find out about a country, the Scarecrow series is what you need. They have titles on virtually every African country, covering names, places and events in detail.

Aujourd'hui (Editions JA, France). The *Aujourd'hui* series – *Togo Aujourd'hui*, etc – is available in English translation for Senegal, Mali, Guinea-Bissau, Côte d'Ivoire, Ghana, Togo, Niger and Cameroon. They're tourist-office oriented but good for an initial browse. Check publication dates, as the books are updated sporadically.

Clio World Bibliographies (Clio Press, UK & US). Annotated coverage, mainly of social and natural sciences and humanities. To date, available for every country in West Africa with the exceptions of Guinea and Togo. Catalogue from Clio Press, Old Clarendon Ironworks, 35A Great Clarendon St, Oxford OX2 6AT, UK (☎01865/311350).

Heinemann African Writers Series. AWS books are the vanguard of African publishing in English and add regularly to their list – now some 300 titles, though kept erratically in print. Catalogue from Heinemann, Halley Court, Jordan Hill, Oxford, OX2 8EJ, UK (☎01865/311 366).

Jeune Afrique and **Hachette** both do one- or two-country guides of a more practical nature, in French only, to most of the Francophone countries. *Jeune Afrique* also publishes an excellent and affordable series of thematic **atlases** on the Francophone countries.

BOOKSHOPS AND LIBRARIES

Useful **bookshops** and **libraries** for obtaining African (and out of print) books are detailed on pp.41–43. Any UK resident can make use of the **Inter-Library Loans** system to obtain even the most obscure titles – given time.

If you're seriously interested in keeping up with scholarly or literary African writing, the **African Books Collective** offers thousands of updated titles from over forty independent, state, and university publishers in West Africa. Their bi-annual catalogues – available from *African Books Collective Ltd*, The Jam Factory, 27 Park End Street, Oxford OX1 1HU, UK (☎01865/726686; Fax 01865/793298) – include annotated reviews of new and recent publications.

For **books in French**, *La Page* French bookshop (7 Harrington Rd, London SW7; ☎0171/589 5991) may be able to help. The best African bookshop in Europe, however, is *L'Harmattan* in Paris (16 rue des Ecoles, 5e).

Longman also publishes a good, though much shorter, series of *African Classics*. Catalogue from Longman UK, Fourth Ave, Harlow, Essex, CM19 5AA (☎01729/29655).

TRAVEL BIBLIOGRAPHIES

Oona Strathern, ed, *Traveller's Literary Companion: Africa* (In Print Books, UK, 1994; Passport Books, US, 1995). Brief selections of literature from – or about – virtually every African country, including passages from many of the books included in this bibliography.

Louis Taussig, *Resource Guide to Travel in Sub-Saharan Africa Vol. 1 East and West Africa* (Hans Zell, UK, 1994). The definitive guide to the guides and much more. Extraordinarily detailed country-by-country coverage of every published source of interest to travellers or expatriates, as well as bookstores, libraries, mapping institutes, children's resources and conservation societies, to list just a few. Libraries will obtain it for you.

TRAVELOGUES AND RELATED LITERATURE

Michael Asher, *Impossible Journey: Two Against the Sahara* (Viking Penguin UK, 1987, o/p). Adventurous Mauritanian and Nigérien foretastes are to be gleaned from this account of a first-ever west to east Saharan crossing. Asher, an ex-SAS man, travelled with his wife, plus camels, from Chinguetti to the Nile. **Geoffrey Moorhouse**'s *Fearful Void* (Penguin, 1974; reprinted Sceptre 1994) details his own, unsuccessful, earlier attempt.

Thomas A Bass, *Camping with the Prince and Other Tales of Science in Africa* (Lutterworth, UK, 1992; Viking Penguin, US, 1991). An interesting slant for the travel genre. The author keeps a focus on African solutions to, for example, agricultural problems.

Peter Biddlecombe, *French Lessons in Africa* (Abacus, UK, 1993). Like an uninvited travelling companion, businessman Biddlecombe rattles out his observations on Francophone West Africa so fast, it seems, there's barely the time to notice the stream of contradictions and inconsistencies. Funny, warm and light, and a good book for lone travellers to argue with.

Dea Birkett, *Mary Kingsley: Imperial Adventuress* (Macmillan, UK, 1992). Finely worked and very readable biography written with relish. The same author's *Jella: A Woman at Sea* (Gollancz, UK, 1992) – the account of her return from West Africa as a member of crew on a cargo ship – is superbly funny and instructive.

Thomas Coraghassen Boyle, *Water Music* (Penguin, UK, 1994; Viking Penguin, US, 1983). Lengthy, meticulous, at times outrageously funny, fictionalization of Mungo Park's explorations. TC Boyle's vision of the West Africa (and Britain) of two centuries ago is utterly captivating. Essential in situ reading for those long roadside waits: if you only take one book, take this.

Ferdinand Dennis, *Back to Africa: a Journey* (Sceptre, UK, 1992). Jamaican-born academic and writer returns to former haunts – and to a war-ravaged Liberia.

Geoffrey Gorer, *Africa Dances* (1935; subsequent reprints, o/p). Enduring account of a journey from Dakar to Dahomey (now Benin) and back with Feral Benga, an African dancer from Paris.

Blaine Harden, *Africa: Dispatches from a Fragile Continent* (Fontana, UK, 1992; Houghton Mifflin, US, 1991). The *Washington Post's* former African bureau chief can't shake the arrogant pessimism American journalists seem to thrive on. Coverage of Ghana, Liberia, and Nigeria.

Eddy L Harris, *Native Stranger: A Blackamerican's Journey into the Heart of Africa* (Simon & Schuster, US 1992; Viking Penguin, UK, 1994). Sour and confrontational travelogue that runs out of steam completely after the author's severe disillusionment in West Africa.

Peter Hudson, *Two Rivers: Travels in West Africa on the Trail of Mungo Park* (Chapmans, UK, 1992). Readable and engaging travelogue.

Elspeth Huxley, *Four Guineas* (1954, o/p). This account of Huxley's trip through the four Anglophone colonies on the eve of independence is full of credible conversations – and the occasional lapse into racist angst.

Mary Kingsley, *Travels in West Africa* (1897; reprinted Everyman, UK, 1993; CE Tuttle, US, 1993). The title is misleading these days, as

Kingsley's dauntless travels in search of fetishes and fish took her – with a quick hike up Mount Cameroon – principally to the region of Gabon. But a terrific book: funny, intelligent and a worthy classic.

David Lamb, *The Africans* (Mandarin, 1984, reprinted Random,1989). *The Africans* was a best-seller, but Lamb's fly-in, fly-out technique is a statistical rant couched in cold war rhetoric – and, even when ostensibly uncovering a pearl of wisdom, he can be rebarbatively offensive.

Patrick Marnham, *Dispatches from Africa* (Penguin UK, 1980, o/p). Although now dated, this journalism remains devastatingly sharp – especially on the aid industry. Notable essays on Senegal, Mali and The Gambia.

Mungo Park, *Travels into the Interior of Africa* (1799; reprinted Eland, UK, 1983; Ayer, US, 1977). Absorbing and short-winded account of the then youthful Scottish traveller's two journeys – 1795–1797 and 1805 – along the Niger.

HISTORY

Most histories cover the whole continent, and, inevitably, jump from place to place: Boahen, or Davidson, Buah & Ajayi are the easiest to follow, and are well complemented by various historical and cultural atlases.

THE AFRICAN CONTINENT

AE Ahigbo, RJ Gavin, R Palmer, EA Ayandele and JD Omer-Cooper, *The Making of Modern Africa, Vol. 1 Nineteenth Century, Vol 2 Twentieth Century* (Longman UK & US, 1986). A detailed, illustrated guide, putting West Africa in the continental context up until the first big changes after independence.

Cheik Anta Diop, *Pre-Colonial Black Africa* (Lawrence Hill US, 1987). First published in the 1950s, Diop asserts that the origins of western civilization, as well as African, began in Africa. The work encouraged a whole generation to reinterpret the past from an African perspective.

Basil Davidson, *Africa in Modern History* (1978, o/p). Lucidly argued and readable summary of Africa's dominant nineteenth- and twentieth-century events.

Christopher Hibbert, *Africa Explored: Europeans in the Dark Continent, 1769–1889* (1984, o/p). Entertaining read, devoted in large part to the "discovery" of West Africa.

UNESCO, *General History of Africa* (Heinemann, UNESCO, University of California Press & UNIPUB). For serious scholarship, this twelve- volume series recounts over three million years of Africa's past. Written by some of the continent's leading historians, it attempts to break from western analysis to give a clearer picture of African peoples in the sociocultural context.

WEST AFRICA

Adu Boahen, with JF Ade Ajayi and Michael Tidy, *Topics in West African History* (Longman, US, 1986). An excellent introduction to basic themes in West African history, written in a clear and concise fashion by one of Ghana's most respected historians.

George E Brooks, *Landlords and Strangers: Ecology, Society and Trade in Western Africa, 1000–1630* (Westview, UK & US, 1993). This dense and fascinating account of the history of western West Africa, shows, among much else, how drought affected trade, including the slave trade.

Basil Davidson, FK Buah and JFA Ajayi, *A History of West Africa 1000–1800* (Longman UK & US, 1977). Clear, wide-ranging and readable.

AG Hopkins, *An Economic History of West Africa* (Longman UK, 1973). Well-written grounding, offering an invaluable economic perspective.

Patrick Manning, *Francophone sub-Saharan Africa 1880–1985* (Cambridge UP, UK, 1988). A rare book on the subject in English.

JB Webster et al., *West Africa Since 1800: The Revolutionary Years* (Longman UK & US, 1980). An excellent follow-up companion to Davidson et al. above.

Kaye Whiteman, ed, *West Africa Over 75 Years: Selections from the Raw Material of History* (West Africa Publishing Company, 1994). A trawl – often fascinating and revealing – through the magazine's archives.

Paul Tiyambe Zeleza, *History of Africa: Vol. 1, The Nineteenth Century* (Codesria, Senegal, 1993). Winner of the NOMA Award 1994.

HISTORICAL ATLASES

Brian Catchpole and LA Akinjogbin, *A History of West Africa in Maps and Diagrams* (Collins Educational, 1984, o/p). A remarkable and highly recommended encapsulation of the region's history from ancient times to the 1980s. Its only flaw is an utterly inadequate index.

Colin McEvedy, *Penguin Atlas of African History* (Penguin UK, 1995; Penguin US, 1980). Useful for placing West Africa, and the whole continent, in context, and for getting to grips with some of the names and themes. Fifty-nine maps of Africa with facing text.

Jocelyn Murray, ed, *Cultural Atlas of Africa* (Facts on File UK & US, 1981). An attractive, highly polished book, if also an inevitably over-simplified view of the continent.

LAND, PEOPLE AND SOCIETY

Donal Cruise O'Brien, *Contemporary West African States* (Cambridge UP, US, 1990). Survey of Burkina Faso, Cameroon, Chad, Côte d'Ivoire, Ghana, Liberia, Nigeria and Senegal.

RJ Harrison Church, *West Africa* (1979, o/p). Formerly the standard geography reference – traditional in approach but much updated from its 1957 original edition. Excellent and unexpectedly absorbing.

Keletigui Mariko, *Les Touaregs Ouelleminden* (Karthala, France, 1984). French survey of the Tuareg nomads who live in Algeria, Niger and Mali.

John S Mbiti, *African Religions and Philosophies* (Heinemann, US, 1989). A good compendium.

Patrick R McNaughton, *The Mande Blacksmiths: Knowledge, Power, and Art in West Africa* (Indiana UP, US, 1988). Accessible scholarship that deals both with the aesthetic qualities of ironworking and its social implications for Mande peoples.

Claire Robertson and Iris Berger, eds, *Women and Class in Africa* (Holmes & Meier, UK & US, 1986). An assessment of gender, money, and socioeconomic power with case studies from across the continent, including Ghana and Nigeria.

Robert Farris Thompson, *Flash of the Spirit: African and Afro-American Art and Philosophy* (Random, US, 1984). "Art history to dance by" in the words of the *Philadelphia Inquirer*'s reviewer, and this is a unique book, illuminating the art and philosophy that connects the black worlds on both sides of the Atlantic. Big on Yoruba and Dan-Homey roots. Lots of illustrations.

Claudia Zaslavsky, *Africa Counts: Number and Pattern in African Culture* (Lawrence Hill, US, 1979). A unique, extraordinary book, with a chapter on "Warri" games (see p.63).

LANGUAGE

There is little available on West African – or even African – languages in the sense of general background, but you will find various phrase books and some language-learning material.

Pierre Alexandre, *Languages and Language in Africa* (Heinemann UK, 1972). Surprisingly entertaining tour of the arcane world of African linguistics, led by a magnificently enthusiastic French professor.

EC Rowlands, *Teach Yourself Yoruba* and **Charles H Kraft and HM Kirk-Greene** *Teach Yourself Hausa* (Teach Yourself Books, UK, 1989; McKay, US, 1979). Serious application required.

US State Department Foreign Service Institute This department has developed a number of self-instructional language courses available through Audio-Forum, Suite LA30A, 96 Broad Street, Guilford, Connecticut 06437 (☎1-800/243-1234; Fax 203/453-9774). The average price is around $200 and each one comes with a textbook and cassettes. Languages available include the Senegambian dialect of Fula (20hr of cassettes); Hausa (15hr); Igbo (12hr); More(18hr); Twi (6hr); and Yoruba (36hr).

ARTS

Most works dealing with the arts cover the whole continent. For books on West African music, see the box on p.1265.

Nigel Barley, *Smashing Pots: Feats of Clay from Africa* (British Museum Press, UK, 1994;

Smithsonian, US, 1994). Stimulating and well-illustrated pottery survey, with much from West Africa, by the anthropologist and director of the Museum of Mankind.

Roy Braverman, *Islam and Tribal Art* (Cambridge UP, 1974). A useful if somewhat specialist paperback text.

Caren Caraway, *African Designs of the Congo, Nigeria, The Cameroons and the Guinea Coast* (Stemmer, 1986). Black and white designs from masks, fetishes and textiles.

Margaret Courtney-Clarke, *African Canvas* (Rizzoli, 1990). Sumptuous colour photos bring out vivid details of exterior and interior house painting by women in a number of countries.

Susan Denyer, *African Traditional Architecture* (Africana Publishing Co UK, 1978; Holmes & Meier US, 1978). Rewarding study, featuring hundreds of photos (most of them old) and a wealth of detailed line drawings.

Werner Gillon, *A Short History of African Art* (Penguin UK, 1991; Viking Penguin US, 1987). A substantial study despite the name, though inevitably still very selective.

Elian Girard, Brigitte Kernel and Eric Megret, *Colons: Statuettes Habillées d'Afrique de l'Ouest* (Syros Alternatives, France, 1993). Fascinating illustrations of a little-known genre of sculpture: statues of Africans dressed in European clothes.

Michael Huet, *The Dance, Art and Ritual of Africa* (Random House, 1978). Remarkable photos of ceremonies and costume, captured with an exceptional clarity and power.

David Kerr, *African Popular Theatre: From Pre-Colonial Times to the Present Day* (James Currey, UK, 1995). Includes sections on masquerade and concert party.

Jean-Marie Lerat and Jean Seisser, *Ici, Bon Coiffeur* (Syros Alternatives, France, 1992). French text accompanies photos of the colourful barbershop boards displaying hairstyles, so characteristic of West African towns.

Labelle Prussin, *African Nomadic Architecture* (Smithsonian Institution Press, UK & US, 1995). A specialist volume, but also a fine, richly illustrated book, thick with symbols, which includes accounts of Tuareg and Moorish architecture.

Esi Sagay, *African Hairstyles* (Heinemann, 1988). What they're called, and how to do them; a wonderful little book.

Jan Vansina, *Art History in Africa* (Longman, UK & US, 1984). Readable theorizing by an interesting French anthropologist.

Frank Willett, *African Art* (Thames and Hudson, 1994). A cheaper, more accessible and better illustrated volume.

Geoffrey Williams, *African Designs From Traditional Sources* (Dover, 1971). A designer's and enthusiast's sourcebook, from the copyright-free publishers.

FOOD

Daniel K Abbiw, *Useful Plants of Ghana* (ITP 1990). Unusual reference guide to plants, organized by use – as food, fuel, medicine. Highly recommended for impoverished volunteers.

Frances Bissel and Christine Hanscomb, *Sainsbury's Book of Food* (Websters, UK, 1989). Excellent photos of the majority of the exotic foodstuffs you're likely to come across, together with pertinent facts and culinary opinion.

Dorinda Hafner, *A Taste of Africa* (Channel 4/Headline, UK, 1994; Ten Speed Press, US, 1995). Enthusiastically conveyed recipes, but not a very practical book outside the region – "take half a pound of lemon grass . . ."

GB Masefield, M Wallis, BE Nicholson and SG Harrison, *The Oxford Book of Food Plants* (Oxford UP, 1976). A good, traditional guide, covering most of the fruit and veg that will come your way.

NATURAL HISTORY

The following field guides are invaluable.

B Bousquet, *Guide des Parc Nationaux d'Afrique: Afrique de l'Ouest* (Delachaux, Lausanne, 1992). French coverage of the important national parks of Francophone West Africa.

T Haltenorth and H Diller, *A Field Guide to the Mammals of Africa* (Collins, 1981).

W Serle and G Morel, *A Field Guide to the Birds of West Africa* (Collins, 1977).

John G Williams, *A Field Guide to the Butterflies of Africa* (Collins, 1969, o/p).

COUNTRY BY COUNTRY

MAURITANIA

Literature in English on Mauritania is minimal. There's a good account of the Adrar in Michael Asher's *Impossible Journey* (see p.1222).

Catherine Belvaude, *La Mauritanie* (Karthala, France, 1989). Describes peoples, the state, religion, economy, fishing, arts, and society. The French reader's essential starting point.

Tony Hodges, *The Western Saharans* (Minority Rights Group report No. 40, 1984). Trenchant background on the situation in Western Sahara. *Western Sahara: the Routes of a Desert War* (Croom Helm, UK; Chicago Review, US) amplifies the analysis and brings the coverage more up to date.

Peter Hudson, *Travels in Mauritania* (1990, o/p). Tale of a two-month trek.

Odette du Puigaudeau, *Barefoot in Mauritania* (1937, o/p). The author and his female companion took camels across "the land of death" – an entertaining ramble through a Mauritania that hardly knew it existed.

SENEGAL

There are several books by Senegalese writers in the Heinemann and Longman series. Other, mostly academic English-language works, are only likely to be available in libraries. In French, there's a very wide range of literature – by both French and Senegalese – and a steady output of glossy tomes to whet travellers' appetites.

Lucy C Behrman, *Muslim Brotherhoods and Politics in Senegal* (Harvard UK & US, 1970). Fascinating, though dated study with interesting statistical information about the marabouts at the turn of the century.

Michael Crowder, *Senegal: A Study of French Assimilation Policy* (1962, o/p). Concise, fairly unacademic look at how the French colonized African minds.

Donal B Cruise O'Brien, *Saints and Politicians: Essays in the Organization of a Senegalese Peasant Society* (1975, o/p); *The Murides of Senegal: The Political and Economic Organization of an Islamic Brotherhood* (1971, o/p). This latter work is the definitive text in English on the Mouride brotherhood.

Rita Cruise O'Brien, *White Society in Black Africa: the French of Senegal* (1972, o/p); *The Political Economy of Underdevelopment: Dependence in Senegal* (1979, o/p).

Sheldon Gellar, *Senegal – An African Nation Between Islam and the West* (Gower UK, 1983; Westview US, 1995). A condensed and very readable survey.

Maureen Mackintosh, *Gender, Class and Rural Transition* (Zed Books UK, 1989; Humanities US, 1989). An alternative view of the effects of development, agribusiness and the food crisis.

Christian Saglio, *Sénégal* (Petite Planète, Editions Seuil, France, 1980). A good introduction to the country, if you read French, full of incisive commentary. Saglio was instrumental in setting up the *campement integré* network.

Robin Sharp, *Senegal: a State of Change* (Oxfam, UK, 1994). Basic, but up-to-date primer, written for students or inquisitive visitors. Illustrated.

Janet G Vailant, *Black, French and African* (Harvard UP, UK & US, 1990). The latest biography of Léopold Senghor.

NOVELS AND POETRY

Mariama Bâ, *So Long a Letter* (Heinemann UK & US, 1981). Dedicated to "all women and to men of good will", this is the story of a woman's life shattered by her husband's sudden, second marriage to a younger woman. Bâ's second book, *The Scarlet Song* (Longman UK, 1995), published posthumously, eloquently traces the relationship between a French woman and a poor, Senegalese man.

Nafissatou Diallo, *A Dakar Childhood* (1982, o/p). Short and sweet; a middle-class girl growing up in the postwar years. Illuminating on family life.

Birago Diop, *Tales of Amadou Koumba* (1966, o/p). A collection of short stories based on the tales of a griot, and rooted in Wolof tradition.

Cheikh Hamidou Kane, *Ambiguous Adventure* (Heinemann UK, 1963; Heinemann

US, 1972). The autobiographical tale of a man torn between Tukulor, Islam and the West. Recommended.

Sembène Ousmane (or Ousmane Sembène), *God's Bits of Wood* (1960), *Xala* (1973), *The Last of the Empire* (1981), and others; all since reprinted by Heinemann UK & US. A committed, political and very immediate writer (and film-maker, see "Cinema" p.1239) who can also be very funny, as in *Xala*, the satirical tale of a wealthy Dakarois' loss of virility. The best of these, by far, is *God's Bits of Wood*, the story of the rail strike of 1947.

Leopold Sédhar Senghor, *Nocturnes* and *Prose and Poetry* (Okpaku Communications, US). Collections of poems and writings by the country's ex-president, and member of the Académie Française. *Leopold Senghor: Collected Poetry* (University Press of Virginia, 1991) gathers poems from the *negritude* era, including *Songs of Darkness* and *Nocturnes*.

Aminata Sow Fall, *The Beggars' Strike, or the Dregs of Society* (Longman UK, 1987). Scorchingly describes the mental health of the Dakar elite when their consciences can no longer be salved.

THE GAMBIA

For general works on The Gambia, and fiction by Gambian writers, the in-print choice is limited.

JM Gray, *History of The Gambia* (1966, reprinted by International Specialist Book Services). This aquarium-style account (peering in from the outside) is heavy going and finishes before World War II.

Mark Hudson, *Our Grandmothers' Drums* (Mandarin UK, 1990). Rich, absorbing story of Hudson's stay in the village of "Dulaba" (Keneba) in the proposed Kiang National Park area.

Arnold Hughes and David Perfect, *A Political History of The Gambia, 1816–1994* (C Hurst & Co, 1995). The most up-to-date history of the country.

Berkeley Rice, *Enter Gambia: the Birth of an Improbable Nation* (1967, o/p). A digestible work, but marred by an unpleasantly derisory tone.

Patience Sonko-Godwin, *Ethnic Groups of the Senegambia* (1985, o/p). A brief and graspable social history of the region.

FICTION

William Conton is a writer from the colonial era, heavily influenced by his Sierra Leonean upbringing. *The African* (Heinemann UK, 1965) is a classic rags-to-premiership story.

Ebou Dibba, *Chaff in the Wind* (Macmillan UK, 1986). Highly accomplished author, now living in Britain, decribes lives and loves in the 1930s. *Fafa* (1989, o/p) tells of goings-on at a remote trading post on the Gambia River.

Alex Haley, *Roots!* (1976; reprinted by Vintage UK, 1994; Dell US, 1980). Good honest "faction", and a reasonably entertaining American saga to read on the beach, though only the first few dozen pages are set in Kunta Kinte's semi-mythical Gambian homeland.

Lenrie Peters, *Selected Poetry* (Heinemann UK, 1981). *The Second Round* (1966, o/p) is a readable, if somewhat downbeat, story.

MALI

There's very little accessible writing in English from, or about, Mali.

Ibn Battuta, *Travels in Asia and Africa* (Routledge UK, 1983). Selections from the writings of the great fourteenth-century wanderer, including his travels along the Niger.

Brian Gardner, *The Quest for Timbuktoo* (1968, o/p). An easily digested, though old-fashioned and not altogether reliable, collection of explorers' biographies; can often be found in second-hand bookshops.

Jean Marie Gibbal, *Genii of the River Niger* (University of Chicago Press, UK & US, 1994). The French author's personal account of travels by *pirogue* through eastern Mali. Some of the more interesting passages depict healing ceremonies, which revolve around the river.

Pascal James Imperato, *Mali: A Search for Direction* (Westview, US, 1989). The author of the *Historical Dictionary of Mali* (Scarecrow, UK & US, 1987) here devotes himself even more extensively to the country's history, society, economy and politics.

Stephen Pern and Bryan Alexander, *Masked Dancers of West Africa: The Dogon* (Time-Life Books, 1982, o/p). Fine photography and good text. Highly recommended pre-visit (or even carry-around) reading.

William Seabrook, *The White Monk of Timbuctoo* (1934, o/p). It's worth checking libraries and second-hand bookshops for this biography of Père Yakouba, a white priest who married a Timbuktu woman and changed his vocation.

Bettina Selby, *Frail Dream of Timbuktu* (1991; reprinted Ulverscroft large print, UK & US, 1993). Selby's account of her bicycle journey from Niamey to Bamako is beautifully written and covers much more than just the journey – with interest-filled deviations and asides.

Fa-Diga Sissoko, translated by John William Johnson, *The Epic of Son-Jara* (Indiana UP, UK & US, 1992). A new translation (and a new spelling for Sundiata/Sunjata) of the 800-year-old story of the Mali empire's founder.

Richard Trench, *Forbidden Sands* (1978, o/p). Stodgy travelogue, but an unusual route: Tindouf–Taoudenni–Timbuktu.

FICTION

You'll be lucky to find much of the following in English translation but Malian literature in French repays the effort.

Seydou Badian, *Le Sang des Masques* (Laffont, France, 1976). Nightmarish vision of the city, in this follow-up to Badian's earlier novel *Sous l'Orage* (Presence Africaine, France, 1963), in which the young generation – formed by Western education – criticize traditional practices of religion and authority.

Mandé-Alpha Diarra, *Sahel! Sanglante Sécheresse* (Présence Africaine, France, 1981). The story of a doomed village schoolboy's life during the drought – a kind of documentary fiction.

Amadou Hampate Ba, *Fortunes of Wangrin* (New Horn US, 1987). An administrative interpreter tells of the colonial period from 1900 to 1945, and his successful collusion with it. Hampate Ba, born in Bandiagara, was a Fula academic and transcriber of oral literature (he died in1991). His *Kaïdara*, an esoteric Fula cosmological epic poem, has also been translated into English (Three Continents Press US, 1988).

Mamadou Kouyaté, *Sundiata: an Epic of Old Mali*, transcribed into French and annotated by DT Niane (translated into English by GD Pickett, Longman, 1995). Slim and fascinating transcription of a griot's history of Mali.

Yambo Ouologuem is Mali's only writer to have achieved international recognition. In *Bound to Violence* (trans. Ralph Manheim, Heinemann UK & US, 1971), his treatment of brutality and deceit in an invented African empire, Nakem, insists that West African society rests on foundations as bloody and self-destructive as any other and screams for a new, re-humanizing look at the liberal romantic version of black history – a position that upset the earnest *negritude* movement. Most of Ouologuem's works excite controversy – he specializes in unabashed plagiarism, pornography (*Les Mille et une Bibles du Sexe*, 1969) and cudgel-like satire – but he can also be very funny (see the poem on p.351). He's been out of circulation for a number of years.

Fily-Dabo Sissoko was one of Mali's earliest contributors to written literature. *Crayons et Portraits* (Mulhouse, France, 1953) recounts his idyllic childhood in rural "Soudan"; *La Savane Rouge* (Presses Universelles, France, 1962) offers further reminiscences; *Sagesse Noire* (Editions de la Tour du Guet, France, 1955) is a collection of over 500 African proverbs and axioms.

CAPE VERDE

Cape Verde is one of the least documented countries in the world. Sources of information in English are few, and most are technical, research-based studies that you'll find only in university libraries.

Antonio Carreira, *The People of the Cape Verde Islands* (Hurst, 1982). An indigestible analysis of a very important subject – the forced labour policy of the Portuguese in Cape Verde.

Basil Davidson, *The Fortunate Isles – a Study in African Transformation* (Hutchinson UK, 1989, o/p). The most recent book on Cape Verde by one of its most ardent supporters, this is a positive and not unduly critical survey, mixing impression with historical accounts to the present.

AB Ellis, *West African Islands* (1885, o/p). Adventures from Madeira to Ascension with a couple of lively chapters on "St Vincent" and "San Antonio". Entertaining stuff.

Colm Foy, *Cape Verde: Politics, Economics and Society* (Pinter Publishers UK, 1986; St Martins Press, US, 1988). The first and only contemporary survey of Cape Verde – very comprehensive on politics and economics, sparser on society.

Anne Hammick and Nicholas Heath, *Atlantic Islands* (RCC Pilotage Foundation, Imray, Laurie, Norie and Wilson, 2nd edition, 1994). A comprehensive sailors' pilot, with a healthy chunk on the Cape Verdes and plenty of navigational charts and photos.

Archibald Lyall, *Black and White Make Brown: An Account of a Journey to the Cape Verde Islands and Portuguese Guinea* (Heinemann, 1938, o/p). Very hard to obtain – but well worth trying.

Deidre Meintel, *Race, Culture and Portuguese Colonialism in Cabo Verde* (Maxwell School of Citizenship and Public Affairs, Syracuse University, New York, 1984). An expanded PhD thesis, this fascinating study of race and self-image gets right inside the psychological effects of Portuguese colonialism.

GUINEA-BISSAU

Again, works in English are extremely sparse – and there's no Guinea-Bissauan literature in translation.

Amílcar Cabral, *Unity and Struggle* (Heinemann, 1980, o/p). Cabral speaks well. Such was his immense popularity, there seems little doubt his assassination marked a point of turning back for the country, and for the whole of Africa.

Basil Davidson, *No Fist is Big Enough to Hide the Sky: The Liberation of Guiné and Cape Verde* (Zed Books UK, 1981). Enthusiastic, quirky account of the war and its aftermath. The late Davidson's close and sympathetic involvement with the liberation fighters, particularly Amílcar Cabral himself, gives a rosy picture, tarnished by subsequent events.

Joshua B Forrest, *Guinea-Bissau: Power, Conflict and Renewal in a West African Nation* (Westview, US, 1992). Most up-to-date English-language profile.

Rosemary E Galli and Jocelyn Jones, *Guinea-Bissau: Politics, Economics and Society* (Pinter Publishers UK, 1987). A well-researched, rather gloomy survey, which found parallels between the independent governments and the fascist New State regime in their alienation of the rural people.

Ole Gjorstad and Chantal Sarrazin, *Sowing the First Harvest: National Reconstruction in Guinea-Bissau* (LSM Press, PO Box 2077, Oakland, CA 94604, USA; 1978, o/p). Dated and rhetorical; but sounded good at the time. See extract on p.436.

Carlos Lopes, *Guinea Bissau: From Liberation Struggle to Independent Statehood* (Zed Books UK, 1986). A survey that brings the story up to the end of the period of stagnation.

Joch McCulloch, *In the Twilight of Revolution: the Political Theory of Amilcar Cabral* (1983, o/p).

Walter Rodney, *A History of the Upper Guinea Coast 1545–1800* (Oxford UP, UK, 1970; Monthly Review, US, 1980). An Afro-centric history covering the region from the Casamance to Sierra Leone, dealing in depth with the area the Portuguese moved into and providing a mass of fascinating material on its social complexity.

Stepanie Urdang, *Fighting Two Colonialisms: Women in Guinea-Bissau* (Monthly Review Press, UK, 1979). Journalistic essays on escorted travels through the liberated zones and after the war. Detailed and interesting but with much wishful thinking.

GUINEA

There's again little published in English, though libraries may reveal some of the following.

Politique Africaine, Guinée: L'après-Sékou Touré (Karthala, France, 1989). A useful collection of articles (in French) looking at political and economic change since the death of Sékou Touré in 1984.

Ladipo Adamolekun, *Sékou Touré's Guinea: an Experiment in Nation Building* (Methuen, UK, 1976). One of the less credulous studies, but too old to be very useful as a retrospective.

Anonymous, *Sékou Touré* (Panaf Great Lives Series, UK, 1978; Humanities, US, 1978). Read now, a naïve tribute to an obsessive despot, yet interesting for putting the ruler's case better than he himself did. Clearly and readably delivered.

FICTION

Camara Laye, *The African Child* (1954; reprinted Fontana, UK, 1989). One of the best-known books by an African writer, these sweet-scented memoirs of a privileged rural childhood are a homage to the author's parents. Other translations of works by Laye include *The Radiance of the King* (1954; reprinted Random, US, 1989), *A Dream of Africa* (1966, o/p) and *The Guardian of the Word* (1978, o/p).

Alioum Fantouré, *Tropical Circle* (1972; translated Longman UK, 1981, o/p). A "novel" about Guinea between the end of World War II and the reign of terror. The build-up to independence is a muddle but the second half is illuminating, despite a dire, anglicized translation.

SIERRA LEONE

Sierra Leone has never had as much literary or scholarly attention as its Anglophone neighbours, Ghana and Nigeria, though there are works to be found if you're prepared to scour libraries.

BACKGROUND AND TRAVELOGUES

Graham Greene, *The Heart of the Matter* (1948; reprinted Penguin UK & US, 1991). Set in Freetown during World War II, Greene's novel uses the town as a seedy web in which his protagonists struggle. No great insights on Sierra Leone, but it touches illuminatingly on the racism and repression then present in the colony. Enduring, and still worth reading as wry introduction or *in situ* mental scenery. *Journey without Maps* (1936; reprinted Penguin UK 1991, Penguin US 1992) includes several dozen atmospheric pages narrating Greene's progress towards the Liberian border in 1935.

FWH Migeod, *View of Sierra Leone* (1926, o/p). Fascinating and readably scatty account of a six-month trek through the country, with interesting appendices on secret societies and Mende songs.

Christophe and Emmanuel Valentin, *Sierra Leone* (Editions Xavier Richer, France, 1986). *The* coffee-table book of Sierra Leone. Nice pictures, mostly of Freetown and the peninsula (some interesting older B&Ws, too) but the feeble French/English text is at tour brochure level.

HISTORY AND SOCIETY

Joe AD Alie, *A New History of Sierra Leone* (Macmillan, UK, 1990; St Martins Press, US, 1990). A recent, accessible and copiously illustrated general history from early times to the present. Explores social and economic as well as political developments.

Sylvia Ardyn Boone, *Radiance from the Waters: Ideals of Feminine Beauty in Mende Art* (Yale UP, UK & US, 1990). Circumspect account of the Mende women's Sande society by an art historian who promised not to reveal all.

Adelaide M Cromwell, *An African Victorian Feminist – the Life and Times of Adelaide Smith Casely Hayford 1868–1960* (Frank Cass, UK, 1986; Harvard UP, US, 1992). A remarkable, epoch-bridging biography on a figure from the Krio elite.

Christopher Fyfe, *A Short History of Sierra Leone* (Longman, US, 1979). School text for West Africa, useful as an introduction, good on the nineteenth century but hazy post-independence, and deliberately written down to pupils.

John W Nursley, *Moving with the Face of the Devil* (University of Illinois Press, US, 1987). A sociology of Freetown's contemporary masquerade societies complemented by brilliant photos.

Olayinka Koso-Thomas, *The Circumcision of Women – a Strategy for Eradication* (Zed Books UK & US, 1987). Just what the Sande secret society matriarchs would prefer to avoid being discussed in public. Focusing on Sierra Leone, and in the Sande context, this includes detailed survey results.

E Frances White, *Sierra Leone's Settler Women Traders* (University of Michigan Press, US, 1987). A study of the central economic role of Freetown's "Big Market" women in the nineteenth century.

FICTION

Syl Cheney-Coker, *The Last Harmattan of Alusine Dunbar* (Heinemann, UK & US, 1990). American-educated professor's first novel – a black comedy of life in a neo-colonial state. Honesty versus Ali Baba and his forty thieves.

R Sarif Easmon, *The Feud* (1981, o/p). A dozen short stories.

Yema Lucilda Hunter, *Road to Freedom* (African Universities Press, 1982). A historical novel about the early Krio settlements in Sierra

Leone. Tracing the expedition of thirteen-year-old Deannie, who leaves Nova Scotia with her family to resettle in Sierra Leone, Hunter provides a vivid and elegant description of Freetown in the late eighteenth century.

Yulisa Amadu Maddy, *No Past, No Present, No Future* (Heinemann, 1973, o/p). Three Sierra Leonean boys in Europe make up for, and make the most of, their different backgrounds. Maddy's *Obasai and Other Plays* (Heinemann, 1971, o/p) is worth looking out for too.

Prince Dowu Palmer, *The Mocking Stones* (Longman, 1982, o/p). Palmer uses a mixed-race love affair as a backdrop for an examination of social and economic exploitation in this novel about the Kono diamond business.

People's Educational Association, *Fishing in Rivers of Sierra Leone* (PEA, 1987, o/p: Private Mail Bag 705, 50 Siaka Stevens St, Freetown). A work of the German-funded organization, this is a major collection of oral literature – stories and songs – from thirteen Sierra Leonean language groups with hundreds of colour and B&W photos of the performers in action. Highly recommended.

Robert Wellesley Cole, *Kossoh Town Boy* (Cambridge UP, 1960, o/p). Classic novel of a childhood in pre-World War 1 and early 1920s Freetown.

LIBERIA

Liberia does have a modest literature, but much of it is American socio-political and development analysis – and hardly screaming out to be read.

Liberia: a Promise Betrayed (Lawyers Committee for Human Rights, New York, 1986). Deeply disturbing background on the nature of the Liberian state under Samuel Doe, setting the present mess in its bloody context.

Anthony Daniels, *Monrovia Mon Amour* (John Murray, UK, 1992, o/p). Interesting and surprisingly enjoyable account of the author's sojourn in the city in 1991.

John Gay, *Red Dust on Green Leaves: a Kpelle Twin's Childhood* (Thompson CN, Interculture Associates, 1973, o/p). Recommended background.

Graham Greene, *Journey without Maps* (see above, under "Sierra Leone"). Acid account of the author's walk in 1936 from Foya to Buchanan, via Ganta. He was accompanied by a cousin (hardly mentioned) and a line of porters.

Barbara Greene, *Too Late to Turn Back* (Settle & Bendall, UK, 1981; Penguin, US, 1991). Revenge of the above-mentioned cousin. "It sounded fun", she writes of her anticipation, but evidently it wasn't.

JG Liebenow, *Liberia: The Quest for Democracy* (Indiana UP, 1987). A detailed, if rather dry political history.

Alice Walker, *The Color Purple* (The Women's Press, UK, 1993; Pocket Books, US, 1990). Part of the story offers an oblique glance at the conditions that led to the creation of America's Liberian colony.

CÔTE D'IVOIRE

Books in English on – or deriving from – Côte d'Ivoire are few, though the French publishers *Karthala* (22–24 Bd Arago, 75013 Paris) publish a number of titles.

Marcel Amdonji, *Félix Houphouët-Boigny: L'envers d'un légende* (Karthala, France, 1985). A hard look at the man.

Laurent Gbagbo, *Histoire d'un Retour* (L'Harmattan, France, 1989). Senior opposition figure putting the case for an alternative to the status quo.

VS Naipaul, *Finding the Centre: Two Narratives* (Penguin, UK, 1985). Includes a long, characteristically interesting and perceptive essay "The Crocodiles of Yamoussoukro".

Abdou Touré, *Les petits métiers d'Abidjan: L'imagination au secours de la "conjoncture"* (Karthala, France, 1985). A series of lucid interviews giving a remarkable inside view of survival strategies on the city's streets.

FICTION

Jean-Marie Adiaffi, *The Identity Card* (1984, o/p). Search for identity in colonial Côte d'Ivoire.

Bernard Dadié, *Climbié* (1956; reprinted Holmes & Meier, 1971). A sedately elegant portrayal of growing up in colonial Côte d'Ivoire and Senegal, shot through with occasional flashes of bitterness against the *colons*. Dadié, who was for many years the Minister of Cultural Affairs, has also edited *The Black*

Cloth (1968, o/p), a collection of tales from the oral tradition.

Ahmadou Kourouma, *The Suns of Independence* (Heinemann, 1981, o/p). A very African novel, full of imagery and suspended reality. His second novel, *Monnew* (Mercury House, US, 1993), comes after a long sabbatical.

BURKINA FASO

There is next to nothing published in English on Burkina – and nothing very digestible in French either. A handful of locally published French-language novels are available in Burkina.

Politique Africaine: Retour au Burkina (Karthala, France, 1989). Survey of changes since the death of Sankara.

Thomas Sankara Speaks (Pathfinder Press, UK & US, 1988). Collection of the revolutionary's speeches – worth dipping into to see where the revolution was supposed to be going.

Pierre Englebert, *La Révolution Burkinabé* (L'Harmattan, France, 1986). Thorough look at the country's modern history by a political scientist.

Ben O Nnaji, *Blaise Compaoré: The Architect of the Burkina Faso Revolution* (Spectrum, 1989). Unashamedly propagandist offering, with some general information on the country.

Robin Sharp, *Burkina Faso: New Life for the Sahel* (Oxfam Publications, 1990). Shows the depth of the country's difficulties without being patronizing.

GHANA

Ghana has an established literary tradition with a number of widely available works.

HISTORY, SOCIETY AND ART

Mike Adjei, *Death and Pain: Rawlings' Ghana, the Inside Story* (Black Line, UK, 1994). Highly crtical of the Rawlings regime, cataloguing alleged political murders.

Peter Adler and Nicholas Barnard, *Asafo! African Flags of the Fante* (Thames & Hudson, UK, 1992). Affordable and striking photo collection of Asafo flags and details.

FK Buah, *History of Ghana* (Macmillan, UK, 1980). A basic text, with a fair amount of illustration.

Gracia Clark, *Onions Are My Husband: Survival and Accumulation by West African Market Women* (University of Chicago Press, UK & US, 1994). Insightful portrait of Kumasi market women.

Jeff Crisp, *Story of an African Working Class: Ghanaian Miners' Struggle* (Zed Books, UK, 1984). Epic struggle retold.

Emmanuel Hansen *Ghana Under Rawlings: Early Years* (Malthouse, UK, 1991).

Eboe Hutchful, *IMF and Ghana* (Zed Books, UK, 1987). Collection of original IMF documents, displaying the Fund with its pants down.

Kofi Kodzi, *Worse than South Africa* (Moreto, UK, 1991). Along the same lines as Adjei's, *Death and Pain*.

Kwame Nkrumah, *Kwame Nkrumah: the Conakry Years*, ed. June Milne (Zed Books, 1990). Fascinating and remarkably large collection of correspondence, both weighty and trivial, from the complex mind of the exiled ex-president.

Thierry Secretan, *Going into Darkness: Fantastic Coffins from Africa* (Thames & Hudson, UK & US, 1995). A photo-documentary about a visually exciting artform – the model coffins (in the form of a boat for a fisherman, a Merc for market woman, etc) of the Ga in Ghana.

FICTION

Maya Angelou, *All God's Children Need Travelling Shoes* (Virago, UK, 1986; Random, US, 1991). The story of American black activist Angelou's emigration to newly independent Ghana and her growing sense of disillusion, picked out in dialogue.

Ama Ata Aidoo, *The Dilemma of a Ghost* and *Anowa* (Longman, UK, 1995). Aidoo, one of Africa's relatively few female writers, deals in *Dilemma* with the unusual theme of a black American girl married into a Ghanaian family and in *Anowa* with a Ghanaian legend about a girl who refuses her parents' chosen suitors. *No Sweetness Here* (Longman, UK, 1995; NOK Pubs, US, 1979) is a collection of short stories, most of which handle the theme of conflict between traditional and urban life in Ghana. *Our Sister Killjoy* (Longman, UK, 1988; Feminist Press, US, 1995), Aidoo's first novel, explores, in an experimental fashion, the thoughts and experience of a Ghanaian girl on a voyage of self-discovery in Germany. *Changes* (The Women's Press, US, 1992) is a love story, used to portray urban African women – and the social forces that combine to make them both powerful and vulnerable.

Ayi Kwei Armah, *The Beautiful Ones Are Not Yet Born* (1968; reprinted Heinemann, UK, 1988; Heinemann, US, 1989). Politics, greed and corruption in newly independent Africa, seen through the life of a railway clerk; Armah beautifully captures the sense of frustration and crisis that befell Ghana after the fall of Nkrumah. Armah's second novel, *Fragments* (Heinemann, UK, 1974), is the story of a young African who comes home to Ghana after five years in the USA. *The Healers* (Heinemann, UK, 1978), a compulsive historical novel set in the Asante empire at the time of its demise, retains an optimistic vision.

Joseph Casely-Hayford, *Ethiopia Unbound* (1911; reprinted Frank Cass, UK, 1969). Generally considered the first West African novel, *Ethiopia Unbound* treats a theme that later became familiar in African literature: the student who goes to study in London, and returns home to find he's a stranger. Early suggestions of what later became "negritude".

Amma Darko, *Beyond the Horizon* (Heinemann, UK, 1995). Provocative story of a Ghanaian woman's prostitution in Germany.

Amu Djoleto, *Hurricane of Dust* (Longman, UK, 1987). A vital, rap-paced tale, set in a post-coup Accra.

Efua Sutherland, *The Marriage of Anansewa* (Longman, UK, 1987). Sutherland – writer and director of numerous plays and founder of Ghana's foremost experimental theatre group – uses the traditional Ananse folktale to examine current social issues.

TOGO

Very little devoted to Togo has ever been published in English.

Tete Michel Kpomassie, *An African in Greenland* (Ulverscroft large print, US, 1988). The narrative of a Togolese explorer on a whimsical journey among the Innuit. Never quite transcends the basic oddity of its theme, and begs a few questions along the way, but entertaining nonetheless.

George Packer, *The Village of Waiting* (Random, US, 1988). An informative book, recounting the experiences of a Peace Corps volunteer.

Comi M Toulabor, *Le Togo sous Eyadema* (Karthala, France, 1986). A solid discussion of 1980s politics – and about the only one to appear.

FICTION

David Ananou, *Le Fils du Fétiche* (Nouvelle Editions Latine, France, 1955). Intended to combat the racism of its time by a portrayal of a typical Togolese family, the effort is confounded by Ananou's rejection of traditional beliefs for the "lofty" tenets of Christianity.

Yves-Emmanuel Dogbé, *La Victime* (Editions Akpagnon, France, 1979). A treatment of the inter-racial theme in West Africa: a white girl's parents come to recognize the error of their prejudice, but too late.

BENIN

With the exception of Chatwin, who also contributed a memorable piece to *The Best of Granta Travel* (1991) on the coup that installed Kérékou, there is little available from, or about Benin.

Bruce Chatwin, *The Viceroy of Ouidah* (Pan, UK, 1982; Viking Penguin, US, 1988). Without a doubt the first book to read on Benin – gripping, in Chatwin's inimitable style, from the prologue on.

Robert Cornevin, *La République Populaire du Bénin* (Editions G-P Maisonneuve et Larose, 1984). A complete, if dryly chronological, history, with a French nationalist slant.

Patrick Manning, *Slavery, Colonialism and Economic Growth in Dahomey 1640–1960* (o/p). Heavy scholarship, but well done.

Dov Ronen, *Dahomey: Between Tradition and Modernity* (Cornell UP, UK & US, 1975). Unfortunately, the publication date means the Kérékou era is largely left out.

FICTION

Olympe Bhêly-Quénum, *Snares Without End* (trans. Dorothy S Blair, Longman 1981, o/p, from *Un Piège sans Fin*, 1978). The only Béninois writer to have been translated into English.

Paul Hazoumé, *Doguicimi* (Larose, 1938, o/p). The essence of the Dan-Homey kingdom is captured in this carefully documented work of realist-romantic fiction, unfortunately not yet translated from French.

Maximilian Quénum, *Légendes Africaines* (1946, o/p). One of the earliest African writers inspired by the doctrine of "negritude". The legends include an account of the founding of the Dan-Homey empire along with that of kingdoms in Côte d'Ivoire and the Soudan (Mali).

NIGER

Published material in English on Niger is really limited: if you want more than the handful of volumes devoted to the country, you'll need to read French.

The late **Boubou Hama** was one of Niger's most prolific writers, publishing numerous historical works on the empires of Gao, Gobir and Songhai. A former president of the National Assembly, he also wrote works on politics, philosophy and folklore.

Politique Africaine: Le Niger (Karthala, 1990). Survey of Nigérien politics, aid and economics – and the Sahara.

Carol Beckwith and Mario Van Offelen, *Nomads of Niger* (Collins, UK, 1984; Abrams, US, 1993). Superbly illustrated essay on the Wodaabe Bororo.

Robert B Charlick, *Niger: Personal Rule and Survival in the Sahel* (Westview, US, 1991). Fairly recent profile of the nation.

Finn Fuglestad, *A History of Niger 1850–1960* (Cambridge UP, 1983, o/p). Somewhat inaccessible, but there's no English alternative.

Paul Stoller and Cheryl Olkes, *In Sorcery's Shadow: a Memoir of Apprenticeship among the Songhay* and *Fusion of the Worlds: An Ethnography of Possession among the Songhay of Niger* (University of Chicago Press, UK & US, 1987 & 1989). Stoller is a kind of Nigérien answer to Carlos Castaneda – apprenticed to a sorcerer, taking drugs. All interesting stuff.

FICTION

Ibrahim Issa, *Grandes Eaux Noires*. The first Nigérien novel to be published (before independence), this manages to describe humorously the travails of second-century BC Mediterranean explorers south of the Sahara.

More recent writers include:

Idé Oumarou, *Gros Plan*. This won the *grand prix de l'Afrique Noire* award in 1978.

Halilou Sabbo Mahamadou, *Abokki ou l'Appel de la Côte, Les Caprices du Destin*.

Amadou Ousmane, *Quinze ans, ça suffit*. Aspects of contemporary Nigérien society illuminated. Kicks off with the food aid-hoarding scandal (see p.954).

NIGERIA

There's a vast body of books on and from Nigeria in print – and more being published all the time.

COUNTRY AND STATE

Nigeria, the Land, its Art and its People (Studio Vista, 1977, o/p). A brief, good-value anthology of prose, with photographs.

Chinua Achebe, *The Trouble with Nigeria* (Heinemann, UK & US, 1983). A brief and immensely useful insight into the complexity of Nigerian society and politics.

William D Graf, *Nigerian State: Political Economy, State, Class and Political System in the Post-Colonial Era* (James Currey, UK, 1988; Heinemann, US, 1990). An overview analysing political, social and economic shifts over the last 25 years.

Peter Holmes, *Nigeria: Giant of Africa* (Oregon Press, 1985, o/p). Coffee-table format with nearly 200 photos. Detailed and interesting notes; nothing else on Nigeria of this type compares.

Adewale Maja-Pearce, *In My Father's Country* (1987, o/p). A curiously flat and brief travelogue. Maja-Pearce (back in Nigeria for the first time in a long while) seems afraid of commitment, travelling to Maiduguri "only to be able to say I'd been there".

Ken Saro-Wiwa, *Genocide in Nigeria: the Ogoni Tragedy* (Saros, Nigeria, 1992). Sets out the disastrous effects of government policy and the oil industry on a region in Rivers State.

ART AND PEOPLE

JS Boston, *Ikenga* (Ethnographica Press, 1977). Explores the symbolism of carvings amongst varied peoples of Nigeria.

TJH Chappel, *Decorated Gourds in North Eastern Nigeria* (Ethnographica Press, 1977, o/p).

A substantial survey of their use, decoration and symbolism.

Henry J Drewal and John Pemberton III, *Yoruba: Nine Centuries of African Art and Thought* (Abrams, US, 1990). Sumptuous and terribly expensive – a majestic, detailed photo and essay documentary on various Yoruba states and their individual artistic traditions.

Edward Fox, *Obscure Kingdoms* (Penguin, UK, 1995). Excitingly written and brilliantly evocative accounts of journeys to the world's remoter royal corners, including a sizeable chapter on meetings in Nigeria with various onis, obas and emirs.

Bryan Freyer, *Royal Benin Art* (Smithsonian Institute, US, 1987). Illustrated and informative catalogue from a major exhibition of the art of the Benin Empire.

Berkare Gbadamosi and Ulli Beier, *Not Even God Is Ripe Enough* (Heinemann, 1968, o/p). Full of amusing stories.

Paula Girshick Ben-Amos, *The Art of Benin* (British Museum Press, UK, 1995). Plenty of photos of bronzes and more.

Barry Hallen and JO Sodipo, *Knowledge, Belief and Witchcraft* (Ethnographica Press, 1977). A survey of Yoruba philosophical ideas.

GI Jones, *Ibo Art* (Shire, UK, 1989; State Mutual, US, 1989). Well-illustrated survey of arts and their role in Ibo (Igbo) society.

FICTION

Nigeria's post-colonial literature has been the continent's most prolific and most outspoken, its writers enjoying a greater liberty than most of their African counterparts. Today, by far the most influential Nigerian writers are Chinua Achebe and the Nobel prize-winning novelist and playwright Wole Soyinka. One of the greatest impetuses to national writing, however, was Onitsha Market Literature, which emerged between 1947 and 1966. At the time, Onitsha was one of Nigeria's most important commercial centres, with a long history of mission education and cosmopolitan influence. Dozens of spare-time writers – teachers, office clerks and journalists – turned out some 200 books that were printed in the market itself.

Chinua Achebe, *Things Fall Apart* (1958), *No Longer at Ease* (1960), *The Arrow of God* (1964), *A Man of the People* (1966), *Anthills of the Savannah* (1987); all published (and in print) by Heinemann in the UK and Doubleday in the US. One of Africa's best-known novelists, Achebe gained international fame with his classic first novel *Things Fall Apart*, which deals with the encounter, at the turn of the century, between missionaries, colonial officers and an Igbo village. Okwonkwo, a self-made man, rises to respected seniority, then falls, inexorably and tragically. It's a brilliant, moving book – universal in what it says on pride, and on fathers and sons. With it, the three following novels form part of a loose quartet: in *No Longer at Ease*, Okwonkwo's grandson, Obi, is a corrupt Lagos civil servant, trapped in his head between home and ambition; in *Arrow of God*, set in the 1920s, there's direct confrontation between an Igbo priest and a colonial officer; and in *A Man of the People*, Achebe adopts a more satirical approach, setting up an idealist against a rogue-and showing how close their paths run. Achebe's characters bend and sweat with life and develop unexpected traits just as you thought you had the measure of them. His last novel, a humanist fable, *Anthills of the Savannah*, was shortlisted for the Booker Prize.

Zainab Alkali, *A Virtuous Woman, The Stillborn* (Longman, 1984, o/p). Alkali is unusual in being a woman writer from the conservative north of the country. "I see myself as a typical Nigerian woman who wants to get married, raise a family and live according to the expected norms of the society . . . A woman can never be anything else but a woman".

TM Aluko, *One Man, One Wife* (Heinemann, 1967, o/p). Entertaining tale of Yoruba villagers' disillusionment with the missionaries' God and their return to traditional worship. *One Man, One Matchet* (Heinemann, 1965, o/p) is written in a similarly crafted and satirical style as it portrays conflict in a Western cocoa community. *Chief the Honourable Minister* (Heinemann, 1970, o/p) is the less amusing story of a schoolmaster appointed minister in a corrupt government. His latest book, *Conduct Unbecoming* (Heinemann Nigeria, 1993), is a parable about corruption and sanctimoniousness.

Tafawa Balewa, *Shaihu Umar* (1968; reprinted Wiener, US, 1989; translated from the Hausa). Portrayal of a Hausa family at the turn of the century by Nigeria's first prime minister.

Simi Bedford, *Yoruba Girl Dancing* (Mandarin, UK, 1991; Viking, US, 1994). A British Nigerian's depiction of early life in Nigeria, adjustment to the UK, and the getting of wisdom.

John Pepper Clark Three of Clark's books, *A Reed in the Tide* (1965, o/p), *Casualties* (Longman, UK, 1970; Holmes & Meier, US, 1970; a lament written during the civil war), and *A Decade of Tongues* (o/p) are poetry collections with which Clark first gained recognition. He is now better known as a playwright – for *Ozidi* (Harvard UP, US, 1991), a play based on an Ijaw saga, *State of the Nation*, a piece of social criticism written in 1985 (o/p), and *America, Their America* (o/p), a biting indictment of values in the United States where he studied in the early 1960s.

T Obinkaram Echewa, *I Saw the Sky Catch Fire* (NAL-Dutton, US, 1993). Fictional accounts of the effects of war, especially as it touches the lives of women. Powerful and moving, from the author of *The Land's Lord*.

Cyprian Ekwensi, *Jagua Nana* (1961; reprinted Heinemann, UK & US, 1987). Superbly captures the life and rhythm of 1950s Lagos using a style resembling that of the traditional storyteller. *Burning Grass* (1962; Heinemann, UK & US, 1990) is set in the north among Fula herders (an unusual setting for Ekwensi). One of Nigeria's most popular novelists, Ekwensi started his writing career at Onitsha market. *Lokotown and other stories* (o/p) is a collection of short tales, again set in the city, while *Survive the Peace* (o/p) is his most political novel, set in the aftermath of the defeat of Biafra, a secession he had supported. His most recent book was *Jagua Nana's Daughter* (Spectrum, 1986).

Buchi Emecheta, *Slave Girl, Second Class Citizen, In The Ditch, Head Above Water, Joys Of Motherhood, Double Yoke, The Bride Price, Destination Biafra, Gwendolen* and *Rape Of Shavi* (all in print, mostly in Ogwugwu or Heinemann, UK, and Brazillier, US). Emecheta writes, with a humour that refuses to be submerged, about the struggle to be a Nigerian woman and an independent person – in Nigeria and the UK. Her latest, *Kehinde* (Heinemann, UK, 1994), is the sharp tale of a westernized woman who leaves London to return to Nigeria with her husband.

Olaudah Equiano, *The Life of Olaudah Equiano* (1789; reprinted Longman, UK, 1995). Classic autobiography and one of the earliest West African books. Equiano was born in Igboland in 1745 and captured by slavers at the age of ten. Highly recommended reading.

Festus Ijayi, *Violence* (Longman, 1979, o/p), *Heroes* (Longman, 1986, o/p). A commitedly political writer, Ijayi was detained in 1988 for protesting against the government's human rights abuses. *Violence* is a howl of anguish at the inhumanity of urban survival in Africa. *Heroes* is set in the dark backyard of Nigeria's soul, the civil war of 1967–69.

Vincent Chukwuemeka Ike, *Toads for Supper* (o/p), *The Naked Gods* (o/p), *Chicken Chasers* (o/p) and *Sunset at Dawn* (o/p). A series of entertaining, critical novels by a brilliant comic writer. Recent works include *The Search* (Heinemann Nigeria, 1991) and *Our Children are Coming* (Spectrum, 1990).

Eddie Iroh, *Forty Eight Guns for the General* (Heinemann, 1976, o/p), *Toads of War* (Heinemann, US, 1979) and *The Sirens in the Night* (Heinemann, 1982, o/p). Three thrillers that rode in on the wave of writing following the Biafran War.

Adewale Maja Pearce, *Loyalties* (Longman, 1987). Evocative short stories and vignettes set in a society always on the brink of chaos (Nigeria) by a writer based in Britain.

Flora Nwapa, *Efuru* (Heinemann, UK & US, 1966). The first African woman to publish a novel. As in the later *Idu* (Heinemann, UK, 1970), Nwapa looks at women's roles – not always in a traditional way – in a society precariously balanced between the traditional and the new. *This is Lagos* (African World Press, UK & US, 1992) is Nwapa's follow-up to her novels portraying women at odds with society – a collection of effective short stories on life in the metropolis. Flora Nwapa died in 1993.

Ben Okri, *Flowers and Shadows* (1980; reprinted Longman, UK, 1989). Okri's excellent first novel was published when he was only twenty. The angry, hallucinatory short story collections, *Incidents at the Shrine* (1986; reprinted Vintage, UK, 1993) and *Stars of the New Curfew* (Penguin, UK, 1989; Viking, US, 1990) propelled Nigerian literature into a new wide audience. Okri, based in Britain, provides razor-sharp dialogue and settings, fine evocations of character (male and female) and an angular wit. With his Booker prize-winning *The Famished Road* (Jonathan Cape, UK, 1991; Anchor Books, US, 1993), he comes home to the themes of tradition and of

Yoruba mythology. It was followed by a sequel, *Songs of Enchantment* (Vintage, UK, 1994; Doubleday, US, 1994) and then by *Astonishing the Gods* (Phoenix House, UK, 1995).

Niyi Osundare, *Moonsongs* (Spectrum, UK, 1988); *Songs of the Season* (Heinemann Nigeria, 1990); *Waiting Laughters* (Malthouse, UK, 1991); *Midlife* (Heinemann Nigeria, 1993). One of Africa's best-known poets, committed to performance of poetry together with drumming and dancing, Osundare is a Commonwealth Prize winner, who received the NOMA Award in 1991 for *Waiting Laughters*. His most easily obtained collection is *Selected Poems* (Heinemann, UK).

Ken Saro-Wiwa, *Sozaboy* (1985; reprinted Longman, UK, 1994); *A Forest of Flowers* (1986; reprinted Longman, UK, 1994; Three Continents, US, 1995); *Basi & Company: A Modern African Folktale* (Saros, Nigeria, 1987); *The Prisoner of Jebs* (Saros, 1988); *Pita Dumbrok's Prison* (Saros, 1991). Saro-Wiwa is a major figure on the Nigerian literary and political scene, in jail, as this book goes to press, for his campaigning work on behalf of his fellow Ogoni people. Saro-Wiwa fought on the Federal side in the Nigerian civil war and his maverick career has spanned publishing, TV and political activism.

Wole Soyinka When Soyinka won the Nobel Prize for Literature in 1986, he not only gained international recognition for himself (becoming the first African to be so honoured), but for the writers of his continent. Known primarily as a playwright, his early works include *The Lion and the Jewel* (1963), *A Dance of the Forests* (1963) – an exercise in demythologizing Africa's historic idyll – and *Kongi's Harvest* (1967). Oxford UP publish UK and US editions of these plays. He later published poetry, sketching beautiful images in *Idanre, and Other Poems* (1967; reprinted Hill & Wang, US, 1987). He has also worked substantially as a novelist with *The Interpreters* (Heinemann, UK & US, 1970) – in which a group of young intellectuals living in Lagos attempts to "interpret" their role in traditional and modern Nigeria – and the luminous, dream-like *Ake* (Arrow, UK, 1983; Random, US, 1989) – an autobiographical account of his childhood in Abeokuta. *Isara* (Minerva, UK, 1991; Random, US, 1989) is a biographical account of Nigeria in the times of his father, the memorable schoolmaster "Essay" from *Ake*. His latest novel, the sequel to *Isara*, is *Ibadan: the Penkelmes Years* (Methuen, UK, 1994), focusing on his fight against the everyday repression of early post-independence Nigeria. As a writer of even greater prominence than Achebe, Soyinka's work is denser and less easy-going. He is also politically more outspoken, and has recently (1995) helped organize a major opposition group in exile.

Amos Tutuola, *Palm Wine Drinkard* (1952; reprinted Faber, UK, 1995; Greenwood, US, 1970). This, the first West African novel, is heavily under the spell of Yoruba oral tradition as it recounts a journey into the "Dead Towns" of the supernatural. It was followed by *My Life in the Bush of Ghosts* (Faber, 1954).

CAMEROON

A fair number of books dealing with Cameroon have been published, and the country has the advantage of a dual linguistic heritage which has inspired a relatively rich literature, though predominantly in French.

GENERAL/TRAVELOGUES

Nigel Barley, *Innocent Anthropologist: Notes from a Mud Hut* (Penguin, UK, 1986), *A Plague of Caterpillars* (Penguin, UK, 1986). The books that did for anthropology what Durrell did for animal collecting – and infuriated anthropologists.

Gerald Durrell, *The Overloaded Ark* (1953; reprinted Faber, UK, 1995, & US, 1987), *The Bafut Beagles* (1954; reprinted Penguin, UK, 1970), *A Zoo in my Luggage* (1960; reprinted Penguin, UK, 1970). Durrell's animal-collecting exploits in the British Cameroons – first freelance, and then for his Jersey Conservation Trust zoo – are delightfully recounted and still funny, with exceptions made for an unexceptionally colonial attitude to quaint native behaviour. But it's hard indeed to recognize the present town of Mamfé – even less Bafut – in his misty pictures.

Dervla Murphy, *In Cameroon with Egbert* (Arrow, UK, 1990; Overlook Press, US, 1991). Murphy and daughter with a horse.

HISTORY/POLITICS/ART/SOCIETY

Mark DeLancey, *Cameroon: Dependence and Independence* (Dartmouth, UK, 1989). Survey of history, economics and politics.

Philippe Gaillard, *Le Cameroun* (L'Harmattan, France, 1989, two volumes). General political and economic survey in French from colonial times to the late 1980s.

TE Mbuagbaw, R Brain, R Palmer, *A History of Cameroon* (Longman, 1987). Useful school text.

Albert Mukong, *Prisoner without a Crime* (Nubia, 1989). The darker side of political life under Biya, this tells the story of six years of imprisonment with graphic details of arbitrary justice, brutality and torture. Leave at home.

Tamara Northern, *Art Of Cameroon* (Smithsonian Institute, UK & US, 1984). Large-format colour-illustrated survey of regions and their art.

Joseph Sheppherd, *Leaf of Honey* (Bahai, US, 1988). An American anthropologist's study of the Ntuumu people of Cameroon, laced with their proverbs and their views about life.

Colin Turnbull, *The Forest People* (1961; reprinted Pimlico, UK, 1994, Simon & Schuster, US, 1987). An account of the Ituri forest Bambuti ("Pygmies") in Zaire; the best writing in English on the oldest African people. Essential, delightful reading for forest stays in Cameroon.

FICTION

Léon-Marie Ayissi, *Contes et Berceuses Béti* (1966). A satisfying collection of Beti folktales.

Francis Bebey, *Agatha Moudio's Son* (trans. from *Le fils d'Agatha Moudio*, Heinemann, 1971, o/p). Better known as a musician (see p.1264), this was Bebey's first novel, a tragi-comic study of human relations in a traditional village society.

Mongo Beti, *The Poor Christ of Bomba* (trans. Heinemann, UK & US, 1971). One of the senior figures of African literature – living in exile since 1959 – Beti's novels combine political satire with more basic human conflict. *Poor Christ*, the most cynical of his novels, deals with the perverse efforts of a French priest to convert the whole village, with disastrously ironic consequences. Later works, *Mission to Kala* (1957; trans. from *Mission terminée*; reprinted Heinemann, UK & US, 1970) and *King Lazurus* (trans. from *Le Roi Miraculé*, o/p) established his mastery of social satire. After independence, Beti embarked on a long period of silence until the publication of his critique of the Ahidjo regime – *Main basse sur le Cameroon* (F Maspero, 1972), which he followed with *Remember Ruben* and *Perpetua and the Habit of Unhappiness* (trans. John Reed and Clive Wake, Heinemann, UK, 1978).

Benjamin Matip, *Afrique nous t'ignorons* (1954). Matip contemplates the past from a young African's perspective – separated from tradition by Western education and World War II. The novel also hits out at the exploitation of Cameroonian planters: it contributed to an outpouring of anti-colonial literature in the 1950s. Matip's *A la Belle Etoile: Contes et nouvelles d'Afrique* (Presence Africaine, France, 1962) is a classic collection of folktales.

Ndeley Mokoso, *Man Pass Man!* (Longman, 1987, o/p). A string of darkly funny short stories. The subject of the title tale – maraboutic meddling on the football pitch – was rumoured as an explanation for Cameroon's success in the 1990 World Cup.

Jacques Mariel Nzouankeu, *Le Souffle des Ancêtres* (Edit CLE, 1965). Tales that illustrate the conflict between humans and the metaphysical forces that are believed to dominate their destinies.

Ferdinand Oyono, *Houseboy* (trans. from *Une Vie de Boy*, 1956; reprinted Heinemann, UK & US, 1990). Oyono was one of the first satirical writers of the anti-colonial period to break from an autobiographical form in this scathing satire about colonialism. *The Old Man and the Medal* (trans. from *Le Vieux Negre et la Médaille*, Heinemann, 1967) is less caustic, but equally effective, both in its criticism of colonial insensitivity, and of blind adherence to tradition. Oyono is now Foreign Minister in Biya's government.

Guillaume Oyônô-Mbia, *Three Suitors, One Husband* and *Until Further Notice* (both o/p). Comic masterpieces, written in English. His later play in French, *Notre Fille ne se mariera pas*, like *Three Suitors*, deals with the familiar theme of the brideprice in a changing African society. It was made into the 1980 film *Notre Fille* by Daniel Kamwa (see p.1245).

René Philombe, *Lettres de ma Cambuse* (Editions CLE, 1964). Life in the urban slums described – even on the basis of personal experience – with humour. Subsequent work includes an inspired collection of short stories *Histoires queue de chat: quelques scènes de la vie camerounaise* (Editions CLE, 1971).

CINEMA

West African cinema provides a stimulating way into the complexities of the region's culture and concerns. This short introduction maps out its history and highlights some of the better-known films and film-makers.

THE BEGINNINGS

In 1963 a short film by the acclaimed novelist **Ousmane Sembène** – *Borom Sarret* – managed to get onto the screens of Africa and Europe. Well received by the critics, this work laid the foundations for what, by the end of the 1960s, had become a great cinematic movement south of the Sahara. In 1968, Sembène released *Mandabi* (The Money Order), the first movie by a Black African to reach a large audience; critics also hailed the film, which won the Silver Lion at the 1969 Venice Film Festival.

The success of *Mandabi* inspired a whole generation of West African film-makers, and the 1970s turned out to be the region's most prolific decade. Early directors, many of them trained in the Soviet Union, were aware of their power to reach the masses and of Lenin's assertion that "the most important of all the arts is cinema". From the beginning they perceived their craft as a functional art form, which could break down stereotypes by giving a realistic portrayal of Africa from an African perspective, and could take an active part in national development by adapting film to the needs and aspirations of their newly independent countries.

Though early West African films were the products of many different cultures and looked at the continent in various historical, political and social stages, they were remarkably similar in their **themes**. Most commonly, they dealt with the conflict that arose from traditional values and those imported from the West. Typically, the opposition between the old and the new is expressed by the opposition between **the city and the country** – the implication being that the process of rural migration has contributed to a loss of cultural identity. Among numerous examples of films of this type are *Kwami* by Quenum Do-Kokou from Togo (1974), *Sous le signe de Vaudou* by Pascal Abikanlou from Benin (1973), and *Le Bracelet du Bronze* by Tidiane Aw from Senegal (1974). Other topics include the **alienation** faced by African emigrants abroad, the **exploitation** of the masses by a corrupt and unscrupulous elite, the weight of **social traditions**, and the **injustices** of colonial or neo-colonial systems.

African film-makers also struggled with the limitations imposed by a film language that has evolved in the West. Thematic inspiration that derived from **African tales and legends** necessitated a new style capable of breaking down a story, of using digression to accept the irrational within the logical structure of a tale. There has thus been a tendency to move away from the slow-paced linear narrative of early films in order to forge an authentic African aesthetic, based on the conventions of oral literature.

FESPACO

As the cinematic movement progressed, **Burkina Faso** (called Upper Volta then) emerged as the "capital" of African cinema. In 1969, Ouagadougou hosted the first **Festival Panafricain du Cinema** (FESPACO), a forum for African film-makers held every other February. Winners of the "Yenenga" – the African Oscar – have increasingly achieved international plaudits, and though participation in the main event is limited to Africans, an increasing number of entries from the diaspora – the United States, Latin America and the Caribbean – have gained recognition through presentation in a special category. Burkina Faso has produced its own notable directors too: **Gaston Kaboré**, whose *Wend Kuuni* (The Gift of God) won the Grand Prix at the 1985 FESPACO; **Samon Emmanuel**, who won acclaim for his 1985 film *Dessé Bagato*; and

Idrissa Ouédraogo, whose *Yaaba* earned a prize at the 1989 Cannes festival.

RECENT SETBACKS

Throughout West Africa, the remarkable creativity that characterized the 1970s, began a **decline** by the end of the decade that continued into the 1980s and 1990s. A major reason for the stagnation can be found in the system of film production and distribution. With few exceptions, films are made with state subsidies, which limits creative possibilities in countries where the treasury doesn't give high priority to cinema. Most people in business consider film a risky investment. Movie-going is popular in towns but the gate receipts are small, and imported **videos** are increasingly driving cinemas out of business. Adding to the frustration, most countries lack film industries of a technical level that would permit post-production control (laboratories, synchro, editing). Most post-production work for African-produced films is still carried out in Europe.

Distribution has proved a further stumbling block. Although mostly nationalized in West African countries, distribution companies still depend on larger European and American firms which control the African screens. Sadly, they exhibit minimal enthusiasm for national products, and films made in Africa have little or no chance of being shown in their countries of origin. Today, in fact, it is easier to see African films in Paris, London, Rome and New York than in Abidjan, Conakry, Lagos or Lomé.

THE NEW GENERATION

Despite these difficulties, independent film continues to progress, and the early pioneers are being followed by a hopeful new generation. Recent FESPACO festivals have pointed to the growing diversity of African cinema and the emergence of a new generation of film-makers. They put their own spin on the **social realism** films of predecessors, drawing from local theatre (Yoruba theatre in Nigeria, or Koteba theatre in Mali and Côte d'Ivoire), oral tradition, and song and dance. Like Sembène and Cissé, new filmmakers treat issues of class, gender, tradition or religion, yet tend to be less didactic in the way they view oppressive forces. Often comedic, the youthful exuberance of films like *Bal Poussiere* (Henri Duparc, Côte d'Ivoire, 1988), *Quartier Mozart* (Jean-Pierre Bekolo, Cameroon, 1991) or even *Finzan* (Cheikh Oumar Sissoko, Mali, 1989) have made them some of the most talked about films in recent festivals. Contemporary, almost hip, new social realist films commonly incorporate popular music stars in the scoring or acting – *Les Guerrisseurs* (Sijiri Bakaba, Côte d'Ivoire, 1988), for example, which featured performances by Alpha Blondy, Salif Keita and Nayanka Bell. Still, there is a commitment to addressing societal malaises and the heroes are workers, women, or children – those commonly marginalized by the elites of modernity and tradition.

Another trend is towards "**return to source**" films, which re-examine African rural life. Souleyman Cissé, whose early works were highly political, embarked on this course with *Yeelen* (Mali, 1987) – a young boy's initiation journey that reveals the oral cultures and traditions of the Bamana, Dogon and Fulani. More recently, Burkina Faso's Idrissa Ouédraogo has been the most prominent proponent with films like *Tilai* (1990). Critics sometimes charge these films with aesthetic excess and with romanticizing village life. But adherents defend efforts to reclaim local history, religion, and

OUSMANE SEMBÈNE

Senegal's **Ousmane Sembène**, a Marxist whose films are explicitly political, remains the "papa" of West African cinema. Since his debut in 1963, he has made over a dozen films, of which several are considered classics. Besides *Borom Sarret* ("Cart-driver", 1963) and *Mandabi* ("The Money Order", 1968), his most famous works are **Xala** (1974) – a satire that gets darker and darker about a corrupt Dakar bureaucrat who loses touch with the people and thereby becomes impotent – and the less accessible *Ceddo*, which deals with the three-way conflict in the the nineteenth century between the jihadists, the traditionalists and the French. More recently, he made **Camp Thiaroye** (1986), the story of a massacre, by French troops, of African soldiers who had mutinied on their return from fighting for France during World War II.

humanism, and to explore African value systems on their own terms, disregarding Western ethnocentric understandings.

Anti-colonial films also remain popular, as witnessed by Sembène's *Camp de Thiaroye* (Senegal, 1988), or Kwaw Ansah's *Heritage Africa* (Ghana, 1987). These films position viewers to identify with national and personal resistance to European political domination and cultural imperialism and to reconsider **history from the African perspective**. Recent films in this tradition also focus on post-independence regimes, calling into question "official" versions of national histories. David Aschkar thus probes the injustices of Sekou Touré's Guinea in *Allah Tanto* (Guinea, 1991) while in *Afrique, Je te Plummerai* (Cameroon, 1992), Jean-Marie Teno points out the connections between colonial exploitation and the kind that continues under the Biya government.

SENEGAL

Senegalese directors, notably Ousmane Sembène, **Pape B Seck** *(Afrique sur Rhin,* 1984), **Djibril Diop Mambety** (*Touki Bouki* – a groundbreaking anti-modernization film from 1973), and one of the continent's first women film-makers, **Safi Faye** (*Lettre Paysan*, 1975; *Mossane*, 1991), have relied heavily on the state for funds. But film-makers have also attempted to diversify the image of African cinema through Le Collectif l'Oeil Vert, an association that aims at increasing cooperation between African film-makers and decreasing dependency on the state. The collective was founded by **Cheikh N'Gaido Bah** who advocates a greater commercialization of film and who cast box office draws like Jean-Paul Belmondo from France and Isaak de Bankolé from Côte d'Ivoire in his latest project, *La Vie en Spirale*. Bah's film *Xew Xew* (1983) dealt with the popular culture of Senegalese music and featured well-known artists like Xalam and Youssou N'Dour. **Moussa Bathily** partly financed his popular film *Petits Blancs au Mainioc et à la Sauce Gombo* (1989) with personal savings and profits from his earlier films. Senegalese film-makers were highly visible at the 1993 FESPACO with **Ahmed Diallo** winning the category for best short for *Boxumaleen* (1991). **Mansour Sora Wade** (*Picc Mi*, 1991), Djibril Diop Mambety (*Hyenes*, 1991) and **Clarence Delgado** (*Niiwan*, 1988) were all honoured with special prizes. But one of the best known of the new generation is **Amadou Seck**, whose film *Saaraba* (1988) – an indictment of a corrupt older generation that provides a tough portrayal of African urban youth – is already something of a classic in the neo-realist tradition.

MALI

The most famous name in Malian cinema is **Souleymane Cissé**, who studied film in the Soviet Union, before returning to Mali and launching his career (see box). His first full-length feature, *Baara*, was followed by *Finye* ("The Wind", 1982). This was filmed entirely in the Bamana language, yet became an international success, and was presented at Cannes, Carthage, and Ouagadougou, where it won first prize.

Two other early Malian film-makers also received their training in the USSR – **Djibral Kouyaté** and **Kalifa Dienta**. Kouyaté was the first Malian to make a fiction film, *Le Retour de Tiéman* (1970) – the story of a young agriculturalist who runs into the resistance of traditionalists when he tries to implement modern methods in his village. Dienta is best known for his feature *A Banna*, in which the main character, Yadji, takes his new bride from Bamako to meet his family in the village. The clash between urban and rural values comes into focus as Yadji's wife has to contend with everything from the authority of the griot to old-fashioned divisions between men and women.

Alkaly Kaba was another pioneer, best known for films portraying the conflict between Western and African worlds. Early films (1970s) in this vein include *Wallanda* and *Wamba*.

Sega Coulibaly comes from a new generation of film-makers whose experiences are rooted in post-independence society. Born in 1950, he briefly studied film in Paris before returning to Mali where he helped Kaba shoot *Wamba*. Coulibaly's first feature, *Mogho Dakan* (1976) follows a city teacher stationed in a village. His success with women (because of his status), backfires when one of them gets pregnant. Coulibaly's second feature, *Kasso Den*, is all-action, a prisoner wrongly jailed seeking vengeance on the men who framed him. **Issa Falaba Traoré** gained recognition for *An Be Nodo* (1980), the story of a promising student. Too poor to continue her studies, she brings shame on her family when she drops out of school and becomes pregnant.

Cheik Oumar Sissoko emerged in the late 1980s as a new film-maker in the social realist tradition. An early documentary, *Rural Exodus* (1984) considered the plight of peasants displaced by drought, while *Nyamanton* ("Garbage Boys", 1986) focused on the condition of urban children. Sissoko gained international recognition for *Finzan* (1989), a fictional piece that uses the theme of genital excision to address wider social issues of women's rights and the struggle for freedom. Titles at the beginning of the film remind the viewer that women do two thirds of the world's work, receive only one tenth of the reward and only one percent of the property. Sissoko won the best picture award at the 1995 FESPACO for *Guimba*, the tale of a chief whose obsession for power drives him to make a dangerous pact with the devil. Sissoko describes the film as an allegory about the downfall of Malian president Amadou Traoré.

Other names to emerge in recent years are **Draba Adama**, whose film *Ta Dona* (1991) fuses elements of ancient mysticism and modern corruption, and **Mahamadou Cissé**, a novelist who shot his second feature *Yelema* in 1990.

GUINEA

Even under Sekou Touré, when cinema took on a propagandist role, Guinea produced some fine films, most notably *Naitou* (1982) by **Diakité Moussa Kemoko.** Featuring the Ballet National de Guinée, the film recounts an African folk tale exclusively through music and dance – a radical, and universally comprehensible, attempt to deal with the issue of appropriate language for African cinema.

Among the newer film-makers, **Mohammed Camara**, who trained as an actor, made an impressive entry at the 1993 FESPACO with a short, *Denko*. Camara tackles his difficult subject with sensitivity: a mother commits incest to restore sight to her blind son and reveals the hypocrisy of society through her transgression. **David Aschkar** also created a stir with his 1991 experimental documentary *Allah Tanto* – the story of the director's father, Maroff Aschkar, who was Guinea's ambassador to the United Nations until his imprisonment and death in one of Sekou Touré's infamous political prisons.

BURKINA FASO

The government of Upper Volta/Burkina Faso, has long been active in promoting the cinema in West Africa. To gain more control over the

SOULEYMANE CISSÉ

Souleymane Cissé, from Mali, was trained, like Sembène Ousmane, at the famous Moscow film school. Since the early 1970s, he has been as prolific as Sembène and has made a good number of films which have gone on to commercial and critical success in Africa and Europe. Unlike Sembène, however, his craft always leads his message, not the other way round.

In addition to well-known early works like *Cinqs jours d'une vie* (1972) and *Baara* ("The Porter", 1977) – a full-length look at the relationship between workers and *patron* in a textile factory – he has made perhaps the two best films to come from Africa. In the first, *Finyé* ("The Wind", 1982), about the overweening pressures of seniority on youth, the wind symbolizes a new generation of post-independence youth, struggling against the repression of the military government. The second, *Yeelen* ("Brightness" 1986), at last saw his recognition as a major film-maker. Through the conflict of the main character, Nianankoro – an initiate possessed of magical powers – with his father, *Yeleen* looks at the conflict of generations in Africa and gives non-African movie-goers a spine-tingling insight into traditional values. With its deft visual impact and atemporality – and a deliberate ambiguity about the level of reality at which the images operate – the metaphysical world of the old West Africa comes alive and is as real as any drought or slave trade. For this lyricism – which made the film an arthouse hit in the West – Cissé is inevitably running into criticism from those who would prefer a more realist cinema talking about exploitation, colonialism and repression. *Yeelen* went on to win the Grand Prix du Jury at the 1987 Cannes Film Festival.

Cissé's latest film, *Waati* (Mali/South Africa, 1994) is an epic set in South Africa. But like all his movies, the making of *Waadi* was clouded in secrecy and, although screened in Cannes in 1995, it hadn't been released in Europe or the USA by the time this book went to press.

film industry, the country nationalized movie theatres in 1979, the first nation besides Guinea to do so. In its early days, the national film company helped finance mainly educational films. It also produced **Djim Mamadou Kola's** *Le Sang de parias* (1971), the first national feature. Kola is still an active film-maker; his award-winning *Etrangers* was released in 1993.

In 1981, a private businessman, Martial Ouédraogo, invested in CINAFRIC – a production company with 16mm and 35mm cameras. The only private film company of its kind in Africa, CINAFRIC has been criticized as "Hollywood on the Volta", yet despite its commercial intent, it has helped free local film-makers from dependence on the West. Within a year, CINAFRIC produced its first feature, *Paweogo* (Burkina, 1981), and thus launched one of the country's most prolific film-makers, **Sanou Kollo**.

Burkina Faso was thrust into the spotlight by **Gaston Kaboré**, who won a French César in 1985 for *Wend Kuuni* – a rural tale that demonstrates how traditional values can heal a modern African state. A prominent figure in Burkinabe, and indeed in pan-African cinema (he is currently director of the Pan-African Federation of Film-makers), Kaboré has gone on to make numerous features including *Zan Boko* (Burkina, 1988) – about the problems of urbanization, its impact on people and their relationship to the environment – and *Rabi* (1991). But **Idrissa Ouédraogo** is probably the country's best known film-maker in the West. *Yaaba* (1988), *Tilai* (1990), and *Samba Traoré* (1992) are strongly rooted in the African rural experience.

Today, the government continues to be supportive and new film-makers continue to emerge. **Drissa Touré** was widely acclaimed for his first feature *Laada* (1991), while **Pierre Yameogo's** film *Wendemi* (1992) received several awards at the 1993 FESPACO.

CÔTE D'IVOIRE

Many Ivoirian film-makers got their start in television, since the country had facilities as early as 1963, a good deal sooner than most neighbours. In 1964, **Timoté Bassori** made a short film for television, *Sur la Lune de la Solitude*, an adaptation of the popular Mamy Wata folktale about the spirit of the waters. In the same year, **George Keita** directed *Korogo*, based on the national heroine Queen Poku. Many film historians regard this two-hour epic as the most important television film made in Africa to date.

Gnoan M'Bala also got his start directing short films for television. He was one of the earliest African directors to use comedy and satire in films such as *La Biche* (1971) – in which a woman pretends to be a married man's sister so that she can have an affair with him while living in the same house with his wife – and *Amanié* (1972) – the story of a peasant who moves to the city and cons people into believing he's a rich diplomat. Some of M'Bala's recent films deal with more serious issues. His latest work, *Au Nom du Christ* (1992), received the award for best picture at the 1993 FESPACO.

The national film industry, however, didn't begin picking up steam until the late 1960s when a new name in Ivoirian film emerged. **Henri Duparc** was one of the early directors to receive support from the Société Ivoirienne du Cinéma (SIC). His first films were mainly documentaries, but in 1969 he directed his debut feature *Mouna, ou Le Rêve d'un Artiste*. In *Abusuan* ("The Family", 1972), Duparc probes the parasitic relationships in a family where a successful member's resources are drained by those who depend on him. In Europe, Duparc is best known for *Bal Poussière* (1988), a comic look at the patriarchal excesses of polygamy.

A few Ivoirian film-makers have managed to make pictures with little or no government support. **Lanciné Kramo Fadika** produced his first feature, *Djeli* (1981), with personal finances and borrowed money. The film – which considers the inequalities of traditional social hierarchies in Côte d'Ivoire – went on to win the best picture award at FESPACO. **Jean-Louis Koula** and **Leo Kozoloa** began their own production company, Les Films de la Montagne, in the late 1970s, though it's been mainly an advertising firm. The two have also produced their own documentaries, Koula's, *Adjo Tio* (1980), on traditional inheritance, and Kozoloa's *Petangin* (1983), on corruption.

More recently, **Sijiri Bakaba**, a prominent actor who appeared in dozens of regional films including Sembène's *Camp de Thiaroye*, directed *Les Guerrisseurs* (1988), a highly popular venture that featured stars of television and music. **Kitia Touré** has won acclaim for his feature *Ça n'arrive qu'ux autres* (1991), a film on Aids.

NIGER

Nigérien cinema has been dominated by three film-makers. **Oumarou Ganda** began his career as an actor in Jean Rouch's *Moi, un Noir*, after he was discovered by the noted French *cinéaste* on the docks in Abidjan. After appearing in other Rouch films, notably *La pyramide humaine*, he went on to become a film-maker in his own right and one of the great cultural archivists of African cinema, with works such as the autobiographical *Cabascabo*, *Wazzou polygame* (1971), *Saitane* (1973) – which looks critically at the authority of the Muslim marabouts – and *L'Exilé*. In 1981, he died unexpectedly at the age of 46, while filming his last work, *Gani Kouré, le vainqueur de Gourma*. Reflecting a distribution problem faced by most contemporary African film-makers, you're more likely to see his works abroad or possibly at Niamey's Franco-Nigérien Cultural Centre than in any ordinary Nigérien movie theatre.

Jean Rouch also inspired another relatively well-known film-maker, **Moustapha Alassane**. After studying at the Institut Nigérien de Recherche en Sciences Humaines, Alassane made a number of shorts, including *Aouré* (1962), and *La Bague du Roi Koda* (1963). His most famous feature film is *Femme, Villa, Voiture, Argent* (1972) a popular comedy dealing with the issue of cultural identity.

The third director to gain international acclaim is **Djingary Maïga**, producer of *l'Etoile Noire*, in which he also starred. Like many early African film-makers, Djingary's movies deal with the clash between Western values and traditional wisdom.

GHANA

The wave of productivity that swept the Francophone countries generally bypassed the English-speaking states, only two of which – Ghana and Nigeria – have gone beyond government-sponsored documentaries to create an independent cinema. In Ghana, independent film-makers began producing features that combined comedy and melodrama.

Ghana is the best equipped of the West African states and the government branches of the film industry have left their mark on some of the country's top film-makers. The documentary style of the state-run Ghana Film Industry Corporation, for example, has influenced the style of such well-known directors as **Sam Aryete** (*No Tears for Ananse*, 1968), **King Ampaw** (*They Call It Love*, 1972; *Kukurantumi*, 1983 and *Juju*, 1986), **Kwate Nee Owo** (*You Hide Me*, 1971; *Struggle for Zimbabwe*, 1974; and *Angela Davis*, 1976), and **Kwaw Ansah** (*Love Brewed in the African Pot*, 1981).

Ghana's film industry does not rely on state funding and some of the best-known filmmakers finance their projects through local and international backing. Kwaw Ansah, for example, produced his latest film, *Heritage Africa* – which won the grand prize at the 1989 FESPACO – with the backing of the Ghana Commercial Bank, the National Investment Bank and other financial institutions. The films of these more independent directors have produced a good box-office return both in and outside Ghana. *Love Brewed in the African Pot*, for example, conveys its narrative through musical performances, wedding ceremonies and sports events – all popular with African audiences – and drew record attendances not only in Ghana, but also in Sierra Leone, Liberia, Kenya and Nigeria.

NIGERIA

Francis Oladele was one of the producers of Nigeria's first film, *Kongi's Harvest*, based on the play by Wole Soyinka. He also co-produced *Bullfrog in the Sun*, adapted from Chinua Achebe's novels *Things Fall Apart* and *No Longer at Ease*. Because of the sensitive political subject matter, this latter film was never properly distributed in Nigeria.

The director **Eddie Ugbomah** also draws his inspiration from current political events but turns them into Hollywood-style popular movies. In *The Rise and Fall of Dr Oyenusi* (1977), he considers the true story of a Lagos gangster who was arrested and publicly executed in the early 1970s. *The Mask* (1979) follows the adventures of a Nigerian secret agent sent to Britain to take back a Benin mask stolen by the British and housed in a London museum. *The Death of a Black President* (1983) treated the events that led to the traumatizing assassination of the popular General Murtala Muhammed.

Other Nigerian directors include the late **Hubert Ogunde** whose films, such as *Aiye* (with Ola Balogun) and its sequel *Jaiyesinmi*, often deal with witchcraft or with the significance of tradition. Ogunde set up a "film village" at Ijebu Ososa near Lagos, to encourage Nigerian film-makers. And in the field of comedy, **Moses Olaiya** – better known as Baba-Sala – is a new arrival from the world of Nigerian TV, now making a name for himself in cinema with films like *Orun Mooru* (It's not easy) and *Mosebolatan* (I thought my wealth was finished).

The most prolific film-maker in West Africa is Nigeria's **Ola Balogun**, who has released a steady stream of documentaries and feature films since the early 1970s. His 1975 production of *Amadi* was the first film in the Igbo language, while the 1976 *Ajani Ogun* was the first in Yoruba.

Yoruba cinema emerged in the early 1970s out of the Yoruba theatre tradition (see p.1011). Its success was partly due to the huge home market – over twenty million Yoruba-speaking Nigerians in the southwest of the country – though films in mother-tongue languages are still a novelty in Africa. In 1978, Balogun's film, *Black Goddess*, dealt with the African-Brazilians who returned to Nigeria after being freed from slavery. But some of Balogun's biggest hits in Nigeria draw their inspiration directly from Yoruba popular theatre. In 1976, *Ajani Ogun* starred one of the country's top theatre performers, **Ade Folayan**, in a story about a young man who runs up against a conniving rich buffoon as he struggles to keep both his fiancée and his inheritance. The popularity of *Ajani Ogun* led to *Ija Ominira* (1977), a popular tale of a tyrannical king in which Ade Folayan again starred. Outside Africa, films such as *Cry Freedom* (1981) and *Money Power* (1982) secured Balogun's international reputation.

CAMEROON

Jean-Paul Ngassa was one of the pioneers of Cameroonian cinema with his production of *Aventures en France* in 1962, followed by *La Grand Case Bamilékeé* in 1965. After *Une Nation est Née*, in 1970, Cameroonian production went into a lull until **Daniel Kamwa** brought a new spark with his 1972 prize-winning short *Boubou Cravatte*. The 1977 production of *Pousse Pousse* – a comical look at the conflict between traditional customs and modern urban lifestyles as expressed through the issue of bride price – established him as a producer with wide public appeal, even if the movie got a mediocre reception in Europe. *Pousse Pousse* was seen by some 700,000 movie-goers, making it one of the most popular African films of the period. The success was followed by *Notre Fille* in 1980.

During the same period **Jean Pierre Dikongue-Pipa** began making waves. *Muno Moto*, made in 1975, won encouraging reviews in France although it was hardly as popular at home as *Pousse Pousse*. Pipa's other productions include *Prix de la Liberté* (1978), *Badiaga* (1983), and *Music Music* (1983).

Although Kamwa and Dikongue-Pipa are still the best-known Cameroonian producer/directors, a new generation seems to be emerging. After studying at the *Ecole Supérieure d'Etudes Cinématographiques* in Paris, **Louis Balthazar Amadangoleda** made his first full-length film, *Les trois petits cireurs*, in 1985. Based on the novel of the same name by Francis Bebey, it looks at delinquency and its consequences.

A former professor of literature, **Arthur Si Bita** turned to film in 1978 and made a couple of shorts, including *No Time to Say Goodbye* shot in Ouagadougou. His first feature-length film, *Les Cooperants*, traces the adventures of six youths from the city who decide to return to the village.

With his first feature-length film, *L'Appat du Gain* (1982), **Jules Takam** breaks away from common themes of bride price, marriage and traditional custom and offers instead a fast-paced political intrigue based in Paris.

Jean-Claude Tchuilen came out with a promising first feature film in 1984 – *Suicides* – a well-paced psycho-drama, also set in Paris. It was banned for being inflammatory when first released in Cameroon and never bounced back commercially after the ban was lifted.

Of the new generation, **Jean-Marie Teno** is considered one of the brightest prospects. Early shorts – *Schubbah* (1984), *Hommage* (1985), and *La caresse et la gifle* (1987) – earned him acclaim, but his feature, *Afrique, Je te Plummerai* (1991), thrust him into the spotlight.

A documentary on the abuses of the Biya government, the film was one of the most popular releases after the 1993 FESPACO.

Critics are also keeping an eye on **Jean-Pierre Bekolo**, who directed his first feature, *Quartier Mozart* (1992), at the age of 25. The imaginative story treats a young girl with magical gifts who transforms herself into a virile male, Mister Guy, and has a lot of fun with gender roles in the process. Bekolo's background in music video, producing and directing for the likes of Manu Dibango, is on show with his quick and unconventional camera work.

RECOMMENDED FILMS

The following filmography provides a good overview of the styles and interests of African filmmakers over the last four decades.

Kwaw P Ansah *Love Brewed in the African Pot* (Ghana, 1981). In English. Comedy, social satire and commercial success – a big hit across Anglophone Africa.

Ola Balogun *Ajani Ogun* (Nigeria, 1976) in Yoruba. A comedy, based on a man's struggle to keep both his inheritance and his fiancée, derived from Yoruba theatre.

Jean-Pierre Bekolo *Quartier Mozart* (Cameroon, 1992). New social realism, up-beat and hip, with a style influenced by both oral tradition and music video.

Ferid Boughedir *Camera d'Afrique: 20 Years of African Cinema* (Morocco, 1983). A valuable documentary and early evaluation of film on the continent. Contains interviews with Ola Balogun, Oumarou Ganda, Souleymane Cissé, Gaston Kaboré, Ousmane Sembène and others, along with extracts of important films.

Souleyman Cissé *Yeelen* ("Brightness", Mali, 1987), in Bamana with English subtitles. A coming-of-age story rooted in oral tradition.

Henri Duparc *Bal Poussière* (Côte d'Ivoire, 1988). A comic investigation of polygamy's social consequences.

Gaston Kaboré *Wend Kuuni* (Burkina, 1982), in the More language with English subtitles, portrays a boy's traumatic experiences after losing his family. *Zan Boko* ("Homeland", 1988), in More with English subtitles, shows how modern culture subverts traditional society.

Djibril Diop Mambety *Touki Bouki* ("The Hyena's Journey", Senegal, 1973) in Wolof with English subtitles. An avant-garde film that remains true to the narrative structure of traditional storytelling while breaking the conventions of film structure.

Idrissa Ouédraogo *Yaaba* (Burkina, 1988) in the More language. A classic of the "back to the roots" genre.

Ousmane Sembène *Mandabi*, ("The Money Order", Senegal, 1967). The first West African film to be distributed commercially outside Africa, this film marks the beginning of an era. *Xala* (1974) in French and Wolof, is an allegorical tale of corruption that succinctly combines many important motifs of African film.

Cheik Oumar Sissoko *Finzan* ("A Dance for the Heroes", Mali, 1989) in Bamana with English subtitles. Socially engaged storytelling dedicated to the status of African women. *Guimba* (Mali, 1994) is an award-winning film about power and arrogance.

BOOKS

Manthia Diawara *African Cinema: Politics and Culture* (Indiana University Press, 1992). One of the leading voices in African film criticism outlines the key figures in African cinema, their works, and the complex relationship between politics, economics, and culture.

Paul Stoller *The Cinematic Griot: The Ethnography of Jean Rouch* (University of Chicago Press, 1992). A re-evaluation of the prolific and controversial ethnographer and of his impact on West African cinema.

Nwachukwu Frank Ukadike *Black African Cinema* (University of California Press, 1994). A historical overview of African film from early colonial works to the new generation.

JOURNALS

Black Film Review (PO Box 18655, Washington DC 20036). An excellent quarterly magazine devoted to film-makers throughout the diaspora. Special issues on African cinema.

Ecrans d'Afrique (International Quarterly of African Film, COE, Communicazione & Media, via Lazaroni 8, 20124 Milan, Italy). The official publication of the Pan-African Federation of Film-makers, in French with full English translations.

Black Film Bulletin (21 Stephen Street, London W1P 1PL; ☎0171/255-1444). The British Film Institute's quarterly on black cinema and film-makers.

FILM AND VIDEO RENTALS

In the USA, screenings of African films except in special festivals are extremely rare, and even the classics are virtually impossible to find in most video stores. Groups or individuals can, however, rent or buy films and videocassettes from the **California Newsreel** (149 9th St, San Francisco, CA 94103; ☎415/621-6196; Fax 415/621-6522). Their catalogue lists an impressive collection, including all of the most important films produced in the last thirty years.

For documentary works about Africa, **Films for the Humanities and Sciences** (PO Box 2053, Princeton NJ 0853-2053; ☎0800/257-5126; Fax 609/275-3767) distributes a reasonable collection of short films on video.

In London, the **African Video Centre** (7 Balls Pond Rd, Dalston, London N1 4AX; ☎0171/923-4224) can oblige. They're particularly hot on Yoruba releases and music videos but also have a full range of Francophone and subtitled films.

FILM INDEX

Further brief accounts of cinema and its theatrical antecedents can be found under:

Burkina Faso p.699
Ghana p.766
Guinea p.477
Mali p.305
Mauritania p.103
Niger p.951
Nigeria p.1011
Senegal p.161
Sierra Leone p.542

MUSIC IN WEST AFRICA: AN INTRODUCTION TO THE FEAST

Nowhere in the world can match the rhythm, melody and musical colour of West Africa. You can hardly fail to come back with at least one tune in your head, and probably a handful of tapes in your luggage.

The question is: where to start? You'll usually hear the cassette stalls when you arrive in any town, and if you want to meet local musicians you'll often find artists glad to play if you can pay something. Your interest may surprise people, so let them know!

Notices about dances and concerts are often posted up but they're most likely to take place around the end of the month – when people have some money in their pockets – and at public holidays, epecially Christmas and Muslim feasts.

This introduction to West African music kicks off with a section on Manding music, the sound of much of the western part of West Africa, particularly Mali and Guinea. This is followed by short pieces on Tuareg, Hausa and Fula music. These, like influential Manding, easily transcend national boundaries. There then follows a country-by-country roundup of national styles and artists, of Mauritania, Senegal and The Gambia, Sierra Leone, Liberia, Côte d'Ivoire, Burkina Faso, Ghana, Togo, Benin, Niger, Nigeria and Cameroon.

"+" indicates a CD release. If there's no "+" it means the entry is only available on vinyl or tape.

The division in several of the country sections into "folk" and "modern" categories is somewhat arbitrary – and much of what you might hear played by local musicians is likely to fall somewhere in between – but it serves as a useful cut-off point. "Folk", embedded in traditional society, whose artists don't as a rule have record deals or tour Europe, includes much that's disappearing; "modern" includes the whole gamut of recording artists, most with devoted local followings. But it also includes a number of styles and performers tearing away from their roots in the attempt to present music that stands alone.

THE REALM OF MANDING MUSIC

"Manding" music is about sweet melodies and hypnotic rhythms. You'll find this broad genre from The Gambia to Mali and down through Guinea – an area roughly corresponding to the spread of the Mande languages. The music of the Mande-speaking peoples (the Malinké, Mandinka, and a number of others; see p.85) is largely untouched by Western influences and has a swingalong quality, to which you can either dance or daydream.

Manding musicians are easy enough to track down. Only certain families – notably Konté or Konteh, Kouyaté or Kuyateh and Diabaté or Jobarteh (note the French/English variations) carry the title of **jali** or hereditary musician, often called a **griot** in French. They have been around since at least the thirteenth-century origins of the Mali empire, based in the northeast of what is now Guinea, under Emperor **Sundiata Keita**. Traditionally, the **kora** – a harp-lute – and most other instruments are restricted to them.

A jali's reputation is built upon humility and correct behaviour as well as his knowledge of history and family genealogies. Originally, the job was to do with the preservation of oral history. Mostly, this meant singing the praises of the noble and wealthy (no occasion – a wedding or child-naming ceremony for example – would be complete without a jali), but now they're just as likely to have business or civil service patrons. Jalis, moreover, are personalities who have the ears of the people and any corrupt politician or civil servant has to reckon with them.

Jalis call on a great **repertoire of songs**. If you have the chance to hear a number of artists, however, you'll start to recognize lyrical variations on common melodic themes. Classic songs like "Sundiata Faso", "Tutu Jara", "Lambang", "Koulanjan", "Duga", "Tara" and "Sori" are heard time and time again, interspersed with songs from this century, often with a regional flavour, such as "Alla l'aa ke" from The Gambia and "Kaira" from Mali. A jali's skill lies in the improvised flourishes and ornamentation – the *birimintingo* – that he brings to the recurrent theme or core melody, called the *donkili*.

In Mande-speaking society **men** always play the instruments. **Women artists** are considered the better singers and often receive extraordinary gifts, especially in Mali – planes and houses aren't unknown. Even at "ordinary" live shows, women commonly receive gold. Moved by a particular song, people in the audience just shed their jewellery there and then.

Traditional Manding music is a lasting influence on the modern music of Mali and Guinea. **Mory Kanté**, **Salif Keita** and **Kasse Mady** all derive artistic sustenance from it, and popular bands like **Bembeya Jazz** and **Les Amazones** reinterpret Manding songs.

THE MANDING JALIS

Some of the great jalis of the Manding region are introduced below, though there are many other, almost equally famous, kora musicians and female singers.

• **Dembo Konteh and Kausu Kouyaté** Although there are hundreds of wonderful jalis in the region, Dembo and Kausu are, after numerous tours, probably the best known overseas. Dembo is the son of the late great **Alhaji Bai Konteh**, one of The Gambia's most revered jalis, several of whose albums are available.

+***Alhaji Bai Konteh*** *Alhaji Bai Konteh* (Rounder, USA). Atmospheric 1972 recordings made at the Konteh home in Brikama. The Gambia's finest exponent of Casamance-style kora, with bluesy tuning and lightning-fast variations.

• **Sidiki Diabaté**, from Mali, toured with his ensemble in 1987, when they recorded a beautiful LP, *Ba Togoma*, which features the talents of **Kandia Kouyaté, Djelimadi Sissoko, Mariama Kouyaté** and Sidiki's son, **Toumani** – who has also made a name for himself as a soloist, with an album of solo kora, *Kaira*.

+***Toumani Diabaté*** *Kaira* (Hannibal, UK). Instrumental solo kora music at its finest, including melodies like "Alla l'aa ke" and "Jarabi". Toumani has worked widely with non-African musicians, including the unconventional flamenco band, Ketama, and Danny Thompson on *Songhai* and *Songhai 2*. His latest is *Djelika* (Rykodisc, UK).

• **Sékou Batourou Kouyaté**, probably the most famous of all Malian kora players, was born about 1920 in Kita. Entirely self-taught, he evolved a unique, highly staccato style and went on to make his reputation as the accompanist to the singer Fanta Damba. His collaboration with Sidiki Diabaté resulted in the first instrumental record of kora music and an all-time classic, still available on market-cassette copies – *Cordes Anciennes* (1970).

• **Jali Musa Jawara** made one of the all-time classic African albums, repeatedly re-released under different titles.

+***Jali Musa Jawara*** *Yasimika* (Hannibal, UK). First prize for the most-released kora recording: formerly issued as *Jali Musa Jawara* by Tangent (France, 1983); as *Fote Mogoban* on Oval (UK, 1986); then as *Direct from West Africa* (Go Discs, UK) before its current release. Fully justified attention for a superb, ethereal, all-acoustic guitar, kora and balafon set, with luscious choruses (Djanka Diabaté and Djenné Doumbia) and soaring vocals from JMJ.

• **Tata Bambo Kouyaté** is one of Mali's leading female vocalists. She claims that everything she has – and she has a lot – came to her because of her voice. She's one of the new breed of jalis who travel between patrons with a portable PA system.

+***Tata Bambo Kouyaté*** *Jatigui* (GlobeStyle, UK). Stunning praise-singing from 1985 by one of Mali's most accomplished female artists. Entirely acoustic accompaniment from the full range of instruments, plus Fulani flute.

MODERN MALIAN MUSIC

Mali's music is steeped in tradition. Even in the modern popular music there's very little influence from cultures outside Mali. The musics of the Mande-speaking Bamana and Malinké, Fula, Songhai and Dogon have all helped to give today's Malian music its flavour and colour.

After **independence**, there was a renaissance of popular music in Mali. The bands, who had for many years been playing latin styles, became aware that people wanted to hear music from their own cultures. The government supported this search for roots and a number of groups received state sponsorship. Orchestras were at last able to afford modern instruments. "Janfa", a popular song of the time, recorded by the **Orchestre National Formation "A"**, made a plea to people not to betray their traditions.

One of the most famous venues in Mali is the **Buffet Hôtel de la Gare** in Bamako, a venue which emerged from the hotel's quest for financial salvation. The director of Mali's state railway in the 1960s, **Djibril Diallo**, was crazy about music and decided to create a station orchestra. The *Buffet Hôtel* soon became the hottest spot in Bamako and the **Rail Band**, as they became known, rapidly acquired legendary status, mixing plaintive vocal styles over traditional Manding rhythms played with electric instruments.

Over the years the Rail Band – still going today – has provided a launch pad for many talented musicians, including **Salif Keita** and **Mory Kanté**. There are two highly recommended Rail Band albums in the **Mali Stars** series.

• **Salif Keita** has become huge in Europe – his album, **Soro**, has sold over 100,000 copies in Europe alone. An albino, Salif Keita started out singing in bars for loose change, evidently to the disgrace of his family. In 1970 he joined the Rail Band, which gave him an opportunity to modernize traditional songs. After being ousted from the *Buffet Hôtel* by the then balafon (xylophone) player Mory Kanté, Salif joined the **Ambassadeurs** – who had immediate success with hits like "Primpin" – and recorded three albums for Safari Ambience. In 1978 he moved to Abidjan and, with **Kanté Manfila**, formed **Ambassadeurs Internationaux**, who recorded the wonderful song "Mandjou" – dedicated, ironically, to the despotic ruler of Guinea, Sekou Touré. Then he left for Paris, international stardom and outer space with the high-tech *Soro*, *Ko-Yan* and *Amen* albums.

• **Kasse Mady Diabaté**, one of the leading vocalists of modern Manding music, made his name playing with **National Badema** for twelve years. There's a great album from this period – part of the Mali Stars series released by Syllart. Kasse Mady's latest album, *Fode* has seen a move into the big sound of Paris production but the next promises a return to more traditional Malinké roots. Keyla, where Kasse Mady Diabaté was born, is a Malinké village in the west of Mali, almost entirely inhabited by jalis of the **Diabaté** family.

• **Super Biton de Ségou** have been around since the early 1960s – when they were one of the state-payrolled regional bands – under the leadership of trumpeter **Amadu Ba**. They successfully transferred Bamana sound onto guitars and horns.

+***Super Biton de Ségou*** *Afro-Jazz du Mali* (Bolibana, France). Hard-hitting early 1980s recording of Bamana music by the pioneering roots band.

• **Zani Diabaté and the Super Djata band** follow in the Super Biton tradition and are much appreciated in Mali. Although from a famous jali family, Zani draws inspiration for his rhythms from the songs of Bamana hunters and Bozo fishermen and laces it with Peul and Manding melodies and an almost psychedelic, Hendrix-style guitar. Although the group have been around since 1969 there's only one album available, released in 1985 on the French Milady label and three years later by Mango, the wonderful *Fadinga Kouma*, which introduces the *balo* to electric instruments. You may find other albums in Senegal or Mali: the *Black Album* – much less refined than the European LP – is worth hearing.

• **Ali Farka Touré** is an oddity, as he'd be the first to admit. Not from one of the traditional families of hereditary musicians, he started playing purely for his own pleasure and doing so in a style which – although he had never heard the Blues until he was already firmly established – resonates with American Blues affinities. He caused a sensation when he came to Europe in the late 1980s. One of a kind and never to be repeated.

+***Ali Farka Touré*** *The River* (World Circuit, UK). Guests on this part-electric set include

Rory McLeod, Chieftains Sean Keane and Kevin Conneff, and Steve Williamson.

+***Ali Farka Touré & Ry Cooder*** *Talking Timbuktu* (World Circuit, UK). A World Music record out of left field that actually sounds like people playing together in a room – a miracle of 1994 and top of many of the indie charts within days of release.

GUINEAN FOLK MUSIC

Traditional music in Guinea can be roughly divided into four areas. In the lowland coastal forest of the west the musics of the Mande-speaking **Susu** and **Jalonke** are related to the **Manding** tradition. The Fouta Djalon highlands of the centre and north are mainly inhabited by the **Fula** (see separate account). In the northern Fouta Djalon, near the frontier with Senegal, the **Konyagi** people play a variety of wind instruments, including long, bamboo flutes, short flutes (usually played in pairs), and a stick-zither, similar to a mouth bow.

The eastern savannah, towards the Niger River, is mainly occupied by the **Malinké**, whose cultural domain spreads into eastern Mali. But the Guinean Malinké use a number of instruments not usually associated with Manding tradition (though possibly more traditional, as this is the area where the Mali empire first emerged) including **slit-drums** (usually a hollowed log with a single longitudinal gash). **Ground bows** (in which a hollow in the earth acts as the soundboxs, are now only used as child's toys.

In Guinea's southeast highland forest region the **Kissi**, **Toma**, **Guerze** and **Kono** use single- and double-headed drums, slit-drums and xylophone-drums. Xylophone-drums are made either from hollowed logs or from bamboo stems, slit to produce vibrating "keys" of different lengths.

MODERN GUINEAN MUSIC

With independence in 1958 and Sékou Touré's *Authenticité* campaign, the government actively encouraged the development of modern musical styles, based on traditional music, but using electric instruments. Local radio was directed to play authentic Guinean music, and state-sponsored national festivals became a focus for the new Guinean sound.

Many new bands were formed, including **Bembeya Jazz**, **Les Balladins** and **Les Amazones**. The Guinean label, Syliphone, reissued some of these albums in the late 1980s. Three well worth listening to are the **Tropical Djoli Band**, **Orchestre Nimba Jazz** and, especially, **Tele-Jazz de Télimélé**.

+***Balla et ses Balladins*** *Reminiscin' in Tempo with...* (World Circuit, UK; Popular African Music, Germany). A compilation album of greats by one of the top regional bands, with the old-time rumba-sound of the 1960s and 70s. Includes two superb examples of the love song "Sara".

• **Bembeya Jazz** were formed in 1961 by singer **Aboubacar Demba Camera**. They mixed Malinké praise songs with Congolese musical threads and Islamic traditions with Cuban rumba. The death in 1973 of Aboubacar Camera robbed Africa of one of its greatest singers. The band is now led by lead guitarist, **Sekou "diamond fingers" Diabate**.

+***Bembeya Jazz*** *Live – 10 Ans de Succès* (Bolibana, France). Atmospheric recording from 1971 of Guinea's most famous band at their finest hour. Wild solos from "diamond fingers" Diabaté measure up to the unforgettable voice of Aboubacar Demba Camera.

• **Les Amazones de Guinée**, also formed in 1961, featured between fifteen and twenty female musicians – all of them supposedly members of the Guinean police force. An album is available on Syliphone, *Au Coeur de Paris*.

• **Mory Kanté** started playing music at the age of seven, later joining the Rail Band in Bamako before embarking on a stupendously successful solo career playing what he describes as **kora funk**. Loathed by purists, his music has a global village feel that makes him a star of the world stage. He still plays the occasional solo kora piece as part of his stage show and he played the instrument on **Kanté Manfila**'s *Tradition*.

+***Mory Kanté*** *10 Cola Nuts* (Barclay, France). Heavy on the drum kit and synth, but this includes some fine material, including the beautiful "Teriya". *Akwaba Beach* (Barclay, France) was his breakthrough album, with his dance floor-shaking version of "Yeke Yeke".

+***Kanté Manfila*** (Manfila Kanté) *Diniya* (Sonodisc, France). Some fine melodies buried beneath a full-blown, high tech production. His earlier *Tradition* (Mélodie, France), with its lovely rolling Kankan melodies and kora by cousin Mory, proves what a fine carrier of that tradition he is.

TRADITIONAL INSTRUMENTS OF WESTERN WEST AFRICA

MANDING INSTRUMENTS

Kora 21-stringed harp-lute made with a large decorated half-gourd covered with a skin. The strings – which used to be twisted leather, but tend now to be various gauges of fishing line – are attached with leather thongs to a rosewood pole put through the gourd. The top of the body has a large sound hole that doubles as a collection point for money from the audience.

Balo Rosewood xylophone with between 17 and 20 keys, known to have been around since the fourteenth century.

Kontingo Small, oval lute with 5 strings.

Bolom (or *bolombato*) Lute with 3 or 4 strings and an arched neck that used to be played for warriors going into battle. It's now an instrument played by men who are not jalis.

MAURITANIAN INSTRUMENTS

Tidinit Lute with 2 long strings on which the melody is played, and 2 short ones which give a fixed drone-like rhythm; played by men.

Ardin 10- to 14-stringed women's harp.

Tbol Large kettledrum.

Daghumma Less common, a slender, hollowed-out gourd with a necklace, which acts as a rattle.

SENEGAMBIAN INSTRUMENTS

The most widespread instruments are plucked **lutes**, known generically in Wolof as *khalem* or *xalam*.

Molo The most common variety, a single-string lute with a half-gourd, skin-covered soundbox.

Diassare 5-stringed, roughly boat-shaped lute with a carved wooden soundbox.

Bappe and **ndere**, often played as a pair, are similar to the *diassare*.

Riti Single-stringed Wolof lute played with a bow.

Gnagnour The Tukulor *riti*.

Paly-yela Sets of gourds of different shapes and sizes, bumped on the ground to produce different notes and tones to accompany Tukulor women's songs.

Tama Small, hourglass-shaped talking drum, which produces an amazing series of tones.

Sabar Large, free-standing cylindrical drums.

TUAREG FOLK MUSIC

The Tuareg have put up with a somewhat embattled existence over the past decade. Drought in the early 1980s pushed them away from a nomadic lifestyle and towards the towns at the edge of the desert. And then in the early 1990s a simmering Tuareg uprising took place against the military regimes in Mali and Niger.

Although Tuareg men and women both make music, they have separate forms and styles. Women's songs include **tinde nomnas** (praise songs), **tinde nguma** (songs of exorcism) and **ezele** (dance songs). The **tinde**, used to accompany women's songs, is a drum made from a goatskin stretched over a mortar.

Other instruments used by women include the **assakhalebo** water drum, made from a half-gourd floating upside down in a bowl of water, and the **tabl** – a kettledrum (traditionally a battle drum) with a broad camel-skin top.

The men's songs, or **tichiwe**, are, in striking contrast to the women's, essentially lyrical. They sing about the beauty of the women they love or celebrate some happy event. The songs are performed by soloists – whose virtuosity lies as ever in improvisation – either with or without an accompaniment. This is usually provided by a single-stringed fiddle, the **inzad**, which consists of a half-gourd, goatskin-covered resonator and a horsehair string stretched over a bridge in the form of a small wooden cross.

The Tuareg also use an end-blown **flute**, called the *sarewa*, constructed from a sorghum stem in which four holes are made, with leather thongs tied round its body for ornamentation and protection.

HAUSA MUSIC

The **Hausa**, whose communities are concentrated in the cities of Niger and northern Nigeria, have spread right across West and Central Africa, setting up shops in the smallest towns, content to live among strangers. They have long been famous for their art and music which has flourished since the sixteenth century and the fall of the Songhai empire, with whose music Hausa has many parallels.

Hausa music splits into **urban music** of the court and state, and **rural music**. State ceremonial state music – *rokon fada* – still plays a great part (though not a very musical one) in Hausa traditions, while court praise singers still play for the amusement of emirs and sultans, usually in private. The emirates of **Katsina** and **Kano** together with the sultanate of **Sokoto**, and to a lesser extent **Zaria** and **Bauchi** (all in Nigeria), are the major creative centres.

The instruments of **ceremonial music** are largely seen as prestige symbols of authority, and ceremonial musicians tend to be chosen for their family connections rather than any musical ability: they don't present the most dulcet of tones. **Court musicians**, on the other hand, are always chosen for their musical skills. Exclusively dependent on a single wealthy patron, it's hardly surprising that the most talented players are rarely seen in public. The greatest praise singer was **Narambad**, who lived and worked in Sokoto; he died in 1960 and it's doubtful if you can still get his recordings.

The most impressive of the state **instruments** is the elongated state trumpet called **kakakai**, which was originally used by the Songhai cavalry and was taken by the rising Hausa states as a symbol of military power. *Kakakai* are usually accompanied by **tambura**, large state drums. Lesser instruments include the **farai**, a small double-reed woodwind instrument, the **kafo**, an animal horn, and the **ganga**, a small snare drum. Ceremonial music can always be heard at the **sara**, the weekly statement of authority which takes place outside the emir's palace on a Thursday evening.

The principal instruments accompanying praise songs are percussive – small kettledrums, **banga** and **tabshi**, and talking drums, **jauje** and **kotso**.

Traditional **rural music** appears to be dying out in favour of modern popular music which still draws inspiration from the traditional roots. The last expressions of rural music are to be found in traditional dances like the **asauwara**, for young girls, and the **bori**, the dance of the spirit possession cult, which dates back to a time before Islam became the accepted religion and continues to thrive parallel with the teachings of the Koran. Zaria is the main stronghold of the *bori*.

Popular music thrives in town and countryside and although very little seems to be of interest outside Hausaland, musicians can still make a good living satisfying local needs and, as ever, expressing, and sometimes moulding, public opinion. The leading Hausa singer, **Muhamman Shata**, is always accompanied by a troupe of virtuoso drummers who play **kalangu**, small talking drums. There's a fair number of other worthy artists such as **Dan Maraya**, leading exponent on the *kontigi* one-stringed lute, **Ibrahim Na Habu**, who popularized a type of small fiddle called the **kukkuma**, and **Audo Yaron Goge** who plays (not surprisingly) the **goge** or fiddle.

There are two excellent records available on Barenreiter Musicaphon.

FULA MUSIC

The Fula are commonly called Fulani in Nigeria where they form a large and powerful community. This name has tended to be used as the standard form in English. The same people, however, are Fullah in Sierra Leone, Peul or Peulh in Senegal and Mali, and Pulaar in Mauritania. Nomadic Fula-speaking groups in Niger include the Bororo and the Wodaabe, while in Senegal, the Tukulor are a Fula-speaking ethnic group who have been Muslims for nearly a thousand years.

With their wide geographical distribution and considerable cultural diversity (most fundamentally between the traditional cattle herders – the Fula stereotype – and the urban communities) it's hard to generalize about **Fula music**. There are, however, two distinct genres. The first is pure Fula music, composed and played by them or their recognized professional musicians; the second consists of the hymns and songs which, though mostly still in the Fula language, have been passed down and evolved from the Islamic tradition.

TRADITIONS AND INSTRUMENTS

There are three **classes of professional musician** in Fula society. The **wammbaabe** and the **maabube** were, and in some cases still are, court musicians, singing the praises of chiefs and wealthy patrons and telling tales of their ancestors and epic stories of the Fula past. The **awlube** are less closely associated with the court and more often found praising and entertaining the people in general, using a wider frame of reference and a wider range of **instruments**. The instrument used most by the *wammbaabe* and *maabube* is the **hoddu**, a three-stringed lute. The *wammbaabe* also play the **nyaanyooru**, a one-stringed fiddle. The *awlube* play everything, but their main instruments are drums.

In some areas – for example The Gambia, where Fula live in proximity to Mandinka – you also find a three- or four-stringed lute, the **bolon**, very similar to the Mandinka *bolombato*. At the other end of West Africa, in Cameroon, the instruments used in court music are similar to those used by the Hausa court musicians of Nigeria.

Professional troupes – and the Fula are famous for their bands of entertainers, which play in all communities – nearly always use at least one **percussion** instrument. The most common is the **horde**, a half-gourd vessel with a rattling metal plate attached inside. The player holds the open end towards his chest and beats the outside with his hands or uses rings on his fingers. The *horde* player is usually the acrobat of the troupe. Another percussive instrument is the **lala**, a pair of L-shaped stick-rattles. Each one has three or four calabash discs which move up and down on the stick.

Lastly, the **instruments of the pastoral Fula** – flutes of wood, bamboo or corn stalks, two-stringed lutes, single-stringed fiddles and jew's harps – are mainly played for their own enjoyment. They have a range of songs for pleasure, similar to that of many other African peoples – work songs, lullabies, love songs and herders' songs (often in praise of cattle, sung at them as they graze).

MODERN FULA SOUNDS – WASSOULOU

Of modern Fula music, try to hear **Dourah Barry** from Guinea, and the stunning voice of **Sali Sidibe** from the **Wassoulou** region of southwest Mali. The people of Wassoulou do not have jalis, and their music is based on an ancient tradition of hunters' songs, with pentatonic (five-note) melodies. This tends to be viewed as music played by people in their teens: only a few decades ago such songs were regarded as slightly subversive, and forbidden by the elders. Sali Sidibe uses traditional instruments like the *nyaanyooru* and *bolon*, which create a hypnotic bass beat, together with what sounds like a Casio keyboard complete with drum machine.

The best-known exponent of the Wassoulou sound is **Oumou Sangaré**, whose passionate style ("I sing of love, not praises") has shaken up the musical status quo in Mali, dominated, as it is, by the fat-cat jalis and Paris-based elite.

+***Oumou Sangaré*** *Ko Sira* (World Circuit, UK). A breath of fresh air from a young woman singer whose impact on traditional musical culture could hardly have been greater, wielding her voice like a weapon, and deploring, as she puts it, the male-dominated status quo. Beautifully produced, this is Wassoulou music at its best.

+***Various*** *The Wassoulou Sound: Women of Mali* and *The Wassoulou Sound: Vol. 2* (Stern's, UK). Excellent compilations featuring a range of female voices and Wassoulou styles, including the pioneers of "Wassoulou electric", Kagbe Sidibé and Coumba Sidibé. Buy the CDs as a set as the notes were written for both.

MAURITANIA

Until the ethnic conflict of 1989, it was easier to hear Mauritanian music in Senegal than in its homeland. This situation has now changed but it's still true that very little Mauritanian music is heard outside the region.

MAURITANIAN FOLK MUSIC

The professional musical caste in Mauritania are called **igaouen** or *iggiw*. In the past they depended, like the jalis, on the patronage of big men and nobles. The more flexible modern *igaouen* repertoire includes complex songs of Middle Eastern character and others simple enough to be taken up in chorus by the audience. The music is based on a sophisticated modal system – sometimes referred to as the "black and white ways" – derived from Arab musical theory.

There are a few **albums** of traditional music available: two of Ocora's feature the black and white ways on the double album *Hodh Oriental*, and a variety of sounds on *Musique Maure*. Three Safari Ambience albums featuring **Saidou Ba** – a musician who plays the *hodou* or African guitar in a bluesy style – are harder to find.

You may also see a group of performers led by **Dimi Mint Abba** and **Seidoum Ould Eide**, who made their first tour of the UK in 1989.

+***Seidoum Ould Eide & Dimi Mint Abba*** *Moorish Music from Mauritania* (World Circuit, UK). Beautiful and evocative. If you haven't seen them on tour then this goes some of the way to giving an insight to their special sound. Notice the flamenco-style hand-clapping.

MODERN MUSIC FROM MAURITANIA

There's very little **modern music** coming out of Mauritania, but one singer – **Tahra Mint Hembara** – is worth listening out for. Her eerie vocal style is given a funky backing on her only available release.

+***Tahra*** *Yamen Yamen* (EMI, France). Baffling album of Mooro-tech with Jean-Philippe Rykiel on synth. Strange mix but very intriguing, like Tahra Mint Hembara herself.

SENEGAL AND THE GAMBIA

Senegal and The Gambia share a common musical heritage and are heavily influenced by the traditions of the Mande heartland to the east. You're most likely to hear Wolof, Fula, Tukulor (Toucouleur) and Serer music north of the Gambia River, and Mandinka, Jola and Balanta music in The Gambia itself and the Casamance region of southern Senegal.

FOLK MUSIC OF SENEGAMBIA

In the south, listen out for the huge double xylophones or **balo** of the **Balanta**, played by two people facing each other. You may hear them, but you'll have difficulty seeing them, because they're invariably surrounded by a jostle of whooping and clapping women.

The best-known **drums** are the Wolof **tama** and **sabar** (both used to great effect by Youssou Ndour and his band). Drums of all shapes and sizes are in great abundance in the Senegambia region and are the only instruments that can be played by absolutely anyone. Wrestling matches are fine opportunities to hear some first-class drumming – in snatches. The wrestlers bring their own drummers to support them and the drum teams jog and pace around the arena, competing with each other with cacophonous dedication.

MODERN SENEGAMBIAN MUSIC

Modern music in the region is essentially Senegalese, largely because of the country's cultural domination of the tiny Gambia and the inevitable magnetism for musicians of Dakar's big audiences and serious money.

• The scene has been dominated for some years by the soaring voice of **Youssou Ndour** backed by his band, the **Super Etoile de Dakar**. **Youssou** plays **mbalax**, a style rooted in the Wolof tradition, featuring frenetic rhythms with bursts of *tama* (battered by **Assane Thiam**) and complex time signatures.

+***Youssou Ndour*** *Immigrés* (Earthworks/ Virgin, UK). The immigrants in question are Senegalese migrant workers in France. The track and the LP hinted at the international success to come. *Eyes Open* (Sony/Columbia, USA) is a rich and satisfying CD, with songs in Wolof, French and English. *The Guide* (Sony/ Columbia, USA) offers Youssou Ndour and the Super Etoile in mature, innovative mode, with collaborations both successful (Branford Marsalis) and successful but mushy (Neneh Cherry). There's also a cut-price introductory compilation CD, "Hey You!" (Music Club, UK).

+***Etoile de Dakar*** *Vols 1–10* (Stern's, UK). A major series of on-going releases, the collected works of one of Senegal's seminal bands, featuring Youssou Ndour. Near-essential.

• **Baaba Maal** is the rising star of Senegalese music. He sings in the Tukulor language (a dialect of Fula), accompanied by guitarist Mansour Seck and electric band **Dande Lenol** (which means "The Voice of the People").

+***Baaba Maal*** *Djam Leelii* (Rogue, UK). Playing acoustic guitar and singing with childhood friend, Mansour Seck, Baaba Maal interprets the traditional tunes and themes of the Senegal River region where he was born. This is music to be transported by. *Lam Toro* (Mango, UK) is the most personal of all Maal's albums, dedicated to his mother who died young but who remains the guiding spirit in all his art. The similarly packaged US version is subtitled "The Remix Album" and has the dubious benefit of geography lesson rapping from Macka B.

• **Orchestre Baobab** were formed in 1971 by saxophonist **Issi Cissokho** and vocalist **Laye M'Boup**. They were one of the first groups to use Wolof and Mandinka songs as the basis for electric music. World Circuit have released the legendary 1982 sessions, but if you find any other old Baobab tapes, buy them; you won't be disappointed.

+***Orchestre Baobab*** *Pirate's Choice* (World Circuit, UK). Blissfully good 1982 session from the best Senegalese band of the 1970s. How did they come up with these songs? *On Verra Ça* (World Circuit, UK) is almost as hot; *Bamba* (Stern's, UK) is definitely third choice.

• **Thione Seck**, the one-time singer with Baobab has been building a reputation in Europe for his rousing, up-tempo *mbalax*.

Thione Seck & le Raam Daan *UNESCO* (local cassette, Senegal). Offering the bravest *mbalax* in the business with almost hysterically up-tempo rhythms against his robust, measured vocals, Seck is a musician's musician par excellence. The LP-release, *Le Pouvoir d'un Coeur Pur* (Stern's, UK), is a good vehicle for his voice, most emotive on the silky ballad "Yeen", but the rhythms are less to the fore.

• **Super Diamono de Dakar** call their style Afro-feeling music. Quite different from *mbalax*, Super Diamono go for a much harder sound with heavy bass and powerful kit drums. Try to hear the early album, *Ndaxona*, which features the wailing vocals of **Omar Pene**.

Omar Pene & Super Diamono *Sai Sai* (Syllart, France). LP featuring strong *mbalax* beat with cheeky lyrics and the winning combination of Pene's dulcet tones and the Super Diamono sound. There's also a CD release available on Stern's, *Fari*.

• **Ismael Lô**, harmonica-player and guitarist, was a member of Super Diamono during their early days in the late 1970s. "Super Diamono's manager asked if I wanted to join them and go with them on tour. I was with them for four years. My pay was a packet of cigarettes a day, and if you wanted something like shoes or something, you asked the boss."

+***Ismael Lô*** *Diawar* (Stern's, UK). Features one of Lô's best tracks, "Sophia", a 1989 interpretation of the song "On Verra Ça" previously recorded by Orchestra Baobab. +*Tajabone* (Barclay, France) is a soulful and highly accessible excursion into a more commercial sphere.

SIERRA LEONE

Although relatively small, Sierra Leone has a rich variety of music and its influence, through the spread of people and ideas from Freetown over the last 200 years, has been large. Elements of early highlife can be traced back to the prewar Krio dance halls. Inland, a much less cosmopolitan scene still prevails: folk music is closely connected with dance, storytelling and drama. Praise songs are also widespread and one unusual characteristic is that male soloists tend to sing in a high register while women sing in low voices.

SIERRA LEONEAN FOLK MUSIC

To list the enormous number of Sierra Leonean **instruments** would take pages. **Thumb pianos** are common in the north, among the Temne, Limba and Loko. **Xylophones and lutes** are used in the north by the Susu, Mandingo, Yalunka, Temne and Koranko. A good selection of traditional music is available on the Ocora label.

MODERN MUSIC OF SIERRA LEONE

In popular music the two main styles, which developed during the Fifties, were acoustic guitar **palm-wine music** (music for drinking with) and **maringa**, a peculiarly Krio style. The *maringa* singer **Ebenezer Calender** was one of the most popular; he played guitar and trumpet and wrote all his own songs. While the Freetown recording industry died in the Seventies, a number of **dance bands** struggle on in concert parties and at public holidays and the odd hotel residence. Local percussive sounds are still popular, but today the best music is heard abroad.

+***Various*** *Sierra Leone Music* (Zensor, Germany). Lovingly packaged compilation of Krio and up-country tracks, recorded for the radio in Freetown in the 1950s and early 60s, a real collector's item. Excellent accompanying booklet.

• **SE Rogie**, the doyen of Sierra Leonean musical entertainers, picked up the trail led by two great guitarists, Ekundaio and Joboynor, and had hits in the 1960s all along the West African coast. He had sell-out gigs in Britain, too, shortly before his death in 1994, confirming the enduring appeal of his palm-wine style.

+***SE Rogie*** *Dead Men Don't Smoke Marijuana* (Real World, UK). The last outing by the ever-cool Sooliman is a delicious piece of music-cake – so long as you like his one tune, the basis of nearly all the tracks.

LIBERIA

Liberian music can be put into three rough and ready groups: music of the indigenous people, music from the freed slave tradition of repatriated Africans, and modern, more de-cultured, popular music. The "Congos" – people with connections with the freed slave heritage – sing a lot of religious music, which bears close comparison with American gospel.

Most indigenous Liberian peoples incorporate "music" within a broader term that describes an event involving music, dancing and celebration. The **Kpelle** call this the **pelee**, and its songs the **wule**. In traditional **Kpelle** and **Gio** culture, a wide variety of flutes, xylophones and drums are used. The coastal **Kru** people also play the guitar and may have been partly responsible for the creation of highlife guitar playing.

Liberian **pop music** was in a parlous state of disarray even before the war. It's hard to say what might be going on there now.

CÔTE D'IVOIRE

Côte d'Ivoire, with Abidjan's high-quality studios, has long been a musical centre for the Francophone states, but has very few international stars of its own. But Ivoirians have no lack of traditions to call upon. In the north the Senoufo and Lobi people are famous for their xylophone music; while in the centre and east, the Akan peoples – Baoulé, Abron, Agni, and Atié – together with the Bété of the southwest, have produced most of Côte d'Ivoire's popular musicians. All have strong, under-recognized, folk music heritages.

In the 1940s, there were **Akan street groups** who played a traditional dance called **Akpombo**. Gradually they started introducing guitars and accordions to their line-up. After independence it was these street groups that became the first popular dance bands. In the 1960s these bands would play cover versions of European and American hits over traditional rhythms like the Bété **gbegbe**. The best-known groups of the day were **Agnebi Jazz, Souers Comoé, Anoma Barou Felix** and, much later, **Ernesto Djedje**, who updated the Bété dance, the *ziglibithy*.

• **Gnaoré Djimi**'s fourteen-member band play an amazingly fast version of a traditional beat called *polihet*, a variation of *ziglibithy*.

+***Gnaoré Djimi*** *All Polihet Up* (GlobeStyle, UK). Forthcoming special: alternative title sought.

• **Zagazougou**'s local cassette release of their German recording surprised local industry bosses by outselling the slicker, Ivoirian electric bands.

+***Zagazougou*** *Zagazougou Coup* (Piranha, Germany). Ivory Coast unplugged, all accordions and percussion. Very, very fast.

• **Sery Simplice** is one the chief modernizers of *gbegbe* music and has made about a dozen records. Try to hear his second and third albums *Gbolou* and *Atrikakou*, on which he tells people to stop playing funk and reggae and listen to the sound of their own culture.

• **Alpha Blondy** has become one of West Africa's most successful musical exports with his form of reggae.

+***Alpha Blondy*** *Apartheid is Nazism* (Stern's, UK). Probably his best to date: a mostly on-target album from a sometimes very off-beam artist.

• **Daouda**, singer and composer, mixes Zairian *soukous* with Cameroonian *makossa* and local rhythms. He's recorded a string of albums in London and Paris.

Daouda *Le Sentimental* (Stern's, UK). Slick, slushy music from a superstar crooner. "La Femme de Mon Patron" (a massive hit all over West Africa, and later covered in English) is its one redeeming feature.

BURKINA FASO

Very little Burkinabe music reaches the ears of other West Africans, let alone Europeans. Yet the country has a rich

musical heritage and an annual percussion festival in Bobo-Dioulasso.

Various *Musiques du Pays Lobi* (Ocora, France). Side 1 is mostly xylophone music with sweet melodies; Side 2 more varied, with some Gan music for mouth bow and some nice Dagarti xylophone tracks.

Various *Musiques Bisa* (Ocora, France). Thumb pianos, fiddles, lutes, flutes and a wide range of percussion gear blended together under unique quavering vocals. Very interesting.

A few **traditional groups** have made tours of Europe. Dance is an important part of their acts so they tend to get booked at outdoor festivals.

- One such group is the **Coulibaly Twins** whose ethnic background is **Bobo Bwa** – Voltaic-speaking people from around Burkina's second largest (and nicest) town, Bobo-Dioulasso. They play together as a duo or as part of the renowned dance and music group the **Kouledafourour Band**.
- The other famous group is drum and dance troupe **Farafina**. They were formed in 1978 by **Mahama Konaté** (also from Bobo) who is rated one of the best balafon players in West Africa. Apart from the balafon they also use the *jembe, tama* (the Wolof hourglass drum), *bara* (calabash drums) and flutes.
- The only other major artist is **Hamidou Ouédraogo**, a Fula singer and accordionist, and master of the *Gumbe* dance. He has released two solo albums on Sonafric.

GHANA

Ghana's "town music" is well known abroad but the country has a strong tradition of rural music still commonly performed, which continues to influence urban sounds.

GHANAIAN FOLK MUSIC

The main types of music you can hear are **court music** played for chiefs, **ceremonial music** and **work songs** – and of course music for its own sake. It's probably clearest to explain traditions region by region.

Northeastern Ghana is home to a cluster of Voltaic-speaking peoples – best known of whom are the **Dagomba**, **Mamprusi** and **Frafra**. In this area you find mostly fiddles, lutes and wonderful hourglass talking-drum ensembles. It's customary for musicians to perform frequently for the local chief – in the Dagomba country each Monday and Friday. In towns like **Tamale** and **Yendi** you might find something going on, because professional musicians, although attached to chiefs, regularly perform for the general public. Dagomba drummers are always a great spectacle, their flowing tunics fanning out as, hands flying, they dance the *takai*.

In the northwest, the main instrument of the **Lobi**, **Wala**, **Dagarti** and **Sissala** is the xylophone – either played alone or with a small group of drums and percussion instruments. Finger bells and ankle bells are often worn by the dancers.

The **Ewe** are the main people of eastern Ghana. Their music is closer to the traditions of Togo and Benin than to that of other Ghanaian peoples and with their enthusiasm for music associations and dance clubs they've developed many different kinds of recreational music.

In the southern part of central Ghana the **Akan** peoples, notably the **Asante** and **Fante**, have an elaborate court music using large drum ensembles and groups of horns. Another great spectacle is that of the huge log xylophones played in **asonko**, a form of recreational music.

PALM-WINE MUSIC

Palm-wine is the popular music of the Asante. Primarily solo guitar music, it originated in the palm-wine bars – usually under a

GHANAIAN INSTRUMENTS

NORTHEAST

Gonge One-stringed fiddle.

Kologo Two-stringed lute.

Donno Talking drums, in an ensemble.

EWE

Sogo and **kidi** Drums.

Atsimewu Master drum.

Axatse Rattles.

Gankogui Double bells.

ASANTE

Atumpane Sets of twin drums.

Ntahera Ensemble of ivory horns.

big tree. A musician would turn up with his guitar and play for as long as people wanted to buy him drinks. This is very much good-time music and such palm-wineists tend to be comedians as well as parodists of the local scene.

Palm-wine guitar music is slowly dying out partly because musicians are being enticed into the guitar bands and concert party groups, and partly due to the lack of instruments in Ghana. In any town someone will be able to point you in the direction of a palm-wine player but you may have to find an instrument for him to play on. Buy the man a drink and you may well find your name included in the current song.

GHANAIAN HIGHLIFE

Highlife originated in Ghana and Sierra Leone and has proved to be one of the most popular and enduring African styles. Originally a fusion of traditional percussion and melodies, with European influences like brass bands, sea shanties and hymns, it started in the early 1920s with the growth of major ports along the West African coast. The term itself is no more than a reference to the kind of European-derived evening of dressing up and dancing (the "highlife") to which new immigrants to the towns of West Africa between the wars were quite unaccustomed – but which they soon made their own.

The first 78rpm records were released in the 1930s and highlife's international reputation started to grow. There are about a dozen **different styles of highlife** but the two main ones are the guitar band and dance band styles. Guitar band highlife is basically a more organized, less horizontal form of palm-wine music. It became known as concert party when exponents added other elements – dance routines and comic turns. "Dance band" highlife, in its extreme form, was all toppers and tails and as much brass as possible. There's a wonderful highlife variation in "Gospel Highlife" – do everything possible to hear something recorded by the **Genesis Gospel Singers**.

• **ET Mensah** was the "King of Highlife". Mensah had a musical childhood and developed his skills on the guitar, organ, sax and trumpet. During World War II he came into contact with British and American styles like calypso, swing and cha-cha, and in 1948 he formed the **Tempos Band**, then the only professional dance band in Ghana. After a string of hits, including "Donkey Calypso", "School Girl" and "All for You", the group went international with frequent tours of West Africa – a golden age of highlife. Soon there were hundreds of bands imitating their style and, in the 1950s and 1960s, a host of exciting groups including **The Uhurus**, **Broadway** and the **Black Beats**. Mensah's popularity declined during the 1970s, but he made a comeback towards the end of the decade.

+***ET Mensah*** *All For You* (Retroafic, UK). All the classics from the 1950s are here, including the wacky "Inflation Calypso", "Sunday Mirror" and the title track. Never mind the crackles, everyone likes it.

+***Various*** *Giants of Danceband Highlife 1950s–1970s* (Original Music, USA). A great stack of fine old dancehall numbers from ET Mensah and the Tempos, the Ramblers International and Professional Uhuru. Grand listening, recalling the golden era when the genre reigned supreme – a good place to start any collection.

+***Various*** *I've Found My Love* (Original Music, USA). Guitar band highlife from the 1950s and 60s. Relaxed shuffles based on the prototype highlife tune, "Yaa Amponsah".

• **African Brothers International Band**, formed in 1963 by **Nana Kwame Ampadu**, are still one of the country's most innovative and enduring guitar groups. They had their earliest and one of their best-loved hits in 1967 with "Ebi Tie Ye" – a plea for democracy in the dark days following the fall of Nkrumah – and had released over 100 discs before 1970 and the release of their first LP. Since then they've released over twenty albums and countless singles. Always a group to mix street wisdom with thinly veiled political comment, they never let this interfere with good music, and are forever trying something new. During the 1970s they experimented with a variety of styles including reggae, rumba and what they called **Afro-hili**, a James Brown-inspired beat which was a challenge to Fela Kuti's Afrobeat.

• **Daniel Amponsah**, aka **Koo Nimo**, is a guitarist who has done as much as anyone to enrich and preserve Ghana's traditional guitar music. Now in his late fifties, he still performs regularly at concerts and festivals with his all-acoustic **Adadam band** and commands huge respect among Ghanaians at home and abroad.

+***Koo Nimo*** *Osabarima* (Adasa/Stern's, UK). Now acknowledged as one of the masters of palm-wine music, Koo Nimo originally recorded this in 1976, his only commercial recording to date.

• **AB Crentsil's Sweet Talks** were one of Ghana's most successful highlife bands in the 1970s. The group gained national popularity after a string of hit albums, the first of which was *Adam and Eve*. In 1978 they went to the USA and recorded their classic *Hollywood Highlife Party*.

+***Sweet Talks and AB Crentsil*** *Hollywood Highlife Party/Moses* (Adasa/Stern's, UK). Recorded in 1978, this is beyond a doubt the best Ghanaian album of the last twenty years. The Sweet Talks split soon after, spawning a host of solo stars.

• **Osibisa** were formed in London by three Ghanaians, **Teddy Osei, Mac Tontoh** and **Sol Amarfino**. Their Afro-rock singles climbed the British charts in the 1970s with three of them, "Dance the Body Music", "Sunshine Day" and "Coffee Song", rising to the top ten. Perhaps they were five years too early, but by the time Sunny Ade was making headlines with undiluted *juju*, they had melted away.

Osibisa *Double Album* (Celluloid, France). All the hits are here, from "The Coffee Song" to "Sunshine Day". In terms both of sales and influence, Osibisa's international impact has never been surpassed by any subsequent African band. If you're too young to remember, then don't delay. Move heaven and earth for this collection. A new triple-CD retrospective is also in the offing.

• **Alex Konadu** is today the uncrowned king of guitar band highlife. He plays music firmly rooted in Ghanaian traditions and has enjoyed massive sales all over West Africa. He claims to have played in every town and village in Ghana.

+***Alex Konadu*** *One Man Thousand Live in London* (World Circuit, UK). The master of sweaty, good-time music – infectious tunes that come back to you months later.

TOGO

Traditional music tends to split into two: Kabyé in the north, "Ghanaian Folk Music", and Ewe/Mina in the south (see above).

The **Kabyé** have a rich musical culture. Some of the most interesting instruments are only used for special celebration, like the **picancala**, a xylophone-like instrument made of stones and rocks – a "lithophone" – and the unusual **water flutes**. There's music played on horns, flutes and whistles and even a trumpet – the **xokudu** – made from the fruit of the baobab tree.

Ocora has an album of Kabyé music. There's a less recherché selection on *Togo: Music from West Africa* on Rounder Records, released a few years back, which has a good mixture of traditional and modern styles and features some nice acoustic guitar songs from **Ali Bawa**.

Modern music in Togo has not thrown up any great stars and most of the few singers seem content to imitate external styles. Togo's urban music was greatly influenced by Congolese styles during the 1960s and 1970s and reggae, soul, highlife and Latin music have all dominated the local scene at some time or other.

Bella Bellow was the leading singer in the late 1960s. She toured Europe and America and made an album, with the help of **Manu Dibango**, *Album Souvenir* which is on Safari Ambience. **Afia Mala** recorded an album in 1984 called Lonlon Viye. A couple of other local stars are included in the Togo chapter on p.846.

BENIN

Benin has a variety of cultures and a diverse musical tradition, with the Hausa, Kabyé and Bariba in the north, and the Yoruba, Gun and Fon people in the south. The music of the Fon played a crucial ceremonial role in the court at Abomey, capital of the country's major pre-colonial state Dan-Homey. The Gun people use a wide variety of instruments including a huge double log xylophone, percussion pots and raft zithers. Benin's best-known musical export, however, is the dynamic voice of Angelique Kidjo.

Modern music of Benin mixes indigenous rhythms and melodies with Congolese styles. During the 1970s Benin's popular music scene was severely impeded by government curfews, but orchestras carried on somehow, the most successful being **Orchestre Poly-Rythmo**, led by horn player **Ignace de Souza**, **Disc Afrique** and **Les Astronauts**.

• **Angélique Kidjo**, a singer of extraordinary power and grace, is the first African woman since Miriam Makeba to achieve real international stardom. An irrepressible figure, she hates artistic ghettoization ("world rock") and despises purists who would curtail her freedom to record as she likes.

+***Angélique Kidjo*** *Parakou* (Mango, UK). From 1989, the first and best of her modern output, with stylish arrangements, intriguing percussion and vocals allowed full rein. *Logozo* (Mango, UK) tore away from Benin roots, while the 1994 *Ayé* (Mango, UK) seemed bound for every dancefloor and beyond.

NIGER

Not much is heard in Europe about music from Niger. A few records of traditional music are available, but little of its modern music travels far.

Niger's major ethnic groups are the **Tuareg**, **Bororo**, **Songhai** and **Hausa**. The Bororo are nomads closely related to the Fula. They have no musical instruments and all their songs are for voices only.

There's a good instrumental ensemble in **Niamey**, which features musicians from all the major ethnic groups, and a national dance troupe called **Karaka**.

Pop artists you may well hear include Hausa singers **Mahaman Garba** and **Yan Ouwa** – both use mostly percussive backing – and the African reggae of **Amadou Hamza**. In Niamey, listen out for female singer, **Madelle Iddari**, Saadou Bori and Moussa Poussy.

+***Saadou Bori & Moussa Poussy*** *Niamey Twice* (Stern's, UK). A double helping of modern Niger, in the shape of Djerma Poussy and Hausa Bori, happily swinging along, mostly in Manding style.

NIGERIA

As far as the music industry is concerned, Nigeria is the centre of African music. The industry is well developed here, with numerous recording studios and pressing plants and, in spite of recession and poverty, a huge home market. Of more intrinsic interest, Nigeria also has a big enough population to sustain artists who sing in regional languages and experiment with indigenous styles. Drawing from traditional sources and outside influences, three main types of modern music have developed – *juju*, highlife and *fuji*. Both *juju* and *fuji* are almost entirely sung in local languages, principally Yoruba.

IGBO MUSIC

The Igbo people of the southeast have always been receptive to cultural change. This ease is reflected in their music and in the incredible variety of instruments played in Igboland. No local occasion would be complete without musicians and you should find them at any event associated with the *obi* (chief). The other major occasions would be seasonal festivals, wrestling matches, a visit by a high-ranking official or the funeral of a prominent citizen.

In more traditional communities, royal music is played every day, when the **ufie** slit drum is used to wake the chief and to tell him when meals are ready. A group, known as **egwu ota**, which consists of slit-drums, drums and bells, performs when the *obi* is leaving the palace and again when he returns.

One of the most pleasing Igbo instruments is the **obo**, a thirteen-stringed raft zither, which can be heard at many a nostalgic palm-wine drinking session.

YORUBA MUSIC

Yoruba instrumental traditions are mostly based on drumming. The most popular form of traditional music today is **dundun**, played on hourglass tension drums of the same name. The usual *dundun* ensemble consists of tension drums of various sizes together with small kettledrums called **gudugudu**. The leading drum of the group is the *iyaalu* ("mother of the drums"), which talks by imitating the tone patterns of Yoruba speech. It's used to play out praise poetry, proverbs and other oral texts. Another important part of Yoruba musical life is **music theatre**, which mixes traditional music with storytelling or live drama.

JUJU

The origins of *juju* music are not very clear, but it's said to have emerged as a Lagosian variation of palm-wine music. The word *juju* is thought to be a corruption of the **Yoruba** word *jo jo*, meaning "dance" – or may just be a dismissive epithet coined by colonial officers and retained, defensively, by its exponents. The first records of this dreamy style started coming out in the early 1930s but it really took off just after World War II with the introduction of amplified sound. The major stars of the pre-war period were **Irewolede Denge** ("grandfather of *juju*") and **Tunde King**; and after the war, **Ayinde Bakara** and the **Jolly Orchestra**.

+***Various*** *Juju Roots, 1930s–1950s* (Rounder, USA). Excellent introduction to the early *juju* years with comprehensive sleeve notes. Featuring Irewolede Denge, Tunde King and Ojoge Daniel – essential.

The **1960s** saw the emergence of a great number of new *juju* singers and bands. Three came to dominate the scene; **IK Dairo**, **Ebenezer Obey** and, in the later 1960s, **Sunny Ade**. During and after the Nigerian civil war (1967–70) *juju* thrived at home as highlife artists from the eastern region either went to Biafra or fled abroad, and highlife as a whole lost its popularity.

• **IK Dairo** had been playing in bands for a good part of his life when he formed the **Morning Star Orchestra** in 1957. By 1961, he had set up the popular **Blue Spots** and rose to become the best-known *juju* player in Nigeria.

+***IK Dairo*** *Juju Master* (Original Music, USA). Singer, composer and band leader, Dairo was responsible for the consolidation of *juju* music among the Yoruba and introduced the accordion to the style. This is a classic round-up of Decca West Africa 45s. IK's new CD, *Ashiko* (Xenophile/ Green Linnet, USA) has him in tune, at last. The talking drums are really speaking here.

• **Ebenezer Obey** formed his first group, **The International Brothers**, in 1964. Since then the man-mountain has released over fifty LPs. The success of his blend of talking drums, percussion and guitar had already caught on by the time he renamed his group **The InterReformers** in 1970. With guaranteed advance sales of over 100,000 records, he went international in 1980.

+***Ebenezer Obey*** *Get Yer Jujus Out* (Rykodisc, USA). Lengthy, live *juju*. Alternatively, the *Solution* LP (Stern's, UK) is fully representative of Obey at his best and really easy to get hold of.

• **King Sunny Ade** started his musical career playing with highlife bands in Lagos before making the transition to *juju*. He went solo in 1966 when he formed **The Green Spots**, and struck gold with *Challenge Cup* the following year. He changed the name of the group to the **African Beats** in 1974 and released hit albums including *The Late General Murtala Muhammed, Sound Vibration* and *The Royal Sound*. By the end of the decade, Ade was one of the most popular musicians in the country. In the 1980s he broke into the intenational scene with tours of Europe, Japan and the USA, and signed to Island records, with whom he released three albums.

King Sunny Ade *Juju Music* (Island, UK). The record that launched a million passions for African sounds. Still wonderful after all these years, *Juju Music* includes many of Ade's best songs, among them the sweet "365 is My Number". On *Bobby* (Sunny Alade, Nigeria) probably the best *juju* album of all time – Ade runs through all the classic riffs in a flowing 1983 tribute to legendary band leader Bobby Benson.

In the 1980s, as *juju* fractured into several strands, Yoruba pop music – **Yo-pop** – crashed onto the scene in the person of **Segun Adewale**. All speed, thunder and lightning, Yo-pop found a huge young audience, especially in Lagos. The latest star in this evolution is **Sir Shina Peters**.

Sir Shina Peters *Afro-Juju I* (Columbia, Nigeria). Creator of ShinaMania, Shina has over twenty albums to his credit and is still in his early thirties. This album was a landmark in the evolution of *juju* music, combining it with elements of Afro-beat and *fuji*.

APALA AND FUJI

Though never knowing the international success of *juju* and highlife, the wall-of-percussion sound of *fuji* has been popular in Nigeria since the 1970s. It has its roots in the Yoruba styles of *apala* and *sakara*, themselves products of Muslim influence on older musical forms in northern Yorubaland. Some of *fuji*'s leading exponents include:

• **Haruna Ishola**. One of Nigeria's greatest *apala* performers, Ishola's music helped pave the way for *fuji*. Before he died in 1983, he had produced some 25 LPs and opened his own recording studio. It's still relatively easy to find many of his later records like *Apala Songs* or *Haruna Ishola and his Apala group*.

• **Sikiru Ayinde**, better known as **Barrister**, is the leading Yoruba *fuji* singer. He started singing *were*, the singing alarm clock songs performed for early breakfast and prayers during Ramadan, at the age of ten. After a brief army career, he turned back to music and, in the early 1970s, formed the **Supreme Fuji Commander**, a 25-piece outfit. They soon became one of Nigeria's top bands, firing off a battery of hit records.

+***Barrister*** *New Fuji Garbage* (GlobeStyle, UK). A recording which is likely to define *fuji* for Western ears for years to come. Barrister's voice here is slightly mellower than usual and the band surround it with a pounding panoply.

• **Ayinla Kollington** – the source of social commentary in the Yoruba Muslim music scene – is ranked second in the *fuji* popularity stakes behind Barrister. His lyrics can be razor-sharp – though he rarely puts himself on the front line with Fela Kuti.

Ayinla Kollington *Ijoba Ti Tun* (KRLPS, Nigeria). *Fuji's* "Man of the People". Challenging lyrics, driving percussion and a touch of Hawaiian guitar.

NIGERIAN HIGHLIFE

Highlife came to Nigeria from Ghana in the 1950s, but it was quickly moulded by indigenous styles and influences from Cameroon and the Congo so that it came to have a flavour that was unmistakably Nigerian. Extra polish, and western instruments – brass sections, electric keyboards and guitars – were added to home-grown rhythms and, by the 1960s, highlife was in the forefront of popular urban music. It lost its universal appeal during the civil war, when it retained mass popularity only in Igboland, and quite quickly lost ground to *juju* among the Yoruba.

• Old albums from the early highlife stars are rarities these days although it is still possible to lay your hands on 1970s and 80s material by the fabulous **Oriental Brothers** (and offshoots Dr Sir Warrior and Kabaka). Meanwhile a steady trickle of re-releases continues to refresh the style.

+***Oriental Brothers*** *Heavy on the Highlife* (Original Music, USA). After dozens of Nigeria-only releases, this wonderful burn-up of a guitar-highlife album sets the standard. Relentless, sexy grooves.

• **Prince Nico Mbarga and Rocafil Jazz** are reckoned to have sold some thirteen million copies of "Sweet Mother", making it the biggest-selling African song of all time. Hundreds of bands copied it; radio stations played it incessantly; vinyl copies could only be had at twenty times the normal price.

+***Prince Nico Mbarga & Rocafil Jazz*** *Aki Special* (Rounder, USA). A bumper CD with nearly two LPs' worth on it – including the global hit "Sweet Mother" –which makes as good a starting point as any for a collection of Nigerian music.

Sweet mother, I no go forget you,
For the suffer wey you suffer for me, yeah,
Sweet mother, I no go forget you,
For the suffer wey you suffer for me, yeah.

When I de cry, my mother go carry me.
She go say, "My pickin, wetin you de cry?, oh,
Stop, stop, stop, stop, stop, stop
Make you no go cry again, oh".

When I want sleep, my mother go bed me,
She go lie me well well for bed, oh.
She cover me clothes, say "Make you sleep,
Sleep, sleep, my pickin, oh".

AFRO-BEAT

Afro-beat was almost solely the creation of one extraordinary musician, **Fela Anikulapo-Kuti**. The style has its own distinctive beats and rhythms which provide a flexible vehicle for Fela's political lyrics and call-and-response vocal style. He chose to sing in the lingua franca of pidgin English to avoid limiting his audience, and his eruptive performances and defiant lifestyle have found him huge following and brought him into constant conflict with the Nigerian authorities. He has released a steady stream of hits including "Black President", "Perambulator", "Coffin for Head of State" and "Expensive Shit".

+***Fela Kuti*** *The 69 Los Angeles Sessions* (Stern's, UK). First release for some vintage numbers from Black Panther days – and ten tracks all under seven minutes make it unique in the Fela oeuvre!

+*Beasts of No Nation* (JDEUR, UK). Even the cover makes an unmissable statement. Confounding critics who felt Fela was past it, he entered the 1990s (his sixth decade) in great shape, howling against Thatcher and Reagan.

CAMEROON

In Cameroon there are hundreds of ethnic groups, many of them with a distinctive musical culture and dances. More than two hundred different dances are still performed on a whole range of occasions and the majority are accompanied by instrumental ensembles.

FOLK MUSIC

In the south the **Bakweri**, **Bamiléké**, **Bamoun** and **Beti** have mostly xylophone or drum ensembles and their masked dance dramas are well worth seeing. The Sultan of Bamoun's Musical Theatre (see p.1175) is a remarkable institution. Also in the south live the **Bulu**, **Fang**, **Eton** and **Mvele**, who play a wide diversity of musical instruments including the **ngkul**, a slit-drum formerly used to send messages but now only to accompany the **ozila** or initiation dance; the **mendzan**, a small xylophone; and the **mvet**, a long stick zither (*mvet* refers not only to the instrument but also the pantomime and dances associated with it).

• The career of **Francis Bebey** won't fit into any category. Multi-talented, Bebey is a writer and storyteller, film-maker and musician. As a guitarist and composer, he sings in English, French and Douala, experimenting with styles ranging from classical guitar and traditional rhythms to *makossa* and plain pop. He has released some twenty albums since 1969 and you never know what you'll find on any of them.

+***Francis Bebey*** *Nandolo/With Love – Works 1963–1994* (Original Music, US). A fine sampling of Bebey's talents, from skill on the bamboo flute to wonderful guitar and thumb piano pieces. Recommended.

MAKOSSA AND OTHER POP MUSIC

Makossa, the pop music of Cameroon, was created in the 1950s but has its roots in the 1930s. Mission schools created their own bands to usher the pupils into assembly, using xylophones and percussion instruments. These bands performed at dances outside school hours, playing a mixture of Western and local styles. Guitars were introduced before the war and guitarists would perform accompanied by a bottle player. There were three main dance styles at the time: *asiko* – percussion and xylophone music; *ambasse bey* – a guitar-based dance with much faster rhythms; and the fledgling makossa, a popular folk dance, named after the word for "to strip off".

Although *makossa* endures, other styles are more ephemeral. The huge publicity given to **bikutsi** – the war rhythm of the Beti people zapped up for amps and guitars – in the early 1990s was at least partly due to the ethnic provenance of the president. For a few months it looked as if **Les Têtes Brulées** would make it big on the world stage. **Bend-skin** is a new kind of street-credible percussion-led folk music, of which Kouchoum Mbada are the main protagonists. On their album *Bend Skin* (cassette only) they have Sam Fan Thomas on keyboards. Lastly, listen out for **Gibraltar Drakus**, ex-Têtes singer, and currently "Le Roi du Bantowbol". This is a style which owes something to folk roots and something to *bol* – from "bal" accordion-playing.

• *Makossa* gained international appeal with the coming of **Manu Dibango**. A sax-player, composer, singer, pianist and arranger, Dibango's inspirations are diverse. He has lived and recorded in Brussels, Paris, Zaire, the United States, Jamaica and Côte d'Ivoire. He started a whole wave of urban popular music with the release of his album *Soul Makossa* in 1973 (somewhat confusingly named, as it contains nothing that a Cameroonian musician would recognise as *makossa*). This record paved the way for a new generation of artists who now rely on a combination of traditional inspiration and high-tech recording facilities to produce the highly exportable dance music that has turned Douala into one of the dynamos of African music. Now in the superstar class – nearly thirty years after his first single – Manu Dibango is one of the few African artists guaranteed to draw a full house anywhere in the world.

+***Manu Dibango*** *Live '91* (Stern's, UK). The output of Africa's foremost jazz-sax-player is so vast, it's hard to know where to begin. If you find nothing to please among the variety on this CD you can be sure you don't like him.

• **André Marike Tala** is a singer/songwriter discovered by Manu Dibango. Blind since the age of thirteen, this didn't stop him going to France where he recorded several singles that became hits in Cameroon such as "Potaksima" and "Sikata". Mixing traditional and modern styles, he is also recognized for the creation of the *tchamassi* rhythm.

+**André Marike Tala** *Si Tcha* (MST Productions, France). Sam Fan Thomas's *makassi* style is virtually indistinguishable from *zouk* on this brief, bouncy release.

• **Sam Fan Thomas** recorded with Tala for over eight years before going solo in 1976. He recorded several albums with minor hits, but had to wait until 1984 and the release of *Makassi* to achieve a wider reputation. The album's single "African Typic Collection" instantly ignited his reputation when it became an international dance hit.

• **Moni Bile**'s career has ignited in the 1980s to make him one of the hottest *makossa* singers in Cameroon. Using the best session men, he's known for his sophistication and driving dance melodies.

+**Moni Bile** *10th Anniversary: Best of ...* (MAD Productions/Sonodisc, France). Bilé really maximized the excitement potential of *makossa*. This includes his great, dance-floor stirrers, "Bijou" and "O Si Tapa Lambo Lam".

• **Anne-Marie Nzie**, "La voix d'or du Cameroun", started singing at the age of eight and was a national star by the 1950s. Though no longer a chart-topper, she remains one of the most respected and popular female singers in the country. 1984 saw the release of her album, *Liberté*.

• **Lapiro de Mbanga**, a master of political rap, is hugely controversial – a tough blend of politics, rhythm and language and a big name in Cameroon. He's comfortable with a range of styles from *makossa* to Zairian *soukous*.

MUSIC BOOKS

Frances Bebey, *African Music: A People's Art* (Lawrence Hill, 1975). First published in French in 1969, this is an excellent and well-illustrated ethnomusicological survey, concentrating on Francophone Africa.

Wolfgang Bender, *Sweet Mother: Modern African Music* (University of Chicago Press, 1991). A cultural history of African urban music. Includes an extensive bibliography and discography.

Broughton, Ellingham, Muddyman & Trillo, eds, *The Rough Guide to World Music* (Rough Guides, 1994). Detailed, lengthy chapter on West African music, complete with interviews and hundreds of CD and record reviews.

Jenny Cathcart, *Hey You!* (Fine Line Books, 1989). A detailed biography of Youssou Ndour, with translations of many of his lyrics.

Samuel Charters, *The Roots of the Blues* (Quartet, 1982). A bit of a classic, Charter's serendipitous journey (The Gambia, Senegal, Mali) aimed to find the Blues' roots in West Africa. While he failed, his other discoveries make great reading. Two illustrative LPs were released with the book.

John Miller Chernoff, *African Rhythm and African Sensibility* (University of Chicago Press, 1980). A travelogue and easy-to-read analysis of Ghanaian drumming, music's spiritual meaning and the place of art in African society. Beautifully written.

John Collins, *Musicmakers of West Africa* (Three Continents Press, 1985). A collection of articles and interviews, mostly on highlife and its offspring, by a committed veteran of the Ghana music scene.

Manu Dibango and Danielle Rouard, *Three Kilos of Coffee: An Autobiography* (University of Chicago Press, 1994). West Africa's most famous musician traces his own story from childhood outside Douala to international success.

Graeme Ewens, *Africa Oyé!* (Guinness, 1992). The best Africa-only music book published to date, with a mass of colour and black and white photos.

Ronnie Graham, *Stern's Guide to Contemporary African Music Vol. 1 and Vol. 2* (Pluto Press, 1989). An invaluable, country-by-country survey of styles, artists and releases.

Chris May and Chris Stapleton. *African All Stars: the Pop Music of a Continent* (Paladin, 1989). An indispensable, and highly readable, account of the development of African music's many and diverse strands.

Christopher Alan Waterman, *Juju: A Social History and Ethnography of an African Popular Music* (University of Chicago Press, 1990). A detailed account of the origins, evolution and social significance of Juju, tracing the roots back more than fifty years.

+***Lapiro de Mbanga*** *Ndinga Man Contre-Attaque: na wou go pay?* (Label Bleu, France). Here – with a hard mix of *makossa, zouk, soukous* and Afro-beat – Lapiro rebuts the criticism that he sold out to the powers that be. Recommended.

Thanks to Dave Muddyman for the version of this article which appeared in the first edition, and to Jenny Cathcart, Lucy Duran and Ben Mandelson for passages from the Rough Guide to World Music.

INDEX

Entries in italics apply to West Africa as a whole. Bold entries are mapped. For individual chapter indexes see key below:

A

B

C

D

DIRECT ORDERS IN THE UK

Title	ISBN	Price
Amsterdam	1858280869	£7.99
Andalucia	185828094X	£8.99
Australia	1858281415	£12.99
Barcelona & Catalunya	1858281067	£8.99
Berlin	1858281296	£8.99
Big Island of Hawaii	185828158X	£8.99
Brazil	1858281024	£9.99
Brittany & Normandy	1858281261	£8.99
Bulgaria	1858280478	£8.99
California	1858280907	£9.99
Canada	185828130X	£10.99
Classical Music on CD	185828113X	£12.99
Corsica	1858280893	£8.99
Crete	1858281326	£8.99
Cyprus	185828032X	£8.99
Czech & Slovak Republics	185828029X	£8.99
Egypt	1858280753	£10.99
England	1858280788	£9.99
Europe	185828077X	£14.99
Florida	1858280109	£8.99
France	1858281245	£10.99
Germany	1858281288	£11.99
Goa	1858281563	£8.99
Greece	1858281318	£9.99
Greek Islands	1858281636	£8.99
Guatemala & Belize	1858280451	£9.99
Holland, Belgium & Luxembourg	1858280877	£9.99
Hong Kong & Macau	1858280664	£8.99
Hungary	1858281237	£8.99
India	1858281040	£13.99
Ireland	1858280958	£9.99
Italy	1858280311	£12.99
Jazz	1858281377	£16.99
Kenya	1858280435	£9.99
London	1858291172	£8.99
Mediterranean Wildlife	0747100993	£7.95
Malaysia, Singapore & Brunei	1858281032	£9.99
Mexico	1858280443	£10.99
Morocco	1858280400	£9.99
Moscow	185828118 0	£8.99
Nepal	185828046X	£8.99
New York	1858280583	£8.99
Nothing Ventured	0747102082	£7.99
Pacific Northwest	1858280923	£9.99
Paris	1858281253	£7.99
Poland	1858280346	£9.99
Portugal	1858280842	£9.99
Prague	185828015X	£7.99
Provence & the Côte d'Azur	1858280230	£8.99
Pyrenees	1858280931	£8.99
Romania	1858280974	£9.99
St Petersburg	1858281334	£8.99
San Francisco	1858280826	£8.99
Scandinavia	1858280397	£10.99
Scotland	1858280834	£8.99
Sicily	1858280370	£8.99
Singapore	1858281350	£8.99
Spain	1858280818	£9.99
Thailand	1858281407	£10.99
Tunisia	1858280656	£8.99
Turkey	1858280885	£9.99
Tuscany & Umbria	1858280915	£8.99
USA	185828080X	£12.99
Venice	1858281709	£8.99
Wales	1858280966	£8.99
West Africa	1858280141	£12.99
More Women Travel	1858280982	£9.99
World Music	1858280176	£14.99
Zimbabwe & Botswana	1858280419	£10.99

Rough Guide Phrasebooks

Title	ISBN	Price
Czech	1858281482	£3.50
French	185828144X	£3.50
German	1858281466	£3.50
Greek	1858281458	£3.50
Italian	1858281431	£3.50
Spanish	1858281474	£3.50

Rough Guides can be obtained directly in the UK* from Penguin by contacting: Penguin Direct, Penguin Books Ltd, Bath Road, Harmondsworth, West Drayton, Middlesex UB7 0DA; or telephone our credit line on 0181-899 4036 (9am–5pm) and ask for Penguin Direct. Visa, Access and Amex accepted. Delivery will normally be within 14 working days. Penguin Direct ordering facilities are only available in the UK.

The availability and published prices quoted are correct at the time of going to press but are subject to alteration without prior notice.

DIRECT ORDERS IN THE USA

Title	ISBN	Price
Amsterdam	1858280869	$13.59
Andalucia	185828094X	$14.95
Australia	1858281415	$19.95
Barcelona & Catalunya	1858281067	$17.99
Berlin	1858281296	$14.95
Big Island of Hawaii	185828158X	$12.95
Brazil	1858281024	$15.95
Brittany & Normandy	1858281261	$14.95
Bulgaria	1858280478	$14.99
California	1858280907	$14.95
Canada	185828130X	$14.95
Classical Music on CD	185828113X	$19.95
Corsica	1858280893	$14.95
Crete	1858281326	$14.95
Cyprus	185828032X	$13.99
Czech & Slovak Republics	185828029X	$14.95
Egypt	1858280753	$17.95
England	1858280788	$16.95
Europe	185828077X	$18.95
Florida	1858280109	$14.95
France	1858281245	$16.95
Germany	1858281288	$17.95
Goa	1858281563	$14.95
Greece	1858281318	$16.95
Greek Islands	1858281636	$14.95
Guatemala & Belize	1858280451	$14.95
Holland, Belgium & Luxembourg	1858280877	$15.95
Hong Kong & Macau	1858280664	$13.95
Hungary	1858281237	$14.95
India	1858281040	$22.95
Ireland	1858280958	$16.95
Italy	1858280311	$17.95
Jazz	1858281377	$24.95
Kenya	1858280435	$15.95
London	1858291172	$12.95
Mediterranean Wildlife	0747100993	$15.95
Malaysia, Singapore & Brunei	1858281032	$16.95
Mexico	1858280443	$16.95
Morocco	1858280400	$16.95
Moscow	1858281180	$14.95
Nepal	185828046X	$13.95
New York	1858280583	$13.95
Nothing Ventured	0747102082	$19.95
Pacific Northwest	1858280923	$14.95
Paris	1858281253	$12.95
Poland	1858280346	$16.95
Portugal	1858280842	$15.95
Prague	1858281229	$14.95
Provence & the Côte d'Azur	1858280230	$14.95
Pyrenees	1858280931	$15.95
Romania	1858280974	$15.95
St Petersburg	1858281334	$14.95
San Francisco	1858280826	$13.95
Scandinavia	1858280397	$16.99
Scotland	1858280834	$14.95
Sicily	1858280370	$14.99
Singapore	1858281350	$14.95
Spain	1858280818	$16.95
Thailand	1858281407	$17.95
Tunisia	1858280656	$15.95
Turkey	1858280885	$16.95
Tuscany & Umbria	1858280915	$15.95
USA	185828080X	$18.95
Venice	1858281709	$14.95
Wales	1858280966	$14.95
West Africa	1858280141	$24.95
More Women Travel	1858280982	$14.95
World Music	1858280176	$19.95
Zimbabwe & Botswana	1858280419	$16.95

Rough Guide Phrasebooks

Title	ISBN	Price
Czech	1858281482	$5.00
French	185828144X	$5.00
German	1858281466	$5.00
Greek	1858281458	$5.00
Italian	1858281431	$5.00
Spanish	1858281474	$5.00

In the USA charge your order by Master Card or Visa ($15.00 minimum order): call 1-800-253-6476; or send orders, with name, address and zip code, and list price, plus $2.00 shipping and handling per order to: Consumer Sales, Penguin USA, PO Box 999 – Dept #17109, Bergenfield, NJ 07621. No COD. Prepay foreign orders by international money order, a cheque drawn on a US bank, or US currency. No postage stamps are accepted. All orders are subject to stock availability at the time they are processed. Refunds will be made for books not available at that time. Please allow a minimum of four weeks for delivery.

The availability and published prices quoted are correct at the time of going to press but are subject to alteration without prior notice.

Czech

French

Greek

Italian

Spanish

AFRICAN TRAILS